From the knowledge leader since 1768

ENCYCLOPÆDIA
Britannica
ALMANAC
2006

ENCYCLOPÆDIA
Britannica®

Jacob E. Safra, *Chairman of the Board*
Jorge Aguilar-Cauz, *President*

Chicago · London · New Delhi · Paris · Seoul · Sydney · Taipei · Tokyo

Economics & Business

Arts, Entertainment, & Leisure

Sports

Year in Review

The Deadliest Tsunami

On 26 Dec 2004, at 7:59 AM local time, an undersea earthquake with a magnitude of 9.0 struck off the coast of the Indonesian island of Sumatra. Over the next seven hours, a tsunami— a series of immense ocean waves— triggered by the quake reached out across the Indian Ocean, devastating coastal areas as far away as East Africa. (See map below). Some locations reported that the waves had even reached a height of 9 m (30 ft) or more when they hit the shoreline. At least 280,000 people were killed across a dozen countries, with Indonesia, Sri Lanka, India, Maldives, and Thailand sustaining massive damage. Indonesian officials estimated that the death toll there could exceed 200,000, particularly in northern Sumatra's Aceh province. Tens of thousands were reported dead or missing in Sri Lanka and India, a large number of

them from the Indian Andaman and Nicobar islands. The low-lying island nation of Maldives reported more than a hundred casualties and economic damage that could exceed the country's gross domestic product. Several thousand non-Asian tourists vacationing in the region also were reported dead or missing. The lack of food, clean water, and medical treatment—combined with the Herculean task faced by relief workers trying to get supplies into some remote areas where roads had been destroyed or where civil war raged—increased the likelihood that the casualty list would continue to grow. Long-term environmental damage was almost as unimaginable as the loss of life, with tourist resorts, villages, farmland, and fishing grounds demolished or inundated with debris, bodies, and plant-killing salt water.

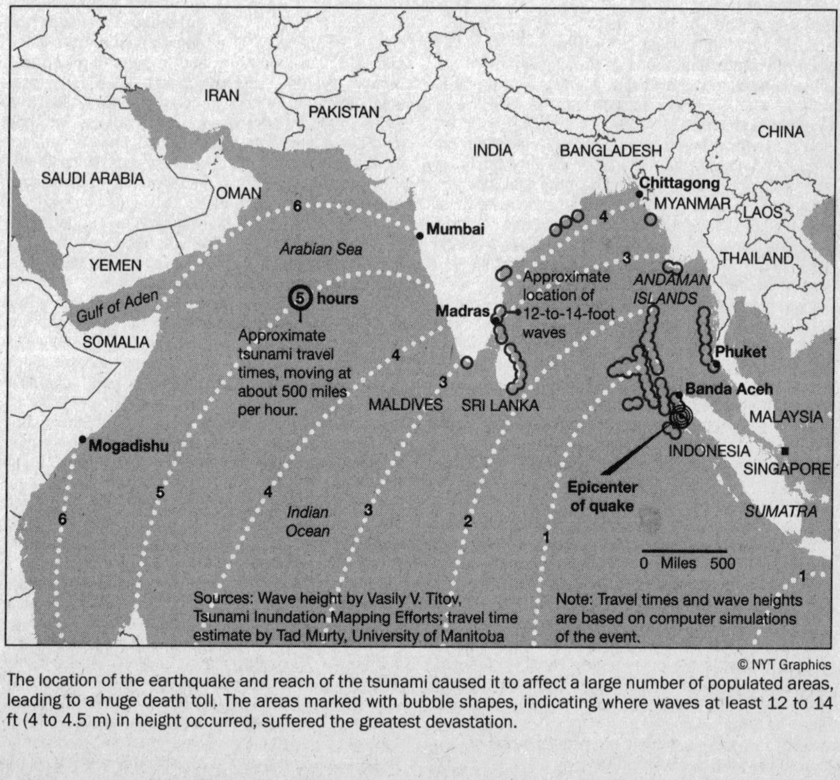

IRAN

PAKISTAN

CHINA

SAUDI ARABIA

OMAN

INDIA

BANGLADESH

Chittagong

MYANMAR

LAOS

6

Mumbai

Arabian Sea

THAILAND

YEMEN

⑤ hours

ANDAMAN ISLANDS

Gulf of Aden

Madras

Approximate location of 12-to-14-foot waves

Phuket

SOMALIA

Approximate tsunami travel times, moving at about 500 miles per hour.

4

Banda Aceh

MALDIVES

SRI LANKA

MALAYSIA

Mogadishu

INDONESIA

SINGAPORE

5

4

Epicenter of quake

SUMATRA

6

Indian Ocean

3

2

1

0   Miles   500

Sources: Wave height by Vasily V. Titov, Tsunami Inundation Mapping Efforts; travel time estimate by Tad Murty, University of Manitoba

Note: Travel times and wave heights are based on computer simulations of the event.

© NYT Graphics

The location of the earthquake and reach of the tsunami caused it to affect a large number of populated areas, leading to a huge death toll. The areas marked with bubble shapes, indicating where waves at least 12 to 14 ft (4 to 4.5 m) in height occurred, suffered the greatest devastation.

The US Election of 2004

by David C. Beckwith

When a US president seeks reelection, the outcome is usually decisive. A consensus emerges on whether the incumbent deserves to be kept on, and the sitting president is either dismissed or, more often, reelected—and by a substantial margin. Incumbent George W. Bush, however, won a second term in 2004 over Sen. John F. Kerry of Massachusetts by 3.3 million votes, with the narrowest popular-ballot percentage of any incumbent since 1916, in an election that was remarkable for an extremely polarized electorate, unprecedented spending, and high voter turnout.

As the year began, former Vermont governor Howard Dean was the front-runner for the Democratic nomination, but he faded rapidly, in part because some party leaders thought he was too liberal to defeat a wartime president. Dean was knocked out in the first major event, the 19 January Iowa caucuses. Dean fielded thousands of volunteer workers nationwide but finished with only 18% of the caucus vote, compared with 32% for first-term Sen. John Edwards of North Carolina and 38% for Kerry. Dean sealed his fate that evening, capping a defiant address to a raucous crowd of supporters with a primal yell in what became known as the "I Have a Scream" speech.

Kerry went on to win all but three Democratic primaries, sewing up the nomination by mid-March. He eventually selected as his running mate rival Edwards, a former trial lawyer who had gained good reviews for his populist "two Americas" message. Early on, independent candidate Ralph Nader appeared poised again to be a spoiler, but Democrats successfully kept him off the general-election ballot in 16 states.

The president's reelection strategy was overseen by Karl Rove, a canny longtime Bush aide from Texas. Bush pointed to significant domestic accomplishments during his first term: a major tax reduction, prescription-drug assistance for seniors, an expansion of federal assistance to public schools, and a real if less-than-robust recovery from the 2001 recession. In contrast to Kerry, Bush also endorsed a constitutional amendment banning same-sex marriage, which energized religious and conservative voters.

Kerry faulted the administration's health and education spending records as puny, vowed to raise taxes on the wealthiest Americans to finance a more muscular expansion, and taunted Bush repeatedly as the first president since Herbert Hoover to preside over a net loss of jobs during his term.

The central campaign issue was Bush's response to the 11 Sep 2001 terrorist attacks, an aggressive approach that split the country virtually down the middle. Bush claimed the strategy was working and promised continuity. Kerry's position was critical of Bush and more nuanced.

Kerry had been launched into politics by his opposition to the Vietnam War in the early 1970s. As a US senator, he had voted against the 1991 Gulf War, for the resolution authorizing the 2003 US-led invasion of Iraq, but against an appropriation bill funding Iraq's occupation and rebuilding. At one point, attempting to explain, he noted that he had voted both for and against that funding bill—playing into Bush campaign charges that Kerry was an inveterate "flip-flopper."

Many of his supporters opposed the Iraq incursion, but a majority of Americans favored tough antiterrorism policies, so Kerry walked a narrow ledge. His campaign settled on a strategy: Kerry would underscore his decorated 1968–69 service as a navy lieutenant in Vietnam, background that contrasted favorably with President Bush's service in the Texas Air National Guard, to demonstrate that Kerry had superior qualifications to be in charge during perilous times.

> " *Bush's margin of victory, while narrow for a reelection contest, was larger than predicted by public opinion polls.* "

The late July Democratic convention in Boston became a paean to Kerry's role in Vietnam. Kerry traveled accompanied by his "band of brothers," shipmates from his Vietnam experience. After he strode on stage to accept the nomination, Kerry saluted and said, "I'm John Kerry, and I'm reporting for duty."

In early August, as Kerry nursed a small lead in public opinion polls, a new ad hoc group, Swift Boat Veterans for Truth, composed of navy officers who had also served in Vietnam, produced anti-Kerry television ads in three states. The commercials challenged Kerry's account of his medal-winning experiences and blasted his later antiwar activism as disloyalty to his comrades in arms. Many major news outlets were slow to cover the Swift Boaters, but conservative Internet "bloggers," writers of so-called Web logs, helped whip up attention to their claims.

This was the first election contested under the 2002 McCain-Feingold campaign-finance-reform legislation, designed to reduce the role of money in politics. The law made "soft-money" contributions from corporations and unions to party organizations illegal but opened the door to "527" groups such as the Swift Boaters operating independently of the campaign. By one estimate total election spending increased by nearly a third, to $3.9 billion, since 2000. Democratic-oriented groups were far quicker to organize under the new rules, and 527s poured about $400 million into the race, helping Democrats overcome a marked Republican-funding advantage.

By late August, when Republicans gathered in New York City for their convention, Bush had regained a significant polling lead. Moderate Republican stars, including California Gov. Arnold Schwarzenegger and former New York City mayor Rudy Giuliani, and disaffected Democrats such as US Sen. Zell Miller of Georgia extolled Bush's conduct of the war on terrorism and attacked Kerry's leadership ability.

Kerry's campaign floundered under the assault, and Bush seemed headed to a comfortable victory—until

the two candidates met on 30 September in Miami FL for the first of three debates. Bush's aides had insisted that the first debate cover foreign policy, thought to be Bush's strong suit. The strategy backfired when Bush appeared on the defensive, finding it difficult to explain his positions and often repeating himself. Of the war on terrorism, Bush said some version of "It's hard work" on 11 occasions. Kerry, by contrast, spoke smoothly and authoritatively and, for the first time, emerged as a plausible alternative.

Within days Bush's lead had almost entirely evaporated. The two candidates spent the final campaign weeks fighting in 14 "battleground" states, with imperceptible movement in the polls. Bush stepped up his game markedly in the second and third debates and thereby halted his slide in the polls and stabilized the race. Potential voters in the 14 battlegrounds were bombarded with repeated candidate visits, saturation media advertising, and multiple phone calls and mail from both campaigns and allied groups.

To all indications the country was heading toward a second consecutive 50–50 election, and both sides moved in the final days to turn out their voters. Kerry's operation, aided significantly by 527s such as America Coming Together, used a small army of paid staffers to register new voters, identify sympathizers, and get them to the polls. Bush's campaign was more centralized, relying heavily on volunteers who worked their own neighborhoods to identify and turn out Republican voters.

Of the most closely watched battlegrounds, Pennsylvania went to Kerry by a small but comfortable margin. Florida, well organized by Gov. Jeb Bush, the president's brother, went clearly for the incumbent. That left Ohio, ordinarily GOP-leaning but hard hit by manufacturing job losses, as the decisive major swing state. Shortly after midnight it appeared that Ohio belonged to Bush by about 135,000 votes—but tens of thousands of "provisional ballots" cast by voters whose registration was in question made the results "within the margin of litigation." As most voters went to bed, it appeared possible the election would again be decided only after court battles. By Wednesday morning, however, the Bush advantage appeared insurmountable, and Kerry delivered a gracious concession speech.

Political maps again popularized the terms "red states" for Republicans and "blue states" for Democrats. Only three states switched color from 2000 to 2004: New Hampshire went from red to blue, and Iowa and New Mexico shifted from blue to red. Bush won 8 of the 14 battleground states. Nader, whose 2.9 million votes in 2000 might have cost Democrat Al Gore the race, was not a factor in 2004.

In the end Kerry and allies were wildly successful in turning out voters to oppose Bush. The Democrat won 57.3 million votes, nearly 7 million more than Gore in 2000 and significantly more than any previous presidential candidate of either party in US history. Nonetheless, Kerry received only 48% of the vote; it was the seventh consecutive presidential election in which the Democratic candidate had failed to top 50%.

The GOP turnout effort was even better. Targeting infrequent voters in suburban, exurban, and rural areas, Bush attracted 60.6 million votes, some 10.2 million more than he had earned in 2000, a 51% share of the electorate. The 120.3 million total votes was nearly 15 million more than in 2000. Bush's margin of victory, while narrow for a reelection contest, was larger than predicted by public opinion polls.

In another unusual result, the incumbent's party added seats in both houses of Congress, increasing the number of Republican US senators from 51 to 55. Bush had surprised many analysts by pursuing an aggressive agenda following his narrow 2000 win. At year's end Bush reshuffled his cabinet, replacing 9 of its 15 members, and again claimed a mandate for an activist agenda, including self-sustaining private accounts in social security, reform of the income-tax system, and staying the course in Iraq.

David C. Beckwith is Vice President of the National Cable Television Association.

Offshoring

by Christopher O'Leary

By 2004 offshoring—the practice of companies outsourcing operations overseas, usually to less-developed countries (LDCs) with the intention of reducing costs—had already become one of the major economic controversies of the decade. While the ultimate impact of offshoring had yet to be measured, surveys estimated that in 2004 some 14 million Americans, 10% of the nation's workforce, held positions that could be outsourced.

Offshoring jobs and infrastructure to countries with more lax regulations and far lower standards of living was nothing new. Many manufacturing jobs, for example, were exported from the US to nations such as China during the 1960s and '70s. What had changed, however, was the nature of the work being exported. With the advent of Internet-based communications technology and improved education in many LDCs, increasing numbers of highly skilled jobs in such areas as information technology (IT) and financial management were heading overseas each year.

The practice had its proponents, who claimed that offshoring's impact was being overstated and that employers, able to use offshoring to reduce overhead costs, were then able to free up capital for new investment and thus create new jobs. Some advocates of this argument included the president of the US Chamber of Commerce, Thomas Donohue, and Federal Reserve Chairman Alan Greenspan. Detractors, however, claimed that the practice had greatly hurt the working class and could decimate the American middle class.

Unsurprisingly, the issue became a battleground in the 2004 presidential election. Sen. John Kerry, the Democratic Party's candidate, denounced CEOs whose companies engaged in outsourcing as traitorous "Benedict Arnolds." He introduced a bill that would require call-center employees to disclose their physical locations to consumers and proposed a plan to eliminate all tax breaks to American companies that export jobs. Kerry's proposals had parallels at the state legislative level; as analysts estimated that at least 13 bills that would ban some form of offshore outsourcing had been introduced in states, including New Jersey, Michigan, and Indiana. Pres. George W.

Bush, while a far-less-severe critic of offshoring than his opponent, also felt political pressure to slow its pace. In January 2004 the president signed an appropriations bill that contained an amendment forbidding some government divisions to use foreign companies when outsourcing work.

Actual data about offshoring's impact on the US economy was preliminary and at times contradictory. In 2004 general estimates were that 250,000-300,000 jobs were leaving the US annually, while some surveys found that about 240,000 technology jobs had gone offshore since January 2001 and about 830,000 general service-sector jobs would have gone overseas by the end of 2005. Some studies were quite grim in their future predictions; Forrester Research Inc. estimated that 3.4 million service-sector jobs (which included most IT positions) would leave the US by 2015. Although outsourcing was not as far advanced in Europe, especially in non-English-speaking countries, Forrester reported that spending on offshoring by European businesses was expected to increase from €82 billion (almost $100 billion) in 2002 to some €129 billion (about $156 billion) in 2008.

A report released in June 2004 by the US Department of Labor downplayed offshoring's effects, stating that in the first quarter of 2004 offshoring represented only 2.5% of the total US job losses posted in that period. Critics said that the report understated the impact of offshoring because the study's results came from asking companies if their layoffs were due to offshoring—something many executives would not care to disclose publicly. The same month, a joint survey by Roland Berger Strategy Consultants and the UN Conference on Trade and Development revealed that more than 40% of the European companies canvassed planned to offshore jobs, primarily to save money.

New Frontiers.

Perhaps the most contentious area of offshoring was in IT, which had been one of the best-paying and fastest-growing job sectors in the US during the previous 20 years. Ironically, massive IT job transfers overseas were possible only because of the advances made by the technology industry in the past decade. Technology consultants estimated that 10% of American computer service and software jobs would have moved offshore by the end of 2004, while other surveys predicted that up to 25% of all IT jobs in Western countries would relocate offshore by 2010.

In the past, companies had focused their outsourcing efforts mainly on transplanting low-skilled jobs, including customer-service call centers. More recently, companies were tapping the growing pool of university-trained technology graduates in countries that included India, the Philippines, and Malaysia for such tasks as software engineering, computer chip design, and code writing. For example, General Electric Corp. offshored about 70% of its technology needs; Motorola was increasing the staff in its technology research operations in Beijing, while Intel was doing the

same in Russia. Aetna planned to cut up to 10% of its IT staff while likely increasing outsourcing agreements with Indian companies such as Infosys Technologies Ltd. Even Infosys CEO Narayana Murthy was compelled to address the issue.

A major factor driving IT offshoring was the vast disparity between highly paid US tech workers and their counterparts in LDCs. Analysts estimated that the average Indian IT worker earned roughly $10 per hour, 13% of his or her American counterpart's salary.

Similar factors were spurring offshoring's growth in the financial services industry, ranging from banking to insurance to securities trading. Within the past year, financial institutions in North America and Europe had increased offshoring to an average of 1,500 positions per firm, a massive increase from the 300-positions-per-firm average estimated in 2003. Surveys calculated that 80% of the world's largest financial institutions—those companies with market capitalizations of $10 billion or greater—currently had offshore operations or agreements. Among the top financial institutions with offshore operations were GE Capital, which had roughly 15,000 employees in India; HSBC, with 8,000 employees scattered around the Pacific Rim; and Citigroup, with 3,200 employees located in India, according to estimates from research firm Celent Communications.

> *Increasing numbers of highly skilled jobs in such areas as information technology (IT) and financial management were heading overseas each year.*

Some observers predicted that by 2010 more than 20% of the financial industry's global cost base, approximately $400 billion, would have been outsourced to LDCs. Analysts estimated that about 2.3 million jobs in the banking and securities industries were at risk for offshoring in the next six years and predicted that in the same period about 30% of the banking industry's operations and technology spending would shift to offshore locations. Again, the wage disparity between Western nations and LDCs was enormous. In 2003 the average Indian financial service industry employee with an MBA earned roughly 14% of his or her American equivalent's wages. Analysts estimated that the financial and insurance industries had saved $11.6 billion in the past four years via offshoring.

Is Offshoring Inevitable?

Given offshoring's potential to generate massive savings, it seemed unlikely that the practice would fade any time soon. Offshoring's future was not entirely assured, however, and not every business was enamored of the practice. Companies such as Capital One and Lehman Brothers had canceled outsourcing contracts with Indian firms, citing poor employee training, inadequate support levels, and security concerns, among other reasons. Furthermore, if more and more job losses could be attributed to offshoring practices, pressure would certainly increase for politicians to enact anti-offshoring legislation.

As the standard of living improved in countries to which Western firms had exported jobs, however, that improvement in turn could diminish the savings companies gained. For example, India's daily wages were expected to rise by more than 150% by 2007,

and in 2004 Indian call-center companies were already facing high attrition rates and were being forced to raise wages and improve employee conditions. While these rising costs had made rival countries such as China (where English was mandatory in all schools) and West African nations such as Ghana more attractive offshoring prospects, American and European companies also were finding that the farther down the economic-development scale they went, the greater the potential for cultural conflicts, government corruption, and employee inefficiency.

Thus, in 2004 the practice of offshoring stood at a crossroads—it could become a primary method of doing business in the US and could radically reshape the American labor market, or it could simply be a limited cost-cutting trend that at some point would stop making economic sense. The years ahead would determine which scenario would prove true.

Christopher O'Leary is Assistant Managing Editor of Investment Dealers Digest.

Text Messaging: WAN2TLK?

by Alan Stewart

In 2005 some 45 billion text messages were expected to be sent by cellular-phone users in the United States. The sending of messages to and from mobile phones via Short Messaging Service (SMS) had been developed in the United Kingdom in the late 1980s, and the first text message was sent on 3 Dec 1992. An SMS commercial service was launched in the UK in 1995. Text messaging, also called "texting" or TXT, did not take off until 1998, however, when it became possible to send messages between the four main British cell phone networks. The number of messages sent in the UK grew from one billion in 1999 to an expected 30 billion in 2005, according to the Mobile Data Association. In the US, text messaging emerged later but expanded rapidly. Though only 30 million messages were sent in the US in June 2001, the number grew to 14 billion in all of 2003 and skyrocketed to 25 billion in 2004.

Because tapping text into a telephone keypad was cumbersome and the number of characters in a text message was limited, a form of shorthand evolved, especially among young people. This included such shortcuts as UR for "your" or "you're," IMHO for "in my humble opinion," BTW for "by the way," and CUL8R for "see you later," as well as the employment of "emoticons," or "smileys," to express emotions. While educators were banning cell phones from the classroom to discourage cheating, there was also concern that standards of English would drop as text abbreviations entered the mainstream.

In addition to basic communication and entertainment, texters developed a wide variety of more serious uses, including the announcement by activists of demonstrations on the streets of China, Ukraine, and Kuwait, as well as clandestine flirting in societies in which informal contact with the opposite sex was frowned on. In South Africa counselors were sending information on patients' use of antiretroviral drugs to combat HIV/AIDS via text message to researchers at Cape Town University. Indian politicians were being summoned by staff members via text message to vote on new laws or make up a quorum in parliament.

A new computer system was being rolled out in the UK that would enable text reminders of criminal court sessions to be sent to witnesses. In May 2005 AMBER Alert warnings of US child abductions began to be sent by text to those who opted to receive them, while Indonesia planned to use text messaging to spread early warnings of impending disasters. Individual politicians around the world—even the pope— were making use of text messaging. Shortly after his inauguration in April 2005, Pope Benedict XVI sent a "thought of the day" text message, a service that had been started by his predecessor, Pope John Paul II, in 2003.

With so many messages being sent, it came as no surprise that overactive texters around the world were developing a form of repetitive strain injury. The American Society of Hand Therapists warned in January 2005 that overuse of handheld devices could lead to carpal tunnel syndrome and tendinitis and advised users to switch hands frequently and take hourly breaks.

> " *Though only 30 million messages were sent in the US in June 2001, the number grew to 14 billion in 2003 and skyrocketed to 25 billion in 2004.* "

Alan Stewart is a freelance journalist and author of Gathering the Clans: Tracing Scottish Ancestry on the Internet *(2004).*

The Alarming State of the US Electricity Grid

by Christopher O'Leary

The massive power blackout of 14 Aug 2003, which affected the midwestern and northeastern United States and parts of Canada, highlighted the precarious condition of the US electricity grid, but a full year after the blackout, only recommendations but no new regulations or major changes to the grid's infrastructure had been made. The US electricity grid, which was described by former US energy secretary Bill Richardson after the 2003 blackout as a "third-world electrical grid," was widely considered to be overburdened and in serious need of new infrastructure. For many years it had suffered sporadic failures, ranging from major blackouts to the minor brownouts that had become commonplace during summer months, especially in the west. Furthermore, during the previous 10 years the demand for electric power in the United States had grown at the same time that the nature of delivering electrical power had radically changed as policies for the deregulation of the electric power industry were implemented. With deregulation, independent suppliers began delivering most of the electric power to utility companies and, for economic reasons, could contract to deliver the electric power from distant locations. Thus, a utility that owned a segment of the electricity grid often served more as a conduit for transmitting electric power between third parties than as a supplier of electric power to its own customers.

Much of the infrastructure for transmitting electric power in the United States was built in the 1960s and early '70s, and few significant improvements had been made since. Estimates of the cost to upgrade the grid lay between $50 billion and $100 billion. Individual utility companies had little incentive to make large-scale investments to improve their segments of the grid for several reasons, including a confusing mix of government regulations and deregulation policies for the utilities and the patchwork nature of the grid that resulted from its being owned by a host of competing regional utilities. Government regulations mandated a cap on the rate of return for many utilities and on the amount they could charge consumers, which thereby limited—in the utilities' view—their ability to recoup costs for any major structural improvements they might make. In addition, the organizations that oversaw the electricity grid, such as the utility industry's North American Electric Reliability Council (NERC) and the government's Federal Energy Regulatory Commission (FERC), had little power to enforce their own recommendations.

A joint US and Canadian task force established to examine the causes of the August 2003 blackout issued a report in April 2004 that called for such reforms as making reliability standards mandatory (thereby giving FERC greater power to enforce the standards), increasing the role of regional reliability councils, and improving the data collection and cooperation of various regional utilities. Despite the favorable attention these recommendations received, various energy bills concerning electric power languished in subcommittees of the House of Representatives. Lacking any federal legislation for energy-related reform in 2004, the US electricity grid was left in essentially the same condition it was in at the time of the 2003 blackout.

> ❝ *Much of the infrastructure for transmitting electric power in the United States was built in the 1960s and early '70s, and few significant improvements had been made since.* ❞

Christopher O'Leary is Assistant Managing Editor of Investment Dealers Digest.

The Legal Debate over Same-Sex Marriages

by Andrew Koppelman

Same-sex marriage came to the United States in 2004. The Massachusetts Supreme Court decided in November 2003 that the denial of marriage licenses to same-sex couples violated the state constitution and gave the state six months to comply with its order. The state consequently started issuing the licenses on 17 May 2004.

The question of whether couples of the same sex should be allowed to marry has roiled American politics since a 1993 Hawaii Supreme Court decision seemed to indicate that that state would shortly have to recognize such marriages. Americans, however, have consistently opposed same-sex marriage by wide margins. In 1996 Congress enacted the federal Defense of Marriage Act, which declared that no same-sex marriage would be recognized for federal purposes, such as filing joint tax returns, the award of Social Security survivors' benefits, or medical insurance for the families of federal employees. The act also indicated (in a restatement of existing law) that no state (or other US territory) was required to recognize marriages from another state when it had strong public policies to the contrary. To date, 43 states have enacted laws declaring that they will not recognize same-sex marriages from other states.

The Hawaii court decision was overruled by a state constitutional amendment in 1998, but other states moved toward recognition of same-sex couples. In 1999 the Vermont Supreme Court declared that same-sex couples were entitled under the state constitution to the same legal rights as married heterosexual couples, and the legislature shortly thereafter enacted a law creating the status of "civil unions," with all the rights of marriage but not the name. In 2003 California enacted a similar statute, calling the relationships "domestic partnerships." Officials in some smaller jurisdictions, notably San Francisco, joined the controversy in early 2004 by issuing marriage licenses in defiance of local prohibitions. All of these were soon held to be invalid.

The Massachusetts decision was not the first legal recognition of same-sex marriage. The Netherlands (in April 2001), Belgium (June 2003), and Canada (July 2003) had already recognized such unions. Like the earlier Hawaii court decision, however, the Massachusetts ruling provoked a negative response in the

US. The Massachusetts legislature narrowly passed a state constitutional amendment banning same-sex marriages and creating civil unions in their place, but the amendment would have to be considered again in 2005 and then be voted on by the electorate—so even if it succeeds, the ban cannot take effect before 2006. In the November 2004 elections, supporters of same-sex marriage gained seats in the Massachusetts legislature, and the new House speaker was a supporter of same-sex marriage who indicated that he might not even bring the bill up again. Pres. George W. Bush endorsed a constitutional amendment banning same-sex marriage throughout the US, but it failed in both houses of Congress. Another bill, to deny federal courts the right to hear same-sex marriage cases, passed the House of Representatives but got no farther.

A Two-Pronged Debate.

Part of the complexity of the issue is that the debate over same-sex marriage is really two different debates. The first is a normative debate about what relationships to value or even to sanctify. The second is a debate about administration—that is, which relationships ought to have legal consequences.

The normative debate, which contains religious dimensions for many people, concerns what relationships are intrinsically valuable. The key question is one about objective moral reality: are same-sex relationships as such morally equal to heterosexual relationships, or do heterosexual relationships partake of a good that homosexual relationships cannot possibly share?

On this issue, Americans are divided, with different groups adhering to two very different moral visions. According to the anti-same-sex-marriage vision, sex can be morally worthy precisely and only because of its place in procreation. Even the marriages of infertile heterosexual couples take their meaning from the fact that they form a union of the procreative kind. From this perspective the movement for same-sex marriage is a misguided attempt to deny fundamental moral distinctions. According to the other moral vision, sex is valuable, either in itself or because it draws people toward friendship of a singular degree and kind. This bringing together of persons has intrinsic worth, whether or not it leads to childbearing or child rearing. On this account, sexuality is linked to the flourishing of the next generation only to the extent that it is one of a number of factors that can bond adults together into stable familial units in which children are likely to thrive. From this perspective it is the devaluation of same-sex intimacy that is immoral, because it reflects arbitrary and irrational discrimination.

The administrative debate concerns what relationships between persons ought to be given legal recognition. Here the issue is more mundane: how should resources be allocated and unfair disruption of people's lives be prevented? Households, of whatever kind, and relationships of dependency exist, and members of those households have wants and needs if some unprovided-for contingency arises, such as the illness or death of one member. Financial issues such as inheritance rights and employer benefits for dependents of employees also come into play.

Are "Civil Unions" the Answer?

Because the moral and the administrative questions are distinct, many jurisdictions besides Vermont and California have opted to grant same-sex couples some or all of the rights of married couples without the honorific of "marriage." Denmark, Sweden, Norway, Finland, Iceland, and New Zealand have legalized partnerships that are nearly identical to marriage, while more limited rights and responsibilities are available to same-sex couples in France, Germany, Austria, Hungary, South Africa, and Portugal, as well as in parts of Australia, Spain, and Switzerland. The US constitutional amendment failed in part because it was so broadly worded that it seemed to some to prohibit civil unions as well as same-sex marriages.

Civil unions, however, are also controversial. Many conservatives believe that same-sex relationships are morally wrong and should not be given any recognition at all by the state, while gay rights advocates object that withholding the name of "marriage" implies an inferior status. Finally, gay men and lesbians are not unanimous in support of same-sex marriage. Some gay rights proponents contend that their movement should focus instead on AIDS prevention, HIV and health care, antigay violence, immigration, employment discrimination, and the military's exclusion of gay service members.

Many legal scholars have developed defensible arguments that same-sex marriage should be protected under the federal constitution, under either the guarantee of equal protection of the laws or the fundamental right to marry. It seems unlikely, however, that the US Supreme Court will adopt these arguments in the near future. In *Lawrence* v. *Texas*, a 2003 decision that struck down laws criminalizing homosexual sex, the Court made clear that it was not about to touch the marriage question. Even if the court is inclined to support same-sex marriage—which is far from clear—it appears to understand that any such decision would almost certainly be overruled by a constitutional amendment.

Future Prospects.

Same-sex marriage is likely to remain part of the American scene for a long time, but it is not likely to spread very widely any time soon. Massachusetts law cannot change until 2006, and even if the state court is overruled, it is not clear that marriages already in

> *The question of whether couples of the same sex should be allowed to marry has roiled American politics since a 1993 Hawaii Supreme Court decision seemed to indicate that that state would shortly have to recognize such marriages.*

existence will not continue. Other states are beginning to sort out what effect Massachusetts marriages will have elsewhere. It is unclear what will happen if the validity of a same-sex marriage comes into question when a Massachusetts resident is visiting—or moves to—another state, or when a same-sex spouse from another country moves to the US. Meanwhile, a poll by the National Annenberg Election Survey reflected a generational divide on the issue; most Americans oppose same-sex marriage, but most 18-to-29-year-olds do not. The long-term goals of the same-sex-marriage movement are perhaps the most powerful reason why opponents are so eager to cement their position into the law now—while conservative political forces still dominate.

Andrew Koppelman is Professor of Law and Political Science at Northwestern University, Chicago IL, and the author of The Gay Rights Question in Contemporary American Law.

Graphic Novels: *Not* Just Comic Books

by Michael Ray

Long a fixture on the fringes of American popular culture, the graphic novel has made notable forays into the literary mainstream in recent years. The year 2004 saw the film adaptation of Harvey Pekar's *American Splendor* nominated for an Academy Award, the final issues of both Dave Sim's 6,000-page magnum opus *Cerebus* and Jeff Smith's influential *Bone*, and the long-awaited debut of Alan Moore's *Lost Girls*. With collected volumes of *Sandman* by Neil Gaiman and Japanese *manga* titles becoming a common sight on public library shelves and film versions of landmark books such as *Sin City, Watchmen*, and *Batman: Year One* in production, the graphic novel had reached levels of respectability and marketability that transcended the disparaging label "comic book."

While the graphic novel format had a long tradition in Europe (albums collecting Belgian artist Hergé's Tintin stories appeared as early as the 1930s) and Japan (with *manga* publications aimed at every age and interest), it struggled to take hold in the United States. One reason for this was the creation of the Comics Code Authority in 1954. The Authority, created by the comics industry to police itself, had a chilling effect on creativity. Publishers dared run only the tamest of stories; sales plummeted; and a once-thriving medium was soon seen as disposable entertainment for children. By the late 1980s, however, most major publishers had dropped the code's certification stamp from their books, and, not coincidentally, a flood of creativity had followed.

The other difficulty faced by the medium is the necessarily vague answer to the question "What is a graphic novel?" Most loosely defined, it is an illustrated story that stands alone or as part of a limited series (a distinction that sets it apart from monthly comic books or serials). The book frequently cited as the first modern graphic novel, Will Eisner's *A Contract with God* (1978), is actually a collection of four semiautobiographical novellas. Art Spiegelman's *Maus* (1986) is perhaps the most critically acclaimed graphic novel, and yet it is not a novel at all but a work of nonfiction that uses animal characters to depict the horrors of the Holocaust. The conflict in the Balkans produced notable works that could most accurately be called illustrated journalism. Joe Kubert's *Fax from Sarajevo* (1996) and Joe Sacco's *Safe Area Gorazde* (2000) stretched the boundaries of the medium by offering uniquely personal accounts of life in a modern war zone. Eisner has suggested the term *sequential art* to more accurately describe this evolving genre, but it appears that, however inaccurate it may be, the current label will stick.

With the advent of direct marketing to bookstores and specialty shops (thus bypassing the Comics Code and the newsstand comics vendors), publishers are far more open to the graphic novel format than they were in the past. The continued interest in groundbreaking titles such as Moore's *Watchmen* (1987), Frank Miller's *Batman: The Dark Knight Returns* (1986), and Gaiman's *Black Orchid* (1988) has opened the door for the next generation of graphic novelists. Craig Thompson's *Good-bye, Chunky Rice* (1999), Chris Ware's *Jimmy Corrigan: The Smartest Kid on Earth* (2000), and Marjane Satrapi's *Persepolis* (2003) eschew the superheroic to focus on human stories of friendship, hope, and despair. Critical acclaim has led to increased sales and a more prominent place in the retail landscape. Although graphic novels still account for less than one percent of the book trade in the United States, they represent one of the fastest-growing markets, with over $120 million in sales in 2003.

Michael Ray is a freelance writer and copy editor at Encyclopædia Britannica.

Chronology, July 2004—June 2005

A day-by-day listing of important and interesting events, adapted from Britannica Book of the Year. See also Disasters.

July 2004

1 Jul The presidency of the European Union rotates from Ireland's prime minister, Bertie Ahern, to the prime minister of The Netherlands, Jan Peter Balkenende.

▶ The International Ship and Port Facility Security Code, intended to help safeguard the world's ports from terrorism, comes into force; two of the busiest ports, in Hong Kong and Singapore, report no major delays or difficulties.

▶ Hundreds of thousands of people demonstrate in Hong Kong, demanding greater democracy from the government of China.

▶ Sir Peter Davis resigns as chairman of J Sainsbury, the oldest supermarket chain in Great Britain, as a result of a dispute over a large bonus granted to him in spite of the poor financial performance of the company.

▶ The Motion Picture Association of America chooses Dan Glickman, a former secretary of Agriculture and a former representative in Congress, to replace Jack Valenti as president of the organization.

▶ To the astonishment of prognosticators, the Colombian club Once Caldas defeats the defending champions Boca Juniors of Argentina to win the South American association football (soccer) Libertadores Cup.

2 Jul Outbreaks of violence leave 22 people dead in several incidents in Kashmir.

▶ A rocket attack is launched against two hotels in Baghdad that housed foreign workers and journalists; three Iraqi security guards are injured.

▶ After the resignation of Vladimir Spidla as prime minister of the Czech Republic in the wake of a no-confidence vote, Pres. Vaclav Klaus names Stanislav Gross to the position.

▶ The Cassini spacecraft returns its first close-up (from about 322,000 km [200,000 mi] away) pictures of Saturn's giant moon Titan; analysis of the photos throws into doubt many assumptions about the nature of the satellite.

3 Jul Pres. Omar Hassan Ahmad al-Bashir of The Sudan pledges to UN Secretary-General Kofi Annan that his government will take steps to disarm the Arab Janjaweed militia and any other militias that have been attacking black Africans in the Darfur region and will send government troops to protect the displaced.

▶ Russian tennis player Mariya Sharapova defeats defending champion Serena Williams to take the All-England (Wimbledon) women's tennis championship; the following day Roger Federer of Switzerland wins the men's title for the second consecutive year when he defeats American Andy Roddick.

4 Jul The cornerstone of Freedom Tower is ceremonially laid at the site of the former World Trade Center in New York City; the tower is expected to be completed in 2008.

▶ The team from Greece defeats the heavily favored team from Portugal to win the UEFA association football (soccer) European Championship in Lisbon.

▶ American golfer Meg Mallon wins the US Women's Open golf tournament in South Hadley MA; Stephen Ames defeats Steve Lowery by two strokes to win the Western Open golf tournament in Lemont IL; and in Straffan, Ireland, Retief Goosen wins the European Open golf tournament two weeks after winning the US Open.

5 Jul Indonesia's first-ever direct presidential election results in no candidate's receiving a majority of votes; the top two vote getters, Susilo Bambang Yudhoyono and Pres. Megawati Sukarnoputri, will contest a runoff election.

▶ José Manuel Durão Barroso resigns as prime minister of Portugal, in preparation for assuming the presidency of the European Commission.

6 Jul Iraqi Prime Minister Awad Allawi signs a law giving him the power to declare emergency martial law anywhere in the country.

▶ During the African Union summit in Addis Ababa, Ethiopia, Pres. Teodoro Obiang Nguema Mbasogo of Equatorial Guinea and Pres. Omar Bongo of Gabon agree to conduct joint explorations for oil in Corisco Bay while UN mediators decide on the border dispute in the bay.

▶ The archdiocese of Portland OR files for bankruptcy protection in the face of growing claims from victims of sexual abuse at the hands of priests; it is the first Roman Catholic diocese in the US to take this step.

▶ Japan's defense agency announces plans to publish its annual defense White Paper in the form of a *manga*, or comic book, in order to increase public understanding.

7 Jul The Parliament of the World's Religions meets for the fourth time since 1893, in Barcelona, Spain; organizers expect thousands of representatives of the world's major religions as well as less well-recognized belief systems and hope to address the issues of refugees, water shortages, religious violence, and rising debt

▶ Charges relating to the collapse of the energy company Enron Corp. are brought against Kenneth Lay, its former chairman and CEO.

▶ The painting *Young Woman Seated at the Virginals*, believed for decades to be a fake but recently discovered to be a genuine painting by Dutch master Johannes Vermeer, is sold at auction by Sotheby's for $30 million.

8 Jul Heinz Fischer becomes president of Austria two days after the death of his predecessor, Thomas Klestil.

9 Jul It is reported that the number of military deaths in the US-led coalition in Iraq since the invasion began in March 2003 has passed 1,000.

▶ The International Court of Justice rules that most of the barrier that Israel is building to wall itself off from the West Bank violates international law because it is built on Palestinian land; it also rules that Palestinians on whose land the wall is built must be compensated.

▶ Portuguese Pres. Jorge Sampaio announces that he will appoint Pedro Santana Lopes, mayor of Lisbon, prime minister.

▸ In a US federal court the dominant diamond company De Beers agrees to plead guilty to charges of price fixing; the admission is expected to allow De Beers to reenter the US market, from which it had departed almost 50 years ago.

▸ In a general cabinet shake-up, Atef Ebeid resigns as prime minister of Egypt, and Pres. Hosni Mubarak chooses Ahmed Nazif to replace him.

▸ Paul Klebnikov, the editor in chief of *Forbes Russia*, a Russian version of the American business magazine, and an investigative journalist who had written extensively on the business climate in Russia, is shot and killed outside the magazine's offices.

10 Jul The World Health Organization's first progress report on the so-called 3 by 5 program, intended to deliver antiretroviral treatment to 3 million people infected with HIV by the end of 2005, estimates that 440,000 worldwide are receiving treatment, about 60,000 behind target, though the organization believes it can achieve its overall goal.

11 Jul Boris Tadic, a supporter of democratic change, takes office as the first president in two years of the republic of Serbia in Serbia and Montenegro.

▸ The 15th International AIDS Conference opens in Bangkok, with speeches by Thai Prime Minister Thaksin Shinawatra and UN Secretary-General Kofi Annan.

12 Jul Minutes before the trial is to start, the major securities company Morgan Stanley agrees to settle a sex-discrimination suit for $54 million.

▸ In Serbia and Montenegro, the legislature in Montenegro adopts a flag, national anthem, and statehood day; the flag, the same one used during Montenegro's independence (1878–1918) is ceremonially raised three days later.

▸ In the Ardoyne section of Belfast, Northern Ireland, a Protestant march to commemorate the Battle of the Boyne (1690) erupts in stone-throwing violence between Protestants and Roman Catholics, marring what had been a remarkably peaceful marching season in Northern Ireland.

13 Jul A bomb explodes as the motorcade of Sergey Abramov, acting president of the separatist Russian republic of Chechnya, passes in Grozny; Abramov, who is unhurt, became acting president after the previous president was killed in a terrorist attack.

▸ Rustam Kasimjanov of Uzbekistan wins two tie-breaking matches against Michael Adams of England to win the FIDE world chess championship in Tripoli, Libya; almost all the world's top players boycotted or were barred from the tournament, however.

14 Jul In response to threats by Iraqi insurgents that they will behead a Filipino hostage unless Philippine troops are withdrawn from Iraq earlier than planned, the Philippines begins pulling out its 51 troops.

▸ A suicide car bombing at the gates of the American-occupied zone in Baghdad kills at least 10 people, while elsewhere the governor of the province of Nineveh is assassinated.

▸ Afghani Pres. Hamid Karzai issues a decree ordering severe punishments for those who fail to cooperate with the UN disarmament program or retain allegiance to private militias rather than Afghanistan's official armed forces.

▸ Swedish director Ingmar Bergman announces his retirement from the theater; his last production, for the Royal Dramatic Theatre in Stockholm, was in 2002.

15 Jul Hun Sen is formally approved as Cambodia's prime minister by the National Assembly almost a year after legislative elections that gave no party a majority.

▸ Officials of the World Food Programme say that the organization has an agreement with Libya that will allow it to transport food through Libya to Sudanese refugees in Chad and in the Darfur area.

▸ Collapsed and disgraced energy giant Enron wins approval to emerge from bankruptcy protection as a much smaller collection of assets to be known as Primsa Energy International.

16 Jul Amid increasing lawlessness in the Gaza Strip, Palestinian militants briefly kidnap and hold four French aid workers and two Palestinian security officials, including the chief of police; the following day the Palestinian National Security Council declares a state of emergency in Gaza.

▸ In the wake of the disappearance of two computer storage devices containing classified information as well as several other security and safety lapses, all work at the Los Alamos NM nuclear research facility is halted, pending a thorough security review.

▸ Chess great Bobby Fischer is arrested in Tokyo for trying to travel on an expired passport; he has been in exile from the US since his indictment on charges of violating sanctions against Yugoslavia for playing a chess match there in 1992.

▸ Lifestyle entrepreneur Martha Stewart is sentenced to five months in prison and five months of house arrest, the minimum possible; she remains free pending an appeal of her conviction.

▸ In downtown Chicago, the long-awaited Millennium Park, featuring gardens, theaters, and public sculpture, has its grand opening.

17 Jul Palestinian Prime Minister Ahmad Qurei submits his resignation, but Palestinian leader Yasir Arafat refuses to accept it.

18 Jul In a referendum in Bolivia, voters approve Pres. Carlos Mesa Gisbert's plan for development of the country's hydrocarbon reserves, which includes leaving them in the hands of foreign energy companies.

▸ Iraqi Prime Minister Ayad Allawi approves a US air strike against insurgents in Fallujah and reopens *Al-Hawza*, the newspaper affiliated with rebel cleric Moktada al-Sadr that US administrators shut down in March.

▸ Three American men—Jack Idema, Brent Bennett, and Edward Caraballo—appear in court on charges of running a private jail and acting as vigilantes in Afghanistan; the men claim to be working for the US and Afghani governments, but officials of both deny it.

▸ The relatively unknown American golfer Todd Hamilton wins the British Open golf tournament in Troon, Scotland, defeating Ernie Els of South Africa in a four-hole playoff.

▸ In the Nagoya Basho in Japan, Asashoryu defeats Kaio to win his fourth consecutive Emperor's Cup in sumo.

▸ In Taipei, Taiwan, Alex Pagulayan of Canada wins the World Pool-Billiard Association world nine-ball championships.

19 Jul Russian Pres. Vladimir Putin dismisses Gen. Anatoly Kvashnin, chief of the general staff of armed services, and three top officials in charge of security in the Caucasus.

▸ Officials of the Aredor mining company in Guinea confirm that a good-quality 182-carat diamond, four times the size of the Hope diamond, has been found.

▶ India's Supreme Court rules that the $325 million compensation for the catastrophic gas leak at a Union Carbide plant in Bhopal in 1984 that killed at least 5,000 people should be paid directly to the victims rather than continue being held by the government.

20 Jul The UN General Assembly passes a resolution calling on Israel to obey the World Court ruling requiring it to remove the barrier being built on the West Bank.

▶ Greece agrees to allow US Special Forces soldiers to carry arms under NATO auspices at the Olympic Games in Athens in August.

21 Jul The cosmologist Stephen Hawking concedes at a conference in Dublin that he lost a bet he made with the physicist John Preskill in 1997 regarding his assertion that information about matter that disappears into a black hole is destroyed when the black hole evaporates, which violates the laws of quantum physics; Hawking says he has since concluded that information can escape from a black hole.

QUOTE OF THE MONTH

❝ *I'm sorry to disappoint science fiction fans, but if information is preserved, there is no possibility of using black holes to travel to other universes.* ❞

—cosmologist Stephen Hawking, addressing the 17th International Conference of General Relativity and Gravitation in Dublin, 21 July

---

▶ A lesbian couple who married in Ontario on 18 Jun 2003 files for divorce; Canada's Divorce Act, however, does not take into account same-sex marriages, which are legal in several provinces.

22 Jul After a 19-month investigation, the congressional 9/11 Commission, headed by Thomas Kean, releases its final report; it finds that the terrorist attacks on 11 Sep 2001 "should not have come as a surprise" and that a thorough overhaul of US intelligence services should be undertaken.

▶ In response to the kidnapping in Iraq of three Kenyans, the government of Kenya orders all of its nationals in Iraq to leave the country.

▶ A court in Germany acquits Deutsche Bank CEO Josef Ackermann and five other defendants of betraying stockholders by granting excessive bonuses to the management of the communications conglomerate Mannesmann; the court does not look kindly on the bonuses, however.

▶ A merger is announced between the US beer company Adolph Coors Co. and Canada's largest brewer, Molson.

23 Jul Celebrations including dancers, high divers, and fireworks mark the reopening of the Stari Most, the 16th-century bridge at Mostar, Bosnia and Herzegovina; rebuilding of the bridge, which had been blown up in 1993 during the civil war, made use of much the same materials and methods used by its original Ottoman Turkish builders.

24 Jul A group that identifies itself as the European branch of al-Qaeda says that both Italy and Aus-

tralia can expect to be attacked if they do not end their military presence in Iraq.

▶ It is revealed that Mohammad Reza Aghdam Ahmadi has been acquitted of the killing in 2003 of Canadian photojournalist Zahra Kazemi; four days later the Iranian judiciary declares that the acquittal means the death must have been the result of an accident.

25 Jul Spain's Banco Santander Central Hispano reaches an agreement to buy Great Britain's Abbey National Bank; the combined entity will be the eighth biggest bank in the world.

▶ American Lance Armstrong becomes the first person to win the Tour de France six times as he coasts to his sixth consecutive victory in the bicycle race 6 min 19 sec ahead of German Andreas Klöden.

▶ In an exciting game, Brazil defeats Argentina in a penalty shoot-out in Lima, Peru, to win the Copa América in association football (soccer) for the 7th time.

▶ The National Baseball Hall of Fame in Cooperstown NY inducts pitcher Dennis Eckersley and hitter Paul Molitor; broadcaster Lon Simmons and sportswriter Murray Chass are honored for their contributions to baseball.

26 Jul In Iraq a kidnapped Egyptian diplomat is freed, two Jordanian truck drivers are kidnapped, an official of the Ministry of the Interior and two of his bodyguards are killed, two Iraqi cleaning women with British employers are killed, and three Iraqis are killed by a car bomb outside an American base.

▶ AltaVista, Lycos, Yahoo!, and Google search engines are disrupted by the latest version of the MyDoom computer worm, which queries search engines to identify valid e-mail addresses.

27 Jul Spain announces that a joint Spanish-Moroccan peacekeeping mission will be sent to Haiti; it is the first ever joint mission between the two countries, which have frequently been at odds.

▶ In the Chilean embassy in San José, Costa Rica, a Costa Rican guard takes 10 people hostage; after hours of negotiation, police storm the embassy and find that the hostage taker has killed four people, including himself.

▶ Four French citizens who have been held for more than two years at the US military base in Guantánamo Bay, Cuba, are released to France, which detains them under antiterrorism laws.

28 Jul A suicide bombing in a public square near a police station kills at least 70 people in Ba'qubah, Iraq, while fighting in south-central Iraq between insurgents and Iraqi and foreign forces leave some 42 people dead.

▶ The operational director of Doctors Without Borders announces that it is withdrawing from Afghanistan, where it has provided assistance for 24 years, because of the failure of the government to prosecute those who killed five of the organization's staffers in June, and because of fears for the safety of its remaining workers.

▶ China opens its first Arctic research station, the Yellow River Station, on Spitsbergen in Norway.

29 Jul Democratic Party delegates, meeting at their national convention in Boston, nominate John Kerry, senator from Massachusetts, and John Edwards, senator from North Carolina, as the party's candidates for president and vice president of the US.

30 Jul The UN Security Council passes a resolution demanding that The Sudan show progress in disarming and bringing to justice Arab militias in the Darfur region with 30 days or face punitive measures.

▸ During a World Trade Organization meeting in Geneva that is part of the Doha Round, the US and other wealthy nations agree to cut some of their farm subsidies by 20%.

31 Jul The government of Iran confirms that it has resumed building centrifuges for the purpose of enriching uranium in view of the failure of France, Germany, and the UK to resolve questions about Iranian compliance with the International Atomic Energy Agency.

August 2004

1 Aug The World Trade Organization agrees that its new framework for global trade rules will include the elimination of farm subsidies in rich countries, including the US

▸ In Iraq, bombs explode near four Christian churches in Baghdad and one in Mosul, all during Sunday services; at least 12 people are killed.

▸ US government officials announce that several financial institutions in and around New York City and Washington DC have been found to be in imminent danger of terrorist attack; it later emerges that the information had originally been received several years previously.

▸ The Warsaw Rising Museum, commemorating the 63-day rebellion against the Nazis in which 200,000 died in summer 1944, opens in Warsaw.

▸ Karen Stupples of England defeats Rachel Teske of Australia to win the British Women's Open golf tournament.

2 Aug The government of Colombia offers to create a safe haven for two rival right-wing paramilitary groups if they declare a cease-fire and begin to disarm.

3 Aug Voters in Missouri approve an amendment to the state constitution that permits only a marriage between a man and a woman to be legally recognized.

▸ NASA launches the space probe *Messenger*, which is scheduled to enter orbit around Mercury in 2011 and spend a year collecting data.

▸ US Pres. George W. Bush signs a free trade agreement with Australia.

4 Aug The African Union agrees to expand its peacekeeping mission in the Darfur region of The Sudan, while tens of thousands of people in Khartoum demonstrate against the United Nations, which has threatened to take action if the ethnic cleansing does not stop.

▸ Swarms of locusts, which have been devastating large areas of North Africa and West Africa this summer, inundate Nouakchott, the capital of Mauritania.

▸ Over the objections of Spain, the inhabitants of Gibraltar celebrate 300 years of British ownership of the peninsula.

5 Aug Israel pulls back its troops in northern Gaza and says that it will open the border checkpoint between Gaza and Egypt, where some 2,000 Palestinians have been stranded since Israel closed the crossing in mid-July.

▸ The World Trade Organization issues a preliminary ruling that subsidies paid by the European Union to assist its sugar producers violate trade rules.

▸ Peruvian Pres. Alejandro Toledo formally inaugurates a 731-km (462-mi) gas pipeline that links the gas field at Camisea to Lima; the gas it carries is intended for industrial and residential use within Peru.

6 Aug After two days of battle in Najaf, Iraq, against forces loyal to rebel cleric Moktada al-Sadr, US military spokesmen report that some 300 Iraqis have been killed.

▸ At a ceremony in the village of Igaliku in Greenland, the US signs an agreement with Denmark and the home rule government of Greenland to upgrade the early warning radar system at the base at Thule, near the North Pole; the US intends Thule to be part of its missile shield plan.

7 Aug Windsong's Legacy, driven by Trond Smedshammer, wins the Hambletonian, the first contest in harness racing's Trotting Triple Crown.

▸ Violent anti-Japanese protests erupt outside Worker's Stadium in Beijing after Japan defeats China 3–1 there to win the Asian Cup title in association football (soccer).

▸ Iraqi Prime Minister Ayad Allawi orders the TV station al-Jazeera to close its Baghdad bureau for at least a month, saying the network's coverage of kidnappings and executions has encouraged the terrorists.

8 Aug A magistrate in Iraq orders the arrest of former American protégé Ahmad Chalabi on charges of counterfeiting.

▸ The Pro Football Hall of Fame in Canton OH inducts offensive tackle Bob Brown, defensive end Carl Eller, quarterback John Elway, and running back Barry Sanders.

9 Aug Steam leaks from a turbine after a pipe burst at the Mihama nuclear power plant in Fukui prefecture, Japan, killing four people; officials say that no radiation escaped and there is no danger to the surrounding area.

▸ The power-sharing cabinet of Côte d'Ivoire meets for the first time since opposition ministers walked out in late March, but the country remains divided in half by civil strife.

▸ The bankrupt Italian dairy conglomerate Parmalat files suit against the Italian branch of Deutsche Bank, seeking to recover money it paid back to the bank on credit lines.

▸ The Velebit Speleological Society announces that what is believed to be the world's deepest vertical drop has been found in a cave in the Velebit mountain range in Croatia; the drop has been measured at 516 m (1,693 ft).

10 Aug The US Department of Homeland Security announces plans to give border patrol agents power to deport illegal aliens arriving over the borders with Mexico and Canada without judicial oversight.

▸ Election officials in Afghanistan approve a total of 18 candidates to contest the presidential election scheduled for 9 October.

▸ Chad and Niger ask for international aid in fighting the locust infestation, which threatens the area with food shortages.

11 Aug South Korean Prime Minister Lee Hai Chan announces that the government has chosen the Yeongi-Kunju region of South Ch'ungch'ong province as the location for the new administrative capital of the country; construction is planned to begin in 2007, with completion set for 2030.

▶ Residents of Pitcairn Island, a British dependency in the Pacific Ocean, are ordered to surrender their firearms by 7 September; authorities fear that the upcoming trial of seven men on sex-crime charges could lead to violence.

▶ The head of Brazil's anti-AIDS program announces that the government plans to distribute three billion free condoms annually in order to decrease the transmission of HIV/AIDS.

12 Aug A tentative accord is reached for Mitsubishi Tokyo Financial Group, the second biggest bank in Japan, to acquire UFJ Holdings; the combined company would be the largest bank in the world.

▶ Lee Hsien Loong is sworn in as prime minister of Singapore.

▶ Gov. James E. McGreevey of New Jersey announces that he is a practicing homosexual and that he will resign; his administration has been beset by several colorful scandals, including accusations that he had hired his paramour for a state job.

▶ The Vatican shuts down the Roman Catholic seminary of Sankt Pölten, Austria; in recent months the seminary, founded in 1455, had been revealed to have become a hotbed of forbidden sexual activity.

▶ California's Supreme Court rules that the 4,000 same-sex marriages that took place in San Francisco in February and March are legally invalid.

▶ Two bombs explode in Spain, one in downtown Santander and one at a beach in Gijón; coupled with two other bombs four days previous, this marks the return to violence by the Basque separatist group ETA for the first time since the terrorist train bombing in Madrid on 11 March.

▶ James H. Billington, the US Librarian of Congress, announces the appointment of Ted Kooser of Nebraska as poet laureate, replacing Louise Glück.

13 Aug Opening ceremonies for the Olympic Games thrill 75,000 spectators in Athens, Greece.

▶ A refugee camp in Burundi housing ethnic Tutsi who fled from the Democratic Republic of the Congo is attacked by a Burundian Hutu militia, who kill nearly 200 of the refugees.

▶ Hurricane Charley, with 233-km/hr (145-mph) winds, makes landfall in western Florida; by the time it has left the state the next day 22 people have died, and the hardest hit towns, Punta Gorda and Port Charlotte, have been devastated.

▶ A powerful typhoon makes landfall in China, leaving 115 people dead and a trail of destruction in its wake.

14 Aug The Iraqi interim government declares that truce talks with forces loyal to rebel cleric Moktada al-Sadr have failed.

▶ Officials in Afghanistan say the fighting has broken out in Herat province as forces have invaded in an attempt to dislodge the governor and warlord Ismail Khan; 21 people have died in the fighting.

▶ At a ceremony in Namibia, a German government official for the first time offers a formal apology for the massacre of some 65,000 Herero in response to a Herero rebellion against German rule in 1904 and describes the massacre as genocide.

▶ At the Olympic Games in Athens, American swimmer Michael Phelps sets a new world record in the 400-meter individual medley with a time of 4 min 8.26 sec; he held the previous record as well.

15 Aug The referendum to recall Pres. Hugo Chávez

in Venezuela fails; Chavez wins the right to remain in office by a wide margin in a vote that international observers certify as free and fair.

▶ In rowing heats in rough waters at the Olympic Games in Athens, the US men's eights break the 2,000-meter race record with a time of 5 min 19.85 sec, and the women's eights do the same, in 5 min 56.55 sec.

▶ At the Whistling Straits golf course in Haven WI, Vijay Singh defeats Justin Leonard and Chris Di-Marco in a three-hole playoff to win his second Professional Golfers' Association of America Championship.

▶ Jane Park, age 17, wins the US Women's Amateur Golf Championship in Erie PA.

▶ With his win at the Hungarian Grand Prix Formula 1 auto race, Michael Schumacher has won a record seven consecutive races as well as a record 12 of the 13 races held so far this season.

16 Aug US Pres. George W. Bush announces plans to realign the deployment of US troops around the world, with some 70,000 troops currently stationed in Europe and Asia expected to be moved and about half the installations in Europe expected to be closed or shrunk.

▶ Leonel Fernández is sworn in as president of the Dominican Republic for the second time; he previously served as president in 1996–2000.

▶ Prince Hans-Adam II, ruler of Liechtenstein transfers day-to-day responsibility to his son, Prince Alois, though Prince Hans-Adam does not intend to abdicate.

▶ Kalkot Mataskelekele is elected president of Vanuatu.

▶ NASA scientists report that the Cassini spacecraft has discovered two previously unseen small moons orbiting Saturn, bringing the number of Saturn's known moons to 33.

17 Aug Delegates from the national conference in Baghdad are turned away from Najaf by Moktada al-Sadr; they had come to ask him to join the political process.

▶ Serbia's legislature replaces its coat of arms and national anthem, which were those of Yugoslavia, with the ones it had used before 1918, when it was an independent kingdom.

18 Aug In Baghdad, Iraq's national conference succeeds in choosing an interim national congress.

▶ Maoist rebels in Nepal declare a blockade on all roads leading to Kathmandu; though no roadblocks are set up, the blockade is universally observed because of fear of reprisal.

▶ After a men's gymnastics event featuring an unusually large number of mistakes, American gymnast Paul Hamm surprisingly wins the men's all-around competition, becoming the first US competitor to take the Olympic gold medal in this event.

▶ At the Olympics, the US women's relay swim team sets a new record in the 4 x 200-m freestyle event of 7 min 53.42 sec; the old record, 7 min 55.80 sec, was set by East Germany in 1987.

19 Aug After an unexpectedly low-priced IPO, shares of Google skyrocket on the first day of trading, making it the third richest IPO in Nasdaq history.

20 Aug Mongolia's Great Hural (legislature) elects Tsakhiagiyn Elbegdorj prime minister.

▶ A Chinese health official reports to a World Health Organization conference in Beijing that the strain of avian influenza that killed 23 people in Asia has been found in pigs at several farms; pigs are believed to be the source of influenza pandemics such as the Spanish flu in 1918–19.

21 Aug Several bombs explode at a rally for the opposition Awami League Party in Dhaka, Bangladesh; at least 19 people are killed, and the following day violence spreads to other cities in Bangladesh.

▶ At the Olympics, Yuliya Nesterenko of Belarus wins the women's 100-meter gold medal in track, becoming the first woman to defeat Americans in the event since before 1980.

▶ The American men's swim team sets a new world record in the 4 x 100-meter medley relay of 3 min 30.68 sec, winning the Olympic gold medal.

22 Aug The Transitional Federal Assembly, Somalia's new provisional legislature, is sworn in in Nairobi, Kenya, where peace negotiations among the warring factions in Somalia have been taking place.

▶ Thieves steal *The Scream* and *Madonna,* Edvard Munch's best-known paintings, from the wall of the Munch Museum in Oslo in front of startled patrons.

▶ The 45th Edward MacDowell Medal for outstanding contribution to the arts is awarded to video artist Nam June Paik at the MacDowell Colony in Peterborough NH.

23 Aug Israel announces plans to expand its settlements in the Jerusalem area; earlier it had issued tenders for increased housing in settlements in the West Bank.

▶ Controversial new rules governing who is eligible for overtime pay go into effect in the US.

▶ The National Underground Railroad Freedom Center, a museum and learning center, is ceremonially opened in Cincinnati.

24 Aug Within three minutes, two passenger planes that departed the same airfield in Moscow are blown up and crash, killing 90 people; the incidents are later discovered to have been caused by Chechen terrorists.

▶ Police in Nairobi, Kenya, turn back Masai demonstrators attempting to march to the British High Commission to protest white ownership of land that was taken from the Masai during the colonial era.

25 Aug Meeting in Tripoli, Libya, Italian Prime Minister Silvio Berlusconi and Libyan leader Muammar al-Qaddafi agree on measures to stop the flow of illegal immigrants from Africa through Libya.

▶ The wealthy businessman Ferenc Gyurcsany is named to replace Peter Medgyessy as prime minister of Hungary.

▶ Interim Prime Minister Chaudhary Shujaat Hussein of Pakistan resigns to make place for Shaukat Aziz, who is approved two days later.

▶ Sir Mark Thatcher, the son of former British prime minister Margaret Thatcher, is arrested in South Africa on suspicion of providing financial support for a plot to overthrow the government of Equatorial Guinea in March.

26 Aug Hours after returning to Iraq after medical treatments abroad, Grand Ayatollah Ali al-Sistani proposes an agreement that is accepted by the interim Iraqi government and rebel cleric Moktada al-Sadr, to end the fighting in Najaf.

▶ The Chiron Corp., a California-based company that manufactures influenza vaccines in a plant in Liverpool, England, and supplies about half of the vaccine used in the US, announces that it has

detected contamination in its new supply; it expects the problem will delay delivery of vaccine by about a month, until mid-October.

27 Aug It is reported that Enzo Baldoni, an Italian journalist working for *Diario della Settimana* who was kidnapped in Iraq while traveling to Najaf, has been beheaded by his captors.

▶ An icon known as *Our Lady of Kazan,* first seen in the town of Kazan in what is now the autonomous Russian republic of Tatarstan, is returned to Aleksey II, patriarch of the Russian Orthodox Church; the icon disappeared from Russia about 1917 and had hung in the private chapel of the Roman Catholic pope since the 1970s.

28 Aug The day after a large anti-American demonstration against the proposed visit, US Secretary of State Colin Powell cancels plans to attend the closing ceremonies of the Olympic Games in Athens.

29 Aug A car bomb explodes at the offices of an American contractor in Kabul, Afghanistan, that provides security guards and training for the Afghani police force; at least seven people are killed.

▶ The XXVIII Olympiad comes to a close in Athens, marred by a strange incident where a man from the crowd pushes the frontrunner in the men's marathon, Vanderlei de Lima of Brazil, off the course; the eventual winner is Meb Keflesighi of the US.

QUOTE OF THE MONTH

❝ These have been unforgettable dream Games. These Games were held in peace and brotherhood. These were the Games where it became increasingly difficult to cheat and where clean athletes were better protected. ❞

— IOC Pres. Jacques Rogge,
at the closing ceremonies of the XXVIII
Olympiad in Athens, 29 August

▶ The Pabao Little League team from Willemstad, Curaçao, Netherlands Antilles, becomes the first team from the Caribbean to win the Little League World Championship when it defeats the Conejo Valley Little League team from Thousand Oaks CA 5–2.

30 Aug The UN-imposed deadline for The Sudan to begin credibly disarming the Janjaweed in the Darfur region passes without significant progress.

31 Aug A suicide bomber blows herself up outside a subway station in Moscow, killing at least 9 people and injuring 50; like last week's twin airplane attacks, this is claimed by a Chechen group.

▶ Fighting erupts when some 2,000 police officers attempt to evict some 3,000 armed squatters occupying a ranch near Champerico, Guatemala; at least seven people are killed.

▶ The UN Convention on the International Trade in Endangered Species of Wild Fauna and Flora bans exports of caviar from countries bordering the Caspian Sea, as the countries have not complied with a 2001 agreement to protect sturgeon stocks.

▶ Cambodia joins the World Trade Organization.

September 2004

1 Sep At the Republican National Convention in New York City, US Pres. George W. Bush and Vice Pres. Richard Cheney are nominated as the party's candidates in the upcoming presidential election.

▶ On the first day of school at Middle School No. 1, serving students from age 6 to 16 in Beslan, North Ossetia, Russia, some 30 terrorists invade the school and take all 1,200 people inside hostage, rigging the building with explosives.

▶ Millions of Sikhs, including Prime Minister Manmohan Singh, gather in their holy city of Amritsar in northern India to celebrate the 400th anniversary of their scripture, the Adi Granth, which is believed to have been placed in the Golden Temple on this date in 1604 by the fifth Guru, Arjun, who compiled the book.

▶ Martin Torrijos is sworn in as president of Panama.

▶ Microsoft introduces MSN Music, its first entry into the digital music download market that is dominated by Apple's iTunes.

2 Sep On the first day of the new school year in France, the controversial ban on the wearing of religious symbols in school, including headscarves by Muslim girls, goes into effect, although two French reporters have been kidnapped in Iraq and their captors threaten to behead them if the ban is not repealed.

▶ Malaysia's High Court overturns the conviction of former deputy prime minister Anwar Ibrahim on sodomy charges and he is released.

▶ The judges in the UN war crimes tribunal trying former Yugoslav president Slobodan Milosevic revoke his right to conduct his own defense, imposing on him the two British lawyers who had been his assigned advisers heretofore.

3 Sep In Middle School No. 1 in Beslan, North Ossetia, Russia, two explosions lead to a gun battle that ends the hostage siege; at least 330 people, mostly students, teachers, and parents, are killed.

> ### QUOTE OF THE MONTH
>
> " *We are dealing with the direct intervention of international terror against Russia, with total and full-scale war. In these conditions, we simply cannot, we should not, live as carelessly as before.*
>
> —Russian Pres. Vladimir Putin, "
> addressing the country after viewing the carnage at Middle School No. 1 in Beslan, North Ossetia, 4 September

▶ Lebanon's parliament passes an amendment to the constitution extending the term of the president by three years, a move dictated by Syria but opposed by all segments of society in Lebanon.

4 Sep In the worst of several attacks in Iraq, a car bomb kills at least 17 people, 14 of them policemen, outside a police academy in Kirkuk.

▶ The huge and slow-moving Hurricane Frances makes landfall in Florida, working its way across the state over the next two days.

5 Sep Two earthquakes with magnitudes of 6.9 and 7.3 shake sparsely populated areas of western Japan; the following day a strong typhoon hits Japan.

▶ The inaugural Rally of Japan automobile race, in Tokachi, Hokkaido, is won by Norwegian Petter Solberg.

6 Sep Former US president Bill Clinton undergoes a quadruple coronary bypass operation.

▶ Vijay Singh of Fiji surpasses Tiger Woods to become the top-ranked golfer in the World Golf Ranking with his win in the Deutsche Bank championship; Woods had held the position for five years, since 8 Aug 1999.

7 Sep NASA officials report that Hurricane Frances caused major damage to several buildings at the Kennedy Space Center in Cape Canaveral FL in particular the hangar in which space shuttles are prepared for flight.

▶ Hurricane Ivan lays waste to Grenada, leaving half the population homeless, destroying the cocoa and nutmeg crops, and killing at least 39 people.

8 Sep Families of victims of the Washington-area sniper attacks in 2002 win a large settlement with the manufacturer and dealer of the gun used in the attacks; it is the third time (all in the past few months) that a gun dealer has paid for allowing a gun to fall into the hands of a criminal and the first time that a manufacturer has paid for such negligence.

▶ NASA's Genesis space capsule, which spent more than two years collecting samples of solar wind, returns to Earth as scheduled, but its parachutes fail to deploy and it crashes into the ground at Dugway Proving Ground in Utah, shattering the plates that contained the samples.

9 Sep Costa Rica withdraws from the US-led coalition for Iraq after a court ruling that such inclusion violates a constitutional prohibition against military action not authorized by the UN.

▶ Al-Muhtadee Billah Bolkiah, crown prince of Brunei, marries Sarah Salleh, the 17-year-old daughter of a Brunei royal and a European, in an opulent ceremony in Bandar Seri Begawan.

▶ A car bomb explodes outside the Australian embassy in Jakarta, Indonesia; at least nine people, all Indonesian, are killed.

▶ US Secretary of State Colin Powell says that he has concluded that genocide has taken place and may continue to take place in the Darfur region of The Sudan; it is the first time that a member of the administration in the US has applied the term in this situation.

10 Sep Hurricane Ivan reaches Jamaica, roaring along the southern coast during the night and next morning and leaving at least 15 people dead; though Kingston is hit hard, the storm changed course to spare the island a direct hit.

▶ Embattled CEO of Walt Disney Co. Michael Eisner announces that he will retire at the end of his contract, in September 2006.

11 Sep A helicopter carrying a religious delegation headed by Patriarch Petros VII of Alexandria, Egypt, head of the Greek Orthodox Church in Africa, from Athens to the monastery of Mt. Athos in Greece crashes shortly before its scheduled landing, killing all 12 on board.

▶ In an unusually bold move, Afghanistan's interim government removes long-standing warlord Ismail Khan as governor of Herat; violent protests greet the arrival of Sayed Muhammad Khairkhwa as his replacement the following day.

▶ Svetlana Kuznetsova of Russia defeats her countrywoman Yelena Dementyeva to win the US Open tennis championship; the following day Roger Federer of Switzerland defeats Lleyton Hewitt of Australia to win the men's tournament.

12 Sep A series of mortar attacks and suicide bombings throughout Baghdad leave at least 25 people dead in the city, with some 34 others being killed elsewhere in the country.

▶ US Airways files for bankruptcy protection for the second time; it filed previously in August 2002.

▶ Rubens Barrichello of Brazil wins the Italian Grand Prix; his Ferrari teammate Michael Schumacher of Germany comes in second.

13 Sep Russian Pres. Vladimir Putin demands enormous changes to the country's political system, including ending the popular election of governors and putting congressional elections on national party rather than district slates.

▶ The 1994 ban on the private ownership of military-style assault weapons in the US is allowed to lapse without a vote in Congress; though supported by most citizens, the ban was opposed by the National Rifle Association.

▶ A consortium with Sony Corp. of America at its head and including the cable company Comcast reaches an agreement to buy the movie studio Metro-Goldwyn-Mayer, shortly before it was to have been sold to Time Warner.

▶ US Secretary of the Interior Gale Norton signs documents turning the Great Sand Dunes National Monument in the Sangre de Cristo Mountains in Colorado into the Great Sand Dunes National Park, with increased acreage and resources.

14 Sep A suicide car bomb kills at least 47 people outside a police station in Baghdad, many of them waiting to apply for jobs; 12 other people, 11 of them Iraqi police, are killed in an ambush in Ba'qubah.

▶ A committee of the US Food and Drug Administration advises placing warnings on antidepressant drugs about increased risk of suicide when the drugs are given to teenagers and children.

▶ Canada defeats Finland 3–2 to win the World Hockey Cup in Toronto.

15 Sep Hurricane Ivan achieves Category 4 strength and makes landfall on the Gulf Coast of the US, and Alabama, Florida, Louisiana, and Mississippi declare states of emergency; by the end of the following day at least 23 people have lost their lives.

16 Sep South Africa announces that it has opened full diplomatic relations with Western Sahara, which is nominally under Moroccan administration.

▶ Peace talks between leaders of the Protestant and Roman Catholic factions in Northern Ireland open in Leeds Castle in England with an eye toward reviving the power-sharing government.

▶ Manitoba becomes the fourth province in Canada to legalize same-sex marriage; Nova Scotia does so too on 24 September.

17 Sep In Mexico City, Mexican Pres. Vicente Fox and Japanese Prime Minister Junichiro Koizumi sign a free-trade agreement.

▶ Argentine Pres. Néstor Kirchner surprises analysts by sacking Alfonso Prat-Gay as head of the country's central bank, replacing him with Martín Redrado, and making other personnel changes as well.

18 Sep Flooding caused by Tropical Storm Jeanne leaves at least 1,500 people dead in Haiti, most of them in and around Gonaïves.

▶ The International Atomic Energy Agency adopts a resolution calling on Iran to stop enriching uranium; the following day Iran announces its refusal.

▶ In the worst of several attacks around the country, a suicide car bomb kills 19 people when it explodes within a group of people looking for work with the Iraqi National Guard in Kirkuk.

▶ Chinese Pres. Hu Jintao succeeds Jiang Zemin as head of country's military, making him leader of the country in fact as well as name, in an unusually orderly transition.

18 Sep Bernard Hopkins defeats Oscar de la Hoya in a knockout in the ninth round to retain the undisputed world middleweight boxing championship in Las Vegas.

▶ Miss Alabama, Deidre Downs, wins the title of Miss America in Atlantic City NJ; on 20 October, ABC TV announces that it will no longer broadcast the Miss America Pageant, imperiling the survival of annual gala.

19 Sep After cutting a swathe of destruction through the Caribbean, the remnants of Hurricane Ivan cause flooding in southern Pennsylvania that leaves six people dead; the region was already waterlogged from rains emanating from the remains of Hurricane Frances earlier in the month.

▶ At the World Athletics Final in Monte-Carlo, the IAAF Athletes of the Year are runner Kenenisa Bekele of Ethiopia and pole-vaulter Yelena Isinbayeva of Russia.

▶ In golf's Ryder Cup competition, Europe defeats the US with a record-breaking 18.5–9.5 margin of victory.

▶ The Emmy Awards are presented in Los Angeles; winners include the TV shows *Arrested Development* and *The Sopranos*, the miniseries *Angels in America*, and the actors Kelsey Grammer, James Spader, Sarah Jessica Parker, Allison Janney, David Hyde Pierce, Michael Imperioli, Cynthia Nixon, and Drea de Matteo.

20 Sep Susilo Bambang Yudhoyono handily defeats Megawati Sukarnoputri in runoff presidential elections in Indonesia.

▶ US Pres. George W. Bush ends all economic sanctions against Libya, and two days later the European Union follows suit.

▶ The first criminal trial resulting from the meltdown of Enron Corp. opens in Houston; though the defendants are mid-level executives from Merrill Lynch and Enron and only one of many transactions is at issue, the charges are emblematic of all other indictments against the company.

21 Sep US Pres. George W. Bush addresses the UN General Assembly, pushing for the advancement of democracy to counter terrorism and defending the war in Iraq as doing the UN's work, though it was unsanctioned by the UN.

▶ The National Museum of the American Indian opens on the National Mall in Washington DC with a ceremonial Native Nations Procession of 20,000 people from some 500 tribes, followed by a six-day First Americans Festival of music, dance, and storytelling.

22 Sep The US Securities and Exchange Commission opens an investigation into the activities of the mortgage backer Fannie Mae.

▶ Interstate Bakeries, maker of Hostess products and Wonder bread, files for bankruptcy protection.

▶ It is reported that China has for the first time set out fuel-economy rules for automobiles in an attempt to lessen its dependence on foreign supplies of oil.

23 Sep A racketeering case against the tobacco

industry in the US begins, with attorneys for the US government declaring that the industry hid what it knew about the link between cancer and smoking for 50 years.

▸ After briefly insisting that a new penal code contain provisions making adultery punishable by law, Turkish Prime Minister Recep Tayyip Erdogan assures officials of the European Union that his government has abandoned that demand, which might derail the country's efforts to join the EU.

▸ Olusegun Obasanjo, president of Nigeria and head of the African Union, says that the union intends to send some 4,000 peacekeeping troops to the Darfur region of The Sudan early in October in response to a UN Security Council resolution.

24 Sep Porter Goss, a former US Congressman from Florida, becomes director of the US Central Intelligence Agency two days after his confirmation in the post by the Senate.

▸ Hurricane Jeanne makes landfall in Florida; this is the fourth hurricane to hit the state since August.

25 Sep In Iraq, an ambush kills seven men applying for jobs with the Iraqi National Guard in Baghdad, and the US conducts an air strike in Fallujah.

▸ The Port Adelaide Power wins its first Australian Football League championship, defeating the defending Brisbane Lions 17.11 (113)–10.123 (73).

26 Sep In a victory for the anti-immigration Swiss People's Party, voters in Switzerland reject a proposal that would have made it easier for Swiss-born children of immigrants to acquire Swiss passports and another that would give passports automatically to third-generation immigrants in Switzerland.

▸ The winners of the 2004 Albert Lasker Medical Research Awards are announced.

▸ The man who is believed to have been behind the two assassination attempts against Pakistani Pres. Pervez Musharraf and is also thought to have been involved in the killing of American reporter Daniel Pearl, Amjad Hussain Farooqi, is killed by Pakistani law enforcement.

▸ In Formula 1 auto racing, Rubens Barrichello of Brazil wins the inaugural Grand Prix of China race in Shanghai.

27 Sep Hundreds of UN peacekeepers are sent to flood-ravaged Gonaïves, Haiti, to try to restore order so food can be distributed; some 300,000 people have been left homeless by the flooding.

▸ The mortgage backer Fannie Mae agrees after negotiations with its federal regulator to reform its accounting and management practices, which have made the company appear in better shape that it was and have made top executives wealthy.

▸ Sir Richard Branson announces plans to form a company called Virgin Galactic that will sell suborbital rocket rides beginning in 2007.

▸ The TV channel NBC announces that Conan O'Brien, host of *Late Night*, will succeed Jay Leno as the host of *The Tonight Show* in 2009.

28 Sep In Cuzco, Peru, 20 foreign tourists who had been kidnapped by coca growers who want the government to end coca eradication efforts are freed by Peruvian authorities.

▸ Health officials in Thailand say that they believe human-to-human transmission of A(H5N1) avian influenza has occurred; a woman died of the disease who had no known contact with birds but visited her daughter, who worked with chickens, in the hospital when the daughter was dying of the disease.

▸ A magnitude-6 earthquake takes place in rural Parkfield CA, which is located on the San Andreas Fault.

29 Sep A US federal judge rules that a section of the USA PATRIOT Act that permits the government to order an Internet service provider to turn over personal information about subscribers and not notify anyone that it had received the order is in violation of the Constitution.

▸ In Yemen two men are sentenced to death for the attack on the USS *Cole* in 2000, and four others are sentenced to a maximum of 10 years in prison.

▸ Hungary's legislature elects Ferenc Gyurcsany prime minister.

▸ In New Zealand the trial of seven men from Pitcairn Island on numerous sex abuse charges begins; the defendants comprise nearly half the adult male population of Pitcairn.

▸ Bud Selig, commissioner of Major League Baseball, announces that the Montreal Expos team will move to Washington DC next season; Washington has been without a baseball team since 1971.

▸ The Cendant Corp., owner of Avis car rental and Days Inn motels, agrees to buy Orbitz, the online travel service that was created by a consortium of airlines in 2000.

▸ The dumbbell-shaped asteroid Toutatis passes within a million miles of the Earth; revolving around the Sun every four years in an orbit that regularly crosses that of Earth, it is the largest asteroid—about five km (three mi) long—to come close to the planet since astronomers developed the means to observe them, and another such opportunity is not expected in this century.

30 Sep Israeli security forces move into a refugee camp in northern Gaza; in the ensuing battle at least 28 Palestinians and 3 Israelis are killed; it is the highest death toll in two years.

▸ At a celebration for the opening of a new sewage plant in Baghdad, two car bombs kill at least 41 Iraqis, the majority of them children gathered to receive candy from US soldiers.

▸ With Russia's endorsement of the Kyoto Protocol on global warming, it becomes possible for the agreement to take effect.

▸ The pharmaceutical company Merck withdraws its extremely popular prescription pain and arthritis medicine Vioxx from the market after finding in testing it for a further use that it increases the risk of heart attack and stroke.

▸ Jazz at Lincoln Center announces the induction of the first 14 people into the Ertegun Jazz Hall of Fame, which will open to the public on 21 October; they include Louis Armstrong, Bix Beiderbecke, Miles Davis, and Charlie Parker.

October 2004

1 Oct Some 5,000 US and Iraqi troops begin a major battle to retake the Iraqi city of Samarra' from insurgent forces; they regain control of the city on 3 October.

▶ A bomb explodes in a Shi'ite mosque in Sialkot, Pakistan, as worshippers attend the Friday sermon; at least 23 people are killed.

▶ The World Health Organization announces a campaign to immunize more than 80 million children in 23 countries in Africa against polio, its largest such project to date.

▶ Seattle Mariners hitter Ichiro Suzuki sets a new record for number of hits in a single baseball season with his 258th hit; the previous record was set by George Sisler of the St. Louis Browns in 1920.

2 Oct Three bombs explode in the town of Dimapur in the Indian state of Nagaland, killing 26 people, while bombs and gunfire in attacks by separatists in Assam state leave 19 people dead.

▶ Violence continues for a third straight day in Port-au-Prince, Haiti; the death toll so far is seven.

3 Oct Parliamentary elections in Slovenia lead to a surprising victory for the opposition Slovenian Democratic Party; the Liberal Democratic Party had held power since the country's independence in 1991.

▶ Pope John Paul II beatifies five people, among them Charles, the last emperor of Austria-Hungary, whose reign coincided with the end of World War I and concluded with the dissolution of the kingdom.

4 Oct Two car bombs in downtown Baghdad and one in Mosul leave at least 26 people dead in Iraq.

▶ Cambodia's lower house of parliament ratifies an agreement made in 2003 with the United Nations to form a tribunal to try Khmer Rouge figures for atrocities committed during the late 1970s; this was considered the last major obstacle to the formation of a tribunal.

▶ The Nobel Prize for Physiology or Medicine is awarded to Americans Richard Axel and Linda B. Buck for their work in unraveling the workings of the human olfactory system.

▶ The private rocket ship *SpaceShipOne* achieves an altitude of 112.17 km (about 70 mi) and safely returns to Earth in the Mojave Desert in California, thus exceeding 100 km twice within a week and winning the $10 million Ansari X Prize.

5 Oct In Stockholm the Nobel Prize for Physics is awarded to Americans David J. Gross, H. David Politzer, and Frank Wilczeck for their work investigating the strong force, which binds quarks in the atomic nucleus; their discoveries led to the theory of quantum chromodynamics.

▶ US health officials announce that British authorities have suspended the license of the Liverpool laboratory of Chiron Corp. that manufactures about half of the US supply of vaccine against influenza because of contamination discovered in August.

▶ Niger produces its first gold bar, from a mine in a goldfield discovered some 15 years ago, in a ceremony attended by Pres. Tandja Mamadou; it is expected that the mine will produce 5,000 ounces of gold annually for the next six years.

6 Oct The Nobel Prize for Chemistry is awarded to Israelis Aaron Ciechanover and Avram Hershko and American Irwin Rose for their discovery of the chemical process by which cells mark proteins for degradation.

▶ The European Commission rules that Turkey has met the criteria for talks to begin about Turkey becoming a member of the European Union.

7 Oct King Norodom Sihanouk abdicates the throne of Cambodia, citing ill health and asking that a council be formed to select the next king.

▶ At a rally of Sunni Muslims in Multan, Pakistan, two bombs go off, killing at least 39 people.

▶ Three resorts popular with Israeli tourists in the Sinai Peninsula in Egypt are destroyed by bombs, leaving at least 33 people dead.

▶ The Nobel Prize for Literature is awarded to Elfriede Jelinek of Austria.

▶ Italian Prime Minister Silvio Berlusconi visits Tripoli, Libya, to join Libyan leader Muammar al-Qaddafi in opening of an oil pipeline between the countries and to discuss the curbing of illegal immigration of Africans through Libya to Italy.

8 Oct The Nobel Peace Prize is awarded to Kenyan environmentalist Wangari Maathai; the committee cites her work combining science with social engagement and politics.

▶ News organizations receive a video showing the beheading of British engineer Kenneth Bigley, who had been kidnapped in Iraq the previous month; he is the first British hostage to be executed in Iraq.

▶ Miguel Angel Rodríguez resigns as secretary-general of the Organization of American States (OAS) after being accused of accepting bribes when he was president of Costa Rica (1998–2002).

▶ The Council on Tall Buildings and Urban Habitat formally certifies the skyscraper Taipei 101, in Taiwan, as the tallest building in the world; it is 56 m (184 ft) taller than Petronas Towers, in Kuala Lumpur, Malaysia, previously the tallest building.

9 Oct Afghanistan's presidential election takes place peacefully; it is expected to be several weeks before the votes are tallied.

▶ In parliamentary elections in Australia, Prime Minister John Howard's Liberal Party wins decisively.

▶ With his win in two straight heats of the Kentucky Futurity, Windsong's Legacy becomes the first horse to win the Trotting Triple Crown since 1972.

10 Oct A suicide bomber kills himself and at least three others outside a Shi'ite mosque in Lahore, Pak.

▶ Meeting in Nigeria, Somalia's transitional parliament elects Abdullahi Yusuf Ahmed the interim president of the war-torn country.

11 Oct Members of rebel Shi'ite cleric Moktada al-Sadr's Mahdi Army begin surrendering their weapons, in accordance with an agreement made between the group and the Iraqi government and US military commanders in Baghdad.

▶ The European Union lifts sanctions, including an arms embargo, against Libya.

▶ The Nobel Memorial Prize in Economic Sciences goes to Norwegian Finn Kydland and American Edward Prescott.

12 Oct For the first time the Romanian government admits that Romania took part in the Holocaust during World War II and concedes that some 240,000 Jews died at that time in Romania.

13 Oct The discount supermarket and retailing chain Daiei in Japan agrees to accept a government bailout; Daiei is considered the epitome of the troubles Japanese banks have had with bad loans.

▶ The Seattle Storm defeats the Connecticut Sun 74–60 to win the Women's National Basketball

Association championship, in Seattle WA.

▸ The official beginning of the National Hockey League season passes with no hockey; the lockout of the players' union by the owners has continued for almost a month.

14 Oct A hastily constituted throne council in Cambodia chooses Norodom Sihamoni, a son of King Norodom Sihanouk and his choice, to succeed his father as king.

▸ In Beijing, Russian Pres. Vladimir Putin and Chinese Pres. Hu Jintao sign an agreement demarcating the 4,345-km (2,700-mi) border between Russia and China for the first time.

▸ Astronauts Leroy Chiao of the US and Salizhan Sharipov of Russia, escorted by Yury Shargin, blast off from the Baikonur Cosmodrone in Kazakhstan; Chiao and Sharipov will replace American Mike Finke and Russian Gennady Padalka as the crew of the International Space Station.

15 Oct Muslims around the world begin observations of the holy month of Ramadan.

▸ The High Court in Harare, Zimbabwe, acquits political opposition leader Morgan Tsvangirai of treason charges.

16 Oct Israeli military forces complete a redeployment from built-up areas of the Gaza Strip to hills overlooking the major refugee camps.

▸ The Royal Institute of British Architects announces that the Stirling Prize for 2004 goes to Lord Norman Foster for the London skyscraper 30 St. Mary Axe, popularly known as the Gherkin.

▸ Italian cyclist Paolo Bettini becomes the only person ever to win the World Cup of cycling three times in spite of not winning a single race, after a 28th place showing in the Tour of Lombardy.

17 Oct In a blatantly manipulated referendum in Belarus an amendment to the constitution allowing the president to seek an unlimited number of terms in office is passed, and in legislative elections supporters of Pres. Alyaksandr Lukashenka win every seat.

▸ The first UN peacekeepers from China ever deployed in the Western Hemisphere arrive in Haiti; Haitian interim prime minister Gérard Latortue publicly accuses deposed president Jean-Bertrand Aristide of orchestrating the violence in Haiti from his exile in South Africa.

▸ Russia opens its largest foreign military base, in Tajikistan, where it will station 5,000 soldiers and an air force unit.

▸ French driver Sébastien Loeb wins the world rally championship with two races to go when he comes in second at the Rally of Corsica, behind Markko Märtin of Estonia.

18 Oct A roadside explosion kills five people, one of them an election official, in an election commission jeep in southeastern Afghanistan.

▸ The notorious bandit Veerappan, thought to have killed more than 100 people, is killed in a shootout with police in India.

▸ The Lambeth Commission, convened by Rowan Williams, archbishop of Canterbury, issues a report calling on the Episcopal Church USA to refrain from ordaining gay clergy and blessing gay unions and to express regret for the difficulties taking these actions has caused within the Anglican Communion.

19 Oct Opposition leader Anatoly V. Lebedko is arrested and beaten on the second night of demonstrations against official, but widely disbelieved, election results in Belarus.

▸ Myanmar announces that Khin Nyunt has been replaced as prime minister by Soe Win; Khin Nyunt seems to have been seen as too liberal for the ruling junta.

▸ Margaret Hassan, the British-Iraqi head of CARE International, a relief organization, and a 30-year resident of Iraq is kidnapped in Baghdad.

▸ The Man Booker Prize for Fiction, Great Britain's top literary award, goes to British writer Alan Hollinghurst for his gay-themed novel *The Line of Beauty.*

20 Oct Susilo Bambang Yudhoyano is inaugurated as Indonesia's first directly elected president.

QUOTE OF THE MONTH

" *Indonesia will be a democratic country, open, modern, pluralistic, and tolerant.* "

—Indonesian Pres. Susilo Bambang Yudhoyano, at his inauguration, 20 October

---

▸ Rafiq al-Hariri resigns as prime minister of Lebanon; the following day the pro-Syrian Omar Karami is named to replace him.

▸ A record 10th typhoon for the season hits Japan, leaving at least 77 dead, in addition to the more than 102 people killed by the previous nine typhoons; Japan's storm records go back to 1551.

21 Oct South Korea's constitutional court rules that the plan to move the country's capital (see 11 August) is illegal; either a national referendum or an amendment to the constitution would be required in order to make the move.

▸ Authorities in Costa Rica arrest Rafael Angel Calderón on charges of having accepted bribes during his presidency of the country (1990–94).

▸ The Court of Arbitration for Sport rules that American Paul Hamm retains his Olympic gold medal in the men's all-around gymnastics in spite of the fact that judges had wrongly deducted a tenth of a point from the score of South Korean competitor Yang Tae Young.

22 Oct A gargantuan mosque opens in the village of Kipchak, the birthplace of Turkmenistan's Pres. Saparmurat Niyazov; in part a monument to Niyazov, the structure features inscriptions from his writings as well as from the Koran.

▸ Avianca Airlines, the national carrier of Colombia, reaches a settlement with the US Department of Justice, which believes that the airline knowingly allowed itself to be used to transport cocaine and heroin; a monitoring agency selected by US authorities will henceforth be allowed to inspect cargo loaded onto US-bound planes.

23 Oct Legislative elections in the UN-administered province of Kosovo in Serbia and Montenegro are boycotted by Serbs, who fear participating will aid ethnic Albanians in making the province independent.

▸ Insurgents dressed as police officers ambush and kill some 50 newly trained members of the Iraqi National Guard.

24 Oct The US government acknowledges that some 380 tons of explosives disappeared from a facility called al-Qaqaa in Iraq some time after the 2003 US-led invasion.

▸ Israel's cabinet approves a formula for the financial compensation of Israeli settlers to be removed from the Gaza Strip under Prime Minister Ariel Sharon's plan.

▸ The New England Patriots set a new National Football League record for consecutive wins with their 18th straight regular-season victory (21 wins overall), against the New York Jets; the previous record had been set by the Chicago Bears in the 1933–34 season.

25 Oct International Steel Group, the biggest US steel manufacturer, announces a complex transaction in which it will be acquired by a Dutch company controlled by Lakshmi Mittal to form a new company, Mittal Steel Co. NV, which will be the largest steel concern in the world.

▸ Jeffrey W. Greenberg resigns as chairman and CEO of Marsh & McLennan Co., the world's biggest insurance broker, in the wake of a suit brought by New York attorney general Eliot Spitzer for false dealing.

▸ The Seibu Lions defeat the Chunichi Dragons 7–2 in the decisive game seven to win the Japan Series baseball championship.

▸ The seventh annual Mark Twain Prize for American Humor is presented to Lorne Michaels, the creator and producer of the TV show *Saturday Night Live,* in a ceremony at the John F. Kennedy Center for the Performing Arts in Washington, DC

▸ In France, Pink TV, a gay and lesbian cable and satellite TV channel, begins broadcasting.

26 Oct The Cassini spacecraft passes within 1,172 km (728 mi) of Saturn's large moon Titan and returns close-up pictures and radar data to Earth.

▸ Officials in Thailand reveal that at least 78 people of the more than 1,300 arrested during a ruthlessly suppressed demonstration in heavily Muslim Narathiwat province died of suffocation while being transported in trucks to a military barracks.

▸ In a crucial vote, the Israeli Knesset (legislature) approves Prime Minister Ariel Sharon's proposal to remove all Israeli settlements from the Gaza Strip.

27 Oct The Federation Council, the upper house of Russia's legislature, votes to ratify the Kyoto Protocol, a treaty to limit greenhouse gases, five days after the State Duma, the lower house approved it.

▸ The Boston Red Sox defeat the St. Louis Cardinals 3–0 in St. Louis in the fourth game of the World Series to win the Major League Baseball championship for the first time since 1918 in a sweep; Red Sox slugger Manny Ramirez is named series Most Valuable Player.

28 Oct The defection of a coalition partner causes the government of Latvia to collapse; Prime Minister Indulis Emsis resigns.

▸ The journal *Nature* publishes a report revealing the discovery on the Indonesian island of Flores of what appears to be a population of miniaturized hominids, approximately three feet in height, that lived there as recently as 18,000 years ago; the species, named *Homo floresiensis,* astonishes anthropologists.

▸ Palestinian officials announce that Yasir Arafat will be flown the following day to Paris to be hospitalized; the nature and severity of Arafat's illness are unclear.

29 Oct The leaders of the countries of the European Union ceremonially sign the new EU constitution in the same building in Rome in which Treaty of Rome, establishing the European Community, was signed in 1957.

▸ The TV network al-Jazeera broadcasts a videotape of al-Qaeda leader Osama bin Laden addressing the US to warn against interference in Muslim affairs; it is the first videotape from bin Laden since 10 Sep 2003.

▸ In a traditional Buddhist ceremony, Norodom Sihamoni is crowned king of Cambodia.

▸ On Pitcairn Island, sentences ranging from community service to six years in prison are pronounced for six men convicted of various sexual assaults over a period of 40 years; the sentences, issued by judges from New Zealand, are suspended pending an appeal of jurisdiction.

30 Oct A car bomb kills eight US Marines near Abu Ghraib prison, outside Baghdad, and another car bomb kills seven people outside the Baghdad offices of the TV network al-Arabiyah.

31 Oct Tabaré Vázquez Rosas of the Socialist Party wins the presidential election in Uruguay; it is the first time a leftist politician has won the office in the country.

▸ A very contentious presidential election in Ukraine, with 24 candidates, results in the need for a runoff between Viktor Yushchenko and Viktor Yanukovych.

▸ After two days of fighting in Henan province in China between ethnic Han and Muslim Hui touched off by a traffic accident have resulted in some 150 deaths, martial law is declared.

▸ The Terra Museum of American Art in Chicago closes permanently, its entire collection of works on paper and 50 of its most important paintings are loaned to the Art Institute of Chicago for 15 years.

November 2004

1 Nov In separate incidents in Baghdad the deputy governor of Baghdad province is assassinated, and four foreign workers are kidnapped.

▸ Japan introduces a redesigned currency for the first time in 20 years in an attempt to thwart forgery.

2 Nov In an extremely close presidential election in the US, Pres. George W. Bush wins with 51% of the popular vote and 286 electoral votes, against challenger John Kerry's 48% and 251 electoral votes, though the results are not clear until the following day.

▸ Dutch filmmaker Theo van Gogh is murdered in Amsterdam by a Muslim extremist, apparently provoked by a short TV film van Gogh had made that painted Muslims as misogynists.

▸ Pres. Sheikh Zayid ibn Sultan Al Nahyan of the United Arab Emirates dies; the following day his son, Sheikh Khalifa ibn Zayid Al Nahyan, is chosen to replace him in the presidency.

▸ The British mare Makybe Diva wins the Melbourne Cup in thoroughbred racing in Australia for the second consecutive year.

3 Nov Hamid Karzai is officially declared the winner of Afghanistan's presidential election.

▸ Hungary announces that it will withdraw its troops from Iraq by March 2005.

4 Nov Russian Pres. Vladimir Putin signs the country's ratification of the Kyoto Protocol governing greenhouse emissions; 90 days after the documents are submitted to the UN, the treaty will go into effect.

▸ After a year-long cease-fire, the government of Côte d'Ivoire conducts bombing raids against two rebel strongholds, in violation of a UN-sponsored truce.

▸ The US announces that it will recognize Macedonia's formal name as the Republic of Macedonia; the country is recognized by the UN as the Former Yugoslav Republic of Macedonia because Greece, which has a province of Macedonia, objects to the formal name.

5 Nov The chief of Chile's army, Gen. Juan Emilio Cheyre, declares publicly that the army accepts collective and institutional responsibility for the human rights violations that occurred during the 1974–90 dictatorship of Augusto Pinochet.

▸ A court in the Canadian province of Saskatchewan rules that laws banning same-sex marriage are unconstitutional.

▸ Voters on the island of Saba express their preference to break away from the Netherlands Antilles to become a direct dependency of The Netherlands.

6 Nov Four car bombs and three attacks on police stations in Samarra', Iraq, leave some 40 people dead.

▸ On the third day of government attacks against the rebel-held areas, eight French peacekeepers are killed and 23 wounded in the town of Bouaké, Côte d'Ivoire.

▸ Australian Rachael Grinham wins the women's British Open Squash championship for the second consecutive year, and Australian David Palmer takes the men's championship, also for the second straight year.

7 Nov US troops begin an expected siege of Fallujah, Iraq, by seizing control of two bridges and a hospital.

▸ British runner Paula Radcliffe is the fastest woman at the New York Marathon with a time of 2 hrs 23 min 10 sec; the winner of the race is Hendrik Ramaala of South Africa with a time of 2 hrs 9 min 28 sec.

8 Nov An assault force of 6,500 US troops and 2,000 Iraqi soldiers enters Fallujah, Iraq, over a railroad embankment at the north end of the city.

▸ The International Rescue Committee becomes the third aid organization, after Doctors Without Borders and CARE International, to cease operations in Iraq because of the danger to aid workers in the country.

▸ A US federal judge rules that military commissions convened to try war detainees at Guantánamo Bay are unconstitutional, immediately ending the first trial before such a tribunal.

▸ It is announced at the International Supercomputer Conference in Pittsburgh that IBM's prototype Blue Gene/L has surpassed Japan's NEC Earth Simulator as the fastest computer in the world, with a speed of 70.72 teraflops (trillion operations per second); capable of 35.86 teraflops, the Japanese computer had held the position since June 2002.

▸ The ice hockey Hall of Fame in Toronto inducts defensemen Ray Bourque, Paul Coffey, and Larry Murphy and manager Cliff Fletcher.

9 Nov The Supreme Court of Belgium rules that the Vlaams Blok party has violated antiracism laws and is thus not a legal political party; the party, very popular in Flanders, campaigns against immigration and in favor of Flemish independence.

▸ The US Supreme Court rules that immigrants may not be deported for driving under the influence of alcohol even if injury is caused; a number of people have been deported because the government has defined such conduct as a "crime of violence."

▸ Tim McGraw and Kenny Chesney each win two Country Music Association Awards, McGraw for song of the year and single of the year for "Live Like You Were Dying" and Chesney for entertainer of the year and album of the year for When the Sun Goes Down.

10 Nov US Pres. George W. Bush nominates Alberto Gonzales to replace John Ashcroft as attorney general; Ashcroft had announced his resignation the previous day, declaring that the US was now safe from terror and crime.

▸ Swaziland's High Court convenes for the first time since all its members resigned in November 2002 in protest over the refusal of the monarchy to recognize a ruling; King Mswati III has agreed to abide by the court's rulings henceforth.

11 Nov After days of conflicting reports on his condition, Palestinian leader Yasir Arafat dies in a hospital in Paris; hours later, Mahmoud Abbas is chosen to succeed him as head of the Palestine Liberation Organization.

▸ Minnesota Twins pitcher Johan Santana is unanimously chosen winner of Major League Baseball's American League Cy Young Award.

12 Nov In a highly publicized five-month trial in California, fertilizer salesman Scott Peterson is found guilty of having murdered his wife, Laci, and their unborn child in 2002.

13 Nov Violence grows in the Iraqi cities of Mosul and Ramadi, as US and Iraqi forces fight their way into the last insurgent-held area of Fallujah; the takeover of Fallujah is completed the following day.

▸ A mosque in Limburg province in The Netherlands is burned down; it is the 20th incident in which either a mosque or a church has been set on fire since the murder of filmmaker Theo van Gogh.

14 Nov DC United wins its fourth Major League Soccer title in nine years with a 3–2 victory over the Kansas City Wizards in the MLS Cup game.

▸ R&B artist Usher wins four awards and hip-hop duo OutKast wins three at the American Music Awards in Los Angeles.

15 Nov Colin Powell announces his resignation as US secretary of state.

▸ In negotiations with France, Great Britain, and Germany, Iran agrees to freeze its uranium-enrichment program while negotiations continue over inducements.

▸ Major League Baseball's National League names Barry Bonds Most Valuable Player for a record fourth consecutive year, and seventh time overall; no other player has won the award more than three times.

▸ The UN Security Council imposes an immediate arms embargo on Côte d'Ivoire, with further sanctions to come into force on 15 December if the cease-fire agreement has not been restored by that time.

16 Nov US Pres. George W. Bush nominates his national security adviser, Condoleezza Rice, to replace Colin Powell as secretary of state.

▸ The unmanned NASA scramjet X-43A reaches approximately Mach 9.6, a new speed record, in a test flight over the Pacific Ocean.

▸ Major League Baseball's American League Most Valuable Player award for the 2004 season is awarded to Vladimir Guerrero of the Anaheim (CA) Angels.

17 Nov The retailers Kmart and Sears announce a merger in which Kmart will buy Sears and become Sears Holdings, the third biggest retailing entity in the US

▸ The US National Medal of Arts is awarded to Ray Bradbury, Carlisle Floyd, Frederick Hart, Anthony Hecht, John Ruthven, Vincent Scully, Twyla Tharp, and the Andrew W. Mellon Foundation.

▸ The National Book Awards are presented.

▸ Archaeologist Albert Goodyear reports that his investigation of flint tools found in Allendale county SC have led him to conclude that humans occupied the site some 50,000 years ago; it is generally believed that humans first reached the Americas only about 12,000 years ago.

18 Nov The European Parliament approves a new incoming European Commission several weeks after the incoming commission's president, José Manuel Barroso, was forced to withdraw a proposed team because the parliament objected to Barroso's choice of justice commissioner.

▸ In Chile a new law comes into effect that for the first time permits divorce; Malta and the Philippines are the only countries where divorce remains illegal.

▸ Google announces the inauguration of a search service specifically for scientists and academic researchers called Google Scholar.

▸ In a ceremony attended by former US presidents George Bush and Jimmy Carter and Pres. George W. Bush, among other celebrities, the presidential library of former president Bill Clinton opens in Little Rock AR.

19 Nov During a meeting of the UN Security Council in Nairobi, Kenya—only the fourth time the body has met outside of UN Headquarters in New York City—the government of The Sudan and the Sudan People's Liberation Movement/Army pledge to reach a peace agreement before the end of the year.

▸ Speaking before the Nairobi UN Security Council meeting, the newly installed Somali president, Abdullahi Yusuf Ahmed, requests an international peacekeeping force for his country; the Security Council declines on the grounds that there is as yet no peace to keep.

▸ UN Secretary-General Kofi Annan announces that he is sending an investigative team immediately to look into allegations of sexual abuse of women and children by UN peacekeeping troops in the Democratic Republic of the Congo.

▸ Thousands of protesters march in the streets of Santiago, Chile, as the Asia-Pacific Economic Cooperation conference (APEC) holds its annual meeting in the city for the first time.

20 Nov In fighting between government forces and Maoist rebels in Pandon, Nepal, at least 26 people are killed.

▸ NASA, in conjunction with the space programs of Italy and Great Britain, successfully launches Swift, a satellite observatory that will find and record enigmatic cosmic explosions known as gamma ray bursts, which may signal the birth of black holes or the collision of neutron stars.

▸ New York City's Museum of Modern Art celebrates its opening in its redesigned gallery after two years of construction; the new gallery, designed by Yoshio Taniguchi, has twice the space of the museum's former home.

21 Nov Ukraine holds its runoff presidential election between Viktor Yanukovych and Viktor Yushchenko; the following day Yanukovych declares victory, international observers release a preliminary report finding the elections undemocratic, and supporters of Yushchenko fill Independence Square in Kiev, believing their candidate to have won.

▸ The Paris Club of creditor countries agrees to cancel 80% of the debt owed to its members by Iraq.

▸ The Toronto Argonauts defeat the British Columbia Lions 27–19 in Ottawa to capture the 92nd Canadian Football League Grey Cup.

22 Nov In accordance with its agreement with Germany, France, and Great Britain, Iran suspends its uranium-enrichment operations.

▸ Sheikh Muhammad Amin al-Faidhi, a prominent Sunni cleric, is killed in Mosul, Iraq, and the bodies of four Iraqi soldiers are found.

▸ US, Iraqi, and British forces begin a major offensive in the area south of Baghdad that has become known as the "triangle of death."

23 Nov Wal-Mart Stores in China issues a statement saying it would respect a request from employees to form a union, in accordance with the law in China; Wal-Mart has steadfastly opposed unionization throughout its stores heretofore.

24 Nov The government of Ukraine declares Viktor Yanukovych the winner of the presidential election, in spite of international reports of fraud and growing demonstrations by supporters of Viktor Yushchenko.

▸ Pakistani Prime Minister Shaukat Aziz travels to India to continue peace talks with Indian Prime Minister Manmohan Singh; it is the first time in 13 years that a Pakistani prime minister has gone to India.

25 Nov Ukraine's Supreme Court rules that the results of the presidential election cannot be made final until the allegations of electoral fraud and intimidation have been investigated; crowds of supporters of opposition candidate Viktor Yushchenko have filled Kiev's Independence Square since the night of the election.

> ### QUOTE OF THE MONTH
>
> ❝ *I feel awful, it's horrible. First it was euphoria, and now the people are yelling in the streets...You see, they have let this genie out of the bottle.* ❞
>
> —Oleksandra Ruzhel, a member of Ukrainian presidential candidate Viktor Yanukovych's staff, on the Supreme Court's ruling delaying the election results, 25 November

▸ Marwan Barghouti, who has been frequently mentioned as a possible candidate for president of the Palestinian Authority although he is serving five life sentences in prison in Israel, agrees not to run and puts his support behind Mahmoud Abbas.

▸ Dozens of defendants are convicted of having planned to overthrow the government of Equatorial Guinea in March and are sentenced to long prison terms.

27 Nov Ukraine's Supreme Council (legislature) meets in a special session and declares the results of the presidential election invalid; the body does not have legal authority to overturn an election, however.

▸ In Vatican City, Pope John Paul II ceremonially delivers to Ecumenical Patriarch Bartholomew I of the Eastern Orthodox Church relics of St. John Chrysostom and St. Gregory of Nazianzus; the relics had been removed from Constantinople many centuries ago.

▸ Sumo wrestling grand champion Asashoryu becomes the first person in 18 years to win five tournaments in a single year when his defeat of Chiyotaikai at the Kyushu Basho brings him his ninth Emperor's Cup.

28 Nov Nicolas Sarkozy is elected leader of the Gaullist Union for a Popular Movement Party, the dominant political party in France.

▸ King Abdullah of Jordan rescinds the title of crown prince from his half-brother, Hamza ibn Hussein.

29 Nov At a meeting in Vientiane, Laos, China and the members of ASEAN sign an agreement to create the largest free-trade zone in the world.

▸ Pres. Ricardo Lagos of Chile announces that the government will give a lifetime stipend and other benefits to compensate the victims of torture during the dictatorship of Augusto Pinochet; the claims of 27,255 people were recognized.

▸ Edwy Plenel resigns as editor-in-chief of Le Monde, France's leading newspaper.

30 Nov A general strike over government economic policy brings Italy to a halt, while tens of thousands of protesters march in cities throughout the country.

▸ A report commissioned by Secretary-General Kofi Annan recommends a number of changes to the UN, most notably an expansion of the Security Council to 24 members, from its current 15.

▸ Tom Ridge announces his resignation as US secretary of homeland security.

▸ Kweisi Mfume surprises observers by announcing his resignation as president of the National Association for the Advancement of Colored People (NAACP).

▸ US Pres. George W. Bush makes his first official visit to Canada.

▸ After an astonishing 74-game winning streak, Ken Jennings finally loses on the TV game show Jeopardy! after having won more than $2 million.

December 2004

1 Dec Rallies are held in cities throughout South Asia in observance of World AIDS Day; AIDS is a growing problem in the region, with India now second only to South Africa in numbers of people infected by HIV.

▸ The US government announces plans to increase the number of troops in Iraq by about 12,000 to a total of 150,000 in the next several weeks in order to provide security for the national election scheduled for 30 Jan 2005.

▸ In spite of having agreed in November not to run for the presidency of the Palestinian Authority, imprisoned Palestinian leader Marwan Barghouti announces through his wife his candidacy.

▸ The second John W. Kluge Prize in the Human Sciences, established by the US Library of Congress to honor lifetime achievement, is awarded to American intellectual historian Jaroslav Pelikan and French philosopher Paul Ricoeur.

2 Dec The European Union officially takes over peacekeeping duties in Bosnia and Herzegovina from NATO; it is the largest peacekeeping force the EU has fielded.

3 Dec To the jubilation of the huge crowds in Independence Square in Kiev, Ukraine's Supreme Court rules that the presidential runoff election on 21 November had been fraudulent and overturns the results, ordering a new runoff be held no later than 26 December.

▸ Tommy G. Thompson steps down as US secretary of health and human services, expressing disagreement with some government policies and concern over the lack of oversight of the country's food supply.

▸ In the enclave of Kosovo in Serbia and Montenegro, the legislature chooses former ethnic Albanian guerrilla leader Ramush Haradinaj to be prime minister, though he is being investigated by the UN war crimes tribunal.

▸ In a number of attacks in both Baghdad and Mosul in Iraq, mostly against police stations, 27 Iraqi police and civilians are killed.

4 Dec In the runoff presidential election in Niger, Pres. Tandja Mamadou wins reelection.

▸ A suicide car bomb destroys a police station in Baghdad, while another one hits a convoy of Kurdish soldiers in Mosul; at least 25 Iraqis are killed in the two attacks, while several US soldiers are killed in smaller skirmishes.

▸ On Hainan Island, China, Miss Peru, María Julia Mantilla García, wins the Miss World beauty pageant.

5 Dec An attack on a busload of Iraqi contractors working for US forces in Tikrit, Iraq, brings the death toll for the past three days to 80.

▸ In municipal elections across Bolivia, Indian and peasant reform parties win most races against traditional party candidates.

▸ The annual Kennedy Center Honors are presented in Washington to actors Warren Beatty, Ossie Davis, and Ruby Dee, musicians Sir Elton John and Dame Joan Sutherland, and composer John Williams.

▸ Carlos Moya leads Spain's tennis team to victory over the US and the Davis Cup title in Seville, Spain.

▸ The book trade magazine Publishers Weekly names America (the Book): A Citizen's Guide to Democracy Inaction, by Jon Stewart and the other writers of TV's The Daily Show with Jon Stewart, as the Book of the Year.

6 Dec Five men attack the US consulate in Jiddah, Saudi Arabia, leading to a three-hour gun battle in which four of the attackers and five consulate employees are killed; the attackers are believed to be members of al-Qaeda.

▸ The Basque separatist organization ETA explodes seven small bombs, one in each of seven cities, in Spain; because the organization phoned in warnings, there are no serious casualties.

▸ Britain's Turner Prize is presented to installation artist Jeremy Deller, who wins on the strength of his film Memory Bucket: A Film About Texas.

▸ In the United Arab Emirates, the city of Dubai opens its first international film festival, to run for six days and include 75 movies from Arab and South Asian countries.

7 Dec Hamid Karzai is sworn in as president of Afghanistan.

▸ John Kufuor wins a second term as president of Ghana.

▶ IBM announces that it has reached a deal to sell its personal computer business to the biggest PC maker in China, Lenovo; the computers will continue to be made in the US, however.

▶ La Scala opera house in Milan has a gala reopening after being closed since 31 Dec 2001 for renovation; it opens with the opera that first opened the theatre in 1778: Antonio Salieri's *Europa riconosciuta*.

8 Dec In Cuzco, Peru, representatives of 12 countries sign an agreement to create the South American Community of Nations.

▶ US Secretary of Defense Donald Rumsfeld holds a question-and-answer session in Kuwait with soldiers headed for Iraq and is apparently surprised to be asked about the shortage of armor for vehicles used in the conflict.

▶ During a concert by the heavy metal band Damageplan in a nightclub in Columbus OH, a man leaps onto the stage and shoots to death the respected guitar player "Dimebag" Darrell Abbott and three more people; he is apparently distraught over the breakup of Abbott's more successful previous band, Pantera.

9 Dec The House of Assembly, Zimbabwe's legislature, approves a law that will ban foreign-based and foreign-supported organizations, including churches, that support greater human rights in the country.

▶ New Zealand's Parliament passes a law that gives same-sex partners the same civil rights enjoyed by married couples.

▶ The crew aboard the International Space Station is asked to cut back on food until the arrival of the next supply ship, scheduled for 25 December; keeping adequate supplies on the station has become more difficult with the grounding of the US space shuttle fleet.

▶ The Right Livelihood Awards are presented in Stockholm to Indian religious figures Swami Agnivesh and Asghar Ali Engineer, for their work promoting harmony among communities; Memorial, a Russian human-rights organization; Bianca Jagger, a Nicaraguan human-rights and environmental activist; and Raúl Montenegro, an Argentine scientist and environmentalist.

10 Dec A panel of judges in criminal court in Milan acquits Italian Prime Minister Silvio Berlusconi of three corruption charges and dismisses a fourth charge after a trial that had dragged on for four years.

▶ A bomb goes off in a crowded outdoor market in Quetta, Pakistan, killing at least 10 people; ethnic nationalists in Baluchistan, the province of which Quetta is the capital, are believed responsible.

▶ Japan adopts a new military plan that focuses more on defense against China and North Korea and less on defense against Russia; the plan also permits some military exporting.

11 Dec Tests by doctors in Vienna confirm that opposition Ukrainian presidential candidate Viktor Yushchenko was poisoned by dioxin.

▶ Legislative elections in Taiwan give a slim majority to the Nationalist Party and its allies, which downplay the issue of Taiwan's independence from mainland China.

▶ The 2004 Heisman Trophy for college football is awarded to University of Southern California quarterback Matt Leinart.

▶ The German-Turkish film *Gegen die Wand* is named the best picture at the European Film Awards in Barcelona, Spain.

12 Dec The presidential election in Romania is unexpectedly won by the opposition candidate, Traian Basescu, who defeats Adrian Nastase, the candidate supported by outgoing president Ion Iliescu.

▶ Having again announced his candidacy on 1 December, Marwan Barghouti bows out of the race for president of the Palestinian Authority for the second time.

▶ Under pressure from the US and the European Union, China agrees to impose tariffs on some of its textile exports.

▶ A bomb explodes in a busy market in General Santos, Philippines, killing at least 15 people.

13 Dec A judge in Chile rules that Augusto Pinochet is mentally fit to stand trial for human rights abuses during his 1974–90 dictatorship and orders him placed on house arrest; the order is immediately appealed.

▶ The day after two Sudanese employees of the charity Save the Children are killed in the Darfur region of The Sudan, the UN suspends relief operations in the area.

▶ In Brussels, representatives of Iran, France, Germany, the UK, and the European Union begin a new round of negotiations to solve the impasse over Iran's nuclear policy.

▶ Sean O'Keefe announces his resignation as head of NASA.

▶ The business database company Oracle acquires the business software company PeopleSoft in a hostile takeover after a long battle.

14 Dec The US Department of Commerce reports that the US reached a all-time record trade deficit of $55.5 billion in October, breaking the record set in June.

▶ Google announces an agreement with several major research libraries to digitize and make available through its regular search service the contents of millions of books that are no longer protected by copyright.

▶ The US Presidential Medal of Freedom is awarded to Gen. Tommy R. Franks, the commander of the US-led forces that invaded Iraq in 2003; L. Paul Bremer III, the US administrator of occupied Iraq; and George Tenet, former CIA director.

15 Dec The US Securities and Exchange Commission, finding the mortgage broker Fannie Mae in violation of accounting rules, orders it to restate its earnings for the past four years.

▶ In an attempt to prevent the auction of its prize oil-producing unit, the Russian energy company Yukos files for bankruptcy protection in Houston, where it says it has some assets.

▶ The cellular phone companies Sprint and Nextel Communications announce plans to merge to create the third biggest carrier in the US.

▶ The first full flight test since 2002 of the US missile defense system, a basic version of which was originally supposed to have been in place by September 2004, fails when the interceptor missile shuts down just before its planned launch against an in-flight simulated ICBM; the previous test had also failed.

▶ Researchers report the existence of a species of macaque previously unknown to science, a stocky, brown-haired, short-tailed primate in living in Arunachal Pradesh state, India, that they have named *Macaca munzala*.

16 Dec An audiotape from Osama bin Laden is posted on a Web site; on it he excoriates the rulers of Saudi Arabia for their association with the US and praised the attackers of the US embassy in Jiddah.

▸ A bomb explodes outside a major Shi'ite shrine in Karbala', Iraq, killing at least 9 people and injuring 40, among them an aide to Ayatollah Ali al-Sistani; the aide may have been the target.

▸ In an enormous child sex abuse scandal that has been rocking Portugal, the first defendant to go on trial, Carlos Silvino, who is charged with 634 offenses, including child rape and procuring, pleads guilty and says all the other defendants, one of whom is a TV star, are also guilty.

▸ In France the Millau bridge, at 270 m (886 ft) the world's highest bridge and at 2,460 m (8,071 ft) the world's longest all-span cable-stayed bridge, opens to the public.

17 Dec Armando Guebuza, of the ruling Frelimo party, is declared the winner of the presidential election that took place in Mozambique 1–2 December.

18 Dec A two-week international conference on global warming in Buenos Aires, concludes with an agreement to hold an informal workshop in 2005 to discuss the matter; the US is accused of foot-dragging and preventing a more substantive agreement.

▸ Representatives of the African Union say that The Sudan has begun withdrawing government troops from the Darfur region hours before a deadline the union had imposed to repair leaks in the ceasefire, but an incident the following day prompts the AU to declare that the government did not meet the deadline.

19 Dec A previously unknown company, the Baikal Finans Group, which registered a last-minute bid, wins the auction for the huge oil-producing unit of the energy company Yukos in Russia, after well-known entities either withdraw or fail to bid.

▸ Car bombs go off in the Iraqi cities of Najaf and Karbala', killing at least 61 people between them, and three election workers in Baghdad are pulled from their cars and executed.

20 Dec A Gulf Cooperation Council meeting in Manama, Bahrain, is notable for the absence of Saudi Arabia's Crown Prince Abdullah; he is said to be upset over a recent free-trade agreement between Bahrain and the US

▸ In Zürich, Switzerland, Brazilian Ronaldinho, who plays for Barcelona, Spain, and Birgit Prinz of Germany are named FIFA World Player and FIFA Women's World Player of the Year in association football (soccer).

21 Dec British Prime Minister Tony Blair makes an unexpected visit to Baghdad, where he meets with interim Iraqi prime minister Ayad Allawi before going to Basra to meet with British troops; the last British prime minister to visit Baghdad was Winston Churchill.

▸ An explosion in a mess tent in an American military base in Mosul, Iraq, at lunchtime, kills at least 24 people, among them 14 US soldiers and 4 American contractors.

▸ UN peacekeeping troops begin moving into the North Kivu region of the Democratic Republic of the Congo, hoping to create a buffer zone between government and rebel forces.

▸ Astronomers announce that a NASA satellite, the Galaxy Evolution Explorer, has found, to their surprise and delight, some three dozen massive, recently formed galaxies that may resemble our own Milky Way Galaxy in its youth; it had been thought new galaxies were no longer being created.

⬩▸ The Washington Post Company announces its purchase from Microsoft of the pioneering online magazine *Slate*.

22 Dec The World Health Organization announces that blood tests performed on poultry workers in Japan have uncovered at least one, and probably five, cases of asymptomatic infections in people of the frequently fatal A(H5N1) strain of avian influenza.

▸ It is revealed that Conrack International Inc., which had contracted to do road and bridge reconstruction in Iraq, has canceled its contract, citing the difficult security situation and problems with supplies that made it almost impossible to operate.

▸ Saudi Arabia withdraws its ambassador from Libya and expels the Libyan ambassador in Riyadh, believing it has found evidence that Libya had plotted to assassinate Crown Prince Abdullah.

▸ Scientists say that Martian volcanoes photographed by the European Space Agency spacecraft Mars Express show signs of geologically recent eruptions, which leads to speculation that they may still be active.

23 Dec The US dollar reaches a record low against the euro and declines against other major currencies; the dollar has fallen about 7% since early November.

▸ Afghani Pres. Hamid Karzai announces his new cabinet; unlike the cabinet he chose as interim president, this one is composed largely of technocrats rather than warlords.

24 Dec US Secretary of Defense Donald Rumsfeld makes a Christmas Eve visit to US soldiers in Iraq.

▸ A tanker truck loaded with butane gas and wired with explosives apparently headed for the Jordanian embassy in Baghdad explodes, destroying a house and killing nine people.

25 Dec In St. Peter's Square in Vatican City, Pope John Paul II delivers Christmas greetings in 62 languages to the crowds and prays for peace.

▸ Ukraine's Constitutional Court allows all the changes to electoral law to stand, save one, the restriction on voting at home; while this practice was the source of much of the fraud in the previous election, the court fears disenfranchising the homebound.

26 Dec A magnitude-9 earthquake, the strongest in 40 years, under the Indian Ocean unleashes a powerful tsunami that kills hundreds of thousands of people in more than 10 countries and destroys coastlines in Indonesia, Sri Lanka, Thailand, Malaysia, the Maldives, and India.

> **QUOTE OF THE MONTH**
>
> ❝ *All the planet is vibrating.* ❞
>
> —Enzo Boschi, director of Italy's National Geophysics Institute, describing the effects of the 9.0 earthquake that unleashed the horrific Indian Ocean tsunami, 26 December

▸ In the repeat runoff presidential election in Ukraine, opposition candidate Viktor Yushchenko wins a convincing victory.

▸ Legislative elections are held in Uzbekistan that international observers say offer the voters no serious choice, as opposition groups were barred from the ballot.

27 Dec Israel releases 159 Palestinian prisoners in a move that Palestinian leaders say they welcome, while calling for more substantive progress.

▸ A large explosion occurs in Baghdad outside the headquarters of the biggest Shi'ite political party in Iraq; 9 people are killed and 67 injured, but the party leader, Abdul Aziz al-Hakim, is unhurt.

28 Dec Several attacks in the region north of Baghdad, kill at least 23 Iraqi police and national guard members.

▸ The pro-commonwealth Aníbal Acevedo-Vilá is certified as the winner of the 2 November election for governor of Puerto Rico; his victory in the original count was so narrow it automatically triggered the need for a hand recount.

29 Dec The US partially lifts its ban on the importation of cattle from Canada, in place since May 2003, when a cow in Alberta was found to have mad cow disease.

▸ An agreement to stop people from immigrating to one country to seek asylum in another goes into effect, closing all border points between Canada and the US to refugees.

30 Dec Senegal signs a peace agreement with separatist rebels in the Casamance region; thousands of people, bedeviled by 20 years of violence in the region, cheer.

▸ The legislature of the Basque Country, an autonomous community of Spain, surprises observers by approving a plan that says the region has the right to secede from Spain.

▸ Democrat Christine Gregoire is certified as the winner of the 2 November election for governor of the US state of Washington; the original results showed Republican Dino Rossi as the winner, a machine recount showed him as the winner by a much smaller margin, but a hand recount gave the race to Gregoire.

▸ Ethiopia's Ministry of Culture and Sports announces that the 1,700-year-old Obelisk of Axum, taken by Italian forces after Italy, under Benito Mussolini, conquered Ethiopia in 1937, will be returned in 2005.

▸ An audience member at the overcrowded Republica Cromagnon nightclub in Buenos Aires sets off fireworks as the band, Los Callejeros, begins its first set, setting the club on fire; 188 people are killed and 700 injured.

31 Dec Promises of aid for the victims of the Indian Ocean tsunami pour in, and the US raises its pledge 10-fold to $350 million.

▸ A peace accord is signed in Nairobi, Kenya, between the government of The Sudan and representatives of rebel groups in the south of the country; the agreement should end the longest-running civil war in Africa.

▸ In Ukraine, losing presidential candidate Viktor Yanukovych resigns as prime minister, a post he held for two years under Pres. Leonid Kuchma.

▸ The British yacht *Aera*, skippered by Jez Fanstone, is named the overall winner of Australia's 60th Sydney-Hobart race.

January 2005

1 Jan With the beginning of the new year, Prime Minister Jean-Claude Juncker of Luxembourg assumes the presidency of the European Union.

▸ A new currency goes into effect in Turkey, replacing the 1,000,000-lira note with a 1-new-lira note and including a return of the kurus coin.

2 Jan A car bomb goes off near Balad, Iraq, killing 18 members of the Iraqi National Guard and a civilian.

▸ Four Peruvian police officers die in a battle to retake the town of Andahuaylas, which was seized the previous day by an armed group led by Antauro Humala that demands the resignation of Pres. Alejandro Toledo.

3 Jan Attacks in various places in Iraq leave at least 20 people dead, including 3 British citizens and a US civilian; insurgent attacks on military and civilian targets in Iraq have become daily and continuing occurrences.

▸ In the Circus Tavern in Purfleet, England, Phil Taylor wins an astonishing 12th world darts title when he defeats Mark Dudbridge in the final of the Ladbrokes World Championship.

4 Jan The governor of Baghdad province in Iraq is assassinated; in four other attacks, 15 people, including 5 US soldiers, are killed.

▸ The University of Southern California defeats the University of Oklahoma 55–19 in college football's annual Orange Bowl to win the Bowl Championship Series trophy and the national Division I-A championship.

▸ Infielder and hitter Wade Boggs and second baseman Ryne Sandberg are elected to the National Baseball Hall of Fame.

5 Jan Officials of the International Atomic Energy Agency announce that Iran has agreed to allow the agency to inspect the Parchin military complex, which the US believes has been used for nuclear weapons development.

▸ The African Union agrees to send troops to Somalia to facilitate the move of Somalia's government from Kenya to the Somalian capital of Mogadishu.

6 Jan The pro forma counting of electoral college votes in the US Congress takes place, and US Pres. George W. Bush is officially certified as the winner of the presidential election.

▸ Edgar Ray Killen, a longtime Ku Klux Klan leader, is arrested in Philadelphia MS and charged with murder in the 1964 killings of three voter-registration workers.

▸ Nelson Mandela, former president of South Africa, announces that his son, Makgatho Mandela, has died of AIDS; it is considered very courageous of him to admit publicly that AIDS was the cause of death.

7 Jan A fire breaks out in a garment factory in Siddhirganj, Bangladesh, killing 22 people who were trapped inside because of locked exits.

8 Jan Riots break out in Gilgit, in the Pakistan-administered Northern Areas, after a prominent Shi'ite cleric is ambushed and shot; 15 people die in the violence.

▸ In assorted attacks in Iraq, at least five Iraqis are killed, and four Iraqi government officials are kidnapped.

9 Jan In the first Palestinian election since 1996, former prime minister Mahmoud Abbas is elected president of the Palestinian Authority; the elections are regarded as free and fair.

▸ In a ceremony in Nairobi, Kenya, a final peace agreement calling for a six-year transitional period is signed between the government of The Sudan and a rebel group from the south of the country led by John Garang.

▸ Storms bring very high winds and flooding to northern Europe, leaving close to 2 million people without electricity and killing at least 11 people, 7 in Sweden and 4 in Denmark.

10 Jan A law banning cigarette smoking in all indoor public places, including restaurants and bars, except in walled-off and ventilated areas, goes into effect in Italy.

▸ An independent panel investigating a CBS News story that was broadcast on *60 Minutes* in September 2004 about US Pres. George W. Bush's service in the Texas Air National Guard during the Vietnam War concludes that the segment had been rushed onto the air without adequate vetting; CBS responds by firing four top journalists.

11 Jan US Pres. George W. Bush nominates Michael Chertoff, who headed the criminal division of the Department of Justice at the time of the 9/11 terrorist attacks, to replace Tom Ridge as secretary of homeland security.

▸ Officials announce that an agreement has been reached for the release of the last four Britons and one Australian citizen being detained at the US military base in Guantánamo Bay, Cuba; the men have been held there for about three years.

▸ A cow infected with mad cow disease is reported found in Alberta, Canada; this is somewhat alarming, because the cow was born after a ban on certain animal protein in cattle feed went into effect.

12 Jan A new constitution for the European Union is signed by a large majority of the European Parliament in Strasbourg, France; it must now be ratified by each of the EU's 25 members, a process expected to take about two years.

▸ NASA's Deep Impact spacecraft is launched from Cape Canaveral FL; it is expected to reach Comet Tempel 1 in July and release an impactor that will penetrate the comet's nucleus.

▸ The US Supreme Court rules that sentencing guidelines imposed on judges in federal courts by Congress in 1994 must be regarded as advisory only and not as mandatory.

▸ It is announced that the US has abandoned the search for weapons of mass destruction in Iraq, having concluded long ago that the former Iraqi government did not possess such weapons at the time of the US-led invasion.

13 Jan Sir Mark Thatcher, son of former British prime minister Margaret Thatcher, pleads guilty in Cape Town, South Africa, to having helped finance mercenaries involved in a coup plot against the president of Equatorial Guinea.

▸ A coordinated Palestinian attack on an Israeli checkpoint in the Gaza Strip leaves six Israeli civilians and three Palestinian militants dead.

14 Jan The European Space Agency spacecraft Huygens, released from the NASA orbiter Cassini, successfully lands on the surface of Saturn's moon Titan and begins transmitting photographs and data.

▸ Israeli Prime Minister Ariel Sharon orders Israel's government officials to cut all contacts with the Palestinian Authority and orders the Gaza Strip sealed off.

▸ Specialist Charles Graner, believed to be the leader of the US soldiers responsible for the abuse of prisoners at the prison in Abu Ghraib, Iraq, is found guilty of all six charges in a court-martial in Fort Hood TX.

15 Jan As has been happening increasingly for the past several days, large demonstrations take place in several cities in Russia protesting against a law that went into effect on 1 January which replaced several state benefits and subsidies for pensioners with small cash stipends.

▸ China and Taiwan reach an agreement to allow charter flights between the mainland and Taiwan to fly nonstop over the Chinese New Year holidays, from 29 January to 20 February; they will be the first nonstop flights between the two entities since 1949.

▸ Michelle Kwan wins her ninth women's title at the US Figure Skating Championships in Portland OR.

16 Jan Stipe Mesic wins reelection as president of Croatia with two-thirds of the votes cast.

▸ As part of a reconciliation program in which the government of Afghanistan will grant amnesty to former Taliban supporters who are willing to give up violence and resume living peacefully, 81 Afghan prisoners are released by the US military from a detention facility in Bagram.

▸ At the Golden Globe Awards in Beverly Hills CA best picture honors go to *The Aviator* and *Sideways* and best director goes to Clint Eastwood for *Million Dollar Baby*.

17 Jan Expatriate Iraqis living in places throughout the US begin arriving in Chicago, Detroit, Los Angeles, Washington DC, and Nashville TN, to register to vote in the upcoming Iraqi national elections.

▸ In the field of children's literature, the Newbery Medal is awarded to Cynthia Kadohata for *Kira-Kira*, and Kevin Henkes wins the Caldecott Medal for illustration for his book *Kitten's First Full Moon*.

18 Jan Ann Veneman, the outgoing US secretary of agriculture, is named to replace Carol Bellamy as head of UNICEF.

▸ A gala unveiling at the Jean-Luc Lagardère hangar in France introduces the first production model of the "superjumbo" Airbus A380 airplane, a double-decker capable of carrying as many as 850 passengers.

19 Jan In a ceremony at the German Historical Museum in Berlin, German Chancellor Gerhard Schröder initiates a yearlong celebration of the centennial of Albert Einstein's publication of the theory of relativity.

▸ A Moscow city official announces a plan to build a monument to leaders in the war against Nazi Germany; the monument will include a representation of Joseph Stalin, the first statue of the former dictator to be publicly displayed in Moscow in some 40 years.

▸ Three British soldiers go on trial at a court-martial in Osnabrück, Germany, on charges of having abused Iraqi prisoners in May 2003.

20 Jan George W. Bush is sworn in for his second term as president of the United States.

▸ The heaviest flooding in more than a century leads the government of Guyana to declare Georgetown and the surrounding area a disaster zone and plead for international help in dealing with the situation.

21 Jan For the second consecutive day, protesters in Beslan, North Ossetia, Russia, block a nearby highway, demanding the resignation of Aleksandr S. Dzasokhov as president of the southern republic, believing the investigation into the school siege that killed more than 300 people in September 2004 is being mishandled.

22 Jan Parliamentary elections, postponed from 31 Dec 2004 because of the Indian Ocean tsunami, take place in Maldives.

23 Jan Viktor Yushchenko is inaugurated as president of Ukraine in a ceremony in Kiev.

▶ Sébastien Loeb of France, the 2004 world champion of automobile rally racing, wins the Monte-Carlo Rally for the third consecutive year.

24 Jan The US Supreme Court rules that the use of a trained drug-sniffing dog during a traffic stop in the absence of any suspicion of the presence of drugs does not constitute an unreasonable search and is thus permissible under the Constitution.

▶ In Thoroughbred horse racing's 2004 Eclipse Awards, Ghostzapper is named Horse of the Year.

25 Jan As hundreds of thousands of pilgrims approach the hilltop Mandher Devi temple near the town of Wai, Maharashtra state, India, a stampede erupts, and relatives of victims begin setting fires in anger; 258 pilgrims are killed.

▶ Andrea Levy wins the 2004 Whitbread Book of the Year Award for her novel *Small Island;* she previously had won the Orange Prize for the same work.

26 Jan Condoleezza Rice is sworn in as US secretary of state.

4 A US Marine helicopter crashes in a sandstorm near Rutba, Iraq, killing all 31 aboard, while four US soldiers are killed in battle in Anbar, another is killed in an attack in Duluiyah, and another is killed by a roadside bomb in Baghdad; this is the highest one-day death toll for the US military in the war to date.

▶ The inaugural Story Prize, given to honor a previously unpublished work of short fiction in the US, is awarded to Haitian-born Edwidge Danticat for *The Dew Breaker.*

27 Jan A bomb goes off at a rally of the opposition Awami League in Laskarpur, Bangladesh, killing four people, among them a former finance minister.

▶ A new 120-km- (75-mi-) long road between Herat, Afghanistan, and a post in the Dogharoun region of Iran is ceremonially opened by Pres. Hamid Karzai of Afghanistan and Pres. Mohammad Khatami of Iran.

28 Jan Israel orders its army to cease offensive operations in the Gaza Strip and open the checkpoints into the region and also to cut back operations in the West Bank.

▶ Consumer products companies Procter & Gamble and the Gillette Company announce a friendly merger.

▶ The annual Ernst von Siemens Music Prize, which honors outstanding achievement in contemporary music, is awarded to French composer Henri Dutilleux.

29 Jan American Serena Williams defeats her countrywoman Lindsay Davenport to win the Australian Open tennis tournament; the following day Marat Safin of Russia defeats Lleyton Hewitt of Australia to win the men's title.

▶ Winning films at the Sundance Film Festival awards ceremony in Park City UT include *Why We Fight, Forty Shades of Blue, Murderball,* and *Hustle & Flow.*

30 Jan Elections take place in Iraq for provincial legislatures and a national assembly empowered to write a new constitution; in spite of attacks that kill 35 people, turnout is estimated at 60%.

▶ A transport plane for the British Royal Air Force crashes in central Iraq; 10 British soldiers are killed, the highest single-day death toll for British forces since the beginning of the war.

31 Jan A commission appointed by UN Secretary-General Kofi Annan to investigate the situation in the Darfur region of The Sudan reports that it found war crimes and crimes against humanity but not genocide; it recommends that the crimes be tried in the International Criminal Court.

▶ The fifth annual World Social Forum, which grew out of the antiglobalization movement and is intended to counterbalance the World Economic Forum, wraps up after six days and thousands of workshops in Pôrto Alegre, Brazil; a record 100,000 people attended.

February

▶ **1 Feb** In a virtual coup, King Gyanendra of Nepal dismisses the government, suspends much of the constitution, and cuts off communication to and within the country.

▶ While visiting Argentina, Pres. Hugo Chávez of Venezuela says that he plans to sell his country's interests in US oil refineries as part of a plan to distance his government from that of the US.

2 Feb Armando Guebuza is sworn in as president of Mozambique.

▶ US Pres. George W. Bush delivers his fourth state of the union address; he emphasizes a plan to rein-

vent Social Security, citing the creation of a system of privately held accounts.

▶ Vietnam appeals to the World Health Organization and the Food and Agriculture Organization for help in dealing with the A(H5N1) avian flu, which is ravaging poultry in the country and has killed 13 of the 14 people infected in the past five weeks.

▶ The Irish Republican Army formally withdraws from peace negotiations in Northern Ireland with the governments of the UK and Ireland.

3 Feb The UN-appointed committee investigating the oil-for-food program in pre-occupation Iraq releases an interim report in which it cites Benon V. Sevan, the head of the program in 1997–2003, for favoritism and conflict of interest.

4 Feb Ukraine's Supreme Council approves the appointment of Yuliya Tymoshenko as prime minister.

5 Feb Gnassingbé Eyadéma, president of Togo, dies in office, and the country's military immediately installs his son Faure E. Gnassingbé in his place, in contravention of the country's constitution; the following day the National Assembly revises the constitution to allow Gnassingbé to remain in office until 2008.

▶ Leaders of the Group of Seven industrialized coun-

> **QUOTE OF THE MONTH**
>
> ❝ *As we fix Social Security, we also have the responsibility to make the system a better deal for younger workers. And the best way to reach that goal is through voluntary personal retirement accounts.* ❞
>
> —US Pres. George W. Bush, in his state of the union address, 2 February

tries meeting in London agree to pursue a plan to allow the entire debt owed by the poorest countries to multilateral institutions such as the World Bank to be written off.

▸ Quarterbacks Benny Friedman, Dan Marino, and Steve Young and halfback Fritz Pollard are elected to the Pro Football Hall of Fame.

6 Feb In parliamentary elections in Thailand, the political party of Prime Minister Thaksin Shinawatra wins lopsidedly.

▸ In Jacksonville FL the New England Patriots defeat the Philadelphia Eagles 24–21 to win Super Bowl XXXIX.

▸ The Mazatlán Venados (Deer) of Mexico defeat the Águilas (Eagles) from the Dominican Republic to win baseball's Caribbean Series, with a tournament record of 5–1.

7 Feb British yachtswoman Ellen MacArthur breaks the solo around-the-world sailing record, completing the journey in 71 days 14 hours.

▸ In the World Allround Speed Skating Championships in Moscow, the top overall female competitor is Anni Friesinger of Germany, and the top male competitor is Shani Davis of the US.

8 Feb At a summit meeting in Egypt, Israeli Prime Minister Ariel Sharon and Palestinian leader Mahmoud Abbas agree to a formal cease-fire.

▸ Greece's parliament elects Karolos Papoulias, a founder of the socialist party PASOK, to the largely ceremonial post of president.

9 Feb A court in Kazakhstan bans the country's second-biggest opposition party, saying that its protests against a parliamentary election in 2004 (which was called unfair by international observers) were an incitement to public disorder.

▸ The board of directors of the computer company Hewlett-Packard forces Carly Fiorina to resign as CEO.

10 Feb In the process of announcing its withdrawal from the six-party talks on the country's nuclear development plans, North Korea for the first time states publicly that it has developed nuclear weaponry.

▸ Voters in Saudi Arabia take part in the country's first-ever general election; only men are allowed to vote or run for office.

11 Feb As protests take place in Togo, the leaders of ECOWAS (Economic Community of West African States) order the newly installed president, Faure E. Gnassingbé, to meet with them the following day in Niger; he had previously refused to meet with ECOWAS in Lomé, Togo's capital.

▸ A judge in Pinellas county, Florida, rules that Terri Schiavo, a severely brain-damaged woman who is being sustained by a feeding tube against what her husband says are her wishes, has not been denied fair legal representation; the case has stirred public controversy for several years.

▸ The 61st Gold Medal of the American Institute of Architects is presented to Spanish architect Santiago Calatrava.

12 Feb A car bomber kills 17 people in front of a hospital south of Baghdad, bringing the death toll for the week to 104.

▸ Dorothy Stang, an American nun, environmentalist, and land rights activist, is murdered in Pará state, Brazil, igniting a storm of outrage.

▸ A public art project by Christo and Jeanne-Claude called *The Gates, Central Park, New York City, 1979–2005* goes on display in New York City's Central Park; it consists of 7,503 gates hung with saf-fron-colored fabric along 37 km (23 mi) of walkway and remains on display until 27 February.

▸ For the first time the European Space Agency's Arianespace successfully launches its most powerful rocket, the Ariane 5-ECA, from the spaceport at Kourou, French Guiana, and places two satellites in orbit.

13 Feb Results of the 30 January election in Iraq are reported: the United Iraqi Alliance, a Shi'ite alliance approved by Grand Ayatollah Ali al-Sistani, won 48% of the popular vote and 140 of the 275 seats in the assembly, a slim majority.

▸ At the Grammy Awards in Los Angeles, the top winner is the late Ray Charles, who wins eight awards, including record of the year for "Here We Go Again," a duet with Norah Jones, and album of the year for *Genius Loves Company;* the song of the year is John Mayer's "Daughters," and the best new artist is Maroon5.

▸ In the new event of team skiing at the World Skiing Championships in Italy, Germany surpasses favorite Austria to win the gold medal.

14 Feb Rafik Hariri, who resigned as Lebanon's prime minister in October 2004, is killed, along with 16 others, by a car bomb that destroys his motorcade in Beirut.

▸ A flight test of the US missile defense system fails when the interceptor missile does not launch; the previous two tests also failed.

▸ Following the suspension of democracy in Nepal the US, the UK, and France recall their ambassadors.

15 Feb The US recalls its ambassador to Syria because of its belief that Syria was involved in the assassination of former Lebanese prime minister Rafik Hariri.

16 Feb A ceremony is held in Kyoto, Japan, to mark the coming into force of the Kyoto Protocol, initialed in 1997; the agreement requires that the industrialized world cut emissions of greenhouse gases by 5.2% below 1990 levels by 2012.

▸ Israel's Knesset (legislature) approves a plan to give $870 million in compensation to settlers required to leave the Gaza Strip to relocate without losing their accustomed living standards.

▸ The Association for Computing Machinery announces that the recipients of the 2004 A.M. Turing Award are Vincent G. Cerf and Robert E. Kahn, who created the structure for TCP/IP, or transmission control protocol and Internet protocol, which allows computer networks to communicate with one another.

▸ The Bollingen Prize in American poetry is awarded to Jay Wright.

▸ National Hockey League commissioner Gary Bettman announces that negotiations between the owners and the players' union have been fruitless and that the entire 2004–05 season is canceled.

17 Feb US Pres. George W. Bush nominates John D. Negroponte, the ambassador to Iraq, as the country's first national intelligence director.

18 Feb Under international pressure, the newly installed president of Togo, Faure E. Gnassingbé, agrees to hold presidential elections within 60 days, as the constitution at the time of his installation required, but not to give up power to the speaker of the legislature, as also required by the constitution.

▸ Scientists at a NASA news conference report that on 27 Dec 2004 they detected a burst of light energy from interstellar space only a fraction of a second long but so powerful that it exceeded the total energy emitted from the Sun in 150,000 years; the source was identified as a distant magnetar, a rapidly spinning neutron star with an extremely intense magnetic field.

19 Feb Suicide bombers target celebrations of the Shi'ite holy day Ashura throughout Iraq, killing some 30 people; on the previous day suicide bombers at various religious gatherings and one police checkpoint killed at least 35 people in Baghdad alone.

20 Feb In legislative elections in Portugal, the Socialist Party defeats the ruling coalition, winning its first-ever absolute majority; José Sócrates becomes prime minister on 12 March.

▶ Spain, the first country to vote on the EU constitution in a national referendum, approves the constitution handily.

▶ In London, *The Producers* wins three Laurence Olivier Awards—best new musical, best actor in a musical (Nathan Lane), and best supporting actor in a musical (Conleth Hill)—and *The History Boys* also wins three awards—best new play, best director (Nicholas Hytner), and best actor (Richard Griffiths); Alan Bennett, the playwright of *The History Boys*, wins a special award for contributions to British theater.

▶ In Daytona Beach FL, Jeff Gordon wins the Daytona 500, NASCAR's premier race, for the third time.

21 Feb Tens of thousands of people—Muslim, Christian, and Druze—march in Beirut, Lebanon, in anti-Syrian protests, while Syrian Pres. Bashar al-Assad tells the secretary-general of the Arab League that Syria intends, as it has since 1989, to withdraw its troops.

▶ The British Royal Navy announces that it is planning to actively recruit gay enlistees to join the service.

22 Feb An early-morning earthquake of magnitude 6.4 centered on the city of Zarand kills at least 490 people in central Iran; many villages are destroyed.

▶ Emerging victorious in the elections, the United Iraqi Alliance chooses Ibrahim al-Jaafari as its candidate for prime minister of Iraq.

23 Feb Shigeru Omi of the World Health Organization warns that a deadly form of avian flu spreading throughout Asia, which has killed 14 people in Vietnam so far in 2005, threatens the world with a pandemic should it mutate into a form that can be transmitted easily from human to human.

▶ US diplomats reveal that Canada has decided against participating with the US in a North American missile defense system.

▶ In a British military court in Germany, two British soldiers, Mark Cooley and Daniel Kenyon, are convicted on charges of having abused Iraqi prisoners near Basra, Iraq, in May 2003.

24 Feb The Palestinian legislature approves a new cabinet that is largely purged of allies of the late Yasir Arafat, though Ahmed Qurei retains his post as prime minister.

▶ Somalian Pres. Abdullahi Yusuf Ahmed and Prime Minister Ali Muhammad Ghedi visit Somalia for the first time since attaining their posts; they are as-

sessing conditions for moving the Somalian government-in-exile from Kenya.

▶ Pope John Paul II is hospitalized for the second time this month and undergoes a tracheotomy because of difficulty breathing.

25 Feb Bowing to internal and international pressure, Faure E. Gnassingbé resigns as president of Togo; Abass Bonfoh becomes interim president until a presidential election, in which Gnassingbé will be a candidate, is held.

▶ For the first time since it was booed off the stage in 1931, the ballet *The Bolt*, with a score by Dmitry Shostakovich, is performed by the Bolshoi Ballet in Moscow.

26 Feb Egyptian Pres. Hosni Mubarak asks the parliament to amend the constitution to permit for the first time in the country's history direct, multiparty presidential elections to be held.

▶ Japan's space agency successfully returns its H-2A heavy-lift rocket to service with a launch from its Tanegashima space center and deploys a geostationary air-traffic/weather satellite; the previous launch, in November 2003, failed to orbit two spy satellites.

▶ Wichita KS police announce that they have arrested a man, Dennis L. Rader, in suburban Park City whom they believe to be the serial killer known as B.T.K., who is responsible for at least eight murders over a 30-year period.

27 Feb Parliamentary elections are held in Kyrgyzstan and Tajikistan; international observers in both countries say the polling fell short of international standards of fairness, and runoff elections for each district in Kyrgyzstan are scheduled for 13 March, while the ruling party retains power in Tajikistan.

▶ The Framework Convention on Tobacco Control, signed by 168 countries but ratified by only 57, comes into effect; it asks those countries to take steps to reduce tobacco smoking, which kills an estimated five million people annually.

▶ At the 77th Academy Awards presentations, hosted by comedian Chris Rock, Oscars are won by, among others, *Million Dollar Baby* and its director, Clint Eastwood, and actors Jamie Foxx, Hilary Swank, Morgan Freeman, and Cate Blanchett.

28 Feb In by far the deadliest bombing since the start of the war in Iraq, a car bomber detonates his weapons in a crowd of police and army recruits outside a medical clinic across the street from a market in Hilla; at least 122 people are killed.

▶ As tens of thousands of people demonstrate in Beirut against Syrian involvement in Lebanon, the pro-Syrian Omar Karami resigns as Lebanese prime minister.

▶ In a referendum, more than 90% of voters in Burundi approve a new constitution that lays the groundwork for a government in which the Hutu majority and the Tutsi minority would share power.

▶ Federated Department Stores, the owner of Macy's and Bloomingdale's, announces that it plans to buy May Department Stores, which owns Lord & Taylor and Marshall Field's.

March

1 Mar Tabaré Vázquez Rosas is inaugurated as president of Uruguay.

▶ In a gun battle in Ituri province in the Democratic Republic of the Congo, UN peacekeepers kill 50 members of an ethnic Lendu militia that has been

terrorizing the area; also, the government says that three militia leaders have been arrested in the ambush killing and mutilation of nine UN peacekeepers in Ituri province.

▶ The US Supreme Court rules that the execution of

people for crimes that they committed when they were younger than 18 years old is unconstitutional; the ruling immediately affects 72 condemned prisoners.

2 Mar Elmar Huseynov, the founder and editor of the Azerbaijani opposition magazine *Monitor,* is shot and killed in Baku.

3 Mar American adventurer Steve Fossett becomes the first person to fly solo nonstop around the world when he lands in Salina KS 67 hr 2 min after taking off; his plane, called the *GlobalFlyer,* was designed and built by Burt Rutan's Scaled Composites company, which also built SpaceShipOne.

▸ A trial involving 39 men and 27 women accused of pedophile crimes begins in Angers, France.

4 Mar A car carrying Giuliana Sgrena, an Italian journalist who had been kidnapped on 4 February in Baghdad, and Nicola Calipari, an Italian intelligence agent who had negotiated her release, is fired on by US soldiers as it approaches a checkpoint on the way to the Baghdad airport; Calipari is killed and Sgrena is wounded.

▸ Yury F. Kravchenko, who was interior minister of Ukraine under former president Leonid Kuchma in 1995–2001, dies in an apparent suicide hours before he is to talk to government prosecutors about the 2000 murder of journalist Georgy Gongadze in which there was widely believed to have been government involvement.

▸ American lifestyle entrepreneur Martha Stewart completes a five-month prison sentence and is released to begin five months of home confinement.

5 Mar Syrian Pres. Bashar al-Assad makes a speech in which he declares that Syrian troops in Lebanon will gradually withdraw to border areas near Syria, but he gives no timetable.

QUOTE OF THE MONTH

❝ *A Syrian pullout from Lebanon does not mean that Syria will vanish from Lebanon.* ❞

—Syrian Pres. Bashar al-Assad in a speech announcing a pullback of Syrian troops, 5 March

---

6 Mar In parliamentary elections in Moldova, the ruling Communist Party retains its majority.

▸ In the first Formula 1 race of the season, Giancarlo Fisichella of Italy wins the Australian Grand Prix for Renault.

7 Mar The Sony Corp. of Japan names Sir Howard Stringer, head of the Sony Corp. of America, its new chairman and CEO, succeeding Nobuyuki Idei.

▸ Harry Stonecipher, who was made CEO of the aerospace company Boeing in order to restore its good name after an era of ethical missteps, is forced to resign when it is revealed that he had engaged in an adulterous liaison with an executive at the company.

8 Mar Bolivia's National Congress refuses to accept the offer of resignation given the day before by Pres. Carlos Mesa; the president reaches an agreement with most opposition parties for a plan that includes increased autonomy for the states and the drafting of a new constitution.

▸ The prime minister of the province of Kosovo in Serbia and Montenegro, Ramush Haradinaj, surprises observers by resigning in order to surrender to the UN war crimes tribunal in The Hague.

▸ In Beirut, Lebanon, a huge demonstration by Shi'ite supporters of the militant group Hezbollah in favor of a continued Syrian presence in Lebanon greatly outnumbers the anti-Syria demonstrations that preceded it.

9 Mar Omar Karami, the pro-Syrian who resigned as prime minister of Lebanon on 28 February, is reelected prime minister by the legislature.

▸ The US Department of State announces that the country has withdrawn from the protocol that gives the International Court of Justice jurisdiction to hear cases involving foreigners arrested and denied the right to contact the embassies of their home countries.

▸ The LexisNexis Group, which compiles personal, legal, and consumer information, reveals that unauthorized access to the information of some 30,000 people has occurred; in recent weeks the data broker ChoicePoint inadvertently sold the information of some 145,000 people to scam artists, and the Bank of America lost backup files containing the information of more than a million people.

▸ Charles H. Townes, a winner of the 1964 Nobel Prize for Physics, is named the winner of the Templeton Prize for Progress Toward Research or Discoveries About Spiritual Realities.

▸ CBS news anchor Dan Rather signs off after his final broadcast, concluding a career of 42 years.

10 Mar Tung Chee-hwa resigns as chief executive of Hong Kong two years before the end of his term; deputy Donald Tsang will serve in his place until the next election.

▸ After winning a tournament in Linares, Spain, Russian chess grandmaster Garry Kasparov announces his retirement from professional chess.

11 Mar The US government announces an agreement with the UK, France, and Germany in which the US will support Iran's entry into the World Trade Organization and sell the country airplane parts if Iran agrees to a permanent end to the enrichment of uranium; the European countries pledge to bring the issue before the UN Security Council if Iran does not agree.

▸ The British Parliament passes a controversial antiterrorism bill that, among other things, allows the government to put suspected terrorists under strict house arrest without trial.

12 Mar UN envoy Terje Roed-Larsen secures an agreement from Syrian Pres. Bashar al-Assad to withdraw Syrian troops from Lebanon completely and to set a timetable for the withdrawal.

▸ Muhammad Ghazal announces that the militant Palestinian organization Hamas will participate in the Palestinian legislative elections that are to take place on 17 July; the organization had boycotted the previous legislative elections.

▸ At the Alpine World Cup skiing competition in Lenzerheide, Switzerland, Bode Miller becomes the first American in 22 years to win the overall men's World Cup championship; the following day Anja Pärson of Sweden wins the women's title for the second consecutive year.

13 Mar Runoff legislative elections in Kyrgyzstan are widely viewed as fraudulent as domestic election observers are prevented from doing their jobs.

▸ The Walt Disney Co. announces that Robert A. Iger, the company's president, will take over from Michael D. Eisner as CEO.

▸ Canada sets a new world record time of 6 min 39.990 sec in the 5,000-m relay at the world short-track speed-skating championships in Beijing.

14 Mar The National People's Congress of China

passes a law that authorizes the use of force against Taiwan should Taiwan declare itself independent of China.

▸ Some 800,000 Lebanese—mostly Sunni Muslims, Druze, and Christians—rally in Beirut against Syrian influence in Lebanon; it is the biggest demonstration ever seen in Lebanon.

▸ In its 20th induction ceremony, the Rock and Roll Hall of Fame in Cleveland inducts the solo performers Buddy Guy and Percy Sledge, the bands the O'Jays, the Pretenders, and U2, booking agency founder Frank Barsalona, and Sire Records founder Seymour Stein.

▸ A state judge in California rules that a state law that limits marriage to opposite-sex couples violates the state's constitution.

15 Mar People protesting elections they believe were rigged march in the streets and occupy government offices in several cities in Kyrgyzstan.

▸ Italian Prime Minister Silvio Berlusconi says that by September he intends to begin withdrawing Italian troops from Iraq, where Italy has some 3,000 troops.

▸ Bernard J. Ebbers, the former CEO of the disgraced telecommunications company WorldCom (now MCI), is found guilty of securities fraud, conspiracy, and seven counts of filing false reports.

16 Mar Iraq's newly elected national assembly conducts its first meeting, in the heavily guarded central Green Zone in Baghdad.

17 Mar During a brief visit to Afghanistan, US Secretary of State Condoleezza Rice reveals that upcoming parliamentary elections in the country are being postponed for a third time, from May until September; meanwhile, in Kandahar, in the worst attack in seven months, a bomb kills at least 5 people and injures 32.

▸ The European Union decides to ban broadcasts by al-Manar, the satellite television channel run by the Lebanese militant group Hezbollah.

18 Mar Wal-Mart Stores agrees to a record $11 million settlement with the federal government, which had accused the retail giant of hiring illegal immigrants as cleaning staff.

▸ The military in Israel announces that henceforth no Israeli citizen may move to any settlement in the Gaza Strip.

▸ John G. Rowland, the former governor of Connecticut, is sentenced to more than a year in prison for having secretly accepted gifts from people doing business with the state while he was governor; he had pled guilty in December 2004.

▸ In accordance with what her husband says would have been her wishes, in Pinellas Park FL the feeding tube keeping the severely brain-damaged Terri Schiavo alive is removed.

▸ The US government suspends military aid to Nicaragua, complaining that the country has failed to destroy its cache of Soviet-made SA-7 shoulder-launched antiaircraft missiles, which the US fears could fall into the hands of terrorists.

19 Mar A bomb goes off at a Shi'ite Muslim religious gathering in Gandhawa, Pakistan, killing at least 44 people.

▸ Irina Slutskaya of Russia wins the women's world figure skating championship in Moscow; two days earlier Stéphane Lambiel became the first Swiss since 1947 to claim the men's title.

▸ In the Six Nations rugby union championship, Wales defeats Ireland 32–20 to win the title and its first grand slam in 27 years.

20 Mar Insurgents attack a US military patrol in Salman Pak, Iraq; at least 24 insurgents are killed, while assorted attacks elsewhere in Iraq leave at least 7 other people dead.

▸ The US Senate passes a bill that would give federal courts jurisdiction over whether it was legal to remove the feeding tube from a severely brain-damaged woman, Terri Schiavo; the House of Representatives calls a special session to consider the measure; Pres. George W. Bush quickly returns to Washington DC from vacation in Texas in order to sign the bill into law.

▸ Thousands of protesters upset by unfair elections rampage in Jalal-Abad, Kyrgyzstan, occupying government offices and burning down a police station.

▸ Fernando Alonso of Spain wins the Malaysian Grand Prix automobile race.

21 Mar Hifikepunye Pohamba is sworn in as president of Namibia; he is the country's first president elected since independence and succeeds Sam Nujoma.

▸ Antigovernment demonstrators take over Osh, the second largest city in Kyrgyzstan.

▸ American architect Thom Mayne is named the winner of the 2005 Pritzker Architecture Prize.

▸ Former world chess champion Bobby Fischer is granted Icelandic citizenship; under indictment by the US government, Fischer has been living in detention in Japan for eight months.

22 Mar Germany's national airline, Deutsche Lufthansa, announces a deal to take over Switzerland's troubled Swiss International Airlines.

23 Mar The Arab League concludes a two-day summit in Algiers; leaders of only 13 of the 22 member countries attended the conference, at which it was decided to create an Arab parliament.

▸ Health officials warn travelers to stay out of Uíge province in Angola, where an outbreak of the Marburg virus, which is related to the Ebola virus and is fatal with no known cure, has killed at least 95 people since October 2004.

24 Mar Thousands of demonstrators storm the presidential palace in Bishkek, Kyrgyzstan, forcing Pres. Askar Akayev to flee the country.

▸ The UN Security Council passes a resolution to send 10,000 peacekeeping troops to The Sudan, some to maintain the peace agreement in the south and some to reinforce African Union troops in the Darfur region.

▸ US Secretary of Defense Donald Rumsfeld announces that the country will resume giving military aid to Guatemala; aid had been suspended in 1990 in the face of atrocities committed by the Guatemalan military, including the killing of an American citizen.

25 Mar Outside Manama, Bahrain, tens of thousands of people march in a demonstration demanding democratic reforms, including more powers for the elected legislative assembly.

26 Mar A half million people march in Taipei, Taiwan, angered and frightened by the antisecession law passed in China on 14 March.

▸ After two days of looting by antigovernment protesters in Kyrgyzstan, a new government, led by Kurmanbek Bakiyev as interim acting president, gains control.

▸ Roses in May wins the Dubai World Cup, the world's richest horse race, by three lengths.

▸ Yokozuna Asashoryu defeats *ozeki* Kaio at the spring grand sumo tournament in Osaka, Japan, to win his 11th Emperor's Cup.

27 Mar Pope John Paul II appears at his window in St.

Peter's Square in the Vatican to deliver his traditional Easter blessing; because of his illnesses, however, he is unable to speak.

▶ Police in Cairo arrest 100 people in preventing a demonstration by thousands of people organized by the Muslim Brotherhood to demand an end to emergency laws that have been in place in Egypt since 1981.

▶ At the Nabisco Championship in Rancho Mirage CA, Annika Sörenstam of Sweden wins her fifth consecutive Ladies Professional Golf Association Tour tournament, tying a record set by American Nancy Lopez in 1978.

▶ Oxford defeats Cambridge by two lengths in the 151st University Boat Race; Cambridge leads the series 78–72.

28 Mar It is reported that King Jigme Singye Wangchuk of Bhutan has unveiled a draft of a new constitution that would establish parliamentary rule and multiparty democracy to replace what is presently a monarchy.

▶ An earthquake measured at magnitude-8.7 occurs with an epicenter about 200 km (125 mi) from the Indonesian island of Sumatra, killing at least 905 people, most on the island of Nias.

▶ A law is passed in Ireland that outlaws the use of English on street signs and official maps in the Gaeltacht region of the country's west coast; in more than 2,000 places signs will appear exclusively in Gaelic.

▶ Maud Fontenoy of France becomes the first woman to row across the Pacific Ocean when she arrives in Hiva Oa, Marquesas Islands, French Polynesia, 73 days after leaving the port of Callao in Peru.

29 Mar The commission investigating misconduct in the oil-for-food program in Iraq reports having found no evidence that UN Secretary-General Kofi Annan had any involvement in the awarding of a contract to a company that employed his son.

▶ Lord Ashdown, the international administrator of Bosnia and Herzegovina, removes the Croat member of the tripartite presidency, Dragan Covic, from office; Covic had refused to resign after being indicted for corruption.

30 Mar After Palestinian Pres. Mahmoud Abbas expels members of al-Aqsa Martyrs Brigades from the presidential compound for refusing to disarm and join the Palestinian Authority security forces, the gunmen run riot in Ram Allah.

▶ Syrian Pres. Bashar al-Assad releases 312 Kurdish prisoners who had been arrested in March 2004 after antigovernment demonstrations.

31 Mar In legislative elections in Zimbabwe that independent observers say are fraudulent, the ruling ZANU-PF is said to have won handily.

▶ The UN Security Council passes a resolution to refer war crimes suspects from the Darfur region of The Sudan to the International Criminal Court in The Hague.

▶ The Vatican reports that Pope John Paul II has suffered a heart attack.

April

1 Apr Overnight, members of the state military police shoot up the streets and sidewalks of two crime-ridden suburbs of Rio de Janeiro, killing 30 people.

2 Apr Pope John Paul II dies in his apartment in Vatican City.

▶ After months of discord that led to many canceled performances, Riccardo Muti resigns as music director of La Scala opera house in Milan.

3 Apr In its first step toward forming a government and following months of debate, the Iraqi National Assembly appoints a Sunni as speaker and a Shi'ite and a Kurd as deputy speakers.

▶ The Museum of the Shenandoah Valley opens in Winchester VA; the historical and cultural museum was designed by the architect Michael Graves.

4 Apr Askar Akayev resigns as president of Kyrgyzstan after receiving assurances that he will not be prosecuted for anything that occurred during his administration.

▶ In New York City the winners of the 2005 Pulitzer Prizes are announced; journalistic awards go to, among others, the *Los Angeles Times* and *The Wall Street Journal*, which each win two awards; winners in arts and letters include Marilynne Robinson in fiction and Ted Kooser in poetry.

▶ The National Collegiate Athletic Association (NCAA) championship in men's basketball is won by the University of North Carolina, which defeats the University of Illinois 75–70; the following day Baylor University defeats Michigan State 84–62 for its first women's NCAA title.

5 Apr Armando Falcon announces his resignation as head of the Office of Federal Housing Enterprise Oversight, the agency that oversees the mortgage companies Fannie Mae and Freddie Mac.

6 Apr Europe's longest-reigning monarch, Prince Rainier III of Monaco, dies after 55 years as ruler; he is succeeded by his son, Prince Albert II.

▶ The Iraqi National Assembly names Kurdish militia leader Jalal Talabani president of Iraq.

▶ In Pretoria, South Africa, the leaders of Côte d'Ivoire's government, the opposition, and rebel forces sign an agreement to cease hostilities, begin disarmament, and make plans to hold elections.

7 Apr Newly named Iraqi Pres. Jalal Talabani appoints Shi'ite leader Ibrahim al-Jaafari as Iraq's new prime minister.

▶ George Foster Peabody Awards for excellence in electronic media are won by, among 30 others, the CBS newsmagazine show *60 Minutes II* and Comedy Central's *The Daily Show with Jon Stewart*.

8 Apr Pope John Paul II is buried after what is by far the largest papal funeral ever held; in the previous week more than two million people had viewed the pope's body as it lay in state.

▶ In a presidential election that is boycotted by the opposition, Pres. Ismail Omar Guelleh, running unopposed, is reelected president of Djibouti.

9 Apr Officially sanctioned anti-Japanese demonstrations in Beijing degenerate into riots in which Japanese-owned businesses are attacked before riot police gain control of the situation.

▶ In Windsor, England, Charles, prince of Wales, marries Camilla Parker Bowles, who hereafter will be called Camilla, duchess of Cornwall.

▶ The winner of the Grand National steeplechase horse race in Aintree, England, by 14 lengths, is Hedgehunter, ridden by Ruby Walsh and trained by Willie Mullins.

10 Apr At the place in Jerusalem that is revered as the Temple Mount by Jews and as Al-Haram al-Sharif by Muslims, a huge deployment of Israeli police prevents a planned rally by a right-wing Israeli organization from taking place.

▸ Anti-Japanese rallies take place in the Chinese cities of Guangzhou and Shenzhen; Japan lodges an official protest with China.

▸ After police break up a roadblock set up weeks earlier by a group of elderly women in Huaxi village, Zhejiang province, China, to protest pollution from nearby factories, thousands of villagers riot in defense of the protesters, destroying police cars and driving police away.

▸ Tiger Woods defeats Chris DiMarco on the first playoff hole to win the Masters golf tournament in Augusta GA for the fourth time.

▸ Canada defeats Scotland 11–4 to win its 29th world men's curling championship since 1959.

11 Apr After several days of delay, Kyrgyzstan's legislature accepts the resignation of Askar Akayev as president and sets a new presidential election for 10 July.

▸ In New Delhi, Chinese Prime Minister Wen Jiabao and Indian Prime Minister Manmohan Singh sign documents on a number of subjects; of special note is an agreement to resolve the 3,540-km (2,200-mi) border between the countries, which has been a source of friction since 1962.

▸ MG Rover, the last major car manufacturer in the UK, sends 6,000 factory workers home and ceases production.

12 Apr The World Health Organization and the US Centers for Disease Control and Prevention observe the 50th anniversary of the introduction of the polio vaccine.

13 Apr The EU agrees to allow Bulgaria and Romania to become members of the association; it is expected that they would enter the union in 2007.

▸ The UN General Assembly passes a nuclear-terrorism treaty that requires its signatories to prosecute or extradite individuals in possession of nuclear devices or materials.

▸ Omar Karami for the second time resigns as prime minister of Lebanon, saying he has been unable to form a government.

▸ In the Indian state of Manipur, members of a group demanding the use of the Mayek system of writing, which has not been widely used in three centuries, set fire to the central library in the capital city of Imphal; about 145,000 books, including many ancient texts, are destroyed.

14 Apr Two suicide bombers in Baghdad kill 14 people, 13 of them civilians, outside the Interior Ministry, while attacks elsewhere in Iraq kill 5 others; also, Iraqi officials describe the discovery of mass graves in al-Nasiriyah, al-Samawah, and Basra, the latter thought to contain as many as 5,000 bodies.

▸ In the heaviest fighting since a five-year-old ceasefire was rescinded, 24 Kurdish rebels and 3 Turkish soldiers are killed in Turkey's southeastern Anatolia region.

▸ Oregon's Supreme Court rules that the same-sex marriage licenses issued by Multnomah county in 2004 are invalid; the ruling affects some 3,000 couples.

▸ In the first Major League Baseball game played in Washington DC in 33 years, the new home team, the Washington Nationals, defeats the Arizona Diamondbacks 5–3 at R.F.K. Stadium.

15 Apr Pres. Émile Lahoud of Lebanon appoints as prime minister Najib Mikati, a pro-Syrian businessman who has won the trust of the opposition.

▸ Pres. Lucio Gutiérrez of Ecuador fires the Supreme Court; it is the second time in four months that the country's top court has been sacked.

16 Apr A bomb goes off in a restaurant in Ba'qubah, Iraq, killing at least 13 people; in attacks elsewhere in Iraq an additional 5 people are killed.

17 Apr Mehmet Ali Talat is elected Turkish Cypriot president, replacing Rauf Denktash.

▸ Ecuador's National Congress dismisses the Supreme Court, making legal the dismissal ordered earlier by the president.

▸ In the UK, Bafta TV Awards are won by *Little Britain*, *Sex Traffic*, *I'm a Celebrity... Get Me Out of Here!*, *Coronation Street*, *Omagh*, *Black Books*, and *Green Wing*.

18 Apr In Vatican City the conclave of 115 cardinals gathers to choose a new pope.

▸ Having earlier refused the help of the UN High Commissioner for Refugees, Indonesia announces the formation of a new agency that will take over the reconstruction of the rebellious province of Aceh, which was particularly hard hit by the Indian Ocean tsunami of December 2004.

▸ The 109th Boston Marathon is won by Hailu Negussie of Ethiopia with a time of 2 hr 11 min 45 sec; Catherine Ndereba of Kenya is the women's winner for the fourth time, finishing in 2 hr 25 min 13 sec.

19 Apr On its third ballot the Roman Catholic Church conclave chooses Joseph Cardinal Ratzinger, a German theologian who served for many years in the Roman Curia as defender of the faith, to be the next pope; he announces his papal name as Benedict XVI.

QUOTE OF THE MONTH

❝ *After the great Pope John Paul II, the cardinals have elected me, a simple, humble worker in the Lord's vineyard.* ❞

—Pope Benedict XVI, in his first public address after his election, 19 April

---

▸ Greece's parliament ratifies the European Union constitution.

▸ Seventeen men return to Afghanistan after being freed from the US military prison in Guantánamo Bay, Cuba; a tribunal had determined that they were not enemy combatants.

20 Apr Ecuador's National Congress dismisses Pres. Lucio Gutiérrez from office, and he flees to the Brazilian embassy; Vice Pres. Alfredo Palacio replaces him.

▸ Connecticut becomes the second US state to permit same-sex couples to enter into civil unions, a status that entails the same statutory rights and responsibilities as marriage.

▸ The first-ever Islamic Solidarity Games, featuring 18 individual and team sports, conclude in Mecca, Saudi Arabia; 54 countries sent some 6,500 male athletes to compete.

▸ The New York Stock Exchange and the Archipelago Exchange announce an agreement to merge in the largest-ever securities-exchange merger.

21 Apr John Negroponte is sworn in as the first US director of national intelligence.

▸ The lower house of the Cortes Generales (legislature) in Spain approves a bill that gives same-sex couples the same marriage rights that opposite-sex couples now have and approves another bill making divorce easier to obtain.

22 Apr At a regional summit meeting in Jakarta, Indonesia, Japanese Prime Minister Junichiro Koizumi apologizes for the suffering and damage caused by Japan during World War II.

▸ Zacarias Moussaoui, the only person charged in the US with complicity in the 11 Sep 2001 terrorist attacks, pleads guilty—but not exactly to what he is charged with.

23 Apr Italian Prime Minister Silvio Berlusconi forms a new coalition government three days after resigning because of the collapse of the previous government.

24 Apr Pope Benedict XVI is formally invested with the symbols of office and installed as the 265th pope.

▸ Faure E. Gnassingbé wins the presidential election in Togo; the result of the ballot is accepted by international observers but not by the opposition.

▸ Pres. Hugo Chávez of Venezuela announces that he is cutting all military ties with the US and ordering US military instructors to leave the country.

25 Apr Stanislav Gross resigns as prime minister of the Czech Republic following weeks of questions about the financing of his luxury apartment; Jiri Paroubek is appointed in his place.

▸ A Soyuz space capsule lands safely in Kazakhstan, bringing home cosmonaut Salizhan Sharipov and astronauts Leroy Chiao and Roberto Vittori; the new crew members replacing them aboard the International Space Station are Russian Sergey Krikalev and American John Phillips.

▸ The final piece of the 1,700-year-old Obelisk of Axum, which had been removed from Ethiopia by Italian troops in 1937, is returned to its home in Axum; it will be reerected in September.

26 Apr Syria formally withdraws the last of its troops from Lebanon; Syria had maintained a military presence in the country for 29 years.

▸ UN Secretary-General Kofi Annan appoints Kemal Dervis, a Turkish economist, to replace Mark Malloch Brown as head of the United Nations Development Programme.

27 Apr China rules that the chief executive to be chosen by the election committee in July to replace Tung Chee-hwa can serve only for the remainder of the term that Tung was elected to, not a full five-year term.

28 Apr Scientists report that an ivory-billed woodpecker, a bird thought to have been extinct since 1944, has been sighted in the Cache River National Wildlife Refuge in Arkansas.

29 Apr In Beijing a meeting between the leader of the Communist Party of China, Hu Jintao, and the leader of the Chinese Nationalist Party, Lien Chan, marks the first time leaders of the two parties have met in 60 years; they pledge to work together against the independence movement in Taiwan.

▸ King Gyanendra of Nepal announces the lifting of emergency rule.

▸ A coordinated series of 12 car bombs in the Baghdad area and other attacks in Iraq leave at least 40 people, most of them Iraqi police or military, dead.

30 Apr A suicide bomber kills himself and injures seven people outside the popular Egyptian Museum in Cairo, and his sister and girlfriend fire guns at a tourist bus.

▸ A parade is held in Ho Chi Minh City (formerly Saigon), Vietnam, to celebrate the 30th anniversary of the fall of that city.

May

1 May At least 35 Iraqis are killed in attacks that include a car bomb at a Kurdish funeral near Mosul and another at a scene in Baghdad where US soldiers are handing out candy to children.

2 May A cache of explosives stored at the home of a commander of a recently disarmed and demobilized regiment in the Afghan village of Kohna Deh explodes, leveling a portion of the village and killing at least 34 people, mostly women and children.

▸ Six car bombs in Baghdad and one in Mosul kill at least 13 Iraqis, and American soldiers engage in a firefight near the Syrian border, killing 12.

▸ A socialist, José Miguel Insulza of Chile, a candidate initially opposed by the US, is elected secretary-general of the Organization of American States.

3 May Iraq's newly appointed cabinet is sworn in, though seven posts remain vacant, including that of minister of defense.

▸ A bomb explodes and kills at least 15 people in a stadium in Mogadishu, Somalia, where the interim prime minister, Ali Muhammad Ghedi, is speaking; top Somali officials have been living outside the country, and this is Ghedi's first visit to the capital since he was elected to office.

4 May A suicide bomber kills at least 60 Kurdish Iraqis at a police recruiting station in Irbil, Iraq, in the worst single attack since early March.

▸ The FBI announces that it plans to exhume from its grave in Alsip IL the body of Emmett Till, whose lynching in Mississippi as a teenager 50 years ago was a catalyst for the US civil rights movement, in hopes that new forensic evidence will make it possible to clarify the circumstances of his death.

▸ Paleontologists in Salt Lake City announce their discovery of a new birdlike, feathered dinosaur species, *Falcarius utahensis*, that lived about 125 million years ago and appears to represent an evolutionary link between carnivorous dinosaurs and later herbivorous groups.

▸ Astronomers report that they have observed 12 tiny previously undiscovered moons orbiting Saturn, all but one in a direction opposite to that of its larger moons, bringing the number of Saturn's known moons to 46; a 47th moon, discovered by the Cassini spacecraft, is announced on May 6.

5 May Elections in the UK return Prime Minister Tony Blair to office for a third term of office—unprecedented for a Labour Party leader—but with his smallest majority so far.

▸ A suicide bomber at an Iraqi army base in Baghdad kills at least 13 people, and a further 9 are killed in other attacks elsewhere in Iraq.

▸ On Holocaust Remembrance Day 60 years after the liberation of the Nazi death camps, some 18,000 people, including the Israeli, Polish, and Hungarian prime ministers, participate in the annual March of the Living from Auschwitz to Birkenau, former concentration camps in southern Poland; on 10 May the Memorial to the Murdered Jews of Europe, designed by Peter Eisenman, opens with a solemn ceremony in Berlin.

6 May Having failed to oust Labour in the British elections, Michael Howard surprises observers by announcing that he will step down as leader of the Conservative Party before the next election.

‣ A car bombing in Tikrit, Iraq, drives his car into a bus, killing at least 10 people, and a car bomber in Suwayrah kills a further 16 people.

‣ Patriarch Irineos I, head of the Greek Orthodox Church in the Holy Land, flees the patriarchate after a number of bishops and archimandrites declare him *persona non grata*, accusing him of having allowed the leasing of two church-owned hotels in Jerusalem to Jewish renters.

‣ In the world table tennis championships in Shanghai, Wang Liqin of China wins the men's singles title to give the host country a clean sweep of the championships.

7 May A bombing in Baghdad kills at least 22 people; in a period of 10 minutes in Yangon, Myanmar, bombs go off at a trade fair in a convention center and in two supermarkets, killing at least 11 people; and another bomb kills at least 3 people at an Internet cafe in Kabul, Afghanistan.

‣ The virtually unknown horse Giacomo, a 50-to-1 shot, wins the Kentucky Derby, the first race of Thoroughbred horse racing's Triple Crown; favorite Afleet Alex finishes third.

‣ A new museum of contemporary art, the MARTa Museum, designed by Frank Gehry, opens in Herford, near Hanover, Germany.

‣ *Margaret Garner*, an opera inspired by the true story of a fugitive slave that was the basis of Toni Morrison's novel *Beloved*, with music composed by Richard Danielpour and book by Morrison, has its premiere at the Detroit Opera House; the lead role is sung by Denyce Graves.

8 May Israeli Prime Minister Ariel Sharon freezes plans for an expected release of 400 Palestinian prisoners; earlier in the week Israeli officials halted plans to transfer security control of three more towns in the West Bank to the Palestinian Authority.

‣ A grand council of more than 1,000 representatives from throughout Afghanistan called by Pres. Hamid Karzai agrees that the country requires the continued presence of international troops but calls on the US to operate in cooperation with Afghanistan's government and army.

‣ Germany commemorates the 60th anniversary of the end of World War II in Europe; the following day world leaders gather in Moscow to celebrate the event.

QUOTE OF THE MONTH

❝ *We Germans look back with shock and shame at World War II, which was unleashed by Germany, and at the Holocaust, which was a breakdown of civilization for which Germans are responsible.* ❞

—*German Pres. Horst Köhler in a speech to Parliament commemorating the end of World War II, 8 May*

---

9 May A large offensive by 1,000 troops led by US Marines has reportedly swept through an area of western Iraq near Syria where it is believed the insurgency is receiving logistical support; the offensive is said to have left 4 Americans and 100 insurgents dead.

‣ Israeli Prime Minister Ariel Sharon announces that the official date for the beginning of the evacuation of Jewish settlements in the Gaza Strip will be pushed back about four weeks from 25 July to avoid a mourning period ending with the Jewish fast day of Tisha be-Av.

‣ Several of Tokyo's rail companies introduce women-only cars on commuter trains as a means of alleviating the problem of men groping women on overcrowded trains.

10 May Russian Pres. Vladimir Putin signs an agreement with the European Union to cooperate in economic and political matters including trade and fighting terrorism and crime.

‣ A US federal bankruptcy court grants United Airlines the right to default on its four employee pension plans, the largest-ever such default.

‣ The World Health Organization announces that more than 40 new cases of polio have been confirmed in Yemen.

‣ Iraq's National Assembly names a committee of 55 members to write a new permanent constitution for the country.

‣ Zahi Hawass, secretary-general of the Supreme Council of Antiquities in Egypt, releases photographs of computer reconstructions of the face of the pharaoh Tutankhamen based on CT scans of his mummy.

11 May In Tikrit, Iraq, a car bomber kills at least 38 people, most of them casual laborers, while in Hawijah a suicide bomber kills at least 32 people; smaller attacks in Baghdad bring the day's death toll to 79.

‣ A demonstration in Jalalabad, Afghanistan, by students upset at a report in *Newsweek* magazine that US interrogators in Guantánamo Bay, Cuba, had flushed a copy of the Koran down a toilet turns into violent rioting; 4 people are killed and 63 are wounded.

‣ In Andijon, Uzbekistan, hundreds of people take part in a protest, seeking the release of 23 Muslim prisoners charged with religious extremism.

‣ A judge in Mali sentences 11 Muslim men to prison for refusing to allow their daughters to be vaccinated against polio for fear it would make them sterile.

‣ Slovakia's legislature ratifies the European constitution.

‣ In Brasilia, Brazil, heads of state and officials representing 34 countries conclude the first Summit of South American–Arab Countries; the two-day meeting is intended to form an alternative grouping that is not dominated by developed countries.

12 May Several bombings in Baghdad kill at least 21 people; the worst of the assaults appear not to have had a military target, unlike the vast majority of attacks.

‣ A US federal judge rules that an amendment to Nebraska's constitution banning same-sex marriage is unconstitutional and was written so broadly as to threaten the rights of foster and adoptive parents and people in other living arrangements.

‣ In honor of the 60th birthday of Pippi Longstocking, Swedish writer Astrid Lindgren's child heroine, the ballet *Pippi Longstocking* has its debut at the Royal Swedish Opera of Stockholm.

13 May Anti-American protests gain in intensity in Afghanistan and Pakistan and spread to Indonesia and Palestine; at least eight protesters in Afghanistan are killed.

‣ Government troops fire on an uprising that had turned violent in Andijon, Uzbekistan, killing possibly as many as 500 people.

‣ Australia and East Timor reach an agreement to divide equally the revenue from the Greater Sunrise gas field, in the Timor Sea between the two countries, and to defer a decision on the maritime boundary between the two for 50 years.

‣ Reporting in the periodical *Science*, geneticists present DNA evidence from the Orang Asli people of Malaysia in support of a proposal that humans migrated out of Africa some 65,000 years ago, taking a southern coastal route into India, Southeast Asia, and Australia, while an offshoot moved north and west eventually to populate the Middle East and Europe.

‣ Archbishop William J. Levada of San Francisco is named by Pope Benedict XVI to head the Congregation for the Doctrine of the Faith, the post the new pope occupied for many years before succeeding Pope John Paul II.

14 May Protests erupt in Karasu, Uzbekistan, as hundreds of Uzbeks attempt to flee to Kyrgyzstan.

‣ The PEN/Faulkner Award for Fiction is presented to Ha Jin for his novel *War Trash;* he also won the award in 2000 for *Waiting*.

15 May *Newsweek* magazine apologizes for printing an item describing the desecration of the Koran that seems to have triggered massive rioting throughout the Muslim world and, on the following day, the magazine retracts the item.

‣ In Vienna, the Czech Republic defeats Canada 3–0 to win the gold medal in the ice hockey men's world championship tournament.

‣ China defeats Indonesia 3–0 to win the Sudirman Cup in badminton, giving China all three of the major team championship trophies in the sport.

16 May Kuwait's National Assembly passes a law that for the first time gives women the right to vote and to run for office.

‣ The head of the last rebel group to remain outside the peace process in Burundi signs an agreement to end hostilities in Dar es Salaam, Tanzania.

‣ A celebration is held in Kinshasa to celebrate the ratification by the legislature of the Democratic Republic of the Congo of a new constitution; the document must still be approved in a public referendum.

17 May The Paris Club of creditor countries announces that it has agreed to seek from its member governments agreement to relieve Rwanda of debts of about $90 million.

‣ Antonio Villaraigosa is elected mayor of Los Angeles and becomes the city's first Latino mayor since 1872.

18 May When a Hamas group begins firing on a Jewish settlement in the Gaza Strip, Israel carries out an air strike on the group, its first since the beginning of the truce three months earlier.

‣ Russia and Estonia sign a treaty ending a border dispute between the two countries; on 27 July, however, days after the Estonian parliament's ratification of the accord, Russia revokes its signature.

‣ A jury in Florida orders the investment firm Morgan Stanley to pay $850 million in punitive damages to financier Ronald O. Perelman, in addition to the $604 million in compensatory damages previously awarded; Perelman had sued the company for defrauding him.

‣ The Russian association football (soccer) club CSKA Moscow defeats Sporting Lisbon to win the UEFA Cup in Lisbon; it is Russia's first European trophy.

‣ The American Academy of Arts and Letters inducts as members architects Maya Lin and James Stewart Polshek, landscape architect Laurie Olin, artists Cindy Sherman and Kiki Smith, writers Tony Kushner and Rosanna Warren, and composer T.J. Anderson and awards the Gold Medal for Belles Lettres (given every six years) to author Joan Didion, the Howells Medal (given every five years) to writer Shirley Hazzard, and the Award for Distinguished Service to the Arts to conductor James Levine.

19 May After a four-day meeting, representatives of North and South Korea announce that they have agreed to hold a cabinet-level meeting on 15 June in Pyongyang, North Korea.

‣ Germany begins repatriating the first of some 35,000 Roma (Gypsies) to the Kosovo region of Serbia and Montenegro, where they face an uncertain future.

‣ US Airways and America West Airlines announce plans to merge under the US Airways name to become the fifth largest carrier in the US.

20 May Charges are filed in Uruguay against former president Juan María Bordaberry (1972–76) and his foreign minister in the 1976 murder of two prominent opposition politicians in Argentina, where they were living in exile.

‣ Zagir Arukhov, minister of information, ethnic policy, and external relations for the Russian republic of Dagestan, is killed by a bomb outside his home in Makhachkala; his predecessor was killed in 2003.

‣ A US federal judge orders the oil and gas company Exxon Mobil Corp. to pay some 10,000 gas-station owners damages for having overcharged them for gasoline for a period of more than 10 years.

‣ Trump Hotels and Casino Resorts emerges from bankruptcy, which it had entered in November 2004, and changes its name to Trump Entertainment Resorts.

‣ South Korean researchers report in the periodical *Science* that they have developed an efficient method to clone human embryos using the DNA of individual patients in order to procure tailor-made stem cells for therapeutic purposes and that they have already developed 11 stem cell lines using this method.

21 May Members of Hamas reach an agreement with the Palestinian Authority to cease rocket and mortar attacks on Jewish settlements and towns in and near the Gaza Strip, salvaging the three-month-old truce.

‣ Afleet Alex recovers from a stumble to win the Preakness Stakes, the second event in Thoroughbred racing's Triple Crown, by 4¾ lengths; Kentucky Derby winner Giacomo is third.

‣ At the Cannes Film Festival, Belgian directors Jean-Pierre Dardenne and Luc Dardenne celebrate as their film *L'Enfant* wins the Palme d'Or; the Grand Prix goes to American director Jim Jarmusch's *Broken Flowers*.

‣ In Kiev, Ukraine, singer Helena Paparizou of Greece emerges number one in the Eurovision Song Contest with "My Number One."

22 May German Chancellor Gerhard Schröder surprises observers by calling for national elections to be held in the fall of 2005, a year earlier than scheduled.

‣ Nambaryn Enkhbayar is elected president of Mongolia.

▸ *Yokozuna* Asashoryu defeats *ozeki* Tochiazuma on the final day to win sumo's Natsu Basho with an undefeated record; it is his 12th Emperor's Cup.

▸ Finnish driver Kimi Räikkönen wins the Monaco Grand Prix.

23 May Two suicide car bombers kill 15 people in Tal Afar, Iraq, two attacks in Baghdad kill at least 18 people, and 5 more are killed in Tuz Khurmatu.

▸ The government of Zimbabwe reports that authorities have detained 9,600 people in Harare for black-market peddling and lawlessness.

24 May UN Secretary-General Kofi Annan appoints António Guterres, a former prime minister of Portugal, to replace Ruud Lubbers as High Commissioner for Refugees.

▸ NATO Secretary-General Jaap de Hoop Scheffer announces that NATO will offer logistical support to the increasing numbers of African Union forces attempting to bring peace to the Darfur region of The Sudan.

▸ At a synod of the leaders of the Orthodox Church in Istanbul, it is decided that the organization will withdraw recognition from Patriarch Irineos I as head of the Greek Orthodox Church in the Holy Land in view of his loss of the support of his subordinates.

▸ Warren Buffett's Berkshire Hathaway buys the electric utility PacifiCorp.

▸ *Star Wars: Episode III—Revenge of the Sith,* which opened worldwide on 21 May, breaks box-office records in the UK and the US for the first four days of its run.

▸ Televisora del Sur (Telesur) begins broadcasting; the 24-hour satellite news channel is owned by Venezuela, Argentina, Cuba, and Uruguay.

25 May In talks with the UK, France, and Germany, Iran agrees to extend its freeze on uranium enrichment.

▸ A referendum in Egypt approves an amendment to the constitution to allow multiparty presidential elections.

▸ The 1,762-km (1,094-mi)-long Baku-Tbilisi-Ceyhan oil pipeline, bringing oil from Azerbaijan in the Caspian basin to the Mediterranean Sea in Turkey, is ceremonially opened; the first drops of what is expected to reach a million barrels a day of oil begin to flow.

▸ Donald Tsang, acting chief executive of Hong Kong, resigns as is required by law in order to become a candidate in the 10 July election.

▸ In association football (soccer) Liverpool defeats AC Milan on penalty kicks to win the UEFA Champions League championship in Istanbul.

26 May Germany's legislature ratifies the proposed European Union constitution.

▸ Pascal Lamy of France, the former European Union trade minister, is selected as new director-general of the World Trade Organization.

27 May Near Islamabad, Pakistan, a suicide bomber at a Muslim shrine kills 20 people and injures 67; on 30 May, in an attack on a Shi'ite mosque in Karachi, two people are killed and at least 24 are injured.

28 May Prime Minister Hama Amadou of Niger makes an emergency food aid request; drought and the 2004 locust plague decimated farming in the poverty-stricken country.

▸ In Christchurch, New Zealand, the Canterbury (New Zealand) Crusaders defeat the New South Wales (Australia) Waratahs 35–25 to win the annual tri-nation Super 12 Rugby Union championship for the fifth time in 10 years.

29 May In a national referendum on the ratification of the European constitution, France votes no; the document cannot take effect until all 25 members of the European Union ratify it.

▸ The 89th Indianapolis 500 auto race is won by Dan Wheldon, the first British driver to do so since 1966; popular favorite Danica Patrick places fourth, the highest place a woman driver has ever achieved in the race.

▸ Spaniard Fernando Alonso, driving for Renault, wins the European Grand Prix in Germany after Kimi Räikkönen of Finland, driving for McLaren-Mercedes, crashes in the last lap.

30 May In negotiations with Georgia, Russia agrees to withdraw by 2008 its troops and equipment from two military bases in Georgia, one near Turkey and one on the Black Sea.

31 May In response to France's rejection of the European constitution, Pres. Jacques Chirac replaces Jean-Pierre Raffarin with Dominique de Villepin as prime minister.

▸ Mikhail Khodorkovsky, the founder of Yukos oil company and once one of the richest men in Russia, is found guilty on tax charges and sentenced to nine years in prison.

▸ *Vanity Fair* magazine reports that W. Mark Felt, who was second in command at the FBI in the early 1970s, has said publicly that he was the anonymous source known as "Deep Throat" who assisted *Washington Post* reporters Carl Bernstein and Bob Woodward in unraveling the Watergate story that led to the resignation of then-president Richard Nixon.

▸ The US Supreme Court overturns the 2002 conviction of the once huge but now all but defunct accounting firm Arthur Andersen for obstruction of justice, ruling that the jury instructions were flawed.

June 2005

1 Jun In a national referendum in The Netherlands, voters reject ratification of the proposed European constitution.

▸ Paul Wolfowitz takes office as the president of the World Bank, declaring that his top priority will be reducing poverty in Africa.

2 Jun Israel releases 398 Palestinian prisoners as part of an agreement that Israeli Prime Minister Ariel Sharon made with Palestinian leader Mahmoud Abbas.

▸ In Vladivostok, Russia, the foreign ministers of Russia and China sign an agreement demarcating the last stretch of the border between the two countries.

▸ Three car bombs, a suicide motorcycle bomb, and a suicide attack leave at least 44 people, including 10 Sufi Muslims, dead in Iraq.

▸ In the Scripps National Spelling Bee, Anurag Kashyap of San Diego spells *appoggiatura* correctly to win the contest.

3 Jun It is reported that torrential rains in three provinces in southern China have caused flooding that may have left hundreds of people dead.

▸ Murder charges are brought against a man accused

of killing Robert McCartney outside a bar in Belfast, Northern Ireland; the attack, which horrified citizens, is believed to have been an act of the Provisional Irish Republican Army against Sinn Féin, the political wing of the IRA.

4 Jun Palestinian leader Mahmoud Abbas announces that the legislative elections scheduled for 17 July will be postponed; the new date will be announced later.

▸ Justine Henin-Hardenne of Belgium defeats Mary Pierce of France to win the women's French Open tennis title; the following day rising star Rafael Nadal of Spain defeats Mariano Puerta of Argentina in the finals to win the men's title.

▸ The Derby, in its 226th year at Epsom Downs in Surrey, England, is won by Motivator, ridden by Johnny Murtagh.

5 Jun A spokesman for the Afghan armed forces reports that the army has captured two Taliban commanders who are believed to be responsible for much of the violence in western Afghanistan.

▸ The second round of legislative elections in Lebanon produces victories for Hezbollah and Amal, parties associated with Syria.

▸ It is reported that Taiwan has for the first time made a successful test-fire of a cruise missile capable of reaching targets in China.

▸ The 59th annual Tony Awards are presented in New York City; winners include the productions *Doubt*, *Monty Python's Spamalot*, *Glengarry Glen Ross*, and *La Cage aux Folles* and the actors Bill Irwin, Cherry Jones, Norbert Leo Butz, and Victoria Clark.

6 Jun In the face of growing and unremitting protests, Carlos Mesa Gisbert resigns as president of Bolivia.

▸ Student protesters in Addis Ababa, Ethiopia, challenging the results of the 15 May legislative elections are met with violence by police, who arrest hundreds of protesters.

▸ The US Supreme Court rules that the constitutional right of Congress to regulate commerce among states gives the federal government the right to enforce laws prohibiting the possession and use of marijuana even in those states that permit the use of the drug for medical purposes.

▸ A land mine destroys a bus in Nepal; at least 37 of the passengers are killed.

7 Jun Google becomes the largest media company in the world by stock market value when its shares reach a level on stock exchanges in New York City that make the Internet search engine company worth $80 billion.

▸ Gary McKinnon, who is believed to have hacked into many of the most secure computers of the Pentagon and NASA in 2001 and 2002, causing $1 billion in damage, in an attempt to prove that the US government was covering up knowledge of UFO visits, is arrested at his home in London.

▸ In Hawijah, Iraq, three simultaneous suicide bombs at checkpoints kill at least 20 Iraqis; elsewhere in the country at least 7 people are killed or found dead.

▸ The Orange Prize for Fiction, an award for women authors, is presented to American writer Lionel Shriver for *We Need to Talk About Kevin*.

8 Jun Security forces in Addis Ababa, Ethiopia, open fire on the continuing election protests, killing at least 22 people.

9 Jun The National Congress of Bolivia accepts the resignation of Carlos Mesa Gisbert as president, naming Eduardo Rodríguez Veltzé, head of the Supreme Court, to replace him.

▸ An appeals court in Mexico overturns the 1999 conviction of Raúl Salinas, brother of former Mexican president Carlos Salinas, for ordering the 1994 murder of a politician.

▸ Clementina Cantoni, an Italian worker for CARE International who was kidnapped in Kabul, Afghanistan, on 16 May, is released unharmed.

10 Jun In Iraq a roadside bomb kills 5 US Marines, a car bomb kills at least 10 Iraqis, 4 Iraqi security officers are gunned down in ambushes, and some 20 bound and blindfolded bodies are found.

▸ The banking company Citigroup settles a lawsuit by investors in Enron Corp. who accused the bank of helping Enron defraud them; Citigroup agrees to a $2 billion payment.

▸ Pius Langa takes office as South Africa's first black chief justice.

11 Jun François Bozizé is sworn in as elected president of the Central African Republic.

▸ The Group of Eight industrialized countries agrees to cancel at least $40 billion of the debt owed by the poorest 18 countries in the world to international lending agencies such as the IMF and the African Development Bank.

▸ In a boxing match with Kevin McBride in Washington DC, former heavyweight champion Mike Tyson fails to return to the ring after the sixth round and declares that he has retired from fighting.

▸ Louise Stahle of Sweden becomes the first person in 30 years to win the Ladies' British Amateur Championship in golf for two successive years when she defeats Claire Coughlan of Ireland to win the 2005 championship at Littlestone, England.

▸ Daniel Sánchez of Spain wins the 58th UMB world championship in three-cushion billiards in Lugo, Spain.

▸ Preakness winner Afleet Alex comes from behind to win the Belmont Stakes, the last event in Thoroughbred horse racing's Triple Crown, by seven lengths.

▸ At the International Indian Film Academy awards, popularly known as the Bollywood awards, in Amsterdam, the film *Veer-Zaara* wins six awards, including best picture, best director, best actor, and best supporting actress.

12 Jun The third round of legislative elections in Lebanon brings victory to candidates aligned with Maronite Christian leader and former prime minister Gen. Michel Aoun.

▸ Massouma al-Mubarak is named Kuwait's minister of planning and minister of state for administrative development affairs; she is the first woman ever to hold a position in that country's cabinet.

▸ Hundreds of women demonstrate in favor of women's rights in Tehran in the first such demonstration since Iran's Islamic revolution of 1979.

▸ Annika Sörenstam of Sweden wins the Ladies Professional Golf Association championship for the third consecutive year, defeating teenage amateur Michelle Wie of the US by three strokes.

13 Jun A car bomb explodes near a security base and a high school in the town of Pulwama in Indian-administered Kashmir, killing at least 14 people and injuring 50.

▸ The US Senate formally apologizes for failing ever to enact a law making lynching a federal crime, though three bills passed by the House of Representatives were sent to it, and seven presidents asked for the legislation; some 5,000 lynchings have been recorded in US history.

▸ After a 14-week trial in Santa Maria CA that became

something of a media circus, pop star Michael Jackson is acquitted of child molestation charges.

▸ Philip J. Purcell announces his retirement as head of the troubled financial concern Morgan Stanley.

▸ The European Union makes the Irish language Gaelic its 21st official language.

▸ Jan Eliasson of Sweden is elected president of the UN General Assembly; he will replace Jean Ping of Gabon.

14 Jun A suicide bomber detonates his weapon among a crowd of retired people lined up to get their pensions from a bank in Kirkuk, Iraq; at least 22 people are killed.

▸ South African Pres. Thabo Mbeki dismisses Deputy Pres. Jacob Zuma, who has been implicated in a bribery scandal.

▸ Argentina's Supreme Court rules that the laws passed in 1986 and 1987 forbidding prosecutions of anyone in connection with the 1976–83 "Dirty War" against those who opposed the military junta then ruling the country are unconstitutional.

15 Jun The first autonomous government of the Papua New Guinean province of Bougainville, headed by newly elected president Joseph Kabui, is sworn in.

▸ The annual International IMPAC Dublin Literary Award goes to *The Known World*, by American author Edward P. Jones.

16 Jun Donald Tsang is officially declared the new leader of Hong Kong; China appoints him chief executive on 21 June.

▸ At a meeting of the leaders of the members of the European Union in Brussels, it is decided that a "period of reflection" and the abandonment of the goal of ratification of the constitution by November 2006 are called for by the rejection of the constitution by France and The Netherlands.

▸ The first case of avian flu in a human in Indonesia is confirmed by health officials.

▸ The blockbuster exhibit from Egypt "Tutankhamun and the Golden Age of the Pharaohs" opens at the Los Angeles County Museum of Art.

▸ Leigh Ann Hester of the Kentucky National Guard becomes the first woman since World War II to be awarded the Silver Star; she and seven other members of her unit are decorated for their roles in stopping an insurgent attack on a convoy in March near Salman Pak, Iraq.

17 Jun MasterCard International reveals that a computer security breach at a payment processing company may have exposed the information of more than 40 million credit card accounts to theft.

▸ L. Dennis Kozlowski, the former CEO of Tyco International, and Mark H. Swartz, the company's former chief financial officer, are found guilty of fraud, conspiracy, and grand larceny.

▸ Australian Prime Minister John Howard announces a loosening of restrictions on illegal immigrants, including no more than six weeks in detention for women and children and no more than six months before claims for asylum are adjudicated.

18 Jun A firefight takes place between US armed forces and insurgents in Karabila, Iraq; US Marine commanders report that at least 30 insurgents were killed.

▸ Hundreds of thousands of people march in downtown Madrid to protest a bill passed by the legislature that would legalize same-sex marriage.

19 Jun A suicide bomber attacks a restaurant in Baghdad that is popular with police officers; at least 23 persons are killed, 16 of them policemen.

▸ A US military spokesman reports that after an American patrol is attacked in Helmand province of Afghanistan, an air strike is called in and as many as 20 possibly Taliban insurgents are killed.

▸ Vietnamese Prime Minister Phan Van Khai arrives in the US for a weeklong visit; it is the first visit to the US by a leader of unified Vietnam.

▸ Denmark's Tom Kristensen, driving with J.J. Lehto and Marco Werner for Audi, wins the Le Mans 24-hour endurance race for a record seventh time.

▸ After tire manufacturer Michelin says it cannot guarantee the safety of its tires under race conditions, leading all 14 drivers using Michelin tires at the US Grand Prix in Indianapolis to withdraw, Michael Schumacher wins the event over the remaining 5 drivers.

▸ In a surprising turn of events, Michael Campbell of New Zealand wins the US Open golf tournament, besting American Tiger Woods by two strokes.

20 Jun A car bomb explodes in a field behind a police station in Irbil, Iraq, killing some 15 police recruits, most of them Kurdish; other attacks in the country kill approximately 15 more people.

▸ The Zentrum Paul Klee, designed by Italian Renzo Piano to house the works of the Swiss artist, opens in Bern, Switzerland; it includes a music hall and will host workshops and a summer academy.

▸ The speed record of Mach 9.6 achieved by NASA's X-43A scramjet in November 2004 is recognized by Guinness World Records.

21 Jun In Beirut a car bomb kills George Hawi, the former head of the Lebanese Communist Party who had campaigned for the anti-Syria slate that won the majority of the seats in the parliament.

▸ At a contentious meeting of the International Whaling Commission in Ulsan, South Korea, a proposal by Japan to loosen the moratorium on whale fishing is firmly voted down.

▸ In Philadelphia MS, 80-year-old Edgar Ray Killen, a former member of the Ku Klux Klan, is found guilty of manslaughter in the 1964 deaths of civil rights workers Michael Schwerner, James Earl Chaney, and Andrew Goodman; two days later he is sentenced to 60 years in prison, the maximum allowed.

22 Jun After a two-day offensive by US and Afghan military forces in response to an attack on district police in Kandahar province, at least 40 of the insurgents have been killed.

▸ Colombia's legislature passes a law that grants leaders of right-wing paramilitaries freedom from severe punishment for atrocities or drug trafficking in return for disarmament of up to 20,000 fighters.

▸ South African Pres. Thabo Mbeki chooses Phumzile Mlambo-Ngcuka, minister of minerals and energy, to replace Jacob Zuma as deputy president.

23 Jun Four car bombs explode in the space of a few minutes in a commercial district of Baghdad, leaving at least 17 people dead and bringing to 700 Baghdad's death toll in the violence of the past month.

▸ The World Customs Organization endorses a new set of standards intended to increase the inspection and tracking of freight cargo throughout the world to decrease the possibility of terrorists making use of the cargo shipping system.

▸ The US Supreme Court rules that governments may exercise the power of eminent domain over private property and cede the property to private developers to promote economic growth, so long as a carefully formulated plan to provide significant benefits to the community provides a rational basis for the seizure of the property.

▸ US prices for light sweet crude oil reach a record level of $60 a barrel.

▸ The San Antonio Spurs defeat the Detroit Pistons 81–74 to win the NBA championship; Tim Duncan of the Spurs is named Most Valuable Player of the finals.

24 Jun The presidential runoff election in Iran is won by the hard-line mayor of Tehran, Mahmoud Ahmadinejad.

▸ The insurance company Aetna announces plans to acquire the regional health-care provider HMS Healthcare.

▸ The *Times Literary Supplement* of London publishes a 12-line poem written by the 6th-century-BC poet Sappho that was discovered a year ago by German researchers on a papyrus once wrapped around a mummy.

25 Jun In parliamentary elections in Bulgaria, the coalition led by the Bulgarian Socialist Party wins the majority of seats.

▸ The NAACP appoints Bruce S. Gordon, a former business executive, to replace Kweisi Mfume as president of the organization; Gordon indicates his emphasis will be on economic equality.

▸ At the 43rd World Outdoor Target Archery Championships in Madrid, Chung Jae Hun of South Korea wins the men's gold medal in recurve, while Lee Sung Jin of South Korea wins the women's recurve competition.

26 Jun Four suicide bomb attacks in 16 hours leave 38 people dead in Iraq.

▸ Birdie Kim of South Korea wins the 60th US Women's Open golf tournament.

▸ Three-year-old Hurricane Run, at 4–5 the favorite, comes from behind to win the Irish Derby horse race.

27 Jun The Lebanese government decides that Palestinians born in Lebanon may henceforth be permitted to hold certain jobs in the country; this is the first time in over 50 years that Palestinian immigrants or their families have been allowed to work.

▸ In two split decisions, the US Supreme Court rules that long-standing outdoor displays of the Ten Commandments on government property are permissible under the Constitution, but newer indoor displays of the Ten Commandments in courthouses violate the prohibition against government establishment of religion.

▸ Ismail Kadare, an Albanian novelist, is awarded the first Man Booker International Prize in Edinburgh.

28 Jun Canada's House of Commons approves a bill permitting same-sex marriage throughout Canada, and easy approval by the Senate was expected; eight provinces and one territory already recognize same-sex marriage.

▸ Emperor Akihito of Japan visits Saipan in the Northern Mariana Islands, the scene of one of the most horrific battles of World War II, to honor the war dead of Japan, Korea, the islands, and the US; it is the first time a Japanese ruler has visited an overseas battle site.

▸ The European Union, the US, Russia, Japan, South Korea, and China reach an agreement to build the International Thermonuclear Experimental Reactor (ITER), the world's largest fusion reactor, in Cadarache, France.

▸ US Pres. George W. Bush makes a televised speech to the country intended to shore up support for the war in Iraq; it draws fewer viewers than any of his previous televised speeches.

▸ With maritime parades, a naval battle reenactment, and fireworks, the 200th anniversary of the Battle of Trafalgar, in which the British navy vanquished that of Napoleon, is celebrated in the Solent in the English Channel.

▸ Uganda's legislature approves a change to the constitution removing a limit on the number of terms a president may serve.

29 Jun Venezuelan Pres. Hugo Chávez Frias announces the formation of an energy alliance of 15 Caribbean countries to be called Petrocaribe, in which Venezuela will offer the other members oil at low prices.

▸ Philippines Pres. Gloria Macapagal Arroyo announces that her husband, José Miguel Arroyo, who is accused of having taken bribes, will go into exile.

▸ California's Supreme Court permits a new law granting domestic partners most of the benefits conferred by marriage to stand.

▸ Brazil defeats Argentina 4–1 to win the FIFA Confederations Cup in association football (soccer).

▸ The 2005 Prince of Asturias Award for the arts is given to ballerinas Maya Plisetskaya and Tamara Rojo; it is the first time the Spanish prize has been awarded to dancers.

30 Jun Spain becomes the third European country, after The Netherlands and Belgium, to grant full marriage rights to same-sex couples; Spain's new law is the most liberal, recognizing no distinctions between same-sex and opposite-sex unions.

QUOTE OF THE MONTH

" *We are not legislating, ladies and gentlemen, for remote unknown people. We are expanding opportunities for the happiness of our neighbors, our work colleagues, our friends, our relatives.* "

—Spanish Prime Minister José Luis Zapatero, addressing the Congress of Deputies ahead of the vote legalizing same-sex marriage, 30 June

---

▸ Police in Zimbabwe finish destroying a squatter settlement that had been home to some 10,000 people, in the process killing several people; since mid-May the government has been carrying out wholesale demolitions of such settlements and flea markets, and within six weeks some half million poor people have become homeless.

▸ The World Food Programme reports that pirates have seized a ship carrying 850 metric tons of rice in food aid that was intended for tsunami victims in Somalia.

Disasters

Listed here are major disasters between July 2004 and June 2005. The list includes natural and nonmilitary mechanical disasters that claimed 15 or more lives and/or resulted in significant damage to property.

July 2004

1 Jul   Agri province, Turkey. An earthquake collapses village houses, leaving 18 people dead.

5 Jul   Taiwan. The worst flooding in a quarter century kills at least 21 people, with a further 14 missing.

5 Jul   India. A landslide sweeps away a section of highway in the Himalayas, taking with it a busload of pilgrims on their way to the shrine at Badrinath; 18 people die and 2,500 are left stranded.

Early July   China. Heavy rains lead to flooding and landslides in the southwestern regions of the country; at least 288 people die as a result.

15 Jul   India. A boat capsizes in a river running high from monsoon rains, drowning 25 people.

16 Jul   Kumbakonam, Tamil Nadu state, India. A fire destroys the Lord Krishna School, a private school, killing at least 90 children; the building lacked fire escapes and had a thatched roof.

19 Jul   Ukraine. An explosion at the Krasnolimanska coal mine leaves at least 31 workers dead, with 5 missing.

19 Jul   West Bengal state, India. The driver of a bus loses control, and the bus falls into a canal; at least 37 people are killed.

22 Jul   Near Pamukova, Turkey. A recently inaugurated high-speed train running between Istanbul and Ankara derails, killing 37 people; the train ran on old tracks, which some saw as a recipe for disaster.

Late July   Peru. Officials declare a state of emergency as unusually cold weather in the Andes Mountains leaves at least 46 children dead.

30 Jul   Ath, Belgium. In Belgium's worst industrial disaster since 1967, a gas pipeline in an industrial park explodes, engulfing two factories, killing at least 18 people, including some firefighters, and injuring more than 100; construction workers said they had accidentally pierced the gas line.

August 2004

1 Aug   Asunción, Paraguay. An intense fire, possibly triggered by a gas leak, breaks out in a supermarket, and at least 464 people are incinerated; it appears that emergency exits were locked to prevent theft after the fire broke out.

2 Aug   Tehri, Uttaranchal state, India. A tunnel being built as part of a controversial hydroelectric dam project caves in, most likely because of floods; 29 of the more than 80 workers in the tunnel are killed.

6 Aug   South Asia. An unusually bad monsoon season leaves some 1,931 people dead in the region from drowning, landslides, electrocution, and waterborne diseases; the hardest hit country is Bangladesh.

7 Aug   Mediterranean Sea. A container ship rescues more than 70 would-be migrants from a drifting boat trying to reach Sicily from North Africa; some 28 of the refugees had died during the previous nine days.

10 Aug   Nagua, Dominican Republic. Fisherman find some 33 survivors of the approximately 80 people who left the country in a boat headed for Puerto Rico; the others died during a horrific two weeks adrift at sea after the boat's motor failed.

11 Aug   Turkey. Two passenger trains crash head-on after one of them runs through a stop signal some 50 miles east of Istanbul; at least 27 people are killed.

12 Aug   Zhejiang province, China. Typhoon Rananim makes landfall and proceeds inland, leaving a path of destruction and killing at least 164 people; it is the most powerful typhoon to hit China in seven years.

12 Aug   Adamawa state, Nigeria. Flash floods caused by days of heavy rain drown at least 23 people as they sleep.

13 Aug   Sierra de Calderona National Park, Spain. A forest fire that has destroyed more than 16,200 ha (40,000 ac) forces 7,000 people near Valencia to evacuate their homes.

13 Aug   Southwestern Florida. Hurricane Charley roars into Charlotte Harbor and across the state, devastating Punta Gorda and Port Charlotte and leaving 27 people dead.

14 Aug   Near Carolina, El Salvador. A bus carrying members of a church group through a mountainous region goes into a ravine; at least 35 of the passengers are killed and the remainder injured.

21 Aug   Central Venezuela. A military plane carrying civilians as well as military personnel from a base on Orchila Island to Maracay crashes into a mountainside; all 25 aboard are killed, among them five children.

24 Aug   Taiwan. Typhoon Aere hits the northern part of the island, leaving 15 people dead; it goes on to claim the lives of 35 people in China and at least 32 in the Philippines.

September 2004

2 Sep   Weimar, Germany. A fire breaks out in the Duchess Anna Amalia Library, a UNESCO World Heritage site housing mostly German manuscripts from 1750 to 1850; some 50,000 books are destroyed, and a further 60,000 are damaged by smoke or water.

4 Sep   Chongqing, China. A bus is swept off a bridge and away in a flooding river; it is feared that some 30 passengers are drowned.

7–17 Sep   Caribbean. Hurricane Ivan devastates Grenada, killing 39 people and destroying its two main crops, then kills at least 18 in Jamaica, and finally strengthens to hit the Gulf Coast of the US, leaving some 33 people dead in several states.

8 Sep Southwestern China. Catastrophic flooding after a week of torrential storms leaves at least 177 people dead.

11 Sep Greece. A helicopter traveling from Athens to the monastery of Mt. Athos crashes into the sea; all 12 passengers, including the head of the Greek Orthodox Church in Africa, Patriarch Petros VII of Alexandria, are killed.

13 Sep Near Kusma, Nepal. A bus carrying at least 50 people, some of them tourists, falls into a river; at least 16 people die.

15 Sep China. At the end of the three-month rainy season, the official death toll is 1,029.

16 Sep Chittagong, Bangladesh. A bus carrying a party returning from a wedding collides with a truck; at least 22 people are killed and 30 are critically injured.

17 Sep Near Lagos, Nigeria. People attempting to steal oil from a state-owned pipeline cause an explosion and fire that kill some 50 people.

18 Sep Haiti. Hurricane Jeanne makes landfall in the area of Gonaïves, already devastated by flooding in May; the death toll from the resultant flooding is more than 3,000.

18 Sep Uttar Pradesh state, India. After heavy rains fall for more than 24 hours, flash flooding sweeps away homes, leading to the death of at least 44 people.

October 2004

4 Oct Off the coast of Tunisia. A boat carrying illegal immigrants attempting to reach Italy from Morocco and Tunisia sinks off the coast of Tunisia shortly after departure; at least 22 are drowned and another 42 are missing.

9 Oct Assam state, India. After a week of heavy rains, flash flooding sweeps down hills, inundating dozens of villages and leaving more than 100 people dead; flooding has also killed at least 44 in Bangladesh and Nepal.

10 Oct Lake Kivu, Democratic Republic of the Congo. In separate incidents, two large overloaded canoes bound for Goma overturn in windy weather; at least 41 die on one canoe and at least 27 on the second, and it is estimated that at least 50 people are still missing.

20 Oct Xinme, Henan province, China. A gas explosion in the Daping coal mine kills 148 of the more than 400 miners working there at the time.

20 Oct Japan. Typhoon Tokage, an unusually large storm and the 10th to hit the country this year, a new record, causes the death of at least 83 people.

23 Oct Niigata prefecture, Japan. A series of earthquakes, the strongest measured at magnitude 6.8, kills at least 37 people; thousands are injured.

November 2004

7 Nov Near Minya, Egypt. A bus carrying Egyptian pilgrims back from Mecca in Saudi Arabia collides with a truck attempting to pass a car; there are 33 fatalities.

9 Nov Kyzil, Siberia, Russia. In a hostel, a fire kills at least 25 people; it is thought that it may have been caused by an illegal attempt at a power connection in the bitter cold, as the power had been discontinued for nonpayment.

11 Nov Liangwa, Henan province, China. The Xinsheng coal mine suffers an explosion that results in the death of 29 workers.

11 Nov Near Maurelandia, Brazil. The driver of a truck carrying cooking gas canisters veers into oncoming traffic, causing a head-on collision with a bus carrying 20 workers, of whom 19 are killed.

12 Nov Alor, Indonesia. A 6.0 earthquake kills at least 21 people and leaves some 8,000 homeless.

17 Nov Off the coast of the Dominican Republic. A boat attempting to carry refugees from the Dominican Republic to Puerto Rico capsizes; at least 8 people die and 15 are missing.

20 Nov Shahe, Hebei province, China. An electric cable starts a fire in an iron ore mine that leaves at least 61 people dead.

21 Nov Baotou, Inner Mongolia, China. A China Eastern Airlines commuter plane bursts into flames shortly after takeoff and falls into a frozen lake; all 53 aboard and 2 people on the ground are killed.

28 Nov Shaanxi province, China. In one of China's worst coal-mining accidents in recent years, 166 miners perish in an explosion in the Chenjishan coal mine.

29 Nov Near Zakhu, Iraq. A large flat-bottomed boat crowded with Kurdish migrant workers trying to reach Turkey overturns in the Tigris River, and at least 40 passengers drown; the workers had recently learned that the border crossings between the countries had been reopened.

29 Nov Philippines. Typhoon Winnie brings flooding and landslides, with a death toll of at least 412.

30 Nov Solo, Indonesia. A Lion Air MD-82 passenger plane skids off a runway and breaks in two after landing in heavy rain, killing at least 62 of the 146 aboard.

December 2004

2 Dec Philippines. Rescue efforts addressing the effects of Typhoon Winnie have hardly begun when the country is hit by the even stronger Typhoon Nanmadol; more than 1,000 people are dead or missing.

2 Dec Guizhou province, China. A mountain landslide destroys dozens of houses, killing 32 people.

5 Dec Near Karaganda, Kazakhstan. An explosion in the Shakhtinskaya coal mine kills 23 miners.

9 Dec Near Yangquan, Shanxi province, China. A gas explosion at the Dazian Sanking coal mine kills 28 miners and 5 rescuers.

10 Dec Near El Junquito, Venezuela. An airplane belonging to the National Guard and bound for an airbase in Caracas crashes into a mountain, killing all 16 personnel, some of them high-ranking officers.

14 Dec Punjab state, India. An express train and a local train crash head-on, killing at least 31 people and injuring 50; the stationmasters of the stations the trains had left and an engineer are fired.

19 Dec   Peru. A passenger bus goes off a bridge in heavy rain; 49 passengers are killed.

21 Dec Sanki-Ilado, Nigeria. As thieves who damaged an oil pipeline to steal from it run from police, the pipeline explodes, and more than 20 people are killed.

25 Dec   Near Jeblum, Pakistan. A passenger bus goes off the road and falls into a ravine; 18 people are killed and 39 injured.

26 Dec   Indian Ocean. A magnitude-9.0 earthquake, the strongest in 40 years, unleashes a powerful tsunami that kills hundreds of thousands of people in more than 10 countries and destroys coastlines in Indonesia, Sri Lanka, Thailand, Malaysia, the Maldives, and India.

26 Dec Mulhouse, France. A gas leak leads to an explosion that destroys a five-story apartment building; 17 of residents are killed and 15 injured.

27 Dec   Colombia. Two buses carrying holidaymakers collide, leaving at least 17 dead.

28 Dec   Mumbai (Bombay), India. Indian authorities report that illegal liquor sold in a suburb the previous weekend has killed at least 37 people, with close to 100 still hospitalized and victims still appearing.

30 Dec   Buenos Aires, Argentina. In an overcrowded nightclub, an audience member sets off a flare, igniting the ceiling and leading to an inferno in which at least 188 people die and more than 700 are injured; it is reported that many fire exits were sealed.

January 2005

3 Jan Qinghai province, China. A truck carrying Tibetan passengers from a pilgrimage to Lhasa in the autonomous region of Tibet overturns, killing at least 54 of the pilgrims.

3 Jan Paulomajra, Punjab state, India. A private minibus carrying girls to work at a factory in Ludhiana collides head-on with another private minibus traveling in the opposite direction; 14 girls and a bus driver are killed.

4 Jan Near Bujumbura, Burundi. An overloaded bus crashes on a hillside road, killing at least 25 people, including at least 6 bicyclists.

6 Jan Graniteville NC. A freight train carrying liquid chlorine crashes into a parked train outside a textile factory; at least 8 people are killed and hundreds made sick by the poison chlorine gas, and some 5,400 residents are evacuated.

7 Jan Siddhirganj, Bangladesh. A fire breaks out in a garment factory, killing at least 22 people who were trapped inside because of locked exits; it is believed that faulty wiring caused the fast-moving fire.

7 Jan Near Bologna, Italy. A passenger train from Verona collides head-on with a freight train in heavy fog; at least 17 people are killed, including the engineers.

10 Jan La Conchita CA. After two weeks of unusually relentless and heavy rain and snow that leave some 20 people dead in southern California, a hillside gives way, burying 4 blocks of houses and leaving at least 10 people dead.

10 Jan Bijapur district, Karnataka state, India. A bus driver loses control of his vehicle, and it falls into a canal; 57 passengers are killed.

11 Jan Southwestern Nigeria. A speeding passenger bus veers into oncoming traffic and collides head-on into another bus, and a third bus plows into the wreckage; at least 21 people are killed.

12 Jan Northern Shanxi province, China. An explosion in a fireworks factory kills at least 25 workers, most of them young women.

13 Jan Colombia. A helicopter provided by the US as part of a drug-eradication system crashes during a nighttime mission; 20 Colombian soldiers are killed.

15 Jan Near Sabana de Torres, Colombia. A passenger bus attempting to pass another vehicle on a curve late at night crashes into a truck stopped at the side of the road because of a mechanical failure; at least 27 people die.

17 Jan Bangkok, Thailand. An empty subway train collides with a crowded one during the morning rush and 212 passengers are injured; Bangkok's subway was initiated only six months previously.

19 Jan Democratic Republic of the Congo. An overcrowded ferry traveling on the Kasai River between Ilebo and Tshikapa capsizes; at least 150 people are believed lost.

19 Jan Lagos, Nigeria. Two buses collide and are then hit by a fuel tanker truck; at least 30 commuters are burned to death.

Late January Guyana. The heaviest flooding in 100 years leaves Georgetown and the surrounding area in a disastrous condition; thousands of people are forced to evacuate, and 34 lives are lost, many from disease.

24 Jan Thailand. A speedboat carrying tourists to the resort island of Koh Samui after a full-moon beach party capsizes; at least 15 people are killed and possibly the same number are missing.

25 Jan Medina, Saudi Arabia. An unusually bad storm brings heavy rain and flash floods on the last day of the Hajj; some 29 people lose their lives.

25 Jan Near Wai, Maharashtra state, India. As hundreds of thousands of pilgrims, mostly women, approach the hilltop Mandhar Devi temple, some begin slipping on coconut oil from devotional offerings, which leads to a panic; angry relatives of victims begin setting fires, worsening the stampede, and a total of 257 pilgrims are killed.

27 Jan Central Vietnam. A Russian-made military helicopter crashes shortly after takeoff from Me island; all 16 aboard, including 2 generals, are killed.

February 2005

3 Feb Afghanistan. A Kam Air Boeing 737 flying from Herat to Kabul in a snowstorm crashes shortly after receiving permission to land at Kabul; all 104 aboard are lost.

3 Feb Maharashtra state, India. A trailer carrying wedding guests that is being pulled across an unmarked railroad crossing by a tractor is hit by a train; 55 of the passengers in the trailer are killed.

6 Feb Todolella, Spain. Butane gas leaking from a heating cylinder kills 18 people who had been attending a weekend party at a 15th-century guesthouse.

8 Feb Lubango, Angola. The brakes on a truck fail and it plows into a crowd of people celebrating Carnival; at least 20 people are killed.

9 Feb Kemerovo region, Siberia, Russia. A methane gas explosion in a coal mine kills at least 21 miners.

early February Venezuela and Colombia. Flooding caused by days of torrential rains sweeps away thousands of homes and leaves at least 86 people dead, 53 in Venezuela and 33 in Colombia.

10 Feb Baluchistan province, Pakistan. Heavy rainfall in the drought-stricken province causes the Shadikor Dam to give way; at least 60 people are reported dead, with more than 500 missing.

14 Feb Tehran, Iran. A fire caused by a kerosene oil heater in a mosque kills 59 people, some of them dying as people stampede to escape.

14 Feb Fuxin, Liaoning province, China. In an unusually deadly mining accident, an explosion in the Sunjiawan coal mine kills at least 209 miners; an earthquake is reported to have occurred in the area 10 minutes before the explosion.

14 Feb North West Frontier Province, Pakistan. Authorities report 260 deaths attributed to heavy rain and snow.

18 Feb Ituri district, Democratic Republic of the Congo. The World Health Organization reports that an airborne form of pneumonic plague has killed at least 61 diamond miners since December 2004, with as many as 300 more possibly also infected.

19 Feb Near Dhaka, Bangladesh. An overcrowded ferry, the *MV Maharaj*, sinks on the Buriganga River in a storm; at least 120 people drown.

19 Feb Indian-administered Kashmir. Avalanches destroy several Himalayan villages, leaving at least 278 people dead; hundreds more have perished in the region owing to frigid temperatures.

21 Feb Western Java, Indonesia. Heavy rainfall causes a hilltop municipal dump to collapse, triggering a landslide that buries much of the village of Cimahi under tons of garbage and soil, leaving some 120 people either dead or missing.

22 Feb Kerman province, Iran. Some 500 people are killed early in the morning when a magnitude-6.4 earthquake centered on the town of Zarand flattens several villages.

23 Feb Juba, The Sudan. High temperatures cause an explosion at an ammunition dump, causing the deaths of at least 24 people.

26 Feb Afghanistan. Officials report that the death toll from an unusually bitter winter is a minimum of 580.

March 2005

2 Mar Kecheng, Shanxi province, China. A cache of explosives being stored at the home of a coal-mine manager explodes, killing at least 20 children in an adjacent elementary school as well as the mine manager.

9 Mar Mabini, Philippines. At least 27 schoolchildren die after eating cassava roots served at an elementary school; it is initially believed that the roots were undercooked and therefore poisonous, but later testing suggests that the children were poisoned by pesticides on the roots.

10 Mar Karachi, Pakistan. A fireball engulfs the *PNS Moawin*, a naval logistics ship, during routine maintenance in port; at least 35 of those aboard are killed and 24 critically injured.

16 Mar Russia. A Russian Antonov-24 airplane carrying oil workers and Lukoil subcontractors crashes near the Arctic port of Varandey; at least 28 people are killed.

17 Mar Jiangxi province, China. A bus traveling near the city of Shangrao is destroyed when a nearby truck carrying explosives and fireworks explodes violently; at least 30 people are killed.

18 Mar Punjab province, India. Floodwaters wash a tractor trailer from the road, killing 41 pilgrims in

the trailer who were returning from a visit to a shrine.

19 Mar Shuozhou, Shanxi province, China. An explosion at the Xishui coal mine leaves at least 59 miners dead; it is reported that the mine had resumed operation illegally, after having been ordered to suspend work because of safety problems.

20 Mar Northern Bangladesh. A tornado in Gaibandha district leaves at least 56 people dead and thousands homeless; storms over the next few days raise the death toll in the region above 80.

20 Mar Afghanistan. The death toll reaches at least 200 as a result of flooding from snowmelt following the worst winter in years.

20 Mar The Sudan. The government reports that 21 people have died and another 6 gone blind after drinking illegally produced alcohol.

28 Mar Nias island, Indonesia. An earthquake with a magnitude of 8.7 and centered deep under the seabed kills at least 905 people.

29 Mar Eastern China. A tanker truck carrying liquid chlorine suffers a tire blowout, causing it to collide with a truck and overturn; chlorine fumes kill at least 27 people, and nearly 300 are hospitalized.

April 2005

6 Apr Afghanistan. A US military helicopter crashes in a dust storm near Ghazni, killing 18 people.

7 Apr Madhya Pradesh state, India. A dam on the Narmada River, the second holiest river in India, releases a barrage of water, inundating some 300,000 Hindu pilgrims who were observing an annual ritual of bathing in the river; at least 62 of them drown; officials say it was a routine release of water by workers unaware of the religious gathering downstream.

10 Apr Savar, Bangladesh. A nine-story garment factory collapses, leaving at least 73 people dead.

10 Apr Kawambwa, Zambia. A truck carrying students home from a high school at the end of term overturns on a curve, killing at least 44 students.

15 Apr Paris, France. A fire started by a candle flame destroys the Paris-Opéra Hotel, leaving 24 people dead, most of them African immigrants placed in the hotel by social service agencies.

20 Apr Zambia. An explosion at a Chinese-owned explosives factory on the grounds of a copper mine kills at least 50 people.

21 Apr Turkey. A gas explosion in a coal mine causes a cave-in and a fire, killing 17 miners.

21 Apr Samlaya, Gujarat state, India. A passenger train traveling from Varanasi to Ahmedabad crashes into a stationary freight train and derails; at least 24 people are killed.

21 Apr Kon Tum province, Vietnam. A bus carrying veterans of the Vietnam War from Hanoi to Ho Chi Minh City along the highway built on the old Ho Chi Minh Trail to celebrate the 30th anniversary of the end of the war goes off a mountain road and falls into the valley below; 30 veterans and the bus driver are killed.

23 Apr Somali region, Ethiopia. The Shebeli River overflows its banks, inundating the area and leaving at least 134 people dead, some 20 of whom were eaten by crocodiles.

23 Apr Khurd, Madhya Pradesh state, India. A truck carrying Hindu pilgrims to a religious meeting goes off the road and falls into a ditch, killing 23 of the passengers and injuring 38; police believe the driver fell asleep.

25 Apr Amagasaki, Japan. An elevated commuter train that is running 90 seconds behind schedule derails while going around a curve, crashing into an adjacent apartment building; at least 107 people are killed.

27 Apr Near Polgahawela, Sri Lanka. The driver of a bus ignores closed gates at a railroad crossing and the bus is hit by a passenger train; at least 35 of the bus passengers are killed.

28 Apr Jiddah, Saudi Arabia. Storms and flash flooding kill some 30 people as houses collapse, cars are swept off roads, and power lines fall.

May 2005

2 May Afghanistan. A cache of explosives stored at the home of a commander of a recently disarmed and demobilized regiment in the village of Kohna Deh explodes, leveling a portion of the village and killing at least 34 people, mostly women and children.

3 May Lahore, Pakistan. A gas explosion causes an apartment and factory building and several houses to collapse, killing at least 28 people.

6 May Delhi, India. It is reported that 15 people have died of a rare strain of bacterial meningitis that has not occurred in India in more than 10 years; by 1 July the outbreak was declared over, but by then 60 people had died and 441 others had been diagnosed with the disease.

7 May Queensland, Australia. A twin-engine propeller airplane traveling from Bamaga to Lockhart River, a remote Aboriginal township, crashes into a hillside; all 15 aboard are killed in the worst civil aviation disaster in the country since 1968.

7 May Near Pampa, Peru. A bus goes off the road and falls some 300 m (1,000 ft) into a ravine; at least 40 passengers are killed.

11 May Northern Philippines. The brakes on a passenger bus traveling from the resort town of Baguio to Dagupan City fail on a mountain road, and the bus crashes into a retaining wall, killing at least 27 people.

15 May Near Golapchipa, Bangladesh. An overloaded ferry sinks; close to 60 people are found dead, and a further 20 are missing.

17 May Manikganj district, Bangladesh. A double-decker ferry sinks in a storm on the Padma River; at least 58 people die, with an unknown number missing.

17 May Panzhihua, Sichuan province, China. A gas explosion kills 21 workers in a coal mine; 10 miners survive.

17 May Near Rudraprayag, Uttaranchal state, India. A bus carrying the bridegroom's party to a wedding in Chamoli falls into a gorge; at least 36 of the passengers die.

18 May Chile. A blizzard overtakes army troops on a training march in the Andes Mountains, leaving at least 26 of them dead and a further 19 missing.

19 May Angola. World Health Organization officials report that the death toll from the outbreak of the Marburg virus, which is incurable and often quickly fatal, has reached 311.

21 May Near Jauja, Peru. A bus goes through a guardrail and falls from a bridge; at least 35 people lose their lives.

June 2005

June South Asia. A heat wave throughout the region is responsible for hundreds of deaths.

3 Jun Southern China. After several days of torrential rain, the death toll reaches 204, with 79 people still missing and tens of thousands of farm animals and homes also destroyed.

7 Jun Alexandria, Egypt. A six-story building collapses, leaving at least 16 people dead; it is believed that the top three floors had been built illegally.

10 Jun Shantou, Guangdong province, China. A fire breaks out at the Huanan Hotel, engulfing the top three floors of the four-story building and killing at least 31 people.

10 Jun Shalan, Heilongjiang province, China. Flash flooding caused when some 8 inches of rainfall in 40 minutes leads to the drowning of at least 92 people, at least 88 of them children in a primary school.

13 Jun Northern Andes, Chile. An earthquake with a magnitude of 7.9 occurs in a sparsely populated area, killing at least 11 people and causing damage to roads and water supply lines.

16 Jun San Antonio Senahu, Guatemala. At least 23 people are killed when a mudslide buries homes in several neighborhoods.

21 Jun Afghanistan. A government official reports that flooding in the north caused by snowmelt has killed 51 people.

24 Jun China. Chinese officials report that the death toll from flooding in the past two weeks has reached 536.

25 Jun Machakos, Kenya. After drinking homebrew made with methanol at a drinks stall, at least 51 people die and several are made blind.

26 Jun El Salvador. Floodwaters wash away a bus, killing 21 people aboard.

30 Jun Northern Italy. Italian news sources report that the death toll from a heat wave has reached 21.

Personalities

Celebrities & Newsmakers

These mini-biographies are intended to provide background information about people in the news. See also the Obituaries (below) for recently deceased persons as well as the presidential biographies and the Britannica lists elsewhere in the Britannica Almanac.

Magdalena Abakanowicz (20 Jun 1930, Falenty, Poland), Polish artist known for her innovative metal sculptures of human and animal figures, usually presented in groups.

Mahmoud (Ridha) Abbas (nom de guerre Abu Mazen; 1935, Zefat, Palestine), Palestinian politician; secretary general of the PLO executive committee and cofounder (with Yasir Arafat) of the Fatah movement; he served as the first prime minister of the Palestine Authority from 30 Apr to 9 Sep 2003.

A.P.J. Abdul Kalam (Avul Pakir Jainulabdeen Abdul Kalam; 15 Oct 1931, Rameswaram, Tamil Nadu state, British India), Indian aeronautical engineer and president of India from 2002.

King Abdullah ('Abdallah ibn 'Abd al-'Aziz Al Saud; 1923, Riyadh, Saudi Arabia), Saudi royal who was de facto ruler from the time that his half-brother, King Fahd, suffered a stroke 1995; Abdullah became king upon Fahd's death on 1 Aug 2005.

King Abdullah II (Abdallah ibn al-Hussein al-Hashimi; 30 Jan 1962, Amman, Jordan), Jordanian royal, the oldest son of King Hussein and king from 1999.

Roger Abiut (1972?), Vanuatuan politician and president from 24 Mar 2004 to 12 Apr 2004 and again from 11 May 2004 during a time of constitutional crisis.

John (Philip) Abizaid (1 Apr 1951, Coleville CA), American military officer (lieutenant general, US Army) who was named commander in chief of the US Central Command and supreme commander of occupation forces in Iraq as of 7 Jul 2003.

Spencer Abraham (12 Jun 1952, Lansing MI), American Republican senator from Michigan (1995–2001) who served as secretary of energy from 2001 to 2005.

Alexei A. Abrikosov (Aleksey Alekseyevich Abrikosov; 25 Jun 1928, Moscow, USSR [now in Russia]), Russian-born American theoretical physicist who explained how certain materials develop their unusual properties of superconductivity and superfluidity when chilled to very low temperatures; he provided a theoretical explanation for type II superconductivity; Abrikosov shared the 2003 Nobel Prize for Physics with Vitaly L. Ginzburg and Anthony J. Leggett.

Nasr Hamid Abu Zayd (7 Oct 1943, Tanta, Egypt), Egyptian scholar and religious reformer who observed how Islam was being interpreted by fundamentalists in Egypt and elsewhere in ways that served political ends, a position he opposed in his 1992 book Naqd al-khitab al-dini ("Critique of Religious Discourse"); he lost his job, and he and his wife were forced into exile.

Aníbal Acevedo Vilá (13 Feb 1962, Hato Rey, Puerto Rico), American governor of Puerto Rico from 2 Jan 2005.

Joe Ackermann (Josef Ackermann; 7 Feb 1948, Mels, Sankt Gallen, Switzerland), Swiss corporate executive and CEO of Deutsche Bank AG from 1997.

Valdas V. Adamkus (Valdas V. Adamkevicius; 3 Nov 1926, Kaunas, Lithuania), Lithuanian politician and president, 1998–2003; following the impeachment of Pres. Rolandas Paksas, in the second-round elections on 27 Jun 2004 Adamkus was re-elected president.

Gerry Adams (Gerard Adams; 6 Oct 1948, Belfast, Northern Ireland), Northern Irish resistance leader; president of Sinn Féin, the political wing of the Irish Republican Army.

John (Coolidge) Adams (15 Feb 1947, Worcester MA), American composer who works in a wide range of genres and is noted for the operas *Nixon in China* (1987) and *The Death of Klinghoffer* (1991); he won the 2003 Pulitzer Prize for Music and three 2004 Grammys for *On the Transmigration of Souls*, written to commemorate the 11 Sep 2001 terrorist attacks.

Scott Adams (8 Jun 1957, Windham NY), American cartoonist, creator of *Dilbert*.

Thomas Adès (27 Jun 1971, London, England), English composer, pianist, and conductor; his compositions are known for their wit and wide-ranging styles; he won the 2000 Grawemeyer Award for Music for *Asyla*.

Ben Affleck (Benjamin Geza Affleck; 15 Aug 1972, Berkeley CA), American actor, director, and writer known for commercially successful films such as *Good Will Hunting* (1997).

Isaias Afwerki (2 Feb 1946, Asmara, Ethiopia [now in Eritrea]), Eritrean independence leader, secretary-general of the Provisional Government, and first president of Eritrea (from 1993).

Andre (Kirk) Agassi (29 Apr 1970, Las Vegas NV), American tennis player who won Wimbledon (1992), the US Open (1994, 1999), the Australian Open (1995, 2000, 2001, 2003), the French Open (1999), and an Olympic gold medal (1996).

Peter (Courtland) Agre (30 Jan 1949, Northfield MN), American chemist who shared (with Roderick MacKinnon) the 2003 Nobel Prize for Chemistry for discoveries about the structure and operation of the many crucial porelike channels that perforate the outer surface of cells in humans and other living things; Agre was recognized for the discovery of water channels in cell membranes.

Christina (Maria) Aguilera (18 Dec 1980, Staten Island NY), American pop singer who won the Grammy for best new artist in 1999; the adult content of her 2002 album *Stripped* marked a change from her former teen-oriented material; in 2003 she was selected to represent the fashion house Versace.

Bertie Ahern (Bartholomew Patrick Ahern; 12 Sep 1951, Dublin, Ireland), Irish politician; prime minister (*taoiseach*) of Ireland from 1997.

Iajuddin Ahmed (1 Feb 1931, Nayagaon, Bengal state, British India [now in Bangladesh]), Bangladeshi scientist and educator; president of Bangladesh from 6 Sep 2002.

Ahn Hyun Soo (23 Nov 1985, South Korea), South Korean short-track speed skater who won the men's 1,000-m, 1,500-m, and 3,000-m events at the 2004 world championships.

Clay Aiken (Clayton Grissom Aiken; 30 Nov 1978, Raleigh NC), American entertainer who won second place in the American Idol competition on TV and whose first album, *Measure of a Man*, shot to the top of the Billboard charts in October 2003.

Askar Akayev (10 Nov 1944, Kyzyl-Bairak, Kirghiz SSR, USSR [now Kyrgyzstan]), Kyrgyz politician and president from 1990 until he was forced out of office on 11 Apr 2005.

Emperor Akihito (original name Tsugu Akihito; era name Heisei; 23 Dec 1933, Tokyo, Japan), Japanese royal who was emperor of Japan from 1989.

Akil Akilov (1944, Tajikistan?), Tajik politician and prime minister from 1999.

Albert II (Albert Félix Humbert Théodore Christian Eugène Marie of Saxe-Coburg-Gotha; 6 Jun 1934, Brussels, Belgium), Belgian king from 1993.

Prince Albert II (Albert Alexandre Louis Pierre; 14 Mar 1958, Monaco), Monegasque royal who became ruler of Monaco upon the death of his father, Rainier III, on 6 Apr 2005.

Bruce (Michael) Alberts (14 Apr 1938, Chicago IL), American molecular biologist; president of the US National Academy of Sciences from 1993 to 2005.

Karl (1920, Germany) and **Theo Albrecht** (28 Mar 1922, Germany) German business executives who founded the Aldi supermarket chain; in 2004 they were number 3 and number 14, respectively, on *Forbes* magazine's annual list of the richest persons in the world.

Alan Alda (Alphonso Joseph D'Abruzzo; 28 Jan 1936, New York NY), American film and TV actor best known for playing Hawkeye Pierce in the TV version of *M*A*S*H*.

Sherman J. Alexie, Jr. (7 Oct 1966, Wellpinit, Spokane Indian Reservation, Washington), American poet and novelist who writes of his Native American upbringing.

Alexis II (Aleksey Mikhaylovich Ridiger; 23 Feb 1929, Tallinn, Estonia), Russian religious leader; Orthodox Patriarch of Moscow and All Russia, the 15th primate of Russia, from 1990.

Monica Ali (20 Oct 1967, Dacca, Pakistan [now Dhaka, Bangladesh]), Bangladesh-born British writer who, though unpublished at the time, was included on the once-a-decade *Granta* list of the 20 best young British writers (2003); her first novel, *Brick Lane*, was short-listed for the 2003 Man Booker Prize.

Muhammad Ali (Cassius Marcellus Clay, Jr., until 1964; 17 Jan 1942, Louisville KY), American boxer, the first to win the heavyweight championship three separate times; his quick reflexes and defensive speed in the ring, combined with his engaging (sometimes outrageous) personality and his refusal on religious grounds to be inducted into the army made him a cultural icon during his 20-year career and long after his final retirement.

Ilham Aliyev (Ilham Geidar ogly Aliev; 24 Dec 1961, Baku, Azerbaijani SSR, USSR [now in Azerbaijan]), Azerbaijani politician and son of Pres. Heydar Aliyev; he was prime minister from 2003.

Mari Alkatiri (26 Nov 1946, Dili, Portuguese East Timor), Timorese politician; first prime minister of independent East Timor (from 2002).

Iyad Allawi (1945?, Iraq?), Iraqi neurologist who was a member of the Iraqi Governing Council in 2003 and became prime minister on 1 Jun 2004; he had been a member of Saddam Hussein's Ba'th Party before he went into exile in the UK, where he was a prominent anti-Saddam activist.

Paul G. Allen (21 Jan 1953, Mercer Island WA), American corporate executive who cofounded Microsoft Corp. (1975) and owned several professional sports teams, including basketball's Portland Trail Blazers and football's Seattle Seahawks, among other enterprises.

Woody Allen (Allen Stewart Konigsberg; 1 Dec 1935, Brooklyn NY), American filmmaker, actor, and comedian best known for absurdly comic but sympathetic works; he won Academy Awards for direction (*Annie Hall*, 1977) and best original screenplay (*Hannah and Her Sisters*, 1986).

Isabel Allende (2 Aug 1942, Lima, Peru), Chilean writer in the magic realist tradition who is considered one of the first successful women novelists in Latin America.

Kirstie Alley (12 Jan 1951, Wichita KS), American film and TV actress who appeared on the TV sitcom *Cheers* (1987–93), for which she won Golden Globe (1990) and Emmy (1991) awards; she won a second Emmy for the TV movie *David's Mother* (1994).

Pedro Almodóvar (24 Sep 1949, Calzada de Calatrava, Spain), Spanish film director specializing in melodrama; his first success was *Women on the Verge of a Nervous Breakdown* (1988).

Prince Alois (Alois Philipp Maria Prince von und zu Liechtenstein; 11 Jun 1968, Zürich, Switzerland), Liechtenstein royal and heir to the throne.

Marin Alsop (1957?, New York NY), American conductor, the first woman to lead a major British orchestra when she was appointed principal conductor of the Bournemouth Symphony Orchestra from the 2002–03 season and was equally controversial when she was named to lead the Baltimore Symphony Orchestra in July 2005.

Robert Altman (20 Feb 1925, Kansas City MO), American filmmaker noted for his unconventional and independent style; his films have included *Nashville* (1975) and *Gosford Park* (2001).

Viswanathan Anand ("Vishy"; 11 Dec 1969, Madras [now Chennai], Tamil Nadu state, India), Indian chess world grandmaster and FIDE world champion in 2000.

Anastacia (Newkirk) (7 Sep 1973, Chicago IL), American pop singer, songwriter, dancer, producer, and breast cancer activist.

Pamela (Denise) Anderson (1 Jul 1967, Ladysmith, BC, Canada), Canadian-born model and actress who has appeared nine times on the cover of *Playboy* magazine.

Tadao Ando (13 Sep 1941, Osaka, Japan), Japanese architect; winner of the 1995 Pritzker Prize.

Marc Andreessen (July 1971, New Lisbon WI), American computer innovator, cofounder (1994) of Mosaic Communications Corp., and developer of Netscape, a software system for browsing the Internet.

Prince Andrew (19 Feb 1960, Buckingham Palace, London, England), British royal; duke of York, the second son of Queen Elizabeth II and Prince Philip, duke of Edinburgh.

Maya Angelou (Marguerite Annie Johnson; 4 Apr 1928, St. Louis MO), American poet whose several volumes of autobiography explore the themes of economic, racial, and sexual oppression.

Jennifer Aniston (Jennifer Linn Anistassakis; 11 Feb

1969, Sherman Oaks CA), American TV and film actress who starred as Rachel Green on TV's *Friends* (1994-2004).

Kofi (Atta) Annan (18 Apr 1938, Kumasi, Gold Coast [now Ghana]), Ghanaian diplomat; UN secretary-general from 1997; cowinner, with the UN, of the 2001 Nobel Peace Prize.

Princess Anne (Elizabeth Alice Louise; 15 Aug 1950, Clarence House, London, England), British princess royal, the daughter of Queen Elizabeth II and Prince Philip, duke of Edinburgh.

Kristi S. Anseth (1968, Minneapolis MN), American biochemical engineer; she won the A.T. Waterman Award in 2004 "for her research at the interface of biology and engineering, resulting in the design of innovative biomaterials that significantly facilitate tissue engineering and regeneration."

Andrus Ansip (1 Oct 1956, Tartu, Estonian SSR, USSR [now in Estonia]), Estonian politician who was confirmed as prime minister on 12 Apr 2005.

Kenny D. Anthony (8 Jan 1951, Saint Lucia), Saint Lucia politician and prime minister from 1997.

Marc Anthony (Marco Antonio Muñiz; 16 Sep 1968, Spanish Harlem, New York NY), American salsa singer.

Severino Antinori (1945?, Rome, Italy), Italian gynecologist and specialist in human fertility; he is the leader of a project to clone humans.

Shizuka Arakawa (29 Dec 1981, Shinagawa, Tokyo, Japan), Japanese figure skater who won the women's 2004 world championship.

Louise Arbour (10 Feb 1947, Montreal, QC, Canada), Canadian judge who served as chief prosecutor for the International Criminal Tribunals for the former Yugoslavia and Rwanda from October 1996 to September 1999, justice on the Supreme Court of Canada, 1999-2004, and, from June 2004, UN High Commissioner for Human Rights.

Denys Arcand (25 Jun 1941, Deschambault, QC, Canada), Canadian film director and screenwriter known first for his documentary films and later for gritty intellectual fare such as *Le Déclin de l'empire américain* (1986; *The Decline of the American Empire*), *Jésus de Montréal* (1989; *Jesus of Montreal*), and *Les Invasions barbares* (2003; *The Barbarian Invasions*; best foreign-language film Academy Award, 2003).

Vladislav Ardzinba (14 May 1945, Abkhazia?, Georgian SSR, USSR [now Georgia]), Abkhaz politician; president of Georgia's secessionist republic of Abkhazia from 1990 to 12 Feb 2005.

Martha Argerich (5 Jun 1941, Buenos Aires, Argentina), Argentine concert pianist with a wide-ranging repertoire, from Bach to Ginastera, who performs solo and chamber music.

Francis Cardinal Arinze (1 Nov 1932, Eziowelle, British Nigeria), Nigerian Roman Catholic churchman who served as president of the Pontifical Council for Inter-religious Dialogue (1984-2002) and as prefect of divine worship and discipline of sacraments (from 2002); he was named cardinal in 1985.

Jean-Bertrand Aristide (15 Jul 1953, Port Salut, Haiti), Haitian politician; president of Haiti, 1991, 1993-94 (in exile), 1994-96, and again from 2001 until he was deposed and fled the country on 29 Feb 2004.

Richard K. Armey (7 Jul 1940, Cando ND), American politician and nine-term Republican congressman from Texas; he was House Republican leader, 1994-2003.

Billie Joe Armstrong (17 Feb 1972, Rodeo CA), American punk rock vocalist and guitarist (of Green Day).

C. Michael Armstrong (18 Oct 1938, Detroit MI), American corporate executive; CEO of AT&T, 1997-2002; head of AT&T Comcast Corp. from 2002.

Lance Armstrong (18 Sep 1971, Plano TX), American cyclist who won the Tour de France seven years in succession (1999-2005) after recovering from cancer in the mid-1990s.

Gerald Arpino (14 Jan 1928, Staten Island NY), American ballet choreographer, a cofounder and leader of the Joffrey Ballet from its founding in 1956 and its artistic director from 1988.

Courteney Cox Arquette (15 Jun 1964, Birmingham AL), American TV and film actress who was featured as Monica Geller Bing on TV's *Friends* (1994-2004).

Rosalía Arteaga (Serrano de Fernández de Córdova; 5 Dec 1956, Cuenca, Ecuador), Ecuadoran government and international official who served as vice president in 1996-98 and briefly as Ecuador's president during a constitutional crisis in February 1997; from May 2004 she was secretary-general of the Amazon Cooperation Treaty Organization.

Owen Seymour Arthur (17 Oct 1949, Barbados), Barbadian politician and prime minister from 1994.

Asashoryu (Dolgorsuren Dagvadorj; 27 Sep 1980, Ulaanbaatar, Mongolia), Mongolian-born sumo wrestler, only the third foreign-born *yokozuna* (from January 2003); he won five of the top contests from 2002 through early 2004.

Ashanti (Ashanti S. Douglas; 13 Oct 1980, Glen Cove NY), American hip-hop singer who had the distinction of having three songs in the top 10 of *Billboard* magazine's Hot 100 in spring 2003.

John (David) Ashcroft (9 May 1942, Chicago IL), American Republican senator from Missouri (1995-2000) and US attorney general, 2001-05.

Paddy Ashdown (Jeremy John Durham Ashdown; Baron Ashdown of Norton-sub-Hamdon in the County of Somerset; 27 Feb 1941, New Delhi, British India), British politician and diplomat who was the first chairman of the Liberal Democratic Party (1988-99) and international high representative in Bosnia and Herzegovina from 27 May 2002.

Hanan Ashrawi (8 Oct 1946, Ram Allah, Palestine), Palestinian academic and spokeswoman for Palestine.

Bashar al-Assad (11 Sep 1965, Damascus, Syria), Syrian statesman and president from 2000.

Azali Assoumani (1959, Grand Comoro Island, Comoros), Comoran politician who was president from 1999 to January 2002, and again from 26 May 2002.

Alaa Al Aswany (1957, Egypt), Egyptian dentist and popular writer known especially for his best-selling novel *The Yacoubian Building* (English version, 2005).

Richard C(hatham) Atkinson (19 Mar 1929, Oak Park IL), American psychologist, a specialist on cognition and memory; he served as director of the National Science Foundation, 1977-80; chancellor of the University of California, San Diego, 1980-95; and president of the University of California from 1995.

Abdul Rahman ibn Hamad al-Attiyah (1950, Qatar), Qatari international official; secretary-general of the Gulf Cooperation Council from March 2002.

Margaret (Eleanor) Atwood (18 Nov 1939, Ottawa,

ON, Canada), Canadian poet, novelist, and critic, noted for her Canadian nationalism and her feminism; she won the 2000 Booker Prize for The Blind Assassin.

Daw Aung San Suu Kyi (19 Jun 1945, Rangoon, Burma [now Yangôn, Myanmar]), Burmese human rights activist and opposition leader, daughter of Aung San (a martyred national hero of independent Burma) and Khin Kyi (a prominent Burmese diplomat), and winner in 1991 of the Nobel Peace Prize.

Geno Auriemma (Luigi Auriemma; 1954, Montella, Italy), Italian-born American women's basketball coach, the successful coach of the University of Connecticut Huskies team, which won the national championship five times from 1995 to 2004, including three years in succession, 2002–04.

Mary Ellen Avery (6 May 1927, Camden NJ), American pediatrician and pharmacologist who is a specialist in respiratory problems of newborns; she was awarded the National Medal of Science in 1991 and served as president of the American Association for the Advancement of Science for the year beginning February 2003.

Richard Axel (2 Jul 1946, New York NY), American immunologist who shared the 2004 Nobel Prize for Physiology or Medicine with Linda B. Buck for their work in olfactory receptors.

Dan Aykroyd (1 Jul 1952, Ottawa, ON, Canada), Canadian-born comic actor best known for TV's Saturday Night Live (1975–79) and the film The Blues Brothers (1980).

Hank Azaria (25 Apr 1964, Forest Hills NY), American actor best known for comic film roles and for providing voices for TV's The Simpsons.

José María Aznar López (25 Feb 1953, Madrid, Spain), Spanish politician and prime minister, 1996–2004.

B-Real (Louis Freese; 2 Jun 1970, Los Angeles CA), American Latino rap artist (of Cypress Hill).

'Abd al-Qadir al-Ba Jamal (1946, Yemen?), Yemeni politician; prime minister from 2001.

Juan N. Babauta (7 Sep 1953, Tanapag, Saipan, Northern Mariana Islands), American Republican politician; governor of the Northern Mariana Islands from January 2002.

Kevin Bacon (8 Jul 1958, Philadelphia PA), American film and theater actor best known for his breakthrough role in Footloose (1984).

Datuk Seri Abdullah Ahmad Badawi (26 Nov 1939, Penang state, Malaysia), Malaysian politician who succeeded Mahathir bin Mohamad as prime minister on 30 Oct 2003.

Erykah Badu (Erica Wright; 26 Feb 1972, Dallas TX), American singer-songwriter appreciated for the phrasing and emotive qualities of her smooth, jazz-inflected vocals.

Bob Baffert (13 Jan 1953, Nogales AZ), American trainer of Thoroughbred horses, including winners of the Preakness Stakes four times, the Kentucky Derby three times, and the Belmont Stakes once.

Natsagiyn Bagabandi (22 Apr 1950, Yaruu Soum, Mongolia), Mongolian politician and president from 1997.

Sergey Bagapsh (1949, Sukhumi, Abkhazian ASSR, USSR [now in Abkhazia, Georgia]), Abkhaz politician and president of Georgia's secessionist republic of Abkhazia from 12 Feb 2005.

Jerry D. Bailey (29 Aug 1957, Dallas TX), American jockey, two-time winner of both the Kentucky Derby (1993, 1996) and the Preakness Stakes (1991, 2000); in January 2004 he won his seventh Eclipse Award.

Anita Baker (26 Jan 1958, Toledo OH), American singer whose three-octave range and powerful, emotional delivery brought her international acclaim in the 1980s and '90s; she was one of the most popular artists in urban contemporary music.

John Elias Baldacci (30 Jan 1955, Bangor ME), American Democratic politician and governor of Maine from 2003.

John Baldessari (17 Jun 1931, National City CA), American conceptual artist.

Alec Baldwin (Alexander Rae Baldwin III; 3 Apr 1958, Massapequa NY), American film and TV actor noted for both dramatic and comic roles.

Jan Peter Balkenende (7 May 1956, Kapelle, The Netherlands), Dutch Christian-Democratic politician and prime minister from 2002.

Steven A. Ballmer (24 Mar 1956, Detroit? MI), American corporate executive who was CEO of Microsoft Corp. from 2000.

Ed(ward) Balls (25 Feb 1967, Norwich, England), British public official; chief economic adviser to the treasury.

David Baltimore (7 Mar 1938, New York NY), American microbiologist who was awarded (with Renato Dulbecco and Howard M. Temin) the 1975 Nobel Prize in Physiology or Medicine for research on how certain viruses affect the genes of cancer cells; he received a 1999 National Medal of Science and has been president of the California Institute of Technology since 1997.

Enric Banda (1948, Girona, Spain), Catalan geophysicist; secretary general of the European Science Foundation from 1998.

Antonio Banderas (José António Domínguez Banderas; 10 Oct 1960, Málaga, Spain), Spanish actor and director who successfully crossed over to make American films such as The Mambo Kings (1992), Philadelphia (1993), Evita (1996), and The Mask of Zorro (1998) and its sequel (2005).

John Bennett Bani (1940, Pentecost Island, New Hebrides [now Vanuatu]), Vanuatu Anglican priest and president from 1999 to 24 Mar 2004.

Tyra Banks (4 Dec 1973, Los Angeles CA), American model and actress best known for Victoria's Secret ads; she was host of the TV show America's Next Top Model (from 2003).

Patricia Barber (8 Nov 1955, Lisle IL), American jazz singer and pianist.

Haley Barbour (22 Oct 1947, Yazoo City MS), American Republican politician and governor of Mississippi from 13 Jan 2004.

Daniel Barenboim (15 Nov 1942, Buenos Aires, Argentina), Israeli pianist and conductor; music director of the Chicago Symphony Orchestra from 1989.

Matthew Barney (25 Mar 1967, San Francisco CA), American installation artist who won the first (1996) Hugo Boss Prize of the Guggenheim Museum; his multimedia exhibition "Matthew Barney: The Cremaster Cycle" opened at the Guggenheim Museum in New York City in 2003.

Hector V. Barreto, Jr. (1962?, Kansas City MO), American government official who was head of the US Small Business Administration from 2001.

Craig R. Barrett (29 Aug 1939, San Francisco CA), American materials scientist and corporate executive; he was CEO of Intel Corp. from 1997.

Dave Barry (3 Jul 1947, Armonk NY), American humorist, syndicated newspaper columnist, and author of multiple best sellers.

Drew Barrymore (Andrew Blythe Barrymore; 22 Feb 1975, Culver City CA), American film actress successful both as a child star (*E.T. the Extra-Ter-restrial*; 1982) and as an adult in such films as *Boys on the Side* (1995), *The Wedding Singer* (1998), *Never Been Kissed* (1999), and two *Charlie's Angels* pictures (2000 and 2003).

Frederick Barthelme (10 Oct 1943, Houston TX), American writer of short stories and novels featuring characters who are shaped by the impersonal suburban environments in which they live.

Cecilia Bartoli (4 Jun 1966, Rome, Italy), Italian operatic mezzo-soprano praised for her supple voice, with its wide, even range, and for her vivaciousness as an actress in comic roles.

Mikhail (Nikolayevich) Baryshnikov (28 Jan 1948, Riga, Latvian SSR, USSR [now Latvia]), Soviet-born American ballet dancer who was the preeminent male classical dancer of the 1970s and '80s; he subsequently became a noted dance director.

Shamil (Salmanovich) Basayev (14 Jan 1965, near Vedeno, Chechen-Ingush ASSR, USSR [now in Chechnya, Russia]), Chechen separatist, guerrilla leader, and terrorist who claimed responsibility for the takeover of a Moscow theater and ensuing siege in 2002 and for the school massacre at Beslan in 2004.

Georg Baselitz (Hans-Georg Kern; 23 Jan 1938, Deutschbaselitz, Germany), German painter principally concerned with the postwar period in Germany; he won a 2004 Praemium Imperiale.

Omar Hassan Ahmad al-Bashir (1944, Hosh Bannaga, Anglo-Egyptian Sudan [now The Sudan]), Sudanese military leader and president from 1989.

Angela Bassett (16 Aug 1958, New York NY), American film actress noted for strong characters, including Tina Turner in *What's Love Got to Do with It* (1993); she was named a celebrity ambassador for the US fund for UNICEF in 2003.

Jorge Batlle Ibáñez (25 Oct 1927, Uruguay?), Uruguayan politician and president from 1 Mar 2000 to 1 Mar 2005.

Kathleen Battle (Kathleen Deanne Battle; 13 Aug 1948, Portsmouth OH), American operatic soprano, among the finest coloraturas of her time; her roles included Susanna in *The Marriage of Figaro*, Rosina in *The Barber of Seville*, and Sophie in *Der Rosenkavalier*.

Rick Bayless (1953, Oklahoma City OK), American chef and owner (from 1987) of Frontera Grill and (from 1989) Topolobampo restaurants in Chicago; he is also a cookbook author, a TV personality, and an expert on Mexican cuisine.

Queen Beatrix (31 Jan 1938, Soestdijk, The Netherlands), Dutch royal and queen of The Netherlands from 1980.

(Henry) Warren Beatty (30 Mar 1937, Richmond VA), American film actor who has also produced, directed, and written screenplays and is best known for politically charged portrayals; his films include *Splendor in the Grass* (1961), *Bonnie & Clyde* (1967), *Bugsy* (1991), and *Bulworth* (1998); he received a Kennedy Center Honor in 2004.

Beck (Beck Hansen; 8 Jul 1970, Los Angeles CA), American singer and songwriter who won Grammys for best male rock vocal performance in 1996 with "Where It's At" and for best alternative music album with *Odelay* (1996) and *Mutations* (1999).

David Beckham (2 May 1975, Leytonstone, East London, England), British association football (soccer) player, star midfielder for Manchester United, and captain of England's national team in the 2002 World Cup; he was also known for his celebrity marriage to Victoria Adams (of the Spice Girls); he was made OBE in 2003, a few days before he agonized fans by being traded to Spain's Real Madrid football club.

Victoria Beckham (Victoria Caroline Adams; 7 Apr 1975, Goff's Oak, Hertfordshire, England), British pop singer ("Posh Spice" of the Spice Girls); also known for her marriage to David Beckham.

Kate Beckinsale (26 Jul 1973, London, England), British actress who has starred in British and American films, both modern and period pieces.

Bei Dao (original name Zhao Zhenkai; 2 Aug 1949, Peking [now Beijing], China), Chinese poet and writer of fiction whose works were published underground for most of his career.

Kenenisa Bekele (13 Jun 1982, near Bekoji, Ethiopia), Ethiopian cross-country runner who, at the 2002 International Association of Athletics Federations (IAAF) world cross country championships in Dublin, won the senior long-course (12-km [7.5-mi]) and short-course (4-km [2.5-mi]) titles—a feat never before accomplished by a male runner—and was world champion in the short and long races in 2002 and 2003.

Marek Belka (9 Jan 1952, Lodz, Poland), Polish economics professor and government domestic and international financial official; he was prime minister from 2 May 2004.

Joshua Bell (9 Dec 1967, Bloomington IN), American violinist who won a Grammy for his world premiere recording of Nicholas Maw's *Concerto for Violin* (2000).

Carol Bellamy (14 Jan 1942, Plainfield NJ), American politician and international official who was director of the US Peace Corps (1993–95) and executive director of UNICEF from 1995 to 2005.

Carlos Filipe Ximenes Belo (3 Feb 1948, Wailacama, Portuguese East Timor), Timorese Roman Catholic bishop and advocate of independence for East Timor who was the cowinner, with José Ramos-Horta, of the 1996 Nobel Peace Prize.

Arden L. Bement, Jr. (22 May 1932, Pittsburgh PA), American materials scientist; director of the National Institute of Standards and Technology, 2001–04; he was named acting director of the National Science Foundation from 22 Feb 2004 and director from 24 Nov 2004.

Zine al-Abidine Ben Ali (3 Sep 1936, Hammam-Sousse, Tunisia), Tunisian politician and president from 1987.

Nicola Benedetti (1987, Scotland), Scottish violinist who was named BBC Young Musician of the Year in May 2004 and whose debut recording of Szymanowski's *Violin Concerto No. 1* was number two on the British classical charts in its first week of release in 2005.

Benedict XVI (Joseph Alois Ratzinger; 16 Apr 1927, Marktl am Inn, Bavaria, Germany), German Roman Catholic churchman; named archbishop of Munich and Freising on 24 Mar 1977 and cardinal on 27 Jun 1977; he served as Prefect for the Congregation for the Doctrine of the Faith from 25 Nov 1981 until his election as pope on 19 Apr 2005.

Luciano Benetton (13 May 1935, Treviso, Italy), Italian retailer and cofounder (1965) of the Benetton company noted for sportswear and provocative advertisements.

Annette Bening (29 May 1958, Topeka KS), American film actress who won critical acclaim for *American Beauty* (1999) and *Being Julia* (2004).

Alan Bennett (9 May 1934, Leeds, England), British

dramatist and writer known especially for his low-key, unpretentious subject matter.

Craig Benson (8 Oct 1954, New York NY), American businessman and Republican politician and governor of New Hampshire from 2003 to 6 Jan 2005.

Paul Bérenger (26 Mar 1945, Quatre Bornes, Mauritius), Mauritian politician, prime minister from 30 Sep 2003.

Yelena Berezhnaya (11 Oct 1977, Nevinnomyssk, Russian SFSR, USSR [now in Russia]), Russian pairs skater (with Anton Sikharulidze); shared the 2002 Olympic gold medal with Canadians Jamie Salé and David Pelletier.

Óscar Berger Perdomo (11 Aug 1946, Guatemala City, Guatemala), Guatemalan politician and president from 14 Jan 2004.

Jorge Mario Cardinal Bergoglio (17 Dec 1936, Buenos Aires, Argentina), Argentine Roman Catholic churchman; archbishop of Buenos Aires from 1998; he was named cardinal in 2001.

Silvio Berlusconi (29 Sep 1936, Milan, Italy), Italian businessman and politician; prime minister of Italy, 1994–95, and again from 2001.

Gael García Bernal (30 Oct 1978, Guadalajara, Mexico), Mexican actor who scored big film hits in three successive years—*Amores perros* (2000), *Y tu mamá también* (2001), and *El crimen del padre Amaro* (2002)—and had two more in 2004: *Diarios de motocicleta* (*The Motorcycle Diaries*) and *La Mala educación* (*Bad Education*).

Tim Berners-Lee (Timothy J. Berners-Lee; 8 Jun 1955, London, England), British inventor of the World Wide Web and director, from 1994, of the World Wide Web Consortium (W3C) at the MIT Laboratory for Computer Science.

Chuck Berry (Charles Edward Anderson Berry; 18 Oct 1926, St. Louis MO), American singer, songwriter, and guitarist who was one of the most popular and influential performers in rhythm-and-blues and rock-and-roll music in the 1950s, '60s, and '70s.

Halle (Maria) Berry (14 Aug 1968, Cleveland OH), American actress and model who received an Academy Award for her role in *Monster's Ball* (2001) and much publicity for starring in the James Bond film *Die Another Day* (2002).

Guy Berryman (12 Apr 1978, Kirkcaldy, Fife, Scotland), British rock bassist (of Coldplay).

Liliane Bettencourt (October 1922, France), French daughter of the founder of the L'Oreal cosmetics company and the wealthiest person in France.

Beyoncé (Knowles) (4 Sep 1981, Houston TX), American R&B singer, formerly of Destiny's Child, whose 2003 album, *Dangerously in Love*, established her as a successful solo act; she won five Grammy Awards in 2004.

Jeffrey P. Bezos (12 Jan 1964, Albuquerque NM), American corporate executive; founder and CEO of Amazon.com from 1995.

King Bhumibol Adulyadej (Rama IX; 5 Dec 1927, Cambridge MA), Thai royal; king of Thailand from 1946, the ninth of the Chakkri dynasty.

Carlos Bianchi (26 Apr 1949, Buenos Aires, Argentina), Argentine association football (soccer) coach whose team, the Boca Juniors, in July 2003 won him a record fourth Libertadores Cup.

Joseph R(obinette) Biden, Jr. (20 Nov 1942, Scranton PA), American Democratic politician and senator from Delaware from 1973.

Big Boi (Antwan Andre Patton; 1 Feb 1975, Savannah GA), American hip-hop artist and a member of the duo OutKast.

James H(adley) Billington (1 Jun 1929, Bryn Mawr PA), American cultural historian and librarian of Congress from 1987.

Osama bin Laden (also spelled Usamah ibn Ladin; 10 Mar 1957, Riyadh, Saudi Arabia), Saudi Arabian–born terrorist leader, alleged mastermind of the 1993 bombing of the World Trade Center and the 11 Sep 2001 attacks on the World Trade Center and the Pentagon; his al-Qaeda network was linked to many international terrorist acts from 2001 as well.

Pat Binns (8 Oct 1948, Weyburn, SK, Canada), Canadian politician; premier of Prince Edward Island from 1996.

Juliette Binoche (9 Mar 1964, Paris, France), French film actress famous for complex characterizations; her breakthrough performance was in *The English Patient* (1996; Academy Award for best supporting actress).

Harrison Birtwistle (15 Jul 1934, Accrington, Lancashire, England), British composer of operas, chamber music, and orchestral music in a contemporary, avant-garde style; he won the 1987 Grawemeyer Award for Music for *The Mask of Orpheus*.

J(ohn) Michael Bishop (22 Feb 1936, York PA), American microbiologist who (with Harold E. Varmus) was awarded the 1989 Nobel Prize for Physiology or Medicine for research on cancer-causing genes called oncogenes; he received a National Medal of Science in 2003.

Paul Biya (13 Feb 1933, Mvomeka'a, Cameroon), Cameroonian politician; president from 1982.

Jonas Bjorkman (23 Mar 1972, Vaxjo, Sweden), Swedish tennis player best known for doubles play, especially with Todd Woodbridge; Bjorkman won the doubles championships at the Australian Open in 1998, 1999, and 2001, at Wimbledon in 2002, 2003, and 2004, and at the US Open in 2003.

Ole Einar Bjørndalen (27 Jan 1974, Drammen, Norway), Norwegian biathlete and cross-country skier who swept the Olympic biathlon (four golds) in 2002.

Conrad (Moffat) Black (25 Aug 1944, Montreal, QC, Canada), Canadian financier and press baron, an icon of capitalism in Canada who built a media empire of almost 250 newspapers worldwide; among other newspapers, Black controlled the London *Daily Telegraph*, the Fairfax Group in Australia, the *Jerusalem Post*, Southam Press in Canada, and nearly 100 local dailies in the US.

Jack Black (28 Aug 1969, Hermosa Beach CA), American TV and film actor and comic rock bandleader known for his portrayal of offbeat characters; films include *High Fidelity* (2000) and *School of Rock* (2003).

Rubén Blades (16 Jul 1948, Panama City, Panama), Panamanian salsa singer and songwriter, actor, and politician.

Rod R. Blagojevich (10 Dec 1956, Chicago IL), American Democratic politician and governor of Illinois from 2003.

David Blaine (David Blaine White; 4 Apr 1973, Brooklyn NY), American magician known for his endurance stunts; in 2003, for example, he spent 44 days without food in a Plexiglas box hanging over the Thames River in London.

Tony Blair (Anthony Charles Lynton Blair; 6 May 1953, Edinburgh, Scotland), British politician, Labour Party leader, and prime minister of the UK from 1997.

Robert Blake (Michael James Vijencio Gubitosi; 18

Sep 1933, Nutley NJ), American film and TV actor best known for the 1970s cop show *Baretta*; he was charged with the 2001 murder of his wife but was acquitted in 2005.

Cate Blanchett (Catherine Elise Blanchett; 14 May 1969, Melbourne, VIC, Australia), Australian film actress known for dramatic parts, including her roles in *Elizabeth* (1998; Golden Globe Award) and *The Talented Mr. Ripley* (1999); she won an Academy Award for best supporting actress in 2005 for her performance in *The Aviator*.

Kathleen Babineaux Blanco (15 Dec 1942, Coteau LA), American Democratic politician and governor of Louisiana from 12 Jan 2004.

Sir Christopher Bland (29 May 1938, Japan), British corporate executive; chairman of British Telecom from 2001.

Mary J. Blige (11 Jan 1971, New York NY), American hip-hop soul singer.

Christoph Blocher (11 Oct 1940, Schaffhausen, Switzerland), Swiss billionaire chemical company executive and right-wing politician (Schweizerische Volkspartei) who opposed Swiss membership in the European Union and foreign immigration into the country; he was named to the seven-member Swiss federal executive in December 2003.

Harold (Irving) Bloom (11 Jul 1930, New York NY), American literary critic known for his innovative interpretations of literary history and of the creation of literature, and for his unconventional approach to writing as in, for example, *The Western Canon* (1994).

Orlando Bloom (13 Jan 1977, Canterbury, Kent, England), British film actor who was first noticed for his portrayal of Legolas in the *Lord of the Rings* trilogy.

Michael R. Bloomberg (14 Feb 1942, Medford MA), American businessman, philanthropist, and Republican politician; he was mayor of New York City from 1 Jan 2002.

David Blunkett (6 Jun 1947, Sheffield, England), British politician, blind from birth; he was British home secretary, 2001–04, and work and pensions secretary from 2005.

Matt Blunt (20 Nov 1970, Springfield MO), American Republican politician and governor of Missouri from 10 Jan 2005.

Andrea Bocelli (22 Sep 1958, Lajatico, Italy), Italian operatic tenor, blind from age 12.

Steven Bochco (16 Dec 1943, New York NY), American writer, producer, and creator of TV series that have included *Hill Street Blues*, *L.A. Law*, and *NYPD Blue*.

Samuel Wright Bodman (26 Nov 1938, Chicago IL), American chemical engineer, corporate leader, and official in the Departments of Commerce and Treasury; he became secretary of energy on 1 Feb 2005.

Enrique Bolaños Geyer (13 May 1928, Masaya, Nicaragua), Nicaraguan politician and president from 2002.

Sir Haji Hassanal Bolkiah Mu'izzadin Waddaulah (15 Jul 1946, Brunei Town [now Bandar Seri Begawan], Brunei), Bruneian royal; the 29th sultan, from 1967.

Joshua B. Bolten (6 Aug 1954, Washington DC?), American international lawyer and government official in the presidential administrations of George H.W. Bush and George W. Bush; director of the Office of Management and Budget from June 2003.

John R. Bolton (20 Nov 1948, Baltimore MD), American lawyer, official in the Departments of State and Justice, and specialist in arms control; on 1 Aug 2005 he was appointed US representative to the United Nations.

Kjell Magne Bondevik (3 Sep 1947, Molde, Norway), Norwegian politician who was prime minister in 1997–2000, and again from 2001.

Barry (Lamar) Bonds (24 Jul 1964, Riverside CA), American baseball player who tallied a record 73 home runs and 177 walks in 2001; he was the only six-time National League MVP (1990, 1992, 1993, 2001–03) and the only player with more than 500 home runs and 500 stolen bases.

Abass Bonfoh (1948, Kabou, French Togo), Togolese acting president from 25 Feb to 4 May 2005.

Omar Bongo (Albert-Bernard Bongo; 30 Dec 1935, Lewai, Gabon), Gabonese politician and president from 1967.

Bono (Paul David Hewson; also known as Bono Vox; 10 May 1960, Dublin, Ireland), Irish lead singer and songwriter of the rock band U2; he is also a human rights activist and mediator.

Cherie Booth (23 Sep 1954, Bury, Lancashire, England), British barrister, the wife of prime minister Tony Blair.

Umberto Bossi (19 Sep 1941, Cassano Magnano, Italy), Italian politician and leader of the separatist Northern League from 1991.

Fernando Botero (19 Apr 1932, Medellín, Colombia), Colombian painter and sculptor of monumental bronze pieces known for his exaggerated representations of human and animal forms.

Lucien Bouchard (22 Dec 1938, Saint-Coeur-de-Marie, QC, Canada), French Canadian politician, an advocate of the separation of Quebec from the rest of Canada.

Pierre Boulez (26 Mar 1925, Montbrison, France), French composer, conductor, and music theorist whose complex, serialist music is marked by a sensitivity to the nuances of instrumental texture and color.

Ray Bourque (28 Dec 1960, Montreal, QC, Canada), American ice hockey defenseman and five-time James Norris Trophy winner.

Abdelaziz Bouteflika (2 Mar 1937, Tlemcen, Algeria), Algerian politician, diplomat, and president from 1999.

T. Coraghessan Boyle (Thomas John Boyle; 2 Dec 1948, Peekskill NY), American short-story writer and novelist.

François Bozizé (14 Oct 1946, Mouila, French Equatorial Africa [now in Gabon]), Central African Republic politician who became president following a successful coup on 15 Mar 2003.

Peter Brabeck-Letmathe (13 Nov 1944, Villach, Austria), Austrian-born corporate executive; as CEO of Nestlé, the world's largest food company, from 1997, he was responsible for significant international expansion of the company and acquisition of other companies, including the pet-food company Ralston Purina in 2001 for $11 billion.

Ray (Douglas) Bradbury (22 Aug 1920, Waukegan IL), American author of science-fiction short stories and novels, nostalgic tales, poetry, radio drama, and TV and film screenplays; his most famous works include the novel *Fahrenheit 451* (1953) and the short-story collections *The Martian Chronicles* (1950) and *The Illustrated Man* (1951); he was awarded a National Medal of Arts in 2004.

Ed Bradley (Edward Riley Bradley; 22 Jun 1941, Philadelphia PA), American TV journalist.

Tom Brady (Thomas Brady; 3 Aug 1977, San Mateo

CA), American professional football quarterback for the NFL New England Patriots who led the team to Super Bowl wins in 2002 and 2004 and was named MVP in both games.

Lakhdar Brahimi (1 Jan 1934, Algeria), Algerian statesman and diplomat; he was foreign minister, 1991–93, later serving as UN special representative for South Africa (1993–94), Haiti (1994–96), and Afghanistan (1997–99, 2001–03); in early 2004 he was appointed special adviser on Iraq.

Kenneth (Charles) Branagh (10 Dec 1960, Belfast, Northern Ireland), British theater and film actor, director, and writer best known for screen adaptations of Shakespeare plays.

Brandy (Brandy Norwood; 11 Feb 1979, McComb MS), American rhythm-and-blues singer and TV actress (on *Moesha*).

Richard (Charles Nicholas) Branson (18 Jul 1950, Shamley Green, Surrey, England), British entrepreneur who founded the Virgin empire in 1973.

Benjamin Bratt (16 Dec 1963, San Francisco CA), American TV and motion picture actor who first gained fame in the series *Law & Order* (1995–99); his film credits include *Miss Congeniality* (2000) and *The Next Best Thing* (2000).

Anthony Braxton (4 Jun 1945, Chicago IL), American reed player and composer whose idiosyncratic style partook of the classical avant-garde (composers such as Karlheinz Stockhausen and John Cage) as well as the classical jazz saxophone repertory and confounded exponents of both styles.

Toni Braxton (7 Oct 1968, Severn MD), American rhythm-and-blues singer.

Algirdas Mykolas Brazauskas (22 Sep 1932, Rokiskis, Lithuanian SSR, USSR [now Lithuania]), Lithuanian politician who was president, 1992–98, and prime minister from 2001.

Phil Bredesen (Philip Norman Bredesen; 21 Nov 1943, Oceanport NJ), American Democratic politician, mayor of Nashville TN, and governor of Tennessee from 2003.

L. Paul Bremer III ("Jerry"; 30 Sep 1941, Hartford CT), American diplomat; US ambassador to The Netherlands (1983–86) and ambassador-at-large for counterterrorism (1986–89); he was appointed on 6 May 2003 to replace Lieut. Gen. (Ret.) Jay Garner as chief administrator following the coalition occupation of Iraq and returned to the US in late June 2004.

Sydney Brenner (13 Jan 1927, Germiston, South Africa), British cowinner of the 2002 Nobel Prize for Physiology or Medicine for his work on the life of a cell.

Thierry Breton (15 Jan 1955, Paris, France), French corporate head; he was executive chairman of Thompson Multimedia to 2002, and executive chairman of France Télécom from 2002.

Stephen (Gerald) Breyer (15 Aug 1938, San Francisco CA), American jurist; associate justice of the US Supreme Court from 1994.

Jeff Bridges (4 Dec 1949, Los Angeles CA), American actor whose breakthrough performance came in *The Last Picture Show* (1971) and who starred in *Seabiscuit* (2003).

Sarah Brightman (14 Aug 1960, Berkhampstead, Hertfordshire, England), British soprano who made her reputation appearing in stage musicals such as *The Phantom of the Opera* and *Cats* and has gone on to issue successful light classical albums.

Sergey Brin (1973, Moscow, USSR [now in Russia]), Russian-born computer scientist and Internet en-

trepreneur who cofounded (with Lawrence Page) in 1998 the Google Internet search engine.

Matthew Broderick (21 Mar 1962, New York NY), American comic actor of stage and screen who gained widespread fame following the film *Ferris Bueller's Day Off* (1986) and starred in the Broadway musical *The Producers* (2001–02).

Adrien Brody (14 Apr 1973, New York NY), American film actor who won a best actor Academy Award in 2002 for *The Pianist*.

Tom Brokaw (Thomas John Brokaw; 6 Feb 1940, Webster SD), American TV newsman and chief anchorman for NBC News until his retirement on 1 Dec 2004.

Edgar M. Bronfman (20 Jun 1929, Montreal, QC, Canada), Canadian-born American businessman; he was chairman of The Seagram Co. Ltd. and, following that company's merger with Vivendi Universal, served on the board of Vivendi; he is equally well known as president of the World Jewish Congress (from 1979) and officer of other Jewish organizations.

Yefim Bronfman (10 Apr 1958, Tashkent, Uzbek SSR, USSR [now Uzbekistan]), Soviet-born American pianist; winner of the Avery Fisher Prize in 1991 and a Grammy Award in 1997 for his recording of the Bartok piano concertos.

Garth Brooks (Troyal Garth Brooks; 7 Feb 1962, Tulsa OK), American country-and-western singer known for his cowboy hats and the commercialism (and great commercial success) of his music from the early 1990s.

Kix Brooks (Leon Eric Brooks; 12 May 1955, Shreveport LA), American country-and-western singer in the duo Brooks & Dunn.

Pierce (Brendan) Brosnan (16 May 1953, Navan, County Meath, Ireland), Irish actor known for portrayal of handsome, suave leading men, including Remington Steele and James Bond.

Dan Brown (22 Jun 1964, Exeter NH), American novelist and author of the number-one best-selling work of fiction *The Da Vinci Code*.

Gordon Brown (20 Feb 1951, Glasgow, Scotland), British politician and chancellor of the Exchequer from 1997.

James Brown (3 May 1933, Barnwell SC), American singer, songwriter, arranger, and dancer who was one of the most important and influential entertainers in 20th-century popular music.

Sir John Browne (Edmund John Phillip Browne; Lord Browne of Maddingly; 20 Feb 1948, Hamburg, West Germany [now in Germany]), British corporate executive; group CEO of British Petroleum/Amoco from 1998.

Dave Brubeck (David Warren Brubeck; 6 Dec 1920, Concord CA), American pianist-composer who brought elements of classical music into jazz.

Jerry Bruckheimer (21 Sep 1945, Detroit MI), American film and TV producer who scored big hits with three *CSI* (Crime Scene Investigation) TV series (from 2000), the series *Without a Trace* (2002), *Cold Case* (2003), and others, as well as films that included *Beverly Hills Cop* (1984), *Black Hawk Down* (2001), and the *Pirates of the Caribbean* series (from 2003).

Gro Harlem Brundtland (20 Apr 1939, Oslo, Norway), Norwegian politician and international official; prime minister, 1981, 1986–89, and 1990–96; and director-general of the World Health Organization, 1998–2003.

Charles Gyude Bryant (17 Jan 1949, Monrovia,

Liberia), Liberian businessman and president from 2003.

Kobe Bryant (23 Aug 1978, Philadelphia PA), American basketball player who won three straight NBA titles (2000–02) with the Los Angeles Lakers; he was a four-time NBA all star.

Bill Bryson (1951, Des Moines IA), American-born British journalist and travel writer whose 1995 *Notes from a Small Island* was voted in a 2003 poll in Great Britain as the book that best represents England.

Patrick J(oseph) Buchanan (2 Nov 1938, Washington DC), American conservative journalist who held positions in the administrations of three presidents and who three times sought nomination as a candidate for the presidency of the US.

Linda B. Buck (29 Jan 1947, Seattle WA), American immunologist who shared the 2004 Nobel Prize for Physiology or Medicine with Richard Axel for their work in olfactory receptors.

Jon Buckland (11 Sep 1977, London, England), British rock guitarist (of Coldplay).

Christopher (Taylor) Buckley (1952, New York NY), American political and satiric novelist and magazine editor; in 2004 he was the winner of the biennial Thurber Prize for American Humor for his novel *No Way To Treat a First Lady* (2002).

Warren (Edward) Buffett (30 Aug 1930, Omaha NE), American investor; CEO of Berkshire Hathaway Inc. since 1965 and chairman of the board of Salomon Brothers Inc. from 1991; in 2004 he was listed second on *Forbes* magazine's annual list of the richest persons in the world.

Sandra (Annette) Bullock (26 Jul 1964, Arlington VA), American film actress who achieved fame after her performance in *Speed* (1994) and became a top box office draw; later films included *Miss Congeniality* and its sequel (2000, 2005), *Murder by Numbers* (2002), and *Divine Secrets of the Ya-Ya Sisterhood* (2002).

Gisele Bündchen (Gisele Caroline Nonnenmacher Bündchen; 20 Jul 1980, Horizontina, Rio Grande do Sul state, Brazil), Brazilian fashion model.

Carol (Creighton) Burnett (26 Apr 1933, San Antonio TX), American comedian, actress, and musician; she starred in the popular variety series *The Carol Burnett Show* (1967–78); she received a Kennedy Center Honor in 2003.

Mark Burnett (17 Jul 1960, Myland, East London, England), English-born American TV producer who made his mark with reality TV shows, notably *Survivor* (2000) and its sequels.

Ken Burns (Kenneth Lauren Burns; 29 Jul 1953, Brooklyn NY), American documentary filmmaker who directed and cowrote the TV miniseries *The Civil War*, *Baseball*, and *Jazz*, among others.

Gary Burton (23 Jan 1943, Anderson IN), American jazz vibraphonist and composer.

Tim Burton (Timothy William Burton; 25 Aug 1958, Burbank CA), American director and writer known for offbeat, imaginative films such as *Edward Scissorhands* (1990), *Big Fish* (2003), and *Charlie and the Chocolate Factory* (2005).

Steve Buscemi (13 Dec 1957, Brooklyn NY), American film actor known for off-center characters, as in *Fargo* (1996) and *The Big Lebowski* (1998).

Barbara Bush (Barbara Pierce; 8 Jun 1925, Rye NY), American first lady; wife of Pres. George H.W. Bush (married 6 Jan 1945).

Barbara Bush (25 Nov 1981, Dallas TX), American personality; daughter of Pres. George W. Bush.

George Herbert Walker Bush (12 Jun 1924, Milton MA), American statesman, vice president, 1981–89, and 41st president, 1989–93; he is the father of Pres. George W. Bush (*see full biography at Presidents*).

George Walker Bush (6 Jul 1946, New Haven CT), American statesman and 43rd president from 2001; he is the son of Pres. George H.W. Bush (*see full biography at Presidents*).

Jeb Bush (John Ellis Bush; 11 Feb 1953, Midland TX), American Republican politician, governor of Florida from 1999, and brother of Pres. George W. Bush.

Jenna Bush (25 Nov 1981, Dallas TX), American personality; daughter of Pres. George W. Bush.

Laura Bush (Laura Lane Welch; 4 Nov 1946, Midland TX), American first lady; wife of Pres. George W. Bush (married 5 Nov 1977).

Eugene C. Butcher (6 Jun 1950, St. Louis MO), American immunologist and pathologist who specialized in the movement and transport of white blood cells in the circulatory system; he shared the 2004 Crafoord Prize with Timothy Springer.

Chief Mangosuthu Gatsha Buthelezi (27 Aug 1928, Mahlabatini, Natal [now KwaZulu Natal] province, South Africa), South African Zulu chief, the head (1972–94) of the nonindependent black South African state of KwaZulu and leader of the Inkatha Freedom Party.

Norbert Leo Butz (St. Louis MO), American actor who won a Tony Award in 2005 for leading actor in a musical for his performance in *Dirty Rotten Scoundrels*.

A.S. Byatt (Antonia Susan Drabble; 24 Aug 1936, Sheffield, England), English scholar, literary critic, and novelist known for her erudite works in which the characters are often academics or artists commenting on the intellectual process; she won the 1990 Booker Prize for *Possession*, and her *Little Black Book of Stories* was published to great acclaim in 2004.

James Caan (26 Mar 1939, New York NY), American actor best remembered as Sonny Corleone in the *Godfather* films (1972, 1974, and 1990) and also featured in the TV series *Las Vegas* (from 2003).

Nicolas Cage (Nicholas Kim Coppola; 7 Jan 1964, Long Beach CA), American film actor who garnered critical acclaim for his performance in *Leaving Las Vegas* (1995; best actor Academy Award).

Santiago Calatrava (28 Jul 1951, Valencia, Spain), Spanish architect noted for his soaring designs for bridges and public buildings, including several in Valencia, Seville, and Bilbao, Spain; the Milwaukee Art Museum in Wisconsin (2001); and the Tenerife Opera House in the Canary Islands (2002).

Sila María Calderón (23 Sep 1942, San Juan, Puerto Rico), Puerto Rican politician and governor of Puerto Rico from 2001.

Félix Pérez Camacho (30 Oct 1957, Camp Zama, Japan), American Republican politician and governor of Guam from 6 Jan 2003.

Camilla, duchess of Cornwall (Camilla Parker Bowles; Camilla Shand; 17 Jul 1947, London, England), English celebrity, the wife, from 9 Apr 2005, of Charles, prince of Wales.

Louis C. Camilleri (1955, Alexandria, Egypt), American corporate executive; president and CEO of Philip Morris Companies Inc. from 2002.

Naomi Campbell (22 May 1970, London, England), British runway and photographic model.

Jennifer Capriati (29 Mar 1976, New York NY), American tennis player; the youngest US player to turn professional (1989, at age 13), she won the Australian Open in 2001 and 2002 and the French Open in 2001.

Don Carcieri (16 Dec 1942, East Greenwich RI), American banker and Republican politician who was governor of Rhode Island from 7 Jan 2003.

Drew (Allison) Carey (23 May 1958, Cleveland OH), American comic TV actor known for his everyman portrayal in *The Drew Carey Show* (1995–2004) and improvisational skills in *Whose Line Is It Anyway?* (from 1998).

Mariah Carey (27 Mar 1970, Huntington, Long Island, NY), American pop singer whose "We Belong Together" topped the *Billboard* singles charts in the summer of 2005.

Peter (Philip) Carey (7 May 1943, Bacchus Marsh, VIC, Australia), Australian author who was the winner of the Booker Prize in 1988 (*Oscar and Lucinda*) and 2001 (*True History of the Kelly Gang*).

King Carl XVI Gustaf (Carl Gustaf Folke Hubertus; 30 Apr 1946, Stockholm, Sweden), Swedish royal and king from 1973.

Richard H. Carmona (22 Nov 1949, Harlem NY), American physician; surgeon general of the US from 2002.

Robert A. Caro (30 Oct 1935, New York NY), American biographer who won Pulitzer Prizes in 1975 and 2003, respectively, for *The Power Broker,* about New York City politician Robert Moses, and *Master of the Senate,* the third of a planned four-volume biography of Lyndon B. Johnson.

Princess Caroline (Caroline Louise Margaret Grimaldi; 23 Jan 1957, Monte Carlo, Monaco), Monegasque royal, the elder daughter of Prince Rainier III and Princess Grace.

José Carreras (Josep Carreras; 5 Dec 1946, Barcelona, Spain), Spanish Catalan operatic tenor, noted for his great all-around musicianship and his special mastery of Verdi roles.

Jim Carrey (James Eugene Carrey; 17 Jan 1962, Newmarket, ON, Canada), Canadian-born American comic actor originally known for his rubber-faced visual comedy; he graduated to more serious roles in *The Truman Show* (1998), *The Majestic* (2001), and *Eternal Sunshine of the Spotless Mind* (2004).

Edwin W. Carrington (1938, Tobago), Trinidadian international official who was the secretary-general of the Caribbean Community (CARICOM) from 1992.

Jimmy Carter (James Earl Carter, Jr.; 1 Oct 1924, Plains GA), American statesman and 39th president of the US, 1977–81; he was the winner of the Nobel Prize for Peace, 2002 (*see full biography at Presidents*).

Ron Carter (4 May 1937, Ferndale MI), American jazz bassist.

Rosalynn Carter (Eleanor Rosalynn Smith; 18 Aug 1927, Plains GA), American first lady (1977–81), the wife of Pres. Jimmy Carter, and mental health advocate.

David Caruso (7 Jan 1956, Forest Hills NY), American actor, mostly in TV, who starred on *NYPD Blue* (1993–94) and *CSI: Miami* (from 2002).

James Carville, Jr. (25 Oct 1944, Carville LA), American political strategist and commentator who guided Bill Clinton's presidential campaign in 1992; he is married to Mary Matalin, a conservative political strategist.

Steve Case (Stephen McDonnell Case; 21 Aug 1958, Honolulu HI), American corporate executive; founder (1991) and CEO of America Online and chairman of AOL Time Warner (2001–03).

Rosanne Cash (24 May 1955, Memphis TN), American country-and-western singer and songwriter, the daughter of Johnny Cash.

Darío Cardinal Castrillón Hoyos (4 Jul 1929, Medellín, Colombia), Colombian Roman Catholic churchman who served as archbishop of Bucaramanga, Colombia, from 1992 to 1996 and from 1998 as prefect of clergy in the Roman Curia; he was named cardinal in 1998.

Fidel Castro Ruz (13 Aug 1926, near Birán, Cuba), Cuban revolutionary and leader of Cuba from 1959, who became a symbol of communist revolution in Latin America.

Helio Castroneves (10 May 1975, São Paulo, Brazil), Brazilian race-car driver who won the Indy 500 in 2001 and 2002 and came in second in 2003.

Kim Cattrall (21 Aug 1956, Liverpool, England), British-born film actress of the 1980s who made a comeback in the 1990s as Samantha Jones on TV's *Sex and the City* (1998–2004).

Luigi Luca Cavalli-Sforza (25 Jan 1922, Genoa, Italy), Italian-American expert on human genetic diversity who, by collecting and analyzing DNA samples from around the world, was instrumental in reconstructing the origins and migration patterns of humans.

Jim Caviezel (James Patrick Caviezel; 26 Sep 1968, Mount Vernon WA), American film actor who starred as Jesus in the controversial 2004 hit *The Passion of the Christ.*

Riccardo Chailly (20 Feb 1953, Milan, Italy), Italian orchestra conductor; chief conductor of the Royal Concertgebouw Orchestra of Amsterdam (1989–2004), after which he became music director of the Leipzig (Germany) Opera.

Wendy J. Chamberlin (12 Oct 1948, Bethesda MD), American diplomat and international official; she was ambassador to Laos (1996–99) and later to Pakistan (2001–02) and was acting UN High Commissioner for Refugees from 24 Feb to 15 Jun 2005.

John T. Chambers (23 Aug 1949, Cleveland OH), American corporate executive; president and CEO of Cisco Systems, Inc., from 1997.

Pierre Chambon (7 Feb 1931, Mulhouse, France), French geneticist and molecular biologist who shared (with Ronald M. Evans and Elwood V. Jensen) the 2004 Lasker Award for Basic Medical Research for "the discovery of the superfamily of nuclear hormone receptors and elucidation of a unifying mechanism that regulates embryonic development and diverse metabolic pathways."

Will Champion (31 Jul 1978, Southampton, England), British rock drummer (of Coldplay).

Jackie Chan (Chan Kwong-Sang; 7 Apr 1954, Hong Kong), Chinese actor and director whose martial arts and acrobatic skills, combined with on-screen comedy, made him an international movie star; in April 2004 he was named a UNICEF goodwill ambassador.

Elaine Chao (26 Mar 1953, Taipei, Taiwan), American government official; US secretary of labor from 2001.

Manu Chao (Oscar Tramor; 26 Jun 1961, Paris, France), French-born Spanish international rock musician noted for his politics and his unstructured approach to the business side of music.

David Chappelle (24 Aug 1973, Washington DC), American film and TV comedian and actor who starred in TV's *Chappelle's Show* from 2003.

Jean Charest (John James Charest; 24 Jun 1958, Sherbrooke, QC, Canada), French Canadian politician and leader of the Quebec Liberal Party from 1998.

Prince Charles (Prince of Wales; 14 Nov 1948, Buckingham Palace, London, England), British royal, the eldest son of Queen Elizabeth II and Prince Philip, duke of Edinburgh, and heir apparent to the throne.

Hugo Chávez Frías (28 Jul 1954, Sabaneta, Venezuela), Venezuelan military leader, politician, and president of Venezuela from 1999 (with a one-day interruption in April 2002); internal turbulence in Venezuela preceded a referendum in August 2004 to force Chavez's resignation, but he won easily.

Don Cheadle (29 Nov 1964, Kansas City MO), American film and TV actor who was praised for his performances in *Devil in a Blue Dress* (1995) and *Hotel Rwanda* (2004).

Chen Kaige (12 Aug 1952, Peking [now Beijing], China), Chinese film director known in the West for his *Farewell My Concubine* (1993).

Chen Shui-bian (Ch'en Shui-pian; 18 Feb 1951, Hsichuang village, Tainan county, Taiwan), Taiwanese politician and president from 2000.

Dick Cheney (Richard Bruce Cheney; 30 Jan 1941, Lincoln NE), American politician, secretary of defense, 1989–93, and vice president from 2001.

Lynne V. Cheney (Lynne Ann Vincent; 14 Aug 1941, Casper WY), American political commentator; she is the wife of Vice Pres. Dick Cheney (married 1964).

Cher (Cherilyn Sarkasian LaPier; 20 May 1946, El Centro CA), American pop singer and film actress; she won an Academy Award for best actress (*Moonstruck* [1987]) and a Grammy in 2000 for her hit dance single "Believe."

Taïeb Chérif (29 Dec 1941, Kasr El Boukhari, Algeria), Algerian international official; secretary-general of the International Civil Aviation Organization (ICAO) from 2003.

Michael Chertoff (28 Nov 1953, Elizabeth NJ), American attorney, judge on the US Court of Appeals, and secretary of homeland security from 15 Feb 2005.

Kenny Chesney (26 Mar 1968, Luttrell TN), American country-and-western singer.

Judy Chicago (Judy Cohen; 20 Jul 1939, Chicago IL), American feminist artist; creator (with Miriam Schapiro) of the controversial installation *Womanhouse*, 1972; she is especially well known for her triangular multimedia installation *The Dinner Party* (1979) with "place settings" for historical women.

Dale Chihuly (20 Sep 1941, Tacoma WA), American glassblower and glass artist known for his vibrantly colored organic sculptures designed for large spaces.

Michael Chiklis (30 Aug 1963, Lowell MA), American TV actor; star of the award-winning TV series *The Shield* from 2002.

Jacques (René) Chirac (29 Nov 1932, Paris, France), French politician; prime minister of France, 1974–76 and 1986–88, and president from 1995.

Joaquim (Alberto) Chissanó (22 Oct 1939, Malehice, Portuguese Mozambique), Mozambican politician and president from 1986 to 2005.

Fujio Cho (1937, Tokyo, Japan), Japanese corporate executive; president of Toyota Motor Corp. from 1999.

(Avram) Noam Chomsky (7 Dec 1928, Philadelphia PA), American linguist, writer, educator, and political activist; one of the founders of transformational, or generative, grammar.

Deepak Chopra (22 Oct 1946, New Delhi, British India), Indian-born American endocrinologist, alternative-medicine advocate, and best-selling author.

Chow Yun-Fat (Zhou Runfa; 18 May 1955, Lamma Island, Hong Kong), Hong Kong actor wildly popular in Hong Kong; famous in the West for films such as *Crouching Tiger, Hidden Dragon* (2000).

Jean Chrétien (Joseph Jacques Jean Chrétien; 11 Jan 1934, Shawinigan, QC, Canada), Canadian lawyer, Liberal Party politician, and prime minister, 1993–2003.

Perry (Gladstone) Christie (21 Aug 1943, Nassau, The Bahamas), Bahamian politician and prime minister from 2002.

Christo (Khristo Yavachev; 13 Jun 1935, Gabrovo, Bulgaria), Bulgarian-born American conceptual artist and environmental sculptor; in February 2005 he and his partner/wife, Jeanne-Claude, made headlines with their installation of 7,500 orange "gates" in New York City's Central Park, touted as the largest artwork since the Sphinx.

Warren (Minor) Christopher (27 Oct 1925, Scranton ND), American lawyer, diplomat, and government official; he served as US secretary of state 1993–97.

Steven Chu (28 Feb 1948, St. Louis MO), American physicist; corecipient of the 1997 Nobel Prize for Physics for the development of techniques that use laser light to cool atoms to extremely low temperatures; he became head of the Lawrence Berkeley National Laboratory on 1 Aug 2004.

Chung Mong Joon (17 Oct 1951, Seoul, South Korea), Korean businessman and politician, CEO of the Hyundai Group from 1987, and cochairman of the Korean Organizing Committee for the 2002 FIFA World Cup.

Carlo Azeglio Ciampi (9 Dec 1920, Livorno, Italy), Italian politician, prime minister, 1993–94, and president from 1999.

Ralph J(ohn) Cicerone (2 May 1943, New Castle PA), American electrical engineer and atmospheric scientist specializing in ozone depletion and the effects of greenhouse gases on the Earth; he served as chancellor of the University of California, Irvine, 1998–2005 and as president of the National Academy of Sciences from July 2005.

Aaron Ciechanover (1 Oct 1947, Haifa, Israel), Israeli biochemist who was corecipient (with Avram Hershko and Irwin Rose) of the 2004 Nobel Prize in Chemistry for their discovery of an ingenious mechanism by which the cells of most living organisms cull unwanted proteins.

Sandra Cisneros (20 Dec 1954, Chicago IL), American short-story writer and poet best known for her evocation of Mexican American life in Chicago.

Tom Clancy (Thomas L. Clancy, Jr.; 12 Apr 1947, Baltimore MD), American best-selling writer on military-tinged current affairs topics; his novels include *The Hunt for Red October*, *Patriot Games*, *Clear and Present Danger*, *Rainbow Six*, and *Red Rabbit*.

Eric Clapton (Eric Patrick Clapp; 30 Mar 1945, Ripley, Surrey, England), British guitarist, singer, and songwriter.

Helen Clark (26 Feb 1950, Hamilton, New Zealand), New Zealand Labour politician and prime minister from 1999.

Mary Higgins Clark (24 Dec 1931, New York NY), American writer of best-selling books, including stories of suspense and historical novels.

Vern Clark (7 Sep 1944, Sioux City IA), American military official; chief of naval operations, US Navy, from 2000.

Victoria Clark (10 Oct 19??, Dallas TX), American

actress who won the 2005 Tony Award for leading actress in a musical for her work in *The Light in the Piazza*.

Wesley Clark (Wesley Kanne; 23 Dec 1944, Chicago IL), American general who served as Supreme Allied Commander of NATO (1997–2000) and Commander-in-Chief of the United States European Command; he was a Democratic candidate for president in 2003–04.

Adrienne Clarkson (10 Feb 1939, Hong Kong), Canadian journalist, publisher, and governor-general of Canada from 1999.

Kelly Clarkson (24 Apr 1982, Burleson TX), American celebrity; winner of Fox TV's *American Idol* competition in 2002.

John (Marwood) Cleese (27 Oct 1939, Weston-super-Mare, England), British comic actor best known for his TV work on *Monty Python's Flying Circus* and *Fawlty Towers*.

Van Cliburn (Harvey Lavan Cliburn, Jr.; 12 Jul 1934, Shreveport LA), American pianist who burst onto the scene in 1958 when he was the first American to win the Tchaikovsky competition in Moscow; he received a lifetime Grammy Award in February 2004.

Kim Clijsters (8 Jun 1983, Bilzen, Belgium), Belgian tennis player who was a finalist in the French Open in 2001 and 2003, and won the women's doubles in the French Open and at Wimbledon in 2003.

Bill Clinton (William Jefferson Blythe IV; 19 Aug 1946, Hope AR), American statesman and 42nd president of the US, 1993–2000 (*see full biography at Presidents*).

Hillary Rodham Clinton (Hillary Diane Rodham; 26 Oct 1947, Chicago IL), American politician; wife of Pres. Bill Clinton; Democratic senator from New York from 2001.

George Clooney (6 May 1961, Lexington KY), American film and TV actor who achieved widespread fame with his TV role on *ER*; his later movie successes included *The Perfect Storm* (2000), *O Brother, Where Art Thou?* (2002), *Ocean's Eleven* (2001), and *Ocean's Twelve* (2004).

Chuck (Thomas) Close (Charles Thomas Close; 5 Jul 1940, Monroe WA), American painter noted for his highly inventive techniques used to paint the human face; he is best known for his large-scale, Photo-realist portraits.

Glenn Close (19 Mar 1947, Greenwich CT), American actress perhaps best known for her motion pictures *The Big Chill* (1983) and *Fatal Attraction* (1987); she won a Tony Award in 1995 for *Sunset Boulevard* and joined the cast of TV's *The Shield* in 2005.

Richard J. Codey (27 Nov 1946, Orange NJ), American Democratic politician and acting governor of New Jersey from 16 Nov 2004.

Paulo Coelho (August 1947, Rio de Janeiro, Brazil), Brazilian author of best-selling novels, including *The Alchemist* (1988).

Ethan (21 Sep 1958, St. Louis Park MN) and **Joel Coen** (29 Nov 1955, St. Louis Park MN), American filmmakers known for off-center creations such as *Raising Arizona* (1987), *Fargo* (1996), *The Big Lebowski* (1998), *O Brother, Where Art Thou?* (2000), and *The Ladykillers* (2004).

J(ohn) M(axwell) Coetzee (9 Feb 1940, Cape Town, South Africa), South African novelist, critic, and translator noted for his novels about the effects of apartheid; he was the first writer to receive the Booker Prize twice (for *Life & Times of Michael K*, 1983, and *Disgrace*, 1999), and he won the 2003 Nobel Prize for Literature.

Leonard Cohen (21 Sep 1934, Montreal, QC, Canada), Canadian singer and songwriter.

Alina Cojocaru (27 May 1981, Bucharest, Romania), Romanian ballerina with the Royal Ballet, London, from 1999.

Natalie (Maria) Cole (Stephanie Natalie Maria Cole; 6 Feb 1950, Los Angeles CA), American pop singer.

Pierluigi Collina (13 Feb 1960, Bologna, Italy), Italian association football (soccer) referee who is one of the most powerful men in the sport.

Billy Collins (1941, New York NY), American poet who was 11th poet laureate of the US, 2001–03.

Marva Collins (Marva Delores Knight; 31 Aug 1936, Monroeville AL), American educator who broke with a public school system she found to be failing inner-city children and established her own rigorous system and practice to cultivate her students' independence and accomplishment; she was awarded a National Humanities Medal in 2004.

Alan Colmes (24 Sep 1950, Long Island NY), American liberal radio and TV journalist and commentator, cohost (with conservative Sean Hannity) of Fox News Channel's political talk show *Hannity and Colmes*; his book *Red, White & Liberal: How Left Is Right and Right Is Wrong* came out in 2003.

Rita Rossi Colwell (23 Nov 1934, Beverly MA), American marine microbiologist and epidemiologist; director of the National Science Foundation, 1998–2004.

Sean Combs (Puffy; Puff Daddy; P. Diddy; 4 Nov 1970, Harlem, New York, NY), American rap artist, impresario, fashion plate, and TV actor.

Blaise Compaoré (1951, Ziniare, Upper Volta [now Burkina Faso]), Burkinabe politician and president of Burkina Faso from 1987.

Philip M. Condit (2 Aug 1941, Berkeley CA), American aerospace engineer and corporate executive; chairman and CEO of the Boeing Co. from 1996.

Bill Condon (22 Oct 1955, New York NY), American screenwriter and film director whose work includes *Gods and Monsters* (1998; best adapted screenplay Academy Award—he also directed) and *Kinsey* (2004; Directors Guild of Great Britain international award).

Jennifer Connelly (12 Dec 1970, Catskill Mountains NY), American fashion model and film actress; she won an Academy Award for best supporting actress in *A Beautiful Mind* (2001).

Sir Sean Connery (Thomas Connery; 25 Aug 1930, Edinburgh, Scotland), Scottish film actor of enduring attraction who is known for portrayals of rugged leading men, including James Bond; he won a best supporting actor Academy Award for *The Untouchables* (1987); he is also active in Scottish nationalist politics.

Lansana Conté (1934, Moussayah Loumbaya, French West Africa [now in Guinea]), Guinean military leader and president from 1984.

Ry Cooder (Ryland Peter Cooder; 15 Mar 1947, Los Angeles CA), American musician and musicologist whose wide-ranging musical curiosity has led to the popularity of many overlooked idioms, most recently traditional Cuban son music through his Buena Vista Social Club project.

Matthew Coon Come (1956, Mistissini, QC, Canada), Canadian Cree grand chief of the James Bay Cree, from 1987, and first-nations and environmental activist; in 1994 he was awarded the Goldman environmental prize and in 2000 was elected national chief of the Assembly of First Nations.

Cynthia Cooper (14 Apr 1963, Chicago IL), American

collegiate, Olympic, and professional basketball player and coach.

Stephen F. Cooper (23 Oct 1946, Gary IN), American corporate executive and turnaround specialist; he was CEO of Enron from 2002.

Francis Ford Coppola (7 Apr 1939, Detroit MI), American film director, writer, and producer whose films ranged from sweeping epics to small-scale character studies; best known for the *Godfather* trilogy (1972, 1974, and 1990) and *Apocalypse Now* (1979); he won a best director Academy Award for *The Godfather Part II* (1974).

Sofia Coppola (14 May 1971, New York NY), American film actress, designer, writer, and director whose original screenplay for *Lost in Translation* (2003), which she also directed, won the Academy Award.

Chick Corea (Armando Anthony Corea; 12 Jun 1941, Chelsea MA), American classically trained jazz pianist, composer, and bandleader whose piano style and tunes were extensively imitated during the 1970s and '80s.

John Corigliano (16 Feb 1938, New York NY), American composer of lyrical, tonal, expressive works in orchestral music, opera, chamber music, and film scores; he won the 1991 Grawemeyer Award for Music for *Symphony No. 1.*

Patricia Cornwell (Patricia Daniels; 9 Jun 1956, Miami FL), American author of mystery novels notably featuring medical examiner Kay Scarpetta.

Karen Corr (10 Nov 1969, Ballymoney, Northern Ireland), Northern Ireland–born billiards player; WPBA national champion in 2002 and number-two ranked player (after Allison Fisher) in mid-2005.

Bill Cosby (William Henry Cosby, Jr.; 12 Jul 1937, Philadelphia PA), American comedian and actor beloved for the groundbreaking TV series *The Cosby Show* (1984–92).

Bob Costas (Robert Quinlan Costas; 22 Mar 1952, New York NY), American TV sportscaster and host.

Kevin (Michael) Costner (18 Jan 1955, Lynwood CA), American film actor and director whose movies range from comic to serious; his most critically acclaimed work was *Dances with Wolves* (1990), which he starred in and directed (Academy Award).

Ann (Hart) Coulter (8 Dec 1961, New Canaan CT), American attorney, syndicated political columnist, and right-wing author of best-selling books, which have included *High Crimes and Misdemeanors: The Case Against Bill Clinton* (1998); *Slander: Liberal Lies About the American Right* (2002); and *Treason: Liberal Treachery from the Cold War to the War on Terrorism* (2003).

David Coulthard (27 Mar 1971, Twynholm, Scotland), Scottish Formula 1 race-car driver; winner of the Monte Carlo Grand Prix, 2002.

Katie Couric (7 Jan 1957, Arlington VA), American TV talk-show host (*Today*, from 1991) who received UNICEF's 2003 Danny Kaye Humanitarian Award.

Larry E(dwin) Craig (20 Jul 1945, Council ID), American Republican politician and senator from Idaho from 1991.

(John) Michael Crichton (23 Oct 1942, Chicago IL), American best-selling writer and director who specializes in novels on scientific themes such as *The Andromeda Strain* (1969), *Jurassic Park* (1990), and *Disclosure* (1993).

Walter (Leland) Cronkite, Jr. (4 Nov 1916, St. Joseph MO), American TV journalist, commentator, and TV news anchor, one of the most influential and authoritative broadcast journalists of his generation.

Stanley Crouch (14 Dec 1945, Los Angeles CA), American journalist and critic noted for his range of interests and for his outspoken essays on African American arts, politics, and culture.

Sheryl Crow (11 Feb 1962, Kennett MO), American pop singer-songwriter, whose 1993 album *Tuesday Night Music Club* won three Grammy Awards (she has won four more Grammys since).

Russell (Ira) Crowe (7 Apr 1964, Wellington, New Zealand), New Zealand–Australian film actor who won a best actor Academy Award for *Gladiator* (2000).

Tom Cruise (Thomas Cruise Mapother IV; 3 Jul 1962, Syracuse NY), American actor, one of the highest-paid film stars of the late 1990s and early 2000s; his breakthrough performance occurred in *Risky Business* (1983), and he followed with *Top Gun* (1986), *Born on the Fourth of July* (1989), two *Mission Impossible* films (1996 and 2000), and *War of the Worlds* (2005).

Gastão Cruz (20 Jul 1941, Faro, Portugal), Portuguese poet and literary critic; he was the winner of the Great Prize in Poetry of the Association of Portuguese Writers in 2004.

Nilo Cruz (1962?, Matanzas, Cuba), Cuban-born American playwright who won the 2003 Pulitzer Prize for Drama for *Anna in the Tropics*.

Penélope Cruz (Sánchez) (28 Apr 1974, Madrid, Spain), Spanish film actress whose first international success came in Pedro Almodóvar's *Todo sobre mi madre* (*All About My Mother*; 1999) and has since distinguished herself in *All the Pretty Horses* (2000), *Blow* (2001), and *Vanilla Sky* (2002).

Branko Crvenkovski (12 Oct 1962, Sarajevo, Yugoslavia [now in Bosnia and Herzegovina]), Macedonian politician and prime minister, 1992–98, and again from 2002 to 12 May 2004, when he took over as president following the death of Pres. Boris Trajkovski in February.

Billy Crystal (14 Mar 1947, Long Beach NY), American comedic actor popular for light dramatic comedies; his recent films include *Monsters, Inc.* (2001, voice), *Analyze This* (1999), and *Analyze That* (2002).

Mihaly Csikszentmihalyi (1934, Fiume, Italy), American psychologist and sociologist who specializes in studies of creativity, especially in art, and social behavior and socialization; a researcher with very wide interests, he has developed his theory of "flow," the intense concentration that accompanies creation, and studies some of the world's most creative minds.

Merce Cunningham (16 Apr 1919, Centralia WA), American modern dancer and choreographer who developed new forms of abstract dance movement; he was awarded the NEA's National Medal of Arts in 1990 and the Edward MacDowell Medal for outstanding contributions to the arts in 2003.

Ben Curtis (26 May 1977, Ostrander OH), American golfer who amazed the public when, as a rookie, he won the 2003 British Open.

Joan Cusack (11 Oct 1962, New York NY), American film actress best known for a stint on TV's *Saturday Night Live* (1985–86) and humorous supporting roles in movies.

Willem Dafoe (William Dafoe, Jr.; 22 Jul 1955, Appleton WI), American actor known for his complex, passionate portrayals; his films include *Platoon* (1986), *The Last Temptation of Christ* (1988), *The English Patient* (1996), and two *Spider-Man* movies (2002 and 2004).

Robert Alan Dahl (1915, Inwood IA), American professor of political science for many years at Yale University and specialist in the American political process; his *Who Governs?* (1961), a study of politics in New Haven CT, is considered a classic, as is his most recent work, *How Democratic Is the American Constitution?* (2001); Dahl was also president of the American Political Science Association.

Dalai Lama (the 14th Dalai Lama, Tenzin Gyatso, birth name Lhamo Dhondrub; 6 Jul 1935, Takster, Amdo province, Tibet [now Tsinghai province, China]), Tibetan spiritual leader (enthroned in 1940) and ruler-in-exile who is the head of the Tibetan Buddhists, who recognize him as a manifestation of the Bodhisattva of Compassion and the reincarnation of the previous Dalai Lama; he has led the Tibetan government-in-exile from India since 1959, and he won the 1989 Nobel Peace Prize.

Richard M. Daley (24 Apr 1942, Chicago IL), American Democratic politician; mayor of Chicago from 1989.

Roméo A. Dallaire (25 Jun 1946, Denekamp, The Netherlands), Canadian military officer, humanitarian, and author; he commanded the UN forces in Rwanda during the civil war and genocide (1993-94) and is considered a national hero for his management of an impossible position between a UN Security Council that sought to reduce UN presence and the worst of the killings among Hutu and Tutsi; in 2005 he was made a senator.

G(ary) Brent Dalrymple (9 May 1937, Alhambra CA), American geochemist with the US Geological Survey (1963-94) and Oregon State University (1994-2001) and president of the American Geophysical Union (1990-92); a specialist in geochronology, he won a 2003 National Medal of Science.

Matt Damon (Matthew Paige Damon; 8 Oct 1970, Cambridge MA), American film actor and writer whose breakthrough acting performance in *Good Will Hunting* (1997) led to roles in *Saving Private Ryan* (1998), *The Talented Mr. Ripley* (1999), and *Ocean's Eleven* (2001) and *The Bourne Identity* (2002)—both with sequels in 2004.

John (Claggett) Danforth (5 Sep 1936, St. Louis MO), American government official who served 18 years as senator from Missouri (1976-95); he was briefly (1 Jul 2004-20 Jan 2005) US ambassador to the United Nations.

Mitchell E. Daniels, Jr. (7 Apr 1949, Monongahela PA), American businessman and politician; he was director of the US Office of Management and Budget (2001-03) and Republican governor of Indiana from 10 Jan 2005.

Ted Danson (Edward Bridge Danson III; 29 Dec 1947, San Diego CA), American film and TV actor best known for playing Sam "Mayday" Malone on the TV series *Cheers* (1982-93) and Dr. John Becker on *Becker* (1998-2004).

Edwidge Danticat (19 Jan 1969, Port-au-Prince, Haiti), Haitian-born American author whose works focus on the lives of women and their relationships and address issues of power, injustice, and poverty; her collection of short fiction *The Dew Breaker* won the inaugural Story Prize in 2005.

Mahmoud Darwish (13 Mar 1942, Birwa, Palestine), Palestinian nationalist poet, probably the most acclaimed poet of the Arab world; his *Halat hisar* (2002; "A State of Seige") dealt with the ordeal of the people of the city of Ram Allah.

Thomas Andrew Daschle (9 Dec 1947, Aberdeen SD), American Democratic politician and senator from South Dakota; he was Senate minority leader (1995-2001, 2003-05) and majority leader (2001-03) but was not reelected in 2004.

Lindsay Davenport (8 Jun 1976, Palos Verdes CA), American tennis player who was the top woman player in the world in July 2005; she won an Olympic gold medal (1996), the US Open (1998), Wimbledon (1999), and the Australian Open (2000).

Larry David (2 Jul 1947, Brooklyn NY), American writer for some of the leading comedy shows in TV, including *Saturday Night Live* (1984-85) and *Seinfeld* (1990-98), which he cocreated; his program on cable, *Curb Your Enthusiasm* (from 2000), polarized audiences for its cinema verité approach and strong language and situations.

Mario Davidovsky (4 Mar 1934, Médanos, Buenos Aires, Argentina), Argentine-born American composer best known for his electronic and electroacoustic works, especially his 10 *Synchronisms* for instruments or voices and tape (1962-92).

Patrick Day (13 Oct 1953, Brush CO), American jockey, the all-time top North American money winner with more than 8,000 career victories.

Carl R. de Boor (3 Dec 1937, Stolp, Germany), German-born American mathematician and computer scientist who specializes in numerical analysis, especially spline functions, which has applications in aircraft and automotive design; he was awarded a 2003 National Medal of Science.

Inge De Bruijn (24 Aug 1973, Barendrecht, The Netherlands), Dutch swimmer who set numerous world records after returning from a hiatus in the mid-1990s and won three Olympic golds (and set three world records) and one silver in 2000.

Jaap de Hoop Scheffer (Jakob Gijsbert de Hoop Scheffer; 3 Apr 1948, Amsterdam, The Netherlands), Dutch international official who served as chairman-in-office of the Organization for Security and Cooperation in Europe from 2003 and secretary-general of NATO from 2004.

Robert De Niro (17 Aug 1943, New York NY), American film actor famous for his uncompromising portrayals of violent and abrasive characters, particularly in gangster films like the *Godfather* trilogy (1972, 1974, 1990), *The Untouchables* (1987), and *GoodFellas* (1990); he won a best actor Academy Award for *Raging Bull* (1979), a best supporting actor Oscar for *The Godfather Part II*, and the 2003 Lifetime Achievement Award of the American Film Institute.

Dominique (Galouzeau) de Villepin (14 Nov 1953, Rabat, Morocco), French diplomat and close political associate of French Pres. Jacques Chirac; he was named foreign minister in 2002 and soon distinguished himself by holding the political line against the US, especially on the question of Iraq, in the UN and other international venues; he was named prime minister on 31 May 2005.

Idriss Déby (1952, Fada, Chad, French Equatorial Africa [now in Chad]), Chadian politician and president from 1990.

Ruby Dee (Ruby Ann Wallace; 27 Oct 1924, Cleveland OH), American film and TV actress who was awarded the NEA's National Medal of Arts in 1995 and a Kennedy Center Honor in 2004.

Ellen DeGeneres (26 Jan 1958, Metairie LA), American comedian and TV personality best known for her TV series *Ellen* (1994-98) and her syndicated talk show, *The Ellen DeGeneres Show* (from 2003; Daytime Emmy Award, 2005).

Joseph Deiss (18 Jan 1946, Fribourg, Switzerland), Swiss president in 2004.

Carla Del Ponte (9 Feb 1947, Lugano, Switzerland), Swiss jurist who has served as prosecutor for the International Criminal Tribunal for the former Yugoslavia (ICTY) from 1999 and the International Criminal Tribunal for Rwanda (ICTR), 1999–2003.

Benicio Del Toro (19 Feb 1967, San Turce, Puerto Rico), American film actor who won a best supporting actor Academy Award for *Traffic* (2000).

Bertrand Delanoë (30 May 1950, Tunis, Tunisia), French politician and mayor of París from 2001.

Michael S. Dell (23 Feb 1965, Houston TX), American businessman; founder and CEO of Dell Computer Corp. from 1984; in the summer of 2003 he was believed to have been the highest-paid US executive; he is also a noted philanthropist.

Yelena Dementyeva (also spelled Elena Dementieva; 15 Oct 1981, Moscow, USSR [now in Russia]), Russian tennis player who was ranked number five in the world in July 2005.

Patrick Dempsey (13 Jan 1966, Lewiston ME), American film and TV actor, who starred in TV's *Grey's Anatomy* from 2005.

Dame Judi Dench (Judith Olivia Dench; 9 Dec 1934, York, England), British actress known for her powerful stage, TV, and screen roles; she won a best supporting actress Academy Award for *Shakespeare in Love* (1998) and starred in *Ladies in Lavender* (2004).

Rauf Denktash (Turkish spelling Denktas; 24 Jan 1924, Baf [Paphos], Cyprus), Turkish Cypriot politician; president of the Turkish Republic of Northern Cyprus, 1975–2005.

Robert H. Dennard (5 Sep 1932, Terrell TX), American electrical engineer and inventor of dynamic random access memory (DRAM), a computer memory system.

Brian Dennehy (9 Jul 1938, Bridgeport CT), American TV, film, and stage actor known for serious dramatic roles; he won the 2003 Tony Award for best actor in a play for his role in *Long Day's Journey into Night*.

Carl Dennis (17 Sep 1939, St. Louis MO), American poet who won the 2000 Ruth Lilly Poetry Prize and the 2002 Pulitzer Prize for Poetry for *Practical Gods*.

Gérard Depardieu (27 Dec 1948, Châteauroux, France), French film actor of international renown who is able to project both sensitivity and great physicality on screen; his films include *The Return of Martin Guerre* (1982), *Jean de Florette* (1986), and *Cyrano de Bergerac* (1990).

Johnny Depp (John Christopher Depp II; 9 Jun 1963, Owensboro KY), American film and TV actor known for eccentric, brooding roles; he starred in *Edward Scissorhands* (1990), *What's Eating Gilbert Grape* (1993), and *Chocolat* (2000) and received Academy Award nominations for *Pirates of the Caribbean: The Curse of the Black Pearl* (2003) and *Finding Neverland* (2004); in November 2003 he was named *People* magazine's "sexiest man alive."

Luis Ernesto Derbez (1 Apr 1947, Mexico City, Mexico), Mexican foreign minister from 2003.

Thierry Desmarest (1945), French corporate executive who was CEO of TotalFinaElf SA from 1995.

Frankie Dettori (Lanfranco Dettori; 15 Dec 1970, Milan, Italy), Italian-born English jockey; winner of more than 2,000 flat races in England and Europe since the mid-1980s.

Danny DeVito (Daniel Michaeli; 17 Nov 1944, Neptune NJ), American actor, director, and producer specializing in supporting comic roles.

Cameron M. Diaz (30 Aug 1972, San Diego CA), American model and actress whose roles have included the hit comedy *There's Something about Mary* (1998), *Being John Malkovich* (1999), *Gangs of New York* (2002), and two *Charlie's Angels* films (2000 and 2003).

Kate DiCamillo (25 Mar 1965, Philadelphia PA), American author of children's books and winner of the 2004 Newbery Medal for *The Tale of Despereaux* (2003).

Leonardo (Wilhelm) DiCaprio (11 Nov 1974, Los Angeles CA), American actor and heartthrob who achieved box-office success with *Titanic* (1997) and critical success with *The Aviator* (2004).

Dido (Florian Cloude de Bourneville Armstrong; 25 Dec 1971, Islington, London, England), British pop singer.

Vin Diesel (Mark Vincent; 18 Jul 1967, New York NY), American film actor who appeared in a self-made film, *Multi-Facial* (1994), which was well received at the Cannes Film Festival, and in *Saving Private Ryan* (1998); *The Fast and the Furious* (2001) was his first big hit, and in 2003 Diesel starred in *A Man Apart*.

Barry Diller (2 Feb 1942, San Francisco CA), American corporate executive; CEO of USA Interactive and Vivendi Universal Entertainment to 2003.

Matt Dillon (18 Feb 1964, New Rochelle NY), American film actor first known as a teen heartthrob; he often plays alienated, dark characters; he starred in *There's Something about Mary* (1998) and *City of Ghosts* (2002), among others.

Fatou Diome (1968, Niodior island, Senegal), Senegalese novelist who writes in French; her first novel, *Le Ventre de l'Atlantique* (2003), won literary prizes and was a best seller in France.

Céline Dion (30 Mar 1968, Charlemagne, QC, Canada), French Canadian pop singer; she received the Diamond Award at the World Music Awards in 2004 as the top-selling female vocalist of all time.

El Hadj Diouf (15 Jan 1981, Dakar, Senegal), Senegalese association football (soccer) star for French clubs and the Senegalese national team who in 2003 was named African Football Confederation (CAF) Player of the Year for the second straight season.

Waris Dirie (1967?, Somalia), Somali supermodel and women's rights activist.

Milo Djukanovic (15 Feb 1962, Niksic, Montenegro, Yugoslavia [now in Serbia and Montenegro]), Montenegrin politician, president of the Yugoslav Republic of Montenegro, 1998–2002, and prime minister of Montenegro, as part of Serbia and Montenegro, from 2003.

Domenico Dolce (13 Aug 1958, Polizzi Generosa, near Palermo, Italy), Italian fashion designer, along with partner Stefano Gabbana, whose designs are inspired by the Mediterranean region.

Plácido Domingo (21 Jan 1941, Madrid, Spain), Spanish-born Mexican operatic tenor, one of the most popular tenors of the second half of the 20th century.

Mary Donaldson (5 Feb 1972, Hobart, TAS, Australia), Australian-born marketing executive who wed Crown Prince Frederik of Denmark on 14 May 2004.

Sam Donaldson (Samuel Andrew Donaldson; 11 Mar 1934, El Paso TX), American TV newsman, one of the leading domestic political correspondents for the ABC network and cohost (with Diane Sawyer) of the weekly news analysis program *PrimeTime Live* from its inception in 1989.

William Henry Donaldson (1931, Buffalo NY), American banker and corporate executive who was chairman of the New York Stock Exchange (1990–95) and chairman of the Security and Exchanges Commission from 2003.

Wendy Doniger (married name O'Flaherty; 20 Nov 1940, New York NY), American scholar and leading authority in international religious studies, especially Eastern religions, myth, and gender issues; she is Mircea Eliade Distinguished Service Professor of the History of Religions, University of Chicago.

Vincent D'Onofrio (30 Jul 1959, Brooklyn NY), American TV actor starring in *Law & Order: Criminal Intent* from 2001.

Mathias Döpfner (15 Jan 1963, Bonn, Germany), German publishing executive who has been chairman and CEO of Axel Springer AG from 2002.

David W. Dorman (c. 1955), American corporate executive who was chairman and CEO of AT&T Corp. from 2002.

José Eduardo dos Santos (28 Aug 1942, Luanda, Angola), Angolan statesman and president from 1979.

James H. Douglas (21 Jun 1951, Springfield MA), American Republican politician who was governor of Vermont from 2003.

Michael Douglas (25 Sep 1944, New Brunswick NJ), American film actor and producer who is best known for his intense portrayals of flawed heroes; he won a best actor Academy Award for *Wall Street* (1987).

Philippe Douste-Blazy (1 Jan 1953, Lourdes, France), French medical doctor and government minister; he was minister of culture (1995–97) in the government of Alain Juppé, minister of health and social protection (2004), minister of solidarity, health, and the family (2004–05), and, from 2 Jun 2005, minister of foreign affairs.

Rita (Frances) Dove (28 Aug 1952, Akron OH), American writer and teacher who won the 1977 Pulitzer Prize for Poetry for *Thomas and Beulah* and served as poet laureate of the US, 1993–95.

Deidre Downs (7 Jul 1980, Birmingham AL), American beauty queen who was Miss Alabama 2004 and Miss America 2005.

Jim Doyle (23 Nov 1945, Washington DC), American attorney and Democratic politician who was governor of Wisconsin from 2003.

Kimberly Dozier (6 Jul 1966, Honolulu HI), American TV journalist and foreign correspondent.

Dr. Dre (Andre Young; 18 Feb 1965, Los Angeles CA), American rap musician and impresario, considered the pioneer of gangsta rap.

Stacy Dragila (25 Mar 1971, Auburn CA), American pole vaulter who won the gold medal in the first-ever Olympic women's pole vault, 2000.

E. Linn Draper, Jr., American energy engineer and corporate executive; he was chairman, president, and CEO of American Electric Power, Inc., from 1992.

Deborah Drattell (1956, Brooklyn NY), American composer of operas; her *Nicholas and Alexandra*, commissioned by the Los Angeles Opera for its 2003–04 season, was well received.

Dré (Andre Benjamin; Andre 3000; 27 May 1975, Atlanta GA), American hip-hop artist and a member of the duo OutKast.

Paquito D'Rivera (Francisco Dejesus Rivera; 4 Jun 1948, Havana, Cuba), Cuban-born American jazz reed player and Afro-Cuban bandleader.

Janez Drnovsek (17 May 1950, Celje, Yugoslavia [now Slovenia]), Slovene politician, prime minister, 1992–2000 and 2000–02, and president from 2002.

Matt Drudge (27 Oct 1967, Maryland), American Internet journalist, editor of the *Drudge Report.*

Andres Duany (7 Sep 1949, New York NY), American urban planner and a leading exponent of New Urbanism who collaborates with his wife, Elizabeth Plater-Zyberk.

Nicanor Duarte Frutos (11 Oct 1956, Coronel Oviedo, Paraguay), Paraguayan politician and president from 2003.

David Duchovny (David William Ducovny; 7 Aug 1960, New York NY), American TV and film actor, best known as Fox Mulder on *The X-Files* (1993–2001 and 2002).

Hilary Duff (28 Sep 1987, Houston TX), American TV and film actress, the star of *Lizzie McGuire* (2001–04) on TV's Disney Channel and *The Lizzie McGuire Movie* (2003).

Eduardo Duhalde (5 Oct 1941, Lomas de Zamora, Argentina), Argentine politician and president, 2002–03.

Avery Robert Cardinal Dulles (24 Aug 1918, Auburn NY), American Roman Catholic Jesuit theologian; he was named cardinal in 2001.

(Dorothy) Faye Dunaway (14 Jan 1941, Bascom FL), American actress known for her tense, absorbing performances; she enjoyed early success on stage and then gained international stardom for her work in films; she won a best actress Academy Award for her performance in *Network* (1976).

Iain Duncan Smith (9 Apr 1954, Edinburgh, Scotland), British politician and leader of the Conservative Party from 2001.

Ronnie Gene Dunn (1 Jun 1953, Coleman TX), American country-and-western singer, a member of the popular vocal duo Brooks & Dunn.

Kirsten Dunst (30 Apr 1982, Point Pleasant NJ), American actress who has appeared in a string of successful films, notably two *Spider-Man* movies (2002 and 2004).

José Manuel Durão Barroso (23 Mar 1956, Lisbon, Portugal), Portuguese politician and prime minister (6 Apr 2002–17 Jul 2004); he was president of the European Commission from 2004.

Henri Dutilleux (22 Jan 1916, Angers, France), French composer who in 2005 added the Ernst von Siemens Music Prize to multiple other awards for his work.

Robert Duvall (5 Jan 1931, San Diego CA), American actor, producer, and screenwriter noted for portrayals of average working people; he won a best actor Academy Award for *Tender Mercies* (1983).

Bob Dylan (Robert Allen Zimmerman; 24 May 1941, Duluth MN), American singer and songwriter who moved from folk to rock music in the 1960s, infusing the lyrics of rock and roll—which had previously been concerned mostly with boy-girl romantic innuendo—with the intellectualism of classic literature and poetry.

Esther Dyson (14 Jul 1951, Zürich, Switzerland), American economist and journalist specializing in computer and cyberspace issues.

Freeman (John) Dyson (15 Dec 1923, Crowthorne, Berkshire, England), British-born American physicist and educator best known for his speculative work on extraterrestrial civilizations; he was the 2000 Templeton Prize winner.

Mikulas Dzurinda (4 Feb 1955, Spissky Stvrtok, Czechoslovakia [now in Slovakia]), Slovak politician and prime minister from 1998.

(Ralph) Dale Earnhardt, Jr. (10 Oct 1974, Concord NC), American NASCAR race car driver (the son of Dale Earnhardt, Sr.) who the Daytona 500 race in 2004.

Michael F. Easley (23 Mar 1950, Nash county NC), American Democratic politician who was governor of North Carolina from 2001.

Clint Eastwood (Clinton Eastwood, Jr.; 31 May 1930, San Francisco CA), American film actor and moviemaker, originally famous for tough guy roles such as *Dirty Harry*; he won Academy Awards for directing for *Unforgiven* (1991) and *Million Dollar Baby* (2004).

Shirin Ebadi (1947, Hamadan, Iran), Iranian lawyer, writer, and teacher who gained prominence as an advocate for democracy and human rights; she was known particularly for her efforts to establish and protect the rights of women and children in the face of a hostile Iranian government; for her work she was awarded the 2003 Nobel Prize for Peace.

Atef Mohamed Ebeid (14 Apr 1932, Gharbiya, Egypt), Egyptian politician and prime minister from 1999.

Roger Ebert (18 Jun 1942, Urbana IL), American film critic who is one of America's leading tastemakers through his newspaper columns and TV programs; he is best known for his work on TV with fellow critics Gene Siskel (until Siskel's death in 1999) and Richard Roeper.

Rolf Eckrodt (25 Jun 1942, Gronau, Germany), German business executive; CEO of Mitsubishi Motors Corp. from 2001 until his resignation on 26 Apr 2004.

Umberto Eco (5 Jan 1932, Alessandria, Italy), Italian literary critic, novelist, and semiotician.

Marian Wright Edelman (6 Jun 1939, Bennettsville SC), American attorney and civil rights advocate who founded the Children's Defense Fund.

Prince Edward (Edward Anthony Richard Louis; 10 Mar 1964, Buckingham Palace, London, England), British royal, third son of Queen Elizabeth II and Prince Philip, Duke of Edinburgh, and Earl of Wessex.

John Edwards (10 Jun 1953, Seneca SC), American Democratic politician, senator from North Carolina from 1999 to 3 Jan 2005, and candidate for vice president in the 2004 elections.

Edward Michael Cardinal Egan (2 Apr 1932, Oak Park IL), American Roman Catholic church leader who was archbishop of New York from 2000 and made cardinal in 2001.

Robert L. Ehrlich, Jr. (25 Nov 1957, Arbutus MD), American Republican politician and governor of Maryland from 2003.

Luigi R. Einaudi (1 Mar 1936, Cambridge MA), American diplomat and international official; he served as acting secretary-general of the Organization of American States from 16 Oct 2004 to 26 May 2005.

Michael D(ammann) Eisner (7 Mar 1942, Mount Kisco NY), American corporate executive who was CEO and chairman of the Walt Disney Co. from 1984 to 2004; he was expected to remain as CEO until fall 2005.

Hicham El Guerrouj (14 Sep 1974, Berkane, Morocco), Moroccan runner who holds world records in the 1,500-m, 2,000-m, and 1-mile races.

Mohamed ElBaradei (Muhammad al-Baradei; 17 Jun 1942, Cairo, Egypt), Egyptian international official who was director-general of the International Atomic Energy Agency from 1997.

Carmen Electra (Tara Leigh Patrick; 20 Apr 1972, Sharonville OH), American model, TV and film actress, and prominent celebrity.

Danny Elfman (29 May 1943, Los Angeles CA), American pop musician (of Oingo Boingo) and composer of scores for films and TV, known especially for his collaborations with director Tim Burton.

Olafur Eliasson (1967, Copenhagen, Denmark), Danish artist whose installation, *The Weather Project*, was a blockbuster for the Tate Modern gallery in London in 2003–04.

Queen Elizabeth II (21 Apr 1926, London, England), British royal; queen of the United Kingdom of Great Britain and Northern Ireland from 1952.

Missy Elliott (Melissa Elliott; 1 Jul 1971, Portsmouth VA), American rapper, singer, and songwriter.

George F.R. Ellis (George Francis Rayner Ellis; 11 Aug 1939, Johannesburg, South Africa), South African applied mathematician and professor of the University of Cape Town who was awarded the 2004 Templeton Prize for Progress Toward Research or Discoveries About Spiritual Realities for his work in synthesizing cosmology, social sciences, and theology into a coherent whole.

Lawrence J. Ellison (17 Aug 1944, Chicago IL), American corporate executive; founder and CEO of Oracle Corp. from 1977.

James Ellroy (Lee Earle Ellroy; 4 Mar 1948, Los Angeles CA), American mystery writer.

Ernie Els (Theodore Ernest Els; 17 Oct 1969, Johannesburg, South Africa), South African golfer who won the US Open (1994 and 1997), the British Open (2002), and numerous other tournaments.

Eminem (Marshall Bruce Mathers III; 17 Oct 1973, St. Joseph MO), American entertainer, hip-hop artist.

Emmanuel III Delly (Emmanuel-Karim Delly; 6 Oct 1927, Telkaif, Iraq), Iraqi churchman, patriarch of Babylonia and the Chaldeans (leader of the Chaldean Catholic Church) from 2003.

Indulis Emsis (2 Jan 1952, Salacas, Latvian SSR, USSR [now in Latvia]), Latvian politician of the Union of Greens and Farmers party; he was sworn in as prime minister on 9 Mar 2004.

Robert F(ry) Engle (November 1942, Syracuse NY), American mathematical economist who shared (with Clive W.J. Granger) the 2003 Nobel Memorial Prize in Economic Sciences for the improved mathematical techniques he developed for the evaluation and more accurate forecasting of risk, which had particular relevance in financial market analysis.

Nambaryn Enkhbayar (1 Jun 1958, Ulaanbaatar, Mongolia), Mongolian politician; prime minister of Mongolia from 26 Jul 2000 until 13 Aug 2004, when he was elected chairman (speaker) of the State Great Hural.

Enya (Eithne Ní Bhraonáin; 17 May 1961, Gweedore, Ireland), Irish New Age singer in the Celtic tradition who was a member of the Irish group Clannad (1980–82) before striking out on a highly successful solo career; her albums won Grammys in 1992, 1996, and 2001.

Recep Tayyip Erdogan (26 Feb 1954, Istanbul, Turkey), Turkish politician, the leader of the Justice and Development Party, and prime minister from 14 Mar 2003.

Andreas Eschbach (15 Sep 1959, Ulm, Germany), German science fiction writer with more than one million books in print in 2003; *Das Jesus Video* (1998; *The Jesus Video*, 1999) was a best seller in 2000.

Christoph Eschenbach (20 Feb 1940, Wroclaw, Poland), Polish-born pianist and conductor; he was named music director of the Philadelphia Orchestra beginning in 2003.

Rafe Esquith, American arts educator at the Hobart Boulevard Elementary School in inner-city Los Angeles who established the Hobart Shakespeareans, a student acting troupe, as a springboard for his disadvantaged students; topping off his many awards was a 2003 National Medal of Arts.

Gloria Estefan (Gloria Maria Milagrosa Fajardo; 1 Sep 1957, Havana, Cuba), Cuban-born American salsa singer and lyricist who, with her backup group the Miami Sound Machine, is one of the leaders of Afro-Cuban music.

Melissa Etheridge (29 May 1961, Leavenworth KS), American rock singer and songwriter.

Robin Eubanks (25 Oct 1955, Philadelphia PA), American jazz trombone player.

Jeffrey Eugenides (8 Mar 1960, Detroit MI), American novelist, author of *The Virgin Suicides* (1993) and *Middlesex* (2002), which won the 2003 Pulitzer Prize for Fiction.

Donald Evans (27 Jul 1946, Houston TX), American government official who was US secretary of commerce, 2001–05.

Ronald M. Evans (17 Apr 1949, East Los Angeles CA), American medical researcher who shared (with Pierre Chambon and Elwood V. Jensen) the 2004 Lasker Award for Basic Medical Research for "the discovery of the superfamily of nuclear hormone receptors and elucidation of a unifying mechanism that regulates embryonic development and diverse metabolic pathways."

Sara Evans (5 Feb 1971, Boonville MO), American country-and-western musician.

Eve (Eve Jihan Jeffers; Eve of Destruction; 10 Nov 1979, Philadelphia PA), American rapper who won the Breakthrough Style award at the VH1/Vogue Fashion Awards in 2002.

Richard D. Fairbank (18 Sep 1950, Menlo Park CA), American corporate executive who was the founder, chairman, and CEO of Capital One Financial Corp. from 1988.

Leo Amy Falcam (20 Nov 1935, Pohnpei Island, Micronesia), Micronesian politician and president of the Federated States of Micronesia, 1999–2003.

Edie Falco (Edith Falco; 5 Jul 1963, Brooklyn NY), American film and TV actress, the award-winning star, as Carmela Soprano, of the TV drama *The Sopranos* (from 1999); in 2003 she won an Emmy Award, a Golden Globe Award, and a SAG Award for best actress in a dramatic series.

Lord Falconer of Thoroton (Charles Leslie Falconer; 19 Nov 1951, Edinburgh, Scotland), Scottish lord high chancellor and keeper of the great seal who is the 259th and last to hold the office; the day after he was appointed, British Prime Minister Tony Blair abolished the post (first created in 605).

Sean Faris (25 Mar 1982, Parma OH), American film and TV actor who was featured in the TV series *Life As We Know It* (2004–05).

Paul (Edward) Farmer (1959, North Adams MA), American medical anthropologist and physician who specializes in diseases that disproportionately affect the poor; he divides his time between the Harvard Medical School and a clinic in rural Haiti.

Louis (Abdul) Farrakhan (Louis Eugene Walcott; 11 May 1933, Bronx NY), American leader of the Nation of Islam (Black Muslims) from 1978.

Colin (James) Farrell (31 May 1976, Dublin, Ireland), Irish actor who has had lead roles in *Phone Booth* (2002), *Hart's War* (2002), and *S.W.A.T.* (2003).

Suzanne Farrell (Roberta Sue Ficker; 16 Aug 1945, Cincinnati OH), American dancer especially known for her performances with the New York City Ballet; she was awarded a 2003 National Medal of Arts.

Roger Federer (8 Aug 1981, Basel, Switzerland), Swiss tennis player who won the British (Wimbledon) men's singles title in 2003, 2004, and 2005 and the Australian Open and the US Open in 2004.

Marc Feldmann (1944, Poland), Polish-born Australian immunologist who was corecipient (with Sir Ravinder N. Maini) of the 2000 Crafoord Prize as well as the 2003 Albert Lasker Clinical Medical Research Award for the discovery of drugs that ease pain in persons afflicted with rheumatoid arthritis.

Prince Felipe (Felipe de Borbón y Grecia; 30 Jan 1968, Madrid, Spain), Spanish royal, prince of Asturias, and heir to the throne.

W. Mark Felt (17 Aug 1913, Twin Falls ID), American law-enforcement official and deputy associate director of the FBI until 1973 who was uncovered in May 2005 as "Deep Throat," the secretive source of information for reporters Bob Woodward and Carl Bernstein about the 1972 Watergate break-in, which eventually led to the resignation of Pres. Richard M. Nixon.

Eddie Fenech Adami (7 Feb 1934, Birkirkara, Malta), Maltese politician who served as prime minister 1987–96 and 1998–2004; he was sworn in as president on 4 Apr 2004.

Svetlana Feofanova (16 Jul 1980, Moscow, USSR [now in Russia]), Russian pole vaulter who set several world indoor records in succession during 2002 and 2003, and set the standing world record (4.88 m) at the Summer Olympic Games in Athens in 2004.

Craig Ferguson (17 May 1962, Glasgow, Scotland), Scottish film and TV actor who was featured as Nigel Wick on *The Drew Carey Show* (1996–2003) and who took over as host of *The Late Late Show* in January 2005.

Sarah (Margaret) Ferguson (15 Oct 1959, London, England), British royal, duchess of York after her marriage (23 Jul 1986) to Prince Andrew; they separated in 1992 and divorced in 1996.

Lawrence Ferlinghetti (Lawrence Ferling; 24 Mar 1919, Yonkers NY), American poet who was one of the founders of the Beat movement and cofounder (1953) of the City Lights bookstore, a San Francisco cultural landmark.

Leonel Fernández Reyna (26 Dec 1953, Santo Domingo, Dominican Republic), Dominican politician and president, 1996–2000 and again from 16 Aug 2004.

Gil de Ferran (11 Nov 1967, Paris, France), French-born Brazilian race-car driver who was CART (Indy Car) champion in 2000 and 2001 and winner of the Indy 500 in 2003.

Will Ferrell (16 Jul 1967, Irvine CA), American comedian and actor who was a member of the cast of TV's *Saturday Night Live* (1995–2002) and star of the 2003 film *Elf*.

Cy Feuer (15 Jan 1911, Brooklyn NY), American stage and film producer who received a special award for lifetime achievement at the 2003 Tony Awards presentation.

Ralph (Nathaniel) Fiennes (22 Dec 1962, Suffolk,

England), British dramatic actor known for intense roles; his films include *Schindler's List* (1993), *The English Patient* (1996), and *The End of the Affair* (1999).

Harvey (Forbes) Fierstein (6 Jun 1954, Brooklyn NY), American playwright (*La Cage aux Folles, Torch Song Trilogy*) and performer; he won the 2003 Tony Award for best actor in a musical for his performance in *Hairspray*.

50 Cent (Curtis Jackson; 6 Jul 1976, Jamaica, Queens, NY), American hardcore rapper with a troubled upbringing whose *Get Rich or Die Tryin'* (2003) was the fastest-selling album in history.

Luis (Filipe Madeira Caeiro) Figo (4 Nov 1972, Almada, Portugal), Portuguese association football (soccer) player; he was FIFA player of the year, 2001.

Harvey V. Fineberg (15 Sep 1945, Pittsburgh PA), American public-health physician and medical administrator; he was president of the Institute of Medicine from 2002.

Carly Fiorina (Cara Carleton Sneed; 6 Sep 1954, Austin TX), American corporate executive; chairman and CEO of Hewlett-Packard Co. and Compaq Computer (which merged in 2002) from 1999 until she was forced out in February 2005.

Heinz Fischer (9 Oct 1938, Graz, Austria), Austrian Social Democratic politician and president of Austria from 8 Jul 2004.

Joschka Fischer (Joseph Martin Fischer; 12 Apr 1948, Gerabronn, West Germany [now in Germany]), German politician and Green/Alliance 90 leader; he was foreign minister of Germany from 1998.

Julia Fischer (15 Jun 1983, Munich, Germany), German violinist who was the winner of the 1995 International Yehudi Menuhin Violin Competition.

Dietrich Fischer-Dieskau (28 May 1925, Berlin, Germany), German operatic baritone and lieder singer who is distinguished by his lyrical voice, commanding presence, and superb artistry; he won a Japanese Praemium Imperiale award for music in 2002.

Allison Fisher (24 Feb 1968, Cheshunt, Hertfordshire, England), British pocket billiards champion; she won the WPA nine-ball world championships in 1996, 1997, 1998, and 2001 and was the top-ranked female player in mid-2005.

Osbourne Berlington Fleming (18 Feb 1940, East End, Anguilla), Anguillan politician and chief minister from 2000.

Renée Fleming (14 Feb 1959, Indiana PA), American operatic soprano.

Ernie Fletcher (12 Nov 1952, Mt. Sterling KY), American physician and Republican governor of Kentucky from 9 Dec 2003.

Francisco Flores Pérez (19 Oct 1959, El Salvador?), Salvadoran politician and president from 1999 to 1 Jun 2004.

Juan Diego Flórez (13 Jan 1973, Lima, Peru), Peruvian bel canto tenor especially admired for his interpretations of Rossini heroes.

Carlisle Floyd (11 Jun 1926, Latta SC), American opera composer and librettist who often bases his operas on American works of fiction; he was awarded a National Medal of Arts in 2004.

Larry (Claxton) Flynt (1 Nov 1942, Magoffin county KY), American publisher of *Hustler Magazine* and freedom of the press advocate; he was a candidate for governor of California in the recall election of October 2003.

William H(erbert) Foege (12 Mar 1936, Decorah IA), American epidemiologist who was a leader of the smallpox eradication campaign in Africa in the 1960s; he later directed the Centers for Disease Control and worked with the Carter Center and the Bill & Melinda Gates Foundation on various disease eradication initiatives; he received the 2005 Public Welfare Medal of the US National Academy of Sciences.

Ken Follett (also published as Zachary Stone and Simon Myles; 5 Jun 1949, Cardiff, Wales), Welsh author of political thrillers; his first novel, *Eye of the Needle* (1978), was a best seller and won the Mystery Writers of America's Edgar Award.

Jean-Martin Folz (11 Jan 1947, Strasbourg, France), French corporate executive; he was CEO of PSA Peugeot Citroën, Europe's second largest automaker, from 1997.

Phil Fontaine (Larry Phillip Fontaine; "Buddy"; 20 Sep 1944, Fort Alexander Reserve, MB, Canada), Canadian Ojibway first-nations activist, grand chief of the Assembly of Manitoba Chiefs, 1989–97, and national chief of the Assembly of First Nations from 1997.

Gerald Rudolph Ford (Leslie Lynch King, Jr.; 14 Jul 1913, Omaha NE), American statesman; 38th president of the US, 1974–77 (*see full biography at Presidents*).

Harrison Ford (13 Jul 1942, Chicago IL), American film actor, a strong leading man, known especially for his work in action films; he achieved immense popularity for playing Han Solo in the *Star Wars* film series (1977, 1980, and 1983) and Indiana Jones in the film series of the same name (1981, 1984, 1989, and another scheduled for 2006).

Tom Ford (27 Aug 1961, Austin TX), American fashion designer who revamped the image of the house of Gucci in the 1990s; he won Designer of the Year at the Vogue Fashion Awards, 2002.

William Clay Ford, Jr. (3 May 1957, Detroit MI), American corporate executive; he was chairman and CEO of Ford Motor Co. from 2001.

Marc Forné Molné (1946, Andorra?), Andorran politician and head of government from 1994.

William Forsythe (1949, New York NY), American ballet dancer, choreographer, and director; he danced with and choreographed for the Stuttgart Ballet for several years and was artistic director of The Forsythe Company (formerly the Frankfurt Ballet) from 1984.

Steve Fossett (22 Apr 1944, Jackson TN), American commodities trader and global circumnavigator who holds three major records: he was the first to circle the globe solo in a hot-air balloon (2002), he made the fastest transatlantic sailboat crossing in 2001, and he was the first to circle the globe solo in an airplane (the *Virgin Atlantic GlobalFlyer*) without refueling in 2005; he also holds dozens of other world speed and distance records.

Jodie Foster (Alicia Christian Foster; 19 Nov 1962, Los Angeles CA), American actress widely respected for her intense performances; her breakthrough came at age 13 in the film *Taxi Driver* (1976); she won Academy Awards for best actress in 1988 (*The Accused*) and 1991 (*The Silence of the Lambs*).

Sir Norman (Robert) Foster (1 Jun 1935, near Manchester, England), British architect who is noted for his conceptual work in corporate, institutional, and transportation structures, such as the Hong Kong Airport (1998) and the Swiss Re tower (2004); he won the 1999 Pritzker Prize and a Japanese

Praemium Imperiale award for excellence in arts in 2002.

Vicente Fox Quesada (2 Jul 1942, Mexico City, Mexico), Mexican politician, businessman, and president from 2000.

Jamie Foxx (Eric Bishop; 13 Dec 1967, Terrell TX), American actor and comedian who won a Critics' Choice Award and an Academy Award for his title role in *Ray* (2004).

Mikhail Fradkov (1 Sep 1950, near Kuybyshev, Russian SSR, USSR [now Samara, Russia]), Russian politician and prime minister from 5 Mar 2004.

Don Francisco (Mario Kreutzberger; 28 Dec 1940, Talca, Chile), Chilean-born American TV personality; host of the popular show *Sábado Gigante,* which has been on the air since 1962 and is by far the longest-running TV show with the same host.

Al Franken (21 May 1951, New York NY), American comedian and writer who worked for more than a decade on TV's *Saturday Night Live* and later made a career with his liberal political comedy and best-selling books such as *Rush Limbaugh Is a Big Fat Idiot and Other Observations* (1996) and *Oh, the Things I Know: A Guide to Success, or, Failing That, Happiness* (2002).

Tommy R. Franks (17 Jun 1945, Wynnewood OK), American four-star general in the US Army; as commander in chief of the US Central Command from 2000 to July 2003, he was in charge of US operations in Afghanistan, against al-Qaeda, and in Iraq.

Dennis Franz (Dennis Schlachta; 28 Oct 1944, Maywood IL), American TV actor famous for police dramas, notably his role as Detective Andy Sipowicz on *NYPD Blue* (1993–2005).

Jonathan Franzen (17 Aug 1959, Western Springs IL), American author whose *The Corrections* won a National Book Award in 2001.

Charles Frazier (1950, Asheville NC), American novelist and winner of the 1997 National Book Award for *Cold Mountain.*

Crown Prince Frederik (Frederik André Henrik Christian; 26 May 1968, Copenhagen, Denmark), Danish royal and heir to the throne; he married Australian Mary Donaldson on 14 May 2004.

Morgan Freeman (1 Jun 1937, Memphis TN), American prolific theater and film actor most famous for the films *Driving Miss Daisy* (1989) and *The Shawshank Redemption* (1994); he won an Academy Award for best supporting actor for his role in *Million Dollar Baby* (2004).

Dawn French (11 Oct 1957, Holyhead, Wales), British actress, comedian, and writer known for her work in the TV series *French & Saunders* (with Jennifer Saunders) and *The Vicar of Dibley;* she also appeared as the Fat Lady, a talking painting, in *Harry Potter and the Prisoner of Azkaban* (2004).

Lucian Freud (8 Dec 1922, Berlin, Germany), German-born British painter renowned for his portraits and nudes, often rendered in extreme close-up; he is the grandson of Sigmund Freud.

Dave Freudenthal (12 Oct 1950, Thermopolis WY), American attorney and Democratic politician; governor of Wyoming from 2003.

Benjamin M. Friedman, American political economist and expert on economic policy who is William Joseph Maier Professor of Political Economy at Harvard University; his books include *The Moral Consequences of Economic Growth* (2005).

Milton Friedman (31 Jul 1912, Brooklyn NY), American laissez-faire economist, professor at the University of Chicago, and one of the leading conservative economists in the second half of the 20th century; he was awarded the 1976 Nobel Memorial Prize for Economic Science.

Stephen E. Friedman (c. 1939), American financier and economist who was named assistant to the president and director of the National Economic Council (chief economic adviser) in 2002.

Thomas L. Friedman (20 Jul 1953, Minneapolis MN), American newspaper columnist and author, prominent foreign affairs columnist for the *New York Times.*

Bill Frisell (18 Mar 1951, Baltimore MD), American jazz guitarist who has worked in a variety of genres—most recently country and world music—both as a soloist and with acclaimed bands; he has a unique, heavily electrified synthesizer-like sound.

Bill Frist (22 Feb 1952, Nashville TN), American cardiac surgeon and politician, Republican senator from Tennessee, and Senate majority leader from 2003.

Pierre Frogier (16 Nov 1950, Nouméa, New Caledonia), New Caledonian politician and president from 2001.

Akira Fujishima (3 Aug 1941, Tokyo, Japan), Japanese biologist, educator, and developer, with Kenichi Honda, of the Honda-Fujishima effect, a photosynthetic method to split water into hydrogen and oxygen, i.e., artificial photosynthesis; both won a 2004 Japan Prize; Fujishima was chairman of the Kanagawa Academy of Science and Technology.

Takeo Fukui (28 Nov 1944, Tokyo, Japan), Japanese corporate executive who was president and CEO of Honda Motor Co., Ltd., from June 2003.

Toshihiko Fukui (7 Sep 1935, Japan), Japanese banker who was governor of the Bank of Japan from 2003.

Richard S. Fuld, Jr. (26 Apr 1946), American corporate executive who was CEO of Lehman Brothers Holdings from 1993.

Nelly (Kim) Furtado (2 Dec 1978, Victoria, BC, Canada), Canadian singer and songwriter.

Stefano Gabbana (14 Nov 1962, Milan, Italy), Italian fashion designer, along with partner Domenico Dolce, whose designs are inspired by the Mediterranean region.

Neil (Richard) Gaiman (10 Nov 1960, Portchester, England), British author of the multiple-award-winning *Sandman* series and of other graphic novels.

John (Charles) Galliano (28 Nov 1960, Gibraltar), British fashion designer and designer in chief at Christian Dior.

Christopher B. Galvin (21 Mar 1950, Chicago IL), American corporate executive who was CEO from 1997 of the Motorola Corp. (which was founded in 1928 by his grandfather, Paul Galvin); he is the son of Robert W. Galvin.

Robert W. Galvin (1922, Marshfield WI), American CEO of Motorola, Inc., from 1959 to 1990; he oversaw the development of the company for the manufacture of semiconductor technology, especially the cell-phone industry; he was given the 2005 Vannevar Bush Award of the National Science Board for lifetime contribution to the nation in science and technology.

Sonia Gandhi (Sonia Maino; 9 Dec 1947, Turin, Italy), Italian-born widow of Rajiv Gandhi and political force in India.

James Gandolfini (18 Sep 1961, Westwood NJ), American TV and film actor, star of the TV series *The Sopranos* (from 1999).

Gao Xingjian (Kao Hsing-chien; 4 Jan 1940, Ganzhou, Jiangxi province, China), Chinese-born

French novelist, playwright, critic, stage director, and artist awarded the 2000 Nobel Prize for Literature for "an oeuvre of universal validity, bitter insights, and linguistic ingenuity."

Mario Garcia (1947?, Cuba), Cuban-born American newspaper designer.

Gabriel García Márquez (6 Mar 1928, Aracataca, Colombia), Colombian novelist and short-story writer, a central figure in the magic realism movement in Latin American literature; he won the 1972 Neustadt Prize and the 1982 Nobel Prize for Literature.

Rulon Gardner (16 Aug 1971, Afton WY), American Greco-Roman wrestler who won the Olympic gold medal in 2000 and a bronze in 2004.

Jay M(ontgomery) Garner (15 Apr 1938, Arcadia FL), American military officer, a lieutenant general (retired) in the US Army who served briefly (March–May 2003) as military governor of Iraq following the coalition occupation.

Jennifer (Anne) Garner (17 Apr 1972, Houston TX), American TV actress, star of the series *Alias* (from 2001).

Jean-Pierre Garnier (31 Oct 1947, France), Swiss corporate executive who was head of GlaxoSmithKline PLC from 2000.

Kenny Garrett (9 Oct 1960, Detroit MI), American jazz alto saxophone player.

Ivan Gasparovic (27 Mar 1941, Poltar, Czechoslovakia [now in Slovakia]), Slovak politician who served as speaker of parliament and was inaugurated as president on 15 Jun 2004.

Bill Gates (William Henry Gates III; 28 Oct 1955, Seattle WA), American computer programmer, businessman and cofounder of the Microsoft Corp., and philanthropist; he is usually considered the richest person in the world.

Henry Louis Gates, Jr. ("Skip"; 16 Sep 1950, Keyser WV), American scholar of African American studies.

Jean-Paul Gaultier (24 Apr 1952, Arcueil, France), French fashion designer known for his unusual and extravagant creations.

Maumoon Abdul Gayoom (29 Dec 1937, Malé, Maldives), Maldive politician and president from 1978.

Laurent Gbagbo (31 May 1945, Gagnoa, French West Africa [now in Côte d'Ivoire]), Ivorian politician and president from 2000.

Haile Gebrselassie (18 Apr 1973, Assela, Ethiopia), Ethiopian runner and world record holder in the 5,000-m and 10,000-m distances.

Frank O(wen) Gehry (28 Feb 1929, Toronto, ON, Canada), Canadian-born American architect and designer whose original, sculptural, often audacious work won him worldwide renown; he was awarded the Pritzker Prize in 1989.

Leslie H(oward) Gelb (4 Mar 1937, New Rochelle NY), American journalist and government official who was columnist, deputy editor of the editorial page, editor of the op-ed page, and national security correspondent at the *New York Times* (Pulitzer Prize, 1985), assistant secretary of state in Pres. Jimmy Carter's administration (1977–79) and director of policy planning and arms control for international security affairs at the Department of Defense (1967–69), and president of the Council on Foreign Relations (1993–2003).

Sir Bob Geldof (5 Oct 1954, Dublin, Ireland), Irish musician (of The Boomtown Rats) who was knighted for his humanitarian work, notably arranging large-scale rock events (Live Aid [1985], Live 8 [2005]) for the benefit of the world's poor.

Murray Gell-Mann (15 Sep 1929, New York NY), American physicist who discovered that particles, including neutrons and protons, are composed of smaller, more fundamental building blocks and with others developed the quantum field theory called quantum chromodynamics; he also suggested the name "quark" to refer to the fundamental particles; Gell-Mann won the 1969 Nobel Prize for Physics.

Sarah Michelle Gellar (14 Apr 1977, New York NY), American TV actress, star of *Buffy the Vampire Slayer* (1997–2003).

Francis (Eugene) Cardinal George (16 Jan 1937, Chicago IL), American Roman Catholic churchman who served as archbishop of Portland OR, 1996–97, and archbishop of Chicago from 1997; he was named cardinal in 1998.

(Susan) Elizabeth George (26 Feb 1949, Warren OH), American mystery writer who found great success with her novels set in England beginning with *A Great Deliverance* (1988), which was filmed for British TV in 2000; *With No One as Witness* was published in 2005.

Richard Gephardt (31 Jan 1941, St. Louis MO), American Democratic politician, congressman from Missouri (1977–2005), and House Democratic leader (1989–2003).

Richard (Tiffany) Gere (31 Aug 1949, Philadelphia PA), American film actor made famous for his performances in *American Gigolo* (1980), *An Officer and a Gentleman* (1982), *Pretty Woman* (1990), and *Chicago* (2002); he is also known for his work for Tibetan cultural and Buddhist causes.

Valery Gergiev (2 May 1953, Moscow, USSR [now in Russia]), Russian conductor, the director of the Kirov Opera from 1998.

Mordicai Gerstein (1935, Los Angeles CA), American painter, designer, and writer and illustrator of children's books; he was awarded the 2004 Caldecott Medal for *The Man Who Walked Between the Towers*.

Louis Gerstner (1 Mar 1942, Mineola NY), American corporate executive; he was president of the IBM Corp. from 1993.

Ricky Gervais (25 Jun 1961, Reading, Berkshire, England), British comedian and actor who was the star of the British TV hit *The Office* (2001–03) and winner of the 2003 O.K. Comedy Award.

Mohamed Ghannouchi (18 Aug 1941, Al-Hamma, Tunisia), Tunisian politician and prime minister from 1999.

Angela Gheorghiu (7 Sep 1965, Adjud, Romania), Romanian operatic soprano.

Nicolas Ghesquiere (9 May 1971, Loudun, France), French fashion designer, creative director of the house of Balenciaga from 1997; he was named International Designer of the Year at the 2001 Fashion Designers of America awards.

Jamal al-Ghitani (1945, Suhag, Egypt), Egyptian writer.

Riccardo Giacconi (6 Oct 1931, Genoa, Italy), Italian-born American X-ray astronomer who was cowinner of the 2002 Nobel Prize for Physics for his studies of solar X-ray radiation using rocketry and telescopes and, later, the Chandra X-Ray Observatory; he won a 2003 National Medal of Science.

Mossimo Giannulli (4 Jun 1963 California), American fashion designer known for his Mossimo line of sportswear and casual clothing for Target stores.

Mel Gibson (Mel Columcille Gerard Gibson; 3 Jan 1956, Peekskill NY), Australian American actor, producer, and director, one of Hollywood's biggest box-office draws in films that include *Hamlet* (1990), *Braveheart* (1995; best director Academy Award), *The Patriot* (2000), and *We Were Soldiers* (2002); in 2004 he created a firestorm with a film he wrote, produced, and directed, *The Passion of the Christ*.

H.R. Giger (Hans Rudi Giger; 5 Feb 1940, Chur, Switzerland), Swiss illustrator, painter, sculptor, and film designer perhaps best known for his designs for the *Alien* film series.

Romeo Gigli (1950, Faenza, Italy), Italian fashion designer whose soft, fluid creations exhibit rich fabrics and detailing.

Gilberto Gil (Gilberto Passos Gil Moreira; 26 Jun 1942, Salvador, Bahia state, Brazil), Brazilian pop singer and songwriter.

Melissa Gilbert (8 May 1964, Los Angeles CA), American film and TV actress beloved for her role as Laura on TV's *Little House on the Prairie*; she was president of the Screen Actors Guild from 2002.

João Gilberto (do Prado Pereira de Oliveira) (10 Jun 1931, Juazeiro, Bahia state, Brazil), Brazilian bossa-nova singer, songwriter, and guitarist.

Vince Gill (Vincent Grant Gill; 12 Apr 1957, Norman OK), American country and progressive-bluegrass instrumentalist and singer who steadily won Nashville's top music awards through the 1990s.

Raymond V. Gilmartin (6 Mar 1941, Sayville NY), American corporate executive who was CEO of Merck & Co. from 1994 until he stepped down in May 2005.

Ruth Bader Ginsburg (15 Mar 1933, Brooklyn NY), American jurist and associate justice of the US Supreme Court from 1993.

Vitaly L(azarevich) Ginzburg (21 Sep [4 Oct, New Style] 1916, Moscow, Russia), Russian theoretical physicist who helped explain how certain materials develop their unusual properties of superconductivity and superfluidity when chilled to very low temperatures; he shared the 2003 Nobel Prize for Physics.

Dana Gioia (24 Dec 1950, Los Angeles CA), American poet and critic who was chairman of the US National Endowment for the Arts from 2003.

Nikki Giovanni (Yolande Cornelia Giovanni, Jr.; 7 Jun 1943, Knoxville TN), American poet whose writings range from calls for violent revolution to poems for children and intimate personal statements.

Ira Glass (3 Mar 1959, Baltimore MD), American radio broadcaster, creator (1995) and host of *This American Life* on public radio.

Philip Glass (31 Jan 1937, Baltimore MD), American composer of innovative minimalist instrumental, vocal, and operatic music.

Natalie Glebova (1982?, Tuapse, Russian SFSR, USSR [now in Russia]), Canadian beauty queen who was Miss Canada and Miss Universe 2005.

Danny (Lebern) Glover (22 Jul 1947, San Francisco CA), American film and TV actor mostly cast in supporting roles, including the *Lethal Weapon* films (1987, 1989, 1992, and 1998).

Savion Glover (19 Nov 1973, Newark NJ), American dancer and choreographer known for a style of dance called "hitting," a combination of the rhythms of hip-hop music and the pounding of tap dancing.

Louise (Elisabeth) Glück (22 Apr 1943, New York NY), American poet who won the 1993 Pulitzer Prize for Poetry for *The Wild Iris* and the 2001 Bollingen Prize; she was poet laureate of the US (2003–04).

Faure (Essozimna) Gnassingbé (Eyadéma) (6 Jun 1966, Afagnan, Togo), Togolese head of the National Assembly and president, 5–25 Feb 2005 and again, following elections, from 4 May 2005; he is the son of the deceased president Gnassingbé Eyadéma.

Jean-Luc Godard (3 Dec 1930, Paris, France), French film director who came to prominence with the New Wave group in France during the late 1950s and the 1960s; he won a Japanese Praemium Imperiale award for excellence in arts in 2002.

Whoopi Goldberg (Caryn Elaine Johnson; 13 Nov 1955, New York NY), American comedian and film actress who starred in a solo Broadway show, *Whoopi Goldberg* (1984–85), in films that included *The Color Purple* (1985; Golden Globe Award) and *Ghost* (1990; best supporting actress Academy Award and Golden Globe), and on TV (*Whoopi*, 2003–04).

Osvaldo Golijov (5 Dec 1960, La Plata, Argentina), Argentine composer of Eastern European Jewish heritage who has found success with his passionate and expressive music.

Gong Li (31 Dec 1965, Shenyang, Liaoning province, China), Chinese film actress who starred in Zhang Yimou's films *Hong gao liang* (1987; *Red Sorghum*), *Ba wang bie ji* (1993; *Farewell My Concubine*), and *Zhou Yu de huo che* (2002; *Zhou Yu's Train*).

Ralph E. Gonsalves (8 Aug 1946, Colonarie, Saint Vincent), St. Vincent politician and prime minister of Saint Vincent and the Grenadines from 2001.

Alberto R. Gonzales (4 Aug 1955, San Antonio TX), American attorney and judge who was White House counsel (2001–05) and attorney general from 3 Feb 2005.

Alejandro González Iñárritu (15 Aug 1963, Mexico City, Mexico), Mexican film director whose hits have included *Amores perros* (2000) and *21 Grams* (2003).

Lawrence Gonzi (1 Jul 1953, Valletta, Malta), Maltese politician, leader of the Nationalist Party, and prime minister from 23 Mar 2004.

Cuba Gooding, Jr. (2 Jan 1968, Bronx NY), American film actor who won a best supporting actor Academy Award in 1996 for *Jerry Maguire*.

John Goodman (20 Jun 1952, Affton MO), American film and TV actor who broke through with the TV comedy *Roseanne* (1988–97) and has played numerous and widely varied roles in major films, including voice work in animated films such as *Monsters, Inc.* (2001) and *Jungle Book 2* (2003).

Al Gore (Albert A. Gore, Jr.; 31 Mar 1948, Washington DC), American Democratic politician, vice president of the US, 1993–2001, and presidential candidate, 2000.

Henryk (Mikolaj) Górecki (6 Dec 1933, Czernica, Poland), Polish composer whose often atonal early compositions gave way to works characterized by folk songs, medieval music, and Roman Catholicism.

R.C. Gorman (Rudolph Charles Gorman; 26 Jul 1931, Chinle AZ), American Navajo painter and printmaker with an international reputation; he is especially noted for his soft, vivid portraits of Indian women.

Porter J. Goss (26 Nov 1938, Waterbury CT), American Republican congressman from Florida (1989–2004) who was confirmed on 22 Sep 2004 as CIA director; Goss was a CIA operative during the Cold War, served as chairman of the House Intelligence Committee, and was a cosponsor in Congress of the USA PATRIOT Act.

Louis Gossett, Jr. (27 May 1936, Brooklyn NY), American film, stage, and TV actor who had roles in *An Officer and a Gentleman* (1982; best supporting actor Academy Award), *Iron Eagle* (1986), and *Return to Lonesome Dove* (1993).

Victoria Gotti (married name Agnello; 196?), American author and media figure who was named editor in chief of *Red Carpet,* a celebrity magazine, from 2004; she is the daughter of organized crime boss John Gotti.

Bill Graham (1939, Montreal, QC, Canada), Canadian politician and foreign minister from 2002.

Jorie Graham (9 May 1951, New York NY), American poet whose abstract, intellectual verse is known for its visual imagery, complex metaphors, and philosophical content.

(Allen) Kelsey Grammer (21 Feb 1955, St. Thomas, Virgin Islands), American TV actor, writer, and producer especially known for the TV series *Frasier* (1993–2004).

Clive W(illiam) J(ohn) Granger (4 Sep 1934, Swansea, Wales), Welsh economist who was awarded (with Robert F. Engle) the 2003 Nobel Memorial Prize in Economic Sciences for his development of concepts and analytic methods to establish meaningful relationships between nonstationary variables, such as exchange rates and inflation rates.

Jennifer Granholm (5 Feb 1959, Vancouver, BC, Canada), Canadian-born American attorney and Democratic politician; she was governor of Michigan from 2003.

Hugh Grant (9 Sep 1960, London, England), British-born film actor whose characters range from awkward to sexy.

Günter (Wilhelm) Grass (16 Oct 1927, Danzig, Germany [now Gdansk, Poland]), German poet, novelist, playwright, sculptor, and printmaker who became a literary spokesman for the German generation that grew up in the Nazi era and survived the war; he won the 1999 Nobel Prize for Literature.

Michael Graves (9 July 1934, Indianapolis IN), American architect and housewares designer in the Postmodernist style, known for his signature creations for Target stores.

Sir Guy (Stephen Montague) Green (26 Jul 1937, Launceston, TAS, Australia), Australian attorney, jurist, and statesman who served as administrator of the Commonwealth for Australia from 2003.

Philip Green (15 Mar 1952, London, England), British entrepreneur, owner of the Bhs retail chain.

Tom Green (30 Jul 1971, Pembroke, ON, Canada), Canadian comedian who started a new series, *The New Tom Green Show,* on MTV in 2003.

Richard Greenberg (1958, Long Island NY), American playwright whose *Take Me Out* won the 2003 Tony Award for best play.

Alan Greenspan (6 Mar 1926, New York NY), American monetary policymaker who has been chairman of the Board of Governors of the US Federal Reserve Bank since 1987.

Colin (26 Jun 1969, Oxford, England) and **Jonny Greenwood** (Jonathan Richard Guy Greenwood; 5 Nov 1971, Oxford, England), British rock bassist and guitarist, respectively, who are brothers and member of the pioneering band Radiohead (formed in 1987).

Christine Gregoire (24 Mar 1947, Auburn WA), American politician and Democratic governor of Washington from 12 Jan 2005.

Grégoire III Laham (Lutfi Laham; 15 Dec 1933, Daraya, Syria), Syrian church leader who was patriarch of Antioch in the Greek Melkite Catholic Church from 2000.

Vartan Gregorian (8 Apr 1934, Tabriz, Iran), Armenian American historian of the Middle East and educator who served as president of Brown University (1989–97) and president of the Carnegie Corporation of New York (from 1997); he was awarded a Presidential Medal of Freedom in 2004.

Rogan Gregory, American furniture and fashion designer.

Brad Grey (1958?, Bronx NY), American talent agent, producer, and film executive who was named chairman and CEO of Paramount Motion Picture Group in 2005.

Ólafur Ragnar Grímsson (14 May 1943, Ísafjördhur, Iceland), Icelandic politician and president from 1996.

Rachael Grinham (22 Jan 1977, Toowoomba, QLD, Australia), Australian squash player who was ranked the world number one women's player from August 2004.

John Grisham (8 Feb 1955, Jonesboro AR), American lawyer and best-selling novelist.

Renate (Tizia) Groenewold (8 Oct 1976, Veendam, The Netherlands), Dutch speed skater who won the women's 2004 all-around world speed-skating championship.

Matt Groening (Matthew Abram Groening; 15 Feb 1954, Portland OR), American cartoonist and creator of TV's *The Simpsons* (1989–).

David J. Gross (19 Feb 1941, Washington DC), American quantum physicist who shared the 2004 Nobel Prize in Physics with H. David Politzer and Frank Wilczek for their studies of the force that binds quarks together and their development of a new physical theory called quantum chromodynamics.

Stanislav Gross (30 Oct 1969, Prague, Czechoslovakia [now in the Czech Republic]), Czech Social Democratic politician and prime minister of the Czech Republic from 26 Jul 2004 to 25 Apr 2005.

Gilbert M. Grosvenor (1933?), American chairman of the board of the National Geographic Society; he was awarded a Presidential Medal of Freedom in 2004.

Andrew S. Grove (Andras Grof; 2 Sep 1936, Budapest, Hungary), Hungarian-born American corporate executive who was CEO of Intel Corp. from 1997.

Jon Gruden (17 Aug 1963, Sandusky OH), American professional football coach, the youngest in the National Football League, who in his first year with the team helped to lift the Tampa Bay Buccaneers, once the laughingstock of the NFL, to their first championship and to a 48–21 rout of the Oakland Raiders in Super Bowl XXXVII.

Sofia (Asgatovna) Gubaidulina (24 Oct 1931, Chistopol, Tatar ASSR, USSR [now Tatarstan, Russia]), Russian Tatar composer whose works are polytonal and characterized by dualities and strongly accented rhythms but also employ traditional genres.

Armando (Emílio) Guebuza (20 Jan 1943, Marrupula, Portuguese Mozambique), Mozambican secretary-general of the Frelimo political party from 2002 and president from 2 Feb 2005.

Ismail Omar Guelleh (27 Nov 1947, Diré-Dawa, Ethiopia), Djibouti politician and president from 1999.

Grand Duke Guillaume (Guillaume Jean Joseph Marie, Prince of Nassau and Bourbon-Parma; 11 Nov 1981, Château de Betzdorf, Luxembourg), Luxembourgian royal and heir to the throne.

Gilbert Guillaume (4 Dec 1930, Bois-Colombes, France), French jurist; president of the International Court of Justice from 2000.

Kenny C. Guinn (24 Aug 1936, Garland AR), American Republican politician who was governor of Nevada from 1999.

James Edward Gunn (21 Oct 1938, Livingstone TX), American cosmologist who was the cowinner (with James Peebles and Martin Rees) of the 2005 Crafoord Prize for their research into the evolution of the universe.

Xanana Gusmão (José Alexandre Gusmão; 20 Jun 1946, Laleia, [Portuguese] East Timor), Timorese independence leader who was first president of independent East Timor from 20 May 2002.

António (Manuel de Oliveira) Guterres (30 Apr 1949, Lisbon, Portugal), Portuguese Socialist politician who was prime minister of Portugal 1995–2002 and became UN High Commissioner for Refugees on 15 Jun 2005.

David Guterson (4 May 1956, Seattle WA), American novelist who followed his best-selling *Snow Falling on Cedars* (1994; PEN/Faulkner Award) and *East of the Mountains* (1999) with *Our Lady of the Forest* (2003).

Carlos M. Gutierrez (1953, Havana, Cuba), Cuban-born American corporate executive, former chairman and CEO of Kellogg Company, and secretary of commerce from 7 Feb 2005.

Lucio (Edwin) Gutiérrez Borbúa (23 Mar 1957, Quito, Ecuador), Ecuadorian politician who, three years after he had been imprisoned for having taken part in a failed uprising, won a resounding mandate in the presidential elections of 2002 and served as president of Ecuador from 15 Jan 2003 to 20 Apr 2005.

Buddy Guy (George Guy; 30 Jul 1936, Lettsworth LA), American traditional guitarist and singer in the delta blues tradition; his Chicago nightclub, Buddy Guy's Legends, is a blues landmark. Guy was awarded a 2003 NEA National Medal of Arts; *Blues Singer* (2003), his 24th album, won a Grammy Award in 2004; and he was inducted into the Rock and Roll Hall of Fame in 2005.

King Gyanendra Bir Bikram Shah Dev (7 Jul 1947, Kathmandu, Nepal), Nepalese king, 1950–51, and again from 2001; on 1 Feb 2005 he fired the government and took over the prime ministership himself.

Jake Gyllenhaal (Jacob Benjamin Gyllenhaal; 19 Dec 1980, Los Angeles CA), American film actor who was featured in *Donnie Darko* (2001), *The Good Girl* (2002), and *Jarhead* (2005).

Ferenc Gyurcsány (4 Jun 1961, Pápa, Hungary), Hungarian multimillionaire, politician, and prime minister from 27 Aug 2004.

Crown Prince Haakon (Haakon Magnus; 20 Jul 1973, Oslo, Norway), Norwegian royal and heir to the throne.

Jürgen Habermas (18 Jun 1929, Düsseldorf, Germany), German philosopher, sociologist, and originator of the theory of communication ethics; he won the 2004 Kyoto Prize in the arts and philosophy category.

Charlie Haden (6 Aug 1937, Shenandoah IA), American jazz bass player.

Zaha Hadid (31 Oct 1950, Baghdad, Iraq), Iraqi-born architect who won a number of important international prizes before gaining acclaim for her design of the Vitra Fire House in Weil am Rhein, Germany (1993), and the Lois and Richard Rosenthal Center for Contemporary Art in Cincinnati OH (2003); she was awarded the 2004 Pritzker Prize, the first woman to be so honored.

Michael W. Hagee (1945, Hampton VA), American US Marine Corps general; commandant of the USMC from 2003.

Håkan Hagegard (25 Nov 1945, Karlstad, Sweden), Swedish operatic baritone.

Hilary Hahn (27 Nov 1979, Lexington VA), American violinist whose 2001 recording of the concertos of Johannes Brahms and Igor Stravinsky won a Grammy Award.

James K. Hahn (3 Jul 1950, Los Angeles CA), American Democratic politician; mayor of Los Angeles from 1 Jul 2001 to 1 Jul 2005.

Jörg Haider (26 Jan 1950, Bad Giosern, Austria), Austrian ultra-right-wing politician.

Zoltán Haiman (8 May 1971, Budapest, Hungary), Hungarian-born American cosmologist working on the early history of the universe, especially the development of dark matter and galaxies that consist of a few very large stars.

Stelios Haji-Ioannou (14 Feb 1967, Athens, Greece), Greek entrepreneur and corporate executive who gave up leadership of Troodos Shipping, the family empire, to found his own company, easyJet, in 1995 and the umbrella company easyGroup in 1998.

Lasse Hallström (2 Jun 1946, Stockholm, Sweden), Swedish film director and screenwriter who reached international fame (and garnered Academy Award nominations) for *My Life as a Dog* (1986) and *The Cider House Rules* (1999); more recent successes include *Chocolat* (2000) and *The Shipping News* (2001).

Tarja (Kaarina) Halonen (24 Dec 1943, Helsinki, Finland), Finnish politician and president from 2000.

Ayumi Hamasaki (2 Oct 1978, Fukuoka, Japan), Japanese singer and songwriter, one of the top recording artists in Japan in the early 21st century.

Sam Hamill (1943, northern California?), American poet, editor, translator, and essayist; founder of Copper Canyon Press and catalyst of the Poets Against the War movement in 2003.

Mia Hamm (Mariel Margaret Hamm; 17 Mar 1972, Selma AL), American association football (soccer) player who led the US women's team to an Olympic gold medal in 1996, the world championship in 1991, and the Women's World Cup in 1999; she was named FIFA Player of the Year in 2001 and 2002.

Herbie Hancock (Herbert Jeffrey Hancock; 12 Apr 1940, Chicago IL), American jazz keyboardist and composer, a prolific recording artist who achieved success as an incisive, harmonically provocative jazz pianist, then went on to gain wide popularity as a leader of electric jazz-rock groups; he was named an NEA Jazz Master for 2004.

Daniel Handler (pen name Lemony Snicket; 28 Feb 1970, San Francisco CA), American children's book author whose works include the book series *A Series of Unfortunate Events;* his works were adapted as the 2004 film *Lemony Snicket's A Series of Unfortunate Events,* for which he wrote the screenplay.

Tom Hanks (9 Jul 1956, Concord CA), American film actor and director who won Academy Awards for best actor in 1993 (*Philadelphia*) and 1994 (*Forrest Gump*).

Daryl (Christine) Hannah (3 Dec 1960, Chicago IL), American film actress, director, and producer who first garnered attention for playing a mermaid in *Splash* (1984) and later appeared in the two *Kill Bill* movies (2003 and 2004).

Prince Hans Adam II (14 Feb 1945, Vaduz, Liechtenstein), Liechtenstein prince from 1989.

Harald V (21 Feb 1937, Skaugum, Norway), Norwegian king from 1991.

John Harbison (20 Dec 1938, Orange NJ), American composer of expressive music in a wide range of forms; he won the Pulitzer Prize in 1987 for his cantata *The Flight into Egypt*.

Marcia Gay Harden (14 Aug 1959, La Jolla CA), American film actress who won an Academy Award for best supporting actress for *Pollock* (2000) and was nominated for best supporting actress for *Mystic River* (2003).

Roy Hargrove (16 Oct 1969, Waco TX), American jazz trumpeter.

Joy Harjo (9 May 1951, Tulsa OK), American poet, musician, and Native American (Muskogee) activist; her *How We Became Human: New and Selected Poems* was published in 2002.

Nikolaus Harnoncourt (6 Dec 1929, Berlin, Germany), Austrian conductor, cellist, and viol player who in the 1950s founded, with his wife, Alice, the Concentus Musicus Wien, an early-music group that plays on historically authentic instruments; he won the 2005 Kyoto Prize in arts and philosophy for his work in recreating early musical works by studying their historical contexts.

Ofra Harnoy (31 Jan 1965, Hadera, Israel), Israeli-born Canadian cellist who has appeared in concerts and recorded widely; she has performed important new concertos for the cello by Giovanni Batista Viotti and Sir Arthur Bliss as well as works by Vivaldi and Offenbach.

Stephen (Joseph) Harper (30 Apr 1959, Toronto, ON, Canada), Canadian politician who was cofounder and leader of the united opposition Conservative Party from the 2004 election.

Ed Harris (Edward Allen Harris; 28 Nov 1950, Englewood NJ), American film and stage actor and director known for the range and depth of his work, especially in *Pollock* (2000).

Emmylou Harris (2 Apr 1947, Birmingham AL), American folk and country singer who ranged effortlessly among folk, pop, rock, and country-and-western styles, added old-time sensibilities to popular music and sophistication to country music, and established herself as "the queen of country rock."

Louis Harris (6 Jan 1921, New Haven CT), American pollster and public opinion analyst.

René Harris (1948), Nauruan politician and president four times, most recently from 8 Aug 2003 to 22 Jun 2004.

William B. Harrison, Jr. (1943, Rocky Mount NC), American corporate executive; CEO of J.P. Morgan Chase & Co. from 2001.

Prince Harry (Henry Charles Albert David; 15 Sep 1984, London, England), British royal, son of Charles and Diana, prince and princess of Wales, and third in line to the British throne.

Mary Hart (Mary Johanna Harum; 8 Nov 1950, Madison SD), American actress and TV hostess, of *Entertainment Tonight* from 1982.

Dominik Hasek (29 Jan 1965, Pardubice, Czechoslo-

vakia [now in the Czech Republic]), Czech ice hockey goalie, two-time NHL MVP, and five-time all star; he led the NHL in saves for six seasons and won the 2002 Stanley Cup with the Detroit Red Wings.

Robert Hass (1 Mar 1941, San Francisco CA), American poet and translator with a deep conviction that poetry, as one critic put it, "is what defines the self"; he served as US poet laureate 1995–97.

Abdiqasim Salad Hassan (1942, Somaliland?), Somali politician and head of the Transitional National Government of Somalia from 2000.

J(ohn) Dennis Hastert (2 Jan 1942, Aurora IL), American politician, Republican congressman from Illinois, and speaker of the House of Representatives from 1999.

Tony Hawk (Anthony Frank Hawk; 12 May 1968, San Diego CA), American professional skateboarder and actor.

Stephen W. Hawking (8 Jan 1942, Oxford, Oxfordshire, England), British theoretical physicist, a specialist in cosmology and quantum gravity; although severely disabled by ALS (amyotrophic lateral sclerosis, or Lou Gehrig's disease), Hawking remains active in science, publishing theoretical papers, and explaining complex phenomena to lay persons in such best-selling books as *A Brief History of Time* (1988) and *The Universe in a Nutshell* (2001).

Issa Hayatou (9 Aug 1945, Garoua, [French] Cameroun [now Cameroon]), Cameroonian sports executive, president of African Football Confederation, vice president of FIFA from 1988, and member of the IOC from 2001.

Salma Hayek (Salma Hayek-Jiménez; 2 Sep 1966, Coatzacoalcos, Veracruz, Mexico), Mexican-born actress who started her career in Mexican TV soap operas before she went to Hollywood; she starred as her countrywoman, the artist Frida Kahlo, in the 2002 film *Frida*.

Roy Haynes (13 Mar 1926, Roxbury, Boston MA), American jazz drummer and bandleader.

Seamus (Justin) Heaney (13 Apr 1939, near Castledáwson, County Londonderry, Northern Ireland), Irish poet whose works evoke events in Irish history and allude to Irish myths; he won the 1995 Nobel Prize for Literature.

Chad Hedrick (17 Apr 1977, Spring TX), American speed skater who was a champion inline (wheels) skater before switching to ice skating; he won the men's 2004 all-around world speed-skating championship.

George H(arry) Heilmeier (22 May 1936, Philadelphia PA), American electronics engineer who led the team that developed the liquid-crystal display (LCD) screen; he was awarded the 2005 Kyoto Prize in advanced technology.

Dave Heineman (12 May 1948, Falls City NE), American politician and Republican governor of Nebraska from 21 Jan 2005.

Heloise (Ponce Kiah Marchelle Heloise Cruse Evans; 15 Apr 1951, Waco TX), American newspaper columnist who took over the popular "Hints from Heloise" syndicated column from her mother in 1977; the household-help feature is now syndicated in more than 500 newspapers and has spawned spinoffs in magazines and radio.

Justine Henin-Hardenne (1 Jun 1982, Liège, Belgium), Belgian tennis player who was ranked number 1 in the world in 2003–04 and won the women's singles in the French Open and the US Open in 2003 and the Australian Open in 2004.

Jill Hennessy (Jillian Hennessy; 25 Nov 1969,

Edmonton, AB, Canada), Canadian-born American TV actress starring in *Crossing Jordan* from 2001.

Grand Duke Henri (16 Apr 1955, Château de Betzdorf, Luxembourg), Luxembourgian grand duke from 2000.

Brad Henry (10 Jun 1963, Shawnee OK), American attorney and Democratic politician; he was governor of Oklahoma from 2003.

Thierry (Daniel) Henry (17 Aug 1977, Châtillon, near Paris, France), French association football (soccer) player who was European Footballer of the Year in 2002 and 2003, winner of the 2003–04 Golden Shoe as Europe's best goal-scorer, and one of the 125 players selected by Pelé to mark FIFA's 100th anniversary in March 2004.

Nat Hentoff (10 Jun 1925, Boston MA), American music critic and journalist; he was named a National Endowment of the Arts Jazz Master for 2004.

Carolina Herrera (María Carolina Josefina Pacanins y Niño; 8 Jan 1939, Caracas, Venezuela), Venezuelan-born American fashion designer and perfume creator whose designs exhibit simple elegance.

Seymour M(yron) Hersh (8 Apr 1937, Chicago IL), American investigative reporter and writer, notably for *The New Yorker* magazine, on topics of the excesses and mistakes in US military and foreign policy (e.g., the My Lai massacre in Vietnam, 1969, Pulitzer Prize for International Reporting; and the mistreatment of Iraqi prisoners by US troops at Abu Ghraib prison, 2004).

Avram Hershko (31 Dec 1937, Karcag, Hungary), Hungarian-born Israeli biochemist who was a corecipient (with Aaron Ciechanover and Irwin Rose) of the 2004 Nobel Prize in Chemistry for their discovery of an ingenious mechanism by which the cells of most living organisms cull unwanted proteins.

Gen. Mohamud Muse Hersi ("Adde"), Somali president of the secessionist republic of Puntland from 8 Jan 2005.

Jacques Herzog (19 Apr 1950, Basel, Switzerland), Swiss architect; cowinner, with Pierre de Meuron, of the 2001 Pritzker Prize.

Lleyton Hewitt (24 Feb 1981, Adelaide, SA, Australia), Australian tennis player, the top-ranked competitor in 2001 and 2002, when he won the Australian Open and the US Open (2001) and Wimbledon (2002).

Tommy Hilfiger (Thomas Jacob Hilfiger; 24 Mar 1951, Elmira NY), American fashion designer whose sportswear and jeans collections express an all-American theme.

Faith Hill (Audrey Faith Perry; 21 Sep 1967, Jackson MS), American country singer.

Julia "Butterfly" Hill (18 Feb 1974, Mount Vernon MO), American environmental activist.

Lauryn Hill (25 May 1975, South Orange NJ), American hip-hop singer and actress.

Tony Hillerman (27 May 1925, Sacred Heart OK), American mystery writer whose best-selling novels usually take place in and around the Four Corners area of the American Southwest and feature Navajo detectives.

Paris Hilton (17 Feb 1981, New York NY), American socialite, the heiress of the Hilton Hotel fortune, and star (with Nicole Richie) of a reality-TV series, *The Simple Life,* from 2003.

Gertrude Himmelfarb (8 Aug 1922, Brooklyn NY), American historian and biographer who most often focuses on Victorian England and contemporary moral and cultural history; she was awarded a National Humanities Medal in 2004.

Gordon B(itner) Hinckley (23 Jun 1910, Salt Lake City UT), American church official who has been president of the Church of Jesus Christ of Latter-day Saints from 1995; he was awarded a Presidential Medal of Freedom in 2004.

Sam Hinds (1943), Guyanese politician who was president in 1997 and prime minister 1992–97, 1997–99, and again from 1999.

Damien Hirst (1965, Bristol, England), British artist whose work appeared in the show, *Sensation: Young British Artists from the Saatchi Collection.*

Christopher Hitchens (26 Apr 1949, Portsmouth, England), American cultural and political critic and journalist.

Stanley Ho (Ho Hung-sun; 25 Nov 1921, Hong Kong), Macanese gaming magnate and multibillionaire who controlled gambling casinos in Macau until 2002, when the territory's gambling concessions were granted to multiple owners, and was the leading casino owner thereafter.

Susan Hockfield (1951, Chicago IL), American neuroscientist and university official who was dean of the graduate school and later provost of Yale University and who became the first woman president of MIT on 6 Dec 2004.

John Hoeven (13 Mar 1957, Bismarck ND), American Republican politician who was governor of North Dakota from 2001.

James P. Hoffa (19 May 1941, Detroit MI), American labor leader who has been the head of the International Brotherhood of Teamsters since 1999.

Dustin Hoffman (8 Aug 1937, Los Angeles CA), American film and stage actor of great range and endurance; his major films include *The Graduate* (1967) and *All the President's Men* (1976); he won best actor Academy Awards for *Kramer vs. Kramer* (1979) and *Rain Man* (1988).

"Hollywood" Hulk Hogan (Terry Gene Bollea; 11 Aug 1953, Augusta GA), American professional wrestler and actor.

Richard (Charles Albert) Holbrooke (24 Apr 1941, New York NY), American diplomat; US permanent representative to the UN, 1999–2001.

Bob Holden (24 Aug 1949, Kansas City MO), American Democratic politician and governor of Missouri (2001–05).

Dave Holland (1 Oct 1946, Wolverhampton, England), English-born American jazz bassist.

Alan Hollinghurst (26 May 1954, Stroud, Gloucestershire, England), English novelist whose 1994 novel, *The Folding Star,* was shortlisted for the Booker Prize; he won the 2004 prize for *The Line of Beauty.*

Katie (Noelle) Holmes (18 Dec 1978, Toledo OH), American TV and film actress who gained notice on the TV series *Dawson's Creek* (1998–2003).

Kelly Holmes (19 Apr 1970, Pembury, Kent, England), British middle-distance runner who won the 800-m and the 1,500-m gold medals at the Athens Olympics in 2004.

Evander Holyfield (19 Oct 1962, Atmore AL), American boxer and four-time heavyweight champion, 1990–92 (WBA, WBC, IBF), 1993–94 (WBA, IBF), 1996–99 (WBA, IBF from 1997), 2000–01 (WBA).

Kenichi Honda (23 Aug 1925, Tokyo, Japan), Japanese biologist, educator, and developer, with Akira Fujishima, of the Honda-Fujishima effect, a photosynthetic method to split water into hydrogen and oxygen, i.e., artificial photosynthesis; both won a 2004 Japan Prize. Honda was president of Tokyo Polytechnic University.

Gerardus 't Hooft (5 Jul 1946, Den Helder, The

Netherlands), Dutch physicist; shared the 1999 Nobel Prize for Physics for developing a way to predict mathematically the properties both of subatomic particles and the forces that hold them together.

Bernard Hopkins (15 Jan 1965, Philadelphia PA), American middleweight boxer who won the unified title in 2001 by defeating favored Félix Trinidad; he successfully defended the title an unprecedented 20 consecutive times.

Sir (Philip) Anthony Hopkins (31 Dec 1937, Margam, West Glamorgan, Wales), British film and stage actor often in intense roles; his credits include *The Elephant Man* (1980), *The Silence of the Lambs* (1991; best actor Academy Award), *Howards End* (1992), *The Remains of the Day* (1993), and *The Human Stain* (2003).

H. Robert Horvitz (8 May 1947, Chicago IL), American cell biologist, cowinner of the 2002 Nobel Prize for Physiology or Medicine for his work on the life of a cell.

Whitney (Elizabeth) Houston (9 Aug 1963, Newark NJ), American pop singer and film actress.

John Winston Howard (26 Jul 1939, Sydney, NSW, Australia), Australian politician, Liberal Party chairman, and prime minister from 1996.

Michael Howard (7 Jul 1941, Llanelli, Wales), British Conservative politician who served as home secretary (1993–97) and shadow chancellor (2001–05).

Ron Howard (1 Mar 1954, Duncan OK), American TV and film actor famous for his role on TV's *Happy Days* (1974–80) and as a movie director; he won a best director Academy Award in 2001 for *A Beautiful Mind* and was awarded a 2003 NEA National Medal of Arts.

Frank Hsieh (18 May 1946, Taipei, Taiwan, China [now in Taiwan]), Taiwanese politician who was Kaohsiung mayor and prime minister from 1 Feb 2005.

Hu Jintao (25 Dec 1942, Jixi, Anhui province, China), Chinese statesman; he was general secretary of the Communist Party of China, president of China from March 2003, and vice chairman of the Military Commission.

Jan Huber (Johannes Huber; 1947?, The Netherlands), Dutch foreign ministry official who was named the first executive secretary of the Antarctic Treaty system, on 1 Sep 2004, 45 years after the treaty was concluded.

Mike Huckabee (24 Aug 1955, Hope AR), American Republican politician and governor of Arkansas from 1996.

Dolores Huerta (Dolores Fernández; 10 Apr 1930, Dawson NM), American labor leader and activist whose work on behalf of migrant farmworkers led to the establishment of the United Farm Workers of America.

Arianna Huffington (Ariana Stassinopoulos; 1953?, Athens, Greece), Greek-born American political commentator, syndicated newspaper columnist, and author who declared herself a candidate for governor of California in the campaign to recall Gov. Gray Davis in late 2003.

Robert (Studley Forrest) Hughes (28 Jul 1938, Sydney, NSW, Australia), Australian art critic and author.

Sarah Hughes (2 May 1985, Great Neck NY), American figure skater who was a gold medalist at the 2002 Winter Olympic Games.

H. Wayne Huizenga (29 Dec 1939, Evergreen Park IL), American corporate executive and sports club owner who founded Waste Management, Inc., Blockbuster Entertainment, and other companies; he is also owner of the Miami Dolphins pro football team.

John Hume (18 Jan 1937, Londonderry, Northern Ireland), Northern Ireland politician; cowinner of the Nobel Peace Prize in 1998 and winner of the Gandhi Peace Prize in 2002.

Cláudio Cardinal Hummes (8 Aug 1934, Montenegro, Brazil), Brazilian Roman Catholic churchman who was archbishop of Fortaleza from 29 May 1996 and archbishop of São Paulo from 15 Apr 1998; he was named cardinal in 2001.

Hun Sen (4 Apr 1951, Kompong Chom province, Cambodia), Cambodian politician and leader of the government from 1985.

Helen (Elizabeth) Hunt (15 Jun 1963, Culver City CA), American film and TV actress made popular by the series *Mad About You;* she went on to star in major films, including *As Good As It Gets* (1997; best actress Academy Award) and *What Women Want* (2000).

(Nelson) Bunker Hunt (22 Feb 1926, El Dorado TX), American business executive, oil heir, and speculator.

Holly Hunter (20 Mar 1958, Conyers GA), American film actress who won an Academy Award for best actress in 1993 (*The Piano*); she starred in *Thirteen* in 2003.

Charlayne Hunter-Gault (27 Feb 1942, Due West SC), American TV journalist especially noted for her work with *The MacNeil/Lehrer Report* and *The NewsHour with Jim Lehrer.*

Lubomyr Cardinal Husar (26 Feb 1933, Lwow, Poland [now Lviv, Ukraine]), Ukrainian Greek Catholic Church leader and patriarch of Lviv from 2000; he was named cardinal in 2001.

Saddam Hussein (in full Saddam Hussein Al-Tikriti; 28 Apr 1937, near Tikrit, Iraq), Iraqi military leader and politician; president of Iraq from 1979 until 2003, when he was deposed by the invasion of Iraq by US-UK coalition forces; he was awaiting trial in mid-2005.

Pierre Huyghe (1962, Paris, France), French artist whose work explores the relationship between reality and fiction; he was the recipient of the 2002 Hugo Boss Prize of the Guggenheim Museum.

Hwang Woo Suk (15 Dec 1953, South Korea), Korean theriogenologist at Seoul National University; he and Shin Yong Moon successfully cloned the first human embryo in February 2004.

Nicholas Hytner (7 May 1956, Didsbury, near Manchester, England), British theater director who took over as artistic director of the Royal National Theatre in April 2003.

Ice Cube (O'Shea Jackson; 15 Jun 1969), American rap singer, songwriter, and actor.

Ice-T (Tracy Morrow; 16 Feb 1958, Newark NJ), American hip-hop artist, a founder of gangsta rap, and TV and film actor (*Law & Order: Special Victims Unit* from 2000).

Nobuyuki Idei (22 Nov 1937, Tokyo, Japan), Japanese corporate executive; he has been CEO of Sony Corp. from 1998 and chairman from 2000.

Eric Idle (29 Mar 1943, South Shields, Durham, England), British TV actor and author, a founding member of the Monty Python Flying Circus troupe; his musical revue, *Monty Python's Spamalot,* was the hottest ticket on Broadway in early 2005 and won the Tony Award for best musical.

Enrique V(alentín) Iglesias (García) (1931, Asturias, Spain), Spanish-born Uruguayan international trade expert, government official, and president of the Inter-American Development Bank from 1988 to 30 Sep 2005.

Ion Iliescu (3 Mar 1930, Oltenita, Romania), Romanian politician and president, 1989–96, and again from 2000.

Ratu Josefa Iloilo (29 Dec 1920, Fiji?), Fijian politician and president from 2000.

Im Kwon-taek (2 May 1936, Jansung, Korea [now in South Korea]), Korean film director, winner of the best director award at the Cannes Film Festival in 2002 for *Chihwaseon*.

Iman (Iman Mohamed Abdulmajid; 25 Jul 1955, Mogadishu, Somalia), Somali fashion model of the 1970s and '80s, actress, and cosmetics executive.

Natalie (Jane) Imbruglia (4 Feb 1975, Sydney, NSW, Australia), Australian pop singer who scored a huge success with her first single, "Torn" (1997), and followed with a well-received album, *Left of the Middle*, in 1998.

Jeffrey R. Immelt (19 Feb 1956, Cincinnati OH), American corporate executive and CEO of the General Electric Co. from 2001.

India.Arie (India Arie Simpson; 3 Oct 1976, Denver CO), American singer and songwriter; her debut album, *Acoustic Soul* (2001), received seven Grammy nominations.

Daisuke Inoue (10 May 1940, Osaka, Japan), Japanese pop drummer and inventor (1971) of the karaoke machine.

Shinya Inoué (5 Jan 1921, London, England), Japanese American cell biologist who developed techniques of microscopy to study intracellular structures; he was awarded the 2003 International Prize for Biology of the Japan Society for the Promotion of Science.

José Miguel Insulza (2 Jun 1943, Santiago, Chile), Chilean Socialist government official who was secretary-general of the Organization of American States from 26 May 2005.

Kathy Ireland (8 Mar 1963, Glendale CA), American fashion model, designer, and actress whose clothing and home-furnishings collections are noted for their affordability.

Bill Irwin (11 Apr 1950, Santa Monica CA), American actor and choreographer who won a 2005 Tony Award for leading actor in a play for his performance in *Who's Afraid of Virginia Woolf?*

Steve Irwin (Stephen Robert Irwin; 22 Feb 1962, Melbourne, VIC, Australia), Australian TV nature-show host.

Walter Isaacson (20 May 1952, New Orleans LA), American corporate executive, chairman and CEO of the Cable News Network (CNN) from 2001.

Riduan Isamuddin (Encep Nurjaman; "Hambali"; 4 Apr 1966, Pamokolan, West Java, Indonesia), Indonesian militant and leader of the Jemaah Islamiya group believed to be associated with the al-Qaeda network and responsible for a number of bombings, including that in Bali, Indonesia, in October 2002; he was arrested in Thailand on 11 Aug 2003.

Kazuo Ishiguro (8 Nov 1954, Nagasaki, Japan), Japanese-born British novelist known for his lyrical tales of regret fused with subtle optimism; he won the 1989 Booker Prize for *The Remains of the Day*.

Shintaro Ishihara (30 Sep 1932, Kobe, Japan), Japanese author and nationalist politician whose first novel, *Taiyo no kisetsu* ("Season of Violence"), won the Akutagawa Prize in 1956; he served in the legislature, in government posts, and as governor of Tokyo from 1999.

Yelena Isinbayeva (3 Jun 1982, Volgograd, Russian SFSR, USSR [now in Russia]), Russian pole vaulter who simultaneously held the women's indoor (4.86 m, set on 6 Mar 2004) and outdoor records (4.82 m, set on 13 Jul 2003).

Jonathan Ive (February 1967, Chingford, England), British industrial designer who was named the 2003 Designer of the Year by the Design Museum in London in recognition of his pioneering designs for the 2002 flat-panel iMac computer and the 2002 iPod, Apple Computer's digital music player.

Allen (Ezail) Iverson (7 Jun 1975, Hampton VA), American basketball player; he was a 2001 six-time all-star (2000–05) and was NBA MVP in 2001; he led the NBA in points per game and steals per game in 2001–02.

Molly Ivins (30 Aug 1944, Monterey CA), American political commentator and columnist.

James (Francis) Ivory (7 Jun 1928, Berkeley CA), American film director famous for his collaboration with producer Ismail Merchant (*see* Obituaries) on many period pieces, including *A Room with a View* (1986), *Howards End* (1992), and *The Remains of the Day* (1993).

Ja Rule (Jeffrey Atkins; 29 Feb 1976, Queens NY), American rap performer.

Ibrahim (al-Eshaiker) al-Jaafari (1947, Karbala, Iraq), Iraqi Shi'ite politician and prime minister from 3 May 2005.

Alan (Eugene) Jackson (17 Oct 1958, Newnan GA), American country music singer and guitarist.

Alphonso Jackson (Texas), American secretary of housing and urban development from 31 Mar 2004.

Janet (Damita Jo) Jackson (16 May 1966, Gary IN), American singer and film and TV actress.

Jesse (Louis) Jackson (8 Oct 1941, Greenville SC), American civil rights leader, Baptist minister, and politician who was the first African American to make a significant bid for the US presidency (in the Democratic Party's nomination races in 1983–84 and 1987–88).

Michael (Joseph) Jackson (29 Aug 1958, Gary IN), American singer, songwriter, and dancer who was the most popular entertainer in the world in the early and mid-1980s.

Peter Jackson (31 Oct 1961, Pukerua Bay, New Zealand), New Zealand film director and producer who directed the *Lord of the Rings* trilogy (2001–03); the third in the series, *The Return of the King*, won 11 Academy Awards in 2003, including that for best picture.

Phil Jackson (Philip Douglas Jackson; 17 Sep 1945, Deer Lodge MT), American basketball player and coach; as coach, he won nine NBA titles with the Chicago Bulls (1991–93, 1996–98) and the Los Angeles Lakers (2000–02), and he holds the record for most NBA playoff coaching wins (175).

Samuel L(eroy) Jackson (21 Dec 1948, Washington DC), American film actor whose breakthrough performance in *Jungle Fever* (1991) launched a successful career.

Marc Jacobs (9 Apr 1963, New York NY), American fashion designer known for his sartorial interpretations of trends in contemporary art, modeling, and the rock music scene; he was the creator of his own signature lines and artistic director for Louis Vuitton.

Jadakiss (Jason Phillips; 25 May 1975, Yonkers NY), American rapper.

Bharrat Jagdeo (23 Jan 1964, Unity village, Demarara, Guyana), Guyanese politician and president from 1999.

Sir Mick Jagger (Michael Philip Jagger; 26 Jul 1943, Dartford, Kent, England), British rock musician and lead singer of the Rolling Stones; he was knighted in 2003.

Helmut Jahn (4 Jan 1940, Nürnberg, Germany), German-born architect known especially for his use of light and color.

Zsuzsanna Jakab (17 May 1951, Hungary), Hungarian epidemiologist and science official who was nominated in December 2004 to be the first director of the European Centre for Disease Prevention and Control (ECDC) in Stockholm.

LeBron James (30 Dec 1984, Akron OH), American basketball player who was the top NBA draft pick in 2003; he played guard for the Cleveland Cavaliers.

Judith Jamison (10 May 1944, Philadelphia PA), American dancer and choreographer who became artistic director of the Alvin Ailey American Dance Theater in 1989.

Yahya Jammeh (Alphonse Jamus Jebulai Jammeh; 25 May 1965, Kanilai village, The Gambia), Gambian politician and president from 1994.

Mariss Jansons (14 Jan 1943, Riga, Latvia), Latvian-born American conductor and music director of the Pittsburgh Symphony Orchestra from 1997 and, from 2004, conductor of the Royal Concertgebouw Orchestra of Amsterdam.

Jim Jarmusch (22 Jan 1953, Akron OH), American avant-garde filmmaker.

Keith Jarrett (8 May 1945, Allentown PA), American jazz pianist, composer, and saxophonist considered to be one of the most original and prolific jazz musicians of the late 20th century.

Tom Jarriel (Thomas Edwin Jarriel; 29 Dec 1934, LaGrange GA), American broadcast journalist, long-time reporter and anchor on ABC TV newscasts and news journals, notably 20/20.

Neeme Järvi (7 Jun 1937, Tallinn, Estonia), Estonian conductor and music director of the Detroit Symphony Orchestra from 1990.

Jay-Z (Shawn Corey Carter; 4 Dec 1970, Brooklyn NY), American rap performer.

Elfriede Jelinek (20 Oct 1946, Mürzzuschlag, Austria), Austrian playwright, novelist, and poet whose works are harshly critical of patriarchal domination and the exploitation of nature; her novel Die Klavierspielerin (1983; The Piano Teacher (1988); filmed 2001), the story of a musician dominated by her possessive mother, is a terrifying story of family violence told from a feminist perspective; Jelinek was awarded the Georg Büchner Prize in 1998 and the Nobel Prize for Literature in 2004.

Elwood V(ernon) Jensen (13 Jan 1920, Fargo ND), American endocrinologist who shared (with Pierre Chambon and Ronald M. Evans) the 2004 Lasker Award for Basic Medical Research for his work on the interaction of hormones and cells, especially in the estrogen receptor; his work led to the development of the drug tamoxifen, which is used in the treatment of breast cancer.

Jewel (Kilcher) (23 May 1974, Payson UT), American pop singer and songwriter.

Ruth Prawer Jhabvala (7 May 1927, Cologne, Germany), German-born writer of short stories and novels especially known for her collaboration as screenwriter with filmmakers Ismail Merchant (see Obituaries) and James Ivory.

Jiang Zemin (17 Aug 1926, Yang-chou [now Yangzhou], Kiangsu [now Jiangsu] province, China), Chinese politician, general secretary of the Communist Party, and president of China, 1993–2003; he became powerful following the Tiananmen Square massacre and promoted an "open door" economic policy for China.

Ha Jin (Xuefei Jin; 21 Feb 1956, Jinzhou, Liaoning province, China), Chinese American writer whose novel Waiting won the 1999 National Book Award and the PEN/Faulkner Award for fiction in 2000; War Trash won the 2005 PEN/Faulkner Award.

Sumi Jo (1962, Seoul, South Korea), Korean operatic soprano.

Steven (Paul) Jobs (24 Feb 1955, San Francisco CA), American corporate executive, cofounder of Apple Computer, and CEO of Apple Computer, Inc., from 1997.

Billy Joel (William Joseph Martin Joel; 9 May 1949, Hicksville NY), American pop singer, pianist, and songwriter.

Mike Johanns (18 Jun 1950, Osage IA), American Republican politician who was governor of Nebraska (1999–2005) and US secretary of agriculture from 21 Jan 2005.

Scarlett Johansson (22 Nov 1984, New York NY), American film actress who appeared in Lost in Translation (2003) and Girl with a Pearl Earring (2003); she won the Palm Springs International Film Festival's Rising Star award in January 2004.

Sir Elton John (Reginald Kenneth Dwight; 25 Mar 1947, Pinner, Middlesex, England), British singer, composer, and pianist who was one of the most popular and enduring entertainers of the late 20th century; he received a Kennedy Center Honor in 2004.

Jasper Johns (15 May 1930, Augusta GA), American painter and graphic artist, a pioneer of Pop art; he raised commonplace subjects (such as numbers, letters, and flags) to the status of icons by rendering them in simple colors and with purposeful, ironic banality.

Robert L. Johnson (8 Apr 1946, Hickory MS), American entrepreneur; creator (1980) of BET (Black Entertainment Television) and the company's chairman and CEO, even after it was sold to Viacom in 2000; he later formed an umbrella company, RLJ Companies, and purchased a number of sports franchises, including a National Basketball Association expansion team, the Charlotte (NC) Bobcats.

Stephen L. Johnson (21 Mar 1951, Washington DC), American government official sworn in as director of the US Environmental Protection Agency on 2 May 2005.

Angelina Jolie (Angelina Jolie Voight; 4 Jun 1975, Los Angeles CA), American film actress best known for the starring role in Lara Croft: Tomb Raider (2001, with a sequel released in 2003) and her work in Girl, Interrupted (1999; Academy Award for best supporting actress).

Cherry Jones (21 Nov 1956, Paris TN), American stage actress who won the 2005 Tony Award for leading actress in a play for her role in Doubt.

James Earl Jones (17 Jan 1931, Arkabutla MS), American actor best known for his leading roles in Shakespeare's Othello and in The Great White Hope (1970); he is also famous as the voice of Darth Vader in the Star Wars films.

James L. Jones (19 Dec 1943, Kansas City MO), American Supreme Allied Commander, Europe (SACEUR) and the Commander of the United States European Command (COMUSEUCOM) from January 2003.

Norah Jones (30 Mar 1979, New York NY), American jazz-pop vocalist and pianist who won five Grammy Awards for her 2002 debut album, *Come Away with Me,* and her song "Don't Know Why"; her 2004 album *Feels Like Home* jumped to the top of the charts as well.

Quincy Jones (Quincy Delight Jones, Jr.; 14 Mar 1933, Chicago IL), American jazz and pop arranger, composer, and producer who has been nominated for a Grammy Award more often than any other person (79 times, winning 27 Grammys, including a lifetime achievement award).

Roy Jones, Jr. (16 Jan 1969, Pensacola FL), American boxer, the undisputed light-heavyweight champion (1999–2004) and WBA heavyweight champ (2003–04) after his victory over John Ruiz on 1 Mar 2003.

Tommy Lee Jones (15 Sep 1946, San Saba TX), American actor whose films include *Coal Miner's Daughter* (1980), *The Executioner's Song* (TV, 1982), *The Fugitive* (1993; Academy Award for best supporting actor), and the popular *Men in Black* (1997 and 2002) movies.

Michael (Jeffrey) Jordan (17 Feb 1963, Brooklyn NY), American basketball player; playing for the Chicago Bulls, he led NBA in scoring, 1987–93, 1996–98; he was MVP in 1988, 1991–92, 1996, 1998; he was voted ESPN's Athlete of the Century and is believed by many to be the best basketball player in the history of the sport.

King Juan Carlos I (Juan Carlos Alfonso Víctor María de Borbón y Borbón; 5 Jan 1938, Rome, Italy), Spanish king from 1975.

Juanes (Juan Esteban Aristizábal Vásquez; 9 Aug 1972, Medellín, Colombia), Colombian singer, songwriter, and guitarist whose first album, *Fíjate bien* (2000), and a later single, "A Dios le pido," won several Latin Grammy awards and spent a year on the top of the Latin pop charts; his *Un Día normal* was Latin Grammy album of the year in 2003.

Ashley Judd (Ashley Tyler Ciminella; 19 Apr 1968, Granada Hills CA), American actress and star of popular motion pictures.

Wynonna Judd (Christina Claire Ciminella; 30 May 1964, Ashland KY), American country-and-western singer.

Sir Anerood Jugnauth (29 Mar 1930, Mauritius), Mauritian politician; he was prime minister, 1982–95 and again 2000–03, and president from 7 Oct 2003.

Jean-Claude Juncker (9 Dec 1954, Rédange-sur-Attert, Luxembourg), Luxembourgian politician and prime minister from 1995.

Andrea Jung (1959, Toronto, ON, Canada), Canadian-born American business executive and CEO of Avon Products, Inc., from 1999.

Ahmad Tejan Kabbah (16 Feb 1932, Pendembu, Sierra Leone), Sierra Leonean politician and president, 1996–97, and again from 1998.

Joseph Kabila (4 Jun 1971, Sud-Kivu province, Dem. Rep. of the Congo), Congolese politician and president of the Dem. Rep. of the Congo from 17 Jan 2001.

Ismail Kadare (28 Jan 1938, Gjirokastër, Albania), Albanian novelist and poet, renowned in Albania for his poetry and internationally for his prose fiction; he won the first Man Booker International Prize in 2005.

Paul Kagame (October 1957, Gitarama, Ruanda-Urundi [now Rwanda]), Rwandan politician and president from 2000.

Dahir Riyale Kahin (1952), Somali politician; president of the secessionist Republic of Somaliland from 3 May 2002.

Daniel Kahneman (5 Mar 1934, Tel Aviv, British Palestine [now in Israel]), Israeli-born American economist; cowinner of the 2002 Nobel Memorial Prize for Economic Science for his work in integrating psychology and economic theory and shared (with Amos Tversky) the 2003 Grawemeyer Award for Psychology.

Stephen Kakfwi (1950, near Fort Good Hope, NWT, Canada), Canadian politician and premier of Northwest Territories from 17 Jan 2000.

Michiko Kakutani (9 Jan 1955, New Haven CT), American journalist who was a reporter for the *Washington Post* and staff writer for *Time* magazine before joining the *New York Times* in 1979; since January 1983 she has been a book critic at that newspaper and become one of the most influential voices in American book publishing.

Dean Kamen (1951, Rockville Centre NY), American engineer and inventor of the Segway Human Transporter (unveiled in December 2001).

Ingvar Kamprad (1926, Småland province, Sweden), Swedish businessman and founder of the home-furnishing company IKEA who created merchandise that could be packaged flat and later put together by the customer; by the early 21st century, IKEA was the world's largest furniture retailer, with stores in some 30 countries.

Hitomi Kanehara (8 Aug 1983, Tokyo, Japan), Japanese novelist and the cowinner, at age 20, of the 2004 Akutagawa Prize for literature, Japan's top award for fiction, for her *Hebi ni piasu* ("Snakes and Earrings").

Radovan Karadzic (19 Jun 1945, Petnijca, Yugoslavia [now in Serbia and Montenegro]), Bosnian Serb politician and president of Republika Srpska (Bosnia and Herzegovina), 1992–96; he was wanted as a war criminal and was still at large in 2005.

Konstantinos Karamanlis (Kostas; 14 Sep 1956, Athens, Greece), Greek politician and leader of the conservative New Democracy party; he became prime minister on 10 Mar 2004.

Omar Karami (1 May 1935, Al Nouri, near Tripoli, Lebanon), Lebanese prime minister, 1990–92 and again from 21 Oct 2004 to 19 Apr 2005.

Donna Karan (Donna Faske; 2 Oct 1948, Forest Hills NY), American fashion designer known for the simplicity of her predominately black- and neutral-colored designs.

Islam Karimov (30 Jan 1938, Samarkand, Uzbek SSR, USSR [now Uzbekistan]), Uzbek politician and president from 1990.

Mel Karmazin (Melvin Alan Karmazin; 24 Aug 1943, New York NY), American media executive; he was president and CEO of CBS and president and chief operating officer of Viacom from May 2000 following the merger of Viacom and CBS.

Hamid Karzai (24 Dec 1957, Karz, Afghanistan), Afghan statesman who was head of the interim administration following the ousting of the Taliban and president of Afghanistan from 2001.

Casey Kasem (Kemal Amin Kasem; 27 Apr 1932, Detroit MI), American radio personality, the host of radio's *American Top 40,* a program that mixed background information about the performers with the countdown format that he devised for the hit songs of the day; after 34 years he retired from the show in January 2004.

Garry Kasparov (Garri Kimovich Kasparov, original name Garri Weinstein or Harry Weinstein; 13 Apr 1963, Baku, Azerbaijan SSR, USSR [now in Azerbaijan]), Azerbaijani-born Russian chess champion of the world from 1985 to 2000.

Moshe Katsav (1945, Iran), Iranian-born Israeli politician and president of Israel from 2000.

Jeffrey Katzenberg (21 Dec 1950, New York NY), American film producer (*Chicken Run* [2000]; *Shrek* [2001]) and a cofounder (1994) of DreamWorks SKG.

Fred Kavli (Fridtjof Kavli; 1927, Norway), Norwegian-born American physicist who founded the Kavlico Corp., a leading manufacturer of sensor technology; after selling his company in 2000, he founded two philanthropic organizations to underwrite basic research in the service of humanity.

Yoriko Kawaguchi (14 Jan 1941, Tokyo, Japan), Japanese politician and foreign minister from 2002.

Nobuhiko Kawamoto (3 Mar 1936, Tokyo, Japan), Japanese corporate executive who was president of Honda Motor Co., Ltd., from 1990.

Alan (Curtis) Kay (1940, Springfield MA), American computer scientist who was instrumental in developing the personal computer, the local area network (LAN), and the graphical user interface (GUI), among other innovations; he received the 2003 Association of Computing Machinery's Turing Award for his development of Smalltalk (an object-oriented programming environment), shared the 2004 Charles Stark Draper Award of the National Academy of Engineering, and was awarded a 2004 Kyoto Prize.

Keb' Mo' (Kevin Moore; 3 Oct 1951, Los Angeles CA), American blues musician.

Garrison Keillor (Gary Edward Keillor; 7 Aug 1942, Anoka MN), American humorist and writer best known for his long-running radio variety show, *A Prairie Home Companion.*

Toby Keith (Toby Keith Covel; 8 Jul 1961, Clinton OK), American country-and-western singer who won top male vocalist awards in 2000 and 2001 and was the CMA entertainer of the year in 2003.

Bill Keller (18 Jan 1949), American journalist who was managing editor of the *New York Times* from 1997 to 2001 and was appointed executive editor in mid-June 2003.

David E. Kelley (4 Apr 1956, Waterville ME), American TV screenwriter (for *L.A. Law*) who created the hit TV series *The Practice* (1997), *Ally McBeal* (1997), and *Boston Legal* (2004).

Ellsworth Kelly (31 May 1923, Newburgh NY), American painter and sculptor who was a leading exponent of the hard-edge style, in which abstract contours are sharply and precisely defined.

R. Kelly (Robert S. Kelly; 8 Jan 1969, Chicago IL), American rhythm-and-blues performer.

Sir Allan Kemakeza (1951, Panueli village, Savo Island, Solomon Islands), Solomon Islands politician and prime minister from 2001.

Yashar Kemal (Kemal Sadik Göğçeli; 1922, Hemite, Turkey), Turkish novelist of Kurdish descent best known for his stories of village life and for his outspoken advocacy on behalf of the dispossessed.

Dirk Kempthorne (29 Oct 1951, San Diego CA), American Republican politician and governor of Idaho from 1999.

Thomas (Michael) Keneally (also published as William Coyle; 7 Oct 1935, Sydney, NSW, Australia), Australian novelist who was shortlisted for the Booker Prize four times, winning it in 1982 with his journalistic novel *Schindler's Ark,* later made into the award-winning film *Schindler's List* (1993).

Anthony (McCleod) Kennedy (23 Jul 1936, Sacramento CA), American jurist who was an associate justice of the US Supreme Court from 1988.

Charles Kennedy (25 Nov 1959, Inverness, Scotland), British politician and leader of the Liberal Democratic Party from 1999.

Edward M(oore) Kennedy (22 Feb 1932, Brookline MA), American Democratic politician and senator from Massachusetts from 1962.

Mathieu Kérékou (2 Sep 1933, Kouarfa, Dahomey [now Benin]), Beninese politician and president of Benin, 1972–91, and again from 1996.

Joseph E. Kernan (8 Apr 1946, Chicago IL), American Democratic politician who succeeded to the governorship of Indiana in 2003 upon the death of Gov. Frank O'Bannon and held that post until 10 Jan 2005.

John F. Kerry (11 Dec 1943, Fitzsimons Army Hospital [now in Aurora CO]), American Democratic politician and senator from Massachusetts from 1985; he was the Democratic candidate for president in 2004.

Alicia Keys (Alicia Augello Cook; 25 Jan 1981, New York NY), American rhythm-and-blues singer; she was the winner of five Grammy Awards in 2002.

Cheb Khaled (Khaled Hadj Brahim; 29 Feb 1960, Sidi-El-Houri, near Oran, French Algeria), Algerian *rai* performer.

Sheikh Hamad ibn 'Isa al-Khalifah (28 Jan 1950, Bahrain), Bahraini emir and chief of state from 1999; he proclaimed himself king on 14 Feb 2002.

Zalmay Khalilzad (1951, Mazar-i-Sharif, Afghanistan), Afghanistan-born American government official and diplomat who served as US ambassador to Afghanistan (2003–05) and to Iraq (from 2005).

Hojatolislam Sayyed Ali Khamenei (15 Jul 1939, Meshed, Iran), Iranian Shi'ite clergyman and politician who served as president (1981–89) and as that country's *rahbar,* or leader, from 1989; a religious figure of some significance, Khamenei was generally addressed with the honorific *ayatollah.*

Khamtay Siphandone (8 Feb 1924, Champassak province, Laos), Laotian politician; general secretary of the Lao People's Revolutionary Party from 1992 and president of Laos from 1998.

Abdul Qadeer Khan (1935, Bhopal, Madhya Pradesh, British India), Pakistani nuclear engineer who was given the charge of developing a program to produced enriched uranium for nuclear weapons for Pakistan and was so successful in doing so that he became a multimillionaire and a national hero, called "the father of the Islamic bomb"; in 2003–04 it was disclosed that he had freely provided nuclear technology and material to other Muslim states, notably Iran and Libya, as well as to North Korea.

Shahrukh Khan (2 Nov 1965, Peshawar, Pakistan), Pakistani-born Indian film and TV actor and Bollywood heartthrob who is one of the top actors in India.

Hojatoleslam Mohammad Khatami (29 Sep 1943, Ardakan, Iran), Iranian politician and president of Iran (1997–2005).

Mikhail (Borisovich) Khodorkovsky (26 Jun 1963, Moscow, USSR [now in Russia]), Russian businessman, former billionaire head of Yukos Oil Co., who was found guilty of various economic crimes in May 2005 and sentenced to nine years in prison.

Abbas Kiarostami (22 Jun 1940, Tehran, Iran), Iranian director director-writer known for experimenting with the boundaries between reality and fiction; he enjoys perhaps the greatest international reputation among filmmakers in his country.

Mwai Kibaki (15 Nov 1931, Gatuyaini village, Central province, Kenya), Kenyan politician and president from 2002.

Sue Monk Kidd (1949?, South Carolina), American author of two best-selling titles, *The Dance of the Dissident Daughter* (1996) and *The Secret Life of Bees* (2002), about what she calls the "sacred feminine."

Angelique Kidjo (14 Jul 1960, Ouidah, Dahomey [now Benin]), Beninese pop singer who won international acclaim with her blend of musical styles from Africa, Europe, and the Americas.

Nicole (Mary) Kidman (20 Jun 1967, Honolulu HI), American-born Australian actress who in recent years has risen to become one of Hollywood's most popular stars; she won the Academy Award for best actress for her work in *The Hours* (2003) and was given the 2003 Fashion Icon Award by the Council of Fashion Designers of America.

Anselm Kiefer (8 Mar 1945, Donaueschingen, Germany), German painter in the Neo-Expressionist movement known for works that deal ironically with 20th-century German history.

Val (Edward) Kilmer (31 Dec 1959, Los Angeles CA), American film actor who broke through in *Top Gun* (1986) and *The Doors* (1991), in which he played Jim Morrison; recent films have included *Pollock* (2000) and a number of thrillers, including *Blind Horizon* (2003).

Jeong H. Kim (1961?, Seoul, South Korea), Korean-born American electronics industry executive who was founder (1992) of Yurie Systems, Inc., and president of Lucent Technologies' Bell Labs from 2005.

Kim Jong Il (16 Feb 1941, near Khabarovsk, Russian SFSR, USSR [now Russia]), North Korean leader and successor to his father, Kim Il-Sung, as general secretary of the Central Committee of the Worker's Party of Korea (North Korea) from 1997.

Kim Soon Kwon (1 May 1945, Ulsan, Korea [now in South Korea]), Korean agricultural scientist specializing in developing high-yield, disease-resistant strains of corn; prominent for his work in aiding Korean reunification.

Kim Woo Choong (19 Dec 1936, Taegu, Korea [now in South Korea]), Korean businessman; founder and chairman of the Daewoo Group; chairman of the Federation of Korean Industries from 1998.

Jimmy Kimmel (13 Nov 1967, Brooklyn NY), American comedian and TV talk show host, anchor of Comedy Central's *The Man Show* (1999–2003) and of the late-night *Jimmy Kimmel Show* on ABC (from 2002).

Mick Kinane (22 Jun 1959, County Tipperary, Ireland), Irish jockey with a highly successful career in European Thoroughbred racing.

Jamaica Kincaid (Elaine Potter Richardson; 25 May 1949, St. Johns, Antigua), Antiguan American writer whose essays, stories, and novels are evocative portrayals of family relationships and her native Antigua.

B.B. King (Riley B. King; 16 Sep 1925, Itta Bena, near Indianola MS), American guitarist and singer, a principal figure in the development of blues; many leading popular musicians have drawn inspiration from his style.

Carole King (Carole Klein; 9 Feb 1942, Brooklyn NY), American pop singer and songwriter.

Coretta Scott King (27 Apr 1927, Marion AL), American lecturer, writer, and widow of the Rev. Dr. Martin Luther King, Jr.; together with her late husband, she was the recipient of the 2004 Congressional Gold Medal.

Larry King (Lawrence Harvey Zeigler; 19 Nov 1933, Brooklyn NY), American TV journalist, longtime host of CNN's *Larry King Live* interview program.

Stephen (Edward) King (pseudonym Richard Bachman; 21 Sep 1947, Portland ME), American writer; author of novels combining horror, fantasy, and science fiction; his best sellers include *Carrie, The Shining,* and *Misery.*

Galway Kinnell (1 Feb 1927, Providence RI), American poet whose poems examine the effects of personal confrontation with violence and inevitable death, attempts to hold death at bay, the plight of the urban dispossessed, and the regenerative powers of love and nature; he won the 1983 Pulitzer Prize for Poetry for *Selected Poems* (1982).

Michael Kinsley (9 Mar 1951, Detroit MI), American political commentator and editor; originator (1996) of the on-line magazine *Slate* and its editor 1996–2002.

Néstor Kirchner (25 Feb 1950, Río Gallegos, Argentina), Argentine politician and president from 2003.

Yevgeny Kissin (10 Oct 1971, Moscow, USSR [now in Russia]), Russian concert pianist.

Takeshi Kitano ("Beat" Takeshi; 18 Jan 1947, Tokyo, Japan), Japanese actor-writer-director and one of Japan's most prominent media personalities who appeared weekly in up to eight prime-time shows on Japanese TV and was also active as a newspaper columnist and as a stand-up comedian; in addition, he had published numerous novels and collections of short stories and poetry and had even made successful forays into music and art.

Vaclav Klaus (19 Jun 1941, Prague, Czechoslovakia [now in the Czech Republic]), Czech politician of the Civic Democratic Party who served as prime minister, 1992–97, and president for one month in January 1993 and again from 2003.

Calvin (Richard) Klein (19 Nov 1942, Bronx NY), American fashion designer noted for his classic, elegant, and easy-to-wear clothing.

Ralph Klein (1 Nov 1942, Calgary, AB, Canada), Canadian politician and leader of the Progressive Conservative Party from 1992.

August Kleinzahler (1949, Jersey City NJ), American poet, winner of the 2004 international Griffin Poetry Prize for *The Strange Hours Travelers Keep.*

Vitali Klitschko (Vitaly Klichko; 19 Jul 1971, Belovodsk, Kirghiz SSR, USSR [now Kyrgyzstan]), Ukrainian boxer, WBC heavyweight champion from 2004; also the brother of Wladimir Klitschko.

Wladimir Klitschko (Vladimir Klichko; 25 Mar 1976, Semipalatinsk, Kazakh SSR, USSR [now Kazakhstan]), Ukrainian heavyweight boxer who was the WBO world champion in 2003 but was TKO'd by Lamon Brewster in April 2004; he is the brother of Vitali Klitschko.

Yana Klochkova (7 Aug 1982, Simferopol, Ukrainian SSR, USSR [now Ukraine]), Ukrainian swimmer who broke the world record in 400-m individual medley in 2002.

Heidi Klum (1 Jun 1973, Bergisch Gladbach, Germany), German supermodel.

Evel Knievel (17 Oct 1938, Butte MT), American motorcycle stunt performer.

Bobby Knight (Robert Montgomery Knight; 25 Oct 1940, Massillon OH), American collegiate basketball coach who led Indiana University to NCAA titles in 1976, 1981, and 1987 and led the US Olympic team to a gold medal in 1984.

Gladys Knight (28 May 1944, Atlanta GA), American rhythm-and-blues singer (of Gladys Knight and the Pips).

Philip H. Knight (24 Feb 1938, Portland OR), American business executive and former CEO of Nike (1972–2004).

Keira Knightley (26 Mar 1985, Teddington, London, England), British film actress who appeared in *Bend It Like Beckham* (2002) and *Pirates of the Caribbean: The Curse of the Black Pearl* (2003).

Alfred G(eorge) Knudson, Jr. (9 Aug 1922, Los Angeles CA), American geneticist and cancer researcher who developed the theory of tumor-suppressor genes; he received the 2004 Kyoto Prize in the basic sciences section.

Samuel Kobia (20 Mar 1947, Miathene, Kenya Colony), Kenyan minister of the Methodist Church who served as general secretary of the World Council of Churches from January 2004.

Robert (Sedraki) Kocharyan (31 Aug 1954, Stepanakert, Nagorno-Karabakh, Azerbaijani SSR, USSR [now Azerbaijan]), Armenian politician and president from 1998.

Horst Köhler (22 Feb 1943, Skierbieszow, Poland), German international economic official who served as president of the European Bank for Reconstruction and Development (1988–2000) and executive director of the International Monetary Fund (2000 to 2004); he has been president of Germany since 1 Jul 2004.

Jun'ichiro Koizumi (8 Jan 1942, Yokosuka, Kanagawa prefecture, Japan), Japanese politician and prime minister from 2001.

Leszek Kolakowski (23 Oct 1927, Radom, Poland), Polish-born philosopher and adviser to the Solidarity opposition movement in Poland; in November 2003 he was awarded the first John W. Kluge Prize (for lifetime achievement in anthropology, history, philosophy, and religion) for showing "the intellectual bankruptcy of the Marxist ideology and the necessity of freedom, tolerance, and diversity."

Willem J. Kolff (14 Feb 1911, Leyden, The Netherlands), Dutch-born American biomechanical engineer and physician, a pioneer in artificial organ technology who invented the artificial kidney, devised the clinical membrane oxygenator, and helped develop the artificial heart; Kolff was awarded the 2003 Fritz J. and Dolores H. Russ Prize of the National Academy of Engineering.

Yusef Komunyakaa (29 Apr 1947, Bogalusa LA), American poet, a prolific writer who won the Ruth Lilly Poetry Prize in 2001 and Pulitzer Prize for Poetry in 1994 for *Neon Vernacular: New and Selected Poems*.

Alpha Oumar Konaré (2 Feb 1946, Kayes, French West Africa [now in Mali]), Malian statesman who served as president of Mali (1992–2002) and chairman of the Commission of the African Union from 2003.

Tim Koogle (1951?, Alexandria VA), American corporate executive and CEO of Yahoo! Inc. from 1995.

Rem Koolhaas (17 Nov 1944, Rotterdam, The Netherlands), Dutch architect known especially for his concepts of large-scale structures; he was awarded the 2000 Pritzker Prize.

Jeff Koons (21 Jan 1955, York PA), American Pop-art painter and sculptor.

Dean (Ray) Koontz (9 Jul 1945, Everett PA), American writer of novels often with a grotesque or science fiction atmosphere; seven of his books have topped the *New York Times* best-seller list.

Ted Kooser (Theodore Kooser; 25 Apr 1939, Ames IA), American poet known for his deft use of images in describing rural Nebraska, where he lives; he was named poet laureate, effective October 2004.

Ted Koppel (Edward James Koppel; 8 Feb 1940, Lancashire, England), British-born American TV news broadcaster and anchor of the news analysis show *Nightline* from 1980; in March 2005 he announced he would leave the show in December, at the end of his contract.

Michael Kors (Karl Anderson, Jr.; 1959, Merrick, Long Island NY), American fashion designer, creator of his own signature lines and artistic director for Celine.

Janica Kostelic ("The Croatian Sensation"; 5 Jan 1982, Zagreb, Yugoslavia [now in Croatia]), Croatian Alpine skier who won three gold medals and one silver at the 2002 Winter Olympic Games and the overall Alpine World Cup in 2001 and 2003.

Roman Kostomarov (8 Feb 1977, Moscow, USSR [now in Russia]), Russian ice dancer who, with his partner, Tatyana Navka, won the 2004 world championship.

Hari Kostov (13 Nov 1959, Pisnica, Macedonia, Yugoslavia [now in Macedonia]), Macedonian politician and prime minister from 2 Jun 2004.

Vojislav Kostunica (24 Mar 1944, Belgrade, Yugoslavia [now Serbia and Montenegro]), Yugoslavian politician and president of Yugoslavia from 2000 until that country's dissolution, 7 Mar 2003; he was approved as Serbian prime minister on 3 Mar 2004.

Diana Krall (16 Nov 1964, Nanaimo, BC, Canada), Canadian jazz pianist and singer.

Hilton Kramer (1928, Gloucester MA), American art critic most notably (1965–82) for the *New York Times*; he was awarded a National Humanities Medal in 2004.

Vladimir Kramnik (25 Jun 1975, Tuapse, Russian SFSR, USSR [now Russia]), Russian chess grand master who defeated Garry Kasparov to become world chess champion in 2000.

Alison Krauss (23 Jul 1971, Decatur IL), American bluegrass fiddle player and singer successful in several award categories; by 2004 she had racked up more Grammys—17—than any other female recording artist.

Lenny Kravitz (26 May 1964, Brooklyn NY), American rock performer.

Gidon Kremer (27 Feb 1947, Riga, Latvian SSR, USSR [now Latvia]), Latvian-born violinist and conductor known for his explorations of the far reaches of the violin repertory, promotion of contemporary music, and his work with chamber orchestras.

Léon Krier (1946, Luxembourg), Luxembourgian architect and urban planner in the New Urbanism style and consultant to Charles, prince of Wales; he was the inaugural recipient of the Richard H. Driehaus Prize for Classical Architecture, 2003.

William Kristol (23 Dec 1952, New York NY), American editor and columnist.

Leonid (Danylovych) Kuchma (9 Aug 1938, Chaykyne, Ukrainian SSR, USSR [now Ukraine]),

Ukrainian engineer, politician, prime minister, 1992–93, and president, 1994–2005.

Dennis J. Kucinich (8 Oct 1946, Cleveland OH), American Democratic politician who was mayor of Cleveland from 1977 to 1979 and a congressman from Ohio from 1996.

John (Kofi Agyekum) Kufuor (8 Dec 1938, Kumisi, Gold Coast [now Ghana]), Ghanaian politician and president from 2001.

Ted Kulongoski (5 Nov 1940 Missouri), American Democratic politician and governor of Oregon from 2003.

Chandrika (Bandaranaike) Kumaratunga (29 Jun 1945, Colombo, Ceylon [now Sri Lanka]), Sri Lankan politician and president from 1994.

Harumi Kurihara (7 Mar 1947, Shimoda, Japan), Japanese chef, lifestyle celebrity, and cookbook author.

Raymond Kurzweil (12 Feb 1948, Queens NY), American computer scientist and visionary, a specialist in pattern recognition, whose work resulted in inventions of flatbed scanners, speech-recognition devices, and reading machines for the blind.

Tony Kushner (16 Jul 1956, New York NY), American playwright; author of the unconventional but highly regarded *Angels in America*, a play in two parts: *Millennium Approaches* (1992; Pulitzer Prize and Tony Award) and *Perestroika* (1993; Tony).

Michelle Kwan (Kwan Shan Wing; 7 Jul 1980, Torrance CA), American figure skater; US (1996, 1998–2004), world (1996, 1998, 2000, 2001, 2003), and Olympic medalist champion (silver medal in 1998 and bronze in 2002).

Aleksander Kwasniewski (15 Nov 1954, Dojlidy, near Bialystok, Poland), Polish politician and president from 1995.

Finn E. Kydland (December 1943, Ålgård, near Stavanger, Norway), Norwegian economist who was the corecipient (with Edward C. Prescott) of the 2004 Nobel Memorial Prize in Economic Sciences "for their contributions to dynamic macroeconomics: the time consistency of economic policy and the driving forces behind business cycles."

Madeleine L'Engle (Madeleine Camp; married name Franklin; 29 Nov 1918, New York NY), American author of imaginative juvenile literature that was often concerned with such themes as the conflict of good and evil, the nature of God, individual responsibility, and family life; she was awarded a National Humanities Medal in 2004.

Patti LaBelle (Patricia Louise Holt; 4 Oct 1944, Philadelphia PA), American soul and rock singer.

Richard Lachmann (1957?), American sociologist of culture and collective behavior whose book, *Capitalists in Spite of Themselves: Elite Conflict and Economic Transitions in Early Modern Europe* (2000) was awarded the American Sociological Association's 2003 Distinguished Scholarly Publication Award.

Andrew Lack (16 May 1947, New York NY), American communications executive; chairman and CEO of Sony Music Entertainment Corp. from 2003.

Christian Lacroix (17 May 1951, Arles, France), French fashion designer known for his ostentatious, extravagant, and colorful creations.

Emeril (John) Lagasse (15 Oct 1959, Fall River MA), American chef, restaurateur, and media personality known for his energetic TV cooking shows; his name was associated with nine restaurants in five US cities, seven cookbooks that had sold more than two million copies, two daily cable TV shows, and his own lines of food and cooking merchandise.

Karl Lagerfeld (10 Sep 1938, Hamburg, Germany), German-born French fashion designer known for his highly feminine creations for the houses of Chloé and Chanel.

Ricardo (Froilán) Lagos Escobar (2 Mar 1938, Santiago, Chile), Chilean economist, Socialist Party leader, and president of Chile from 2000.

Émile Jamil Lahoud (12 Jan 1936, Baabdat, Lebanon), Lebanese politician and president of Lebanon from 1998.

Guy Laliberté (1959, Quebec City, QC, Canada), Canadian circus performer and founder of Cirque de Soleil.

Princess Lalla Salma (Lalla Salma Bennani; 10 May 1978, Fes, Morocco), Moroccan royal, consort of King Muhammad VI of Morocco (married 21 Mar 2002).

Edward S. Lampert (1963?), American business executive and chairman of ESL Investments and Kmart Holding Corp. who engineered the takeover of Sears in 2005.

Pascal Lamy (8 Apr 1947, Levallois-Perret, Paris, France), French financial and government official; he served as EU trade commissioner (1999–2004) and was selected to be director-general of the World Trade Organization to begin on 1 Sep 2005.

Bernard Landry (9 Mar 1937, Saint-Jacques-de-Montcalm, QC, Canada), Canadian politician and premier of Quebec from 2001.

Nathan Lane (Joseph Lane; 3 Feb 1956, Jersey City NJ), American comedic actor of stage and screen; starred with Matthew Broderick in *The Producers* on Broadway (2001–02).

Helmut Lang (10 Mar 1956, Vienna, Austria), Austrian fashion designer whose simple creations are changed very little from season to season.

kd lang (Kathryn Dawn Lang; 2 Nov 1961, Consort, AB, Canada), Canadian singer and songwriter, originally in the country-rock style, but later (after her album *Ingenue* [1992]) in the adult contemporary style.

Lang Lang (1982, Shenyang, Liaoning, China), Chinese classical pianist.

Jessica Lange (Jesse Lange; 20 Apr 1949, Cloquet MN), American actress whose films include *Tootsie* (1982; Academy Award for best supporting actress), *Crimes of the Heart* (1986), and *Blue Sky* (1994; Academy Award for best actress).

Sherry Lansing (Sherry Lee Heimann; 31 Jul 1944, Chicago IL), American actress and film executive who was named president of 20th Century Fox in 1980 and who was chairman of Paramount Motion Picture Group from 1992 to 2005.

Anthony M. LaPaglia (31 Jan 1959, Adelaide, SA, Australia), Australian film and TV actor who appeared in the film *Lantana* (2001) and starred on TV's *Without a Trace* (from 2002).

Lewis H. Lapham (8 Jan 1935, San Francisco CA), American liberal political commentator, author, and influential editor of *Harper's Magazine* from 1983.

Lyndon (Hermyle) LaRouche, Jr. (8 Sep 1922, Rochester NH), American economist and populist politician and a frequent candidate for US president.

John Larroquette (25 Nov 1947, New Orleans LA), American film and TV actor who appeared in TV's *Night Court* (1984–92) and starred in *Happy Family* (2003–04).

Mark Latham (28 Feb 1961, Sydney, NSW, Australia), Australian Labor politician and party leader in the

2004 elections, which were a misfortune for him and the party.

Matt(hew Todd) Lauer (30 Dec 1957, New York NY), American TV journalist and news anchor; host of the *Today* show from 1994.

Ralph Lauren (Ralph Lipschitz; 14 Oct 1939, New York NY), American fashion designer who, by developing his brand around the image of an elite, American lifestyle, built one of the world's most successful fashion empires; he is known for his ready-to-wear collections and his use of unconventional materials.

Paul C. Lauterbur (6 May 1929, Sidney OH), American chemist and a pioneer of magnetic resonance imagery (MRI), which spares medical patients the use of potentially harmful ionizing radiation; he shared the 2003 Nobel Prize for Physiology or Medicine with fellow MRI researcher Sir Peter Mansfield.

Avril (Ramona) Lavigne (27 Sep 1984, Napanee, ON, Canada), Canadian pop singer; her first album, *Let Go* (2002), sold more than six million copies.

Sergey (Viktorovich) Lavrov (21 Mar 1950), Russian politician and foreign minister from 9 Mar 2004.

Bernard Francis Cardinal Law (4 Nov 1931, Torreón, Mexico), American Roman Catholic archbishop of Boston (1984–2002), cardinal from 1985, and senior Catholic leader in the US; he resigned in December 2002 following allegations of sexual misconduct among priests and inadequate response to the crisis on the part of the Church hierarchy.

Jude Law (29 Dec 1972, Blackheath, London, England), British stage and screen actor who rose to prominence after appearing in the film *The Talented Mr. Ripley* (1999); his more recent work includes *Cold Mountain* (2003) and *The Aviator* (2004).

Martin Lawrence (16 Apr 1965, Frankfurt am Main, West Germany [now in Germany]), American TV and film actor and comedian, star of the TV series *Martin* (1992–97) and the film series *Bad Boys* (1995, 2003).

Nigella (Lucy) Lawson (6 Jan 1960), British cook and author of food-related books such as *How to Be a Domestic Goddess* (2000) and *Nigella Bites* (2002) as well as hostess of the TV show *Nigella Bites*.

John H. Lawton (24 Sep 1943), British ecologist, head of the Natural Environment Research Council and winner of a 2004 Japan Prize for his studies and preservation of biodiversity.

Kenneth (Lee) Lay (15 Apr 1942, Tyrone MO), American business executive and CEO of Enron Corp. until his resignation on 23 Jan 2002; he was indicted by a federal jury in Houston on 7 Jul 2004 for his role in the catastrophic crash of the company in 2002.

John Le Carré (David John Moore Cornwell; 19 Oct 1931, Poole, Dorset, England), English novelist who created suspenseful, realistic spy novels based on a wide knowledge of international espionage.

Ursula K. Le Guin (Ursula Kroeber; 21 Oct 1929, Berkeley CA), American author best known for tales of science fiction and fantasy distinctive for their character development and use of language, including *The Left Hand of Darkness* (1969) and *The Beginning Place* (1980); she received a lifetime achievement award from the American Library Association in January 2004.

Richard (Erskine Frere) Leakey (19 Dec 1944, Nairobi, Kenya), Kenyan physical anthropologist, paleontologist, conservationist, and politician.

Matt LeBlanc (25 Jul 1967, Newton MA), American TV actor who played Joey Tribbiani on the TV sitcom *Friends* (1994–2004) and its spin-off, *Joey* (from 2004).

Ang Lee (23 Oct 1954, P'ing-Tung county, Taiwan), Taiwanese-born film director of extraordinary versatility most famous for *Crouching Tiger, Hidden Dragon* (2000).

Spike Lee (Shelton Lee; 20 Mar 1957, Atlanta GA), American filmmaker known for his uncompromising, provocative approach to controversial subject matter; his works include *Do the Right Thing* (1989), *Mo' Better Blues* (1990), *Malcolm X* (1992), and *25th Hour* (2002).

Stan Lee (Stanley Lieber; 1922, New York NY), American comic-book artist and creator of Spider-Man and Stripperella.

Lee Hsien Loong (10 Feb 1952, Singapore), Singaporean politician and economic expert who was deputy prime minister of Singapore and took over as prime minister on 12 Aug 2004.

Lee Hun Jai (17 Apr 1944, Shanghai, China), South Korean government official who served as prime minister of South Korea for three days in 2000 and was acting prime minister from 25 May 2004 to 30 Jun 2004.

Lee Jong Wook (12 Apr 1945, Seoul, Korea [now in South Korea]), South Korean epidemiologist and public-health expert who served as director general of the World Health Organization from 21 Jul 2003.

Lee Kun Hee (9 Jan 1942, Uiryung, Korea [now in South Korea]), Korean corporate executive and chairman of the Samsung Group from 1987.

Lee Myung-bak (19 Dec 1941, Yeongil-gun, Korea), South Korean politician, mayor of Seoul from 1 Jul 2002.

Anthony J(ames) Leggett (26 Mar 1938, London, England), British physicist who shared the 2003 Nobel Prize for Physics with Alexei A. Abrikosov and Vitaly L. Ginzburg for their explanation of how certain materials develop their unusual properties of superconductivity and superfluidity when chilled to very low temperatures.

John Leguizamo (22 Jul 1964, Bogotá, Colombia), Colombian-born American comedian and actor; he won a 2004 Hispanic Heritage Award.

Jim Lehrer (James C. Lehrer; 19 May 1934, Wichita KS), American TV journalist and author who was co-host, with Robert MacNeil, of *The MacNeil/Lehrer Report* from 1976 and, after MacNeil's retirement in 1995, the host of *The NewsHour with Jim Lehrer*.

Annie Leibovitz (Anna-Lou Leibovitz; 2 Oct 1949, Westbury CT), American photographer and photojournalist known for her intense, often intimate portraits of celebrities.

Jean Lemierre (6 Jun 1950, Sainte Adresse, France), French international banking executive and president of the European Bank for Reconstruction and Development from 2000.

Jay Leno (James Douglas Muir Leno; 28 Apr 1950, Short Hills NJ), American comedian; host of *The Tonight Show with Jay Leno* from 1992.

Robert Lepage (12 Dec 1957, Quebec, QC, Canada), Canadian actor, director, and playwright.

King Letsie III (David Mohato; 17 Jul 1963, Morija, Lesotho), Lesotho king, 1990–95 and again from 1996.

David (Michael) Letterman (12 Apr 1947, Indianapolis IN), American TV personality; host of the *Late Show with David Letterman* from 1993.

Simon Asher Levin (22 Apr 1941, Baltimore MD),

American biologist who specializes in the application of mathematics to problems in ecology; the director of the Center for Biocomplexity, Princeton University, he received the 2005 Kyoto Prize for basic sciences for his role in establishing the field of spacial ecology.

James Levine (23 Jun 1943, Cincinnati OH), American conductor and pianist, especially noted for his work with the Metropolitan Opera of New York City; he was principal conductor of the Boston Symphony Orchestra from 2004.

Bernard-Henri Lévy (5 Nov 1948, Béni-Saf, French Algeria), Algerian-born French media darling and author of best-selling "enhanced nonfiction" books; his 2003 work *Qui a tué Daniel Pearl?* (*Who Killed Daniel Pearl?*) was especially provocative.

Eugene Levy (17 Dec 1946, Hamilton, ON, Canada), Canadian comedian and writer, a cast member of the TV comedy show *SCTV* (1976–81, plus some spin-offs); his quirky films include *American Pie* (1999 and sequels in 2001 and 2003), *Best in Show* (2000), and *A Mighty Wind* (2003).

Kenneth D. Lewis (9 Apr 1947, Meridian MS), American corporate executive, CEO of the Bank of America Corp. from 1999.

Lennox (Claudius) Lewis (2 Sep 1965, West Ham, London, England), British boxer, world heavyweight champion in the WBC from 1997 and the IBF from 1999; he retired in early 2004.

(Diane) Monique Lhuillier (1971, Cebu, Philippines), American couturier known for her bridal gowns for the stars.

Jet Li (Li Lian Jie; 26 Apr 1963, Beijing, China), Chinese-born wushu (acrobatic martial arts) champion who has starred in numerous martial arts films in China and the West, including the blockbuster *Ying xiong* (2002; *Hero*, 2004) .

Li Hongzhi (7 Jul 1952, Jilin province, China), Chinese religious leader who developed the Falun Dafa system, a cultivation of five meditation exercises (known as Falun Gong) that were based on ancient Chinese methods of spiritual healing and enlightenment.

Li Ka-shing (13 Jun 1928, Chaozhou, Guangdong province, China), Chinese (Hong Kong) corporate executive, chairman of Hutchison Whampoa Ltd. and Cheung Kong Holdings, and the richest man in Asia; Li was tied for 19th on *Forbes* magazine's 2004 list of the richest persons in the world.

Li Zhaoxing (October 1940, Shandong province, China), Chinese politician and foreign minister from 2003.

Daniel Libeskind (12 May 1946, Lodz, Poland), Polish-born Israeli-American architect noted for his design of the Jewish Museum in Berlin; in February 2003 he won the design competition for the former site of New York City's World Trade Center.

Joseph I. Lieberman (24 Feb 1942, Stamford CT), American Democratic politician, US senator from Connecticut, vice-presidential contender in 2000, and presidential candidate in 2004.

Lil Jon (Jonathan Smith; 1970, Atlanta GA), American "crunk" rapper and producer.

Lil' Kim (Kimberly Denise Jones; 11 Jul 1975, Bedford-Stuyvesant, Brooklyn NY), American hip-hop performer.

Rush Limbaugh (12 Jan 1951, Cape Girardeau MO), American radio talk-show host and conservative commentator.

Thierry Lincou (2 Apr 1976, Réunion), Réunion-born French squash player who was runner-up in the World Open championship in 2003 and world number one throughout the first half of 2005.

Linda Lingle (4 Jun 1953, St. Louis MO), American Republican politician, mayor of Maui county, and governor of Hawaii from 2002.

John Lithgow (19 Oct 1945, Rochester NY), American film and TV actor known for his skill at comic and dramatic roles; he won multiple awards for his work on the TV sitcom *3rd Rock from the Sun* (1996–2001).

Lucy (Alexis) Liu (2 Dec 1968, Jackson Heights, Queens NY), American TV and film actress who gained fame for playing Ling on TV's *Ally McBeal* (1998–2002) and for her role in two *Charlie's Angels* films (2000 and 2003).

Nicholas (Joseph Orville) Liverpool (1934, Dominica?), Dominican politician and president of Dominica from 2003.

Kenneth Livingstone (17 Jun 1945, Lambeth, London, England), British politician and Labour mayor of London from 2000.

LL Cool J (James Todd Smith; 14 Jan 1968, Queens NY), American hip-hop artist and actor.

Sir Andrew Lloyd Webber (22 Mar 1948, London, England), British composer whose eclectic stage musicals such as *Jesus Christ Superstar*, *Evita*, *Cats*, and *The Phantom of the Opera* blended pop, rock, and classical forms and helped revitalize musical theater.

Gary Locke (21 Jan 1950, Seattle WA), American Democratic politician and governor of Washington (1997–2005).

Keith Alan Lockhart (7 Nov 1959, Poughkeepsie NY), American conductor of the Boston Pops from 1993.

Heather Locklear (25 Sep 1961, Westwood CA), American TV actress best known for her work on *Melrose Place* (1993–99), *Spin City* (1999–2002), and *LAX* (2004).

Sébastien Loeb (26 Feb 1974, Haguenau, France), French rally driver who won the Monte-Carlo Rally in 2003 and 2004.

Elizabeth F. Loftus (Elizabeth Fishman; 1944, Los Angeles CA), American psychologist and specialist on human memory and how it can be altered; she was the winner of the 2005 Grawemeyer Award for Psychology.

Lindsay (Morgan) Lohan (2 Jul 1986, New York NY), American teen actress and starlet in daytime TV and films.

Bjørn Lomborg (6 Jan 1965, Copenhagen, Denmark), Danish statistician and controversial environmentalist, author of *Verdens sande tilstand* (1998; *The Skeptical Environmentalist* [2001]) and director of Denmark's Environmental Assessment Institute (from 2002); Lomborg's book was a trenchant attack on the proposition that the world is heading for ecological catastrophe.

Jonah Tali Lomu (12 May 1975, Auckland, New Zealand), New Zealand rugby winger of Tongan heritage; perhaps the most famous rugby player in the world.

Jeannie Longo (Jeannie Longo-Ciprelli; 31 Oct 1958, Saint-Gervais, France), French cyclist who was world champion 12 times and broke the women's record for distance traveled in one hour (44.767 km) in 2000.

Jennifer Lopez (24 Jul 1970, Bronx NY), American pop singer, actress, and fashion designer; she won the Most Influential award at the Vogue Fashion Awards, 2002.

Andrés Manuel López Obrador (13 Nov 1953, Tepetitán, Mexico), Mexican politician and mayor of

Mexico City and tipped as a top candidate for president.

Bernard Lord (27 Sep 1965, Moncton?, NB, Canada), Canadian politician and premier of New Brunswick from 1999.

Trent Lott (9 Oct 1941, Grenada MS), American Republican politician; senator from Mississippi from 1989 and Senate Republican leader to 2003.

Joe Lovano (29 Dec 1952, Cleveland OH), American jazz tenor saxophone player, bandleader, and composer.

Courtney Love (Love Michelle Harrison; 9 Jul 1964, San Francisco CA), American pop-rock singer and actress.

Patty Loveless (Patricia Lee Ramey; 4 Jan 1957, Pikeville KY), American country-and-western singer who has won top recording awards since 1994; she returned to her roots in bluegrass with her albums *Mountain Soul* (2001) and *On Your Way Home* (2003).

Lyle (Pierce) Lovett (1 Nov 1957, Klein TX), American country-and-western singer.

Rob Lowe (17 Mar 1964, Charlottesville VA), American actor and heartthrob of the 1980s whose career was revitalized by his role on TV's *The West Wing* (1999–2003).

Henri Loyrette (31 May 1952, Neuilly-sur-Seine, France), French director of the Louvre museum in Paris from 2001.

Ruud Lubbers (Rudolphus Franciscus Marie Lubbers; 7 May 1939, Rotterdam, The Netherlands), Dutch politician who was prime minister of The Netherlands (1982–94), and UN High Commissioner for Refugees from 2001 to 20 Feb 2005.

Jane Lubchenco (4 Dec 1947, Denver CO), American marine ecologist and science administrator, president of the American Association for the Advancement of Science, 1996–97, and president of the International Council of Scientific Unions from 2002.

George Lucas (George Walton Lucas, Jr.; 14 May 1944, Modesto CA), American film producer.

Susan Lucci (23 Dec 1947, Scarsdale NY), American TV soap opera star; she has played Erica Kane on *All My Children* since its premiere in 1970.

R. Duncan Luce (16 May 1925, Scranton PA), American cognitive scientist specializing in mathematical psychology and psychometrics; he was awarded a 2003 National Medal of Science.

Lya Luft (15 Sep 1938, Santa Cruz do Sul, Rio Grande do Sul, Brazil), Brazilian poet who published her first poetry collection, *Canções de Limiar* ("Songs of Threshold") in 1964 and whose 2003 romance novel *Perdas & Ganhos* ("Losses and Gains") rode the top of the Brazilian fiction bestseller list in early 2004.

Baz Luhrmann (Bazmark Anthony Luhrmann; 17 Sep 1962, near Sydney, NSW, Australia), Australian film and stage director and producer known for his showy spectacles, often theatrical classics rewritten in 20th-century terms.

Alyaksandr (Hrygorevich) Lukashenka (30 Aug 1954, Kopys, Vitebsk oblast, Belorussian SSR, USSR [now Belarus]), Belarusian politician and president from 1994.

Luiz Inácio Lula da Silva ("Lula"; 27 Oct 1945, Garanhuns, Pernambuco state, Brazil), Brazilian labor leader and socialist politician; he helped found the Workers Party in 1980 and was elected president of Brazil in 2002.

Sidney Lumet (25 Jun 1924, Philadelphia PA), American film, TV, and stage director whose urban, gritty films often take place in New York City; his film credits include *The Pawnbroker* (1964), *Serpico* (1973), *Dog Day Afternoon* (1975), and *Prince of the City* (1981); he was awarded an honorary Academy Award in 2004.

Hilary Lunke (7 Jun 1979, Edina MN), American golfer who won the US Women's Open tournament in 2003.

Uri Lupolianski (1951, Haifa, Israel), Israeli politician; mayor of Jerusalem from February 2003; he is the first ultra-Orthodox Jew to hold the position.

Yury (Mikhaylovich) Luzhkov (21 Sep 1936, Moscow, USSR [now in Russia]), Russian politician and mayor of Moscow from 1992.

John Lynch (25 Nov 1952, Waltham MA), American businessman and Democratic politician who was governor of New Hampshire from 6 Jan 2005.

Loretta Lynn (Loretta Webb; 14 Apr 1935, Butcher Hollow KY), American country-and-western singer, a pioneer among women in country music and one of its greatest stars ever; she was inducted into the Country Music Hall of Fame in 1988 and received a Kennedy Center Honor in 2003.

Sghair Ould M'Bareck (1957, Néma region, Mauritania), Mauritanian politician and former slave who served as prime minister from 2003.

Yo-Yo Ma (7 Oct 1955, Paris, France), American cellist noted for impeccable technique, fine interpretations of the classical repertoire, the large number of commissions of new works he has attracted, and the breadth of his musical interests.

Ma Lin (19 Feb 1980, Liaoning province, China), Chinese table tennis player who alternated with Wang Liqin as top-ranked men's player in the world in 2004–05.

Baaba Maal (13 Jun 1953, Podor, French West Africa [now in Senegal]), Senegalese world-music performer whose songs are grounded in the village life of his native Senegal River region but also incorporate styles from Europe and the Caribbean as well as rap from North America.

Wangari (Muta) Maathai (1 Apr 1940, Nyeri, British Kenya), Kenyan environmental activist who campaigned against the deforestation of Africa; she is best known for having founded the Green Belt movement, which among other things was responsible for the planting of more than 30 million trees in Kenya and elsewhere in Africa.

Lorin Maazel (6 Mar 1930, Neuilly, France), French-born American conductor and violinist; he was music director of the Cleveland Orchestra, 1972–82, and of the New York Philharmonic from 2002.

Bernie Mac (Bernard Jeffrey McCollough; 5 Oct 1958, Chicago IL), American TV and film entertainer; he stars in TV's *The Bernie Mac Show* (from 2001) and had a featured role in the film *Charlie's Angels: Full Throttle* (2003).

Gloria (Macaraeg) Macapagal Arroyo (5 Apr 1947, San Juan, Philippines), Philippine politician and president from 2001.

Dame Ellen MacArthur (8 Jul 1976, Derbyshire, England), British sailor who in February 2005 set the round-the-world solo sailing record in her 23-m (75-ft) trimaran, *B&Q*; she traveled 43,500 km (27,000 mi) in 71 days 14 hr 18 min 33 sec.

Roderick MacKinnon (19 Feb 1956, Burlington MA), American chemist who shared (with Peter Agre) the 2003 Nobel Prize for Chemistry for discoveries about the structure and operation of the many crucial porelike channels that perforate the outer surface of cells in humans and other living things; MacKinnon was recognized for research on ion channels.

Alistair MacLeod (1936, North Batteford, SK, Canada), Canadian writer who won the Dublin IMPAC award in 2001 for his novel *No Great Mischief.*

Elle Macpherson (Eleanor Gow; 29 Mar 1964, Cronulla, Sydney, NSW, Australia), Australian fashion model, actress, and lingerie designer.

Ferenc Mádl (29 Jan 1931, Band, Hungary), Hungarian politician and president from 2000 to 5 Aug 2005.

Madonna (Madonna Louise Veronica Ciccone; 16 Aug 1958, Bay City MI), American singer, songwriter, actress, and entrepreneur whose immense popularity in the 1980s and '90s allowed her to achieve levels of power and control unprecedented for a woman in the entertainment industry.

Ricardo Maduro (20 Apr 1946, Panama), Panamanian-born Honduran politician and president from 2002.

João Magueijo (1967?, Portugal), Portuguese-born cosmologist who developed a controversial theory that in the first instant of the creation of the universe, light must have traveled at a speed much faster than that generally accepted by physicists.

Martie Maguire (Martha Elenor Erwin; Martie Seidel; 12 Oct 1969, York PA), American country musician and a member of the Dixie Chicks (Academy of Country Music Entertainers of the Year, 2000).

Tobey Maguire (Tobias Vincent Maguire; 27 Jun 1975, Santa Monica CA), American film actor known for playing unconventional leads; he found great success in *Spider-Man* (2002), *Seabiscuit* (2003), and *Spider-Man 2* (2004).

Bill Maher (20 Jan 1956, New York NY), American TV comedian and personality, host of *Politically Incorrect*, an often controversial TV talk show (that was canceled in 2002 after Maher's politically incorrect observations on the 9/11 attacks), and from February 2003 the host of *Real Time with Bill Maher* on HBO.

Roger Michael Cardinal Mahony (27 Feb 1936, Hollywood CA), American Roman Catholic churchman who was appointed archbishop of Los Angeles in 1985 and was named cardinal in 1991.

Hermann Maier (7 Dec 1972, Flachau, Austria), Austrian Alpine skier who dominated the sport in the late 1990s and who may be Austria's greatest downhill racer ever; in 2003–04 he made a comeback after a career-threatening broken leg.

Natalie Maines (14 Oct 1974, Lubbock TX), American country musician; member of the Dixie Chicks.

Sir Ravinder N. Maini (1937, Ludhiana, Punjab, British India), Indian-born British immunologist and rheumatologist; he was a coreipient (with Marc Feldmann) of the 2000 Crafoord Prize as well as the 2003 Lasker Clinical Medical Research Award for the discovery of drugs that ease pain in persons afflicted with rheumatoid arthritis.

Sheikh Maktum ibn Rashid al-Maktum (1943?, Dubai [now in United Arab Emirates]), UAE royal; prime minister of the UAE, 1971–79 and again from 1990.

Sheikh Mohammed ibn Rashid al-Maktum (1949, Dubai? [now in United Arab Emirates]), UAE royal who was named crown prince of Dubai in 1995; he is also a noted horse breeder and runs Godolphin Stables with his brothers.

Tuilaepa Sailele Malielegaoi (14 Apr 1945, Lepa, Samoa), Samoan politician and prime minister from 1998.

John (Gavin) Malkovich (9 Dec 1953, Christopher IL), American film actor and filmmaker.

David (George Joseph) Malouf (20 Mar 1934, Brisbane, QLD, Australia), Australian poet and novelist of Lebanese and English descent whose work reflects his ethnic background as well as his Queensland childhood and youth; winner of the Neustadt Prize in 2000.

Tandja Mamadou (1938), Nigerois politician and president of Niger from 1999.

David (Alan) Mamet (30 Nov 1947, Chicago IL), American playwright, director, and screenwriter noted for his often desperate working-class characters and for his distinctive and colloquial dialogue that is frequently profane.

Joe Manchin III (24 Aug 1947, Farmington WV), American businessman and Democratic politician who was governor of West Virginia from 17 Jan 2005.

Ange Mancini (15 Jun 1944, Beausoleil, France), French Guianan politician and prefect of French Guiana from 2002.

Nelson (Rolihlahla) Mandela (18 Jul 1918, Umtata, Cape of Good Hope, South Africa), South African black nationalist leader and statesman; he was a political prisoner, 1962–90, president of South Africa (1994–99), and coreipient of the 1993 Nobel Peace Prize.

Winnie Madikizela Mandela (original name Nomzamo Winifred, original Xhosa name Nkosikazi Nobandle Nomzamo Madikizela; 26 Sep 1934/36, Pondoland district, Transkei, South Africa), South African social worker and black nationalist leader; second wife of Nelson Mandela; in April 2003 she was sentenced to five years in prison on charges of fraud and theft from a women's political organization.

Peter (Benjamin) Mandelson (21 Oct 1953, London, England), British Labour politician, cabinet minister, and international official who was EU commissioner for trade from 23 Nov 2004.

Barry Manilow (Barry Alan Pincus; 17 Jun 1946, Brooklyn NY), American pop singer and songwriter.

Henning Mankell (3 Feb 1948, Härjedalen, Sweden), Swedish international best-selling detective novelist, the author of psychological mysteries featuring Swedish police officer Kurt Wallander.

John Manley (5 Jan 1950, Ottawa, ON, Canada), Canadian Liberal politician who became minister of foreign affairs in 2000 and minister of finance and deputy prime minister in 2002; in 2003, after Paul Martin became the Liberal Party leader, Manley announced his resignation from politics.

Michael Mann (1942?, Manchester, England), British-born sociologist and writer who was the author of the multivolume study *The Sources of Social Power* (1986, 1993, and 2006 [projected]).

Patrick (Augustus Merving) Manning (17 Aug 1946, San Fernando, Trinidad), Trinidadian politician and prime minister of Trinidad and Tobago, 1991–95 and again from 2001.

Preston Manning (10 Jun 1942, Edmonton, AB, Canada), Canadian politician and leader of the Reform Party.

Harvey C. Mansfield, Jr. (1932, New Haven CT), American political philosopher and professor of government at Harvard University; he was awarded a National Humanities Medal in 2004.

Sir Peter Mansfield (9 Oct 1933, London, England), British physicist and a pioneer of magnetic resonance imaging (MRI); he shared the 2003 Nobel

Prize for Physiology or Medicine with fellow MRI researcher Paul C. Lauterbur.

Marilyn Manson (Brian Hugh Warner; 5 Jan 1969, Canton OH), American shock-rock performer who styles himself the "Antichrist Superstar."

John H. Marburger III (1941?, Staten Island NY), American physicist who was presidential science adviser and head of the Office of Science and Technology Policy from 2001.

Guido de Marco (22 Jul 1931, Valletta, Malta), Maltese politician and president from 1999 to 4 Apr 2004.

Geoffrey W. Marcy (29 Sep 1954, St. Clair Shores MI), American astronomer; discoverer of planetary systems outside the solar system.

Brice Marden (15 Oct 1938, Bronxville NY), American painter and printmaker who combines the techniques of Abstract Expressionism with the philosophies of Minimalism.

Queen Margrethe II (Margrethe Alexandrine Thorhildur Ingrid; 16 Apr 1940, Copenhagen, Denmark), Danish royal, queen from 1972.

Maksim Marinin (23 Mar 1971, Volgograd, Russian SFSR, USSR [now in Russia]), Russian pairs figure skater who, with Tatyana Totmyanina, won the world championship in 2004.

Mariza (Mariza Nunes; 1974?, Mozambique), Portuguese fado singer.

Mary Ellen Mark (20 Mar 1940, Philadelphia PA), American photojournalist whose compelling, empathetic images document the lives of marginalized people in the US and other countries.

Andranik Markaryan (12 Jun 1951, Yerevan, Armenian SSR, USSR [now in Armenia]), Armenian politician and prime minister from 2000.

Svetozar Marovic (31 Mar 1955, Kotor, Montenegro, Yugoslavia), Serbian politician and president of Serbia and Montenegro from 2003.

Branford Marsalis (26 Aug 1960, Breaux Bridge LA), American jazz saxophonist and bandleader.

Wynton Marsalis (18 Oct 1961, New Orleans LA), American jazz trumpeter.

Yann Martel (1963, Spain), Spanish-born Canadian novelist whose *Life of Pi* won the 2002 Man Booker Prize.

Chris Martin (2 Mar 1977, Exeter, Devon, England), British rock vocalist, guitarist, and pianist (of Coldplay).

Paul Martin (28 Aug 1938, Windsor, ON, Canada), Canadian lawyer and businessman who succeeded Jean Chrétien as prime minister of Canada; Martin, who had headed a multinational shipping company and had also served as one of the most successful ministers of finance (1993–2002) in Canada's history, took office on 12 Dec 2003.

Steve Martin (14 Aug 1945, Waco TX), American comedic actor known for many popular films, including *The Jerk* (1979) and *Dirty Rotten Scoundrels* (1988); he has also written screenplays and stage plays, including *Picasso at the Lapin Agile* (1993), as well as books such as *Shopgirl* (2000).

Valerie (Metcalf) Martin (1948, Sedalia MO), American novelist whose *Property* won the 2003 Orange Prize for fiction.

Mel Martinez (Melquiades Rafael Martinez; 23 Oct 1946, Sagua la Grande, Cuba), Cuban-born American government official who served as US secretary of housing and urban development (2001–03) and Republican senator from Florida from 2005.

Tomás Eloy Martínez (16 Jul 1934, Tucumán, Argentina), Argentine writer and journalist, winner of the 2002 Alfaguara Prize for his novel *El vuelo de la reina*.

Peter Martins (27 Oct 1946, Copenhagen, Denmark), Danish dancer and choreographer known for his work with the New York City Ballet as principal dancer (1969), choreographer (1977), and ballet master in chief (from 1989).

Princess Masako (Masako Owada; 9 Dec 1963, Tokyo, Japan), Japanese royal, consort of Crown Prince Naruhito.

Master P (Percy Miller; 29 Apr 1970, New Orleans LA), American gangsta rap performer and producer.

Mary Matalin (19 Aug 1953, Chicago IL), American political commentator and activist; a conservative, she is famously married to liberal commentator James Carville.

Princess Mathilde (Mathilde d'Udekem d'Acoz; 21 Jan 1973, Uccle, Belgium), Belgian royal, the consort of Prince Philippe, and heir to the throne (married 4 Dec 1999).

Hideki Matsui (12 Jun 1974, Ishikawa prefecture, Japan), Japanese baseball outfielder known for his hitting; he led Japan's Central League in the 2002 season in home runs (50) and RBIs (107); he joined the New York Yankees in 2003.

Koichiro Matsuura (1937, Tokyo, Japan), Japanese international official who was director-general of UNESCO from 1999.

Dave Matthews (David John Matthews; 9 Jan 1967, Johannesburg, South Africa), South African–born American rock musician and songwriter; he is the leader of the Dave Matthews Band.

Princess Máxima (Máxima Zorreguieta Cerruti; 17 May 1971, Buenos Aires, Argentina), Argentine-born Dutch investment banker and consort of Crown Prince Willem-Alexander (married 2 Feb 2002).

Maxwell (23 May 1973, Brooklyn NY), American rhythm-and-blues and soul singer.

John (Dayton) Mayer (1979, Fairfield CT), American singer and songwriter who won a Grammy for best male pop vocalist in 2003.

Thom Mayne (19 Jan 1944, Waterbury CT), American architect, a cofounder (1972) of the architectural studio Morphosis, which specializes in schools and commercial buildings; Mayne won the Pritzker Prize in 2005.

Kiran Mazumdar-Shaw (1954?, Bangalore, India), Indian business executive and founder (1978) of Biocon India, India's first biotechnology company; known as the "Biotech Queen," she is India's richest woman.

Thabo (Mvuyelwa) Mbeki (18 Jun 1942, Idutywa, Transkei, South Africa), South African politician and president from 1999.

Mary Patricia McAleese (27 Jun 1951, Belfast, Northern Ireland), Irish politician and president from 1997.

Christian McBride (31 May 1972, Philadelphia PA), American jazz bassist.

Martina McBride (Martina Maria Schiff; 29 Jul 1966, Sharon KS), American country singer who was voted Country Music Association Female Vocalist of the Year in 1999 and 2002; she was also Academy of Country Music Top Female Vocalist, 2001.

John McCain (John Sidney McCain III; 29 Aug 1936, Panama Canal Zone), American Republican politician and senator from Arizona.

Theodore Edgar Cardinal McCarrick (7 Jul 1930, New York NY), American Roman Catholic churchman who was appointed archbishop of Newark NJ in

1986 and archbishop of Washington DC in 2000; he was named cardinal in 2000.

Chris McCarron (27 Mar 1955, Dorchester MA), American jockey who won the Kentucky Derby, Preakness Stakes, and Belmont Stakes each two times and who was the leading jockey in earnings in four seasons; he retired in 2002 and managed Santa Anita Racetrack.

Cormac McCarthy (Charles McCarthy, Jr.; 20 Jul 1933, Providence RI), American writer in the Southern gothic tradition whose novels about wayward characters in the rural American South and Southwest are noted for their dark violence.

Sir Paul McCartney (James Paul McCartney; 18 Jun 1942, Liverpool, England), British singer, songwriter, and member of the Beatles.

Stella (Nina) McCartney (13 Sep 1971, London, England), British fashion designer who gained fame at a young age as a designer for Chloé and for her own signature line.

Delbert McClinton (4 Nov 1940, Lubbock TX), American country-and-western singer and harmonica player, a pioneer of the Texas roots music revival.

Mitch McConnell (20 Feb 1942, Sheffield AL), American Republican politician, senator from Kentucky, and Senate majority whip from 2002.

Eric McCormack (18 Apr 1963, Toronto, ON, Canada), American TV actor who has played Will Truman on Will & Grace from 1998.

David McCullough (7 Jul 1933, Pittsburgh PA), American biographer and historian, the author of Truman (1992), John Adams (2001)—both of which won Pulitzer Prizes—and 1776, a best seller in 2005.

Audra (Ann) McDonald (3 Jul 1970, Berlin, Germany), American actress and singer on Broadway, on TV, and in classical music who received her fourth Tony Award in 2004 for her performance in A Raisin in the Sun.

Frances McDormand (23 Jun 1957, Chicago IL), American film actress of great versatility whose works include Fargo (1996, best actress Academy Award), Wonder Boys (2000), and Laurel Canyon (2003).

Malcolm McDowell (Malcolm Taylor; 13 Jun 1943, Leeds, England), British film actor especially known for his work in A Clockwork Orange (1971); in 2003 he was featured in The Company.

John McEnroe (John Patrick McEnroe, Jr.; 16 Feb 1959, Wiesbaden, West Germany [now in Germany]), American tennis player and TV sportscaster, a leading competitor in the late 1970s and the '80s; he won 154 professional matches, 77 in singles (including 7 Grand Slam events) and 77 in doubles (9 in Grand Slams) and was ranked in the top 10 for 10 years.

Reba McEntire (28 Mar 1954, McAlester OK), American country singer and TV and film actress.

Ian (Russell) McEwan (21 Jun 1948, Aldershot, England), British writer who won the Booker Prize in 1998 for Amsterdam; his best-selling ninth novel, Atonement (2001), was nominated for the Booker Prize and the International IMPAC Dublin Literary Award.

Daniel L. McFadden (29 Jul 1937, Raleigh NC), American economist who shared (with James J. Heckman) the 2000 Nobel Memorial Prize for Economic Science for work in solving problems of analysis of microdata.

Bobby McFerrin (11 Mar 1950, New York NY), American jazz and pop vocalist.

Patrick McGovern (1952?), American founder and chairman of International Data Group (IDG), a market-research and technology media company, and major philanthropist.

Phil McGraw (Phillip C. McGraw; "Dr. Phil"; 1 Sep 1950, Vinita OK), American talk-show host, author, and psychologist-educator who was the host of Dr. Phil (from 2002), a TV program on which he dispensed real solutions to real problems in his characteristic blunt but caring manner.

Tim McGraw (Samuel Timothy McGraw; 1 May 1967, Delhi LA), American country-and-western singer who numbered among his many awards the Country Music Association's male vocalist of the year in 1999, 2000, and 2001.

James E. McGreevey (6 Aug 1957, Jersey City NJ), American Democratic politician and governor of New Jersey from 2002 until 2004, when he announced that he was a homosexual and resigned.

Dalton McGuinty (19 Jul 1955, Ottawa, ON, Canada), Canadian Liberal politician and premier of Ontario from 2003.

Mark David McGwire (1 Oct 1963, Pomona CA), American baseball player considered one of the most powerful hitters in the history of the game; in 1998 he set a major league record for most home runs in a season (70), breaking Roger Maris's mark of 61, set in 1961; he retired in 2001 with 583 home runs, fifth on the all-time list.

Dan Peter McKenzie (21 Feb 1942, Cheltenham, England), British geophysicist; winner of the 2002 Crafoord Prize "for fundamental contributions to the understanding of the dynamics of the lithosphere, particularly plate tectonics, sedimentary basin formation and mantle melting."

Kevin McKenzie (29 Apr 1954, Burlington VT), American ballet dancer, choreographer, and director who danced with the American Ballet Theatre (1979–91) and became its artistic director in October 1992.

Don McKinnon (Donald Charles McKinnon; 27 Feb 1939, Greenwich, England), New Zealand international official and secretary-general of the Commonwealth from 2000.

Sarah McLachlan (28 Jan 1968, Halifax, NS, Canada), Canadian singer and songwriter; she was the organizer and headliner of the Lilith Fair, a traveling summer concert tour featuring female performers; her album Afterglow debuted in late 2003.

Beverley McLachlin (7 Sep 1943, Pincher Creek, AB, Canada), Canadian Supreme Court justice from 1989 and chief justice from 2000.

Vince McMahon (Vincent Kennedy McMahon, Jr.; 24 Aug 1945, Pinehurst NC), American wrestling promoter, owner of World Wrestling Entertainment, Inc., from 1982.

Larry McMurtry (3 Jun 1936, Wichita Falls TX), American writer noted for his novels set on the frontier, in contemporary small towns, and in increasingly urbanized and industrial areas of Texas.

Marian McPartland (Margaret Marian Turner; 20 Mar 1918, Slough, England), English-born jazz pianist and composer, host of Piano Jazz, a weekly music and talk show on America's National Public Radio (from 1978).

James M. McPherson (11 Oct 1936, Valley City ND), American historian of slavery and the antislavery movement whose work has been successful both among scholars and with the general public; he won the Pulitzer Prize in History for Battle Cry of Freedom: The Civil War Era (1988).

Alexander McQueen (Lee McQueen; 1969, London, England), British fashion designer known for his rebellious style and his bizarre, extravagant runway shows.

Ian McShane (29 Sep 1942, Blackburn, Lancashire, England), British film and TV actor who starred in the TV series *Lovejoy* (1986–94) and *Deadwood* (from 2004).

Russell (Charles) Means (10 Nov 1939, Pine Ridge SD), American Lakota Sioux activist who was a leader of the American Indian Movement (AIM); he is best known for leading a 71-day siege at Wounded Knee SD to focus attention on rights for Native Americans.

Péter Medgyessy (1942, Budapest, Hungary), Hungarian politician and prime minister from 2002 to 29 Sep 2004.

Brad Mehldau (23 Aug 1970, Jacksonville FL), American jazz pianist and composer.

Zubin Mehta (29 Apr 1936, Bombay [now Mumbai], British India), Indian-born orchestral conductor; he was music director of the Los Angeles Philharmonic, 1962–78, the New York Philharmonic, 1978–91, and the Israel Philharmonic from 1968.

Rafael Hipólito Mejía Domínguez (22 Feb 1941, Gurabo, Dominican Republic), Dominican politician and president of the Dominican Republic, 2000–04.

John Mellencamp (Johnny Cougar; John Cougar Mellencamp; 7 Oct 1951, Seymour IN), American singer-songwriter who became popular in the 1980s by creating basic, often folk-inflected hard rock and presenting himself as a champion of small-town values.

Sam Mendes (Samuel Alexander Mendes; 1 Aug 1965, Reading, England), British film director who won a best director Academy Award for *American Beauty* (1999).

Fradique de Menezes (1942), São Tomé and Príncipe politician; president of São Tomé and Príncipe from 2001 to 2003 and again from 23 Jul 2003.

Angela Merkel (Angela Dorothea Kasner; 17 Jul 1954, Hamburg, West Germany [now in Germany]), German politician; leader of the Christian Democratic Union and parliament leader.

W.S. Merwin (William Stanley Merwin; 30 Sep 1927, New York NY), American poet and translator known for the spare style of his poetry, in which he expressed his concerns about the alienation of humans from their environment; he won the 1971 Pulitzer Prize for Poetry for *The Carrier of Ladders* (1970) and the 1979 Bollingen Prize in Poetry.

Carlos (Diego) Mesa Gisbert (12 Aug 1953, La Paz, Bolivia), Bolivian historian and journalist who became president in 2003 after his predecessor, Gonzalo Sánchez de Lozada, was forced from office and fled the country; Mesa himself was forced out of office on 9 Jun 2005.

Matthew Stanley Meselson (24 May 1930, Denver CO), American molecular biologist who was the recipient of the 2004 Albert Lasker Special Achievement Award "for a lifetime career that combines penetrating discovery in molecular biology with creative leadership in the public policy of chemical and biological weapons."

Stipe Mesic (Stjepan Mesic; 24 Dec 1934, Orahovica, Yugoslavia [now in Croatia]), Croatian politician and president from 2000.

Jean-Marie Messier (13 Dec 1956, Grenoble, France), French corporate executive and chairman and CEO of Vivendi Universal, 1996–2002.

Debra Messing (15 Aug 1968, Brooklyn NY), American TV actress who plays Grace Adler on *Will & Grace* (from 1998) and won a best comedy actress Emmy for the role in 2003.

Tammy Faye Messner (Tammy Faye LaValley, previous married name Bakker; 7 Mar 1942, International Falls MN), American TV evangelist and personality.

Pat Metheny (12 Aug 1954, Lee's Summit MO), American jazz guitarist and bandleader.

Princess Mette-Marit (Mette-Marit Tjessem Høiby; 19 Aug 1973, Kristiansand, Norway), Norwegian royal, consort of Crown Prince Haakon of Norway.

Pierre de Meuron (8 May 1950, Basel, Switzerland), Swiss architect; cowinner, with Jacques Herzog, of the 2001 Pritzker Prize.

Michael (Michael Hohenzollern-Sigmaringen; ruled as Mihai I; 25 Oct 1921, Sinaia, Romania), Romanian king, 1927–30 (under regency) and 1940–47; he resides in Switzerland but his Romanian citizenship was restored in 1997.

Lorne Michaels (Lorne Michael Lipowitz; 17 Nov 1944, Toronto, ON, Canada), Canadian-born TV and film producer who was the originator and executive producer of TV's *Saturday Night Live* from its inception in 1975 (except for 1980–85) and executive producer of *Late Night with Conan O'Brien* from 1993; he received the 2004 Mark Twain Prize for American Humor at the John F. Kennedy Center for the Performing Arts in Washington DC.

Shaun Micheel (5 Jan 1970, Orlando FL), American professional golfer who won the PGA Championship in 2003; it was his first win on the PGA tour.

James (Alix) Michel (16 Aug 1944, Mahe Island, Seychelles), Seychelles politician and president from 14 Apr 2004.

Empress Michiko (Michiko Shoda; 20 Oct 1934, Tokyo, Japan), Japanese royal, consort of Emperor Akihito of Japan.

Thomas Middelhoff (11 May 1953, Düsseldorf, West Germany [now in Germany]), German corporate executive who was chairman and CEO of Bertelsmann AG, 1998–2002.

Midori (Midori Goto; 25 Oct 1971, Osaka, Japan), Japanese-born American violinist.

(Muhammad) Najib (Azmi) Mikati (24 Nov 1955, Tripoli, Lebanon), Lebanese businessman and Sunni politician who held various government positions before becoming prime minister on 19 Apr 2005.

Dennis Miller (3 Nov 1953, Pittsburgh PA), American TV comedian and writer; he was a member of the cast of TV's *Saturday Night Live* (1985–91) and hosted his own TV show (1994–2002, 2004–05).

(Samuel) Bode Miller (12 Oct 1977, Easton NH), American Alpine skier who took two silver medals at the 2002 Olympics and won the 2005 overall World Cup title, the first American to do so in 22 years.

Shannon (Lee) Miller (10 Mar 1977, Rolla MO), American gymnast who won five medals in the 1992 Summer Olympic Games and two more in the 1996 Games.

Slobodan Milosevic (29 Aug 1941, Pozarevac, Yugoslavia [now in Serbia and Montenegro]), Serbian nationalist leader, president of Serbia, 1989–97, and of Yugoslavia, 1997–2000.

Norman (Yoshio) Mineta (12 Nov 1931, San Jose CA), American government official, secretary of commerce, 2000–01, and secretary of transportation from 2001.

Ming-Na (Wen) (20 Nov 1963, Macau), Macanese-born American TV actress who appeared in *ER* (1995 and 2000–04).

Anthony Minghella (6 Jan 1954, Ryde, Isle of Wight, England), British film director and screenwriter who won an Academy Award for directing (*The English Patient*, 1996); his other films include *The Talented Mr. Ripley* (1999), and *Cold Mountain* (2003).

Ruth Ann Minner (17 Jan 1935, Milford DE), American Democratic politician and governor of Delaware from 2001.

Kylie (Ann) Minogue (28 May 1968, Melbourne, VIC, Australia), Australian actress and pop singer who was first noticed in Australia and Great Britain in a soap opera, *Neighbours*, in 1985–88, but left TV for a singing career; she was initially successful but her career sagged in the mid-1990s before she again rocketed to the top in the early 2000s.

Dame Helen Mirren (Ilyena Lydia Mironoff; 26 Jul 1945, Chiswick, London, England), British stage and film actress best known for the TV series *Prime Suspect*; she was knighted in 2003.

Rohinton Mistry (3 Jul 1952, Bombay [now Mumbai], India), Indian-born Canadian novelist whose stories are often set in metropolitan Mumbai and evoke the lives of lower-middle-class people of the Parsi community.

Andrea Mitchell (30 Oct 1946, New York NY), American TV foreign affairs correspondent.

Joni Mitchell (Roberta Joan Anderson; 7 Nov 1943, Fort MacLeod, AB, Canada), Canadian pop singer and songwriter.

Keith (Claudius) Mitchell (12 Nov 1946, Grenada), Grenadan politician and prime minister from 1995.

Lakshmi Mittal (15 Jun 1950, Sadulpur, Rajastan state, India), Indian-born British steel magnate and one of the richest men in the world; he is the owner of the LMN Group, the world's largest steel producer, and holder of a three-quarters interest in Ispat International; recently he has been working on a plan to merge these two companies with the International Steel Group in the US.

Issey Miyake (22 Apr 1938, Hiroshima, Japan), Japanese fashion designer whose creations are a blend of Eastern and Western elements.

Shigeru Miyamoto (16 Nov 1952, Sonobe, Kyoto prefecture, Japan), Japanese video game designer and corporate official at Nintendo; he is credited with designing many of the seminal video games such as Donkey Kong, the Mario Brothers titles, and the Legend of Zelda series.

Hayao Miyazaki (5 Jan 1941, Tokyo, Japan), Japanese animation film director whose *Sen to chihiro no kamikakushi* (2002; *Spirited Away*) captured the top prize at the Berlin Film Festival and was a surprise winner of the Academy Award for best animated feature film in 2003.

Jun'ichiro Miyazu, Japanese corporate executive and CEO of Nippon Telephone & Telegraph from 2002.

Isaac Mizrahi (14 Oct 1961, Brooklyn NY), American fashion designer and TV personality.

Benjamin (William) Mkapa (12 Nov 1938, Masasi, Tanganyika [now Tanzania]), Tanzanian politician and president from 1995.

Ratko Mladic (12 Mar 1943, Kalinovik village, Bosnia, Yugoslavia [now in Bosnia and Herzegovina]), Bosnian Serb military officer who led the Bosnian Serb army during the breakup of the Yugoslav Federation and who was sought as a war criminal in the 1990s and 2000s.

Phumzile Mlambo-Ngcuka (3 Nov 1955, Claremont,

Natal [now KwaZulu Natal] province, South Africa), South African politician and government official who was named deputy president by Pres. Thabo Mbeki on 22 Jun 2005; she is the first woman to hold such a high post in South Africa.

Festus (Gontebanye) Mogae (23 Jul 1939, Kanye, Botswana), Botswanan politician and president from 1998.

Alfred (Spiro) Moisiu (1 Dec 1929, Shkodër, Albania), Albanian military engineer, goverment official, and president from 2002.

N(avarre) Scott Momaday (27 Feb 1934, Lawton OK), American author of many works centered on his Kiowa heritage.

Jane Monheit (3 Nov 1977, Oakdale, Long Island NY), American jazz singer.

Meredith (Jane) Monk (20 Nov 1942, Lima, Peru), American performance artist, a pioneer in the avant-garde, whose work skillfully integrates diverse disciplines and media, including singing, film-making, choreography, and acting.

Tim Montgomery (25 Jan 1975, Gaffney SC), American sprinter who set a world record for the 100 m, 9.78 sec, at the IAAF Grand Prix final in Paris on 14 Sep 2002.

Sir Mark Moody-Stuart (1941, Antigua, West Indies), British corporate executive and CEO of the Royal Dutch/Shell Group (UK).

Moon Shin Yong (1 Apr 1948, Kongju, South Korea), Korean professor of obstetrics and specialist of in vitro fertilization at Seoul National University; he and Woo Suk Hwang successfully cloned the first human embryo in February 2004.

Alan Moore (18 Nov 1953), British author and creator of graphic novels (comic books), such as the *Watchmen* series (1987), with intellectual, adult-oriented content.

Julianne Moore (Julie Anne Smith; 3 Dec 1960, Fayetteville NC), American film actress whose recent works include *Magnolia* (1999), *Far from Heaven* (2002), *The Hours* (2002), and *Laws of Attraction* (2004).

Lorrie Moore (Marie Lorena Moore; 13 Jan 1957, Glens Falls NY), American short story writer and novelist; she was the recipient of the 2005 PEN/Malamud Award for Short Fiction.

Mandy Moore (Amanda Leigh Moore; 10 Apr 1984, Nashua NH), American pop singer and actress.

Michael Moore (23 Apr 1954, Davison MI), American film director and author; his book *Stupid White Men ... and Other Sorry Excuses for the State of the Nation!* (2002) topped the nonfiction best-seller lists in 2002, and his film *Bowling for Columbine* won an Academy Award for best documentary in 2003; his film *Fahrenheit 9/11*, an exposé of the US government's handling of the terrorist attacks of 11 Sep 2001, broke box-office records when it opened in June 2004.

Jason Moran (21 Jan 1975, Houston TX), American jazz pianist and bandleader who was named *Downbeat Magazine*'s jazz artist rising star in 2003.

Airto Moreira (5 Aug 1941, Itaiopolis, Santa Catarina state, Brazil), Brazilian jazz percussionist.

Luis Moreno Ocampo (4 Jun 1952, Buenos Aires, Argentina), Argentine lawyer who in 2003 became the first chief prosecutor of the International Criminal Court, based in The Hague.

Rhodri Morgan (29 Sep 1939, Cardiff, Wales), Welsh Labour politician and first minister of Wales from 2000.

Yasumasa Morimura (1951, Osaka, Japan), Japanese photographer especially known for his large-scale self-portraits.

Alanis Morissette (1 Jun 1974, Ottawa, ON, Canada), Canadian-born American pop singer and songwriter.

Mark Morris (29 Aug 1956, Seattle WA), American dancer and leading choreographer for several international dance companies; he founded the Mark Morris Dance Group in 1980.

Toni Morrison (Chloe Anthony Wofford; 18 Feb 1931, Lorain OH), American novelist noted for her examination of black experience (particularly black female experience) within the African American community; she won the 1993 Nobel Prize for Literature.

Viggo (Peter) Mortensen (20 Oct 1958, New York NY), American film actor who portrayed Aragorn in the three *Lord of the Rings* films (2001–03) and starred in *Hidalgo* (2004).

Mireya Elisa Moscoso de Gruber (1 Jul 1946, Pedasi, Panama), Panamanian politician of the Arnulfista party and president, 1999–2004.

Walter Mosley (12 Jan 1952, Los Angeles CA), American writer of science fiction and mystery novels interwoven with a progressive voice on social matters; he is best known for his *Easy Rawlins* mystery series, as in *Little Scarlet* (2004).

Kate Moss (16 Jan 1974, Croydon, Surrey, England), British fashion model known for her work for Calvin Klein and for introducing the "waif" look to fashion.

Andrew Motion (26 Oct 1952, London, England), English poet, teacher, editor, and biographer; poet laureate of England from 1999; his biography of Philip Larkin won the 1994 Whitbread Prize.

Bill Moyers (Billy Don Moyers; 5 Jun 1934, Hugo OK), American TV journalist, government official, and author.

Ms. Dynamite (Niomi McLean-Daley; 1982, London, England), British rhythm-and-blues singer, the first black female artist to win a Mercury Music Prize (2002); she also won the 2003 Brit Award for female solo artist.

King Mswati III (19 Apr 1968, Swaziland), Swazi royal; king of Swaziland from 1986.

Cándido Muatetema Rivas (1961, Equatorial Guinea?), Equatorial Guinean politician and prime minister from 2001 to 14 Jun 2004.

(Muhammed) Hosni Mubarak (4 May 1928, Al-Minufiyah governorate, Egypt), Egyptian politician and president from 1981.

Lisel Mueller (Lisel Neumann; 8 Feb 1924, Hamburg, Germany), German-born American poet who won the 1997 Pulitzer Prize for Poetry for her collection *Alive Together: New and Selected Poems*.

Robert S(wan) Mueller III (7 Aug 1944, New York NY), American government official who was FBI director from 2001.

Robert (Gabriel) Mugabe (21 Feb 1924, Kutama, Southern Rhodesia [now Zimbabwe]), Zimbabwean politician; he was the first prime minister (1980–87) of the reconstituted state of Zimbabwe and president from 1987.

Thierry Mugler (1948, Strasbourg, France), French fashion designer known for his varied, innovative style and theatrical fashion shows.

King Muhammad VI (Muhammad ibn al-Hassan; 21 Aug 1963, Rabat, Morocco), Moroccan king from 1999.

Paul Muldoon (20 Jun 1951, Portadown, Northern Ireland), Irish-born American poet known for his ingenious verses and flashy wordplay that left read-

ers at once amused and unsettled; he won the Pulitzer Prize for Poetry and the Canadian Griffin Poetry Prize for an international writer for his collection *Moy Sand and Gravel* (2002).

Marcia Muller (28 Sep 1944, Detroit MI), American mystery writer; author of a series of novels (from 1977) featuring a female detective, Sharon McCone.

Viktoria Mullova (27 Nov 1959, Moscow, USSR [now in Russia]), Russian-born violinist who specialized in chamber music and founded (1994) the Mullova Chamber Ensemble but has explored music ranging from Baroque to modern jazz.

Bakili Muluzi (17 Mar 1943, Machinga, Nyasaland [now Malawi]), Malawian politician and president from 1994 to 24 May 2004.

Alice Munro (10 Jul 1931, Wingham, ON, Canada), Canadian short-story writer who gained international recognition with her exquisitely drawn stories, usually set in southwestern Ontario, peopled by characters of Scotch-Irish stock.

Takashi Murakami (1962, Tokyo, Japan), Japanese artist trained in the classic Nihon-ga style who shifted his focus to contemporary art and a mixture of Eastern and Western styles, drawing heavily on decorative arts and animé; he is the leader of the "superflat" movement.

Muttiah Muralitharan (17 Apr 1972, Kandy, Sri Lanka), Sri Lankan cricket spin bowler who was the third cricketer in history to take 450 Test wickets.

(Keith) Rupert Murdoch (11 Mar 1931, Melbourne, VIC, Australia), Australian-born British newspaper publisher and media entrepreneur, founder and head of the global media holding company the News Corporation Ltd., which governed News Limited (Australia), News International (UK), and News America Holdings Inc. (US).

Frank Hughes Murkowski (28 Mar 1933, Seattle WA), American politician, four-term senator, and governor of Alaska from 2002.

Eddie Murphy (3 Apr 1961, Brooklyn NY), American comedian and film actor first famous from his work on TV's *Saturday Night Live* (1980–84) and later a string of highly successful film comedies, including the *Beverly Hills Cop* (1984 and 1987) and *Nutty Professor* (1996 and 2000) series.

Cormac Cardinal Murphy-O'Connor (24 Aug 1932, Reading, Berkshire, England), British church leader; archbishop of Westminster (leader of the Roman Catholic church in the UK) from 2000; he was named cardinal in 2001.

Bill Murray (21 Sep 1950, Wilmette IL), American comedian and film actor known for eccentric characterizations; he was a cast member of TV's *Saturday Night Live* (1977–80); his films include *Caddyshack* (1980), *What About Bob?* (1991), *Rushmore* (1998), *Lost in Translation* (2003), and *Broken Flowers* (2005).

Said Wilbert Musa (19 Mar 1944, San Ignacio, British Honduras [now Belize]), Belizean politician and prime minister from 1998.

Yoweri (Kaguta) Museveni (15 Aug 1944, Mbarra district, Uganda), Ugandan politician and president from 1986.

Ronnie Musgrove (29 Jul 1956, Tocowa MS), American Democratic politician and governor of Mississippi, 2000–04.

Pervez Musharraf (11 Aug 1943, New Delhi, British India), Pakistani military leader and politician; he was head of Pakistan's government, 1999–2001, and president from 2001.

Riccardo Muti (28 Jul 1941, Naples, Italy), Italian conductor of both opera and the symphonic repertory; he has held the posts of music director of the Philadelphia Orchestra (1980–92) and principal conductor of La Scala Orchestra in Milan (from 1987).

Halil Mutlu (Huben Hubenov; "Little Dynamo"; 14 Jul 1973, Postnik, Bulgaria), Bulgarian-born Turkish weightlifter in the 54/56-kg class who has set more than 20 world records during his career; he was a gold medalist at the 1999 and 2003 world championships, the 2000 European championships, and the 1996, 2000, and 2004 Olympic Games.

Anne-Sophie Mutter (29 Jun 1963, Rheinfelden, West Germany [now in Germany]), German violinist known for her striking onstage appearance, impeccable technique, and idiosyncratic interpretations of the standard repertoire.

Levy Patrick Mwanawasa (3 Sep 1948, Mufulira, Southern Rhodesia [now Zambia]), Zambian politician and president from 2002.

Mike Myers (25 May 1963, Scarborough, ON, Canada), Canadian comedian and actor famous for offbeat comedy; he is best known as a member of the cast of TV's *Saturday Night Live* (1989–95) and for his starring role in the *Austin Powers* film series (1997, 1999, and 2002).

Richard B. Myers (1 Mar 1942, Kansas City MO), American military official, general in the US Air Force, and chairman of the Joint Chiefs of Staff from 2001 until his retirement in September 2005.

Youssou N'Dour (1 Oct 1959, Dakar, French West Africa [now in Senegal]), Senegalese singer and songwriter.

James Nachtwey (14 Mar 1948, Syracuse NY), American photojournalist known especially for his award-winning work typically in zones of war and other turmoil.

Ralph Nader (27 Feb 1934, Winsted CT), American social activist and politician; he was a presidential candidate in 2000 and 2004.

Makoto Nagao (4 Oct 1936, Mie prefecture, Japan), Japanese information scientist and specialist in machine translation of languages; he was awarded the 2005 Japan Prize in Information and Communications Technology for his "pioneering contributions to natural language processing and intelligent image processing."

Thomas Nagel (4 Jul 1937, Belgrade, Yugoslavia [now in Serbia and Montenegro]), American philosopher and writer whose range of interests includes political philosophy, ethics, epistemology, and philosophy of mind; in addition to his professional work, Nagel is the author of many books on real-world problems.

Parminder K. Nagra (5 Oct 1975, Leicester, Leicestershire, England), British film and TV actress who attracted attention with her lead role in *Bend It Like Beckham* (2002) and went on to join the cast of TV's *ER* in 2003.

V.S. Naipaul (Vidiadhar Surajprasad Naipaul; 17 Aug 1932, Chaguanas, Trinidad), Trinidadian-born British writer known for his pessimistic novels concerned with exile and alienation among postcolonial peoples; he won the 1971 Booker Prize for *In a Free State* and the 2001 Nobel Prize for Literature.

Mira Nair (15 Oct 1957, Bhubaneshwar, Orissa state, India), Indian film director and screenwriter known for controversial documentary and feature films; her works include *Kama Sutra: A Tale of Love* (1996), *Monsoon Wedding* (2001), and *Vanity Fair* (2004).

Fatos Nano (16 Sep 1952, Tirana, Albania), Albanian politician who was prime minister in 1991, 1997–98, and again from 2002.

Janet Napolitano (29 Nov 1957, New York NY), American Democratic politician and governor of Arizona from 2003.

Yoshitomo Nara (1959, Hirosaki, Japan), Japanese graphic artist, a major figure in the "superflat" movement of the 1990s and 2000s.

Murthy Narayana (20 Aug 1946, Karnataka state, British India), Indian international business executive and pioneer in India's high-tech industry; he was cofounder and CEO of Infosys Technologies Ltd., a technology and consulting firm.

Robert Louis Nardelli (17 May 1948, Old Forge PA), American corporate executive and CEO of The Home Depot, Inc., from 2000.

Crown Prince Naruhito (23 Feb 1960, Tokyo, Japan), Japanese royal and heir to the throne.

Milton Nascimento (1942, Rio de Janeiro, Brazil), Brazilian pop singer and songwriter.

Taslima Nasrin (25 Aug 1962, Mymensingh, Bangladesh), Bangladeshi Islamic feminist writer.

Adrian Nastase (22 Jun 1950, Bucharest, Romania), Romanian politician and prime minister from 2000 to 21 Dec 2004.

S.R. Nathan (Sellapan Ramanathan Nathan; 3 Jul 1924, Singapore?), Singaporean diplomat and president (from 1999).

Bruce (Lee) Nauman (1941, Fort Wayne IN), American sculptor and installation and performance artist.

Tatyana Navka (13 Apr 1975, Dnepropetrovsk, Ukrainian SSR, USSR [now Dnipropetrovsk, Ukraine]), Russian ice dancer who, with her partner, Roman Kostomarov, won the 2004 world championship.

Nursultan Nazarbayev (6 Jul 1940, Chemolgan, Kazakh SSR, USSR [now Kazakhstan]), Kazakh statesman and president of Kazakhstan from 1990.

Domitien Ndayizeye (2 May 1953, Murango, Belgian Ruanda-Urundi [now in Burundi]), Burundian Hutu politician and president of the transitional government of Burundi from 2003.

Liam Neeson (William Neeson; 7 Jun 1952, Ballymena, Northern Ireland), British film actor respected for his lead roles in *Schindler's List* (1993) and *Kinsey* (2004).

John D(imitri) Negroponte (21 Jul 1939, London, England), British-born American diplomat, US representative to the United Nations 2001–04, and US ambassador to Iraq from June 2004; he was appointed the first director of national intelligence on 17 Feb 2005.

Nelly (Cornell Haynes, Jr.; 2 Nov 1978, Austin TX), American rap artist.

Willie (Hugh) Nelson (30 Apr 1933, Fort Worth TX), American songwriter and guitarist, one of the most popular country-music performers of the late 20th century.

Silje Nergaard (1969?, Norway), Norwegian jazz singer and songwriter.

Nerses Bedros XIX (Boutros Tarmouni; 17 Jan 1940, Cairo, Egypt), Armenian churchman and patriarch of the Catholic Armenians from 1999.

Anna Netrebko (18 Sep 1971, Krasnodar, Russian SFSR, USSR [now Russia]), Russian operatic soprano.

Randy Newman (Randall Stuart Newman; 28 Nov 1943, Los Angeles CA), American composer, songwriter, singer, and pianist whose character-driven, ironic, and often humorous compositions won him a cult audience and praise from critics.

(Carson) Wayne Newton (3 Apr 1942, Roanoke VA), American pop singer.

Teodoro Obiang Nguema Mbasogo (1942, Acoacan, Río Muni [now Equatorial Guinea]), Equatorial Guinean politician and president of Equatorial Guinea from 1979.

Ngugi wa Thiong'o (James Thiong'o Ngugi; 5 Jan 1938, Limuru, Kenya), Kenyan author and East Africa's leading novelist, whose popular *Weep Not, Child* (1964) was the first major novel in English by an East African; as he became sensitized to the effects of colonialism in Africa, he adopted his traditional name and wrote in the Bantu language of Kenya's Kikuyu people.

Mike Nichols (Michael Igor Peschkowsky; 6 Nov 1931, Berlin, Germany), American film and stage director whose productions focus on the absurdities and horrors of modern life as revealed in personal relationships; he won a best director Academy Award for *The Graduate* (1967), was awarded the NEA's National Medal of the Arts in 2001, received a Kennedy Center Honor in 2003, and won a Tony in 2005 for directing *Monty Python's Spamalot*.

Jim Nicholson (R. James Nicholson; 4 Feb 1938, near Struble IA), American army officer and lawyer who served as chairman of the Republican National Committee, 1997–2000; ambassador to the Vatican, 2001–04; and secretary of veterans affairs from 1 Feb 2005.

Uichiro Niwa (c. 1941, Aichi prefecture, Japan), Japanese corporate executive who was CEO and president of Itochu Corp. from 1998.

Saparmurad Niyazov ("Turkmenbashi"; 19 Feb 1940, Kipchak, near Ashkhabad [now Ashgabat], Turkmen SSR, USSR [now in Turkmenistan]), Turkmenistani politician and autocratic president from 1990 and through the time during which Turkmenistan quit the Soviet Union).

Christopher (Jonathan James) Nolan (30 Jul 1970, London, England), British film director known for his psychologically challenging pictures *Following* (1998), *Memento* (2000), and *Insomnia* (2002).

Donald A. Norman (25 Dec 1935, New York NY), American cognitive scientist specializing in problems of systems and design; he is an advocate of human-centered design who helps companies make products that appeal to the emotions as well as to reason; Norman is cofounder of the Nielsen Norman Group, an executive consulting firm that helps companies produce human-centered products and services, and a professor of computer science, psychology, and cognitive science at Northwestern University.

Norodom Sihamoni (14 May 1953, Phnom Penh, Cambodia), Cambodian royal trained in classical dance and filmmaking; he was crowned king on 14 Oct 2004 following the abdication of his father, King Norodom Sihanouk.

Prince Norodom Sihanouk (Preah Baht Samdach Preah Norodom Sihanuk Varman; 31 Oct 1922, Phnom Penh, Cambodia), Cambodian king from 1941 to 1955 and again 1993–2004; he was head of state 1960–70 and again in 1991–93.

Elwood "Woody" Norris (1942?), American inventor of HyperSonic Sound, a device to focus sound waves, the AirScooter, a personal helicopter, and other devices; he won the 2005 Lemelson–Massachusetts Institute of Technology prize.

Gale Norton (11 Mar 1954, Wichita KS), American government official; US secretary of the interior from 2001.

Deborah Norville (8 Aug 1958, Dalton GA), American TV anchor on NBC's *Today* show (1989–91), ABC's *Inside Edition* (1995–), and MSNBC's *Deborah Norville Tonight* (2004–05).

Kessai H. Note (1950, Ailinglaplap atoll, Marshall Islands), Marshallese politician and president from 2000.

Richard C. Notebaert (1948?, Montreal, QC, Canada), Canadian-born corporate executive; he was chairman and CEO of Ameritech Corp., 1993–99, and of Qwest Communications International Inc. from 2002.

Dries van Noten (1958, Antwerp, Belgium), Belgian fashion designer who mixes opposing elements, such as classic and contemporary, within a single creation.

Chris Noth (13 Nov 1954, Madison WI), American film and TV actor most recognized for his roles on *Law & Order* (1990–95) and *Sex and the City* (1998–2004).

Lynn Nottage (1971?, Brooklyn NY), American playwright whose works include *Por'knockers* (1994), *Crumbs from the Table of Joy* (1998), and *Intimate Apparel* (2003); she received the 2004 PEN/Laura Pels Foundation Award for Drama.

Robert Novak (26 Feb 1931, Joliet IL), American newspaper and TV journalist.

Antonia Novello (Antonia Coello; 23 Aug 1944, Fajardo, Puerto Rico), American physician and public official; the first woman and the first Hispanic to serve as surgeon general of the US (1990–93).

Sam Nujoma (Samuel Daniel Shafiishuna Nujoma; 12 May 1929, Owambo, South West Africa [now Namibia]), Namibian independence leader and president from 1990 to 21 Mar 2005.

Khin Nyunt (11 Oct 1939, Kyauktan, Burma [now Myanmar]), Burmese army intelligence officer and prime minister from 2003.

Conan O'Brien (18 Apr 1963, Brookline MA), American TV personality; host of *Late Night with Conan O'Brien* (from 1993).

Ed O'Brien (Edward John O'Brien; 15 Apr 1968, Oxford, England), British rock guitarist and member of the pioneering band Radiohead.

Mark O'Connor (5 Aug 1961, Seattle WA), American country fiddle player.

Sandra Day O'Connor (26 Mar 1930, El Paso TX), American jurist and associate justice of the US Supreme Court from 1981 to 2005, the first woman appointed to the court; on 1 Jul 2005 she announced her retirement, immediately setting off a storm of speculation about whom the president might nominate to replace this justice who had cast the decisive vote in so many high court rulings during her tenure.

Rosie O'Donnell (Rosanne O'Donnell; 21 Mar 1962, Commack NY), American TV personality; host of *The Rosie O'Donnell Show,* 1996–2002; in February 2004 she and her partner, along with thousands of other same-sex couples, were married in San Francisco.

Sean (Charles) O'Keefe (27 Jan 1956, Monterey CA), American public official who served as secretary of the navy under Pres. George H.W. Bush and as the 10th administrator of NASA, 2001–05.

Sean Patrick O'Malley (29 Jun 1944, Lakewood OH), American Roman Catholic churchman who was archbishop of Boston from 2003.

Shaquille (Rashaun) O'Neal (6 Mar 1972, Newark NJ), American professional basketball center who led the Los Angeles Lakers to NBA titles in 2000, 2001, and 2002; he was only the third player in history to be named MVP of the regular season, the all-star game, and the finals in the same season (1999–2000).

Bill O'Reilly (William James O'Reilly, Jr.; 10 Sep 1949, New York NY), American TV journalist and talk-show host; executive producer and anchorman of *The O'Reilly Factor* on cable TV's Fox News Channel from 1996; he is also the author of several books, including the best-selling *Who's Looking Out for You?* (2003).

David J. O'Reilly (January 1947, Dublin, Ireland), Irish-born American corporate executive who was chairman and CEO of ChevronTexaco Corp. from 2001.

P.J. O'Rourke (Patrick Jake O'Rourke; 14 Nov 1947, Toledo OH), American political satirist.

Peter (Seamus) O'Toole (2 Aug 1932, Connemara, County Galway, Ireland), British stage and film actor of great range famous for Shakespearean roles and the film *Lawrence of Arabia* (1962).

Joyce Carol Oates (16 Jun 1938, Lockport NY), American novelist, short-story writer, and essayist noted for her depictions of violence and evil in modern society.

Thoraya Obaid (2 Mar 1945, Baghdad, Iraq), Iraqi-born Saudi Arabian civil servant who was executive director of the UN Population Fund from 2001.

Barack Obama (4 Aug 1961, Honolulu HI), American Democratic politician and senator from Illinois from 2005.

Olusegun Obasanjo (5 Mar 1937, Abeokuta, Nigeria), Nigerian military leader and politician and president from 1999.

Piermaria J. Oddone (26 Mar 1944, Arequipa, Peru), Peruvian-born American experimental particle physicist and administrator; he was director of the Fermi National Accelerator Laboratory, Batavia IL, from 1 Jul 2005.

David Oddson (17 Jan 1948, Reykjavík, Iceland), Icelandic politician and prime minister from 1991 to 15 Sep 2004.

Kenzaburo Oe (31 Jan 1935, Ose, Ehime prefecture, Japan), Japanese novelist whose works express the disillusionment and rebellion of his post-World War II generation; he won the 1994 Nobel Prize for Literature.

Sadaharu Oh (20 May 1940, Tokyo, Japan), Japanese baseball player who holds the world record for most professional career home runs (868) and holds the Japanese single-season home-run record (55).

Paul Okalik (26 May 1964, Pangnirtung, NWT [now in Nunavut], Canada), Canadian politician and premier of Nunavut from 1999.

Claes (Thure) Oldenburg (28 Jan 1929, Stockholm, Sweden), Swedish-born Pop-art sculptor, best known for his giant soft sculptures of everyday objects.

Sharon Olds (19 Nov 1942, San Francisco CA), American poet best known for her powerful, often erotic, imagery of the body and her examination of her family.

Jamie Oliver (27 May 1975, Essex, England), British chef and TV personality who is known by the title of his TV program, *The Naked Chef,* and for his hip, down-to-earth, and fun style of food preparation.

Ashley (Fuller) and **Mary-Kate Olsen** (13 Jun 1986, Sherman Oaks CA), American twin child stars and a marketing phenomenon in modeling, films, TV, and music videos.

Omarion (Omari Ishmael Grandberry; 12 Nov 1984, Los Angeles CA), American soul-pop singer, originally of the group B2K but beginning in 2005 also a successful solo act.

(Philip) Michael Ondaatje (12 Sep 1943, Colombo, Ceylon [now Sri Lanka]), Canadian novelist and poet whose musical prose and poetry are created from a blend of myth, history, jazz, memoir, and other forms; he was a cowinner of the 1992 Booker Prize for *The English Patient.*

Ong Keng Yong (1954), Singaporean diplomat and international official, secretary general of the Association of Southeast Asian Nations from 6 Jan 2003.

Makoto Ooka (16 Feb 1931, Mishima, Shizuoka prefecture, Japan), Japanese poet and literary critic, a prolific writer largely responsible for bringing contemporary Japanese poetry to the attention of the Western world.

Suze Orman (5 Jun 1951, Chicago IL), American financial adviser and best-selling author.

Amancio Ortega (March 1936, León, Spain), Spanish fashion and textile tycoon; reportedly one of Europe's richest men.

Yury (Sergeyevich) Osipov (7 Jul 1936, Tobolsk, Russian SFSR, USSR [now Russia]), Russian mathematician and computer scientist and president of the Russian Academy of Sciences from 1991.

Joel Osteen (5 Mar 1963, Houston TX), American evangelist who in 1999 took over as head of the Lakewood Church in Houston, which, with weekly attendance estimated at 30,000, is one of the largest congregations in the US; the church broadcasts on TV and is active in foreign missions as well.

Albert Osterhaus (1949?, The Netherlands), Dutch virologist famed for his knack for isolating and identifying pathogenic human and animal viruses, including, in March–April 2003, the SARS (severe acute respiratory syndrome) virus.

Anne Sofie von Otter (9 May 1955, Stockholm, Sweden), Swedish operatic mezzo-soprano.

Ahmed Ouyahia (2 Jul 1952, Bouadnane, Algeria), Algerian politician who was prime minister, 1995–98 and again from 2003.

Michael Ovitz (14 Dec 1946, Encino CA), American entertainment executive; cofounder of the Creative Artists Agency (1975).

Bill Owens (22 Oct 1950, Fort Worth TX), American Republican politician and governor of Colorado from 1999.

Carol Owens (4 Jun 1971, Melbourne, VIC, Australia), Australian-born New Zealand squash player who won the World Open championships in 2000 and 2003; she retired in early 2004.

Amos Oz (4 May 1939, Jerusalem, British mandate of Palestine), Israeli novelist, short-story writer, and essayist.

Cynthia Ozick (17 Apr 1928, New York NY), American novelist, short story writer, and playwright.

Makoto Ozone (25 Mar 1961, Kobe, Japan), Japanese jazz pianist known for his performances with vibraphonist Gary Burton as well as his solo work.

Peter Pace (1945, Brooklyn NY), American military officer, a general in the US Marine Corps, who was named chairman of the Joint Chiefs of Staff from 1 Oct 2005.

Rajendra K. Pachauri (20 Aug 1940, Nainital, Uttar Pradesh [now in Uttaranchal] state, British India), Indian businessman and head of the Intergovernmental Panel on Climate Change from 2002.

Abel Pacheco de la Espriella (22 Dec 1933, San José, Costa Rica), Costa Rican politician and president from 2002.

Al Pacino (Alfredo James Pacino; 25 Apr 1940, New York NY), American film actor known for intense, explosive roles; he won an Academy Award for best actor for *Scent of a Woman* (1992) and was hailed for his portrayal of Shylock in *The Merchant of Venice* (2004).

Lawrence Page (1972, East Lansing MI), American computer scientist and Internet entrepreneur who cofounded (with Sergey Brin) in September 1998 the Google Internet search engine; he was the founding CEO and in 2001 became Google, Inc.'s president of products.

Roderick R. Paige (17 Jun 1933, Monticello MS), American government official and secretary of education (2001–05).

Nam June Paik (20 Jul 1932, Seoul, Korea [now in South Korea]), Korean-born German sculptor and performance artist who is called the father of video art.

Michael Palin (5 May 1943, Sheffield, Yorkshire, England), British comedian and film and TV actor; a founding member of the Monty Python comedy troupe.

Eddie Palmieri (15 Dec 1936, New York NY), American jazz-salsa pianist.

Samuel J. Palmisano (29 Jul 1951), American corporate executive, who was president and CEO of the International Business Machines (IBM) Corp. from 2002.

Gwyneth Paltrow (28 Sep 1972, Los Angeles CA), American film and stage actress who gained a best actress Academy Award in 1998 for the film *Shakespeare in Love.*

Orhan Pamuk (7 Jun 1952, Istanbul, Turkey), Turkish novelist, a prizewinning and best-selling author in his own country and abroad; his works include *Benim adim kirmizi* (1998; *My Name Is Red* [2001]), a historical murder mystery, and *Kar* (2002; *Snow* [2004]).

Supachai Panitchpakdi (30 May 1946, Bangkok, Thailand), Thai financial official, politician, and statesman who was named director-general of the World Trade Organization in 2002.

Queen Paola (Paola dei Principi Ruffo di Calabria; 11 Sep 1937, Forte dei Marmi, Italy), Italian-born Belgian queen consort of King Albert II (married 2 Jul 1959).

Tassos Papadopoulos (7 Jan 1934, Nicosia, Cyprus), Cypriot lawyer, politician, and government official who was president of the Republic of Cyprus from 2003.

Karolos Papoulias (4 Jun 1929, Ioannina, Greece), Greek PASOK politician and government minister who served as president from 12 Mar 2005.

Anna (Helene) Paquin (24 Jul 1982, Winnipeg, MB, Canada), New Zealand film actress whose work includes *The Piano* (1993; Academy Award), *Jane Eyre* (1996), *Fly Away Home* (1996), and *X2* (2003).

Sara Paretsky (8 Jun 1947, Ames IA), American mystery writer who created the detective Victoria Iphigenia Warshawski.

Sir Alan (William) Parker (14 Feb 1944, Islington, London, England), British advertising copywriter and film director whose movie credits include *Evita* (1996) and *Angela's Ashes* (1999).

Eugene N(ewman) Parker (10 Jun 1927, Houghton MI), American physicist and astronomer who was awarded the 2003 Kyoto Prize in the basic science section for his prediction of the existence of the solar wind; he received a National Medal of Science in 1989.

Mary-Louise Parker (2 Aug 1964, Fort Jackson SC), American actress successful in equal measure on stage (*Proof* [2001], Tony Award), in film (*Fried Green Tomatoes* [1991]), and on TV (*Angels in America* [2003]).

Sarah Jessica Parker (25 Mar 1965, Nelsonville OH), American TV and film actress and model popular since the 1980s; she reestablished her reputation as star of TV's *Sex and the City* (1998–2004).

Trey Parker (Randolph Severn Parker III; 19 Oct 1969, Conifer CO), American animator and cocreator (with Matt Stone) of *South Park,* an animated TV show.

Bradford W. Parkinson (1935, Wisconsin), American aerospace engineer and developer of the NAVSTAR global positioning system; he was the corecipient (with Ivan A. Getting) of the 2003 Charles Stark Draper Prize of the National Academy of Engineering.

Suzan-Lori Parks (10 May 1963, Fort Knox KY), American playwright who won a MacArthur Foundation grant in 2001 and the Pulitzer Prize for Drama in 2002 for *Topdog/Underdog.*

Jiri Paroubek (21 Aug 1952, Olomouc, Czechoslovakia [now in Czech Republic]), Czech politician of the Czech Social Democratic Party who was prime minister from 25 Apr 2005.

Richard D(ean) Parsons (4 Apr 1949, Bedford-Stuyvesant, Brooklyn NY), American corporate executive, CEO of AOL Time Warner from 2002, and chairman from May 2003.

Timothy (Richard) Parsons (1 Nov 1932, Colombo, Ceylon [now Sri Lanka]), Canadian oceanographer who won the 2001 Japan Prize for his work in fisheries management.

Arvo Pärt (11 Sep 1935, Paide, Estonia), Estonian composer whose works display a simplicity and a medieval liturgical sound.

Dolly (Rebecca) Parton (19 Jan 1946, Locust Ridge TN), American country-and-western singer, songwriter, and actress; she won country-music awards frequently in the 1970s and '80s; in 2004 she received the US Library of Congress's Living Legend award.

Juhan Parts (27 Aug 1966, Tallinn, Estonian SSR, USSR [now in Estonia]), Estonian politician and prime minister from 2003 to 24 Mar 2005.

Amy Pascal (1959, Los Angeles CA), American film executive; president of Turner Pictures from 1994 and, from Turner's merger in 1996 with Time Warner, president of Sony Corp.'s Columbia Pictures; she was named *Variety* magazine's Showman of the Year in 2002.

George E. Pataki (24 Jun 1945, Peekskill NY), American Republican politician and governor of New York from 1995.

Ann Patchett (2 Dec 1963, Los Angeles CA), American novelist whose *Bel Canto* won the PEN/Faulkner Award and the Orange Prize in 2002.

Percival (Noel James) Patterson (10 Apr 1935, Goodwill, Jamaica), Jamaican politician and prime minister from 1992.

Arnall Patz (14 Jun 1920), American ophthalmologist and researcher on the causes and treatment of eye disease, especially among children; he was awarded a Presidential Medal of Freedom in 2004.

Sean Paul (Sean Paul Henriques; 8 Jan 1973, St.

Andrew, Jamaica), Jamaican musician who first became a hit with his reggae music in his home country and scored in the American market beginning in 1999 with his rap single "Hot Gal Today."

(Margaret) Jane Pauley (31 Oct 1950, Indianapolis IN), American TV personality, coanchor of the *Today* show from 1976 to 1989 and host of *Dateline NBC* from 1992 to 2003.

Luciano Pavarotti (12 Oct 1935, Modena, Italy), Italian operatic tenor of worldwide reputation as perhaps the leading tenor of his generation; he is celebrated for the purity of his voice and his ability to reach the highest notes in a tenor's range; in March 2004 he gave his final performance on the operatic stage in a production of *Tosca* at the Met in New York City.

Tim Pawlenty (Timothy James Pawlenty; 21 Nov 1960, St. Paul MN), American Republican politician and governor of Minnesota from 2003.

Peaches (Merrill Nisker; 1968, Toronto, ON, Canada), Canadian electro-techno rapper known for her brash, sexually explicit material.

Claudia Pechstein (22 Feb 1972, East Berlin, East Germany [now Berlin, Germany]), German speed skater who was 2002 Olympic gold medalist in the 3,000-m and 5,000-m races and winner of the latter race in the two previous Olympics as well (and the bronze in 1992).

Amanda Peet (11 Jan 1972, New York NY), American film actress whose breakthrough came in *The Whole Nine Yards* (2000); she appeared in *Identity* (2003) and on the stage in *This Is How It Goes* (2005).

Harvey Pekar (1939, Cleveland OH), American file clerk and alternative comic-book artist whose American Book Award–winning (1987) serial publication *American Splendor* (from 1976) served as the basis for an equally well received film (in which Pekar appeared) of the same name in 2003.

Pelé (Edson Arantes do Nascimento; 23 Oct 1940, Três Corações, Minas Gerais state, Brazil), Brazilian soccer (association football) inside-forward who was revered as much for his sportsmanship as for his extraordinary skill and innovative style; in his time he was probably the most famous and possibly the best-paid athlete in the world; Pelé led Brazil to three World Cup victories (1958, 1962, and 1970) and permanent possession of the trophy.

Viktor (Olegovich) Pelevin (22 Nov 1962, Moscow, USSR [now in Russia]), Russian novelist especially popular among young readers.

Jaroslav Jan Pelikan (17 Dec 1923, Akron OH), American religious, intellectual, and cultural historian specializing in the history of Eastern and Western Christianity; he was Sterling Professor of History at Yale University (from 1972) and dean of Yale's graduate school (1973–78); he was the recipient of a 2004 John W. Kluge Prize in the Human Sciences.

David Pelletier (22 Nov 1974, Sayabec, QC, Canada), Canadian pairs figure skater (with Jamie Salé); he and Salé shared the 2002 Olympic gold medal with Russian pairs skaters Yelena Berezhnaya and Anton Sikharulidze.

Cesar Pelli (12 Oct 1926, Tucumán, Argentina), Argentine architect known for the lightweight, almost tentlike, appearance of his buildings, which are often surfaced in glass or with a thin stone veneer.

Nancy Pelosi (Nancy D'Alesandro; 26 Mar 1940, Baltimore MD), American Democratic politician; congresswoman from California (1987–), minority whip, 2002–03, and House Democratic leader from 2003.

Leonard Peltier (12 Sep 1944, Grand Forks ND), American Ojibwa and Lakota activist and a leader in the American Indian Movement; his conviction in 1977 and imprisonment for the murder of two FBI agents at South Dakota's Pine Ridge Reservation in 1975 became a cause célèbre.

Krzysztof Penderecki (23 Nov 1933, Debica, Poland), Polish composer and a leader of the European avant-garde whose works exhibit a novel and masterful treatment of orchestration; he won the 1992 Grawemeyer Award for Music for *Adagio for Large Orchestra* and a Praemium Imperiale in 2004.

Sean (Justin) Penn (17 Aug 1960, Santa Monica CA), American film actor in intense, brooding roles; his film credits include *Fast Times at Ridgemont High* (1982), *Dead Man Walking* (1995), *The Thin Red Line* (1998), *I Am Sam* (2001), and *Mystic River* (2003), for which he won the Academy Award for best actor.

Murray Perahia (19 Apr 1947, New York NY), American concert pianist who returned to the concert stage and the recording studio after a hand injury and impressed critics and fans with a series of outstanding recordings, notably of the music of J.S. Bach.

Sonny Perdue (20 Dec 1946, Perry GA), American agribusinessman, Republican politician, and governor of Georgia from 2003.

Arturo Pérez Reverte (24 Nov 1951, Cartagena, Spain), Spanish TV journalist and novelist who has won an international audience for his novels, often historical mysteries; his *La reina del sur* (2002; *The Queen of the South* [2004]) was a best seller in Spain and Latin America.

Kieran Perkins (14 Aug 1973, Brisbane, QLD, Australia), Australian swimmer who held 12 world records in distance freestyle events.

Grayson Perry (24 Mar 1960, Chelmsford, Essex, England), British transvestite artist who was awarded the 2003 Turner Prize for ceramic pots decorated with his drawings.

Matthew Perry (19 Aug 1969, Williamstown MA), American TV actor who appeared as Chandler Bing on the hit TV sitcom *Friends* (1994–2004).

Rick Perry (4 Mar 1950, West Texas), American Republican politician and governor of Texas from 2000.

Göran Persson (20 Jan 1949, Vingaker, Sweden), Swedish politician and prime minister from 1996.

Joe Pesci (9 Feb 1943, Newark NJ), American film actor best known for roles in gangster movies and comedies; he won a best supporting actor Academy Award in 1990 for *GoodFellas*.

Bernadette Peters (Bernadette Lazzaro; 28 Feb 1948, Queens NY), American singer and actress on Broadway, on TV, and in films.

Jürgen Peters (17 Mar 1944, Bolko, Germany [now Oppeln, Poland]), German trade union leader and chairman of IG Metall, the most powerful German trade union, from 2003.

Tom Petty (20 Oct 1953, Gainesville FL), American singer and songwriter whose roots-oriented guitar rock arose from the new-wave movement of the late 1970s and resulted in a string of hit singles and albums.

Madeleine Peyroux (1973, Athens GA), American jazz singer.

Michelle Pfeiffer (29 Apr 1958, Santa Ana CA), American leading actress of great talent and beauty; her films include *Dangerous Liaisons*

(1988), *The Age of Innocence* (1993), *Dangerous Minds* (1995), and *What Lies Beneath* (2000).

Liz Phair (Elizabeth Clark Phair; 17 Apr 1967, New Haven CT), American rock singer and songwriter first noticed for her debut album, *Exile in Guyville* (1993).

Michael Phelps (30 Jun 1985, Baltimore MD), American swimmer who won three gold medals and one silver medal (including firsts in three different strokes, a record) at the 2003 US nationals and set five world records (itself a record) at the 2003 FINA World Championships; he set seven world records overall in 2003 and took home eight medals from the 2004 Olympic Games; he was awarded the 2003 Sullivan Award.

Regis (Francis Xavier) Philbin (25 Aug 1934, New York NY), American TV personality, host of *Live with Regis and Kathie Lee/Kelly* (from 1989) and *Who Wants to Be a Millionaire?* (1999–2002).

Prince Philip (Prince Philip of Greece; 3rd Duke of Edinburgh; 10 Jun 1921, Corfu, Greece), British royal; consort of Queen Elizabeth II (married 20 Nov 1947).

Crown Prince Philippe (Philippe Leopold Louis Marie; 15 Apr 1960, Brussels, Belgium), Belgian royal, duke of Brabant, and heir to the throne.

Stone Phillips (2 Dec 1954, Texas City TX), American TV host and anchorman for *Dateline NBC* (from 1992).

Phoebe Philo (1973, Paris, France), British fashion designer who is creative director of the Chloé fashion house; she was named Designer of the Year at the 2004 British Fashion Awards.

Renzo Piano (14 Sep 1937, Genoa, Italy), Italian architect; winner of the 1998 Pritzker Prize and the 2002 UIA Gold Medal for Architecture.

Heinrich von Pierer (26 Jan 1941, Erlangen, Germany), German corporate executive and CEO of Siemens AG from 1992.

D.B.C. Pierre (Peter Finlay; June 1961, Australia), Australian-born British novelist who won the 2003 Man Booker Prize for *Vernon God Little*.

Stefano Pilati (10 Dec 1965, Milan, Italy), Italian fashion designer who became creative director at the fashion house YSL Rive Gauche in 2004.

Laffit Pincay, Jr. (29 Dec 1946, Panama City, Panama), Panamanian-born American jockey, the sport's leading money-winner in 1970–74, 1979, 1985; he retired in 2003 with a record 9,530 wins.

Pink (Alecia Moore; 8 Sep 1979, Doylestown PA), American pop vocalist.

Steven Pinker (18 Sep 1954, Montreal, QC, Canada), Canadian-born American experimental psychologist and author of scholarly and popular books on language.

Trevor Pinnock (16 Dec 1946, Canterbury, England), English harpsichordist and conductor.

Robert Pinsky (20 Oct 1940, Long Branch NJ), American poet and critic whose poems searched for the significance underlying everyday acts; he was poet laureate of the US, 1997–2000, and winner of the 2004 PEN/Voelcker Award for Poetry.

Harold Pinter (10 Oct 1930, London, England), English playwright regarded as one of the most complex and challenging post-World War II dramatists; his plays are noted for their use of understatement, small talk, reticence, and even silence to convey the substance of their characters.

Pedro Verona Rodrigues Pires (April 1934, Ilha do Fogo, Cape Verde), Cape Verdean politician and president from 2001.

Bernd Pischetsrieder (15 Feb 1948, Munich, West Germany [now in Germany]), German corporate executive and CEO of Volkswagen AG from September 2001.

Brad Pitt (William Bradley Pitt; 18 Dec 1963, Shawnee OK), American actor and one of the biggest box-office draws in America; his films include *A River Runs Through It* (1992), *Interview with the Vampire* (1994); *Ocean's Eleven* (2001), and *Mr. & Mrs. Smith* (2005).

Harvey Pitt (28 Feb 1945, Brooklyn NY), American securities lawyer who was chairman of the Securities and Exchange Commission from 2001 to November 2002.

Ronald Plasterk (12 Apr 1957, The Hague, The Netherlands), Dutch molecular geneticist and media commentator.

Elizabeth Plater-Zyberk (20 Dec 1950, Bryn Mawr PA), American urban planner who collaborates with her husband, Andres Duany.

Yevgeny (Viktorovich) Plushchenko (also written Evgeni Plushenko; 3 Nov 1982, Solnechny, Russian SFSR, USSR [now in Russia]), Russian figure skater, world champion in 2001, 2003, and 2004, and silver medalist at the 2002 Winter Olympics.

Norman Podhoretz (16 Jan 1930, Brooklyn NY), American political commentator and editor of the journal *Commentary* (1960–95); he was awarded a Presidential Medal of Freedom in 2004.

Sylvia Poggioli (194?, Providence RI), American foreign correspondent for National Public Radio.

Hifikepunye (Lucas) Pohamba (18 Aug 1935, Okanghudi, South West Africa [now Namibia]), Namibian independence leader and politician who was president from 21 Mar 2005.

Sidney Poitier (20 Feb 1927?, Miami FL), Bahamian American stage and film actor and director who won an Academy Award for best actor for *Lilies of the Field* (1963); he was awarded a lifetime achievement award at the 2001 Oscar ceremony.

Roman Polanski (Raimund Liebling; 18 Aug 1933, Paris, France), Polish film director, scriptwriter, and actor; known especially for *Noz w wodzie* (1962; *Knife in the Water*), *Repulsion* (1965); *Rosemary's Baby* (1968), *Macbeth* (1971), and *Chinatown* (1974); his film *The Pianist* (2002) won a French César award, a British BAFTA, and the Palme d'Or at the 2002 Cannes Film Festival and brought Polanski a best director Oscar.

Judit Polgar (23 Jul 1976, Budapest, Hungary), Hungarian chess player, the youngest of the three chess-playing Polgar sisters; she achieved the rank among male chess players of grand master in December 1991 at the age of 15.

H. David Politzer (31 Aug 1949, New York NY), American quantum physicist who shared the 2004 Nobel Prize in Physics with David J. Gross and Frank Wilczek for their studies of the force that binds quarks together and their development of a new physical theory called quantum chromodynamics.

Sigmar Polke (13 Feb 1941, Oels, Germany [now Olesnica, Poland]), German painter who was one of the founders of Capitalist Realism, a movement that depicts popular and mundane cultural artifacts with ironic seriousness; he won a Japanese Praemium Imperiale Award for excellence in arts in 2002.

John (Charlton) Polkinghorne (16 Oct 1930, Weston-super-Mare, Somerset, England), British Anglican priest and particle physicist who won the 2002 Templeton Prize.

Ruslan Ponomaryov (11 Oct 1983, Gorlovka, Ukrainian SSR, USSR [now Horlivka, Ukraine]), Ukrainian chess master who won the FIDE world chess championship in 2002.

Natalie Portman (Natalie Hershlag; 9 Jun 1981, Jerusalem, Israel), Israeli-born American film actress whose credits include *Where the Heart Is* (2000) and *Star Wars* episodes I, II, and III (1999, 2002, and 2005).

Zac Posen (Zachary E. Posen; 24 Oct 1980, New York NY), American fashion designer whose first independent show in February 2002 featured 1930s-inspired fashions.

John E. Potter (195?), American corporate executive who was CEO and postmaster general of the US Postal Service from 2001.

Colin (Luther) Powell (5 Apr 1937, New York NY), American military officer and government official who was national security adviser, 1987–89; chairman of the Joint Chiefs of Staff, 1989–93; and US secretary of state, 2001–05.

Earl A. ("Rusty") Powell, III (24 Oct 1943, Spartanburg SC), American museum official; director of the National Gallery of Art in Washington DC from 1992.

Michael K. Powell (23 Mar 1963, Birmingham AL), American lawyer who was chairman of the Federal Communications Commission from January 2001 to March 2005; he is the son of Colin Powell.

Samantha Power (1970, Ireland), Irish-born American writer; author of *A Problem from Hell* (2002), a study of US inaction against genocide in the 20th century, which won the 2003 Pulitzer Prize for General Nonfiction.

Velupillai Prabhakaran (26 Nov 1954, Jaffna, Sri Lanka), Sri Lankan secessionist, the founder and leader of Liberation Tigers of Tamil Eelam (Tamil Tigers) from the early 1970s.

Miuccia Prada (1949, Milan, Italy), Italian fashion designer whose clothing, footwear, and accessories designs are characterized by casual luxury.

John M(ichael) Prausnitz (1928, Berlin, Germany), German-born American applied physical chemist who specialized in the design of industrial-scale chemical separation processes to make them more efficient and environmentally sound; he won a 2003 National Medal of Science.

Azim Hasham Premji (24 Jul 1945, Bombay [now Mumbai], British India), Indian corporate executive who was chairman of the Wipro Corp. of Bangalore, India, from 1977.

Edward C. Prescott (26 Dec 1940, Glens Falls NY), American economist who was the corecipient (with Finn E. Kydland) of the 2004 Nobel Memorial Prize in Economic Sciences "for their contributions to dynamic macroeconomics: the time consistency of economic policy and the driving forces behind business cycles."

André (George) Previn (6 Apr 1929, Berlin, Germany), German-born American pianist, composer, and conductor who was music director of the Los Angeles Philharmonic, 1985–89, and the Oslo Symphony Orchestra from 2002.

Prince (Prince Rogers Nelson; 7 Jun 1958, Minneapolis MN), American singer and songwriter who is considered one of the most talented and influential musicians of his generation.

Anthony Principi (16 Apr 1944, Bronx NY), American government official and secretary of veterans affairs, 2001–05.

Richard B. Priory (15 May 1946, Lakehurst NJ), American energy engineer, corporate executive, and CEO of Duke Energy from 1997.

Romano Prodi (9 Aug 1939, Scandiano, Italy), Italian politician, prime minister, 1996–98, and president of the European Commission from 1999 to 31 Oct 2004.

E(dna) Annie Proulx (22 Aug 1935, Norwich CT), American writer whose darkly comic yet sad fiction is peopled with quirky, memorable individuals and unconventional families.

Stanley Ben Prusiner (28 May 1942, Des Moines IA), American biochemist who discovered the prion; he was awarded the 1997 Nobel Prize for Physiology or Medicine.

Georgi Purvanov (28 Jun 1957, Kovachevtsi, Bulgaria), Bulgarian politician and president from 2002.

Vladimir (Vladimirovich) Putin (7 Oct 1952, Leningrad, Russian SFSR, USSR [now St. Petersburg, Russia]), Russian intelligence officer, politician, and president from 1999.

(Sayyid) Qabus ibn Saʿid (18 Nov 1940, Salalah, Oman), Omani sultan from 1970.

Muammar al-Qaddafi (also spelled Muammar Khadafy, Moammar Gadhafi, or Muʿammar al-Qadhdhafi; spring 1942, near Surt, Libya), Libyan military leader and controversial Arab statesman; he has been de facto chief of state from 1969.

Dennis Quaid (9 Apr 1954, Houston TX), American film actor who won notice in *The Right Stuff* (1983), *The Big Easy* (1987), and *The Alamo* (2004).

Thomas Quasthoff (9 Nov 1959, Hildesheim, Germany), German bass-baritone who overcame being severely disabled to become one of the world's preeminent classical music artists.

Queen Latifah (Dana Elaine Owens; 18 Mar 1970, Newark NJ), American rap musician, film actress, and TV personality.

Anna Quindlen (8 Jul 1953, Philadelphia PA), American political commentator and author whose *Blessings* was a best seller in 2002.

Ahmed Qurei (Abu Ala; 1937, Abu Dis, near Jerusalem, Palestine), Palestinian businessman and core member of the Palestine Liberation Organization; he served as prime minister of the Palestinian Authority from 2003.

Daniel Radcliffe (23 July 1989, London, England), British actor who played the title character in the highly successful *Harry Potter* series of films (from 2001).

Paula Radcliffe (17 Dec 1973, Northwich, Cheshire, England), British long-distance runner, the world women's record holder at 2 hr 15 min 25 sec, who won her third London Marathon in April 2005.

Teimour Radjabob (12 Mar 1987, Baku, Azerbaijani SSR, USSR [now in Azerbaijan]), Azerbaijani chess player; one of the youngest (at 14 years and 14 days) ever to win the title of grandmaster.

Jean-Pierre Raffarin (3 Aug 1948, Poitiers, France), French politician and prime minister of France from 2002 to 31 May 2005.

A.R. Rahman (Muslim name Allah Rakha Rahman; A.S. Dileep Kumar; 6 Jan 1966, Madras [now Chennai], India), Indian composer of Bollywood film music.

Aishwarya Rai (1 Nov 1973, Mangalore, Karnataka state, India), Indian beauty queen (Miss World of 1994) and film actress.

Sam Raimi (Samuel M. Raimi; 23 Oct 1959, Franklin MI), American cult filmmaker who struck it big with *Spider-Man* (2002) and its sequel (2004).

Franklin D. Raines (14 Jan 1949, Seattle WA), American corporate executive and CEO of Fannie Mae from 1999.

Konrad Raiser (25 Jan 1938, Magdeburg, Germany), German church official and general secretary of the World Council of Churches from 1993.

Bonnie Raitt (8 Nov 1949, Burbank CA), American singer and bottleneck guitarist remarkable for her gutsy blend of blues and rhythm-and-blues styles, her full head of red hair, and the two decades in which she paid her dues in the music business before achieving popular success (and a Grammy) with her 1989 album, *Nick of Time*.

Mahinda Rajapakse (18 Nov 1945, British Ceylon [now Sri Lanka]), Sri Lankan politician and prime minister from 6 Apr 2004.

Imomali Rakhmonov (5 Oct 1952, Dangara, Tadzhik SSR, USSR [now Tajikistan]), Tajik politician and president from 1992.

Samuel Ramey (28 Mar 1942, Colby KS), American bass, one of the operatic stars of his generation, known for his mastery of the repertory and commanding stage presence.

Sara Ramirez (1976, Mazatlán, Mexico), Mexican-born actress and singer who won a 2005 Tony Award for best actress in a musical for her work in *Monty Python's Spamalot*.

Don Michael Randel (1941?, Oklahoma), American scholar of medieval music and university official; he is a leading expert in music of the Middle Ages and Renaissance in Spain and France and has been president of the University of Chicago since 2000.

Queen Rania, al-Abdullah (Rania al-Yaseen; 31 Aug 1970, Kuwait), Kuwaiti-born Jordanian royal, the consort of King Abdullah II.

Ian Rankin (28 Apr 1960, Cardenden, Fife, Scotland), Scottish author, one of the top-selling crime writers in the UK and creator of Inspector John Rebus; Rankin won the 2004 best novel Edgar Award of the Mystery Writers of America.

Anders Fogh Rasmussen (26 Jan 1953, Ginnerup, Denmark), Danish politician and prime minister from 2001.

Dan Rather (31 Oct 1931, Wharton TX), American TV journalist and news anchor; he was the anchorman for the *CBS Evening News* from 1981 (when he took over from Walter Cronkite) until his retirement in 2005.

Aleksei Ratmansky (1968, Leningrad, USSR [now St. Petersburg, Russia]), Russian dancer, choreographer, and director who was a principal dancer with the Royal Danish Ballet before being named artistic director of the Bolshoi Ballet in May 2003 to replace Boris Akimov.

Rodrigo de Rato y Figaredo (18 Mar 1949, Madrid, Spain), Spanish government and international official; he was Spain's minister of finance (1996–2004) before becoming (7 Jun 2004) managing director and chairman of the International Monetary Fund.

Sir Simon (Denis) Rattle (19 Jan 1955, Liverpool, England), British orchestra conductor who was principal conductor and artistic director of the Berlin Philharmonic from the 2002–03 season.

Marc Ravalomanana (1949, near Atananarivo, [French] Madagascar), Malagasy politician and president of Madagascar from 2002.

Lee R. Raymond (1938, Waterstown SD), American corporate executive and chairman and CEO of Exxon Mobil Corp. from 1994.

Giovanni Battista Cardinal Re (30 Jan 1934, Borno, Italy), Italian Roman Catholic churchman and official of the Roman Curia; named cardinal in 2001.

Nancy Davis Reagan (Anne Frances Robbins; 6 Jul 1921, New York NY), American first lady; second wife and widow of Pres. Ronald Reagan.

Robert Redford (18 Aug 1937, Santa Monica CA), American film actor and director and founder of the Sundance Institute and Film Festival; he won a best director Academy Award in 1980 for *Ordinary People*.

Lynn Redgrave (8 Mar 1943, London, England), British stage, screen, and TV actress whose breakthrough came in the film *Georgy Girl* (1966).

Vanessa Redgrave (30 Jan 1937, London, England), British stage and screen actress and political activist; she won the best supporting actress Academy Award for *Julia* (1977) and the Tony Award for best actress in a play for her role in *Long Day's Journey into Night* (2003).

Joshua Redman (1 Feb 1969, Berkeley CA), American jazz-saxophone player.

Sumner Redstone (Sumner Rothstein; 27 May 1923, Boston MA), American corporate executive and chairman of the board (from 1987) and CEO (from 1996) of Viacom Inc.

John S. Reed (1939, Chicago IL), American financial official who was chairman and CEO of Citibank, Citicorp, and Citigroup from 1984 to 2000 and served as chairman of the New York Stock Exchange from 2003 to April 2005.

David Rees (1973?), American comic artist, creator (2001) of the topical (some say subversive), profane *Get Your War On* comic strip on the Internet.

Sir Martin J(ohn) Rees (23 Jun 1942, Shropshire, England), British astronomer royal whose controversial book *Our Final Century* (2003; published in the US as *Our Final Hour*) argued that the pace of technological change threatened to outstrip the ability of humans to control it.

Keanu (Charles) Reeves (2 Sep 1964, Beirut, Lebanon), American actor known for many popular films, including *Bill & Ted's Excellent Adventure* (1989), *Speed* (1994), *The Replacements* (2000), and the *Matrix* series (1999 and 2003).

William (Hubbs) Rehnquist (1 Oct 1924, Milwaukee WI), American jurist; associate justice of the US Supreme Court from 1972 and chief justice from 1986.

Harry Reid (2 Dec 1939, Searchlight NV), American Democratic politician, senator from Nevada (from 1987), Senate minority whip (1998–2005), and minority leader from 2005.

Tara Reid (8 Nov 1975, Wyckoff NJ), American film actress and host of E! Entertainment Television's *Wild On* series (from 2005).

Rob Reiner (6 Mar 1947, Bronx NY), American actor, director, writer, and producer of critically and commercially successful films.

M(argaret) Jodi Rell (16 Jun 1946, Norfolk VA), American Republican politician and governor of Connecticut from 1 Jul 2004.

Thomas Esang Remengesau, Jr. (1956), Palauan politician and president from 2001.

Edward Gene Rendell (5 Jan 1944, New York NY), American Democratic politician, mayor of Philadelphia, 1992–2000, and governor of Pennsylvania from 2003.

Ruth Rendell (Baroness Rendell of Babergh; pseudonym Barbara Vine; 17 Feb 1930, London, England), British mystery novelist and creator of Chief Inspector Wexford.

Einars Repse (9 Dec 1961, Jelgava, Latvian SSR, USSR [now Latvia]), Latvian politician and prime minister from 2002 to 9 Mar 2004.

Yasmina Reza (1 May 1959, Paris, France), French playwright of international acclaim, best known for her play *Art*.

Busta Rhymes (Trevor Smith, Jr.; 20 May 1972, Brooklyn NY), American rap performer.

Anne Rice (Howard Allen O'Brien; pseudonyms A.N. Roquelaure and Anne Rampling; 4 Oct 1941, New Orleans LA), American gothic novelist known especially for her six-volume *Vampire Chronicles*.

Condoleezza Rice (14 Nov 1954, Birmingham AL), American academic and government official; she was national security adviser (2001–05) and US secretary of state from 26 Jan 2005.

Adrienne (Cecile) Rich (16 May 1929, Baltimore MD), American poet, scholar, teacher, and critic whose many volumes of poetry trace a stylistic transformation from formal, well-crafted but imitative poetry to a more personal and powerful style informed by a lesbian-feminist aesthetic; she was the recipient of the 2003 Bollingen Prize for American Poetry.

Denise (Lee) Richards (17 Feb 1971, Downers Grove IL), American model and TV and film actress; she starred in the James Bond film *The World Is Not Enough* (1999).

Keith Richards (18 Dec 1943, Dartford, Kent, England), British guitarist and singer with the Rolling Stones.

(George) Maxwell Richards (1931, San Fernando, Trinidad), Trinidadian chemical engineer and university professor who was president of Trinidad and Tobago from 2003.

Bill Richardson (15 Nov 1947, Pasadena CA), American government official, former secretary of energy, ambassador to the UN, and congressman from New Mexico; he was governor of New Mexico from 2003.

Lionel B. Richie, Jr. (20 Jun 1949, Tuskegee AL), American rhythm-and-blues songwriter and singer.

Nicole Richie (15 Sep 1981, Berkeley CA), American celebrity entertainer, daughter of Lionel Richie, and costar (with Paris Hilton) of the reality-TV series *The Simple Life* from 2003.

Gerhard Richter (9 Feb 1932, Dresden, Germany), German artist and cofounder of the movement known as Capitalist Realism, in which ordinary objects such as furniture and food, and sometimes the artists themselves, are depicted as art.

Kai-Uwe Ricke (Oct 1961, Krefeld, West Germany [now in Germany]), German corporate executive and CEO of Deutsche Telekom from 2002.

Sally K(risten) Ride (26 May 1951, Encino CA), American astronaut and astrophysicist who was the first American woman to fly in space (1983).

Tom Ridge (Thomas Joseph Ridge; 26 Aug 1945, Munhall PA), American politician and governor of Pennsylvania (1995–2001) who was designated in 2002 to be secretary of homeland security, a new cabinet office; he served until 2005.

Robert R. Riley (3 Oct 1944, Ashland AL), American Republican politician and governor of Alabama from 20 Jan 2003.

LeAnn Rimes (28 Aug 1982, Jackson MS), American country-and-western singer.

Pipilotti Rist (Charlotte Rist; 21 Jun 1962, Grabs, Sankt Gallen canton, Switzerland), Swiss video-installation artist.

Rivaldo (Vitor Borba Ferreira; 19 Apr 1972, Recife, Brazil), Brazilian association football (soccer) player who was named FIFA World Footballer of the Year in 1999 and was a key player on the Brazilian national team in the 1998 and 2002 World Cup competitions.

Geraldo (Miguel) Rivera (4 Jul 1943, Brooklyn NY), American TV journalist and talk-show host.

Tim Robbins (16 Oct 1958, West Covina CA), American actor whose films include *Bull Durham* (1988), *The Player* (1992), *The Shawshank Redemption* (1994), and *Mystic River* (2003; best supporting actor Academy Award).

Cecil E(dward) Roberts, Jr. (31 Oct 1946, Kayford WV), American labor leader; president of the United Mine Workers of America from 1995.

John G(lover) Roberts (27 Jan 1955, Buffalo NY), American trial lawyer and federal appeals court judge who was nominated in July 2005 by Pres. George W. Bush to fill the seat on the US Supreme Court vacated by retiring Associate Justice Sandra Day O'Connor.

Julia Roberts (Julie Fiona Roberts; 28 Oct 1967, Smyrna GA), American actress, one of the biggest names in Hollywood since her performance in the film *Pretty Woman* (1990); she won a best actress Academy Award for *Erin Brockovich* (2000).

Nora Roberts (Eleanor Marie Robertson; 10 Oct 1950, Silver Spring MD), American author of best-selling novels that blur the distinction between the romance, fantasy, and suspense genres; she is a prolific writer, producing several novels a year; her first was *Irish Thoroughbred* (1981).

David (Maurice) Robinson (6 Aug 1965, Key West FL), American basketball player, a center who led the San Antonio Spurs to NBA championships in 1999 and 2003.

Smokey Robinson (William Robinson, Jr.; 19 Feb 1940, Detroit MI), American rhythm-and-blues singer and songwriter.

Emily Robison (Emily Burns Erwin; 16 Aug 1972, Pittsfield MA), American country musician, a member of the Dixie Chicks.

Chris Rock (7 Feb 1966, Georgetown SC), American stand-up performer and actor known for his brash style.

Kid Rock (Robert James Ritchie; 17 Jan 1971, Romeo MI), American rap-rock artist.

The Rock (Dwayne Douglas Johnson; 2 May 1972, Hayward CA), American professional wrestler turned actor.

Andy Roddick (30 Aug 1982, Omaha NE), American tennis player who won the 2003 US Open; he finished 2004 ranked second in the world.

Anita (Lucia) Roddick (23 Oct 1942, Littlehampton, West Sussex, England), British businesswoman and cofounder of The Body Shop in 1976.

Alex Rodriguez (27 Jul 1975, New York NY), American baseball player, a shortstop known as a fine all-around player who signed the largest salary deal in history ($252 million over 10 years) in 2000; named the 2003 American League MVP; he switched to third base when he was traded to the New York Yankees in early 2004.

Narciso Rodríguez (1961, New Jersey), American fashion designer who rose quickly to fame when he designed Carolyn Bessette's dress for her 1996 wedding to John F. Kennedy, Jr.; he was named the best women's-wear designer by the Council of Fashion Designers of America in 2002 and 2003.

Oscar Andrés Cardinal Rodríguez Maradiaga (29 Dec 1942, Tegucigalpa, Honduras), Honduran Roman

Catholic churchman, archbishop of Tegucigalpa from 1993; he was named cardinal in 2001.

Eduardo Rodríguez Veltzé (2 Mar 1956, Cochabamba, Bolivia), Bolivian jurist and head of the Supreme Court who became president on 9 Jun 2005.

Robert G. Roeder (1942, Boonville IN), American biochemist; recipient of the 2003 Lasker Award for Basic Medical Research for his investigations into DNA/RNA transcription.

Jacques Rogge (2 May 1942, Ghent, Belgium), Belgian Olympic yachtsman, surgeon, and sports executive; he has been president of the International Olympic Committee since 2001.

Roh Moo Hyun (6 Aug 1946, near Pusan, Korea [now in South Korea]), Korean politician; he was president of the Republic of Korea from 2003 but was suspended from office for two months in 2004 after a vote in the legislature to impeach him.

Sonny Rollins (Theodore Walter Rollins; 7 Sep 1930, Harlem, New York NY), American jazz tenor and soprano saxophonist; he received a lifetime achievement Grammy Award in February 2004.

Holmes Rolston III (19 Nov 1932, Staunton VA), American Presbyterian minister and environmental ethicist; leading scholar of the philosophical, scientific, and religious conceptions of nature and founder of the journal *Environmental Ethics* (1979); he was the winner of the 2003 Templeton Prize for Progress Toward Research or Discoveries About Spiritual Realities.

Ray Romano (21 Dec 1957, Queens NY), American comic actor best known for the award-winning TV series *Everybody Loves Raymond* (1996–2005).

Mitt Romney (12 Mar 1947, Bloomfield MI), American businessman, sports executive (CEO of the group that organized the 2002 Winter Olympics in Salt Lake City), and Republican governor of Massachusetts from 2 Jan 2003.

Ronaldo (Ronaldo Luiz Nazario de Lima; 22 Sep 1976, Itaguai, Rio de Janeiro state, Brazil), Brazilian association football (soccer) player; he was the FIFA Player of the Year in 1996, 1997, and 2002 and star of Brazil's national team in the 2002 World Cup.

Andy Rooney (14 Jan 1919, Albany NY), American TV journalist, well known for his ironic and mordant observations on life in a regular segment at the end of the weekly *60 Minutes* program (from 1978; three Emmy Awards) and for a series of books collecting these commentaries.

Anton Rop (27 Dec 1960, Ljubljana, Yugoslavia [now in Slovenia]), Slovene politician and prime minister from 2002 to 9 Nov 2004.

Henrique Rosa (1946?, Guinea-Bissau?), Guinea-Bissau politician and interim president from 2003.

Charlie Rose (5 Jan 1942, Henderson NC), American TV journalist and interviewer who has hosted *The Charlie Rose Show* since 1991.

Irwin A. Rose (16 Jul 1926, Brooklyn NY), American biochemist who was corecipient (with Aaron Ciechanover and Avram Hershko) of the 2004 Nobel Prize in Chemistry for their discovery of an ingenious mechanism by which the cells of most living organisms cull unwanted proteins.

Roseanne (Roseanne Cherrie Barr; Roseanne Arnold; 3 Nov 1952, Salt Lake City UT), American TV, film, stage, and nightclub comedian and actress who is best known for her TV series *The Roseanne Barr Show* (1987) and *Roseanne* (1988–97).

Wilbur Ross (28 Nov 1937, North Bergen NJ), American financier and turnaround specialist who is chairman of International Steel Group, Inc.

Philip (Milton) Roth (19 Mar 1933, Newark NJ), American novelist and short-story writer whose works are characterized by an acute ear for dialogue, a concern with Jewish middle-class life, and the painful entanglements of sexual and familial love.

Mike Rounds (24 Oct 1954, Huron SD), American Republican politician and governor of South Dakota from 2003.

Karl Rove (25 Dec 1950, Denver CO), American right-wing political operative and chief strategist for Pres. George W. Bush.

J.K. Rowling (Joanne Rowling; 31 Jul 1965, Chipping Sodbury, near Bristol, Gloucestershire, England), British author, creator of the popular and critically acclaimed *Harry Potter* series about a young sorcerer in training; the sixth book in the series, *Harry Potter and the Half-Blood Prince,* was released in July 2005.

Arundhati Roy (24 Nov 1961, Shillong, Bengal state, India), Indian novelist who won the Booker Prize in 1998 for *The God of Small Things* (1997).

Patrick Roy (5 Oct 1965, Quebec City, QC, Canada), Canadian ice-hockey goalie; he is the only three-time NHL play-offs MVP, winning the Conn Smythe Trophy in 1986, 1993, and 2001.

Ibrahim Rugova (2 Dec 1944, Istok, Kosovo, Yugoslavia [now in Serbia and Montenegro]), Kosovar (Albanian) nationalist leader and officer in the opposition government of Kosovo.

Louis Rukeyser (30 Jan 1933, New York NY), American TV journalist and financial analyst.

Donald (Henry) Rumsfeld (9 Jul 1932, Chicago IL), American government official who was US secretary of defense, 1975–77 and again from 2001.

Erkki Ruoslahti (16 Feb 1940, Helsinki, Finland), Finnish-born American cell biologist and distinguished professor at the Burnham Institute, La Jolla CA; he shared (with Masatoshi Takeichi) the 2005 Japan Prize in Cell Biology for "fundamental contribution in elucidating the molecular mechanisms of cell adhesion."

Ed Ruscha (Edward Joseph Ruscha; 16 Dec 1937, Omaha NE), American artist known for his deadpan take on American pop culture; he enjoyed a major retrospective at the Hirshhorn Museum and Sculpture Garden in Washington DC in 2000 and another at the Whitney Museum of American Art in New York City in 2004.

Geoffrey Rush (6 Jul 1951, Toowoomba, QLD, Australia), Australian film actor whose credits include *Shine* (1996; Academy Award for best actor), *Shakespeare in Love* (1998), and *Quills* (2000).

(Ahmed) Salman Rushdie (19 Jun 1947, Bombay [now Mumbai], British India), Anglo-Indian novelist who won the 1981 Booker Prize for *Midnight's Children*; he was condemned to death by leading Iranian Muslim clerics in 1989 for allegedly having blasphemed Islam in his novel *The Satanic Verses* (1988).

Tim Russert (7 May 1950, Buffalo NY), American TV talk-show host and moderator of *Meet the Press* (from 1991).

Patricia F(iorello) Russo (12 Jun 1952, Trenton NJ), American business executive and CEO of Lucent Technologies from 2002; she was credited with the company's financial turnaround.

Burt Rutan (Elbert L. Rutan; 17 Jun 1943, Portland OR), American test pilot, aerospace engineer, and designer of specialized aircraft.

John A. Ruthven (1927, Cincinnati OH), American wildlife artist; he received a National Medal of Arts in 2004.

John Rutter (24 Sep 1945, London, England), British composer and conductor; he is the founder (1981) and leader of the Cambridge Singers, a professional chamber choir.

Arnold Rüütel (10 May 1928, Saaremaa, Estonia), Estonian politician, chairman of the Supreme Council, 1990–92, and president from 2001.

Kay Ryan (11 Sep 1945, San Jose CA), American poet who won the 2004 Ruth Lilly Poetry Prize.

Meg Ryan (Margaret Mary Emily Anne Hyra; 19 Nov 1961, Fairfield CT), American film star known mostly for upbeat romantic comedies.

Winona Ryder (Winona Laura Horowitz; 29 Oct 1971, Winona MN), American film actress noticed for her roles in *The Age of Innocence* (1993) and *Little Women* (1994).

Mikhail Saakashvili (21 Dec 1967, Tbilisi, Georgian SSR, USSR [now in Georgia]), Georgian politician and president from 25 Jan 2004.

Charles Saatchi (9 Jun 1943, Baghdad, Iraq), Iraqi-born British advertising executive who, with his younger brother Maurice, founded the Saatchi & Saatchi firm in London; he is equally well known as an art collector and patron and owner of the Saatchi Gallery, which has specialized in contemporary British art.

Sheikh Jabir al-Ahmad al-Jabir Al Sabah (29 Jun 1928, Kuwait City, Kuwait), Kuwaiti emir from 1977.

Sheikh Saad al-Abdullah al-Salim al Sabah (1930, Kuwait), Kuwaiti crown prince who was prime minister, 1978–2003.

Sheikh Sabah al-Ahmad al-Jabir Al Sabah (1929?, Kuwait), Kuwaiti royal, the fourth son of Emir Ahmad al-Jabir Al Sabah, who was prime minister from 2003.

Antonio Saca (Antonio Elías Saca González; 9 Mar 1965, Usulután, El Salvador), Salvadoran communications executive and politician of the Nationalist Republican Alliance; he was inaugurated as president on 1 Jun 2004.

Oliver (Wolf) Sacks (9 Jul 1933, London, England), British-born American neurologist and best-selling author.

Sade (Helen Folasade Adu; 16 Jan 1959, Ibadan, Nigeria), Nigerian-born British singer and songwriter.

Moqtada al-Sadr (1974?, Baghdad, Iraq), Iraqi Muslim junior cleric, the son of influential Shiʻa religious leader Mohammad Sadeq al-Sadr, and a charismatic figure in the anti-American and anti-Western insurrection in Iraq, especially Baghdad, following the US-led occupation of March 2003.

Keith J. Sainsbury (22 Feb 1951, Christchurch, NZ), New Zealand-born ecologist who researched marine-shelf ecosystems and their sustainable use; he was the winner of a Japan Prize in 2004.

Yves Saint Laurent (Yves-Henri-Donat-Mathieu Saint Laurent; 1 Aug 1936, Oran, Algeria), French fashion designer noted for his popularization of women's trousers for all occasions.

Jamie Salé (21 Apr 1977, Calgary, AB, Canada), Canadian pairs figure skater (with David Pelletier); shared the 2002 Olympic gold medal with Russians Yelena Berezhnaya and Anton Sikharulidze.

ʻAli ʻAbdullah Saleh (21 Mar 1942, Beit al-Ahmar, Yemen), Yemeni politician, president of Yemen (Sanʻa) 1978–90, and of the unified Yemen thereafter.

Sebastião (Ribeiro) Salgado (8 Feb 1944, Aimorés, Minas Gerais state, Brazil), Brazilian photographer whose work powerfully expresses the suffering of the homeless and downtrodden.

Esa-Pekka Salonen (30 Jun 1958, Helsinki, Finland), Finnish conductor and musical director of the Los Angeles Philharmonic from 1992.

Jorge (Fernando Branco de) Sampaio (18 Sep 1939, Lisbon, Portugal), Portuguese politician and president from 1996.

Ivo Sanader (8 Jun 1953, Split, Croatia, Yugoslavia), Croatian scholar, politician, and prime minister from 2003.

Pedro A. Sanchez (1940, Havana, Cuba), Cuban-born American soil scientist who was awarded the 2002 World Food Prize; Sanchez developed programs to help individual farmers in tropical regions to utilize natural material instead of imported fertilizers to boost crop yields; he is chair of the UN Millennium Project Task Force on World Hunger.

Jil Sander (Heidemarie Jiline Sander; 27 Nov 1943, Wesselburen, Germany), German fashion designer known for simple, sophisticated, classic creations.

Adam Sandler (9 Sep 1966, Brooklyn NY), American comic actor and *Saturday Night Live* cast member (1991–95) who is known for playing flawed but endearing comic characters.

Mark Sanford (15 Jan 1960, Fort Lauderdale FL), American Republican politician and governor of South Carolina from 2003.

Carlos Santana (20 Jul 1947, Autlán de Navarro, Mexico), Mexican-born American guitarist and bandleader.

Pedro Santana Lopes (29 Jun 1956, Lisbon, Portugal), Portuguese Social Democratic politician and prime minister from 17 Jul 2004 to 12 Mar 2005.

Alejandro Sanz (Alejandro Sánchez Pizarro; 18 Dec 1968, Madrid, Spain), Spanish pop singer-songwriter and flamenco-pop artist who won multiple Latin Grammy awards in 2001 and 2002.

Cristina Saralegui (29 Jan 1948, Havana, Cuba), Cuban-born American Spanish-language TV talk-show host.

José Saramago (16 Nov 1922, Azinhaga, Portugal), Portuguese novelist and man of letters who was awarded the 1998 Nobel Prize for Literature.

Susan Sarandon (Susan Abigail Tomalin; 4 Oct 1946, New York NY), American film actress who won an Academy Award for best actress for *Dead Man Walking* (1995) and whose other works include *Thelma & Louise* (1991) and *Anywhere but Here* (1999).

Paul S. Sarbanes (3 Feb 1933, Salisbury MD), American Democratic politician and senator from Maryland from 1977.

Nicolas Sarkozy (Nicolas Paul-Stéphane Sarközy de Nagy-Bocsa; 28 Jan 1955, Paris, France), French politician, the chairman (from 2004) of the conservative Union pour un Mouvement Populaire (UMP) party, and parliamentary deputy; he was appointed interior minister on 2 Jun 2005.

Mikio Sasaki (1937?), Japanese corporate executive who was president and CEO of Mitsubishi Motors Corp. from 1998.

Denis Sassou-Nguesso (1943, Edou, French Equatorial Africa [now in the Republic of the Congo]), Congolese politician and president of the Republic of the Congo, 1979–92 and again from 1997.

Jennifer Saunders (6 Jul 1958, Sleaford, Lincolnshire, England), British TV actress and comedian, best known for her work in the TV series

French & Saunders (with Dawn French) and *Absolutely Fabulous*.

Michael Savage (Michael Alan Weiner; 31 Mar 1942, Bronx NY), American nutrition expert who published several books on homeopathy and herbal medicine but much better known as the popular, populist host of radio talk shows and author of the best-selling book *The Savage Nation* (2003) and a 2004 follow-up, *The Enemy Within*.

Felix Savon (Félix Savón Fabré; 22 Sep 1967, San Vicente, Cuba), Cuban heavyweight boxer, three-time Olympic gold medalist.

Diane K. Sawyer (Lila Sawyer; 22 Dec 1945, Glasgow KY), American TV journalist.

Antonin Scalia (11 Mar 1936, Trenton NJ), American jurist and associate justice of the US Supreme Court from 1986.

Dame Marjorie Scardino (Marjorie Morris; 25 Jan 1947, Flagstaff AZ), American-born British CEO (from 1997) of the media firm Pearson PLC, which owns the *Financial Times* newspaper among others.

Claudia Schiffer (25 Aug 1970, Düsseldorf, West Germany [now in Germany]), German fashion model who appeared on hundreds of magazine covers and in advertisements.

Samuel Schmid (8 Jan 1947, Rüti bei Büren, Switzerland), Swiss president in 2005.

Eric E. Schmidt (1955?), American computer scientist and corporate executive who was CTO of Sun Microsystems, Inc., chairman and CEO of Novell, Inc., and chairman and CEO of Google, Inc., from 2001.

Eric-Emmanuel Schmitt (28 Mar 1960, St.-Foy-les-Lyon, France), French writer of plays, dramatic monologues, screenplays, and novels; his plays include *Le visiteur* (1994), for which he won three Molière awards, and *Monsieur Ibrahim et les fleurs du Coran* (2001; *Monsieur Ibrahim and the Flowers of the Koran*).

Maria (Lynn) Schneider (27 Nov 1960, Windom MN), American jazz composer and arranger.

Christoph Cardinal Schönborn (22 Jan 1945, Skalsko, Czechoslovakia [now in the Czech Republic]), Austrian Roman Catholic churchman, archbishop of Vienna from 1995 and bishop of Austria for the Faithful of Eastern Rite (Byzantine) from 1995; he was appointed cardinal in 1998.

Daniel Schorr (31 Aug 1916, New York NY), American TV and radio journalist and political commentator.

Jürgen Schrempp (14 Sep 1944, Freiburg im Breisgau, Germany), German executive and chairman of DaimlerChrysler from 1998.

Gerhard Schröder (7 Apr 1944, Mossenberg, Germany), German Socialist politician who served as defense minister and, from 1998, as chancellor.

Dieter Schulte (13 Jan 1940, Duisberg, Germany), German labor leader and head of the German Trade Union Federation from 1994.

Henning Schulte-Noelle (26 Aug 1942, Essen, Germany), German corporate executive and CEO of Allianz AG from 1991.

Howard Schultz (19 Jul 1953, Brooklyn NY), American businessman, moving spirit behind Starbucks Corp. (CEO from 1987) and principal owner of the Seattle SuperSonics pro basketball team (from 2001).

Michael Schumacher (3 Jan 1969, Hürth-Hermülheim, West Germany [now in Germany]), German Formula 1 race-car driver who dominated Grand Prix racing in the early 2000s and whose sports winnings, approaching $1 billion, were reportedly the highest of any athlete.

Wolfgang Schüssel (7 Jun 1945, Vienna, Austria), Austrian politician (Austrian People's Party) and chancellor from 2000.

Rudolf Schuster (4 Jan 1934, Kosice, Czechoslovakia [now Slovakia]), Slovak politician and president, 1999–2004.

Arnold (Alois) Schwarzenegger (30 Jul 1947, Thal bei Graz, Austria), Austrian-born American bodybuilder who became a Hollywood star with the film *The Terminator* (1984) and governor of California in 2003.

Brian Schweitzer (4 Sep 1955, Havre MT), American politician and Democratic governor of Montana from 3 Jan 2005.

David Schwimmer (2 Nov 1966, Astoria, Queens NY), American TV and film actor best known for his portrayal of Ross Geller on the TV comedy *Friends* (1994–2004).

Walter Schwimmer (16 Jun 1942, Vienna, Austria), Austrian international executive and secretary-general of the Council of Europe from 1999 to 31 Aug 2004.

John Scofield (26 Dec 1951, Dayton OH), American jazz electric guitarist, composer, and bandleader.

Martin Scorsese (17 Nov 1942, Flushing, Long Island NY), American film director, writer, and producer known for harsh, violent depictions; his works include *Taxi Driver* (1976), *Raging Bull* (1980), *GoodFellas* (1990), and *Gangs of New York* (2002).

H. Lee Scott, Jr. (1949?, Joplin MO), American executive who was named president and CEO of Wal-Mart Stores in January 2000.

Sir Ridley Scott (30 Nov 1937, South Shields, Durham, England), British film director and producer known for visual style and rich details; his films include *Alien* (1979), *Blade Runner* (1982), *Thelma & Louise* (1991), and *Gladiator* (2000).

Kristin Scott Thomas (24 May 1960, Redruth, Cornwall, England), British actress whose film credits include *The English Patient* (1996), *The Horse Whisperer* (1998), *Life as a House* (2001), and *Gosford Park* (2001).

Ludwig Scotty, Nauruan politician and president, May–August 2003 and again from 22 Jun 2004.

Vincent J. Scully, Jr. (New Haven CT), American architectural historian and critic; he received a National Medal of Arts in 2004.

Seal (Sealhenry Olusegun Olumide Samuel; 19 Feb 1963, Kilburn, London, England), British soul singer who found success in the adult contemporary market in the UK and the US.

Son Seals (13 Aug 1942, Osceola AR), American blues singer.

John (Rogers) Searle (31 Jul 1932, Denver CO), American philosopher of language and professor at the University of California, Berkeley; he was awarded a National Humanities Medal in 2004.

Kathleen Sebelius (15 May 1948, Cincinnati OH), American Democratic politician and governor of Kansas from 2003.

Alice Sebold (1963, Madison WI), American author whose first published novel, *The Lovely Bones* (2002), was a best seller.

David Sedaris (26 Dec 1956, Johnson City NY), American writer and humorist who has written a number of acclaimed books including *Naked* (1997) and *Dress Your Family in Corduroy and Denim* (2004).

Ivan G. Seidenberg (1947?, Bronx NY), American corporate executive and CEO of Verizon Communications from 2002.

Jerry Seinfeld (29 Apr 1954, Brooklyn NY), American

comic and TV personality made famous by his series *Seinfeld* (1990–98).

Monica Seles (2 Dec 1973, Novi Sad, Yugoslavia [now in Serbia and Montenegro]), Yugoslav-born tennis player who holds nine Grand Slam titles.

Bud Selig (Allan H. Selig; 30 Jul 1934, Milwaukee WI), American sports executive; Major League Baseball commissioner from 1998 (and de facto commissioner for six years before that).

Tom Selleck (29 Jan 1945, Detroit MI), American film and TV actor best remembered as star of the TV series *Magnum, P.I.* (1980–88).

Phil Selway (23 May 1967, Hemingford Grey, Cambridgeshire, England), British rock drummer and member of Radiohead.

Amartya (Kumar) Sen (3 Nov 1933, Santiniketan, Bengal state, British India), Indian economist who won the 1998 Nobel Memorial Prize for Economic Science for his contributions to welfare economics and social choice and his interest in the problems of society's poorest members.

Senait (Senait G. Mehari; 3 Dec 1976, Asmara, Ethiopia [now Eritrea]), Eritrean-born German singer who was a child soldier during the Eritrean war of independence, was later homeless in Hamburg, and became a pop star in Germany; her book *Feuerherz* came out in 2004.

Paul Sereno (11 Oct 1957, Aurora IL), American paleontologist credited with a number of significant dinosaur finds.

Jean-Pierre Serre (15 Sep 1926, Bages, France), French mathematician, a specialist in algebraic topology; he was the 1954 Fields medalist and the first winner (2003) of the Abel Prize.

Vikram Seth (20 Jun 1952, Calcutta [now Kolkata], India), Indian poet, novelist, and travel writer known for his verse novel *The Golden Gate* (1986) and his epic novel *A Suitable Boy* (1993).

Ahmed Necdet Sezer (13 Sep 1941, Ayfon, Turkey), Turkish politician and president from 2000.

Nasrallah Pierre Cardinal Sfeir (Nasrallah Boutros Pierre Sfeir; 15 May 1920, Reyfoun, Lebanon), Lebanese (Maronite Catholic) Patriarch of Antioch and All the East and Roman Catholic cardinal from 1994.

Shaggy (Orville Richard Burrell; 22 Oct 1968, Rae Town, Kingston, Jamaica), Jamaican reggae artist.

Gil Shaham (19 Feb 1971, Champaign-Urbana IL), American violinist often heard in concerts and recordings; he is known for his musicianship and broad repertory.

Shakira (Shakira Isabel Mebarak Ripoll; 2 Feb 1977, Barranquilla, Colombia), Colombian-born pop singer; she was appointed a UNICEF goodwill ambassador in 2003.

Tony Shalhoub (9 Oct 1953, Green Bay WI), American TV actor, who won an Emmy Award (2003) for best comedy actor for his work in the popular cable TV detective show *Monk* (from 2002).

Gene Shalit (25 Mar 1932, New York NY), American film critic.

Silvan Shalom (1958, Tunisia), Tunisian-born Israeli foreign minister from 2003.

John Patrick Shanley (1950, Bronx NY), American screenwriter and playwright who won an Academy Award in 1987 for his screenplay for *Moonstruck* and both a Pulitzer Prize for Drama and a Tony Award in 2005 for *Doubt*.

Natan Sharansky (Anatoly Borisovich Shcharansky; 20 Jan 1948, Stalino, Ukrainian SSR, USSR [now Donetsk, Ukraine]), Ukrainian-born Soviet dissident and political activist who turned to politics after immigration to Israel; he was deputy prime minister of Israel (2001–03) and, from 2003, minister without portfolio; his 2004 book, *The Case for Democracy*, reportedly influenced the administration of US Pres. George W. Bush.

Mariya Sharapova (19 Apr 1987, Nyagan, USSR [now in Russia]), Russian tennis player who surprised the world in 2004 by defeating two-time tournament women's champion Serena Williams 6–1, 6–4 to win the Wimbledon title; she was ranked second in the world in June 2005.

Ariel Sharon (Ariel Sheinerman; 26 Feb 1928, Kefar Malal, Palestine), Israeli politician and prime minister of Israel from 2001.

Al Sharpton (3 Oct 1954, New York NY), American Democratic political activist, civil-rights leader, and a presidential candidate in 2003–04.

William Shatner (22 Mar 1931, Montreal, QC, Canada), Canadian TV actor, author, and personality famous as Captain Kirk in the *Star Trek* TV series and films; he appeared in a new show, *Boston Legal*, from 2004.

Jim Shea, Jr. (10 Jun 1968, Hartford CT), American skeleton slider and third-generation Olympic competitor; he won the gold medal in the 2002 Winter Games.

Charlie Sheen (Carlos Irwin Estevez; 3 Sep 1965, New York NY), American film and TV actor.

Martin Sheen (Ramon Estevez; 3 Aug 1940, Dayton OH), American stage, film, and TV actor who plays the president in the award-winning TV series *The West Wing* (from 1999).

Judith Sheindlin (21 Oct 1942, Brooklyn NY), American TV judge (*Judge Judy*).

Sam Shepard (Samuel Shepard Rogers; 5 Nov 1943, Fort Sheridan IL), American playwright and actor whose plays adroitly blend images of the American West, Pop motifs, science fiction, and other elements of popular and youth culture.

Cindy Sherman (Cynthia Morris Sherman; 19 Jan 1954, Glen Ridge NJ), American photographer who is known for her elaborately disguised self-portraits that comment on social role-playing and sexual stereotypes.

Eric K. Shinseki (28 Nov 1942, Lihue HI), American military official and chief of staff of the US Army from 1999.

Vandana Shiva (1952, Dehra Dun, Uttar Pradesh [now in Uttaranchal] state, India), Indian biologist and social activist against the "biological theft" of the resources of poor countries by the richer ones; director of the Research Foundation on Science, Technology, and Ecology in India.

Martin Short (26 Mar 1950, Hamilton, ON, Canada), Canadian actor and comedian who won, among many other awards, a Tony in 1999 for his role in the play *Little Me*.

Will Shortz (1952), American "enigmatologist" and "puzzlemaster"; crossword-puzzle editor at the *New York Times*.

Etsuhiko Shoyama (c. 1937), Japanese corporate executive and CEO of Hitachi, Ltd., from 1999.

Maria (Owings) Shriver (6 Nov 1955, Chicago IL), American TV journalist with *Dateline NBC* (1989–2004) and wife of actor and California governor Arnold Schwarzenegger.

M. Night Shyamalan (6 Aug 1970, Pondicherry, India), Indian-born film director and screenwriter made famous by *The Sixth Sense* (1999) and *Signs* (2002).

John W. Sidgmore (1950?), American corporate executive; CEO of WorldCom, Inc., from 2002.

Thomas M. Siebel (February 1953, Chicago IL), American corporate executive, the founder and CEO of Siebel Systems from 1993.

Anton Sikharulidze (25 Oct 1976, Leningrad, USSR [now St. Petersburg, Russia]), Russian pairs figure skater (with Yelena Berezhnaya); they shared the 2002 Olympic gold medal with Canadians Salé and Pelletier.

Alicia Silverstone (4 Oct 1976, San Francisco CA), American film and TV actress.

Queen Silvia (Silvia Renate Sommerlath; 23 Dec 1943, Heidelberg, Germany), Swedish royal and social activist, queen consort of King Carl XVI Gustaf (married 19 Jun 1976).

Simeon II (Simeon Saxecoburggotski; 16 Jun 1937, Sofia, Bulgaria), Bulgarian royal, the last king of Bulgaria (Simeon II, 1943–46), and prime minister of the country from 2001.

Charles Simic (9 May 1938, Belgrade, Yugoslavia [now in Serbia and Montenegro]), Yugoslav-born American poet who evoked his Eastern European heritage and his childhood experiences during World War II to comment poetically on the dearth of spirituality in contemporary life.

Kostas Simitis (Konstantinos Georgiou Simitis; 23 Jun 1936, Athens, Greece), Greek politician and prime minister, 1996–2004.

Russell Simmons ("Rush"; 4 Oct 1957, Queens NY), American hip-hop impresario and cofounder (with Rick Rubin) of Def Jam Records.

Paul Simon (13 Oct 1941, Newark NJ), American singer and songwriter known first for his folk-rock albums with partner Art Garfunkel and later for his innovative solo work.

Anne Simpson (1956, Toronto, ON, Canada), Canadian poet and writer, winner of the 2004 Canadian Griffin Poetry Prize for *Loop.*

Ashlee Simpson (3 Oct 1984, Dallas TX), American singer and TV and film actress, the younger sister of Jessica Simpson.

Jessica Simpson (10 Jul 1980, Dallas TX), American dance-pop singer and star of MTV's *Newlyweds* (from 2003).

Manmohan Singh (26 Sep 1932, Gah, Punjab, British India [now in Pakistan]), Indian Sikh economist, professor, and government official; he was prime minister from 22 May 2004.

Gary Sinise (17 Mar 1955, Blue Island IL), American TV and film actor and director first noticed for his work in the TV miniseries *The Stand* (1994) and for his work in the film *Forrest Gump* (1994).

(Sayyid) Ali (Hussaini) al-Sistani (4 Aug 1930?, near Meshed, Iran), Iranian Shi'ite Muslim cleric, a grand ayatollah, and one of the top two religious and legal authorities in Shi'i Islam.

Ricky Skaggs (18 Jul 1954, Cordell KY), American bluegrass and country musician, a top award-winner and concert draw in the 1980s and '90s.

Antonio Skármeta (7 Nov 1940, Antofagasta, Chile), Chilean novelist and screenwriter.

Jeffrey S. Skoll (16 Jan 1965, Montreal, QC, Canada), Canadian entrepreneur, a cofounder of eBay and, from 1999, the president of the philanthropic Skoll Foundation.

Leonard (Edward) Slatkin (1 Sep 1944, Los Angeles CA), American conductor; music director of the National Symphony Orchestra from 1996; he was awarded a 2003 National Medal of Arts.

Carlos Slim Helú (1940, Mexico?), Mexican investor; head of Grupo Carso, SA de CV, and longtime owner of the national telephone monopoly, Teléfonos de México (Telmex); he was 17th on *Forbes* magazine's 2004 list of the world's richest persons.

Irina Slutskaya (9 Feb 1979, Moscow, USSR [now in Russia]), Russian figure skater, six-time European champion and twice world champion (2002 and 2005).

Lawrence M. Small (14 Sep 1941, New York NY), American businessman who was president and COO of Fannie Mae, the housing finance company, and served as secretary of the Smithsonian Institution from 2000.

Tavis Smiley (13 Sep 1964, Gulfport MS), American advocacy journalist, the host of *The Tavis Smiley Show* on Public Radio International and *Tavis Smiley* on PBS, as well as a daily radio feature on urban contemporary stations.

Emmitt Smith (Emmitt James Smith III; 15 May 1969, Pensacola FL), American football player, a Dallas Cowboys running back who on 27 Oct 2002 surpassed Walter Payton's record 16,726 yd rushing.

Marc (Kelly) Smith ("Slampapi"; 195?, Chicago IL), American poet and originator of the "poetry slam"—performance-poetry competitions—in the mid-1980s.

Michael W. Smith (7 Oct 1957, Kenova WV), American Christian singer.

Patti Smith (30 Dec 1946, Chicago IL), American musician, poet, and visual artist.

Vernon L. Smith (1 Jan 1927, Wichita KS), American economist; cowinner of the 2002 Nobel Memorial Prize for Economic Science for developing experimental methods that have been key to empirical economic analysis.

Will Smith (Willard Christopher Smith, Jr.; 25 Sep 1968, Philadelphia PA), American rapper and actor on TV (*The Fresh Prince of Bel Air*, 1990–96) and in films, such as *Men in Black* (1997) and *Men in Black II* (2002).

Zadie Smith (Sadie Smith; 1975, Willesden Green, London, England), British novelist whose work is acclaimed for its eccentric characters, savvy humor, and snappy dialogue and for addressing such serious issues as race, religion, and cultural identity.

Jimmy Smits (9 Jul 1955, Brooklyn NY), American TV and film actor who starred in *NYPD Blue* (1994–98) and *The West Wing* (from 2004).

Aleksandr Pavlovich Smolensky (1954), Russian banker and president of Stolichny Bank Sberezhny (SBS; now SBS-Agro).

Wesley Snipes (31 Jul 1962, Orlando FL), American film actor, principally in action movies, including two *Blade* films (1998 and 2002).

Snoop Dogg (Calvin Broadus; 20 Oct 1972, Long Beach CA), American gangsta rap musician whose private life often seemed to be an extension of his violent and sexist lyrics.

John W. Snow (2 Aug 1939, Toledo OH), American businessman and government official who was secretary of the treasury from 2003.

Gary (Sherman) Snyder (8 May 1930, San Francisco CA), American poet early identified with the Beat movement and, from the late 1960s, a spokesman for the concerns of communal living and ecological activism.

Solomon Halbert Snyder (26 Dec 1938, Washington DC), American neuroscientist who discovered opiate receptors in the brain and determined that gases can serve as neural messengers; he was honored with a Lasker Award in 1978 and a 2003 National Medal of Science.

José Sócrates (Carvalho Pinto de Sousa) (6 Sep 1957, Vilar de Maçada, Portugal), Portuguese civil engineer and Socialist politician who served as prime minister from 4 March 2005.

Angelo Cardinal Sodano (23 Nov 1927, Isola d'Asto, Italy), Italian Roman Catholic churchman who was secretary of state of the Vatican from 1991 and was elevated to cardinal in the same year.

Steven Soderbergh (14 Jan 1963, Atlanta GA), American film director who has won commercial success and critical acclaim; he received an Academy Award for directing *Traffic* in 2000.

Queen Sofia (Princess Sophie of Greece; Sofia de Grecia y Hannover; 2 Nov 1938, Athens, Greece), Spanish royal, the queen consort of King Juan Carlos I of Spain (married 12 May 1962).

Javier Solana Madariaga (14 Jul 1942, Madrid, Spain), Spanish statesman who was NATO secretary-general, 1995–99, and secretary-general of the Western European Union from 1999.

Howard Solomon (12 Aug 1927, New York NY), American corporate executive and CEO of Forest Laboratories, Inc., from 1977.

Susan Solomon (19 Jan 1956, Chicago IL), American photochemist specializing in the chemistry of the stratosphere, especially the science of the Antarctic ozone hole; she was the recipient of a National Medal of Science in 2000 and the 2002 Weizmann Women & Science Award.

László Sólyom (3 Jan 1942, Pécs, Hungary), Hungarian jurist and environmentalist who was president from 5 Aug 2005.

Sir Michael (Thomas) Somare (9 Apr 1936, Rabaul, [Australian-mandated] New Guinea [now Papua New Guinea]), politician who was the first prime minister of independent Papua New Guinea, 1975–80, served a second time, 1982–85, and again from 2002.

Ron Sommer (29 Jul 1949, Haifa, Israel), Israeli-born German corporate executive who was the CEO of Deutsche Telekom AG, 1995–2002.

Stephen (Joshua) Sondheim (22 Mar 1930, New York NY), American composer and lyricist for musical theater; he won eight Tony Awards as well as the 1985 Pulitzer Prize for Drama.

Queen Sonja (Sonja Haraldsen; 4 Jul 1937, Oslo, Norway), Norwegian royal, the queen consort of King Harald V (married 29 Aug 1968).

Sophie, countess of Wessex (Sophie Helen Rhys-Jones; 20 Jan 1965, Oxford, England), British royal, the wife of Prince Edward, earl of Wessex.

Annika Sörenstam (9 Oct 1970, Stockholm, Sweden), Swedish golfer who was the LPGA top golfer in 2001, 2002, and 2003; she completed a career grand slam on 3 Aug 2003 by winning the British Open, having previously won the US Open (2002), the LPGA championship (2003), and the Kraft Nabisco competition (2001). In 2003 she also competed in a PGA (normally all-men) Tour event, the first woman in 58 years to do so.

Aaron Sorkin (9 Jun 1961, Scarsdale NY), American screenwriter, playwright, and TV producer.

Mira Sorvino (28 Sep 1967, Tenafly NJ), American film actress who gained fame with *Mighty Aphrodite* (1995; best supporting actress Academy Award).

Sammy Sosa (Samuel Sosa Peralta; 12 Nov 1968, San Pedro de Macoris, Dominican Republic), Dominican baseball outfielder for the Baltimore Ori-

oles and, from 1992 to 2004, the Chicago Cubs; he was the only player to hit more than 60 home runs three times (1998, 1999, 2001).

David H(ackett) Souter (17 Sep 1939, Melrose MA), American jurist and associate justice of the US Supreme Court from 1990.

Wole Soyinka (Akinwande Oluwole Soyinka; 13 Jul 1934, Abeokuta, Nigeria), Nigerian playwright, poet, novelist, and critic who received the 1986 Nobel Prize for Literature; he wrote of modern West Africa in a satirical style and with a tragic sense of the obstacles to human progress.

Kevin Spacey (Kevin Matthew Fowler; 26 Jul 1959, South Orange NJ), American stage and film actor who won an Oscar for best supporting actor for *The Usual Suspects* (1995) and for best actor for *American Beauty* (1999).

James (Todd) Spader (7 Feb 1960, Boston MA), American film and TV actor who won a best actor award at the Cannes Film Festival in 1989 for his work in *Sex, Lies, and Videotape*; he joined the cast of the TV series *The Practice* (2003–04) and continued as the same character in *Boston Legal* (from 2004).

Nicholas Sparks (31 Dec 1965, Omaha NE), American author of best-selling novels including *Nights in Rodanthe* (2002) and *The Guardian* (2003).

Britney (Jean) Spears (2 Dec 1981, Kentwood LA), American pop singer, film star, and teen idol.

Aaron Spelling (22 Apr 1923, Dallas TX), American TV producer.

Margaret Spellings (30 Nov 1957, Michigan), American political adviser, education expert (she helped draft the No Child Left Behind Act), and US secretary of education from 31 Jan 2005.

W(inston) Baldwin Spencer (8 Oct 1948), Antigua and Barbuda politician and prime minister of Antigua and Barbuda from 24 Mar 2004.

Steven Spielberg (18 Dec 1947, Cincinnati OH), American film director and producer, one of the foremost of all time; he won Academy Awards for directing in 1993 (*Schindler's List*) and 1998 (*Saving Private Ryan*); his other works include *Jaws* (1975), *E.T. the Extra-Terrestrial* (1982), *The Color Purple* (1985), *Catch Me If You Can* (2002), and *War of the Worlds* (2005).

Eliot Spitzer (10 Jun 1959, Riverdale, Bronx NY), American attorney and politician who, as attorney general of New York from 1999, doggedly pursued irregularities in the activities and accounting practices of some of the largest American stock brokerage firms and secured actions against them in the courts and through the US Securities and Exchange Commission.

Jerry Springer (Gerald N. Springer; 13 Feb 1944, London, England), American TV personality and politician; he served as mayor of Cincinnati OH (1977–78) and ran in the primary race for governor of Ohio before becoming a TV journalist and commentator in 1982; he launched the sensationalist and often physical *The Jerry Springer Show* on TV in 1991.

Timothy A. Springer (23 Feb 1948, Fort Benning GA), American pathologist who shared the 2004 Crafoord Prize with Eugene C. Butcher "for their studies on the molecular mechanisms involved in migration of white blood cells in health and disease."

Bruce Springsteen ("The Boss"; 23 Sep 1949, Freehold NJ), American rock singer and songwriter who became the archetypal rock performer of the 1970s and '80s and who enjoyed a new surge of popularity in 2002 with a concert tour and a new album, *The Rising*, that treated the aftermath of 9/11.

Sylvester Stallone (Michael Sylvester Enzio Stallone; "Sly," "The Italian Stallion"; 6 Jul 1946, New York NY), American film actor and director best known for macho acting roles such as in four *Rocky* films (1976, 1979, 1982, and 1985) and the *Rambo* series (1982, 1985, and 1988).

Mavis Staples (1940, Chicago IL), American gospel vocalist, the lead singer of the Staples Singers.

Danielle Steel (Danielle Fernande Schuelein-Steel; 14 Aug 1947, New York NY), American romance novelist.

Shelby Steele (1 Jan 1946, Chicago IL), American critic and scholar of race issues who opposed quota-based affirmative action; he was awarded a National Humanities Medal in 2005.

Gwen Stefani (3 Oct 1969, Fullerton CA), American rock vocalist who led the group No Doubt from 1987 and later established herself as a successful solo artist.

Frank P(hilip) Stella (12 May 1936, Malden MA), American painter, a leading figure in the Minimal art movement, known especially for paintings that were austere yet monumental in the simplicity of their design.

Princess Stephanie (Stéphanie Marie Elizabeth Grimaldi; 1 Feb 1965, Monaco), Monegasque royal, the youngest child of Prince Rainier III and Grace Kelly.

George Stephanopoulos (10 Feb 1961, Fall River MA), American journalist, political commentator, and presidential adviser.

Konstantinos Dimitriou ("Kostis") Stephanopoulos (15 Aug 1926, Patras, Greece), Greek politician; president of the Second Hellenic Republic from 1995 to 12 Mar 2005.

Stéphanos II (Amba Andraos Ghattas; Stéphanos Cardinal Ghattas; 16 Jan 1920, Cheikh Zein-el-Dine, Egypt), Egyptian churchman, patriarch of Alexandria of the Coptics from 1986; he was named Roman Catholic cardinal in 2001.

Howard Stern (12 Jan 1954, Roosevelt NY), American radio and TV "shock jock," actor, and author.

Karl O. Stetter (16 Jul 1941, Munich, Germany), German microbiologist, a specialist in hyperthermophiles, or organisms that live in high-temperature environments; he was the recipient of the 2003 Leeuwenhoek Medal of the Dutch Royal Academy of Sciences.

John Paul Stevens (20 Apr 1920, Chicago IL), American jurist; associate justice of the US Supreme Court from 1975.

Ted Stevens (18 Nov 1923, Indianapolis IN), American Republican politician, senator from Alaska, and president pro tempore of the Senate from 2003.

Jon Stewart (Jonathan Stewart Leibowitz; 28 Nov 1962, New York NY), American actor, writer, and comedian; he was the anchor of TV's *The Daily Show with Jon Stewart* from 1999.

Martha Stewart (Martha Helen Kostyra; 3 Aug 1941, Nutley NJ), American homemaking adviser, TV personality, and entrepreneur.

Rod Stewart (Roderick David Stewart; 10 Jan 1945, London, England), British singer whose soulful, raspy voice has graced rock and pop hits since the late 1960s.

Joseph E. Stiglitz (9 Feb 1943, Gary IN), American economist; cowinner of the 2001 Nobel Memorial Prize for Economic Science for work in the theory of markets with asymmetrical information.

Ben Stiller (30 Nov 1965, New York NY), American comedian, actor, and film director.

Sting (Gordon Matthew Sumner; 2 Oct 1951, Wallsend, Newcastle upon Tyne, England), British musician, singer, songwriter, and actor; he was made CBE in 2003.

Hannah Stockbauer (7 Jan 1982, Nürnberg, West Germany), German swimmer who took three first place medals in distance freestyle events at the 2003 world championships and was named *Swimming World*'s 2003 World Female Swimmer of the Year.

Edmund Stoiber (28 Sep 1941, Oberaudorf, Bavaria, Germany), German politician, Christian Socialist Union party leader, premier of Bavaria, and unsuccessful candidate for the German chancellorship in 2002.

Joss Stone (Joscelyn Eve Stoker; 11 Apr 1987, Dover, Kent, England), English soul singer.

Matt Stone (26 May 1971, Houston TX), American cocreator (with Trey Parker) of *South Park,* an animated TV show.

Oliver (William) Stone (15 Sep 1946, New York NY), American director, writer, and producer of films with often politically controversial content; he won Academy Awards for directing *Platoon* (1986) and *Born on the Fourth of July* (1989).

Sharon (Vonne) Stone (10 Mar 1958, Meadville PA), American fashion model and film actress who broke through in the movies in 1990 with *Total Recall* and hit it big with *Basic Instinct* (1992); other notable performances include those in *Casino* (1995) and *Cold Creek Manor* (2003).

Sir Tom Stoppard (Tomas Straussler; 3 Jul 1937, Zlin, Czechoslovakia [now in the Czech Republic]), British playwright and screenplay writer whose work is marked by verbal brilliance, ingenious action, and structural dexterity.

Mark Strand (11 Apr 1934, Summerside, PE, Canada), Canadian writer whose poetry, noted for its surreal quality, explores the boundaries of the self and the external world.

Jozef Straus (1946, Velke Kapusany, Czechoslovakia [now in Slovakia]), American corporate executive who was CEO of JDS Uniphase, Inc., from 1999.

Jack Straw (3 Aug 1946, Essex, England), British politician; foreign secretary from 2001.

Meryl Streep (Mary Louise Streep; 22 Jun 1949, Summit NJ), American film actress who won Academy Awards for best supporting actress in *Kramer vs. Kramer* (1979) and best actress in *Sophie's Choice* (1982); she received the American Film Institute's Life Achievement Award in 2004.

John F. Street (1943, Norristown PA), American Democratic politician; mayor of Philadelphia from 2000.

Barbra Streisand (Barbara Joan Streisand; 24 Apr 1942, Brooklyn NY), American singer, actress, and film director who is renowned for her compelling interpretations of popular songs on stage and screen and for her tour de force performances in films; Streisand has received two Academy Awards, 10 Grammys, 6 Emmys, a Tony Award, 11 Golden Globes, 2 CableACEs, 2 Peabody Awards, and the American Film Institute's Life Achievement Award (2001).

Sir Howard Stringer (19 Feb 1942, Cardiff, Wales), Welsh-born business executive who in 2005 was named chairman and CEO of Sony Corp., the first non-Japanese to hold those posts.

Susan Stroman (17 Oct 1954, Wilmington DE),

American theater director, winner of two Tony Awards in 2001 for *The Producers*.

(Christopher) Ruben Studdard (12 Sep 1978, Frankfurt am Main, West Germany [now in Germany]), American singer who won the 2003 TV competition *American Idol*; his debut CD, *Soulful*, was released in December 2003 and went immediately to the top of the charts.

Yevgeny Sudbin (19 Apr 1980, Leningrad, USSR [now St. Petersburg, Russia]), Russian concert pianist.

Hiroshi Sugimoto (1948, Tokyo, Japan), Japanese-born American photographer who achieved a striking, meditative quality in his very-long-exposure black-and-white photographs of architectural subjects and in his portraits of wax models.

Anna Sui (1955, Dearborn MI), American fashion designer whose clothing and cosmetics reflect a rock-music style mixed with vintage-inspired designs.

Megawati Sukarnoputri (23 Jan 1947, Jakarta, Indonesia), Indonesian politician and president from 2001 to 20 Oct 2004; she is the daughter of Sukarno, the founder of independent Indonesia.

Raman Sukumar (3 Apr 1955, Madras [now Chennai], India), Indian animal ecologist who has spent more than two decades studying Asian elephants in the wild in an effort to preserve the species; he was presented with the 2003 Whitley Gold Award in recognition of his commitment to conservation.

John E. Sulston (27 Mar 1942, Cambridge, England), British cell biologist; he was cowinner of the 2002 Nobel Prize for Physiology or Medicine for his work on the life of a cell.

Arthur Ochs Sulzberger, Jr. (22 Sep 1951, Mt. Kisco NY), American newspaper executive, publisher of the *New York Times* from 1992 and CEO from 1997.

Frederick Sumaye (29 May 1950, Hanang district, Tanganyika [now Tanzania]), Tanzanian politician and prime minister from 1995.

Lawrence H. Summers (30 Nov 1954, New Haven CT), American university and government official; he was US secretary of the treasury, 1999–2001, and president of Harvard University from 2001; his brash personal style led to clashes with faculty members and public controversy over the role of the modern American university.

Pat Summitt (Patricia Head; 14 Jun 1952, Henrietta TN), American basketball coach; longtime coach of the University of Tennessee Lady Volunteers teams, which won six national championships during her tenure.

Kiefer Sutherland (William Frederick Dempsey George Sutherland; 21 Dec 1966, London, England), Canadian film and TV actor whose first success was in the movie *The Bay Boy* (1984) before his hit turn on TV (from 2001) as American counterterrorist agent Jack Bauer in *24*.

Lord Sutherland of Houndwood (25 Feb 1941, Aberdeen, Scotland), Scottish historian and philosopher of religion; he was knighted in 1995, raised to the peerage as Baron Sutherland of Houndwood in 2001, made president of the Royal Society of Edinburgh in 2002, and inducted into the Order of the Thistle in 2002.

Ichiro Suzuki (22 Oct 1973, Kasugai, Aichi prefecture, Japan), Japanese baseball player, right fielder for the Orix BlueWave of Japan's Pacific League, who moved to the US to play with the Seattle Mariners in 2000 and was named American League MVP and Rookie of the Year in 2001.

Esbjörn Svensson (1964, Västeras, Sweden), Swedish jazz pianist whose group, the Esbjörn Svensson Trio (or "e.s.t."), has won numerous awards in Sweden and internationally for its creative fusion of jazz, rock, and classical traditions and for the equality of roles given to the piano, bass, and drums.

Hilary Swank (30 Jul 1974, Lincoln NE), American film actress most noted for her Academy Award-winning performance for best actress in *Boys Don't Cry* (1999); she won a best actress Oscar again for *Million Dollar Baby* (2004).

John J. Sweeney (5 May 1934, New York NY), American labor leader and president of the AFL-CIO from 1995.

Tuanku Syed Sirajuddin ibni al-Marhum Syed Putra Jamalullail (16 May 1943, Arau, British Malaya [now Malaysia]), Malaysian royal; *yang di-pertuan agong* (paramount ruler) of Malaysia from 2001.

Azadeh Tabazadeh (1965?, Iran), Iranian-born American atmospheric scientist whose work was instrumental in proving that naturally produced materials cannot be responsible for the degradation of the Earth's ozone layer.

Antonio Tabucchi (23 Sep 1943, Pisa, Italy), Italian novelist and educator.

Keiji Tachikawa (27 May 1939, Ogaki, Gifu prefecture, Japan), Japanese communications executive, president of DoCoMo, a wireless provider operated by Nippon Telegraph & Telephone, Japan's main telecommunications carrier.

Bob Taft (8 Jan 1942, Boston MA), American Republican politician and governor of Ohio from 1999.

Paul Tagliabue (24 Nov 1940, Jersey City NJ), American sports executive and commissioner of the National Football League from 1989.

Masatoshi Takeichi (27 Nov 1943, Nagoya, Japan), Japanese developmental biologist, professor, and director of the RIKEN Center for Developmental Biology; he shared (with Erkki Ruoslahti) the Japan Prize in Cell Biology in 2005 for "fundamental contributions in elucidating the molecular mechanisms of cell adhesion."

Jalal Talabani (1933, Kalkan, Iraq), Iraqi Kurdish politician who created (1976) and led the Patriotic Union of Kurdistan and was the first democratically elected president of Iraq, from 7 Apr 2005.

Mehmet Ali Talat (6 Jul 1952, Girne, Cyprus), Turkish Cypriot politician and prime minister of the Turkish Republic of Northern Cyprus (2004-05), and president from 24 Apr 2005.

Ryoko Tamura (married name Tani; 6 Sep 1975, Fukuoka, Japan), Japanese judoka who, at the 2004 Games, won a second straight Olympic gold medal in judo, the first woman to win two medals in the sport; she was also world champion for six consecutive seasons.

Koichi Tanaka (3 Aug 1959, Toyama, Toyama prefecture, Japan), Japanese chemist; cowinner of the 2002 Nobel Prize for Chemistry for his work in the study of macromolecules.

Malietoa Tanumafili II (4 Jan 1913, Apia, Western Samoa [now Samoa]), Samoan royal, *O le Ao o le Malo* (elective monarch) of Samoa from 1963.

Quentin (Jerome) Tarantino (27 Mar 1963, Knoxville TN), American film director who gained attention with *Reservoir Dogs* (1992) and widespread recognition for *Pulp Fiction* (1994; Palme d'Or at Cannes) and the two *Kill Bill* films (2003 and 2004).

Vasile Tarlev (9 Oct 1963, Bascalia, Moldavian SSR, USSR [now Moldova]), Moldovan politician and prime minister from 2001.

Ibrahim Tatlises (Ibrahim Tatli; "Ibo"; 1954, Urfa, Turkey), Turkish singer, actor, and TV host.

King Taufa'ahau Tupou IV (4 Jul 1918, Nuku'alofa, Tonga), Tongan king from 1965.

Sir John Tavener (28 Jan 1944, London, England), British composer whose works were inspired by sacred and spiritual texts and drew from Russian, Byzantine, and Greek influences.

Maaouya Ould Sidi Ahmed Taya (1941, Atar, Mauritania), Mauritanian politician and president from 1992.

Cecil (Percival) Taylor (15 Mar 1933, New York NY), American jazz pianist and composer, a leading exponent of free jazz.

Charles (McArthur Ghankay) Taylor (27 Jan 1948, Athington, Liberia), Liberian coup leader and president of Liberia from 1997 until 2003, when he stepped down and went into exile.

Elizabeth Taylor (27 Feb 1932, London, England), American film actress of great distinction noted for emotionally volatile characters; she won Academy Awards for best actress for *Butterfield 8* (1960) and *Who's Afraid of Virginia Woolf?* (1966).

Te Ata-i Rangi-Kahu Koroki Te Rata Mahuta Tawhiao Potatau Te Wherowhero (1931, New Zealand?), New Zealand Maori royal; queen of the Maori community from 1966.

Oscar Temaru (1 Nov 1944, Faa'a district, Tahiti, French Polynesia), French Polynesian politician and president from 19 Jun 2004.

Sachin Ramesh Tendulkar (24 Apr 1973, Bombay [now Mumbai], India), Indian cricket batsman who scored 673 runs in the 2003 World Cup, breaking his own world record for the tournament.

George (John) Tenet (5 Jan 1953, Queens NY), American government official who was director of central intelligence and CIA director from 1997 to 11 Jul 2004.

Bryn Terfel (Bryn Terfel Jones; 9 Nov 1965, near Pant Glas, Wales), Welsh operatic bass-baritone.

Studs Terkel (Louis Terkel; 16 May 1912, New York NY), American author, radio host, and oral historian.

Adnan Terzic (1960, Zagreb, Croatia, Yugoslavia [now in Croatia]), Bosnian and Herzegovinian politician and chairman of the Council of Ministers (prime minister) from 23 Dec 2002.

Mario Testino (1954, Lima, Peru), Peruvian fashion photographer.

Dionigi Cardinal Tettamanzi (14 Mar 1934, Renate, Italy), Italian Roman Catholic churchman; archbishop of Genoa, from 1995 and archbishop of Milan from 2002; he was named cardinal in 1998.

Bal (Keshav) Thackeray (23 Jan 1927), Indian political cartoonist and newspaper publisher who started (1966) the ultra-Hindu-nationalist Shivsena party; he holds no government post but as president of Shivsena controls politics in Maharashtra state; he is known as the "Tiger" and the "godfather of Bombay."

John A. Thain (1955?), American financial official appointed CEO of the New York Stock Exchange from 15 Jan 2004.

Thaksin Shinawatra (26 Jul 1949, Chiangmai, Thailand), Thai politician and prime minister from 2001.

Sheikh Hamad ibn Khalifah al-Thani (1950, Doha, Qatar), Qatari emir from 1995.

Twyla Tharp (1 Jul 1941, Portland IN), American dancer, director, and choreographer noted for her innovation and for the humor she brought to much

of her work; she received a National Medal of Arts in 2004.

Charlize Theron (7 Aug 1975, Benoni, South Africa), South African actress whose films included *The Cider House Rules* (1999), *Reindeer Games* (2000), *The Legend of Bagger Vance* (2000), and *Monster* (2003; best actress Academy Award).

Olivier Theyskens (4 Jan 1977, Brussels, Belgium), Belgian-born fashion designer whose first collection for Maison Rochas in March 2003 drew wide attention.

Thich Nhat Hanh (1926, central Vietnam), Vietnamese Buddhist monk, pacifist, and teacher.

Clarence Thomas (23 Jun 1948, Pinpoint community, near Savannah GA), American jurist; associate justice of the US Supreme Court from 1991.

Michael Tilson Thomas (21 Dec 1944, Hollywood CA), American conductor and composer; music director of the San Francisco Symphony from 1995.

Emma Thompson (15 Apr 1959, London, England), British film actress known especially for serious dramatic roles and period pieces; she won an Academy Award for best actress for *Howards End* (1992).

Jenny Thompson (26 Feb 1973, Danvers MA), American swimmer who held the record for the most Olympic medals ever won by an American (12, including 8 golds, in the 1992, 1996, 2000, and 2004 Games).

Tommy G. Thompson (19 Nov 1941, Elroy WI), American government official, governor of Wisconsin, 1987–2001, and US secretary of health and human services from 2001 to 2005.

James Thomson (20 Dec 1958, Chicago IL), American cell biologist and stem-cell researcher, the first person to isolate stem cells from human embryos.

Robert Thomson (11 Mar 1961, Echuca, VIC, Australia), Australian journalist; editor of *The Times* of London from February 2002 and the first non-Briton ever to hold the post.

Billy Bob Thornton (4 Aug 1955, Hot Springs AR), American director and actor whose work includes *Sling Blade* (1996), *Monster's Ball* (2001), and *Levity* (2003).

Ian Thorpe ("The Thorpedo"; 13 Oct 1982, Sydney, NSW, Australia), Australian swimmer who won three gold and one silver medal in the 2000 Games, then won six gold medals and set four world records in the 2001 world championships.

Uma (Karuna) Thurman (29 Apr 1970, Boston MA), American film actress often cast in sultry roles; she appeared in *Pulp Fiction* (1994), *Les Miserables* (1998), *Sweet and Lowdown* (1999), and two *Kill Bill* films (2003 and 2004).

Justin (Randall) Timberlake (31 Jan 1981, Memphis TN), American singer at the forefront of the teen-pop movement of the 1990s; he was a member of the group *NSYNC and, after 2001, performed as a solo artist and released a successful solo album, *Justified* (2002).

Rirkrit Tiravanija (1961, Buenos Aires, Argentina), Thai interactive artist who seeks to involve his audience in the creation and experiencing of the artwork in a maximal way; he was awarded the Hugo Boss Prize of the Guggenheim Museum in 2004.

Maatia Toafa (Nanumea island, Tuvalu), Tuvalu politician and prime minister from 27 Aug 2004 (acting until 11 October).

Alejandro Toledo (Manrique) (28 Mar 1946, Cabana, Peru), Peruvian politician and president of Peru from 2001.

Claire Tomalin (Claire Delavenay; 20 Jun 1933, London, England), English biographer and journalist.

Anote Tong (1952), Kiribati politician and president from 2003.

Martín Torrijos Espino (18 Jul 1963, Panama City, Panama), Panamanian politician and president from 1 Sep 2004; he is the son of former military dictator Omar Torrijos.

Linus (Benedict) Torvalds (28 Dec 1969, Helsinki, Finland), Finnish-born computer scientist who developed the Linux operating system.

Tatyana Totmyanina (2 Nov 1981, Perm, Russian SFSR, USSR [now in Russia]), Russian pairs figure skater who, with Maksim Marinin, won the world championship in 2004.

Amadou Toumani Touré (4 Nov 1948, Mpoti, French Sudan [now in Mali]), Malian politician and president, 1991–92, and again from 2002.

Charles H(ard) Townes (28 Jul 1915, Greenville SC), American physicist who received (with N.G. Basov and A.M. Prokhorov) the 1964 Nobel Prize for Physics for developing masers and lasers; he was awarded the 2005 Templeton Award for Progress Toward Research or Discoveries about Spiritual Realities.

Tran Duc Luong (5 May 1937, Quang Ngai province, French Indochina [now in Vietnam]), Vietnamese politician and president from 1997.

Tomas Tranströmer (15 Apr 1931, Stockholm, Sweden), Swedish lyrical poet noted for his resonant and strangely suggestive imagery.

Randy Travis (Randy Traywick; 4 May 1959, Marshville NC), American country-and-western singer, songwriter, and actor.

John (Joseph) Travolta (18 Feb 1955, Englewood NJ), American actor known for TV roles and trendsetting films such as *Saturday Night Fever* (1977) and *Grease* (1978); he later began a career revival with *Pulp Fiction* (1994).

Jean-Claude Trichet (20 Dec 1942, Lyons, France), French banker, two-term governor of the Banque de France, and president of the European Central Bank from 2003.

Calvin Trillin (5 Dec 1935, Kansas City MO), American author, commentator, and occasional poet.

(William) David Trimble (15 Oct 1944, Belfast, Northern Ireland), Northern Irish politician and first minister of Northern Ireland from 1998 (with a three-week interruption in October–November 2001); cowinner of the 1998 Nobel Peace Prize.

Travis Tritt (9 Feb 1963, Marietta GA), American country-and-western singer who found great success from 1990 onward with a blues- and rock-tinged style.

Garry Trudeau (21 Jul 1948, New York NY), American cartoonist, creator of the durable *Doonesbury* syndicated comic strip.

Donald (John) Trump (14 Jun 1946, New York NY), American real-estate developer known for his high-profile real-estate developments, including New York City's Trump Tower and Atlantic City's Trump Taj Mahal casino; he also starred in a reality-TV series, *The Apprentice* (from 2004).

Morgan Tsvangirai (10 Mar 1952, Buhera, Southern Rhodesia [now Zimbabwe]), Zimbabwean labor leader and politician, head of the Movement for Democratic Change (from 2002), and major opposition leader to the regime of Pres. Robert Mugabe.

Kostya Tszyu (Konstantin Tszyu; "The Thunder from Down Under"; 19 Sep 1969, Serov, Russian SFSR, USSR [now in Russia]), Russian-born Australian boxer, the undisputed junior welterweight (super-lightweight) champion from 2001 (although the WBA took away his title in June 2004).

Togiola Tulafono (28 Feb 1947, American Samoa), American Democratic politician and governor of American Samoa from 2003.

Tommy Tune (28 Feb 1939, Wichita Falls TX), American musical comedy dancer and actor noted especially for his work on Broadway; he was awarded a 2003 NEA National Medal of Arts.

Tung Chee-hwa (29 May 1937, Shanghai, China), Chinese businessman and chief executive of Hong Kong (later the Hong Kong Special Administrative Region of China) from 1997 until his resignation on 10 Mar 2005.

Christy Turlington (2 Jan 1969, Oakland CA), American fashion model.

Charles Wesley Turnbull (5 Feb 1935, St. Thomas, Virgin Islands), American Democratic politician and governor of the US Virgin Islands from 1999.

Ted Turner (Robert Edward Turner III; 19 Nov 1938, Cincinnati OH), American TV executive, the founder of Turner Broadcasting System and owner of Cable News Network (CNN), a pioneer in the use of satellite and cable technology; he is also a sports club owner (Atlanta Braves and others), a noted yachtsman, and a philanthropist.

Scott Turow (12 Apr 1949, Chicago IL), American best-selling novelist, the creator of a genre of crime and suspense novels dealing with law and the legal profession.

Steve Turre (12 Sep 1948, Omaha NE), American jazz trombone and conch-shell player and arranger.

James Turrell (6 May 1943, Los Angeles CA), American installation artist especially known for his explorations of light and sky.

John Turturro (27 Feb 1957, Brooklyn NY), American stage, film, and TV actor, often cast as disturbed or eccentric characters.

Desmond (Mpilo) Tutu (7 Oct 1931, Klerksdorp, South Africa), South African Anglican cleric who in 1984 received the Nobel Peace Prize for his role in the opposition to apartheid in South Africa.

Shania Twain (Eileen Regina Edwards; 28 Aug 1965, Windsor, ON, Canada), Canadian country singer whose 1997 *Come On Over* is the best-selling album by a female solo artist.

Cy Twombly (Edwin Parker Twombly, Jr.; 25 Apr 1928, Lexington VA), American abstract artist and sculptor.

Anne Tyler (25 Oct 1941, Minneapolis MN), American novelist and short-story writer whose comedies of manners are marked by compassionate wit and precise details of domestic life; she won a Pulitzer Prize for *Breathing Lessons* (1989).

Liv Tyler (Liv Rundgren; 1 Jul 1977, Portland ME), American actress and model.

Steven Tyler (Steven Tallarico; 26 Mar 1948, New York NY), American rock vocalist (of Aerosmith).

Yuliya Tymoshenko (Yuliya Telegina; 27 Nov 1960, Dnipropetrovsk, Ukrainian SSR, USSR [now in Ukraine]), Ukrainian businesswoman and politician, the founder (2001) of the Yuliya Tymoshenko Bloc, which opposed the government of Pres. Leonid Kuchma; she was made prime minister on 4 Feb 2005.

(Alfred) McCoy Tyner (later Sulaimon Saud; 11 Dec 1938, Philadelphia PA), American jazz pianist and composer.

Mike Tyson (Michael Gerard Tyson; 30 Jun 1966, Brooklyn NY), American boxer who was undisputed heavyweight champion, 1987–90.

João Ubaldo Ribeiro (João Ubaldo Osório Pimentel Ribeiro; 23 Jan 1941, Itaparica, Bahia state, Brazil), Brazilian novelist whose *Diário do farol*—about a morally corrupt priest—was a best seller.

Robert J. Ulrich (Minneapolis MN), American corporate executive and CEO of Target Corp. from 1994.

"Country" Carrie Underwood (10 Mar 1983, Muskogee OK), American country singer who was named the 2005 American Idol on the Fox TV show of that name.

John (Hoyer) Updike (18 Mar 1932, Shillington PA), American writer of novels, short stories, and poetry, known for his careful craftsmanship and realistic, subtle depiction of American, Protestant, small-town, middle-class life.

Dawn Upshaw (17 Jul 1960, Nashville TN), American concert and operatic soprano noted for the beauty of her voice and her musical sensibility, particularly in contemporary music; she is especially associated with the work of composer John Harbison.

Álvaro Uribe Vélez (4 Jul 1952, Medellín, Colombia), Colombian politician and president from 2002.

Joseph J. Urusemal (19 Mar 1952, Woleai, Yap, Trust Territory of the Pacific Islands [now in the Federated States of Micronesia]), Micronesian politician and president of the Federated States of Micronesia from 2003.

Greg Urwin (1947?, Lithgow, NSW, Australia), Australian diplomat and international official who was secretary-general of the Pacific Islands Forum from 16 Jan 2004.

Usher (Usher Raymond IV; 14 Oct 1978, Chattanooga TN), American rhythm-and-blues singer.

Jørn Utzon (9 Apr 1918, Copenhagen, Denmark), Danish architect best known for his dynamic, imaginative, but problematic design for the Sydney Opera House, Australia; he won the 2003 Pritzker Prize.

Jochem Uytdehaage (9 Jul 1976, Utrecht, The Netherlands), Dutch speed skater who was the 2002 Olympic gold medalist in the 5,000-m race and all-around world champion in the same year.

Atal Bihari Vajpayee (25 Dec 1924, Gwalior, Madhya Pradesh state, British India), Indian politician; prime minister of India in 1996 and again from 1998 to May 2004.

Dick Van Dyke (13 Dec 1925, West Plains MO), American actor and comedian best remembered as the star on TV of *The Dick Van Dyke Show* (1961–66) and, more recently (1993–2001), the *Diagnosis Murder* series.

Martine Van Hamel (16 Nov 1945, Brussels, Belgium), Belgian dancer and leading choreographer for the American Ballet Theatre.

Gus van Sant (24 Jul 1952, Louisville KY), American film director whose recent work includes the films *Finding Forrester* (2002) and *Elephant* (2003).

Vanessa Mae (Vanessa-Mae Vanakorn Nicholson; 27 Oct 1978, Singapore), Singapore-born British violinist who has made headlines with her exotic (half-Thai, half-Chinese) beauty and her determination to add contemporary pop music styles to her mastery of the classical repertory.

Matti Vanhanen (4 Nov 1955, Jyväskylä, Finland), Finnish politician and prime minister from 2003.

(Jorge) Mario (Pedro) Vargas Llosa (28 Mar 1936, Arequipa, Peru), Peruvian-born Spanish novelist and presidential candidate; he won the Cervantes Prize in 1994.

Harold (Eliot) Varmus (18 Dec 1939, Oceanside NY), American virologist; cowinner of 1989 Nobel Prize for Physiology or Medicine for research on oncogenes; he was director of the National Institutes of Health, 1993–99, and president of Memorial Sloan-Kettering Cancer Center in New York City from 2000.

Daniel Lucius Vasella (1953, Fribourg?, Switzerland), Swiss corporate executive and CEO of the Novartis Group (from merger, 1996).

Gaddi H. Vasquez (22 Dec 1955, Carrizo Springs TX), American government official, director of the US Peace Corps from 2002.

Tabaré (Ramón) Vázquez Rosas (17 Jan 1940, Barrio La Teja, Montevideo, Uruguay), Uruguayan physician and Socialist mayor of Montevideo (1990–1994) who served as president from 1 Mar 2005; he is the first leftist to hold this position.

Jeroen van der Veer (1947, Utrecht, The Netherlands), Dutch corporate executive; CEO of Royal Dutch Shell Group (Netherlands).

Jaci Velasquez (Jacquelyn Davette Velasquez; 15 Oct 1979, Houston TX), American Latin and gospel singer.

Caetano Veloso (7 Aug 1942, Santo Amaro da Purificacão, Bahia state, Brazil), Brazilian singer with an international reputation and one of the originators of the *tropicália* movement in Brazilian popular music.

Helen (Hennessy) Vendler (1933, Boston MA), American university professor and influential poetry critic.

Ann M. Veneman (29 Jun 1949, Modesto CA), American government official who was US secretary of agriculture (2001–05).

(Runaldo) Ronald Venetiaan (18 Jun 1936, Paramaribo, Dutch Guiana [now Suriname]), Surinamese politician who was president, 1991–96, and again from 2000.

Maxim Vengerov (20 Aug 1974, Novosibirsk, Russian SFSR, USSR [now Russia]), Russian-born concert violinist known for his mastery of technique and his ardent, lyrical playing.

J. Craig Venter (14 Oct 1946, Salt Lake City UT), American geneticist and researcher into the human genome; he was the founder of Celera Genomics.

Guy Verhofstadt (11 Apr 1953, Dendermonde, Belgium), Belgian politician and prime minister from 1999.

Donatella Versace (2 May 1955, Reggio di Calabria, Italy), Italian fashion designer who took over as creative director at her brother Gianni Versace's design house after he was murdered in 1997.

Ben Verwaayen (Feb 1952), Dutch corporate executive and CEO of British Telecommunications PLC from 2002.

Jack Vettriano (Jack Hoggan; 17 Nov 1951, St. Andrews, Fife, Scotland), British painter of realistic natural scenes, sometimes with erotic overtones; he is one of the most popular contemporary British artists.

Crown Princess Victoria (Victoria Ingrid Alice Desirée; 14 Jul 1977, Stockholm, Sweden), Swedish royal and heiress to the throne.

Vaira Vike-Freiberga (1 Dec 1937, Riga, Latvia), Canadian Latvian folklorist and politician; she was president of Latvia from 1999.

Antonio Villaraigosa (Antonio Villar; 23 Jan 1953, East Los Angeles CA), American Democratic politician and mayor of Los Angeles from 1 Jul 2005; he is the first Hispanic to hold the post since 1872.

Thomas Vilsack (13 Dec 1950, Pittsburgh PA), American Democratic politician and governor of Iowa from 1999.

Vladimir (Viktorovich) Vinogradov (1955, Ufa, Bashkir ASSR, USSR [now Bashkortostan, Russia]), Russian industrialist and banker, chairman of the Moscow Banking Union; he is both wealthy and politically connected.

Nora D. Volkow (1956?, Mexico City, Mexico), American biochemist and specialist in the use of PET imaging to record the biochemical effects of drugs on the brain; she was director of the National Institute for Drug Addiction from 2003.

William T. Vollmann (28 Jul 1959, Los Angeles CA), American historical novelist who writes of the interactions of ethnic cultures in North America.

Diane von Fürstenberg (Diane Simone Michelle Halfin; 31 Dec 1946, Brussels, Belgium), Belgian-born American fashion designer who made her name in the 1970s with the wrap dress; she received a lifetime achievement award from the Council of Fashion Designers of America in June 2005.

Lars von Trier (30 Apr 1956, Copenhagen, Denmark), Danish film director and cinematographer known for his avant-garde approach to filmmaking.

Kurt Vonnegut, Jr. (11 Nov 1922, Indianapolis IN), American novelist and short-story writer noted for his pessimistic and satirical works that use fantasy and science fiction to highlight the horrors and ironies of 20th-century civilization.

Carol Vorderman (24 Dec 1960, Prestatyn, Wales), British TV personality and author of instructional books for children and adults.

Vladimir Voronin (25 May 1941, Corjova, Moldavian SSR, USSR [now Moldova]), Moldovan politician and president from 2001.

Rem (Ivanovich) Vyakhirev (23 Aug 1934, Bolshaya Chernigovka, Russian SFSR, USSR [now Russia]), Russian billionaire head (1992–2001) of Gazprom, the largest company in Russia, with interests chiefly in petroleum and the media, and chairman (from 1996) of Siberia Oil Co.

Linda Wachner (3 Feb 1946, New York NY), American apparel industry executive; she was CEO (from 1987) and chairwoman (from 1991) of Warnaco Group, Inc., and Authentic Fitness Corp. until November 2001; Wachner was the first woman to lead a Fortune 500 company.

Norio Wada (17 Nov 1949, Osaka, Japan), Japanese corporate executive; president and CEO of Nippon Telegraph & Telephone from 2002.

Abdoulaye Wade (29 May 1926, Kébémer, Senegal, French West Africa), Senegalese politician and president from 2000.

G. Richard Wagoner, Jr. (9 Feb 1953, Wilmington DE), American corporate executive and CEO of General Motors Corp. from 2000.

Rufus Wainwright (22 Jul 1973, Rhinebeck NY), Canadian pop singer whose classically grounded and theatrically delivered material drew critical and popular acclaim.

Ted Waitt (18 Jan 1963, Sioux City IA), American computer executive and philanthropist; cofounder of Gateway Inc. in 1985 and chairman and CEO of the charitable Waitt Family Foundation from its foundation in 1993.

Derek (Alton) Walcott (23 Jan 1930, Castries, Saint Lucia), Saint Lucia–born poet and playwright noted for works that explored the Caribbean cultural experience; he won the 1992 Nobel Prize for Literature.

Jimmy (Donal) Wales (7 Aug 1966, Huntsville AL), American Internet publisher and founder of Wikipedia, an alternative, "open source" encyclopedia.

Lech Walesa (29 Sep 1943, Popowo, near Wloclawek, Poland), Polish labor activist who helped form and led (1980–90) communist Poland's first independent trade union, Solidarity; the charismatic leader of millions of Polish workers, he went on to become the president of Poland (1990–95) and received the Nobel Prize for Peace in 1983.

Prince al-Walid ibn Talal ibn Abdulaziz al-Saud (1954, Riyadh, Saudi Arabia), Saudi Arabian businessman who saved EuroDisney; a majority stockholder in CitiGroup, he was listed fourth on *Forbes* magazine's 2004 list of influential billionaires.

Alice (Malsenior) Walker (9 Feb 1944, Eatonton GA), American writer whose novels, short stories, and poems are noted for their insightful treatment of African American culture; her novels, most notably *The Color Purple* (1982; National Book Award, 1983), focus on women.

Olene S. Walker (15 Nov 1930, Ogden UT), American businesswoman, Republican politician, and governor of Utah from 2003.

Mike Wallace (Myron Leon Wallace; 9 May 1918, Brookline MA), American TV journalist, interviewer, and coeditor of CBS's *60 Minutes*.

Immanuel Wallerstein (28 Sep 1930, New York NY), American sociologist of systems theory.

Mark J. Walport (1953, England), British immunologist and specialist in lupus and other autoimmune diseases; director of The Wellcome Trust from 2003.

Courtney (Andrew) Walsh (30 Oct 1962, Kingston, Jamaica), Jamaican cricket bowler who in 2000 became the highest wicket-taker in Test history; he retired in 2001 with 519 Test wickets.

Barbara Walters (25 Sep 1931, Boston MA), American broadcast journalist known especially as an interviewer, first on TV's *Today* show, then on the *Barbara Walters Special*; in 1976 she became the first woman to anchor a network news program (*ABC Evening News*).

Alice L. (c. 1949), **Helen R.** (c. 1920), and **Jim C.** (c. 1948) **Walton**, American heirs to the Wal-Mart fortune left by Sam Walton, who died in 1992; each appears prominently on *Forbes* magazine's 2004 list of the world's richest persons.

Michael Waltrip (30 Apr 1963, Owensboro KY), American NASCAR race car driver and winner of the Daytona 500 race in 2001 and 2003.

Vera Wang (27 June 1949, New York NY), American fashion designer known for her elegant and luxurious wedding gowns.

Wang Liqin (18 Jun 1978, Haerbin [Harbin], China), Chinese table tennis player, the top-ranked male in the world in 2004–05.

Jigme Singye Wangchuk (11 Nov 1955, Dechenchholing Palace, Thimphu, Bhutan), Bhutanese king from 1972.

Lloyd Ward (1949, Romulus MI), American corporate executive, CEO of Maytag Co. from 1999, and CEO of the US Olympic Commission from 2001.

Shane Keith Warne (13 Sep 1969, Ferntree Gully, VIC, Australia), Australian cricketer, a spin bowler named one of Wisden's Five Cricketers of the Century.

Mark R. Warner (15 Dec 1954, Indianapolis IN), American Democratic politician and governor of Virginia from 2002.

Rick Warren (1954, San Jose CA), American evangelist minister whose Saddleback Church in Lake Forest CA (established in 1980) enjoys a membership of 50,000, reportedly the largest church in the Southern Baptist Convention and possibly the fastest growing congregation anywhere.

Denzel Washington (28 Dec 1954, Mount Vernon NY), American film and TV actor who won Academy Awards for best supporting actor in *Glory* (1989) and best actor in *Training Day* (2001).

(Chaudhry) Wasim Akram (3 Jun 1966, Lahore, Pakistan), Pakistani cricketer, called the greatest left-handed fast bowler, pioneer of "reverse swing" bowling; he retired in 2003.

Risa Wataya (1 Feb 1984, Kyoto, Japan), Japanese novelist, cowinner (with Hitomi Kanehara), at age 19, of the 2004 Akutagawa Prize, Japan's top award for fiction, for *Keritai senaka* ("The Back One Wants to Kick").

John Waters (22 Apr 1946, Baltimore MD), American filmmaker who first transcended his Baltimore upbringing in 1972 with the celluloid monument to bad taste, *Pink Flamingos*, and went on to write, direct, and produce mainstream film successes such as *Hairspray* (1988; made into a Tony-winning Broadway musical in 2002), *Cry-Baby* (1990), and *A Dirty Shame* (2004).

Sara Watkins (8 Jun 1981), American progressive bluegrass fiddler (of Nickel Creek).

Charlie Watts (2 Jun 1941, Islington, England), British rock drummer (of the Rolling Stones).

J.C. Watts, Jr. (Julius Caesar Watts; 18 Nov 1957, Eufaula OK), American Republican politician, US congressman from Oklahoma and chair of the Republican Conference.

Naomi Watts (28 Sep 1968, Shoreham, Kent, England), Australian film actress.

Keenen Ivory Wayans (8 Jun 1958, New York NY), American TV and film actor, the host of *The Keenen Ivory Wayans Show* (1997–98); he later worked as a film writer, director, and producer of such hits as *Scary Movie* (2000), *Scary Movie 2* (2001), and *White Chicks* (2004).

George Weah (George Manneh Oppong Ousman Weah; 1 Oct 1966, Monrovia, Liberia), Liberian-born association football (soccer) star who in 1995–96 achieved the triple honor of being elected European, African, and FIFA World Footballer of the Year, the first player ever to win three such titles in one year; in 1998 Weah was named African Player of the Century.

Sigourney Weaver (Susan Alexandra Weaver; 8 Oct 1949, New York NY), American film actress; a strong leading lady most recognized for the *Alien* films (1979, 1986, 1992, and 1997).

Hugo Weaving (4 Apr 1960, Austin, Nigeria), Australian film actor whose credits included *Proof* (1991) and *The Interview* (1998) as well as three *Matrix* films (1999, 2003) and three *Lord of the Rings* films (2001, 2002, and 2003).

Karrie Webb (21 Dec 1974, Ayr, QLD, Australia), Australian golfer who won the Women's British Open in 2002, completing a round of wins in the top six major women's tournaments.

Andrew Thomas Weil (8 Jun 1942, Philadelphia PA), American physician and champion of alternative medicine.

Sandy Weill (Sanford I. Weill; 16 Mar 1933, Brooklyn NY), American corporate executive; CEO of Travelers Group and, after its merger in 1998 with Citicorp, CEO of Citigroup.

Harvey Weinstein (19 Mar 1952, Queens NY), American film executive; as cochairman (with his brother Bob) of Miramax Films from 1979, he was known for producing high-quality films.

Alek Wek (16 Apr 1977, Wau, The Sudan), Sudanese-born fashion model.

Gillian Welch (1967, New York NY), American folk and country-and-western singer who often teams with singer, songwriter, and instrumentalist David Rawlings on bluegrass-inflected contemporary music.

Wen Jiabao (September 1942, Tianjin, China), Chinese geologist and party and state official who became premier of China in 2003.

Jann S. Wenner (7 Jan 1946, New York NY), American journalist, originator (1967), and publisher of *Rolling Stone* magazine and other periodicals.

Kanye West (8 Jun 1977, Atlanta GA), American rapper and music producer who won three 2004 Grammys.

Randy Weston (Randolph Edward Weston; 6 Apr 1926, Brooklyn NY), American jazz pianist and composer.

Vivienne Westwood (Vivienne Swire; 8 Apr 1941, Tintwistle, Derbyshire, England), British fashion designer whose radical, antiestablishment creations started the 1970s punk fashion trend; she was the subject of a retrospective, "Vivienne Westwood: 34 Years in Fashion," at the Victoria and Albert Museum in London in 2004.

Christopher Wheeldon (22 Mar 1973, Yeovil, Somerset, England), British dancer and choreographer with the New York City Ballet.

Meg Whitman (Margaret C. Whitman; 4 Aug 1956, Cold Spring Harbor NY), American corporate executive and president and CEO of eBay, the Internet auction house, from 1998.

Ranil Wickremesinghe (24 Mar 1949), Sri Lankan politician and prime minister, 1993–94 and again 2001–04.

John Edgar Wideman (14 Jun 1941, Washington DC), American writer regarded for his intricate literary style in novels about the experiences of black men in contemporary urban America.

Carl E. Wieman (26 Mar 1951, Corvallis OR), American physicist; cowinner of the 2001 Nobel Prize for Physics for work in the creation of the Bose-Einstein condensate.

Richard (Purdy) Wilbur (1 Mar 1921, New York NY), American poet associated with the New Formalist movement and poet laureate of the US, 1987–88.

Frank A. Wilczek (15 May 1951, New York NY), American quantum physicist who shared the 2004 Nobel Prize in Physics with David J. Gross and H. David Politzer for their studies of the force that binds quarks together and their development of a new physical theory called quantum chromodynamics.

George F(rederick) Will (4 May 1941, Champaign IL), American political commentator and columnist known for his conservative commentary on national and international events in print and broadcast media.

Crown Prince Willem-Alexander (27 Apr 1967, Utrecht, The Netherlands), Dutch royal and heir to the throne of The Netherlands.

Prince William (William Arthur Philip Louis; 21 Jun 1982, London, England), British royal, son of Charles and Diana, prince and princess of Wales, and second in line to the British throne.

C(harles) K(enneth) Williams (4 Nov 1936, Newark NJ), American poet who won the 2000 Pulitzer Prize for Poetry for *Repair*.

John Williams (24 Apr 1941, Melbourne, VIC, Australia), Australian-born classical guitarist.

John (Towner) Williams (8 Feb 1932, Queens NY), American conductor and composer; conductor of the Boston Pops Orchestra (1980–93), known especially for composing scores for films such as *Jaws*, *Star Wars*, *E.T. the Extraterrestrial*, and *Schindler's List*; he was awarded a Kennedy Center Honor in 2004.

Lucinda Williams (26 Jan 1953, Lake Charles LA), American contemporary folk and country singer and songwriter.

Montel (Brian Anthony) Williams (3 Jul 1956), American TV personality, host (from 1991) of *The Montel Williams Show*, a talk show.

Robbie Williams (Robert Peter Maximillian Williams; 13 Feb 1974, Tunstall, Stoke-on-Trent, Staffordshire, England), British rock performer (with Take That) who has enjoyed great success in Britain.

Robin Williams (21 Jul 1952, Chicago IL), American comedian and actor known for his eccentricity, rapid-fire wit, and energy; his works include the TV series *Mork and Mindy* (1978–82) and the films *Good Morning, Vietnam* (1987), *Dead Poets Society* (1989), *Good Will Hunting* (1997; Academy Award for best supporting actor), and *Insomnia* (2002).

Rowan Williams (14 Jun 1950, Swansea, Wales), Welsh-born Anglican clergyman who was enthroned as the 104th archbishop of Canterbury in 2003.

Serena Williams (26 Sep 1981, Saginaw MI), American tennis player, an Olympic and Grand Slam champion; she won Wimbledon in 2002 and 2003 and the Australian Open in 2003; she was ranked number four in the world in June 2005.

Treat Williams (Richard Williams; 1 Dec 1951, Rowayton CT), American TV and film actor who starred in the TV series *Everwood* from 2002.

Venus Williams (17 Jun 1980, Lynwood CA), American tennis player who won both the US Open and Wimbledon in 2000 and 2001 and Wimbledon again in 2005; she is the sister of Serena Williams, with whom she has also won doubles titles.

Walter Ray Williams, Jr. (6 Oct 1959, San Jose CA), American bowler who bowled four perfect games in one tournament and was five-time PBA Bowler of the Year (1986, 1993, 1996–98, and 2003).

Bruce Willis (Walter Willison; 19 Mar 1955, Idar-Oberstein, West Germany [now in Germany]), American actor first famous as the star of TV's *Moonlighting*; he is also aclaimed for the *Die Hard* movies and *The Sixth Sense* (1999).

August Wilson (27 Apr 1945, Pittsburgh PA), American playwright who created a cycle of plays, each set in a different decade of the 20th century, about black American life; he won Pulitzer Prizes for *Fences* (1986) and *The Piano Lesson* (1990).

Cassandra Wilson (4 Dec 1955, Jackson MS), American jazz singer who applies her wide-ranging "smoky contralto" voice to jazz standards, folk songs, Delta blues, and pop classics.

Lanford Wilson (13 Apr 1937, Lebanon MO), American playwright, a pioneer of the Off-Off-Broadway and regional theater movements; he won the 2004 PEN/Laura Pels Foundation Award for Drama.

Nancy Wilson (20 Feb 1937, Chillicothe OH), American pop and jazz singer; she was named a National Endowment of the Arts Jazz Master for 2004.

Robert Wilson (4 Oct 1941, Waco TX), American avant-garde theater director with a vast range.

William Julius Wilson (20 Dec 1935, Derry township, Westmoreland county PA), American sociologist of race and urban society; government adviser.

Oprah Winfrey (29 Jan 1954, Kosciusko MS), American TV personality; host and producer of *The Oprah Winfrey Show* from 1985.

Kate Winslet (5 Oct 1975, Reading, England), British film actress made famous by her performance in *Titanic* (1997).

Anna Wintour (3 Nov 1949, London, England), British-born fashion magazine editor, editor in chief of American *Vogue* from 1988.

Bob Wise (6 Jan 1948, Washington DC), American Democratic politician and governor of West Virginia (2001–05).

Reese Witherspoon (Laura Jean Reese Witherspoon; 22 Mar 1976, Baton Rouge LA), American film actress whose credits included *Pleasantville* (1998), two *Legally Blonde* films (2001 and 2003), *The Importance of Being Earnest* (2002), and *Vanity Fair* (2004).

Carl R. Woese (15 Jul 1928, Syracuse NY), American microbiologist and winner of the 2003 Crafoord Prize for his discovery of archaea, a third domain of life (besides eukaryotes and prokaryotes [bacteria]) that live in extreme environments lacking in oxygen, such as the deep-sea bottoms.

Girma Wolde-Giorgis (December 1924, Addis Ababa, Ethiopia), Ethiopian military officer and president from 2001.

Tom Wolfe (Thomas Kennerly Wolfe, Jr.; 2 Mar 1930, Richmond VA), American novelist, journalist, and social commentator who is a leading critic of contemporary life and a proponent of New Journalism (the application of fiction-writing techniques to journalism).

James D. Wolfensohn (1 Dec 1933, Sydney, NSW, Australia), Australian-born American banker who served two terms as president of the World Bank (1995–2005).

Tobias (Jonathan Ansell) Wolff (19 Jun 1945, Birmingham AL), American writer primarily known for his short stories, in which many voices and a wide range of emotions are skillfully depicted.

Paul Wolfowitz (22 Dec 1943, New York NY), American scholar and government official; he was US deputy secretary of defense from 2001–05 and president of the World Bank from 1 Jun 2005.

Stephen Wolfram (29 Aug 1959, London, England), British-born American physicist whose book *A New Kind of Science* (2002) suggested the inadequacy of math-based science and proposed "cellular automata" as a better key to understanding the patterns of nature.

Lee Ann Womack (19 Aug 1966, Jacksonville TX), American country singer.

Stevie Wonder (Steveland Judkins, later Steveland Morris; 13 May 1950, Saginaw MI), American pop composer, singer, and pianist.

Elijah (Jordan) Wood (28 Jan 1981, Cedar Rapids IA), American film actor who cinched his already impressive career by playing Frodo in the *Lord of the Rings* trilogy (2001, 2002, 2003).

Todd Woodbridge (2 Apr 1971, Sydney, NSW, Australia), Australian tennis player best known for doubles play, especially with Jonas Bjorkman.

Tiger Woods (Eldrick Woods; 30 Dec 1975, Cypress CA), American golfer, perhaps the greatest of all time; among his many honors, in 2001 he was the first to hold all four major golf championships at the same time.

Bob Woodward (Robert Upshur Woodward; 26 Mar 1943, Geneva IL), American journalist and author of nonfiction political best sellers.

Stephen Wozniak (11 Aug 1950, San Jose CA), American electrical engineer, cofounder of Apple Computer Corp., and youth leader.

Wu Bangguo (Jul 1941, Feidong, Anhui province, China), Chinese Communist Party official, Politburo member from 1992, and chairman of the National People's Congress Standing Committee from 2003.

William A. Wulf (8 Dec 1939, Chicago IL), American computer scientist who was president of the National Academy of Engineering from 1997.

Kurt Wüthrich (4 Oct 1938, Aarberg, Bern canton, Switzerland), Swiss chemist; cowinner of the 2002 Nobel Prize for Chemistry for his work in the study of macromolecules.

Xie Jun (30 Oct 1970, Baoding, Hebei province, China), Chinese women's chess champion of the world, 1991–96 and 1999–2001.

Aleksey (Konstantinovich) Yagudin (18 Mar 1980, Leningrad, USSR [now St. Petersburg, Russia]), Russian figure skater; he was a four-time world champion and 2002 Olympic gold medalist.

Yohji Yamamoto (3 Oct 1943, Tokyo, Japan), Japanese fashion designer known for his simple and sophisticated creations.

Yang Yang (A) (24 Aug 1976, Heilongjiang province, China), Chinese short-track speed skater, a five-time world champion.

Charles Yanofsky (17 Apr 1925, New York NY), American geneticist who demonstrated the colinearity of gene and protein structures; he was awarded a 2003 National Medal of Science.

Viktor (Fedorovych) Yanukovych (9 Jul 1950, Yenakiyevo, Ukrainian SSR, USSR [now Ukraine]), Ukrainian politician and prime minister (2002–05).

Yao Ming (12 Sep 1980, Shanghai, China), Chinese basketball player, 7 ft 5 in (2.26 m) tall; he starred with the Shanghai Sharks from 1997 to 2001 and became a national icon; he was the first overall pick in the 2002 NBA Draft (by the Houston Rockets).

Yury (Fyodorvich) Yarov (2 Apr 1942, Leningrad, USSR [now St. Petersburg, Russia]), Russian international official and executive secretary of the Commonwealth of Independent States from 1999.

Catherine Yass (1963, London, England), British photographic artist whose work often combines positive and negative photographic images to eerie effect.

Ghazi (Mash'al Ujail) al-Yawer (1958?, Mosul, Iraq), Iraqi civil engineer and businessman who was president of Iraq from 30 Jun 2004.

Trisha Yearwood (Patricia Lynn Yearwood; 19 Sep 1964, Monticello GA), American country singer.

A(braham) B. Yehoshua (9 Dec 1936, Jerusalem), Israeli novelist and playwright.

Michelle Yeoh (Yang Zi Chong or Yeoh Chu-keng; 6 Aug 1962, Ipoh, Malaysia), Malaysian-born film actress, best known in the West for her appearance in the James Bond film *Tomorrow Never Dies* (1997) and for playing the lead role in *Crouching Tiger, Hidden Dragon* (2000); she was named actress of the year in the 2003 MTV Style Awards in Shanghai.

Gloria Yerkovich (1942), American founder of CHILDFIND, a nationwide organization that helps locate missing children.

Frances Yip (Frances Yip Lai Yee; 1948, Hong Kong), Hong Kong popular singer.

Dwight (David) Yoakam (23 Oct 1956, Pikesville KY), American country-and-western singer, songwriter, and actor.

Thom Yorke (7 Oct 1968, Wellingborough, Northamptonshire, England), British rock vocalist and member of the band Radiohead.

Banana Yoshimoto (Yoshimoto Mahoko; 24 Jul 1964, Tokyo, Japan), Japanese writer of best-selling fiction.

Will Young (William Robert Young; 20 Jan 1979, Hungerford, Berkshire, England), British rock singer who won the 2002 Pop Idol contest and whose 2002 single "Anything Is Possible/Evergreen" was the fastest-selling record in British history.

Étienne (Nestor) Ys (26 Feb 1962, Curaçao, Netherlands Antilles?), Netherlands Antilles politician and prime minister from 2002.

Yu Miri (22 Jun 1968, Yokohama, Japan), Japanese writer of Korean ancestry who won the Akutagawa Prize in 1997 for her novel *Kazoku shinema* (1996; "Family Cinema").

Yu Shyi-kun (25 Apr 1948, Taiho, Taiwan), Taiwanese politician and prime minister (2002–05).

Susilo Bambang Yudhoyono (9 Sep 1949, Pacitan, East Java, Indonesia), Indonesian military officer and politician; he was president from 20 Oct 2004.

Viktor (Andriyovych) Yushchenko (23 Feb 1954, Khoruzhivka, Sumska oblast, Ukrainian SSR, USSR [now in Ukraine]), Ukrainian banker and politician; he was prime minister (1999–2001), founder (2002) of the Our Ukraine party, and, following a tumultuous election in late 2004, president from 23 Jan 2005.

Sadi Yusuf (1934, near Basra, Iraq), Iraqi-born poet, a collection of whose work, *Without an Alphabet, Without a Face: Selected Poems,* appeared in late 2002.

Raúl Yzaguirre (22 Jul 1939, south Texas), American Hispanic rights activist; president and CEO of the National Council of La Raza from 1974.

Adam Zagajewski (21 Jun 1945, Lwow, Poland [now Lviv, Ukraine]), Polish poet, novelist, and essayist who gained attention as a member of the Generation of '68, or the Polish New Wave; he won the 2004 Neustadt Prize.

Paula Zahn (24 Feb 1956, Omaha NE), American TV anchorwoman and journalist, host of CNN's primetime evening program *Paula Zahn Now* and of its *People in the News.*

José Luis Rodríguez Zapatero (4 Aug 1960, Valladolid, Spain), Spanish politician, general secretary of the Socialist Workers' Party of Spain from 2000, and prime minister from 17 Apr 2004.

Renée (Kathleen) Zellweger (25 Apr 1969, Katy TX), American actress first famous for her role in *Jerry Maguire* (1996) and who went on to win a loyal following for *Nurse Betty* (2000, Golden Globe Award), *Bridget Jones's Diary* (2001; sequel, 2004), *Chicago* (2002, Golden Globe Award), and *Cold Mountain* (2003; best supporting actress Academy Award).

Robert Zemeckis (14 May 1952, Chicago IL), American director and producer of popular mainstream films, including *Forrest Gump* (1994; best director Academy Award).

Meles Zenawi (8 May 1955, Adoua, Ethiopia), Ethiopian politician and prime minister from 1995.

Zeng Qinghong (Jul 1939, Jian, Jiangxi province, China), Chinese Communist Party official and director of the Organization Department of the CPC Central Committee from 1999.

Elias (Adam) Zerhouni (1 Apr 1951, Nedroma, Algeria), Algerian-born American radiologist and medical administrator; he was director of the National Institutes of Health from 2002.

Catherine Zeta-Jones (Catherine Jones; 25 Sep 1969, Swansea, West Glamorgan, Wales), Welsh-born American actress first recognized in *The Mask of Zorro* (1998); her films include *Entrapment* (1999), *Traffic* (2000), *America's Sweethearts*

(2001), and *Chicago* (2002; best supporting actress Academy Award).

Zhang Yimou (14 Nov 1951, Xi'an, Shaanxi province, China), Chinese film director of international reputation who made such films as *Red Sorghum* (1987), *The Story of Qiu Ju* (1992), and *Hero* (2002).

Zhang Yining (5 Oct 1982, China), Chinese table tennis player, the top-ranked woman in 2004–05.

Zhang Ziyi (9 Feb 1979, Beijing, China), Chinese actress who came to international fame in the film *Crouching Tiger, Hidden Dragon* (2000) and who followed up that success with *House of Flying Daggers* (2004).

Zhou Guangzhao (May 1929, Changsha, Hunan province, China), Chinese mechanical engineer, president of the Chinese Academy of Sciences, 1987–97, and chairman of the China Association of Science and Technology from 1996.

Zhu Chen (16 Mar 1976, China), Chinese chess grandmaster who was women's world champion from 2001.

Zhu Rongji (1 Oct 1928, Changsha, Hunan province, China), Chinese politician and premier, 1998–2003.

Begum Khaleda Zia (ur-Rahman) (Khaleda Majumdar; 15 Aug 1945, Dinâjpur, West Bengal state, British India [now in Bangladesh]), Bangladeshi politician who was prime minister, 1991–96, and again from 2001; she was the first woman to serve as prime minister of Bangladesh.

Zinedine Zidane (23 Jun 1972, Marseille, France), French association football (soccer) player, star of the French team that won the FIFA World Cup in 1998; FIFA World Footballer of the Year, 1998, 2000, and 2003.

Mary (Alice) Zimmerman (23 Aug 1960, Lincoln NE), American stage director who won a Tony Award for best director in 2002 for *Metamorphoses*; she contributed the libretto to the opera *Galileo Galilei*, which opened in Chicago in 2002.

Zoran Zivkovic (22 Dec 1960, Nis, Serbia, Yugoslavia [now in Serbia and Montenegro]), Serbian politician and former Yugoslav interior minister who served as prime minister of Serbia (part of Serbia and Montenegro) from 18 Mar 2003, in the wake of the assassination of reformist premier Zoran Djindjic, until 3 Mar 2004.

Robert B. Zoellick (25 Jul 1953, Evergreen Park IL), American businessman and government official and US Trade Representative from 2001.

Armin Zöggeler (4 Jan 1974, Merano?, Italy), Italian luger, Olympic (2002) and World Cup (2000, 2001, and 2004) champion.

Mortimer B. Zuckerman (4 Jun 1937, Montreal, QC, Canada), Canadian-born American publisher, columnist, and editor in chief of *U.S. News & World Report.*

Jacob (Gedleyihlekisa) Zuma (12 Apr 1942, Inkandla, Natal [now KwaZulu Natal] province, South Africa), South African politician who was deputy president of the African National Congress (from 1997) and deputy president of South Africa from 1999 until his dismissal on 14 Jun 2005 by Pres. Thabo Mbeki under suspicion of corruption.

Obituaries

Death of notable people since 1 July 2004

Philip (Hauge) Abelson (27 Apr 1913, Tacoma WA—1 Aug 2004, Bethesda MD), American physical chemist who proposed the gas diffusion process for separating uranium-235 from uranium-238 and was codiscoverer of the element neptunium; awarded the National Medal of Science in 1987.

Max Abramovitz (23 May 1908, Chicago IL—12 Sep 2004, Pound Ridge NY), American architect who partnered with Wallace K. Harrison to influence the development of modernist architecture and helped shape the Manhattan skyline with his designs for a number of midtown buildings; he collaborated on such high-profile projects as the United Nations complex in New York City and the Central Intelligence Agency headquarters in Langley VA, but he was best known for his work on Philharmonic Hall (later Avery Fisher Hall) at Lincoln Center, New York City.

Red Adair (Paul Neal Adair; 18 Jun 1915, Houston TX—7 Aug 2004, Houston TX), American firefighter who demonstrated remarkable daring and creativity in fighting oil blowouts and fires; his reputation as an exceptionally talented firefighter was established in 1962 when his team extinguished the "Devil's Cigarette Lighter," a gas fire that had been raging in the desert of Algeria for six months.

Eddie Adams (Edward Thomas Adams; 12 Jun 1933, New Kensington PA—19 Sep 2004, New York NY), American photojournalist who won hundreds of awards during his 45-year career and counted 13 wars among the events he covered but was most renowned for the Pulitzer Prize-winning photograph he took in 1968 at the moment a South Vietnamese general shot a Viet Cong prisoner to death on the streets of Saigon.

Eddie Albert (Edward Albert Heimberger; 22 Apr 1906, Rock Island IL—26 May 2005, Pacific Palisades CA), American actor who was best remembered for his starring role as Oliver Wendell Douglas, a lawyer intent on leaving the trappings of city life to become a gentleman farmer, in the popular TV series *Green Acres* (1965–71); he was featured in numerous Broadway productions and more than 100 films; he received Academy Award nominations for his roles in *Roman Holiday* (1953) and *The Heartbreak Kid* (1972).

Shana Alexander (Shana Ager; 6 Oct 1925, New York NY—23 Jun 2005, Hermosa Beach CA), American journalist and author who battled conservative columnist James Kilpatrick on "Point-Counterpoint," a political debate segment during the 1970s on the TV program *60 Minutes*; she began her career as a reporter and in 1951 became the first woman staff writer at *Life* magazine; she also authored several nonfiction books, many of them about notable trials.

Dave Allen (David Tynan O'Mahoney; 6 Jul 1936, Tallaght, County Dublin, Ireland—10 Mar 2005, London, England), Irish comedian who mocked the absurdities of society, politics, and religion—particularly the Roman Catholic Church and its clergy; he offered his wry comedy monologues and introduced filmed satiric sketches on *Dave Allen at Large* (1971–76 and 1978–79) and other British TV programs from the late 1960s until the mid-1990s.

Mulk Raj Anand (12 Dec 1905, Peshawar, British India [now in Pakistan]—28 Sep 2004, Pune, India), Indian author of novels, short stories, and critical essays in English who was a founder of the English-language novel in India and is best known for his works that focused on the injustices of India's caste system, especially the exploitation of the poor.

Victoria de los Ángeles (Victoria Gómez Cima; 1 Nov 1923, Barcelona, Spain—14/15 Jan 2005, Barcelona, Spain), Spanish soprano who was one of the most celebrated singers of her generation. Her voice was warm and rich, with a wide range, and her repertoire was extraordinarily broad. She sometimes ended recitals with Spanish and Catalan songs, accompanying herself on the guitar.

Yasir Arafat (Muhammad 'Abd al-Rauf al-Qudwah al-Husayni; 24? Aug 1929, Cairo, Egypt?—11 Nov 2004, Paris, France), Palestinian statesman and president of the Palestinian Authority from 1996 who was credited with creating the Palestinian nationalist movement, but he never wholly cut his ties to terrorism and failed in the goal of establishing an independent state; he was the cowinner of the 1994 Nobel Peace Prize.

Thea (Beatrice May) Astley (25 Aug 1925, Brisbane, QLD, Australia—17 Aug 2004, NSW, Australia), Australian writer and teacher who used satire to examine the lives of repressed and isolated people, especially those living in small towns; considered one of Australia's leading writers, she was praised for her caustic wit, keen observations, and lyrical prose.

Richard Avedon (15 May 1923, New York NY—1 Oct 2004, San Antonio TX), American photographer who gained renown as the revolutionary fashion photographer who placed his models in candid and dramatic yet casual situations instead of the rigid, formal poses that had been the norm and in the process introduced the concept of the supermodel.

Julius Axelrod (30 May 1912, New York NY—29 Dec 2004, Rockville MD), American biochemist who discovered biochemical processes that play a crucial role in the mechanisms by which chemicals called neurotransmitters carry nerve impulses between cells in the nervous system and for this work shared the Nobel Prize for Physiology or Medicine in 1970 with British biophysicist Sir Bernard Katz and Swedish physiologist Ulf von Euler.

Anne Bancroft (Anna Maria Louisa Italiano; 17 Sep 1931, Bronx NY—6 Jun 2005, New York NY), American actress, a versatile performer whose half-century-long career was studded with renowned successes on stage, screen, and TV; she won both a Tony Award and an Academy Award for one of her most physically and emotionally demanding roles, that of Helen Keller's teacher, Annie Sullivan, in *The Miracle Worker* (Broadway, 1959; film, 1962), but it was for another Oscar-nominated film role, the seductive Mrs. Robinson in *The Graduate* (1967), that she was most identified.

John Drew Barrymore (John Blythe Barrymore, Jr.; 4 Jun 1929, Beverly Hills CA—29 Nov 2004, Los Angeles CA), American actor who was a fourth-generation member of one of the most famous American theatrical families—and the father of actress Drew Barrymore—but lifestyle and substance-abuse difficulties prevented him from attaining the success he might have enjoyed.

Geoffrey Beene (Samuel Albert Bozeman, Jr.; 30 Aug

1927, Haynesville LA—28 Sep 2004, New York NY), American fashion designer who revolutionized the American fashion industry with minimalist designs that incorporated a variety of materials and emphasized comfort over couture.

Saul Bellow (Solomon Bellow; 10 Jun 1915; Lachnine, near Montreal, QC, Canada—5 Apr 2005, Brookline MA), Canadian-born American novelist who wrote picaresque, often comic tales of thoughtful modern urbanites and was a leading exponent of Jewish American literature after World War II; *The Adventures of Augie March,* published in 1953, was a best seller and won a National Book Award, an honor he received again for *Herzog* (1964) and *Mr. Sammler's Planet* (1970); he won the Pulitzer Prize for *Humboldt's Gift* (1975), and in 1976 he was the recipient of the Nobel Prize for Literature.

Peter (James Henry Solomon) Benenson (31 Jul 1921, London, England—25 Feb 2005, Oxford, England), British attorney and human rights activist who founded Amnesty International (AI) in 1961 after reading in a news story that two students in Portugal had been imprisoned by that country's dictatorial government for proposing a toast to freedom; by 2005 AI was the world's largest human rights organization, with membership soaring to 1.8 million in more than 160 countries; in recognition of its humanitarian efforts, AI was awarded the Nobel Prize for Peace in 1977.

Obie Benson (Renaldo Benson; 14 Jun 1936, Detroit MI—1 Jul 2005, Detroit MI), American singer and songwriter who lent his powerful bass vocals to the legendary Motown group the Four Tops.

Jacques Benveniste (12 Mar 1935, Paris, France—4 Oct 2004, Paris, France), French immunologist who was responsible for numerous advances in allergy medicine and immunology, gaining prominence as part of the research team that isolated platelet-activating factor (an important blood-clotting protein).

Sune K(arl Detlof) Bergström (10 Jan 1916, Stockholm, Sweden—15 Aug 2004, Stockholm, Sweden), Swedish biochemist who laid the groundwork for chemical research on prostaglandins, an important group of natural hormone-like substances that affect blood pressure, body temperature, allergic reactions, and other physiological functions; for his work on prostaglandins Bergström shared the 1982 Nobel Prize for Physiology or Medicine.

Prince Bernhard (Bernhard Leopold Frederik Everhard Julius Coert Karel Godfried Pieter, Prince of The Netherlands, Prince of Lippe-Biesterfeld; 29 Jun 1911, Jena, Germany—1 Dec 2004, Utrecht, The Netherlands), German-born Dutch royal who was the husband of one Dutch queen, Juliana, and the father of another, Beatrix; Bernhard gained international respect as a Dutch patriot (especially during World War II) and as the founding president (1961–77) of the World Wildlife Fund.

Elmer Bernstein (4 Apr 1922, New York NY—18 Aug 2004, Ojai CA), American composer who created the scores for more than 200 motion pictures during a career that spanned half a century and produced some of Hollywood's most memorable film music, fashioning its style to reflect the mood and action of its film.

Pierre Berton (12 Jul 1920, Whitehorse, YT, Canada—30 Nov 2004, Toronto, ON, Canada), Canadian print and broadcast journalist who wrote popular works on national history, such as *Klondike* (1958), which chronicled the gold rush; *The National Dream* (1970), a story about the Canadian Pacific Railway; and *The Invasion of Canada* (1980), which recounted the War of 1812.

Hans Albrecht Bethe (2 Jul 1906, Strassburg, Germany [now Strasbourg, France]—6 Mar 2005, Ithaca NY), German-born American theoretical physicist who helped to shape classical physics into quantum physics and increased the understanding of the atomic processes responsible for the properties of matter and of the forces governing the structures of atomic nuclei; he received a National Medal of Science in 1975, the Nobel Prize for Physics in 1967 for his work on the production of energy in stars, and the 2001 Bruce Gold Medal for lifetime achievement in astronomy.

Norbert Brainin (12 Mar 1923, Vienna, Austria—10 Apr 2005, London, England), Austrian-born British violinist and teacher who founded the Amadeus Quartet; in 1938 he emigrated with his family to England, where, while interned as a refugee, he met two of the members of the future quartet; the group had its debut, as the Brainin Quartet, in 1947, becoming the Amadeus Quartet in 1948, and remained together for 40 years.

Marlon Brando, Jr. (3 Apr 1924, Omaha NE—1 Jul 2004, Los Angeles CA), American actor who brought a revolutionary new attitude to film acting in the 1950s—finding small details that added dimension to and insight into his characters and employing a raw, visceral, spontaneous, and naturalistic delivery—and became an icon for generations of Method actors; he won his first best actor Oscar for his performance in *On the Waterfront* (1954) and won another for *The Godfather* (1972)—though he refused that award in protest against Hollywood's treatment of Native Americans.

D(avid) Allan Bromley (4 May 1926, Westmeath, ON, Canada—10 Feb 2005, New Haven CT), Canadian-born American physicist and government official who was the founding director (1963–89) of Yale University's A.W. Wright Nuclear Structure Laboratory, where he conducted pioneering research in heavy-ion physics, and was nationally known as the most influential science adviser in US history as the architect (1989–93) of Pres. George H.W. Bush's science and technology policy.

Edward Maurice Bronfman (1 Nov 1927, Montreal, PQ, Canada—4 Apr 2005, Toronto, ON, Canada), Canadian businessman who founded, with his brother Peter, Edper Investments, Ltd., after the two were forced out of their stake in distilling giant Seagram; Edper, later known as the Brascan Corp., grew into a vast financial empire that became Canada's largest and included the Labatt brewing company and the Montreal Canadiens franchise of the National Hockey League; Bronfman ended his active involvement in Brascan in the 1990s and focused on charitable activities; he was awarded the Order of Canada in 2000.

Herbert Charles Brown (Herbert Brovarnik; 22 May 1912, London, England—19 Dec 2004, Lafayette IN), British-born American chemist who did extensive research into the chemical element boron and advanced the field of organic chemistry with the development of a class of chemicals called organoboranes—compounds of boron, carbon, and hydrogen; organoboranes proved to be extremely useful in synthesizing carbon compounds, both for laboratory research and for industrial purposes, including the production of pharmaceutical and agricultural chemicals; he was awarded the Nobel Prize for Chemistry in 1979 together with Georg Wittig.

Oscar (Cicero) Brown, Jr. (10 Oct 1926, Chicago IL—29 May 2005, Chicago IL), American jazz artist, actor, and activist who became noted during the civil rights movement for the songs he created and sang celebrating black American life and history; "Brown Baby," "The Snake," and "Signifyin' Monkey" were among his best-known compositions, and the lyrics he wrote to jazz standards such as "All Blues," "Dat Dere," and "Work Song" were covered by many other singers.

R(obert) W(illiam) Burchfield (27 Jan 1923, Wanganui, New Zealand—5 Jul 2004, Abingdon, Oxfordshire, England), New Zealand-born British scholar and lexicographer who ushered into print the four-volume Supplement to the *Oxford English Dictionary* (1972–86); he was personally responsible for adding words and phrases of non-British origin as well as controversial vulgarisms to the OED.

Guillermo Cabrera Infante (22 Apr 1929, Gibara, Cuba—21 Feb 2005, London, England), Cuban novelist and essayist who wrote the acclaimed novel *Tres tristes tigres* (1965; *Three Trapped Tigers* [1971]), a comic and loving portrait of Havana nightlife in the years before the 1959 Cuban Revolution; he received the Cervantes Prize in 1998.

James Callaghan, Baron Callaghan (of Cardiff; Leonard James Callaghan; 27 Mar 1912, Portsmouth, Hampshire, England—26 Mar 2005, Ringmer, East Sussex, England), British Labour Party politician who served in a succession of top ministerial posts in Harold Wilson's Labour government before succeeding him as prime minister, from 1976 to 1979.

Jim Capaldi (Nicola James Capaldi; 24 Aug 1944, Evesham, Worcestershire, England—28 Jan 2005, London, England), British rock musician who played drums for and was a founding member of the psychedelic rock band Traffic; he won several songwriting awards, and Traffic was inducted into the Rock and Roll Hall of Fame in 2004.

Chico Carrasquel (Alfonso Colón Carrasquel; 23 Jan 1928, Caracas, Venezuela—26 May 2005, Caracas, Venezuela), Venezuelan-born professional baseball player who was the first in a long line of outstanding Venezuelan shortstops to play in Major League Baseball and the first Latin American player to appear (1951) in an All-Star Game.

Johnny Carson (John William Carson; 23 Oct 1925, Corning IA—23 Jan 2005, Los Angeles CA), American comedian who served as host of *The Tonight Show* for nearly 30 years, during which he established the standard format for TV chat shows—including the guest couch and the studio band—and came to be considered the king of late-night TV; he won four Emmy Awards, was inducted into the Television Hall of Fame (1987), and was given the Presidential Medal of Freedom (1992) and a Kennedy Center Honor (1993).

Henri Cartier-Bresson (22 Aug 1908, Chanteloup, France—3 Aug 2004, Céreste, France), French photographer whose humane, spontaneous photographs helped establish photojournalism as an art form; his theory that photography can capture the meaning beneath outward appearance in instants of extraordinary clarity is perhaps best expressed in his book *Images à la sauvette* (1952; *The Decisive Moment*).

Jean Cayrol (Jean-Raphaël-Marie-Noël Cayrol; 6 Jun 1911, Bordeaux, France—9 Feb 2005, Bordeaux, France), French poet, novelist, and essayist who was a pioneer in the French avant-garde *nouveau roman* of the 1950s; he was elected to the Académie Goncourt in 1974.

Iris Chang (28 Mar 1968, Princeton NJ—9 Nov 2004, near Los Gatos CA), American historian who documented, in the best-selling book *The Rape of Nanking: The Forgotten Holocaust of World War II* (1997), the mass atrocities of murder and rape committed by the Japanese military while destroying the Chinese city during the Nanking Massacre of 1937–38.

Shiing-shen Chern (26 Oct 1911, Jiaxing, Zhejiang province, China—3 Dec 2004, Tianjin, China), Chinese-American mathematician who advanced the field of differential geometry with new insights into the curvature of objects; his study of the "characteristic classes" of surfaces had resonance in such disparate fields as physics and computer graphics.

Julia Child (Julia Carolyn McWilliams; 15 Aug 1912, Pasadena CA—13 Aug 2004, Montecito CA), American chef, TV personality, and author who brought the art of French cookery to a vast number of Americans through her books and, especially, her programs on public TV.

Shirley Chisholm (Shirley Anita St. Hill; 30 Nov 1924, Brooklyn NY—1 Jan 2005, Ormond Beach FL), American politician who was the first black woman to serve (1969–83) as a representative in the US Congress and in 1972 became the first woman to enter the Democratic presidential primaries; self-described as "unbought and unbossed," she challenged the seniority system for committee assignments in Congress in order to champion the rights of minorities and women and help improve the lives of the underprivileged.

Jerome Chodorow (10 Aug 1911, New York NY—12 Sep 2004, Nyack NY), American playwright who authored more than a dozen successful Broadway plays, most notably the comedy *My Sister Eileen* (1940) and its musical adaptation *Wonderful Town* (1953).

Chung Se Yung (6 Aug 1928, Tongchon, Kangwon province, Korea [now in South Korea]—21 May 2005, Seoul, South Korea), Korean industrialist who established the Hyundai Motor Co. in 1967, which, under his leadership grew into one of the world's largest automobile manufacturers.

Kenneth (Bancroft) Clark (24 Jul 1914, Panama Canal Zone—1 May 2005, Hastings-on-Hudson NY), American psychologist who conducted pioneering research into the impact of racial segregation on children; in the 1940s and '50s he administered to African American schoolchildren the "doll test," in which a child was presented with a black doll and a white doll and asked to choose a favorite; in the segregated South, the black children preferred the white doll by a wide margin, with many children identifying the black doll as "bad."

Johnnie L. Cochran, Jr. (2 Oct 1937, Shreveport LA—29 Mar 2005, Los Angeles CA), American trial lawyer who gained international prominence with his skillful (and controversial) defense of O.J. Simpson, a football star charged with (but later acquitted of) a double murder in 1994; Cochran showed his skill for connecting with jurors and for putting the prosecution and police on the defensive.

Isidore Cohen (16 Dec 1922, Brooklyn NY—23 Jun 2005, Bronx NY), American violinist and teacher who, from 1958 to 1968, was second violinist in the Juilliard String Quartet; he then joined the Beaux Arts Trio, the most celebrated piano trio of its time, where he remained until his retirement in 1992; from 1966 he was affiliated with the Marlboro (VT) Music School and Festival.

Cy Coleman (Seymour Kaufman; 14 Jun 1929, New York NY—18 Nov 2004, New York NY), American jazz pianist and composer who was at first a classical pianist but then turned to jazz and began partnering with lyricists to write songs. Many of them became popular standards, as did songs from his numerous Broadway musicals and motion picture scores.

Frank Conroy (15 Jan 1936, New York NY—6 Apr 2005, Iowa City IA), American author who first came to prominence with the publication of *Stop-Time* (1967), a memoir of his nomadic childhood; he taught writing at several universities before joining the staff of the University of Iowa Writers' Workshop as director, a position he held for 18 years (1987–2004).

L(eroy) Gordon Cooper, Jr. (6 Mar 1927, Shawnee OK—4 Oct 2004, Ventura CA), American astronaut who was one of seven pilots chosen for the Mercury series of one-man spacecraft; on 15 May 1963 he piloted the capsule Faith 7 on the final Mercury mission, during which he set a US record by completing 22 orbits of the Earth and remaining in space for 34 hours and 20 minutes; he made history again on 21 Aug 1965, when he commanded the Gemini 5 mission and became the first person to reach orbit twice.

Robert (White) Creeley (21 May 1926, Arlington MA—30 Mar 2005, Odessa TX), American poet and founder of the Black Mountain movement; he was the winner of the Bollingen Prize in Poetry in 1999, a Before Columbus Lifetime Achievement Award in 2000, and a Lannan Lifetime Achievement Award in 2001.

Francis (Harry Compton) Crick (8 Jun 1916, Northampton, England—28 Jul 2004, San Diego CA), British biophysicist, who, with James Watson and Maurice Wilkins *(q.v.)*, received the 1962 Nobel Prize for Physiology or Medicine for their determination of the molecular structure of deoxyribonucleic acid (DNA).

Harold Wright Cruse (8 Mar 1916, Petersburg VA—25 Mar 2005, Ann Arbor MI), American social and cultural critic who authored *The Crisis of the Negro Intellectual* (1967); Cruse argued for black Americans to embrace their own distinctive economic, political, and cultural institutions; with LeRoi Jones (now Amiri Baraka), Cruse founded the Black Arts Repertory Theatre/School in Harlem, New York City.

Álvaro (Barreirinhas) Cunhal (10 Nov 1913, Coimbra, Portugal—13 Jun 2005, Lisbon, Portugal), Portuguese politician and general secretary of the Portuguese Communist Party (from 1961) who was instrumental in the 1974 overthrow of the long dictatorship established by António Salazar; he was also a journalist and literary scholar.

Hubert Curien (30 Oct 1924, Cornimont, France—6 Feb 2005, Loury, France), French scientist and public servant who pioneered France's space program and supervised the debut launch of the European Space Agency's Ariane series of rockets in 1979; he was the first chairman of the European Space Agency and president of the French Academy of Sciences.

Lloyd Norton Cutler (10 Nov 1917, New York NY—8 May 2005, Washington DC), American lawyer and White House counsel; from 1979 to 1981 he helped Pres. Jimmy Carter navigate difficult situations such as the Soviet invasion of Afghanistan and the hostage crisis in Iran, and in 1994 he helped Pres. Bill Clinton answer charges emanating from the Whitewater scandal; later he was asked by Pres. George W. Bush to join the commission investigating intelligence failures leading up to the 2003 invasion of Iraq.

Katharina Dorothea Kuipers Dalton (11 Nov 1916, London, England—17 Sep 2004, Poole, Dorset, England), British gynecologist who identified the symptoms suffered by women before and during their menstrual cycles as those of an actual physical disorder, which she called premenstrual syndrome, or PMS.

Rodney Dangerfield (Jacob Cohen; 22 Nov 1921, Babylon NY—5 Oct 2004, Los Angeles CA), American comedian and film actor who immortalized the line "I don't get no respect" as part of his stand-up comedy act.

George B(ernard) Dantzig (8 Nov 1914, Portland OR—13 May 2005, Palo Alto CA), American mathematician who devised the simplex algorithm, a method for solving problems that involve numerous conditions and variables, in the process founding the field of linear programming; he was awarded the Von Neumann Theory Prize in Operations Research (1975), the National Medal of Science (1976), and the National Academy of Sciences Award in Applied Mathematics and Numerical Analysis (1977).

Paula Danziger (18 Aug 1945, Washington DC—8 Jul 2004, New York NY), American children's author who wrote more than 30 books, notably the popular Amber Brown series, that presented serious issues with humor and honesty.

Glenn Woodward Davis (26 Dec 1924, Claremont CA—9 Mar 2005, La Quinta CA), American football player who teamed with Doc Blanchard to form arguably the greatest rushing tandem in the history of American collegiate football; the fast and elusive Davis was "Mr. Outside" to Blanchard's "Mr. Inside" on the great Army teams of the mid-1940s; Davis was a three-time all-American, and he won the Heisman Trophy in 1946; his career average of 8.26 yards per carry remains a collegiate record.

Ossie Davis (Raiford Chatman Davis; 18 Dec 1917, Cogdell GA—4 Feb 2005, Miami Beach FL), American actor, writer, director, producer, and social activist who had a stately presence and a mellifluous voice that both enriched his stage, film, and TV performances and gave extra power to his work on behalf of civil rights and peace; he was also noted for his partnership with his wife, Ruby Dee, which was considered one of the theater and film world's most distinguished; Davis and Dee were awarded a National Medal of Arts in 1995 and a Kennedy Center Honor in 2004.

Skeeter Davis (Mary Francis Penick; 30 Dec 1931, Dry Ridge KY—19 Sep 2004, Nashville TN), American country music singer who began performing on the Grand Ole Opry radio program in 1959 and remained a regular for more than 40 years; her best-known hit, "The End of the World," climbed high on the pop charts in 1963.

Tyrone Davis (4 May 1938, Greenville MS—9 Feb 2005, Hinsdale IL), American rhythm-and-blues singer who helped shape Chicago soul music in the 1960s and '70s; known for his warm, smooth delivery, he scored hits with "Can I Change My Mind," "Turn Back the Hands of Time," and "Turning Point."

Gerard Debreu (4 Jul 1921, Calais, France—31 Dec

2004, Paris, France), French-born American economist who was the winner of the 1983 Nobel Memorial Prize for Economic Science for economics for his development of a mathematical model that proved the theory of supply and demand; Debreu's use of mathematical modeling in economics was somewhat uncommon and proved influential in the field.

Sandra Dee (Alexandra Cymboliak Zuck; 23 Apr 1942, Bayonne NJ—20 Feb 2005, Thousand Oaks CA), American actress who was best known as the perky star of such films as *Gidget* (1959), *Tammy Tell Me True* (1961), and *Tammy and the Doctor* (1963) and as the wife (1960–67) of pop idol Bobby Darin.

John (Zachary) DeLorean (6 Jan 1925, Detroit MI—19 Mar 2005, Summit NJ), American automobile manufacturer and entrepreneur who established the DeLorean Motor Co. in Northern Ireland; in 1981 the company produced the stainless-steel, gull-winged DeLorean DMC-12 sports coupe that sparked the imagination of millions of filmgoers after being featured as a time machine in the movie *Back to the Future* (1985).

Arnold Sheldon Denker (21 Feb 1914, New York NY—2 Jan 2005, Fort Lauderdale FL), American chess master who was a top player during the 1940s and later a respected administrator and promoter of chess; he was made an honorary grandmaster in 1981, in 1992 he was inducted into the US Chess Hall of Fame, and in 2004 the US Chess Federation named him a dean of American chess.

Martin Denny (10 Apr 1911, New York NY—2 Mar 2005, Hawaii Kai, near Honolulu HI), American bandleader who specialized in exotica—music that combined jazz, Polynesian rhythms and instrumentation, and jungle sounds—which had a wave of popularity in the 1950s and '60s; the first of his 39 albums, *Exotica*, topped the charts in 1959, and the single "Quiet Village" made it to the number-two spot.

Jacques Derrida (Jackie Derrida; 15 Jul 1930, El Biar, French Algeria—8 Oct 2004, Paris, France), French philosopher who played a leading role in popularizing the controversial method of reading philosophical texts known as deconstruction; considered by its opponents a subversive instrument of relativism and nihilism, deconstruction was seen by its adherents as a tool for uncovering, by close reading, hidden blind spots and contradictions (*aporia*) in the texts that could serve as the starting point for going beyond conventional readings.

Carlo Di Palma (17 Apr 1925, Rome, Italy—9 Jul 2004, Rome, Italy), Italian cinematographer who created masterful illusions of lighting and color in order to portray an altered sense of reality in his films.

David (Leo) Diamond (9 Jul 1915, Rochester NY—13 Jun 2005, Rochester NY), American composer who left a large body of work that included 11 symphonies, 10 string quartets, and many songs; his music was characterized by its classic structures and its strong melodic sense.

Sacha Distel (Alexandre Distel; 29 Jan 1933, Paris, France—22 Jul 2004, Rayol-Canadel, France), French musician and entertainer who established himself as the best jazz guitarist in France by the time he reached his early 20s; his debonair appearance and suave voice also made him popular in the US, where he performed alongside such jazz greats as Miles Davis and Dizzy Gillespie.

Elisabeth Domitien (1925, Lobaye region, Ubangi-

Shari [now Central African Republic]—26 Apr 2005, Bimbo, Central African Republic), Central African Republic prime minister, 1975–76, who was the first woman to hold that post in an African country.

Piero Dorazio (Piero D'Orazio; 29 Jun 1927, Rome, Italy—17 May 2005, Perugia, Italy), Italian painter who was originally a Cubist, but who gradually adopted Abstract and Futurist styles; he was one of the leading modern artists in Italy.

Spencer Dryden (7 Apr 1938, New York NY—11 Jan 2005, Petaluma CA), American rock drummer who helped create the sound of the psychedelic rock band Jefferson Airplane during its heyday in the late 1960s.

Wim Duisenberg (Willem Frederik Duisenberg) (9 Jul 1935, Heerenveen, The Netherlands—31 Jul 2005, Faucon, France), Dutch economist and first president (1998–2003) of the European Central Bank; he was a leading proponent of the European common currency, the euro.

(Otis) Dudley Duncan (2 Dec 1921, Nocona TX—16 Nov 2004, Santa Barbara CA), American sociologist who showed that education was more influential than social status in determining future success.

Sunil Dutt (Balraj Dutt; 6 Jun 1929, Khurd, Jhelum district, British India [now in Pakistan]—25 May 2005, Mumbai [Bombay], India), Indian film actor and politician who starred in more than 100 Bollywood motion pictures between 1955 and 1993, notably the Oscar-nominated *Mother India* (1957); in 2004 he was appointed sports minister.

Andrea Rita Dworkin (26 Sep 1946, Camden NJ—9 Apr 2005, Washington DC), American feminist writer, activist, and public figure who worked to end violence against women and the subjugation of women; her book *Scapegoat: The Jews, Israel, and Women's Liberation* won the 2001 American Book Award.

Fred Ebb (8 Apr 1928?, New York NY—11 Sep 2004, New York NY), American lyricist who collaborated with composer John Kander for more than 40 years, and together they created enduring music for a number of classic Broadway shows including *Cabaret* (1966), *Chicago* (1975), *New York, New York* (1977), *Woman of the Year* (1981), and *Kiss of the Spider Woman* (1993).

Richard (Ghormley) Eberhart (5 Apr 1904, Austin MN—9 Jun 2005, Hanover NH), American poet, playwright, and teacher who received numerous awards for his lyric verse that combined a modern style with elements of Romanticism; from 1959 to 1961 he was consultant in poetry at the Library of Congress (poet laureate), and he was a cowinner of the 1961 Bollingen Prize for Poetry.

(Evert) Sixten Ehrling (3 Apr 1918, Malmö, Sweden—13 Feb 2005, New York NY), Swedish-born American conductor who directed orchestras with passion and precision that led to his reputation as one of the most respected conductors of his era; he was musical director (1963–73) of the Detroit Symphony Orchestra and later was associated with the Juilliard School and the Manhattan School of Music in New York City.

Will Eisner (William Erwin Eisner; 6 Mar 1917, Brooklyn NY—3 Jan 2005, Fort Lauderdale FL), American comic-book artist who created the influential comic strip *The Spirit* and whose *A Contract with God* (1978) is often cited as the first modern graphic novel.

(Richard) Gwynfor Evans (1 Sep 1912, Barry, Co. Glamorgan, Wales—21 Apr 2005, Pencarreg, Carmarthenshire, Wales), Welsh politician who devoted his life to the peaceful cause of Welsh nationalism, as vice president (1943–45), president (1945–81), and honorary president (from 1982) of Plaid Cymru, the Welsh nationalist political party.

(Étienne) Gnassingbé Eyadéma (26 Dec 1935, Pya village, Togoland [now Togo]–5 Feb 2005, en route from Togo to France), Togolese soldier and president who was, at the time of his death, Africa's longest serving political leader, having ruled Togo with near dictatorial power for more than 37 years.

Fahd ibn 'Abd al-'Aziz al-Sa'ud (1923, Riyadh, Arabia [now Saudi Arabia]–31 Jul 2005, Riyadh), king of the Saudi Arabians from 1982; he was a consistent advocate of modernization and established a corps of Western-trained technicians to oversee the country's industrial diversification; in the 1970s and '80s, he was also the principal architect of Saudi Arabia's foreign policy, which sought to counterbalance Soviet influence in the Middle East by providing financial aid to moderate states, notably Egypt.

Frederick Fennell (2 July 1914, Cleveland OH–7 Dec 2004, Siesta Key FL), American conductor and founder of the Eastman Wind Ensemble, one of the major chamber music groups in America.

Geraldine (Mary) Fitzgerald (24 Nov 1913, Greystones, Co. Wicklow, Ireland–17 Jul 2005, New York NY), Irish-born actress, a versatile performer whose long career was especially notable for her supporting roles in films that included *Wuthering Heights* (1939), *Dark Victory* (1939), *Watch on the Rhine* (1943), *Ten North Frederick* (1958), *The Pawnbroker* (1964), *Harry and Tonto* (1974), and *Arthur* (1981).

Cyril Fletcher (25 Jun 1913, Watford, Hertfordshire, England–2 Jan 2005, St. Peter Port, Guernsey, Channel Islands), British entertainer who appeared regularly on BBC radio and TV for more than six decades.

Shelby Foote (17 Nov 1916, Greenville MS–27 Jun 2005, Memphis TN), American novelist and historian who wrote a masterly history of the American Civil War and who also wrote a number of well-regarded novels, each set in the American South; he devoted two decades to completing the work for which he is best known, *The Civil War: A Narrative* (1958–74), in three volumes; the work earned Foote a prominent role on filmmaker Ken Burns's widely acclaimed TV documentary *The Civil War* (1990).

James (Rufus) Forman (4 Oct 1928, Chicago IL–10 Jan 2005, Washington DC), American civil rights activist who served as executive secretary of the Student Nonviolent Coordinating Committee (1961–66); in that position he was a pivotal figure in the struggle for racial equality, especially in the organization of the Freedom Rides in the South and of the 1963 March on Washington.

Frank Kelly Freas (27 Aug 1922, Hornell NY–2 Jan 2005, Los Angeles CA), American illustrator who earned the title "the most popular illustrator in the history of science fiction" with his stylized depictions of fantastic landscapes, alien women, and painstakingly detailed robots.

Edward David Freis (13 May 1912, Chicago IL–1 Feb 2005, Washington DC), American physician and medical researcher who successfully demonstrated the benefits of treating hypertension by administration of drugs and also revealed the health risks associated with hypertension, such as heart attack and stroke, and disproved the established theory that high blood pressure was necessary for circulating blood to the heart, brain, and other vital parts of the body.

Christopher Fry (Christopher Harris; 18 Dec 1907, Bristol, Gloucestershire, England–30 Jun 2005, Chichester, England), British writer of verse plays who gained fame as a playwright with *The Lady's Not for Burning* (1948); he also collaborated on the screenplays of the epic films *Ben Hur* (1959) and *Barabbas* (1962), and he wrote both radio and TV plays.

Antonio Gades (Antonio Esteve Ródenas; 14 Nov 1936, Elda, Spain–20 Jul 2004, Madrid, Spain), Spanish dancer and choreographer who popularized flamenco and other Spanish dances with his elegant performances and powerful choreography.

Gemini Ganesan (17 Nov 1920, Madras [now Chennai], British India–22 Mar 2005, Chennai, India), Indian film actor who was the "Kadhal Mannan" ("King of Romance") in southern India's Tamil-language cinema; he appeared in more than 200 films, beginning with a small role in *Miss Malini* (1947); his last screen appearance was in *Avvai Shanmugi* (1996), a Tamil remake of *Mrs. Doubtfire*.

John Garang (de Mabior) (23 Jun 1945, Bor district, Anglo-Egyptian Sudan–31 Jul 2005, southern Sudan), Sudanese military officer, rebel leader, and government official who formed the Sudan People's Liberation Movement in the southern part of the country in 1983; the Christian and animist south was involved in a 22-year-long civil war with the Muslim north that cost an estimated two million lives; after the war Garang was named Sudanese vice president, but three weeks later he perished in a helicopter crash.

Hank Garland (Walter Louis Garland; 11 Nov 1930, Cowpens SC–27 Dec 2004, Orange Park FL), American musician who was a legendary country, jazz, and rock guitarist, best known for his studio work with such performers as Elvis Presley, Roy Orbison, the Everly Brothers, and Patsy Cline.

J(ohn) Donald MacIntyre Gass (2 Aug 1928, Prince Edward Island, Canada–26 Feb 2005, Nashville TN), American ophthalmologist who conducted groundbreaking research on diseases of the retina, which led to treatments that saved the eyesight of thousands of patients.

Sir Harry Talbot Gibbs (7 Feb 1917, Sydney, NSW, Australia–25 Jun 2005, Sydney, NSW, Australia), Australian jurist who was appointed to the High Court of Australia in 1970 and served as its chief justice from 1981 to 1987; he was knighted in 1970 and became a privy councillor in 1972.

Carlo Maria Giulini (9 May 1914, Barletta, Italy–13 Jun 2005, Brescia, Italy), Italian conductor esteemed for his skills in directing both Italian opera and symphony orchestras; he was music director of the Vienna Symphony Orchestra, 1973–76, and music director of the Los Angeles Philharmonic, 1978–84.

Jerry Goldsmith (Jerrald King Goldsmith; 10 Feb 1929, Los Angeles CA–21 Jul 2004, Beverly Hills CA), American composer who demonstrated his versatility and originality in more than 300 scores for movies and TV programs; notable among his film scores were those for *Planet of the Apes* (1968), *Chinatown* (1974), *The Omen* (1976), for which he won an Academy Award, *Total Recall* (1990), and

L.A. Confidential (1997); for his TV work he won five Emmy Awards.

Vasco dos Santos Gonçalves (3 May 1921, Sintra, Portugal—11 Jun 2005, Almancil, Algarve, Portugal), Portuguese military officer, Socialist Party politician, and prime minister (1974–75); like his Communist colleague, Álvaro Cunhal *(q.v.)* he was instrumental in bringing to an end the 30-year dictatorship established by António Salazar.

Andrew J(ackson) Goodpaster (12 Feb 1915, Granite City IL—16 May 2005, Washington DC), American military leader and scholar, a four-star general in the US Army who wielded great influence during a lengthy military career in which he served as a presidential adviser (1954–61); commander of NATO forces in Europe (1969–74); and superintendent of the US Military Academy at West Point (1977–81); in 1984 he received the Presidential Medal of Freedom.

Frank Gorshin (5 Apr 1933, Pittsburgh PA—17 May 2005, Burbank CA), American actor and comedian who was best known for his manic portrayal of the arch-villain the Riddler on the 1960s TV series *Batman.*

Joseph Grant (15 May 1908, New York NY—6 May 2005, Glendale CA), American animator who served as both a designer and a writer on some of the classic works of the Disney studios; he joined Disney in 1933 and created the wicked queen/witch of *Snow White and the Seven Dwarfs* (1937), played a central creative role in *Pinocchio* and *Fantasia* (both 1940), and cowrote *Dumbo* (1941) and *The Lady and the Tramp* (1955).

L(ouis) Patrick Gray, III (18 Jul 1916, St. Louis MO—6 Jul 2005, Atlantic Beach FL), American lawyer and government official who served as interim director of the Federal Bureau of Investigation after the death of J. Edgar Hoover in 1972.

Henry Grunwald (2 Dec 1922, Vienna, Austria—26 Feb 2005, New York NY), Austrian-born American magazine editor who introduced extensive innovations to the format of *Time* magazine when he became its managing editor in 1968; the magazine also loosened its conservative political views; Grunwald later served as *Time*'s editor in chief (1979–87); after retiring he was appointed American ambassador to Austria in 1988.

Lalo Guerrero (Eduardo Guerrero, Jr.; 24 Dec 1916, Tucson AZ—17 Mar 2005, Rancho Mirage CA), Mexican American singer-songwriter who captured the spirit of daily Mexican American life and embraced the social diversity of these communities in bilingual songs and parodies; dubbed "the father of Chicano music" due to his variety of musical styles, during his six-decade career he recorded more than 700 songs; he was awarded a National Medal of Arts in 1996.

Karl Haas (6 Dec 1913, Speyer-am-Rhein, Germany—6 Feb 2005, Royal Oak MI), American musicologist and music broadcaster who hosted a daily radio program, *Adventures in Good Music,* which he originated on a Detroit radio station in 1959; the show was syndicated nationally in 1970 and continued on the air until 2002; it won many honors, including two Peabody Awards for excellence in broadcasting.

David Haskell Hackworth (11 Nov 1930, Venice CA—4 May 2005, Tijuana, Mexico), American military leader who was a highly decorated soldier who earned a reputation as a brilliant but rebellious battlefield commander; he was the youngest American full colonel during the Vietnam War but incurred the wrath of senior officers for his harsh public criticism of US strategy and policies; in 1990 he was hired by *Newsweek* magazine to report on the First Persian Gulf War and again became a severe critic of US military policy.

Horace Hagedorn (18 Mar 1915, New York NY—31 Jan 2005, Sands Point NY), American businessman who founded Miracle-Gro Products, Inc., and used his marketing acumen to make Miracle-Gro the most widely used home plant fertilizer in the world.

Gunder Hägg (31 Dec 1918, Sörbygden, Sweden—27 Nov 2004, Malmö, Sweden), Swedish middle-distance runner who set 15 world records during his career, 10 of which were registered during a three-month period in 1942; "Gunder the Wonder" was the first athlete to run the 5,000 m in under 14 minutes (in 1942) and the last runner to hold a world record of more than 4 minutes in the mile.

Arthur Hailey (5 Apr 1920, Luton, Bedfordshire, England—24 Nov 2004, Lyford Cay, New Providence Island, Bahamas), British-born author who enjoyed a string of best-selling novels in the 1960s and '70s that included *Hotel* (1965), *Airport* (1968), *Wheels* (1971), and *The Moneychangers* (1975), and helped launch the disaster-movie genre when *Airport* was made into a motion picture in 1970.

Mary Agnes Hallaren (4 May 1907, Lowell MA—13 Feb 2005, McLean VA), American soldier who helped to integrate women into the military in the 1940s and '50s; she was the first woman outside of the Medical Corps to be commissioned into the US Army; during World War II she commanded the first battalion to go overseas, a unit attached to the 8th and 9th Air Forces, and earned the Legion of Merit, the Bronze Star, and the Croix de Guerre (France); she served as director of the Women's Army Corps (WAC) until 1953.

Joseph Hansen (19 Jul 1923, Aberdeen SD—24 Nov 2004, Laguna Beach CA), American mystery writer and gay rights activist who featured as his protagonist a homosexual detective, considered to be one of the first such characters in the genre; the fictional Dave Brandstetter appeared in a dozen hard-boiled detective novels, from *Fadeout* (1970) to *A Country of Old Men* (1991).

James Edward Hanson, Baron Hanson of Egerton (20 Jan 1922, Huddersfield, Yorkshire, England—1 Nov 2004, Newbury, Berkshire, England), British business magnate who cofounded, with his partner Gordon White (later Lord White of Hull), Hanson PLC and, through a succession of aggressive business takeover deals throughout Britain and the US, built it into one of the UK's biggest conglomerates; Hanson's billion-dollar empire earned him the nickname "Lord Moneybags."

Billy James Hargis (3 Aug 1925, Texarkana TX—27 Nov 2004, Tulsa OK), American evangelist who founded the Christian Crusade, an international ministry with a special interest in battling communism; he built a powerful media empire, reaching millions through TV, radio, books, and pamphlets; in 1970 he founded the American Christian Crusade College in Tulsa OK.

Rafiq (Baha al-Din) al-Hariri (1 Nov 1944, Sidon, Lebanon—14 Feb 2005, Beirut, Lebanon), Lebanese business tycoon, politician, and philanthropist who used his personal wealth, international business contacts, and charismatic personality to help broker the end of the Lebanese civil war and rebuild the country's economy and infrastructure, first as an unofficial representative of the

Saudi government and then as prime minister of Lebanon (1992–98 and 2000–04).

June Haver (June Stovenour; 10 Jun 1926, Rock Island IL–4 Jul 2005 Brentwood CA), American actress in film musicals of the 1940s; she was married to actor Fred MacMurray.

Vijay Hazare (11 Mar 1915, Sangli, Maharashtra, British India–18 Dec 2004, Baroda, Gujarat, India), Indian cricketer who was a solid right-handed batsman and medium-pace bowler, he played in 30 Test matches (14 as India's captain) between 1946 and 1953, scoring 2,192 runs (average 47.65) and seven centuries, including two in one Test against Don Bradman's formidable national side in Adelaide, Australia, in 1947–48.

Percy (Leroy) Heath (30 Apr 1923, Wilmington NC–28 Apr 2005, Southampton NY), American jazz musician who became renowned for his melodic bass playing in the Modern Jazz Quartet and in the popular Heath Brothers combos.

Anthony (Evan) Hecht (16 Jan 1923, New York NY–20 Oct 2004, Washington DC), American poet who served as consultant in poetry to the Library of Congress (poet laureate) from 1982 to 1984; a formalist, he mastered a wide range of poetic forms and was noted for both the elegance and the intelligence of his work; he received, posthumously, a National Medal for Arts in 2004.

Robert Louis Heilbroner (24 Mar 1919, New York NY–4 Jan 2005, New York NY), American economist who was the author of several of the most widely read books on economics in the US; he viewed economics broadly, as a system in context with political and social systems.

James Aloysius Cardinal Hickey (11 Oct 1920, Midlean MI–24 Oct 2004, Washington DC), American Roman Catholic prelate who held to conservative theological policies while serving (1980–2000) as archbishop of Washington DC; during his tenure Hickey also took activist roles in support of gun control and nuclear disarmament and in opposition to right-wing military groups in Central America.

Hildegarde (Hildegarde Loretta Sell; 1 Feb 1906, Adell WI–29 Jul 2005, New York NY), American singer of sophisticated popular songs and nightclub entertainer whose hits in the 1940s included "Darling, Je Vous Aime Beaucoup" and "The Last Time I Saw Paris."

Maurice Ralph Hilleman (30 Aug 1919, Miles City MT–11 Apr 2005, Philadelphia PA), American microbiologist who developed some 40 vaccines, including those for chicken pox, hepatitis A, hepatitis B, measles, meningitis, mumps, and rubella; his work was credited with having saved tens of millions of lives by making possible the virtual elimination from many countries of once-common deadly childhood diseases.

Justin Hinds (7 May 1942, Steer Town, Jamaica–17 Mar 2005, Steer Town, Jamaica), Jamaican reggae singer who enjoyed a four-decade-long career beginning in the 1960s when his group the Dominoes recorded the ska classic "Carry Go Bring Come"; his unique vocal style reflected his rural roots and sustained him as a solo act through the ska, rocksteady, and roots reggae periods; in the 1990s he gained international acclaim through projects with Keith Richards of the Rolling Stones and with the Jamaica All Stars.

Red Horner (Reginald Horner; 28 May 1909, Lynden, ON, Canada–27 Apr 2005, Toronto, ON, Canada), Canadian ice hockey player who had a reputation as the toughest and most intimidating player of his era; as a defenseman for the Toronto Maple Leafs (1928–40), he accrued 1,264 penalty minutes, leading the National Hockey League in that category eight times.

Sir Godfrey Newbold Hounsfield (28 Aug 1919, Newark, Nottinghamshire, England–12 Aug 2004, Kingston upon Thames, Surrey, England), British electrical engineer who invented the CT (computed tomography) scanner, also known as the CAT (computerized axial tomography) scanner, a medical imaging device that revolutionized medical diagnosis; he shared the 1979 Nobel Prize for Physiology or Medicine with Allan M. Cormack.

Emlyn Walter Hughes (28 Aug 1947, Barrow-in-Furness, Lancashire, England–9 Nov 2004, Sheffield, England), British association football (soccer) player who was one of England's finest footballers of the 1970s; during 12 years (1967–79) with Liverpool, the exuberant left-half known as "Crazy Horse" led that club to the Football Association Cup (1974), four league championships (1973, 1976–77, 1979), two Union des Associations Européennes de Football Cups (1973, 1976), and two European Cups (1977–78); he was named Player of the Year in 1977.

Evan Hunter (Salvatore Albert Lombino; noms de plume included Ed McBain, Curt Cannon, Hunt Collins, Ezra Hannon, Richard Marsten, and John Abbott; 15 Oct 1926, New York NY–6 Jul 2005, Weston CT), American writer who specialized in crime fiction and was best remembered for his series of 87th Precinct novels written under the name Ed McBain, which numbered more than 50 and introduced the gritty realism of police procedure to the genre.

Robert Hunter (13 Oct 1941, St. Boniface, MB, Canada–2 May 2005, Toronto, ON, Canada), Canadian environmental activist who was a cofounder (1971) and president (1973–77) of Greenpeace, the international organization devoted to preserving the environment; as Greenpeace president he steered the organization toward high-profile media-driven campaigns against whale and seal hunting as well as toxic-waste dumping in the oceans.

Ruth Hussey (Ruth Carol O'Rourke; 30 Oct 1911, Providence RI–19 Apr 2005, Newbury Park CA), American actress who appeared onstage, on TV, and in more than 40 films, usually in roles that called for a witty, sophisticated, and worldly-wise beauty.

Frances Hyland (25 Apr 1927, Shaunavon, SK, Canada–11 Jul 2004, Toronto, ON, Canada), Canadian actress who concentrated mostly on stage work, starring in and directing productions at the Stratford and Shaw festivals in Ontario in addition to performing in numerous theaters across Canada and occasionally on Broadway and in London during her 50-year career.

Iakovos (Aghioi Theodoroi; Demetrios Coucouzis; 29 Jul 1911, Imbrosz [Imbros] Island, Ottoman Empire [now Gökçeada, Turkey]–10 Apr 2005, Stamford CT), Greek Orthodox archbishop who promoted the ecumenical movement and gained broader acceptance for the Eastern Church in the US during his long tenure (1959–96) as primate of the Greek Orthodox Archdiocese in North and South America; during the 1960s he served as president of the World Council of Churches; he was the recipient of the Presidential Medal of Freedom in 1980.

Kenneth E(ugene) Iverson (17 Dec 1920, Camrose,

AB, Canada—19 Oct 2004, Toronto, ON, Canada), Canadian-born American mathematician and computer scientist who pioneered a very compact high-level computer programming language called APL (the initials of his book *A Programming Language* [1962]); the language made efficient use of the slow communication speeds of the computer terminals of that time, and APL enjoyed an enthusiastic following.

Rick James (James Ambrose Johnson; 1 Feb 1948, Buffalo NY—6 Aug 2004, Hollywood CA), American musician and singer who was the creator of such classic funk hits as "Super Freak" and "Give It to Me."

Elizabeth Janeway (Elizabeth Ames Hall; 7 Oct 1913, New York NY—15 Jan 2005, Rye NY), American writer who was a best-selling novelist in the 1940s and transformed herself into a critic, social historian, and feminist; her popular novels included *The Walsh Girls* (1943), *Daisy Kenyon* (1945), and *Leaving Home* (1953).

Peter (Charles) Jennings (29 Jul 1938, Toronto, ON, Canada—7 Aug 2005, New York NY), Canadian-born American broadcast journalist and news anchor of *ABC's World News Tonight with Peter Jennings* from 1983 until April 2005.

Sir Robert Yewdall Jennings (19 Oct 1913, Idle, West Yorkshire, England—4 Aug 2004, Cambridge, England), British lawyer and jurist who served as Whewell Professor of International Law at the University of Cambridge (1955–82) and as a judge on the International Court of Justice (1982–95, president 1991–94) at The Hague.

Grant Johannesen (30 Jul 1921, Salt Lake City UT—27 Mar 2005, near Munich, Germany), American pianist who championed American and French piano works by Aaron Copland, Peter Mennin, Gabriel Fauré, and Francis Poulenc; throughout his career he toured extensively, particularly with the New York Philharmonic and the Cleveland Orchestra.

John Paul II (Karol Józef Wojtyla; 18 May 1920, Wadowice, Poland—2 Apr 2005, Vatican City State), Polish-born pope of the Roman Catholic Church who served as the spiritual leader of the world's 1.1 billion Roman Catholics for more than 26 years—one of the longest papal reigns in church history; installed on 22 Oct 1978, John Paul II was the first non-Italian pope in 455 years and the first ever from a Slavic country; he became known for his energy and charisma as well as for his widely publicized crusades against political oppression; within the church, he maintained a steadfastly conservative stance on theological issues and appointed bishops and cardinals who shared his views; while he failed to reverse a decline in vocations and church attendance, he made extraordinary efforts to reach out to people around the world, Catholics and non-Catholics alike.

John H(arold) Johnson (19 Jan 1918, Arkansas City AR—8 Aug 2005), American magazine and book publisher; creator of *Ebony* (1945), *Jet* (1951), and other periodicals aimed at an African American readership; *Ebony* was the first black-oriented magazine in the country to attain mass circulation.

Philip C(ortelyou) Johnson (8 Jul 1906, Cleveland OH—25 Jan 2005, New Canaan CT), American architect; an exponent of the International Style and the principle of space unification he later designed in a postmodernist style; he was the winner of the first (1979) Pritzker Architecture Prize.

E(uine) Fay Jones (31 Jan 1921, Pine Bluff AR—30 Aug 2004, Fayetteville AR), American architect who designed Thorncrown Chapel in Eureka Springs AR, which the American Institute of Architects rated among the five best American buildings of the 20th century; in the many houses and chapels that he designed, Jones relied on natural materials such as stone and wood.

Georgeanna Seegar Jones (6 Jul 1912, Baltimore MD—26 Mar 2005, Norfolk VA), American physician who pioneered (with her husband, Howard W. Jones, Jr.) the development of in vitro fertilization; the couple had spent more than 40 years teaching and conducting research in gynecology and obstetrics.

Donald (Rodney) Justice (12 Aug 1925, Miami FL—6 Aug 2004, Iowa City IA), American poet and editor who was best known for finely crafted verse that frequently illuminates the pain of loss and the desolation of an unlived life.

Howard Keel (Harold Clifford Leek; 13 Apr 1919, Gillespie IL—7 Nov 2004, Palm Desert CA), American actor-singer who had a booming baritone voice that, combined with his good looks, gained him the lead roles in a succession of Hollywood musicals in the early 1950s opposite the leading musical ingenues of the day.

Charles David Keeling (20 Apr 1928, Scranton PA—20 Jun 2005, Hamilton MT), American atmospheric scientist who presented the first evidence that carbon dioxide produced by automobiles and factories was negatively affecting the Earth's climate; in 2002 he was awarded a National Medal of Science.

John Adelbert Kelley (6 Sep 1907, West Medford MA—6 Oct 2004, South Yarmouth MA), American marathoner who ran the Boston Marathon a record 61 times; he ran his first Boston Marathon in 1928, won it in 1935 and 1945, and finished 18 times in the top 10; he was the first road runner inducted into the National Track and Field Hall of Fame and was named Runner of the Century by *Runner's World* magazine.

Margaret Kelly (24 Jun 1910, Dublin, Ireland—11 Sep 2004, Paris, France), Irish-born French dancer and choreographer who was a professional chorus-line dancer by the time she was 14 and in 1932 formed what became the Bluebell Girls cabaret dance troupe; for more than half a century, she led the troupe, which dazzled its audiences with energetic high-kicking routines.

George Frost Kennan (16 Feb 1904, Milwaukee WI—17 Mar 2005, Princeton NJ), American diplomat who defined US foreign policy during the Cold War as principal architect of the "containment policy" against the expansionism of the Soviet Union; he also helped shape the Marshall Plan for the reconstruction of Europe following World War II; Kennan undertook brief ambassadorships in Moscow (1952–53) and Yugoslavia (1961–63) and was awarded the Presidential Medal of Freedom (1989).

Rosemary Kennedy (13 Sep 1918, Brookline MA—7 Jan 2005, Jefferson WI), American personality, the mentally challenged sister of Pres. John F. Kennedy who at age 23 was given a prefrontal lobotomy, a procedure that left her in an infantlike state and needing institutional care for most of the rest of her life; her younger sister, Eunice Kennedy Shriver, founded the Special Olympics in her honor.

Gibson Kente ("Bra Gib"; 23 Jul 1932, East London,

South Africa—7 Nov 2004, Soweto, South Africa), South African playwright who introduced musical theater to the impoverished townships of South Africa; considered the founding father of black township theater, Kente connected with local audiences not only by entertaining them with laughter, music, and dance but also by dealing with social issues such as crime, poverty, and apartheid.

Ancel Keys (26 Jan 1904, Colorado Springs CO—20 Nov 2004, Minneapolis MN), American physiologist who created the ready-to-eat portable meals known as K rations that were used by American soldiers during World War II.

Jack S(t. Clair) Kilby (8 Nov 1923, Jefferson City MO—20 Jun 2005, Dallas TX), American electronics engineer who invented the integrated circuit, which allowed the development of the personal computer and the cell phone and was also used in radios, televisions, and microwave ovens; for this work he was awarded the 2000 Nobel Prize for Physics; among his other honors were a National Medal of Science (1969), induction into the National Inventors Hall of Fame (1982), and a National Medal of Technology (1990).

Edward Abel Killingsworth (4 Nov 1917, Taft CA—6 Jul 2004, Long Beach CA), American architect who designed elegant modernist houses in southern California and luxury hotels in Hawaii, Indonesia, and South Korea.

Ephraim Kishon (Ferenc Hoffman; 23 Aug 1924, Budapest, Hungary—29 Jan 2005, Appenzell, Switzerland), Hungarian-born Israeli satirist who after surviving the Holocaust and emigrating to Israel, wrote prolifically and gained a large and appreciative audience, notably in Israel and Germany; he was awarded the Israel Prize for lifetime achievement in 2002.

Carlos Kleiber (3 Jul 1930, Berlin, Germany—13 Jul 2004, Slovenia), German conductor who was widely regarded as one of the most important opera and symphony concert conductors of the latter half of the 20th century—despite a strictly controlled repertory, infrequent public performances, capricious behavior, and a limited number of commercial recordings.

Thomas Klestil (4 Nov 1932, Vienna, Austria—6 Jul 2004, Vienna, Austria), Austrian diplomat and politician who worked to earn international respect for Austria, serving as an ambassador, as foreign minister, and, finally, as president (1992–2004).

Elisabeth Kübler-Ross (8 Jul 1926, Zürich, Switzerland—24 Aug 2004, Scottsdale AZ), Swiss-born American psychiatrist who specialized in the needs of the dying and who was a founder of the hospice movement in the US; she is best known for her 1969 book *On Death and Dying*, which revolutionized the way Americans look at death.

(Abubakar) Sangoulé Lamizana (31 Jan 1916, Dianra, Upper Senegal–Niger (now Burkina Faso)—26 May 2005, Ouagadougou, Burkina Faso), Burkinabe military officer who served as the second president of Upper Volta (now Burkina Faso), from 3 Jan 1966 until he was overthrown in a coup on 25 Nov 1980.

Frances Langford (Frances Newbern; 4 Apr 1914, Lakeland FL—11 Jul 2005, Jensen Beach FL), American singer and actress who acted in some 30 motion pictures and starred as the combative wife, Blanche, opposite Don Ameche, in the 1940s radio series *The Bickersons*; she gained her greatest fame as an entertainer with Bob Hope's USO tours during World War II and the Korean and Vietnam wars.

(Nathaniel) Lester Lanin (26 Aug 1907, Philadelphia PA—27 Oct 2004, New York NY), American bandleader who provided the music for several decades' worth of high-society parties and balls with his tasteful mix of music types, including his debutante ball standard "Pink Petal Waltz."

Ruth Laredo (Ruth Meckler; 20 Nov 1937, Detroit MI—25 May 2005, New York NY), American pianist who was a recitalist and accompanist and also performed with orchestras and chamber groups.

Frederick Cheney LaRue (11 Oct 1928, Athens TX—24 Jul 2004, Biloxi MS), American businessman and political figure who served as an aide to Pres. Richard M. Nixon and was a prominent figure in the cover-up of the Watergate break-in during the re-election campaign in 1972; he was the "bagman" who delivered the payoff money to the burglars to encourage their silence and served 136 days in prison after pleading guilty to obstruction of justice.

Lynda Lee-Potter (Lynda Higginson; 2 May 1935, Leigh, Lancashire, England—20 Oct 2004, Stoborough, Dorset, England), British journalist who was admired for her sharp wit, notorious for her derisive criticism of celebrities and other notable persons, and controversial for her attacks on such social targets as single mothers and political correctness, particularly in her weekly column for the *Daily Mail* newspaper from 1972.

Ernest Lehman (8 Dec 1915, New York NY—2 Jul 2005, Los Angeles CA), American screenwriter and film producer who wrote screenplays for some of the most enduring Hollywood films of the 1950s and '60s; he proved adept at both original screenplays, including his Academy Award-nominated work on *North by Northwest* (1959), and adapted screenplays, including notably his Oscar-nominated work for *Sabrina* (1954), *West Side Story* (1961) and *Who's Afraid of Virginia Woolf?* (1966).

Janet Leigh (Jeanette Helen Morrison; 6 Jul 1927, Merced CA—3 Oct 2004, Beverly Hills CA), American actress who had a half-century-long career that comprised some 60 motion pictures as well as TV appearances, but it was for one role in particular that she was most remembered, Marion Crane in Alfred Hitchcock's *Psycho* (1960).

(Henry) Bernard Levin (19 Aug 1928, London, England—7 Aug 2004, London, England), British journalist who applied his acerbic wit for almost 40 years as a political columnist and entertainment critic for British newspapers, especially *The Times*, where he was chief columnist from 1971 to 1997.

Edward B. Lewis (20 May 1918, Wilkes-Barre PA—21 Jul 2004, Pasadena CA), American geneticist who discovered how certain genes control early development in embryos; for this work Lewis was awarded the 1995 Nobel Prize for Physiology or Medicine jointly with Christiane Nüsslein-Volhard and Eric F. Wieschaus.

Bella Lewitzky (13 Jan 1916, Los Angeles CA—16 Jul 2004, Pasadena CA), American dancer and choreographer who formed (1966) the Bella Lewitzky Dance Company in Los Angeles, which she danced with until 1978 and directed until she disbanded it in 1997.

Sol Myron Linowitz (7 Dec 1913, Trenton NJ—18 Mar 2005, Washington DC), American diplomat, attorney, and businessman who served as a highly influential adviser to US Presidents Lyndon B. Johnson, Jimmy Carter, and Bill Clinton and was a key negotiator of the Panama Canal treaties during the late 1970s; he was (with Joseph C. Wilson) a founder of the Xerox Corp. and was US ambassador to the Organization of American States and representative to the Inter-American Committee of the Alliance for Progress; in 1998 he was awarded a Presidential Medal of Freedom.

Mario Egidio Vincenzo Luzi (20 Oct 1914, Castello, near Florence, Italy—28 Feb 2005, Florence, Italy), Italian poet, essayist, and translator who was an exponent of Hermeticism, an Italian modernist poetic movement, and whose works were characterized by unorthodox structure, illogical sequences, and highly subjective language; in 2004 Italian Pres. Carlo Ciampi named Luzi a senator for life.

Dame Moura Lympany (Mary Johnstone; 18 Aug 1916, Saltash, Cornwall, England—28 Mar 2005, Menton, France), British concert pianist who enjoyed a career of 65 years and was known particularly for her interpretations of the romantic repertoire.

Saunders Mac Lane (4 Aug 1909, Taftville CT—14 Apr 2005, San Francisco CA), American mathematician who made significant contributions to modern algebra and topology and, with Samuel Eilenberg, was a cofounder of category theory, which established a general framework for understanding how mathematical structures, and systems of structures, relate to one another and has since been applied in many areas of mathematics, as well as to computer science and theoretical physics; in 1989 he was awarded a National Medal of Science.

Achille Maramotti (7 Jan 1927, Reggio Emilia, Italy—12 Jan 2005, Albinea, Italy), Italian fashion entrepreneur who founded the fashion house Max Mara and was credited with introducing high-quality ready-to-wear fashion to Italy; by the time he retired in 1989, Max Mara had more than 20 labels, among them Sportmax, I Blue, and Marella, and hundreds of retail shops throughout the world.

Gladys Marín Millié (16 Jul 1941, Curepto, Chile—6 Mar 2005, Santiago, Chile), Chilean political figure who opposed the regime of Augusto Pinochet Ugarte through her work as a leader of the Communist Party of Chile.

Dame Alicia Markova (Lilian Alicia Marks; 1 Dec 1910, London, England—2 Dec 2004, Bath, England), English ballet dancer who was the first true British prima ballerina and one of the finest dancers of the 20th century and as such helped establish a ballet tradition in her country.

Agnes (Bernice) Martin (22 Mar 1912, Macklin, SK, Canada—16 Dec 2004, Taos NM), Canadian-American painter who developed a spare, meticulously drawn, and meditative style that made her one of the giants of 20th-century Abstract Expressionism.

Bill Martin (20 Mar 1916, Hiawatha KS—11 Aug 2004, Commerce TX), American author who wrote more than 300 children's books in his career; his first book, *The Little Squeegy Bug* appeared in 1948; his best books, such as *Brown Bear, Brown Bear, What Do You See?* (1967) and *Chicka, Chicka, Boom, Boom* (1989), contained an adventurous spirit and rhythmic wordplay.

Jimmy Martin (James Henry Martin; 10 Aug 1927, Sneedville TN—14 May 2005, Nashville TN), American singer and guitarist who pioneered the "high lonesome sound" of bluegrass music with his high-ranging, heart-piercing vocals; he was the subject of the documentary film *King of Bluegrass* (2003).

Aslan Maskhadov (21 Sep 1951, Shakai, Kazakh SSR, USSR [now Kazakhstan]—8 Mar 2005, Tolstoy-Yurt, Chechen republic, Russia), Chechen separatist leader who was president of the Russian republic of Chechnya from 1997 until he was killed by Russian soldiers.

Robert Takeo Matsui (17 Sep 1941, Sacramento CA—1 Jan 2005, Bethesda MD), American politician who served as congressman from the 5th district of California from 1979; he worked for the passage of the North American Free Trade Agreement in the 1990s and helped create the State Children's Health Insurance Program; he also helped create a fund for reparations for the 120,000 Japanese Americans who, like his own family, had spent time in internment camps during World War II.

Virginia Mayo (Virginia Clara Jones; 30 Nov 1920, St. Louis MO—17 Jan 2005, Thousand Oaks CA), American actress who appeared in more than 40 movies, many of them comedies and adventure films, but was most memorable for her dramatic portrayals of an unfaithful wife of a World War II veteran in *The Best Years of Our Lives* (1946) and of James Cagney's gun-moll wife in *White Heat* (1949).

Ernst (Walter) Mayr (5 Jul 1904, Kempten, Germany—3 Feb 2005, Bedford MA), German-born American biologist whose work in avian taxonomy provided insights into evolution and led to his becoming one of the leading evolutionary biologists of the 20th century; in the 1940s he presented the now widely accepted definition of species as "groups of interbreeding natural populations that are reproductively isolated from other such groups," and he showed how geographical isolation played an important role in the origin of new species; among the honors he received were the US National Medal of Science (1970) and the Royal Swedish Academy's Craoford Prize in biology (1999).

Maclyn McCarty (9 Jun 1911, South Bend IN—2 Jan 2005, New York NY), American microbiologist and physician who, together with colleagues Oswald Avery and Colin MacLeod, provided the first evidence that genes are composed of DNA, a discovery that made possible the later development of molecular biology and genetic engineering; in 1994 he received an award for special achievement in medical science from the Lasker Foundation.

Vaughn Meader (20 Mar 1936, Waterville ME—29 Oct 2004, Auburn ME), American comedian whose album of impersonations of Pres. John F. Kennedy, *The First Family,* was the fastest-selling record ever in 1962, but whose career ended abruptly with the assassination of Kennedy the following year.

Ismail Merchant (Ismail Noormohamed Abdul Rehman; 25 Dec 1936, Bombay [now Mumbai], British India—25 May 2005, London, England), Indian-born British film producer famous for his collaboration with James Ivory on many period pieces, including *A Room with a View* (1986; three Academy Awards), *Howards End* (1992), and *The Remains of the Day* (1993).

Robert Merrill (Moishe Miller; 4 Jun 1917, Brooklyn NY—23 Oct 2004, New Rochelle NY), American opera singer who employed his powerful, precise baritone voice for some 31 seasons (1945–75) at New York City's Metropolitan Opera, where he was especially noted for his performances in the operas of Giuseppe Verdi.

Dale Messick (Dalia Messick; 11 Apr 1906, South Bend IN—5 Apr 2005, Penngrove CA), American artist who created one of the top-rated comic strips of all time, *Brenda Starr, Reporter,* which featured a fiery-haired heroine modeled after actress Rita Hayworth; the strip debuted on 30 Jun 1940, and by 1945 it began appearing as a daily; while encountering thrilling adventures, the glamorous Brenda paraded high fashion, presented impeccably coiffed hair, and captivated readers of both sexes; she later sketched a single-panel strip, *Granny Glamour,* until age 92.

Russ Meyer (Russell Albion Meyer; 21 Mar 1922, Oakland CA—18 Sep 2004, Hollywood Hills CA), American filmmaker whose movies usually featured big-busted women; he was considered a pioneer of the adult-movie, "skin-flick" genre; his best-known films include *Vixen* (1968) and *Beyond the Valley of the Dolls* (1970).

Rinus Michels (9 Feb 1928, Amsterdam, The Netherlands—3 Mar 2005, Aalst, Belgium), Dutch association football (soccer) player and coach who was credited with creating "total football," an aggressive style of play in which players adapt, shift positions, and improvise on the field as needed.

George (Lawrence) Mikan (18 Jun 1924, Joliet IL—1 Jun 2005, Scottsdale AZ), American basketball player who transformed basketball as the game's first outstanding big man and emerged as the game's first superstar; his dominating play resulted in several rule changes and led the Minneapolis (now Los Angeles) Lakers to six championships (1948-50; 1952-54); in nine seasons of professional play, he scored 11,764 points in 520 regular games, averaging 22.6 points a game; after retiring in 1956, he briefly coached (1957–58) the Lakers and served as the first commissioner (1967–69) of the American Basketball Association.

Arthur Miller (17 Oct 1915, New York NY—10 Feb 2005, Roxbury CT), American playwright who combined social awareness with a searching concern for his characters' inner lives; he was widely recognized as one of the most important playwrights of the mid-20th century, and Willy Loman, the tragic figure at the center of Miller's Pulitzer Prize-winning masterpiece, *Death of a Salesman* (1949; filmed 1951), gained iconic status as a symbol of a common man destroyed by the failure of the American dream and the false values at the heart of the society in which he lives; Miller's highly publicized five-year marriage (1956–61) to motion picture star Marilyn Monroe figured in two of his plays, *After the Fall* (1964) and *Finishing the Picture* (2004).

Keith Ross Miller (28 Nov 1919, Sunshine, VIC, Australia—11 Oct 2004, Melbourne, VIC, Australia), Australian cricketer who was one of the best all-rounders of the 20th century and a key member of Don Bradman's Australian team that was unbeaten on its 1948 tour of England; a glamorous middle-order right-hand batsman and right-arm fast bowler, he scored 181 runs for Victoria on his first-class debut.

Sir John Mills (Lewis Ernest Watts Mills; 22 Feb 1908, Watts Naval Training College, North Elmham, Norfolk, England—23 Apr 2005, Denham, Buckinghamshire, England), British actor who appeared in more than 100 motion pictures and dozens of stage plays and TV programs during a career that spanned some seven decades; his ability to portray "everyman" characters sincerely and believably endeared him to audiences; his films included *Great Expectations* (1946), *Scott of the Antarctic* (1948), and *Ryan's Daughter* (1970; best supporting actor Academy Award).

Czeslaw Milosz (30 Jun 1911, Sateiniai, Lithuania, Russian Empire [now in Lithuania]—14 Aug 2004, Kraków, Poland), Polish-American author, translator, and critic who was noted for his classical style and preoccupation with philosophical and political issues; he won the 1978 Neustadt Prize and the 1980 Nobel Prize for Literature for his poems.

Marvin (Morris) Mitchelson (7 May 1928, Detroit MI—18 Sep 2004, Beverly Hills CA), American lawyer who established the concept of palimony—the right of a longtime, but unmarried, live-in partner to sue for alimony—in the 1976 California Supreme Court case *Marvin v. Marvin.*

Philip Morrison (7 Nov 1915, Somerville NJ—22 Apr 2005, Cambridge MA), American physicist who helped transport the plutonium core of the first atomic bomb by car to the Trinity test site near Alamogordo NM in 1945; a protégé of J. Robert Oppenheimer, Morrison joined the Manhattan Project in 1942 and helped build the atomic bomb that was dropped on Nagasaki; after witnessing the devastation of the bomb, he became an advocate for arms control.

John Cullen Murphy (3 May 1919, New York NY—2 Jul 2004, Greenwich CT), American illustrator who drew the finely detailed comic strip *Prince Valiant* from 1970 until March 2004.

Carl (Mayer) Mydans (20 May 1907, Boston MA—16 Aug 2004, Larchmont NY), American photojournalist who was on the staff of *Life* magazine from 1936 to 1972 and one of the best-known photographers of World War II; Mydan's signature photo was of Gen. Douglas MacArthur returning to the Philippines in 1945.

Sheikh Zayid ibn Sultan Al Nahyan (1918?, Al Ain, British protectorate of Abu Dhabi—2 Nov 2004, Abu Dhabi, United Arab Emirates), United Arab Emirates political leader who, as the chief architect and first president (1971–2004) of the United Arab Emirates, was responsible for modernizing the country and helped to make it one of the wealthiest in the world.

Joe Nash (Joseph V. Nash; 5 Oct 1919, New York NY—13 Apr 2005, New York NY), American dancer, historian, and archivist who performed in stage musicals, danced with the early notable figures in modern dance, and for 25 years was involved with the Christian liturgical dance known as praise dancing.

Gaylord (Anton) Nelson (4 Jun 1916, Clear Lake WI—3 Jul 2005, Kensington MD), American Democratic politician and conservationist who founded (1970) the first Earth Day to draw attention to the importance of preserving the planet's natural resources; Nelson was governor of Wisconsin (1959–62) and then served three terms as a US senator (1963–80), during which time he sponsored numerous conservation bills; he received the Presidential Medal of Freedom in 1995.

Nigel Nicolson (19 Jan 1917, London, England—23 Sep 2004, Sissinghurst, Kent, England), British biographer, publisher, and politician who created a furor in 1973 with *Portrait of a Marriage,* a frank and—to many—shocking analysis of the unorthodox 50-year marriage of his parents, writer-gardener Vita Sackville-West and diplomat Sir Harold Nicolson.

Andriyan Grigoryevich Nikolayev (5 Sep 1929, Shorshely, Chuvash ASSR, USSR [now Chuvashiya, Russia]—3 Jul 2004, Cheboksary, Chuvashia, Russia), Soviet Russian cosmonaut, who piloted the *Vostok 3* spacecraft, launched 11 Aug 1962.

Paul H(enry) Nitze (16 Jan 1907, Amherst MA—19 Oct 2004, Washington DC), American diplomat and scholar who was a specialist in nuclear arms control and international relations; he served in many government posts including as secretary of the navy and was a cofounder of the School of Advanced International Studies (SAIS) of Johns Hopkins University.

Fumio Niwa (22 Nov 1904, Yokkaichi, Mie prefecture, Japan—20 Apr 2005, Tokyo, Japan), Japanese novelist who was one of his country's most prolific authors and a leading literary figure known for his popular and religious novels; from 1966 to 1972 he served as president of the Japan Writers Association.

Andre Norton (Alice Mary Norton; 17 Feb 1912, Cleveland OH—17 Mar 2005, Murfreesboro TN), American author who led many young readers into the realm of science fiction with her fantasy adventure novels of the 1950s and '60s; she later concentrated on fantasy, notably with her popular Witch World series, launched in 1963.

Jan Nowak-Jezioranski (13 May 1913, Warsaw, Poland, Russian Empire—20 Jan 2005, Warsaw, Poland), Polish Resistance courier during World War II and later the authoritative voice of independent Poland as a broadcaster on Radio Free Europe (1952–76).

Dan(iel) Peter O'Herlihy (1 May 1919, Wexford, Ireland—17 Feb 2005, Malibu CA), Irish actor on stage, screen, and TV who earned an Academy Award nomination for his starring performance in Luis Buñuel's film *The Adventures of Robinson Crusoe* (1954); his TV work included the programs *Bonanza, Murder She Wrote,* and *Twin Peaks.*

Betty Oliphant (Nancy Elizabeth Oliphant; 5 Aug 1918, London, England—12 Jul 2004, St. Catherines, ON, Canada), British-born Canadian dance educator who became a ballet dancer in London and, after moving to Canada in 1947, opened her own school in Toronto; she became ballet mistress of the National Ballet of Canada in 1951 and from 1969 to 1975 served as associate artistic director of the company.

Alfred, Freiherr von Oppenheim (5 May 1934, Cologne, Germany—5 Jan 2005, Cologne, Germany), German banker and financier who was the chairman of Sal Oppenheim, Germany's largest private bank, which had been owned by his family since 1789.

Jerry Orbach (Jerome Bernard Orbach; 20 Oct 1935, Bronx NY—28 Dec 2004, New York NY), American actor and singer who made his mark in the theater world as a Broadway song-and-dance man, originating such roles as El Gallo in the Off-Broadway *The Fantasticks* (1960), but later became better known to the American TV-viewing public as Detective Lennie Briscoe in 12 seasons of *Law & Order* and to movie audiences as the father in *Dirty Dancing* (1987).

Bruce Palmer (9 Sep 1946, Liverpool, NS, Canada—1 Oct 2004, Belleville, ON, Canada), Canadian bass guitarist who was a founding member of the influential folk-rock band Buffalo Springfield.

Frank Pantridge (James Francis Pantridge; 3 Oct 1916, Hillsborough, County Down, Ireland—26 Dec 2004), Irish-born cardiologist who developed (1965) the first portable heart defibrillator, a life-

saving device for providing rapid emergency treatment to heart-attack victims.

Sir Eduardo (Luigi) Paolozzi (7 Mar 1924, Edinburgh, Scotland—22 Apr 2005, London, England), British sculptor and artist whose early work dealt with questions of popular culture and consumerism, though his later public commissions, such as the cast-iron *Piscator* (1981) that graces London's Euston Station or the celebrated bronze sculpture [Isaac] *Newton* (1997, after a watercolor by William Blake) that stands in front of the British Museum, were more in a Surrealist mode.

Carlos Paredes (16 Feb 1925, Coimbra, Portugal—23 Jul 2004, Lisbon, Portugal), Portuguese guitarist and composer who mastered the distinctive round-shaped Portuguese guitar, a 12-string mandolin-like instrument usually associated with the national style of music known as fado.

Mimi Parent (Marie Parent; 8 Sep 1924, Montreal, QC, Canada—14 Jun 2005, Switzerland), French Canadian painter and engraver who participated in most of the major Surrealist exhibitions of the mid-20th century, including the 1959 show "Eros."

Ed Paschke (Edward Francis Paschke, Jr.; 22 Jun 1929, Chicago IL—25 Nov 2004, Chicago IL), American artist who created outlandish works of Pop Art, breaking through with the Chicago Imagists (a figurative movement) of the 1960s; Paschke rendered images from popular culture in garish fluorescent colors and the staticky lines of electronic video.

John Arthur Passmore (9 Sep 1914, Manly, NSW, Australia—25 Jul 2004, Canberra, ACT, Australia), Australian philosopher who was a leading figure in the field of applied philosophy, in which philosophical research is applied to practical matters, such as medical ethics and the environment.

Tom Patterson (Harry Thomas Patterson; 11 Jun 1920, Stratford, ON, Canada—23 Feb 2005, Toronto, ON, Canada), Canadian theatrical producer who founded (1953) the Stratford Festival of Canada, which grew into the largest repertory theater in North America.

Niels-Henning Ørsted Pedersen (27 May 1946, Osted, Denmark—19 Apr 2005, Ishøj, Denmark), Danish bassist noted for his innovative style and who played with some of the greatest jazz musicians of the 20th century; he was especially noted for his duo work with pianist Kenny Drew in the 1970s and his concerts and recordings with the Oscar Peterson Trio.

John Peel (John Robert Parker Ravenscroft; 30 Aug 1939, Heswall, Cheshire, England—25 Oct 2004, Cuzco, Peru), British disc jockey who fueled the independent music scene in Britain by debuting such performers as David Bowie, Joy Division, and the Smiths.

Frank(lin) Parsons Perdue (9 May 1920, near Salisbury MD—31 Mar 2005, Salisbury MD), American business executive who created widespread recognition for his chicken brand with his homespun advertisements in which he delivered his trademark line, "It takes a tough man to make a tender chicken"; he was one of the first CEOs to become an advertising spokesperson for his own company.

Petros VII (Petros Papapetrou; 3 Sep 1949, Sichari, [Northern] Cyprus—11 Sep 2004, off the coast of Greece), Cypriot-born patriarch of Alexandria (1997–2004), the spiritual leader of Greek Orthodox Christians in Africa; he was killed in a helicopter crash en route to the monastic community on Mount Athos, Greece.

Maria de Lourdes Ruivo da Silva Pintasilgo (18 Jan 1930, Abrantes, Portugal—10 Jul 2004, Lisbon, Portugal), Portuguese politician who was prime minister—the first woman to hold the post—for 149 days in 1979–80; she later unsuccessfully ran for president of Portugal.

Fernando Poe, Jr. (Ronald Allan Kelley Poe; 20 Aug 1939, San Carlos City, Philippines—13 Dec 2004, Manila, Philippines), Filipino actor and politician who starred in nearly 300 films in his 46-year career as the Philippines' premier action star and earned the nickname "Da King" for his portrayal of rugged underdog heroes; he was the main opposition candidate in the 2004 presidential elections, but he lost to incumbent Gloria Macapagal Arroyo.

Amrish Puri (22 Jun 1932, Hoshiapur district, Punjab state, India—12 Jan 2005, Mumbai [Bombay], India), Indian movie actor who epitomized the Bollywood villain and made more than 200 movies over 30 years.

Prince Rainier III (Rainier-Louis-Henri-Maxence-Bertrand de Grimaldi; 31 May 1923, Monaco—6 Apr 2005, Monaco), Monegasque head of state who carried on the long Grimaldi family dynasty over the tiny European principality, maintaining Monaco's sense of glamour and intrigue; he diversified the longstanding monoculture of casino tourism to include banking and finance and oversaw huge construction projects; he led Monaco into the United Nations in 1993 and adopted the international currency of the euro in 2002; Rainier's 1956 marriage to American actress Grace Kelly struck many as a fairy-tale wedding, with its dashing prince and beautiful princess.

John (Emmet) Raitt (29 Jan 1917, Santa Ana CA—20 Feb 2005, Pacific Palisades CA), American actor and singer who employed his lyrical baritone voice and strong good looks to create a powerful presence in leading roles on the musical stage; his success in the role of Curly in the road company of *Oklahoma!* led to his being cast as Billy Bigelow in the Broadway production of *Carousel* (1945); in later years he frequently collaborated with his daughter, singer Bonnie Raitt.

David Raksin (4 Aug 1912, Philadelphia PA—9 Aug 2004, Los Angeles CA), American film composer who created the music for some 400 motion pictures and TV series, the most notable of which was the haunting score for the film *Laura* (1944).

Raja Ramanna (28 Jan 1925, Tumkur, India—24 Sep 2004, Mumbai [Bombay], India), Indian nuclear physicist who played a key role in the development of India's nuclear weapons program; as director (1972–78, 1981–83) of the Bhabha Atomic Research Centre, India's top nuclear research facility, Ramanna oversaw the country's first nuclear weapons test in 1974; he also headed India's atomic energy commission (1984–87) and served as secretary of defense (1990–92).

Johnny Ramone (John Cummings; 8 Oct 1948, Long Island NY—15 Sep 2004, Los Angeles CA), American rock musician who cofounded the legendary punk band the Ramones in 1974.

Nell Rankin (3 Jan 1924, Montgomery AL—13 Jan 2005, New York NY), American mezzo-soprano who was known for her warm tones in recitals and marquee opera roles during a 25-year career; especially associated with the role of Amneris in *Aida*,

she enjoyed worldwide success until she retired in the mid-1970s.

P.V. Narasimha Rao (Pamulaparti Venkata Narasimha Rao; 28 Jun 1921, Karimnagar, Andhra Pradesh, British India—23 Dec 2004, New Delhi, India), Indian politician who, as leader of the Congress (I) Party and prime minister (1991–96), saved India from bankruptcy, moving it away from its semisocialistic economic program; Rao's shift toward market capitalism encouraged domestic growth and foreign investment but incurred higher deficits and inflation.

Jef Raskin (9 Mar 1943, New York NY—26 Feb 2005, Pacifica CA), American computer scientist who revolutionized the personal computer industry by pioneering the Apple Macintosh computer, which featured a user-friendly graphical interface rather than the standard text-based commands that were common in the late 1970s.

Lawrence G. Rawl (4 May 1928, Lyndhurst NJ—13 Feb 2005, Fort Worth TX), American business executive who served as chairman and chief executive officer of Exxon Corp. from 1987 to 1993, during which time he consolidated the company's assets and enlarged its oil and gas reserves by exploring new drilling sites; he also directed the company through a public relations crisis when on 24 Mar 1989 the *Exxon Valdez* tanker struck a reef and spilled a huge amount of crude oil into Prince William Sound, Alaska.

Christopher Reeve (25 Sep 1952, New York NY—10 Oct 2004, Mt. Kisco NY), American film actor who was best known for having played Superman; following a severe injury in a horse-riding accident he became a crusader for spinal-cord-injury research, for which he was awarded the Lasker Award for Public Service in 2003.

Paul Ricoeur (27 Feb 1913, Valence, France—20 May 2005, Châtenay Malabry, France), French philosopher and historian who studied various linguistic and psychoanalytic theories of interpretation; he was the recipient of a 2004 John W. Kluge Prize in the Human Sciences.

Augusto Antonio Roa Bastos (13 Jun 1917, Iturbe, Paraguay—26 Apr 2005, Asunción, Paraguay), Paraguayan novelist and poet who wrote his masterpiece, *Yo el supremo* (1974; *I, the Supreme*; in bilingual edition), which recounted the life of the dictator José Gaspar Rodríguez de Francia and covered more than 100 years of Paraguayan history; in 1989 he was awarded the Cervantes Prize.

Louis Joseph Robichaud (21 Oct 1925, Saint-Antoine, NB, Canada—6 Jan 2005, Saint-Antoine, NB, Canada), Canadian politician who introduced far-reaching reforms as the premier (1960–70) of New Brunswick; he was the first Acadian elected to the premiership of any of the Maritime Provinces; from 1973 until 2000 he served in the Senate of Canada.

George Rochberg (5 Jul 1918, Paterson NJ—29 May 2005, Bryn Mawr PA), American composer whose works included symphonies, string quartets, and songs.

Laurance S(pelman) Rockefeller (26 May 1910, New York NY—11 Jul 2004, New York NY), American philanthropist, venture capitalist, and conservationist who, as a member of one of the richest families in the US, used his business acumen to fund start-up companies, greatly augmenting his wealth, and promoted conservation, notably by donating land to the National Park Service.

Peter Rodino (Peter Wallace Rodino, Jr.; 7 Jun 1909, Newark NJ–7 May 2005, West Orange NJ), American politician who as chairman of the US House of Representatives judiciary committee steered the 1974 impeachment hearings of Pres. Richard Nixon; he was widely praised for his patient and even-handed leadership of the politically charged proceedings; in his 40 years as a congressman (1949–89) Rodino was known for his advocacy of civil and immigrants' rights and for introducing the bill that made Columbus Day a national holiday.

Patsy Rowlands (Patricia Rowlands; 19 Jan 1934, London, England–22 Jan 2005, Hove, East Sussex, England), British actress who was a successful character actress on stage and screen for 50 years, but she was best remembered for her roles in 9 of the 31 raucous, double entendre–laden Carry On film comedies.

Stanley John Sadie (30 Oct 1930, London, England–21 Mar 2005, Cossington, Somerset, England), British musicologist and Mozart scholar who was editor of The New Grove Dictionary of Music and Musicians (1980) and other reference works.

Françoise Sagan (Françoise Quoirez; 21 Jun 1935, Cajarc, France–24 Sep 2004, Honfleur, France), French novelist and dramatist who created an international sensation as a teenager with the publication of her first novel, Bonjour tristesse (1954), a precocious story of amorality, seduction, and infidelity that she wrote in only a few weeks after having failed her exams at the Sorbonne.

Pierre (Emil George) Salinger (14 Jun 1925, San Francisco CA–16 Oct 2004, Avignon, France), American journalist and political figure who served as press secretary (1961–64) to Presidents John F. Kennedy and Lyndon B. Johnson; he later was a Paris-based international correspondent for ABC News (1978–93).

Anthony Terrell Seward Sampson (3 Aug 1926, Billingham-on-Tees, Durham, England–18 Dec 2004, Wardour, Wiltshire, England), British journalist and author who scrutinized political power and influence, especially in the UK and South Africa, and highlighted human rights issues in his many works; he contributed to several newspapers and wrote more than 20 books.

Isabel Sanford (29 Aug 1917, New York NY–9 Jul 2004, Los Angeles CA), American TV actress who played Louise on The Jeffersons (1975–85) and was the first black woman to receive a best actress Emmy Award (1981).

Lucia de Jesus dos Santos (Lucia Abobora; 22 Mar 1907, Aljustrel, Portugal–13 Feb 2005, Coimbra, Portugal), Portuguese nun who was the oldest of the three shepherd children who claimed to have seen visions of the Virgin Mary near Fátima, Portugal, one each month between 13 May and 13 Oct 1917.

Trina Schart Hyman (8 Apr 1939, Philadelphia PA–19 Nov 2004, Lebanon NH), American artist who illustrated more than 150 children's books, including Caldecott Medal winner St. George and the Dragon (1984; written by Margaret Hodges).

Albert Schatz (2 Feb 1920, Norwich CT–17 Jan 2005, Philadelphia PA), American microbiologist who, along with Selman Waksman, discovered streptomycin, the first antibiotic that effectively treated a multitude of deadly diseases such as tuberculosis, typhoid, tularemia, brucellosis, cholera, and bubonic plague; denied a share of the 1952 Nobel Prize for Physiology or Medicine that was awarded solely to Waksman, Schatz was recognized in 1994 when he was awarded the Rutgers University Medal.

Maria (Margarethe Anna) Schell (15 Jan 1926, Vienna, Austria–26 Apr 2005, Preitenegg, Austria), Austrian actress who was acclaimed for her work in German-language films and stage productions in the 1940s and '50s, winning the best actress award at the Cannes Film Festival for Die letzte Brücke (1954; The Last Bridge) and at the Venice Film Festival for Gervaise (1956).

Terri Schiavo (Theresa Marie Schindler; 3 Dec 1963, near Philadelphia PA–31 Mar 2005, Pinellas Park FL), American woman who remained in "a persistent vegetative state" following cardiac arrest in 1990; she was the center of an ethical and legal battle, from 1998 until her death, over a patient's right to die and the question of which family members, medical authorities, and government bodies may be permitted to intervene.

Max Schmeling (Maximilian Adolph Otto Siegfried Schmeling; 28 Sep 1905, Klein Luckow, Brandenburg, Germany–2 Feb 2005, Hollenstedt, Germany), German heavyweight who was the first European boxer to become heavyweight champion of the world when he captured the title from Jack Sharkey on 12 Jun 1930; Schmeling held the championship until 21 Jun 1932, when he lost a rematch with Sharkey on a highly controversial split decision; Schmeling's two most notable fights, however, came later against emerging heavyweight great Joe Louis.

Peter K. Schoening (30 Jul 1927, Seattle WA–22 Sep 2004, Kenmore WA), American mountaineer who single-handedly averted the loss in 1953 of an entire expedition on K2, the world's second highest peak; after his climbing team experienced a chain-reaction series of falls, Schoening displayed almost superhuman strength by anchoring the entire group and pulling four of the five to safety.

Bernard A(dolph) Schriever (10 Sep 1910, Bremen, Germany–20 Jun 2005, Washington DC), German-born American military leader, a general in the US Air Force, who led the intercontinental ballistic missile (ICBM) and military space programs during the Cold War; he established a new management technique known as concurrency, which entailed designing all subsystems of a weapon simultaneously, rather than sequentially as had been done previously; Schriever thus expedited development of the Atlas, Titan, and Minuteman ICBMs.

George Lewis Scott (18 Mar 1929, Notasulga AL–9 Mar 2005, Durham NC), American gospel singer who contributed his driving baritone to the celebrated gospel group the Blind Boys of Alabama, who pioneered the jubilee style of gospel music, incorporating jazz and blues elements into their rich harmonizing; they won the first of their four consecutive Grammy awards for the album Spirit of the Century (2001).

William T(homas) Seawell (27 Jan 1918, Pine Bluff AR–20 May 2005, Pine Bluff AR), American military officer and businessman who served in the US Air Force for 22 years—rising to the rank of brigadier general and serving as commandant of cadets at the Air Force Academy (1961-63)—before embarking on a business career; as CEO and chairman of Pan American World Airways (1972–81) he proved unable to turn around the fortunes of the now-defunct company.

Liber Seregni (13 Dec 1916, Montevideo, Uruguay–

31 Jul 2004, Montevideo, Uruguay), Uruguayan general and politician who was a cofounder and the first president of Frente Amplio, a leftist political party formed in 1971 to break the hegemony of Uruguay's two controlling political parties, the Colorados and the Blancos.

Maurice Shadbolt (4 Jun 1932, Auckland, New Zealand—10 Oct 2004, Taumarunui, New Zealand), New Zealand author who was celebrated for historical novels about his native country. His trilogy on the Maori wars of the 19th century—*Season of the Jew* (1986), *Monday's Warriors* (1990), and *The House of Strife* (1993)—was widely regarded as his best work.

Moshe Shamir (15 Sep 1921, Zefat, British Palestine—20 Aug 2004, Rishon LeZiyyon, Israel), Israeli novelist and politician championed the socialist ideals of kibbutz life in his novels; in the 1960s he launched a political career as a member of the conservative Likud Party, but after the 1979 peace treaty with Egypt was negotiated, he quit to form a more right-wing party.

Artie Shaw (Abraham Isaac Arshawasky; 23 May 1910, New York NY—30 Dec 2004, Newbury Park CA), American clarinetist and bandleader who played soaring melodic solos and created many of the Swing era's most popular records.

Hugh Lawson Shearer (18 May 1923, Martha Brae, Jamaica—5 Jul 2004, Kingston, Jamaica), Jamaican trade unionist and politician who served as independent Jamaica's third prime minister (1967–72) and thereafter was a trade union president.

David (Stuart) Sheppard (6 Mar 1929, Reigate, Surrey, England—5 Mar 2005, Wirral, Merseyside, England), British cricket right-handed batsman who enjoyed a first-class career (1947–62) with 45 centuries and played in Test matches from 1950 through 1963, totaling 15,838 runs; known for his antiapartheid views, he was also an ordained Anglican priest and rose in the hierarchy to become bishop of Liverpool in 1975.

Bobby Short (Robert Waltrip Short; 15 Sep 1924, Danville IL—21 Mar 2005, New York NY), American cabaret singer who began a legendary 36-year run at the Café Carlyle in Manhattan in 1968 and established himself as a New York institution, winning fans and friends among the city's social and artistic elite.

Ota Sik (11 Sep 1919, Plzen, Czechoslovakia [now in Czech Republic]—22 Aug 2004, Sankt Gallen, Switzerland), Czech economist who laid the economic groundwork for the reforms of the Prague Spring of 1968. By proposing a "third way" between free-market capitalism and a Soviet-style planned economy, he sought to bring "socialism with a human face" to the Czechoslovak government; in April 1968 he was named vice-premier and economics minister.

George Silk (17 Nov 1916, Levin, New Zealand—23 Oct 2004, Norwalk CT), New Zealand-born American photographer who worked for Life magazine from 1943 until 1972; he at first was a combat photographer and was one of the first to photograph Nagasaki, Japan, after the atomic bomb was dropped on it in 1945, but he later turned to sports photography and pioneered the adaptation of a racetrack photo-finish camera for use in capturing shots of athletes in motion.

Claude (-Eugène-Henri) Simon (10 Oct 1913, Tananarive, Madagascar—6 Jul 2005, Paris, France), French novelist whose works are among the most authentic representatives of the French *nouveau roman* that emerged in the 1950s; his style is a mixture of narration and stream of consciousness, lacking all punctuation and heavy with 1,000-word sentences; his novels remain readable despite their seeming chaos; he won the 1985 Nobel Prize for Literature.

Simone Simon (23 Apr 1910, Béthune, France—22 Feb 2005, Paris, France), French actress who was much admired for her innocent appearance and on-screen sensuality, notably in Jean Renoir's *La Bête humaine* (1938), but she was best known to American audiences for the stylish low-budget thriller *Cat People* (1942).

Jaime (Lachica) Cardinal Sin (31 Aug 1928, New Washington, Philippines—21 Jun 2005, Greenhills, San Juan, Philippines), Philippine spiritual leader of Roman Catholics as archbishop of Manila from 1974 to 2003; his tenure was marked by his influential involvement in Philippine politics.

Joseph John Sisco (31 Oct 1919, Chicago IL—23 Nov 2004, Chevy Chase MD), American diplomat who shaped American foreign policy in the Middle East as the chief mediator for that region from 1968 to 1976; widely regarded as Secretary of State Henry Kissinger's top aide, Sisco used his influence to contain a number of conflicts, most notably when he prevented the military leadership of Greece from responding to the Turkish invasion of Cyprus in 1974.

(Enrique) Omar Sivori (2 Oct 1935, San Nicolas, Argentina—17 Feb 2005, San Nicolas, Argentina), Argentine-born association football (soccer) player who was revered for his audacious and brilliant play in both his homeland and his adopted country, Italy, although his cocky attitude earned him the sobriquet El Cabezón ("Bighead"); Sivori was named European Footballer of the Year in 1961.

Jeff Smith (Jeffrey L. Smith; 22 Jan 1939, Tacoma WA—7 Jul 2004, Seattle WA), American host of the extremely popular TV cooking show *The Frugal Gourmet* on PBS from 1983 until accusations of sexual misconduct derailed his career in 1997; Smith was ordained a minister in the United Methodist Church in 1965; his TV career began in 1973, and he delighted viewers with his low-key, humorous, and educational approach.

Jimmy Smith (James Oscar Smith; 8 Dec 1925, Norristown PA—found dead 8 Feb 2005, Scottsdale AZ), American musician who made the previously scorned electric organ into one of the most popular instruments in jazz; his biggest hit was "Walk on the Wild Side" (1962).

Leslie Charles Smith (6 Mar 1918, Enfield, Middlesex, England—26 May 2005, London, England), British toy manufacturer who, as joint founder of Lesney Products, in 1953 pioneered Matchbox toys—scale-model, die-cast metal replicas small enough to fit inside a British cardboard match box; the phenomenally popular miniatures, which featured realistic detail and movable parts, were marketed around the world, with as many as 50 million sold annually by 1962.

Sammi Smith (Jewel Fay Smith; 5 Aug 1943, Orange CA—12 Feb 2005, Oklahoma City OK), American country singer who was the Academy of Country Music's top new female vocalist in 1970; she won a Grammy Award for her single number-one hit, "Help Me Make It Through the Night" (1971).

Susan Sontag (Susan Rosenblatt; 16 Jan 1933, New

York NY—28 Dec 2004, New York NY), American essayist, critic, and novelist who was a leading intellectual in the US, best known for her provocative essays on modern culture; her reputation was established in 1964 with "Notes on 'Camp,'" a seminal essay that examined certain sensibilities toward popular culture, especially within the gay community.

Jesús-Rafael Soto (5 Jul 1923, Ciudad Bolívar, Venezuela—17 Jan 2005, Paris, France), Venezuelan-born French artist who attached himself to avant-garde modernism immediately after World War II and by the late 1960s became known as a leader in optical and kinetic art, with works that were remarkable for their illusions of sensory vibrations.

Gérard Souzay (Gérard Marcel Tisserand; 8 Dec 1918, Angers, France—17 Aug 2004, Antibes, France), French concert and operatic baritone who performed in concerts and recitals around the world for more than three decades and made hundreds of recordings; he was best known for his sensitive interpretation of French and German art songs.

(John) Humphrey Spender (19 Apr 1910, London, England—11 Mar 2005, Ulting, Essex, England), British photojournalist and artist who chronicled the everyday lives of working-class Britons during the 1930s and '40s in a series of candid, often surreptitiously taken photographs for the Mass-Observation Project, the journals *Left Review* and *Picture Post,* and the *Daily Mirror.*

Sister Dorothy Stang (7 Jun 1931, Dayton OH—12 Feb 2005, Anapu, Pará state, Brazil), American missionary and activist who was a staunch champion of peasant farmers in the Amazon rainforest during her 22 years spent helping them to attain a sustainable living; she was the victim of a contract killing, which prompted Brazilian Pres. Luiz Inácio Lula da Silva to create two vast Amazonian forest preserves and to deploy troops to the troubled Pará state.

James B(ond) Stockdale (23 Dec 1923, Abingdon IL—5 Jul 2005, Coronado CA), American naval aviator who received the Medal of Honor in 1976 for his bravery in the face of torture and imprisonment during the Vietnam War; he flew more than 200 missions over Vietnam before he was shot down in 1965; he was imprisoned for over seven years, during the first four of which he endured torture and isolation by drawing on lessons learned from his studies of ancient Greek philosophy; after his release, he remained in the Navy and rose to the rank of vice admiral; in 1992 he was the running mate of the independent presidential candidate H. Ross Perot.

Ezra Stoller (16 May 1915, Chicago IL—29 Oct 2004, Williamstown MA), American photographer who captured the beauty of modern architecture through his black-and-white photography; architects revered his work, and he photographed buildings designed by such noted ones as Frank Lloyd Wright, Eero Saarinen, and Louis Kahn.

Ross Stretton (6 Jun 1952, Canberra, ACT, Australia—16 Jun 2005, Melbourne, VIC, Australia), Australian dancer who was noted for his elegance and pure technique and enjoyed performance careers with the Australian Ballet, the Joffrey Ballet, and American Ballet Theatre; he later served as artistic director of the Australian Ballet (1997–2001) and Britain's Royal Ballet (2001–02).

Raisa (Stepanovna) Struchkova (5 Oct 1925, Moscow, USSR [now in Russia]—2 May 2005, Moscow, Russia), Russian dancer and teacher who was noted for her brilliant, expressive technique in classical and dramatic ballets during her more than 30-year career with the Bolshoi Ballet; especially in the West she was also known for her virtuosity and athleticism in bravura pas de deux with her husband, Aleksandr Lapauri.

Zenko Suzuki (11 Jan 1911, Yamada, Iwate prefecture, Japan—19 Jul 2004, Tokyo, Japan), Japanese politician who served as prime minister from 1980 to 1982.

Charles William Sweeney (27 Dec 1919, Lowell MA—16 Jul 2004, Boston MA), American pilot who flew the B-29 bomber that dropped the atomic bomb on Nagasaki, Japan, 9 Aug 1945.

Kenzo Tange (4 Sep 1913, Imabari, Ehime prefecture, Japan—22 Mar 2005, Tokyo, Japan), Japanese architect and teacher who embodied the Japanese reverence for the past while embracing the future in such breathtaking structures as his sports stadiums—known together as Yoyogi National Stadium—for the 1964 Tokyo Olympic Games; he received the Pritzker Prize in 1987.

Luis Taruc (21 Jun 1913, San Luis, Philippines—4 May 2005, Quezon City, Philippines), Philippine freedom fighter and social reformer who was the leader (1948–54) of the communist Huk movement, which began in 1942 as the Hukbalahap ("People's Anti-Japanese Army") and evolved in the late 1940s into the antigovernment Hukbong Magapayang Bayan ("People's Liberation Army"); Taruc and his Huk insurgents led an unsuccessful armed rebellion in the early 1950s; he surrendered to authorities in 1954 and was tried for revolt and terrorism and sentenced to 12 years' imprisonment; after his release, he became active in the land-reform movement and served in the national legislature.

Kenneth Taylor (8 May 1917, Portland OR—10 Jun 2005, Wheaton IL), American publisher who founded (1962) Tyndale House Publishers but was best known as the creator of *The Living Bible* (1971), which featured paraphrasing of the King James Version of the Bible in an attempt to make readings more accessible to a broader audience.

Theodore B(rewster) Taylor (11 Jul 1925, Mexico City, Mexico—28 Oct 2004, Silver Spring MD), American nuclear physicist and weapons designer who devised the most powerful fission explosives in the US arsenal as well as the smallest and lightest (the 23-kg [51-lb] Davy Crockett in 1961); later, however, he worried about the dangers of small nuclear weapons of the type he had created falling into the wrong hands and became deeply concerned about his country's readiness to use nuclear weapons.

Renata Tebaldi (1 Feb 1922, Pesaro, Italy—19 Dec 2004, San Marino), Italian soprano who was one of the foremost opera singers of the post-World War II period; with a rich and powerful voice, over which she exercised great control, she was especially identified with works by Italian composers.

William John Thaler (4 Dec 1925, Baltimore MD—5 Jun 2005, Centreville VA), American physicist who, in the late 1950s, pioneered the development of over-the-horizon radar for the US Navy, an innovation that enabled early detection of Soviet ballistic missile launches and nuclear explosions up to 8,000 km (5,000 mi) away, far beyond the range of conventional radar systems.

Frank Thomas (5 Sep 1912, Santa Monica CA—8 Sep 2004, Flintridge CA), American animator who created some of the most memorable moments in animated film history, most notably the spaghetti dinner scene in Walt Disney's *The Lady and the Tramp* (1955); one of Disney's core circle of master animators—a group that Disney referred to as his "Nine Old Men"—Thomas drew praise for his ability to convey emotion through his characters without straying into excessive sentimentality.

Alice Thomas Ellis (Anna Margaret Lindholm Haycraft; 9 Sep 1932, Liverpool, England—8 Mar 2005, Powys, Wales?), British novelist and editor who published 21 books mostly concerned with faith (she was a devout Roman Catholic) and the darker side of the human soul and usually told in a domestic setting; perhaps her best-known novels were the Summerhouse trilogy—*The Clothes in the Wardrobe* (1987), *The Skeleton in the Cupboard* (1988), and *The Fly in the Ointment* (1989; trilogy televised in 1992).

Hunter S(tockton) Thompson (18 Jul 1937, Louisville KY—20 Feb 2005, Woody Creek CO), American journalist and author who blurred the line between reporting and storytelling with a signature brand of highly subjective writing that he dubbed gonzo journalism; his first book, *Hell's Angels* (1967), recounted the time he spent with the motorcycle gang and established him as a story unto himself.

Ron(ald) Todd (11 Mar 1927, Walthamstow, London, England—30 Apr 2005, Romford, Essex, England), British trade unionist who was active at the Ford Motor Co. facilities in Walthamstow and Dagenham before joining the staff of the Transport and General Workers Union; he worked his way up through the T&G ranks and served as the union's general secretary from 1985 to 1992; he was also active in antiwar and antiapartheid affairs.

Andrew Toti (24 Jul 1915, Visalia CA—20 Mar 2005, Modesto CA), American inventor who developed (at age 16) the "Mae West" life vest, an innovation that saved thousands of World War II pilots and sailors from drowning; during his career Toti patented more than 500 inventions, including a mechanical poultry-feather plucker (1951), a grape-harvesting machine for wine producers Ernest and Julio Gallo (1972), pull tabs for beverage cans, lightweight construction beams, and various types of venetian blinds.

Rigo Tovar (Rigoberto Tovar García; 29 Mar 1946, Matamoros, Mexico—27 Mar 2005, Mexico City, Mexico), Mexican singer who rose from poverty to reach the greatest heights of stardom not only in his home country but also in Latin America and the US during a career in which he sold more than 25 million albums; he formed his band Costa Azul in 1972 and played a central role in popularizing the Colombian *cumbia* in Mexico by introducing synthesizers, electric guitars, and elements of rock and roll.

Alex Trotman (Alexander James Trotman, Lord Trotman of Osmotherly; 22 Jul 1933, Isleworth, Middlesex, England—25 Apr 2005, Northallerton, Yorkshire, England), British business executive who spent 43 years employed by the Ford Motor Co. and served as the company's CEO and chairman from 1993 to 1998; he was credited with pulling Ford out of a deep financial slump in the early 1990s through a cost-cutting program and bringing the company to one of the most profitable periods in its history.

Theodor Uppman (12 Jan 1920, San Jose CA—17 Mar 2005, New York NY), American baritone who originated the title role of Benjamin Britten's opera *Billy Budd* at its premiere at Covent Garden, London, in 1951; his performance was widely praised, and he reprised the role for an NBC TV broadcast.

Jay Van Andel (3 Jun 1924, Grand Rapids MI—7 Dec 2004, Ada MI), American entrepreneur who in 1959 cofounded (with Richard DeVos) Amway, a direct-sales company that generated billion-dollar revenues around the world; the company originally sold vitamins and quickly expanded its business into soaps and other household products.

Mona Van Duyn (9 May 1921, Waterloo IA—2 Dec 2004, University City MO), American poet who wrote about ordinary middle-class suburban life with clarity and humor; she used the rigor of formal technique to examine moments of domesticity in an unpretentious manner; in 1991 she won the Pulitzer Prize for poetry for *Near Changes,* and the following year she was selected as US poet laureate, the first woman to be named to the post.

Luther (Ronzoni) Vandross (20 Apr 1951, New York NY—1 Jul 2005, Edison NJ), American singer, songwriter, and record producer who dominated the rhythm-and-blues charts in the 1980s with his smooth, romantic vocals and sold more than 25 million albums; his big break came in 1975 when he sang backup and did vocal arrangements for David Bowie's *Young Americans* album; his solo career took off in 1981 with the release of *Never Too Much;* he won eight Grammy awards in his career.

John Robert Vane (29 Mar 1927, Tardebigg, Worcestershire, England—19 Nov 2004, Farnborough, Kent, England), English pharmacologist who conducted pioneering research in the study of hormone-like substances in the body called prostaglandins; he shared the 1982 Nobel Prize for Physiology or Medicine with Swedish biochemists Sune K. Bergström and Bengt I. Samuelsson.

Max Velthuijs (22 May 1923, The Hague, The Netherlands—25 Jan 2005, The Hague, The Netherlands), Dutch children's author and illustrator who was best known for his series of Kikker ("Frog") books; in his "moral fables" Velthuijs used simple illustrations and childlike characters—notably the playful, striped shorts–wearing Frog and his friends Pig, Duck, and Hare—to introduce young children to such themes as friendship, loyalty, prejudice, fear, love, and death.

Hans Vonk (18 Jun 1942?, Amsterdam, The Netherlands—29 Aug 2004, Amsterdam, The Netherlands), Dutch conductor who excelled in the works of Romantic composers; he was much respected for his musicianship and for his many fine recordings; he served as conductor of major European orchestras from 1973; he was chief conductor of the St. Louis Symphony Orchestra from 1996 to 2002.

Charlie Waller (Charles Otis Waller; 19 Jan 1935, Joinerville TX—18 Aug 2004, Gordonsville VA), American bluegrass vocalist, guitarist, and songwriter who was a founding member (1957) of the Country Gentlemen, a group that began the "new grass revival," modernizing and bringing bluegrass music to wider audiences, especially on college campuses and at urban nightclubs.

Rodger Ward (10 Jan 1921, Beloit KS—5 Jul 2004, Anaheim CA), American race car driver who won the Indianapolis 500 twice (1959, 1962) and was a racing star in the late 1950s and early '60s.

Ruth Warrick (29 Jun 1915, St. Joseph MO—15 Jan

2005, New York NY), American actress who had her best screen role in the first of her more than 30 films when she played the frosty first wife of newspaper magnate Charles Foster Kane in Orson Welles's *Citizen Kane* (1941); she later became better known as Phoebe Tyler Wallingford on the TV daytime soap opera *All My Children,* a role she played from the show's debut in 1970 until nearly the end of her life.

Al(bert) Wasserman (9 Feb 1921, Bronx NY—31 Mar 2005, New York NY), American filmmaker who produced award-winning TV and film documentaries that examined world affairs topics ranging from civil rights to travel by rail; Wasserman launched his own production company before returning to CBS as a producer (1976–86) of the series *60 Minutes.*

Yuko Watanabe (12 Jul 1953, Fukuoka, Japan—15 Jul 2004, Milan, Italy), Japanese opera singer who made her professional debut on the opera stage in 1978 and over the next 22 years became renowned for the intensity of her portrayals of the major heroines, most notably Cio-Cio-San in Puccini's Madama Butterfly.

Dick Weber (Richard Anthony Weber; 23 Dec 1929, Indianapolis IN—14 Feb 2005, Florissant MO), American bowler who reigned, along with Don Carter and Earl Anthony, as one of the top bowlers of the 20th century and captivated TV audiences during the sport's heyday in the 1960s.

Wee Kim Wee (4 Nov 1915, Singapore—2 May 2005, Singapore), Singaporean journalist, diplomat, and statesman who worked as a correspondent for the United Press Association before becoming Singapore's high commissioner to Malaysia and later his country's ambassador to Japan and South Korea; he served as head of state from 1985 to 1993 and was known as "the people's president" because of his efforts to make the high office accessible to all citizens.

Ezer Weizman (15 Jun 1924, Tel Aviv, British Mandate of Palestine [now Tel Aviv–Yafo, Israel]—24 Apr 2005, Caesarea, Israel), Israeli politician (a nephew of Chaim Weizmann, the first president of Israel) who, in 1958–69, as commander of the Israeli Air Force and deputy chief of staff, was instrumental in making the Israeli military a modern fighting force that successfully concluded the 1967 Six-Day War; a pragmatic politician, he served as president from 1993 to 2000.

William C(hilds) Westmoreland (26 Mar 1914, Spartanburg county SC—18 Jul 2005, Charleston SC), American military leader who commanded US forces in the Vietnam War from 1964 to 1968, a period during which American involvement increased to more than 500,000 troops; he implemented a strategy of attrition, using overwhelming firepower to try to kill enemy troops at a rate faster than they could be replaced; his continuing requests for additional troops, however, were not welcomed by senior officials in the administration of Pres. Lyndon B. Johnson, who now came to see the war as unwinnable; Westmoreland was given the post of Army chief of staff.

Sy Wexler (Simon Wexler; 6 Oct 1916, New York NY—10 Mar 2005, Los Angeles CA), American filmmaker who produced more than 300 training, educational, and documentary films for students and physicians; recognized for their quality and superb ability to explain difficult scientific information in an easily understandable and entertaining way, Wexler's films won several awards from the International Scientific Film Festival and the Biological Photographers Association.

(John) Harvey Wheeler (17 Oct 1918, Waco TX—6 Sep 2004, Carpinteria CA), American political scientist and writer who was the author of numerous nonfiction political science books but was best known for the work of fiction he co-wrote with Eugene Burdick, *Fail-Safe* (1962), which—with its theme of accidental nuclear attack—struck a chord with a nervous public upon its release at a time of heightened Cold War tensions.

Fred L(awrence) Whipple (9 May 1906, Red Oak IA—30 Aug 2004, Cambridge MA), American astronomer who was an expert on meteors, meteorites, and comets; in 1950 he hypothesized that a comet has a nucleus that is made up of a mixture of dust and frozen water, ammonia, methane, and carbon dioxide and that some of the frozen material is vaporized by solar energy as the comet passes through the inner solar system; this idea, which became known as the dirty-snowball theory, was confirmed in 1986 by close-up space-probe images of Halley's Comet and was an important contribution to the understanding of the solar system.

Reggie White (Reginald Howard White; 19 Dec 1961, Chattanooga TN—26 Dec 2004, Huntersville NC), American professional football player who was considered one of the best defensive linemen in the history of the National Football League; during a 15-year career, which included stints with the Philadelphia Eagles (1985–92) and the Green Bay Packers (1993–98), a franchise he helped lead to a Super Bowl title in 1997, White set a record for career sacks (198) and was selected to the Pro Bowl an unprecedented 13 consecutive times (1986–98).

Thelma White (Thelma Wolpa; 4 Dec 1910, Lincoln NE—11 Jan 2005, Los Angeles CA), American actress who was best remembered for her role in the docudrama *Reefer Madness* (1936), which became a cult classic in the 1970s because of the unintentional hilarity of the way-over-the-top exaggeration of its propaganda against the "demon weed," marijuana.

(John) Richard Whiteley (28 Dec 1943, Bradford, Yorkshire, England—26 Jun 2005, Leeds, West Yorkshire, England), British journalist and TV personality best known as the host of the TV game show *Countdown* on BBC Channel 4 beginning in 1982.

Maurice (Hugh Frederick) Wilkins (15 Dec 1916, Pongaroa, New Zealand—5 Oct 2004, London, England), New Zealand-born British biophysicist whose X-ray diffraction studies of deoxyribonucleic acid (DNA) proved crucial to the determination of DNA's molecular structure by James Watson and Sir Francis Crick *(q.v.);* for this work the three scientists were jointly awarded the 1962 Nobel Prize for Physiology or Medicine.

Paul Winchell (Paul Wilchin; 21 Dec 1922, New York NY—24 Jun 2005, Moorpark CA), American ventriloquist and voice-over artist who was a familiar presence on TV in the 1950s and '60s, appearing first with his wisecracking dummy Jerry Mahoney and later adding the dim-witted puppet Knucklehead Smiff to his act.

Henry Wolf (23 May 1925, Vienna, Austria—14 Feb 2005, New York NY), Austrian-born American graphic designer and photographer who influenced and energized magazine design during the 1950s and '60s with his bold layouts, elegant typography, and whimsical cover photographs while serving as art director at *Esquire, Harper's Bazaar,* and *Show* magazines.

Robert C(oldwell) Wood (16 Sep 1923, St. Louis MO—1 Apr 2005, Boston MA), American political scientist, professor, and president of the University of Massachusetts who was briefly secretary of housing and urban development in 1969.

Rose Mary Woods (26 Dec 1917, Sebring OH—22 Jan 2005, Alliance OH), American personality who served as personal secretary for Richard M. Nixon from 1951, when he entered the Senate, until some time after he resigned the presidency in 1974 because of the Watergate scandal; she achieved notoriety when it was discovered that an 18 1/2-minute segment of one of the White House tapes she was transcribing had been mysteriously erased; she claimed that the erasure had to have been accidental.

(Vina) Fay Wray (15 Sep 1907, near Cardston AB—8 Aug 2004, New York NY), Canadian-born American actress who was made famous in the 1933 film *King Kong,* in which she struggled to escape from the paw of the enormous ape-like beast who was scaling the Empire State Building.

Sir Edward (Maitland) Wright (13 Feb 1906, Farnley, near Leeds, England—2 Feb 2005, Reading, England), British mathematician and university official who was a largely self-taught specialist in analytic number theory; he coauthored (with G.H. Hardy) the standard textbook, *An Introduction to the Theory of Numbers* (1938), and was one of the first to work on problems of differential equations.

(Muriel) Teresa Wright (27 Oct 1918, New York NY—6 Mar 2005, New Haven CT), American actress who had the distinction of being the only person to receive an Academy Award nomination for each of her first three films—*The Little Foxes* (1941), *The Pride of the Yankees* (1942), and *Mrs. Miniver* (1942), for which she was awarded the best supporting actress Oscar.

Walter B(igelow) Wriston (3 Aug 1919, Middletown CT—19 Jan 2005, New York NY), American banker who, as head of the company now known as Citigroup, transformed the American banking industry through a series of innovations in financing and technology; he was awarded the Presidential Medal of Freedom in 2004.

George Harry Yardley (23 Nov 1928, Hollywood CA—12 Aug 2004, Newport Beach CA), American basketball player who was the first person in the National Basketball Association (NBA) to score over 2,000 points in one season; this feat was accomplished while he was a member of the Detroit Pistons during the 1957–58 season.

Akira Yoshizawa (14 Mar 1911, Kaminokawa, Tochigi prefecture, Japan—14 Mar 2005, Ogikubo, near Tokyo, Japan), Japanese artist who revived the ancient craft of origami, or paper folding, and gave it an international appeal; he used his geometry skills, precise technique, and fine design concepts to create sensational dragons, birds, and elephants from a single sheet of paper, and he invented "wet folding," the dampening of paper to mold it into sculptural forms.

Ahmed Zaki ("the Black Tiger"; 18 Nov 1949, Zaqaziq, Egypt—27 Mar 2005, Cairo, Egypt), Egyptian actor who broke the unspoken color barrier in Egyptian cinema as the first dark-skinned actor to play leading roles.

Zhang Chunqiao (1917, Juye, China—21 Apr 2005, Shanghai, China), Chinese government official who played a leading role in the Cultural Revolution (1966–76); when Communist Party of China chairman Mao Zedong called for a new class struggle in order to stave off opposition to his failed policies, Zhang quickly moved to the front of the Cultural Revolution, forming an alliance with Mao's wife, Jiang Qing; Jiang and Zhang enjoyed unprecedented power during this period, and as the revolution began to wind down they launched new attacks on senior party members; their plan failed, and in October 1976, Zhang, Jiang, and two others, known as the Gang of Four, were arrested for treason.

Zhao Ziyang (or Chao Tzu-yang; 17 Oct 1919, Hua county, Henan province, China—17 Jan 2005, Beijing, China), Chinese politician who rose to prominence as an economic reformer and served as premier of China (1980–87) and general secretary of the Communist Party of China (1987–89); a political centrist, he split from extremist party leaders who sought to suppress prodemocracy demonstrations forcibly in the spring of 1989; Zhao's dramatic, conciliatory visit to student protestors in Tiananmen Square shortly before the crackdown was his last appearance in public.

Zurab Zhvania (9 Dec 1963, Tbilisi, Georgian SSSR, USSR [now in Georgia]—3 Feb 2005, Tbilisi, Georgia), Georgian politician who was viewed as a liberal moderating influence and who, in the shuffle that followed Pres. Eduard Shevardnadze's departure from office in 2004, became prime minister; he reportedly died from accidental carbon monoxide poisoning from a faulty space heater.

Eddison Zvobgo (2 Oct 1935, near Fort Victoria, Southern Rhodesia [now Masvingo, Zimbabwe]—22 Aug 2004, Harare, Zimbabwe), Zimbabwean politician who was one of the founding fathers of independent Zimbabwe; in 1978 he joined Robert Mugabe in exile in Mozambique, and in 1979 Zvobgo acted as spokesman of the Zimbabwe African National Union in the independence negotiations in London; he served in Mugabe's cabinet from 1980 until 2000.

Awards

The Nobel Prizes

The Alfred B. Nobel Prizes are widely regarded as the world's most prestigious awards given for intellectual achievement. They are awarded annually from a fund bequeathed for that purpose by the Swedish inventor and industrialist Alfred Bernhard Nobel and administered by the Nobel Foundation. Nobel's 1895 will established five of the six prizes: those for physics, chemistry, literature, physiology or medicine, and peace. The prize for economic sciences was added in 1969. Country given is the citizenship of recipient at the time award was made. Prizes may be withheld or not awarded in years when no worthy recipient can be found or when the world situation (e.g., World Wars I and II) prevents the gathering of information needed to reach a decision. Prizes are announced in mid-October and awarded in December in Stockholm and Oslo. Web site: <www.nobel.se>

Physics

YEAR	WINNER(S)	COUNTRY	ACHIEVEMENT
1901	Wilhelm Conrad Röntgen	Germany	discovery of X rays
1902	Hendrik Antoon Lorentz	Neth.	investigation of the influence
	Pieter Zeeman	Neth.	of magnetism on radiation
1903	Henri Becquerel	France	discovery of spontaneous radioactivity
	Marie Curie	France	investigations of radiation phenomena
	Pierre Curie	France	discovered by Becquerel
1904	John William Strutt, 3rd Baron Rayleigh (of Terling Place)	UK	discovery of argon
1905	Philipp Lenard	Germany	research on cathode rays
1906	Sir J.J. Thomson	UK	researches into electrical conductivity of gases
1907	A.A. Michelson	US	spectroscopic and metrological investigations
1908	Gabriel Lippmann	France	photographic reproduction of colors
1909	Ferdinand Braun	Germany	development of
	Guglielmo Marconi	Italy	wireless telegraphy
1910	Johannes Diederik van der Waals	Neth.	research concerning the equation of state of gases and liquids
1911	Wilhelm Wien	Germany	discoveries regarding laws governing heat radiation
1912	Nils Dalén	Sweden	invention of automatic regulators for lighting coastal beacons and light buoys
1913	Heike Kamerlingh Onnes	Neth.	investigation into the properties of matter at low temperatures; production of liquid helium
1914	Max von Laue	Germany	discovery of diffraction of X rays by crystals
1915	Sir Lawrence Bragg	UK	analysis of crystal structure
	Sir William Bragg	UK	by means of X rays
1917	Charles Glover Barkla	UK	discovery of characteristic X-radiation of elements
1918	Max Planck	Germany	discovery of the elemental quanta
1919	Johannes Stark	Germany	discovery of Doppler effect in positive ion rays and division of spectral lines in electric field
1920	Charles Édouard Guillaume	Switz.	discovery of anomalies in alloys
1921	Albert Einstein	Switz.	work in theoretical physics
1922	Niels Bohr	Denmark	investigation of atomic structure and radiation
1923	Robert Andrews Millikan	US	work on elementary electric charge and the photoelectric effect
1924	Karl Manne Georg Siegbahn	Sweden	work in X-ray spectroscopy
1925	James Franck	Germany	discovery of the laws governing the
	Gustav Hertz	Germany	impact of an electron upon an atom
1926	Jean Perrin	France	work on discontinuous structure of matter
1927	Arthur Holly Compton	US	discovery of wavelength change in diffused X rays
	C.T.R. Wilson	UK	method of making visible the paths of electrically charged particles
1928	Sir Owen Willans Richardson	UK	work on electron emission by hot metals
1929	Louis-Victor, 7e duc (duke) de Broglie	France	discovery of the wave nature of electrons

Physics (continued)

YEAR	WINNER(S)	COUNTRY	ACHIEVEMENT
1930	Sir Chandrasekhara Venkata Raman	India	work on light diffusion; discovery of Raman effect, light wavelength variation that occurs when a light beam is deflected by molecules
1932	Werner Heisenberg	Germany	creation of quantum mechanics
1933	P.A.M. Dirac	UK	} introduction of wave equations
	Erwin Schrödinger	Austria	} in quantum mechanics
1935	Sir James Chadwick	UK	discovery of the neutron
1936	Carl David Anderson	US	discovery of the positron
	Victor Francis Hess	Austria	discovery of cosmic radiation
1937	Clinton Joseph Davisson	US	} experimental demonstration of the interference
	Sir George Paget Thomson	UK	} phenomenon in crystals irradiated by electrons
1938	Enrico Fermi	Italy	disclosure of artificial radioactive elements produced by neutron irradiation
1939	Ernest Orlando Lawrence	US	invention of the cyclotron
1943	Otto Stern	US	discovery of the magnetic moment of the proton
1944	Isidor Isaac Rabi	US	resonance method for registration of various properties of atomic nuclei
1945	Wolfgang Pauli	Austria	discovery of the exclusion principle of electrons
1946	Percy Williams Bridgman	US	discoveries in the domain of high-pressure physics
1947	Sir Edward V. Appleton	UK	discovery of Appleton layer in upper atmosphere
1948	Patrick M.S. Blackett	UK	discoveries in the domain of nuclear physics and cosmic radiation
1949	Hideki Yukawa	Japan	prediction of the existence of mesons
1950	Cecil Frank Powell	UK	photographic method of studying nuclear processes; discoveries concerning mesons
1951	Sir John D. Cockcroft	UK	} work on transmutation of atomic nuclei
	Ernest T.S. Walton	Ireland	} by accelerated particles
1952	Felix Bloch	US	} discovery of nuclear magnetic
	E.M. Purcell	US	} resonance in solids
1953	Frits Zernike	Neth.	method of phase-contrast microscopy
1954	Max Born	UK	statistical studies of atomic wave functions
	Walther Bothe	W.Ger.	invention of coincidence method
1955	Polykarp Kusch	US	measurement of magnetic moment of electron
	Willis Eugene Lamb, Jr.	US	discoveries in the hydrogen spectrum
1956	John Bardeen	US	} investigations on
	Walter H. Brattain	US	} semiconductors and
	William B. Shockley	US	} invention of the transistor
1957	Tsung-Dao Lee	China	} discovery of violations of the principle of parity, the
	Chen Ning Yang	China	} symmetry between phenomena in coordinate systems
1958	Pavel Alexeyevich Cherenkov	USSR	discovery and interpretation of the Cherenkov effect, which indicates that electrons emit light as they
	Ilya Mikhaylovich Frank	USSR	pass through a transparent medium at a speed
	Igor Yevgenyevich Tamm	USSR	higher than the speed of light in that medium
1959	Owen Chamberlain	US	} confirmation of the existence
	Emilio Segrè	US	} of the antiproton
1960	Donald A. Glaser	US	development of the bubble chamber
1961	Robert Hofstadter	US	determination of shape and size of atomic nucleons
	Rudolf Ludwig Mössbauer	W.Ger.	discovery of the Mössbauer effect, a nuclear process permitting the resonance absorption of gamma rays
1962	Lev Davidovich Landau	USSR	contributions to the understanding of condensed states of matter
1963	J. Hans D. Jensen	W.Ger.	} development of shell model theory of
	Maria Goeppert Mayer	US	} the structure of the atomic nuclei
	Eugene Paul Wigner	US	principles governing interaction of protons and neutrons in the nucleus
1964	Nikolay G. Basov	USSR	work in quantum electronics leading to
	Aleksandr M. Prokhorov	USSR	construction of instruments based on
	Charles Hard Townes	US	maser-laser principles
1965	Richard P. Feynman	US	basic principles of quantum electrodynamics, which
	Julian Seymour Schwinger	US	describes mathematically all interactions of light with
	Shin'ichiro Tomonaga	Japan	matter and of charged particles with one another
1966	Alfred Kastler	France	discovery of optical methods for studying Hertzian resonances in atoms
1967	Hans Albrecht Bethe	US	discoveries concerning the energy production of stars
1968	Luis W. Alvarez	US	work with elementary particles, discovery of resonance states
1969	Murray Gell-Mann	US	classification of elementary particles and their interactions

Physics (continued)

YEAR	WINNER(S)	COUNTRY	ACHIEVEMENT
1970	Hannes Alfvén	Sweden	work in magnetohydrodynamics and
	Louis-Eugène-Félix Néel	France	in antiferromagnetism and ferrimagnetism
1971	Dennis Gabor	UK	invention of holography
1972	John Bardeen	US	development of thetheory of superconductivity, the
	Leon N. Cooper	US	disappearance of electrical resistancein various
	John Robert Schrieffer	US	solids when they are cooled below certain temperature
1973	Leo Esaki	Japan	experimental disoveries in tunneling in
	Ivar Giaever	US	semiconductors and superconductors
	Brian D. Josephson	UK	predictions of supercurrent properties through a tunnel barrier
1974	Antony Hewish	UK	work in radio
	Sir Martin Ryle	UK	astronomy
1975	Aage N. Bohr	Denmark	work on the atomic nucleus
	Ben R. Mottelson	Denmark	that paved the way for nuclear
	James Rainwater	US	fusion
1976	Burton Richter	US	discovery of new class of
	Samuel C.C. Ting	US	elementary particles (psi, or J)
1977	Philip W. Anderson	US	contributions to understanding the
	Sir Nevill F. Mott	UK	behavior of electrons in
	John H. Van Vleck	US	magnetic, noncrystalline solids
1978	Pyotr L. Kapitsa	USSR	research in magnetism and low-temperature physics
	Arno Penzias	US	discovery of cosmic microwave background
	Robert Woodrow Wilson	US	radiation, providing support for the big-bang theory
1979	Sheldon Lee Glashow	US	unification of electromagnetism and
	Abdus Salam	Pakistan	the weak interactions of
	Steven Weinberg	US	subatomic particles
1980	James Watson Cronin	US	demonstration of simultaneous violation of both
	Val Logsdon Fitch	US	charge-conjugation and parity-inversion symmetries
1981	Nicolaas Bloembergen	US	applications of lasers
	Arthur L. Schawlow	US	in spectroscopy
	Kai M. B. Siegbahn	Sweden	electron spectroscopy for chemical analysis
1982	Kenneth G. Wilson	US	analysis of continuous phase transitions
1983	Subrahmanyan Chandrasekhar	US	contributions to understanding the evolution and devolution of stars
	William A. Fowler	US	studies of nuclear reactions key to the formation of chemical elements
1984	Simon van der Meer	Neth.	discovery of subatomic particles W and Z
	Carlo Rubbia	Italy	which supports the electroweak theory
1985	Klaus von Klitzing	W.Ger.	discovery of the quantized Hall effect, permitting exact measurements of electrical resistance
1986	Gerd Binnig	W.Ger.	development of the scanning tunnelling
	Heinrich Rohrer	Switz.	electron microscopes
	Ernst Ruska	W.Ger.	development of the electron microscope
1987	J. Georg Bednorz	W.Ger.	discoveries of superconductivity in
	Karl Alex Müller	Switz.	ceramic materials
1988	Leon Max Lederman	US	research in
	Melvin Schwartz	US	subatomic
	Jack Steinberger	US	particles
1989	Hans Georg Dehmelt	US	development of methods to isolate atoms
	Wolfgang Paul	W.Ger.	and subatomic particles for study
	Norman Foster Ramsey	US	development of the atomic clock
1990	Jerome Isaac Friedman	US	discovery of
	Henry Way Kendall	US	atomic
	Richard E. Taylor	Canada	quarks
1991	Pierre-Gilles de Gennes	France	discovery of general rules for behavior of molecules
1992	Georges Charpak	France	inventor of detector that traces subatomic particles
1993	Russell Alan Hulse	US	identifying
	Joseph H. Taylor, Jr.	US	binary pulsars
1994	Bertram N. Brockhouse	Canada	development of
	Clifford G. Shull	US	neutron-scattering techniques
1995	Martin Lewis Perl	US	discovery of tau subatomic particle
	Frederick Reines	US	discovery of neutrino subatomic particle
1996	David M. Lee	US	discovery of
	Douglas D. Osheroff	US	superfluidity in
	Robert C. Richardson	US	isotope helium-3
1997	Steven Chu	US	process of
	Claude Cohen-Tannoudji	France	cooling and trapping atoms with
	William D. Phillips	US	laser light

Physics (continued)

YEAR	WINNER(S)	COUNTRY	ACHIEVEMENT
1998	Robert B. Laughlin	US	} discovery of fractional quantum Hall effect, demonstrating that electrons in a powerful low-temperature magnetic field can form a quantum fluid whose particles have fractional electric charges
	Horst L. Störmer	US	
	Daniel C. Tsui	US	
1999	Gerardus 't Hooft	Neth.	} study of quantum structure of electroweak interactions
	Martinus J.G. Veltman	Neth.	
2000	Zhores I. Alferov	Russia	} development of fast semiconductors for use in microelectronics
	Herbert Kroemer	Germany	
	Jack S. Kilby	US	development of the integrated circuit (microchip)
2001	Eric A. Cornell	US	} achievement of Bose-Einstein condensation in dilute gases of alkali atoms, and for early fundamental studies of the properties of the condensates
	Wolfgang Ketterle	Germany	
	Carl E. Wieman	US	
2002	Raymond Davis, Jr.	US	} pioneering contributions to astrophysics, in particular for the detection of cosmic neutrinos
	Masatoshi Koshiba	Japan	
	Riccardo Giacconi	US	pioneering contributions to astrophysics, which have led to the discovery of cosmic X-ray sources
2003	Alexei A. Abrikosov	US, Russia	} pioneering contributions to the theory of superconductors and superfluids
	Vitaly L. Ginzburg	Russia	
	Anthony J. Leggett	UK, US	
2004	David J. Gross	US	} discovery of asymptotic freedom in the theory of the strong interaction
	H. David Politzer	US	
	Frank Wilczek	US	

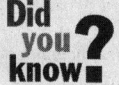

Did you know? In 2003 the longest prime number yet confirmed, 6,320,430 digits long and requiring 1,400 to 1,500 pages to print out, was discovered.

Chemistry

YEAR	WINNER(S)	COUNTRY	ACHIEVEMENT
1901	Jacobus H. van 't Hoff	Neth.	laws of chemical dynamics and osmotic pressure
1902	Emil Fischer	Germany	work on sugar and purine syntheses
1903	Svante Arrhenius	Sweden	theory of electrolytic dissociation
1904	Sir William Ramsay	UK	discovery of inert gas elements and their places in the periodic system
1905	Adolf von Baeyer	Germany	work on organic dyes, hydroaromatic compounds
1906	Henri Moissan	France	isolation of fluorine; introduction of Moissan furnace
1907	Eduard Buchner	Germany	discovery of noncellular fermentation
1908	Ernest Rutherford	UK	investigations into the disintegration of elements and the chemistry of radioactive substances
1909	Wilhelm Ostwald	Germany	pioneer work on catalysis, chemical equilibrium, and reaction velocities
1910	Otto Wallach	Germany	pioneer work in alicyclic combinations
1911	Marie Curie	France	discovery of radium and polonium; isolation of radium
1912	Victor Grignard	France	discovery of the Grignard reagents
	Paul Sabatier	France	method of hydrogenating organic compounds
1913	Alfred Werner	Switz.	work on the linkage of atoms in molecules
1914	Theodore W. Richards	US	accurate determination of the atomic weights of numerous elements
1915	Richard Willstätter	Germany	research in plant pigments, especially chlorophyll
1918	Fritz Haber	Germany	synthesis of ammonia
1920	Walther Hermann Nernst	Germany	work in thermochemistry
1921	Frederick Soddy	UK	chemistry of radioactive substances; occurrence and nature of isotopes
1922	Francis William Aston	UK	work with mass spectrograph; whole-number rule
1923	Fritz Pregl	Austria	method of microanalysis of organic substances
1925	Richard Zsigmondy	Austria	elucidation of the heterogeneous nature of colloidal solutions
1926	Theodor H.E. Svedberg	Sweden	work on disperse systems
1927	Heinrich Otto Wieland	Germany	researches into the constitution of bile acids
1928	Adolf Windaus	Germany	constitution of sterols and their connection with vitamins

Chemistry (continued)

YEAR	WINNER(S)	COUNTRY	ACHIEVEMENT
1929	Hans von Euler-Chelpin	Sweden	investigations in the fermentation of sugars
	Sir Arthur Harden	UK	and the enzyme action involved
1930	Hans Fischer	Germany	hemin, chlorophyll research; synthesis of hemin
1931	Friedrich Bergius	Germany	invention and development of
	Carl Bosch	Germany	chemical high-pressure methods
1932	Irving Langmuir	US	discoveries and investigations in surface chemistry
1934	Harold C. Urey	US	discovery of heavy hydrogen
1935	Frédéric and Irène Joliot-Curie	France	synthesis of new radioactive elements
1936	Peter Debye	Neth.	work on dipole moments and diffraction of X rays and electrons in gases
1937	Sir Norman Haworth	UK	research on carbohydrates and vitamin C
	Paul Karrer	Switz.	research on carotenoids, flavins, and vitamins
1938	Richard Kuhn (declined)	Germany	carotenoid and vitamin research
1939	Adolf Butenandt (declined)	Germany	work on sexual hormones
	Leopold Ruzicka	Switz.	work on polymethylenes and higher terpenes
1943	Georg Charles von Hevesy	Hungary	use of isotopes as tracers in chemical research
1944	Otto Hahn	Germany	discovery of the fission of heavy nuclei
1945	Artturi Ilmari Virtanen	Finland	invention of fodder preservation method
1946	John Howard Northrop	US	preparation of enzymes and
	Wendell M. Stanley	US	virus proteins in pure form
	James B. Sumner	US	discovery of enzyme crystallization
1947	Sir Robert Robinson	UK	investigation of alkaloids and other plant products
1948	Arne Tiselius	Sweden	researches in electrophoresis and adsorption analysis; serum proteins
1949	William Francis Giauque	US	behavior of substances at extremely low temperatures
1950	Kurt Alder	W.Ger.	discovery and development of
	Otto Paul Hermann Diels	W.Ger.	diene synthesis
1951	Edwin M. McMillan	US	discovery of and research on
	Glenn T. Seaborg	US	transuranium elements
1952	A.J.P. Martin	UK	development of partition
	R.L.M. Synge	UK	chromatography
1953	Hermann Staudinger	W.Ger.	work on macromolecules
1954	Linus Pauling	US	study of the nature of the chemical bond
1955	Vincent du Vigneaud	US	first synthesis of a polypeptide hormone
1956	Sir Cyril N. Hinshelwood	UK	work on the kinetics of
	Nikolay N. Semyonov	USSR	chemical reactions
1957	Alexander Robertus Todd, Baron Todd (of Trumpington)	UK	work on nucleotides and nucleotide coenzymes
1958	Frederick Sanger	UK	determination of the structure of the insulin molecule
1959	Jaroslav Heyrovsky	Czecho-slovakia	discovery and development of polarography
1960	Willard Frank Libby	US	development of radiocarbon dating
1961	Melvin Calvin	US	study of chemical steps that take place during photosynthesis
1962	Sir John C. Kendrew	UK	determination of the structure of
	Max Ferdinand Perutz	UK	hemoproteins
1963	Giulio Natta	Italy	structure and synthesis of polymers
	Karl Ziegler	W.Ger.	in the field of plastics
1964	Dorothy M.C. Hodgkin	UK	determining the structure of biochemical compounds essential in combating pernicious anemia
1965	R.B. Woodward	US	synthesis of sterols, chlorophyll, and other substances
1966	Robert S. Mulliken	US	work concerning chemical bonds and the electronic structure of molecules
1967	Manfred Eigen	W.Ger.	studies of extremely fast chemical reactions
	Ronald G. W. Norrish	UK	studies of extremely fast
	Sir George Porter	UK	chemical reactions
1968	Lars Onsager	US	work on theory of thermodynamics of irreversible processes
1969	Sir Derek H.R. Barton	UK	work in determining actual
	Odd Hassel	Norway	three-dimensional shape of molecules
1970	Luis Federico Leloir	Argentina	discovery of sugar nucleotides and their role in the biosynthesis of carbohydrates

Chemistry (continued)

YEAR	WINNER(S)	COUNTRY	ACHIEVEMENT
1971	Gerhard Herzberg	Canada	research in the structure of molecules
1972	Christian B. Anfinsen	US	fundamental contributions to enzyme chemistry
	Stanford Moore	US	} fundamental contributions
	William H. Stein	US	} to enzyme chemistry
1973	Ernst Otto Fischer	W.Ger.	} organometallic
	Sir Geoffrey Wilkinson	UK	} chemistry
1974	Paul J. Flory	US	studies of long-chain molecules
1975	Sir John W. Cornforth	UK	} work in
	Vladimir Prelog	Switz.	} stereochemistry
1976	William N. Lipscomb, Jr.	US	structure of boranes
1977	Ilya Prigogine	Belgium	widening the scope of thermodynamics
1978	Peter Dennis Mitchell	UK	formulation of a theory of energy transfer processes in biological systems
1979	Herbert Charles Brown	US	introduction of compounds of boron and phosphorus in the synthesis of organic substances
	Georg Wittig	W.Ger.	introduction of compounds of boron and phosphorus in the synthesis of organic substances
1980	Paul Berg	US	first preparation of a hybrid DNA
	Walter Gilbert	US	} development of chemical and
	Frederick Sanger	UK	} biological analyses of DNA structure
1981	Kenichi Fukui	Japan	} orbital symmetry interpretation
	Roald Hoffmann	US	} of chemical reactions
1982	Aaron Klug	UK	determination of structure of biological substances
1983	Henry Taube	US	study of electron transfer reactions
1984	Bruce Merrifield	US	development of a method of polypeptide synthesis
1985	Herbert A. Hauptman	US	} development of a way to map the
	Jerome Karle	US	} chemical structure of small molecules
1986	Dudley R. Herschbach	US	} development of methods
	Yuan T. Lee	US	} for analyzing basic
	John C. Polanyi	Canada	} chemical reactions
1987	Donald J. Cram	US	} development of molecules
	Jean-Marie Lehn	France	} that can link with
	Charles J. Pedersen	US	} other molecules
1988	Johann Deisenhofer	W.Ger.	} discovery of structure
	Robert Huber	W.Ger.	} proteins needed
	Hartmut Michel	W.Ger.	} in photosynthesis
1989	Sidney Altman	US	} discovery of certain
	Thomas Robert Cech	US	} basic properties of RNA
1990	Elias James Corey	US	development of retrosynthetic analysis for synthesis of complex molecules
1991	Richard R. Ernst	Switz.	improvements in nuclear magnetic resonance spectroscopy
1992	Rudolph A. Marcus	US	explanation of how electrons transfer between molecules
1993	Kary B. Mullis	US	} inventors of techniques for
	Michael Smith	Canada	} gene study and manipulation
1994	George A. Olah	US	development of techniques to study hydrocarbon molecules
1995	Paul Crutzen	Neth.	} explanation of process
	Mario Molina	US	} that deplete Earth's
	F. Sherwood Rowland	US	} ozone layer
1996	Robert F. Curl, Jr.	US	} discovery of new
	Sir Harold W. Kroto	UK	} carbon compounds
	Richard E. Smalley	US	} called fullerenes
1997	Paul D. Boyer	US	} explanation of the enzymatic conversion of
	John E. Walker	UK	} conversion of adenosine triphosphate
	Jens C. Skou	Denmark	discovery of sodium-potassium-activated adenosine triphosphatase
1998	Walter Kohn	US	development of the density-functional theory
	John A. Pople	UK	development of computational methods in quantum chemistry
1999	Ahmed H. Zewail	Egypt/US	study of the transition states of chemical reactions using femtosecond spectroscopy
2000	Alan J. Heeger	US	} discovery of plastics
	Alan G. MacDiarmid	US	} that conduct
	Hideki Shirakawa	Japan	} electricity

Chemistry (continued)

YEAR	WINNER(S)	COUNTRY	ACHIEVEMENT
2001	William S. Knowles	US	} work on chirally catalyzed
	Ryoji Noyori	Japan	} hydrogenation reactions
	K. Barry Sharpless	US	work on chirally catalyzed oxidation reactions
2002	John B. Fenn	US	development of soft desorption ionization methods
	Koichi Tanaka	Japan	for mass spectrometric analyses of biological macromolecules
	Kurt Wüthrich	Switz.	development of nuclear magnetic resonance spectroscopy for determining the three-dimensional structure of biological macromolecules in solution
2003	Peter Agre	US	} cell membrane channel
	Roderick MacKinnon	US	} discoveries; discovery of water channels (Agre); ion channel studies (MacKinnon)
2004	Aaron Ciechanover	Israel	discovery of
	Avram Hershko	Israel	} ubiquitin-mediated
	Irwin Rose	US	protein degradation

Physiology or Medicine

YEAR	WINNER(S)	COUNTRY	ACHIEVEMENT
1901	Emil von Behring	Germany	work on serum therapy
1902	Sir Ronald Ross	UK	discovery of how malaria enters an organism
1903	Niels Ryberg Finsen	Denmark	treatment of skin diseases with light
1904	Ivan Petrovich Pavlov	Russia	work on the physiology of digestion
1905	Robert Koch	Germany	tuberculosis research
1906	Camillo Golgi	Italy	} work on the structure
	Santiago Ramón y Cajal	Spain	} of the nervous system
1907	Alphonse Laveran	France	discovery of the role of protozoa in diseases
1908	Paul Ehrlich	Germany	} work on
	Élie Metchnikoff	Russia	} immunity
1909	Emil Theodor Kocher	Switz.	physiology, pathology, and surgery of the thyroid gland
1910	Albrecht Kossel	Germany	researches in cellular chemistry
1911	Allvar Gullstrand	Sweden	work on dioptrics of the eye
1912	Alexis Carrel	France	work on vascular suture; transplantation of organs
1913	Charles Richet	France	work on anaphylaxis
1914	Robert Bárány	Austria-Hungary	work on vestibular apparatus
1919	Jules Bordet	Belgium	work on immunity factors in blood serum
1920	August Krogh	Denmark	discovery of capillary motor-regulating mechanism
1922	A.V. Hill	UK	discoveries concerning heat production in muscles
	Otto Meyerhof	Germany	work on metabolism of lactic acid in muscles
1923	Sir Frederick G. Banting	Canada	} discovery of
	J.J.R. Macleod	UK	} insulin
1924	Willem Einthoven	Neth.	discovery of electrocardiogram mechanism
1926	Johannes Fibiger	Denmark	contributions to cancer research
1927	Julius Wagner-Jauregg	Austria	work on malaria inoculation in dementia paralytica
1928	Charles-Jules-Henri Nicolle	France	work on typhus
1929	Christiaan Eijkman	Neth.	discovery of antineuritic vitamin
	Sir Frederick Gowland Hopkins	UK	discovery of growth-stimulating vitamins
1930	Karl Landsteiner	US	grouping of human blood
1931	Otto Warburg	Germany	discovery of nature and action of respiratory enzyme
1932	Edgar Douglas Adrian, 1st Baron Adrian (of Cambridge)	UK	discoveries regarding function of neurons
	Sir Charles Scott Sherrington	UK	discoveries regarding function of neurons
1933	Thomas Hunt Morgan	US	heredity transmission functions of chromosomes
1934	George Richards Minot	US	} discoveries concerning
	William P. Murphy	US	} liver treatment
	George H. Whipple	US	for anemia
1935	Hans Spemann	Germany	organizer effect in embryo
1936	Sir Henry Dale	UK	} work on chemical
	Otto Loewi	Germany	} transmission of nerve impulses

Physiology or Medicine (continued)

YEAR	WINNER(S)	COUNTRY	ACHIEVEMENT
1937	Albert Szent-Gyorgyi	Hungary	work on biological combustion
1938	Corneille Heymans	Belgium	discovery of role of sinus and aortic mechanisms in respiration regulation
1939	Gerhard Domagk (declined)	Germany	antibacterial effect of Prontosil
1943	Henrik Dam	Denmark	discovery of vitamin K
	Edward Adelbert Doisy	US	discovery of chemical nature of vitamin K
1944	Joseph Erlanger	US	researches on differentiated
	Herbert S. Gasser	US	functions of nerve fibers
1945	Sir Ernst Boris Chain	UK	discovery of penicillin
	Sir Alexander Fleming	UK	and its curative value
	Howard Walter Florey, Baron Florey	Australia	discovery of penicillin and its curative value
1946	Hermann Joseph Muller	US	production of mutations by X-ray irradiation
1947	Carl and Gerty Cori	US	discovery of how glycogen is catalytically converted
	Bernardo A. Houssay	Argentina	pituitary hormone function in sugar metabolism
1948	Paul Hermann Müller	Switz.	properties of DDT
1949	António Egas Moniz	Portugal	therapeutic value of leucotomy in psychoses
	Walter Rudolf Hess	Switz.	discovery of function of interbrain
1950	Philip Showalter Hench	US	research on adrenal cortex
	Edward Calvin Kendall	US	hormones, their structure and
	Tadeus Reichstein	Switz.	biological effects
1951	Max Theiler	South Africa	yellow fever discoveries
1952	Selman A. Waksman	US	discovery of streptomycin
1953	Sir Hans Adolf Krebs	UK	discovery of coenzyme A citric acid cycle in
	Fritz Albert Lipmann	US	metabolism of carbohydrates
1954	John Franklin Enders	US	cultivation of the
	Frederick C. Robbins	US	poliomyelitis virus in
	Thomas H. Weller	US	tissue cultures
1955	Axel H.T. Theorell	Sweden	nature and mode of action of oxidation enzymes
1956	André F. Cournand	US	discoveries concerning
	Werner Forssmann	W.Ger.	heart catheterization and
	Dickinson W. Richards	US	circulatory changes
1957	Daniel Bovet	Italy	production of synthetic curare
1958	George Wells Beadle	US	genetic regulation of
	Edward L. Tatum	US	chemical processes
	Joshua Lederberg	US	genetic recombination
1959	Arthur Kornberg	US	work on producing nucleic
	Severo Ochoa	US	acids artificially
1960	Sir Macfarlane Burnet	Australia	acquired immunity to
	Sir Peter B. Medawar	UK	tissue transplants
1961	Georg von Békésy	US	functions of the inner ear
1962	Francis H.C. Crick	UK	discoveries concerning
	James Dewey Watson	US	the molecular structure
	Maurice Wilkins	UK	of DNA
1963	Sir John Carew Eccles	Australia	study of the transmission
	Sir Alan Hodgkin	UK	of impulses along
	Sir Andrew F. Huxley	UK	a nerve fiber
1964	Konrad Bloch	US	discoveries concerning
	Feodor Lynen	W.Ger.	cholesterol and fatty-acid metabolism
1965	François Jacob	France	discoveries concerning
	André Lwoff	France	regulatory activities
	Jacques Monod	France	of the body cells
1966	Charles B. Huggins	US	research on causes and
	Peyton Rous	US	treatment of cancer
1967	Ragnar Arthur Granit	Sweden	discoveries about chemical
	Haldan Keffer Hartline	US	and physiological visual
	George Wald	US	processes in the eye
1968	Robert William Holley	US	deciphering
	Har Gobind Khorana	US	of the
	Marshall W. Nirenberg	US	genetic code
1969	Max Delbrück	US	research and discoveries
	A.D. Hershey	US	concerning viruses and
	Salvador Luria	US	viral diseases

Physiology or Medicine (continued)

YEAR	WINNER(S)	COUNTRY	ACHIEVEMENT
1970	Julius Axelrod	US	discoveries concerning
	Ulf von Euler	Sweden	the chemistry of
	Sir Bernard Katz	UK	nerve transmission
1971	Earl W. Sutherland, Jr.	US	action of hormones
1972	Gerald M. Edelman	US	research on the chemical
	Rodney Robert Porter	UK	structure of antibodies
1973	Karl von Frisch	Austria	discoveries in
	Konrad Lorenz	Austria	animal behavior
	Nikolaas Tinbergen	UK	patterns
1974	Albert Claude	US	research on structural
	Christian René de Duve	Belgium	and functional organization
	George E. Palade	US	of cells
1975	David Baltimore	US	interaction between
	Renato Dulbecco	US	tumor viruses and the genetic
	Howard Martin Temin	US	material of the cell
1976	Baruch S. Blumberg	US	studies of origin and
	D. Carleton Gajdusek	US	spread of infectious diseases
1977	Roger C.L. Guillemin	US	research on pituitary
	Andrew Victor Schally	US	hormones
	Rosalyn S. Yalow	US	development of radioimmunoassay
1978	Werner Arber	Switz.	discovery and application
	Daniel Nathans	US	of enzymes that
	Hamilton O. Smith	US	fragment DNA
1979	Allan M. Cormack	US	development of
	Sir Godfrey N. Hounsfield	UK	the CAT scan
1980	Baruj Benacerraf	US	investigations of genetic
	Jean-Baptiste-Gabriel-	France	control of the response of the
	George Davis Snell	US	immune system to foreign substances
1981	David Hunter Hubel	US	processing of visual
	Torsten Nils Wiesel	Sweden	information by the brain
	Roger Wolcott Sperry	US	functions of the cerebral hemispheres
1982	Sune K. Bergström	Sweden	biochemistry and
	Bengt I. Samuelsson	Sweden	physiology of
	John Robert Vane	UK	prostaglandins
1983	Barbara McClintock	US	discovery of mobile plant genes that affect heredity
1984	Niels K. Jerne	Denmark	theory and development
	Georges J.F. Köhler	W.Ger.	of a technique
	César Milstein	UK-	for producing
		Argentina	monoclonal antibodies
1985	Michael S. Brown	US	discovery of cell receptors relating to
	Joseph L. Goldstein	US	cholesterol metabolism
1986	Stanley Cohen	US	discovery of chemical agents
	Rita Levi-Montalcini	Italy	that help regulate the growth of cells
1987	Susumu Tonegawa	Japan	study of genetic aspects of antibodies
1988	Sir James Black	UK	development of new
	Gertrude Belle Elion	US	classes of drugs for
	George H. Hitchings	US	combating disease
1989	J. Michael Bishop	US	study of cancer-causing
	Harold Varmus	US	genes called oncogenes
1990	Joseph E. Murray	US	development of kidney and
	E. Donnall Thomas	US	bone-marrow transplants
1991	Erwin Neher	Germany	discovery of how cells
	Bert Sakmann	Germany	communicate, as related to diseases
1992	Edmond H. Fischer	US	discovery of class of enzymes
	Edwin Gerhard Krebs	US	called protein kinases
1993	Richard J. Roberts	UK	discovery of "split," or
	Phillip A. Sharp	US	interrupted, genetic structure
1994	Alfred G. Gilman	US	discovery of cell signalers
	Martin Rodbell	US	called G-proteins
1995	Edward B. Lewis	US	identification of genes
	Christiane	Germany	that control the body's
	Nüsslein-Volhard		early structural
	Eric F. Wieschaus	US	development
1996	Peter C. Doherty	Australia	discovery of how the immune
	Rolf M. Zinkernagel	Switz.	system recognizes virus-infected cells
1997	Stanley B. Prusiner	US	discovery of the prion, a type of disease-causing protein

Physiology or Medicine (continued)

YEAR	WINNER(S)	COUNTRY	ACHIEVEMENT
1998	Robert F. Furchgott	US	discovery that nitric oxide (NO)
	Louis J. Ignarro	US	acts as a signaling molecule in
	Ferid Murad	US	the cardiovascular system
1999	Günter Blobel	US	discovery that proteins have signals governing cellular organization
2000	Arvid Carlsson	Sweden	discovery of how signals
	Paul Greengard	US	are transmitted between nerve
	Eric Kandel	US	cells in the brain
2001	Leland H. Hartwell	US	discovery of key
	R. Timothy Hunt	UK	regulators of
	Sir Paul M. Nurse	UK	the cell cycle
2002	Sydney Brenner	UK	discoveries concerning how genes
	H. Robert Horvitz	US	regulate and program organ
	John E. Sulston	UK	development and cell death
2003	Paul C. Lauterbur	US	discoveries concerning magnetic
	Sir Peter Mansfield	UK	resonance imaging
2004	Richard Axel	US	discoveries of odorant receptors and the
	Linda B. Buck	US	organization of the olfactory system

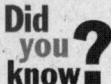

Did you know? In 1604 the first purely English dictionary to be issued as a separate work appeared in London, entitled *A Table Alphabeticall, conteyning and teaching the true writing and understanding of hard usuall English wordes, borrowed from the Hebrew, Greeke, Latine, or French &c.*, by Robert Cawdrey, a schoolmaster.

Literature

YEAR	WINNER(S)	COUNTRY	FIELD
1901	Sully Prudhomme	France	poetry
1902	Theodor Mommsen	Germany	history
1903	Bjørnstjerne Martinus Bjørnson	Norway	prose fiction, poetry, drama
1904	José Echegaray y Eizaguirre	Spain	drama
	Frédéric Mistral	France	poetry
1905	Henryk Sienkiewicz	Poland	prose fiction
1906	Giosuè Carducci	Italy	poetry
1907	Rudyard Kipling	UK	poetry, prose fiction
1908	Rudolf Christoph Eucken	Germany	philosophy
1909	Selma Lagerlöf	Sweden	prose fiction
1910	Paul Johann Ludwig von Heyse	Germany	poetry, prose fiction, drama
1911	Maurice Maeterlinck	Belgium	drama
1912	Gerhart Hauptmann	Germany	drama
1913	Rabindranath Tagore	India	poetry
1915	Romain Rolland	France	prose fiction
1916	Verner von Heidenstam	Sweden	poetry
1917	Karl Gjellerup	Denmark	prose fiction
	Henrik Pontoppidan	Denmark	prose fiction
1918	Erik Axel Karlfeldt (declined)	Sweden	poetry
1919	Carl Spitteler	Switz.	poetry, prose fiction
1920	Knut Hamsun	Norway	prose fiction
1921	Anatole France	France	prose fiction
1922	Jacinto Benavente y Martínez	Spain	drama
1923	William Butler Yeats	Ireland	poetry
1924	Wladyslaw Stanislaw Reymont	Poland	prose fiction
1925	George Bernard Shaw	Ireland	drama
1926	Grazia Deledda	Italy	prose fiction
1927	Henri Bergson	France	philosophy
1928	Sigrid Undset	Norway	prose fiction
1929	Thomas Mann	Germany	prose fiction
1930	Sinclair Lewis	US	prose fiction
1931	Erik Axel Karlfeldt (posthumous award)	Sweden	poetry
1932	John Galsworthy	UK	prose fiction
1933	Ivan Alekseyevich Bunin	USSR	poetry, prose fiction

Literature (continued)

YEAR	WINNER(S)	COUNTRY	FIELD
1934	Luigi Pirandello	Italy	drama
1936	Eugene O'Neill	US	drama
1937	Roger Martin du Gard	France	prose fiction
1938	Pearl Buck	US	prose fiction
1939	Frans Eemil Sillanpää	Finland	prose fiction
1944	Johannes V. Jensen	Denmark	prose fiction
1945	Gabriela Mistral	Chile	poetry
1946	Hermann Hesse	Switz.	prose fiction
1947	André Gide	France	prose
1948	T.S. Eliot	UK	poetry, criticism
1949	William Faulkner	US	prose fiction
1950	Bertrand Russell	UK	philosophy
1951	Pär Lagerkvist	Sweden	prose fiction
1952	François Mauriac	France	poetry, prose fiction, drama
1953	Sir Winston Churchill	UK	history, oration
1954	Ernest Hemingway	US	prose fiction
1955	Halldór Laxness	Iceland	prose fiction
1956	Juan Ramón Jiménez	Spain	poetry
1957	Albert Camus	France	prose fiction, drama
1958	Boris L. Pasternak (declined)	USSR	prose fiction, poetry
1959	Salvatore Quasimodo	Italy	poetry
1960	Saint-John Perse	France	poetry
1961	Ivo Andric	Yugoslavia	prose fiction
1962	John Steinbeck	US	prose fiction
1963	George Seferis	Greece	poetry
1964	Jean-Paul Sartre (declined)	France	philosophy, drama
1965	Mikhail A. Sholokhov	USSR	prose fiction
1966	S.Y. Agnon	Israel	prose fiction
	Nelly Sachs	Sweden	poetry
1967	Miguel Ángel Asturias	Guatemala	prose fiction
1968	Yasunari Kawabata	Japan	prose fiction
1969	Samuel Beckett	Ireland	prose fiction, drama
1970	Aleksandr I. Solzhenitsyn	USSR	prose fiction
1971	Pablo Neruda	Chile	poetry
1972	Heinrich Böll	W.Ger.	prose fiction
1973	Patrick White	Australia	prose fiction
1974	Eyvind Johnson	Sweden	prose fiction
	Harry Martinson	Sweden	prose fiction, poetry
1975	Eugenio Montale	Italy	poetry
1976	Saul Bellow	US	prose fiction
1977	Vicente Aleixandre	Spain	poetry
1978	Isaac Bashevis Singer	US	prose fiction
1979	Odysseus Elytis	Greece	poetry
1980	Czeslaw Milosz	US	poetry
1981	Elias Canetti	Bulgaria	prose
1982	Gabriel García Márquez	Colombia	prose fiction, journalism, social criticism
1983	Sir William Golding	UK	prose fiction
1984	Jaroslav Seifert	Czechoslovakia	poetry
1985	Claude Simon	France	prose fiction
1986	Wole Soyinka	Nigeria	drama, poetry
1987	Joseph Brodsky	US	poetry, prose
1988	Naguib Mahfouz	Egypt	prose fiction
1989	Camilo José Cela	Spain	prose fiction
1990	Octavio Paz	Mexico	poetry, prose
1991	Nadine Gordimer	South Africa	prose fiction
1992	Derek Walcott	St. Lucia	poetry
1993	Toni Morrison	US	prose fiction
1994	Kenzaburo Oe	Japan	prose fiction
1995	Seamus Heaney	Ireland	poetry
1996	Wislawa Szymborska	Poland	poetry
1997	Dario Fo	Italy	drama
1998	José Saramago	Portugal	prose fiction
1999	Günter Grass	Germany	prose fiction
2000	Gao Xingjian	France	prose fiction, drama
2001	Sir V.S. Naipaul	UK	prose fiction
2002	Imre Kertész	Hungary	prose fiction
2003	J.M. Coetzee	South Africa	prose fiction
2004	Elfriede Jelinek	Austria	prose fiction, drama

Peace

YEAR	WINNER(S)	COUNTRY
1901	Henri Dunant	Switzerland
	Frédéric Passy	France
1902	Élie Ducommun	Switzerland
	Charles-Albert Gobat	Switzerland
1903	Sir Randal Cremer	UK
1904	Institute of International Law	(founded 1873)
1905	Bertha, Freifrau von Suttner	Austria-Hungary
1906	Theodore Roosevelt	US
1907	Ernesto Teodoro Moneta	Italy
	Louis Renault	France
1908	Klas Pontus Arnoldson	Sweden
	Fredrik Bajer	Denmark
1909	Auguste-Marie-François Beernaert	Belgium
	Paul-H.-B. d'Estournelles de Constant	France
1910	International Peace Bureau	(founded 1891)
1911	Tobias Michael Carel Asser	Netherlands
	Alfred Hermann Fried	Austria-Hungary
1912	Elihu Root	US
1913	Henri-Marie Lafontaine	Belgium
1917	International Committee of the Red Cross	(founded 1863)
1919	Woodrow Wilson	US
1920	Léon Bourgeois	France
1921	Karl Hjalmar Branting	Sweden
	Christian Lous Lange	Norway
1922	Fridtjof Nansen	Norway
1925	Sir Austen Chamberlain	UK
	Charles G. Dawes	US
1926	Aristide Briand	France
	Gustav Stresemann	Germany
1927	Ferdinand-Édouard Buisson	France
	Ludwig Quidde	Germany
1929	Frank B. Kellogg	US
1930	Nathan Söderblom	Sweden
1931	Jane Addams	US
	Nicholas Murray Butler	US
1933	Sir Norman Angell	UK
1934	Arthur Henderson	UK
1935	Carl von Ossietzky	Germany
1936	Carlos Saavedra Lamas	Argentina
1937	Robert Gascoyne-Cecil, 1st Viscount Cecil (of Chelwood)	UK
1938	Nansen International Office for Refugees	(founded 1931)
1944	International Committee of the Red Cross	(founded 1863)
1945	Cordell Hull	US
1946	Emily Greene Balch	US
	John R. Mott	US
1947	American Friends Service Committee	US
	Friends Service Council (FSC)	UK
1949	John Boyd Orr, Baron Boyd-Orr of Brechin Mearns	UK
1950	Ralph Bunche	US
1951	Léon Jouhaux	France
1952	Albert Schweitzer	Alsace
1953	George C. Marshall	US
1954	Office of the United Nations High Commissioner for Refugees	(founded 1951)
1957	Lester B. Pearson	Canada

YEAR	WINNER(S)	COUNTRY
1958	Dominique Pire	Belgium
1959	Philip John Noel-Baker, Baron Noel-Baker (of the City of Derby)	UK
1960	Albert John Luthuli	South Africa
1961	Dag Hammarskjöld	Sweden
1962	Linus Pauling	US
1963	International Committee of the Red Cross	(founded 1863)
	League of Red Cross Societies	
1964	Martin Luther King, Jr.	US
1965	United Nations Children's Fund	(founded 1946)
1968	René Cassin	France
1969	International Labour Organisation	(founded 1919)
1970	Norman Ernest Borlaug	US
1971	Willy Brandt	West Germany
1973	Henry Kissinger	US
	Le Duc Tho (declined)	North Vietnam
1974	Seán MacBride	Ireland
	Eisaku Sato	Japan
1975	Andrey Dmitriyevich Sakharov	USSR
1976	Mairéad Corrigan	Northern Ireland
	Betty Williams	Northern Ireland
1977	Amnesty International	(founded 1961)
1978	Menachem Begin	Israel
	Anwar el-Sadat	Egypt
1979	Mother Teresa	India
1980	Adolfo Pérez Esquivel	Argentina
1981	Office of the United Nations High Commissioner for Refugees	(founded 1951)
1982	Alfonso García Robles	Mexico
	Alva Myrdal	Sweden
1983	Lech Walesa	Poland
1984	Desmond Tutu	South Africa
1985	International Physicians for the Prevention of Nuclear War	(founded 1980)
1986	Elie Wiesel	US
1987	Oscar Arias Sánchez	Costa Rica
1988	United Nations Peace-keeping Forces	
1989	Dalai Lama	Tibet
1990	Mikhail Gorbachev	USSR
1991	Aung San Suu Kyi	Myanmar
1992	Rigoberta Menchú	Guatemala
1993	F.W. de Klerk	South Africa
	Nelson Mandela	South Africa
1994	Yasir 'Arafat	Palestinian
	Shimon Peres	Israel
	Yitzhak Rabin	Israel
1995	Pugwash Conferences	(founded 1957)
	Joseph Rotblat	UK
1996	Carlos Filipe Ximenes Belo	Timorese
	José Ramos-Horta	Timorese
1997	International Campaign to Ban Landmines	(founded 1992)
	Jody Williams	US
1998	John Hume	Northern Ireland

Peace (continued)

YEAR	WINNER(S)	COUNTRY	YEAR	WINNER(S)	COUNTRY
	David Trimble	Northern Ireland	2003	Shirin Ebadi	Iran
			2004	Wangari Maathai	Kenya
1999	Doctors Without Borders	(founded 1971)			
2000	Kim Dae Jung	South Korea			
2001	Kofi Annan	Ghana			
2002	Jimmy Carter	US			

Economics

YEAR	WINNER(S)	COUNTRY	ACHIEVEMENT
1969	Ragnar Frisch Jan Tinbergen	Norway Neth.	work in econometrics
1970	Paul Samuelson	US	work in scientific analysis of economic theory
1971	Simon Kuznets	US	extensive research on the economic growth of nations
1972	Kenneth J. Arrow Sir John R. Hicks	US UK	contributions to general economic equilibrium theory and welfare theory
1973	Wassily Leontief	US	input-output analysis
1974	Friedrich von Hayek Gunnar Myrdal	UK Sweden	pioneering analysis of the interdependence of economic, social, and institutional phenomena
1975	Leonid V. Kantorovich Tjalling C. Koopmans	USSR US	contributions to the theory of optimum allocation of resources
1976	Milton Friedman	US	consumption analysis, monetary theory, and economic stabilization
1977	James Edward Meade Bertil Ohlin	UK Sweden	contributions to theory of international trade
1978	Herbert A. Simon	US	decision-making processes in economic organizations
1979	Sir Arthur Lewis Theodore W. Schultz	UK US	analyses of economic processes in developing nations
1980	Lawrence Robert Klein	US	development and analysis of empirical models of business fluctuations
1981	James Tobin	US	portfolio selection theory of investment
1982	George J. Stigler	US	economic effects of governmental regulation
1983	Gerard Debreu	US	mathematical proof of supply and demand theory
1984	Sir Richard Stone	UK	development of national income accounting system
1985	Franco Modigliani	US	analyses of household savings and financial markets
1986	James M. Buchanan	US	public-choice theory bridging economics and political science
1987	Robert Merton Solow	US	contributions to the theory of economic growth
1988	Maurice Allais	France	contributions to the theory of markets and efficient use of resources
1989	Trygve Haavelmo	Norway	development of statistical techniques for economic forecasting
1990	Harry M. Markowitz Merton H. Miller William F. Sharpe	US US US	study of financial markets and investment decision making
1991	Ronald Coase	US	application of economic principles to the study of law
1992	Gary S. Becker	US	application of economic theory to social sciences
1993	Robert William Fogel Douglass C. North	US US	contributions to economic history
1994	John C. Harsanyi John F. Nash Reinhard Selten	US US Germany	development of game theory
1995	Robert E. Lucas, Jr.	US	incorporation of rational expectations in macroeconomic theory
1996	James A. Mirrlees William Vickrey	UK US	contributions to theory of incentives under conditions of asymmetric information
1997	Robert C. Merton Myron S. Scholes	US US	method for determining the value of stock options and other derivatives
1998	Amartya Sen	India	contribution to welfare economics
1999	Robert A. Mundell	Canada	analysis of optimum currency areas and of policy under different exchange rate regimes
2000	James J. Heckman Daniel L. McFadden	US US	development of methods of statistical analysis of individual and household behavior
2001	George A. Akerlof A. Michael Spence Joseph E. Stiglitz	US US US	analyses of markets with asymmetric information

Economics (continued)

YEAR	WINNER(S)	COUNTRY	ACHIEVEMENT
2002	Daniel Kahneman	US, Israel	integration of psychological research into economics, particularly concerning decision-making under circumstances of uncertainty
	Vernon L. Smith	US	establishment of laboratory experiments for empirical economic analysis, particularly in the area of alternative market mechanisms
2003	Robert F. Engle	US	methods of analysis of economic time series with time-varying volatility
	Clive W.J. Granger	UK	methods of analysis of economic time series with common trends
2004	Finn E. Kydland	Norway	} macroeconomic analysis of time consistency of economic policy and the driving forces behind business cycles
	Edward C. Prescott	US	

Special Achievement Awards

Templeton Prize Winners

Formerly the Templeton Prize for Progress in Religion, the Templeton Prize for Progress Toward Research or Discoveries about Spiritual Realities was established in 1972 by American-born British businessman and philanthropist Sir John Templeton. It recognizes the diversity of and rewards advancement in the ideas and perceptions of divinity. Each year an international interfaith group of judges chooses a winner from any of the world's religions. Award amount: £795,000 (about $1.5 million). Templeton Prize Web site: <www.templetonprize.org>

YEAR	NAME	FIELD
1973	Mother Teresa	founder, Missionaries of Charity
1974	Brother Roger	founder, Taizé Community
1975	Sir Sarvepalli Radhakrishnan	president of India, 1962–67
1976	Leon Joseph Cardinal Suenens	pioneer, Charismatic Renewal Movement
1977	Chiara Lubich	founder, Focolare Movement
1978	Thomas F. Torrance	educator, writer on religion and science
1979	Nikkyo Niwano	founder, Rissho Kosei-Kai
1980	Ralph Wendell Burhoe	founder and editor, Zygon, Journal of Religion and Science
1981	Dame Cicely Saunders	founder, Hospice and Palliative Care Movement
1982	Billy Graham	Christian evangelist
1983	Aleksandr Solzhenitsyn	writer, dissident
1984	Michael Bourdeaux	scholar, religious freedom activist
1985	Sir Alister Hardy	scientist, educator
1986	James McCord	chancellor, Center of Theological Inquiry; president, Princeton Theological Seminary
1987	Stanley L. Jaki	Benedictine monk, professor of astrophysics
1988	Inamullah Khan	interfaith peace activist; founder, Modern World Muslim Congress
1989	Lord George MacLeod	founder, Iona Community
	Carl Friedrich von Weizsäcker	physics and theology scholar
1990	Baba Amte	social activist, philanthropist
	L. Charles Birch	natural scientist
1991	Lord Immanuel Jakobovits	Chief Rabbi of Great Britain and the Commonwealth, 1967–91
1992	Kyung-Chik Han	founder, Young Nak Presbyterian Church
1993	Charles W. Colson	prison ministry founder
1994	Michael Novak	theologian, writer on theology and economics
1995	Paul Charles William Davies	mathematical physicist
1996	William R. Bright	founder, Campus Crusade for Christ
1997	Pandurang Shastri Athavale	founder, swadhyaya self-study
1998	Sir Sigmund Sternberg	philanthropist, businessman
1999	Ian Graeme Barbour	technology ethicist
2000	Freeman J. Dyson	physicist, social activist
2001	Arthur Peacocke	founder, Society of Ordained Scientists
2002	John C. Polkinghorne	Anglican priest, mathematical physicist
2003	Holmes Rolston III	Presbyterian minister, environmental ethicist
2004	George Ellis	cosmologist, scholar of the relationship between science and faith
2005	Charles Townes	physicist, proponent of exploring commonalities between science and religion

Congressional Gold Medal

Individuals, institutions, or events of distinguished achievement are honored by the Congressional Gold Medal. The medal was first awarded in 1776, and 132 others have since been given out. Early medals went primarily to military figures; beginning in the mid-19th century, they were given to a wide variety of people. Past recipients include George Washington, Zachary Taylor, the Wright Brothers, inventor Thomas Edison, entertainer Bob Hope, singers Marion Anderson and Frank Sinatra, Queen Beatrix I of The Netherlands, human rights activist Elie Wiesel, South African President Nelson Mandela, cartoonist Charles M. Schulz, and the Navajo code talkers of World War II. In 2004 Congress awarded the medal to to civil rights advocates Reverend Dr. Martin Luther King, Jr., and Coretta Scott King.

Did you know? The title role in *Dirty Harry* (1971) was offered to Frank Sinatra, Steve McQueen, John Wayne, and Paul Newman before finally being accepted by Clint Eastwood.

The Kennedy Center Honors

The Kennedy Center Honors are bestowed annually by the John F. Kennedy Center for the Performing Arts in Washington DC. First conferred in 1978, the honors salute five artists each year for lifetime achievement in the performing arts and are celebrated by a televised gala in December. Web site: <www.kennedy-center.org/programs/specialevents/honors/>.

YEAR	NAME	FIELD
1978	Marian Anderson	opera singer
	Fred Astaire	dancer, actor
	George Balanchine	choreographer
	Richard Rodgers	composer
	Arthur Rubenstein	pianist
1979	Aaron Copland	composer
	Ella Fitzgerald	singer
	Henry Fonda	actor
	Martha Graham	dancer, choreographer
	Tennessee Williams	playwright
1980	Leonard Bernstein	conductor
	James Cagney	actor
	Agnes de Mille	dancer, choreographer
	Lynn Fontanne	actress
	Leontyne Price	opera singer
1981	Count Basie	jazz pianist
	Cary Grant	actor
	Helen Hayes	actress
	Jerome Robbins	dancer, choreographer
	Rudolf Serkin	pianist
1982	George Abbott	theater producer, director, writer
	Lillian Gish	actress
	Benny Goodman	swing musician
	Gene Kelly	dancer, actor
	Eugene Ormandy	conductor
1983	Katherine Dunham	dancer, choreographer
	Elia Kazan	theater and film director
	Frank Sinatra	singer, actor
	James Stewart	actor
	Virgil Thomson	composer, music critic
1984	Lena Horne	singer, actress
	Danny Kaye	actor, comedian
	Gian Carlo Menotti	composer
	Arthur Miller	playwright
	Isaac Stern	violinist

YEAR	NAME	FIELD
1985	Merce Cunningham	dancer, choreographer
	Irene Dunne	actress
	Bob Hope	entertainer, actor
	Alan Jay Lerner	playwright, lyricist
	Frederick Loewe	composer
	Beverly Sills	opera singer
1986	Lucille Ball	actress
	Ray Charles	soul musician
	Hume Cronyn	actor
	Jessica Tandy	actress
	Yehudi Menuhin	violinist
	Antony Tudor	choreographer
1987	Perry Como	singer
	Bette Davis	actress
	Sammy Davis, Jr.	singer, dancer, entertainer
	Nathan Milstein	violinist
	Alwin Nikolais	choreographer
1988	Alvin Ailey	dancer, choreographer
	George Burns	actor, comedian
	Myrna Loy	actress
	Alexander Schneider	violinist, conductor
	Roger L. Stevens	arts administrator
1989	Harry Belafonte	folk singer, actor
	Claudette Colbert	actress
	Alexandra Danilova	ballet dancer
	Mary Martin	actress, singer
	William Schuman	composer
1990	Dizzy Gillespie	jazz musician
	Katharine Hepburn	actress
	Risë Stevens	opera singer
	Jule Styne	composer
	Billy Wilder	film director
1991	Roy Acuff	country musician
	Betty Comden	theater and film writer
	Adolph Green	theater and film writer
	Fayard Nicholas	dancer

The Kennedy Center Honors (continued)

YEAR	NAME	FIELD
1991 (cont.)	Harold Nicholas	dancer
	Gregory Peck	actor
	Robert Shaw	choral and orchestral conductor
1992	Lionel Hampton	swing musician
	Paul Newman	actor
	Joanne Woodward	actress
	Ginger Rogers	dancer, actress
	Mstislav Rostropovich	musician, conductor
	Paul Taylor	dancer, choreographer
1993	Johnny Carson	television entertainer
	Arthur Mitchell	dancer, choreographer
	George Solti	conductor
	Stephen Sondheim	composer, lyricist
	Marion Williams	gospel singer
1994	Kirk Douglas	actor
	Aretha Franklin	soul singer
	Morton Gould	composer
	Harold Prince	theater director, producer
	Pete Seeger	folk musician
1995	Jacques d'Amboise	dancer, choreographer
	Marilyn Horne	opera singer
	B.B. King	blues musician
	Sidney Poitier	actor
	Neil Simon	playwright
1996	Edward Albee	playwright
	Benny Carter	jazz musician
	Johnny Cash	country musician
	Jack Lemmon	actor
	Maria Tallchief	ballet dancer
1997	Lauren Bacall	actress
	Bob Dylan	singer, songwriter
	Charlton Heston	actor
	Jessye Norman	opera singer
	Edward Villella	dancer, choreographer
1998	Bill Cosby	actor, comedian
	Fred Ebb and John Kander	lyricist and composer
	Willie Nelson	country musician

YEAR	NAME	FIELD
1998 (cont.)	André Previn	pianist, composer, conductor
	Shirley Temple Black	actress
1999	Victor Borge	pianist, comedian
	Sean Connery	actor
	Judith Jamison	dancer, choreographer
	Jason Robards	actor
	Stevie Wonder	musician
2000	Mikhail Baryshnikov	dancer
	Chuck Berry	musician
	Plácido Domingo	opera singer
	Clint Eastwood	actor, director
	Angela Lansbury	actress
2001	Julie Andrews	actress
	Van Cliburn	pianist
	Quincy Jones	music producer, composer
	Jack Nicholson	actor
	Luciano Pavarotti	opera singer
2002	James Earl Jones	actor
	James Levine	conductor
	Chita Rivera	musical theater performer
	Paul Simon	singer
	Elizabeth Taylor	actress
	Chuck Berry	musician
	Plácido Domingo	opera singer
	Clint Eastwood	film actor, director
	Angela Lansbury	actress
2003	James Brown	musician
	Carol Burnett	actress
	Loretta Lynn	musician
	Mike Nichols	director
	Itzhak Perlman	musician
2004	Warren Beatty	film actor, director
	Ossie Davis and Ruby Dee	actors, writers, producers
	Elton John	musician
	Joan Sutherland	opera singer
	John Williams	composer

The National Medal of Arts

The National Medal of Arts, awarded annually since 1985 by the National Endowment for the Arts (NEA) and the president of the United States, honors artists and art patrons for remarkable contributions to American arts. As many as 12 medals may be given out each year. Both the NEA and the president choose candidates for the award, and the winners are selected by the president. Web site: <www.nea.gov/honors/medals/medalists_year.html>.

YEAR	NAME	FIELD
1985	Elliott Carter, Jr.	composer
	Ralph Ellison	writer
	José Ferrer	actor
	Martha Graham	dancer, choreographer
	Louise Nevelson	sculptor
	Georgia O'Keeffe	painter
	Leontyne Price	opera singer
	Dorothy Buffum Chandler	patron
	Lincoln Kirstein	patron
	Paul Mellon	patron
	Alice Tully	patron
	Hallmark Cards, Inc.	patron

YEAR	NAME	FIELD
1986	Marian Anderson	opera singer
	Frank Capra	film director
	Aaron Copland	composer
	Willem de Kooning	painter
	Agnes de Mille	dancer, choreographer
	Eva Le Gallienne	actress, theater producer
	Alan Lomax	ethnomusicologist
	Lewis Mumford	architectural critic, historian
	Eudora Welty	writer
	Dominique de Menil	patron
	Exxon Corporation	patron
	Seymour H. Knox	patron

The National Medal of Arts (continued)

YEAR	NAME	FIELD
1987	Romare Bearden	painter
	Ella Fitzgerald	singer
	Howard Nemerov	writer, scholar
	Alwin Nikolais	choreographer
	Isamu Noguchi	sculptor
	William Schuman	composer
	Robert Penn Warren	writer
	J.W. Fisher	patron
	Armand Hammer	patron
	Sydney and Frances Lewis	patrons
1988	Saul Bellow	writer
	Helen Hayes	actress
	Gordon Parks	photographer, writer
	I.M. Pei	architect
	Jerome Robbins	dancer, choreographer
	Rudolf Serkin	pianist
	Virgil Thomson	composer, music critic
	Sydney J. Freedberg	art historian, museum curator
	Roger L. Stevens	arts administrator
	Brooke Astor	patron
	Francis Goelet	patron
	Obert C. Tanner	patron
1989	Leopold Adler	historic preservationist, civic leader
	Katherine Dunham	dancer, choreographer
	Alfred Eisenstaedt	photojournalist
	Martin Friedman	museum director
	Leigh Gerdine	civic leader, patron
	Dizzy Gillespie	jazz musician
	Walker Kirtland Hancock	sculptor
	Vladimir Horowitz[1]	pianist
	Czeslaw Milosz	writer
	Robert Motherwell	painter
	John Updike	writer
	Dayton Hudson Corporation	patron
1990	George Abbott	theater producer, director, writer
	Hume Cronyn	actor, director
	Jessica Tandy	actress
	Merce Cunningham	dancer, choreographer
	Jasper Johns	painter, sculptor
	Jacob Lawrence	painter
	B.B. King	blues musician
	Beverly Sills	opera singer
	Ian McHarg	landscape architect
	Harris & Carroll Sterling Masterson	patrons
	David Lloyd Kreeger	patron
	Southeastern Bell Corporation	patron
1991	Maurice Abravanel	conductor, music director
	Roy Acuff	country musician
	Pietro Belluschi	architect
	J. Carter Brown	museum director
	Charles "Honi" Coles	tap dancer
	John O. Crosby	opera director, conductor
	Richard Diebenkorn	painter
	Isaac Stern	violinist
	Kitty Carlisle Hart	actress, singer, arts administrator
	R. Philip Hanes, Jr.	patron

YEAR	NAME	FIELD
1991 (cont.)	Pearl Primus	choreographer, anthropologist
	Texaco Inc.	patron
1992	Marilyn Horne	opera singer
	James Earl Jones	actor
	Allan Houser	sculptor
	Minnie Pearl	Grand Ole Opry performer
	Robert Saudek	television producer, museum director
	Earl Scruggs	banjo player
	Robert Shaw	choral and orchestral conductor
	Billy Taylor	jazz pianist
	Robert Venturi and Denise Scott Brown	architects
	Robert Wise	film director
	AT&T	patron
	Lila Wallace–Reader's Digest Fund	patron
1993	Cabell "Cab" Calloway	jazz musician
	Ray Charles	soul musician
	Bess Lomax Hawes	folklorist, musician
	Stanley Kunitz	poet
	Robert Merrill	opera singer
	Arthur Miller	playwright
	Robert Rauschenberg	painter
	Lloyd Richards	theater director
	William Styron	writer
	Paul Taylor	dancer, choreographer
	Billy Wilder	film director, producer, writer
	Walter and Leonore Annenberg	patrons
1994	Harry Belafonte	folk singer, actor
	Dave Brubeck	jazz musician
	Celia Cruz	salsa singer
	Dorothy DeLay	violin instructor
	Julie Harris	actress
	Erick Hawkins	dancer, choreographer
	Gene Kelly	dancer, actor
	Pete Seeger	folk musician
	Wayne Thiebaud	painter
	Richard Wilbur	poet
	Young Audiences	arts organization
	Catherine Filene Shouse	patron
1995	Licia Albanese	opera singer
	Gwendolyn Brooks	poet
	Ossie Davis and Ruby Dee	actors
	David Diamond	composer
	James Ingo Freed	architect
	Bob Hope	entertainer
	Roy Lichtenstein	painter
	Arthur Mitchell	dancer, choreographer
	William S. Monroe	bluegrass musician
	Urban Gateways	arts education organization
	B. Gerald and Iris Cantor	patrons
1996	Edward Albee	playwright
	Sarah Caldwell	opera conductor, producer
	Harry Callahan	photographer
	Zelda Fichandler	theater founder, director

The National Medal of Arts (continued)

YEAR	NAME	FIELD
1996 (cont.)	Eduardo "Lalo" Guerrero	Chicano musician
	Lionel Hampton	swing musician
	Bella Lewitzky	dancer, choreographer
	Robert Redford	actor, film director
	Maurice Sendak	illustrator, writer
	Stephen Sondheim	composer, lyricist
	Boys Choir of Harlem	youth performance group
	Vera List	patron
1997	Louise Bourgeois	sculptor
	Betty Carter	jazz singer
	Daniel Urban Kiley	landscape architect
	Angela Lansbury	actress
	James Levine	opera conductor, pianist
	Tito Puente	jazz and mambo musician
	Jason Robards	actor
	Edward Villella	dancer, choreographer
	Doc Watson	folk and country musician
	MacDowell Colony	artists' colony
	Agnes Gund	patron
1998	Jacques d'Amboise	dancer, choreographer
	Antoine "Fats" Domino	rock-and-roll musician
	Ramblin' Jack Elliott	folk musician
	Frank O. Gehry	architect
	Agnes Martin	painter
	Gregory Peck	actor
	Roberta Peters	opera singer
	Philip Roth	writer
	Gwen Verdon	actress, dancer
	Steppenwolf Theatre Company	arts organization
	Sara Lee Corporation	patron
	Barbara Handman	patron
1999	Aretha Franklin	soul singer
	Michael Graves	architect, designer
	Odetta	folk singer
	Norman Lear	television producer, writer
	Rosetta LeNoire	actress, theater founder
	Harvey Lichtenstein	arts administrator
	Lydia Mendoza	Tejano musician
	George Segal	sculptor
	Maria Tallchief	ballet dancer
	The Juilliard School	performing arts school
	Irene Diamond	patron
2000	Maya Angelou	poet, writer
	Eddy Arnold	country musician
	Mikhail Baryshnikov	dancer, dance company director
	Benny Carter	jazz musician
	Chuck Close	painter

YEAR	NAME	FIELD
2000 (cont.)	Horton Foote	dramatist
	Claes Oldenburg	sculptor
	Itzhak Perlman	violinist
	Harold Prince	theater director, producer
	Barbra Streisand	singer, actress, film director
	Lewis Manilow	patron
	NPR Cultural Programming Division	broadcaster
2001	Alvin Ailey Dance Foundation	modern dance company and school
	Rudolfo Anaya	writer
	Johnny Cash	country musician
	Kirk Douglas	actor
	Helen Frankenthaler	painter
	Judith Jamison	dancer, choreographer
	Yo-Yo Ma	cellist
	Mike Nichols	theater and film director
2002	Florence Knoll Bassett	designer, architect
	Trisha Brown	dancer, choreographer
	Philippe de Montebello	museum director
	Uta Hagen	actress, educator
	Lawrence Halprin	landscape architect
	Al Hirschfeld[1]	artist, caricaturist
	George Jones	singer, songwriter
	Ming Cho Lee	painter, stage designer
	William "Smokey" Robinson, Jr.	singer, songwriter
2003	*Austin City Limits*	television show
	Beverly Cleary	children's book author
	Rafe Esquith	arts educator
	Suzanne Farrell	dancer, artistic director, arts educator
	Buddy Guy	blues musician
	Ron Howard	actor, director, writer, producer
	The Mormon Tabernacle Choir	choir
	Leonard Slatkin	conductor
	George Strait	singer, songwriter
	Tommy Tune	director, actor
2004	Andrew W. Mellon Foundation	arts patron
	Ray Bradbury	writer
	Carlisle Floyd	opera composer
	Frederick "Rick" Hart[1]	sculptor
	Anthony Hecht[1]	poet
	John Ruthven	painter
	Vincent Scully	architectural historian
	Twyla Tharp	dancer, choreographer

[1]Awarded posthumously.

 **Did you know?** Barbra Streisand was the first person ever to receive a Grammy, an Emmy, an Oscar, and a Tony. She won her first Grammy of ten in 1964, her first Emmy of six in 1965, her first Oscar of two in 1969, and her one Tony in 1970.

American Academy of Arts and Letters

Each year the American Academy of Arts and Letters, a 250-member organization founded in 1898, elects new members to fill vacancies in the academy's membership. Election to the academy is considered the country's highest formal recognition of artistic merit. The members elected in 2005 were as follows: ▶ **Art**, Maya Lin, Laurie Olin, James Stewart Polshek, Cindy Sherman, and Kiki Smith; ▶ **Literature**, Tony Kushner and Rosanna Warren; ▶ **Music**, T.J.

Anderson. The academy also confers some two dozen awards for excellence in the fields of art, music, musical theater, literature, and architecture. Of the prizes, the Academy Awards in each field are the most prestigious. Winners receive $7,500; music winners receive an additional $7,500 to be used for the recording of a musical piece.

Web site: <www.artsandletters.org>

National Humanities Medal

The National Humanities Medal (originally known as the Charles Frankel Prize, 1988–96) is awarded by the National Endowment for the Humanities for notable contributions to Americans' understanding of and involvement with the humanities. As many as 12 medals may be conferred each year. The recipients for 2004 were Marva Collins, educator; Gertrude Himmelfarb, author; Hilton

Kramer, author and art critic; Madeleine L'Engle, author; Harvey Mansfield, scholar; John Searle, philosopher; Shelby Steele, scholar; and the United States Capitol Historical Society.

Web site: <www.neh.gov/whoweare/awards.html>

The Spingarn Medal

The National Association for the Advancement of Colored People (NAACP) presents the medal for distinguished achievement among African Americans. The medal is named for early NAACP activist Joel E. Spingarn.

YEAR	NAME	FIELD
1915	Ernest Everett Just	zoologist, marine biologist
1916	Charles Young	army officer
1917	Harry Thacker Burleigh	singer, composer
1918	William Stanley Braithwaite	poet, literary critic
1919	Archibald Henry Grimké	lawyer, diplomat, social activist
1920	W.E.B. Du Bois (William Edward Burghardt Du Bois)	sociologist, social activist
1921	Charles S. Gilpin	actor
1922	Mary Burnett Talbert	civil rights activist
1923	George Washington Carver	agricultural chemist
1924	Roland Hayes	singer, composer
1925	James Weldon Johnson	writer, diplomat, anthologist
1926	Carter G. Woodson	historian
1927	Anthony Overton	businessman
1928	Charles W. Chesnutt	writer
1929	Mordecai W. Johnson	minister, university president
1930	Henry Alexander Hunt	educator, government official
1931	Richard B. Harrison	actor
1932	Robert Russa Moton	educator, civil rights leader
1933	Max Yergan	civil rights leader
1934	William T.B. Williams	educator
1935	Mary McLeod Bethune	educator, social activist
1936	John Hope	educator
1937	Walter White	civil rights leader
1938	*no medal awarded*	
1939	Marian Anderson	opera singer
1940	Louis T. Wright	surgeon, civil rights leader
1941	Richard Wright	writer
1942	A. Philip Randolph	labor and civil rights leader
1943	William H. Hastie	lawyer, judge
1944	Charles Richard Drew	surgeon, research scientist
1945	Paul Robeson	actor, singer, social activist
1946	Thurgood Marshall	lawyer, US Supreme Court justice
1947	Percy L. Julian	chemist
1948	Channing H. Tobias	civil rights leader
1949	Ralph Bunche	diplomat, scholar
1950	Charles Hamilton Houston	lawyer
1951	Mabel Keaton Staupers	nurse, social activist
1952	Harry T. Moore	civil rights activist, educator
1953	Paul R. Williams	architect
1954	Theodore K. Lawless	dermatologist, philanthropist
1955	Carl Murphy	journalist, civil rights activist
1956	Jackie Robinson (Jack Roosevelt Robinson)	baseball player
1957	Martin Luther King, Jr.	civil rights leader
1958	Daisy Bates and the Little Rock Nine	school integration activists
1959	Duke Ellington (Edward Kennedy Ellington)	jazz musician
1960	Langston Hughes	writer
1961	Kenneth Bancroft Clark	educator
1962	Robert C. Weaver	economist, government official
1963	Medgar Evers	civil rights activist
1964	Roy Wilkins	civil rights leader
1965	Leontyne Price	opera singer
1966	John H. Johnson	publisher
1967	Edward W. Brooke III	lawyer, US senator

The Spingarn Medal (continued)

YEAR	NAME	FIELD
1968	Sammy Davis, Jr.	singer, dancer, entertainer
1969	Clarence M. Mitchell, Jr.	civil rights lobbyist
1970	Jacob Lawrence	painter
1971	Leon H. Sullivan	minister, civil rights activist
1972	Gordon Parks	photographer, writer
1973	Wilson C. Riles	educator
1974	Damon Keith	lawyer, judge
1975	Hank Aaron	baseball player
1976	Alvin Ailey	dancer, choreographer
1977	Alex Haley	writer
1978	Andrew Young	politician, civil rights leader
1979	Rosa Parks	civil rights activist
1980	Rayford W. Logan	educator, writer
1981	Coleman A. Young	labor activist, politician
1982	Benjamin E. Mays	educator, minister
1983	Lena Horne	singer, actress
1984	Thomas Bradley	politician
1985	Bill Cosby	actor, comedian
1986	Benjamin L. Hooks	civil rights leader, government official
1987	Percy Ellis Sutton	civil rights activist, politician
1988	Frederick Douglass Patterson	educator

YEAR	NAME	FIELD
1989	Jesse Jackson	minister, politician, civil rights leader
1990	L. Douglas Wilder	politician
1991	Colin Powell	army general, government official
1992	Barbara Jordan	lawyer, politician
1993	Dorothy I. Height	social activist
1994	Maya Angelou	poet
1995	John Hope Franklin	historian, educator
1996	A. Leon Higginbotham	lawyer, judge, scholar
1997	Carl T. Rowan	journalist, commentator
1998	Myrlie Evers-Williams	civil rights activist
1999	Earl G. Graves	publisher
2000	Oprah Winfrey	television host, media personality
2001	Vernon E. Jordan, Jr.	lawyer, civil rights activist
2002	John Lewis	politician, civil rights activist
2003	Constance Baker Motley	judge, lawyer, civil rights activist
2004	Robert L. Carter	judge, lawyer, civil rights activist
2005	Oliver W. Hill	lawyer, civil rights activist

Science Honors

Fields Medal

The Fields Medal, officially known as the International Medal for Outstanding Discoveries in Mathematics, is granted every four years to between two and four mathematicians for outstanding or groundbreaking research. It is traditionally given to mathematicians under the age of 40. Prize: $1,500.

YEAR	NAME	BIRTHPLACE	PRIMARY RESEARCH
1936	Lars Ahlfors	Helsinki, Finland	Riemann surfaces
1936	Jesse Douglas	New York NY	Plateau problem
1950	Laurent Schwartz	Paris, France	functional analysis
1950	Atle Selberg	Langesund, Norway	number theory
1954	Kunihiko Kodaira	Tokyo, Japan	algebraic geometry
1954	Jean-Pierre Serre	Bages, France	algebraic topology
1958	Klaus Roth	Breslau, Germany	number theory
1958	René Thom	Montbéliard, France	topology
1962	Lars Hörmander	Mjällby, Sweden	partial differential equations
1962	John Milnor	Orange NJ	differential topology
1966	Michael Atiyah	London, England	topology
1966	Paul Cohen	Long Branch NJ	set theory
1966	Alexandre Grothendieck	Berlin, Germany	algebraic geometry
1966	Stephen Smale	Flint MI	topology
1970	Alan Baker	London, England	number theory
1970	Heisuke Hironaka	Yamaguchi prefecture, Japan	algebraic geometry
1970	Sergey Novikov	Gorky, Russia	topology
1970	John Thompson	Ottawa KS	group theory
1974	Enrico Bombieri	Milan, Italy	number theory
1974	David Mumford	Worth, Sussex, UK	algebraic geometry
1978	Pierre Deligne	Brussels, Belgium	algebraic geometry
1978	Charles Fefferman	Washington DC	classical analysis
1978	Gregory Margulis	Moscow, Russia	Lie groups
1978	Daniel Quillen	Orange NJ	algebraic K-theory
1983	Alain Connes	Darguignan, France	operator theory
1983	William Thurston	Washington DC	topology
1983	Shing-Tung Yau	Swatow, China	differential geometry

Fields Medal (continued)

YEAR	NAME	BIRTHPLACE	PRIMARY RESEARCH
1986	Simon Donaldson	Cambridge, UK	topology
1986	Gerd Faltings	Gelsenkirchen, West Germany	Mordell conjecture
1986	Michael Freedman	Los Angeles CA	Poincaré conjecture
1990	Vladimir Drinfeld	Kharkov, Ukraine	algebraic geometry
1990	Vaughan Jones	Gisborne, New Zealand	knot theory
1990	Shigefumi Mori	Nagoya, Japan	algebraic geometry
1990	Edward Witten	Baltimore MD	superstring theory
1994	Jean Bourgain	Ostend, Belgium	analysis
1994	Pierre-Louis Lions	Grasse, France	partial differential equations
1994	Jean-Christophe Yoccoz	France	dynamical systems
1994	Yefim Zelmanov	Khabarovsk, Russia	group theory
1998	Richard Borcherds	Cape Town, South Africa	mathematical physics
1998	William Gowers	Marlborough, Wiltshire, UK	functional analysis
1998	Maksim Kontsevich	Khimki, Russia	mathematical physics
1998	Curt McMullen	Berkeley CA	chaos theory
2002	Laurent Lafforgue	Antony, France	number theory and analysis
2002	Vladimir Voevodsky	Russia	algebraic geometry

Japan Prize

The Science and Technology Foundation of Japan awards the Japan Prize annually to living individuals or small groups whose achievements in science and technology have advanced knowledge and promoted human peace and prosperity. A cash award of ¥50 million (about $465,000), a certificate of merit, and a commemorative medal are also given for each prize category. Web site: <www.japanprize.jp>.

YEAR	LAUREATE	COUNTRY	AREA OF ACHIEVEMENT
1985	John R. Pierce	US	electronics and communications technologies
	Ephraim Katchalski-Katzir	Israel	basic theory of immobilized enzymes
1986	David Turnbull	US	new materials technology such as amorphous solids
	Willem J. Kolff	US	artificial organs
1987	Henry M. Beachell	US	high-yield rice
	Gurdev S. Khush	India	hardy rice
	Theodore H. Maiman	US	lasers
1988	Georges Vendryes	France	fast breeder reactor technology
	Donald A. Henderson	US	
	Isao Arita	Japan	} eradication of smallpox
	Frank Fenner	Australia	
	Luc Montagnier	France	discovery of HIV
	Robert C. Gallo	US	isolation of HIV and development of AZT
1989	Frank Sherwood Rowland	US	stratospheric ozone depletion by chlorofluorocarbons
	Elias James Corey	US	syntheses of prostaglandins and related compounds
1990	Marvin Minsky	US	Artificial Intelligence
	William Jason Morgan	US	
	Dan Peter Mckenzie	UK	} plate tectonics
	Xavier Le Pichon	France	
1991	Jacques-Louis Lions	France	analysis and control of distributed systems, applied analysis
	John Julian Wild	US	ultrasound imaging
1992	Gerhard Ertl	Germany	chemistry and physics of solid surfaces
	Ernest John Christopher Polge	UK	cryopreservation of semen and embryos in farm animals
1993	Frank Press	US	seismology and disaster science
	Kary B. Mullis	US	polymerase chain reaction
1994	William Hayward Pickering	US	space travel and unmanned space exploration
	Arvid Carlsson	Sweden	dopamine's role in mental and motor functions
1995	Nick Holonyak, Jr.	US	light emitting diodes and lasers
	Edward F. Knipling	US	pest management
1996	Charles K. Kao	Hong Kong	wide-band, low-loss optical fiber communications
	Masao Ito	Japan	cerebellum function
1997	Takashi Sugimura	Japan	} cancer
	Bruce N. Ames	US	
	Joseph F. Engelberger	US	} robotics
	Hiroyuki Yoshikawa	Japan	
1998	Leo Esaki	Japan	man-made superlattice crystals
	Jozef S. Schell	Belgium	} transgenic plants
	Marc C. E. Van Montagu	Belgium	

Japan Prize (continued)

YEAR	LAUREATE	COUNTRY	AREA OF ACHIEVEMENT
1999	W. Wesley Peterson	US	algebraic coding theory
	Jack L. Strominger	US	human histocompatibility
	Don C. Wiley	US	antigens and their bound peptides
2000	Ian L. McHarg	US	ecological city planning and land use evaluation
	Kimishige Ishizaka	Japan	Immunoglobulin E and IgE-mediated allergic reactions
2001	John B. Goodenough	US	environmentally benign electrode materials for rechargeable lithium batteries
	Timothy R. Parsons	Canada	fishery resources and marine environment conservation
2002	Timothy John Berners-Lee	UK	World Wide Web
	Anne McLaren	UK	study and manipulation of early-
	Andrzej K. Tarkowski	Poland	stage mammalian embryos
2003	Benoit B. Mandelbrot	France	fractals
	James A. Yorke	US	concept of chaos in complex systems
	Seiji Ogawa	Japan	magnetic resonance imaging
2004	Kenichi Honda	Japan	photochemical
	Akira Fujishima	Japan	catalysis
	Keith Sainsbury	New Zealand	sustainable usage of seabed shelf ecosystems
	John H. Lawton	UK	conservation of biodiversity
2005	Makoto Nagao	Japan	contributions to natural language processing and intelligent image processing
	Masatoshi Takeichi	Japan	contributions to clarifying the molecular mechanisms
	Erkki Ruoslahti	US	of cell adhesion

National Medal of Science

The National Medal of Science was established by Congress in 1959. Awarded annually since 1962 by the National Science Foundation and the president of the United States, it recognizes notable achievements in mathematics, engineering, and the physical, natural, and social sciences. A presidentially appointed committee selects the winners from a pool of nominees. Medals have been given out in the second year after the date of the award: e.g. 2003 medals were awarded in March 2005. For more information, see the National Science Foundation Web site at <www.nsf.gov/nsb/awards/nms/medal.htm>.

YEAR	NAME	FIELD
1962	Theodore von Karman	aerospace engineering
1963	Luis W. Alvarez	physics
	Vannevar Bush	electrical engineering
	John Robinson Pierce	communications engineering
	Cornelius Barnardus van Niel	biology
	Norbert Wiener	mathematics
1964	Roger Adams	chemistry
	Othmar Herman Ammann	bridge design engineering
	Theodosius Dobzhansky	genetics
	Charles Stark Draper	aerospace engineering
	Solomon Lefschetz	mathematics
	Neal Elgar Miller	psychology
	H. Marston Morse	mathematics
	Marshall Warren Nirenberg	biochemistry
	Julian Seymour Schwinger	physics
	Harold C. Urey	chemistry
	Robert Burns Woodward	chemistry
1965	John Bardeen	physics
	Peter J.W. Debye	physical chemistry
	Hugh L. Dryden	physics

YEAR	NAME	FIELD
1965 (cont.)	Clarence L. Johnson	aerospace engineering
	Leon M. Lederman	physics
	Warren K. Lewis	chemical engineering
	Francis Peyton Rous	pathology
	William W. Rubey	geology
	George Gaylord Simpson	paleontology
	Donald D. Van Slyke	chemistry
	Oscar Zariski	mathematics
1966	Jacob A.B. Bjerknes	meteorology
	Subrahmanyan Chandrasekhar	astrophysics
	Henry Eyring	chemistry
	Edward F. Knipling	entomology
	Fritz Albert Lipmann	biochemistry
	John Willard Milnor	mathematics
	William C. Rose	biochemistry
	Claude E. Shannon	mathematics, electrical engineering
	John H. Van Vleck	physics
	Sewall Wright	genetics
	Vladimir Kosma Zworykin	electrical engineering
1967	Jesse W. Beams	physics
	Francis Birch	geophysics
	Gregory Breit	physics
	Paul Joseph Cohen	mathematics
	Kenneth S. Cole	biophysics

National Medal of Science (continued)

YEAR	NAME	FIELD
1967 (cont.)	Louis P. Hammett	chemistry
	Harry F. Harlow	psychology
	Michael Heidelberger	immunology
	George B. Kistiakowsky	chemistry
	Edwin Herbert Land	physics
	Igor I. Sikorsky	aircraft design
	Alfred H. Sturtevant	genetics
1968	Horace A. Barker	biochemistry
	Paul D. Bartlett	chemistry
	Bernard B. Brodie	pharmacology
	Detlev W. Bronk	biophysics
	J. Presper Eckert, Jr.	engineering, computer science
	Herbert Friedman	astrophysics
	Jay L. Lush	livestock genetics
	Nathan M. Newmark	civil engineering
	Jerzy Neyman	mathematics, statistics
	Lars Onsager	chemistry
	B.F. Skinner	psychology
	Eugene Paul Wigner	mathematical physics
1969	Herbert C. Brown	chemistry
	William Feller	mathematics
	Robert J. Huebner	virology
	Jack Kilby	electrical engineering
	Ernst Mayr	biology
	Wolfgang K.H. Panofsky	physics
1970	Richard Dagobert Brauer	mathematics
	Robert H. Dicke	physics
	Barbara McClintock	genetics
	George E. Mueller	physics
	Albert Bruce Sabin	medicine, vaccine development
	Allan R. Sandage	astronomy
	John C. Slater	physics
	John Archibald Wheeler	physics
	Saul Winstein	chemistry
1971	no awards given	
1972	no awards given	
1973	Daniel I. Arnon	biochemistry
	Carl Djerassi	chemistry
	Harold E. Edgerton	electrical engineering, photography
	Maurice Ewing	geophysics
	Arie Jan Haagen-Smit	biochemistry
	Vladimir Haensel	chemical engineering
	Frederick Seitz	physics
	Earl W. Sutherland, Jr.	biochemistry
	John Wilder Tukey	statistics
	Richard T. Whitcomb	aerospace engineering
	Robert Rathbun Wilson	particle physics
1974	Nicolaas Bloembergen	physics
	Britton Chance	biophysics
	Erwin Chargaff	biochemistry
	Paul J. Flory	physical chemistry
	William A. Fowler	nuclear astrophysics
	Kurt Gödel	mathematics
	Rudolf Kompfner	physics
	James Van Gundia Neel	genetics

YEAR	NAME	FIELD
1974 (cont.)	Linus Pauling	chemistry
	Ralph Brazelton Peck	geotechnical engineering
	Kenneth Sanborn Pitzer	physical chemistry
	James Augustine Shannon	physiology
	Abel Wolman	sanitary engineering
1975	John W. Backus	computer science
	Manson Benedict	nuclear engineering
	Hans Albrecht Bethe	theoretical physics
	Shiing-shen Chern	mathematics
	George B. Dantzig	mathematics
	Hallowell Davis	physiology
	Paul Gyorgy	medicine, vitamin research
	Sterling Brown Hendricks	chemistry
	Joseph O. Hirschfelder	chemistry
	William Hayward Pickering	physics
	Lewis H. Sarett	chemistry
	Frederick Emmons Terman	electrical engineering
	Orville Alvin Vogel	research agronomy
	Wernher von Braun	aerospace engineering
	E. Bright Wilson, Jr.	chemistry
	Chien-Shiung Wu	physics
1976	Morris Cohen	materials science
	Kurt Otto Friedrichs	mathematics
	Peter C. Goldmark	communications engineering
	Samuel Abraham Goudsmit	physics
	Roger Charles Louis Guillemin	physiology
	Herbert S. Gutowsky	chemistry
	Erwin W. Mueller	physics
	Keith Roberts Porter	cell biology
	Efraim Racker	biochemistry
	Frederick D. Rossini	chemistry
	Verner E. Suomi	meteorology
	Henry Taube	chemistry
	George Eugene Uhlenbeck	physics
	Hassler Whitney	mathematics
	Edward O. Wilson	biology
1977	no awards given	
1978	no awards given	
1979	Robert H. Burris	biochemistry
	Elizabeth C. Crosby	neuroanatomy
	Joseph L. Doob	mathematics
	Richard P. Feynman	theoretical physics
	Donald E. Knuth	computer science
	Arthur Kornberg	biochemistry
	Emmett N. Leith	electrical engineering
	Herman F. Mark	chemistry
	Raymond D. Mindlin	mechanical engineering
	Robert N. Noyce	computer science
	Severo Ochoa	biochemistry
	Earl R. Parker	materials science
	Edward M. Purcell	physics
	Simon Ramo	electrical engineering
	John H. Sinfelt	chemical engineering
	Lyman Spitzer, Jr.	astrophysics
	Earl Reece Stadtman	biochemistry

National Medal of Science (continued)

YEAR	NAME	FIELD
1979 (cont.)	George Ledyard Stebbins	botany, genetics
	Victor F. Weisskopf	physics
	Paul Alfred Weiss	biology
1980	no awards given	
1981	Philip Handler	biochemistry
1982	Philip W. Anderson	physics
	Seymour Benzer	molecular biology
	Glenn W. Burton	genetics
	Mildred Cohn	biochemistry
	F. Albert Cotton	chemistry
	Edward H. Heinemann	aerospace engineering
	Donald L. Katz	chemical engineering
	Yoichiro Nambu	theoretical physics
	Marshall H. Stone	mathematics
	Gilbert Stork	organic chemistry
	Edward Teller	nuclear physics
	Charles Hard Townes	physics
1983	Howard L. Bachrach	biochemistry
	Paul Berg	biochemistry
	E. Margaret Burbidge	astronomy
	Maurice Goldhaber	physics
	Herman H. Goldstine	computer science
	William R. Hewlett	electrical engineering
	Roald Hoffmann	chemistry
	Helmut E. Landsberg	climatology
	George M. Low	aerospace engineering
	Walter H. Munk	oceanography
	George C. Pimentel	chemistry
	Frederick Reines	physics
	Wendell L. Roelofs	chemistry, entomology
	Bruno B. Rossi	astrophysics
	Berta V. Scharrer	neuroscience
	John Robert Schrieffer	physics
	Isadore M. Singer	mathematics
	John G. Trump	electrical engineering
	Richard N. Zare	chemistry
1984	no awards given	
1985	no awards given	
1986	Solomon J. Buchsbaum	physics
	Stanley Cohen	biochemistry
	Horace R. Crane	physics
	Herman Feshbach	physics
	Harry Gray	chemistry
	Donald A. Henderson	medicine, public health
	Robert Hofstadter	physics
	Peter D. Lax	mathematics
	Yuan Tseh Lee	chemistry
	Hans Wolfgang Liepmann	aerospace engineering
	T.Y. Lin	civil engineering
	Carl S. Marvel	chemistry
	Vernon B. Mountcastle	neurophysiology
	Bernard M. Oliver	electrical engineering
	George Emil Palade	cell biology
	Herbert A. Simon	social science
	Joan A. Steitz	molecular biology
	Frank H. Westheimer	chemistry
	Chen Ning Yang	theoretical physics
	Antoni Zygmund	mathematics
1987	Philip Hauge Abelson	physical chemistry

YEAR	NAME	FIELD
1987 (cont.)	Anne Anastasi	psychology
	Robert Byron Bird	chemical engineering
	Raoul Bott	mathematics
	Michael E. DeBakey	heart surgery
	Theodor O. Diener	plant pathology
	Harry Eagle	cell biology
	Walter M. Elsasser	physics
	Michael H. Freedman	mathematics
	William S. Johnson	chemistry
	Har Gobind Khorana	biochemistry
	Paul C. Lauterbur	chemistry
	Rita Levi-Montalcini	neurology
	George E. Pake	research, physics
	H. Bolton Seed	civil engineering
	George J. Stigler	economics
	Walter H. Stockmayer	chemistry
	Max Tishler	chemistry
	James Alfred Van Allen	physics
	Ernst Weber	electrical engineering
1988	William O. Baker	chemistry
	Konrad E. Bloch	biochemistry
	David Allan Bromley	physics
	Michael S. Brown	molecular genetics
	Paul C.W. Chu	physics
	Stanley N. Cohen	genetics
	Elias James Corey	chemistry
	Daniel C. Drucker	engineering education
	Milton Friedman	economics
	Joseph L. Goldstein	molecular genetics
	Ralph E. Gomory	mathematics, research
	Willis M. Hawkins	aerospace engineering
	Maurice R. Hilleman	vaccine research
	George W. Housner	earthquake engineering
	Eric Kandel	neurobiology
	Joseph B. Keller	mathematics
	Walter Kohn	physics
	Norman Foster Ramsey	physics
	Jack Steinberger	physics
	Rosalyn S. Yalow	medical physics
1989	Arnold O. Beckman	chemistry
	Richard B. Bernstein	chemistry
	Melvin Calvin	biochemistry
	Harry G. Drickamer	chemistry, physics
	Katherine Esau	botany
	Herbert E. Grier	aerospace engineering
	Viktor Hamburger	biology
	Samuel Karlin	mathematics
	Philip Leder	genetics
	Joshua Lederberg	genetics
	Saunders Mac Lane	mathematics
	Rudolph A. Marcus	chemistry
	Harden M. McConnell	chemistry
	Eugene N. Parker	theoretical astrophysics
	Robert P. Sharp	geology
	Donald C. Spencer	mathematics
	Roger Wolcott Sperry	neurobiology
	Henry M. Stommel	oceanography
	Harland G. Wood	biochemistry

National Medal of Science (continued)

YEAR	NAME	FIELD
1990	Baruj Benacerraf	pathology, immunology
	Elkan R. Blout	chemistry
	Herbert W. Boyer	biochemistry, genetics
	George F. Carrier	mathematics
	Allan MacLeod Cormack	physics
	Mildred S. Dresselhaus	physics
	Karl August Folkers	chemistry
	Nick Holonyak, Jr.	electrical engineering
	Leonid Hurwicz	economics
	Stephen Cole Kleene	mathematics
	Daniel E. Koshland, Jr.	biochemistry
	Edward B. Lewis	developmental genetics
	John McCarthy	computer science
	Edwin Mattison McMillan	nuclear physics
	David G. Nathan	pediatrics
	Robert V. Pound	physics
	Roger R.D. Revelle	oceanography
	John D. Roberts	chemistry
	Patrick Suppes	philosophy and statistics education
	E. Donnall Thomas	medicine
1991	Mary Ellen Avery	pediatrics
	Ronald Breslow	chemistry
	Alberto P. Calderon	mathematics
	Gertrude B. Elion	pharmacology
	George H. Heilmeier	electrical engineering
	Dudley R. Herschbach	chemistry
	G. Evelyn Hutchinson	zoology
	Elvin A. Kabat	immunology
	Robert W. Kates	geography
	Luna B. Leopold	hydrology, geology
	Salvador Luria	biology
	Paul A. Marks	hematology, cancer research
	George A. Miller	psychology
	Arthur L. Schawlow	physics
	Glenn T. Seaborg	nuclear chemistry
	Folke K. Skoog	botany
	H. Guyford Stever	aerospace engineering
	Edward C. Stone	physics
	Steven Weinberg	nuclear physics
	Paul C. Zamecnik	molecular biology
1992	Eleanor J. Gibson	psychology
	Allen Newell	computer science
	Calvin F. Quate	electrical engineering
	Eugene M. Shoemaker	planetary geology
	Howard E. Simmons, Jr.	chemistry
	Maxine F. Singer	biochemistry, administration
	Howard Martin Temin	virology
	John Roy Whinnery	electrical engineering
1993	Alfred Y. Cho	electrical engineering
	Donald J. Cram	chemistry
	Val Logsdon Fitch	particle physics
	Norman Hackerman	chemistry
	Martin D. Kruskal	mathematics

YEAR	NAME	FIELD
1993 (cont.)	Daniel Nathans	microbiology
	Vera C. Rubin	astronomy
	Salome G. Waelsch	molecular genetics
1994	Ray W. Clough	civil engineering
	John Cocke	computer science
	Thomas Eisner	chemical ecology
	George S. Hammond	chemistry
	Robert K. Merton	sociology
	Elizabeth F. Neufeld	biochemistry
	Albert W. Overhauser	physics
	Frank Press	geophysics, administration
1995	Thomas Robert Cech	biochemistry
	Hans Georg Dehmelt	physics
	Peter M. Goldreich	astrophysics
	Hermann A. Haus	electrical engineering
	Isabella L. Karle	chemistry
	Louis Nirenberg	mathematics
	Alexander Rich	molecular biology
	Roger N. Shepard	psychology
1996	Wallace S. Broecker	geochemistry
	Norman Davidson	chemistry, molecular biology
	James L. Flanagan	electrical engineering
	Richard M. Karp	computer science
	C. Kumar N. Patel	electrical engineering
	Ruth Patrick	limnology
	Paul Samuelson	economics
	Stephen Smale	mathematics
1997	William K. Estes	psychology
	Darleane C. Hoffman	chemistry
	Harold S. Johnston	chemistry
	Marshall N. Rosenbluth	theoretical plasma physics
	Martin Schwarzschild	astrophysics
	James Dewey Watson	genetics, biophysics
	Robert A. Weinberg	biology, cancer research
	George W. Wetherill	planetary science
	Shing-Tung Yau	mathematics
1998	Bruce N. Ames	biochemistry, cancer research
	Don L. Anderson	geophysics
	John N. Bahcall	astrophysics
	John W. Cahn	materials science
	Cathleen Synge Morawetz	mathematics
	Janet D. Rowley	medicine, cancer research
	Eli Ruckenstein	chemical engineering
	George M. Whitesides	chemistry
	William Julius Wilson	sociology
1999	David Baltimore	virology, administration
	Felix E. Browder	mathematics
	Ronald R. Coifman	mathematics
	James Watson Cronin	particle physics
	Jared Diamond	physiology
	Leo P. Kadanoff	theoretical physics
	Lynn Margulis	microbiology
	Stuart A. Rice	chemistry
	John Ross	chemistry
	Susan Solomon	atmospheric science
	Robert M. Solow	economics
	Kenneth N. Stevens	electrical engineering, speech
2000	Nancy C. Andreasen	psychiatry

National Medal of Science (continued)

YEAR	NAME	FIELD
2000 (cont.)	John D. Baldeschwieler	chemistry
	Gary S. Becker	economics
	Yuan-Cheng B. Fung	bioengineering
	Ralph F. Hirschmann	chemistry
	Willis Eugene Lamb, Jr.	physics
	Jeremiah P. Ostriker	astrophysics
	Peter H. Raven	botany
	John Griggs Thompson	mathematics
	Karen K. Uhlenbeck	mathematics
	Gilbert F. White	geography
	Carl R. Woese	microbiology
2001	Andreas Acrivos	chemical engineering
	Francisco J. Ayala	molecular biology
	George F. Bass	nautical archaeology
	Mario R. Capecchi	genetics
	Marvin L. Cohen	materials science
	Ernest R. Davidson	chemistry
	Raymond Davis, Jr.	chemistry, astrophysics
	Ann M. Graybiel	neuroscience
	Charles D. Keeling	oceanography
	Gene E. Likens	ecology
	Victor A. McKusick	medical genetics

YEAR	NAME	FIELD
2001 (cont.)	Calyampudi R. Rao	mathematics, statistics
	Gabor A. Somorjai	chemistry
	Elias M. Stein	mathematics
	Harold Varmus	virology, administration
2002	Leo L. Beranek	engineering
	John I. Brauman	chemistry
	James E. Darnell	biological sciences
	Richard L. Garwin	physical sciences
	James G. Glimm	mathematics and computer science
	W. Jason Morgan	physical sciences
	Evelyn M. Witkin	biological sciences
	Edward Witten	physical sciences
2003	J. Michael Bishop	biological sciences
	G. Brent Dalrymple	physical sciences
	Carl R. de Boor	mathematics and computer science
	Riccardo Giacconi	physical sciences
	R. Duncan Luce	behavioral and social science
	John M. Prausnitz	engineering
	Solomon H. Snyder	biological sciences
	Charles Yanofsky	biological sciences

The National Inventor of the Year Award

The National Inventor of the Year Award is given by the Intellectual Property Owners Association, a trade organization established in 1972. Patented American inventions from the preceding four years are eligible for nomination annually; runners-up receive recognition as Distinguished Inventors. The winners for 2005 were scientists Duane Burnett, John Clader, Sundeep Dugar, Brian McKittrick, and Stuart Rosenblum, part of a Schering-Plough team responsible for the discovery and development of a new treatment for reducing cholesterol levels. Award amount: $10,000.

Web site: <www.ipo.org>.

Intel Science Talent Search

The Intel Science Talent Search encourages American high school seniors to pursue careers in the sciences by awarding scholarships for outstanding science projects. Created in 1942 by Science Service, a nonprofit organization devoted to public appreciation of science, and Westinghouse Electric Corporation, the contest brings 40 finalists each year to exhibit their projects at the Science Talent Institute in Washington DC and compete for the top prizes. Since 1998 the talent search has been sponsored by Intel Corp. The highest-place winners for 2005 were **David Vigliarolo Bauer** of Bronx NY (first prize, $100,000), **Timothy Frank Credo** of Highland Park IL (second prize, $75,000), and **Kelley Harris** of Sacramento CA (third prize, $50,000).

Bauer designed a process for rapidly screening for exposure to toxic agents that affect the nervous system. Credo developed a method of measuring time more precisely at extremely brief intervals (picoseconds, or trillionths of a second), contributing to the measurement of the movement of charged secondary particles of light. Harris explored the role Z-DNA binding proteins might play in the response of cells to some viral infections.

Web site: <www.sciserv.org/sts>.

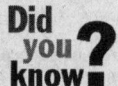

Did you know? Pharmacist John S. Pemberton invented Coca-Cola in 1886; Caleb Bradham invented Pepsi-Cola 12 years later.

Nature, Science, Medicine, & Technology

Time

Measuring Time

The measurement of time is an ancient science, though many of its discoveries are relatively recent. The **Cro-Magnons** recorded the phases of the Moon some 30,000 years ago—but the first minutes were counted accurately only 400 years ago, and the atomic clocks that allow us to track time to the billionth of a second are less than 50 years old. Timekeeping has been both a lens through which humanity has observed the heavens and a mirror reflecting the progress of science and civilization.

Our millennia-long struggle to **define and calibrate** time through calendars and clocks has meant trying to bring the register of human affairs in line with natural cycles—of the Earth, Sun, Moon, and stars, the physics of matter—but always, cycles. What vary are the cultural values and goals that dictate which cycles are significant.

With a religious culture dominated by gods of the Sun and sky, and a civilization dependent on the annual cycle of a river, the **ancient Egyptians** were expert astronomers who studied the Sun's recurrent movements and their effects on the Earth very closely. By plotting the beginning of the Nile's flood each year, a reliable harbinger of seasonal change, they measured a cycle 365 days long—a reasonable approximation of the duration of the tropical solar year. Observations of the star Sirius eventually allowed Egyptian astronomers to adjust the solar year to 365.25 days.

About 127 BC the **Greek astronomer Hipparchus** further refined the year. His adjustments centered on the equinoxes—which he discovered to be shifting to the west at the barely perceptible rate of two degrees in 150 years. Because of this discovery Hipparchus realized that the solar year was slightly shorter than the accepted 365.25 days. His calculation of 365.242 days was remarkably close to the present calculation of 365.242199 days.

Unfortunately for civic and religious leaders of the next 1,600 years, Hipparchus's discoveries were virtually ignored by calendar makers. **Julius Caesar's** calendrical reforms in 46 BC left the calendar year at 365.25 days—more than 11 minutes too long. By the 1500s the Julian calendar was 10 days behind the solar year. The shortfall alarmed Christian religious leaders because it meant that holy days, including Easter, were being observed at the wrong times. In 1582, **Pope Gregory XIII** officially revised the accepted length of the year to 365.2422 days, adjusted the leap-year rule, and lopped off the 10 extra days, creating in the process the calendar in most widespread use today.

Meanwhile, the quest to measure time accurately on a much smaller scale was still in its early phases. The invention of the **weight-driven mechanical clock** some 200 years earlier had revolutionized timekeeping, making it possible to count equal units of time.

This leap forward in precision radically changed the way people thought about time and the best ways to measure it.

Calendars are deemed accurate according to how well they accommodate the variations in larger celestial cycles. Clocks, on the other hand, have historically been judged accurate in relation to the average duration of the Earth's rotation around the Sun—that is, by how well they keep "**mean time.**" While calendrical standards have remained fairly stable, however, the clock's units of measure have gradually shifted away from using the Earth-Sun relationship as a norm. With the introduction of mechanical clocks in the late 13th or early 14th century, clock time became increasingly removed from cyclical events in the sky, for the cycles on which mechanical clocks base their measures are independent of Earth and Sun. A pendulum clock, for example, measures only the beat of its pendulum, not any part of a "real" day.

The **pendulum clock** kicked off the modern search for the perfect clock, a timepiece governed by a naturally cycling period—like a pendulum's—that operated free from mechanical friction and fatigue. Another 300 years would pass before any clock came close. In 1927 W.A. Marrison invented a clock that operated via a tiny **quartz crystal**. The crystal vibrated at an ultrasonic frequency when exposed to an electric field. These vibrations were constant and delivered a virtually frictionless beat to the counting mechanism of the clock. Accurate to thousandths of a second, quartz clocks led scientists to make the belated discovery that the Earth was not a reliable clock to begin with. Disparities between the measurements of quartz clocks and the rotation of the Earth revealed unpredictable irregularities in the rotation, which had to that point defined the duration of a second (1/86,400 of the mean solar day).

In 1967 the **definition of a second** was officially divorced from the Earth's rotation. That year, the 13th General Conference of Weights and Measures redefined the second as "9,192,631,770 periods of the radiation corresponding to the transition between the two hyperfine levels of the ground state of the cesium-133 atom." **Cesium atoms** are superior to quartz crystals because they do not wear out. These atoms have cycles that comprise oscillations between precisely defined energy states; these cycles can oscillate forever without any distortion whatsoever. Furthermore, each atom of cesium oscillates at exactly the same frequency as all others, making each one a perfect timekeeper—too perfect, even. To keep solar time and atomic time from drifting too far apart, the two were combined in 1964 to form **Coordinated Universal Time**, which is based on the atomic second and kept within 0.9 second of solar time by adding a leap second as needed.

Time Zone Map

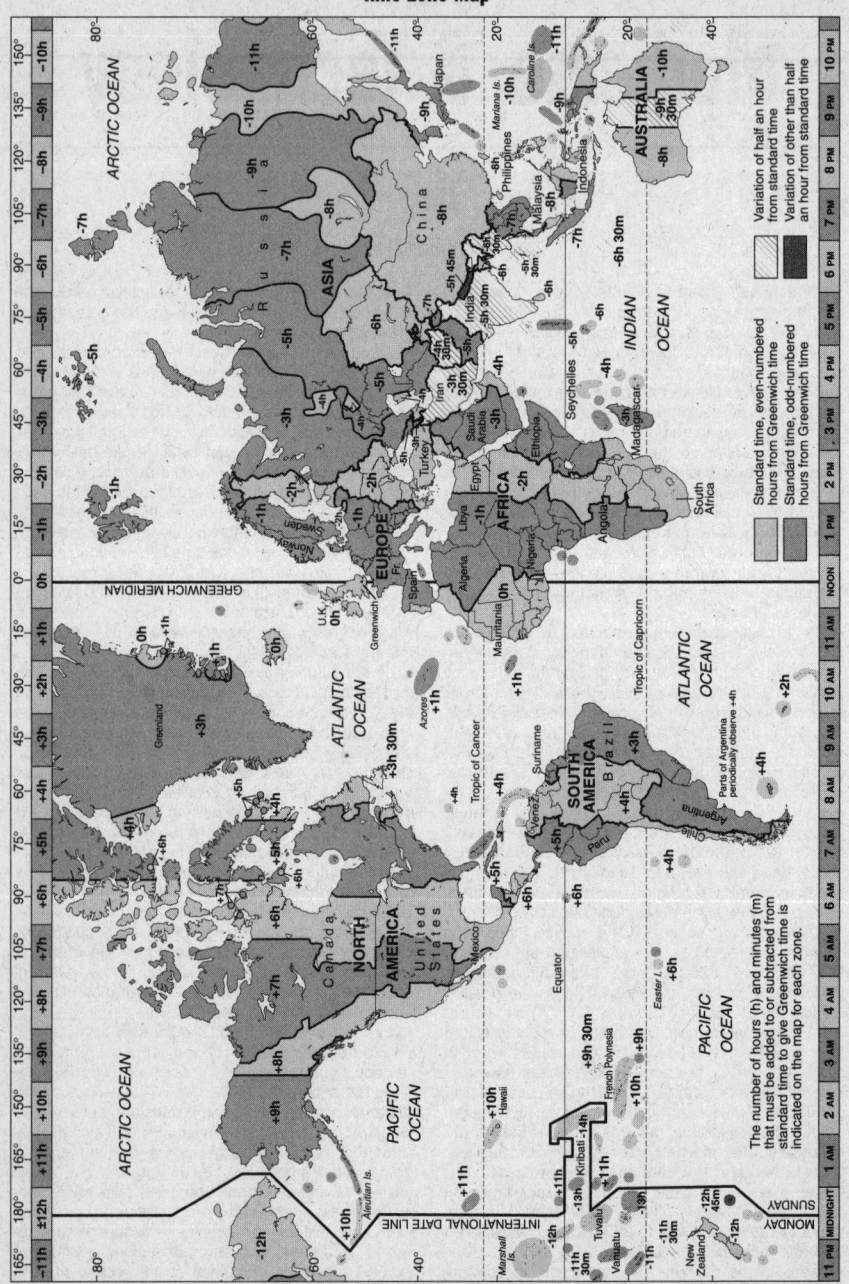

Based on data from the US Defense Mapping Agency Hydrographic/Topographic Center

Daylight Saving Time

Also called **summer time, daylight saving time** is a system for uniformly advancing clocks, especially in summer, so as to extend daylight hours during conventional waking time. In the Northern Hemisphere, clocks are usually set ahead one hour in late March or in April and are set back one hour in late September or in October; most Southern Hemisphere countries that observe daylight saving time set clocks ahead in October or November and reset them in March or April. Equatorial countries do not observe daylight saving time because daylight hours stay about the same from season to season in the lower latitudes.

The practice was first suggested in a whimsical essay by **Benjamin Franklin** in 1784. In 1907 an Englishman, William Willett, campaigned for setting the clock ahead by 80 minutes in four moves of 20 minutes each during the spring and summer months. In 1908 the House of Commons rejected a bill to advance the clock by one hour in the spring and return to Greenwich Mean (standard) Time in the autumn.

Several countries, including Australia, Great Britain, Germany, and the United States, adopted **summer daylight saving time** during World War I to conserve fuel by reducing the need for artificial light. During World War II, clocks were kept continuously advanced by an hour in some nations—e.g., in the US from 9 Feb 1942 to 30 Sep 1945; and England used "double summer time" during part of the year, advancing clocks two hours from the standard time during the summer and one hour during the winter months.

In 2005 the US Congress changed the law governing daylight saving time, moving the start of daylight saving time to the second Sunday in March from the first Sunday in April, while moving the end date from the last Sunday in October to the first Sunday in November starting in 2007. In most of the countries of Western Europe, daylight saving time starts on the last Sunday in March and ends on the last Sunday in October.

Julian and Gregorian Calendars

The **Julian calendar,** also called the Old Style calendar, is a dating system established by Julius Caesar as a reform of the Roman republican calendar. Caesar, advised by the Alexandrian astronomer Sosigenes, made the new calendar solar, not lunar, and he took the length of the solar year as 365¼ days. The year was divided into 12 months, all of which had either 30 or 31 days except February, which contained 28 days in common (365-day) years and 29 in every fourth year (a leap year, of 366 days). Because of misunderstandings, the calendar was not established in smooth operation until AD 8. Further, Sosigenes had overestimated the length of the year by 11 minutes 14 seconds, and by the mid-1500s, the cumulative effect of this error had shifted the dates of the seasons by about 10 days from Caesar's time.

This inaccuracy led **Pope Gregory XIII** to reform the Julian calendar. His **Gregorian calendar,** also called the **New Style calendar,** is still in general use. Gregory's proclamation in 1582 restored the calendar to the seasonal dates of AD 325, an adjustment of 10 days. Although the amount of regression was some 14 days by Pope Gregory's time, Gregory based his reform on restoration of the vernal equinox, then falling on 11 March, to the date (21 March) it had in AD 325, the time of the Council of Nicaea. Advancing the calendar 10 days after 4 Oct 1582, the day following being reckoned as 15 October, effected the change.

The Gregorian calendar differs from the Julian only in that no century year is a leap year unless it is exactly divisible by 400 (e.g., 1600, 2000). A further refinement, the designation of years evenly divisible by 4,000 as common (not leap) years, will keep the Gregorian calendar accurate to within one day in 20,000 years.

Jewish Calendar

The **Jewish calendar** is **lunisolar**—i.e., regulated by the positions of both the Moon and the Sun. It consists usually of 12 alternating lunar months of 29 and 30 days each (except for Heshvan and Kislev, which sometimes have either 29 or 30 days), and totals 353, 354, or 355 days per year. The average lunar year (354 days) is adjusted to the solar year (365¼ days) by the periodic introduction of leap years in order to assure that the major festivals fall in their proper season. The leap year consists of an additional 30-day month called **First Adar,** which always precedes the month of (Second) Adar. (During leap year, the Adar holidays are postponed to Second Adar.) A leap year consists of either 383, 384, or 385 days and occurs seven times during every 19-year period (the so-called Metonic cycle). Among the consequences of the lunisolar structure are these: (1) The number of days in a year may vary considerably, from 353 to 385 days. (2) The first day of a month can fall on any day of the week, that day varying from year to year. Consequently, the days of the week upon which an annual Jewish festival falls vary from year to year despite the festival's fixed position in the Jewish month. The months of the Jewish calendar and their Gregorian equivalents are as follows:

JEWISH MONTH	GREGORIAN MONTH(S)	JEWISH MONTH	GREGORIAN MONTH(S)
Tishri	September–October	Nisan	March–April
Heshvan, or Marheshvan	October–November	Iyyar	April–May
Kislev	November–December	Sivan	May–June
Tevet	December–January	Tammuz	June–July
Shevat	January–February	Av	July–August
Adar	February–March	Elul	August–September

Muslim Calendar

The **Muslim calendar** (also called the **Islamic calendar**, or **Hijrah**) is a dating system used in the Muslim world that is based on a year of 12 months. Each month begins approximately at the time of the New Moon. The **months** of the Muslim calendar are: Muharram, Safar, Rabi I, Rabi II, Jumada I, Jumada II, Rajab, Sha'ban, Ramadan, Shawwal, Dhu al-Qa'dah, and Dhu al-Hijjah.

In the standard Muslim calendar the months are alternately 30 and 29 days long except for the 12th month, Dhu al-Hijjah, the length of which is varied in a 30-year cycle intended to keep the calendar in step with the true phases of the Moon. In 11 years of this cycle, Dhu al-Hijjah has 30 days, and in the other 19 years it has 29. Thus the year has either 354 or 355 days. No months are intercalated, so that the named months do not remain in the same seasons but retrogress through the entire solar, or seasonal, year (of about 365.25 days) every 32.5 solar years.

There are some exceptions to this calendar in the Muslim world. **Turkey** uses the Gregorian calendar, while the **Iranian Muslim calendar** is based on a solar year. The Iranian calendar still begins from the same dating point as other Muslim calendars (that is, some 10 years prior to the death of Muhammad in AD 632). Thus, the Gregorian year AD 2000 corresponded to the Hijrah year of AH 1420/1421.

Chinese Calendar

The **Chinese calendar** is a dating system used concurrently with the Gregorian (Western) calendar in China and Taiwan and in neighboring countries (e.g., Japan). The calendar consists of 12 months of alternately 29 and 30 days, equal to 354 or 355 days, or approximately 12 full lunar cycles. Intercalary months have been inserted to keep the calendar year in step with the solar year of about 365 days. **Months** have no names but are instead referred to by numbers within a year and sometimes also by a series of 12 animal names that from ancient times have been attached to years and to hours of the day.

The calendar also incorporates a **meteorologic cycle** that contains 24 points, each beginning one of the periods named. The establishment of this cycle required a fair amount of astronomical understanding of the Earth as a celestial body. Modern scholars acknowledge the superiority of pre-Sung **Chinese astronomy** (at least until about the 13th century AD) over that of other, contemporary nations.

The **24 points** within the meteorologic cycle coincide with points 15° apart on the ecliptic (the plane of the Earth's yearly journey around the Sun or, if it is thought that the Sun turns around the Earth, the apparent journey of the Sun against the stars). It takes about 15.2 days for the Sun to travel from one of these points to another (because the ecliptic is a complete circle of 360°), and the Sun needs 365¼ days to finish its journey in this cycle. Supposedly, each of the 12 months of the year contains two points, but, because a lunar month has only 29½ days and the two points share about 30.4 days, there is always the chance that a lunar month will fail to contain both points, though the distance between any two given points is only 15°. If such an occasion occurs, the intercalation of an extra month takes place. For instance, one may find a year with two "Julys" or with two "Augusts" in the Chinese calendar. In fact, the exact length of the month in the Chinese calendar is either 30 days or 29 days—a phenomenon that reflects its lunar origin.

SOLAR TERMS—CHINESE (ENGLISH EQUIVALENTS)	GREGORIAN DATE (APPROXIMATE)	LUNAR MONTH (CORRESPONDENCE OF LUNAR AND SOLAR MONTHS APPROXIMATE)
Lichun (spring begins)	5 February	
Yushui (rain water)	19 February	1—tiger
Jingzhe (excited insects)	5 March	
Chunfen (vernal equinox)	20 March	2—rabbit/hare
Qingming (clear and bright)	5 April	
Guyu (grain rains)	20 April	3—dragon
Lixia (summer begins)	5 May	
Xiaoman (grain fills)	21 May	4—snake
Mangzhong (grain in ear)	6 June	
Xiazhi (summer solstice)	21 June	5—horse
Xiaoshu (slight heat)	7 July	
Dashu (great heat)	23 July	6—sheep/ram
Liqiu (autumn begins)	7 August	
Chushu (limit of heat)	23 August	7—monkey
Bailu (white dew)	8 September	
Qiufen (autumn equinox)	23 September	8—chicken/rooster
Hanlu (cold dew)	8 October	
Shuangjiang (hoar frost descends)	24 October	9—dog
Lidong (winter begins)	8 November	
Xiaoxue (little snow)	22 November	10—pig/boar
Daxue (heavy snow)	7 December	
Dongzhi (winter solstice)	22 December	11—rat
Xiaohan (little cold)	6 January	
Dahan (severe cold)	20 January	12—cow/ox

Chinese Calendar (continued)

CHINESE NEW YEAR	GREGORIAN DATE	ANIMAL	CHINESE NEW YEAR	GREGORIAN DATE	ANIMAL
4698	5 Feb 2000	dragon	4705	18 Feb 2007	pig/boar
4699	24 Jan 2001	snake	4706	7 Feb 2008	rat
4700	12 Feb 2002	horse	4707	26 Jan 2009	cow/ox
4701	1 Feb 2003	sheep/ram	4708	14 Feb 2010	tiger
4702	22 Jan 2004	monkey	4709	3 Feb 2011	rabbit/hare
4703	9 Feb 2005	chicken/rooster	4710	23 Jan 2012	dragon
4704	29 Jan 2006	dog	4711	10 Feb 2013	snake

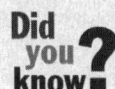

Did you know? Saint Lucy (Santa Lucia in Italian) was one of the earliest Christian saints to achieve popularity, having a widespread following before the 5th century. She is the patron saint of the city of Syracuse (Sicily). She came to be thought of as the patron of sight. St. Lucy is venerated on her feast day, December 13. In Sweden, St. Lucia's Day marks the beginning of the Christmas celebration. On that day the eldest daughter of the family traditionally dresses in a white robe and wears as a crown an evergreen wreath studded with candles.

Religious and Traditional Holidays

The word holiday comes from "holy day," and it was originally a day of dedication to religious observance; in modern times a holiday may be of either religious or secular commemoration. All dates in this article are Gregorian.

Jewish holidays—The major holidays are the Pilgrim Festivals: **Pesach** (Passover), **Shavuot** (Feast of Weeks, or Pentecost), and **Sukkot** (Tabernacles); and the High Holidays: **Rosh Hashana** (New Year) and **Yom Kippur** (Day of Atonement).

Pesach commemorates the Exodus from Egypt and the servitude that preceded it. As such, it is the most significant of the commemorative holidays, for it celebrates the very inception of the Jewish people—i.e., the event that provided the basis for the covenant between God and Israel. The term Pesach refers originally to the paschal (Passover) lamb sacrificed on the eve of the Exodus, the blood of which marked the Jewish homes to be spared from God's plague. Leaven (se'or) and foods containing leaven (hametz) are neither to be owned nor consumed during Pesach. Aside from meats, fresh fruits, and vegetables, it is customary to consume only those foods prepared under rabbinic supervision and labeled "kosher for Passover." The unleavened bread (matzo) consists entirely of flour and water. On the eve of Pesach families partake of the Seder, an elaborate festival meal. The table is bedecked with an assortment of foods symbolizing the passage from slavery (e.g., bitter herbs) into freedom (e.g., wine). Pesach will begin at sundown on 12 April and end on 20 April in 2006. (All Jewish holidays begin at sundown.)

A distinctive **Rosh Hashana** observance is the sounding of the ram's horn (shofar) at the synagogue service. Symbolic ceremonies, such as eating bread and apples dipped in honey, accompanied by prayers for a "sweet" and propitious year, are performed at the festive meals. In 2006 Rosh Hashana will begin at sundown on 21 September and will end on 23 September. **Yom Kippur** is a day when sins are confessed and expiated and man and God are reconciled. It is the holiest and most solemn day of the Jewish year. It is marked by fasting, penitence, and prayer. Working, eating, drinking, washing, anointing one's body, engaging in sexual intercourse, and donning leather shoes are all forbidden. Yom Kippur begins at sundown on 1 October in 2006.

Though not as important theologically, the feast of **Hanukka** has become socially significant, especially in western cultures. Hanukka commemorates the rededication (164 BCE) of the Second Temple of Jerusalem after its desecration three years earlier. Though modern Israel tends to emphasize the military victory of the general Judas Maccabeus, the distinctive rite of lighting the menorah also recalls the Talmud story of how the small supply of nondesecrated oil—enough for one day—miraculously burned in the Temple for eight full days until new oil could be obtained. During Hanukka, in addition to the lighting of the ceremonial candles, gifts are exchanged and children play holiday games. The festival occurs 25 Dec 2005 through 2 Jan 2006, subsequently spanning 15 through 23 Dec 2006.

Christian holidays—The major holidays celebrated by nearly all Christians are **Easter** and **Christmas**.

Easter celebrates the Resurrection of Jesus on the third day after his Crucifixion. In the Christian liturgical year, Easter is preceded by the period of **Lent**, the 40 days (not counting Sundays) before Easter, which traditionally were observed as a period of penance and fasting. Lent begins on **Ash Wednesday**, a day devoted to penitence. Holy Week precedes **Easter Sunday** and includes **Maundy Thursday**, the commemoration of Jesus' last supper with his disciples; **Good Friday**, the day of his Crucifixion; and **Holy Saturday**, the transition between Crucifixion and Resurrection. Easter shares with Christmas the presence of numerous customs, some of which have little to do with the Christian celebration of the resurrection but clearly derive from folk customs. In 2006 the western churches (nearly all Christian denominations) will observe Ash Wednesday on 1 March and Easter on 16 April. For Eastern Orthodox Christians, Lent begins on 6 March and Easter will be observed on 23 Apr 2006.

Christmas commemorates the birth of Jesus Christ. Since the early part of the 20th century, Christmas has also become a secular family holiday, observed by non-Christians, devoid of Christian elements, and marked by an increasingly elaborate exchange of gifts. In this secular Christmas celebration, a mythical figure named Santa Claus plays the pivotal role. Christmas is held on 25 December in most Christian cultures, but occurs on the following 7 January in some Eastern Orthodox churches.

Islamic holidays—Ramadan is the holy month of fasting for Muslims. The Islamic ordinance prescribes abstention from evil thoughts and deeds as well as from food, drink, and sexual intercourse from dawn until dusk throughout the month. The beginning and end of Ramadan are announced when one trustworthy witness testifies before the authorities that the new moon has been sighted; a cloudy sky may, therefore, delay or prolong the fast. The end of the fast is celebrated as the feast of 'Id al-Fitr. Ramadan begins on 24 September in 2006 and 'Id al-Fitr falls on 24 October of that year (all Islamic holidays begin at sundown). The Muslim New Year, **Hijra**, is on 31 January in 2006.

After 'Id al-Fitr, the second major Islamic festival is **'Id al-Adha**. Throughout the Muslim world, all who can sacrifice sheep, goats, camels, or cattle and then divide the flesh equally among themselves, the poor, and friends and neighbors, to commemorate the ransom of Ishmael with a ram. This festival falls at the end of the hajj, the pilgrimage to the holy city of Mecca in Saudi Arabia, which every adult Muslim of either sex must make at least once in his or her lifetime. 'Id al-Adha will be observed on 10–13 January in 2006.

Ashura was originally designated in AD 622 by Muhammad as a day of fasting from sunset to sunset, probably patterned on the Jewish Day of Atonement, Yom Kippur. Among the Shi'ites, Ashura is a major festival that commemorates the death of Husayn (Hussein), son of Ali and grandson of Muhammad. It is a period of expressions of grief and of pilgrimage to Karbala (the site of Husayn's death, now in present-day Iraq). Ashura is on 9 February in 2006.

Buddhist holidays—Holidays practiced by a large number of Buddhists are *uposatha* days and days that commemorate events in the life of the Buddha.

The four monthly holy days of ancient Buddhism continue to be observed in the Theravada countries of Southeast Asia. These *uposatha* days—the new moon and full moon days of each lunar month and the eighth day following the new and full moons—have their origin, according to some scholars, in the fast days that preceded the Vedic soma sacrifices.

The three major events of the Buddha's life—his birth, Enlightenment, and entrance into final nirvana—are commemorated in all Buddhist countries but not everywhere on the same day. In the Theravada countries the three events are all observed together on **Vesak**, the full moon day of the sixth lunar month, which usually occurs in May. In Japan and other Mahayana countries, the three anniversaries of the Buddha are observed on separate days (in some countries the birth date is 8 April, the Enlightenment date is 8 December, and the death date is 15 February).

Chinese holidays—The **Chinese New Year** is celebrated with a big family meal, and presents of cash are given to children in red envelopes. In 2006 the Chinese New Year will be on 29 January.

During the **Chinese Moon Festival**, on the 15th day of the 8th month of the lunar calendar, people return to their homes to visit with their family. The traditional food is moon cakes, round pastries stuffed with food such as red bean paste. The Moon Festival will occur on 6 October in 2006.

Japanese holidays—The Japanese celebrate **3-5-7 day** (Shichigosan no hi) in which parents bring children of those ages to the Shinto shrine to pray for their continued health. This day is held on 15 November.

In mid-July (or mid-August, in some areas) the Japanese celebrate **Obon** (also known as Bon Matsuri, or Urabon). The festival honors the spirits of deceased householders and of the dead generally. Memorial stones are cleaned, community dances are performed, and paper lanterns and fires are lit to welcome the dead and to bid them farewell at the end of their visit. The Shinto New Year, **Gantan-sai**, is celebrated on 1–3 January.

Hindu holidays—Dussehra celebrates the victory of Rama over Ravana, the symbol of evil on earth. In 2006 Dussehra falls on 2 October. **Diwali** is a festival of lights devoted to Laksmi, the goddess of wealth. During the festival, small earthenware lamps filled with oil are lighted and placed in rows along the parapets of temples and houses and set adrift on rivers and streams. Diwali is on 21 October in 2006. **Sivaratri**, the most important sectarian festival of the year for devotees of the Hindu god Shiva, occurs on 26 February in 2006. **Holi** is a spring festival, probably of ancient origin. Participants throw colored waters and powders on one another, and, on this day, the usual restrictions of caste, sex, status, and age are disregarded. It will be on 14 March in 2006.

Sikh holidays—Sikhs observe all festivals celebrated by the Hindus of northern India. In addition, they celebrate the birthdays of the first and the last Gurus and the martyrdom of the fifth (Arjun) and the ninth (Tegh Bahadur). In 2006 **Guru Nanak Dev Sahib's birthday** is celebrated on 5 November, and that of **Guru Gobind Singh Sahib** is celebrated on 5 January. On 16 June **Arjun's martyrdom** is observed. *Kachi lassi* (sweetened milk) is offered to passersby to commemorate his death. On 24 November the **martyrdom of Tegh Bahadur** is observed.

Baha'i holidays—The Baha'i New Year (**Naw Ruz**) in 2006 will fall on 21 March. Other important observances include the **declaration of the Bab** on 23 May, the **Baha 'Ullah's birth** (12 November), and **Ascension** (29 May).

Zoroastrian holidays—Noruz (New Day) is on 21 March for 2006, and the 26th of that month is **Khordad Sal**, the birth of the prophet Zarathustra.

The **African American holiday** of **Kwanzaa** (Swahili for "First Fruits") is celebrated each year from 26 December to 1 January and is patterned after various African harvest festivals. Maulana Karenga, a black-studies professor, created Kwanzaa in 1966 as a nonreligious celebration of family and social values. Each day of Kwanzaa is dedicated to one of seven principles: unity (*umoja*), self-determination (*kujichagulia*), collective responsibility (*ujima*), cooperative economics (*ujamaa*), purpose (*nia*), creativity (*kuumba*), and faith (*imani*).

Perpetual Calendar

The perpetual calendar is a type of dating system that makes it possible to find the correct day of the week for any date over a wide range of years. Aspects of the perpetual calendar can be found in the Jewish religious and the Julian calendars, and some form of it has appeared in many proposed calendar reforms.

To find the day of the week for any Gregorian or Julian date in the perpetual calendar provided in this table, first find the proper dominical letter (one of the letters A through G) for the year in the upper table. Leap years have two dominical letters, the first applicable to dates in January and February, the second to dates in the remaining months. Then find the same dominical letter in the lower table, in whichever column it appears opposite the month in question. The days then fall as given in the lowest section of the column.

YEAR				CENTURY										
				JULIAN CALENDAR								GREGORIAN CALENDAR			
				0	100	200	300	400	500	600	1500**	1600	1700	1800	1900
				700	800	900	1000	1100	1200	1300		2000	2100	2200	2300
				1400	1500*										
0				DC	ED	FE	GF	AG	BA	CB	...	BA	C	E	G
1	29	57	85	B	C	D	E	F	G	A	F	G	B	D	F
2	30	58	86	A	B	C	D	E	F	G	E	F	A	C	E
3	31	59	87	G	A	B	C	D	E	F	D	E	G	B	D
4	32	60	88	FE	GF	AG	BA	CB	DC	ED	CB	DC	FE	AG	CB
5	33	61	89	D	E	F	G	A	B	C	A	B	D	F	A
6	34	62	90	C	D	E	F	G	A	B	G	A	C	E	G
7	35	63	91	B	C	D	E	F	G	A	F	G	B	D	F
8	36	64	92	AG	BA	CB	DC	ED	FE	GF	ED	FE	AG	CB	ED
9	37	65	93	F	G	A	B	C	D	E	C	D	F	A	C
10	38	66	94	E	F	G	A	B	C	D	B	C	E	G	B
11	39	67	95	D	E	F	G	A	B	C	A	B	D	F	A
12	40	68	96	CB	DC	ED	FE	GF	AG	BA	GF	AG	CB	ED	GF
13	41	69	97	A	B	C	D	E	F	G	E	F	A	C	E
14	42	70	98	G	A	B	C	D	E	F	D	E	G	B	D
15	43	71	99	F	G	A	B	C	D	E	C	D	F	A	C
16	44	72		ED	FE	GF	AG	BA	CB	DC	...	CB	ED	GF	BA
17	45	73		C	D	E	F	G	A	B	...	A	C	E	G
18	46	74		B	C	D	E	F	G	A	...	G	B	D	F
19	47	75		A	B	C	D	E	F	G	...	F	A	C	E
20	48	76		GF	AG	BA	CB	DC	ED	FE	...	ED	GF	BA	DC
21	49	77		E	F	G	A	B	C	D	...	C	E	G	B
22	50	78		D	E	F	G	A	B	C	...	B	D	F	A
23	51	79		C	D	E	F	G	A	B	...	A	C	E	G
24	52	80		BA	CB	DC	ED	FE	GF	AG	...	GF	BA	DC	FE
25	53	81		G	A	B	C	D	E	F	...	E	G	B	D
26	54	82		F	G	A	B	C	D	E	C	D	F	A	C
27	55	83		E	F	G	A	B	C	D	B	C	E	G	B
28	56	84		DC	ED	FE	GF	AG	BA	CB	AG	BA	DC	FE	AG

MONTH	DOMINICAL LETTER						
January, October	A	B	C	D	E	F	G
February, March, November	D	E	F	G	A	B	C
April, July	G	A	B	C	D	E	F
May	B	C	D	E	F	G	A
June	E	F	G	A	B	C	D
August	C	D	E	F	G	A	B
September, December	F	G	A	B	C	D	E
1 8 15 22 29	Sunday	Saturday	Friday	Thursday	Wednesday	Tuesday	Monday
2 9 16 23 30	Monday	Sunday	Saturday	Friday	Thursday	Wednesday	Tuesday
3 10 17 24 31	Tuesday	Monday	Sunday	Saturday	Friday	Thursday	Wednesday
4 11 18 25	Wednesday	Tuesday	Monday	Sunday	Saturday	Friday	Thursday
5 12 19 26	Thursday	Wednesday	Tuesday	Monday	Sunday	Saturday	Friday
6 13 20 27	Friday	Thursday	Wednesday	Tuesday	Monday	Sunday	Saturday
7 14 21 28	Saturday	Friday	Thursday	Wednesday	Tuesday	Monday	Sunday

*On and before 1582, 4 October only.   **On and after 1582, 15 October only.
Source: Smithsonian Physical Tables, 9th edition, rev. 1956.

Civil Holidays

DAY	EVENT
1 January	New Year's Day, the first day of the modern calendar (various countries)
20 January	Inauguration Day, for quadrennial inauguration of US president
26 January	Australia Day, commemorates the establishment of the first British settlement in Australia
3rd Monday in January	Martin Luther King Day, for birth of US civil-rights leader
2nd new moon after winter solstice (at the earliest 21 January and at the latest 19 February)	New Year, for Chinese lunar year, inaugurating a 15-day celebration
6 February	Waitangi Day, for Treaty of Waitangi, granting British sovereignty (New Zealand)
11 February	National Foundation Day, for founding by first emperor (Japan)
14 February	St. Valentine's Day, celebrating the exchange of love messages and named for either of two 3rd-century Christian martyrs (various)
3rd Monday in February	Presidents' Day, Washington-Lincoln Day, or Washington's Birthday, for birthdays of US Presidents George Washington and Abraham Lincoln
8 March	International Women's Day, celebration of the women's liberation movement
17 March	St. Patrick's Day, for patron saint of Ireland (Ireland and various)
21 or 22 March	Vernal Equinox Day, for beginning of spring (Japan)
25 March	Independence Day, for proclamation of independence from the Ottoman Empire (Greece)
4th Sunday in Lent	Mothering Day (UK)
1 April	April Fools' Day, or All Fools' Day, day for playing jokes, falling one week after the old New Year's Day of 25 March (various)
5 April	Ching Ming (Qingming), for sweeping tombs and honoring the dead (China)
7 April	World Health Day, for founding of World Health Organization
22 April	Earth Day, for conservation and reclaiming of the natural environment (various)
25 April	ANZAC Day, for landing at Gallipoli (Australia/New Zealand/Samoa/Tonga)
29 April	Green Day, national holiday for environment and nature (Japan)
30 April	Queen's Birthday, for Queen Beatrix's investiture and former queen Juliana's birthday (The Netherlands)
1 May	May Day, celebrated as labor day or as festival of flowers (various)
3 May	Constitution Memorial Day, for establishment of democratic government (Japan)
5 May	Children's Day, honoring children (Japan/South Korea)
5 May	Cinco de Mayo, anniversary of Mexico's victory over France in the Battle of Puebla (Mexico)
8/9 May	V-E Day, or Liberation Day, for end of World War II in Europe (various)
2nd Sunday in May	Mother's Day, honoring mothers (US)
Monday on or preceding 25 May	Victoria Day, for Queen Victoria's birthday (Canada)
30 or last Monday in May	Memorial Day, or Decoration Day, in honor of the deceased, especially the war dead (US)
2 June	Anniversary of the Republic, for referendum establishing republic (Italy)
5 June	Constitution Day (Denmark)
6 June	National Day, for Gustav I Vasa's ascension to the throne and adoption of Constitution (Sweden)
10 June	Portugal's Day, or Camões Memorial Day, anniversary of Luis de Camões's death
14 June	Flag Day, honoring flag (US)
3rd Saturday in June	Queen's Official Birthday, for Queen Elizabeth II (UK/New Zealand)
3rd Sunday in June	Father's Day, honoring fathers (US)
23 June	National Day, for Grand Duke Jean's official birthday (Luxembourg)
23–24 June	Midsummer Eve and Midsummer Day, celebrating the return of summer (various European)
last Sunday in June	Gay and Lesbian Pride Day, final day of weeklong advocacy of rights of gay men and lesbians (international)
1 July	Canada Day (formerly Dominion Day), for establishment of dominion
4 July	Independence Day, for Declaration of Independence from Britain (US)
12 July	Orangemen's Day, or Orange Day, anniversary of the Battle of the Boyne (Northern Ireland)
14 July	Bastille Day, for fall of the Bastille and onset of French Revolution (France)
21 July	National Day, for separation from The Netherlands (Belgium)
1 August	National Day, anniversary of the founding of the Swiss Confederation (Switzerland)
6 August	Hiroshima Day, for dropping of atomic bomb (Japan)
full-moon day of 8th lunar month	Chusok, harvest festival (Korea)
1st Monday in September	Labor Day, tribute to workers (US/Canada)
15 September	Respect-for-the-Aged Day, for the elderly (Japan)
16 September	Independence Day, for independence from Spain (Mexico)
23 or 24 September	Autumnal Equinox Day, for beginning of autumn; in honor of ancestors (Japan)

Civil Holidays (continued)

DAY	EVENT
two weeks ending on 1st Sunday in October	Oktoberfest, festival of food and drink, formerly commemorating marriage of King Louis (Ludwig) I (Germany)
3 October	Day of German Unity, for reunification of Germany
5 October	Republic Day, for founding of the republic (Portugal)
12 or 2nd Monday in October	Hispanic Day, Columbus Day, Discovery Day, or Day of the Race, for Christopher Columbus's discovery of the New World on behalf of Spain (Spain and various)
2nd Monday in October	Thanksgiving Day, harvest festival (Canada)
24 October	United Nations Day, for effective date of UN Charter (international)
26 October	National Day, for end of postwar occupation and return of sovereignty (Austria)
31 October	Halloween, or All Hallows' Eve, festive celebration of ghosts and spirits, on eve of All Saints' Day (various)
5 November	Guy Fawkes Day, anniversary of the Gunpowder Plot to blow up the king and Parliament (UK)
11 November	Armistice Day, Remembrance Day, or Veterans' Day, honoring participants in past wars and recalling the Armistice of World War I (various)
23 November	Labor Thanksgiving Day, honoring workers (Japan)
4th Thursday in November	Thanksgiving Day, harvest festival (US)
16 December	Day of Reconciliation, for promoting national unity (South Africa)
23 December	Emperor's Birthday, for birthday of Emperor Akihito (Japan)
26 December	Boxing Day, second day of Christmas, for giving presents to service people (various)
31 December	New Year's Eve, celebration ushering out the old year and in the new year (various)

The Universe

Cosmogony (Theories of the Origin of the Universe)

Three great ages of scientific thinking about the universe can be distinguished. The first began in Greece in the 6th century BC when the **Pythagoreans** introduced the concept of a **spherical Earth** and postulated a universe in which the motions of heavenly bodies were governed by natural laws. The **infinite atomist universe** of Leucippus and Democritus followed, wherein countless worlds, teeming with life, were the result of chance aggregations of atoms. The **geocentric Aristotelian universe** arose in the 4th century BC. It consisted of a central Earth surrounded by revolving, translucent spheres to which were attached the Sun and the planets; the outermost sphere supported the fixed stars.

The **Copernican revolution** ushered in the second great age. In the 16th century, Nicolaus Copernicus revived ancient ideas and proposed a heliocentric universe, which during the following century was transformed into the mechanistic, infinite **Newtonian universe** that flourished until the early 1900s. In the mid-18th century, Thomas Wright proposed the influential notion of a universe composed of numerous **galaxies**, and William Herschel, followed by many other astronomers, made rapid strides in the study of stars and the Milky Way Galaxy, of which the Earth is a component.

The third great age began in the early years of the 20th century, with the discovery of **special relativity** and its development into **general relativity** by Albert Einstein. These years also saw momentous developments in astronomy: extragalactic redshifts were detected by Vesto Slipher; extragalactic nebulae were shown to be galaxies comparable with the Milky Way; and **Edwin Hubble** began to estimate the distances of these galactic systems. Such discoveries and the application of general relativity to cosmology eventually gave rise to the view that the **universe is expanding**. The basic premise of modern thinking on the universe is the principle that asserts that the universe is homogeneous in space (on the average all places are alike at any time) and that the laws of physics are everywhere the same.

Two theories of the origin of the universe have been the most influential during the last century—the steady state theory and the big bang theory. The **steady state theory** posits that the universe is always expanding but maintains a constant average density, matter being continuously created to form new stars and galaxies at the same rate that old ones become unobservable as a consequence of their increasing distance and velocity of recession. A steady-state universe has no beginning or end in time; and from any point within it the view on the grand scale—i.e., the average density and arrangement of galaxies—is the same. Galaxies of all possible ages are intermingled. Observations since the 1950s have produced much evidence contradictory to the steady-state picture and supportive of the big-bang model.

The essential feature of the widely-held **big bang theory** is the emergence of the universe from a state of extremely high temperature and density—the so-called big bang that occurred at least 10,000,000,000 years ago. Although this type of universe was proposed by Alexander Friedmann and Abbé Georges Lemaître in the 1920s, the modern version was developed by George Gamow and colleagues in the 1940s.

One current problem that scientists are studying is the **amount of matter in the universe**. Based upon such things as the rate of the motion of galaxies, scientists realized that there is some 90% more matter in the universe than can be seen. Scientists refer to the matter that can be observed as "**bright matter**" and this other 90% is called "**dark matter**." Whether dark matter is of a different and exotic nature from the matter with which we are familiar, or whether dark matter is just like luminous matter (and for some reason we cannot detect it), is something a large number of scientists are studying.

Astronomical Constants

QUANTITY	SYMBOL	VALUE
astronomical unit	AU	length of the semimajor axis of the Earth's orbit around the Sun—149,597,870 km (92,955,808 mi)

measures large distances in space; equals the average distance from the Earth to the Sun

parsec　　　　　　　　　pc　　　　　　one parsec equals 3.26 light-years
measures the distance at which the radius of the Earth's orbit subtends an angle of one second of arc

light-year　　　　　　　ly　　　　　9.46089×10^{12} km (5.8787×10^{12} mi)
measures the distance traveled by light moving in a vacuum in the course of one year

solar parallax　　　　　　　　　　　　8.79414 seconds of arc
quantifies the angular difference in direction of the Sun as seen from the Earth's center and a point one Earth radius away

lunar parallax　　　　　　　　　　　　57 minutes 02.608 seconds of arc
quantifies the angular difference in direction of the Moon as seen from the Earth's center and a point one Earth radius away

general precession　　　　　　　　　50.29 seconds of arc per year
measures the cyclic wobbling in the orientation of the Earth's axis of rotation with a period of almost 26,000 years

constant of aberration　　　　　　　about 20.49 seconds of arc
the maximum amount of the apparent yearly aberrational displacement of a star or other celestial body, resulting from the Earth's orbital motion around the Sun

constant of nutation　　　　　　　　9.202 seconds of arc
a small irregularity in the Earth's axial precession of that occurs over a period of 18.6 years

speed of light (in a vacuum)　　　c　　　$2.99792458 \times 10^{10}$ cm per sec
　　　　　　　　　　　　　　　　　　　　　(186,282 mi per sec)

radius of the Sun　　　　　Sun $R_\odot$　　6.96×10^8 m (109 times the radius of Earth)

mass of the Sun　　　　　Sun $M_\odot$　　1.989×10^{30} kg (330,000 times the mass of the Earth)

Earth's mean radius　　　　　　　　6,378 km (3,963 mi)

sidereal day (on Earth)　　　　　23 h 56 min 4.10 sec of mean solar time
defined by the period between two successive passages of a star across the same meridian; it is the time required for the Earth to rotate once relative to the distant stars

mean solar day (on Earth)　　　　24 h 3 min 56.55 sec of mean sideral time
the interval between two successive passages of the Sun across the same meridian is a solar day; in practice, since the rate of the Sun's motion varies with the seasons, use is made of a fictitious Sun that always moves across the sky at an even rate

tropical (or solar) year (on Earth)　　　　365.242 days
the time required for the Earth's orbital motion to return the Sun's position to the spring equinoctial point

sidereal year (on Earth)　　　　　365.256 days
the time required for the Earth in its orbit to return to the longitude of a distant star

synodic month (on Earth)　　　　29.53 days
the time required for the Moon to pass through one complete cycle of phases

sidereal month (on Earth)　　　　27.32 days
the time required for the Moon to return to the same place in relation to distant stars

---

Did you know? Antimatter is a substance composed of atoms made up of elementary particles that have the mass and charge of electrons, protons, or neutrons—their counterparts in ordinary matter—but for which the charge is opposite in sign. Such particles are called *positrons* (e^+), *antiprotons* ($\bar{p}$), and *antineutrons* ($\bar{n}$), or, collectively, *antiparticles*. Matter and antimatter cannot coexist at close range for more than a small fraction of a second because they annihilate each other with release of large quantities of energy. It has been suggested that some distant galaxies may be composed entirely of antimatter.

Definitions of Astronomical Positions

A conjunction is an apparent meeting or passing of two or more celestial bodies. For example, the Moon is in conjunction with the Sun at the phase of new Moon, when it moves between the Earth and Sun and the side turned toward the Earth is dark. Inferior planets—those with orbits smaller than the Earth's (namely, Venus and Mercury)—have two kinds of conjunctions with the Sun. An **inferior conjunction** occurs when the planet passes approximately between Earth and Sun; if it passes exactly between them, moving across the Sun's face as seen from Earth, it is said to be in transit (*see* below). A **superior conjunction** occurs when Earth and the other planet are on opposite sides of the Sun, but all three bodies are again nearly in a straight line. Superior planets, those with orbits larger than the Earth's can have only superior conjunctions with the Sun.

When celestial bodies appear in opposite directions in the sky they are said to be in **opposition**. The Moon, when full, is said to be in opposition to the Sun (the Earth is then approximately between them). A superior planet (one with an orbit farther from the Sun than Earth's) is in opposition when Earth passes between it and the Sun. The opposition of a planet is a good time to observe it, because the planet is then at its nearest point to the Earth and in its full phase. The inferior planets, Venus and Mercury, can never be in opposition to the Sun.

When a celestial body as seen from the Earth makes a right angle with the direction of the Sun it is said to be in **quadrature**. The Moon at first or last quarter is said to be at east or west quadrature, respectively. A superior planet is at west quadrature when its position is 90° west of the Sun.

The east–west coordinate by which the position of a celestial body is ordinarily measured is known as the **right ascension**. Right ascension in combination with **declination** defines the position of a celestial object. Declination is the angular distance of a body north or south of the celestial equator. North declination is considered positive and south, negative. Thus, +90° declination marks the north celestial pole, 0° the celestial equator, and −90° the south celestial pole. The symbol for right ascension is the Greek letter α (alpha) and for declination the lowercase Greek letter Δ (delta).

The angular distance in celestial longitude separating the Moon or a planet from the Sun is known as **elongation**. The greatest elongation possible for the two inferior planets is about 48° in the case of Venus and about 28° in that of Mercury. Elongation may also refer to the angular distance of any celestial body from another around which it revolves or from a particular point in the sky; e.g., the extreme east or west position of a star with reference to the north celestial pole.

The point at which a planet is closest to the Sun is called the **perihelion**, and the most distant point in that planet's orbit is the **aphelion**. The term helion refers specifically to the Sun as the primary body about which the planet is orbiting.

Occultation refers to the obscuring of the light of an astronomical body, most commonly a star, by another astronomical body, such as a planet or a satellite. Hence, a solar eclipse is the occultation of the Sun by the Moon. From occultations of stars by planets, asteroids, and satellites, astronomers are able to determine the precise sizes and shapes of the latter bodies in addition to the temperatures of planetary atmospheres. For example, astronomers unexpectedly discovered the rings of Uranus during a stellar occultation on 10 Mar 1977.

A complete or partial obscuring of a celestial body by another is an **eclipse**; these occur when three celestial objects become aligned. The Sun is eclipsed when the Moon comes between it and the Earth; the Moon is eclipsed when it moves into the shadow of the Earth cast by the Sun. Eclipses of natural or artificial satellites of a planet occur as the satellites move into the planet's shadow. When the apparent size of the eclipsed body is much smaller than that of the eclipsing body, the phenomenon is known as an **occultation** (*see* above). Examples are the disappearance of a star, nebula, or planet behind the Moon, or the vanishing of a natural satellite or space probe behind some body of the solar system. A **transit** (*see* above) occurs when, as viewed from the Earth, a relatively small body passes across the disk of a larger body, usually the Sun or a planet, eclipsing only a very small area: Mercury and Venus periodically transit the Sun, and a satellite may transit its planet.

When an object orbiting the Earth is at the point in its orbit that is the greatest distance from the center of the Earth, this point is known as **apogee**; the term is also used to describe the point farthest from a planet or a satellite (as the Moon) reached by an object orbiting it. **Perigee** is the opposite of apogee.

The difference in direction of a celestial object as seen by an observer from two widely separated points is termed **parallax**. The measurement of parallax is used directly to find the distance of the body from the Earth (geocentric parallax) and from the Sun (heliocentric parallax). The two positions of the observer and the position of the object form a triangle; if the base line between the two observing points is known and the direction of the object as seen from each has been measured, the apex angle (the parallax) and the distance of the object from the observer can be determined.

An **hour angle** is the angle between an observer's meridian (a great circle passing over his head and through the celestial poles) and the hour circle (any other great circle passing through the poles) on which some celestial body lies. This angle, when expressed in hours and minutes, is the time elapsed since the celestial body's last transit of the observer's meridian. The hour angle can also be expressed in degrees, 15° of arc being equal to one hour.

Constellations

C onstellations are certain groupings of stars that were imagined—at least by those who named them—to form conspicuous configurations of objects or creatures in the sky. Constellations are useful in tracking artificial satellites and in assisting astronomers and navigators to locate certain stars.

From the earliest times the star groups known as constellations, the smaller groups (parts of constellations) known as **asterisms**, and, also, **individual stars** have received names connoting some meteorological phenomena or symbolizing religious or mythological beliefs. At one time it was held that the constellation

Constellations (continued)

names and myths were of Greek origin; this view has now been disproved. It is now thought that the Greek constellation system and the cognate legends are primarily of Semitic or even pre-Semitic origin and that they came to the Greeks through the Phoenicians.

The Alexandrian astronomer **Ptolemy** lists the names and orientation of the 48 constellations in his *Almagest*, and, with but few exceptions, they are iden-

tical with those used at the present time. The majority of the remaining 40 constellations that are now accepted were added by European astronomers in the 17th and 18th centuries. In the 20th century the delineation of precise boundaries for all the 88 constellations was undertaken by a committee of the International Astronomical Union. By 1930 it was possible to assign any star to a constellation.

NAME	GENITIVE	MEANING	NOTES
Constellations described by Ptolemy: the zodiac			(First-magnitude stars are given in italics in this column)
Aries	Arietis	Ram	
Taurus	Tauri	Bull	*Aldebaran* is the constellation's brightest star. Taurus also contains the Pleiades star cluster and the Crab Nebula.
Gemini	Geminorum	Twins	The brightest stars in Gemini are Castor and *Pollux*.
Cancer	Cancri	Crab	Cancer contains the well-known star cluster Praesepe.
Leo	Leonis	Lion	*Regulus* is the brightest star in Leo.
Virgo	Virginis	Virgin	*Spica* is the brightest star in Virgo.
Libra	Librae	Balance	
Scorpius	Scorpii	Scorpion	*Antares* is the brightest star of Scorpius, which also contains many star clusters.
Sagittarius	Sagittarii	Archer	The center of the Milky Way Galaxy lies in Sagittarius, with the densest star clouds of the galaxy.
Capricornus	Capricorni	Sea-goat	
Aquarius	Aquarii	Water-bearer	
Pisces	Piscium	Fishes	
Other Ptolemaic constellations			
Andromeda	Andromedae	Andromeda (an Ethiopian princess of Greek legend, daughter of Cepheus and Cassiopeia)	The constellation's most notable feature is the great spiral galaxy Andromeda (also called M31).
Aquila	Aquilae	Eagle	The brightest star in Aquila is *Altair*.
Ara	Arae	Altar	
Argo Navis	Argus Navis	the ship *Argo*	Argo Navis is now divided into smaller constellations that include Carina, Puppis, Pyxis, and Vela.
Auriga	Aurigae	Charioteer	The brightest star in Auriga is *Capella*. The constellation also contains open star clusters M36, M37, and M38.
Boötes	Boötis	Herdsman	*Arcturus* is the brightest star in Boötes.
Canis Major	Canis Majoris	Greater Dog	*Sirius* is the brightest star in Canis Major.
Canis Minor	Canis Minoris	Smaller Dog	*Procyon* is the brightest star in Canis Minor.
Cassiopeia	Cassiopeiae	Cassiopeia was a legendary queen of Ethiopia	Tycho's nova, one of the few recorded supernovae in the Galaxy, appeared in Cassiopeia in 1572.
Centaurus	Centauri	Centaur (possibly represents Chiron)	*Alpha Centauri* in Centaurus contains Proxima, the nearest star to the Sun.
Cepheus	Cephei	Cepheus (legendary king of Ethiopia)	Delta Cephei was the prototype for cepheid variables (a class of variable stars).
Cetus	Ceti	Whale	Mira Ceti was the first recognized variable star.
Corona Austrina	Coronae Austrinae	Southern Crown	
Corona Borealis	Coronae Borealis	Northern Crown	
Corvus	Corvi	Raven	
Crater	Crateris	Cup	
Cygnus	Cygni	Swan	Cygnus contains the asterism (grouping of stars) known as the Northern Cross; the constellation's brightest star is *Deneb*.
Delphinus	Delphini	Dolphin	Delphinus contains the asterism known as Job's Coffin.
Draco	Draconis	Dragon	Draco contains the star Thuban, which was the polestar in 3000 BC.

Constellations (continued)

NAME	GENITIVE	MEANING	NOTES
Other Ptolemaic constellations (continued)			
Equuleus	Equulei	Little Horse	
Eridanus	Eridani	River Eridanus or river god	*Achernar* is the brightest star in Eridanus.
Hercules	Herculis	Hercules (Greek hero)	Hercules contains the great globular star cluster M13.
Hydra	Hydrae	Water Snake	
Lepus	Leporis	Hare	
Lupus	Lupi	Wolf	
Lyra	Lyrae	Lyre	The brightest star in Lyra is *Vega*. In some 10,000 years, *Vega* will become the polestar. Lyra also contains the Ring Nebula (M57).
Ophiuchus	Ophiuchi	Serpent-bearer	When the Zodiac was conceived of, Ophiuchus was not in the Sun's path, but the Sun does now pass through Ophiuchus each December.
Orion	Orionis	Hunter	*Rigel* is the brightest star in Orion, followed closely by *Betelgeuse;* M42 (the Great Nebula) resides in Orion.
Pegasus	Pegasi	Pegasus (winged horse)	The constellation contains stars of the Great Square of Pegasus.
Perseus	Persei	Perseus (legendary Greek hero)	
Piscis Austrinus	Piscis Austrini	Southern Fish	The brightest star in Piscis Austrinus is *Fomalhaut*.
Sagitta	Sagittae	Arrow	
Serpens	Serpentis	Serpent	
Triangulum	Trianguli	Triangle	The constellation contains M33, a nearby spiral galaxy.
Ursa Major	Ursae Majoris	Great Bear	The seven brightest stars of this constellation are the Big Dipper (also called the Plough).
Ursa Minor	Ursae Minoris	Lesser Bear	Ursa Minor contains Polaris (the north polestar).
Southern constellations, added c. 1600			
Apus	Apodis	Bird of Paradise	
Chamaeleon	Chamaeleontis	Chameleon	
Dorado	Doradus	Swordfish	The most notable object in Dorado is the Large Magellanic Cloud.
Grus	Gruis	Crane	
Hydrus	Hydri	Water Snake	
Indus	Indi	Indian	
Musca	Muscae	Fly	
Pavo	Pavonis	Peacock	
Phoenix	Phoenicis	Phoenix (mythical bird)	
Triangulum Australe	Trianguli Australis	Southern Triangle	
Tucana	Tucanae	Toucan	The most notable object in Tucana is the Small Magellanic Cloud.
Volans	Volantis	Flying Fish	
Constellations of Bartsch, 1624			
Camelopardalis	Camelopardalis	Giraffe	
Columba	Columbae	Dove	The constellation was formed by Petrus Plancius in the early 1600s.
Monoceros	Monocerotis	Unicorn	
Constellations of Hevelius, 1687			
Canes Venatici	Canum Venaticorum	Hunting Dogs	The constellation contains M51 (the Whirlpool Galaxy).
Lacerta	Lacertae	Lizard	
Leo Minor	Leonis Minoris	Lesser Lion	
Lynx	Lyncis	Lynx	
Scutum	Scuti	Shield	Scutum contains the Scutim star cloud in the Milky Way.
Sextans	Sextantis	Sextant	
Vulpecula	Vulpeculae	Fox	Vulpecula contains M27 (the Dumbbell Nebula).

Constellations (continued)

NAME	GENITIVE	MEANING	NOTES
Ancient asterisms that are now separate constellations			
Carina	Carinae	Keel [of the legendary ship the *Argo*]	The brightest star in Carina is *Canopus*.
Coma Berenices	Comae Berenices	Berenice's Hair	The constellation contains both a coma (star cluster) and the north galactic pole (a point that lies perpendicular to the Milky Way).
Crux	Crucis	[Southern] Cross	
Puppis	Puppis	Stern [of the *Argo*]	
Pyxis	Pyxidis	Compass [of the *Argo*]	
Vela	Velorum	Sails [of the *Argo*]	
Southern constellations of Lacaille, c. 1750			
Antlia	Antliae	Pump	
Caelum	Caeli	[Sculptor's] Chisel	
Circinus	Circini	Drawing Compasses	
Fornax	Fornacis	[Chemical] Furnace	
Horologium	Horologii	Clock	
Mensa	Mensae	Table [Mountain]	
Microscopium	Microscopii	Microscope	
Norma	Normae	Square	
Octans	Octantis	Octant	Octans contains the south celestial pole.
Pictor	Pictoris	Painter's [Easel]	
Reticulum	Reticuli	Reticle	
Sculptor	Sculptoris	Sculptor's [Workshop]	Sculptor contains the south galactic pole.
Telescopium	Telescopii	Telescope	

Astrology: The Zodiac

Signs of the zodiac are popularly used for divination as well as for designation of constellations.

NAME	SYMBOL	DATES	SEX/NATURE	TRIPLICITY	HOUSE	EXALTATION
Aries the Ram	♈	21 Mar–19 Apr	masculine/moving	fire	Mars	Sun (19°)
Taurus the Bull	♉	20 Apr–20 May	feminine/fixed	earth	Venus	Moon (3°)
Gemini the Twins	♊	21 May–21 Jun	masculine/common	air	Mercury	
Cancer the Crab	♋	22 Jun–22 Jul	feminine/moving	water	Moon	Jupiter (15°)
Leo the Lion	♌	23 Jul–22 Aug	masculine/fixed	fire	Sun	
Virgo the Virgin	♍	23 Aug–22 Sep	feminine/common	earth	Mercury	Mercury (15°)
Libra the Balance	♎	23 Sep–23 Oct	masculine/moving	air	Venus	Saturn (21°)
Scorpius the Scorpion	♏	24 Oct–21 Nov	feminine/fixed	water	Mars	
Sagittarius the Archer	♐	22 Nov–21 Dec	masculine/common	fire	Jupiter	
Capricorn the Goat	♑	22 Dec–19 Jan	feminine/moving	earth	Saturn	Mars (28°)
Aquarius the Water Bearer	♒	20 Jan–18 Feb	masculine/fixed	air	Saturn	
Pisces the Fish	♓	19 Feb–20 Mar	feminine/common	water	Jupiter	Venus (27°)

Classification of Stars

The spectral sequence O–M represents stars of essentially the same chemical composition but of different temperatures and atmospheric pressures. Stars belonging to other, more rare types of spectral classifications differ in chemical composition from O–M stars.

Each spectral class is additionally subdivided into 10 spectral types. For example, spectral class A is subdivided into spectral types A0–A9 with 0 being the hottest and 9 the coolest. (Spectral class O is unusual in that it is subdivided into O4–O9.) Between two stars of the same spectral type, the more luminous star will also be larger in diameter. Thus the Yerkes system of luminosity also tells something of a star's radius, with Ia being the largest and V the smallest. Approximately 90% of all stars are main sequence, or type V, stars.

Based upon these systems, the Sun would be a G2 V star (a yellow, relatively hot dwarf star).

SPECTRAL CLASS	COLOR	APPROXIMATE SURFACE TEMP (°C)	EXAMPLES
O	blue	30,000 or greater	These stars are relatively rare
B	blue-white	20,000 to 30,000	Rigel, Alpha Crucis, Beta Crucis
A	white	10,000 to 20,000	Sirius, Vega, Fomalhaut
F	yellow-white	7,000 to 10,000	Canopus, Procyon

Classification of Stars (continued)

SPECTRAL CLASS	COLOR	APPROXIMATE SURFACE TEMP (°C)	EXAMPLES
G	yellow	6,000 to 7,000	Sun
K	orange	4,500 to 6,000	Arcturus, Aldebaran
M	red	3,000 to 4,500	Betelgeuse, Antares

LUMINOSITY CLASSES (BASED UPON THE YERKES SYSTEM)	
Ia	most luminous supergiants
Ib	luminous supergiants
II	bright giants
III	normal giants
IV	subgiants
V	main sequence stars (dwarfs)

The 20 Brightest Stars in the Night Sky

This table lists the stars in descending order from brightest to less bright, based on apparent visual magnitude. Formal names of stars, such as Alpha Carinae, refer to the constellation in which the star appears (Carina) and to which star appears the brightest in that constellation; the second highest would be designated Beta, etc. Some anomalies exist within the naming convention: Betelgeuse, for example, is the Alpha star of Orion, though Rigel appears brighter.

On the scale of brightness, negative magnitudes are brightest, and one magnitude difference corresponds to a difference in brightness of 2.5 times; e.g., a star of magnitude −1 is 10 times brighter than one of magnitude +1.5.

Apparent magnitude is a measure of how bright a star appears to a viewer on Earth. Absolute magnitude is the brightness one would perceive if all stars were at the same distance from Earth. The distance from Earth that scientists assume when computing absolute magnitude is 10 parsecs (about 32.6 light-years; one light-year equals about 9.46×10^{12} km). With absolute magnitude a comparison can be made between a star such as Rigel, which is very bright but very distant, and a star such as Sirius, which is less bright but is fairly close to Earth. The Sun, for purposes of comparison with the stars in the table, has an apparent magnitude of −26.8 and an actual magnitude of +4.8; it is a yellow dwarf star that is 8.3 light-minutes from Earth.

STAR	APPARENT VISUAL MAGNITUDE/ABSOLUTE VISUAL MAGNITUDE	DISTANCE FROM THE SOLAR SYSTEM (LIGHT-YEARS)	CONSTELLATION
Sirius (Alpha Canis Majoris, or Dog Star)	−1.46/+1.43	8.6	Canis Major

Sirius is a blue-white dwarf with a white-dwarf companion; among the ancient Romans, the hottest part of the year was associated with the time in which the Dog Star rose just before dawn; this connection survives in the expression "dog days."

Canopus (Alpha Carinae)	−0.72/around −3.1 (reported values vary)	74 (reported values vary)	Carina

A yellow-white supergiant, Canopus is sometimes used as a guide in the attitude control of spacecraft because of its angular distance from the Sun and the contrast of its brightness among nearby celestial objects.

Alpha Centauri (Rigel Kentaurus)	−0.01/+4.5	4.3	Centaurus

Alpha Centauri is a triple star—a binary yellow dwarf circled by a red dwarf with a much smaller red dwarf; the faintest of Alpha Centauri's three stars, Proxima, is the star closest to the Sun.

Arcturus (Alpha Boötis)	−0.04/−0.3	34	Boötes

An orange-colored giant, Arcturus lies in an almost direct line with the tail of Ursa Major (the Great Bear); hence its name, derived from the Greek words for "bear guard."

Vega (Alpha Lyrae)	+0.03/+0.58	25.3	Lyra

A blue dwarf, Vega will become the northern polestar by about AD 14,000 because of the precession of the equinoxes.

Capella (Alpha Aurigae)	+0.08/−0.48	41	Auriga

Capella is actually four stars, two yellow giants and two red-dwarf companion stars. Scientists are studying Capella to determine why it emits more X-rays than other stars of its type.

Rigel (Beta Orionis)	+0.12 (variable)/−6.4	815	Orion

Rigel is a blue-white supergiant with two smaller companion stars. The name Rigel derives from an Arabic term meaning "the left leg of the giant," referring to the figure of Orion.

The 20 Brightest Stars in the Night Sky (continued)

STAR	APPARENT VISUAL MAGNITUDE/ABSOLUTE VISUAL MAGNITUDE	DISTANCE FROM THE SOLAR SYSTEM (LIGHT-YEARS)	CONSTELLATION
Procyon (Alpha Canis Minoris)	+0.38/+2.7	11.4	Canis Minor

Procyon is a yellow-white subgiant with a faint white-dwarf companion. The name Procyon apparently derives from Greek words for "before the dog," as in northern latitudes the star rises just before Sirius, the Dog Star.

Achernar (Alpha Eridani)   +0.46/−2.6   69   Eridanus
Achernar is a blue dwarf. The name Achernar probably derives from an Arabic phrase meaning "the end of the river," in which the river referred to is the constellation.

Betelgeuse (Alpha Orionis)   +0.50 (variable)/−5.1   650   Orion
A red supergiant, Betelgeuse has a diameter that varies between 430 and 625 times the diameter of the Sun over a period of 5.8 years.

Beta Centauri (Hadar)   +0.61/−3.1   320   Centaurus
Beta Centauri is a blue-white supergiant with two smaller companion stars; the constellation Centaurus most likely is meant to represent the centaur Chiron. In Greek mythology Chiron was renowned for his wisdom and knowledge of medicine. He renounced his immortality to escape a painful wound, and Zeus placed him in the Southern sky.

Altair (Alpha Aquilae)   +0.77/+2.2   16.8   Aquila
A blue dwarf, Altair spins nearly 470,000 mph, as compared with Earth, which spins some 1,000 mph. This rapid spinning flattens Altair from a spherical into an oblate shape.

Aldebaran (Alpha Tauri)   +0.85/−0.63   60   Taurus
A red giant, Aldebaran has a name derived from the Arabic for "the follower," perhaps because it rises after the Pleiades cluster of stars.

Antares (Alpha Scorpii)   +0.96/−5.28   425   Scorpio
Antares is a red supergiant. The name Antares seems to come from a Greek phrase meaning "rival of Ares" (i.e., rival of the planet Mars) and was probably given because of the star's color and brightness.

Spica (Alpha Virginis)   +0.98/−3.55   220   Virgo
A binary blue-white dwarf with a nonvisible companion, Spica has a name derived from the Latin for "ear of wheat"; the star is said to represent the wheat being held by the Virgin.

Pollux (Beta Geminorum)   +1.14/+1.09   40   Gemini
A red giant, Pollux is named for one of the twins of ancient Greek mythology (the other is Castor).

Fomalhaut (Alpha Piscis Austrini)   +1.16/+1.74   22   Piscis Austrinus
The blue-white dwarf Fomalhaut's name is derived from the Arabic for "mouth of the fish."

Deneb (Alpha Cygni)   +1.25/−8.73   1,630   Cygnus
A blue-white supergiant, Deneb gained its name from an Arabic word meaning "tail," as it is considered the tail of the swan Cygnus.

Becrux (Beta Crucis, or Mimosa)   +1.25/−3.92   460   Crux (The Southern Cross)
A blue-white giant, Becrux forms the eastern tip of the Southern Cross.

Regulus (Alpha Leo)   +1.35/−0.3   69   Leo
Regulus is a blue-white main sequence star; its name is the diminutive form of the Latin *rex* ("king").

Data for apparent visual magnitudes taken from The Astronomical Almanac for 2003, issued jointly by the Nautical Almanac Office of the United States Naval Observatory and Her Majesty's Nautical Almanac Office of the United Kingdom.

 **Did you know?**

The Hubble Space Telescope is the most sophisticated optical observatory ever placed into orbit around the Earth. Stationed in outer space and entirely above the Earth's atmosphere, it receives images of much greater brightness, clarity, and detail than do ground-based telescopes with comparable optics. The HST was placed into orbit about 600 km (370 miles) above the Earth by the crew of the space shuttle Discovery on 25 Apr 1990.

Astronomical Phenomena for 2006

Source: The Astronomical Almanac 2006.

MONTH	DAY	HOUR (GMT)	EVENT	MONTH	DAY	HOUR (GMT)	EVENT
January	1	10	Venus 7° N of Moon	March	21	03	Antares 0.°3 N of Moon[1]
	1	23	Moon at perigee		22	19	last quarter
	2	12	Neptune 7° N of Moon		24	12	Mercury stationary
	4	00	Uranus 2° N of Moon		25	07	Venus greatest elongation W (47°)
	4	15	Earth at perihelion				
	5	23	Vesta at opposition		25	12	Ceres 0.°8 S of Moon[1]
	6	19	first quarter		25	23	Venus 6° N of Moon
	8	20	Mars 1.°3 S of Moon		26	01	Neptune 4° N of Moon
	14	00	Venus in inferior conjunction		26	21	Venus 1.°9 N of Neptune
	14	10	full moon		27	15	Uranus 1.°4 N of Moon[1]
	15	13	Saturn 4° S of Moon		27	17	Mercury 2° N of Moon
	16	20	Juno stationary		28	07	Moon at perigee
	17	19	Moon at apogee		29	10	new moon[2]
	21	22	Spica 0.°6 S of Moon[1]		29	15	Pluto stationary
	22	15	last quarter	April	3	20	Mars 4° S of Moon
	23	20	Jupiter 5° N of Moon		5	12	first quarter
	25	12	Antares 0.°02 S of Moon[1]		5	12	Saturn stationary
	26	22	Mercury in superior conjunction		6	23	Saturn 6° S of Moon
	27	23	Saturn at opposition		8	19	Mercury greatest elongation W (28°)
	28	00	Venus 12° N of Moon		9	13	Moon at apogee
	29	14	new moon		13	17	full moon
	30	08	Moon at perigee		13	17	Spica 0.°03 S of Moon[1]
	31	12	Uranus 1.°7 N of Moon		15	15	Jupiter 5° N of Moon
February	3	07	Venus stationary		17	09	Antares 0.°02 N of Moon[1]
	5	06	first quarter		18	12	Venus 0.°3 N of Uranus
	5	22	Mars 2° S of Moon		21	03	last quarter
	6	06	Neptune in conjunction with Sun		22	09	Neptune 4° N of Moon
	11	15	Saturn 4° S of Moon		24	02	Uranus 1.°2 N of Moon[1]
	13	05	full moon		24	14	Venus 0.°5 N of Moon[1]
	14	01	Moon at apogee		25	11	Moon at perigee
	17	20	Venus greatest illuminated extent		26	08	Mercury 4° S of Moon
	18	05	Spica 0.°4 S of Moon[1]		27	20	new moon
	20	08	Jupiter 5° N of Moon	May	2	11	Mars 4° S of Moon
	21	07	last quarter		3	03	Pallas stationary
	21	21	Antares 0.°2 N of Moon[1]		4	09	Saturn 4° S of Moon
	23	08	Vesta stationary		4	15	Jupiter at opposition
	24	05	Mercury greatest elongation E (18°)		5	05	first quarter
	24	21	Venus 10° N of Moon		7	07	Moon at apogee
	25	10	Ceres 0.°8 N of Moon[1]		11	00	Spica 0.°3 S of Moon[1]
	26	13	Neptune 4° N of Moon		12	16	Jupiter 5° N of Moon
	27	20	Moon at perigee		13	07	full moon
	28	01	new moon		14	15	Antares 0.°1 N of Moon[1]
March	1	02	Mercury 4° N of Moon		18	20	Mercury in superior conjunction
	1	11	Uranus in conjunction with Sun		19	15	Neptune 4° N of Moon
	2	07	Mercury stationary		20	09	last quarter
	5	00	Jupiter stationary		21	10	Uranus 1.°0 N of Moon[1]
	6	07	Mars 3° S of Moon		22	15	Moon at perigee
	6	20	first quarter		22	17	Neptune stationary
	10	18	Saturn 4° S of Moon		24	08	Venus 4° S of Moon
	11	00	Mars 7° N of Aldebaran		25	05	Mars 5° S of Pollux
	12	03	Mercury in inferior conjunction		27	05	new moon
	13	02	Moon at apogee		31	03	Mars 3° S of Moon
	15	00	full moon[3]		31	12	Vesta 0.°9 S of Moon[1]
	17	11	Spica 0.°3 N of Moon[1]		31	21	Saturn 4° S of Moon
	19	14	Jupiter 5° N of Moon	June	3	23	first quarter
	20	18	equinox		4	02	Moon at apogee
					7	09	Spica 0.°1 S of Moon[1]
					8	19	Jupiter 5° N of Moon
					10	23	Antares 0.°1 N of Moon[1]
					11	18	full moon

Astronomical Phenomena for 2006 (continued)

MONTH	DAY	HOUR (GMT)	EVENT	MONTH	DAY	HOUR (GMT)	EVENT
June	15	21	Neptune 3° N of Moon	August	28	08	Spica 0°5 N of Moon[1]
	16	17	Moon at perigee		30	01	Jupiter 5° N of Moon
	16	17	Pluto at opposition		31	23	first quarter
	17	17	Uranus 0°6 N of Moon[1]	September	1	02	Antares 0°5 N of Moon[1]
	17	23	Mars 0°6 N of Saturn				
	18	14	last quarter		1	05	Mercury in superior conjunction
	19	16	Uranus stationary				
	20	20	Mercury greatest elongation E (25°)		2	06	Juno in conjunction with Sun
					5	11	Pluto stationary
	20	23	Mercury 6° S of Pollux		5	11	Uranus at opposition
	21	12	Solstice		5	22	Neptune 3° N of Moon
	23	03	Venus 6° S of Moon		5	23	Venus 0°8 N of Regulus
	25	16	new moon				
	26	12	Ceres stationary		7	15	Uranus 0°4 N of Moon[1]
	27	14	Mercury 5° S of Moon		7	19	full moon[2]
	28	11	Saturn 3° S of Moon		8	03	Moon at perigee
	28	19	Vesta 0°2 N of Moon[1]		11	01	Vesta in conjunction with Sun
	28	21	Mars 2° S of Moon				
July	1	20	Moon at apogee		14	11	last quarter
	1	20	Pallas at opposition		19	03	Saturn 2° S of Moon
	2	20	Venus 4° N of Aldebaran		22	05	Moon at apogee
	3	17	first quarter		22	12	new moon[2]
	3	23	Earth at aphelion		23	04	Equinox
	4	02	Mercury stationary		24	04	Mercury 1°8 N of Moon
	4	17	Spica 0°1 N of Moon[1]				
	6	02	Jupiter 5° N of Moon		24	14	Spica 0°5 N of Moon[1]
	6	19	Jupiter stationary		26	16	Jupiter 5° N of Moon
	8	08	Antares 0°2 N of Moon[1]		27	15	Mercury 1°3 N of Spica
	11	03	full moon		28	08	Antares 0°5 N of Moon[1]
	13	04	Neptune 3° N of Moon				
	13	18	Moon at perigee		30	11	first quarter
	14	23	Uranus 0°4 N of Moon[1]	October	3	07	Neptune 3° N of Moon
	17	19	last quarter		5	00	Uranus 0°5 N of Moon[1]
	18	07	Mercury in inferior conjunction		5	20	Ceres stationary
	22	06	Mars 0°7 N of Regulus		6	14	Moon at perigee
	23	00	Venus 6° S of Moon		7	03	full moon
	25	05	new moon		14	00	last quarter
	27	17	Mars 1°1 S of Moon[1]		16	14	Saturn 2° S of Moon
	28	17	Mercury stationary		17	04	Mercury greatest elongation E (25°)
	29	13	Moon at apogee				
August	1	01	Spica 0°4 N of Moon[1]		19	10	Moon at apogee
	2	09	first quarter		19	18	Juno 0°3 N of Moon[1]
	2	12	Jupiter 5° N of Moon		22	05	new moon
	4	18	Antares 0°4 N of Moon[1]		23	07	Mars in conjunction with Sun
	6	12	Mercury 9° S of Pollux				
	7	01	Mercury greatest elongation W (19°)		24	08	Jupiter 5° N of Moon
					24	08	Mercury 1°4 N of Moon
	7	12	Saturn in conjunction with Sun		25	14	Antares 0°4 N of Moon[1]
	8	08	Venus 7° S of Pollux		25	22	Mercury 4° S of Jupiter
	9	11	full moon		27	18	Venus in superior conjunction
	9	12	Neptune 3° N of Moon				
	10	18	Moon at perigee		28	14	Mercury 4° S of Jupiter
	11	05	Neptune at opposition		29	00	Mercury stationary
	11	06	Uranus 0°3 N of Moon[1]		29	07	Neptune stationary
	12	15	Ceres at opposition		29	21	first quarter
	16	02	last quarter		30	14	Neptune 3° N of Moon
	22	03	Venus 3° S of Moon	November	1	08	Uranus 0°5 N of Moon[1]
	23	19	new moon		4	00	Moon at perigee
	24	10	Pallas stationary		5	13	full moon
	25	14	Mars 0°6 N of Moon[1]		8	22	Mercury in inferior conjunction, transit over Sun
	26	01	Moon at apogee				
	26	23	Venus 0°07 N of Saturn		12	18	last quarter

Astronomical Phenomena for 2006 (continued)

MONTH	DAY	HOUR (GMT)	EVENT	MONTH	DAY	HOUR (GMT)	EVENT
November	13	01	Saturn 1°6 S of Moon	December	12	00	Mars 0°8 S of Jupiter
	15	23	Moon at apogee		12	15	last quarter
	17	19	Mercury stationary		13	19	Moon at apogee
	18	03	Spica 0°6 N of Moon[1]		14	08	Mercury 5° N of Antares
	19	13	Mercury 6° N of Moon				
	20	14	Uranus stationary		15	11	Spica 0°8 N of Moon[1]
	20	22	new moon		18	15	Pluto in conjunction with Sun
	21	23	Jupiter in conjunction with Sun		18	21	Jupiter 6° N of Moon
	25	13	Mercury greatest elongation W (20°)		19	03	Mars 4° N of Antares
					19	04	Antares 0°8 N of Moon[1]
	26	21	Neptune 3° N of Moon		19	04	Mars 5° N of Antares
	28	06	first quarter		20	14	new moon
	28	15	Uranus 0°3 N of Moon[1]		22	00	solstice
December	2	00	Moon at perigee		24	03	Neptune 3° N of Moon
	5	00	full moon		25	21	Uranus 0°08 S of Moon[1]
	6	20	Saturn stationary				
	10	11	Saturn 1°2 S of Moon[1]		27	15	first quarter
	10	16	Mercury 0°1 N of Jupiter		28	02	Moon at perigee

[1]Occultation. [2]Eclipse. [3]Penumbral eclipse.

Morning and Evening Stars

This table gives the morning and evening stars for autumn 2005 through 2006. The morning and evening stars are actually planets visible to the naked eye during the early morning and at evening twilight.

PLANET	MORNING STAR	EVENING STAR
Mercury	December 2005; 1–12 Jan, 19 Mar–11 May, 26 Jul–24 Aug, and 15 Nov–21 Dec 2006	30 Sep–19 Nov 2005; 8 Feb–6 Mar, 26 May–11 Jul, and 12 Sep–3 Nov 2006
Venus	19 Jan–19 Sep 2006	9 May 2005–8 Jan 2006; 8 Dec–31 Dec 2006
Mars	10–31 Dec 2006	7 Nov 2005–7 Sep 2006
Jupiter	5 Nov 2005–4 May 2006 and 5–31 Dec 2006	4 May–9 Nov 2006
Saturn	11 Aug 2005–27 Jan 2006 and 26 Aug–31 Dec 2006	27 Jan–20 Jul 2006
Uranus	late March–fall 2006	December 2005–early February 2006 and December 2006
Neptune	late February 2006–fall 2006	November 2005–early January 2006 and mid-November–31 Dec 2006

Meteors, Meteorites, and Meteor Showers

A meteor (also called a **shooting star** or **falling star**) is a streak of light in the sky that results when a particle or small chunk of stony or metallic matter enters the Earth's atmosphere and vaporizes. The term is sometimes applied to the falling object itself, but the latter is properly called a **meteoroid**. The vast majority of meteoroids burn up in the upper atmosphere, but occasionally one of relatively large mass survives its fiery plunge and reaches the surface as a solid body. Such an object is known as a **meteorite**.

On any clear night in the countryside beyond the bright lights of cities, one can observe with the naked eye several meteors per hour as they streak through the sky. Quite often they vary in brightness along the path of their flight, appear to emit "sparks" or flares, and sometimes leave a luminous train that lingers after their flight has ended. These meteors are the result of the high-velocity collision of meteoroids with the Earth's atmosphere. Nearly all such interplanetary bodies are small fragments derived from comets or asteroids.

The brightest meteor (possibly of cometary origin) for which historical documentation exists—called the **Tunguska event**—struck on 30 Jun 1908 in central Siberia and rivaled the Sun in brightness. The energy delivered to the atmosphere by this impact was roughly equivalent to that of a 10-megaton thermonuclear explosion and caused the destruction of forest over an area of about 2,000 sq km (772.2 sq mi). The geologic record of cratering attests to the impact of much more massive meteoroids. Fortunately, impacts of this magnitude occur only once or twice every 100 million years. It is hypothesized that large impacts of this kind may have played a major role in determining the course of biological evolution by causing simultaneous **mass extinctions** of many species of organisms, possibly including the dinosaurs some 65 million years ago. If so, the replacement of reptiles by mammals as the dominant land animals, the eventual consequence of which was the rise of the human species, would be the result of a grand example of a phenomenon observable every clear night.

The **visibility of meteors** is a consequence of the high velocity of meteoroids in interplanetary space. Before entering the region of the Earth's gravitational influence, their **velocities** range from a few kilometers per second up to as high as 72 km (44.7 mi) per second. As they approach the Earth, the Earth's gravitational field accelerates them to even higher velocities. This great release of energy destroys meteoroids of small mass—particularly those with relatively high ve-

locities—very quickly. Numerous meteors end their observed flight at altitudes above 80 km (49.7 mi), and penetration to as low as 50 km (31 mi) is unusual.

"Showers" of meteors have been known since ancient times. On rare occasions, these showers are very dramatic, with thousands of meteors falling per hour. More often, the background hourly rate of roughly 5 observed meteors increases up to about 10–50. Some of the best-known meteor showers are listed below, with their average date of maximum strength and associated comet, if known: **Quadrantid** (3 January); **Lyrid** (22 April; 1861 I [Thatcher]); **Eta Aquarid** (3 May; Halley); **S. Delta Aquarid** (29 July); **Capricornid** (30 July); **Perseid** (12 August; Swift-Tuttle); **Andromedid** (3 October; Biela); **Draconid** (9 October; Giacobini-Zinner); **Orionid** (21 October; Halley); **Taurid** (8 November; Encke); **Leonid** (17 November; Temple-Tuttle); **Germinid** (14 December; 3200 Phaeton [this body exhibits no cometary activity and may be of asteroidal rather than cometary origin]).

Auroras

Auroras are **luminous phenomena** of the upper atmosphere that occur primarily in high latitudes of both hemispheres; auroras in the Northern Hemisphere are called **aurora borealis**, or **northern lights**; in the Southern Hemisphere, **aurora australis**, or **southern lights**.

Auroras are caused by the interaction of energetic particles (electrons and protons) from outside the atmosphere with atoms of the upper atmosphere. Such interaction occurs in zones surrounding the Earth's magnetic poles. During periods of intense solar activity, auroras occasionally extend to the middle latitudes; for example, the aurora borealis has been seen at latitudes as far south as 40° in the US.

Auroras take many **forms**, including luminous curtains, arcs, bands, and patches. The uniform arc is the most stable form of aurora, sometimes persisting for hours without noticeable variation. In a great display, however, other forms appear, commonly under-

going dramatic variation. The lower edges of the arcs and folds are usually much more sharply defined than the upper parts. Greenish rays may cover most of the sky poleward of the magnetic zenith, ending in an arc that is usually folded and sometimes edged with a lower red border that may ripple like drapery. The display ends with a poleward retreat of the auroral forms, the rays gradually degenerating into diffuse areas of white light.

The **mechanisms** that produce auroral displays are not completely understood. It is known, however, that charged particles arriving in the vicinity of Earth as part of the solar wind are captured by the Earth's magnetic field and conducted downward toward the magnetic poles. They collide with oxygen and nitrogen atoms, knocking away electrons to leave ions in excited states. These ions emit radiation at various wavelengths, creating the characteristic colors (red or greenish blue) of the aurora.

Eclipses

An **eclipse** is a complete or partial obscuring of one celestial body by another; this event occurs when three celestial objects become aligned.

The Sun is eclipsed when the Moon comes between it and the Earth. (Hence, a **solar eclipse** can only occur during a new moon.) The Moon's shadow sweeps across the Earth, darkening the sky, while the Moon blocks out some portion of the view of the Sun. During a total eclipse of the Sun, the Moon's elliptical orbit brings the satellite closer to Earth and causes it to appear larger than the Sun. When the Moon's orbit places it at its farthest distance from Earth, the Moon appears smaller than the Sun and the eclipse will appear as a ring or "annulus" of bright sunlight around the Moon.

A **lunar eclipse** occurs when the Moon moves into the shadow of the Earth cast by the Sun. A lunar eclipse can only occur during a full moon. Lunar eclipses can be penumbral, partial, or total. The first type is of interest to astronomers but is difficult to detect because the Moon's dimming is so slight. With the next two types either a portion of the Moon or the entire Moon passes through Earth's umbral shadow.

It is safe to watch a lunar eclipse, but solar eclipses must be viewed via a projection onto another surface or through protective filters designed specially for eclipses.

The eclipses for 2006 are given in the table below.

	DATE	TYPE	VISIBLE IN
Solar eclipses	29 March	total eclipse	western Asia, Europe, northern and western Africa, eastern Brazil
	22 September	annular eclipse	South America, western and southern Africa, Antarctica
Lunar eclipses	14–15 March	penumbral eclipse	North America, western Oceania, South America, Europe, Africa, Asia
	7 September	partial eclipse	Asia, Oceania, Europe, Africa, eastern Brazil

Characteristics of Celestial Bodies

Mean orbital velocity indicates the average speed with which a planet orbits the Sun unless otherwise specified. *Inclination of orbit to ecliptic* indicates the angle of tilt between a planet's orbit and the plane of the Earth's orbit (essentially the plane of the solar system). *Orbital period* indicates the planet's sidereal year (in Earth days except where noted). *Rotation period* indicates the planet's sidereal day (in Earth days except where noted). *Inclination of equator to orbit* indicates the angle of tilt between a planet's orbit and its equator. *Gravitational acceleration* is a measure of the body's gravitational pull on other objects. *Escape velocity* is the speed needed at the surface to escape the planet's gravitational pull.

Sun
diameter (at equator): 1,390,000 km (863,705 mi)
mass (in 10^{20} kg): 19.8 billion
density (mass/volume, in kg/m³): 1,408
mean orbital velocity: the Sun orbits the Milky Way's center at around 220 km/sec (136.7 mi/sec)
orbital period: the Sun takes approximately 250 million Earth years to complete its orbit around the Milky Way's center
rotation period: 25–36 Earth days
gravitational acceleration: 275 m/sec² (902.2 ft/sec²)
escape velocity: 618.02 km/sec (384.01 mi/sec)
mean temperature at visible surface: 5,527 °C (9,980 °F)
probes and space missions: US—Pioneer 5-9, launched 1959-87; Skylab, launched 1973; Ulysses, 1990; Genesis, 2001; Japan—Yohkoh, 1991; US/European Space Agency (ESA)—SOHO, 1995.

Mercury
average distance from Sun: 58 million km (36 million mi)
diameter (at equator): 4,879 km (3,032 mi)
mass (in 10^{20} kg): 3,300
density (mass/volume, in kg/m³): 5,427
eccentricity of orbit*: 0.205
mean orbital velocity: 47.9 km/sec (29.7 mi/sec)
inclination of orbit to ecliptic: 7.0°
orbital period: 88 Earth days
rotation period: 58.6 Earth days
inclination of equator to orbit: probably 0°
gravitational acceleration: 3.7 m/sec² (12.1 ft/sec²)
escape velocity: 4.3 km/sec (2.7 mi/sec)
mean temperature at surface†: 167 °C (333 °F)
satellites: none known
probes and space missions: US—Mariner 10, 1973; Messenger, 2004.

Venus
average distance from Sun: 108.2 million km (67.2 million mi)
diameter (at equator): 12,104 km (7,521 mi)
mass (in 10^{20} kg): 48,700
density (mass/volume, in kg/m³): 5,243
eccentricity of orbit*: 0.007
mean orbital velocity: 35.0 km/sec (21.8 mi/sec)
inclination of orbit to ecliptic: 3.4°
orbital period: 224.7 Earth days
rotation period: 243.0 Earth days (retrograde)
inclination of equator to orbit: 177.4°
gravitational acceleration: 8.9 m/sec² (29.1 ft/sec²)
escape velocity: 10.4 km/sec (6.4 mi/sec)
mean temperature at surface†: 464 °C (867 °F)
satellites: none known
probes and space missions: USSR—Venera 1-16, 1961-83; Vega 1 and 2, 1984; US—Mariner 2, 5, and 10, 1962, 1967, and 1973; Pioneer Venus 1 and 2, 1978; Galileo, 1989; Magellan, 1989.

Earth
average distance from Sun: 149.6 million km (93 million mi)
diameter (at equator): 12,756 km (7,926 mi)
mass (in 10^{20} kg): 59,700
density (mass/volume, in kg/m³): 5,515
eccentricity of orbit*: 0.017
mean orbital velocity: 29.8 km/sec (18.5 mi/sec)
inclination of orbit to ecliptic: 0.00°
orbital period: 365.25 days
rotation period: 23 hours, 56 minutes, and 4 seconds of mean solar time
inclination of equator to orbit: 23.5°
gravitational acceleration: 9.8 m/sec² (32.1 ft/sec²)
escape velocity: 11.2 km/sec (7.0 mi/sec)
mean temperature at surface†: 15 °C (59 °F)
satellites: 1 known—the Moon.

Moon (of Earth)
average distance from Earth: 384,401 km (238,855.7 mi)
diameter (at equator): 3,475 km (2,159 mi)
mass (in 10^{20} kg): 730
density (mass/volume, in kg/m³): 3,340
eccentricity of orbit*: orbital eccentricity of Moon around Earth is 0.055
mean orbital velocity: the Moon orbits Earth at 1.0 km/sec (0.64 mi/sec)
inclination of orbit to ecliptic: 5.1°
orbital period: the Moon revolves around the Earth in 27.32 Earth days
rotation period: the Moon rotates on its axis every 27.32 Earth days (synchronous with orbital period)
inclination of equator to orbit: 6.7°
gravitational acceleration: 1.6 m/sec² (5.3 ft/sec²)
escape velocity: 2.4 km/sec (1.5 mi/sec)
mean temperature at surface†: daytime: 107 °C (224.6 °F); nighttime: –153 °C (–243.4 °F)
probes and space missions: USSR, US, ESA, Japan—collectively about 70 missions since 1959, including 9 manned missions by the US. On 20 Jul 1969 humans first set foot on the Moon, from NASA's Apollo 11.

Mars
average distance from Sun: 227.9 million km (141.6 million mi)
diameter (at equator): 6,794 km (4,222 mi)
mass (in 10^{20} kg): 6,420
density (mass/volume, in kg/m³): 3,933
eccentricity of orbit*: 0.094
mean orbital velocity: 24.1 km/sec (15 mi/sec)
inclination of orbit to ecliptic: 1.9°
orbital period: 687 Earth days (1.88 Earth years)
rotation period: 24.6 Earth hours
inclination of equator to orbit: 24.9°
gravitational acceleration: 3.7 m/sec² (12.1 ft/sec²)
escape velocity: 5.0 km/sec (3.1 mi/sec)
mean temperature at surface†: –65 °C (–85 °F)
satellites: 2 known—Phobos and Deimos

probes and space missions: US—Mariner 4, 6, 7, and 9, 1964–71; Viking 1 and 2, 1975; Mars Global Surveyor, 1996; Mars Pathfinder, 1996; 2001 Mars Odyssey, 2001; Mars Exploration Rovers, 2003; USSR—Mars 2–7, 1971–73; Phobos 1 and 2, 1988; ESA—Mars Express, 2003.

asteroids

(several hundred thousand small rocky bodies, about 1,000 km [610 mi] or less in diameter, that orbit the Sun primarily between the orbits of Mars and Jupiter)

distance from Sun: between approximately 300 million km (190 million mi) and 600 million km (380 million mi), with notable outlyers

estimated mass: 2.3×10^{21} kg

probes and space missions: US—Galileo, 1989; Ulysses, 1990; NEAR Shoemaker, 1996; Deep Space 1, 1998; Stardust, 1999; US/ESA/Italy—Cassini-Huygens, 1997; ESA—Rosetta, 2004; Japan—Hayabusa, 2003.

Jupiter

average distance from Sun: 778.6 million km (483.8 million mi)

diameter (at equator): 142,984 km (88,846 mi)

mass (in 10^{20} kg): 18,990,000

density (mass/volume, in kg/m^3): 1,326

eccentricity of orbit*: 0.049

mean orbital velocity: 13.1 km/sec (8.1 mi/sec)

inclination of orbit to ecliptic: 1.3°

orbital period: 11.86 Earth years

rotation period: 9.9 Earth hours

inclination of equator to orbit: 3.1°

gravitational acceleration: 23.1 m/sec^2 (75.9 ft/sec^2)

escape velocity: 59.5 km/sec (37.0 mi/sec)

mean temperature at surface†:–110 °C (–166 °F)

satellites: more than 60 moons—including Callisto, Ganymede, Europa, and Io—plus rings

probes and space missions: US—Pioneer 10 and 11, 1972–73; Voyager 1 and 2, 1977; Galileo, 1989; Ulysses, 1990; US/ESA/Italy—Cassini-Huygens, 1997.

Saturn

average distance from Sun: 1.433 billion km (890.8 million mi)

diameter (at equator): 120,536 km (74,897 mi)

mass (in 10^{20} kg): 5,680,000

density (mass/volume, in kg/m^3): 687

eccentricity of orbit*: 0.057

mean orbital velocity: 9.7 km/sec (6 mi/sec)

inclination of orbit to ecliptic: 2.5°

orbital period: 29.43 Earth years

rotation period: 10.7 Earth hours

inclination of equator to orbit: 26.7°

gravitational acceleration: 9.0 m/sec^2 (29.4 ft/sec^2)

escape velocity: 35.5 km/sec (22.1 mi/sec)

mean temperature at surface†: –140 °C (–220 °F)

satellites: more than 45 moons—including Titan—plus rings

probes and space missions: US—Pioneer 11, 1973; Voyager 1 and 2, 1977; US/ESA/Italy—Cassini-Huygens, 1997.

Uranus

average distance from Sun: 2.872 billion km (1.784 billion miles)

diameter (at equator): 51,118 km (31,763 mi)

mass (in 10^{20} kg): 868,000

density (mass/volume, in kg/m^3): 1,270

eccentricity of orbit*: 0.046

mean orbital velocity: 6.8 km/sec (4.2 mi/sec)

inclination of orbit to ecliptic: 0.8°

orbital period: 84.01 Earth years

rotation period: 17.2 Earth hours (retrograde)

inclination of equator to orbit: 97.8°

gravitational acceleration: 8.7 m/sec^2 (28.5 ft/sec^2)

escape velocity: 21.3 km/sec (13.2 mi/sec)

mean temperature at surface†: –195 °C (–320 °F)

satellites: at least 27 moons, plus rings

probes and space missions: US—Voyager 2, 1977.

Neptune

average distance from Sun: 4.495 billion km (2.793 billion mi)

diameter (at equator): 49,528 km (30,775 mi)

mass (in 10^{20} kg): 1,020,000

density (mass/volume, in kg/m^3): 1,638

eccentricity of orbit*: 0.009

mean orbital velocity: 5.4 km/sec (3.4 mi/sec)

inclination of orbit to ecliptic: 1.8°

orbital period: 164.79 Earth years

rotation period: 16.1 Earth hours

inclination of equator to orbit: 28.3°

gravitational acceleration: 11.0 m/sec^2 (36.0 ft/sec^2)

escape velocity: 23.5 km/sec (14.6 mi/sec)

mean temperature at surface†: –200 °C (–330 °F)

satellites: at least 13 moons, plus rings

probes and space missions: US—Voyager 2, 1977.

Pluto

average distance from Sun: 5.910 billion km (3.67 billion mi); Pluto lies within the Kuiper belt and can be considered its largest known member.

diameter (at equator): 2,344 km (1,485 mi)

mass (in 10^{20} kg): 125

density (mass/volume, in kg/m^3): about 2,000

eccentricity of orbit*: 0.249

mean orbital velocity: 4.72 km/sec (2.93 mi/sec)

inclination of orbit to ecliptic: 17.2°

orbital period: 248 Earth years

rotation period: 6.4 Earth days (retrograde)

inclination of equator to orbit: 122.5°

gravitational acceleration: 0.6 m/sec^2 (1.9 ft/sec^2)

escape velocity: 1.1 km/sec (0.7 mi/sec)

mean temperature at surface†: –225 °C (–375 °F)

satellites: 1 known—Charon.

Charon (moon of Pluto)

average distance from Pluto: 19,600 km (12,178.8 mi)

diameter (at equator): 1,250 km (777 mi)

mass (in 10^{20} kg): 19

density (mass/volume, in kg/m^3): about 1,700

eccentricity of orbit*: 0

mean orbital velocity: Charon orbits Pluto at 0.23 km/sec (0.142 mi/sec)

inclination of orbit to Pluto's equator: close to 0°

orbital period: 6.3873 Earth days

rotation period: 6.3873 Earth days

gravitational acceleration: 0.21 m/sec^2 (0.69 ft/sec^2)

escape velocity: 0.58 km/sec (0.36 mi/sec)

mean temperature at surface†: as low as –240 °C (–400 °F).

Comet 1P Halley
distance from Sun at closest point of orbit is 87.8 million km (54 million mi). Farthest distance from Sun is 5.2 billion km (3.2 billion mi).
diameter (at equator): 16 x 8 x 8 km (9.9 x 4.9 x 4.9 mi)
density (mass/volume, in kg/m³): possibly as low as 200
eccentricity of orbit*: 0.967
inclination of orbit to ecliptic: 18°
orbital period: 76.1 to 79.3 Earth years. The next appearance will be 2061. The comet's orbit is retrograde.
rotation period: 52 Earth hours
probes and space missions: ESA—Giotto, 1985; USSR—Vega 1 and 2, 1985; Japan—Sakigake and Suisei, 1985.

Comet 2P Encke
distance from Sun at closest point of orbit is 50 million km (31 million mi). Farthest distance from Sun is 658 million km (408 million mi).
eccentricity of orbit*: 0.847
orbital period: 3.3 Earth years (shortest known for a comet); next closest pass of Sun is on 19 Apr 2007.

Comet 9P Tempel 1
distance from Sun at closest point of orbit is 225 million km (140 million mi). Farthest distance from Sun is 708 million km (440 million mi).
eccentricity of orbit*: 0.52
orbital period: 5.52 Earth years; next closest pass of Sun is in January 2011.
rotation period: 41 Earth hours
probes and space missions: US—Deep Impact, 2005

Comet 81P Wild 2
distance from Sun at closest point of orbit is 236.8 million km (147.1 million mi). Farthest distance from Sun is 10 billion km (6.2 billion mi).
eccentricity of orbit*: 0.54
orbital period: 6.39 Earth years; next closest pass of Sun is in February 2010.
probes and space missions: US—Stardust, 1999.

Comet Hale-Bopp
distance from Sun at closest point of orbit is 136 million km (84.5 million mi). Farthest distance from Sun is 74.7 billion km (46.4 billion mi).
eccentricity of orbit*: 0.995
orbital period: 4,000 Earth years; last closest pass of Sun was on 31 Mar 1997.

Comet Hyakutake
distance from Sun at closest point of orbit is 34 million km (21 million mi). Farthest distance from Sun is 344 billion km (213 billion mi).
eccentricity of orbit*: 0.9998
orbital period: about 40,000 Earth years; last closest pass of Sun was on 1 May 1996.

Kuiper belt
(a huge flat ring located beyond Neptune containing residual icy material from the formation of the outer planets)
average distance from Sun (main concentration): 4.5–7.5 billion km (2.8–4.7 billion mi)
mass: Scientists estimate there may be as many as 100,000 icy, cometlike bodies of a size greater than 100 km in the Kuiper belt; the belt is estimated to have a mass of 6,000 x 10²⁰ kg.

Oort cloud
(an immense, roughly spherical cloud of icy, cometlike bodies inferred to orbit Sun at distances roughly 1,000 times that of the orbit of Pluto)
average distance from Sun: 3–7 trillion km (1.9–4.3 trillion mi)
mass: some trillions of the cloud's icy objects have an estimated total mass of at least 600,000 x 10²⁰ kg (10 times the mass of Earth).

*Eccentricity of orbit measures circularity or elongation of an orbit; 0 indicates circular orbits, and closer to 1 more elliptical ones.   †For planets with no surface, temperature given is at a level in the atmosphere equal to 1 bar of pressure.

Solar System Superlatives

Largest planet in solar system: Jupiter (142,984 km [88,846 mi] diameter); all of the other planets in the solar system could fit inside Jupiter.
Largest moon in the solar system: Jupiter's moon Ganymede (5,270 km [3,275 mi]).
Smallest planet in solar system: Pluto (2,390 km [1,485 mi] diameter).
Smallest moons in the solar system: Saturn and Jupiter both have numerous satellites that are smaller than 10 km (6 mi) in diameter.
Planet closest to the Sun: Mercury (average distance from the Sun 58 million km [36 million mi]).
Planet farthest from the Sun: usually Pluto (average distance from the Sun 5.91 billion km [3.67 billion mi]); for 20 years of its 248-year orbital period, Pluto travels within Neptune's orbit, temporarily allowing Neptune to hold the title of farthest planet.

Planet with the most eccentric (least circular) orbit: Pluto (eccentricity of 0.249).
Moon with the most eccentric orbit: Neptune's moon Nereid (eccentricity of 0.75).
Planet with the least eccentric orbit: Venus (eccentricity of 0.007).
Moon with the least eccentric orbit: Pluto's moon, Charon (eccentricity of 0.0).
Planet most tilted on its axis: Uranus (axial tilt of 98° from its orbital plane).
Planet with the most moons: Jupiter (more than 60).
Planets with the fewest moons: Mercury and Venus (no moons).
Planet with the longest day: Venus (1 day on Venus equals 243 Earth days).
Planet with the shortest day: Jupiter (1 day on Jupiter equals 9.9 hours).

Planet with the longest year: Pluto (1 year on Pluto equals 248 Earth years).

Planet with the shortest year: Mercury (1 year on Mercury equals 88 Earth days).

Fastest orbiting planet in the solar system: Mercury (47.9 km per second [29.7 mi per second] average orbital speed).

Slowest orbiting planet in the solar system: Pluto (4.72 km per second [2.93 mi per second] average orbital speed).

Hottest planet in solar system: Venus (464 °C [867 °F] average temperature); although Mercury is closer to the Sun, Venus is hotter because Mercury has no atmosphere, whereas the atmosphere of Venus traps heat via a strong greenhouse effect.

Coldest planet in the solar system: Pluto (–225 °C [–375 °F] average temperature).

Brightest visible star in the night sky: Sirius (–1.46 apparent visual magnitude).

Brightest planet in the night sky: Venus (apparent visual magnitude –4.5 to –3.77).

Densest planet: Earth (density of 5,515 kg/m³).

Least dense planet: Saturn (density of 687 kg/m³); Saturn in theory would float in water.

Planet with strongest gravity: Jupiter (more than twice the gravitational force of Earth at an altitude at which 1 bar of atmospheric pressure is exerted).

Planet with weakest gravity: Pluto (about 1/17 the gravitational force of Earth).

Planet with the largest mountain: Mars (Olympus Mons, an extinct volcano, stands some 21 km [13 mi] above the planet's mean radius and 540 km [335 mi] across).

Planet with deepest valley: Mars (Valles Marineris, a system of canyons, is some 4,000 km [2,500 mi] long and from about 2 to 9 km [1 to 5.6 mi] deep).

Largest known impact crater: Valhalla, a crater on Jupiter's moon Callisto, has a bright central area that is about 600 km (370 mi) across with sets of concentric ridges extending about 1,500 km (900 mi) from the center. For contrast, the largest crater on Earth believed to be of impact origin is the Vredefort ring structure in South Africa, which is about 300 km (190 mi) across.

The Sun

The Sun is the star around which the Earth and the other components of the solar system revolve. It is the dominant body of the system, constituting more than 99% of the system's entire mass. The Sun is the source of an enormous amount of energy, a portion of which provides the Earth with the light and heat necessary to support life. The geologic record of the Earth and Moon reveals that the Sun was formed about 4.5 billion years ago. The energy radiated by the Sun is produced during the conversion of hydrogen atoms to helium. The Sun is at least 90% hydrogen by number of atoms, so the fuel is readily available.

The Sun is classified as a G2 V star, where G2 stands for the second hottest stars of the yellow G class—of surface temperature about 5,500 °C (10,000 °F)—and V represents a main sequence, or dwarf, star, the typical star for this temperature class (see also "Classification of Stars"). The Sun exists in the outer part of the Milky Way Galaxy and was formed from material that had been processed inside other stars and supernovas.

The mass of the Sun is 743 times the total mass of all the planets in the solar system and 330,000 times that of the Earth. All the interesting planetary and interplanetary gravitational phenomena are negligible effects in comparison to the gravitational force exerted by the Sun. Under the force of gravity, the great mass of the Sun presses inward, and to keep the star from collapsing, the central pressure outward must be great enough to support its weight. The Sun's core, which occupies approximately 25% of the star's radius, has a density about 100 times that of water (roughly 6 times that at the center of the Earth), but the temperature at the core is at least 15 million °C (27 million °F), so the central pressure is at least 10,000 times greater than that at the center of the

Earth. In this environment atoms are completely stripped of their electrons, and at this high temperature the bare nuclei collide to produce the nuclear reactions that are responsible for generating the energy vital to life on Earth.

The temperature of the Sun's surface is so high that no solid or liquid can exist; the constituent materials are predominantly gaseous atoms, with a very small number of molecules. As a result, there is no fixed surface. The surface viewed from Earth, the photosphere, is approximately 400 km (250 mi) thick and is the layer from which most of the radiation reaches us; the radiation from below the photosphere is absorbed and reradiated, while the emission from overlying layers drops sharply, by about a factor of six every 200 km (124 mi).

While the temperature of the Sun drops from 15 million °C (27 million °F) at the core to around 5,500 °C (10,000 °F) at the photosphere, a surprising reversal occurs above that point; the temperature begins to rise in the chromosphere, a layer several thousand kilometers thick. Temperatures there range from 4,200 °C (7,600 °F) to 100,000 °C (180,000 °F). Above the chromosphere is a comparatively dim, extended halo called the corona, which has a temperature of 1 million °C (1.8 million °F) and reaches far past the planets. Beyond a distance of around 3.5 million km (2.2 million mi) from the Sun, the corona flows outward at a speed (near the Earth) of 400 km/sec (250 mi/sec); this flow of charged particles is called the solar wind.

The Sun is a very stable source of energy. Superposed on this stability, however, is an interesting 11-year cycle of magnetic activity manifested by regions of transient strong magnetic fields called sunspots. The largest sunspots can be seen on the solar surface even without a telescope.

Mercury

Mercury is the planet closest to the Sun, revolving around it at an average distance of 58 million km (36 million mi). In Sumerian times, some 5,000 years ago, it was already known

in the night sky. In classical Greece the planet was called Apollo when it appeared as a morning star and Hermes, for the Greek equivalent of the Roman god Mercury, when it appeared as an evening star.

Mercury's orbit lies inside the orbit of the Earth and is more elliptical than those of most of the other planets. At its closest approach (perihelion), Mercury is only 46 million km (28.5 million mi) from the Sun, while its greatest distance (aphelion) approaches 70 million km (43.5 million mi). Mercury orbits the Sun in 88 Earth days at an average speed of 48 km per second (29.8 mi per sec), allowing it to overtake and pass Earth every 116 Earth days (synodic period).

Because of its proximity to the Sun, the surface of Mercury can become extremely hot. High temperatures at "noon" may reach 400 °C (755 °F) while the "predawn" lowest temperature is –173 °C (–280 °F). Mercury's equator is almost exactly in its orbital plane (its spin axis inclination is nearly zero), and thus Mercury does not have seasons as does the Earth. Because of its elliptical orbit and a peculiarity of its rotational period (see below), however, certain longitudes experience cyclical variations in temperatures on a "yearly" as well as on a "diurnal" basis.

Mercury is about 4,879 km (3,032 mi) in diameter, smaller than any other planet with the exception of Pluto. Mercury is only a bit larger than the Moon. Its mass, as measured by the gravitational perturbation of the path of the Mariner 10 spacecraft during close fly-bys in 1974 and 1975, is about one-eighteenth of the mass of the Earth. Escape velocity, the speed needed to escape from a planet's gravitational field, is about 4.3 km per second (2.7 mi per second)—compared with 11.2 km per sec (7 mi per sec) for the Earth.

The mean density of Mercury, calculated from its mass and radius, is about 5.43 grams per cubic cm, nearly the same as that of the Earth (5.52 grams per cubic cm).

Photographs relayed by the Mariner 10 spacecraft showed that Mercury spins on its axis (rotates) once every 58.646 Earth days, exactly two-thirds of the orbital period of 87.9694 Earth days. This observation confirmed that Mercury is in a 3:2 spin-orbit tidal resonance—i.e., that tides raised on Mercury by the Sun have forced it into a condition that causes it to rotate three times on its axis in the same time it takes to revolve around the Sun twice. The 3:2 spin-orbit coupling combines with Mercury's eccentric orbit to create very unusual temperature effects.

Although Mercury rotates on its axis once every 58.646 Earth days, one rotation does not bring the Sun back to the same part of the sky, because during that time Mercury has moved partway around the Sun. A solar day on Mercury (for example, from one sunrise to another, or one noon to another) is 176 Earth days (exactly two Mercurian years).

Mercury's low escape velocity and high surface temperatures do not permit it to retain a significant atmosphere.

Venus

Venus is the second planet from the Sun and the planet whose orbit is closest to that of the Earth. When visible, Venus is the brightest planet in the sky. Viewed through a telescope, it presents a brilliant, yellow-white, essentially featureless face to the observer. The obscured appearance results because the surface of the planet is hidden from sight by a continuous and permanent cover of clouds.

Venus's orbit is the most nearly circular of that of any planet, with a deviation from perfect circularity of only about 1 part in 150. The period of the orbit—that is, the length of the Venusian year—is 224.7 Earth days. The rotation of Venus is unusual in both its direction and speed. Most of the planets in the solar system rotate in a counterclockwise direction when viewed from above their north poles; Venus, however, rotates in the opposite, or retrograde, direction. Were it not for the planet's clouds, an observer on Venus's surface would see the Sun rise in the west and set in the east.

Venus spins on its axis very slowly, taking 243 Earth days to complete one rotation. Venus's spin and orbital periods are nearly synchronized with the Earth's orbit such that Venus presents almost the same face toward the Earth when the two planets are at their closest approach.

Venus is nearly the Earth's twin in terms of size and mass. Venus's equatorial diameter is about 95% of the Earth's diameter, while its mass is 81.5% that of the Earth. The similarities to the Earth in size and mass also produce a similarity in density; Venus's density is 5.24 grams per cubic cm, as compared with 5.52 for the Earth.

In terms of its shape, Venus is more nearly a perfect sphere than are most planets. A planet's rotation generally causes a slight flattening at the poles and bulging at the equator, but Venus's very slow rotation rate allows it to maintain its highly spherical shape.

Venus has the most massive atmosphere of all the terrestrial planets (Mercury, Venus, Earth, and Mars). Its atmosphere is composed of 96.5% carbon dioxide and 3.5% nitrogen. The atmospheric pressure at the planet's surface varies with the surface elevation but averages about 90 bars, or 90 times the atmospheric pressure at the Earth's surface. This is the same pressure found at a depth of about one kilometer in the Earth's oceans. Temperatures range between a minimum temperature of –45 °C (–49 °F) and a maximum temperature of 500 °C (932 °F); the average temperature is 464 °C (867 °F).

Earth

The Earth is the third planet in distance outward from the Sun. It is the only planetary body in the solar system that has conditions suitable for life, at least as known to modern science.

The average distance of the Earth from the Sun—149.6 million km (93 million mi)—is designated as the distance of the unit of measurement known as the AU (astronomical unit). The Earth orbits the Sun at a speed of 29.8 km (18.5 mi) per second, making one complete revolution in 365.25 days. As it revolves around the Sun, the Earth spins on its axis and rotates completely once every 23 hr 56 min 4 sec. The Earth has a single natural satellite, the Moon.

The fifth largest planet of the solar system, the Earth has a total surface area of roughly 509.6 million sq km (197 million sq mi), of which about 29%, or 148 million square km (57 million square mi), is land. Oceans and smaller seas cover the balance of the surface. The Earth is the only planet known to have liquid water. Together with ice, the liquid water constitutes the hydrosphere. Seawater makes up more than 98% of the total mass of the hydrosphere and covers about 71% of the Earth's surface. Significantly, seawater constituted the environment of the earliest terrestrial life forms.

The Earth's atmosphere consists of a mixture of gases, chiefly nitrogen (78%) and oxygen (21%). Argon makes up much of the remainder of the gaseous envelope, with trace amounts of water vapor, carbon dioxide, and various other gases also present.

The Earth's structure consists of an inner core of nearly solid iron, surrounded by successive layers of molten metals and solid rock, and a thin layer at the surface comprising the continental crust.

The Earth is surrounded by a magnetosphere, a region dominated by the Earth's magnetic field and extending upward from about 140 km (90 mi) in the upper atmosphere. In the magnetosphere, the magnetic field of the Earth traps rapidly moving charged particles (mainly electrons and protons), the majority of which flow from the Sun (as solar wind). If it were not for this shielding effect, such particles would bombard the terrestrial surface and destroy life. High concentrations of the trapped particles make up two doughnut-shaped zones called the Van Allen radiation belts. These belts play a key role in certain geophysical phenomena, such as auroras.

The Moon

The Moon is the sole natural satellite of the Earth. It revolves around the planet from west to east at a mean distance of about 384,400 km (238,900 mi). The Moon is less than one-third the size of the Earth, having a diameter of only about 3,475 km (2,159 mi) at its equator. The Moon shines by reflecting sunlight, but its albedo—i.e., the fraction of light received that is reflected—is only 0.073.

The Moon rotates about its own axis about 27.32 days, which is virtually identical to the time it takes to complete its orbit around the Earth. As a result, the Moon always presents nearly the same face to the Earth. The rate of actual rotation is uniform, but the arc through which the Moon moves from day to day varies somewhat, causing the lunar globe (as seen by a terrestrial observer) to oscillate slightly over a period nearly equal to that of revolution.

The surface of the Moon has been a subject of continuous telescopic study from the time of Galileo's first observation in 1609. The Italian Jesuit astronomer Giovanni B. Riccioli designated the dark areas on the Moon as seas (maria), with such fanciful names as Mare Imbrium ("Sea of Showers") and Mare Nectaris ("Sea of Nectar"). This nomenclature continues to be used even though it is now known that the Moon is completely devoid of surface water. During the centuries that followed the publication of these early studies, more detailed maps and, eventually, photographs were produced. A Soviet space probe photographed the side of the Moon facing away from the Earth in 1959. By the late 1960s the US Lunar Orbiter missions had yielded close-up photographs of the entire lunar surface. On 20 Jul 1969, Apollo 11 astronauts Neil Armstrong and Edwin ("Buzz") Aldrin set foot on the Moon.

The most striking formations on the Moon are its craters. These features, which measure up to about 200 km (320 mi) or more in diameter, are scattered over the surface in great profusion and often overlap one another. Meteorites hitting the lunar surface at high velocity produced most of the large craters. Many of the smaller ones—those measuring less than 1 km (0.6 mi) across—appear to have been formed by explosive volcanic activity, however. The Moon's maria have relatively few craters. These lava outpourings spread over vast areas after most of the craters had already been formed.

Various theories for the Moon's origin have been proposed. At the end of the 19th century, the English astronomer Sir George H. Darwin advanced a hypothesis stating that the Moon had been originally part of the Earth but had broken away as a result of tidal gravitational action and receded from the planet. This was proved unlikely in the 1930s. A theory that arose during the 1950s postulated that the Moon had formed elsewhere in the solar system and was then later captured by the Earth. This idea was also proved to be physically implausible and was dismissed. Today, most investigators favor an explanation known as the giant-impact hypothesis, which postulates that a Mars-sized body struck the proto-Earth early in the history of the solar system. As a result, a cloud of fragments from both bodies was ejected into orbit around the Earth, and this later accreted into the Moon.

Moon Phases, 2005–2006

As the Moon orbits the Earth, more or less of the half of the Moon illuminated by the Sun is visible on Earth. During the lunar month the Moon's appearance changes from dark (the new moon) to being illuminated more and more on the right side (waxing crescent, first quarter, and waxing gibbous) to the full disc being illuminated (the full moon). The phases of the Moon are completed by the Moon being illuminated less and less on the left side (waning gibbous, last quarter, and waning crescent) and end with another new moon. The cycle of the Moon takes place over a period of around 29 days; the time from new moon to new moon is referred to as a lunation.

The phases of the Moon are caused by the positions of the Sun in relationship to the Moon. Thus, when the Sun and Moon are close in the sky a dark new moon is the result (the Sun is lighting the half of the Moon not visible to Earth). When the Sun and Moon are at opposition (in opposite parts of the sky) the full moon occurs (the Sun illuminates fully the half of the Moon seen on Earth). When the Sun and Moon are at about a 90-degree angle, one sees either a first quarter or last quarter moon.

The dates for the new moon, first quarter, full moon, and last quarter for July 2005–December 2006 are given in the table below.

Moon Phases, 2005–2006 (continued)

	NEW MOON	FIRST QUARTER	FULL MOON	LAST QUARTER
July 2005	6	14	21	28
August 2005	5	13	19	26
September 2005	3	11	18	25
October 2005	3	10	17	25
November 2005	2	9	16	23
December 2005	1	8	15	23
January 2006	(31 December)	6	14	22
February 2006	(29 January)	5	13	21
March 2006	(28 February)	6	15	22
April 2006	(29 March)	5	13	21
May 2006	(27 April)	5	13	20
June 2006	(27 May)	3	11	18
July 2006	(25 June)	3	11	17
August 2006	(25 July)	2	9	16
September 2006	(23 August)	(31 August)	7	14
October 2006	(22 September)	(30 September)	7	14
November 2006	(22 October)	(29 October)	5	12
December 2006	(20 November)	(28 November)	5	12
	20	27		

Moon's Apogee and Perigee, 2006

The distance between the centers of mass of the Earth and the Moon varies rather widely due to the combined gravity of the Earth, the Sun, and the planets. For example, during the period 1969–2000, apogee (when the Moon is at the greatest distance from Earth) varied from 404,063 to 406,711 km (251,073 to 252,719 mi), while perigee (when the Moon is closest to Earth) varied from 356,517 to 370,354 km (221,529 to 230,127 mi). Tidal interactions have braked the Moon's spin so that presently the same side always faces the Earth. Dates are Universal Time/GMT.

	Moon at apogee
DATE	NEAREST PHASE OF MOON
17 January	between full moon and last quarter
14 February	between full moon and last quarter
13 March	between first quarter and full moon
9 April	between first quarter and full moon
7 May	between first quarter and full moon
4 June	between first quarter and full moon
1 July	between new moon and first quarter
29 July	between new moon and first quarter
26 August	between new moon and first quarter
22 September	between last quarter and new moon
19 October	between last quarter and new moon
15 November	between last quarter and new moon
13 December	between last quarter and new moon

	Moon at perigee
DATE	NEAREST PHASE OF MOON
1 January	between new moon and first quarter
30 January	between new moon and first quarter
27 February	between last quarter and new moon
28 March	between last quarter and new moon
25 April	between last quarter and new moon
22 May	between last quarter and new moon
16 June	between full moon and last quarter
13 July	between full moon and last quarter
10 August	between full moon and last quarter
8 September	between full moon and last quarter
6 October	between first quarter and full moon
4 November	between first quarter and full moon
2 December	between first quarter and full moon
28 December	between first quarter and full moon

Mars

Mars is the fourth planet in order of distance from the Sun and the seventh in order of diminishing size and mass. It orbits the Sun once in 687 Earth days and spins on its axis once every 24 hr and 37 min.

Owing to its blood-red color, Mars has often been associated with warfare and slaughter. It is named for the Roman god of war; as far back as 3,000 years ago, Babylonian astronomer-astrologers called the planet Nergal for their god of death and pestilence. The Greeks called it Ares for their god of battle; the planet's two satellites, Phobos (Fear) and Deimos (Terror), were later named for the two sons of Ares and Aphrodite.

Mars moves around the Sun at a mean distance of approximately 1.52 times that of the Earth from the Sun. Because the orbit of Mars is relatively elongated, the distance between Mars and the Sun varies from 206.6 to 249.2 million km (128.4 to 154.8 million mi). Mars completes a single orbit in roughly the time in which the Earth completes two. At its closest approach, Mars is less than 56 million km (34.8 million mi) from the Earth, but it recedes to almost 400 million km (248.5 million mi). Mars is a small planet. Its equatorial radius is about half that of Earth, and its mass is only one-tenth the terrestrial value.

The axis of rotation is inclined to the orbital plane at an angle of 24.9°, and, as for the Earth, the tilt gives rise to the seasons on Mars. The Martian year consists of 668.6 Martian solar days (called sols). The orientation and eccentricity of the orbit (eccentricity denotes how much the orbit deviates from a perfect circle, the more elongated the more eccentric) leads to seasons that are quite uneven in length.

The Martian atmosphere is composed mainly of carbon dioxide. It is very thin (less than 1% of the Earth's atmospheric pressure). Evidence suggests that the atmosphere was much denser in the remote past and that water was once much more abundant at the surface. Only small amounts of water are found in the lower atmosphere today, occasionally forming thin ice clouds at high altitudes and, in several localities, morning ice fogs. Mars's polar caps consist of frozen carbon dioxide and water ice. Intriguing spacecraft observations confirm that water ice also is present under large areas of the Martian surface and hint that liquid water may have flowed in geologically recent times.

The characteristic temperature in the lower atmosphere is about –70 °C (–100 °F). Unlike that of Earth, the total mass (and pressure) of the atmosphere experiences large seasonal variations, as carbon dioxide "snows out" at the winter pole.

The surface of Mars shows some of the most dramatic variation in the solar system: the massive extinct volcano Olympus Mons stands some 21 km (13 mi) above the planet's mean radius and is 540 km (335 mi) across, and Valles Marineris, a system of canyons, is some 4,000 km (2,500 mi) long and from about 2 to 9 km (1 to 5.6 mi) deep.

The two satellites of Mars, Phobos and Deimos, were discovered in 1877 by Asaph Hall of the United States Naval Observatory. Little was known about these bodies until observations were made by orbiting spacecraft a century later. The moons of Mars cannot be seen from all locations on the planet because of their small size, proximity to the planet, and near-equatorial orbits.

Special Report: The Mystique of Mars

by Dave Dooling

On 27 Aug 2003, thousands of people lined up at telescopes to glimpse Mars during its closest approach to Earth in more than 60,000 years (at a distance of 56 million km [35 million mi]). Even though more highly detailed images were readily available from robotic spacecraft, why did people want a firsthand view? Simple: Mars attracts. Of all the planets, it is the most similar to Earth in many ways. It has a transparent atmosphere (though thin and consisting largely of carbon dioxide), a day that is only 37 minutes longer than that of Earth, and even an ice cap that waxes and wanes with the seasons. Most important of all, Mars might harbor life.

In the 1960s and '70s, the robot surrogates of the Space Age brought Mars closer to its human observers. NASA's Mariner 4, the first spacecraft to fly by Mars (July 1965), sent back pictures of a bleak, cratered world. The Mariner 6 and 7 flyby missions (July and August 1969) reaffirmed this view. When Mariner 9 went into Martian orbit (November 1971), a planet-wide dust storm was at its height, but as the dust settled, the improved imaging devices on the probe revealed dazzling geologic features, from towering extinct volcanoes to gaping dry valleys.

Mars 3, launched by the USSR, was the first Mars lander (2 Dec 1971), but it went silent after only 20 seconds on the surface. The Viking 1 and 2 landers, NASA spacecraft designed to detect life on Mars, touched down successfully (20 Jul and 3 Sep 1976). Over the next few years, onboard labs did not detect life as it is known on Earth, but they did reveal some unusual chemistry in the surface material they analyzed. The inconclusive results stirred controversy for many years.

In the mid-1990s the public was showered anew with images of Mars. These images were provided by the Mars Global Surveyor, which went into orbit around Mars (September 1997), and the Sojourner rover, which landed on (4 Jul 1997) and traveled over its surface. Exploration of Mars suffered a setback with the back-to-back failures of the Mars Climate Orbiter (launched 1998) and the Mars Polar Lander (1999) and its Deep Space 2 surface-penetration probes. (About a third of all space missions sent to Mars have failed for a variety of reasons.) After a thorough reassessment, NASA pressed on successfully with the Mars Odyssey orbiter and the twin Mars Exploration Rovers, Spirit (landed 3 Jan 2004) and Opportunity (25 Jan 2004). Europe had success with the Mars Express orbiter (2003) but lost its Beagle 2 lander (2003).

A common finding for all of these missions was evidence that Mars once had plentiful water. The Mars Odyssey orbiter and the Mars Express orbiter sent back to Earth thousands of images revealing outflow channels and valley networks that apparently had been formed by flowing water. Among the discoveries of Opportunity, which was equipped with tools to assay chemicals in rocks, were the mineral jarosite (which is typically formed in acidic lakes or hot springs), rock indentations called vugs (which are typically formed when crystals dissolve from rocks), and spherules (which are sometimes formed by minerals emerging from porous rock). Images of the Martian surface taken by cameras on Opportunity showed types of sand banding called festooning and cross-bedding, which led American scientists to announce that the landing site might once have been the shore of a salty sea. Data from the Mars Global Surveyor indicated that the sea would have been as large as the Great Lakes or the Baltic Sea. A separate finding by the Mars Express orbiter was the existence of traces of methane in the Martian atmosphere. Because the methane would normally have become oxidized within a few hundred years, scientists believed it undergoes replenishment, with the mostly likely sources being volcanoes or living organisms.

Even as it was reaching the Moon, NASA sketched plans for human expeditions to Mars. In September 1969 a presidential task group envisioned expeditions with two separate ships under nuclear propulsion, each carrying six astronauts. The first landings were to come as early as 1982, but no funding was forthcoming. Indeed, the US pulled back from plans to explore Mars and canceled the Apollo program as well, ending exploration of the Moon. Several false starts followed, most notably the high-priced proposals of the "90-Day Study" commissioned by Pres. George H.W. Bush in 1989. The loss of space shuttle *Columbia* on 1 Feb 2003, seemed to serve as a turning point in returning to plans for the human exploration of Mars. In the wake of the tragedy, the administration of Pres. George W. Bush moved to retire the shuttle program around 2010 and to discontinue US participation aboard the International Space Station at that time. NASA was directed

© Bruno Fert/Corbis

26 Dec 2004, Nagappattinam, India: tsunami survivor Vasenti cradles her child Rithis on the beach. Vasenti was able to save Rithis but lost her three other children and her husband.

PLATE 2   **WORLD EVENTS**

© Lynsey Addario/Corbis

18 Aug 2004, Bahai, Chad: a sandstorm blows near the Chad-Sudan border. Fighting in the Darfur region of The Sudan has forced thousands of refugees into Chad.

© Stephanie Sinclair/Corbis

© Viktor Korotayev/Reuters/Corbis

© Alexander Natruskin/Reuters/Corbis

2 May 2005, Meerwala, Pakistan: *(above left)* Muchtaran Mai (right) and her best friend Naseem Akhter visit with relatives. Muchtaran Mai defied Pakistani tradition requiring that she commit suicide after a group of men carried out a village council sentence upon her to be gang-raped for an alleged breach of honor by her brother and became an outspoken advocate of women's rights.

2 Sep 2004, Beslan, Russia: *(above)* a member of Russia's special forces carries an infant to safety from a school seized by Chechen insurgents. At least 330 died in the confrontation.

30 May 2005, Moscow: *(left)* Oil billionaire and Yukos chairman Mikhail Khodorkovsky (left) awaits sentencing in his trial for fraud and tax evasion.

© Rick Wilking/Reuters/Corbis

29 Aug 2005, New Orleans LA: a survivor makes his way through the flooded Treme neighborhood after Hurricane Katrina devastated the US Gulf Coast. The hurricane's wind, rain, and storm surge caused overwhelming levee breaches in New Orleans, flattened structures in low-lying areas, left thousands missing or dead, and displaced hundreds of thousands.

© Dylan Martinez/Reuters/Corbis

7 Jul 2005, London: a bomb destroyed a double-decker bus in Tavistock Square, one of four detonated dur-

PLATE 4 WORLD EVENTS

7 Aug 2004, Baghdad, Iraq: *(right)* a masked Iraqi Shi'ite militiaman rushes across a street wielding a rocket-propelled grenade launcher. The grafitti behind him reads "No Bush" in Arabic.

1 Jun 2005, Xinshao County, China: *(below)* a villager rests after floods destroyed her home in central China. At least 22 died in the flooding.

26 Jun 2005, Shirat Hayamin, Gaza Strip: *(center right)* Israeli soldiers and police confront Jewish settlers in the run-up to Israel's planned pull-out from the Gaza Strip.

30 Jan 2005, Al Anbar province, Iraq: *(lower right)* an Iraqi villager demonstrates that she is not armed during a security check while waiting to vote in the national elections.

© Ali Jasim/Reuters/Corbis

AP/Wide World Photos

Getty Images

© Erik de Castro/Reuters/Corbis

© Jason Reed/Reuters/Corbis

3 Mar 2005, Crawford TX: Canadian Prime Minister Paul Martin (left) and Mexican President Vicente Fox ight) walk with US Pres. George W. Bush on a tour of Bush's ranch.

© MAL Langsdon/Reuters/Corbis

4 Jun 2005, Paris: *(above)* French President acques Chirac (center) and UN Secretary-eneral Kofi Annan greet British Prime Minister ony Blair at the Elysée Palace.

2 Nov 2004, Kiev, Ukraine: *(right)* Opposition ader Viktor Yushchenko waits for results of the an-off voting for prime minister. Poisoned with oxin earlier in the year, Yushchenko suffers om a disfiguring illness that creates a stark ntrast to his campaign poster image.

© Korea News Service/Reuters/Corbis

6 May 2005, Wonsan, North Korea: North Korean leader Kim Jong Il (fifth from right) poses with officials at im's inspection of the Wonsan Youth power station construction site.

© Damir Sagolj/Reuters/Corbis

4 Mar 2005, Beirut, Lebanon: a demonstrator

© Darren Whiteside/Reuters/Corbis

1 Oct 2004, Jakarta, Indonesia: Indonesia's newly elected members of parliament are sworn in.

11 Sep 2004, Hong Kong, Ch
pro-democracy activist and le
didate Leung Kwok-hung dist
paign leaflets the day before

13 Dec 2004, Havana, Cuba:
President Fidel Castro (left) g
Venezuelan President Hugo C
Chavez's arrival at José Martí
Airport.

PLATE 8 | ART & ARCHITECTURE

© Fred Prouser/Reuters/Corbis

15 Jun 2005, Los Angeles CA: *(above)* a cosmetic jar featuring a recumbent lion on its lid goes on display at the Los Angeles County Museum of Art's exhibit "Tutankhamun and the Golden Age of Pharaohs."

10 May 2005, Berlin, Germany: *(below)* 2,751 concrete slabs on a sloping area of land the size of two football fields form the Memorial to the Murdered Jews of Europe, designed by American architect Peter Eisenman.

© Molly Riley/Reuters/Corbis

17 Sep 2004, Washington DC: the National Museum of the American Indian, the last museum to be built on the Mall, is built of undulating forms and houses art and artifacts from a variety of cultures indigenous to the western hemisphere.

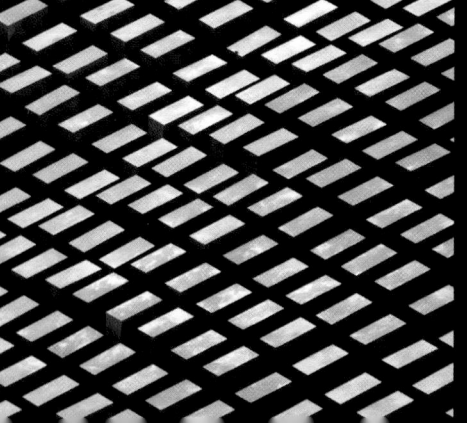

AFP/Getty Images

30 Sep 2004, Dubai, UAE: *(above)* a graphic image illustrates the plan for a luxury retreat being built in the Persian Gulf near Dubai. Three hundred man-made islands are to be laid out in the shape of a world map.

© Kristine Strom Photography

18 Jul 2004, Chicago IL: Anish Kapoor's sculpture *Cloud Gate* attracts throngs of visitors to the new Millennium Park, as does the Jay Pritzker Pavilion (right; designed by Frank O. Gehry) for free outdoor music performances.

© James Leynse/Corbis

15 Nov 2004, New York NY: architect Yoshio Tanichi designed the expanded and renovated Museum of Modern Art at a cost of $425 million; the main floor is shown from the outside.

AFP/Getty Images

3 Jun 2005, Bilbao, Spain: monumental works by American sculptor Richard Serra appear at the Guggenheim Bilbao Museum exhibition, "The Matter of Time."

PLATE 10   SCIENCE & TECHNOLOGY

1 Sep 2004, Ilulissat, Greenland: an iceberg floats in the Ilulissat fjord on Greenland's western coast. The town of Ilulissat risks losing the support of tourists because the Sermeq Kujalleq glacier is receding.

14 Apr 2005, Cremona, Italy: Pieraz-Cryozootech-Stallion, a 48-day-old clone of Pieraz, an Arab gelding and endurance champion, runs in a field in northern Italy. The foal was cloned to make a breeding animal from a sterile one.

1 Sep 2004, Dakar, Senegal: children run as locusts spread into the Senegalese capital after engulfing other areas of North Africa.

NASA/JP

5 May 2005, Pasadena CA: engineers at NASA's Jet Propulsion Laboratory explore options for helping the Mars rover Opportunity get out of a Martian sand pit.

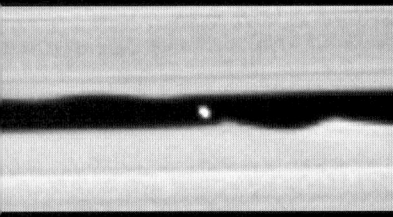

NASA/JPL/Space Science Institute

1 May 2005: The Cassini probe captures images of S/2005 S1, a previously undetected moon orbiting Saturn within the space of the rings' Keeler gap. The moon is 6.4 km (4 mi) in diameter.

AP/Wide World Photos/NOA

12 Aug 2004: Tropical Storm Bonnie (top) moves over northwest Florida and Hurricane Charley (bottom) swirls across Cuba in this NOAA satellite image

9 Jun 2005, Nagakute, Japan: two Partner Ballroom Dance Robots face the audience with a human dancer during a demonstration at the Prototype Robot Exhibition.

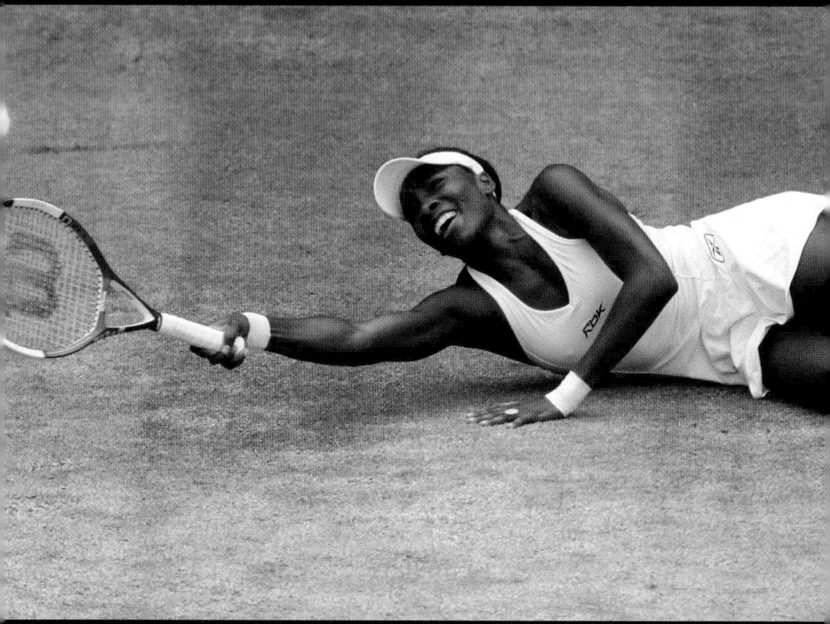

Carl De Souza/AFP/Getty Images

Jul 2005, Wimbledon, England: Venus Williams defeated Lindsay Davenport 4-6, 7-6 (4), 9-7 in the longest omen's final in the history of the Wimbledon tennis tournament, finally prevailing after 2 hours and 45 ninutes of play.

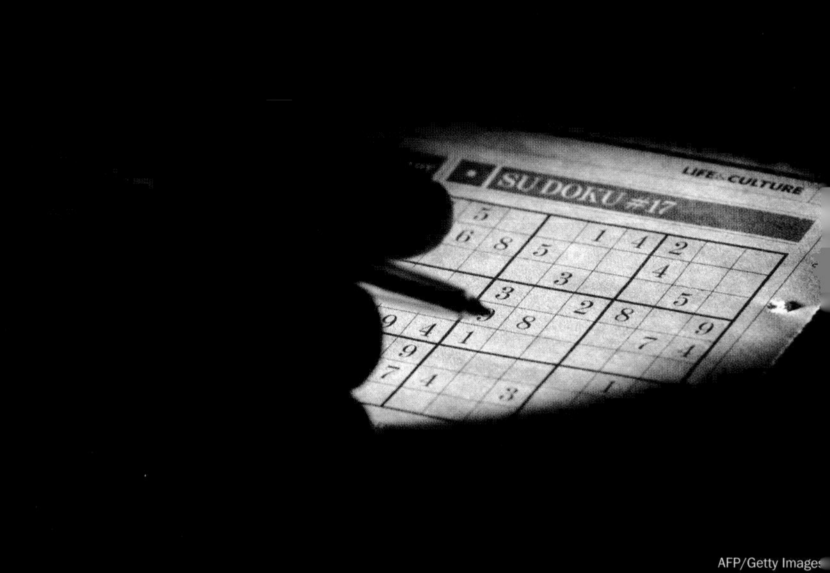

AFP/Getty Images

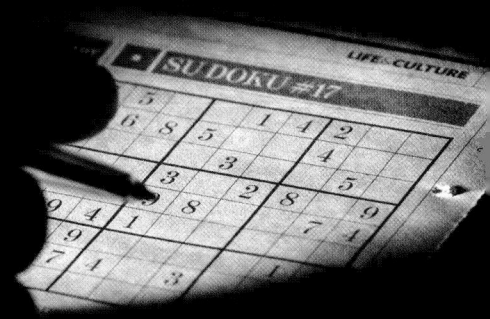

1 May 2005, London: the newly popular game Sudoku appears in *The Independent* newspaper. Players fill

Getty Images

5 May 2005, Indianapolis IN: Danica Patrick, age 23, poses after finishing her qualifying run for the 89th Indy 500 race. Patrick is the driver of the #16 Rahal Letterman Racing Argent Pioneer Panoz Honda.

© John Sommers/Reuters/Corbi

19 Jun 2005, Pinehurst NC: Michael Campbell of New Zealand chips onto the fourth hole during the final round of the US Open golf tournament.

PLATE 14   **ENTERTAINMENT**

© Kimberly White/Corbis

5 Jun 2005, Madrid, Spain: *(below)* singer Shakira performs at the Puerta de Alcalá during the Madrid 2012 Sunday 5th Party.

13 Jun 2005, Santa Maria CA: *(above)* pop singer Michael Jackson leaves the Santa Barbara county courthouse after his acquittal on all child molestation charges.

Getty Images

©Tim Shaffer/Reuters/Corbis

2 Jul 2005, Philadelphia PA: the Dave Matthews Band performs at the Live 8 concert, part of ten shows around the world staged to appl[y] pressure on G8 leaders to address poverty in Africa.

© 20th Century Fox/ZUMA/Corbis

19 May 2005, in a galaxy far, far away: *(above)* Jedi Master Yoda appears in *Star Wars: Revenge of the Sith*.

17 Jan 2005, Los Angeles CA: Clint Eastwood and Hilary Swank celebrate winning Golden Globe awards for best director and best actress

© Jeff Christensen/Reuters/Corbis

5 Jun 2005, New York NY: actress Adriane Lenox accepts the 2005 Tony Award for best featured actress in a play for *Doubt*.

CANAL+/TVE /The Kobal Collection

Gael García Bernal appears in Pedro Almodóvar's film *Bad Education*.

Photo by Bride Productions/ZUMA Press. © 2004 by courtesy of Bride Productions

Aishwarya Rai stars in *Bride and Prejudice*.

© Mike Blake/Reuters/Corbis

14 Nov 2004, Los Angeles CA: Gwen Stefani performs "What You Waiting For?" at the American Music Awards ceremony.

AP/Wide World Photo

12 May 2005, Cannes, France: a giant version of Nick Park's clay-animated character Gromit is unveiled at the Cannes film festival.

PLATE 16 | **OBITUARIES**

© Bassouls Sophie/Corbis Sygma

American writer Susan Sontag

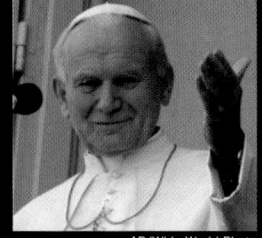

AP/Wide World Photo

Pope John Paul II

The Kobal Collection

American actress Anne Bancroft in the role of Mrs. Robinson in *The Graduate*, with Dustin Hoffman

Hulton Archive/Getty Images

American actor Christopher Reeve in the title role of *Superman*

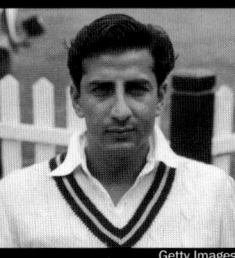

Getty Images

Pakistani cricket player Fazal Mahmood

Mike Hutchings/Reuters

South African rain queen Makobo Modjadji

Remembering Palestinian leader Yasir Arafat

© Eric Gaillard/Reuters/Corbis

© Bettmann/Corbis

Monaco's Prince Rainier, with Grace Kelly

© Reuters/Corbis

Indian bandit Koose Muniswamy Veerappan

AP/Wide World Photo

American legislator Robert T. Matsui

© Manuel Zambrana/Corbis

American chef Julia Child

instead to start planning exploration programs that would take humans back to the Moon by 2020, setting the stage for going onward to Mars. A new Crew Exploration Vehicle would be designed to carry humans to space starting in 2014. A wide range of technologies would need to be developed, including nuclear rockets, which had been abandoned in the 1970s, and advanced radiation shielding to protect astronauts living for years in space.

"Mankind is drawn to the heavens for the same reason we were once drawn into unknown lands and across the open sea," President Bush said at the White House ceremony on 14 Jan 2004 announcing the new direction in the US space program. "We choose to explore space because doing so improves our lives and lifts our national spirit. So let us continue the journey."

Dave Dooling is the Education and Public Outreach Officer at the National Solar Observatory, Sacramento Peak NM, and coauthor of Engineering Tomorrow.

Small Celestial Bodies

Small bodies are defined as all the natural objects in the solar system other than the Sun and the major planets and their satellites. The solar system is populated by vast numbers of these small bodies, which can be grouped as asteroids, comets, and meteoroids (at times, however, the distinctions between these groupings can be somewhat blurred).

Small bodies in stable orbits are found in several regions of the solar system. Most asteroids reside in a belt between Mars and Jupiter at approximately 300–600 million km (190–380 million mi). Others, called Trojan asteroids, are found at gravitationally stable points near the orbits of Mars and Jupiter.

The trans-Neptunian objects (considered comets) are located outside the orbit of Neptune, from around 4.5 billion km (2.8 billion mi) to 7.5 billion km (4.7 billion mi) in the area known as the Kuiper belt. A spherical cloud known as the Oort cloud also contains comets at a distance of some 3–15 trillion km (1.8–9 trillion mi).

Other small bodies travel in unstable paths which cross planetary orbits. These include: all observed comets; near-Earth asteroids, whose orbits either cross or closely approach Earth's orbit; and other planet-crossing objects (a mixture of both asteroids and icy cometlike bodies). All objects on planet-crossing orbits will eventually collide with the Sun or a planet or be permanently ejected from the solar system, although some of these objects do survive for long periods of time due to stabilizing orbital resonances.

Comets originate, and most are still located, in the Kuiper belt and Oort cloud. Even though comets are brief visitors to the inner solar system, their population is constantly replenished through perturbations of the comets in these areas.

There are several characteristics that traditionally have distinguished asteroids, comets, and meteoroids. These are based upon origin, orbital, and physical differences. An object is classified as a comet when it displays a coma or tail (or any evidence of gas or dust coming from it). In addition, the icy objects found in the Kuiper belt (and the Oort cloud, though none of these are observable) are also considered to be comets. They do not display cometary activity because of their great distance from the Sun. Nevertheless, they are believed to be made up of the same volatile material—primarily water and carbon dioxide—as the nuclei of observed comets, and it is the presence of these volatiles on the surface that is responsible for cometary activity. Finally, objects on parabolic or hyperbolic (nonreturning) orbits are generally considered to be comets.

Meteoroids are defined as any small object in space, especially one less than a few tens of meters in size. When a meteoroid enters the Earth's atmosphere, the heat of friction creates a glowing trail of hot gases called a meteor. Should any part of a meteoroid reach the ground without being completely vaporized, that object is termed a meteorite. The term asteroid is traditionally reserved for the larger rocky bodies in solar orbit, which range up to nearly 1,000 km (600 mi) in size.

Asteroids and the Asteroid Belt

Asteroids are any of a host of small rocky bodies, about 1,000 km (600 mi) or less in diameter, that orbit the Sun. About 95% of the known asteroids move in orbits between those of Mars and Jupiter in an area known as the asteroid belt. The orbits of the asteroids, however, are not uniformly distributed within the asteroid belt, but exhibit "gaps." Known as Kirkwood gaps, these asteroid-less areas are maintained by the gravitational force exerted by Jupiter upon asteroids in certain orbits.

The vast majority of asteroids have orbital periods between three years and six years—i.e., between one-fourth and one-half of Jupiter's orbital period. These asteroids are said to be main-belt asteroids. Within the main belt are asteroids that share certain traits. Known as families, about 40% of all known asteroids belong to such groupings. Families are usually assigned the name of the lowest numbered (first discovered) asteroid in the family. The three largest families (Eos, Koronis, and Themis) have been

determined to be compositionally homogeneous; each is thought to comprise fragments from a larger parent body that broke apart in a collision.

Besides the few asteroids in highly unusual orbits, there are a number of groups that fall outside the main belt. Those that have orbital periods greater than one-half that of Jupiter are called outer-belt asteroids. There are four such groups: the Cybeles, Hildas, Thule, and Trojan groups.

There is only one known group of inner-belt asteroids—namely, the Hungarias. The Hungaria asteroids have orbital periods that are less than one-fourth that of Jupiter. Finally, asteroids that pass inside the orbit of Mars are said to be near-Earth asteroids. There are two groups of near-Earth asteroids that deeply cross the Earth's orbit on an almost continuous basis. The first of these to be discovered were the Apollo asteroids. The other group of Earth-crossing asteroids is named Atens. A third group, the Amors, comprises part-time Earth crossers.

Asteroids are thought to be made of the same rocky (stony, metallic, and carbon-rich) material that formed the planets. Scientists believe that at the time the planets were forming the gravitational influence of what became Jupiter kept the asteroids from aggregating into a single planet. Since that time they have been evolving through ongoing collisions so that most of the present-day asteroids are remnants or fragments of larger bodies. As of 2005 astronomers had detected and numbered almost 100,000 asteroids.

Jupiter

Jupiter is the most massive of the planets and is 5th in distance from the Sun. When ancient astronomers named the planet Jupiter for the ruler of the gods in the Greco-Roman pantheon, they had no idea of the planet's true dimensions, but the name is appropriate, for Jupiter is larger than all the other planets combined. It has a narrow ring system and more than 60 known satellites, 3 larger than the Earth's Moon. Jupiter also has an internal heat source—i.e., it emits more energy than it receives from the Sun. This giant has the strongest magnetic field of any planet, with a magnetosphere so large that, if it could be seen from Earth, its apparent diameter would exceed that of the Moon. Jupiter's system is the source of intense bursts of radio noise, at some frequencies occasionally radiating more energy than the Sun.

Of special interest concerning Jupiter's physical properties is the low mean density of 1.33 grams per cubic cm—in contrast with Earth's 5.52 grams/cm³—coupled with the large dimensions and mass and the short rotational period. The low density and large mass indicate that Jupiter's composition and structure are quite unlike those of the Earth and the other inner planets, a deduction that is supported by detailed investigations of the giant planet's atmosphere and interior.

Jupiter has no solid surface; the transition from the atmosphere to its highly compressed core occurs gradually at great depths. The close-up views of Jupiter from the Voyager spacecraft revealed a variety of cloud forms, with a predominance of elliptical features reminiscent of cyclonic and anticyclonic storm systems on the Earth. All these systems are in motion, appearing and disappearing on time scales dependent on their sizes and locations. Also observed to vary are the pastel shades of various colors present in the cloud layers—from the tawny yellow that seems to characterize the main layer, through browns and blue-grays, to the well-known salmon-colored Great Red Spot, Jupiter's largest, most prominent, and longest-lived feature.

Because Jupiter has no solid surface it has no topographic features, and latitudinal currents dominate the planet's large-scale circulation. The lack of a solid surface with physical boundaries and regions with different heat capacities makes the persistence of these currents and their associated cloud patterns all the more remarkable. The Great Red Spot, for example, moves in longitude with respect to Jupiter's rotation, but it does not move in latitude.

The Voyager 1 spacecraft verified the existence of a ring system surrounding Jupiter when it crossed the planet's equatorial plane. Subsequently, images from the Galileo spacecraft revealed that the ring system consists principally of 4 concentric components whose boundaries are associated with the orbits of Jupiter's 4 innermost moons. The ring system is comprised of large numbers of micrometer-sized particles that produce strong forward scattering of incident sunlight. The presence of such small particles requires a source, and the association of the ring boundaries with the 4 moons makes the source clear. The particles are generated by impacts on these moons (and on still smaller bodies within the main part of the ring) by micrometeoroids, cometary debris, and possibly volcanically produced material from Jupiter's moon Io.

Jovian Moons

The satellites orbiting Jupiter are numerous; there are more than 60 known Jovian moons and likely additional ones to be discovered.

The first objects in the solar system discovered by means of a telescope (by Galileo in 1610) were the four brightest moons of Jupiter. Now known as the Galilean satellites, they are (in order of increasing distance from Jupiter) Io, Europa, Ganymede, and Callisto. Each is a unique world in its own right. Callisto and Ganymede, for example, are as large or larger than the planet Mercury, but, while Callisto's icy surface is ancient and heavily cratered from impacts, Ganymede's appears to have been extensively modified by internal activity. Europa may still be geologically active and may harbor an ocean of liquid water, and possibly even life, beneath its frozen surface. Io is the most volcanically active body in the solar system; its suface is a vividly colored landscape of erupting vents, pools and solidified flows of lava, and sulfurous deposits.

Data for the first 16 known Jovian moons (discovered 1610–1979) are summarized below. The orbits of the inner eight satellites have low inclinations (they are not tilted relative to the planet's equator) and low eccentricities (their orbits are relatively circular). The orbits of the outer eight have much higher inclinations and eccentricities, and four of them are retrograde (they are opposite to Jupiter's spin and orbital motion around the Sun). The innermost four satellites are thought to be intimately associated with Jupiter's ring and are the sources of the fine particles within the ring itself.

Beginning in 1999 some 47 tiny moons (including one seen in 1975 and then lost) were discovered photographically in observations from Earth. All have high orbital eccentricities and inclinations and large orbital radii; nearly all of the orbits are retrograde. Rough size estimates based on their brightness place them between 2 and 8 km (1.2 and 5 mi) in diameter. They were assigned provisional numerical designations on discovery; many also have received official names.

In the table, "sync" denotes that the orbital period and rotational period are the same, or synchronous; hence, the moon always keeps the same face toward Jupiter. "R" following the orbital period indicates a retrograde orbit. Unspecified quantities are unknown.

Jovian Moons (continued)

NAME (DESIGNATION)	MEAN DISTANCE FROM JUPITER	DIAMETER	MASS (10^{20} KG)	ORBITAL PERIOD (EARTH DAYS)	ROTATIONAL PERIOD (EARTH DAYS)
Metis (JXVI)	128,000 km (79,500 mi)	40 km (25 mi)	0.001	0.295	sync
Adrastea (JXV)	129,000 km (80,000 mi)	20 km (12 mi)	0.0002	0.298	sync
Amalthea (JV)[1]	181,000 km (112,500 mi)	189 km (117 mi)	0.075	0.498	sync
Thebe (JXIV)	222,000 km (138,000 mi)	100 km (62 mi)	0.008	0.675	sync
Io (JI)[1]	422,000 km (262,000 mi)	3,630 km (2,256 mi)	893.2	1.769	sync
Europa (JII)[1]	671,000 km (417,000 mi)	3,130 km (1,945 mi)	480.0	3.551	sync
Ganymede (JIII)[1]	1,070,000 km (665,000 mi)	5,268 km (3,273 mi)	1,482.0	7.155	sync
Callisto (JIV)[1]	1,883,000 km (1,170,000 mi)	4,806 km (2,986 mi)	1,076.0	16.689	sync
Leda (JXIII)	11,127,000 km (6,914,000 mi)	10 km (6 mi)	0.00006	234	
Himalia (JVI)	11,480,000 km (7,133,000 mi)	170 km (106 mi)	0.095	251	0.4
Lysithea (JX)	11,686,000 km (7,261,300 mi)	24 km (15 mi)	0.0008	258	0.5
Elara (JVII)	11,737,000 km (7,293,000 mi)	80 km (50 mi)	0.008	256	0.5
Ananke (JXII)	21,269,000 km (13,216,000 mi)	20 km (12.5 mi)	0.0004	634 R	0.4
Carme (JXI)	23,350,000 km (14,509,000 mi)	30 km (18.6 mi)	0.001	729 R	0.4
Pasiphae (JVIII)	23,500,000 km (14,602,000 mi)	36 km (22.3 mi)	0.003	735 R	
Sinope (JIX)	23,700,000 km (14,726,500 mi)	28 km (17.3 mi)	0.0008	758 R	0.5

[1]Densities are known for these moons. They are: Amalthea (0.86 grams/cm³), Io (3.53 grams/cm³), Europa (3.01 grams/cm³), Ganymede (1.94 grams/cm³), Callisto (1.83 grams/cm³).

Jovian Ring

Jupiter's complex ring was discovered and first studied by the twin Voyager spacecraft during their flybys of the giant planet in 1979. It is now known to consist of four main components: an outer gossamer ring, whose outer radius coincides with the orbital radius of the Jovian moon Thebe (222,000 km; 138,000 mi); an inner gossamer ring bounded on its outer edge by the orbit of Amalthea (181,000 km; 112,500 mi); the main ring, extending inward some 6,000 km (3,700 mi) from the orbits of Adrastea (129,000 km; 80,000 mi) and Metis (128,000 km; 79,500 mi); and a halo of particles with a thickness of 25,000 km (15,500 mi) that extends from the main ring inward to a radius of about 95,000 km (59,000 mi). For comparison, Jupiter's visible surface lies at a radius of about 71,500 km (44,400 mi) from its center. The four moons involved with the ring are believed to supply the fine particles that compose it.

Saturn

Saturn is the 6th planet in order of distance from the Sun and the second largest of the planets in mass and size. Its dimensions are almost equal to those of Jupiter, while its mass is about a third as large; it has the lowest mean density of any object in the solar system.

Both Saturn and Jupiter resemble stellar bodies in that the light gas hydrogen dominates their bulk chemical composition. Saturn's atmosphere is 91% hydrogen by mass and is thus the most hydrogen-rich atmosphere in the solar system. Saturn's structure and evolutionary history, however, differ significantly from those of its larger counterpart. Like the other giant planets, Jupiter, Uranus, and Neptune, Saturn has extensive satellite and ring systems, which may provide clues to its origin and evolution. The planet has at least 47 moons, including 5 that are more than 1,000 km (600 mi) in diameter. Saturn's dense and extended rings, which lie in its equatorial plane, are the most impressive in the solar system.

Saturn has no single rotation period. Cloud motions in its massive upper atmosphere can be used to trace out a variety of rotation periods, with periods as short as about 10 hours, 10 minutes near the equator and increasing with some oscillation to about 30 minutes longer at latitudes higher than 40°. The rotation period of Saturn's deep interior can be determined from the rotation period of the magnetic field, which is presumed to be rooted in an outer core of hydrogen compressed to a metallic state. The "surface" of Saturn that is seen through telescopes and in spacecraft images is actually a complex layer of clouds.

The **atmosphere** of Saturn shows many smaller-scale time-variable features similar to those found in Jupiter,

such as red, brown, and white spots, bands, eddies, and vortices. The atmosphere generally has a much blander appearance than Jupiter's, however, and is less active on a small scale. A spectacular exception occurred during September–November 1990, when a large white spot appeared near the equator, expanded to a size exceeding 20,000 km (12,400 mi), and eventually spread around the equator before fading.

Saturnian Moons

At least 47 natural satellites are known to circle the planet Saturn. Data for the first 18 Saturnian moons (discovered 1655–1990) are summarized below. As with the other giant planets, those satellites closest to Saturn are mostly regular, meaning that their orbits are fairly circular and not greatly inclined (tilted) with respect to the planet's equator. All of the satellites in the table except distant Phoebe are regular.

Titan is Saturn's largest moon and the only satellite in the solar system known to have clouds and a dense atmosphere (composed mostly of nitrogen and methane). The moon is also enveloped in a reddish haze, which is thought to be composed of complex organic compounds that are produced by the action of sunlight on its clouds and atmosphere. That organic molecules may have been settling out of the haze onto Titan's surface for much of its history has encouraged some scientists to speculate on the possibility that life may have evolved there. Observations by the Cassini-Huygens spacecraft showed Titan to have a varied surface sculpted by rains of hydro-

carbon compounds, flowing liquids, wind, impacts, and possibly volcanic and tectonic activity. Saturn's second largest moon is **Rhea**, followed by **Iapetus** and **Dione**.

An unusual Saturnian satellite is **Hyperion**. Owing to its highly irregular shape and eccentric orbit, it does not rotate stably about a fixed axis. Unlike any other known object in the solar system, Hyperion rotates chaotically, alternating unpredictably between periods of tumbling and seemingly regular rotation.

Between 2000 and 2005 about 30 additional tiny moons occupying various (mostly distant) orbits were discovered. Like the numerous outer moons of Jupiter, nearly all of the recent finds around Saturn belong to the irregular class, meaning that their orbits are highly inclined and elliptical. More than half of them, plus Phoebe, are in retrograde orbits (they move opposite to Saturn's spin and orbital motion around the Sun).

In the table, "sync" denotes that the orbital period and rotational period are the same, or synchronous. Unspecified quantities are unknown.

NAME (DESIGNATION)	MEAN DISTANCE FROM SATURN	DIAMETER	MASS (10^{20} KG)	DENSITY (GRAMS/CM³)	ORBITAL PERIOD (EARTH DAYS)	ROTATIONAL PERIOD (EARTH DAYS)
Pan (SXVIII)	133,580 km (83,000 mi)	20 km (12 mi)	0.00003	0.63	0.5750	
Atlas (SXV)	137,670 km (85,540 mi)	28 km (17 mi)	0.0001	0.63	0.6019	
Prometheus (SXVI)	139,350 km (86,590 mi)	92 km (57 mi)	0.0033	0.63	0.6130	
Pandora (SXVII)	141,700 km (88,050 mi)	92 km (57 mi)	0.002	0.63	0.6285	
Epimetheus (SXI)	151,420 km (94,090 mi)	114 km (71 mi)	0.0054	0.60	0.6942	sync
Janus (SX)	151,470 km (94,120 mi)	178 km (111 mi)	0.0192	0.65	0.6945	sync
Mimas (SI)	185,520 km (115,280 mi)	392 km (244 mi)	0.375	1.14	0.94	sync
Enceladus (SII)	238,020 km (147,900 mi)	520 km (323 mi)	0.7	1.0	1.37	sync
Tethys (SIII)	294,660 km (183,090 mi)	1,060 km (659 mi)	6.27	1.0	1.88	sync
Telesto (SXIII)*	294,660 km (183,090 mi)	30 km (19 mi)	0.00007	1.0	1.88	
Calypso (SXIV)*	294,660 km (183,090 mi)	26 km (16 mi)	0.00004	1.0	1.88	
Dione (SIV)	377,400 km (234,510 mi)	1,120 km (696 mi)	11	1.5	2.73	sync
Helene (SXII)†	377,400 km (234,510 mi)	32 km (20 mi)	0.0003	1.5	2.73	
Rhea (SV)	527,040 km (327,490 mi)	1,530 km (951 mi)	23.1	1.24	4.51	sync
Titan (SVI)	1,221,830 km (759,210 mi)	5,150 km (3,200 mi)	1,350	1.881	15.94	sync
Hyperion (SVII)	1,481,100 km (920,310 mi)	286 km (178 mi)	0.2	1.50	21.27	chaotic

Saturnian Moons (continued)

NAME (DESIGNATION)	MEAN DISTANCE FROM SATURN	DIAMETER	MASS (10^{20} KG)	DENSITY (GRAMS/CM³)	ORBITAL PERIOD (EARTH DAYS)	ROTATIONAL PERIOD (EARTH DAYS)
Iapetus (SVIII)	3,561,300 km (2,212,890 mi)	1,460 km (907 mi)	16	1.02	79.33	sync
Phoebe (SIX)	12,952,000 km (8,048,000 mi)	220 km (137 mi)	0.004	1.3	550.5 (retrograde)	0.4

*Telesto and Calypso occupy the same orbit as Tethys but about 60° ahead and behind, respectively.
†Helene occupies the same orbit as Dione but about 60° behind.

Saturnian Rings

Saturn's rings rank among the most spectacular phenomena in the solar system. They have intrigued astronomers ever since they were discovered telescopically by Galileo in 1610, and their mysteries have only deepened since they were photographed and studied by Voyagers 1 and 2 in the early 1980s. The **particles** that make up the rings are composed primarily of water ice and range from dust specks to car- and house-sized chunks. The rings exhibit a great amount of structure on many scales, from the broad **A, B, and C rings** visible from Earth down to myriad narrow component ringlets. Odd structures resembling spokes, braids, and spiral waves are also present. Some of this detail is explained by gravitational interaction with a number of Saturn's many moons (the orbits of well more than a dozen known moons, from Pan to Dione and Helene, lie within the rings), but much of it remains unaccounted for.

Numerous divisions or **gaps** are seen in the major ring regions. A few of the more prominent ones are named for famous astronomers who were associated with studies of Saturn.

The major rings and gaps, listed outward from Saturn, are given below. For comparison, Saturn's visible surface lies at a radius of about 60,300 km (37,500 mi).

RING (OR DIVISION)	RADIUS OF RING'S INNER EDGE	WIDTH	COMMENTS
D ring	66,900 km (41,600 mi)	7,500 km (4,700 mi)	faint, visible only in reflected light
(Guerin division)			
C ring	74,500 km (46,300 mi)	17,500 km (10,900 mi)	also called Crepe ring
(Maxwell division)			
B ring	92,000 km (57,200 mi)	25,500 km (15,800 mi)	brightest ring
(Cassini division, Huygens gap)			Cassini division is the largest ring gap
A ring	122,200 km (75,900 mi)	14,600 km (9,100 mi)	the outermost ring visible from Earth
(Encke division)			located within the A ring, near its outer edge
F ring	140,200 km (87,100 mi)	30–500 km (20–300 mi)	faint, narrowest major ring
G ring	165,800 km (103,000 mi)	8,000 km (5,000 mi)	faint
E ring	180,000 km (111,800 mi)	300,000 km (186,400 mi)	faint

Uranus

Uranus is the seventhth planet in order of distance from the Sun. Its low density and large size place it among the four giant planets, all of which are composed primarily of hydrogen, helium, water, and other volatile compounds and which thus are without solid surfaces. Absorption of red light by methane gas gives the planet a blue-green color. The planet has at least 27 satellites, ranging up to 789 km (490 mi) in radius, and 10 narrow rings.

Uranus spins on its side; its **rotation axis** is tipped at an angle of 98° relative to its orbit axis. The 98° tilt is thought to have arisen during the final stages of planetary accretion when bodies comparable in size to the present planets collided in a series of violent events that knocked Uranus onto its side.

Although Uranus is nearly featureless, extreme contrast enhancement of images taken by the Voyager spacecraft reveals faint bands oriented parallel to circles of constant latitude. Apparently the rotation of the planet and not the distribution of absorbed sunlight controls the cloud patterns.

Wind is the motion of the atmosphere relative to the rotating planet. At high latitudes on Uranus, as on the Earth, this relative motion is in the direction of the planet's rotation. At low (that is, equatorial) latitudes, the relative motion is in the opposite direction. On the Earth these directions are called east and west, respectively, but the more general terms are prograde and retrograde. The winds that exist on Uranus are several times stronger than are those of the Earth. The wind is 200 m (656 ft) per second (prograde) at a latitude of 55° S and 110 m (360.8 ft) per second (retrograde) at the equator. Neptune's equatorial winds are also retrograde, although those of Jupiter and Saturn are prograde. No satisfactory theory exists to explain these differences.

Uranus has no large **spots** like the Great Red Spot of Jupiter or the Great Dark Spot of Neptune. Since the giant planets have no solid surfaces, the spots represent atmospheric storms. For reasons that are not clear, Uranus seems to have the smallest number of storms of any of the giant planets. Most of the mass of Uranus (roughly 80%) is in the form of a liquid core made primarily of icy materials (water, methane, and ammonia).

Uranus was discovered in 1781 by the English astronomer **William Herschel,** who had undertaken a survey of all stars down to eighth magnitude—i.e., those about five times fainter than stars visible to the naked eye. Herschel suggested naming the new planet the Georgian Planet after his patron, King George III of England, but the planet was eventually named according to the tradition of naming planets for the gods of Greek and Roman mythology; Uranus

is the father of Saturn, who is in turn the father of Jupiter.

After the discovery, Herschel continued to observe the planet with larger and better telescopes and eventually discovered its two largest satellites, Titania and Oberon, in 1787. Two more satellites, Ariel and Umbriel, were discovered by the British astronomer William Lassell in 1851. The names of the four satellites come from English literature—they are characters in works by Shakespeare and Pope—and were proposed by Herschel's son, John Herschel. A fifth satellite, Miranda, was discovered by Gerard P. Kuiper in 1948. The tradition of naming the satellites after characters in Shakespeare's and Pope's works continues to the present.

Uranian Moons and Rings

Uranus has 27 known **satellites** forming three distinct groups: 13 small moons orbiting quite close to the planet, 5 large moons located somewhat farther out, and finally another 9 small and much more distant moons. The members of the first two groups are in nearly circular orbits with low inclinations with respect to the planet.

The densities of the 4 largest satellites, **Ariel, Umbriel, Titania,** and **Oberon,** suggest that they are about half (or more) water ice and the rest rock. Oberon and Umbriel are heavily scarred with large impact craters dating back to the very early history of the solar system, evidence that their surfaces probably have been stable since their formation. In contrast, Titania and Ariel have far fewer large craters, indicating relatively young surfaces shaped over time by internal geological activity. Miranda, though small compared with the other major moons, has a unique jumbled patchwork of varied surface terrain revealing surprisingly extensive past activity. Data for the major satellites are summarized below.

The 5 major moons were **discovered** telescopically from Earth between 1787 and 1948. Eleven of the 13 innermost moons, with diameters of about 40–160 km (25–100 mi), were found in Voyager 2 images. The rest of the moons, with diameters of 10–200 km (6–120 mi), were detected in Earth-based observations between 1997 and 2003; the orbital motion of nearly all of the outermost moons is retrograde (opposite to the direction of Uranus's spin and revolution around the Sun).

Ten very narrow rings are known to encircle Uranus, with radii from 41,800 to 51,100 km (26,000 to 31,800 mi), for the most part within the orbits of the innermost moons. For comparison, Uranus's visible surface lies at a radius of about 25,600 km (15,900 mi). The ring system was first detected in 1977 during Earth-based observations of Uranus when the planet was passing in front of a star. Subsequent observations from Earth and images from Voyager 2 clarified the number and other features of the rings.

NAME (DESIGNATION)	MEAN DISTANCE FROM URANUS	DIAMETER	MASS (10^{20} KG)	DENSITY (GRAMS/CM³)	ORBITAL PERIOD/ ROTATIONAL PERIOD (EARTH DAYS)*
Miranda (V)	129,390 km (80,400 mi)	472 km (293 mi)	0.66	1.2	1.41
Ariel (I)	191,020 km (118,690 mi)	1,158 km (720 mi)	13.5	1.67	2.52
Umbriel (II)	266,300 km (165,470 mi)	1,169 km (726 mi)	11.7	1.4	4.14
Titania (III)	435,910 km (270,860 mi)	1,578 km (981 mi)	35.2	1.71	8.70
Oberon (IV)	583,520 km (362,580 mi)	1,523 km (946 mi)	30.1	1.63	13.46

*The orbital period and rotational period are the same, or synchronous, for the listed moons.

Neptune

Neptune is the 8th planet in average distance from the Sun. It was named for the Roman god of the sea. The sea god's trident serves as the planet's astronomical symbol.

Neptune's **distance** from the Sun varies between 29.8 and 30.4 astronomical units (AUs). Its **diameter** is about 4 times that of the Earth, but because of its great distance Neptune cannot be seen from the Earth without the aid of a telescope. Neptune's deep blue **color** is due to the absorption of red light by methane gas in its atmosphere. It receives less than

half as much sunlight as Uranus, but heat escaping from its interior makes Neptune slightly warmer than the latter. The heat released may also be responsible for Neptune's stormier **atmosphere,** which exhibits the fastest winds seen on any planet in the solar system.

Neptune's **orbital period** is 164.8 Earth years. It has not completely circled the Sun since its discovery in 1846, so some refinements in calculations of its orbital size and shape are still expected. The planet's orbital eccentricity of 0.009 means that its orbit is very nearly circular; among the 9 planets in the solar system, only Venus has a smaller eccentricity. Neptune's seasons (and the seasons of its moons) are therefore of nearly equal length, each about 41 Earth years in duration. The length of Neptune's day, as determined by Voyager 2, is 16.11 hours.

As with the other giant planets of the outer solar system, Neptune's atmosphere is composed predominantly of hydrogen and helium. The **temperature** of Neptune's atmosphere varies with altitude. A minimum temperature of about −223 °C (−369 °F) occurs at pressure near 0.1 bar. The temperature increases with altitude to about 477 °C (891 °F) at 2,000 km (1,240 mi, which corresponds to a pressure of 10^{-11} bar) and remains uniform above that altitude. It also increases with depth to about 6,730 °C (12,140 °F) near the center of the planet.

As with the other giant planets of the outer solar system, the **winds** on Neptune are constrained to blow generally along lines of constant latitude and are relatively invariable with time. Winds on Neptune vary from about 100 m/sec (328 ft/sec) in an easterly (prograde) direction near latitude 70° S to as high as 700 m/sec (2,300 ft/sec) in a westerly (retrograde) direction near latitude 20° S.

The high winds and relatively large contribution of escaping internal heat may be responsible for the observed turbulence in Neptune's visible atmosphere. Two large dark ovals are clearly visible in images of Neptune's southern hemisphere taken by Voyager 2 in 1989, although they are not present in Hubble Space Telescope images made 2 years later. The largest, called the **Great Dark Spot** because of its similarity in latitude and shape to Jupiter's Great Red Spot, is comparable to the entire Earth in size. It was near this feature that the highest wind speeds were measured. Atmospheric storms such as the Great Dark Spot may be centers where strong upwelling of gases from the interior takes place.

Neptune's mean **density** is about 30% of the Earth's; nevertheless, it is the densest of the giant planets. Neptune's greater density implies that a larger percentage of its interior is composed of melted ices and molten rocky materials than is the case for the other gas giants.

Neptunian Moons and Rings

Neptune has at least 13 natural satellites, but Earth-based observations had found only 2 of them, Triton in 1847 and Nereid in 1949, before Voyager 2 flew by the planet. The spacecraft observed 5 small moons orbiting close to Neptune and verified the existence of a 6th that had been detected from Earth in 1981. Data for these 8 moons are summarized in the table below. In 2002–03, 5 additional small moons (diameters roughly 30–60 km [20–40 mi]) were discovered telescopically from Earth; they all occupy highly inclined and elliptical orbits that are comparatively far from Neptune.

Triton is Neptune's only large moon and the only large satellite in the solar system to orbit its planet in the retrograde direction (opposite the planet's rotation and orbital motion around the Sun). Thus, as is also suspected of the solar system's other retrograde moons, Triton likely was captured by its planet rather than formed in orbit with its planet from the solar nebula. Its density (2 grams/cm³) suggests that it is about 25% water ice and the rest rock. Triton has a tenuous atmosphere, mostly of nitrogen. Its varied icy surface, imaged by Voyager 2, contains giant faults and dark markings that have been interpreted as the product of geyserlike "ice volcanoes" in which the eruptive material may be gaseous nitrogen and methane. Nereid has the most elliptical orbit of any planet or moon in the solar system; it also is probably a captured object.

Neptune's system of several faint rings, with radii from about 42,000 to 63,000 km (26,000–39,000 mi), straddles the orbits of its 4 innermost moons. (Neptune's visible surface lies at a radius of 24,800 km, or 15,400 mi.) The outermost ring, named Adams, is unusual in that it contains several clumps, or concentrations of material, that before Voyager 2's visit had been interpreted incorrectly as independent ring arcs. What created and has maintained this structure has not yet been fully explained; it has been suggested that the clumps resulted from the relatively recent breakup of a small moon and are being temporarily held together by the gravitational effects of the nearby moon Galatea.

NAME (DESIGNATION)	MEAN DISTANCE FROM NEPTUNE	DIAMETER	MASS (10^{20} KG)	ORBITAL PERIOD (EARTH DAYS)
Naiad (III)	48,230 km (29,970 mi)	58 km (36 mi)	0.002	0.294
Thalassa (IV)	50,070 km (31,110 mi)	80 km (50 mi)	0.004	0.311
Despina (V)	52,530 km (32,640 mi)	148 km (92 mi)	0.02	0.335
Galatea (VI)	61,950 km (38,490 mi)	158 km (98 mi)	0.04	0.429
Larissa (VII)	73,550 km (45,700 mi)	192 km (119 mi)	0.05	0.555
Proteus (VIII)	117,640 km (73,100 mi)	416 km (258 mi)	0.5	1.122
Triton (I)*	354,800 km (220,460 mi)	2,700 km (1,678 mi)	214	5.877 (retrograde)
Nereid (II)	5,509,100 km (3,423,200 mi)	340 km (211 mi)	0.2	359.632

*Among the rotational periods of Neptune's moons, only Triton's has been established; it is the same as (synchronous with) the orbital period.

Pluto

Pluto is the planet normally farthest from the Sun. It is named for the god of the underworld in Roman mythology (Greek: Hades). Pluto has a single natural satellite, Charon. Because their dimensions are sufficiently similar and they orbit around a common center of gravity, it has become common to speak of the Pluto-Charon system as a double planet.

Pluto was the third planet to be discovered, as opposed to the six planets that had been visible in the sky to the naked eye since ancient times. Pluto is so distant that sunlight traveling at 299,792 km/sec (186,282.1 mi/sec) takes more than five hours to reach the planet. An observer standing on the planet's surface would see the Sun as an extremely bright star in the dark sky, providing Pluto with only 1/1600 the amount of sunlight reaching the Earth.

Pluto's average **distance** from the Sun (39.6 astronomical units, or AU), as well as its orbital eccentricity (0.249) and inclination (17.2°), are the greatest of any of the planets in the solar system. In traveling in its highly eccentric orbit, Pluto varies in distance from the Sun from 29.7 AU at perihelion to 49.5 AU at aphelion. Thus, Pluto at times is actually closer to the Sun than Neptune, which has a nearly circular orbit at approximately 30 AU. A 3:2 resonance between the orbital periods of Neptune and Pluto prevents the two planets from ever passing closer than about 17 AU to one another. The most recent perihelion of Pluto occurred on 5 Sep 1989, so that Neptune was the most distant planet from the Sun from 1979 through 1999.

Pluto is by far the smallest planet, having a **diameter** less than half that of Mercury; it is about two-thirds the size of the Moon. Pluto's physical characteristics are unlike those of any other planet. Pluto resembles most closely Neptune's icy satellite Triton, which implies a similar origin for these two bodies. Most scientists now believe that Pluto and Charon are large icy planetesimals left over from the formation of the giant outer planets of the solar system. Accordingly, Pluto can be interpreted to be the largest known member of the Kuiper belt (which, significantly, includes the outer part of Pluto's orbit). Observations of Pluto show that it appears slightly red, although not as red as Mars or Io. Thus, the surface of Pluto cannot be composed simply of pure ices. Its overall reflectivity, or albedo, ranges from 0.3 to 0.5, as compared with 0.1 for the Moon and 0.8 for Triton.

The surface **temperature** of Pluto has proved very difficult to measure. Observations made from the Infrared Astronomical Satellite suggest values in the range of −228 to −215 °C (−379 to −355 °F), whereas measurements at radio wavelengths imply a range of −238 to −223 °C (−397 to −370 °F). The temperature certainly must vary over the surface, depending on the local reflectivity and solar zenith angle. There is also expected to be a seasonal decrease in incident solar energy by a factor of roughly three as Pluto moves from perihelion to aphelion.

The detection of methane ice on the planet's surface made scientists confident that Pluto had an **atmosphere** before one was actually discovered. The atmosphere was finally detected in 1988 when Pluto passed in front of a star as observed from the Earth. The light of the star was dimmed before disappearing entirely behind the planet during the occultation. This proved that a thin, greatly distended atmosphere was present. Because Pluto's atmosphere must consist of vapors in equilibrium with their ices, small changes in temperature will have a large effect on the amount of gas in the atmosphere.

Pluto's only known **satellite** was discovered as a small bump on images of the planet that were recorded photographically at the US Naval Observatory in Flagstaff AZ near the site of Pluto's discovery nearly 50 years earlier. The new satellite was named **Charon**, after the boatman who ferries dead souls across the River Styx to the underworld in Greek mythology. Subsequent observations showed that Charon's period of revolution around Pluto is exactly equal to the period of rotation of the planet itself. In other words, Pluto is the only planet in the solar system with a natural satellite in a synchronous orbit. As a result, Charon is only visible from one hemisphere of Pluto. In addition, as with most planetary satellites, Charon is in a state of synchronous rotation—i.e., it always presents the same face to its primary planet.

Comets

Comets are a class of small bodies orbiting the Sun and developing diffuse gaseous envelopes. They also often form long luminous tails when near the Sun. The comet makes a transient appearance in the sky and is often said to have a "hairy" tail. In fact, the word comes from the Greek *kometes*, meaning "hairy one," a description that fits the bright comets noticed by the ancients.

Despite their name, many comets do not develop tails. Moreover, a comet is not surrounded by nebulosity during most of its lifetime. The only permanent feature of a comet is its **nucleus**, which is a small body that may be seen as a starlike object in large telescopes when tail and nebulosity do not exist, particularly when the comet is still far away from the Sun. Two characteristics differentiate the cometary nucleus from a rocky body such as an asteroid or meteoroid—its orbit and its chemical nature. A comet's **orbit** is more eccentric (less circular); therefore, its distance to the Sun varies considerably. Its material contains more volatile components, with water ice the predominant compound. They have been described as "dirty snowballs" or "icy mudballs." When far from the Sun, however, a comet remains in its pristine state for eons without losing any volatile components because of the deep cold of space. For this reason, astronomers believe that pristine cometary nuclei may represent the oldest and best-preserved material in the solar system.

During a close passage near the Sun, the nucleus of a comet loses water vapor and other more volatile compounds, as well as dust dragged away by the sublimating gases. It is then surrounded by a transient dusty "atmosphere" that is steadily lost to space. This feature is the **coma**, which gives a comet its nebulous appearance.

The astronomer **Edmond Halley**, a friend of Isaac Newton, endeavored to compute the orbits of 24 comets for which he had found fairly accurate historical documents. Applying a method Newton had developed, Halley predicted that the comet that now bears his name would return to Earth in 1758, and that proved correct. Since its prediction by astronomers and its appearance in 1758/59, Comet Halley has reappeared three times—in 1835, 1910, and 1986.

Each century, a score of comets brighter than Comet Halley have been discovered. Many are **periodic** (returning) **comets** like Comet Halley, but their periods are extremely long (millennia or even scores or hundreds of millennia), and they have not left any identifiable trace in prehistory. Bright Comet Bennett (1970) will return in 17 centuries, whereas the spectacular Comet West (1976) will reappear in about 500,000 years. Among the comets that can easily be seen with the unaided eye, Comet Halley is the only one that returns in a single lifetime. About 200 comets whose periods are between 3 and 200 years are known, however. Unfortunately, they are or have become too faint to be readily seen without the aid of telescopes.

For faraway objects that contain volatile ices, the distinction between **asteroids and comets** becomes a matter of semantics because many orbits are unstable; an asteroid that comes closer to the Sun than usual may become a comet by producing a transient atmosphere that gives it a fuzzy appearance and that may develop into a tail. Some objects have been reclassified as a result of such occurrences. For example, asteroid 1990 UL3, which crosses the orbit of Jupiter, was reclassified as Comet P/Shoemaker-Levy 2 late in 1990. Conversely, it is suspected that some of the Earth-approaching asteroids (Amors, Apollos, and Atens) could be the extinct nuclei of comets that have now lost most of their volatile ices.

Measurements and Numbers

The International System of Units (SI)

Rapid advances in science and technology in the 19th and 20th centuries fostered the development of several overlapping systems of units of measurements as scientists improvised to meet the practical needs of their disciplines. The **General Conference on Weights and Measures** was chartered by international convention in 1875 to produce standards of physical measurement based upon an earlier international standard, the meter-kilogram-second (MKS) system. The convention calls for regular General Conference meetings to consider improvements or modifications in standards, an International Committee of Weights and Measures elected by the Conference (meets annually), and several consultative committees. **The International Bureau of Weights and Measures** (Bureau International des Poids et Mesures) at Sèvres, France, serves as a depository for the primary international standards and as a laboratory for certification and intercomparison of national standard copies.

The 1960 **International System** (universally abbreviated as **SI**, from *système international*) builds upon the MKS system. Its **seven basic units**, from which other units are derived, are currently defined as

follows: the **meter**, defined as the distance traveled by light in a vacuum in 1/299,792,458 second; the **kilogram** (about 2.2 pounds avoirdupois), which equals 1,000 grams as defined by the international prototype kilogram of platinum-iridium in the keeping of the International Bureau of Weights and Measures; the **second**, the duration of 9,192,631,770 periods of radiation associated with a specified transition of the cesium-133 atom; the **ampere**, which is the current that, if maintained in two wires placed one meter apart in a vacuum, would produce a force of 2×10^{-7} newton per meter of length; the **candela**, defined as the intensity in a given direction of a source emitting radiation of frequency 540×10^{12} hertz and that has a radiant intensity in that direction of 1/683 watt per steradian; the **mole**, defined as containing as many elementary entities of a substance as there are atoms in 0.012 kilogram of carbon-12; and the **kelvin**, which is 1/273.16 of the thermodynamic temperature of the triple point (equilibrium among the solid, liquid, and gaseous phases) of pure water.

International Bureau of Weights and Measures Web site: <www.bipm.fr>.

Elemental and Derived SI Units and Symbols

Quantity	SI Units		
	UNIT	FORMULA/EXPRESSION IN BASE UNITS	SYMBOL
elemental units			
length	meter	—	m
mass	kilogram	—	kg
time	second	—	s
electric current	ampere	—	A
luminous intensity	candela	—	cd
amount of substance	mole	—	mol
thermodynamic temperature	kelvin	—	K
derived units			
acceleration	meter/second squared	m/s^2	
area	square meter	m^2	
capacitance	farad	$A \times s/V$	F
charge	coulomb	$A \times s$	C
Celsius temperature	degree Celsius	K	°C
density	kilogram/cubic meter	kg/m^3	
electric field strength	volt/meter	V/m	
electrical potential	volt	W/A	V

Elemental and Derived SI Units and Symbols (continued)

Quantity	SI Units		
	UNIT	FORMULA/EXPRESSION IN BASE UNITS	SYMBOL
derived units (continued)			
energy	joule	$N \times m$	J
force	newton	$kg \times m/s^2$	N
frequency	hertz	s^{-1}	Hz
illumination	lux	lm/m^2	lx
inductance	henry	$V \times s/A$	H
kinematic viscosity	square meter/second	m^2/s	
luminance	candela/square meter	cd/m^2	
luminous flux	lumen	$cd \times sr$	lm
magnetic field strength	ampere/meter	A/m	
magnetic flux	weber	$V \times s$	Wb
magnetic flux density	tesla	Wb/m^2	T
plane angle	radian	$m \times m^{-1}=1$	rad
power	watt	J/s	W
pressure	pascal (newton/square meter)	N/m^2	Pa
resistance	ohm	V/A	Ω
solid angle	steradian	$m^2 \times m^{-2}=1$	sr
stress	pascal (newton/square meter)	N/m^2	Pa
velocity	meter/second	m/s	
viscosity	newton-second/square meter	$N \times s/m^2$	
volume	cubic meter	m^3	

Conversion of Metric Weights and Measures

The International System of Units is a decimal system of weights and measures derived from and extending the metric system of units. Adopted by the 11th General Conference on Weights and Measures in 1960, it is abbreviated "SI" in all languages. Below are common equivalents and conversion factors for US customary and SI systems.

approximate common equivalents		conversions accurate within 10 parts per million	
1 inch	= 25 millimeters	inches × 25.4[1]	= millimeters
1 foot	= 0.3 meter	feet × 0.3048[1]	= meters
1 yard	= 0.9 meter	yards × 0.9144[1]	= meters
1 mile	= 1.6 kilometers	miles × 1.60934	= kilometers
1 square inch	= 6.5 sq. centimeters	square inches × 6.4516[1]	= square centimeters
1 square foot	= 0.09 square meter	square feet × 0.0929030	= square meters
1 square yard	= 0.8 square meter	square yards × 0.836127	= square meters
1 acre	= 0.4 hectare[2]	acres × 0.404686	= hectares
1 cubic inch	= 16 cubic centimeters	cubic inches × 16.3871	= cubic centimeters
1 cubic foot	= 0.03 cubic meter	cubic feet × 0.0283168	= cubic meters
1 cubic yard	= 0.8 cubic meter	cubic yards × 0.764555	= cubic meters
1 quart (liq)	= 1 liter[2]	quarts (liquid) × 0.946353	= liters
1 gallon	= 0.004 cubic meter	gallons × 0.00378541	= cubic meters
1 ounce (avdp)[3]	= 28 grams	ounces (avdp)[3] × 28.3495	= grams
1 pound (avdp)[3]	= 0.45 kilogram	pounds (avdp)[3] × 0.453592	= kilograms
1 horsepower	= 0.75 kilowatt	horsepower × 0.745700	= kilowatts
1 millimeter	= 0.04 inch	millimeters × 0.0393701	= inches
1 meter	= 3.3 feet	meters × 3.28084	= feet
1 meter	= 1.1 yards	meters × 1.09361	= yards
1 kilometer	= 0.6 mile (statute)	kilometers × 0.621371	= miles (statute)
1 square centimeter	= 0.16 square inch	square centimeters × 0.155000	= square inches
1 square meter	= 11 square feet	square meters × 10.7639	= square feet
1 square meter	= 1.2 square yards	square meters × 1.19599	= square yards
1 hectare[2]	= 2.5 acres	hectares × 2.47105	= acres
1 cubic centimeter	= 0.06 cubic inch	cubic centimeters × 0.0610237	= cubic inches
1 cubic meter	= 35 cubic feet	cubic meters × 35.3147	= cubic feet
1 cubic meter	= 1.3 cubic yards	cubic meters × 1.30795	= cubic yards
1 liter[2]	= 1 quart (liq)	liters × 1.05669	= quarts (liq)
1 cubic meter	= 264 gallons	cubic meters × 264.172	= gallons
1 gram	= 0.035 ounce (avdp)[3]	grams × 0.0352740	= ounces (avdp)[3]
1 kilogram	= 2.2 pounds (avdp)[3]	kilograms × 2.20462	= pounds (avdp)[3]
1 kilowatt	= 1.3 horsepower	kilowatts × 1.34102	= horsepower

[1]Exact.   [2]Common term not used in SI.   [3]avdp = avoirdupois.
Source: National Institute of Standards and Technology.

British/US system (ft-lb-second, fps)

length
1 statute mi	= 5,280 ft	= 1,760 yd	= 320 rods	= 8 furlongs
1 nautical mi	= 6,076 ft	= 1.151 mi		
1 furlong	= 660 ft	= 220 yd	= 40 rods	= 1/8 mi
1 chain (Gunter's)	= 66 ft	= 22 yd	= 100 links	= 4 rods
1 rod	= 16.5 ft	= 5.5 yd	= 25 links	
1 fathom	= 6 ft	= 72 in		
1 yd	= 3 ft	= 36 in		
1 ft	= 12 in			
1 link (Gunter's)	= 0.66 ft	= 7.92 in		
1 hand	= 4 in			
1 mil	= 0.001 in			

area
1 sq mi	= 640 acres	= 102,400 sq rods	= 3,097,600 sq yd	= 27,878,400 sq ft
1 acre	= 10 sq chains	= 160 sq rods	= 4,840 sq yd	= 43,560 sq ft
1 sq ft	= 144 sq in			

volume
1 cu ft	= 1/27 cu yd	= 12 board ft	= 1,728 cu in
1 cu in	= 1/46,656 cu yd	= 1/1,728 cu ft	
1 acre-ft	= 43,560 cu ft	= 1,613 cu yd	
1 board ft	= 144 cu in	= 1/12 cu ft	= 1 super ft (lumber)
1 cord (US)	= 128 cu ft		

capacity
1 cu ft	= 7.481 gal (US)	= 6.229 gal (British)

liquid measure (US)
1 barrel, oil	= 42 gal (US)	= 34.97 gal (British)		
1 gal	= 0.833 gal (British)	= 4 quarts	= 231.00 cu in	= 128 fl oz
1 quart	= 1/4 gal	= 2 pints	= 57.75 cu in	= 32 fl oz
1 pint	= 1/8 gal	= 1/2 quart	= 28.88 cu in	= 16 fl oz
1 gill	= 1/32 gal	= 1/4 pint	= 7.22 cu in	= 4 fl oz
1 fl oz	= 1/128 gal	= 1/16 pint	= 1.80 cu in	

dry measure (US)
1 bushel	= 0.97 bushel (British)	= 4 pecks	= 2,150.4 cu in	= 1.24 cu ft
1 peck	= 1/4 bushel	= 8 quarts	= 537.6 cu in	= 0.31 cu ft
1 quart	= 1/32 bushel	= 2 pints	= 67.2 cu in	= 1/8 peck
1 pint	= 1/64 bushel	= 1/2 quart	= 33.6 cu in	

liquid and dry measure (British)
1 bushel	= 1.03 bushels (US)	= 8 gal	= 4 pecks	= 2,219.36 cu in	= 1.284 cu ft
1 peck	= 0.25 bushel	= 2 gal	= 8 quarts	= 554.84 cu in	
1 gal	= 1.20 gal (US)	= 4 quarts		= 277.42 cu in	
1 quart	= 0.30 gal	= 2 pints	= 1/8 peck	= 69.36 cu in	
1 pint	= 4.80 gills (US)	= 4 gills		= 34.68 cu in	= 20 fl oz
1 gill	= 1.20 gills (US)			= 8.67 cu in	= 5 fl oz
1 fl oz	= 0.96 fl oz (US)			= 1.73 cu in	

weight
1 short ton (US)	= 0.89 long ton	= 2,000 lbs	= 20 short cwt*
1 long ton (British)	= 1.12 short tons	= 2,240 lbs	= 22.4 short cwt*
1 short cwt* (US)	= 0.05 short ton	= 100 lbs	
1 long cwt* (British)	= 0.05 long ton	= 112 lbs	
1 stone (person)	= 0.14 short cwt*	= 14 lbs	
1 lb	= 0.07 stone (British)		
1 oz avdp†	= 437.50 grains	= 1/16 lb	= 0.911 oz troy
1 oz troy	= 480.00 grains	= 1/12 lb	= 1.097 oz
1 grain		= 0.0023 oz	= 0.0021 oz troy

*cwt = hundredweight.   †avdp = avoirdupois.

Tables of Equivalents: Metric System Units and Prefixes

base unit*

QUANTITY	NAME OF UNIT	SYMBOL
length	meter	m
area	square meter	square m, or m^2
	are (100 square meters)	a
volume	cubic meter	cubic m, or m^3
	stere (1 cubic meter)	s
mass	gram	g
	metric ton (1,000,000 grams)	t
capacity	liter	l
temperature	degree Celsius	°C

prefixes designating multiples and submultiples

PREFIX	SYMBOL	FACTOR BY WHICH UNIT IS MULTIPLIED		EXAMPLES
exa-	E	10^{18}	= 1,000,000,000,000,000,000	
peta-	P	10^{15}	= 1,000,000,000,000,000	
tera-	T	10^{12}	= 1,000,000,000,000	
giga-	G	10^9	= 1,000,000,000	
mega-	M	10^6	= 1,000,000	megaton (Mt)
kilo-	k	10^3	= 1,000	kilometer (km)
hecto-, hect-	h	10^2	= 100	hectare (ha)
deca- dec-	da	10	= 10	decastere (das)
			1	
deci-	d	10^{-1}	= 0.1	decigram (dg)
centi-, cent-	c	10^{-2}	= 0.01	centimeter (cm)
milli-	m	10^{-3}	= 0.001	milliliter (ml)
micro-, micr-	μ	10^{-6}	= 0.000001	microgram (μg)
nano-	n	10^{-9}	= 0.000000001	
pico-	p	10^{-12}	= 0.000000000001	
femto-	f	10^{-15}	= 0.000000000000001	
atto-	a	10^{-18}	= 0.000000000000000001	

The metric system of bases and prefixes has been applied to many other units, such as decibel (0.1 bel), kilowatt (1,000 watts), and microhm (one-millionth of an ohm).

Electrical Units

UNIT	SYMBOL	ATTRIBUTE MEASURED	EXPRESSION IN OTHER UNITS (S = SECOND)
ampere	A	current	C/s or V/Ω

the basic electrical unit of the International System of Units (SI), since 1948 defined by the International Bureau of Weights and Measures as the constant current which, if maintained in two straight parallel conductors of infinite length, of negligible circular cross section, and placed one meter apart in a vacuum, would produce between these conductors a force equal to 2×10^{-7} newton per meter of length. One ampere is equal to a flow of one coulomb of electricity per second; or, the flow produced in a conductor with a resistance of one ohm by a potential difference of one volt.

farad	F	capacitance (ability to hold a charge)	A × s/V or C/V

the ability of two parallel, oppositely charged plates (a capacitor) to hold an electric charge equals one farad when one coulomb of electricity changes the potential between the plates by one volt.

coulomb	C	charge	A × s

the quantity of electricity transported in one second by a current of one ampere. Approximately equal to 6.24×10^{18} electrons.

watt	W	power	J/s or V × A

one joule of work performed per second; or, the power dissipated in an electrical conductor carrying one ampere current between points at one volt potential difference.

ohm	Ω	resistance	V/A or W/A^2

resistance of a circuit in which a potential difference of one volt produces a current of one ampere; or, the resistance in which one watt of power is dissipated when one ampere flows through it.

volt	V	potential	W/A or A × Ω

the difference in potential between two points in a conductor carrying one ampere current when the power dissipated between the points is one watt; or, the difference in potential between two points in a conductor across a resistance of one ohm when one ampere is flowing through it.

Temperature Equivalents

Instructions for converting °F into °C or K*, and °C into °F: Find the figure you wish to convert in the second column. If this figure is in °F, the corresponding temperature in °C and K will be found in the third and fourth columns; if the figure is in °C, the corresponding temperature in °F will be found in the first column. To convert a temperature range between two scales, rather than finding equivalent temperatures, see the temperature conversion instructions, below.

°FAHRENHEIT (°F)	FIGURE TO BE CONVERTED	°CELSIUS (°CENTIGRADE) (°C)	KELVIN (K)
...	−459.67	−273.15	0
...	−400	−240.00	+33.15
...	−300	−184.44	+88.71
−459.67	−273.15	−169.53	+103.62
−328.0	−200	−128.89	+144.26
−148.0	−100	−73.33	+199.82
−130.0	−90	−67.78	+205.37
−112.0	−80	−62.22	+210.93
−94.0	−70	−56.67	+216.48
−76.9	−60	−51.11	+222.04
−58.0	−50	−45.56	+227.59
−40.0	−40	−40.00	+233.15
−22.0	−30	−34.44	+238.71
−4.0	−20	−28.89	+244.26
+14.0	−10	−23.33	+249.82
+32.0	0	−17.78	+255.37
+33.8	+1	−17.22	+255.93
+35.6	+2	−16.67	+256.48
+37.4	+3	−16.11	+257.04
+39.2	+4	−15.56	+257.59
+41.0	+5	−15.00	+258.15
+42.8	+6	−14.44	+258.71
+44.6	+7	−13.89	+259.26

°FAHRENHEIT (°F)	FIGURE TO BE CONVERTED	°CELSIUS (°CENTIGRADE) (°C)	KELVIN (K)
+46.4	+8	−13.33	+259.82
+48.2	+9	−12.78	+260.37
+50.0	+10	−12.22	+260.93
+68.0	+20	−6.67	+266.48
+86.0	+30	−1.11	+272.04
+89.6	+32	0.00	+273.15
+104.0	+40	+4.44	+277.59
+122.0	+50	+10.00	+283.15
+140.0	+60	+15.56	+288.71
+158.0	+70	+21.11	+294.26
+176.0	+80	+26.67	+299.82
+194.0	+90	+32.22	+305.37
+212.0	+100	+37.78	+310.93
+392.0	+200	+93.33	+366.48
+572.0	+300	+148.89	+422.04
+752.0	+400	+204.44	+477.59
+932.0	+500	+260.00	+533.15
+1112.0	+600	+315.56	+588.71
+1292.0	+700	+371.11	+644.26
+1472.0	+800	+426.67	+699.82
+1652.0	+900	+482.22	+755.37
+1832.0	+1000	+537.78	+810.93
+3632.0	+2000	+1093.33	+1366.45
+5432.0	+3000	+1648.89	+1922.05

All systems of measuring temperature in degrees or units (kelvins) on a scale are based on the interval between the freezing and boiling points of water and differ only in the number of degrees or units into which this interval is divided.

Fahrenheit: interval is divided into 180 degrees (32° to 212°); 0° is at 32° below the freezing point of water.

Rankine: degree is the same as the Fahrenheit degree; 0° is at absolute zero (the theoretical point at which a thermodynamic system has the lowest energy, −459.67 °F). Once common in engineering applications in the US, the Rankine scale is now rarely used.

Celsius: interval is divided into 100 degrees; 0° is at the freezing point of water.

Kelvin: interval is the same as the Celsius degree; 0 K is at absolute zero (the theoretical point at which a thermodynamic system has the lowest energy, −273.15 °C).

Réaumur: interval is divided into 80 degrees; 0° is at the freezing point of water. One of the earliest (1730) temperature scales in widespread use, the Réaumur scale had been supplanted by other scales by the late 19th century.

*temperature conversion instructions:***
°Fahrenheit	into	°Celsius	subtract 32, divide by 1.8**
°Celsius	into	°Fahrenheit	multiply by 1.8, add 32**
°Celsius	into	kelvin	add 273.15

*Because a kelvin is itself a unit of measurement, it is incorrect to use "degree" or the ° symbol with it, as is necessary with the units of the Rankine, Fahrenheit, Celsius, and Réaumur scales. One kelvin is equal to one degree Celsius.

**Instructions are for finding equivalent temperatures; to find the equivalent number of degrees in a temperature range (e.g., tomorrow's temperature will be 11.0 °F, or 6.1 °C, warmer than today's temperature), omit the step of adding or subtracting 32.

Melting and Boiling Points of Selected Substances

Values are in °C at a pressure of 1 atmosphere (atm.; 101.325 kPa), except when a substance has a triple-point pressure greater than 1 atm.; in those cases the triple-point temperature and sublimation temperature are given and noted accordingly (see footnotes 1 and 2); figures are given only for those temperatures for which measurements or reliable estimates are available.

SUBSTANCE	MELTING POINT (°C)	BOILING POINT (°C)
common compounds		
ammonia (H_3N)	-77.74	-33.34
carbon dioxide (CO_2)	-56.57[1]	-78.5[2]
ethyl alcohol (C_2H_5OH)	-114.1	78.5
heavy water (D_2O)	3.82	101.42
hydrogen chloride (HCl)	-114	-85
hydrogen peroxide (H_2O_2)	-0.43	150.2
methane (CH_4)	-182.5	-162
ozone (O_3)	-251.4	-112
propane (C_3H_8)	-187.6	-42.1
sulfuric acid (H_2SO_4)	10.37	338
water (H_2O)	0.00	100.00
selected elements		
aluminum (Al)	660.32	2,519
argon (Ar)	-189.35	-185.85
arsenic (As)	817[1]	614[2]
bromine (Br)	-7.2	58.8
cadmium (Cd)	321.07	767
calcium (Ca)	842	1,484
carbon (C)	4,492[1]	3,642[2]
chlorine (Cl)	-101.5	-34.04
cobalt (Co)	1,495	2,927
copper (Cu)	1,084.62	2,562
fluorine (F)	-219.62	-188.12
gold (Au)	1,064.18	2,856
helium (He)		-268.93
hydrogen (H)	-259.34	-252.87

SUBSTANCE	MELTING POINT (°C)	BOILING POINT (°C)
selected elements (continued)		
iodine (I)	113.7	184.4
iron (Fe)	1,538	2,861
lead (Pb)	327.46	1,749
lithium (Li)	180.5	1,342
magnesium (Mg)	650	1,090
manganese (Mn)	1,246	2,061
mercury (Hg)	-38.83	356.73
molybdenum (Mo)	2,623	4,639
neon (Ne)	-248.59	-246.08
nickel (Ni)	1,455	2,913
nitrogen (N)	-210	-195.79
oxygen (O)	-218.79	-182.95
phosphorus (P)	44.15	280.5
platinum (Pt)	1,768.4	3,825
plutonium (Pu)	640	3,228
potassium (K)	63.38	759
radon (Rn)	-71	-61.7
silicon (Si)	1,414	3,265
silver (Ag)	691.78	2,162
sodium (Na)	97.80	883
sulfur (S)	115.21	444.6
tin (Sn)	231.93	2,602
titanium (Ti)	1,668	3,287
uranium (U)	1,135	4,131
xenon (Xe)	-111.75	-108.04
zinc (Zn)	419.53	907

[1]Triple-point temperature (equilibrium between the solid, liquid, and gaseous phases).   [2]Sublimation temperature at 1 atm. (substance passes directly from solid to gaseous phase at a pressure of 1 atm.).

Selected Physical Properties of Water

molar mass	18.0151 g/mol
melting point	0.00 °C
boiling point	100.00 °C
vapor pressure (25 °C)	23.75 torr
heat of fusion (0 °C)	6.010 kJ/mol

heat of vaporization (100 °C)	0.65 kJ/mol
heat of formation (25 °C)	-285.85 kJ/mol
entropy of vaporization (25 °C)	118.8 J/°C mol
surface tension (25 °C)	71.97 dynes/cm
viscosity	0.8903 centipoise

density

freshwater

ice	0.92 g/cm³
0 °C	0.99987 g/cm³
3.98 °C	1.0000 g/cm³ (maximum density)
20 °C	0.99823 g/cm³
25 °C	0.99701 g/cm³
100 °C	0.95841 g/cm³

seawater (salinity 35 parts/thousand, at 0 °C)

DEPTH (M)	PRESSURE (DECIBARS)	DENSITY (G/CM³)
0	0	1.02813
1,000	1,000	1.03285
2,000	2,000	1.03747
4,000	4,000	1.04640
6,000	6,000	1.05495
8,000	8,000	1.06315
10,000	10,000	1.07104

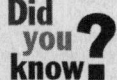 **Did you know?** The national dish of St. Vincent and the Grenadines is pickled flying fish.

Playing Cards and Dice Chances

Blackjack

Number of two-card combinations in a 52-card deck (where aces equal 11 and face cards equal 10) for each number between 13 and 21

TOTAL WITH TWO CARDS	POSSIBLE COMBINATIONS FROM 52 CARDS
21	64
20	136
19	80
18	86
17	96
16	86
15	96
14	102
13	118

Approximate chances of various hands reaching or exceeding 21

TOTAL IN HAND BEFORE DEAL (TWO OR MORE CARDS)	CHANCE OF REACHING A COUNT OF 17 TO 21 (%)	CHANCE OF EXCEEDING 21: ONE CARD (%)	CHANCE OF EXCEEDING 21: ANY NUMBER OF CARDS (%)
16	38	62	62
15	42	54	58
14	44	46	56
13	48	38	52

Poker

Number of ways to reach and odds of reaching various five-card combinations on a single deal (52-card deck, no wild cards)

HAND	NUMBER OF COMBINATIONS	ODDS OF RECEIVING ON A SINGLE DEAL
royal flush	4	1 in 649,740
straight flush	36	1 in 72,193
four of a kind	624	1 in 4,165
full house	3,744	1 in 694
flush	5,108	1 in 509
straight	10,200	1 in 255
three of a kind	54,912	1 in 47
two pairs	123,552	1 in 21
one pair	1,098,240	1 in 2

Dice

Probabilities of two-die totals

TWO-DIE TOTAL	NUMBER OF COMBINATIONS	PROBABILITY (%)	TWO-DIE TOTAL	NUMBER OF COMBINATIONS	PROBABILITY (%)
2	1	2.78	8	5	13.89
3	2	5.56	9	4	11.11
4	3	8.33	10	3	8.33
5	4	11.11	11	2	5.56
6	5	13.89	12	1	2.78
7	6	16.67	**total**	**36**	**100[1]**

[1] *Detail does not add to total because of rounding.*

Spirits Measure

From smallest to largest. Many specific volumes have varied over time and from place to place, but the proportional relationships within the various families of measures have generally remained the same.

MEASURE	CONVENTIONAL EQUIVALENTS*	METRIC EQUIVALENT†
pony	0.75 oz = ¾ shot= ½ jigger	22.17 ml
shot/ounce/finger	1 oz = 1⅓ ponies = ⅔ jigger	29.57 ml
jigger	1.5 oz = 2 ponies = 1½ shots	44.36 ml
double	2 oz = 2 shots	59.15 ml
triple	3 oz = 3 shots	88.72 ml
noggin/imperial gill/drink (whiskey)	4.8 oz	142.1 ml
pint	16 oz = ⅝ fifth = ½ quart	473.2 ml
quarter yard	20 oz = 1¼ pints	591.5 ml
bottle (champagne or other wine)	about 25.5 oz or ⅙ imperial gallon	about 750 ml†
fifth	25.6 oz = ⅘ quart = ⅕ gallon	757.1 ml
quart	32 oz = ½ magnum = ¼ gallon	946.3 ml
half yard	40 oz = 2½ pints	1.182 l
magnum	2 bottles (champagne or other wine)	1.5 l
magnum	64 oz = 2 quarts = ½ gallon	1.893 l
yard	80 oz = 5 pints	2.365 l
jeroboam	4 bottles (champagne or other wine)	3 l

Spirits Measure (continued)

MEASURE	CONVENTIONAL EQUIVALENTS*	METRIC EQUIVALENT†
gallon/double magnum	128 oz = 4 quarts = 5 fifths = 2 magnums	3.785 l
rehoboam	6 bottles (champagne or other wine)	4 l
imperial gallon	1.20 gallons = ⅖ barn gallon = ⅒ anker	4.546 l
ale/beer gallon	1.22 gallons	4.620 l
methuselah	8 bottles (champagne or other wine)	6 l
salmanazar	12 bottles (champagne or other wine)	9 l
barn gallon	2½ imperial gallons = ¼ anker	11.37 l
balthazar	16 bottles (champagne or other wine)	12 l
half keg	5 gallons (type varies)	varies
nebuchadnezzar	20 bottles (champagne or other wine)	15 l
firkin	9 gallons	34.07 l
keg	10 gallons (type varies)	varies
anker	60 bottles = 10 imperial gallons = 4 barn gallons	45.46 l
runlet/rundlet/rudlet	144 pints = 72 quarts = 18 gallons = 2 firkins	68.14 l
octave	15.75 imperial gallons = ⅛ butt (wine)	71.60 l
British bottle	126 bottles = 21 imperial gallons	95.47 l
aum	120 quarts = 30 gallons	113.6 l
barrel (wine)	126 quarts = 31½ gallons = ¾ tierce	119.2 l
barrel (ale/beer)	144 quarts = 36 gallons = ½ puncheon (ale/beer)	136.3 l
tierce	168 quarts = 42 gallons = ½ puncheon (wine)	159.0 l
British hogshead (ale/beer)	54 imperial gallons = ½ butt (ale/beer) = ¼ tun (ale/beer)	245.5 l
puncheon (ale/beer)	72 gallons = 2 barrels (ale/beer)	272.5 l
British hogshead (wine)	63 imperial gallons = ½ butt (wine) = ¼ tun (wine)	286.4 l
puncheon (wine)	84 gallons = 2 tierces	318.0 l
butt/pipe (ale/beer)	108 imperial gallons = ½ tun (ale/beer)	491.0 l
butt/pipe (wine)	126 imperial gallons = ½ tun (wine)	572.8 l
tun (ale/beer)	216 imperial gallons = 4 British hogsheads (ale/beer) = 2 butts (ale/beer)	982.0 l
tun (wine)	252 imperial gallons = 12 British bottles = 2 butts (wine)	1,146 l

*All ounce measures are in US fluid ounces.   †Wine bottle sizes have varied from 700 to 800 ml in various countries; industry standard is 750 ml.

Cooking Measurements

MEASURE	CONVENTIONAL EQUIVALENTS*	METRIC EQUIVALENT
drop	⅟₆₀ teaspoon	0.08 ml
dash	⅛ teaspoon	0.62 ml
teaspoon	8 dashes; ⅓ tablespoon; ⅙ fluid ounce	4.93 ml
tablespoon	3 teaspoons; ½ fluid ounce	14.79 ml
ounce (weight)	⅟₁₆ pound	28.35 g
fluid ounce (volume)	2 tablespoons	29.57 ml
cup	8 fluid ounces; 16 tablespoons; ½ pint	236.59 ml
pound	16 ounces	453.6 g
pint	16 fluid ounces; 2 cups; ½ quart	473.18 ml
quart	32 fluid ounces; 4 cups; 2 pints; ¼ gallon	946.36 ml
gallon	128 fluid ounces; 16 cups; 8 pints; 4 quarts	3.785 l
peck	2 gallons	7.57 l
bushel	8 gallons; 4 pecks	30.28 l

*All ounce measurements are in US ounces or fluid ounces.

		OVEN TEMPERATURE EQUIVALENTS		
		AMERICAN OVEN TEMPERATURE	FRENCH OVEN TEMPERATURE TERMS AND THERMOSTAT	BRITISH "GAS MARK" OVEN THERMOSTAT
°F	°C	TERMS	SETTINGS	SETTINGS
160	71		#1	
170	77			
200	93		très doux; étuve	
212	100			
221	105		#2	
225	107	very slow	doux	
230	110		#3	#¼ (241 °F)
250	121			

Cooking Measurements (continued)

OVEN TEMPERATURE EQUIVALENTS (CONTINUED)

°F	°C	AMERICAN OVEN TEMPERATURE TERMS	FRENCH OVEN TEMPERATURE TERMS AND THERMOSTAT SETTINGS	BRITISH "GAS MARK" OVEN THERMOSTAT SETTINGS
275	135			#½ (266 °F)
284	140	slow	moyen; modéré	#1 (291 °F)
300	149			
302	150		#4	
320	160			#2 (313 °F)
325	163			
350	177	moderate	assez chaud; bon four	#3 (336 °F)
356	180			#4 (358 °F)
375	190		#5	
390	200			#5 (379 °F)
400	205			#6 (403 °F)
410	210	hot	chaud	
425	218		#6	#7 (424 °F)
428	220			
437	225			
450	232			#8 (446 °F)
475	246	very hot	très chaud; vif	#9 (469 °F)
500	260		#7	
525	274		#8	
550	288		#9	

Large Numbers

The American system of numeration for denominations above one million was modeled on the French system, but more recently the French system has been changed to correspond to the German and British systems. In the American system each of the denominations above 1,000 millions (the American *billion*) is 1,000 times the preceding one (one trillion = 1,000 billions; one quadrillion = 1,000 trillions). In the British system the first denomination above 1,000 millions (the British *milliard*) is 1,000 times the preceding one, but each of the denominations above 1,000 milliards (the British *billion*) is 1,000,000 times the preceding one (one trillion = 1,000,000 billions; one quadrillion = 1,000,000 trillions).

Source: *Merriam-Webster's Collegiate Dictionary*, Tenth Edition, Merriam-Webster, Inc., 1993.

AMERICAN NAME	VALUE IN POWERS OF TEN	NUMBER OF ZEROS	BRITISH NAME	VALUE IN POWERS OF TEN	NUMBER OF ZEROS
billion	10^9	9	milliard	10^9	9
trillion	10^{12}	12	billion	10^{12}	12
quadrillion	10^{15}	15	trillion	10^{18}	18
quintillion	10^{18}	18	quadrillion	10^{24}	24
sextillion	10^{21}	21	quintillion	10^{30}	30
septillion	10^{24}	24	sextillion	10^{36}	36
octillion	10^{27}	27	septillion	10^{42}	42
nonillion	10^{30}	30	octillion	10^{48}	48
decillion	10^{33}	33	nonillion	10^{54}	54
undecillion	10^{36}	36	decillion	10^{60}	60
duodecillion	10^{39}	39	undecillion	10^{66}	66
tredecillion	10^{42}	42	duodecillion	10^{72}	72
quattuordecillion	10^{45}	45	tredecillion	10^{78}	78
quindecillion	10^{48}	48	quattuordecillion	10^{84}	84
sexdecillion	10^{51}	51	quindecillion	10^{90}	90
septendecillion	10^{54}	54	sexdecillion	10^{96}	96
octodecillion	10^{57}	57	septendecillion	10^{102}	102
novemdecillion	10^{60}	60	octodecillion	10^{108}	108
vigintillion	10^{63}	63	novemdecillion	10^{114}	114
centillion	10^{303}	303	vigintillion	10^{120}	120
			centillion	10^{600}	600

Roman Numerals

Seven numeral-characters compose the Roman numeral system. When a numeral appears with a line above it, it represents the base value multiplied by 1,000. However, because Roman numerals are now seldom utilized for values beyond 4,999, this convention is no longer in use.

Roman Numerals (continued)

ARABIC	ROMAN	ARABIC	ROMAN	ARABIC	ROMAN	ARABIC	ROMAN
1	I	15	XV	70	LXX	1,000	M
2	II	16	XVI	80	LXXX	1,001	MI
3	III	17	XVII	90	XC	1,002	MII
4	IV	18	XVIII	100	C	1,003	MIII
5	V	19	XIX	101	CI	1,900	MCM
6	VI	20	XX	102	CII	2,000	MM
7	VII	21	XXI	200	CC	2,001	MMI
8	VIII	22	XXII	300	CCC	2,002	MMII
9	IX	23	XXIII	400	CD	2,100	MMC
10	X	24	XXIV	500	D	3,000	MMM
11	XI	30	XXX	600	DC	4,000	MMMM or MV̄
12	XII	40	XL	700	DCC	5,000	V̄
13	XIII	50	L	800	DCCC		
14	XIV	60	LX	900	CM		

Ancient Measures

The standard unit of measure is listed first, with a rough modern equivalent in parentheses. Often, standard units varied over time, so a range is sometimes given. The subdivisions below relate to the standard unit of measure given first.

CULTURE	LENGTH	WEIGHT	LIQUID
Egyptian	cubit (524 mm; 20.62 in)	kite (4.5–29.9 g; 0.16–1.05 oz)	cubic cubit (0.14 cubic m; 37 gal)[1]
	digit (1/28 of a cubit)	deben (10 kites)	khar
	palm (4 digits)	sep (10 debens)	hekat
	hand (5 digits)		hin
	small span (12 digits, or 3 palms)		ro
	large span (14 digits, or 1/2 cubit)		
	t'ser (16 digits, or 4 palms)		
	small cubit (24 digits, or 6 palms)		
Babylonian	kus[2] (530 mm; 20.9 in)	mina (640–978 g; 23–34 oz)	ka (99–102 cubic mm; 3.9–4.0 cubic in)
	foot (2/3 kus)	shekel	gur (300 ka)
	shusi (1/30 kus)		
Hebrew[3]		sacred mina (60 shekels)	bat[4]
		sacred talent (3,000 shekels, or 50 sacred minas)	hin
		Talmudic mina (25 shekels)	log
		Talmudic talent (1,500 shekels, or 60 Talmudic minas)	
Greek	finger (19.3 mm; 0.76 in)	talent (25.8 kg; 56.9 lb)	metretes (39.4 l; 10.4 gal)
	foot (16 fingers)		
	Olympic cubit (24 fingers)		
Roman	foot (subdivided into the uncia [plural unciae; 1/12 ft])	libra (327.45 g; 11.55 oz)	sextarius (0.53 l; 0.14 gal)
	pace, or double step (5 ft)	uncia (1/12 lb)	amphora (48 sextarii)
	mille passus (1,000 paces)		
Chinese[5]	chih (25 cm; 9.8 in)	shih, or tan (60 kg; 132 lb)	
	chang (3 m; 9.8 ft)		

[1]Measures given below the cubic cubit run from small to large.   [2]Also called the Babylonian cubit.   [3]The Hittites, Assyrians, Phoenicians, and Hebrews derived their systems from the Babylonians and Egyptians. Hebrew standards were based on the relationship between the mina, the talent (the basic unit), and the shekel.   [4]Volumes are not definitely known but are listed from largest to smallest.   [5]The Chinese system of measurement exhibited all the principal characteristics of the Western. It was, however, fundamentally chaotic in that there was no relationship between different types of units, such as those of length and those of volume. It also fluctuated from region to region and according to use. The first emperor of China, Shi Huangdi (221–210/09 BC), fixed the basic units given here.

Prime Numbers

A prime number is a positive integer greater than 1 that is divisible only by itself and 1. Every positive integer greater than 1 can be expressed as the product of only a single set of prime numbers. Primes have been recognized since at least 300 BC, when they were studied by the Greek mathematicians Euclid and Eratosthenes. They have always fascinated mathematicians, and even today there remain certain open questions regarding them. The first 100 prime numbers are: 2, 3, 5, 7, 11, 13,

17, 19, 23, 29, 31, 37, 41, 43, 47, 53, 59, 61, 67, 71, 73, 79, 83, 89, 97, 101, 103, 107, 109, 113, 127, 131, 137, 139, 149, 151, 157, 163, 167, 173, 179, 181, 191, 193, 197, 199, 211, 223, 227, 229, 233, 239, 241, 251, 257, 263, 269, 271, 277, 281, 283, 293, 307, 311, 313, 317, 331, 337, 347, 349, 353, 359, 367, 373, 379, 383, 389, 397, 401, 409, 419, 421, 431, 433, 439, 443, 449, 457, 461, 463, 467, 479, 487, 491, 499, 503, 509, 521, 523, and 541.

For more numbers, see <www.utm.edu/research/primes>

Decimal Equivalents of Common Fractions

4THS	8THS	16THS	32NDS	DECIMAL		3RDS	6THS	12THS	DECIMAL
				0.015625				1	0.833334
			1	0.03125			1	2	0.166667
		1	2	0.0625				3	0.25
			3	0.09375		1	2	4	0.333334
	1	2	4	0.125				5	0.416667
			5	0.15625			3	6	0.5
		3	6	0.1875				7	0.583333
			7	0.21875		2	4	8	0.666667
1	2	4	8	0.25				9	0.75
			9	0.28125			5	10	0.833333
		5	10	0.3125				11	0.916667
			11	0.34375			6	12	1
	3	6	12	0.375					
			13	0.40625					
		7	14	0.4375			5THS		DECIMAL
			15	0.46875			1		0.2
2	4	8	16	0.5			2		0.4
			17	0.53125			3		0.6
		9	18	0.5625			4		0.8
			19	0.59375			5		1
	5	10	20	0.625					
			21	0.65625					
		11	22	0.6875			7THS		DECIMAL
			23	0.71875			1		0.142857
3	6	12	24	0.75			2		0.285714
			25	0.78125			3		0.428571
		13	26	0.8125			4		0.571428
			27	0.84375			5		0.714285
	7	14	28	0.875			6		0.857142
			29	0.90625			7		1
		15	30	0.9375					
			31	0.96875					
4	8	16	32	1					

Mathematical Formulas

The ratio of the circumference of a circle to its diameter is π (3.141592653589793238462643383279..., generally rounded to ²²/₇ or 3.1416). It occurs in various mathematical problems involving the lengths of arcs or other curves, the areas of surfaces, and the volumes of many solids.

	ACTION	FORMULA
circumference		
circle	multiply diameter by π	πd
area		
circle	multiply radius squared by π	πr^2
rectangle	multiply height by length	hl
sphere surface	multiply radius squared by π by 4	$4\pi r^2$
square	length of one side squared	s^2
trapezoid	parallel side length A + parallel side length B multiplied by height and divided by 2	$(A+B)h/2$
triangle	multiply base by height and divide by 2	$hb/2$
volume		
cone	multiply base radius squared by π by height and divide by 3	$br^2\pi h/3$
cube	length of one edge cubed	$a3$
cylinder	multiply base radius squared by π by height	$br^2\pi h$
pyramid	multiply base area by height and divide by 3	$hb/3$
sphere	multiply radius cubed by π by 4 and divide by 3	$4\pi r^3/3$

Encyclopædia Britannica's Selected Culturally Pivotal Inventions

INVENTION	YEAR	INVENTOR	COUNTRY
air-conditioning	1902	Willis Haviland Carrier	US
airplane, engine-powered	1903	Wilbur & Orville Wright	US
alphabet	c. 1700–1500 BC	Semitic-speaking peoples	eastern Mediter-ranean coast
American Sign Language	1817	Thomas H. Gallaudet	US
answering machine, telephone	1898	Valdemar Poulsen	Denmark
aspirin	1897	Felix Hoffmann (Bayer & Co.)	Germany
assembly line	1913	Henry Ford	US
astrolabe	c. 2nd century	—	—
automated teller machine (ATM)	1968	Don Wetzel	US
automobile	1889	Gottlieb Daimler	Germany
barometer	1643	Evangelista Torricelli	Italy
battery, electric storage	1800	Alessandro Volta	Italy
beer	before 6000 BC	Sumerians, Babylonians	Mesopotamia
bicycle	1818	Baron Karl von Drais de Sauerbrun	Germany
blood bank	late 1930s	Charles Richard Drew	US
bomb, atomic	1945	J. Robert Oppenheimer, et al.	US
button	c. 700 BC	Greeks, Etruscans	Greece, Italy
buttonhole	13th century	—	Europe
calculator, electronic handheld	1967	Jack S. Kilby	US
calculus	c. 1670	Sir Isaac Newton and Gottfried Wilhelm Leibniz (invented separately)	England; Germany
calendar, modern (Gregorian)	1582	Pope Gregory XIII	Italy
camera, portable photographic	1888	George Eastman	US
candle	c. 3000 BC	—	Egypt, Crete
canning, food	1809	Nicolas Appert	France
cardboard, corrugated	1871	Albert Jones	US
cards, playing	c. 10th century	—	China
cash register	1879	James Ritty	US
catalog, mail-order	1872	Aaron Montgomery Ward	US
cement, portland	1824	Joseph Aspdin	England
chocolate	c. 3rd–10th century	Maya, Aztecs	Central America, Mexico
clock, pendulum	1656	Christiaan Huygens	The Netherlands
cloning, animal	1970	John B. Gurdon	The Netherlands, UK
coins	c. 650 BC	Lydians	Turkey
compact disc (CD)	1980	Philips Electronics, Sony Corp.	The Netherlands, Japan
compass, magnetic	c. 12th century	—	China, Europe
computed tomography (CT scan, CAT scan)	1972	Godfrey Hounsfield, Allan Cormack	UK, US
computer, electronic digital	1939	John V. Atanasoff, Clifford E. Berry	US
computer, personal	1974	MITS (Micro Instrumentation Telemetry Systems)	US
concrete, reinforced	1867	Joseph Monier	France
condom, latex	c. 1930	—	—
contraceptives, oral	early 1950s	Gregory Pincus, et. al.	US
cotton gin	1793	Eli Whitney	US
coupon, grocery	1894	Asa Candler	US
credit card, universal	1950	Frank McNamara, Ralph Schneider (Diners' Club)	US
diapers, disposable	1950	Marion Donovan	US
DNA fingerprinting	1984	Alec Jeffreys	UK
dynamite	1867	Alfred Nobel	Sweden
electrocardiogram (ECG, EKG)	1903	Willem Einthoven	The Netherlands
electronic mail (e-mail)	1971	Ray Tomlinson	US
encyclopedia	c. 4th century BC or 77 AD	Speusippus (compliation of Plato's teachings) or Pliny the Elder (comprehensive work)	Greece or Rome
engine, internal-combustion	1859	Étienne Lenoir	France
engine, steam	1698	Thomas Savery	England
eyeglasses	1280s	Salvino degli Armati or Alessandro di Spina	Italy
genetic engineering	1973	Stanley N. Cohen, Herbert W. Boyer	US
glass	c. 2500 BC	Egyptians or Phoenicians	Egypt or Lebanon
guitar, electric	1941	Les Paul	US
gunpowder	c. 10th century	—	China or Arabia
hypodermic syringe	1853	Charles Gabriel Pravaz	France

Encyclopædia Britannica's Selected Culturally Pivotal Inventions (continued)

INVENTION	YEAR	INVENTOR	COUNTRY
ink	c. 2500 BC	—	Egypt, China
insulin, extraction and preparation of	1921	Sir Frederick Grant Banting, Charles H. Best	Canada
integrated circuit	1958	Jack S. Kilby	US
jeans	1873	Levi Strauss, Jacob Davis	US
lamp, incandescent	1879	Thomas Alva Edison	US
laser	1958	Gordon Gould; Charles Hard Townes and Arthur L. Schawlow (invented separately)	US
lock and key	c. 2000 BC	Assyrians	Mesopotamia
magnetic resonance imaging (MRI)	early 1970s	Raymond Damadian, Paul Lauterbur	US
microscope, compound optical	c. 1600	Hans & Zacharias Jansen	The Netherlands
microwave oven	1945	Percy L. Spencer	US
mirror, glass	c. 1200	Venetians	Italy
missile, guided	1942	Wernher von Braun	Germany
money, paper	late 900s	—	China
Morse code	1838	Samuel F.B. Morse	US
motor, electric	1834	Thomas Davenport	US
nail, construction	c. 3300 BC	Sumerians	Mesopotamia
nuclear reactor	1942	Enrico Fermi	US
oil-drilling well	1859	Edwin Drake	US
paper	c. 105	Ts'ai Lun	China
particle accelerator	1929	Sir John Douglas Cockcroft, Ernest Thomas Sinton Walton	UK
pacemaker, cardiac	1952	Paul M. Zoll	US
pasteurization	1864	Louis Pasteur	France
pencil	1565	Conrad Gesner	Switzerland
periodic table	1871	Dmitry Mendeleyev	Russia
phonograph	1877	Thomas Alva Edison	US
plow, steel	1836	John Deere	US
pocket watch	c. 1500	Peter Henlein	Germany
printing press, movable type	c. 1450	Johannes Gutenberg	Germany
projector, motion picture	1891	Thomas Alva Edison, William K.L. Dickson	US
Prozac	1972	Bryan B. Molloy, et al.	Scotland
radar	c. 1904	Christian Hülsmeyer	Germany
radio	1896	Guglielmo Marconi	Italy
refrigerator	1842	John Gorrie	US
rubber, vulcanized	1839	Charles Goodyear	US
saddle	c. 200 BC	—	China
satellite, successful artificial Earth	1957	Sergey Korolyov, et al.	USSR
satellite, communications	1960	John Robinson Pierce	US
sewing machine	1841	Barthélemy Thimonnier	France
shoelaces	1790	—	England
skyscraper, steel-frame	1884	William Jenney	US
soap	600 BC	Phoenicians	Lebanon
stamps, postage	1840	Sir Rowland Hill	UK
steel, mass-production	1856	Henry Bessemer	UK
stethoscope	1819	René-Théophile-Hyacinthe Laënnec	France
stove, gas	1826	James Sharp	UK
telephone, wired-line	1876	Alexander Graham Bell	Scotland/US
telescope, optical	1608	Hans Lippershey	The Netherlands
television	1923, 1927	Vladimir Zworykin, Philo Farnsworth	Russia/US, US
thermometer	1592	Galileo	Italy
toilet, flush	c. 1591	Sir John Harington	England
toothbrush	1498	—	China
typewriter	1868	Christopher Latham Sholes	US
vaccination	1796	Edward Jenner	England
video games	1972	Nolan Bushnell	US
washing machine, electric	1907	Alva J. Fisher	US
wheel	c. 3500 BC	proto-Aryan people or Sumerians	central Asia or Mesopotamia
windmill	644	—	Persia
wine	before 4000 BC	—	Middle East
World Wide Web	1989	Tim Berners-Lee	UK
X-ray imaging	1895	Wilhelm Röntgen	Germany
zipper	1893	Whitcomb L. Judson	US

Periodic Table of the Elements

The periodic table arranges the elements into groups (vertically) of elements sharing common physical and chemical characteristics and into periods (horizontally) of sequentially increasing atomic number and electron-shell configuration. Elements 111–116 have been created experimentally and have temporary names. Atomic weights in parentheses indicate the number of the most stable isotope of a radioactive element.

1	2	3	4	5	6	7	8	9	10	11	12	13	14	15	16	17	18
1 H																	2 He
3 Li	4 Be											5 B	6 C	7 N	8 O	9 F	10 Ne
11 Na	12 Mg											13 Al	14 Si	15 P	16 S	17 Cl	18 Ar
19 K	20 Ca	21 Sc	22 Ti	23 V	24 Cr	25 Mn	26 Fe	27 Co	28 Ni	29 Cu	30 Zn	31 Ga	32 Ge	33 As	34 Se	35 Br	36 Kr
37 Rb	38 Sr	39 Y	40 Zr	41 Nb	42 Mo	43 Tc	44 Ru	45 Rh	46 Pd	47 Ag	48 Cd	49 In	50 Sn	51 Sb	52 Te	53 I	54 Xe
55 Cs	56 Ba	57 La	72 Hf	73 Ta	74 W	75 Re	76 Os	77 Ir	78 Pt	79 Au	80 Hg	81 Tl	82 Pb	83 Bi	84 Po	85 At	86 Rn
87 Fr	88 Ra	89 Ac	104 Rf	105 Db	106 Sg	107 Bh	108 Hs	109 Mt	110 Ds	111 Uuu	112 Uub	113 Uut	114 Uuq	115 Uup	116 Uuh		

Lanthanide Series

58 Ce	59 Pr	60 Nd	61 Pm	62 Sm	63 Eu	64 Gd	65 Tb	66 Dy	67 Ho	68 Er	69 Tm	70 Yb	71 Lu

Actinide Series

90 Th	91 Pa	92 U	93 Np	94 Pu	95 Am	96 Cm	97 Bk	98 Cf	99 Es	100 Fm	101 Md	102 No	103 Lr

Element	Symbol	Atomic no.	Atomic weight	Element	Symbol	Atomic no.	Atomic weight
Actinium	Ac	89	227.028	Molybdenum	Mo	42	95.94
Aluminum	Al	13	26.9815	Neodymium	Nd	60	144.24
Americium	Am	95	(243)	Neon	Ne	10	20.180
Antimony	Sb	51	121.75	Neptunium	Np	93	(237.0482)
Argon	Ar	18	39.948	Nickel	Ni	28	58.69
Arsenic	As	33	74.9216	Niobium	Nb	41	92.9064
Astatine	At	85	(210)	Nitrogen	N	7	14.0067
Barium	Ba	56	137.33	Nobelium	No	102	(259)
Berkelium	Bk	97	(247)	Osmium	Os	76	190.2
Beryllium	Be	4	9.01218	Oxygen	O	8	15.9994
Bismuth	Bi	83	208.9804	Palladium	Pd	46	106.42
Bohrium	Bh	107	(264)	Phosphorus	P	15	30.97376
Boron	B	5	10.81	Platinum	Pt	78	195.08
Bromine	Br	35	79.904	Plutonium	Pu	94	(244)
Cadmium	Cd	48	112.41	Polonium	Po	84	(209)
Calcium	Ca	20	40.08	Potassium	K	19	39.0983
Californium	Cf	98	(251)	Praseodymium	Pr	59	140.9077
Carbon	C	6	12.011	Promethium	Pm	61	(145)
Cerium	Ce	58	140.12	Protactinium	Pa	91	231.0359
Cesium	Cs	55	132.9054	Radium	Ra	88	(226.0254)
Chlorine	Cl	17	35.453	Radon	Rn	86	(222)
Chromium	Cr	24	51.996	Rhenium	Re	75	186.207
Cobalt	Co	27	58.9332	Rhodium	Rh	45	102.9055
Copper	Cu	29	63.546	Rubidium	Rb	37	85.4678
Curium	Cm	96	(247)	Ruthenium	Ru	44	101.07
Darmstadtium	Ds	110	(271)	Rutherfordium	Rf	104	(261)
Dubnium	Db	105	(262)	Samarium	Sm	62	150.36
Dysprosium	Dy	66	162.50	Scandium	Sc	21	44.9559
Einsteinium	Es	99	(252)	Seaborgium	Sg	106	(266)
Erbium	Er	68	167.26	Selenium	Se	34	78.96
Europium	Eu	63	151.96	Silicon	Si	14	28.0855
Fermium	Fm	100	(257)	Silver	Ag	47	107.868
Fluorine	F	9	18.9984	Sodium	Na	11	22.98977
Francium	Fr	87	(223)	Strontium	Sr	38	87.62
Gadolinium	Gd	64	157.25	Sulfur	S	16	32.07
Gallium	Ga	31	69.72	Tantalum	Ta	73	180.9479
Germanium	Ge	32	72.61	Technetium	Tc	43	(98)
Gold	Au	79	196.9665	Tellurium	Te	52	127.60
Hafnium	Hf	72	178.49	Terbium	Tb	65	158.9254
Hassium	Hs	108	(277)	Thallium	Tl	81	204.383
Helium	He	2	4.00260	Thorium	Th	90	232.0381
Holmium	Ho	67	164.930	Thulium	Tm	69	168.9342
Hydrogen	H	1	1.0079	Tin	Sn	50	118.71
Indium	In	49	114.82	Titanium	Ti	22	47.867
Iodine	I	53	126.9045	Tungsten (wolfram)	W	74	183.85
Iridium	Ir	77	192.22	Ununbium	Uub	112	(285)
Iron	Fe	26	55.845	Ununhexium	Uuh	116	(292)
Krypton	Kr	36	83.80	Ununpentium	Uup	115	(288)
Lanthanum	La	57	138.9055	Ununquadium	Uuq	114	(289)
Lawrencium	Lr	103	(262)	Ununtrium	Uut	113	(284)
Lead	Pb	82	207.2	Unununium	Uuu	111	(272)
Lithium	Li	3	6.941	Uranium	U	92	238.029
Lutetium	Lu	71	174.967	Vanadium	V	23	50.9415
Magnesium	Mg	12	24.305	Xenon	Xe	54	131.29
Manganese	Mn	25	54.9380	Ytterbium	Yb	70	173.04
Meitnerium	Mt	109	(268)	Yttrium	Y	39	88.9059
Mendelevium	Md	101	(258)	Zinc	Zn	30	65.39
Mercury	Hg	80	200.59	Zirconium	Zr	40	91.224

Applied Science

Chemistry

Chemistry is the science that deals with the properties, composition, and structure of substances (defined as elements and compounds), the transformations that they undergo, and the energy that is released or absorbed during these processes. Every substance, whether naturally occurring or artificially produced, consists of one or more of the hundred-odd species of atoms that have been identified as elements. Although these atoms, in turn, are composed of more elementary particles, they are the basic building blocks of chemical substances; there is no quantity of oxygen, mercury, or gold, for example, smaller than an atom of that substance. Chemistry, therefore, is concerned not with the subatomic domain but with the properties of atoms and the laws governing their combinations and with how the knowledge of these properties can be used to achieve specific purposes.

Common Alloys

ALLOY	COMPOSITION	ALLOY	COMPOSITION
brass	55% copper, 45% zinc	pewter	tin, antimony, copper
bronze	copper, tin	solder	tin, lead
cast iron	iron, carbon, silicon, manganese, trace impurities	stainless steel	iron, carbon, chromium, nickel
cupronickel	copper, nickel	steel	iron, carbon
		sterling silver	silver, copper

Physics

Physics is the science that deals with the structure of matter and the interactions between the fundamental constituents of the observable universe. The basic physical science, its aim is the discovery and formulation of the fundamental laws of nature. In the broadest sense, physics (from the Greek *physikos*) is concerned with all aspects of nature on both the macroscopic and submicroscopic levels. Its scope of study encompasses not only the behavior of objects under the action of given forces but also the nature and origin of gravitational, electromagnetic, and nuclear force fields. Its ultimate objective is the formulation of a few comprehensive principles that bring together and explain all such disparate phenomena. Physics can, at base, be defined as the science of matter, motion, and energy. Its laws are typically expressed with economy and precision in the language of mathematics.

Weight, Mass, and Density

Mass, strictly defined, is the quantitative measure of inertia, the resistance a body offers to a change in its speed or position when force is applied to it. The greater the mass of a body, the smaller the change produced by an applied force. In more practical terms, it is the measure of the amount of material in an object, and in common usage is often expressed as weight. However, the mass of an object is constant regardless of its position, while weight varies according to gravitational pull.

In the International System of Units (SI, the metric system), the kilogram is the standard unit of mass, defined as equaling the mass of the international prototype of the kilogram, currently a platinum-iridium cylinder kept at Sèvres, near Paris, France; it is roughly equal to the mass of 1,000 cubic centimeters of pure water at the temperature of its maximum density. In the US customary system, the unit is the slug, defined as the mass which a one pound force can accelerate at a rate of one foot per second per second, which is the same as the mass of an object weighing 32.17 pounds on the earth's surface.

Weight is the gravitational force of attraction on an object, caused by the presence of a massive second object, such as the Earth or Moon. Weight is the product of an object's mass and the acceleration of gravity at the point where the object is located. A given object will have the same mass on the Earth's surface, on the Moon, or in the absence of gravity, while its weight on the Moon would be about one sixth of its weight on the Earth's surface, because of the Moon's smaller gravitational pull (due in turn to the Moon's smaller mass and radius), and in the absence of gravity the object would have no weight at all.

Weight is measured in units of force, not mass, though in practice units of mass (such as the kilogram) are often substituted because of mass's relatively constant relation to weight on the Earth's surface. The weight of a body can be obtained by multiplying the mass by the acceleration of gravity. In SI, weight is expressed in newtons, or the force required to impart an acceleration of one meter per second per second to a mass of one kilogram. In the US customary system, it is expressed in pounds.

Density is the mass per unit volume of a material substance. It offers a convenient means of obtaining the mass of a body from its volume, or vice versa; the mass is equal to the volume multiplied by the density, while the volume is equal to the mass divided by the density. In SI, density is expressed in kilograms per cubic meter.

Communications

Introduction to the Internet

The **Internet** is a dynamic collection of computer networks that has revolutionized communications and methods of commerce by enabling those networks around the world to interact with each other. Sometimes referred to as a "**network of networks**," the Internet was developed in the United States in the 1970s but was not widely used by the general public until the early 1990s. By the beginning of the 21st century approximately 360 million people, or roughly 6% of the world's population, were estimated to have access to the Internet. It is widely assumed that at least half of the world's population will have some form of Internet access by 2010 and that wireless access will play a growing role.

The Internet is so powerful and general that it can be used for almost any purpose that depends on the processing of information, and it is accessible by every individual who connects to one of its constituent networks. It supports human communication via **electronic mail** (e-mail), as well as real-time "chat rooms," newsgroups, and audio and video transmission and allows people to work collaboratively at many different locations. It supports access to information by many applications, including the **World Wide Web**, which uses text and graphical presentations. Publishing has been revolutionized, as whole novels and reference works are available on the Web, and periodicals, including data prepared daily for an individual subscriber (such as stock market reports or news summaries), are also common. The Internet has attracted a large and growing number of "e-businesses" (including subsidiaries of traditional "brick-and-mortar" companies) that carry out most of their sales and services over the Internet.

While the precise structure of the future Internet is not yet clear, many directions of growth seem apparent. One is the increased availability of wireless access, enabling better real-time use of web-managed information. Another future development is toward higher backbone and network access speeds. Backbone data rates of 10 billion bits (10 gigabits) per second are readily available today, but data rates of 1 trillion bits (1 terabit) per second or higher will eventually become commercially feasible. At very high data rates, high-resolution video, for example, would occupy only a small fraction of available bandwidth, and remaining bandwidth could be used to transmit auxiliary information about the data being sent, which in turn would enable rapid customization of displays and prompt resolution of certain local queries.

Communications connectivity will be a key function of a future Internet as more machines and devices are interconnected. Since the Internet Engineering Task Force published its 128-bit IP address standard in 1998, the number of available addresses (2^{128}, as opposed to 2^{32} under the previous standard), almost every electronic device imaginable may be assigned a unique address. Thus the expressions "wired" office, home, and car may all take on new meanings, even if the access is really wireless.

Growth of Internet Use

Sources: International Telecommunications Union Yearbook of Statistics, CIA World Factbook.

YEAR	US USERS	WORLD USERS	YEAR	US USERS	WORLD USERS
1992	4,500,000	12,300,000	1998	73,000,000	160,000,000
1993	5,500,000	15,000,000	1999	102,000,000	270,000,000
1994	8,500,000	17,500,000	2000	124,000,000	385,000,000
1995	20,000,000	23,700,000	2001	143,000,000	496,000,000
1996	30,000,000	55,000,000	2002	159,000,000	627,000,000
1997	45,000,000	101,000,000	2003	161,632,400	693,424,400

Worldwide Cellular Mobile Telephone Subscribers, 2003

Source: International Telecommunication Union Yearbook of Statistics.

COUNTRY	SUBSCRIBERS	SUBSCRIBERS PER 1,000 RESIDENTS	COUNTRY	SUBSCRIBERS	SUBSCRIBERS PER 1,000 RESIDENTS
China	269,953,000	215	India	26,154,000	25
United States	158,722,000	546	Mexico	30,098,000	295
Japan	86,655,000	679	Taiwan	25,800,000	1,141
Germany	64,800,000	785	Russia	36,500,000	249
Italy	55,918,000	1,018	Indonesia	18,800,000	87
United Kingdom	52,984,000	912	Poland	17,401,000	451
			South Africa	16,860,000	364
Brazil	46,373,000	264	Thailand	24,864,000	394
France	41,683,000	696	Philippines	21,860,000	270
Spain	37,507,000	916	Australia	14,347,000	720
South Korea	33,592,000	701	Canada	13,291,000	419
Turkey	27,887,500	394	The Netherlands	12,500,000	768

Growth of Cell Phone Use in the US

*Estimated number of cellular mobile telephone subscribers in the US, 1993–2004. Source: CTIA-
The Wireless Association's Annualized Wireless Industry Survey Results December 1985–December 2004.*

YEAR	SUBSCRIBERS	YEAR	SUBSCRIBERS	YEAR	SUBSCRIBERS	YEAR	SUBSCRIBERS
1993	16,009,000	1996	44,043,000	1999	86,047,000	2002	140,767,000
1994	24,134,000	1997	55,312,000	2000	109,478,000	2003	158,722,000
1995	33,786,000	1998	69,209,000	2001	128,375,000	2004	182,140,000

Aerospace Technology

Space Exploration

Three men were the first scientists to conceive pragmatically of spaceflight: the Russian **Konstantin Tsiolkovsky**, the American **Robert Goddard**, and the German **Hermann Oberth**. Technology in the early 20th century, however, was a long way from the level required for rocket-powered flight. Nonetheless, the theory and dynamics of such flights were rigorously studied. By the end of World War II, the German development of rocket propulsion for aircraft and guided missiles (notably the V-2) had reached a high level. With the German surrender in 1945, the US and its Allies fell heir to the technical knowledge of rocket power developed by the Germans. The technical director of the German missile effort, **Wernher von Braun**, and some 150 of his top aides surrendered to US troops. Most emigrated to the US, where they assembled and launched V-2 missiles that had been captured and shipped there. The USSR carried out an unpublicized but extensive and likely similar program; Britain and France conducted smaller programs.

In both the US and the USSR the development of **military missile technology** was essential to the achievement of satellite flight. Preparations for the International Geophysical Year (IGY, 1957–58) stimulated discussion of the possibility of launching **artificial Earth satellites** for scientific investigations. Both the US and the USSR became determined to prepare scientific satellites for launching during the IGY. While the US was still developing a space launch vehicle, the USSR startled the world by placing **Sputnik 1** in orbit on 4 Oct 1957. This was followed a month later by **Sputnik 2** carrying a live dog. The failure by the US to launch its small payload on 6 Dec 1957 heightened that nation's political discomfiture in view of its supposed advanced status in science. Following debates on the necessity of achieving parity, the US government established the **National Aeronautics and Space Administration (NASA)** in 1958. Since that time, NASA has conducted virtually all major aspects of the US space program.

The first successful US satellite, **Explorer 1**, was launched about 4 months after Sputnik 1. During the next decades the two nations participated in a space race, conducting thousands of successful launches of spacecraft of all varieties including scientific research,

communications, meteorological, remote-sensing, military reconnaissance, early warning, and navigation satellites, lunar and planetary probes, and manned craft. The USSR launched the first human, **Yury Gagarin**, into orbit around Earth on 12 Apr 1961. On 20 July 1969, the US landed two men, **Neil Armstrong** and **Edwin ("Buzz") Aldrin**, on the surface of the Moon as part of the **Apollo 11** mission. On 12 Apr 1981, the 20th anniversary of manned space flight, the US launched the first reusable manned space transportation system, the space shuttle. From the 1960s the European nations, Japan, India, and other countries have formed their own agencies for space exploration and development. The **European Space Agency (ESA)**, consists of 15 member nations. Private corporations, too, offer space launches for communications and remote sensing satellites.

In the post-Apollo decades, while the US focused much of its manned space program on the **shuttle**, the USSR concentrated on launching a series of increasingly sophisticated Earth-orbiting **space stations**, beginning with the world's first in 1971. Station crews, who were carried up in two- and three-person spacecraft, carried out mostly scientific missions while gaining experience in living and working for long periods in the space environment. After the USSR was dissolved in 1991, its space program was continued by Russia on a much smaller scale owing to economic constraints. The US launched a space station in 1973 using surplus Apollo hardware and conducted shuttle missions to a Russian station, Mir, in the 1990s. In 1998, at the head of a 16-nation consortium and with Russia as a major partner, it began in-orbit assembly of the **International Space Station (ISS)**, using the shuttle and Russian expendable launch vehicles to ferry the facility's modular components and crews into space. In addition to manned and unmanned lunar exploration, space exploration programs have included deep-space robotic missions to the planets, their moons, and smaller bodies such as comets and asteroids. Also important has been the development of unmanned space-based astronomical observatories, which allow observation of near and distant cosmic objects above the filtering and distorting effects of Earth's atmosphere.

Significant space programs and missions:

Sputnik (Russian for "fellow traveler")
Years launched: 1957–58. **Country or space agency:** USSR. **Designation:** 1 through 3 (first series). **Not Manned. Events of note:** Sputnik 1 was the first satellite to be successfully launched into space; Sputnik 2 carried a small dog named Laika ("Barker"); Sputnik 3 became the first multipurpose space-science satellite.

Vanguard
Years launched: 1958–59. **Country or space agency:** US. **Designation:** 1 through 3. **Not Manned. Events of note:** The first attempted Vanguard launch, hastily mounted in December 1957 after the USSR's Sputnik successes, failed with the launch vehicle's explosion.

Explorer
Years launched: 1958–75. **Country or space agency:** US. **Designation:** 1 through 55. **Not Manned. Events of note:** Explorer 1, the first successful US satellite,

discovered Earth's inner radiation belt. Other Explorers in this long series conducted pioneering studies over a broad spectrum of Earth and space sciences.

Pioneer

Years launched: 1958–78. **Country or space agency:** US. **Designation:** 1 through 13. **Not Manned. Events of note:** Pioneer 10 was the first spacecraft to travel through the asteroid belt, to fly by Jupiter, and to escape the solar system; Pioneer 11 was the first to visit Saturn. Complementary Pioneer 12 and 13 spacecraft (also called Pioneer Venus) explored Venus, one conducting radar mapping of the planet's cloud-shrouded surface from orbit while the other dropped atmospheric probes.

Luna (Russian for "Moon")

Years launched: 1959–76. **Country or space agency:** USSR. **Designation:** 1 through 24. **Not Manned. Events of note:** Luna 2 was the first spacecaft to crash-land on the lunar surface; Luna 3 took the first photographs of the Moon's far side; three Lunas (16, 20, and 24) returned with samples of lunar soil.

Mercury

Years launched: 1961–63 (manned missions). **Country or space agency:** US. **Designation:** Manned Mercury spacecraft had program designations, but they became better known by the individual names bestowed on them, such as "Freedom," followed by a "7" to honor the seven NASA astronauts chosen for the program. **Manned. Events of note:** Some 20 preliminary unmanned Mercury missions took place between 1959 and 1961. Of the six manned missions, Freedom 7 was launched in 1961 with Alan Shepard (the first American in space) aboard; Liberty Bell 7 in 1961 with Virgil "Gus" Grissom; Friendship 7 in 1962 with John Glenn (the first American to orbit Earth); Aurora 7 in 1962 with Scott Carpenter; Sigma 7 in 1962 with Walter Schirra; and Faith 7 in 1963 with Gordon Cooper.

Vostok (Russian for "east")

Years launched: 1961–63. **Country or space agency:** USSR. **Designation:** 1 through 6. **Manned. Events of note:** The first man in space and to orbit Earth was Soviet cosmonaut Yury Gagarin in Vostok 1, launched on 12 April 1961. Vostok 2 was launched with Gherman Titov in 1961, Vostok 3 with Andriyan Nikolayev in 1962, Vostok 4 with Pavel Popovich in 1962, Vostok 5 with Valery Bykovsky in 1963, and Vostok 6 with Valentina Tereshkova, the first woman in space, in 1963.

Venera (Russian for "Venus")

Years launched: 1961–83. **Country or space agency:** USSR. **Designation:** 1 through 16. **Not Manned. Events of note:** Venera 1 carried out the first Venus flyby. Venera 3 was the first spacecraft to impact on another planet, and Venera 7 was the first to softland on another planet. Venera 9 and 10 sent back the first closeup pictures of Venus's surface.

Ranger

Years launched: 1961–65. **Country or space agency:** US. **Designation:** 1 through 9. **Not Manned. Events of note:** Ranger 4 was the first US spacecraft to crash-land on the Moon; the last three Rangers returned thousands of images of the lunar surface before impacting the lunar surface as planned.

Mariner

Years launched: 1962–73. **Country or space agency:** US. **Designation:** 1 through 10. **Not Manned. Events of note:** Various Mariners in the program flew by Venus, Mercury, and Mars. Mariner 9 mapped Mars in detail from orbit, becoming the first spacecraft to orbit another planet. Mariner 10 is the only spacecraft to have visited the vicinity of Mercury.

Voskhod (Russian for "sunrise" or "ascent")

Years launched: 1964–65. **Country or space agency:** USSR. **Designation:** 1 and 2. **Manned. Events of note:** Voskhod 1 was the first spacecraft to carry more than one person; Aleksey Leonov performed the first space walk, from the Voskhod 2 spacecraft, on 18 Mar 1965.

Gemini

Years launched: 1965–66. **Country or space agency:** US. **Designation:** 1 through 12. **Manned. Events of note:** Ten two-person manned missions followed two unmanned test flights. Gemini 8 was the first spacecraft to dock with another craft, an unmanned launcher stage. The Gemini program showed that astronauts could carry out rendezvous and docking maneuvers and could live and work in space for the time needed for a round-trip to the Moon.

Lunar Orbiter

Years launched: 1966–67. **Country or space agency:** US. **Designation:** 1 through 5. **Not Manned. Events of note:** Five consecutive spacecraft made detailed photographic surveys of most of the Moon's surface, providing the mapping essential for choosing landing sites for the manned Apollo missions.

Soyuz (Russian for "union")

Years launched: 1967–present. **Country or space agency:** USSR. **Designation:** 1 through 40 (first series). Three subsequent series of upgraded spacecraft received the additional suffix letters T, TM, or TMA and were renumbered from 1. **Manned. Events of note:** On 24 Apr 1967 cosmonaut Vladimir Komarov conducted the inaugural test flight (Soyuz 1) of this multiperson transport craft but died returning to Earth after the parachute system failed, becoming the first fatality during a spaceflight. Soyuz 11 ferried the crew of the first space station, Salyut 1. Soyuz TM-2 made the inaugural manned flight of this TM upgrade while transporting the second crew of the Mir space station. Soyuz TM-31 carried up the International Space Station's first three-man crew. An automated unmanned cargo ferry, called Progress, was derived from the Soyuz design.

Apollo

Years launched: 1968–72. **Country or space agency:** US. **Designation:** 7 through 17. **Manned. Events of note:** Several unmanned test flights preceded 11 manned Apollo missions, including two in Earth orbit (7 and 9), two in lunar orbit (8 and 10), one lunar swingby (13), and six lunar landings (11, 12, and 14–17) in which a total of 12 astronauts walked on the Moon. Apollo 11, crewed by Neil Armstrong, Michael Collins, and Buzz Aldrin, was the first mission to land humans on the Moon, on 20 Jul 1969. Apollo 13, planned as a lunar landing mission, experienced an onboard explosion en route to the Moon; after a swing around the Moon, the crippled spacecraft made a harrowing but safe return journey to Earth with its crew, James Lovell, John Swigert, and Fred Haise. The six landing missions collectively returned almost 382 kg (842 pounds) of lunar rocks and soil for study on Earth.

Salyut (Russian for "salute")
Years launched: 1971–82. Country or space agency: USSR. Designation: 1 through 7 (two designs). Manned. Events of note: Salyut 1, launched 19 Apr 1971, was the world's first space station; its crew, cosmonauts Georgy Dobrovolsky, Vladislav Volkov, and Viktor Patsayev, died returning to Earth when their Soyuz spacecraft depressurized. Salyut 6, the first of an improved design, operated as a highly successful scientific space platform, supporting a series of crews and international visitors over a four-year period.

Skylab
Year launched: 1973. Country or space agency: US. Manned. Events of note: Skylab, based on the outfitted and pressurized upper stage of a Saturn V Moon rocket, was the first US space station. Three successive astronaut crews carried out solar astronomy studies, materials-sciences research, and biomedical experiments on the effects of weightlessness.

Apollo-Soyuz
Year launched: 1975. Countries or space agencies: US and USSR. Manned. Events of note: As a sign of improved US-Soviet relations, an Apollo spacecraft carrying three astronauts docked in Earth orbit with a Soyuz vehicle carrying two cosmonauts. It was the first cooperative multinational space mission and the last use of an Apollo craft.

Viking
Year launched: 1975. Country or space agency: US. Designation: 1 and 2. Not Manned. Events of note: Both space probes traveled to Mars, released landers, and took photographs of large expanses of Mars from orbit. The Viking 1 lander transmitted the first pictures from the Martian surface; both landers carried experiments designed to detect living organisms or life processes but found no convincing signs of life.

Voyager
Years launched: 1977. Country or space agency: US. Designation: 1 and 2. Not Manned. Events of note: Both Voyager spacecraft flew past Jupiter and Saturn, transmitting measurements and photographs; Voyager 2 went on to Uranus in 1986 and then to Neptune. Both craft continued out of the solar system, with Voyager 1 overtaking Pioneer 10 in 1998 to become the most distant human-made object in space.

space shuttle (Space Transportation System, or STS)
Years launched: 1981–present. Country or space agency: US. Designation: Individual missions were designated STS with a number (and sometimes letter) suffix, although the orbiter spacecraft themselves were reused. Manned. Events of note: The first flight of a manned space shuttle, STS-1, was on 12 Apr 1981 with the orbiter Columbia. Other original operational orbiters included Challenger, Discovery, and Atlantis. During shuttle mission STS-51-L, Challenger exploded after liftoff on 28 Jan 1986, killing all seven astronauts aboard including a private citizen, Christa McAuliffe; the orbiter Endeavour was built as a replacement vehicle. Space shuttle missions were used to deploy satellites, space observatories, and planetary probes; to carry out in-space repairs of orbiting spacecraft; and to take US astronauts to the Russian space station Mir. Beginning in 1998 a series of shuttle missions ferried components, supplies, and crews to the International Space Station during its assembly and operation. In 2003 the orbiter Columbia disintegrated while returning from a space mission, claiming the lives of its seven-person crew including Ilan Ramon, the first Israeli astronaut to go into space.

Giotto (named for the Italian artist)
Year launched: 1985. Countries or space agency: ESA. Not Manned. Events of note: This first deep-space probe launched by ESA made a close flyby of Halley's Comet, collecting data and transmitting images of the icy nucleus. It was then redirected to a second comet, using a gravity-assist flyby of Earth, the first time that a spacecraft coming back from deep space had made such a maneuver.

Mir (Russian for "peace" and "world")
Years launched: 1986–96. Country or space agency: USSR/Russia. Manned. Events of note: The core of this modular space station was launched on 20 Feb 1986; five additional modules were added over the next decade to create a large, versatile space laboratory. Although intended for a 5-year life, it supported human habitation between 1986 and 2000, including an uninterrupted stretch of occupancy of almost 10 years, and it hosted a series of US astronauts as part of a Mir–space shuttle cooperative endeavor. In 1995, Mir cosmonaut Valery Polyakov set a space endurance record of nearly 438 days.

Magellan
Year launched: 1989. Country or space agency: US. Not Manned. Events of note: Magellan was the first deep-space probe deployed by the space shuttle. During four years in orbit above Venus, it mapped some 98% of the surface of the cloud-covered planet with radar at high resolution. At the end of its mission, it was sent on a gradual dive into the Venusian atmosphere, where it measured various properties before burning up.

Galileo
Year launched: 1989. Country or space agency: US. Not Manned. Events of note: En route to Jupiter, Galileo took the first detailed pictures of two asteroids and returned unique images of a comet as it impacted Jupiter's atmosphere. Near the Jovian system, it released an atmospheric probe and then went into orbit around Jupiter for an extended study of the giant planet and its Galilean moons. Among many discoveries, Galileo found evidence of a liquid water ocean below the moon Europa's icy surface.

Ulysses
Year launched: 1990. Countries or space agency: US and ESA. Not Manned. Events of note: Ulysses traveled first to Jupiter in order to use the giant planet's gravity to sling the probe out of the plane of the planets. Ulysses successively passed over the Sun's south and north poles, studying properties of the corona, solar wind, and interplanetary space at high solar latitudes.

Clementine
Year launched: 1994. Country or space agency: US. Not Manned. Events of note: This probe was designed to test new imaging sensors in space for defense applications. It mapped the Moon in various wavelengths from lunar orbit, determining mineral content of the surface and producing tantalizing hints

of the existence of frozen water in permanently shadowed craters near the Moon's south pole.

NEAR Shoemaker (Near Earth Asteroid Rendezvous Shoemaker)

Year launched: 1996. **Country or space agency:** US. **Not Manned. Events of note:** This spacecraft, targeted to the Earth-approaching asteroid Eros, was the first to orbit a small body and to touch down on its surface. It studied Eros for a year with cameras and instruments, then made a slow descent and a soft landing and transmitted gamma-ray data from the surface for more than two weeks.

Mars Global Surveyor (MGS)

Year launched: 1996. **Country or space agency:** US. **Not Manned. Events of note:** MGS conducted long-term mapping from Martian orbit of the planet's entire surface and studies of its magnetic, atmospheric, and internal properties. Close-up images suggested, controversially, that liquid water may have flowed on or near the planet's surface in geologically recent times and still may exist in protected areas. They also showed that the "face on Mars" formation first photographed by Viking 1 was of natural origin and not a product of alien intelligence, as some had purported.

Mars Pathfinder

Year launched: 1996. **Country or space agency:** US. **Not Manned. Events of note:** The first spacecraft to land on Mars since the 1976 Viking missions, Pathfinder descended to the Martian surface using a novel combination of parachutes, rockets, and air bags. The lander and its six-wheeled robotic surface rover, called Sojourner, which together successfully collected 17,000 images and other data, added to evidence that ancient Mars was much more Earth-like than it is today.

Cassini-Huygens

Year launched: 1997. **Country or space agency:** US, ESA, and Italy. **Not Manned. Events of note:** Consisting of an orbiter (Cassini) and a descent probe (Huygens), the spacecraft traveled seven years to the Saturnian system. En route, it flew by Jupiter and returned detailed images. At Saturn, Cassini established an orbit around the planet for several years of studies, while its detached Huygens probe parachuted through the veiling atmosphere of the moon Titan to a soft landing, transmitting pictures and other data for about three hours during its descent and once on the moon's surface.

Lunar Prospector

Year launched: 1998. **Country or space agency:** US. **Not Manned. Events of note:** Equipped with radiation- and particle-measuring equipment to assay the geochemistry of the Moon's surface from orbit, the probe strengthened the evidence for water (first found by Clementine) in the south polar region. It later was deliberately crashed into a permanently shadowed crater at the south pole in an unsuccessful attempt to liberate water vapor, which could be detected from Earth.

International Space Station (ISS)

Years launched: 1998–present. **Countries or space agencies:** US, Russia, ESA, Canada, Japan, and Brazil. **Manned. Events of note:** A large modular complex of habitat modules and laboratories powered by solar arrays, the ISS continued to be assembled in Earth orbit by means of space-shuttle and Proton and Soyuz rocket flights that ferried components, crews, and supplies between Earth and the station. The first component, a US-funded, Russian-built module called Zarya, was launched on 20 Nov 1998. The ISS received its first resident crew on 2 Nov 2000.

2001 Mars Odyssey

Year launched: 2001. **Country or space agency:** US. **Not Manned. Events of note:** This spacecraft was launched to study Mars from orbit and serve as a communications relay for future US and multinational landers. Its instruments mapped the distribution of various elements on or near the surface; some of its data suggested the presence of huge subsurface reservoirs of frozen water in both polar regions.

Mars Express

Year launched: 2003. **Country or space agency:** ESA. **Not Manned. Events of note:** Carrying instruments to study the atmosphere, surface, and subsurface from Mars orbit, the spacecraft detected vast fields of water ice as well as carbon dioxide ice at the planet's south pole. Its lander, Beagle 2, which was designed to examine the rocks and soil for signs of past or present life, failed to establish radio contact after presumably reaching the Martian surface.

Mars Exploration Rover Mission

Year launched: 2003. **Country or space agency:** US. **Designation:** Spirit and Opportunity. **Not Manned. Events of note:** Twin six-wheeled robotic rovers, each equipped with cameras, a microscopic imager, a rock-grinding tool, and other instruments, landed on opposite sides of Mars at sites chosen because they seemed to have been affected by water in the planet's history. Both rovers found evidence of past water; particularly dramatic was the discovery by Opportunity of rocks that appeared to have been laid down at the shoreline of an ancient body of salty water.

Deep Impact

Year launched: 2005. **Country or space agency:** US. **Not Manned. Events of note:** Deep Impact was the first spacecraft designed to study the interior composition of a comet. As it traveled past Comet Tempel 1, it released a 370-kg (820-lb) instrumented impactor into the path of the comet's icy nucleus. A high-resolution camera and other apparatus on the flyby portion of the probe studied the impact and the resulting crater and excavated debris. The collision occurred at a relative speed of about 37,000 km/hr (23,000 mi/hr).

Space Exploration Firsts

EVENT	DETAILS	COUNTRY OR AGENCY	DATE ACCOMPLISHED
earliest known person to write about spaceflight	Lucian, in his satire *True History*, which includes a visit to the Moon	ancient Greece	2nd century

Space Exploration Firsts (continued)

EVENT	DETAILS	COUNTRY OR AGENCY	DATE ACCOMPLISHED
earliest appearance of rocket-propulsion technology	recorded use of gunpowder-propelled arrows in battle	China	by 13th century
first publication of fictional works employing scientific principles to describe human space travel and encounters with alien life	examples: Jules Verne's *From the Earth to the Moon* (1865); H.G. Wells's *The War of the Worlds* (1898) and *The First Men in the Moon* (1901)	—	late 19th and early 20th centuries
first person to study in detail the use of rockets for spaceflight	Konstantin Tsiolkovsky	Russia	late 19th and early 20th centuries
first rigorous mathematical analysis of rocketry and its application to rocket design	Hermann Oberth, in "The Rocket into Interplanetary Space" (1923) and *Ways to Spaceflight* (1929)	Germany	1920s
first launch of a liquid-fueled rocket	Robert Goddard	US	16 Mar 1926
first launch of the V-2 ballistic missile, the forerunner of modern space rockets	Wernher von Braun	Germany	3 Oct 1942
first artificial Earth satellite	Sputnik 1	USSR	4 Oct 1957
first animal launched into space	dog Laika aboard Sputnik 2	USSR	3 Nov 1957
first spacecraft to hard-land on another celestial object (the Moon)	Luna 2	USSR	14 Sep 1959
first pictures of the far side of the Moon	Luna 3	USSR	7 Oct 1959
first applications satellite launched	Tiros 1 (weather observation)	US	1 Apr 1960
first recovery of a payload from Earth orbit	Discoverer 13 (part of Corona reconnaissance satellite program)	US	11 Aug 1960
first human to orbit Earth	Yury Gagarin on Vostok 1	USSR	12 Apr 1961
first data transmitted to Earth from vicinity of another planet (Venus)	Mariner 2	US	14 Dec 1962
first woman in space	Valentina Tereshkova on Vostok 6	USSR	16 Jun 1963
first satellite to operate in geostationary orbit	Syncom 2 (telecommunications satellite)	US	26 Jul 1963
first space walk	Aleksey Leonov on Voskhod 2	USSR	18 Mar 1965
first spacecraft pictures of Mars	Mariner 4	US	14 Jul 1965
first spacecraft to soft-land on the Moon	Luna 9	USSR	3 Feb 1966
first death during a space mission	Vladimir Komarov on Soyuz 1	USSR	24 Apr 1967
first humans to orbit the Moon	Frank Borman, James Lovell, and William Anders on Apollo 8	US	24 Dec 1968
first human to walk on the Moon	Neil Armstrong on Apollo 11	US	20 Jul 1969
first unmanned spacecraft to carry lunar samples back to Earth	Luna 16	USSR	24 Sep 1970
first soft landing on another planet (Venus)	Venera 7	USSR	15 Dec 1970
first space station launched	Salyut 1	USSR	19 Apr 1971
first spacecraft to orbit another planet (Mars)	Mariner 9	US	13 Nov 1971
first spacecraft to soft-land on Mars	Mars 3	USSR	2 Dec 1971
first spacecraft to fly by Jupiter	Pioneer 10	US	3 Dec 1973
first international docking in space	Apollo and Soyuz spacecraft during Apollo-Soyuz Test Project	US/USSR	17 Jul 1975
first pictures transmitted from the surface of Mars	Viking 1	US	20 Jul 1976
first spacecraft to fly by Saturn	Pioneer 11	US	1 Sep 1979
first reusable spacecraft launched and returned from space	space shuttle Columbia	US	12–14 Apr 1981
first spacecraft to fly by Uranus	Voyager 2	US	24 Jan 1986
first spacecraft to make a close flyby of a comet's nucleus	Giotto at Halley's Comet	European Space Agency	13 Mar 1986
first spacecraft to fly by Neptune	Voyager 2	US	24 Aug 1989
first large optical space telescope launched	Hubble Space Telescope	US/European Space Agency	25 Apr 1990
first spacecraft to orbit Jupiter	Galileo	US	7 Dec 1995
first resident crew to occupy the International Space Station	William Shepherd, Yury Gidzenko, Sergey Krikalyov	US/Russia	2 Nov 2000
first spacecraft to orbit and land on an asteroid	NEAR at the asteroid Eros	US	14 Feb 2000/ 12 Feb 2001
first privately funded human spaceflight (to 100 km [62 mi])	SpaceShipOne, piloted by Michael W. Melvill (private venture)	US	21 Jun 2004
first spacecraft to strike a comet's nucleus and study its interior composition	Deep Impact at Comet Tempel 1	US	4 Jul 2005

Air Travel
Flight History

Humanity has been fascinated with the possibility of flight for millennia; a myriad of myths and stories feature humans with the ability to fly. Indeed, an important characteristic of the history of flight is the pervasive human interest in the subject; inventors from many countries took up the challenge over the years, achieving varying degrees of success. The history of flight began at least as early as about AD 400 with historical references to a Chinese kite that used a rotary wing as a source of lift. Other toys using the principle of the helicopter—in this case a rotary blade turned by the pull of a string—were known during the Middle Ages. During the latter part of the 15th century, Leonardo da Vinci made drawings pertaining to flight. In the 1700s experiments were made with the ornithopter, a machine with flapping wings.

The history of successful flight begins with the hot-air balloon. In southwestern France, two brothers, Joseph and Étienne Montgolfier, papermakers, experimented with a large cell contrived of paper in which they could collect heated air. On 19 Sep 1783 the Montgolfiers sent aloft a balloon with a rooster, a duck, and a sheep, and on 21 November the first manned flight was made. Balloons gained importance as their flights increased into hundreds of miles, but they were essentially unsteerable.

A former military man, Count Ferdinand von Zeppelin, spent much of his life after retiring in 1890 working with balloons, particularly on the steering problem. As his experimentation continued, hydrogen and illuminating gas were substituted for hot air, and a motor was mounted on a bag filled with gas that had been fitted with propellers and rudders. It was Zeppelin who first saw clearly that maintaining a steerable shape was essential, so he created a rigid but light frame. On 2 Jul 1900 Zeppelin undertook the first experimental flight of what he called an airship. The development of the dirigible went well until the docking procedure at Lakehurst NJ on 6 May 1937, when the *Hindenburg* burst into flames and exploded, with a loss of 36 lives. Public feeling about the craft made further development futile.

It should be remembered, however, that neither balloons or dirigibles had produced true flight: what they had done was harness the dynamics of the atmosphere to lift a craft off the ground, using what power (if any) they supplied primarily to steer. The first scientific exposition of the principles that ultimately led to the successful flight with a heavier-than-air device came in 1843 from Sir George Cayley, who is also regarded by many as the father of fixed-wing flight. It was Cayley who built the successful man-carrying

glider that came closest to permitting real flight. Cayley's work was built upon in the experiments and writings on gliders from the late 1800s by aviation pioneers Otto Lilienthal of Germany and Octave Chanute of the United States. The works of Cayley, Lilienthal, and Chanute would eventually inspire and form the basis of the Wright brothers' work.

The Americans Wilbur and Orville Wright by 1902 had developed a fully practical biplane glider that could be controlled in every direction. Fitting a small engine and two propellers to another biplane, the Wrights on 17 Dec 1903 made the world's first successful flight of a man-carrying, engine-powered, heavier-than-air craft at a site near Kitty Hawk NC.

The Wright brothers' success soon inspired successful aircraft designs and flights by others, and World War I (1914–18) further accelerated the expansion of aviation. Though initially used for aerial reconnaissance, aircraft were soon fitted with machine guns to shoot at other aircraft and with bombs to drop on ground targets; military aircraft with these types of missions and armaments became known, respectively, as fighters and bombers.

By the 1920s the first small commercial airlines had begun to carry mail, and the increased speed and range of aircraft made nonstop flights over the world's oceans, poles, and continents possible. In the 1930s more efficient monoplane aircraft with an all-metal fuselage and a retractable undercarriage became standard. Aircraft played a key role in World War II (1939–45), developing in size, weight, speed, power, range, and armament. The war marked the high point of piston-engined propeller craft while also introducing the first aircraft with jet engines, which could fly at higher speeds. Jet-engined craft became the norm for fighters in the late 1940s and proved their superiority as commercial transports beginning in the '50s. The high speeds and low operating costs of jet airliners led to a massive expansion of commercial air travel in the second half of the 20th century.

The next great aviation innovation after the jet engine was aircraft able to fly at supersonic speeds. The first was a Bell XS-1 rocket-powered research plane piloted by Maj. Charles E. Yeager of the US Air Force on 14 Oct 1947. The XS-1 broke the sound barrier at 1,066 km/hr (662 mph) and attained a top speed of 1,126 km/hr (700 mph). Thereafter many military aircraft capable of supersonic flight were built. The first supersonic, passenger-carrying, commercial airplane, the Concorde, was built jointly by aircraft manufacturers in Great Britain and France and was in regular commercial service between 1976 and 2003.

Airlines in the US: Best On-Time Arrival Performance
Source: US Department of Transportation, April 2005.

	AIRLINE	% OF ALL FLIGHTS		AIRLINE	% OF ALL FLIGHTS		AIRLINE	% OF ALL FLIGHTS
1	Hawaiian	95.6	8	Independence Air[1]	84.6	14	Continental	80.4
2	ATA	89.0				15	US Airways	80.0
3	Skywest	87.6	9	American	84.4	16	AirTran Airways	78.8
4	Southwest	86.7	10	Northwest	83.7	17	Atlantic Southeast	77.3
5	Comair	85.5	11	Delta	82.6			
6	America West	85.2	12	American Eagle	82.1	18	JetBlue Airways	77.0
7	United	84.8	13	ExpressJet	81.7	19	Alaska Airlines	77.0

[1]*Formerly Atlantic Coast Airlines.*

US Aviation Safety, 1985–2004

2004 data are preliminary.
Source: US National Transportation Safety Board.

	US AIRLINES[1]				US GENERAL AVIATION			
YEAR	NO. OF ACCIDENTS	NO. OF ACCIDENTS WITH FATALITIES	TOTAL NO. OF DEATHS	HOURS FLOWN	ALL ACCIDENTS	FATAL ACCIDENTS	TOTAL FATALITIES	HOURS FLOWN
1985	21	7	526	8,709,894	2,739	498	956	28,322,000
1986	24	3	8	9,976,104	2,581	474	967	27,073,000
1987	34	5	232	10,645,192	2,495	446	837	26,972,000
1988	30	3	285	11,140,548	2,388	460	797	27,446,000
1989	28	11	278	11,274,543	2,242	432	769	27,920,000
1990	24	6	39	12,150,116	2,242	444	770	28,510,000
1991	26	4	62	11,780,610	2,197	439	800	27,678,000
1992	18	4	33	12,359,715	2,111	451	867	24,780,000
1993	23	1	1	12,706,206	2,064	401	744	22,796,000
1994	23	4	239	13,124,315	2,022	404	730	22,235,000
1995	36	3	168	13,505,257	2,056	413	735	24,906,000
1996	37	5	380	13,746,112	1,908	361	636	24,881,000
1997	49	4	8	15,838,109	1,845	350	631	25,591,000
1998	50	1	1	16,816,555	1,905	365	625	25,518,000
1999	51	2	12	17,555,208	1,905	340	619	29,246,000
2000	56	3	92	18,299,257	1,837	345	596	27,838,000
2001	46	6	531	17,814,191	1,727	325	562	25,431,000
2002	41	0	0	16,986,088	1,715	345	581	25,545,000
2003	54	2	22	17,433,964	1,741	352	632	25,705,000
2004	28	2	14	17,575,000	1,614	312	556	25,900,000

[1]Scheduled and nonscheduled service.

World's Busiest Airports

Ranked by total aircraft movement (takeoffs and landings), 2004.
Source: Airports Council International (preliminary statistics). Web site: <www.airports.org>.

RANK	AIRPORT	LOCATION	AIRPORT CODE	TOTAL MOVEMENTS
1	O'Hare International Airport	Chicago IL	ORD	992,427
2	Hartsfield-Jackson Atlanta International Airport	Atlanta GA	ATL	964,858
3	Dallas/Fort Worth International Airport	Dallas/Ft. Worth TX	DFW	801,941
4	Los Angeles International Airport	Los Angeles CA	LAX	654,677
5	Denver International Airport	Denver CO	DEN	558,609
6	Phoenix Sky Harbor International Airport	Phoenix AZ	PHX	546,763
7	McCarran International Airport	Las Vegas NV	LAS	544,679
8	Minneapolis–St. Paul International Airport	Minneapolis/St. Paul MN	MSP	540,645
9	Paris Charles de Gaulle International Airport	Paris, France	CDG	534,561
10	Detroit Metropolitan Wayne County Airport	Detroit MI	DTW	519,624
11	Cincinnati/Northern Kentucky International Airport	Cincinnati OH	CVG	517,520
12	George Bush Intercontinental Airport	Houston TX	IAH	517,197
13	Philadelphia International Airport	Philadelphia PA	PHL	486,164
14	Frankfurt Airport	Frankfurt, Germany	FRA	477,475
15	London Heathrow Airport	London, UK	LHR	475,999
16	Washington Dulles International Airport	Washington DC	IAD	469,634
17	Charlotte/Douglas International Airport	Charlotte NC	CLT	468,464
18	Van Nuys Airport	Los Angeles CA	VNY	448,681
19	Newark International Airport	Newark NJ	EWR	433,296
20	Amsterdam Airport Schiphol	Amsterdam, The Netherlands	AMS	418,611
21	Salt Lake City International Airport	Salt Lake City UT	SLC	411,978
22	Logan International Airport	Boston MA	BOS	405,263
23	Toronto Pearson International Airport	Toronto, ON, Canada	YYZ	403,424
24	Madrid Barajas International Airport	Madrid, Spain	MAD	401,514
25	Miami International Airport	Miami FL	MIA	400,864
26	LaGuardia Airport	New York NY	LGA	395,198
27	Memphis International Airport	Memphis TN	MEM	387,968
28	Munich International Airport	Munich, Germany	MUC	383,110
29	Seattle-Tacoma International Airport	Seattle/Tacoma WA	SEA	357,434
30	Orlando Sanford International Airport	Orlando FL	SFB	357,076

Meteorology

Global Temperatures and Precipitation

Listed in alphabetical order by city. For more information see <www.weatherbase.com>.

CITY	AVERAGE TEMPERATURE °F (°C)				AVERAGE ANNUAL PRECIPITATION LEVELS IN INCHES (MM)
	JAN	APR	JUL	OCT	
Ankara, Turkey	27 (-2)	49 (9)	69 (20)	52 (11)	13.6 (346)
Beijing, China	26 (-3)	57 (13)	79 (26)	57 (13)	25.1 (630)
Buenos Aires, Argentina	75 (23)	62 (16)	50 (10)	61 (16)	38.5 (970)
Cairo, Egypt	57 (13)	71 (21)	83 (28)	75 (23)	1 (25)
Casablanca, Morocco	55 (12)	60 (15)	73 (22)	66 (18)	16.1 (400)
Christchurch, New Zealand	63 (17)	54 (12)	44 (6)	53 (11)	25.5 (640)
Colombo, Sri Lanka	81 (27)	84 (28)	83 (28)	82 (27)	87.8 (2,230)
Doha, Qatar	63 (17)	80 (26)	96 (35)	85 (29)	3.2 (80)
Hanoi, Vietnam	62 (16)	76 (24)	86 (30)	78 (25)	66.2 (1,682)
Havana, Cuba	71 (21)	76 (24)	82 (27)	78 (25)	48.2 (1,225)
Jerusalem, Israel	46 (7)	59 (15)	73 (22)	66 (18)	23 (580)
Johannesburg, South Africa	69 (20)	61 (16)	52 (11)	64 (17)	28.7 (720)
Kandahar, Afghanistan	44 (6)	68 (19)	89 (31)	64 (17)	7.4 (180)
Lima, Peru	74 (23)	71 (21)	64 (17)	65 (18)	0.3 (7.6)
Lisbon, Portugal	51 (10)	58 (14)	73 (22)	64 (17)	27.9 (708)
London, UK	39 (3)	46 (7)	62 (16)	51 (10)	29.7 (750)
Mbarara, Uganda	69 (20)	69 (20)	68 (20)	69 (20)	35.3 (890)
Moscow, Russia	16 (-8)	42 (5)	63 (17)	39 (3)	23.6 (590)
Nice, France	48 (8)	55 (12)	74 (23)	62 (16)	32.4 (820)
Nuuk, Greenland	17 (-8)	25 (-3)	45 (7)	31 (0)	23.9 (600)
Pala, Chad	77 (25)	87 (31)	77 (25)	78 (26)	40.4 (1,027)
Reykjavík, Iceland	31 (0)	37 (2)	52 (11)	40 (4)	32.2 (810)
Rotterdam, The Netherlands	38 (3)	47 (8)	63 (17)	52 (11)	N/A
Santiago, Chile	70 (21)	59 (15)	47 (8)	58 (14)	13.4 (340)
São Paulo, Brazil	74 (23)	70 (21)	63 (17)	69 (20)	53.2 (1,350)
South Pole, Antarctica	-16 (-26)	-69 (-56)	-74 (-58)	-58 (-50)	0.1 (2.5)
Sydney, Australia	72 (22)	65 (18)	53 (11)	64 (17)	44.5 (1,130)
Tokyo, Japan	42 (5)	57 (13)	77 (25)	64 (17)	60.2 (1,520)
Toronto, ON, Canada	21 (-6)	44 (6)	70 (21)	48 (8)	30.1 (760)
Vilnius, Lithuania	23 (-5)	41 (5)	62 (17)	42 (6)	26.3 (669)

N/A: not available.

World Temperature Extremes

REGION	highest recorded air temperature			lowest recorded air temperature		
	PLACE (ELEVATION)	°F	°C	PLACE (ELEVATION)	°F	°C
Africa	Al-'Aziziyah, Libya (112 m [367 ft]; 13 Sep 1922)	136	57.7	Ifrane, Morocco (1,635 m [5,364 ft]; 11 Feb 1935)	−11	−23.9
Antarctica	Vanda Station, Scott Coast (15 m [49 ft]; 5 Jan 1974)	59	15	Vostok, 78° 27′ S, 106° 52′ E (3,420 m [11,220 ft]; 21 Jul 1983)	−129	−89.4
Asia	Tirat Zevi, Israel (−220 m [−722 ft]; 21 Jun 1942)	129	53.9	Oymyakon, Russia (806 m [2,625 ft]; 6 Feb 1933)	−90	−67.7
Australia	Cloncurry, Queensland (190 m [622 ft]; 16 Jan 1889)	128	53.3	Charlotte Pass, New South Wales (1,755 m [5,758 ft]; 29 Jun 1994)	−9.4	−23
Europe	Seville, Spain (8 m [26 ft]; 4 Aug 1881)	122	50	Ust-Shchuger, Russia (85 m [279 ft]; exact date unknown)	−67	−55
North America	Greenland Ranch, Death Valley, California (−54 m [−178 ft]; 10 Jul 1913)	134	56.6	Snag, Yukon (646 m [2,120 ft]; 3 Feb 1947)	−81.4	−63
South America	Rivadavia, Argentina (206 m [676 ft]; 11 Dec 1905)	120	48.9	Colonia, Sarmiento, Argentina (268 m [879 ft]; 1 Jun 1907)	−27	−33
Tropical Pacific	Tuguegarao, Philippines (22 m [72 ft]; 29 Apr 1912)	108	42.2	Haleakala, Hawaii (2,972 m [9,750 ft]; 17 May 1979)	12	−11

Normal Temperatures and Precipitation for Selected US Cities

Statistics from city airports, 1971–2000. Alphabetical by state.
Source: National Oceanic and Atmospheric Administration, National Climatic Data Center, Asheville NC.

CITY	MEAN TEMPERATURE (°F)				ANNUAL PRECIPITATION (IN)
	JAN	APR	JUL	OCT	
Montgomery AL	46.6	64.3	81.8	65.4	54.77
Anchorage AK	15.8	36.3	58.4	34.1	16.08
Phoenix AZ	54.2	70.2	92.8	74.6	8.29
Little Rock AR	40.1	61.4	82.4	63.3	50.93
Los Angeles CA	57.1	60.8	69.3	66.9	13.15
San Francisco CA	49.4	56.2	62.8	61.0	20.11
Denver CO	29.2	47.6	73.4	51.0	15.81
Hartford CT	25.7	48.9	73.7	51.9	46.16
Wilmington DE	31.5	52.4	76.6	55.8	42.81
Miami FL	68.1	75.7	83.7	78.8	58.53
Atlanta GA	42.7	61.6	80.0	62.8	50.20
Honolulu HI	73.0	75.6	80.8	80.2	18.29
Boise ID	30.2	50.6	74.7	52.8	12.19
Chicago IL[1]	22.0	47.8	73.3	52.1	36.27
Indianapolis IN	26.5	52.0	75.4	54.6	40.95
Des Moines IA	20.4	50.6	76.1	52.8	34.72
Topeka KS	27.2	54.5	78.4	56.6	35.64
Louisville KY	33.0	56.4	78.4	58.5	44.54
New Orleans LA	52.6	68.2	82.7	70.0	64.16
Portland ME	21.7	43.7	68.7	47.7	45.83
Baltimore MD	32.3	53.2	76.5	55.4	41.94
Boston MA	29.3	48.3	73.9	54.1	42.53
Detroit MI	24.5	48.1	73.5	51.9	32.89
Minneapolis MN	13.1	46.6	73.2	48.7	29.41
Jackson MS	45.0	63.4	81.4	64.4	55.95
St. Louis MO	29.6	56.6	80.2	58.3	38.75
Missoula MT	23.5	45.2	66.9	44.4	13.82
Lincoln NE	22.4	51.2	77.8	53.5	28.37
Las Vegas NV	47.0	66.0	91.2	68.7	4.49
Concord NH	20.1	44.6	70.0	47.8	37.60
Newark NJ	31.3	52.3	77.2	56.4	46.25
Albuquerque NM	35.7	55.6	78.5	57.3	9.47
New York NY[2]	31.8	50.1	74.8	56.5	42.46
Charlotte NC	41.7	60.9	80.3	61.7	43.51
Fargo ND	6.8	43.5	70.6	45.3	21.19
Cleveland OH	25.7	47.6	71.9	52.2	38.71
Tulsa OK	36.4	60.8	83.5	62.6	42.42
Portland OR	39.9	51.2	68.1	54.3	37.07
Philadelphia PA	32.3	53.1	77.6	57.2	42.05
Providence RI	28.7	48.6	73.3	53.0	46.45
Charleston SC	47.9	64.2	81.7	66.2	51.53
Rapid City SD	22.4	44.7	71.7	48.2	16.64
Memphis TN	39.9	62.1	82.5	63.8	54.65
Dallas TX[3]	44.1	65.0	85.0	67.2	34.73
Salt Lake City UT	29.2	50.0	77.0	52.5	16.50
Burlington VT	18.0	43.5	70.6	47.7	36.05
Richmond VA	36.4	57.1	77.9	58.3	43.91
Seattle WA	40.9	50.2	65.3	52.7	37.07
Charleston WV	33.4	54.3	73.9	55.1	44.05
Milwaukee WI	20.7	45.2	72.0	51.4	34.81
Casper WY	22.3	42.7	70.0	45.7	13.03

[1]Data from O'Hare International Airport. [2]Data from John F. Kennedy International Airport. [3]Data from Dallas/Fort Worth International Airport.

Hurricane and Tornado Classifications

The Saffir/Simpson Hurricane Scale[1] is used to rank tropical cyclones in the North Atlantic Ocean and the eastern North Pacific.

Category 1. *Barometric pressure:* 28.91 in or more; *wind speed:* 74–95 mph; *storm surge:* 4–5 ft; *damage:* minimal.

Category 2. *Barometric pressure:* 28.50–28.91 in; *wind speed:* 96–110 mph; *storm surge:* 6–8 ft; *damage:* moderate.

Category 3. *Barometric pressure:* 27.91–28.47 in; *wind speed:* 111–130 mph; *storm surge:* 9–12 ft; *damage:* extensive.

Category 4. *Barometric pressure:* 27.17–27.88 in; *wind speed:* 131–155 mph; *storm surge:* 13–18 ft; *damage:* extreme.

Category 5. *Barometric pressure:* less than 27.17 in; *wind speed:* 155 mph or more; *storm surge:* 18 ft or more; *damage:* catastrophic.

Tornado classifications.

Tornado intensity is commonly estimated after the fact by analyzing damaged structures and then correlating the damage with the wind speeds known to produce various degrees of damage. Tornadoes are assigned specific values on the Fujita Scale, or F-Scale, of tornado intensity established by meteorologist T. Theodore Fujita.

Categories:

F0. *Wind speed:* 40–72 mph; *damage:* light.

F1. *Wind speed:* 73–112 mph; *damage:* moderate.

F2. *Wind speed:* 113–157 mph; *damage:* considerable.

F3. *Wind speed:* 158–206 mph; *damage:* severe.

F4. *Wind speed:* 207–260 mph; *damage:* devastating.

F5. *Wind speed:* 261–318 mph; *damage:* incredible.

[1]*Published by permission of Herbert Saffir, consulting engineer, and Robert Simpson, meteorologist.*

Indexes

Wind Chill Table

The wind chill index is based upon a formula that determines how cold the atmosphere feels by combining the temperature and wind speed and applying other factors. For more information, see <www.nws.noaa.gov/om/windchill/index.shtml>.

		TEMPERATURE (°F)														
	CALM	**40**	**35**	**30**	**25**	**20**	**15**	**10**	**5**	**0**	**-5**	**-10**	**-15**	**-20**	**-25**	**-30**
WIND SPEED (MPH)	**5**	36	31	25	19	13	7	1	-5	-11	-16	-22	-28	-34	-40	-46
	10	34	27	21	15	9	3	-4	-10	-16	-22	-28	-35	-41	-47	-53
	15	32	25	19	13	6	0	-7	-13	-19	-26	-32	-39	-45	-51	-58
	20	30	24	17	11	4	-2	-9	-15	-22	-29	-35	-42	-48	-55	-61
	25	29	23	16	9	3	-4	-11	-17	-24	-31	-37	-44	-51	-58	-64
	30	28	22	15	8	1	-5	-12	-19	-26	-33	-39	-46	-53	-60	-67
	35	28	21	14	7	0	-7	-14	-21	-27	-34	-41	-48	-55	-62	-69
	40	27	20	13	6	-1	-8	-15	-22	-29	-36	-43	-50	-57	-64	-71
	45	26	19	12	5	-2	-9	-16	-23	-30	-37	-44	-51	-58	-65	-72
	50	26	19	12	4	-3	-10	-17	-24	-31	-38	-45	-52	-60	-67	-74
	55	25	18	11	4	-3	-11	-18	-25	-32	-39	-46	-54	-61	-69	-75
	60	25	17	10	3	-4	-11	-19	-26	-33	-40	-48	-55	-62	-69	-76

Heat Index

The Heat Index shows the effects of the combination of heat and humidity. Apparent temperature is the temperature as it feels to your body. For more information see <www.jeonet.com/heat.htm>.

	AIR TEMPERATURE (°F)										
relative	70	75	80	85	90	95	100	105	110	115	120
humidity	apparent temperature										
0%	64	69	73	78	83	87	91	95	99	103	107
10%	65	70	75	80	85	90	95	100	105	111	116
20%	66	72	77	82	87	93	99	105	112	120	130
30%	67	73	78	84	90	96	104	113	123	135	148
40%	68	74	79	86	93	101	110	123	137	151	
50%	69	75	81	88	96	107	120	135	150		
60%	70	76	82	90	100	114	132	149			
70%	70	77	85	93	106	124	144				
80%	71	78	86	97	113	136	157				
90%	71	79	88	102	122	150	170				
100%	72	80	91	108	133	166					

	HEAT INDEX/HEAT DISORDERS
Heat Index	Possible heat disorders for people in higher risk groups*
130°F or higher	Heatstroke/sunstroke highly likely with continued exposure.
105°-130°F	Sunstroke, heat cramps, or heat exhaustion likely, and heatstroke possible with prolonged exposure and/or physical activity.
90°-105°F	Sunstroke, heat cramps, and heat exhaustion possible with prolonged exposure and/or physical activity.
80°-90°F	Fatigue possible with prolonged exposure and/or physical activity.

**Small children, the elderly, the chronically ill, those on certain medications or drugs (especially tranquilizers and anticholinergics), and persons with weight and alcohol problems are particularly susceptible to heat reactions, especially during heat waves in areas where moderate climate usually prevails.*

Ultraviolet (UV) Index

The Ultraviolet (UV) Index predicts the intensity of the sun's ultraviolet rays. It was developed by the National Weather Service and the US Environmental Protection Agency to provide a daily forecast of the expected risk of overexposure to the sun. The Index is calculated on a next-day basis for dozens of cities across the US. Other local conditions, such as cloud cover, are taken into account in determining the UV Index number. UV Index numbers are: 0–2 (minimal exposure); 3–4 (low exposure); 5–6 (moderate exposure); 7–9 (high exposure); and 10 and over (very high exposure).

Some simple precautions can be taken to reduce the risk of sun-related illness: limit time in the sun between 10 AM and 4 PM, when rays are generally the strongest; seek shade whenever possible; use a broad spectrum sunscreen with an SPF of at least 15; wear a wide-brimmed hat and, if possible, tightly woven, full-length clothing; wear UV-protective sunglasses; avoid sunlamps and tanning salons; and watch for the UV Index daily. The UV Index should not be used by seriously sun-sensitive individuals, who should consult their doctors and take additional precautions regardless of the exposure level.

National Weather Service Watches, Warnings, and Advisories

For more information, see *National Weather Service Web site:* <www.nws.noaa.gov>.

Blizzard warning. Winter storms with sustained winds or frequent gusts of 35 mph (56 km/hr) or greater and considerable falling and/or blowing snow; visibility reduced to less than ¼ mile (0.4 km). Conditions expected to last at least three hours.

Excessive heat warning. Heat index is expected to equal or exceed 115 °F (46 °C) for three hours or more. In these cases, the heat becomes dangerous for a large portion of the population.

Flash flood. *Watch:* Flash flooding is possible in and close to the watch area. Those in the affected area are urged to be ready to take quick action if a flash flood warning is issued or flooding is observed. *Warning:* Rapid flooding of small rivers, streams, creeks, or urban areas is imminent or already occurring.

Flood. *Watch:* Widespread flooding is possible in and close to the watch area. Those in the affected area are urged to be ready to take quick action if a flood warning is issued or flooding is observed. Issued for general flooding that is expected to occur during or within 12 hours after heavy rain has ended. *Warning:* Issued for life- or property-threatening general flooding that occurs during or within 12 hours after heavy rainfall has ended. Can be issued for rural or urban areas as well as for areas along small streams and creeks. **Coastal flood.** *Watch:* Alerts coastal residents to the possibility of flooding. *Warning:* Flooding is imminent or occurring. Coastal waters extend out 100 nautical miles (115 mi; 185 km). **River flood.** *Warning:* Alerts residents of long-term flooding (more than 12 hours) along major streams and rivers that is a threat to life and/or property. Usually contains river stage forecast, crest information, and the history and impact of the flood.

Gale warning. Sustained winds of 34 to 47 knots (39 to 54 mph; 63 to 87 km/hr) are expected or occurring (not directly associated with tropical cyclones).

Health warning. Ground level ozone readings are expected to be in the unhealthful range. The elderly and persons with heart or respiratory problems should stay indoors near a fan or circulating air and reduce physical activity. Motorists are asked to reduce unnecessary driving by carpooling or using public transportation.

Heavy snow warning. Snowfall amounts of four inches (10 cm) or more in 12 hours or six inches (15 cm) or more in 24 hours are expected.

Heavy surf advisory. Describes all tropical cyclone watches and warnings in effect along with details concerning locations, intensity, movement, and precautions. Also issued to describe tropical cyclones and subtropical cyclones prior to the issuance of watches and warnings. High surf may pose a threat to life or property. May be issued alone or in conjunction with coastal flood watches or warnings.

High wind warning. Sustained winds of 40 mph (64 km/hr) or more are expected to last for at least one hour, or for nonthunderstorm winds of 58 mph (93 km/hr) or greater for any duration.

Hurricane. *Local statement:* A public release in or near the threatened area giving specific details on weather conditions, evacuation decisions made by local officials, and other necessary precautions to protect life and property. *Watch:* An announcement for specific locations that a hurricane poses a possible threat, generally within 36 hours. *Warning:* A warning that sustained surface winds of 64 knots (74 mph; 119 km/hr) or higher are expected in specified coastal areas within 24 hours or less. A hurricane warning can remain in effect when dangerously high water and/or exceptionally high waves continue even though winds may be less than hurricane force. *Watch:* Issued for inland locations when hurricane force winds are anticipated beyond the coastal areas, though the actual occurrence, timing, and location are still uncertain.

Ice storm warning. Damaging ice accumulations are expected during freezing rain situations; walking and driving becomes extremely dangerous. Ice accumulations are usually ¼ inch (0.6 cm) or greater.

Severe thunderstorm. *Watch:* Conditions are favorable for the development of severe thunderstorms in and close to the watch area. Usually in effect for several hours. *Warning:* Issued when a thunderstorm produces hail ¾ inch (2 cm) or larger in diameter and/or winds of 58 mph (93 km/hr) or more.

Sleet warning. Accumulations of sleet covering the ground to a depth of ½ inch (1.3 cm) or more are expected.

Special tropical disturbance statement. Issued to furnish information on strong formative, nondepression systems. Focuses on major threats of the disturbance, such as the potential for torrential rains on island or inland areas.

Storm warning (coastal, oceanic, or marine). Sustained winds of 48 knots (55 mph; 89 km/hr) or greater are expected or occurring and are not directly associated with tropical cyclones.

Strike probability forecast of tropical cyclone conditions. The probability that the cyclone center will pass within 50 miles (80 km) to the right or 75 miles (121 km) to the left of the listed locations within the indicated time period when looking at the coast in the direction of the cyclone's movement.

Tornado. *Watch:* Conditions are favorable for the development of tornadoes in and close to the watch area. Usually in effect for several hours. *Warning:* A tornado is indicated by radar or sighted by storm spotters. The warning will include where the tornado is and what towns will be in its path.

Tropical storm. *Watch:* An announcement that a tropical storm or tropical storm conditions pose a threat to coastal areas, generally within 36 hours. A tropical storm watch is not usually issued if a tropical cyclone is expected to attain hurricane strength. *Warning:* Sustained winds of 34 to 63 knots (39 to

73 mph; 63 to 118 km/hr) inclusive are expected in specified coastal areas within 24 hours.

Wind chill warning. Wind chill temperatures are expected to reach −35 °F (−37 °C) or colder, with a minimum wind speed of about 10 mph (16 km/hr).

Winter storm. *Watch:* Conditions are favorable for the development of hazardous weather elements, such as heavy snow or sleet, blizzard conditions, significant accumulations of freezing rain or drizzle, or any combination thereof. Usually issued 12 to 48 hours in advance of an event. *Warning:* Hazardous winter weather conditions are imminent or very likely, including any occurrence or combination of heavy snow, wind-driven snow, sleet, or freezing rain or drizzle. Usually issued for up to 12 hours, but can be extended to 24 hours. The term "near-blizzard" may be incorporated into the winter storm warning for serious situations which fall just short of official blizzard conditions.

Meteorological Phenomena

Tides

"Tides" refer to any of the cyclic deformations of one astronomical body caused by the gravitational forces exerted by others. The most familiar are the **periodic variations in sea level** on the Earth that correspond to changes in the relative positions of the Moon and the Sun.

At the surface of the Earth the gravitational force of the Moon is about 2.2 times greater than that of the Sun. The tide-producing action of the Moon arises from the variations in its gravitational field over the surface of the Earth as compared with its strength at the Earth's center. The effect is that the water tends to accumulate on the parts of the Earth's surface directly toward and directly opposite the Moon and to be depleted elsewhere. The regions of accumulation move over the surface as the position of the Moon varies relative to the Earth, mainly because of the Earth's rotation but also because of the Moon's orbital motion around the Earth. There are approximately two high and two low tides per day at any given place, but they occur at times that change from day to day; the average interval between consecutive high tides is 12 hours 25 minutes. The effect of the Sun is similar and additive to that of the Moon. Consequently, the tides of largest range or amplitude (**spring tides**) occur at New Moon, when the Moon and the Sun are in the same direction, and at Full

Moon, when they are in opposite directions; the tides of smallest range (**neap tides**) occur at intermediate phases of the Moon.

Although the observed tides possess the broad features discussed above, this pattern does not correspond to a pair of bulges that move around the Earth. The inertia of the water, the existence of continents, and effects associated with the water depth result in much more complicated behavior. For the main oceans, a combination of theory and observation indicates the existence of **amphidromic points**, at which the tidal rise and fall is zero: patterns of high and low tides rotate around these points (either clockwise or counterclockwise). Amplitudes are typically less than a meter.

Tides are most easily observed—and of greatest practical importance—along **seacoasts**, where the amplitudes are exaggerated. When tidal motions run into the shallow waters of the continental shelf, their rate of advance is reduced, energy accumulates in a smaller volume, and the rise and fall is amplified. The details of tidal motions in coastal waters, particularly in channels, gulfs, and estuaries, depend on the details of coastal geometry and water-depth variation. Tidal amplitudes, the contrast between spring and neap tides, and the variation of times of high and low tide all vary widely from place to place.

Monsoons

A monsoon is a type of major wind system that seasonally reverses its direction—e.g., one that blows for approximately six months from the northeast and six months from the southwest. The most prominent examples of such seasonal winds occur in southern Asia and in Africa. Monsoonal tendencies also are apparent along the Gulf Coast of the United States and in central Europe, as well as in various other areas. The **primary cause** of monsoons lies in the difference in the annual temperature trends over land and sea. Seasonal changes in temperature are large over land but small over ocean waters. A monsoon blows from cold toward warm

regions: from sea toward land in summer and from land toward sea in winter. Atmospheric pressure is high in cold regions and low in warm ones, permitting the movement of air to occur. Most **summer monsoons** have a dominant westerly component and a strong tendency to ascend and produce copious amounts of rain (because of the condensation of water vapor in the rising air). The intensity and duration, however, are not uniform from year to year. **Winter monsoons**, by contrast, have a dominant easterly component and a strong tendency to diverge, subside, and cause drought.

El Niño

In oceanography and climatology, **El Niño** ("The Christ Child" in Spanish) is the anomalous appearance, every few years, of unusually warm ocean conditions along the tropical west coast of South America. This event is associated with adverse effects on fishing, agriculture, and local weather from Ecuador to Chile and with far-field climatic anomalies in the equatorial Pacific and occasionally in Asia and North America as well.

The **name El Niño** was originally used during the 19th century by the fishermen of northern Peru in reference to the annual flow of warm equatorial waters southward around Christmastime. Peruvian scientists later noted that more intense changes occurred at intervals of several years and were associated with catastrophic seasonal flooding along the normally arid coast, while the thermal anomalies lasted for a year or more. The more unusual episodes gained world attention during the 20th century, and the original annual connotation of the name was replaced by that of the anomalous occurrence.

The **timing and intensity** of El Niño events vary widely. The first recorded occurrence of unusual desert rainfall was in 1525, when the Spanish conquistador Francisco Pizarro landed in northern Peru.

Historians suggest that the desert rains and vegetation encountered by the Spaniards may have facilitated their conquest of the Inca empire. The intensity of El Niño episodes varies from weak thermal anomalies (2–3 °C [about 4–5 °F]) with only moderate local effects to very strong anomalies (8–10 °C [14–18 °F]) associated with worldwide climatic perturbations. El Niño events typically occur at **three- to four-year intervals**, with the strong events being less common. The intermittency varies widely, however, and the phenomenon is neither periodic nor predictable in the sense that ocean tides are.

The warm ocean conditions in the equatorial Pacific induce large-scale anomalies in the atmosphere. **Rainfall** increases manyfold in Ecuador and northern Peru, causing coastal flooding and erosion and consequent hardships in transportation and agriculture. Additionally, strong El Niño events are associated with **droughts** in Indonesia, Australia, and northeastern South America and with altered patterns of tropical storms in the tropical belt. During the stronger El Niño episodes, the atmospheric "teleconnections" are extensive enough to cause unusually severe winter weather at the higher latitudes of North and South America.

Environmental Change

Pollution

Pollution is the addition of any substance or form of energy to the environment at a rate faster than the environment can accommodate it by dispersion, breakdown, recycling, or storage in some harmless form. All living things exert some pressure on the natural environment, but modern efforts to improve the standard of living for humans—through the control of nature and the development of new consumer products—have partially contaminated much of the world's air, water, and land with chemical wastes. As a result, governments have passed laws to limit or reverse the threat of environmental pollution.

The branch of science that deals with how living things, including humans, are related to their surroundings is called **ecology**. The Earth supports some five million species of plants, animals, and microorganisms that form a vast network of interrelated environmental systems called **ecosystems**. The arctic tundra is an ecosystem and so is a Brazilian rain forest.

If left undisturbed, natural environmental systems tend to achieve **balance or stability** among the various species of plants and animals. Sudden changes in the relative population of a particular species can begin a kind of chain reaction among other elements of the ecosystem. For example, eliminating a species of insect through the use of a chemical pesticide also may eliminate a bird species that depends upon the

insect as a source of food. As another example, overhunting by humans caused the extinction of the passenger pigeon in 1914.

Environmental pollution has existed since people began to congregate in towns and cities; ancient Athenians and Romans stored garbage outside city walls, a practice that may have contributed to outbreaks of viral diseases. The adverse effects of pollution became more noticeable as cities grew during the Middle Ages, as the human population grew steadily after 1650, and with the advent of the Industrial Revolution in the 19th century. The reduction of the Earth's resources has been closely linked to the rise in human population.

In 1997 representatives from 160 nations signed the **Kyoto Protocol**, an international agreement that called for the gradual reduction of greenhouse-gas emissions. These are emissions that increase atmospheric carbon dioxide and contribute to the greenhouse effect, an overwarming of the Earth's surface and lower atmosphere. Originally a supporter of the Protocol, the US, shortly after George W. Bush became president, in 2001, opted not to participate.

The various **kinds of pollution** are most conveniently considered under three headings: air, ground, and water.

Air Pollution

Air pollution is the release into the atmosphere of gases, finely divided solids, or finely dispersed liquid aerosols at rates that exceed the capacity of the atmosphere to dissipate them or to dispose of them through incorporation into the biosphere.

Dust storms in desert areas and **smoke** from forest and grass fires contribute to particulate and chemical air pollution. **Volcanic activity** is the major natural source of air pollution, pouring huge amounts of ash and toxic fumes into the atmosphere.

Air pollution may affect humans directly, causing irritation of the eyes or coughing. More indirectly, its effects can be measured far from the source, as, for example, the fallout of tetraethyl lead from automobile exhausts, which has been observed in the oceans and on the Greenland ice sheet. Still less direct are possible effects on global climates.

Though not generally categorized as air pollution, **noise pollution**, or excessively loud noises, is another form of airborne contamination that has deleterious effects on the environment.

Ground Pollution

Ground pollution occurs when the land is unable to accommodate in a natural manner the addition of substances to the soil, such as solid wastes that can't be broken down quickly, or, in some instances, at all. It can also refer to the unintended removal of needed components from the earth, such as topsoil. In many areas, the overuse of croplands in the quest to maximize yields results in the erosion of topsoil, which, in turn, causes the over-silting or sedimentation of rivers and streams.

One of the most hazardous forms of pollution comes from **agricultural pesticides**. These chemicals are designed to deter or kill insects, weeds, fungi, or rodents that pose a threat to crops. When airborne pesticides drift with the wind or become absorbed into the fruits and vegetables they are meant to protect, they can become a source of many illnesses, including cancer and birth defects. Pesticides are often designed to withstand rain, which means they are not always water-soluble, and therefore they may persist in the environment for long periods of time. In addition, some pests have developed a genetic resistance

to these chemicals, forcing farmers to increase the amounts or types of pesticide.

Some urban areas are experiencing serious problems regarding the disposal of **garbage and hazardous wastes,** such as solvents and industrial dyes and inks. In many areas landfill sites have reached full capacity, forcing municipalities to consider alternative disposal methods, including incineration. Giant high-temperature incinerators have become another source of air pollution, however, because incineration ashes sometimes contain very high concentrations of metals as well as dioxins, a dangerous family of chemical poisons.

One step toward solving the garbage problem is **recycling.** Some towns have passed ordinances that encourage or require residents to separate glass and aluminum cans and bottles from other refuse so that these substances can be melted down and reused. Although lightweight steel, cardboard, and paper are also economically recyclable, most industries and cities still burn or bury large amounts of scrap metal and paper products.

Water Pollution

Water pollution occurs when substances are released into a body of water, where they become dissolved or suspended or deposited on the bottom, accumulating to the extent that they overwhelm the body of water's capacity to absorb, break down, or recycle them, and thus interfere with the functioning of aquatic ecosystems.

Contributions to water pollution include substances drawn from the air (such as **acid rain**), silt from **soil erosion**, chemical **fertilizers** and **pesticides**, runoff from **septic tanks**, outflow from **livestock feedlots**, **chemical wastes** from industries, and **sewage** and other urban wastes. A community far upstream in a watershed may thus receive relatively clean water,

whereas one farther downstream receives a partly diluted mixture of urban, industrial, and rural wastes.

When organic matter exceeds the capacity of microorganisms in the water to break it down and recycle it, the excess of nutrients in such matter encourages **algal water blooms**. When these algae die, their remains add further to the organic wastes already in the water, and eventually the water becomes deficient in oxygen. Organisms that do not require oxygen then attack the organic wastes, releasing gases such as methane and hydrogen sulfide, which are harmful to the oxygen-requiring forms of life. The result is a foul-smelling, waste-filled body of water.

Natural Disasters

Geologic Disasters

Major Historical Earthquakes

Magnitudes given for pre-20th-century events are generally estimations from intensity data. When no magnitude was available, the earthquake's maximum intensity, written as a Roman numeral from I to XII, is given.

YEAR (AD)	AFFECTED AREA	MAGNITUDE OR INTENSITY	DEATHS	YEAR (AD)	AFFECTED AREA	MAGNITUDE OR INTENSITY	DEATHS
365	Knossos, Crete (Greece)	XI	50,000	893	Caucasus	unknown	82,000
				893	Daipur, India	unknown	180,000
526	Antioch, Syria	unknown	250,000	893	Ardabil, Iran	unknown	150,000
844	Damascus, Syria	VIII	50,000	1042	Palmyra, Baalbek, Syria	X	50,000
847	Mosul, Iraq	unknown	50,000				
847	Damascus, Syria	X	70,000	1138	Ganzah, Aleppo, Syria	XI	230,000
856	Qumis, Damghan, Iran	unknown	200,000				

Major Historical Earthquakes (continued)

YEAR (AD)	AFFECTED AREA	MAGNITUDE OR INTENSITY	DEATHS	YEAR (AD)	AFFECTED AREA	MAGNITUDE OR INTENSITY	DEATHS
1201	Upper Egypt or Syria	IX	1,100,000	1970	northern Peru	7.8	66,794
				1972	Managua, Nicaragua	6.2	5,000
1268	Cilicia, Anatolia (Turkey)	unknown	60,000	1976	Guatemala City, Guatemala	7.5	22,778
1290	China	6.7	100,000	1976	northeastern Italy	6.5	929
1556	Shaanxi province, China	IX	830,000	1976	Tangshan, China	7.8	240,000
1667	Shemakha, Azerbaijan	6.9	80,000	1977	Bucharest, Romania	7.2	1,581
				1978	Khorasan, Iran	7.4	25,000
1668	Shandong province, China	XII	50,000	1979	Colombia; Ecuador	7.9	579
1693	Sicily, Catania (Italy)	XI	100,000	1980	El-Asnam (Ech-Cheliff), Algeria	7.7	5,000
1703	Jeddo, Japan	unknown	200,000	1980	southern Italy	6.9	3,114
1727	Tabriz, Iran	VIII	77,000	1983	eastern Turkey	6.9	1,400
1730	Hokkaido, Japan	unknown	137,000	1985	Mexico City, Mexico	8.1	9,500
1731	Beijing, China	unknown	100,000	1986	San Salvador, El Salvador	5.4	1,000
1737	Kolkata (Calcutta), India	unknown	300,000	1988	Leninakan (Kumayri), Armenia	6.8	25,000
1739	China	X	50,000	1989	northern California	7.1	62
1755	Lisbon, Portugal; Spain; Morocco	XI	62,000	1990	Rasht, Iran	7.6	50,000
				1990	Luzon, Philippines	7.7	1,600
1780	Tabriz, Iran	unknown	100,000	1991	northern India	7.1	2,000
1811	New Madrid MO	8.6	unknown	1992	Flores Island, Indonesia	7.5	2,500
1835	northern Japan	7.6	28,300	1993	southern India	6.4	30,000
1857	Tejon Pass (Palmdale) CA	8.3	unknown	1995	Kobe, Japan	7.2	5,000
1868	Ecuador; Colombia	7.7	70,000	1995	Sakhalin Island, Russia	7.1	2,000
1883	Java, Indonesia	unknown	100,000	1997	northwestern Iran	5.5	1,000
1905	Jammu and Kashmir, India	8.6	19,000	1997	eastern Iran	7.1	1,560
1906	San Francisco CA	8.3	700	1998	Takhar province, Afghanistan	6.1	4,000
1906	Valparaíso, Chile	8.6	1,500	1999	Colombia	6.2	1,185
1908	Calabria, Messina, Italy	7.5	58,000	1999	Turkey	7.6	17,000
1915	Abruzzi, Italy	7.5	32,600	1999	Taiwan	7.7	2,400
1920	Gansu province, China	8.5	200,000	2001	El Salvador	7.7	844
				2001	India	7.7	20,085
1923	Tokyo; Yokohama, Japan	8.3	142,800	2001	El Salvador	6.6	315
1927	Nan Ling, China	8.0	40,900	2002	Hindu Kush region, Afghanistan	7.4	150
1932	Gansu province, China	7.6	70,000	2002	Hindu Kush region, Afghanistan	6.1	1,000
1935	Quetta, India	7.5	30,000	2003	northern Algeria	6.8	2,266
1939	Chillán, Chile	8.3	28,000	2003	southeastern Iran	6.6	43,200
1939	Erzincan, Turkey	8.0	32,700	2003	southern Xinjiang, China	6.3	261
1948	Ashkhabad, Turkmenistan	7.3	19,800	2003	eastern Turkey	6.4	177
1950	Assam, India	8.7	574	2004	Strait of Gibraltar	6.4	628
1960	Agadir, Morocco	5.9	12,000	2004	off the west coast of northern Sumatra, Indonesia	9.0	283,100
1960	Puerto Montt, Valdivia, Chile	8.5	5,700	2005	central Iran	6.4	612
1963	Skopje, Macedonia	6.0	1,070	2005	northern Sumatra, Indonesia	8.7	1,000
1964	Prince William Sound AK	8.3	131				
1970	southern Yunnan province, China	7.7	10,000				

Measuring Earthquakes

The seismologists Beno Gutenberg and Charles Francis Richter introduced measurement of the seismic energy released by earthquakes on a magnitude scale in 1935. Each increase of one unit on the scale represents a 10-fold increase in the magnitude of an earthquake. Seismographs are designed to measure different components of seismic waves, such as wave type, intensity, and duration. This table shows the typical effects of earthquakes in various magnitude ranges. For further information, see <www.seismo.unr.edu/ftp/pub/louie/class/100/magnitude.html>.

MAGNITUDE	EARTHQUAKE EFFECTS
Less than 3.5	Generally not felt, but recorded.
3.5–5.4	Often felt, but rarely causes damage.

Measuring Earthquakes (continued)

MAGNITUDE	EARTHQUAKE EFFECTS
Less than 6.0	At most, slight damage to well-designed buildings. Can cause major damage to poorly constructed buildings over small regions.
6.1–6.9	Can be destructive in areas up to about 100 km (61 mi) across where people live.
7.0–7.9	Major earthquake. Can cause serious damage over larger areas.
8 or greater	Great earthquake. Can cause serious damage in areas several hundred km across.

Tsunami

A tsunami is a catastrophic ocean wave, usually caused by a submarine earthquake occurring less than 30 mi (50 km) beneath the seafloor, with a magnitude greater than 6.5. Underwater or coastal landslides or volcanic eruptions also may cause a tsunami. The often-used term tidal wave is a misnomer: the wave has no connection with the tides. After the earthquake or other generating impulse, a train of simple, progressive oscillatory waves is propagated great distances at the ocean surface in ever-widening circles, much like the waves produced by a pebble falling into a shallow pool. In deep water, the wavelengths are enormous, about 60 to 125 mi (100 to 200 km), and the wave heights are very small, only 1 to 2 ft (0.3 to 0.6 m). The resulting wave steepness is extremely low; coupled with the waves' long periods that vary from five minutes to an hour, this enables normal wind waves and swell to completely obscure the waves in deep water. Thus, a ship in the open ocean experiences the passage of a tsunami as an insignificant rise and fall. As the waves approach the continental coasts, friction with the increasingly shallow bottom reduces the velocity of the waves. The period must remain constant; consequently, as the velocity lessens, the wavelengths become shortened and the wave amplitudes increase, coastal waters rising as high as 100 feet (30 m) in 10 to 15 minutes. By a poorly understood process, the continental shelf waters begin to oscillate after the rise in sea level. Between three and five major oscillations generate most of the damage; the oscillations cease, however, only several days after they begin. Occasionally, the first arrival of a tsunami at a coast may be a trough, the water receding and exposing the shallow seafloor.

Avalanches

An avalanche is a large mass of rock debris or snow that moves rapidly down a mountain slope, sweeping and grinding everything in its path. An avalanche begins when a mass of material overcomes frictional resistance of the sloping surface, often after its foundation is loosened by spring rains or is rapidly melted by a warm, dry wind. Vibrations caused by loud noises, such as artillery fire, thunder, or blasting, can start the mass in motion. Rock avalanches (rockfalls) are commonly composed of bedrock fragments a few centimeters (an inch or so) in diameter and include much soil and dust; they are thought to ride on a cushion of compressed air that allows them to travel long distances. A debris avalanche usually occurs in unconsolidated earth materials when weakened by moisture. Snow avalanches may develop during heavy snowstorms and slide while the snow is still falling, but more often they occur after the snow has accumulated at a given site. One of the causes of snow avalanches is the slow formation of depth hoar (hexagonal cuplike ice crystals that begin to form at ground level) under the snowpack. Depth-hoar crystals develop in loose array from the evaporation of the original snow particles and the simultaneous vapor deposition of larger, denser ice crystals near the ground; thus a zone of weakness occurs within the snowpack near the ground, the particles of which act as a lubricant when the upper layers of the snow start sliding down the mountain. The wet snow avalanche is perhaps the most dangerous because of its great weight, heavy texture, and tendency to solidify as soon as it stops moving. The dry type is also dangerous because its entraining of great amounts of air makes it act like a fluid; this kind of avalanche may flow up the opposite side of a narrow valley. Avalanches can carry a considerable amount of rock debris with the snow.

Deadly Volcano Eruptions

Casualty figures are approximate.

VOLCANO (LOCATION)	YEAR	CASUALTIES	VOLCANO (LOCATION)	YEAR	CASUALTIES
Tambora (Indonesia)	1815	92,000[1]	Raung (Indonesia)	1730	3,000
Krakatoa (Indonesia)	1883	36,000[1]	Lamington (Papua New Guinea)	1951	3,000
Pelée (Martinique)	1902	30,000	Awu (Indonesia)	1856	2,800
Ruiz (Colombia)	1985	25,000[2]	Taal, Luzon (Philippines)	1906	1,500
Etna (Italy)	1669	20,000	Taal, Luzon (Philippines)	1911	1,300
Unzen (Japan)	1792	15,000	Etna (Italy)	1536	1,000
Kélud (Indonesia)	1586	10,000	Paricutín (Mexico)	1949	1,000
Laki (Iceland)	1783	9,000	Purace (Colombia)	1949	1,000
Kelud (Indonesia)	1919	5,000	Pinatubo (Philippines)	1991	350
Vesuvius (Italy)	79	3,360	El Chichón (Mexico)	1982	100
Awu (Indonesia)	1711	3,200	St. Helens (Washington, US)	1980	66[3]
Raung (Indonesia)	1638	3,000			

[1]Includes tidal wave triggered by eruption.   [2]Includes mudflow triggered by eruption.   [3]Includes persons missing.

Weather-Related Disasters

Storms

A storm is simply a disturbed state of the atmosphere. The term strongly implies destructive or unpleasant weather conditions characterized by strong winds, heavy rain, snow, sleet, hail, lightning, or a combination of these occurrences. Each type of storm—thunderstorms, cyclonic· storms and tornadoes, hurricanes and typhoons—follows a particular cycle and occurs in specific seasons when atmospheric conditions are right for its creation.

Thunderstorms arise when layers of warm, moist air rise in a large, swift updraft to cooler regions of the atmosphere. There the moisture contained in the updraft condenses to form towering cumulonimbus clouds and, eventually, precipitation. Columns of cooled air then sink earthward, striking the ground with strong downdrafts and horizontal winds. At the same time, electrical charges accumulate on cloud particles (water droplets and ice). **Lightning** discharges occur when the accumulated electric charge becomes sufficiently large. Lightning heats the air it passes through so intensely and quickly that shock waves are produced; these shock waves are heard as claps and rolls of **thunder**. On occasion, severe thunderstorms are accompanied by swirling vortices of air that become concentrated and powerful enough to form·tornadoes. The temperate and tropical regions of the world are the most prone to thunderstorms.

A **tornado** is a small-diameter column of violently rotating air developed within a convective cloud and in contact with the ground. Tornadoes occur most often in association with thunderstorms during the spring and summer in the mid-latitudes of both the Northern and Southern Hemispheres. These whirling atmospheric vortices can generate the strongest winds known on Earth: wind speeds in the range of 500 km/h (300 mph) have been estimated. When winds of this magnitude strike a populated area, they can cause fantastic destruction and great loss of life, mainly through injuries from flying debris and collapsing structures. Most tornadoes, however, are comparatively weak events that occur in sparsely populated areas and cause minor damage.

A **cyclone** is any large system of winds that rotates about a center of low atmospheric pressure in a counterclockwise direction north of the Equator and in a clockwise direction to the south. Cyclonic winds move across nearly all regions of the Earth except the equatorial belt and are generally associated with rain or snow. In the Atlantic and Caribbean regions, tropical cyclones are commonly called **hurricanes**, while in the western Pacific and China Sea the term **typhoon** is applied.

Hurricanes are characterized by very strong winds and torrential rains; severe thunderstorms and waterspouts are embedded in the storm's cloud system. **Storm surge**, similar to a tidal wave, is sometimes created by the storm's high winds and by variations in air pressure. When a storm surge slams into a coastline, it usually inflicts severe damage.

Typhoons in the western Pacific are generally much stronger and more deadly than their Atlantic hurricane counterparts. This is because the Pacific Ocean is much larger than the Atlantic, and the typhoons have more time to develop before striking land.

A **blizzard** is a severe weather condition that is distinguished by low temperatures, strong winds, and large quantities of snow. The US Weather Service defines a blizzard as a storm with winds of more than 51 km/h (32 mph) and enough snow to limit visibility to 150 m (500 ft) or less. A severe blizzard has winds of over 72 km/h (about 45 mph), visibility near zero, and temperatures of −12 °C (10 °F) or lower. The name originated in the central US, where blizzards are brought by northwesterly winds following winter depressions, or low-pressure systems. In the US and in England, the term is commonly used for any strong, heavy snowstorm. In Antarctica, blizzards are associated with winds spilling over the edge of the ice plateau at an average velocity of 160 km/h (about 100 mph).

Floods

A flood occurs when water overflows its natural or artificial banks onto normally dry land. The effects of floods on human well-being range from unqualified blessings to catastrophes. The regular seasonal spring floods of the **Nile River** prior to construction of the Aswan High Dam, for example, were depended upon to provide moisture and soil enrichment for the fertile floodplains of its delta. The uncontrolled floods of the **Yangtze River** and the **Huang Ho** (Yellow River) in China, however, have repeatedly wrought disaster when these rivers habitually rechart their courses. Uncontrollable floods likely to cause considerable damage commonly result from excessive rainfall over brief periods of time, as, for example, the floods of Paris (1658 and 1910), of Warsaw (1861 and 1964), and of Rome (1530 and 1557). Potentially disastrous floods may also result from ice jams during the spring rise, as with the Danube River (1342, 1402, 1501, and 1830); from storm tides such as those of 1099 and 1953 that flooded the coasts of England, Belgium, and The Netherlands; and from **tsunamis**, the mountainous sea waves caused by earthquakes, as in Lisbon (1755) and Hawaii (Hilo, 1946).

Floods can be measured for height, peak discharge, area inundated, and volume of flow. These factors are important to judicious land use, construction of bridges and dams, and prediction and control of floods. Common measures of flood control include the improvement of channels, the construction of protective levees and storage reservoirs, and, indirectly, the implementation of programs of soil and forest conservation to retard and absorb runoff from storms.

The discharge volume of an individual stream·is often highly variable from month to month and year to year. A particularly striking example of this variability is the **flash flood**, a sudden, unexpected torrent of muddy and turbulent water rushing down a canyon or a gulch. It is uncommon, of relatively brief duration, and generally the result of summer **thunderstorms** in mountains. A flash flood can take place in a single tributary while the rest of the drainage basin remains dry. The suddenness of its occurrence makes a flash flood extremely dangerous.

Wildfires

Fire danger in a wildland setting varies with weather conditions: drought, heat, and wind participate in drying out the timber or other fuel, making it easier to ignite. Once a fire is burning, these factors all increase its intensity. Topography also affects wildland fire, which spreads quickly uphill and slowly downhill.

In the past, a combination of high summer temperatures, strong winds, late summer drought, and accumulations of dead vegetation set the stage for many naturally caused **prairie fires**, which prevented trees from becoming abundant in prairie vegetation. Now the fertile prairie soils are cultivated or grazed.

Peat bogs, which cover vast areas in the tundra and boreal forest regions of Canada, northern Europe, Russia, and Britain, are also prone to potentially dangerous fires. Although usually moist, peat may dry out and then burns easily. Peat bog fires are especially hazardous, as they emit carbon monoxide and carbon dioxide and burn deep underground. They may smolder for years, nearly impossible to extinguish.

Dried grass, leaves, and light branches are considered **flash fuels**; they ignite readily and fire spreads quickly in them, often generating enough heat to ignite heavier fuels such as tree stumps, heavy limbs, and the matted duff of the forest floor. Such fuels, ordinarily slow to kindle, are difficult to extinguish. **Green fuels**—growing vegetation—are not considered flammable, but an intense fire can dry out leaves and needles quickly enough to allow ready ignition. Green fuels sometimes carry a special danger: evergreens, such as pine, cedar, fir, and spruce, contain flammable oils that burst into flames when heated sufficiently by the searing drafts of a forest fire.

Tools for fighting wildland fires range from the standard equipment of urban fire departments to portable pumps, tank trucks, and earth-moving equipment. **Firefighting forces** specially trained to deal with wildland fires are maintained by public and private owners of forestlands. Such a force may attack a fire directly by spraying water, beating out flames, and removing vegetation at the edge of the fire to contain it behind a **firebreak** (or fire line). When the edge is too hot to approach, a firebreak is built at a safe distance, sometimes using **strip burning** or **backfire** to eliminate fuel in the path of the uncontrolled fire or to change the fire's direction or slow its progress. Backfiring is used only as a last resort.

Aircraft were first used in fighting wildland fires in California in 1919. Airplanes and helicopters are primarily used for dumping water, for observation, and occasionally for assisting in communication and transporting personnel, supplies, and equipment.

Humans cause most of the nation's wildfires, either intentionally or through negligence. In the summer of 2003 enormous wildfires burned in several western US states, including one in Arizona that consumed nearly 100,000 acres and destroyed hundreds of homes and buildings in the Santa Catalina Mountains before being contained. In the summer of 2005 wildfires broke out in California, Utah, Arizona, and Nevada, some caused by lightning strikes.

Deadliest Hurricanes in the US

Listed below, in order of number of deaths, are the 30 deadliest hurricanes to hit the US mainland 1900–2001. Hurricane names are given in parentheses after the location, when applicable. The list includes Atlantic/Gulf Coast hurricanes only. Source: National Hurricane Center. Web site: <www.nhc.noaa.gov/pastdead.html>.

	HURRICANE LOCATION	YEAR	CATEGORY	DEATHS		HURRICANE LOCATION	YEAR	CATEGORY	DEATHS
1	Galveston TX	1900	4	8,000[1]	17	SC; NC (Hazel)	1954	4	95
2	Lake Okeechobee FL	1928	4	1,836	18	southeast FL; southeast LA (Betsy)	1965	3	75
3	south TX; FL Keys	1919	4	600[2]					
4	New England	1938	3	600	19	northeast US (Carol)	1954	3	60
5	FL Keys	1935	5	408	20	eastern US (Floyd)	1999	2	56
6	southwest LA/ north TX (Audrey)	1957	4	390	21	southeast FL; LA; MS	1947	4	51
7	northeast US	1944	3	390[3]	22	FL; eastern US (Donna)	1960	4	50
8	Grand Isle LA	1909	4	350					
9	New Orleans LA	1915	4	275	23	GA; SC; NC	1940	2	50
10	Galveston TX	1915	4	275	24	TX (Carla)	1961	4	46
11	MS; LA (Camille)	1969	5	256	25	Velasco TX	1909	3	41
12	FL; LA; MS; AL	1926	4	243	26	east Texas; southeast US (Allison)	2001	TS[4]	41
13	northeast US (Diane)	1955	1	184					
14	southeast Florida	1906	2	164	27	Freeport TX	1932	4	40
15	FL; MS; AL	1906	3	134	28	south TX	1933	3	40
16	northeast US (Agnes)	1972	1	122	29	LA (Hilda)	1964	3	38
					30	southwest LA	1918	3	34

[1]Death toll may actually have been as high as 12,000.   [2]More than 500 of these lost on ships at sea; 600–900 estimated deaths.   [3]344 of these lost on ships at sea.   [4]Tropical storm.

Costliest Hurricanes in the US

This table shows cyclones that caused the most damage on the US mainland. For more information see <www.nhc.noaa.gov/pastcost.shtml>. Note: ranking numbers 17 and 26 on the main list are repeated due to the equal damage amount in dollars of multiple separate hurricanes.

RANK	HURRICANE (LOCATION)	YEAR	CATEGORY	ESTIMATED DAMAGE ($), NOT ADJUSTED	DAMAGE IN CONSTANT 2000 DOLLARS
1	Andrew (southeastern FL/southeastern LA)	1992	5	26,500,000,000	34,954,825,000
2	Ivan (southeastern US)	2004	5	15,000,000,000	13,673,900,000
3	Charley (parts of FL/other southern states)	2004	4	14,000,000,000	12,762,300,000
4	Frances (southeastern US)	2004	2	8,860,000,000	8,076,720,000
5	Hugo (SC)	1989	4	7,000,000,000	9,739,820,675
6	Jeanne (southeastern US)	2004	3	6,900,000,000	6,289,000,000
7	Allison (eastern TX/ southeastern US)	2001	TS[2]	5,000,000,000	4,861,660,000
8	Floyd (midatlantic and northeastern US)	1999	2	4,500,000,000	4,666,817,360
9	Isabel (NC/eastern US)	2003	2	3,370,000,000	3,153,880,000
10	Fran (NC)	1996	3	3,200,000,000	3,670,400,000
11	Opal (northwestern FL/AL)	1995	3	3,000,000,000	3,520,596,085
12	Dennis (FL/AL)	2005	3-4	3–5,000,000,000	2.6–4,426,740,000
13	Georges (Florida Keys, MS, AL)	1998	2	2,310,000,000	2,494,800,000
14	Frederic (AL/MS)	1979	3	2,300,000,000	4,965,327,332
15	Agnes (northeastern US)	1972	1	2,100,000,000	8,602,500,000
16	Alicia (northern TX)	1983	3	2,000,000,000	3,421,660,182
17	Bob (NC/northeastern US)	1991	2	1,500,000,000	2,004,635,258
	Juan (LA)	1985	1	1,500,000,000	2,418,795,844
18	Camille (MS/AL)	1969	5	1,420,700,000	6,992,441,549
19	Betsy (FL/LA)	1965	3	1,420,500,000	8,516,866,023
20	Elena (MS/AL/ northwestern FL)	1985	3	1,250,000,000	2,015,663,203
21	Gloria (eastern US)	1985	3[1]	900,000,000	1,451,277,506
22	Lili (LA/MS)	2002	1	860,000,000	908,500,000
23	Diane (northeastern US)	1955	1	831,700,000	5,540,676,187
24	Bonnie (NC/VA)	1998	2	720,000,000	760,638,000
25	Erin (central and northwestern FL/AL)	1995	2	700,000,000	790,945,000
26	Allison (northern TX)	1989	TS[2]	500,000,000	694,355,000
	Alberto (northwestern FL/GA/AL)	1994	TS[2]	500,000,000	580,972,000
	Frances (TX)	1998	TS[2]	500,000,000	528,221,000
27	Eloise (northwestern FL)	1975	3	490,000,000	1,489,250,000
28	Carol (northeastern US)	1954	3[1]	461,000,000	3,134,443,557
29	Celia (southern TX)	1970	3	453,000,000	2,015,663,203
non-Atlantic or non-Gulf Coast systems					
9	Georges (USVI/Puerto Rico)	1998	3	3,600,000,000	3,888,000,000
16	Iniki (Kauai, Hawaii)	1992	unknown[3]	1,800,000,000	2,190,600,000
17	Marilyn (USVI/eastern Puerto Rico)	1995	2	1,500,000,000	1,624,110,320
21	Hugo (USVI/Puerto Rico)	1989	4	1,000,000,000	1,283,755,274
26	Hortense (Puerto Rico)	1996	1	500,000,000	548,760,000

[1]Moving more than 30 mph.   [2]Of tropical storm intensity but included because of high damage.   [3]Intensity not sufficiently known to establish category.

Hurricane Names

Source: National Hurricane Center.

In 1953, the National Hurricane Center developed a list of given names for Atlantic tropical storms. This list is now maintained by the World Meteorological Organization (WMO). Until 1979, only women's names were used, but since then men's and women's names have alternated. There are six lists currently in rotation, so names are reused every six years. Any country affected by a hurricane, however, can request its name be retired for ten years. Also, if a storm has been particularly destructive, the WMO can remove it from the list and replace it with a different name.

Civil Engineering

History of Civil Engineering

Civil engineering describes the design and construction of public structures. The term first came into use in the 18th century, though the discipline has been in practice since antiquity. Civil engineering is generally distinguished from military engineering and often times from architecture. It is the oldest of the four traditional disciplines of engineering: civil, mechanical, electrical, and chemical.

The first engineer known by name and achievement is **Imhotep**, builder of the **Step Pyramid** at Saqqarah, Egypt, (c. 2550 BC). Imhotep's successors—Egyptian, Persian, Greek, and Roman—carried civil engineering to remarkable heights on the basis of empirical methods aided by arithmetic, geometry, and a smattering of physical science. The lighthouse **Pharos** of Alexandria, **Solomon's Temple** in Jerusalem, the **Colosseum** in Rome, the **Persian Royal Road** and **Roman road systems**, the **Pont du Gard** aqueduct in France, and many other large structures testify to their skill, imagination, and daring. Of many treatises written by them, one in particular survives to provide a picture of engineering education and practice in classical times: *De architectura* by Vitruvius of Rome, published in the 1st century AD.

In construction, medieval European engineers carried technique, in the form of the **Gothic arch** and the **flying buttress**, to a height unknown to the Romans. The sketchbook of the 13th-century French engineer **Villard de Honnecourt** reveals a wide knowledge of mathematics, geometry, natural and physical science, and draftsmanship.

In Asia, engineering had a separate but very similar development, with more and more sophisticated techniques of construction, hydraulics, and metallurgy helping to create advanced civilizations such as the **Mongol empire**, whose large, beautiful cities impressed Marco Polo in the 13th century.

The appearance of civil engineering as a distinct discipline began in France in 1747 with the establishment of the **École Nationale des Ponts et Chaussées** ("National School of Bridges and Highways"), whose faculty and students helped to define the emerging field. Soon, craftsmen, stonemasons, and toolmakers from France and England became civil engineers. In Britain, **James Brindley** began as a millwright and became the foremost canal builder of the century; **John Rennie** was a millwright's apprentice who eventually built the new London Bridge; **Thomas Telford**, a stonemason, became Britain's leading road builder; and **John Smeaton**, an instrument maker, built the Eddystone Lighthouse (1756–59), before founding the Society of Civil Engineers (1771; now known as the **Smeatonian Society**). Other institutions included the **École Polytechnique** in Paris (1794), the **Bauakademie** in Berlin (1799) and the **Institution of Civil Engineers** in London (1818).

Today civil engineering is taught in universities across the world and national organizations of civil engineers have been formed widely.

The Seven Wonders of the Ancient World

The seven wonders of the ancient world were considered to be the preeminent architectural and sculptural achievements of the Mediterranean and Middle East. The best known are those of the 2nd-century-BC writer Antipater of Sidon. Some early lists included the Walls of Babylon or the Palace of King Cyrus of Persia, but the established list usually contained the following:

Pyramids of Giza. The oldest of the wonders and the only one substantially in existence today, the pyramids of Giza were erected c. 2575–c. 2465 BC on the west bank of the Nile River near Al-Jizah in northern Egypt. The designations of the pyramids—Khufu, Khafre, and Menkaure—correspond to the kings for whom they were built. Khufu (also called the Great Pyramid) is the largest of the three, the length of each side at the base averaging 230 m (755 ¾ ft). Its original height was 147 m (481.4 ft); none of the pyramids reach their original heights because they have been almost entirely stripped of their outer casings of smooth white limestone. According to Herodotus, the Great Pyramid took 20 years to construct and demanded the labor of 100,000 men.

Hanging Gardens of Babylon. A series of landscaped terraces ascribed to either Queen Sammu-ramat (810–783 BC) or King Nebuchadrezzar II (c. 605–c. 561 BC), the gardens were built within the walls of the royal palace at Babylon (in present-day southern Iraq). They did not actually "hang" but were instead "up in the air"—that is, they were roof gardens laid out on a series of ziggurat terraces that were irrigated by pumps from the Euphrates River. Although no traces of the Hanging Gardens have been found, classical authors related that the terraces were roofed with stone balconies on which were layered various materials, such as reeds, bitumen, and lead, so that the irrigation water would not seep through them.

Statue of Zeus. A large, ornate figure of Zeus on his throne, this wonder was made around 430 BC by Phidias of Athens. It was placed in the huge Temple of Zeus at Olympia in western Greece. The statue, almost 12 m (40 ft) high and plated with gold and ivory, represented the god sitting on an elaborate cedarwood throne ornamented with ebony, ivory, gold, and precious stones. On his outstretched right hand was a statue of Nike (Victory), and in the god's left hand was a scepter on which an eagle was perched. The statue, which took eight years to construct, may have been destroyed along with the temple in AD 426, or in a fire at Constantinople (Istanbul) about 50 years later.

Temple of Artemis. The great temple was built by Croesus, king of Lydia, in about 550 BC and was rebuilt after being burned by a madman named Herostratus in 356 BC. The artemesium was famous not only for its great size (over 110 by 55 m [350 by 80 ft]) but also for the magnificent works of art that adorned it. It was destroyed by invading Goths in AD 262 and was never rebuilt. Little remains of the temple, but excavation has revealed traces of it, and copies survive of the famous statue of Artemis. A mummylike figure, this early representation of the goddess stands stiffly straight, with her hands extended outward. The original statue was made of gold, ebony, silver, and black stone, the legs and hips covered by a garment decorated with reliefs of animals and bees and the head adorned with a high-pillared headdress.

Mausoleum of Halicarnassus. Monumental tomb of Mausolus, the tyrant of Caria in southwestern Asia Minor, the mausoleum was built between about 353 and 351 BC by Mausolus' sister and widow, Artemisia. The architect was Pythius (Pytheos), and the sculptures that adorned the building were the work of four leading Greek artists. According to the description of Pliny the Elder, the monument was almost square, with a total periphery of 125 m (411 ft). It was bounded by 36 columns, and the top formed a 24-step pyramid surmounted by a four-horse marble chariot. Fragments of the mausoleum's sculpture are preserved in the British Museum. The mausoleum probably destroyed by an earthquake between the 11th and 15th century AD, and the stones were reused in local buildings.

Colossus of Rhodes. This huge bronze statue was built at the harbor of Rhodes in ancient Greece in commemoration of the raising of the siege of Rhodes (305–304 BC). The sculptor was Chares of Lyndus, and the statue was made of bronze, reinforced with iron, and weighted with stones. The Colossus was said to be 70 cubits (32 m [105 ft]) high and stood beside Mandrákion harbor. It is technically impossible that the statue could have straddled the harbor entrance, and the popular belief that it did so dates only from the Middle Ages. The Colossus took 12 years to build (c. 294–282 BC) and was toppled by an earthquake about 225 BC. The fallen Colossus was left in place until AD 654, when Arabian forces raided Rhodes and had the statue broken up and the bronze sold for scrap.

Pharos of Alexandria. The most famous lighthouse of the ancient world, it was built by Sostratus of Cnidus, perhaps for Ptolemy I Soter, but was finished during the reign of his son, Ptolemy II of Egypt, about 280 BC. The lighthouse stood on the island of Pharos off Alexandria and is said to have been more than 100 m (350 ft) high; the only taller man-made structures at the time would have been the pyramids of Giza. It was a technological triumph and is the archetype of all lighthouses since. According to ancient sources, a broad spiral ramp led to the top, where a fire burned at night. The lighthouse was destroyed by an earthquake in the 1300s. In 1994 a large amount of masonry blocks and statuary was found in the waters off Pharos.

25 Tallest Buildings in the World

Building height equals the distance from the sidewalk level of the main entrance to the structural top of the building, including spires. Sources: Council on Tall Buildings and Urban Habitat and Emporis Data.

RANK	BUILDING	CITY	YEAR COMPLETED	HEIGHT IN FT/M	STORIES
1	Taipei 101	Taipei, Taiwan	2004	1,670/509	101
2	Petronas Tower 1	Kuala Lumpur, Malaysia	1998	1,483/452	88
3	Petronas Tower 2	Kuala Lumpur, Malaysia	1998	1,483/452	88
4	Sears Tower	Chicago IL	1974	1,450/442	110
5	Jin Mao Building	Shanghai, China	1998	1,381/421	88
6	Two International Finance Centre	Hong Kong, China	2003	1,362/415	88
7	CITIC Plaza	Guangzhou, China	1997	1,283/391	80
8	Shun Hing Square	Shenzhen, China	1996	1,260/384	69
9	Empire State Building	New York NY	1931	1,250/381	102
10	Central Plaza	Hong Kong, China	1992	1,227/374	78
11	Bank of China Tower	Hong Kong, China	1990	1,204/367	70
12	Emirates Office Tower	Dubai, UAE	1999	1,165/355	55
13	Tuntex Sky Tower	Kaohsiung, Taiwan	1997	1,140/348	85
14	Aon Center	Chicago IL	1973	1,136/346	83
15	The Center	Hong Kong, China	1998	1,135/346	73
16	John Hancock Center	Chicago IL	1969	1,127/344	100
17	Shimao International Plaza	Shanghai, China	2005	1,093/333	60
18	Wuhan International Securities	Wuhan, China	2005	1,087/331	68
19	Ryugyong Hotel	Pyongyang, North Korea	1992	1,083/330	105
20	Burj Al Arab	Dubai, UAE	1999	1,053/321	60
21	Chrysler Building	New York NY	1930	1,046/319	77
22	Nina Tower I	Hong Kong, China	2005	1,046/319	80
23	Bank of America Plaza	Atlanta GA	1992	1,023/312	55
24	US Bank Tower	Los Angeles CA	1989	1,018/310	73
25	Menara Telekom	Kuala Lumpur, Malaysia	2001	1,017/310	55

Notable Towers

A tower is any structure that is relatively tall in proportion to the dimensions of its base. It may be either freestanding or attached to a building or wall. Modifiers frequently denote a tower's function (e.g., watchtower, water tower, church tower, and so on).

Historically, there are several types of structures particularly implied by the name. **Defensive towers** served as platforms from which a defending force could rain missiles down upon an attacking force. The Romans, Byzantines, and medieval Europeans built such towers along their city walls and adjoining important gates. The Romans and other peoples also used offensive, or **siege**, towers as raised platforms for attacking troops to overrun high city walls. **Military towers** often gave their name to an entire fortress; the **Tower of London**, for example, includes the entire complex of buildings contiguous with the **White Tower** of William I the Conqueror.

Towers were an important feature of the **churches and cathedrals** built during the Romanesque and Gothic periods. Some Gothic church towers were designed to carry a spire, while others had flat roofs. Many church towers were used as belfries, though the most famous **campanile**, or bell tower, the **Leaning Tower of Pisa** (1174), is a freestanding structure. In civic architecture, towers were often used to hold clocks, as in town halls in France and Germany. The use of towers declined somewhat during the Renaissance but reappeared in the more flamboyant Baroque architecture of the 17th and 18th centuries.

The use of **steel frames** enabled buildings to reach unprecedented heights in the late 19th and 20th centuries; the **Eiffel Tower** (1889) in Paris was the first structure to reveal the true vertical potential of steel construction. The ubiquity of modern skyscrapers has robbed the word *tower* of most of its meaning, though the **Petronas Twin Towers** in Kuala Lumpur, Malaysia, the **Sears Tower** in Chicago, and other skyscrapers still bear the term in their official names.

The world's **tallest freestanding structure** is the CN Tower (1976), an observation and broadcasting tower in Toronto that rises to more than 553 m (1,815 ft). Construction of a taller (1,830-ft) structure, the Jakarta Tower in Indonesia, began in 1997 and resumed in 2004. **The tallest supported structure** is a 629-m (2,063-ft) stayed television broadcasting tower, completed in 1963 and located between Fargo and Blanchard ND.

Bridges

A bridge is a structure that spans horizontally between supports to allow pedestrians and vehicles to cross a void, such as a river or a valley. The bridge supports must be strong enough to hold the structure up, and the span between the supports must be strong enough to carry the vertical loads. Spans are generally made as short as possible; long spans are justified where good foundations are limited—for example, over estuaries with deep water.

The loads that bridges transfer to their vertical supports are of various kinds. Dead load is the weight of the bridge, live load is the weight of the traffic on it, and wind load is the pressure of the wind against the bridge. Major bridges are usually built with public money, and bridge-building can achieve a high level of prominence. Civil engineers often design a bridge to be elegant, as well as efficient and economical.

Beam bridge

The simplest bridge is the beam (or girder) bridge, consisting of straight, rigid beams placed across a span (e.g., a tree trunk laid across a stream). A more complex example is a plate girder bridge over a highway; a plate girder is a built-up beam consisting of a steel plate to which angles are riveted or welded. Because a simple beam tends to bend down at its middle, particularly over a long chasm, the beam may rest on more than one support to form a continuous beam.

Another beam bridge is the **truss bridge**, made up of members forming rigid triangles. Trusses are popular because they use a relatively small amount of material to carry relatively large loads. A variation of the beam principle is used in the **cantilever bridge**. A cantilever is a beam that extends beyond its support. Sometimes two cantilever arms meet at mid-span or are connected by a light suspended span.

Arch bridge

Based on a different principle than the beam is the arch bridge. In the beam bridge the load is transmitted vertically to the supports, whereas the arch bridge pushes outward against its supports, which must be heavy to resist the horizontal thrust of the arch. The arch may be fixed, with each end rigid; two-hinged, with a hinge at each support; or three-hinged, with a third hinge at its crown. The hinges permit movement because of loads or temperature changes.

Suspension bridge

In the suspension bridge huge cables are hung over two high towers. The cable ends are fastened to heavy concrete or masonry anchorages. Suspender cables hanging from the main cables support the roadway. As in the arch, the thrust on the suspension bridge is horizontal. Instead of horizontal compression, or push, however, there is horizontal tension, or pull, upon the anchorages.

Cable-stayed bridge

Cable-stayed bridges carry the vertical main-span loads by nearly straight diagonal cables in tension. The towers transfer the cable forces to the foundations through vertical compression. The tensile forces in the cables also put the deck into horizontal compression.

Other bridges

A **drawbridge** over the moat of a medieval castle is an example of a movable bridge. The **bascule bridge**, in either single-leaf or double-leaf, is the modern-day version. Bascule in French means "a seesaw;" a counterweight balances the span in every open position.

The **swing span** bridge turns about a vertical axis to allow ships to pass. It is balanced on a pivot pier, usually in its center. Its span is measured by including the length of both arms. The vertical lift bridge has a tower at each end of its span. Cables attached to ends of the span pass over pulleys at the top of the towers and are fastened to counterweights that equal the weight of the span. The span moves up and down like an elevator.

In the **floating bridge**, boats or pontoons support the road. The bridge retracts or swings aside to allow ships to pass. The **transporter bridge** has two towers supporting a fixed span from which a moving platform or car is hung.

Early history of bridgebuilding

The earliest bridges were made from materials at hand. The Swiss lake dwellers built their timber houses by driving piles into the lake bed. From this evolved the timber pile and trestle railroad bridge. In warmer parts of the world bridgebuilders erected suspension bridges. In one Chinese type the traveler sat in a basket or saddle suspended from a cable and slid to the opposite bank. Bridgemakers in the Himalayas threw ropes across a chasm and from these hung thinner ropes to carry the road. This was the origin of the modern suspension bridge. The cantilever bridge also originated in Asia, in India; wooden planks, weighted down by abutment stones, were projected from the two banks until they met in the center.

Basic Types of Bridges

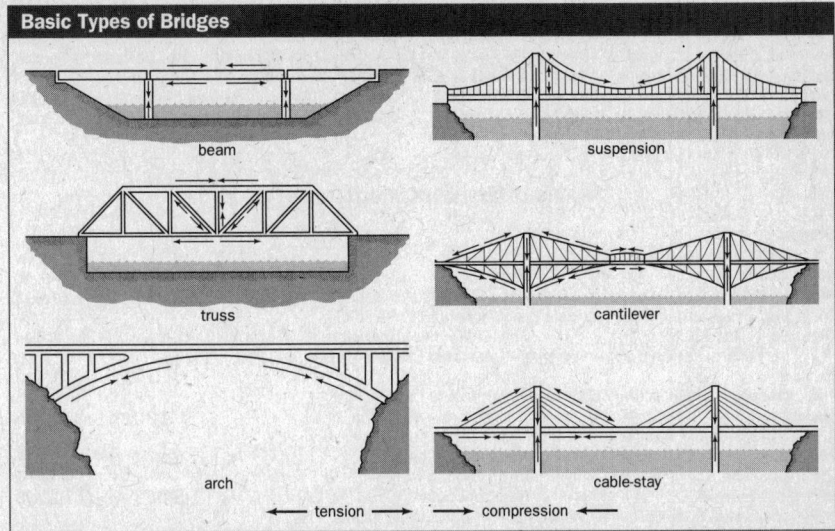

beam

suspension

truss

cantilever

arch

cable-stay

←——— tension ———→ · ←— compression —←

The ancient **Romans** were notable bridgebuilders. Six of their masonry arch bridges over the Tiber River still stand in Rome. The most beautiful of the existing Roman bridges is the **Ponte di Augusto**, built at Rimini about 5 BC. The greatest Roman aqueduct is the **Pont du Gard** at Nîmes, France. It has three tiers of arches, which rise 47 m (155 ft) above the Gard River.

Medieval bridges
During the Middle Ages the church became the chief builder of bridges. Churchmen formed the **Brotherhood of Bridgebuilders** in Italy and France at the end of the 12th century. St. Bénézet built a beautiful stone bridge over the Rhone at Avignon, in southern France. Four arches still remain.

Monks also built the old **London Bridge** (1209) over the River Thames, in London. By the 16th century more than a hundred shops and dwellings had been erected on it. Another covered bridge with shops along the sides was the **Ponte Vecchio** (1345), which still stands over the Arno River, at Florence, Italy.

A major contribution of the Renaissance was the theory of the truss. **Andrea Palladio** of Italy wrote about truss design in *The Four Books of Architecture* (1570). Typical of the bridgebuilding of this period is the stone arch **Rialto Bridge** over the Grand Canal, in Venice. Two Renaissance stone bridges remain over the Seine in Paris—the **Pont Notre Dame** (1505) and the **Pont Neuf** (1606).

The 18th century
In the 18th century, bridge design came to be considered a science. **Hubert Gautier**, a French engineer, wrote a treatise on bridgebuilding. The first engineering school was founded in Paris. Its director, **Jean Perronet**, is called the father of modern bridgebuilding. He perfected the masonry arch, using a flat arch and slender piers. One of his finest bridges is the **Pont de la Concorde**, in Paris.

Also in the 1700s the **wooden truss bridge** was rediscovered, and the covered wooden bridge began to appear in Switzerland. The **Grubenmann brothers**, Swiss carpenters, built a 200-ft (60-m) span at Wettin-

gen. The picturesque covered bridge was highly developed in the American Colonies. **Col. Enoch Hale** built the first framed **timber bridge** in the United States, over the Connecticut River at Bellows Falls VT, in 1785.

The invention of the steam locomotive changed bridgebuilding, for stronger spans were needed. Iron was first used for chain cables of a suspension over the Tees River, in England, in 1741. Abraham Darby and John Wilkinson built the first **iron bridge** over the Severn River at Coalbrookdale, England, in 1779.

Modern bridges
Thomas Telford built the first modern iron arch bridge in 1813–Craig Ellachie Bridge over the River Spey at Banffshire, Scotland. In the 1820s Telford built the forerunner of the modern suspension bridge–the 570-foot span over **Menai Strait**, in Wales. It had wrought-iron chains for cables. The first to design railroad bridges was George Stephenson, who with his son Robert invented the Rocket, the first practical locomotive. Many truss designs were patented in the 1850s for railroad bridges. After numerous failures of cast-iron bridges, wrought iron was used, then steel.

The first bridge to use steel extensively was the triple-arched **Eads Bridge** over the Mississippi at St. Louis MO, in 1874. The first major use of pneumatic caissons for large piers was made in this bridge. It was an important link in the transcontinental railroad and made St. Louis a crossroads.

At the turn of the 20th century, the construction of **masonry arch bridges** reached its peak. Then the more economical and easier to use concrete became common for arch bridges. Later, reinforced concrete and then prestressed concrete were used.

The first **modern cantilever bridge** was built in 1867 by **Heinrich Gerber** over the Main River at Hassfurt, Germany. The first major example of the cantilever, however, was the **Firth of Forth Bridge**, in Scotland. It was built in 1882–90 with two 1,700-ft (510-m) spans and steel truss members that are tubular in shape.

As the suspension bridge replaced the cantilever, the United States became the world leader in this type of long-span bridgebuilding. One reason was the peninsula sites of two of its major cities—New York and San Francisco. **John A. Roebling**'s greatest achievement was his design of the Brooklyn Bridge over the East River in New York City in 1883. In 1937 San Francisco's **Golden Gate Bridge** was completed with a span of 1280 m (4,200 ft).

After World War II, bridges of note included the **Mackinac Bridge** (1957), linking the upper and lower peninsulas of Michigan; the **Verrazano-Narrows Bridge** (1964) connecting Brooklyn with Staten Island; and the **Akashi Kaikyo Bridge** (1998), bringing together the islands of Honshu and Shikoku, Japan.

World's Longest-Span Structures by Type

Bridges

SUSPENSION	LOCATION	YEAR OF COMPLETION	MAIN SPAN (M)
Akashi Kaikyo	Kobe–Awaji Island, Japan	1998	1,991
part of eastern link between islands of Honshu and Shikoku			
Store Bælt (Great Belt)	Zealand–Funen, Denmark	1998	1,624
part of link between Copenhagen and mainland Europe			
Humber	near Hull, England	1981	1,410
crosses Humber estuary between Yorkshire and Lincolnshire			
Jiangyin	Jiangsu province, China	1999	1,385
crosses Chang Jiang (Yangtze River) near Shanghai			
Tsing Ma	Hong Kong, China	1997	1,377
connects Hong Kong city with airport on Landao Island			
Verrazano-Narrows	New York NY	1964	1,298
spans New York Harbor between Brooklyn and Staten Island			
Golden Gate	San Francisco CA	1937	1,280
spans entrance to San Francisco Bay			
Höga Kusten (High Coast)	Kramfors, Sweden	1997	1,210
crosses Angerman River on scenic coastal route in northern Sweden			
Mackinac	Mackinaw City–St. Ignace MI	1957	1,158
spans Mackinac Straits between upper and lower peninsulas of Michigan			
Minami Bisan-Seto	Sakaide, Japan	1988	1,100
part of central link between islands of Honshu and Shikoku			
Bosporus II (Fatih Sultan Mehmet)	Istanbul, Turkey	1988	1,090
spans strait from Rumeli Fortress on European side to Anadolu Fortress on Asian side			
Bosporus I	Istanbul, Turkey	1973	1,074
provides highway link between European Turkey (Thrace) and Asian Turkey (Anatolia)			
George Washington	New York NY	1931	1,067
crosses Hudson River between New Jersey and Manhattan Island			
Kurushima-3	Onomichi–Imabari, Japan	1999	1,030
part of western link between islands of Honshu and Shikoku			
Kurushima-2	Onomichi–Imabari, Japan	1999	1,020
part of western link between islands of Honshu and Shikoku			
Ponte 25 de Abril (Salazar)	Lisbon, Portugal	1966	1,013
provides main crossing over Tagus River into Lisbon			
Forth Road	Queensferry, Scotland	1964	1,006
carries automobile traffic over Firth of Forth			
Kita Bisan-Seto	Kojima–Sakaide, Japan	1988	990
part of central link between islands of Honshu and Shikoku			
Severn	near Bristol, England	1966	988
crosses Severn estuary between England and Wales			
Yichang	Hubei province, China	2001	960
crosses Chang Jiang (Yangtze River) downstream of Three Gorges Dam			
CABLE-STAYED (STEEL)			
Tatara	Onomichi–Imabari, Japan	1999	890
part of western link between islands of Honshu and Shikoku			
Normandie	near Le Havre, France	1995	856
crosses Seine estuary between upper and lower Normandy			
Nancha	Nanjing, China	2001	628
southern span of Second Nanjing Yangtze Bridge			
Wuhan Baishazhou	Hubei province, China	2000	618
provides third crossing of Chang Jiang (Yangtze River) in city of Wuhan			
Qingzhou Minjiang	Fuzhou, China	2001	605
connects Fuzhou with airport across Minjiang (Min River)			
Yangpu	Shanghai, China	1993	602
crosses Huangpujiang (Huang-p'u River) between northeast Shanghai and Pudong New District			
Xupu	Shanghai, China	1997	590
crosses Huangpujiang (Huang-p'u River) between southwest Shanghai and Pudong New District			

World's Longest-Span Structures (continued)

CABLE-STAYED (STEEL)	LOCATION	YEAR OF COMPLETION	MAIN SPAN (M)
Meikouchuou (Meiko Central)	Nagoya, Japan	1998	590
middle of three spans crossing Nagoya's port			
Skarnsundet	near Trondheim, Norway	1991	530
crosses scenic Trondheimsfjorden between northern and southern Norway			
Queshi	Shantou, China	1998	518
carries highway traffic across Shantou's harbor			
Tsurumi Tsubasa	Yokohama, Japan	1994	510
one of two spans crossing Yokohama's harbor			
Jingsha Yangtze River North	Jingzhou, China	2002	500
part of multispan crossing of Chang Jiang (Yangtze River) on north-south highway			
Ikuchi	Onomichi–Imabari, Japan	1991	490
part of western link between islands of Honshu and Shikoku			
Øresund (Öresund)	Copenhagen– Malmö	2000	490
part of link across The Sound between Denmark and Sweden			

ARCH
steel

Lupu	Shanghai, China	2003	550
crosses Huangpujiang (Huang-p'u River) between central Shanghai and Pudong New District			
New River Gorge	Fayetteville WV	1977	518
provides road link through scenic New River Gorge National River area			
Bayonne	Bayonne NJ–New York NY	1931	504
spans the Kill Van Kull between New Jersey and Staten Island			
Sydney Harbour	Sydney, Australia	1932	503
links the City of Sydney with North Sydney			
Fremont	Portland OR	1973	383
links interstate highways over Willamette River			
Port Mann	Vancouver, BC, Canada	1964	366
carries TransCanada Highway across Fraser River			

concrete

Wanxian	Sichuan province, China	1997	420
crosses Chang Jiang (Yangtze River) in Three Gorges area			
Krk I	Krk Island, Croatia	1980	390
links scenic Krk Island with mainland Croatia			
Jiangjiehe	Guizhou province, China	1995	330
spans gorge of Wujiang (Wu River)			
Yongning	Guangxi province, China	1996	312
crosses Yongjiang (Yung River) near Nanning			
Gladesville	Sydney, Australia	1964	305
spans Parramatta River upstream from Sydney Harbour			

CANTILEVER
steel truss

Pont de Québec	Quebec City, QC, Canada	1917	549
provides rail crossing over St. Lawrence River			
Forth	Queensferry, Scotland	1890	2 spans, each 521
provides rail crossing over Firth of Forth			
Minato	Osaka–Amagasaki, Japan	1974	510
carries road traffic across Osaka's harbor			
Commodore John J. Barry	Bridgeport NJ–Chester PA	1974	501
provides road crossing over Delaware River			
Greater New Orleans-1	New Orleans LA	1958	480
connects highway traffic across Mississippi River			
Greater New Orleans-2	New Orleans LA	1988	480
provides parallel service to Greater New Orleans-1 Bridge			
Howrah	Calcutta	1943	457
provides automobile and pedestrian crossing of Hooghly River			

PRESTRESSED CONCRETE

Stolmasundet	Austevoll, Norway	1998	301
links islands of Stolmen and Sjelbörn south of Bergen			
Raftsundet	Lofoten, Norway	1998	298
crosses Raft Sound in arctic Lofoten Islands			
Sundøy	Leirfjord, Norway	2003	298
links Alsten Island to mainland Norway			
Boca Tigris-2	Humen, China	1997	270
part of multispan link across Tiger's Mouth (Boca Tigris) of Pearl River Delta			

World's Longest-Span Structures (continued)

	LOCATION	YEAR OF COMPLETION	MAIN SPAN (M)
PRESTRESSED CONCRETE			
Gateway	Brisbane, Australia	1986	260
provides highway link between Queensland's Sunshine Coast and Gold Coast			
BEAM			
steel truss			
Ikitsuki Ohashi	Nagasaki prefecture, Japan	1991	400
connects islands of Iki and Hirado off of northwest Kyushu			
Astoria	Astoria OR	1966	376
carries Pacific Coast Highway across Columbia River between Oregon and Washington			
Francis Scott Key	Baltimore MD	1977	366
spans Patapsco River at Baltimore Harbor			
Oshima	Yamaguchi prefecture, Japan	1976	325
links Yanai City and Oshima Island			
Tenmon	Kumamoto prefecture, Japan	1966	295
part of Amakusa Gokyo (Five Bridges of Amakusa) linking islands in southwestern Kumamoto			
steel plate and box girder			
Presidente Costa e Silva	Rio de Janeiro State, Brazil	1974	300
crosses Guanabara Bay between Rio de Janeiro and suburb of Niterói			
Neckartalbrücke-1	Weitingen, Germany	1978	263
carries highway across Neckar River Valley			
Brankova	Belgrade, Serbia	1956	261
provides road crossing of Sava River between Old and New Belgrade			
Ponte de Vitória-3	Espírito Santo State, Brazil	1989	260
provides road link to state capital on Vitória Island			
Zoobrücke (Zoo Bridge)	Cologne, Germany	1966	259
spans Rhine River between old city on left bank and convention centre on right bank			
MOVABLE			
vertical lift			
Arthur Kill	Elizabeth NJ–New York NY	1959	170
provides rail link between port of Elizabeth and Staten Island			
Cape Cod Canal	Cape Cod MA	1935	166
provides rail crossing over waterway near Buzzard's Bay			
Delair	Delair NJ–Philadelphia PA	1960	165
provides rail link across Delaware River between Philadelphia and South Jersey shore			
Marine Parkway-Gil Hodges Memorial	New York NY	1937	165
carries road traffic over mouth of Jamaica Bay between Brooklyn and the Rockaways, Queens			
swing span			
Al-Firdan (El-Ferdan)	Suez Canal, Egypt	2001	340
provides road and rail link between Sinai Peninsula and eastern Nile Delta region			
Santa Fe	Fort Madison IA–Niota IL	1927	160
provides road and rail crossing of Mississippi River			
BASCULE			
South Capitol Street/Frederick Douglass Memorial	Washington DC	1949	118
carries road traffic over Anacostia River			
Sault Sainte Marie	Sault Sainte Marie MI–Ontario	1941	102
connects rail systems of United States and Canada			
Charles Berry	Lorain OH	1940	101
carries road traffic over Black River			
Market Street/Chief John Ross	Chattanooga TN	1917	94
carries road traffic over Tennessee River			
Causeways[1]			
Lake Pontchartrain-2	Metairie–Mandeville LA	1969	38,422
carries northbound road traffic from suburbs of New Orleans to north lakeshore			
Lake Pontchartrain-1	Mandeville–Metairie LA	1956	38,352
carries southbound road traffic from north lakeshore to suburbs of New Orleans			
King Fahd Causeway	Bahrain–Saudi Arabia	1986	24,950
carries road traffic across Gulf of Bahrain in Persian Gulf			
Confederation Bridge	Borden-Carleton, PE–Cape Jourimain, NB	1997	12,900
carries road traffic over Northumberland Strait			

[1] *Defined here as fixed link over water consisting almost entirely of multiple spans of identical beam or cantilever construction. Does not include links containing tunnels or bridges of suspension, cable-stayed, or arch construction.*

Roads

A road is the traveled way on which people, animals, or wheeled vehicles move. The term **street** implies an urban roadway, **boulevard** denotes a broad landscaped road, and **highway** suggests a high-speed or heavily traveled route, with controlled points of entrance and exit. **Thruway, expressway, motorway, tollway,** and **freeway** are variations of highway.

The earliest roads developed from paths and trails and appeared with the invention of wheeled vehicles, around 3000 BC. Road systems developed to facilitate trade in early civilizations. The **Persian Royal Road,** the first major road, extended 1,775 miles (2,857 km) from the Persian Gulf to the Aegean Sea and was used c. 3500–300 BC.

The **Romans** used roads to maintain control of their empire, with over 53,000 miles (85,000 km) of roadways extending across its lands. Their roads were often several feet thick, characteristically straight, and composed of layers of flintlike lava, gravel mixed with lime, flat stones, and sand or mortar—all stacked on a graded soil foundation. Roman construction techniques and design remained the most advanced until the late 1700s.

In the 19th century, invention of **macadam** road construction provided a quick and durable method for building roads, and **asphalt** and **concrete** also began to be used. The widespread use of bicycles created a demand for roads with smoother surfaces. New types of pavement were developed, in both flexible and rigid varieties.

Motorized traffic in the 20th century led to the **limited-access highway,** the first of which was the Bronx River Parkway in New York City (1925). In the 1930s superhighways also appeared in Italy, as the autostrada, and in Germany, as the autobahn. Military use was an important design feature of these highways, which could accommodate heavy traffic at high speeds. In the 1950s the **US interstate highway system** was inaugurated to link the country's major cities. It included toll roads, for which users pay in increments while traveling on them.

In industrialized nations, roadway planners must account for existing traffic congestion, future traffic needs, and the effects of urban sprawl, in addition to the measures of affordability, quality, and project duration. Engineers must consider material durability, local climatic conditions, drainage patterns, and safety improvements, such as reflective markings, rumble strips, guardrails, and crash cushions.

Notable Tunnels

A tunnel is a horizontal underground or underwater passageway, generally produced by excavation. Tunnels are used for mining, as passageways for trains and motor vehicles, for diverting rivers around damsites, for housing underground installations such as power plants and military bases, and for conducting water.

When natural obstacles—such as mountains, hills, or rivers—block the path proposed for a railway, highway, or pipeline, engineers bore tunnels through or under the obstacles. Structures built as trenches and later covered are also often called tunnels. A tunnel that carries water from reservoirs to cities for drinking and irrigation is an aqueduct, while those transporting water-borne freight through hillsides are canals. Mass-transit railway tunnels constructed under cities to relieve crowded streets are known as subways.

Excavation of a drift, or horizontal shaft, can begin from a hill or mountain slope, in which case the entrance is called a portal. Work can also begin from a vertical shaft, in which workers and equipment are raised and lowered and out of which rubble or muck is removed. All tunnels need some form of ventilation to supply air to workers and, later, to traffic. Ventilation also draws out potentially dangerous fumes from blasting or from gas deposits and prevents temperatures from getting too high. Tunnels can be divided into four general categories, depending on the material through which they pass: soft ground, solid rock, soft rock, and under water.

Tunneling in soft ground

Soft-ground tunnels are generally shallow and are often built for use as subways, water-supply systems, and sewers. Excavation in soft ground is much easier than it is in solid rock, but the stand-up time—that is, the time an excavated section will safely stand up without support—is very short. To prevent the tunnel from collapsing, a support structure is continuously built around the heading, or excavation face. A circu-

lar or arch-shaped design has been found to be the best at bearing the ground load from above. Brick and stone were used for support in early tunnels, but in modern tunneling steel is generally used to provide temporary support until a concrete lining can be installed.

Soft-soil excavation can be accomplished by a number of methods, from simple hand mining with shovel and pickax to full-face boring with sophisticated machinery. One such device, the tunneling mole, utilizes a rotating wheel set with teeth that continuously excavates material and loads it onto a conveyor belt. When the ground being excavated is extremely soft or a tunnel of large diameter is being constructed, it is sometimes necessary to use what is called the multiple-drift method: a number of small, parallel drifts are bored and connected to create the sides and crown, or top, of the tunnel; the core can then be safely excavated.

Soft-ground tunnels can be built under rivers or in water-bearing strata by using a tunneling shield. The problem of tunneling under a river had defied the engineering imagination for centuries because of the difficulty of preventing mud and water from seeping in and causing the tunnel to collapse. In 1818 Marc Isambard Brunel, a former French naval officer who had immigrated to England, observed the action of a tiny marine borer, the shipworm. The animal's shell plates permitted it to bore through timber and push the sawdust out behind it. Brunel built a giant iron casing, or shield, that could be pushed forward through soft ground by means of screw jacks, while miners dug through shutter openings in the face.

Brunel's rectangular shield was used successfully in driving the world's first underwater tunnel beneath the River Thames in London in 1825–42. Later improvements on Brunel's shield included that of Peter Barlow in 1865, perfected by James Henry Greathead to burrow under the Thames. In the 1880s Greathead used compressed air behind a shield in a

London subway tunnel to prevent flooding while the lining was being installed. Modern tunneling shields are essentially the same as the Greathead design—that is, strong steel cylinders shoved forward by hydraulic jacks.

Tunneling through rock

Although tunnels through solid rock can be excavated at only about half the rate of tunnels through soft earth, rock bores have much longer stand-up times. If a tunnel is pushed through unfractured blocks, it may need little or no additional support. Tunnelers, however, must be able to change their method of tunneling quickly to suit the conditions. Jointed rock exists in much larger sections and may not settle or shift for several days. Rock bolts, which are rods driven into the joints and kept under tension with nuts, provide extra support.

The introduction of gunpowder blasting in the 17th century marked a great advance in solid-rock excavation. Railroad and, later, motor-vehicle transportation in the 19th–20th centuries led to a tremendous expansion in the number and length of tunnels. Brick and stone were used for support in early tunnels, but in modern tunneling steel is generally used until a concrete lining can be installed. A common method of lining involves spraying a cement mixture called shotcrete onto the tunnel crown immediately after excavation. A permanent shield can then be built by thickening the concrete lining; steel ribs can be used for additional support.

The problem of water inflow can occur in any type of tunneling operation; it is a constant danger during the construction of underwater tunnels. An early solution involved using a pressurized excavation chamber that held back incoming water. Alternative methods include the construction of drainage tunnels and the use of prefabricated sections that can be floated into position, sunk, and attached to other sections.

History

Ancient civilizations used tunnels to divert water for consumption and farming, and cave dwellers cut short passageways through clay or soft rock to connect adjacent caves or burrow into the sides of hills. In about 2180–60 BC the Babylonians built a tunnel for pedestrian traffic under the Euphrates River. An early Greek tunnel was completed in 687 BC on the island of Samos as part of an aqueduct system.

Initial tunnel-building techniques varied. The Egyptians used copper saws that were capable of cutting soft rock, while the Babylonians constructed masonry tunnels. The Romans built aqueduct tunnels through mountains by heating the rock face with fire and rapidly cooling it with water, causing the rock to crack.

Their greatest feat was a 3.5-mile (5.6-kilometer) tunnel to drain Lake Fucino in Italy to create Fucino Basin.

The first tunnel that can rightly be called modern was built near Malpas, France, as part of the Canal du Midi, or Languedoc Canal. More than 500 feet (150 meters) long, the tunnel was completed in the late 1600s. The Union Canal Tunnel in Pennsylvania, several hundred miles long and completed in 1826, is the oldest existing transportation tunnel in the US. The Hoosac Tunnel, drilled for a railroad through the Berkshire Mountains in Massachusetts in 1851–75, contributed advances in tunneling, including the first use of nitroglycerin as a blasting agent, the first use of electric firing of explosives, and the introduction of power drills—initially steam and later air, from which there ultimately developed a compressed-air industry.

Simultaneously, more spectacular railroad tunnels were being started through the Alps, beginning with the Mont Cenis Tunnel (1857–71). Its engineer, Germain Sommeiller, introduced pioneering techniques such as rail-mounted drill carriages, hydraulic ram air compressors, and construction camps for workers. Subsequent Alpine railroad tunnels were the 9-mile St. Gotthard (1872–82), the 12-mile Simplon (1898–1906), and the 9-mile Lötschberg (1906–11). Nearly 7,000 feet below the mountain crest, Simplon encountered major problems from highly stressed rock bursting off the walls; from high pressure in weak schists and gypsum, requiring 10-foot-thick masonry lining to resist swelling; and from high-temperature water (130 °F [54 °C]), which was partly treated by spraying from cold springs. Driving Simplon as two parallel tunnels with frequent crosscut connections considerably aided ventilation and drainage. The Mont Blanc Tunnel, which links France and Italy through the Alps, was at its opening in 1965 the world's longest vehicular tunnel.

Other tunnels of note include the Cascade Tunnel (1925–29) in Washington, at 7.8 miles (12.5 km) in length, and the Kanmon Tunnel (1936–44), connecting the Japanese islands of Honshu and Kyushu—the first tunnel built under an ocean. The Seikan Tunnel (1964–88) links Honshu to Hokkaido and is the longest tunnel in the world, with a length of 33.5 miles (53.9 km). A series of passageways, extending the Italian high-speed railway system through the Apennine Range between Bologna and Florence, Italy, is projected to top Seikan as the world's longest, with 41 miles (66 km) of tunnel scheduled to be driven by 2006. One of the most famous tunnels, opened in 1994, is the Eurotunnel, or Channel Tunnel (or Chunnel), a 31-mile (50-kilometer) route beneath the English Channel, connecting Folkestone, England, with Sangatte (near Calais), France.

The World's 25 Longest Tunnels

TUNNEL	LOCATION	LENGTH IN KM (MI)	COMPLETED	USE
Seikan	Japan	53.9 (33.5)	1988	railway
passes under the Tsugaru Strait between islands of Honshu and Hokkaido				
Channel Tunnel (Eurotunnel)	UK–France	50.5 (31.4)	1994	railway
passes under English Channel between Folkestone (UK) and Sangatte (France)				
Iwate-Ichinohe	Japan	25.8 (15.7)	2002	railway
carries Tohoku high-speed line through mountains between Tokyo and northern Honshu				
Lærdal	Norway	24.5 (15.3)	2000	highway
carries main cross-country highway through mountains in central Norway				
Daishimizu	Japan	22.2 (13.8)	1982	railway
on Joetsu Line across Honshu between Tokyo and Niigata				

The World's 25 Longest Tunnels (continued)

TUNNEL	LOCATION	LENGTH IN KM (MI)	COMPLETED	USE
Simplon II	Italy–Switzerland	19.8 (12.3)	1922	railway
Simplon I	Italy–Switzerland	19.8 (12.3)	1906	railway
rail links under Simplon Pass, traditional divide between northern and southern Europe				
Vereina	Switzerland	19.1 (11.9)	1999	railway
rail link under Flüela Pass between upper Rhine and lower Engadin valleys				
Shin-Kanmon	Japan	18.7 (11.6)	1975	railway
carries Sanyo high-speed line under Kanmon Strait between islands of Honshu and Kyushu				
Great Apennine	Italy	18.5 (11.5)	1934	railway
rail link through mountains between Bologna and Florence				
Qinling	China	18.5 (11.5)	2001	railway
traverses Qinling (Tsinling) Mountains, historic barrier between northern and southern China				
Saint Gotthard	Switzerland	16.9 (10.5)	1980	highway
links Uri and Ticino cantons under St. Gotthard Pass				
Rokko	Japan	16.3 (10.1)	1972	railway
carries Sanyo high-speed line through Rokko Mountains near Kobe				
Furka	Switzerland	15.4 (9.6)	1982	railway
carries scenic Glacier Express line under Furka Pass				
Haruna	Japan	15.4 (9.6)	1982	railway
on Joetsu Line across Honshu between Tokyo and Niigata				
Saint Gotthard	Switzerland	15 (9.3)	1882	railway
carries Luzern–Milan line under St. Gotthard Pass between Uri and Ticino cantons				
Nakayama	Japan	14.9 (9.2)	1982	railway
on Joetsu Line across Honshu between Tokyo and Niigata				
Lötschberg	Switzerland	14.6 (9.1)	1913	railway
rail link under Lötschen Pass between Bern and Valais cantons				
Mount MacDonald	British Columbia	14.6 (9.1)	1988	railway
carries Canadian Pacific Railway under Rogers Pass in Glacier National Park				
Dayaoshan (Ta-yao Shan)	China	14.3 (8.9)	1988	railway
carries dual-track line through Nan Mountains, northern Guangdong province				
Arlberg	Austria	14 (8.7)	1978	highway
provides road link under Arlberg Pass between Tirol and Vorarlberg provinces				
Hokuriku	Japan	13.9 (8.6)	1962	railway
on Hokuriku Line along Sea of Japan				
Romeriks	Norway	13.9 (8.6)	1999	railway
on high-speed rail line between Oslo and airport at Gardermoen				
Mount Cenis	France–Italy	13.7 (8.5)	1871	railway
carries main Paris–Turin line through Alps At Fréjus Pass				
Shin-Shimizu	Japan	13.5 (8.4)	1967	railway
on Joetsu Line across Honshu between Tokyo and Niigata				

World's Largest Dams

Source: International Water Power and Dam Construction Yearbook *(1996).*

NAME	TYPE*	DATE OF COMPLETION	RIVER	COUNTRY	
by height					**height (m)**
Nurek	E	1980	Vakhsh	Tajikistan	300
Grand Dixence	G	1961	Dixence	Switzerland	285
Inguri	A	1980	Inguri	Georgia	272
Vaiont[1]	A	1961	Vaiont	Italy	262
Chicoasen	ER	1980	Grijalva	Mexico	261
Tehri	ER	2002[2]	Bhagirathi	India	261
Mauvoisin	A	1957	Drance de Bagnes	Switzerland	250
Guavio	ER	1989	Guavio	Colombia	246
Sayano-Shushensk	AG	1989	Yenisey	Russia	245
Mica	ER	1973	Columbia	Canada	242
Ertan	A	1999	Yalong (Ya-lung)	China	240
Chivor	ER	1957	Batá	Colombia	237
					volume
by volume					**('000 cubic m)**
Syncrude Tailings	E	N/A	...[3]	Canada	540,000
New Cornelia Tailings	E	1973	Ten Mile Wash	US	209,500
Tarbela	ER	1976	Indus	Pakistan	106,000
Fort Peck	E	1937	Missouri	US	96,050
Lower Usuma	E	1990	Usuma	Nigeria	93,000

World's Largest Dams (continued)

NAME	TYPE*	DATE OF COMPLETION	RIVER	COUNTRY	
by volume (continued)					volume ('000 cubic m)
Tucurui	EGR	1984	Tocantins	Brazil	85,200
Ataturk	ER	1990	Euphrates	Turkey	84,500
Guri	EGR	1986	Caroni	Venezuela	77,971
Oahe	E	1958	Missouri	US	66,517
Gardiner	E	1968	Saskatchewan	Canada	65,400
Mangla	E	1967	Jhelum	Pakistan	65,379
Afsluitdijk	E	1932	IJsselmeer	The Netherlands	63,430
by size of reservoir					reservoir capacity ('000 cubic m)
Owen Falls	G	1954	Victoria Nile	Uganda	2,700,000,000[4]
Kakhovsk	EG	1955	Dnieper	Ukraine	182,000,000
Kariba	A	1959	Zambezi	Zimbabwe–Zambia	180,600,000
Bratsk	EG	1964	Angara	Russia	169,270,000
Aswan High	ER	1970	Nile	Egypt	168,900,000
Akosombo	ER	1965	Volta	Ghana	153,000,000
Daniel Johnson	M	1968	Manicouagan	Canada	141,852,000
Guri (Raúl Leoni)	EGR	1986	Caroní	Venezuela	138,000,000
Krasnoyarsk	G	1967	Yenisey	Russia	73,300,000
W.A.C. Bennett	E	1967	Peace	Canada	70,309,000
Zeya	B	1978	Zeya	Russia	68,400,000
Cabora Bassa	A	1974	Zambezi	Mozambique	63,000,000
by power capacity					power capacity (megawatts)
Itaipú	EGR	1983	Paraná	Brazil–Paraguay	13,320
Guri (Raúl Leoni)	EGR	1986	Caroní	Venezuela	10,055
Grand Coulee	G	1942	Columbia	US	6,809
Sayano-Shushenskoye	GA	1989	Yenisey	Russia	6,400
Krasnoyarsk	G	1968	Yenisey	Russia	6,000
Churchill Falls	E	1971	Churchill	Canada	5,428
La Grande 2	R	1979	LaGrande	Canada	5,328
Three Gorges	G	2003	Yangtze	China	4,970
Bratsk	EG	1961	Angara	Russia	4,500
Ust-Ilim	R	1977	Angara	Russia	4,320
Tucurui (Raúl G. Lhano)	EGR	1984	Tocantins	Brazil	4,240
Ertan	A	1999	Yalong (Ya-lung)	China	3,492

*Key: A, arch; B, buttress; E, earth fill; G, gravity; M, multi-arch; R, rock fill.   N/A indicates "not available." [1]Vaiont Dam was the scene of a massive landslide and flood in 1963 and no longer operates. [2]Diversion tunnels closed and reservoir filling begun December 2002. [3]Near Fort McMurray AB. [4]Most of this reservoir is a natural lake.

Lighthouses

A lighthouse is a structure, usually with a tower, built onshore or on the seabed to signal danger or to help those on ships determine location. Lighthouses have been built for centuries in areas where naval or commercial vessels sail. They have guided marine navigators through busy and often tortuous coastal waters and harbor approaches. Lighthouses were initially manned by lighthouse keepers, who lived in or nearby the structure in order to keep the light shining. Most modern lighthouses, however, have automatic lights that need little tending.

History
The first known lighthouse was built on the island of Pharos, near Alexandria, Egypt, about 280 BC. It was regarded as one of the seven wonders of the ancient world. The modern lighthouse dates only from the early 18th century. Initially made of **wood**, these towers were often washed away in severe storms.

The first lighthouse made of **interlocking masonry** blocks was built on the treacherous Eddystone Rocks reef, off Plymouth, England. Celebrated in ballad and folklore, it endured four successive constructions: in timber (1696–99), until it was swept out to sea in 1703; in oak and iron (1708), until it was destroyed by fire in 1755; in interlocking stone (1756–59), until its foundation deteriorated; and again in stone (1882). Interlocking masonry blocks remained the principal material of construction until they were replaced by **concrete** and **steel** in the 20th century.

Lighthouse construction
Modern construction techniques have facilitated the building of lighthouses in the open sea. On soft ground, the **submerged caisson** method is used, a system applied first in the late 19th century in Germany and the United States. With this method a large steel caisson is sunk deep into the seabed, then

pumped dry and filled with concrete to form a solid base on which the lighthouse proper is built. Where the seabed is suitable, it is possible to build a **float-out lighthouse**, consisting of a cylindrical tower—constructed on shore, towed out to sea, and sunk into position—with a broad concrete base that is fillled with sand. This design was pioneered largely in Sweden.

Another design, which is more independent of seabed conditions, is the **conventional steel-piled structure** used for offshore oil and gas rigs. Piles may be driven as deep as 46 m (150 ft) into the seabed, depending on the underlying strata. Helicopters are widely employed in the servicing and maintenance of offshore towers, so that modern designs normally include a helipad.

Lighthouse illumination
Historically illuminants included **wood** fires, discontinued c. 1800, and **coal**, begun c. 1550. In 1782 Swiss scientist Aimé Argand invented an **oil lamp** with a steady smokeless flame. It had a circular wick with a glass chimney that ensured an adequate current of air up the center and the outside of the wick for even combustion of the oil. These lamps originally burned **fish oil**, later **vegetable oil**, and by 1860 **mineral oil**. The Argand lamp became the principal lighthouse illuminant for more than 100 years. In 1901 the Briton Arthur Kitson invented the **vaporized oil burner**, which was subsequently improved by David Hood of Trinity House and others. This burner utilized **kerosene** vaporized under pressure, mixed with air, and burned to heat an incandescent mantle.

Early proposals to use **coal gas** at lighthouses did not meet with great success. However, **acetylene gas**, generated in situ from calcium carbide and water and safe to compress for storage, was pioneered by Gustaf Dalén of Sweden between 1900 and 1910. Its great advantage was that it could be readily controlled; thus, for the first time automatic unattended lights were possible. Its main use today is in buoys, which inherently have to operate unattended. **Floating lights** (i.e., lightships and buoys) have an important function in coastal waters, guiding both passing ships and those making for or leaving harbor.

Liquefied petroleum gas, such as propane, has also found use as an illuminant, although both oil and gas lamps have largely been superseded by **electricity**.

Electric illumination in the form of **carbon arc lamps** was first employed at Dungeness, England, in 1862, even while oil lamps were still in vogue. The **electric-filament lamp**, which came into general use in the 1920s, is now the standard illuminant. Most lamps are of the **tungsten-halogen** type for better efficiency and longer life.

Optical equipment
With the advent of the **Argand lamp**, a reliable and steady illuminant, it became possible to develop effective optical apparatuses for increasing the intensity of the light. In the first equipment of this type, known as the **çatoptric system**, paraboloidal reflectors concentrated the light into a beam. In 1777 William Hutchinson of Liverpool, England, produced the first practical mirrors for lighthouses. The first revolving-beam lighthouse was at Carlsten, near Marstrand, Sweden, in 1781.

In 1828 Augustin Fresnel of France produced the first apparatus using the refracting properties of glass, now known as the **dioptric system**. On a lens panel he surrounded a central bull's-eye lens with a series of concentric glass prismatic rings. The panel collected light emitted by the lamp over a wide horizontal angle and also the light that would otherwise escape to the sky or to the sea, concentrating it into a narrow, horizontal pencil beam, which he later expanded to be several revolving beams and then a fixed all-around light. Thus emerged the full **Fresnel catadioptric system**, the basis of all lighthouse lens systems today, although many have been converted to electric lamps with electric-motor drives.

Other innovations
The limitations of purely visual navigation very early led to the idea of supplementary audible warning in lighthouses. Early **sound signals** included cannonfire and bells, but at the beginning of the 20th century, **compressed-air** fog signals, which sounded a series of blasts, were developed. The most widely used were the siren and the diaphone. A later compressed-air signal was the tyfon, employing a metal diaphragm vibrated by differential air pressure. Modern fog signals are almost invariably electric.

Radio and **satellite-based** navigation systems have greatly reduced the need for large lighthouses in sighting land.

Notable Civil Engineering Projects (in progress or completed as of December 2004)

NAME	LOCATION	terminal area (sq m)	YEAR OF COMPLETION	NOTES
airports				
Suvarnabhumi	near Bangkok, Thailand	563,000	2005	to replace Don Muang
Barajas International Airport (new Terminal 4)	northeast of Madrid, Spain	470,000	2005	new terminal in leading airport for Europe–Latin America flights
Changi International (new Terminal 3)	eastern Singapore	430,000	2006	new terminal in Asia's 4th largest airport
Toronto Pearson International (new Terminal 1)	Toronto, ON, Canada	340,000	2004	opened 6 Apr 2004; new terminal at Canada's busiest airport
Baiyun ("White Cloud") International (replacement)	near Guangzhou, China	305,000	2004	opened 5 Aug 2004; main hub airport of south China (excluding Hong Kong)

Notable Civil Engineering Projects (in progress or completed as of December 2004) (continued)

NAME	LOCATION	terminal area (sq m)	YEAR OF COMPLETION	NOTES
airports (continued)				
Ben-Gurion International (new Terminal 3)	southeast of Tel Aviv, Israel	223,000	2004	opened 2 Nov 2004; new international terminal at the Middle East's busiest airport
Central Japan International	artificial island off Nagoya, Japan	220,000	2005	to be Japan's 3rd largest airport
Dallas/Fort Worth International (new Terminal D)	Irving TX	195,000	2005	new international terminal
Heathrow (new Terminal 5)	southwest of London	70,000	2008	biggest construction project in the UK from 2002

NAME	LOCATION	length (main span; m)	YEAR OF COMPLETION	NOTES
bridges				
Hangzhou Bay	near Jiaxing, China– near Cixi, China	2,600	2009	to be world's longest transoceanic bridge/ causeway; begun 2003
I-95 (Woodrow Wilson #2)	Alexandria VA– Maryland suburbs of Washington DC	1,829 each	2005–08	2 bascule spans forming higher inverted V shape for ships; begun 2000
Nancha (1 bridge of 2-section Runyang)	Zhenjiang, China (across the Yangtze)	1,490	2005	to be world's third longest suspension bridge
Sutong	Nantong, China (100 km from Yangtze mouth)	1,088	2008	to be world's longest cable-stayed bridge
Stonecutters	Tsing Yi-Sha Tin, Hong Kong, China	1,018	2008	to be world's 2nd longest cable-stayed bridge
Tacoma Narrows (#3)	the Narrows of Puget Sound, Tacoma WA	853	2008	built over collapsed Tacoma Narrows #1; longest US suspension bridge since 1964
Rion–Antirion	near Patrai, Greece (across Gulf of Corinth)	560	2004	opened 8 Aug 2004; 2nd longest all-span cable-stayed (2,252 m)
(New) Cooper River	Charleston– Mt. Pleasant SC	471	2005	to be longest cable-stayed bridge in North America
Millau Viaduct	Tarn Gorge, west of Millau, France	342	2004	opened 14 Dec 2004; world's highest (270 m) bridge; longest all-span cable-stayed (2,460 m) bridge
Shibanpe	Chongqing, China (across the Yangtze)	330	2005	to be world's longest pre-stressed-concrete box girder bridge

NAME	LOCATION	height (m)	YEAR OF COMPLETION	NOTES
buildings				
Burj ("Tower") Dubai	Dubai, United Arab Emirates	805	2008	To be the world's tallest building
Taipei 101 (Taipei Financial Center)	Taipei, Taiwan	508	2003	declared world's tallest building 15 Apr 2004; opened in stages from November 2003
Shanghai World Financial Center	Shanghai, China	492	2007	begun 1997, resumed 2003; to be the world's 2nd tallest building
Union Square Phase 7	Hong Kong	474	2007	begun 2002; 16-building complex
Federation Tower A	Moscow, Russia	340	2007	to be tallest building in Europe
Eureka Tower	Melbourne, Australia	300	2005	to be the 2nd tallest residential building in the world

NAME	LOCATION	crest length (m)	YEAR OF COMPLETION	NOTES
dams and hydrologic projects				
Three Gorges (3rd of 3 phases)	west of Yichang, China	1,983	2009	to create world's largest reservoir (620 km long) beginning 2003 and ⅑th of national total generated power
Sardar Sarovar (Narmada) Project	Narmada River, Madhya Pradesh, India	1,210	2007	largest dam of controversial 30-dam project; drinking water for Gujarat

Notable Civil Engineering Projects (in progress or completed as of December 2004) (continued)

NAME	LOCATION		YEAR OF COMPLETION	NOTES
dams and hydrologic projects (continued)		crest length (m)		
Bakun Dam	Balui River, Sarawak, Borneo, Malaysia	740	2007	will bring hydroelectricity to peninsular Malaysia via world's longest submarine cable
Caruachi (3rd of 5-dam Lower Caroní Development scheme)	Caroní River, northern Bolívar, Venezuela	360	2003–06	hydroelectric generation began 28 Feb 2003
Belo Monte	Xingù River, Pará, Brazil	?	2008	to be 3rd largest dam in the world in terms of electricity output
Tucuruí (upgrade)	Tocantins River, eastern Pará, Brazil	?	2005	generating capacity to be doubled; 1st Brazilian Amazon dam (1984)
Project Moses (flood-protection plan)	Venice, Italy	–	2010	79 submerged gates in 3 lagoon openings will rise in flood conditions
highways		length (km)		
Golden Quadrilateral superhighway	Mumbai–Chennai–Kolkata–Delhi, India	5,846	2005–07	upgrade to 4 lanes; Mumbai–Delhi (2005), Delhi–Kolkata (2007)
Trans-Siberian highway (final stage)	Khabarovsk–Chita, Russia	2,165	2004	opened 26 Feb 2004; last link in 10,000-km Moscow–Vladivostok highway
Highway 1	Kabul–Kandahar–Herat, Afghanistan	1,048	2005	final, 566-km Kandahar–Herat section to open in September
Egnatia Motorway	Igoumenitsa–Kipi, Greece	680	2006	first Greek highway at international standards; 76 tunnels, 1,650 bridges
Croatian Motorway	Zagreb–Split, Croatia	380	2005	mountainous terrain with unstable slopes, caves, and unexploded ordnance
land reclamation		area (sq km)		
Palm Jumeirah and Palm Jebel Ali islands	in the Persian Gulf, near Dubai, UAE	20–40	2006–09	date-palm-tree-shaped islands ("two 17 fronds + trunk" and one 41 fronds + trunk); ultraexclusive
railways (heavy)		length (km)		
Trans-Kazakhstan	Dostyq (Druzhba), Kazakhstan–Gorgan, Iran	3,943	2008	China to Europe link, bypassing Russia and Uzbekistan; 3,083 km in Kazakhstan
Qinghai–Tibet	China: Golmud, Qinghai–Lhasa, Tibet	1,142	2007	world's highest railway (5,072 m at summit); 86% above 4,000 m
Xi'an–Nanjing	China: Xi'an, Shaanxi–Nanjing, Jiangsu	1,129	2007	for economic growth in interior; 954-km Xi'an-Hefei section finished 2003
Ferronorte (extension to Rondonópolis)	Alto Araguaia–Rondonópolis, Brazil	270	2007	for agricultural exports from Mato Grosso (Brazil interior)
Bothnia Line (Botniabanan)	Nyland–Umeå, Sweden	190	2010	along north Swedish coast; difficult terrain with 25 km of tunnels
railways (high speed)		length (km)		
Spanish high speed (second line)	Madrid, Spain–France (via Barcelona)	719	2009	to reach Barcelona in 2007?; Madrid–Lleida corridor opened 11 Oct 2003
Korea Train Express (KTX)	Seoul–Pusan, South Korea	412	2008	will connect largest and 2nd largest cities; to Taegu as of 1 Apr 2004

Notable Civil Engineering Projects (in progress or completed as of December 2004) (continued)

NAME	LOCATION		YEAR OF COMPLETION	NOTES
railways (high speed) (continued)		length (km)		
Taiwan high speed	Hsi-chih–Tso-ying, Taiwan	345	2005	links Taiwan's 2 largest cities (Taipei and Kao-hsiung) along west coast
Eastern France high speed	eastern outskirts of Paris–near Metz, France	300	2007	106-km extension to Strasbourg in planning stage
Italian high speed (second line)	Rome–Naples, Italy	205	2005	entire Turin–Naples high-speed routes (844 km) to be completed 2009?
Channel Tunnel Rail Link	near Folkestone, England–central London	109	2007	74-km section (Folkestone–north Kent) opened 16 Sep 2003
subways/metros/light rails		length (km)		
Shanghai Metro	Shanghai, China	99.9	2005-06	length of 4 lines under construction in late 2004
Barcelona Metro (Line 9)	airport–northeast Barcelona, Spain	47	2008	connects to other metro lines and future high-speed rail
Guangzhou (Canton) Metro (Line 3)	Guangzhou, China (north-south line)	36.1	2006	15-line system planned; 83 km in 4 lines under construction in 2004
Shenzhen Metro (phase 1; Lines 1 and 4)	Shenzhen, China (adjacent to Hong Kong)	21.8	2004	phase 1 of both lines began operation 28 Dec 2004
Delhi Metro (Line 1)	Delhi, India	21.3	2004	opened 31 Mar 2004; 30.2 km of lines 2 and 3 to in open 2005
Copenhagen Metro (last extension)	Copenhagen, Denmark	21	2007	connects city center to airport
Bangkok Blue Line	north-south line in central Bangkok, Thailand	20	2004	opened to the public 3 Jul 2004; Thailand's first underground system
Hiawatha Light Rail	downtown Minneapolis–Bloomington MN	19.3	2004	opened 4 Dec 2004
Las Vegas Monorail	Las Vegas NV (east side of the Strip)	6.1	2004	opened 14 Jul 2004, temp. closure 8 Sep–23 Dec 2004; 5-km extension by 2007?
tunnels		length (m)		
Apennine Range tunnels (9)	Bologna–Florence, Italy (high-speed railway)	73,400	2008	longest tunnel (Vaglia, 18.6 km); tunnels to cover 93% of railway
Lötschberg #2	Frutigen–Raron, Switzerland	34,577	2007	to be world's 3rd longest rail tunnel; France–Italy link
Guadarrama	50 km north-northwest of Madrid, Spain	28,377	2007	to be world's 4th longest rail tunnel; Valladolid high-speed link
Södra Länken ("Southern Link")	part of Stockholm, Sweden, ring road	16,600	2004	opened 24 Oct 2004; complex of underground interchanges
Hsüeh-shan ("Snow Mountain")	near Taipei, Taiwan	12,900	2005	breakthrough 16 Sep 2004; world's 4th longest road tunnel
East and West tunnels of A86 ring road	western outskirts of Paris, France	10,000/ 7,500	2007	two tunnels under Versailles and nearby protected woodlands

1 m=3.28 ft; 1 km=0.62 mi

Life on Earth

Taxonomy

Taxonomy is the classification of living and extinct organisms. The term is derived from the Greek *taxis* ("arrangement") and *nomos* ("law") and refers to the methodology and principles of systematic botany and zoology and sets up arrangements of the kinds of plants and animals in hierarchies of superior and subordinate groups.

Popularly, classifications of living organisms arise according to need and are often superficial; for example, although the term fish is common to the names shellfish, crayfish, and starfish, there are more anatomical differences between a shellfish and a starfish than there are between a bony fish and a human. Also, vernacular names vary widely. Biologists have attempted to view all living organisms with equal thoroughness and thus have devised a formal classification. A formal classification supports a relatively uniform and internationally understood nomenclature, thereby simplifying cross-referencing and retrieval of information.

Carolus Linnaeus, who is usually regarded as the founder of modern taxonomy and whose books are considered the beginning of modern botanical and zoological nomenclature, drew up rules for assigning names to plants and animals and was the first to use binomial nomenclature consistently, beginning in 1758. Classification since Linnaeus has incorporated newly discovered information and more closely approaches a natural system, and the process of clarifying relationships continues to this day. The table below shows the seven ranks that are accepted as obligatory by zoologists and botanists and sample listings for animals and plants.

	ANIMALS	PLANTS
Kingdom	Animalia	Plantae
Phylum/Division	Chordata	Tracheophyta
Class	Mammalia	Pteropsida
Order	Primates	Coniferales
Family	Hominidae	Pinaceae
Genus	*Homo*	*Pinus*
Species	*Homo sapiens* (human)	*Pinus strobus* (white pine)

Animals

Notable Venomous Animals

Instances where the exact chemical makeup of a toxin has not been established are indicated as "unknown."

REPRESENTATIVE VENOMOUS ANIMALS THAT INFLICT A STING

Marine animals

crown-of-thorns starfish (*Acanthaster planci*; Indo-Pacific): unknown (penetration of spines produces a painful wound, redness, swelling, vomiting, numbness, and paralysis)

long-spined sea urchin (*Diadema setosum*; Indo-Pacific): unknown (penetration of spines produces an immediate and intense burning sensation, redness, swelling, numbness, muscular paralysis)

Portuguese man-of-war (*Physalia* species; tropical seas): tetramine, 5-hydroxytryptamine (immediate stinging, throbbing, or burning sensation; inflammatory rash; blistering; shock; collapse; death in very rare cases)

scorpion fish (*Scorpaena* species; temperate and tropical seas): unknown (fin spines can inflict painful stings and intense, immediate pain, followed by redness, swelling, loss of consciousness, ulceration of the wound, paralysis, cardiac failure, delirium, convulsions, nausea, prostration, and respiratory distress, but rarely death; no known antidote)

sea anemone (*Actinia equina*; Mediterranean, Black Sea, etc.): unknown (burning or stinging sensation, itching, swelling, redness, ulceration, nausea, vomiting, prostration; no specific antidote)

sea urchin (*Toxopneustes pileolus*; Indo-Pacific): unknown (bites from stinging jaws or small pincerlike organs produce an immediate, intense, radiating pain, faintness, numbness, muscular paralysis, respiratory distress, and occasionally death)

spotted octopus (*Octopus maculosus*; Indo-Pacific, Indian Ocean): cephalotoxin, a neuromuscular poison (sharp stinging pain, numbness of mouth and tongue, blurred vision, loss of tactile sensation, difficulty in speech and swallowing, paralysis of legs, nausea, prostration, coma, death in a high percentage of cases)

stingray (*Dasyatis* species; warm temperate and tropical seas): cardiotoxin (penetration of tail spines inflicts jagged wounds that produce sharp, shooting, throbbing pain, fall in blood pressure, nausea, vomiting, cardiac failure, muscular paralysis, and rarely death; no known antidote; stingrays are among the most common causes of envenomizations in the marine environment)

stonefish (*Synanceja* species; Indo-Pacific region): unknown (produces an extremely painful sting by means of the dorsal fin spines; symptoms similar to other scorpion fish stings but more serious)

weever fish (*Trachinus draco*; Mediterranean Sea): unknown (penetration of opercular and dorsal fin spines can produce instant pain, burning, stabbing, or crushing sensation; pain spreads and becomes progressively more intense, causing victim to lose consciousness; numbness around the wound, swelling, redness, nausea, delirium, difficulty breathing, convulsions, and death; no known antidote)

Arthropods

kissing bug (*Triatoma* species; Latin America, US): unknown (bite usually painless; later itching, edema around the bite, nausea, palpitation, redness; the bite is of minor importance but spreads Chagas' disease caused by a trypanosome)

honeybee (*Apis* species; worldwide): neurotoxin, hemolytic, melittin, hyaluronidase, phospholipase A, histamine, and others (acute local pain or burning sensation, blanching at site of sting surrounded by redness, and itching; local symptoms usually disappear after 24 hours; severe cases may develop massive swelling, shock, prostration, vomiting, rapid heartbeat, respiratory distress, trembling, coma, and death; estimated that 500 stings in a short period of time can produce a lethal dose; bee stings kill more people in the US than do venomous reptiles)

bumblebee (*Bombus* species; temperate regions): similar to (*Apis*) honeybee venom (stings are similar to honeybee stings; bumblebees are not as vicious as honeybees)

yellow jacket, hornet (*Vespula* species; temperate regions): similar to bee venom; also acetylcholine (yellow jackets are quite aggressive and can both bite and sting; the sting is similar to a honeybee's but more painful and may be fatal)

wasp (*Polistes* and *Vespa* species; worldwide): similar to bee venom; also acetylcholine (wasps are less aggressive than hornets, and their stings are similar to the honeybee's but generally less painful than the hornet's; stings may be fatal)

harvester ant (*Pogonomyrmex* species; US): bradykinin, formic acid, hyaluronidase, hemolytic, phospholipase A, and others (immediate intense burning, pain, blanched area at site of sting surrounded by redness, ulceration, fever, blistering, itching, hemorrhaging into the skin, eczematoid dermatitis, pustules, respiratory distress, prostration, coma, and death in some instances)

fire ant (*Solenopsis* species; US, Latin America): similar to harvester ant venom

millipede (*Apheloria* species [and others]; temperate areas): hydrogen cyanide and benzaldehyde (toxic liquid or gas from lateral glands causes inflammation, swelling, and blindness in contact with eyes; brown stain, swelling, redness, and vesicle formation in contact with skin)

centipede (*Scolopendra* species; temperate and tropical regions): hemolytic phospholipase and serotonin (local pain, swelling, and redness at bite site)

brown spider (*Loxosceles* species; US, South America, Europe, Asia): cytotoxic, hyaluronidase, hemolytic, and others (bite causes stinging or burning, blanching at site of bite surrounded by redness, blistering, hemorrhaging into the skin and internal organs, ulceration, vomiting, fever, cardiovascular collapse, convulsions, and sometimes death)

black widow (*Latrodectus* species; tropical and temperate regions): neurotoxin (bite may be painful; two tiny red dots at site, localized swelling after a few minutes; intense cramping pain of abdomen, legs, chest, back; rigidity of muscles lasting 12–48 hours, nausea, sweating, respiratory distress, abnormal and painful erection of the penis, chills, skin rash, restlessness, fever, numbness, tingling; about 4% are fatal; antiserum is available)

tarantula (*Dugesiella* and *Lycosa* species; temperate and tropical regions): venom varies, usually mild (most of the large tarantulas found in the US, Mexico, and Central America are harmless to humans;

some of the large tropical species may be more poisonous, but their effects are largely localized)

scorpion (species of *Centruroides*, *Tityus*, and *Leiurus*; warm temperate and tropical regions): neurotoxin, cardiotoxin, hemolytic, lecithinase, hyaluronidase, and others (symptoms vary depending upon species; sting from the tail causes a sharp burning sensation, swelling, sweating, restlessness, salivation, confusion, vomiting, abdominal pain, chest pain, numbness, muscular twitching, respiratory distress, convulsions, and often death; the mortality rate from certain species of scorpions is very high; antiserum is available)

Reptiles

Gila monster (*Heloderma suspectum*; southwestern US): heloderma venom, primarily a neurotoxin (all of the teeth are venomous; bite causes local pain, swelling, weakness, ringing of the ears, nausea, respiratory distress, and cardiac failure; may cause death; no antiserum available)

REPRESENTATIVE CRINOTOXIC ANIMALS (THOSE THAT RELEASE POISON THROUGH A PORE)

Sponges

red moss (*Microciona prolifera*; eastern US coastal waters): unknown (contact produces chemical irritation of the skin, redness, stiffness of finger joints, swelling, blisters, and pustules)

Flatworms

flatworm (*Leptoplana tremellaris*; European coastal waters): unknown (poison is produced by epidermal skin glands; no human intoxications recorded, but extracts from the skin injected into laboratory animals produces cardiac arrest)

Arthropods

blister beetles (*Cantharis vesicatorea*; US): cantharidin (toxic substance is found throughout the body of the beetle; no discomfort from initial contact; after about 8–10 hours large blisters on the skin accompanied by slight burning or tingling; swallowing of the beetles may cause kidney damage; cantharidin is used as an aphrodisiac known as Spanish Fly, a very dangerous substance; ingestion can cause severe gastroenteritis, kidney damage, blood in the urine, abnormal and painful erection of the penis, profound collapse, and death)

venomous ticks (species of *Ixodes* and *Ornithodoros*; temperate and tropical regions): unknown (bites result in swelling, redness, intense pain, headache, muscle cramps, loss of memory)

Fishes

sea lamprey (*Petromyzon marinus*; Atlantic Ocean): unknown (slime is toxic; ingestion may cause diarrhea)

soapfish (*Rypticus saponaceus*; tropical and subtropical Atlantic): neurotoxin (slime is toxic; produces irritation of the mucous membrane)

Amphibians

European earth salamander (*Salamandra maculosa*; Europe): skin glands are poisonous; contain the alkaloids samandarine, samandenone, samandine, samanine, samandarone, samandaridine, and others (effects on humans not known; affects the heart and nervous system; in animals causes convulsions, cardiac irregularity, paralysis, and death)

toads (*Bufo* species; temperate and tropical regions):

bufotoxin, bufogenins, and 5-hydroxytryplanime; poison includes a complex of many substances (produces a poisonous secretion in parotid glands and skin; handling of some toads may cause skin irritation; ingestion causes nausea, vomiting, numbness of mouth and tongue, and tightness of chest; the poison has a digitalis-like action)

frogs (some species of *Dendrobates*, *Physalaemus*, and *Rana*; northern South America and Central America): skin secretions are poisonous; histamine, bufotenine, physalaemin, serotonin, and other substances; composition varies with the species (secretions produce a burning sensation; used by indigenous peoples as an arrow poison)

SELECTED HIGHLY VENOMOUS SNAKES

inland taipan (*Oxyuranus microlepidotus*): Australia
eastern brown snake (*Pseudonaja textilis*): Australia
Malayan krait (*Bungarus candidus*): Southeast Asia and Indonesia
coastal taipan (*Oxyuranus scutellatus*): Australia
tiger snake (*Notechis scutatus*): Australia
beaked sea snake (*Enhydrina schistosa*): South Asian waters
saw-scaled viper (*Echis carinatus*): Middle East, Asia
eastern coral snake (*Micrurus fulvius*): North America
boomslang (*Dispholidus typus*): Africa
death adder (*Acanthophis antarcticus*): Australia and New Guinea

Period of Gestation and Longevity of Selected Mammals

ANIMAL	AVERAGE GESTATION (DAYS)	AVERAGE LONGEVITY (YEARS)	ANIMAL	AVERAGE GESTATION (DAYS)	AVERAGE LONGEVITY (YEARS)
bear (black)	219	18	horse	330	20
bear (grizzly)	225	25	human (worldwide)	266–70	Men: 64.7; Women: 68.9
bear (polar)	240	20			
cat (domestic)	63	12	monkey (rhesus)	164	15
dog (domestic)	61	12	mouse (domestic white)	19	3
elephant (Asian)	645	40	pig (domestic)	112	10
fox (red)	52	7	rabbit (domestic)	31	5
guinea pig	68	4	sheep (domestic)	154	12
hippopotamus	238	25–30	squirrel (gray)	44	9–10

Names of the Male, Female, Young, and Group of Animals

ANIMAL	MALE	FEMALE	YOUNG	GROUP
ape	male	female	baby	shrewdness
bear	boar	sow	cub	sleuth, sloth
camel	bull	cow	calf	flock
cattle	bull	cow	calf	drift, drove, herd, mob
chicken	rooster	hen	chick, pullet (hen), cockrell (rooster)	flock, brood (hens), clutch & peep (chicks)
deer	buck, stag	doe	fawn	herd
donkey	jack, jackass	jennet, jenny	colt, foal	drove, herd
elephant	bull	cow	calf	herd, parade
ferret	hob	jill	kit	business, fesynes
fox	reynard	vixen	kit, cub, pup	skulk, leash
giraffe	bull	doe	calf	herd, corps, tower, group
goat	buck, billy	doe, nanny	kid, billy	herd, tribe, trip
gorilla	male	female	infant	band
hamster	buck	doe	pup	horde
hippopotamus	bull	cow	calf	herd, bloat
horse	stallion, stud	mare, dam	foal, colt (male), filly (female)	stable, harras, herd, team (working) string or field (racing)
human	man	woman	baby, infant, toddler	clan (related), crowd, family (closely related), community, gang, mob, tribe, etc.
lion	lion	lioness	cub	pride
louse	male	female	nymph	lice, colony, infestation
mouse	buck	doe	pup, pinkie, kitten	horde, mischief
ostrich	cock	hen	chick	flock
pig	boar	sow	piglet, shoat, farrow	drove, herd, litter (of pups), sounder
quail	cock	hen	chick	bevy, covey, drift
rhinoceros	bull	cow	calf	crash
seal	bull	cow	pup	herd, pod, rookery, harem
sheep	buck, ram	ewe, dam	lamb, lambkin, cosset	drift, drove, flock, herd, mob, trip
turkey	tom	hen	poult	rafter
turtle	male	female	hatchling	bale
whale	bull	cow	calf	gam, grind, herd, pod, school
wolf	dog	bitch	pup, whelp	pack, rout
zebra	stallion	mare	colt, foal	herd, crossing

Plants

Notable Medicinal Plants

Sources: <http://world.std.com/~krahe/html1.html>; <www.hort.purdue.edu/newcrop/med-aro/toc.html>.

PLANT	NATIVE REGION	MAIN PROPERTIES (USES)
angelica	Europe	antispasmodic, promotes menstrual flow
basil (holy basil)	India	antispasmodic, analgesic, fungicidal, lowers blood pressure, lowers blood sugar, reduces fever, anti-inflammatory
chamomile	Europe, Western Asia, North America, Africa	anti-inflammatory, antispasmodic, relaxant, carminative, bitter, nervine
chicory	Europe	digestive, liver tonic, anti-rheumatic, mild laxative
cinnamon	Sri Lanka	warming stimulant, carminative, antispasmodic, antiseptic, anti-viral
coriander	Europe, Mediterranean	digestive, antispasmodic, anti-rheumatic
cymbopogon (lemon grass)	Sri Lanka, south India	digestive, antispasmodic, analgesic
dandelion	Asia	diuretic, digestive, antibiotic, bitter
eucalyptus	Australia	antiseptic, expectorant, stimulates local blood flow, anti-fungal
fennel	Mediterranean	digestive, antispasmodic, anti-inflammatory
garlic	Central Asia	antibiotic, expectorant, diaphoretic, hypotensive, antispasmodic, expels worms
ginger	Southeast Asia	diaphoretic, carminative, circulatory stimulant, anti-inflammatory, antiseptic, inhibits coughing
ginkgo	China	anti-asthmatic, antispasmodic, anti-allergenic, anti-inflammatory, circulatory stimulant and tonic
ginseng	northeastern China, eastern Russia, Korea	tonic, stimulant, physical and mental revitalizer
gumplant	Southwestern US, Mexico	antispasmodic, expectorant, hypotensive
hamamelis (witch hazel)	eastern North America	astringent, anti-inflammatory, stops external and internal bleeding
hyssop	Mediterranean	antispasmodic, expectorant, diaphoretic, anti-inflammatory, hepatic
jasmine	Iran	aromatic, antispasmodic, expectorant
lavender	Mediterranean	carminative, antidepressant, antiseptic, antibacterial, stimulates blood flow, relieves muscle spasms
marjoram (wild marjoram)	Asia	antiseptic, antispasmodic, digestive
melissa (lemon balm)	Mediterranean	relaxant, antispasmodic, carminative, anti-viral, nerve tonic, increases sweating
myrrh	northeast Africa	stimulant, antiseptic, anti-inflammatory, astringent, expectorant, antispasmodic, carminative
nettle	Eurasia	diuretic, tonic, astringent, anti-allergenic, prevents hemorrhaging, reduces prostate enlargement (root)
parsley	North & Central Europe, Western Asia	digestive, diuretic
passiflora (passion flower)	North America	anti-inflammatory, antispasmodic, hypotensive, sedative, tranquilizing
peppermint	unknown	carminative, antiseptic, relieves muscle spasms, increases sweating, stimulates secretion of bile
rosemary	Mediterranean	tonic, stimulant, astringent, nervine, anti-inflammatory, carminative
rue	southern Europe	antispasmodic, increases peripheral blood circulation, relieves eye tension
sesame	Africa	digestive, aromatic, antispasmodic
St. John's wort	Europe	antidepressant, antispasmodic, astringent, sedative, anti-viral, relieves pain
thyme	western Mediterranean, southwest Italy	antiseptic, expectorant, tonic, relieves muscle spasm
turmeric	India, southern Asia	anti-inflammatory, antioxidant, antibacterial, eases stomach pain, stimulates secretion of bile
valerian	Europe, Western Asia	sedative, relaxant, relieves muscle spasm, relieves anxiety, lowers blood pressure
verbena	Europe	nervine, tonic, mild sedative, stimulates bile secretion, mild bitter
wormwood	Europe	aromatic bitter, anti-inflammatory, mild antidepressant, stimulates bile secretion, eliminates worms, eases stomach pains

Notable Medicinal Plants (continued)

PLANT	NATIVE REGION	MAIN PROPERTIES (USES)
yarrow	Europe	antispasmodic, astringent, bitter tonic, mild diuretic, urinary antiseptic, increases sweating, lowers blood pressure, reduces fever

World's Oldest Trees and Flowering Plants

	MAXIMUM AGE IN YEARS		
	ESTIMATED	VERIFIED	LOCATION
trees			
bristlecone pine		4,900	Wheeler Peak, Humboldt National Forest, Nevada
Sierra redwood	4,000	2,200–2,300	northern California
Swiss stone pine	1,200	750	Riffel Alp, Switzerland
common juniper	2,000	544	Kola Peninsula, northeastern Russia
European larch	700	417	Riffel Alp, Switzerland
Norway spruce	1,200	350–400	Eichstätt, Bavaria, Germany
flowering plants			
bo tree	2,000–3,000		Buddh Gaya, India; Anuradhapura, Ceylon
English oak	2,000	1,500	Hasbruch Forest, Lower Saxony, Germany
linden		815	Lithuania
European beech	900	250	Montigny, Normandy, France
English ivy	440		Ginac, near Montpellier, France
dragon tree	200		Tenerife, Canary Islands
dwarf birch		80	eastern Greenland

Endangerment

Selected Endangered Species: Flora

For a complete list of endangered and threatened flora, see
<http://endangered.fws.gov/wildlife.html#Species>.

Flowering plants
Akoko, Ewa Plains
Alani (*Melicope reflexa*)
Arrowhead, bunched
Avens, spreading
Ayenia, Texas
Bird's-beak, salt marsh
Bittercress, small-anthered
Bladderpod, Missouri
Bluegrass, Hawaiian
Bluet, Roan Mountain
Boxwood, Vahl's
Buckwheat, steamboat
Bulrush, Northeastern
Cactus, Key tree
Cactus, Knowlton
Cactus, Pima pineapple
Cactus, Sneed pincushion
Cactus, star
Campion, fringed
Chaffseed, American
Checker-mallow, pedate
Clarkia, Pismo
Clover, running buffalo
Clover, showy Indian
Coneflower, smooth
Desert-parsley, Bradshaw's
Dropwort, Canby's
Flannelbush, Mexican
Frankenia, Johnston's
Geranium, Hawaiian
  red-flowered
Gerardia, sandplain
Grass, Tennessee yellow-eyed

Flowering plants (continued)
Ha'iwale (*Cyrtandra munroi*)
Haha (*Cyanea superba*)
Harperella
Hau kuahiwi (*Hibiscadelphus giffardianus*)
Iagu, Hayun
Ipomopsis, Holy Ghost
Jewelflower, California
Kamakahala (*Labordia lanaiensis*)
Koki'o, Cooke's
Larkspur, San Clemente Island
Lau'ehu
Lily, Western
Liveforever, Santa Barbara Island
Loosestrife, rough-leaved
Lo'ulu (*Pritchardia munroi*)
Lousewort, Furbish
Love grass, Fosberg's
Lupine, scrub
Manioc, Walker's
Mesa-mint, Otay
Milk-vetch, Jesup's
Milk-vetch, Mancos
Mint, longspurred
Monardella, willowy
Na'ena'e (*Dubautia herbstobatae*)
Nehe (*Lipochaeta lobata*)
Niterwort, Amargosa
'Oha wai (*Clermontia mauiensis*)
Orcutt grass, California
Penstemon, blowout

Flowering plants (continued)
Phacelia, clay
Pinkroot, gentian
Pitcher-plant, green
Pitcher-plant, mountain sweet
Pondberry
Prairie-clover, leafy
Prickly-ash, St. Thomas
Rock-cress, Hoffmann's
Rock-cress, McDonald's
Rock-cress, shale barren
Rosemary, short-leaved
Sandwort, Cumberland
Sandwort, Marsh
Spineflower, slender-horned
Sumac, Michaux's
Sunflower, Schweinitz's
Thistle, Chorro Creek bog
Trillium, persistent
Trillium, relict
Wallflower, Contra Costa
Walnut, West Indian or nogal
Water-umbel, Huachuca

Conifers and cycads
Cypress, Santa Cruz
Torreya, Florida

Ferns and allies
Diellia, asplenium-leaved
Fern, Aleutian shield
Fern, Elfin tree
Fern, pendant kihi
Ihi'ihi

Selected Endangered Species: Flora (continued)

Ferns and allies (continued)
Pauoa
Quillwort, black spored
Quillwort, Louisiana

Ferns and allies (continued)
Quillwort, mat-forming
Wawae'iole (*Huperzia mannii*)
Wawae'iole (*Lycopodium nutans*)

Lichens
Lichen, rock gnome

The World's Forests

This table shows the 50 countries that either lost or gained the most forest area between 1990 and 2000 as well as forest losses or gains by continent. Source: State of the World's Forests 2001.
1 hectare (ha) = x .01 sq km, .004 sq mi. Web site: <www.fao.org/forestry>.

COUNTRY/AREA	LAND AREA ('000 HA)	TOTAL FOREST, 1990 ('000 HA)	TOTAL FOREST IN 2000 ('000 HA)	PERCENTAGE OF LAND AREA IN 2000 (%)	% CHANGE 1990-2000
Burundi	2,568	241	94	3.7	−61.00
Haiti	2,756	158	88	3.2	−44.30
Micronesia	69	24	15	21.7	−37.50
El Salvador	2,072	193	121	5.8	−37.31
Saint Lucia	61	14	9	14.8	−35.71
Comoros	186	12	8	4.3	−33.33
Rwanda	2,466	457	307	12.4	−32.82
Niger	126,670	1,945	1,328	1	−31.72
Togo	5,439	719	510	9.4	−29.07
Côte d'Ivoire	31,800	9,766	7,117	22.4	−27.12
Nicaragua	12,140	4,450	3,278	27	−26.34
Sierra Leone	7,162	1,416	1,055	14.7	−25.49
Mauritania	102,522	415	317	0.3	−23.61
Nigeria	91,077	17,501	13,517	14.8	−22.76
Malawi	9,409	3,269	2,562	27.2	−21.63
Zambia	74,339	39,755	31,246	42	−21.40
Belize	2,280	1,704	1,348	59.1	−20.89
Benin	11,063	3,349	2,650	24	−20.87
Samoa	282	130	105	37.2	−19.23
Liberia	11,137	4,241	3,481	31.3	−17.92
Uganda	19,964	5,103	4,190	21	−17.89
Yemen	52,797	541	449	0.9	−17.01
Nepal	14,300	4,683	3,900	27.3	−16.72
Ghana	22,754	7,535	6,335	27.8	−15.93
Guatemala	10,843	3,387	2,850	26.3	−15.85
Greece	12,890	3,299	3,599	27.9	9.09
The Gambia	1,000	436	481	48.1	10.32
China	932,743	145,417	163,480	17.5	12.42
Swaziland	1,721	464	522	30.3	12.50
Cuba	10,982	2,071	2,348	21.4	13.38
Azerbaijan	8,359	964	1,094	13.1	13.49
Armenia	2,820	309	351	12.4	13.59
Bangladesh	13,017	1,169	1,334	10.2	14.11
Algeria	238,174	1,879	2,145	0.9	14.16
Libya	175,954	311	358	0.2	15.11
Liechtenstein	15	6	7	46.7	16.67
Portugal	9,150	3,096	3,666	40.1	18.41
Guadeloupe	169	67	82	48.5	22.39
Iceland	10,025	25	31	0.3	24.00
Kazakhstan	267,074	9,758	12,148	4.5	24.49
Kyrgyzstan	19,180	775	1,003	5.2	29.42
United Arab Emirates	8,360	243	321	3.8	32.10
Ireland	6,889	489	659	9.6	34.76
Belarus	20,748	6,840	9,402	45.3	37.46
Egypt	99,545	52	72	0.1	38.46
Cyprus	925	119	172	18.6	44.54
Israel	2,062	82	132	6.4	60.98
Uruguay	17,481	791	1,292	7.4	63.34
Kuwait	1,782	3	5	0.3	66.67
Cape Verde	403	35	85	21.1	142.86
Africa	2,978,394	702,502	649,866	21.8	−7.5
Asia	3,084,746	551,448	547,793	17.8	−0.7

The World's Forests (continued)

COUNTRY/AREA	LAND AREA ('000 HA)	TOTAL FOREST, 1990 ('000 HA)	TOTAL FOREST IN 2000 ('000 HA)	PERCENTAGE OF LAND AREA IN 2000 (%)	% CHANGE 1990–2000
Europe	2,259,957	1,030,475	1,039,251	46	0.9
North and Central America	2,136,966	555,002	549,304	25.7	–1.0
Oceania	849,096	201,271	197,623	23.3	–1.8
South America	1,754,741	922,731	885,618	50.5	–4.0
World	13,063,900	3,963,429	3,869,455	29.6	–2.4

Selected Endangered Species: Fauna

For a complete list of endangered and threatened fauna, see
<http://endangered.fws.gov/wildlife.html#Species>.

Vertebrate animals
Mammals
Bat, gray
Bat, Indiana
Caribou, woodland
Deer, Columbian white-tailed
Deer, Key
Ferret, black-footed
Fox, San Joaquin kit
Jaguar
Manatee, West Indian
Mouse, Perdido Key beach
Ocelot
Panther, Florida
Pronghorn, Sonoran
Puma (cougar), eastern
Rabbit, Lower Keys marsh
Rabbit, pygmy
Rat, rice
Seal, Caribbean monk
Seal, Hawaiian monk
Sea-lion, Steller
Sheep, bighorn (two varieties)
Shrew, Buena Vista Lake ornate
Squirrel, Carolina northern flying
Squirrel, Delmarva Peninsula fox
Vole, Amargosa
Vole, Hualapai Mexican
Whale, blue
Whale, humpback
Whale, sperm
Wolf, gray
Wolf, red
Woodrat, Key Largo
Woodrat, riparian (San Joaquin Valley)

Birds
Albatross, short-tailed
Blackbird, yellow-shouldered
Bobwhite, masked (quail)
Condor, California
Coot, Hawaiian
Crane, whooping
Creeper, Molokai
Crow, Mariana
Crow, white-necked
Curlew, Eskimo
Duck, Hawaiian
Duck, Laysan
Elepaio, Oahu
Falcon, northern aplomado
Finch, Laysan

Birds (continued)
Finch, Nihoa
Flycatcher, southwestern willow
Goose, Hawaiian
Hawk, Hawaiian
Hawk, Puerto Rican broad-winged
Honeycreeper, crested
Kingfisher, Guam Micronesian
Kite, Everglade snail
Megapode, Micronesian
Millerbird, Nihoa (Old World warbler)
Parrot, Puerto Rican
Pelican, brown
Pigeon, Puerto Rican plain
Plover, piping
Pygmy-owl, cactus ferruginous
Rail, Yuma clapper
Sparrow, Cape Sable seaside
Stilt, Hawaiian
Stork, wood
Swiftlet, Mariana gray
Tern, least
Thrush, large Kauai
Thrush, small Kauai
Vireo, black-capped
Vireo, least Bell's
Warbler (wood), Bachman's
Warbler (wood), golden-cheeked
Warbler (wood), Kirtland's
White-eye, bridled
Woodpecker, ivory-billed
Woodpecker, red-cockaded

Reptiles
Anole, Culebra Island giant
Boa, Puerto Rican
Boa, Virgin Islands tree
Crocodile, American
Gecko, Monito
Lizard, blunt-nosed leopard
Lizard, St. Croix ground
Sea turtle, green
Sea turtle, hawksbill
Sea turtle, Kemp's ridley
Sea turtle, leatherback
Snake, San Francisco garter
Turtle, Alabama red-belly
Turtle, Plymouth redbelly

Amphibians
Frog, Mississippi gopher
Salamander, California tiger

Amphibians (continued)
Salamander, desert slender
Salamander, Santa Cruz long-toed
Salamander, Shenandoah
Salamander, Sonoran tiger
Salamander, Texas blind
Toad, arroyo (arroyo southwestern)
Toad, Houston
Toad, Wyoming

Fish
Chub, bonytail
Chub, humpback
Dace, Moapa
Darter, amber
Darter, boulder
Darter, Maryland
Gambusia, Pecos
Gambusia, San Marcos
Goby, tidewater
Logperch, Conasauga
Madtom, Scioto
Minnow, Rio Grande silvery
Pikeminnow (squawfish), Colorado
Pupfish, desert
Salmon, Atlantic
Salmon, sockeye
Shiner, palezone
Shiner, Topeka
Sturgeon, pallid
Sturgeon, shortnose
Sucker, Lost River
Sucker, razorback
Topminnow, Gila (incl. Yaqui)
Trout, Gila
Woundfin

Invertebrate animals
Clams
Acornshell, southern
Bean, Cumberland (pearlymussel)
Bean, purple
Blossom, tubercled (pearlymussel)
Blossom, turgid (pearlymussel)
Catspaw (purple cat's paw pearlymussel)
Catspaw, white (pearlymussel)
Clubshell
Clubshell, southern
Combshell, Cumberlandian

Selected Endangered Species: Fauna (continued)

Invertebrate Animals (continued)
Clams (continued)
Combshell, upland
Elktoe, Appalachian
Elktoe, Cumberland
Fanshell
Heelsplitter, Carolina
Higgins eye (pearlymussel)
Kidneyshell, triangular
Lampmussel, Alabama
Lilliput, pale (pearlymussel)
Mapleleaf, winged (mussel)
Moccasinshell, Coosa
Moccasinshell, Gulf
Monkeyface, Appalachian (pearly-mussel)
Monkeyface, Cumberland (pearly-mussel)
Mussel, oyster
Mussel, scaleshell
Pearlymussel, cracking
Pearlymussel, littlewing
Pigtoe, finerayed
Pigtoe, rough
Pimpleback, orangefoot (pearly-mussel)
Pocketbook, fat
Pocketbook, shinyrayed
Rabbitsfoot, rough
Riffleshell, northern
Riffleshell, tan
Ring pink (mussel)

Clams (continued)
Spinymussel, James
Stirrupshell
Three-ridge, fat (mussel)
Wartyback, white (pearlymussel)
Wedgemussel, dwarf

Snails
Ambersnail, Kanab
Riversnail, Anthony's
Snail, Iowa Pleistocene
Snail, Utah valvata
Springsnail, Idaho

Insects
Beetle, American burying
Beetle, Helotes mold
Beetle, Hungerford's crawling water
Butterfly, Karner blue
Butterfly, Mitchell's satyr
Dragonfly, Hine's emerald
Fly, Delhi Sands flower-loving
Grasshopper, Zayante band-winged
Ground beetle (unnamed, *Rhadine exilis*)
Ground beetle (unnamed, *Rhadine infernalis*)
Moth, Blackburn's sphinx
Skipper, Carson wandering
Tiger beetle, Ohlone

Arachnids
Harvestman, Bee Creek Cave
Harvestman, Bone Cave
Meshweaver, Madla's cave
Meshweaver, Robber Baron Cave
Pseudoscorpion, Tooth Cave
Spider, Government Canyon cave
Spider, Kauai cave wolf (pe'e pe'e maka 'ole)
Spider, spruce-fir moss
Spider, Tooth Cave

Crustaceans
Amphipod, Hay's Spring
Amphipod, Illinois cave
Amphipod, Kauai cave
Amphipod, Peck's cave
Crayfish, cave (*Cambarus aculabrum*)
Crayfish, cave (*Cambarus zophonastes*)
Crayfish, Nashville
Crayfish, Shasta
Fairy shrimp, Conservancy
Fairy shrimp, Riverside
Isopod, Lee County cave
Isopod, Socorro
Shrimp, Alabama cave
Shrimp, California freshwater
Shrimp, Kentucky cave
Tadpole shrimp, vernal pool

Geology

The Continents

Figures given are approximate. Area and population as of 2004. Lowest points listed are all below sea level.

CONTINENT	POPULATION	AREA	% OF TOTAL LAND AREA[1]	HIGHEST/LOWEST POINT
Africa	852,637,200	30,263,037 sq km 11,684,711 sq mi	20.2	Mt. Kilimanjaro (Tanzania): 5,895 m (19,340 ft) Lake Assal (Djibouti): −157 m (−515 ft)
Antarctica	N/A	14,000,000 sq km 5,400,000 sq mi	9.4	Vinson Massif: 4,897 m (16,066 ft) Bentley Subglacial Trench: −5,538 m (−8,327 ft)
Asia	3,879,428,240	44,887,537 sq km 17,331,069 sq mi	30.0	Mount Everest (China, Nepal): 8,848 m (29,028 ft) Dead Sea (Israel, Jordan): −400 m (−1,312 ft)
Europe	691,509,155	9,859,691 sq km 3,806,906 sq mi	6.6	Mt. Elbrus (Russia): 5,642 m (18,510 ft) Caspian Sea (Russia): −27 m (−90 ft)
North America	509,198,900	24,238,486 sq km 9,358,532 sq mi	16.2	Mt. McKinley (Alaska): 6,194 m (20,320 ft) Death Valley (California): −86 m (−282 ft)
Oceania	32,813,267	8,514,986 sq km 3,287,656 sq mi	5.7	Mt. Wilhelm (Papua New Guinea): 4,509 m (14,793 ft) Lake Eyre: −15 m (−50 ft)
South America	364,018,500	17,822,497 sq km 6,881,304 sq mi	11.9	Mt. Aconcagua (Argentina): 6,959 m (22,831 ft) Valdés Peninsula (Argentina): −40 m (−131 ft)

[1]*Together, the continents make up about 29.2% of the Earth's surface.*

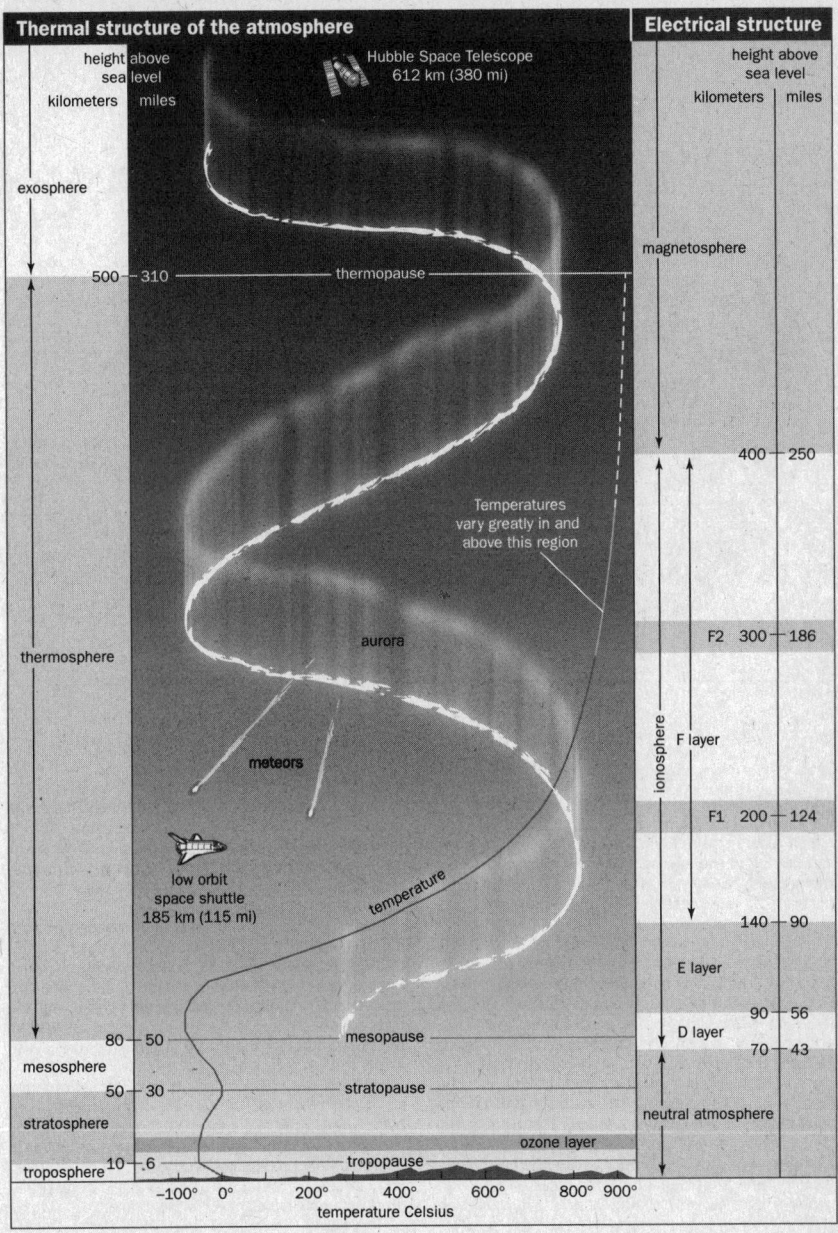

Thermal structure of the atmosphere

height above sea level
kilometers   miles

Hubble Space Telescope
612 km (380 mi)

exosphere

500 — 310 ———— thermopause ————

thermosphere

Temperatures
vary greatly in and
above this region

aurora

meteors

low orbit
space shuttle
185 km (115 mi)

temperature

80 — 50 ———— mesopause ————

mesosphere

50 — 30 ———— stratopause ————

stratosphere

ozone layer

troposphere   10 — 6 ———— tropopause ————

−100° 0° 200° 400° 600° 800° 900°
temperature Celsius

Electrical structure

height above
sea level
kilometers   miles

magnetosphere

400 — 250

F2 300 — 186

ionosphere   F layer

F1 200 — 124

140 — 90

E layer

90 — 56
D layer   70 — 43

neutral atmosphere

Earth's interior layers (depths below surface)

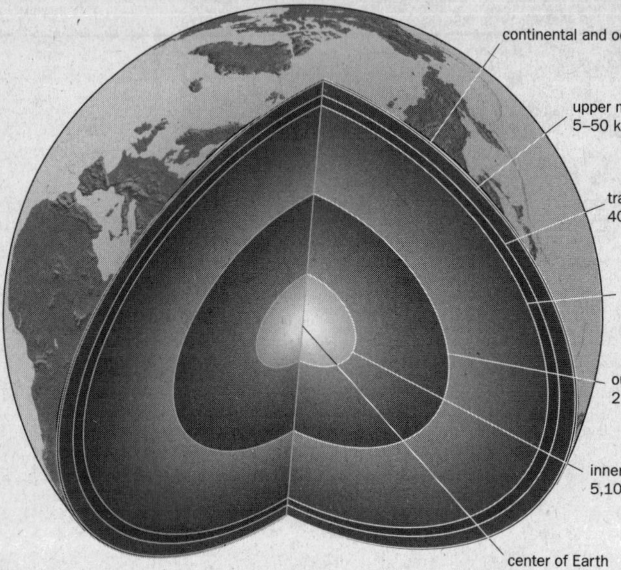

continental and oceanic crust

upper mantle (solid rock)
5–50 km (3–30 mi)

transition zone (solid rock)
400 km (240 mi)

lower mantle (solid rock)
650 km (400 mi)

outer core (molten metals)
2,900 km (1,800 mi)

inner core (nearly solid iron)
5,100 km (3,200 mi)

center of Earth
6,378 km (3,961 mi)

Geologic Time and Geochronology

The extensive interval of time occupied by the Earth's geologic history is called "geologic time." It extends from about 3.9 billion years ago (corresponding to the age of the oldest known rocks) to the present day. It is, in effect, that segment of Earth history that is represented by and recorded in rock strata.

The geologic time scale is the "calendar" for events in Earth history. It subdivides all time since the end of the Earth's formative period as a planet (nearly 4 billion years ago) into named units of abstract time: the latter, in descending order of duration, are eons, eras, periods, and epochs. The enumeration of these geologic time units is based on stratigraphy, which is the correlation and classification of rock strata. The fossil forms that occur in these rocks provide the chief means of establishing a geologic time scale. Because living things have undergone evolutionary changes over geologic time, particular kinds of organisms are characteristic of particular parts of the geologic record. By correlating the strata in which cer-

tain types of fossils are found, the geologic history of various regions (and of the Earth as a whole) can be reconstructed. The relative geologic time scale developed from the fossil record has been numerically quantified by means of absolute dates obtained with radiometric dating methods.

The field of scientific investigation concerned with determining the age and history of the Earth's rocks and rock assemblages is called "geochronology." Such time determinations are made and the record of past geologic events is deciphered by studying the distribution and succession of rock strata, as well as the character of the fossil organisms preserved within the strata.

The Earth's surface is a complex mosaic of exposures of different rock types that are assembled in an astonishing array of geometries and sequences. Individual rocks in the myriad of rock outcroppings (or in some instances shallow subsurface occurrences) contain certain materials or mineralogic information that can provide insight as to their "age."

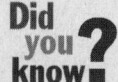

Did you know? In May 2003 the Pacific Ocean republic of Vanuatu opened the world's first underwater post office, an event that provided an opportunity for divers to post waterproof postcards. A commemorative stamp was issued for the occasion.

Geologic Time Scale

Cenozoic Era

mya*	period		epoch		age	boundaries*
	Quaternary		Holocene			0.01
5			Pleistocene		Calabrian	1.8
	Tertiary	Neogene	Pliocene	L	Piacenzian	3.6
				E	Zanclean	5.3
			Miocene	L	Messinian	7.1
10					Tortonian	11.2
15				M	Serravallian	14.8
					Langhian	16.4
20				E	Burdigalian	20.5
					Aquitanian	23.8
25		Paleogene	Oligocene	L	Chattian	28.5
30				E	Rupelian	33.7
35			Eocene	L	Priabonian	37.0
40				M	Bartonian	41.3
45					Lutetian	49.0
50				E	Ypresian	54.8
55			Paleocene	L	Thanetian	57.9
60					Selandian	61.0
65				E	Danian	65.0

Mesozoic Era

mya*	period	epoch	age	boundaries*
	Cretaceous	L	Maastrichtian	65.0
70				71.3
80			Campanian	83.5
			Santonian	85.8
			Coniacian	89.0
90			Turonian	93.5
			Cenomanian	99.0
100		E	Albian	112
110				
120		(Neocomian)	Aptian	121
			Barremian	127
130			Hauterivian	132
			Valanginian	137
140			Berriasian	144
150	Jurassic	L	Tithonian	151
			Kimmeridgian	154
			Oxfordian	159
160			Callovian	164
170		M	Bathonian	169
			Bajocian	176
180			Aalenian	180
190		E	Toarcian	190
			Pliensbachian	195
200			Sinemurian	202
			Hettangian	206
210	Triassic	L	Rhaetian	210
220			Norian	221
			Carnian	227
230		M	Ladinian	234
240			Anisian	242
		E	Olenekian	245
			Induan	248

Paleozoic Era

mya*	period	epoch	age	boundaries*
	Permian	L	Tatarian	248
			Ufimian-Kazanian	256
260			Kungurian	260
		E	Artinskian	269
280			Sakmarian	282
			Asselian	290
	Pennsylvanian	L	Gzelian S.	296
300			Kasimovian W.	303
			Moscovian N.	311
320		E	Bashkirian	323
	Mississippian	L	Serpukhovian	327
340			Visean	342
		E	Tournaisian	354
360	Devonian	L	Famennian	364
			Frasnian	370
380		M	Givetian	380
			Eifelian	391
400		E	Emsian	400
			Praghian	412
	Silurian	L	Lochkovian	417
420			Pridoli	419
			Ludlow	423
		E	Wenlockian	428
440			Llandoverian	443
	Ordovician	L	Ashgilian	449
460			Caradocian	458
		M	Llandeilian	464
			Llanvirnian	470
480	Cambrian**	E	Arenigian	485
			Tremadocian	490
			Sunwaptan**	495
500		D	Steptoean**	500
		C	Marjuman**	506
			Delamaran**	512
		B	Dyeran**	516
520			Montezuman**	520
540		A		543

Precambrian time

mya*	eon	era	boundaries*
	Proterozoic	L	543
750			900
1,000		M	
1,250			
1,500			1,600
1,750		E	
2,000			
2,250			
2,500	Archean	L	2,500
2,750			
3,000		M	3,000
3,250			
3,500		E	3,400
3,750			---3,800?

* Millions of years before the present.
** International ages have not been established. These are regional (Laurentian) only.

Published with permission of the Geological Society of America.

Largest Islands of the World

NAME AND LOCATION	CONTINENT	AREA* SQ MI	AREA* SQ KM
Greenland	North America	822,700	2,130,800
New Guinea, Papua New Guinea–Indonesia	Oceania	309,000	800,000
Borneo, Indonesia–Malaysia–Brunei	Asia	283,400	734,000
Madagascar	Africa	226,658	587,041
Baffin, Nunavut, Canada	North America	195,928	507,451
Sumatra, Indonesia	Asia	167,600	434,000
Honshu, Japan	Asia	87,805	227,414
Victoria, Northwest Territories–Nunavut, Canada	North America	83,897	217,291
Great Britain	Europe	83,698	216,777
Ellesmere, Nunavut, Canada	North America	75,767	196,236
Celebes, Indonesia	Asia	69,100	179,000
South Island, New Zealand	Oceania	58,676	151,971
Java, Indonesia	Asia	49,000	126,900
North Island, New Zealand	Oceania	44,204	114,489
Newfoundland, Canada	North America	42,031	108,860
Cuba	North America	40,519	104,945
Luzon, Philippines	Asia	40,420	104,688
Iceland	Europe	39,699	102,819
Mindanao, Philippines	Asia	36,537	94,630
Ireland, Ireland–UK	Europe	32,589	84,406
Hokkaido, Japan	Asia	30,144	78,073
Sakhalin, Russia	Asia	29,500	76,400
Hispaniola, Haiti–Dominican Republic	North America	29,418	76,192
Banks, Northwest Territories, Canada	North America	27,038	70,028
Sri Lanka, Ceylon	Asia	25,332	65,610
Tasmania, Australia	Oceania	24,868	64,409
Devon, Nunavut, Canada	North America	21,331	55,247
Severny, Novaya Zemlya, Russia	Europe	18,882	48,904
Tierra del Fuego, Argentina–Chile	South America	18,530	47,992
Alexander I	Antarctica	16,700	43,200
Axel Heiberg, Nunavut, Canada	North America	16,671	43,178
Melville, Northwest Territories–Nunavut, Canada	North America	16,274	42,149
Southampton, Nunavut, Canada	North America	15,913	41,214
Marajó, Pará, Brazil	South America	15,500	40,100
Spitsbergen, Svalbard, Norway	Europe	15,075	39,044
Kyushu, Japan	Asia	14,114	36,554
New Britain, Papua New Guinea	Oceania	14,100	36,500
Taiwan, Formosa	Asia	13,851	35,873
Hainan, China	Asia	12,962	33,572
Prince of Wales, Nunavut, Canada	North America	12,872	33,339
Yuzhny, Novaya Zemlya, Russia	Europe	12,848	33,275
Vancouver, British Columbia, Canada	North America	12,079	31,285
Timor, Indonesia–East Timor	Asia	11,883	30,777
Sicily, Italy	Europe	9,830	25,460
Somerset, Nunavut, Canada	North America	9,570	24,786
Sardinia, Italy	Europe	9,194	23,813
Bananal, Tocantins, Brazil	South America	7,700	20,000
Shikoku, Japan	Asia	7,049	18,256
Halmahera, Indonesia	Asia	6,865	17,780
Seram, Indonesia	Asia	6,621	17,148

*Area given may include small adjoining islands. Conversions for rounded figures are rounded to nearest hundred.

Highest Mountains of the World

"I" in the name of a peak refers to the highest in a group of numbered peaks of the same name.

NAME AND LOCATION	HEIGHT IN M	HEIGHT IN FT	YEAR FIRST CLIMBED
Africa			
Kilimanjaro (Kibo peak), Tanzania	5,895	19,340	1889
Mt. Kenya (Batian peak), Kenya	5,199	17,058	1899
Margherita, Ruwenzori Range, Zaire–Uganda	5,119	16,795	1906
Ras Dashen, Simen Mtns., Ethiopia	4,620	15,157	1841
Meru, Tanzania	4,565	14,978	N/A
Lageda, Ethiopia	4,532	14,869	N/A

Highest Mountains of the World (continued)

NAME AND LOCATION	HEIGHT IN M	HEIGHT IN FT	YEAR FIRST CLIMBED
Africa (continued)			
Karisimbi, Virunga Mtns., Zaire–Rwanda	4,507	14,787	1903
Analu, Ethiopia	4,480	14,698	N/A
Weynober, Ethiopia	4,472	14,672	N/A
Mikeno, Virunga Mtns., Zaire–Rwanda	4,437	14,557	1927
Antarctica			
Vinson Massif, Sentinel Range, Ellsworth Mtns.	4,897	16,066	1966
Tyree, Sentinel Range, Ellsworth Mtns.	4,852	15,919	1967
Shinn, Sentinel Range, Ellsworth Mtns.	4,801	15,751	1966
Kirkpatrick, Queen Alexandra Range	4,528	14,856	N/A
Markham, Queen Elizabeth Range	4,350	14,272	N/A
Asia			
Everest, Chomolungma), Himalayas, Nepal–Tibet, China	8,848	29,028	1953
K2 (Godwin Austen) (Chogori), Karakoram Range, Pakistan–Sinkiang, China	8,611	28,251	1954
Kanchenjunga I (Gangchhendzonga), Himalayas, Nepal–India	8,586	28,169	1955
Lhotse I, Himalayas, Nepal–Tibet, China	8,516	27,940	1956
Makalu I, Himalayas, Nepal–Tibet, China	8,463	27,766	1955
Cho Oyu, Himalayas, Nepal–Tibet, China	8,201	26,906	1954
Dhaulagiri I, Himalayas, Nepal	8,167	26,795	1960
Manaslu I, Himalayas, Nepal	8,163	26,781	1956
Nanga Parbat I, Himalayas, Pakistan	8,126	26,660	1953
Annapurna I, Himalayas, Nepal	8,091	26,545	1950
Caucasus			
Elbrus, Russia	5,642	18,510	1874
Dykh–Tau, Russia	5,204	17,073	1888
Koshtan–Tau, Russia	5,151	16,900	1889
Shkhara, Russia–Georgia	5,068	16,627	1888
Dzhangi–Tau, Russia–Georgia	5,058	16,594	1903
Kazbek, Georgia	5,033	16,512	1868
Shota Rustaveli, Russia–Georgia	4,960	16,273	N/A
Dzhimara, Georgia	4,780	15,682	N/A
Ushba, Georgia	4,700	15,420	1888
Uilpata, Russia	4,649	15,253	N/A
Europe			
Mont Blanc, Alps, France–Italy	4,807	15,771	1786
Dufourspitze (Monte Rosa), Alps, Switzerland–Italy	4,634	15,203	1855
Dom (Mischabel), Alps, Switzerland	4,545	14,911	1858
Weisshorn, Alps, Switzerland	4,505	14,780	1861
Matterhorn, Alps, Switzerland–Italy	4,478	14,692	1865
Mont Maudit, Alps, France–Italy	4,471	14,669	N/A
Dent Blanche, Alps, Switzerland	4,357	14,295	1862
Grand Combin, Alps, Switzerland	4,314	14,154	1859
Dôme du Goûter, Alps, France	4,304	14,121	1784
Finsteraarhorn, Alps, Switzerland	4,274	14,022	1812
North America			
McKinley, Alaska Range, Alaska	6,194	20,320	1913
Logan, St. Elias Mtns., Yukon, Canada	5,951	19,524	1925
Citlaltépetl (Orizaba), Cordillera Neo-Volcánica, Mexico	5,610	18,406	1848
St. Elias, St. Elias Mtns., Alaska–Canada	5,489	18,009	1897
Popocatépetl, Cordillera Neo-Volcánica, Mexico	5,465	17,930	1519
Foraker, Alaska Range, Alaska	5,304	17,400	1934
Iztaccíhuatl (Ixtacihuatl), Cordillera Neo-Volcánica, Mexico	5,230	17,159	1889
Lucania, St. Elias Mtns., Yukon, Canada	5,226	17,146	1937
King, St. Elias Mtns., Yukon, Canada	5,173	16,972	1952
Steele, St. Elias Mtns., Yukon, Canada	5,073	16,644	1935

Highest Mountains of the World (continued)

NAME AND LOCATION	HEIGHT IN M	HEIGHT IN FT	YEAR FIRST CLIMBED
Oceania			
Jaya (Sukarno, Carstensz), Sudirman Range, Indonesia	5,030	16,500[1]	1962
Pilimsit (Idenburg), Sudirman Range, Indonesia	4,800	15,750[1]	1962
Trikora (Wilhelmina), Jayawijaya Mtns., Indonesia	4,750	15,580[1]	1912
Mandala (Juliana), Jayawijaya Mtns., Indonesia	4,700	15,420[1]	1959
Wisnumurti (Jan Pieterszoon Coen), Jayawijaya, Mtns., Indonesia	4,595	15,080[1]	N/A
Wilhelm, Bismarck Range, Papua New Guinea	4,509	14,793	N/A
Giluwe, Hagen Range, Papua New Guinea	4,368	14,331	N/A
Kubor, Kubor Range, Papua New Guinea	4,359	14,301	N/A
Herbert, Bismarck Range, Papua New Guinea	4,267	13,999	N/A
Mauna Kea, Hawaii, US	4,205	13,796	N/A
South America			
Aconcagua, Andes, Argentina-Chile	6,959	22,831	1897
Ojos del Salado, Andes, Argentina-Chile	6,893	22,615	1937
Bonete, Andes, Argentina	6,872	22,546	1913
Tupungato, Andes, Argentina-Chile	6,800	22,310	1897
Pissis, Andes, Argentina	6,779	22,241	1937
Mercedario, Andes, Argentina	6,770	22,211	1934
Huascarán, Cordillera Blanca, Andes, Peru	6,768	22,205	1908
Tres Cruces, Andes, Argentina-Chile	6,753	22,156	1937
Llullaillaco, Cordillera Occidental, Andes, Argentina-Chile	6,723	22,057	1952
Cachi (El Libertador), Sierra de Pastos Grandes, Andes, Argentina	6,720	22,047	1904

[1]Conversions rounded to the nearest 10 ft.

Major Caves and Cave Systems of the World by Continent

NAME AND LOCATION	DEPTH[1]		LENGTH[2]	
	FEET	M	MILES	KM
Africa				
Achra Lemoun, Algeria	1,060	323	N/A	N/A
Ambatoanjahana, Madagascar	N/A	N/A	6.7	10.8
Ambatoharanana, Madagascar	N/A	N/A	11.2	18.1
Apocalypse Pothole, South Africa	279	85	7.5	12.1
Boussouil, Algeria	2,641	805	2	3.2
Ifflis, Algeria	3,802	1,159	1	1.6
Jabal As-Sarj, Tunisia	876	267	1.1	1.7
Leviathani, Kenya	1,526	465	7	11.2
Sof 'Umar, Ethiopia	N/A	N/A	9.4	15.1
Tafna (Bou Maʾza), Algeria	N/A	N/A	11.4	18.4
Toghobeït, Morocco	2,339	713	2.3	3.7
Antarctica: no significant caves				
Asia				
Air Jernih, Malaysia	1,165	355	32.1	51.6
Bilremos, South Korea	N/A	N/A	7.3	11.7
Byakuren, Japan	1,476	450	0.7	1.1
Faouar Dara, Lebanon	2,041	622	1.5	2.5
Kap-Kutan/Promezhutochnaya, Uzbekistan	N/A	N/A	31.3	50.3
Kiev, Uzbekistan	3,248	990	1.1	1.8
Manjung, South Korea	N/A	N/A	8.3	13.3
Omi-senri, Japan	1,198	365	N/A	N/A
Oreshnaya, Russia	623	190	25.5	41
Parau, Iran	2,464	751	0.9	1.4
Sallukan Kallang, Indonesia	673	205	7.6	12.3
Ural, Uzbekistan	1,854	565	1.5	2.5
Wu-chia, China	1,430	436	N/A	N/A
Europe				
Arañonera, Spain	3,888	1,185	4	6.5
Berger, France	4,072	1,241	12.9	20.7

Major Caves and Cave Systems of the World (continued)

NAME AND LOCATION	DEPTH[1]		LENGTH[2]	
	FEET	M	MILES	KM
Europe (continued)				
Coumo d'Hyouernèdo, France	3,294	1,004	56.2	90.5
Dachstein-Mammut, Austria	3,871	1,180	23.9	38.5
Dent de Crolles, France	1,978	603	33.6	54.1
Ease Gill, United Kingdom	N/A	N/A	32.6	52.5
Ffynnon Ddu, United Kingdom	1,010	308	26.7	43
Fighiera-Farolfi-Antro del Corchia, Italy	3,986	1,215	28	45
Hirlatz, Austria	2,008	612	35.4	57
Hölloch, Switzerland	2,844	867	82.7	133.1
Jean Bernard, France	5,036	1,535	11.1	17.9
L'Alpe, France	2,014	614	28.7	46.2
Laminako Ateak (Illamina), Spain	4,619	1,408	7.4	11.9
Ojo Guareña, Spain	N/A	N/A	55.4	89.1
Optimisticheskaya, Ukraine	N/A	N/A	102.5	165
Ozernaya, Ukraine	N/A	N/A	66.5	107
Pierre Saint-Martin, France-Spain	4,403	1,342	32.3	52
Raucherkar, Austria	2,379	725	29.8	48
Red del Río Silencio, Spain	1,614	492	32.9	53
Schwer, Austria	3,999	1,219	3.8	6.1
Siebenhengste-Hohgant-Höhlen, Switzerland	3,346	1,020	68.4	110
Snezhnoye-Mezhonnogo, Georgia	4,495	1,370	11.8	19
Trave, Spain	4,528	1,380	1.8	2.9
Vyacheslav Pantyukhin, Georgia	4,948	1,508	N/A	N/A
Xitu, Spain	3,766	1,148	4.7	7.5
Zolushka, Moldova	N/A	N/A	51	82
Oceania				
Atea, Papua New Guinea	1,148	350	21.4	34.5
Bulmer, New Zealand	2,388	728	6.8	11
Cora-Lynn, Australia	N/A	N/A	8.3	13.3
Gardners Gut, New Zealand	N/A	N/A	7.4	11.9
H.H. Hole, New Zealand	2,044	623	N/A	N/A
Honeycomb, New Zealand	N/A	N/A	8.1	13.1
Ipaku-Kukumbu, Papua New Guinea	1,273	388	6.8	11
Kavakuna II, Papua New Guinea	1,499	457	2.2	3.5
Mamo, Papua New Guinea	1,732	528	34.1	54.8
Mini-Martin-Exit, Australia	722	220	9.9	16
Muruk, Papua New Guinea	2,090	637	2.9	4.6
Nettlebed, New Zealand	2,917	889	15.2	24.4
Selminum, Papua New Guinea	N/A	N/A	12.7	20.5
North America				
Aztotempa, Mexico	2,297	700	2.5	4
Binkley's, Indiana	N/A	N/A	19.1	30.7
Butler-Sinking Creek, Virginia	623	190	20	32.2
Carlsbad Caverns, New Mexico	1,027	313	20.8	33.5
Crevice, Missouri	N/A	N/A	28.2	45.4
Cuicateca, Mexico	4,035	1,230	5.8	9.3
Cumberland Caverns, Tennessee	N/A	N/A	27.6	44.4
Fisher Ridge, Kentucky	N/A	N/A	44.4	71.5
Friars Hole, West Virginia	617	188	42.8	68.8
Guixani Ndia Guinjao, Mexico	3,084	940	1.2	2
The Hole, West Virginia	N/A	N/A	22.9	36.8
Huautla, Mexico	4,439	1,353	32.4	52.1
Jewel, South Dakota	443	135	76.9	123.8
Lechuguilla, New Mexico	1,503	458	32.9	53
Mammoth-Flint Ridge, Kentucky	360	110	329.3	530
Organ, West Virginia	N/A	N/A	37.6	60.5
Purificación, Mexico	2,936	895	44.5	71.6
Sloan's Valley, Kentucky	N/A	N/A	24.6	39.6
Sonyance, Mexico	2,444	745	1.1	1.8
Tilaco, Mexico	2,129	649	N/A	N/A
Trinidad, Mexico	2,736	834	N/A	N/A
Whigpistle, Kentucky	N/A	N/A	22.5	36.2
Xanadu, Tennessee	N/A	N/A	24	38.6

Major Caves and Cave Systems of the World (continued)

NAME AND LOCATION	DEPTH[1]		LENGTH[2]	
	FEET	M	MILES	KM
South America				
Angélica, Brazil	N/A	N/A	4	6.4
Aonda, Venezuela	1,188	362	N/A	N/A
Auyantepuy Norte, Venezuela	1,050	320	N/A	N/A
Brejões, Brazil	N/A	N/A	4.8	7.8
Guácharo, Venezuela	164	50	6.3	10.2
Guarataro, Venezuela	1,001	305	N/A	N/A
Kaukiran, Peru	1,335	407	1.3	2.1
Major de Sarisarinama, Venezuela	1,030	314	N/A	N/A
Ôlhos d'Água, Brazil	N/A	N/A	3.9	6.3
San Andrés, Peru	1,096	334	N/A	N/A
São Mateus-Imbira, Brazil	N/A	N/A	12.7	20.5

[1]Below highest entrance.   [2]Explored portion of cave.
Source: Paul Courbon et al., Atlas of the Great Caves of the World (1989).

Major Deserts of the World by Continent

DESERT (LOCATION)	AREA		DESERT (LOCATION)	AREA	
	SQ KM	SQ MI		SQ KM	SQ MI
Africa			**Australia**		
Sahara, northern Africa	8,600,000	3,320,000	Great Victoria, Western and South Australia	647,000	250,000
Libyan, Libya, Egypt, and Sudan	N/A	N/A	Great Sandy, northern Western Australia	400,000	150,000
Kalahari, southwestern Africa	930,000	360,000	Gibson, Western Australia	N/A	N/A
Namib, southwestern Africa	135,000	52,000	Simpson, Northern Territory	145,000	56,000
Asia			**North America**		
Arabia, southwestern Asia	2,330,000	900,000	Great Basin, southwestern US	492,000	190,000
Rub'al-Khali, southern Arabian Peninsula	650,000	250,000	Chihuahuan, northern Mexico	450,000	175,000
Gobi, Mongolia and northeastern China	1,300,000	500,000	Sonoran, southwestern US and Baja California	310,000	120,000
Kyzylkum, Kazakhstan-Uzbekistan	300,000	115,000	Colorado, California and northern Mexico	N/A	N/A
Takla Makan, northern China	270,000	105,000	Yuma, Arizona and Sonora, Mexico	N/A	N/A
Karakum, Turkmenistan	350,000	135,000	Mojave, southwestern US	65,000	25,000
Kavir, central Iran	260,000	100,000			
Syrian, Saudi Arabia, Jordan, Syria, and Iraq	260,000	100,000	**South America**		
Thar, India and Pakistan	200,000	77,000	Patagonian, southern Argentina	673,000	260,000
Lut, eastern Iran	52,000	20,000	Atacama, northern Chile	140,000	54,000

Major Volcanoes of the World by Continent

VOLCANO, LOCATION	ELEVATION		FIRST RECORDED ERUPTION	MOST RECENT ERUPTION
	M	FT		
Africa				
Kilimanjaro, Tanzania[1]	5,895	19,340	N/A	N/A[2]
Cameroon, Cameroon	4,100	13,451	1650	2000
Teide (Tenerife), Canary Islands	3,718	12,198	N/A	1909
Nyiragongo, Dem. Rep. of the Congo	3,475	11,400	1884	2002
Nyamuragira, Dem. Rep. of the Congo	3,055	10,023	1882	2001
Fogo, Cape Verde	2,829	9,281	1500	1995
Karthala, Comoros	2,361	7,745	1828	1991
Fournaise, Reunion Islands	1,823	5,981	1640	2001
Antarctica				
Erebus, Ross Island	3,743	12,280	1841	1991
Darnley, Sandwich Islands	1,100	3,608	1823	N/A

Major Volcanoes of the World (continued)

VOLCANO, LOCATION	ELEVATION M	ELEVATION FT	FIRST RECORDED ERUPTION	MOST RECENT ERUPTION
Asia-Oceania-Pacific				
Klyuchevskaya, Kamchatka, Russia[3]	4,750	15,584	1697	2002
Mauna Kea, Hawaii[4]	4,205	13,796	N/A	*dormant*
Mauna Loa, Hawaii	4,169	13,678	1750	1984
Kerinci, Sumatra, Indonesia	3,800	12,467	1838	1970
Fuji, Honshu, Japan	3,776	12,388	1050 BC	1708
Rinjani, Lombok, Indonesia	3,726	12,224	1847	1994
Tolbachik, Kamchatka, Russia	3,682	12,080	1740	1976
Semeru, Java, Indonesia	3,676	12,060	1818	2002
Ichinskaya, Kamchatka, Russia	3,621	11,880	N/A	N/A
Slamet, Java, Indonesia	3,428	11,247	1772	1988
Raung, Java, Indonesia	3,332	10,932	1586	2000
Shiveluch, Kamchatka, Russia	3,283	10,771	1793	2002
Dempo, Sumatra, Indonesia	3,159	10,364	1817	1974
Sundoro, Java, Indonesia	3,151	10,338	1818	1971
Ontake, Honshu, Japan	3,063	10,049	1979	1979
Papandayan, Java, Indonesia	2,987	9,802	1772	1998
Gede, Java, Indonesia	2,958	9,705	1747	1957
Zhupanovsky, Kamchatka, Russia	2,958	9,705	1776	1959
Merapi, Java, Indonesia	2,911	9,551	1006	2002
Bezymianny, Kamchatka, Russia	2,900	9,514	1055	2001
Marapi, Sumatra, Indonesia	2,891	9,485	1770	1994
Ruapehu, North Island, New Zealand	2,797	9,177	1861	1999
Peuet Sague, Sumatra, Ipdonesia	2,780	9,121	1918	1998
Avachinskaya, Kamchatka, Russia	2,751	9,026	1737	1991
Mayon, Luzon, Philippines	2,421	7,943	1616	2001
Alaid, Kuril Islands, Russia	2,335	7,662	1790	1981
Ulawun, New Britain, Papua New Guinea	2,296	7,532	1700	2002
Kelud, Java, Indonesia	1,731	5,679	1000	2001
Pinatubo, Luzon, Philippines	1,460	4,800	1380	1991
Lopevi, Vanuatu	1,364	4,755	1864	2001
Unzen, Kyushu, Japan	1,360	4,462	860	1991
Awu, Pulau Sangihe, Indonesia	1,320	4,331	1640	1966
Kilauea, Hawaii	1,243	4,077	1750	2002
Krakatoa, Krakatau, Indonesia	813	2,667	1680	2001
Suwanose-jima, Ryukyu Islands, Japan	799	2,621	1813	1996
Taal, Luzon, Philippines	400	1,312	1572	1999
Europe and the Atlantic				
Etna, Italy	3,323	10,899	N/A	2002
Beerenberg, Norway	2,277	7,470	1558	N/A
Tristan da Cunha, South Atlantic	2,060	6,760	1700	N/A
Askja, Iceland	1,570	5,149	1875	1961
Hekla, Iceland	1,491	4,890	1104	2000
Vesuvius, Italy	1,280	4,198	N/A	1944
Stromboli, Italy	926	3,038	N/A	2002
Krafla, Iceland	818	2,683	1300	1984
North America				
Citlaltépetl, Mexico	5,610	18,406	N/A	N/A
Popocatépetl, Mexico	5,465	17,930	1347	2002
Rainier, Washington	4,392	14,410	N/A	c. 200 BC
Shasta, California	4,317	14,160	N/A	1786 (?)
Colima, Mexico	4,240	13,911	1576	2002
Tajumulco, Guatemala	4,220	13,845	1821	N/A
Acatenango, Guatemala	3,976	13,041	1924	1972
Fuego, Guatemala	3,763	12,342	1524	2002
Hood, Oregon	3,424	11,235	1800	c. 1800
Spurr, Alaska	3,374	11,067	1953	1992
Baker, Washington	3,285	10,775	1820	1880
Lassen, California	3,187	10,457	1650	1921
Redoubt, Alaska	3,108	10,194	1778	1990
Iliamna, Alaska	3,053	10,016	1768	1953
Shishaldin, Alaska	2,857	9,371	1775	2000
Parícutin, Mexico	2,807	9,210	1943	1952
Pavlof, Alaska	2,714	8,902	1790	1997

Major Volcanoes of the World (continued)

VOLCANO, LOCATION	ELEVATION M	FT	FIRST RECORDED ERUPTION	MOST RECENT ERUPTION
North America (continued)				
Poas, Costa Rica	2,704	8,869	1834	N/A
Pacaya, Guatemala	2,552	8,371	1565	2001
St. Helens, Washington	2,549	8,360	1500	1998
Veniaminof, Alaska	2,507	8,223	c. 1750	1993
San Miguel, El Salvador	2,180	7,150	1586	1976
Chiginagak, Alaska	2,126	6,973	1852	1997
Katmai, Alaska	2,047	6,714	1912	1912
Makushin, Alaska	2,035	6,674	1786	1987
Izalco, El Salvador	1,965	6,445	1770	1966
San Cristóbal, Nicaragua	1,745	5,724	1522	2001
Great Sitkin, Alaska	1,737	5,697	1760	1974
Arenal, Costa Rica	1,633	5,356	1968	2001
Pelée, Martinique	1,397	4,582	1792	1932
Momotombo, Nicaragua	1,280	4,198	1550	1996
Kiska, Alaska	1,220	4,001	1907	1969
Telica, Nicaragua	1,060	3,477	1527	1999
South America				
Guallatiri, Chile	6,060	19,876	1825	1985
Cotopaxi, Ecuador[5]	5,897	19,347	1532	1904
Tupungatito, Chile	5,640	18,499	1829	1986
Lascar, Chile	5,592	18,342	1848	2000
Ruiz, Colombia	5,400	17,716	1595	1985
Sangay, Ecuador	5,230	17,154	1628	1983
Tolima, Colombia	5,215	17,105	c. 1600 BC	1822
Tungurahua, Ecuador	5,033	16,512	1534	2002
Purace, Colombia	4,800	15,744	1827	1977
Guagua Pichincha, Ecuador	4,794	15,724	1533	2000
Lautaro, Chile	3,380	11,115	1878	N/A
Llaima, Chile	3,125	10,250	1640	1995
Villarrica, Chile	2,840	9,318	1558	2000
Hudson, Chile	2,615	8,580	1971	1991

[1]Includes three dormant volcanoes (Kibo, Mawensi, and Shira) that have not erupted in historic times.   [2]Has not erupted in historic times.   [3]Highest active volcano on the Kamchatka Peninsula.   [4]Usually snowcapped dormant volcano.   [5]The world's highest continuously active volcano.

Oceans & Seas

	AREA SQ KM	SQ MI	VOLUME CU KM	CU MI
Pacific Ocean				
without marginal seas	165,250,000	63,800,000	707,600,000	169,900,000
with marginal seas	179,680,000	69,370,000	723,700,000	173,700,000
Atlantic Ocean				
without marginal seas	82,440,000	31,830,000	324,600,000	77,900,000
with marginal seas	106,460,000	41,100,000	354,700,000	85,200,000
Indian Ocean				
without marginal seas	73,440,000	28,360,000	291,000,000	69,900,000
with marginal seas	74,920,000	28,930,000	291,900,000	70,100,000
Arctic Ocean	14,090,000	5,440,000	17,000,000	4,100,000
Australasian Central Sea	8,140,000	3,140,000	9,900,000	2,400,000
Gulf of Mexico and Caribbean Sea	4,320,000	1,670,000	9,600,000	2,300,000
Mediterranean and Black Seas	2,970,000	1,150,000	4,200,000	100,000
Bering Sea	2,304,000	890,000	3,330,000	80,000
Sea of Okhotsk	1,583,000	611,000	1,300,000	30,000
Hudson Bay	1,230,000	470,000	160,000	40,000
North Sea	570,000	220,000	50,000	10,000
Baltic Sea	420,000	160,000	20,000	5,000
Irish Sea	100,000	40,000	6,000	1,000
English Channel	75,000	29,000	4,000	1,000

Oceans & Seas (continued)

	AVERAGE DEPTH		
	M	FT	DEEPEST POINT
Pacific Ocean			
without marginal seas	4,280	14,040	Mariana Trench
with marginal seas	4,030	13,220	(11,034 m; 36,201 ft)
Atlantic Ocean			
without marginal seas	3,930	12,890	Puerto Rico Trench
with marginal seas	3,330	10,920	(8,380 m; 27,493 ft)
Indian Ocean			
without marginal seas	3,960	10,040	Sunda Deep of the Java
with marginal seas	3,900	12,790	Trench (7,450 m; 24,442 ft)
Arctic Ocean	1,205	3,950	(5,502 m; 18,050 ft)
Australasian Central Sea	1,210	3,970	N/A
Gulf of Mexico and	2,220	7,280	Cayman Trench
Caribbean Sea			(7,686 m; 25,216 ft)
Mediterranean and	1,430	4,690	Ionian Basin
Black Seas			(4,900 m; 16,000 ft)
Bering Sea	1,440	4,720	Bowers Basin (4,097 m; 13,442 ft)
Sea of Okhotsk	838	2,750	Kuril Basin (2,499 m; 8,200 ft)
Hudson Bay	128	420	(867 m; 2,846 ft)
North Sea	94	310	Skagerrak (700 m; 2,300 ft)
Baltic Sea	55	180	Landsort Deep (459 m; 1,506 ft)
Irish Sea	60	200	Mull of Galloway (175 m; 576 ft)
English Channel	54	180	Hurd Deep (172 m; 565 ft)

Major Natural Lakes of the World

Conversions for figures have been rounded, thousands to the nearest hundred and hundreds to the nearest ten.

NAME	LOCATION	AREA		NAME	LOCATION	AREA	
		SQ MI	SQ KM			SQ MI	SQ KM
Caspian Sea	Central Asia	149,200	386,400	Nyasa (Malawi)	eastern Africa	11,430	29,604
Superior	Canada-US	31,700	82,100	Great Slave	Northwest	11,031	28,570
Victoria	eastern Africa	26,828	69,485		Territories,		
Huron	Canada-US	23,000	59,600		Canada		
Michigan	US	22,300	57,800	Erie	Canada-US	9,910	25,667
Aral Sea[1]	Central Asia	13,000	33,800	Winnipeg	Manitoba,	9,417	24,390
Tanganyika	eastern Africa	12,700	32,900		Canada		
Great Bear	Northwest	12,028	31,153	Ontario	Canada-US	7,340	19,010
	Territories,						
	Canada						

[1]*Salt lake.*

Longest Rivers of the World

This list includes both rivers and river systems. Conversions of rounded figures are rounded to nearest 10 or 100 miles or kilometers.

NAME	OUTFLOW	LENGTH	
		MI	KM
Africa			
Nile	Mediterranean Sea	4,132	6,650
Congo	South Atlantic Ocean	2,900	4,700
Niger	Bight of Biafra	2,600	4,200
Zambezi	Mozambique Channel	2,200	3,500
Kasai	Congo River	1,338	2,153
Orange	South Atlantic Ocean	1,300	2,100
White Nile (al-Bahr al-Abyad)	Nile River	1,295	2,084
Lualaba	Congo River	1,100	1,800
Limpopo	Mozambique Channel	1,100	1,800
Jubba (Juba)	Indian Ocean	1,030	1,658
Asia			
Yangtze	East China Sea	3,915	6,300
Yenisey-Baikal-Selenga	Kara Sea	3,442	5,540
Huang Ho (Yellow)	Gulf of Chihli	3,395	5,464

Longest Rivers of the World (continued)

NAME	OUTFLOW	LENGTH MI	LENGTH KM
Asia (continued)			
Ob–Irtysh	Gulf of Ob	3,362	5,410
Amur–Argun	Sea of Okhotsk	2,761	4,444
Lena	Laptev Sea	2,734	4,400
Mekong	South China Sea	2,700	4,350
Ob–Katun	Gulf of Ob	2,696	4,338
Irtysh–Chorny Irtysh	Ob River	2,640	4,248
Yenisey	Kara Sea	2,549	4,102
Europe			
Volga	Caspian Sea	2,193	3,530
Danube	Black Sea	1,770	2,850
Ural	Caspian Sea	1,509	2,428
Dnieper	Black Sea	1,367	2,200
Don	Sea of Azov	1,162	1,870
Pechora	Barents Sea	1,124	1,809
Kama	Volga River	1,122	1,805
Oka	Volga River	932	1,500
Belaya	Kama River	889	1,430
Dniester	Black Sea	840	1,352
North America			
Mississippi–Missouri–Red Rock	Gulf of Mexico	3,710	5,971
Mackenzie–Slave–Peace	Beaufort Sea	2,635	4,241
Missouri–Red Rock	Mississippi River	2,540	4,090
St. Lawrence–Great Lakes	Gulf of St. Lawrence	2,500	4,000
Mississippi	Gulf of Mexico	2,340	3,770
Missouri	Mississippi River	2,315	3,726
Yukon–McNeil	Bering Sea	1,980	3,190
Rio Grande	Gulf of Mexico	1,900	3,060
Yukon	Bering Sea	1,875	3,018
Nelson–Saskatchewan	Hudson Bay	1,600	2,575
Oceania			
Darling	Murray River	1,702	2,739
Murray	Great Australian Bight	1,609	2,589
Murrumbidgee	Murray River	981	1,579
Lachlan	Murrumbidgee River	922	1,484
Cooper Creek	Lake Eyre	882	1,420
South America			
Amazon–Ucayali–Apurimac	South Atlantic Ocean	4,000	6,400
Paraná	Río de la Plata	3,032	4,880
Madeira–Mamoré–Guaporé	Amazon River	2,082	3,350
Jurua	Amazon River	2,040	3,283
Purus	Amazon River	1,995	3,211
São Francisco	South Atlantic Ocean	1,811	2,914
Japurá (Caquetá)	Amazon River	1,750	2,816
Ucayali–Apurimac	Amazon River	1,701	2,738
Orinoco	South Atlantic Ocean	1,700	2,736
Tocantins	Pará River	1,677	2,699

Glaciers

A glacier is a large mass of perennial ice that originates on land by the recrystallization of snow or other forms of solid precipitation and that shows evidence of past or present flow. The term **ice sheet** is commonly applied to a glacier that occupies an extensive tract of relatively level land and that flows from the center outward. Exact limits for glaciers cannot be set. Except in size, a small snow patch that persists for more than one season is hydrologically indistinguishable from a true glacier.

Glaciers occur where snowfall in winter exceeds melting in summer, conditions that prevail only in high mountain areas and polar regions. Glaciers occupy about 11% of the earth's land surface but hold roughly three-fourths of its fresh water; 99% of glacier ice lies in Antarctica and Greenland. At the end of the 20th century, scientists became increasingly concerned with **glacial melting**, which is often linked to **global warming** trends and may lead to changes in sea level and weather patterns.

Preserving Nature

US National Parks

Dates in parentheses indicate when the area was first designated a park, in most cases under a different name. Web site: <www.nps.gov/parks.html>.

PARK	LOCATION	DESIGNATION DATE	SQ MI	SQ KM
Acadia	Bar Harbor ME	1929 (1916)	74	192
American Samoa	American Samoa	1993 (1988)	14	36
Arches	Moab UT	1971 (1929)	120	311
Badlands	southwestern South Dakota	1978 (1939)	379	982
Big Bend	curve of the Rio Grande river, Texas	1944	1,252	3,243
Biscayne	near Miami FL	1980 (1968)	270	699
Black Canyon of the Gunnison	near Montrose CO	1999 (1933)	43	112
Bryce Canyon	Bryce Canyon, Utah	1928 (1923)	56	145
Canyonlands	near Moab UT	1964	527	1,366
Capitol Reef	near Torrey UT	1971 (1937)	379	982
Carlsbad Caverns	near Carlsbad NM	1930 (1923)	73	189
Channel Islands	Ventura CA	1980 (1938)	75	194
Congaree	Hopkins SC	2003	34	88
Crater Lake	Crater Lake OR	1902	286	741
Cuyahoga Valley	near Cleveland and Akron OH	2000 (1974)	51	133
Death Valley	Death Valley, California	1994 (1933)	5,219	13,518
Denali	central Alaska	1980 (1917)	9,492	24,584
Dry Tortugas	Key West FL	1992 (1935)	101	262
Everglades	southern Florida	1947	2,358	6,107
Gates of the Arctic	Bettles AK	1980 (1978)	13,238	34,287
Glacier	northwest Montana	1910	1,584	4,102
Glacier Bay	Gustavus AK	1980 (1925)	5,130	13,287
Grand Canyon	Grand Canyon, Arizona	1919 (1908)	1,902	4,927
Grand Teton	Moose WY	1950 (1929)	484	1,255
Great Basin	near Baker NV	1986 (1922)	121	313
Great Sand Dunes	Mosca CO	2000 (1932)	132	343
Great Smoky Mountains	Tennessee and North Carolina	1934	815	2,110
Guadalupe Mountains	Salt Flat TX	1972	135	350
Haleakala	Kula, Maui HI	1960 (1916)	47	121
Hawaii Volcanoes	near Hilo HI	1961 (1916)	328	849
Hot Springs	Hot Springs AR	1921 (1832)	9	22
Isle Royale	Houghton MI	1940 (1931)	893	2,314
Joshua Tree	near Palm Springs CA	1994 (1936)	1,591	4,120
Katmai	near King Salmon AK	1980 (1918)	7,385	19,128
Kenai Fjords	Seward AK	1980 (1978)	1,047	2,711
Kobuk Valley	Kotzebue AK	1980 (1978)	2,672	6,920
Lake Clark	Port Alsworth AK	1980 (1978)	6,297	16,309
Lassen Volcanic	Mineral CA	1916 (1907)	166	430
Mammoth Cave	Mammoth Cave, Kentucky	1941	83	214
Mesa Verde	near Cortez and Mancos CO	1906	81	211
Mount Rainier	near Ashford WA	1899	368	954
North Cascades	near Marblemount WA	1968	1,069	2,769
Olympic	near Port Angeles WA	1938	1,442	3,734
Petrified Forest	Arizona	1962 (1906)	146	379
Redwood	Crescent City CA	1994	172	445
Rocky Mountain	near Estes Park and Grand Lake CO	1915	415	1,076
Saguaro	Tucson AZ	1994 (1933)	143	370
Sequoia & Kings Canyon	near Three Rivers CA	1940 (1890)	1,351	3,498
Shenandoah	near Luray VA	1935	311	805
Theodore Roosevelt	Medora ND (south unit); near Watford City ND (north unit)	1978 (1947)	110	285
Virgin Islands	St. John, US Virgin Islands	1956	23	59
Voyageurs	International Falls MN	1975	341	883
Wind Cave	near Hot Springs SD	1903	44	115
Wolf Trap	Vienna VA	2002 (1966)	130 acres	
Wrangell–St. Elias	near Copper Center AK	1980	20,587	53,320
Yellowstone	Idaho, Montana, and Wyoming	1872	3,468	8,983
Yosemite	in the Sierra Nevada, California	1890 (1864)	1,189	3,081
Zion	Springdale UT	1919 (1909)	229	593

The 100 Largest City Parks in the US

Source: Trust for Public Land, Center for City Park Excellence, Washington DC. Web site: <www.tpl.org>.

RANK	PARK NAME	ACRES	LOCATION	PARK TYPE
1	Franklin Mountains State Park	24,000	El Paso TX	state, county, or regional
2	South Mountain Preserve	16,283	Phoenix AZ	municipal park
3	Carvins Cove Natural Reserve	12,700	Roanoke VA	municipal park
4	McDowell Sonoran Preserve	11,250	Scottsdale AZ	municipal park
5	Cullen Park	8,270	Houston TX	municipal park
6	George Bush Park	7,800	Houston TX	municipal park
7	North Mountain Preserve	7,500	Phoenix AZ	municipal park
8	Gateway National Recreation Area	7,138	New York NY	national park, or national wildlife refuge
9	Jefferson Memorial Forest	5,650	Louisville KY	municipal park
10	William B. Umstead State Park	5,554	Raleigh NC	state, county, or regional park
11	Mission Trails Preserve	4,323	San Diego CA	municipal park
12	False Cape State Park	4,321	Virginia Beach VA	state, county, or regional park
13	Forest Park	4,317	Portland OR	municipal park
14	Eagle Creek Park	4,279	Indianapolis IN	municipal park
15	Griffith Park	4,171	Los Angeles CA	municipal park
16	Fairmount Park-Wissahickon Valley	4,167	Philadelphia PA	municipal park
17	Walter Long Park	3,802	Austin TX	municipal park
18	Bidwell Park	3,670	Chico CA	municipal park
19	Mountain Creek Lake Park	3,643	Dallas TX	municipal park
20	Don Edwards San Francisco Bay National Wildife Refuge	3,586	San Jose CA	national park, or national wildlife refuge
21	Fort Worth Nature Center/ Wildlife Refuge	3,331	Fort Worth TX	municipal park
22	Trinity River Park	3,173	Dallas TX	municipal park
23	Anderson County Park	3,109	San Jose CA	state, county, or regional park
24	Bear Creek Pioneers Park	3,080	Houston TX	state, county, or regional park
25	Mohawk Park and Golf Course	2,820	Tulsa OK	municipal park
26	Pelham Bay Park	2,766	New York NY	municipal park
27	Sheldon State Park	2,718	Houston TX	state, county, or regional park
28	Otter Creek Park	2,600	Lousiville KY	municipal park
29	Los Penasquitos Canyon	2,405	San Diego CA	municipal park
30	Tilden Park	2,077	Berkeley CA	municipal park
31	Percy Warner Park	2,058	Nashville TN	municipal park
32	Sepulveda Basin Recreation Area	2,031	Los Angeles CA	municipal park
33	Floyd Lamb State Park	2,027	Las Vegas NV	state, county, or regional park
34	Galveston Island State Park	2,013	Galveston TX	state, county, or regional park
35	Smith and Bybee Lakes Wildlife Area	1,973	Portland OR	state, county, or regional park
36	White Rock Lake Park	1,952	Dallas TX	municipal park
37	Rock Creek Park	1,949	Washington DC	national park, or national wildlife refuge
38	Greenbelt Park	1,778	New York NY	municipal park
39	Barton Creek Greenway	1,771	Austin TX	municipal park
40	Swope Park	1,769	Kansas City MO	municipal park
41	Mission Bay Park	1,756	San Diego CA	municipal park
42	Coyote Creek Parkchain	1,662	San Jose CA	state, county, or regional park
43	Fort Harrison State Park	1,640	Indianapolis IN	state, county, or regional park
44	Pennypack Park	1,618	Philadelphia PA	municipal park
45	Burns Park	1,575	North Little Rock AR	municipal park

The 100 Largest City Parks in the US (continued)

RANK	PARK NAME	ACRES	LOCATION	PARK TYPE
46	Memorial Park	1,503	Houston TX	municipal park
47	City Park	1,500	New Orleans LA	municipal park
48	Hansen Dam Recreation Center	1,437	Los Angeles CA	municipal park
49	Mt. Airy Forest	1,420	Cincinnati OH	municipal park
50	Garden of the Gods Park	1,367	Colorado Springs CO	municipal park
51	Forest Park	1,293	St. Louis MO	municipal park
52	Black Mountain Park	1,284	San Diego CA	municipal park
53	Latta Plantation Nature Preserve	1,282	Charlotte NC	municipal park
54	North Cheyenne Canyon Park	1,260	Colorado Springs CO	municipal park
55	Flushing Meadows/ Corona Park	1,255	New York NY	municipal park
56	Martin Luther King Shoreline Park	1,220	Oakland CA	state, county, or regional park
57	Koko Head Regional Park	1,218	Honolulu HI	state, county, or regional park
58	Anacostia Park	1,215	Washington DC	national park, or national wildlife refuge
59	Lincoln Park	1,212	Chicago IL	municipal park
60	Cave Buttes Recreation Area I & II	1,200	Phoenix AZ	municipal park
61	Gwynns Falls/Leakin Park	1,200	Baltimore MD	municipal park
62	San Jacinto State Historical Park	1,200	La Porte TX	state, county, or regional park
63	River Rouge Park	1,181	Detroit MI	municipal park
64	McClay Gardens State Park	1,179	Tallahassee FL	state, county, or regional park
65	Red Mountain	1,146	Mesa AZ	municipal park
66	Van Cortlandt Park	1,146	New York NY	municipal park
67	Emma Long Park	1,137	Austin TX	municipal park
68	McDowell Nature Preserve	1,098	Charlotte NC	municipal park
69	Balboa Park	1,091	San Diego CA	municipal park
70	Rochester Park	1,032	Dallas TX	municipal park
71	Golden Gate Park	1,018	San Francisco CA	municipal park
72	Olmos Basin	1,010	San Antonio TX	municipal park
73	Stinchcomb Wildlife Refuge	988	Oklahoma City OK	municipal park
74	Richmond Parkway	984	New York NY	municipal park
75	Belle Isle Park	982	Detroit MI	municipal park
76	Riverfront Park	955	Kansas City MO	municipal park
77	Eisenhower Park	930	East Meadow NY	state, county, or regional park
78	Papago Park	895	Phoenix AZ	municipal park
79	McAllister Park	856	San Antonio TX	municipal park
80	Central Park	840	New York NY	municipal park
81	Scripps Miramar Open Space	822	San Diego CA	municipal park
82	Tierrasanta Open Space	818	San Diego CA	municipal park
83	William T. Davis Wildlife Refuge	814	New York NY	municipal park
84	Robert H. Hodge Park	801	Kansas City MO	municipal park
85	Tres Rios	800	Phoenix AZ	municipal park
86	Gerritsen Beach (Marine Park)	798	New York NY	municipal park
87	Hamilton Creek Park	790	Nashville TN	municipal park
88	Cobb's Creek Park	786	Philadelphia PA	municipal park
89	Sabre Springs Open Space	780	San Diego CA	municipal park
90	White Rock Creek Greenbelt	773	Dallas TX	municipal park
91	Bear Creek Canyon Park	769	Colorado Springs CO	municipal park
92	Leif Ericson Drive (Shore Parkway)	760	New York NY	municipal park
93	Cullinan Park	755	Houston TX	municipal park
94	McNeely Lake Park	746	Louisville KY	municipal park
95	Iroquois Park	739	Louisville KY	municipal park
96	Palmer Park	737	Colorado Springs CO	municipal park
97	Forest Park	735	Springfield MA	municipal park
98	Brooks Tract	730	Wichita KS	municipal park
99	Penasquitos Creek Park	725	San Diego CA	municipal park
100	Alum Rock Park	719	San Jose CA	municipal park

Major World Zoos

Numbers given for species and animals are approximate.

ZOO (LOCATION)	FOUNDED	NUMBER OF SPECIES	NUMBER OF ANIMALS	FEATURES OF INTEREST
Antwerp Zoo (Belgium)	1843	1,160	6,450	Père David's deer, white rhinoceroses, okapi, Congo peafowl
Bronx Zoo (New York)	1899	700	6,000	largest US metropolitan zoo, Wildlife Conservation Society headquarters, snow leopards, Congo Gorilla Forest
Brookfield Zoo (Illinois)	1934	500	2,300	Wolf Woods exhibit, Habitat Africa exhibit, Wild Encounters program
Cincinnati Zoo (Ohio)	1875	510	17,000	red pandas, Vanishing Giants exhibit, Wings of the World exhibit
Columbus Zoo (Ohio)	1927	700	6,000	first lowland gorilla born in captivity, bonobos, koalas
Denver Zoo (Colorado)	1896	750	4,000	conservation center, Primate Panorama, Dragons of Komodo exhibit
Hagenbeck Zoo (Hamburg, Germany)	1907	360	2,500	first zoo with natural animal habitats
Indianapolis Zoo (Indiana)	1964	360	3,800	incorporates zoo, aquarium, and botanical garden; five biomes; Dolphin Adventure exhibit
Lincoln Park Zoo (Chicago IL)	1868	400	2,400	Primate House, wildlife conservation department
London Zoo (England)	1828	650	8,000	largest zoological library of any zoo, apes and monkeys, giant pandas
National Zoological Gardens of South Africa (Pretoria)	1899	640	5,500	antelope, cheetah-breeding area
Philadelphia Zoo (Pennsylvania)	1874	400	1,800	first white lions and blue-eyed lemurs exhibited in the US
Phoenix Zoo (Arizona)	1962	N/A	1,200	wildlife relief program, reptile exhibit
Leningrad Zoo (St. Petersburg, Russia)	1865	410	2,000	polar bears, ornithological exhibit, 130 threatened species
San Diego Zoo (California)	1916	800	4,000	international conservation program, koalas, white rhinoceroses
Edinburgh Zoo (Scotland)	1913	150	1,500	largest penguin colony in Europe
National Zoological Park (Washington DC)	1889	435	2,700	giant pandas, Sumatran tigers
Dehiwala Zoo (Sri Lanka)	1936	330	3,890	elephant orphanage
Taronga Zoological Park (Sydney, Australia)	1884	340	2,600	native Australian wildlife, mountain pygmy possum, bird collection
Toronto Zoo (Ontario, Canada)	1974	460	5,000	gorillas, Siberian tigers, African bush elephants
Ueno Zoological Garden (Japan)	1882	464	2,600	insectarium, giant salamander, rare pheasants and wallabies, giant pandas

Major World Botanical Gardens

Most botanical gardens are concerned primarily with exhibiting ornamental plants, insofar as possible in a scheme that emphasizes natural relationships. A major contemporary objective of botanical gardens is to maintain extensive collections of plants, labeled with common and scientific names and regions of origin. Numbers given for species are approximate.

GARDEN (LOCATION)	FOUNDED	NUMBER OF SPECIES	FEATURES OF INTEREST
Atlanta Botanical Garden (Georgia)	1976	N/A	plant conservation
Australian National Botanic Gardens (Canberra)	1970	6,800	Australian flora
The Botanical Garden of the University of Vienna (Austria)	1754	9,000	woody tropical plants, teaching and research
The Botanic Garden of Padua (Italy)	1545	6,000	oldest university garden, medicinal plants
Brooklyn Botanic Garden (New York)	1911	12,000	rose, cactus, and orchid collections; garden for the blind
Cheyenne Botanic Gardens (Wyoming)	1977	N/A	solar heated conservatory, solar energy research
Chicago Botanic Garden (Illinois)	1890	8,310 taxa	23 gardens, ornamentals, Midwest plant conservation
Denver Botanic Gardens (Colorado)	1951	17,000	Rocky Mountain region plants

Major World Botanical Gardens (continued)

GARDEN (LOCATION)	FOUNDED	NUMBER OF SPECIES	FEATURES OF INTEREST
Fort Worth Botanic Garden (Texas)	1933	2,500	21 specialty gardens
Missouri Botanical Garden (St. Louis)	1859	N/A	Climatron conservatory, EarthWays Center (previously Gateway Center for Resource Efficiency), Shaw Nature Reserve
National Botanic Gardens, Glasnevin (Dublin, Ireland)	1795	20,000	palms, native strawberry trees, Atlantic cedar
National Botanic Garden of Belgium (Meise)	1829	18,000	classical herbarium studies
The New York Botanical Garden (Bronx NY)	1891	12,000	48 gardens and plant collections, 50-acre forest, International Plant Science Center
Peradeniya Botanic Gardens (Sri Lanka)	1821	4,000	orchids, gymnosperms, flowering trees
Royal Botanic Garden Edinburgh (Scotland)	1670	17,000	botanical library, among largest collections of living plants
Royal Botanic Gardens, Kew (London, England)	1759	33,400 taxa	alpines, junipers, seed conservation
Santa Barbara Botanic Garden (California)	1939	1,000 taxa	native California vegetation
Singapore Botanic Gardens	1859	2,700	orchids, bromeliads, palms
Tower Hill Botanic Garden (Boylston MA)	1986	N/A	apples, flowering bulbs
University of Copenhagen Botanic Garden (Denmark)	1759	13,000	Palm House, research and education
United States Botanic Garden (Washington DC)	1820	13,000 taxa	conservatory, large greenhouse

Health

Worldwide Health Indicators

*Column data as follows: **Life expectancy** in 2003; **Doctors** = persons per doctor, latest data[1]; **Infant mortality** per 1,000 births in 2003; **Water** = percentage (%) of population with access to safe drinking water (2000); **Food** = percentage (%) of the FAO recommended minimum (2002)[2].*

REGION/BLOC	LIFE EXPECTANCY MALE	LIFE EXPECTANCY FEMALE	DOCTORS	INFANT MORTALITY	WATER	FOOD
World	65.5	69.5	730	39.6	82	119
Africa	**51.0**	**53.2**	**2,560**	**78.1**	**64**	**103**
Central Africa	45.7	49.1	12,890	102.1	46	82
East Africa	45.1	46.5	13,620	93.6	50	86
North Africa	66.4	70.4	890	42.6	87	123
Southern Africa	44.1	45.3	1,610	64.1	85	119
West Africa	49.2	50.6	6,260	81.7	65	110
Americas	**71.0**	**77.3**	**520**	**18.8**	**91**	**135**
Anglo-America[3]	74.6	80.4	370	6.6	100	158
Canada	76.4	83.4	540	5.0	100	135
United States	74.4	80.1	360	6.8	100	143
Latin America	68.9	75.4	690	26.1	86	120
Caribbean	67.1	71.4	380	29.3	79	99
Central America	66.9	70.9	950	29.5	88	107
Mexico	71.9	77.6	810	17.4	88	135
South America	68.4	75.7	710	27.9	86	120
Andean Group	68.9	75.0	830	26.5	86	108
Brazil	67.2	75.3	770	31.8	87	128
Other South America	71.5	78.9	410	17.7	82	123
Asia	**66.6**	**69.7**	**970**	**41.8**	**81**	**117**
Eastern Asia	70.9	74.6	610	23.4	78	123
China	70.1	73.3	620	26.4	75	125
Japan	78.4	85.3	530	3.0	97	118
South Korea	71.7	79.3	740	7.3	92	130
Other Eastern Asia	71.3	76.9	500	14.1	94	92

Worldwide Health Indicators (continued)

REGION/BLOC	LIFE EXPECTANCY MALE	LIFE EXPECTANCY FEMALE	DOCTORS	INFANT MORTALITY	WATER	FOOD
Asia (continued)						
South Asia	62.3	63.7	2,100	63.4	85	107
India	62.9	64.4	1,920	59.6	84	111
Pakistan	61.3	63.2	1,840	76.6	90	105
Other South Asia	60.0	60.3	5,080	73.7	85	85
Southeast Asia	66.1	71.0	3,120	36.2	78	123
Southwest Asia	66.4	70.5	610	43.1	85	117
Central Asia	62.0	68.7	330	55.9	82	94
Gulf Cooperation Council	68.5	72.2	620	39.3	95	120
Iran	68.0	70.7	1,200	44.2	92	128
Other Southwest Asia	66.9	70.8	690	39.1	82	119
Europe	**70.0**	**78.3**	**300**	**9.2**	**98**	**130**
Eastern Europe	61.3	72.7	290	16.4	95	119
Russia	58.5	71.9	240	13.3	99	120
Ukraine	61.1	72.2	330	20.8	98	119
Other Eastern Europe	67.2	74.8	370	20.1	84	118
Western Europe	76.0	82.0	385	4.7	100	133
European Union (EU)	74.8	81.3	290	5.2	100	136
France	75.6	83.1	330	4.4	100	145
Germany	75.5	81.6	290	4.2	100	131
Italy	76.5	82.5	180	6.2	100	146
Spain	75.7	83.1	240	3.6	99	137
United Kingdom	75.7	80.7	720	5.3	100	135
Other EU	72.8	79.7	320	6.2	100	131
Non-EU	77.2	82.6	480	4.2	100	130
Oceania	**73.4**	**79.1**	**480**	**15.0**	**87**	**119**
Australia	77.0	83.1	400	4.8	100	115
Pacific Ocean Islands	67.7	72.7	770	31.3	67	128

[1]Latest data available for individual countries. [2]The Food and Agriculture Organization of the United Nations (FAO) calculates this percentage by dividing the caloric equivalent to the known average daily supply of foodstuffs for human consumption in a given country by its population, thus arriving at a minimum daily per capita caloric intake. The higher the percentage, the more calories consumed. [3]Includes Canada, the US, Greenland, Bermuda, and St. Pierre and Miquelon.

Causes of Death, Worldwide, by Sex

Global estimates for 2002 as published in the World Health Organization World Health Report 2003. *Data are percentages of total deaths in each category. Ranking is based on categories defined by the International Classification of Diseases, Tenth Revision. All other causes of death (mostly residual) make up approximately 3.7 percent of all deaths.*

	LEADING CAUSES OF DEATH	ALL CATEGORIES (%)	MALES (%)	FEMALES (%)
1	Major cardiovascular diseases	29.2	27.0	31.7
	Ischemic heart diseases	12.6	12.6	12.5
	Cerebrovascular diseases	9.6	8.5	10.9
	Hypertensive heart disease	1.6	1.4	1.8
2	Infectious and parasitic diseases	19.5	19.9	19.0
	HIV/AIDS	4.9	5.1	4.8
	Diarrheal diseases	3.1	3.1	3.1
	Tuberculosis	2.8	3.5	2.0
	Childhood diseases	2.4	2.3	2.5
	Malaria	2.1	2.0	2.4
3	Malignant neoplasms	12.5	13.2	11.6
	Trachea, bronchus, and lung	2.2	3.0	1.3
	Stomach	1.5	1.7	1.2
	Colon, rectum, and anus	1.1	1.1	1.1
	Liver	1.1	1.4	0.7
4	Respiratory infections	6.7	6.4	7.1
5	Respiratory diseases	6.5	6.4	6.6
	Chronic obstructive pulmonary disease	4.8	4.7	4.9

Causes of Death, Worldwide, by Sex (continued)

	LEADING CAUSES OF DEATH	ALL CATE-GORIES (%)	MALES (%)	FEMALES (%)
6	Accidents (unintentional injuries)	6.2	7.7	4.6
	Road traffic injuries	*2.1*	*2.9*	*1.2*
	Falls	*0.7*	*0.8*	*0.6*
7	Perinatal conditions	4.3	4.6	4.0
8	Digestive diseases	3.4	3.6	3.2
	Chronic liver disease and cirrhosis of the liver	*1.4*	*1.7*	*1.0*
9	Neuropsychiatric disorders	1.9	1.9	2.0
	Alzheimer and other dementias	*0.7*	*0.5*	*0.9*
10	Diabetes mellitus	1.7	1.5	2.0
11	Nephritis, nephrotic syndrome, and nephrosis	1.2	1.2	1.2
12	Intentional injuries	2.9	3.9	1.7
	Intentional self-harm (suicide)	*1.5*	*1.8*	*1.2*
	Violence (assault)	*1.0*	*1.5*	*0.4*

Causes of Death, Worldwide, by Region

Global estimates for 2001 as published in the World Health Organization (WHO) World Health Report 2002. Regions are as defined by the WHO. Numbers are in thousands ('000).

	LEADING CAUSES OF DEATH	ALL CATE-GORIES (%)	ALL CATE-GORIES	AFRI-CAN	AMER-ICAN	EASTERN MEDITER-RANEAN	EURO-PEAN	SOUTHEAST ASIAN	WESTERN PACIFIC
1	Ischemic heart disease	12.7	7,181	333	967	523	2,423	1,972	963
2	Cerebrovascular disease	9.6	5,454	307	454	218	1,480	1,070	1,926
3	Lower respiratory infections	6.8	3,871	1,026	225	383	298	1,355	586
4	HIV disease	5.1	2,866	2,197	88	58	26	445	53
5	Chronic obstructive pulmonary disease	4.7	2,672	116	222	88	285	614	1,347
6	Perinatal conditions	4.4	2,504	577	167	313	70	1,023	353
7	Diarrheal diseases	3.5	2,001	703	76	326	21	802	74
8	Tuberculosis	2.9	1,644	336	46	133	77	701	351
9	Road traffic accidents	2.1	1,194	179	141	103	125	353	292
10	Trachea, bronchus, lung cancers	2.1	1,213	23	227	30	371	162	399
11	Malaria	2.0	1,124	963	1	55	0	95	10
12	Diabetes mellitus	1.6	895	55	230	52	141	238	179
13	Hypertensive heart disease	1.5	874	54	131	91	175	138	285
14	Stomach cancer	1.5	850	37	76	21	172	65	480
15	Self-inflicted injuries	1.5	849	28	65	35	168	234	318
16	Cirrhosis of the liver	1.4	796	70	104	60	166	214	183
17	Measles	1.3	745	426	0	85	6	193	32
18	Nephritis and nephrosis	1.1	625	80	95	61	77	155	157
19	Liver cancer	1.1	616	64	39	14	64	65	371
20	Colon and rectum cancers	1.1	615	27	108	15	235	58	174
21	Congenital anomalies	0.9	507	67	62	75	38	149	116
22	Violence	0.9	500	116	150	22	70	77	65
23	Breast cancer	0.8	479	38	90	28	154	90	79
24	Esophagus cancer	0.8	438	27	31	13	50	80	236
25	Drowning	0.7	403	92	24	27	37	91	132
26	Alzheimer's and other dementias	0.7	368	5	94	10	97	100	62
27	Poisoning	0.6	343	37	17	18	104	95	73
28	Mouth and oropharynx cancers	0.6	326	34	22	21	52	144	54
29	Whooping cough	0.5	285	157	7	59	0	60	2
30	Tetanus	0.5	282	110	0	53	0	101	18
31	Prostate cancer	0.5	269	45	77	8	95	26	19
32	Cervix uteri cancer	0.5	258	59	30	12	27	99	33
33	War	0.4	230	122	11	59	16	20	3

Did you know? The modern idea of a population census as a complete enumeration of all the people and their important characteristics for purposes of understanding the basic structure and trends of the society rather than for identifying and controlling particular individuals (e.g., to identify who should be taxed, inducted into military service, or forced to work) slowly arose in the 17th and 18th centuries. There is no such thing as "the first census" because, although early efforts embodied one or another modern feature, none of them embodied all modern features. Perhaps the first effort in an area larger than a city to count everyone at successive intervals was made in New France (Quebec) and Acadia (Nova Scotia), where 16 enumerations were made between 1665 and 1754.

Ten Leading Causes of Death in the US, by Age

Preliminary data for 2003. Numbers in thousands. Rates per 100,000 population. Numbers are based on weighted data rounded to the nearest individual, so category percentages and rates may not add to totals. Source: National Vital Statistics Report, <www.cdc.gov/nchs>.

CAUSE	NUMBER	RATE	%
1–4 YEARS			
1 Accidents	1,679	10.6	34.2%
Motor vehicle accidents	591	3.7	12.0%
All other accidents	1,088	6.9	22.2%
2 Congenital malformations, deformations, and chromosomal abnormalities	514	3.3	10.5%
3 Malignant neoplasms	383	2.4	7.8%
4 Assault (homicide)	342	2.2	7.0%
5 Diseases of heart	186	1.2	3.8%
6 Influenza and pneumonia	151	1.0	3.1%
7 Septicemia	82	0.5	1.7%
8 Conditions of perinatal origin	76	0.5	1.5%
9 Nonmalignant/unknown neoplasms	53	0.3	1.1%
10 Chronic lower respiratory diseases	47	0.3	1.0%
All other causes	1,398	8.9	28.5%
All causes, 1–4 years	**4,911**	**31.1**	**100.0%**
5–14 YEARS			
1 Accidents	2,561	6.3	37.0%
Motor vehicle accidents	1,592	3.9	23.0%
All other accidents	970	2.4	14.0%
2 Malignant neoplasms	1,060	2.6	15.3%
3 Congenital malformations, deformations, and chromosomal abnormalities	370	0.9	5.3%
4 Assault (homicide)	310	0.8	4.5%
5 Intentional self-harm (suicide)	255	0.6	3.7%
6 Diseases of heart	252	0.6	3.6%
7 Influenza and pneumonia	77	0.2	1.1%
8 Chronic lower respiratory diseases	134	0.3	1.9%
9 Septicemia	107	0.3	1.5%
10 Nonmalignant/unknown neoplasms	76	0.2	1.1%
All other causes	1,728	4.2	24.9%
All causes, 5–14 years	**6,930**	**16.9**	**100.0%**
15–24 YEARS			
1 Accidents	14.966	36.3	45.3%
Motor vehicle accidents	10,857	26.3	32.9%
All other accidents	4,109	10.0	12.4%
2 Assault (homicide)	5,148	12.5	15.6%

CAUSE	NUMBER	RATE	%
15–24 YEARS (CONTINUED)			
3 Intentional self-harm (suicide)	3,921	9.5	11.9%
4 Malignant neoplasms	1,628	4.0	4.9%
5 Diseases of heart	1,083	2.6	3.3%
6 Congenital malformations, deformations, and chromosomal abnormalities	425	1.0	1.3%
7 Influenza and pneumonia	216	0.5	0.7%
8 Cerebrovascular diseases	204	0.5	0.6%
9 Chronic lower respiratory diseases	172	0.4	0.5%
10 HIV disease	171	0.4	0.5%
All other causes	5,088	12.3	15.4%
All causes, 15–24 years	**33,022**	**80.1**	**100.0%**
25–44 YEARS			
1 Accidents	27,844	33.1	22.0%
Motor vehicle accidents	13,582	16.1	10.5%
All other accidents	14,261	16.9	11.1%
2 Malignant neoplasms	19,041	22.6	14.8%
3 Diseases of heart	16,283	19.3	12.6%
4 Intentional self-harm (suicide)	11,251	13.4	8.7%
5 Assault (homicide)	7,367	8.7	5.7%
6 HIV disease	6,879	8.2	5.3%
7 Chronic liver disease and cirrhosis	3,288	3.9	2.6%
8 Cerebrovascular diseases	3,004	3.6	2.3%
9 Diabetes mellitus	2,662	3.2	2.1%
10 Influenza and pneumonia	1,337	1.6	1.0%
All other causes	29,968	35.6	23.2%
All causes, 25–44 years	**128,924**	**153.0**	**100.0%**
45–64 YEARS			
1 Malignant neoplasms	144,936	211.0	33.2%
2 Diseases of heart	101,713	148.0	23.3%
3 Accidents	23,669	34.5	5.4%
Motor vehicle accidents	9,891	14.4	2.3%
All other accidents	13,778	20.1	3.2%
4 Diabetes mellitus	16,326	23.8	3.7%
5 Cerebrovascular diseases	15,971	23.2	3.7%

Ten Leading Causes of Death in the US, by Age (continued)

CAUSE	NUMBER	RATE	%
45–64 YEARS (CONTINUED)			
6 Chronic lower respiratory diseases	15,409	22.4	3.5%
7 Chronic liver disease and cirrhosis	13,649	19.9	3.1%
8 Intentional self-harm (suicide)	10,057	14.6	2.3%
9 HIV disease	5,917	8.6	1.4%
10 Septicemia	5,827	8.5	1.3%
All other causes	83,584	121.7	19.1%
All causes, 45–64 years	**437,058**	**636.1**	**100.0%**

CAUSE	NUMBER	RATE	%
65 YEARS AND OVER			
1 Diseases of heart	564,204	1570.8	31.3%
2 Malignant neoplasms	387,475	1078.7	21.5%
3 Cerebrovascular diseases	138,397	385.3	7.7%

CAUSE	NUMBER	RATE	%
65 YEARS AND OVER (CONTINUED)			
4 Chronic lower respiratory diseases	109,199	304.0	6.1%
5 Alzheimer disease	62,707	174.6	3.5%
6 Influenza and pneumonia	57,507	160.1	3.2%
7 Diabetes mellitus	54,770	152.5	3.0%
8 Nephritis, nephrotic syndrome, and nephrosis	35,392	98.5	2.0%
9 Accidents	26,597	94.6	1.5%
Motor vehicle accidents	7,379	20.5	0.4%
All other accidents	26,597	74.0	1.5%
10 Septicemia	26,609	74.1	1.5%
All other causes	333,895	929.6	18.5%
All causes, 65 years and over	**1,804,131**	**5022.8**	**100.0%**

Twenty Leading Causes of Death in the US for All Ages

Data for 2001. Rates per 100,000 population. Source: National Vital Statistics Report, <www.cdc.gov/nchs>.

	CAUSE	NUMBER	RATE	TOTAL %	% MALE (RANK)	% FEMALE (RANK)
1	Diseases of heart	700,142	245.8	29.0	28.7(1)	29.3 (1)
	Ischemic heart disease	502,189	176.3	20.8	21.5	20.1
	Heart failure	56,934	20.0	2.4	1.8	2.9
2	Malignant neoplasms	553,768	194.4	22.9	24.3 (2)	21.6 (2)
	Neoplasms of the trachea, bronchus, and lung	156,058	54.8	6.5	7.6	5.3
	Neoplasms of the colon, rectum, and anus	56,887	20.0	2.4	2.4	2.3
3	Cerebrovascular diseases	163,538	57.4	6.8	5.3 (4)	8.1 (3)
4	Chronic lower respiratory diseases	123,013	43.2	5.1	5.0 (5)	5.1 (4)
	Emphysema	16,242	5.7	0.7	0.7	0.6
5	Accidents	101,537	35.7	4.2	5.6 (3)	2.9 (7)
	Motor vehicle accidents	43,788	15.4	1.8	2.5	1.1
	Accidental poisoning and exposure to noxious substances	14,078	4.9	0.6	0.8	0.3
6	Diabetes mellitus	71,372	25.1	3.0	2.8 (6)	3.1 (5)
7	Influenza and pneumonia	62,034	21.8	2.6	2.3 (7)	2.8 (8)
	Pneumonia	61,777	21.7	2.6	2.3	2.8
8	Alzheimer disease	53,852	18.9	2.2	1.3 (11)	3.1 (6)
9	Nephritis, nephrotic syndrome, and nephrosis	39,480	13.9	1.6	1.6 (9)	1.7 (9)
10	Septicemia	32,238	11.3	1.3	1.2 (13)	1.5 (10)
11	Intentional self-harm (suicide)	30,622	10.8	1.3	2.1 (8)	0.5
	by discharge of firearms	16,869	5.9	0.7	1.2	0.2
12	Chronic liver disease and cirrhosis	27,035	9.5	1.1	1.5 (10)	0.8 (12)
13	Assault (homicide)	20,308	7.1	0.8	1.3 (12)	0.4 (21)
	by discharge of firearms	11,348	4.0	0.5	0.8	0.1
14	Essential (primary) hypertension and hypertensive renal disease	19,250	6.8	0.8	0.6 (19)	1.0 (11)
15	Pneumonitis due to solids and liquids	17,301	6.1	0.7	0.7 (17)	0.7 (14)
16	Parkinson disease	16,544	5.8	0.7	0.8 (15)	0.6 (15)
17	Aortic aneurysm and dissection	15,234	5.3	0.6	0.8 (16)	0.5 (17)
18	HIV disease	14,175	5.0	0.6	0.9 (14)	0.3 (22)
19	Atherosclerosis	14,086	4.9	0.6	0.4 (22)	0.7 (13)
20	Conditions of perinatal origin	13,887	4.9	0.6	0.7 (18)	0.5 (18)

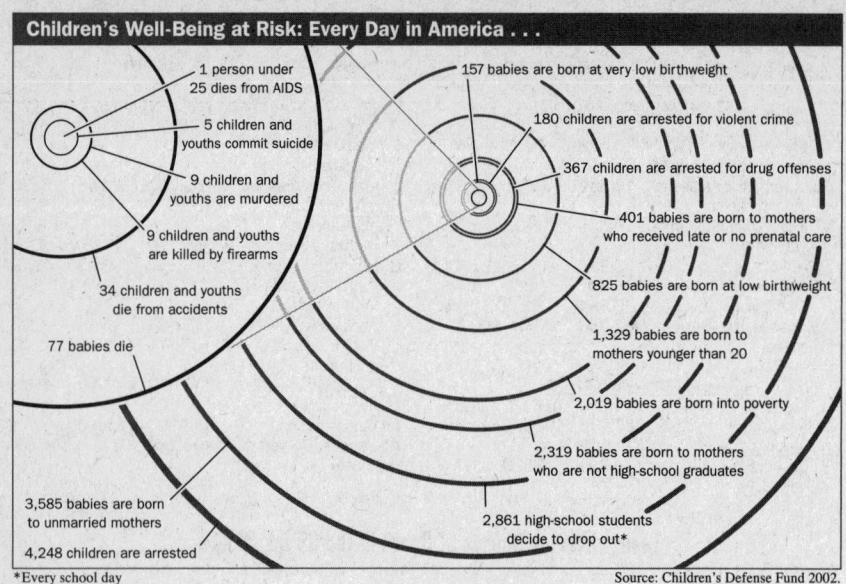

Children's Well-Being at Risk: Every Day in America . . .

- 1 person under 25 dies from AIDS
- 5 children and youths commit suicide
- 9 children and youths are murdered
- 9 children and youths are killed by firearms
- 34 children and youths die from accidents
- 77 babies die
- 3,585 babies are born to unmarried mothers
- 4,248 children are arrested

- 157 babies are born at very low birthweight
- 180 children are arrested for violent crime
- 367 children are arrested for drug offenses
- 401 babies are born to mothers who received late or no prenatal care
- 825 babies are born at low birthweight
- 1,329 babies are born to mothers younger than 20
- 2,019 babies are born into poverty
- 2,319 babies are born to mothers who are not high-school graduates
- 2,861 high-school students decide to drop out*

*Every school day

Source: Children's Defense Fund 2002.

Infectious Diseases

Infectious diseases are caused by microscopic organisms, including viruses, bacteria, fungi, and animal parasites, that invade the body and multiply. Some infections, such as measles and malaria, affect the entire body; other infections affect only one body organ or system. **Infectious agents** may enter the body in a variety of ways, including inhalation of airborne microbes, skin-to-skin or sexual contact, ingestion of contaminated food or water, insect bites, and transmission from women to their unborn children. The outcome of any infection depends on the number and virulence of infectious agents, as well as on the response of the immune system.

Although progress has been made in the **eradication** of many infectious diseases, new diseases are emerging and many previously controlled diseases are making a resurgence. Unprecedented population growth, an increase in international travel, worldwide transport of animals and food products, and human encroachment on wilderness habitats all play a role in the spread of infectious diseases. In addition, microbial evolution has led to new strains of disease that are resistant to the antibiotics available to treat them. This has led to a call for a decrease in the use of antibiotics by health professionals, as the more often these drugs are administered, the more likely it is that antibiotic-resistant strains of microorganisms will emerge. **Immunization**, increased public health measures, and the development of new treatments are all crucial to controlling infectious diseases.

Autoimmune Diseases

In **autoimmune diseases**, the immune system mistakenly attacks the cells, tissues, or organs of a person's own body. The cells that normally work to defend against infection effectively misrecognize parts of one's own body as alien. Autoimmune diseases are not contagious; genetic makeup increases one's chances of developing an autoimmune disease, but other environmental triggers may also play a role in disease onset. Many autoimmune diseases are rare, but as a group they afflict millions of Americans. For 2001 it was estimated that 50 million Americans (or one in five people) suffered from one or more than 80 autoimmune diseases. Women of childbearing age are most often afflicted.

Each autoimmune disease affects the body in a different way. Some of the most common diseases are listed by main target organs in the table below. All involve a collection of immune system cells and molecules at a target site, broadly referred to as **inflammation**. For example, in multiple sclerosis the autoimmune reaction is directed against the brain, and in inflammatory bowel diseases (Crohn's disease and ulcerative colitis) the immune system attacks the gut. In autoimmune diseases such as lupus, affected tissues and organs vary among individuals.

Autoimmune diseases are often difficult to **diagnose**, particularly in the early stages. Laboratory tests and close supervision are necessary for proper diagnosis and treatment. The majority of autoimmune diseases are **chronic**; health professionals seek to manage the inflammation caused by the disease rather than to cure it. Research into the intricate workings of the immune system and pathways of inflammation is being conducted in the hopes of future disease prevention.

Autoimmune Diseases

For information on specific autoimmune diseases, see <www.niaid.nih.gov>.

Blood
Autoimmune hemolytic anemia
Autoimmune thrombocytopenia
Pernicious anemia

Blood vessels
Anti-phospholipid syndrome
Behcet's disease
Temporal artertis
Vasculitides (such as Wegener's granulomatosis)

Endocrine glands
Autoimmune disease of the adrenal gland
Autoimmune oophoritis and orchitis
Diabetes mellitus (type I or immune mediated)
Graves' disease
Hashimoto's thyroiditis

Gastrointestinal system
Autoimmune hepatitis
Crohn's disease
Primary biliary cirrhosis
Ulcerative colitis

Multiple organs (including the musculoskeletal systems)
Polymyositis, dermatomyositis
Rheumatoid arthritis
Scleroderma
Sjogren's syndrome
Spondyloarthropathies (such as ankylosing spondylitis)
Systemic lupus erythematosus

Nervous systems
Autoimmune neuropathies (such as Guillain-Barré)
Autoimmune ureitis
Multiple sclerosis
Myasthenia gravis

Skin
Dermatitis herpetiformis
Pemphigus vulgaris
Psoriasis
Vitiligo

Cardiovascular Diseases

Cardiovascular diseases are the leading cause of death in the US, accounting for more than 40% of fatalities each year. There are many different diseases that can lead to congestive **heart failure**, a condition in which the heart muscle is less able to pump blood. Some of the common cardiovascular diseases are:

Ischemic Heart Disease (coronary heart disease)—the effect of an inadequate supply of oxygen-rich blood to the heart muscle because of narrowing or blocking of a coronary artery by fatty and fibrous tissue (arteriosclerosis). If the oxygen depletion is extreme, the effect may be the death of a section of heart muscle (myocardial infarction); if the deprivation is insufficient to cause infarction, the effect may be angina pectoris. Both conditions can be fatal because they can cause left ventricular failure or ventricular fibrillation—an uncontrolled and uncoordinated twitching of the ventricle muscle that induces sudden cardiac death. Coronary bypass surgery or balloon angioplasty are indicated if medication and diet do not control progressive coronary heart disease and if the myocardial damage is not too extensive.

Pulmonary Heart Disease—enlargement and eventual failure of the right ventricle of the heart because of disorders of the lungs, disorders of the blood vessels of the lungs, or abnormalities of the chest wall. The most common causes are chronic bronchitis and emphysema. The condition is such that the network of capillaries in the lungs is progressively destroyed, causing pressure in the pulmonary artery to be increased. The resultant back pressure on the right ventricle increases the work and the size of the chamber, leading to heart enlargement and eventually, if uncorrected, heart failure. The disease is characterized by a chronic cough, difficulty in breathing after exertion, wheezing, and weakness and fatigue. Treatment of the acute form of the disease is often by removal of the pulmonary blockage. Other treatment may include the use of antibiotics to combat respiratory infection; the use of a respirator to ease breathing; the restriction of sodium intake; and the administration of diuretics and digitalis.

Heart Malformation (congenital heart disease)—any deformity of the heart that develops within the first two months of fetal life. After birth, some of these deformities impair the supply of oxygen to the tissues and may cause disability or death. Approximately 40,000 children are born with a heart defect each year. These malformations can be repaired by modern surgical procedures with varying degrees of success.

Other cardiovascular-related conditions that may increase one's likelihood of heart disease include arrhythmias and blood pressure irregularities:

Arrhythmias are disorders of the rhythmic beating of the heart and are fairly common. Although often relatively harmless, they may indicate a more serious heart problem.

Blood pressure is the force originating in the pumping action of the heart, exerted by the blood against the walls of the blood vessels. It is usually measured indirectly over the brachial or femoral artery. The highest (systolic) pressure, normally about 120, occurs during contraction of the ventricles; the lowest (diastolic) pressure, normally about 80, occurs during ventricular relaxation. **Hypertension**, or high blood pressure, occurs when the blood vessels lose their flexibility or the muscles surrounding them force them to contract. As a result, the heart must pump more forcefully to move the same amount of blood through the narrowed vessels into the capillaries, thereby increasing blood pressure. The increased risk of death from congestive heart failure, kidney failure, or stroke is the chief danger of hypertension. **Hypotension**, or low blood pressure, is a condition in which the blood pressure is abnormally low, either because of reduced blood volume or because of increased blood-vessel capacity. Although not in itself an indication of ill health, it often accompanies disease conditions. Some causes are extensive bleeding or burns and exposure to cold.

To help prevent heart disease, the American Heart Association recommends maintaining a healthy diet, exercising, keeping cholesterol low, and managing stress.

Internet resources: <www.americanheart.org>

Stroke

A stroke is a sudden impairment of brain function resulting either from a substantial reduction in blood flow to some part of the brain or from intracranial bleeding. The consequences may include transient or lasting paralysis on one or both sides of the body, difficulties in using words or in eating, and a loss in muscular coordination. A stroke may cause cerebral infarctions (dead sections of brain tissue).

Stroke occurs in conjunction with at least one of the following four events:

A blood clot forms within a blood vessel of the brain (thrombosis). This is the most common cause.

A blood clot lodges in an artery supplying brain tissue after originating in another portion of the body (embolism). A heart attack, damage to a valve, and an irregular heartbeat can cause blood clots that·may reach the brain.

An intermittent insufficiency in the flow of blood results temporarily from a spasm of the arteries or the sludging of the blood as it passes through segments of vessels that have been narrowed by arteriosclerosis.

Hemorrhage occurs after an artery ruptures, usually as a result of a weakening of the arterial wall because of arteriosclerosis or because of a thinning of the wall along with bulging (an aneurysm), which may be congenital or develop later in life. The walls of arteries in the brain can become weakened by the assault of **high blood pressure**.

So-called "little strokes" result when long, thin arteries penetrating deep into the brain become blocked by arteriosclerosis, causing areas of surrounding tissue to lose their blood supply. Whereas the initial onset of stroke may be massive in its effects, producing widespread paralysis within several hours, the onset may also be manifested by a series of transient little strokes during which the patient may experience weakness and numbness of an arm, a leg, or a side of the face.

Precise history and physical examination are essential to differentiate stroke from a tumor and from brain injury resulting from other causes. Examination of spinal fluid for evidence of blood and diagnostic imaging may clarify the **diagnosis**. Surgery may be attempted to remove the obstruction or to insert a graft or synthetic bypass. Physical and speech therapy may also help prevent deformity. Many victims of stroke may live for a further 10 to 20 years or longer after the occurrence.

Smoking, high cholesterol, aging, diabetes, and heritable defects are among the major **risk factors** for stroke. Statistically, men and African Americans also have a higher stroke risk.

The National Stroke Association recommends maintaining a healthy diet that is low in sodium and fat, exercising, keeping cholestorol and alcohol consumption low, and not smoking.

Internet resources: <www.stroke.org>

Diabetes

Diabetes mellitus is a disease in which the body does not produce or properly use insulin, a hormone that is needed to convert sugar, starches, and other food into energy. Two common problems thus caused by diabetes are hyperglycemia (high blood sugar) and hypoglycemia (low blood sugar). There are two types of diabetes: type I, insulin-dependent diabetes (formerly referred to as juvenile-onset diabetes as it usually arises in childhood); and type II, non-insulin-dependent diabetes (formerly referred to as adult-onset diabetes, as it usually occurs after 40 years of age). Despite their former classifications, either type of diabetes can occur at any age. Type II diabetes is by far the most common type of the disease, accounting for about 90% of all cases.

Type I diabetes is an **autoimmune disorder** in which the diabetic's immune system produces antibodies that destroy insulin-producing beta cells. People with type I diabetes require insulin injections to stay alive. Meal planning and exercise also help keep blood sugar levels regular.

Type II diabetes arises from either sluggish pancreatic secretion of insulin or reduced responsiveness in target cells of the body to secreted insulin, or both. It is linked to genetics and obesity. Some cases of type II diabetes can be controlled through diet and exercise, but often medication or insulin shots are needed as well.

It is estimated that 17 million Americans have diabetes, and one in three does not know it. Often diabetes goes undiagnosed because its symptoms seem harmless at first. Diabetes is also more common in African Americans, Latinos, Native Americans, Asian Americans, and Pacific Islanders. Some of the early **warning signs** of diabetes are: frequent urination, excessive thirst, extreme hunger, unusual weight loss, increased fatigue, irritability, and blurry vision.

Diabetes is the sixth leading cause of death by disease in the US. Each year, at least 190,000 people die as a result of complications associated with diabetes. Possible complications include:

Blindness. Each year, 12,000 to 24,000 people lose their sight due to diabetes. It is the leading cause of new blindness in people 20–74 years of age.

Kidney disease. Diabetic nephropathy, the most common cause of end-stage renal disease, requires dialysis or a kidney transplant to prevent death; 10–21% of all people with diabetes develop kidney disease.

Heart disease and stroke. People with diabetes are two to four times more likely to have heart disease, to die from heart disease, or to suffer a stroke.

Nerve disease and amputations. Approximately 70% of people with diabetes have mild to severe forms of diabetic nerve damage, which can lead to lower limb amputation. Diabetes is the most frequent cause of non-traumatic lower limb amputations in the US.

Impotence. Approximately 13% of men with Type I diabetes and 8% of men with Type II report problems with impotence.

Diabetes is a serious condition, but with proper treatment patients can lead productive lives. To avoid complications, people with diabetes should keep blood-sugar levels close to normal, control their weight, eat a healthy diet, exercise, see a doctor regularly, check their feet carefully for abnormalities, and refrain from smoking.

Internet resources: <www.diabetes.org>

Cancer

Cancer is any of a group of related diseases characterized by uncontrolled multiplication and disorganized growth of the affected cells; it may arise in any of the body's tissues. If left untreated, cancer cells infiltrate and destroy adjacent tissues, eventually gain access to the circulatory system, are transported to distant parts of the body, and ultimately destroy the host. Not all abnormal growths are **malignant**, however; those that are not are referred to as **benign** tumors.

Cancer was known as far back as antiquity, and malignant tumors have been found in mummies 5,000 years old. It is estimated that nearly 1.3 million new cases will arise in the US in 2002. The disease can be caused by a variety of factors, including chemical substances, ionizing radiation, and viruses. Although much is known about how cancer is caused, the precise mechanism involved continues to elude researchers. Certain cancers have the ability to spread from their sites of origin, rendering their treatment and eradication difficult; this results either from direct extension from the primary site as a consequence of growth and tumor cell movement or from the cancer cells entering the vascular system by invading lymphatics or blood vessels (**metastasis**). The more the cancer spreads, the more difficult it is to treat, making early diagnosis of utmost importance.

Some of the major types of cancer are listed below, along with cancer-detection guidelines from the American Cancer Society.

Breast cancer. Breast cancer is the leading cause of death from cancer in women, afflicting approximately 192,200 US women in 2001. *Treatment:* Most patients will require some type of surgery to treat the tumor, possibly in combination with chemotherapy, hormone therapy, or radiation therapy. *Prevention:* Women age 20 and over should perform monthly breast self-exams. Women between the ages of 20 and 39 should have a clinical breast exam every 3 years; women over 40 should have one annually. Women 40 and over should also have a mammogram each year.

Colorectal cancer. Colorectal cancer is very common in the Western world, with an equal incidence in men and women. Generally, the tumors metastasize to the liver, lungs, and other distant sites. *Treatment:* Surgery is the most favored treatment, although chemotherapy and radiation may also be used. *Prevention:* There are five tests to detect colorectal cancer. Individuals 50 and over should choose one of the following options, even if they have no symptoms of the disease:

Fecal occult blood test (every year)
Flexible sigmoidoscopy (every 5 years)
Fecal occult blood test every year plus sigmoidoscopy every 5 years (preferred to either of the above treatments alone)
Double-contrast barium enema (every 5 years)
Colonoscopy (every 10 years)

Leukemias. Leukemias are a heterogeneous group of malignancies of the blood-forming tissues, which include the bone marrow, lymph nodes, and spleen. The acute form of the disease in adults is rapidly fatal, with infiltration of bone marrow and other blood-forming tissues by the malignant cells, while the acute form in children has yielded to treatment and a number of cures are documented. The best established cause involves chronic exposure to ionizing radiation. Other factors, including congenital disorders such as Down syndrome, viruses, and certain chemicals and drugs, have also been implicated. Patients afflicted with leukemia are rendered anemic and are susceptible to infection. *Treatment:* Treatment involves attempts to correct leukemia-related complications by transfusion of normal blood, as well as antibiotics to combat infection and chemotherapy to destroy malignant cells. *Prevention:* There are no special tests that can detect any form of leukemia and no known way to prevent most cases, as the disease is not linked to lifestyle risk factors.

Lung cancer. The most common forms of lung cancer are squamous-cell carcinomas, which arise in bronchial glandular epithelium that has been altered by long exposure to cigarette smoke. Cancers of the lung tend to metastasize widely; the average survival of persons with untreated lung cancer is about 9 months after diagnosis, and the spreading to regional or distant lymph nodes has already occurred in the majority of cases. *Treatment:* Removal of the tumor may prolong life for a number of months. *Prevention:* Do not smoke and avoid second-hand smoke as well as cancer-causing chemicals such as radon gas.

Ovarian cancer. Very common in the industrialized Western world, ovarian cancer may be linked to environmental factors. Many different types of ovarian cancer have been identified, arising either in the epithelium or in connective tissue components. *Treatment:* Tumors may be treated successfully through surgery if diagnosed early. Extension of the disease may require radiation or chemotheraphy. *Prevention:* Only 25% of ovarian cancers are found at an early stage, as they often manifest no symptoms early on. Therefore, women 18 and over should have a yearly pelvic exam. If symptoms do present, imaging studies or biopsy may be used to properly diagnose the disease.

Prostate cancer. A common form of cancer in men, prostate cancer commonly metastasizes to the bones and, together with involvement of nerves in the pelvis, creates considerable pain and discomfort. Fortunately, prostate cancer differs from other cancers in its slow rate of growth; if the cancer does not spread, the 5-year survival rate is nearly 100%, even if it remains untreated. *Treatment:* Surgery, radiation, and chemotherapy are the most-frequently used treatments. PSA blood tests and digital rectal exams can help diagnose the disease. *Prevention:* The exact cause of prostate cancer is not known, but a diet low in animal fat and high in vegetables, fruits, and grains is recommended for overall health.

Skin cancer. Approximately 82% of skin cancer arises from basal cells in the deepest layer of the skin, resulting in basal-cell carcinoma. This type of cancer grows slowly and rarely metastasizes, but does invade locally and can cause considerable destruction of adjacent tissues, which can result in disfigurement. Squamous-cell carcinoma arises from the platelike flat cells that constitute the major cellular component of skin, and these cells may metastasize to regional lymph nodes. *Treatment*: Surgical excision or radiation therapy is often successful. *Prevention:* The best way to lower one's risk of skin cancer is to avoid UV light. A sunscreen with an SPF of 15 or above is recommended, even on cloudy days. A self-exam each month should reveal any new or changing spots or blemishes on the skin; anything unusual should be reported to a health care provider.

Internet resources: <www.cancer.org>

Alzheimer Disease

Alzheimer disease is the most common form of dementia—it is estimated that up to 4 million Americans are currently afflicted. An irreversible, progressive brain disorder that involves the death of brain cells and the breakdown of the connections between them, Alzheimer usually begins gradually, with symptoms increasing as the disease progresses. On average, patients live for 8 to 10 years after diagnosis, but some have been known to survive for as long as 20.

Scientists are still trying to understand the underlying mechanisms of Alzheimer; the disease develops differently among individuals, and this suggests that more than one pathological process may lead to the same outcome. One key element is the presence in the brain of two abnormalities—amyloid plaques and neurofibrillary tangles. Unfortunately, these growths can be detected only during an autopsy, and it is not known whether the plaques and tangles are a cause or a consequence of the disease. The majority of cases of Alzheimer occur after age 60, but about 10% of those who develop the disease are younger. These cases, referred to as early-onset familial Alzheimer disease, result from an inherited genetic mutation.

The Alzheimer Association recognizes 10 **warning signs** of disease onset: memory loss; difficulty performing familiar tasks; problems with language; disorientation to time and place; poor or decreased judgment; problems with abstract thinking; misplacing things; changes in mood or behavior; changes in personality; and loss of initiative. These symptoms become progressively more severe, and eventually people with Alzheimer lose all memory, thinking, and reasoning abilities and become dependent on others for their daily needs.

No single diagnostic test can detect if a person has Alzheimer. Standard clinical methods of **diagnosis** involve a complete medical history, various medical and neuropsychological tests, a mental status evaluation, a neurological examination, and a psychiatric evaluation. These procedures help rule out other diseases and enable physicians to make a positive clinical diagnosis of Alzheimer with approximately 90% accuracy.

There is currently no **treatment** to prevent or reverse the effects of Alzheimer disease; however, four FDA-approved drugs may help prevent worsening of some symptoms for a limited time. Other medications may help control the behavioral symptoms of the disease and make patients more comfortable and easier to care for.

Internet resources: <www.alz.org>

Arthritis

There are more than 100 different medical conditions that fall under the category "arthritis," a blanket term for inflammation of the joints. Arthritis is the number one cause of disability in the US; nearly 43,000,00 (1 in 6) Americans are affected by it, including almost 300,000 children. Arthritis is generally a chronic condition that requires ongoing treatment. Many forms of arthritis are initially difficult to diagnose; health professionals will generally perform a physical exam, conduct various medical tests, and order X rays to confirm a **diagnosis.**

Osteoarthritis, the most common joint disease, is characterized by progressive deterioration of the articular cartilage and afflicts more than 80% of those who reach the age of 70. It often affects the hands and the weight-bearing joints, such as the knees, hips, feet, and back, resulting in stiffness, pain, and a limitation in movement as the disease progresses. The genesis of this disorder is not completely understood, but biomechanical forces that place stress on the joints are thought to interact with biochemical and genetic factors to contribute to the degenerative process. Obesity, joint injury owing to sports, and work-related activities may place individuals at increased risk for developing osteoarthritis. Corticosteroids and NSAIDS are commonly prescribed for **treatment**; glucocorticoids may be injected into the affected joints; and surgery may be needed to relieve chronic pain and improve joint function. In addition, joint protection, weight control, and non-weight-bearing exercise are recommended.

Rheumatoid arthritis is an **autoimmune** disease that typically affects many different joints and may also affect other internal organs. Inflammation and thickening of the synovial membranes can result in irreversible damage to the joint as the inflamed joint lining invades and damages bone and cartilage. In addition to joint swelling, redness, warmth, stiffness, and pain, symptoms may include loss of appetite or energy, fever, anemia, and the development of rheumatoid nodules. Rheumatoid arthritis is about three times as common in women as in men and afflicts about 1% of the adult population in developed nations. Although the exact cause of the disease remains unknown, approximately 80% of individuals with rheumatoid arthritis have characteristic autoantibodies in their blood that are collectively called rheumatoid factor, and there is evidence that such individuals have a genetic susceptibility to some environmental agent related to disease onset. Rheumatoid arthritis is generally chronic, often with periods of disease flare-up and remission. There are a variety of drugs available for **treatment.** Symptomatic medications such as NSAIDS, analgesics, and glucocorticoids help reduce joint pain, stiffness, and swelling, while disease-modifying anti-rheumatic medications, including methotrexate, antimalarials, and biologic agents, may actually help stop disease progression.

Fibromyalgia is an arthritis-related syndrome that is characterized by widespread musculoskeletal pain, fatigue, and tenderness in precise areas of the body. It affects approximately 2% of Americans, primarily women of childbearing age. It was not until 1990 that fibromyalgia was officially recognized as a distinct syndrome. **Treatment** often includes a combination of exercise, medication (including antidepressants), physical therapy, and relaxation.

Other conditions related to arthritis include lupus, ankylosing spondylitis, gout, and psoriatic arthritis.

Internet resources: <www.arthritis.org>

Allergies

An allergy is a hypersensitive reaction by the body to foreign substances that in similar amounts and circumstances are harmless within the bodies of other people.

Antigens that provoke allergic reactions are called **allergens**. Typical allergens include pollens, drugs, lints, bacteria, foods, and dyes or chemicals. Allergies tend to run in families and are common among children. Skin testing is often used to determine the source of the allergen.

Allergic reactions can be the result of inhaled allergens, such as weed, tree, and grass pollen, mold spores, animal dander, or house dust. These generally result in runny nose, sneezing, and watery and itchy eyes (allergic rhinitis). Eczema and contact dermatitis are common skin allergies that may result in a variety of problems, including rashes, hives, and itching. Certain foods, most frequently milk, fish, eggs, nuts, and wheat, tend to produce allergic reactions that result in intestinal disturbances.

Anaphylactic shock is the most severe allergic reaction and often occurs in individuals sensitive to stinging insects, penicillin, nuts, or shellfish. Anaphylaxis causes swelling of body tissues, vomiting, cramps, and a drop in blood pressure.

The most effective **treatment** is avoidance of the allergen. Additionally, allergy shots allow patients to build an immunity to the allergen. Antihistamines, decongestants, bronchodilators, and anti-inflammatory agents may also be used.

Internet resources: <www.aaaai.org>

Asthma

Asthma is a chronic lung disorder affecting 12–17 million Americans, including approximately 5 million children. During an **asthmatic episode,** the airways become inflamed and may constrict, causing episodes of breathlessness, wheezing, coughing, and chest tightness that range in severity from mild to life-threatening. Although the mechanisms underlying an asthmatic episode are not fully understood, in general it is known that exposure to an inciting factor stimulates the release of chemicals from the immune system that cause spasmodic contraction of the smooth muscle surrounding the bronchi, swelling and inflammation of the bronchial tubes, and excessive secretion of mucus. The inflamed, mucus-clogged airways act as a one-way valve, preventing air from being expired.

Asthma is classified into four categories depending on severity and frequency: mild intermittent, mild persistent, moderate persistent, and severe persistent. Childhood asthma is often associated with an inherited susceptibility to **allergens,** substances such as pollen or dust mites. In adults, asthma also may develop in response to allergens, but viral infections, aspirin, exercise, and exposure to certain materials in the workplace may cause the disease as well.

Asthma sufferers are encouraged to minimize their exposure to substances that may trigger an attack. A number of **medications** are available to prevent and control the symptoms of asthma, including long-term and quick-relief prescriptions. A prolonged asthma attack that does not respond to medication may require hospitalization and administration of oxygen. Individuals can also monitor their level of airflow obstruction by using a pocket-size device called a **peak-flow meter.**

Internet resources: <www.aaaai.org>

HIV/AIDS

Acquired Immunodeficiency Syndrome, or AIDS, is a fatal transmissable disorder of the immune system that is caused by the human immunodeficiency virus (HIV). HIV was first isolated in 1983. In most cases, HIV slowly attacks and destroys the **immune system**, leaving the infected individual vulnerable to malignancies and infections that eventually cause death. AIDS is the last stage of HIV infection, during which time these diseases arise. An average interval of 10 years exists between infection with HIV and development of the conditions typical of AIDS. **Pneumonia** and **Kaposi's sarcoma** are two of the most common diseases seen in AIDS patients.

HIV is contracted through semen, vaginal fluid, breast milk, blood, or other body fluids containing blood. Health care workers may come into contact with other body fluids that may transmit the HIV virus, including amniotic and synovial fluids. Although it is a transmissable virus, it is not contagious and it cannot be spread through coughing, sneezing, or casual physical contact. Other **STDs**, such as genital herpes, may increase the risk of contracting AIDS through sexual contact.

The main **cellular target** of HIV is a special class of white blood cells critical to the immune system known as T4 helper cells. Once HIV has entered a helper T cell, it can cause the cell to function poorly or it can destroy the cell. A hallmark of the onset of AIDS is a drastic reduction in the number of helper T cells in the body. Two predominant strains of the virus, designated HIV-1 and HIV-2, are known. World-wide the most common strain is HIV-1, with HIV-2 more common primarily in western Africa; the two strains act in a similar manner, but the latter causes a form of AIDS that progresses much more slowly.

Diagnosis is made on the basis of blood tests approved by the CDC that may be administered by a doctor or at a local health department. Alternately, a home collection kit may be purchased at many pharmacies. No vaccine or cure has yet been developed that can prevent HIV infection. Several **drugs** are now used to slow the development of AIDS, including azidothymidine (AZT). **Protease inhibitors**, such as ritonavir and indinavir, have been shown to block the development of AIDS, at least temporarily. Protease inhibitors are most effective when used in conjunction with two different reverse transcriptase inhibitors—the so-called "triple-drug therapy."

HIV/AIDS is a major problem in developing countries, particularly sub-Saharan Africa. At the end of 2001, 40 million people were estimated to have contracted HIV, with 95% of those living in the developing world.

For information on **prevention**, see "Safer Sex Defined," below.

For confidential information on HIV/AIDS, call 1-800-342-AIDS.

Internet resources: <www.cdc.gov/hiv>

Sexually Transmitted Diseases (STDs)

A sexually transmitted disease (STD) is usually passed from person to person by direct sexual contact. It may also be transmitted from a mother to her child before or at birth or, less frequently, may be passed from person to person in non-sexual contact. STDs usually initially affect the genitals, the reproductive tract, the urinary tract, the oral cavity, the anus, or the rectum but may mature in the body to attack various organs and systems. Following are some of the major STDs:

Syphilis was first widely reported by European writers in the 16th century, and a virtual epidemic swept Europe around the year 1500. Syphilis is spread through direct contact with a syphilis sore (chancre); development of this sore is the first stage of the disease. The second stage manifests itself as a rash on the palms and the bottoms of the feet. In the last stage, symptoms disappear, but the disease remains in the body and may damage internal organs and lead to paralysis, blindness, dementia, and even death. For individuals infected less than a year, a single dose of penicillin will cure the disease. Larger doses are needed for those who have had it for a longer period of time.

Gonorrhea, a form of urethritis (an infection and inflammation of the urethra), is one of the most common STDs. Although spread through sexual contact, the gonorrhea infection can also be spread to other parts of the body after touching the infected area. Men manifest symptoms, which include discharge and a burning sensation when urinating, more often than women. If gonorrhea is left untreated, women may develop pelvic inflammatory disease (PID) and men may become infertile. The disease can also spread to the blood or joints and is potentially life-threatening.

Chlamydia, another form of urethritis, can be transmitted during vaginal, anal, or oral sex. Since there are frequently no symptoms, most infected individuals do not know they have the disease until complications develop. Untreated chlamydia can cause urethral infection in men and PID in women. Antibiotics can successfully cure the disease.

Genital herpes, a disease that became especially widespread in the 1960s and 1970s, often presents minimal symptoms upon infection. The most common sign, however, is blistering in the genital area; outbreaks can occur over many years but generally decrease in severity and number. Genital herpes is caused by the herpes simplex viruses type 1 (HSV-1) and type 2 (HSV-2). The former causes infections on and around the mouth but may be spread through the saliva to the genitals; the latter is transmitted during sexual contact with someone who has a genital infection. The HSV-2 infection can cause problems for people with suppressed immune systems and for infants who contract the disease upon delivery. Herpes can also leave individuals more susceptible to HIV infection and make those carrying the disease more infectious. A variety of treatments, including antiviral medications, have been used to help manage genital herpes, but currently there is no cure for the disease.

Almost all STDs have reasonably effective drug cures. For information on STD **prevention**, see below, "Safer Sex Defined." For information on **HIV disease**, see individual entry.

Internet resources: <www.cdc.gov/nchstp/od/nchstp.html>

Safer Sex Defined

Defining risky sexual behavior. Any activity involving the exchange of body fluids—vaginal secretions, semen, or blood—could result in the transmission of HIV and other STDs. Unprotected vaginal and anal intercourse present the highest risks for contraction of STDs. Women are at greater risk than men of developing an infection as a result of heterosexual intercourse, and many STDs present fewer symptoms in women than in men. However, men and women of all sexual orientations should practice safer sex to reduce their risk of contracting an STD.

HIV testing. It can take years to develop symptoms of HIV disease, so it is important to be tested for HIV after any behavior that might have resulted in infection. The CDC recommends undergoing two separate HIV-antibody tests, six months apart. If the second test is negative, there is a reasonable certainty that HIV is not present.

STD testing. It is important to get checked for other STDs at least once a year. Do not assume that STD testing is part of a routine checkup.

Abstinence. Refraining from any sexual activity that would allow the exchange of body fluids is by far the most effective method of birth control and disease prevention.

Monogamous intercourse. Sexual intercourse with only one partner can be as effective as abstinence in preventing disease transmission, if both partners have been properly tested for HIV and other STDs. Most health professionals, however, recommend continuing to practice safer sex, even in monogamous relationships, as there is no way to be sure a partner is being faithful.

Condoms. Using a latex or female condom correctly and consistently significantly reduces the chance of unplanned pregnancy. Condoms also reduce the risk of transmission of HIV, vaginitis, chlamydia, honeymoon cystitis, syphilis, pelvic inflammatory disease, chancroid, and gonorrhea. Condoms may be less effective in preventing genital warts, herpes, cervical cancer, and hepatitis B. Male and female condoms should not be worn simultaneously.

Birth control. There are many methods of birth control for women that can help prevent unwanted pregnancy, including birth control pills, Norplant, Depo-Provera, condoms, diaphragms, and cervical caps. However, of these, only condoms protect against STDs. Emergency contraception, including the "morning-after" pill, should be used only when necessary and not relied upon as a regular method of birth control. Withdrawal and family planning are not recommended forms of birth control.

Internet resources: <www.sexualhealth.com>

Contraceptive Use by US Women

Percent distribution by age. Source: Fertility, Family Planning, and Women's Health: New Data From the 1995 National Survey of Family Growth (CDC/National Center for Health Statistics)

	AGE 15-44	AGE 15-19	20-24	25-29	30-34	35-39	40-44
Using contraception							
Pill	17.3	13.0	33.1	27.0	20.7	8.1	4.2
Condom	13.1	10.9	16.7	16.8	13.4	12.3	8.8
Female sterilization	17.8	0.1	2.5	11.8	21.4	29.8	35.6
Male sterilization	7.0	0.0	0.7	3.1	7.6	13.6	14.5
Implant	0.9	0.8	2.4	1.4	0.5	0.2	0.1
Injectable	1.9	2.9	3.9	2.9	1.3	0.8	0.2
Intrauterine device (IUD)	0.5	0.0	0.2	0.5	0.6	0.7	0.9
Diaphragm	1.2	...[1]	0.4	0.6	1.7	2.2	1.9
Female condom	...[1]	0.0	0.1	0.0	0.0	0.0	0.0
Periodic abstinence	1.5	0.4	0.6	1.2	2.3	2.1	1.8
Natural family planning	0.2	0.0	0.1	0.2	0.3	0.4	0.2
Withdrawal	2.0	1.2	2.1	2.6	2.1	2.3	1.4
Other[2]	1.0	0.3	0.9	1.2	1.3	0.9	1.8
Total using contraception[3]	**64.2**	**29.8**	**63.4**	**69.3**	**72.7**	**72.9**	**71.5**
Not using contraception							
Surgically sterile female	3.0	0.1	0.1	0.6	1.7	5.1	9.6
Nonsurgically sterile female	1.3	0.7	0.5	0.7	1.2	2.3	1.9
Pregnant or postpartum	4.6	4.5	7.3	8.4	5.6	2.1	0.4
Seeking pregnancy	4.0	0.9	3.4	6.1	6.2	4.6	2.2
Other							
Never had intercourse	10.9	49.8	12.1	4.2	2.7	1.4	1.4
No intercourse in last 3 months	6.2	7.1	6.8	5.7	4.9	6.2	6.8
Had intercourse in last 3 months	5.2	7.1	6.0	4.7	4.4	4.3	5.1
Total not using contraception[3]	**35.8**	**70.2**	**36.6**	**30.7**	**27.3**	**27.1**	**28.5**

[1]*Less than 0.05.*   [2]*Includes morning-after pill, cervical cap, Today™ sponge, suppository, and other methods.*   [3]*Includes other categories not listed. Totals may not add to 100% due to rounding.*

Complementary and Alternative Medicine and Treatment

In the past decade, the use of **alternative therapy** has doubled in North America and Europe, where conventional Western medicine generally had been the only accepted form of treatment. Alternative therapy encompasses both remedies and practices, including the use of herbs, homeopathy, therapeutic massage, acupuncture, hypnotism, and traditional Oriental medicine. Also called **complementary medicine** (as it may be used in conjunction with conventional practices), alternative medicine approaches are often **holistic**, or focused on the whole person, including physical, mental, emotional, and spiritual aspects. Related to alternative therapies in their treatment of the body as whole, **osteopathy** and **chiropractic** have also enjoyed greater acceptance in recent years, particularly in the US.

In 1998 Congress established the National Center for Complementary and Alternative Medicine as a division of the **NIH** to develop and support research on alternative medicine. In May 2002 WHO announced the development of a **global strategy** for researching and regulating alternative treatments; it is currently compiling reports on more than 100 medicinal plants. At issue is the safety and usefulness of alternative medicine, which remains largely unregulated. Often patients pursue treatment without the advice of a health care professional; as with conventional medicines, if used incorrectly alternative treatments can cause injury or even death. WHO is urging member states to adopt regulations to license providers and determine the authenticity and safety of alternative products. Only China, Vietnam, North Korea, and South Korea have integrated traditional medicines into their official health care systems.

Internet resources: <http://nccam.nih.gov>

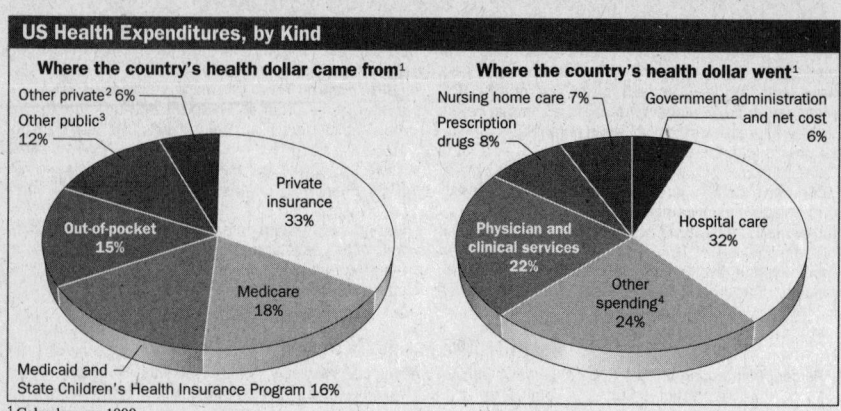

US Health Expenditures, by Kind

Where the country's health dollar came from[1]

- Other private[2] 6%
- Other public[3] 12%
- Out-of-pocket 15%
- Private insurance 33%
- Medicare 18%
- Medicaid and State Children's Health Insurance Program 16%

Where the country's health dollar went[1]

- Nursing home care 7%
- Prescription drugs 8%
- Government administration and net cost 6%
- Physician and clinical services 22%
- Hospital care 32%
- Other spending[4] 24%

[1] Calendar year 1999.

[2] Other private includes industrial in-plant, privately funded construction, and non-patient revenues, including philanthropy.

[3] Other public includes programs such as workers' compensation, public health activity, US Department of Defense, US Department of Veterans Affairs, Indian Health Service, state and local hospital subsidies, and school health.

[4] Other spending includes dentist and other professional services, home health care, durable medical equipment, other nondurable medical products, government public health activities, and research and construction.

Source: Centers for Medicare & Medicaid Services, Office of the Actuary, National Health Statistics Group.

The Centers for Disease Control and Prevention (CDC) and the National Institutes of Health (NIH)

Both the CDC and the NIH are part of the US Department of Health and Human Services.
CDC Web site: <www.cdc.gov>
NIH Web site: <www.nih.gov>

Centers for Disease Control. *Mission:* To promote health and quality of life by preventing and controlling disease, injury, and disability. *Location:* Atlanta, GA. *Acting Director:* Julie L. Gerberding. *Budget:* FY 2004 (requested) $6.5 billion. *Functions:* Monitors health problems and infectious diseases worldwide; conducts research to enhance disease prevention; develops public health policy; provides leadership and training; assists state and local health departments.

National Institutes of Health. *Mission:* To uncover new knowledge that will lead to better health for everyone. *Location:* Bethesda MD. *Director:* Elias A. Zerhouni. *Budget:* FY 2004 (requested) $27.9 billion. *Functions:* Supports and conducts biomedical research, both in its own laboratories and through research grants to universities, medical schools, hospitals, and research institutes. Future research will center on disease treatment and prevention in a variety of areas, including mental illness, cancer, AIDS, arthritis, and other unconquered diseases; improving the health of children, women, and minorities; and better understanding the aging process.

Mental Health

Diagnostic and Statistical Manual of Mental Disorders (DSM)

The *Diagnostic and Statistical Manual of Mental Disorders* (DSM) is the standard reference work on the subject for mental health professionals in the US (worldwide, the World Health Organization's *International Classification of Diseases* is used). Published by the American Psychiatric Association (APA), the *DSM* sets forth diagnostic criteria, descriptions, and other information to help classify and diagnose mental disorders.

There are three main components of the *DSM*. The **diagnostic classification** is a list of mental disorders that are officially recognized by the APA. These labels include diagnostic codes, which are used by institutions for data collection and billing. For each of these disorders, **diagnostic criteria** indicate what symptoms must be present and what others must not be present in order to make a particular diagnosis. A **descriptive text** also follows each disorder and includes information on subtypes, specific age and gender features, prevalence, and familial patterns, among other categories.

The *DSM-I* was published in 1952, at a time when little empirical data existed for the evaluation of mental illness; its primary purpose was to standardize this data collection and establish a consensus among clinicians. Today the *DSM* is used mainly as a diagnostic, rather than a statistical, tool, but it is still an evolving entity, and changes are made with every new edition. One example of the way the *DSM* has evolved involves the classification of homosexuality as a mental disorder. Facing mounting empirical data, changing social norms, and pressure from the gay community, the board of trustees of the APA removed homosexuality from the *DSM* in 1973; it was subsequently replaced with a more refined diagnosis, egodystonic homosexuality, which was marked by a lack of heterosexual arousal despite the desire for such and by unwanted homosexual impulses. This disorder was in turn criticized, and homosexuality was entirely removed from the *DSM* in 1987.

The most recent edition, *DSM-IV*, was completed in 1994; a text revision, **DSM-IV-TR**, was made available in July 2000 (changes to the diagnostic criteria for Tourette's Disorder and Alzheimer's Disease were among the revisions). The *DSM-V* is slated for publication in 2010.

Anxiety Disorders

Anxiety is defined as a feeling of fear, dread, or apprehension that arises without a clear or appropriate real-life justification. Generally, intense, persistent, or chronic anxiety that is not justified and that interferes with daily functioning is classified as a manifestation of a mental disorder. The most common anxiety disorders are:

Panic disorder. Panic disorder is characterized by recurrent panic attacks, with at least one of the attacks followed by persistent fear of having another attack, worry about the implications or consequences of the attack, or a change in behavior related to the attack; these feelings last for one month or more. A **panic attack** is the sudden onset of intense apprehension, fear, or terror and at least four of the following conditions: shortness of breath or a smothering sensation; palpitations or accelerated heart rate; chest pain or discomfort; choking; dizziness or faintness; trembling or shaking; sweating; nausea or abdominal distress; a feeling of unreality; numbness or tingling; hot flashes or chills; fear of dying; and fear of "going crazy" or losing control. A panic attack is unexpected and does not immediately precede or follow a stressful situation, although the person who experiences the attack usually is in a period of increased stress. It is easy to mistake the attack for other problems such as heart disease, as somatic symptoms play a prominent role. There is a close association between panic disorder and **depression**, and a large percentage of persons suffering from panic disorder go on to experience a major depression within the next few years. *Treatment:* Short-term individual psychotherapy is usually helpful, during which relaxation and imagery techniques may be taught. For more severe cases, benzodiazepines or selective serotonin reuptake inhibitor antidepressants may be prescribed.

Generalized anxiety disorder. Generalized anxiety disorder is characterized as the unrealistic or excessive worry about two or more life circumstances that is experienced more days than not for a period of six months or longer. Examples are excessive worry about finances or danger to one's child when there is no reason for this concern. The anxious behavior indicative of this disorder includes symptoms such as trembling, muscle soreness, restlessness, shortness of breath, palpitations, dizziness, difficulty concentrating, and an exaggerated startle response. *Treatment:* The first stage of treatment should be a full medical exam to rule out a biological or environmental cause. If the anxiety is found to be a psychological disorder, there are a number of treatment options, including cognitive-behavioral therapy, which often teaches relaxation techniques; hypnotherapy and self-help treatments can also be useful. Medication is often used in treatment as well. Traditionally, benzodiazepines were used, but they are often habit-forming and sedating; Buspar (buspirone) does not have these side effects and is now often prescribed. Some antidepressant medications may also relieve the symptoms of anxiety.

Post-traumatic stress disorder. The result of exposure to a very distressing event that elicits feelings of intense terror, fear, or helplessness, post-traumatic stress disorder often results in frequent flashbacks, nightmares, or an exaggerated startle response. Events that may cause this disorder include witnessing a murder, participating in a military battle, or being raped. *Treatment:* Three main psychotherapy treatments are used: stress inoculation, in which the patients learn coping skills to conquer their fears; prolonged exposure, in which the event is talked about repeatedly and thus rendered less threatening; and cognitive processing, in which memories of the event are written about and discussed with the therapist in order to reevaluate the emotions affected by the trauma. Medication is not generally used to treat this disorder except when specific symptoms, such as anxiety or depression, are also present. Self-help and a good support network are also valuable in the healing process.

Phobias. A phobic disorder involves the persistent and irrational fear of a specific object, activity, or situation that results in avoidance. Individuals with phobias recognize that their fear is excessive or unreasonable but cannot control the anxiety associated with it. **Specific phobias** usually develop in adolescence or adulthood and affect more than 1 in 10 people. Examples include fear of dogs, water, or flying; some of the most severe types are **agoraphobia** (characterized by a fear of being in open or public places) and **claustrophobia** (fear of confined spaces). The immediate response often resembles a panic attack. *Treatment:* Behavioral approaches are used, including desensitization, in which the patient is gradually exposed to a phobic object or situation, and emotive imagery, in which relaxation techniques help guide the patient through an imagined phobic encounter. **Social phobia** is the fear of social situations in which the individual dreads being criticized or humiliated. *Treatment:* Cognitive-behavioral therapy is widely used; tricyclic antidepressants can be useful in combatting panic attacks.

Obsessive-compulsive disorder. This disorder is marked by recurrent obsessions or compulsions that cause extreme distress and interfere with the normal activities of daily life. **Obsessions** are persistent ideas, thoughts, impulses, or images that are experienced as intrusive, senseless, and generally repugnant but which cannot be ignored or suppressed. Common obsessions include thoughts about committing violent acts, worries about contamination, and doubt (as in wondering whether one had turned off the stove before leaving the house). **Compulsions** are repetitive, intentional behaviors performed in a ritualized manner in an attempt to neutralize the obsession and control the anxiety associated with it. Persistent hand washing, counting, or touching are common compulsive behaviors. *Treatment:* Behavioral therapy, including systematic desensitization and flooding techniques, is common. The antidepressant drugs clomipramine (Anafranil), fluoxetine (Prozac), and fluvoxamine (Luvox) are helpful in relieving symptoms for the majority of sufferers.

Internet resources: <www.nimh.nih.gov/anxiety/anxietymenu.cfm>

Autism

Autism is a neurobiological disorder that affects physical, social, and language skills. The term was first used by the psychiatrist Leo Kanner in the 1940s to describe children who appeared to be excessively withdrawn and self-preoccupied. The syndrome usually appears before 2½ years of age. According to the Autism Society of America, the following areas may be affected by autism:

Social interaction. Autistic infants generally appear indifferent or averse to affection and physical contact, though attachment to caregivers often develops later. Children are less responsive to eye contact or other social cues. Inappropriate attachment to objects may occur.

Communication. Speech develops slowly and abnormally or not at all. It may be characterized by meaningless repetition or strange mechanical sounds.

Sensory impairment. There may be underemphasized reaction to sound, no reaction to pain, or no recognition of genuine danger, as well as sensitivities in the areas of sight, touch, hearing, smell, and taste.

Play. Autistic children do not play spontaneously, imitate the play of others, or imagine their own games.

Behaviors. Usually the syndrome is accompanied by an obsessive desire to prevent environmental change, and frequently, rhythmic body movements such as rocking or hand-clapping. The behavior of children with autism varies greatly, from overactivity to passivity.

About 25% of autistic children develop **seizures** by late adolesence. Some individuals with autism also have other disorders of the brain, including epilepsy, Down syndrome, or mental retardation, or genetic disorders such as Tourette's syndrome, thus making the disease very difficult to diagnose. There are no medical tests for the **diagnosis** of autism, but tests may help rule out other diseases. Initial diagnosis may include a number of different health care professionals, including a psychologist, neurologist, developmental pediatrician, speech and language therapist, learning consultant, or other autism specialist.

The **cause** of autism remains unknown and the disease is incompletely understood. Recent research has revealed abnormalities in the brain structure of autistic individuals, abnormalities likely to have occurred during early brain development. Researchers also have noted a deficiency of large nerve cells called Purkinje cells and an excess of serotonin. There appears to be a complex genetic component as well. Since the early 1990s the global rate of autism has increased greatly; researchers speculate that over-vaccination has contributed to this disturbing rise.

Treatment of autism centers on helping the patient, as well as caregivers, to understand and cope with the disorder. Whereas most sufferers were previously institutionalized, children and adults with autism are now living more independently and becoming integrated into mainstream society. Some autistic individuals display remarkable talents, such as enhanced musical or mathematical prowess. Currently, there is no prescribed medical regime for autistic individuals.

Depression

Clinical depression usually involves one or more of the following symptoms consistently for at least a two-week period: feelings of sadness, hopelessness, or pessimism; lowered self-esteem and heightened self-depreciation; a decrease or loss of ability to enjoy daily life; reduced energy and vitality; slowness of thought or action; loss of appetite; suicidal ideation; and disturbed sleep or insomnia. Depression differs from simple grief or mourning, which are appropriate emotional responses to the loss of loved persons or objects. Where there are clear grounds for a person's unhappiness, depression is considered to be present if the depressed mood is disproportionately long or severe.

Depression is probably the most common psychiatric complaint; the rate of incidence increases with age in men, while the peak for women is between the ages of 35 and 45 (women in general suffer from depression more often than men). Most professionals now agree that biological, social, and psychological factors all contribute to depression. The chief biochemical cause seems to be the defective regulation of the release of one or more naturally occurring monoamines in the brain, particularly norepinephrine and serotonin. Reduced quantities or reduced activity of these chemicals is linked to depression.

Treatment of depression has been a controversial topic in recent years as new drugs have been approved by the Food and Drug Administration. Many types of psychotherapy, both individual and group, are used to treat depressed patients; the medications most often prescribed are selective serotonin reuptake inhibitors (SSRIs), which regulate serotonin. A combination of psychotherapy and medication is generally the preferred choice for treatment. Hospitalization may be necessary if a patient is contemplating **suicide**. Although most depressed individuals are only mildly suicidal, poorly monitored administration of medications may actually increase the risk of suicide. The energizing effects of an anti-depressant can empower patients to act on suicidal thoughts, whereas they previously lacked the energy or will to do so; an inadequate or incomplete trial of a medication has also been correlated with increased suicide rates. An alternate or complementary approach to the treatment of depression involves the use of self-help techniques, including depression-oriented support groups.

Internet resources: <www.nimh.nih.gov/publicat/depressionmenu.cfm>

Bipolar Disorder

Bipolar disorder, or **manic-depression,** is characterized by alternating periods of extreme moods, from excessive irritability or elation (manic state) to despondency or severe tension (depressed state), often with periods of normal mood in between. The frequency and duration of this cycling of moods varies between individuals but usually begins in adolescence or early adulthood. Bipolar disorder may also feature such psychotic symptoms as delusions and hallucinations. **Depression** is the more common symptom, and many patients never develop a genuine manic phase, although they may experience a brief period of overoptimism and mild euphoria while recovering from a depression. Patients in a manic state are highly sociable, gregarious, and optimistic and have grandiose notions and an inflated sense of self-esteem.

At any given time, at least two million Americans suffer from bipolar disorder. The first manic episode may be caused by some external stress the patient has experienced, but ensuing cycles are beyond control. Statistical studies have suggested a hereditary predisposition to the disorder, and this has now been linked to a defect on a dominant gene located on chromosome 11. In a physiological sense, it is believed that bipolar disorder is caused by the faulty regulation of one or more amines at sites in the brain where the transmission of nerve impulses takes place; a deficiency of the amines results in depression, and an excess of them causes mania. However, there is no single known cause for the disorder, and the best **treatment** involves individual or group therapy and medication. The two complement one another, as follow-up care can help ensure medical compliance, often an issue for manic-depressive patients: one of the main causes of a return of the disorder is the patient's discontinuance of medication. **Lithium** is the drug of choice and is generally prescribed long-term. However, if a patient first presents in a depressive state, appropriate antidepressants may be used initially. If left untreated, the disease worsens and the patient eventually experiences full-fledged mania and clinical depression. With proper treatment, people with bipolar disorder can lead productive, functional lives.

Eating Disorders

Eating disorders are characterized by an unhealthy relationship with food in which normal eating habits are disrupted or polarized. They most often afflict women in adolescence or early adulthood and are linked to low self-esteem and poor body image rather than any biomedical cause. The main eating disorders are:

Anorexia nervosa. The most defining feature of anorexia is starvation, accompanied by the patients' misperception that they are actually overweight. Emotional manifestations may range from a neurotic overreaction to a weight-reduction diet to full-blown schizophrenic delusions resulting in the abhorrence of food. As with bulimia, **binging** (extreme overindulgence in food) may be part of this destructive eating cycle. These patterns are related to a preoccupation with self-control through starvation, and loss of that control leads to shame and self-loathing. Sufferers are often able to maintain their strength and daily activities at approximately normal levels; they appear characteristically unconcerned with their undernourished state. Associated symptoms include vomiting and, in women, failure to menstruate. *Treatment:* A complete medical examination is needed to assess any possible physical damage done during the course of the disease. In severe cases hospitalization may be necessary. Since people suffering from anorexia often rationalize their behavior, they may be unwilling to seek help. A trusting relationship with a therapist is key, though patients may relapse during the course of treatment. Group therapy may also prove useful. Often, specific childhood trauma triggers the patient's negative self-image; exploring these issues may help reach the goal of an improved self-evaluation. Medications, particularly anti-depressants, may be prescribed.

Bulimia nervosa. Bulimia is characterized by periods of **binging** followed by **purging** via one or more of the following: self-induced vomiting, unnecessary ingestion of laxatives, or exercising too much. Binging is often done in secret and is followed by a shame and self-loathing similar to that experienced by anorexic individuals, which results in the subsequent purging. Although sufferers are also obsessed with body image, unlike anorexic patients the majority are close to their proper weight. If left untreated, bulimia can result in serious medical complications, such as dental decay, stomach rupture, and dehydration, and can also be fatal. *Treatment:* Like anorexia, a prominent feature of bulimia is a negative self-image, and treatment options are the same. Since bulimic patients may purge medication, careful monitoring is necessary.

A new diagnostic category, **binge-eating disorder**, was recently classified as a medical condition. Patients with this disorder also overindulge in food but do not follow the cycle of purging.

Personality Disorders

Personality disorders are marked by deeply ingrained and lasting patterns of inflexible, maladaptive, or antisocial behavior. A personality disorder is an accentuation of one or more personality traits. It need not disrupt a person's daily functioning, but in times of extreme stress symptoms increase and may interfere with psychological and emotional functioning. Individuals with personality disorders generally have difficulty with interpersonal relationships, range of emotion, self-perception, and impulse control. There are many different types of personality disorders, classified below according to the **DSM-IV**. All manifest themselves by early adulthood.

Antisocial personality disorder. Individuals follow a pattern of behavior that disregards and often violates the rights of others, including at least three of the following symptoms: failure to conform to social norms and the law (frequent arrests are common); deceitfulness, including lying, using aliases, and deceiving others for profit; impulsivity (failure to plan ahead); irritability and aggressiveness (physical fights); reckless disregard for individual's own safety or the safety of others; consistent irresponsibility, including failure to sustain work or be financially responsible; and a lack of remorse concerning mistreatment of others. *Treatment:* Psychotherapy is the usual treatment, with medication being used to help with mood swings or other specific problems. Many individuals will be mandated to therapy by the court, though not all people who commit crimes can be classified as having antisocial personality disorder, and thorough psychological testing is needed. Proper therapy may help individuals realize greater emotional depth. Group therapy centered around the disorder may also be useful in exploring these issues and establishing relationships.

Avoidant personality disorder. This disorder involves extreme social inhibition, hypersensitivity, and feelings of inadequacy. Four or more of the following symptoms must be present: avoidance of occupational activities involving significant interpersonal contact; unwillingness to become involved with people socially unless certain of being accepted; restraint within intimate relationships; preoccupation with social criticism or rejection; inhibition in new interpersonal situations; negative self-perception (views self as inferior and unappealing to others); and a reluctance to take risks or participate in new activities due to fear of embarrassment. *Treatment:* Short-term individual psychotherapy is the preferred treatment, though some patients may attend group therapy later in the process. Medication is not useful unless there is a concurrent disorder that requires it.

Borderline personality disorder. Individuals with this disorder experience unstable interpersonal relationships, self-image, and emotions and display impulsive behaviors. These problems are present in social, familial, and occupational settings. Five or more of the following are necessary for diagnosis: frantic efforts to avoid real or imagined abandonment; a pattern of unstable but intense interpersonal relationships characterized by alternating idealization and devaluation (a person is either "good" or "bad"); identity disturbance (unstable self-image); impulsivity in at least two areas that are potentially self-damaging (including spending, substance abuse, reckless driving, binge eating, and sexual activity); recurrent suicidal behavior or threats, or self-mutilation; emotional instability owing to a marked reactivity of mood (intense episodic irritability or anxiety usually lasting a few hours); long-term feelings of emptiness; inappropriate, intense anger and lack of control over this emotion; and transient, stress-related paranoia or severe dissociative symptoms. *Treatment:* People with this disorder are notoriously difficult to treat, as they place a considerable emotional burden on a therapist. Fairly long-term psychotherapy is the preferred treatment, and the use of medication is controversial. Suicidal feelings may require hospitalization and should always be evaluated by the therapist. A popular new treatment called dialectical behavior therapy teaches patients how to better control their emotions and lives through regulation and self-knowledge.

Dependent personality disorder. This disorder is characterized by a fear of separation or abandonment and manifests itself in submissive and clinging behavior. Five or more of the following symptoms are present: difficulty making everyday decisions; the need for others to assume responsibility over the patient's life; difficulty expressing disagreement; difficulty initiating projects or doing things alone; going to excessive lengths to garner other's support; discomfort or helplessness when left alone; need to seek a new relationship as soon as a close relationship ends; and fears of being left to care for oneself. *Treatment:* Psychotherapy is preferred, though the relationship between therapist and patient is often a delicate one given the latter's need for constant reassurance and support. Long-term therapy is generally not recommended, and ending therapy may be

an indication of how well the patient has progressed. Assertiveness training and group therapy later in treatment may also be useful. Medication is generally avoided, as drug abuse and overdose are common in individuals with this disorder.

Histrionic personality disorder. Individuals exhibit excessive emotionality and seek attention. Five or more of the following symptoms are present: discomfort in situations in which the individual is not the center of attention; interaction with others that is often characterized by sexually seductive behavior; rapidly shifting emotions that appear shallow; use of physical appearance to draw attention; excessively impressionistic speech that lacks detail; self-dramatization, theatricality, and exaggerated emotional expression; suggestibility (easily influenced by criticism); and relationships that the individual deems more intimate than they actually are. *Treatment:* Individual psychotherapy is preferred, as group therapy may exacerbate the patients' needs to dramatize and draw attention to themselves. Boundary issues between therapist and client are key, and solution-focused treatment dedicated to helping the individual view social interactions objectively is usually helpful. Medication is generally prescribed with great caution, as suicidal behavior is common.

Narcissistic personality disorder. This disorder is characterized by a pattern of grandiosity, the need for admiration, and a lack of empathy; patients manifest five or more of the following symptoms: grandiose sense of self-importance; preoccupation with fantasies of unlimited success, power, brilliance, beauty, or ideal love; belief that they are unique and can only associate with or be understood by others who are equally special; need for excessive admiration; sense of entitlement (unreasonable expectations of favorable treatment or compliance with wishes); exploitation of interpersonal relationships; difficulty identifying with others' needs and a lack of empathy; envy of others or the belief that others envy them; and arrogance or haughtiness. *Treatment:* Frequently, patients with narcissistic personality disorder are hospitalized. Individual therapists will often be devalued by clients in an attempt to gain dominance and maintain their fragile sense of grandeur. In extreme cases, treatment may be symptom-oriented; less-resistant patients often are taught how to acknowledge the needs and ideas of others while maintaining a healthier sense of self (this goal may be aided by group therapy).

Obsessive-compulsive personality disorder. Defined as a pervasive preoccupation with orderliness, perfectionism, and mental and interpersonal control, individuals with this disorder engage in behaviors even when they impair flexibility, openness, and efficiency. Four or more of the following symptoms are present: preoccupation with details, rules, lists, order, organization, or schedules; perfectionism that interferes with task completion; excessive devotion to work and productivity (to the exclusion of leisure activities); inflexibility about morals, ethics, or values to the point of being overly scrupulous or conscientious; inability to discard worn-out objects; reluctance to delegate authority or to work with others; hoarding of money; and rigidity and stubbornness. *Treatment:* Psychotherapy is often focused on short-term symptom relief and coping mechanisms, as well as helping the patient identify and realize more complex emotions. Patients are usually resistent to long-term therapy with the goal of personality change. Group therapy and medication are not often used, though newer medications such as Prozac may provide some relief.

Paranoid personality disorder. Persons with this disorder are distrustful and suspicious of others and interpret others' motives as malevolent. Four or more of the following symptoms are present: suspicion that others are exploiting, harming, or deceiving them (without sufficient cause); preoccupation with the trustworthiness or loyalty of friends or associates; reluctance to confide in others (with the fear that this information will be used against them); misinterpretation of benign remarks or events; persistance in bearing a grudge; perception of character attacks that do not exist; and suspicions regarding the fidelity of a sexual partner. *Treatment:* Paranoid personality disorder is very difficult to treat, as individuals with this disorder rarely seek help and usually suffer from it their whole lives. There has been no substantive work done to determine a course of treatment, but a straightforward, trusting relationship with a therapist may prove promising. Clients often view medication with suspicion, and there is no specific drug used to treat this condition.

Schizoid personality disorder. A pervasive detachment from social relationships and a restricted range of emotions in interpersonal settings characterize this disorder, which may manifest itself in four or more of the following symptoms: lack of desire to form close relationships; limitation to solitary activities; little interest in sexual experiences; little plea-sure in most activities; no close friends other than immediate relatives; indifference to praise or criticism; and emotional coldness and detachment. *Treatment:* Psychotherapy is usually best kept short-term, with clear and simple goals in mind. Individuals may attempt group therapy following initial treatment. No medication has proven effective for this disorder.

Schizotypal personality disorder. Individuals with this disorder exhibit acute discomfort with close relationships as well as cognitive or perceptual distortions and eccentricities of behavior. Five or more of the following symptoms are present: ideas of reference; odd beliefs or magical thinking that influences behavior; unusual perceptual experiences, including bodily illusions; odd thinking and speech; suspiciousness or paranoid ideation; inappropriate or constricted emotions; behavior or appearance that is eccentric; lack of close friends other than immediate relatives; and excessive social anxiety that does not diminish with familiarity and tends to be associated with paranoia. *Treatment:* Psychotherapy usually focuses on developing a supportive, non-threatening relationship with the client as well as social skills training and other behavioral approaches. Group therapy may be appropriate after the initial treatment. Antipsychotic medications may be useful for treating the more acute phases of this disorder.

Schizophrenia

Schizophrenia refers to any of a group of severe mental disorders that have in common such symptoms as hallucinations, delusions, blunted emotions, disordered thinking, and a withdrawal from reality. The most common psychotic disorder, schizophrenia affects approximately 1% of the world's population; it is estimated that between one third and one half of all homeless Americans have schizophrenia. There is no known cause, but scientists are currently researching possible genetic and hereditary factors (the disorder tends to run in families). There are four main types of this disorder:

Paranoid type. This type of schizophrenia usually arises later in life than others and is characterized primarily by delusions of persecution and grandeur combined with unrealistic, illogical thinking, often accompanied by hallucinations.

Catatonic type. Characterized by striking motor behavior, patients with this form may remain in a state of almost complete immobility, often assuming statuesque positions. Mutism (the inability to talk), extreme incompliance, and absence of almost all voluntary actions are also common. This state of inactivity is at times preceded or interrupted by episodes of excessive motor activity and excitement, generally of an impulsive, unpredictable nature.

Disorganized (hebephrenic) type. Patients display shallow and inappropriate emotional responses, fool-ish or bizarre behavior, disorganized speech, delusions, and hallucinations.

Undifferentiated type. The simplest form of schizophrenia, it manifests as an insidious and gradual reduction in external relations and interests. A lack of emotional depth, a simplicity of ideation, a relative absence of mental activity, a progressive lessening in the use of inner resources, and a retreat to simpler or sterotyped behavior is common.

These types are not mutually exclusive, and schizophrenic patients may display a combination of symptoms that defy convenient classification. There may also be a mixture of schizophrenic symptoms with those of other psychoses, notably those of **bipolar disorder.**

Treatment always focuses on medication. Unfortunately, patients often relapse after failing to take their medications; therapy, including family therapy, may aid in support and help prevent such a relapse. A combination of antipsychotic, antianxiety, and antidepressant medications are often combined. Newer antipsychotics, which block both serotonin and dopamine receptors, prove promising, as they effectively treat a fuller range of symptoms with fewer side effects.

Internet resources: <www.nimh.nih.gov/publicat/schizmenu.cfm>

Alcohol and Substance Abuse

Alcoholism. Simply defined, alcoholism is the excessive and repeated use of alcoholic beverages that causes harm to the drinker; this harm may be physical, mental, social, or economic. It has recently been accepted that alcoholism is a disease, a compulsive behavior out of the user's control akin to other substance abuse problems. Unlike other addictions, however, alcoholics do not need increased doses to produce the desired effect. Although consciousness of the disease is high, the nature and causes of alcoholism remain marginally understood.

Many theories of the **cause** of alcoholism rest on the limited perspectives of specialists in particular disciplines or professions, most of which have their own definitions of the disease. The most comprehensive conceptions recognize that alcoholism may have a genetic or constitutional underlying factor—not a fateful heredity but a predisposition that renders some people more disposed to alcoholism than others. Other factors, such as childhood trauma, may also make a person more vulnerable to addiction. Some evidence links alcoholism to other mental illness and hypothesizes that alcohol intake is a form of self-medicating behavior that masks a different condition, such as depression or anxiety.

Because of the lack of a precise definition, it is difficult to rely on statistics regarding alcoholism. However, in the US rates are generally higher in urban and industrialized areas and among men, and alcoholism is certainly in the front rank of public-health problems. Suicide rates are 2.5 times higher; accidental death rates are seven times higher; and there is an enormously higher rate of general morbidity among alcoholics.

Treatment may be physiological (with drugs that cause vomiting and a feeling of panic when alcohol is consumed); psychological (with therapy and rehabilitation); or social (group therapy). These may take place in or out of an institutional setting, though there is a growing trend in the US toward detoxification centers. Suddenly stopping heavy drinking can lead to **withdrawal** symptoms, including delirium tremens. Many professionals recommend a variety of treatments pursued simultaneously, and even clients in individual therapy are encouraged to attend Alcoholics Anonymous (AA) meetings. AA was founded in 1935 and is based on Twelve Steps, a nonsectarian spiritual program the central points of which are reliance on God or a higher power as each individual understands that concept and the value of help to other alcoholics. AA is thought by many to be the single most successful method yet devised for coping with alcoholism.

Substance abuse. Abused substances include anabolic steroids, which are used by some athletes to enhance performance, and psychotropic agents, substances that affect the user's mental state and are mood- and perception-altering. The latter category, which has a much longer history of abuse, includes opium (and the derivative heroin), hallucinogens, barbiturates, cocaine, amphetamines, tranquilizers, and cannabis (alcohol is also often included in this group). Dependence on prescribed drugs is increasingly common, particularly with tranquilizers and hypnotics. Ecstasy abuse and solvent abuse became increasingly popular among young people in the late 1990s.

Like alcoholics, individuals addicted to drugs are compelled to use them despite the deterioration in health, work, or social activities they may cause. This dependence varies from drug to drug in its extent and effect; it can be physical or psychological or both. Physical dependence becomes apparent only when the drug intake is decreased or stopped and **withdrawal** occurs. Psychological dependence is indicated when the user relies on a drug to produce a feeling of well-being. Another related phenomenon is **tolerance**, a gradual decrease in the effect of a certain dose as the drug is repeatedly taken, causing the user to consume larger doses to produce the desired effect (most marked with habitual opiate users). **Treatment** is similar to that for alcoholism and involves an initial process of detoxification, which should be medically supervised.

Internet resources:
<www.niaaa.nih.gov> (alcohol abuse)
<www.samhsa.gov> (substance abuse)

Suicide

Suicide prevention hotline: 1-800-SUICIDE; Suicide prevention online: <www.samaritans.org>;
Other Internet resources: <www.nimh.nih.gov/suicideprevention/index.cfm>.

Every year approximately 30,000 Americans commit suicide, making it the 11th leading cause of death in 2001. Suicide has historically been condoned by some groups, including the Brahmans of India and the samurai of Japan. In some countries suicide attempts are punishable by law, but in many there is now a greater readiness to sympathize with rather than condemn suicide, though a tendency to conceal suicidal acts still persists.

Although not classified as a distinct mental disorder, suicide is closely linked to **depression** and **bipolar disorder**. It is estimated that approximately 60% of people who commit suicide have had some form of mood disorder. In younger people, substance abuse often plays a role as well. Early recognition and treatment of mental disorders is thus an important deterrent.

Over half of all suicides occur in men aged 25–65; men are often more deliberate in their suicide intentions, are less likely to confide in someone about their plans, and often use measures that are more certain to be lethal.

Among the **warning signs** of suicide are: suicidal talk, including threats of self-harm; previous suicide attempts; preoccupation with death; signs of depression, including social withdrawal, agitation, and behavioral changes; a recent life crisis, such as divorce or the loss of a loved one; and disposal of possessions. Friends and relatives who suspect a person of suicidal ideation are encouraged to get help from agencies specializing in suicide prevention and to always take seriously the threat of suicide.

Assisted suicide, or euthanasia, is currently illegal in the US. The exception is Oregon, where physician-assisted suicide is permitted under tightly controlled conditions. Those in favor of assisted suicide argue that the terminally ill have a right to die with dignity and on their own terms. Many in the medical profession oppose physician-assisted suicide on ethical grounds, as health care workers are bound to prevent injury, even if it is self-induced. Others note that depression, and thus suicidal ideation, is a natural response to a debilitating disease.

Incidence of Suicide in the US, 1900–2002

Age-adjusted rates per 100,000 population. Figures based on death registration data.
Courtesy of National Center for Injury Prevention and Control.

YEAR	MALE	FEMALE	TOTAL	YEAR	MALE	FEMALE	TOTAL
1900	17.7	5.0	11.3	1954	16.3	4.1	10.1
1906	22.0	6.2	14.3	1960	16.5	4.9	10.6
1912	26.0	7.9	17.3	1966	16.1	5.9	10.9
1918	20.0	6.9	13.6	1972	17.4	6.7	11.9
1924	20.2	6.2	13.4	1978	18.7	6.2	12.3
1930	26.2	7.4	17.0	1984	18.6	5.2	11.6
1936	22.4	7.0	14.8	1990	19.0	4.5	11.5
1942	18.0	5.8	11.8	1996	18.0	4.1	10.8
1948	16.7	5.1	10.8	2002	18.4	4.2	10.9

Diet and Exercise

The Food and Drug Administration (FDA)

The FDA is a division of the US Department of Health and Human Services. FDA Web site: <www.fda.gov>.

Mission: To promote and protect the public health by helping safe and effective products reach the market in a timely way and monitoring products for continued safety after they are in use. **Location:** Rockville, MD. **Commissioner of Food and Drugs:** Mark B. McClellan. **Budget:** FY 2004 (requested) $1.4 billion. **Functions:** The FDA is the agency of the US federal government authorized by Congress to inspect, test, approve, and set safety standards for foods and food additives, drugs, chemicals, cosmetics, and household and medical devices. Generally, the FDA is empowered to prevent untested products from being sold and to take legal action to halt sale of undoubtedly harmful products or of products which involve a health or safety risk. Through court procedure, the FDA can seize products and prosecute the persons or firms responsible for legal violation. FDA authority is limited to interstate commerce. The agency cannot control prices nor directly regulate advertising except of prescription drugs and medical devices.

Vitamins, with Daily Recommendations

Vitamins are organic substances that are usually divided into two types: water-soluble and fat-soluble. Small quantities are necessary for normal health and growth in higher forms of animal life, as they work to regulate reactions that occur in metabolism (in contrast to macronutrients such as fats, carbohydrates, and proteins, which are the compounds utilized in the reactions regulated by vitamins). Absence of a vitamin blocks one or more specific metabolic reactions in a cell; thus, vitamin deficiency may result in specific diseases. As they generally cannot be synthesized by humans, vitamins must be obtained from the diet or from a synthetic source.

The name of each vitamin is followed by its alternative name and usual pharmaceutical preparation, respectively. Amounts shown indicate recommended daily consumption.

Abbreviations—mg: milligram; mcg: microgram; RE: retinol equivalent; IU: international unit

Water-soluble vitamins

Thiamin (vitamin B_1; thiamine hydrochloride)
  Purpose: energy metabolism and initiation of nerve impulses. **Dietary sources:** pork, nuts, peas. **Men over 14:** 1.2 mg; **women over 18:** 1.1 mg; **pregnant women:** 1.4 mg; **lactating women:** 1.5 mg.

Riboflavin (vitamin B_2; riboflavin)
  Purpose: release of energy from carbohydrates, fats, and proteins; maintaining integrity of red blood cells. **Dietary sources:** milk, eggs, kidney, liver, peas, soybeans, leafy vegetables. **Men over 14:** 1.3 mg; **women over 18:** 1.0 mg; **pregnant women:** 1.4 mg; **lactating women:** 1.6 mg.

Niacin (nicotonic acid; nicotinamide; nicotinamide)
  Purpose: release of energy from carbohydrates and fats; red blood cell formation; metabolism of proteins. **Dietary sources:** cereal grains, nuts, green vegetables, liver, kidney. **Men over 14:** 16.0 mg; **women over 18:** 14.0 mg; **pregnant women:** 18.0 mg; **lactating women:** 17.0 mg.

Pantothenic acid (vitamin B_5; calcium pantothenate)
  Purpose: metabolism of carbohydrates; synthesis and degradation of fats; synthesis of sterols and other compounds. **Dietary sources:** liver, kidney, eggs, avocados, bananas. **All adults:** 4.0–7.0 mg.

Vitamins, with Daily Recommendations (continued)

Water-soluble vitamins (continued)

Vitamin B6 (pyroxidine; pyroxidine hydrochloride)
   Purpose: amino acid, carbohydrate, and fat metabolism. **Dietary sources:** bananas, cereal grains, fish, nuts, spinach. **Men 14–50:** 1.3 mg; **men over 50:** 1.7 mg; **women 19–50:** 1.3 mg; **women over 50:** 1.5 mg; **pregnant women:** 1.9 mg; **lactating women:** 2.0 mg.

Biotin (N/A; biotin)
   Purpose: carbohydrate and fat metabolism. **Dietary sources:** beef liver, yeast, oatmeal. **All adults:** 0.3 mg.

Folate (folacin; vitamin B9; folic acid)
   Purpose: cellular metabolism, including synthesis of DNA components; normal red blood cell formation. **Dietary sources:** chicken, liver, green leafy vegetables, wheat bran and germ, citrus fruits, cereals, beans, asparagus. **Adults over 13:** 400 mcg; **pregnant women:** 600 mcg; **lactating women:** 500 mcg.

Vitamin B12 (cobalamin; cyanocobalamin; hydroxocobalamin)
   Purpose: proper functioning of many enzymes involved in carbohydrate, fat, and protein metabolism; synthesis of the insulating sheath around nerve cells; cell reproduction and normal growth; red blood cell formation. **Dietary sources:** eggs, meat, milk, nutritional yeast, fortified cereals. **Adults:** 2.4 mcg; **pregnant women:** 2.6 mcg; **lactating women:** 2.8 mcg.

Vitamin C (ascorbic acid; ascorbic acid)
   Purpose: prevention of oxidative damage to DNA, membrane lipids, and proteins; synthesis of collagen, hormones, transmitters of the nervous sytem, lipids, and proteins; proper immune function. **Dietary sources:** citrus fruits, green peppers, broccoli, cantaloupe, green leafy vegetables. **Adults over 14:** 60 mg; **pregnant women:** 70 mg; **lactating women** (first 6 months): 95 mg; (second 6 months): 90 mg.

Fat-soluble vitamins

Vitamin A (retinol; retinol)
   Purpose: functioning of the retina; growth and maturation of epithelial cells; growth of bone; reproduction and embryonic development. **Dietary sources:** fish and fish-liver oils, liver, butter, orange vegetables and fruits, dark green leafy vegetables; tomatoes. **Men over 10:** 1000 RE; **women over 10:** 800 RE; **pregnant women:** 800 RE; **lactating women** (first 6 months): 1300 RE; (second 6 months): 1200 RE.

Vitamin D (vitamins D2 and D3; [ergo] calciferol)
   Purpose: promotes formation of bone by increasing the blood levels of calcium and phosphorus. **Dietary sources:** fish-liver oils, eggs, milk enriched with Vitamin D. **All adults:** 400 IU.

Vitamin E (N/A; tocopherol)
   Purpose: protection of cell membranes and prevention of damage to membrane-associated enzymes. **Dietary sources:** nuts, vegetable oils, margarine, cereal grains. **Men over 10:** 15 IU. **women over 10:** 12 IU; **pregnant women:** 15 IU; **lactating women** (first 6 months): 18 IU; (second 6 months): 16.5 IU.

Vitamin K (N/A; vitamin K1)
   Purpose: formation of several blood clotting factors. **Dietary sources:** green leafy vegetables, vegetable oils. *No recommended daily allowance.*

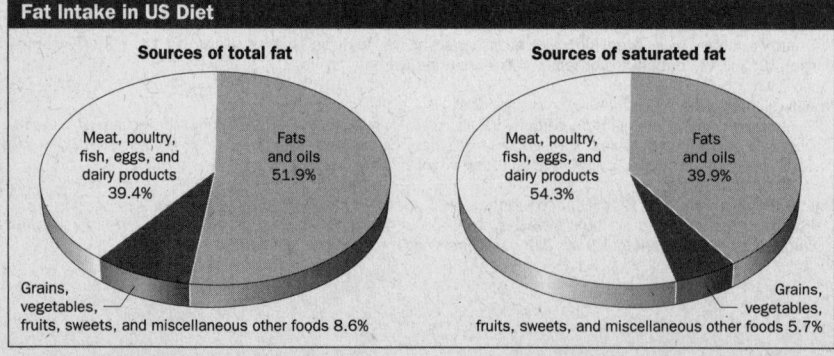

Fat Intake in US Diet

Sources of total fat

Meat, poultry, fish, eggs, and dairy products 39.4%

Fats and oils 51.9%

Grains, vegetables, fruits, sweets, and miscellaneous other foods 8.6%

Sources of saturated fat

Meat, poultry, fish, eggs, and dairy products 54.3%

Fats and oils 39.9%

Grains, vegetables, fruits, sweets, and miscellaneous other foods 5.7%

Food Guide Pyramid

In 2005 the USDA released an update of its food-pyramid guide to a healthy diet. It is designed to help individuals get proper nutrients while at the same time consuming the appropriate amount of calories necessary to maintain healthy weight. The 2005 pyramid also provides information about exercise and weight loss. Diets should be low in added sugars, salt, saturated fat and cholesterol and moderate in overall fat.

Find your balance between food and physical activity:

- Be sure to stay within your daily calorie needs.
- Be physically active for at least 30 minutes most days of the week.
- About 60 minutes a day of physical activity may be needed to prevent weight gain.
- For sustaining weight loss, at least 60 to 90 minutes a day of physical activity may be required.
- Children and teenagers should be physically active for 60 minutes every day or most days.

Recommended daily intake
These amounts are appropriate for individuals who get less than 30 minutes per day of moderate physical activity, beyond normal daily activities. Those who are more physically active may be able to consume more because they may have greater calorie needs.

MyPyramid.gov

	Grains	Vegetables	Fruits	Fats and Oils—limit your intake	Milk	Meat and Beans
Children 2–3 years old	3 ounce equivalents[1]	1 cup[2]	1 cup[3]		2 cups[4]	2 ounce equivalents[5]
Children 4–8 years old	4–5 ounce equivalents[1]	1.5 cups[2]	1–1.5 cups[3]		2 cups[4]	3–4 ounce equivalents[5]
Girls 9–13 years old	5 ounce equivalents[1]	2 cups[2]	1.5 cups[3]		3 cups[4]	5 ounce equivalents[5]
Boys 9–13 years old	6 ounce equivalents[1]	2.5 cups[2]	1.5 cups[3]		3 cups[4]	5 ounce equivalents[5]
Girls 14–18 years old	6 ounce equivalents[1]	2.5 cups[2]	1.5 cups[3]		3 cups[4]	5 ounce equivalents[5]
Boys 14–18 years old	7 ounce equivalents[1]	3 cups[2]	2 cups[3]		3 cups[4]	6 ounce equivalents[5]
Women 19–30 years old	6 ounce equivalents[1]	2.5 cups[2]	2 cups[3]		3 cups[4]	5.5 ounce equivalents[5]
Men 19–30 years old	8 ounce equivalents[1]	3 cups[2]	2 cups[3]		3 cups[4]	6.5 ounce equivalents[5]
Women 31–50 years old	6 ounce equivalents[1]	2.5 cups[2]	1.5 cups[3]		3 cups[4]	5 ounce equivalents[5]
Men 31–50 years old	7 ounce equivalents[1]	3 cups[2]	2 cups[3]		3 cups[4]	6 ounce equivalents[5]
Women 51+ years old	5 ounce equivalents[1]	2 cups[2]	1.5 cups[3]		3 cups[4]	5 ounce equivalents[5]
Men 51+ years old	6 ounce equivalents[1]	2.5 cups[2]	2 cups[3]		3 cups[4]	5.5 ounce equivalents[5]

[1] 1 slice of bread, 1 cup of ready-to-eat cereal, or ½ cup of cooked rice, cooked pasta, or cooked cereal can be considered as 1 ounce equivalent from the grains group.
[2] 1 cup of raw or cooked vegetables or vegetable juice or 2 cups of raw leafy greens can be considered as 1 cup from the vegetable group.
[3] 1 cup of fruit or 100% fruit juice or ½ cup of dried fruit can be considered as 1 cup from the fruit group.
[4] 1 cup of milk or yogurt, 1½ ounces of natural cheese, or 2 ounces of processed cheese can be considered as 1 cup from the milk group.
[5] 1 ounce of meat, poultry, or fish, ¼ cup cooked dry beans, 1 egg, 1 tablespoon of peanut butter, or ½ ounce of nuts or seeds can be considered as 1 ounce equivalent from the meat and beans group.

Source: USDA.

Individuals Meeting Dietary Guidelines
1977-78 and 1994-96.

Percentages of US population that meet or exceed the minimum dietary guidelines given in *Nutrition and Your Health: Dietary Guidelines for Americans, 5th edition (2000)*, a joint publication of the depart- ments of Health and Human Services and Agriculture. To view the complete publication or to order a print copy, visit <www.health.gov/dietaryguidelines>. Next update: 2005.

AGE AND GENDER	CALORIES	TOTAL FAT	SATURA- TED FAT	CHOL- ESTEROL	SODIUM	FIBER	CALCIUM	IRON
			1977-78					
Children (2–17)	33	14	N/A	N/A	N/A	N/A	37	39
Adults (18 and over)	23	13	N/A	N/A	N/A	N/A	15	43
Males 60 and over	29	12	N/A	N/A	N/A	N/A	11	66
Females 60 and over	18	17	N/A	N/A	N/A	N/A	4	40
All individuals 2 and over	**26**	**13**	**N/A**	**N/A**	**N/A**	**N/A**	**22**	**42**
			1994-96					
AGE AND GENDER								
Children (2–17)	38	37	31	77	39	39	37	59
Adults (18 and over)	27	37	43	69	34	20	21	60
Males 60 and over	28	36	43	65	30	26	16	77
Females 60 and over	18	41	49	79	54	35	6	56
All individuals 2 and over	**30**	**37**	**40**	**71**	**35**	**25**	**25**	**59**

N/A indicates data not available.

Nutrient Composition of Selected Fruits and Vegetables

Values shown are approximations for 100 grams (3.57 oz.). Foods are raw unless otherwise noted. Source: USDA Nutrient Data Laboratory. kcal: kilocalorie; g: gram; mg: milligram; IU: international unit.

	ENERGY (KCAL)	WATER (G)	CARBO- HYDRATE (G)	PROTEIN (G)	FAT (G)	VITAMIN A (IU)	VITAMIN C (MG)	THIAMINE (MG)	RIBO- FLAVIN (MG)	NIACIN (MG)
Fruits										
Apple	59	83.93	15.25	0.19	0.36	53	5.7	0.017	0.014	0.077
Apricot	48	86.35	11.12	1.40	0.39	2,612	10.0	0.030	0.040	0.600
Avocado	161	74.27	7.39	1.98	15.32	61	7.9	0.108	0.122	1.921
Banana	92	74.26	23.43	1.03	0.48	81	9.1	0.045	0.100	0.540
Blackberries	52	85.64	12.76	0.72	0.39	165	21.0	0.030	0.040	0.400
Blueberries	56	84.61	14.13	0.67	0.38	100	13.0	0.048	0.050	0.359
Cantaloupe	35	89.78	8.36	0.88	0.28	3,224	42.2	0.036	0.021	0.574
Cherries (sweet)	72	80.76	16.55	1.20	0.96	214	7.0	0.050	0.060	0.400
Grapes	67	81.30	17.15	0.63	0.35	100	4.0	0.092	0.057	0.300
Grapefruit	32	90.89	8.08	0.63	0.10	124	34.4	0.036	0.020	0.250
Kiwi	61	83.05	14.88	0.99	0.44	175	98.0	0.020	0.050	0.500
Lemon	29	88.98	9.32	1.10	0.30	29	53.0	0.040	0.020	0.100
Lime	30	88.26	10.54	0.70	0.20	10	29.1	0.030	0.020	0.200
Mango	65	81.71	17.00	0.51	0.27	3,894	27.7	0.058	0.057	0.584
Nectarine	49	86.28	11.78	0.94	0.46	736	5.4	0.017	0.041	0.990
Orange	47	86.75	11.75	0.94	0.12	205	53.2	0.087	0.040	0.282
Peach	43	87.66	11.10	0.70	0.09	535	6.6	0.017	0.041	0.990
Pear	59	83.81	15.11	0.39	0.40	20	4.0	0.020	0.040	0.100
Pineapple	49	86.50	12.39	0.39	0.43	23	15.4	0.092	0.036	0.420
Plum	55	85.20	13.01	0.79	0.62	323	9.5	0.043	0.096	0.500
Raspberries	49	86.57	11.57	0.91	0.55	130	25.0	0.030	0.090	0.900
Strawberries	30	91.57	7.02	0.61	0.37	27	56.7	0.020	0.066	0.230
Tangerine	44	87.60	11.19	0.63	0.19	920	30.8	0.105	0.022	0.160
Watermelon	32	91.51	7.18	0.62	0.43	366	9.6	0.080	0.020	0.200
Vegetables										
Artichoke[1]	50	83.97	11.18	3.48	0.16	177	10.0	0.065	0.066	1.001
Asparagus[1]	24	92.20	4.23	2.59	0.31	539	10.8	0.123	0.126	1.082
Beans (snap, green)	31	90.27	7.14	1.82	0.12	668	16.3	0.084	0.105	0.752
Beet	43	87.58	9.56	1.61	0.17	38	4.9	0.031	0.040	0.334
Broccoli	28	90.69	5.24	2.98	0.35	1,542	93.2	0.065	0.119	0.638
Brussels sprout	43	86.00	8.96	3.38	0.30	883	85.0	0.139	0.090	0.745
Cabbage	25	92.15	5.43	1.44	0.27	133	32.2	0.050	0.040	0.300
Carrot	43	87.79	10.14	1.03	0.19	28,129	9.3	0.097	0.059	0.928
Cauliflower	25	91.91	5.20	1.98	0.21	19	46.4	0.057	0.063	0.526

Nutrient Composition of Selected Fruits and Vegetables (continued)

	ENERGY (KCAL)	WATER (G)	CARBO-HYDRATE (G)	PROTEIN (G)	FAT (G)	VITAMIN A (IU)	VITAMIN C (MG)	THIAMINE (MG)	RIBO-FLAVIN (MG)	NIACIN (MG)
Vegetables (continued)										
Celery	16	94.64	3.65	0.75	0.14	134	7.0	0.046	0.045	0.323
Collards[1]	26	91.86	4.90	2.11	0.36	3,129	18.2	0.040	0.106	0.575
Corn (sweet, yellow)[1]	108	69.57	25.11	3.32	1.28	217	6.2	0.215	0.072	1.614
Cucumber	13	96.01	2.76	0.69	0.13	215	5.3	0.024	0.022	0.221
Eggplant[1]	28	91.77	6.64	0.83	0.23	64	1.3	0.076	0.020	0.600
Lettuce (iceberg)	12	95.89	2.09	1.01	0.19	330	3.9	0.046	0.030	0.187
Mushroom[1]	27	91.08	5.14	2.17	0.47	0	4.0	0.073	0.300	4.460
Okra[1]	32	89.91	7.21	1.87	0.17	575	16.3	0.132	0.055	0.871
Onion[1]	44	87.86	10.15	1.36	0.19	0	5.2	0.042	0.023	0.165
Pepper (sweet, green)	27	92.19	6.43	0.89	0.19	632	89.3	0.066	0.030	0.509
Pepper (sweet, red)	27	92.19	6.43	0.89	0.19	5,700	190.0	0.066	0.030	0.509
Potato[2]	93	75.42	21.56	1.96	0.10	0	12.8	0.105	0.021	1.395
Spinach	22	91.58	3.50	2.86	0.35	6,715	28.1	0.078	0.189	0.724
Sweet potato[2]	103	72.85	24.27	1.72	0.11	21,822	24.6	0.073	0.127	0.604
Tomato (red)	21	93.76	4.64	0.85	0.33	623	19.1	0.059	0.048	0.628

[1]Boiled. [2]Baked.

Nutritional Value of Selected Foods

Values shown are approximations. Source: Home and Garden Bulletin No. 72, USDA. kcal: kilocalorie; g: gram; mg: milligram; oz: ounce; fl oz: fluid ounce.

FOOD	AMOUNT	GRAMS	ENERGY (KCAL)	CARBO-HYDRATE (G)	PROTEIN (G)	TOTAL FAT (G)	SATU-RATED FAT (G)	CALCIUM (MG)	IRON (MG)	SODIUM (MG)
Beverages										
Beer	12 fl oz	360	150	13	1	0	0	14	0.1	18
Cola, regular	12 fl oz	369	160	41	0	0	0	11	0.2	18
Cola, diet (w/aspartame and saccharine)	12 fl oz	355	0	0	0	0	0	14	0.2	32
Coffee, brewed	6 fl oz	180	0	0	0	0	0	4	0	2
Orange juice, canned	8 fl oz	249	105	25	1	0	0	20	1.1	5
Tea, instant, prepared, un-sweetened	8 fl oz	241	0	1	0	0	0	1	0	1
Wine, table, red	3.5 fl oz	102	75	3	0	0	0	8	0.4	5
Dairy										
Butter, salted	4 oz	113	810	0	1	92	57.1	27	0.2	933
Cheese, American (pasteurized, processed)	1 oz	28.35	105	0	6	9	5.6	174	0.1	406
Cheese, cheddar	1 oz	28.35	115	0	7	9	6	204	0.2	176
Cheese, mozzarella (whole milk)	1 oz	28.35	80	1	6	6	3.7	147	0.1	106
Cheese, swiss	1 oz	28.35	105	1	8	8	5	272	0	74
Cottage cheese, small curd	8 oz	210	215	6	26	9	6	126	0.3	850
Cream cheese	1 oz	28.35	100	1	2	10	6.2	23	0.3	84
Cream, half and half	0.5 oz	15	20	1	0	2	1.1	16	0	6
Cream, sour	8 oz	230	495	10	7	48	30	268	0.1	123
Eggs, cooked, fried	1 egg	46	90	1	6	7	1.9	25	0.7	162
Eggs, cooked, hard-cooked	1 egg	50	75	1	6	5	1.6	25	0.6	62
Eggs, cooked, scrambled	1 egg	61	100	1	7	7	2.2	44	0.7	171
Ice cream, vanilla, 11% fat	8 oz	133	270	32	5	14	8.9	176	0.1	116
Milk, whole, 3.3% fat	8 oz	244	150	11	8	8	5.1	291	0.1	120
Milk, low fat, 2% fat	8 oz	244	120	12	8	5	2.9	297	0.1	122
Milk, skim	8 oz	245	85	12	8	0	0.3	302	0.1	126
Milk, chocolate	8 oz	250	210	26	8	8	5.3	280	0.6	149
Yogurt, plain, low fat	8 oz	227	145	16	12	4	2.3	415	0.2	159
Fats, oils										
Lard	0.5 oz	13	115	0	0	13	5.1	0	0	0
Margarine, hard, 80% fat	0.5 oz	14	100	0	0	11	2.2	4	0	132

Nutritional Value of Selected Foods (continued)

FOOD	AMOUNT	GRAMS	ENERGY (KCAL)	CARBO-HYDRATE (G)	PROTEIN (G)	TOTAL FAT (G)	SATU-RATED FAT (G)	CALCIUM (MG)	IRON (MG)	SODIUM (MG)
Fats, oils (continued)										
Olive oil	0.5 oz	14	125	0	0	14	1.9	0	0	0
Vegetable shortening	0.5 oz	13	115	0	0	13	3.3	0	0	0
Fish										
Crabmeat, canned	8 oz	135	135	1	23	3	0.5	61	1.1	1350
Fish sticks, frozen	1 piece	28	70	4	6	3	0.8	11	0.3	53
Ocean perch, breaded, fried	1 piece	85	185	7	16	11	2.6	31	1.2	138
Oysters, raw	8 oz	240	160	8	20	4	1.4	226	15.6	175
Salmon, baked, red	3 oz	85	140	0	21	5	1.2	26	0.5	55
Shrimp, fried	3 oz	85	200	11	16	10	2.5	61	2	384
Trout, broiled, w/butter and lemon juice	3 oz	85	175	0	21	9	4.1	26	1	122
Tuna, canned, white, in water	3 oz	85	135	0	30	1	0.3	17	0.6	468
Fruits, fruit products										
Apples, peeled, sliced	8 oz	110	65	16	0	0	0.1	4	0.1	0
Applesauce, canned, sweetened	8 oz	255	195	51	0	0	0.1	10	0.9	8
Apricots	3 apricots	106	50	12	1	0	0	15	0.6	1
Bananas	1 banana	114	105	27	1	1	0.2	7	0.4	1
Blackberries	8 oz	144	75	18	1	1	0.2	46	0.8	0
Blueberries	8 oz	145	80	20	1	1	0	9	0.2	9
Grapefruit, pink	½ grapefruit	120	40	10	1	0	0	14	0.1	0
Grapes, European, Thompson	10 grapes	50	35	9	0	0	0.1	6	0.1	1
Oranges	1 orange	131	60	15	1	0	0	52	0.1	0
Peaches	1 peach	87	35	10	1	0	0	4	0.1	0
Pears, Bartlett	1 pear	166	100	25	1	1	0	18	0.4	0
Pineapple, canned, heavy syrup	8 oz	255	200	52	1	0	0	36	1	3
Plums, 2⅛-in. diam.	1 plum	66	35	9	1	0	0	3	0.1	0
Prunes, dried, large	5 prunes	49	115	31	1	0	0	25	1.2	2
Raisins	8 oz	145	435	115	5	1	0.2	71	3	17
Strawberries	8 oz	149	45	10	1	1	0	21	0.6	1
Watermelon	1 piece	482	155	35	3	2	0.3	39	0.8	10
Grains										
Bagels, plain	1 bagel	68	200	38	7	2	0.3	29	1.8	245
Bread, rye, light	1 slice	25	65	12	2	1	0.2	20	0.7	175
Bread, wheat	1 slice	25	65	12	2	1	0.2	32	0.9	138
Bread, white	1 slice	25	65	12	2	1	0.3	32	0.7	129
Bread, whole wheat	1 slice	28	70	13	3	1	0.4	20	1	180
Cereal, Cheerios	1 oz	28.35	110	20	4	2	0.3	48	4.5	307
Cereal, Kellogg's Corn Flakes	1 oz	28.35	110	24	2	0	0	1	1.8	351
Cereal, Lucky Charms	1 oz	28.35	110	23	3	1	0.2	32	4.5	201
Cereal, Post Raisin Bran	1 oz	28.35	85	21	3	1	0.1	13	4.5	185
Cake, white, w/white frosting, commercial	1 piece	71	260	42	3	9	2.1	33	1	176
Cheesecake	1 piece	92	280	26	5	18	9.9	52	0.4	204
Chocolate chip cookies, commercial	4 cookies	42	180	28	2	9	2.9	13	0.8	140
Cornmeal, whole-ground, dry	8 oz	122	435	90	11	5	0.5	24	2.2	1
Doughnuts, cake, plain	1 doughnut	50	210	24	3	12	2.8	22	1	192
English muffins, plain	1 muffin	57	140	27	5	1	0.3	96	1.7	378
Oatmeal, instant, cooked, w/salt	8 oz	234	145	25	6	2	0.4	19	1.6	374
Macaroni, cooked, firm	8 oz	130	190	39	7	1	0.1	14	2.1	1
Muffins, blueberry, commercial mix	1 muffin	45	140	22	3	5	1.4	15	0.9	225
Pancakes, plain, commercial mix	1 pancake	27	60	8	2	2	0.5	36	0.7	160
Pie, apple	1 piece	158	405	60	3	18	4.6	13	1.6	476

Nutritional Value of Selected Foods (continued)

FOOD	AMOUNT	GRAMS	ENERGY (KCAL)	CARBO-HYDRATE (G)	PROTEIN (G)	TOTAL FAT (G)	SATU-RATED FAT (G)	CALCIUM (MG)	IRON (MG)	SODIUM (MG)
Grains (continued)										
Popcorn, air-popped, unsalted	8 oz	8	30	6	1	0	0	1	0.2	0
Pretzels, stick	10 pieces	3	10	2	0	0	0	1	0.1	48
Rice, brown, cooked	8 oz	195	230	50	5	1	0.3	23	1	0
Rice, white, instant, cooked	8 oz	165	180	40	4	0	0.1	5	1.3	0
Saltines	4 pieces	12	50	9	1	1	0.5	3	0.5	165
Spaghetti, cooked, tender	8 oz	140	155	32	5	1	0.1	11	1.7	1
Waffles, from commercial mix	1 waffle	75	205	27	7	8	2.7	179	1.2	515
Meat, poultry										
Bacon, regular, cooked	3 slices	19	110	0	6	9	3.3	2	0.3	303
Beef, chuck, lean, cooked	2.2 oz	62	170	0	19	9	3.9	8	2.3	44
Chicken, breast, roasted	3 oz	86	140	0	27	3	0.9	13	0.9	64
Chicken, drumstick, floured, fried	1.7 oz	49	120	1	13	7	1.8	6	0.7	44
Ground beef, broiled	3 oz	85	245	0	20	18	6.9	9	2.1	70
Ham, roasted, lean and fat	3 oz	85	205	0	18	14	5.1	6	0.7	1009
Hamburger	4-oz patty	174	445	38	25	21	7.1	75	4.8	763
Lamb chops, braised, lean	1.7 oz	48	135	0	17	7	2.9	12	1.3	36
Turkey, roasted, light and dark	8 oz	140	240	0	41	7	2.3	35	2.5	98
Veal cutlet, med. fat, braised or broiled	3 oz	85	185	0	23	9	4.1	9	0.8	56
Nuts, legumes, seeds										
Mixed nuts w/peanuts, dry, salted	1 oz	28.35	170	7	5	15	2	20	1	190
Peanuts, oil-roasted, unsalted	8 oz	145	840	27	39	71	9.9	125	2.8	22
Peanut butter	0.5 oz	16	95	3	5	8	1.4	5	0.3	75
Pinto beans, dry, cooked	8 oz	180	265	49	15	1	0.1	86	5.4	3
Sunflower seeds	1 oz	28.35	160	5	6	14	1.5	33	1.9	1
Tofu	1 piece	120	85	3	9	5	0.7	108	2.3	8
Sauces, dressings, condiments										
Catsup	0.5 oz	15	15	4	0	0	0	3	0.1	156
Cheese sauce w/milk, from mix	8 fl oz	279	305	23	16	17	9.3	569	0.3	1565
Honey	0.5 oz	21	65	17	0	0	0	1	0.1	1
Jams/preserves	0.5 oz	20	55	14	0	0	0	4	0.2	2
Mayonnaise	0.5 oz	14	100	0	0	11	1.7	3	0.1	80
Mustard, yellow	0.17 oz	5	5	0	0	0	0	4	0.1	63
Salad dressing, French	0.5 oz	16	85	1	0	9	1.4	2	0	188
Salad dressing, Italian, low calorie	0.5 oz	15	5	2	0	0	0	1	0	136
Syrup, table	1 oz	42	122	32	0	0	0	1	0	19
Sugars, sweets, miscellaneous snacks										
Caramels, plain or chocolate	1 oz	28.35	115	22	1	3	2.2	42	0.4	64
Chocolate, milk, candy, w/almonds	1 oz	28.35	150	15	3	10	4.8	65	0.5	23
Chocolate, dark, sweet	1 oz	28.35	150	16	1	10	5.9	7	0.6	5
Gelatin dessert, prepared	4 oz	120	70	17	2	0	0	2	0	55
Hard candy	1 oz	28.35	110	28	0	0	0	0	0.1	7
Popsicle	1 popsicle	95	70	18	0	0	0	0	0	11
Potato chips	10 chips	20	105	10	1	7	1.8	5	0.2	94
Pudding, chocolate, instant	4 oz	130	155	27	4	4	2.3	130	0.3	440
Sugar, brown	8 oz	220	820	212	0	0	0	187	4.8	97
Sugar, white, granulated	8 oz	200	770	199	0	0	0	3	0.1	5
Vegetables										
Beans, snap, yellow, canned, no salt	8 oz	135	25	6	2	0	0	35	1.2	3
Broccoli	1 spear	151	40	8	4	1	0.1	72	1.3	41

Nutritional Value of Selected Foods (continued)

FOOD	AMOUNT	GRAMS	ENERGY (KCAL)	CARBO-HYDRATE (G)	PROTEIN (G)	TOTAL FAT (G)	SATU-RATED FAT (G)	CALCIUM (MG)	IRON (MG)	SODIUM (MG)
Vegetables (continued)										
Carrots, cooked from frozen	8 oz	146	55	12	2	0	0	41	0.7	86
Cauliflower, cooked from raw	8 oz	125	30	6	2	0	0	34	0.5	8
Celery, Pascal, raw	1 stalk	40	5	1	0	0	0	14	0.2	35
Corn, yellow, cooked from frozen	8 oz	165	135	34	5	0	0	3	0.5	8
Cucumber, w/peel	6 slices	28	5	1	0	0	0	4	0.1	1
Lettuce, crisphead	1 wedge	135	20	3	1	0	0	26	0.7	12
Mushrooms	8 oz	70	20	3	1	0	0	4	0.9	3
Onions, sliced	8 oz	115	40	8	1	0	0.1	29	0.4	2
Peas, green, cooked from frozen	8 oz	160	125	23	8	0	0.1	38	2.5	139
Potatos, boiled, peeled after	1 potato	136	120	27	3	0	0	7	0.4	5
Tomatoes, raw	1 tomato	123	25	5	1	0	0	9	0.6	10

Reading Food Labels

The FDA requires most food manufacturers to provide standardized information about certain nutrients. Within strict guidelines the nutritional labels are designed to **aid the consumer in making informed dietary decisions** as well as to **regulate claims made by manufacturers** about their products.

The percent daily value is based on a 2,000-calorie-per-day diet. Some larger packages will have listings for both 2,000-calorie and 2,500-calorie diets. For products that require additional preparation before eating, such as dry cake mixes, manufacturers often provide two columns of nutritional information, one with the values of the food as purchased, the other with the values of the food as prepared.

The FDA selects mandatory label components (see sample label at right) based on current understanding of nutrition concerns, and **component order on the label is consistent with the priority of dietary recommendations.** Components that may appear in addition to the mandatory components are limited to the following: calories from saturated fat; polyunsaturated fat; monounsaturated fat; potassium; soluble fiber; insoluble fiber; sugar alcohol (for example, the sugar substitutes xylitol, mannitol, and sorbitol); other carbohydrate (the difference between total carbohydrate and the sum of dietary fiber, sugars, and sugar alcohol if declared); percent of vitamin A present as beta-carotene; and other essential vitamins and minerals. Any of these optional components that form the basis of product claims, fortification, or enrichment must appear in the nutrition facts. By 2006 labels must specify amounts of trans fatty acids.

Certain key descriptions are also regulated by the FDA. They include the following, in amounts per serving:

Low fat: 3 g or less
Low saturated fat: 1 g or less
Low sodium: 140 mg or less
Low cholesterol: 20 mg or less and 2 g or less of saturated fat
Low calorie: 40 calories or less

US FDA Center for Food Safety & Applied Nutrition Web site: <www.cfsan.fda.gov>.

Nutrition Facts

Serving Size ½ cup (114g)
Servings Per Container 4

Amount Per Serving

Calories 90   Calories from Fat 30

	%Daily Value*
Total Fat 3g	**5%**
Saturated Fat 0g	**0%**
Cholesterol 0mg	**0%**
Sodium 300mg	**13%**
Total Carbohydrate 13g	**4%**
Dietary Fiber 3g	**12%**
Sugars 3g	
Protein 3g	

Vitamin A 80%	•	Vitamin C 60%
Calcium 4%	•	Iron 4%

* Percent Daily Values are based on a 2,000 calorie diet. Your daily values may be higher or lower depending on your calorie needs:

	Calories	2,000	2,500
Total Fat	Less than	65g	80g
Sat. Fat	Less than	20g	25g
Cholesterol	Less than	300mg	300mg
Sodium	Less than	2,400mg	2,400mg
Total Carbohydrate		300g	375g
Dietary Fiber		25g	30g

Calories per gram:
Fat 9   •   Carbohydrate 4   •   Protein 4

Americans and Physical Activity

This table shows selected data illustrating the number of leisure-time periods of vigorous physical activity per week (lasting 10 minutes or longer) among persons 18 years of age and over. Numbers are in thousands ('000). Figures may not add to totals due to rounding. Data from the Centers for Disease Control and Prevention National Center for Health Statistics National Health Interview Survey, 2002.

SELECTED CHARACTERISTIC	ALL PERSONS 18 YEARS OF AGE AND OVER	NEVER	LESS THAN 1	1-2	3-4	5 OR MORE
Total	205,825	119,634	6,022	24,914	26,655	24,911
Age						
18-44 years	108,114	52,714	3,901	16,583	17,183	15,671
45-64 years	64,650	40,137	1,746	6,957	7,718	6,931
65-74 years	17,809	13,513	238	1,038	1,174	1,566
75 years and over	15,252	13,270	138	336	580	743
Sex and ethnicity						
Hispanic male or Latino	11,145	6,738	239	1,500	1,112	1,341
Hispanic female or Latina	11,546	8,632	180	852	928	790
Not Hispanic or Latino						
White male	71,855	35,539	2,689	10,554	10,495	11,216
White female	77,729	47,741	1,980	8,351	10,227	8,139
Black male	10,292	5,617	249	1,281	1,543	1,389
Black female	12,773	9,225	320	1,139	1,009	829
Education (respondents 25 and older)						
Less than a high school diploma	28,248	23,044	372	1,451	1,154	1,821
High school diploma or GED	52,556	35,412	1,263	5,008	4,479	5,384
Some college	48,091	26,867	1,595	6,230	6,894	5,694
Bachelor's degree or higher	47,197	20,254	1,892	8,013	9,455	7,083
Family income						
Less than $20,000	37,369	27,175	618	2,856	2,788	3,465
$20,000 or more	155,166	83,864	5,174	20,835	22,758	20,288
$20,000-$34,999	29,671	19,443	731	2,978	2,974	3,278
$35,000-$54,999	31,814	17,666	987	4,425	4,279	4,139
$55,000-$74,999	23,984	12,212	985	3,661	3,666	3,254
$75,000 or more	41,572	17,538	1,789	7,021	8,429	6,341
Marital status						
Married	118,960	69,003	3,693	15,198	15,219	13,618
Widowed	13,093	11,004	148	444	626	735
Divorced or separated	21,203	13,386	529	2,083	2,580	2,230
Never married	39,981	19,103	1,327	5,492	6,695	6,791
Living with a partner	11,978	6,842	312	1,648	1,473	1,497

Ways to Burn 150 Calories

Values shown are approximations. Activities are listed from more to less vigorous—the more vigorous an activity, the less time it takes to burn a calorie. When specific distances are given, the activity must be performed in the time shown (for example, one must run 1.5 miles in 15 minutes to burn 150 calories).

ACTIVITY	DURATION (MINUTES)
Climbing stairs	15
Shoveling snow	15
Running 1.5 miles (10 minutes/mile)	15
Jumping rope	15
Bicycling 4 miles	15
Playing basketball	15-20
Playing wheelchair basketball	20
Swimming laps	20
Performing water aerobics	30
Walking 2 miles (15 minutes/mile)	30
Raking leaves	30
Pushing a stroller 1.5 miles	30
Dancing fast	30
Bicycling 5 miles	30
Shooting baskets	30
Walking 1.75 miles (20 minutes/mile)	35
Wheeling oneself in a wheelchair	30-40
Gardening (standing)	30-45
Playing touch football	30-45
Playing volleyball	45
Washing windows or floors	45-60
Washing and waxing a car or boat	45-60

Target Heart Rate Training Zones

Measuring **target heart rate** involves monitoring your pulse periodically as you exercise. To use the Target Heart Rate chart:

1. Calculate your maximum heart rate by subtracting your age from 220.
2. Determine your target heart rate zone (50–70% of your maximum heart rate).
3. While exercising, monitor your pulse regularly. Count the number of beats for 10 seconds, then multiply by 6 to determine in what zone you are working.

The American Heart Association recommends using the target heart rate scale when participating in more vigorous athletic activity, such as jogging or aerobics. If your activity is moderate or taking your pulse is too bothersome, a "talk test" can be used as a substitute. If you can converse with someone with minimal effort, you are not working too hard. Alternately, if you can sing without difficulty, you are not working hard enough.

Note: For optimal cardiovascular fitness, you should work toward the middle of your 50 and 70% zones. Always check with your physician before starting any fitness routine, especially if you have heart or respiratory concerns.

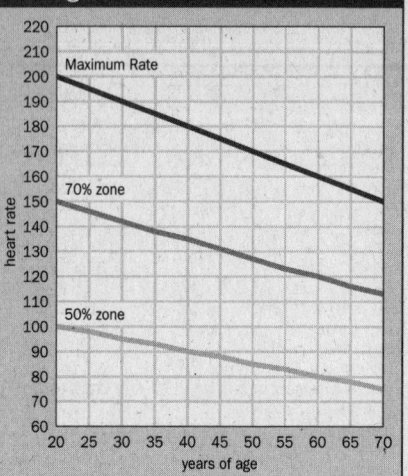

Body Mass Index (BMI)

The BMI is a measure expressing the relationship of weight to height determined by dividing body weight in kilograms by the square of height in meters (for convenience, the information has been converted to standard US measurements in the table below). It is more highly correlated with body fat than any other indicator of height and weight. The National Institutes of Health recommend using the BMI scale to help assess the risk of diseases and disabilities associated with an unhealthy weight. Individuals with a BMI below 18.5 are considered underweight; those with a BMI from 18.5 to 24.9 are considered normal; those with a BMI between 25.0 and 29.9 are considered overweight; and those with a BMI of 30.0 or more are considered obese. The BMI may overestimate body fat in athletes and others who have a muscular build, and it may underestimate body fat in older persons and others who have lost muscle mass. Source: <www.nhlbi.nih.gov>.

HEIGHT (INCHES)	BODY WEIGHT (POUNDS)																				
58	91	96	100	105	110	115	119	124	129	134	138	143	148	153	158	162	167	172	177	181	186
59	94	99	104	109	114	119	124	128	133	138	143	148	153	158	163	168	173	178	183	188	193
60	97	102	107	112	118	123	128	133	138	143	148	153	158	163	168	174	179	184	189	194	199
61	100	106	111	116	122	127	132	137	143	148	153	158	164	169	174	180	185	190	195	201	206
62	104	109	115	120	126	131	136	142	147	153	158	164	169	175	180	186	191	196	202	207	213
63	107	113	118	124	130	135	141	146	152	158	163	169	175	180	186	191	197	203	208	214	220
64	110	116	122	128	134	140	145	151	157	163	169	174	180	186	192	197	204	209	215	221	227
65	114	120	126	132	138	144	150	156	162	168	174	180	186	192	198	204	210	216	222	228	234
66	118	124	130	136	142	148	155	161	167	173	179	186	192	198	204	210	216	223	229	235	241
67	121	127	134	140	146	153	159	166	172	178	185	191	198	204	211	217	223	230	236	242	249
68	125	131	138	144	151	158	164	171	177	184	190	197	203	210	216	223	230	236	243	249	256
69	128	135	142	149	155	162	169	176	182	189	196	203	209	216	223	230	236	243	250	257	263
70	132	139	146	153	160	167	174	181	188	195	202	209	216	222	229	236	243	250	257	264	271
71	136	143	150	157	165	172	179	186	193	200	208	215	222	229	236	243	250	257	265	272	279
72	140	147	154	162	169	177	184	191	199	206	213	221	228	235	242	250	258	265	272	279	287
73	144	151	159	166	174	182	189	197	204	212	219	227	235	242	250	257	265	272	280	288	295
74	148	155	163	171	179	186	194	202	210	218	225	233	241	249	256	264	272	280	287	295	303
75	152	160	168	176	184	192	200	208	216	224	232	240	248	256	264	272	279	287	295	303	311
76	156	164	172	180	189	197	205	213	221	230	238	246	254	263	271	279	287	295	304	312	320
BMI	19	20	21	22	23	24	25	26	27	28	29	30	31	32	33	34	35	36	37	38	39
			NORMAL				OVERWEIGHT					OBESE									

The World

The information about the countries of the world that follows has been assembled and analyzed by Encyclopædia Britannica editors from hundreds of private, national, and international sources. Included are all the sovereign states of the world as well as the major dependent, or nonsovereign, areas. The historical background sketches have been adapted, augmented, and updated from *Britannica Concise Encyclopedia* and the statistical sections from *Britannica World Data*, which is published annually in conjunction with *Britannica Book of the Year*. The section called "Recent Developments" also has been adapted from material appearing in recent issues of the yearbook, as well as from other sources inside and outside Britannica. The locator maps have been prepared by Britannica's Cartography Department, and the recommended Web sites are from Britannica Online.

All information is the latest available to Britannica, although it must be understood that in many cases it takes several years for the various countries or agencies to gather and process statistics, such that the most current data available will normally be dated several years earlier.

A few definitions of terms used in the articles may be useful. **Gross domestic product** (GDP) is the total value of goods and services produced in a country during a given accounting period, usually a year. Unless otherwise noted, the value is given in current prices of the year indicated. **Gross national product** (GNP) is essentially GDP plus income from foreign transactions minus payments made outside the country. **Imports** are material goods legally entering a country (or customs area) and subject to customs regulations and exclude financial movements. The value of goods imported is given free on board (f.o.b.) unless otherwise specified. The principal alternate basis for valuation of goods in international trade is that of cost, insurance, and freight (c.i.f.); its use is restricted to imports, as it comprises the principal charges needed to bring the goods to the customs house in the country of destination. **Exports** are material goods legally leaving a country and subject to customs regulations. Valuation of goods exported is free on board (f.o.b.) unless otherwise specified; the value of goods exported and imported f.o.b. is calculated from the cost of production and excludes the cost of transport. The **FAO recommended daily per capita caloric requirement** varies by region and is calculated from age and sex distributions, average body weights, and environmental temperatures.

The symbol $ indicates US dollars unless otherwise indicated. "**CFA franc**" stands for Communauté Financière Africaine franc. A few helpful **conversions** for the statistical section are given at the foot of the left-hand pages.

Afghanistan

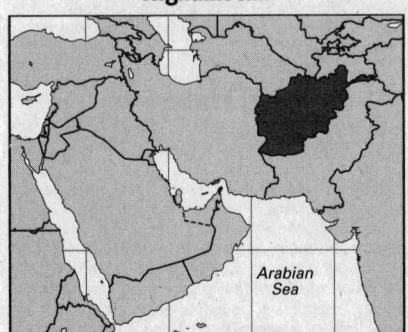

Arabian
Sea

Official name: Islamic Republic of Afghanistan (Jomhuri-ye Eslami-ye Afghanestan [Dari (Persian)] Da Afghanestan Eslami Jamhuriyat [Pashto]). **Form of government:** Islamic republic. **Chief of state and head of government:** President Hamid Karzai (from 2002). **Capital:** Kabul. **Official languages:** Dari (Persian); Pashto; six additional local languages have official status per the 2004 constitution. **Official religion:** Islam. **Monetary unit:** 1 (new) afghani (Af) = 100 puls (puli); valuation (7 Jul 2005) $1 = Af 42.79.

Demography

Area: 249,347 sq mi, 645,807 sq km. **Population** (2004): 20,869,000 (excludes Afghan refugees in Pakistan and Iran and other Afghans abroad). **Density** (2004): persons per sq mi 83.7, persons per sq km 32.3. **Urban** (2003): 22.4%. **Sex distribution** (2003): male 51.17%; female 48.83%. **Age breakdown** (2003): under 15, 44.8%; 15–29, 26.8%; 30–44, 15.9%; 45–59, 8.5%; 60–74, 3.4%; 75 and over, 0.6%. **Ethnolinguistic composition** (early 1990s): Pashtun 52.4%; Tajik 20.4%; Hazara 8.8%; Uzbek 8.8%; Chahar Aimak 2.8%; Turkmen 1.9%; other 4.9%. **Religious affiliation** (2000): Sunni Muslim 89.2%; Shi'i Muslim 8.9%; Zoroastrian 1.4%; Hindu 0.4%; other 0.1%. **Major cities** (2003–04): Kabul 2,799,300 (urban agglomeration); Kandahar (Qandahar) 323,900; Herat 254,800; Mazar-e Sharif 187,700; Jalalabad 97,900. **Location:** southern Asia, bordering Uzbekistan, Tajikistan, China, Pakistan, Iran, and Turkmenistan.

Vital statistics

Birth rate per 1,000 population (2003): 47.5 (world avg. 21.3). **Death rate** per 1,000 population (2003): 21.5 (world avg. 9.1). **Total fertility rate** (avg. births per childbearing woman; 2003): 6.8. **Life expectancy** at birth (2003): male 41.8 years; female 42.2 years.

National economy

Budget (2003–04). *Revenue:* $208,000,000 (domestic revenue only; excludes heavy reliance on foreign assistance; tax revenue 63.0%, of which import duties 53.4%; nontax revenue 37.0%). *Expenditures:* $2,826,000,000 (development expenditure 84.0%; current expenditure 16.0%). **Gross domestic product** (2003): $7,000,000,000 (one-third of which is illegal opiate receipts; $340 per capita). **Public debt** (external, outstanding; 2000): $5,319,000,000. **Production** (metric tons except as noted). *Agriculture,* *forestry, fishing* (2002): wheat 2,686,000, rice 388,000, grapes 365,000, opium poppy 3,400 (represents 74% of world production); livestock (number of live animals; 2003) 8,700,000 sheep, 7,200,000 goats, 3,600,000 cattle; roundwood (2002) 1,404,-208 cu m; fish catch (2001) 2,000. *Mining and quarrying* (2000): salt 13,000; copper (metal content) 5,000. *Manufacturing* (by production value in Af '000,000; 1988–89): food products 4,019; leather and fur products 2,678; textiles 1,760. *Energy production (consumption):* electricity (kW-hr; 2002) 557,000,000 ([2000] 480,000,000); coal (metric tons; 2000) 2,000 (2,000); petroleum products (metric tons; 2000) none (206,000); natural gas (cu m; 2000) 116,603,000 (116,603,000). **Household income and expenditure** (2003). Average household size 8.0; sources of income: wages and salaries 49%, self-employed 47%, other 4%. **Population economically active** (1994; based on settled population only): total 5,557,000; activity rate of total population 29.4% (participation rates: female 9.0%; unemployed [1995] c. 8%). **Tourism** (1997): receipts $1,000,000; expenditures $1,000,000. **Land use** as % of total land area (2000): in temporary crops 12.1%, in permanent crops 0.2%, in pasture 46.0%; overall forest area 2.1%.

Foreign trade

Imports (2002–03-c.i.f.): $880,000,000 (machinery 36.8%, consumer goods and medicine 26.8%, clothing 14.9%, food 8.9%). *Major import sources:* Pakistan 23.5%; South Korea 12.8%; Japan 9.7%; Kenya 6.5%; Turkmenistan 5.6%; Germany 5.6%. **Exports** (2002–03-f.o.b.): $97,000,000 (carpets and rugs 47.4%, dried fruits and nuts 40.5%). *Major export destinations:* India 27.8%; Pakistan 23.7%; Germany 6.2%; Finland 6.2%; UAE 5.2%.

Transport and communications

Transport. *Roads* (2001): total length 20,720 km (paved 12%). *Vehicles* (2000): passenger cars 39,707; trucks and buses 7,000. *Air transport* (Ariana Afghan Airlines only): passenger-km (1999) 129,000,000; metric ton-km cargo 19,000,000; airports (2002) 2. **Communications,** in total units (units per 1,000 persons). Daily newspaper circulation (2000): 129,000 (5); radios (2000): 2,950,000 (114); televisions (2000): 362,000 (14); telephone main lines (2002): 33,100 (1.6); cellular telephone subscribers (2002): 12,000 (0.6); Internet users (2002): 1,000 (0.04).

Education and health

Literacy (2003; based on settled population only): total population age 15 and over literate 29%; males 43%; females 14%. **Health:** physicians (2002) 2,880 (1 per 7,128 persons); infant mortality rate per 1,000 live births (2003) 115.0. **Food** (1999): daily per capita caloric intake 1,755 (vegetable products 79%, animal products 21%); 72% of FAO recommended minimum.

Military

Total active duty personnel (2004): 13,000 (army 100%); size of planned army is 65,000, size of

planned air force 8,000. Foreign troops (2004): 8,000-member, NATO-controlled, 31-nation International Security Assistance Force (ISAF) and more than 18,000-member, non-ISAF US troops searching for al-Qaeda and Taliban fighters.

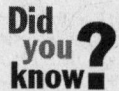

Did you know? The town of Bamian is northwest of Kabul, the nation's capital, in the Bamian Valley. Two great figures of Buddha were erected there in the 4th and 5th centuries. Despite international pleas to preserve them, the statues were destroyed in early 2001 after the Taliban condemned them as idolatrous.

Background

The area was part of the Persian empire in the 6th century BC and was conquered by Alexander the Great in the 4th century BC. Hindu influence entered with the Hephthalites and Sasanians; Islam became entrenched during the rule of the Saffarids, c. AD 870. Afghanistan was divided between the Mughal empire of India and the Safavid empire of Persia until the 18th century, when other Persians under Nadir Shah took control. Great Britain and Russia fought several wars in the area in the 19th century. From the 1930s Afghanistan had a stable monarchy; it was overthrown in the 1970s. The rebels' intention was to institute Marxist reforms, but the reforms sparked rebellion, and troops from the USSR invaded to establish order. Afghan guerrillas prevailed, and the Soviet Union withdrew in 1988–89. In 1992 rebel factions overthrew the government and established an Islamic republic, but fighting among factions continued. In 1996 the government was taken over by the Taliban faction.

Recent Developments

Following the overthrow of the Taliban in December 2001, Hamid Karzai, a Pashtun tribal leader and supporter of the former King Zahir Shah, was installed in Afghanistan, and on 13 Jun 2002 he was elected president. The government continued to struggle against warlordism, ethnic rivalry, and terrorism. The most serious worry was the general deterioration of security in parts of the country beyond the reach of the central government. Operation Enduring Freedom, a US-led coalition of 12,500 soldiers, battled against terrorist opposition thought to be grouped around al-Qaeda loyalists of Osama bin Laden, followers of ousted Taliban leader Mohammad Omar, and Hezbi Islami forces of Gulbuddin Hekmatyar. All three leaders continued to elude capture. On 26 Jan 2004 President Karzai signed a new constitution for Afghanistan that made provision for a strong presidency with two vice presidents, a bicameral legislature, and an independent judiciary. It declared Afghanistan an Islamic republic and prohibited laws that were contrary to the tenets of Islam. During early 2005 preparations were under way for legislative elections, which were set for 18 September.

Internet resources: <www.afghan-web.com/politics>.

1 metric ton = about 1.1 short tons;   1 kilometer = 0.6 mi (statute);   1 metric ton-km cargo = about 0.68 short ton-mi cargo;   c.i.f.: cost, insurance, and freight;   f.o.b.: free on board

Albania

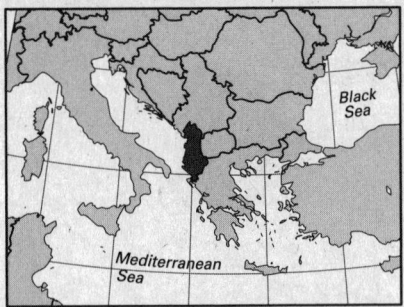

Black
Sea

Mediterranean
Sea

Official name: Republika e Shqipërisë (Republic of Albania). **Form of government:** unitary multiparty republic with one legislative house (Assembly [140]). **Chief of state:** President Alfred Moisiu (from 2002). **Head of government:** Prime Minister Fatos Nano (from 2002). **Capital:** Tirana (Tiranë). **Official language:** Albanian. **Official religion:** none. **Monetary unit:** 1 lek = 100 qindars; valuation (7 Jul 2005) $1 = 103.10 leks.

Demography

Area: 11,082 sq mi, 28,703 sq km. **Population** (2004): 3,136,000. **Density** (2004): persons per sq mi 283.0, persons per sq km 109.3. **Urban** (2001): 42.1%. **Sex distribution** (2001): male 49.88%; female 50.12%. **Age breakdown** (2003): under 15, 27.1%; 15–29, 26.0%; 30–44, 20.6%; 45–59, 14.6%; 60–74, 8.8%; 75 and over, 2.9%. **Ethnic composition** (2000): Albanian 91.7%; Vlach (Aromanian) 3.6%; Greek 2.3%; other 2.4%. **Religious affiliation** (2000): Muslim 38.8%; Roman Catholic 16.7%; nonreligious 16.6%; Albanian Orthodox 10.4%; other Orthodox 5.7%; other 11.8%. **Major cities** (2001): Tirana (Tiranë) 343,078; Durrës 99,546; Elbasan 87,797; Shkodër 82,455. **Location:** southeastern Europe, bordering Serbia and Montenegro, Macedonia, Greece, and the Mediterranean Sea.

Vital statistics

Birth rate per 1,000 population (2002): 18.6 (world avg. 21.3). **Death rate** per 1,000 population (2002): 6.5 (world avg. 9.1). **Natural increase rate** per 1,000 population (2002): 12.1 (world avg. 12.2). **Total fertility rate** (avg. births per childbearing woman; 2002): 2.3. **Marriage rate** per 1,000 population (1998): 7.4. **Life expectancy** at birth (2002): male 69.3 years; female 75.1 years.

National economy

Budget (2002). *Revenue:* 149,487,000,000 leks (taxes 86.3%, of which value-added tax 30.8%, social security contributions 17.1%, income tax 14.0%, import duties and export taxes 9.0%, other taxes 15.4%; nontax revenue 13.7%). *Expenditures:* 196,549,000,000 leks (current expenditure 78.7%, of which wages 21.4%, social security 20.4%, interest on debt 12.6%, government operations 10.4%, other 13.9%; capital expenditure 21.3%). **Public debt** (2002): $1,187,000,000. **Production** (metric tons except as noted). *Agriculture, forestry, fishing* (2002): vegetables and melons 650,000 (mainly beans, peas, onions,

tomatoes, cabbage, eggplants, and carrots), cereals 472,500, watermelons 293,000; livestock (number of live animals) 1,844,000 sheep, 929,000 goats, 690,000 cattle; roundwood (2002) 304,800 cu m; fish catch (2001) 3,596. *Mining and quarrying* (2001): chromium ore 165,000; copper ore 45,000. *Manufacturing* (value added in $'000,000; 2001): textiles 17; glass products 14; leather (all forms) 11. *Energy production (consumption):* electricity (kW-hr; 2002) 3,880,000,000 (3,880,000,000); lignite (metric tons; 2001) 17,300 (17,300); crude petroleum (barrels; 2001) 2,136,000 ([2000] 2,090,000); petroleum products (metric tons; 2000) 228,000 (390,000); natural gas (cu m; 2001) 10,000,000 (10,000,000). **Gross national product** (2003): $5,517,000,000 ($1,740 per capita). **Population economically active** (2001): total 1,244,000; activity rate of total population 40.3% (participation rates: ages 15–64, 55.4%; female 49.8%; unemployed [2002] 15.8%). **Households.** Average household size (2002): 4.2. **Tourism** (2002): receipts $487,000,000; expenditures $366,000,000. **Land use** as % of total land area (2000): in temporary crops 21.1%, in permanent crops 4.4%, in pasture 16.2%; overall forest area 36.2%.

Foreign trade

Imports (2002): $1,487,000,000 (food and beverages 20.0%; nonelectrical and electrical machinery 16.2%; mineral fuels 12.9%; textiles and clothing 11.0%; base and fabricated metals 8.9%). *Major import sources:* Italy 47.9%; Greece 34.3%; Germany 6.3%; UK 3.6%. **Exports** (2002): $330,000,000 (textiles and clothing 37.7%; footwear and related products 28.9%; base and fabricated metals 9.3%). *Major export destinations:* Italy 71.7%; Greece 12.8%; Germany 5.5%; Yugoslavia 1.5%.

Transport and communications

Transport. *Railroads* (2001): length 670 km; passenger-km 138,000,000; metric ton-km cargo 19,000. *Roads* (2000): total length 18,000 km (paved 30%). *Vehicles* (2001): passenger cars 133,533; trucks and buses 70,413. *Air transport* (2001; Albanian Air only): passenger-km 82,298,000; airports (2002) 1. **Communications,** in total units (units per 1,000). Daily newspaper circulation (2000): 109,000 (35); radios (2000): 756,000 (243); televisions (2001): 480,000 (157); telephone main lines (2003): 255,000 (83); cellular telephone subscribers (2003): 1,100,000 (358); Internet users (2003): 30,000 (9.8).

Education and health

Educational attainment (1989). Population age 10 and over having: primary education 65.3%; secondary 29.1%; higher 5.6%. **Literacy** (2001): total population age 10 and over literate 85.3%; males 92.5%; females 77.8%. **Health** (1999): physicians 4,325 (1 per 724 persons); hospital beds 10,237 (1 per 306 persons); infant mortality rate per 1,000 live births (2002) 38.6. **Food** (2001): daily per capita caloric intake 2,900 (vegetable products 72%, animal products 28%); 110% of FAO recommended minimum.

Military

Total active duty personnel (2003): 22,000 (army 72.7%, navy 11.4%, air force 15.9%). **Military expen-**

diture as percentage of GNP (1999): 1.3% (world 2.4%); per capita expenditure $21.

Background

The Albanians are descended from the Illyrians, an ancient Indo-European people who lived in central Europe and migrated south by the beginning of the Iron Age. Of the two major Illyrian migrating groups, the Ghegs settled in the north and the Tosks in the south, along with Greek colonizers. The area was under Roman rule by the 1st century BC; after AD 395 it was connected administratively to Constantinople. Turkish invasion began in the 14th century and continued into the 15th century; though the national hero, Skanderbeg, was able to resist them for a time, after his death (1468) the Turks consolidated their rule. The country achieved independence in 1912 and was admitted into the League of Nations in 1920. It was briefly a republic in 1925–28, then became a monarchy under Zog I, whose initial alliance with Benito Mussolini led to Italy's invasion of Albania in 1939. After the war a socialist government under Enver Hoxha was installed. Gradually Albania cut itself off from the nonsocialist international community and eventually from all nations, including China, its last political ally. By 1990 economic hardship had produced antigovernment demonstrations, and in 1992 a non-Communist government was elected and Albania's international isolation ended. In 1997 it plunged into chaos, brought on by the collapse of pyramid investment schemes. In 1999 it was overwhelmed by ethnic Albanians seeking refuge from Yugoslavia.

Recent Developments

The Albanian Socialists, under their leader Prime Minister Fatos Nano, and the rival Democratic Party, under former president Sali Berisha, continued their squabbling into 2005 and, in fact, were joined by a splinter of the Socialists, the Socialist Movement for Integration, which planned to run against them in the elections later in the year. Albania was cooperating within NATO programs but was disappointed when no news was received from the Istanbul summit about a date for Tirana to join.

Internet resources: <www.albanian.com>.

Algeria

Official name: Al-Jumhuriyah al-Jazairiyah al-Dimuqratiyah al-Sha'biyah (Arabic) (People's Democratic Republic of Algeria). Form of government: multiparty republic with two legislative bodies (Council of the Nation [144; includes 48 nonelected seats appointed by the president]; National People's Assembly [389]). Chief of state: President Abdelaziz Bouteflika (from 1999). Head of government: Prime Minister Ahmed Ouyahia (from 2003). Capital: Algiers. Official languages: Arabic; Tamazight is designated as a national language. Official religion: Islam. Monetary unit: 1 Algerian dinar (DA) = 100 centimes; valuation (7 Jul 2005) $1 = DA 73.45.

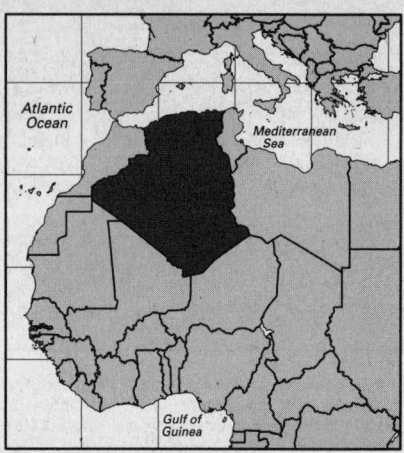

Demography

Area: 919,595 sq mi, 2,381,741 sq km. Population (2004): 32,322,000. Density (2004): persons per sq mi 35.1, persons per sq km 13.6. Urban (1998): 80.8%. Sex distribution (2003): male 50.40%; female 49.60%. Age breakdown (1998): under 15, 29.9%; 15–29, 30.6%; 30–44, 17.7%; 45–59, 8.9%; 60–74, 5.1%; 75 and over, 1.5%. Ethnic composition (2000): Algerian Arab 59.1%; Berber 26.2%, of which Arabized Berber 3.0%; Bedouin Arab 14.5%; other 0.2%. Religious affiliation (2000): Muslim 99.7%, of which Sunni 99.1%, Ibadiyah 0.6%; Christian 0.3%. Major cities (1998): Algiers 1,519,570; Oran 692,516; Constantine 462,187; Annaba 348,554; Batna 242,514. Location: northern Africa, bordering the Mediterranean Sea, Tunisia, Libya, Niger, Mali, Mauritania, Western Sahara, and Morocco.

Vital statistics

Birth rate per 1,000 population (2003): 18.3 (world avg. 21.3). Death rate per 1,000 population (2003): 4.6 (world avg. 9.1). Natural increase rate per 1,000 population (2003): 13.7 (world avg. 12.2). Total fertility rate (avg. births per childbearing woman; 2003): 2.2. Marriage rate per 1,000 population (2000): 5.8. Life expectancy at birth (2003): male 71.0 years; female 74.0 years.

National economy

Budget (2002). Revenue: DA 1,603,200,000,000 (taxes on hydrocarbons 62.9%, value-added taxes 7.0%, other 30.1%). Expenditures: DA 1,550,-600,000,000 (current expenditure 70.8%, development expenditure 29.2%). Land use as % of total land area (2000): in temporary crops 3.2%, in permanent crops 0.2%, in pasture 13.4%, overall forest area 0.9%. Production (metric tons except as noted). Agriculture, forestry, fishing (2002): wheat 1,502,000, potatoes 1,000,000, tomatoes 830,000; livestock (number of live animals) 17,300,000 sheep, 3,200,000 goats; roundwood (2002) 7,526,000 cu m; fish catch (2001) 100,300. Mining and quarrying (2002): iron ore 1,202,000; phosphate rock 740,000;

1 metric ton = about 1.1 short tons;   1 kilometer = 0.6 mi (statute);   1 metric ton-km cargo = about 0.68 short ton-mi cargo;   c.i.f.: cost, insurance, and freight;   f.o.b.: free on board

zinc (metal content) 8,576. *Manufacturing* (value added in $'000,000; 1997): food products 463; cement, bricks, and tiles 393. *Energy production (consumption):* electricity (kW-hr; 2001) 24,690,000,000 (22,900,000,000); coal (metric tons; 2000) 25,000 (583,000); crude petroleum (barrels; 2001) 305,-599,000 ([2000] 168,338,000); petroleum products (metric tons; 2000) 44,689,000 (10,584,000); natural gas (cu m; 2001) 80,300,000,000 (22,320,000,000). **Household income and expenditure.** Average household size (2000) 6.3; income per household (2001) c. $6,700; sources of income (2001): wages and salaries 39.9%, self-employment 39.2%, transfers 20.9%; expenditure (2001): food and beverages 44.1%, clothing and footwear 11.6%, transportation and communications 11.5%, furniture 6.8%, education 6.5%. **Gross national product** (2003): $60,221,000,000 ($1,890 per capita). **Population economically active** (2002): total 9,303,000; activity rate of population 29.2% (participation rates: ages 15–64 [1998] 52.6%; unemployed [2002] 25.9%). **Public debt** (external, outstanding; 2002): $21,255,000,000. **Tourism:** receipts from visitors (2002) $133,000,000; expenditures by nationals abroad (2000) $193,000,000.

Foreign trade

Imports (2001-c.i.f.): $9,482,000,000 (industrial equipment 34.7%, food 24.7%, semifinished products 18.4%, consumer goods 14.8%). *Major import sources* (2002): France 22.7%; US 9.8%; Italy 9.6%; Germany 7.2%; Spain 5.3%. **Exports** (2001-f.o.b.): $19,091,000,000 (crude petroleum 38.9%, natural and manufactured gas 36.6%, refined petroleum 17.1%). *Major export destinations* (2002): Italy 20.1%; US 14.2%; France 13.6%; Spain 12.1%; The Netherlands 9.0%; Turkey 5.1%; Canada 5.0%.

Transport and communications

Transport. *Railroads* (2003): route length 3,973 km; (2000) passenger-km 1,142,000,000; metric ton-km cargo 2,029,000,000. *Roads* (1999): total length 104,000 km (paved 69%). *Vehicles* (2001): passenger cars 1,692,148; trucks and buses 948,553. *Air transport* (2003; Air Algérie only): passenger-km 3,343,000,000; metric ton-km cargo 19,091,000; airports (1996) 28. **Communications,** in total units (units per 1,000 persons). Daily newspaper circulation (2000): 817,000 (27); radios (2000): 7,380,000 (244); televisions (2000): 3,300,000 (110); telephone main lines (2003): 2,199,600 (69); cellular telephone subscribers (2003): 1,447,310 (45); personal computers (2003): 242,000 (7.6); Internet users (2002): 500,000 (16).

Education and health

Educational attainment (1998). Percentage of economically active population age 6 and over having: no formal schooling 30.1%; primary education 29.9%; lower secondary 20.7%; upper secondary 13.4%; higher 4.3%; other 1.6%. **Literacy** (1998): total population age 10 and over literate 15,314,109 (68.1%); males literate 8,650,719 (76.3%); females literate 6,663,392 (59.7%). **Health** (1996): physicians 27,650 (1 per 1,015 persons); hospital beds 34,544 (1 per 812 persons); infant mortality rate per 1,000 live births (2003) 33.4. **Food** (2000): daily per capita caloric intake 2,987 (vegetable products 90%, animal products 10%); 124% of FAO recommended minimum.

Military

Total active duty personnel (2003): 127,500 (army 86.3%, navy 5.9%, air force 7.8%). **Military expenditure as percentage of GNP** (1999): 4.0% (world 2.4%); per capita expenditure $60.

 **Did you know?** Algeria is Africa's only producer of mercury and produces about one-tenth of the world's supply.

Background

Phoenician traders settled the area early in the 1st millennium bc; several centuries later the Romans invaded, and by ad 40 they had control of the Mediterranean coast. The fall of Rome in the 5th century led to invasion by the Vandals and later by Byzantium. The Islamic invasion began in the 7th century; by 711 all of northern Africa was under the control of the Umayyad caliphate. Several Islamic Berber empires followed, most prominently the Almoravid (c. 1054–1130), which extended its domain to Spain, and the Almohad (c. 1130–1269). The Barbary Coast pirates, operating in the area, had menaced Mediterranean trade for centuries, and France seized this pretext to enter Algeria in 1830. By 1847 France had established control in the region, and by the late 19th century it had instituted civil rule. Popular movements resulted in the bloody Algerian War (1954–62); independence was achieved following a referendum in 1962. In the 1990s Islamic fundamentalists opposing the military brought Algeria to a state of virtual civil war.

Recent Developments

In 2004–05 the violence that had plagued Algeria for the past decade declined. An explosion at the liquefied natural gas shipping terminal at Skikda on 19 Jan 2004—the worst such accident in three decades—cost 30 lives and caused worldwide concern about the safety of such facilities. The country's first presidential elections in 12 years were held in April 2004, and the incumbent, Abdelaziz Bouteflika, was reelected with 85% of the vote.

Internet resources: <www.algeria.com>.

American Samoa

Official name: American Samoa (English); Amerika Samoa (Samoan). **Political status:** unincorporated and unorganized territory of the US with two legislative houses (Senate [18]; House of Representatives [20; excludes nonvoting delegate representing Swains Island]). **Chief of state:** President George W. Bush (from 2001). **Head of government:** Governor Togiola Tulafono (from 2003). **Capital:** Fagatogo (legislative and judicial) and Utulei (executive). **Official languages:** English; Samoan. **Official religion:** none. **Monetary unit:** 1 US dollar ($) = 100 cents.

Demography

Area: 84.4 sq mi, 218.6 sq km. **Population** (2004): 62,700. **Density** (2004): persons per sq mi 811.1,

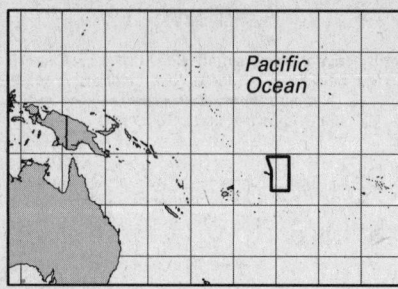

Pacific Ocean

persons per sq km 313.2. **Urban** (2000): 53.4%. **Sex distribution** (2000): male 51.08%; female 48.92%. **Age breakdown** (2000): under 15, 38.8%; 15–29, 25.5%; 30–44, 19.4%; 45–59, 10.8%; 60–74, 4.5%; 75 and over, 1.0%. **Ethnic composition** (2000): Samoan 88.2%; Tongan 2.8%; Asian 2.8%; Caucasian 1.1%; other 5.1%. **Religious affiliation** (1995): 4 major Protestant groups 60.1%; Roman Catholic 19.4%; Mormon 12.5%; other 8.0%. **Major villages** (2000): Tafuna 8,406; Nu'uuli 5,154; Pago Pago 4,278 (urban agglomeration [2001] 15,000); Leone 3,568; Fagatogo 2,096 (within Pago Pago). **Location:** group of islands in the south Pacific Ocean.

Vital statistics

Birth rate per 1,000 population (2003): 25.9 (world avg. 21.3); legitimate (2001) 71.7%; illegitimate 28.3%. **Death rate** per 1,000 population (2003): 3.4 (world avg. 9.1). **Natural increase rate** per 1,000 population (2003): 22.5 (world avg. 12.2). **Total fertility rate** (avg. births per childbearing woman; 2003): 3.6. **Marriage rate** per 1,000 population (2000): 4.7. **Divorce rate** per 1,000 population (1993): 0.5. **Life expectancy** at birth (2003): male 71.8 years; female 79.2 years.

National economy

Budget (1997). *Revenue:* $144,438,095 (US government grants 67.4%; taxes 23.6%; insurance claims 4.9%; other 4.1%). *Expenditures:* $152,912,308 (education and culture 28.5%; health and welfare 27.3%; general government 14.1%; public works and parks 12.8%; public safety 6.9%; economic development 6.1%; capital projects 3.4%; debt 0.9%). **Gross national product** (1997): $253,000,000 ($4,300 per capita). **Production** (metric tons except as noted). *Agriculture, forestry, fishing* (2002): coconuts 4,700, taros 1,500, fruits (excluding melons) 1,200; livestock (number of live animals; 2002) 10,700 pigs, 37,000 chickens; fish catch (2000) 866, of which tunas, bonitos, and billfish 820. *Manufacturing* (value of export in $; 2003): canned tuna 467,700,-000; pet food 9,800,000; other manufactures include garments, handicrafts, soap, and alcoholic beverages. *Energy production* (consumption): electricity (kW-hr; 2001) 171,101,000 (148,109,000); petroleum products (1999) none (93,000). **Population economically active** (2000): total 17,664, activity rate of total population 30.8% (participation rates: ages 16 and over 52.0%; female 41.5%; unemployed 5.1%). **Household income and expenditure.** Average household size (2000) 6.0; income per household (2000): $24,000; expenditure (1995): food and beverages 30.9%, housing and furnishings 25.8%, church donations 20.7%, transportation and communications 9.4%, clothing 2.9%, other 10.3%. **Tourism:** receipts from visitors (1997) $10,000,000; expenditures by nationals abroad (1996) $2,000,000. **Land use** as % of total land area (2000): in temporary crops 10%, in permanent crops 15%; overall forest area 60%.

Foreign trade

Imports (2001): $520,000,000 (fish for cannery 50.9%, consumer goods 16.4%, other food 12.8%, mineral fuels 5.0%). *Major import sources* (2000): US 56.7%; Australia 14.9%; New Zealand 11.1%; Fiji 5.7%; Samoa 3.1%. **Exports** (2001; to the US only): $317,000,000 (tuna in airtight containers 86.3%, fish meal 8.9%, pet food 4.8%). *Major export destinations* (2000): US 99.6%.

Transport and communications

Transport. *Roads* (1991): total length 350 km (paved 43%). *Vehicles* (2001): passenger cars 6,579; trucks and buses 625. *Air transport* (2001): incoming flights 7,805; incoming passengers 74,543; incoming cargo 890 metric tons; airports (2000) with scheduled flights 3. **Communications,** in total units (units per 1,000 persons). Daily newspaper circulation (1996): 5,000 (85); radios (1997): 57,000 (929); televisions (2000): 13,200 (211); telephone main lines (2002): 14,700 (252); cellular telephone subscribers (2001): 2,156 (38).

Education and health

Educational attainment (2000). Percentage of population age 25 and over having: no formal schooling to some secondary education 33.9%; completed secondary 39.3%; some college 19.4%; undergraduate degree 4.8%; graduate degree 2.6%. **Literacy** (2000): total population age 10 and over literate 33,993 (99.4%); males literate 17,704 (99.4%); females literate 16,589 (99.5%). **Health** (1991): physicians 26 (1 per 1,888 persons); hospital beds (1995) 140 (1 per 4.7 persons); infant mortality rate per 1,000 live births (2003) 9.7.

Military

Military defense is the responsibility of the United States.

Background

The Samoan islands were probably inhabited by Polynesians 2,500 years ago. Dutch explorers first arrived in 1722. A haven for runaway sailors and escaped convicts, the islands were ruled by native chiefs until c. 1860. The US gained the right to establish a naval station at Pago Pago in 1878, and the US, Britain, and Germany administered a tripartite protectorate in 1889–99. The islands were ceded to the US in 1904 and 1925. The first constitution was approved in 1960, and in 1977 the territory's first elected governor took office.

1 metric ton = about 1.1 short tons; 1 kilometer = 0.6 mi (statute); 1 metric ton-km cargo = about 0.68 short ton-mi cargo; c.i.f.: cost, insurance, and freight; f.o.b.: free on board

Recent Developments

Military activity on American Samoa was under focus with the US involvement in Iraq and Afghanistan. A local initiative that would require US military personnel to present a passport upon entering American Samoa was being opposed by the local congressman.

Internet resources: <www.amsamoa.com/tourism>.

Andorra

Official name: Principat d'Andorra (Principality of Andorra). **Form of government:** parliamentary coprincipality with one legislative house (General Council [28]). **Chiefs of state:** President of France Jacques Chirac (from 1995); Bishop of Urgell, Spain, Joan Enric Vives Sicília (from 2003). **Head of government:** Chief Executive Marc Forné Molné (from 1994). **Capital:** Andorra la Vella. **Official language:** Catalan. **Official religion:** none (Roman Catholicism enjoys special recognition in accordance with Andorran tradition). **Monetary unit:** 1 euro (€) = 100 cents; valuation (7 Jul 2005) $1 = €0.84.

Demography

Area: 179 sq mi, 464 sq km. **Population** (2004): 67,600. **Density** (2004): persons per sq mi 377.7, persons per sq km 145.7. **Urban** (2003): 93%. **Sex distribution** (2002): male 51.82%; female 48.18%. **Age breakdown** (2002): under 15, 15.1%; 15–29, 18.0%; 30–44, 29.1%; 45–59, 20.5%; 60–74, 11.1%; 75 and over, 6.2%. **Ethnic composition** (by nationality; 2000): Spanish 40.6%; Andorran 36.0%; Portuguese 10.2%; French 6.5%; British 1.4%; Moroccan 0.7%; German 0.5%; other 4.1%. **Religious affiliation** (2000): Roman Catholic 89.1%; other Christian 4.3%; Muslim 0.6%; Hindu 0.5%; nonreligious 5.0%; other 0.5%. **Major urban areas** (2002): Andorra la Vella 20,787; Les Escaldes–Engordany 15,519; Encamp 10,627. **Location:** southwestern Europe, between France and Spain.

Vital statistics

Birth rate per 1,000 population (2002): 11.1 (world avg. 21.3). **Death rate** per 1,000 population (2002): 3.3 (world avg. 9.1). **Natural increase rate** per 1,000 population (2002): 7.8 (world avg. 12.2). **Total fertility rate** (avg. births per childbearing woman; 2003):

1.3. **Marriage rate** per 1,000 population (2002): 2.8. **Life expectancy** at birth (2003): male 80.6 years; female 86.6 years.

National economy

Budget (2003). *Revenue:* €246,610,000 (indirect taxes 75.0%, taxes from government enterprises 15.6%, revenue from capital 9.4%). *Expenditures:* €253,835,000 (current expenditures 51.3%, of which education 13.9%, tourism 7.7%, public order 6.5%, health 4.3%, environment 3.5%; development expenditures 48.7%). **Production.** *Agriculture* (2002): tobacco 321 metric tons; other traditional crops include hay, potatoes, and grapes; livestock (number of live animals; 2002) 2,683 sheep, 1,194 cattle, 741 horses. *Quarrying:* small amounts of marble are quarried. *Manufacturing* (value of recorded exports in €'000; 2000): electrical machinery and apparatus 11,090; motor vehicles and parts 8,500; newspapers and periodicals 4,690. *Energy production (consumption):* electricity (kW-hr; 1997) 116,000,000 ([2002] 463,000,000); petroleum products, none ([2000] 201,677,000 liters). **Household expenditure** (1997): food, beverages, and tobacco 25.5%, housing and energy 19.4%, transportation 17.7%, clothing and footwear 9.2%. **Land use** as % of total land area (2000): in temporary and permanent crops 4%, in pasture 45%; overall forest area 35%. **Population economically active** (2002): total 44,058; activity rate of total population 66.4% (participation rate: ages 15–64 [2000] 72.6%). **Gross domestic product** (at current market prices; 2001): $1,462,000,000 ($22,120 per capita). **Public debt** (1995): c. $500,000,000. **Tourism** (2002): 11,500,698 visitors; number of hotels 271.

Foreign trade

Imports (2002): €1,269,200,000 (food, beverages, and tobacco 19.2%; machinery and apparatus 19.1%; chemicals and chemical products 10.0%; transport equipment 9.9%; textiles and wearing apparel 8.4%; photographic and optical goods and watches and clocks 5.7%). *Major import sources:* Spain 50.0%; France 24.5%; Germany 5.1%; Italy 3.2%; UK 2.0%. **Exports** (2002): €64,900,000 (motor vehicles and parts 29.7%; optical and photo equipment 17.7%; electrical machinery and apparatus 16.3%; chemicals and chemical products 7.0%; clothing 4.8%). *Major export destinations:* Spain 54.8%; France 30.3%; Germany 9.8%; Hong Kong 3.2%.

Transport and communications

Transport. *Railroads:* none; however, both French and Spanish railways stop near the border. *Roads* (1999): total length 269 km (paved 74%). *Vehicles* (2002): passenger cars 63,616; trucks and buses 4,809. **Communications**, in total units (units per 1,000 persons). Daily newspaper circulation (1996): 4,000 (62); radios (1997): 16,000 (247); televisions (2000): 30,400 (458); telephones (2002): 43,561 (653); cellular telephone subscribers (2002): 31,323 (469); Internet users (2001): 7,000 (88).

Education and health

Educational attainment (mid-1980s). Percentage of population age 15 and over having: no formal schooling 5.5%; primary education 47.3%; secondary education 21.6%; postsecondary education 24.9%; unknown 0.7%. **Literacy:** resident population is virtually 100% literate. **Health** (1999): physicians 218 (1 per 303 persons); hospital beds 203 (1 per 323 persons); infant mortality rate per 1,000 live births (1999–2001 avg.) 4.1.

Military

France and Spain are responsible for Andorra's external security; the police force is assisted in alternate years by either French gendarmerie or Barcelona police.

Did you know? Andorra has the world's highest life expectancy rate: 83.5 years overall, with 80.6 for males and 86.6 for females.

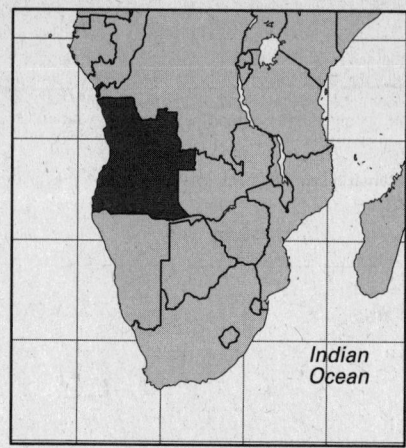

Indian Ocean

Background

Andorra's independence is traditionally ascribed to Charlemagne, who recovered the region from the Muslims in 803. It was placed under the joint suzerainty of the French counts of Foix and the Spanish bishops of the See of Urgell in 1278, and it was subsequently governed jointly by the Spanish bishop of Urgell and the French head of state. This feudal system of government, the last in Europe, lasted until 1993, when a constitution was adopted that transferred most of the coprinces' powers to the Andorran General Council, a body elected by universal suffrage. Andorra has long had a strong affinity with Catalonia; its institutions are based in Catalonian law, and it is part of the diocese of the See of Urgell (Spain). The traditional economy was based on sheep raising, but tourism has been very important since the 1950s.

Recent Developments

Andorra in 2004 worked to develop more modern institutions in order to achieve fuller alignment with those of the EU, members of which completely surrounded Andorra. Only one-third of Andorran residents were actual citizens of the country, and residency of 25 years was required for citizenship eligibility.

Internet resources: <www.turisme.ad>.

Angola

Official name: República de Angola (Republic of Angola). **Form of government:** unitary multiparty republic with one legislative house (National Assembly [220]). **Head of state and government:** President José Eduardo dos Santos (from 1979), assisted by Prime Minister Fernando da Piedade Dias dos Santos (from 2002). **Capital:** Luanda. **Official language:** Portuguese. **Official religion:** none. **Monetary unit:** 1 refloated kwanza = 100 lwei; valuation (7 Jul 2005) $1 = refloated kwanza 89.19.

Demography

Area: 481,354 sq mi, 1,246,700 sq km. **Population** (2004): 10,979,000. **Density** (2004): persons per sq mi 22.8, persons per sq km 8.8. **Urban** (2001): 34.9%. **Sex distribution** (2003): male 50.53%; female 49.47%. **Age breakdown** (2003): under 15, 43.5%; 15–29, 26.5%; 30–44, 16.8%; 45–59, 8.5%; 60–74, 4.1%; 75 and over, 0.6%. **Ethnic composition** (2000): Ovimbundu 25.2%; Kimbundu 23.1%; Kongo 12.6%; Lwena (Luvale) 8.2%; Chokwe 5.0%; Kwanyama 4.1%; Nyaneka 3.9%; Luchazi 2.3%; Ambo (Ovambo) 2.0%; Mbwela 1.7%; Nyemba 1.7%; other 10.2%. **Religious affiliation** (2001): Christian 94.1%, of which Roman Catholic 62.1%, Protestant 15.0%; traditional beliefs 5.0%; other 0.9%. **Major cities** (2004): Luanda 2,783,000; Huambo 173,600; Lobito 137,400; Benguela 134,500; Namibe 132,900. **Location:** southern Africa, bordering Democratic Republic of the Congo, Zambia, Namibia, and the Atlantic Ocean.

Vital statistics

Birth rate per 1,000 population (2003): 45.6 (world avg. 21.3). **Death rate** per 1,000 population (2003): 25.8 (world avg. 9.1). **Natural increase rate** per 1,000 population (2003): 19.8 (world avg. 12.2). **Total fertility rate** (avg. births per childbearing woman; 2003): 6.4. **Life expectancy** at birth (2003): male 36.1 years; female 37.8 years.

National economy

Budget (2002). *Revenue:* $4,367,000,000 (oil revenue 76.7%; non-oil revenue 23.3%, of which tax on goods 7.7%, income tax 6.6%, import duties 5.6%, other 3.4%). *Expenditure:* $5,370,000,000 (defense and internal security 15.0%, social security 7.0%, education 6.0%, economic services 5.2%, health 4.0%, interest payment 2.1%, other 60.7%). **Public debt** (external, outstanding; 2002): $8,883,000,000. **Household.** Average household size (2000) 4.7. **Production** (metric tons except as noted). *Agriculture, forestry, fishing* (2002): cassava 5,400,000, corn (maize) 430,000, sugarcane 360,000; livestock (number of

---

1 metric ton = about 1.1 short tons;   1 kilometer = 0.6 mi (statute);   1 metric ton-km cargo = about 0.68 short ton-mi cargo;   c.i.f.: cost, insurance, and freight;   f.o.b.: free on board

live animals) 4,150,000 cattle, 2,050,000 goats, 780,000 pigs; roundwood (2002) 4,436,271 cu m; fish catch (2001) 252,518. *Mining and quarrying* (2002): diamonds 5,022,000 carats. *Manufacturing* (1999): bread 87,500; frozen fish 57,700; wheat flour 57,500. *Energy production (consumption):* electricity (kW-hr; 2002) 1,710,000,000 ([2000] 1,235,000,-000); crude petroleum (barrels; 2001) 270,800,000 ([2000] 14,114,000); petroleum products (2000) 1,658,000 (976,000); natural gas (cu m; 2001) 710,000,000 (710,000,000). **Tourism:** receipts from visitors (2002) $60,000,000; expenditures by nationals abroad (2001) $66,000,000. **Gross national product** (at current market prices; 2003): $10,004,000,-000 ($740 per capita). **Population economically active** (1999): total 5,729,000; activity rate of total population 57.7% (participation rates over age 10 [1991] 60.1%; female 38.4%; unemployed [2002] 70%). **Land use** as % of total land area (2000): in temporary crops 2.4%, in permanent crops 0.2%, in pasture 43.3%; overall forest area 56.0%.

Foreign trade

Imports (2001): $3,179,000,000 (consumer goods 68.4%, capital goods 22.1%, intermediate goods 9.5%). *Major import sources* (2001): South Korea 22.4%; Portugal 14.5%; South Africa 12.3%; US 8.9%; France 4.8%. **Exports** (2001): $6,534,000,000 (crude petroleum 90.5%, diamonds 7.6%, refined petroleum 1.4%, coffee 0.1%). *Major export destinations* (2001): US 44.3%; China 18.7%; France 9.0%; Belgium 8.8%; Taiwan 6.8%.

Transport and communications

Transport. *Railroads* (2001): route length 2,771 km; (1991) passenger-km 246,200,000; metric ton-km cargo 45,300,000. *Roads* (1998): total length 72,626 km (paved 25%). *Vehicles* (1997): passenger cars 207,000; trucks and buses 25,000. Air transport (2001; TAAG airline): passenger-km 732,-968,000; metric ton-km cargo 57,662,000; airports (1999) with scheduled flights 17. **Communications,** in total units (units per 1,000 persons). Daily newspaper circulation (2000): 111,000 (11); televisions (2000): 193,000 (19); telephones (2003): 96,300 (6.7); cellular telephone subscribers (2002): 130,-000 (9.3); personal computers (2002): 27,000 (1.9); Internet users (2002): 41,000 (2.9).

Education and health

Literacy (1998): percentage of population age 15 and over literate 41.7%; males literate 55.6%; females literate 28.5%. **Health** (1997): physicians 736 (1 per 12,985 persons); hospital beds (1990) 11,857 (1 per 845 persons); infant mortality rate per 1,000 live births (2003) 193.8. **Food** (2000): daily per capita caloric intake 1,953 (vegetable products 92%, animal products 8%); 81% of FAO recommended minimum.

Military

Total active duty personnel (2003): 131,000 (army 91.6%, navy 2.3%, air force 6.1%). **Military expenditure as percentage of GNP** (1999): 21.2% (world 2.4%); per capita expenditure $248.

Background

An influx of Bantu-speaking peoples in the 1st millennium AD led to their dominance in the area by c. 1500. The most important Bantu kingdom was the Kongo; south of the Kongo was the Ndongo kingdom of the Mbundu people. Portuguese explorers arrived in 1483 and over time gradually extended their rule. Angola's frontiers were largely determined with other European nations in the 19th century, but not without severe resistance by the indigenous peoples. Its status as a Portuguese colony was changed to that of an overseas province in 1951. Resistance to colonial rule led to the outbreak of fighting in 1961, which led ultimately to independence in 1975. Rival factions continued fighting after independence; although a peace accord was reached in 1994, forces led by Jonas M. Savimbi continued to resist government control. The killing of Savimbi in February 2002 changed the political balance and led to the signing of a cease-fire agreement in Luanda in April that effectively ended the civil war.

Recent Developments

Instability continued in the exclave of Cabinda, where local leaders were demanding independence. In March 2004, Roman Catholic clergy in Cabinda who sought to interpose themselves between secessionists and government troops formed an association called Mpalabanda. The association sought an accommodation with the government by negotiation rather than by forceful means. Mpalabanda was not, they said, attempting to seize control of the province's rich oil resources, but felt that the population derived little benefit from the profits from oil production. By March 2005 the death toll had risen to 122 in a months-long outbreak of Marburg virus, a hemorrhagic, Ebola-like illness.

Internet resources: <www.angola.org>.

Antigua and Barbuda

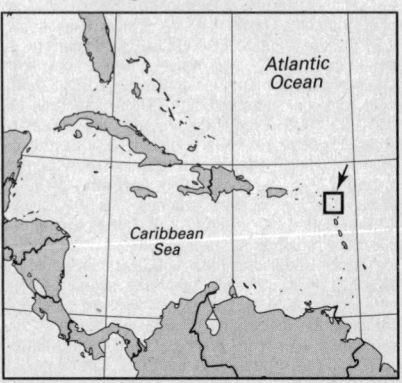

Official name: Antigua and Barbuda. **Form of government:** constitutional monarchy with two legislative houses (Senate [17]; House of Representatives [17 directly elected seats; attorney general and speaker may serve ex officio if they are not elected to House of Representatives]). **Chief of state:** British Monarch Queen Elizabeth II (from 1952), represented by Governor-General Sir James B. Carlisle (from 1993). **Head of government:** Prime Minister Baldwin Spencer (from 24 Mar 2004). **Capital:** Saint John's. **Official language:** English. **Official religion:** none. **Monetary unit:** 1 Eastern Caribbean dollar (EC$) = 100 cents; valuation (7 Jul 2005) US$1 = EC$2.67.

Demography

Area: 170.5 sq mi, 441.6 sq km. **Population** (2004): 68,300. **Density** (2004): persons per sq mi 399.4, persons per sq km 154.5. **Urban** (2001): 36.9%. **Sex distribution** (2001): male 48.25%; female 51.75%. **Age breakdown** (2001): under 15, 26.4%; 15–29, 25.4%; 30–44, 23.9%; 45–59, 13.9%; 60 and over, 10.4%. **Ethnic composition** (2000): black 82.4%; US white 12.0%; mulatto 3.5%; British 1.3%; other 0.8%. **Religious affiliation** (1991): Protestant 73.7%, of which Anglican 32.1%, Moravian 12.0%, Methodist 9.1%, Seventh-day Adventist 8.8%; Roman Catholic 10.8%; Jehovah's Witness 1.2%; Rastafarian 0.8% (increased to more than 3% of population by 2000); other religion/no religion/not stated 13.5%. **Major city** (2004): Saint John's 23,600. **Location:** eastern Caribbean Sea.

Vital statistics

Birth rate per 1,000 population (2003): 18.2 (world avg. 21.3). **Death rate** per 1,000 population (2003): 5.6 (world avg. 9.1). **Natural increase rate** per 1,000 population (2003): 12.6 (world avg. 12.2). **Total fertility rate** (avg. births per childbearing woman; 2003): 2.3. **Marriage rate** per 1,000 population (1995): 22.1. **Divorce rate** per 1,000 population (1988): 0.2. **Life expectancy** at birth (2003): male 69.0 years; female 73.8 years.

National economy

Budget (2002). *Revenue:* EC$418,000,000 (tax revenue 92.9%, of which taxes on international transactions 49.8%, consumption taxes 18.9%, corporate income taxes 14.7%; grants 4.3%; other 2.8%). *Expenditures:* EC$535,500,000 (current expenditures 94.5%, of which interest payments 10.8%; development expenditures 5.5%). **Public debt** (external, outstanding; 2004): more than US$740,000,000. **Production** (metric tons except as noted). *Agriculture, forestry, fishing* (2002): tropical fruit (including papayas, guavas, soursops, and oranges) 6,750, mangoes 1,400, eggplants 270; livestock (number of live animals) 18,500 sheep, 13,800 cattle; fish catch (2000) 1,481. *Mining and quarrying:* crushed stone for local use. *Manufacturing* (1994): beer and malt 166,000 cases; T-shirts 179,000 units; other manufactures include cement, handicrafts, and furniture, as well as electronic components for export. *Energy production (consumption):* electricity (kW-hr; 2002) 110,000,000 (110,000,000); petroleum products (2000) negligible (115,000). **Population economically active** (1991): total 26,753; activity rate of total population 45.1% (participation rates: ages 15–64, 69.7%; female 45.6%; unemployed [2000] 11.0%). **Households.** Average household size (2001) 3.1.

Gross national product (2003): US$719,000,000 (US$9,160 per capita). **Land use** as % of total land area (2000): in temporary crops c. 18%, in permanent crops c. 5%, in pasture c. 9%; overall forest area c. 20%. **Tourism:** receipts from visitors (2001) US$272,000,000; expenditures by nationals abroad US$32,000,000.

Foreign trade

Imports (1999): US$356,000,000 (machinery and equipment 32.2%, agricultural products 24.7%, basic manufactures 15.4%, petroleum products 10.5%). *Major import sources:* US 49.5%; Japan 10.2%; UK 6.3%; Trinidad and Tobago 6.0%; Netherlands Antilles 5.5%. **Exports** (1999): US$37,800,000 (reexports [significantly, petroleum products reexported to neighboring islands] 60.3%, domestic exports 39.7%). *Major export destinations* (1998): Barbados 9.5%; Trinidad and Tobago 7.3%; St. Lucia 7.3%; UK 6.1%; unspecified 52.5%.

Transport and communications

Transport. *Roads* (1998): total length 250 km. *Vehicles* (1995): passenger cars 13,588; trucks and buses 1,342. *Air transport* (1999): passenger-km 276,300,000; metric ton-km cargo 300,000; airports (2001) with scheduled flights 2. **Communications,** in total units (units per 1,000 persons). Daily newspaper circulation (1996): 6,000 (87); radios (1997): 36,000 (523); televisions (1999): 33,000 (501); telephones (2002): 38,000 (488); cellular telephone subscribers (2002): 38,200 (490); Internet users (2002): 10,000 (128).

Education and health

Educational attainment (1991). Percentage of population age 25 and over having: no formal schooling 1.1%; primary education 50.5%; secondary 33.4%; higher (not university) 5.4%; university 6.2%; other/unknown 3.4%. **Literacy** (2000): percentage of total population age 15 and over literate 86.6%. **Health** (1996): physicians 75 (1 per 915 persons); hospital beds 255 (1 per 269 persons); infant mortality rate per 1,000 live births (2003) 20.9. **Food** (2000): daily per capita caloric intake 2,381 (vegetable products 67%, animal products 33%); 102% of FAO recommended minimum.

Military

Total active duty personnel (2003): a 170-member defense force (army 73.5%, navy 26.5%) is part of the Eastern Caribbean regional security system. **Military expenditure as percentage of GNP** (1998): 0.7% (world 2.5%); per capita expenditure US$57.

 Antigua, the "gateway to the Caribbean," is home to Nelson's Dockyard, named for British Adm. Horatio Nelson. The collection of buildings, most built between 1785 and 1792, is considered an architectural treasure and is a major tourist attraction.

---

1 metric ton = about 1.1 short tons;   1 kilometer = 0.6 mi (statute);   1 metric ton-km cargo = about 0.68 short ton-mi cargo;   c.i.f.: cost, insurance, and freight;   f.o.b.: free on board

Background

Christopher Columbus visited Antigua in 1493 and named it after a church in Seville, Spain. It was colonized in 1632 by English settlers, who imported African slaves to grow tobacco and sugarcane. Barbuda was colonized by the English in 1678. In 1834 its slaves were emancipated. Antigua (with Barbuda) was part of the British colony of the Leeward Islands from 1871 until that colony was defederated in 1956. The islands achieved full independence in 1981.

Recent Developments

Lester Bird, whose family had dominated politics in Antigua and Barbuda since the 1950s and who had himself been prime minister for a decade, conceded defeat to Baldwin Spencer in the election on 23 Mar 2004. In the same month the tiny Caribbean country won a ruling against the United States from the World Trade Organization; the US had sought a prohibition on Internet gambling, while Antigua and Barbuda held that such a ban would be against normal international trade.

Internet resources: <www.antigua-barbuda.org>.

Argentina

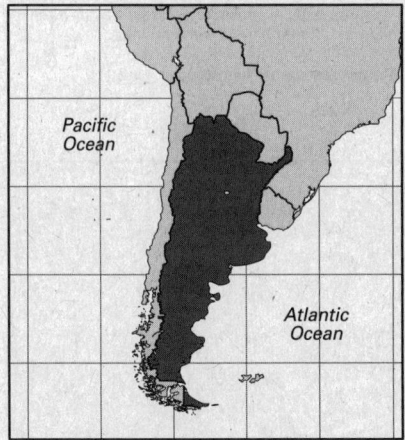

Pacific Ocean

Atlantic Ocean

Official name: República Argentina (Argentine Republic). **Form of government:** federal republic with two legislative houses (Senate [72]; Chamber of Deputies [257]). **Head of state and government:** President Néstor Kirchner (from 2003), assisted by Cabinet Chief Alberto Fernández (from 2003). **Capital:** Buenos Aires. **Official language:** Spanish. **Official religion:** Roman Catholicism. **Monetary unit:** 1 peso (pl. pesos) (Arg$) = 100 centavos; valuation (7 Jul 2005) US$1 = Arg$2.88.

Demography

Area: 1,073,400 sq mi, 2,780,092 sq km. **Population** (2004): 39,145,000. **Density** (2004): persons per sq mi 36.5, persons per sq km 14.1. **Urban** (2000): 89.6%. **Sex distribution** (2001): male 48.70%; female 51.30%. **Age breakdown** (2001):

under 15, 28.3%; 15–29, 25.0%; 30–44, 18.6%; 45–59, 14.7%; 60–74, 9.3%; 75 and over, 4.1%. **Ethnic composition** (2000): European extraction 86.4%; mestizo 6.5%; Amerindian 3.4%; Arab 3.3%; other 0.4%. **Religious affiliation** (2000): Roman Catholic 79.8%; Protestant 5.4%; Muslim 1.9%; Jewish 1.3%; other 11.6%. **Major cities** (2001): Buenos Aires 2,768,772 (16,603,341 combined population of Gran Buenos Aires and Buenos Aires city); Córdoba 1,267,774; San Justo 1,256,724; Rosario 906,004; La Plata 553,002. **Location:** southern South America, bordering Bolivia, Paraguay, Brazil, Uruguay, the South Atlantic Ocean, and Chile.

Vital statistics

Birth rate per 1,000 population (2003): 17.5 (world avg. 21.3). **Death rate** per 1,000 population (2003): 7.6 (world avg. 9.1). **Natural increase rate** per 1,000 population (2003): 9.9 (world avg. 12.2). **Total fertility rate** (avg. births per childbearing woman; 2003): 2.3. **Life expectancy** at birth (2003): male 71.7 years; female 79.4 years.

National economy

Budget (2001). *Revenue:* Arg$37,093,900,000 (tax revenue 90.3%, of which sales tax 36.0%, social security tax 22.8%, income tax 17.9%, property tax 9.3%; nontax revenue 9.7%). *Expenditure:* Arg$46,013,400,000 (social security 47.8%; debt service 22.1%; education 5.7%; defense 3.8%; health 1.8%). **Public debt** (external, outstanding; 2002): US$74,661,000,000. **Gross national product** (at current market prices; 2003): US$140,113,000,000 (US$3,650 per capita). **Production** (metric tons except as noted). *Agriculture, forestry, fishing* (2002): soybeans 30,000,000, sugarcane 16,500,000, corn (maize) 14,710,000; livestock (number of live animals) 50,669,000 cattle, 14,000,000 sheep; roundwood (2002) 9,307,000 cu m; fish catch (2001) 924,700. *Mining and quarrying* (2001): silver 152,802 kg; gold 30,630 kg. *Manufacturing* (value added in US$'000,000; 1999): food products 5,601; beverages 2,146; refined petroleum products 1,361. *Energy production (consumption):* electricity (kW-hr; 2002) 81,390,000,000 ([2000] 89,014,000,000); coal (2000) 259,000 (1,058,000); crude petroleum (barrels; 2001) 277,000,000 ([2000] 191,379,000); petroleum products (2000) 23,197,000 (20,460,000); natural gas (cu m; 2001) 53,298,000,000 ([2000] 40,817,400,000). **Land use** as % of total land area (2000): in temporary crops 12.2%, in permanent crops 0.5%, in pasture 51.9%; overall forest area 12.7%. **Tourism** (2002): receipts US$1,476,000,000; expenditures US$2,256,000,000. **Population economically active** (2001): total 15,264,783; activity rate of total population 42.1% (participation rates: ages 14 and over 57.2%; female 40.9%; unemployed [2004] c. 12%). **Households.** Average household size (2001) 3.6.

Foreign trade

Imports (2001-f.o.b. in balance of trade and c.i.f. in commodities and trading partners): US$20,311,600,000 (chemicals and chemical products 17.8%, nonelectrical machinery 17.4%, electrical machinery 12.6%, transport equipment 10.5%). *Major import sources:* Brazil 26.0%; US 18.6%; Germany 5.2%; China 5.2%; Italy 4.1%; Japan 3.8%. **Exports** (2001):

US$26,655,200,000 (food products and live animals 44.2%, crude petroleum and petroleum products 16.9%, road vehicles 8.3%, nonelectrical machinery 4.3%). *Major export destinations:* Brazil 23.3%; US 10.9%; Chile 10.7%; China 4.2%; Spain 4.1%.

Transport and communications

Transport. *Railroads:* (2000) route length 35,753 km; (2001) passenger-km 7,934,000,000; (2001) metric ton-km cargo 8,989,000,000. *Roads* (1999): total length 215,471 km (paved 29%). *Vehicles:* passenger cars (2000) 5,386,700; commercial vehicles and buses (1998) 1,496,567. *Air transport* (2003; Aerolineas Argentinas): passenger-km 9,514,000,000; metric ton-km cargo 103,435,000. **Communications,** in total units (units per 1,000 persons). Daily newspaper circulation (2000): 1,320,000 (37); radios (2000): 24,300,000 (681); televisions (2000): 10,500,000 (293); telephones (2002): 8,009,400 (219); cellular telephone subscribers (2002): 6,500,000 (178); personal computers (2002): 3,000,000 (82); Internet users (2002): 4,100,000 (112).

Education and health

Educational attainment (2001). Percentage of population age 15 and over having: no formal schooling 3.7%; incomplete primary education 14.2%; complete primary 28.0%; secondary 37.1%; some higher 8.3%; complete higher 8.7%. **Literacy** (2001): percentage of total population age 10 and over literate 97.4%; males literate 97.4%; females literate 97.4%. **Health:** physicians (1992) 88,800 (1 per 376 persons); hospital beds (1996) 115,803 (1 per 304 persons); infant mortality rate (2003) 16.2. **Food** (2001): daily per capita caloric intake 3,171 (vegetable products 70%, animal products 30%); 135% of FAO recommended minimum.

Military

Total active duty personnel (2003): 71,400 (army 58.0%, navy 24.5%, air force 17.5%). **Military expenditure as percentage of GNP** (1999): 1.6% (world 2.4%); per capita expenditure US$118.

Background

Little is known of Argentina's indigenous population before the Europeans' arrival. The area was explored for Spain by Sebastian Cabot in 1526–30; by 1580, Asunción, Santa Fe, and Buenos Aires had been settled. At first attached to the viceroyalty of Peru (1620), it was later included with regions of modern Uruguay, Paraguay, and Bolivia in the viceroyalty of La Plata, or Buenos Aires (1776). With the establishment of the United Provinces of the Plate River in 1816, Argentina achieved its independence from Spain, but its boundaries were not set until the early 20th century. In 1943 the government was overthrown by the military; Col. Juan Perón took control in 1946. He in turn was overthrown in 1955. He returned to power in 1973 after two decades of turmoil. His second wife, Isabel, became president on his death in 1974 but lost power after a military coup in 1976. The military government tried to take the Falkland Islands (Islas Malvinas) in 1982 but

was defeated by the British, with the result that the government returned to civilian rule in 1983. The government of Raúl Alfonsín worked to end the human rights abuses that characterized the former regimes. Hyperinflation led to public riots and Alfonsín's electoral defeat in 1989; his Peronist successor, Carlos Menem, instituted laissez-faire economic policies. In 1999 Fernando de la Rúa of the Alliance coalition was elected president, and his administration struggled with rising unemployment, foreign debt, and government corruption until the collapse of the government late in 2001.

Recent Developments

January 2004 marked the two-year anniversary of Argentina's historic economic and political collapse. Compared with the dark days of December 2001 and January 2002, Argentina functioned quite well throughout 2004. The Argentine economy experienced robust growth in 2004, fueled by the success of the agricultural sector (particularly soybean exports), an increase in local industrial production as consumers substituted locally manufactured products for imports (which were now prohibitively expensive, owing to the three-to-one exchange rate with the US dollar), and the boom experienced by the construction sector. The country's GDP increased by a healthy 8% in 2004. Crime emerged as a salient issue for the Argentine public during the year, with mounting popular pressure on Pres. Néstor Kirchner to adopt a harder line toward criminals.

Internet resources: <www.sectur.gov.ar>.

Armenia

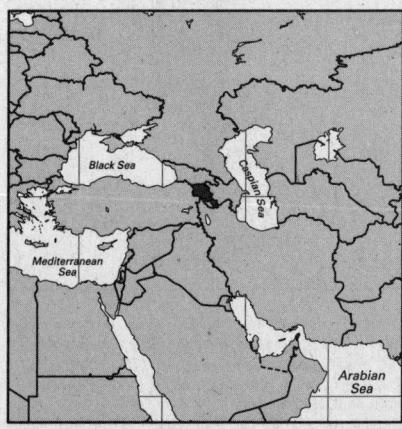

Official name: Hayastani Hanrapetut'yun (Republic of Armenia). **Form of government:** unitary multiparty republic with a single legislative body (National Assembly [131]). **Head of state:** President Robert Kocharyan (from 1998). **Head of government:** Prime Minister Andranik Markaryan (from 2000). **Capital:** Yerevan. **Official language:** Armenian. **Official religion:** none, but the Armenian Apostolic Church (Armenian Orthodox

---

1 metric ton = about 1.1 short tons;   1 kilometer = 0.6 mi (statute);   1 metric ton-km cargo = about 0.68 short ton-mi cargo;   c.i.f.: cost, insurance, and freight;   f.o.b.: free on board

Church) has special status per 1991 religious law. **Monetary unit:** 1 dram = 100 lumas; valuation (7 Jul 2005) $1 = 452.50 drams.

Demography

Area: 11,484 sq mi, 29,743 sq km; in addition, about 16% of neighboring Azerbaijan (including the 1,700-sq mi [4,400-sq km] geographic region of Nagorno-Karabakh [Armenian: Artsakh]) has been occupied by Armenian forces since 1993. **Population** (2004): 2,991,000. **Density** (2004): persons per sq mi 260.4, persons per sq km 100.6. **Urban** (2001): 64.8%. **Sex distribution** (2001): male 46.87%; female 53.13%. **Age breakdown** (2001): under 15, 24.8%; 15–29, 24.9%; 30–44, 21.8%; 45–59, 13.6%; 60–74, 12.1%; 75 and over, 2.8%. **Ethnic composition** (2001): Armenian 97.9%; Kurdish 1.3%; Russian 0.5%; other 0.3%. **Religious affiliation** (1995): Armenian Apostolic 64.5%; other Christian 1.3%; other (mostly nonreligious) 34.2%. **Major cities** (2001): Yerevan 1,091,235; Gyumri 150,917; Vanadzor (Kirovakan) 107,394; Vagharshapat 56,388; Hrazdan 52,808. **Location:** southwestern Asia, bordering Georgia, Azerbaijan, Iran, and Turkey.

Vital statistics

Birth rate per 1,000 population (2002): 10.1 (world avg. 21.3); legitimate 86.8%; illegitimate 13.2%. **Death rate** per 1,000 population (2002): 8.0 (world avg. 9.1). **Natural increase rate** per 1,000 population (2002): 2.1 (world avg. 12.2). **Total fertility rate** (avg. births per childbearing woman; 2001): 1.1. **Marriage rate** per 1,000 population (2002): 4.3. **Divorce rate** per 1,000 population (2002): 0.5. **Life expectancy** at birth (2002): male 70.0 years; female 76.1 years.

National economy

Budget (2002). *Revenue:* 228,317,000,000 drams (tax revenue 87.0%, of which value-added tax 41.6%, excise tax 15.5%, enterprise profit tax 7.6%, stamp duties 5.8%; nontax revenue 13.0%). *Expenditures:* 263,912,000,000 drams (public services and social welfare 18.2%, defense 13.9%, education 11.0%, housing and energy 6.4%, public health 6.0%, unspecified 27.2%). **Public debt** (external, outstanding; 2002): $920,000,000. **Tourism** (2002): receipts from visitors $162,000,000; expenditures by nationals abroad $54,000,000. **Land use** as % of total land area (2000): in temporary crops 17.6%, in permanent crops 2.3%, in pasture 28.4%; overall forest area 12.4%. **Gross national product** (2003): $2,910,-000,000 ($950 per capita). **Production** (metric tons except as noted). *Agriculture, forestry, fishing* (2002): potatoes 374,263, wheat 280,477, tomatoes 171,000; livestock (number of live animals) 546,136 sheep, 514,244 cattle, 97,884 pigs; roundwood (2002) 54,000 cu m; fish catch (2001) 2,100. *Mining and quarrying* (2000): copper (metal content) 14,000; molybdenum (metal content) 6,044; gold (metal content) 400 kg. *Manufacturing* (value of production in '000,000 drams; 2001): food products 109,300; metals 24,600; jewelry 16,600. *Energy production (consumption):* electricity (kW-hr; 2002) 5,519,000,000 (5,519,000,000); coal (2001) none (5,000); crude petroleum (barrels; 1998) none (1,035,000); petroleum products (2000) none (273,000); natural gas (cu m; 2000) none (1,336,000,000). **Population economically active:** total (2003) 1,232,400; activity rate of total population (2001) 49.5% (participation rates [2001]: ages 15–64, 72.1%; female [2003] 49.5%; unemployed [2003] 10.1%). **Household income and expenditure.** Average household size (2001) 4.1; income per household (2002) 750,400 drams; sources of income (1999): agricultural income 32.1%, wages and salaries 24.6%, transfers 19.3%, help from abroad 12.8%, self-employment 10.6%, other 0.6%; expenditure (1999): food 67.0%, beverages and tobacco 19.2%, services 12.4%, other 1.4%.

Foreign trade

Imports (2001-f.o.b. in balance of trade and c.i.f. in commodities and trading partners): $877,434,000 (2000; mineral fuels 20.8%; food 20.6%, of which cereals 9.8%; rough diamonds 11.0%; nonelectrical machinery 10.9%). *Major import sources* (2001): Russia 19.5%; UK 10.4%; US 9.6%; Iran 8.9%; UAE 5.4%; Belgium 4.8%. **Exports** (2001): $341,836,000 (2000; cut diamonds 33.5%; alcoholic beverages 7.5%; electric current 7.0%; metal scrap 6.8%; nonelectrical machinery 6.4%). *Major export destinations* (2001): Russia 17.7%; US 15.3%; Belgium 13.6%; Iran 9.5%; UK 5.9%.

Transport and communications

Transport. *Railroads* (2003): length 711 km; (2002) passenger-km 48,400,000; metric ton-km cargo 451,800,000. *Roads* (2003): length 7,527 km (paved 100%). *Vehicles* (1996): passenger cars 1,300; trucks and buses 4,460. *Air transport* (2002): passenger-km 755,300,000; metric ton-km cargo 5,800,000; airports (2003) 1. **Communications**, in total units (units per 1,000 persons). Daily newspaper circulation (2000): 18,700 (6.2); radios (2000): 700,000 (225); televisions (2000): 759,000 (244); telephone main lines (2003): 562,600 (148); cellular telephone subscribers (2003): 114,400 (30); personal computers (2002): 60,000 (16); Internet users (2003): 150,000 (39).

Education and health

Educational attainment (2001). Percentage of population age 26 and over having: no formal schooling 0.7%; primary education 13.0%; completed secondary and some postsecondary 66.0%; higher 20.3%. **Literacy** (2001): total population age 15 and over literate 99.4%; male 99.7%; female 99.2%. **Health** (2002): physicians 11,508 (1 per 279 persons); hospital beds 13,968 (1 per 230 persons); infant mortality rate per 1,000 live births (2002) 14.0. **Food** (2001): daily per capita caloric intake 1,991 (vegetable products 84%, animal products 16%); 80% of FAO recommended minimum.

Military

Total active duty personnel (2003): 44,660 (army 92.9%, air force 7.1%; Russian troops (August 2004) 3,500. **Military expenditure as percentage of GNP** (1999): 5.8% (world 2.4%); per capita expenditure $170.

Did you know? Though first historically recorded in AD 607, Armenia's capital, Yerevan, dates by archaeological evidence to a settlement on the site in the 6th-3rd millennia BC.

Background

Armenia is a successor state to a historical region in southwestern Asia. Historical Armenia's boundaries have varied considerably, but the region extended over what is now northeastern Turkey and the Republic of Armenia. The area was later conquered by the Medes and Macedonia and still later allied with the Roman Empire. Armenia adopted Christianity as its national religion in AD 303. It came under the rule of the Ottoman Turks in 1514. Over the next centuries, as parts were ceded to other rulers, nationalism arose among the scattered Armenians; by the late 19th century it was causing widespread disruption. Fighting between Turks and Russians escalated when part of Armenia was ceded to Russia in 1878, and it continued through World War I, leading to Armenian deaths on a genocidal scale. With the Turkish defeat, the Russian-controlled part of Armenia was set up as a Soviet republic in 1921. Armenia became a constituent republic of the USSR in 1936. With the latter's dissolution in the late 1980s, Armenia declared its independence in 1990. It fought Azerbaijan for control over Nagorno-Karabakh until a cease-fire in 1994. About one-fifth of the population left the country beginning in 1993 because of an energy crisis. Political tension escalated, and in 1999 the prime minister and some legislators were killed in a terrorist attack on the legislature.

Recent Developments

The antagonism between the Armenian three-party coalition government and the opposition generated by the flawed elections in 2003 continued to pervade domestic politics in 2004. On 4 February opposition deputies walked out of the parliament to protest the majority's refusal to debate proposed constitutional amendments that would have paved the way for a referendum of confidence in Pres. Robert Kocharyan. An agreement was signed on 8 September on the construction of a 140-km (87-mi) pipeline to export Iranian gas to Armenia.

Internet resources: <www.armeniaemb.org>.

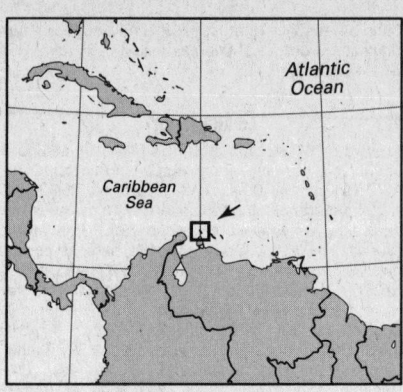

over, 2.7%; unknown 0.1%. **Linguistic composition** (2000): Papiamento 69.4%; Spanish 13.2%; English 8.1%; Dutch 6.1%; Portuguese 0.3%; other 2.0%; unknown 0.9%. Most Arubans are racially and ethnically mixed; ethnic composition (1998): Amerindian/other 80%; other (primarily Dutch, Spanish and/or black) 20%. **Religious affiliation** (2000): Christian 96.2%, of which Roman Catholic 81.9%, Protestant 7.3%, other Christian (Jehovah's Witness) 1.3%; Spiritist 1.0%; nonreligious 1.4%; other 1.4%. **Major urban areas** (2000): Oranjestad 26,355; San Nicolas 15,848. **Location:** southern Caribbean, north of Venezuela.

Vital statistics

Birth rate per 1,000 population (2002): 14.6 (world avg. 21.3); legitimate 52.5%; illegitimate 47.5%. **Death rate** per 1,000 population (2002): 5.2 (world avg. 9.1). **Natural increase rate** per 1,000 population (2002): 9.4 (world avg. 12.2). **Total fertility rate** (avg. births per childbearing woman; 2002): 1.8. **Marriage rate** per 1,000 population (2002): 6.9. **Divorce rate** per 1,000 population (2002): 5.2. **Life expectancy** at birth (2002): male 70.0 years; female 76.0 years.

National economy

Budget (2002). *Revenue:* Af. 751,200,000 (tax revenue 81.2%, of which taxes on income and profits 40.1%, sales tax 28.4%; nontax revenue 13.8%; grants 5.0%). *Expenditures:* Af. 816,400,000 (wages 32.1%, goods and services 18.3%, subsidies 13.2%, social security contributions 8.1%). **Production** (metric tons except as noted). *Agriculture, forestry, fishing:* aloes are cultivated for export; small amounts of tomatoes, beans, cucumbers, gherkins, watermelons, and lettuce are grown on hydroponic farms; divi-divi pods, sour orange fruit, sorghum, and peanuts (groundnuts) are nonhydroponic crops of limited value; fish catch (2001) 163. *Mining and quarrying:* excavation of sand for local use. *Manufacturing:* rum, cigarettes, aloe products, and soaps. Service facilities include a free zone, offshore corporate banking facilities, casino/resort complexes, a petroleum transshipment terminal, a cruise ship terminal, and ship repair and bunkering facilities. *Energy production (consumption):* electricity (kW-hr; 2002) 824,649,000 (690,129,000); crude petroleum (barrels; 2000) none (2,382,000); petroleum

Aruba

Official name: Aruba. **Political status:** nonmetropolitan territory of The Netherlands with one legislative house (States of Aruba [21]). **Chief of state:** Dutch Monarch Queen Beatrix (from 1980), represented by Governor-General Fredis Refunjol (from 11 May 2004). **Head of government:** Prime Minister Nelson O. Oduber (from 2001). **Capital:** Oranjestad. **Official language:** Dutch. **Official religion:** none. **Monetary unit:** 1 Aruban florin (Af.) = 100 cents; pegged to the US dollar at a fixed rate of Af. 1.79 = $1.

Demography

Area: 75 sq mi, 193 sq km. **Population** (2004): 95,600. **Density** (2004): persons per sq mi 1,274.7, persons per sq km 495.3. **Urban** (2001): 67.0%. **Sex distribution** (2002): male 47.81%; female 52.19%. **Age breakdown** (2002): under 15, 22.9%; 15–29, 19.4%; 30–44, 27.5%; 45–59, 18.7%; 60–74, 8.7%; 75 and

1 metric ton = about 1.1 short tons; 1 kilometer = 0.6 mi (statute); 1 metric ton-km cargo = about 0.68 short ton-mi cargo; c.i.f.: cost, insurance, and freight; f.o.b.: free on board

products (2000) none (302,000). **Gross domestic product** (2003): $2,011,000,000 ($21,160 per capita). **Population economically active** (2000): total 45,036; activity rate of total population 49.5% (participation rates: ages 15–64, 71.9%; female 46.6%; unemployed [2003] 8.0%). **Public debt** (external, outstanding; 2003): $407,800,000. **Household income and expenditure** (1999): average household size 3.6; average annual income per household: Af. 39,000; expenditure (1994): transportation and communications 20.7%, food and beverages 18.4%, clothing and footwear 11.3%, household furnishings 10.4%, housing 9.8%. **Tourism:** receipts from visitors (2003) $844,000,000; expenditures by nationals abroad (2002) $154,000,000. **Land use** as % of total land area (2000): in temporary crops c. 11%, in pasture, negligible; overall forest area, negligible.

Foreign trade

Imports (2001): $2,362,000,000 (petroleum [all forms] and free-zone imports 68.8%, food and beverages 7.1%, electrical and nonelectrical machinery 5.5%). *Major import sources* (excludes petroleum [all forms] and free-zone trade): US 61.9%; The Netherlands 11.6%; Netherlands Antilles 3.6%; Venezuela 3.1%. **Exports** (2001): $2,439,000,000 (petroleum [all forms] and free-zone exports 98.8%, food and beverages 0.5%). *Major export destinations:* US 25.9%; Venezuela 21.3%; Netherlands Antilles 19.8%; The Netherlands 14.5%.

Transport and communications

Transport. *Roads* (1995): total length 800 km (paved 64%). *Vehicles* (2002): passenger cars 42,802; trucks and buses 1,072. *Air transport* (2001; Air Aruba only): passenger-km 800,000,000; airports (2001) with scheduled flights 1. **Communications,** in total units (units per 1,000 persons). Daily newspaper circulation (1996): 73,000 (851); radios (2000): 51,000 (562); televisions (2000): 20,000 (224); telephone main lines (2001): 37,100 (350); cellular telephone subscribers (2001): 53,000 (500); Internet users (2001): 24,000 (226).

Education and health

Educational attainment (2000). Percentage of population age 25 and over having: no formal schooling or incomplete primary education 9.7%; primary education 33.9%; secondary/vocational 39.2%; advanced vocational/higher 16.2%; unknown status 1.0%. **Literacy** (2000): percentage of total population age 13 and over literate 97.3%. **Health** (2002): physicians 99 (1 per 944 persons); hospital beds 305 (1 per 306 persons); infant mortality rate per 1,000 live births (2000) 6.5.

Military

Total active duty personnel (2003): a small Dutch naval/coast guard contingent is stationed in Aruba and the Netherlands Antilles to combat organized crime and drug smuggling.

Background

Aruba's earliest inhabitants were Arawak Indians, whose cave drawings can still be seen. Though the Dutch took possession of Aruba in 1636, they did not

begin to develop it aggressively until 1816. In 1986 Aruba seceded from the Federation of the Netherlands Antilles in an initial step toward independence.

Recent Developments

An agreement to exchange tax information signed in November 2003 by the US Treasury and the Dutch government was aimed at curbing crime and tax evasion on Aruba and elsewhere. A 315,000-barrels-per-day oil refinery, one of Aruba's principal sources of revenue, changed hands in February 2004 when it was sold by El Paso Corp. to Valero Energy Corp. for $365 million.

Internet resources: <www.aruba.com>.

Australia

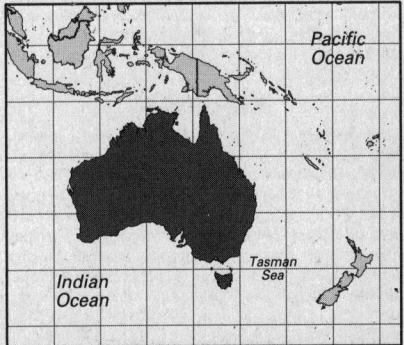

Official name: Commonwealth of Australia. **Form of government:** federal parliamentary state (formally a constitutional monarchy) with two legislative houses (Senate [76]; House of Representatives [150]). **Chief of state:** British Monarch Queen Elizabeth II (from 1952), represented by Governor-General Michael Jeffery (from 2003). **Head of government:** Prime Minister John Howard (from 1996). **Capital:** Canberra. **Official language:** English. **Official religion:** none. **Monetary unit:** 1 Australian dollar ($A) = 100 cents; valuation (7 Jul 2005) US$1 = $A 1.35.

Demography

Area: 2,969,978 sq mi, 7,692,208 sq km. **Population** (2004): 20,141,000. **Density** (2004): persons per sq mi 6.8, persons per sq km 2.6. **Urban** (2002): 85.0%. **Sex distribution** (2003): male 49.80%; female 50.20%. **Age breakdown** (2003): under 15, 20.3%; 15–29, 20.7%; 30–44, 22.7%; 45–59, 19.3%; 60–74, 11.0%; 75 and over, 6.0%. **Ethnic composition** (2001): white c. 92%; Asian c. 6%; aboriginal c. 2%. **Religious affiliation** (2001): Christian 68.0%, of which Roman Catholic 26.6%, Anglican Church of Australia 20.7%, other Protestant 15.8% (Uniting Church 6.7%, Presbyterian 3.4%), Orthodox 2.8%, other Christian 2.1%; Buddhist 1.9%; Muslim 1.5%; Hindu 0.5%; Jewish 0.4%; no religion 15.5%; other 12.2%. **Metropolitan areas** (2001): Sydney 3,997,321; Melbourne 3,366,542; Brisbane 1,627,535; Perth 1,339,993; Adelaide 1,072,585; Newcastle 470,610; Gold Coast 444,077; Canberra 353,149; Wollongong 257,510;

Caloundra 192,397; Hobart 191,169. **Location:** Oceania; a continent between the Indian Ocean and the South Pacific Ocean. **Place of birth** (2001): 76.9% native-born; 23.1% foreign-born, of which Europe 9.7% (UK and Republic of Ireland 5.5%, Italy 1.2%, Greece 0.7%, Germany 0.7%, The Netherlands 0.5%, other Europe 1.1%), Asia and Middle East 3.9%, New Zealand 1.9%, Africa, the Americas, and other 7.6%. **Mobility** (1995–96). Population age 15 and over living in the same residence as in 1994: 81.6%; different residence between states, regions, and neighborhoods 18.4%. **Households** (2000). Total number of households 7,510,000. Average household size 3.0; 1 person 25.1%, 2 persons 33.4%, 3 or more persons 41.5%. Family households 5,367,000 (71.5%), nonfamily 2,143,000 (28.5%), of which 1-person 25.1%. **Immigration** (2001–02): permanent immigrants admitted 88,900, from New Zealand 17.6%, UK and Ireland 10.4%, China 7.5%, India 5.7%, Indonesia 4.7%, South Africa 4.0%, Vietnam 2.3%, Philippines 2.3%, former Yugoslavia 2.3%, Sri Lanka 2.3%. Refugee arrivals (2001–02): 12,349. Emigration (2001–02): 48,241.

Vital statistics

Birth rate per 1,000 population (2003): 12.6 (world avg. 21.3); (2000) legitimate 69.3%; illegitimate 30.7%. **Death rate** per 1,000 population (2003): 7.3 (world avg. 9.1). **Natural increase rate** per 1,000 population (2003): 5.3 (world avg. 12.2). **Total fertility rate** (avg. births per childbearing woman; 2003): 1.8. **Marriage rate** per 1,000 population (2001): 5.3. **Divorce rate** per 1,000 population (2001): 2.8. **Life expectancy** at birth (2003): male 77.3 years; female 83.1 years.

Social indicators

Educational attainment (1999). Percentage of population age 15 to 64 having: no formal schooling and incomplete secondary education 38.0%; completed secondary 18.3%; postsecondary, technical, or other certificate/diploma 28.3%; university 15.4%. **Quality of working life** (2003). Average workweek: 34.7 hours. Working 50 hours a week or more 28.8%. Annual rate per 100,000 workers for: accidental injury and industrial disease, 3,200 (1992–93). Proportion of employed persons insured for damages or income loss resulting from: injury 100%; permanent disability 100%; death 100%. Working days lost to industrial disputes per 1,000 employees (2000): 52. Means of transportation to work (2000): private automobile 76.0%; public transportation 12.0%; motorcycle, bicycle, and foot 12.0%. Discouraged job seekers (2002): 78,000 (0.8% of labor force). **Social participation.** Eligible voters participating in last national election (2001): 95.0%; voting is compulsory. Trade union membership in total workforce (2002): 23.1%. **Social deviance** (2003). Offense rate per 100,000 population for: murder 1.5; sexual assault 92; assault 798; auto theft 497; burglary and housebreaking 1,776; armed robbery 99. Incidence per 100,000 in general population of: prisoners 139 (2001); suicide 13.0 (2001).

National economy

Gross national product (2003): US$430,533,000,000 (US$21,650 per capita). **Budget** (2002–03). *Revenue:*

$A 175,014,000,000 (tax revenue 93.2%, of which individual 52.5%, corporate 19.1%, excise duties and sales tax 15.6%; nontax revenue 6.8%). *Expenditures:* $A 169,247,000,000 (social security and welfare 42.1%; health 17.4%; defense 7.9%; public services 7.7%; economic services 7.5%; education 7.2%; interest on public debt 2.7%; other 7.5%). **Public debt** (2002–03): $A 69,926,000,000. **Tourism** (2002): receipts from visitors US$8,087,000,000; expenditures by nationals abroad US$6,116,000,000. **Production** (gross value in $A '000 except as noted). *Agriculture, forestry, fishing* (1999–2000): livestock (slaughtered value) 7,946,900 (cattle 5,050,900, sheep and lambs 1,053,900, poultry 1,031,000, pigs 791,700); wheat 4,831,200, wool 2,149,000, vegetables 1,861,900, fruits and nuts 1,761,100, seed cotton 1,400,000, grapes 1,118,200, sugarcane 881,900, barley 864,- 800, canola 638,000, oats 118,400, sunflower seeds 74,000, corn (maize) 60,000, tobacco 40,000, other cereal crops 4,735,100; livestock (number of live animals; 2002) 113,000,000 sheep, 30,500,000 cattle, 2,912,000 pigs, 93,000,000 poultry; roundwood (2002) 31,212,000 cu m; fish catch (2001) 236,300 metric tons. *Mining and quarrying* (metric tons except as noted; 2001): iron ore 112,592,000 (world rank: 2), bauxite 53,285,000 (world rank: 1), ilmenite 2,017,- 000, zinc (metal content) 1,519,000, copper (metal content) 873,000 (world rank: 4), lead (metal content) 432,000, rutile 206,000, nickel (metal content) 205,000, cobalt (metal content) 6,100, opal (value of production) US$140,000,000, sapphire (value of production) US$40,000,000; gem diamonds 14,397,000 carats, gold 285,030 kilograms (world rank: 3). *Manufacturing* (value added in $A '000,000; 2000–01): food products 11,026; printing and publishing 6,599; chemicals and chemical products 5,756; nonferrous base metals 5,678; fabricated metal products 5,402; motor vehicles and parts 4,657; electrical machinery and apparatus 3,366; beverages 3,185. **Population economically active** (2003): total 10,066,000; activity rate of total population 50.6% (participation rates: ages 15–64, 74.2%; female 44.8%; unemployed [September 2003–August 2004] 5.7%). **Household income and expenditure** (1999–2000). Average household size (2002) 3.0; average annual income per household $A 37,752; sources of income: wages and salaries 56.7%, transfer payments 28.0%, self-employment 6.0%, other 9.3%; expenditure (1998–99): food and nonalcoholic beverages 18.2%, transportation and communications 16.9%, housing 13.9%, recreation 12.7%, household durable goods 6.0%. *Energy production (consumption):* electricity (kW-hr; 2002) 210,320,000,000 (210,320,000,000); hard coal (metric tons; 2001) 264,680,000 ([1999] 60,643,- 000); lignite (metric tons; 2001) 70,000,000 (70,000,- 000); crude petroleum (barrels; 2000) 187,500,000 (224,810,000); petroleum products (metric tons; 1999) 34,381,000 (32,001,000); natural gas (cu m; 2002) 31,188,000,000 ([2000] 24,095,000,000). **Land use** as % of total land area (2000): in temporary crops 6.5%, in permanent crops 0.04%, in pasture 52.7%; overall forest area 20.1%.

Foreign trade

Imports (2000–01-f.o.b.): $A 118,264,000,000 (machinery and transport equipment 45.2%, of which road motor vehicles 12.1%, office machines and au-

---

1 metric ton = about 1.1 short tons;   1 kilometer = 0.6 mi (statute);   1 metric ton-km cargo = about 0.68 short ton-mi cargo;   c.i.f.: cost, insurance, and freight;   f.o.b.: free on board

tomatic data-processing equipment 7.0%, telecommunications equipment 6.7%; chemicals and related products 12.0%, of which medicines and pharmaceuticals 3.7%; mineral fuels and lubricants 8.9%; food and live animals 3.6%). *Major import sources:* US 18.9%; Japan 13.0%; China 8.4%; UK 5.3%; Germany 5.2%; South Korea 4.0%; New Zealand 3.9%; Malaysia 3.5%; Singapore 3.3%; Taiwan 2.8%. **Exports** (2000–01): $A 119,602,000,000 (mineral fuels 21.1%, of which coal [all forms] 9.1%, petroleum products and natural gas 9.1%; crude materials excluding fuels 19.7%, of which metalliferous ores and metal scrap [mostly iron ore and alumina] 12.3%, textile fibers 4.7%; food 16.8%, of which meat and meat preparations 4.8%, cereals and cereal preparations 4.5%; nonferrous metals 7.9%). *Major export destinations:* Japan 19.6%; US 9.7%; South Korea 7.7%; China 5.7%; New Zealand 5.7%; Singapore 5.0%; Taiwan 4.9%; UK 3.9%; Hong Kong 3.3%; Indonesia 2.6%.

Transport and communications

Transport. *Railroads* (1999–2000; government railways only): route length 35,780 km; passengers carried 629,200,000; metric ton-km cargo 134,200,000,000. *Roads* (2000): total length 808,465 km (paved 40%). *Vehicles* (2002): passenger cars 10,100,000; trucks and buses 2,355,400. *Air transport* (2002; Qantas only): passenger-km 72,890,571,000; metric ton-km cargo 1,466,937,000; airports (1996) with scheduled flights 400. **Communications,** in total units (units per 1,000 persons). Daily newspaper circulation (2000): 5,630,000 (293); radios (2000): 36,700,000 (1,908); televisions (2000): 14,200,000 (738); telephone main lines (2003): 10,815,000 (542); cellular telephone subscribers (2003): 14,347,000 (720); personal computers (2002): 11,100,000 (564); Internet users (2002): 9,472,000 (482).

Education and health

Literacy (1996): total population literate, virtually 100% (a national survey conducted in 1996 put the number of persons who had very poor literacy and numeracy skills at about 17% of the total population [age 15 to 64]). **Health:** physicians (2001) 48,211 (1 per 404 persons); hospital beds (2001) 79,900 (1 per 244 persons); infant mortality rate per 1,000 live births (2003) 4.8. **Food** (2001): daily per capita caloric intake 3,126 (vegetable products 66%, animal products 34%); 117% of FAO recommended minimum.

Military

Total active duty personnel (2003): 53,650 (army 49.5%, navy 24.0%, air force 26.5%). **Military expenditure as percentage of GNP** (1999): 1.8% (world 2.4%); per capita expenditure US$372.

Did you know? Ayers Rock, which the Aboriginals of the region call Uluru, is a tor (an isolated mass of weathered rock) in southwestern Northern Territory, Australia. It is perhaps the world's largest monolith, rising 1,100 ft (335 m) above the surrounding desert plain.

Background

Australia has long been inhabited by Aborigines, who arrived on the continent 40,000–60,000 years ago. Estimates of the population at the time of European settlement in 1788 range from 300,000 to more than 1,000,000. Widespread European knowledge of Australia began with 17th-century explorations. The Dutch landed in 1616 and the British in 1688, but the first large-scale expedition was that of James Cook in 1770, which established Britain's claim to Australia. The first English settlement, at Port Jackson (1788), consisted mainly of convicts and seamen; convicts were to make up a large proportion of the incoming settlers. By 1859 the colonial nuclei of all Australia's states had been formed, but with devastating effects on the Aborigines, whose population declined sharply with the introduction of European diseases and weaponry. Britain granted its colonies limited self-government in the mid-19th century, and Australia achieved federation in 1901. Australia fought alongside the British in World War I, notably at Gallipoli, and again in World War II, preventing the occupation of Australia by the Japanese. It joined the US in the Korean and Vietnam wars. Since the 1960s the government has sought to deal more fairly with the Aborigines, and a loosening of immigration restrictions has led to a more heterogeneous population. Constitutional links allowing British interference in government were formally abolished in 1968, and Australia has assumed a leading role in Asian and Pacific affairs. During the 1990s it experienced several debates about giving up its British ties and becoming a republic.

Recent Developments

Australian Prime Minister John Howard won his fourth general election in a row on 9 Oct 2004. The Liberal–Country Party coalition went into the campaign in a political climate that was overwhelmingly hostile to conservative political views, and every state government was in the hands of the Australian Labor Party (ALP). The ALP went into battle with an untried leader, Mark Latham. Both parties saw trust and integrity as key issues. Howard argued that the ALP could not be trusted to keep the economy strong, protect family interests, and lead the fight against international terrorism. Latham accused the prime minister of dishonesty and deceit. Taxation and health rather than the war on terrorism became the key issues.

The Australian economy remained solid in 2004. While global restructuring by Mitsubishi Motors Corp. cost Australian jobs, the yearly unemployment rate remained below 6%. Despite the growing balance-of-payments deficits, the Reserve Bank kept interest rates low.

The Howard government stressed its experience and reliability as the manager of Australian foreign policy. A series of diplomatic misunderstandings undermined this strategy, however. A diplomatic row was triggered after Foreign Minister Alexander Downer told Chinese Premier Wen Jiabao that under the ANZUS Treaty in any potential conflict with China over Taiwan, Australia might not support the US. Howard quickly repudiated Downer's view that Australia's ANZUS commitment applied to attacks on US territory but stressed that while only the US could guarantee Australia's ultimate security, Australia had its own interests in Asia and a strong and growing separate relationship with China. Downer also increased tensions with North Korea by noting that Pyongyang had developed the capacity to hit Sydney with intercontinental ballistic missiles. Relations with Malaysia improved and a free-trade agreement was signed with Thailand. Australia for the first time received an invitation to the ASEAN summit, which was held in Vientiane, Laos, in November.

Internet resources: <www.australia.com>.

Austria

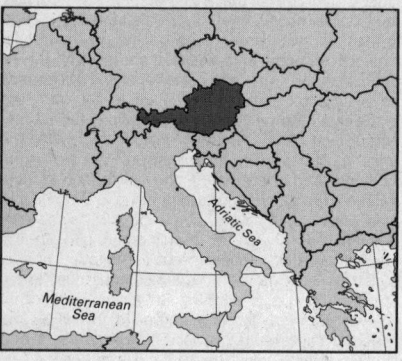

Official name: Republik Österreich (Republic of Austria). **Form of government:** federal state with two legislative houses (Federal Council [64]; National Council [183]). **Chief of state:** President Heinz Fischer (from 8 Jul 2004). **Head of government:** Chancellor Wolfgang Schüssel (from 2000). **Capital:** Vienna. **Official language:** German. **Official religion:** none. **Monetary unit:** 1 euro (€) = 100 cents; valuation (7 Jul 2005) $1 = €0.84; the Austrian Schilling (S) was the former monetary unit; on 1 Jan 2002, S13.76 = €1.

Demography

Area: 32,383 sq mi, 83,871 sq km. **Population** (2004): 8,105,000. **Density** (2004): persons per sq mi 250.3, persons per sq km 96.6. **Urban** (2001): 66.8%. **Sex distribution** (2001): male 48.41%; female 51.59%. **Age breakdown** (2001): under 15, 16.9%; 15–29, 18.6%; 30–44, 24.9%; 45–59, 18.6%; 60–74, 13.8%; 75 and over, 7.2%. **Ethnic composition** (national origin; 1998): Austrian 91.2%; citizens of former Yugoslavia 4.0%; Turkish 1.6%; other 3.2%. **Religious affiliation** (1995): Roman Catholic 75.1%; nonreligious and atheist 8.6%; Protestant (mostly Lutheran) 5.4%; Muslim 2.1%; Eastern Orthodox 0.7%; Jewish 0.1%; other 1.9%; unknown 6.1%. **Major cities** (2001): Vienna 1,550,123 (2003; urban agglomeration 2,179,-000); Graz 226,244; Linz 183,504; Salzburg 142,662; Innsbruck 113,392. **Location:** central Europe, bordering the Czech Republic, Slovakia, Hungary, Slovenia, Italy, Switzerland, Liechtenstein, and Germany.

Vital statistics

Birth rate per 1,000 population (2002): 9.7 (world avg. 21.3); (2002) legitimate 73.6%; illegitimate 26.4%. **Death rate** per 1,000 population (2002): 9.5 (world avg. 9.1). **Natural increase rate** per 1,000 population (2002): 0.2 (world avg. 12.2). **Total fertility rate** (avg. births per childbearing woman; 2002): 1.3. **Marriage rate** per 1,000 population (2002): 4.5. **Divorce rate** per 1,000 population (2002): 2.5. **Life expectancy** at birth (2002): male 75.8 years; female 81.7 years.

National economy

Budget (2003). *Revenue:* €57,414,000,000 (tax revenue 93.6%, of which individual income taxes 29.3%, turnover tax 28.4%, corporate income tax 7.1%, other taxes 28.8%; nontax revenue 6.4%). *Expenditures:* €61,355,000,000 (social security, health, and welfare 34.3%; education 14.3%; interest 14.2%; transportation 9.9%; public safety 6.6%; defense 2.6%). **Public debt** (2001): $117,420,000,000. **Production** (metric tons except as noted). *Agriculture, forestry, fishing* (2002): sugar beets 3,005,000, corn (maize) 2,000,000, wheat 1,460,000; livestock (number of live animals) 3,440,405 pigs, 2,118,454 cattle, 11,000,000 chickens; roundwood (2002) 14,845,000 cu m; fish catch (2001) 2,755. *Mining and quarrying* (2002): iron ore 1,941,800; magnesite 728,200; talc 140,000. *Manufacturing* (value added in $'000,000; 2000): nonelectrical machinery and apparatus 3,907; electrical machinery and apparatus 3,786; food products and beverages 3,112. *Energy production (consumption):* electricity (kW-hr; 2002) 58,490,000,000 ([2001] 62,250,000,000); hard coal (2002) negligible ([2000] 3,710,000); lignite (2002) 1,411,800 ([2000] 1,290,000); crude petroleum (barrels; 2001) 7,139,000 ([2000] 58,639,000); petroleum products (2000) 7,461,000 (10,297,000); natural gas (cu m; 2002) 2,014,-600,000 ([2001] 7,333,000,000). **Tourism** ($'000,-000; 2002): receipts $11,237; expenditures $9,391. **Population economically active** (2002): total 3,996,-700; activity rate of total population 49.6% (participation rates: ages 15–64 [2001] 72.0%; female 44.4%; unemployed [April 2003–March 2004] 7.1%). **Gross national product** (2003): $215,372,000,000 ($26,720 per capita). **Household income and expenditure.** Average household size (2001) 2.4; sources of income (1995): wages and salaries 54.8%, transfer payments 25.9%; expenditure (2001): housing and energy 19.3%, transportation 12.6%, food and nonalcoholic beverages 12.6%, cafe and hotel expenditures 12.2%, recreation 11.5%, household furnishings 8.3%. **Land use** as % of total land area (2000): in temporary crops 16.9%, in permanent crops 0.9%, in pasture 23.2%; overall forest area 47.0%.

Foreign trade

Imports (2002-c.i.f.): €77,104,000,000 (machinery and transport equipment 38.9%, of which road vehicles 11.2%, electrical machinery and apparatus 7.6%; chemicals and related products 11.3%; mineral fuels 7.4%; food products 5.2%). *Major import sources:* Germany 40.3%; Italy 7.2%; US 4.8%;

1 metric ton = about 1.1 short tons;   1 kilometer = 0.6 mi (statute);   1 metric ton-km cargo = about 0.68 short ton-mi cargo;   c.i.f.: cost, insurance, and freight;   f.o.b.: free on board

France 3.9%; Hungary 3.3%; Switzerland 3.3%. **Exports** (2002-f.o.b.): €77,400,000,000 (machinery and apparatus 32.9%; chemical products 10.2%; transportation equipment 9.8%; paper and paper products 4.6%; fabricated metals 4.3%; iron and steel 4.1%). *Major export destinations:* Germany 32.0%; Italy 8.5%; Switzerland 5.3%; US 5.2%; UK 4.7%; France 4.4%; Hungary 4.3%.

Transport and communications

Transport. *Railroads:* (2002) length 5,616 km; (2000) passenger-km 8,206,000,000; (2001) metric ton-km cargo 17,387,000,000. *Roads* (2001): total length 210,483 km (paved 100%). *Vehicles* (2002): passenger cars 3,987,093; trucks and buses 313,434. *Air transport* (2003; Austrian Airlines Group): passenger-km 17,965,000,000; metric ton-km cargo 442,549,000; airports (2002) with scheduled flights 6. **Communications**, in total units (units per 1,000 persons). Daily newspaper circulation (2000): 2,380,000 (296); radios (2000): 6,050,000 (753); televisions (2000): 4,310,000 (536); telephone main lines (2003): 3,881,000 (481); cellular telephone subscribers (2003): 7,094,500 (879); personal computers (2002): 3,013,000 (374); Internet users (2003): 3,730,000 (462).

Education and health

Educational attainment (1993). Percentage of population age 25 and over having: lower-secondary education 37.5%; vocational education ending at secondary level 44.6%; completed upper secondary 6.1%; higher vocational 5.5%; higher 6.3%. **Literacy:** virtually 100%. **Health:** physicians (2003) 36,531 (1 per 213 persons); hospital beds (2002) 66,299 (1 per 118 persons); infant mortality rate per 1,000 live births (2002) 4.1. **Food** (2001): daily per capita caloric intake 3,799 (vegetable products 67%; animal products 33%); 144% of FAO recommended minimum.

Military

Total active duty personnel (2003): 34,600 (army 80.2%; air force 19.8%). **Military expenditure as percentage of GNP** (1999): 0.8% (world 2.4%); per capita expenditure $208.

Background

Settlement in Austria goes back some 3,000 years, when Illyrians were probably the main inhabitants. The Celts invaded c. 400 BC and established Noricum. The Romans arrived after 200 BC and established the provinces of Raetia, Noricum, and Pannonia; prosperity followed and the population became romanized. With the fall of Rome in the 5th century AD, many tribes invaded, including the Slavs; they were eventually subdued by Charlemagne, and the area became ethnically Germanic. The distinct political entity that would become Austria emerged in 976 with Leopold I of Babenberg as margrave. In 1278 Rudolf I of the Holy Roman Empire (formerly Rudolf IV of Habsburg) conquered the area; Habsburg rule lasted until 1918. While in power the Habsburgs created a kingdom centered on Austria, Bohemia, and Hungary. The Napoleonic Wars brought about the creation of the Austrian empire (1804) and the end of the Holy Roman Empire (1806). Count von Metternich tried to assure Austrian supremacy among Germanic states, but war with Prussia led Austria to divide the empire into the Dual Monarchy of Austria-Hungary. Nationalist sentiment plagued the kingdom, and the assassination of Francis Ferdinand by a Serbian nationalist in 1914 triggered World War I, which destroyed the Austrian empire. In the postwar carving up of Austria-Hungary, Austria became an independent republic. It was annexed by Nazi Germany in 1938 and joined the Axis powers in World War II. The republic was restored in 1955 after 10 years of Allied occupation. Austria became a member of the European Union in 1995.

Recent Developments

Austria's political polarization was underscored in spring 2004 when the right-wing populist Jörg Haider was unexpectedly reelected as governor of Carinthia and a Social Democrat, Heinz Fischer, was elected president, an event interpreted as a vote against the center-right/populist–far right coalition government. Relations between the coalition partners, the Austrian People's Party (ÖVP) and the Freedom Party (FPÖ), improved. The appointment of Hubert Gorbach, a notable representative of the FPÖ's liberal wing, as vice-chancellor in late 2003 brought stability to the coalition, as did the appointment of Ursula Haubner, Haider's sister and a popular and respected junior minister, as the FPÖ's new leader in June. In April 2005, however, all three FPÖ notables quit the party to form a new Alliance for Austria's Future.

Internet resources: <www.austria.org>.

Azerbaijan

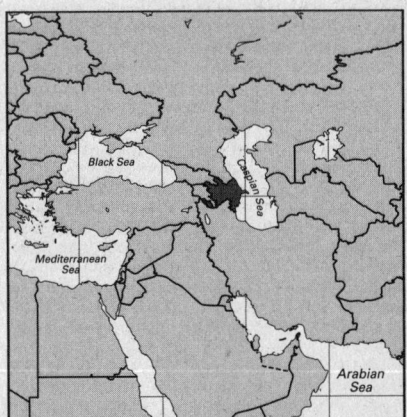

Official name: Azerbaycan Respublikasi (Republic of Azerbaijan). **Form of government:** unitary multiparty republic with a single legislative body (National Assembly [124, excluding one vacant seat reserved for Nagorno-Karabakh representative]). **Head of state and government:** President Ilham Aliyev (from 2003), assisted by Prime Minister Artur Rasizade (from 2003). **Capital:** Baku. **Official language:** Azerbaijani. **Official religion:** none. **Monetary unit:** 1 manat (A.M.) = 100 gopik; valuation (7 Jul 2005) free rate, $1 = A.M. 4,719.50.

Demography

Area: 33,400 sq mi, 86,600 sq km. **Population** (2004): 8,343,000. **Density** (2004): persons per sq mi 249.8, persons per sq km 96.3. **Urban** (2004): 50.6%. **Sex distribution** (2001): male 48.94%; female 51.06%. **Age breakdown** (2004): under 15, 27.4%; 15–29, 27.1%; 30–44, 24.5%; 45–59, 11.5%; 60 and over, 9.5%. **Ethnic composition** (1995): Azerbaijani 89.0%; Russian 3.0%; Lezgian 2.2%; Armenian 2.0%; other 3.8%. **Religious affiliation** (1995): Muslim 93.4%, of which Shi'i 65.4%, Sunni 28.0%; Russian Orthodox 1.1%; Armenian Apostolic (Orthodox) 1.1%; other 4.4%. **Major cities** (2003): Baku 1,828,800; Ganca 302,200; Sumqayit (Sumgait) 289,700; Mingacevir (Mingechaur) 94,900. **Location:** eastern Transcaucasia, bordering Russia, the Caspian Sea, Iran, Turkey, Armenia, and Georgia.

Vital statistics

Birth rate per 1,000 population (2004): 14.0 (world avg. 21.3); (2003) legitimate 92.4%; illegitimate 7.6%. **Death rate** per 1,000 population (2004): 6.0 (world avg. 9.1). **Natural increase rate** per 1,000 population (2004): 8.0 (world avg. 12.2). **Total fertility rate** (avg. births per childbearing woman; 2001): 1.6. **Life expectancy** at birth (2003): male 69.5 years; female 75.1 years.

National economy

Budget (2003). *Revenue:* A.M. 6,131,900,000,000 (tax revenue 82.5%, of which value-added tax 33.4%, enterprise profits tax 14.5%, personal income tax 12.3%, import duties 7.6%, excise taxes 5.5%; nontax revenue 17.5%). *Expenditures:* A.M. 6,173,000,-000,000 (national economy 19.7%; education 19.0%; social security 17.3%; defense 9.8%; health 5.0%). **Public debt** (external, outstanding; 2002): $964,000,000. **Production** (metric tons except as noted). *Agriculture, forestry, fishing* (2003): cereals 2,057,800, vegetables (except potatoes) 1,046,300, potatoes 769,000; livestock (number of live animals) 7,280,100 sheep and goats, 2,241,800 cattle; roundwood (2002) 13,500 cu m; fish catch (2001) 11,063. *Mining and quarrying* (2000): alumina 200,000; gypsum 60,000. *Manufacturing* (gross value of production in A.M. '000,000; 2003): food, beverages, and tobacco products 4,216,600; petroleum products 3,162,800; chemicals and chemical products 697,000. *Energy production (consumption):* electricity (kW-hr; 2002) 18,708,000,000 ([2001] 19,193,000,000); coal (2002) none (1,000); crude petroleum (barrels; 2002) 113,418,000 (63,384,-000); petroleum products (2003) 5,476,000 ([1999] 5,030,000); natural gas (cu m; 2003) 5,100,000,000 (5,100,000,000). **Households.** Average household size (2000) 5.3; income per household (2000) $460; sources of money income (2003): self-employment 55.2%, wages and salaries 7.5%, transfers 7.5%, other 29.8%. **Tourism** (2002): receipts $51,000,000; expenditures $106,000,000. **Gross national product** (at current market prices; 2003): $6,709,000,000 ($810 per capita). **Population economically active** (2003): total 3,801,400; activity rate of total population 46.3% (participation rates: ages 15–64, 75.6%; female 47.7%; unemployed 1.4%). **Land use** as % of

total land area (2000): in temporary crops 19.2%, in permanent crops 2.8%, in pasture 29.6%; overall forest area 13.1%.

Foreign trade

Imports (2002): $1,665,000,000 (machinery and equipment 23.8%, natural gas 12.9%, iron and steel 11.6%, food 10.3%, transport equipment 7.4%). *Major import sources* (2002): Russia 16.9%; Turkey 9.4%; Kazakhstan 9.0%; Turkmenistan 7.2%; France 7.1%; US 5.9%. **Exports** (2002): $2,167,000,000 (crude petroleum 68.1%, refined petroleum 19.6%, food products 1.8%). *Major export destinations* (2002): Italy 50.0%; France 7.7%; Israel 7.1%; Spain 4.8%; Russia 4.4%.

Transport and communications

Transport. *Railroads* (2003): length 2,116 km; passenger-km 636,000,000; metric ton-km cargo 7,696,000,000. *Roads* (2002): total length 45,870 km (paved 94%). *Vehicles* (2003): passenger cars 370,439; trucks and buses 95,800. *Air transport* (2003; Azerbaijan Airlines): passenger-km 755,-000,000; metric ton-km cargo 67,109,000; airports (2002) 3. **Communications,** in total units (units per 1,000 persons). Daily newspaper circulation (2000): 217,000 (27); radios (2000): 177,000 (22); televisions (2000): 2,080,000 (259); telephone main lines (2003): 976,500 (119); cellular telephone subscribers (2003): 1,055,000 (128); Internet users (2002): 300,000 (37).

Education and health

Educational attainment (1995). Percentage of population age 15 and over having: primary education or no formal schooling 12.1%; some secondary 9.1%; completed secondary and some postsecondary 27.5%; higher 7.6%. **Literacy** (1995): percentage of total population 15 and over literate 99.6%. **Health** (2003): physicians 29,500 (1 per 280 persons); hospital beds 68,600 (1 per 120 persons); infant mortality rate per 1,000 live births (2003) 12.8. **Food** (2001): daily per capita caloric intake 2,474 (vegetable products 86%, animal products 14%); 96% of FAO recommended minimum.

Military

Total active duty personnel (2003): 66,490 (army 85.5%, navy 2.6%, air force 11.9%). **Military expenditure as percentage of GNP** (1999): 6.6% (world 2.4%); per capita expenditure $120.

Background

Azerbaijan adjoins the Iranian region of the same name, and the origin of their respective inhabitants is the same. By the 9th century AD the area had come under Turkish influence, and in ensuing centuries it was fought over by Arabs, Mongols, Turks, and Iranians. Russia acquired the territory of what is now independent Azerbaijan in the early 19th century. After the Russian Revolution of 1917, Azerbaijan declared its independence; it was subdued by the Red Army in 1920 and became a soviet socialist

---

1 metric ton = about 1.1 short tons;   1 kilometer = 0.6 mi (statute);   1 metric ton-km cargo = about 0.68 short ton-mi cargo;   c.i.f.: cost, insurance, and freight;   f.o.b.: free on board

republic. It declared independence from the collapsing Soviet Union in 1991. Azerbaijan has two geographic peculiarities. The exclave Nakhichevan is separated from the rest of Azerbaijan by Armenian territory. Nagorno-Karabakh, which lies within Azerbaijan and is administered by it, has a Christian Armenian majority. Azerbaijan and Armenia went to war over both territories in the 1990s, causing great economic disruption. Though a cease-fire was declared in 1994, the political situation remained unresolved.

Recent Developments

Despite persistent rumors of a rift within Azerbaijan's top leadership, both veteran Prime Minister Artur Rasizade and presidential administration head Ramiz Mekhtiyev retained their posts in 2004. In September the weakened and demoralized opposition rejected an invitation from Pres. Ilham Aliyev to seek national reconciliation through dialogue. Opposition candidates fared poorly in local elections on 17 Dec 2004 that were marred by allegations of fraud. Elmar Huseynov, the editor in chief of Baku's leading opposition magazine, *Monitor,* was gunned down in front of his apartment in March 2005.

Internet resources: <www.president.az>.

The Bahamas

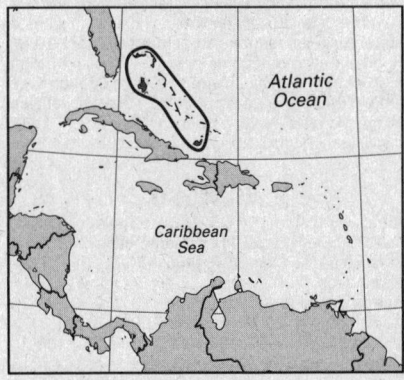

Atlantic Ocean

Caribbean Sea

Official name: The Commonwealth of The Bahamas. Form of government: constitutional monarchy with two legislative houses (Senate [16]; House of Assembly [40]). Chief of state: Queen Elizabeth II, represented by Governor-General Dame Ivy Dumont (from 2001). Head of government: Prime Minister Perry Christie (from 2002). Capital: Nassau. Official language: English. Official religion: none. Monetary unit: 1 Bahamian dollar (B$) = 100 cents; valuation (7 Jul 2005) US$1 = B$1.00.

Demography

Area: 5,382 sq mi, 13,939 sq km. Population (2004): 317,000. Density (2004): persons per sq mi 81.5, persons per sq km 31.5. Urban (2000): 88.4%. Sex distribution (2000): male 48.65%; female 51.35%. Age breakdown (2000): under 15, 29.6%; 15–29, 25.8%; 30–44, 24.2%; 45–59, 12.6%; 60–74, 5.9%; 75 and over, 1.9%. Ethnic composition (2000): local

black 67.5%; mulatto 14.2%; British 12.0%; Haitian black 3.0%; US white 2.4%; other 0.9%. Religious affiliation (1995): non-Anglican Protestant 45.4%, of which Baptist 17.5%; Roman Catholic 16.8%;.Anglican 10.8%; nonreligious 5.3%; Spiritist 1.5%; other (mostly independent and unaffiliated Christian) 20.2%. Major cities (2002): Nassau 179,300; Freeport 42,600; West End 7,800; Cooper's Town 5,700; Marsh Harbour 3,600. Location: chain of islands in the Caribbean Sea, southeast of Florida.

Vital statistics

Birth rate per 1,000 population (2003): 18.6 (world avg. 21.3); (2000) legitimate 43.2%; illegitimate 56.8%. Death rate per 1,000 population (2003): 8.7 (world avg. 9.1). Natural increase rate per 1,000 population (2003): 9.9 (world avg. 12.2). Total fertility rate (avg. births per childbearing woman; 2003): 2.3. Marriage rate per 1,000 population (2000): 7.8. Life expectancy at birth (2003): male 62.3 years; female 69.2 years.

National economy

Budget (2003). *Revenue:* B$991,503,000 (import taxes 45.0%, stamp taxes from imports 11.3%, departure taxes 6.6%, business and professional licenses 5.5%). *Expenditures:* B$1,088,643,000 (education 19.2%, health 15.9%, public order 11.6%, interest on public debt 10.3%, defense 3.1%). National debt (2003): US$1,647,600,000. Production (value of production in B$'000 except as noted). *Agriculture, forestry, fishing* (2001): crayfish 56,500, poultry products 28,300 (1998), citrus and other fruit 21,300 (1998); roundwood (2002) 17,000 cu m. *Mining and quarrying* (value of export production; 2000): aragonite 26,086; salt 12,447. *Manufacturing* (value of export production; 2000): chemical products 42,787; rum 18,856. *Energy production (consumption):* electricity (kW-hr; 2003) 1,797,-029,000 (1,656,600,000); petroleum products (metric tons; 2000) none (584,000). Tourism (US$'000,-000): receipts (2003) 1,763; expenditures (2001) 297. Household income and expenditure. Average household size (2000) 3.5; income per household (1996) B$27,252; expenditure (1995): housing 32.8%, transportation and communications 14.8%, food and beverages 13.8%, household furnishings 8.9%. Gross national product (at current market prices; 2002): US$4,684,000,000 (US$14,920 per capita). Population economically active (2000): total 154,396; activity rate of total population 50.9% (participation rates: ages 15–64, 76.6%; female 47.5%; unemployed [2001] 6.9%). Land use as % of total land area (2000): in temporary crops 0.7%, in permanent crops 0.4%, in pasture 0.2%; overall forest area 84.1%.

Foreign trade

Imports (2001-c.i.f.): B$1,927,000,000 (machinery and apparatus 16.0%; food products 14.2%; refined petroleum 14.1%; transport equipment 10.3%). *Major import sources:* US 83.3%; Venezuela 5.5%; Netherlands Antilles 2.6%; Japan 1.2%. Exports (2001-f.o.b.): B$376,000,000 (crustaceans and mollusks [primarily crayfish] 19.1%; polystyrene 19.1%; refined petroleum 18.3%; alcoholic beverages 10.5%). *Major export destinations:* US 77.5%; France 5.7%; Germany 3.9%; Spain 3.3%.

Transport and communications

Transport. *Roads* (2000): total length 2,693 km (paved 57%). *Vehicles* (1998): passenger cars 67,400; trucks and buses 16,800. *Air transport* (2001; Bahamasair only): passenger-km 374,-000,000; metric ton-km cargo 1,764,000; airports (1997) with scheduled flights 22. **Communications,** in total units (units per 1,000 persons). Daily newspaper circulation (1996): 28,000 (99); radios (1997): 215,000 (744); televisions (2000): 75,200 (247); telephone main lines (2003): 131,700 (419); cellular telephone subscribers (2002): 121,800 (390); Internet users (2003): 84,000 (264).

Education and health

Educational attainment (2000). Percentage of population age 15 and over having: no formal schooling 1.5%; primary education 8.7%; incomplete secondary 19.9%; complete secondary 53.7%; incomplete higher 8.1%; complete higher 7.1%; not stated 1.0%. **Literacy** (2001): total percentage age 15 and over literate 95.5%; males literate 94.6%; females literate 96.3%. **Health** (2001): physicians 458 (1 per 672 persons); hospital beds 1,540 (1 per 200 persons); infant mortality rate per 1,000 live births (2000) 17.0. **Food** (2001): daily per capita caloric intake 2,777 (vegetable products 67%, animal products 33%); 104% of FAO recommended minimum.

Military

Total active duty personnel (2003): 860 (paramilitary coast guard 100%). **Military expenditure as percentage of GNP** (2000): 0.6% (world, n.a.); per capita expenditure US$85.

Background

The islands were inhabited by Lucayan Indians when Christopher Columbus sighted them on 12 Oct 1492. He is thought to have landed on San Salvador (Watling) Island. The Spaniards made no attempt to settle but carried out slave raids that depopulated the islands; when English settlers arrived in 1648 from Bermuda, the islands were uninhabited. They became a haunt of pirates, and few of the ensuing settlements prospered. The islands enjoyed some prosperity following the American Revolution, when Loyalists fled the US and established cotton plantations. The islands were a center for blockade runners during the American Civil War. Not until the development of tourism after World War II did permanent economic prosperity arrive. The Bahamas was granted internal self-government in 1964 and became independent in 1973.

Recent Developments

In a report published in February 2003, the US Department of State identified The Bahamas as a "major" Caribbean transit route for Colombian cocaine headed for the US. The Bahamas government announced in March 2004 that it had made "significant progress" on a key aspect of the fight against money laundering—mutual legal assistance treaties with other countries.

Internet resources: <www.bahamas.com>.

Bahrain

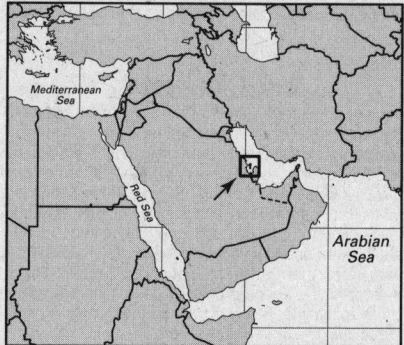

Official name: Mamlakat al-Bahrayn (Kingdom of Bahrain). **Form of government:** constitutional monarchy (declared 14 Feb 2002) with two legislative houses (Chamber of Deputies [40; elected] and Consultative Council [40; appointed by the king]). **Chief of state:** King Hamad ibn 'Isa al-Khalifah (from 1999). **Head of Government:** Prime Minister Sheikh Khalifah ibn Sulman al-Khalifah (from 1970). **Capital:** Manama. **Official language:** Arabic. **Official religion:** Islam. **Monetary unit:** 1 Bahrain dinar (BD) = 1,000 fils; valuation (7 Jul 2005) $1 = BD 0.38.

Demography

Area: 277.0 sq mi, 717.5 sq km. **Population** (2004): 709,000. **Density** (2004): persons per sq mi 2,559.6, persons per sq km 988.2. **Urban** (2001): 88.4%. **Sex distribution** (2002): male 57.46%; female 42.54%. **Age breakdown** (2001): under 15, 27.9%; 15–29, 27.5%; 30–44, 29.6%; 45–59, 11.0%; 60–74, 3.2%; 75 and over, 0.8%. **Ethnic composition** (2000): Bahraini Arab 63.9%; Indo-Pakistani 14.8%, of which Urdu 4.5%, Malayali 3.5%; Persian 13.0%; Filipino 4.5%; British 2.1%; other 1.7%. **Religious affiliation** (2000): Muslim 82.4%, of which Shi'i c. 41%, Sunni c. 41%; Christian 10.5%; Hindu 6.3%; other 0.8%. **Major urban areas** (2001): Manama 143,035; Muharraq 91,307; Ar-Rifa' 79,550; Madinat Hamad 52,718; Madinat 'Isa 36,833. **Location:** Middle East, archipelago in the Persian Gulf, east of Saudi Arabia.

Vital statistics

Birth rate per 1,000 population (2002): 20.2 (world avg. 21.3). **Death rate** per 1,000 population (2002): 3.0 (world avg. 9.1). **Natural increase rate** per 1,000 population (2002): 17.2 (world avg. 12.2). **Total fertility rate** (avg. births per childbearing woman; 2002): 3.0. **Marriage rate** per 1,000 population (2002): 7.3. **Divorce rate** per 1,000 population (2002): 1.2. **Life expectancy** at birth (2002): male 73.2 years; female 76.2 years.

---

1 metric ton = about 1.1 short tons;   1 kilometer = 0.6 mi (statute);   1 metric ton-km cargo = about 0.68 short ton-mi cargo;   c.i.f.: cost, insurance, and freight;   f.o.b.: free on board

National economy

Budget (2002). *Revenue:* BD 1,026,800,000 (petroleum revenue 67.3%, non-petroleum revenue 32.7%). *Expenditures:* BD 1,031,000,000 (infrastructure 35.4%, general administration and public order 26.3%, social services 18.3%, transfers 12.9%, economic services 5.8%, other 1.3%). **Production** (metric tons except as noted). *Agriculture, forestry, fishing* (2002): dates 16,508, fruit (excluding dates) 8,336, vegetables 7,922 (of which tomatoes 2,048, onions 1,213); livestock (number of live animals; 2003) 17,500 sheep, 16,000 goats, 13,000 cattle; fish catch (2002) 11,204. *Manufacturing* (barrels; 2002): gas oil 31,575,000; fuel oil 18,878,000; kerosene and jet fuel 18,804,000. *Energy production (consumption):* electricity (kW-hr; 2002) 7,278,000,000 (6,454,658,000); crude petroleum (barrels; 2003) 68,900,000 ([2000] 93,886,000); petroleum products (2000) 11,105,000 (913,000); natural gas (cu m; 2002) 9,429,000,000 (9,429,000,000). **Public debt** (2001): BD 773,600,000 ($2,057,800,000). **Gross national product** (2002): $7,977,000,000 ($11,900 per capita). **Population economically active** (2002): total 319,000; activity rate of total population 46.3% (participation rates: ages 15 and over 64.1%; female 21.7%; unemployed [2001] 5.5%). **Tourism** (2002): receipts from visitors $741,000,000; expenditures by nationals abroad $378,000,000. **Household income and expenditure.** Average household size (2001) 6.2; expenditure (1984): food and tobacco 33.3%, housing 21.2%, household durable goods 9.8%, transportation and communications 8.5%, recreation 6.4%, clothing and footwear 5.9%. **Land use** as % of total land area (2000): in temporary crops 3%, in permanent crops 6%, in pasture 6%; overall forest area, negligible.

Foreign trade

Imports (2002-c.i.f.): BD 1,881,300,000 (petroleum products 33.4%, machinery and transport equipment 23.6%, food, beverages, and tobacco products 11.1%). *Major import sources* (2001; excludes trade in petroleum): Australia 10.0%; Saudi Arabia 9.0%; Japan 8.3%; US 7.8%; UK 6.4%; Germany 6.0%. **Exports** (2002): BD 2,178,800,000 (petroleum products 68.3%, aluminum [all forms] 15.0%, textiles and clothing 7.8%). *Major export destinations* (2001; excludes trade in petroleum): US 23.8%; Saudi Arabia 14.2%; Taiwan 9.8%; Malaysia 4.3%; India 4.2%.

Transport and communications

Transport. *Roads* (2002): total length 3,459 km (paved 79%). *Vehicles* (2002): passenger cars 176,261; trucks and buses 36,231. *Air transport* (2003; one-fourth apportionment of international flights of Gulf Air [jointly administered by the governments of Bahrain, Oman, Qatar, and the UAE]): passenger-km 3,369,800,000; metric ton-km cargo 140,000,000; airports (2002) with scheduled flights 1. **Communications,** in total units (units per 1,000 persons). Daily newspaper circulation (1996): 67,000 (117); radios (2000): 48,500 (76); televisions (2000): 256,000 (402); telephone main lines (2003): 185,800 (268); cellular telephone subscribers (2003): 443,100 (638); personal computers (2002): 108,000 (159); Internet users (2003): 195,700 (282).

Education and health

Educational attainment (2001). Percentage of population age 15 and over having: no formal education 24.0%; primary education 37.1%; secondary 26.4%; higher 12.5%. **Literacy** (2001): percentage of population age 15 and over literate 87.7%; males literate 92.5%; females literate 83.0%. **Health** (2002): physicians 1,189 (1 per 565 persons); hospital beds 1,814 (1 per 371 persons); infant mortality rate per 1,000 live births (2001) 8.7.

Military

Total active duty personnel (2003): 11,200 (army 75.9%, navy 10.7%, air force 13.4%); US troops in Bahrain (2004): 4,500. **Military expenditure as percentage of GNP** (1999): 8.1% (world 2.4%); per capita expenditure $666.

Background

The area has long been an important trading center and is mentioned in Persian, Greek, and Roman references. It was ruled by Arabs from the 7th century AD but was then occupied by the Portuguese 1521–1602. Since 1783 it has been ruled by the Khalifah family, though through a series of treaties its defense remained a British responsibility from 1820 to 1971. After Britain withdrew its forces from the Persian Gulf (1968), Bahrain declared its independence in 1971. It served as a center for the allies in the First Persian Gulf War (1990–1991). Since 1994 it has experienced bouts of political unrest, mainly by Shi'ites, who attempted to get the government to restore the parliament (abolished in 1975).

Recent Developments

In 2004 Bahrain, lacking important oil resources, continued to establish itself as a center of trade and finance. During the year efforts were made to attract foreign investment and encourage the establishment of private companies by offering advantages such as nondiscriminatory financial regulations and more efficient procedures for investment.

Internet resources: <www.bahraintourism.com>.

Bangladesh

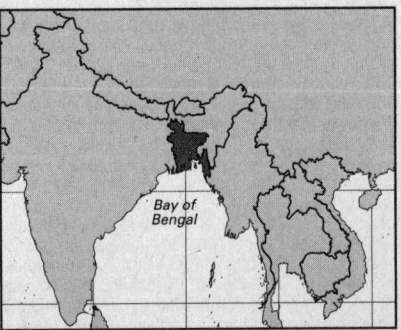

Official name: Gana Prajatantri Bangladesh (People's Republic of Bangladesh). **Form of government:**

unitary multiparty republic with one legislative house (Parliament [300 seats, excluding 45 reserved for women to be reinstated as of 2006 elections]). **Chief of state:** President Iajuddin Ahmed (from 2002). **Head of government:** Prime Minister Khaleda Zia (from 2001). **Capital:** Dhaka. **Official language:** Bengali. **Official religion:** Islam. **Monetary unit:** 1 Bangladesh taka (Tk) = 100 paisa; valuation (7 Jul 2005) $1 = Tk 64.00.

Demography

Area (including river area): 56,977 sq mi, 147,570 sq km. **Population** (2004): 135,255,000. **Density** (2004): persons per sq mi 2,514.2, persons per sq km 970.7. **Urban** (2001): 23.4%. **Sex distribution** (2003): male 51.30%; female 48.70%. **Age breakdown** (2003): under 15, 34.1%; 15–29, 32.4%; 30–44, 18.0%; 45–59, 10.2%; 60–74, 4.3%; 75 and over, 1.0%. **Ethnic composition** (1997): Bengali 97.7%; tribal 1.9%, of which Chakma 0.4%, Saontal 0.2%, Marma 0.1%; other 0.4%. **Religious affiliation** (2000): Muslim 85.8%; Hindu 12.4%; Christian 0.7%; Buddhist 0.6%; other 0.5%. **Major cities/urban agglomerations** (2001): Dhaka 5,644,235/10,403,-597; Chittagong 2,199,590/3,361,244; Khulna 811,490/1,287,987; Rajshahi 402,646/ 678,728. **Location:** South Asia, bordering India, Myanmar (Burma), and the Bay of Bengal.

Vital statistics

Birth rate per 1,000 population (2003): 29.9 (world avg. 21.3). **Death rate** per 1,000 population (2003): 8.6 (world avg. 9.1). **Natural increase rate** per 1,000 population (2003): 21.3 (world avg. 12.2). **Total fertility rate** (avg. births per childbearing woman; 2003): 3.2. **Marriage rate** per 1,000 population (1998): 9.2. **Life expectancy** at birth (2003): male 61.5 years; female 61.2 years.

National economy

Budget (2002–03). *Revenue:* Tk 326,000,000,000 (value-added tax 39.3%, international trade 36.2%, income taxes 14.7%, other 9.8%). *Expenditures:* Tk 448,000,000,000 (development program 42.4%, wages 16.5%, subsidies 14.7%, interest payments 10.3%, goods and services 8.3%, other 7.8%). **Production** (metric tons except as noted). *Agriculture, forestry, fishing* (2002): paddy rice 38,134,000, sugarcane 6,502,000, potatoes 3,216,000; livestock (number of live animals) 34,400,000 goats, 24,000,-000 cattle, 140,000,000 chickens; roundwood (2002) 28,386,000 cu m; fish catch (2001) 1,687,-000. *Mining and quarrying* (2002): marine salt 350,000; industrial limestone 32,000. *Manufacturing* (value added in $'000,000; 1998): wearing apparel 839; tobacco products 634; textiles 567. *Energy production (consumption):* electricity (kW-hr; 2002) 17,021,000,000 (17,021,000,000); coal (2000 none (660,000); crude petroleum (barrels; 2000) none (10,054,000); petroleum products (2002) 1,323,000 (3,769,000); natural gas (cu m; 2002) 6,568,000,000 (3,096,000,000). **Household income and expenditure.** Average household size (2000) 5.7; average annual income per household Tk 52,389; sources of income: self-employment 56.9%,

wages and salaries 28.1%, transfer payments 9.1%, other 5.9%; expenditure (2002–03): food and drink 64.5%, housing and energy 15.0%, clothing and footwear 5.9%, transport 3.3%, other 11.3%. **Population economically active** (2000): total 52,847,000; activity rate of total population 47.3% (participation rates: over age 15, 58.8%; female 37.5%; unemployed 2.0%). **Public debt** (external, outstanding; 2002): $16,445,000,000. **Gross national product** (2003): $54,587,000,000 ($400 per capita). **Land use** as % of total land area (2000): in temporary crops 62.5%, in permanent crops 2.7%, in pasture 4.6%; overall forest area 10.2%. **Tourism** (2002): receipts $57,000,000; expenditures $202,000,000.

Foreign trade

Imports (2002–03-f.o.b. in balance of trade and c.i.f, in commodities and trading partners): $9,648,-000,000 (capital goods 28.3%; textile yarn, fabrics, and made-up articles 14.3%; imports for export processing zone 7.5%; rice and wheat 4.3%; cotton 4.1%). *Major import sources* (2001): China 11.0%; India 10.9%; Singapore 8.1%; Japan 7.3%; South Korea 6.5%; Hong Kong 6.2%. **Exports** (2002–03): $6,548,000,000 (ready-made garments 49.8%; hosiery and knitwear 25.3%; frozen fish and shrimp 4.9%; jute manufactures 3.9%). *Major export destinations* (2001): US 39.0%; Germany 11.1%; UK 8.8%; France 5.7%; The Netherlands 5.3%.

Transport and communications

Transport. *Railroads* (1998–99): route length 2,734 km; passenger-km 4,980,000,000; metric ton-km cargo 828,000,000. *Roads* (1999): total length 207,486 km (paved 10%). *Vehicles* (1999): passenger cars 66,723; trucks and buses 82,025. *Air transport* (2002; Bangladesh Biman only): passenger-km 4,584,000,000; metric ton-km cargo 205,896,000; airports with scheduled flights (2001) 8. **Communications,** in total units (units per 1,000 persons). Daily newspaper circulation (2000): 6,880,000 (53); radios (2000): 6,360,000 (49); televisions (2000): 909,000 (7); telephone main lines (2003): 740,000 (5.5); cellular telephone subscribers (2003): 1,365,-000 (10.1); personal computers (2002): 450,000 (3); Internet users (2003): 243,000 (1.8).

Education and health

Educational attainment (1991). Percentage of population age 25 and over having: no formal schooling 65.4%; primary education 17.1%; secondary 13.8%; postsecondary 3.7%. **Literacy** (2000): total population age 15 and over literate 41.3%; males literate 52.3%; females literate 29.9%. **Health** (1999): physicians 30,864 (1 per 4,150 persons); hospital beds 44,374 (1 per 2,886 persons); infant mortality rate per 1,000 live births (2002) 68.0. **Food** (2001): daily per capita caloric intake 2,187 (vegetable products 97%, animal products 3%); 95% of FAO recommended minimum.

Military

Total active duty personnel (2003): 125,500 (army 87.6%, navy 7.2%, air force 5.2%). **Military expendi-**

---

1 metric ton = about 1.1 short tons; 1 kilometer = 0.6 mi (statute); 1 metric ton-km cargo = about 0.68 short ton-mi cargo; c.i.f.: cost, insurance, and freight; f.o.b.: free on board

ture as percentage of GNP (1999): 1.4% (world 2.4%); per capita expenditure $5.

The Sundarbans is a vast tract of forests and saltwater swamps in Bangladesh that forms the lower part of the Ganges delta, extending about 160 mi (260 km) along the Bay of Bengal. The Sundarbans is one of the last preserves of the Bengal tiger.

Background

In its early years Bangladesh was known as Bengal. When the British left the subcontinent in 1947, the area that was East Bengal became the part of Pakistan called East Pakistan. Bengali nationalist sentiment increased after the creation of an independent Pakistan. In 1971 violence erupted; some one million Bengalis were killed, and millions more fled to India, which finally entered the war on the side of the Bengalis, ensuring West Pakistan's defeat. East Pakistan became the independent nation of Bangladesh. Little of the devastation caused by the war has been repaired, and political instability, including the assassination of two presidents, has continued. In addition, the low-lying country has been repeatedly battered by natural disasters, notably tropical storms and flooding.

Recent Developments

Tumult and violence characterized politics in Bangladesh in 2004, with the division and mutual mistrust between the ruling Bangladesh Nationalist Party and the main opposition Awami League deepening. The political situation took on an even more sinister edge with the emergence of a Taliban-like anticommunist Islamist group named Jagrata Muslim Janata Bangladesh, in the northwest of the country. This group, led by Azizur Rahman, called "Bangla Bhai," was reportedly responsible for a wave of vigilante-style terrorism and the execution of some 15 persons whom it had deemed "outlaws."

Internet resources: <www.bangladesh.gov.bd/>.

Barbados

Official name: Barbados. Form of government: constitutional monarchy with two legislative houses (Senate [21]; House of Assembly [30]). Chief of state: Queen Elizabeth II, represented by Governor-General Sir Clifford Husbands (from 1996). Head of government: Prime Minister Owen Arthur (from 1994). Capital: Bridgetown. Official language: English. Official religion: none. Monetary unit: 1 Barbados dollar (BDS$) = 100 cents; valuation (7 Jul 2005) US$1 = BDS$1.99.

Demography

Area: 166 sq mi, 430 sq km. Population (2004): 273,000. Density (2004): persons per sq mi 1,645, persons per sq km 634.9. Urban (2001): 50.5%. Sex distribution (2003): male 48.26%; female 51.74%. Age breakdown (2003): under 15, 21.2%; 15–29, 23.1%; 30–44, 25.8%; 45–59, 17.8%; 60–74, 8.1%; 75 and over, 4.0%. Ethnic composition (2000): local black 87.1%; mulatto 6.0%; British expatriates 4.3%;

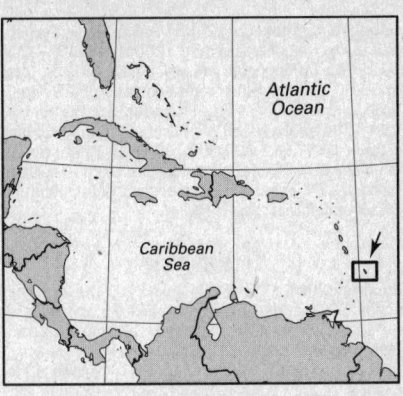

US white 1.2%; Indo-Pakistani 1.1%; other 0.3%. Religious affiliation (1995): Protestant 63.0%, of which Anglican 26.3%, Pentecostal 10.6%, Methodist 5.7%; Roman Catholic 4.8%; other Christian 2.0%; nonreligious/other 30.2%. Major cities (1990): Bridgetown 6,070 (urban agglomeration [2003] 140,000); Speightstown c. 3,500. Location: northeast of Venezuela at the eastern edge of the Caribbean Sea where it adjoins the North Atlantic Ocean.

Vital statistics

Birth rate per 1,000 population (2001): 15.0 (world avg. 21.3). Death rate per 1,000 population (2001): 8.9 (world avg. 9.1). Natural increase rate per 1,000 population (2001): 6.1 (world avg. 12.2). Total fertility rate (avg. births per childbearing woman; 2000): 1.6. Marriage rate per 1,000 population (1995): 13.5. Divorce rate per 1,000 population (1995): 1.5. Life expectancy at birth (2000): male 70.4 years; female 75.6 years.

National economy

Budget (2003). Revenue: BDS$1,843,800,000 (tax revenue c. 94%, of which personal income and company taxes 31.4%, value-added tax 29.8%, import duties 9.3%; nontax revenue c. 6%). Expenditures: BDS$2,009,200,000 (current expenditure 86.4%, of which wages and salaries 31.5%, debt payment 13.5%; capital expenditure 13.6%). Public debt (external, outstanding; 2002): US$958,000,000. Production (metric tons except as noted). Agriculture, forestry, fishing (2002): raw sugar 50,000, sweet potatoes 5,300, yams 1,450; livestock (number of live animals) 41,300 sheep, 35,000 pigs, 21,000 cattle; roundwood (2002) 5,000; fish catch (2001) 2,676. Manufacturing (value added in US$'000,000; 1997): industrial chemicals 87; food products 63; beverages (significantly rum and beer) 58. Energy production (consumption): electricity (kW-hr; 2002) 741,300,000 (741,300,000); crude petroleum (barrels; 2002) 390,600 ([2000] 1,778,000); petroleum products (2000) 1,000 (332,000); natural gas (cu m; 2001) 34,900,000 (34,900,000). Household income and expenditure. Average household size (2000) 2.8; income per household (1988) BDS$13,455; expenditure (1994): food 39.4%, housing 16.8%, transportation 10.5%, household operations 8.1%, alcohol and tobacco 6.4%, fuel and light 5.2%, clothing and footwear 5.0%, other 8.6%. Tourism: receipts from visitors (2002) US$648,000,000; expenditures by nationals abroad (2001) US$101,000,000. **Population economically active** (2002): total 143,200; activity rate of total population 52.8% (participation rates: ages 15 and over, 68.5%; female 48.4%; unemployed 10.3%). **Gross national product** (2003): US$2,512,000,000 (US$9,270 per capita). **Land use** as % of total land area (2000): in temporary crops c. 37%, in permanent crops c. 2%, in pasture c. 5%; overall forest area c. 5%.

Foreign trade

Imports (2003-c.i.f.): BDS$2,050,000,000 (capital goods 20.9%; food and beverages 15.5%; mineral fuels 11.1%; chemicals and chemical products 5.1%). *Major import sources* (2002): US 44.1%; Trinidad and Tobago 11.7%; UK 7.9%; Japan 4.5%; Canada 3.7%. **Exports** (2003-f.o.b.): BDS$542,000,000 (food and beverages 25.3%, of which sugar and molasses 9.2%, rum 7.0%; chemicals and chemical products 8.3%; electrical components 5.2%; other manufactures 17.5%). *Major export destinations* (2002): US 16.5%; UK 11.9%; Trinidad and Tobago 11.0%; Jamaica 7.0%; bunkers and ships' stores 9.3%.

Transport and communications

Transport. *Roads* (2000): total length 1,600 km (paved 99%). *Vehicles* (2001): passenger cars 64,900; trucks and buses 11,400. *Air transport:* (2001) passenger arrivals and departures 1,760,000; (2000) cargo unloaded and loaded 14,000 metric tons; airports (2002) with scheduled flights 1. **Communications,** in total units (units per 1,000 persons). Daily newspaper circulation (1996): 53,000 (199); radios (2001): 202,000 (749); televisions (2001): 83,700 (310); telephone main lines (2003): 134,000 (497); cellular telephone subscribers (2003): 140,000 (519); personal computers (2002): 28,000 (104); Internet users (2003): 100,000 (371).

Education and health

Educational attainment (1990). Percentage of population age 25 and over having: no formal schooling 0.4%; primary education 23.7%; secondary 60.3%; higher 11.2%; other 4.4%. **Literacy** (1995): total population age 15 and over literate 97.4%; males literate 98.0%; females literate 96.8%. **Health:** physicians (2002) 376 (1 per 721 persons); hospital beds (1992) 1,966 (1 per 134 persons); infant mortality rate per 1,000 live births (2002) 12.6. **Food** (2001): daily per capita caloric intake 2,992 (vegetable products 75%, animal products 25%); 124% of FAO recommended minimum.

Military

Total active duty personnel (2003): 500 (army 82.0%, navy 18.0%). **Military expenditure as percentage of GNP** (1999): 0.5% (world 2.4%); per capita expenditure US$44.

Background

The island of Barbados was probably inhabited by Arawak Indians who originally came from South America. Spaniards may have landed by 1518, and by 1536 they had apparently wiped out the Indian population. Barbados was settled by the English in the 1620s. Slaves were brought in to work the sugar plantations, which were especially prosperous in the 17th–18th centuries. The British Empire abolished slavery in 1834, and all the Barbados slaves were freed by 1838. In 1958 Barbados joined the West Indies Federation. When the latter dissolved in 1962, Barbados sought independence from Britain; it achieved it and joined the Commonwealth in 1966.

Recent Developments

In early 2005 Prime Minister Owen Arthur repeated a pledge he had made during the 2003 election campaign to replace the country's existing monarchical constitution with a republican one. This would result in the replacement of the governor-general (who represents the queen of England) with a nonexecutive president as head of state.

Internet resources: <www.barbados.org>.

Belarus

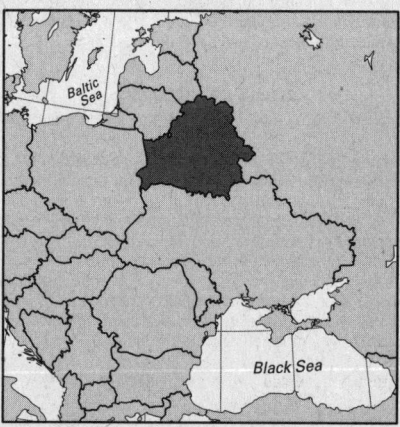

Official name: Respublika Belarus (Republic of Belarus). **Form of government:** republic with two legislative bodies (Council of the Republic [64]; House of Representatives [110]). **Head of state and government:** President Alyaksandr H. Lukashenka (from 1994), assisted by Prime Minister Syarhey Sidorski (from 2003). **Capital:** Minsk. **Official languages:** Belarusian; Russian. **Official religion:** none. **Monetary unit:** rubel (Rbl; plural rubli); valuation (7 Jul 2005) $1 = (new) Rbl 2,164.50; rubel re-denominated 1 Jan 2000; as of that date 1,000 (old) rubli = 1 (new) rubel.

Demography

Area: 80,153 sq mi, 207,595 sq km. **Population** (2004): 9,828,000. **Density** (2004): persons per sq mi 122.6, persons per sq km 47.3. **Urban** (2004): 71.5%. **Sex distribution** (2004): male 46.61%; fe-

---

1 metric ton = about 1.1 short tons;   1 kilometer = 0.6 mi (statute);   1 metric ton-km cargo = about 0.68 short ton-mi cargo;   c.i.f.: cost, insurance, and freight;   f.o.b.: free on board

male 53.39%. **Age breakdown** (2003): under 15, 16.8%; 15–29, 23.5%; 30–44, 22.7%; 45–59, 18.1%; 60–74, 13.4%; 75 and over, 5.5%. **Ethnic composition** (1999): Belarusian 81.2%; Russian 11.4%; Polish 3.9%; Ukrainian 2.4%; Jewish 0.3%; other 0.8%. **Religious affiliation** (1995): Belarusian Orthodox 31.6%; Roman Catholic 17.7%; other (mostly nonreligious) 50.7%. **Major cities** (2004): Minsk 1,682,900; Homyel 497,200; Mahilyow 365,400; Vitsyebsk 355,200; Hrodna 315,500. **Location:** Eastern Europe, bordering Latvia, Russia, Ukraine, Poland, and Lithuania.

Vital statistics

Birth rate per 1,000 population (2003): 10.1 (world avg. 21.3); (2000) legitimate 81.4%; illegitimate 18.6%. **Death rate** per 1,000 population (2003): 14.1 (world avg. 9.1). **Natural increase rate** per 1,000 population (2003): –4.0 (world avg. 12.2). **Total fertility rate** (avg. births per childbearing woman; 2003): 1.3. **Marriage rate** per 1,000 population (2000): 6.2. **Divorce rate** per 1,000 population (2000): 4.3. **Life expectancy** at birth (2003): male 62.5 years; female 74.6 years.

National economy

Budget (2003). *Revenue:* Rbl 12,154,223,000,000 (tax revenue 76.8%, of which value-added tax 23.8%, income tax 8.4%, profit tax 7.7%, excise tax 6.9%, property tax 6.0%, other 24.0%; nontax revenue 23.2%). *Expenditures:* Rbl 12,646,135,000,000 (education 18.5%, target budgetary fund 15.3%, health 14.3%, subsidies 7.4%, public order 5.2%, capital expenditure 4.2%, defense 3.0%). **Public debt** (external, outstanding; 2002): $709,500,000. **Household income and expenditure.** Average household size (2000) 3.4; sources of money income (2003): wages and salaries 49.2%, business activities 31.6%, transfers 18.1%; expenditure (2001): food and nonalcoholic beverages 53.6%, clothing and footwear 9.4%, housing and energy 7.2%, transport 6.3%, alcoholic beverages and tobacco products 5.9%. **Population economically active** (2003): 4,446,000; activity rate of total population 45.1% (participation rate: ages 16–59 [male], 16–54 [female] 74.0%; female 53.5%; unemployed 3.1%). **Production** (metric tons except as noted). *Agriculture, forestry, fishing* (2003): potatoes 8,649,000, maize for forage 6,500,000, sugar beets 1,920,000; livestock (number of live animals) 3,921,000 cattle, 3,277,000 pigs, 30,600,-000 poultry; roundwood (2002) 6,947,000 cu m; fish catch (2001) 5,609. *Mining and quarrying* (2000): potash 3,400,000; peat 2,211,000. *Manufacturing* (value of production in [old] Rbl '000,000; 1994): machine-building equipment 1,086,650; chemical products 659,438; food products 562,438. *Energy production (consumption):* electricity (kW-hr; 2003) 26,615,000,000 (33,228,000,000); coal (2000) none (504,000); crude petroleum (barrels; 2000) 13,600,000 (98,640,000); petroleum products (2003) 15,774,000 (6,240,000); natural gas (cu m; 2003) 254,000,000 (18,448,000,000). **Gross national product** (2003): $15,700,000,000 ($1,590 per capita). **Tourism** (2002): receipts $193,000,000; expenditures $559,000,000. **Land use** as % of total land area (2000): in temporary crops 29.6%, in permanent crops 0.6%, in pasture 14.4%; overall forest area 45.3%; 25% of Belarusian territory severely affected by radioactive fallout from Chernobyl.

Foreign trade

Imports (2002-c.i.f.): $8,980,000,000 (crude petroleum 16.8%, machinery and apparatus 15.5%, chemicals and chemical products 10.2%, food and beverages 8.8%, natural and manufactured gas 6.3%, iron and steel 6.2%). *Major import sources:* Russia 65.1%; Germany 7.7%; Ukraine 3.2%; Poland 2.4%; Italy 2.4%. **Exports** (2002-f.o.b.): $8,098,000,000 (refined petroleum 18.3%, road vehicles 8.9%, nonelectrical machinery 8.3%, food 6.7%, potassium chloride 5.7%, electrical machinery 5.7%). *Major export destinations:* Russia 50.1%; Latvia 6.4%; UK 6.1%; Germany 4.3%; The Netherlands 3.4%.

Transport and communications

Transport. *Railroads* (2002): length 5,533 km; passenger-km 14,349,000,000; metric ton-km cargo 34,169,000,000. *Roads* (2000): total length 74,400 km (paved 89%). *Vehicles* (2001): passenger cars 1,448,461; trucks and buses 85,791. *Air transport* (2002): passenger-km 553,000,000; metric ton-km cargo 37,000,000; airports 1. **Communications,** in total units (units per 1,000 persons). Daily newspaper circulation (2000): 1,550,000 (155); radios (2000): 2,990,000 (299); televisions (2000): 3,420,000 (342); telephone main lines (2003): 3,071,300 (311); cellular telephone subscribers (2003): 1,118,000 (113); Internet users (2003): 1,391,900 (141).

Education and health

Literacy (2001): total population age 15 and over literate 99.7%; males literate 99.8%; females literate 99.6%. **Health:** physicians (2003) 44,800 (1 per 220 persons); hospital beds (2000) 126,209 (1 per 79 persons); infant mortality rate per 1,000 live births (2003) 7.7. **Food** (2001): daily per capita caloric intake 2,925 (vegetable products 72%, animal products 28%); 113% of FAO recommended minimum.

Military

Total active duty personnel (2003): 72,940 (army 40.6%, air force and air defense 24.9%, other 34.5%). **Military expenditure as percentage of GNP** (1999): 1.3% (world 2.4%); per capita expenditure $89.

Background

While Belarusians share a distinct identity and language, they did not enjoy political sovereignty until the late 20th century. The territory that is now Belarus underwent partition and changed hands often; as a result its history is entwined with those of its neighbors. In medieval times the region was ruled by Lithuanians and Poles. Following the Third Partition of Poland, it was ruled by Russia. After World War I, the western part was assigned to Poland and the eastern part became Soviet Russian territory. After World War II, the Soviets expanded what had been the Belorussian SSR by annexing more of Poland. Much of the area suffered contamination from the Chernobyl accident in 1986, forcing many to evacuate. Belarus declared its independence in 1991 and later joined the Commonwealth of Independent States. Amid increasing political turmoil in the 1990s, it proposed a union with Russia in 1997 that was still being debated at the start of the 21st century.

Recent Developments

Politics in Belarus focused on the increasing authoritarianism of the president, Alyaksandr Lukashenka, and the repressive measures the government was taking to keep any opposition in check. A referendum was held on 17 Oct 2004, the day of the parliamentary election, to change the constitution to allow Lukashenka to run for a third term in office. The government prevailed with almost 80% voting in favor, but there was widespread dissatisfaction with the conduct of the election. In April 2004, Mikhail Marynich, a former minister, was arrested for illegal storage of firearms, and criminal charges were brought against him in August. On 28 July the authorities closed the European Humanities University, the only university in Belarus outside state control.

Internet resources: <www.belarusembassy.org>.

Belgium

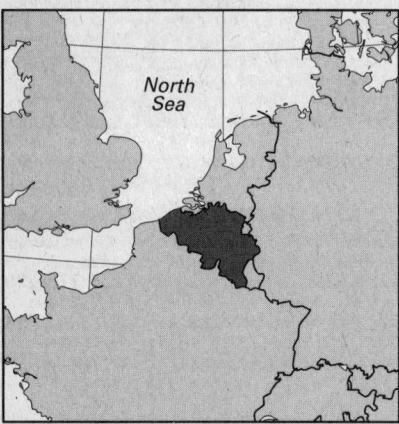

Official name: Koninkrijk België (Dutch); Royaume de Belgique (French) (Kingdom of Belgium). **Form of government:** federal constitutional monarchy with a Parliament composed of two legislative chambers (Senate [71, excluding children of the monarch serving ex officio from age 18]; House of Representatives [150]). **Chief of state:** King Albert II (from 1993). **Head of government:** Prime Minister Guy Verhofstadt (from 1999). **Capital:** Brussels. **Official languages:** Dutch; French; German. **Official religion:** none. **Monetary unit:** 1 euro (€) = 100 cents; $1 = €0.84 (7 Jul 2005). The Belgian franc (BF) was the former monetary unit; at conversion on 1 Jan 2002, €1 = BF40.34.

Demography

Area: 11,787 sq mi, 30,528 sq km. **Population** (2004): 10,416,000. **Density** (2004): persons per sq mi 883.7, persons per sq km 341.9. **Urban** (2002): 97.0%. **Sex distribution** (2003): male 48.95%; female 51.05%. **Age breakdown** (2003): under 15, 17.2%; 15–29, 18.2%; 30–44, 22.5%; 45–59,

20.1%; 60–74, 14.1%; 75 and over, 7.9%. **Ethnic composition** (2000): Flemish 53.7%; Walloon (French) 31.6%; Italian 2.6%; French 2.0%; Arab 1.8%; German 1.5%; Berber 0.9%; other 5.9%. **Religious affiliation** (1995): Roman Catholic 87.9%; Muslim 2.5%; other Christian 2.4%, of which Protestant 1.0%; Jewish 0.3%; other 6.9%. **Major cities** (2004): Brussels 999,899; Antwerp 455,148; Ghent 229,344; Charleroi 200,608; Liège 185,488. **Location:** western Europe, bordering The Netherlands, Germany, Luxembourg, France, and the North Sea.

Vital statistics

Birth rate per 1,000 population (2003): 10.7 (world avg. 21.3). **Death rate** per 1,000 population (2003): 10.2 (world avg. 9.1). **Natural increase rate** per 1,000 population (2003): 0.5 (world avg. 12.2). **Total fertility rate** (avg. births per childbearing woman; 2003): 1.6. **Marriage rate** per 1,000 population (2001): 4.1. **Divorce rate** per 1,000 population (2000): 2.6. **Life expectancy** at birth (2002): male 75.1 years; female 81.6 years.

National economy

Budget (2003). *Revenue:* €137,781,000,000 (social security contributions 28.4%, income tax 24.5%, taxes on goods and services 21.9%, property tax 6.7%). *Expenditures:* €137,348,000,000 (social security payments 25.7%, wages 23.5%, health 12.1%, interest on debt 11.0%, capital expenditure 6.1%). **Public debt** (2001): $244,540,000,000. **Production** (metric tons except as noted). *Agriculture, forestry, fishing* (2003): sugar beets 6,450,000, potatoes 2,522,000, wheat 1,640,000; livestock (number of live animals) 6,539,000 pigs, 2,778,000 cattle; roundwood (2002) 4,500,000 cu m; fish catch (2001; includes Luxembourg) 31,839. *Mining and quarrying* (2002): limestone 30,000,000; granite (Belgium bluestone) 1,200,000 cu m. *Manufacturing* (value added in $'000,000; 1997): chemicals and chemical products 7,702; food products 4,513; motor vehicles and parts 3,287; electrical machinery 3,278; base metals 3,126; value of traded diamonds handled in Antwerp (2002) €26,000,-000,000. *Energy production (consumption):* electricity (kW-hr; 2002) 76,580,000,000 ([2000] 88,225,000,000); coal (2000) 375,000 (11,266,-000); crude petroleum (barrels; 2000) none (248,700,000); petroleum products (2000) 29,525,-000 (15,991,000); natural gas (cu m; 2000) 3,017,000 (19,544,000,000). **Household income and expenditure.** Average household size (2000) 2.5; sources of income (2003): wages and transfer payments 69.3%, property income 11.1%, mixed income 19.6%; expenditure (1992): food 18.0%, housing 17.0%, transportation 13.3%, health 11.8%, durable goods 10.7%, clothing 7.7%. **Tourism** (2002): receipts $6,892,000,000; expenditures $10,435,000,000. **Population economically active** (2003): total 4,708,000; activity rate 45.5% (participation rates: ages 15–64, 69.3%; female [2000] 43.1%; unemployed 11.4%). **Gross national product** (2003): $267,227,000,000 ($25,820 per capita). **Land use** as % of total land area (2000): in temporary crops 25.6%, in permanent crops 0.7%, in pasture 20.5%; overall forest area 21.1%.

---

1 metric ton = about 1.1 short tons;   1 kilometer = 0.6 mi (statute);   1 metric ton-km cargo = about 0.68 short ton-mi cargo;   c.i.f.: cost, insurance, and freight;   f.o.b.: free on board

Foreign trade

Imports (2002-c.i.f.): €209,720,700,000 (machinery and apparatus 16.3%, road vehicles 12.0%, medicine and pharmaceuticals 10.6%, food 6.8%). *Major import sources:* Germany 17.3%; The Netherlands 15.8%; France 12.6%; UK 7.5%; Ireland 7.0%. **Exports** (2002-f.o.b.): €228,561,700,000 (machinery and apparatus 14.0%, road vehicles 13.8%, pharmaceuticals 10.1%, food 7.6%, organic chemicals 5.9%). *Major export destinations:* Germany 18.6%; France 16.3%; The Netherlands 11.7%; UK 9.6%; US 7.8%.

Transport and communications

Transport. *Railroads* (2001): route length 3,380 km; passenger-km 8,038,000,000; metric ton-km cargo 7,080,000,000. *Roads* (1997): total length 143,800 km (paved 97%). *Vehicles* (2001): passenger cars 4,739,850; trucks and buses 541,056. *Air transport* (2000; Sabena airlines only; shut down November 2001. SN Brussels Airlines was founded in February 2002): passenger-km 19,378,689,000; metric ton-km cargo 568,244,000; airports 2. **Communications**, in total units (units per 1,000 persons). Daily newspaper circulation (2000): 1,640,000 (160); radios (2000): 8,130,000 (793); televisions (2000): 5,550,000 (541); telephone main lines (2002): 5,120,400 (494); cellular telephone subscribers (2002): 8,135,500 (786); personal computers (2002): 2,500,000 (242); Internet users (2002): 3,400,000 (329).

Education and health

Educational attainment (1991). Percentage of population age 18 and over having: less than secondary education 46.8%; lower secondary 16.6%; upper secondary 21.6%; teacher's college 3.7%; university 11.3%. **Health:** physicians (2002) 46,268 (1 per 223 persons); hospital beds (2001) 71,907 (1 per 143 persons); infant mortality rate (2001) 5.1. **Food** (2001; includes Luxembourg): daily per capita caloric intake 3,682 (vegetable products 69%, animal products 31%); 140% of FAO recommended minimum.

Military

Total active duty personnel (2003): 40,800 (army 60.8%, navy 6.0%, air force 25.1%, medical service 4.4%, other 3.7%). **Military expenditure as percentage of GNP** (1999): 1.4% (world 2.4%); per capita expenditure $352.

Background

Inhabited in ancient times by the Belgae, a Celtic people, the area was conquered by Caesar in 57 BC; under Augustus it became the Roman province of Gallia Belgica. Conquered by the Franks, it later broke up into semi-independent territories, including Brabant and Luxembourg. By the late 15th century, the territories of the Netherlands, of which the future Belgium was a part, had gradually united and passed to the Habsburgs. In the 16th century, it was a center for European commerce. The basis of modern Belgium was laid in the southern Catholic provinces that split from the northern provinces after the Union of Utrecht in 1579. Overrun by the French and incorporated into France in 1801, it was reunited to Holland and with it became the independent Kingdom of The Netherlands in 1815. After the revolt of its citizens in 1830, it became the independent Kingdom of Belgium. Under Léopold II it acquired vast lands in Africa. Overrun by the Germans in World Wars I and II, Belgium was the scene of the Battle of the Bulge. Internal discord led to legislation in the 1970s and 1980s that created three nearly autonomous regions in accordánce with language distribution: Flemish Flanders, French Wallonia, and bilingual Brussels. In 1993 it became a federation comprising the three regions. It is a member of the European Union.

Recent Developments

Elections in mid-June 2004 in Belgium's three regions—Flanders, Wallonia, and Brussels—brought major strains to Prime Minister Guy Verhofstadt's Liberal-Socialist federal coalition government less than a year after it had come into office. Verhofstadt's own Dutch-speaking Liberal party, VLD-Vivant, was pushed into third place in Flanders, overtaken even by the extreme right-wing Vlaams Blok. In November, however, the Supreme Court of Belgium ruled that Vlaams Blok had violated antiracism laws and was thus not a legal party. Elsewhere the main victor was the French-speaking Socialist Party, which consolidated its leading position in Wallonia and overtook the French-speaking Liberals to become the main political force in Brussels. In January 2004 Belgium extended existing legislation on same-sex marriages to allow gay Belgians to marry foreign partners. Previously, the right covered only nationals from countries where same-sex marriages were legal and thus effectively enabled only Belgians and Dutch to benefit.

Internet resources: <www.visitbelgium.com>.

Belize

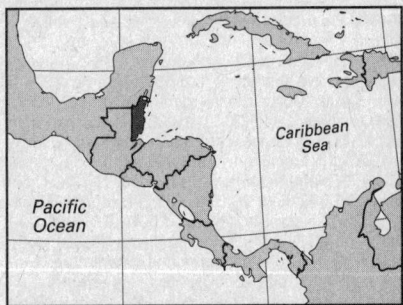

Official name: Belize. **Form of government:** constitutional monarchy with two legislative houses (Senate [8, excluding president of the Senate]; House of Representatives [29, excluding speaker of the House of Representatives]). **Chief of state:** Queen Elizabeth II, represented by Governor-General Sir Colville Young (from 1993). **Head of government:** Prime Minister Said Musa (from 1998). **Capital:** Belmopan. **Official language:** English. **Official religion:** none. **Monetary unit:** 1 Belize dollar (BZ$) = 100 cents; valuation (7 Jul 2005) US$1 = BZ$1.97 (pegged to the US dollar).

Demography

Area: 8,867 sq mi, 22,965 sq km (includes offshore cays totaling 266 sq mi (689 sq km). **Population** (2004): 283,000. **Density** (2004): persons per sq mi 31.9, persons per sq km 12.3. **Urban** (2004): 49.9%. **Sex distribution** (2004): male 50.50%; female 49.50%. **Age breakdown** (2004): under 15, 40.8%; 15–29, 27.7%; 30–44, 17.4%; 45–59, 8.1%; 60–74, 4.3%; 75 and over, 1.7%. **Ethnic composition** (2000): mestizo (Spanish-Indian) 48.7%; Creole (predominantly black) 24.9%; Mayan Indian 10.6%; Garifuna (black-Carib Indian) 6.1%; white 4.3%; East Indian 3.0%; other or not stated 2.4%. **Religious affiliation** (2000): Roman Catholic 49.6%; Protestant 31.8%, of which Pentecostal 7.4%, Anglican 5.3%, Seventh-day Adventist 5.2%, Mennonite 4.1%; other Christian 1.9%; nonreligious 9.4%; other 7.3%. **Major cities** (2004): Belize City 59,400; San Ignacio/Santa Elena 16,100; Orange Walk 15,000; Belmopan 12,300; Dangriga 10,400. **Location:** Central America, bordering Mexico, the Caribbean Sea, and Guatemala.

Vital statistics

Birth rate per 1,000 population (2002): 27.7 (world avg. 21.3); (1997) legitimate 40.3%; illegitimate 59.7%. **Death rate** per 1,000 population (2002): 4.8 (world avg. 9.1). **Natural increase rate** per 1,000 population (2002): 22.9 (world avg. 12.2). **Total fertility rate** (avg. births per childbearing woman; 2003): 3.9. **Marriage rate** per 1,000 population (2002): 6.1. **Divorce rate** per 1,000 population (2002): 0.2. **Life expectancy** at birth (2003): male 65.2 years; female 69.6 years.

National economy

Budget (2002–03). *Revenue:* BZ$431,300,000 (tax revenue 83.4%, of which import duties 38.3%, general sales tax 26.3%, income tax 18.3%; nontax revenue 12.2%; grants 4.4%). *Expenditures:* BZ$600,900,000 (current expenditure 60.2%; capital expenditure 39.8%). **Production** (metric tons except as noted). *Agriculture, forestry, fishing* (2002): sugarcane 1,150,656, oranges 168,652, grapefruits 44,762; livestock (number of live animals; 2002) 56,949 cattle, 22,874 pigs, 1,400,000 chickens; roundwood (2002) 187,600 cu m; fish catch (2001) 18,830, of which marine fish 10,155, crustaceans 4,983. *Mining and quarrying* (2002): limestone 700,000; sand and gravel 415,000. *Manufacturing* (2002): sugar 107,209; molasses 35,633; flour 26,078. *Energy production (consumption):* electricity (kW-hr; 2000) 137,000,000 (162,000,000); petroleum products (2000) none (258,000). **Household income and expenditure.** Average household size (2000) 4.5; average annual income of employed head of household (1993) BZ$6,450 (estimated); expenditure (1990): food, beverages, and tobacco 34.0%, transportation 13.7%, energy and water 9.1%, housing 9.0%, clothing and footwear 8.8%, household furnishings 8.0%. **Tourism** (2002): receipts from visitors US$132,800,000; expenditures by nationals abroad US$43,000,000. **Land use** as % of total land area (2000): in temporary crops 2.8%, in permanent crops 1.7%, in pasture 2.2%; overall forest area 59.1%. **Population economically active** (2002): total 94,172; activity rate of total population 35.5% (participation rates: ages 14 and over 58.4%; female [2001] 29.6%; unemployed 10.0%). **Gross national product** (2002): US$807,000,000 (US$3,190 per capita). **Public debt** (external, outstanding; 2002): US$789,600,000.

Foreign trade

Imports (2002): BZ$995,900,000 (machinery and transport equipment 19.4%; mineral fuels and lubricants 13.0%; manufactured goods 11.9%; food 10.0%; chemicals and chemical products 7.9%). *Major import sources:* US 43.3%; EU 7.9%; Mexico 7.8%; Canada 3.1%; Caricom 3.0%. **Exports** (2002): BZ$619,400,000 (domestic exports 51.6%, of which seafood products [significantly shrimp] 11.8%, raw sugar 11.3%, citrus concentrate 9.3%, bananas 7.0%, garments 5.1%; reexports [principally to Mexico] 48.4%). *Major export destinations* (domestic exports only): US 49.0%; UK 22.7%; other EU 8.6%; Caricom 6.5%.

Transport and communications

Transport. *Roads* (1999): total length 2,872 km (paved 18%). *Vehicles* (1998): passenger cars 9,929; trucks and buses 11,755. *Air transport* (2001; Belize international airport only): passenger arrivals 256,564, passenger departures 240,900; cargo loaded 186 metric tons, cargo unloaded 1,272 metric tons. Airports (1997) with scheduled flights 9. **Communications,** in total units (units per 1,000 persons). Radios (1997): 133,000 (571); televisions (1998): 42,000 (183); telephone main lines (2003): 33,300 (113); cellular telephone subscribers (2003): 60,400 (205); personal computers (2002): 35,000 (138); Internet users (2002): 30,000 (109).

Education and health

Educational attainment (2000). Percentage of population age 25 and over having: no formal schooling 36.6%; primary education 40.9%; secondary 11.7%; postsecondary/advanced vocational 6.4%; university 3.8%; other/unknown 0.6%. **Literacy** (2001): total population age 14 and over literate 93.4%; males 93.6%; females 93.3%. **Health** (1998): physicians 155 (1 per 1,558 persons); hospital beds 554 (1 per 435 persons); infant mortality rate per 1,000 live births (2003) 27.1. **Food** (2001): daily per capita caloric intake 2,885 (vegetable products 79%, animal products 21%); 128% of FAO recommended minimum.

Military

Total active duty personnel (2003): 1,050 (army 100%); British army 30. **Military expenditure as percentage of GNP** (1999): 1.6% (world 2.4%); per capita expenditure US$47.

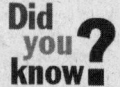

Did you know? The Maya Mountains form a plateau in southern Belize. The range's highest point is Victoria Peak, which rises to 3,681 ft. (1,122 m) in a spur of the Maya range.

---

1 metric ton = about 1.1 short tons;   1 kilometer = 0.6 mi (statute);   1 metric ton-km cargo = about 0.68 short ton-mi cargo;   c.i.f.: cost, insurance, and freight;   f.o.b.: free on board

Background

The area was inhabited by the Maya c. 300 BC–AD 900; the ruins of their ceremonial centers, including Caracol and Xunantunich, can still be seen. The Spanish claimed sovereignty from the 16th century but never tried to settle Belize, though they regarded as interlopers the British who did. British logwood cutters arrived in the mid-17th century; Spanish opposition was finally overcome in 1798. When settlers began to penetrate the interior they met with Indian resistance. In 1871 British Honduras became a crown colony, but an unfulfilled provision of a 1859 British-Guatemalan treaty led Guatemala to claim the territory. The situation had not been resolved when Belize was granted its independence in 1981. A British force, stationed there to ensure the new nation's security, was withdrawn after Guatemala officially recognized the territory's independence in 1991.

Recent Developments

The primary concerns in Belize in 2004 were the heightened public debt and the manner in which the government responded to it. The government attempted to float a bond of $225 million on the international market but was unsuccessful. More than half the cabinet resigned in the public uproar that ensued, but they soon returned to their posts.

Internet resources: <www.belize.gov.bz>.

Benin

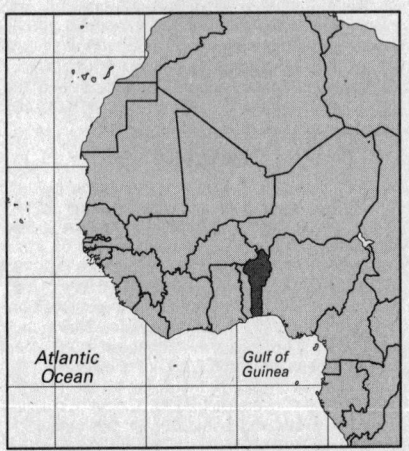

Atlantic Ocean

Gulf of Guinea

Official name: République du Bénin (Republic of Benin). Form of government: multiparty republic with one legislative house (National Assembly [83]). Head of state and government: President Mathieu Kérékou (from 1996). Capital: Porto-Novo (official capital and seat of legislature; administrative seat in Cotonou). Official language: French. Official religion: none. Monetary unit: 1 CFA franc (CFAF) = 100 centimes; valuation (7 Jul 2005) $1 = CFAF 549.50 (formerly pegged to the French franc and since 1 Jan 2002 to the euro at €1 = CFAF 655.96).

Demography

Area: 43,483 sq mi, 112,622 sq km. Population (2004): 7,250,000. Density (2004): persons per sq mi 166.7, persons per sq km 64.4. Urban (2002): 43.0%. Sex distribution (2003): male 49.36%; female 50.64%. Age breakdown (2003): under 15, 47.1%; 15–29, 27.7%; 30–44, 14.5%; 45–59, 7.0%; 60–74, 3.1%; 75 and over, 0.6%. Ethnic composition (1992): Fon 39.7%; Yoruba (Nago) 12.1%; Adjara 11.1%; Bariba 8.6%; Aizo 8.6%; Somba (Otomary) 6.6%; Fulani 5.6%; other 7.7%. Religious affiliation (1992): Christian 35.4%, of which Roman Catholic 25.9%, Protestant 9.5%; traditional beliefs, including voodoo 35.0%; Muslim 20.6%; other 9.0%. Major cities (2004): Cotonou 818,100; Porto-Novo 234,-300; Parakou 227,900; Djougou 206,500; Abomey 126,800. Location: western Africa, bordering Burkina Faso, Niger, Nigeria, the Atlantic Ocean, and Togo.

Vital statistics

Birth rate per 1,000 population (2003): 43.2 (world avg. 21.3). Death rate per 1,000 population (2003): 13.7 (world avg. 9.1). Natural increase rate per 1,000 population (2003): 29.5 (world avg. 12.2). Total fertility rate (avg. births per childbearing woman; 2003): 6.0. Life expectancy at birth (2003): male 50.4 years; female 51.8 years.

National economy

Budget (2002). Revenue: CFAF 300,200,000,000 (tax revenue 80.5%, of which tax on international trade 44.3%, income tax 19.8%, sales tax 16.3%; nontax revenue 12.8%; grants 6.7%). Expenditures: CFAF 352,800,000,000 (current expenditures 61.6%, of which salaries 22.9%, pensions and other transfers 17.6%, interest on debt 4.3%; development expenditure 38.4%). Production (metric tons except as noted). Agriculture, forestry, fishing (2002): cassava 2,452,050; yams 1,785,000; corn (maize) 622,136; livestock (number of live animals; 2002) 1,550,000 cattle, 1,270,000 goats, 10,000,000 chickens; roundwood (2002) 6,297,969 cu m; fish catch (2001) 38,415. Mining (2002): gold 20 kg. Manufacturing (value added in $'000,000; 1999): food products 74; textiles 42; beverages 36. Energy production (consumption): electricity (kW-hr; 2001) 55,888,000 (413,587,000); crude petroleum (barrels; 2001) 365,000 (negligible); petroleum products (2001) none (150,000). Gross national product (2003): $2,990,000,000 ($440 per capita). Public debt (external, outstanding; 2002): $1,690,000,000. Population economically active (1997): total 2,608,-000; activity rate of total population 44.2% (participation rates: ages 15–64, 84.3%; female 48.3%). Households. Average household size (2000) 6.1. Land use as % of total land area (2000): in temporary crops 17.6%, in permanent crops 2.4%, in pasture 5.0%; overall forest area 24.0%. Tourism (2002): receipts from visitors $60,000,000; expenditures by nationals abroad $7,000,000.

Foreign trade

Imports (2002-f.o.b. in balance of trade and commodities and c.i.f. in trading partners): CFAF 389,-800,000,000 (food products 27.6%; petroleum products 22.4%; machinery and transport equipment 18.0%). Major import sources (2001): France c. 23%;

China c. 8%; free-trade zones c. 6%; Côte d'Ivoire c. 5%; Ghana c. 5%; Nigeria c. 5%. **Exports** (2002): CFAF 261,400,000,000 (domestic exports 60.2%, of which cotton yarn 33.3%; reexports 39.8%). *Major export destinations* (2001): India c. 31%; Brazil c. 6%; Indonesia c. 6%; Ghana c. 6%; Nigeria c. 5%.

Transport and communications

Transport. *Railroads* (2000): length 578 km; passenger-km 156,600,000; metric ton-km cargo 153,200,000. *Roads* (1999): total length 6,787 km (paved 20.0%). *Vehicles* (1996): passenger cars 37,772; trucks and buses 8,058. *Air transport*: Air Afrique, an airline jointly owned by 11 African countries (including Benin) was declared bankrupt in February 2002; airports (2002) with scheduled flights 1. **Communications**, in total units (units per 1,000 persons). Daily newspaper circulation (2000): 12,900 (2); radios (2000): 2,820,000 (439); televisions (2000): 289,000 (45); telephone main lines (2003): 66,500 (9.5); cellular telephone subscribers (2003): 236,200 (34); personal computers (2003): 26,000 (3.7); Internet users (2003): 70,000 (10.0).

Education and health

Educational attainment (1992). Percentage of population age 25 and over having: no formal schooling 78.5%; primary education 10.8%; some secondary 8.2%; secondary 1.2%; postsecondary 1.3%. *Literacy* (1998): total percentage of population age 15 and over literate 37.7%; males literate 53.8%; females literate 22.6%. **Health:** physicians (1995) 313 (1 per 17,520 persons); hospital beds (1994) 1,230 (1 per 4,342 persons); infant mortality rate per 1,000 live births (2003) 86.7. **Food** (2001): daily per capita caloric intake 2,455 (vegetable products 96%, animal products 4%); 107% of FAO recommended minimum.

Military

Total active duty personnel (2003): 4,550 (army 94.5%, navy 2.2%, air force 3.3%). **Military expenditure as percentage of GNP** (1999): 1.4% (world 2.4%); per capita expenditure $5.

Background

In southern Benin, the Dahomey, or Fon, established the Abomey kingdom in 1625. In the 18th century, the kingdom became known as Dahomey when it expanded to include Allada and Ouidah, where French forts had been established in the 17th century. In 1857 the French reestablished themselves in the area, and eventually fighting ensued. In 1894 Dahomey became a French protectorate; it was incorporated into the federation of French West Africa in 1904. It achieved independence in 1960. The area called Dahomey was renamed Benin in 1975. At the end of the 20th century, its chronically weak economy produced tension between laborers and the government.

Recent Developments

Benin's economic performance continued to worsen in 2004. The government's goal of a 7% growth rate in 2004 proved wildly optimistic, prices of staple foodstuffs doubled, and the price of cotton, the country's main export good, tumbled. In March 2005 Titan, an American defense corporation, admitted to having violated US anti-bribery laws in connection with a telecommunications project in Benin.

Internet resources:
<www.siftthru.com/benintrav.htm>.

Bermuda

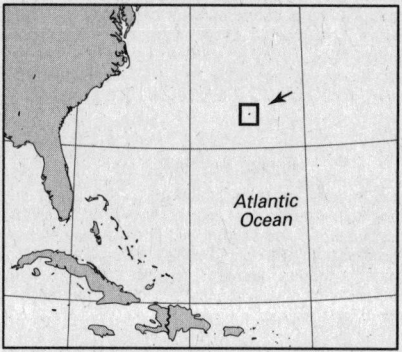

Atlantic Ocean

Official name: Bermuda. **Political status:** colony (UK) with two legislative houses (Senate [11]; House of Assembly [36]). **Chief of state:** Queen Elizabeth II, represented by Governor Sir John Vereker (from 2002). **Head of government:** Premier Alex Scott (from 2003). **Capital:** Hamilton. **Official language:** English. **Official religion:** none. **Monetary unit:** 1 Bermuda dollar (Bd$) = 100 cents; valuation (7 Jul 2005) US$1 = Bd$1.00.

Demography

Area: 20.5 sq mi, 53.1 sq km. **Population** (2004): 64,000. **Density** (2004): persons per sq mi 3,048, persons per sq km 1,185. **Urban** (2003): 100%. **Sex distribution** (2000): male 48.03%; female 51.97%. **Age breakdown** (2000): under 15, 19.1%; 15–29, 18.4%; 30–44, 27.9%; 45–59, 19.6%; 60–74, 10.9%; 75 and over, 4.1%. **Ethnic composition** (2000): black 50.4%; British expatriates 29.0%; mulatto 10.0%; US white 6.0%; Portuguese 4.5%; other 0.1%. **Religious affiliation** (2000): Protestant 64.3%, of which Anglican 22.6%, Methodist 14.9%; Roman Catholic 14.9%; nonreligious 13.8%; other 6.0%; unknown 1.0%. **Major cities** (2000): St. George 1,752; Hamilton 969. **Location:** North Atlantic Ocean, east of North Carolina (US).

Vital statistics

Birth rate per 1,000 population (2001): 13.2 (world avg. 21.3); legitimate 62.3%. **Death rate** per 1,000 population (2001): 7.0 (world avg. 9.1). **Natural increase rate** per 1,000 population (2001): 6.2 (world avg. 12.2). **Total fertility rate** (avg. births per childbearing woman; 2000): 1.8. **Marriage rate** per 1,000

1 metric ton = about 1.1 short tons; 1 kilometer = 0.6 mi (statute); 1 metric ton-km cargo = about 0.68 short ton-mi cargo; c.i.f.: cost, insurance, and freight; f.o.b.: free on board

population (2001): 14.6. **Divorce rate** per 1,000 population (2000): 3.5. **Life expectancy** at birth (2000): male 74.9 years; female 78.9 years.

National economy

Budget (2002). *Revenue:* Bd$631,100,000 (customs duty 30.1%; payroll tax 27.1%; tax on international companies 7.2%; land tax 6.3%; stamp duties 4.5%; other 24.8%). *Expenditures:* Bd$607,500,000 (current expenditure 89.4%, of which wages 41.9%, goods and services 25.6%, grants and contributions 21.9%; development expenditure 10.6%). **Production** (value in Bd$'000 except as noted). *Agriculture, forestry, fishing* (1999): vegetables 3,000, milk 1,657, fruits 900; livestock (number of live animals; 2002) 900 horses, 600 cattle, 45,000 chickens; fish catch (metric tons; 2001) 315, of which crustaceans and mollusks 25. *Mining and quarrying:* crushed stone for local use. *Manufacturing:* industries include pharmaceuticals, cosmetics, and electronics. *Energy production (consumption):* electricity (kW-hr; 2003) 664,000,000 (664,000,000); petroleum products (metric tons; 2000) none (151,000). **Tourism:** receipts from visitors (2003) US$342,000,000; expenditures by nationals abroad (1997) US$148,000,000. **Population economically active** (2002): total 37,815; activity rate of total population 59.1% (participation rates [2000]: ages 15–64, 88.1%; female 49.0%; unemployed 2.9%). **Gross domestic product** (at current market prices; 2000–01): US$3,023,000,000 (US$48,580 per capita). **Household income and expenditure.** Average household size (2000) 2.4; average annual income per household (2001) Bd$72,500; sources of income (1993): wages and salaries 65.3%, imputed income from owner occupancy 10.6%, self-employment 9.0%, net rental income 4.8%, other 10.3%; expenditure (2002): housing 26.1%, food and nonalcoholic beverages 16.0%, household furnishings 15.0%, clothing and footwear 4.2%, other goods and services 38.7%.

Foreign trade

Imports (2002): Bd$746,000,000 (food, beverages, and tobacco 20.2%; machinery 16.5%; chemicals and chemical products 13.9%; mineral fuels 7.8%; transport equipment 6.0%). *Major import sources:* US 76%; Canada 5%; UK 5%; Caribbean countries (mostly Netherlands Antilles) 3%. **Exports** (2002): Bd$57,000,000 (nearly all reexports; diamond market was established in 1990s). *Major export destinations* (2002): mostly US, UK, Norway, and Spain.

Transport and communications

Transport. *Roads* (2000): total length 225 km (paved 100%). *Vehicles* (2002): passenger cars 21,594; trucks and buses 3,768. *Air transport* (2001): passenger arrivals 826,000, passenger departures 826,000; cargo loaded and unloaded 4,200 metric tons; airports (2002) with scheduled flights 1. **Communications,** in total units (units per 1,000 persons). Daily newspaper circulation (1996): 17,000 (277); radios (1997): 82,000 (1,328); televisions (1997): 66,000 (1,069); telephone main lines (2001): 56,300 (872); cellular telephone subscribers (2001): 13,300 (206); personal computers (2001): 32,000 (495); Internet users (2001): 30,000 (464).

Education and health

Educational attainment (2000). Percentage of total population age 16 and over having: no formal schooling 0.4%; primary education 7.0%; secondary 39.3%; postsecondary technical 25.7%; higher 26.8%; not stated 0.8%. **Literacy** (1997): total population age 15 and over literate 98%. **Health** (2002): physicians 122 (1 per 524 persons); hospital beds 226 (1 per 283 persons); infant mortality rate per 1,000 live births (2003) 9.1. **Food** (2001): daily per capita caloric intake 2,904 (vegetable products 74%, animal products 26%); 115% of FAO recommended minimum.

Military

Total active duty personnel (2003): 700; part-time defense force assists police and is drawn from Bermudian conscripts.

Background

The Bermuda archipelago was named for Juan de Bermúdez, who may have visited the islands in 1503. Colonized by the English in 1612, Bermuda became a crown colony in 1684 and a British overseas territory in 2002. Its economy is based on tourism and international finance; its per capita gross national product is among the world's highest.

Recent Developments

In late 2004 Premier Alex Scott created the Bermuda Independence Commission, raising the question of sovereignty for Bermuda. Polls over the years showed that about two-thirds of Bermudans did not favor changing the island's status from British overseas territory to independent republic, yet the question has continued to be raised periodically over the past 40 years.

Internet resources: <www.bermudatourism.org>.

Bhutan

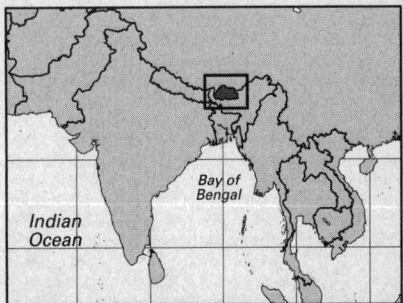

Bay of Bengal

Indian Ocean

Official name: Druk-Yul (Kingdom of Bhutan). **Form of government:** de facto constitutional monarchy with one legislative house (National Assembly [152 seats, including 36 nonelective seats representing the king and religious groups]). **Chief of state:** King Jigme Singye Wangchuk (from 1972). A constitution commissioned by the monarch is to become effective in 2005; reforms in July 1998 curtailed the powers of the monarchy. **Head of government:** Prime Minister

Yeshey Zimba (from 18 Aug 2004). **Capital:** Thimphu. **Official language:** Dzongkha (a Tibetan dialect). **Official religion:** Mahayana Buddhism. **Monetary unit:** 1 ngultrum (Nu) = 100 chetrum; valuation (7 Jul 2005) $1 = Nu 43.61; the Indian rupee is also accepted legal tender.

Demography

Area: 14,824 sq mi, 38,394 sq km. **Population** (2004): 700,000. **Density** (2004): persons per sq mi 47.2, persons per sq km 18.2. **Urban** (2000): 21.0%. **Sex distribution** (2003): male 50.50%; female 49.50%. **Age breakdown** (2003): under 15, 42.1%; 15–29, 23.7%; 30–44, 16.4%; 45–59, 10.6%; 60–74, 5.9%; 75 and over, 1.3%. **Ethnic composition** (1993): Bhutia (Ngalops) 50.0%; Nepalese (Gurung) 35.0%; Sharchops 15.0%. **Religious affiliation** (2000): Buddhist 74.0%; Hindu 20.5%; other 5.5%. **Major cities** (2002): Thimphu 45,000; Phuntsholing (1997) 45,000. **Location:** southern Asia, bordering China and India.

Vital statistics

Birth rate per 1,000 population (2002): 34.9 (world avg. 21.3). **Death rate** per 1,000 population (2002): 8.7 (world avg. 9.1). **Natural increase rate** per 1,000 population (2002): 26.2 (world avg. 12.2). **Total fertility rate** (avg. births per childbearing woman; 2003): 4.9. **Life expectancy** at birth (2002): male 62.0 years; female 64.0 years.

National economy

Budget (2003–04). *Revenue:* Nu 11,154,500,000 (domestic revenue 46.8%, grants 44.6%, other 8.6%). *Expenditures:* Nu 11,537,700,000 (capital expenditures 54.4%, current expenditures 43.3%, repayments 2.3%). **Public debt** (external, outstanding; 2002): $376,900,000. **Production** (metric tons except as noted). *Agriculture, forestry, fishing* (2002): corn (maize) 48,500, rice 44,300, oranges 30,000; livestock (number of live animals) 355,400 cattle, 41,400 pigs, 31,300 goats; roundwood (2002) 4,482,000 cu m; fish catch (2001) 330. *Mining and quarrying* (2001): limestone 434,900; dolomite 283,700; gypsum 87,000. *Manufacturing* (value in Nu '000,000; 2000): cement 696.7; chemical products 474.6; alcoholic beverages 255.0. *Energy production (consumption):* electricity (kW-hr; 2002) 2,059,400,000 (489,260,000); coal (2000) 50,000 (66,000); petroleum products (2000) none (47,000). **Households.** Average household size (2000) 5.5. **Population economically active** (1999): total 358,950; activity rate of total population 52.9% (participation rates: ages 15 and over 69.6%; unemployed 1.4%). **Gross national product** (2003): $578,000,000 ($660 per capita). **Tourism** (2002): receipts from visitors $8,000,000. **Land use** as % of total land area (2000): in temporary crops 3.0%, in permanent crops 0.4%, in pasture 8.8%; overall forest area 64.2%.

Foreign trade

Imports (2001-c.i.f.): $188,300,000 (1999; machinery and transport equipment 41.7%, of which computers and related goods 11.0%, road vehicles 10.5%; food 13.9%, of which cereals 7.6%; refined petroleum 7.2%). *Major import sources* (2001): India 81.1%; Japan 7.2%; Thailand 3.4%; Singapore 2.5%. **Exports** (2001-f.o.b.): $97,700,000 (electricity 48.1%, calcium carbide 13.3%, ferro-silicon 12.6%, cement 9.6%). *Major export destinations* (2001): India 94.1%; Bangladesh 4.5%; Nepal 0.8%.

Transport and communications

Transport. *Roads* (2003): total length 4,007 km (paved 60%). *Vehicles* (2003): passenger cars 10,574; trucks and buses 3,852. *Air transport* (1999): passenger-km 49,000,000; metric ton-km cargo 4,000,000; airports (2002) with scheduled flights 1. **Communications,** in total units (units per 1,000 persons). Radios (1997): 37,000 (19); televisions (1999): 13,000 (20); telephone main lines (2002): 20,168 (33); personal computers (2002): 10,000 (15); Internet users (2002): 17,980 (27).

Education and health

Literacy (1995): total population age 15 and over literate 42.2%; males literate 56.2%; females literate 28.1%. **Health** (2002): physicians 122 (1 per 6,019 persons); hospital beds 1,023 (1 per 696 persons); infant mortality rate per 1,000 live births 55.0.

Military

Total active duty personnel (2002): about 6,000 (army 100%).

Background

Bhutan's mountains and forests long made it inaccessible to the outside world, and its feudal rulers banned foreigners until well into the 20th century. It nevertheless became the object of foreign invasions; in 1865 it came under British influence, and in 1910 it agreed to be guided by Britain in its foreign affairs. It later became oriented toward British-ruled India, though much of its trade was with Tibet. India took over Britain's role in 1949, and Communist China's 1950 occupation of neighboring Tibet further strengthened Bhutan's ties with India. The apparent Chinese threat made Bhutan's rulers aware of the need to modernize, and it embarked on a program to build roads and hospitals and to create a system of secular education.

Recent Developments

Virtually untouched by terrorist activities in the past, Bhutan began 2004 with a small-scale war as its 8,000-man army was sent to flush out Indian insurgent groups hiding in Bhutanese territory. More than 100,000 Bhutanese refugees continued to languish in camps in Nepal. In February 2005, two months after the government prohibited the sale of tobacco in the country, it also banned smoking in public places. A draft constitution presented in March committed to transforming one of the world's few remaining absolute monarchies into a two-party democracy.

Internet resources: <www.kingdomofbhutan.com>.

---

1 metric ton = about 1.1 short tons;   1 kilometer = 0.6 mi (statute);   1 metric ton-km cargo = about 0.68 short ton-mi cargo;   c.i.f.: cost, insurance, and freight;   f.o.b.: free on board

Bolivia

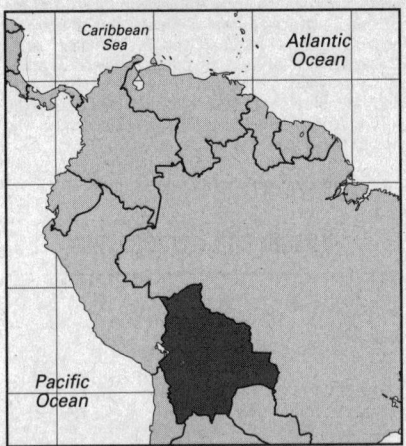

Official name: República de Bolivia (Republic of Bolivia). **Form of government:** unitary multiparty republic with two legislative houses (Chamber of Senators [27]; Chamber of Deputies [130]). **Head of state and government:** President Eduardo Rodríguez (from 9 Jun 2005). **Capitals:** La Paz (administrative); Sucre (judicial). **Official languages:** Spanish, Aymara, Quechua. **Official religion:** Roman Catholicism. **Monetary unit:** 1 boliviano (Bs) = 100 centavos; valuation (7 Jul 2005) $1 = Bs 8.09.

Demography

Area: 424,164 sq mi, 1,098,581 sq km. **Population** (2004): 8,724,000. **Density** (2004): persons per sq mi 20.6, persons per sq km 7.9. **Urban** (2001): 62.4%. **Sex distribution** (2003): male 49.81%; female 50.19%. **Age breakdown** (2001): under 15, 38.6%; 15–29, 27.4%; 30–44, 17.0%; 45–59, 10.0%; 60–74, 5.2%; 75 and over, 1.8%. **Ethnic composition** (2000): Amerindian 65%, of which Quechua 40%, Aymara 24%; mestizo 27%; white 8%, of which German 3%. **Religious affiliation** (1995): Roman Catholic 88.5%; Protestant 9.0%; other 2.5%. **Major cities** (2001): Santa Cruz 1,116,059; La Paz 789,585 (urban agglomeration [2003] 1,477,000); El Alto 647,350 (within La Paz agglomeration); Cochabamba 516,683; Oruro 201,230. **Location:** central South America, bordering Brazil, Paraguay, Argentina, Chile, and Peru.

Vital statistics

Birth rate per 1,000 population (2003): 25.5 (world avg. 21.3). **Death rate** per 1,000 population (2003): 7.9 (world avg. 9.1). **Natural increase rate** per 1,000 population (2003): 17.6 (world avg. 12.2). **Total fertility rate** (avg. births per childbearing woman; 2003): 3.2. **Life expectancy** at birth (2003): male 62.2 years; female 67.4 years.

National economy

Budget (2002). *Revenue:* Bs 13,558,000,000 (tax revenue 74.3%, of which value-added taxes 25.2%, taxes on hydrocarbons 19.3%, import duties 12.7%; nontax revenue 11.3%; foreign grants 9.4%; other 5.0%). *Expenditures:* Bs 18,857,000,000 (current expenditure 75.1%; capital expenditure 24.9%). **Production** (metric tons except as noted). *Agriculture, forestry, fishing* (2002): sugarcane 4,320,784, soybeans 1,166,660, potatoes 944,216; livestock (number of live animals) 8,901,631 sheep, 6,576,277 cattle, 2,850,547 pigs; roundwood (2002) 10,237,753 cu m; fish catch (2001) 6,260. *Mining and quarrying* (pure metal; 2003): zinc 145,490; tin 16,386; lead 9,353. *Manufacturing* (value added in $'000,000; 1998): petroleum products 399; food products 222; beverages 141. *Energy production (consumption):* electricity (kW-hr; 2003) 4,318,000,000 (2,905,000,000); crude petroleum (barrels; 2000) 11,877,000 (11,877,000); petroleum products (2000) 1,345,000 (1,641,000); natural gas (cu m; 2000) 3,904,000,000 (1,815,000,000). **Population economically active** (2002): total 3,823,500; activity rate of total population 44.5% (participation rates: ages 10 and over 78.2%; female 45.9%; unemployed [2000] 7.4%). **Tourism:** receipts (2002) $104,000,000; expenditures (2001) $118,000,000. **Gross national product** (at current market prices; 2003): $7,985,000,000 ($890 per capita). **Public debt** (external, outstanding; 2002): $3,378,000,000. **Household income and expenditure.** Average household size (2000): 4.0; expenditure (1988): food 35.5%, transportation and communications 17.7%, housing 14.8%, household durable goods 7.3%, clothing and footwear 5.1%, beverages and tobacco 4.5%, recreation 2.7%, health 2.1%. **Land use** as % of total land area (2000): in temporary crops 2.7%, in permanent crops 0.2%, in pasture 31.2%; overall forest area 48.9%.

Foreign trade

Imports (2001-f.o.b. in balance of trade and c.i.f. for commodities and trading partners): $1,706,800,000 (machinery and transport equipment 27.6%; chemicals and chemical products 17.0%; food 11.4%; refined petroleum 6.2%; iron and steel 5.8%). *Major import sources:* Argentina 16.9%; US 16.6%; Brazil 16.2%; Chile 8.4%; Peru 6.3%. **Exports** (2001): $1,351,200,000 (food 20.7%, of which soybean oilcake 13.7%; natural gas 17.9%; zinc ores and concentrates 8.9%; soybean oil 5.5%; gold 3.7%). *Major export destinations:* Brazil 22.1%; Colombia 14.1%; US 13.9%; Switzerland 13.0%; Venezuela 7.3%.

Transport and communications

Transport. *Railroads* (2000): route length 3,608 km; (1997) passenger-km 224,900,000; metric ton-km cargo 838,900,000. *Roads* (2001): total length 53,259 km (paved 6%). *Vehicles* (2001): passenger cars 254,175; trucks and buses 194,510. *Air transport* (2003): passenger-km 1,704,000,000; metric ton-km cargo 24,348,000; airports (2000) with scheduled flights 14. **Communications,** in total units (units per 1,000 persons). Daily newspaper circulation (2000): 448,000 (65); radios (2000): 5,510,000 (676); televisions (2000): 970,000 (119); telephone main lines (2003): 600,100 (71); cellular telephone subscribers (2003): 1,401,500 (167); personal computers (2002): 190,000 (23); Internet users (2002): 270,000 (32).

Education and health

Educational attainment (1992). Percentage of population age 25 and over having: no formal schooling 23.3%; some primary 20.3%; primary education 21.7%; some secondary 9.0%; secondary 6.5%; some higher 5.0%; higher 4.8%; not specified 9.4%. **Literacy** (2001): total population age 15 and over literate 86.0%; males literate 92.3%; females literate 79.9%. **Health** (2002): physicians 2,987 (1 per 2,827 persons); hospital beds 11,921 (1 per 708 persons); infant mortality rate per 1,000 live births (2003) 56.1. **Food** (2001): daily per capita caloric intake 2,267 (vegetable products 84%, animal products 16%); 95% of FAO recommended minimum.

Military

Total active duty personnel (2003): 31,500 (army 79.4%, navy 11.1%, air force 9.5%). **Military expenditure as percentage of GNP** (1998): 1.8% (world 2.5%); per capita expenditure $18.

 **Did you know?** Lake Titicaca, the world's highest lake navigable to large vessels, lies 12,500 ft (3,810 m) above sea level in the Andes Mountains of South America, astride the Peru-Bolivia border.

Background

The Bolivian highlands were the location of the advanced Tiwanaku culture in the 7th–11th centuries and, with its passing, became the home of the Aymara, an Indian group conquered by the Incas in the 15th century. The Incas were overrun by the invading Spanish under Francisco Pizarro in the 1530s. By 1600 Spain had established the cities of Charcas (now Sucre), La Paz, Santa Cruz, and what would become Cochabamba, and had begun to exploit the silver wealth of Potosí. Bolivia flourished in the 17th century, and for a time Potosí was the largest city in the Americas. By the end of the century, the mineral wealth had dried up. Talk of independence began as early as 1809, but not until 1825 were Spanish forces finally defeated. Bolivia shrank in size when it lost Atacama province to Chile in 1884 at the end of the War of the Pacific, and again in 1939 when it lost most of Gran Chaco to Paraguay. One of South America's poorest countries, it was plagued by governmental instability for much of the 20th century. By the 1990s Bolivia had become one of the world's largest producers of coca, from which cocaine is derived. The government subsequently instituted a largely successful program to eradicate the crop, although such efforts were resisted by the many poor farmers who depended on coca.

Recent Developments

The rollercoaster of Bolivian politics started down another steep slope in early 2005. Social and economic pressures converged: the combination of widespread poverty, squabbling over natural gas development, a restive Indian population highly dependent on the cultivation of coca leaf, resentment and mistrust of the US and its strong-arm war on drugs, and an inexperienced president—historian and TV journalist Carlos Mesa Gisbert—created an atmosphere of volatility. Mesa resigned in June, and, after the vice president and National Assembly speaker declined the job, he was replaced by the Supreme Court chief justice, who was to call elections within six months.

Internet resources: <www.boliviabiz.com>.

Bosnia and Herzegovina

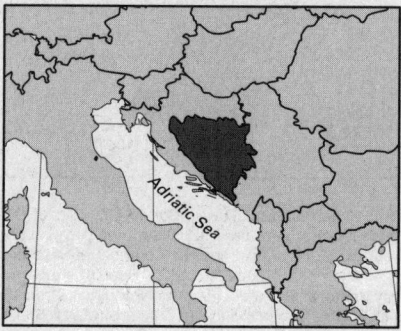

Official name: Bosna i Hercegovina (Bosnia and Herzegovina). **Form of government:** federal multiparty republic with bicameral legislature (House of Peoples [15; all seats are nonelective]; House of Representatives [42]). **Chiefs of state:** Tripartite presidency with 8-month-long rotating chairmanship (final authority rests with International High Representative Paddy Ashdown, Baron Ashdown [from 2002]). **Head of government:** Prime Minister Adnan Terzic (chairman of Council of Ministers; from 2002). **Capital:** Sarajevo. **Official language:** Bosnian (Serbo-Croatian). **Official religion:** none. **Monetary unit:** 1 marka (KM) = 100 fenning; valuation (7 Jul 2005) $1 = KM 1.64 (pegged to the euro from 1 Jan 2002; the euro also circulates as semiofficial legal tender).

Demography

Area: 19,767 sq mi, 51,197 sq km. **Population** (2004; excludes refugees in adjacent countries and western Europe): 3,870,000. **Density** (2004): persons per sq mi 195.7, persons per sq km 75.6. **Urban** (2002): 43.4%. **Sex distribution** (2002): male 48.80%; female 51.20%. **Age breakdown** (2002): under 15, 18.4%; 15–29, 21.8%; 30–44, 23.0%; 45–59, 18.5%; 60–74, 15.2%; 75 and over, 3.1%. **Ethnic composition** (1999): Bosniac 44.0%; Serb 31.0%; Croat 17.0%; other 8.0%. **Religious affiliation** (1999): Sunni Muslim 43.0%; Serbian Orthodox 30.0%; Roman Catholic 18.0%; other (mostly nonreligious) 9.0%. **Major cities** (2004): Sarajevo 428,600 (urban agglomeration 602,500); Banja Luka 170,000; Zenica 139,800; Tuzla 123,500; Mostar 94,100. **Location:** southeastern Europe, bordered by Croatia, Serbia and Montenegro, and the Adriatic Sea.

---

1 metric ton = about 1.1 short tons;   1 kilometer = 0.6 mi (statute);   1 metric ton-km cargo = about 0.68 short ton-mi cargo;   c.i.f.: cost, insurance, and freight;   f.o.b.: free on board

Vital statistics

Birth rate per 1,000 population (2002): 9.5 (world avg. 21.3); (2001) legitimate 89.4%. **Death rate** per 1,000 population (2002): 8.0 (world avg. 9.1). **Natural increase rate** per 1,000 population (2002): 1.5 (world avg. 12.2). **Total fertility rate** (avg. births per childbearing woman; 2002): 1.4. **Marriage rate** per 1,000 population (2002): 5.4. **Life expectancy** at birth (2001): male 64.6 years; female 70.2 years.

National economy

Budget (2001). *Revenue:* KM 1,653,100,000 (tax revenue 90.8%, nontax revenue 6.4%, grants 2.8%). *Expenditures:* KM 1,887,600,000 (wages and contributions 24.1%, transfers to households 22.6%, defense 15.4%). **Gross national product** (2003): $6,386,000,000 ($1,540 per capita). **Production** (metric tons except as noted). *Agriculture, forestry, fishing* (2002): corn (maize) 530,000, potatoes 310,000, wheat 297,000; livestock (number of live animals) 670,000 sheep, 440,000 cattle, 300,000 pigs; roundwood (2002) 4,226,000 cu m; fish catch (2001) 2,500. *Mining* (2001): iron ore (gross weight) 100,000; bauxite 75,000; kaolin 3,000. *Manufacturing* (2001): cement 300,000; crude steel 80,000; pig iron 60,000. *Energy production (consumption):* electricity (kW-hr; 2000) 10,429,000,000 (9,365,-000,000); hard coal (2000) 3,553,000 (3,553,000); lignite (2000) 5,330,000 (5,330,000); petroleum products (2000) none (842,000); natural gas (cu m; 2000) none (276,800,000). **Public debt** (external, outstanding; 2002): $2,282,000,000. **Population economically active** (2001): total 1,015,169; activity rate of total population 27.4% (participation rates: ages 15–64 [1991] 35.6%; female [1990] 37.7%; unemployed [2002] 42.7%). **Households.** Average household size (1991) 3.4; sources of income (1990): wages 53.2%, transfers 18.2%, self-employment 12.0%, other 16.6%. **Tourism** (2002): receipts from visitors $112,000,000; expenditures by nationals abroad $49,000,000. **Land use** as % of total land area (2000): in temporary crops 13.0%, in permanent crops 3.0%, in pasture 23.7%; overall forest area 44.6%.

Foreign trade

Imports (2003): KM 7,920,191,000. *Major import sources:* Croatia 17.3%; Germany 13.2%; Italy 9.6%; Slovenia 9.6%; Serbia and Montenegro 7.6%. **Exports** (2003): KM 2,349,189,000. *Major export destinations:* Croatia 17.9%; Germany 15.4%; Serbia and Montenegro 15.3%; Italy 13.4%; Slovenia 9.7%.

Transport and communications

Transport. *Railroads* (2001): length 1,031 km; passenger-km 38,740,000; metric ton-km cargo 239,138,000. *Roads* (2001): total length 21,846 km (paved 64%). *Vehicles* (1996): passenger cars 96,182; trucks and buses 10,919. *Air transport* (2000): passenger-km 48,000,000; airports (2000) with scheduled flights 1. **Communications,** in total units (units per 1,000 persons). Daily newspaper circulation (2000): 563,000 (152); radios (2000): 900,000 (243); televisions (2000): 411,000 (111); telephone main lines (2003): 938,000 (244); cellular telephone subscribers (2003): 1,050,000 (274); Internet users (2002): 100,000 (24).

Health

Health: physicians (2000) 5,293 (1 per 714 persons); hospital beds (1999) 13,783 (1 per 270 persons); infant mortality rate per 1,000 live births (2002) 23.5. **Food** (2001): daily per capita caloric intake 2,845 (vegetable products 85%, animal products 15%); 112% of FAO recommended minimum.

Military

Total active duty personnel: EU peacekeeping troops (also includes Canadian and Turkish troops; 2004) 7,000. **Military expenditure as percentage of GNP** (1999): 4.5% (world 2.4%); per capita expenditure $75.

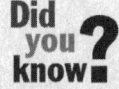

Did you know? Slivovitz, distilled from plums, particularly those from the Posavina region in the far north of Bosnia and Herzegovina, is the liquor of choice for men here and in many other Balkan countries.

Background

Habitation long predates the era of Roman rule, when much of the country was included in the province of Dalmatia. Slav settlement began in the 6th century AD. For the next several centuries, parts of the region fell under the rule of Serbs, Croats, Hungarians, Venetians, and Byzantines. The Ottoman Turks invaded Bosnia in the 14th century, and after many battles it became a Turkish province in 1463. Herzegovina, then known as Hum, was taken in 1482. In the 16th–17th century the area was an important Turkish outpost, constantly at war with the Habsburgs and Venice. During this period much of the native population converted to Islam. At the Congress of Berlin after the Russo-Turkish War of 1877–78, Bosnia and Herzegovina was assigned to Austria-Hungary and annexed in 1908. Growing Serb nationalism resulted in the 1914 assassination of the Austrian Archduke Francis Ferdinand at Sarajevo by a Bosnian Serb, an event that precipitated World War I. After the war the area was annexed to Serbia. Following World War II the twin territory became a republic of communist Yugoslavia. With the collapse of communist regimes in Eastern Europe, Bosnia and Herzegovina declared its independence in 1992; its Serb population objected, and conflict ensued among Serbs, Croats, and Muslims. The 1995 peace accord established a loosely federated government roughly divided between a Muslim-Croat federation and a Serb Republic (Republika Srpska). In 1996 a NATO peacekeeping force was installed there.

Recent Developments

Efforts to reintegrate and reform the two entities that make up Bosnia and Herzegovina—the Muslim-Croat Federation and the Serb Republika Srpska—were pushed through by international pressure in 2004. The continuing weakness of the state and the failure of the Serbs to arrest a single suspect wanted by the International War Crimes Tribunal were the major obstacles blocking the country's eligibility for membership in NATO's Partnership for Peace program. At the end of 2004 NATO turned over command of peace-keeping activities to the 7,000-strong EU force.

Internet resources: <www.bhembassy.org>.

Botswana

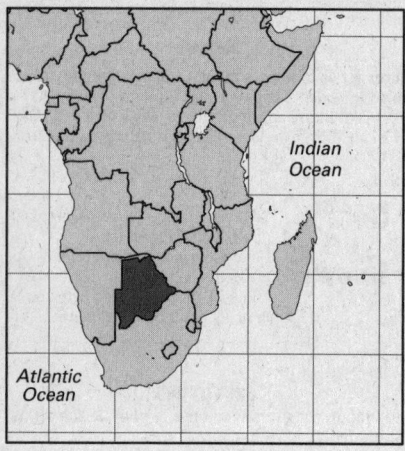

Indian
Ocean

Atlantic
Ocean

Official name: Republic of Botswana. **Form of government:** multiparty republic with one legislative body (National Assembly [63]) and a 15-member advisory board, the House of Chiefs. **Head of state and government:** President Festus Mogae (from 1998). **Capital:** Gaborone. **Official language:** English (Tswana is the national language). **Official religion:** none. **Monetary unit:** 1 pula (P) = 100 thebe; valuation (7 Jul 2005) $1 = P 5.62.

Demography

Area: 224,848 sq mi, 582,356 sq km. **Population** (2004): 1,661,000. **Density** (2004): persons per sq mi 7.3, persons per sq km 2.9. **Urban** (2002): 49.4%. **Sex distribution** (2001): male 48.40%; female 51.60%. **Age breakdown** (2000): under 15, 40.6%; 15–29, 30.8%; 30–44, 15.0%; 45–59, 7.7%; 60–74, 4.3%; 75 and over, 1.6%. **Ethnic composition** (2000): Tswana 66.8%; Kalanga 14.8%; Ndebele 1.7%; Herero 1.4%; San (Bushman) 1.3%; Afrikaner 1.3%. **Religious affiliation** (2000): traditional beliefs 38.8%; African Christian 30.7%; Protestant 10.9%; Roman Catholic 3.7%. **Major cities** (2001): Gaborone 186,007; Francistown 83,023; Molepolole 54,561; Selebi-Pikwe 49,849; Maun 43,776. **Location:** southern Africa, bordered by Namibia, Zimbabwe, and South Africa.

Vital statistics

Birth rate per 1,000 population (2002): 28.0 (world avg. 21.3). **Death rate** per 1,000 population (2002): 26.3 (world avg. 9.1). **Natural increase rate** per 1,000 population (2002): 1.7 (world avg. 12.2). **Total fertility rate** (avg. births per childbearing woman; 2002): 3.6. **Life expectancy** at birth (2002): male 36.9 years;

female 37.6 years. **Adult population** (ages 15–49) **living with HIV** (2004): 37.3% (world avg. 1.1%).

National economy

Budget (2002–03). *Revenue:* P 14,311,000,000 (tax revenue 85.7%, of which mineral royalties 52.4%, income tax 12.9%, value-added tax 8.8%; nontax revenue 13.7%, of which property income 7.4%; grants 0.6%). *Expenditures:* P 15,710,100,000 (education 22.6%, health 8.8%, defense 8.3%, public order 4.0%). **Public debt** (external, outstanding; 2002): $463,900,000. **Population economically active** (2000): total 574,160; activity rate of total population 35.1% (participation rates: ages 15–64, 58.3%; female 44.3%; unemployed 15.8%). **Production** (metric tons except as noted). *Agriculture, forestry, fishing* (2002): sorghum 32,298, pulses 17,500, corn (maize) 10,000; livestock (number of live animals) 2,250,000 goats, 1,700,000 cattle, 370,000 sheep; roundwood 749,515 cu m; fish catch (2001) 118. *Mining and quarrying* (2003): soda ash 234,520; nickel ore (metal content) 27,400; copper ore (metal content) 24,289. *Manufacturing* (value added in $'000,000; 1997): motor vehicles 33; beverages 26; bricks, cement, and tiles 20. *Energy production (consumption):* electricity (kW-hr; 2003) 624,000,000 [2000] 1,450,000,000); coal (2003) 822,780 ([2000] 971,000). **Tourism:** receipts (2002) $309,-000,000; expenditures $184,000,000. **Gross national product** (at current market prices; 2003): $5,911,000,000 ($3,430 per capita). **Household expenditure.** Average household size (2001) 4.2; expenditure (2000): food and nonalcoholic beverages 30.6%, housing and energy 13.4%, alcoholic beverages and tobacco 12.3%, education 7.0%, transportation 5.7%. **Land use** as % of total land area (2000): in temporary crops 0.7%, in permanent crops 0.01%, in pasture 45.2%, overall forest area 21.9%.

Foreign trade

Imports (2002-c.i.f.): P 10,169,000,000 (machinery and apparatus 19.6%; food, beverages, and tobacco 13.9%; transport equipment 12.1%; chemical and rubber products 10.3%; wood and paper products 8.8%). *Major import sources* (2001): Customs Union of Southern Africa (CUSA) 77.6%; Europe 12.3%, of which UK 4.4%; Zimbabwe 3.2%; US 1.8%. **Exports** (2002-f.o.b.): P 14,983,000,000 (diamonds 83.3%; copper-nickel matte 3.2%; textiles 2.0%; meat products 1.9%). *Major export destinations* (2001): UK 85.9%; CUSA 6.5%; Zimbabwe 2.6%.

Transport and communications

Transport. *Railroads* (2000–01): length 1,135 km; passenger-km 106,000,000; metric ton-km cargo 747,000. *Roads* (2002): total length 10,528 km (paved 55%). *Vehicles* (2003): passenger cars 64,681; trucks and buses 70,923. *Air transport* (2002; Air Botswana only): passenger-km 96,000,-000; metric ton-km cargo 300,000; airports (1998) 7. **Communications,** in total units (units per 1,000 persons). Daily newspaper circulation (2000): 44,200 (27); radios (2000): 254,000 (155); televisions (2000): 40,900 (25); telephone main lines (2002): 142,400 (83); cellular telephone subscribers

1 metric ton = about 1.1 short tons;   1 kilometer = 0.6 mi (statute);   1 metric ton-km cargo = about 0.68 short ton-mi cargo;   c.i.f.: cost, insurance, and freight;   f.o.b.: free on board

(2002): 435,000 (253); personal computers (2002): 70,000 (41); Internet users (2002): 60,000 (35).

Education and health

Educational attainment (1993). Percentage of population age 25 and over having: no formal schooling 34.7%; primary education 44.1%; some secondary 19.8%; postsecondary 1.4%. **Literacy** (2001): total population over age 15 literate 78.1%; males literate 75.3%; females literate 80.6%. **Health** (2003): physicians 510 (1 per 3,261 persons); hospital beds 3,088 (1 per 539 persons); infant mortality rate per 1,000 live births (2002) 64.7. **Food** (2001): daily per capita caloric intake 2,292 (vegetable products 83%, animal products 17%); 99% of FAO recommended minimum.

Military

Total active duty personnel (2003): 9,000 (army 94.4%, air force 5.6%). **Military expenditure as percentage of GNP** (1999): 4.7% (world 2.4%); per capita expenditure $142.

Did you know? Gaborone is the capital of Botswana. The seat of government was transferred there from Mafeking, South Africa, in 1965, one year before Botswana became independent of Great Britain. It is the seat of the University of Botswana (founded 1976), and it also has a national museum and art gallery (1968).

Background

The region's earliest inhabitants were the Khoekhoe and San (Bushmen). Sites were settled as early as AD 190 during the southerly migration of Bantu-speaking farmers. Tswana dynasties, which developed in the western Transvaal in the 13th–14th century, moved into Botswana in the 18th century and established several powerful states. European missionaries arrived in the early 19th century, but it was the discovery of gold in 1867 that excited European interest. In 1885 the area became the British Bechuanaland Protectorate. The next year the region south of the Molopo River became a crown colony, and it was annexed by the Cape Colony 10 years later. Bechuanaland itself continued as a British protectorate until the 1960s. In 1966 the Republic of Bechuanaland (later Botswana) was proclaimed an independent member of the British Commonwealth. Independent Botswana tried to maintain a delicate balance between its economic dependence on South Africa and its relations with the surrounding black countries; the independence of Namibia in 1990 and South Africa's rejection of apartheid eased tensions.

Recent Developments

Beginning in January 2004, all patients at doctors' offices in Botswana who did not object were automatically tested for HIV. Gaborone had the largest HIV/AIDS clinic in the world; antiretroviral drugs were dispensed there free of charge in a program paid for by government and international donor agencies. In April the first cases of polio in 13 years were de-tected, near Maun and Francistown. The affected children were successfully treated, however, and an emergency national immunization campaign followed. The polio strain was identical with the one that was infecting northern Nigeria.

Internet resources: <www.botswana-tourism.gov.bw>.

Brazil

Caribbean Sea

Atlantic Ocean

Pacific Ocean

Official name: República Federativa do Brasil (Federative Republic of Brazil). **Form of government:** multiparty federal republic with two legislative houses (Federal Senate [81]; Chamber of Deputies [513]). **Chief of state and government:** President Luiz Inácio Lula da Silva (from 2003). **Capital:** Brasília. **Official language:** Portuguese. **Official religion:** none. **Monetary unit:** 1 real (R$) = 100 centavos; valuation (7 Jul 2005) US$1 = 2.39 reais.

Demography

Area (including inland water): 3,287,612 sq mi, 8,514,877 sq km. **Population** (2004): 180,542,000. **Density** (2004): persons per sq mi 54.9, persons per sq km 21.2. **Urban** (2000): 81.2%. **Sex distribution** (2000): male 49.21%; female 50.79%. **Age breakdown** (2000): under 15, 29.6%; 15–29, 28.2%; 30–44, 21.1%; 45–59, 12.5%; 60–74, 6.5%; 75 and over, 2.1%. **Racial composition** (1999; excludes rural population of Acre, Amapá, Amazonas, Pará, Rondônia, and Roraima): white 54.0%; mulatto and mestizo 39.9%; black and black/Amerindian 5.4%; Asian 0.5%; Amerindian 0.2%. **Religious affiliation** (1995): Catholic 74.3%, of which Roman Catholic 72.3%; Protestant 23.2%, of which Pentecostal 19.1%; other Christian 0.9%; New-Religionist 0.3%; Buddhist 0.3%; Jewish 0.2%; Muslim 0.1%; other 0.7%. **Major cities and metropolitan areas** (2003): São Paulo 10,041,500 (18,628,444); Rio de Janeiro 5,974,100 (11,226,729); Salvador 2,555,400 (3,183,327); Belo Horizonte 2,305,800 (5,100,359); Fortaleza 2,256,200 (3,164,225); Brasília 2,094,100 (3,199,-451); Curitiba 1,671,200 (2,930,772); Manaus 1,517,500 (1,527,314); Recife 1,461,300 (3,466,214); Porto Alegre 1,353,300 (3,815,447); Belém 1,333,500 (1,916,982); Goiânia 1,138,600

(1,766,588); Guarulhos 1,135,500 (within São Paulo metropolitan area); Campinas 990,100 (2,483,594). **Location:** eastern South America, bordered by Venezuela, Guyana, Suriname, French Guiana, Uruguay, Argentina, Paraguay, Bolivia, Peru, and Colombia. **Families** (1999). Average family size 3.3; (1996) 1–2 persons 25.2%, 3 persons 20.3%, 4 persons 22.2%, 5–6 persons 23.3%, 7 or more persons 9.0%. **Number of emigrants/immigrants** (1986–96): 2,355,057/169,303. Emigrants' most popular destinations in order of preference are the US, Japan, and the UK.

Vital statistics

Birth rate per 1,000 population (2003): 19.5 (world avg. 21.3). **Death rate** per 1,000 population (2003): 6.7 (world avg. 9.1). **Natural increase rate** per 1,000 population (2003): 12.8 (world avg. 12.2). **Total fertility rate** (avg. births per childbearing woman; 2003): 2.2. **Marriage rate** per 1,000 population (2002): 4.1. **Divorce rate** per 1,000 population (2001): 0.7. **Life expectancy** at birth (2003): male 67.2 years; female 75.3 years.

Social indicators

Quality of working life. Proportion of employed population receiving minimum wage (2002): 53.5%. Number and percentage of children (age 5–17) working: 5,400,000 (12.6% of age group). **Access to services** (1999; excludes rural population of Acre, Amapá, Amazonas, Pará, Rondônia, and Roraima). Proportion of households having access to: electricity 94.8%, of which urban households having access 99.2%, rural households having access 75.4%; safe public (piped) water supply 79.8%, of which urban households having access 92.3%, rural households having access 24.9%; public (piped) sewage system 43.6%, of which urban households having access 52.5%, rural households having access 4.5%; no sewage disposal 8.5%, of which urban households having no disposal 2.9%, rural households having no disposal 32.9%. **Social participation.** Voting is mandatory for national elections; abstention is punishable by a fine. Trade union membership in total workforce (2001): 19,500,000. Practicing Roman Catholic population in total affiliated Roman Catholic population (2000): large cities 10–15%; towns and rural areas 60–70%. **Social deviance.** Annual murder rate per 100,000 population (1996): Brazil 23, Rio de Janeiro only 69, São Paulo only 55. **Leisure.** Favorite leisure activities include: playing soccer, dancing, rehearsing all year in neighborhood samba groups for celebrations of Carnival, and competing in water sports, volleyball, and basketball. **Material well-being** (1999; excludes rural population of Acre, Amapá, Amazonas, Pará, Rondônia, and Roraima). Households possessing: television receiver 87.7%, of which urban 93.2%, rural 63.8%; refrigerator 82.8%, of which urban 89.7%, rural 52.5%; washing machine 32.8%, of which urban 38.0%, rural 10.0%.

National economy

Gross national product (at current market prices; 2003): US$478,922,000,000 (US$2,710 per capita). **Budget** (1998). *Revenue:* R$237,187,- 000,000 (current revenue 95.8%, of which social contributions 32.6%, sales tax 20.3%, tax on income and profit 19.4%, nontax revenue 16.3%; capital revenue 4.2%). *Expenditures:* R$245,- 032,100,000 (social security and welfare 47.3%; interest on debt 14.3%; defense and public order 6.6%; health 6.2%; education 6.1%; economic affairs 4.8%; other 14.7%). **Public debt** (external, outstanding; 2002): US$96,565,000,000. **Production** ('000 metric tons except as noted). *Agriculture, forestry, fishing* (2002): sugarcane 360,566, soybeans 41,903, corn (maize) 35,479, cassava 23,108, oranges 18,694, rice 10,489, bananas 6,369, tomatoes 3,518, dry beans 3,017, wheat 2,926, potatoes 2,865, coconuts 2,695, coffee 2,390, seed cotton 2,172, cashew apples 1,600, papayas 1,500, pineapples 1,469, onions 1,132, grapes 1,099, apples 858, sorghum 814, tobacco 654, lemons and limes 580, maté 535, oil palm fruit 450, peanuts (groundnuts) 192, cashews 184, sisal 177, cacao beans 172, garlic 113, natural rubber 96, Brazil nuts 26; livestock (number of live animals) 176,000,000 cattle, 30,000,000 pigs, 15,000,000 sheep, 5,900,000 horses; roundwood (2002) 237,467,063 cu m, of which fuelwood 134,473,063 cu m, sawlogs and veneer logs 49,290,000 cu m, pulpwood 45,860,000 cu m; fish catch (2001) 847, of which freshwater fishes 299. *Mining and quarrying* (value of export production in US$'000,000; 1998): iron ore 3,066; ferroniobium 242; silicon 135; bauxite 122; kaolin (clay) 106; ferrosilicon 101; granite (1996) 97; copper 89; manganese 52; nickel 52; gold production for both domestic use and export 1,594,000 troy oz; Brazil is also a world-leading producer of high-quality grade quartz and tantalum. *Manufacturing* (value added in US$'000,000; 2001): food products 15,387; petroleum products 11,046; transport equipment 10,632, of which cars 8,103; electrical machinery 7,248; iron, steel, and nonferrous metals 7,209; industrial chemicals 5,457; paper and paper products 4,740; printing and publishing 4,304; plastics and rubber products 4,201. *Energy production (consumption):* electricity (kW-hr; 2000) 349,000,000,000 (393,000,000,000); coal (metric tons; 2001) 6,600,000 ([2000] 20,270,000); crude petroleum (barrels; 2002) 536,000,000 ([2000] 583,000,000); petroleum products (metric tons; 2000) 67,910,000 (71,664,000); natural gas (cu m; 2002) 15,517,000,000 ([2000] 7,938,000,- 000). **Land use** as % of total land area (2000): in temporary crops 6.8%, in permanent crops 0.9%, in pasture 23.2%; overall forest area 64.3%. **Population economically active** (2000; excludes rural population of Acre, Amapá, Amazonas, Pará, Rondônia, and Roraima): total 77,467,473; activity rate of total population 45.6% (participation rates: ages 15–59, 73.8%; female [1999] 40.2%; unemployed [2004] 11.2%). **Tourism** (2002): receipts from visitors US$3,120,000,000; expenditures by nationals abroad US$2,380,000,000. **Households.** Average household size (2002) 3.8. **Family income and expenditure.** Average family size (1999; excludes rural population of Acre, Amapá, Amazonas, Pará, Rondônia, and Roraima) 3.3; annual income per family (1999) R$10,500 (excludes rural population of Acre, Amapá, Amazonas, Pará, Rondônia, and Roraima); expenditure (1995–96; based on survey

---

1 metric ton = about 1.1 short tons; 1 kilometer = 0.6 mi (statute); 1 metric ton-km cargo = about 0.68 short ton-mi cargo; c.i.f.: cost, insurance, and freight; f.o.b.: free on board

of 11 metropolitan areas only): housing, energy, and household furnishings 28.8%, food and beverages 23.4%, transportation and communications 13.8%, health care 9.2%, education and recreation 8.4%.

Foreign trade

Imports (2001-f.o.b.): US$55,581,000,000 (machinery and apparatus 43.0%; chemicals and chemical products 18.1%; mineral fuels 14.4%; motor vehicles 9.5%; food products 5.0%). *Major import sources* (2002): US 21.8%; Argentina 10.1%; Germany 9.3%; Japan 5.0%; Italy 3.7%; France 3.7%; China 3.3%; UK 2.8%; Algeria 2.3%; South Korea 2.3%. Exports (2001): US$58,223,000,000 (food products 20.0%, of which meat 5.0%, sugar 4.1%, animal food 3.7%, coffee 3.0%; transportation equipment 13.6%, of which road vehicles 7.4%; machinery and apparatus 13.1%; iron and steel 5.5%; chemicals and chemical products 5.4%; iron ore and concentrates 5.0%; soybeans 4.7%). *Major export destinations* (2002): US 25.4%; The Netherlands 5.3%; Germany 4.2%; China 4.2%; Argentina 3.9%; Mexico 3.9%; Japan 3.5%; Belgium 3.1%; UK 2.9%; France 2.5%.

Transport and communications

Transport. *Railroads* (2000): route length 29,283 km; passenger-km 5,852,000,000; metric ton-km cargo 154,870,000,000. *Roads* (2000): total length 1,724,924 km (paved 10%). *Vehicles* (2001): passenger cars 23,241,966; trucks and buses 3,897,140. *Air transport* (2002; TAM, VARIG, and VASP airlines only): passenger-km 40,861,000,000; metric ton-km cargo 1,327,000,000; airports (1995) with scheduled flights 139. Communications, in total units (units per 1,000 persons). Daily newspaper circulation (2000): 7,390,000 (43); radios (2000): 74,400,000 (433); televisions (2000): 58,900,000 (343); telephone main lines (2002): 38,810,000 (223); cellular telephone subscribers (2003): 46,373,000 (264); personal computers (2002): 13,000,000 (75); Internet users (2002): 14,300,000 (82).

Education and health

Educational attainment (1996). Percentage of population age 25 and over having: no formal schooling or less than one year of primary education 17.7%; lower primary only 19.1%; upper primary 30.7%; complete primary to some secondary 11.6%; complete secondary to some higher 13.9%; complete higher 6.2%; unknown 0.8%. Literacy (2000): total population age 15 and over literate 86.4%. Health: physicians (1999) 429,808 (1 per 395 persons); hospital beds (1999) 484,945 (1 per 343 persons); infant mortality rate per 1,000 live births (2002) 31.8. Food (2001): daily per capita caloric intake 3,002 (vegetable products 80%, animal products 20%); 126% of FAO recommended minimum.

Military

Total active duty personnel (2003): 287,600 (army 65.7%, navy 16.9%, air force 17.4%). Military expenditure as percentage of GNP (1999): 1.9% (world 2.4%); per capita expenditure US$59.

Did you know? Iguaçu Falls is a series of cataracts on the Iguaçu River, 14 miles (23 km) above its confluence with the Alto Paraná River, at the Argentina-Brazil border. The falls resemble an elongated horseshoe that extends for 1.7 miles (2.7 km)—nearly three times wider than Niagara Falls in North America. In 1897 Edmundo de Barros, a Brazilian army officer, envisaged the establishment of a national park at Iguaçu Falls. Following boundary rectifications between Brazil and Argentina, two separate national parks were established, one by each country—Iguaçu National Park (1939) in Brazil and Iguazú National Park (1934) in Argentina.

Background

Little is known about Brazil's early indigenous inhabitants. Though the area was theoretically allotted to Portugal by the 1494 Treaty of Tordesillas, it was not formally claimed by discovery until Pedro Alvares Cabral accidentally touched land in 1500. It was first settled by the Portuguese in the early 1530s on the southeastern coast and at São Vicente (near modern São Paulo); the French and Dutch created small settlements over the next century. A viceroyalty was established in 1640, and Rio de Janeiro became the capital in 1763. In 1808 Brazil became the refuge and seat of the government of John VI of Portugal when Napoleon invaded Portugal; ultimately the Kingdom of Portugal, Brazil, and the Algarves was proclaimed, and John ruled from Brazil in 1815–21. On John's return to Portugal, his son Pedro I proclaimed Brazilian independence. In 1889 his successor, Pedro II, was deposed, and a constitution mandating a federal republic was adopted. The 20th century saw increased immigration and growth in manufacturing along with frequent military coups and suspensions of civil liberties. Construction of a new capital at Brasília, intended to spur development of the country's interior, worsened the inflation rate. After 1979 the military government began a gradual return to democratic practices, and in 1989 the first popular presidential election in 29 years was held.

Recent Developments

Pres. Luiz Inácio Lula da Silva, despite his long history of leftist militancy, generally continued the economic goals of his more conservative predecessor, such as achieving a primary budget surplus in accordance with an IMF agreement, keeping inflation in check, and pushing for budget cuts. With an eye toward the midterm municipal elections held in October 2004, however, the government advanced little through an agenda that included a biosecurity law, reform of the regulatory agencies, judicial reform, a public-private partnership law, independence for the central bank, an increase in the minimum wage, a bankruptcy law, and an informatics law. Instead, the federal government negotiated cabinet positions and political accords in order to advance its candidates. Clashes involving illegal miners, government forces, Indians, and landless workers took place throughout 2004 and resulted in numerous deaths. President Lula led a historic mission to China in late May during which several investment agreements were negotiated; a reciprocal visit to Brazil in mid-November was led by Chinese Pres. Hu Jintao.

Internet resources: <www.embratur.gov.br>.

Brunei

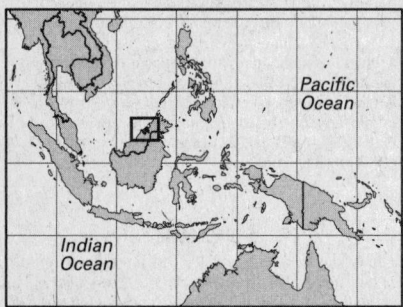

Official name: Negara Brunei Darussalam (State of Brunei, Abode of Peace). **Form of government:** monarchy (monarch is advised on legislative matters by a 21-member appointed body). **Head of state and government:** Sultan Haji Hassanal Bolkiah Muʻizzadin Waddaulah (from 1967). **Capital:** Bandar Seri Begawan. **Official language:** Malay. **Official religion:** Islam. **Monetary unit:** 1 Brunei dollar (B$) = 100 cents; valuation (7 Jul 2005) US$1 = B$1.70.

Demography

Area: 2,226 sq mi, 5,765 sq km. **Population** (2004): 351,000. **Density** (2004): persons per sq mi 157.7, persons per sq km 60.9. **Urban** (2002): 73.0%. **Sex distribution** (2002): male 52.35%; female 47.65%. **Age breakdown** (2002): under 15, 30.2%; 15–29, 27.0%; 30–44, 25.2%; 45–59, 13.2%; 60–74, 3.6%; 75 and over, 0.8%. **Ethnic composition** (2001): Malay 66.8%; Chinese 11.1%; other indigenous 3.5%; other 18.6%. **Religious affiliation** (2000): Muslim 64.4%; traditional beliefs 11.2%; Buddhist 9.1%; Christian 7.7%; other religions and nonreligious 7.6%. **Major cities:** Bandar Seri Begawan (2001) 27,285 (urban agglomeration [2002] 74,700); Kuala Belait (2002) 27,200; Seria (2002) 23,200. **Location:** southeastern Asia, bordering the South China Sea and Malaysia.

Vital statistics

Birth rate per 1,000 population (2002): 20.1 (world avg. 21.3). **Death rate** per 1,000 population (2002): 3.4 (world avg. 9.1). **Natural increase rate** per 1,000 population (2002): 16.7 (world avg. 12.2). **Total fertility rate** (avg. births per childbearing woman; 2002): 2.4. **Marriage rate** per 1,000 population (2000): 6.7. **Divorce rate** per 1,000 population (2000): 1.1. **Life expectancy** at birth (2002): male 71.7 years; female 76.6 years.

National economy

Budget (2000). *Revenue:* B$5,084,000,000 (nontax revenue 52.1%, of which government property in-

come 39.7%, commercial receipts 12.4%; tax revenue 47.6%). *Expenditures:* B$4,196,000,000 (current expenditure 83.5%; capital expenditure 9.1%; other 7.4%). **Public debt** (external, outstanding; 1999): US$902,000,000. **Tourism** (1998): receipts from visitors US$37,000,000; expenditures by nationals abroad US$1,000,000. **Production** (metric tons except as noted). *Agriculture, forestry, fishing* (2002): vegetables and melons 9,800, fruits (excluding melons) 4,150, cassava 1,800; livestock (number of live animals) 7,000 buffalo, 6,500 pigs, 12,500,000 chickens; roundwood (2001) 228,550 cu m; fish catch (2001) 1,591. *Mining and quarrying:* sand and gravel for construction. *Manufacturing* (2003): gasoline 1,717,000 barrels;' kerosene 634,000 barrels; distillate fuel oils 1,195 barrels. *Energy production (consumption):* electricity (kW-hr; 2000) 2,434,000,000 (2,434,000,000); crude petroleum (barrels; 2003) 75,600,000 ([2000] 1,700,000); petroleum products (2000) 985,000 (987,000); natural gas (cu m; 2003) 12,000,000,000 ([2001] 1,371,000,000). **Gross national product** (at current market prices; 2001): US$8,169,000,000 (US$24,630 per capita). **Population economically active** (2001): total 145,600; activity rate of total population 43.9% (participation rates: ages 15–64, 65.9%; female 41.4%; unemployed [2002] 4.6%). **Households.** Average household size (2000) ; expenditure (1990): food 38.7%, transportation and communications 19.9%, housing 18.6%, clothing 6.4%, other 16.4%. **Land use** as % of total land area (2000): in temporary crops 0.6%, in permanent crops 0.8%, in pasture 1.1%; overall forest area 83.9%.

Foreign trade

Imports (2001-c.i.f.): B$2,076,000,000 (basic manufactures 30.7%, machinery and transport equipment 30.3%, food and live animals 16.4%, chemicals and chemical products 7.6%). *Major import sources:* Singapore 23.4%; Malaysia 22.0%; US 9.2%; Japan 6.4%; Hong Kong 5.0%. **Exports** (2001-f.o.b.): B$6,522,000,000 ([1999] crude petroleum and partly refined petroleum 43.4%, natural gas 37.7%, petroleum products 2.2%). *Major export destinations* (2001): Japan 46.0%; South Korea 11.9%; Thailand 11.8%; Singapore 8.4%; US 7.5%.

Transport and communications

Transport. *Railroads:* length 19 km. *Roads* (2000): total length 3,272 km (paved 73%). *Vehicles* (2000): passenger cars 188,720; trucks and buses 17,828. *Air transport* (2003; Royal Brunei Airlines): passenger-km 3,588,000,000; metric ton-km cargo 148,703,000; airports (2001) with scheduled flights 1. **Communications,** in total units (units per 1,000 persons). Daily newspaper circulation (2002): 72,000 (213); radios (2000): 362,712 (1,120); televisions (2000): 216,223 (668); telephone main lines (2002): 90,000 (256); cellular telephone subscribers (2001): 137,000 (401); personal computers (2002): 27,000 (77); Internet users (2001): 35,000 (102).

Education and health

Educational attainment (1991). Percentage of population age 25 and over having: no formal schooling

---

1 metric ton = about 1.1 short tons; 1 kilometer = 0.6 mi (statute); 1 metric ton-km cargo = about 0.68 short ton-mi cargo; c.i.f.: cost, insurance, and freight; f.o.b.: free on board

17.0%; primary education 43.3%; secondary 26.3%; postsecondary and higher 12.9%; not stated 0.5%. **Literacy** (2000): percentage of total population age 15 and over literate 91.5%; males literate 95.0%; females literate 88.0%. **Health** (2001): physicians 371 (1 per 929 persons); hospital beds 908 (1 per 379 persons); infant mortality rate per 1,000 live births (2002) 14.0. **Food** (2001): daily per capita caloric intake 2,814 (vegetable products 80%, animal products 20%); 120% of FAO recommended minimum.

Military

Total active duty personnel (2003): 7,000 (army 70.0%, navy 14.3%, air force 15.7%). British troops (a Gurkha batallion): 1,100. **Military expenditure as percentage of GNP** (1999): 4.0% (world 2.4%); per capita expenditure US$897.

Background

Brunei traded with China in the 6th century AD. Through allegiance to the Javanese Majapahit kingdom (13th–15th century), it came under Hindu influence. In the early 15th century, with the decline of the Majapahit kingdom, many people converted to Islam, and Brunei became an independent sultanate. When Ferdinand Magellan's ships visited in 1521, the sultan of Brunei controlled almost all of Borneo and its neighboring islands. Beginning in the late 16th century, Brunei lost power because of the Portuguese, Dutch, and, later, British activities in the region. By the 19th century, the sultanate of Brunei included Sarawak (present-day Brunei) and part of North Borneo (now part of Sabah). In 1841 a revolt took place against the sultan, and a British soldier, James Brooke, helped put it down; he was later proclaimed governor. In 1847 the sultanate entered into a treaty with Great Britain and by 1906 had yielded all administration to a British Resident. Brunei rejected membership in the Federation of Malaysia in 1963, negotiated a new treaty with Britain in 1979, and achieved independence in 1984, with membership in the Commonwealth.

Recent Developments

On 15 Jul 2004, Brunei's Sultan Haji Hassanal Bolkiah MuAizzaddin Waddaulah announced that the Legislative Council, which was suspended in 1984, would be revitalized. He also stated that the 1959 constitution was being reviewed and draft amendments would soon be debated by the Legislative Council. The sultan appointed 21 Legislative Council members on 6 September; 11 were state officials, including the sultan himself. A gala royal wedding took place on 9 September as Crown Prince Haji Al-Muhtadee Billah Bolkiah married Sarah binti Pengiran Salleh Ab Rahaman, the daughter of a Bruneian father and a Swiss-born mother.

Internet resources: <www.brunei.gov.bn>.

Bulgaria

Official name: Republika Bulgariya (Republic of Bulgaria). **Form of government:** unitary multiparty republic with one legislative body (National Assembly [240]). **Chief of state:** President Georgi Purvanov

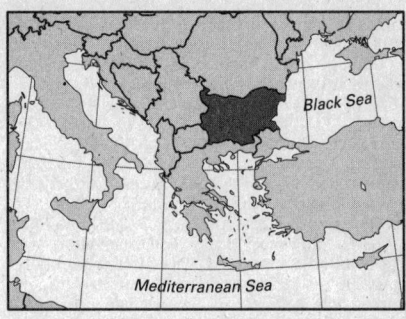

(from 2002). **Head of government:** Prime Minister Simeon Saxecoburggotski (from 2001). **Capital:** Sofia. **Official language:** Bulgarian. **Official religion:** none. **Monetary unit:** 1 lev (Lw; leva) = 100 stotinki; valuation (7 Jul 2005) $1 = 1.64 (new) leva (re-denominated in 1999 to 1 new lev = 1,000 old leva).

Demography

Area: 42,858.1 sq mi, 111,002 sq km. **Population** (2004): 7,715,000. **Density** (2004): persons per sq mi 180.0, persons per sq km 69.5. **Urban** (2001): 69.0%. **Sex distribution** (2002): male 48.68%; female 51.32%. **Age breakdown** (2002): under 15, 15.0%; 15–29, 21.3%; 30–44, 20.4%; 45–59, 20.9%; 60–74, 16.1%; 75 and over, 6.3%. **Ethnic composition** (2001): Bulgarian 83.9%; Turkish 9.4%; Rom (Gypsy) 4.7%; other 2.0%. **Religious affiliation** (2001): Christian 83.7%, of which Bulgarian Orthodox c. 72%, independent Christian c. 7%; Sunni Muslim 12.2%; other/nonreligious 4.1%. **Major cities** (2001): Sofia 1,099,507; Plovdiv 340,122; Varna 313,408; Burgas 193,316; Ruse 162,128. **Location:** southeastern Europe, bordering Romania, the Black Sea, Turkey, Greece, Macedonia, and Serbia and Montenegro.

Vital statistics

Birth rate per 1,000 population (2001): 8.6 (world avg. 21.3). **Death rate** per 1,000 population (2001): 14.2 (world avg. 9.1). **Natural increase rate** per 1,000 population (2001): –5.6 (world avg. 12.2). **Total fertility rate** (avg. births per childbearing woman; 2001): 1.2. **Life expectancy** at birth (2001): male 68.5 years; female 75.2 years.

National economy

Budget (2003). *Revenue:* 13,222,000,000 leva (tax revenue 77.7%, of which value-added tax 23.5%, social insurance 21.2%, income and profit tax 16.8%; nontax revenue 20.0%; grants 2.3%). *Expenditures:* 13,221,000,000 leva (social insurance 35.0%; capital expenditure 10.3%; health 9.5%; administration and defense 8.4%; interest on debt 5.5%). **Public debt** (external, outstanding; 2002): $7,474,000,000. **Gross national product** (2003): $16,639,000,000 ($2,130 per capita). **Production** (metric tons except as noted). *Agriculture, forestry, fishing* (2002): wheat 4,888,648, corn (maize) 1,206,000, barley 1,187,-859; livestock (number of live animals) 2,418,490 sheep, 1,013,740 pigs, 898,559 goats; roundwood (2002) 4,833,000 cu m; fish catch (2001) 8,100. *Mining and quarrying* (2000): iron (metal content)

178,000; copper (metal content) 107,000; gold 2,347 kg. *Manufacturing* (value added in $'000,000; 2001): nonelectrical machinery and apparatus 188; wearing apparel 168; food products 158. *Energy production (consumption):* electricity (kW-hr; 2001) 43,968,000,000 (43,968,000,000); hard coal (2000) 118,000 (3,379,000); lignite (2003) 27,156,000 ([2000] 25,844,000); crude petroleum (barrels; 2000) 308,000 (39,100,000); petroleum products (2000) 4,459,000 (3,064,000); natural gas (cu m; 2000) 16,313,000 (3,883,-000,000). **Household income and expenditure.** Average household size (2001) 3.0; income per household (2001) 4,532 leva ($2,280); sources of income: wages and salaries 37.8%, transfer payments 24.4%, self-employment in agriculture 14.2%; expenditure (2001): food 42.7%, housing and energy 11.5%, transportation 5.0%, health 3.7%, clothing 3.4%. **Population economically active** (2003): total 3,237,100; activity rate of total population 41.5% (participation rates [2001] age 16–59 [male], 16–54 [female] 54.2%; female [2001] 46.4%; unemployed 12.7%). **Tourism** (2002): receipts $1,344,-000,000; expenditures $616,000,000. **Land use** as % of total land area (2000): in temporary crops 40.0%, in permanent crops 1.9%, in pasture 14.6%; overall forest area 33.4%.

Foreign trade

Imports (2003-f.o.b. in balance of trade and c.i.f. for commodities and trading partners): $10,836,-000,000 (textiles 13.7%; crude petroleum and natural gas 13.6%; machinery and apparatus 13.1%; transport equipment 9.4%; plastics and rubber 4.6%. *Major import sources:* Germany 14.3%; Russia 12.6%; Italy 10.2%; Turkey 6.1%; France 5.6%. **Exports** (2003): $7,520,000,000 (clothing and footwear 21.9%; base and fabricated metals 16.1%, of which iron and steel 8.1%; machinery and transport equipment 10.3%; mineral fuels 8.4%, of which petroleum products 5.8%). *Major export destinations:* Italy 14.0%; Germany 10.8%; Greece 10.4%; Turkey 9.2%; Belgium 6.1%; France 5.1%.

Transport and communications

Transport. *Railroads* (2002): track length 6,384 km; passenger-km 2,598,000,000; metric ton-km cargo 4,628,000,000. *Roads* (2001): length 37,296 km (paved 92%). *Vehicles* (2001): cars 2,085,730; trucks and buses 288,832. *Air transport* (2001): passenger-km 1,795,400,000; metric ton-km cargo 2,335,000; airports (2000) with scheduled flights 3. **Communications,** in total units (units per 1,000 persons). Daily newspaper circulation (2000): 2,060,000 (257); radios (2001): 4,340,000 (543); televisions (2002): 3,620,000 (453); telephone main lines (2002): 2,868,200 (368); cellular telephone subscribers (2002): 2,597,500 (330); personal computers (2002): 405,000 (52); Internet users (2002): 630,000 (81).

Education and health

Educational attainment (1992). Percentage of population age 25 and over having: no formal schooling 4.7%; incomplete primary education 12.5%; primary 31.9%; secondary 35.7%; higher 15.0%. **Literacy** (2001): total population age 15 and over literate 98.5%; males 99.0%; females 98.0%. **Health** (2001): physicians 27,186 (1 per 290 persons); hospital beds 56,984 (1 per 138 persons); infant mortality rate per 1,000 live births (2001) 13.5. **Food** (2001): daily per capita caloric intake 2,626 (vegetable products 73%, animal products 27%); 105% of FAO recommended minimum.

Military

Total active duty personnel (2003): 51,000 (army 49.0%, navy 8.6%, air force 25.7%, other 16.7%). **Military expenditure as percentage of GNP** (1999): 3.0% (world 2.4%); per capita expenditure $158.

Background

Evidence of human habitation in Bulgaria dates from prehistoric times. Thracians were its first recorded inhabitants, dating from c. 3500 BC, and their first state dates from about the 5th century BC; the area was subdued by the Romans, who divided it into the provinces of Moesia and Thrace. In the 7th century AD the Bulgars took the region to the south of the Danube. The Byzantine Empire in 681 formally recognized Bulgar control over the area between the Balkans and the Danube. In the second half of the 14th century, Bulgaria fell to the Turks and ultimately lost its independence. At the end of the Russo-Turkish War (1877–78), Bulgaria rebelled. The ensuing Treaty of San Stefano was unacceptable to the Great Powers, and the Congress of Berlin (1878) resulted. In 1908 the Bulgarian ruler, Ferdinand, declared Bulgaria's independence. After its involvement in the Balkan Wars (1912–13), Bulgaria lost territory. It sided with the Central Powers in World War I and with Germany in World War II. A communist coalition seized power in 1944, and in 1946 a people's republic was declared. Like other eastern European countries in the late 1980s, Bulgaria experienced political unrest; its communist leader resigned in 1989. A new constitution proclaiming a republic was implemented in 1991. The rest of the decade brought economic turmoil.

Recent Developments

Bulgarians were pleased when, on 19 Feb 2004, the European Parliament's Foreign Affairs Committee reported favorably on Bulgaria's progress toward accession to the European Union. By the middle of June, negotiations had been completed, and Bulgaria's accession to the EU on 1 Jan 2007 was virtually guaranteed. At the end of March, Bulgaria was admitted to NATO. There was a much less happy outcome at the end of the trial of five Bulgarian nurses who, with a Palestinian doctor, were accused on the basis of questionable evidence of having deliberately infected 426 Libyan children with HIV. The accused had been in detention since 1998 and had been maltreated in prison. Sentences were delivered on 6 May, and the accused were condemned to death. The Libyan Supreme Court agreed to hear an appeal in November 2005.

Internet resources: <www.bulgaria-embassy.org>.

---

1 metric ton = about 1.1 short tons; 1 kilometer = 0.6 mi (statute); 1 metric ton-km cargo = about 0.68 short ton-mi cargo; c.i.f.: cost, insurance, and freight; f.o.b.: free on board

Burkina Faso

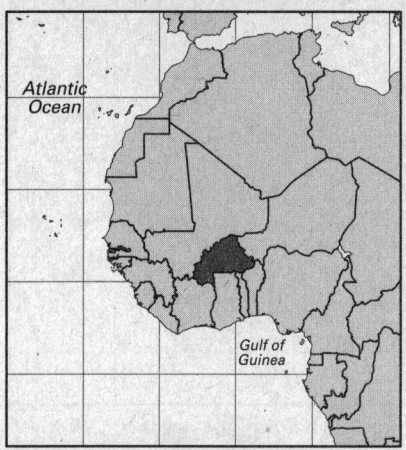

Official name: Burkina Faso. **Form of government:** multiparty republic with one legislative body (National Assembly [111]). **Chief of state:** President Blaise Compaoré (from 1987). **Head of government:** Prime Minister Ernest Paramanga Yonli (from 2000). **Capital:** Ouagadougou. **Official language:** French. **Official religion:** none. **Monetary unit:** 1 CFA franc (CFAF) = 100 centimes; valuation (7 Jul 2005) $1 = CFAF 549.50 (formerly pegged to the French franc and since 1 Jan 2002 to the euro (€) at €1 = CFAF 655.96).

Demography

Area: 103,456 sq mi, 267,950 sq km. **Population** (2004): 13,575,000. **Density** (2004): persons per sq mi 131.2, persons per sq km 50.7. **Urban** (2002): 16.9%. **Sex distribution** (2003): male 49.26%; female 50.74%. **Age breakdown** (2003): under 15, 46.1%; 15–29, 27.4%; 30–44, 14.8%; 45–59, 7.4%; 60–74, 3.7%; 75 and over, 0.8%. **Ethnic composition** (1995): Mossi 47.9%; Fulani 10.3%; Lobi 6.9%; Bobo 6.9%; Mande 6.7%; Senufo 5.3%; Grosi 5.0%; Gurma 4.8%; Tuareg 3.1%. **Religious affiliation** (2000): Muslim 48.6%; traditional beliefs 34.1%; Christian 16.7%, of which Roman Catholic 9.5%. **Major cities** (1996): Ouagadougou 709,736; Bobo-Dioulasso 309,771; Koudougou 72,490; Ouahigouya 52,193; Banfora 49,724. **Location:** western Africa, bordering Mali, Niger, Benin, Togo, Ghana, and Côte d'Ivoire.

Vital statistics

Birth rate per 1,000 population (2003): 44.8 (world avg. 21.3). **Death rate** per 1,000 population (2003): 18.8 (world avg. 9.1). **Natural increase rate** per 1,000 population (2003): 26.0 (world avg. 12.2). **Total fertility rate** (avg. births per childbearing woman; 2003): 6.3. **Life expectancy** at birth (2003): male 43.0 years; female 45.9 years. **Adult population** (ages 15–49) **living with HIV** (2004): 4.2% (world avg. 1.1%).

National economy

Budget (2002). *Revenue:* CFAF 377,000,000,000 (tax revenue 63.9%, of which sales tax 34.5%, in-

come taxes 16.4%, import duties 11.2%; grants 31.5%; nontax revenue 4.6%). *Expenditures:* CFAF 489,100,000,000 (current expenditure 52.9%, of which wages and salaries 21.1%, transfers 14.3%, goods and services 12.8%, debt service 3.4%; investment expenditure 47.1%). **Public debt** (external, outstanding; 2002): $1,399,000,000. **Households.** Average household size (2000) 6.0; expenditure (1998; Ouagadougou only): food 33.9%, transportation 15.6%, electricity and fuel 10.5%, clothing 6.4%, health 4.2%, education 3.4%. **Production** (metric tons except as noted). *Agriculture, forestry, fishing* (2002): sorghum 1,373,300, millet 994,700, corn (maize) 653,100; livestock (number of live animals) 9,450,000 goats, 7,411,000 sheep, 23,000,000 chickens; roundwood (2002) 11,994,000 cu m; fish catch (2001) 8,505. *Mining and quarrying* (2002): gold 624 kg (does not include substantial illegal production). *Manufacturing* (2002): sugar 47,743; edible oils 19,636; flour 10,005. *Energy production (consumption):* electricity (kW-hr; 2002) 361,000,000 (361,000,000); petroleum products (2001) none (294,000). **Tourism:** receipts (2002) $39,000,000; expenditures (1994) $23,000,000. **Population economically active** (1996): total 5,075,615; activity rate 49.2% (participation rates: over age 10, 70.0%; female 48.2%; unemployed 1.4%). **Gross national product** (at current market prices; 2003): $3,587,000,000 ($300 per capita). **Land use** as % of total land area (2000): in temporary crops 13.9%, in permanent crops 0.2%, in pasture 21.9%; overall forest area 25.9%.

Foreign trade

Imports (2002): CFAF 381,700,000,000 (capital equipment 32.6%, petroleum products 18.6%, food products 12.7%, raw materials 10.1%). *Major import sources:* France 19.6%; Côte d'Ivoire 18.8%; Japan 9.3%; Germany 6.0%; US 3.3%. **Exports** (2002): CFAF 164,200,000,000 (raw cotton 54.1%, hides and skins 11.0%, live animals 8.8%, shea nuts 2.6%, gold 2.0%). *Major export destinations:* France 45.3%; Côte d'Ivoire 9.2%; Singapore 5.1%; Mali 4.0%; Japan 3.0%.

Transport and communications

Transport. *Railroads:* (2002) route length 622 km; (1995) passenger-km 202,000,000; (1995) metric ton-km cargo 45,000,000. *Roads* (1999): total length 10,469 km (paved 19%). *Vehicles* (1999): passenger cars 26,300; trucks and buses 19,600. *Air transport* (2000; Air Afrique, an airline jointly owned by 11 African countries including Burkina Faso, was declared bankrupt in February 2002): passenger-km 247,000,000; airports 2. **Communications**, in total units (units per 1,000 persons). Daily newspaper circulation (2000): 12,200 (1); radios (2000): 428,000 (35); televisions (2000): 147,000 (12); telephone main lines (2003): 65,400 (5.3); cellular telephone subscribers (2003): 227,000 (19); personal computers (2003): 26,000 (2.1); Internet users (2003): 48,000 (3.9).

Education and health

Educational attainment (1985). Percentage of population age 10 and over having: no formal schooling 86.1%; some primary 7.3%; general secondary 2.2%; specialized secondary and postsecondary 3.8%; other 0.6%. **Literacy** (2000): percentage of total population age 15 and over literate 23.9%; males literate 33.9%; females literate 14.1%. **Health** (1995): physicians 361 (1 per 29,385 persons); hospital beds (1991) 5,041 (1 per 1,837 persons); infant mortality rate per 1,000 live births (2003) 99.8. **Food** (2001): daily per capita caloric intake 2,485 (vegetable products 95%, animal products 5%); 105% of FAO recommended minimum.

Military

Total active duty personnel (2003): 10,800 (army 98.1%, air force 1.9%). **Military expenditure as percentage of GNP** (1999): 1.6% (world 2.4%); per capita expenditure $4.

Background

Probably in the 14th century, the Mossi and Gurma peoples established themselves in eastern and central areas of what is now Burkina Faso. The Mossi kingdoms of Yatenga and Ouagadougou existed into the early 20th century. A French protectorate was established over the region (1895–97), and its southern boundary was demarcated through an Anglo-French agreement. It was part of the Upper Senegal–Niger colony, then became a separate colony in 1919. Named Upper Volta, it was constituted an overseas territory within the French Union in 1947, became an autonomous republic within the French Community in 1958, and achieved total independence in 1960. Since then, the country has been ruled primarily by the military and has experienced several coups; following one in 1983, the country received its present name. A new constitution, adopted in 1991, restored multiparty rule.

Recent Developments

Preparations for the 2005 presidential elections got off to an early start after a cabinet minister revealed in January 2004 that Pres. Blaise Compaoré would be a candidate. A 2000 amendment to Burkina Faso's constitution was ambiguous as to whether the provisions for a renewable term were applicable to the incumbent, i.e., Compaoré. On 27 Apr 2004 the National Assembly, dominated by the ruling Congress for Democracy and Progress Party, adopted a new electoral code that opposition parties claimed would make it more difficult for small parties to contest legislative and municipal elections.

Internet resources: <www.burkinaembassy-usa.org>.

Burundi

Official name: Republika y'u Burundi (Rundi); République du Burundi (French) (Republic of Burundi). **Form of government:** transitional regime with one legislative body (Transitional Assembly [178]). **Head of state and government:** President Domitien Ndayizeye (from 2003), assisted by Vice President Frederic Ngenzebuhoro (from 11 Nov 2004). **Capital:** Bujumbura. **Official languages:** Rundi; French. **Official religion:** none. **Monetary unit:** 1 Burundi franc (FBu) = 100 centimes; valuation (7 Jul 2005) $1 = FBu 1,086.25.

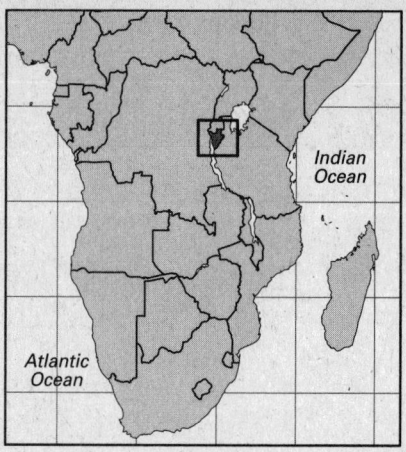

Demography

Area: 10,740 sq mi, 27,816 sq km. **Population** (2004): 6,231,000. **Density** (2004): persons per sq mi 621.9, persons per sq km 243.5. **Urban** (2002): 9.3%. **Sex distribution** (2003): male 49.57%; female 50.43%. **Age breakdown** (2003): under 15, 46.7%; 15–29, 28.8%; 30–44, 13.4%; 45–59, 7.1%; 60–74, 3.1%; 75 and over, 0.9%. **Ethnic composition** (2000): Hutu 80.9%; Tutsi 15.6%; Lingala 1.6%; Twa Pygmy 1.0%; other 0.9%. **Religious affiliation** (2000): Roman Catholic 57.2%; Protestant 19.5%; unaffiliated Christian 14.7%; traditional beliefs 6.7%; Muslim 1.4%; other 0.5%. **Major cities** (2004): Bujumbura 340,300; Gitega 46,900; Muyinga 45,300; Ngozi 40,200; Ruyigi 36,800. **Location:** central Africa, bordering Rwanda, Tanzania, Lake Tanganyika, and the Democratic Republic of the Congo.

Vital statistics

Birth rate per 1,000 population (2003): 39.7 (world avg. 21.3). **Death rate** per 1,000 population (2003): 17.8 (world avg. 9.1). **Natural increase rate** per 1,000 population (2003): 21.9 (world avg. 12.2). **Total fertility rate** (avg. births per childbearing woman; 2003): 6.0. **Life expectancy** at birth (2003): male 42.5 years; female 43.9 years. **Adult population** (ages 15–49) **living with HIV** (2004): 6.0% (world avg. 1.1%).

National economy

Budget (2002). *Revenue:* FBu 118,400,000,000 (tax revenue 88.5%, of which taxes on goods and services 43.8%, income tax 24.8%, taxes on international trade 19.6%; nontax revenue 11.5%). *Expenditures:* FBu 151,600,000,000 (current expenditure 79.0%; capital expenditure 21.0%). **Public debt** (external, outstanding; 2002): $1,095,000,000. **Production** (metric tons except as noted). *Agriculture, forestry, fishing* (2003): bananas 1,600,000, sweet potatoes 835,000, cassava 750,000; livestock (number of live animals) 750,000 goats, 325,000 cattle, 4,300,000 chickens; roundwood (2002) 8,428,000 cu m; fish catch (2001) 9,064. *Mining and quarrying* (2001): gemstones 16,500 kg; gold 415 kg. *Manufacturing*

1 metric ton = about 1.1 short tons;   1 kilometer = 0.6 mi (statute);   1 metric ton-km cargo = about 0.68 short ton-mi cargo;   c.i.f.: cost, insurance, and freight;   f.o.b.: free on board

(2003): beer 580,226 hectoliters; carbonated beverages 82,367 hectoliters; cottonseed oil 25,000 liters. **Energy production (consumption):** electricity (kW-hr; 2001) 107,774,000 (108,800,000); petroleum products (2001) none (48,093); peat (2000) 12,000 (12,000). **Households.** Average household size (2000) 5.1; expenditure: (1991) food 51.9%, energy and housing 27.0%, transportation 5.3%, clothing 5.3%. **Land use** as % of total land area (2000): in temporary crops 35.0%, in permanent crops 14.0%, in pasture 36.4%; overall forest area 3.7%. **Gross national product** (at current market prices; 2003): $702,000,000 ($100 per capita). **Population economically active** (1997): total 3,475,000; activity rate of total population 63.1% (participation rates [1991]: ages 15–64, 91.4%; female 48.9%). **Tourism** (2002): receipts from visitors $1,100,000; expenditures by nationals abroad $14,000,000.

Foreign trade

Imports (2002): $103,900,000 (consumption goods 45.0%, of which food and food products 12.4%; capital goods 30.8%; petroleum products 15.3%). *Major import sources:* Belgium 16.4%; Kenya 12.1%; Tanzania 10.3%; France 7.0%; Japan 5.7%. **Exports** (2002): $31,200,000 (coffee 53.9%, tea 28.5%, manufactured products 12.9%). *Major export destinations:* UK 18.9%; Kenya 18.7%; Rwanda 10.1%; Belgium 8.5%; The Netherlands 5.2%.

Transport and communications

Transport. *Roads* (1999): total length 14,480 km (paved 7%). *Vehicles* (1999): passenger cars 6,900; trucks and other vehicles 9,300. *Air transport* (2000; Bujumbura airport only): passenger arrivals and departures 58,402; cargo loaded and unloaded 3,905 metric tons; airports (2002) 1. **Communications,** in total units (units per 1,000 persons). Daily newspaper circulation (1996): 20,000 (3.2); radios (2000): 1,260,000 (220); televisions (2002): 220,000 (31); telephone main lines (2003): 23,900 (3.4); cellular telephone subscribers (2003): 64,000 (9); Internet users (2003): 14,000 (1.8).

Education and health

Literacy (2000): percentage of total population age 15 and over literate 48.0%; males literate 56.2%; females literate 40.4%. **Health** (1999): physicians 357 (1 per 15,695 persons); hospital beds 3,380 (1 per 1,657 persons); infant mortality rate per 1,000 live births (2003) 71.5. **Food** (2001): daily per capita caloric intake 1,612 (vegetable products 98%, animal products 2%); 72% of FAO recommended minimum.

Military

Total active duty personnel (2003): 50,500 (army 100%); UN peacekeeping troops (2004) 2,700. **Military expenditure as percentage of GNP** (1999): 7.0% (world 2.4%); per capita expenditure $8.

Background

Original settlement by the Twa people was followed by Hutu settlement, which occurred gradually and was completed by the 11th century. The Tutsi arrived 300–400 years later; though a minority, they established the kingdom of Burundi in the 16th century. In the 19th century the area came within the German sphere of influence, but the Tutsi remained in power. Following World War I the Belgians took control of the area, which became a UN trusteeship after World War II. Colonial-period conditions had intensified Hutu-Tutsi ethnic animosities, and as independence neared, hostilities flared. Independence was granted in 1962 in the form of a kingdom ruled by the Tutsi. In 1965 the Hutu rebelled but were brutally repressed. The rest of the 20th century saw violent clashes between the two groups, leading to charges of genocide in the 1990s. The very unstable government that existed in these surroundings was overthrown by the military in 1996.

Recent Developments

A political timetable to restore peace and stability to Burundi was agreed upon by the government and the largest insurgency group, the Forces for Defense of Democracy, although a major Hutu rebel group kept on fighting. A new constitution under which power would be divided according to a formula between Hutu and Tutsi was overwhelmingly approved on schedule by voters in February 2005, but the presidential elections slated for late April had to be postponed until August.

Internet resources: <www.burundi.gov.bi>.

Cambodia

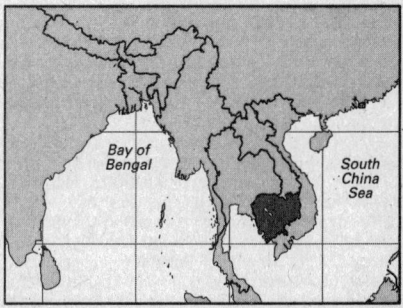

Bay of Bengal   *South China Sea*

Official name: Preah Reach Ana Pak Kampuchea (Kingdom of Cambodia). **Form of government:** constitutional monarchy with two legislative houses (Senate [61; all seats appointed in 1999; all seats to be elected in future]; National Assembly [123]). **Chief of state:** King Norodom Sihamoni (from 14 Oct 2004). **Head of government:** Prime Minister Hun Sen (from 1998). **Capital:** Phnom Penh. **Official language:** Khmer. **Official religion:** Buddhism. **Monetary unit:** 1 riel = 100 sen; valuation (7 Jul 2005) $1 = 4,109 riels.

Demography

Area: 69,898 sq mi, 181,035 sq km. **Population** (2004): 13,470,000. **Density** (2004): persons per sq mi 196.0, persons per sq km 75.7. **Urban** (2002): 17.0%. **Sex distribution** (2003): male 48.60%; female 51.40%. **Age breakdown** (2003): under 15, 39.3%; 15–29, 28.8%; 30–44, 18.5%; 45–59, 8.8%; 60–74, 3.7%; 75 and over, 0.9%. **Ethnic composition** (2000): Khmer 85.2%; Chinese 6.4%; Vietnamese 3.0%; Cham 2.5%; Lao 0.6%; other 2.3%. **Religious affiliation** (2000): Buddhist 84.7%; Chinese folk religionist 4.7%; traditional beliefs 4.3%; Muslim 2.3%; Christian 1.1%; other 2.9%. **Major urban areas** (1998): Phnom Penh (2003) 1,157,000; Bat Dambang 124,290; Sisophon 85,382; Siem Reab 83,715; Preah Sihanouk 66,723. **Location**: southeastern Asia, bordering Thailand, Laos, Vietnam, and the Gulf of Thailand.

Vital statistics

Birth rate per 1,000 population (2003): 27.3 (world avg. 21.3). **Death rate** per 1,000 population (2003): 9.3 (world avg. 9.1). **Natural increase rate** per 1,000 population (2003): 18.0 (world avg. 12.2). **Total fertility rate** (avg. births per childbearing woman; 2003): 3.7. **Life expectancy** at birth (2003): male 55.5 years; female 60.5 years.

National economy

Budget (2001). *Revenue*: 1,520,000,000,000 riels (indirect taxes 37.6%, of which value-added taxes 26.5%; taxes on international trade 24.7%; nontax revenue 27.9%). *Expenditures*: 2,329,000,000,000 riels (current expenditure 58.1%, of which civil administration 30.2%, defense and security 16.7%; development expenditure 41.9%). **Public debt** (external, outstanding; 2002): $2,594,000,000. **Production** (metric tons except as noted). *Agriculture, forestry, fishing* (2002): rice 3,740,002, cassava 186,800, corn (maize) 168,700; livestock (number of live animals) 2,924,457 cattle, 2,105,435 pigs, 625,912 buffalo; roundwood (2002) 9,858,000 cu m; fish catch (2001) 412,700. *Mining and quarrying*: legal mining is confined to fertilizers, salt, and construction materials. *Manufacturing* (value added in $'000,000; 2000): wearing apparel 626; textiles 479; leather products 105. *Energy production (consumption)*: electricity (kW-hr; 2000) 229,000,000 (229,000,000); petroleum products (2000) negligible (173,000). **Households**. Average household size (2000) 5.7; household expenditure (2002): food, beverages, and tobacco 62.6%, housing and energy 19.7%, health 6.0%, transportation and communications 3.4%. **Gross national product** (2003): $4,105,-000,000 ($310 per capita). **Population economically active** (2002): total 6,399,677; activity rate of total population 48.8% (participation rates [2000]: ages 15 and over, 69.9%; female 54.6%; unemployed 5.3%). **Tourism** (2002): receipts $379,000,000; expenditures $38,000,000. **Land use** as % of total land area (2000): in temporary crops 21.0%, in permanent crops 0.6%, in pasture 8.5%; overall forest area 52.9%.

Foreign trade

Imports (2001): $1,951,000,000 (retained imports 91.1%; imports for reexport 8.9%). *Major import sources* (2002): Thailand 30.2%; Singapore 21.5%; Hong Kong 10.2%; China 7.7%; Vietnam 6.6%. **Exports** (2001): $1,475,000,000 (domestic exports 87.8%, of which garments c. 75%, rubber 3.4%, sawn timber and logs 2.2%; reexports 12.2%). *Major export destinations* (2002): US 61.4%; Germany 8.9%; UK 7.2%.

Transport and communcations

Transport. *Railroads* (1999): length 649 km; passenger-km 49,894,000; metric ton-km 76,171,000.

Roads (1999): total length 35,769 km (paved 12%). *Vehicles* (2002): passenger cars 209,128; trucks and buses 33,164. *Air transport* (2002; combined total of Imtrec Aviation, Phnom Penh Airways, President Airlines, and Siem Reap Airways): passenger-km 60,900,000; metric ton-km cargo 4,100,000; airports (1997) with scheduled flights 8. **Communications**, in total units (units per 1,000 persons). Daily newspaper circulation (2000): 24,000 (2); radios (2000): 1,480,000 (119); televisions (2000): 99,500 (8); telephone main lines (2002): 35,400 (2.6); cellular telephone subscribers (2002): 380,000 (28); personal computers (2002): 27,000 (2); Internet users (2002): 30,000 (2.2).

Education and health

Educational attainment (1998). Percentage of population age 25 and over having: no formal schooling 2.1%; some primary education 56.6%; primary 24.7%; some secondary 11.8%; secondary and above 4.8%. **Literacy** (2000): percentage of total population age 15 and over literate 68.5%; males literate 79.8%; females literate 57.1%. **Health** (2001): physicians 2,047 (1 per 5,862 persons); hospital beds 10,900 (1 per 1,100 persons); infant mortality rate per 1,000 live births (2003) 75.9. **Food** (2001): daily per capita caloric intake 1,967 (vegetable products 91%, animal products 9%); 89% of FAO recommended minimum.

Military

Total active duty personnel (2003; excludes paramilitary forces): 125,000 (army 60.0%, navy 2.4%, air force 1.6%, provincial forces 36.0%). **Military expenditure as percentage of GNP** (1999): 4.0% (world 2.4%); per capita expenditure $28.

Did you know? Angkor was the capital of the Khmer (Cambodian) empire from the 9th to the 15th century AD. Its most imposing monuments are Angkor Wat, a temple complex built in the 12th century by King Suryavarman II (reigned 1113-c. 1150), and Angkor Thom, a temple complex built about 1200 by King Jayavarman VII.

Background

In the early Christian era, what is now Cambodia was under Hindu and, to a lesser extent, Buddhist influence. The Khmer state gradually spread in the early 7th century and reached its height under Jayavarman II and his successors in the 9th–12th centuries, when it ruled the Mekong Valley and the tributary Shan states and built Angkor. Widespread adoption of Buddhism occurred in the 13th century, resulting in a script change from Sanskrit to Pali. From the 13th century Cambodia was attacked by Annam and Siamese city-states and was alternately a province of one or the other. The area became a French protectorate in 1863. It was occupied by the Japanese in World War II and became independent in 1954. Cambodia's borders were the scene of fighting in the Vietnam War from 1961, and in 1970 its northeast-

---

1 metric ton = about 1.1 short tons; 1 kilometer = 0.6 mi (statute); 1 metric ton-km cargo = about 0.68 short ton-mi cargo; c.i.f.: cost, insurance, and freight; f.o.b.: free on board

ern and eastern areas were occupied by the North Vietnamese and penetrated by US and South Vietnamese forces. An indiscriminate US bombing campaign alienated much of the population, enabling the communist Khmer Rouge under Pol Pot to seize power in 1975. Their regime of terror resulted in the deaths of at least one million Cambodians. Vietnam invaded in 1979 and drove the Khmer Rouge into the western hinterlands, but it was unable to effect reconstruction of the country, and Cambodian infighting continued. A peace accord was reached by most Cambodian factions under UN auspices in 1991, and elections were held in 1993. Civil and military unrest continued, however. In 1997 King Norodom Sihanouk left the country, which was on the verge of civil war.

Recent Developments

Political deadlock between the majority Cambodian People's Party (CPP) of Prime Minister Hun Sen and the two other major royalist parties began in Cambodia after the July 2003 elections. It lasted nearly a year. Although it did not seem to affect the everyday workings of the government, it meant that the National Assembly did not meet and no new ministers were appointed. On 7 Oct 2004 King Norodom Sihanouk abdicated. The 81-year-old king was in poor health, complained of being insufficiently consulted in the formation of the government, and pushed for a clearer legal definition of royal succession to be put in place before his death. The National Assembly quickly enacted legislation to create a throne council, which in turn named as king Norodom Sihamondi, Sihanouk's son, who was formerly a ballet dancer and Cambodian representative to UNESCO.

Internet resources: <www.cambodia.org>.

Cameroon

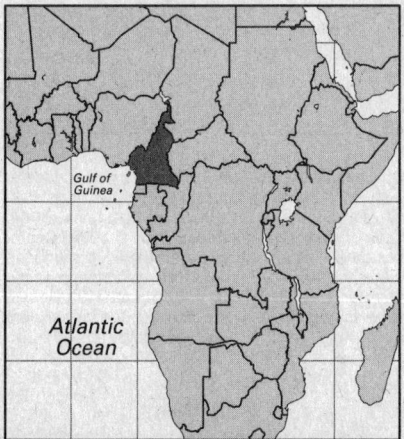

Gulf of
Guinea

Atlantic
Ocean

Official name: République du Cameroun (French); Republic of Cameroon (English). Form of government: unitary multiparty republic with one legislative house (National Assembly [180]). Chief of state: President Paul Biya (from 1982). Head of government: Prime Minister Ephraïm Inoni (from 8 Dec 2004). Capital: Yaoundé. Official languages: French; English. Official

religion: none. Monetary unit: 1 CFA franc (CFAF) = 100 centimes; valuation (7 Jul 2005) $1 = CFAF 549.50 (formerly pegged to the French franc and, since 1 Jan 2002, to the euro [€] at the rate of €1 = CFAF 655.96).

Demography

Area: 183,569 sq mi, 475,442 sq km. Population (2004): 16,064,000. Density (2004; based on land area): persons per sq mi 89.5, persons per sq km 34.5. Urban (2002): 49.7%. Sex distribution (2003): male 50.27%; female 49.73%. Age breakdown (2003): under 15, 42.3%; 15–29, 29.0%; 30–44, 15.3%; 45–59, 8.4%; 60–74, 4.0%; 75 and over, 0.9%. Ethnic composition (1983): Fang 19.6%; Bamileke and Bamum 18.5%; Duala, Luanda, and Basa 14.7%; Fulani 9.6%; Tikar 7.4%; Mandara 5.7%; Maka 4.9%; Chamba 2.4%; Mbum 1.3%; Hausa 1.2%; French 0.2%; other 14.5%. Religious affiliation (2000): Roman Catholic 26.4%; traditional beliefs 23.7%; Muslim 21.2%; Protestant 20.7%. Major cities (2002): Douala 1,239,100; Yaoundé 1,122,500; Garoua 185,800; Maroua 169,200; Bafoussam 151,800. Location: western Africa, bordering Chad, Central African Republic, Republic of the Congo, Gabon, Equatorial Guinea, the Bight of Biafra and Nigeria.

Vital statistics

Birth rate per 1,000 population (2003): 35.5 (world avg. 21.3). Death rate per 1,000 population (2003): 15.3 (world avg. 9.1). Natural increase rate per 1,000 population (2003): 20.2 (world avg. 12.2). Total fertility rate (avg. births per childbearing woman; 2003): 4.6. Life expectancy at birth (2003): male 47.2 years; female 49.0 years. Adult population (ages 15–49) living with HIV (2004): 6.9% (world avg. 1.1%).

National economy

Budget (2000–01). Revenue: CFAF 1,326,000,-000,000 (oil revenue 33.0%; taxes on goods and services 32.9%; income tax 16.6%; customs duties 11.2%). Expenditures: CFAF 1,175,000,000,000 (current expenditure 80.9%, of which wages and salaries 28.8%, debt service 20.9%, goods and services 20.0%, transfers 11.3%; capital expenditure 19.1%). Public debt (external, outstanding; 2002): $7,240,-000,000. Gross national product (2003): $10,287,-000,000 ($640 per capita). Households. Average household size (2000) 5.5; expenditure (1993): food 49.1%, housing 18.0%, transportation and communications 13.0%, health 8.6%, clothing 7.6%, recreation 2.4%. Tourism (2000): receipts $39,000,000; expenditures (1995) $105,000,000. Population economically active (1991): total 4,740,000; activity rate of total population 40.0% (participation rates [1985]: ages 15–69, 66.3%; female 38.5%). Production (metric tons except as noted). Agriculture, forestry, fishing (2002): cassava 1,900,000; sugarcane 1,350,000, plantains 1,200,000; livestock (number of live animals) 5,900,000 cattle, 4,400,000 goats, 3,800,000 sheep; roundwood (2002) 10,526,000 cu m; fish catch (2001) 111,100. Mining and quarrying (2002): pozzolana 620,000; aluminum 80,000; gold 1,000 kg. Manufacturing (value added in $'000; 1999): beverages 182; food products 149; textiles 112. Energy production (consumption): electricity (kW-hr; 2000) 3,441,000,000 (3,441,000,000); coal (2000) 1,000 (1,000); crude petroleum (barrels; 2000) 52,000,000

(10,700,000); petroleum products (2000) 1,530,000 (898,000). **Land use** as % of total land area (2000): in temporary crops 12.8%, in permanent crops 2.6%, in pasture 4.3%; overall forest area 51.3%.

Foreign trade

Imports (2000–01): CFAF 1,157,800,000,000 (minerals and other raw materials c. 21%, semifinished goods c. 16%, industrial equipment c. 13%, food and beverages c. 11%, transport equipment c. 10%). *Major import sources:* France c. 24%; Nigeria c. 20%; Germany c. 5%; US c. 5%; Japan c. 5%; Belgium-Luxembourg c. 5%. **Exports** (2000–01): CFAF 1,540,200,-000,000 (crude petroleum c. 50.6%, lumber c. 13.4%, cocoa beans c. 6.3%, aluminum c. 4.6%, cotton c. 4.2%, coffee c. 3.7%). *Major export destinations:* Italy c. 24%; France c. 9%; Spain c. 9%; The Netherlands c. 7%; China c. 7%; Taiwan c. 7%.

Transport and communications

Transport. *Railroads* (2001): route length 1,016 km; passenger-km 237,800,000; metric ton-km cargo 854,600,000. *Roads* (1999): total length 49,300 km (paved 8%). *Vehicles* (1997): passenger cars 98,000; trucks and buses 64,350. *Air transport* (2001): passenger-km 796,567,000; metric ton-km cargo 23,255,000; airports (1998) with scheduled flights 5. **Communications,** in total units (units per 1,000 persons). Daily newspaper circulation (2000): 104,-000 (7); radios (2000): 2,410,000 (163); televisions (2000): 503,000 (34); telephone main lines (2002): 110,900 (7); cellular telephone subscribers (2003): 1,077,000 (66); personal computers (2002): 90,000 (5.7); Internet users (2002): 60,000 (3.8).

Education and health

Literacy (2001): percentage of total population age 15 and over literate 72.5%; males literate 79.9%; females literate 65.1%. **Health:** physicians (1996) 1,031 (1 per 13,510 persons); hospital beds (1988) 29,285 (1 per 371 persons); infant mortality rate per 1,000 live births (2003) 70.1. **Food** (2001): daily per capita caloric intake 2,242 (vegetable products 94%, animal products 6%); 97% of FAO recommended minimum.

Military

Total active duty personnel (2003): 14,100 (army 88.7%, navy 9.2%, air force 2.1%). **Military expenditure as percentage of GNP** (1999): 1.8% (world 2.4%); per capita expenditure $10.

Background

The Cameroon area had long been inhabited before European colonization. Bantu speakers from equatorial Africa settled in the south, followed by Muslim Fulani from the Niger River basin, who settled in the north. Portuguese explorers visited in the late 15th century and established a foothold, but they lost control to the Dutch in the 17th century. In 1884 the Germans took control and extended their protectorate over Cameroon. In World War I joint French-British action forced the Germans to retreat, and after the war the region was divided into French and British admin-

istrative zones. After World War II the two areas became UN trusteeships. In 1960 the French trust territory became an independent republic. In 1961 the southern part of the British trust territory voted for union with the new republic of Cameroon, and the northern part for union with Nigeria. In recent decades economic problems have produced unrest in the country.

Recent Developments

Cameroon's main opposition parties once again faced failure in their efforts to defeat Pres. Paul Biya's bid for a third term in the election held on 11 Oct 2004. Election turnout was high, and Biya won handily with about 75% of the vote. Biya attended ceremonies on 15 August marking the 60th anniversary of the World War II liberation of Provence in southern France, in which Cameroonians, serving in the Tirailleurs Sénégalais alongside thousands of other West African troops, played a major role.

Internet resources:
<www.cameroon.net/cameroon-guide.php>.

Canada

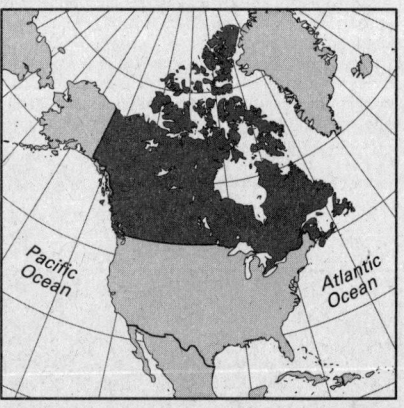

Official name: Canada. **Form of government:** federal multiparty parliamentary state with two legislative houses (Senate [105]; House of Commons [308]). **Chief of state:** Queen Elizabeth II (from 1952). **Representative of chief of state:** Governor-General Adrienne Clarkson (from 1999). **Head of government:** Prime Minister Paul Martin (from 2003). **Capital:** Ottawa. **Official languages:** English; French. **Official religion:** none. **Monetary unit:** 1 Canadian dollar (Can$) = 100 cents; valuation (7 Jul 2005) US$1 = Can$1.24.

Demography

Area: 3,855,103 sq mi, 9,984,670 sq km. **Population** (2004): 31,876,000. **Density** (2004; based on land area of 3,551,023 sq mi [9,093,507 sq km]): persons per sq mi 9.0, persons per sq km 3.5. **Urban** (2001): 78.9%. **Sex distribution** (2003): male 49.51%; female 50.49%. **Age breakdown** (2003):

1 metric ton = about 1.1 short tons;   1 kilometer = 0.6 mi (statute);   1 metric ton-km cargo = about 0.68 short ton-mi cargo;   c.i.f.: cost, insurance, and freight;   f.o.b.: free on board

under 15, 18.3%; 15–29, 20.3%; 30–44, 23.4%; 45–59, 20.7%; 60–74, 11.3%; 75 and over, 6.0%. **Ethnic origin** (2000): Anglo-Canadian 45.5%; French-Canadian 23.5%; Chinese 3.4%; British expatriates 3.3%; Indo-Pakistani 2.6%, of which Punjabi 2.3%; German 2.4%; Italian 2.2%; US white 1.8%; Métis (part-Indian) 1.8%; Indian 1.5%, of which detribalized 0.5%; Jewish 1.4%; Arab 1.3%; Ukrainian 1.2%; Eskimo (Inuit) 0.1%; other 8.0%. **Religious affiliation** (2001): Christian 77.1%, of which Roman Catholic 43.2%, Protestant 28.3%, unspecified Christian 2.6%, Orthodox 1.7%, other Christian 1.3%; Muslim 2.0%; Jewish 1.1%; Hindu 1.0%; Buddhist 1.0%; Sikh 0.9%; nonreligious 16.5%; other 0.4%. **Major metropolitan areas** (2002): Toronto 5,029,900; Montreal 3,548,800; Vancouver 2,122,700; Ottawa-Hull 1,128,900; Calgary 993,200; Edmonton 967,200; Quebec 697,800; Hamilton 686,900; Winnipeg 685,500; Kitchener 438,000. **Location:** northern North America, bordering the Arctic Ocean, the North Atlantic Ocean, the US, and the North Pacific Ocean. **Place of birth** (2001): 81.6% native-born; 18.4% foreign-born, of which UK 2.0%, other European 5.7%, Asian countries 5.8%, US 0.8%, other 4.1%. **Mobility** (2001). Population living in the same residence as in 1996: 58.1%; different residence, same municipality 22.4%; same province, different municipality 3.3%; different province 12.7%; different country 3.5%. **Households.** Total number of households (2002) 11,657,730. Average household size (2002) 2.7; 1 person (1997) 25.2%, 2 persons 33.0%, 3 persons 16.7%, 4 persons 16.3%, 5 or more persons 8.8%. Family households (2001): 8,371,020 (72.4%), nonfamily 3,191,955 (27.6%, of which 1 person 75.6%). **Immigration** (2002): permanent immigrants admitted 222,447; (2000) from Asia 62.1%, of which India 11.6%, Philippines 5.6%, Vietnam 0.7%, Hong Kong 0.3%; US 2.4%; UK 2.1%; refugee arrivals (2002) 27,899.

Vital statistics

Birth rate per 1,000 population (2003): 10.5 (world avg. 21.3); (1997) legitimate 72.3%. **Death rate** per 1,000 population (2003): 7.2 (world avg. 9.1). **Natural increase rate** per 1,000 population (2003): 3.3 (world avg. 12.2). **Total fertility rate** (avg. births per childbearing woman; 2002): 1.6. **Marriage rate** per 1,000 population (2003): 4.8. **Divorce rate** per 1,000 population (2003): 2.2. **Life expectancy** at birth (2003): male 76.4 years; female 83.4 years.

Social indicators

Quality of working life. Average workweek (2000): 31.6 hours. Annual rate per 100,000 workers for (1997): injury, accident, or industrial illness 1,330; death 2.7. Average days lost to labor stoppages per 1,000 employee-workdays (2001): 0.7. Average commuting distance (2001): 4.5 mi, 7.2 km; mode of transportation: automobile 80.7%, public transportation 10.5%, walking 6.6%, other 2.2%. Labor force covered by a pension plan (2001): 33.6%. **Access to services.** Proportion of households having access to: electricity (2002) 100.0%; public water supply (1996) 99.8%; public sewage collection (1996) 99.3%. **Social participation.** Eligible voters participating in last national election (June 2004): 60.5%. Population over 18 years of age participating in voluntary work (2000): 26.7%. Union membership as percentage of civilian labor force (2003) 25.0%. Attendance at reli-

gious services on a weekly basis (2001): 20.0%. **Social deviance** (2003). Offense rate per 100,000 population for: violent crime 962.8, of which assault 746.5, sexual assault 74.1, homicide 1.7; property crime 4,121, of which auto theft 541, burglary 900. **Leisure** (1998). Favorite leisure activities (hours weekly): television (2002) 21.6; social time 13.3; reading 2.8; sports and entertainment 1.4. **Material well-being** (1999). Households possessing: automobile 64.4%; telephone 98.2%; cellular phone 31.9%; color television 99.9%; central air conditioner 34.0%; cable television 73.3%; home computers 49.8%; Internet access 33.1%.

National economy

Gross national product (2003): US$756,770,-000,000 (US$23,930 per capita). **Budget** (2003–04; federal revenues and expenditures). *Revenue:* Can$204,075,000,000 (income tax 60.8%, sales tax 21.6%, contributions to social security 10.8%, other 6.8%). *Expenditures:* Can$197,296,000,000 (social services and welfare 37.9%, defense and social protection 13.0%, public debt interest 12.1%, economy 3.9%, health 3.1%, education 2.4%). **Public debt** (2001): US$406,000,000,000. **Tourism** (2002): receipts US$9,700,000,000; expenditures US$9,929,-000,000. **Production** (metric tons except as noted). *Agriculture, forestry, fishing* (2002): wheat 15,689,-000, corn (maize) 9,069,000, barley 7,282,600, potatoes 4,645,000, rapeseed 3,577,100, oats 2,748,000, vegetables 2,435,000 (of which tomatoes 690,000, carrots 280,000, onions 190,000, cabbage 160,000), soybeans 2,334,000, dry peas 1,365,000, linseed 679,400, sugar beets 540,000, apples 460,000; livestock (number of live animals) 14,367,100 pigs, 13,699,500 cattle, 993,600 sheep; roundwood (2002) 193,168,000 cu m; fish catch (2001) 1,116,902. *Mining and quarrying* (value of production in Can$'000,000; 2002): gold 2,292; nickel 1,883; potash 1,598; copper 1,419; iron ore 1,392; zinc 1,090; sand and gravel 1,047; stone 972; diamonds 802. *Manufacturing* (value of shipments in Can$'000,000; 2002): transportation equipment 119,746; food 62,911; chemicals 37,679; paper products 32,726; petroleum and coal 32,250; primary metals 32,216; wood industries 29,498; fabricated metal products 27,510; machinery 24,113; rubber and plastic products 23,002; computers and electronic products 21,255. *Energy production (consumption):* electricity (kW-hr; 2000) 590,134,000,000 (554,411,000,000); hard coal (2000) 33,804,000 (21,620,000); lignite (2000) 35,359,000 (40,459,000); crude petroleum (barrels; 2000) 655,400,000 (554,300,000); petroleum products (2000) 103,972,000 (88,296,000); natural gas (cu m; 2000) 164,352,000,000 (76,277,000,000). **Population economically active** (2003): total 17,046,800; activity rate of total population 54.0% (participation rates: ages 15 and over 67.5%; female 46.4%; unemployed [August 2004] 7.2%). **Household income and expenditure** (2002). Average household size 2.6; average annual income per family (2002) Can$73,200; sources of income (1995): wages and salaries 57.0%, transfer payments 20.7%, property and entrepreneurial income 13.7%, profits 8.6%; expenditure (2002): housing 25.9%, food, alcohol, and tobacco 18.9%, transportation and communications 19.5%, recreation 8.2%, utilities 6.4%, clothing 5.7%, household durable goods 4.1%, health 3.7%, education 2.1%, other 5.5%. **Land use** as % of total land area (2000): in temporary crops 4.9%, in permanent crops 0.02%, in pasture 3.1%; overall forest area 26.5%.

Foreign trade

Imports (2002): Can$348,198,000,000 (machinery and apparatus 27.8%; transport equipment 21.5%, of which road vehicles 19.1%; chemicals and chemical products 9.4%; food products 5.1%; crude petroleum 3.4%). *Major import sources:* US 62.6%; China 4.6%; Japan 4.4%; Mexico 3.6%; UK 2.8%; Germany 2.4%; France 1.7%. **Exports** (2002): Can$396,020,-000,000 (transport equipment 24.8%, of which road vehicles 21.4%; machinery and apparatus 13.3%; food products 6.4%; chemicals and chemical products 5.9%; natural gas 5.2%; wood and wood pulp 4.7%; crude petroleum 4.5%; paper and paperboard 4.4%). *Major export destinations:* US 87.2%; Japan 2.1%; UK 1.1%; China 1.0%; Germany 0.7%.

Transport and communications

Transport. *Railroads* (2000): length 65,403 km; passenger-km 1,571,000,000; metric ton-km cargo 319,382,000,000. *Roads* (1999): total length 901,-903 km (paved 35%). *Vehicles* (1998): passenger cars 13,887,270; trucks and buses 3,694,125. *Air transport* (2003): passenger-km 59,016,000,000; metric ton-km cargo 1,284,800,000; airports (1997) 269. **Communications,** in total units (units per 1,000 persons). Daily newspaper circulation (2000): 4,890,000 (159); radios (2000): 32,200,000 (1,047); televisions (2000): 21,700,000 (691); telephone main lines (2003): 19,950,900 (658); cellular telephone subscribers (2003): 13,221,800 (417); personal computers (2002): 15,300,000 (487); Internet users (2002): 16,110,000 (513).

Education and health

Educational attainment (2001). Percentage of population age 15 and over having: incomplete primary education 2.2%; complete primary education 7.6%; some secondary and complete secondary 49.5%; postsecondary 25.3%; undergraduate degree 10.1%; graduate degree 5.3%. **Literacy** (2003): total population age 15 and over literate virtually 100%. **Health:** physicians (2000) 60,559 (1 per 508 persons); hospital beds (1997) 161,867 (1 per 185 persons); infant mortality rate per 1,000 live births (2001) 5.0. **Food** (2001): daily per capita caloric intake 3,176 (vegetable products 70%, animal products 30%); 121% of FAO recommended minimum.

Military

Total active duty personnel (2003): 52,300 (army 36.9%, navy 17.2%, air force 25.8%, not identified by service 20.1%). **Military expenditure as percentage of GNP** (1999): 1.4% (world 2.4%); per capita expenditure US$269.

Background

Originally inhabited by American Indians and Inuit, Canada was visited c. AD 1000 by Scandinavian explorers, whose discovery is confirmed by archaeological evidence from Newfoundland. Fishing expeditions off Newfoundland by the English, French, Spanish, and Portuguese began as early as 1500. The French claim to Canada was made in 1534 when Jacques Cartier entered the Gulf of St. Lawrence. A small settlement was made in Nova Scotia (Acadia) in 1605, and in 1608 Samuel de Champlain founded Quebec. Fur trading was the impetus behind the early colonizing efforts. In response to French activity, the English in 1670 formed the Hudson's Bay Company.

The British-French rivalry for the interior of upper North America lasted almost a century. The first French loss occurred in 1713 at the conclusion of Queen Anne's War (War of the Spanish Succession) when Nova Scotia and Newfoundland were ceded to the British. The Seven Years' War (French and Indian War) resulted in France's expulsion from continental North America in 1763. After the US War of Independence, the population was augmented by Loyalists fleeing the US, and the increasing number arriving in Quebec led the British to divide the colony into Upper and Lower Canada in 1791. The British reunited the two provinces in 1841. Canadian expansionism resulted in the confederation movement of the mid-19th century, and in 1867 the Dominion of Canada, comprising Nova Scotia, New Brunswick, Quebec, and Ontario, came into existence. After confederation, Canada entered a period of westward expansion.

The prosperity that accompanied Canada into the 20th century was marred by continuing conflict between the English and French communities. Through the Statute of Westminster (1931), Canada was recognized as an equal of Great Britain. With the Constitution Act of 1982, the British gave Canada total control over its constitution and severed the remaining legal connections between the two countries. French Canadian unrest continued to be a major concern, with a movement growing for Quebec separatism in the late 20th century. Referendums for more political autonomy for Quebec were rejected in 1992 and 1995, but the issue remained unresolved. In 1999 Canada formed the new territory of Nunavut, and on 6 Dec 2001 Newfoundland was renamed Newfoundland and Labrador.

Recent Developments

After having won three successive majority governments since 1993, Canada's Liberal Party (LP) was humbled in a general election held on 28 Jun 2004. Jean Chrétien's retirement as prime minister in December 2003 had led to the selection of Paul Martin as his successor, and the LP's poor showing at the polls forced Martin to form a minority government. Martin was in a difficult position. He could not dwell on his success as finance minister, since he wanted to disassociate his government from the scandal of the previous Chrétien administration. Martin's conduct of the election campaign was uncertain, appearing to lack focus. He dwelled on his government's priority to strengthen public health care, vowed to improve the infrastructure of cities, pledged to spend more on defense and homeland security, and declared that he would accomplish all this while balancing the federal budget. For the first time since the election of 1993, the Liberals faced a united conservative opposition. In late 2003 the two parties of the right—the historic Progressive Conservative Party

---

1 metric ton = about 1.1 short tons;　1 kilometer = 0.6 mi (statute);　1 metric ton-km cargo = about 0.68 short ton-mi cargo;　c.i.f.: cost, insurance, and freight;　f.o.b.: free on board

and a newer group representing Western discontent, the Canadian Alliance—had merged into the Conservative Party of Canada (CP). The Alliance, formed in 2000, grew out of the Reform Party, which had been a voice for the West since 1987. On 20 Mar 2004, just three months before the election, the CP chose Stephen Harper of the Alliance as its new leader. Harper attempted to establish a moderate tone for the new party but was hampered by extreme statements, mostly on social issues, made by some of the Western members of his organization. There was also the impression, which Harper tried to dispel, that the CP was sympathetic to introducing private medical care into the public system.

Despite Martin's best efforts, the scandal (which involved alleged Liberal government payments to an advertising firm in Quebec for no work) that had undermined Chrétien's government continued to fester and grow. By spring 2005 Martin's government was seen to be in real trouble, and the several political parties were sensing that an election could be called as early as summer.

The Canadian economy performed well in 2004 following the shocks of the previous year. The recovery resulted from expanded trade with Canada's leading partners, the US, China, and Japan. High crude oil prices gave an added boost to Canada's trade position. By the middle of the year, the trade surplus had reached a three-year high and continued to grow into 2005. Economic growth of 2.9% was forecast for 2004. Inflation was under control, although rising energy prices were worrisome. In September the consumer price index showed an increase of 1.8% on a year-over-year basis. Employment was steady, with an unemployment rate of 7.1% recorded in September.

Prime Minister Martin made his first official visit to Washington for discussions with US Pres. George W. Bush on 29–30 Apr 2004. No action was taken on bilateral commercial issues such as the US duties imposed on Canadian softwood lumber and the ban on beef imports from Canada because of the mad cow disease scare in 2003 (a second case was reported in late December). President Bush had announced in an earlier meeting that Canada would be allowed to bid on reconstruction projects in Iraq.

Internet resources: <www.travelcanada.ca>.

Cape Verde

Official name: República de Cabo Verde (Republic of Cape Verde). Form of government: multiparty republic with one legislative house (National Assembly [72]). Chief of state: President Pedro Pires (from 2001). Head of government: Prime Minister José Maria Neves (from 2001). Capital: Praia. Official language: Portuguese. Official religion: none. Monetary unit: 1 escudo (C.V.Esc.) = 100 centavos; valuation (7 Jul 2005) $1 = C.V.Esc. 93.07 (formerly pegged to the Portuguese escudo and, since 1 Jan 2002, to the euro [€] at the rate of €1 = C.V.Esc. 110.27).

Demography

Area: 1,557 sq mi, 4,033 sq km. Population (2004): 454,000. Density (2004): persons per sq mi 291.6, persons per sq km 112.6. Urban (2002) 63.5%. Sex distribution (2003): male 48.39%; female 51.61%. Age breakdown (2003): under 15, 41.0%; 15–29, 26.7%; 30–44, 17.0%; 45–59, 6.8%; 60–74, 5.8%;

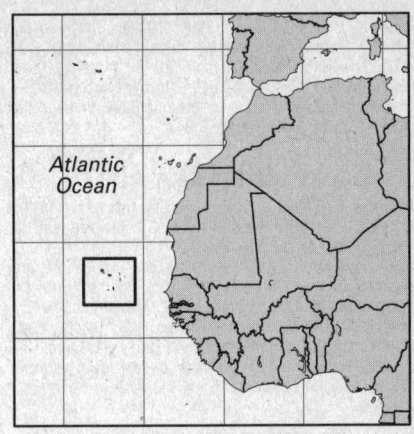

75 and over, 2.7%. Ethnic composition (2000): Cape Verdean *mestico* (black-white admixture) 69.6%; Fulani 12.2%; Balanta 10.0%; Mandyako 4.6%; Portuguese white 2.0%; other 1.6%. Religious affiliation (2000): Roman Catholic 91.4%; Muslim 2.8%; other 5.8%. Major cities (2000): Praia 94,757; Mindelo 62,970; São Filipe 7,894. Location: off the coast of western Africa; consists of 10 islands in the North Atlantic Ocean.

Vital statistics

Birth rate per 1,000 population (2003): 27.0 (world avg. 21.3); (1989) legitimate 28.9%. Death rate per 1,000 population (2002): 6.9 (world avg. 9.1). Natural increase rate per 1,000 population (2002): 20.1 (world avg. 12.2). Total fertility rate (avg. births per childbearing woman; 2003): 3.8. Marriage rate per 1,000 population (1994): 3.1. Life expectancy at birth (2003): male 66.5 years; female 73.2 years.

National economy

Budget (2001). *Revenue:* C.V.Esc. 14,900,000,000 (tax revenue 87.2%, of which taxes on international trade 35.6%, income taxes 32.2%, sales taxes 14.1%; nontax revenue 12.8%). *Expenditures:* C.V.Esc. 21,200,000,000 (current expenditure 69.8%, of which wages and salaries 31.1%, transfers 26.9%, public debt 6.6%, goods and services 2.9%; capital expenditure 30.2%). Public debt (external, outstanding; 2002): $385,000,000. Production (metric tons except as noted). *Agriculture, forestry, fishing* (2002): corn (maize) 20,000, sugarcane 14,000, bananas 6,000; livestock (number of live animals) 200,000 pigs, 112,000 goats, 22,000 cattle; fish catch (2000) 10,821. *Mining and quarrying* (2000): salt 2,000. *Manufacturing* (1999): flour 15,901; bread 5,628 (1995); soap 833. *Energy production (consumption):* electricity (kW-hr; 2001) 43,000,000 (43,000,000); petroleum products (2001) none (101,619). Tourism (2002): receipts from visitors $66,000,000; expenditures by nationals abroad $56,000,000. Land use as % of total land area (2000): in temporary crops 9.7%, in permanent crops 0.5%, in pasture 6.2%; overall forest area 21.1%. Gross national product (2003): $701,000,000 ($1,490 per capita). Population economically active (2000): total 174,644; activity rate of total population 40.2% (participation rates: ages

15–64 [1990] 64.3%; female 39.0%; unemployed 17.4%). **Households.** Average household size (2000) 4.6; expenditure (1988): food 51.1%, housing, fuel, and power 13.5%, beverages and tobacco 11.8%, transportation and communications 8.8%, household durable goods 6.9%, other 7.9%.

Foreign trade

Imports (2000-c.i.f.; excludes reexports of fuel): C.V.Esc. 27,585,000,000 (food 32.8%, machinery and apparatus 16.1%, transport equipment 9.5%, base and fabricated metals 6.5%). *Major import sources* (2001–02): Portugal 54.8%; The Netherlands 13.4%; Spain 4,9%; Belgium 4.1%; Brazil 3.6%. **Exports** (2000-f.o.b.; excludes reexports of fuel): C.V.Esc. 1,272,000,000 (shoes and shoe parts 51.8%, clothing 35.1%, fish 4.8%). *Major export destinations* (2001–02): Portugal 91.7%; US 2.1%; Germany 1.6%.

Transport and communications

Transport. *Roads* (1999): total length 1,100 km (paved [1996] 78%). *Vehicles* (2000): passenger cars 13,473; trucks and buses 3,085. *Air transport* (2001; TACV airline only): passenger-km 276,000,-000; metric ton-km cargo 26,000,000; airports (1997) with scheduled flights 9. **Communications,** in total units (units per 1,000 persons). Radios (1997): 71,000 (179); televisions (2000): 2,000 (4.6); telephone main lines (2003): 71,700 (156); cellular telephone subscribers (2003): 53,300 (116); personal computers (2002): 35,000 (78); Internet users (2003): 20,400 (44).

Education and health

Educational attainment (1990). Percentage of population age 25 and over having: no formal schooling 47.9%; primary 40.9%; incomplete secondary 3.9%; complete secondary 1.4%; higher 1.5%; unknown 4.4%. **Literacy** (2000): total population age 15 and over literate 73.8%; males 84.5%; females 65.7%. **Health** (2000): physicians 102 (1 per 4,274 persons); hospital beds 689 (1 per 631 persons); infant mortality rate per 1,000 live births (2002) 50.5. **Food** (2001): daily per capita caloric intake 3,308 (vegetable products 85%, animal products 15%); 141% of FAO recommended minimum.

Military

Total active duty personnel (2003): 1,200 (army 83.3%, air force 8.3%, coast guard 8.4%). **Military expenditure as percentage of GNP** (1999): 0.9% (world 2.4%); per capita expenditure $13.

Background

When visited by the Portuguese in 1456–60, the islands were uninhabited. In 1460 Diogo Gomes sighted and named Maio and São Tiago, and in 1462 the first settlers landed on São Tiago, founding the city of Ribeira Grande. The city's importance grew with the development of the slave trade, but its wealth attracted pirates so often that it was abandoned after 1712. The prosperity of the Portuguese-controlled islands vanished with the decline of the

slave trade in the 19th century but later improved because of their position on the great trade routes between Europe, South America, and southern Africa. In 1951 the colony became an overseas province of Portugal. Many islanders preferred outright independence, and it was finally granted in 1975. At one time associated politically with Guinea-Bissau, Cape Verde split from it in 1981.

Recent Developments

In 2004, because of Cape Verde's political stability and reputation for efficient government and an economy that had provided annual GDP growth averaging 7% a year for a decade, the UN Economic and Social Council decided to review its status as a "least developed country." Cape Verde's main sources of income remained aid, overseas remittances (more Cape Verdeans lived abroad than in the country itself), and fish exports. The government aimed to establish a more broadly based economy.

Internet resources: <www.ine.cv>.

Central African Republic

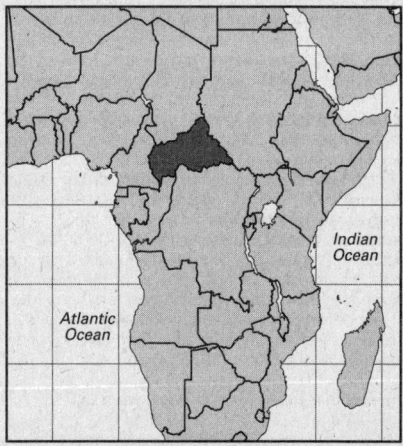

Official name: République Centrafricaine (Central African Republic). **Form of government:** military regime with one advisory body (National Transitional Council [63]). **Chief of state:** President François Bozizé (from 2003). **Head of government:** Prime Minister Célestin Gaombalet (from 2003). **Capital:** Bangui. **Official languages:** French; Sango. **Official religion:** none. **Monetary unit:** 1 CFA franc (CFAF) = 100 centimes; valuation (7 Jul 2005) $1 = CFAF 549.50 (formerly pegged to the French franc and, since 1 Jan 2002, to the euro [€] at the rate of €1 = CFAF 655.96).

Demography

Area: 240,324 sq mi, 622,436 sq km. **Population** (2004): 3,742,000. **Density** (2004): persons per sq mi 15.6, persons per sq km 6.0. **Urban** (2002): 41.7%. **Sex distribution** (2003): male 49.47%; female

---

1 metric ton = about 1.1 short tons;   1 kilometer = 0.6 mi (statute);   1 metric ton-km cargo = about 0.68 short ton-mi cargo;   c.i.f.: cost, insurance, and freight;   f.o.b.: free on board

50.53%. **Age breakdown** (2003): under 15, 43.1%; 15–29, 28.9%; 30–44, 14.6%; 45–59, 8.2%; 60–74, 4.2%; 75 and over, 1.0%. **Ethnolinguistic composition** (1988): Gbaya (Baya) 23.7%; Banda 23.4%; Mandjia 14.7%; Ngbaka 7.6%; Sara 6.5%; Mbum 6.3%; Kare 2.4%; French 0.1%; other 15.3%. **Religious affiliation** (2000): Christian 67.8%, of which Roman Catholic 18.4%, Protestant 14.4%, African Christian 11.6%, other Christian 23.4%; Muslim 15.6%; traditional beliefs 15.4%; other 1.2%. **Major cities** (1994): Bangui 524,000; Berbérati 47,000; Bouar 43,000; Bambari 41,000; Carnot 41,000. **Location:** central Africa, bordering Chad, The Sudan, Democratic Republic of the Congo, Republic of the Congo, and Cameroon.

Vital statistics

Birth rate per 1,000 population (2003): 35.9 (world avg. 21.3). **Death rate** per 1,000 population (2003): 19.7 (world avg. 9.1). **Natural increase rate** per 1,000 population (2003): 16.2 (world avg. 12.2). **Total fertility rate** (avg. births per childbearing woman; 2003): 4.7. **Life expectancy** at birth (2003): male 40.2 years; female 43.3 years. **Adult population** (ages 15–49) living with HIV (2004): 13.5% (world avg. 1.1%).

National economy

Budget (2001). *Revenue:* CFAF 63,200,000,000 (1999; taxes 88.0%, of which international trade tax 38.0%, indirect domestic tax 30.1%, taxes on income and profits 19.9%; nontax receipts 12.0%). *Expenditures:* CFAF 97,200,000,000 (current expenditure 61.2%, of which wages 30.5%; public investment program 38.8%). **Public debt** (external, outstanding; 2002): $980,000,000. **Production** (metric tons except as noted). *Agriculture, forestry, fishing* (2002): cassava 563,000, yams 400,000, peanuts (groundnuts) 127,800; livestock (number of live animals; 2002) 3,273,000 cattle, 2,921,000 goats, 4,575,000 chickens; roundwood (2001) 3,058,000 cu m; fish catch (2001) 15,125. *Mining and quarrying* (2002): gold 20 kg, diamonds 415,000 carats (official figure; at least an equal amount was smuggled out of the country in 2002). *Manufacturing* (value added in $'000; 1994): food, beverages, and tobacco 19,000; chemical products 3,000; wood products 2,000. *Energy production (consumption):* electricity (kW-hr; 2000) 107,000,000 (107,000,000); petroleum products (2000) none (88,000). **Household income and expenditure.** Average household size (2000) 5.9; average annual income per household (1988) CFAF 91,985; expenditure (1991): food 70.5%, clothing 8.5%, other manufactured products 7.6%, energy 7.3%, services (including transportation and communications, recreation, and health) 6.1%. **Gross national product** (2003): $1,019,000,000 ($260 per capita). **Population economically active** (2000): total 1,752,000; activity rate of total population 50.0% (participation rates [1988]: ages 15–64, 78.3%; female 46.8%). **Land use** as % of total land area (2000): in temporary crops 3.1%, in permanent crops 0.1%, in pasture 5.0%; overall forest area 36.8%. **Tourism** (2002): receipts $3,000,000; expenditures $29,000,000.

Foreign trade

Imports (2001): CFAF 84,800,000,000 (1996; road vehicles 18.3%, machinery and apparatus 15.8%, raw cotton 9.7%, refined petroleum 8.0%, food 7.0%).

Major import sources (1999): France 34%; Cameroon 12%; Belgium 7%; UK 4%; Japan 3%. **Exports** (2001): CFAF 100,500,000,000 (wood 41.3%, diamonds 41.0%, cotton 7.4%, coffee 1.8%). *Major export destinations* (1999): Belgium 65%; Spain 6%; Indonesia 4%; France 3%; UK 3%.

Transport and communications

Transport. *Roads* (1999): total length 23,810 km (paved 3%). *Vehicles* (1996): passenger cars 8,900; trucks and buses 7,000. *Air transport* (1998; Air Afrique, an airline jointly owned by 11 African countries [including the Central African Republic], was declared bankrupt in February 2002): passenger-km 258,000,000; metric ton-km cargo 38,000,000; airports (2001) 1. **Communications,** in total units (units per 1,000 persons). Daily newspaper circulation (2000): 7,000 (2); radios (2000): 280,000 (80); televisions (2002): 22,800 (6); telephone main lines (2002): 9,000 (2.3); cellular telephone subscribers (2002): 13,000 (3.1); personal computers (2002): 8,000 (2); Internet users (2002): 5,000 (1.3).

Education and health

Educational attainment (1988). Percentage of population age 10 and over having: no formal schooling 59.3%; primary education 29.6%; lower secondary 7.5%; upper secondary 2.3%; higher 1.3%. **Literacy** (2000): total population age 15 and over literate 46.7%; males literate 59.7%; females literate 34.9%. **Health** (1995): physicians 112 (1 per 28,600 persons); hospital beds (1998) 3,044 (1 per 1,111 persons); infant mortality rate per 1,000 live births (2003) 93.3. **Food** (2002): daily per capita caloric intake 1,980 (vegetable products 90%, animal products 10%); 86% of FAO recommended minimum.

Military

Total active duty personnel (2003): 2,550 (army 54.9%; air force 5.9%; paramilitary [gendarmerie] 39.2%). **Military expenditure as percentage of GNP** (1999): 2.8% (world 2.4%); per capita expenditure $8.

Background

For several centuries before the arrival of Europeans, the territory was subjected to slave traders. The French explored and claimed central Africa and in 1889 established a post at Bangui. In 1898 they partitioned the colony among commercial concessionaires. United with Chad in 1906 to form the French colony of Ubangi-Shari, it later became part of French Equatorial Africa. It was separated from Chad in 1920 and became an overseas territory in 1946. Named an autonomous republic within the French Community in 1958, the country achieved independence in 1960. In 1966 the military overthrew a civilian government and installed Jean-Bédel Bokassa, who in 1976 declared himself Emperor Bokassa I and renamed the country the Central African Empire. He was overthrown in 1979, but the military again seized power in the 1980s. Elections in 1993 led to the installation of a civilian government.

Recent Developments

Under increasing international pressure to restore democratic institutions to the Central African Republic

(CAR), in May 2004 Pres. François Bozizé appointed 30 people to sit on the newly created commission formed to oversee legislative and presidential elections scheduled for early 2005. The first round of voting, on March 13, led to a runoff in May in which Bozizé won a comfortable victory over former Prime Minister Martin Ziguele. Another candidate, former president Gen. André Kolingba, called the earlier balloting fraudulent and sought nullification of the elections. A shooting spree outside Kolingba's house on 22 March was seen as a possible assassination attempt on him.

Internet resources:
<www.sas.upenn.edu/African_Studies/Country_Specific/CAR.html>.

Chad

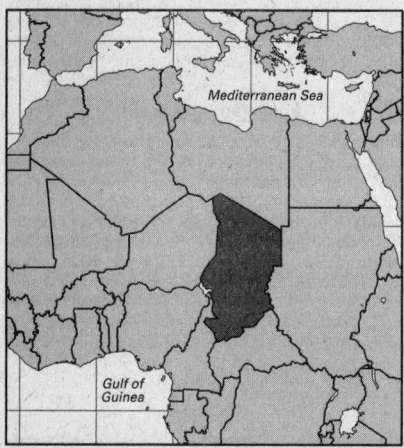

Official name: Jumhuriyah Tshad (Arabic); République du Tchad (French) (Republic of Chad). **Form of government:** unitary republic with one legislative body (National Assembly [155]). **Chief of state:** President Idriss Déby (from 1990). **Head of government:** Prime Minister Pascal Yoadimnadji (from 3 Feb 2005). **Capital:** N'Djamena. **Official languages:** Arabic; French. **Official religion:** none. **Monetary unit:** 1 CFA franc (CFAF) = 100 centimes; valuation (7 Jul 2005) $1 = CFAF 549.50 (formerly pegged to the French franc and, since 1 Jan 2002, to the euro [€] at the rate of €1 = CFAF 655.96).

Demography

Area: 495,755 sq mi, 1,284,000 sq km. **Population** (2004): 9,539,000. **Density** (2004): persons per sq mi 19.2, persons per sq km 7.4. **Urban** (2002): 24.1%. **Sex distribution** (2002): male 48.62%; female 51.38%. **Age breakdown** (2002): under 15, 47.8%; 15–29, 26.2%; 30–44, 14.1%; 45–59, 7.5%; 60–74, 3.6%; 75 and over, 0.8%. **Ethnolinguistic composition** (1993): Sara 27.7%; Sudanic Arab 12.3%; Mayo-Kebbi peoples 11.5%; Kanem-Bornu peoples 9.0%; Ouaddaï peoples 8.7%; Hadjeray (Had-

jaraï) 6.7%; Tangale (Tandjilé) peoples 6.5%; Gorane peoples 6.3%; Fitri-Batha peoples 4.7%; Fulani (Peul) 2.4%; other 4.2%. **Religious affiliation** (1993): Muslim 53.9%; Christian 34.7%, of which Roman Catholic 20.3%, Protestant 14.4%; traditional beliefs 7.4%; other 4.0%. **Major cities** (1993): N'Djamena 530,-965; Moundou 282,103; Bongor 196,713; Sarh 193,753; Abéché 187,936. **Location:** central Africa, bordered by Libya, The Sudan, Central African Republic, Cameroon, Nigeria, and Niger.

Vital statistics

Birth rate per 1,000 population (2003): 47.1 (world avg. 21.3). **Death rate** per 1,000 population (2003): 16.4 (world avg. 9.1). **Natural increase rate** per 1,000 population (2003): 30.7 (world avg. 12.2). **Total fertility rate** (avg. births per childbearing woman; 2003): 6.4. **Life expectancy** at birth (2003): male 47.0 years; female 50.1 years. **Adult population** (ages 15–49) **living with HIV** (2004): 4.8% (world avg. 1.1%).

National economy

Budget (2000). *Revenue:* CFAF 128,200,000,000 (tax revenue 53.3%, of which income tax 19.0%, taxes on international trade 17.0%, taxes on goods and services 14.7%, other taxes 2.6%; grants 37.4%; nontax revenue 9.3%). *Expenditures:* CFAF 203,200,000,000 (current expenditure 49.2%, of which government salaries 19.7%, materials and supply 10.2%, defense 7.5%, transfer payments 5.9%, debt service 5.1%, other 0.8%; capital expenditure 50.8%). **Tourism** (2001): receipts from visitors $23,000,000; expenditures by nationals abroad $56,000,000. **Production** (metric tons except as noted). *Agriculture, forestry, fishing* (2002): peanuts (groundnuts) 448,089, sorghum 428,000, millet 369,000; livestock (number of live animals) 5,900,000 cattle, 5,500,000 goats, 5,000,000 chickens; roundwood (2001) 6,761,676 cu m; fish catch (2001) 84,000. *Mining and quarrying* (1997): aggregate (gravel) 170,000; limited commercial production of natron (10,000) and salt; artisanal gold production. *Manufacturing* (2000): cotton fiber (1998) 86,260; refined sugar 27,000; gum arabic 3,420. *Energy production (consumption):* electricity (kW-hr; 2000) 92,000,000 (92,000,000); crude petroleum (barrels; 2003) production began in 2003 at 50,000 barrels per day and was expected to increase to 225,000 barrels per day by the end of the first quarter 2004 (none); petroleum products (2000) none (41,000). **Household income and expenditure.** Average household size (2000) 4.2; average annual income per household (1993) CFAF 96,806; sources of income (1995–96; urban): informal-sector employment and entrepreneurship 36.7%, transfers 24.8%, wages 23.6%, ownership of real estate 8.6%; expenditure (1983; capital city only): food 45.3%, health 11.9%, energy 5.8%, clothing 3.3%. **Population economically active** (1997): total 3,433,000; activity rate of total population 47.9% (participation rates: over age 15, 72.3%; female 44.5%; unemployed [1993] 0.6%). **Public debt** (external, outstanding; 2002): $1,148,000,000. **Gross national product** (2003): $2,104,000,000 ($250 per capita). **Land use** as % of total land area (2000): in temporary crops 2.8%, in permanent crops 0.02%, in pasture 35.7%; overall forest area 10.1%.

---

1 metric ton = about 1.1 short tons;   1 kilometer = 0.6 mi (statute);   1 metric ton-km cargo = about 0.68 short ton-mi cargo;   c.i.f.: cost, insurance, and freight;   f.o.b.: free on board

Foreign trade

Imports (2001): CFAF 328,700,000,000 (petroleum sector 61.3%; non-petroleum sector 38.7%). *Major import sources* (1999): France 37%; Cameroon 22%; Nigeria 10%; India 4%. **Exports** (2001): CFAF 129,600,000,000 (cattle, sheep, and goats 39.5%; cotton fiber 37.2%; other 23.3%). *Major export destinations* (1999): Portugal 29%; Germany 15%; Taiwan 8%; US 7%; France 5%; Brazil 5%.

Transport and communications

Transport. *Roads* (1999): total length 33,400 km (paved 1%). *Vehicles* (1996): passenger cars 10,560; trucks and buses 14,550. *Air transport* (1996; data represent 1/11 of the total traffic of Air Afrique; Air Afrique, an airline jointly owned by 11 African countries [including Chad], was declared bankrupt in 2002): passenger-km 233,000,000; metric ton-km cargo 37,000,000; airports (2000) with scheduled flights 1. **Communications**, in total units (units per 1,000 persons). Daily newspaper circulation (1997): 2,000 (0.2); radios (2000): 1,990,000 (236); televisions (2002): 16,600 (2); telephone main lines (2002): 11,800 (1.5); cellular telephone subscribers (2003): 65,000 (8); personal computers (2002): 13,000 (1.7); Internet users (2002): 15,000 (1.9).

Education and health

Educational attainment (1993). Percentage of economically active population age 15 and over having: no formal schooling 81.1%; Koranic education 4.2%; primary education 11.2%; secondary education 2.7%; higher education 0.3%; professional education 0.5%. **Literacy** (2000): percentage of total population age 15 and over literate 42.6%; males literate 51.6%; females literate 34.0%. **Health** (2000): physicians 1,667 (1 per 4,471 persons); hospital beds (1993) 3,962 (1 per 1,521 persons); infant mortality rate per 1,000 live births (2002) 96.7. **Food** (2001): daily per capita caloric intake 2,245 (vegetable products 94%, animal products 6%); 94% of FAO recommended minimum.

Military

Total active duty personnel (2003): 30,350 (army 82.4%; air force 1.2%; paramilitary [gendarmerie] 16.4%); French peacekeeping troops (August 2004) 1,000. **Military expenditure as percentage of GNP** (1999): 2.4% (world 2.4%); per capita expenditure $5.

Background

Around AD 800 the kingdom of Kanem was founded in north-central Africa, and by the early 1200s its borders had expanded to form a new kingdom, Kanem-Bornu, in the northern regions of the area. Its power peaked in the 16th century with its command of the southern terminus of the trans-Sahara trade route to Tripoli. Around this time the rival kingdoms of Baguirmi and Wadai evolved in the south. In the years 1883–93 all three kingdoms fell to the Sudanese adventurer Rabih al-Zubayr, who was in turn pushed out by the French in 1900. Extending their power, the French in 1910 made Chad a part of French Equatorial Africa. Chad became a separate colony in 1920 and was made an overseas territory in 1946. The country achieved independence in 1960. This was followed by decades of civil war and frequent intervention by France and Libya.

Recent Developments

In 2004 Chad received the first share of royalties from the large oil project that went onstream in 2003. Estimated at about $100 million, these royalties added another 40% to the government's revenues. The government had used much of the $25 million signing bonus it got before the completion of the pipeline to Cameroon to purchase arms. After an abortive army uprising in the capital, which Pres. Idriss Déby claimed had been organized to overthrow him, the parliament in May and the people in June approved the idea of amending the constitution to allow him to seek a third term as president. Chad's domestic and international politics were focused on the critical situation in the Darfur region of The Sudan and the tens of thousands of refugees who had fled to Chad.

Internet resources: <www.chadembassy.org>.

Chile

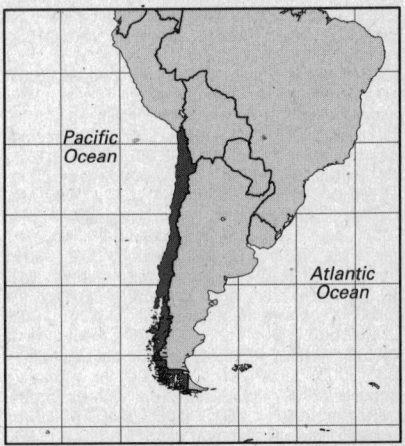

Pacific Ocean

Atlantic Ocean

Official name: República de Chile (Republic of Chile). **Form of government:** multiparty republic with two legislative houses (Senate [48, including 9 nonelective seats and excluding one senator-for-life]; Chamber of Deputies [120]). **Head of state and government:** President Ricardo Lagos Escobar (from 2000). **Capital:** Santiago (legislative bodies meet in Valparaíso). **Official language:** Spanish. **Official religion:** none. **Monetary unit:** 1 peso (Ch$) = 100 centavos; valuation (7 Jul 2005) US$1 = Ch$586.25.

Demography

Area: 291,930 sq mi, 756,096 sq km. **Population** (2004): 15,824,000. **Density** (2004): persons per sq mi 54.2, persons per sq km 20.9. **Urban** (2002): 86.6%. **Sex distribution** (2002): male 49.27%; female 50.73%. **Age breakdown** (2002): under 15, 25.7%; 15–29, 24.3%; 30–44, 23.6%; 45–59, 15.0%; 60–74, 8.3%; 75 and over, 3.1%. **Ethnic composition** (2000): mestizo 72.4%; local white 20.8%; Araucanian (Mapuche) 4.7%; European 1.0%; other

1.1%. **Religious affiliation** (2002; for population age 15 and older): Roman Catholic 70.0%; Protestant 15.4%; other Christian 2.1%; atheist/nonreligious 4.6%; other 7.9%. **Major cities** (2002): Greater Santiago 4,647,444; Puente Alto 501,042; Concepción 376,043; Viña del Mar 298,828; Antofagasta 298,153. **Location:** southern South America, bordering Peru, Bolivia, Argentina, the South Atlantic Ocean, and the South Pacific Ocean.

Vital statistics

Birth rate per 1,000 population (2003): 16.1 (world avg. 21.3). **Death rate** per 1,000 population (2003): 5.7 (world avg. 9.1). **Natural increase rate** per 1,000 population (2003): 10.4 (world avg. 12.2). **Total fertility rate** (avg. births per childbearing woman; 2003): 2.1. **Life expectancy** at birth (2003): male 72.9 years; female 79.6 years.

National economy

Budget (2001). *Revenue:* Ch$9,537,200,000,000 (income from taxes 76.2%, nontax revenue 23.5%, capital 0.3%). *Expenditures:* Ch$9,932,200,000,000 (pensions 29.5%, wages 19.0%, capital expenditure 15.0%, interest 2.1%). **Population economically active** (1999): total 5,822,700; activity rate of total population 38.6% (participation rates [1995]: ages 15–64, 58.6%; female 32.4%; unemployed [2002] 9.0%). **Production** (metric tons except as noted). *Agriculture, forestry, fishing* (2003): sugar beets 2,100,000, wheat 1,797,084, grapes 1,750,000; livestock (number of live animals) 4,105,000 sheep, 3,927,000 cattle, 3,100,000 pigs; roundwood (2001) 37,790,000 cu m; fish catch (2001) 3,717,000. *Mining* (metal content; 2002): iron ore (2001) 5,520,000; copper 4,580,600; molybdenum 29,500. *Manufacturing* (value added in US$'000,000; 2000): food products 3,251; nonferrous base metals 1,947; paints, soaps, pharmaceuticals 1,206. *Energy production (consumption):* electricity (kW-hr; 2001) 41,292,000,000 (41,292,000,000); coal (2001) 480,000 ([2000] 4,590,000); crude petroleum (barrels; 2000) 2,027,000 (72,771,000); petroleum products (2000) 8,943,000 (10,270,000); natural gas (cu m; 2000) 2,188,300,000 (6,407,400,000). **Gross national product** (2003): US$69,193,000,000 (US$4,390 per capita). **Public debt** (external, outstanding; 2002): US$6,792,000,000. **Household income and expenditure.** Average household size (2002) 3.4; average annual income per household (1994) Ch$5,981,706 at November prices; sources of income (1990): wages and salaries 75.1%, transfer payments 12.0%, other 12.9%; expenditure (1989): food 27.9%, clothing 22.5%, housing 15.2%, transportation 6.4%. **Tourism** (2002): receipts US$845,000,000; expenditures US$793,000,000. **Land use** as % of total land area (2000): in temporary crops 2.6%, in permanent crops 0.4%, in pasture 17.3%; overall forest area 20.7%.

Foreign trade

Imports (2001-f.o.b. in balance of trade and c.i.f. in commodities and trading partners): US$17,181,000,000 (machinery and fabricated metals 29.4%; chemical products and mineral fuels 19.7%; copper

12.5%). *Major import sources:* Argentina 17.8%; US 16.8%; Brazil 8.7%; Germany 4.0%; Japan 3.3%. **Exports** (2001): US$17,620,000,000 (copper 37.9%; food products 24.8%, of which raw fruit 7.8%; paper and paper products 6.4%). *Major export destinations:* US 19.4%; Japan 12.1%; UK 7.0%; Brazil 4.8%; France 3.4%.

Transport and communications

Transport. *Railroads* (2001): route length 8,501 km; passenger-km 870,836,000; metric ton-km cargo 3,318,000,000. *Roads* (1996): total length 79,800 km (paved 14%). *Vehicles* (2001): passenger cars 1,351,900; trucks and buses 693,000. *Air transport* (1999): passenger-km 10,650,500,000; metric ton-km cargo 2,107,000,000; airports (1998) with scheduled flights 23. **Communications**, in total units (units per 1,000 persons). Daily newspaper circulation (2000): 1,450,000 (98); radios (2000): 5,230,000 (354); televisions (2000): 3,580,000 (242); telephone main lines (2002): 3,467,200 (230); cellular telephone subscribers (2002): 6,446,000 (428); personal computers (2002): 1,796,000 (119); Internet users (2002): 3,575,000 (236).

Education and health

Educational attainment (1992). Percentage of population age 25 and over having: no formal schooling 5.7%; primary education 44.2%; secondary 42.2%; higher 7.9%. **Literacy** (1995): total population age 15 and over literate 95.2%; males literate 95.4%; females literate 95.0%. **Health:** physicians (2000) 17,720 (1 per 834 persons); hospital beds (1999) 42,163 (1 per 346 persons); infant mortality rate per 1,000 live births (2003) 9.3. **Food** (2001): daily per capita caloric intake 2,868 (vegetable products 78%, animal products 22%); 118% of FAO recommended minimum.

Military

Total active duty personnel (2003): 77,300 (army 61.7%, navy 24.6%, air force 13.7%). **Military expenditure as percentage of GNP** (1999): 3.0% (world 2.4%); per capita expenditure US$133.

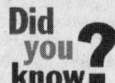

Did you know? Some 2,200 miles west of Chile is the island known to its original inhabitants as Rapa Nui ("Great Rapa") or Te Pito te Henua ("Navel of the World"). Its first European visitors, the Dutch, named it Paaseiland ("Easter Island") in memory of their own day of arrival.

Background

Originally inhabited by native peoples, including the Mapuche, the Chilean coast was invaded by the Spanish in 1536. A settlement begun at Santiago in 1541 was governed under the viceroyalty of Peru but became a separate captaincy general in 1778. It revolted against Spanish rule in 1810; its independence was finally assured by the victory of José de

---

1 metric ton = about 1.1 short tons;   1 kilometer = 0.6 mi (statute);   1 metric ton-km cargo = about 0.68 short ton-mi cargo;   c.i.f.: cost, insurance, and freight;   f.o.b.: free on board

San Martín in 1818, and the area was then governed by Bernardo O'Higgins to 1823. In the War of the Pacific against Peru and Bolivia, it won the rich nitrate fields on the coast of Bolivia, effectively forcing that country into a landlocked position. Chile remained neutral in World War I and in World War II but severed diplomatic ties with the Axis in 1943. In 1970 Salvador Allende was elected president, becoming the first avowed Marxist to be elected chief of state in Latin America. Following economic upheaval, he was ousted in 1973 in a coup led by Gen. Augusto Pinochet, whose military junta for many years harshly suppressed all internal opposition. A national referendum in 1988 rejected Pinochet, and elections held in 1989 returned the country to civilian rule.

Recent Developments

The affair of former president Gen. Augusto Pinochet Ugarte continued to dominate headlines in 2004 and 2005. In July 2004 a US Senate committee reported that between 1994 and 2002 the Washington DC–based Riggs Bank had helped Pinochet hide millions of dollars in at least six secret bank accounts (many more were later revealed) and apparently aided him in setting up phony offshore companies and illegally transferring funds to them. These unlawful activities helped change Pinochet's image in Chile and opened the way for his prosecution for human rights crimes. Even right-wing supporters could no longer claim that he had acted only to help his country during a turbulent time. Pinochet also damaged his case against prosecution on medical grounds by giving a lucid interview to a Miami FL–based television station. As a result, Chile's Supreme Court lifted his immunity in late August, and on 13 December Pinochet was ruled fit for trial.

Internet resources: <www.visit-chile.org>.

China

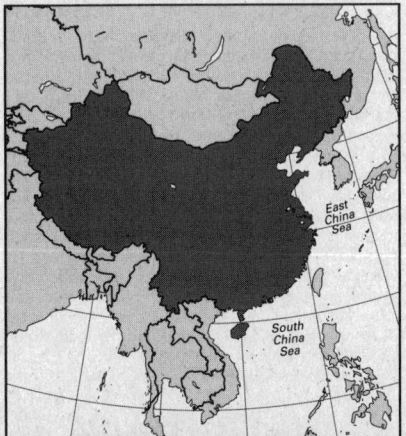

East China Sea

South China Sea

Official name: Zhonghua Renmin Gongheguo (People's Republic of China). **Form of government:** single-party people's republic with one legislative house (National People's Congress [2,985; 36 seats are allotted to Hong Kong and 12 to Macau]). **Chief of**

state: President Hu Jintao (from 2003). **Head of government:** Premier Wen Jiabao (from 2003). **Capital:** Beijing (Peking). **Official language:** Mandarin Chinese. **Official religion:** none. **Monetary unit:** 1 Renminbi (yuan) (Y) = 10 jiao = 100 fen; valuation (7 Jul 2005) $1 = Y 8.28 (devalued on 21 Jul 2005 to 8.11).

Demography

Area: 3,696,100 sq mi, 9,572,900 sq km. **Population** (2004): 1,298,848,000. **Density** (2004): persons per sq mi 351.4, persons per sq km 135.7. **Urban** (2002): 37.7%. **Sex distribution** (2002): male 51.46%; female 48.54%. **Age breakdown** (2000): under 15, 22.9%; 15–29, 25.4%; 30–44, 25.6%; 45–59, 15.7%; 60–74, 8.2%; 75 and over, 2.2%. **Ethnic composition** (2000): Han (Chinese) 91.53%; Chuang 1.30%; Manchu 0.86%; Hui 0.79%; Miao 0.72%; Uighur 0.68%; Tuchia 0.65%; Yi 0.62%; Mongolian 0.47%; Tibetan 0.44%; Puyi 0.24%; Tung 0.24%; Yao 0.21%; Korean 0.15%; Pai 0.15%; Hani 0.12%; Kazakh 0.10%; Li 0.10%; Tai 0.09%; other 0.54%. **Religious affiliation** (2000): nonreligious 42.1%; Chinese folk-religionist 28.5%; Buddhist 8.4%; atheist 8.1%; Christian 7.1%; traditional beliefs 4.3%; Muslim 1.5%. **Major cities** (2003): Shanghai 10,030,800; Beijing 7,699,300; Tianjin 4,933,100; Guangzhou 4,653,100; Wuhan 4,593,400; Chongqing 4,239,700; Shenyang 3,995,500; Nanjing 2,966,000; Harbin 2,735,100; Chengdu 2,664,000; Xi'an 2,657,900; Jinan 2,346,000; Changchun 2,283,800; Dalian 2,181,-600; Hangzhou 2,059,800; Shijiazhuang 1,971,000; Taiyuan 1,970,300; Qingdao 1,930,200; Zhengzhou 1,770,800; Kunming 1,597,800; Lanzhou 1,576,-400; Changsha 1,562,200; Zibo 1,519,300. **Location:** eastern Asia, bordering Mongolia, Russia, North Korea, the Yellow Sea, the East China Sea, the South China Sea, Vietnam, Laos, Myanmar (Burma), India, Bhutan, Nepal, Pakistan, Afghanistan, Tajikistan, Kyrgyzstan, and Kazakhstan. **Households.** Average household size (2000) 3.4; total households 351,-233,698, of which family households 340,491,197 (96.9%), collective 10,742,501 (3.1%).

Vital statistics

Birth rate per 1,000 population (2003): 13.0 (world avg. 21.3). **Death rate** per 1,000 population (2003): 6.9 (world avg. 9.1). **Natural increase rate** per 1,000 population (2003): 6.1 (world avg. 12.2). **Total fertility rate** (avg. births per childbearing woman; 2003): 1.7. **Marriage rate** per 1,000 population (2001): 6.3. **Divorce rate** per 1,000 population (2001): 1.0. **Life expectancy** at birth (2003): male 70.1 years; female 73.3 years.

Social indicators

Educational attainment (2000). Percentage of population age 15 and over having: no schooling and incomplete primary 15.6%; completed primary 35.7%; some secondary 34.0%; complete secondary 11.1%; some postsecondary through advanced degree 3.6%. **Quality of working life.** Average workweek (1998): 40 hours. Annual rate per 100,000 workers for (1997): injury or accident 0.7; death 1.4. Funds for pensions and social welfare relief (2001): Y 26,668,000,000. **Access to services.** Proportion of communes having access to electricity (1979) 87.1%. Percentage of urban population with: safe public water supply (1996) 95.0%. **Social participation.** Trade union membership in total labor force (1996): 14.7%. **Social deviance.** Annual reported arrest rate per 100,000 population (1986) for: property violation 20.7; infringing personal rights 7.2; disruption of social administration 3.3; endangering public security 1.0 (excludes arrests for anti-Communist activities). **Material well-being.** Urban households possessing (number per household; 2002): bicycles 1.6; color televisions 1.2; washing machines 0.9; refrigerators 0.8; cameras 0.4; rural families possessing (number per family; 2002): bicycles 1.2; color televisions 0.5; washing machines 0.3; refrigerators 0.1; cameras 0.03.

National economy

Gross national product (2003): $1,417,301,000,-000 ($1,100 per capita). **Budget** (2001). *Revenue:* Y 1,638,604,000,000 (tax revenue 93.4%, of which VAT 32.7%, corporate income taxes 12.6%, consumption tax 5.6%; nontax revenue 6.6%). *Expenditures:* Y 1,890,258,000,000 (economic development 34.2%; education, health, and science 27.6%; administration 18.9%; debt payment 10.6%; defense 7.6%; other 1.1%). **Public debt** (external, outstanding; 2002): $88,531,000,000. **Tourism** (2001): receipts from visitors $20,385,000,000; expenditures by nationals abroad $15,398,000,000. **Production** (metric tons except as noted). *Agriculture, forestry, fishing* (2002): grains—rice 176,553,000, corn (maize) 123,175,000, wheat 91,290,000, sorghum 2,731,000, barley 2,470,000, millet 2,071,000; oilseeds—soybeans 16,900,000, peanuts (groundnuts) 15,006,000, rapeseed 10,530,000, sunflower seeds 1,900,000; fruits and nuts—watermelons 57,554,000, apples 20,435,000, pears 9,091,000, cantaloupes 8,631,000, oranges 3,676,000; other—sweet potatoes 114,289,000, sugarcane 82,278,-000, potatoes 65,052,000, cabbage 26,812,000, tomatoes 25,466,000, cucumbers 22,924,000, onions 15,622,000, eggplants 15,430,000, seed cotton 14,760,000, sugar beets 11,562,000, garlic 8,694,000, tobacco leaves 2,394,000, tea 760,000; livestock (number of live animals) 464,695,000 pigs, 161,492,000 goats, 136,972,000 sheep, 106,175,-000 cattle, 22,249,000 water buffalo, 8,815,000 asses, 8,262,000 horses, 3,923,600,000 chickens, 661,250,000 ducks; roundwood (2001) 284,910,-000 cu m; fish catch (2002) 44,320,000, of which aquaculture 27,767,000. *Mining and quarrying* (2002): metal content of mine output—zinc 1,550,000, lead 641,000, copper 568,000, antimony 100,000, tin 62,000, tungsten 49,500; metal ores—iron ore 231,000,000, bauxite 11,000,000, manganese ore 4,500,000, vanadium 33,000, silver 2,950, gold 192; nonmetals—salt 36,024,000, soda ash 10,330,000, gypsum 6,850,000, magnesite 3,700,000, talc 3,600,000, barite 3,100,000, fluorspar 2,450,000, asbestos 270,000. *Manufacturing* (2001): cement 661,040,000; steel products 160,676,000; pig iron 155,554,000; rolled steel 151,634,000; paper and paperboard 37,771,000; chemical fertilizer 33,830,000; sulfuric acid 22,300,-000; cotton fabrics 11,716,000; cotton yarn 7,606,-000; sugar 6,531,000; color television sets 40,937,000 units; bicycles 29,023,000 units; household refrigerators 13,513,000 units; household washing machines 13,416,000 units; motor vehicles 2,342,000 units. Distribution of industrial production

(percentage of total value of output by sector; 2001): state-operated enterprises 26.8%; urban collectives 16.6%; rural collectives 23.2%; privately operated enterprises 33.4%. Retail sales (percentage of total sales by sector; 2001): state-operated enterprises 25.3%; collectives 29.8%; privately operated enterprises 44.9%. *Energy production (consumption):* electricity (kW-hr; 2003) 1,838,748,000,000 ([2002] 1,602,156,000,000); coal (2003) 1,315,224,000 ([2000] 981,776,000); crude petroleum (barrels; 2003) 1,247,679,000 ([2000] 1,565,236,000); petroleum products (2000) 157,629,000 (174,016,-000); natural gas (cu m; 2003) 34,243,412,000 ([2000] 33,542,000,000). **Household income and expenditure.** Average household size (2001) 3.5; rural households 4.4, urban households 3.1. Average annual per capita income of household (2001): rural households Y 2,366, urban households Y 6,907. Sources of income (2001): rural households—income from household businesses 77.9%, wages 16.6%, transfers 4.3%, other 1.2%; urban households—wages 73.9%, transfers 19.7%, business income 5.8%, other 0.6%. Expenditure: rural (urban) households—food 47.7% (37.9%), housing 16.0% (10.3%), education and recreation 11.1% (13.0%), transportation and communications 6.3% (8.6%), clothing 5.7% (10.1%), health and personal effects 5.6% (6.5%), household furnishings 4.4% (8.3%). **Population economically active** (2001): total 744,320,000; activity rate of total population 58.5% (participation rates: over age 15, 77.7%; female 37.8%; registered unemployed in urban areas 3.6%). Urban employed workforce (2001): 239,400,000; by sector: state enterprises 76,400,000, collectives 28,130,000, self-employment or privately run enterprises 134,870,-000. Rural employed workforce 490,850,000. **Land use** as % of total land area (2000): in temporary crops 14.7%, in permanent crops 1.2%, in pasture 42.9%; overall forest area 17.5%.

Foreign trade

Imports (2000-f.o.b. in balance of trade and c.i.f. in commodities and trading partners): $225,094,-000,000 (machinery and apparatus 38.0%, of which transistors/microcircuits 9.4%, telecommunications equipment 5.5%; crude petroleum 6.6%; artificial resins and plastic materials 5.8%; textile yarn, fabrics, and made-up articles 5.8%; iron and steel 4.4%). *Major import sources:* Japan 18.4%; unspecified Asia (mostly Taiwan) 11.3%; South Korea 10.3%; US 9.9%; Germany 4.6%; Hong Kong 4.2%; free zones 3.2%; Russia 2.6%; Malaysia 2.4%; Singapore 2.2%. **Exports** (2000): $249,203,000,000 (machinery and apparatus 29.5%, of which computers and related units 7.5%, telecommunications equipment and related parts 5.0%; wearing apparel 14.5%; textile yarn, fabrics, and made-up articles 6.5%; toys, games, and sporting goods 4.1%). *Major export destinations:* US 20.9%; Hong Kong 17.9%; Japan 16.7%; South Korea 4.5%; Germany 3.7%; The Netherlands 2.7%; UK 2.5%; Singapore 2.3%.

Transport and communications

Transport. *Railroads* (2001): route length 70,057 km; passenger-km 476,680,000,000; metric ton-km cargo 1,457,510,000,000. *Roads* (2001): total

---

1 metric ton = about 1.1 short tons; 1 kilometer = 0.6 mi (statute); 1 metric ton-km cargo = about 0.68 short ton-mi cargo; c.i.f.: cost, insurance, and freight; f.o.b.: free on board

length 1,698,012 km. *Vehicles* (2001): passenger cars 9,939,600; trucks and buses 7,652,400. *Air transport* (2001): passenger-km 109,140,000,000; metric ton-km cargo 4,372,000,000; airports (1996) with scheduled flights 113. **Communications,** in total units (units per 1,000 persons). Daily newspaper circulation (1994): 27,790,000 (23); radios (2000): 428,000,000 (339); televisions (2000): 448,000,000 (350); telephone main lines (2003): 263,000,000 (209); cellular telephone subscribers (2003): 269,000,000 (214); personal computers (2002): 35,500,000 (28); Internet users (2003): 79,500,000 (63).

Education and health

Literacy (2000): total population age 15 and over literate 90.9%; males literate 95.1%; females literate 86.5%. **Health** (2004): physicians 1,830,000 (1 per 708 persons); hospital beds 2,900,000 (1 per 447 persons); infant mortality rate per 1,000 live births (2003) 26.4. **Food** (2002): daily per capita caloric intake 2,951 (vegetable products 79%, animal products 21%); 125% of FAO recommended minimum.

Military

Total active duty personnel (2003): 2,250,000 (army 75.6%, navy 11.1%, air force 13.3%). **Military expenditure as percentage of GNP** (1999): 2.3% (world 2.4%); per capita expenditure $71.

Did you know? The Forbidden City is the imperial palace complex at the heart of Beijing, China. Commissioned in 1406 by the Yung-lo emperor of the Ming dynasty, it was first officially occupied by the court in 1420. It was so named because access to the area was barred to most of the subjects of the realm.

Background

The discovery of Peking man (*Homo erectus*) in 1927 dated the advent of early humans in what is now China to the Middle Pleistocene, about 900,000 to 130,000 years ago. Chinese civilization probably spread from the Huang He (Yellow River) valley, where it existed c. 3000 BC. The first dynasty for which there is definite historical material is the Shang (c. 16th century BC), which had a writing system and a calendar. The Zhou, a subject state of the Shang, overthrew its Shang rulers in the 11th century BC and ruled until the 3rd century BC. Taoism and Confucianism were founded in this era.

A time of conflict, called the Warring States Period, lasted from the 5th century BC until in 221 BC the Qin (Ch'in) dynasty (from whose name China is derived) was established after its rulers had conquered rival states and created a unified empire. The Han dynasty was established in 206 BC and ruled until AD 220. A time of turbulence followed, and Chinese reunification was not achieved until the Sui dynasty was established in 581.

After the founding of the Song dynasty in 960, the capital was moved to the south because of northern invasions. In 1279 this dynasty was overthrown and Mongol (Yuan) domination began. During this time Marco Polo visited Kublai Khan. The Ming dynasty followed the period of Mongol rule and lasted from 1368 to 1644, cultivating antiforeign feelings to the point that China closed itself off from the rest of the world.

Peoples from Manchuria overran China in 1644 and established the Qing (Manchu) dynasty. Ever-increasing incursions by Western and Japanese interests led in the 19th century to the Opium Wars, the Taiping Rebellion, and the Sino-Japanese War, all of which weakened the Manchus.

The dynasty fell in 1911, and a republic was proclaimed in 1912 by Sun Yat-sen. The power struggles of warlords weakened the republic. Under Sun's successor, Chiang Kai-shek, some national unification was achieved in the 1920s, but Chiang soon broke with the Communists, who then formed their own armies. Japan invaded northern China in 1937; its occupation lasted until 1945. The Communists gained support after the Long March (1934–35), in which Mao Zedong emerged as their leader.

Upon Japan's surrender at the end of World War II, a fierce civil war began; in 1949 the Nationalists fled to Taiwan and the Communists proclaimed the People's Republic of China. The Communists undertook extensive reforms, but pragmatic policies alternated with periods of revolutionary upheaval, most notably in the Great Leap Forward and the Cultural Revolution. The chaos of the latter led, after Mao's death in 1976, to a turn to moderation under Deng Xiaoping, who undertook economic reforms and renewed China's ties to the West. The government established diplomatic ties with the US in 1979. It suppressed the Tiananmen Square student demonstration in 1989. The economy has been in transition since the late 1970s, moving from central planning and state-run industries to a mixture of state-owned and private enterprises in manufacturing and services. The death of Deng in 1997 marked the end of a political era, but power passed peacefully to Jiang Zemin. In 1997 Hong Kong reverted to Chinese rule, as did Macao in 1999.

Recent Developments

The transition of power from the third to the fourth generation of Communist Party of China (CPC) leadership had begun with the 16th party Congress, when Jiang Zemin passed his title of CPC general secretary to party Political Bureau member and Vice Pres. Hu Jintao. In March 2003 Hu became president when Jiang retired, yet Jiang retained the key position of chairman of the CPC Central Military Commission, or de facto head of the armed forces. In March 2004 the People's National Congress adopted landmark revisions to the 1982 constitution that would protect private property for the first time since the Communists took power in 1949—and thereby apparently abandoned one of the key pillars of communism. In other new text the state committed itself to respecting human rights, but in weak and ambiguous wording.

Much attention was given to the question of how to ensure a soft landing for China's economy and improve the energy supply. Although China enjoyed a robust 9.1% GDP growth rate in 2003, it had to import about 50% of its crude oil to fuel the overheated manufacturing sector and meet residential demand. Oil imports rose by nearly 40% year-on-year in the first eight months of 2004. At the beginning of 2004, the State Council injected $45 billion into the Bank of China and the China Construction Bank to encourage corporate reconstruction by transferring assets into stocks. The goal was to introduce hard budget constraint to the banking system and, among intended other results, to implement more fully the central "financial retrenchments" policy.

The Dalai Lama openly acknowledged that Tibet was a part of China and sent high-level envoys to Beijing in September 2004 to discuss the possibility of the Buddhist leader's return home. In early 2005 there was news of a new law that would allow China to use force against Taiwan if necessary, while at the same time the first nonstop flights between Taiwan and the mainland seemed to indicate a softening of relations. China's relationship with Japan was strained in the spring of 2005 by semiofficial anti-Japanese demonstrations in China, differences over possible Japanese membership in the UN Security Council, and other issues.

Internet resources: <www.chinaonline.com>.

Colombia

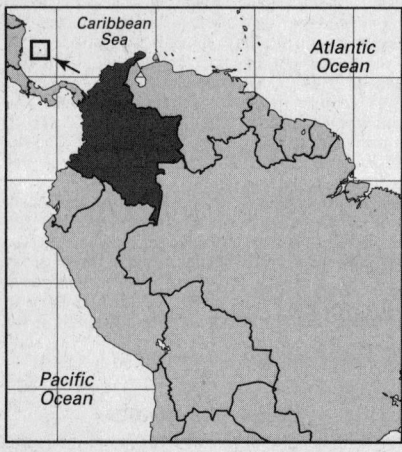

Official name: República de Colombia (Republic of Colombia). **Form of government:** unitary, multiparty republic with two legislative houses (Senate [102]; House of Representatives [166, including two representatives from indigenous communities]). **Head of state and government:** President Álvaro Uribe Vélez (from 2002). **Capital:** Bogotá. **Official language:** Spanish. **Official religion:** none. **Monetary unit:** 1 peso (Col$) = 100 centavos; valuation (7 Jul 2005) US$1 = Col$2,337.50.

Demography

Area: 440,762 sq mi, 1,141,568 sq km. **Population** (2004): 42,311,000. **Density** (2004): persons per sq mi 96.0, persons per sq km 37.1. **Urban** (2003) 76.5%. **Sex distribution** (2003): male 49.08%; female 50.92%. **Age breakdown** (2003): under 15, 31.3%; 15–29, 25.8%; 30–44, 22.8%; 45–59, 12.8%; 60–74, 5.8%; 75 and over, 1.5%. **Ethnic composition** (2000): mestizo 47.3%; mulatto 23.0%; white 20.0%; black 6.0%; black-Amerindian 1.0%; Amerindian/other 2.7%. **Religious affiliation** (1995): Roman Catholic 91.9%; other 8.1%. **Major cities** (1999): Bogotá, D.C., 6,276,428; Cali 2,110,571;

Medellín 1,957,928; Barranquilla 1,226,292; Bucaramanga 520,874. **Location:** northern South America, bordering the Caribbean Sea, Venezuela, Brazil, Peru, Ecuador, the Pacific Ocean, and Panama.

Vital statistics

Birth rate per 1,000 population (2003): 21.6 (world avg. 21.3). **Death rate** per 1,000 population (2003): 5.6 (world avg. 9.1). **Natural increase rate** per 1,000 population (2003): 16.0 (world avg. 12.2). **Total fertility rate** (avg. births per childbearing woman; 2003): 2.6. **Life expectancy** at birth (2003): male 67.3 years; female 75.1 years.

National economy

Budget (1999). *Revenue:* Col$41,457,000,000,000 (tax revenue 61.7%, nontax revenue 38.3%). *Expenditures:* Col$50,441,000,000,000 (current expenditure 73.6%, capital expenditure 26.4%). **Public debt** (external, outstanding; 2002): US$21,177,000,000. **Population economically active** (2000): total 15,417,000; activity rate 38.8% (participation rates: ages 15–69, 64.3%; female 38.0%; unemployed 20.2%). **Production** (metric tons except as noted). *Agriculture, forestry, fishing* (2002): sugarcane 38,200,000, plantains 2,827,024, potatoes 2,697,980; livestock (number of live animals) 27,000,000 cattle, 2,260,000 sheep, 2,150,000 pigs; roundwood (2001) 12,501,000 cu m; fish catch (2001) 190,000. *Mining and quarrying* (2001): nickel (metal content) 52,962; gold 21,813 kg; emeralds 5,500,000 carats. *Manufacturing* (value added in Col$'000,000; 1997): processed food 11,133,000; beverages 3,165,400; petroleum products 2,483,600. *Energy production (consumption):* electricity (kW-hr; 2000) 43,943,000,000 (43,983,-000,000); coal (2000) 38,365,000 (4,551,000); crude petroleum (barrels; 2001) 243,208,000 ([2000] 110,482,000); petroleum products (2000) 13,050,000 (8,656,000); natural gas (cu m; 2000) 7,337,400,000 (7,337,400,000). **Gross national product** (2003): US$80,488,000,000 (US$1,810 per capita). **Land use** as % of total land area (2000): in temporary crops 2.7%, in permanent crops 1.7%, in pasture 39.4%; overall forest area 47.8%. **Households.** Average household size (2000) 5.0; expenditure (1992): food 34.2%, transportation 18.5%, housing 7.8%, health care 6.4%. **Tourism** (2002): receipts US$962,-000,000; expenditures US$1,072,000,000.

Foreign trade

Imports (2002-c.i.f.): US$12,690,000,000 (capital goods 32.5%, consumer goods 21.3%). *Major import sources:* US 31.7%; Venezuela 6.2%; Mexico 5.3%; Brazil 5.1%; Japan 4.9%. **Exports** (2002-f.o.b.): US$11,900,000,000 (crude and refined petroleum 27.5%, chemicals and chemical products 12.4%, coal 8.3%, food, beverages, and tobacco 7.9%, machinery and equipment 7.6%, coffee 6.5%). *Major export destinations:* US 43.0%; Venezuela 9.4%; Ecuador 6.8%; Peru 2.9%; Germany 2.8%.

Transport and communications

Transport. *Railroads* (2000): route length 3,154 km; passenger-km (1992) 15,524,000; metric ton-km

1 metric ton = about 1.1 short tons;   1 kilometer = 0.6 mi (statute);   1 metric ton-km cargo = about 0.68 short ton-mi cargo;   c.i.f.: cost, insurance, and freight;   f.o.b.: free on board

cargo (1999) 473,000,000. *Roads* (1999): total length 114,912 km (paved 14%). *Vehicles* (1999): cars 762,000; trucks 672,000. *Air transport* (2001): passenger-km 5,858,369,000; metric ton-km cargo 33,037,000; airports (1998) 43. **Communications,** in total units (units per 1,000 persons). Daily newspaper circulation (1996): 1,800,000 (46); radios (2001): 25,968,000 (549); televisions (2002): 13,241,000 (303); telephone main lines (2003): 8,768,000 (200); cellular telephone subscribers (2003): 6,186,000 (141); personal computers (2002): 2,133,000 (49); Internet users (2003): 2,732,000 (62).

Education and health

Educational attainment (1985). Percentage of population age 25 and over having: no schooling 15.3%; primary education 50.1%; secondary 25.4%; higher 6.8%; not stated 2.4%. **Literacy** (2002): population age 15 and over literate 92.1%; males literate 92.1%; females literate 92.2%. **Health** (2003): physicians 57,000 (1 per 729 persons); hospital beds 49,000 (1 per 850 persons); infant mortality rate per 1,000 live births 24.2. **Food** (2001): daily per capita caloric intake 2,580 (vegetable products 84%, animal products 16%); 111% of FAO recommended minimum.

Military

Total active duty personnel (2003): 200,000 (army 89.0%, navy 7.5%, air force 3.5%). **Military expenditure as percentage of GNP** (1999): 3.2% (world 2.4%); per capita expenditure US$68.

Background

The Spanish arrived in what is now Colombia c. 1500 and by 1538 had defeated the area's Chibchan-speaking Indians and made the area subject to the viceroyalty of Peru. After 1740 authority was transferred to the newly created viceroyalty of New Granada. Parts of Colombia threw off Spanish jurisdiction in 1810, and full independence came after Spain's defeat by Simón Bolívar in 1819. Civil war in 1840 checked development. Conflict between the Liberal and Conservative parties led to the War of a Thousand Days (1899–1903). Years of relative peace followed, but hostility erupted again in 1948; the two parties agreed in 1958 to a scheme for alternating governments. A new constitution was adopted in 1991, but democratic power remained threatened by civil unrest. Many leftist rebels and right-wing paramilitary groups funded their activities through kidnappings and narcotics trafficking.

Recent Developments

In 2004 the government of Pres. Álvaro Uribe Vélez pushed ahead with its hard-line stance toward armed groups on the left and the right. The left-wing Revolutionary Armed Forces of Colombia (FARC) appeared unprepared for the more vigorous government approach; they had lost control over much of the countryside that the government had ceded to them, and they now chose to fight a more urban battle. The government's Patriot Plan took the fight to members of the FARC surrounding the capital, then pushed into the southeastern states of Caquetá and Guaviare. Observers were alarmed, however, by what they saw as ever-increasing human rights violations by the government in its war on the FARC and other groups.

President Uribe was seen as more interested in security than democracy; still, he enjoyed widespread popularity, and there were continued efforts to revise the constitution to allow him to seek reelection in 2006.

Internet resources: <www.dane.gov.co>.

Comoros

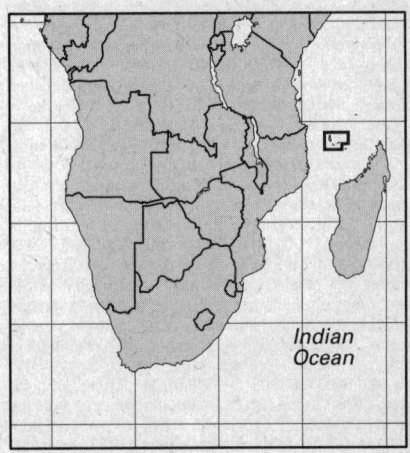

Indian Ocean

Official name: Udzima wa Komori (Comorian); L'Union des Comores (French) (Union of the Comoros). **Form of government:** federal republic with one legislative house (Federal Assembly [33, including 15 non-elected seats]). **Head of state and government:** President Azali Assoumani (from 2002), assisted by vice presidents. **Capital:** Moroni. **Official languages:** Comorian (Shikomor); Arabic; French. **Official religion:** Islam. **Monetary unit:** 1 Comorian franc (formerly pegged to the French franc and, since 1 Jan 2002, to the euro [€] at the rate of €1 = CF 491.97) (CF) = 100 centimes; valuation (7 Jul 2005) $1 = CF 412.58.

Demography

Area: 719 sq mi, 1,862 sq km. **Population** (2004): 596,000 (includes Comorians living abroad in France or Mayotte). **Density** (2004): persons per sq mi 828.9, persons per sq km 320.1. **Urban** (2002): 33.8%. **Sex distribution** (2002): male 49.62%; female 50.38%. **Age breakdown** (2002): under 15, 42.9%; 15–29, 27.8%; 30–44, 16.6%; 45–59, 8.1%; 60–74, 3.9%; 75 and over, 0.7%. **Ethnic composition** (2000): Comorian (a mixture of Bantu, Arab, Malay, and Malagasy peoples) 97.1%; Makua 1.6%; French 0.4%; Arab 0.1%; other 0.8%. **Religious affiliation** (2000): Sunni Muslim 98.0%; Christian 1.2%; other 0.8%. **Major cities** (1991): Moroni (2003) 41,557 (urban agglomeration [2001] 49,000); Mutsamudu 16,785; Domoni 10,400; Fomboni 5,633. **Location:** western Indian Ocean, lying between Madagascar and Mozambique.

Vital statistics

Birth rate per 1,000 population (2003): 38.5 (world avg. 21.3). **Death rate** per 1,000 population (2003): 8.9 (world avg. 9.1). **Natural increase rate** per 1,000 population (2003): 29.6 (world avg. 12.2). **Total fertility rate (avg. births per childbearing woman; 2002): 5.2. **Marriage rate** per 1,000 population: n.a. (in the early 1990s, 20% of adult men had more than one wife). **Life expectancy** at birth (2003): male 58.9 years; female 63.5 years.

National economy

Budget (2000). *Revenue:* CF 15,557,000,000 (tax revenue 62.5%, of which taxes on international trade 40.9%, income and profit taxes 12.2%, sales tax 7.7%; grants 29.2%; nontax revenue 8.3%). *Expenditures:* CF 17,649,000,000 (current expenditures 68.4%, of which wages 34.5%, goods and services 23.3%, interest on debt 5.4%, transfers 4.8%; development expenditures 31.6%). **Public debt** (external, outstanding; 2002): $239,900,000. **Production** (metric tons except as noted). *Agriculture, forestry, fishing* (2002): coconuts 76,000, bananas 60,000, cassava 55,000; livestock (number of live animals; 2002) 115,000 goats, 52,000 cattle, 21,000 sheep; roundwood (2001) 8,650; fish catch (2002) 12,200. *Mining and quarrying:* sand, gravel, and crushed stone from coral-mining for local construction. *Manufacturing:* products of small-scale industries include processed vanilla and ylang-ylang, cement, handicrafts, soaps, soft drinks, woodwork, and clothing. *Energy production (consumption):* electricity (kW-hr; 2001) 36,578,000 (19,780,000); petroleum products (2000) none (26,000). **Population economically active** (2000): total 156,000; activity rate of total population 28.4% (participation rates: [1991] ages 10 years and over, 57.8%; female 40.0%; unemployed [2000] 20%). **Tourism:** receipts from visitors (2002) $11,000,000; expenditures by nationals abroad (1998) $3,000,000. **Household income and expenditure.** Average household size (1995) 6.3; average annual income per household (1995) CF 188,985; expenditure (1993): food and beverages 67.3%, clothing and footwear 11.6%, tobacco and cigarettes 4.1%, energy 3.8%, health 3.2%, education 2.5%, transportation 2.2%, other 5.3%. **Gross national product** (at current market prices; 2003): $269,000,000 ($450 per capita). **Land use** as % of total land area (2000; includes Mayotte): in temporary crops 36%, in permanent crops 22%, in pasture 7%; overall forest area 4%.

Foreign trade

Imports (2001-c.i.f.): CF 27,776,000,000 (food products 28.1%, of which rice 11.3%, meat and fish 8.0%; vehicles 15.6%; petroleum products 15.3%; unspecified 30.1%). *Major import sources:* EU 49%; UAE 11%; South Africa 10%; Pakistan 9%. **Exports** (2001-f.o.b.): CF 9,144,000,000 (vanilla 59.1%, cloves 26.6%, ylang-ylang 10.9%). *Major export destinations:* France 47%; US 30%.

Transport and communications

Transport. *Roads* (1996): total length 900 km (paved 76%). *Vehicles* (1996): passenger cars 9,100; trucks and buses 4,950. *Air transport* (1996): passenger-km 3,000,000; airports (2002) with scheduled flights 4. **Communications,** in total units (units per 1,000 persons). Radios (1997): 90,000 (170); televisions (1997): 1,000 (1.8); telephone main lines (2003): 13,200 (17); cellular telephone subscribers (2003):

2,000 (2.5); personal computers (2003): 5,000 (5.8); Internet users (2003): 5,000 (5.8).

Education and health

Educational attainment (1980). Percentage of population age 25 and over having: no formal schooling 56.7%; Koranic school education 8.3%; primary 3.6%; secondary 2.0%; higher 0.2%; not specified 29.2%. **Literacy** (2000): total population age 15 and over literate 55.9%; males literate 63.2%; females literate 48.7%. **Health** (1995): physicians 64 (1 per 7,800 persons); hospital beds 1,450 (1 per 342 persons); infant mortality rate per 1,000 live births (2003) 79.5. **Food** (2002): daily per capita caloric intake 1,754 (vegetable products 95%, animal products 5%); 75% of FAO recommended minimum.

Military

Total active duty personnel (1997): 1,500.

Elaborate public wedding celebrations, some lasting as long as 3 weeks, are common in the Comoros, and tourists are generally welcome to attend.

Background

The Comoros islands were known to European navigators from the 16th century. In 1843 France officially took possession of Mayotte and in 1886 placed the other three islands under protection. Subordinated to Madagascar in 1912, the Comoros became an overseas territory of France in 1947. In 1961 they were granted autonomy. In 1974 majorities on three of the islands voted for independence, which was granted in 1975. The following decade saw several coup attempts, which culminated in the assassination of the president in 1989. French intervention permitted multiparty elections in 1990, but the country remained in a state of chronic instability. Anjouan seceded from the Comoros federation in 1997. The army took control of the government in 1999. A referendum at the end of 2001 renamed the country the Union of the Comoros and granted the three main islands partially autonomous status.

Recent Developments

The island country had suffered more than 20 coups since gaining independence from France in 1975. Elections that had been postponed for more than a year owing to disagreements over the devolution process on the Comoros's three islands—Anjouan, Grande Comore, and Mohéli—were held in April 2004. The party of federal president Azali Assoumani lost heavily, and the majority of the elected national assembly seats went to the parties of the autonomous islands' presidents. The new assembly finally opened in June but not without continuing tensions between the parties.

Internet resources:
<http://travel.state.gov/comoros>.

---

1 metric ton = about 1.1 short tons;   1 kilometer = 0.6 mi (statute);   1 metric ton-km cargo = about 0.68 short ton-mi cargo;   c.i.f.: cost, insurance, and freight;   f.o.b.: free on board

Democratic Republic of the Congo

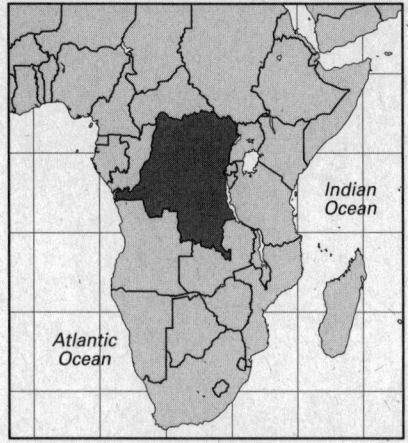

Official name: République Democratique du Congo (Democratic Republic of the Congo). **Form of government:** transitional regime (five-year civil war began in 1998; peace accord and transitional constitution effective from 5–6 Apr 2003 created a two-year interim administration) with two legislative bodies (Senate [120]; National Assembly [500]). **Head of state and government:** President Joseph Kabila (from 2001), assisted by vice presidents. **Capital:** Kinshasa. **Official languages:** French; English. **Official religion:** none. **Monetary unit:** Congo franc (FC); valuation (7 Jul 2005) $1 = FC 419.00.

Demography

Area: 905,354 sq mi, 2,344,858 sq km. **Population** (2004): 54,417,000. **Density** (2004): persons per sq mi 60.1, persons per sq km 23.2. **Urban** (2002): 30.7%. **Sex distribution** (2002): male 49.38%; female 50.62%. **Age breakdown** (2002): under 15, 48.3%; 15–29, 27.2%; 30–44, 13.6%; 45–59, 6.9%; 60–74, 3.2%; 75 and over, 0.8%. **Ethnic composition** (1983): Luba 18.0%; Kongo 16.1%; Mongo 13.5%; Rwanda 10.3%; Azande 6.1%; Bangi and Ngale 5.8%; Rundi 3.8%; Teke 2.7%; Boa 2.3%; Chokwe 1.8%; Lugbara 1.6%; Banda 1.4%; other 16.6%. **Religious affiliation** (1995): Roman Catholic 41.0%; Protestant 32.0%; indigenous Christian 13.4%, of which Kimbanguist 13.0%; other Christian 0.8%; Muslim 1.4%; traditional beliefs and other 11.4%. **Major cities** (1994): Kinshasa 4,655,313; Lubumbashi 851,381; Mbuji-Mayi 806,475; Kolwezi 417,800; Kisangani 417,517. **Location:** central Africa, bordering the Central African Republic, The Sudan, Uganda, Rwanda, Burundi, Tanzania, Zambia, Angola, the South Atlantic Ocean, and the Republic of the Congo.

Vital statistics

Birth rate per 1,000 population (2003): 45.1 (world avg. 21.3). **Death rate** per 1,000 population (2003): 14.9 (world avg. 9.1). **Natural increase rate** per 1,000 population (2003): 30.2 (world avg. 12.2). **Total fertility rate** (avg. births per childbearing woman; 2003): 6.7. **Life expectancy** at birth (2003): male 46.8 years; female 51.1 years. **Adult popula-**tion (ages 15–49) living with HIV (beginning of 2004): 4.2% (world avg. 1.1%).

National economy

Budget (2000). *Revenue:* FC 15,091,000,000 (tax revenue 83.3%, of which sales tax 24.4%, taxes on international trade 23.8%, corporate tax 23.8%; nontax revenue 16.7%). *Expenditures:* FC 32,988,000,000 (goods and services 45.4%; wages and salaries 22.2%; interest on debt 18.7%). **Public debt** (external, outstanding; 2002): $7,391,000,000. **Production** (metric tons except as noted). *Agriculture, forestry, fishing* (2002): cassava 14,929,410, sugarcane 1,550,000, plantains 1,200,000; livestock (number of live animals) 4,003,880 goats, 953,066 pigs; roundwood (2001) 69,733,688 cu m; fish catch (2001) 208,848. *Mining and quarrying* (2002): copper (metal content) 30,000; cobalt (metal content) 3,000; diamonds 18,556,000 carats. *Manufacturing* (2000): butter 2,052,000; steel 259,000; explosives 246,000. *Energy production (consumption):* electricity (kW-hr; 2000) 5,458,000,000 (4,414,000,000); coal (2000) 986,000 (136,000); crude petroleum (barrels; 2000) 9,553,000 (1,358,000); petroleum products (2000) 176,000 (612,000). **Households.** Average household size (1998) 2.3; expenditure (1985): food 61.7%, housing and energy 11.5%, clothing and footwear 9.7%, transportation 5.9%, furniture and utensils 4.9%. **Gross national product** (at current market prices; 2002): $5,369,000,000 ($100 per capita). **Population economically active** (2000): total 20,686,000; activity rate 42.6%. **Tourism** (1998): receipts $2,000,000; expenditures (1997) $7,000,000. **Land use** as % of total land area (2000): in temporary crops 3.0%, in permanent crops 0.5%, in pasture 6.6%, overall forest area 59.6%.

Foreign trade

Imports (2000): $680,000,000 (non-petroleum sector 92.9%, petroleum sector 7.1%). *Major import sources* (2001): Belgium 17.5%; South Africa 15.9%; Nigeria 10.3%; France 5.1%; Kenya 5.0%. **Exports** (2000): $892,000,000 (diamonds 52.5%, crude petroleum 22.8%, cobalt 8.0%, coffee 6.2%, copper 4.8%, gold 2.4%). *Major export destinations* (2001): Belgium 62.1%; US 14.7%; Finland 8.0%; India 4.8%; Italy 2.0%.

Transport and communications

Transport. *Railroads* (1996; Zaire National Railway only): length 5,138 km; passenger-km (1994) 29,000,000; metric ton-km cargo (1994) 176,000,-000. *Roads* (1996): total length 154,027 km (paved 2%). *Vehicles* (1996): passenger cars 787,000; trucks and buses 60,000. *Air transport* (1996): passenger-km 279,000,000; metric ton-km cargo 42,000,000; airports (1997) with scheduled flights 22. **Communications**, in total units (units per 1,000 persons). Daily newspaper circulation (1996): 124,000 (2.7); radios (2000): 18,700,000 (386); televisions (1997): 6,478,000 (135); telephone main lines (2002): 10,000 (0.2); cellular telephone subscribers (2003): 1,000,000 (19); Internet users (2002): 50,000 (0.9).

Education and health

Literacy (2000): percentage of total population age 15 and over literate 61.4%; males literate 73.1%;

females literate 50.2%. **Health:** physicians (1996) 3,129 (1 per 14,494 persons); infant mortality rate per 1,000 live births (2003) 96.6. **Food** (2001): daily per capita caloric intake 1,535 (vegetable products 98%, animal products 2%); 68% of FAO recommended minimum.

Military

Total active duty personnel: new national army being created from August 2003; UN peacekeepers (August 2004): 10,000. **Military expenditure as percentage of GNP** (1997): 14.4% (world 2.4%); per capita expenditure $102.

Background

Prior to European colonization, several native kingdoms had emerged in the Congo region, including the 16th-century Luba kingdom and the Kuba federation, which reached its peak in the 18th century. European development began late in the 19th century when King Léopold II of Belgium financed Henry Morton Stanley's exploration of the Congo River. The 1884–85 Berlin West Africa Conference recognized the Congo Free State with Léopold as its sovereign. The growing demand for rubber helped finance the exploitation of the Congo, but abuses against native peoples outraged Western nations and forced Léopold to grant the Free State a colonial charter as the Belgian Congo (1908). Independence was granted in 1960, and the country's name was changed to Zaire. The post-independence period was marked by unrest, culminating in a military coup that brought Gen. Mobutu Sese Seko to power in 1965. Mismanagement, corruption, and increasing violence devastated the infrastructure and economy. Mobutu was deposed in 1997 by Laurent Kabila, who restored the country's name to Congo. Regional instability and desire for Congo's mineral wealth led to military involvement by numerous African countries. Kabila was assassinated in 2001 and succeeded by his son Joseph.

Recent Developments

The kaleidoscope of attacks, coup attempts, ceasefire agreements, and peacekeeping interventions continued in the Democratic Republic of the Congo in 2004 and 2005. Violence by Mai-Mai fighters in Katanga province was reported in February 2004; a possible coup was quashed by the government in Kinshasa in March; two militant groups agreed to stop fighting in Ituri district, Orientale province, in May but then did not do so; Bukavu city, South Kivu province, was seized by two dissident army officers on 2 June; a second coup was attempted on 11 June; killings of Congolese Tutsi in Burundi heightened tensions in South Kivu in August; and fierce fighting was reported in North Kivu in December after reports were circulated that Rwandan troops had entered the area. In early 2005 UN peacekeepers were ambushed and nine were killed in the Ituri region, and nearby a week later UN troops killed some 50 militiamen in a campaign to stop wanton violence in the region.

Internet resources: <www.un.int/drcongo>.

Republic of the Congo

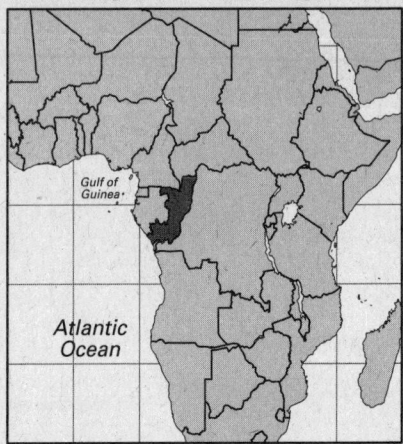

Official name: République du Congo (Republic of the Congo). **Form of government:** republic with two legislative houses (Senate [66]; National Assembly [137]). **Chief of state and government:** President Denis Sassou-Nguesso (from 1997). **Capital:** Brazzaville. **Official language:** French (Lingala and Monokutuba are "functional" national languages). **Official religion:** none. **Monetary unit:** 1 CFA franc (CFAF) = 100 centimes; valuation (7 Jul 2005) $1 = CFAF 549.50 (formerly pegged to the French franc and, since 1 Jan 2002, to the euro at the rate of €1 = CFAF 655.96).

Demography

Area: 132,047 sq mi, 342,000 sq km. **Population** (2004): 3,818,000. **Density** (2004): persons per sq mi 28.9, persons per sq km 11.2. **Urban** (2002): 66.1%. **Sex distribution** (2002): male 49.36%; female 50.64%. **Age breakdown** (2002): under 15, 38.9%; 15–29, 29.6%; 30–44, 17.7%; 45–59, 8.4%; 60–74, 4.4%; 75 and over, 1.0%. **Ethnic composition** (1983): Kongo 51.5%; Teke 17.3%; Mboshi 11.5%; Mbete 4.9%; Punu 3.0%; Sango 2.7%; Maka 1.8%; Pygmy 1.5%; other 5.8%. **Religious affiliation** (2000): Roman Catholic 49.3%; Protestant 17.0%; African Christians 12.6%; unaffiliated Christians 11.9%; traditional beliefs 4.8%; other 4.4%. **Major cities** (1992): Brazzaville (urban agglomeration; 2001) 1,360,000; Pointe-Noire (1996) 455,131; Dolisie (known as Loubomo between 1980 and 2000) 83,605; Nkayi 42,465; Mossendjo 16,405. **Location:** west-central Africa, bordering Cameroon, the Central African Republic, the Democratic Republic of the Congo, Angola, the South Atlantic Ocean, and Gabon.

Vital statistics

Birth rate per 1,000 population (2003): 29.5 (world avg. 21.3). **Death rate** per 1,000 population (2003): 14.2 (world avg. 9.1). **Natural increase rate** per 1,000 population (2002): 15.3 (world avg. 12.2). **Total fertility rate** (avg. births per childbearing

---

1 metric ton = about 1.1 short tons;   1 kilometer = 0.6 mi (statute);   1 metric ton-km cargo = about 0.68 short ton-mi cargo;   c.i.f.: cost, insurance, and freight;   f.o.b.: free on board

woman; 2003): 3.7. **Life expectancy** at birth (2003): màle 49.0 years; female 51.0 years. **Adult population** (ages 15–49) **living with HIV** (beginning of 2004): 4.9% (world avg. 1.1%).

National economy

Budget (2001). *Revenue:* CFAF 631,800,000,000 (petroleum revenue 68.2%; nonpetroleum receipts 31.2%; grants 0.6%). *Expenditures:* CFAF 645,900,-000,000 (current expenditure 68.2%, of which debt service 23.5%, salaries 18.3%, transfers and subsidies 11.3%; capital expenditure 31.8%). **Public debt** (external, outstanding; 2002): $3,974,000,000. **Households.** Average household size (1984) 5.2. **Gross national product** (at current market prices; 2002): $2,407,000,000 ($640 per capita). **Production** (metric tons except as noted). *Agriculture, forestry, fishing* (2002): cassava 862,000, sugarcane 459,000, oil palm fruit 90,000; livestock (number of live animals) 294,000 goats, 96,000 sheep, 93,000 cattle; roundwood (2001) 2,420,000 cu m; fish catch (2002) 43,000. *Mining and quarrying* (2002): gold 10 kg; diamonds, no reported production (annual volume of large-scale diamond smuggling as of July 2004 equaled 5,200,000 carats). *Manufacturing* (2000): residual fuel oil 262,000; distillate fuel oils 96,000; refined sugar 74,726. *Energy production (consumption):* electricity (kW-hr; 2000) 300,000,000 (490,000,000); crude petroleum (barrels; 2000) 99,200,000 (4,444,000); petroleum products (2001) 383,000 (165,400); natural gas (cu m; 2000) 124,983,000 (124,983,000). **Population economically active** (2000): total 1,232,000; activity rate of total population 35.7% (participation rates [1984]: ages 15–64, 54.0%; female [1997] 43.4%). **Land use** as % of total land area (2000): in temporary crops 0.5%, in permanent crops 0.1%, in pasture 29.3%; overall forest area 64.6%. **Tourism** (2002): receipts $25,000,000; expenditures $70,000,000.

Foreign trade

Imports (2001): CFAF 486,200,000,000 (nonpetroleum sector 84.0%; petroleum sector 16.0%). *Major import sources* (1999): France 23%; US 8%; Italy 8%; Hong Kong 5%; Belgium 4%. **Exports** (2001): CFAF 1,443,200,000,000 (crude petroleum 89.6%, wood and wood products 5.1%, petroleum products 1.3%, sugar 0.7%). *Major export destinations* (1999): Taiwan 32%; US 23%; South Korea 15%; Germany 7%; China 3%.

Transport and communications

Transport. *Railroads:* (1998) length 894 km; passenger-km 242,000,000; metric ton-km cargo 135,-000,000. *Roads* (2001): total length 17,244 km (paved 7%). *Vehicles* (1997): passenger cars 37,240; trucks and buses 15,500. *Air transport* (1998; represents 1/11 of the traffic of Air Afrique; Air Afrique, an airline jointly owned by 11 African countries [including Republic of the Congo], was declared bankrupt in February 2002): passenger-km 258,272,000; metric ton-km cargo 13,524,000; airports (1998) with scheduled flights 10. **Communications**, in total units (units per 1,000 persons). Daily newspaper circulation (2000): 10,300 (3); radios (2000): 403,300 (109); televisions (2000): 114,000 (13); telephone main lines (2003): 7,000 (2); cellular telephone subscribers (2003): 330,000

(94); personal computers (2003): 15,000 (4.3); Internet users (2003): 15,000 (4.3).

Education and health

Educational attainment (1984). Percentage of population age 25 and over having: no formal schooling 58.7%; primary education 21.4%; secondary education 16.9%; postsecondary 3.0%. **Literacy** (2000): total population age 15 and over literate 80.7%; males literate 87.5%; females literate 74.4%. **Health:** physicians (1995) 632 (1 per 4,083 persons); hospital beds (1989) 4,817 (1 per 446 persons); infant mortality rate per 1,000 live births (2003) 95.3. **Food** (2002): daily per capita caloric intake 2,162 (vegetable products 94%, animal products 6%); 97% of FAO recommended minimum.

Military

Total active duty personnel (2003): 10,000 (army 80.0%, navy 8.0%, air force 12.0%). **Military expenditure as percentage of GNP** (1999): 3.5% (world 2.4%); per capita expenditure $21.

Background

In precolonial days the Congo area was home to several thriving kingdoms, including the Kongo, which had its beginnings in the 1st millennium AD. The slave trade began in the 15th century with the arrival of the Portuguese; it supported the local kingdoms and dominated the area until its suppression in the 19th century. The French arrived in the mid-19th century and established treaties with two of the kingdoms, placing them under French protection prior to their becoming part of the colony of French Congo. In 1910 the French possessions were renamed French Equatorial Africa, and Congo became known as Middle (Moyen) Congo. In 1946 Middle Congo became a French overseas territory and in 1958 voted to become an autonomous republic within the French Community. Full independence came two years later. The area has suffered from political instability since independence. Congo's first president was ousted in 1963. A Marxist party, the Congolese Labor Party, gained strength, and in 1968 another coup, led by Maj. Marien Ngouabi, created the People's Republic of the Congo. Ngouabi was assassinated in 1977. A series of military rulers followed, at first militantly socialist but later oriented toward social democracy. Fighting between local militias that began in 1997 badly disrupted the economy.

Recent Developments

The IMF opened consultations with the Republic of the Congo government on 24 May 2004 and announced in July that it would undertake a three-year program designed to reduce poverty and increase economic growth. The government admitted on 5 June that a large trade in illegal diamonds existed in the country but disclaimed all responsibility on the grounds that the diamonds were being illegally imported from neighboring countries and then smuggled out to Switzerland and the United Arab Emirates.

Internet resources:
<www.cia.gov/cia/publications/factbook/geos/cf.html>.

Costa Rica

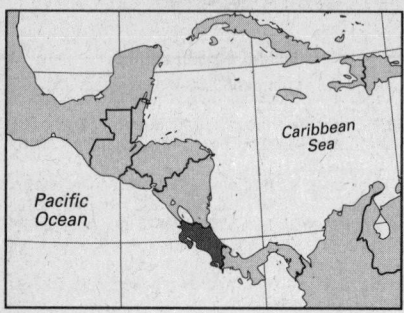

Official name: República de Costa Rica (Republic of Costa Rica). **Form of government:** unitary multiparty republic with one legislative house (Legislative Assembly [57]). **Head of state and government:** President Abel Pacheco de la Espriella (from 2002). **Capital:** San José. **Official language:** Spanish. **Official religion:** Roman Catholicism. **Monetary unit:** 1 Costa Rican colón (₡) = 100 céntimos; valuation (7 Jul 2005) $1 = ₡478.90.

Demography

Area: 19,730 sq mi, 51,100 sq km. **Population** (2004): 4,252,000. **Density** (2004): persons per sq mi 215.5, persons per sq km 83.2. **Urban** (2003): 60.6%. **Sex distribution** (2003): male 50.86%; female 49.14%. **Age breakdown** (2002): under 15, 30.7%; 15–29, 27.3%; 30–44, 21.7%; 45–59, 12.5%; 60–74, 5.7%; 75 and over, 2.1%. **Ethnic composition** (2000): white 77.0%; mestizo 17.0%; black/mulatto 3.0%; East Asian (mostly Chinese) 2.0%; Amerindian 1.0%. **Religious affiliation** (1995): Roman Catholic 86.0%; Protestant 9.3%, of which Pentecostal 4.9%; other Christian 2.4%; other 2.3%. **Major cities** (2000): San José 309,672 (San José canton; urban agglomeration 983,000 [2001]); Limón 60,298 (district population); Alajuela 42,889 (district population); San Isidro de El General 41,221 (district population); Cartago 39,958 (three districts). **Location:** Central America, bordering Nicaragua, the Caribbean Sea, Panama, and the North Pacific Ocean.

Vital statistics

Birth rate per 1,000 population (2003): 19.4 (world avg. 21.3); (1999) legitimate 51.0%. **Death rate** per 1,000 population (2003): 4.3 (world avg. 9.1). **Natural increase rate** per 1,000 population (2003): 15.1 (world avg. 12.2). **Total fertility rate** (avg. births per childbearing woman; 2003): 2.4. **Marriage rate** per 1,000 population (1999): 7.1. **Divorce rate** per 1,000 population (1995): 1.4. **Life expectancy** at birth (2003): male 73.9 years; female 79.1 years.

National economy

Budget (2000). *Revenue:* ₡610,138,000,000 (taxes on goods and services 63.8%, income and profit taxes 21.8%, import duties 7.7%, other 6.7%). *Ex-* penditures: ₡761,306,000,000 (current expenditures 90.1%, of which transfers 30.5%, wages 29.7%, interest on debt 23.0%; development expenditures 9.9%). **Public debt** (external, outstanding; 2002): $3,139,000,000. **Gross national product** (2003): $17,157,000,000 ($4,280 per capita). **Production** (metric tons except as noted). *Agriculture, forestry, fishing* (2003): sugarcane 3,923,870, bananas 1,862,978, green coffee 731,126; livestock (number of live animals) 1,150,000 cattle, 500,000 pigs, 18,500,000 chickens; roundwood (2001) 5,140,781 cu m; fish catch (2001) 35,000. *Mining and quarrying* (2002): limestone 900,000; gold 100 kg. *Manufacturing* (value added in $'000,000; 2001): food products 777; beverages 211; paints, soaps, and pharmaceuticals 148. *Energy production (consumption):* electricity (kW-hr; 2000) 7,227,000,000 (7,226,000,000); crude petroleum (barrels; 2000) none (80,630); petroleum products (2000) 6,000 (1,597,000). **Population economically active** (2000): total 1,390,560; activity rate of total population 39.9% (participation rates: ages 12–59, 53.4%; female 32.1%; unemployed 5.2%). **Tourism** (2002): receipts $1,078,000,000; expenditures $367,000,-000. **Household income and expenditure.** Average household size (2000) 4.1; average annual household income (1997) ₡1,468,597; sources of income (1987–88): wages and salaries 61.0%, self-employment 22.6%, transfers 9.6%; expenditure (1987–88): food and beverages 39.1%, housing and energy 12.1%, transportation 11.6%, household furnishings 10.9%. **Land use** as % of total land area (2000): in temporary crops 4.4%, in permanent crops 5.9%, in pasture 45.8%; overall forest area 38.5%.

Foreign trade

Imports (2000-c.i.f.): $6,380,000,000 (estimated figures: general merchandise 68%; goods for reassembly 32%). *Major import sources:* US 53.1%; Mexico 6.2%; Venezuela 5.3%; Japan 3.4%; Spain 2.3%. **Exports** (2000-f.o.b.): $5,897,000,000 (components for microprocessors 28.0%, bananas 9.0%, processed food and tobacco products 6.5%, coffee 4.7%, tropical fruit 3.4%). *Major export destinations:* US 51.8%; The Netherlands 6.7%; UK 5.1%; Guatemala 3.3%; Nicaragua 3.0%.

Transport and communications

Transport. *Roads* (1999): total length 35,876 km (paved 17%). *Vehicles* (1999): passenger cars 326,524; trucks and buses 181,272. *Air transport* (2001; Lacsa [Costa Rican Airlines] only): passenger-km 2,143,000,000; metric ton-km cargo 84,697,-000; airports (1996) 14. **Communications,** in total units (units per 1,000 persons). Daily newspaper circulation (1996): 320,000 (94); radios (2000): 3,200,000 (816); televisions (2000): 907,000 (231); telephone main lines (2002): 1,038,000 (251); cellular telephone subscribers (2003): 459,800 (141); personal computers (2002): 800,000 (193); Internet users (2002): 817,000 (197).

Education and health

Educational attainment (1996). Percentage of population age 5 and over having: no formal schooling

---

1 metric ton = about 1.1 short tons; 1 kilometer = 0.6 mi (statute); 1 metric ton-km cargo = about 0.68 short ton-mi cargo; c.i.f.: cost, insurance, and freight; f.o.b.: free on board

11.7%; incomplete primary education 28.5%; complete primary 25.8%; incomplete secondary 16.0%; complete secondary 9.0%; higher 8.5%; other/unknown 0.5%. **Literacy** (2002): total population age 15 and over literate 95.8%; males literate 95.7%; females literate 95.9%. **Health** (2003): physicians (2000) 6,800 (1 per 625 persons); hospital beds 6,000 (1 per 700 persons); infant mortality rate per 1,000 live births 10.6. **Food** (2001): daily per capita caloric intake 2,761 (vegetable products 80%, animal products 20%); 123% of FAO recommended minimum.

Military

Paramilitary expenditure as percentage of GNP (1999): 0.5% (world 2.4%); per capita expenditure $19. The army was officially abolished in 1948. Paramilitary (police) forces had 8,400 members in 2003.

Background

Christopher Columbus landed in Costa Rica in 1502 in an area inhabited by a number of small, independent Indian tribes. These peoples were not easily dominated, and it took almost 60 years for the Spanish to establish a permanent settlement. Ignored by the Spanish crown because of its lack of mineral wealth, the colony grew slowly. Coffee exports and the construction of a rail line improved its economy in the 19th century. It joined the short-lived Mexican Empire in 1821, was a member of the United Provinces of Central America 1823–38, and adopted a constitution in 1871. In 1890 Costa Ricans held what is considered to be the first free and honest election in Central America, beginning a tradition of democracy for which Costa Rica is renowned. In 1987 then president Oscar Arias Sánchez was awarded the Nobel Peace Prize. During the 1990s Costa Rica struggled with its economic policies. It suffered severe damage from a hurricane in 1996.

Recent Developments

National attention in Costa Rica was riveted on the Central American Free Trade Agreement (CAFTA) with the United States. By late 2003 bilateral negotiations had reached an impasse, and there were growing hints that Costa Rica would be excluded from the agreement. In January 2004, however, the differences were smoothed over, and the agreement was signed in May 2004. The main sticking point had been the US insistence that Costa Rica's state-run monopolies in telecommunications—including cell phones and the Internet—as well as electric power and insurance, be opened to competition. Still, in early 2005, when the question of ratification began to be discussed, Costa Rica was again seen to be dragging its feet.

Internet resources: <www.casapres.go.cr>.

Côte d'Ivoire

Official name: République de Côte d'Ivoire (Republic of Côte d'Ivoire). **Form of government:** republic with one legislative house (National Assembly [225, including unoccupied seats]); constitutional referendum approved July 2000, but status of new constitution unclear in 2004. **Chief of state and government:** President Laurent Gbagbo (from 2000), assisted by

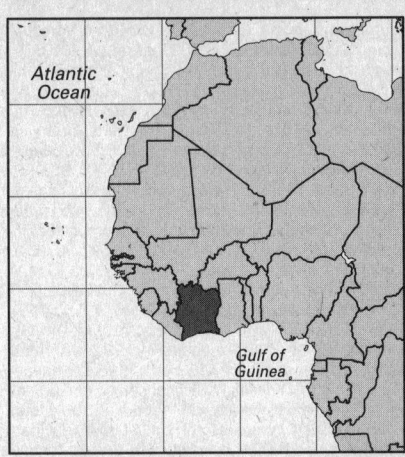

Prime Minister Seydou Diarra (from 2003). **Capital:** Abidjan. **Official language:** French. **Official religion:** none. **Monetary unit:** 1 CFA franc (CFAF) = 100 centimes; valuation (7 Jul 2005) $1 = CFAF 549.50 (formerly pegged to the French franc and, since 1 Jan 2002, to the euro at the rate of €1 = CFAF 655.96).

Demography

Area: 123,863 sq mi, 320,803 sq km. **Population** (2004): 16,897,000. **Density** (2004): persons per sq mi 136.4, persons per sq km 52.7. **Urban** (2003): 44.9%. **Sex distribution** (2002): male 50.28%; female 49.72%. **Age breakdown** (2002): under 15, 45.6%; 15–29, 28.7%; 30–44, 14.4%; 45–59, 7.6%; 60–74, 3.0%; 75 and over, 0.7%. **Ethnolinguistic composition** (1998; local population only; foreigners constituted 26% of the population and two-thirds of all foreigners were from Burkina Faso): Akan 42.1%; Mande 26.5%; other 31.4%. **Religious affiliation** (1998): Muslim 38.6%; Christian 30.4%; nonreligious 16.7%; animist 11.9%; other 2.4%. **Major cities** (1998): Abidjan (1999) 3,199,000; Bouaké 462,000; Daloa 173,000; Yamoussoukro 110,000. **Location:** western Africa, bordering Mali, Burkina Faso, Ghana, the Atlantic Ocean, Liberia, and Guinea.

Vital statistics

Birth rate per 1,000 population (2002): 40.4 (world avg. 21.3). **Death rate** per 1,000 population (2001): 18.4 (world avg. 9.1). **Natural increase rate** per 1,000 population (2002): 22.0 (world avg. 12.2). **Total fertility rate** (avg. births per childbearing woman; 2002): 5.6. **Life expectancy** at birth (2002): male 40.4 years; female 45.3 years. **Adult population** (ages 15–49) **living with HIV** (2004): 7.0% (world avg. 1.1%).

National economy

Budget (2000). *Revenue:* CFAF 1,237,100,000,000 (tax revenue 87.1%, of which import taxes and duties 29.2%, export taxes 13.2%, taxes on profits 11.6%, income tax 10.2%; nontax revenue 12.9%). *Expenditures:* CFAF 1,358,200,000,000 (wages and salaries 33.0%; debt service 22.7%; capital expenditure 15.4%; transfers 13.1%; other 15.8%). **Production**

(metric tons except as noted). *Agriculture, forestry, fishing* (2002): yams 3,000,000, cassava 1,700,000, plantains 1,410,000; livestock (number of live animals) 1,522,000 sheep, 1,476,000 cattle, 32,625,-000 chickens; roundwood (2001) 12,083,092 cu m; fish catch (2001) 74,581. *Mining and quarrying* (2002): gold 2,000 kg; diamonds 306,500 carats. *Manufacturing* (value added in CFAF '000,000,000; 1997): food 156.6, of which cocoa and chocolate 72.4, vegetable oils 62.7; chemicals 60.2; wood products 55.9. *Energy production (consumption)*: electricity (kW-hr; 2000) 3,619,000,000 (3,619,000,000); crude petroleum (barrels; 2000) 11,270,000 (30,087,000); petroleum products (2000) 2,801,000 (1,242,000); natural gas (cu m; 2000) 1,510,400,-000 (1,510,400,000). **Households.** Average household size (2000) 7.8; expenditure (1992–93): food 48.0%, transportation 12.2%, clothing 10.1%, energy and water 8.5%, housing 7.8%, household equipment 3.4%. **Population economically active** (2000): total 6,531,000; activity rate of total population 40.9% (participation rates [1994] over age 10, 64.3%; female 33.0%; unemployed [1996] 38.8%). **Gross national product** (2003): $11,159,000,000 ($660 per capita). **Public debt** (external, outstanding; 2002): $9,110,-000,000. **Tourism** (2001): receipts $48,000,000; expenditures $192,000,000. **Land use** as % of total land area (2000): in temporary crops 9.7%, in permanent crops 13.8%, in pasture 40.9%; overall forest area 22.4%.

Foreign trade

Imports (2001-f.o.b. in balance of trade and commodities and c.i.f. for trading partners): CFAF 1,768,000,000,000 (crude and refined petroleum 28.8%, food products 22.5%, machinery and transport equipment 20.4%). *Major import sources* (2000): Nigeria 26.6%; France 20.3%; Belgium 4.0%; Italy 3.6%; Germany 3.6%. **Exports** (2001): CFAF 2,891,000,000,000 (cocoa beans and products 33.2%, crude petroleum and petroleum products 13.7%, wood and wood products 7.1%, coffee beans 3.6%). *Major export destinations* (2000): France 14.9%; The Netherlands 9.7%; US 8.3%; Mali 5.7%; Italy 4.8%; Senegal 4.0%.

Transport and communications

Transport. *Railroads* (1999): route length 655 km; passenger-km 93,100,000; metric ton-km cargo 537,600,000. *Roads* (1999): total length 50,400 km (paved 9.7%). *Vehicles* (1999): passenger cars 109,600; trucks and buses 54,100. *Air transport* (1998): passenger-km 318,000,000; metric ton-km cargo 44,000,000; airports (1999) 5. **Communications**, in total units (units per 1,000 persons). Daily newspaper circulation (2000): 1,440,000 (91); radios (2001): 3,053,000 (185); televisions (2002): 1,007,000 (61); telephone main lines (2003): 328,000 (20); cellular telephone subscribers (2003): 1,236,000 (74); personal computers (2002): 154,000 (9.3); Internet users (2002): 90,000 (5.5).

Education and health

Educational attainment (1988). Percentage of population age 6 and over having: no formal schooling

60.0%; Koranic school 3.6%; primary education 24.8%; secondary 10.7%; higher 0.9%. **Literacy** (2000): percentage of population age 15 and over literate 46.8%; males 54.5%; females 38.6%. **Health:** physicians (1996) 1,318 (1 per 11,111 persons); hospital beds (1993) 7,928 (1 per 1,698 persons); infant mortality rate per 1,000 live births (2001) 99.6. **Food** (2001): daily per capita caloric intake 2,594 (vegetable products 97%, animal products 3%); 112% of FAO recommended minimum.

Military

Total active duty personnel: New national army to be created pending final resolution of 2002–03 civil war. Peacekeeping troops (August 2004): UN 5,800; French 4,000. **Military expenditure as percentage of GNP** (1999): 0.8% (world avg. 2.4%); per capita expenditure $5.

Background

Europeans came to the area to trade in ivory and slaves beginning in the 15th century, and local kingdoms gave way to French influence in the 19th century. The French colony of Côte d'Ivoire was founded in 1893, and full occupation took place 1908–18. In 1946 it became a territory in the French Union. Côte d'Ivoire achieved independence in 1960, when Félix Houphouët-Boigny was elected president. The country's first multiparty presidential elections were held in 1990.

Recent Developments

In 2004 Côte d'Ivoire remained effectively split in two as a result of the civil war that erupted in September 2002. Members of the rebellious New Force alliance (FN) continued to hold the north, while the government, assisted by 4,000 French troops and about 5,800 United Nations peacekeepers, controlled the south. Spasmodic outbreaks of ethnic and religious violence dominated the year. Political proposals for resolving the conflict seemed to win little support. In November violence flared after France, responding to an Ivorian air strike that killed nine French soldiers, destroyed Côte d'Ivoire's air force. Anti-French riots ensued, and thousands of Ivorians and French nationals and other foreigners fled the country. Another peace accord was signed by the government and FN representatives in April 2005.

Internet resources: <www.africaonline.co.ci>.

Croatia

Official name: Republika Hrvatska (Republic of Croatia). **Form of government:** multiparty republic with one legislative house (House of Representatives [152, including six seats representing Croatians living abroad and two seats for minorities]). **Head of state:** President Stipe Mesic (from 2000). **Head of government:** Prime Minister Ivo Sanader (from 2003). **Capital:** Zagreb. **Official language:** Croatian (Serbo-Croatian). **Official religion:** none. **Monetary unit:** 1 kuna (HrK; plural kune) = 100 lipa; valuation (7 Jul 2005) $1 = HrK 6.13.

---

1 metric ton = about 1.1 short tons;   1 kilometer = 0.6 mi (statute);   1 metric ton-km cargo = about 0.68 short ton-mi cargo;   c.i.f.: cost, insurance, and freight;   f.o.b.: free on board

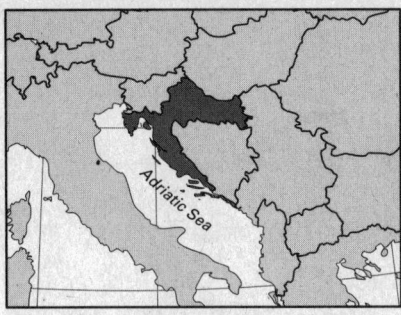

Demography

Area: 56,542 sq km. **Population** (2004): 4,497,000. **Density** (2004): persons per sq mi 206.0, persons per sq km 79.5. **Urban** (2002): 59.0%. **Sex distribution** (2001): male 48.13%; female 51.87%. **Age breakdown** (2001): under 15, 17.1%; 15–29, 20.4%; 30–44, 21.4%; 45–59, 19.5%; 60–74, 16.3%; 75 and over, 5.3%. **Ethnic composition** (2001): Croat 89.6%; Serb 4.5%; Bosniac 0.5%; Italian 0.4%; Hungarian 0.4%; other 4.6%. **Religious affiliation** (2000): Christian 95.2%, of which Roman Catholic 88.5%, Eastern Orthodox 5.6%, Protestant 0.6%; Sunni Muslim 2.3%; nonreligious/atheist 2.5%. **Major cities** (2001): Zagreb 691,724; Split 175,140; Rijeka 143,360; Osijek 90,411; Zadar 69,556. **Location:** southeastern Europe, bordering Slovenia, Hungary, Serbia and Montenegro, Bosnia and Herzegovina, and the Adriatic Sea.

Vital statistics

Birth rate per 1,000 population (2003): 9.5 (world avg. 21.3); (1999) legitimate 91.8%. **Death rate** per 1,000 population (2003): 11.2 (world avg. 9.1). **Natural increase rate** per 1,000 population (2001): –1.7 (world avg. 12.2). **Total fertility rate** (avg. births per childbearing woman; 2003): 1.4. **Marriage rate** per 1,000 population (2001): 5.0. **Divorce rate** per 1,000 population (2001): 1.1. **Life expectancy** at birth (2003): male 69.6 years; female 78.3 years.

National economy

Budget (2001). *Revenue:* HrK 55,303,800,000 (tax revenue 84.9%, of which sales tax 40.7%, excise taxes 14.2%, income tax 6.8%; nontax revenue 15.1%). *Expenditures:* HrK 57,308,100,000 (social security and welfare 43.2%; education 10.7%; public order 8.3%; defense 7.4%). **Population economically active** (2001): total 1,728,503; activity rate 39.0% (participation rates: ages 15–64, 57.9%; female 43.0%; unemployed 22.0%). **Production** (metric tons except as noted). *Agriculture, forestry, fishing* (2002): corn (maize) 2,502,000, sugar beets 1,183,000, wheat 988,000; livestock (number of live animals) 1,286,000 pigs, 580,000 sheep, 11,665,000 poultry; roundwood (2001) 3,468,000 cu m; fish catch (2002) 30,000. *Mining and quarrying* (2002): gypsum 145,000; ornamental stone 1,128,000 sq m. *Manufacturing* (value added in $'000,000; 1996): food products 895; transport equipment 425; electrical machinery 362. *Energy production (consumption):* electricity (kW-hr; 2001) 11,674,000,000 ([2000] 14,702,000,000); hard coal (2000) none (623,000); lignite (2000) none

(80,000); crude petroleum (barrels; 2000) 8,158,000 (37,845,000); petroleum products (2000) 4,827,000 (3,534,000); natural gas (cu m; 2001) 2,009,000,000 ([2000] 2,633,994,000). **Gross national product** (2003): $23,839,000,000 ($5,350 per capita). **Public debt** (external, outstanding; 2002): $7,679,000,000. **Household income and expenditure.** Average household size (2001) 3.0; income per household HrK 64,288; sources: wages 42.8%, self-employment 22.5%, pension 20.6%, other 14.1%; expenditure (2001): food and nonalcoholic beverages 33.7%, housing and energy 13.4%, transportation 11.5%, clothing 9.1%, recreation and culture 5.9%, household furnishings 5.6%, alcoholic beverages and tobacco 4.1%, other 16.7%. **Tourism** (2002): receipts $3,811,000,000; expenditures $781,000,000. **Land use** as % of total land area (2000): in temporary crops 26.1%, in permanent crops 2.3%, in pasture 28.1%; overall forest area 31.9%.

Foreign trade

Imports (2001-f.o.b. in balance of trade and c.i.f. for commodities and trading partners): $9,044,000,000 (machinery and transport equipment 33.2%, chemical products 11.5%, base and fabricated metals 10.1%, crude and refined petroleum 9.2%). *Major import sources:* Germany 17.1%; Italy 16.9%; Slovenia 7.9%; Russia and other countries of former USSR 7.2%; Austria 7.0%. **Exports** (2001): $4,659,000,000 (machinery and transport equipment 29.4%, chemical and chemical products 10.6%, clothing 10.5%, crude petroleum and petroleum products 7.4%, food 6.9%). *Major export destinations:* Italy 23.7%; Germany 14.8%; Bosnia and Herzegovina 12.0%; Slovenia 9.1%; Austria 5.7%.

Transport and communications

Transport. *Railroads* (2001): length 2,726 km; passenger-km 1,234,000,000; metric ton-km cargo 2,148,000,000. *Roads* (2001): total length 28,275 km (paved 82%). *Vehicles* (2001): passenger cars 1,195,450; trucks and buses 124,669. *Air transport* (2001): passenger-km 921,053,000; metric ton-km cargo 3,597,000; airports (2001) 4. **Communications,** in total units (units per 1,000 persons). Daily newspaper circulation (1996): 515,000 (118); radios (2000): 1,120,000 (252); televisions (2000): 1,693,000 (380); telephone main lines (2002): 1,825,000 (417); cellular telephone subscribers (2003): 2,553,000 (584); personal computers (2002): 760,000 (174); Internet users (2003): 1,014,000 (232).

Education and health

Educational attainment (1991). Percentage of population age 15 and over having: no schooling or unknown 10.1%; less than full primary education 21.2%; primary 23.4%; secondary 36.0%; postsecondary and higher 9.3%. **Literacy** (1999): population age 15 and over literate 98.2%; males 99.3%; females 97.1%. **Health** (1999): physicians 8,046 (1 per 529 persons); hospital beds 27,000 (1 per 158 persons); infant mortality rate per 1,000 live births (2003) 7.1. **Food** (2002): daily per capita caloric intake 2,799 (vegetable products 81%, animal products 19%); 110% of FAO recommended minimum.

Military

Total active duty personnel (2003): 20,800 (army 67.5%, navy 12.0%, air force and air defense 11.1%, headquarters staff 9.4%). **Military expenditure as percentage of GNP** (1999): 6.4% (world 2.4%); per capita expenditure $491.

Did you know? The seaport and resort of Split is the chief city of Dalmatia, Croatia. The city is best known for the ruins of the Palace of Diocletian (built AD 295–305).

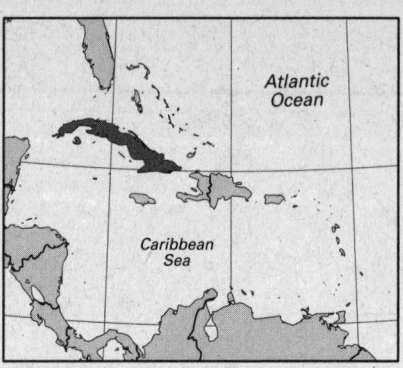

Atlantic Ocean

Caribbean Sea

Background

The Croats, a southern Slavic people, arrived in the area in the 7th century AD and in the 8th century came under Charlemagne's rule. They converted to Christianity soon afterward and formed a kingdom in the 10th century. Most of Croatia was taken by the Turks in 1526; the rest voted to accept Austrian rule. In 1867 it became part of Austria-Hungary, with Dalmatia and Istria ruled by Vienna and Croatia-Slavonia a Hungarian crown land. In 1918, after the defeat of Austria-Hungary in World War I, it joined other south Slavic territories to form the Kingdom of Serbs, Croats, and Slovenes, renamed Yugoslavia in 1929. During World War II an independent state of Croatia was established by Germany and Italy, embracing Croatia-Slavonia, part of Dalmatia, and Bosnia and Herzegovina; after the war Croatia was rejoined to Yugoslavia as a people's republic. It declared its independence in 1991, sparking insurrections by Croatian Serbs, who carved out autonomous regions with Serbian-led Yugoslav army help; Croatia had taken back most of these regions by 1995. With some stability returning, Croatia's economy began to revive in the late 1990s.

Recent Developments

Croatia's new, center-right government assumed power on 22 Dec 2003, following the victory of the Croatian Democratic Union (HDZ) over the incumbent center-left coalition. Despite fears among some domestic and foreign observers that the HDZ would take the country back to the undemocratic and isolationist politics of the recent past, the new prime minister, Ivo Sanader, pursued a moderate agenda. One of the government's first actions was to initiate dialogue with the country's Serb minority, which resulted in measures aimed at facilitating the return of Serb refugees. Relations between Croatia and the International Criminal Tribunal for the Former Yugoslavia also saw significant improvement. The government played a key role in securing the voluntary departure of indicted Croatian citizens to The Hague. Pres. Stipe Mesic easily won reelection in the voting in January 2005.

Internet resources: <www.croatia.hr>.

Cuba

Official name: República de Cuba (Republic of Cuba). **Form of government:** unitary socialist republic with one legislative house (National Assembly of the People's Power [609]). **Head of state and government:** President Fidel Castro (from 1976). **Capital:** Havana. **Official language:** Spanish. **Official religion:** none. **Monetary unit:** 1 Cuban peso (CUP) = 100 centavos; valuation (7 Jul 2005) $1 = 0.93 CUP.

Demography

Area: 42,804 sq mi, 110,861 sq km. **Population** (2004): 11,300,000. **Density** (2004): persons per sq mi 264.0, persons per sq km 101.9. **Urban** (2003): 75.6%. **Sex distribution** (2003): male 50.02%; female 49.98%. **Age breakdown** (2003): under 15, 20.5%; 15–29, 21.2%; 30–44, 27.7%; 45–59, 16.5%; 60–74, 9.9%; 75 and over, 4.2%. **Ethnic composition** (1994): mixed 51.0%; white 37.0%; black 11.0%; other 1.0%. **Religious affiliation** (1995): Roman Catholic 39.5%; Protestant 2.4%; other Christian 0.2%; other (mostly Santería) 57.9%. **Major cities** (1999): Havana (2002) 2,175,900; Santiago de Cuba 441,524; Camagüey 306,049; Holguín 259,300; Santa Clara 210,100. **Location:** island southeast of Florida, US, between the North Atlantic Ocean and the Caribbean Sea.

Vital statistics

Birth rate per 1,000 population (2003): 12.4 (world avg. 21.3). **Death rate** per 1,000 population (2003): 7.2 (world avg. 9.1). **Natural increase rate** per 1,000 population (2003): 5.2 (world avg. 12.2). **Total fertility rate** (avg. births per childbearing woman; 2003): 1.7. **Marriage rate** per 1,000 population (2001): 4.8. **Divorce rate** per 1,000 population (2001): 2.3. **Life expectancy** at birth (2003): male 74.6 years; female 79.2 years.

National economy

Budget (2000). *Revenue:* CUP 14,505,000,000. *Expenditures:* CUP 15,243,000,000 (capital expenditure 18.0%, education 13.9%, health 11.3%, defense 6.1%, other 50.7%). **Public debt** (external, outstanding; 2002): $12,300,000,000. **Production** (metric tons except as noted). *Agriculture, forestry, fishing* (2003): sugarcane 22,901,600, fresh vegetables 1,930,870, plantains 797,200; livestock (number of live animals) 4,025,000 cattle, 3,121,000 sheep, 23,210,000 chickens; roundwood (2003) 3,597,000 cu m; fish catch (2001) 110,330. *Mining and quarrying* (2001):

---

1 metric ton = about 1.1 short tons; 1 kilometer = 0.6 mi (statute); 1 metric ton-km cargo = about 0.68 short ton-mi cargo; c.i.f.: cost, insurance, and freight; f.o.b.: free on board

nickel (metal content) 72,619; cobalt (metal content) 3,910. *Manufacturing* (value added in $'000,000; 1990): tobacco products 2,629; food products 1,033; beverages 358. *Energy production (consumption):* electricity (kW-hr; 2001) 15,301,000,000 (15,301,-000,000); coal (2000) none (15,000); crude petroleum (2003) 26,020,000 ([2000] 28,240,000); petroleum products (2000) 2,068,000 (5,888,000); natural gas (cu m; 2003) 653,000,000 ([2000] 574,000,-000). **Population economically active** (2002): total 4,300,000; activity rate 38.2% (participation rates: female [1998] 37.0%; unemployed [2002] 3.5%). **Gross domestic product** (2002): $25,900,000,000 ($2,300 per capita). **Households.** Average household size (2000) 3.6. **Tourism** (2002): $1,633,000,000. **Land use** as % of total land area (2000): in temporary crops 33.1%, in permanent crops 7.6%, in pasture 20.0%; overall forest area 21.4%.

Foreign trade

Imports (1996-f.o.b. in balance of trade and trading partners and c.i.f. for commodities): $3,481,000,000 (refined petroleum 20.2%; food and live animals 19.8%, of which cereals 11.4%; machinery and transport equipment 16.1%, of which power-generating machinery 7.4%; crude petroleum 7.2%). *Major import sources* (2001): Spain 12.7%; France 6.5%; Canada 5.7%; China 5.3%; Italy 5.0%. **Exports** (1996): $1,849,000,000 (raw sugar 51.5%; nickel [all forms] 22.6%; fresh and frozen fish 6.7%; raw tobacco and tobacco products 5.9%; medicinal and pharmaceutical products 2.8%). *Major export destinations* (2001): The Netherlands 22.4%; Russia 13.3%; Canada 13.3%; Spain 7.3%; China 6.2%.

Transport and communications

Transport. *Railroads* (2001): length 4,807 km; (1997) passenger-km 1,684,000; metric ton-km cargo 821,500,000. *Roads* (1997): total length 60,858 km (paved 49%). *Vehicles* (1998): passenger cars 172,574; trucks and buses 185,495. *Air transport* (2000): passenger-km 2,769,162,000; metric ton-km cargo 49,294,000; airports with scheduled flights (1999) 14. **Communications,** in total units (units per 1,000 persons). Daily newspaper circulation (2000): 1,280,000 (114); radios (2001): 2,091,000 (185); televisions (2000): 3,580,000 (242); telephone main lines (2001): 574,000 (51); cellular telephone subscribers (2002): 179,000 (1.6); personal computers (2002): 359,000 (32); Internet users (2001): 120,000 (11).

Education and health

Literacy (2004): total population age 15 and over literate 96.9%; males 97.0%; females 96.8%. **Health** (2002): physicians 67,000 (1 per 168 persons); hospital beds 70,424 (1 per 161 persons); infant mortality rate per 1,000 live births 6.5. **Food** (2001): daily per capita caloric intake 2,564 (vegetable products 86%, animal products 14%); 111% of FAO recommended minimum.

Military

Total active duty personnel (2003): 46,000 (army 76.1%, navy 6.5%, air force 17.4%). **Military expenditure as percentage of GDP** (1999): 1.9% (world 2.4%); per capita expenditure: $57.

 Located on Cuba's north coast, Havana is the country's capital and one of the great treasuries of colonial architecture in the Western Hemisphere.

Background

Several Indian groups, including the Ciboney, the Taino, and the Arawak, inhabited Cuba at the time of the first Spanish contact. Christopher Columbus claimed the island for Spain in 1492, and the Spanish conquest began in 1511, when the settlement of Baracoa was founded. The native Indians were eradicated over the succeeding centuries, and African slaves, from the 18th century until slavery was abolished in 1886, were imported to work the sugar plantations. Cuba revolted unsuccessfully against Spain in the Ten Years' War (1868–78); a second war of independence began in 1895. In 1898 the US entered the war; Spain relinquished its claim to Cuba, which was occupied by the US for three years before gaining its independence in 1902. The US invested heavily in the Cuban sugar industry in the first half of the 20th century, and this, combined with tourism and gambling, caused the economy to prosper. Inequalities in the distribution of wealth persisted, however, as did political corruption. In 1958–59 the communist revolutionary Fidel Castro overthrew Cuba's longtime dictator, Fulgencio Batista, and established a socialist state aligned with the Soviet Union, abolishing capitalism and nationalizing foreign-owned enterprises. Relations with the US deteriorated, reaching a low point with the 1961 Bay of Pigs invasion and the 1962 Cuban missile crisis. In 1980 about 125,000 Cubans, including many that their government officially labeled "undesirables," were shipped to the US in the so-called Mariel Boat Lift. When communism collapsed in the USSR, Cuba lost important financial backing and its economy suffered greatly. The latter gradually improved in the 1990s with the encouragement of tourism, though diplomatic relations with the US were not resumed.

Recent Developments

Tensions between Cuba and the United States mounted in May 2004 when the administration of Pres. George W. Bush released the 423-page report of the Commission for Assistance to a Free Cuba. The report led to Washington's further tightening of travel restrictions to Cuba, eliminating many types of educational travel, limiting family visits, and restricting remittances to relatives. The US also increased funding for anti-Castro broadcasts by Radio and TV Martí, aid to dissidents on the island, and an international public diplomacy campaign to promote the US view that Cuba was a dangerous rogue state. Cuba's ties with Latin America were strained when Cuba narrowly lost a UN vote on its human rights conditions. In May Castro lashed out at Mexico, and in August he broke off relations with Panama when that country pardoned four Cuban exiles convicted of having plotted to kill him. Ties with Venezuela, Argentina, and other states in the region remained warm, however, and the election of socialist governments in several Latin American countries in 2004 and 2005 augured well for Cuba.

Internet resources: <www.cubatravel.cu>.

Cyprus

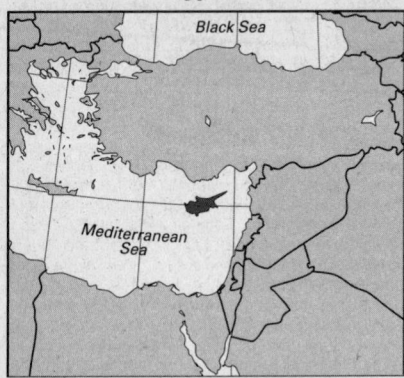

Two de facto states currently exist on the island of Cyprus: the Republic of Cyprus (ROC), predominantly Greek in character, occupying the southern two-thirds of the island, which is the original and still the internationally recognized de jure government of the whole island; and the Turkish Republic of Northern Cyprus (TRNC), proclaimed unilaterally 15 Nov 1983, on territory originally secured for the Turkish Cypriot population by the 20 Jul 1974 intervention of Turkey. Only Turkey recognizes the TRNC, and the two ethnic communities have failed to reestablish a single state. Provision of separate data below does not imply recognition of either state's claims but is necessitated by the lack of unified data.

Area: 3,572 sq mi, 9,251 sq km. **Population** (2004): 937,000; includes 80,000 "settlers" from Turkey and 38,000 Turkish military in the TRNC; excludes 3,300 British military in the Sovereign Base Areas (SBA) in the ROC and 1,200 UN peacekeeping forces. **Location:** Middle East, island in the Mediterranean Sea, south of Turkey.

Republic of Cyprus

Official name: Kipriakí Dhimokratía (Greek); Kibris Cumhuriyeti (Turkish) (Republic of Cyprus). **Form of government:** unitary multiparty republic with a unicameral legislature (House of Representatives [80; 24 seats reserved for Turkish Cypriots are not occupied]). **Head of state and government:** President Tassos Papadopoulos (from 2003). **Capital:** Lefkosia (Nicosia). **Official languages:** Greek; Turkish. **Monetary unit:** 1 Cyprus pound (£C) = 100 cents; valuation (7 Jul 2005) $1 = £C 0.48.

Demography

Area (includes 99 sq mi [256 sq km] of British military SBA and c. 107 sq mi (c. 278 sq km) of the UN Buffer Zone): 2,276 sq mi, 5,896 sq km. **Population** (2004; excludes British and UN military forces): 726,000. **Urban** (2001): 68.8%. **Age breakdown** (2002): under 15, 21.5%; 15–29, 22.6%; 30–44, 22.0%; 45–59, 17.8%; 60–74, 11.2%; 75 and over, 4.9%. **Ethnic composition** (2000): Greek Cypriot 91.8%; Armenian 3.3%; Arab 2.9%, of which Lebanese 2.5%; British 1.4%; other 0.6%. **Religious affiliation** (2001): Greek Orthodox 94.8%; Roman Catholic 2.1%, of which Maronite 0.6%; Anglican 1.0%; Muslim 0.6%; other 1.5%. **Urban areas** (2001): Lefkosia 200,686 (ROC only); Limassol 156,939; Larnaca 70,502.

Vital statistics

Birth rate per 1,000 population (2003): 11.2 (world avg. 21.3). **Death rate** per 1,000 population (2003): 7.2 (world avg. 9.1). **Natural increase rate** per 1,000 population (2003): 4.0 (world avg. 12.2). **Life expectancy** at birth (2002–03): male 77.0 years; female 81.4 years.

National economy

Budget (2001). *Revenue:* £C 2,073,100,000 (indirect taxes 34.8%, direct taxes 31.8%, social security contributions 19.7%). *Expenditures:* £C 2,239,700,000 (current expenditures 90.0%, development expenditures 10.0%). **Tourism** (2002): receipts $1,863,000,000; expenditures $424,000,000. **Household expenditure** (2000): housing and energy 21.3%, food and beverages 20.0%, transportation and communications 19.2%. **Gross national product** (2003): $9,373,000,000 ($12,320 per capita). **Production.** *Agriculture* (in '000 metric tons; 2002): potatoes 142.0, barley 125.7, grapes 88.0. *Manufacturing* (value added in £C '000,000; 1999): food 102.7; cement, bricks, and tiles 47.1; tobacco products 46.3. *Energy production:* electricity (kW-hr; 2001) 3,552,000,000.

Foreign trade

Imports (2001-c.i.f.): £C 2,528,700,000 (consumer goods 24.4%; for reexport 13.9%; mineral fuels 10.5%; capital goods 10.2%). *Major import sources:* US 9.4%; Greece 8.9%; UK 8.8%; Italy 8.8%; Germany 6.8%; Japan 6.1%. **Exports** (2001-f.o.b.): £C 628,000,000 (reexports 53.7%; domestic exports 37.2%, of which pharmaceuticals 6.3%, clothing 3.1%; ships' stores 9.1%). *Major export destinations:* UK 18.7%; Russia 8.6%; Greece 8.4%; UAE 7.8%; Syria 6.0%.

Transport and communications

Transport. *Roads* (2001): total length 11,408 km (paved 58%). *Vehicles* (2001): cars 268,200; trucks and buses 136,200. *Air transport* (2002; Cyprus Airways): passenger-km 3,276,000,000; metric ton-km cargo 40,392,000; airports (2000) 2. **Communications,** in total units (units per 1,000 persons). Televisions (1999): 120,000 (180); telephone main lines (2002): 492,000 (688); cellular telephone subscribers (2002): 417,900 (597); personal computers (2002): 193,000 (270); Internet users (2002): 210,000 (294).

Education and health

Educational attainment (2001). Percentage of population age 15 and over having: no formal schooling 2.1%; incomplete primary 6.4%; complete primary

---

1 metric ton = about 1.1 short tons;   1 kilometer = 0.6 mi (statute);   1 metric ton-km cargo = about 0.68 short ton-mi cargo;   c.i.f.: cost, insurance, and freight;   f.o.b.: free on board

20.6%; secondary 48.3%; higher education 22.3%; not stated 0.3%. **Health** (2002): physicians 1,864 (1 per 381 persons); hospital beds 3,092 (1 per 229 persons); infant mortality rate per 1,000 live births (2003) 4.1.

Turkish Republic of Northern Cyprus

Official name: Kuzey Kibris Türk Cumhuriyeti (Turkish Republic of Northern Cyprus). **Capital:** Lefkosa (Nicosia). **Official language:** Turkish. **Monetary unit:** 1 Turkish lira (TL) = 100 kurush; valuation (7 Jul 2005) $1 = TL 1,356,000. **Population** (2004; includes 80,000 "settlers" from Turkey and 38,000 Turkish military in the TRNC; excludes 3,300 British military in the Sovereign Base Areas (SBA) in the ROC and 1,200 UN peacekeeping forces): 211,000 (Lefkosa 39,176 [1996]; Gazimagusa [Famagusta] 27,637 [1996]; Girne [Kyrenia] 14,205 [1996]). **Ethnic composition** (1996): Turkish Cypriot/Turkish 96.4%; other 3.6%. **Budget** (2001). *Revenue:* $418,200,000 (foreign aid 46.8%, direct taxes 24.2%, indirect taxes 18.8%, loans 6.4%). *Expenditures:* $418,200,000 (wages 32.9%, social transfers 29.8%, defense 8.3%, investments 8.2%). **Imports** (2001): $272,000,000 (machinery and transport equipment 21.7%, food 21.7%). *Major import sources:* Turkey 63.7%; UK 10.5%. **Exports** (2001): $34,600,000 (ready-made garments 32.1%, citrus fruits 28.6%). *Major export destinations:* Turkey 37.0%; UK 33.2%. **Health** (2002): physicians 523 (1 per 408 persons); hospital beds 1,121 (1 per 190 persons); infant mortality rate per 1,000 live births (1999) 3.7.

Internet resources:
<www.visitcyprus.org.cy>; <www.trncwashdc.org>.

Background

Cyprus was inhabited by the early Neolithic Age; by the late Bronze Age it had been visited and settled by Mycenaeans and Achaeans, who introduced Greek culture and language, and it became a trading center. By 800 BC Phoenicians had begun to settle there. Ruled over the centuries by the Assyrian, Persian, and Ptolemaic empires, it was annexed by Rome in 58 BC. It was part of the Byzantine empire in the 4th–12th centuries AD. Cyprus was conquered by the English king Richard I in 1191. A part of the Venetian empire from 1489, it was taken by Ottoman Turks in 1571. In 1878 the British assumed control, and Cyprus became a British crown colony in 1925. It gained independence in 1960. Conflict between Greek and Turkish Cypriots led to the establishment of a UN peacekeeping mission in 1964. In 1974, fearing a movement to unite Cyprus with Greece, Turkish soldiers occupied the northern third of the country and Turkish Cypriots established a functioning government, which obtained recognition only from Turkey. Conflict has continued to the present, and the UN peacekeeping mission has remained in place. Reunification talks have remained deadlocked.

Recent Developments

Reunification of the Greek and Turkish parts of Cyprus was still the main topic of discussion in 2005. Despite hopes and favorable developments as late as February 2004, the two sides were ultimately unable to reach agreement; the Greek part of Cyprus joined the European Union on 1 May 2004. Despite contin-

ued partition, Cyprus Turks were considered EU members. Some voted in the European elections, and international agencies planned economic relief for them. Moreover, movement between the zones eased, and telephone contact opened. The election of Mehmet Ali Talat as president of the Turkish Republic of Northern Cyprus in April 2005 was also promising. Unlike his predecessor, Rauf Denktash, Talat was seen as both pro-unification and pro-European.

Czech Republic

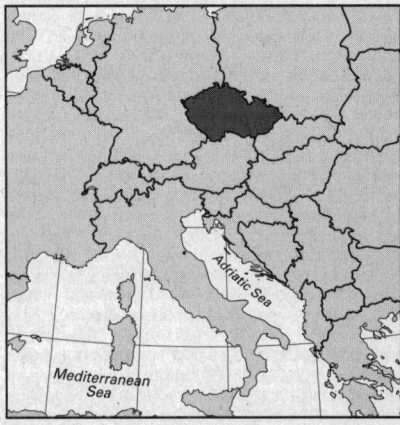

Official name: Ceska Republika (Czech Republic). **Form of government:** unitary multiparty republic with two legislative houses (Senate [81]; Chamber of Deputies [200]). **Chief of state:** President Vaclav Klaus (from 2003). **Head of government:** Prime Minister Jiri Paroubek (from 25 Apr 2005). **Capital:** Prague. **Official language:** Czech. **Official religion:** none. **Monetary unit:** 1 koruna (Kc) = 100 halura; valuation (7 Jul 2005) $1 = 25.36 Kc.

Demography

Area: 30,450 sq mi, 78,866 sq km. **Population** (2004): 10,212,000. **Density** (2004): persons per sq mi 335.4, persons per sq km 129.5. **Urban** (2003): 74.3%. **Sex distribution** (2002): male 48.68%; female 51.32%. **Age breakdown** (2001): under 15, 16.3%; 15–29, 23.5%; 30–44, 20.1%; 45–59, 21.8%; 60–74, 12.8%; 75 and over, 5.5%. **Ethnic composition** (2001): Czech 90.4%; Moravian 3.7%; Slovak 1.9%; Polish 0.5%; German 0.4%; Silesian 0.1%; Rom (Gypsy) 0.1%; other 2.9%. **Religious affiliation** (2000): Catholic 43.8%, of which Roman Catholic 40.4%, Hussite Church of the Czech Republic 2.2%; nonreligious 31.9%; atheist 5.0%; Protestant 3.1%; Orthodox Christian 0.6%; Jewish 0.1%; other (mostly unaffiliated Christian) 15.5%. **Major cities** (2003): Prague 1,161,938; Brno 370,505; Ostrava 314,102; Plzen 163,791; Olomouc 101,624. **Location:** central Europe, bordering Germany, Poland, Slovakia, and Austria.

Vital statistics

Birth rate per 1,000 population (2003): 9.2 (world avg. 21.3); (2002) legitimate 74.5%. **Death rate** per

1,000 population (2003): 10.9 (world avg. 9.1). **Natural increase rate** per 1,000 population (2003): −1.7 (world avg. 12.2). **Total fertility rate** (avg. births per childbearing woman; 2001): 1.1. **Marriage rate** per 1,000 population (2003): 4.8. **Divorce rate** per 1,000 population (2003): 3.2. **Life expectancy** at birth (2002): male 72.1 years; female 78.5 years.

National economy

Budget (2001). *Revenue:* Kc 626,216,000,000 (tax revenue 95.6%, of which social security contributions 37.4%, value-added tax 18.6%, personal income tax 13.4%, corporate tax 9.4%, excise tax 9.3%; nontax revenue 4.4%). *Expenditures:* Kc 693,920,000,000 (social security and welfare 39.3%; education 11.6%; health 6.1%; defense 5.4%; police 3.9%). **Production** (metric tons except as noted). *Agriculture, forestry, fishing* (2002): cereals 6,771,000 (of which wheat 3,867,000, barley 1,793,000, corn [maize] 616,000), sugar beets 3,833,000, potatoes 901,000; livestock (number of live animals) 3,363,000 pigs, 1,474,000 cattle, 16,564,000 chickens; roundwood (2001) 14,374,000 cu m; fish catch (2002) 24,000. *Mining and quarrying* (2001): kaolin 6,300,000; feldspar 410,000. *Manufacturing* (value added in Kc '000,000,000; 1998): nonelectrical machinery and apparatus 47.0; food products 37.4; fabricated metals 35.2. *Energy production (consumption):* electricity (kW-hr; 2001) 74,647,000,000 (65,108,000,000); hard coal (2001) 15,138,000 (15,138,000); lignite (2001) 50,968,000 (50,968,000); crude petroleum (barrels; 2000) 1,186,500 (39,771,000); petroleum products (2000) 6,132,000 (7,998,000); natural gas (cu m; 2000) 238,462,000 (10,564,000,000). **Household income and expenditure.** Average household size (2001) 2.5; disposable income per household (2000) Kc 286,920; sources of income (2001): wages and salaries 67.4%, transfer payments 21.5%, self-employment 6.7%, other 4.4%; expenditure (2001): food and beverages 25.3%, housing and utilities 19.8%, transportation and communications 14.4%, recreation 10.5%, household furnishings 6.9%. **Population economically active** (2002): total 4,769,727; activity rate of total population 46.6% (participation rates: ages 15–64, 60.9%; female 44.3%; unemployed [2003] 9.9%). **Public debt** (external, outstanding; 2002): $6,904,000,000. **Gross national product** (2003): $68,711,000,000 ($6,740 per capita). **Tourism** (2002): receipts from visitors $2,941,000,000; expenditures by nationals abroad $1,575,000,000. **Land use** as % of total land area (2000): in temporary crops 39.9%, in permanent crops 3.1%, in pasture 12.4%; overall forest area 34.1%.

Foreign trade

Imports (2002): Kc 1,326,339,000,000 (machinery and apparatus 31.2%; base and fabricated metals 10.9%; chemicals and chemical products 10.4%; motor vehicles 9.7%). *Major import sources:* Germany 32.5%; Italy 5.4%; Slovakia 5.2%; France 4.8%; China 4.6%; Russia 4.5%. **Exports** (2002): Kc 1,251,884,000,000 (machinery and apparatus 31.9%, of which computers 6.2%; motor vehicles 16.7%; fabricated metals 6.5%; base metals 5.4%; chemicals and chemical products 5.4%). *Major export destinations:*

Germany 36.5%; Slovakia 7.7%; UK 5.8%; Austria 5.5%; Poland 4.7%; France 4.7%.

Transport and communications

Transport. *Railroads* (2001): length 9,444 km; passenger-km 7,299,000,000; metric /ton-km cargo 16,882,000,000. *Roads* (2001): total length 125,905 km. *Vehicles* (2001): passenger cars 3,529,791; trucks and buses 381,876. *Air transport* (2001): passenger-km 6,398,920,000; metric ton-km 29,209,000; airports (2001) with scheduled flights 2. **Communications**, in total units (units per 1,000 persons). Daily newspaper circulation (2000): 1,210,000 (118); televisions (2000): 3,289,000 (341); telephone main lines (2003): 3,626,000 (360); cellular telephone subscribers (2003): 9,709,000 (965); personal computers (2002): 1,800,000 (177); Internet users (2003): 2,700,000 (268).

Education and health

Educational attainment (2001). Percentage of population age 15 and over having: no formal schooling 0.2%; primary education 21.6%; secondary 68.7%; higher 9.5%. **Literacy** (2001): 99.8%. **Health** (2002): physicians 43,824 (1 per 233 persons); hospital beds 66,668 (1 per 153 persons); infant mortality rate per 1,000 live births (2003) 3.9. **Food** (2002): daily per capita caloric intake 3,171 (vegetable products 73%, animal products 27%); 128% of FAO recommended minimum.

Military

Total active duty personnel (2003): 57,050 (army 69.9%, air force 23.0%, ministry of defense 7.1%). **Military expenditure as percentage of GNP** (1999): 2.3% (world 2.4%); per capita expenditure: $292.

Background

Until 1918 the history of what is now the Czech Republic was largely that of Bohemia. In that year the independent republic of Czechoslovakia was born through the union of Bohemia and Moravia with Slovakia. Czechoslovakia came under the domination of the Soviet Union after World War II, and from 1948 to 1989 it was ruled by a communist government. Its growing political liberalization was suppressed by a Soviet invasion in 1968. After communist rule collapsed in 1989–90, separatist sentiments emerged among the Slovaks, and in 1992 the Czechs and Slovaks agreed to break up their federated state. On 1 Jan 1993 the Czechoslovakian republic was peacefully dissolved and replaced by two new countries, the Czech Republic and Slovakia, with the region of Moravia remaining in the former. In the late 1990s the Czech Republic started membership talks with the EU, and in 1999 it entered NATO.

Recent Developments

The year 2004 was marked by political upheaval and an economic upturn as the Czech Republic finally "rejoined Europe." Like its counterparts in Poland and Hungary, the center-left Czech government collapsed

---

1 metric ton = about 1.1 short tons;   1 kilometer = 0.6 mi (statute);   1 metric ton-km cargo = about 0.68 short ton-mi cargo;   c.i.f.: cost, insurance, and freight;   f.o.b.: free on board

after the country's accession to the European Union on 1 May, with Vladimir Spidla resigning as prime minister in July and handing over the reigns to the youthful Stanislav Gross. The new government consisted of all the same parties and most of the same ministers as the previous cabinet. Moreover, it faced all of the same problems, particularly those relating to public finance reform. Gross's government, in fact, lasted only nine months, until April 2005, undone ultimately by allegations of spending improprieties, including the financing of Gross's own luxury apartment. He was replaced by the left-leaning Jiri Paroubek.

Internet resources: <www.czechtourism.com>.

Denmark

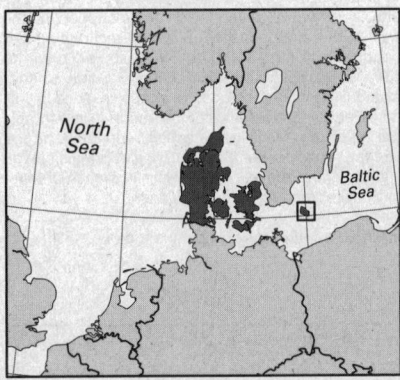

Official name: Kongeriget Danmark (Kingdom of Denmark). **Form of government:** parliamentary state and constitutional monarchy with one legislative house (Folketing [179]). **Chief of state:** Queen Margrethe II (from 1972). **Head of government:** Prime Minister Anders Fogh Rasmussen (from 2001). **Capital:** Copenhagen. **Official language:** Danish. **Official religion:** Evangelical Lutheran. **Monetary unit:** 1 Danish krone (Dkr; plural kroner) = 100 øre; valuation (7 Jul 2005) $1 = Dkr 6.25.

Demography

Area: 16,640 sq mi, 43,098 sq km (excludes the Faroe Islands and Greenland). **Population** (2004): 5,401,000. **Density** (2004): persons per sq mi 324.6, persons per sq km 125.3. **Urban** (2003): 85.3%. **Sex distribution** (2003): male 49.46%; female 50.54%. **Age breakdown** (2003): under 15, 18.8%; 15–29, 17.9%; 30–44, 22.3%; 45–59, 20.9%; 60–74, 13.1%; 75 and over, 7.0%. **Ethnic composition** (2001; based on nationality): Danish 95.2%; Asian 1.7%, of which Turkish 0.7%; residents of pre-1992 Yugoslavia 0.7%; African 0.5%; German 0.2%; English 0.2%; other 1.5%. **Religious affiliation** (1998): Christian 87.5%, of which Evangelical Lutheran 85.8%; Muslim 2.2%; other/nonreligious 10.3%. **Major urban areas** (2003): Greater Copenhagen 1,085,813; Århus 222,559; Odense 145,374; Ålborg 121,100; Esbjerg 72,613. **Location:** northern Europe, bordering the North Sea, the Baltic Sea, and Germany.

Vital statistics

Birth rate per 1,000 population (2003): 12.0 (world avg. 21.3). **Death rate** per 1,000 population (2003): 10.7 (world avg. 9.1). **Natural increase rate** per 1,000 population (2003): 1.3 (world avg. 12.2). **Total fertility rate** (avg. births per childbearing woman; 2003): 1.8. **Marriage rate** per 1,000 population (2003): 6.5. **Divorce rate** per 1,000 population (2003): 2.9. **Life expectancy** at birth (2003): male 74.9 years; female 79.5 years.

National economy

Budget (2002). *Revenue:* Dkr 498,382,000,000 (tax revenue 82.8%, nontax revenue 11.9%, other 5.3%). *Expenditures:* Dkr 482,437,000,000 (health and social protection 39.6%, education 12.9%, economic affairs 7.1%, defense 4.8%, public order 2.7%). **National debt** (end of year; 2001): Dkr 679,957,-000,000. **Tourism** (2002): receipts $5,785,000,000; expenditures $6,856,000,000. **Population economically active** (2002): total 2,892,800; activity rate of total population 53.9% (participation rates: ages 16–66, 77.8%; female 46.9%; unemployed 3.8%). **Household income and expenditure.** Average household size (2001) 2.2; annual disposable income per household (2000) Dkr 259,589; expenditure (2000): housing 22.3%, transportation and communications 16.1%, food 11.3%, recreation 11.1%, energy 6.8%, household furnishings 6.3%. **Production** (in Dkr '000,000 except as noted). *Agriculture, forestry, fishing* (value added; 2001): meat 24,884 (of which pork 21,069, beef 2,178), milk 11,327, cereals 8,095 (of which wheat 4,012, barley 3,469); livestock (number of live animals) 12,732,035 pigs, 1,796,118 cattle; roundwood (2002) 1,446,000 cu m; fish catch (2001) 1,552,000 metric tons. *Mining and quarrying* (2001): sand and gravel 23,000,000 cu m; chalk 410,000 metric tons. *Manufacturing* (value added in $'000,000; 1998): nonelectrical machinery and apparatus 3,874; food products 3,848; fabricated metals 2,228. *Energy production (consumption):* electricity (kW-hr; 2003) 43,752,000,000 ([2000] 44,284,000,000); coal (metric tons; 2001) none (6,984,000); crude petroleum (barrels; 2003) 140,-800,000 ([2000] 61,812,000); petroleum products (metric tons; 2001) 8,860,000 (7,547,000); natural gas (cu m; 2001) 4,427,000,000 ([2001] 4,366,-000,000). **Gross national product** (2003): $181,-825,000,000 ($33,750 per capita). **Land use** as % of total land area (2000): in temporary crops 53.8%, in permanent crops 0.2%, in pasture 8.4%; overall forest area 10.7%.

Foreign trade

Imports (2001-c.i.f.): Dkr 369,582,000,000 (machinery and apparatus [including parts] 22.9%; transport equipment and parts 10.5%; food, beverages, and tobacco 8.5%; clothing and footwear 5.0%; fuels 4.7%). *Major import sources:* Germany 22.0%; Sweden 12.0%; UK 7.5%; The Netherlands 7.0%; France 5.7%. **Exports** (2001-f.o.b.): Dkr 422,877,000,000 (machinery and apparatus 27.5%; agricultural products 19.2%, of which swine 5.7%; mineral fuels and lubricants 6.8%; pharmaceuticals 6.7%; furniture 3.8%). *Major export destinations:* Germany 19.7%; Sweden 11.7%; UK 9.4%; US 7.0%; Norway 5.6%; France 5.1%.

Transport and communications

Transport. *Railroads* (2001): route length 2,743 km; passenger-km 5,318,000,000; metric ton-km cargo 2,025,000,000. *Roads* (2001): total length 71,663 km (paved 100%). *Vehicles* (2001): passenger cars 1,854,060; trucks and buses 335,690. *Air transport* (2001; Danish share of Scandinavian Airlines System [scheduled air service only] and Maersk Air): passenger-km 8,942,000,000; metric ton-km cargo 183,152,000; airports (1996) with scheduled flights 13. **Communications,** in total units (units per 1,000 persons). Daily newspaper circulation (2000): 1,510,000 (283); radios (2000): 7,200,000 (1,349); televisions (2000): 4,310,000 (807); telephone main lines (2003): 3,610,100 (669); cellular telephone subscribers (2003): 4,785,300 (887); personal computers (2002): 2,756,000 (513); Internet users (2002): 3,100,000 (577).

Education and health

Educational attainment (2000). Percentage of population age 25–69 having: completed lower secondary or not stated 34.6%; completed upper secondary or vocational 42.3%; undergraduate 17.6%; graduate 5.5%. **Literacy:** 100%. **Health:** physicians (2002) 19,600 (1 per 276 persons); hospital beds (2001) 22,604 (1 per 239 persons); infant mortality rate per 1,000 live births (2003) 4.0. **Food** (2001): daily per capita caloric intake 3,454 (vegetable products 60.5%, animal products 39.5%); 128% of FAO recommended minimum.

Military

Total active duty personnel (2003): 22,880 (army 64.2%, navy 17.5%, air force 18.3%). **Military expenditure as percentage of GNP** (1999): 1.6% (world 2.4%); per capita expenditure $524.

Did you know? The city of Copenhagen, located on the islands of Zealand and Amager, has been the capital of Denmark since 1445. It is the residence of the Danish royal family and is a cultural center of northern Europe.

Background

The Danes, a Scandinavian branch of the Teutons, settled the area in c. 6th century AD. During the Viking period the Danes expanded their territory, and by the 11th century the united Danish kingdom included parts of what are now Germany, Sweden, England, and Norway. Scandinavia was united under Danish rule from 1397 until 1523, when Sweden became independent; a series of debilitating wars with Sweden in the 17th century resulted in the Treaty of Copenhagen (1660), which established the modern Scandinavian frontiers. Denmark gained and lost various other territories, including Norway, in the 19th and 20th centuries; it went through three constitutions between 1849 and 1915 and was occupied by Nazi Germany in 1940–45. A founding member of NATO (1949), Denmark adopted its current constitution in 1953. It became a member of the European Community in 1973 and modified its membership during the 1990s. The island of Zealand, on which Copenhagen stands, was connected to the central island of Funen by a rail tunnel and bridge in 1997. This ended more than 100 years of ferry service and cut the crossing time from an hour to under 10 minutes.

Recent Developments

Denmark's involvement in Iraq, where it had 500 troops under UK command, continued to divide Danes in 2004. The general feeling of unease about Denmark's pro-Washington stance was exacerbated by allegations by a Danish national that he was tortured and humiliated by American soldiers in Afghanistan prior to being sent to the US base at Guantánamo Bay in Cuba for two years of detention. In a vote seen as a backlash against the ruling Liberal-Conservative government for its support of the war in Iraq, the opposition Social Democrats almost doubled their support in the European Parliament in June. Council of Europe Human Rights Commissioner Álvaro Gil-Robles concluded in a report issued in July that Denmark's restrictive immigration laws—notably the notorious family-reunification requirements preventing young people from marrying or bringing in foreigners under the age of 24—were in breach of international human rights conventions.

Internet resources: <www.denmark.dk>.

Djibouti

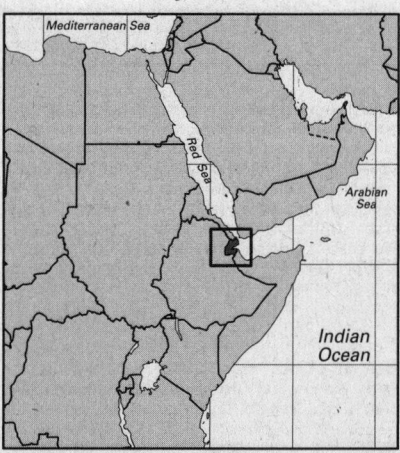

Official name: Jumhuriyah Jibuti (Arabic); République de Djibouti (French) (Republic of Djibouti). **Form of government:** multiparty republic with one legislative house (National Assembly [65]). **Chief of state and head of government:** President Ismail Omar Guelleh (from 1999), assisted by Prime Minister Dileita Muhammad Dileita (from 2001). **Capital:** Djibouti. **Official languages:** Arabic; French. **Official religion:** none. **Monetary unit:** 1 Djibouti franc (DF) = 100 centimes; valuation (7 Jul 2005) $1 = DF 174.46.

---

1 metric ton = about 1.1 short tons; 1 kilometer = 0.6 mi (statute); 1 metric ton-km cargo = about 0.68 short ton-mi cargo; c.i.f.: cost, insurance, and freight; f.o.b.: free on board

Demography

Area: 8,950 sq mi, 23,200 sq km. **Population** (2004): 467,000. **Density** (2004): persons per sq mi 52.2, persons per sq km 20.1. **Urban** (2003): 83.7%. **Sex distribution** (2002): male 51.55%; female 48.45%. **Age breakdown** (2002): under 15, 43.0%; 15–29, 28.1%; 30–44, 13.2%; 45–59, 10.5%; 60–74, 4.6%; 75 and over, 0.6%. **Ethnic composition** (2000): Somali 46.0%; Afar 35.4%; Arab 11.0%; mixed African and European 3.0%; French 1.6%; other/unspecified 3.0%. **Religious affiliation** (1995): Sunni Muslim 97.2%; Christian 2.8%, of which Roman Catholic 2.2%, Orthodox 0.5%, Protestant 0.1%. **Major city and towns** (1991): Djibouti 465,300 (2004); 'Ali Sabih 8,000; Tadjoura 7,500; Dikhil 6,500. **Location:** eastern Africa, bordering Eritrea, the Red Sea, the Gulf of Aden, Somalia, and Ethiopia.

Vital statistics

Birth rate per 1,000 population (2003): 40.8 (world avg. 21.3). **Death rate** per 1,000 population (2003): 19.5 (world avg. 9.1). **Natural increase rate** per 1,000 population (2003): 21.3 (world avg. 12.2). **Total fertility rate** (avg. births per childbearing woman; 2003): 5.6. **Life expectancy** at birth (2003): male 41.8 years; female 44.5 years.

National economy

Budget (2000). *Revenue:* DF 23,739,000,000 (tax revenue 91.2%, of which indirect taxes 45.3%, direct taxes 38.9%, income and profit tax 6.7%; non-tax revenue 8.8%). *Expenditures:* DF 32,813,-,000,000 (current expenditures 92.0%, of which general administration 22.7%, defense 13.7%, education 10.0%, health 4.6%; capital expenditures 8.0%). **Tourism** (1998): receipts from visitors $4,000,000; expenditures by nationals abroad $4,000,000. **Production** (metric tons except as noted). *Agriculture, forestry, fishing* (2002): vegetables and melons 24,000 (of which tomatoes 1,100, onions 110, eggplant 33), lemons and limes 1,800, tropical fruit 1,100; livestock (number of live animals) 512,000 goats, 475,000 sheep, 270,000 cattle; fish catch (2001) 350. *Mining and quarrying:* mineral production limited to locally used construction materials and evaporated salt (2001) 173,000. *Manufacturing* (2000): main products include furniture, nonalcoholic beverages, meat and hides, light electromechanical goods, and mineral water. *Energy production (consumption):* electricity (kW-hr; 2001) 235,262,000 (182,870,000); petroleum products (2000) none (126,000); geothermal, wind, and solar resources are substantial but largely undeveloped. **Population economically active** (1991): total 282,000; activity rate of total population 61.5% (participation rates: over age 10, 70.4%; female 40.8%; unemployed [2000] c. 50%). **Households.** Average household size (2000) 5.3; expenditure (expatriate households; 1984): food 50.3%, energy 13.1%, recreation 10.4%, housing 6.4%, clothing 1.7%, personal effects 1.4%, health care 1.0%, household goods 0.3%, other 15.4%. **Gross national product** (2003): $643,000,000 ($910 per capita). **Public debt** (external, outstanding; 2002): $305,200,000. **Land use** as % of total land area (2000): in temporary crops, negligible, in permanent crops, negligible, in pasture 56.1%; overall forest area 0.3%.

Foreign trade

Imports (1999; excludes Ethiopian trade via rail): $152,700,000 (food and beverages 25.0%; machinery and electric appliances 12.5%; khat 12.2%; petroleum products 10.9%; transport equipment 10.3%). *Major import sources* (2001): Saudi Arabia 18.5%; France 16.1%; Ethiopia 10.3%; China 8.1%; Italy 3.8%. **Exports** (2001; excludes Ethiopian trade via rail): $10,200,000 (aircraft parts 24.5%; hides and skins of cattle, sheep, goats, and camels 20.6%; unspecified special transactions 8.8%; leather 7.8%; live animals 6.9%). *Major export destinations* (2001): Somalia 44.8%; France 23.5%; Yemen 19.2%; Ethiopia 3.5%; UAE 3.3%.

Transport and communications

Transport. *Railroads* (2000): length 100 km; (1999) passenger-km 81,000,000; metric ton-km cargo 266,100,000. *Roads* (1999): total length 2,890 km (paved 13%). *Vehicles* (1996): passenger cars 9,200; trucks and buses 2,040. *Air transport* (2001): passengers handled 94,590; metric tons of freight handled 6,652; airports (2000) with scheduled flights 1. **Communications,** in total units (units per 1,000 persons). Daily newspaper circulation (1995): 500 (0.8); radios (1997): 52,000 (84); televisions (2000): 45,000 (104); telephone main lines (2003): 9,500 (14); cellular telephone subscribers (2003): 23,000 (34); personal computers (2003): 15,000 (22); Internet users (2003): 6,500 (9.7).

Education and health

Literacy (2000): percentage of population age 15 and over literate 64.6%; males literate 75.6%; females literate 54.4%. **Health:** physicians (1996) 60 (1 per 7,100 persons); hospital beds (1990; public health facilities only) 930 (1 per 394 persons); infant mortality rate per 1,000 live births (2003) 107.0. **Food** (2002): daily per capita caloric intake 2,220 (vegetable products 87%, animal products 13%); 96% of FAO recommended minimum.

Military

Total active duty personnel (2003; excludes foreign troops): 9,850 (army 81.3%, navy 2.0%, air force 2.5%, paramilitary 14.2%). Foreign troops (March 2004): French 2,700; US 1,800; German 800. **Military expenditure as percentage of GNP** (1999): 4.3% (world 2.4%); per capita expenditure $51.

 **Did you know?** Djibouti, virtually a city-state, is a deepwater port city and railhead bordered on three sides by a sparsely-populated hot, arid landscape. In 1985 this small country won the first world cup men's team marathon.

Background

Settled around the 3rd century BC by the Arab ancestors of the Afars, Djibouti was later populated by Somali Issas. In AD 825 Islam was brought to the area by missionaries. Arabs controlled the trade in this region until the 16th century; it became the French protectorate of French Somaliland in 1888. In 1946 it became a French overseas territory, and in 1977 it gained its independence. In the late 20th century, the country received refugees from the Ethiopian-Somali war and from civil conflicts in Eritrea. In the 1990s it suffered from political unrest.

Recent Developments

An initiative to repatriate refugees and illegal immigrants from Djibouti began in July 2003 after government officials told the country's estimated 100,000 illegal immigrants to either apply for asylum or leave. During February and March 2004 more than 430 Somalis returned to the self-declared Republic of Somaliland, and by June efforts to move more than 3,000 Ethiopian returnees over the border were under way. Pres. Ismail Omar Guelleh won reelection on 8 Apr 2005 in an election that was boycotted by the opposition.

Internet resources: <www.office-tourisme.dj>.

Dominica

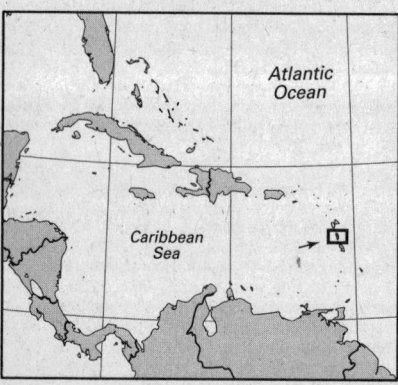

Atlantic
Ocean

Caribbean
Sea

Official name: Commonwealth of Dominica. **Form of government:** multiparty republic with one legislative house (House of Assembly [32; includes 22 seats that are elective [including speaker if elected from outside of the House of Assembly] and 10 seats that are nonelective [including 9 appointees of the president and the attorney general serving ex officio]). **Chief of state:** President Nicholas Liverpool (from 2003). **Head of government:** Prime Minister Roosevelt Skerrit (from 8 Jan 2004). **Capital:** Roseau. **Official language:** English. **Official religion:** none. **Monetary unit:** 1 East Caribbean dollar (EC$) = 100 cents; valuation (7 Jul 2005) US$1 = EC$2.67.

Demography

Area: 290 sq mi (750 sq km). **Population** (2004): 69,300. **Density** (2004): persons per sq mi 239.0, persons per sq km 92.4. **Urban** (2003): 72.0%. **Sex distribution** (2003): male 50.33%; female 49.67%. **Age breakdown** (2002): under 15, 27.8%; 15–29, 24.8%; 30–44, 26.3%; 45–59, 10.7%; 60–74, 7.0%; 75 and over, 3.4%. **Ethnic composition** (2000): black

88.3%; mulatto 7.3%; black-Amerindian 1.7%; British expatriates 1.0%; Indo-Pakistani 1.0%; other 0.7%. **Religious affiliation** (1991): Roman Catholic 70.1%; six largest Protestant groups 17.2%, of which Seventh-day Adventist 4.6%, Pentecostal 4.3%, Methodist 4.2%; other 8.9%; nonreligious 2.9%; unknown 0.9%. **Major towns** (1991): Roseau 15,853; Portsmouth 3,621; Marigot 2,919. **Location:** island in the southern Caribbean Sea, south of Guadeloupe and north of Martinique.

Vital statistics

Birth rate per 1,000 population (2003): 17.8 (world avg. 21.3); (1991) legitimate 24.1%. **Death rate** per 1,000 population (2003): 7.0 (world avg. 9.1). **Natural increase rate** per 1,000 population (2003): 10.8 (world avg. 12.2). **Total fertility rate** (avg. births per childbearing woman; 2003): 2.0. **Marriage rate** per 1,000 population (1996): 3.1. **Divorce rate** per 1,000 population (1996): 0.7. **Life expectancy** at birth (2002): male 71.0 years; female 75.8 years.

National economy

Budget (2000–01). *Revenue:* EC$194,900,000 (tax revenue 79.2%, of which consumption taxes on imports 39.1%, income taxes 19.9%; nontax revenue 13.8%; grants 7.0%). *Expenditures:* EC$270,800,000 (current expenditures 84.2%, of which wages 42.8%, debt payment 13.6%; development expenditures 15.8%). **Tourism:** receipts from visitors (2002) US$45,000,000; expenditures by nationals abroad (2001) US$9,000,000. **Gross national product** (2003): US$239,000,000 (US $3,360 per capita). **Land use** as % of total land area (2000): in temporary crops 7%, in permanent crops 19%, in pasture 3%; overall forest area 61%. **Public debt** (external, outstanding; 2002): US$178,300,000. **Population economically active** (1997): total 33,420; activity rate of total population 45.8% (participation rates: ages 15–64 [1991] 62.4%; female 45.8%; unemployed 23.1%). **Households.** Average household size (1991) 3.6; expenditure (1984): food and nonalcoholic beverages 43.1%, housing and utilities 16.1%, transportation 11.6%, clothing and footwear 6.5%, household furnishings 6.0%. **Production** (metric tons except as noted). *Agriculture, forestry, fishing* (2003): bananas 29,000, root crops 23,750 (of which taro 11,200, yams 8,000, yautia 4,550), grapefruit and pomelos 17,000; livestock (number of live animals; 2003) 13,400 cattle, 9,700 goats, 7,600 sheep; fish catch (2001) 1,157. *Mining and quarrying:* pumice, limestone, and sand and gravel are quarried primarily for local consumption. *Manufacturing* (value of production in EC$'000; 2000): toilet and laundry soap 18,815; toothpaste 10,063; crude coconut oil 1,758. *Energy production (consumption):* electricity (kW-hr; 2000) 77,000,000 (77,000,000); petroleum products (2000) none (33,000).

Foreign trade

Imports (2000-c.i.f.): EC$397,700,000 (food and beverages 19.3%; machinery and apparatus 17.7%; refined petroleum 8.6%; road vehicles 8.3%). *Major import sources:* US 37.5%; Trinidad and Tobago 16.3%; UK 7.7%; Japan 6.3%; Canada 4.2%. **Exports**

---

1 metric ton = about 1.1 short tons;   1 kilometer = 0.6 mi (statute);   1 metric ton-km cargo = about 0.68 short ton-mi cargo;   c.i.f.: cost, insurance, and freight;   f.o.b.: free on board

(2000-f.o.b.): EC\$147,300,000 (agricultural exports 37.5%, of which bananas 25.9%; coconut-based soaps 25.0%; perfumery and cosmetics 13.7%). *Major export destinations:* UK 24.8%; Jamaica 23.7%; France (significantly Guadeloupe) 8.5%; US 7.4%; Antigua and Barbuda 7.4%.

Transport and communications

Transport. *Roads* (1999): total length 780 km (paved 50%). *Vehicles* (1998): passenger cars 8,700; trucks and buses 3,400. *Air transport:* (1997) passenger arrivals and departures 74,100; (1997) cargo unloaded 575 metric tons, cargo loaded 363 metric tons; airports (1996) with scheduled flights 2. **Communications,** in total units (units per 1,000 persons). Radios (1997): 46,000 (608); televisions (2000): 15,700 (220); telephone main lines (2002): 23,700 (265); cellular telephone subscribers (2002): 9,400 (120); personal computers (2002): 7,000 (90); Internet users (2002): 12,500 (160).

Education and health

Educational attainment (1991). Percentage of population age 25 and over having: no formal schooling 4.2%; primary education 78.4%; secondary 11.0%; higher vocational 2.3%; university 2.8%; other/unknown 1.3%. **Literacy** (1996): total population age 15 and over literate, 94.0%. **Health** (2002): physicians 34 (1 per 2,041 persons); hospital beds 270 (1 per 257 persons); infant mortality rate per 1,000 live births 15.9. **Food** (2001): daily per capita caloric intake 2,995 (vegetable products 77%, animal products 23%); 124% of FAO recommended minimum.

Military

Total active duty personnel (2003): none; 300-member police force includes a coast guard unit.

Background

At the time of the arrival of Christopher Columbus in 1493, Dominica was inhabited by the Caribs. With its steep coastal cliffs and inaccessible mountains, it was one of the last islands to be explored by Europeans, and the Caribs remained in possession until the 18th century; it was then settled by the French and ultimately taken by Britain in 1783. Subsequent hostilities between the settlers and the native inhabitants resulted in the Caribs' near extinction. Incorporated with the Leeward Islands in 1883 and with the Windward Islands in 1940, it became a member of the West Indies Federation in 1958. Dominica became independent in 1978.

Recent Developments

Prime Minister Pierre Charles died in January 2004 and was succeeded by Roosevelt Skerrit, who also took over control of the Finance Ministry. The IMF came to Dominica's aid in January 2004 with a three-year, \$11.4 million credit from its Poverty Reduction and Growth Facility, which was designed, among other purposes, to help restore economic growth and preserve the public-sector investment program.

Internet resources: <www.ndcdominica.dm>.

Dominican Republic

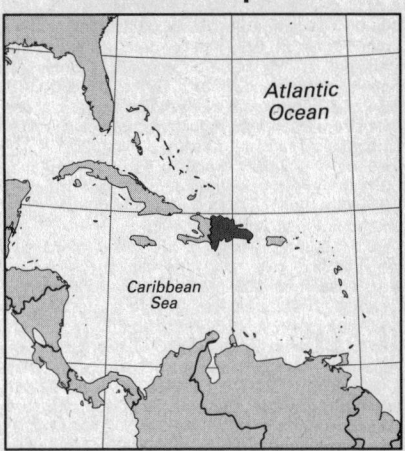

Atlantic Ocean

Caribbean Sea

Official name: República Dominicana (Dominican Republic). **Form of government:** multiparty republic with two legislative houses (Senate [32]; Chamber of Deputies [150]). **Head of state and government:** President Leonel Fernández Reyna (from 16 Aug 2004). **Capital:** Santo Domingo. **Official language:** Spanish. **Official religion:** none (Roman Catholicism is the state religion per concordat with Vatican City). **Monetary unit:** 1 Dominican peso (RD\$) = 100 centavos; valuation (7 Jul 2005) US\$1 = RD\$28.38.

Demography

Area: 18,792 sq mi, 48,671 sq km. **Population** (2004): 8,834,000. **Density** (2004): persons per sq mi 470.1, persons per sq km 181.5. **Urban** (2002): 63.6%. **Sex distribution** (2002): male 49.81%; female 50.19%. **Age breakdown** (2002): under 15, 34.0%; 15–29, 27.1%; 30–44, 20.2%; 45–59, 11.2%; 60–74, 5.9%; 75 and over, 1.6%. **Ethnic composition** (2000): mulatto 69.5%; white 17.0%; local black 9.4%; Haitian black 2.4%; other/unknown 1.7%. **Religious affiliation** (1995): Roman Catholic 81.8%; Protestant 6.4%; other Christian 0.6%; other 11.2%. **Major urban centers** (2004): Santo Domingo 1,817,754; Santiago 505,600; La Romana 171,500; San Francisco de Macorís 152,600; San Cristóbal 120,200. **Location:** eastern two-thirds of the island of Hispaniola, bordered by the North Atlantic Ocean, the Caribbean Sea, and Haiti.

Vital statistics

Birth rate per 1,000 population (2003): 23.0 (world avg. 21.3). **Death rate** per 1,000 population (2003): 7.2 (world avg. 9.1). **Natural increase rate** per 1,000 population (2003): 15.8 (world avg. 12.2). **Total fertility rate** (avg. births per childbearing woman; 2003): 2.7. **Marriage rate** per 1,000 population (2001): 2.9. **Divorce rate** per 1,000 population (2001): 1.0. **Life expectancy** at birth (2003): male 66.4 years; female 69.6 years.

National economy

Budget (2002). *Revenue:* RD\$67,009,000,000 (tax revenue 94.5%, of which taxes on goods and services

45.5%, income taxes 25.0%, import duties 21.2%; nontax revenue 5.5%. *Expenditures:* RD$75,789,-000,000 (current expenditures 63.1%; development expenditures 36.9%). **Public debt** (external, outstanding; 2002): US$4,035,000,000. **Gross national product** (2003): US$18,078,000,000 (US$2,070 per capita). **Households.** Average household size (2002) 3.5. **Production** (metric tons except as noted). *Agriculture, forestry, fishing* (2002): sugarcane 4,846,000, rice 731,000, bananas 503,000; livestock (number of live animals) 2,160,000 cattle, 577,000 pigs, 46,000,000 chickens; roundwood (2001) 562,000 cu m; fish catch (2001) 15,864. *Mining* (2002): nickel (metal content) 38,859; gold, none (the mining of gold was suspended from 1999 through late 2003). *Manufacturing* (1998; excludes free-zone sector for reexport employing [2000] 195,000): cement 1,872,000; refined sugar 105,000; beer 2,990,000 hectoliters. *Energy production (consumption):* electricity (kW-hr; 2002) 10,449,000,000 (6,808,-000,000); coal (2000) none (193,000); crude petroleum (barrels; 2002) none (14,400,000); petroleum products (2000) 1,859,000 (7,325,000). **Tourism** (2002): receipts US$2,738,000,000; expenditures US$295,000,000. **Population economically active** (1997): total 3,155,500; activity rate of total population 39.5% (participation rates: ages 15–64 [1993] 54.3%; female [1993] 24.9%; unemployed [2002] 16.1%). **Land use** as % of total land area (2000): in temporary crops 22.7%, in permanent crops 10.3%, in pasture 43.4%; overall forest area 28.4%.

Foreign trade

Imports (2002): US$8,882,000,000 (imports for free zones 29.8%, refined petroleum 14.6%, machinery and apparatus 11.4%, transport equipment 10.5%, food 5.4%). *Major import sources* (1998): US 65%; Venezuela 6%; Mexico 4%; Japan 3%. **Exports** (2002): US$5,183,000,000 (reexports of free zones 83.6%, ferronickel 3.0%, ships' stores 2.2%, raw sugar 1.4%, cacao and cocoa 1.3%). *Major export destinations* (1998): US 87%; Belgium-Luxembourg 2%; UK 2%.

Transport and communications

Transport. *Railroads* (1997; most track is privately owned and serves the sugar industry only): route length 1,743 km. *Roads* (1999): total length 12,600 km (paved 49%). *Vehicles* (1998): passenger cars 353,177; trucks and buses 200,347. *Air transport* (1997; Aerochago and Dominair airlines): passenger-km, 15,808,000; metric ton-km cargo 11,624,000; airports (2002) 6. **Communications,** in total units (units per 1,000 persons). Daily newspaper circulation (1996): 416,000 (53); radios (2000): 1,510,000 (181); televisions (2000): 810,000 (97); telephone main lines (2003): 901,800 (115); cellular telephone subscribers (2003): 2,120,400 (271); Internet users (2003): 500,000 (64).

Education and health

Literacy (1995): total population age 15 and over literate, 4,164,000 (82.1%); males literate, 2,118,000

(82.0%); females literate, 2,046,000 (82.2%). **Health** (1999): physicians 15,422 (1 per 526 persons); hospital beds 16,234 (1 per 500 persons); infant mortality rate per 1,000 live births (2003) 34.2. **Food** (2002): daily per capita caloric intake 2,347 (vegetable products 85%, animal products 15%); 104% of FAO recommended minimum.

Military

Total active duty personnel (2003): 24,500 (army 61.2%, navy 16.3%, air force 22.4%). **Military expenditure as percentage of GNP** (1999): 0.7% (world 2.4%); per capita expenditure US$15.

Did you know? The island of Hispaniola was the first area in the New World to receive the full imprint of Spanish colonial policy. The oldest cathedral, monastery, and hospital in the Americas were established on the island, and the first university was chartered in Santo Domingo in 1538.

Background

The Dominican Republic was originally part of the Spanish colony of Hispaniola. In 1697 the western third of the island, which later became Haiti, was ceded to France; the remainder of the island passed to France in 1795. The eastern two-thirds of the island were returned to Spain in 1809, and the colony declared its independence in 1821. Within a matter of weeks it was overrun by Haitian troops and occupied until 1844. Since then the country has been under the rule of a succession of dictators, except for short interludes of democratic government, and the US has frequently been involved in its affairs. The termination of the dictatorship of Rafael Trujillo in 1961 led to civil war in 1965 and US military intervention. The country suffered from severe hurricanes in 1979 and 1998.

Recent Developments

To the surprise of almost no one, Leonel Fernández Reyna, head of the Dominican Liberation Party, defeated incumbent Pres. Hipólito Mejía Domínguez of the Dominican Revolutionary Party in the 16 May 2004 elections in the Dominican Republic. Mejía had presided over the largest contraction in the economy in more than a decade. Corruption was unchecked, and a massive banking scandal continued to damage the country's fiscal credibility. Inflation at the end of his term was running at an annualized rate of approximately 52%, and a deteriorating power infrastructure left many areas of the country without electricity for more than 12 hours a day. Without support from the IMF, the government had been unable to cover overdue payments to private energy suppliers. The poor and lower-middle classes were hard hit; the percentage of citizens living below the poverty line had risen above 50%.

Internet resources: <www.dominicana.com.do>.

---

1 metric ton = about 1.1 short tons;   1 kilometer = 0.6 mi (statute);   1 metric ton-km cargo = about 0.68 short ton-mi cargo;   c.i.f.: cost, insurance, and freight;   f.o.b.: free on board

East Timor

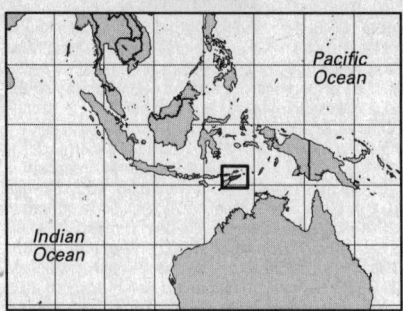

Pacific Ocean

Indian Ocean

Official name: Repúblika Demokrátika Timor Lorosa'e (Tetum); República Democrática de Timor-Leste (Portuguese) (Democratic Republic of Timor-Leste). **Form of government:** republic with one legislative body (National Parliament [88]). **Chief of State:** President Xanana Gusmão (from 2002). **Head of government:** Prime Minister Mari Alkatiri (from 2002). **Capital:** Dili. **Official languages:** Tetum and Portuguese; Indonesian and English are "working" languages. **Official religion:** none. **Monetary unit:** 1 US dollar ($) = 100 centavos (minor currency coins introduced in November 2003 at par with US coins).

Demography

Area: 5,639 sq mi, 14,604 sq km. **Population** (2004): 925,000. **Density** (2004): persons per sq mi 164.0, persons per sq km 63.3. **Urban** (2001): 24.0%. **Sex distribution** (2003): male 50.94%; female 49.06%. **Age breakdown** (2003): under 15, 38.7%; 15–29, 26.9%; 30–44, 19.0%; 45–59, 10.6%; 60–74, 4.0%; 75 and over, 0.7%. **Ethnic composition** (1999): East Timorese 80%; other (nearly all Indonesian, and particularly West Timorese) 20%. **Religious affiliation** (2000): Roman Catholic 87%; Protestant 5%; Muslim 3%; traditional beliefs 3%; other 2%. **Major cities** (2000): Dili 48,200; Dare 17,100; Baucau 14,200; Maliana 12,300; Ermera 12,000. **Location:** southeast Asia, eastern end of the island of Timor plus an exclave on the western end, bordering the Timor Sea and Indonesia.

Vital statistics

Birth rate per 1,000 population (2003): 27.7 (world avg. 21.3). **Death rate** per 1,000 population (2003): 6.4 (world avg. 9.1). **Natural increase rate** per 1,000 population (2003): 21.3 (world avg. 12.2). **Total fertility rate** (avg. births per childbearing woman; 2003): 3.8. **Marriage rate** per 1,000 population (1997–98): 0.4. **Divorce rate** per 1,000 population (1997–98): 0.1. **Life expectancy** at birth (2003): male 63.0 years; female 67.0 years.

National economy

Budget (2002–03). *Revenue:* $77,100,000 (tax revenue 52.0%, grants 42.8%; nontax revenue 5.2%). *Expenditures:* $70,500,000 (education 24.3%, economic affairs 23.3%, general public services 17.0%, public order 13.9%, health 10.5%, defense 7.0%). **Production** (metric tons except as noted). *Agriculture, forestry, fishing* (2003): corn (maize) 70,200, rice

65,400, cassava 41,500; livestock (number of live animals; 2003) 345,000 pigs, 170,000 cattle, 1,300,000 chickens; fish catch (2001) 356. *Mining and quarrying* (2001): commercial quantities of marble are exported. *Manufacturing* (2001): principally the production of textiles, garments, handicrafts, bottled water, and processed coffee. *Energy production (consumption):* electricity (kW-hr; 1998) 40,000,000 (n.a.). **Households.** Average household size (1995) 4.9. **Population economically active** (2001): total 232,000; activity rate of total population 28% (participation rates: ages 15–64, 57%). **Gross national product** (2003): $351,000,000 ($430 per capita). **Tourism:** available beds for tourists (1998) 580. **Land use** as % of total land area (2000): in temporary crops 4.7%, in permanent crops 0.7%, in pasture 10.1%; overall forest area 34.3%.

Foreign trade

Imports (1998): $135,000,000 (foodstuffs 26%, of which rice 10%; construction materials 15%; petroleum products 10%; unspecified 49%). *Major import sources* (2003): Australia 44.0%, Indonesia 16.8%, Singapore 12.9%, Japan 7.3%, Portugal 4.3%. **Exports** (1998): $55,000,000 (agricultural products 93%, of which nonfood crops [nearly all coffee] 51%, livestock 22%, food crops 15%; garments, bottled water, handicrafts, and other manufactured goods 5%). *Major export destination:* Indonesia 96%.

Transport and communications

Transport. *Roads* (December 1999): total length 1,414 km (57% of paved roads were in poor or damaged condition in late 1999; gravel roads were not usable for most vehicles). *Vehicles* (1998): passenger cars 3,156; trucks and buses 7,140. *Air transport:* airports (2001) with scheduled flights 2. **Communications,** in total units (units per 1,000 persons). Daily newspaper circulation (2002): 1,500 (1.8); telephone main lines (1996): 6,600 (8).

Education and health

Educational attainment (2001). Percentage of adult population having: no formal education 57%, primary education 23%, secondary 18%, higher 1.4%. **Literacy** (2001): total population age 15 and over literate 203,000 (48%). **Health:** physicians (1996–97) 122 (1 per 6,590 persons); hospital beds (1999) 560 (1 per 1,277 persons); infant mortality rate per 1,000 live births (2003) 50.5.

Military

Total active duty personnel (2003): 650 (army 94.3%, naval element 5.7%); UN peacekeeping troops (August 2004) 425; UN presence slated to end in May 2005 per May 2004 announcement.

Background

The Portuguese first settled on the island of Timor in 1520 and were granted rule over Timor's eastern half in 1860. The Timor political party Fretilin declared East Timor independent in 1975 after Portugal withdrew its troops. It was invaded by Indonesian forces and was incorporated as a province of Indonesia in 1976. The takeover, which resulted in thousands of East Timorese deaths during the next two decades, was disputed by the UN. In 1999 an independence referendum won overwhelmingly; civilian militias, armed by the military and led by local supporters of integration, then rampaged through the province, killing 1,000–2,000 people. The Indonesian parliament rescinded Indonesia's annexation of the territory, and East Timor was returned to its preannexation status as a non-self-governing territory, though this time under UN supervision. Preparation for independence got under way in 2001, with East Timorese voting by universal suffrage in August for a Constituent Assembly of 88 members. Independence was declared on 20 May 2002 and was followed by the swearing in of Xanana Gusmão as the first president of the world's newest country.

Recent Developments

In December 2003 East Timor opened an embassy in Canberra, Australia, to strengthen the new nation's close ties with its most important neighbor, but ongoing disputes over offshore gas and oil revenue kept bilateral relations strained in 2004. Relations were somewhat better with another important neighbor, Indonesia, whose new president made a symbolically significant visit to Dili in the spring of 2005 and signed a border demarcation agreement on 8 April.

Internet resources: <www.gov.east-timor.org>.

Ecuador

Caribbean Sea

Pacific Ocean

Official name: República del Ecuador (Republic of Ecuador). **Form of government:** unitary multiparty republic with one legislative house (National Congress [125]). **Head of state and government:** President Alfredo Palacio (from 20 Apr 2005). **Capital:** Quito. **Official language:** Spanish (Quechua and Shuar are also official languages for the indigenous peoples). **Official religion:** none. **Monetary unit:** the US dollar ($) was formally adopted as the national currency on 9 Sep 2000; the pegged value of the sucre (S/.), the former national currency, was $1 = S/. 25,000.

Demography

Area: 105,037 sq mi, 272,045 sq km (includes 884 sq mi [2,289 sq km] in nondelimited areas). **Population** (2004): 13,213,000. **Density** (2004): persons per sq mi 125.8, persons per sq km 48.6. **Urban** (2003): 61.8%. **Sex distribution** (2003): male 49.99%; female 50.01%. **Age breakdown** (2003): under 15, 34.4%; 15–29, 28.6%; 30–44, 19.1%; 45–59, 10.9%; 60–74, 5.1%; 75 and over, 1.9%. **Ethnic composition** (2000): mestizo 42.0%; Amerindian 40.8%; white 10.6%; black 5.0%; other 1.6%. **Religious affiliation** (2000): Roman Catholic 94.1%; Protestant 1.9%; other 4.0%. **Major cities** (2001): Guayaquil 1,985,-379; Quito 1,399,378; Cuenca 277,374; Machala 204,578; Santo Domingo de los Colorados 200,421. **Location:** northwestern South America, bordering Colombia, Peru, and the Pacific Ocean.

Vital statistics

Birth rate per 1,000 population (2003): 23.7 (world avg. 21.3; excludes nomadic Indian tribes). **Death rate** per 1,000 population (2003): 4.3 (world avg. 9.1; excludes nomadic Indian tribes). **Natural increase rate** per 1,000 population (2003): 19.4 (world avg. 12.2; excludes nomadic Indian tribes). **Total fertility rate** (avg. births per childbearing woman; 2003): 2.8. **Life expectancy** at birth (2003): male 73.0 years; female 78.8 years.

National economy

Budget (2002). *Revenue:* $4,526,000,000 (nonpetroleum revenue 72.4%, of which value-added tax 33.8%, income tax 14.8%; petroleum revenue 27.6%). *Expenditures:* $4,694,000,000 (current expenditure 73.9%; capital expenditure 26.1%). **Public debt** (external, outstanding; 2002): $13,828,000,000. **Production** (metric tons except as noted). *Agriculture, forestry, fishing* (2002): sugarcane 5,690,895, bananas 5,609,460, fruit palm oil 1,450,000; livestock (live animals) 4,794,000 cattle, 3,007,000 pigs, 142,000,000 chickens; roundwood (2001) 10,919,709 cu m; fish catch (2001) 654,539. *Mining and quarrying* (2000): limestone 3,147,000; gold 2,823 kg. *Manufacturing* (value added in $'000,000; 1999): food products 497; refined petroleum 413; beverages 223. *Energy production (consumption):* electricity (kW-hr; 2000) 10,607,000,000 (10,607,000,000); crude petroleum (barrels; 2001) 146,200,000 ([2000] 61,026,-000); petroleum products (2000) 7,567,000 (5,723,000); natural gas (cu m; 2000) 569,500,000 (569,500,000). **Household income and expenditure.** Average household size (2001) 4.1; average annual income per household (1995) S/. 9,825,610; sources of income (1995): self-employment 70.9%, wages 16.0%, transfer payments 6.7%, other 6.4%; expenditure (1995): food and tobacco 37.9%, transportation and communications 15.0%, clothing 9.2%, household furnishings 6.5%. **Population economically active** (2001): total 4,124,185; activity rate of total population 49.6% (participation rates: ages 15 and over, 72.8%; female 42.3%; unemployed 13.3%). **Gross national product** (2003): $23,347,000,000 ($1,790 per capita). **Land use** as % of total land area (2000): in temporary crops 5.8%, in permanent crops 4.9%, in pasture 18.4%; overall forest area 38.1%. **Tourism**

---

1 metric ton = about 1.1 short tons;   1 kilometer = 0.6 mi (statute);   1 metric ton-km cargo = about 0.68 short ton-mi cargo;   c.i.f.: cost, insurance, and freight;   f.o.b.: free on board

(2002): receipts $447,000,000; expenditures $364,000,000.

Foreign trade

Imports (2000-f.o.b. in balance of trade and c.i.f. for commodities and trading partners): $3,446,000,000 (chemicals and chemical products 23.5%; machinery and apparatus 21.1%; mineral fuels and lubricants 8.2%; food and live animals 7.6%). *Major import sources* (2001): US 29.4%; Colombia 10.3%; Japan 8.2%; Venezuela 4.7%; Chile 4.5%. **Exports** (2000): $4,822,000,000 (mineral fuels and lubricants 50.7%, of which crude petroleum 44.5%; food 35.7%, of which bananas 17.0%, fish and crustaceans 11.8%; cut flowers 3.2%). *Major export destinations* (2001): US 36.2%; Colombia 5.0%; South Korea 4.6%; Germany 4.3%; Japan 4.0%.

Transport and communications

Transport. *Railroads* (2000): route length 956 km; passenger-km 5,000,000; metric ton-km cargo, less than 500,000. *Roads* (1999): total length 43,197 km (paved 19%). *Vehicles* (1999): passenger cars 322,300; trucks and buses 272,000. *Air transport* (2001; Ecuatoviana and TAME airlines): passenger-km 901,000,000; metric ton-km cargo 14,344,000. **Communications**, in total units (units per 1,000 persons). Daily newspaper circulation (1996): 820,000 (70); radios (2001): 5,130,000 (422); televisions (2002): 3,034,000 (237); telephone main lines (2003): 1,549,000 (119); cellular telephone subscribers (2003): 2,394,400 (184); personal computers (2002): 403,000 (31); Internet users (2003): 569,700 (44).

Education and health

Educational attainment (1990). Percentage of population age 25 and over having: no formal schooling 2.2%; incomplete primary 54.3%; primary 28.0%; postsecondary 15.5%. **Literacy** (2001): total population age 15 and over literate 91.0%; males 92.3%; females 89.7%. **Health** (2000): physicians 18,335 (1 per 456 persons); hospital beds 19,564 (1 per 427 persons); infant mortality rate per 1,000 live births (2003) 25.4. **Food** (2001): daily per capita caloric intake 2,333 (vegetable products 86%, animal products 14%); 103% of FAO recommended minimum.

Military

Total active duty personnel (2003): 59,500 (army 84.0%, navy 9.3%, air force 6.7%). **Military expenditure as percentage of GNP** (1999): 3.7% (world 2.4%); per capita expenditure $38.

Background

Ecuador was conquered by the Incas in AD 1450 and came under Spanish control in 1534. Under the Spaniards it was a part of the viceroyalty of Peru until 1740, when it became a part of the viceroyalty of New Granada. It gained its independence from Spain in 1822 as part of the republic of Gran Colombia, and in 1830 it became a sovereign state. A succession of authoritarian governments ruled into the mid-20th century, and economic hardship and social unrest prompted the military to take a strong role. Border disputes led to war between Peru and Ecuador in 1941; the two fought periodically until agreeing to a final demarcation in 1998. The economy, booming in the 1970s with petroleum profits, was depressed in the 1980s by reduced oil prices and earthquake damage. A new constitution was adopted in 1979. In the 1990s social unrest caused political instability and several changes of heads of state. In a controversial move to help stabilize the economy, the US dollar replaced the sucre as the national currency in 2000.

Recent Developments

Lucio Gutiérrez Borbúa took over as president of Ecuador in 2003. By 2004 he found himself increasingly at odds with his people and Congress and came under accusations of nepotism and corruption. In November 2004 Gutiérrez was almost impeached on corruption charges, and the following month, with the assistance of Congress, he purged most of the country's Supreme Court judges, accusing them of being tools of the opposition. Following months of constitutional turmoil, in April 2005 Gutiérrez again dissolved the Court and declared a state of emergency. Congress supported the judicial dismissals but repeatedly called for Gutierrez's resignation. On 20 April they voted to remove the president, and Gutiérrez fled into exile. He was replaced by the vice president, Alfredo Palacio.

Internet resources: <www.ecuador.com>.

Egypt

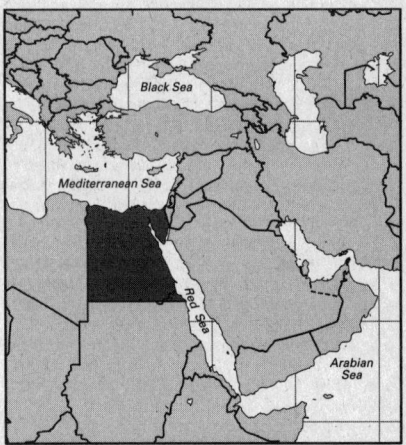

Official name: Jumhuriah Misr al-'Arabiyah (Arab Republic of Egypt). **Form of government:** republic with one legislative house (People's Assembly [454, including 10 nonelective seats]). **Chief of state:** President Hosni Mubarak (from 1981). **Head of government:** Prime Minister Ahmed Nazif (from 14 Jul 2004). **Capital:** Cairo. **Official language:** Arabic. **Official religion:** Islam. **Monetary unit:** 1 Egyptian pound (£E) = 100 piastres; valuation (7 Jul 2005) $1 = £E 5.78.

Demography

Area: 385,229 sq mi, 997,739 sq km. **Population** (2004): 69,261,000. **Density** (2004): persons per sq mi 179.8, persons per sq km 69.4. **Urban** (2002): 45.0%. **Sex distribution** (2003): male 50.46%; female 49.54%. **Age breakdown** (2003): under 15, 33.9%; 15–29, 28.1%; 30–44, 19.4%; 45–59, 12.0%; 60–74, 5.5%; 75 and over, 1.1%. **Ethnic composition** (2000): Egyptian Arab 84.1%; Sudanese Arab 5.5%; Arabized Berber 2.0%; Bedouin 2.0%; Rom (Gypsy) 1.6%; other 4.8%. **Religious affiliation** (2000): Muslim 84.4% (nearly all Sunni); Christian 15.1%, of which Orthodox 13.6%, Protestant 0.8%, Roman Catholic 0.3%; nonreligious 0.5%. **Major cities** ('000; 1996): Cairo 6,789 (10,834; 2003 urban agglomeration); Alexandria 3,328; Al-Jizah 2,222; Shubra al-Khaymah 871; Port Said 470. **Location:** northern Africa, bordering the Mediterranean Sea, the Gaza Strip, Israel, the Red Sea, The Sudan, and Libya.

Vital statistics

Birth rate per 1,000 population (2003): 24.4 (world avg. 21.3). **Death rate** per 1,000 population (2003): 5.4 (world avg. 9.1). **Natural increase rate** per 1,000 population (2003): 19.0 (world avg. 12.2). **Total fertility rate** (avg. births per childbearing woman; 2003): 3.0. **Life expectancy** at birth (2003): male 67.9 years; female 73.0 years.

National economy

Budget (2000–01). *Revenue:* £E 97,938,000,000 (income and profits taxes 28.4%, sales taxes 18.4%, customs duties 13.3%, oil revenue 4.7%, Suez Canal fees 3.6%). *Expenditures:* £E 111,669,000,000 (current expenditure 76.7%; capital expenditure 23.3%). **Public debt** (external, outstanding; 2002): $26,624,000,000. **Population economically active** (1999–2000): total 18,818,000; activity rate 29.7% (participation rates [1998]: ages 15–64, 45.9%; female 21.4%; unemployed 8.1%). **Production** ('000; metric tons except as noted). *Agriculture, forestry, fishing* (2003): sugarcane 12,000, corn (maize) 6,400, tomatoes 6,350; livestock ('000; number of live animals) 4,672 sheep, 3,810 cattle, 3,560 buffalo; roundwood (2003) 16,905,059 cu m; fish catch (2001) 772. *Mining and quarrying* (1999–2000): gypsum 3,027; iron ore 2,932; salt 1,990. *Manufacturing* (value added in $'000,000; 1998): chemicals (all forms) 1,535; food products 958; textiles 828. *Energy production (consumption):* electricity ('000,000 kW-hr; 2000) 76,282 (76,282); coal (2000) none (458); crude petroleum ('000 barrels; 2001) 243,400 ([2000] 239,400); petroleum products (2000) 28,815 (21,512); natural gas ('000,000 cu m; 2000) 21,000 (21,000). **Gross national product** (2003): $93,850,000,000 ($1,390 per capita). **Land use** as % of total land area (2000): in temporary crops 2.8%, in permanent crops 0.5%; overall forest area 0.1%. **Households.** Average household size (2000) 4.7. **Tourism** (2002): receipts $3,764,000,000; expenditures $1,278,000,000.

Foreign trade

Imports (1999-c.i.f.): $15,962,000,000 (machinery and apparatus 22.6%; food 18.3%, of which cereals 8.1%; chemicals and chemical products 11.5%; iron and steel 5.6%). *Major import sources* (2001): US

18.6%; Italy 6.6%; Germany 6.5%; France 4.9%; China 4.4%. **Exports** (1999-f.o.b.): $3,501,000,000 (crude petroleum 27.4%; refined petroleum 8.4%; food 7.9%; wearing apparel 7.9%; raw cotton 6.8%). *Major export destinations* (2001): Italy 15.0%; US 14.4%; UK 9.3%; France 4.7%; Germany 4.1%.

Transport and communications

Transport. *Railroads* (1999): length 4,810 km; passenger-km (1998) 56,667,000,000; metric ton-km cargo (1996) 4,117,000,000. *Roads* (1999): length 64,000 km (paved 78%). *Vehicles* (1998): passenger cars 1,154,753; trucks and buses 510,766. *Inland water* (2000): Suez Canal, number of transits 14,141; metric ton cargo 438,962,000. *Air transport* (2001): passenger-km 8,892,000,000; metric ton-km cargo 239,040,000; airports (1998) 11. **Communications,** in total units (units per 1,000 persons). Daily newspaper circulation (2000): 2,780,000 (43); radios (2000): 21,900,000 (418); televisions (2002): 15,206,000 (229); telephone main lines (2003): 8,735,700 (127); cellular telephone subscribers (2003): 5,797,500 (85); personal computers (2003): 1,500,000 (22); Internet users (2003): 2,700,000 (39).

Education and health

Literacy (2000): total population age 15 and over literate 55.3%; males 66.6%; females 43.8%. **Health** (2002–03): physicians 145,000 (1 per 464 persons); hospital beds 143,100 (1 per 470 persons); infant mortality rate per 1,000 live births (2003) 35.3. **Food** (2001): daily per capita caloric intake 3,385 (vegetable products 92%, animal products 8%); 133% of FAO recommended minimum.

Military

Total active duty personnel (2003): 450,000 (army 71.1%, navy 4.4%, air force [including air defense] 24.5%). **Military expenditure as percentage of GNP** (1999): 2.7% (world 2.4%); per capita expenditure $36.

Background

Egypt is home to one of the world's oldest continuous civilizations. Upper and Lower Egypt were united c. 3000 BC, beginning a period of cultural achievement and a line of native rulers that lasted nearly 3,000 years. Egypt's ancient history is divided into the Old, Middle, and New Kingdoms, spanning 31 dynasties and lasting to 332 BC. The pyramids date from the Old Kingdom; the cult of Osiris and the refinement of sculpture, from the Middle Kingdom; and the era of empire and the Exodus of the Jews, from the New Kingdom. An Assyrian invasion occurred in the 7th century BC, and the Persian Achaemenids established a dynasty in 525 BC. The invasion by Alexander the Great in 332 BC inaugurated the Macedonian Ptolemaic period and the ascendancy of Alexandria. The Romans held Egypt from 30 BC to AD 395; later it was placed under the control of Constantinople. Constantine's granting of tolerance in 313 to the Christians began the development of a formal Egyptian (Coptic) church. Egypt came under Arab control in 642 and ultimately was transformed into an Arabic-speaking

---

1 metric ton = about 1.1 short tons;   1 kilometer = 0.6 mi (statute);   1 metric ton-km cargo = about 0.68 short ton-mi cargo;   c.i.f.: cost, insurance, and freight;   f.o.b.: free on board

state, with Islam as the dominant religion. Held by the Umayyad and Abbasid dynasties, in 969 it became the center of the Fatimid dynasty. In 1250 the Mamluks established a dynasty that lasted until 1517, when Egypt fell to the Ottoman Turks. An economic decline ensued, and with it a decline in Egyptian culture. Egypt became a British protectorate in 1914 and received nominal independence in 1922, when a constitutional monarchy was established. A coup overthrew the monarchy in 1952, with Gamal Abdel Nasser taking power. Following three wars with Israel, Egypt, under Nasser's successor, Anwar al-Sadat, ultimately played a leading role in Middle East peace talks. Sadat was succeeded by Hosni Mubarak, who followed Sadat's peace initiatives and in 1982 regained Egyptian sovereignty (lost in 1967) over the Sinai peninsula. Although Egypt took part in the coalition against Iraq during the Persian Gulf War (1991), it later made peace overtures to Iraq and other countries in the region.

Recent Developments

Egypt's planned October 2005 presidential elections took on significance beyond simply marking the end of the tenure in office of Hosni Mubarak, who had led the country for 24 years. Initially it seemed that Gamal Mubarak, Hosni's son and chair of the ruling National Democratic Party's Policies Committee, was being groomed to succeed his father, but in March 2005 he said he was not a candidate for president. A month earlier President Mubarak had asked Parliament to amend the constitution to allow direct, multiparty elections; they would be the first in Egypt's history. Other signs of increasing democracy were seen as well, as opposition rallies were more or less permitted.

Internet resources: <www.touregypt.net>.

El Salvador

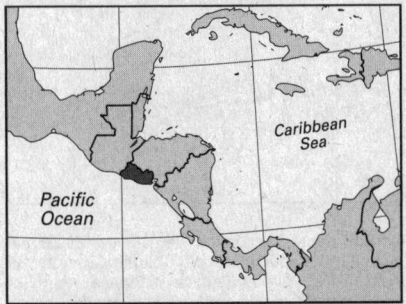

Caribbean Sea

Pacific Ocean

Official name: República de El Salvador (Republic of El Salvador). **Form of government:** republic with one legislative house (Legislative Assembly [84]). **Chief of state and government:** President Antonio Saca (from 1 Jun 2004). **Capital:** San Salvador. **Official language:** Spanish. **Official religion:** none (Roman Catholicism, although not official, enjoys special recognition in the constitution). **Monetary units:** 1 colón (₡) = 100 centavos; valuation (7 Jul 2005; pegged rate) $1 = ₡8.75 (colón rarely in use; the US dollar has also been legal tender since 1 Jan 2001).

Demography

Area: 8,124 sq mi, 21,042 sq km. **Population** (2004): 6,698,000. **Density** (2004): persons per sq mi 824.5, persons per sq km 318.3. **Urban** (2003): 59.6%. **Sex distribution** (2002): male 48.67%; female 51.33%. **Age breakdown** (2002): under 15, 37.1%; 15–29, 28.7%; 30–44, 17.2%; 45–59, 9.8%; 60–74, 5.0%; 75 and over 2.2%. **Ethnic composition** (2000): mestizo 88.3%; Amerindian 9.1%, of which Pipil 4.0%; white 1.6%; other/unknown 1.0%. **Religious affiliation** (1995): Roman Catholic 78.2%; Protestant 17.1%, of which Pentecostal 13.3%; other Christian 1.9%; other 2.8%. **Major cities** (2000): San Salvador 479,600 (urban agglomeration 1,959,036); Soyapango 285,300 (within San Salvador agglomeration); Mejicanos 172,500 (within San Salvador urban agglomeration); Santa Ana 164,500; San Miguel 159,700. **Location:** Central America, bordering Guatemala, Honduras, and the North Pacific Ocean.

Vital statistics

Birth rate per 1,000 population (2003): 27.9 (world avg. 21.3); (1998) legitimate 27.2%. **Death rate** per 1,000 population (2003): 6.0 (world avg. 9.1). **Natural increase rate** per 1,000 population (2003): 21.9 (world avg. 12.2). **Total fertility rate** (avg. births per childbearing woman; 2003): 3.2. **Marriage rate** per 1,000 population (2001): 4.6. **Life expectancy** at birth (2003): male 67.0 years; female 74.4 years.

National economy

Budget. Revenue (2001): $1,499,400,000 (sales taxes 57.2%, corporate taxes 13.1%, individual income taxes 11.4%, import duties 9.7%). *Expenditures:* $1,968,600,000 (education 23.3%, police 15.7%, economic services 14.7%, social services 12.7%, health 11.1%, defense 6.6%). **Public debt** (external, outstanding; 2002): $4,712,000,000. **Production** (metric tons except as noted). *Agriculture, forestry, fishing* (2002): sugarcane 4,933,000, corn (maize) 637,000, sorghum 139,000; livestock (number of live animals) 1,392,000 cattle, 153,000 pigs; roundwood (2001) 5,200,000 cu m; fish catch (2001) 18,142. *Mining and quarrying* (2002): limestone 3,200,000. *Manufacturing* (value added in $'000,000; 1998): food products 306; wearing apparel 249; drugs and medicines 128. *Energy production (consumption):* electricity (kW-hr; 2000) 3,546,000,000 (4,242,000,000); crude petroleum (barrels; 2000) none (7,147,000); petroleum products (2000) 901,000 (1,723,000). **Household income and expenditure.** Average household size (2000) 4.5; average income per household (1992–93) ₡22,930; expenditure (1990–91): food and beverages 37.0%, housing 12.1%, transportation and communications 10.2%, clothing and footwear 6.7%. **Land use** as % of total land area (2000): in temporary crops 30.9%, in permanent crops 12.1%, in pasture 38.3%; overall forest area 5.8%. **Population economically active** (1999): total 2,444,900; activity rate of total population 40.1% (participation rates: ages 15–64 (1995) 62.9%; female 40.7%; unemployed 7.0%). **Gross national product** (2003): $14,387,000,000 ($2,200 per capita). **Tourism** (2002): receipts $342,000,000; expenditures $229,000,000.

Foreign trade

Imports (2000-c.i.f.): $4,947,000,000 (Imports for reexport 23.3%; machinery and apparatus 15.5%; chemicals and chemical products 11.2%; food 10.4%; petroleum [all forms] 10.3%). *Major import sources* (2002): US 49.6%; Guatemala 8.1%; Honduras 3.0%; Costa Rica 2.9%; unspecified 30.4%. **Exports** (2000-f.o.b.): $2,941,000,000 (reexports [mostly clothing] 54.4%; coffee 10.1%; paper and paper products 2.8%; yarn, fabrics, made-up articles 2.7%). *Major export destinations:* US 67.0%; Guatemala 11.5%; Honduras 5.9%; Nicaragua 3.8%; unspecified 6.9%.

Transport and communications

Transport. *Railroads* (2001): operational route length 283 km; (1999) passenger-km 8,000,000; metric ton-km cargo 19,000,000. *Roads* (1999): total length 10,029 km (paved 20%). *Vehicles* (2000): passenger cars 148,000; trucks and buses 250,800. *Air transport* (2001; TACA International Airlines only): passenger-km 6,150,000,000; metric ton-km cargo 379,000; airports (2001) with scheduled flights 1. **Communications,** in total units (units per 1,000 persons). Daily newspaper circulation (2000): 217,000 (35); radios (2000): 2,970,000 (478); televisions (2000): 1,250,000 (201); telephone main lines (2003): 752,600 (116); cellular telephone subscribers (2003): 1,149,800 (177); personal computers (2002): 163,000 (25); Internet users (2003): 550,000 (84).

Education and health

Educational attainment (1992). Percentage of population over age 25 having: no formal schooling 34.7%; incomplete primary education 37.6%; complete primary (through ninth grade) 10.8%; secondary 9.4%; higher technical 2.4%; incomplete undergraduate 1.1%; complete undergraduate 2.9%; other/unknown 1.1%. **Literacy** (1999): total population age 15 and over literate 78.3%; males literate 81.3%; females literate 75.6%. **Health** (2002): physicians 8,212 (1 per 794 persons); hospital beds 4,562 (1 per 1,429 persons); infant mortality rate per 1,000 live births (2003) 26.8. **Food** (2002): daily per capita caloric intake 2,584 (vegetable products 87%, animal products 13%); 113% of FAO recommended minimum.

Military

Total active duty personnel (2003): 15,500 (army 89.4%, navy 4.5%, air force 6.1%). **Military expenditure as percentage of GNP** (1999): 0.9% (world 2.4%); per capita expenditure $18.

Background

The Spanish arrived in the area in 1524 and subjugated the Pipil Indian kingdom of Cuzcatlán by 1539. The country was divided into two districts, San Salvador and Sonsonate, both attached to Guatemala. When independence came in 1821, San Salvador was incorporated into the Mexican Empire; upon its collapse in 1823, Sonsonate and San Salvador combined to form the new state of El Salvador within the United Provinces of Central America. From its founding, El Salvador experienced a high degree of political turmoil and was under military rule from 1931 to 1979, when the government was ousted in a coup. Elections held in 1982 set up a new government, and in 1983 a new constitution was adopted, but civil war continued through the 1980s. An accord in 1992 brought an uneasy truce.

Recent Developments

El Salvador's presidential elections in March 2004 were a pitched battle between the right and the left, but the right-wing National Republican Alliance was victorious for the fourth straight time, sending former sports commentator Tony Saca to the presidential palace. Saca promised to continue the pro-business and pro-US policies of his predecessor, Francisco Flores Pérez, to increase foreign investment, and not to privatize the country's social security and health care systems. On 28 May 2004 El Salvador signed the Central American Free Trade Agreement, along with other Central American countries and the US.

Internet resources: <www.elsalvadorturismo.gob.sv>.

Equatorial Guinea

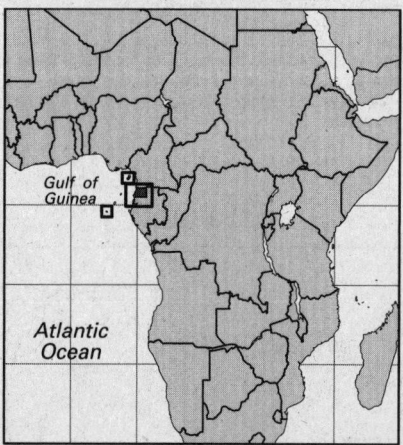

Official name: República de Guinea Ecuatorial (Spanish); République du Guinée Équatoriale (French) (Republic of Equatorial Guinea). **Form of government:** republic with one legislative house (House of Representatives of the People [100]). **Chief of state:** President Teodoro Obiang Nguema Mbasogo (from 1979). **Head of government:** Prime Minister Miguel Abia Biteo Borico (from 14 Jun 2004). **Capital:** Malabo. **Official languages:** Spanish; French. **Official religion:** none. **Monetary unit:** 1 CFA franc (CFAF) = 100 centimes; valuation (7 Jul 2005) $1 = CFAF 549.50; the CFAF is pegged to the euro (€) at €1 = CFAF 655.96 from 1 Jan 2002.

1 metric ton = about 1.1 short tons;   1 kilometer = 0.6 mi (statute);   1 metric ton-km cargo = about 0.68 short ton-mi cargo;   c.i.f.: cost, insurance, and freight;   f.o.b.: free on board

Demography

Area: 10,831 sq mi, 28,051 sq km. **Population** (2004): 507,000. **Density** (2004): persons per sq mi 46.8, persons per sq km 18.1. **Urban** (2003): 48.1%. **Sex distribution** (2002): male 48.77%; female 51.23%. **Age breakdown** (2002): under 15, 42.4%; 15–29, 27.0%; 30–44, 16.2%; 45–59, 8.3%; 60–74, 4.8%; 75 and over, 1.3%. **Ethnic composition** (1995): Fang 82.9%; Bubi 9.6%; other 7.5%. **Religious affiliation** (2000): Roman Catholic 80.1%; Muslim 4.0%; African Christian 3.7%; Protestant 3.1%; other 9.1%. **Major cities** (2003): Malabo 92,900; Bata 66,800; Mbini 11,600; Ebebiyin 9,100; Luba 6,800. **Location:** western Africa, the mainland portion bordering Cameroon, Gabon, and the Bight of Biafra (inlet of the Atlantic Ocean).

Vital statistics

Birth rate per 1,000 population (2003): 36.9 (world avg. 21.3). **Death rate** per 1,000 population (2003): 12.5 (world avg. 9.1). **Natural increase rate** per 1,000 population (2003): 24.4 (world avg. 12.2). **Total fertility rate** (avg. births per childbearing woman; 2003): 4.7. **Life expectancy** at birth (2003): male 52.6 years; female 56.9 years.

National economy

Budget (2002). *Revenue:* CFAF 414,484,000,000 (oil revenue 81.6%, of which royalties 41.5%; tax revenue 15.3%; nontax revenue 3.1%). *Expenditures:* CFAF 227,236,000,000 (capital expenditure 55.7%; current expenditure 44.3%). **Public debt** (external, outstanding; 2002): $209,100,000. **Gross national product** (at current market prices; 2003): $2,200,-000,000 ($4,400 per capita). **Production** (metric tons except as noted). *Agriculture, forestry, fishing* (2002): roots and tubers 105,000 (of which cassava 45,000, sweet potatoes 36,000), palm oil 35,000, bananas 20,000; livestock (number of live animals) 38,000 sheep, 9,000 goats, 6,100 pigs; roundwood (2003) 811,000 cu m, of which saw logs and veneer logs 364,000; fish catch (2001) 3,500. *Mining and quarrying:* gold (2002) 500 kg. *Manufacturing:* methanol (2002) 719,000. *Energy production (consumption):* electricity (kW-hr; 2000) 23,000,000 (23,000,000); crude petroleum (barrels; 2003) 97,601,000 ([2000] 102,600); petroleum products (2000) none (53,000); natural gas (2002) 1,050,-000,000 (n.a.). **Population economically active** (1997): total 177,000; activity rate of total population 40.0% (participation rates: ages 15–64, 74.7%; female 35.4%). **Household income and expenditure.** Sources of income (1988): wages and salaries 57.0%, business income 42.0%, other 1.0%; expenditure (2000): food and beverages 60.4%; clothing 14.7%; household furnishings 8.6%. **Tourism:** tourism is a government priority but remains undeveloped. **Land use** as % of total land area (2000): in temporary crops 4.6%, in permanent crops 3.6%, in pasture 3.7%; overall forest area 62.5%.

Foreign trade

Imports (2001-c.i.f.): CFAF 593,400,000,000 (for petroleum sector 80.8%; other machinery and apparatus 11.6%; petroleum products 4.8%). *Major import sources* (1999): US 60%; France 12%; Spain 8%; Italy 6%; Cameroon 3%. **Exports** (2001-f.o.b.): CFAF 1,346,700,000,000 (crude petroleum 91.6%; methanol 4.5%; wood 2.9%; cocoa beans 0.1%). *Major export destinations* (1999): Spain 46%; China 24%; Japan 7%; US 7%; Chile 5%.

Transport and communications

Transport. *Roads* (1999): total length 2,880 km (paved 13%). *Vehicles* (1994): passenger cars 6,500; trucks and buses 4,000. *Air transport* (1998): passenger-km 4,000,000; airports (2003) with scheduled flights 3. **Communications,** in total units (units per 1,000 persons). Daily newspaper circulation (1996): 2,000 (4.9); radios (1997): 180,000 (428); televisions (1997): 4,000 (9.8); telephone main lines (2003): 9,600 (18); cellular telephone units (2003): 41,500 (76); personal computers (2002): 4,000 (6.9); Internet users (2002): 1,800 (3.6).

Education and health

Educational attainment (1983). Percentage of population age 15 and over having: no schooling 35.4%; some primary education 46.6%; primary 13.0%; secondary 2.3%; postsecondary 1.1%; not specified 1.6%. **Literacy** (2000): percentage of total population age 15 and over literate 83.2%; males literate 92.5%; females literate 74.4%. **Health:** physicians (1996) 106 (1 per 4,065 persons); hospital beds (1990) 992 (1 per 350 persons); infant mortality rate per 1,000 live births (2003) 89.0.

Military

Total active duty personnel (2003): 1,320 (army 83.3%, navy 9.1%, air force 7.6%). **Military expenditure as percentage of GNP** (1999): 3.2% (world 2.4%); per capita expenditure $40.

Background

The first inhabitants of the mainland region appear to have been Pygmies. The now-prominent Fang and Bubi reached the mainland region in the 17th-century Bantu migrations. Equatorial Guinea was ceded by the Portuguese to the Spanish in the late 18th century; it was frequented by slave traders, as well as by British, German, Dutch, and French merchants. Bioko was administered by British authorities (1827–58) before the official takeover by the Spanish. The mainland (Río Muni) was not effectively occupied by the Spanish until 1926. Independence was declared in 1968, followed by a reign of terror and economic chaos under the dictatorial president Macías Nguema, who was overthrown by a military coup in 1979 and later executed. A new constitution was adopted in 1982, but political unrest persisted.

Recent Developments

In December 2003 news of a power struggle in Equatorial Guinea began to emerge; the situation seemed to be related to the illness of Pres. Teodoro Obiang Nguema Mbasogo and his plans to hand over power to his playboy son Teodorin. Various members of the armed forces, including relatives of the president, were sacked, and others were arrested. In March 2004 Obiang learned that a coup was being planned to oust him. A group of alleged mercenaries were arrested and charged with plotting to install his rival,

Severo Moto, who lived in exile. Another 70 members of the alleged plot were arrested in Zimbabwe en route to Equatorial Guinea. The mercenaries were brought to trial in August, but after the arrest in South Africa of Mark Thatcher—son of the former British prime minister—for helping to finance the attempted coup (he pleaded guilty in January 2005), the trial was suspended indefinitely.

Internet resources:
<www.cia.gov/cia/publications/factbook/geos/ek.html>.

Eritrea

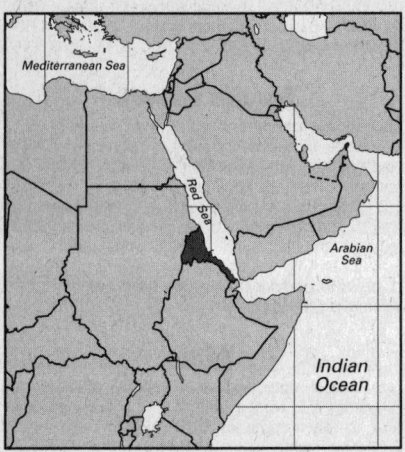

Mediterranean Sea

Red Sea

Arabian Sea

Indian Ocean

Official name: State of Eritrea. **Form of government:** transitional regime with one interim legislative body (Transitional National Assembly [150]). Constitution adopted in May 1997 was still not implemented in mid-2005. **Head of state and government:** President Isaias Afwerki (from 1993). **Capital:** Asmara. **Official language:** none. **Official religion:** none. **Monetary unit:** 1 nakfa (Nfa) = 100 cents; valuation (7 Jul 2005) $1 = Nfa 13.50.

Demography

Area: 46,760 sq mi, 121,100 sq km. **Population** (2004): 4,297,000. **Density** (2004; based on land area only): persons per sq mi 110.2, persons per sq km 42.5. **Urban** (2003): 19.9%. **Sex distribution** (2003): male 49.75%; female 50.25%. **Age breakdown** (2003): under 15, 44.7%; 15–29, 27.2%; 30–44, 14.1%; 45–59, 8.7%; 60–74, 4.3%; 75 and over, 1.0%. **Ethnolinguistic composition** (2000): Tigrinya (Tigray) 51.8%; Tigré 17.9%; Afar 8.1%; Saho 4.3%; Kunama 4.1%; other 13.8%. **Religious affiliation** (2000): Christian 50.5%, of which Eritrean Orthodox 46.1%; Muslim 44.7%; other 4.8%. **Major cities** (2000): Asmara (2001) 503,000; Keren 70,000; Mendefera 65,000; Asseb (2003) 56,300; Massawa 35,000. **Location:** the Horn of eastern Africa, bordering The Sudan, the Red Sea, Djibouti, and Ethiopia.

Vital statistics

Birth rate per 1,000 population (2003): 39.4 (world avg. 21.3). **Death rate** per 1,000 population (2003): 13.2 (world avg. 9.1). **Natural increase rate** per 1,000 population (2003): 26.2 (world avg. 12.2). **Total fertility rate** (avg. births per childbearing woman; 2003): 5.7. **Marriage rate** per 1,000 population (1992): 6.8. **Life expectancy** at birth (2003): male 51.5 years; female 54.9 years.

National economy

Budget (2001). *Revenue:* Nfa 3,361,900,000 (grants 40.9%; tax revenue 38.0%, of which direct taxes 17.0%, import duties 12.2%; nontax revenue 15.9%; extraordinary revenue 5.2%). *Expenditures:* Nfa 4,545,300,000 (current expenditure 72.3%; capital expenditure 27.7%). **Production** (metric tons except as noted). *Agriculture, forestry, fishing* (2003): roots and tubers 85,000, sorghum 64,000, potatoes 33,000; livestock (number of live animals; 2003) 2,100,000 sheep, 1,927,500 cattle, 1,700,000 goats; roundwood (2003) 2,366,117; fish catch (2001) 8,820. *Mining and quarrying* (2001): salt 200,000; marble and granite are quarried, as are sand and aggregate (gravel) for construction. *Manufacturing* (value added in $'000,000; 2001): beverages 17; food products 6; tobacco products 5. *Energy production (consumption):* electricity (kW-hr; 2002) 249,117,000 (194,-161,000); petroleum products (2000) n.a. (191,000). **Gross national product** (at current market prices; 2002): $850,000,000 ($190 per capita). **Public debt** (external, outstanding; 2002): $496,400,000. **Households.** Average household size (2000) 5.3. **Population economically active** (1996): 1,649,000; activity rate of total population 41.4%. **Tourism** (2002): receipts from visitors $73,000,000. **Land use** as % of total land area (2000): in temporary crops 5.0%, in permanent crops 0.03%, in pasture 69.0%; overall forest area 13.5%.

Foreign trade

Imports (2002-c.i.f.): $538,000,000 (food and live animals 28.4%, of which cereals [all forms] 11.0%; raw sugar 7.9%; machinery and apparatus 17.5%; road vehicles 11.5%; chemicals and chemical products 6.6%; iron and steel 6.2%). *Major import sources* (2001): Italy 18.7%; Saudi Arabia 16.6%; UAE 15.3%; US 4.8%. **Exports** (2002-f.o.b.): $52,000,000 (raw sugar 60.8%; synthetic woven fabrics 4.4%; vegetables and fruits 3.3%; fish 2.9%; sesame 2.7%). *Major export destinations* (2001): The Sudan 48.9%; Italy 8.2%; Germany 3.5%.

Transport and communications

Transport. *Railroads* (2001): part of the 306-km rail line that formerly connected Massawa and Agordat is under reconstruction; the 118-km section between Massawa and Asmara was reopened in 2003. *Roads* (1999): total length 4,010 km (paved 22%). *Vehicles* (1996): automobiles 5,940. *Air transport* (2001; Asmara airport only): passenger arrivals 39,266, passenger departures 46,448; freight loaded 202 metric tons, freight unloaded 1,548 metric tons; airports (2000) with scheduled flights 2. **Communications,** in total units (units per 1,000 persons). Daily newspaper

---

1 metric ton = about 1.1 short tons; 1 kilometer = 0.6 mi (statute); 1 metric ton-km cargo = about 0.68 short ton-mi cargo; c.i.f.: cost, insurance, and freight; f.o.b.: free on board

circulation (2000): 104,000 (28); radios (2001): 1,763,000 (464); televisions (2002): 215,000 (50); telephone main lines (2003): 38,100 (9.2); personal computers (2003): 12,000 (2.9); Internet users (2003): 9,500 (2.3).

Education and health

Literacy (2003): total population age 15 and over literate, 58.6%; males 69.9%; females 47.6%. **Health** (2000): physicians 173 (1 per 21,457 persons); hospital beds: 3,126 (1 per 1,187 persons); infant mortality rate per 1,000 live births (2003) 76.3. **Food** (2001): daily per capita caloric intake 1,690 (vegetable 94%, animal products 6%); 76% of FAO recommended minimum.

Military

Total active duty personnel (2002): 172,200 (army 98.7%, navy 0.8%, air force 0.5%). UN peacekeeping force along Eritrean-Ethiopian border (September 2004) 3,900. **Military expenditure as percentage of GNP** (1999): 27.4% (world 2.4%); per capita expenditure $52.

Did you know? The Eritrean cities of Massawa and Asmara are notable for their rich Italianate architecture and urban design, legacies of the Italian occupation of the region from the 1880s until 1941. After the end of the war of independence from Ethiopia in the 1990s, restoration returned the cities to their earlier grandeur.

Background

As the site of the main ports of the Aksumite empire, Eritrea was linked to the beginnings of the Ethiopian kingdom, but it retained much of its independence until it came under Ottoman rule in the 16th century. In the 17th and 19th centuries, control of the territory was disputed among Ethiopia, the Ottomans, the kingdom of Tigray, Egypt, and Italy; it became an Italian colony in 1890. Eritrea was used as the main base for the Italian invasions of Ethiopia (1896 and 1935–36) and in 1936 became part of Italian East Africa. It was captured by the British in 1941, federated to Ethiopia in 1952, and made a province of Ethiopia in 1962. Thirty years of guerrilla warfare by Eritrean secessionist groups ensued. A provisional Eritrean government was established in 1991 after the overthrow of the Ethiopian government, and independence came in 1993. A new constitution was ratified in 1997.

Recent Developments

In 2004 Eritrea settled, albeit uneasily, into a no-war–no-peace stalemate with Ethiopia. Dismayed by what it saw as yet another betrayal by the international community, the government sent delegations abroad to express its displeasure to countries as varied as Australia, Benin, Kuwait, The Gambia, Saudi Arabia, and Switzerland. The failure to attain a fair hearing internationally for its grievances against Ethiopia was due less to the merits of its case, however, than to Eritrea's deteriorating international standing—the result of violations of regional and in-

ternational norms, which in turn were deftly manipulated by Ethiopia, a country that still enjoyed the esteem of African and international bodies.

Internet resources: <http://allafrica.com/eritrea>.

Estonia

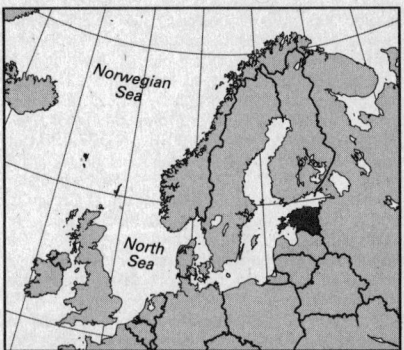

Official name: Eesti Vabariik (Republic of Estonia). **Form of government:** unitary multiparty republic with a single legislative body (Riigikogu [101]). **Chief of state:** President Arnold Ruutel (from 2001). **Head of government:** Prime Minister Andrus Ansip (from 13 Apr 2005). **Capital:** Tallinn. **Official language:** Estonian. **Official religion:** none. **Monetary unit:** 1 kroon (EEK) = 100 senti; valuation (7 Jul 2005) $1 = EEK 13.12.

Demography

Area: 16,769 sq mi, 43,431 sq km. **Population** (2004): 1,342,000. **Density** (2004): persons per sq mi 76.9, persons per sq km 29.7. **Urban** (2002): 69.4%. **Sex distribution** (2003): male 46.09%; female 53.91%. **Age breakdown** (2002): under 15, 15.8%; 15–29, 22.7%; 30–44, 21.5%; 45–59, 19.1%; 60–74, 14.9%; 75 and over, 6.0%. **Ethnic composition** (2000): Estonian 67.9%; Russian 25.6%; Ukrainian 2.1%; Belarusian 1.3%; Finnish 0.9%; other 2.2%. **Religious affiliation** (1995): Christian 38.1%, of which Orthodox 20.4%, Evangelical Lutheran 13.7%; other (mostly nonreligious) 61.9%. **Major cities** (2003): Tallinn 400,378; Tartu 101,169; Narva 67,752; Kohtla-Jarve 46,765; Pärnu 44,781. **Location:** eastern Europe, bordering the Gulf of Finland, Russia, Latvia, the Gulf of Riga, and the Baltic Sea.

Vital statistics

Birth rate per 1,000 population (2002): 9.6 (world avg. 21.3); legitimate 43.7%. **Death rate** per 1,000 population (2002): 13.5 (world avg. 9.1). **Natural increase rate** per 1,000 population (2002): –3.9 (world avg. 12.2). **Total fertility rate** (avg. births per childbearing woman; 2002): 1.4. **Marriage rate** per 1,000 population (2002): 4.3. **Divorce rate** per 1,000 population (2002): 3.0. **Life expectancy** at birth (2002): male 64.4 years; female 76.6 years.

National economy

Budget (2001). *Revenue:* EEK 36,881,000,000 (social security contributions 31.2%, value-added taxes

23.4%, personal income taxes 19.2%, excise taxes 9.3%). *Expenditures:* EEK 36,548,000,000 (social security and welfare 31.5%, health 16.3%, education 7.3%, police 7.2%, defense 5.0%). **Public debt** (external, outstanding; 2002): $482,000,000. **Production** (metric tons except as noted). *Agriculture, forestry, fishing* (2002): barley 249,400, potatoes 210,900, wheat 74,400; livestock (number of live animals) 345,000 pigs, 260,500 cattle; roundwood (2001) 10,200,000 cu m; fish catch (2001) 105,634. *Mining and quarrying* (2002): oil shale 12,400,000; peat 1,518,600. *Manufacturing* (value of production in EEK '000,000; 2001): food products 9,282; wood products (excluding furniture) 7,321; fabricated metal products 4,251. *Energy production (consumption):* electricity (kW-hr; 2002) 8,527,000,000 (5,686,000,000); hard coal (2002) none (60,000); lignite (2000) 11,727,000 (13,232,000); petroleum products (2000) none (736,000); natural gas (cu m; 2002) none (743,000,000). **Tourism** (2002): receipts $555,000,000; expenditures $231,000,000. **Population economically active** (2002): total 652,700; activity rate of total population 48.0% (participation rates: ages 15–74, 62.3%; female 48.9%; unemployed 10.3%). **Household income and expenditure** (2002). Average household size (2000) 2.2; average disposable income per household (1998) EEK 53,049; sources of income: wages and salaries 64.5%, transfers 25.0%, self-employment 5.2%, other 5.3%; expenditure: food and beverages 32.6%, housing 15.7%, transportation and communications 13.1%, clothing and footwear 6.2%. **Gross national product** (2003): $6,699,000,000 ($4,960 per capita). **Land use** as % of total land area (2000): in temporary crops 26.5%, in permanent crops 0.3%, in pasture 7.1%; overall forest area 48.7%.

Foreign trade

Imports (2001-c.i.f.): EEK 75,073,000,000 (electrical and nonelectrical machinery 33.5%, textiles and apparel 10.3%, foodstuffs 9.4%, transport equipment 8.9%). *Major import sources:* Finland 29.9%; Germany 11.2%; Sweden 10.0%; Russia 7.8%; Latvia 4.0%. **Exports** (2001-f.o.b.): EEK 57,832,000,000 (electrical and nonelectrical machinery 33.1%, wood and paper products 15.2%, textiles and apparel 14.0%). *Major export destinations:* Finland 33.9%; Sweden 14.0%; Germany 6.9%; Latvia 6.9%; UK 4.2%.

Transport and communications

Transport. *Railroads* (2002): route length 963 km; passenger-km 177,000,000; metric ton-km cargo 9,697,000,000. *Roads* (2000): total length 16,430 km (paved 51%). *Vehicles* (2002): passenger cars 400,700; trucks and buses 85,700. *Air transport* (2002; Estonian Air): passenger-km 355,000,000; metric ton-km cargo 5,000,000; airports (2001) 1. **Communications,** in total units (units per 1,000 persons). Daily newspaper circulation (1996): 255,000 (174); radios (2001): 1,590,000 (1,136); televisions (2002): 702,000 (502); telephone main lines (2003): 464,000 (343); cellular telephone subscribers (2003): 1,050,200 (776); personal computers (2002): 285,000 (210); Internet users (2002): 444,000 (328).

Health and nutrition

Health (2002): physicians 4,190 (1 per 324 persons); hospital beds 8,088 (1 per 168 persons); infant mortality rate per 1,000 live births (2002) 5.7. **Food** (2001): daily per capita caloric intake 3,048 (vegetable products 75%, animal products 25%); 119% of FAO recommended minimum.

Military

Total active duty personnel (2003): 5,510 (army 88.0%, navy 8.0%, air force 4.0%). **Military expenditure as a percentage of GNP** (1999): 1.5% (world 2.4%); per capita expenditure $120.

Background

The lands on the eastern shores of the Baltic Sea were invaded by Vikings in the 9th century AD and later by Danes, Swedes, and Russians, but the Estonians were able to withstand the assaults until the Danes took control in 1219. In 1346 the Danes sold their sovereignty to the Teutonic Order, which was then in possession of Livonia (southern Estonia and Latvia). In the mid-16th century Estonia was once again divided, with northern Estonia capitulating to Sweden and Poland gaining Livonia, which it surrendered to Sweden in 1629. Russia acquired Livonia and Estonia in 1721. Nearly a century later, serfdom was abolished, and from 1881 Estonia underwent intensive Russification. In 1918 Estonia obtained independence from Russia, which lasted until the Soviet Union occupied the country in 1940 and forcibly incorporated it into the USSR. Germany held the region (1941–44) during World War II, but the Soviet regime was restored in 1944, after which Estonia's economy was collectivized and integrated into that of the Soviet Union. In 1991, along with other parts of the former USSR, it proclaimed its independence and subsequently held elections. Estonia continued negotiations with Russia to settle their common border.

Recent Developments

The center-right coalition government of Prime Minister Juhan Parts resigned on 21 Mar 2005 following a no-confidence vote on an anticorruption plan proposed by the justice minister. Andrus Ansip took over as prime minister and formed a new government. Foreign Minister Kristiina Ojuland had been dismissed a month earlier after a number of sensitive documents went missing.

Internet resources: <http://visitestonia.com>.

Ethiopia

Official name: Federal Democratic Republic of Ethiopia. **Form of government:** federal republic with two legislative houses (Federal Council [108]; Council of People's Representatives [546]). **Chief of state:** President Girma Wolde-Giorgis (from 2001). **Head of government:** Prime Minister Meles Zenawi (from 1995). **Capital:** Addis Ababa. **Official language:** none (Amharic is the "working" language). **Official religion:**

---

1 metric ton = about 1.1 short tons;   1 kilometer = 0.6 mi (statute);   1 metric ton-km cargo = about 0.68 short ton-mi cargo;   c.i.f.: cost, insurance, and freight;   f.o.b.: free on board

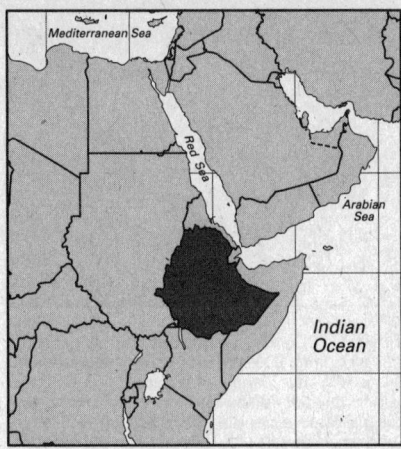

none. **Monetary unit:** 1 birr (Br) = 100 cents; valuation (7 Jul 2005) $1 = Br 8.71.

Demography

Area: 435,186 sq mi, 1,127,127 sq km. **Population** (2004): 67,851,000. **Density** (2004): persons per sq mi 155.0, persons per sq km 59.8. **Urban** (2002): 15.6%. **Sex distribution** (2002): male 50.14%; female 49.86%. **Age breakdown** (2002): under 15, 44.9%; 15–29, 28.0%; 30–44, 14.5%; 45–59, 8.2%; 60–74, 3.7%; 75 and over, 0.7%. **Ethnolinguistic composition** (1994): Oromo 31.8%; Amharic 29.3%; Somali 6.2%; Tigrinya 5.9%; Walaita 4.6%; Gurage 4.2%; Sidamo 3.4%; Afar 1.9%; Hadya-Libide 1.7%; other 11.0%. **Religious affiliation** (1994): Ethiopian Orthodox 50.3%; Muslim 32.9%; Protestant 10.1%; traditional beliefs 4.8%; Roman Catholic 0.6%; other 1.3%. **Major cities** (1994): Addis Ababa 2,112,737; Dire Dawa 164,851; Nazret 127,842; Gonder 112,249; Dese 97,314. **Location:** the Horn of eastern Africa, bordering Eritrea, Djibouti, Somalia, Kenya, and The Sudan.

Vital statistics

Birth rate per 1,000 population (2003): 39.9 (world avg. 21.3). **Death rate** per 1,000 population (2003): 15.5 (world avg. 9.1). **Natural increase rate** per 1,000 population (2003): 24.4 (world avg. 12.2). **Total fertility rate** (avg. births per childbearing woman; 2003): 5.6. **Life expectancy** at birth (2003): male 47.3 years; female 49.7 years. **Adult population** (ages 15–49) **living with HIV** (beginning of 2004): 4.4% (world avg. 1.1%).

National economy

Budget (1999–2000). *Revenue:* Br 11,222,000,000 (tax revenue 57.8%, of which import duties 22.5%, income and profit tax 19.3%, sales tax 12.8%, export duties 1.3%; nontax revenue 26.9%; grants 15.3%). *Expenditures:* Br 17,184,000,000 (current expenditure 80.0%, of which defense 39.8%, wages 20.5%, education and health 12.2%, debt payment 6.5%; capital expenditure 20.0%). **Public debt** (external, outstanding; 2002): $6,313,000,000. **Tourism** (2002): receipts $77,000,000; expenditures $45,-

000,000. **Gross national product** (2003): $6,325,-000,000 ($90 per capita). **Production** (metric tons except as noted). *Agriculture, forestry, fishing* (2002): corn (maize) 2,600,000, sugarcane 2,500,000, sorghum 1,820,000; livestock (number of live animals) 35,500,000 cattle, 11,438,000 sheep, 9,622,-000 goats; roundwood (2001) 91,283,000 cu m; fish catch (2001) 15,390. *Mining and quarrying* (2001–02): rock salt 61,000; tantalum 37,000 kg; niobium 6,100 kg. *Manufacturing* (value added in $'000,000; 2001): food products 143; beverages 95; nonmetallic mineral products 38. *Energy production (consumption):* electricity (kW-hr; 2000) 1,700,-000,000 (1,700,000,000); crude petroleum (barrels; 2000) none (5,498,000); petroleum products (2000) 611,000 (1,508,000). **Land use** as % of total land area (2000): in temporary crops 10.0%, in permanent crops 0.7%, in pasture 20.0%; overall forest area 4.2%. **Population economically active** (2000): total 27,781,000; activity rate of total population 44.3% (participation rates [1999]: ages over 15, 80.5%; female [1999] 45.5%). **Households.** Average household size (2000) 5.2.

Foreign trade

Imports (2000-f.o.b. in balance of trade and c.i.f. for commodities and trading partners): $1,260,000,000 (machinery and apparatus 19.8%, refined petroleum 19.6%, road vehicles 12.0%, chemicals and chemical products 11.3%, iron and steel 5.6%). *Major import sources:* Yemen 19.1%; Italy 8.9%; Japan 8.2%; China 7.7%; India 5.2%; Germany 5.2%. **Exports** (2000): $482,000,000 (coffee 53.0%, leather 8.5%, nonmonetary gold 5.7%, sesame seeds 4.6%). *Major export destinations:* Germany 19.6%; Japan 11.7%; Djibouti 10.7%; Saudi Arabia 8.1%; Italy 6.7%; Somalia 6.1%.

Transport and communications

Transport. *Railroads* (2001): length 681 km (length of Ethiopian segment of Addis Ababa–Djibouti railroad); (1998–99) passenger-km 151,000,000 (includes Djibouti part of Addis Ababa–Djibouti railroad); (1998–99) metric ton-km cargo 90,000,000 (includes Djibouti part of Addis Ababa–Djibouti railroad). *Roads* (2001): total length 29,799 km (paved 13%). *Vehicles* (1999): passenger cars 54,240; trucks and buses 34,333. *Air transport* (2003; Ethiopian Airlines only): passenger-km 3,573,-000,000; metric ton-km cargo 93,000,000; airports (1997) 31. **Communications,** in total units (units per 1,000 persons). Daily newspaper circulation (1997): 86,000 (1.5); radios (2000): 11,800,000 (189); televisions (2000): 376,000 (6); telephone main lines (2003): 435,000 (6.3); cellular telephone subscribers (2003): 97,800 (1.4); personal computers (2003): 150,000 (2.2); Internet users (2003): 75,000 (1.1).

Education and health

Literacy (2000): total population age 15 and over literate 39.1%; males 47.2%; females 30.9%. **Health** (2001–02): physicians 1,833 (1 per 35,604 persons); hospital beds 11,367 (1 per 5,740 persons); infant mortality rate per 1,000 live births (2003) 98.6. **Food** (2002): daily per capita caloric intake 1,857 (vegetable products 95%, animal products 5%); 80% of FAO recommended minimum.

Military

Total active duty personnel (2003): 162,500 (army 98.5%, air force 1.5%); UN peacekeeping personnel along Ethiopian-Eritrean border (August 2004) 3,900. **Military expenditure as percentage of GNP** (1999): 8.8% (world 2.4%); per capita expenditure $9.

Background

Ethiopia, the Biblical land of Cush, was inhabited from earliest antiquity and was once under ancient Egyptian rule. Geez-speaking agriculturalists established the kingdom of Daamat in the 2nd millennium BC. After 300 BC they were superseded by the kingdom of Aksum, whose King Menilek I, according to legend, was the son of King Solomon and the Queen of Sheba. Christianity was introduced in the 4th century AD and became widespread. Ethiopia's prosperous Mediterranean trade was cut off by the Muslim Arabs in the 7th and 8th centuries, and the area's interests were directed eastward. Contact with Europe resumed in the late 15th century with the arrival of the Portuguese. Modern Ethiopia began with the reign of Tewodros II, who began the consolidation of the country. In the wake of European encroachment, the coastal region was made an Italian colony in 1890, but under Emperor Menilek II the Italians were defeated and ousted in 1896. Ethiopia prospered under his rule, and his modernization programs were continued by Emperor Haile Selassie in the 1930s. In 1936 Italy again gained control of the country, and it was held as part of Italian East Africa until 1941, when it was liberated by the British. Ethiopia incorporated Eritrea in 1952. In 1974 Haile Selassie was deposed, and a Marxist government, plagued by civil wars and famine, controlled the country until 1991. In 1993 Eritrea gained its independence, but border conflicts with Ethiopia and neighboring Somalia continued in the 1990s.

Recent Developments

Foreign affairs in 2004 were dominated by the ongoing diplomatic crisis with Eritrea. The border demarcation between Ethiopia and Eritrea necessitated by the 1998–2000 war between the two countries was still not finalized, and tensions remained high. Ethiopia rejected the border determined by the UN Boundary Commission because it was unhappy with the award of the town of Badme to Eritrea. Ethiopia called for further talks to resolve the crisis, but Eritrea wanted the demarcation to occur first. The Axum obelisk, which was carved some 1,700 years ago and had been looted by Mussolini's troops from Ethiopia in 1937 to adorn a piazza in Rome, was returned home in April 2005.

Internet resources: <www.ethiopians.com>.

Faroe Islands

Official name: Føroyar (Faroese); Færøerne (Danish) (Faroe Islands; English-language alternative spelling is Faeroe Islands). **Political status:** self-governing region of the Danish realm with a single legislative body (Lagting [32]). **Chief of state:** Danish Queen Margrethe

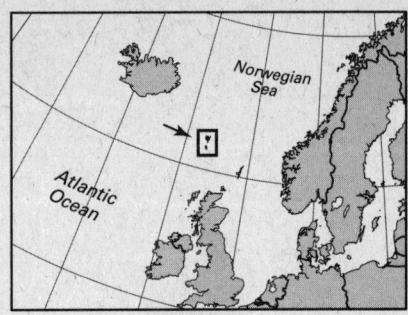

II (from 1972), represented by High Commissioner Birgit Kleis (from 2001). **Head of home government:** Prime Minister Jóannes Eidesgaard (from 3 Feb 2004). **Capital:** Tórshavn (Thorshavn). **Official languages:** Faroese; Danish. **Official religion:** Evangelical Lutheran. **Monetary unit:** 1 Danish krone (Dkr) = 100 øre; valuation (7 Jul 2005) $1 = Dkr 6.25. The local currency, the Faroese króna (Fkr), is equivalent to the Danish krone. Banknotes used are Faroese or Danish; coins are Danish.

Demography

Area: 540.1 sq mi, 1,398.8 sq km. **Population** (2004): 48,500. **Density** (2004): persons per sq mi 89.8, persons per sq km 34.7. **Urban** (2003): 38.6%. **Sex distribution** (2003): male 51.90%; female 48.10%. **Age breakdown** (2003): under 15, 23.6%; 15–29, 19.4%; 30–44, 20.9%; 45–59, 18.4%; 60–74, 11.3%; 75 and over, 6.4%. **Ethnic composition** (2000): Faroese 97.0%; Danish 2.5%; other Scandinavian 0.4%; other 0.1%. **Religious affiliation** (1995): Evangelical Lutheran Church of Denmark 80.8%; Plymouth Brethren 10.1%; Roman Catholic 0.2%; other (mostly nonreligious) 8.9%. **Major towns** (2003): Tórshavn 18,420; Klaksvík 4,794; Runavík 2,557; Tvøroyri 1,867. **Location:** island group north of the British Isles between the Norwegian Sea and the North Atlantic Ocean.

Vital statistics

Birth rate per 1,000 population (2002): 15.0 (world avg. 21.3); (1998) legitimate 62.0%. **Death rate** per 1,000 population (2002): 8.3 (world avg. 9.1). **Natural increase rate** per 1,000 population (2002): 6.7 (world avg. 12.2). **Total fertility rate** (avg. births per childbearing woman; 2002): 2.5. **Marriage rate** per 1,000 population (2002): 5.2. **Divorce rate** per 1,000 population (2002): 1.1. **Life expectancy** at birth (2003): male 75.4 years; female 82.4 years.

National economy

Budget (2002). *Revenue:* Dkr 3,762,060,000 (income taxes 44.5%, customs and excise duties 32.9%, transfers from the Danish government 16.7%). *Expenditures:* Dkr 3,586,220,000 (health and social welfare 46.6%, education 17.6%, debt service 10.5%, agriculture, fishing, and commerce 4.1%). **Gross national product** (at current market prices; 2002): $1,290,000,000 ($27,270 per capita). **Production**

1 metric ton = about 1.1 short tons;   1 kilometer = 0.6 mi (statute);   1 metric ton-km cargo = about 0.68 short ton-mi cargo;   c.i.f.: cost, insurance, and freight;   f.o.b.: free on board

(metric tons except as noted). *Agriculture, forestry, fishing* (2002): potatoes 1,500, other vegetables, grass, hay, and silage are produced; livestock (number of live animals) 70,000 sheep, 2,398 cattle; fish catch (2001) 524,837 (of which blue whiting 259,761, saithe 45,792, cod 38,706, herring 35,172, capelin 32,110, mackerel 24,005, prawns, shrimps, and other crustaceans 20,239). *Mining and quarrying:* negligible (the maritime boundary demarcation agreement between the Shetland Islands [UK] and the Faroes in May 1999 allowed for the exploration of deep-sea petroleum). *Manufacturing* (value added in Dkr '000,000; 1999): processed fish 393; all other manufacturing 351; important products include handicrafts and woolen textiles and clothing. *Energy production (consumption):* electricity (kW-hr; 2002) 239,644,000 ([2001] 223,000,000); petroleum products (2001) none (285,603). **Population economically active** (2002): total 29,540; activity rate of total population 62% (participation rates: female [1997] 46%; unemployed 2%). **Public debt** (to Denmark; end of 2001): none. **Households.** Expenditure (1998): food and beverages 25.1%, transportation and communications 17.7%, housing 12.5%, recreation 11.9%, energy 7.7%. **Land use** as % of total land area (1997): in temporary crops 2%, in pasture 93%; overall forest area, negligible.

Foreign trade

Imports (2002): Dkr 3,896,000,000 (goods for household consumption 28.3%, machinery and transport equipment 21.3%, goods for industries 19.0%). *Major import sources:* Denmark 31.4%; Norway 18.7%; Germany 7.6%; Sweden 6.5%; UK 4.6%. **Exports** (2002): Dkr 4,107,000,000 (chilled and frozen fish [excluding salmon] 50.4%, salted fish 16.3%, salmon 14.8%, prawns 5.7%, fish meal and fish oil 4.8%, trout 3.2%). *Major export destinations:* UK 24.4%; Denmark 20.5%; Spain 11.7%; France 8.2%; Germany 6.9%; Norway 6.5%.

Transport and communications

Transport. *Roads* (2001): total length 464 km. *Vehicles* (2001): passenger cars 15,615; trucks, vans, and buses 3,698. *Air transport* (2001): airports with scheduled flights 1. **Communications,** in total units (units per 1,000 persons). Daily newspaper circulation (1996): 6,000 (136); radios (2000): 102,000 (2,222); televisions (2000): 46,800 (1,022); telephone main lines (2002): 23,000 (482); cellular telephone subscribers (2002): 30,700 (644); Internet users (2002): 25,000 (524).

Health

(2001): physicians 90 (1 per 518 persons); hospital beds (2002) 290 (1 per 163 persons); infant mortality rate per 1,000 live births (2003) 6.5.

Military

Defense responsibility lies with Denmark.

Background

First settled by Irish monks (c. 700), the islands were colonized by the Vikings (c. 800) and were ruled by Norway from the 11th century until 1380, when they passed to Denmark. They unsuccessfully sought independence in 1946 but received self-government in 1948.

Recent Developments

A divided vote in the 20 Jan 2004 general election in the Faroe Islands led to intense negotiations to form a new government. Although the pro-independence Republican Party had the most seats (8) in the 32-seat Løgting (parliament), on 3 February the Union, Social Democratic, and People's parties—each with 7 seats— formed a broad-based coalition, with Social Democrat leader Jóannes Eidesgaard as prime minister.

Internet resources: <www.tourist.fo>.

Fiji

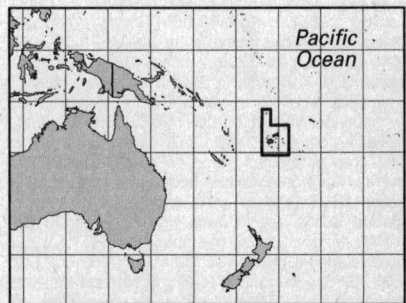

Official name: Republic of the Fiji Islands; Kai Vakarairai ni Fiji (Fijian). **Form of government:** multiparty republic with two legislative houses (Senate [32; all seats are nonelected]; House of Representatives [72]). **Chief of state:** President Ratu Josefa Iloilo (from 2000). **Head of government:** Prime Minister Laisenia Qarase (from 2001). **Capital:** Suva. **Official languages:** English, Fijian, and Hindustani have equal status per constitution. **Official religion:** none. **Monetary unit:** 1 Fiji dollar (F$) = 100 cents; valuation (7 Jul 2005) US$1 = F$1.73.

Demography

Area: 7,055 sq mi, 18,272 sq km. **Population** (2004): 839,000. **Density** (2004): persons per sq mi 118.9, persons per sq km 45.9. **Urban** (2003): 51.7%. **Sex distribution** (2003): male 50.21%; female 49.79%. **Age breakdown** (2003): under 15, 32.1%; 15–29, 28.8%; 30–44, 19.9%; 45–59, 12.8%; 60–74, 5.6%; 75 and over, 0.8%. **Ethnic composition** (2000): Fijian 52.0%; Indian 41.5%; other 6.5%. **Religious affiliation** (2000): Christian 56.8%, of which Protestant 37.1%, independent Christian 8.5%, Roman Catholic 8.4%; Hindu 33.3%; Muslim 6.9%; nonreligious 1.3%; Sikh 0.7%; other 1.0%. **Major cities** (1996; "urban centers"): Suva 167,421; Lautoka 42,917; Nadi 30,791; Labasa 24,187; Nausori 21,645. **Location:** archipelago in the South Pacific Ocean, between Hawaii (US) and New Zealand.

Vital statistics

Birth rate per 1,000 population (2003): 23.1 (world avg. 21.3). **Death rate** per 1,000 population (2003): 5.7 (world avg. 9.1). **Natural increase rate** per 1,000 population (2003): 17.4 (world avg. 12.2). **Total fertility rate** (avg. births per childbearing woman; 2003): 2.8. **Life expectancy** at birth (2003): male 66.4 years; female 71.4 years.

National economy

Budget (2002). *Revenue:* F$949,388,000 (customs duties 54.9%, income and estate taxes 29.0%, fees and royalties 5.6%). *Expenditures:* F$1,345,300,000 (goods and services 42.5%, debt redemption 14.2%, education 12.5%, defense 4.2%). **Production** (metric tons except as noted). *Agriculture, forestry, fishing* (2003): sugarcane 3,300,000, coconuts 170,000, taro 38,000; livestock (number of live animals) 320,000 cattle, 248,000 goats, 139,000 pigs; roundwood (2003) 383,000 cu m; fish catch (2001) 44,689. *Mining and quarrying* (2003): gold 3,517 kg; silver 1,247 kg. *Manufacturing* (2002): raw sugar 317,000; cement 102,000; flour 59,000. *Energy production (consumption):* electricity (kW-hr; 2000) 545,000,000 (545,000,000); coal (2000) none (18,000); petroleum products (2000) none (205,000). **Tourism:** receipts from visitors (2002) US$261,000,000; expenditures by nationals abroad (2000) US$78,000,000. **Land use** as % of total land area (2000): in temporary crops 10.9%, in permanent crops 4.7%, in pasture 9.6%; overall forest area 44.6%. **Population economically active** (1996): total 297,770; activity rate of total population 38.4% (participation rates: ages 15–64, 60.6%; female 32.8%; unemployed [2000] 12.2%). **Gross national product** (2003): US$1,969,000,000 (US$2,360 per capita). **Public debt** (external, outstanding; 2002): US$165,400,000. **Households**. Average household size (2000) 6.1; expenditure (1991): food, beverages, and tobacco 41.5%, housing and energy 21.4%, transportation and communications 12.9%, household durable goods 6.5%.

Foreign trade

Imports (2003-c.i.f.): F$2,215,000,000 (transport equipment 16.1%, mineral fuels 15.0%, machinery and apparatus 13.8%, textiles and wearing apparel 10.7%, live animals and animal products 6.2%). *Major import sources:* Australia 37.5%; New Zealand 18.8%; US 9.2%; Singapore 6.4%; Japan 5.4%. **Exports** (2003-f.o.b.): F$1,273,000,000 (reexports [mostly petroleum products] 26.0%, clothing 19.8%, sugar 18.1%, fish 6.7%, gold 6.0%). *Major export destinations:* Australia 27.4%; US 24.5%; UK 19.5%; New Zealand 5.6%; Japan 4.5%.

Transport and communications

Transport. *Railroads* (1999): length 595 km. *Roads* (1999): total length 3,440 km (paved 49%). *Vehicles* (2000): passenger cars 50,005; trucks and buses 35,038. *Air transport* (2003; Air Pacific only): passenger-km 2,190,000,000; metric ton-km cargo 62,692,000; airports (1997) with scheduled flights 13. **Communications**, in total units (units per 1,000 persons). Daily newspaper circulation (2001): 49,000 (60); radios (1997): 500,000 (636); televisions (2000): 92,000 (114); telephone main lines (2003): 102,000 (124); cellular telephone subscribers (2003): 109,900 (133); personal computers (2002): 40,000 (49); Internet users (2003): 55,000 (67).

Education and health

Educational attainment (1996): Percentage of population age 25 and over having: no formal schooling 4.4%; some education 22.3%; incomplete secondary 47.7%; complete secondary 17.0%; some higher 6.7%; university degree 1.9%. **Literacy** (2001): total population age 15 and over literate 93.2%; males 95.2%; females 91.2%. **Health** (2003): physicians 373 (1 per 2,229 persons); hospital beds (1999) 2,097 (1 per 385 persons); infant mortality rate per 1,000 live births 13.4. **Food** (2002): daily per capita caloric intake 2,894 (vegetable products 84%, animal products 16%); 127% of FAO recommended minimum.

Military

Total active duty personnel (2003): 3,500 (army 91.4%, navy 8.6%). **Military expenditure as percentage of GNP** (1999): 2.0% (world 2.4%); per capita expenditure US$42.

Did you know? The Fijian flag features the Union Jack, reflecting its history as a British colony, and includes Fiji's coat of arms. The arms includes a white shield bearing symbols of England, the Cross of St. George and a lion. Local symbols also appear: sugar cane, coconuts, bananas, and a dove are featured, and the lion holds a coconut.

Background

Archaeological evidence shows that the islands of Fiji were occupied in the late 2nd millennium BC and that the inhabitants had developed pottery by c. 1300 BC. The first European sighting was by the Dutch in the 17th century; in 1774 the islands were visited by Capt. James Cook, who found a mixed Melanesian-Polynesian population with a complex society. Traders and the first missionaries arrived in 1835. In 1857 a British consul was appointed, and in 1874 Fiji was proclaimed a crown colony. It became independent as a member of the Commonwealth in 1970 and was declared a republic in 1987 following a military coup. Elections in 1992 restored civilian rule. A new constitution was approved in 1997.

Recent Developments

Businessmann George Speight's 2000 coup cast a shadow long after it was peacefully resolved after 56 days; four serving politicians, including the vice president and deputy speaker, were convicted of treason in 2004 and imprisoned for having taken illegal oaths of office during the coup. Courts-martial of soldiers for mutiny, also during the coup, led to several convictions. Fiji mourned the death in April 2004 of Ratu Sir Kamisese Mara, the country's first prime minister (1970–92; except for a few months in 1987) and president from 1994 until he was deposed in the coup in 2000.

Internet resources: <www.fiji.org.nz>.

1 metric ton = about 1.1 short tons;   1 kilometer = 0.6 mi (statute);   1 metric ton-km cargo = about 0.68 short ton-mi cargo;   c.i.f.: cost, insurance, and freight;   f.o.b.: free on board

Finland

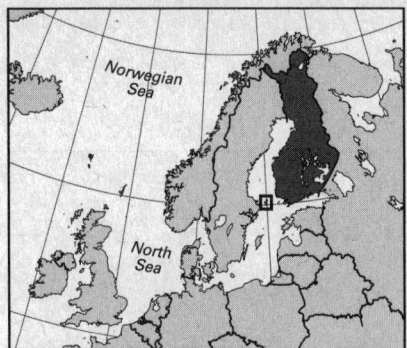

Official names: Suomen Tasavalta (Finnish); Republiken Finland (Swedish) (Republic of Finland). **Form of government:** multiparty republic with one legislative house (Parliament [200]). **Chief of state:** President Tarja Halonen (from 2000). **Head of government:** Prime Minister Matti Vanhanen (from 2003). **Capital:** Helsinki. **Official languages:** none (Finnish and Swedish are national languages). **Official religion:** none. **Monetary unit:** 1 euro (€) = 100 cents; valuation (7 Jul 2005) $1 = €0.84; at conversion on 1 Jan 2002, €1 = 5.95 Finnish markka (Fmk).

Demography

Area (includes inland water area of 13,001 sq mi [33,672 sq km]): 130,559 sq mi; 338,145 sq km. **Population** (2004): 5,226,000. **Density** (2004; based on land area only): persons per sq mi 44.5, persons per sq km 17.2. **Urban** (2003): 83.3%. **Sex distribution** (2003): male 48.88%; female 51.12%. **Age breakdown** (2003): under 15, 17.8%; 15–29, 18.6%; 30–44, 20.6%; 45–59, 22.5%; 60–74, 13.6%; 75 and over, 6.9%. **Ethnic composition** (2000): Finnish 91.9%; Swedish 5.9%; Karelian 0.8%; Russian 0.2%; other 1.2%. **Religious affiliation** (2002): Evangelical Lutheran 84.9%; Finnish (Greek) Orthodox 1.1%; nonreligious 12.9%; other 1.1%. **Major cities** (2003): Helsinki 559,716 (urban agglomeration 1,075,000); Espoo 221,097 (within Helsinki urban agglomeration); Tampere 199,823; Vantaa 181,890 (within Helsinki urban agglomeration); Turku 174,618. **Location:** northern Europe, bordering Norway, Russia, the Gulf of Finland, the Baltic Sea, the Gulf of Bothnia, and Sweden.

Vital statistics

Birth rate per 1,000 population (2002): 10.7 (world avg. 21.3); (2000) legitimate 60.8%. **Death rate** per 1,000 population (2002): 9.5 (world avg. 9.1). **Natural increase rate** per 1,000 population (2002): 1.2 (world avg. 12.2). **Total fertility rate** (avg. births per childbearing woman; 2002): 1.7. **Marriage rate** per 1,000 population (2002): 5.3. **Divorce rate** per 1,000 population (2002): 2.6. **Life expectancy** at birth (2002): male 74.6 years; female 81.6 years.

National economy

Budget (2003). *Revenue:* €35,755,000,000 (income and property taxes 36.6%, value-added taxes 27.4%, excise duties 13.7%). *Expenditures:* €35,755,000,000 (social security and health 23.8%, education 16.4%, interest on state debt 9.6%, agriculture and forestry 7.2%, defense 5.5%). **Production** (metric tons except as noted). *Agriculture, forestry, fishing* (2002): silage 6,842,500, barley 1,738,700, oats 1,507,800; livestock (number of live animals; 2002) 1,315,000 pigs, 1,025,400 cattle, 200,000 reindeer; roundwood (2002) 52,210,000 cu m; fish catch (2001) 165,835. *Mining and quarrying* (2002): chromite (concentrate) 340,000; zinc (metal content) 61,580; gold 4,666 kg. *Manufacturing* (value added in €'000,000; 2000): radio, television, and communications equipment 6,289; wood pulp, paper, and paper products 5,472; nonelectrical machinery and equipment 3,183. *Energy production (consumption):* electricity (kW-hr; 2001) 71,229,000,000 (81,188,000,000); coal (2000) none (5,131,000); crude petroleum (barrels; 2000) none (78,409,000); petroleum products (2000) 12,131,000 (9,305,000); natural gas (cu⁻ m; 2000) none (4,079,844,000). **Population economically active** (2002): total 2,610,000; activity rate of total population 50.2% (participation rates: ages 15–64, 74.5%; female 47.9%; unemployed 9.1%). **Household income and expenditure** (2001). Average household size 2.2; disposable income per household €28,807; sources of gross income (2000): wages and salaries 55.4%, transfer payments 24.3%, other 20.3%; expenditure: housing and energy 28.7%, transportation and communications 18.0%, food, beverages, and tobacco 16.0%. **Gross national product** (2003): $140,755,000,000 ($27,020 per capita). **Public debt** (2001): $52,850,000,000. **Tourism** (in $'000,000; 2002): receipts 1,573; expenditures 2,002. **Land use** as % of total land area (2000): in temporary crops 7.2%, in permanent crops 0.03%, in pasture 0.07%; overall forest area 72.0%.

Foreign trade

Imports (2001-c.i.f.): €35,891,000,000 (electrical machinery and apparatus 18.2%; nonelectrical machinery and apparatus 13.8%; mineral fuels 11.6%; automobiles 7.0%). *Major import sources:* Germany 14.5%; Sweden 10.2%; Russia 9.5%; US 6.8%; UK 6.4%; France 4.5%. **Exports** (2001-f.o.b.): €47,800,000,000 (electrical machinery and apparatus 24.3%; paper and paper products 18.8%; nonelectrical machinery and apparatus 11.6%; wood and wood products [excluding furniture] 5.1%). *Major export destinations:* Germany 12.3%; US 9.7%; UK 9.6%; Sweden 8.4%; Russia 5.9%; France 4.6%.

Transport and communications

Transport. Railroads: route length (2002) 5,850 km; passenger-km 3,305,000,000; metric ton-km cargo 9,664,000,000. Roads (2002; excludes Åland Islands): total length 78,137 km (paved 64%). *Vehicles* (2002): passenger cars 2,194,683; trucks and buses 319,699. *Air transport* (2003; Finnair): passenger-km 12,971,000,000; metric ton-km cargo 314,500,000; airports (2001) 27. **Communications,** in total units (units per 1,000 persons). Daily newspaper circulation (2000): 2,360,000 (456); radios (2000): 8,400,000 (1,623); televisions (2000): 3,580,000 (692); telephone main lines (2002): 2,850,000 (547); cellular telephone subscribers (2002): 4,400,000 (845); personal computers (2002): 2,300,000 (442); Internet users (2002): 2,650,000 (509).

Education and health

Educational attainment (end of 2000). Percentage of population age 25 and over having: incomplete upper-secondary education 38.6%; complete upper secondary or vocational 34.5%; higher 26.9%. **Literacy:** virtually 100%. **Health** (2002): physicians 16,446 (1 per 316 persons); hospital beds 38,025 (1 per 137 persons); infant mortality rate per 1,000 live births 3.6. **Food** (2001): daily per capita caloric intake 3,202 (vegetable products 64.3%, animal products 35.7%); 118% of FAO recommended minimum.

Military

Total active duty personnel (2003): 27,000 (army 71.1%, navy 18.5%, air force 10.4%). **Military expenditure as percentage of GNP** (1999): 1.4% (world 2.4%); per capita expenditure $344.

 The *Kalevala*, Finland's national epic, was compiled from oral sources in the early 19th century. Kalevala, the dwelling place of the poem's chief characters, is a poetic name for Finland, meaning "land of heroes."

Background

Recent archaeological discoveries have led some to suggest that human habitation in Finland dates back at least 100,000 years. Ancestors of the Sami apparently were present in Finland by about 7000 BC. The ancestors of the present-day Finns came from the southern shore of the Gulf of Finland in the 1st millennium BC. The area was gradually Christianized from the 11th century. From the 12th century Sweden and Russia contested for supremacy in Finland, until in 1323 Sweden ruled most of the country. Russia was ceded part of Finnish territory in 1721; in 1808 Alexander I of Russia invaded Finland, which in 1809 was formally ceded to Russia. The subsequent period saw the growth of Finnish nationalism. Russia's losses in World War I and the Russian Revolution of 1917 set the stage for Finland's independence in 1917. It was defeated by the Soviet Union in the Russo-Finnish War (1939–40) but then sided with Nazi Germany against the Soviets during World War II and regained the territory it had lost. Facing defeat again by the advancing Soviets in 1944, it reached a peace agreement with the USSR, ceding territory and paying reparations. Finland's economy recovered after World War II. It joined the EU in 1995.

Recent Developments

Finnish Pres. Tarja Halonen spoke on the international stage in September 2004 when she told the UN General Assembly that she thought the US-led military intervention in Iraq was not in line with international law. Prime Minister Matti Vanhanen's government, after prompting from Halonen, had earlier announced that the country would join the Ottawa Agreement against land mines, scrapping its own mines, which had not yet been deployed, and replacing them with comparable anti-infantry systems. A well-known newspaper commentator remarked that Finland should not scrap its infantry mines until neighboring Russia had scrapped its infantry.

Internet resources: <www.finland-tourism.com>.

France

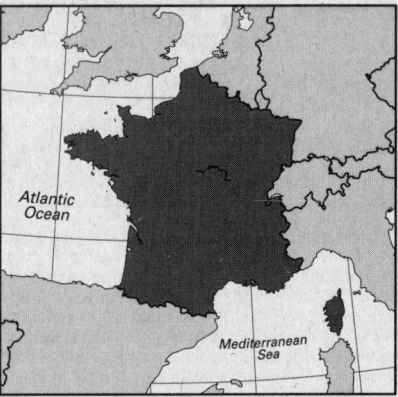

Official name: République Française (French Republic). **Form of government:** republic with two legislative houses (Parliament; Senate [321], National Assembly [577]). **Chief of state:** President Jacques Chirac (from 1995). **Head of government:** Prime Minister Dominique de Villepin (from 31 May 2005) **Capital:** Paris. **Official language:** French. **Official religion:** none. **Monetary unit:** 1 euro (€) = 100 cents; valuation (7 Jul 2005) $1 = €0.84; at conversion on 1 Jan 2002, €1 = 6.56 French francs (F).

Demography

Area: 210,026 sq mi, 543,965 sq km. **Population** (2004): 60,044,000. **Density** (2004): persons per sq mi 285.9, persons per sq km 110.4. **Urban** (2003): 76.3%. **Sex distribution** (2003): male 48.77%; female 51.23%. **Age breakdown** (2003): under 15, 18.6%; 15–29, 19.4%; 30–44, 21.6%; 45–59, 19.8%; 60–74, 12.8%; 75 and over, 7.8%. **Ethnic composition** (2000): French 76.9%; Algerian and Moroccan Berber 2.2%; Italian 1.9%; Portuguese 1.5%; Moroccan Arab 1.5%; Fleming 1.4%; Algerian Arab 1.3%; Basque 1.3%; Jewish 1.2%; German 1.2%; Vietnamese 1.0%; Catalan 0.5%; other 8.1%. **Religious affiliation** (2000): Roman Catholic 82.3%; Muslim 7.1%; atheist 4.4%; Protestant 3.7%; Orthodox 1.1%; Jewish 1.0%; other 0.4%. **Major cities** (1999): Paris 2,125,246 (metropolitan area 9,644,507); Marseille 798,430 (1,349,772); Lyon 445,452 (1,348,832); Toulouse 390,350 (761,090); Nice 342,738 (888,784); Nantes 270,251 (544,932); Strasbourg 264,115 (427,245); Montpellier 225,392 (287,981); Bordeaux 215,363 (753,931); Rennes 206,229 (272,263); Le Havre 190,905 (248,547); Reims 187,206 (215,581); Lille 184,493 (1,000,900); Saint-Étienne 180,210 (291,960); Toulon 160,639 (519,640). **Location:** western Europe, bordering the

---

1 metric ton = about 1.1 short tons;   1 kilometer = 0.6 mi (statute);   1 metric ton-km cargo = about 0.68 short ton-mi cargo;   c.i.f.: cost, insurance, and freight;   f.o.b.: free on board

North Atlantic Ocean, Belgium, Luxembourg, Germany, Switzerland, Italy, the Mediterranean Sea, Spain, and Andorra. **Dependent territories:** French Guiana, French Polynesia, Guadeloupe, Martinique, Mayotte, New Caledonia, Réunion, Saint Pierre and Miquelon, and Wallis and Futuna. **Mobility** (1990). Population living in same residence as in 1982: 51.4%; same region 89.0%; different region 8.8%; different country 2.2%. **Households** (1999). Average household size 2.4; 1 person 31.0%, 2 persons 31.1%, 3 persons 16.2%, 4 persons 13.8%, 5 persons or more 7.9%. Family households (1999): 15,942,369 (67.0%); nonfamily 7,865,703 (33.0%). **Immigration** (2000): immigrants admitted 53,879 (from Africa 56.0%, of which Algerian 16.9%; from Europe 23.1%; from Asia 12.4%).

Vital statistics

Birth rate per 1,000 population (2003): 12.5 (world avg. 21.3); (2002) legitimate 54.8%; illegitimate 45.2%. **Death rate** per 1,000 population (2003): 9.1 (world avg. 9.1). **Natural increase rate** per 1,000 population (2003): 3.4 (world avg. 12.2). **Total fertility rate** (avg. births per childbearing woman; 2003): 1.9. **Marriage rate** per 1,000 population (2002): 4.7. **Divorce rate** per 1,000 population (2002): 2.2. **Life expectancy** at birth (2003): male 75.6 years; female 83.1 years.

Social indicators

Quality of working life. Average workweek (2001): 38.4 hours. Annual rate per 100,000 workers for (1999): injury or accident 4,432 (deaths 0.1%); accidents in transit to work (1994) 708 (deaths 68.3). Average days lost to labor stoppages per 1,000 workers (1994): 21.0. Trade union membership (2001): 1,900,000 (8% of labor force). **Access to services** (1992). Proportion of dwellings having: central heating 86.0%; piped water 97.0%; indoor plumbing 95.8%. **Social participation.** Eligible voters participating in last (June 2002) national election: 64.4%. Population over 15 years of age participating in voluntary associations (1997): 28.0%. **Social deviance.** Offense rate per 100,000 population (1998) for: murder 1.6, rape 13.4, other assault 583.8; theft (including burglary and housebreaking) 6,107.6. Incidence per 100,000 in general population of: homicide (2000) 0.9; suicide (2000) 16.8. **Material well-being** (2002). Households possessing: automobile 79%; color television 94%; VCR (2001) 70%; microcomputer 37%; washing machine 91%; microwave 68%; dishwasher (2001) 39%.

National economy

Gross national product (2003): $1,523,025,000,000 ($24,770 per capita). **Budget** (2001). *Revenue:* €244,846,800,000 (value-added taxes 55.7%, personal income tax 21.8%, corporate income tax 20.1%). *Expenditures:* €268,669,600,000 (current expenditure 89.9%, of which public debt 14.9%, pensions 11.3%, social services 11.3%; development expenditure 10.1%). **Public debt** (2001): $756,080,000,000. **Production** (metric tons except as noted). *Agriculture, forestry, fishing* (2003): corn (maize) 59,170,000, wheat 30,582,000, sugar beets 29,238,000, barley 9,818,000, potatoes 6,235,000, grapes 6,178,000, rapeseed 3,341,000, apples 2,402,000, dry peas 1,617,000, sunflower seeds

1,494,000, triticale 1,291,000, tomatoes 834,000, carrots 682,000, oats 555,000, lettuce 426,000, green peas 396,000, dry onions 393,000, cauliflower 390,000, string beans 373,000; livestock (number of live animals) 19,517,000 cattle, 15,058,000 pigs, 9,204,000 sheep, 220,000,000 chickens; roundwood 36,850,000 cu m; fish catch 877,995. *Mining and quarrying* (2001): gypsum 4,500,000; kaolin 375,000; potash 257,000; gold 80,700 troy oz. *Manufacturing* (value added in $'000,000; 2000; data unavailable for production of food, beverages, and tobacco products): motor vehicles, trailers, and motor vehicle parts 17,157; pharmaceuticals, soaps, and paints 16,360; fabricated metal products 12,996; general purpose machinery 7,064; basic chemicals 6,378; aircraft and spacecraft 6,045; plastic products 6,014; publishing 5,184; medical, measuring, and testing appliances 4,765; telecommunications equipment 4,615. *Energy production* (consumption; consumption data includes Monaco): electricity (kW-hr; 2001) 520,000,000,000 ([2000] 477,288,000,000); hard coal (2001; last coal-producing mine closed in April 2004) 2,400,000 ([2000] 21,090,000); lignite (2000) 296,000 (335,000); crude petroleum (barrels; 2001) 11,027,000 ([1999] 608,200,000); petroleum products (2000) 76,665,000 (71,631,000); natural gas (cu m; 2001) 1,982,000,000 ([2000] 43,555,000,000). **Population economically active** (2001): total 27,812,600; activity rate of total population 47.0% (participation rates: ages 15–64 [1994] 67.6%; female [2001] 47.9%; unemployed 12.1%). **Household income and expenditure.** Average household size (1999) 2.5; average disposable income per household (2001) €26,570; sources of income (1995): wages and salaries 70.0%, self-employment 24.4%, social security 5.6%; expenditure (2001): housing and energy 23.4%, transportation 15.2%, food and nonalcoholic beverages 14.4%, recreation 8.9%, restaurants and hotels 7.6%. **Tourism** (in $'000,000; 2002): receipts $32,329; expenditures $19,460. **Land use** as % of total land area (2000): in temporary crops 33.5%, in permanent crops 2.1%, in pasture 18.4%; overall forest area 27.9%.

Foreign trade

Imports (2002-c.i.f.; includes Monaco): $303,800,000,000 (machinery and apparatus 24.2%; transport equipment 13.5%; chemicals and chemical products 12.9%; petroleum [all forms] 9.2%; food 7.0%). *Major import sources:* Germany 17.2%; Italy 9.0%; US 8.0%; UK 7.3%; Spain 7.2%; Belgium 6.6%; The Netherlands 4.7%; China 3.5%; Japan 3.2%; Switzerland 2.2%; Ireland 2.0%. **Exports** (2002-f.o.b.; includes Monaco): $304,900,000,000 (machinery and apparatus 23.2%; transport equipment 20.5%, of which road vehicles 14.0%, aircraft and spacecraft 5.6%; chemicals and chemical products 14.9%, of which pharmaceuticals 4.9%; food 7.9%; iron and steel 3.2%; perfumes, cosmetics, and toiletries 2.9%). *Major export destinations:* Germany 14.5%; UK 10.3%; Spain 9.7%; Italy 9.1%; US 8.1%; Belgium 7.2%; The Netherlands 4.0%; Switzerland 3.2%; Japan 1.7%; Portugal 1.5%.

Transport and communications

Transport. *Railroads* (2002): route length 32,008 km; (2000) passenger-km 69,870,000,000; metric ton-km cargo 55,370,000,000. *Roads* (1999): total length 893,300 km (paved 100%). *Vehicles* (2000): passenger cars 28,060,000; trucks and buses 5,673,000. *Air transport* (2003; Air France only): passenger-km 99,122,000,000; metric ton-km cargo 4,875,000,000; airports (1996) 61. **Communications,** in total units (units per 1,000 persons). Daily newspaper circulation (2000): 11,800,000 (201); radios (2000): 55,900,000 (950); televisions (2000): 37,000,000 (628); telephone main lines (2003): 33,905,400 (566); cellular telephone subscribers (2003): 41,683,100 (696); personal computers (2002): 20,700,000 (347); Internet users (2003): 21,900,000 (366).

Education and health

Educational attainment (2001). Percentage of population age 25–64 with at least upper secondary education 63.2%. **Health:** physicians (2002) 199,000 (1 per 301 persons); hospital beds (2001) 477,000 (1 per 126 persons); infant mortality rate (2003) 4.4. **Food** (2001): daily per capita caloric intake 3,629 (vegetable products 63%, animal products 37%); 129% of FAO recommended minimum.

Military

Total active duty personnel (2003): 259,050 (army 52.9%, navy 17.1%, air force 24.7%, unallocated 5.3%). **Military expenditure as percentage of GNP** (1999): 2.7% (world 2.4%); per capita expenditure $658.

Did you know? The Loire is the longest river in France, rising in the southern Massif Central and flowing north and west for 634 mi (1,020 km) to the Atlantic Ocean, which it enters south of the Bretagne (Brittany) peninsula.

Background

Archaeological excavations in France indicate continuous settlement from Paleolithic times. About 1200 BC the Gauls migrated into the area, and in 600 BC Ionian Greeks established several settlements, including one at Marseille. Julius Caesar completed the Roman conquest of Gaul in 50 BC. During the 6th century AD the Salian Franks ruled; by the 8th century power had passed to the Carolingians, the greatest of whom was Charlemagne. The Hundred Years' War (1337–1453) resulted in the return to France of land that had been held by the British; by the end of the 15th century, France approximated its modern boundaries. The 16th century was marked by the Wars of Religion between Protestants (Huguenots) and Roman Catholics. Henry IV's Edict of Nantes (1598) granted substantial religious toleration, but this was revoked in 1685 by Louis XIV, who helped to raise monarchical absolutism to new heights. In 1789 the French Revolution proclaimed the rights of the individual and destroyed the ancient regime. Napoleon ruled from 1799 to 1814, after which a limited monarchy was restored until 1871, when the Third Republic was created. World War I (1914–18)

ravaged the northern part of France. After Nazi Germany's invasion during World War II, the collaborationist Vichy regime governed. Liberated by Allied and Free French forces in 1944, France restored parliamentary democracy under the Fourth Republic. A costly war in Indochina and rising nationalism in French colonies during the 1950s overwhelmed the Fourth Republic. The Fifth Republic was established in 1958 under Charles de Gaulle, who presided over the dissolution of most of France's overseas colonies. In 1981 François Mitterrand became France's first elected Socialist president. During the 1990s the French government, balancing right- and left-wing forces, moved toward solidifying European unity.

Recent Developments

The year in France was dominated by domestic politics. The predominant mood was a feeling of fin de règne for Jacques Chirac, even though the Gaullist president's term ran until 2007. The main events of 2004 were the double electoral hammering meted out to his ruling Union for a Popular Movement in the regional elections in March and the European Parliament elections in June and the growing unpopularity of everyone on the center-right with the notable exception of Nicolas Sarkozy, whose determination to challenge Chirac for the presidency became ever more marked as the year wore on. These internal tensions helped distract the government of Prime Minister Jean-Pierre Raffarin from progress on difficult health and privatization reforms. Equally controversial was the ban on the wearing of Muslim headscarves and other ostentatious religious symbols in schools. The year was relatively undramatic for foreign policy, though French troops came under fire and suffered casualties in Côte d'Ivoire as France found it increasingly hard to keep the peace there. On the diplomatic level, Chirac once again demonstrated his belief in the desirability of a multipolar world, using various diplomatic summits to maintain his distance from US policy in the Middle East and to seek rapprochement with China.

In early 2005 attention shifted to a massive pedophile case—said to be the largest trial ever in France, involving 66 adults and 45 children—that opened in Angers in March. Later that month the center-right National Assembly voted revisions to the nation's vaunted 35-hour work week, making it legal for French employees to work as many as 48 hours a week, the EU-sanctioned maximum. Ignoring pleas by Chirac, including a prime time TV appearance, the citizenry voted "non" in a referendum to accept the draft European Constitution on 29 May, essentially shelving, for the present, plans for a united Europe. Chirac replaced the prime minister two days later.

Internet resources: <www.franceguide.com>.

French Guiana

Official name: Département de la Guyane française (Department of French Guiana). **Political status:** overseas department of France with two legislative houses (General Council [19]; Regional Council [31]).

---

1 metric ton = about 1.1 short tons;   1 kilometer = 0.6 mi (statute);   1 metric ton-km cargo = about 0.68 short ton-mi cargo;   c.i.f.: cost, insurance, and freight;   f.o.b.: free on board

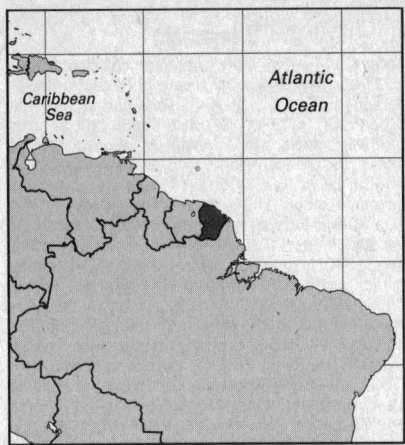

Atlantic Ocean

Caribbean Sea

Chief of state: President Jacques Chirac of France (from 1995). **Heads of government:** Prefect Ange Mancini (from 2002), President Pierre Désert of the General Council (from 4 Apr 2004), and President Antoine Karam of the Regional Council (from 1992). **Capital:** Cayenne. **Official language:** French. **Official religion:** none. **Monetary unit:** 1 euro (€) = 100 cents; valuation (7 Jul 2005) $1 = €0.84; at conversion on 1 Jan 2002, €1 = 6.56 French francs (F).

Demography

Area: 32,253 sq mi, 83,534 sq km. **Population** (2004): 182,000. **Density** (2004): persons per sq mi 5.6, persons per sq km 2.2. **Urban** (2003): 75.4%. **Sex distribution** (1999): male 50.36%; female 49.64%. **Age breakdown** (1999): under 15, 34.0%; 15–29, 24.2%; 30–44, 23.3%; 45–59, 12.5%; 60–74, 4.3%; 75 and over, 1.7%. **Ethnic composition** (2000): Guianese Mulatto 37.9%; French 8.0%; Haitian 8.0%; Surinamese 6.0%; Antillean 5.0%; Chinese 5.0%; Brazilian 4.9%; East Indian 4.0%; other (other West Indian, Hmong, other South American) 21.2%. **Religious affiliation** (2000): Christian 84.6%, of which Roman Catholic 80.0%, Protestant 3.9%; Chinese folk-religionist 3.6%; Spiritist 3.5%; nonreligious/atheist 3.0%; traditional beliefs 1.9%; Hindu 1.6%; Muslim 0.9%; other 0.9%. **Major cities** (1999 [commune pop.]): Cayenne 50,594 (urban agglomeration 84,181); Saint-Laurent-du-Maroni 19,211; Kourou 19,107; Matoury 18,032 (within Cayenne urban agglomeration); Rémire-Montjoly 15,555 (within Cayenne urban agglomeration). **Location:** northern South America, bordering the Atlantic Ocean, Brazil, and Suriname.

Vital statistics

Birth rate per 1,000 population (2003): 21.3 (world avg. 21.3); (2000) legitimate 17.6%. **Death rate** per 1,000 population (2003): 4.8 (world avg. 9.1). **Natural increase rate** per 1,000 population (2003): 16.5 (world avg. 12.2). **Total fertility rate** (avg. births per childbearing woman; 2003): 3.1. **Marriage rate** per 1,000 population (1999): 3.5. **Divorce rate** per 1,000 population (1998): 1.0. **Life expectancy** at birth (2003): male 73.4 years; female 80.2 years.

National economy

Budget (2000). *Revenue:* €141,000,000 (direct taxes 32.6%, indirect taxes 29.8%, revenue from French central government 17.7%, development receipts 15.6%). *Expenditures:* €141,000,000 (current expenditures 83.0%, capital expenditures 17.0%). **Production** (metric tons except as noted). *Agriculture, forestry, fishing* (2002): rice 19,900, cassava 10,375, cabbages 6,350; livestock (number of live animals) 10,500 pigs, 9,200 cattle; roundwood (2001) 139,000 cu m; fish catch (2001) 5,231. *Mining and quarrying* (2001): stone, sand, and gravel 1,500; gold 127,671 troy oz. *Manufacturing* (2001): pork 1,245; chicken meat 560; finished wood products (1996) 3,172 cu m. *Number of satellites launched from the Kourou Space Center* (2002): 12. *Energy production (consumption):* electricity (kW-hr; 2000) 455,000,000 (455,000,000); petroleum products (2000) none (292,000). **Household income and expenditure.** Average household size (1999) 3.3; income per household (1997) €31,203; sources of income (1997): wages and salaries and self-employed 72.9%, transfer payments 20.2%; expenditure (1994): food and beverages 28.7%, housing 11.7%, energy 9.0%, clothing and footwear 6.4%, health 2.7%, other 41.5%. **Land use** as % of total land area (2000): in temporary crops 0.14%, in permanent crops 0.05%, in pasture 0.08%; overall forest area 89.9%. **Gross national product** (2000): $2,360,000,000 ($14,370 per capita). **Population economically active** (1999): total 62,634; activity rate of total population 39.4% (participation rates: age 15 and over 60.5%; female 43.8%; unemployed [March 2003] 22.8%). **Tourism** (2002): receipts $45,000,000.

Foreign trade

Imports (2002): €643,000,000 (food products 21.8%, road vehicles 12.8%, refined petroleum 9.0%, nonelectrical machinery 8.6%). *Major import sources:* France 51.5%; Trinidad and Tobago 8.7%; The Netherlands 2.5%; Germany 2.5%; Japan 2.5%. **Exports** (2002): €129,000,000 (nonferrous metals [nearly all gold] 70.5%, food products [mostly fish, shrimp, and rice] 12.5%, parts for air and space vehicles 3.1%). *Major export destinations:* France 62.8%; Belgium 10.1%; Switzerland 9.3%; Brazil 3.9%; Guadeloupe 3.1%.

Transport and communications

Transport. *Roads* (1996): total length 1,245 km. *Vehicles* (1999): passenger cars 32,900; trucks and buses 11,900. *Air transport* (2002): passenger arrivals 186,920; passenger departures 192,764; cargo unloaded 4,569 metric tons, cargo loaded 2,119 metric tons; airports (2001) with scheduled flights 1. **Communications,** in total units (units per 1,000 persons). Daily newspaper circulation (1996): 2,000 (14); radios (1997): 104,000 (702); televisions (1998): 37,000 (202); telephone main lines (1999): 49,000 (308); cellular telephone subscribers (2002): 138,200 (781); personal computers (1999): 23,000 (145); Internet users (2001): 3,200 (17).

Education and health

Educational attainment (1990). Percentage of population age 25 and over having: incomplete primary education or no declaration 61.7%; completed primary

5.3%; some secondary 15.9%; completed secondary 8.2%; some higher 4.9%; completed higher 4.0%. **Health** (2000): physicians 219 (1 per 737 persons); hospital beds 750 (1 per 215 persons); infant mortality rate per 1,000 live births (2003) 12.8. **Food** (1992): daily per capita caloric intake 2,900 (vegetable products 70%, animal products 30%); 128% of FAO recommended minimum.

Military

Total active duty personnel (2003): French troops 3,100.

Background

Originally settled by the Spanish, French, and Dutch, the territory of French Guiana was awarded to France in 1667, and the inhabitants were made French citizens after 1877. By 1852 the French began using the territory as a penal colony with one locale, on Devils Island, being especially notorious. It became an overseas territory of France in 1946; the penal colonies were closed by 1939.

Recent Developments

The European Space Agency has regularly launched communication satellites from French Guiana, and the space center near Kourou, completed in 1968, is a major factor in the local economy. Under an agreement signed in November 2003, the facility would launch space vehicles for Rosaviakosmos, the Russian Aviation and Space Agency, beginning in 2006.

Internet resources:
<www.countryreports.org/french.htm>.

French Polynesia

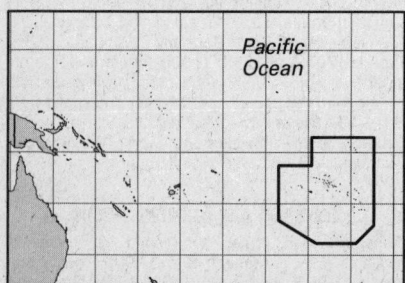

Pacific Ocean

Official name: Polynésie française (French); Polynesia Farani (Tahitian) (French Polynesia). **Political status:** overseas country of France with one legislative house (Assembly [57]). **Chief of state:** President Jacques Chirac of France (from 1995). **Head of government:** President Oscar Temaru (from 3 Mar 2005). **Capital:** Papeete. **Official languages:** French; Tahitian. **Official religion:** none. **Monetary unit:** 1 Franc de la Comptoirs française du pacifique (CFPF) = 100 centimes; valuation (7 Jul 2005) $1 = CFPF 100.02; the CFPF is pegged to the euro (€) at €1 = CFPF 119.25 from 1 Jan 2002.

Demography

Area: 1,544 sq mi, 4,000 sq km. **Population** (2004): 252,000. **Density** (2004; based on land area only): persons per sq mi 185.4, persons per sq km 71.6. **Urban** (2002): 52.1%. **Sex distribution** (2002): male 51.39%; female 48.61%. **Age breakdown** (2002): under 15, 29.9%; 15–29, 26.0%; 30–44, 23.5%; 45–59, 13.3%; 60–74, 5.9%; 75 and over, 1.4%. **Ethnic composition** (1996): Polynesian and part-Polynesian 82.8%; European (mostly French) 11.9%; Asian (mostly Chinese) 4.7%; other 0.6%. **Religious affiliation** (1995): Protestant 50.2%, of which Evangelical Church of French Polynesia (Presbyterian) 46.1%; Roman Catholic 39.5%; other Christian 9.9%, of which Mormon 5.9%; other 0.4%. **Major communes** (2002): Faaa 28,339 (part of Papeete urban agglomeration); Papeete 26,181 (urban agglomeration [2002] 124,864); Punaauia 23,706 (part of Papeete urban agglomeration); Moorea-Maiao 14,550; Pirae 14,499 (part of Papeete urban agglomeration). **Location:** Oceania, an archipelago in the South Pacific Ocean, about midway between South America and Australia.

Vital statistics

Birth rate per 1,000 population (2002): 19.6 (world avg. 21.3); (1996) legitimate 35.4%. **Death rate** per 1,000 population (2002): 4.5 (world avg. 9.1). **Natural increase rate** per 1,000 population (2002): 15.1 (world avg. 12.2). **Total fertility rate** (avg. births per childbearing woman; 2003): 2.1. **Marriage rate** per 1,000 population (2000): 4.6. **Life expectancy** at birth (2003): male 73.1 years; female 77.9 years.

National economy

Budget (2001). *Revenue:* CFPF 108,036,000,000 (indirect taxes 55.1%, direct taxes and nontax revenue 44.9%). *Expenditures:* CFPF 140,709,000,000 (current expenditure 68.1%, capital expenditure 31.9%). **Public debt** (external, outstanding; 1999): $542,000,000. **Production** (metric tons except as noted). *Agriculture, forestry, fishing* (2002): coconuts 88,000, copra 9,416, cassava 6,000; livestock (number of live animals) 34,000 pigs, 16,500 goats, 10,800 cattle; fish catch (2001) 15,470; export production of black pearls (1998) 6,050 kg. *Mining and quarrying:* estimated annual production of phosphates ranges from 1,000,000 to 1,200,000 tons. *Manufacturing* (1999): coconut oil 6,386; other manufactures include monoï oil (primarily refined coconut and sandalwood oils), beer, printed cloth, and sandals. *Energy production (consumption):* electricity (kW-hr; 2001) 495,000,000 (495,000,000); petroleum products (2000) none (177,000). **Population economically active** (1996): total 87,121; activity rate of total population 39.7% (participation rates: ages 14 and over, 68.3%; female 38.7%; unemployed 13.2%). **Tourism** (1999): receipts from visitors $394,000,000. **Gross national product** (at current market prices; 2001): $4,100,000,000 ($17,290 per capita). **Household income and expenditure** (1986). Average household size (1996) 4.3; average annual income per household CFPF 2,153,112; sources of income (1993): salaries 61.9%, self-employment 21.5%, transfer payments 16.6%; expendi-

---

1 metric ton = about 1.1 short tons;   1 kilometer = 0.6 mi (statute);   1 metric ton-km cargo = about 0.68 short ton-mi cargo;   c.i.f.: cost, insurance, and freight;   f.o.b.: free on board

ture: food and beverages 32.1%, household furnishings 12.3%, transportation 12.2%, energy 8.1%, recreation and education 6.9%, clothing 6.3%. **Land use** as % of total land area (2000): in temporary crops 0.8%, in permanent crops 5.5%, in pasture 5.5%; overall forest area 28.7%.

Foreign trade

Imports (2001-c.i.f.): CFPF 135,569,000,000 (machinery and apparatus 19.7%; consumer goods 16.0%; mineral fuels 8.5%). *Major import sources* (2000): France 35.9%; US 13.9%; Australia 9.3%; New Zealand 7.4%; Germany 4.8%. **Exports** (2001-f.o.b.): CFPF 18,677,000,000 (pearl products 80.0%, of which black cultured pearls 76.1%; fish 7.3%; *nono* fruit 4.6%; coconut oil 1.6%; *monoï* oil 0.8%). *Major export destinations* (2000): Japan 36.9%; Hong Kong 20.9%; France 14.5%; US 12.1%; New Caledonia 5.0%.

Transport and communications

Transport. *Roads* (1996): total length 884 km (paved 44%). *Motor vehicles:* passenger cars (1996) 47,300; trucks and buses (1993) 15,300. *Air transport* (2001): passengers carried 1,453,513; freight handled 9,834 metric tons; airports (1994) with scheduled flights 17. **Communications,** in total units (units per 1,000 persons). Daily newspaper circulation (1996): 24,000 (110); radios (1997): 128,000 (574); televisions (2000): 44,500 (189); telephone main lines (2002): 52,000 (219); cellular telephone subscribers (2002): 90,000 (375); personal computers (2002): 70,000 (292); Internet users (2002): 35,000 (146).

Education and health

Educational attainment (1996). Percentage of population age 15 and over having: no formal schooling 4.9%; primary education 37.4%; secondary 49.0%; higher 8.7%. **Literacy** (2000): total population age 15 and over literate, almost 100%. **Health** (2002): physicians 429 (1 per 568 persons); hospital beds (2003) 971 (1 per 256 persons); infant mortality rate per 1,000 live births 9.0. **Food** (2001): daily per capita caloric intake 2,889 (vegetable products 72%, animal products 28%); 127% of FAO recommended minimum.

Military

Total active duty personnel (2003): 2,400 French military personnel.

Background

European contact with the islands of French Polynesia was gradual. Portuguese navigator Ferdinand Magellan sighted Pukapuka in the Tuamotu group in 1521. The southern Marquesas Islands were discovered in 1595. Dutch explorer Jacob Roggeveen in 1722 discovered Makatea, Bora-Bora, and Maupiti. Captain Samuel Wallis in 1767 discovered Tahiti, Moorea, and Maiao Iti. The Society Islands were named after the Royal Society, which had sponsored the expedition under Capt. James Cook that observed from Tahiti the 1769 transit of the planet Venus. Tubuai was discovered on Cook's last voyage, in 1777. The islands became French protectorates in

the 1840s, and in the 1880s the French colony of Oceania was established. French Polynesia became an overseas territory of France after World War II and was granted partial autonomy in 1977.

Recent Developments

Effective 2 Mar 2004, the status of French Polynesia changed from that of a French Overseas Territory to that of a French Overseas Country that "governs itself freely and democratically through its elected representatives and by way of local referendum." A pro-independence coalition government led by veteran politician Oscar Temaru was elected in June, but this government lasted less than four months. France refused to allow new elections, and former leader Gaston Flosse was returned to power. New Caledonia's economy benefited from strong nickel prices as well as a stable tourism market.

Internet resources:
<www.polynesianislands.com/fp>.

Gabon

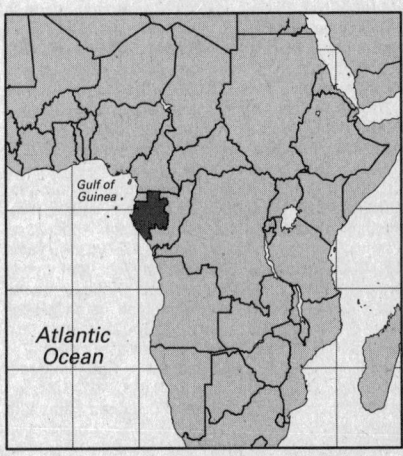

Official name: République Gabonaise (Gabonese Republic). **Form of government:** unitary multiparty republic with a Parliament comprising two legislative houses (Senate [91]; National Assembly [120]). **Chief of state:** President Omar Bongo Ondimba (from 1967). **Head of government:** Prime Minister Jean-François Ntoutoume Emane (from 1999). **Capital:** Libreville. **Official language:** French. **Official religion:** none. **Monetary unit:** 1 CFA franc (CFAF) = 100 centimes; valuation (7 Jul 2005) $1 = CFAF 549.50; the CFAF is pegged to the euro (€) at €1 = 655.96 from 1 Jan 2002.

Demography

Area: 103,347 sq mi, 267,667 sq km. **Population** (2004): 1,351,000. **Density** (2004): persons per sq mi 13.1, persons per sq km 5.0. **Urban** (2003): 83.8%. **Sex distribution** (2003): male 49.59%; female 50.41%. **Age breakdown** (2003): under 15, 42.3%; 15–29, 26.3%; 30–44, 16.6%; 45–59, 8.7%; 60–74, 4.8%; 75 and over, 1.3%. **Ethnic composition**

(2000): Fang 28.6%; Punu 10.2%; Nzebi 8.9%; French 6.7%; Mpongwe 4.1%. **Religious affiliation** (2000): Christian 90.6%, of which Roman Catholic 56.6%, Protestant 17.7%; Muslim 3.1%; traditional beliefs 1.7%. **Major cities** (2003): Libreville 420,000; Port-Gentil 88,000; Franceville (1993) 30,246; Oyem 23,000; Moanda (1993) 21,921. **Location**: western Africa, bordering Cameroon, Republic of the Congo, the South Atlantic Ocean, and Equatorial Guinea.

Vital statistics

Birth rate per 1,000 population (2003): 36.5 (world avg. 21.3). **Death rate** per 1,000 population (2003): 11.2 (world avg. 9.1). **Natural increase rate** per 1,000 population (2003): 25.3 (world avg. 12.2). **Total fertility rate** (avg. births per childbearing woman; 2003): 4.8. **Life expectancy** at birth (2003): male 55.5 years; female 58.8 years. **Adult population** (ages 15–49) **living with HIV** (2004): 8.1% (world avg. 1.1%).

National economy

Budget (2001). *Revenue:* CFAF 1,190,100,000,000 (oil revenues 65.7%; taxes on international trade 17.7%; income tax 8.3%; value-added tax 5.1%; other revenues 3.2%). *Expenditures:* CFAF 976,200,-000,000 (current expenditure 81.0%, of which service on public debt 31.0%, wages and salaries 21.9%, transfers 14.3%; capital expenditure 19.0%). **Public debt** (external, outstanding; 2002): $3,231,-000,000. **Tourism:** receipts from visitors (2001) $7,000,000; expenditures by nationals abroad (2002) $219,000,000. **Gross national product** (2003): $4,813,000,000 ($3,580 per capita). **Production** (metric tons except as noted). *Agriculture, forestry, fishing* (2003): plantains 170,000, yams 155,000, sugarcane 135,000; livestock (number of live animals) 212,000 pigs, 195,000 sheep; roundwood (2003) 3,106,710 cu m; fish catch (2001) 40,559. *Mining and quarrying* (2002): manganese ore 1,816,000; gold 70 kg (excludes about 400 kg of illegally mined gold smuggled out of Gabon). *Manufacturing* (value added in $'000,000; 1995): wood products (excluding furniture) 44; refined petroleum products 25; food products 22. *Energy production (consumption):* electricity (kW-hr; 2000) 1,354,-000,000 (1,354,000,000); crude petroleum (barrels; 2002) 108,000,000 ([2000] 5,610,000); petroleum products (2000) 593,400 (590,000); natural gas (cu m; 2000) 810,000,000 (810,000,000). **Population economically active** (2000): total 555,000; activity rate of total population 44.1% (participation rates [1985] ages 15–64, 68.2%; female 44.5%; unemployed [1996] 20%). **Households.** Average household size (2000) 6.1. **Land use** as % of total land area (2000): in temporary crops 1.3%, in permanent crops 0.7%, in pasture 18.1%; overall forest area 84.7%.

Foreign trade

Imports (2003): CFAF 602,000,000,000 (for petroleum sector 27.9%, other unspecified 72.1%). *Major import sources* (2000): France 44%; US 11%; The Netherlands 5%; Germany 3%; Spain 3%. **Exports** (2003): CFAF 1,842,000,000,000 (crude petroleum and petroleum products 80.5%, wood

10.2%, manganese ore and concentrate 4.8%). *Major export destinations* (2000): US 63%; China 7%; Australia 6%; France 4%; South Korea 4%.

Transport and communications

Transport. *Railroads* (2002): route length 814 km; (2002) passenger-km 97,500,000; (2002) metric ton-km cargo carried 1,553,000,000. *Roads* (1996): total length 7,670 km (paved 8%). *Vehicles* (1997): passenger cars 24,750; trucks and buses 16,490. *Air transport* (2000): passenger-km 1,204,000,000; airports (1997) 17. **Communications,** in total units (units per 1,000 persons). Daily newspaper circulation (1997): 33,000 (30); radios (2000): 630,000 (501); televisions (2002): 400,000 (308); telephone main lines (2003): 38,400 (29); cellular telephone subscribers (2003): 300,000 (224); personal computers (2003): 30,000 (22); Internet users (2003): 35,000 (26).

Education and health

Educational attainment of economically active population (1993): no formal schooling and incomplete primary education 37.7%; complete primary 32.1%; complete secondary 16.4%; postsecondary certificate or degree 13.8%. **Literacy** (2000): total population age 15 and over literate 71%; males literate 80%; females literate 62%. **Health:** physicians (1995) 321 (1 per 3,455 persons); hospital beds (1995) 4,631 (1 per 240 persons); infant mortality rate per 1,000 live births (2003) 55.1. **Food** (2001): daily per capita caloric intake 2,602 (vegetable products 87%, animal products 13%); 111% of FAO recommended minimum.

Military

Total active duty personnel (2003): 4,700 (army 68.1%, navy 10.6%, air force 21.3%); French troops (2003) 800. **Military expenditure as percentage of GNP** (1999): 2.4% (world 2.4%); per capita expenditure $78.

Did you know? The top green stripe on Gabon's flag represents the extensive forests in the country. The yellow stripe in the center symbolizes the equator, which bisects the country, and the bottom blue stripe symbolizes the Atlantic Ocean.

Background

Artifacts dating from late Paleolithic and early Neolithic times have been found in Gabon, but it is not known when the Bantu speakers who established Gabon's ethnic composition arrived. Pygmies were probably the original inhabitants. The Fang arrived in the late 18th century and were followed by the Portuguese and by French, Dutch, and English traders. The slave trade dominated commerce in the 18th and much of the 19th century. The French then took control, and Gabon was administered (1843–86)

---

1 metric ton = about 1.1 short tons;   1 kilometer = 0.6 mi (statute);   1 metric ton-km cargo = about 0.68 short ton-mi cargo;   c.i.f.: cost, insurance, and freight;   f.o.b.: free on board

with French West Africa. In 1886 the colony of French Congo was established to include both Gabon and the Congo; in 1910 Gabon became a separate colony within French Equatorial Africa. An overseas territory of France from 1946, it became an autonomous republic within the French Community in 1958 and declared its independence in 1960. Rule by a sole political party was established in the 1960s, but discontent with it led to riots in Libreville in 1990. Legalization of opposition parties led to new elections in 1990. Peace negotiations with neighboring Chad rebels and with the Republic of the Congo were ongoing in the 1990s.

Recent Developments

On 2 Feb 2004 visiting Pres. Hu Jintao of China signed an agreement to import large quantities of Gabonese oil. China had funded and built Gabon's parliamentary complex and in July announced it would construct a national media center in Libreville. On 6 September, Pres. Omar Bongo left for a weeklong state visit to China, where he held talks with Hu at the Great Hall of the People in Beijing.

Internet resources: <www.gabonnews.com>.

The Gambia

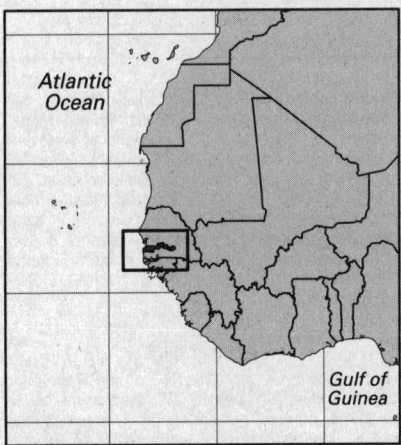

Atlantic Ocean

Gulf of Guinea

Official name: The Republic of The Gambia. Form of government: multiparty republic with one legislative house (National Assembly [53, including 5 nonelective seats]). Head of state and government: President Col. Yahya Jammeh (from 1994). Capital: Banjul. Official language: English. Official religion: none. Monetary unit: 1 dalasi (D) = 100 butut; valuation (7 Jul 2005) $1 = D 28.25.

Demography

Area (including inland water area of 802 sq mi [2,077 sq km]): 4,127 sq mi, 10,689 sq km. Population (2004): 1,405,000. Density (2004; based on land area only): persons per sq mi 422.6, persons per sq km 163.1. Urban (2003): 26.1%. Sex distribution (2003): male 49.59%; female 50.41%. Age breakdown (2003): under 15, 44.9%; 15–29, 26.4%;

30–44, 15.5%; 45–59, 8.8%; 60–74, 3.6%; 75 and over, 0.8%. Ethnic composition (1993): Malinke 34.1%; Fulani 16.2%; Wolof 12.6%; Diola 9.2%; Soninke 7.7%; other 20.2%. Religious affiliation (1993): Muslim 95.0%; Christian 4.1%; traditional beliefs and other 0.9%. Major cities/urban areas (2003): Kanifing 322,410 (Kanifing includes the urban areas of Serekunda and Bakau); Brikama 63,000; Banjul 34,828 (Greater Banjul 523,589 [Kanifing and Banjul make up most of Greater Banjul]). Location: western Africa, bordering Senegal on three sides and the North Atlantic Ocean.

Vital statistics

Birth rate per 1,000 population (2003): 40.8 (world avg. 21.3). Death rate per 1,000 population (2003): 12.4 (world avg. 9.1). Natural increase rate per 1,000 population (2003): 28.4 (world avg. 12.2). Total fertility rate (avg. births per childbearing woman; 2002): 5.5. Life expectancy at birth (2003): male 52.4 years; female 56.4 years.

National economy

Budget (2002). Revenue: D 1,528,700,000 (tax revenue 68.0%, of which taxes on international trade 39.1%, corporate taxes 11.6%; grants 21.4%; nontax revenue 10.6%). Expenditures: D 1,870,700,000 (current expenditure 70.5%, of which interest payments 19.8%; capital expenditure 29.5%). Production (metric tons except as noted). Agriculture, forestry, fishing (2002): millet 84,618, peanuts (groundnuts) 71,526, paddy rice 20,452; livestock (number of live animals) 327,000 cattle, 262,000 goats, 146,000 sheep; roundwood (2001) 724,000 cu m; fish catch (2001) 34,527, of which Atlantic Ocean 32,037, inland water 2,490. Mining and quarrying: sand, clay, and gravel are excavated for local use. Manufacturing (value added in $; 1995): food products and beverages 6,000,000; textiles, clothing, and footwear 750,000; wood products 550,000. Energy production (consumption): electricity (kW-hr; 2001) 134,000,000 (134,000,000); petroleum products (2000) none (88,000). Population economically active (1998): total 575,140; activity rate of total population 47.3% (participation rates: ages 15–64, 86.6%; female 40.0%). Tourism (2000): receipts from visitors $48,000,000; expenditures by nationals abroad (1997) $16,000,000. Households. Average household size (2000) 7.9; expenditure (1991; low-income population in Banjul and Kanifing only): food and beverages 58.0%, clothing and footwear 17.5%, energy and water 5.4%, housing 5.1%, education, health, transportation and communications, recreation, and other 14.0%. Public debt (external, outstanding; 2002): $503,600,000. Gross national product (at current market prices; 2003): $442,000,-000 ($310 per capita). Land use as % of total land area (2000): in temporary crops 23.0%, in permanent crops 0.5%, in pasture 45.9%; overall forest area 48.1%.

Foreign trade

Imports (2002-c.i.f.): $160,100,000 (imports for re-export comprise 36.0% of total; food and live animals 23.5%; machinery and transport equipment 17.0%; petroleum products 10.6%). Major import sources: EU 31.0%; China 22.3%; Senegal 9.2%. Exports (2002-f.o.b.): $111,000,000 (reexports 70.4%;

peanuts [groundnuts] 21.6%; fruits and vegetables 3.7%; fish and fish products 2.6%). *Major export destinations:* EU 76.6%; Asian countries 16.7%.

Transport and communications

Transport. *Roads* (1999): total length 2,700 km (paved 35%). *Vehicles* (1997): passenger cars 7,267; trucks and buses (1996) 9,000. *Air transport* (2001; Yumdum International Airport at Banjul): passenger arrivals 300,000, passenger departures 300,000; cargo loaded and unloaded 2,700 metric tons; airports (2000) with scheduled flights 1. **Communications,** in total units (units per 1,000 persons). Daily newspaper circulation (2000): 39,400 (30); radios (2000): 520,000 (396); televisions (2000): 3,940 (3); telephone main lines (2002): 38,400 (29); cellular telephone subscribers (2002): 100,000 (75); personal computers (2002): 19,000 (14); Internet users (2002): 25,000 (19).

Education and health

Literacy (1998): total population age 15 and over literate 34.6%; males literate 41.9%; females literate 27.5%. **Health** (2000): physicians 105 (1 per 12,977 persons); hospital beds 1,140 (1 per 1,199 persons); infant mortality rate per 1,000 live births (2003) 74.9. **Food** (2002): daily per capita caloric intake 2,273 (vegetable products 94%, animal products 6%); 96% of FAO recommended minimum.

Military

Total active duty personnel (2003): 800 (army 100%). **Military expenditure as percentage of GNP** (1999): 1.3% (world 2.4%); per capita expenditure $12.

Background

Beginning about the 13th century AD, the Wolof, Malinke, and Fulani peoples settled in different parts of what is now The Gambia and established villages and then kingdoms in the region. European exploration began when the Portuguese sighted the Gambia River in 1455. Britain and France both settled in the area in the 17th century. The British Fort James, on an island about 20 mi (32 km) from the river's mouth, was an important collection point for the slave trade. In 1783 the Treaty of Versailles reserved the Gambia River for Britain. After the British abolished slavery in 1807, they built a fort at the mouth of the river to block the continuing slave trade. In 1889 The Gambia's boundaries were agreed upon by Britain and France; the British declared a protectorate over the area in 1894. Independence was proclaimed in 1965, and The Gambia became a republic within the Commonwealth in 1970. It formed a limited confederation with Senegal in 1982 that was dissolved in 1989. During the 1990s the government was in turmoil.

Recent Developments

On 13 Feb 2004 Gambian Pres. Yahya Jammeh announced the discovery of "very large quantities of oil" in Gambian waters; test drilling began in the summer. In July Jammeh celebrated 10 years in office. Opposition leader Lamin Juwara took the occasion to accuse the government of forcing many young people to flee the country because of a lack of employment opportunities and an oppressive political climate.

Internet resources: <www.visitthegambia.gm>.

Georgia

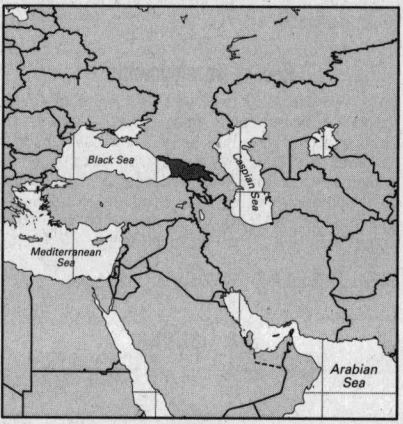

Official name: Sak'art'velo (Georgia). **Form of government:** unitary multiparty republic with a single legislative body (Parliament [235]). **Head of state and government:** President Mikhail Saakashvili (from 25 Jan 2004), assisted by Prime Minister Zurab Nogaideli (from 17 Feb 2005). **Capital:** Tbilisi. **Official language:** Georgian (locally Abkhazian, in Abkhazia). **Official religion:** none; but special recognition is given to the Georgian Orthodox Church. **Monetary unit:** 1 Georgian lari = 100 tetri; valuation (7 Jul 2005) $1 = 1.81 lari.

Demography

Area: 27,086 sq mi, 70,152 sq km. **Population** (2004): 4,694,000. **Density** (2004): persons per sq mi 174.4, persons per sq km 67.3. **Urban** (2002): 52.3%. **Sex distribution** (2002): male 47.16%; female 52.84%. **Age breakdown** (2002): under 15, 21.0%; 15–29, 22.8%; 30–44, 21.9%; 45–59, 15.6%; 60–74, 14.6%; 75 and over, 4.1%. **Ethnic composition** (2000): Georgian 57.9%; Mingrelian 9.1%; Armenian 8.1%; Russian 6.3%; Azerbaijani 5.7%; Ossetian 3.0%; Greek 1.9%; Abkhazian 1.8%; other 6.2%. **Religious affiliation** (1995): Christian 46.2%, of which Georgian Orthodox 36.7%, Armenian Apostolic 5.6%, Russian Orthodox 2.7%, other Christian 1.2%; Sunni Muslim 11.0%; other (mostly nonreligious) 42.8%. **Major cities** (2002): Tbilisi 1,081,679; K'ut'aisi 185,965; Bat'umi 121,806; Rust'avi 116,348; Sokhumi (1994) 112,000. **Location:** Caucasus region of southwestern Asia, bordering Russia, Azerbaijan, Armenia, Turkey, and the Black Sea.

---

1 metric ton = about 1.1 short tons; 1 kilometer = 0.6 mi (statute); 1 metric ton-km cargo = about 0.68 short ton-mi cargo; c.i.f.: cost, insurance, and freight; f.o.b.: free on board

Vital statistics

Birth rate per 1,000 population (2003): 10.0 (world avg. 21.3). **Death rate** per 1,000 population (2003): 8.9 (world avg. 9.1). **Natural increase rate** per 1,000 population (2003): 1.1 (world avg. 12.2). **Total fertility rate** (avg. births per childbearing woman; 2003): 1.4. **Marriage rate** per 1,000 population (2001): 2.7. **Divorce rate** per 1,000 population (2001): 0.4. **Life expectancy** at birth (2003): male 72.1 years; female 79.2 years.

National economy

Budget (2002). *Revenue:* 928,600,000 lari (tax revenue 83.1%, of which value-added tax 40.4%, social security tax 17.4%, excise tax 11.3%; nontax revenue 8.5%; grants 8.4%). *Expenditures:* 920,500,000 lari (current expenditure 99.7%, of which social security and welfare 30.0%, public order 9.1%, health 4.5%, defense 4.4%, education 4.1%; capital expenditure 0.3%). **Public debt** (external, outstanding; 2002): $1,444,000,000. **Population economically active** (2000): total 1,748,800 (excludes informal sector, which was about 750,000 persons in 1998); activity rate of total population 35.1% (participation rates [1993]: ages 16–65 [male], 16–60 [female] 55.6%; female 47.8%; unemployed [2000] 12.0%). **Production** (metric tons except as noted). *Agriculture, forestry, fishing* (2002): potatoes 414,000, wheat 306,000, corn (maize) 290,000; livestock (number of live animals) 1,180,000 cattle, 568,000 sheep; fish catch (2001) 1,910. *Mining and quarrying* (2001): manganese ore 98,300. *Manufacturing* (value of production in $'000,000; 2001; excludes Abkhazia and South Ossetia): food products 139.6, basic metals 36.5, transport equipment 27.0. *Energy production (consumption):* electricity (kW-hr; 2001) 5,700,000,-000 (5,700,000,000); coal (2000) 7,000 (27,000); crude petroleum (barrels; 2001) 719,000 (719,000); petroleum products (2000) 10,600 (1,305,000); natural gas (cu m; 2000) 59,019,000 (1,002,000,000). **Gross national product** (2003): $3,780,000,000 ($830 per capita). **Household income and expenditure.** Average household size (2000) 4.6; sources of income (1993): wages and salaries 34.5%, benefits 21.9%, agricultural income 21.6%, other 22.0%; expenditure (1993): taxes 42.5%, retail goods 32.3%, savings 16.4%, transportation 4.2%. **Tourism** ($'000,000; 2002): receipts 472; expenditures 174. **Land use** as % of total land area (2000): in temporary crops 11.4%, in permanent crops 3.9%, in pasture 27.9%; overall forest area 43.7%.

Foreign trade

Imports (2001-c.i.f.): $684,000,000 (food [all forms] 23.8%; mineral fuels 22.7%; machinery and apparatus 18.3%; transport equipment 7.1%). *Major import sources:* Turkey 15.4%; Russia 13.3%; Azerbaijan 10.7%; Germany 10.1%; Ukraine 7.2%. **Exports** (2001-f.o.b.): $320,000,000 (beverages [including wine] 16.7%; iron and steel 15.9%; aircraft and parts 11.3%; food [all forms] 8.8%; mineral fuels 8.6%). *Major export destinations:* Russia 23.0%; Turkey 21.5%; Turkmenistan 9.0%; UK 7.2%; Switzerland 4.9%.

Transport and communications

Transport. *Railroads* (2001): 1,546 km; passenger-km 398,000,000; metric ton-km cargo 4,473,000,-000. *Roads* (2001): 20,215 km (paved 93.5%). *Vehicles* (1999): passenger cars 247,872; trucks and buses 43,421. *Air transport* (2001): passenger-km 241,000,000; metric ton-km cargo 3,000,000; airports with scheduled flights 1. **Communications,** in total units (units per 1,000 persons). Radios (2000): 2,790,000 (556); televisions (2002): 1,856,000 (357); telephone main lines (2003): 650,500 (133); cellular telephone subscribers (2003): 522,300 (107); personal computers (2002): 156,000 (31); Internet users (2003): 150,500 (31).

Health and nutrition

Health (2001): physicians 22,000 (1 per 213 persons); hospital beds 24,520 (1 per 208 persons); infant mortality rate per 1,000 live births (2002) 23.3. **Food** (2002): daily per capita caloric intake 2,354 (vegetable products 82%, animal products 18%; 92% of FAO recommended minimum.

Military

Total active duty personnel (2003): 17,500 (army 49.3%, air force 7.1%, navy 10.5%, paramilitary 33.1%). About 3,000 Russian troops acting as a buffer force between Georgians and Abkhazians were in Abkhazia in August 2004 along with about 125 UN peacekeeping troops. **Military expenditure as percentage of GNP** (1999): 1.2% (world 2.4%); per capita expenditure $33.

Did you know? The world's deepest known cave is Krubera, in the Georgian republic of Abkhazia. In October 2004 a Ukrainian spelelogical expedition descended to more than 2,000 m (6,560 ft). South African gold miners, however, routinely descend below 3,400 m (11,000 ft).

Background

Ancient Georgia was the site of the kingdoms of Iberia and Colchis, whose fabled wealth was known to the ancient Greeks. The area was part of the Roman empire by 65 BC and became Christian in AD 337. For the next three centuries it was involved in the conflicts between the Byzantine and Persian empires; after 654 it was controlled by Arab caliphs, who established an emirate in Tbilisi. It was controlled by the Bagratids from the 8th to the 12th century, and the zenith of Georgia's power was reached in the reign of Queen Tamara, whose realm stretched from Azerbaijan to Circassia, forming a pan-Caucasian empire. Invasions by Mongols and Turks in the 13th and 14th centuries disintegrated the kingdom, and the fall of Constantinople (now Istanbul) to the Ottoman Turks in 1453 isolated it from western Christendom. The next three centuries saw repeated invasions by the Armenians, Turks, and Persians. Georgia sought Russian protection in 1783, and in 1801 it was annexed to Russia. After the Russian Revolution of 1917, the area was briefly independent; in 1921 a Soviet regime was installed, and in 1936 Georgia became the Georgian SSR, a full member of the Soviet Union. In 1990 a noncommunist coalition came to power in the first free elections ever held in Soviet Georgia, and in 1991 Georgia declared independence. In the 1990s, while Pres. Eduard Shevardnadze tried to steer a middle course, internal dissension resulted in conflicts with the northwestern republic of Abkhazia, and external distrust of Russian motives in the area grew. In 1992 Abkhazia reinstated its 1925 constitution and declared independence, which Georgia refused to recognize.

Recent Developments

Following Georgia's "Rose Revolution" in late 2003, the presidential ballot on 4 Jan 2004 saw a young and charismatic Mikhail Saakashvili win some 96% of the votes. Saakashvili moved quickly to remodel his administration along Western European parliamentary lines, but attempts to reunify the country were challenged by forces in the restive republics of Ajaria, Abkhazia, and South Ossetia. The public was shocked and saddened by the accidental death in February 2005 of popular Prime Minister Zurab Zhvania; he was replaced by former finance minister Zurab Nogaideli. The visit to Tbilisi in May by US Pres. George W. Bush—the first ever by a US president—was a landmark with extraordinary significance for this fiercely nationalistic Caucasian state that historically had been in the sway of Russia.

Internet resources:
<www.parliament.ge/gotoGeorgia.htm>.

Germany

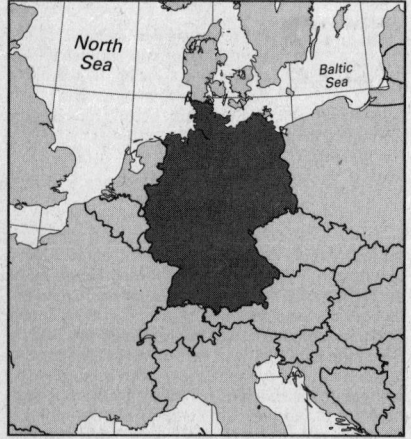

Official name: Bundesrepublik Deutschland (Federal Republic of Germany). **Form of government:** federal multiparty republic with two legislative houses (Federal Council [69]; Federal Diet [603]). **Chief of state:** President Horst Köhler (from 1 Jul 2004). **Head of government:** Chancellor Gerhard Schröder (from 1998). **Capital:** Berlin; some ministries remain in Bonn. **Official language:** German. **Official religion:** none. **Monetary unit:** 1 euro (€) = 100 cents; valuation (7 Jul 2005) $1 = €0.84; at conversion on 1 Jan 2002, €1= 1.96 Deutsche Marks (DM).

Demography

Area: 137,847 sq mi, 357,023 sq km. **Population** (2004): 82,561,000. **Density** (2004): persons per sq mi 598.9, persons per sq km 231.2. **Urban** (2003): 88.1%. **Major cities** (2002; urban agglomerations [2000]): Berlin 3,388,434 (city population coextensive with urban agglomeration); Hamburg 1,726,363 (2,664,000); Munich 1,227,958 (2,291,000); Cologne 967,940 (3,050,000); Frankfurt am Main 641,076 (3,681,000); Essen 591,889 (6,531,000; part of the Rhine-Ruhr North urban agglomeration); Dortmund 589,240 (6,531,000; part of the Rhine-Ruhr North urban agglomeration); Stuttgart 587,152 (2,672,000); Düsseldorf 570,765 (3,233,000); Bremen 540,950 (880,000); Hannover 516,415 (1,283,000); Duisburg 512,030 (6,531,000; part of the Rhine-Ruhr North urban agglomeration); Leipzig 493,052; Nuremberg (Nürnberg) 491,307 (1,189,-000). **Location:** central Europe, bordering Denmark, the Baltic Sea, Poland, the Czech Republic, Austria, Switzerland, France, Luxembourg, Belgium, The Netherlands, and the North Sea. **Sex distribution** (2003): male 48.78%; female 51.22%. **Ethnic composition** (by nationality; 2000): German 88.2%; Turkish 3.4% (including Kurdish 0.7%); Italian 1.0%; Greek 0.7%; Serb 0.6%; Russian 0.6%; Polish 0.4%; other 5.1%. **Age breakdown** (2003): under 15, 14.9%; 15–29, 17.0%; 30–44, 24.3%; 45–59, 19.3%; 60–74, 16.9%; 75 and over, 7.6%. **Religious affiliation** (2000): Christian 75.8%, of which Protestant 35.6% (including Lutheran 33.9%), Roman Catholic 33.5%, Orthodox 0.9%, independent Christian 0.9%, other Christian 4.9%; Muslim 4.4%; Jewish 0.1%; nonreligious 17.2%; atheist 2.2%; other 0.3%. **Households** (2000). Number of households 38,124,000; average household size 2.2; 1 person 36.0%, 2 persons 33.4%, 3 persons 14.7%, 4 persons 11.5%, 5 or more persons 4.4%.

Vital statistics

Birth rate per 1,000 population (2003): 8.6 (world avg. 21.3); legitimate 73.0%; illegitimate 27.0%. **Death rate** per 1,000 population (2003): 10.3 (world avg. 9.1). **Natural increase rate** per 1,000 population (2003): −1.7 (world avg. 12.2). **Total fertility rate** (avg. births per childbearing woman; 2003): 1.4. **Marriage rate** per 1,000 population (2003): 4.6. **Divorce rate** per 1,000 population (2003): 2.6. **Life expectancy** at birth (2003): male 75.5 years; female 81.6 years.

Social indicators

Quality of working life. Average workweek (2002): 37.9 hours. Annual rate per 100,000 workers (1993) for: injuries or accidents at work 4,808; deaths, including commuting accidents, 6.7. Proportion of labor force insured for damages of income loss resulting from: injury, virtually 100%; permanent disability, virtually 100%; death, virtually 100%. Average days lost to labor stoppages per 1,000 workers (2000): 0.3. **Access to services.** Proportion of dwellings (2002) having: electricity, virtually 100%; piped water supply, virtually 100%; flush sewage disposal (1993) 98.4%; public fire protection, virtually 100%. **Social participation.** Eligible voters participating in last (September

1 metric ton = about 1.1 short tons;　1 kilometer = 0.6 mi (statute);　1 metric ton-km cargo = about 0.68 short ton-mi cargo;　c.i.f.: cost, insurance, and freight;　f.o.b.: free on board

2002) national election 79.1%. Trade union membership in total workforce (2003): c. 18%. Practicing religious population (1994): 5% of Protestants and 25% of Roman Catholics "regularly" attend religious services. **Social deviance** (2000). Offense rate per 100,000 population for: murder and manslaughter 3.8; sexual abuse 37.0, of which rape and forcible sexual assault 11.7, child molestation 10.2; assault and battery 153.2; theft 754.2. **Material well-being** (2001; median income). Households possessing: automobile 75.1%; telephone 96.4%; mobile telephone 55.7%; color television 95.9%; washing machine 95.1%; clothes dryer 33.3%; personal computer 53.4%; dishwasher 51.3%; high-speed Internet access 12.0%.

National economy

Budget (2001). *Revenue:* €922,472,000,000 (taxes 87.9%, loan interest 2.7%, other 9.4%). *Expenditures:* €972,104,000,000 (current expenditure 66.1%, of which purchase of current goods and services 22.2%, personnel costs 18.6%; capital expenditure 33.9%). **Total public debt** (2001): $1,109,680,-000,000. **Production** (value of production in € except as noted; 2002). *Agriculture, forestry, fishing:* cereal grains 4,265,000,000, fodder plants 4,148,-000,000, flowers and ornamental plants 2,797,-000,000, vegetables 1,334,000,000, sugar beets 1,267,000,000, potatoes 939,000,000, grapes for wine 929,000,000, oilseeds 876,000,000, fruits 628,000,000; livestock (number of live animals; 2003) 26,251,000 pigs, 13,732,000 cattle, 2,658,-000 sheep, 110,000,000 chickens; roundwood 42,380,000 cu m; fish catch (metric tons; 2001) 266,000. *Mining and quarrying* (metric tons; 2001): potash (potassium oxide content) 3,549,000; feldspar 500,000. *Manufacturing* (value added in $'000,000; 2000): motor vehicles 72,300; nonelectrical machinery and apparatus 71,800; chemicals (including pharmaceuticals) 62,900; food and beverages 44,700; electrical machinery and apparatus [excluding telecommunications, electronics] 38,600; fabricated metal products 37,000; petroleum products and coal derivatives 28,200; printing and publishing 25,400; rubber products and plastic products 23,700; base metals 22,100. *Energy production (consumption):* electricity (kW-hr; 2001) 565,284,-000,000 ([2000] 583,415,000,000); hard coal (2002) 26,364,000 ([2000] 64,357,000); lignite (2002) 181,416,000 ([2000] 169,942,000); crude petroleum (barrels; 2003) 30,003,000 ([2000] 775,820,000); petroleum products (2000) 98,024,-000 (104,149,000); natural gas (cu m; 2002) 24,158,000,000 ([2000] 109,387,000,000). **Gross national product** (at current market prices; 2003): $2,084,631,000,000 ($25,250 per capita). **Household income and expenditure.** Average annual income per household (1998) DM 75,144 ($42,702); sources of take-home income (1997): wages 77.6%, self-employment 12.0%, transfer payments 10.4%; expenditure (2001): housing and energy 24.5%, transportation 14.2%, food and nonalcoholic beverages 12.3%, recreation and culture 9.7%, household furnishings 7.1%, clothing and footwear 6.4%, restaurants and hotels 4.9%. **Tourism** (2002): receipts $19,158,000,000; expenditures $53,196,000,000. **Population economically active** (2002): total 40,607,000; activity rate of total population 49.3% (participation rates: ages 15–64 [2001] 71.5%; female 44.3%; unemployed 10.0%). **Land use** as % of

total land area (2000): in temporary crops 33.8%, in permanent crops 0.6%, in pasture 14.5%; overall forest area 30.7%.

Foreign trade

Imports (2002-c.i.f.): €522,062,000,000 (machinery and equipment 22.6%, of which televisions, telecommunications equipment, and electronic components 6.0%, office machinery and computers 5.3%; transport equipment 14.3%, of which road vehicles 10.2%; chemicals and chemical products 10.6%; crude petroleum and natural gas 6.0%; food products and beverages 5.0%; base metals 4.8%; wearing apparel 3.1%). *Major import sources:* France 9.5%; The Netherlands 8.3%; US 7.7%; UK 6.4%; Italy 6.4%; Belgium 5.2%; Austria 4.1%; China 4.0%; Switzerland 3.7%; Japan 3.6%. **Exports** (2002-f.o.b.): €648,306,000,000 (machinery and equipment 26.3%, of which nonelectrical machinery 14.1%, televisions, telecommunications equipment, and electronic components 4.8%; transport equipment 23.4%, of which road vehicles 19.1%; chemicals and chemical products 11.8%; base metals 4.5%; medical and precision instruments and watches and clocks 4.0%). *Major export destinations:* France 10.8%; US 10.3%; UK 8.4%; Italy 7.3%; The Netherlands 6.1%; Austria 5.1%; Belgium 4.8%; Spain 4.6%; Switzerland 4.1%; Poland 2.5%.

Transport and communications

Transport. *Railroads* (2001): length 85,653 km; (2002) passenger-km 70,814,000,000; (2002) metric ton-km cargo 72,014,000,000. *Roads* (2002): total length 230,800 km (paved 99%). *Vehicles* (2002): passenger cars 44,383,300; trucks and buses 2,735,600. *Air transport* (2003; Lufthansa Group, Condor, and Eurowings only): passenger-km 112,089,000,000; metric ton-km cargo 7,088,600,000; airports (1997) 35. **Communications,** in total units (units per 1,000 persons). Daily newspaper circulation (2000): 25,100,000 (305); radios (2000): 77,900,000 (948); televisions (2002): 54,533,000 (661); telephone main lines (2003): 54,350,000 (658); cellular telephone subscribers (2003): 64,800,000 (785); personal computers (2002): 35,921,000 (435); Internet users (2003): 39,000,000 (473).

Education and health

Educational attainment (2000). Percentage of population age 25 and over having: primary and lower secondary 50.6%; intermediate secondary 17.9%; vocational secondary 8.7%; postsecondary and higher (all levels) 22.8%. **Health:** physicians (2001) 298,000 (1 per 276 persons); hospital beds (2001) 552,680 (1 per 150 persons); infant mortality rate per 1,000 live births (2002) 4.2. **Food** (2001): daily per capita caloric intake 3,567 (vegetable products 71%, animal products 29%); 134% of FAO recommended minimum.

Military

Total active duty personnel (2003): 284,500 (army 67.3%, navy 9.0%, air force 23.7%); German peacekeeping troops abroad (May 2004) 7,700; US troops in Germany (August 2004) 75,600. **Military expenditure as percentage of GNP** (1999): 1.6% (world 2.4%); per capita expenditure $395.

Background

Germanic tribes entered the region about the 2nd century BC, displacing the Celts. The Romans failed to conquer the region, which became a political entity only with the division of the Carolingian Empire in the 9th century AD. The monarchy's control was weak, and power increasingly devolved upon the nobility, organized in feudal states. The monarchy was restored under Saxon rule in the 10th century, and the Holy Roman Empire, centering on Germany and northern Italy, was revived. Continuing conflict between the Holy Roman emperors and the Roman Catholic popes undermined the empire, and its dissolution was accelerated by Martin Luther's revolt in 1517, which divided Germany, and ultimately Europe, into Protestant and Roman Catholic camps, culminating in the Thirty Years' War (1618–48). Germany's population and borders were greatly reduced, and its numerous feudal princes gained virtually full sovereignty. In 1862 Otto von Bismarck came to power in Prussia and over the next decade reunited Germany in the German Empire. It was dissolved in 1918 after the German defeat in World War I. Germany was stripped of much of its territory and all of its colonies. In 1933 Adolf Hitler became chancellor and established a totalitarian state, the Third Reich, dominated by the Nazi Party. Hitler's invasion of Poland in 1939 plunged the world into World War II. Following its defeat in 1945, Germany was divided by the Allied Powers into four zones of occupation. Disagreement with the USSR over the reunification of the zones led to the creation in 1949 of the Federal Republic of Germany (West Germany) and the German Democratic Republic (East Germany). Berlin, the former capital, remained divided. West Germany became a prosperous parliamentary democracy, East Germany a one-party state under Soviet control. The East German Communist government was brought down peacefully in 1989, and Germany was reunited in 1990. After the initial euphoria over unity, the former West Germany sought to incorporate the former East Germany both politically and economically, resulting in heavy financial burdens for the wealthier western Germans. The country continued to move toward deeper political and economic integration with western Europe through its membership in the European Union.

Recent Developments

The state of the German economy and the federal government's reform program were the dominant—and closely intertwined—topics of 2004–05. The government's economic woes were compounded by shattering results for the dominant coalition partner, the Social Democratic Party, in state and European Parliament elections. The slight stirrings of economic growth remained stubbornly weak, just as the unemployment rate remained stubbornly strong at over 10% in 2004 and climbing to 12.6%—the highest since the 1930s—by March 2005. Foreign affairs continued to be dominated by the German position on Iraq—and its consequences for Germany's relationship with the US. In the European Union tensions arose from a variety of sources, not least the row over the voting procedures set out in the draft constitutional treaty and the German government's continued

inability to bring its budget deficit under the ceiling set by the euro zone's Stability and Growth Pact. On 12 May 2005 the German Bundestag (lower house) voted overwhelmingly in favor of the new EU Constitution.

Internet resources: <www.germany-tourism.de>.

Ghana

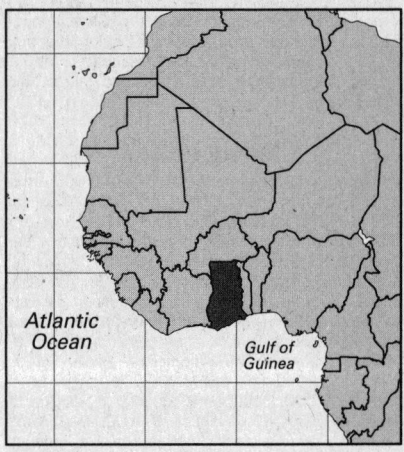

Official name: Republic of Ghana. **Form of government:** unitary multiparty republic with one legislative house (House of Parliament [230]). **Head of state and government:** President John Agyekum Kufuor (from 2001). **Capital:** Accra. **Official language:** English. **Official religion:** none. **Monetary unit:** 1 cedi (₵) = 100 pesewas; valuation (7 Jul 2005) $1 = ₵9,027.50.

Demography

Area: 92,098 sq mi, 238,533 sq km. **Population** (2004): 20,732,000. **Density** (2004): persons per sq mi 225.1, persons per sq km 86.9. **Urban** (2003): 45.4%. **Sex distribution** (2000): male 49.46%; female 50.54%. **Age breakdown** (2000): under 15, 41.2%; 15–29, 28.3%; 30–44, 17.3%; 45–59, 7.9%; 60–74, 4.3%; 75 and over, 1.0%. **Ethnic composition** (2000): Akan 41.6%; Mossi 23.0%; Ewe 10.0%; Ga-Adangme 7.2%; Gurma 3.4%; Nzima 1.8%; Yoruba 1.6%; other 11.4%. **Religious affiliation** (2000): Christian 55.4%, of which Protestant 16.6%, African Christian 14.4%, Roman Catholic 9.5%; traditional beliefs 24.4%; Muslim 19.7%; other 0.5%. **Major cities** (2002): Accra 1,605,400; Kumasi 627,600; Tamale 269,200; Tema 237,700; Obuasi 122,600. **Location:** western Africa, bordering Burkina Faso, Togo, the Atlantic Ocean, and Côte d'Ivoire.

Vital statistics

Birth rate per 1,000 population (2003): 25.8 (world avg. 21.3). **Death rate** per 1,000 population (2003): 10.5 (world avg. 9.1). **Natural increase rate** per 1,000 population (2003): 15.3 (world avg. 12.2).

---

1 metric ton = about 1.1 short tons;　1 kilometer = 0.6 mi (statute);　1 metric ton-km cargo = about 0.68 short ton-mi cargo;　c.i.f.: cost, insurance, and freight;　f.o.b.: free on board

Total fertility rate (avg. births per childbearing woman; 2003): 3.3. Life expectancy at birth (2003): male 55.7 years; female 57.4 years.

National economy

Budget (2000). *Revenue:* ₵5,385,000,000,000 (tax revenue 82.0%, of which indirect taxes 37.5%, direct taxes 26.2%, trade taxes 18.3%; grants 10.7%; non-tax revenue 7.3%). *Expenditures:* ₵7,525,100,-000,000 (current expenditure 66.9%, capital expenditure 33.1%). Public debt (external, outstanding; 2002): $6,129,000,000. Households. Average household size (1999) 4.3. Gross national product (2003): $6,563,000,000 ($320 per capita). Production (metric tons except as noted). *Agriculture, forestry, fishing* (2002): roots and tubers 15,491,000 (of which cassava 9,731,000, yams 3,900,000, taro 1,860,000), bananas and plantains 2,291,000, cereals 2,162,000 (of which corn [maize] 1,407,000, sorghum 316,000, rice 280,000, millet 159,000); livestock (number of live animals) 3,410,000 goats, 2,970,000 sheep, 22,000,000 chickens; roundwood (2001) 21,979,000 cu m; fish catch (2001) 459,000. *Mining and quarrying* (2002): manganese (metal content) 363,000; bauxite 684,000; gold 2,241,000 troy oz. *Manufacturing* (value added in ₵; 1993): tobacco 71,474,700,000; footwear 60,350,600,000; chemical products 40,347,600,000. *Energy production (consumption):* electricity (kW-hr; 2001) 8,321,-000,000 (8,029,000,000); coal (2000) none (3,000); crude petroleum (barrels; 2000) 87,000 (8,210,000); petroleum products (2000) 1,062,000 (1,567,000). Population economically active (1999): total 11,590,000; activity rate of total population 60.5% (participation rates: over age 15 [1984] 82.5%; female 51.1%.). Tourism (2002): receipts $358,000,-000; expenditures $120,000,000. Land use as % of total land area (2000): in temporary crops 15.9%, in permanent crops 9.7%, in pasture 36.7%; overall forest area 27.8%.

Foreign trade

Imports (2000-f.o.b. in balance of trade and c.i.f. for commodities and trading partners): $2,933,000,000 (crude and refined petroleum 18.9%, machinery and apparatus 18.8%, road vehicles 11.6%, food 10.9%). *Major import sources:* Nigeria 10.9%; UK 9.2%; US 7.5%; Germany 7.1%; The Netherlands 6.3%; Italy 5.0%. Exports (2000): $1,671,000,000 (gold 36.7%, cocoa beans 15.5%, aluminum 9.1%, sawn wood 4.9%). *Major export destinations:* Switzerland 23.5%; UK 18.9%; The Netherlands 11.2%; US 5.9%; Germany 5.4%.

Transport and communications

Transport. *Railroads* (2000): route length 953 km; (1996) passenger-km 209,000,000; (1996) metric ton-km cargo 160,000,000. *Roads* (1996): total length 38,700 km (paved 40%). *Vehicles* (1999): passenger cars 90,400; trucks and buses 119,900. *Air transport* (2003; Ghana Airways only): passenger-km 906,000,000; metric ton-km cargo 16,630,000; airports (1996) with scheduled flights 1. Communications, in total units (units per 1,000 persons). Daily newspaper circulation (2000): 273,000 (14); radios (2000): 13,900,000 (710); televisions (2000): 2,300,000 (118); telephone main lines (2003): 302,300 (14); cellular telephone subscribers (2003):

799,900 (36); personal computers (2002): 82,000 (3.8); Internet users (2002): 170,000 (7.8).

Education and health

Educational attainment (1984). Percentage of population age 25 and over having: no formal schooling 60.4%; primary education 7.1%; middle school 25.4%; secondary 3.5%; vocational and other postsecondary 2.9%; higher 0.6%. Literacy (2000): total population age 15 and over literate 8,070,000 (70.2%); males literate 4,520,000 (79.8%); females literate 3,550,000 (61.2%). Health: physicians (1996) 1,058 (1 per 16,129 persons); hospital beds (1998) 26,991 (1 per 667 persons); infant mortality rate per 1,000 live births (2003) 53.0. Food (2002): daily per capita caloric intake 2,667 (vegetable products 95%, animal products 5%); 116% of FAO recommended minimum.

Military

Total active duty personnel (2003): 7,000 (army 71.4%, navy 14.3%, air force 14.3%). Military expenditure as percentage of GNP (1999): 0.8% (world 2.4%); per capita expenditure $3.

Background

The modern state of Ghana is named after the ancient Ghana empire that flourished until the 13th century AD in the western Sudan, about 500 mi (800 km) northwest of the modern state. The Akan peoples then founded their first states in modern Ghana. Gold-seeking Mande traders arrived by the 14th century, and Hausa merchants arrived by the 16th century. During the 15th century the Mande founded the states of Dagomba and Mamprussi in the northern half of the region. The Ashanti, an Akan people, originated in the central forest region and formed a strongly centralized empire that was at its height in the 18th and 19th centuries. European exploration of the region began early in the 15th century, when the Portuguese landed on the Gold Coast; they later established a settlement at Elmina as headquarters for the slave trade. By the mid-18th century the Gold Coast was dominated by numerous forts controlled by Dutch, British, and Danish merchants. Britain made the Gold Coast a crown colony in 1874, and British protectorates over the Ashanti and the northern territories were established in 1901. In 1957 the Gold Coast became the independent state of Ghana. Since independence, numerous political coups have occurred, but that of 1981 produced a government that lasted through the 1990s.

Recent Developments

Turnout was massive for Ghana's elections on 7 Dec 2004, with more than 80% of eligible voters going to the polls. Pres. John Agyekum Kufuor won reelection, garnering nearly 53% of the vote. Despite earlier reports of registration problems, observers said the vote was "transparent and in good order." Accra played host to peace talks and a cease-fire agreement between the Côte d'Ivoire government and warring factions in July.

Internet resources:
<www.africaonline.com.gh/Tourism>.

Greece

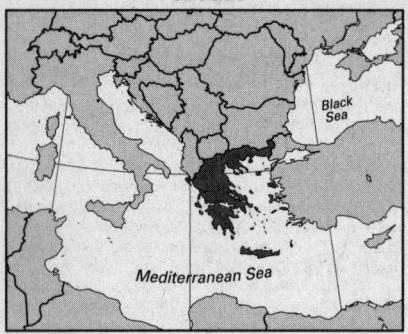

Official name: Elliniki Dhimokratia (Hellenic Republic). **Form of government:** unitary multiparty republic with one legislative house (Greek Chamber of Deputies [300]). **Chief of state:** President Karolos Papoulias (from 12 Mar 2005). **Head of government:** Prime Minister Konstantinos (Kostas) Karamanlis (from 10 Mar 2004). **Capital:** Athens. **Official language:** Greek. **Official religion:** Eastern Orthodox. **Monetary unit:** 1 euro (€) = 100 cents; valuation (7 Jul 2005) $1 = €0.84; at conversion on 1 Jan 2002, €1 = 340.75 Greek drachma (Dr).

Demography

Area: 50,949 sq mi, 131,957 sq km. **Population** (2004): 11,015,000. **Density** (2004): persons per sq mi 216.2, persons per sq km 83.5. **Urban** (2002): 60.3%. **Sex distribution** (2001): male 49.49%; female 50.51%. **Age breakdown** (2002): under 15, 15.2%; 15–29, 22.0%; 30–44, 22.3%; 45–59, 18.0%; 60–74, 16.5%; 75 and over, 6.0%. **Ethnic composition** (2000): Greek 90.4%; Macedonian 1.8%; Albanian 1.5%; Turkish 1.4%; Pomak 0.9%; Roma (Gypsy) 0.8%; other 3.2%. **Religious affiliation** (1995): Christian 95.2%, of which Eastern Orthodox 94.0%, Roman Catholic 0.5%; Muslim 1.3%; other 3.5%. **Major cities** (2001): Athens 745,514 (urban agglomeration 3,120,000); Thessaloniki 363,987 (urban agglomeration [2000] 789,000); Piraeus (Piraievs) 175,697 (within Athens urban agglomeration); Patrai 163,446; Peristerion 137,918 (within Athens urban agglomeration); Iraklion 137,711. **Location:** southern Europe, bordering Albania, Macedonia, Bulgaria, Turkey, and the Mediterranean Sea.

Vital statistics

Birth rate per 1,000 population (2003): 9.7 (world avg. 21.3); (2001) legitimate 95.7%. **Death rate** per 1,000 population (2003): 10.0 (world avg. 9.1). **Natural increase rate** per 1,000 population (2003): –0.3 (world avg. 12.2). **Total fertility rate** (avg. births per childbearing woman; 2002): 1.3. **Marriage rate** per 1,000 population (2001): 5.7. **Life expectancy** at birth (2003): male 76.3 years; female 81.4 years.

National economy

Budget (2001). *Revenue:* Dr 20,596,049,000,000 (indirect taxes 31.9%; direct taxes 22.5%; nontax

revenue 28.9%; other 16.7%). *Expenditures:* Dr 20,596,049,000,000 (current expenditure 86.9%, of which health and social insurance 10.3%, education and culture 6.8%, defense 6.8%; capital expenditure 13.1%). **Public debt** (2001): $116,870,000,000. **Production** (metric tons except as noted). *Agriculture, forestry, fishing* (2002): sugar beets 2,780,000, wheat 2,033,000, corn (maize) 2,014,000; livestock (number of live animals) 9,205,000 sheep, 5,023,000 goats, 938,000 pigs; roundwood (2001) 1,915,930 cu m; fish catch (2001) 192,190. *Mining and quarrying:* bauxite (2001) 1,931,000; crude magnesite 483,-000; marble 200,000 cu m. *Manufacturing* (value added in Dr '000,000,000; 1999): food 573; paints, soaps, varnishes, drugs, and medicines 371; electrical machinery 287. *Energy production (consumption):* electricity (kW-hr; 2000) 49,296,000,000 (49,285,-000,000); hard coal (2000) none (1,121,000); lignite (2000) 63,887,000 (64,564,000); crude petroleum (barrels; 2000) 183,800 (138,800,000); petroleum products (2000) 20,265,000 (16,667,000); natural gas (cu m; 2000) 49,280,000 (2,030,900,000). **Land use** as % of total land area (2000): in temporary crops 21.3%, in permanent crops 8.6%, in pasture 36.3%; overall forest area 27.9%. **Household income and expenditure.** Average household size (2000) 3.0; income per family (1998–99) Dr 6,429,000; sources of income (1998–99): wages and salaries 35.7%, transfer payments 16.7%, self-employment 14.9%, other 32.7%; expenditure (1999): food and beverages 24.9%, transportation and communications 14.3%, cafe/hotel expenditures 9.4%, housing 8.1%, household furnishings 7.3%. **Gross national product** (2003): $146,563,000,000 ($13,720 per capita). **Population economically active** (2001): total 4,362,300; activity rate of total population 42.1% (participation rates: ages 15–64, 56.9%; female 40.2%; unemployed 10.2%). **Tourism** (2002): receipts $9,741,000,000; expenditures $2,450,000,000.

Foreign trade

Imports (2000-c.i.f.): $29,816,000,000 (machinery and apparatus 18.6%, chemicals and chemical products 11.5%, crude petroleum 10.1%, road vehicles 9.5%, food products 9.1%, ships and boats 5.2%). *Major import sources:* Italy 12.9%; Germany 12.8%; France 7.2%; The Netherlands 5.8%; UK 5.0%. **Exports** (2000-f.o.b.): $10,964,000,000 (food 14.6%, of which fruits and nuts 6.0%; clothing and apparel 12.8%; refined petroleum 12.5%; machinery and apparatus 9.8%; aluminum 4.2%). *Major export destinations:* Germany 12.3%; Italy 9.2%; UK 6.3%; US 5.8%; Turkey 5.0%.

Transport and communications

Transport. *Railroads* (2000): route length 2,299 km; passenger-km 1,629,000,000; metric ton-km cargo 427,000,000. *Roads* (1999): total length 117,000 km (paved 92%). *Vehicles* (2001): passenger cars 3,423,704; trucks and buses 1,112,926. *Air transport* (2003: Olympic Airways): passenger-km 6,240,000,000; metric ton-km cargo 55,800,000; airports (1997) 36. **Communications,** in total units (units per 1,000 persons). Daily newspaper circulation (2000): 1,530,000 (140); radios (2000): 5,220,000 (478); televisions (2000): 5,330,000

1 metric ton = about 1.1 short tons;   1 kilometer = 0.6 mi (statute);   1 metric ton-km cargo = about 0.68 short ton-mi cargo;   c.i.f.: cost, insurance, and freight;   f.o.b.: free on board

(488); telephone main lines (2003): 5,205,100 (454); cellular telephone subscribers (2003): 8,936,200 (785); personal computers (2002): 900,000 (82); Internet users (2003): 1,718,400 (150).

Education and health

Educational attainment (2001). Percentage of population age 25 and over having: no formal schooling/preprimary 12.7%; primary education 34.3%; lower secondary 8.5%; upper secondary 25.7%; postsecondary 3.4%; incomplete and complete higher 15.4%. **Literacy** (2000): total population age 15 and over literate 97.2%; males 98.6%; females 96.0%. **Health:** physicians (2001) 46,325 (1 per 221 persons); hospital beds (2000) 49,804 (1 per 205 persons); infant mortality rate per 1,000 live births (2003) 5.7. **Food** (2001): daily per capita caloric intake 3,754 (vegetable products 78%, animal products 22%); 150% of FAO recommended minimum.

Military

Total active duty personnel (2003): 177,600 (army 70.7%, navy 10.7%, air force 18.6%). **Military expenditure as percentage of GNP** (1999): 4.7% (world 2.4%); per capita expenditure $573.

Did you know? Rhodes is the major city of the island of Rhodes and capital of the *nomos* (department) of Dhodhekanisos (in the Dodecanese islands), Greece. In Classical history, Rhodes was a maritime power and the site of the Colossus of Rhodes, a statue that was purportedly more than 100 ft (32 m) tall.

Background

The earliest urban society in Greece was the palace-centered Minoan civilization, which reached its height on Crete c. 2000 BC. It was succeeded by the mainland Mycenaean civilization, which arose c. 1600 BC following a wave of Indo-European invasions. In about 1200 BC a second wave of invasions destroyed the Bronze Age cultures, and a dark age followed, known mostly through the epics of Homer. At the end of this time, classical Greece began to emerge (c. 750 BC) as a collection of independent city-states, including Sparta in the Peloponnese and Athens in Attica. The civilization reached its zenith after repelling the Persians at the beginning of the 5th century BC and began to decline after the civil strife of the Peloponnesian War at the century's end. In 338 BC the Greek city-states were taken over by Philip II of Macedon, and Greek culture was spread by Philip's son Alexander the Great throughout his empire. The Romans, themselves heavily influenced by Greek culture, conquered the Greek states in the 2nd century BC. After the fall of Rome, Greece remained part of the Byzantine empire until the mid-15th century, when it became part of the expanding Ottoman Empire; it gained its independence in 1832. It was occupied by Nazi Germany during World War II. Civil war followed and lasted until 1949, when communist forces were defeated. In 1952 Greece joined NATO. A military junta ruled the country from 1967 to 1974, when democracy was restored and a referendum declared

an end to the Greek monarchy. In 1981 Greece joined the European Community, the first Eastern European country to do so. Upheavals in the Balkans in the 1990s strained Greece's relations with some neighboring states, notably the former Yugoslav entity that took the name Republic of Macedonia.

Recent Developments

In 2004 Greece not only saw significant political developments at home but was also in the international limelight as the host of the 2004 Olympic Games. On 7 March parliamentary elections brought an end to 11 years of rule by the Panhellenic Socialist Movement (PASOK) and the return to power of the center-right New Democracy (ND). With 45.4% of the vote, ND won 165 of the 300 mandates in the parliament, compared with 40.6% and 117 seats for PASOK. Throughout 2004 major infrastructure projects were completed. These included the world's longest (in total length) cable-stayed suspension bridge, which linked the Peloponnesus and western mainland Greece; suburban train, subway, and tram lines in Athens; road projects; and, of course, sport venues.

Internet resources: <www.gnto.gr>.

Greenland

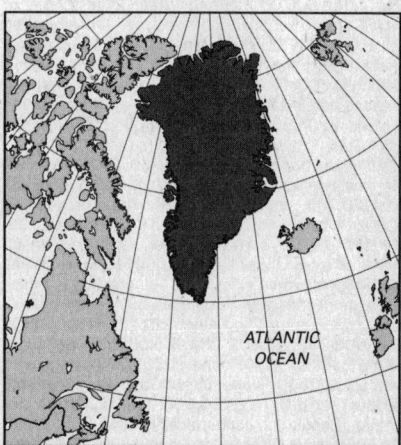

ATLANTIC OCEAN

Official name: Kalaallit Nunaat (Greenlandic); Grønland (Danish) (Greenland). **Political status:** integral part of the Danish realm with one legislative house (Parliament [31]). **Chief of state:** Danish monarch Queen Margrethe II (from 1972). **Heads of government:** High Commissioner (for Denmark) Peter Lauritzen (from 2002); Prime Minister (for Greenland) Hans Enoksen (from 2002). **Capital:** Nuuk (Godthåb). **Official languages:** Greenlandic; Danish. **Official religion:** Evangelical Lutheran (Lutheran Church of Greenland). **Monetary unit:** 1 Danish krone (Dkr) = 100 øre; valuation (7 Jul 2005) $1 = Dkr 6.25.

Demography

Area: 836,330 sq mi, 2,166,086 sq km. **Population** (2004): 56,800. **Density** (2004; ice-free areas only): persons per sq mi 0.36, persons per sq km 0.14.

Urban (2003): 82.2%. **Sex distribution** (2003): male 53.37%; female 46.63%. **Age breakdown** (2003): under 15, 26.2%; 15–29, 19.7%; 30–44, 27.9%; 45–59, 17.4%; 60–74, 7.5%; 75 and over, 1.3%. **Ethnic composition** (2000): Greenland Eskimo 79.1%; Danish 13.6%; other 7.3%. **Religious affiliation** (2000): Protestant 69.2%, of which Evangelical Lutheran 64.2%, Pentecostal 2.8%; other Christian 27.4%; other/nonreligious 3.4%. **Major towns** (2003): Nuuk (Godthåb) 13,884; Sisimiut (Holsteinsborg) 5,263; Ilulissat (Jakobshavn) 4,525. **Location:** North Atlantic Ocean, east of northern Canada.

Vital statistics

Birth rate per 1,000 population (2003): 16.1 (world avg. 21.3); (1993) legitimate 29.2%. **Death rate** per 1,000 population (2003): 7.7 (world avg. 9.1). **Natural increase rate** per 1,000 population (2003): 8.4 (world avg. 12.2). **Total fertility rate** (avg. births per childbearing woman; 2003): 2.4. **Marriage rate** per 1,000 population (1993): 7.1. **Life expectancy** at birth (2003): male 65.4 years; female 72.7 years.

National economy

Budget (2001). *Revenue:* Dkr 7,648,000,000 (block grant from Danish government 37.9%; income tax 30.5%; import duties 8.8%). *Expenditures* (2001): Dkr 7,069,000,000 (current expenditure 92.1%, of which social welfare 24.1%, culture and education 21.1%, health 11.9%, defense 3.7%; capital [development] expenditure 7.9%). **Public debt** (2000): $53,000,000. **Tourism** (2002): number of overnight stays at hotels 179,349, of which visitors from within Greenland 94,552, from Denmark 55,602, from the US 6,227. **Production** (metric tons except as noted). *Fishing, animal products:* fish catch (2001) 292,000 (by local boats 143,000, of which prawn 85,800, halibut 20,700, crab 14,200; by foreign boats 149,000); livestock (number of live animals; 2002) 18,967 sheep, 3,100 reindeer; animal products (value of external sales in Dkr '000; 1998) sealskins 31,044, polar bear skins 579. *Manufacturing:* principally handicrafts and fish processing. *Energy production (consumption):* electricity (kW-hr; 2002) 311,000,000 ([2001] 284,000,000); crude petroleum (barrels; 1999) none (1,307,000); petroleum products (2000) none (181,000). **Gross national product** (1998): $1,150,000,000 ($20,500 per capita). **Population economically active** (2002): total 31,506; activity rate of total population 55.7% (participation rates: ages 15–62, 82.9%; female [1987] 43.4%; unemployed [2002] 6.5%). **Households.** Average household size (1998): 2.6; income per person (1997): Dkr 144,700; expenditure (1994): food, beverages, and tobacco 41.6%, housing and energy 22.4%, transportation and communications 10.2%, recreation 6.4%. **Land use** as % of total land area (2000): in temporary crops, negligible, in pasture 0.6%; overall forest area, negligible.

Foreign trade

Imports (2002): Dkr 2,891,000,000 (goods for trades and industries 19.8%; food, beverages, and tobacco products 16.4%; goods for construction industry 14.8%; mineral fuels 8.9%; machinery 6.8%;

transport equipment 3.1%). *Major import sources:* Denmark 70%; Norway 8%. **Exports** (2002): Dkr 2,140,000,000 (marine products 88.4%, of which shrimp 55.7%, fish 20.6%, crab 10.1%). *Major export destinations:* Denmark 88%; US 4%; UK 2%.

Transport and communications

Transport. *Roads* (1998): total length 150 km (paved 60%). *Vehicles* (2001): passenger cars 2,485; trucks and buses 1,483. *Air transport* (2001; Air Greenland A/S only): passenger-km 211,000,000; metric ton-km cargo 24,000,000; airports (1998) with scheduled flights 18. **Communications,** in total units (units per 1,000 persons). Daily newspaper circulation (1996): 1,000 (18); radios (1997): 27,000 (482); televisions (1997): 22,000 (393); telephone main lines (2002): 25,300 (447); cellular telephone subscribers (2002): 17,700 (313); Internet users (2002): 9,100 (161).

Education and health

Literacy (1999): total population age 15 and over literate: virtually 100%. **Health** (2001): physicians 89 (1 per 634 persons); hospital beds 406 (1 per 139 persons); infant mortality rate per 1,000 live births (2003) 16.8.

Military

Total active duty personnel. Denmark is responsible for Greenland's defense. Greenlanders are not liable for military service.

 **Did you know?** Greenland is the world's largest island, covering 840,000 sq mi (2,175,600 sq km) and lying in the North Atlantic Ocean. Its deeply indented coastline is 24,430 mi (39,330 km) long, a distance roughly equivalent to the Earth's circumference at the Equator.

Background

The Inuit probably crossed to northwestern Greenland from North America, along the islands of the Canadian Arctic, from 4000 BC to AD 1000. The Norwegian Erik the Red visited Greenland in 982; his son, Leif Eriksson, introduced Christianity in the 11th century. Greenland came under joint Danish-Norwegian rule in the late 14th century. The original Norse settlements became extinct in the 15th century, but Greenland was recolonized by Denmark in 1721. In 1776 Denmark closed the Greenland coast to foreign trade; it was not reopened until 1950. Greenland became part of the kingdom of Denmark in 1953. Home rule was established in 1979.

Recent Developments

At a ceremony in Greenland, US Secretary of State Colin Powell, Danish Foreign Minister Per Stig Møller, and Greenland's local home-rule government minister Josef Motzfeldt signed a historic agreement granting

---

1 metric ton = about 1.1 short tons;   1 kilometer = 0.6 mi (statute);   1 metric ton-km cargo = about 0.68 short ton-mi cargo;   c.i.f.: cost, insurance, and freight;   f.o.b.: free on board

the US permission to upgrade its strategically important Thule Radar Station in Greenland as part of an expanded missile-defense program. Inuit who had been evicted from the region in 1953 took their fight to regain the land to the European Court of Human Rights in May 2004.

Internet resources: <www.greenland.com>.

Grenada

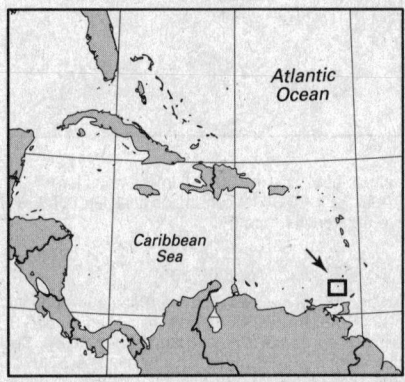

Official name: Grenada. **Form of government:** constitutional monarchy with two legislative houses (Senate [13]; House of Representatives [15, excluding the speaker]). **Chief of state:** Queen Elizabeth II (from 1952), represented by Governor-General Sir Daniel Williams (from 1996). **Head of government:** Prime Minister Keith Mitchell (from 1995). **Capital:** St. George's. **Official language:** English. **Official religion:** none. **Monetary unit:** 1 East Caribbean dollar (EC$) = 100 cents; valuation (7 Jul 2005) US$1 = EC$2.67.

Demography

Area: 133 sq mi, 344 sq km. **Population** (2004): 103,000. **Density** (2004): persons per sq mi 774.4, persons per sq km 299.4. **Urban** (2001): 38.4%. **Sex distribution** (2001): male 49.55%; female 50.45%. **Age breakdown** (2001): under 15, 35.1%; 15–29, 28.1%; 30–44, 17.6%; 45–59, 9.0%; 60 and over, 10.2%. **Ethnic composition** (2000): black 51.7%; mixed 40.0%; Indo-Pakistani 4.0%; white 0.9%; other 3.4%. **Religious affiliation** (1995): Roman Catholic 57.8%; Protestant 37.6%, of which Anglican 14.4%, Pentecostal 8.3%, Seventh-day Adventist 7.0%; other 4.6%, of which Rastafarian c. 3.0%. **Major localities** (2001): St. George's 3,908 (urban agglomeration 35,559); Gouyave (1991) 3,100; Grenville 2,300. **Location:** island between the Caribbean Sea and the Atlantic Ocean, north of Trinidad and Tobago.

Vital statistics

Birth rate per 1,000 population (2003): 22.9 (world avg. 21.3). **Death rate** per 1,000 population (2003): 7.5 (world avg. 9.1). **Natural increase rate** per 1,000 population (2003): 15.4 (world avg. 12.2). **Total fertility rate** (avg. births per childbearing woman; 2003): 2.5. **Marriage rate** per 1,000 population (2001): 5.0.

Divorce rate per 1,000 population (2001): 1.1. **Life expectancy** at birth (2003): male 62.7 years; female 66.3 years.

National economy

Budget (2000). *Revenue:* EC$297,900,000 (tax revenue 89.1%, of which tax on international trade 51.3%, general sales taxes 17.1%, income taxes 17.5%; grants from abroad 10.9%). *Expenditures:* EC$365,700,000 (current expenditure 63.0%, of which wages 31.3%, transfers 13.2%, debt 11.3%; capital expenditure 37.0%). **Public debt** (external, outstanding; 2002): US$268,700,000. **Tourism** (2002): receipts from visitors US$84,000,000; expenditures by nationals abroad US$8,000,000. **Gross national product** (at current market prices; 2003): US$396,000,000 (US $3,790 per capita). **Production** (metric tons except as noted). *Agriculture, forestry, fishing* (2002): sugarcane 7,200, coconuts 6,800, bananas 4,100; livestock (number of live animals) 13,100 sheep, 7,100 goats, 5,850 pigs; fish catch (2001) 2,247. *Mining and quarrying:* excavation of limestone, sand, and gravel for local use. *Manufacturing* (value of production in EC$'000; 1997): wheat flour 13,390; soft drinks 9,798; beer 7,072. *Energy production (consumption):* electricity (kW-hr; 2000) 118,000,000 (118,000,000); petroleum products (2000)* none (69,000). **Household income and expenditure.** Average household size (1991) 3.7; income per household (1988) EC$7,097; expenditure (1987): food, beverages, and tobacco 40.7%, household furnishings and operations 13.7%, housing 11.9%, transportation 9.1%. **Population economically active** (1998): total 41,015; activity rate of total population 46% (participation rate: ages 15–64, 78%; female 43.5%; unemployed 15.2%). **Land use** as % of total land area (2000): in temporary crops 3%, in permanent crops 29%, in pasture 3%; overall forest area 15%.

Foreign trade

Imports (2002-f.o.b. in balance of trade and c.i.f. for commodities and trading partners): US$233,200,000 (machinery and transport equipment 27.4%; food 16.6%; chemicals and chemical products 11.1%; mineral fuels 9.8%). *Major import sources:* US 45.8%; Caricom 25.6%; EU 12.5%, of which UK 6.0%; Venezuela 4.6%. **Exports** (2002): US$59,700,000 (domestic exports 92.1%, of which electronic components 39.2%, nutmeg 21.4%, fish 7.4%, paper products 2.5%, cocoa beans 2.3%; reexports 7.9%). *Major export destinations:* US 38.9%; EU 34.5%, of which UK 1.2%; Caricom 22.2%.

Transport and communications

Transport. *Roads* (1999): total length 1,040 km (paved 61%). *Vehicles* (1991): passenger cars 4,739; trucks and buses 3,068. *Air transport* (2001; Point Salines airport): passengers 331,000; cargo 2,747 metric tons; airports (1998) with scheduled flights 2. **Communications,** in total units (units per 1,000 persons). Radios (1997): 57,000 (615); televisions (1997): 33,000 (353); telephone main lines (2002): 33,500 (317); cellular telephone subscribers (2002): 7,600 (71); personal computers (2002): 14,000 (132); Internet users (2002): 15,000 (142).

Education and health

Educational attainment (1991). Percentage of population age 25 and over having: no formal schooling 1.8%; primary education 74.9%; secondary 15.5%; higher 4.7%, of which university 2.8%; other/unknown 3.1%. **Literacy** (1995): total population age 15 and over literate 50,000 (85.0%). **Health** (1999): physicians 81 (1 per 1,233 persons); hospital beds (2000) 623 (1 per 161 persons); infant mortality rate per 1,000 live births (2003) 14.6. **Food** (2002): daily per capita caloric intake 2,932 (vegetable products 74%, animal products 26%); 121% of FAO recommended minimum.

Military

Total active duty personnel (1997): a 730-member police force includes an 80-member paramilitary unit and a 30-member coast guard unit.

Background

The warlike Carib Indians dominated Grenada when Christopher Columbus sighted the island in 1498 and named it Concepción; they ruled it for the next 150 years. In 1674 it became subject to the French crown and remained so until 1762, when British forces captured it. In 1833 the island's black slaves were freed. Grenada was the headquarters of the government of the British Windward Islands 1885–1958 and a member of the West Indies Federation 1958–62. It became a self-governing state in association with Britain in 1967 and gained its independence in 1974. In 1979 a left-wing government took control in a bloodless coup. Relations with its US-oriented Latin American neighbors became strained as Grenada leaned toward Cuba and the Soviet bloc. In order to counteract this trend, the US invaded the island in 1983; democratic self-government was reestablished in 1984. Its relations with Cuba, once suspended, were restored in 1997.

Recent Developments

A South Korean delegation visited the country in June 2004 to assess investment opportunities and joint ventures, including possible exploration for oil and gas. In January 2005 it was announced that Grenada had established diplomatic relations with China—and severed ties with Taiwan—recognizing "one China."

Internet resources: <www.grenadagrenadines.com>.

Guadeloupe

Official name: Département de la Guadeloupe (Department of Guadeloupe). **Political status:** overseas department (France) with two legislative houses (General Council [42]; Regional Council [41]). **Chief of state:** President Jacques Chirac of France (from 1995). **Heads of government:** Commissioner of the Republic Paul Girot de Langlade (from 17 Aug 2004); President of the General Council Jacques Gillot (from 2001); President of the Regional Council Victorin Lurel (from 2 Apr 2004). **Capital:** Basse-Terre. **Official language:** French. **Official religion:** none. **Monetary**

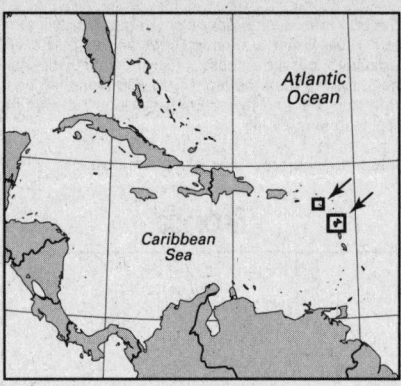

unit: 1 euro (€) = 100 centimes; valuation (7 Jul 2005) $1 = €0.84; at conversion on 1 Jan 2002, €1 = 6.56 French francs (F).

Demography

Area: 658 sq mi, 1,705 sq km. **Population** (2004): 443,000. **Density** (2004): persons per sq mi 673.3, persons per sq km 259.8. **Urban** (2001): 99.6%. **Sex distribution** (2002): male 47.93%; female 52.07%. **Age breakdown** (1999): under 15, 23.6%; 15–29, 22.4%; 30–44, 24.3%; 45–59, 15.7%; 60–74, 9.3%; 75 and over, 4.7%. **Ethnic composition** (2000): Creole (mulatto) 76.7%; black 10.0%; Guadeloupe mestizo (French–East Asian) 10.0%; white 2.0%; other 1.3%. **Religious affiliation** (1995): Roman Catholic 81.1%; Jehovah's Witness 4.8%; Protestant 4.7%; other 9.4%. **Major communes** (1999): Les Abymes 63,054 (within Pointe-à-Pitre urban agglomeration); Saint-Martin (Marigot) 29,078; Le Gosier 25,360 (within Pointe-à-Pitre urban agglomeration); Pointe-à-Pitre 20,948 (urban agglomeration 171,773); Basse-Terre 12,410 (urban agglomeration 54,076). **Location:** islands in the eastern Caribbean Sea, southeast of Puerto Rico.

Vital statistics

Birth rate per 1,000 population (2003): 16.2 (world avg. 21.3); (1997) legitimate 37.0%. **Death rate** per 1,000 population (2003): 6.0 (world avg. 9.1). **Natural increase rate** per 1,000 population (2003): 10.2 (world avg. 12.2). **Total fertility rate** (avg. births per childbearing woman; 2003): 1.9. **Marriage rate** per 1,000 population (2002): 4.1. **Divorce rate** per 1,000 population (1997): 1.3. **Life expectancy** at birth (2003): male 74.4 years; female 80.8 years.

National economy

Budget (1998). *Revenue:* F 4,227,000,000 (tax revenues 69.0%, of which direct taxes 42.5%, value-added taxes 25.1%; advances, loans, and transfers 26.8%). *Expenditures:* F 7,874,000,000 (current expenditures 70.6%, capital [development] expenditures 10.6%; advances and loans 18.8%). **Production** (metric tons except as noted). *Agriculture, forestry, fishing* (2002): sugarcane 798,072, bananas

1 metric ton = about 1.1 short tons;   1 kilometer = 0.6 mi (statute);   1 metric ton-km cargo = about 0.68 short ton-mi cargo;   c.i.f.: cost, insurance, and freight;   f.o.b.: free on board

135,000, yams 10,032; livestock (number of live animals) 85,000 cattle, 28,000 goats; roundwood (2001) 15,300 cu m; fish catch (2001) 10,114. *Mining and quarrying* (2000): pumice 210,000. *Manufacturing* (2002): cement 284,000; raw sugar 51,726; rum 67,151 hectoliters. *Energy production (consumption):* electricity (kW-hr; 2000) 1,220,000,000 (1,220,000,000); petroleum products (2000) none (497,000). **Land use** as % of total land area (2000): in temporary crops 11%, in permanent crops 4%, in pasture 14%; overall forest area 48%. **Population economically active** (1999): total 191,362; activity rate of total population 45.3% (participation rates: ages 15–64 [1995] 73.2%; female 49.1%; unemployed [2003] 24.1%). **Gross national product** (2000): $6,148,000,000 ($14,370 per capita). **Household income and expenditure.** Average household size (1999) 2.9; disposable income per household (1999) €26,938; sources of income (1988): wages and salaries 78.9%, self-employment 12.7%, transfer payments 8.4%; expenditure (1994–95): housing 26.2%, food and beverages 21.4%, transportation and communications 14.1%, household durables 6.0%, culture and leisure 4.2%. **Tourism** (2000): receipts from visitors $418,000,000.

Foreign trade

Imports (2001): €1,835,000,000 (food and agriculture products 19.8%, consumer goods 18.6%, machinery and equipment 15.8%). *Major import sources* (1998): France 63.4%; Germany 4.4%; Italy 3.5%; Martinique 3.4%; US 2.9%. **Exports** (2001): €169,000,000 (food and agricultural products 58.4% [including bananas, sugar, rum, melons, eggplant, and flowers]). *Major export destinations* (1998): France 68.5%; Martinique 9.4%; Italy 4.8%; Belgium-Luxembourg 3.3%; French Guiana 3.0%.

Transport and communications

Transport. *Roads* (1998): total length 3,415 km (paved [1986] 80%). *Vehicles* (1999): passenger cars 117,700; trucks and buses 31,400. *Air transport* (2002): passenger arrivals and departures 1,807,400; cargo handled 16,179 metric tons, cargo unloaded 5,204 metric tons; airports (1997) with scheduled flights 7. **Communications**, in total units (units per 1,000 persons). Daily newspaper circulation (1995): 35,000 (81); radios (1997): 113,000 (258); televisions (1999): 118,000 (262); telephone main lines (2001): 210,000 (457); cellular telephone subscribers (2002): 323,500 (697); personal computers (2001): 100,000 (217); Internet users (2001): 20,000 (43).

Education and health

Educational attainment (1990). Percentage of population age 25 and over having: incomplete primary, or no declaration 59.8%; primary education 14.5%; secondary 19.0%; higher 6.7%. **Literacy** (1992): total population age 15 and over literate 225,400 (90.1%); males literate 108,700 (89.7%); females literate 116,700 (90.5%). **Health** (2001): physicians 835 (1 per 515 persons); hospital beds 2,435 (1 per 177 persons); infant mortality rate per 1,000 live births (2003) 9.1. **Food** (1995): daily per capita caloric intake 2,732 (vegetable products 75%, animal products 25%); 129% of FAO recommended minimum.

Military

Total active duty personnel (2003): French troops in Antilles (Guadeloupe and Martinique) 4,100.

Background

The Carib Indians held off the Spanish and French for a number of years before the islands of Guadeloupe became part of France in 1674. The British occupied Guadeloupe for short periods in the 18th and 19th centuries; the islands became officially French in 1816. In 1946 Guadeloupe was made an overseas territory of France. Tourism has benefited the economy in recent decades.

Recent Developments

Until a 7 Dec 2003 referendum, Guadeloupe administered Saint-Martin (the French part of the island of Saint Martin; Dutch Sint Maarten occupies the other part) and Saint-Barthélemy. The vote was in favor of separate status with France, as distinct from being subprefectures of Guadeloupe. Meanwhile, Guadeloupe and Martinique rejected Paris's proposed merger of their regional and general councils.

Internet resources: <www.guadeloupe-info.com>.

Guam

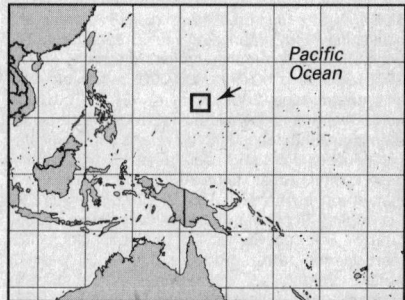

Pacific Ocean

Official name: Teritorion Guam (Chamorro); Territory of Guam (English). **Political status:** self-governing, organized, unincorporated territory of the US with one legislative house (Guam Legislature [15]). **Chief of state:** President of the US George W. Bush (from 2001). **Head of government:** Governor Felix Camacho (from 2003). **Capital:** Hagåtña (Agana). **Official languages:** Chamorro; English. **Official religion:** none. **Monetary unit:** 1 US dollar ($) = 100 cents.

Demography

Area: 209 sq mi, 541 sq km. **Population** (2004): 165,000. **Density** (2004; based on land area): persons per sq mi 789.5, persons per sq km 305.0. **Urban** (2003): 93.7%. **Sex distribution** (2000): male 51.15%; female 48.85%. **Age breakdown** (2000): under 15, 30.5%; 15–29, 24.1%; 30–44, 23.3%; 45–59, 13.9%; 60–74, 6.7%; 75 and over, 1.5%. **Ethnic composition** (2000): Pacific Islander 44.6%, of which Chamorro 37.0%; Asian 32.5%, of which Filipino 26.3%, Korean 2.5%; white 6.8%; black 1.0%; mixed 13.9%; other 1.2%. **Religious affiliation**

(1995): Roman Catholic 74.7%; Protestant 12.8%; other Christian 2.4%; other 10.1%. **Major populated places** (2000): Tamuning 10,833; Mangilao 7,794; Yigo 6,391; Astumbo 5,207; Hagåtña 1,122. **Location:** Oceania, island in the North Pacific Ocean, south of the Northern Mariana Islands.

Vital statistics

Birth rate per 1,000 population (2003): 19.7 (world avg. 21.3); (2000) legitimate 45.4%. **Death rate** per 1,000 population (2003): 4.3 (world avg. 9.1). **Natural increase rate** per 1,000 population (2002): 15.4 (world avg. 12.2). **Total fertility rate** (avg. births per childbearing woman; 2003): 2.6. **Marriage rate** per 1,000 population (2000): 9.7. **Divorce rate** per 1,000 population (2000): 4.0. **Life expectancy** at birth (2003): male 74.8 years; female 81.0 years.

National economy

Budget (2001). *Revenue:* $662,994,000 (local taxes 63.6%, federal contributions 27.4%, other 9.0%). *Expenditures:* $518,433,000 (current expenditures 91.6%, capital expenditures 8.4%). **Production.** *Agriculture, forestry, fishing* (value of production in $'000; 2000): long beans 234, cucumbers 166, watermelons 106; livestock (number of live animals [2002]) 200,000 poultry, 5,000 pigs, 680 goats; fish catch (metric tons; 2001) 507, value of aquaculture production (1996) $1,442,000. *Mining and quarrying:* sand and gravel. *Manufacturing* (value of sales in $'000; 2002): food processing 26,733; printing and publishing 7,382; fabricated metal products 4,052. *Energy production (consumption):* electricity (kW-hr; 2000) 830,000,000 (830,000,000); petroleum products (metric tons; 2000) none (1,327,000). **Households.** Average household size (2000) 3.9 (excludes US military and dependents); average annual income per household $38,983 (excludes US military and dependents). **Gross domestic product** (at current market prices; 2000): $3,419,920,000 ($22,120 per capita). **Population economically active** (2001): total 64,800; activity rate of total population 42% (participation rates: over age 15, 55.8%; female 45.1%; unemployed [September 2001] 13.5%). **Tourism** (1999): receipts from visitors $1,908,-000,000. **Land use** as % of total land area (2000): in temporary crops 9%, in permanent crops 16%, in pasture 15%; overall forest area 38%.

Foreign trade

Imports (2001): $503,000,000 (food products and nonalcoholic beverages 32%; leather products including footwear 20%; motor vehicles and parts 12%; clothing 8%). *Major import sources:* significantly US and Japan. **Exports** (2001): $60,800,000 (food products 52.2%, of which fish 51.4%; petroleum and natural gas products 6.2%; perfumes and colognes 6.0%; tobacco products 5.8%). *Major export destinations:* Japan 50.0%; Palau 9.4%; Federated States of Micronesia 9.1%; Hong Kong 7.4%; Taiwan 4.7%.

Transport and communications

Transport. *Roads* (1999): total length 885 km (paved 76%). *Vehicles* (2001): passenger cars 64,018;

trucks and buses 28,322. *Air transport* (2003; Continental Micronesia only): passenger-km 3,697,-000,000; metric ton-km cargo 61,256,000; airports with scheduled flights 1. **Communications,** in total units (units per 1,000 persons). Daily newspaper circulation (1996): 28,000 (178); radios (1997): 221,000 (1,400); televisions (1997): 106,000 (668); telephone main lines (2002): 76,425 (478); cellular telephone subscribers (2001): 32,600 (207); Internet users (2002): 50,000 (313).

Education and health

Educational attainment (2000). Percentage of population age 25 and over having: no formal schooling to some secondary education 23.7%; completed secondary 31.9%; some higher 24.5%; undergraduate 15.3%; advanced degree 4.6%. **Literacy:** virtually 100%. **Health** (1999): physicians 130 (1 per 1,169 persons); hospital beds 192 (1 per 792 persons); infant mortality rate per 1,000 live births (2003) 7.4.

Military

Total active duty US personnel (2003): 3,293 (army 1.2%; navy 45.5%; air force 53.3%).

Background

Possibly visited by Ferdinand Magellan in 1521, Guam was formally claimed by Spain in 1565. It remained Spanish until it was ceded to the US after the Spanish-American War in 1898. During World War II the Japanese occupied the island (1941–44). It subsequently became a major US air and naval base. In 1950 it was made a US territory.

Recent Developments

Typhoon Pongsana devastated Guam in December 2002, and the island was declared a disaster area in July 2004 following Cyclone Tingting. The government sought compensatory funds from the US for the collateral effects of new Compacts of Free Association reached between the US and the former Trust Territories, especially in regard to costs incurred by migration to Guam from those countries.

Internet resources: <http://ns.gov.gu>.

Guatemala

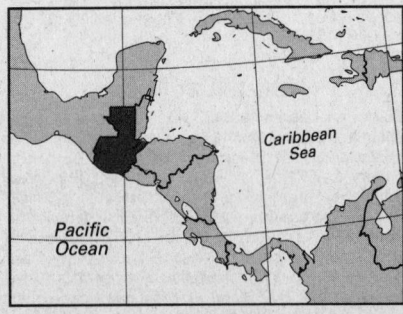

Official name: República de Guatemala (Republic of Guatemala). **Form of government:** republic with one legislative house (Congress of the Republic [158]). **Head of state and government:** President Óscar Berger Perdomo (from 14 Jan 2004). **Capital:** Guatemala City. **Official language:** Spanish. **Official religion:** none. **Monetary unit:** 1 quetzal (Q) = 100 centavos; valuation (7 Jul 2005) $1 = Q 7.60.

Demography

Area: 42,130 sq mi, 109,117 sq km. **Population** (2004): 12,661,000. **Density** (2004): persons per sq mi 300.5, persons per sq km 116.0. **Urban** (2003): 46.3%. **Sex distribution** (2003): male 50.67%; female 49.33%. **Age breakdown** (2003): under 15, 42.9%; 15–29, 27.8%; 30–44, 15.6%; 45–59, 8.7%; 60–74, 4.0%; 75 and over, 1.0%. **Ethnic composition** (2000): mestizo 63.7%; Amerindian 33.1%; black 2.0%; white 1.0%; other 0.2%. **Religious affiliation** (1995): Roman Catholic 75.9%, of which Catholic/traditional syncretist 25.0%; Protestant 21.8%; other 2.3%. **Major cities** (2002): Guatemala City 942,348 (urban agglomeration [2001] 3,366,000); Mixco 277,400 (within Guatemala City urban agglomeration); Villa Nueva 187,700 (within Guatemala City urban agglomeration); Quetzaltenango 106,700; Escuintla 65,400. **Location:** Central America, bordering Mexico, Belize, the Caribbean Sea, Honduras, El Salvador, and the Pacific Ocean.

Vital statistics

Birth rate per 1,000 population (2003): 35.1 (world avg. 21.3). **Death rate** per 1,000 population (2003): 6.8 (world avg. 9.1). **Natural increase rate** per 1,000 population (2003): 28.3 (world avg. 12.2). **Total fertility rate** (avg. births per childbearing woman; 2003): 4.7. **Marriage rate** per 1,000 population (1999): 5.5. **Life expectancy** at birth (2003): male 64.3 years; female 66.2 years.

National economy

Budget (2000). *Revenue:* Q 15,554,320,000 (tax revenue 96.9%, of which VAT 45.2%, income tax 23.7%; grants 2.2%; nontax revenue 0.9%). *Expenditures:* Q 18,220,750,000 (current expenditures 80.6%; capital expenditures 19.4%). **Public debt** (external, outstanding; 2002): $2,972,000,000. **Tourism** (2002): receipts from visitors $612,000,000; expenditures by nationals abroad $267,000,000. **Production** (metric tons except as noted). *Agriculture, forestry, fishing* (2003): sugarcane 17,500,000, corn (maize) 1,053,560, bananas 1,000,000; livestock (number of live animals) 2,540,000 cattle, 780,000 pigs, 27,000,000 chickens; roundwood (2001) 16,069,873 cu m; fish catch (2001) 14,300. *Mining and quarrying* (2001): gypsum 100,000; gold 4,500 kg; marble 3,800 cu m. *Manufacturing* (value added in Q '000,000; 1998): food and beverage products 298; clothing and textiles 119; machinery and metal products 55. *Energy production (consumption):* electricity (kW-hr; 2000) 6,048,000,000 (5,344,000,000); crude petroleum (barrels; 2000) 7,500,000 (6,600,000); petroleum products (2000) 820,000 (2,859,000); natural gas (cu m; 2000) 11,020,000 (11,020,000). **Household income and expenditure.** Average household size (2000) 4.5; income per household (1989) Q 4,306; expenditure (1981): food 64.4%, housing and energy 16.0%, transportation

and communications 7.0%, household furnishings 5.0%, clothing 3.1%. **Gross national product** (at current market prices; 2003): $23,486,000,000 ($1,910 per capita). **Population economically active** (1998–99): total 4,207,946; activity rate of total population 38.9% (participation rates: ages 15–64, 53.4%; female 36.2%; unemployed [1995] 1.4%). **Land use** as % of total land area (2000): in temporary crops 12.5%, in permanent crops 5.0%, in pasture 24.0%; overall forest area 26.3%.

Foreign trade

Imports (2000-f.o.b. in balance of trade and c.i.f. for commodities and trading partners): $4,882,000,000 (machinery and apparatus 22.1%, chemicals and chemical products 16.0%, crude and refined petroleum 11.0%, road vehicles 10.2%). *Major import sources:* US 39.7%; Mexico 11.7%; El Salvador 6.4%; Venezuela 5.4%; Costa Rica 4.1%. **Exports** (2000): $2,699,000,000 (agricultural products 52.1%, of which coffee 21.3%, sugar 7.1%, bananas 6.6%, spices 3.0%; crude petroleum 5.9%). *Major export destinations:* US 36.1%; El Salvador 12.6%; Honduras 8.6%; Costa Rica 4.7%; Mexico 4.5%.

Transport and communications

Transport. *Railroads* (2003): route length 784 km (mostly inoperable in 2003; no passenger service). *Roads* (1999): total length 14,118 km (paved 35%). *Vehicles* (1999): passenger cars 578,733; trucks and buses 53,236. *Air transport* (1998; Aviateca Airlines only): passenger-km 480,000,000; metric ton-km cargo 50,000,000; airports (1996) 2. **Communications,** in total units (units per 1,000 persons). Daily newspaper circulation (2000): 377,000 (33); radios (2000): 902,000 (79); televisions (2000): 697,000 (61); telephone main lines (2002): 846,000 (71); cellular telephone subscribers (2002): 1,577,100 (132); personal computers (2002): 173,000 (14); Internet users (2002): 400,000 (33).

Education and health

Educational attainment (1994). Percentage of population age 25 and over having: no formal schooling 45.2%; incomplete primary education 20.8%; complete primary 18.0%; some secondary 4.8%; secondary 7.2%; higher 4.0%. **Literacy** (2002): total population age 15 and over literate 69.9%; males literate 77.3%; females literate 62.5%. **Health** (2003): physicians 11,700 (1 per 1,053 persons); hospital beds (2002) 6,000 (1 per 2,000 persons); infant mortality rate per 1,000 live births 37.9. **Food** (2001): daily per capita caloric intake 2,203 (vegetable products 91%, animal products 9%); 101% of FAO recommended minimum.

Military

Total active duty personnel (2003): 31,400 (army 93.0%, navy 4.8%, air force 2.2%). **Military expenditure as percentage of GNP** (1999): 0.7% (world 2.4%); per capita expenditure $10.

Background

From simple farming villages dating to 2500 BC, the Maya of Guatemala and the Yucatan developed an impressive civilization. The civilization of the Maya declined after AD 900, and the Spanish began the subjugation of their descendants in 1523. The Central American colonies declared independence from Spain in Guatemala City in 1821, and Guatemala became part of the Mexican Empire until its collapse in 1823. In 1839 Guatemala became an independent republic under the first of a series of dictators who held power almost continuously for the next century. In 1945 a liberal-democratic coalition came to power and instituted sweeping reforms. Attempts to expropriate land belonging to US business interests prompted the US government in 1954 to sponsor an invasion. In the following years Guatemala's social revolution came to an end and most of the reforms were reversed. Chronic political instability and violence thenceforth marked Guatemalan politics; most of the 200,000 deaths that resulted were blamed on government forces. In 1991 the country abandoned its long-standing claims of sovereignty over Belize, and the two established diplomatic relations. It continued to experience violence as guerrillas sought to seize power. A peace treaty was signed in 1996, and the country started slowly to recover from its civil war.

Recent Developments

Newly inaugurated Guatemalan Pres. Óscar Berger promised in 2004 to increase productivity and create jobs in a country where 60% of the population lived in poverty. He also formally recognized the government's responsibility for much of the country's violence by compensating peasants for lands and lives lost during the civil war (1961–96). Nonetheless, murder, violence against women, kidnappings, land conflicts, and violations of human rights continued. Guatemala signed the Central American Free Trade Agreement and also took the lead in a new customs union that would integrate the Central American economies more fully.

Internet resources: <www.terra.com.gt/turismogt>.

Guernsey

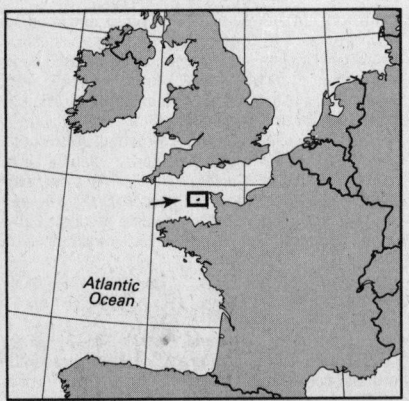

Data exclude Guernsey dependencies (particularly Alderney and Sark) unless otherwise indicated. **Official**

name: Bailiwick of Guernsey. **Political status:** crown dependency (UK) with one legislative house (States of Deliberation [51; includes ex officio members and two representatives from Alderney]); Alderney and Sark have their own parliaments. **Chief of state:** Queen Elizabeth II (from 1952), represented by Lieutenant Governor Sir John Foley (from 2000). **Head of government:** the government of Guernsey is conducted by committees appointed by the States of Deliberation. **Capital:** St. Peter Port. **Official language:** English. **Monetary unit:** 1 Guernsey pound (equivalent to pound sterling) = 100 pence; valuation (7 Jul 2005) $1 = 0.57 Guernsey pound.

Demography

Area: 30.2 sq mi, 78.1 sq km (including areas of Guernsey dependencies, of which Alderney 3.1 sq mi [7.9 sq km], Sark 1.6 sq mi [4.2 sq km], others 1.2 sq mi [3.0 sq km]). **Population** (2004; includes Alderney, Sark, and other dependencies): 63,300. **Density** (2004; includes Alderney, Sark, and other dependencies): persons per sq mi 2,096.0, persons per sq km 810.5. **Urban** (2003; includes Jersey): 30.5%. **Sex distribution** (2001): male 48.72%; female 51.28%. **Age breakdown** (2001): under 15, 17.2%; 15–29, 18.8%; 30–44, 23.2%; 45–59, 20.0%; 60–74, 13.4%; 75 and over, 7.4%. **Population by place of birth** (2001): Guernsey 64.3%; UK 27.4%; Portugal 1.9%; Jersey 0.7%; Ireland 0.7%; Alderney 0.2%; Sark 0.1%; other Europe 3.2%; other 1.5%. **Religious affiliation** (1990): Anglican 65.2%; other 34.8%. **Major cities** (2001; pop. of parish): St. Peter Port 16,488; Vale 9,573; Castel 8,975; St. Sampson 8,592; St. Martin 6,267. **Location:** western Europe, island in the English Channel, northwest of France.

Vital statistics

Birth rate per 1,000 population (2003): 9.4 (world avg. 21.3); (2000) legitimate 65.2%. **Death rate** per 1,000 population (2003): 9.8 (world avg. 9.1). **Natural increase rate** per 1,000 population (2002): −0.4 (world avg. 12.2). **Total fertility rate** (avg. births per childbearing woman; 2003): 1.4. **Marriage rate** per 1,000 population (2000): 5.7. **Divorce rate** per 1,000 population (2000): 2.9. **Life expectancy** at birth (2003): male 77.0 years; female 83.1 years.

National economy

Budget (1999). *Revenue:* £306,991,000 (income tax 79.7%, customs duties and excise taxes 5.7%, document duties 2.7%, corporation taxes 2.1%, automobile taxes 1.9%). *Expenditures:* £244,418,000 (welfare 31.1%, health 26.2%, education 15.9%, administrative services 6.7%, law and order 4.9%, community services 4.1%). **Gross national product** (at current market prices; 2002): $2,116,833,000 ($33,650 per capita). **Production** (metric tons except as noted). *Agriculture, forestry, fishing* (1999): tomatoes (1998) 2,449, flowers 1,154,000 boxes, of which roses 288,000 boxes, freesia 184,000 boxes, carnations 161,000 boxes; livestock (number of live animals) 3,262 cattle; fish catch (2001; includes Jersey): 4,414, of which crustaceans 2,169 (sea spiders and crabs 1,988), mollusks 1,456 (abalones, winkles, and conch 523), marine fish 789. *Manufactur-*

1 metric ton = about 1.1 short tons;   1 kilometer = 0.6 mi (statute);   1 metric ton-km cargo = about 0.68 short ton-mi cargo;   c.i.f.: cost, insurance, and freight;   f.o.b.: free on board

ing (1999): milk 98,830 hectoliters. *Energy production (consumption): electricity* (kW-hr; 1999–2000), n.a. (273,013,000). **Households.** Average household size (2001) 2.6; expenditure (1996): housing 21.6%, food 12.7%, household goods and services 11.2%, recreation services 9.2%, transportation 8.5%, clothing and footwear 5.6%, personal goods 4.9%, energy 4.1%. **Population economically active** (2001): total 32,293; activity rate of total population 51.5% (participation rates: ages 15–64, 80.4%; female 45.3%). **Tourism** (1996): receipts $275,000,000. **Land use** as % of total land area (1999): in pasture 37%; overall forest area 3%.

Foreign trade

Imports (1998): petroleum products are important. *Major import sources* (1998): mostly UK. **Exports** (1998): £93,000,000 (manufactured goods 51%, of which electronic components 18%, printed products 10%; agricultural products 42%, of which flowers 25%, plants 10%; fish, crustaceans, and mollusks 7%). *Major export destinations* (1998): mostly UK.

Transport and communications

Transport. *Vehicles* (2000): passenger cars 37,598; trucks and buses 7,338. *Air transport* (2001; Guernsey airport): passenger arrivals 429,076, passenger departures 430,254; cargo loaded 969 metric tons, cargo unloaded 3,557 metric tons; airports (1999) with scheduled flights 2 (includes one airport on Alderney). **Communications,** in total units (units per 1,000 persons). Daily newspaper circulation (1998): 15,784 (260); telephone main lines (2001): 55,000 (877); cellular telephone subscribers (2001): 31,500 (502); Internet users (2000): 20,000 (320).

Education and health

Literacy (2002): virtually 100%. **Health** (1999): physicians 93 (1 per 654 persons); infant mortality rate per 1,000 live births (2003) 4.9. **Food** (2002; data for the UK): daily per capita caloric intake 3,412 (vegetable products 69%, animal products 31%); 135% of FAO recommended minimum.

Military

Total active duty personnel: The UK is responsible for defense.

Guinea

Official name: République de Guinée (Republic of Guinea). **Form of government:** unitary multiparty republic with one legislative house (National Assembly [114 seats]). **Head of state and government:** President Lansana Conté (from 1984), assisted by Prime Minister Cellou Dalein Diallo (from 9 Dec 2004). **Capital:** Conakry. **Official language:** French. **Official religion:** none. **Monetary unit:** 1 Guinean franc (GF) = 100 cauris; valuation (7 Jul 2005) $1 = GF 3,675.00.

Demography

Area: 94,919 sq mi, 245,836 sq km. **Population** (2004): 8,620,000. **Density** (2004): persons per sq mi 90.8, persons per sq km 35.1. **Urban** (2003): 34.9%. **Sex distribution** (2003): male 49.95%; female

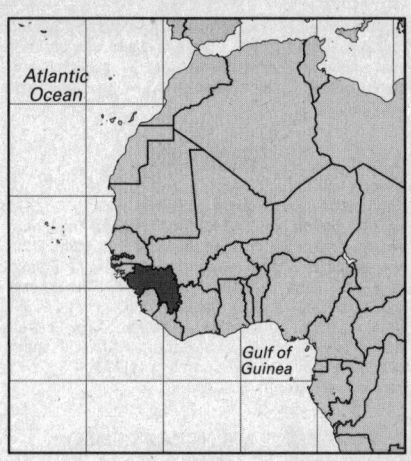

50.05%. **Age breakdown** (2003): under 15, 44.5%; 15–29, 26.4%; 30–44, 15.4%; 45–59, 8.7%; 60–74, 4.1%; 75 and over, 0.9%. **Ethnic composition** (1996): Fulani 38.6%; Malinke 23.2%; Susu 11.0%; Kissi 6.0%; Kpelle 4.6%; other 16.6%. **Religious affiliation** (1996): Muslim 85.0%; Christian 10.0%; other 5.0%. **Major cities** (2001): Conakry 1,565,200; Kankan 88,800; Labé 64,500; Kindia 56,000; Nzérékoré 55,000. **Location:** western Africa, bordering Guinea-Bissau, Senegal, Mali, Côte d'Ivoire, Liberia, Sierra Leone, and the North Atlantic Ocean.

Vital statistics

Birth rate per 1,000 population (2003): 42.5 (world avg. 21.3). **Death rate** per 1,000 population (2003): 15.7 (world avg. 9.1). **Natural increase rate** per 1,000 population (2003): 26.8 (world avg. 12.2). **Total fertility rate** (avg. births per childbearing woman; 2003): 5.9. **Life expectancy** at birth (2003): male 48.3 years; female 50.8 years.

National economy

Budget (2002). *Revenue:* GF 909,700,000,000 (tax revenue 76.2%, of which value-added tax 20.3%, mining sector 16.0%, tax on trade 15.3%, income tax 10.4%; grants 16.0%; nontax revenue 7.8%). *Expenditures:* GF 1,281,800,000 (current expenditure 61.5%, of which defense 14.4%, interest 8.2%; capital expenditure 38.5%). **Production** (metric tons except as noted). *Agriculture, forestry, fishing* (2003): cassava 1,150,000, rice 845,000, oil palm fruit 830,000; livestock (number of live animals) 3,285,-000 cattle, 1,201,000 goats, 13,500,000 chickens; roundwood 12,236,000 cu m; fish catch (2001) 90,000. *Mining and quarrying* (2001): bauxite 17,950,000; alumina 550,000; gold 13,000 kg. *Manufacturing* (2001): cement 300,000. *Energy production (consumption): electricity* (kW-hr; 2000) 569,000,000 (569,000,000); petroleum products (2000) none (373,000). **Households.** Average household size (2000) 4.0; expenditure (1985): food 61.5%, health 11.2%, clothing 7.9%, housing 7.3%. **Gross national product** (2003): $3,372,000,000 ($430 per capita). **Public debt** (external, outstanding; 2002): $2,972,000,000. **Population economically active** (2000): total 4,047,000; activity rate of total population 49.9%. **Tourism** (2002): receipts $43,000,-000; expenditures $31,000,000. **Land use** as % of total land area (2000): in temporary crops 3.6%, in permanent crops 2.4%, in pasture 43.5%; overall forest area 28.2%.

Foreign trade

Imports (2000-f.o.b. in balance of trade and c.i.f. for commodities and trading partners): $612,400,000 (refined petroleum 24.8%, food 18.0%, machinery and apparatus 10.0%, road vehicles 8.7%). *Major import sources* (2000): Côte d'Ivoire 21.4%; France 19.8%; US 7.9%; Belgium 7.7%; Japan 5.6%. **Exports** (2002): $700,400,000 (bauxite 43.6%, gold 20.5%, alumina 18.3%, diamonds 4.9%, fish 4.0%, coffee 2.5%). *Major export destinations* (2002): Spain 10.5%; Belgium 10.1%; Cameroon 10.1%; US 9.6%; France 7.4%; Germany 5.0%.

Transport and communications

Transport. *Railroads* (2000): route length of operational lines for cargo (mostly bauxite) transport 274 km; metric ton-km cargo (1993) 710,000,000. *Roads* (1999): total length 30,500 km (paved 16.5%). *Vehicles* (1996): passenger cars 14,100; trucks and buses 21,000. *Air transport* (1998): passenger-km 50,000,000; metric ton-km cargo 5,000,000; airports (2000) 1. **Communications,** in total units (units per 1,000 persons). Daily newspaper circulation (1988): 13,000 (2); radios (2000): 422,000 (52); televisions (2000): 357,000 (44); telephone main lines (2003): 26,200 (3.4); cellular telephone subscribers (2003): 111,500 (14); personal computers (2003): 43,000 (5.5); Internet users (2003): 40,000 (5.2).

Education and health

Educational attainment of those age 6 and over having attended school (1983): primary 55.2%; secondary 32.7%; vocational 3.4%; higher 8.7%. **Literacy** (2000): percentage of total population age 15 and over literate 41.0%; males literate 55.0%; females literate 27.0%. **Health:** physicians (1995) 920 (1 per 7,693 persons); hospital beds (1990) 3,700 (1 per 1,667 persons); infant mortality rate (2003) 93.3. **Food** (2001): daily per capita caloric intake 2,362 (vegetable products 96%, animal products 4%); 102% of FAO recommended minimum.

Military

Total active duty personnel (2003): 9,700 (army 87.7%, navy 4.1%, air force 8.2%). **Military expenditure as percentage of GNP** (1999): 1.6% (world 2.4%); per capita expenditure $7.

Did you know? Guinea's flag features three vertical stripes echoing France's red-white-blue *Tricouleur*, but with red, yellow, and green, the pan-African colors. Other African flags featuring these colors include Burkina Faso, Cameroon, Ethiopia, Ghana, Guinea-Bissau, and Mali.

Background

About AD 900 successive migrations of the Susu swept down from the desert and pushed the original inhabitants of Guinea, the Baga, to the Atlantic coast. Small kingdoms of the Susu rose in importance in the 13th century and later extended their rule to the coast. In the mid-15th century the Portuguese visited the coast and developed a slave trade. In the 16th century the Fulani established domination over the Fouta Djallon region; they ruled into the 19th century. In the early 19th century the French arrived and in 1849 proclaimed the coastal region a French protectorate. In 1895 French Guinea became part of the federation of French West Africa. In 1946 it was made an overseas territory of France, and in 1958 it achieved independence. Following a military coup in 1984, Guinea began implementing Westernized government systems. A new constitution was adopted in 1991, and the first multiparty elections were held in 1993. During the 1990s Guinea accommodated several hundred thousand war refugees from neighboring Liberia and Sierra Leone.

Recent Developments

Pres. Lansana Conté ran again for office in December 2003 despite his increasingly bad health. He won easily, with more than 90% of the vote, but the opposition parties boycotted the election. Opposition leader Sidya Touré was detained in late April 2004 on suspicion of being involved in a coup plot. Shots were fired at Conté on 19 Jan 2005 in what the president said was a coup attempt.

Internet resources: <www.mirinet.net.gn/ont>.

Guinea-Bissau

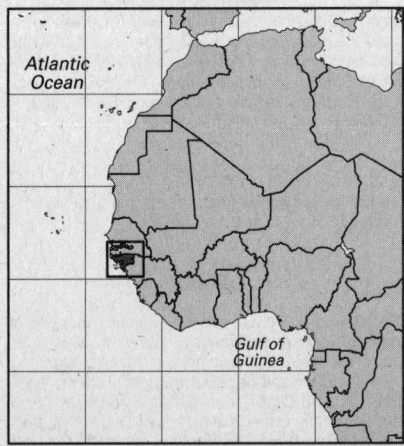

Official name: República da Guiné-Bissau (Republic of Guinea-Bissau). **Form of government:** multiparty republic (reestablished as of March 2004 legislative elections) (National People's Assembly [102]). **Chief of state:** President Henrique Rosa (interim; from

---

1 metric ton = about 1.1 short tons;   1 kilometer = 0.6 mi (statute);   1 metric ton-km cargo = about 0.68 short ton-mi cargo;   c.i.f.: cost, insurance, and freight;   f.o.b.: free on board

2003). **Head of government:** Prime Minister Carlos Gomes, Jr. (from 10 May 2004). **Capital:** Bissau. **Official language:** Portuguese. **Official religion:** none. **Monetary unit:** 1 CFA franc (CFAF) = 100 centimes; valuation (7 Jul 2005) $1 = CFAF 549.50 (formerly pegged to the French franc and since 1 Jan 2002 to the euro at €1 = CFAF 655.96).

Demography

Area: 13,948 sq mi, 36,125 sq km; area figures include water area of about 3,089 sq mi (8,000 sq km). **Population** (2004): 1,388,000. **Density** (2004; based on land area only): persons per sq mi 127.8, persons per sq km 49.4. **Urban** (2003): 34.0%. **Sex distribution** (2003): male 48.52%; female 51.48%. **Age breakdown** (2003): under 15, 41.9%; 15–29, 28.1%; 30–44, 15.9%; 45–59, 9.4%; 60–74, 4.0%; 75 and over, 0.7%. **Ethnic composition** (1996): Balante 30%; Fulani 20%; Mandyako 14%; Malinke 13%; Pepel 7%; nonindigenous Cape Verdean mulatto 2%; other 14%. **Religious affiliation** (2000): traditional beliefs 45.2%; Muslim 39.9%; Christian 13.2%, of which Roman Catholic 9.9%; other 1.7%. **Major cities** (1997): Bissau 200,000 (urban agglomeration [2003] 336,000); Bafatá 15,000; Cacheu 14,000; Gabú 10,000. **Location:** western Africa, bordering Senegal, Guinea, and the North Atlantic Ocean.

Vital statistics

Birth rate per 1,000 population (2003): 38.4 (world avg. 21.3). **Death rate** per 1,000 population (2003): 16.6 (world avg. 9.1). **Natural increase rate** per 1,000 population (2003): 21.8 (world avg. 12.2). **Total fertility rate** (avg. births per childbearing woman; 2003): 5.1. **Life expectancy** at birth (2003): male 45.1 years; female 48.9 years.

National economy

Budget (2001). *Revenue:* CFAF 47,530,000,000 (foreign grants 40.0%; tax revenue 31.0%, of which taxes on international trade 13.6%, general sales tax 7.3%; nontax revenue 29.0%, of which fishing licenses 15.6%). *Expenditures:* CFAF 63,162,000,000 (current expenditures 65.7%, of which scheduled external interest payments 19.4%; capital expenditures 34.3%). **Public debt** (external, outstanding; 2002): $662,100,000. **Production** (metric tons except as noted). *Agriculture, forestry, fishing* (2002): cashew nuts 80,000, oil palm fruit 80,000, rice 79,900; livestock (number of live animals) 515,000 cattle, 350,000 pigs, 325,000 goats; roundwood (1999) 592,000 cu m; fish catch (2001) 5,000. *Mining and quarrying:* extraction of construction materials only. *Manufacturing* (2000): processed wood 11,200; wood products 4,400; dried and smoked fish 3,500. *Energy production (consumption):* electricity (kW-hr; 2000) 58,000,000 (58,000,000); petroleum products (2000) none (88,000). **Population economically active** (1992): total 471,000; activity rate of total population 46.9% (participation rates [1991]: over age 10, 67.1%; female 40.5%). **Households.** Average household size (1996) 6.9. **Gross national product** (at current market prices; 2003): $202,000,000 ($140 per capita). **Land use** as % of total land area (2000): in temporary crops 10.7%, in permanent crops 8.8%, in pasture 38.4%; overall forest area 60.5%.

Foreign trade

Imports (2001-c.i.f.): $96,700,000 (foodstuffs 18.7%, of which rice 6.6%; transport equipment 13.2%; equipment and machinery 7.7%; fuel and lubricants 6.2%; unspecified 39.3%). *Major import sources:* Portugal 30.9%; Senegal 28.3%; China 11.3%; The Netherlands 6.8%; Japan 5.8%. **Exports** (2001-f.o.b.): $47,200,000 (cashews 95.6%; cotton 2.3%; logs 1.5%). *Major export destinations:* India 85.6%; Portugal 3.8%; Senegal 2.5%; France 1.7%.

Transport and communications

Transport. *Roads* (1999): total length 4,400 km (paved 10%). *Vehicles* (1996): passenger cars 7,120; trucks and buses 5,640. *Air transport* (1998): passenger-km 10,000,000; airports (1997) with scheduled flights 2. **Communications,** in total units (units per 1,000 persons). Daily newspaper circulation (2000): 6,390 (5); radios (2001): 56,200 (178); telephone main lines (2002): 10,600 (8.2); cellular telephone subscribers (2003): 1,300 (1); Internet users (2003): 19,000 (15).

Education and health

Literacy (1995): total population age 15 and over literate 54.9%; males literate 68.0%; females literate 42.5%. **Health:** physicians (1996) 193 (1 per 6,024 persons); hospital beds (1998) 1,832 (1 per 667 persons); infant mortality rate per 1,000 live births (2003) 110.3. **Food** (2002): daily per capita caloric intake 2,024 (vegetable products 93%, animal products 7%); 88% of FAO recommended minimum.

Military

Total active duty personnel (2003): 9,250 (army 73.5%, navy 3.8%, air force 1.1%, paramilitary [gendarmerie] 21.6%). **Military expenditure as percentage of GNP** (1999): 2.7% (world 2.4%); per capita expenditure $4.

Background

More than 1,000 years ago the coast of Guinea-Bissau was occupied by iron-using agriculturists. They grew irrigated and dry rice and were also the major suppliers of marine salt to the western Sudan. At about the same time, the region came under the influence of the Mali empire and became a tributary kingdom known as Gabú. After 1546 Gabú was virtually autonomous; vestiges of the kingdom lasted until 1867. The earliest overseas contacts came in the 15th century with the Portuguese, who imported slaves from the Guinea area to the offshore Cape Verde Islands. Portuguese control of Guinea-Bissau was marginal despite claims to sovereignty there. The end of the slave trade forced the Portuguese inland in search of new profits. Their subjugation of the interior was slow and sometimes violent; it was not effectively achieved until 1915, though sporadic resistance continued until 1936. Guerrilla warfare in the 1960s led to the country's independence in 1974, but political turmoil continued and the government was overthrown by a military coup in 1980. A new constitution was adopted in 1984, and the first multiparty elections were held in 1994. A destructive civil war in 1998 was followed by a military coup in 1999.

Recent Developments

In March 2004 12 political parties and three coalitions contested 102 seats in the National People's Assembly of Guinea-Bissau. The vote was a key step toward the restoration of civilian rule, for the winning party was to replace the interim government. The caretaker president, Henrique Pereira Rosa, would remain in power, however, until presidential elections that were held in June and July 2005. The African Party for the Independence of Guinea-Bissau and Cape Verde, which led the country for a quarter century after independence, gained the most seats, with former president Kumba Ialá's Social Renewal Party finishing second.

Internet resources: <www.bissau.com>.

Guyana

Official name: Co-operative Republic of Guyana. **Form of government:** unitary multiparty republic with one legislative house (National Assembly [65]). **Chief of state:** President Bharrat Jagdeo (from 1999). **Head of government:** Prime Minister Sam Hinds (from 1999). **Capital:** Georgetown. **Official language:** English. **Official religion:** none. **Monetary unit:** 1 Guyana dollar (G$) = 100 cents; valuation (7 Jul 2005) US$1 = G$175.01.

Demography

Area: 83,044 sq mi, 215,083 sq km (includes inland water area of c. 7,000 sq mi [18,000 sq km]). **Population** (2004): 752,000. **Density** (2003; based on land area only): persons per sq mi 9.9, persons per sq km 3.8. **Urban** (2003): 37.6%. **Sex distribution** (2002): male 49.30%; female 50.70%. **Age breakdown** (2002): under 15, 27.6%; 15–29, 31.0%; 30–44, 21.3%; 45–59, 12.8%; 60–74, 5.4%; 75 and over, 1.9%. **Ethnic composition** (1992–93): East Indian 49.4%; black (African Negro and Bush Negro) 35.6%; Amerindian 6.8%; Portuguese 0.7%; Chinese 0.4%; mixed 7.1%. **Religious affiliation** (1995): Christian 40.9%, of which Protestant 27.5% (including Anglican 8.6%), Roman Catholic 11.5%, Ethiopian Orthodox 1.1%; Hindu 34.0%; Muslim 9.0%; other 16.1%. **Major cities** (2002): Georgetown 137,330 (urban agglomeration [2003] 231,000); Linden 29,572; New Amsterdam (1997) 25,000; Corriverton (1997) 24,000. **Location:** northern South America, bordering the North Atlantic Ocean, Suriname, Brazil, and Venezuela.

Vital statistics

Birth rate per 1,000 population (2003): 18.7 (world avg. 21.3). **Death rate** per 1,000 population (2003): 8.5 (world avg. 9.1). **Natural increase rate** per 1,000 population (2003): 10.2 (world avg. 12.2). **Total fertility rate** (avg. births per childbearing woman; 2003): 2.1. **Life expectancy** at birth (2003): male 62.1 years; female 67.3 years.

National economy

Budget (1999): *Revenue:* G$36,544,000,000 (tax revenue 91.6%, of which consumption taxes 32.0%, income taxes on companies 22.2%, personal income taxes 15.5%, import duties 11.4%; nontax revenue 8.2%). *Expenditures:* G$41,983,000,000 (current expenditure 71.2%, of which debt charges 13.8%; development expenditure 28.8%). **Production** (metric tons except as noted). *Agriculture, forestry, fishing* (2002): rice 450,000, raw sugar (2001) 284,000, coconuts 45,000; livestock (number of live animals) 130,000 sheep, 100,000 cattle, 12,500,000 chickens; roundwood (2001) 1,188,000 cu m; fish catch (2003) 56,307, of which shrimps and prawns 22,584. *Mining and quarrying* (2003): bauxite 1,716,000; gold 357,000 troy oz; diamonds 413,000 carats. *Manufacturing* (2002): flour 36,570; rum 145,900 hectoliters; beer and stout 108,500 hectoliters. *Energy production (consumption):* electricity (kW-hr; 2000) 894,000,000 (894,000,000); petroleum products (2000) none (521,000). **Population economically active** (1997): total 263,807; activity rate of total population 33.9% (participation rates: ages 15–64 [1992] 59.5%; female 35.2%; unemployed 9.1%). **Gross national product** (2003): US$689,000,000 (US$900 per capita). **Public debt** (external, outstanding; 2003): US$1,084,000,000. **Households.** Average household size (2002) 4.0. **Tourism** (2002): receipts from visitors US$49,000,000; expenditures by nationals abroad US$38,000,000. **Land use** as % of total land area (2000): in temporary crops 2.4%, in permanent crops 0.2%, in pasture 6.2%; overall forest area 78.5%.

Foreign trade

Imports (2002-f.o.b. in balance of trade and commodities and c.i.f. for trading partners): US$563,-100,000 (consumer goods 28.0%, fuels and lubricants 22.3%, capital goods 20.1%). *Major import sources* (2001): US 24%; Netherlands Antilles 17%; Chile 16%; Trinidad and Tobago 13%; UK 6%. **Exports** (2002): US$494,900,000 (gold 27.5%, sugar 24.1%, shrimp 10.6%, rice 9.2%, timber 7.2%, bauxite 7.1%). *Major export destinations* (2001): US 22%; Canada 20%; UK 12%; Netherlands Antilles 12%; Belgium 5%.

---

1 metric ton = about 1.1 short tons;　1 kilometer = 0.6 mi (statute);　1 metric ton-km cargo = about 0.68 short ton-mi cargo;　c.i.f.: cost, insurance, and freight;　f.o.b.: free on board

Transport and communications

Transport. *Roads* (1999): total length 7,970 km (paved 7%). *Vehicles* (1995): passenger cars 24,000; trucks and buses 9,000. *Air transport* (1999; scheduled flights only): passenger-km 276,600,000; metric ton-km cargo 2,200,000; airports (2000) with scheduled international flights 1. **Communications**, in total units (units per 1,000 persons). Daily newspaper circulation (1996): 42,000 (54); radios (1997): 420,-000 (539); televisions (1999): 60,000 (77); telephone main lines (2002): 80,400 (92); cellular telephone subscribers (2002): 87,300 (99); personal computers (2002): 24,000 (27); Internet users (2002): 125,000 (142).

Education and health

Educational attainment (1980). Percentage of population age 25 and over having: no formal schooling 8.1%; primary education 72.8%; secondary 17.3%; higher 1.8%. **Literacy** (2002): total population age 15 and over literate 98.7%; males literate 99.0%; females literate 98.3%. **Health**: physicians (1999) 203 (1 per 3,846 persons); hospital beds (2002) 3,274 (1 per 229 persons); infant mortality rate per 1,000 live births (2003) 35.1. **Food** (2002): daily per capita caloric intake 2,692 (vegetable products 84%, animal products 16%); 119% of FAO recommended minimum.

Military

Total active duty personnel (2003): 1,600 (army 87.5%, navy 6.3%, air force 6.2%). **Military expenditure as percentage of GNP** (1999): 0.8% (world 2.4%); per capita expenditure $7.

Background

Guyana was colonized by the Dutch in the 17th century. During the Napoleonic Wars the British occupied the territory and afterward purchased the colonies of Demerara, Berbice, and Essequibo, united in 1831 as British Guiana. The slave trade was abolished in 1807, but emancipation of the 100,000 slaves in the colonies was not completed until 1838. From the 1840s East Indian and Chinese indentured servants were brought to work the plantations; by 1917 almost 240,000 East Indians had migrated to British Guiana. It was made a crown colony in 1928 and granted home rule in 1953. Political parties began to emerge, developing on racial lines as the People's Progressive Party (largely East Indian) and the People's National Congress (largely black). The PNC formed a coalition government and led the country into independence as Guyana in 1966. In 1970 Guyana became a republic within the Commonwealth; in 1980 it adopted a new constitution. Venezuela has long claimed land west of the Essequibo River, and the UN has continued to arbitrate the issue.

Recent Developments

In February 2004, Guyana formally referred its maritime border dispute with Suriname to the arbitration panel of the UN Convention on the Law of the Sea. The dispute had prevented Guyana from pursuing what was believed to be potentially lucrative oil deposits in the offshore Corentyne region.

Internet resources: <www.guyana.org>.

Haiti

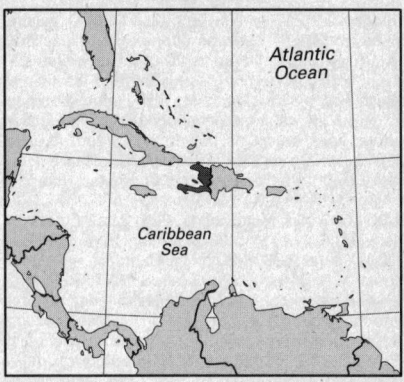

Atlantic Ocean

Caribbean Sea

Official name: Repiblik Dayti (Haitian Creole); République d'Haïti (French) (Republic of Haiti). **Form of government:** interim regime (from February 2004) with two legislative houses (Senate [27]; Chamber of Deputies [83]). **Chief of state:** President Boniface Alexandre (from 29 Feb 2004). **Head of government:** Prime Minister Gérard Latortue (from 12 Mar 2004). **Capital:** Port-au-Prince. **Official languages:** Haitian Creole; French. **Official religions:** Roman Catholicism has special recognition per concordat with the Vatican; voodoo became officially sanctioned per governmental decree of April 2003. **Monetary unit:** 1 gourde (G) = 100 centimes; valuation (7 Jul 2005) $1 = G 40.19.

Demography

Area: 10,695 sq mi, 27,700 sq km. **Population** (2004): 8,074,000. **Density** (2004): persons per sq mi 754.9, persons per sq km 291.5. **Urban** (2003): 37.5%. **Sex distribution** (2003): male 48.35%; female 51.65%. **Age breakdown** (2003): under 15, 42.7%; 15–29, 29.3%; 30–44, 14.2%; 45–59, 8.2%; 60–74, 4.5%; 75 and over, 1.1%. **Ethnic composition** (2000): black 94.2%; mulatto 5.4%; other 0.4%. **Religious affiliation** (1995): Roman Catholic 68.5% (about 80% of all Roman Catholics also practice voodoo); Protestant 24.1%, of which Baptist 5.9%, Pentecostal 5.3%, Seventh-day Adventist 4.6%; other 7.4%. **Major cities** (1999): Port-au-Prince 990,558 (metropolitan area [2003] 1,977,036); Carrefour 336,222 (within Port-au-Prince metropolitan area); Delmas 284,079 (within Port-au-Prince metropolitan area); Cap-Haïtien 113,555; Pétion-Ville (1997) 76,155 (within Port-au-Prince metropolitan area). **Location:** western third of the island of Hispaniola, between the North Atlantic Ocean and the Caribbean Sea.

Vital statistics

Birth rate per 1,000 population (2003): 36.7 (world avg. 21.3). **Death rate** per 1,000 population (2003): 12.7 (world avg. 9.1). **Natural increase rate** per 1,000 population (2003): 24.0 (world avg. 12.2). **Total fertility rate** (avg. births per childbearing woman; 2003): 5.2. **Life expectancy** at birth (2003): male 51.0 years; female 53.7 years. **Adult population** (ages 15–49) **living with HIV** (2004): 5.6% (world avg. 1.1%).

National economy

Budget (2002). *Revenue:* G 7,721,700,000 (general sales tax 31.3%; customs duties 26.8%; individual taxes on income and profits 20.5%). *Expenditures:* G 10,376,700,000 (current expenditure 81.6%, of which wages 33.6%, transfers 4.8%, interest on public debt 1.2%; capital expenditure 18.4%). **Production** (metric tons except as noted). *Agriculture, forestry, fishing* (2002): sugarcane 1,010,000, cassava (manioc) 335,000, bananas 295,000; livestock (number of live animals) 1,943,000 goats, 1,450,000 cattle, 1,001,000 pigs; roundwood (2001) 2,210,000 cu m; fish catch (2001) 5,000. *Mining and quarrying* (2001): sand 2,000,000 cu m. *Manufacturing* (value added in G '000,000; 2001 [at prices of 1986–87]): food and beverages 467.1; textiles, wearing apparel, and footwear 202.4; chemical and rubber products 62.8. *Energy production (consumption):* electricity (kW-hr; 2000) 635,000,000 (635,000,000); petroleum products (2000) none (463,000). **Land use** as % of total land area (2000): in temporary crops 28.3%, in permanent crops 11.6%, in pasture 17.8%; overall forest area 3.2%. **Population economically active** (2002): total 4,100,000; activity rate of total population 55% (participation rates: ages 15–64 [1990] 64.8%; female [1996] 43.0%; unemployed unofficially [1996] 60%). **Household income and expenditure.** Average household size (1982) 4.4; average annual income of urban wage earners (1984): G 1,545; expenditure (1996): food, beverages, and tobacco 49.4%, housing and energy 9.1%, transportation 8.7%, clothing and footwear 8.5%. **Public debt** (external, outstanding; 2002): $1,063,000,000. **Gross national product** (at current market prices; 2003): $3,214,000,000 ($380 per capita). **Tourism** (2001): receipts from visitors $54,000,000; expenditures by nationals abroad (1998) $37,000,000.

Foreign trade

Imports (2002-f.o.b. in balance of trade and c.i.f. in commodities and trading partners): $1,054,200,000 (food and live animals 22.4%, basic manufactures 19.9%, machinery and transport equipment 15.2%, petroleum and derivatives 14.9%). *Major import sources* (1999): US 60%; Dominican Republic 4%; Japan 3%; France 3%; Canada 3%. **Exports** (2002): $274,400,000 (reexports to US 80.8%, of which clothing and apparel 79.1%; mangoes 2.6%; cacao 2.0%; essential oils 1.5%; leather goods 1.1%). *Major export destinations* (1999): US 90%; Canada 3%; Belgium 2%; France 2%.

Transport and communications

Transport. *Roads* (1999): total length 4,160 km (paved 24%). *Vehicles* (1996): passenger cars 32,000; trucks and buses 21,000. *Air transport* (2000; Port-au-Prince Airport only): passenger arrivals and departures 924,000; cargo unloaded and loaded 15,300 metric tons; airports (1997) with scheduled flights 2. **Communications,** in total units (units per 1,000 persons). Daily newspaper circulation (2000): 21,500 (3); radios (2000): 395,000 (55); televisions (2000): 35,900 (5); telephone main lines (2002): 130,000 (16); cellular telephone subscribers (2002): 140,000 (17); Internet users (2002): 80,000 (9.6).

Education and health

Educational attainment (1986–87). Percentage of population age 25 and over having: no formal schooling 59.5%; primary education 30.5%; secondary 8.6%; vocational and teacher training 0.7%; higher 0.7%. **Literacy** (1995): total population age 15 and over literate 1,930,000 (45.0%); males literate 992,000 (48.0%); females literate 938,000 (42.2%). **Health:** physicians (1999) 1,910 (1 per 4,000 persons); hospital beds (1996) 5,241 (1 per 1,242 persons); infant mortality rate per 1,000 live births (2003) 77.0. **Food** (2002): daily per capita caloric intake 2,086 (vegetable products 93%, animal products 7%); 92% of FAO recommended minimum.

Military

Total active duty personnel: The Haitian army was disbanded in 1995. The national police force had 5,300 personnel in 2003; UN peacekeeping troops (October 2004) 3,092.

Background

Haiti gained its independence when the former slaves of the island, initially led by Toussaint-Louverture, and later by Jean-Jacques Dessalines, rebelled against French rule in 1791–1804. The new republic encompassed the entire island of Hispaniola, but the eastern portion was restored to Spain in 1809. The island was reunited under Haitian Pres. Jean-Pierre Boyer (1818–43); after his overthrow the eastern portion revolted and formed the Dominican Republic. Haiti's government was marked by instability, with frequent coups and assassinations. It was occupied by the US in 1915–34. In 1957 the dictator François ("Papa Doc") Duvalier came to power. Despite an economic decline and civil unrest, Duvalier ruled until his death in 1971. He was succeeded by his son, Jean-Claude ("Baby Doc") Duvalier, who was forced into exile in 1986. Haiti's first free presidential elections, held in 1990, were won by Jean-Bertrand Aristide. He was deposed by a military coup in 1991, after which tens of thousands of Haitians attempted to flee to the US in small boats. The military government stepped down in 1994, and Aristide returned from exile and resumed the presidency.

Recent Developments

The 200th anniversary year of Haitian independence, 2004, saw a country still deeply mired in poverty and paralyzed by political turmoil. Beginning in January, huge popular demonstrations were organized to demand the ouster of Pres. Jean-Bertrand Aristide because of corruption, human rights violations, and increasing authoritarian rule. Insurgents captured several large cities in Haiti in the weeks following, and gradually the US, which had installed Aristide as president in 1994, abandoned its support for him. By the end of February the rebels had gained the upper hand. US troops were sent in to assist Aristide in leaving; he was granted asylum in South Africa. A multinational force comprising primarily US, French, Canadian, and Chilean troops was sent in to guarantee the peace, and by early March a new prime minister and an interim president had been sworn in. Throughout

1 metric ton = about 1.1 short tons;   1 kilometer = 0.6 mi (statute);   1 metric ton-km cargo = about 0.68 short ton-mi cargo;   c.i.f.: cost, insurance, and freight;   f.o.b.: free on board

2004 and into 2005 the international peacekeepers proved largely ineffective in controlling roaming armed gangs of thugs, hunger and disease were still widespread, and the shaky government looked to elections scheduled for November 2005.

Internet resources: <www.haiti.org>.

Honduras

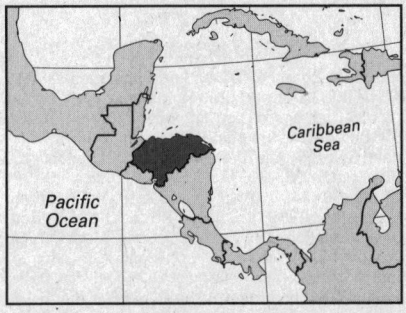

Official name: República de Honduras (Republic of Honduras). **Form of government:** multiparty republic with one legislative house (National Assembly [128]). **Head of state and government:** President Ricardo Maduro (from 2002). **Capital:** Tegucigalpa. **Official language:** Spanish. **Official religion:** none. **Monetary unit:** 1 Honduran lempira (L) = 100 centavos; valuation (7 Jul 2005) $1 = L 18.88.

Demography

Area: 43,433 sq mi, 112,492 sq km. **Population** (2004): 6,948,000. **Density** (2004): persons per sq mi 160.0, persons per sq km 61.8. **Urban** (2003): 47.5%. **Sex distribution** (2002): male 50.09%; female 49.91%. **Age breakdown** (2002): under 15, 41.9%; 15–29, 29.1%; 30–44, 15.3%; 45–59, 8.3%; 60–74, 4.1%; 75 and over, 1.3%. **Ethnic composition** (2000): mestizo 86.6%; Amerindian 5.5%; black (including Black Carib) 4.3%; white 2.3%; other 1.3%. **Religious affiliation** (1995): Roman Catholic 86.7%; Protestant 10.4%, of which Pentecostal 5.7%; other 2.9%. **Major cities** (2001): Tegucigalpa 769,061; San Pedro Sula 439,086; La Ceiba 114,584; El Progreso 90,475; Choluteca 75,600. **Location:** Central America, bordering the Caribbean Sea, Nicaragua, the North Pacific Ocean, El Salvador, and Guatemala.

Vital statistics

Birth rate per 1,000 population (2002): 32.3 (world avg. 21.3). **Death rate** per 1,000 population (2002): 6.3 (world avg. 9.1). **Natural increase rate** per 1,000 population (2002): 26.0 (world avg. 12.2). **Total fertility rate** (avg. births per childbearing woman; 2002): 4.2. **Life expectancy** at birth (2002): male 65.2 years; female 68.7 years.

National economy

Budget (1999). *Revenue:* L 14,621,500,000 (tax revenue 92.6%, of which indirect taxes 72.8%, direct taxes 19.8%; nontax revenue 5.1%; transfers 2.3%). *Expenditures:* L 18,197,700,000 (current expendi-

ture 67.9%; capital expenditure 32.1%). **Public debt** (external, outstanding; 2002): $4,211,000,000. **Production** (metric tons except as noted). *Agriculture, forestry, fishing* (2002): sugarcane 4,300,000, bananas 965,066, oil palm fruit 735,802; livestock (number of live animals) 1,859,737 cattle, 538,033 pigs, 18,648,000 chickens; roundwood (2001) 9,531,959 cu m; fish catch (2001) 16,451. *Mining and quarrying* (2001): gypsum 59,500; zinc (metal content) 48,485; silver 35,000 kg. *Manufacturing* (value added in L '000,000; 1996): food products 1,937; wearing apparel 1,266; beverages 700. *Energy production (consumption):* electricity (kW-hr; 2001) 4,191,600,000 (4,191,600,000); petroleum products (2000) none (1,382,000). **Tourism** (2002): receipts from visitors $342,000,000; expenditures by nationals abroad $185,000,000. **Population economically active** (2001): total 2,438,000; activity rate of total population 38.5% (participation rates: ages 15–64, 64.5%; female 35.7%; unemployed 4.2%). **Gross national product** (at current market prices; 2003): $6,760,000,000 ($970 per capita). **Household income and expenditure.** Average household size (2000) 5.1; sources of income (1985): wages and salaries 58.8%, transfer payments 1.8%, other 39.4%; expenditure (1986): food 44.4%, utilities and housing 22.4%, clothing and footwear 9.0%, household furnishings 8.3%. **Land use** as % of total land area (2000): in temporary crops 9.5%, in permanent crops 3.2%, in pasture 13.5%; overall forest area 48.1%.

Foreign trade

Imports (2001-c.i.f.): $2,984,000,000 (food products and live animals 18.3%, machinery and electrical equipment 15.1%, chemicals and chemical products 14.1%, mineral fuels and lubricants 13.2%). *Major import sources:* US 46.2%; Guatemala 9.9%; El Salvador 6.2%; Mexico 4.7%; Costa Rica 3.5%. **Exports** (2001-f.o.b.): $1,329,000,000 (bananas 15.4%, shrimp 13.3%, coffee 12.1%, nontraditional exports [including African palm oil, decorative plants, and mangoes] 42.2%). *Major export destinations:* US 45.7%; El Salvador 10.2%; Guatemala 9.7%; Belgium 4.7%; Germany 4.3%.

Transport and communications

Transport. *Railroads* (2000): serviceable lines 205 km; most tracks are out of use but not dismantled. *Roads* (2001): total length 13,603 km (paved 20%). *Vehicles* (1999): passenger cars 326,541; trucks and buses 59,322. *Air transport* (1995): passenger-km 341,000,000; metric ton-km cargo 33,000,000; airports (1996) with scheduled flights 8. **Communications,** in total units (units per 1,000 persons). Daily newspaper circulation (2000): 349,000 (55); radios (2000): 2,620,000 (412); televisions (2002): 809,000 (119); telephone main lines (2003): 334,400 (49); cellular telephone subscribers (2002): 326,500 (49); personal computers (2002): 91,000 (14); Internet users (2003): 185,416 (27).

Education and health

Educational attainment (1988). Percentage of population age 10 and over having: no formal schooling 33.4%; primary education 50.1%; secondary education 13.4%; higher 3.1%. **Literacy** (2000): total population age 15 and over literate 74.6%; males literate

74.7%; females literate 74.5%. **Health:** physicians (2000) 5,287 (1 per 1,201 persons); hospital beds (2003) 5,069 (1 per 1,353 persons); infant mortality rate per 1,000 live births (2002) 30.9. **Food** (2001): daily per capita caloric intake 2,405 (vegetable products 85%, animal products 15%); 106% of FAO recommended minimum.

Military

Total active duty personnel (2003): 12,000 (army 69.2%, navy 11.7%, air force 19.1%); US troops (August 2003) 390. **Military expenditure as percentage of GNP** (1999): 0.7% (world 2.4%); per capita expenditure $6.

Background

Early residents of Honduras were part of the Maya civilization that flourished in the 1st millennium AD. Christopher Columbus reached Honduras in 1502, and permanent settlement followed. A major war between the Spanish and the Indians broke out in 1537, culminating in the decimation of the Indian population through disease and enslavement. After 1570 Honduras was part of the captaincy general of Guatemala until Central American independence in 1821. Part of the United Provinces of Central America, Honduras withdrew in 1838 and declared its independence. In the 20th century, under military rule, there was constant civil war and some intervention by the US. A civilian government assumed office in 1982. The military remained in the background, however, as the activity of leftist guerrillas increased.

Recent Developments

The problem of demarcation of Honduras's border with El Salvador was finally resolved, and permanent markers were installed in 2004. The dispute resulted from the 1969 "Soccer War" and remained unsettled until International Court of Justice rulings in 1992 and 2003. Honduras joined its neighbors in May 2004 in signing the Central American Free Trade Agreement.

Internet resources: <www.honduras.com>.

Hong Kong

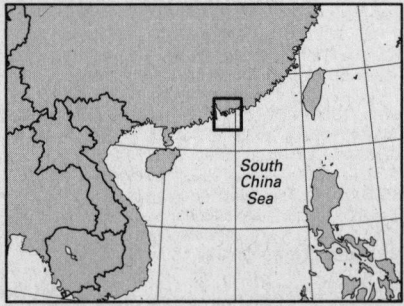

South
China
Sea

Official name: Xianggang Tebie Xingzhengqu (Chinese); Hong Kong Special Administrative Region

(English). **Political status:** special administrative region (People's Republic of China) with one legislative house (Legislative Council [60; 30 seats are directly elected by ordinary voters, and the remaining 30 are elected by special interest groups]). **Chief of state:** President Hu Jintao of China (from 2003). **Head of government:** Chief Executive Donald Tsang (from 12 Mar 2005). **Official languages:** Chinese; English. **Official religion:** none. **Monetary unit:** 1 Hong Kong dollar (HK$) = 100 cents; valuation (7 Jul 2005) US$1 = HK$7.77.

Demography

Area: 425 sq mi, 1,102 sq km. **Population** (2004): 6,848,000. **Density** (2004): persons per sq mi 16,113, persons per sq km 6,214. **Urban** (2003): 100.0%. **Sex distribution** (2003): male 48.42%; female 51.58%. **Age breakdown** (2002): under 15, 16.1%; 15–29, 20.6%; 30–44, 28.9%; 45–59, 19.4%; 60–74, 10.4%; 75 and over, 4.6%. **Ethnic composition** (2003): Chinese 95%; other 5%. **Religious affiliation** (1994): Buddhist and Taoist 73.8%; Christian 8.4%, of which Protestant 4.3%, Roman Catholic 4.1%; New Religionist 3.2%; Muslim 0.8%; Hindu 0.2%; nonreligious/atheist 13.5%; other 0.1%. **Location:** east Asia, bordering China and the South China Sea.

Vital statistics

Birth rate per 1,000 population (2003): 6.8 (world avg. 21.3). **Death rate** per 1,000 population (2003): 5.4 (world avg. 9.1). **Natural increase rate** per 1,000 population (2003): 1.4 (world avg. 12.2). **Total fertility rate** (avg. births per childbearing woman; 2003): 1.3. **Marriage rate** per 1,000 population (2003): 5.2. **Life expectancy** at birth (2003): male 78.6 years; female 84.3 years.

National economy

Budget (2002–03). *Revenue:* HK$173,345,000,000 (earnings and profits taxes 41.2%; indirect taxes 22.6%, of which property taxes 5.1%; capital revenue 12.8%). *Expenditures:* HK$273,055,000,000 (education 14.7%; social welfare 11.9%; housing 10.6%; health 9.1%; police 7.5%; economic services 5.4%). **Gross domestic product** (2003): US$173,306,-000,000 (US$25,430 per capita). **Production** (metric tons except as noted). *Agriculture, forestry, fishing* (2000): vegetables 42,500, fruits and nuts 2,022, field crops 508; livestock (2002; number of live animals) 100,000 pigs, 25,000 cattle, 3,000,000 chickens; fish catch (2001) 179,600. *Manufacturing* (value added in HK$'000,000; 2001): publishing and printed materials 12,309; electronic parts and components 9,945; textiles 6,874. *Energy production (consumption):* electricity (kW-hr; 2000) 31,329,-000,000 (40,351,000,000); coal (2000) none (6,057,000); petroleum products (2000) none (5,070,000). **Population economically active** (2003): total 3,487,800; activity rate of total population 51.3% (participation rates: over age 15, 61.1%; female 43.9%; unemployed 7.3%). **Household income and expenditure.** Average household size (2003) 3.1; annual income per household (1996) HK$210,000; expenditure (2001): housing and energy 22.2%, clothing and footwear 15.2%, food and nonalcoholic beverages 13.5%, household furnishings 12.6%, transportation 11.0%. **Tourism** (2001): receipts US$8,241,000,000; expenditures US$12,494,000,- 000. **Land use** as % of total land area (2000): in temporary and permanent crops 5.4%, in pasture 29.3%; overall forest area 18.0%.

Foreign trade

Imports (2003-c.i.f.): HK$1,805,800,000,000 (consumer goods 31.9%, capital goods 26.7%, foodstuffs 3.2%, mineral fuels and lubricants 2.0%). *Major import sources:* China 43.5%; Japan 11.9%; Taiwan 6.9%; US 5.5%; Singapore 5.0%. **Exports** (2003-f.o.b.): HK$1,742,400,000,000 (reexports 93.0%, of which consumer goods 35.4%, capital goods 26.0%; domestic exports 7.0%, of which clothing accessories and apparel 3.7%). *Major export destinations:* China 42.6%; US 18.6%; Japan 5.2%; UK 3.3%; Germany 3.2%.

Transport and communications

Transport. *Railroads* (2003): route length 64 km (combined length of East Rail and West Rail; West Rail was inaugurated in December 2003); (2002) passenger-km 4,540,000,000 (East Rail only). *Roads* (2003): total length 1,924 km (paved 100%). *Vehicles* (2003): passenger cars 357,000; trucks and buses 137,000. *Air transport* (2003; Cathay Pacific and Dragonair only): passenger-km 46,523,000,000; metric ton-km cargo 6,057,000,000; airports (2003) with scheduled flights 1. **Communications,** in total units (units per 1,000 persons). Daily newspaper circulation (2000): 5,280,000 (792); radios (2000): 4,560,000 (684); televisions (2000): 3,290,000 (493); telephone main lines (2003): 3,820,000 (561); cellular telephone subscribers (2004):·7,625,700 (1,114); personal computers (2002): 2,864,000 (422); Internet users (2003): 3,212,800 (469).

Education and health

Educational attainment (2003). Percentage of population age 15 and over having: no formal schooling 6.9%; primary education 20.4%; secondary 46.2%; matriculation 5.3%; nondegree higher 7.8%; higher degree 13.4%. **Literacy** (2000): total population age 15 and over literate 93.5%; males literate 96.5%; females literate 90.2%. **Health** (2003): physicians 10,884 (1 per 625 persons); hospital beds 35,378 (1 per 192 persons); infant mortality rate per 1,000 live births (2003) 2.3. **Food** (2001): daily per capita caloric intake 3,104 (vegetable products 68%, animal products 32%); 136% of FAO recommended minimum.

Military

Total active duty personnel (2003): 4,000 troops of Chinese army to intervene in local matters only at the request of the Hong Kong government.

 **Did you know?** Hong Kong ("fragrant harbor" in Chinese) developed initially on the basis of its excellent natural harbor and lucrative trade opportunities, particularly opium dealing. It is located to the east of the Pearl River (Zhu Jiang) estuary on the south coast of China.

Background

The island of Hong Kong and adjacent islets were ceded by China to the British in 1842, and the Kowloon Peninsula and the New Territories were later leased by the British from China for 99 years (1898–1997). A joint Chinese-British declaration, signed on 19 Dec 1984, paved the way for the entire territory to be returned to China, which occurred on 1 Jul 1997.

Recent Developments

The 2004 elections in Hong Kong, ostensibly organized under the "one country, two systems" principle, showed more controversy than freedom of choice. Beijing was accused of trying to influence the outcome, using tactics such as recruiting Chinese Olympic medalists to appear at events just before the election to present a positive image of the central government. In the event, the pro-Beijing camp won 34 out of 60 seats. In March 2005 Hong Kong leader Tung Chee-hwa resigned from office two years before the end of his term.

Internet resources: <www.discoverhongkong.com>.

Hungary

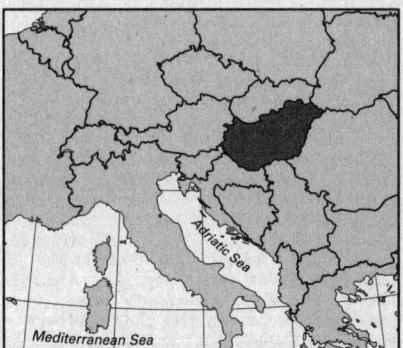

Official name: Magyar Köztársaság (Republic of Hungary). **Form of government:** unitary multiparty republic with one legislative house (National Assembly [386]). **Chief of state:** President Ferenc Mádl (from 2000). **Head of government:** Prime Minister Ferenc Gyurcsány (from 27 Aug 2004). **Capital:** Budapest. **Official language:** Hungarian. **Official religion:** none. **Monetary unit:** 1 forint (Ft) = 100 filler; valuation (7 Jul 2005) $1 = Ft 207.79.

Demography

Area: 35,919 sq mi, 93,030 sq km. **Population** (2004): 10,103,000. **Density** (2004): persons per sq mi 281.3, persons per sq km 108.6. **Urban** (2004): 64.8%. **Sex distribution** (2004): male 47.49%; female 52.51%. **Age breakdown** (2004): under 15, 15.9%; 15–29, 21.9%; 30–44, 19.8%; 45–59, 21.4%; 60–74, 14.5%; 75 and over, 6.5%. **Ethnic composition** (2000): Hungarian 84.4%; Rom (Gypsy) 5.3%; Ruthenian 2.9%; German 2.4%; Romanian 1.0%; Slovak 0.9%; Jewish 0.6%; other 2.5%. **Religious affiliation**

(1998): Roman Catholic 57.8%; Reformed 17.7%; Lutheran 3.9%; Jewish 0.2%; nonreligious 18.5%; other/unknown 1.9%. **Major cities** (2004): Budapest 1,708,000; Debrecen 205,000; Miskolc 178,000; Szeged 163,000; Pécs 158,000. **Location:** central Europe, bordering Slovakia, Ukraine, Romania, Serbia and Montenegro, Croatia, Slovenia, and Austria.

Vital statistics

Birth rate per 1,000 population (2003): 9.3 (world avg. 21.3); (2002) legitimate 68.7%. **Death rate** per 1,000 population (2003): 13.4 (world avg. 9.1). **Natural increase rate** per 1,000 population (2003): –4.1 (world avg. 12.2). **Total fertility rate** (avg. births per childbearing woman; 2003): 1.3. **Marriage rate** per 1,000 population (2003): 4.5. **Life expectancy** at birth (2002): male 68.3 years; female 76.6 years.

National economy

Budget (2002). *Revenue:* Ft 6,338,100,000,000 (social contributions 34.1%, taxes on goods and services 32.1%, personal income taxes 15.1%). *Expenditures:* Ft 7,781,600,000,000 (social protection 30.2%, public debt 8.8%, transport 8.1%, health 5.8%, education 5.2%, defense 3.0%). **Production** (metric tons except as noted). *Agriculture, forestry, fishing* (2003): corn (maize) 4,534,000, wheat 2,920,000, sugar beets 1,802,000; livestock (number of live animals) 4,658,000 pigs, 1,281,000 sheep, 714,000 cattle; roundwood (2002) 5,637,000 cu m; fish catch (2001) 19,694. *Mining and quarrying* (2002): bauxite 720,000. *Manufacturing* (value added in $'000,000; 2000): electrical machinery and apparatus 1,309; motor vehicles and parts 1,105; food products 1,001. *Energy production (consumption):* electricity (kW-hr; 2003) 34,282,000,000 (43,188,000,000); hard coal (2003) 672,000 ([2000] 1,280,000); lignite (2003) 11,984,000 (14,619,000); crude petroleum (barrels; 2003) 7,586,000 ([2000] 45,853,000); petroleum products (2000) 6,202,000 (5,817,000); natural gas (cu m; 2003) 3,087,000,000 (14,558,000,000). **Public debt** (external, outstanding; 2002): $13,551,-000,000. **Population economically active** (2003): total 4,166,400; activity rate of total population 41.1% (participation rates: ages 15–74, 53.8%; female [2002] 44.5%; unemployed 5.9%). **Tourism** ($'000,000; 2002): receipts 3,273; expenditures 1,722. **Gross national product** (2003): $64,028,-000,000 ($6,330 per capita). **Household income and expenditure.** Average household size (2002) 2.5; income per household (2001) Ft 2,898,000; sources of income (2001): wages 48.3%, transfers 25.7%, self-employment 16.3%; expenditure (2002): food products 28.8%, housing and energy 17.6%, transportation and communications 16.5%, recreation 7.0%. **Land use** as % of total land area (2000): in temporary crops 50.0%, in permanent crops 2.2%, in pasture 11.4%; overall forest area 19.9%.

Foreign trade

Imports (2002-c.i.f.): Ft 9,704,000,000,000 (electrical machinery 17.0%, nonelectrical machinery 14.6%, road vehicles 8.1%, mineral fuels 7.0%, telecommunications equipment 6.2%). *Major import sources:* Germany 24.3%; Italy 7.5%; Austria 6.9%;

Russia 6.1%; China 5.5%. **Exports** (2002-f.o.b.): Ft 8,874,000,000,000 (telecommunications equipment 15.5%, electrical machinery 11.2%, power-generating machinery 10.9%, road vehicles 8.7%, office machines and computers 7.1%). *Major export destinations:* Germany 35.5%; Austria 7.1%; Italy 5.8%; France 5.7%; UK 4.7%.

Transport and communications

Transport. *Railroads* (2003): route length 7,898 km; passenger-km (2002) 10,408,000,000; metric ton-km cargo 7,980,000,000. *Roads* (1999): total length 188,203 km (paved 43%). *Vehicles* (2003): passenger cars 2,777,000; trucks and buses 395,000. *Air transport* (2003): passenger-km 3,130,400,000; metric ton-km cargo 46,000,000; airports with scheduled flights 1. **Communications**, in total units (units per 1,000 persons). Daily newspaper circulation (1996): 1,895,000 (186); radios (2000): 7,050,000 (690); televisions (2000): 4,460,000 (437); telephone main lines (2002): 3,666,400 (361); cellular telephone subscribers (2002): 6,862,800 (676); personal computers (2002): 1,100,000 (108); Internet users (2002): 1,600,000 (158).

Education and health

Educational attainment (1990). Population age 25 and over having: no formal schooling 1.3%; primary education 57.9%; secondary 30.7%; higher 10.1%. **Health** (2002): physicians 32,452 (1 per 313 persons); hospital beds 80,340 (1 per 126 persons); infant mortality rate per 1,000 live births (2003) 7.3. **Food** (2001): daily per capita caloric intake 3,520 (vegetable products 69%, animal products 31%); 134% of FAO recommended minimum.

Military

Total active duty personnel (2003): 33,400 (army 70.7%, air force 23.1%, headquarters staff 6.2%). **Military expenditure as percentage of GNP** (1999): 1.7% (world 2.4%); per capita expenditures $185.

Background

The western part of Hungary was incorporated into the Roman Empire in 14 BC. The Magyars, a nomadic people, occupied the middle basin of the Danube River in the late 9th century AD. Stephen I, crowned in 1000, Christianized the country and organized it into a strong and independent state. Invasions by the Mongols in the 13th century and by the Ottoman Turks in the 14th century devastated the country, and by 1568 the territory of modern Hungary had been divided into three parts: Royal Hungary went to the Habsburgs; Transylvania gained autonomy in 1566 under the Turks; and the central plain remained under Turkish control until the late 17th century, when the Austrian Habsburgs took over. Hungary declared its independence from Austria in 1849, and in 1867 the dual monarchy of Austria-Hungary was established. Its defeat in World War I resulted in the dismemberment of Hungary, leaving it only those areas in which Magyars predominated. In an attempt to regain some of this lost territory, Hungary cooperated with the Germans against the Soviet Union during

---

1 metric ton = about 1.1 short tons;   1 kilometer = 0.6 mi (statute);   1 metric ton-km cargo = about 0.68 short ton-mi cargo;   c.i.f.: cost, insurance, and freight;   f.o.b.: free on board

World War II. After the war, a pro-Soviet provisional government was established, and in 1949 the Hungarian People's Republic was formed. Opposition to this Stalinist regime broke out in 1956 but was suppressed. Nevertheless, from 1956 to 1988 communist Hungary grew to become the most tolerant of the Soviet-bloc nations of Eastern Europe. It gained its independence in 1989 and soon attracted the largest amount of direct foreign investment in east-central Europe. In 1999 it joined NATO.

Recent Developments

Following the country's accession to the European Union on 1 May 2004, Hungary experienced a serious government crisis, which saw the resignation of a prime minister for the first time in the post-1989 period. Peter Medgyessy quit in August after losing confidence from the governing Hungarian Socialist Party and its junior coalition partner, the Alliance of Free Democrats. His successor was former minister of children, youth, and sports Ferenc Gyurcsany, a wealthy businessman, who pledged to focus on generating employment and improving social equality. Among other things, he promised to reduce the tax burdens on low-income families and increase taxation on banks and other financial service companies.

Internet resources: <www.hungary.com>.

Iceland

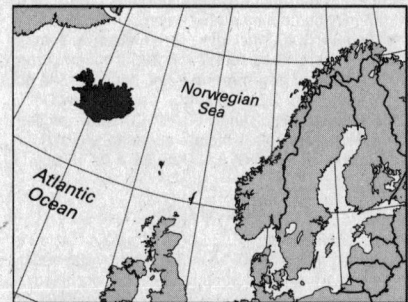

Official name: Lýdhveldidh Ísland (Republic of Iceland). **Form of government:** unitary multiparty republic with one legislative house (Althingi [63]). **Chief of state:** President Ólafur Ragnar Grímsson (from 1996). **Head of government:** Prime Minister Halldór Ásgrímsson (from 15 Sep 2004). **Capital:** Reykjavík. **Official language:** Icelandic. **Official religion:** Evangelical Lutheran. **Monetary unit:** 1 króna (ISK) = 100 aurar; valuation (7 Jul 2005) $1 = ISK 65.86.

Demography

Area: 39,741 sq mi, 102,928 sq km. **Population** (2004): 292,000. **Density** (2004; calculated with reference to 9,191 sq mi [23,805 sq km] area free of glaciers [comprising 4,603 sq mi {11,922 sq km}], lava fields or wasteland [comprising 24,918 sq mi {64,538 sq km}], and lakes [comprising 1,064 sq mi {2,757 sq km}]): persons per sq mi 31.8, persons per sq km 12.3. **Urban** (2003): 93.8%. **Sex distribution** (2003): male 50.02%; female 49.98%. **Age breakdown** (2003): under 15, 22.9%; 15–29, 22.1%;

30–44, 21.9%; 45–59, 17.8%; 60–74, 9.9%; 75 and over, 5.4%. **Ethnic composition** (2003; by citizenship): Icelandic 96.5%; European 2.5%, of which Nordic 0.6%; Asian 0.6%; other 0.4%. **Religious affiliation** (2001): Protestant 92.2%, of which Evangelical Lutheran 87.1%, other Lutheran 4.1%; Roman Catholic 1.7%; other and not specified 6.1%. **Major cities** (2003): Reykjavík 112,554 (urban area 179,992); Kópavogur 25,016 (within Reykjavík urban area); Hafnarfjördhur 20,720 (within Reykjavík urban area); Akureyri 15,867; Gardhabær 8,695 (within Reykjavík urban area). **Location:** northern Europe, an island between the Greenland Sea, the Norwegian Sea, and the North Atlantic Ocean.

Vital statistics

Birth rate per 1,000 population (2002): 14.1 (world avg. 21.3); (2001) legitimate 36.7%. **Death rate** per 1,000 population (2002): 6.3 (world avg. 9.1). **Natural increase rate** per 1,000 population (2002): 7.8 (world avg. 12.2). **Total fertility rate** (avg. births per childbearing woman; 2002): 1.9. **Marriage rate** per 1,000 population (2002): 5.6. **Divorce rate** per 1,000 population (2002): 1.8. **Life expectancy** at birth (2001–02): male 78.4 years; female 82.6 years.

National economy

Budget (2004). *Revenue:* ISK 279,425,000,000 (tax revenue 90.3%, of which value-added tax 30.8%, individual income tax 26.4%, social security contribution 10.4%; nontax revenue 9.7%). *Expenditures:* ISK 273,035,000,000 (social security and health 40.4%, education 11.8%, social affairs 8.4%, interest payment 5.5%). **Public debt** (2003): $3,333,000,000. **Production** (metric tons except as noted). *Agriculture, forestry, fishing* (2002): potatoes 8,800, cereals 4,400, tomatoes 948; livestock (number of live animals) 469,657 sheep, 71,267 horses, 67,225 cattle; fish catch (value in ISK '000,000; 2002) 77,075, of which cod 28,655, redfish 5,918, herring 4,319, halibut 4,129, shrimp 4,110. *Mining and quarrying* (2002): diatomite 31,000. *Manufacturing* (value added in ISK '000,000; 1996): preserved and processed fish 18,114; other food products 10,848; printing and publishing 6,914. *Energy production (consumption):* electricity (kW-hr; 2002) 8,409,000,000 (8,409,000,000); coal (2000) none (101,000); petroleum products (2000) none (560,000). **Land use** as % of total land area (2000): in temporary crops 0.07%, in pasture 22.7%; overall forest area 0.3%. **Population economically active** (2004): total 162,400; activity rate of total population 55.9% (participation rates: ages 16–74, 81.5%; female (2002) 46.9%; unemployed 2.6%). **Gross national product** (2003): $8,813,000,000 ($30,810 per capita). **Household income and expenditure.** Average household size (2002) 2.8; annual employment income per household (2002) ISK 2,330,000; sources of income (2001): wages and salaries 78.6%, pension 10.3%, self-employment 2.0%, other 9.1%; expenditure (2003): housing and energy 20.3%, food, beverages, and tobacco 19.9%, transportation and communications 18.7%, recreation and culture 13.9%, household goods 6.1%. **Tourism** (2002): receipts $250,000,000; expenditures $365,000,000.

Foreign trade

Imports (2002-f.o.b. in balance of trade and c.i.f. in commodities and trading partners): ISK

207,609,000,000 (machinery and apparatus 20.4%; transport equipment 11.9%; food products 9.5%; crude petroleum and petroleum products 7.9%; clothing and footwear 4.4%). *Major import sources:* US 11.1%; Germany 10.7%; Denmark 8.5%; Norway 8.0%; UK 7.4%; The Netherlands 6.0%. **Exports** (2002): ISK 203,394,000,000 (marine products 62.8%, of which cod 23.9%, shrimp 6.3%, redfish 5.3%, haddock 4.0%; aluminum 18.9%; medicinal products 3.0%). *Major export destinations:* Germany 18.5%; UK 17.6%; US 10.8%; The Netherlands 10.8%; Spain 5.3%.

Transport and communications

Transport. *Roads* (2002): total length 12,955 km (paved 33%). *Vehicles* (2003): passenger cars 161,721; trucks and buses 21,977. *Air transport* (2003; Icelandair only): passenger-km 2,999,800,-000; metric ton-km cargo 95,500,000; airports (1996) with scheduled flights 24. **Communications,** in total units (units per 1,000 persons). Daily newspaper circulation (2000): 100,000 (347); radios (2000): 270,000 (960); televisions (2000): 143,000 (509); telephone main lines (2003): 190,700 (660); cellular telephone subscribers (2003): 279,100 (966); personal computers (2002): 130,000 (451); Internet users (2003): 195,000 (675).

Education and health

Educational attainment (2002): Percentage of population ages 25–64 having: primary and some secondary education 34.4%; secondary 45.7%; higher 19.9%. **Literacy:** virtually 100%. **Health:** physicians (2002) 1,029 (1 per 280 persons); hospital beds 2,432 (1 per 118 persons); infant mortality rate per 1,000 live births (2002) 2.2. **Food** (2001): daily per capita caloric intake 3,313 (vegetable products 59%, animal products 41%); 121% of FAO recommended minimum.

Military

Total active duty personnel (2003): 120 coast guard personnel; NATO-sponsored US-manned Iceland Defense Force (August 2004): 1,800. **Military expenditure as percentage of GNP** (1999): none (world average 2.4%).

Background

Iceland was settled by Norwegian seafarers in the 9th century and was Christianized by 1000. Its legislature, the Althing, was founded in 930, making it one of the oldest legislative assemblies in the world. Iceland united with Norway in 1262. It became an independent state of Denmark in 1918 but severed those ties to become an independent republic in 1944. Vigdís Finnbogadóttir became the world's first female elected president in 1980.

Recent Developments

Iceland's economy expanded at a brisk pace in 2004, with GDP growing at a rate of 5%, following 4½% growth in the previous year. Inflation edged up slightly, to an annual rate of 3–4%. The rapid growth

was primarily due to the ongoing construction project in the northeastern part of the country, where a 690-MW hydropower station was being built to provide electricity to an Alcoa aluminum plant. Together these two construction projects, which were scheduled for completion in 2006, would cost $3 billion, almost one-fourth of Iceland's normal annual GDP.

Internet resources: <www.icetourist.is>.

India

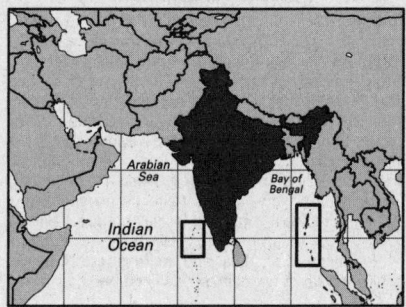

Official name: Bharat (Hindi); Republic of India (English). **Form of government:** multiparty federal republic with two legislative houses (Council of States [245; can have a maximum of 250 members, up to 12 of whom may be nominated by the president], House of the People [545, including 2 nonelective seats]). **Chief of state:** President A.P.J. Abdul Kalam (from 2002). **Head of government:** Prime Minister Manmohan Singh (from 22 May 2004). **Capital:** New Delhi. **Official languages:** Hindi; English. **Official religion:** none. **Monetary unit:** 1 Indian rupee (Re, plural Rs) = 100 paise; valuation (7 Jul 2005) $1 = Rs 43.55.

Demography

Area: 1,222,559 sq mi, 3,166,414 sq km (excludes 46,660 sq mi [120,849 sq km] of territory claimed by India as part of Jammu and Kashmir but occupied by Pakistan or China; inland water constitutes 9.6% of total area of India [including all of Indian-claimed Jammu and Kashmir]). **Population** (2004): 1,081,229,000. **Density** (2004): persons per sq mi 884.4, persons per sq km 341.5. **Urban** (2001): 27.8%. **Sex distribution** (2001): male 51.74%; female 48.26%. **Age breakdown** (2001): under 15, 35.3%; 15–29, 26.6%; 30–44, 19.5%; 45–59, 10.9%; 60–74, 6.0%; 75 and over, 1.4%; unknown 0.3%. **Major cities** (2001; urban agglomerations, 2001): Greater Mumbai (Greater Bombay) 11,914,398 (16,368,084); Delhi 9,817,439 (12,791,458); Kolkata (Calcutta) 4,580,-544 (13,216,546); Bangalore 4,292,223 (5,686,-844); Chennai (Madras) 4,216,268 (6,424,624); Ahmadabad 3,515,361 (4,519,278); Hyderabad 3,449,878 (5,533,640); Pune (Poona) 2,540,069 (3,755,525); Kanpur 2,532,138 (2,690,486); Surat 2,433,787 (2,811,466); Jaipur 2,324,319 (2,324,-319); New Delhi (within Delhi urban agglomeration) 294,783. **Location:** southern Asia, bordering Pakistan, China, Nepal, Bhutan, Myanmar, Bangladesh, and the

1 metric ton = about 1.1 short tons;   1 kilometer = 0.6 mi (statute);   1 metric ton-km cargo = about 0.68 short ton-mi cargo;   c.i.f.: cost, insurance, and freight;   f.o.b.: free on board

Indian Ocean. **Linguistic composition** (1991; mother tongue except as noted): Hindi 27.58% (including associated languages and dialects, 38.58%); Bengali 8.22%; Telugu 7.80%; Marathi 7.38%; Tamil 6.26%; Urdu 5.13%; Gujarati 4.81%; Kannada 3.87%; Malayalam 3.59%; Oriya 3.32%; Punjabi 2.76%; Assamese 1.55%; Bhili/Bhilodi 0.66%; Santhali 0.62%; Kashmiri 0.47% (1981); Gondi 0.25%; Sindhi 0.25%; Nepali 0.25%; Konkani 0.21%; Tulu 0.18%; Kurukh 0.17%; Manipuri 0.15%; Bodo 0.14%; Khandeshi 0.12%; other 3.26%. Hindi (66.00%) and English (19.00%) are also spoken as lingua francas (second languages). **Religious affiliation** (2000): Hindu 73.72%; Muslim 11.96%, of which Sunni 8.97%, Shi'i 2.99%; Christian 6.08%, of which Independent 2.99%, Protestant 1.47%, Roman Catholic 1.35%, Orthodox 0.27%; traditional beliefs 3.39%; Sikh 2.16%; Buddhist 0.71%; Jain 0.40%; Baha'i 0.12%; Zoroastrian (Parsi) 0.02%; other 1.44%. **Households** (2001). Total number of households 191,963,935. Average household size 5.4. Type of household: permanent 51.8%; semipermanent 30.0%; temporary 18.2%. Average number of rooms per household 2.2; 1 room 38.4%, 2 rooms 30.0%, 3 rooms 14.3%, 4 rooms 7.5%, 5 rooms 2.9%, 6 or more rooms 3.7%, unspecified number of rooms 3.2%.

Vital statistics

Birth rate per 1,000 population (2003): 23.3 (world avg. 21.3). **Death rate** per 1,000 population (2003): 8.5 (world avg. 9.1). **Natural increase rate** per 1,000 population (2003): 14.8 (world avg. 12.2). **Total fertility rate** (avg. births per childbearing woman; 2003): 2.9. **Life expectancy** at birth (2003): male 62.9 years; female 64.4 years.

Social indicators

Educational attainment (1991; excludes Jammu and Kashmir); no formal schooling: males 43.3%, females 72.8%; complete secondary or higher education: males 10.6%, females 3.7%. Percentage of population age 25 and over having: no formal schooling 57.5%; incomplete primary education 28.0%; complete primary or some secondary 7.2%; complete secondary or higher 7.3%. **Quality of working life** (the first two statistics apply to the workers employed in the "organized sector" only [27.8 million in 2001, of which 19.1 million were employed in the public sector and 8.7 million were employed in the private sector]); few legal protections exist for the more than 370 million workers in the "unorganized sector"). Average workweek (2001): 46 hours. Rate of fatal injuries per 100,000 employees (2001) 36. Agricultural workers in servitude to creditors (early 1990s) 10–20%. **Access to services** (2001). Percentage of total (urban, rural) households having access to: electricity for lighting purposes 55.8% (87.6%, 43.5%); kerosene for lighting purposes 43.3% (11.6%, 55.6%), water closets 18.0% (46.1%, 7.1%), pit latrines 11.5% (14.6%, 10.3%), no latrines 63.6% (26.3%, 78.1%), closed drainage for waste water 12.5% (34.5%, 3.9%), open drainage for waste water 33.9% (43.4%, 30.3%), no drainage for waste water 53.6% (22.1%, 65.8%). Type of fuel used for cooking in households: firewood 52.5% (22.7%, 64.1%), LPG (liquefied petroleum gas) 17.5% (48.0%, 5.7%), kerosene 6.5% (19.2%, 1.6%), crop residue 10.0% (2.1%, 13.1%), cow dung 9.8% (2.0%, 12.8%), electricity 0.2% (0.3%, 0.1%). Source of drinking water: hand pump or tube well 41.3% (21.3%, 48.9%), piped water 36.7% (68.7%, 24.3%), well

18.2% (7.7%, 22.2%), river, canal, spring, public tank, pond, or lake 2.7% (0.7%, 3.5%). **Social participation.** Eligible voters participating in April/May 2004 national election: 58.1%. Trade union membership (1998): c. 16,000,000 (primarily in the public sector). **Social deviance** (1990). Offense rate per 100,000 population for: murder 4.1; dacoity (gang robbery) 1.3; theft and housebreaking 56.6; riots 12.0. Rate of suicide per 100,000 population (1991): 9.0. **Material well-being** (2001). Total (urban, rural) households possessing: televisions 31.6% (64.3%, 18.9%), telephones 9.1% (23.0%, 3.8%), scooters, motorcycles, or mopeds 11.7% (24.7%, 6.7%), cars, jeeps, or vans 2.5% (5.6%, 1.3%). Households availing banking services 35.5% (49.5%, 30.1%).

National economy

Gross national product (2003): $567,604,000,000 ($530 per capita). **Budget** (2002). Revenue (central government only): Rs 3,088,200,000,000 (tax revenue 76.4%, of which excise taxes 29.5%, taxes on income and profits 29.4%; nontax revenue 23.1%; other 0.5%). Expenditures: Rs 4,239,100,000,000 (general public services 61.0%, of which public debt payments 26.8%; economic affairs 15.3%; defense 15.2%; education 2.5%; health 1.7%). **Public debt** (external, outstanding; 2002): $88,271,000,000. **Production** (in '000 metric tons except as noted). Agriculture, forestry, fishing (2002): cereals 491,174 (of which rice 116,580, wheat 71,814, corn [maize] 10,570, sorghum 7,060, millet 6,150), sugarcane 279,000, fruits 34,720 (of which bananas 16,450, mangoes 11,400, oranges 2,980, apples 1,420, lemons and limes 1,370, pineapples 1,100), oilseeds 16,750 (of which peanuts [groundnuts] 5,400, rapeseed 5,040, soybeans 4,270, sunflower seeds 870, castor beans 590, sesame 580), pulses 10,760 (of which chickpeas 5,320, dry beans 3,000, pigeon peas 2,440), coconuts 9,300, eggplants 8,800, seed cotton 5,580, jute 1,789, tea 826, natural rubber 650, tobacco 575, garlic 497, cashews 460, betel 330, coffee 317, ginger 275, pepper 51; livestock (number of live animals; 2002) 221,-900,000 cattle, 124,000,000 goats, 95,100,000 water buffalo, 58,800,000 sheep, 18,000,000 pigs, 900,000 camels; roundwood 319,418,047 cu m, of which fuelwood 300,564,000 cu m, industrial roundwood 18,854,000; fish catch (2001) 5,965,230, of which freshwater fish 2,950,003, marine fish 2,301,609, crustaceans 498,827. Mining and quarrying (2002–03): limestone 136,224; iron ore 54,432 (approximate metal content); bauxite 9,439; manganese 617 (approximate metal content); chromium (2001–02) 543 (approximate metal content); zinc 299 (approximate metal content); lead 40.6 (approximate metal content); copper 38 (approximate metal content); gold 2,873 kg; gem diamonds (2002) 17,000 carats. Manufacturing (value added in $'000,000; 2000): industrial chemicals 4,274; food products 3,723; paints, soaps, varnishes, drugs, and medicines 3,500; textiles 3,498; iron and steel 2,989; nonelectrical machinery and apparatus 2,457; cements, bricks, and tiles 1,988; refined petroleum 1,870; motor vehicles and parts 1,744. Energy production (consumption): electricity (kW-hr; 2002) 529,692,000,000 (529,698,000,-000); hard coal (2003) 348,432,000 ([2000] 315,583,000); lignite (2003) 26,004,000 ([2000] 22,704,000); crude petroleum (barrels; 2002) 248,520,000 ([2000] 579,300,000); petroleum products (2000) 75,409,000 (79,876,000); natural gas (cu m; 2002) 29,495,000,000 ([2000] 24,315-,000,000). **Land use** as % of total land area (2000): in temporary crops 54.4%, in permanent crops 2.7%, in pasture 3.7%; overall forest area 21.6%. **Population economically active** (2001): total 402,512,190; activity rate of total population 39.2% (female 36.5%; unemployed 10.4%). **Household income and expenditure.** Average household size (2002) 5.4; sources of income (1984–85): salaries and wages 42.2%, self-employed 39.7%, interest 8.6%, profits and dividends 6.0%, rent 3.5%; expenditure (1998–99): food, beverages, and tobacco 52.1%, transportation and **Communications** 13.7%, housing and energy 10.2%, clothing and footwear 5.2%, health 4.4%. **Service enterprises** (net value added in Rs '000,000,000; 1998–99): wholesale and retail trade 1,562; finance, real estate, and insurance 1,310; transport and storage 804; community, social, and personal services 763; construction 545. **Tourism** (2002): receipts from visitors $2,923,000,000; expenditures by nationals abroad $3,449,000,000.

Foreign trade

Imports (2003–04): $77,032,000,000 (crude petroleum and refined petroleum 26.7%; electronic goods [including computer software] 10.2%; precious and semiprecious stones 9.3%; gold and silver 8.8%; nonelectrical machinery and apparatus 6.1%; organic and inorganic chemicals 5.2%). *Major import sources* (2002–03): US 7.2%; Belgium 6.0%; UK 4.5%; China 4.5%; Germany 3.9%; Switzerland 3.8%; South Africa 3.4%; Japan 3.0%; Malaysia 2.4%; Singapore 2.2%. **Exports** (2003–04): $63,454,000,000 (engineering goods 19.2%; cut and polished diamonds and jewelry 16.6%; chemicals and chemical products 14.5%; food and agricultural products 11.7%; cotton ready-made garments 9.6%; petroleum products 5.5%; cotton yarn, fabrics, and thread 5.2%). *Major export destinations* (2002–03): US 20.7%; UAE 6.3%; Hong Kong 5.0%; UK 4.7%; Germany 4.0%; China 3.7%; Japan 3.5%; Belgium 3.2%; Italy 2.5%; Bangladesh 2.2%.

Transport and communications

Transport. *Railroads* (2002): route length 144,647 km; passenger-km 936,037,000,000 (includes Indian Railways and 15 regional railways); metric ton-km cargo 541,783,000,000 (includes Indian Railways and 9 regional railways). *Roads* (2002): total length 3,319,644 km (paved 46%). *Vehicles* (2001): passenger cars 7,058,000; trucks and buses 3,582,000. *Air transport* (2002–03): passenger-km 28,561,922,-000; metric ton-km cargo 567,272,000; airports (2002) with scheduled flights 96. **Communications**, in total units (units per 1,000 persons). Daily newspaper circulation (2000): 61,000,000 (60); radios (2000): 123,000,000 (121); televisions (2000): 79,000,000 (78); telephone main lines (2003): 48,917,000 (46); cellular telephone subscribers (2003): 26,154,400 (24); personal computers (2002): 7,500,000 (7.2); Internet users (2003): 18,481,000 (17).

Education and health

Literacy (2001): percentage of total population age 15 and over literate 64.8%; males literate 75.3%;

females literate 53.7%. **Health** (1999): physicians 519,000 (1 per 1,923 persons); hospital beds 918,000 (1 per 1,087 persons); infant mortality rate per 1,000 live births (2003) 59.6. **Food** (2001): daily per capita caloric intake 2,487 (vegetable products 92%, animal products 8%); 113% of FAO recommended minimum.

Military

Total active duty personnel (2003): 1,325,000 (army 83.0%, navy 4.2%, air force 12.8%); personnel in paramilitary forces 1,089,700. **Military expenditure as percentage of GNP** (1999): 2.5% (world 2.4%); per capita expenditure $11.

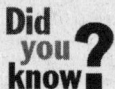 **Did you know?** The city of Simla is the capital of Himachal Pradesh state, northwestern India. It was built by the British on land they retained after the Gurkha War of 1814–16 and was used for resting troops. It gained popularity as a summer resort because of its cool climate and scenic setting, and from 1865 to 1939 it served as India's summer capital.

Background

India has been inhabited for thousands of years. Agriculture dates back to at least the 7th millennium BC, and an urban civilization, that of the Indus Valley, was established by 2600 BC. Buddhism and Jainism arose in the 6th century BC in reaction to the caste-based society created by the Vedic religion and its successor, Hinduism. Muslim invasions began c. AD 1000, establishing the long-lived Delhi sultanate in 1206 and the Mughal dynasty in 1526. Vasco da Gama's voyage to India in 1498 initiated several centuries of commercial rivalry among the Portuguese, Dutch, English, and French. British conquests in the 18th and 19th centuries led to the rule of the British East India Co., and direct administration by the British Empire began in 1858. After Mohandas K. Gandhi helped end British rule in 1947, Jawaharlal Nehru became India's first prime minister and he, his daughter, Indira Gandhi, and his grandson Rajiv Gandhi guided the nation's destiny for all but a few years until 1989. The subcontinent was partitioned into two countries—India, with a Hindu majority, and Pakistan, with a Muslim majority—in 1947. A later clash with Pakistan resulted in the creation of Bangladesh in 1971. In the 1980s and '90s, Sikhs sought to establish an independent state in Punjab, and ethnic and religious conflicts took place in other parts of the country as well.

Recent Developments

Prime Minister Vajpayee decided to call early elections, which proved to be a disaster and a shock for the Bharatiya Janata Party, the principal constituent of the ruling National Democratic Alliance. The voting, held in four stages in late April and early May 2004, resulted in stunning losses for the coalition and corresponding gains for the Congress Party, which had dominated politics in India since independence—although Congress did not win an absolute majority

1 metric ton = about 1.1 short tons;　1 kilometer = 0.6 mi (statute);　1 metric ton-km cargo = about 0.68 short ton-mi cargo;　c.i.f.: cost, insurance, and freight;　f.o.b.: free on board

and so formed a coalition government. A politically low-key candidate, academic economist and former finance minister Manmohan Singh, was tapped for the top job. Peace initiatives moved forward in the troubled state of Jammu and Kashmir and in the northeastern states. The New Delhi government also took initiatives to resume a dialogue with other disaffected groups. The hope for peace was rekindled, and Singh was viewed as a sincere and caring leader who was genuinely committed to a peaceful resolution of the problem of disaffection in those parts of the country. In April 2005 a bridge between the Pakistani- and Indian-controlled portions of Kashmir that had been destroyed 50 years ago was reopened, and bus and rail service between the two sectors was restored.

Internet resources: <www.tourismofindia.com>.

Indonesia

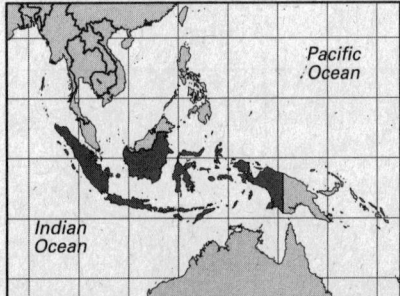

Pacific Ocean

Indian Ocean

Official name: Republik Indonesia (Republic of Indonesia). **Form of government:** unitary multiparty republic with two legislative houses (Regional Representatives Council [128]; House of Representatives [500]). **Head of state and government:** President Susilo Bambang Yudhoyono (from 20 Oct 2004). **Capital:** Jakarta. **Official language:** Indonesian (Bahasa Indonesia). **Official religion:** monotheism. **Monetary unit:** 1 Indonesian rupiah (Rp) = 100 sen; valuation (7 Jul 2005) $1 = Rp 9,800.81.

Demography

Area: 730,024 sq mi, 1,890,754 sq km. **Population** (2004): 222,611,000. **Density** (2004): persons per sq mi 304.9, persons per sq km 117.7. **Urban** (2003): 45.6%. **Sex distribution** (2000): male 50.14%; female 49.86%. **Age breakdown** (2000): under 15, 30.4%; 15–29, 29.3%; 30–44, 21.8%; 45–59, 11.3%; 60–74, 5.8%; 75 and over, 1.4%. **Ethnic composition** (2000): Javanese 36.4%; Sundanese 13.7%; Malay 9.4%; Madurese 7.2%; Han Chinese 4.0%; Minangkabau 3.6%. **Religious affiliation** (2000): Muslim 76.5%; Christian 13.1%, of which Protestant 5.7%, independent Christian 4.0%, Roman Catholic 2.7%; Hindu 3.4%; traditional beliefs 2.5%; nonreligious 1.9%; other 2.6%. **Major cities** (2000): Jakarta 8,347,083 (urban agglomeration [2003] 12,300,000); Surabaya 2,599,796; Bandung 2,136,260; Medan 1,904,273; Bekasi 1,663,802. **Location:** archipelago in southeast Asia, bordering Malaysia, the Pacific Ocean, Papua New Guinea, and the Indian Ocean.

Vital statistics

Birth rate per 1,000 population (2003): 21.5 (world avg. 21.3). **Death rate** per 1,000 population (2003): 6.3 (world avg. 9.1). **Total fertility rate** (avg. births per childbearing woman; 2003): 2.5. **Marriage rate** per 1,000 population (2001; Muslim population only): 8.7. **Life expectancy** at birth (2003): male 66.5 years; female 71.5 years.

National economy

Budget (2002). *Revenue:* Rp 300,190,000,000,000 (tax revenue 70.3%, of which income tax 33.9%, VAT 21.9%; nontax revenue 29.7%, of which revenue from petroleum 15.9%). *Expenditures:* Rp 327,860,-000,000,000 (current expenditure 57.7%; development expenditure 12.3%; expenditure 30.0%). **Public debt** (external, outstanding; 2002): $70,011,-000,000. **Population economically active** (2001): total 98,812,448; activity rate 46.1% (participation rates: over age 15 [2000] 67.8%; unemployed 8.1%). **Households.** Average household size (2000) 3.9. **Production** (metric tons except as noted). *Agriculture, forestry, fishing* (2002): rice 51,604,000, palm fruit oil 40,000,000, sugarcane 23,400,000; livestock (number of live animals) 12,400,000 goats, 11,200,000 cattle, 7,350,000 sheep; roundwood (2001) 119,209,000 cu m; fish catch (2001) 5,068,000. *Mining and quarrying* (2002): bauxite 1,283,000; copper (metal content) 1,172,000; nickel (metal content) 123,000. *Manufacturing* (value added in Rp '000,000,000; 2000): machinery and transport equipment 57,296; food products 44,736; chemicals and plastics 39,168. *Energy production (consumption):* electricity (kW-hr; 2000) 99,511,-000,000 (99,511,000,000); coal (2001) 90,648,000 ([2000] 19,668,000); crude petroleum (barrels; 2003) 452,000,000 ([2000] 385,600,000); petroleum products (2000) 48,518,000 (50,136,000); natural gas (cu m; 2002) 86,400,000,000 ([2000] 21,500,000,000). **Gross national product** (2003): $172,733,000,000 ($810 per capita). **Tourism** (2002): receipts $4,306,000,000; expenditures $3,368,000,000. **Land use** as % of total land area (2000): in temporary crops 11.3%, in permanent crops 7.2%, in pasture 6.2%; overall forest area 58.0%.

Foreign trade

Imports (2000-c.i.f.): $33,515,000,000 (machinery and apparatus 18.8%, refined petroleum 10.6%, food and live animals 8.3%, crude petroleum 7.8%, organic chemicals 7.3%). *Major import sources:* Japan 16.0%; Singapore 11.3%; US 10.1%; South Korea 6.2%; China 6.0%. **Exports** (2000-f.o.b.): $62,124,000,000 (natural gas 10.7%, crude petroleum 9.8%, garments 7.7%, telecommunications equipment 5.6%, wood products 5.2%, computers and parts 4.9%). *Major export destinations:* Japan 23.2%; US 13.7%; Singapore 10.6%; South Korea 7.0%; China 4.5%.

Transport and communications

Transport. *Railroads* (2000): route length 6,458 km; passenger-km 19,228,000,000; metric ton-km cargo 4,997,000,000. *Roads* (1999): length 355,951 km (paved 57%). *Vehicles* (2000): passenger cars 3,038,913; trucks and buses 2,373,414. *Air transport* (1999): passenger-km (2002) 19,690,000,000;

metric ton-km cargo 340,932,000; airports (1996) 81. **Communications,** in total units (units per 1,000 persons). Daily newspaper circulation (2000): 4,870,-000 (23); radios (2000): 33,200,000 (157); televisions (2000): 31,500,000 (149); telephone main lines (2002): 7,750,000 (37); cellular telephone subscribers (2002): 11,700,000 (55); personal computers (2002): 2,519,000 (12); Internet users (2002): 8,000,000 (38).

Education and health

Educational attainment (2000). Percentage of population age 15 and over having: no schooling or incomplete primary 23.9%; primary and some secondary 53.8%; complete secondary 17.9%; some higher 2.2%; complete higher 2.2%. **Literacy** (2000): total population age 15 and over literate 86.9%; males literate 91.8%; females literate 82.0%. **Health** (1999): physicians 31,603 (1 per 6,605 persons); hospital beds 124,834 (1 per 1,671 persons); infant mortality rate per 1,000 live births (2003) 38.1. **Food** (2002): daily per capita caloric intake 2,904 (vegetable products 96%, animal products 4%); 134% of FAO recommended minimum.

Military

Total active duty personnel (2003): 302,000 (army 76.2%, navy 14.9%, air force 8.9%). **Military expenditure as percentage of GNP** (1999): 1.1% (world 2.4%); per capita expenditure $7.

Background

Proto-Malay peoples migrated to Indonesia from mainland Asia before 1000 BC. Commercial relations were established with China in about the 5th century AD, and Hindu and Buddhist cultural influences from India began to take hold. Arab traders brought Islam to the islands in the 13th century; the religion took hold throughout the islands, except for Bali, which retained its Hindu religion and culture. European influence began in the 16th century, and the Dutch ruled Indonesia from the late 17th century until 1942, when the Japanese invaded. Independence leader Sukarno declared Indonesia's independence in 1945, which the Dutch granted, with nominal union to The Netherlands, in 1949; Indonesia dissolved this union in 1954. The suppression of an alleged coup attempt in 1965 resulted in the deaths of more than 300,000 people the government claimed to be communists, and by 1968 Gen. Suharto had taken power. His government forcibly incorporated East Timor into Indonesia in 1975–76, with much loss of life. In the 1990s the country was beset by political, economic, and environmental problems, and Suharto was deposed in 1998.

Recent Developments

Elections dominated Indonesian life during 2004, and the year came to a tragic close with the massive tsunami of 26 December. The elections brought to power a new president, Susilo Bambang Yudhoyono (commonly known as SBY), and changed the dynamics of the nation's politics. The tsunami was the most lethal in modern history and devastated littoral regions of Aceh province in northern Sumatra, killing at least 120,000 people and displacing 300,000 others. Complicating the rebuilding of Aceh was the continuing conflict between Indonesian security forces and the separatist Free Aceh Movement (GAM). The government of Pres. Megawati Sukarnoputri had launched full-scale military operations against GAM in May 2003, and the province had remained in a state of "military emergency" until May 2004. According to official figures, during 2004 more than 1,200 people had died in the conflict by the end of September. SBY had hinted that he would seek to wind back military operations in Aceh and restore full civilian control, but details were not announced. A second large earthquake in March 2005 that killed hundreds of people and the eruption of the Mount Talang volcano in central Sumatra in April kept memories of the tsunami vivid and crippled the tourism industry.

Internet resources: <www.budpar.go.id>.

Iran

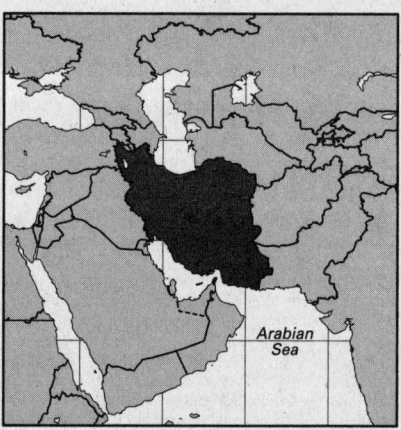

Official name: Jomhuri-ye Eslami-ye Iran (Islamic Republic of Iran). **Form of government:** unitary Islamic republic with one legislative house (Islamic Consultative Assembly [290]). **Supreme political/religious authority:** *Rahbar* (Spiritual Leader; not required to be a supreme theological authority) Ayatollah Sayyed Ali Khamenei (from 1989). **Head of state and government:** President Mahmoud Ahmadinejad (from 3 Aug 2005). **Capital:** Tehran. **Official language:** Farsi (Persian). **Official religion:** Islam. **Monetary unit:** 1 rial (Rls); valuation (7 Jul 2005) $1 = Rls 8,995.00.

Demography

Area (land area only): 629,272 sq mi, 1,629,807 sq km. **Population** (2004; based on total area of 636,400 sq mi [1,648,200 sq km]): 67,503,000. **Density** (2004): persons per sq mi 106.1, persons per sq km 41.0. **Urban** (2003): 66.7%. **Sex distribution** (2003): male 50.99%; female 49.01%. **Age**

1 metric ton = about 1.1 short tons;   1 kilometer = 0.6 mi (statute);   1 metric ton-km cargo = about 0.68 short ton-mi cargo;   c.i.f.: cost, insurance, and freight;   f.o.b.: free on board

breakdown (2003): under 15, 29.4%; 15–29, 34.5%; 30–44, 19.4%; 45–59, 10.0%; 60–74, 5.1%; 75 and over, 1.6%. **Ethnic composition** (2000): Persian 34.9%; Azerbaijani 15.9%; Kurd 13.0%; Luri 7.2%; Gilaki 5.1%; Mazandarani 5.1%; Afghan 2.8%; Arab 2.5%; other 13.5%. **Religious affiliation** (2000): Muslim 95.6% (Shi'i 90.1%, Sunni 5.5%); Zoroastrian 2.8%; Christian 0.5%; other 1.1%. **Major cities** (1996): Tehran 6,758,845; Mashhad 1,887,405; Esfahan 1,266,072; Tabriz 1,191,043; Shiraz 1,053,025. **Location:** Middle East, bordering the Caspian Sea, Turkmenistan, Afghanistan, Pakistan, the Gulf of Oman, the Persian Gulf, Iraq, Turkey, Azerbaijan, and Armenia.

Vital statistics

Birth rate per 1,000 population (2003): 17.2 (world avg. 21.3). **Death rate** per 1,000 population (2003): 5.6 (world avg. 9.1). **Natural increase rate** per 1,000 population (2003): 11.6 (world avg. 12.2). **Total fertility rate** (avg. births per childbearing woman; 2003): 1.9. **Marriage rate** per 1,000 population (2002–03): 9.9. **Life expectancy** at birth (2003): male 68.0 years; female 70.7 years.

National economy

Budget (2001–02). *Revenue:* Rls 180,975,000,000,000 (petroleum and natural gas revenue 57.0%; taxes 23.0%, of which corporate 6.8%, import duties 6.5%; other 20.0%). *Expenditures:* Rls 168,992,000,000,000 (current expenditure 66.6%; development expenditures 15.1%; other 18.3%). **Public debt** (external, outstanding; 2002): $6,578,000,000. **Tourism** (2002): receipts $1,249,000,000; expenditures $2,514,000,000. **Gross national product** (2003): $132,896,000,000 ($2,000 per capita). **Production** (metric tons except as noted). *Agriculture, forestry, fishing* (2003): wheat 12,900,000, sugar beets 5,300,000, sugarcane 3,650,000; livestock (number of live animals) 53,900,000 sheep, 9,000,000 cattle; roundwood (2003) 1,310,751 cu m; fish catch (2001–02) 399,000. *Mining and quarrying* (metal content; 2001): iron ore 5,400,000; copper ore 120,000; manganese 105,000. *Manufacturing* (value added in $'000,000; 2000): basic chemicals 5,871; motor vehicles and parts 5,091; iron and steel 4,199. *Energy production (consumption):* electricity (kW-hr; 2003–04) 146,923,000,000 ([2002–03] 136,231,000,000); coal (2000) 1,394,000 (2,094,000); crude petroleum (barrels; 2003–04) 1,364,000,000 ([2000] 470,000,000); petroleum products (2000) 68,687,000 (54,319,000); natural gas (cu m; 2001–02) 86,300,000,000 (66,600,000,000). **Population economically active** (2002–03): total 19,819,000; activity rate 30.0% (participation rates: over age 15 [1996] 44.0%; female [1996] 12.7%; unemployed [2002–03] 15.7%). **Household income and expenditure.** Average household size (2000) 4.6; annual average income per urban household (1998–99) Rls 15,151,894; sources of urban income (1998–99): wages 32.8%, self-employment 29.6%, other 37.6%; expenditure (1997–98): food, beverages, and tobacco 32.5%, housing and energy 27.0%, transportation 11.4%. **Land use** as % of total land area (2000): in temporary crops 8.8%, in permanent crops 1.2%, in pasture 26.9%; overall forest area 4.5%.

Foreign trade

Imports (2002-f.o.b. in balance of trade and c.i.f. in commodities and trading partners): $20,336,000,000 (nonelectrical machinery and apparatus 22.1%, road vehicles 15.4%, chemicals and chemical products 11.1%, iron and steel 8.0%, food products 7.2%, gold 7.1%). *Major import sources* (2002): Germany 17.1%; Switzerland 9.3%; UAE 9.0%; France 5.9%; Italy 5.8%. **Exports** (2002): $28,356,000,000 (crude and refined petroleum 85.4%, carpets 1.9%, nuts 1.7%). *Major export destinations* (2003): Japan 23.0%; China 10.2%; Italy 6.6%; Taiwan 6.4%; South Korea 5.0%.

Transport and communications

Transport. *Railroads* (2002–03): route length 7,265 km; (2001–02) passenger-km 8,043,000,000; (2001–02) metric ton-km cargo 14,613,000,000. *Roads* (2001–02): length 80,720 km (paved 100%). *Vehicles* (2000–01): passenger cars 1,351,800; trucks and buses 384,900. *Air transport* (2003; Iran Air): passenger-km 7,658,000,000; metric ton-km cargo 99,050,000; airports (1996) 19. **Communications**, in total units (units per 1,000 persons). Daily newspaper circulation (2000): 1,780,000 (28); radios (2000): 17,900,000 (281); televisions (2002): 11,331,500 (173); telephone main lines (2003): 14,571,100 (220); cellular telephone subscribers (2003): 3,376,500 (51); personal computers (2002): 4,900,000 (75); Internet users (2003): 4,300,000 (65).

Education and health

Literacy (2002): total population age 15 and over literate 77.1%; males literate 83.5%; females literate 70.4%. **Health** (2002–03): physicians 17,975 (1 per 3,726 persons; excludes private sector physicians); hospital beds 110,797 (1 per 604 persons); infant mortality rate per 1,000 live births (2003) 44.2. **Food** (2001): daily per capita caloric intake 2,931 (vegetable products 90%, animal products 10%); 122% of FAO recommended minimum.

Military

Total active duty personnel (2003): 540,000 (revolutionary guard corps 22.2%, army 64.9%, navy 3.3%, air force 9.6%). **Military expenditure as percentage of GNP** (1999): 2.9% (world 2.4%); per capita expenditure $106.

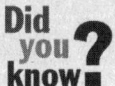

Did you know? Shiraz is the capital of Fars province in south-central Iran, lying at an elevation of 4,875 ft. (1,486 m). Famous for its wine, it is notable for its gardens, shrines, and mosques. Shiraz is the birthplace of the Persian poets Sa'di and Hafez, whose garden tombs, both resplendently renovated, lie on the northern outskirts.

Background

Habitation in Iran dates to c. 100,000 BC, but recorded history began with the Elamites c. 3000 BC. The Medes flourished from c. 728 BC but were overthrown (550 BC) by the Persians, who were in turn conquered by Alexander the Great in the 4th century BC. The Parthians created a Greek-speaking empire that lasted from 247 BC to AD 226, when control passed to the Sasanians. Arab Muslims conquered them in 640 and ruled Iran for 850 years. In 1502 the Safavids established a dynasty that lasted until 1736. The Qajars ruled from 1779, but in the 19th century the country was controlled economically by the Russian and British empires. Reza Khan seized power in a coup (1921). His son Mohammad Reza Shah Pahlavi alienated religious leaders with a program of modernization and Westernization and was overthrown in 1979; Shi'ite cleric Ruhollah Khomeini then set up a fundamentalist Islamic republic, and Western influence was suppressed. The destructive Iran-Iraq War of the 1980s ended in a stalemate. During the 1990s the government gradually moved to a more liberal conduct of state affairs.

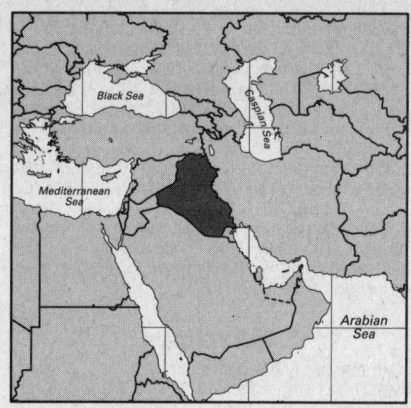

Recent Developments

Elections to Iran's seventh Majlis (parliament) took place on 20 Feb 2004 in a climate of mistrust caused by the Council of Guardians, which debarred thousands of candidates whom it found inadequately committed to Islam. Overall victory was won by conservative groups, and the hard-liners were in undisputed control. Foreign policy remained antagonistic to the West, not least the United States. The US and the EU showed increasing alarm at Iran's nuclear program. In February International Atomic Energy Agency (IAEA) inspectors announced that Iran had failed to disclose fully its program of nuclear development and had traded on the international black market. In September Iran announced a 10-point proposal on nuclear and related security issues, including elimination of all aspects of nuclear weaponry, but this did not deter US demands for immediate abandonment of its nuclear program. Meanwhile, by declining to sign an Additional Safeguard Protocol to the 1968 Nuclear Non-proliferation Treaty, Iran edged ever closer to being subject to UN Security Council economic sanctions. There was serious speculation that either the US or Israel might attack the country's nuclear industry. Negotiations between Iran and three European states dragged on in 2005 but without much satisfaction for any of the parties.

Internet resources: <www.itto.org>.

Iraq

Official name: Al-Jumhuriyah al-Iraqiyah (Republic of Iraq). **Form of government:** transitional regime with one legislative body (National Council [100; all seats are nonelected]). **Head of state:** President Jalal Talabani (from 7 Apr 2005). **Head of government:** Prime Minister Ayad Allawi (from 1 Jun 2004). **Capital:** Baghdad. **Official languages:** Arabic; Kurdish. **Official religion:** Islam. **Monetary unit:** 1 (new) Iraqi dinar (ID); valuation (7 Jul 2005) $1 = ID 1,470.00.

Demography

Area: 167,618 sq mi, 434,128 sq km. **Population** (2004): 25,375,000. **Density** (2004): persons per sq mi 151.4, persons per sq km 58.5. **Urban** (2000):

67.5%. **Sex distribution** (2001): male 50.57%; female 49.43%. **Age breakdown** (2000): under 15, 42.1%; 15–29, 30.4%; 30–44, 15.6%; 45–59, 7.4%; 60–74, 3.5%; 75 and over, 1.0%. **Ethnic composition** (2000): Arab 64.7%; Kurd 23.0%; Azerbaijani 5.6%; Turkmen 1.2%; Persian 1.1%; other 4.4%. **Religious affiliation** (2000): Shi'i Muslim 62.0%; Sunni Muslim 34.0%; Christian (primarily Chaldean rite and Syrian rite Catholic and Nestorian) 3.2%; other (primarily Yazidi syncretist) 0.8%. **Major cities** (2003): Baghdad 5,750,000; Mosul 1,800,000; Al-Basrah 1,400,000; Irbil 850,000; Karkuk 750,000. **Location:** Middle East, bordering Turkey, Iran, the Persian Gulf, Kuwait, Saudi Arabia, Jordan, and Syria.

Vital statistics

Birth rate per 1,000 population (2003): 33.7 (world avg. 21.3). **Death rate** per 1,000 population (2003): 5.8 (world avg. 9.1). **Natural increase rate** per 1,000 population (2003): 27.9 (world avg. 12.2). **Total fertility rate** (avg. births per childbearing woman; 2003): 4.5. **Marriage rate** per 1,000 population (2000): 7.3. **Divorce rate** per 1,000 population (1997): 1.3. **Life expectancy** at birth (2003): male 66.7 years; female 69.0 years.

National economy

Budget (2003). *Revenue:* ID 4,596,000,000,000 (petroleum revenue 89%; other 11%). *Expenditures:* ID 9,233,000,000,000 (current expenditure 79.7%; development expenditure 20.3%). **Production** (metric tons except as noted). *Agriculture, forestry, fishing* (2002): wheat 800,000, dates 650,000, potatoes 625,000; livestock (number of live animals) 6,200,-000 sheep, 1,400,000 cattle; roundwood (2001) 111,294 cu m; fish catch (2001) 22,800. *Mining and quarrying* (2002): phosphate rock 100,000. *Manufacturing* (value added in $'000,000; 1995): refined petroleum 143; bricks, tiles, and cement 103; food products 59. *Energy production (consumption):* electricity (kW-hr; 2000) 30,521,000,000 (30,521,-000,000); crude petroleum (barrels; 2003) 485,-400,000 ([2000] 180,793,000); petroleum products (2000) 20,589,000 (18,644,000); natural gas (cu m; 2002) 2,900,000,000 ([2000] 3,737,000,000).

1 metric ton = about 1.1 short tons;   1 kilometer = 0.6 mi (statute);   1 metric ton-km cargo = about 0.68 short ton-mi cargo;   c.i.f.: cost, insurance, and freight;   f.o.b.: free on board

Household income and expenditure (1988). Average household size 8.9; sources of income: self-employment 33.9%, wages and salaries 23.9%, transfers 23.0%, rent 18.6%; expenditure (1993): food 62%, housing 12%, clothing 10%. **Gross domestic product** (2003): $19,110,000,000 ($770 per capita). **Public debt** (external, outstanding; 1999): $23,000,-000,000. **Population economically active** (1996): total 5,573,000; activity rate of total population 27.6% (participation rates: ages 15–64, 45.7%; female 25.0%). **Tourism** (2001): receipts $14,500,000; expenditures $30,600,000. **Land use** as % of total land area (2000): in temporary crops 12.5%, in permanent crops 0.8%, in pasture 9.1%; overall forest area 1.8%.

Foreign trade

Imports (2003-c.i.f.): $9,933,000,000 (UN oil-for-food program 65.7%, capital goods 17.0%, consumer goods 11.4%). *Major import sources:* EU 36.4%; Asia (excluding Middle East) 25.7%; Arab countries 19.9%. **Exports** (2003-f.o.b.): $10,086,000,000 (crude petroleum 82.8%; food and live animals 5.0%). *Major export destinations:* Western Hemisphere (mostly US) 71.2%; EU 13.3%; Arab countries 8.8%.

Transport and communications

Transport. *Railroads* (1999): route length 2,603 km; passenger-km 499,600,000; metric ton-km cargo 830,200,000. *Roads* (1999): total length 45,550 km (paved 84%). *Vehicles* (1998): passenger cars 735,521; trucks and buses 349,202. *Air transport:* Iraqi Airways resumed international flights in September 2004 after 14 years of being grounded by war and sanctions. **Communications,** in total units (units per 1,000 persons). Daily newspaper circulation (2000): 431,000 (19); radios (2000): 5,030,000 (222); televisions (2000): 1,880,000 (83); telephone main lines (2002): 675,000 (28); cellular telephone subscribers (2002): 20,000 (1); Internet users (2002): 25,000 (1).

Education and health

Educational attainment (1987). Percentage of population age 10 and over having: no formal schooling 52.8%; primary education 21.5%; secondary 11.6%; higher 4.1%; unknown 10.0%. **Literacy** (1995): total population age 15 and over literate 58.0%; males literate 70.7%; females literate 45.0%. **Health:** physicians (1998) 11,046 (1 per 1,937 persons); hospital beds (1999) 26,961 (1 per 817 persons); infant mortality rate per 1,000 live births (2003) 55.2. **Food** (2000): daily per capita caloric intake 2,197 (vegetable products 96%, animal products 4%); 91% of FAO recommended minimum.

Military

Total active duty personnel: US/allied coalition forces (November 2004): 138,000/24,000. **Military expenditure as percentage of GDP** (1999): 5.5% (world 2.4%); per capita expenditure $57.

Background

Called Mesopotamia in classical times, the region gave rise to the world's earliest civilizations, including those of Sumer, Akkad, and Babylon. Conquered by Alexander the Great in 330 BC, the area later became a battleground between Romans and Parthians, then between Sasanians and Byzantines. Arab Muslims conquered it in the 7th century AD and ruled until the Mongols took over in 1258. The Ottomans took control in the 16th century and ruled until 1917. The British occupied the country during World War I and created the kingdom of Iraq in 1921. The British occupied Iraq again during World War II. A king was restored following the war, but a revolution ended the monarchy in 1958. Following a series of military coups, the socialist Ba'th Party, led by Saddam Hussein, took control and established totalitarian rule in 1968. The Iran-Iraq War of the 1980s and the Persian Gulf War (precipitated by the Iraqi invasion of Kuwait in 1990) brought heavy casualties and disrupted the economy. The 1990s were dominated by economic and political turmoil. In response to increasingly willful and autocratic behavior by Saddam Hussein and the contention that Iraq was in possession of weapons of mass destruction (none were ever found), on 19 March 2003 air attacks on Baghdad began, and soon afterward US and British ground forces invaded southern Iraq from Kuwait; within a month most of the country was under the control of coalition forces. Saddam was taken into custody in December. In July US authorities established an Iraqi Governing Council, and a new interim constitution was agreed upon in late February 2004. Almost immediately after the occupation began, however, various forms of Iraqi opposition arose, and resistance grew in tempo and violence in the years that followed.

Recent Developments

The year 2004 in Iraq was marked by a sharp degradation of the security situation while the US-led coalition occupation forces struggled to rebuild the Iraqi nation. The numbers of shadowy underground insurgent groups launching attacks against American forces and Iraqi government targets were legion. Most notorious among them was a group under the control of Abu Musab al-Zarqawi, a Jordanian-born terrorist with ties to the al-Qaeda terrorist network. These groups attracted both homegrown insurgents and non-Iraqi volunteer fighters from Arab and Islamic countries who had entered Iraq across poorly guarded borders, mainly via Syria and Iran. Insurgents also comprised remnants of the old Iraqi Ba'th regime, Arab nationalists, and Sunni Islamic fundamentalists. They were responsible for countless acts of killing, sabotage, destruction of public property, hostage taking, and suicide bombings.

On 20 Mar 2004 the US military charged several members of the US Army police with assault and mistreatment of Iraqi prisoners at Abu Ghraib prison on the outskirts of Baghdad. Shocking photos of American prison guards humiliating Muslim prisoners had circulated widely and were a major embarrassment to the US military. Several of the accused military personnel were brought to trial, and some were found guilty and received punishment.

Under pressure from the resistance movement, the US authorities returned sovereignty to the Iraqis on 28 Jun 2004, earlier than scheduled. An interim administration was appointed with the task of preparing for general elections to be held by 30 Jan 2005. UN Special Adviser Lakhdar Brahimi selected Ghazi al-Yawar, a Sunni sheikh, to be president and head of the interim administration. Subsequently, Ayad Allawi was elected prime minister of the interim government. The Transitional Administrative Law was adopted by the Governing Council on 8 March. The document proclaimed Islam as a source of legislation and granted individual rights to all Iraqis. It did not expand the Kurdish self-governing area.

Despite a turbulent run-up to the ballot, the 30 Jan 2005 elections were held on schedule with a large turnout (at least among the majority Shi'ite population) of 58% and relatively little violence. The main winner (140 seats) was a loose coalition of Shi'ite parties under the influence of the Grand Ayatollah Ali al-Sistani; Prime Minister Allawi's more pro-Western Shi'ite party won 40 seats, and the Kurdistan Alliance showed strongly, taking 75 seats. The new Iraqi parliament convened on 16 March and was immediately plunged into divisive wrangling over the formation of a government and planning for a constitution. A Kurd, Jalal Talabani, emerged as president on 6 April and the leader of a major Shi'ite party, Ibrahim al-Jaafari, was chosen prime minister the following day.

Internet resources:
<www.iraqigovernment.org/index_en.htm >.

Ireland

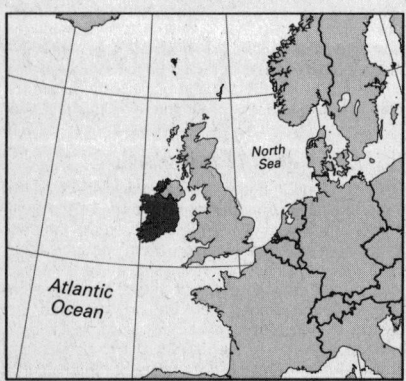

North Sea

Atlantic Ocean

Official name: Éire (Irish); Ireland (English). **Form of government:** unitary multiparty republic with two legislative houses (Senate [60, including 11 nonelective seats]; House of Representatives [166]). **Chief of state:** President Mary McAleese (from 1997). **Head of government:** Prime Minister Bertie Ahern (from 1997). **Capital:** Dublin. **Official languages:** Irish; English. **Official religion:** none. **Monetary unit:** 1 euro (€) = 100 cents; valuation (7 Jul 2005) $1 = €0.84; at conversion on 1 Jan 2002, €1= 0.79 Irish pound (£Ir).

Demography

Area: 27,133 sq mi, 70,273 sq km. **Population** (2004): 4,024,000. **Density** (2004): persons per sq mi 148.3, persons per sq km 57.3. **Urban** (2002): 59.6%. **Sex distribution** (2003): male 49.68%; female 50.32%. **Age breakdown** (2003): under 15, 21.0%; 15–29, 24.1%; 30–44, 22.3%; 45–59, 17.4%; 60–74, 10.3%; 75 and over, 4.9%. **Ethnic composi-**

tion (2000): Irish 95.0%; British 1.7%, of which English 1.4%; Ulster Irish 1.0%; US white 0.8%; other 1.5%. **Religious affiliation** (2002): Roman Catholic 88.4%; Church of Ireland (Anglican) 3.0%; other Christian 1.6%; nonreligious 3.5%; other 3.5%. **Major cities** (2002): Dublin 495,781 (urban agglomeration 1,004,600); Cork 123,062; Galway 65,832; Limerick 54,023; Waterford 44,594. **Location:** western Europe, bordering the UK (Northern Ireland), the Irish Sea, the Celtic Sea, and the North Atlantic Ocean.

Vital statistics

Birth rate per 1,000 population (2003): 15.5 (world avg. 21.3). **Death rate** per 1,000 population (2003): 7.2 (world avg. 9.1). **Natural increase rate** per 1,000 population (2003): 8.3 (world avg. 12.2). **Marriage rate** per 1,000 population (2003): 5.1. **Total fertility rate** (avg. births per childbearing woman; 2003): 2.0. **Life expectancy** at birth (2002): male 75.1 years; female 80.3 years.

National economy

Budget (2000). *Revenue:* £Ir 21,741,000,000 (income taxes 33.0%, value-added tax 27.0%, excise taxes 15.4%). *Expenditures:* £Ir 19,297,000,000 (social welfare 27.9%, health 20.9%, education 14.9%, debt service 10.5%). **Total public debt** (2001): $37,837,410,000. **Gross national product** (2003): $105,160,000,000 ($26,960 per capita). **Tourism** (2002): receipts $3,768,000,000; expenditures $3,741,000,000. **Production** (metric tons except as noted). *Agriculture, forestry, fishing* (2002): sugar beets 1,313,000, barley 963,000, wheat 867,000; livestock (number of live animals) 6,408,000 cattle, 4,807,000 sheep, 1,763,000 pigs; roundwood (2001) 2,455,000 cu m; fish catch (2001) 417,244. *Mining and quarrying* (metal content; 2002): zinc ore 252,700; lead ore 32,500. *Manufacturing* (gross value added in €'000,000; 2001): chemicals and chemical products 12,370; electrical and optical equipment 7,293; food and beverages 6,902. *Energy production (consumption):* electricity (kW-hr; 2000) 23,750,000,000 (23,848,000,000); coal (2000) none (2,828,000); crude petroleum (barrels; 2000) none (24,540,000); petroleum products (2000) 3,197,000 (7,708,000); natural gas (cu m; 2000) 1,120,800,000 (4,019,000,000). **Population economically active** (2002): total 1,827,100; activity rate 46.6% (participation rates: ages 15–64 [2000] 68%; female [2000] 40.3%; unemployed 4.3%). **Household income and expenditure.** Average household size (2002) 2.9; income per household (1994–95): £Ir 16,224; expenditure (1996): food and beverages 35.4%, transportation 13.9%, rent/household goods 11.6%. **Land use** as % of total land area (2000): in temporary crops 15.2%, in permanent crops 0.03%, in pasture 48.6%; overall forest area 9.6%.

Foreign trade

Imports (2000-c.i.f.): €54,858,000,000 (machinery and apparatus 43.4%, of which computers and parts 20.5%, electronic microcircuits 5.1%; chemicals and chemical products 10.8%; road vehicles 7.3%; food 5.1%). *Major import sources:* UK 31.3%; US 16.6%; Germany 5.8%; Japan 4.8%; France 4.7%. **Exports**

---

1 metric ton = about 1.1 short tons;   1 kilometer = 0.6 mi (statute);   1 metric ton-km cargo = about 0.68 short ton-mi cargo;   c.i.f.: cost, insurance, and freight;   f.o.b.: free on board

(2000-f.o.b.): €82,562,000,000 (computers and parts 23.5%; organic chemicals 20.2%; food 7.1%; electronic microcircuits 5.3%; sound-recording devices 5.0%; telecommunications equipment 4.2%). *Major export destinations:* UK 21.8%; US 17.2%; Germany 11.3%; France 7.6%; The Netherlands 5.6%.

Transport and communications

Transport. *Railroads* (2001): route length 1,947 km; passenger-km 1,515,303,000; metric ton-km cargo 515,754,000. *Roads* (1999): length 92,500 km (paved 94%). *Vehicles* (2000): passenger cars 1,269,245; trucks and buses 188,814. *Air transport* (2001; Aer Lingus only): passenger-km 8,901,000-,000; metric ton-km cargo 146,530,000; airports (1996) 9. **Communications,** in total units (units per 1,000 persons). Daily newspaper circulation (2000): 574,000 (150); radios (2000): 2,660,000 (695); televisions (2002): 2,707,000 (694); telephone main lines (2003): 1,955,000 (486); cellular telephone subscribers (2003): 3,400,000 (845); personal computers (2002): 1,654,000 (421); Internet users (2003): 1,260,000 (313).

Education and health

Educational attainment (1999). Percentage of population ages 25–64 and over having: no formal schooling through lower secondary 49%; upper secondary 30%; higher 21%, of which university 11%. **Health:** physicians (1998) 8,114 (1 per 457 persons); hospital beds (2002) 13,020 (1 per 306 persons); infant mortality rate per 1,000 live births (2000) 5.6. **Food** (2001): daily per capita caloric intake 3,666 (vegetable products 69%, animal products 31%); 146% of FAO recommended minimum.

Military

Total active duty personnel (2003): 10,460 (army 81.3%, navy 10.5%, air force 8.2%). **Military expenditure as percentage of GNP** (1999): 1.0% (world 2.4%); per capita expenditure $208.

Did you know? Waterford glass is a heavy cut glassware produced in Waterford, Ireland, since 1729. Waterford glass, is characterized by thick walls, deeply incised geometric cutting, and brilliant polish. The smoky, bluish gray color of early Waterford glass was considered a drawback, and a clear crystal was produced after 1830.

Background

Human settlement in Ireland began c. 6000 BC, and Celtic migration dates from c. 300 BC. St. Patrick is credited with Christianizing the country in the 5th century AD. Norse domination began in 795 and ended in 1014, when the Norse were defeated by Brian Boru. Gaelic Ireland's independence ended in 1171 when English King Henry II proclaimed himself overlord of the island. Beginning in the 16th century, Irish Catholic landowners fled religious persecution by the English and were replaced by English and Scottish Protestant migrants. The United Kingdom of Great Britain and Ireland was established in 1801. The Great Famine of the 1840s led over two million

people to emigrate and built momentum for Irish Home Rule. The Easter Rising (1916) was followed by civil war (1919–21) between the Catholic majority in southern Ireland, who favored complete independence, and the Protestant majority in the north, who preferred continued union with Britain. Southern Ireland was granted dominion status and became the Irish Free State in 1921, and in 1937 it adopted the name Éire and became a sovereign independent nation. It remained neutral during World War II. Britain recognized the status of Ireland in 1949 but declared that cession of the northern six counties could not occur without the consent of the Parliament of Northern Ireland. In 1973 Ireland joined the European Economic Community (later the European Community) and is now a member of the EU. The late 20th century was dominated by sectarian hostilities between the island's Catholics and Protestants.

Recent Developments

In June 2004 the Fianna Fail and Progressive Democrat parties suffered severe reverses in the local and European elections within the Republic. Fianna Fail's vote collapsed as the voters sent strong messages of protest. Poor health services, inadequate public transportation, bad roads, overcrowded schools, and controversial legislation—notably a ban on smoking in the workplace—combined to create strong antigovernment sentiment. The mainstream opposition party, Fine Gael, secured some additional seats, but the bulk of the gains went to Sinn Fein. In November popular Irish Pres. Mary McAleese was returned to office unopposed. Two new laws adopted in March 2005 made Gaelic (Irish) the only legal language for place-names in government documents and signs in parts of western Ireland and called for Gaelic to be used equally with English elsewhere in the country.

Internet resources: <www.ireland.ie>.

Isle of Man

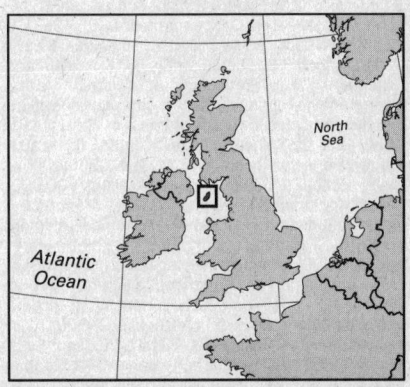

Official name: Isle of Man (Manx Gaelic: Ellan Vannin). **Political status:** crown dependency (UK) with two legislative bodies (collectively named Tynwald; Legislative Council [11, including 3 nonelective seats]; House of Keys [24]). **Chief of state:** Queen Elizabeth II (from 1952), represented by Lieutenant Governor Ian David Macfadyen (from 2000). **Head of government:**

Chief Minister Donald Gelling (14 Dec 2004). **Capital:** Douglas. **Official language:** English. **Official religion:** none. **Monetary unit:** 1 Manx pound (£M) = 100 new pence; valuation (7 Jul 2005) $1 = £M 0.57; the Manx pound is equivalent in value to the pound sterling (£).

Demography

Area: 220.9 sq mi, 572.0 km. **Population** (2004): 77,700. **Density** (2004): persons per sq mi 351.6, persons per sq km 135.8. **Urban** (2001): 72.6%. **Sex distribution** (2001): male 48.97%; female 51.03%. **Age breakdown** (2001): under 15, 17.9%; 15–29, 17.5%; 30–44, 22.6%; 45–59, 20.1%; 60–74, 13.6%; 75 and over, 8.3%. **Population by place of birth** (2001): Isle of Man 48.0%; UK 45.2%, of which England 38.2%, Scotland 3.5%, Northern Ireland 2.3%, Wales 1.2%; Ireland 2.3%; other Europe 1.0%; other 3.5%. **Religious affiliation** (2000): Christian 63.7%, of which Anglican 40.5%, Methodist 9.9%, Roman Catholic 8.2%; other (mostly nonreligious) 36.3%. **Major towns** (2001): Douglas 25,347; Onchan 8,803; Ramsey 7,322; Peel 3,785; Port Erin 3,369. **Location:** Irish Sea, midway between Ireland and Great Britain.

Vital statistics

Birth rate per 1,000 population (2003): 11.1 (world avg. 21.3); (2002) legitimate 64.6%. **Death rate** per 1,000 population (2003): 11.0 (world avg. 9.1). **Natural increase rate** per 1,000 population (2003): 0.1 (world avg. 12.2). **Total fertility rate** (avg. births per childbearing woman; 1999): 1.6. **Marriage rate** per 1,000 population (2002): 5.6. **Divorce rate** per 1,000 population (2000): 3.6. **Life expectancy** at birth (1999): male 73.9 years; female 80.8 years.

National economy

Budget (2001–02). *Revenue:* £466,177,000 (customs duties and excise taxes 64.3%; income taxes 34.8%, of which resident 30.5%, nonresident 4.3%; nontax revenue 0.9%). *Expenditures:* £360,499,000 (health and social security 39.8%; education 19.1%; transportation 6.8%; home affairs 6.0%; tourism and recreation 5.8%). **Production.** *Agriculture, forestry, fishing:* main crops include hay, oats, barley, wheat, and orchard crops; livestock (number of live animals; 2002) 171,000 sheep, 34,000 cattle; fish catch (value of principal catch in £; 2001): 2,200,000, of which scallops 1,600,000, queen scallops 600,000. *Mining and quarrying:* sand and gravel. *Manufacturing* (value added in $; 1996–97): electrical and nonelectrical machinery/apparatus, textiles, other 103,700,000; food and beverages 18,600,000. *Energy production (consumption):* electricity (kW-hr; 2001–02), n.a. (345,000,000). **Household income and expenditure.** Average household size (2001) 2.4; income per household (1981–82) £7,479; sources of income (1981– 82): wages and salaries 64.1%, transfer payments 16.9%, interest and dividends 11.2%, self-employment 6.6%; expenditure (1981–82): food and beverages 31.0%, transportation 14.9%, energy 11.0%, housing 7.9%, clothing and footwear 7.0%. **Gross national product** (at current market prices; 2001–02): $1,770,000,000 ($23,000 per capita).

Population economically active (2001): total 39,685; activity rate of total population 52.0% (participation rates: ages 16 and over 64.2%; female 45.4%; unemployed 1.6%). **Tourism:** receipts from visitors (1999) $90,600,000; number of tourists (2001) 201,300. **Land use** as % of total land area (2000): in temporary crops 8.1%, in permanent crops 0.7%, in pasture 71.5%.

Foreign trade

Imports: n.a. *Major import sources:* mostly the UK. **Exports:** traditional exports include scallops, herring, beef, lambs, and tweeds. *Major export destinations:* mostly the UK.

Transport and communications

Transport. *Railroads* (2001): route length 61 km. *Roads* (2001): total length, more than 805 km. *Vehicles* (2001): passenger cars 45,195; trucks and buses 4,635. *Air transport* (1998; Manx Airlines): passenger-km 846,775,000; metric ton-km cargo 168,000; airports (2001) with scheduled flights 1. **Communications,** in total units (units per 1,000 persons). Newspaper circulation (2001): 2 weekly newspapers and 1 biweekly newspaper (n.a.); televisions (2000): 28,600 (355); telephone main lines (2001): 56,000 (741); cellular telephone subscribers (2001): 32,000 (424).

Health

Physicians (2003) 143 (1 per 540 persons); hospital beds (1998) 505 (1 per 143 persons); infant mortality rate per 1,000 live births (2002) 3.0. **Food** (2002): daily per capita caloric intake 3,412 (vegetable products 69%, animal products 31%); 135% of FAO recommended minimum.

Military

Total active duty personnel: the UK is responsible for defense.

Israel

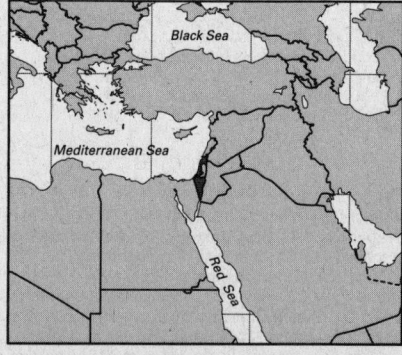

Official name: Medinat Yisrael (Hebrew); Isrāil (Arabic) (State of Israel). **Form of government:** multiparty

1 metric ton = about 1.1 short tons; 1 kilometer = 0.6 mi (statute); 1 metric ton-km cargo = about 0.68 short ton-mi cargo; c.i.f.: cost, insurance, and freight; f.o.b.: free on board

republic with one legislative house (Knesset [120]). **Chief of state:** President Moshe Katzav (from 2000). **Head of government:** Prime Minister Ariel Sharon (from 2001). **Capital:** Jerusalem is the proclaimed capital of Israel and the actual seat of government, but recognition of its status as capital by the international community has largely been withheld. **Official languages:** Hebrew; Arabic. **Official religion:** none. **Monetary unit:** 1 New (Israeli) sheqel (NIS) = 100 agorot; valuation (7 Jul 2005) $1 = NIS 4.61.

Demography

Area: 8,367 sq mi, 21,671 sq km. **Population** (2004): 6,562,000. **Density** (2004): persons per sq mi 784.3, persons per sq km 302.8. **Urban** (2002): 91.6%. **Sex distribution** (2000): male 49.33%; female 50.67%. **Age breakdown** (2000): under 15, 28.6%; 15–29, 25.1%; 30–44, 18.7%; 45–59, 14.5%; 60–74, 8.8%; 75 and over, 4.3%. **Ethnic composition** (2004): Jewish 76.2%; Arab and other 23.8%. **Religious affiliation** (2004): Jewish 76.2%; Muslim (mostly Sunni) 15.7%; Christian 2.1%; Druze 1.6%; other 4.4%. **Major cities** (2003): Jerusalem 680,400; Tel Aviv–Yafo 360,400; Haifa 270,800; Rishon LeZiyyon 211,600; Ashdod 187,500. **Location:** Middle East, bordering Lebanon, Syria, Jordan, the West Bank, Egypt, the Gaza Strip, and the Mediterranean Sea.

Vital statistics

Birth rate per 1,000 population (2002): 21.0 (world avg. 21.3); (2000; Jewish population only) legitimate 97.2%. **Death rate** per 1,000 population (2002): 5.8 (world avg. 9.1). **Natural increase rate** per 1,000 population (2002): 15.2 (world avg. 12.2). **Total fertility rate** (avg. births per childbearing woman; 2002): 2.9. **Marriage rate** per 1,000 population (2001): 5.9. **Divorce rate** per 1,000 population (2001): 1.7. **Life expectancy** at birth (2001): male 77.3 years; female 81.2 years.

National economy

Budget (2003). *Revenue:* NIS 205,703,000,000 (tax revenue 75.4%, of which income tax 35.4%, value-added tax 27.7%; nontax revenue 18.0%; grants 6.6%). *Expenditures:* NIS 220,903,000,000 (defense 21.2%; social security and welfare 19.5%; interest on loans 15.1%; education 14.6%; health 7.2%). **Public debt** (2001): $111,658,000,000. **Gross national product** (2003): $105,160,000,000 ($16,020 per capita). **Production** (metric tons except as noted). *Agriculture, forestry, fishing* (2002): potatoes 375,000, tomatoes 352,000, grapefruit and pomelos 255,000; livestock (number of live animals) 392,000 sheep, 390,000 cattle; roundwood (2002) 27,000 cu m; fish catch (2001) 25,100. *Mining and quarrying* (2001): phosphate rock 3,511,000, potash 1,774,000. *Manufacturing* (value added in $'000,-000; 2000): electronic components 2,243; medical, measuring, and testing appliances 2,103; fabricated metals 1,686. *Energy production (consumption):* electricity (kW-hr; 2001) 43,838,000,000 ([2000] 41,459,000,000); hard coal (2000) none (10,257,-000); lignite (2000) 888,000 (888,000); crude petroleum (barrels; 2000) 29,000 (75,800,000); petroleum products (2000) 9,244,000 (10,428,000); natural gas (cu m; 2000) 8,779,000 (8,779,000). **Population economically active** (2003): total

2,601,000; activity rate 40.2% (participation rates: over age 15, 54.3%; female 46.0%; unemployed 10.7%). **Household income and expenditure** (2002). Average household size 3.4; net annual income per household (2001) NIS 136,332; sources of income (2000): salaries and wages 67.5%, self-employment 11.5%; expenditure (2001): housing 22.6%, transport and communications 20.1%, food and beverages 17.0%, education 13.4%, health 4.9%. **Tourism** (2002): receipts $1,197,000,000; expenditures $2,547,000,000. **Land use** as % of total land area (2000): in temporary crops 16.4%, in permanent crops 4.2%, in pasture 6.9%; overall forest area 6.4%.

Foreign trade

Imports (2002-f.o.b. in balance of trade and c.i.f. in commodities and trading partners; balance of trade data excludes the Gaza Strip and the West Bank): $33,106,000,000 (machinery and apparatus 23.7%; diamonds 21.7%; chemicals and chemical products 9.6%; crude petroleum and refined petroleum 7.7%; road vehicles 5.7%). *Major import sources:* US 18.5%; Belgium 9.1%; Germany 7.1%; UK 6.7%; Switzerland 6.3%. **Exports** (2002): $29,511,000,000 (cut diamonds 28.2%; telecommunications equipment 9.2%; rough diamonds 6.5%; organic chemicals 3.9%; electronic microcircuits 3.6%; aircraft parts 3.6%; pharmaceuticals 3.1%). *Major export destinations:* US 40.2%; Belgium 6.3%; Hong Kong 4.7%; UK 3.9%; Germany 3.5%.

Transport and communications

Transport. *Railroads* (2002): route length 678 km; passenger-km 1,116,000,000, metric ton-km cargo 1,102,000,000. *Roads* (2002): total length 16,903 km (paved 100%). *Vehicles* (2002): passenger cars 1,496,878; trucks and buses 347,566. *Air transport* (2003; El Al only): passenger-km 12,126,000,000; metric ton-km cargo 1,091,342,000; airports (1999) with scheduled flights 7. **Communications,** in total units (units per 1,000 persons). Daily newspaper circulation (2000): 1,770,000 (290); radios (2000): 3,210,000 (526); televisions (2000): 2,040,000 (335); telephone main lines (2002): 3,006,000 (453); cellular telephone subscribers (2002): 6,334,000 (954); personal computers (2002): 1,610,000 (243); Internet users (2002): 2,000,000 (301).

Education and health

Educational attainment (2001). Percentage of population age 15 and over having: no formal schooling 3.1%; primary 1.7%; secondary 56.7%; postsecondary, vocational, and higher 38.5%. **Literacy** (2001): 96.9%. **Health** (2002): physicians 21,800 (1 per 291 persons); hospital beds 40,116 (1 per 158 persons); infant mortality rate per 1,000 live births 11.3. **Food** (2001): daily per capita caloric intake 3,512 (vegetable products 81.1%, animal products 18.9%); 137% of FAO recommended minimum.

Military

Total active duty personnel (2003): 167,600 (army 74.6%, navy 4.5%, air force 20.9%). **Military expenditure as percentage of GNP** (1999): 8.8% (world 2.4%); per capita expenditure $1,510.

Background

The record of human habitation in Israel is at least 100,000 years old. Efforts by Jews to establish a national state there began in the late 19th century. Britain supported Zionism and in 1922 assumed political responsibility for what was Palestine. Migration of Jews there during Nazi persecution led to deteriorating relations with Arabs. In 1947 the UN voted to partition the region into separate Jewish and Arab states, a decision opposed by neighboring Arab countries. The State of Israel was proclaimed in 1948, and Egypt, Transjordan, Syria, Lebanon, and Iraq immediately declared war on it. Israel won this war as well as the 1967 Six-Day War, in which it claimed the West Bank from Jordan and the Gaza Strip from Egypt. Another war with its Arab neighbors followed in 1973, but the Camp David Accords led to the signing of a peace treaty between Israel and Egypt in 1979. Israel invaded Lebanon to quell the Palestine Liberation Organization (PLO) in 1982, and in the late 1980s a Palestinian resistance movement arose in the occupied territories. Peace negotiations between Israel and the Arab states and Palestinians began in 1991. Israel and the PLO agreed in 1993 upon a five-year extension of self-government to the Palestinians of the West Bank and the Gaza Strip. Israel signed a full peace treaty with Jordan in 1994. Israeli soldiers and Lebanon's Hezbollah forces clashed in 1997. Following numerous contentious talks between Israel and Lebanon, Israeli troops abruptly withdrew from Lebanon in 2000.

Recent Developments

Prime Minister Ariel Sharon's plan to withdraw Israeli soldiers and settlers unilaterally from Gaza and part of the West Bank dominated the Israeli-Palestinian agenda in 2004–05. The emergence of a more pragmatic Palestinian leadership after the death in late 2004 of Pres. Yasir Arafat raised hopes that the "disengagement plan" could lead to a negotiated Israeli-Palestinian settlement. The plan, announced in late 2003 as the Palestinian uprising against Israeli occupation entered its fourth year, was presented as a significant step toward a two-state solution, with Israel and Palestine living side by side in accordance with the goals of the internationally approved "road map" to peace. As such, the disengagement plan received extensive international and regional backing. In Israel, however, it encountered angry right-wing opposition, and there were fears of armed clashes between radical Jewish settlers and the Israeli military.

Hopes were reinforced in early 2005 when on 9 January Mahmoud Abbas, an opponent of Palestinian violence against Israel, was elected president of the Palestinian Authority and a day later Sharon received the go-ahead for a new coalition government that was expected to be more amenable to his plans to withdraw Israelis from Gaza. The two sides negotiated a truce on 7 February. Spring 2005 was largely devoted to mutual demonstrations of good faith on the part of the two leaders—for example, Abbas reined in his security leaders, firing several of them along the way, while Sharon moved ahead with plans for withdrawal from Gaza and the West Bank, returned security control of Jericho to the Palestinian Authority, and released a number of Palestinian prisoners. Violence

did not cease, however, as there remained powerful forces on both sides that opposed the détente. One bone of contention was Sharon's insistence on retaining control of the largest Jewish "population blocs" in the West Bank, settlements that were created by Israel after 1967.

Internet Resources: <www.goisrael.com>.

Italy

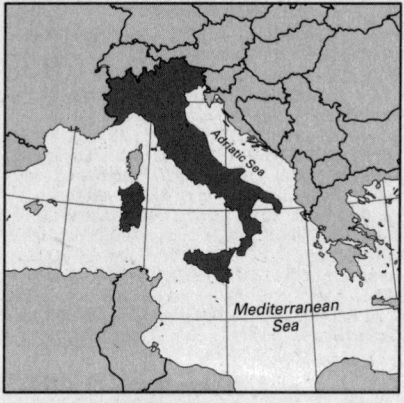

Official name: Repubblica Italiana (Italian Republic). **Form of government:** republic with two legislative houses (Senate [321, including 6 nonelective seats]; Chamber of Deputies [630]). **Chief of state:** President Carlo Azeglio Ciampi (from 1999). **Head of government:** Prime Minister Silvio Berlusconi (from 2001). **Capital:** Rome. **Official language:** Italian. **Official religion:** none. **Monetary unit:** 1 euro (€) = 100 cents; valuation (7 Jul 2005) $1 = €0.84; at conversion on 1 Jan 2002, €1= 1,936.27 Italian lire (Lit).

Demography

Area: 116,343 sq mi, 301,328 sq km. **Population** (2004): 57,537,000. **Density** (2004): persons per sq mi 494.5, persons per sq km 190.9. **Urban** (2003): 67.4%. **Sex distribution** (2003): male 48.44%; female 51.56%. **Age breakdown** (2003): under 15, 14.2%; 15–29, 18.0%; 30–44, 23.5%; 45–59, 19.3%; 60–74, 16.3%; 75 and over, 8.7%. **Ethnolinguistic composition** (2000): Italian 96.0%; North African Arab 0.9%; Italo-Albanian 0.8%; Albanian 0.5%; German 0.4%; Austrian 0.4%; other 1.0%. **Religious affiliation** (2000): Roman Catholic 79.6%; nonreligious 13.2%; Muslim 1.2%; other 6.0%. **Major cities and urban agglomerations** (major city populations are 2001 preliminary census figures; urban agglomeration populations are 2000 estimates by the UN): Rome 2,459,776 (2,649,000); Milan 1,182,693 (4,251,000); Naples 993,386 (3,012,000); Turin 857,433 (1,294,000); Palermo 652,640; Genoa 603,560 (890,000); Bologna 369,955; Florence 352,227 (778,000); Bari 312,452; Catania 306,464; Venice 266,181; Verona 243,474; Messina 236,621; Trieste 209,520. **Location:** southern Europe, bordering Switzerland, Austria, Slovenia, the Mediterranean Sea, and France. **National origin** (1991): Italian 99.3%; foreign-born 0.7%, of which European 0.3%, African 0.2%, Asian 0.1%, other 0.1%. **Households.** Average household size (2000) 2.6; composition of households: 1 person 23.3%, 2 persons 26.1%, 3 persons 23.0%, 4 persons 20.2%, 5 or more persons 7.4%. Family households (1991): 15,538,335 (73.8%); nonfamily 5,527,105 (26.2%), of which 1-person 19.5%. **Immigration** (1997): immigrants 162,857, from Europe 41.1%, of which EU countries 14.2%; Africa 25.5%; Asia 19.0%; Western Hemisphere 14.0%.

Vital statistics

Birth rate per 1,000 population (2003): 9.2 (world avg. 21.3); (2000) legitimate 89.8%; illegitimate 10.2%. **Death rate** per 1,000 population (2003): 10.1 (world avg. 9.1). **Natural increase rate** per 1,000 population (2003): −0.9 (world avg. 12.2). **Total fertility rate** (avg. births per childbearing woman; 2002): 1.3. **Marriage rate** per 1,000 population (2001): 4.7. **Divorce rate** per 1,000 population (2000): 0.7. **Life expectancy** at birth (2003): male 76.5 years; female 82.5 years.

Social indicators

Quality of working life. Average workweek (2001): 39.3 hours. Annual rate per 100,000 workers (2000) for: nonfatal injury 4,030; fatal injury 7. Percentage of labor force insured for damages or income loss (1992) resulting from: injury 100%; permanent disability 100%; death 100%. Number of working days lost to labor stoppages per 1,000 workers (1996): 97. **Material well-being.** Rate per 1,000 of population possessing (1995): telephone 434; automobile 550; television 436. **Social participation.** Eligible voters participating in last national election (13 May 2001): 81.2%. Trade union membership in total workforce (2000): c. 35%. **Social deviance** (2000). Offense rate per 100,000 population for: murder 1.3; rape 4.1; assault 210.4 (1995); theft, including burglary and housebreaking 2,466; drug trafficking 61.1; suicide 6.3 (1996). **Access to services** (2002). Nearly 100% of dwellings have access to electricity, a safe water supply, and toilet facilities. **Leisure** (1998). Favorite leisure activities (as percentage of household spending on culture): cinema 21.8%; sporting events 14.6%; theater 13.8%.

National economy

Gross national product (at current market prices; 2003): $1,242,978,000,000 ($21,560 per capita). **Budget** (2000). *Revenue:* €444,502,000,000 (social security contributions 32.5%, individual income taxes 28.6%, taxes on goods and services 15.9%, corporate income tax 5.9%. *Expenditures:* €462,352,-000,000 (social benefits 41.9%, interest payments 16.0%, grants to general government units 14.9%). **Tourism** (2002): receipts $26,915,000,000; expenditures $16,935,000,000. **Production** (metric tons except as noted). *Agriculture, forestry, fishing* (2003): corn (maize) 8,978,000, sugar beets 8,300,000, grapes 7,484,000, tomatoes 6,634,000, wheat 6,243,000, olives 3,150,000, oranges 1,962,000, apples 1,945,000, potatoes 1,604,000, rice 1,360,000, peaches and nectarines 1,357,000, barley 1,026,000, lettuce 914,000, pears 822,000; live-

stock (number of live animals) 10,950,000 sheep, 9,111,000 pigs, 6,430,000 cattle, 100,000,000 chickens; roundwood (2002) 7,789,000 cu m; fish catch (2001) 528,666. *Mining and quarrying* (2001): loam rock 13,973,000; rock salt 3,281,300; feldspar 3,092,400; barite 10,800; lead 4,000. *Manufacturing* (value added in $'000,000; 2000): nonelectrical machinery and apparatus 25,935; fabricated metal products 22,934; food products 13,468; paints, soaps, pharmaceuticals 10,594; bricks, cement, ceramics 8,418; textiles 8,165; wearing apparel 7,524; motor vehicles and parts 7,254; plastic products 6,627; furniture 5,924; footwear and leather products 5,592; telecommunications equipment 5,374. *Energy production (consumption):* electricity (kW-hr; 2003) 292,632,000,000 ([2000] 320,986,000,-000); hard coal (2000) negligible (18,013,000); lignite (2000) 114,000 (130,000); crude petroleum (barrels; 2001) 27,714,000 ([2000] 599,600,000); petroleum products (2000) 84,900,000 (81,700,-000); natural gas (cu m; 2003) 13,456,000,000 ([2000] 70,770,000,000). **Population economically active** (2001): total 23,901,000; activity rate of total population 42.4% (participation rates: ages 15–64, 63.0%; female 38.7%; unemployed 9.6%). **Household income and expenditure** (2000). Average household size 2.6; sources of income (1996): salaries and wages 38.8%, property income and self-employment 38.5%, transfer payments 22.0%; expenditure (2001): housing 34.9%, food and beverages 18.9%, transportation and communications 16.7%, leisure 6.3%, other 16.2%. **Land use** as % of total land area (2000): in temporary crops 28.2%, in permanent crops 9.7%, in pasture 15.1%; overall forest area 34.0%. **Public debt** (2002): $1,333,669,000,000.

Foreign trade

Imports (2000-c.i.f.): $235,859,000,000 (machinery 20.5%, chemicals 12.0%, road vehicles 11.0%, crude petroleum 7.2%, food 6.9%, iron and steel 3.6%). *Major import sources:* Germany 17.5%; France 11.2%; The Netherlands 5.7%; UK 5.4%; US 5.3%; Spain 4.1%; Belgium 4.0%; Switzerland 3.0%. **Exports** (2000-f.o.b.): $237,640,000,000 (machinery and apparatus 27.7%; chemicals and chemical products 9.1%, road vehicles 8.1%, apparel and clothing accessories 5.6%, textile yarn and fabrics 5.1%, food 4.3%). *Major export destinations:* Germany 15.0%; France 12.5%; US 10.3%; UK 6.8%; Spain 6.2%; Switzerland 3.3%; Belgium 2.7%; The Netherlands 2.6%.

Transport and communications

Transport. *Railroads:* (2002) length 19,786 km; (2001) passenger-km 46,675,000,000; (2001) metric ton-km cargo 24,995,000,000. *Roads* (1997): total length 654,676 km (paved 100%). *Vehicles* (2001): passenger cars 33,129,300; trucks and buses 3,749,200. *Air transport* (2003; Alitalia and Air One only): passenger-km 30,736,000,000; metric ton-km cargo 1,355,000,000; airports (1997) 34. **Communications,** in total units (units per 1,000 persons). Daily newspaper circulation (2000): 5,920,-000 (104); radios (2000): 50,000,000 (878); televisions (2000): 28,100,000 (494); telephone main lines (2003): 26,596,000 (453); cellular telephone subscribers (2003): 55,918,000 (1,018); personal computers (2002): 13,025,000 (231); Internet users (2003): 18,500,000 (337).

Education and health

Educational attainment (1995). Percentage of labor force age 15 and over having: basic literacy or primary education 40.4%; secondary 30.5%; postsecondary technical training 5.1%; some college 19.2%; college degree 4.3%. **Literacy** (2000): total population age 15 and over literate 48,100,000 (98.4%); males literate 23,800,000 (98.9%); females literate 24,300,000 (98.0%). **Health**: physicians (2001) 348,862 (1 per 164 persons); hospital beds (2001) 254,663 (1 per 224 persons); infant mortality rate (2003) 6.2. **Food** (2001): daily per capita caloric intake 3,680 (vegetable products 75%, animal products 25%); 146% of FAO recommended minimum.

Military

Total active duty personnel (2003): 200,000 (army 58.0%, navy 18.0%, air force 24.0%); US military forces (2004) 13,400. **Military expenditure as percentage of GNP** (1999): 2.0% (world 2.4%); per capita expenditure $412.

Did you know? The Blue Grotto is a cave found on the Island of Capri near the Bay of Naples in southern Italy. The most notable of the caves on the island, it was rediscovered in 1826 and is accessible only by boat. Sunlight entering through the water that fills most of the entrance gives it an extraordinary blue light, whence its name.

Background

The Etruscan civilization arose in the 9th century BC and was overthrown by the Romans in the 4th–3rd centuries BC. Barbarian invasions of the 4th and 5th centuries AD destroyed the western Roman empire. Italy's political fragmentation lasted for centuries but did not diminish its impact on European culture, notably during the Renaissance. From the 15th to the 18th century, Italian lands were ruled by France, the Holy Roman Empire, Spain, and Austria. When Napoleonic rule ended in 1815, Italy was again a grouping of independent states. The Risorgimento successfully united most of Italy, including Sicily and Sardinia, by 1861, and the unification of peninsular Italy was completed by 1870. Italy joined the Allies during World War I, but social unrest in the 1920s brought to power the Fascist movement of Benito Mussolini, and Italy allied itself with Nazi Germany in World War II. Defeated by the Allies in 1943, Italy proclaimed itself a republic in 1946. It was a charter member of NATO (1949) and of the European Community. It completed the process of setting up regional legislatures with limited autonomy in the 1970s. Since World War II it has experienced rapid changes of government but has remained socially stable. It worked with other European countries to establish the European Union.

Recent Developments

The government of Prime Minister Silvio Berlusconi took its first steps toward a sweeping reform of Italy's constitution, in keeping with an election pledge to the Northern League, a coalition partner opposed to centralized power as "spendthrift." In March 2004 the Senate passed a bill that would devolve responsibility for health and education from the federal government to the country's 20 regions, transform the Senate into a regional body, substantially diminish the role of the president, and enable Italians to elect directly a prime minister with stronger powers. In October the lower house followed suit. Reform of the judiciary was at the top of the agenda for many after bribery charges were dismissed against Berlusconi in December. The prime minister was obliged to resign in April 2005 after his right-leaning coalition was thrashed in local elections, losing in 11 of 13 contested regions. He promptly formed a new government, however.

Internet resources: <www.italyemb.org>.

Jamaica

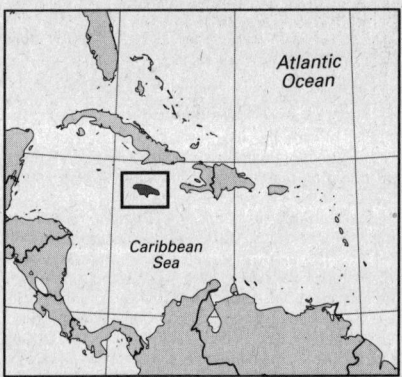

Atlantic Ocean

Caribbean Sea

Official name: Jamaica. **Form of government:** constitutional monarchy with two legislative houses (Senate [21]; House of Representatives [60]). Jamaica is to become a republic by 2007 per announcement of prime minister in September 2003. **Chief of state:** Queen Elizabeth II (from 1952), represented by Governor-General Sir Howard Cooke (from 2001). **Head of government:** Prime Minister Percival James Patterson (from 1992). **Capital:** Kingston. **Official language:** English. **Official religion:** none. **Monetary unit:** 1 Jamaica dollar (J$) = 100 cents; valuation (7 Jul 2005) US$1 = J$61.74.

Demography

Area: 4,244 sq mi, 10,991 sq km. **Population** (2004): 2,649,000. **Density** (2004): persons per sq mi 624.2, persons per sq km 241.0. **Urban** (2001): 52.0%. **Sex distribution** (2001): male 49.22%; female 50.78%. **Age breakdown** (2002): under 15, 32.3%; 15–29, 25.9%; 30–44, 20.6%; 45–59, 11.0%; 60–74, 6.8%; 75 and over, 3.4%. **Ethnic composition** (2001): black 91.6%; mixed race 6.2%; East Indian 0.9%; Chinese 0.2%; white 0.2%; other/unknown 0.9%. **Religious affiliation** (2001): Protestant

61.2%, of which Church of God 23.8%, Seventh-day Adventist 10.8%, Pentecostal 9.5%; Roman Catholic 2.6%; other Christian 1.7%; Rastafarian 0.9%; nonreligious 20.9%; other/unknown 12.7%. **Major cities** (2001): Kingston 96,052 (metro area 579,137); Portmore 161,658; Spanish Town 131,515; Montego Bay 96,488; May Pen 57,334. **Location:** island in the Caribbean Sea south of Cuba.

Vital statistics

Birth rate per 1,000 population (2003): 19.3 (world avg. 21.3). **Death rate** per 1,000 population (2003): 6.4 (world avg. 9.1). **Natural increase rate** per 1,000 population (2003): 12.9 (world avg. 12.2). **Total fertility rate** (avg. births per childbearing woman; 2003): 2.0. **Marriage rate** per 1,000 population (1999): 10.4. **Divorce rate** per 1,000 population (1999): 0.4. **Life expectancy** at birth (2003): male 73.8 years; female 78.0 years.

National economy

Budget (2000–01). *Revenue:* J$101,018,000,000 (tax revenue 86.2%, of which income taxes 35.1%, consumption taxes 26.4%, custom duties 8.4%; nontax revenue 7.7%; bauxite levy 2.7%; capital revenue 1.7%; grants 1.7%). *Expenditures:* J$104,171,000,-000 (current expenditure 91.0%, of which debt interest 41.2%, wages 33.8%; capital expenditure 9.0%). **Production** (metric tons except as noted). *Agriculture, forestry, fishing* (2002): sugarcane 2,400,000, citrus fruits 221,000, vegetables and melons 197,000; livestock (number of live animals) 440,000 goats, 400,000 cattle, 180,000 pigs; roundwood (2002) 867,000 cu m; fish catch (2001) 10,212. *Mining and quarrying* (2003): bauxite 13,443,000; alumina 3,844,000; gypsum 162,000. *Manufacturing* (2001): cement 595,000; animal feeds 385,000; sugar 205,000. *Energy production (consumption):* electricity (kW-hr; 2000) 6,631,000,000 (6,631,000,000); coal (2000) none (72,000); crude petroleum (barrels; 2000) none (7,762,000); petroleum products (2000) 998,000 (3,326,000). **Population economically active** (April 2001): total 1,105,800; activity rate of total population 42.4% (participation rates: ages 14 and over 63.0%; female 43.9%; unemployed 14.8%). **Gross national product** (2003): US$7,285,000,000 (US$2,760 per capita). **Public debt** (external, outstanding; 2002): US$4,592,000,000. **Household income and expenditure.** Average household size (2001) 3.5; average annual income per household (1988) J$8,356; sources of income (1989): wages and salaries 66.1%, self-employment 19.3%, transfers 14.6%; expenditure (1988): food and beverages 55.6%, housing 7.9%, fuel and other household supplies 7.4%, health care 7.0%, transportation 6.4%. **Tourism:** receipts (2002) US$1,200,000,000; expenditures US$258,000,000. **Land use** as % of total land area (2000): in temporary crops 16.1%, in permanent crops 10.2%, in pasture 21.1%; overall forest area 30.0%.

Foreign trade

Imports (2001-c.i.f.): US$3,365,000,000 (consumer goods 29.4%, capital goods 16.8%, refined petroleum and other fuels and lubricants 12.4%, crude petroleum 5.0%). *Major import sources* (2001): US 44.8%; Caricom 12.7%; Latin American countries 10.5%; EU 9.3%, of which UK 3.0%. **Exports** (2001-

f.o.b.): US$1,225,000,000 (alumina 52.5%, bauxite 7.7%, wearing apparel 7.2%, refined sugar 5.8%, coffee 2.5%, rum 2.4%). *Major export destinations:* US 31.1%; Canada 15.6%; UK 12.8%; Norway 7.5%.

Transport and communications

Transport. *Railroads* (2003): route length 201 km (inoperable since 1992 except for 92-km section leased to a mining operator). *Roads* (1999): total length 18,700 km (paved 70%). *Vehicles* (2000–01): passenger cars 168,179, trucks and buses 62,634. *Air transport* (2003; Air Jamaica only): passenger-km 5,005,-000,000; metric ton-km cargo 48,859,000; airports (2000) with scheduled flights 4. **Communications,** in total units (units per 1,000 persons). Daily newspaper circulation (2000): 161,000 (62); radios (2000): 2,030,000 (784); televisions (2000): 502,000 (194); telephone main lines (2002): 444,400 (169); cellular telephone subscribers (2002): 1,400,000 (533); personal computers (2002): 141,000 (54); Internet users (2002): 600,000 (228).

Education and health

Educational attainment (2001). Percentage of population age 15 and over having: no formal schooling 0.9%; primary education 25.5%; secondary 55.5%; higher 12.3%, of which university 4.2%; other/unknown 5.8%. **Literacy** (2000): total population age 15 and over literate 88%; males literate 83%; females literate 91%. **Health** (2000): physicians 435 (1 per 5,988 persons); hospital beds (2001) 3,795 (1 per 686 persons); infant mortality rate per 1,000 live births (2003) 13.3. **Food** (2002): daily per capita caloric intake 2,685 (vegetable products 85%, animal products 15%); 120% of FAO recommended minimum.

Military

Total active duty personnel (2003): 2,830 (army 88.3%, coast guard 6.7%, air force 5.0%). **Military expenditure as percentage of GNP** (1999): 0.8% (world 2.4%); per capita expenditure US$19.

Background

The island of Jamaica was settled by Arawak Indians c. AD 600. It was sighted by Christopher Columbus in 1494; Spain colonized it in the early 16th century but neglected it because it lacked gold reserves. Britain gained control in 1655, and by the end of the 18th century Jamaica had become a prized colonial possession due to the volume of sugar produced by slave laborers. Slavery was abolished in the late 1830s, and the plantation system collapsed. Jamaica gained full internal self-government in 1959 and became an independent country within the British Commonwealth in 1962.

Recent Developments

In September 2004 Hurricane Ivan killed at least 18 people in Jamaica and caused damages totaling $90 million; the estimated losses included 60% of the coffee crop, 30% of the citrus crop, 15% of the sugarcane crop, and 20% of poultry production. In addition, 75% of the homes in one district were damaged.

Internet Resources: <www.visitjamaica.com>.

Japan

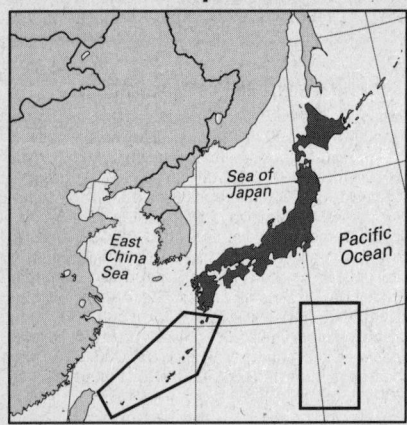

Sea of Japan

East China Sea

Pacific Ocean

Official name: Nihon (Japan). **Form of government:** constitutional monarchy with a national Diet consisting of two legislative houses (House of Councillors [247]; House of Representatives [480]). **Chief of state:** Emperor Akihito (from 1989). **Head of government:** Prime Minister Junichiro Koizumi (from 2001). **Capital:** Tokyo. **Official language:** Japanese. **Official religion:** none. **Monetary unit:** 1 yen (¥) = 100 sen; valuation (7 Jul 2005) $1 = ¥111.92.

Demography

Area: 145,903 sq mi, 377,887 sq km. **Population** (2004): 127,757,000. **Density** (2004): persons per sq mi 875.6, persons per sq km 338.1. **Urban** (2001): 78.9%. **Sex distribution** (2003): male 48.85%; female 51.15%. **Age breakdown** (2003): under 15, 14.1%; 15–29, 18.6%; 30–44, 20.3%; 45–59, 21.3%; 60–74, 17.4%; 75 and over, 8.3%. **Composition** by nationality (2002): Japanese 98.7%; Korean 0.5%; Chinese 0.3%; other 0.5%. **Immigration** (2000): permanent immigrants/registered aliens admitted 1,686,444, from North and South Korea 37.7%, Taiwan, Hong Kong, and China 19.9%, Brazil 15.1%, Philippines 8.6%, Peru 2.7%, US 2.6%, Thailand 1.7%, Indonesia 1.1%, UK 1.0%, Vietnam 0.6%, Canada 0.6%, India 0.6%, Pakistan 0.4%, other 7.4%. **Major cities** (2002): Tokyo 8,025,538; Yokohama 3,433,612; Osaka 2,484,326; Nagoya 2,109,681; Sapporo 1,822,992; Kobe 1,478,380; Kyoto 1,387,-264; Fukuoka 1,302,454; Kawasaki 1,245,780; Hiroshima 1,113,786; Saitama (created in 2001 with the merger of the cities of Urawa, Omiya, and Yono) 1,029,327; Kita-Kyushu 999,806; Sendai 986,713. **Location:** eastern Asia; island chain between the North Pacific Ocean and the Sea of Japan. **Religious affiliation** (1995): Shinto and related religions 93.1% (many Japanese practice both Shintoism and Buddhism); Buddhism 69.6%; Christian 1.2%; other 8.1%. **Households** (2000). Total households 46,782,000; average household size 2.7; composition of households 1 person 27.6%, 2 persons 25.1%, 3 persons 18.8%, 4 persons 16.9%, 5 persons 6.8%, 6 or more persons 4.8%. Family households 33,769,000

(72.2%); nonfamily 13,013,000 (27.8%). **Mobility** (2002). Percentage of total population moving: within a prefecture 2.5%; between prefectures 2.1%.

Vital statistics

Birth rate per 1,000 population (2003): 8.9 (world avg. 21.3). **Death rate** per 1,000 population (2003): 8.0 (world avg. 9.1). **Natural increase rate** per 1,000 population (2003): 0.9 (world avg. 12.2). **Total fertility rate** (avg. births per childbearing woman; 2003): 1.3. **Marriage rate** per 1,000 population (2003): 5.9; average age at first marriage (2003) men 29.4 years, women 27.4 years. **Divorce rate** per 1,000 population (2003): 2.3. **Life expectancy** at birth (2003): male 78.4 years; female 85.3 years.

Social indicators

Quality of working life. Average hours worked per month (2002): 153.1. Annual rate of industrial deaths per 100,000 workers (2001): 2.7. Proportion of labor force insured for damages or income loss resulting from injury, permanent disability, and death (2001): 65.4%. Average man-days lost to labor stoppages per 1,000,000 workdays (1998): 6.8. Average duration of journey to work (1996): 19.0 minutes. Rate per 1,000 workers of discouraged workers (unemployed no longer seeking work: 1997): 89.4. **Access to services** (1989). Proportion of households having access to: gas supply 64.6%; safe public water supply 94.0%; public sewage collection 89.4%. **Social participation.** Eligible voters participating in last national election (November 2003): 52%. Population 15 years and over participating in social-service activities on a voluntary basis (1991): 26.3%. Trade union membership in total workforce (2002): 20.2%. **Social deviance** (2001). Offense rate per 100,000 population for: homicide 0.6; robbery 1.2; larceny and theft 14.2. Incidence in general population of drug and substance abuse per 100,000 population, 0.1. Rate of suicide per 100,000 population: 23.1. **Material well-being** (2001). Households possessing: automobile 84.4%; telephone, virtually 100%; color television 99.3%; refrigerator 98.4%; air conditioner 87.2%; washing machine 99.3%; vacuum cleaner 98.2%; videocassette recorder 79.6%; camera 86.8%; microwave oven 96.2%; compact disc player 60.5%; personal computer 57.2%; cellular phone 78.6%.

National economy

Gross national product (at current market prices; 2003): $4,389,791,000,000 ($34,510 per capita). **Budget** (2002–03). *Revenue:* ¥81,230,000,000,-000 (government bonds 36.9%; income tax 19.5%; corporation tax 13.8%; value-added tax 12.1%; stamp and customs duties 3.9%). *Expenditures:* ¥81,230,000,000,000 (social security 22.5%; debt service 20.5%; public works 10.3%; national defense 6.1%). **Public debt** (March 2004): $6,740,000,-000,000. **Population economically active** (2002): total 66,890,000; activity rate of total population 52.5% (participation rates: age 15 and over, 63.9%; female 40.9%; unemployed 5.4%). **Household income and expenditure** (2002). Average household size 2.7; average annual income per household ¥6,338,000; sources of income (1994): wages and

---

1 metric ton = about 1.1 short tons;   1 kilometer = 0.6 mi (statute);   1 metric ton-km cargo = about 0.68 short ton-mi cargo;   c.i.f.: cost, insurance, and freight;   f.o.b.: free on board

salaries 59.0%, transfer payments 20.5%, self-employment 12.8%, other 7.3%; expenditure (2002): food 23.3%, transportation and communications 12.0%, recreation 10.1%, fuel, light, and water charges 6.9%, housing 6.5%, clothing and footwear 4.7%, education 4.2%, medical care 3.8%, furniture and household utensils 3.4%. **Tourism** (2002): receipts from visitors $3,499,000,000; expenditures by nationals abroad $26,681,000,000. **Production** (metric tons except as noted). *Agriculture, forestry, fishing* (2002): rice 11,111,000, sugar beets 4,098,000, potatoes 2,980,000, cabbages 2,500,-000, sugarcane 1,400,000, onions 1,270,000, sweet potatoes 1,030,000, apples 911,000, wheat 827,800, tomatoes 800,000, cucumbers 740,000, carrots 700,000, watermelons 570,000, lettuce 560,000, eggplant 450,000, pears 375,500, spinach 320,000, cantaloupes 305,000, soybeans 270,200, persimmons 269,300, grapes 231,700, pumpkins 220,000, taro 218,000, barley 217,000, strawberries 210,000, yams 200,000, peaches 175,100, peppers 171,000, cauliflower 115,000, plums 112,700; livestock (number of live animals) 9,612,000 pigs, 4,564,000 cattle, 283,102,000 chickens; roundwood (2001) 16,236,538 cu m; fish catch (2000) 5,752,178, of which squid 671,100, scallops 515,000, cod 398,900, crabs 42,000. *Mining and quarrying* (2001): limestone 182,255,000; silica stone 14,213,000; dolomite 3,389,000; pyrophyllite 403,000; zinc 44,519; lead 4,997; copper 744; silver 80,397 kg; gold 7,815 kg. *Energy production (consumption):* electricity (kW-hr; 2000) 1,091,499,000,000 (1,091,499,000,000); coal (2000) 3,127,000 (147,891,000); crude petroleum (barrels; 2000) 2,500,000 (1,535,900,000); petroleum products (2000) 182,429,000, of which (by volume [1998]) diesel 32.8%, heavy fuel oil 21.7%, gasoline 21.7%, kerosene and jet fuel 12.0% (190,-196,000); natural gas (cu m; 2000) 2,452,600,000 (73,485,300,000). Composition of energy supply by source (1998): crude oil and petroleum products 50.9%, coal 17.0%, nuclear power 14.2%, natural gas 12.8%, hydroelectric power 4.1%, other 1.0%. Domestic energy demand by end use (1998): mining and manufacturing 46.3%, residential and commercial 26.3%, transportation 25.2%, other 2.2%. *Manufacturing* (2001): crude steel 102,866,000; steel products 78,927,000; pig iron 78,836,000; cement 76,550,000; sulfuric acid 6,727,000; plastic products 6,300,000; fertilizers 4,200,000; newsprint 3,210,000; cotton fabrics 710,000,000 sq m; synthetic fabrics 1,920,000 sq m; finished products (in number of units) 420,000,000 watches and clocks, 51,062,000 industrial robots, 46,072,000 cellular phones, 12,421,000 air conditioners, 11,350,000 computers, 9,777,000 passenger cars, 9,112,000 cameras, 8,993,000 video cameras, 5,446,000 vacuum cleaners, 4,184,000 bicycles, 4,059,000 automatic washing machines, 3,875,000 electric refrigerators, 3,130,000 color televisions, 2,675,000 microwave ovens, 2,398,000 photocopy machines, 2,328,000 motorcycles, 1,916,000 facsimile machines, 1,185,000 videocassette recorders. **Land use** as % of total land area (2000): in temporary crops 12.3%, in permanent crops 1.0%, in pasture 1.1%; overall forest area 64.0%.

Foreign trade

Imports (2001-c.i.f.): ¥42,415,500,000,000 (machinery and apparatus 28.5%, of which computers and office machinery 6.5%; crude and refined petroleum 13.3%; food products 12.4%, chemicals and chemical products 7.3%, apparel and clothing accessories 5.5%). *Major import sources:* US 18.1%; China 16.6%; South Korea 4.9%; Indonesia 4.3%; Australia 4.1%; Taiwan 4.1%; Malaysia 3.7%; UAE 3.7%; Germany 3.6%; Saudi Arabia 3.5%. **Exports** (2001-f.o.b.): ¥48,979,200,000,000 (machinery and apparatus 44.4%, of which electronic microcircuits 7.4%, computers and office machinery 5.8%; road vehicles and parts 18.6%; base and fabricated metals 5.9%; precision instruments 5.4%). *Major export destinations:* US 30.0%; China 7.7%; South Korea 6.3%; Taiwan 6.0%; Hong Kong 5.8%; Germany 3.9%; Singapore 3.6%; UK 3.0%; Thailand 2.9%; The Netherlands 2.8%.

Transport and communications

Transport. *Railroads* (2001): length 23,654 km; rolling stock—(1995) locomotives 1,787, (1995) passenger cars 25,973, (1995) freight cars 12,688; passengers carried 21,700,000,000; passenger-km 385,421,000,000; metric ton-km cargo 22,193,-000,000. *Roads* (2002): total length 1,232,000 km (paved 82%). *Vehicles* (2002): passenger cars 42,655,000; trucks and buses 18,200,000. *Air transport* (2000): passengers carried 205,106,000; passenger-km 256,428,000,000; metric ton-km cargo 9,800,000,000; airports (1996) with scheduled flights 73. *Urban transport* (2000; Tokyo, Nagoya, and Osaka metropolis traffic range only): passengers carried 57,719,000, of which by rail 34,020,000, by road 19,466,000, by subway 4,233,000. **Communications**, in total units (units per 1,000 persons). Daily newspaper circulation (2000): 73,300,000 (578); radios (2000): 121,000,-000 (956); televisions (2002): 99,852,000 (785); telephone main lines (2002): 71,149,000 (558); cellular telephone subscribers (2003): 86,659,000 (680); personal computers (2002): 48,700,000 (383); Internet users (2002): 57,200,000 (449). *Radio and television broadcasting* (2001): total radio stations 1,586, of which commercial 707; total television stations 15,088, of which commercial 8,299. Commercial broadcasting hours (by percentage of programs; 2001): reports—radio 12.6%, television 21.4%; education—radio 2.4%, television 12.1%; culture—radio 13.5%, television 24.8%; entertainment—radio 69.0%, television 39.2%. Advertisements (daily average; 2001): radio 158, television 431.

Education and health

Educational attainment (1998). Percentage of population ages 25–64 having: no formal schooling through complete primary education 2.4%; incomplete through complete secondary 79.9%; postsecondary 17.7%. **Literacy:** total population age 15 and over literate, virtually 100%. **Health** (2002): physicians 260,500 (1 per 489 persons); dentists 91,783 (1 per 1,388 persons); nurses 1,096,967 (1 per 116 persons); pharmacists 212,720 (1 per 583 persons); midwives (2000) 24,511 (1 per 5,176 persons); hospital beds 1,642,593 (1 per 78 persons); infant mortality rate per 1,000 live births (2003) 3.0. **Food** (2001): daily per capita caloric intake 2,768 (vegetable products 79%, animal products 21%); 118% of FAO recommended minimum.

Military

Total active duty personnel (2003): 239,900 (army 61.8%, navy 18.5%, air force 19.0%); US troops (August 2004) 40,000. **Military expenditure as percentage of GNP** (1999): 1.0% (world 2.4%); per capita expenditure $342.

Did you know? The last eruption of Mount Fuji took place in 1707. Mount Fuji is the highest mountain in Japan, rising to 12,388 ft (3,776 m) near the Pacific coast in central Honshu, about 60 mi (100 km) west of Tokyo. Although the volcano has been dormant since 1707, it is still generally classified as active.

Background

Japan's history began with the accession of the legendary first emperor, Jimmu, in 660 BC. The Yamato court established the first unified Japanese state in the 4th–5th century AD; during this period Buddhism arrived in Japan by way of Korea. For centuries Japan borrowed heavily from Chinese culture, but it began to sever its links with the mainland by the 9th century. In 1192 Minamoto Yoritomo established Japan's first *bakufu*, or shogunate. Unification was achieved in the late 1500s under the leadership of Oda Nobunaga, Toyotomi Hideyoshi, and Tokugawa Ieyasu. During the Tokugawa shogunate, beginning in 1603, the government imposed a policy of isolation. Under the leadership of Emperor Meiji (1868–1912), it adopted a constitution (1889) and began a program of modernization and Westernization. Japanese imperialism led to war with China (1894–95) and Russia (1904–05) as well as the annexation of Korea (1910) and Manchuria (1931). During World War II Japan attacked US forces in Hawaii and the Philippines (December 1941) and occupied European colonial possessions in South Asia. In 1945 the US dropped atomic bombs on Hiroshima and Nagasaki, and Japan surrendered to the Allied powers. US postwar occupation of Japan led to a new democratic constitution in 1947. In rebuilding Japan's ruined industrial plant, new technology was used in every major industry. A tremendous economic recovery followed, and it was able to maintain a favorable balance of trade into the 1990s.

Recent Developments

The second term of Japanese Prime Minister Junichiro Koizumi continued to be stable following the general election of November 2003, which saw the ruling coalition of the Liberal Democratic Party (LDP) and the New Komeito party lose seats but maintain its majority in the lower house of the Diet (parliament). The growth of Japan's gross domestic product in the first quarter of 2004, in real terms, maintained the momentum of the last quarter of 2003, and a 3.2% growth rate was achieved. In the second and third quarters, however, the vigor disappeared, and the growth rates fell to a less-than-modest level— 0.4% and 0.1%, respectively. The methodology for calculating GDP was to be slightly changed in the last quarter, and a further slowdown was expected for the year as a whole. The Ministry of Finance reported that in 2003, Japan's exports to greater China (China, Hong Kong, and Taiwan) totaled ¥13.7 trillion (about $134 billion) and for the first time exceeded exports to the United States. Imports from greater China had surpassed US imports in 2000. In September Prime Minister Koizumi and Mexican Pres. Vicente Fox Quesada signed a free-trade agreement. It was Japan's second such agreement, following one with Singapore, but the first that covered some agricultural products. The agreement was expected to accelerate similar negotiations with Southeast Asian countries.

Japan's relations with its Asian neighbors topped the foreign policy agenda. In January 2004 Koizumi once again visited the Yasukuni Shrine—and once again aroused China's displeasure. Along with some 2.5 million Japanese war victims, 14 convicted Class A World War II war criminals were interred at the shrine. In August, at the association football (soccer) Asian Cup final held in China, Chinese spectators booed during the Japanese national anthem, and after the game some of them mobbed a car carrying a Japanese embassy minister. In November a Chinese nuclear submarine violated Japan's territorial waters, which caused a minor incident. A new type of friction emerged in the continental shelf area of the East China Sea, where Japanese and Chinese territorial, economic, and scientific research interests overlapped. In early 2005 the Japanese Ministry of Education approved for use in schools a history textbook that many observers, including China and South Korea, felt glossed over Japan's belligerence toward its neighbors during World War II; a series of anti-Japanese protests and demonstrations ensued. An old squabble with South Korea about ownership of two tiny islets in the Sea of Japan (Korea calls it the East Sea) was renewed as well.

Internet Resources: <www.jnto.go.jp>.

Jersey

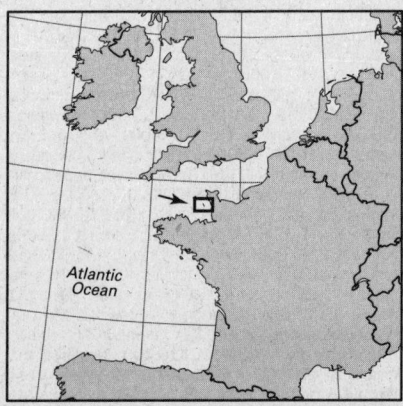

Atlantic Ocean

Official name: Bailiwick of Jersey. **Political status:** crown dependency (UK) with one legislative house (States of Jersey [58, including 53 elected officials and 5 ex officio members with limited legislative rights]). **Chief of state:** British Monarch Queen Elizabeth II (from 1952), represented by Lieutenant Governor Sir John Cheshire (from 2001). **Head of government:** executive committees appointed by the States of Jersey (alternately called States Assembly). **Capital:** Saint Helier. **Official language:** English (until the 1960s French was an official language of Jersey and is still used by the court and legal professions; Jèrriais, a Norman-French dialect, is spoken by a small number of residents). **Official religion:** none. **Monetary unit:** 1 Jersey pound (£J) = 100 pence; valuation (7 Jul 2005) $1 = £J0.57; at par with the British pound (£).

Demography

Area: 45.6 sq mi, 118.2 sq km. **Population** (2004): 87,900. **Density** (2004): persons per sq mi 1,927.6, persons per sq km 743.7. **Urban** (2001; includes Guernsey): 28.9%. **Sex distribution** (2001): male 48.73%; female 51.27%. **Age breakdown** (2001): under 15, 16.9%; 15–29, 18.4%; 30–44, 25.9%; 45–59, 19.7%; 60–74, 12.6%; 75 and over, 6.5%. **Population by place of birth** (2001): Jersey 52.6%; UK, Guernsey, or Isle of Man 35.8%; Portugal 5.9%; France 1.2%; other 4.5%. **Religious affiliation** (2000; includes Guernsey): Christian 86.0%, of which Anglican 44.1%, Roman Catholic 14.6%, other Protestant 6.9%, unaffiliated Christian 20.1%; nonreligious/atheist 13.4%; other 0.6%. **Major cities** (2001; population of parishes): St. Helier 28,310; St. Saviour 12,491; St. Brelade 10,134. **Location:** western Europe, island in the English Channel.

Vital statistics

Birth rate per 1,000 population (2003): 10.4 (world avg. 21.3). **Death rate** per 1,000 population (2003): 9.2 (world avg. 9.1). **Natural increase rate** per 1,000 population (2003): 1.2 (world avg. 12.2). **Total fertility rate** (avg. births per childbearing woman; 2003): 1.6. **Marriage rate** per 1,000 population (2001): 7.6. **Divorce rate** per 1,000 population (2001): 3.2. **Life expectancy** at birth (2003): male 76.5 years; female 81.6 years.

National economy

Budget (2001). *Revenue:* £400,085,000 (income tax 86.8%, import duties 8.7%, interest payment 1.5%, other 3.0%). *Expenditures:* £369,138,000 (current expenditure 79.3%, of which health 25.7%, education 19.0%, social security 18.2%, public services 5.1%; capital expenditure 20.7%). *Production. Agriculture, forestry, fishing:* fruits and vegetables, mostly potatoes and greenhouse tomatoes; greenhouse flowers are important export crops; livestock (number of live animals; 2001) 4,552 mature dairy cattle; fish catch (value of catch in £'000; 2002): 6,053, of which crustaceans (including lobsters and crabs) 3,695, scallops 758, marine fish 713, oysters 607. *Manufacturing:* light industry, mainly electrical goods, textiles and clothing. *Energy production (consumption):* electricity (kW-hr; 2001) 153,000,000 (567,000,000). **Gross national product** (at current market prices; 2003): $4,805,000,000 ($54,810 per capita). **Household income and expenditure.** Average household size (2001) 2.4; average annual income of workers (2001) £22,700; expenditure (1998–99): housing 20.1%, recreation 16.5%, trans-

portation 12.8%, household furnishings 11.6%, food 11.5%, alcoholic beverages 6.0%, clothing and footwear 5.5%. **Population economically active** (2003): total 46,620; activity rate of total population 53.2% (participation rates [2001]: ages 15–64, 81.7%; female 45.5%; unemployed [June 2004] 0.9%). **Tourism** (1996): receipts $429,000,000; number of visitors for at least one night (2001) 470,000. **Land use** as % of total land area (1997): in temporary and permanent crops 29%, in pasture 22%; overall forest area 6%.

Foreign trade

Customs ceased recording imports and exports as of 1980. *Major import sources* (2001): mostly the UK. **Exports:** agricultural and marine exports (2001): £40,626,000 (potatoes 67.4%, greenhouse tomatoes 19.1%, flowers 3.3%, zucchini 3.0%, crustaceans 2.0%, mollusks 2.0%). *Major export destinations:* mostly the UK.

Transport and communications

Transport. *Roads* (1995): total length 557 km (paved 100%). *Vehicles* (2002): passenger cars 74,007; trucks and buses 12,957. *Air transport* (1999; Jersey European Airways): passenger-km 890,438,000; metric ton-km cargo 923,000; airports (2002) with scheduled flights 1. **Communications,** in total units (units per 1,000 persons). Daily newspaper circulation (2002): 22,897 (262); telephone main lines (2002): 74,300 (851); cellular telephone subscribers (2002): 72,000 (824); Internet users (2001): 8,000 (92).

Education and health

Educational attainment (2001). Percentage of male population (16–64), female population (16–59) having: no formal degree 34.1%; undergraduate 7.1%; graduate (advanced degree) 4.1%. **Literacy** (2002): 100.0%. **Health:** physicians (2001) 174 (1 per 500 persons); hospital beds (1995) 651 (1 per 130 persons); infant mortality rate per 1,000 live births (2003) 5.4.

Military

Total active duty personnel (2003): none; defense is the responsibility of the UK.

Jordan

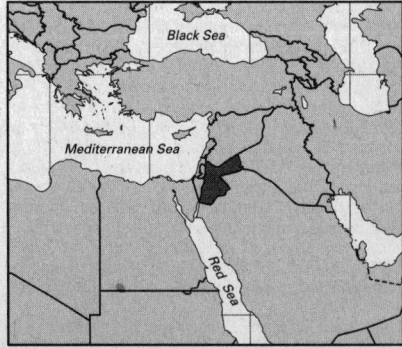

Official name: Al-Mamlakah al-Urdunniyah al-Hashimiyah (Al-Urdun) (Hashemite Kingdom of Jordan). **Form of government:** constitutional monarchy with two legislative houses (Senate [55; all members are appointed by the king]; House of Representatives [110]). **Head of state and government:** King Abdullah II (from 1999), assisted by Prime Minister Adnan Badran (from 7 Apr 2005). **Capital:** Amman. **Official language:** Arabic. **Official religion:** Islam. **Monetary unit:** 1 Jordan dinar (JD) = 1,000 fils; valuation (7 Jul 2005) $1 = JD 0.71.

Demography

Area: 34,495 sq mi, 89,342 sq km. **Population** (2004): 5,543,000. **Density** (2004): persons per sq mi 160.7, persons per sq km 62.0. **Urban** (2003): 78.7%. **Sex distribution** (2003): male 52.30%; female 47.70%. **Age breakdown** (2002): under 15, 36.6%; 15–29, 30.4%; 30–44, 19.8%; 45–59, 8.0%; 60–74, 4.3%; 75 and over, 0.9%. **Ethnic composition** (2000): Arab 97.8%, of which Jordanian 32.4%, Palestinian 32.2%, Iraqi 14.0%, Bedouin 12.8%; Circassian 1.2%; other 1.0%. **Religious affiliation** (2000): Sunni Muslim 93.5%; Christian 4.1%; other 2.4%. **Major cities** (1994): Amman 969,598; Az-Zarqa 350,849; Irbid 208,329; Ar-Rusayfah 137,247; Wadi Essier 89,104. **Location:** the Middle East, bordering Syria, Iraq, Saudi Arabia, the Gulf of Aqaba, Israel, and parts of the Emerging Palestinian Autonomous Areas.

Vital statistics

Birth rate per 1,000 population (2003): 27.4 (world avg. 21.3). **Death rate** per 1,000 population (2003): 3.1 (world avg. 9.1). **Natural increase rate** per 1,000 population (2003): 24.3 (world avg. 12.2). **Total fertility rate** (avg. births per childbearing woman; 2003): 3.7. **Marriage rate** per 1,000 population (2003): 9.0. **Divorce rate** per 1,000 population (2003): 1.7. **Life expectancy** at birth (2003): male 70.6 years; female 72.4 years.

National economy

Budget (2003). *Revenue:* JD 2,511,000,000 (tax revenue 43.1%, of which sales tax 23.7%, custom duties 8.0%, income and profits taxes 7.8%; nontax revenue 32.9%, of which licenses and fees 11.2%; foreign grants 24.0%). *Expenditures:* JD 2,678,000,000 (current expenditure 76.8%, of which defense 23.5%, social security and other transfers 21.7%, wages 15.6%, interest payments 10.1%; capital expenditure 23.2%). **Public debt** (external, outstanding; 2002): $7,076,000,000. **Production** (metric tons except as noted). *Agriculture, forestry, fishing* (2002): tomatoes 359,830, olives 180,900, cucumbers 150,000; livestock (number of live animals) 1,457,910 sheep, 557,260 goats; roundwood (2001) 233,544 cu m; fish catch (2001) 1,060. *Mining and quarrying* (2002): phosphate ore 7,107,200; potash 1,956,200. *Manufacturing* (value added in $'000,000; 2000): chemicals and chemical products 236; tobacco products 184; bricks, cement, ceramics 168. *Energy production (consumption):* electricity (kW-hr; 2003) 7,341,000,000 (7,341,000,000); crude petroleum (barrels; 2002) 14,600 ([2000] 27,789,000); petro-

leum products (2002) 3,627,000 ([2000] 4,481,000); natural gas (cu m; 2002) 269,000,000 ([2000] 283,000,000). **Land use** as % of total land area (2000): in temporary crops 2.7%, in permanent crops 1.8%, in pasture 8.9%; overall forest area 1.0%. **Tourism** (2002): receipts $786,000,000; expenditures $416,000,000. **Population economically active** (2001): total 1,293,000; activity rate of total population 23.6% (participation rates: over age 15, 40.2%; female 14.9%; unemployed 14.5%). **Gross national product** (2003): $9,800,000,000 ($1,850 per capita). **Household income and expenditure.** Average household size (2003) 5.7; income per household (1997) JD 5,464; sources of income (1997): wages and salaries 52.4%, rent and property income 24.5%, transfer payments 12.8%, self-employment 10.3%; expenditure (1997): food and beverages 44.3%, housing and energy 23.5%, transportation 8.2%, clothing and footwear 6.2%, education 4.5%, health care 2.5%.

Foreign trade

Imports (2003-c.i.f.): JD 4,072,000,000 (food products 15.5%; machinery and apparatus 13.4%; crude petroleum 11.5%; chemicals and chemical products 10.9%; transport equipment 9.2%). *Major import sources:* Saudi Arabia 11.3%; Germany 7.9%; China 7.9%; US 6.8%; Iraq 6.5%. **Exports** (2003-f.o.b.): JD 2,185,000,000 (domestic exports 76.7%, of which clothing 20.5%, chemicals and chemical products 17.8% [including medicines and pharmaceuticals 6.0%], potash 6.6%, vegetables 4.6%, phosphates 4.2%; reexports 23.3%). *Major export destinations:* US 29.0%; Iraq 13.4%; India 8.4%; Saudi Arabia 6.5%; Israel 4.1%.

Transport and communications

Transport. *Railroads* (2003): length 788 km; passenger-km 2,100,000; metric ton-km cargo 348,000,000. *Roads* (2000): total length 7,245 km (paved 69%). *Vehicles* (2001): passenger cars 245,357; trucks and buses 110,920. *Air transport* (2003; Royal Jordanian airlines only): passenger-km 4,553,000,000; metric ton-km cargo 200,728,000; airports (1999) 3. **Communications,** in total units (units per 1,000 persons). Daily newspaper circulation (2000): 383,000 (77); radios (2000): 1,850,000 (372); televisions (2002): 138,900 (177); telephone main lines (2003): 622,600 (113); cellular telephone subscribers (2003): 1,325,300 (242); personal computers (2002): 200,000 (38); Internet users (2003): 457,000 (45).

Education and health

Educational attainment (2003). Percentage of population age 15 and over having: no formal schooling 9.9%; primary education 54.8%; secondary 17.8%; postsecondary and vocational 8.1%; higher 9.4%. **Literacy** (2003): percentage of population age 15 and over literate 90.1%; males literate 94.9%; females literate 85.1%. **Health:** physicians (2000) 9,493 (1 per 523 persons); hospital beds (2001) 8,982 (1 per 577 persons); infant mortality rate per 1,000 live births (2003) 22.0. **Food** (2001): daily per capita caloric intake 2,769 (vegetable products 89%, animal products 11%); 113% of FAO recommended minimum.

---

1 metric ton = about 1.1 short tons; 1 kilometer = 0.6 mi (statute); 1 metric ton-km cargo = about 0.68 short ton-mi cargo; c.i.f.: cost, insurance, and freight; f.o.b.: free on board

Military

Total active duty personnel (2003): 100,500 (army 84.6%, navy 0.5%, air force 14.9%). **Military expenditure as percentage of GDP** (1999): 9.2% (world 2.4%); per capita expenditure $150.

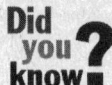 The Dead Sea, actually a landlocked salt lake, lies between Jordan and Israel. Its extreme salinity excludes all animal or vegetable life, allowing only bacteria.

Background

Jordan shares much of its history with Israel, since both occupied the area known historically as Palestine. Much of present-day eastern Jordan was incorporated into Israel under Kings David and Solomon c. 1000 BC. It fell to the Seleucids in 330 BC and to Muslim Arabs in the 7th century AD. The Crusaders extended the kingdom of Jerusalem east of the Jordan River in 1099. Jordan submitted to Ottoman Turkish rule during the 16th century. In 1920 the area comprising Jordan (then known as the Transjordan) was established within the British mandate of Palestine. Transjordan became an independent state in 1927, although the British mandate did not end until 1948. After hostilities with the new state of Israel ceased in 1949, Jordan annexed the West Bank of the Jordan River, administering the territory until Israel gained control of it in the Six-Day War of 1967. In 1970–71 Jordan was wracked by fighting between the government and guerrillas of the Palestine Liberation Organization (PLO), a struggle that ended in the expulsion of the PLO from Jordan. In 1988 King Hussein renounced all Jordanian claims to the West Bank in favor of the PLO. In 1994 Jordan and Israel signed a full peace agreement. Upon the death of King Hussein in 1999, his son Abdullah took over the throne.

Recent Developments

On 27 Jun 2004 the lower house of the Jordanian parliament narrowly rejected the Personal Status Law, which would have given women the right to divorce their husbands in return for monetary compensation. Opponents of the law, which would also have raised the legal age of marriage to 18 for both sexes, argued that it would undermine family values, increase immorality, and contravene Islamic law. In November King Abdullah stripped his half brother and heir apparent, Prince Hamzah, of his duties as crown prince; the new heir to the throne would be Abdullah's eldest son, 10-year-old Hussein.

Internet resources: <www.seejordan.org>.

Kazakhstan

Official name: Qazaqstan Respublikasy (Republic of Kazakhstan). **Form of government:** unitary republic with a parliament consisting of two chambers (Senate [39, including 7 nonelective seats] and Assembly [77]). **Head of state and government:** President Nursultan Nazarbayev (from 1991), assisted by Prime Minister Daniyal Akhmetov (from 2003). **Capital:** Astana. **Official language:** Kazakh (Russian commands

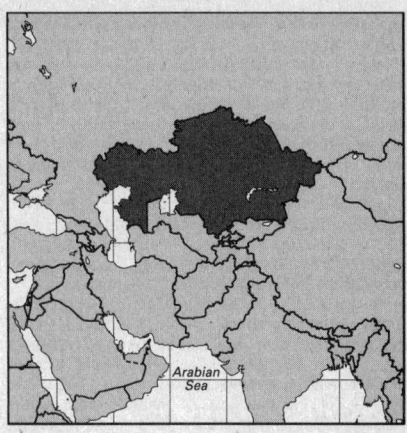

Arabian
Sea

equal status at state-owned organizations and local government bodies). **Official religion:** none. **Monetary unit:** 1 tenge (T) = 100 tiyn; valuation (7 Jul 2005) $1 = 135.47 tenge.

Demography

Area: 1,052,100 sq mi, 2,724,900 sq km. **Population** (2004): 15,144,000. **Density** (2004): persons per sq mi 14.4, persons per sq km 5.6. **Urban** (2001): 55.8%. **Sex distribution** (2003): male 48.35%; female 51.65%. **Age breakdown** (2003): under 15, 25.3%; 15–29, 27.8%; 30–44, 21.3%; 45–59, 14.4%; 60–74, 8.9%; 75 and over, 2.3%. **Ethnic composition** (1999): Kazakh 53.4%; Russian 30.0%; Ukrainian 3.7%; Uzbek 2.5%; German 2.4%; Tatar 1.7%; other 6.3%. **Religious affiliation** (1995): Muslim (mostly Sunni) 47.0%; Russian Orthodox 8.2%; Protestant 2.1%; other (mostly nonreligious) 42.7%. **Major cities** (1999): Almaty 1,130,068; Qaraghandy (Karaganda) 436,900; Shymkent (Chimkent) 360,100; Taraz 330,100; Astana 319,318. **Location:** central Asia, bordering Russia, China, Kyrgyzstan, Uzbekistan, the Aral Sea, Turkmenistan, and the Caspian Sea.

Vital statistics

Birth rate per 1,000 population (2003): 15.3 (world avg. 21.3); (2000) legitimate 76.1%. **Death rate** per 1,000 population (2003): 9.7 (world avg. 9.1). **Natural increase rate** per 1,000 population (2003): 5.6 (world avg. 12.2). **Total fertility rate** (avg. births per childbearing woman; 2003): 1.9. **Life expectancy** at birth (2003): male 65.6 years; female 71.3 years.

National economy

Budget (2001). *Revenue:* 743,550,000,000 tenge (tax revenue 91.1%, of which income and profits taxes 34.8%, sales tax 29.3%, social security 17.5%; nontax revenue 8.9%). *Expenditures:* 749,092,-000,000 tenge (social security 24.9%; education 14.0%; health 8.3%; debt 6.7%; defense 4.3%). **Population economically active** (2001): total 7,479,100; activity rate of total population 50.4% (participation rates: ages 16–59 [male], 16–54 [female] 73.6%; female 46.0%; unemployed 12.8%). **Production** (metric tons except as noted). *Agriculture, forestry, fishing* (2003): wheat 11,519,000, potatoes 2,320,000, barley 2,220,000; livestock (number of live animals) 9,920,200 sheep, 4,559,500 cattle, 23,600,000 chickens; fish catch (2001) 31,071. *Mining and quarrying* (2000): iron ore 13,828,000; bauxite 3,730,000; chromite 2,607,000. *Manufacturing* (value of production in '000,000 tenge; 2002): metallurgy 396,000; food 307,000; oil and nuclear energy 149,000. *Energy production (consumption)*: electricity (kW-hr; 2002) 58,464,000,000 ([2000] 54,616,000,000); hard coal (2002) 70,608,000 ([2000] 45,503,000); lignite (2002) 2,616,000 ([2000] 2,235,000); crude petroleum (barrels; 2002) 348,224,000 ([2000] 18,800,000); petroleum products (2000) 5,961,000 (5,592,000); natural gas (cu m; 2002) 9,112,000,000 ([2000] 11,001,800,000). **Gross national product** (2003): $26,535,000,000 ($1,780 per capita). **Public debt** (external, outstanding; 2002): $3,209,000,000. **Household income and expenditure.** Average household size (1999) 3.6; sources of income (2001): salaries and wages 72.1%, social benefits 9.2%; expenditure (2001): food and beverages 56.0%, housing 11.7%. **Land use** as % of total land area (2000): in temporary crops 8.0%, in permanent crops 0.05%, in pasture 68.6%; overall forest area 4.5%. **Tourism** (2002): receipts $621,000,000; expenditures $756,000,000.

Foreign trade

Imports (2000-c.i.f.): $5,052,000,000 (machinery and apparatus 27.4%; mineral fuels and lubricants 11.5%; chemicals and chemical products 11.4%; transport equipment 11.1%). *Major import sources:* Russia 48.7%; Germany 6.6%; US 5.5%; UK 4.3%; Italy 3.1%. **Exports** (2000-f.o.b.): $9,139,000,000 (crude petroleum 49.4%; nonferrous metals 13.7%, of which copper 7.5%; iron and steel 12.0%; cereals 6.0%). *Major export destinations:* Russia 19.5%; Bermuda 14.9%; British Virgin Islands 11.6%; Italy 9.8%; China 7.3%.

Transport and communications

Transport. *Railroads* (2001): route length 13,500 km; passenger-km 10,384,000,000; metric ton-km cargo 135,653,000,000. *Roads* (1999): total length 109,445 km (paved 90%). *Vehicles* (2001): passenger cars 1,000,298; trucks and buses 278,711. *Air transport* (2001): passenger-km 1,901,100,000; metric ton-km cargo 44,000,000; airports (1999) with scheduled flights 20. **Communications**, in total units (units per 1,000 persons). Radios (2000): 6,270,000 (422); televisions (2000): 3,580,000 (241); telephone main lines (2002): 2,081,900 (130); cellular telephone subscribers (2002): 1,027,000 (64); Internet users (2002): 250,000 (16).

Education and health

Educational attainment (1999). Population age 25 and over having: no formal schooling or some primary education 9.1%; primary education 23.1%; secondary and some postsecondary 57.8%; higher 10.0%. **Literacy** (2002): percentage of total population age 15 and over literate 99.4%; males literate 99.7%; females literate 99.2%. **Health** (2002): physicians 55,800 (1 per 277 persons); hospital beds 108,300 (1 per 143 persons); infant mortality rate

per 1,000 live births (2003) 31.9. **Food** (2001): daily per capita caloric intake 2,477 (vegetable products 73%, animal products 27%); 97% of FAO recommended minimum.

Military

Total active duty personnel (2003): 65,800 (army 71.1%, air force 28.9%). **Military expenditure as percentage of GNP** (1999): 0.9% (world avg. 2.4%); per capita expenditure $40.

Background

Named for its earliest inhabitants, the Kazakhs, the area came under Mongol rule in the 13th century. The Kazakhs consolidated a nomadic empire in the 15th–16th century. Under Russian rule by the mid-19th century, it became part of the Kirgiz Autonomous Republic formed by the Soviets in 1920, and in 1925 its name was changed to the Kazakh Autonomous Soviet Socialist Republic. Kazakhstan obtained its independence from the Soviet Union in 1991, and during the 1990s it attempted to stabilize its economy.

Recent Developments

In July 2004 the World Bank and the IMF advised Kazakhstan to use its oil profits to develop other sectors of the national economy, especially services and small and medium businesses. Pres. Nursultan Nazarbayev continued in his efforts to attract foreign investment to nonextractive sectors of the economy and hoped that Kazakhstan could become a center of high-tech industry. In the first six months of 2004 the US remained the top foreign investor in the Kazakh economy, followed by European states. Economic and security ties with Russia grew during the year, as did ties with China.

Internet resources: <www.president.kz>.

Kenya

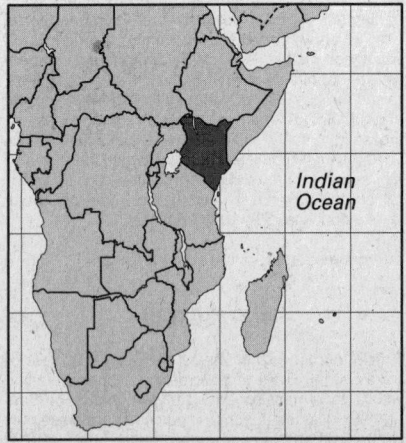

Indian Ocean

Official name: Jamhuri ya Kenya (Swahili); Republic of Kenya (English). **Form of government:** unitary multiparty republic with one legislative house (National Assembly [224, including 14 nonelective seats]). **Head of state and government:** President Mwai Kibaki (from 2002). **Capital:** Nairobi. **Official languages:** Swahili; English. **Official religion:** none. **Monetary unit:** 1 Kenya shilling (K Sh) = 100 cents; valuation (7 Jul 2005) $1 = K Sh 76.30.

Demography

Area: 224,961 sq mi, 582,646 sq km. **Population** (2004): 32,022,000. **Density** (2004): persons per sq mi 142.3, persons per sq km 55.0. **Urban** (2003): 39.4%. **Sex distribution** (2003): male 50.11%; female 49.89%. **Age breakdown** (2003): under 15, 42.4%; 15–29, 31.5%; 30–44, 15.1%; 45–59, 7.3%; 60–74, 3.0%; 75 and over, 0.7%. **Ethnic composition** (1989): Kikuyu 17.7%; Luhya 12.4%; Luo 10.6%; Kalenjin 9.8%; Kamba 9.8%; other 39.7%. **Religious affiliation** (2000): Christian 79.3%, of which Roman Catholic 22.0%, African Christian 20.8%, Protestant 20.1%; Muslim 7.3%; other 13.4%. **Major cities** (1999; pop. of urban core[s]): Nairobi 2,143,354; Mombasa 665,018; Kisumu 322,734; Nakuru 219,366; Eldoret 167,016. **Location:** eastern Africa, bordering Ethiopia, Somalia, the Indian Ocean, Tanzania, Uganda, and The Sudan.

Vital statistics

Birth rate per 1,000 population (2003): 40.2 (world avg. 21.3). **Death rate** per 1,000 population (2003): 15.6 (world avg. 9.1). **Natural increase rate** per 1,000 population (2003): 24.6 (world avg. 12.2). **Total fertility rate** (avg. births per childbearing woman; 2003): 5.0. **Life expectancy** at birth (2003): male 47.4 years; female 45.7 years. **Adult population** (ages 15–49) **living with HIV** (2004): 6.7% (world avg. 1.1%).

National economy

Budget (2001–02). *Revenue:* K Sh 206,665,-600,000 (tax revenue 86.6%, of which income and profit taxes 29.0%, value-added tax 27.2%, import duties 15.3%; nontax revenue 13.4%). *Expenditures:* K Sh 235,832,000,000 (recurrent expenditure 80.4%, of which administration 29.7%, education 22.2%, defense 6.1%, health 6.0%; development expenditure 19.6%). **Public debt** (external, outstanding; 2002): $5,139,000,000. **Production** (metric tons except as noted). *Agriculture, forestry, fishing* (2003): sugarcane 4,500,000, corn (maize) 2,300,000, potatoes 900,000; livestock (number of live animals) 11,500,000 cattle, 11,000,000 goats, 7,700,000 sheep; roundwood (2002) 1,704,250 cu m; fish catch (2001) 165,160, of which freshwater fish 95.5%. *Mining and quarrying* (2000): soda ash 238,200; fluorite 100,100; salt 16,400. *Manufacturing* (value added in K£'000 [Kenya pound (K£) as a unit of account equals 20 K Sh]; 1995): food products 847,000; beverages and tobacco 249,000; machinery and transport equipment 226,000. *Energy production (consumption):* electricity (kW-hr; 2001) 4,338,400,000 (3,654,800,000); coal (2000) none (98,000); crude petroleum (barrels; 2000) none (18,000,000); petroleum products (2001) 1,695,-600 (2,385,200). **Households.** Average household size (1998) 3.4; expenditure (1993–94): food 42.4%,

housing and energy 24.1%, clothing and footwear 9.1%, transportation 6.4%, other 18.0%. **Population economically active** (2001): total 12,952,000; activity rate of total population 42.1% (participation rates [1985]: ages 15–64, 76.2%; female [1997] 46.1%). **Gross national product** (2003): $12,604,000,000 ($390 per capita). **Tourism** (2002): receipts from visitors $297,000,000; expenditures by nationals abroad (2001) $143,000,000. **Land use** as % of total land area (2000): in temporary crops 7.9%, in permanent crops 1.0%, in pasture 37.4%; overall forest area 30.0%.

Foreign trade

Imports (2002-c.i.f.): K Sh 277,275,000,000 (crude petroleum and petroleum products 22.8%, machinery and transport equipment 19.3%, chemicals and chemical products 14.1%). *Major import sources* (2001): US 16.4%; UAE 10.7%; Saudi Arabia 7.8%; South Africa 7.1%; UK 7.1%. **Exports** (2002): K Sh 158,600,000,000 (tea 21.4%, horticultural products [mostly cut flowers] 13.8%, petroleum products 7.6%, coffee 4.1%, other [including nontraditional fruits and vegetables, iron and steel, and fish] 53.1%). *Major export destinations* (2001): Uganda 17.4%; UK 12.5%; The Netherlands 6.5%; Pakistan 6.1%; US 5.6%.

Transport and communications

Transport. *Railroads* (2000): route length 2,700 km; passenger-km 302,000,000; metric ton-km cargo 1,557,000,000. *Roads* (1999): total length 63,800 km (paved 14%). *Vehicles* (2000): passenger cars 244,836; trucks and buses 96,726. *Air transport* (1998): passenger-km 2,091,000,000; metric ton-km cargo 243,000,000; airports (1997) with scheduled flights 11. **Communications,** in total units (units per 1,000 persons). Daily newspaper circulation (2000): 303,000 (10); radios (2001): 6,801,000 (221); televisions (2000): 758,000 (25); telephone main lines (2003): 328,400 (10); cellular telephone subscribers (2003): 1,590,800 (50); personal computers (2002): 204,000 (6.5); Internet users (2002): 400,000 (13). •

Education and health

Literacy (2002): total population over age 15 literate 84.3%; males literate 90.0%; females literate 78.5%. **Health** (2002): physicians 4,740 (1 per 6,623 persons); hospital beds 60,657 (1 per 515 persons); infant mortality rate per 1,000 live births (2003): 65.6. **Food** (2001): daily per capita caloric intake 2,058 (vegetable products 88%, animal products 12%); 89% of FAO recommended minimum.

Military

Total active duty personnel (2003): 24,120 (army 82.9%, navy 6.7%, air force 10.4%). **Military expenditure as percentage of GNP** (1999): 1.9% (world 2.4%); per capita expenditure $7.

Background

The coastal region of East Africa was dominated by Arabs until it was seized by the Portuguese in the 16th century. The Masai people held sway in the north and moved into central Kenya in the 18th century, while the Kikuyu expanded from their home region in south-central Kenya. The interior was explored by European missionaries in the 19th century. After the British took control, Kenya was established as a British protectorate (1890) and a crown colony (1920). The Mau Mau rebellion of the 1950s was directed against European colonialism. In 1963 the country became fully independent, and a year later a republican government under Jomo Kenyatta was elected. In 1992 Kenyan Pres. Daniel arap Moi allowed the country's first multiparty elections in three decades, though the balloting was marred by violence and fraud. Political turmoil occurred over the following years.

Recent Developments

In spring 2004 a commission set up to draft a new constitution recommended the creation of a post of prime minister with strong executive powers, leaving the president with an essentially ceremonial role. The matter went to the High Court, which ruled that the draft constitution had to be approved by a public referendum and not solely by a vote of the members of the parliament. In April Pres. Mwai Kibaki dismissed the police commissioner after a series of complaints in the press about the rising incidence of crime, especially in Nairobi. In May the president continued his anticorruption campaign by suspending four senior officials in connection with scandals in the Immigration Department relating to the sale of passports. Kibaki's top aide for the campaign, former Transparency International official John Githongo, quit in February 2005.

Internet resources: <www.magicalkenya.com>.

Kiribati

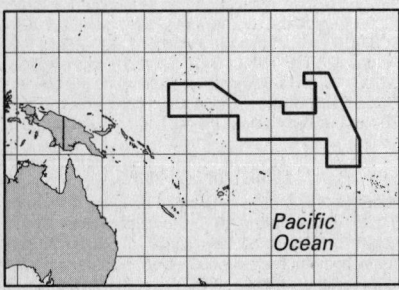

Pacific Ocean

Official name: Republic of Kiribati. **Form of government:** unitary republic with a unicameral legislature (House of Assembly [42, including two nonelective members]). **Head of state and government:** President Anote Tong (from 2003). **Capital:** Bairiki, on Tarawa Atoll. **Official language:** English. **Official religion:** none. **Monetary unit:** 1 Australian dollar ($A) = 100 cents; valuation (7 Jul 2005) US$1 = $A 1.35.

Demography

Area: 312.9 sq mi, 810.5 sq km (including uninhabited islands). **Population** (2004): 89,100. **Density** (2004; based on inhabited island areas [280 sq mi (726 sq km)] only): persons per sq mi 318.2, persons

per sq km 122.7. **Urban** (2003): 47.3%. **Sex distribution** (2003): male 49.65%; female 50.35%. **Age breakdown** (2003): under 15, 39.7%; 15–29, 26.3%; 30–44, 18.8%; 45–59, 10.1%; 60–74, 4.3%; 75 and over, 0.9%. **Ethnic composition** (2000): Micronesian 98.8%; Polynesian 0.7%; European 0.2%; other 0.3%. **Religious affiliation** (2000): Roman Catholic 54.6%; Kiribati Protestant (Congregational) 37.0%; Mormon 2.7%; Baha'i 2.4%; other Protestant 2.3%; other/non-religious 1.0%. **Major city** (2000): Tarawa (urban area) 36,717. **Location:** western Pacific Ocean, south of the Hawaiian Islands (US).

Vital statistics

Birth rate per 1,000 population (2003): 31.2 (world avg. 21.3). **Death rate** per 1,000 population (2003): 8.6 (world avg. 9.1). **Total fertility rate** (avg. births per childbearing woman; 2003): 4.3. **Natural increase rate** per 1,000 population (2003): 22.6 (world avg. 12.2). **Marriage rate** per 1,000 population (1988): 5.2. **Life expectancy** at birth (2003): male 58.0 years; female 64.0 years.

National economy

Budget (2000). *Revenue:* $A 107,800,000 (nontax revenue 59.5%, tax revenue 22.9%, grants 17.6%). *Expenditures:* $A 90,000,000 (current expenditures 87.2%, capital expenditures 12.8%). **Public debt** (external, outstanding; 1999): $9,500,000. **Tourism:** receipts from visitors (2001) US$3,200,000; expenditures by nationals abroad (1999) US$2,000,000. **Land use** as % of total land area (2000): in temporary crops 3%, in permanent crops 51%; overall forest area 38%. **Production** (metric tons except as noted). *Agriculture, forestry, fishing* (2003): coconuts 99,000, roots and tubers 7,300 (of which taro 1,900), fresh vegetables 5,800; livestock (number of live animals) 12,000 pigs, 450,000 chickens; fish catch (2001) 32,393. *Manufacturing* (1996): processed copra 9,321; other important products are processed fish, baked goods, clothing, and handicrafts. *Energy production (consumption):* electricity (kW-hr; 2000) 7,000,000 (7,000,000); petroleum products (2000) none (8,000). **Gross national product** (2003): US$84,000,000 (US$880 per capita). **Population economically active** (1995): total 38,407; activity rate of total population 49.5% (participation rates: over age 15, 84.0%; female 47.8%; unemployed [2000] 1.5%). **Households.** Average household size (1995) 6.5; expenditure (1996): food 45.0%, nonalcoholic beverages 10.0%, transportation 8.0%, energy 8.0%, education 8.0%.

Foreign trade

Imports (1999): $A 63,700,000 (food and live animals 28.3%; machinery and transport equipment 22.6%; mineral fuels 10.3%; beverages and tobacco products 7.7%). *Major import sources* (2001): Australia 26.5%; Poland 15.7%; Fiji 14.8%; US 9.5%; Japan 8.0%. **Exports** (1999): $A 14,000,000 (domestic exports 92.6%, of which copra 63.9%, seaweed 5.1%, other [including fish for food and pet fish] 23.6%; reexports 7.4%). *Major export destinations* (2001): Japan 45.8%; Thailand 24.8%; South Korea 10.7%; Bangladesh 5.5%; Brazil 3.0%.

1 metric ton = about 1.1 short tons;   1 kilometer = 0.6 mi (statute);   1 metric ton-km cargo = about 0.68 short ton-mi cargo;   c.i.f.: cost, insurance, and freight;   f.o.b.: free on board

Transport and communications

Transport. *Roads* (1996): total length 670 km (paved 5%). *Vehicles* (2000; registered vehicles in South Tarawa only): passenger cars 477; trucks and buses 277. *Air transport* (1996): passenger-km 7,000,000; metric ton-km cargo 1,000,000; airports 9. **Communications,** in total units (units per 1,000 persons). Radios (2000): 32,600 (386); televisions (2000): 3,030 (36); telephone main lines (2002): 4,500 (51); cellular telephone subscribers (2002): 500 (5.7); personal computers (2001): 2,000 (25); Internet users (2002): 2,000 (23).

Education and health

Educational attainment (1995). Percentage of population age 25 and over having: no schooling 7.8%; primary education 68.5%; secondary or higher 23.7%. **Literacy** (1998): population age 15 and over literate 92%; males literate 94%; females literate 91%. **Health:** physicians (1998) 26 (1 per 3,378 persons); hospital beds (1990) 306 (1 per 233 persons); infant mortality rate per 1,000 live births (2003) 51.3. **Food** (2001): daily per capita caloric intake 2,922 (vegetable products 88%, animal products 12%); 128% of FAO recommended minimum.

Background

The islands were settled by Austronesian-speaking peoples before the 1st century AD. In 1765 the British discovered the island of Nikunau; the first permanent European settlers arrived in 1837. In 1916 the Gilbert and Ellice islands and Banaba became a crown colony of Britain; they were later joined by the Phoenix and Line islands. In 1979 the colony became the nation of Kiribati.

Did you know? The remote Kiritimati Atoll, part of the Pacific nation Kiribati, is the world's oldest and one of the largest coral formations in the world. Kiritimati was used for British nuclear testing in the 1950s; it now has a large coconut plantation and fish farms.

Recent Developments

Relations remained strained between Kiribati and China. After the newly elected government of Pres. Anote Tong recognized Taiwan in November 2003, China severed diplomatic links and dismantled its satellite-tracking station on South Tarawa Island. The switch of diplomatic allegiance was criticized by the parliamentary opposition led by Harry Tong, the president's brother. Taiwan had offered scholarships and technical assistance to Kiribati, together with aid for infrastructure projects and the development of sports facilities.

Internet Resources: <www.kiribati.spto.org>.

North Korea

Official name: Choson Minjujuui In'min Konghwaguk (Democratic People's Republic of Korea). **Form of**

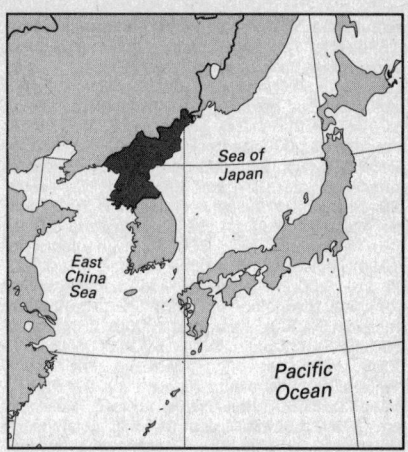

government: unitary single-party republic with one legislative house (Supreme People's Assembly [687]). **Head of state and government:** Chairman of the National Defense Commission Kim Jong Il (from 1998). **Capital:** P'yongyang. **Official language:** Korean. **Official religion:** none. **Monetary unit:** 1 won = 100 chon; valuation (7 Jul 2005) $1 = 2.20 won.

Demography

Area: 47,399 sq mi, 122,762 sq km. **Population** (2004): 22,698,000. **Density** (2004): persons per sq mi 478.9, persons per sq km 184.9. **Urban** (2003): 61.1%. **Sex distribution** (2000): male 48.48%; female 51.52%. **Age breakdown** (2000): under 15, 25.6%; 15–29, 24.5%; 30–44, 24.7%; 45–59, 14.4%; 60–74, 9.0%; 75 and over, 1.8%. **Ethnic composition** (1999): Korean 99.8%; Chinese 0.2%. **Religious affiliation** (2000): nonreligious 55.6%; atheist 15.6%; Ch'ondogyo 12.9%; traditional beliefs 12.3%; Christian 2.1%; Buddhist 1.5%. **Major cities** (1993): P'yongyang (2001) 3,164,000 (urban agglomeration); Namp'o (2000) 1,022,000 (urban agglomeration); Hamhung 709,730; Ch'ongjin 582,480; Kaesong 334,433. **Location:** eastern Asia, bordering China, Russia, the Sea of Japan (East Sea), South Korea, and the Yellow Sea.

Vital statistics

Birth rate per 1,000 population (2003): 17.6 (world avg. 21.3). **Death rate** per 1,000 population (2003): 6.9 (world avg. 9.1). **Natural increase rate** per 1,000 population (2003): 10.7 (world avg. 12.2). **Total fertility rate** (avg. births per childbearing woman; 2003): 2.3. **Marriage rate** per 1,000 population (1987): 9.3. **Divorce rate** per 1,000 population (1987): 0.2. **Life expectancy** at birth (2003): male 68.1 years; female 73.6 years.

National economy

Budget (1999). *Revenue:* 19,801,000,000 won (turnover tax and profits from state enterprises). *Expenditures:* 20,018,200,000 won (1994; national economy 67.8%, social and cultural affairs 19.0%, defense 11.6%). **Population economically active** (1997): total 11,898,000; activity rate of total population 55.8% (participation rates [1988–93]: ages 15–64, 49.5%; female 46.0%). **Production** (metric tons except as noted). *Agriculture, forestry, fishing* (2002): rice 2,190,000, potatoes 1,884,000, corn (maize) 1,651,000; livestock (number of live animals) 3,152,000 pigs, 2,693,000 goats, 575,000 cattle; roundwood (2000) 4,900,000 cu m; fish catch (2001): 264,000. *Mining and quarrying* (2002): iron ore (metal content) 1,150,000; magnesite 1,000,000; phosphate rock 300,000. *Manufacturing* (1999): cement 16,000,000; crude steel 8,100,000; pig iron 6,600,000. *Energy production (consumption):* electricity (kW-hr; 2000) 32,815,000,000 (32,815,000,000); hard coal (2000) 53,873,000 (55,540,000); lignite (2000) 15,728,000 (15,728,000); crude petroleum (barrels; 2000) none (18,000,000); petroleum products (2000) 2,654,000 (4,063,000). **Households.** Average household size (1999) 4.6. **Public debt** (external, outstanding; 1999): $12,000,000,000. **Gross national product** (1999): $9,912,000,000 ($457 per capita). **Land use** as % of total land area (2000): in temporary crops 20.8%, in permanent crops 2.5%, in pasture 0.4%; overall forest area 68.2%.

Foreign trade

Imports (2001): $1,847,000,000 (excludes trade with South Korea; food, beverages, and other agricultural products 23.7%, machinery and apparatus 15.0%, mineral fuels and lubricants 14.3%, textiles and clothing 12.6%). *Major import sources:* China 31.0%; Japan 13.5%; South Korea 12.3%; India 8.4%; Singapore 6.1%. **Exports** (2001): $826,000,000 (excludes trade with South Korea; live animals and agricultural products 30.2%, textiles and wearing apparel 21.6%, machinery and apparatus 15.1%, base and fabricated metals 9.3%). *Major export destinations:* Japan 27.3%; South Korea 21.3%; China 20.2%; Hong Kong 4.6%; Thailand 3.0%.

Transport and communications

Transport. *Railroads* (1999): length 8,533 km. *Roads* (1998): total length 23,407 km (paved 8%). *Vehicles* (1990): passenger cars 248,000. *Air transport* (1997): passenger-km 286,000,000; short ton-mi cargo 18,600,000; metric ton-km cargo 30,000,000; airports (2001) with scheduled flights 1. **Communications**, in total units (units per 1,000 persons). Daily newspaper circulation (2000): 4,500,000 (208); radios (2000): 3,330,000 (154); televisions (2000): 1,170,000 (54); telephone main lines (1999): 1,100,000 (46).

Education and health

Educational attainment (1987–88). Percentage of population age 16 and over having attended or graduated from postsecondary-level school: 13.7%. **Literacy** (1997): 95%. **Health** (1995): physicians 64,039 (1 per 337 persons); hospital beds 293,457 (1 per 73 persons); infant mortality rate (2003) 25.7. **Food** (2002): daily per capita caloric intake 2,142 (vegetable products 94%, animal products 6%); 92% of FAO recommended minimum.

Military

Total active duty personnel (2003): 1,082,000 (army 87.8%, navy 4.3%, air force 7.9%). **Military expenditure as percentage of GNP** (1999): 18.8% (world 2.4%); per capita expenditure $199.

Background

According to tradition, the ancient kingdom of Choson was established in the northern part of the Korean Peninsula, probably by peoples from northern China, in the 3rd millennium BC and was conquered by China in 108 BC. The kingdom was ruled by the Yi dynasty from 1392 to 1910. That year Korea was formally annexed by Japan. It was freed from Japanese control in 1945, at which time the USSR occupied the area north of latitude 38° N and the US occupied the area south of it. The Democratic People's Republic of Korea was established as a communist state in 1948. North Korea launched an invasion of South Korea in 1950, initiating the Korean War, which ended with an armistice in 1953. Under Kim Il-sung, North Korea became one of the most harshly regimented societies in the world, with a state-owned economy that failed to produce adequate food. In the late 1990s, under Kim Il-sung's successor, Kim Jong Il, the country endured a serious famine; as many as a million Koreans may have died.

Recent Developments

The dominant issue in North Korea in 2004–05 was the development of nuclear weapons and negotiations among regional and international powers to abandon that program. The second round of six-party talks was held in February 2004 in Beijing, where the two Koreas, China, the United States, Japan, and Russia met to find a negotiated end to the confrontation over nuclear weapons on the Korean peninsula. The third round was held in June, and the fourth round, planned for October, was postponed and not rescheduled. It appeared that North Korea had decided to wait for the outcome of the US presidential election before meeting again, but the reelection of Pres. George W. Bush sent the message that there would be no changes in the US position. P'yongyang upped the ante on 10 Feb 2005 by announcing for the first time that North Korea possessed nuclear weapons, while refusing to resume the talks. Talks with China in the spring failed to get the Koreans to return to the negotiating table.

Internet resources: <www.kcna.co.jp/index-e.htm>.

South Korea

Official name: Taehan Min'guk (Republic of Korea). **Form of government:** unitary multiparty republic with one legislative house (National Assembly [299]). **Head of state and government:** President Roh Moo Hyun (from 2003), assisted by Prime Minister Lee Hai Chan (from 30 Jun 2004). **Capital:** Seoul. **Official language:** Korean. **Official religion:** none. **Monetary unit:** 1 won (W) = 100 chon; valuation (7 Jul 2005) $1 = W 1,052.14.

---

1 metric ton = about 1.1 short tons;   1 kilometer = 0.6 mi (statute);   1 metric ton-km cargo = about 0.68 short ton-mi cargo;   c.i.f.: cost, insurance, and freight;   f.o.b.: free on board

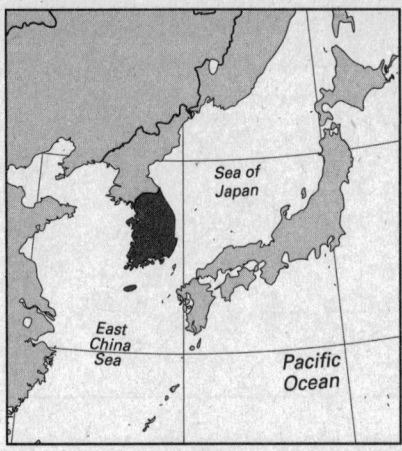

Demography

Area: 38,572 sq mi, 99,900 sq km. **Population** (2004): 48,199,000. **Density** (2004): persons per sq mi 1,249.6, persons per sq km 482.5. **Urban** (2003): 80.3%. **Sex distribution** (2003): male 50.30%; female 49.70%. **Age breakdown** (2003): under 15, 20.2%; 15–29, 23.6%; 30–44, 26.8%; 45–59, 17.5%; 60–74, 9.4%; 75 and over, 2.5%. **Ethnic composition** (2000): Korean 97.7%; Japanese 2.0%; US white 0.1%; Han Chinese 0.1%; other 0.1%. **Religious affiliation** (1995): religious 50.7%, of which Buddhist 23.2%, Protestant 19.7%, Roman Catholic 6.6%, Confucian 0.5%, Wonbulgyo 0.2%, Ch'ondogyo 0.1%, other 0.4%; nonreligious 49.3%. **Major cities** (2003): Seoul 10,280,523; Pusan 3,747,369; Inch'on 2,596,102; Taegu 2,540,647; Taejon 1,424,844. **Location:** northeast Asia, bordering North Korea, the Sea of Japan (East Sea), and the Yellow Sea; Cheju Island lies off the southern coast in the East China Sea.

Vital statistics

Birth rate per 1,000 population (2003): 10.3 (world avg. 21.3). **Death rate** per 1,000 population (2003): 6.0 (world avg. 9.1). **Natural increase rate** per 1,000 population (2003): 4.3 (world avg. 12.2). **Total fertility rate** (avg. births per childbearing woman; 2003): 1.2. **Marriage rate** per 1,000 population (2002): 6.3. **Divorce rate** per 1,000 population (2002): 3.0. **Life expectancy** at birth (2003): male 71.7 years; female 79.3 years.

National economy

Budget (2002). *Revenue:* W 105,876,700,000,000 (tax revenue 88.6%, of which income and profits taxes 34.3%, value-added tax 30.2%; nontax revenue 11.4%). *Expenditures:* W 105,876,700,000,000 (economic services 25.9%, education 17.4%, defense 16.2%, social services 13.1%). **Public debt** (external, outstanding; 2001): $33,742,000,000. **Production** (metric tons except as noted). *Agriculture, forestry, fishing* (2003): rice 6,068,000, cabbages 2,576,000, onions 933,000; livestock (number of live animals) 8,912,000 pigs, 1,935,000 cattle, 98,000,000 chickens; roundwood (2002) 4,062,638 cu m; fish catch (2001) 2,282,486. *Mining and quar-*

rying (2001): iron ore 195,000. *Manufacturing* (units; 2001): transistors 21,126,000,000; mobile phones 89,834,000; color television receivers 15,914,000. *Energy production (consumption):* electricity (kW-hr; 2000) 295,156,000,000 (295,156,000,000); coal (2000) 4,150,000 (66,525,000); crude petroleum (barrels; 2000) none (891,500,000); petroleum products (2000) 97,275,000 (63,447,000); natural gas (cu m; 2000) none (19,833,700,000). **Household income and expenditure** (2001). Average household size 3.5; annual income per household W 31,501,-200; sources of income: wages 84.2%, other 15.8%; expenditure: food and beverages 26.3%, transportation and communications 16.3%, education 11.3%. **Gross national product** (at current market prices; 2003): $576,426,000,000 ($12,030 per capita). **Population economically active** (2001): total 22,181,000; activity rate 46.9% (participation rates: ages 15–64, 64.6%; female 41.3%; unemployed [2002] 3.1%). **Tourism** (2002): receipts $5,919,000,-000; expenditures $9,036,000,000. **Land use** as % of total land area (2000): in temporary crops 17.4%, in permanent crops 2.0%, in pasture 0.5%; overall forest area 63.3%.

Foreign trade

Imports (2001-c.i.f.): $141,098,000,000 (electric and electronic products 19.4%, crude petroleum 15.1%, nonelectrical machinery and transport equipment 14.5%, chemicals and chemical products 9.2%, food and live animals 4.8%). *Major import sources:* Japan 18.9%; US 15.9%; China 9.4%; Saudi Arabia 5.7%; Australia 3.9%. **Exports** (2001-f.o.b.): $150,-439,000,000 (electric and electronic products 25.0%, transport equipment 17.0%, nonelectrical machinery and apparatus 15.6%, chemicals and chemical products 8.3%). *Major export destinations:* US 20.7%; China 12.1%; Japan 11.0%; Hong Kong 6.3%; Taiwan 3.9%.

Transport and communications

Transport. *Railroads* (2001): length 6,819 km; passenger-km 29,172,000,000; metric ton-km cargo 10,492,000,000. *Roads* (2001): total length 91,396 km (paved 77%). *Vehicles* (2001): passenger cars 8,889,000; trucks and buses 3,768,000. *Air transport* (2002; scheduled flights of Asiana and Korean Air only): passenger-km 48,325,000,000; metric ton-km cargo 4,590,000,000; airports (1996) with scheduled flights 14. **Communications**, in total units (units per 1,000 persons). Daily newspaper circulation (2000): 18,500,000 (393); radios (2000): 48,600,-000 (1,033); televisions (2000): 17,100,000 (364); telephone main lines (2003): 22,877,000 (472); cellular telephone subscribers (2003): 33,592,000 (694); personal computers (2003): 26,700,000 (551); Internet users (2003): 29,220,000 (603).

Education and health

Educational attainment (1995). Percentage of population age 25 and over having: no formal schooling 8.5%; primary education or less 17.7%; some secondary and secondary 53.1%; postsecondary 20.6%. **Literacy** (2001): total population age 15 and over literate 97.9%; males literate 99.2%; females literate 96.6%. **Health** (2002): physicians 78,592 (1 per 606 persons); hospital beds 316,015 (1 per 151 persons); infant mortality rate per 1,000 live births (2003) 7.3. **Food** (2001): daily per capita caloric intake 3,055 (vegetable products 85%, animal products 15%); 130% of FAO recommended minimum.

Military

Total active duty personnel (2003): 686,000 (army 81.6%, navy 9.2%, air force 9.2%); US military forces (2004): 40,258. **Military expenditure as percentage of GNP** (1999): 2.9% (world 2.4%); per capita expenditure $246.

Background

Civilization in the Korean Peninsula dates to the 3rd millennium BC (see background of Democratic People's Republic of Korea, above). The Republic of Korea was established in 1948 in the southern portion of the Korean peninsula. In 1950 North Korean troops invaded South Korea, precipitating the Korean War. UN forces intervened on the side of South Korea, while Chinese troops backed North Korea in the war, which ended with an armistice in 1953. The devastated country was rebuilt with US aid, and South Korea prospered in the postwar era, developing a strong export-oriented economy. It experienced an economic downturn in the mid-1990s that affected many economies in the area.

Recent Developments

On 25 Feb 2003, South Korea began a new political era with the inauguration of Pres. Roh Moo Hyun. Roh's campaign attracted young people and many who were openly anti-American. Although he wrapped himself in the cloak of an anticorruption and pro-democracy campaigner, Roh and his cronies themselves soon fell afoul of corruption. By early 2004 six of his close associates and more than a dozen members of parliament had been accused of involvement in political funding scandals. In March two opposition parties inaugurated a parliamentary debate on impeachment of President Roh for what many saw as a minor violation of election regulations. The vote on 12 March, however, was a resounding 193–2 in favor of impeachment, which would take effect if confirmed by the Constitutional Court. In legislative elections in April, the opposition conservatives were turned out of office, and the liberal pro-Roh Uri party won a majority. The Constitutional Court rejected Roh's impeachment on 14 May, and his powers were restored. Prime Minister Goh Kun, who had been acting president, resigned on 24 May. Amid allegations of financial improprieties, three top ministers resigned from the government in the first three months of 2005.

Internet resources: <www.korea.net>.

Kuwait

Official name: Dawlat al-Kuwayt (State of Kuwait). **Form of government:** constitutional monarchy with one legislative body (National Assembly [50, excluding cabinet ministers not elected to National Assembly serving ex officio]). **Head of state and government:** Emir Sheikh Jabir al-Ahmad al-Jabir Al Sabah

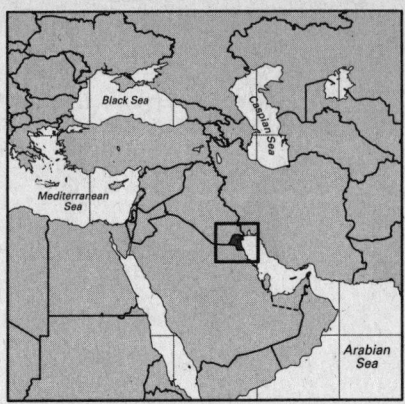

(from 1977), assisted by Prime Minister Sheikh Sabah al-Ahmad al-Jabir Al Sabah (from 2003). **Capital:** Kuwait (city). **Official language:** Arabic. **Official religion:** Islam. **Monetary unit:** 1 Kuwaiti dinar (KD) = 1,000 fils; valuation (7 Jul 2005) $1 = KD 0.29.

Demography

Area: 6,880 sq mi, 17,818 sq km. **Population** (2004): 2,586,000. **Density** (2004): persons per sq mi 375.9, persons per sq km 145.1. **Urban** (2001): 96.1%. **Sex distribution** (2003): male 60.31%; female 39.69%. **Age breakdown** (2003): under 15, 27.9%; 15–29, 31.8%; 30–44, 23.9%; 45–59, 12.1%; 60–74, 3.7%; 75 and over, 0.6%. **Ethnic composition** (2000): Arab 74%, of which Kuwaiti 30%, Palestinian 17%, Jordanian 10%, Bedouin 9%; Kurd 10%; Indo-Pakistani 8%; Persian 4%; other 4%. **Religious affiliation** (1995): Muslim 85%, of which Sunni 45%, Shi'i 30%, other Muslim 10%; other (mostly Christian and Hindu) 15%. **Major cities** (1995): As-Salimiyah 130,215; Qalib ash-Shuyukh 102,178; Hawalli 82,238; Kuwait (city) 28,859 (urban agglomeration [2003] 1,222,000). **Location:** the Middle East, bordering Iraq, the Persian Gulf, and Saudi Arabia.

Vital statistics

Birth rate per 1,000 population (2003): 21.8 (world avg. 21.3). **Death rate** per 1,000 population (2003): 2.5 (world avg. 9.1). **Natural increase rate** per 1,000 population (2003): 19.3 (world avg. 12.2). **Total fertility rate** (avg. births per childbearing woman; 2003): 3.1. **Marriage rate** per 1,000 population (2000): 4.9. **Divorce rate** per 1,000 population (2000): 1.7. **Life expectancy** at birth (2003): male 75.7 years; female 77.6 years.

National economy

Budget (2003–04). *Revenue:* KD 3,397,000,000 (oil revenue 87.5%). *Expenditures:* KD 5,666,000,000 (wages 32.4%, defense 18.5%, social security and welfare 14.8%, health 14.8%, economic development 8.5%, education 6.0%). **Tourism** (2002): receipts from visitors $119,000,000; expenditures by nationals abroad $3,021,000,000. **Gross national product**

1 metric ton = about 1.1 short tons;   1 kilometer = 0.6 mi (statute);   1 metric ton-km cargo = about 0.68 short ton-mi cargo;   c.i.f.: cost, insurance, and freight;   f.o.b.: free on board

(2003): $38,037,000,000 ($16,340 per capita). **Production** (metric tons except as noted). *Agriculture, forestry, fishing* (2002): tomatoes 35,127, cucumbers and gherkins 33,004, eggplants 12,002; livestock (number of live animals) 800,000 sheep, 130,000 goats, 18,000 cattle; fish catch (2001) 6,041. *Mining and quarrying* (2001): sulfur 524,000; lime 40,000. *Manufacturing* (value added in $'000,-000; 1999): refined petroleum products 2,481; food products 170; nonmetallic mineral products 158. *Energy production (consumption):* electricity (kW-hr; 2000) 32,853,000,000 (32,853,000,000); crude petroleum (barrels; 2002) 680,000,000 ([2000] 274,129,000); petroleum products (2000) 33,410,-000 (8,583,000); natural gas (cu m; 2002) 8,297,-000,000 ([2000] 9,177,000,000). **Population economically active** (2003): total 1,466,092, of which Kuwaiti 19.1%, non-Kuwaiti 80.9%; activity rate of total population 57.6% (participation rates: ages 15–59, 73.8%; female [1995] 26.1%; unemployed 1.2%). **Household income and expenditure.** Average household size (2002) 5.0; sources of income (1986): wages and salaries 53.8%, self-employment 20.8%, other 25.4%; expenditure (2000): housing energy 26.7%, food 18.3%, transportation and communications 16.1%, household furnishings 14.7%, clothing and footwear 8.9%. **Land use** as % of total land area (2000): in temporary crops 0.6%, in permanent crops 0.1%, in pasture 7.6%; overall forest area 0.3%.

Foreign trade

Imports (2003-c.i.f.): KD 3,217,000,000 (machinery and apparatus 24.0%, transport equipment 20.5%, food 14.0%, chemicals and chemical products 8.7%). *Major import sources:* US 11.1%; Japan 10.7%; Germany 9.5%; Saudi Arabia 6.6%; Italy 5.5%, China 5.3%. **Exports** (2003-f.o.b.): KD 6,162,000,000 (crude petroleum and petroleum products 91.9%, ethylene products 3.0%, reexports 2.5%). *Major export destinations:* Japan 22.1%; South Korea 13.1%; US 12.0%; Taiwan 10.7%; Singapore 10.2%.

Transport and communications

Transport. *Roads* (1999): total length 4,450 km (paved 81%). *Vehicles* (2001): passenger cars 715,000; trucks and buses 226,000. *Air transport* (2003): passenger-km 6,714,693,000; metric ton-km cargo 219,428,000; airports (2003) with scheduled flights 1. **Communications,** in total units (units per 1,000 persons). Daily newspaper circulation (2000): 836,000 (374); radios (2000): 1,400,000 (624); televisions (2000): 1,090,000 (486); telephone main lines (2003): 486,900 (198); cellular telephone subscribers (2003): 1,420,000 (578); personal computers (2002): 285,000 (121); Internet users (2003): 567,000 (231).

Education and health

Educational attainment (1988). Percentage of population age 25 and over having: no formal schooling 44.8%; primary education 8.6%; some secondary 15.1%; complete secondary 15.1%; higher 16.4%. **Literacy** (2001): total population age 15 and over literate 82.4%; males literate 84.3%; females literate 80.3%. **Health** (2002): physicians 3,780 (1 per 625 persons); hospital beds 5,200 (1 per 455 persons); infant mortality rate per 1,000 live births (2003) 10.7. **Food** (2001): daily per capita caloric intake

3,170 (vegetable products 78%, animal products 22%); 131% of FAO recommended minimum.

Military

Total active duty personnel (2003): 15,500 (army [including central staff] 71.0%, navy 12.9%, air force 16.1%); US and coalition troops (March 2004) 26,000. **Military expenditure as percentage of GNP** (1999): 7.7% (world 2.4%); per capita expenditure $1,410.

Background

Faylakah Island, in Kuwait Bay, had a civilization dating back to the 3rd millennium BC that flourished until 1200 BC. Greek colonists resettled the island in the 4th century BC. Abd Rahim of the Sabah dynasty became sheikh in 1756, the first of a family that continues to rule Kuwait. In 1899, to thwart German and Ottoman influences, Kuwait gave Britain control of its foreign affairs. Following the outbreak of war in 1914, Britain established a protectorate there. In 1961, after Kuwait became independent, Iraq laid claim to it. British troops defended Kuwait, and the Arab League recognized its independence, and Iraq dropped its claim. Iraqi forces invaded and occupied Kuwait in 1990, and a US-led military coalition drove them out in 1991. The destruction of many of Kuwait's oil wells complicated reconstruction efforts.

Recent Developments

The year 2004 saw a major shift in Kuwait's policy toward Iraq. Traditionally, the two neighbors entertained considerable suspicion—even animosity—toward one another, but the changing situation in Iraq induced Kuwait to call for friendly ties. Kuwaiti businesses sought commerce with Iraq and hoped to help in Iraq's reconstruction. At the end of July Iraqi Prime Minister Ayad Allawi made a historic state visit to Kuwait during which he asked for relief of the $15 billion that Iraq owed from its invasion of Kuwait in 1990–91. On 28 June Kuwait's prime minister, Sheikh Sabah al-Ahmad al-Jabir Al Sabah, announced the restoration of full diplomatic ties with Iraq. In May 2005 Kuwait's parliament granted women the right to vote and run for office for the first time in the country's history.

Internet resources: <www.kuwait-info.org>.

Kyrgyzstan

Official name: Kyrgyz Respublikasy (Kyrgyz); Respublika Kirgizstan (Russian) (Kyrgyz Republic). **Form of government:** unitary multiparty republic with two legislative houses (Assembly of People's Representatives [45]; Legislative Assembly [60]). **Head of state and government:** President Kurmanbek Bakiyev (from 25 Mar 2005 [acting until 14 August]). **Capital:** Bishkek. **Official languages:** Kyrgyz; Russian. **Official religion:** none. **Monetary unit:** 1 som (K.S.) = 100 tyiyn; valuation (7 Jul 2005) $1 = K.S. 40.96.

Demography

Area: 77,200 sq mi, 199,945 sq km. **Population** (2004): 5,081,000. **Density** (2004): persons per sq mi 65.8, persons per sq km 25.4. **Urban** (2003): 33.9%. **Sex distribution** (2001): male 48.84%; female

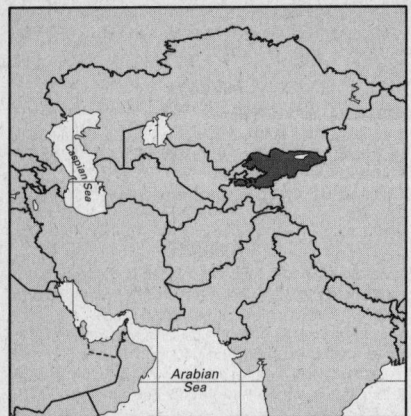

horses; roundwood (2001) 26,000 cu m; fish catch (2001) 201. *Mining and quarrying* (2002): mercury 300; antimony 200; gold (2001) 24,600 kg. *Manufacturing* (value of production in '000,000 som; 2001): ferrous metals 21,268; nonferrous metals 21,243; flour 3,914. *Energy production (consumption)*: electricity (kW-hr; 2001) 13,667,000,000 (11,503,000,000); hard coal (1999) 97,000 (878,-000); lignite (2000) 321,000 (339,000); crude petroleum (barrels; 2001) 553,000 (553,000); petroleum products (2001) 131,000 (387,000); natural gas (cu m; 2001) 32,800,000 (655,700,000). **Household income and expenditure**. Average household size (1999) 4.3; income per household (1994) 4,359 som; sources of income (1999): wages and salaries 29.2%, self-employment 25.6%, other 45.2%; expenditure (1990): food and clothing 48.0%, health care 13.1%, housing 5.9%. **Gross national product** (2003): $1,649,000,000 ($330 per capita). **Tourism** (2002): receipts from visitors, $36,000,000; expenditures by nationals abroad, $10,000,000.

51.16%. **Age breakdown** (2001): under 15, 35.0%; 15–29, 28.1%; 30–44, 18.6%; 45–59, 9.2%; 60–74, 7.0%; 75 and over, 2.1%. **Ethnic composition** (1999): Kyrgyz 64.9%; Uzbek 13.8%; Russian 12.5%; Hui 1.1%; Ukrainian 1.0%; Uighur 1.0%; other 5.7%. **Religious affiliation** (1997): Muslim (mostly Sunni) 75.0%; Christian 6.7%, of which Russian Orthodox 5.6%; other (mostly nonreligious) 18.3%. **Major cities** (1999): Bishkek (Frunze) 750,327; Osh 208,520; Jalal-Abad 70,401; Tokmok 59,409; Kara-Köl 47,159. **Location**: central Asia, bordering Kazakhstan, China, Tajikistan, and Uzbekistan.

Vital statistics

Birth rate per 1,000 population (2003): 21.9 (world avg. 21.3); (1994) legitimate 83.2%. **Death rate** per 1,000 population (2003): 7.3 (world avg. 9.1). **Natural increase rate** per 1,000 population (2003): 14.6 (world avg. 12.2). **Total fertility rate** (avg. births per childbearing woman; 2001): 2.5. **Marriage rate** per 1,000 population (1999): 5.6. **Divorce rate** per 1,000 population (1999): 4.6. **Life expectancy** at birth (2003): male 63.5 years; female 71.7 years.

National economy

Budget (2001). *Revenue:* K.S. 12,544,000,000 (tax revenue 73.2%, of which VAT 33.6%, taxes on income 16.0%, excise taxes 8.8%, other taxes 14.8%; nontax revenue 21.3%; grants 5.5%). *Expenditures:* K.S. 13,133,000,000 (education 21.7%; general public services 16.0%; social security 10.8%; health 10.5%; defense 7.5%). **Public debt** (external, outstanding; 2002): $1,394,000,000. **Land use** as % of total land area (2000): in temporary crops 7.1%, in permanent crops 0.3%, in pasture 48.4%; overall forest area 5.2%. **Population economically active** (2001): total 1,939,000; activity rate of total population 39.2% (participation rates [2000]: ages 16–59 [male], 16–54 [female] 62.0%; female (1999) 44.9%; unemployed [2001] 7.8%). **Production** (metric tons except as noted). *Agriculture, forestry, fishing* (2002): mixed grasses and legumes 2,900,000, wheat 1,306,000, potatoes 1,244,000; livestock (number of live animals) 3,104,000 sheep, 988,000 cattle, 350,000

Foreign trade

Imports (2001-f.o.b. in balance of trade and c.i.f. for commodities and trading partners): $467,200,000 (petroleum and natural gas 22.6%, machinery and apparatus 21.0%, food products 11.7%, chemicals and chemical products 9.5%). *Major import sources:* Russia 18.2%; Kazakhstan 17.5%; Uzbekistan 14.3%; China 10.4%; US 5.7%. **Exports** (2001): $476,-200,000 (nonferrous metals [significantly gold] 51.7%, machinery and apparatus 12.0%, electricity 9.8%, agricultural products [significantly tobacco] 9.5%). *Major export destinations:* Switzerland 26.1%; Germany 19.8%; Russia 13.5%; Uzbekistan 10.1%; Kazakhstan 8.2%.

Transport and communications

Transport. *Railroads* (2000): length 424 km; passenger-km 44,000,000; metric ton-km cargo 348,000,-000. *Roads* (1999): total length 18,500 km (paved 91%). *Vehicles* (2000): passenger cars 187,322. *Air transport* (1999): passenger-km 532,000,000; metric ton-km cargo 56,000,000; airports with scheduled flights 2. **Communications**, in total units (units per 1,000 persons). Daily newspaper circulation (2000): 73,000 (15); radios (2000): 542,000 (111); televisions (2000): 239,000 (49); telephone main lines (2002): 394,800 (79); cellular telephone subscribers (2002): 53,100 (10); personal computers (2002): 65,000 (13); Internet users (2002): 152,000 (30).

Education and health

Educational attainment (1999). Percentage of population age 15 and over having: primary education 6.3%; some secondary 18.3%; completed secondary 50.0%; some postsecondary 14.9%; higher 10.5%. **Literacy** (1999): total population age 15 and over literate 97.5%; males literate 98.5%; females literate 96.5%. **Health** (1997): physicians 15,100 (1 per 307 persons); hospital beds 40,700 (1 per 114 persons); infant mortality rate per 1,000 live births (2003) 38.0. **Food** (2001): daily per capita caloric intake 2,882 (vegetable products 81%, animal products 19%); 111% of FAO recommended minimum.

1 metric ton = about 1.1 short tons;　1 kilometer = 0.6 mi (statute);　1 metric ton-km cargo = about 0.68 short ton-mi cargo;　c.i.f.: cost, insurance, and freight;　f.o.b.: free on board

Military

Total active duty personnel (2003): 10,900 (army 78.0%, air force 22.0%); US troops (July 2004) 1,200. A Russian air base opened in Kyrgyzstan in October 2003. Military expenditure as percentage of GNP (1999): 2.4% (world 2.4%); per capita expenditure $62.

Background

The Kyrgyz, a nomadic people of Central Asia, settled in the Tian Shan region in ancient times. They were conquered by Genghis Khan's son Jochi in 1207. The area became part of the Qing empire of China in the mid-18th century. The region came under Russian control in the 19th century, and its rebellion against Russia in 1916 resulted in a long period of brutal repression. Kirgiziya became an autonomous province of the USSR in 1924 and was made the Kirghiz Soviet Socialist Republic in 1936. Kyrgyzstan gained independence in 1991. In the 1990s it struggled with its democratization process and with establishing a thriving economy.

Recent Developments

Undoubtedly influenced by Ukraine's "Orange Revolution" a few months earlier, the 15-year-old regime of Pres. Askar Akayev in Kyrgyzstan came crashing down with starling rapidity in the country's own "Tulip Revolution" on 24 Mar 2005. Disgruntled by parliamentary elections that were seen as fraudulent, protesters gathered in the central square in Bishkek and elsewhere. Their numbers swelled during the day, and demonstrators overran the presidential compound, forcing officials to flee out the back. The Supreme Court declared the elections invalid and reinstated the previous parliament. Presidential elections originally scheduled for October 2005 were moved forward to 10 July. Acting president Kurmanbek Bakiyev won 89% of the vote.

Internet resources: <www.kyrgyzstan.org>.

Laos

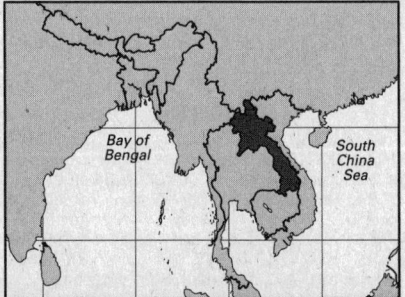

Bay of Bengal

South China Sea

Official name: Sathalanalat Paxathipatai Paxaxon Lao (Lao People's Democratic Republic). Form of government: unitary single-party people's republic with one legislative house (National Assembly [109]). Chief of state: President Khamtai Siphandon (from 1998). Head of government: Prime Minister Boungnang Vorachith (from 2001). Capital: Vientiane (Viangchan). Official language: Lao. Official religion: none. Monetary unit: 1 kip (KN) = 100 at; valuation (7 Jul 2005) $1 = KN 10,390.05.

Demography

Area: 91,429 sq mi, 236,800 sq km. Population (2004): 5,787,000. Density (2004): persons per sq mi 63.3, persons per sq km 24.4. Urban (2002): 25.0%. Sex distribution (2002): male 49.97%; female 50.03%. Age breakdown (2000): under 15, 42.8%; 15–29, 27.0%; 30–44, 16.3%; 45–59, 8.3%; 60–74, 4.6%; 75 and over, 1.0%. Ethnic composition (2000): Lao-Lum (Lao) 53.0%; Lao-Theung (Mon-Khmer) 23.0%; Lao-Tai (Tai) 13.0%; Lao-Soung (Miao [Hmong] and Man [Yao]) 10.0%; other (ethnic Chinese or Vietnamese) 1.0%. Religious affiliation (2000): Buddhist 48.8%; traditional beliefs 41.7%; nonreligious 4.3%; Christian 2.1%; other 3.1%. Major cities (2003): Vientiane 194,200 (urban agglomeration [2001] 663,-000); Savannakhét 58,200; Pakxé 50,100; Xam Nua 40,700; Muang Khammouan 27,300. Location: southeastern Asia, bordering China, Vietnam, Cambodia, Thailand, and Myanmar (Burma).

Vital statistics

Birth rate per 1,000 population (2003): 36.9 (world avg. 21.3). Death rate per 1,000 population (2004): 12.4 (world avg. 9.1). Natural increase rate per 1,000 population (2003): 24.5 (world avg. 12.2). Total fertility rate (avg. births per childbearing woman; 2003): 4.9. Life expectancy at birth (2003): male 52.3 years; female 56.3 years.

National economy

Budget (2001–02). Revenue: KN 2,481,000,000,-000 (tax revenue 82.3%; nontax revenue 17.7%). Expenditures: KN 3,614,000,000,000 (capital expenditure 59.9%, of which foreign-financed 34.8%; current expenditure 40.1%). Public debt (external, outstanding; 2002): $2,620,000,000. Tourism (2002): receipts from visitors $113,000,000; expenditures by nationals abroad (2000) $8,000,000. Population economically active (2000): total 2,625,000; activity rate of total population 50% (participation rates: female 47%; unemployed [1994] 2.6%). Production (metric tons except as noted). Agriculture, forestry, fishing (2002): rice 2,410,000, sugarcane 210,000, corn (maize) 113,000; livestock (number of live animals) 1,425,900 pigs, 1,150,000 cattle, 15,000,000 chickens; roundwood (2001) 6,455,000 cu m; fish catch (2001) 80,000. Mining and quarrying (2002): gypsum 130,000; tin (metal content) 3,000; gold (2003) 115,000 troy oz. Manufacturing (1998): plastic products 3,225; tobacco 1,000; detergent 912. Energy production (consumption): electricity (kW-hr; 2000) 1,225,000,000 (497,000,000); coal (2000) 1,000 (1,000); petroleum products (2000) none (119,000). Gross national product (2003): $1,821,000,000 ($320 per capita). Households. Average household size (1995) 6.1; average annual income per household KN 3,710. Land use as % of total land area (2000): in temporary crops 3.8%, in permanent crops 0.4%, in pasture 3.8%; overall forest area 54.4%.

Foreign trade

Imports (2000-c.i.f.): $569,000,000 (consumption goods 50.6%, mineral fuels 13.9%, materials for garment assembly 10.6%, construction and electrical equipment 7.6%). *Major import sources* (2001): Thailand 52.0%; Vietnam 26.5%; China 5.7%; Singapore 3.3%; Japan 1.5%. **Exports** (2000-f.o.b.): $351,000,-000 (electricity 32.0%, garments 26.1%, wood products [mostly logs and timber] 24.8%, motorcycles 6.3%). *Major export destinations* (2001): Vietnam 41.5%; Thailand 14.8%; France 6.1%; Germany 4.6%; Belgium 2.2%.

Transport and communications

Transport. *Roads* (1999): total length 21,716 km (paved [1995] 45%). *Vehicles* (1996): passenger cars 16,320; trucks and buses 4,200. *Air transport* (1997): passenger-km 48,000,000; metric ton-km cargo 5,000,000; airports (1996) with scheduled flights 11. **Communications,** in total units (units per 1,000 persons). Daily newspaper circulation (2000): 21,100 (4); radios (2000): 781,000 (148); televisions (2000): 52,800 (10); telephone main lines (2002): 61,900 (11); cellular telephone subscribers (2002): 55,200 (10); personal computers (2002): 15,000 (2.7); Internet users (2002): 18,000 (3.3).

Education and health

Educational attainment (1985). Percentage of population age 6 and over having: no schooling 49.3%; primary 41.2%; secondary 9.1%; higher 0.4%. **Literacy** (1995): total population age 15 and over literate 56.6%; males literate 69.4%; females literate 44.4%. **Health:** physicians (1996) 1,167 (1 per 4,115 persons); hospital beds (1990) 10,364 (1 per 402 persons); infant mortality rate per 1,000 live births (2003) 88.9. **Food** (2001): daily per capita caloric intake 2,309 (vegetable products 93%, animal products 7%); (2001) 108% of FAO recommended minimum.

Military

Total active duty personnel (2003): 29,100 (army 88.0%, air force 12.0%). **Military expenditure as percentage of GNP** (1999): 2.0% (world 2.4%); per capita expenditure $5.

Background

The Lao people migrated into Laos from southern China after the 8th century AD, displacing indigenous tribes. In the 14th century Fa Ngum founded the first Laotian state, Lan Xang. Except for a period of rule by Burma (1574–1637), the Lan Xang kingdom ruled Laos until 1713, when it split into three kingdoms. France gained control of the region in 1893. In 1945 Japan seized it and declared Laos independent. The area reverted to French rule after World War II. The Geneva Conference of 1954 unified and granted independence to Laos. Communist forces took control in 1975, establishing the Lao People's Democratic Republic. Laos held its first election in 1989 and promulgated a new constitution in 1991. Although its economy was adversely affected by the mid-1990s Asian monetary crises, it realized a longtime goal in 1997 when it joined the Association of Southeast Asian Nations.

Recent Developments

Issues of regional integration were topmost among the priorities for Laos. In November 2004, for the first time, Laos was host of the annual summit of the Association of Southeast Asian Nations (ASEAN)—an event that was, despite the logistic and financial challenges, a landmark for Laos's relations with its neighbors. In March, the first Thai-Lao joint cabinet retreat took place in Pakse, southern Laos, led by the two countries' prime ministers. The meeting marked the official start of the construction of a second Lao-Thai Friendship Bridge. Earlier in the same month, the Thai government approved partial funding for the construction of a third bridge. The Laotian government hoped that the building of such infrastructure would turn Laos into the transportation hub of mainland Southeast Asia.

Internet resources: <www.visit-laos.com>.

Latvia

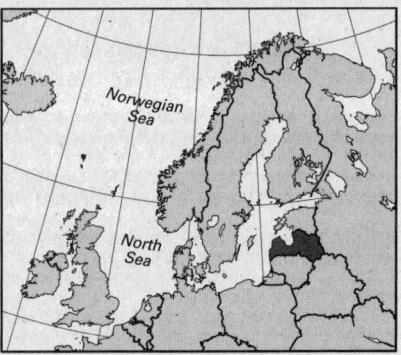

Official name: Latvijas Republika (Republic of Latvia). **Form of government:** unitary multiparty republic with a single legislative body (Parliament, or Saeima [100]). **Chief of state:** President Vaira Vike-Freiberga (from 1999). **Head of government:** Prime Minister Aigars Kalvitis (from 2 Dec 2004). **Capital:** Riga. **Official language:** Latvian. **Official religion:** none. **Monetary unit:** 1 lats (Ls; plural lati) = 100 santimi; valuation (7 Jul 2005) $1 = 0.59 lats.

Demography

Area: 24,938 sq mi, 64,589 sq km. **Population** (2004): 2,312,000. **Density** (2004): persons per sq mi 92.7, persons per sq km 35.8. **Urban** (2002): 67.8%. **Sex distribution** (2002): male 46.03%; female 53.97%. **Age breakdown** (2000): under 15, 18.1%; 15–29, 21.2%; 30–44, 21.4%; 45–59, 18.3%; 60–74, 15.7%; 75 and over, 5.3%. **Ethnic composition** (2002): Latvian 58.2%; Russian 29.2%; Belarusian 4.0%; Ukrainian 2.6%; Polish 2.5%; Lithuanian 1.4%; other 2.1%. **Religious affiliation** (1995): Christian 39.6%, of which Protestant 16.7% (of which Lutheran 14.6%), Roman Catholic 14.9%, Orthodox 8.0%; Jewish 0.6%; other (mostly nonreligious) 59.8%. **Major cities** (2002): Riga 747,157;

---

1 metric ton = about 1.1 short tons;   1 kilometer = 0.6 mi (statute);   1 metric ton-km cargo = about 0.68 short ton-mi cargo;   c.i.f.: cost, insurance, and freight;   f.o.b.: free on board

Daugavpils 113,409; Liepaja 87,505; Jelgava 65,927; Jurmala 55,328. **Location:** eastern Europe, bordering Estonia, Russia, Belarus, Lithuania, and the Baltic Sea.

Vital statistics

Birth rate per 1,000 population (2002): 8.6 (world avg. 21.3); (1998) legitimate 62.9%. **Death rate** per 1,000 population (2002): 13.9 (world avg. 9.1). **Natural increase rate** per 1,000 population (2002): -5.3 (world avg. 12.2). **Total fertility rate** (avg. births per childbearing woman; 2002): 1.2. **Marriage rate** per 1,000 population (2002): 4.2. **Divorce rate** per 1,000 population (2002): 2.5. **Life expectancy** at birth (2002): male 65.4 years; female 76.8 years.

National economy

Budget (2001). *Revenue:* Ls 1,244,100,000 (social security contributions 35.3%, value-added taxes 28.2%, income taxes 14.3%, excises 13.0%, nontax revenue 9.2%). *Expenditures:* Ls 1,399,800,000 (social security and welfare 40.7%, health 11.0%, police 7.0%, education 6.3%, defense 3.1%). **Public debt** (external, outstanding; 2002): $1,124,000,000. **Production** (metric tons except as noted). *Agriculture, forestry, fishing* (2002): grasses for forage and silage 14,000,000, potatoes 768,000, sugar beets 622,000; livestock (number of live animals) 453,000 pigs, 388,000 cattle; roundwood (2001) 14,037,000 cu m; fish catch (2002) 105,000. *Mining and quarrying* (2001): peat 555,000. *Manufacturing* (value added in Ls '000,000; 1998): alcoholic beverages 79.4; sawn wood 64.4; veneer/plywood 37.6. *Energy production (consumption):* electricity (kW-hr; 2001) 4,236,000,000 ([2002] 6,323,000,000); coal (2002) none (102,000); petroleum products (2002) none (1,084,000); natural gas (cu m; 2002) none (1,610,000,000). **Household income and expenditure.** Average household size (2000) 2.7; annual disposable income per household (2002) Ls 2,076; sources of income (1998): wages and salaries 55.8%, pensions and transfers 25.7%; expenditure (2001–02): food, beverages, and tobacco 40.0%, transportation and communications 15.0%, housing and energy 14.0%. **Tourism** (in $'000,000; 2002): receipts 161; expenditures 230. **Gross national product** (2003): $9,441,000,000 ($4,070 per capita). **Population economically active** (2002): total 1,123,000; activity rate of total population 48.1% (participation rates: ages 15–64 [2000] 67.5%; female [2000] 48.5%; unemployed 12.0%). **Land use** as % of total land area (2000): in temporary crops 29.7%, in permanent crops 0.5%, in pasture 9.8%; overall forest area 47.1%.

Foreign trade

Imports (2002-c.i.f.): Ls 2,497,000,000 (machinery and apparatus 21.3%, chemicals and chemical products 10.5%, transport vehicles 9.8%, mineral fuels 9.7%). *Major import sources:* Germany 17.2%; Lithuania 9.8%; Russia 8.8%; Finland 8.0%; Sweden 6.4%. **Exports** (2002-f.o.b.): Ls 1,409,000,000 (wood and wood products [mostly sawn wood] 33.6%, base and fabricated metals [mostly iron and steel] 13.2%, textiles and clothing 12.8%). *Major export destinations:* Germany 15.5%; UK 14.6%; Sweden 10.5%; Lithuania 8.4%; Estonia 6.0%.

Transport and communications

Transport. *Railroads* (2002): length 2,270 km; passenger-km (2000) 715,000,000; metric-km cargo 15,020,000,000. *Roads* (1999): total length 73,227 km (paved 39%). *Vehicles* (2002): passenger cars 552,200; trucks and buses 113,900. *Air transport* (1999): passenger-km 238,000,000; metric ton-km cargo 10,000,000; airports with scheduled flights (2001) 2. **Communications,** in total units (units per 1,000 persons). Daily newspaper circulation (2000): 586,000 (247); radios (2000): 1,650,000 (695); televisions (2002): 1,955,000 (850); telephone main lines (2003): 653,900 (283); cellular telephone subscribers (2003): 1,219,600 (529); personal computers (2002): 400,000 (171); Internet users (2003): 936,000 (406).

Education and health

Educational attainment (2000). Percentage of population age 15 and over having: some and complete primary education 8.5%; lower secondary 26.5%; upper secondary 51.1%; higher 13.9%. **Literacy** (2000): 99.8%. **Health** (2002): physicians 7,900 (1 per 295 persons); hospital beds 18,200 (1 per 128 persons); infant mortality rate per 1,000 live births (2002) 9.9. **Food** (2001): daily per capita caloric intake 2,809 (vegetable products 72%, animal products 28%); 110% of FAO recommended minimum.

Military

Total active duty personnel (2003): 4,880, excluding 3,200 border guards classified as paramilitary (army 82.0%, navy 12.7%, air force 5.3%). **Military expenditure as percentage of GNP** (1999): 0.9% (world 2.4%); per capita expenditure $59.

Background

Latvia was settled by the Balts in ancient times. It was conquered by the Vikings in the 9th century and later dominated by its German-speaking neighbors, who Christianized the people in the 12th–13th centuries. By 1230 German rule was established. From the mid-16th to the early 18th century, the region was split between Poland and Sweden, but by the end of the 18th century all of Latvia had been annexed by Russia. Latvia declared its independence after the Russian Revolution of 1917, but in 1940 the Soviet Red Army invaded. Held by Nazi Germany in 1941–44, the country was recaptured by the Soviets and incorporated into the Soviet Union. Latvia gained its independence in 1991 with the breakup of the Soviet Union; throughout the 1990s it sought to privatize the economy and build ties with Western Europe.

Recent Developments

In joining NATO on 29 March and the European Union on 1 May, Latvia in 2004 achieved its main foreign-policy goals since regaining independence. Riga contributed to international missions in Iraq, Afghanistan, the Balkans, and Georgia and generally maintained good relations with the rest of the world. Relations with Russia remained a challenge, however. Moscow objected to NATO's patrolling airspace over the Baltic States and insisted that EU enlargement and the new EU-Russia Partnership and Cooperation Agreement be contingent upon concessions from both the EU and the Baltic States. The EU rejected Moscow's accusations that the rights of Russian-speaking minorities in Latvia and Estonia were being violated, especially in education.

Internet resources: <www.latviatourism.lv>.

Lebanon

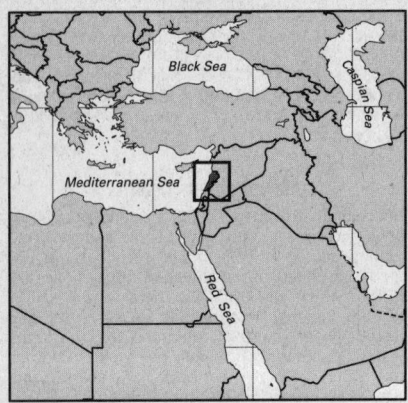

Official name: Al-Jumhuriyah al-Lubnaniyah (Lebanese Republic). **Form of government:** unitary multiparty republic with one legislative house (National Assembly [128]). **Chief of state:** President Émile Lahoud (from 1998). **Head of government:** Prime Minister Najib Mikati (from 19 Apr 2005). **Capital:** Beirut. **Official language:** Arabic. **Official religion:** none. **Monetary unit:** 1 Lebanese pound (£L) = 100 piastres; valuation (7 Jul 2005) $1 = £L 1,507.50.

Demography

Area: 4,016 sq mi, 10,400 sq km. **Population** (2004): 3,777,000 (excludes about 300,000 unnaturalized Palestinian refugees). **Density** (2004): persons per sq mi 940.5, persons per sq km 363.2. **Urban** (2001): 90.1%. **Sex distribution** (2002): male 48.48%; female 51.52%. **Age breakdown** (2002): under 15, 27.4%; 15–29, 32.2%; 30–44, 21.0%; 45–59, 10.1%; 60–74, 7.1%; 75 and over, 2.2%. **Ethnic composition** (2000): Arab 84.5%, of which Lebanese 71.2%, Palestinian 12.1%; Armenian 6.8%; Kurd 6.1%; other 2.6%. **Religious affiliation** (1995): Muslim 55.3%, of which Shi'i 34.0%, Sunni 21.3%; Christian 37.6%, of which Catholic 25.1% (Maronite 19.0%, Greek Catholic or Melchite 4.6%), Orthodox 11.7% (Greek Orthodox 6.0%, Armenian Apostolic 5.2%), Protestant 0.5%; Druze 7.1%. **Major cities** (1998): Beirut 1,100,000 (urban agglomeration 2,115,000 [2001]); Tripoli 200,000; Sidon 140,000; Tyre (Sur) 110,000; An-Nabatiyah 84,000. **Location:** the Middle East, bordering Syria, Israel, and the Mediterranean Sea.

Vital statistics

Birth rate per 1,000 population (2003): 19.7 (world avg. 21.3). **Death rate** per 1,000 population (2003):

6.3 (world avg. 9.1). **Natural increase rate** per 1,000 population (2003): 13.4 (world avg. 12.2). **Total fertility rate** (avg. births per childbearing woman; 2003): 1.9. **Life expectancy** at birth (2003): male 69.6 years; female 74.6 years.

National economy

Budget (2000). *Revenue:* £L 4,091,435,000,000 (1998; tax revenue 74.6%, of which customs revenues 44.1%, income tax 9.0%, taxes on goods and services 8.4%, property tax 8.4%, miscellaneous taxes and fees 2.1%; nontax revenue 25.4%). *Expenditures:* £L 8,190,034,000,000 (current expenditures 81.1%, of which debt service 40.0%, public services 10.3%, defense 9.7%, education 8.3%, social security 6.4%, health 2.6%; capital expenditures 18.9%). **Production** (metric tons except as noted). *Agriculture, forestry, fishing* (2002): potatoes 257,000, tomatoes 247,000, cucumbers and gherkins 161,000; livestock (number of live animals) 385,000 goats, 350,000 sheep, 33,000,000 chickens; roundwood (2001) 89,426 cu m; fish catch (2001) 3,970. *Mining and quarrying* (1996): lime 16,000; salt 4,000; gypsum 2,000. *Manufacturing* (2001): cement 2,727,000; flour 420,000; olive oil 7,000. *Energy production (consumption):* electricity (kW-hr; 2001) 10,452,000,000 ([2000] 10,633,000,000); coal, n.a. (117,000); crude petroleum (barrels; 1998) none (1,358,000); petroleum products (2001) none (4,784,000). **Gross national product** (2003): $18,187,000,000 ($4,040 per capita). **Population economically active** (1997): total 1,362,000; activity rate of total population 39.7% (unemployed 8.5%). **Public debt** (external, outstanding; 2002): $13,829,000,000. **Households.** Average household size (2000) 4.5; average annual income per household (1994; ESCWA estimate for Beirut only) £L 2,400,000. **Tourism** (2002): receipts from visitors $956,000,000. **Land use** as % of total land area (2000): in temporary crops 18.6%, in permanent crops 13.9%, in pasture 1.6%; overall forest area 3.5%.

Foreign trade

Imports (2002-c.i.f.): $6,445,000,000 (mineral products 15.1%, machinery and apparatus 13.4%, food and live animals 13.3%, chemicals and chemical products 9.8%). *Major import sources:* Italy 10.8%; Germany 9.0%; France 8.0%; US 7.2%; China 6.7%. **Exports** (2002): $1,046,000,000 (precious metal [significantly gold] jewelry 20.5%, machinery and apparatus 11.4%, chemicals and chemical products 10.3%, food and beverages 9.8%, paper and paper products 9.4%). *Major export destinations:* Switzerland 12.6%; Saudi Arabia 9.2%; UAE 9.1%; Syria 7.2%; Iraq 6.8%.

Transport and communications

Transport. *Roads* (1996): total length 6,350 km (paved 95%). *Vehicles* (1997): passenger cars 1,299,398; trucks and buses 85,242. *Air transport* (2001; Middle East Airlines and Trans-Mediterranean Airways): passenger-km 1,661,000,000; metric ton-km cargo 216,700,000; airports (1999) 1. **Communications,** in total units (units per 1,000 persons). Daily newspaper circulation (2000): 383,000 (107); radios (2000): 2,460,000 (687); televisions (2000): 1,200,000

1 metric ton = about 1.1 short tons;   1 kilometer = 0.6 mi (statute);   1 metric ton-km cargo = about 0.68 short ton-mi cargo;   c.i.f.: cost, insurance, and freight;   f.o.b.: free on board

(335); telephone main lines (2002): 678,800 (198); cellular telephone subscribers (2002): 775,100 (227); personal computers (2002): 275,000 (81); Internet users (2002): 400,000 (117).

Education and health

Literacy (2000): total population age 15 and over literate 87.4%; males literate 93.1%; females literate 82.2%. **Health** (1997): physicians 7,203 (1 per 476 persons); hospital beds (1995) 11,596 (1 per 319 persons); infant mortality rate per 1,000 live births (2003) 26.4. **Food** (2001): daily per capita caloric intake 3,184 (vegetable products 85%, animal products 15%); 128% of FAO recommended minimum.

Military

Total active duty personnel (2003): Lebanese national armed forces 72,100 (army 97.1%, navy 1.5%, air force 1.4%). External regular military forces include: UN peacekeeping force in Lebanon (August 2004) 2,000; Syrian army (September 2004) 14,000. **Military expenditure as percentage of GNP** (1999): 4.0% (world 2.4%); per capita expenditure $185.

Background

Much of present-day Lebanon corresponds to ancient Phoenicia, which was settled c. 3000 AD. In the 6th century AD, Christians fleeing Syrian persecution settled in what is now northern Lebanon and founded the Maronite Church. Arab tribesmen settled in southern Lebanon and by the 11th century had founded the Druze faith. Lebanon was later ruled by the Mamluks. In 1516 the Ottoman Turks seized control; the Turks ended the local rule of the Druze Shihab princes in 1842. After the massacre of Maronites by Druze in 1860, France forced the Ottomans to form an autonomous province for the Christian area, known as Mount Lebanon. Following World War I, it was administered by the French military, but by late 1946 it was fully independent. After the Arab-Israeli War of 1948–49, Palestinian refugees settled in southern Lebanon. In 1970 the Palestine Liberation Organization (PLO) moved its headquarters there and began raids into northern Israel. The Christian-dominated Lebanese government tried to curb them, and in response the PLO sided with Lebanon's Muslims in their conflict with Christians, sparking a civil war by 1975. In 1982 Israeli forces invaded in an effort to drive Palestinian forces out of southern Lebanon. Israeli troops withdrew from most of Lebanon in 1985, leaving the conflict unresolved, but later returned. A cease-fire, agreed to in 1996, was broken in 1997 when Israeli soldiers and Lebanon's Hezbollah forces clashed.

Recent Developments

The assassination in a terrorist car bombing of Rafik Hariri, a popular, rich, and powerful former prime minister (1992–98 and 2000–04), on 14 Feb 2005 served to catalyze growing anti-Syrian feelings in Lebanon. Western observers, in particular the US, seemed certain of the involvement of Syria, which for decades had exercised great influence on the Lebanese government and currently kept some 15,000 troops in Lebanon. The pro-Syrian prime minister, Omar Karami, resigned on 28 February (he was reinstated on 10 March and resigned again on 13 April). On 5 March, Syrian Pres. Bashar al-Assad agreed to a US demand and promised a "gradual and organized" withdrawal of his forces. The militant Shi-'ite organization Hezbollah, however, opposed this policy and staged a huge pro-Syrian demonstration in Beirut on 8 March; largely as a result, Hezbollah was transformed into a national political force and its leader, Sheikh Hassan Nasrallah, into a Lebanese national leader. By late April all Syrian troops had left Lebanon, and another pro-Syrian, Najib Mikati, had been installed as prime minister. Staggered parliamentary elections took place in late spring. Rafik Hariri's son Saad led a sweep of Beirut's 19 seats, and a complex array of alliances and constituent priorities in other areas of the country set the scene for a challenging next stage in Lebanon's history.

Internet resources: <www.presidency.gov.lb>.

Lesotho

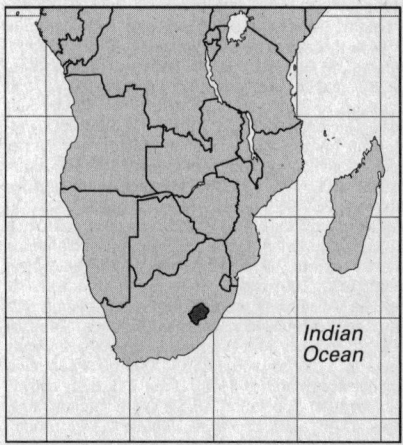

Indian Ocean

Official name: Lesotho (Sotho); Kingdom of Lesotho (English). **Form of government:** constitutional monarchy with 2 legislative houses (Senate [33]; National Assembly [120]). **Chief of state:** King Letsie III (from 1996). **Head of government:** Prime Minister Bethuel Pakalitha Mosisili (from 1998). **Capital:** Maseru. **Official languages:** Sotho; English. **Official religion:** Christianity. **Monetary unit:** 1 loti (plural maloti [M]) = 100 lisente; valuation (7 Jul 2005) $1 = M 6.85.

Demography

Area: 11,720 sq mi, 30,355 sq km. **Population** (2004): 1,800,000. **Density** (2004; de facto): persons per sq mi 153.6, persons per sq km 59.3. **Urban** (2001; de jure figure including absentee miners working in South Africa): 13.4%. **Sex distribution** (2001; de jure figure including absentee miners working in South Africa): male 50.62%; female 49.38%. **Age breakdown** (2001; de jure figure including absentee miners working in South Africa): under 15, 35.3%; 15–29, 31.4%; 30–44, 14.8%; 45–59, 10.0%; 60–74, 5.9%; 75 and over, 2.6%. **Ethnic composition** (2000): Sotho 80.3%; Zulu 14.4%; other 5.3%. **Religious affiliation** (2000): Christian 91.0%, of which

Roman Catholic 37.5%, Protestant (mostly Presbyterian) 13.0%, African Christian 11.8%; other (mostly traditional beliefs) 9.0%. **Major urban centers** (1996): Maseru 137,837 (urban agglomeration [2001] 271,000); Teyateyaneng 48,869; Maputsoe 27,951; Hlotse 23,122; Mafeteng 20,804. **Location:** southern Africa, surrounded by South Africa.

Vital statistics

Birth rate per 1,000 population (2003): 27.3 (world avg. 21.3). **Death rate** per 1,000 population (2003): 24.6 (world avg. 9.1). **Natural increase rate** per 1,000 population (2003): 2.7 (world avg. 12.2). **Total fertility rate** (avg. births per childbearing woman; 2003): 3.5. **Life expectancy** at birth (2003): male 36.8 years; female 37.1 years. **Adult population** (ages 15–49) **living with HIV** (2004): 28.9% (world avg. 1.1%).

National economy

Budget (2000–01). *Revenue:* M 2,752,200,000 (customs receipts 40.9%, grants and nontax revenue 29.4%, income tax 11.4%, sales tax 10.2%). *Expenditures:* M 2,897,900,000 (personal emoluments 31.8%, capital expenditure 17.8%, subsidies and transfers 9.6%, interest payments 9.0%). **Public debt** (external, outstanding; 2002): $611,000,000. **Production** (metric tons except as noted). *Agriculture, forestry, fishing* (2002): corn (maize) 300,000, potatoes 90,000, wheat 51,000; livestock (number of live animals) 850,000 sheep, 650,000 goats, 540,000 cattle; roundwood (2001) 2,028,134 cu m; fish catch (2001) 32. *Mining and quarrying* (2001): diamonds 1,140 carats. *Manufacturing* (value added in $'000,000; 1995): food products 58; beverages 38; textiles 14. *Energy production (consumption):* data for Lesotho included with South Africa. **Tourism** (2002): receipts from visitors $20,000,000; expenditures by nationals abroad $14,000,000. **Population economically active** (1993): total 617,871; activity rate of total population 45.1% (participation rates: ages 15–64 [1986] 79.8%; female 23.7%; unemployed [2001] 40%). **Households.** Average household size (2000) 5.0; expenditure (1989): food 48.0%, clothing 16.4%, household durable goods 11.9%, housing and energy 10.1%, transportation 4.7%. **Gross national product** (at current market prices; 2003): $1,049,000,000 ($590 per capita). **Land use** as % of total land area (2000): in temporary crops 10.9%, in permanent crops 0.1%, in pasture 65.9%; overall forest area 0.5%.

Foreign trade

Imports (2001-f.o.b. in balance of trade and c.i.f. in commodities and trading partners): M 5,824,-000,000 (1999; food products 15.3%, unspecified commodities 84.7%). *Major import sources* (2001): Customs Union of Southern Africa (mostly South Africa) 82.8%; Asian countries 14.9%. **Exports** (2001): M 2,426,000,000 (manufactured goods [mostly clothing] 74.7%, machinery and transport equipment 10.5%, beverages 3.6%, wool 2.5%). *Major export destinations:* North America (mostly the US) 62.8%; Customs Union of Southern Africa (mostly South Africa) 37.0%.

Transport and communications

Transport. *Railroads* (2001): length 2.6 km. *Roads* (1999): total length 5,940 km (paved 18%), *Vehicles* (1996): passenger cars 12,610; trucks and buses 25,000. *Air transport* (1999): passenger-km, negligible (less than 500,000); metric ton-km cargo, negligible; airports (1997) with scheduled flights 1. **Communications,** in total units (units per 1,000 persons). Daily newspaper circulation (2000): 14,300 (8); radios (2000): 94,600 (53); televisions (2002): 63,000 (35); telephone main lines (2002): 28,600 (13); cellular telephone subscribers (2002): 96,800 (45); Internet users (2002): 21,000 (9.7).

Education and health

Educational attainment (1986–87). Percentage of population age 10 and over having: no formal education 22.9%; primary 52.8%; secondary 23.2%; higher 0.6%. **Literacy** (2000–04): total population age 15 and over literate 81.4%; males literate 73.7%; females literate 90.3%. **Health:** physicians (1995) 105 (1 per 18,527 persons); hospital beds (1992) 2,400 (1 per 765 persons); infant mortality rate per 1,000 live births (2003) 86.2. **Food** (2001): daily per capita caloric intake 2,320 (vegetable products 97%, animal products 3%); 102% of FAO recommended minimum.

Military

Total active duty personnel (2003): 2,000 (Royal Lesotho Defence Force). **Military expenditure as percentage of GNP** (1999): 2.6% (world 2.4%); per capita expenditure $14.

Background

Bantu-speaking farmers began to settle the area in the 16th century, and a number of chiefdoms arose. The most powerful organized the Basotho in 1824 and obtained British protection in 1843, as tension between the Basotho and the South African Boers increased. The area became a British territory in 1868 and was annexed to the Cape Colony in 1871. The colony's effort to disarm the Basotho resulted in revolt in 1880, and four years later it separated from the colony and became a British High Commission Territory. In 1966 it declared its independence. A new constitution (1993) ended seven years of military rule. In the late 20th century, Lesotho suffered from internal political problems and a deteriorating economy.

Recent Developments

According to UNAIDS, some 360,000 of the 2,000,-000 people in Lesotho were living with HIV, and 100,000 orphans had lost parents to HIV/AIDS. Another severe blow to the population came in early 2005 when, because of the ending of worldwide textile quotas, six foreign-owned textile factories were closed in Lesotho, resulting in the immediate loss of 6,650 jobs and the likelihood of the loss of many others. Lesotho had been one of Africa's leading textile producers.

Internet resources: <www.lesotho.gov.ls>.

1 metric ton = about 1.1 short tons;   1 kilometer = 0.6 mi (statute);   1 metric ton-km cargo = about 0.68 short ton-mi cargo;   c.i.f.: cost, insurance, and freight;   f.o.b.: free on board

Liberia

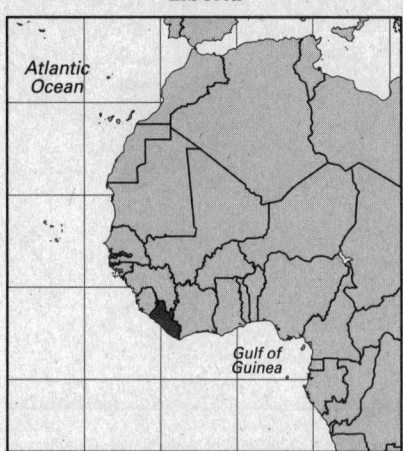

Atlantic Ocean

Gulf of Guinea

Official name: Republic of Liberia. **Form of government:** transitional government established in October 2003 was expected to be in place for two years. **Head of state and government:** Chairman of the National Transitional Government Gyude Bryant (from 2003). **Capital:** Monrovia. **Official language:** English. **Official religion:** none. **Monetary unit:** 1 Liberian dollar (L$) = 100 cents; valuation (7 Jul 2005) US$1 = L$49.00 (par value rate to US$ ineffective from January 1998; the independent free market exchange rate was roughly US$1 = L$60 in August 2001).

Demography

Area: 37,743 sq mi, 97,754 sq km. **Population** (2004): 3,391,000. **Density** (2004): persons per sq mi 89.8, persons per sq km 34.7. **Urban** (2001): 45.5%. **Sex distribution** (2002): male 49.47%; female 50.53%. **Age breakdown** (2001): under 15, 43.2%; 15–29, 27.0%; 30–44, 15.1%; 45–59, 9.4%; 60–74, 4.2%; 75 and over, 1.1%. **Ethnic composition** (2000): Kpelle 18.9%; Bassa 13.1%; Grebo 10.3%; Gio (Dan) 7.4%; Kru 6.9%; Mano 6.1%; Loma 5.3%; Kissi 3.8%; Krahn 3.7%; Americo-Liberians 2.4% (descendants of freed US slaves); other 22.1%. **Religious affiliation** (1995): traditional beliefs 63.0%; Christian 21.0%, of which Protestant 13.5%, African Christian 5.1%, Roman Catholic 2.4%; Muslim 16.0%. **Major cities** (2002): Monrovia 543,000; Zwedru 33,800; Buchanan 27,000; Yekepa 22,500; Harper 19,600. **Location:** western Africa, bordering Guinea, Côte d'Ivoire, the North Atlantic Ocean, and Sierra Leone.

Vital statistics

Birth rate per 1,000 population (2003): 45.3 (world avg. 21.3). **Death rate** per 1,000 population (2003): 17.8 (world avg. 9.1). **Natural increase rate** per 1,000 population (2003): 27.5 (world avg. 12.2). **Total fertility rate** (avg. births per childbearing woman; 2003): 6.2. **Life expectancy** at birth (2003): male 47.0 years; female 49.3 years. **Adult population** (ages 15–49) **living with HIV** (2004): 5.9% (world avg. 1.1%).

National economy

Budget (2002). *Revenue:* US$72,700,000 (tax revenue 96.7%, of which import duties 23.1%, income and profit taxes 19.8%, maritime revenue 18.4%, stamps and land rental 17.9%, petroleum sales tax 8.3%; nontax revenue 3.3%). *Expenditures:* US$80,100,000 (development expenditures [including national security] 67.5%; current expenditures 32.5%, of which wages 16.7%, interest on debt 7.9%, goods and services 7.4%). **Population economically active** (1997): total 1,183,000; activity rate 51.4% (participation rates: ages 10–64 [1994] 64.0%; female 39.5%; unemployed [1996] 95%). **Production** (metric tons except as noted). *Agriculture, forestry, fishing* (2002): cassava 445,000, natural rubber 220,000, rice 187,000; livestock (number of live animals) 220,000 goats, 210,000 sheep, 5,000,000 chickens; roundwood (2001) 5,261,930 cu m; fish catch 11,514. *Mining and quarrying* (2001): diamonds 170,000 carats; gold 1,000 kg. *Manufacturing* (2000): palm oil 42,000; cement 15,000; cigarettes 22,000,000 units (1992). International maritime licensing (fees earned; 2002): more than US$13,000,000. *Energy production (consumption):* electricity (kW-hr; 2000) 524,000,000 (524,000,000); petroleum products (2000) none (128,000). **Public debt** (external, outstanding; 2002): US$1,065,000,000. **Households.** Average household size (1983) 4.3; expenditure (1998): food 34.4%, housing 14.9%, clothing 13.8%, household furnishings 6.1%, beverages and tobacco 5.7%, energy 5.0%. **Gross national product** (2003): US$445,000,000 (US$130 per capita). **Land use** as % of total land area (2000): in temporary crops 3.9%, in permanent crops 2.2%, in pasture 20.8%; overall forest area 31.3%.

Foreign trade

Imports (2001): US$196,900,000 (food and live animals 31.1%, of which rice 14.0%; petroleum and petroleum products 20.7%; machinery and transport equipment 18.0%). *Major import sources* (1999): South Korea 27%; Japan 25%; Germany 14%; Singapore 7%; Croatia 5%. **Exports** (2001): US$127,900,000 (logs and timber 54.1%, rubber 42.2%). *Major export destinations* (2001): Norway 24%; Germany 11%; US 9%; France 8%; Singapore 7%.

Transport and communications

Transport. *Railroads* (2001): route length 490 km; (1998) metric ton-km cargo 860,000,000. *Roads* (1999): total length 10,600 km (paved 6%). *Vehicles* (1996): passenger cars 9,400; trucks and buses 25,000. *Air transport* (1992): passenger-km 7,000,000; metric ton-km cargo 1,000,000; airports (2000) with scheduled flights 2. **Communications,** in total units (units per 1,000 persons). Daily newspaper circulation (2000): 37,800 (12); radios (2000): 863,000 (274); televisions (2000): 78,700 (25); telephone main lines (1999): 6,600 (2.2).

Education and health

Literacy (2000): total population age 15 and over literate 54.0%. **Health:** physicians (1992) 257 (1 per 8,333 persons); infant mortality rate per 1,000 live births (2002) 133.8. **Food** (2001): daily per capita caloric intake 1,946 (vegetable products 97%, animal products 3%); 84% of FAO recommended minimum.

Military

Total active duty personnel: UN peacekeeping troops (September 2004) 14,700; 18,000 of 40,000 former combatants were disarmed by April 2004. **Military expenditure as percentage of GNP** (1999): 1.2% (world 2.4%); per capita expenditure US$2.

 In 1847 a committee of Liberian women had the task of choosing a flag for the new nation. Their design echoed the US flag, but with a single white star in the blue canton symbolizing Liberia's status as the only free, Westernized state in Africa. The 11 stripes represent 11 men who signed the Liberian Declaration of Independence.

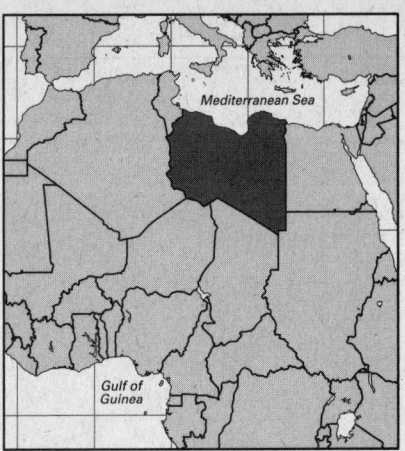

Background

Africa's oldest republic, Liberia was established as a home for freed US slaves under the American Colonization Society, which founded a colony at Cape Mesurado in 1821. In 1822 Jehudi Ashmun, a Methodist minister, became the director of the settlement and Liberia's real founder. Joseph Jenkins Roberts, Liberia's first nonwhite governor, proclaimed Liberian independence in 1847 and expanded its boundaries, which were officially established in 1892. In 1980 a coup led by Samuel K. Doe marked the end of the Americo-Liberians' long political dominance over the descendents of indigenous Africans. A rebellion in 1989 escalated into a destructive civil war in the 1990s. A peace agreement was reached in 1996, and elections were held in 1997.

Recent Developments

Most of 2004 was spent rebuilding Liberia after 14 years of civil war that had killed thousands of people, displaced 300,000, created a generation of child soldiers, destabilized Liberian society, and devastated the national economy. By April more than 18,000 former combatants had been disarmed and 10,600 weapons collected. At a Lagos, Nigeria, conference of international leaders in February, the UN, the US, and the European Union pledged $520 million over a two-year period to rebuild Liberia. The UN Security Council passed a resolution in March freezing the assets of exiled former Liberian president Charles Taylor, and in late May a UN-backed court in Sierra Leone ruled that Taylor could be tried by an international war-crimes tribunal on 17 counts of crimes against humanity for his alleged role in arming and supporting rebels in Sierra Leone.

Internet resources: <www.liberianews.com>.

Libya

Official name: Al-Jamahiriyah al-ʿArabiyah al-Libiyah al-Shaʿbiyah al-Ishtirakiyah al-ʿUzma (Socialist People's Libyan Arab Jamahiriya). **Form of government:** socialist state with one policy-making body (General People's Congress [760]). **Chief of state:** Muammar al-Qaddafi (de facto; from 1969); Secretary of General People's Congress Zentani Muhammad al-Zentani (de jure; from 1992). **Head of government:** Secretary of the General People's Committee (Prime Minister) Shokri Ghanem (from 2003). **Capital:** Tripoli. **Official language:** Arabic. **Official religion:** Islam. **Monetary unit:** 1 Libyan dinar (LD) = 1,000 dirhams; valuation (7 Jul 2005) $1 = LD 1.33.

Demography

Area: 679,362 sq mi, 1,759,540 sq km. **Population** (2004): 5,659,000. **Density** (2004): persons per sq mi 8.3, persons per sq km 3.2. **Urban** (2001): 88.0%. **Sex distribution** (2001): male 51.41%; female 48.59%. **Age breakdown** (2001): under 15, 35.4%; 15–29, 31.7%; 30–44, 19.1%; 45–59, 8.0%; 60–74, 4.5%; 75 and over, 1.3%. **Ethnic composition** (2000): Arab 87.1%, of which Libyan 57.2%, Bedouin 13.8%, Egyptian 7.7%, Sudanese 3.5%, Tunisian 2.9%; Berber 6.8%, of which Arabized 4.2%; other 6.1%. **Religious affiliation** (1995): Sunni Muslim 96.1%; other 3.9%. **Major cities** (1995): Tripoli 1,140,000 (urban agglomeration [2001] 1,776,000); Banghazi 650,000 (urban agglomeration [2000] 829,000); Misratah 280,000; Surt 150,000. **Location:** northern Africa, bordering the Mediterranean Sea, Egypt, The Sudan, Chad, Niger, Algeria, and Tunisia.

Vital statistics

Birth rate per 1,000 population (2003): 27.4 (world avg. 21.3). **Death rate** per 1,000 population (2003): 3.5 (world avg. 9.1). **Natural increase rate** per 1,000 population (2003): 23.9 (world avg. 12.2). **Total fertility rate** (avg. births per childbearing woman; 2003): 3.5. **Life expectancy** at birth (2003): male 73.9 years; female 78.3 years.

National economy

Budget (2001). *Revenue:* LD 5,998,800,000 (oil revenues 60.1%, other 39.9%). *Expenditures:* LD 5,625,600,000 (current expenditures 63.9%, development expenditures 27.3%, extraordinary expenditures 8.8%). **Public debt** (2001): $2,359,000,000.

1 metric ton = about 1.1 short tons;   1 kilometer = 0.6 mi (statute);   1 metric ton-km cargo = about 0.68 short ton-mi cargo;   c.i.f.: cost, insurance, and freight;   f.o.b.: free on board

Production (metric tons except as noted). *Agriculture, forestry, fishing* (2002): watermelons 218,000, potatoes 195,000, dry onions 182,000; livestock (number of live animals; 2001) 4,130,000 sheep, 1,265,000 goats, 25,000,000 chickens; roundwood (2001) 652,000 cu m; fish catch (2001) 33,339. *Mining and quarrying* (2001): lime 250,000; gypsum 150,000; salt 40,000. *Manufacturing* (value of production in LD '000,000; 1996): base metals 212, electrical equipment 208, petrochemicals 175. *Energy production (consumption):* electricity (kW-hr; 2001) 20,180,000,000 (18,770,000,000); coal (2000) none (5,000); crude petroleum (barrels; 2002) 482,000,000 ([2000] 157,000,000); petroleum products (2001) 15,070,700 (6,629,200); natural gas (cu m; 2001) 6,174,000,000 (4,265,-100,000). **Households.** Average household size (2000) 6.3. **Tourism** (2002): receipts $75,000,000; expenditures $548,000,000. **Population economically active** (1996): total 1,224,000; activity rate of total population 26.1% (participation rates [1993]: ages 10 and over, 35.2%; female 9.8%; unemployed [2000] 30.0%). **Gross domestic product** (2000): $38,000,000,000 ($6,200 per capita). **Land use** as % of total land area (2000): in temporary crops 1.0%, in permanent crops 0.2%, in pasture 7.6%; overall forest area 0.2%.

Foreign trade

Imports (2001): $8,700,000,000 (1997; machinery 25.9%, food products 20.0%, road vehicles 10.1%, chemical products 7.5%). *Major import sources* (2001): Italy 28.5%; Germany 12.1%; UK 6.6%; Tunisia 6.0%; France 5.9%. **Exports** (2001): $7,500,000,000 (crude petroleum 85%, refined petroleum 11%, natural gas 2%). *Major export destinations:* Italy 39.8%; Germany 15.6%; Spain 14.1%; Turkey 6.4%; France 5.5%.

Transport and communications

Transport. *Roads* (1999): total length 83,200 km (paved 57%). *Vehicles* (1996): passenger cars 809,514; trucks and buses 357,528. *Air transport* (2001): passenger-km 410,000,000; metric ton-km cargo 259,000. **Communications,** in total units (units per 1,000 persons). Daily newspaper circulation (2000): 78,600 (14); radios (2000): 1,430,000 (259); televisions (2000): 717,000 (133); telephone main lines (2003): 750,000 (136); cellular telephone subscribers (2003): 100,000 (18); personal computers (2002): 130,000 (23); Internet users (2003): 160,000 (29).

Education and health

Educational attainment (1984). Percentage of population age 25 and over having: no formal schooling (illiterate) 59.7%; incomplete primary education 15.4%; complete primary 8.5%; some secondary 5.2%; secondary 8.5%; higher 2.7%. **Literacy** (1998): percentage of total population age 15 and over literate 78.1%; males literate 89.6%; females literate 65.4%. **Health:** physicians (1997) 6,092 (1 per 781 persons); hospital beds (1998) 18,100 (1 per 312 persons; includes beds in clinics); infant mortality rate per 1,000 live births (2003) 26.8. **Food** (2001): daily per capita caloric intake 3,333 (vegetable products 89%, animal products 11%); 141% of FAO recommended minimum.

Military

Total active duty personnel (2003): 76,000 (army 59.2%, navy 10.5%, air force 30.3%). **Military expenditure as percentage of GNP** (1995): 6.1% (world 2.4%); per capita expenditure $342.

Background

Greeks and Phoenicians settled the area in the 7th century BC. It was conquered by Rome in the 1st century BC and by Arabs in the 7th century AD. In the 16th century the Ottoman Turks combined Libya's three regions under one regency in Tripoli. In 1911 Italy claimed control of Libya, and by the outbreak of World War II, 150,000 Italians had immigrated there. The scene of much fighting in the war, it became an independent state in 1951. The discovery of oil in 1959 brought wealth to Libya. A decade later a group of army officers led by Muammar al-Qaddafi deposed the king and made the country an Islamic republic. Under Qaddafi's rule it supported the Palestinian Liberation Organization and terrorist groups, bringing protests from many countries, particularly the US. Intermittent warfare with Chad during the 1970s and '80s ended with Chad's defeat of Libya in 1987. International relations in the 1990s were dominated by the consequences of the 1988 bombing of a US airliner over Lockerbie, Scotland; the US accused Libyan nationalists of the deed and imposed a trade embargo on Libya, endorsed by the UN in 1992.

Recent Developments

In 2004 Libyan leader Muammar al-Qaddafi realized the rapprochement with the United States and its European allies that he had been signaling for more than a decade. Libya's penalty payments included $2.7 billion compensation for the 270 victims of the December 1988 Pan Am disaster over Lockerbie, Scotland, $170 million for the 170 victims of the 1989 UTA flight, and $35 million for more than 160 non-American victims of the 1986 Berlin disco bombing. Following the lifting of sanctions by the UN Security Council in 2003, EU countries had intensified their trading activities in Libya, a process that significantly accelerated in 2004. In September 2004 Pres. George W. Bush lifted the ban on US commercial air services to Libya and released $1.3 billion of frozen assets in recognition of Libya's significant steps in eliminating its weapons programs. Other gestures from Libya, such as its promise in December 2003 to eliminate all weapons of mass destruction, were welcomed by the international community. The initiative prompted a visit to Tripoli by British Prime Minister Tony Blair in the spring of 2004. With world oil prices above $50 a barrel, both the Libyan leadership and the people felt very confident about their immediate economic future.

Internet resources: <www.arab.net/libya>.

Liechtenstein

Official name: Fürstentum Liechtenstein (Principality of Liechtenstein). **Form of government:** constitutional monarchy with one legislative house (Diet [25]). **Chief of state:** Prince Hans Adam II (from 1989); Regent, Prince Alois (from 15 Aug 2004). **Head of government:** Prime Minister Otmar Hasler (from 2001). **Capital:**

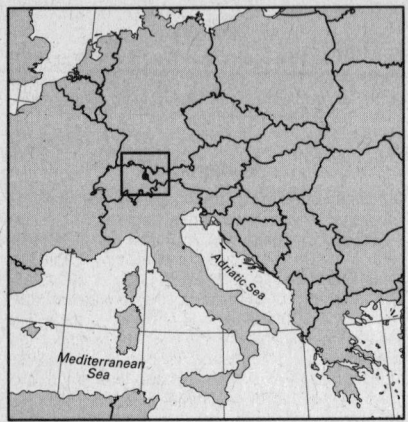

Vaduz. **Official language:** German. **Official religion:** none. **Monetary unit:** 1 Swiss franc (Sw F) = 100 centimes; valuation (7 Jul 2005) $1 = Sw F 1.30.

Demography

Area: 61.8 sq mi, 160.0 sq km. **Population** (2004): 34,500. **Density** (2003): persons per sq mi 556.5, persons per sq km 215.6. **Urban** (2003): 21.6%. **Sex distribution** (2003): male 49.11%; female 50.89%. **Age breakdown** (2003): under 15, 17.0%; 15–29, 20.2%; 30–44, 25.9%; 45–59, 21.2%; 60–74, 10.8%; 75 and over, 4.9%. **Ethnic composition** (2002): Liechtensteiner 65.8%; Swiss 10.9%; Austrian 5.9%; German 3.4%; Italian 3.3%; other 10.7%. **Religious affiliation** (1998): Roman Catholic 80.0%; Protestant 7.5%; Muslim 3.3%; Eastern Orthodox 0.7%; atheist 0.6%; other 7.9%. **Major cities** (2002): Schaan 5,556; Vaduz 4,949. **Location:** central Europe, between Austria and Switzerland.

Vital statistics

Birth rate per 1,000 population (2003): 10.9 (world avg. 21.3); (1997) legitimate 86.0%. **Death rate** per 1,000 population (2003): 6.8 (world avg. 9.1). **Natural increase rate** per 1,000 population (2003): 4.1 (world avg. 12.2). **Total fertility rate** (avg. births per childbearing woman; 2002): 1.5. **Marriage rate** per 1,000 population (2001): 11.5. **Divorce rate** per 1,000 population (1994): 1.4. **Life expectancy** at birth (2003): male 75.6 years; female 82.9 years.

National economy

Budget (2001). *Revenue:* Sw F 804,100,000 (taxes and duties 85.8%, investment income 5.5%, charges and fees 5.0%, real estate capital-gains taxes and death and estate taxes 3.7%). *Expenditures:* Sw F 751,400,000 (financial affairs 34.8%, social welfare 19.5%, education 14.1%, general administration 10.2%, public safety 5.5%, transportation 4.8%). **Tourism** (2001): 123,273 tourist overnight stays. **Population economically active** (2002): total 17,011; activity rate of total population 50.7% (participation rates: ages 15–64, 71.4%;

female 40.4%; unemployed 2.1%). **Households.** Average household size (1990) 2.7. **Production** (metric tons except as noted). *Agriculture and forestry* (2002): significantly market gardening, other crops include cereals and apples; livestock (number of live animals) 6,000 cattle, 3,000 pigs, 2,900 sheep; commercial timber (1999) 22,000 cu m. *Manufacturing* (2000): small-scale precision manufacturing includes optical lenses, electron microscopes, electronic equipment, and high-vacuum pumps; metal manufacturing, construction machinery, and ceramics are important; dairy products and wine are also produced. *Energy production (consumption):* electricity (kW-hr; 2001) 93,282,000 (313,450,000); coal (2000) none (24); petroleum products (2000) none (47,100). **Gross national product** (1999): $2,664,000,000 ($63,550 per capita). **Land use** as % of total land area (2000): in temporary crops 25%, in permanent crops 1%, in pasture 31%; overall forest area 47%.

Foreign trade

Data exclude trade with Switzerland and transshipments through Switzerland. Liechtenstein has formed a customs union with Switzerland since 1923. **Imports** (2000): Sw F 1,456,000,000 (machinery and apparatus 30.4%, glass [all forms] and ceramics 11.0%, fabricated metals 10.0%, iron and steel 5.7%, transport equipment 5.7%). *Major import sources:* Germany 34.6%; Austria 31.8%; Italy 7.9%; US 6.1%; France 3.5%. **Exports** (2000): Sw F 3,032,000,000 (machinery and apparatus [mostly electronic products and precision tools] 35.1%, fabricated metals 15.2%, glass and ceramic products [including lead crystal and specialized dental products] 9.9%, food products 5.3%). *Major export destinations:* Germany 25.8%; US 20.0%; Austria 8.4%; France 7.8%; Italy 6.5%.

Transport and communications

Transport. *Railroads* (1998): length 18.5 km. *Roads* (1999): total length 323 km. *Vehicles* (2002): passenger cars 23,265; trucks and buses 2,824. *Air transport:* the nearest scheduled airport service is through Zürich, Switzerland. **Communications,** in total units (units per 1,000 persons). Daily newspaper circulation (1998): 17,900 (565); radios (1997): 21,000 (658); televisions (1997): 12,000 (364); telephone main lines (2002): 19,900 (583); cellular telephone subscribers (2002): 11,400 (333); Internet users (2002): 20,000 (585).

Education and health

Educational attainment (1990). Percentage of population not of preschool age or in compulsory education having: no formal schooling 0.3%; primary and lower secondary education 39.3%; higher secondary and vocational 47.6%; some postsecondary 7.4%; university 4.2%; other and unknown 1.1%. **Literacy:** virtually 100%. **Health:** physicians (2000) 46 (1 per 714 persons); hospital beds (1997) 108 (1 per 288 persons); infant mortality rate per 1,000 live births (2003) 4.9. **Food** (1999; figures are derived from statistics for Switzerland and Austria): daily per capita caloric intake 3,600 (vegetable products 65%, animal products 35%); 134% of FAO recommended minimum.

---

1 metric ton = about 1.1 short tons;   1 kilometer = 0.6 mi (statute);   1 metric ton-km cargo = about 0.68 short ton-mi cargo;   c.i.f.: cost, insurance, and freight;   f.o.b.: free on board

Military

Total active duty personnel: Liechtenstein has had no standing army since 1868.

Background

The Rhine plain was occupied for centuries by two independent lordships of the Holy Roman Empire, Vaduz and Schellenberg. The principality of Liechtenstein, consisting of these two lordships, was founded in 1719 and remained part of the Holy Roman Empire. It was included in the German Confederation (1815–66). In 1866 it became independent, recognizing Vaduz and Schellenberg as unique regions forming separate electoral districts. An almost 60-year ruling coalition dissolved in 1997, and the prince urged adoption of constitutional reforms.

Recent Developments

On 15 Aug 2004 Prince Hans Adam II, age 59, formally transferred day-to-day governing power in Liechtenstein to his 36-year-old son, Crown Prince Alois. Hans Adam retained overall authority over the country, which his family had ruled for almost 300 years. An international report released in April 2005 alleged that the Liechtenstein royal family was not entirely innocent of war-crimes abuses during World War II.

Internet resources: <www.tourismus.li>.

Lithuania

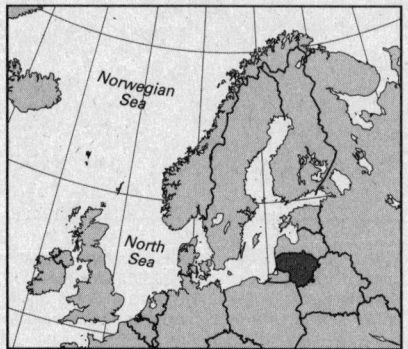

Official name: Lietuvos Respublika (Republic of Lithuania). **Form of government:** unitary multiparty republic with a single legislative body, the Seimas (141). **Head of state:** President Valdas Adamkus (from 12 Jul 2004). **Head of government:** Prime Minister Algirdas Brazauskas (from 2001). **Capital:** Vilnius. **Official language:** Lithuanian. **Official religion:** none. **Monetary unit:** 1 litas (LTL) = 100 centai; valuation (7 Jul 2005) $1 = LTL 2.89.

Demography

Area: 25,212 sq mi, 65,300 sq km. **Population** (2004): 3,439,000. **Density** (2004): persons per sq mi 136.4, persons per sq km 52.7. **Urban** (2003): 66.8%. **Sex distribution** (2003): male 46.70%; female 53.30%. **Age breakdown** (2004): under 15, 17.7%; 15–29, 21.9%; 30–44, 22.4%; 45–59, 17.8%; 60–74, 14.2%; 75 and over, 6.0%. **Ethnic composition** (2001): Lithuanian 83.5%; Polish 6.7%; Russian 6.3%; Belarusian 1.2%; Ukrainian 0.7%; other 1.6%. **Religious affiliation** (2001): Roman Catholic 79.0%; nonreligious 9.5%; Orthodox 4.8%, of which Old Believers 0.8%; Protestant 1.0%; unknown 5.4%; other 0.3%. **Major cities** (2004): Vilnius 553,038; Kaunas 368,917; Klaipeda 190,098; Siauliai 131,184; Panevezys 117,606. **Location:** eastern Europe, bordering Latvia, Belarus, Poland, Russia, and the Baltic Sea.

Vital statistics

Birth rate per 1,000 population (2003): 8.9 (world avg. 21.3); (2001) legitimate 74.6%. **Death rate** per 1,000 population (2003): 11.9 (world avg. 9.1). **Natural increase rate** per 1,000 population (2003): −3.0 (world avg. 12.2). **Total fertility rate** (avg. births per childbearing woman; 2003): 1.3. **Marriage rate** per 1,000 population (2003): 4.9. **Divorce rate** per 1,000 population (2003): 3.1. **Life expectancy** at birth (2003): male 66.5 years; female 77.9 years.

National economy

Budget (2002). *Revenue:* LTL 15,112,000,000 (tax revenue 92.5%, of which value-added tax 25.2%, individual income tax 23.6%, social security tax 22.7%, excise tax 10.6%; nontax revenue 7.5%). *Expenditures:* LTL 15,907,000,000 (current expenditure 90.0%, of which social security and welfare 28.0%, wages 23.2%; capital expenditure 10.0%). **Gross national product** (2003): $15,509,000,000 ($4,490 per capita). **Production** (metric tons except as noted). *Agriculture, forestry, fishing* (2002): hay 2,500,000, potatoes 1,531,300, wheat 1,165,100; livestock (number of live animals) 1,010,800 pigs, 751,500 cattle; roundwood (2001) 5,700,000 cu m; fish catch (2001) 153,932. *Mining and quarrying* (2002): limestone 857,500; peat 262,700. *Manufacturing* (value of production in LTL '000,000; 2000): food and beverages 4,952; refined petroleum products 4,303; wearing apparel 2,034. *Energy production (consumption):* electricity (kW-hr; 2000) 11,424,000,000 (10,088,000,000); coal (2000) none (131,000); crude petroleum (barrels; 2000) 2,316,000 (34,766,000); petroleum products (2002) 6,543,500 (2,756,000); natural gas (cu m; 2000) none (2,462,000,000). **Public debt** (external, outstanding; 2002): $2,486,000,000. **Population economically active** (2001): total 1,745,300; activity rate of total population 50.2% (participation rates: ages 15–64, 69.3%; female 49.8%; registered unemployed 12.7%). **Household income and expenditure.** Average household size (2000) 2.7; average annual household disposable income (1997): LTL 12,914; sources of income (2001): wages and salaries 53.6%, transfers 24.2%, self-employment 11.3%; expenditure (2001): food and beverages 42.4%, housing and energy 13.6%, transportation and communications 11.8%, clothing and footwear 6.5%. **Land use** as % of total land area (2000): in temporary crops 45.3%, in permanent crops 0.9%, in pasture 7.7%; overall forest area 31.9%. **Tourism** (2001): receipts from visitors $513,000,000; expenditures by nationals abroad $341,000,000.

Foreign trade

Imports (2002-c.i.f.): LTL 28,220,000,000 (mineral fuels [mostly crude petroleum] 17.8%, machinery and apparatus 17.5%, transport equipment 16.4%, chemicals and chemical products 8.7%, textiles and clothing 7.9%). *Major import sources:* Russia 21.4%; Germany 17.2%; Italy 4.9%; Poland 4.8%; France 3.9%. **Exports** (2002-f.o.b.): LTL 20,280,000,000 (mineral fuels [mostly refined petroleum] 19.0%, transport equipment [mostly auto components] 15.9%, textiles and clothing 15.0%, agricultural and food products 10.8%, machinery and apparatus 9.9%). *Major export destinations:* UK 13.5%; Russia 12.1%; Germany 10.3%; Latvia 9.6%; Denmark 5.0%.

Transport and communications

Transport. *Railroads* (2001): route length 1,696 km; passenger-km 533,000,000; metric ton-km cargo 7,741,000,000. *Roads* (2002): total length 76,573 km (paved 91%). *Vehicles* (2002): passenger cars 1,133,477; trucks and buses 104,544. *Air transport* (2001): passenger-km 484,000,000; metric ton-km cargo 3,000,000; airports with scheduled flights (2001) 3. **Communications,** in total units (units per 1,000 persons). Daily newspaper circulation (1996): 344,000 (93); radios (2000): 1,750,000 (500); televisions (2002): 1,704,500 (487); telephone main lines (2003): 824,200 (253); cellular telephone subscribers (2003): 2,169,900 (666); personal computers (2003): 380,000 (110); Internet users (2003): 695,700 (213).

Education and health

Educational attainment (2001). Percentage of population age 10 and over having: no schooling and incomplete primary education 5.1%; complete primary 20.8%; incomplete and complete secondary 42.2%; postsecondary 31.9%, of which university 12.6%. **Literacy** (2000): total population age 15 and over literate 99.6%. **Health** (2004): physicians 13,682 (1 per 252 persons); hospital beds 29,990 (1 per 115 persons); infant mortality rate per 1,000 live births (2003) 6.7. **Food** (2001): daily per capita caloric intake 3,384 (vegetable products 76%, animal products 24%); 132% of FAO recommended minimum.

Military

Total active duty personnel (2003): 12,700 (excludes 13,850 in paramilitary; army 62.6%, navy 5.1%, air force 9.1%, volunteer national defense force 13.5%, centrally controlled staff 9.7%). **Military expenditure as percentage of GNP** (1999): 1.3% (world 2.4%); per capita expenditure $87.

Background

Lithuanian tribes united in the mid-13th century to oppose the Teutonic knights. Gediminas, one of the grand dukes, expanded Lithuania into an empire that dominated much of Eastern Europe in the 14th through 16th centuries. In 1386 the Lithuanian grand duke became the king of Poland, and the two countries remained closely associated until Lithuania was acquired by Russia in the Third Partition of Poland in 1795. Occupied by Germany during World War I, it declared its independence in 1918. In 1940 the Red Army gained control of Lithuania. Germany occupied it again in 1941–44, but the USSR regained control in

1944. With the breakup of the USSR, Lithuania became independent in 1991. During the 1990s it sought economic stability and hoped to join the European Union and NATO. It signed a border treaty with Russia in 1997.

Recent Developments

Rolandas Paksas, who had been unexpectedly elected Lithuania's president in January 2003, was impeached 13 months later for breaches of the constitution and was forced out of office in April 2004, just weeks before the country was to join the European Union. Of the states that joined the EU on 1 May 2004, Lithuania was perhaps the most eager and surely the best prepared. Lithuania became a member of NATO on 2 Apr 2004 and proudly hosted a NATO foreign ministers' meeting—the first such gathering in a former Soviet bloc country—in April 2005.

Internet resources: <www.tourism.lt>.

Luxembourg

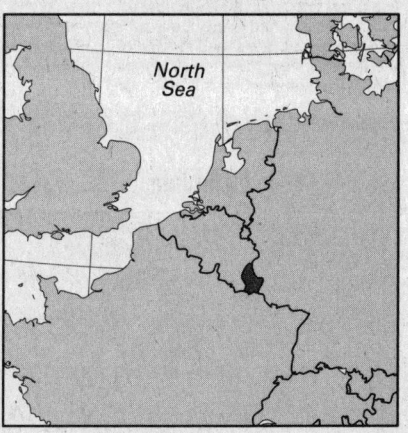

North Sea

Official name: Groussherzogtum Lëtzebuerg (Luxemburgian); Grand-Duché de Luxembourg (French); Grossherzogtum Luxemburg (German) (Grand Duchy of Luxembourg). **Form of government:** constitutional monarchy with two legislative houses (Council of State [21]; Chamber of Deputies [60]). **Chief of state:** Grand Duke Henri (from 2000). **Head of government:** Prime Minister Jean-Claude Juncker (from 1995). **Capital:** Luxembourg. **Official language:** none; Luxemburgian (national); French (used for most official purposes); German (lingua franca). **Official religion:** none. **Monetary unit:** 1 euro (€) = 100 cents; valuation (7 Jul 2005) $1 = €0.84; at conversion on 1 Jan 2002, €1= 40.3 Luxembourg franc (Lux F).

Demography

Area: 999 sq mi, 2,586 sq km. **Population** (2004): 454,000. **Density** (2004): persons per sq mi 454.5, persons per sq km 175.6. **Urban** (2003): 91.9%. **Sex distribution** (2003): male 49.30%; female 50.70%.

1 metric ton = about 1.1 short tons;   1 kilometer = 0.6 mi (statute);   1 metric ton-km cargo = about 0.68 short ton-mi cargo;   c.i.f.: cost, insurance, and freight;   f.o.b.: free on board

Age breakdown (2003): under 15, 18.9%; 15–29, 18.6%; 30–44, 25.5%; 45–59, 18.4%; 60–74, 12.9%; 75 and over, 5.7%. **Ethnic composition** (nationality; 2003): Luxemburger 61.9%; Portuguese 13.5%; French 4.8%; Italian 4.2%; Belgian 3.5%; German 2.3%; English 1.0%; other 8.8%. **Religious affiliation** (2000): Roman Catholic 90.6%; Protestant 2.1%; other Christian 1.1%; Muslim 1.0%; nonreligious 3.7%; other 1.5%. **Major cities** (2001; pops. of localities): Luxembourg 76,688; Esch-sur-Alzette 27,146; Dudelange 17,320; Schifflange 7,849; Bettembourg 7,157. **Location:** western Europe, bordering Belgium, Germany, and France.

Vital statistics

Birth rate per 1,000 population (2003): 11.8 (world avg. 21.3); (2002) legitimate 76.8%. **Death rate** per 1,000 population (2003): 9.0 (world avg. 9.1). **Natural increase rate** per 1,000 population (2003): 2.8 (world avg. 12.2). **Total fertility rate** (avg. births per childbearing woman; 2003): 1.6. **Marriage rate** per 1,000 population (2003): 4.5. **Divorce rate** per 1,000 population (2003): 2.3. **Life expectancy** at birth (2000–02): male 74.9 years; female 81.0 years.

National economy

Budget (2002). *Revenue:* €5,977,200,000 (direct taxes 47.4%, indirect taxes 38.5%, other 14.1%). *Expenditures:* €5,976,100,000 (current expenditure 85.7%, development expenditure 14.3%). **Public debt** (2001): $1,080,000,000. **Production** (metric tons except as noted). *Agriculture and forestry* (2002): corn (maize) 139,000, wheat 67,126, barley 65,000; livestock (number of live animals; 2000) 205,000 cattle, 80,141 pigs; roundwood (2001) 142,000 cu m. *Mining and quarrying* (2002): limited quantities of limestone and slate. *Manufacturing* (2002): rolled steel 4,467,000; crude steel 2,736,000; cement 800,000. *Energy production (consumption):* electricity (kW-hr; 2000) 1,228,000,000 (6,950,000,000); coal (2000) none (171,000); petroleum products (2000) none (1,906,000); natural gas (cu m; 2000) none (782,000,000). **Household income and expenditure.** Average household size (2000) 2.5; income per household (2002) €61,800; sources of income (1992): wages and salaries 67.1%, transfer payments 28.1%, self-employment 4.8%; expenditure (2002): food, beverages, and tobacco 21.0%, housing 20.7%, transportation and communications 19.3%, entertainment and education 8.6%, household goods and furniture 8.3%, clothing and footwear 5.3%. **Gross national product** (2003): $15,509,000,000 ($43,940 per capita). **Population economically active** (2002): total 285,700; activity rate of total population 63.9% (participation rates: ages 15–64 [2001] 64.4%; female [2001] 40.2%; unemployed [2002] 3.0%). **Tourism** (2002): receipts from visitors $2,186,000,000; expenditures $1,896,000,000. **Land use** as % of total land area (2000): in temporary crops 23.6%, in permanent crops 0.5%, in pasture 25.2%; overall forest area 34.3%.

Foreign trade

Imports (2001-c.i.f.): €12,335,000,000 (machinery and apparatus 21.5%, transport equipment 15.2%, base and fabricated metals 11.3%, chemicals and chemical products 10.1%). *Major import sources:* Belgium 34.3%; Germany 25.1%; France 12.8%; The

Netherlands 5.8%; US 5.1%. **Exports** (2001-f.o.b.): €9,082,000,000 (base and fabricated metals [mostly iron and steel] 28.1%, machinery and apparatus 24.0%, chemicals and chemical products 6.3%, transport equipment 4.3%, food products 4.2%). *Major export destinations:* Germany 24.6%; France 19.6%; Belgium 12.3%; UK 8.2%; Italy 6.2%.

Transport and communications

Transport. *Railroads* (2002): route length 274 km; passenger-km 268,000,000; metric ton-km cargo 613,000,000. *Roads* (1999): total length 5,166 km (paved 100%). *Vehicles* (2003): passenger cars 287,245; trucks and buses 22,691. *Air transport* (2002): passengers carried 1,517,000; cargo 578,944 metric tons; airports with scheduled flights 1. **Communications**, in total units (units per 1,000 persons). Daily newspaper circulation (1996): 135,000 (325); radios (2000): 300,000 (685); televisions (2000): 170,000 (391); telephone main lines (2002): 355,400 (797); cellular telephone subscribers (2002): 473,000 (1,061); personal computers (2002): 265,000 (594); Internet users (2002): 165,000 (370).

Education and health

Literacy (2001): virtually 100% literate. **Health** (2002): physicians 1,137 (1 per 393 persons); hospital beds 3,035 (1 per 147 persons); infant mortality rate per 1,000 live births (2003) 5.0. **Food** (1995): daily per capita caloric intake 3,530 (vegetable products 68%, animal products 32%); 134% of FAO recommended minimum.

Military

Total active duty personnel (2003): 900 (army 100%). **Military expenditure as percentage of GNP** (1999): 0.8% (world 2.4%); per capita expenditure $326.

Background

At the time of Roman conquest (57–50 BC), Luxembourg was inhabited by a Belgic tribe. After AD 400, Germanic tribes invaded the region. Made a duchy in 1354, it was ceded to the house of Burgundy in 1443 and to the Habsburgs in 1477. In the mid-16th century it became part of the Spanish Netherlands. It was made a grand duchy in 1815. After an uprising in 1830, its western portion became part of Belgium, while the remainder was held by The Netherlands. In 1867 the European powers guaranteed the neutrality and independence of Luxembourg. In the late 19th century it exploited its extensive iron-ore deposits. It was invaded and occupied by Germany in both world wars. It abandoned its neutrality by joining NATO in 1949; it had joined the Benelux Economic Union in 1944. A member of the European Union, its economy has continued to expand. On 7 Oct 2000, Grand Duke Jean abdicated power in favor of his son, Crown Prince Henri, after 36 years on the throne.

Recent Developments

On 1 Jan 2005 Luxembourg's Prime Minister Jean-Claude Juncker, dubbed "Mr. Euro," took his seat as the first permanent president of the 12 euro-zone countries. This renewable two-year appointment replaced the previous system, in which the chair of the euro group changed every six months along with the EU's rotating presidency.

Internet resources: <www.ont.lu>.

Macau

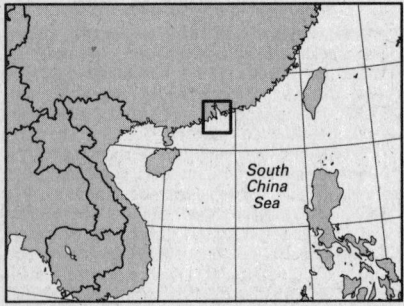

South China Sea

Official name: Aomen Tebie Xingzhengqu (Chinese); Região Administrativa Especial de Macau (Portuguese) (Macau Special Administrative Region). Political status: special administrative region (China) with one legislative house (Legislative Council [27, including 10 directly elected seats, 7 seats appointed by the chief executive, and 10 seats appointed by special-interest groups]). Chief of state: President Hu Jintao of China (from 2003). Head of government: Chief Executive Edmund Ho Hau-wah (from 1999). Capital: Macau. Official languages: Chinese; Portuguese. Official religion: none. Monetary unit: 1 pataca (MOP) = 100 avos; valuation (7 Jul 2005) $1 = MOP 8.01.

Demography

Area: 10.5 sq mi, 27.3 sq km. Population (2004): 451,000. Density (2004): persons per sq mi 42,952, persons per sq km 16,520. Urban (2004): virtually 100% (about 0.5% of Macau's population live on sampans and other vessels). Sex distribution (2003): male 48.07%; female 51.93%. Age breakdown (2003): under 15, 18.7%; 15–29, 22.8%; 30–44, 27.3%; 45–59, 21.0%; 60–74, 6.7%; 75 and over, 3.5%. Nationality (2001; resident pop.): Chinese 95.2%; Portuguese 2.0%; Filipino 1.2%; other 1.6%. Religious affiliation (1998): nonreligious 60.8%; Buddhist 16.7%; other 22.5%. Major city (2000 est.): Macau 437,900. Location: eastern Asia, bordering China and the South China Sea.

Vital statistics

Birth rate per 1,000 population (2003): 7.2 (world avg. 21.3). Death rate per 1,000 population (2003): 3.3 (world avg. 9.1). Natural increase rate per 1,000 population (2003): 3.9 (world avg. 12.2). Total fertility rate (avg. births per childbearing woman; 2002): 1.1. Marriage rate per 1,000 population (2003): 2.9. Divorce rate per 1,000 population (2003): 1.0. Life expectancy at birth (2002): male 77.0 years; female 82.0 years.

National economy

Budget (1998). Revenue: MOP 14,831,099,000 (recurrent receipts 69.1%, autonomous agency receipts 21.4%, capital receipts 2.2%). Expenditures: MOP 14,831,099,000 (recurrent payments 61.1%, autonomous agency expenditures 21.4%, capital payments 17.5%). Production (metric tons except as noted). Agriculture and fishing (1999): eggs 650; livestock (number of live animals) 500,000 chickens; fish catch (2000) 1,500. Quarrying (value added in MOP '000,000; 1997): 13. Manufacturing (value added in MOP '000,000; 2001): wearing apparel 2,090; textiles 522; printing and publishing 95. Energy production (consumption): electricity (kW-hr; 2000) 1,571,000,000 (1,766,000,000); petroleum products (2000) none (500,000). Public debt (long-term, external; 1999): $706,000,000. Population economically active (2001): total 231,266; activity rate of total population 53.1% (participation rates: over age 14, 66.1%; female 46.5%; unemployed 7.0%). Household income and expenditure. Average household size (2001) 3.1; annual income per household MOP 181,884; expenditure (1987–88): food 38.3%, housing 19.7%, education, health, and other services 12.1%, transportation 7.4%, clothing and footwear 6.8%, energy 4.0%, household durable goods 3.7%, other goods 8.0%. Gross domestic product (at current market prices; 2002): $6,731,-246,000 ($15,320 per capita). Tourism: receipts from visitors (2002) $4,415,000,000; expenditures by nationals abroad (1999) $131,000,000. Land use as % of total land area (2000): "green area" 22.4%.

Foreign trade

Imports (2002): MOP 20,323,000,000 (textile materials 32.3%; capital goods 13.8%; clothing and footwear 13.3%; food, beverages, and tobacco 11.4%). Major import sources: China 41.7%; Hong Kong 14.5%; Taiwan 6.7%; Japan 6.7%; France 4.3%. Exports (2002): MOP 18,925,000,000 (domestic exports 78.1%, of which machine-knitted clothing 42.1%, machine-woven clothing 27.4%, footwear 3.6%; reexports 21.9%). Major export destinations: US 48.4%; China 15.6%; Germany 7.5%; Hong Kong 5.8%; UK 5.4%.

Transport and communications

Transport. Roads (2003): total length 345 km (paved 100%). Vehicles (1999): passenger cars 47,776; trucks and buses 5,812. Air transport (2001; Air Macau only): passenger-km 1,907,988,000; metric ton-km cargo 22,616,000. Communications, in total units (units per 1,000 persons). Daily newspaper circulation (2000): 210,100 (488); radios (2000): 215,300 (500); televisions (2000): 123,100 (286); telephone main lines (2003): 174,600 (391); cellular telephone subscribers (2003): 364,000 (815); personal computers (2002): 92,000 (208); Internet users (2003): 120,000 (269).

Education and health

Educational attainment (2001). Population age 25 and over having: no formal schooling 7.6%; incomplete primary education 13.6%; completed primary

1 metric ton = about 1.1 short tons;　1 kilometer = 0.6 mi (statute);　1 metric ton-km cargo = about 0.68 short ton-mi cargo;　c.i.f.: cost, insurance, and freight;　f.o.b.: free on board

26.6%; some secondary 23.9%; completed secondary and post-secondary 28.3%. **Literacy** (2001): percentage of population age 15 and over literate 91.3%; males literate 95.3%; females literate 87.8%. **Health** (2002): physicians 915 (1 per 480 persons); hospital beds 990 (1 per 444 persons); infant mortality rate per 1,000 live births (2003) 0.6. **Food** (1998): daily per capita caloric intake 2,471 (vegetable products 76%, animal products 24%); 108% of FAO recommended minimum.

Military

Total active duty personnel: Chinese troops (2001) 500.

Did you know? Macau's flag features a white lotus flower, its 3 petals symbolizing Macau's 3 areas; 5 yellow stars refer to Chinese rule. The water and bridge below the lotus and the green field suggest the region's geography and fertile land.

Background

Portuguese traders first arrived in Macau in 1513, and it soon became the chief market center for the trade between China and Japan. It was declared a Portuguese colony in 1849 and an overseas territory in 1951. In December 1999 Portugal returned Macau to Chinese rule.

Recent Developments

Vigorous new development in the gaming industry boosted revenue and employment in Macao. Beijing expected some $1.1 billion in tax revenues from the industry in 2004. Plans were under way to bring flashy Las Vegas glamour to the industry and attract the potentially huge number of gamblers in China proper.

Internet resources: <www.macautourism.gov.mo>.

Macedonia

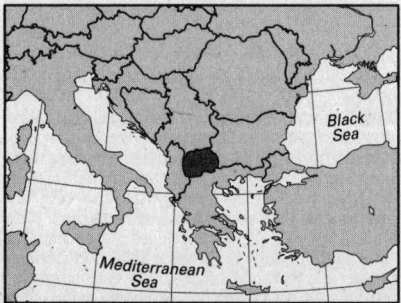

Official name: Republika Makedonija (Macedonian); Republika e Maqedonisë (Albanian) (Republic of Macedonia [member of the UN under the name The Former Yugoslav Republic of Macedonia]). **Form of government:** unitary multiparty republic with a unicameral legislative (Assembly [120]). **Head of state:**

President Branko Crvenkovski (from 12 May 2004). **Head of government:** Prime Minister Vlado Buckovski (from 17 Dec 2004). **Capital:** Skopje. **Official languages:** Macedonian; Albanian. **Official religion:** none. **Monetary unit:** denar; valuation (7 Jul 2005) $1 = 47.85 denar.

Demography

Area: 9,928 sq mi, 25,713 sq km (including inland water area). **Population** (2004): 2,035,000. **Density** (2004): persons per sq mi 205.0, persons per sq km 79.1. **Urban** (2003): 59.5%. **Sex distribution** (2002): male 50.20%; female 49.80%. **Age breakdown** (2002): under 15, 21.1%; 15–29, 23.8%; 30–44, 22.0%; 45–59, 18.1%; 60–64, 11.2%; 65 and over, 3.3%. **Ethnic composition** (2002): Macedonian 64.2%; Albanian 25.2%; Turkish 3.9%; Rom (Gypsy) 2.7%; Serbian 1.8%; Bosniac 0.8%; other 1.5%. **Religious affiliation** (2000): Orthodox 59.3%; Sunni Muslim 28.3%; Roman Catholic 3.5%; nonreligious 6.6%; other 2.3%. **Major cities** (1994): Skopje 440,577; Bitola 75,386; Prilep 67,371; Kumanovo 66,237; Tetovo 50,376. **Location:** southeastern Europe, bordering Serbia and Montenegro, Bulgaria, Greece, and Albania.

Vital statistics

Birth rate per 1,000 population (2003): 11.9 (world avg. 21.3); legitimate (2000) 90.2%. **Death rate** per 1,000 population (2003): 8.8 (world avg. 9.1). **Natural increase rate** per 1,000 population (2003): 3.1 (world avg. 12.2). **Total fertility rate** (avg. births per childbearing woman; 2003): 1.6. **Marriage rate** per 1,000 population (2000): 7.0. **Life expectancy** at birth (2003): male 70.8 years; female 75.8 years.

National economy

Budget (2002). *Revenue:* 53,089,000,000 denar (tax revenue 94.2%, of which value-added tax 33.7%, excise taxes 20.6%, income and profit tax 19.6%, import duties 10.0%; nontax revenue 5.8%). *Expenditure:* 59,979,000,000 denar (wages and salaries 29.5%, pensions 26.1%, goods and services 20.0%, interest 6.1%). **External debt** (2002): $1,262,000,-000. **Production** (metric tons except as noted). *Agriculture, forestry, fishing* (2002): wheat 267,100, potatoes 183,000, corn (maize) 140,200; livestock (number of live animals) 1,233,800 sheep, 259,000 cattle; roundwood (2001) 740,000 cu m; fish catch (2001) 1,181. *Mining and quarrying* (2001; contained metal of ore): lead 11,000; copper 7,000; silver 15,000 kg. *Manufacturing* (1998): cement 461,195; steel sheets 276,464; detergents 21,990. *Energy production (consumption):* electricity (kW-hr; 2000) 6,811,000,000 (6,923,000,000); hard coal (2000) none (155,000); lignite (2000) 7,516,000 (7,702,000); crude petroleum (barrels; 2000) none (5,886,000); petroleum products (2000) 775,000 (838,000); natural gas (cu m; 2000) none (64,503,000). **Household income and expenditure.** Average household size (2002) 3.6; income per household (2000) $3,798; sources of income (2000): wages and salaries 54.2%, transfer payments 22.6%, savings 3.2%, other 20.0%; expenditure: food 38.4%, transportation and communications 9.7%, fuel and lighting 8.2%, beverages and tobacco 7.6%. **Gross national product** (at current market prices; 2003): $4,058,000,000 ($1,980 per capita). **Population economically active** (2000): total 811,000; activity rate 39.9% (participation rates: ages 15–64, 52.9%; female 38.5%; unemployed [2002] 31.9%). **Land use** as % of total land area (2000): in temporary crops 21.8%, in permanent crops 1.7%, in pasture 25.0%; overall forest area 35.6%. **Tourism** (2002): receipts from visitors $39,000,000; expenditures by nationals abroad $45,000,000.

Foreign trade

Imports (2001-c.i.f.): $1,688,000,000 (mineral fuels 13.9%, machinery and apparatus 13.0%, food and live animals 11.5%, chemicals and chemical products 10.2%). *Major import sources* (2002): Germany 14.3%; Greece 12.1%; Yugoslavia 9.4%; Slovenia 6.6%; Bulgaria 6.5%; Italy 6.0%. **Exports** (2001-f.o.b.): $1,155,000,000 (clothing 27.7%, iron and steel 16.9%, tobacco [all forms] 6.5%, nonferrous base metals 6.4%, beverages 4.0%). *Major export destinations* (2002): Yugoslavia 22.1%; Germany 21.0%; Greece 10.4%; Italy 7.1%; US 7.0%.

Transport and communications

Transport. *Railroads* (2002): route length 699 km; passenger-km 98,000,000; metric ton-km cargo 334,000,000. *Roads* (2000): length 12,522 km (paved 58%). *Vehicles* (2002): passenger cars 307,600; trucks and buses 33,000. *Air transport* (2003; Macedonian Airline): passenger-km 294,000,-000; metric ton-km cargo 141,000; airports (2002) with scheduled flights 2. **Communications,** in total units (units per 1,000 persons). Daily newspaper circulation (2000): 89,400 (44); radios (2000): 415,000 (205); televisions (2000): 571,000 (282); telephone main lines (2002): 560,000 (271); cellular telephone subscribers (2002): 365,300 (177); Internet users (2002): 100,000 (48).

Education and health

Educational attainment (1994). Percentage of population age 15 and over having: less than full primary education 25.0%; primary 33.4%; secondary 32.3%; postsecondary and higher 8.7%; unknown 0.6%. **Literacy** (1998): 94.6%. **Health** (2000): physicians 4,455 (1 per 454 persons); hospital beds 10,248 (1 per 198 persons); infant mortality rate per 1,000 live births (2003) 10.7. **Food** (2001): daily per capita caloric intake 2,552 (vegetable products 80%, animal products 20%); 100% of FAO recommended minimum.

Military

Total active duty personnel (2003): 12,850 (army 90.7%, headquarters staff 9.3%). **Military expenditure as percentage of GNP** (1999): 2.5% (world 2.4%); per capita expenditure $112.

Background

Macedonia has been inhabited since before 7000 BC. Part of it was incorporated into a Roman province in AD 29. It was settled by Slavic tribes by the mid-6th century AD. Seized by the Bulgarians in 1185, it was ruled by the Ottoman Empire from 1371 to 1912. The north and center of the region were annexed by Serbia in 1913 and in 1918 became part of what was later known as Yugoslavia. When Yugoslavia was partitioned by the Axis powers in 1941, Yugoslav Macedonia was occupied principally by Bulgaria. Macedonia again became part of Yugoslavia in 1946. After Croatia and Slovenia seceded from Yugoslavia, fear of Serbian dominance drove Macedonia to declare its independence in 1991. Because of Greek objections to the new state using the name of an ancient Greek province, it entered the UN as "the Former Yugoslav Republic of Macedonia."

Recent Developments

Macedonians were shocked when, on 26 Feb 2004, their president, Boris Trajkovski, died in a plane crash in Bosnia en route to a development conference in Mostar, Bosnia and Herzegovina. Trajkovski had been credited with making progess toward a solution to Macedonia's difficult relations between Slavs and ethnic Albanians. In elections in May the prime minister, Branko Crvenkovski, was elected to succeed Trajkovski, while Interior Minister Hari Kostov moved up to the prime ministership.

Internet resources: <www.sinf.gov.mk>.

Madagascar

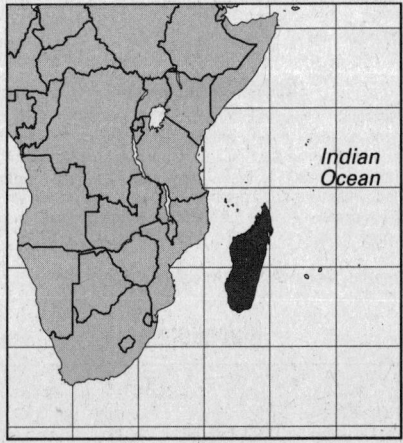

Indian Ocean

Official name: Repoblikan'i Madagasikara (Malagasy); République de Madagascar (French) (Republic of Madagascar). **Form of government:** federal multiparty republic with two legislative houses (Senate [90]; National Assembly [160]). **Heads of state and government:** President Marc Ravalomanana (from 2002), assisted by Prime Minister Jacques Sylla (from 2002). **Capital:** Antananarivo. **Official languages:** none; Malagasy is the national language and French is widely spoken; the two versions of the constitution are in Malagasy and French. **Official religion:** none. **Monetary unit:** 1 ariary (MGA) = 100 centimes; valuation (7 Jul 2005) $1 = MGA 1,800.05. The ariary (MGA), the precolonial currency of Mada-

---

1 metric ton = about 1.1 short tons;   1 kilometer = 0.6 mi (statute);   1 metric ton-km cargo = about 0.68 short ton-mi cargo;   c.i.f.: cost, insurance, and freight;   f.o.b.: free on board

gascar, replaced the Malagasy franc (FMG) in July 2003 at a rate of 1 MGA = FMG 5.

Demography

Area: 226,658 sq mi, 587,041 sq km. **Population** (2004): 17,082,000. **Density** (2004): persons per sq mi 75.4, persons per sq km 29.1. **Urban** (2001): 30.1%. **Sex distribution** (2000): male 49.70%; female 50.30%. **Age breakdown** (2000): under 15, 45.0%; 15–29, 26.5%; 30–44, 15.8%; 45–59, 7.9%; 60–74, 3.8%; 75 and over, 1.0%. **Ethnic composition** (2000): Malagasy 95.9%, of which Merina 24.0%, Betsi-misaraka 13.4%, Betsileo 11.3%, Tsimihety 7.0%, Sakalava 5.9%; Makua 1.1%; French 0.6%; Comorian 0.5%; Reunionese 0.4%; other 1.5%. **Religious affiliation** (2000): Christian 49.5%, of which Protestant 22.7%, Roman Catholic 20.3%; traditional beliefs 48.0%; Muslim 1.9%; other 0.6%. **Major cities** (2001): Antananarivo 1,403,449; Toamasina 179,045; Antsirabe 160,356; Fianarantsoa 144,225; Mahajanga 135,660. **Location:** island in the Indian Ocean, east of the mainland of southern Africa.

Vital statistics

Birth rate per 1,000 population (2003): 42.2 (world avg. 21.3). **Death rate** per 1,000 population (2003): 11.9 (world avg. 9.1). **Natural increase rate** per 1,000 population (2003): 30.3 (world avg. 12.2). **Total fertility rate** (avg. births per childbearing woman; 2003): 5.7. **Life expectancy** at birth (2003): male 53.8 years; female 58.5 years.

National economy

Budget (2000). *Revenue:* FMG 3,068,000,000,000 (taxes 96.9%, of which duties on trade 51.9%, value-added tax 16.7%; income tax 15.2%; nontax receipts 3.1%). *Expenditures:* FMG 4,168,600,000,000 (current expenditure 57.6%, of which general administration 21.1%, debt service 14.7%, education 13.3%, defense 7.7%, health 4.4%, agriculture 2.0%; capital expenditure 42.4%). **Public debt** (external, outstanding; 2002): $4,137,000,000. **Production** (metric tons except as noted). *Agriculture, forestry, fishing* (2002): paddy rice 2,671,000, cassava 2,510,000, sugarcane 2,223,000; livestock (number of live animals) 11,000,000 cattle, 1,600,000 pigs, 1,350,000 goats; roundwood (2001) 10,012,542 cu m; fish catch (2001) 143,000, of which crustaceans (2001) 18,881. *Mining and quarrying* (2002): chromite ore 15,600; graphite 1,300; gold, none (illegally smuggled, c. 3,500 kg). *Manufacturing* (2000): refined sugar 62,487; cement 50,938; soap 15,385. *Energy production (consumption):* electricity (kW-hr; 2000) 807,000,000 (807,000,000); coal (2000) none (10,000); crude petroleum (barrels; 2000) none (3,379,000); petroleum products (2000) 311,000 (568,000). **Population economically active** (1993): total 5,914,000; activity rate of total population 48.9% (participation rates [1995]: over age 10, 59.4%; female 38.4%). **Gross national product** (at current market prices; 2003): $4,848,000,000 ($290 per capita). **Household income and expenditure.** Average household size (1993; Malagasy households only) 4.6; expenditure (1983; Antananarivo only; excludes housing): food 60.4%, fuel and light 9.1%, clothing and footwear 8.6%, household goods and utensils 2.4%. **Land use** as % of total land area (2000): in temporary crops 5.0%, in permanent crops 1.0%, in pasture 41.3%; overall forest area 20.2%.

Tourism (2002): receipts from visitors $36,000,000; expenditures by nationals abroad $91,000,000.

Foreign trade

Imports (2001-f.o.b. in balance of trade and c.i.f. for commodities and trading partners): FMG 7,363,000,000,000 (petroleum [all forms] 15.0%, machinery and apparatus 14.7%, consumer goods 11.8%, other [mostly imports for export-processing zones] 39.3%). *Major import sources:* France 21.5%; China 9.1%; South Africa 5.5%; Japan 4.4%; US 4.2%. **Exports** (2001): FMG 6,356,000,000,000 (export-processing zones exports [mostly textiles and clothing] 35.3%, vanilla 17.0%, cloves 9.9%, shellfish 9.6%). *Major export destinations:* France 29.7%; US 13.9%; Mauritius 2.6%; unspecified countries 34.7%.

Transport and communications

Transport. *Railroads:* route length (2003) 901 km; passenger-km (2000) 24,471,000; metric ton-km cargo (2000) 27,200,000. *Roads* (2000): total length 49,827 km (paved 12%). *Vehicles* (1998): passenger cars 64,000; trucks and buses 9,100. *Air transport* (2003; Air Madagascar): passenger-km 715,920,000; metric ton-km cargo 9,740,000; airports (1994) with scheduled flights 44. **Communications**, in total units (units per 1,000 persons). Daily newspaper circulation (2000): 77,500 (5); radios (2000): 3,350,000 (216); televisions (2002): 410,000 (25); telephone main lines (2003): 59,600 (3.6); cellular telephone subscribers (2003): 279,500 (17); personal computer users (2003): 80,000 (4.9); Internet users (2003): 70,500 (4.3).

Education and health

Literacy (2000): percentage of total population age 15 and over literate 66.5%; males literate 73.6%; females literate 59.7%. **Health** (2000): physicians 1,428 (1 per 10,859 persons); hospital beds (total number of regional and provincial hospital beds) 7,043 (1 per 2,202 persons); infant mortality rate per 1,000 live births (2002) 81.9. **Food** (2001): daily per capita caloric intake 2,072 (vegetable products 91%, animal products 9%); 91% of FAO recommended minimum.

Military

Total active duty personnel (2003): 13,500 (army 92.6%, navy 3.7%, air force 3.7%). **Military expenditure as percentage of GNP** (1999): 1.2% (world 2.4%); per capita expenditure $3.

Did you know? Madagascar is the world's fourth largest island, after Greenland, New Guinea, and Borneo. Because of the island's isolation, many zoologically primitive primates have survived and evolved into unique forms.

Background

Indonesians migrated to Madagascar about AD 700. The first European to visit the island was Portuguese navigator Diogo Dias in 1500. Trade in arms and slaves allowed the development of Malagasy kingdoms at the beginning of the 17th century. The Merina kingdom became dominant in the 18th century and in 1868 signed a treaty granting France control over the northwestern coast. In 1895 French troops took the island, and Madagascar became a French overseas territory in 1946. As the Malagasy Republic, it gained independence in 1960. It severed ties with France in the 1970s, taking its present name in 1975. A new constitution was adopted in 1992. The country has since been both politically and economically unstable.

Recent Developments

Two major cyclones hit Madagascar in January and March 2004, killing 295 people, ruining rice fields, and destroying infrastructure. The island country did not suffer great damage in the Indian Ocean tsunami in December, however. High world oil prices and a collapse of the Malagasy franc helped force up the price of rice, the major staple, which led to mass street demonstrations. With three-quarters of the population living on less than a dollar a day, the government was forced to import cheap rice to try to stabilize prices.

Internet resources:
<www.embassy.org/madagascar>.

Malawi

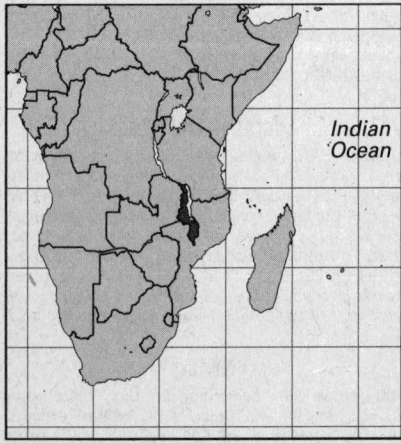

Indian Ocean

Official name: Republic of Malawi. **Form of government:** multiparty republic with one legislative house (National Assembly [193]). **Head of state and government:** President Bingu wa Mutharika (from 24 May 2004). **Capital:** Lilongwe (the judiciary meets in Blantyre). **Official language:** none. **Official religion:** none. **Monetary unit:** 1 Malawi kwacha (MK) = 100 tambala; valuation (7 Jul 2005) $1 = MK 123.82.

Demography

Area: 45,747 sq mi, 118,484 sq km. **Population** (2004): 11,907,000. **Density** (2004): persons per sq mi 327.1, persons per sq km 126.3. **Urban** (2002): 15.1%. **Sex distribution** (2001): male 49.39%; female 50.61%. **Age breakdown** (2001): under 15, 44.4%; 15–29, 30.4%; 30–44, 13.5%; 45–59, 7.2%; 60–74, 3.7%; 75 and over, 0.8%. **Ethnic composition** (2000): Chewa 34.7%; Maravi 12.2%; Ngoni 9.0%; Yao 7.9%; Tumbuka 7.9%; Lomwe 7.7%; Ngonde 3.5%; other 17.1%. **Religious affiliation** (2000): Protestant 38.5%; Roman Catholic 24.7%; Muslim 14.8%; traditional beliefs 7.8%; other 14.2%. **Major cities** (1998): Blantyre 502,053; Lilongwe 440,471; Mzuzu 86,980; Zomba 65,915; Karonga 27,811. **Location:** southeastern Africa, bordering Tanzania, Mozambique, and Zambia.

Vital statistics

Birth rate per 1,000 population (2003): 44.7 (world avg. 21.3). **Death rate** per 1,000 population (2003): 22.6 (world avg. 9.1). **Natural increase rate** per 1,000 population (2003): 22.1 (world avg. 12.2). **Total fertility rate** (avg. births per childbearing woman; 2003): 6.1. **Life expectancy** at birth (2003): male 37.6 years; female 38.4 years. **Adult population** (ages 15–49) **living with HIV** (2004): 14.2% (world avg. 1.1%).

National economy

Budget (2001–02). *Revenue:* MK 22,853,200,000 (tax revenue 72.5%, of which surtax 21.5%, income and profit tax 17.1%, import tax 8.4%; grants 19.8%; nontax revenue 7.7%). *Expenditures:* MK 30,476,300,000 (current expenditure 86.7%; capital expenditure 9.9%; other 3.4%). **Public debt** (external, outstanding; 2002): $2,688,000,000. **Production** (metric tons except as noted). *Agriculture* (2002): sugarcane 1,900,000, corn (maize) 1,603,000, cassava 1,540,000; livestock (number of live animals) 1,700,000 goats, 750,000 cattle, 456,000 pigs; roundwood (2001) 5,515,659 cu m; fish catch (2001) 41,187. *Mining and quarrying* (2002): limestone 175,000; gemstones 16,500 kg. *Manufacturing* (value added in $'000,000; 2001): food products 62; beverages 28; chemicals and chemical products 11. *Energy production (consumption):* electricity (kW-hr; 2002) 1,156,000,000 ([2000] 884,000,000); hard coal (2002) 41,900 ([2000] 17,000); petroleum products (2000) none (209,000). **Land use** as % of total land area (2000): in temporary crops 22.3%, in permanent crops 1.5%, in pasture 19.7%; overall forest area 27.2%. **Population economically active** (1998): total 4,509,290; activity rate 45.4% (participation rates: ages 10 and over 66.9%; female 50.2%). **Gross national product** (2003): $1,832,000,000 ($170 per capita). **Households.** Average household size (1998) 4.3; expenditure (2001): food 55.5%, clothing and footwear 11.7%, housing 9.6%, household goods 8.4%. **Tourism:** receipts (2002) $125,000,000; expenditures (1994) $78,000,000.

Foreign trade

Imports (2001–c.i.f.): MK 39,480,000,000 (1998; food 16.4%, of which cereals 13.1%; machinery and apparatus 15.3%; chemicals and chemical products 13.2%; road vehicles 11.6%; mineral fuels 9.6%). *Major import sources* (2001): South Africa 39.7%;

---

1 metric ton = about 1.1 short tons;   1 kilometer = 0.6 mi (statute);   1 metric ton-km cargo = about 0.68 short ton-mi cargo;   c.i.f.: cost, insurance, and freight;   f.o.b.: free on board

Zimbabwe 16.0%; Zambia 10.9%; India 3.2%; Germany 2.7%. **Exports** (2001-f.o.b.): MK 31,816,-000,000 (tobacco 57.7%; sugar 12.5%; tea 7.7%; apparel 1.7%; coffee 1.4%). *Major export destinations:* South Africa 19.1%; US 15.4%; Germany 11.2%; Japan 7.6%; The Netherlands 5.4%.

Transport and communications

Transport. *Railroads* (1999–2000): route length 797 km; passenger-km 19,000,000; metric ton-km cargo 62,000,000. *Roads* (1998): total length 16,451 km (paved 19%). *Vehicles* (2001): passenger cars 22,500; trucks and buses 57,600. *Air transport* (2003; Air Malawi only): passenger-km 146,900,000; metric ton-km cargo 1,176,000; airports (1998) 5. **Communications,** in total units (units per 1,000 persons). Daily newspaper circulation (1996; circulation for one newspaper only): 22,000 (2.3); radios (2000): 5,426,000 (499); televisions (2000): 32,600 (3); telephone main lines (2003): 85,000 (8.1); cellular telephone subscribers (2003): 135,100 (13); personal computers (2003): 16,000 (1.5); Internet users (2003): 36,000 (3.4).

Education and health

Educational attainment (1998). Percentage of population age 25 and over having: no formal education 40.9%; primary education 48.7%; secondary 9.7%; university 0.7%. **Literacy** (2000): total population age 15 and over literate 60.1%; males literate 74.5%; females literate 46.5%. **Health:** physicians (1989) 186 (1 per 47,634 persons); hospital beds (1998) 14,200 (1 per 746 persons); infant mortality rate per 1,000 live births (2003) 105.2. **Food** (2001): daily per capita caloric intake 2,168 (vegetable products 97%, animal products 3%); 93% of FAO recommended minimum.

Military

Total active duty personnel (2003): 5,300 (army 100%; navy, none; air force, none). **Military expenditure as percentage of GNP** (1999): 0.6% (world 2.4%); per capita expenditure $1.

Background

Inhabited since at least 8000 BC, the region was settled by Bantu-speaking peoples between the 1st and the 4th century AD. About 1480 they founded the Maravi Confederacy, which encompassed most of central and southern Malawi. In northern Malawi the Ngonde people established a kingdom about 1600. The slave trade flourished during the 18th–19th centuries. Britain established colonial authority in 1891, and the area became known as Nyasaland in 1907. The colonies of Northern and Southern Rhodesia and Nyasaland formed a federation (1951–53), which was dissolved in 1963. The next year Malawi achieved independence. In 1966 it became a republic, with Hastings Banda as president. In 1971 Banda was designated president for life, and he ruled until he was defeated in multiparty elections in 1994. A new constitution was adopted in 1995.

Recent Developments

The incumbent regime of the United Democratic Front seemed to be squandering its political capital in 2004–05 in light of widespread discontent over official corruption, the government's inadequate handling of the economy, and its failure to deal with the problem of HIV/AIDS. The party's presidential candidate, Bingu wa Mutharika, won only 36% of the vote in May 2004. In January 2005 he accused his predecessor and fellow party member, Bakili Muluzi, of plotting to murder him, and in February Mutharika quit the UDF, which was considering expelling him for misconduct.

Internet resources: <www.malawi.gov.mw>.

Malaysia

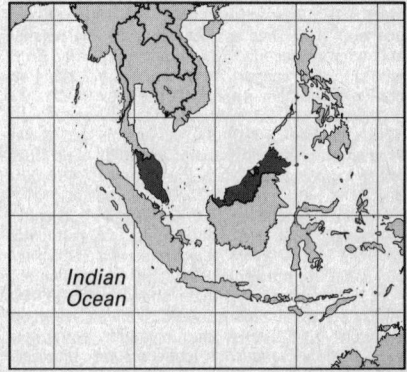

Indian Ocean

Official name: Malaysia. **Form of government:** federal constitutional monarchy with two legislative houses (Senate [70, including 44 appointees of the Paramount Ruler; the remaining 26 are indirectly elected]; House of Representatives [219]). **Chief of state:** Yang di-Pertuan Agong (Paramount Ruler) Tuanku Syed Sirajuddin ibni al-Marhum Tuanku Syed Putra Jamalullail (from 2001). **Head of government:** Prime Minister Datuk Seri Abdullah Ahmad Badawi (from 2003). **Capital:** transferring from Kuala Lumpur to Putrajaya between 1999 and 2012. **Official language:** Malay. **Official religion:** Islam. **Monetary unit:** 1 ringgit, or Malaysian dollar (RM) = 100 cents; pegged since 6 Oct 2000 to the US dollar at the rate of $1 = RM 3.80.

Demography

Area: 127,355 sq mi, 329,847 sq km. **Population** (2004): 25,584,000. **Density** (2004): persons per sq mi 200.9, persons per sq km 77.6. **Urban** (2002): 59.0%. **Sex distribution** (2000): male 50.93%; female 49.07%. **Age breakdown** (2000): under 15, 33.0%; 15–29, 28.3%; 30–44, 21.0%; 45–59, 11.6%; 60–74, 4.9%; 75 and over, 1.2%. **Ethnic composition** (2000): Malay and other indigenous 61.3%; Chinese 24.5%; Indian 7.2%; other nonindigenous 1.1%; noncitizen 5.9%. **Religious affiliation** (2000): Muslim 60.4%; Buddhist 19.2%; Christian 9.1%; Hindu 6.3%; Chinese folk religionist 2.6%; other 2.4%. **Major cities** (2000): Kuala Lumpur 1,297,526; Ipoh 566,211; Klang 563,173; Petaling Jaya 438,084; Johor Bahru 384,613. **Location:** southeastern Asia, on the Malay Peninsula and the northern third of the island of Borneo, bordering Thailand, the South China Sea, Brunei, and Indonesia.

Vital statistics

Birth rate per 1,000 population (2003): 21.9 (world avg. 21.3). **Death rate** per 1,000 population (2003): 4.7 (world avg. 9.1). **Natural increase rate** per 1,000 population (2003): 17.2 (world avg. 12.2). **Total fertility rate** (avg. births per childbearing woman; 2003): 3.1. **Life expectancy** at birth (2003): male 71.0 years; female 75.5 years.

National economy

Budget (2001). *Revenue:* RM 79,567,000,000 (income tax 52.9%, nontax revenue 25.1%, taxes on goods and services 16.9%, taxes on international trade 5.1%). *Expenditures:* RM 63,757,000,000 (education 22.6%, interest payments 15.1%, defense and internal security 13.0%, social security 8.7%, health 7.3%, transport 2.1%, agriculture 2.1%). **Population economically active** (1999): total 9,010,000; activity rate 39.7% (participation rates: ages 15–64, 60.6%; female [2000] 34.7%; unemployed 3.0%). **Production** (metric tons except as noted). *Agriculture, forestry, fishing* (2002): palm fruit oil 67,400,000, rice 2,091,000, coconuts 700,000; livestock (number of live animals) 1,824,000 pigs, 748,000 cattle; roundwood (2001) 16,347,000 cu m; fish catch (2001) 1,393,000. *Mining and quarrying* (2001): iron ore 376,000; struverite 9,657; tin (metal content) 4,973. *Manufacturing* (value added in $'000,000; 2000): electronic products 4,962; refined petroleum products 2,492; telecommunications equipment 2,062. *Energy production (consumption):* electricity (kW-hr; 2003; excludes Sabah and Sarawak) 84,024,000,000 ([2000] 69,268,000,000); coal (2003) 168,000 ([2000] 3,761,000,000); crude petroleum (barrels; 2003; Sabah and Sarawak only) 268,300,000 ([2000] 155,548,000); petroleum products (2000) 19,386,000 (20,495,000); natural gas (cu m; 2003) 51,808,000,000 ([2000] 29,454,000,000). **Gross national product** (2003): $93,683,000,000 ($3,780 per capita). **Public debt** (external, outstanding; 2002): $26,200,000,000. **Household income and expenditure.** Average household size (2000) 4.5; annual income per household (1999) RM 32,784; expenditure (1998–99): food at home 22.2%, housing and energy 21%, food away from home 10.9%. **Tourism** (2002): receipts $6,785,000,000; expenditures $2,618,000,000. **Land use** as % of total land area (2000): in temporary crops 5.5%, in permanent crops 17.6%, in pasture 0.9%; overall forest area 58.7%.

Foreign trade

Imports (2002-c.i.f.): RM 303,510,000,000 (microcircuits, transistors, and valves 29.2%; computers/office machines 6.9%; telecommunications equipment 4.3%; other electrical machinery 6.6%). *Major import sources:* Japan 17.8%; US 16.4%; Singapore 12.0%; China 7.8%; Taiwan 5.6%. **Exports** (2002-f.o.b.): RM 354,480,000,000 (microcircuits, transistors, and valves 20.5%; computers/office machines 18.4%; telecommunications equipment 5.4%; fixed vegetable oils 3.9%; crude petroleum 3.3%). *Major export destinations:* US 20.2%; Singapore 17.1%; Japan 11.2%; Hong Kong 5.7%; China 5.6%.

Transport and communications

Transport. *Railroads* (2000): route length 2,227 km; passenger-km 1,241,000,000 (peninsular Malaysia and Singapore); metric ton-km cargo 918,000,000 (peninsular Malaysia and Singapore). *Roads* (2000): total length 66,445 km (paved 76%). *Vehicles* (2000): passenger cars 4,212,567; trucks and buses 713,946. *Air transport* (2003; Malaysian airline only): passenger-km 36,797,000,000; metric ton-km cargo 2,176,000,000; airports (1997) 39. **Communications**, in total units (units per 1,000 persons). Daily newspaper circulation (2000): 3,672,000 (158); radios (2000): 9,762,000 (420); televisions (2002): 5,103,000 (210); telephone main lines (2003): 4,571,600 (182); cellular telephone subscribers (2003): 11,124,100 (442); personal computers (2002): 3,600,000 (147); Internet users (2003): 8,692,100 (345).

Education and health

Educational attainment (1996). Percentage of population age 25 and over having: no formal schooling 16.7%; primary education 33.7%; secondary 42.8%; higher 6.8%. **Literacy** (2000): total population age 15 and over literate 87.5%; males literate 91.4%; females literate 83.4%. **Health** (2002): physicians 17,442 (1 per 1,406 persons); hospital beds (2001) 41,927 (1 per 570 persons); infant mortality rate per 1,000 live births 7.9. **Food** (2001): daily per capita caloric intake 2,927 (vegetable products 82%, animal products 18%); 131% of FAO recommended minimum.

Military

Total active duty personnel (2003): 104,000 (army 77.0%, navy 13.5%, air force 9.5%). **Military expenditure as percentage of GDP** (1999): 2.3% (world 2.4%); per capita expenditure $78.

Did you know? Kuala Lumpur International Airport, one of the largest airports in the world, is located in the city's Gateway Park, a development that includes a major hotel, golf course, and amusement park.

Background

Malaya has been inhabited for 6,000–8,000 years, and small kingdoms existed in the 2nd–3rd century AD, when adventurers from India first arrived. Sumatran exiles founded the city-state of Malacca about 1400, and it flourished as a trading and Islamic religious center until its capture by the Portuguese in 1511. Malacca passed to the Dutch in 1641. The British founded a settlement on Singapore Island in 1819, and by 1867 they had established the Straits Settlements, including Malacca, Singapore, and Penang. During the late 19th century the Chinese began to migrate to Malaya. Japan invaded in 1941. Opposition to British rule led to the creation of the United Malays National Organization (UNMO) in 1946, and in 1948 the peninsula was federated with

---

1 metric ton = about 1.1 short tons;   1 kilometer = 0.6 mi (statute);   1 metric ton-km cargo = about 0.68 short ton-mi cargo;   c.i.f.: cost, insurance, and freight;   f.o.b.: free on board

Penang. Malaya gained independence in 1957, and the federation of Malaysia was established in 1963. Its economy expanded greatly from the late 1970s, but it suffered from the economic slump that struck the area in the mid-1990s.

Recent Developments

On 2 Sep 2004 the High Court in Malaysia ended one of the country's most wrenching controversies when it released Anwar Ibrahim, the former deputy prime minister imprisoned since 1998 on charges of questionable validity. The court overturned his conviction for sodomy. The action was widely attributed to the anticorruption campaign of Prime Minister Abdullah Ahmad Badawi and was a move that clearly resonated with Malaysians, who gave his United Malays National Organization (UMNO) a landslide victory in general elections held on 21 March. The government was also struggling to combat rising crime rates. In January the government considered introducing public flogging as a punishment for child rape. Flogging demonstrations in Malaysian schools, launched in May to deter juvenile delinquency, were quickly discontinued following warnings that such demonstrations legitimized violence in the eyes of children. In August a royal commission reported that Malaysia's police force was riddled with corruption and brutality.

Internet resources:
<www.geographia.com/malaysia>.

Maldives

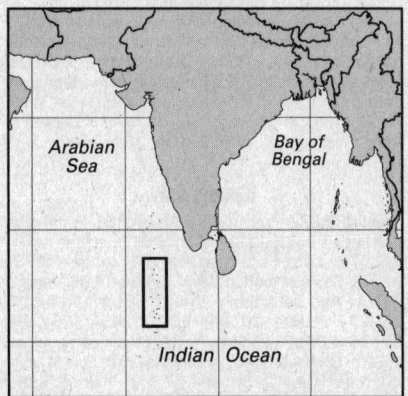

Arabian Sea
Bay of Bengal
Indian Ocean

Official name: Divehi Jumhuriyya (Republic of Maldives). **Form of government:** republic with one legislative house (Majlis [42; excludes eight nonelective seats]). **Head of state and government:** President Maumoon Abdul Gayoom (from 1978). **Capital:** Male. **Official language:** Divehi. **Official religion:** Islam. **Monetary unit:** 1 Maldivian rufiyaa (Rf) = 100 laari; valuation (7 Jul 2005) $1 = Rf 12.80.

Demography

Area: 115 sq mi, 298 sq km. **Population** (2004): 289,000. **Density** (2004): persons per sq mi 2,513, persons per sq km 969.8. **Urban** (2002): 27.0%. **Sex distribution** (2003): male 50.73%; female 49.27%.

Age breakdown (2003): under 15, 36.1%; 15–29, 31.7%; 30–44, 18.0%; 45–59, 7.9%; 60–74, 5.2%; 75 and over, 1.1%. **Ethnic composition** (2000): Maldivian 98.5%; Sinhalese 0.7%; other 0.8%. **Religious affiliation:** virtually 100% Sunni Muslim. **Major city** (2000): Male 74,069. **Location:** islands in the Indian Ocean, south of India.

Vital statistics

Birth rate per 1,000 population (2003): 35.7 (world avg. 21.3). **Death rate** per 1,000 population (2003): 6.0 (world avg. 9.1). **Natural increase rate** per 1,000 population (2003): 29.7 (world avg. 12.2). **Total fertility rate** (avg. births per childbearing woman; 2003): 5.3. **Marriage rate** per 1,000 population (2001): 11.6. **Divorce rate** per 1,000 population (2001): 5.5. **Life expectancy** at birth (2003): male 62.0 years; female 64.6 years.

National economy

Budget (2001). *Revenue:* Rf 2,513,200,000 (nontax revenue 50.8%; taxation 41.4%; foreign aid 7.3%). *Expenditures:* Rf 2,886,200,000 (general public services 42.1%, of which defense 15.2%; education 18.5%; health 10.4%; transportation and communications 8.9%; transfer payments 2.3%). **Public debt** (external, outstanding; 2002): $221,700,000. **Production** (metric tons except as noted). *Agriculture, forestry, fishing* (2001): vegetables and melons 28,000, coconuts 15,000, fruits (excluding melons) 9,000; fish catch 125,814. *Mining and quarrying:* coral for construction materials. *Manufacturing:* details, n.a.; however, major industries include boat building and repairing, coir yarn and mat weaving, coconut and fish processing, lacquerwork, garment manufacturing, and handicrafts. *Energy production (consumption):* electricity (kW-hr; 2000) 104,000,-000 (104,000,000); petroleum products (2000) none (163,000). **Tourism** (2002): receipts from visitors $318,000,000; expenditures by nationals abroad $46,000,000. **Population economically active** (2000): total 87,987; activity rate of total population 32.6% (participation rates: ages 15–64, 58.5%; female 33.8%; unemployed 2.0%). **Household income and expenditure.** Average household size (2000) 6.8; annual income per household (1990) Rf 2,616; expenditure (1995): food, beverages and tobacco 36.9%, housing and energy 14.9%; transportation and communications 11.1%, clothing and footwear 9.8%, education 8.6%, household furnishings 8.3%. **Gross national product** (2003): $674,000,000 ($2,300 per capita). **Land use** as % of total land area (2000): in temporary crops 13%, in permanent crops 17%, in pasture 3%; overall forest area 3%.

Foreign trade

Imports (2001-c.i.f.): $395,400,000 (food products 36.9%; petroleum products 12.1%; transport equipment 10.5%; construction-related goods 10.2%). *Major import sources:* Asian countries 69%, of which Singapore 25%, Sri Lanka 13%, India 10%, Malaysia 9%; European countries 14%. **Exports** (2001-f.o.b.): $110,200,000 (domestic exports 69.1%, of which fish 32.5%, garments 29.3%, live tropical fish 2.8%; reexports 30.9%, of which jet fuel 25.6%). *Major export destinations:* US 39%; Sri Lanka 21%; European countries 15%.

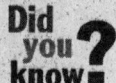

Did you know? The Maldive Islands are a series of coral atolls built up from the crowns of a submerged ancient volcanic mountain range. All the islands are low-lying, none rising to more than 6 ft (1.8 m) above sea level.

Transport and communications

Transport. *Vehicles* (2002): passenger cars 2,594; trucks and buses 644. *Air transport* (2001): passenger-km 385,000,000; airports (1997) with scheduled flights 5. **Communications,** in total units (units per 1,000 persons). Daily newspaper circulation (1996): 5,000 (19); radios (1997): 34,000 (129); televisions (2000): 10,900 (40); telephone main lines (2002): 28,700 (102); cellular telephone subscribers (2002): 41,900 (149); personal computers (2002): 20,000 (71); Internet users (2002): 15,000 (53).

Education and health

Educational attainment (2000). Population age 25 and over 71,937; percentage with university education 0.4%. **Literacy** (1995): total population age 15 and over literate 93.2%; males literate 93.0%; females literate 93.3%. **Health** (2003): physicians 314 (1 per 905 persons); hospital beds 643 (1 per 443 persons); infant mortality rate per 1,000 live births (2002) 38.0. **Food** (2001): daily per capita caloric intake 2,587 (vegetable products 75%, animal products 25%); 117% of FAO recommended minimum.

Military

Total active duty personnel: combined army/police force 700–1,000. **Military expenditure as percentage of GDP** (2002): 6.2%; per capita expenditure $103.

Background

The archipelago was settled in the 5th century BC by Buddhists from Sri Lanka and southern India, and Islam was adopted there in 1153. The Portuguese held sway in Male in 1558–73. The islands were a sultanate under the Dutch rulers of Ceylon (now Sri Lanka) during the 17th century. After the British gained control of Ceylon in 1796, the area became a British protectorate, a status formalized in 1887. The islands won full independence from Britain in 1965, and in 1968 a republic was founded. During the 1990s its economy gradually developed.

Recent Developments

In 2004 the very survival of Maldives was threatened by the tsunami that swept across the Indian Ocean in late December. Waves submerged many of the nation's low-lying coral islands, at least 50 of which were either severely damaged or completely destroyed. Only a sea wall built to protect Male saved the capital city itself from catastrophic damage. Relief workers and government officials believed the death toll would exceed 100 persons. The economic cost of the disaster was estimated at hundreds of

millions of dollars, and socioeconomic development was set back "by at least two decades," a government spokesman said.

Internet resources: <www.visitmaldives.com>.

Mali

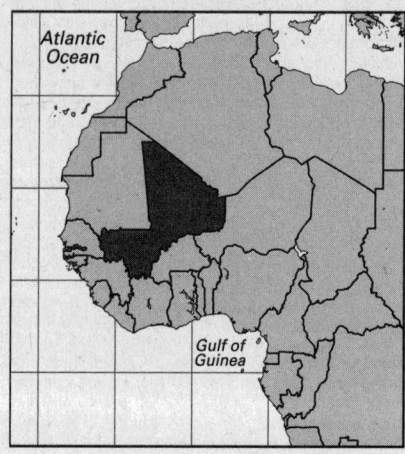

Official name: République du Mali (Republic of Mali). **Form of government:** multiparty republic with one legislative house (National Assembly [147]). **Chief of state:** President Amadou Toumani Touré (from 2002). **Head of government:** Prime Minister Ousmane Issoufi Maïga (from 30 Apr 2004). **Capital:** Bamako. **Official language:** French. **Official religion:** none. **Monetary unit:** 1 CFA franc (CFAF) = 100 centimes; valuation (7 Jul 2005) $1 = CFAF 549.50; the CFAF is pegged to the euro (€) at €1 = 655.96 from 1 Jan 2002.

Demography

Area: 482,077 sq mi, 1,248,574 sq km. **Population** (2004): 11,957,000. **Density** (2004): persons per sq mi 24.8, persons per sq km 9.6. **Urban** (1998): 28.7%. **Sex distribution** (2001): male 48.9%; female 51.1%. **Age breakdown** (2001): under 15, 47.2%; 15–29, 26.8%; 30–44, 13.3%; 45–59, 7.9%; 60–74, 4.0%; 75 and over, 0.8%. **Ethnic composition** (2000): Bambara 30.6%; Senufo 10.5%; Fula Macina (Niafunke) 9.6%; Soninke 7.4%; Tuareg 7.0%; Maninka 6.6%; Songhai 6.3%; Dogon 4.3%; Bobo 3.5%; other 14.2%. **Religious affiliation** (2000): Muslim 82%; traditional beliefs 16%; Christian 2%. **Major cities** (1998): Bamako 1,016,167; Sikasso 113,803; Ségou 90,898; Mopti 79,840; Gao 54,903. **Location:** western Africa, bordering Algeria, Niger, Burkina Faso, Côte d'Ivoire, Guinea, Senegal, and Mauritania.

Vital statistics

Birth rate per 1,000 population (2003): 47.8 (world avg. 21.3). **Death rate** per 1,000 population (2003): 19.2 (world avg. 9.1). **Natural increase rate** per 1,000 population (2003): 28.6 (world avg. 12.2).

---

1 metric ton = about 1.1 short tons;   1 kilometer = 0.6 mi (statute);   1 metric ton-km cargo = about 0.68 short ton-mi cargo;   c.i.f.: cost, insurance, and freight;   f.o.b.: free on board

Total fertility rate (avg. births per childbearing woman; 2003): 6.7. Life expectancy at birth (2003): male 44.7 years; female 46.2 years.

National economy

Budget (2002). Revenue: CFAF 379,400,000,000 (tax revenue 82.7%, nontax revenue 17.3%). Expenditures: CFAF 601,500,000,000 (current expenditure 46.7%, of which wages and salaries 14.9%, education 4.9%, interest on public debt 3.5%; capital expenditure 53.3%). Public debt (external, outstanding; 2002): $2,487,000,000. Tourism (2000): receipts from visitors $71,000,000; expenditures by nationals abroad $41,000,000. Population economically active (2001): total 5,895,000; activity rate of total population 53.7%. Production (metric tons except as noted). Agriculture, forestry, fishing (2002): millet 1,034,211, sorghum 951,417, rice 926,497; livestock (number of live animals) 15,000,000 goats and sheep, 6,818,000 cattle, 700,000 asses; roundwood (2001) 5,200,428 cu m; fish catch (2001) 100,035. Mining and quarrying (1997): limestone 20,000; phosphate 3,000; iron oxide 708. Manufacturing (2000): cement 40,000; sugar 28,000; soap (1995) 10,097. Energy production (consumption): electricity (kW-hr; 2000) 412,000,000 (412,000,000); petroleum products (2000) none (161,000). Gross national product (2003): $3,428,000,000 ($290 per capita). Households. Average household size (2000) 5.6. Land use as % of total land area (2000): in temporary crops 3.8%, in permanent crops, negligible, in pasture 24.6%; overall forest area 10.8%.

Foreign trade

Imports (2001): CFAF 532,900,000,000 (machinery and apparatus 46.0%, petroleum products 25.9%, food products 13.0%). Major import sources (1999): African countries 51%, of which Côte d'Ivoire 20%; France 18%; Germany 3%; Hong Kong 3%. Exports (2001): CFAF 530,500,000,000 (gold 66.7%, raw cotton and cotton products 15.7%, live animals 8.5%). Major export destinations (1999): Italy 12%; Taiwan 10%; Thailand 10%; South Korea 9%; Canada 8%; Portugal 5%.

Transport and communications

Transport. Railroads (1999): route length 729 km; passenger-km 210,000,000; metric ton-km cargo 241,000,000. Roads (1996): total length 15,100 km (paved 12%). Vehicles (1996): passenger cars 26,190; trucks and buses 18,240. Air transport (1999; represents ¹/₁₁ of the traffic of Air Afrique, which was operated by 11 West African states and was declared bankrupt in February 2002): passenger-km 235,000,000; metric ton-km cargo 36,000,000; airports (1999) 9. Communications, in total units (units per 1,000 persons). Daily newspaper circulation (1997): 45,000 (4.6); radios (2001): 1,976,000 (180); televisions (2002): 376,200 (33); telephone main lines (2002): 56,600 (5.3); cellular phone subscribers (2002): 250,000 (23); personal computers (2002): 15,000 (1.5); Internet users (2002): 25,000 (2.3).

Education and health

Literacy (2000): percentage of total population age 15 and over literate 41.5%; males literate 48.9%; females literate 34.4%. Health: physicians (1993) 483

(1 per 18,376 persons); hospital beds (1998) 2,412 (1 per 4,168 persons); infant mortality rate per 1,000 live births (2003) 119.2. Food (2001): daily per capita caloric intake 2,376 (vegetable products 91%, animal products 9%); 101% of FAO recommended minimum.

Military

Total active duty personnel (2003): 7,350 (army 100%). Military expenditure as percentage of GNP (1999): 2.3% (world 2.4%); per capita expenditure $6.

Background

Inhabited since prehistoric times, the region was situated on a caravan route across the Sahara. In the 12th century the Malinke empire of Mali was founded on the Upper and Middle Niger. In the 15th century the Songhai empire in the Timbuktu-Gao region gained control. In 1591 Morocco invaded the area, and Timbuktu remained under the Moors for two centuries. In the mid-19th century the French conquered the area, which became a part of French West Africa known as the French Sudan. In 1946 it became an overseas territory of the French Union. It was proclaimed the Sudanese Republic in 1958, briefly joined with Senegal (1959–60) to form the Mali Federation, and became the Republic of Mali in 1960. The government was overthrown by military coups in 1968 and 1991. Elections were held in 1992 and 1997, but political instability continued.

Recent Developments

The plague of locusts infesting West Africa swept into Mali during the summer of 2004. On 3 September Pres. Amadou Toumani Touré, Prime Minister Ousmane Issoufi Maïga, and all the cabinet ministers donated one month's salary to the fight to eradicate the pests. Despite efforts to control the invasion, it was estimated that one-third of Mali's grain crop would be destroyed.

Internet resources:
<www.oxfam.org.uk/coolplanet/ontheline/explore/jo urney/mali/malindex.htm>.

Malta

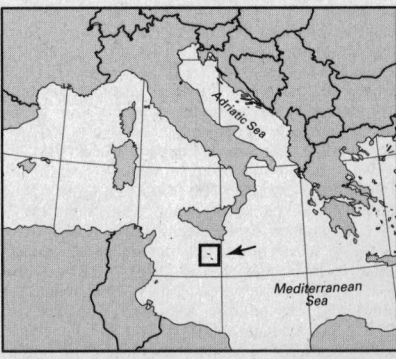

Official name: Repubblikka ta' Malta (Maltese); Republic of Malta (English). Form of government: unitary multiparty republic with one legislative house (House of Representatives [65]). **Chief of state:** President Eddie Fenech Adami (from 4 Apr 2004). **Head of government:** Prime Minister Lawrence Gonzi (from 23 Mar 2004). **Capital:** Valletta. **Official languages:** Maltese; English. **Official religion:** Roman Catholicism. **Monetary unit:** 1 Maltese lira (Lm) = 100 cents = 1,000 mils; valuation (7 Jul 2005) $1 = Lm 0.36.

Demography

Area: 121.7 sq mi, 315.1 sq km. **Population** (2004): 401,000. **Density** (2004): persons per sq mi 3,287, persons per sq km 1,273. **Urban** (2000): 90.5%. **Sex distribution** (2004): male 49.54%; female 50.46%. **Age breakdown** (2004): under 15, 18.2%; 15–29, 22.1%; 30–44, 20.0%; 45–59, 22.3%; 60–74, 12.1%; 75 and over, 5.3%. **Ethnic composition** (2000): Maltese 93.8%; British 2.1%; Arab 2.0%; Italian 1.5%; other 0.6%. **Religious affiliation** (2000): Roman Catholic 94.5%; unaffiliated Christian 2.7%; Protestant 0.8%; Muslim 0.5%; nonreligious 1.0%; other 0.5%. **Major localities** (2004): Birkirkara 22,435; Qormi 18,547; Mosta 18,070; Zabbar 15,134; Valletta 7,137 (urban agglomeration [2003] 83,000). **Location:** islands in the Mediterranean Sea, south of Sicily (Italy).

Vital statistics

Birth rate per 1,000 population (2003): 10.1 (world avg. 21.3); legitimate 83.2%. **Death rate** per 1,000 population (2003): 7.9 (world avg. 9.1). **Natural increase rate** per 1,000 population (2003): 2.2 (world avg. 12.2). **Total fertility rate** (avg. births per childbearing woman; 2003): 1.5. **Marriage rate** per 1,000 population (2003): 6.1. **Life expectancy** at birth (2003): male 76.3 years; female 80.8 years.

National economy

Budget (2001). *Revenue:* Lm 797,400,000 (social security 22.5%; income tax 20.9%; value-added tax 14.4%; grants and loans 13.6%). *Expenditures:* Lm 766,700,000 (recurrent expenditures 80.2%, of which social security 24.1%; education 6.1%; capital expenditure 10.5%; public debt service 9.3%). **Public debt** (2001): $616,000,000. **Production** (metric tons except where noted). *Agriculture, forestry, fishing* (2002): vegetables 49,200 (of which melons 12,800, tomatoes 7,400, onions 4,392, cabbage 3,900, garlic 551), potatoes 27,500, wheat 9,600; livestock (number of live animals; 2002) 79,300 pigs, 18,000 cattle, 6,600 sheep; fish catch (2003) 1,070. *Quarrying* (2002): small quantities of limestone and salt. *Manufacturing* (value added in $'000,000; 1998): telecommunications equipment and electronics 149; food products 69; wearing apparel 63. *Energy production (consumption):* electricity (kW-hr; 2000) 1,875,000,000 (1,875,000,000); coal (2000) none (325,000); petroleum products (2000) none (677,000). **Population economically active** (1998): total 144,824; activity rate of total population 38.4% (participation rates: ages 15–64 [1985] 45.9%; female 27.6%; unemployed [2001] 6.1%). **Household income and expenditure.** Average household size (2001) 3.1; average annual income per household (1982) Lm 4,736; sources of income (1993): wages

and salaries 63.8%, professional and unincorporated enterprises 19.3%, rents, dividends, and interest 16.9%; expenditure (2000): food and beverages 36.6%, transportation and communications 23.4%, recreation, entertainment, and education 9.4%, household furnishings and operations 7.6%. **Tourism** (2002): receipts from visitors $568,000,000; expenditures by nationals abroad $153,000,000. **Gross national product** (2003): $3,678,000,000 ($9,260 per capita). **Land use** as % of total land area (2000): in temporary crops 25%, in permanent crops 3%; overall forest area, negligible.

Foreign trade

Imports (2000-c.i.f.): Lm 1,492,400,000 (electronic microcircuits 37.3%, refined petroleum 7.0%, chemicals and chemical products 6.9%, food 6.0%). *Major import sources* (2001): Italy 17.3%; France 10.3%; Singapore 8.3%; Japan 7.6%; UK 7.5%. **Exports** (2000-f.o.b.): Lm 1,072,400,000 (electronic microcircuits 62.1%, apparel and clothing accessories 5.9%, refined petroleum 4.4%, children's toys and games 4.3%). *Major export destinations* (2001): US 15.2%; Germany 13.4%; Singapore 11.6%; France 8.9%; UK 8.7%.

Transport and communications

Transport. *Roads* (1997): total length 1,961 km (paved 94%). *Vehicles* (2000): passenger cars 202,883; trucks and buses 52,604. *Air transport* (2001): passenger-km 2,364,000,000; (2000) metric ton-km cargo 14,292,000; airports (1999) with scheduled flights 1. **Communications,** in total units (units per 1,000 persons). Daily newspaper circulation (1996): 54,000 (145); radios (1997): 255,000 (680); televisions (2000): 217,000 (556); telephone main lines (2003): 208,300 (521); cellular telephone subscribers (2003): 290,000 (725); personal computers (2002): 101,000 (255); Internet users (2002): 120,000 (303).

Education and health

Educational attainment (2001). Percentage of population age 15 and over having: no formal schooling 4.3%; primary education 34.4%; general secondary 37.6%; vocational secondary 5.7%; some postsecondary 11.8%; undergraduate 5.4%; graduate 0.8%. **Literacy** (2000): total population age 15 and over literate 279,000 (92.1%). **Health** (1996): physicians 925 (1 per 403 persons); hospital beds 2,140 (1 per 174 persons); infant mortality rate per 1,000 live births (2003) 4.0. **Food** (2001): daily per capita caloric intake 3,495 (vegetable products 73%, animal products 27%); 141% of FAO recommended minimum.

Military

Total active duty personnel (2003): 2,140 (army 100%). **Military expenditure as percentage of GNP** (1999): 0.8% (world 2.4%); per capita expenditure $73.

Background

Inhabited as early as 3800 BC, Malta was ruled by the Carthaginians from the 6th century BC until it came

---

1 metric ton = about 1.1 short tons;   1 kilometer = 0.6 mi (statute);   1 metric ton-km cargo = about 0.68 short ton-mi cargo;   c.i.f.: cost, insurance, and freight;   f.o.b.: free on board

under Roman control in 218 BC. In AD 60 the apostle Paul converted the inhabitants to Christianity. It was under Byzantine rule until the Arabs seized control in 870. In 1091 the Normans defeated the Arabs, and Malta was ruled by feudal lords until it came under the Knights of Malta in 1530. Napoleon seized control in 1798, the British took it in 1800, and it was returned to the knights in 1802. The Maltese protested and acknowledged the British as sovereign, an arrangement ratified in 1814. It became self-governing in 1921 but reverted to a colonial regime in 1936. Malta was severely bombed by Germany and Italy during World War II, and in 1942 it received the George Cross, Britain's highest civilian decoration. In 1964 it gained independence within the Commonwealth, and in 1974 became a republic. When its alliance with Britain ended in 1979, Malta proclaimed its neutral status.

Recent Developments

Malta became a member of the European Union on 1 May 2004. On 23 March Eddie Fenech Adami handed in his resignation as prime minister, and Lawrence Gonzi succeeded him; parliament elected Fenech Adami president the following month. Illegal immigration from Libya, mostly of Arabs and black Africans, created a serious problem, and Gonzi led a delegation to Libya to discuss the migration issue and other matters of mutual interest.

Internet resources: <www.mol.net.mt>.

Marshall Islands

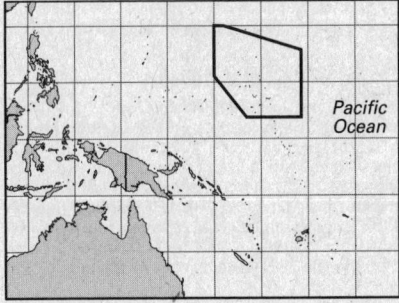

Pacific Ocean

Official name: Majol (Marshallese); Republic of the Marshall Islands (English). **Form of government:** unitary republic with two legislative houses (Council of Iroij [12; advisory body only]; Nitijela [33]). **Head of state and government:** President Kessai Note (from 2000). **Capital:** Majuro (Rita). **Official languages:** Marshallese (Kajin-Majol); English. **Official religion:** none. **Monetary unit:** 1 US dollar ($) = 100 cents.

Demography

Area: 70.05 sq mi, 181.43 sq km. **Population** (2004): 54,600. **Density** (2004): persons per sq mi 780.0, persons per sq km 301.7. **Urban** (2004): 65.0%. **Sex distribution** (2003): male 51.07%; female 48.93%. **Age breakdown** (2003): under 15, 39.2%; 15–29, 30.7%; 30–44, 16.4%; 45–59, 9.6%; 60–74, 3.1%; 75 and over, 1.0%. **Ethnic composition** (nationality; 2000): Marshallese 88.5%; US white

6.5%; other Pacific islanders and East Asians 5.0%. **Religious affiliation** (1995): Protestant 62.8%; Roman Catholic 7.1%; Mormon 3.1%; Jehovah's Witness 1.0%; other 26.0%. **Major towns** (1999): Majuro (Rita) 19,300; Ebeye 9,300; Laura 2,300; Ajeltake 1,200; Enewetak 820. **Location:** Oceania, group of atolls and reefs in the North Pacific Ocean, halfway between Hawaii and Papua New Guinea.

Vital statistics

Birth rate per 1,000 population (2003): 34.2 (world avg. 21.3). **Death rate** per 1,000 population (2003): 5.0 (world avg. 9.1). **Natural increase rate** per 1,000 population (2003): 29.2 (world avg. 12.2). **Total fertility rate** (avg. births per childbearing woman; 2003): 4.1. **Life expectancy** at birth (2003): male 67.4 years; female 71.4 years.

National economy

Budget (2002). *Revenue:* $83,600,000 (US government grants 70.3%, tax revenue 22.2%, nontax revenue 7.5%). *Expenditures:* $74,000,000 (current expenditure 79.3%, capital expenditure 20.7%). **Public debt** (external, outstanding; 1996–97): $124,900,000. **Production** (metric tons except as noted). *Agriculture, forestry, fishing* (value of production for household consumption in $'000; 1999): fish 3,920; pork 1,496; breadfruit 646; fish catch (2002) 38,242, of which skipjack 37,057. *Mining and quarrying:* for local construction only. *Manufacturing* (2002): copra 2,653; coconut oil and processed (chilled or frozen) fish are important products; the manufacture of handicrafts and personal items (clothing, mats, boats, etc.) by individuals is also significant. *Energy production (consumption):* electricity (kW-hr; 2002) 79,764,000 (79,764,000). **Household income and expenditure.** Average household size (2000) 7.8; annual median income per household (1999) $6,840; expenditure (2003): food 35.9%, housing and energy 17.1%, transportation 13.7%, education and communication 6.6%, clothing 4.3%. **Gross national product** (2003): $143,000,000 ($2,710 per capita). **Population economically active** (1999): total 14,677; activity rate of total population 28.9% (participation rates: over age 15, 51.1%; female 34.1%; unemployed 30.9%). **Tourism** (2002): receipts $4,000,000. **Land use** as % of total land area (2000): in temporary crops 17%, in permanent crops 39%, in pasture 22%.

Foreign trade

Imports (2000-c.i.f.): $68,200,000 (mineral fuels and lubricants 43.6%; machinery and transport equipment 16.9%; food, beverages, and tobacco 10.9%). *Major import sources:* US 61.4%; Japan 5.1%; Australia 2.0%; Hong Kong 1.9%; Taiwan 1.3%. **Exports** (2000-f.o.b.): $7,300,000 (copra cake 16.2%; crude coconut oil 14.7%; aquarium fish 6.2%). *Major export destinations:* US 71%; other 29%.

Transport and communications

Transport. *Roads:* only Majuro and Kwajalein have paved roads. *Vehicles:* passenger cars 1,910; trucks and buses 193. *Air transport* (2001; Air Marshall Islands only): passenger-km 24,972,000; metric ton-km cargo 183,000; airports (2002) 32. **Communications,** in total units (units per 1,000 persons).

Telephone main lines (2003): 4,500 (83); cellular telephone subscribers (2003): 600 (11); personal computers (2002): 3,000 (56); Internet users (2003): 1,400 (26).

Education and health

Educational attainment (1999). Percentage of population age 25 and over having: no formal schooling 3.1%; elementary education 35.5%; secondary 46.5%; some higher 12.3%; undergraduate degree 1.7%; advanced degree 0.9%. **Literacy** (latest): total population age 15 and over literate 19,377 (91.2%); males literate 9,993 (92.4%); females literate 9,384 (90.0%). **Health:** physicians (1997) 34 (1 per 1,452 persons); hospital beds (2002) 140 (1 per 380 persons); infant mortality rate per 1,000 live births (2003) 31.6.

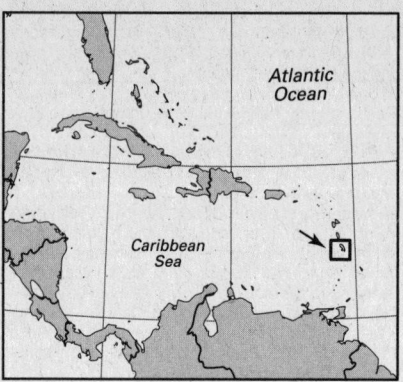

Military

The US provides for the defense of the Republic of the Marshall Islands under the 1984 and 2003 compacts of free association.

Background

The islands were sighted in 1529 by the Spanish navigator Álvaro Saavedra. Germany purchased them from Spain in 1899, and Japan seized them in 1914. During World War II the US took Kwajalein and Enewetak, and the Marshall Islands were made part of a UN trust territory under US jurisdiction in 1947. Bikini and Enewetak atolls served as testing grounds for US nuclear weapons from 1946 to 1958. The country became an internally self-governing republic in 1979. In 1986 it became fully self-governing when it entered into a Compact of Free Association with the US, which was renewed in 2003.

Recent Developments

In a major report in September 2004, the Asian Development Bank identified economic dependence on the US and public health on Majuro Atoll as significant issues for the Marshall Islands. On Majuro, rapid urbanization had led to overcrowding, inadequate infrastructure, contaminated water supplies, and poor waste disposal.

Internet resources: <http://marshall.csu.edu.au>.

Martinique

Official name: Département de la Martinique (Department of Martinique). **Political status:** overseas department (France) with two legislative houses (General Council [45]; Regional Council [41]). **Chief of state:** President Jacques Chirac of France (from 1995). **Head of government:** Prefect (for France) Yves Dassonville (from 9 Feb 2004); President of the General Council (for Martinique) Claude Lise (from 1992). **Capital:** Fort-de-France. **Official language:** French. **Official religion:** none. **Monetary unit:** 1 euro (€) = 100 cents; valuation (7 Jul 2005) $1 = €0.84; at conversion on 1 Jan 2002, €1 = 6.56 French francs (F).

Demography

Area: 436 sq mi, 1,128 sq km. **Population** (2004): 395,000. **Density** (2004): persons per sq mi 906.0, persons per sq km 350.2. **Urban** (2001): 95.2%. **Sex distribution** (2001): male 49.47%; female 50.53%. **Age breakdown** (2001): under 15, 23.1%; 15–29, 23.3%; 30–44, 26.3%; 45–59, 13.8%; 60–74, 9.1%; 75 and over, 4.4%. **Ethnic composition** (2000): mixed race (black/white/Asian) 93.4%; French (metropolitan and Martinique white) 3.0%; East Indian 1.9%; other 1.7%. **Religious affiliation** (1995): Roman Catholic 86.5%; Protestant 8.0% (mostly Seventh-day Adventist); Jehovah's Witness 1.6%; other 3.9%, including Hindu, syncretist, and nonreligious. **Major communes** (1999): Fort-de-France 94,049; Le Lamentin 35,460; Le Robert 21,201; Schoelcher 20,845; Sainte-Marie 20,058. **Location:** island in Atlantic Ocean and the Caribbean Sea, between Dominica and Saint Lucia.

Vital statistics

Birth rate per 1,000 population (2003): 15.0 (world avg. 21.3); (1997) legitimate 31.8%. **Death rate** per 1,000 population (2003): 6.4 (world avg. 9.1). **Natural increase rate** per 1,000 population (2003): 8.6 (world avg. 12.2). **Total fertility rate** (avg. births per childbearing woman; 2003): 1.8. **Marriage rate** per 1,000 population (1999): 4.2. **Divorce rate** per 1,000 population (1999): 0.9. **Life expectancy** at birth (2003): male 79.3 years; female 78.2 years.

National economy

Budget (1999). *Revenue:* F 1,298,000,000 (general receipts from French central government and local administrative bodies 45.0%; tax receipts 34.0%, of which indirect taxes 19.5%, direct taxes 14.5%). *Expenditures:* F 1,298,000,000 (health and social assistance 42.0%; wages and salaries 16.7%; other administrative services 7.2%; debt amortization 5.0%). **Public debt** (1994): $186,700,000. **Production** (metric tons except as noted). *Agriculture, forestry, fishing* (2002): bananas 303,800, sugarcane 207,000, pineapples 18,000; livestock (number of live animals) 35,000 pigs, 34,000 sheep, 25,000 cattle; roundwood (2001) 12,000 cu m; fish catch (2001) 6,251. *Mining and quarrying* (2001): salt 200,000, pumice 130,000. *Manufacturing* (2002): cement

1 metric ton = about 1.1 short tons;   1 kilometer = 0.6 mi (statute);   1 metric ton-km cargo = about 0.68 short ton-mi cargo;   c.i.f.: cost, insurance, and freight;   f.o.b.: free on board

(2001) 220,000; sugar 5,340; rum 91,629 hectoliters. *Energy production (consumption):* electricity (kW-hr; 2000) 1,085,000,000 (1,085,000,000); crude petroleum (barrels; 2000) none (6,000,000); petroleum products (2000) 751,000 (575,000). **Household income and expenditure.** Average household size (1999) 3.0; annual net income per household (1997) €29,516; sources of income (1997): wages and salaries 49.0%, inheritance or endowment 16.4%, self-employment 14.7%, other 19.9%; expenditure (1993): food and beverages 32.1%, transportation and communications 20.7%, housing and energy 10.6%, household durable goods 9.4%, clothing and footwear 8.0%. **Tourism** (2001): receipts from visitors $237,000,000; number of visitors 654,000. **Gross domestic product** (2000): $5,064,-000,000 ($13,160 per capita). **Population economically active** (1998): total 165,900; activity rate of total population 43.7% (participation rates: ages 15–64, 70.7%; female 45.9%; unemployed [March 2003] 22.2%). **Land use** as % of total land area (2000): in temporary crops 10%, in permanent crops 9%, in pasture 11%; overall forest area 44%.

Foreign trade

Imports (2001-c.i.f.): €1,878,000,000 (consumer goods 20%, processed foods, beverages, and tobacco 18%, automobiles 12%). *Major import sources* (2000): France 63.5%; Venezuela 5.8%; Germany 3.9%; Italy 3.1%; Netherlands Antilles 2.3%. **Exports** (2001-f.o.b.): €274,000,000 (bananas 35%, processed foods and beverages [significantly rum] 21%, machinery and apparatus 15%, refined petroleum 9%). *Major export destinations* (2000): France 57.8%; Guadeloupe 21.4%; French Guiana 3.7%; UK 3.4%; Belgium 2.7%.

Transport and communications

Transport. *Roads* (1994): total length 2,077 km (paved [1988] 75%). *Vehicles* (1998): passenger cars 147,589; trucks and buses 35,615. *Air transport* (2001): passenger arrivals 706,929, passenger departures 701,597; cargo loaded 5,656 metric tons; cargo unloaded 9,303 metric tons; airports (2000) 1. **Communications,** in total units (units per 1,000 persons). Daily newspaper circulation (1996): 32,000 (83); radios (1997): 82,000 (213); televisions (1999): 66,000 (168); telephone main lines (2001): 172,192 (417); cellular telephone subscribers (2002): 319,900 (790); personal computers (2001): 52,000 (130); Internet users (2001): 40,000 (100).

Education and health

Educational attainment (1990). Percentage of population age 25 and over having: incomplete primary, or no declaration 54.3%; primary education 18.0%; secondary 20.0%; higher 7.7%. **Health** (2000): physicians 762 (1 per 507 persons); hospital beds 2,674 (1 per 144 persons); infant mortality rate per 1,000 live births (2003) 7.4. **Food** (1998): daily per capita caloric intake 2,865 (vegetable products 75%, animal products 25%); 118% of FAO recommended minimum.

Military

Total active duty personnel (2004): 4,100 French troops.

Background

Carib Indians, who had ousted earlier Arawak inhabitants, resided on the island when Christopher Columbus visited it in 1502. In 1635 the French established a colony there. The British captured and held the island in 1762–63 and again during the Napoleonic Wars, but each time it was returned to France. Made a department of France in 1946, Martinique remains under French rule despite a 1970s independence movement.

Recent Developments

French Pres. Jacques Chirac gave a clear hint in 2000 that the hitherto highly centralized relationship between Paris and French overseas departments might be relaxed and that Martinique might enjoy more local control in the future. As a part of France, Martinique joined in the adoption of the euro in 2002.

Internet resources: <www.martinique.org>.

Mauritania

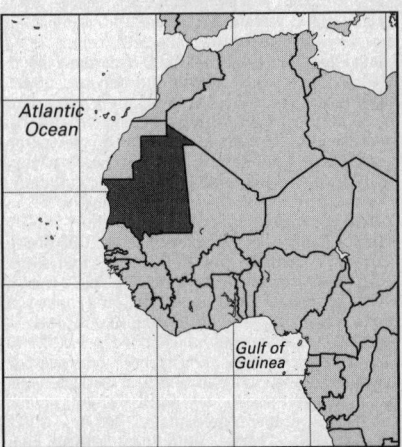

Official name: Al-Jumhuriyah al-Islamiyah al-Muritaniyah (Islamic Republic of Mauritania). **Form of government:** unitary multiparty republic with two legislative houses (Senate [56]; National Assembly [81]). **Head of state and government:** President Maaouya Ould Sid 'Ahmed Taya (from 1984), assisted by Prime Minister Sghair Ould M'Bareck (from 2003). **Capital:** Nouakchott. **Official language:** Arabic (Arabic, Fulani, Soninke, and Wolof are national languages). **Official religion:** Islam. **Monetary unit:** 1 ouguiya (UM) = 5 khoums; valuation (7 Jul 2005) $1 = UM 268.17.

Demography

Area: 398,000 sq mi, 1,030,700 sq km. **Population** (2004): 2,774,000. **Density** (2004): persons per sq mi 7.0, persons per sq km 2.7. **Urban** (2000): 57.7%. **Sex distribution** (2000): male 49.51%; female 50.49%. **Age breakdown** (2000): under 15, 43.9%; 15–29, 27.0%; 30–44, 15.9%; 45–59, 7.7%; 60–74, 4.3%; 75 and over, 1.2%. **Ethnic composition**

(1993): Moor 70% (of which about 40% "black" Moor [Haratin, or African Sudanic] and about 30% "white" Moor [Bidan, or Arab-Berber]); other black African 30% (mostly Wolof, Tukulor, Soninke, and Fulani). **Religious affiliation** (2000): Sunni Muslim 99.1%; traditional beliefs 0.5%; Christian 0.3%; other 0.1%. **Major cities** (2000): Nouakchott 558,195; Nouadhibou 72,337; Rosso 48,922; Boghé 37,531; Adel Bagrou 36,007. **Location:** northern Africa, bordering Western Sahara (annexed by Morocco), Algeria, Mali, Senegal, and the North Atlantic Ocean.

Vital statistics

Birth rate per 1,000 population (2003): 42.1 (world avg. 21.3). **Death rate** per 1,000 population (2003): 13.0 (world avg. 9.1). **Natural increase rate** per 1,000 population (2003): 29.1 (world avg. 12.2). **Total fertility rate** (avg. births per childbearing woman; 2003): 6.1. **Life expectancy** at birth (2003): male 49.7 years; female 54.1 years.

National economy

Budget (2002). *Revenue:* UM 101,000,000,000 (fishing royalties 51.2%; tax revenue 38.7%, of which taxes on goods and services 19.3%, income taxes 12.0%, import taxes 6.2%; revenue from public enterprises 4.8%; capital revenue 2.3%; other 3.0%). *Expenditures:* UM 84,400,000,000 (current expenditure 62.1%, of which goods and services 25.6%, wages and salaries 15.4%, interest on public debt 9.8%, defense 5.8%; capital expenditure 37.9%). **Land use** as % of total land area (2000): in temporary crops 0.5%, in permanent crops 0.01%, in pasture 38.3%; overall forest area 0.3%. **Production** (metric tons except as noted). *Agriculture, forestry, fishing* (2002): rice 67,900, millet 51,500, sorghum 25,405; livestock (number of live animals) 7,600,000 sheep, 5,100,000 goats, 1,500,000 cattle; roundwood (2001) 1,470,448 cu m; fish catch (2001) 83,596, of which octopuses 20,308. *Mining and quarrying* (gross weight; 2002): iron ore 9,553,000; gypsum 100,000. *Manufacturing* (value added in $'000,000; 1997): food, beverages, and tobacco products 5.2; machinery, transport equipment, and fabricated metals 3.8; bricks, tiles, and cement 1.6. *Energy production (consumption):* electricity (kW-hr; 2002) 263,972,000 (191,893,000); coal (2000) none (6,000); crude petroleum (barrels; 2000) none (7,147,000); petroleum products (2000) 860,000 (961,000). **Population economically active** (2001): total 786,000; activity rate of total population 30.9% (participation rates: over age 10 [1991] 45.5%; female [1994] 22.9%; unemployed [1999] 21.0%). **Households.** Average household size (2000): 5.3; expenditure (1990): food and beverages 73.1%, clothing and footwear 8.1%, energy and water 7.7%, transportation and communications 2.0%. **Gross national product** (2003): $1,163,000,000 ($430 per capita). **Public debt** (external, outstanding; 2002): $1,984,000,000. **Tourism** (1999): receipts $28,000,000; expenditures $55,000,000.

Foreign trade

Imports (2002): $418,000,000 (capital goods 26.0%; petroleum products 25.8%; food products

12.8%; vehicles and parts 9.3%; construction materials 9.1%). *Major import sources:* France 20.8%; Belgium-Luxembourg 8.8%; Spain 6.7%; Germany 5.6%; Italy 4.2%. **Exports** (2002): $330,300,000 (iron ore 55.6%; fish 43.4%, of which cephalopods 29.0%). *Major export destinations:* Italy 14.8%; France 14.4%; Spain 12.1%; Germany 10.8%; Belgium-Luxembourg 10.3%; Japan 6.4%.

Transport and communications

Transport. *Railroads* (2000): route length 717 km; passenger-km, negligible; (2000) metric ton-km cargo 7,766,000,000. *Roads* (1999): total length 7,891 km (paved 26%). *Vehicles* (1999): passenger cars 9,900; trucks and buses 17,300. *Air transport* (1999; data represent ¹⁄₁₁ of the total scheduled traffic of Air Afrique; Air Afrique was declared bankrupt in February 2002): passenger-km 290,000,000; metric ton-km cargo (1998) 13,524,000; airports (1997) with scheduled flights 9. **Communications**, in total units (units per 1,000 persons). Daily newspaper circulation (1996): 1,000 (0.4); radios (1997): 360,000 (147); televisions (1999): 247,000 (100); telephone main lines (2002): 31,500 (12); cellular telephone subscribers (2003): 300,000 (109); personal computers (2002): 29,000 (11); Internet users (2002): 10,000 (3.7).

Education and health

Educational attainment (2000). Percentage of population age 6 and over having: no formal schooling 43.9%; no formal schooling but literate 2.5%; Islamic schooling 18.4%; primary education 23.2%; lower secondary 5.3%; upper secondary 4.6%; higher technical 0.4%; higher 1.7%. **Literacy** (2000): percentage of total population age 10 and over literate 52.5%; males literate 60.1%; females literate 45.3%. **Health:** physicians (1994) 200 (1 per 11,085 persons); hospital beds (1988) 1,556 (1 per 1,217 persons); infant mortality rate per 1,000 live births (2003) 73.8. **Food** (2001): daily per capita caloric intake 2,764 (vegetable products 84%, animal products 16%); 120% of FAO recommended minimum.

Military

Total active duty personnel (2003): 15,750 (army 95.2%, navy 3.2%, air force 1.6%). **Military expenditure as percentage of GNP** (1999): 4.0% (world 2.4%); per capita expenditure $14.

Background

Inhabited in ancient times by Sanhadja Berbers, in the 11th and 12th centuries Mauritania was the center of the Berber Almoravid movement, which imposed Islam. Arab tribes arrived in the 15th century and formed powerful confederations; the Portuguese also arrived then. France gained control of the coast in 1817 and in 1903 made the territory a protectorate. In 1904 it was added to French West Africa, and later it became a colony. In 1960 Mauritania achieved independence. Its first president was ousted in a 1978 military coup. After a series of military rulers, in 1991 a new constitution was adopted, and multiparty elections were held in 1992. During

1 metric ton = about 1.1 short tons;   1 kilometer = 0.6 mi (statute);   1 metric ton-km cargo = about 0.68 short ton-mi cargo;   c.i.f.: cost, insurance, and freight;   f.o.b.: free on board

the 1990s relations between the government and opposition groups deteriorated, even as there was some success in liberalizing the economy.

Recent Developments

In August 2004 the government of Mauritania appealed to the global community for planes and insecticides to combat a locust plague; massive infestations of the pests were devastating many of Mauritania's fields and pastures, and a major food crisis seemed inevitable. The United Nations World Food Programme estimated in January 2005 that because of the devastation wreaked by the locusts and a continuing drought some 60% of the country's population would lack sufficient food.

Internet resources: <www.ami.mr/fr/defaultfr.htm>.

Mauritius

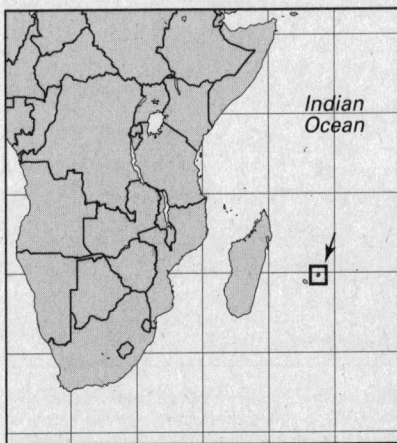

Indian Ocean

Official name: Republic of Mauritius. Form of government: republic with one legislative house (National Assembly [70, including 8 "bonus" seats allocated to minor parties]). Chief of state: President Sir Anerood Jugnauth (from 2003). Head of government: Prime Minister Paul Bérenger (from 2003). Capital: Port Louis. Official language: English. Official religion: none. Monetary unit: 1 Mauritian rupee (Mau Re; plural Mau Rs) = 100 cents; valuation (7 Jul 2005) $1 = Mau Rs 29.25.

Demography

Area: 788 sq mi, 2,040 sq km. Population (2004): 1,233,000. Density (2004): persons per sq mi 1,565, persons per sq km 604.4. Urban (2002): 42.5%. Sex distribution (2003): male 49.49%; female 50.51%. Age breakdown (2000): under 15, 25.2%; 15–29, 26.0%; 30–44, 24.8%; 45–59, 14.9%; 60–74, 6.8%; 75 and over, 2.3%. Ethnic composition (2000): Indo-Pakistani 67.0%; Creole (mixed Caucasian, Indo-Pakistani, and African) 27.4%; Chinese 3.0%; other 2.6%. Religious affiliation (2000): Hindu 49.6%; Christian 32.2%, of which Roman Catholic 23.6%; Muslim 16.6%; Buddhist 0.4%; other 1.2%. Major urban areas (2000): Port Louis

144,303; Beau Bassin-Rose Hill 103,872; Vacoas-Phoenix 100,066; Curepipe 78,920; Quatre Bornes 75,884. Location: island in the Indian Ocean, east of Madagascar.

Vital statistics

Data from 2003 exclude Agalega. Birth rate per 1,000 population (2003): 16.3 (world avg. 21.3). Death rate per 1,000 population (2003): 6.7 (world avg. 9.1). Natural increase rate per 1,000 population (2003): 9.6 (world avg. 12.2). Total fertility rate (avg. births per childbearing woman; 2003): 1.9. Marriage rate per 1,000 population (2003): 8.5. Divorce rate per 1,000 population (2003): 0.9. Life expectancy at birth (2003): male 68.6 years; female 75.5 years.

National economy

Budget (2001–02). Revenue: Mau Rs 28,319,-500,000 (tax revenue 82.2%, of which taxes on goods and services 39.2%, import duties 20.8%, income tax 12.6%; nontax revenue 16.2%; grants 1.1%). Expenditures: Mau Rs 33,385,800,000 (social security 21.8%; government services 18.1%; education 15.4%; economic services 12.3%; interest on debt 10.6%; health 8.7%). Tourism (2001): receipts from visitors $612,000,000; expenditures by nationals abroad $204,000,000. Public debt (external, outstanding; 2002): $832,000,000. Gross national product (2003): $5,012,000,000 ($4,090 per capita). Production (metric tons except as noted). Agriculture, forestry, fishing (2002): sugarcane 4,874,000, vegetables 21,000, roots and tubers 15,000; livestock (number of live animals) 93,000 goats, 28,000 cattle, 14,000 pigs; roundwood (2001) 17,000 cu m; fish catch (2001) 10,753. Manufacturing (value added in Mau Rs '000,000; 2001): apparel 9,651; food products 2,757; beverages and tobacco 1,717. Energy production (consumption): electricity (kW-hr; 2000) 1,777,000,000 (1,777,-000,000); coal (2000) none (254,000); petroleum products (2000) none (724,000). Population economically active (2002): total 541,100; activity rate of total population 44.7% (participation rates: ages 15 and over, 59.8%; female 34.6%; unemployed 9.7%). Household income and expenditure. Average household size (2000) 4.2; annual income per household (2001–02) Mau Rs 170,784; sources of income (1990): salaries and wages 48.4%, entrepreneurial income 41.2%, transfer payments 10.4%; expenditure (2001–02): food and nonalcoholic beverages 31.9%, transportation 12.7%, housing and energy 9.4%, alcoholic beverages and tobacco products 9.1%, clothing and footwear 6.4%. Land use as % of total land area (2000): in temporary crops 49%, in permanent crops 3%, in pasture 3%; overall forest area 8%.

Foreign trade

Imports (2001-c.i.f.): Mau Rs 57,940,000,000 (fabrics and yarn 18.3%; food and live animals 14.3%; machinery and apparatus 14.3%; refined petroleum 9.5%; transport equipment 8.1%). Major import sources: South Africa 13.9%; France 9.3%; India 7.9%; China 7.1%; Germany 5.4%. Exports (2001-f.o.b.): Mau Rs 47,511,000,000 (domestic exports 91.8%, of which clothing 54.4%, sugar 18.0%, fabric, yarn, and made-up articles 4.7%; reexports 4.1%; ships' stores and bunkers 4.1%). Major export destinations: UK

31.3%; US 20.3%; France 18.7%; Madagascar 6.1%; Italy 3.8%.

Transport and communications

Transport. *Roads* (1998): total length 1,905 km (paved 93%). *Vehicles* (2002): passenger cars 61,885; trucks and buses 13,892. *Air transport* (2003; Air Mauritius only): passenger-km 5,213,-000,000; metric ton-km cargo 194,510,000; airports (1998) with scheduled flights 1. **Communications,** in total units (units per 1,000 persons). Daily newspaper circulation (2000): 84,300 (71); radios (2000): 450,000 (379); televisions (2000): 318,000 (268); telephone main lines (2003): 348,200 (285); cellular telephone subscribers (2003): 462,400 (379); personal computers (2002): 180,000 (149); Internet users (2003): 150,000 (123).

Education and health

Educational attainment (2000). Percentage of population age 25 and over having: no formal education 12.3%; primary 44.1%; lower secondary 23.2%; upper secondary/some higher 17.3%; complete higher 2.6%; unknown 0.5%. **Literacy** (2000): percentage of total population age 12 and over literate 85.1%; males literate 88.7%; females literate 81.6%. **Health** (2003): physicians 1,172 (1 per 1,043 persons); hospital beds 3,827 (1 per 320 persons); infant mortality rate per 1,000 live births 13.2. **Food** (2001): daily per capita caloric intake 2,995 (vegetable products 86%, animal products 14%); 132% of FAO recommended minimum.

Military

Total active duty personnel (2003): none; however, a special 2,000-person paramilitary force ensures internal security. **Military expenditure as percentage of GNP** (1999): 0.2% (world 2.4%); per capita expenditure $7.

Did you know? In early 2005, Mauritius launched an initiative to make it the first country in the world to achieve complete wireless broadband access.

Background

The island was visited by the Portuguese in the early 16th century. The Dutch took possession in 1598 and made attempts to settle it (1638–58 and 1664–1710) before abandoning it to pirates. The French East India Company occupied Mauritius in 1721 and administered it until the French government took over in 1767. Sugar production allowed the colony to prosper. The British captured the island in 1810 and were granted formal control in 1814. In the late 19th century, competition from beet sugar and the opening of the Suez Canal caused an economic decline. After World War II, Mauritius adopted political and economic reforms, and in 1968 it became an independent state within the Commonwealth. In 1992 it became a republic. It experienced political unrest during the 1990s.

Recent Developments

A diplomatic row erupted in June 2004 with the United Kingdom over the sovereignty of the Chagos Archipelago, or British Indian Ocean Territory, 60 islands 965 km (600 mi) north of Mauritius, and the right of the Ilois—who had been forcibly removed by the UK after it bought the islands from Mauritius in 1965—to return. The disputed archipelago included Diego Garcia, an atoll that the British had cleared of all inhabitants to enable the construction of a US naval support base.

Internet resources: <www.mauritius.net>.

Mayotte

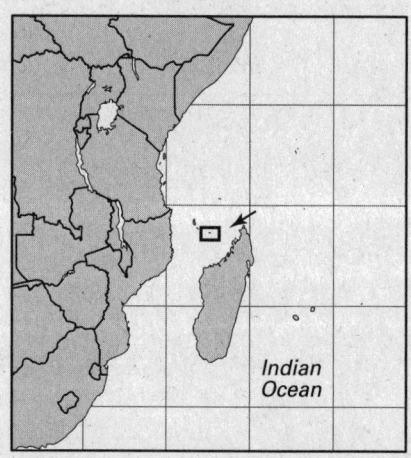

Indian Ocean

Official name: Collectivité Départementale de Mayotte (Departmental Collectivity of Mayotte); known as Mahoré or Maore in Shimaoré, the local Swahili-based language. **Political status:** overseas dependency of France with one legislative house (General Council [19]); claimed by Comoros since 1975. **Chief of state:** President of France Jacques Chirac (from 1995). **Head of government:** President of the General Council Said Omar Oili (from 2 Apr 2004). **Capital:** Mamoudzou. **Official language:** French. **Official religion:** none. **Monetary unit:** 1 euro (€) = 100 cents; valuation (7 Jul 2005) $1 = €0.84; at conversion on 1 Jan 2002, €1 = 6.56 French francs (F).

Demography

Area: 144.1 sq mi, 373.3 sq km. **Population** (2004): 172,000. **Density** (2004): persons per sq mi 1,194, persons per sq km 459.9. **Sex distribution** (2002): male 50.10%; female 49.90%. **Age breakdown** (2002): under 15, 42.0%; 15–29, 29.0%; 30–44, 17.0%; 45–59, 7.0%; 60 and over, 5.0%. **Place of birth** (2002): Mayotte (including 2–4% for metropolitan France) 65.6% (nearly all ethnic Comorian); nearby islands of the Comoros 33.1% (nearly all ethnic Comorian); other 1.3%. **Ethnic composition** (2000): Comorian (Mauri, Mahorais; a mixture of

1 metric ton = about 1.1 short tons;   1 kilometer = 0.6 mi (statute);   1 metric ton-km cargo = about 0.68 short ton-mi cargo;   c.i.f.: cost, insurance, and freight;   f.o.b.: free on board

Bantu, Arab, and Malagasy peoples) 92.3%; Swahili 3.2%; white (French) 1.8%; Makua 1.0%; other 1.7%. **Religious affiliation** (2000): Sunni Muslim 96.5%; Christian, principally Roman Catholic, 2.2%; other 1.3%. **Major communes** (2002): Mamoudzou 45,485; Koungou 15,383; Dzaoudzi 12,308. **Location:** island in the Indian Ocean, between the northern tip of Madagascar and the African mainland.

Vital statistics

Birth rate per 1,000 population (2003): 42.9 (world avg. 21.3). **Death rate** per 1,000 population (2003): 8.3 (world avg. 9.1). **Natural increase rate** per 1,000 population (2003): 34.6 (world avg. 12.2). **Total fertility rate** (avg. births per childbearing woman; 2003): 6.1. **Life expectancy** at birth (2003): male 58.5; female 62.8.

National economy

Budget (1997). *Revenue:* F 1,022,400,000 (1993; current revenue 68.8%, of which subsidies 40.0%, indirect taxes 16.8%, direct taxes 4.9%; development revenue 31.2%, of which loans 11.6%, subsidies 7.9%). *Expenditures:* F 964,200,000 (current expenditure 75.2%; development expenditure 24.8%). **Production** (metric tons except as noted). *Agriculture, forestry, fishing* (1997): bananas 30,200, cassava 10,000, cinnamon 27,533 kg; livestock (number of live animals; 1997) 25,000 goats, 17,000 cattle, 2,000 sheep; fish catch (1999) 1,502. *Manufacturing:* mostly processing of agricultural products and materials used in housing construction (including siding and roofing materials, joinery, and latticework). *Energy production (consumption):* electricity (kW-hr; 2002) 107,056,000 (107,056,000). **Tourism** (number of visitors; 2001): 35,000; receipts (1999) $10,000,000. **Population economically active** (1997): total 42,896; activity rate of total population 32.7% (participation rates: ages 15–64, 58.6%; female 43.4%; unemployed 41.5%). **Gross national product** (2000): $398,000,000 ($2,700 per capita). **Households.** Average household size (1997) 4.6; expenditure (1991): food 42.2%, clothing and footwear 31.5%, household furnishings 8.8%, energy and water 6.8%, transportation 5.1%.

Foreign trade

Imports (2002): €181,800,000 (food products 27.0%; machinery and apparatus 18.9%; transport equipment 16.1%; chemicals 8.7%; metals and metal products 7.4%). *Major import sources* (1997): France 66.0%; South Africa 14.0%; Asia 11.0%. **Exports** (2002): €6,300,000 (ylang-ylang 11.1%; vanilla 3.2%; unspecified commodities 85.7%). *Major export destinations* (1997): France 80.0%; Comoros 15.0%.

Transport and communications

Transport. *Roads* (1998): total length 233 km (paved 77%). *Vehicles* (1998): 8,213. *Air transport* (2002): passenger arrivals and departures 133,686; cargo unloaded and loaded 1,048 metric tons; airports (2002) with scheduled flights 1. **Communications,** in total units (units per 1,000 persons). Radios (1996): 50,000 (427); televisions (1999): 3,500 (30); telephone main lines (2001): 10,000 (70); cellular telephone subscribers (2002): 21,700 (147).

Education and health

Educational attainment (2002). Percentage of population age 15 and over having: no formal education 46%; primary education 25%; lower secondary 16%; upper secondary 8%; higher 5%. **Literacy** (1997): total population age 15 and over literate 63,053 (86.1%). **Health:** physicians (1997) 57 (1 per 2,304 persons); hospital beds 186 (1 per 706 persons); infant mortality rate per 1,000 live births (2003) 65.9.

Military

Total active duty personnel (2003): 3,600 French troops are assigned to Mayotte and Réunion.

Background

Originally inhabited by descendants of Bantu and Malayo-Indonesian peoples, Mayotte was converted to Islam by Arab invaders in the 15th century. Taken by a Malagasy tribe from Madagascar at the end of the 18th century, it came under French control in 1843. Together with the other Comoros islands and Madagascar, it became part of a single French overseas territory in the early 20th century. It has been administered separately since 1975, when the three northernmost islands of the Comoros declared independence.

Recent Developments

Brigitte Girardin, the French minister for overseas territories, visited Mayotte in January 2004 to discuss the struggle against illegal immigration, which the minister intended to stop by increasing the frontier police force by 50%. Girardin also announced plans to build an improved maritime surveillance system. Penalties for the traffickers and the employers of illegal immigrants were also increased. Girardin judged that more than a quarter of the island's population were clandestine arrivals.

Internet resources: <www.mayotte-tourisme.com>.

Mexico

Official name: Estados Unidos Mexicanos (United Mexican States). **Form of government:** federal republic with two legislative houses (Senate [128]; Chamber of Deputies [500]). **Head of state and government:** President Vicente Fox Quesada (from 2000). **Capital:** Mexico City. **Official language:** Spanish. **Official religion:** none. **Monetary unit:** 1 Mexican peso (Mex$) = 100 centavos; valuation (7 Jul 2005) US$1 = Mex$10.80.

Demography

Area: 758,449 sq mi, 1,964,375 sq km. **Population** (2004): 105,447,000. **Density** (2004): persons per sq mi 139.0, persons per sq km 53.7. **Urban** (2002): 74.6%. **Sex distribution** (2002): male 48.82%; female 51.18%. **Age breakdown** (2000): under 15, 34.3%; 15–29, 28.5%; 30–44, 19.5%; 45–59, 10.5%; 60–74, 5.3%; 75 and over, 1.9%. **Ethnic composition** (2000): mestizo 64.3%; Amerindian 18.0%, of which detribalized 10.5%; Mexican white 15.0%; Arab 1.0%; Mexican black 0.5%; Spaniard 0.3%; US white 0.2%; other 0.7%. **Religious affiliation** (2000):

Gulf of
Mexico

Pacific Ocean

Caribbean
Sea

Roman Catholic 90.4%; Protestant (including Evangelical) 3.8%; other 5.8%. **Major cities** (2000): Mexico City 8,605,239 (urban agglomeration [2001] 18,268,000); Guadalajara 1,646,183 (urban agglomeration 3,697,000); Puebla 1,271,673 (urban agglomeration 1,888,000); Ciudad Netzahualcóyotl 1,225,083; Juárez 1,187,275; Tijuana 1,148,681; Monterrey 1,110,909 (urban agglomeration 3,267,000); León 1,020,818; Mérida 662,530; Chihuahua 657,876. **Location:** middle America, bordering the US, the Gulf of Mexico, the Caribbean Sea, Belize, Guatemala, and the North Pacific Ocean. **Place of birth** (1990): 93.1% native-born; 6.9% foreign-born and unknown. **Households.** Total households (2000) 21,954,733; distribution by size (2000): 1 person 6.0%, 2 persons 12.3%, 3 persons 17.2%, 4 persons 21.8%, 5 persons 17.7%, 6 persons 10.9%, 7 or more persons 14.1%. **Emigration** (2000): legal immigrants into the US 173,900.

Vital statistics

Birth rate per 1,000 population (2003): 21.9 (world avg. 21.3). **Death rate** per 1,000 population (2003): 4.7 (world avg. 9.1). **Natural increase rate** per 1,000 population (2003): 17.2 (world avg. 12.2). **Total fertility rate** (avg. births per childbearing woman; 2002): 2.3. **Marriage rate** per 1,000 population (2001): 6.6. **Divorce rate** per 1,000 population (2001): 0.6. **Life expectancy** at birth (2003): male 71.9 years; female 77.6 years.

Social indicators

Access to services (2000). Proportion of dwellings having: electricity 94.8%; piped water supply 83.3%; drained sewage 76.2%. **Quality of working life.** Average workweek (1999): 44.4 hours (manufacturing only). Annual rate (1992) per 100,000 insured workers for: temporary disability 6,426; indemnification for permanent injury 239; death 18. Labor stoppages (2001): 35, involving 23,234 workers. **Social participation.** Eligible voters participating in last national election (July 2000): 41.7%. Practicing religious population in total affiliated population: national average of weekly attendance (1993) 11%. **Social deviance** (1991). Criminal cases tried by local authorities per 100,000 population for: murder 60.3; rape 22.4; other assault 301.0; theft 703.8. Incidence per 100,000 in general population of: alcoholism (2000) 7.6; drug and substance abuse 26.6; suicide (2001) 3.1.

National economy

Gross national product (2003): US$637,159,000,000 (US$6,230 per capita). **Budget** (2001). *Revenue:* Mex$939,114,500,000 (income tax 30.4%, VAT 22.2%, royalties 21.7%, excise tax 11.8%, import duties 3.1%, other 10.8%). *Expenditures:* Mex$996,950,600,000 (current expenditure 63.4%, of which social security and welfare 41.8%, interest on public debt 16.7%; capital expenditure 36.6%). **Public debt** (external, outstanding; 2002): US$76,327,000,000. **Tourism** (2002): receipts from visitors US$8,858,000,000; expenditures by nationals abroad US$6,060,000,000. **Production** (metric tons except as noted). *Agriculture, forestry, fishing* (2002): sugarcane 46,000,000, corn (maize) 17,500,000, sorghum 5,800,000, oranges 3,844,000, wheat 3,273,000, tomatoes 2,084,000, bananas 2,077,000, chilies and green peppers 1,756,000, lemons and limes 1,680,000, dry beans 1,648,000, mangoes 1,413,000, watermelons 1,226,000, coconuts 959,000, avocados 897,000, barley 839,000, papayas 689,000, pineapples 585,000, grapes 446,000, carrots 379,000, coffee (green) 320,000, cauliflower 200,000; livestock (number of live animals) 30,600,000 cattle, 17,000,000 pigs, 9,400,000 goats, 8,100,000 ducks, 6,700,000 sheep, 6,255,000 horses, 5,850,000 turkeys, 3,280,000 mules, 3,260,000 asses, 520,800,000 chickens; roundwood (2001) 45,156,000 cu m; fish catch (2001) 1,475,000. *Mining and quarrying* (2002): bismuth 1,126 (metal content; world rank: 1); celestite 94,015 (world rank: 1); silver 2,747,000 kg (metal content; world rank: 1); fluorite 622,000 (world rank: 2); cadmium 1,609 (metal content; world rank: 4); lead 138,700 (metal content; world rank: 5); gypsum 6,740,000 (world rank: 6); zinc 446,100 (metal content; world rank: 6); sulfur 1,460,000 (world rank: 9); copper 329,900 (metal content; world rank: 12); gold 21,324 kg (world rank: 19); iron ore 5,965,000 (metal content). *Manufacturing* (value added in US$'000,000; 2000): motor vehicles and parts 10,718; food products 8,883; paints, soaps, pharmaceuticals 7,044; beverages 5,422; bricks, cement, ceramics 3,580; iron and steel 2,891; paper and paper products 2,243; basic chemicals 1,682; fabricated metal products 1,518. *Energy production (consumption):* electricity (kW-hr; 2003) 263,488,000,000 ([2000] 229,747,000,000); hard coal (2000) 2,214,000 (2,724,000); lignite (2000) 9,130,000 (9,570,000); crude petroleum (barrels; 2003) 1,244,000,000 ([2000] 467,393,000); petroleum products (2000) 73,045,000 (87,048,000); natural gas (cu m; 2003) 47,377,000,000 ([2000] 36,953,000,000). **Household income and expenditure.** Average household size (2000) 4.4; income per household (2000) Mex$15,762; sources of income (2000): wages and salaries 63.4%, property and entrepreneurship 23.6%, transfer payments 10.0%, other 2.9%; expenditure (2000): food, beverages, and tobacco 29.9%, transportation and communications 17.8%, education 17.3%, housing (includes household furnishings) 16.5%, clothing and footwear 5.8%. **Population economically active** (2001): total 39,682,800; activity rate of total population 39.9% (participation rates: ages 15–64 [1999] 63.4%; female 29.9%; unemployed [2002] 4.4%). **Land use** as % of total land area (2000): in temporary crops 13.0%, in permanent crops 1.3%, in pasture 41.9%; overall forest area 28.9%.

1 metric ton = about 1.1 short tons;   1 kilometer = 0.6 mi (statute);   1 metric ton-km cargo = about 0.68 short ton-mi cargo;   c.i.f.: cost, insurance, and freight;   f.o.b.: free on board

Foreign trade

Imports (2002): US$168,679,000,000 (non-maquiladora sector 64.8%, of which machinery and apparatus 18.9%, transport and communications equipment 13.0%, chemicals and chemical products 7.4%, processed food, beverages, and tobacco 3.7%; maquiladora sector 35.2%, of which electrical machinery, apparatus, and electronics 15.9%, non-electrical machinery and apparatus 5.4%, textiles and clothing 3.3%, rubber and plastic products 3.0%). *Major import sources:* US 63.2%; Japan 5.5%; China 3.7%; Germany 3.6%; Canada 2.7%; Taiwan 2.5%; South Korea 2.3%. **Exports** (2002): US$160,682,000,000 (non-maquiladora sector 51.4%, of which road vehicles and parts 16.0%, machinery and apparatus 8.9%, crude petroleum 8.2%; maquiladora sector 48.6%, of which electrical machinery, apparatus, and electronics 24.2%, nonelectrical machinery and apparatus 10.2%, textiles and clothing 4.3%). *Major export destinations:* US 89.0%; Canada 1.7%; South America 1.5%; Caribbean countries 1.4%; Central America 1.1%; Germany 0.9%; Spain 0.8%.

Transport and communications

Transport. *Railroads* (2003): route length 26,655 km; passenger-km 67,000,000; metric ton-km cargo 54,813,000,000. *Roads* (2003): total length 348,529 km (paved 33%). *Vehicles* (1999): passenger cars 9,842,006; trucks and buses 4,749,789. *Air transport* (2003; AeroMexico and Mexicana only): passenger-km 25,409,000,000; metric ton-km cargo 145,351,000,000; airports (2001) 85. **Communications,** in total units (units per 1,000 persons). Daily newspaper circulation (2000): 9,580,000 (98); radios (2000): 32,300,000 (330); televisions (2000): 27,700,000 (283); telephone main lines (2002): 14,941,600 (147); cellular telephone subscribers (2002): 25,928,000 (254); personal computers (2002): 8,353,000 (83); Internet users (2002): 10,033,000 (98).

Education and health

Educational attainment (2000). Population age 15 and over having: no primary education 10.3%; some primary 18.1%; completed primary 19.4%; incomplete secondary 5.3%; complete secondary 19.1%; some higher 16.8%; higher 11.0%. **Literacy** (2000): total population age 15 and over literate 91.4%; males literate 93.4%; females literate 89.5%. **Health** (2002): physicians 140,286 (1 per 734 persons); hospital beds 76,529 (1 per 1,346 persons); infant mortality rate per 1,000 live births (2002) 17.4. **Food** (2001): daily per capita caloric intake 3,160 (vegetable products 82%, animal products 18%); 136% of FAO recommended minimum.

Military

Total active duty personnel (2003): 192,770 (army 74.7%, navy 19.2%, air force 6.1%). **Military expenditure as percentage of GNP** (1999): 0.6% (world 2.4%); per capita expenditure $27.

Background

Inhabited for more than 20,000 years, Mexico produced great civilizations in AD 100–900, including the Olmec, Toltec, Mayan, and Aztec. The Aztec were conquered in 1521 by Spanish explorer Hernán Cortés, who established Mexico City on the site of the Aztec capital, Tenochtitlán. Francisco de Montejo conquered the remnants of Maya civilization in the mid-16th century, and Mexico became part of the viceroyalty of New Spain. In 1821 rebels negotiated a status quo independence from Spain, and in 1823 a new congress declared Mexico a republic. In 1845 the US voted to annex Texas, initiating the Mexican War. Under the Treaty of Guadalupe Hidalgo in 1848, Mexico ceded a vast territory in what is now the western and southwestern US. The Mexican government endured several rebellions and civil wars in the late 19th and early 20th centuries. During World War II it declared war on the Axis powers (1942), and in the postwar era it was a founding member of the UN (1945) and the Organization of American States (1948). In 1993 it ratified the North American Free Trade Agreement. The election of Vicente Fox to the presidency in 2000 ended 71 years of rule by the Institutional Revolutionary Party.

Recent Developments

The failure of Pres. Vicente Fox Quesada's center-right National Action Party (PAN) to win a congressional majority in the 2003 midterm elections, as well as growing frustration with his inability to secure congressional approval for his principal policy initiatives, eroded Fox's public credibility despite the fact that his personal-approval ratings remained comparatively strong. The greatest controversy was provoked by repeated comments by Martha Sahagún de Fox suggesting that she aspired to succeed her husband in the presidency. The political reaction against Sahagún's possible candidacy proved so strong that in July 2004 she was forced to renounce her presidential ambitions, but other presidential aspirants felt encouraged to initiate their own campaigns scarcely more than halfway through Fox's term in office. The Institutional Revolutionary Party (PRI) regained ground in gubernatorial races in Chihuahua, Durango, Oaxaca, and Veracruz, northern states hitherto identified with the PAN. Another of the year's greatest political controversies involved Andrés Manuel López Obrador, the popular governor of the Federal District. Even in the wake of sensational corruption scandals involving other Party of the Democratic Revolution (PRD) officials, public opinion polls consistently favored López Obrador to win the 2006 presidential race. His candidacy was, however, endangered by judicial charges stemming from his decision—in defiance of a court order—to construct across private land a public-access road to a hospital. In May the federal attorney general initiated legal proceedings against López Obrador by requesting that the Chamber of Deputies lift his immunity from prosecution as an elected public official, an action that might eventually lead to his formal conviction, removal from office, and ineligibility to hold future public office. These actions touched off a political firestorm that continued into mid-2005, with the PRD and its allies arguing that the Fox administration was manipulating the judicial process in order to eliminate its most visible partisan rival (and the PRD's best-ever chance of winning the presidency).

Internet resources: <www.visitmexico.com>.

Micronesia

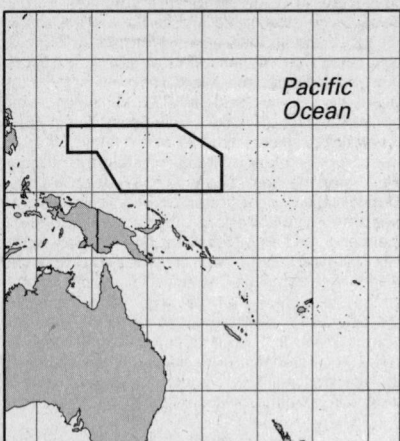

Pacific
Ocean

Official name: Federated States of Micronesia. **Form of government:** federal nonparty republic in free association with the US with one legislative house (Congress [14]). **Head of state and government:** President Joseph J. Urusemal (from 2003). **Capital:** Palikir, on Pohnpei. **Official language:** none. **Official religion:** none. **Monetary unit:** 1 US dollar ($) = 100 cents.

Demography

Area: 270.8 sq mi, 701.4 sq km. **Population** (2004): 114,000. **Density** (2004): persons per sq mi 420.7, persons per sq km 162.6. **Urban** (2000): 28.5%. **Sex distribution** (2000): male 50.64%; female 49.36%. **Age breakdown** (2000): under 15, 40.3%; 15–29, 28.4%; 30–44, 16.9%; 45–59, 9.1%; 60–74, 3.9%; 75 and over, 1.4%. **Ethnic composition** (2000): Chuukese/Mortlockese 33.6%; Pohnpeian 24.9%; Yapese 10.6%; Kosraean 5.2%; US white 4.5%; Asian 1.3%; other 19.9%. **Religious affiliation** (2000): Roman Catholic 52.7%; Protestant 41.7%, of which Congregational 40.1%; Mormon 1.0%; other/unknown 4.6%. **Major towns** (2000): Weno, in Chuuk state 13,900; Tol, in Chuuk state 9,500; Palikir, on Pohnpei 6,227; Kolonia, on Pohnpei 5,681; Colonia, on Yap 3,350. **Location:** Oceania, island group in the North Pacific Ocean, northeast of New Guinea.

Vital statistics

Birth rate per 1,000 population (2003): 26.5 (world avg. 21.3). **Death rate** per 1,000 population (2003): 5.1 (world avg. 9.1). **Natural increase rate** per 1,000 population (2003): 21.4 (world avg. 12.2). **Total fertility rate** (avg. births per childbearing woman; 2003): 3.5. **Life expectancy** at birth (2003): male 67.4 years; female 71.0 years.

National economy

Budget (2001–02). *Revenue:* $160,400,000 (external grants 71.2%, tax revenue 17.7%, nontax revenue [including fishing rights fees] 11.1%). *Expendi-*

tures: $154,800,000 (current expenditures 83.4%, capital expenditure 16.6%). **Public debt** (external, outstanding; 2000): $85,700,000. **Population economically active** (2000): total 37,414; activity rate of total population 35.0% (participation rates: ages 15–64, 61.7%; female 42.9%; unemployed 22.0%). **Production** (metric tons except as noted). *Agriculture, fishing* (2002): coconuts 140,000, cassava 11,800, sweet potatoes 3,000; livestock (number of live animals) 32,000 pigs, 13,900 cattle, 4,000 goats; fish catch (2001) 18,100, of which skipjack tuna 10,300, yellowfin tuna 5,300. *Mining and quarrying:* quarrying of sand and aggregate for local construction only. *Manufacturing:* n.a.; however, copra and coconut oil, traditionally important products, are being displaced by garment production; the manufacture of handicrafts and personal items (clothing, mats, boats, etc.) by individuals is also important. *Energy production (consumption):* electricity (kW-hr; 1997) 100,333,000 (100,333,000); petroleum products (1992) none (77,000). **Household income and expenditure.** Average household size (2000) 6.7; annual income per household $8,944 (median income: $4,618); sources of income (1994): wages and salaries 51.8%, operating surplus 23.0%, social security 2.1%; expenditure (1985): food and beverages 73.5%. **Land use** as % of total land area (2000): in temporary crops 6%, in permanent crops 46%, in pasture 16%; overall forest area 22%. **Gross national product** (at current market prices; 2003): $261,000,000 ($2,090 per capita). **Tourism** (2001): receipts from visitors $13,000,000.

Foreign trade

Imports (1999): $12,328,000 (food and live animals 24.8%, mineral fuels 20.3%, machinery and transport equipment 19.5%, beverages and tobacco products 6.0%). *Major import sources* (2000): US 43.9%; Australia 19.8%; Japan 12.5%. **Exports** (1999): $2,128,000 (fish 92.0%, bananas 1.2%). *Major export destinations* (1996): Japan 79.0%; US 18.3%.

Transport and communications

Transport. *Roads* (1990): total length 226 km (paved 17%). *Vehicles* (1998): passenger cars 2,044; trucks and buses 354. *Air transport:* airports (1997) with scheduled flights 4. **Communications,** in total units (units per 1,000 persons). Radios (1996): 70,000 (667); televisions (1999): 2,400 (21); telephone main lines (2001): 10,000 (93); cellular telephone subscribers (2002): 1,800 (150); Internet users (2000): 6,000 (51).

Education and health

Educational attainment (2000). Percentage of population age 25 and over having: no formal schooling 12.3%; primary education 37.0%; some secondary 18.3%; secondary 12.9%; some college 18.4%. **Literacy** (2000): total population age 10 and over literate 72,140 (92.4%); males literate 36,528 (92.9%); females literate 35,612 (91.9%). **Health** (1998): physicians 68 (1 per 1,677 persons); hospital beds (1997) 260 (1 per 447 persons); infant mortality rate per 1,000 live births (2003) 32.4.

---

1 metric ton = about 1.1 short tons;   1 kilometer = 0.6 mi (statute);   1 metric ton-km cargo = about 0.68 short ton-mi cargo;   c.i.f.: cost, insurance, and freight;   f.o.b.: free on board

Military

External security is provided by the US.

Background

The islands of Micronesia were probably settled by people from eastern Melanesia some 3,500 years ago. Europeans first landed on the islands in the 16th century. Spain took control of the islands in 1886, then sold them to Germany in 1899. The islands came under Japanese rule after World War I. They were captured by US forces during World War II, and in 1947 they became a UN trust territory administered by the US. The group of islands centered on the Caroline Islands became an internally self-governing federation in 1979. In 1986 Micronesia entered into a Compact of Free Association with the US, some provisions of which were set to expire in 2001. In the late 1990s the republic was struggling to solve its economic difficulties.

Recent Developments

The Federated States of Micronesia (FSM) ratified its renegotiated Compact of Free Association with the US in May 2004. The compact provided for an investment fund to be built with US contributions of $800,000 a year until the fund reached an estimated $16 million by 2023, at which time income from the fund was expected to replace grants from the US. The Asian Development Bank had agreed to provide $800,000 in technical assistance for the management of the fund.

Internet resources: <www.fsmgov.org>.

Moldova

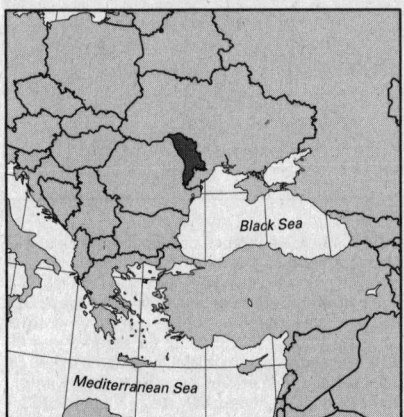

Black Sea

Mediterranean Sea

Official name: Republica Moldova (Republic of Moldova). **Form of government:** unitary parliamentary republic with a single legislative body (Parliament [101]). **Head of state:** President Vladimir Voronin (from 2001). **Head of government:** Prime Minister Vasile Tarlev (from 2001). **Capital:** Chisinau. **Official language:** Romanian (constitutionally designated as Moldovan). **Official religion:** none. **Monetary unit:** 1 Moldovan leu (plural lei) = 100 bani; valuation (7 Jul 2005) free rate, $1 = 12.50 Moldovan lei.

Demography

Area: 13,068 sq mi, 33,845 sq km. **Population** (2004): 4,216,000 (includes Moldovans working abroad). **Density** (2004): persons per sq mi 322.6, persons per sq km 124.6. **Urban** (2002): 45.3%. **Sex distribution** (2002): male 47.84%; female 52.16%. **Age breakdown** (2001): under 15, 22.4%; 15–29, 25.5%; 30–44, 21.1%; 45–59, 16.6%; 60–74, 11.0%; 75 and over, 3.4%. **Ethnic composition** (2000): Moldovan 48.2%; Ukrainian 13.8%; Russian 12.9%; Bulgarian 8.2%; Rom (Gypsy) 6.2%; Gagauz 4.2%; other 6.5%. **Religious affiliation** (1995): Orthodox 46.0%, of which Romanian Orthodox 35.0%, Russian Orthodox 9.5%; Muslim 5.5%; Catholic 1.8%, of which Roman Catholic 0.6%; Protestant 1.7%; Jewish 0.9%; other (mostly nonreligious) 44.1%. **Major cities** (2003; includes Moldovans working abroad): Chisinau 662,400; Tiraspol 185,000; Balti 145,900; Tighina 125,000; Rābnita 62,000. **Location:** eastern Europe, bordering Ukraine and Romania.

Vital statistics

Birth rate per 1,000 population (2002): 9.9 (world avg. 21.3); (1995) legitimate 87.7%. **Death rate** per 1,000 population (2002): 11.5 (world avg. 9.1). **Natural increase rate** per 1,000 population (2002): –1.6 (world avg. 12.2). **Total fertility rate** (avg. births per childbearing woman; 2002): 1.7. **Marriage rate** per 1,000 population (2002): 6.0. **Life expectancy** at birth (2002): male 60.6 years; female 69.4 years.

National economy

Budget (2002). *Revenue:* 6,611,000,000 lei (value-added tax 30.8%; social fund contributions 24.9%; excise taxes 9.9%; personal income tax 7.1%; profits tax 6.5%; duties and customs taxes 5.0%). *Expenditures:* 7,057,000,000 lei (current expenditures 95.3%, of which social fund expenditures 26.9%, education 17.6%, interest payments 6.9%, health care 11.2%; capital expenditure 4.7%). **Production** (metric tons except as noted). *Agriculture, forestry, fishing* (2002): corn (maize) 1,192,770, wheat 1,122,270, sugar beets 1,116,034; livestock (number of live animals) 834,870 sheep, 448,898 pigs, 404,845 cattle; roundwood (2001) 56,800 cu m; fish catch (2001) 1,576. *Mining and quarrying* (2000): sand and gravel 277,000; gypsum 32,100. *Manufacturing* (value of production in $'000,000; 1998; excludes Transnistria [Stonga Nistruli]): food products 299; beverages 194; tobacco products 44. *Energy production (consumption):* electricity (kW-hr; 2000) 3,110,000,000 (5,095,000,000); coal (2000) none (180,000); petroleum products (2000) none (409,000); natural gas (cu m; 2000) none (2,519,000,000). **Population economically active** (2003): total 1,473,580; activity rate of total population 34.8% (participation rates: female [2001] 50.1%; unemployed 7.9%). **Gross national product** (2003): $2,137,000,000 ($590 per capita). **Public debt** (external, outstanding; 2002): $846,000,000. **Tourism** (2002): receipts from visitors $47,000,000; expenditures by nationals abroad $86,000,000. **Household income and expenditure.** Average household size (2002) 3.3; annual average income per household (2002) $1,200; sources of income (1994): wages and salaries 41.2%, social benefits 15.3%, agricultural income 10.4%, other 33.1%; expenditure (2001): food and drink 40.4%, housing

13.5%, utilities 10.5%, transportation 8.9%, clothing 7.6%, health 3.9%. **Land use** as % of total land area (2000): in temporary crops 55.1%, in permanent crops 10.7%, in pasture 11.7%; overall forest area 9.9%.

Foreign trade

Imports (2002): $1,103,000,000 (mineral products 21.7%; machinery and apparatus 14.0%; chemicals and chemical products 10.7%; textiles 10.0%). *Major import sources:* Ukraine 20.4%; Russia 15.3%; Romania 11.4%; Germany 9.2%; Italy 7.5%. **Exports** (2002): $710,000,000 (processed food, beverages [significantly wine], and tobacco products 37.8%; textiles and wearing apparel 16.7%; vegetables, fruits, seeds, and nuts 15.0%). *Major export destinations:* Russia 35.4%; Ukraine 9.1%; Italy 9.1%; Romania 8.4%; Germany 7.4%.

Transport and communications

Transport. *Railroads* (2000): length 2,710 km; passenger-km 315,000,000; metric ton-km cargo 1,513,000,000. *Roads* (2000): total length 12,691 km (paved 86%). *Vehicles* (2001): passenger cars 256,500. *Air transport* (2003; Air Moldova only): passenger-km 238,000,000; metric ton-km cargo 540,-000; airports (2001) 1. **Communications**, in total units (units per 1,000 persons). Daily newspaper circulation (2000): 660,000 (154); radios (2000): 3,250,000 (758); televisions (2000): 1,270,000 (297); telephone main lines (2002): 706,900 (161); cellular telephone subscribers (2002): 338,200 (77); personal computers (2002): 77,000 (18); Internet users (2002): 150,000 (34).

Education and health

Literacy (2000): total population age 15 and over literate 98.9%; males literate 99.5%; females literate 98.3%. **Health** (2001): physicians 12,800 (1 per 334 persons); hospital beds 25,000 (1 per 171 persons); infant mortality rate per 1,000 live births (2002) 41.6. **Food** (2001): daily per capita caloric intake 2,766 (vegetable products 86%, animal products 14%); 108% of FAO recommended minimum.

Military

Total active duty personnel (2003): 6,910 (army 84.1%, air force 15.9%). Opposition forces in Transnistria (excluding militia; 2003) c. 9,500. **Military expenditure as percentage of GNP** (1999): 1.6% (world 2.4%); per capita expenditure $10.

Background

Moldova, once part of the principality of Moldavia, was founded by the Vlachs in the 14th century. In the mid-16th century it was under Ottoman rule. In 1774 it came under Russian control and lost portions of its territory. In 1859 it joined with the principality of Walachia to form the state of Romania, and in 1918 some of the territory it had ceded earlier also joined Romania. Romania was compelled to cede some of the Moldavian area to Russia in 1940, and that area combined with what Russia already controlled to become the Moldavian SSR. In 1991 Moldavia declared independence from the Soviet Union. It adopted the Romanian spelling of Moldova after having legitimized (1989) the use of the Roman rather than the Cyrillic alphabet. During the 1990s the country struggled to find economic equilibrium.

Recent Developments

In July 2004 a serious crisis erupted between the Moldovan government and the self-proclaimed territory of Transnistria, which had seceded in 1992. Although some 40% of Transnistria's population spoke Romanian as its first language, the authorities in Tiraspol, the capital, forcibly closed six schools for teaching Romanian in the Latin rather than the Cyrillic script. Moldova imposed economic sanctions and severed transport links with Transnistria, despite an earlier warning from the Russian Foreign Ministry not to take such steps. The situation had already prompted US Secretary of Defense Donald Rumsfeld to visit Moldova on 26 June, when he added his voice to calls for Russia to abide by a 1999 agreement and withdraw its forces from Transnistria.

Internet resources: <www.turism.md>.

Monaco

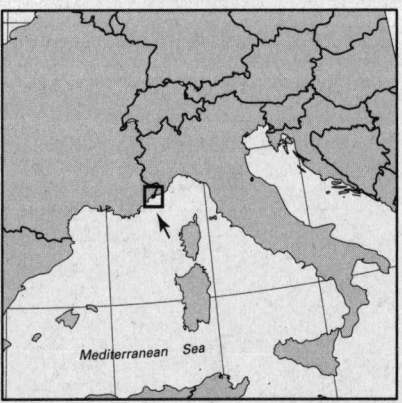

Mediterranean Sea

Official name: Principauté de Monaco (Principality of Monaco). **Form of government:** constitutional monarchy with one legislative body (National Council [24]). **Chief of state:** Prince Albert (from 31 Mar 2005). **Head of government:** Minister of State Patrick Leclercq (from 2000). **Capital:** no separate area is distinguished as such. **Official language:** French. **Official religion:** Roman Catholicism. **Monetary unit:** 1 euro (€) = 100 centimes; valuation (7 Jul 2005) $1 = €0.84; at conversion on 1 Jan 2002, €1 = 6.56 French francs (F).

Demography

Area: 0.75 sq mi, 1.95 sq km. **Population** (2004): 32,600. **Density** (2004): persons per sq mi 43,467, persons per sq km 16,718. **Urban** (2000): 100%. **Sex distribution** (2000): male 48.54%; female 51.4%.

---

1 metric ton = about 1.1 short tons;   1 kilometer = 0.6 mi (statute);   1 metric ton-km cargo = about 0.68 short ton-mi cargo;   c.i.f.: cost, insurance, and freight;   f.o.b.: free on board

Age breakdown (2000): under 15, 13.2%; 15–29, 13.4%; 30–44, 22.1%; 45–59, 22.4%; 60–74, 17.4%; 75 and over, 11.5%. **Ethnic composition** (2000): French 45.8%; Ligurian (Genoan) 17.2%; Monegasque 16.9%; British 4.5%; Jewish 1.7%; other 13.9%. **Religious affiliation** (2000): Christian 93.2%, of which Roman Catholic 89.3%; Jewish 1.7%; nonreligious and other 5.1%. **Location:** western Europe, bordering the Mediterranean Sea and France.

Vital statistics

Birth rate per 1,000 population (2003): 9.5 (world avg. 21.3). **Death rate** per 1,000 population (2003): 12.8 (world avg. 9.1). **Natural increase rate** per 1,000 population (2003): −3.3 (world avg. 12.2). **Total fertility rate** (avg. births per childbearing woman; 2003): 1.8. **Marriage rate** per 1,000 population (2002): 5.4. **Divorce rate** per 1,000 population (2002): 2.1. **Life expectancy** at birth (2003): male 75.4 years; female 83.4 years.

National economy

Budget (2001). *Revenue:* €624,254,804 (value-added taxes 50%, state-run monopolies 20%). *Expenditures:* €621,041,725 (current expenditure 65.5%, capital expenditure 34.5%). **Production**. *Agriculture, forestry, fishing:* some horticulture and greenhouse cultivation; no agriculture as such. *Manufacturing* (value of export sales in €'000,000; 2001): chemicals, cosmetics, perfumery, and pharmaceuticals 347; plastic products 179; light electronics and precision instruments 81. *Energy production (consumption):* electricity (kW-hr; 2001), n.a. (475,000,000 [imported from France]). **Gross national product** (2002): $849,000,000 ($26,300 per capita). **Population economically active** (2001): total 39,543, of which Monegasque 3,471, foreign workers 36,072; female participation in labor force 42.4%. **Households.** Average household size (1998) 2.2. **Tourism** (2002): 2,191 hotel rooms; 263,000 overnight stays; 3 casinos run by the state attract 400,000 visitors annually. **Land use** as % of total land area (2000): public gardens 20%.

Foreign trade

Data exclude trade with France; Monaco has participated in a customs union with France since 1963. **Imports** (2001): €394,000,000 (consumer goods and parts for industrial production [including pharmaceuticals, perfumes, clothing, publishing] 23.8%, food products 22.6%, transport equipment and parts 20.0%). *Major import sources:* EEC 64.0%; US, Japan, Switzerland, and Norway 11.6%; African countries 8.8%. **Exports** (2001): €403,000,000 (rubber and plastic products, glass, construction materials, organic chemicals, and paper and paper products 31.4%, products of automobile industry 21.4%, consumer goods 17.0%). *Major export destinations:* EEC 63.5%; US, Japan, Switzerland, and Norway 10.6%; African countries 8.6%.

Transport and communications

Transport. *Railroads* (2001): length 1.7 km; passengers 2,171,100; cargo 3,357 tons. *Roads* (2001): total length 50 km (paved 100%). *Vehicles* (1997): passenger cars 21,120; trucks and buses 2,770. *Air transport:* airports with scheduled flights; none; fixed-wing service is provided at Nice, France; helicopter service is available at Fontvieille. **Communications**, in total units (units per 1,000 persons). Daily newspaper circulation (1999): 10,000 (300); radios (1997): 34,000 (1,030); televisions (1997): 25,000 (758); telephone main lines (2002): 33,700 (1,040); cellular telephone subscribers (2002): 19,300 (596); Internet users (2002): 16,000 (494).

Education and health

Literacy: virtually 100%. **Health** (2002): physicians 156 (1 per 207 persons); hospital beds 521 (1 per 62 persons); infant mortality rate per 1,000 live births (2003) 5.6. **Food:** daily per capita caloric intake, n.a.; assuming consumption patterns similar to France (2000) 3,591 (vegetable products 62%, animal products 38%); 143% of FAO recommended minimum.

Military

Defense responsibility lies with France according to the terms of the Versailles Treaty of 1919.

Background

Inhabited since prehistoric times, Monaco was known to the Phoenicians, Greeks, Carthaginians, and Romans. In 1191 the Genoese took possession of it; in 1297 the reign of the Grimaldi family began. The Grimaldis allied themselves with France except for the period 1524–1641, when they were under the protection of Spain. France annexed Monaco in 1793, and it remained under French control until the fall of Napoleon, when the Grimaldis returned. In 1815 it was put under the protection of Sardinia. A treaty in 1861 called for the sale of the towns of Menton and Roquebrune to France and the establishment of Monaco's independence. Monaco is one of Europe's most luxurious resorts. In 1997 the 700-year rule of the Grimaldis, then under Prince Rainier III, was celebrated.

Recent Developments

Prince Rainier III of Monaco, the longest-reigning monarch in Europe, died at the age of 81 on 6 Apr 2005. His son, Albert, succeeded him, taking the throne as Prince Albert II.

Internet Resources: <www.visitmonaco.com>.

Mongolia

Official name: Mongol Uls (Mongolia). **Form of government:** unitary multiparty republic with one legislative house (State Great Hural [76]). **Chief of state:** President Natsagiyn Bagabandi (from 1997). **Head of government:** Prime Minister Tsahiagiyn Elbegdorj (from 20 Aug 2004). **Capital:** Ulaanbaatar (Ulan Bator). **Official language:** Khalkha Mongolian. **Official religion:** none. **Monetary unit:** 1 tugrik (Tug) = 100 mongo; valuation (7 Jul 2005) $1 = Tug 1,189.00.

Demography

Area: 603,930 sq mi, 1,564,160 sq km. **Population** (2004): 2,519,000. **Density** (2004): persons per sq mi 4.2, persons per sq km 1.6. **Urban** (2002): 56.4%.

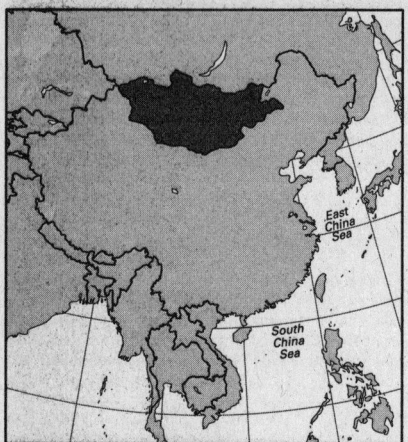

Sex distribution

Sex distribution (2002): male 49.53%; female 50.47%. **Age breakdown** (2002): under 15, 32.7%; 15–29, 31.4%; 30–44, 21.2%; 45–59, 9.2%; 60–69, 3.4%; 70 and over, 2.1%. **Ethnic composition** (2000): Khalkha Mongol 81.5%; Kazakh 4.3%; Dörbed Mongol 2.8%; Bayad 2.1%; Buryat Mongol 1.7%; Dariganga Mongol 1.3%; Zakhchin 1.3%; Tuvan (Uriankhai) 1.1%; other 3.9%. **Religious affiliation** (1995): Tantric Buddhist (Lamaism) 96.0%; Muslim 4.0%. **Major cities** (2000): Ulaanbaatar (Ulan Bator) 760,077; Erdenet 68,310; Darhan 65,791; Choybalsan 41,714; Ulaangom 26,319. **Location**: north-central Asia, bordering Russia and China.

Vital statistics

Birth rate per 1,000 population (2003): 21.4 (world avg. 21.3); legitimate 82.2%. **Death rate** per 1,000 population (2003): 7.2 (world avg. 9.1). **Natural increase rate** per 1,000 population (2003): 14.2 (world avg. 12.2). **Total fertility rate** (avg. births per child-bearing woman; 2003): 2.3. **Marriage rate** per 1,000 population (2001): 5.1. **Divorce rate** per 1,000 population (2001): 1.5. **Life expectancy** at birth (2003): male 61.6 years; female 66.1 years.

National economy

Budget (2002). *Revenue:* Tug 466,527,000,000 (taxes 76.4%, of which VAT 25.2%, income tax 15.2%, social security contributions 11.4%, customs duties 11.2%; nontax revenue 23.6%). *Expenditures:* Tug 536,549,300,000 (education, health, social services 52.3%; wages 19.6%; capital investment 11.9%; interest 3.3%; other 12.9%). **Public debt** (external; 2002): $950,400,000. **Tourism** (2002): receipts $167,000,000; expenditures $119,000,000. **Population economically active** (2002): total 872,600; activity rate of total population 35.7% (participation rates: ages 15 and over 62.2%; female 49.8%; unemployed 4.6%). **Production** (metric tons except as noted). *Agriculture, forestry, fishing* (2002): wheat 149,336, potatoes 65,560, vegetables and melons 45,000; livestock (number of live animals) 11,937,300 sheep, 8,858,000 goats, 3,100,000

horses; roundwood (2001) 631,000 cu m; fish catch (2001) 117. *Mining and quarrying* (2002): copper 376,300; fluorspar concentrate 159,800; molybdenum 3,384. *Manufacturing* (value added by manufacturing in Tug '000,000; 2001): textiles 82,486; food and beverages 81,319; clothing and apparel 23,007. *Energy production (consumption):* electricity (kW-hr; 2001) 3,017,000,000 (3,213,000,000); hard coal (2000) 833,000 (876,000); lignite (2000) 4,178,000 (4,177,000); petroleum products (2000) none (420,000). **Gross national product** (2003): $1,188,000,000 ($480 per capita). **Household income and expenditure** (2001): Average household size 4.4; annual income per household Tug 1,226,000; sources of income: wages 29.2%, self-employment 28.6%, transfer payments 8.0%, other 34.2%; expenditure: food 42.5%, clothing 16.2%, transportation and communications 7.8%, education 7.1%, housing 6.8%, health care 1.7%. **Land use** as % of total land area (2000): in temporary crops 0.7%, in permanent crops, negligible, in pasture 82.5%; overall forest area 6.8%.

Foreign trade

Imports (2002): $659,000,000 (machinery and apparatus 19.5%, food and agricultural products 19.0%, mineral fuels 18.6%, textiles and clothing 12.7%). *Major import sources:* Russia 34.1%; China 24.4%; South Korea 12.2%; Japan 6.2%; Germany 4.5%. **Exports** (2002): $500,900,000 (2001; copper concentrate 28.1%, gold 14.3%, cashmere [all forms] 13.4%, fluorspar 3.8%). *Major export destinations* (2002): China 42.4%; US 31.6%; Russia 8.6%; South Korea 4.4%; Australia 3.5%.

Transport and communications

Transport. *Railroads* (2001): length 1,815 km; passenger-km (2001): 1,062,200,000; metric ton-km cargo 5,287,900,000. *Roads* (2001): total length 49,250 km (paved 4%). *Vehicles* (2001): passenger cars 53,200; trucks and buses 36,600. *Air transport* (2001): passenger-km 538,900,000; metric ton-km cargo 9,500,000; airports with scheduled flights 1. **Communications**, in total units (units per 1,000 persons). Daily newspaper circulation (1996): 68,000 (27); radios (2000): 368,000 (154); televisions (2002): 189,600 (79); telephone main lines (2002): 128,000 (53); cellular telephone subscribers (2002): 216,000 (89); personal computers (2002): 69,000 (21); Internet users (2002): 50,000 (28).

Education and health

Educational attainment (2000). Percentage of population age 10 and over having: no formal education 11.6%; primary education 23.5%; secondary 46.1%; vocational secondary 11.2%; higher 7.6%. **Literacy** (2000): percentage of total population age 15 and over literate 98.9%; males literate 99.1%; females literate 98.8%. **Health** (2001): physicians 6,639 (1 per 365 persons); hospital beds 18,100 (1 per 135 persons); infant mortality rate per 1,000 live births (2003) 23.8. **Food** (2001): daily per capita caloric intake 1,974 (vegetable products 60%, animal products 40%); 81% of FAO recommended minimum.

1 metric ton = about 1.1 short tons;   1 kilometer = 0.6 mi (statute);   1 metric ton-km cargo = about 0.68 short ton-mi cargo;   c.i.f.: cost, insurance, and freight;   f.o.b.: free on board

Military

Total active duty personnel (2003): 8,600 (army 87.2%, air force 12.8%). **Military expenditure as percentage of GNP** (1999): 2.1% (world 2.4%); per capita expenditure $5.

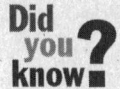

Did you know? The Gobi ("waterless place" in Mongolian) is a great desert and semidesert region of Central Asia. Much of the Gobi is not sandy desert but bare rock, Cars may drive over this surface for long distances in any direction.

Background

In Neolithic times Mongolia was inhabited by small groups of nomads. During the 3rd century BC it became the center of the Xiongnu empire. Turkic-speaking peoples held sway in the 4th–10th centuries AD. In the early 13th century Genghis Khan united the Mongol tribes and conquered central Asia. His successor, Ogodei, conquered the Chin dynasty of China in 1234. Kublai Khan established the Yuan, or Mongol, dynasty in China in 1279. After the 14th century the Ming dynasty of China confined the Mongols to their homeland in the steppes; later they became part of the Chinese Ch'ing dynasty. Inner Mongolia was incorporated into China in 1644. After the fall of the Ch'ing dynasty in 1911, Mongol princes declared Mongolia's independence from China, and in 1921 Russian forces helped drive off the Chinese. The Mongolian People's Republic was established in 1924 and recognized by China in 1946. The nation adopted a new constitution in 1992 and shortened its name to Mongolia.

Recent Developments

The 27 Jun 2004 general elections marked a turning point in Mongolia's post-Soviet history and a challenge to its emerging democracy. With its 72 to 4 majority, the Mongolian People's Revolutionary Party (MPRP) commanded the State Great Hural (parliament), and with its control of the state-owned media it also dominated the election campaign. Nonetheless, the opposition parties joined forces and succeeded in overturning the MPRP's monopoly of power. Neither coalition, however, won enough seats for an overall majority. Eventually they agreed to form a "grand coalition," but there was much mutual antagonism during protracted negotiations.

Internet resources: <www.mongoliatourism.gov.mn>.

Morocco

Official name: Al-Mamlakah al-Maghribiyah (Kingdom of Morocco). **Form of government:** constitutional monarchy with two legislative houses (House of Councillors [270 {indirectly elected seats}]; House of Representatives [325]). **Chief of state and head of government:** King Muhammad VI (from 1999), assisted by Prime Minister Driss Jettou (from 2002). **Capital:** Rabat. **Official language:** Arabic. **Official religion:** Islam. **Monetary unit:** 1 Moroccan dirham (DH) = 100 Moroccan francs; valuation (7 Jul 2005) $1 = DH 9.16.

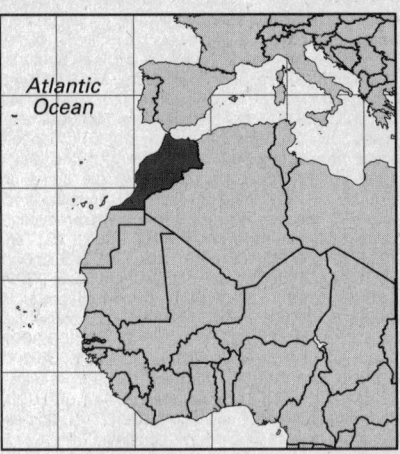

Demography

Area (includes Western Sahara): 274,461 sq mi, 710,850 sq km. **Population** (2004; includes Western Sahara, annexure of Morocco whose unresolved political status [from 1991] is to be eventually decided by an internationally sponsored referendum; Western Sahara area: 97,344 sq mi, 252,120 sq km; Western Sahara population [2004] 267,000): 30,569,000. **Density** (2004): persons per sq mi 111.4, persons per sq km 43.0. **Urban** (2002): 56.6%. **Sex distribution** (2002): male 49.75%; female 50.25%. **Age breakdown** (2002): under 15, 30.9%; 15–29, 30.3%; 30–44, 20.4%; 45–59, 10.9%; 60–74, 5.9%; 75 and over, 1.6%. **Ethnic composition** (2000): Berber 45%, of which Arabized 24%; Arab 44%; Moors originally from Mauritania 10%; other 1%. **Religious affiliation** (2000): Muslim (mostly Sunni) 98.3%; Christian 0.6%; other 1.1%. **Major urban areas** (2003): Casablanca 3,353,000; Rabat-Salé (2000) 1,616,000; Fès 1,053,000; Marrakech (2000) 822,000; Tangier 681,444. **Location:** northern Africa, bordering the Mediterranean Sea, Algeria, the Spanish exclaves of Ceuta and Melilla, and the North Atlantic Ocean.

Vital statistics

Birth rate per 1,000 population (2002): 21.0 (world avg. 21.3). **Death rate** per 1,000 population (2002): 5.6 (world avg. 9.1). **Natural increase rate** per 1,000 population (2002): 15.4 (world avg. 12.2). **Total fertility rate** (avg. births per childbearing woman; 2002): 3.0. **Life expectancy** at birth (2002): male 67.5 years; female 72.1 years.

National economy

Budget. *Revenue* (2003): DH 102,482,000,000 (value-added tax 25.5%; individual income tax 17.2%; excise taxes 15.2%; corporate taxes 14.2%; international trade 12.2%; stamp tax 5.2%). *Expenditures* (2003): DH 128,113,000,000 (current expenditure 76.8%, of which wages 42.1%, debt payment 13.5%; capital expenditure 17.1%; transfers to local governments 6.1%). **Public debt** (external, outstanding; 2002): $15,001,000,000. **Population economically**

active (2001): total 10,230,000; activity rate 35.4% (unemployed [2002] 11.6%). **Production** (metric tons except as noted). *Agriculture, forestry, fishing* (2002): wheat 3,356,000, sugar beets 2,985,900, barley 1,669,000; livestock (number of live animals) 16,335,000 sheep, 5,090,000 goats, 2,669,000 cattle; roundwood (2001) 971,000 cu m; fish catch (2001) 1,083,000, of which sardines 763,000, octopuses 113,000. *Mining and quarrying* (2002): phosphate rock 21,808,000; barite 469,900; zinc (metal content) 178,400. *Manufacturing* (value added in $'000,000; 2001): food products 778; tobacco products 635; wearing apparel 565. *Energy production (consumption):* electricity (kW-hr; 2002) 15,539,-300,000 (14,085,000,000); coal (2001) 135,000 ([2000] 4,029,000); crude petroleum (barrels; 2002) 97,000 ([2000] 52,288,000); petroleum products (2002) 6,339,500 ([2000] 6,553,000); natural gas (cu m; 2002) 48,700,000 ([2000] 49,900,000). **Gross national product** (2003): $39,661,000,000 ($1,320 per capita). **Tourism** (2002): receipts $2,046,000,000; expenditures $444,000,000. **Households.** Average household size (2002) 5.5; expenditure (1994): food 45.2%, housing 12.5%, transportation 7.6%. **Land use** as % of total land area (2000): in temporary crops 19.6%, in permanent crops 2.2%, in pasture 47.1%; overall forest area 6.8%.

Foreign trade

Imports (2002-c.i.f.): DH 129,346,000,000 (machinery and apparatus 19.3%; mineral fuels 15.6%, of which crude petroleum 10.0%; food, beverages, and tobacco 11.8%; cotton fabric and fibers 6.4%). *Major import sources* (2001): France 24.1%; Spain 10.3%; UK 6.2%; Italy 5.0%; Germany 5.0%. **Exports** (2002-f.o.b.; cannabis is an important illegal export): DH 85,653,000,000 (garments 21.4%; food, beverages, and tobacco 20.5%, of which crustaceans and mollusks 6.6%; knitwear 10.4%; phosphoric acid 6.8%; machinery and apparatus 6.6%; phosphates 5.2%). *Major export destinations* (2001): France 32.8%; Spain 15.3%; UK 8.6%; Italy 5.7%; Germany 4.2%.

Transport and communications

Transport. *Railroads* (2002): route length 1,907 km; passenger-km 2,145,000,000; metric ton-km cargo 4,974,000,000. *Roads* (2001): total length 57,226 km (paved 56%). *Vehicles* (2000): passenger cars 1,211,100; trucks and buses 415,700. *Air transport* (2002; Royal Air Maroc only): passenger-km 6,044,800,000; metric ton-km cargo 51,285,000; airports (2002) 15. **Communications,** in total units (units per 1,000 persons). Daily newspaper circulation (2000): 740,000 (26); radios (2000): 6,920,000 (243); televisions (2000): 4,720,000 (166); telephone main lines (2003): 1,219,200 (41); cellular telephone subscribers (2003): 7,332,800 (243); personal computers (2003): 600,000 (20); Internet users (2003): 800,000 (27).

Education and health

Literacy (2000): total population over age 15 literate 48.9%; males literate 61.1%; females literate 35.1%. **Health** (2002): physicians 13,955 (1 per 2,123 persons); hospital beds (1998) 26,153 (1 per 1,062

persons); infant mortality rate per 1,000 live births (2002) 44.0. **Food** (2001): daily per capita caloric intake 3,046 (vegetable products 93%, animal products 7%); 126% of FAO recommended minimum.

Military

Total active duty personnel (2003): 196,300 (army 89.1%, navy 4.0%, air force 6.9%). **Military expenditure as percentage of GNP** (1999): 4.3% (world 2.4%); per capita expenditure $49.

Background

The Berbers entered Morocco near the end of the 2nd millennium BC. Phoenicians established trading posts along the Mediterranean during the 12th century BC, and Carthage had settlements along the Atlantic in the 5th century BC. After the fall of Carthage, Morocco became a loyal ally of Rome, and in AD 42 it was annexed by Rome as part of the province of Mauretania. It was invaded by Muslims in the 7th century. Beginning in the mid-11th century, the Almoravids, Almohads, and Marinids ruled successively. After the fall of the Marinids in the mid-15th century, the Sa'dis ruled for a century after 1550. The French fought Morocco over the Algerian boundary in the 1840s, and the Spanish seized part of Moroccan territory in 1859. It was a French protectorate from 1912 until its independence in 1956. In the mid-1970s it reasserted claim to the Western Sahara, and in 1976 Spanish troops left there. Conflicts with Mauritania and Algeria over the region continued into the 1990s. As the decade wore on, the UN tried to solve the dispute. King Hassan II died in July 1999 after 38 years on the throne and was succeeded by his eldest son, Sidi Muhammad, who took the name Muhammad VI.

Recent Developments

In January 2004 the Moroccan parliament approved the country's new family law, the Mudawwanah, which effectively rendered the status of males and females equal before the law. Morocco was increasingly eager to resolve the Western Sahara dispute and had been pushing Algeria to bring pressure to bear on the Polisario Front, the Western Saharan liberation movement based in Algeria. Regional tensions over the issue hardened as Morocco accused Algeria of supplying military aid to the Polisario Front and South Africa recognized the Saharawi Arab Democratic Republic in September.

Internet resources: <www.mincom.gov.ma>.

Mozambique

Official name: República de Moçambique (Republic of Mozambique). **Form of government:** multiparty republic with a single legislative house (Assembly of the Republic [250]). **Head of state and government:** President Armando Guebuza (from 2 Feb 2005) assisted by Prime Minister Luisa Diogo (from 17 Feb 2004). **Capital:** Maputo. **Official language:** Portuguese. **Official religion:** none. **Monetary unit:** 1 metical (Mt; plural meticais) = 100 centavos; valuation (7 Jul 2005) $1 = Mt 24,413.

---

1 metric ton = about 1.1 short tons;   1 kilometer = 0.6 mi (statute);   1 metric ton-km cargo = about 0.68 short ton-mi cargo;   c.i.f.: cost, insurance, and freight;   f.o.b.: free on board

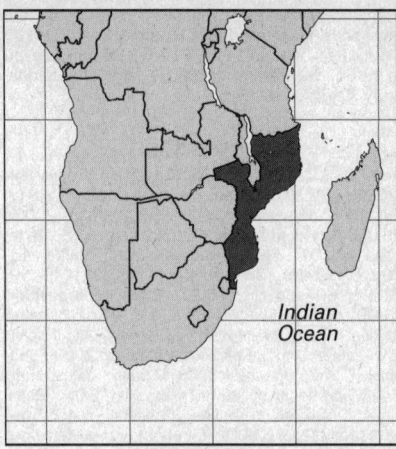

Indian
Ocean

Demography

Area: 313,661 sq mi, 812,379 sq km. **Population** (2004): 18,812,000. **Density** (2004): persons per sq mi 60.0, persons per sq km 23.2. **Urban** (2001): 33.3%. **Sex distribution** (2003): male 49.27%; female 50.73%. **Age breakdown** (2003): under 15, 43.8%; 15–29, 26.5%; 30–44, 16.2%; 45–59, 8.9%; 60–74, 3.8%; 75 and over, 0.7%. **Ethnic composition** (2000): Makuana 15.3%; Makua 14.5%; Tsonga 8.6%; Sena 8.0%; Lomwe 7.1%; Tswa 5.7%; Chwabo 5.5%; other 35.3%. **Linguistic composition** (1997): Makua 26.3%; Tsonga 11.4%; Lomwe 7.6%; Sena 7.0%; Portuguese 6.5%; Chuaba 6.3%; other Bantu languages 33.0%; other 1.9%. **Religious affiliation** (2000): traditional beliefs 50.4%; Christian 38.4%, of which Roman Catholic 15.8%, Protestant 8.9%; Muslim 10.5%. **Major cities** (1997): Maputo 989,386; Matola 440,927; Beira 412,588; Nampula 314,965; Chimoio 177,608. **Location:** southern Africa, bordering Tanzania, the Indian Ocean, South Africa, Swaziland, Zimbabwe, Zambia, and Malawi.

Vital statistics

Birth rate per 1,000 population (2003): 36.9 (world avg. 21.3). **Death rate** per 1,000 population (2003): 23.0 (world avg. 9.1). **Natural increase rate** per 1,000 population (2003): 13.9 (world avg. 12.2). **Total fertility rate** (avg. births per childbearing woman; 2003): 5.0. **Life expectancy** at birth (2003): male 38.9 years; female 37.4 years. **Adult population** (ages 15–49) **living with HIV** (2004): 12.2% (world avg. 1.1%).

National economy

Budget (2002). *Revenue:* Mt 22,077,000,000,000 (tax revenue 48.1%, of which VAT 20.8%, taxes on international trade 8.4%, personal income tax 5.9%; grants 45.1%; nontax revenue 6.8%). *Expenditures:* Mt 29,032,000,000,000 (current expenditures 46.4%; capital expenditures 41.8%; net lending 11.8%). **Public debt** (external, outstanding; 2002): $2,526,000,000. **Production** (metric tons except as noted). *Agriculture, forestry, fishing* (2003): cassava 6,149,897, corn (maize) 1,248,000, sugarcane 400,000; livestock (number of live animals) 1,320,000 cattle, 392,000 goats, 28,000,000 chick-

ens; roundwood (2002) 18,043,000 cu m; fish catch (2001) 32,512. *Mining and quarrying* (2002): tantalite 46,900 kg; gold 17 kg (official figures; unofficial artisanal production is 360–480 kg per year). *Manufacturing* (value added in Mt '000,000,000; 2002): aluminum 13,547; beverages 2,130; food products 1,789. *Energy production (consumption):* electricity (kW-hr; 2000) 6,974,000,000 (1,562,000,000); coal (2001) 17,700 (n.a.); petroleum products (2000) none (334,000); natural gas (cu m; 2000) 563,800 (563,800). **Household income and expenditure.** Average family size (1997) 4.1; source of income (1992–93; city of Maputo only): wages and salaries 51.6%, self-employment 12.5%, barter 11.5%, private farming 7.7%; expenditure (1992–93; city of Maputo only): food, beverages, and tobacco 74.6%, housing and energy 11.7%, transportation and communications 4.7%, clothing and footwear 3.7%, education and recreation 1.4%, health 0.8%. **Tourism** (2002): receipts from visitors $144,000,000; expenditures by nationals abroad $298,000,000. **Population economically active** (2002): total 9,696,000; activity rate 55.3%. **Gross national product** (2003): $3,897,000,000 ($210 per capita). **Land use** as % of total land area (2000): in temporary crops 5.0%, in permanent crops 0.3%, in pasture 56.1%; overall forest area 39.0%.

Foreign trade

Imports (2001-f.o.b. in balance of trade and c.i.f. for commodities and trading partners): $1,063,000,000 (machinery and apparatus 14.9%; refined petroleum 12.5%; food products 11.8%, of which cereals 8.0%; transport equipment 7.0%; unspecified commodities 21.9%). *Major import sources:* South Africa 42%; Australia 7%; Spain 4%; unspecified 23%. **Exports** (2001): $703,000,000 (aluminum 54.5%; food products 20.1%, of which crustaceans and mollusks 13.4%; electricity 8.1%; cotton 2.3%). *Major export destinations:* Belgium 35%; Zimbabwe 10%; Germany 7%; The Netherlands 7%; Spain 5%.

Transport and communications

Transport. *Railroads* (2002): route length 3,123 km; (2001) passenger-km 142,000,000; (2001) metric ton-km cargo 774,500,000. *Roads* (1996): total length 30,400 km (paved 19%). *Vehicles* (1999): passenger cars 78,600; trucks and buses 46,900. *Air transport:* (2001) passenger-km 272,400,000; metric ton-km cargo 6,700,000; airports (1997) with scheduled flights 7. **Communications**, in total units (units per 1,000 persons). Daily newspaper circulation (2000): 53,000 (3); radios (2000): 778,000 (44); televisions (2002): 257,600 (14); telephone main lines (2002): 83,700 (4.6); cellular telephone subscribers (2003): 428,900 (23); personal computers (2002): 82,000 (4.5); Internet users (2002): 50,000 (2.8).

Education and health

Educational attainment (1997). Percentage of population 15 and over having: no formal schooling 78.4%; primary education 18.4%; secondary 2.0%; technical 0.4%; higher 0.2%; other/unknown 0.6%. **Literacy** (2000): percentage of total population age 15 and over literate 43.8%; males literate 59.9%; females literate 28.4%. **Health:** physicians (2003) 500 (1 per 37,000 persons); hospital beds (1997) 12,630 (1 per 1,210 persons); infant mortality rate per 1,000 live births (2003) 137.8. **Food** (2001): daily per capita caloric intake 1,980 (vegetable products 98%, animal products 2%); 85% of FAO recommended minimum.

Military

Total active duty personnel (2003): 8,200 (army 85.4%, navy 2.4%, air force 12.2%). **Military expenditure as percentage of GNP** (1999): 2.5% (world 2.4%); per capita expenditure $5.

Background

Inhabited in prehistoric times, Mozambique was settled by Bantu peoples about the 3rd century AD. Arab traders occupied the coastal region from the 14th century, and the Portuguese controlled the area from the early 16th century. The slave trade later became an important part of the economy. In the late 19th century private trading companies began to administer parts of the inland areas. It became an overseas province of Portugal in 1951. After years of war beginning in the 1960s, the country was granted independence in 1975. It was wracked by civil war in the 1970s and '80s. In 1990 a new constitution was promulgated, and a peace treaty was signed with the rebels in 1992.

Recent Developments

Pascoal Mocumbi, who had served as prime minister since 1994, was dismissed from that post in February 2004; he was selected to lead a new international health care organization based in The Netherlands. Finance Minister Luisa Diogo was named to replace Mocumbi. Armando Guebuza of the ruling Mozambique Liberation Front won the December 2004 presidential elections handily and was sworn in on 2 Feb 2005.

Internet resources: <www.mozambique.mz>.

Myanmar (Burma)

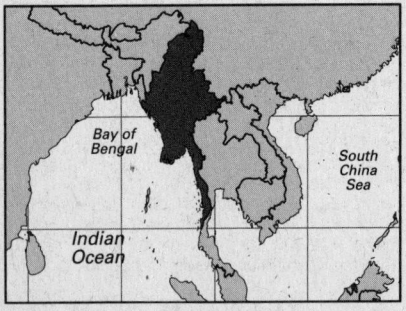

Bay of Bengal

South China Sea

Indian Ocean

Official name: Pyidaungzu Myanma Naingngandaw (Union of Myanmar). **Form of government:** military regime. **Head of state and government:** Chairman of the State Peace and Development Council Gen. Than Shwe (from 1997); assisted by Prime Minister Lt. Gen. Soe Win (from 19 Oct 2004). **Capital:** Yangon (Rangoon). **Official language:** Burmese. **Official religion:** none. **Monetary unit:** 1 Myanmar kyat (K) = 100 pyas; valuation (7 Jul 2005) $1 = K 5.88 (rate pegged to the Special Drawing Right of the International Monetary Fund).

Demography

Area: 261,228 sq mi, 676,577 sq km. **Population** (2004): 42,720,000. **Density** (2004): persons per sq mi 163.5, persons per sq km 63.1. **Urban** (2002): 29.0%. **Sex distribution** (2002): male 49.81%; female 50.19%. **Age breakdown** (2002): under 15, 28.5%; 15–29, 30.8%; 30–44, 22.0%; 45–59, 11.4%; 60 and over, 5.7%. **Ethnic composition** (2000): Burman 55.9%; Karen 9.5%; Shan 6.5%; Han Chinese 2.5%; Mon 2.3%; Yangbye 2.2%; Kachin 1.5%; other 19.6%. **Religious affiliation** (2000): Buddhist 72.7%; Christian 8.3%; Muslim 2.4%; Hindu 2.0%; traditional beliefs 12.6%; other 2.0%. **Major cities** (2004 est.): Yangon (Rangoon) 4,455,500; Mandalay 1,176,900; Moulmein (Mawlamyine) 405,800; Bassein (Pathein) 215,600; Pegu (Bago) 200,900. **Location:** southeastern Asia, bordering China, Laos, Thailand, the Andaman Sea, the Bay of Bengal, Bangladesh, and India.

Vital statistics

Birth rate per 1,000 population (2003): 23.7 (world avg. 21.3). **Death rate** per 1,000 population (2003): 11.2 (world avg. 9.1). **Natural increase rate** per 1,000 population (2003): 12.5 (world avg. 12.2). **Total fertility rate** (avg. births per childbearing woman; 2003): 2.2. **Life expectancy** at birth (2002): male 54.1 years; female 57.6 years.

National economy

Budget (2000–01). *Revenue:* K 134,550,000,000 (revenue from taxes 56.4%, of which taxes on goods and services 32.8%, taxes on income 19.4%; nontax revenue 43.4%; foreign grants 0.2%). *Expenditures:* K 221,255,000,000 (defense 28.7%; agriculture and forestry 17.4%; education 14.2%; public works and housing 9.2%). **Public debt** (external, outstanding; 2002): $5,391,000,000. **Tourism** (2001): receipts from visitors $45,000,000; expenditures by nationals abroad $27,000,000. **Production** (metric tons except as noted). *Agriculture, forestry, fishing* (2002): rice 21,900,000, sugarcane 6,333,000, dry beans 1,467,330; livestock (number of live animals) 11,551,000 cattle, 4,498,680 pigs, 2,252,020 buffalo; roundwood (2001) 39,365,000 cu m; fish catch (2001) 1,288,134. *Mining and quarrying* (2001): copper (metal content) 26,300; jade 1,700,000 kg; rubies, sapphires, and spinel 8,630,000 carats. *Manufacturing* (2001): cement 384,000; refined sugar 101,000; fertilizers 60,100. *Energy production (consumption):* electricity (kW-hr; 2000) 5,076,000,000 (5,076,000,000); hard coal (2000) 51,000 (43,000); lignite (2000) 524,000 (524,000); crude petroleum (barrels; 2001) 3,300,000 ([2000] 7,339,000); petroleum products (2000) 820,000 (1,625,000); natural gas (cu m; 2001) 6,800,300,000 ([2000] 1,427,000,000). **Households.** Average household size (2000) 4.8; expenditure (1994; Yangon only): food and beverages 67.1%, fuel and lighting 6.6%, transportation 4.0%, charitable contributions 3.1%, medical care 3.1%. **Gross national product** (1996): $119,334,000,000 ($2,610 per capita). **Population economically active** (1999): total 23,700,000; activity rate of total population 57.1% (unemployed 4.1%). **Land use** as % of total land area (2000): in temporary crops 15.1%, in permanent crops 0.9%, in pasture 0.5%; overall forest area 52.3%.

Foreign trade

Imports (2000–01-c.i.f.): K 14,900,000,000 (machinery and transport equipment 25.2%, chemicals and chemical products 12.9%, mineral fuels 7.7%, food and live animals 3.9%). *Major import sources* (2001): China 21.8%; Singapore 16.6%; Thailand 13.9%; South Korea 9.1%; Malaysia 8.0%; Japan 7.1%. **Exports** (2000–01-f.o.b.): K 12,262,000,000 (domestic exports 68.6%, of which food 26.1% [including pulses 13.5%], mineral fuels [significantly natural gas] 9.6%, teak and other hardwood 6.5%; re-exports [significantly garments] 31.4%). *Major export destinations* (2001): Thailand 26.0%; US 16.2%; India 10.2%; China 5.0%; Singapore 3.6%.

Transport and communications

Transport. *Railroads* (2000): route length 3,955 km; passenger-km 4,451,000,000; metric ton-km cargo 1,222,000,000. *Roads* (1996): total length 28,200 km (paved 12%). *Vehicles* (1999): passenger cars 171,300; trucks and buses 83,400. *Air transport* (1999): passenger-km 355,000,000; metric ton-km cargo 40,000,000; airports (1996) 19. **Communications**, in total units (units per 1,000 persons). Daily newspaper circulation (2000): 376,000 (9); radios (2001): 2,772,000 (66); televisions (2002): 390,400 (8); telephone main lines (2003): 357,300 (7.2); cellular telephone subscribers (2003): 66,500 (1.3); personal computers (2002): 250,000 (5.1); Internet users (2003): 28,000 (0.5).

Education and health

Literacy (2000): total population age 15 and over literate 84.7%; males literate 89.0%; females literate 80.5%. **Health** (1999): physicians 14,622 (1 per 2,838 persons); hospital beds (1997) 28,943 (1 per 1,433 persons); infant mortality rate per 1,000 live births (2003) 83.0. **Food** (2001): daily per capita caloric intake 2,822 (vegetable products 96%, animal products 4%); 132% of FAO recommended minimum.

Military

Total active duty personnel (2003): 488,000 (army 93.6%, navy 3.3%, air force 3.1%). **Military expenditure as percentage of GNP** (1999): 7.8% (world 2.4%); per capita expenditure $112.

Background

Myanmar, until 1989 known as Burma, has long been inhabited, with the Mon and Pyu states dominant between the 1st century BC and the 9th century AD. It was united in the 11th century under a Burmese dynasty that was overthrown by the Mongols in the 13th century. The Portuguese, Dutch, and English traded there in the 16th–17th centuries. The modern Burmese state was founded in the 18th century. It fell to the British in 1885 and became a province of India. It was occupied by Japan in World War II and became independent in 1948. A military coup took power in 1962 and nationalized major economic sectors. Civilian unrest in the 1980s led to antigovernment rioting. In 1990 opposition parties won in national elections, but the army remained in control. Trying to negotiate for a freer government amid the unrest, Aung San Suu Kyi, the National League for Democracy (NLD) leader, was awarded the Nobel Peace Prize in 1991. She spent extended periods of the 1990s under house arrest.

Recent Developments

In 2004 Myanmar's growing isolation and international pressure for political reform created fissures inside the military junta, known as the State Peace and Development Council, forcing it to consolidate its control over power and neutralize domestic and external threats. The US and the EU imposed tough new sanctions that extended a visa blacklist for all of Myanmar's military leaders, froze their overseas assets, and banned all commercial links; these measures had a severe impact on the garments and textiles sector. Myanmar's ASEAN neighbors, China and India, however, refused to cut off commercial ties with Yangon.

Internet resources: <www.myanmar-tourism.com>.

Namibia

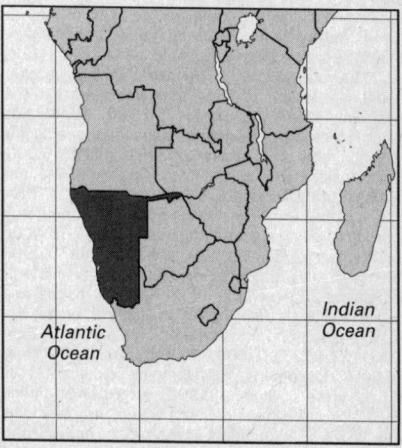

Atlantic Ocean

Indian Ocean

Official name: Republic of Namibia. **Form of government:** republic with two legislative houses (National Council [26]; National Assembly [72 elected and up to 6 appointed members]). **Head of state and government:** President Hifikepunye Pohamba (from 21 Mar 2005), assisted by Prime Minister Nahas Angula (from 21 Mar 2005). **Capital:** Windhoek. **Official language:** English. **Official religion:** none. **Monetary unit:** 1 Namibian dollar (N$) = 100 cents; valuation (7 Jul 2005) US$1 = N$6.84.

Demography

Area: 318,580 sq mi, 825,118 sq km. **Population** (2004): 1,954,000. **Density** (2004): persons per sq mi 6.2, persons per sq km 2.4. **Urban** (2001): 31.4%.

Sex distribution (2001): male 48.73%; female 51.27%. Age breakdown (1999): under 15, 43.2%; 15–29, 28.6%; 30–44, 15.1%; 45–59, 7.7%; 60–74, 4.0%; 75 and over, 1.4%. Ethnic composition (2000): Ovambo 34.4%; mixed race (black/white) 14.5%; Kavango 9.1%; Afrikaner 8.1%; San (Bushmen) and Bergdama 7.0%; Herero 5.5%; Nama 4.4%; Kwambi 3.7%; German 2.8%; other 10.5%. Religious affiliation (2000): Protestant (mostly Lutheran) 47.5%; Roman Catholic 17.7%; African Christian 10.8%; traditional beliefs 6.0%; other 18.0%. Major cities (2001): Windhoek 216,000 (urban agglomeration); Walvis Bay 40,849; Swakopmund 25,442 (population of constituency [second-order administrative subdivision]); Rehoboth 21,782; Rundu 19,597. Location: southwestern Africa, bordering Angola, Zambia, Botswana, South Africa, and the Atlantic Ocean.

Vital statistics

Birth rate per 1,000 population (2003): 27.4 (world avg. 21.3). Death rate per 1,000 population (2003): 16.7 (world avg. 9.1). Natural increase rate per 1,000 population (2003): 10.7 (world avg. 12.2). Total fertility rate (avg. births per childbearing woman; 2003): 3.5. Life expectancy at birth (2003): male 46.0 years; female 46.1 years. Adult population (ages 15–49) living with HIV (2004): 21.3% (world avg. 1.1%).

National economy

Budget (2002–03). Revenue: N$10,256,000,000 (taxes on income and profits 38.5%; taxes on international trade 25.3%; taxes on goods and services 23.6%; nontax revenue 9.7%). Expenditures: N$12,257,000,000 (current expenditure 84.3%; development expenditure 15.7%). Public debt (external, outstanding; 1998): US$747,700,000. Production (metric tons except as noted). Agriculture and fishing (2002): roots and tubers 270,000, millet 65,000, corn (maize) 27,700; livestock (number of live animals) 2,509,000 cattle, 2,370,000 sheep, 1,769,000 goats; fish catch (2001) 547,542. Mining and quarrying (2001): gem diamonds (2002) 1,550,000 carats; fluorite 81,200; zinc (metal content) 31,803 Manufacturing: products include cut gems (primarily diamonds), fur products (from Karakul sheep), and processed foods (fish, meats, and dairy products). Energy production (consumption): electricity (kW-hr; 2001) 27,000,000 (603,000,000); coal (2000) none (3,000). Households. Average household size (2001) 5.1; sources of income (1992): wages and salaries 69.0%, income from property 25.6%, transfer payments 5.4%. Population economically active: total (1991) 493,580; activity rate of total population, 34.9% (participation rates: ages 15–64, 61.3%; female 43.5%; unemployed 20.1%). Gross national product (2003): US$3,771,000,000 (US$1,870 per capita). Tourism (2002): receipts US$219,000,000; expenditures (1998) US$56,000,000. Land use as % of total land area (2000): in temporary crops 1.0%, in permanent crops, negligible, in pasture 46.2%; overall forest area 9.8%.

Foreign trade

Imports (1997-f.o.b. in balance of trade and c.i.f. for commodities and trading partners): N$7,718,000,-

000 (food, beverages, and tobacco 24.1%; machinery and apparatus 15.0%; transport equipment 14.7%; base and fabricated metals 7.5%). Major import sources (2000): South Africa 86.4%; Germany 2.0%; UK 2.0%; US 1.3%. Exports (2001): N$8,901,-000,000 (diamonds 45.4%; metals 18.6%, of which gold 2.3%, zinc 1.5%, other [mostly uranium and copper] 14.8%; fish 10.4%; meat [mostly beef] 7.0%). Major export destinations (1998): UK 43%; South Africa 26%; Spain 14%; France 8%.

Transport and communications

Transport. Railroads: route length (1999) 2,382 km; (1995–96) passenger-km 48,300,000; (1995–96) metric ton-km 1,082,000,000. Roads (2000): total length 66,467 km (paved 7%). Vehicles: passenger cars (1996) 74,875; trucks and buses (1995) 66,500. Air transport (2001; Air Namibia only): passenger-km 624,000,000; metric ton-km cargo 72,575,000; airports (1997) 11. Communications, in total units (units per 1,000 persons). Daily newspaper circulation (2000): 34,700 (19); radios (2000): 258,000 (141); televisions (2000): 69,400 (38); telephone main lines (2003): 127,400 (66); cellular telephone subscribers (2003): 223,700 (116); personal computers (2003): 191,000 (99); Internet users (2003): 65,000 (34).

Education and health

Educational attainment (1991). Percentage of population age 25 and over having: no formal schooling 35.1%; primary education 31.9%; secondary 28.5%; higher 4.5%. Literacy (2000): total population age 15 and over literate 830,200 (82.1%); males literate 416,000 (82.9%); females literate 414,200 (81.2%). Health (2000; public sector only): physicians 244 (1 per 7,500 persons); hospital beds 6,739 (1 per 271 persons); infant mortality rate per 1,000 live births (2003) 50.7. Food (2001): daily per capita caloric intake 2,745 (vegetable products 85%, animal products 15%); 120% of FAO recommended minimum.

Military

Total active duty personnel (2003): 9,000 (army 100.0%). Military expenditure as percentage of GNP (1999): 2.9% (world 2.4%); per capita expenditure $53.

Did you know? A cool, coastal desert, the Namib Desert extends for 1,200 mi (1,900 km) along the entire Atlantic coast of Namibia. It reaches inland 80 to 100 m (130 to 160 km) to the foot of the Great Escarpment. Its name is derived from the Nama language, implying "an area where there is nothing."

Background

Long inhabited by indigenous peoples, Namibia was explored by the Portuguese in the late 15th century. In 1884 it was annexed by Germany as German South West Africa. It was captured in World War I by

---

1 metric ton = about 1.1 short tons;   1 kilometer = 0.6 mi (statute);   1 metric ton-km cargo = about 0.68 short ton-mi cargo;   c.i.f.: cost, insurance, and freight;   f.o.b.: free on board

South Africa, which received it as a mandate from the League of Nations in 1920 and refused to give it up after World War II. A UN resolution in 1966 ending the mandate was challenged by South Africa in the 1970s and '80s. Through long negotiations involving many factions and interests, Namibia achieved independence in 1990.

Recent Developments

Until the South West African People's Organization (SWAPO) held an extraordinary congress in May 2004, there was intense competition over the successor to Sam Nujoma as president of Namibia. One of the leading contenders, Hidipo Hamutenya, was dismissed by Nujoma from his government on the eve of the congress. After Nujoma made clear that he favored Hifikepunye Pohamba as his successor, the congress ratified the decision, and few were surprised that Pohamba won the election held in mid-November. Nujoma, the founding president of Namibia, was voted a very generous retirement package by the parliament and remained SWAPO president. Pohamba was inaugurated on 21 Mar 2005.

Internet resources: <www.namibiatourism.com.na>.

Nauru

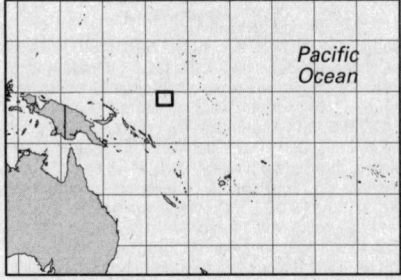

Official name: Naoero (Republic of Nauru). **Form of government:** republic with one legislative house (Parliament [18]). **Head of state and government:** President Ludwig Scotty (from 22 Jun 2004). **Capital:** government offices are located in Yaren district. **Official language:** none; Nauruan is the national language; English is the language of business and government. **Official religion:** none. **Monetary unit:** 1 Australian dollar ($A) = 100 cents; valuation (7 Jul 2005) US$1 = $A 1.35.

Demography

Area: 8.2 sq mi, 21.2 sq km. **Population** (2004): 10,100. **Density** (2004): persons per sq mi 1,232, persons per sq km 476.4. **Urban** (2001): 100%. **Sex distribution** (2001): male 50.50%; female 49.50%. **Age breakdown** (2001): under 15, 40.3%; 15–29, 26.8%; 30–44, 19.0%; 45–59, 10.7%; 60–74, 3.0%; 75 and over, 0.2%. **Ethnic composition** (1992): Nauruan 68.9%; other Pacific Islander 23.7%, of which Kiribati 12.8%, Tuvaluan 8.7%; Asian 5.9%, of which Filipino 2.5%, Chinese 2.3%; other 1.5%. **Religious affiliation** (1995): Protestant 53.5%, of which Congregational 35.3%, Pentecostal 4.8%; Roman Catholic 27.5%; other 19.0%. **Major cities:** none; population of

Yaren district (1996) 700. **Location:** western Pacific Ocean, near the equator east of Papua New Guinea.

Vital statistics

Birth rate per 1,000 population (2002): 21.8 (world avg. 21.3). **Death rate** per 1,000 population (2002): 7.5 (world avg. 9.1). **Natural increase rate** per 1,000 population (2002): 14.3 (world avg. 12.2). **Total fertility rate** (avg. births per childbearing woman; 2003): 3.4. **Marriage rate** per 1,000 population (1995): 5.3. **Life expectancy** at birth (2003): male 58.4 years; female 65.7 years.

National economy

Budget (1999). *Revenue:* $A 38,700,000. *Expenditures:* $A 37,200,000. **Public debt** (external, outstanding; beginning of 1996): US$150,000,000. **Tourism:** receipts from visitors, virtually none. **Gross national product** (at current market prices; 1997): US$128,000,000 (US$11,538 per capita). **Production** (metric tons except as noted). *Agriculture and fishing* (2002): coconuts 1,600, vegetables 450, tropical fruit (including mangoes) 275; livestock (number of live animals) 2,800 pigs; fish catch (2001) 400. *Mining and quarrying* (2001): phosphate rock (gross weight) 400,000. *Manufacturing:* none; virtually all consumer manufactures are imported. *Energy production (consumption):* electricity (kW-hr; 2000) 33,000,000 (33,000,000); petroleum products (2000) none (44,000). **Population economically active** (1992): 2,453 (Nauruan only); activity rate of total population 35.9% (unemployed 18.2%). **Households.** Average household size (1992; employed only) 10.0.

Foreign trade

Imports (1999): US$20,000,000 (agricultural products 65.0%, of which food 45.0%; remainder 35.0%). *Major import sources* (2001): Australia 49.4%; US 16.9%; Indonesia 7.9%; India 4.8%; UK 4.6%. **Exports** (1999): US$40,000,000 (phosphate, virtually 100%). *Major export destinations* (2001): New Zealand 28.6%; Australia 23.6%; Thailand 14.7%; South Korea 11.5%; Japan 9.6%.

Transport and communications

Transport. *Railroads* (2001): length 5 km. *Roads* (2001): total length 30 km (paved 79%). *Vehicles* (1989): passenger cars, trucks, and buses 1,448. *Air transport* (1996): passenger-km 243,000,000; metric ton-km cargo 24,000,000; airports (2001) with scheduled flights 1. **Communications**, in total units (units per 1,000 persons). Radios (1997): 7,000 (609); televisions (1997): 500 (48); telephone main lines (2001): 1,900 (160); cellular telephone subscribers (2001): 1,500 (130); Internet users (2001): 300 (26).

Education and health

Educational attainment (1992; Nauruan only). Percentage of population age 5 and over having: primary education or less 77.4%; secondary education 12.9%; higher 4.1%; not stated 5.6%. **Literacy** (1999): total population age 15 and over literate 99%. **Health** (2003): physicians 5 (1 per 2,016 persons); hospital beds 60 (1 per 168 persons); infant mortality rate per 1,000 live births 10.3. **Food** (2002;

data for Oceania): daily per capita caloric intake 2,952 (vegetable products 70%, animal products 30%); 129% of FAO recommended minimum.

Military

Total active duty personnel (2003): Nauru does not have any military establishment. The defense is assured by Australia, but no formal agreement exists.

Background

Nauru was inhabited by Pacific islanders when British explorers arrived in 1798 and named it Pleasant Island for the friendly welcome they received. Annexed by Germany in 1888, it was occupied by Australia at the start of World War I, and in 1919 it was placed under a joint mandate of Britain, Australia, and New Zealand. During World War II it was occupied by the Japanese. Made a UN trust territory under Australian administration in 1947, it gained independence in 1968. During the mid-1990s Nauru suffered political unrest.

Recent Developments

Constitutional problems combined with a funding crisis to cripple Nauru's economy in 2004. On 22 June Pres. René Harris's government collapsed in a no-confidence vote after one of his supporters changed sides, and former president Ludwig Scotty was returned to office. On 1 October Scotty abruptly dissolved the government, announced a state of emergency, and called a snap election for 23 October. His supporters captured a solid majority with 15 of the 18 seats, and Scotty immediately announced a new cabinet.

Internet resources:
<www.cia.gov/cia/publications/factbook/geos/nr.html>.

Nepal

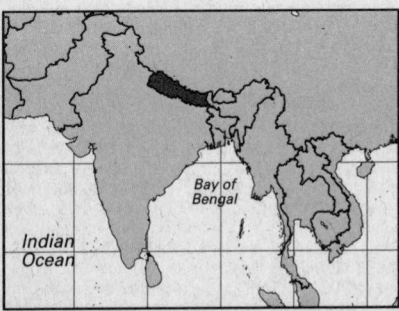

Bay of Bengal

Indian Ocean

Official name: Nepal Adhirajya (Kingdom of Nepal). **Form of government:** constitutional monarchy. **Chief of state:** King Gyanendra Bir Bikram Shah Deva (from 2001). **Head of government:** prime minister. **Capital:** Kathmandu. **Official language:** Nepali. **Official religion:** Hinduism. **Monetary unit:** 1 Nepalese rupee (NRs) = 100 paisa (pice); valuation (7 Jul 2005) $1 = NRs 70.48.

Demography

Area: 56,827 sq mi, 147,181 sq km. **Population** (2004): 24,692,000. **Density** (2004): persons per sq mi 434.5, persons per sq km 167.8. **Urban** (2002): 13.0%. **Sex distribution** (2001): male 49.95%; female 50.05%. **Age breakdown** (2001): under 15, 39.3%; 15–29, 27.0%; 30–44, 17.1%; 45–59, 10.1%; 60–74, 5.2%; 75 and over, 1.3%. **Ethnic composition** (2000): Nepalese 55.8%; Maithili 10.8%; Bhojpuri 7.9%; Tharu 4.4%; Tamang 3.6%; Newar 3.0%; Awadhi 2.7%; Magar 2.5%; Gurkha 1.7%; other 7.6%. **Religious affiliation** (2001): Hindu 80.6%; Buddhist 10.7%; Muslim 4.2%; Kirat (local traditional belief) 3.6%; Christian 0.5%; other 0.4%. **Major cities** (2001): Kathmandu 671,846; Biratnagar 166,674; Lalitpur 162,991; Pokhara 156,312; Birganj 112,484. **Location:** south-central Asia, bordering China and India.

Vital statistics

Birth rate per 1,000 population (2003): 32.5 (world avg. 21.3). **Death rate** per 1,000 population (2003): 9.8 (world avg. 9.1). **Natural increase rate** per 1,000 population (2002): 22.7 (world avg. 12.2). **Total fertility rate** (avg. births per childbearing woman; 2003): 4.4. **Life expectancy** at birth (2003): male 59.4 years; female 58.6 years.

National economy

Budget (2001). *Revenue:* NRs 48,596,000,000 (taxes on goods and services 34.1%, taxes on international trade 28.1%, income taxes 19.0%, state property revenues 1.9%, other 16.9%). *Expenditures:* NRs 74,289,000,000 (current expenditure 59.3%, of which education 14.0%, defense 7.8%, health 2.8%; development expenditure 40.7%, of which economic services 25.7%). **Public debt** (external, outstanding; 2002): $2,913,000,000. **Production** (metric tons except as noted). *Agriculture, forestry, fishing* (2002): rice 4,130,000, sugarcane 2,248,000, corn (maize) 1,511,000; livestock (number of live animals) 6,979,000 cattle, 6,607,000 goats, 3,701,000 buffalo; roundwood (2002) 13,988,000 cu m; fish catch (2002) 33,270. *Mining and quarrying* (2001): limestone 280,000; talc 6,000; salt 2,000. *Manufacturing* (value added in $'000,000; 1996): textiles 99; tobacco products 46; beverages 35. *Energy production (consumption):* electricity (kW-hr; 2000) 1,425,000,000 (1,525,000,000); coal (2000) 18,000 (435,000); petroleum products (2000) none (684,000). **Tourism** (2002): receipts from visitors $107,000,000; expenditures by nationals abroad (2001) $80,000,000. **Population economically active** (2001): total 11,138,000; activity rate of total population 48% (participation rates: ages 10 years and over, 58.2%; female [1991] 45.5%; unemployed 5.1%). **Household income and expenditure** (1984–85). Average household size (2001) 5.4; income per household NRs 14,796; sources of income: self-employment 63.4%, wages and salaries 25.1%, rent 7.5%, other 4.0%; expenditure: food and beverages 61.2%, housing 17.3%, clothing 11.7%, health care 3.7%, education and recreation 2.9%, transportation and communications 1.2%. **Gross national product** (at current market prices; 2003): $5,824,000,000 ($240 per capita). **Land use**

---

1 metric ton = about 1.1 short tons;   1 kilometer = 0.6 mi (statute);   1 metric ton-km cargo = about 0.68 short ton-mi cargo;   c.i.f.: cost, insurance, and freight;   f.o.b.: free on board

as % of total land area (2000): in temporary crops 21.3%, in permanent crops 0.6%, in pasture 12.3%; overall forest area 27.3%.

Foreign trade

Imports (2000–01-c.i.f.): NRs 115,687,000,000 (basic manufactures [including fabrics, yarns, and made-up articles] 35.6%, machinery and transport equipment 19.9%, chemicals and chemical products 11.2%, mineral fuels [mostly refined petroleum] 9.7%). *Major import sources* (2001): India 36.7%; Argentina 15.5%; China 15.3%; UAE 5.8%; Singapore 5.1%. **Exports** (2000–01-f.o.b.): NRs 55,654,000,-000 (ready-made garments 23.6%, carpets 15.4%, pashmina shawls 12.4%, vegetable ghee 6.4%). *Major export destinations* (2001): US 30.7%; India 30.2%; Germany 11.6%; Argentina 7.4%; Japan 2.3%.

Transport and communications

Transport. *Railroads* (2002): route length 59 km; passengers carried 1,600,000; freight handled 22,000 metric tons. *Roads* (1997): total length 7,700 km (paved 42%). *Vehicles* (2000): passenger cars 53,073; trucks and buses 32,065. *Air transport* (2000): passenger-km 1,023,000,000; metric ton-km cargo 108,000,000; airports (1996) with scheduled flights 24. **Communications,** in total units (units per 1,000 persons). Daily newspaper circulation (1996): 250,000 (11); radios (2000): 883,000 (39); televisions (2000): 159,000 (7); telephone main lines (2003): 371,800 (16); cellular telephone subscribers (2003): 50,400 (2.1); personal computers (2002): 85,000 (3.7); Internet users (2002): 80,000 (3.4).

Education and health

Educational attainment (2001). Percentage of population age 6 and over having: no formal schooling 8.7%; primary education 41.9%; incomplete secondary 30.6%; complete secondary and higher 17.6%; unknown 1.2%. **Literacy** (2001): total population age 15 and over literate 53%; males literate 60%; females literate 43%. **Health** (1999): physicians 1,259 (1 per 17,589 persons); hospital beds 5,190 (1 per 4,267 persons); infant mortality rate per 1,000 live births (2003) 70.6. **Food** (2001): daily per capita caloric intake 2,459 (vegetable products 94%, animal products 6%); 112% of FAO recommended minimum.

Military

Total active duty personnel (2003): 63,000 (army 100%). **Military expenditure as percentage of GNP** (1999): 0.8% (world 2.4%); per capita expenditure $2.

Did you know? Junko Tabei of Japan, with Ang Tsering Sherpa of Nepal, was the first woman to reach the summit of Mount Everest (16 May 1975).

Background

Nepal developed under early Buddhist influence, and dynastic rule dates from about the 4th century AD. It was formed into a single kingdom in 1769 and fought border wars with China, Tibet, and British India in the 18th–19th centuries. Its independence was recog-

nized by Britain in 1923. A new constitution in 1990 restricted royal authority and accepted a democratically elected parliamentary government. Nepal signed trade agreements with India in 1997. The Maoist Communist Party of Nepal began an armed insurgency in 1996. On 1 Jun 2001, King Birendra, the queen, and seven other members of the royal family were fatally shot by Crown Prince Dipendra, who then turned the gun on himself.

Recent Developments

Amid increasing street violence, political uncertainty and frustration, and an increasingly stronger position of the Maoist rebels in the western part of the country, on 1 Feb 2005 King Gyanendra seized total power in Nepal and declared a state of emergency, firing the prime minister and the government and suspending the civil rights of citizens. He also cut off telephone, airline, and Internet links with the outside world; in response the major powers recalled their ambassadors and cut off military aid. Both the rebels and domestic political opposition escalated their antigovernment activities. In early May the state of emergency was lifted.

Internet resources: <www.welcomenepal.com>.

The Netherlands

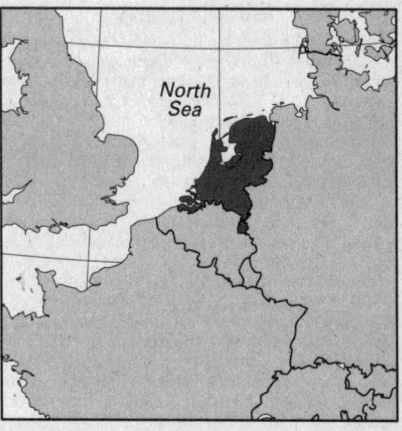

North Sea

Official name: Koninkrijk der Nederlanden (Kingdom of The Netherlands). **Form of government:** constitutional monarchy with a parliament (States General) comprising two legislative houses (First Chamber [75]; Second Chamber [150]). **Chief of state:** Queen Beatrix (from 1980). **Head of government:** Prime Minister Jan Peter Balkenende (from 2002). **Seat of government:** The Hague. **Capital:** Amsterdam. **Official language:** Dutch. **Official religion:** none. **Monetary unit:** 1 euro (€) = 100 cents; valuation (7 Jul 2005) $1 = €0.84; at conversion on 1 Jan 2002, €1 = 2.20 Netherlands guilders (f.).

Demography

Area: 16,034 sq mi, 41,528 sq km (including inland and coastal water area totaling 2,990 sq mi [7,745 sq km]). **Population** (2004): 16,275,000. **Density**

(2004; based on land area only): persons per sq mi 1,248, persons per sq km 481.8. **Urban** (2001): 89.6%. **Sex distribution** (2003): male 49.50%; female 50.50%. **Age breakdown** (2000): under 15, 18.6%; 15–29, 19.3%; 30–44, 24.2%; 45–59, 19.8%; 60–74, 12.1%; 75 and over, 6.0%. **Ethnic composition** (by place of origin [including 2nd generation]; 2002): Netherlander 81.6%; Indonesian 2.5%; German 2.5%; Turkish 2.1%; Surinamese 2.0%; Moroccan 1.8%; Netherlands Antillean/Aruban 0.8%; other 6.7%. **Religious affiliation** (1999): Roman Catholic 31.0%; Reformed (NHK) 14.0%; other Reformed 7.0%; Muslim 4.5%; Hindu 0.5%; nonreligious and other 43.0%. **Major urban agglomerations** (2000): Amsterdam 1,002,868; Rotterdam 989,956; The Hague 610,245; Utrecht 366,186; Eindhoven 302,274. **Location**: northwestern Europe, bordering the North Sea, Germany, and Belgium.

Vital statistics

Birth rate per 1,000 population (2003): 12.4 (world avg. 21.3); legitimate 72.8%. **Death rate** per 1,000 population (2003): 8.7 (world avg. 9.1). **Natural increase rate** per 1,000 population (2003): 3.0 (world avg. 12.2). **Total fertility rate** (avg. births per childbearing woman; 2003): 1.7. **Marriage rate** per 1,000 population (2000): 5.3. **Life expectancy** at birth (2003): male 76.2 years; female 80.9 years.

National economy

Budget (1997). *Revenue:* f. 324,360,000,000 (social security taxes 41.1%, income and corporate taxes 24.8%, value-added and excise taxes 22.7%, property taxes 3.0%). *Expenditures:* f. 337,620,000,000 (social security and welfare 37.4%, health 14.8%, education 10.0%, interest payments 9.1%, defense 3.9%, transportation 3.5%). **Public debt** (2002): $240,951,000,000. **Production** (metric tons except as noted). *Agriculture, forestry, fishing* (2002): potatoes 7,363,000, sugar beets 6,250,000, wheat 1,057,000; livestock (number of live animals; 2002) 11,648,000 pigs, 3,858,000 cattle, 1,186,000 sheep; roundwood (2002) 839,000 cu m; fish catch (2001) 570,226. *Manufacturing* (value added in €'000,000; 2000): food, beverages, and tobacco 11,625; chemicals and chemical products 8,314; electric/electronic machinery 6,429. *Energy production (consumption):* electricity (kW-hr; 2000) 92,110,000,000 (111,025,000,000); coal (2000) negligible (12,972,000); crude petroleum (barrels; 2000) 9,889,000 (377,450,000); petroleum products (2000) 63,322,000 (34,027,000); natural gas (cu m; 2000) 76,741,000,000 (51,469,000,000). **Household income and expenditure.** Average household size (2003) 2.3; disposable income per household (2000) €26,653; sources of income (1996): wages 48.4%, transfers 28.5%, self-employment 11.3%; expenditure (2000): housing and energy 23.2%, food and beverages 14.2%, transportation and communications 11.7%, textiles and clothing 6.4%. **Gross national product** (2003): $426,641,-000,000 ($26,310 per capita). **Population economically active** (1998): total 7,735,000; activity rate of total population 49.3% (participation rates: ages 15–64, 72.9%; female 42.5%; unemployed [February 2001–January 2002] 2.0%). **Tourism** (2002): re-

ceipts $7,706,000,000; expenditures $12,919,-000,000. **Land use** as % of total land area (2000): in temporary crops 26.9%, in permanent crops 1.0%, in pasture 29.9%; overall forest area 11.1%.

Foreign trade

Imports (2001-c.i.f.): €217,151,000,000 (computers and related equipment 11.9%, chemicals and chemical products 11.4%, mineral fuels 10.1%, food 8.2%, road vehicles 7.0%). *Major import sources:* Germany 18.5%; US 9.8%; Belgium-Luxembourg 9.3%; UK 8.9%; France 5.7%. **Exports** (2001-f.o.b.): €240,833,000,000 (chemicals and chemical products 15.4%, food 12.3%, computers and related equipment 11.7%, mineral fuels 9.2%). *Major export destinations:* Germany 25.6%; Belgium-Luxembourg 11.9%; UK 11.2%; France 10.3%; Italy 6.2%.

Transport and communications

Transport. *Railroads* (2001): length 2,809 km; passenger-km 14,392,000,000; metric ton-km cargo 4,293,000,000. *Roads* (1999): total length 116,500 km (paved 90%). *Vehicles* (2002): passenger cars 6,711,000; trucks and buses 997,000. *Air transport* (2001; KLM only): passenger-km 57,848,000,000; metric ton-km cargo 4,464,000,000; airports (1996) 6. **Communications**, in total units (units per 1,000 persons). Daily newspaper circulation (2000): 4,870,000 (306); radios (2000): 15,600,000 (980); televisions (2000): 8,570,000 (538); telephone main lines (2003): 10,004,000 (614); cellular telephone subscribers (2003): 12,500,000 (768); personal computers (2002): 7,557,000 (467); Internet users (2003): 8,500,000 (822).

Education and health

Educational attainment (2001). Percentage of population ages 15–64 having: primary education 14.1%; lower secondary 9.3%; upper secondary/vocational 54.3%; tertiary vocational 15.1%; university 6.9%; unknown 0.3%. **Health** (2000): physicians 27,161 (1 per 586 persons); hospital beds 90,747 (1 per 175 persons); infant mortality rate per 1,000 live births (2003) 5.2. **Food** (2001): daily per capita caloric intake 3,282 (vegetable products 64%, animal products 36%); 117% of FAO recommended minimum.

Military

Total active duty personnel (2003): 53,130 (army 43.6%, navy 22.8%, air force 20.8%, paramilitary 12.8%). **Military expenditure as percentage of GNP** (1999): 1.8% (world 2.4%); per capita expenditure $445.

Background

Celtic and Germanic tribes inhabited The Netherlands at the time of the Roman conquest. Under the Romans, trade and industry flourished, but by the mid-3rd century AD Roman power had waned, eroded by resurgent German tribes and the encroachment of the sea. A Germanic invasion (406–07) ended Roman control. The Merovingian dynasty followed the Romans but was supplanted in the 7th century

---

1 metric ton = about 1.1 short tons;   1 kilometer = 0.6 mi (statute);   1 metric ton-km cargo = about 0.68 short ton-mi cargo;   c.i.f.: cost, insurance, and freight;   f.o.b.: free on board

by the Carolingian dynasty, which converted the area to Christianity. After Charlemagne's death in 814, the area was increasingly the target of Viking attacks. It became part of the kingdom of Lotharingia, which established an Imperial Church. In the 12th–14th centuries dike building occurred on a large scale. The dukes of Burgundy gained control in the late 14th century. By the early 16th century the Low Countries were ruled by the Spanish Habsburgs. In 1581 the seven northern provinces, led by Calvinists, declared their independence from Spain, and in 1648, following the Thirty Years' War, Spain recognized Dutch independence. The 17th century was the golden age of Dutch civilization. The Dutch East India Company secured Asian colonies, and the country's standard of living soared. In the 18th century the region was conquered by the French and became the kingdom of Holland under Napoleon (1806). It remained neutral in World War I and declared neutrality in World War II but was occupied by Germany. It joined NATO in 1949, was a founding member of what is now the European Community, and is part of the EU.

Recent Developments

In 2004, the year that marked the 40th anniversary of the arrival of the first Turkish migrant workers, The Netherlands continued to struggle with issues of diversity and integration. A parliamentary commission in January concluded that government policies and procedures of the past 30 years had been at best only partially effective in accomplishing integration of immigrants. The same month the government announced the one-time approval of 2,334 long-standing applications for residence permits. In a move that was met with widespread consternation, the government also announced that within the next three years some 26,000 rejected asylum seekers who had exhausted all appeals would be returned to countries in which their safety was not deemed endangered. The murder of filmmaker Theo van Gogh, threats against politicians Ayaan Hirsi Ali (van Gogh's collaborator on *Submission*, a film some people considered derisive of Islam) and Geert Wilders (for controversial political proposals about immigration policy), along with the ensuing upheaval—including violent attacks on Muslim and Christian schools and houses of worship—underscored the view that ethnic and religious factions remained a significant concern. On 1 Jun 2005 Dutch voters overwhelmingly rejected the proposed EU constitution. That result, which followed on France's "non" vote three days earlier, effectively halted the ratification process.

Internet resources: <www.holland.com>.

Netherlands Antilles

Official name: Nederlandse Antillen (Netherlands Antilles). **Political status:** nonmetropolitan territory of The Netherlands with one legislative house (States of the Netherlands Antilles [22]). **Chief of state:** Queen Beatrix (from 1980), represented by Governor Frits Goedgedrag (from 2002). **Head of government:** Prime Minister Etienne Ys (from 3 Jun 2004). **Capital:** Willemstad. **Official language:** Dutch. **Official religion:** none. **Monetary unit:** 1 Netherlands Antillean guilder (NA f.) = 100 cents; valuation (7 Jul 2005) $1 = NA f. 1.77.

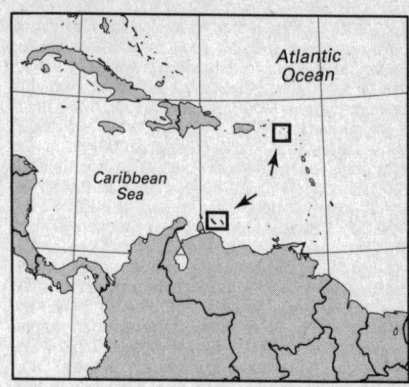

Demography

Area: 308 sq mi, 800 sq km. **Population** (2004): 179,000. **Density** (2004): persons per sq mi 581.1, persons per sq km 223.7. **Urban** (2001): 69.6%. **Sex distribution** (2003): male 46.81%; female 53.19%. **Age breakdown** (2001): under 15, 24.2%; 15–29, 18.2%; 30–44, 25.5%; 45–59, 19.0%; 60–74, 9.4%; 75 and over, 3.7%. **Ethnic composition** (2000): local black-other (Antillean Creole) 81.1%; Dutch 5.3%; Surinamese 2.9%; other (significantly West Indian black) 10.7%. **Religious affiliation** (2001): Roman Catholic 72.0%; Protestant 16.0%; Spiritist 0.9%; Buddhist 0.5%; Jewish 0.4%; Baha'i 0.3%; Hindu 0.2%; Muslim 0.2%; other/unknown 9.5%. **Major cities** (2001): Willemstad (urban agglomeration) 125,000; Kralendijk 7,900; Philipsburg 6,300. **Location:** two separate island groups in the Caribbean Sea, one just north of Venezuela, the other east of Puerto Rico.

Vital statistics

Birth rate per 1,000 population (2001): 13.6 (world avg. 21.3); (1988) legitimate 51.6%. **Death rate** per 1,000 population (2001): 6.4 (world avg. 9.1). **Natural increase rate** per 1,000 population (2001): 7.2 (world avg. 12.2). **Total fertility rate** (avg. births per childbearing woman; 2003): 2.0. **Marriage rate** per 1,000 population (2003): 4.2. **Divorce rate** per 1,000 population (1999): 2.6. **Life expectancy** at birth (2003): male 73.2 years; female 77.7 years.

National economy

Budget (2002). *Revenue:* NA f. 616,500,000 (tax revenue 86.5%, of which sales tax 40.6%, import duties 20.6%, excise on gasoline 12.7%; nontax revenue 11.7%; grants 1.8%). *Expenditures:* NA f. 669,000,-000 (current expenditures 94.7%, of which transfers 32.0%, wages 31.1%, interest payments 16.1%, goods and services 12.9%; development expenditures 5.3%). **Production** (metric tons except as noted). *Agriculture and fishing:* mostly tomatoes, beans, cucumbers, gherkins, melons, and lettuce grown on hydroponic farms; aloes grown for export, divi-divi pods, and sour orange fruit are nonhydroponic crops; livestock (number of live animals; 2002) 13,000 goats, 7,300 sheep, 135,000 chickens; fish catch (2001) 955. *Mining and quarrying* (2001): salt 500,000, sulfur by-product 30,000. *Manufacturing* (2000): residual fuel oil 5,112,000; gas-diesel oils

2,525,000; other manufactures include electronic parts, cigarettes, textiles, rum, and Curaçao liqueur. *Energy production (consumption):* electricity (kW-hr; 2000) 1,120,500,000 (1,120,600,000); crude petroleum (barrels; 2000) none (107,000,000); petroleum products (2000) 10,459,000 (2,052,000). **Land use** as % of total land area (2000): in temporary crops 10.0%; overall forest area 1%. **Tourism** (2001): receipts from visitors $746,000,000; expenditures by nationals abroad (2000) $339,-000,000. **Households.** Average household size (2001) 2.9; expenditure (1996; Curaçao only): housing 26.5%, transportation and communications 19.9%, food 14.7%, household furnishings 8.8%, recreation and education 8.2%, clothing and footwear 7.5%. **Gross domestic product** (at current market prices; 2001): $2,546,000,000 ($14,720 per capita). **Population economically active** (2001): total 81,558; activity rate of total population 46.4% (participation rates: ages 15–64, 68.7%; female 49.0%; unemployed [2002] 14.2%). **Public debt** (2003): $2,458,000,000.

Foreign trade

Imports (2001): NA f. 2,850,000,000 (nonpetroleum domestic imports 67.8%, crude petroleum and petroleum products 17.6%, imports of Curaçao free zone 14.6%). *Major import sources* (2000): US 25.8%; Mexico 20.7%; Gabon 6.6%; Italy 5.8%; The Netherlands 5.5%. **Exports** (2001): NA f. 984,000,000 (goods procured in ports for ships' bunkers 37.7%, re-exports of Curaçao free zone 30.9%, nonpetroleum domestic exports 18.3%). *Major export destinations* (2000): US 35.9%; Guatemala 9.4%; Venezuela 8.7%; France 5.4%; Singapore 2.8%.

Transport and communications

Transport. *Roads* (1992): total length 590 km (paved 51%). *Vehicles* (1999): passenger cars 74,840; trucks and buses 17,415. *Air transport* (2001; Curaçao and Sint Maarten airports): passenger arrivals and departures 2,131,000; freight loaded and unloaded 18,900 metric tons; airports (2000) with scheduled flights 5. **Communications,** in total units (units per 1,000 persons). Daily newspaper circulation (1996): 70,000 (341); radios (1997): 217,000 (1,039); televisions (1997): 69,000 (330); telephone main lines (2001): 81,000 (372); cellular telephone subscribers (1998): 16,000 (77); Internet users (1999): 2,000 (9.3).

Education and health

Educational attainment (2001). Percentage of population 25 and over having: no formal schooling 0.8%; primary education 24.2%; lower secondary 42.8%; upper secondary 16.8%; higher 11.4%; unknown 4.0%. **Literacy** (1995): total population age 15 and over literate 194,900 (96.6%); males literate 93,300 (96.6%); females literate 101,600 (96.6%). **Health** (2001): physicians 333 (1 per 520 persons); hospital beds 1,343 (1 per 129 persons); infant mortality rate per 1,000 live births (2003) 10.7. **Food** (2001): daily per capita caloric intake 2,565 (vegetable products 72%, animal products 28%); 106% of FAO recommended minimum.

Military

Total active duty personnel (2004): 1,000 Dutch naval personnel in Netherlands Antilles and Aruba.

Background

The islands of the Netherlands Antilles were sighted by Christopher Columbus in 1493 and claimed for Spain. In the 17th century the Dutch gained control, and in 1845 the islands became the Netherlands Antilles. In 1954 they became an integral part of The Netherlands, with full autonomy in domestic affairs. Aruba seceded from the group in 1986.

Recent Developments

In April 2004, Netherlands Antilles Prime Minister Mirna Louisa-Godett and Bernard Komproe, the current justice minister and former prime minister, were forced out of office in a parliamentary no-confidence vote. In November, Saba voted in a referendum to break from the Netherlands Antilles and be administered separately, similar to Aruba.

Internet resources:
<www.cia.gov/cia/publications/factbook/geos/nt.html>.

New Caledonia

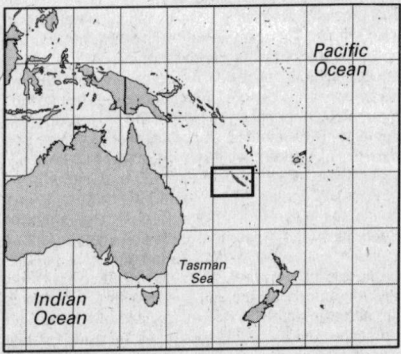

Official name: Nouvelle-Calédonie (New Caledonia). **Political status:** overseas collectivity (France) with one legislative house (Congress [54]; operates in association with 3 provincial assemblies). The Nouméa Accord of 1998 granted New Caledonia limited autonomy with likely independence by 2013. **Chief of state:** President of France Jacques Chirac (from 1995), represented by High Commissioner Daniel Constantin (from 2002). **Head of government:** President Marie-Noëlle Thémereau (from 10 Jun 2004). **Capital:** Nouméa. **Official language:** none; Kanak languages and French have special recognition per the Nouméa Accord. **Official religion:** none. **Monetary unit:** 1 franc of the Comptoirs français du Pacifique (CFPF) = 100 centimes; valuation (7 Jul 2005) $1 = CFPF 100.02; the CFPF is pegged to the euro (€) at €1 = CFPF 119.25 from 1 Jan 2002.

1 metric ton = about 1.1 short tons;   1 kilometer = 0.6 mi (statute);   1 metric ton-km cargo = about 0.68 short ton-mi cargo;   c.i.f.: cost, insurance, and freight;   f.o.b.: free on board

Demography

Area: 7,172 sq mi, 18,575 sq km. **Population** (2004): 224,000. **Density** (2004): persons per sq mi 31.2, persons per sq km 12.0. **Urban** (2002): 79.0%. **Sex distribution** (2003): male 50.33%; female 49.67%. **Age breakdown** (2003): under 15, 29.7%; 15–29, 25.4%; 30–44, 21.6%; 45–59, 13.9%; 60–74, 7.5%; 75 and over, 1.9%. **Ethnic composition** (1996): Melanesian 45.3%, of which local (Kanak) 44.1%, Vanuatuan 1.2%; European 34.1%; Wallisian or Futunan 9.0%; Indonesian 2.6%; Tahitian 2.6%; Vietnamese 1.4%; other 5.0%. **Religious affiliation** (2000): Roman Catholic 54.2%; Protestant 14.0%; Muslim 2.7%; other Christian 2.1%; other 27.0%. **Major cities** (1996): Nouméa 76,293 (urban agglomeration 118,823); Mont-Dore 20,780 (within Nouméa urban agglomeration); Dumbéa 13,888 (within Nouméa urban agglomeration). **Location:** South Pacific Ocean, about 1,100 mi (1,800 km) east of Queensland, Australia.

Vital statistics

Birth rate per 1,000 population (2003): 18.6 (world avg. 21.3); (1996) legitimate 36.4%. **Death rate** per 1,000 population (2003): 5.1 (world avg. 9.1). **Natural increase rate** per 1,000 population (2003): 13.5 (world avg. 12.2). **Total fertility rate** (avg. births per childbearing woman; 2003): 2.4. **Marriage rate** per 1,000 population (2001): 4.3. **Divorce rate** per 1,000 population (1999): 0.8. **Life expectancy** at birth (2003): male 70.6 years; female 76.6 years.

National economy

Budget (2001). *Revenue:* $A 1,184,000,000 (tax revenue 74.7%, nontax revenue 25.3%). *Expenditures:* $A 1,156,000,000 (current expenditure 90.1%, development expenditure 9.9%). **Production** (metric tons except as noted). *Agriculture, forestry, fishing* (2003): coconuts 16,000, yams 11,222, vegetables 3,900; livestock (number of live animals) 110,000 cattle, 25,500 pigs, 510,000 poultry; roundwood (2002) 4,800 cu m; fish catch (2001) 5,197, of which shrimp 1,870, tuna 1,008, sea cucumbers 489. *Mining and quarrying:* nickel ore (2003) 6,625,000, of which nickel content (2002) 59,867; cobalt (2002) 900 (recovered). *Manufacturing* (2003): cement (2002) 100,080; ferronickel (metal content) 50,666; nickel matte (metal content) 10,857. *Energy production (consumption):* electricity (kW-hr; 2002) 1,758,000,000 (1,758,000,000); coal (2000) none (160,000); petroleum products (2000) none (405,-000). **Population economically active** (1996): total 80,589; activity rate of total population 40.9% (participation rates: over age 14, 57.3%; female 39.7%; unemployed 18.6%). **Public debt** (external, outstanding; 1999): $746,000,000. **Gross national product** (at current market prices; 2001): $3,200,000,000 ($15,060 per capita). **Household income and expenditure.** Average household size (2002) 3.9; average annual income per household (1991) CFPF 3,361,233; sources of income (1991): wages and salaries 68.2%, transfer payments 13.7%, other 18.1%; expenditure (1991): food and beverages 25.9%, housing 20.4%, transportation and communications 16.1%, recreation 4.8%. **Tourism:** receipts from visitors (2001) $93,000,000. **Land use** as % of total land area (2000): in temporary crops 0.4%, in permanent crops 0.3%, in pasture 11.8%; overall forest area 20.4%.

Foreign trade

Imports (2002-c.i.f.): CFPF 127,123,000,000 (machinery and apparatus 18.2%, food 15.6%, transportation equipment 15.2%, mineral products [mostly coal and refined petroleum] 13.4%, chemicals and chemical products 8.4%). *Major import sources* (2003): France 50.0%; Singapore 10.4%; Australia 10.2%; New Zealand 4.1%; Germany 3.8%. **Exports** (2002-f.o.b.): CFPF 59,101,000,000 (ferronickel 64.2%, nickel matte 13.0%, nickel ore 12.3%, shrimp 2.3%). *Major export destinations* (2003): France 26.0%; Japan 21.4%; Taiwan 16.6%; Spain 8.8%; Australia 6.4%.

Transport and communications

Transport. *Roads* (2000): total length 5,432 km (paved [1993] 52%). *Vehicles:* passenger cars (2001) 85,500; trucks and buses (1997) 23,000. *Air transport* (2003; Air Calédonie only): passenger-km 46,000,000, metric ton-km cargo 4,115,000; airports (2004) with scheduled flights 11. **Communications,** in total units (units per 1,000 persons). Daily newspaper circulation (1996): 24,000 (121); radios (1997): 107,-000 (533); televisions (1999): 101,000 (480); telephone main lines (2002): 52,000 (232); cellular telephone subscribers (2002): 80,000 (357); Internet users (2003): 60,000 (262).

Education and health

Educational attainment (1996). Percentage of population age 14 and over having: no formal schooling 5.7%; primary education 28.9%; lower secondary 30.2%; upper secondary 24.6%; higher 10.5%. **Health** (1999): physicians 418 (1 per 497 persons); hospital beds 838 (1 per 248 persons); infant mortality rate per 1,000 live births (2003) 8.1. **Food** (2001): daily per capita caloric intake 2,770 (vegetable products 76%, animal products 24%); 120% of FAO recommended minimum.

Military

Total active duty personnel (2003): 2,700 French troops.

Background

Excavations indicate an Austronesian presence in New Caledonia about 2000–1000 BC. The islands were visited by James Cook in 1774 and by various navigators and traders in the 18th–19th centuries. They were occupied by France in 1853 and were a penal colony from 1864 to 1897. During World War II the islands were the site of Allied bases. They became a French overseas territory in 1946. In 1987 residents voted by referendum to remain part of France.

Recent Developments

Political tensions remained high in New Caledonia, with some groups demanding greater recognition of indigenous rights and even independence. The debate was sharpened when the planned census there was dropped after French Pres. Jacques Chirac criticized the inclusion of questions concerning ethnic origin. New Caledonia's economy benefited from strong nickel prices as well as a stable tourism market.

Internet resources:
<www.newcaledoniatourism-south.com>.

New Zealand

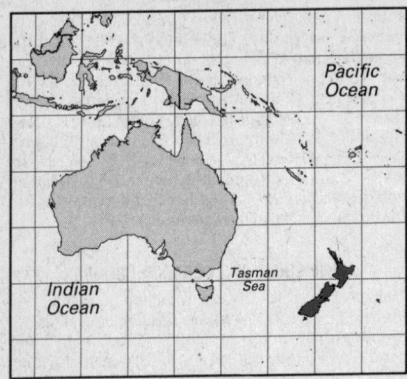

Official name: New Zealand (English); Aotearoa (Maori). **Form of government:** constitutional monarchy with one legislative house (House of Representatives [120, including seven elective seats allocated to Maoris]). **Chief of state:** Queen Elizabeth II (from 1952), represented by Governor-General Dame Silvia Cartwright (from 2001). **Head of government:** Prime Minister Helen Clark (from 1999). **Capital:** Wellington. **Official languages:** English; Maori. **Official religion:** none. **Monetary unit:** 1 New Zealand dollar ($NZ) = 100 cents; valuation (7 Jul 2005) US$1 = $NZ 1.49.

Demography

Area: 104,454 sq mi, 270,534 sq km. **Population** (2004): 4,060,000. **Density** (2004): persons per sq mi 38.9, persons per sq km 15.0. **Urban** (2002): 86.0%. **Sex distribution** (2001): male 49.07%; female 50.93%. **Age breakdown** (2001): under 15, 22.5%; 15–29, 20.4%; 30–44, 23.0%; 45–59, 18.0%; 60–74, 10.7%; 75 and over, 5.4%. **Ethnic composition** (2001): European 73.8%; Maori (local Polynesian) 13.5%; Asian 6.1%; other Pacific Peoples (mostly other Polynesian) 6.0%; other 0.6%. **Religious affiliation** (2001): Christian 55.2%, of which Anglican 15.3%, Roman Catholic 12.7%, Presbyterian 11.3%; nonreligious 26.9%; Buddhist 1.1%; Hindu 1.0%; other religions/not specified 15.8%. **Major urban areas** (2001): Auckland. 1,074,513; Wellington 339,750; Christchurch 334,107; Hamilton 166,128; Dunedin 107,088. **Location:** between the South Pacific Ocean and the Tasman Sea, southeast of Australia.

Vital statistics

Birth rate per 1,000 population (2003): 14.1 (world avg. 21.3); (2001) legitimate 56.3%. **Death rate** per 1,000 population (2003): 7.5 (world avg. 9.1). **Natural increase rate** per 1,000 population (2003): 6.6 (world avg. 12.2). **Total fertility rate** (avg. births per childbearing woman; 2003): 1.8. **Marriage rate** per 1,000 population (2001): 5.1. **Life expectancy** at birth (2003): male 75.3 years; female 81.4 years.

National economy

Budget (2000–01). *Revenue:* $NZ 37,156,000,000 (income taxes 59.4%, taxes on goods and services 34.4%, nontax revenue 6.2%). *Expenditures:* $NZ 37,019,000,000 (social welfare 37.0%, health 19.0%, education 17.6%). **Production** (metric tons except as noted). *Agriculture, forestry, fishing* (2002): apples 537,000, barley 406,000, wheat 355,000; livestock (number of live animals) 43,142,000 sheep, 9,633,000 cattle, 358,000 pigs; roundwood (2000) 20,523,000 cu m; fish catch (2001) 637,000. *Mining and quarrying* (2001): limestone 4,746,000; iron ore and sand concentrate 1,636,000; gold 9,850 kg. *Manufacturing* (1999): wood pulp 1,572,000; chemical fertilizers 1,365,000; wool yarn 23,500. *Energy production (consumption):* electricity (kW-hr; 2000) 39,010,000,000 (39,010,000,000); hard coal (2000) 3,355,000 (1,755,000); lignite (2000) 213,000 (261,000); crude petroleum (barrels; 2000) 13,068,000 (40,001,000); petroleum products (2000) 5,038,000 (5,365,000); natural gas (cu m; 2000) 5,445,000,000 (5,444,000,000). **Household income and expenditure.** Average household size (1998) 2.8; annual gross income per household (2000–01) $NZ 53,076; sources of income (1998): wages and salaries 65.8%, transfer payments 15.2%, self-employment 9.8%, other 9.2%; expenditure (2000–01): housing 23.9%, food 16.5%, transportation 15.9%, household goods 12.8%, clothing 3.2%. **Tourism** (2002): receipts US$2,918,000,000; expenditures US$1,480,000,000. **Gross national product** (2003): US$63,608,000,000 (US$15,870 per capita). **Population economically active** (2000): total 1,923,700; activity rate 50.1% (participation rates: over age 15, 66.2%; female 45.3%; unemployed 5.7%). **Land use** as % of total land area (2000): in temporary crops 5.6%, in permanent crops 6.9%, in pasture 51.7%; overall forest area 29.7%.

Foreign trade

Imports (2001–02-f.o.b. in balance of trade and c.i.f. in commodities and trading partners): $NZ 32,165,000,000 (machinery and apparatus 21.4%, crude and refined petroleum 13.7%, vehicles 13.4%, plastics 3.7%). *Major import sources:* Australia 21.4%; US 13.7%; Japan 10.8%; China 7.2%; Germany 4.7%. **Exports** (2001–02): $NZ 31,676,000,000 (domestic exports 96.2%, of which dairy products 20.6%, beef and sheep meat 12.7%, wood and paper products 10.8%, machinery and apparatus 6.1%, fruits and nuts 3.7%; reexports 3.8%). *Major export destinations:* Australia 19.9%; US 15.3%; Japan 11.5%; UK 4.9%; South Korea 4.5%; China 4.5%.

Transport and communications

Transport. *Railroads* (1999): route length 3,912 km; passengers carried (2001–02) 14,330,000; metric ton-km cargo (1998) 3,960,000,000. *Roads* (1999): total length 92,075 km (paved 62%). *Vehicles* (2002): passenger cars 1,960,503; trucks and buses 374,005. *Air transport* (1999; Air New Zealand only): passenger-km 19,879,000,000; metric ton-km cargo 851,744,000; airports (1997) 36.

---

1 metric ton = about 1.1 short tons;   1 kilometer = 0.6 mi (statute);   1 metric ton-km cargo = about 0.68 short ton-mi cargo;   c.i.f.: cost, insurance, and freight;   f.o.b.: free on board

Communications, in total units (units per 1,000 persons). Daily newspaper circulation (2000): 799,000 (207); radios (2000): 3,850,000 (997); televisions (2000): 2,010,000 (522); telephone main lines (2002): 1,765,000 (448); cellular telephone subscribers (2003): 2,599,000 (648); personal computers (2002): 1,630,000 (414); Internet users (2003): 2,110,000 (526).

Education and health

Educational attainment (2001). Percentage of population ages 25–64 having: no formal schooling to incomplete secondary 26%; secondary 36%; vocational and some undergraduate 24%; completed undergraduate 14%. **Literacy:** virtually 100%. **Health** (2002): physicians 8,403 (1 per 469 persons); hospital beds 23,825 (1 per 165 persons); infant mortality rate per 1,000 live births (2003) 6.1. **Food** (2001): daily per capita caloric intake 3,235 (vegetable products 67%, animal products 33%); 123% of FAO recommended minimum.

Military

Total active duty personnel (2003): 8,610 (army 51.5%, air force 23.0%, navy 25.6%). **Military expenditure as percentage of GNP** (1999): 1.2% (world 2.4%); per capita expenditure $156.

Background

Polynesian occupation of New Zealand dates to about AD 1000. First sighted by Dutch explorer Abel Janszoon Tasman in 1642, the main islands were charted by Capt. James Cook in 1769. Named a British crown colony in 1840, the area was the scene of warfare between colonists and native Maori through the 1860s. In 1907 the colony became the Dominion of New Zealand. It administered Western Samoa during 1919–62 and participated in both world wars. When Britain joined what is now the European Union in the early 1970s, its influence led New Zealand to expand its export markets and diversify its economy.

Recent Developments

Race relations dominated politics in New Zealand after opposition National Party leader Donald Brash alleged that Prime Minister Helen Clark's Labour-led government was running policies with a pro-Maori bias. Responding to opinion polls supporting Brash's stance, Clark appointed Trevor Mallard coordinating minister on race relations to review policies with racial preferences. Having rejected Maori claims to title of the nation's foreshore and seabed and ignored a two-week protest march by thousands of Maori demonstrators that ended on 5 May 2004, Parliament enacted government-sponsored legislation in November confirming public ownership. In protest against the Foreshore and Seabed bill, junior cabinet minister Tariana Turia resigned from the Labour Party and the House of Representatives, forcing a by-election on 10 July, which she won overwhelmingly on behalf of the new Maori Party. Destiny New Zealand, a new church-based political party, organized rallies on family and moral issues in Auckland and Wellington, where police estimated 7,500 attendees. The party also protested legalized prostitution, abortion, and government-sponsored legislation to solemnize and register relationships and civil unions between same-sex couples.

Internet resources: <www.newzealand.com>.

Nicaragua

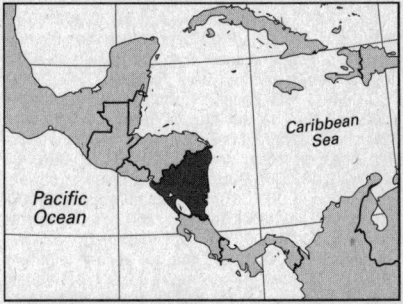

Official name: República de Nicaragua (Republic of Nicaragua). **Form of government:** unitary multiparty republic with one legislative house (National Assembly [92, including two unsuccessful 2001 presidential candidates meeting constitutional requirements for seating]). **Head of state and government:** President Enrique Bolaños Geyer (from 2002). **Capital:** Managua. **Official language:** Spanish. **Official religion:** none. **Monetary unit:** 1 córdoba oro (C$) = 100 centavos; valuation (7 Jul 2005) US$1 = C$16.39.

Demography

Area: 50,337 sq mi, 130,373 sq km; land area alone equals 46,464 sq mi, 120,340 sq km. **Population** (2004): 5,360,000. **Density** (2004; based on land area): persons per sq mi 115.4, persons per sq km 44.5. **Urban** (2001): 56.5%. **Sex distribution** (2003): male 50.01%; female 49.99%. **Age breakdown** (2003): under 15, 38.8%; 15–29, 30.4%; 30–44, 17.5%; 45–59, 8.6%; 60–74, 3.7%; 75 and over, 0.9%. **Ethnic composition** (2000): mestizo (Spanish/Indian) 63.1%; white 14.0%; black 8.0%; multiple ethnicities 5.0%; other 9.9%. **Religious affiliation** (1995): Roman Catholic 85.1%; Protestant 11.6%, of which Evangelical 8.8%; nonreligious 1.3%; other 2.0%. **Major cities** (1995): Managua (urban agglomeration, 2003) 1,098,000; León 123,865; Chinandega 97,387; Masaya 88,971; Granada 71,783. **Location:** Central America, bordering Honduras, the Caribbean Sea, Costa Rica, and the North Pacific Ocean.

Vital statistics

Birth rate per 1,000 population (2003): 26.1 (world avg. 21.3). **Death rate** per 1,000 population (2003): 4.6 (world avg. 9.1). **Natural increase rate** per 1,000 population (2003): 21.5 (world avg. 12.2). **Total fertility rate** (avg. births per childbearing woman; 2003): 3.0. **Life expectancy** at birth (2003): male 67.7 years; female 71.8 years.

National economy

Budget (2002). *Revenue:* C$8,592,400,000 (tax revenue 94.7%, of which sales tax 42.2%, import duties

29.2%, tax on income and profits 18.8%; nontax revenue 5.3%). *Expenditures:* C$11,905,000,000 (current expenditure 67.2%, development expenditure 32.8%). **Public debt** (external, outstanding; 2002): US$5,576,000,000. **Production** (metric tons except as noted). *Agriculture, forestry, fishing* (2002): sugarcane 3,389,000, corn (maize) 483,330, rice 264,000; livestock (number of live animals) 3,350,000 cattle, 420,000 pigs; roundwood 5,920,000 cu m; fish catch (2001) 28,520, of which crustaceans 15,486. *Mining and quarrying* (2001): gold 117,350 troy oz. *Manufacturing* (value added in C$'000,000; 2002 [at 1980 prices]): food 1,975; beverages 1,349; cement, bricks, tiles 576; refined petroleum 222; chemical products 206. *Energy production (consumption):* electricity (kW-hr; 2002) 2,620,000,000 ([2000] 2,403,000,000); crude petroleum (barrels; 2000) none (6,069,000); petroleum products (2000) 785,000 (1,138,000). **Tourism** (2002): receipts from visitors US$110,000,000; expenditures by nationals abroad US$69,000,000. **Land use** as % of total land area (2000): in temporary crops 15.9%, in permanent crops 1.9%, in pasture 39.7%; overall forest area 27.0%. **Population economically active** (2001): total 1,900,400; activity rate of total population 37.7% (participation rates: ages 15–64 [2000] 64.1%; female [2000] 29.5%; unemployed 10.5%). **Gross national product** (2003): US$3,989,000,000 (US$730 per capita). **Households.** Average household size (2002) 5.6; expenditure (1999): food and beverages 41.8%, education 9.8%, housing 9.8%, transportation 8.5%.

Foreign trade

Imports (2003-f.o.b. in balance of trade and c.i.f. in commodities and trading partners): US$1,887,000,000 (nondurable consumer goods 25.9%; mineral fuels 17.4%; capital goods for industry 11.8%; durable consumer goods 7.5%). *Major import sources:* US 24.7%; Venezuela 9.7%; Costa Rica 9.0%; Mexico 8.4%; Guatemala 7.3%. **Exports** (2003): US$605,000,000 (non-marine food products 44.6%, of which coffee 14.1%, meat 13.5%; lobster 6.0%; gold 5.8%; shrimp 5.5%). *Major export destinations:* US 33.4%; El Salvador 17.3%; Costa Rica 8.1%; Honduras 7.2%; Mexico 4.6%.

Transport and communications

Transport. *Roads* (2002): total length 18,709 km (paved 11%). *Vehicles* (2002): passenger cars 83,168; trucks and buses 121,796. *Air transport* (2000): passenger-km 72,000,000; metric ton-km cargo 600,000; airports (1997) with scheduled flights 10. **Communications,** in total units (units per 1,000 persons). Daily newspaper circulation (2000): 152,000 (30); radios (2000): 1,370,000 (270); televisions (2000): 350,000 (69); telephone main lines (2002): 171,600 (32); cellular telephone subscribers (2002): 202,800 (38); personal computers (2002): 90,000 (17); Internet users (2002): 150,000 (28).

Education and health

Educational attainment (1995). Percentage of population age 25 and over having: no formal schooling 30.6%; no formal schooling (literate) 3.9%; primary

education 39.2%; secondary 17.0%; technical 3.1%; incomplete undergraduate 2.2%; complete undergraduate 4.0%. **Literacy** (2000): total population age 15 and over literate 66.5%; males literate 66.3%; females literate 66.8%. **Health:** physicians (2002) 2,066 (1 per 2,491 persons); hospital beds 5,031 (1 per 1,023 persons); infant mortality rate per 1,000 live births (2003) 31.2. **Food** (2001): daily per capita caloric intake 2,256 (vegetable products 92%, animal products 8%); 99% of FAO recommended minimum.

Military

Total active duty personnel (2003): 14,000 (army 85.7%, navy 5.7%, air force 8.6%). **Military expenditure as percentage of GNP** (1999): 1.2% (world 2.4%); per capita expenditure US$5.

Background

Nicaragua has been inhabited for thousands of years, most notably by the Maya. Christopher Columbus arrived in 1502, and Spanish explorers discovered Lake Nicaragua soon thereafter. Nicaragua was governed by Spain until 1821, when it declared its independence. It was part of Mexico and then the United Provinces of Central America until 1938, when full independence was achieved. The US intervened in political affairs by maintaining troops there in 1912–33. Ruled by the dictatorial Somoza dynasty from 1936 to 1979, it was taken over by the Sandinistas after a popular revolt. They were opposed by armed insurgents, the US-backed contras, from 1981. The Sandinista government nationalized several sectors of the economy but lost the national elections in 1990. The new government returned many economic activities to private control, but unrest continued through the 1990s.

Recent Developments

Politics in Nicaragua in 2004 was dominated by a three-way struggle between Pres. Enrique Bolaños Geyer, the Constitutionalist Liberal Party (PLC), and the Sandinista Front (FSLN). In November municipal elections, the FSLN won 87 of the 152 municipalities, including Managua. The PLC won 57 municipalities, and a conservative alliance (APRE) formed to back Bolaños placed a distant third. Under pressure from the US, Bolaños ordered the destruction of all surface-to-air missiles (SAMs) in Nicaragua's arsenal, and by December about half of them had been destroyed. When in early 2005 some SAMs were discovered being sold on the black market, however, and the involvement of the old antagonist of the US, leftist Daniel Ortega, was confirmed, the US suspended military aid to Nicaragua.

Internet resources: <www.intur.gob.ni>.

Niger

Official name: République du Niger (Republic of Niger). **Form of government:** multiparty republic with one legislative house (National Assembly [113]). **Head of state and government:** President Mamadou Tandja (from

---

1 metric ton = about 1.1 short tons; 1 kilometer = 0.6 mi (statute); 1 metric ton-km cargo = about 0.68 short ton-mi cargo; c.i.f.: cost, insurance, and freight; f.o.b.: free on board

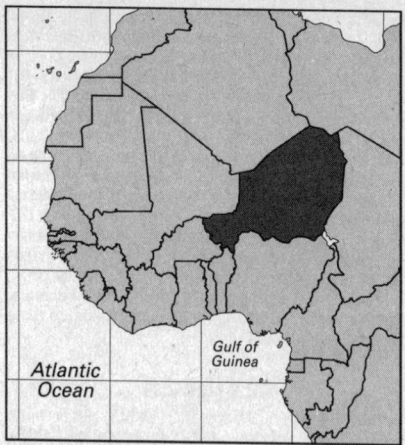

Atlantic
Ocean

Gulf of
Guinea

1999), assisted by Prime Minister Hama Amadou (from 2000). **Capital:** Niamey. **Official language:** French. **Official religion:** none. **Monetary unit:** 1 CFA franc (CFAF) = 100 centimes; valuation (7 Jul 2005) $1 = CFAF 549.50 (earlier pegged to the French franc, after 1 Jan 2002 the CFAF was pegged at 655.96 to the euro).

Demography

Area: 459,286 sq mi, 1,189,546 sq km. **Population (2004):** 11,679,000. **Density (2004):** persons per sq mi 25.4, persons per sq km 9.8. **Urban** (2001): 16.2%. **Sex distribution** (2001): male 49.86%; female 50.14%. **Age breakdown** (2001): under 15, 48.0%; 15–29, 26.3%; 30–44, 14.1%; 45–59, 7.8%; 60–74, 3.2%; 75 and over, 0.6%. **Ethnolinguistic composition** (2000): Zerma- (Djerma-) Songhai 25.7%; Tazarawa 14.9%; Fulani (Peul) 11.1%; Hausa 6.6%; other 41.7%. **Religious affiliation** (2000): Sunni Muslim 90.7%; traditional beliefs 8.7%; Christian 0.5%; other 0.1%. **Major cities** (2001): Niamey 674,950 (urban agglomeration [2003] 890,000); Zinder 170,574; Maradi 147,038; Agadez 76,957; Tahoua 72,446. **Location:** western Africa, bordering Algeria, Libya, Chad, Nigeria, Benin, Burkina Faso, and Mali.

Vital statistics

Birth rate per 1,000 population (2003): 49.5 (world avg. 21.3). **Death rate** per 1,000 population (2003): 21.7 (world avg. 9.1). **Natural increase rate** per 1,000 population (2003): 27.8 (world avg. 12.2). **Total fertility rate** (avg. births per childbearing woman; 2003): 6.9. **Life expectancy** at birth (2003): male 42.3 years; female 42.1 years.

National economy

Budget (2003). *Revenue:* CFAF 221,281,000,000 (taxes 69.3%, external aid and gifts 29.2%, nontax revenue 1.5%). *Expenditures:* CFAF 272,200,-000,000 (current expenditures 57.6%, of which education 10.9%, defense and public order 8.4%, interest 6.4%, health 3.8%; development expenditures 42.4%). **Public debt** (external, outstanding; 2002): $1,604,000,000. **Tourism** (2002): receipts from visi-

tors $28,000,000; expenditures by nationals abroad $16,000,000. **Gross national product** (2003): $2,361,000,000 ($200 per capita). **Production** (metric tons except as noted). *Agriculture, forestry, fishing* (2003): millet 2,567,200, sorghum 669,700, cowpeas 654,200; livestock (number of live animals) 6,900,000 goats, 4,500,000 sheep, 2,260,000 cattle; roundwood (2002) 8,601,400 cu m; fish catch (2001) 20,821. *Mining and quarrying* (2003): uranium 3,143; salt 3,000. *Manufacturing* (value added in CFAF '000,000; 1998): paper and products 3,171; food 1,697; soaps and other chemical products 1,547. *Energy production (consumption):* electricity (kW-hr; 2000) 238,000,000 (451,000,000); coal (2000) 175,000 (175,000); petroleum products (2001) none (138,300). **Population economically active** (1988; excludes nomadic population): total 2,315,694; activity rate of total population 31.9% (participation rates: ages 15–64, 55.2%; female 20.4%). **Households.** Average household size (2002) 6.4; expenditure (1996): food, beverages, and tobacco products 45.1%, housing and energy 13.9%, transportation 12.1%, household furnishings 7.7%, clothing and footwear 5.8%. **Land use** as % of total land area (2000): in temporary crops 3.5%, in permanent crops 0.01%, in pasture 9.5%; overall forest area 1.0%.

Foreign trade

Imports (2003): CFAF 275,700,000,000 (food products 28.6%, capital goods 26.3%, petroleum products 11.5%, intermediate goods 6.7%). *Major import sources:* France 17.1%; Côte d'Ivoire 15.0%; Nigeria 8.1%; Japan 4.6%. **Exports** (2003): CFAF 203,300,-000,000 (uranium 32.2%, reexports 17.9%, cattle 17.5%, onions 7.7%, cowpeas 5.3%). *Major export destinations:* France 37.1%; Nigeria 33.6%; Japan 17.2%; Spain 3.8%.

Transport and communications

Transport. *Roads* (2000): total length 14,000 km (paved 26%). *Vehicles* (1999): passenger cars; 26,000, trucks and buses 35,600. *Air transport* (2000; represents $1/11$ of the traffic of Air Afrique; Air Afrique, an airline jointly owned by 11 African countries [including Niger], was declared bankrupt in 2002): passenger-km 216,000,000; airports (1999) with scheduled flights 6. **Communications,** in total units (units per 1,000 persons). Daily newspaper circulation (1996): 2,000 (0.2); radios (2000): 1,270,000 (121); televisions (2000): 388,000 (37); telephone main lines (2002): 22,400 (1.9); cellular telephone subscribers (2003): 24,000 (2); personal computers (2002): 7,000 (0.6); Internet users (2002): 15,000 (1.3).

Education and health

Educational attainment (1988). Percentage of population age 25 and over having: no formal schooling 85.0%; Koranic education 11.2%; primary education 2.5%; secondary 1.1%; higher 0.2%. **Literacy** (2001): total population age 15 and over literate 16.5%; males literate 24.4%; females literate 8.9%. **Health:** physicians (1997) 324 (1 per 28,117 persons); infant mortality rate per 1,000 live births (2003) 123.6. **Food** (2001): daily per capita caloric intake 2,118 (vegetable products 94%, animal products 6%); 90% of FAO recommended minimum.

Military

Total active duty personnel (2003): 5,300 (army 98.1%, air force 1.9%). Military expenditure as percentage of GNP (1999): 1.2% (world 2.4%); per capita expenditure $2.

Background

On the territory of Niger, there is evidence of Neolithic culture, and several kingdoms existed there before the colonialists arrived. First explored by Europeans in the late 18th century, it became a French colony in 1922. It became an overseas territory of France in 1946 and gained independence in 1960. The first multiparty elections were held in 1993.

Recent Developments

Niger remained one of the poorest countries in the world, but international donors expressed guarded approval of the government's attempts to lift the standard of living of its people, particularly subsistence farmers. On 5 Oct 2004 the first ingot was extracted from the new Samira gold mine in southwestern Niger, marking the launch of modern commercial extraction of the ore.

Internet resources: <www.nigerembassyusa.org>.

Nigeria

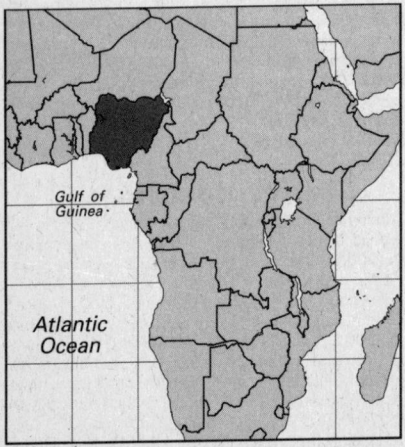

Gulf of Guinea

Atlantic Ocean

Official name: Federal Republic of Nigeria. Form of government: federal republic with two legislative bodies (Senate [109]; House of Representatives [360]). Head of state and government: President Olusegun Obasanjo (from 1999). Capital: Abuja. Official language: English. Official religion: none. Monetary unit: 1 Nigerian naira (N) = 100 kobo; valuation (7 Jul 2005) $1 = N133.75.

Demography

Area: 356,669 sq mi, 923,768 sq km. Population (2004): 128,254,000. Density (2004): persons per sq mi 359.6, persons per sq km 138.8. Urban (2002): 44.9%. Sex distribution (2003): male 50.59%; female 49.41%. Age breakdown (2003): under 15, 43.6%; 15–29, 27.9%; 30–44, 15.4%; 45–59, 8.5%; 60–74, 3.9%; 75 and over, 0.7%. Ethnic composition (2000): Yoruba 17.5%; Hausa 17.2%; Igbo (Ibo) 13.3%; Fulani 10.7%; Ibibio 4.1%; Kanuri 3.6%; Egba 2.9%; Tiv 2.6%; Bura 1.1%; Nupe 1.0%; Edo 1.0%; other 25.0%. Religious affiliation (2000): Christian 45.9%, of which independent Christian 15.0%, Anglican 13.0%, other Protestant 9.0%, Roman Catholic 8.0%; Muslim 43.9%; African indigenous 9.8%; other 0.4%. Major cities (2002): Lagos 8,030,000; Kano 3,250,000; Ibadan 3,080,000; Kaduna 1,460,000; Benin City 1,050,000. Location: western Africa, bordering Niger, Chad, Cameroon, the Gulf of Guinea, and Benin.

Vital statistics

Birth rate per 1,000 population (2003): 38.8 (world avg. 21.3). Death rate per 1,000 population (2003): 13.8 (world avg. 9.1). Natural increase rate per 1,000 population (2003): 25.0 (world avg. 12.2). Total fertility rate (avg. births per childbearing woman; 2003): 5.4. Life expectancy at birth (2003): male 50.9 years; female 51.1 years. Adult population (ages 15–49) living with HIV (2004): 5.4% (world avg. 1.1%).

National economy

Budget (2003). Revenue: N 2,752,107,000,000 (nontax revenue 62.6%, of which crude oil export proceeds 35.1%, crude oil sales to domestic refineries 14.0%; tax revenue 37.4%, of which oil profits tax 15.9%, tax on international trade 8.5%). Expenditures: N 2,853,918,000,000 (state and local governments 40.5%, current expenditure 32.0%, Nigerian National Petroleum Corporation [NNPC] 15.8%, capital expenditure 8.8%). Production (metric tons except as noted). Agriculture, forestry, fishing (2003): cassava 40,927,000, yams 30,439,000, millet 9,974,-000; livestock 27,000,000 goats, 22,500,000 sheep, 15,163,700 cattle; roundwood (2002) 69,482,328 cu m; fish catch (2001) 476,544. Mining and quarrying (2002): limestone 3,400,000; marble 130,000. Manufacturing (value added in N'000,000; 1995): food and beverages 25,415; textiles 16,193; chemical products 11,181. Energy production (consumption): electricity (kW-hr; 2000) 17,757,000,000 (17,757,000,000); coal (2000) 61,000 (61,000); crude petroleum (barrels; 2003) 899,300,000 ([2001] 106,580,000); petroleum products (2000) 4,500,000 (10,199,000); natural gas (cu m; 2000) 12,539,000 (7,123,000). Households. Average household size (2002) 4.9; annual income per household (1992–93) N 15,000. Gross national product (2003): $42,984,000,000 ($320 per capita). Public debt (external, outstanding; 2002): $28,057,000,000. Population economically active (1993–94): total 29,000,000; activity rate 31.0% (participation rates: ages 15–59, 64.4%; female 44.0%). Tourism (2002): receipts $263,000,000; expenditures $950,000,000. Land use as % of total land area (2000): in temporary crops 31.0%, in permanent crops 2.9%, in pasture 43.0%; overall forest area 14.8%.

1 metric ton = about 1.1 short tons;   1 kilometer = 0.6 mi (statute);   1 metric ton-km cargo = about 0.68 short ton-mi cargo;   c.i.f.: cost, insurance, and freight;   f.o.b.: free on board

Foreign trade

Imports (2003-c.i.f.): $10,853,000,000 ([2000] machinery and apparatus 21.1%; chemicals and chemical products 20.1%; food 18.9%, of which cereals 7.1%; road vehicles 10.4%; iron and steel 6.2%). *Major import sources* (2003): China 13.6%; UK 9.3%; France 8.0%; US 7.8%; The Netherlands 6.5%; Germany 5.9%; South Korea 5.8%. **Exports** (2003-f.o.b.): $19,887,000,000 (crude petroleum 99.7%, remainder 0.3%). *Major export destinations* (2003): US 40.2%; Spain 8.3%; Brazil 5.3%; France 5.0%; Indonesia 4.6%; Japan 4.1%; India 4.0%.

Transport and communications

Transport. *Railroads* (2000): length 3,505 km; passenger-km 179,000,000 (1997); metric ton-km cargo 120,000,000 (1997). *Roads* (1999): total length 62,598 km (paved 19%). *Vehicles* (1996): passenger cars 773,000. *Air transport* (2002; Nigeria Airways only): passenger-km 892,720,000; metric ton-km cargo 10,783,000; airports (1998) 12. **Communications**, in total units (units per 1,000 persons). Daily newspaper circulation (2000): 2,770,000 (24); radios (2000): 23,000,000 (200); televisions (2000): 7,840,000 (68); telephone main lines (2003): 853,100 (6.9); cellular telephone subscribers (2003): 3,149,500 (26); personal computers (2002): 853,000 (7.1); Internet users (2003): 750,000 (6.1).

Education and health

Literacy (2002): total population age 15 and over literate 40,700,000 (64.1%); males literate 22,600,000 (62.3%); females literate 18,100,000 (56.2%). **Health** (2002): physicians 25,914 (1 per 4,722 persons); hospital beds 54,872 (1 per 2,230 persons); infant mortality rate per 1,000 live births (2003) 71.3. **Food** (2001): daily per capita caloric intake 2,747 (vegetable products 97%, animal products 3%); 116% of FAO recommended minimum.

Military

Total active duty personnel (2003): 78,500 (army 79.0%, navy 8.9%, air force 12.1%). **Military expenditure as percentage of GNP** (1999): 1.7% (world 2.4%); per capita expenditure $13.

Background

Inhabited for thousands of years, Nigeria was the center of the Nok culture from 500 BC to AD 200 and of several precolonial empires, including the state of Kanem-Bornu and the Songhai, Hausa, and Fulani kingdoms. Visited in the 15th century by Europeans, it became a center for the slave trade. The area began to come under British control in 1861; by 1903 British rule was total. Nigeria gained independence in 1960 and became a republic in 1963. Ethnic strife soon led to military coups, and military groups ruled the country from 1966 to 1979 and from 1983 to 1999. A civil war between the central government and the former Eastern Region—which seceded and called itself Biafra—began in 1967 and ended in 1970 with Biafra's surrender after widespread starvation and civilian deaths. In 1991 the capital was moved from Lagos to Abuja. The government's execution of environmental activist Ken Saro-Wiwa in 1995 led to international sanctions, and civil-

ian rule was finally reestablished in 1999. By far the most populous nation in Africa, Nigeria suffers from rapid population increase, political instability, foreign debt, slow economic growth, a high rate of violent crime, and rampant government corruption.

Recent Developments

During much of 2004, religious violence preoccupied Nigeria. In May the government declared a state of emergency in Plateau state following religious-based violence that left more than 1,000 persons dead and 70,000 displaced. Christian militias in six Plateau villages attacked mosques and killed an estimated 600 people and left more than 1,000, mostly Muslims, wounded; the most horrific atrocities occurred in Yelwa. These attacks led to reprisals by Muslims in Kano, Nigeria's second largest city, where an estimated 600 people, predominantly Christians, were killed. Many observers emphasized that the violence could not be attributed to religion alone and that the causes were complex. Land disputes between Tarok farmers and Fulani cattle herders were cited as one of the causes. Similar but smaller religious attacks occurred in early June in Numan, near the Cameroon border. Kano state was hit hard by a serious polio outbreak that swept across nine West and Central African countries and was believed to have originated in Nigeria. The Kano state government refused to participate in the immunization program led by the World Health Organization, asserting that the shots were unsafe. The boycott resulted in 257 polio-afflicted Nigerian children's becoming paralyzed. Nigeria's oil-rich Niger delta was also fraught with violence and targeted attacks on oil-production sites. Several foreign oil companies operating in Nigeria faced lawsuits and continued attacks, as a result of ongoing conflict over land and extraction rights.

Internet resources: <www.nigeriatourism.net>.

Northern Mariana Islands

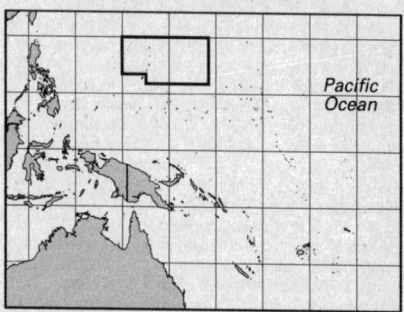

Pacific Ocean

Official name: Commonwealth of the Northern Mariana Islands. **Political status:** self-governing commonwealth in association with the US, having two legislative houses (Senate [9]; House of Representatives [18]; residents elect a nonvoting representative to the US Congress). **Chief of state:** President of the US George W. Bush (from 2001). **Head of government:** Governor Juan N. Babauta (from 2002). **Seat of government:** on Saipan. **Official languages:** Chamorro, Carolinian, and English. **Official religion:** none. **Monetary unit:** 1 US dollar ($) = 100 cents.

Demography

Area: 176.5 sq mi, 457.1 sq km. **Population** (2004): 78,000. **Density** (2004): persons per sq mi 443.2, persons per sq km 170.7. **Urban** (2002; all of Saipan was designated an urban area in 2002): 90.0%. **Sex distribution** (2000): male 46.21%; female 53.79%. **Age breakdown** (2000): under 15, 22.5%; 15–29, 31.8%; 30–44, 32.3%; 45–59, 10.7%; 60–74, 2.3%; 75 and over, 0.4%. **Ethnic composition** (2000; includes aliens): Filipino 26.2%; Chinese 22.1%; Chamorro 21.3%; Carolinian 3.8%; other Asian 7.5%; other Pacific Islander 6.6%; white 1.8%; multiethnic and other 10.7%. **Religious affiliation** (1995): Roman Catholic 59.6%; Protestant 18.7%; other Christian 1.4%; other 20.3%. **Major villages** (2000): San Antonio 4,741; Garapan 3,588; Susupe 2,083. **Location:** Oceania, islands in the North Pacific Ocean, between Hawaii (US) and the Philippines.

Vital statistics

Birth rate per 1,000 population (2002): 20.0 (world avg. 21.3). **Death rate** per 1,000 population (2002): 2.4 (world avg. 9.1). **Natural increase rate** per 1,000 population (2002): 17.6 (world avg. 12.2). **Total fertility rate** (avg. births per childbearing woman; 2002): 1.4. **Life expectancy** at birth (2002): male 72.9 years; female 79.2 years.

National economy

Budget (2002). *Revenue:* $199,713,000 (tax revenue 83.5%, of which income tax 28.5%, corporate tax 24.3%, excise tax 9.4%; nontax revenue 16.5%). *Expenditures:* $212,089,000 (2001; health 20.4%, education 20.1%, general government 15.0%, social services 12.0%, public safety 9.3%). **Public debt** (external, outstanding; 1999): $146,000,000. **Gross national product** (1999): $664,600,000 ($9,600 per capita). **Production** (metric tons except as noted). *Agriculture and fishing* (1998): cucumbers 175, bananas 174, watermelons 134; livestock (number of live animals; 1998) 1,789 cattle, 831 pigs, 29,409 chickens; fish catch (2001) 197. *Mining and quarrying:* negligible amount of quarrying for building material. *Manufacturing* (value of sales in $'000,000; 2002): garments 639; bricks, tiles, and cement 12; printing and related activities 5. **Tourism** (1998): receipts from visitors $394,000,000. **Population economically active** (2000): total 44,471; activity rate of total population 64.2% (participation rates: ages 16 and over, 84.1%; female 49.9%; unemployed 3.9%). **Households.** Average household size (2000) 3.7; average income per household (2000) $37,015; sources of income (1994): wages 83.9%, interest and rental 7.2%, self-employment 7.2%, transfer payments 1.7%. **Land use** as % of total land area (2000): in temporary crops 13%, in permanent crops 4%, in pasture 11%; overall forest area 30%.

Foreign trade

Imports (1997): $836,200,000 (clothing and accessories 37.0%, foodstuffs 9.6%, petroleum and petroleum products 8.2%, transport equipment and parts 5.0%, construction materials 4.2%). *Major import sources:* Guam 35.6%, Hong Kong 24.0%, Japan 14.1%, South Korea 9.6%, US 7.6%. **Exports** (2002): $817,000,000 (garments and accessories 99.8%, of which cotton garments 69.8%; remainder 0.2%). *Major export destinations:* nearly all to the US.

Transport and communications

Transport. *Roads* (1998): total length 360 km (paved, nearly 100%). *Vehicles* (2001): passenger cars 11,019; trucks and buses 4,928. *Air transport* (1999; Saipan International Airport only): aircraft landings 23,853; boarding passengers 562,364; airports (2002) with scheduled flights 2 (international flights are regularly scheduled at Saipan and at Rota; Tinian has nonscheduled domestic service. Additional domestic airports mainly handle charter flights). **Communications,** in total units (units per 1,000 persons). Radios (1999): 10,500 (152); televisions (1999): 4,100 (59); telephone main lines (2000): 20,990 (309); cellular telephone subscribers (2000): 3,000 (57).

Education and health

Educational attainment (2000). Percentage of population age 25 and over having: primary education 14.1%; some secondary 17.5%; completed secondary 35.8%; some postsecondary 12.0%; completed undergraduate or higher 20.6%. **Literacy** (2000): 100%. **Health:** physicians (1999) 31 (1 per 2,170 persons); hospital beds (1998) 74 (1 per 877 persons); infant mortality rate per 1,000 live births (2002): 7.5.

Military

The US is responsible for military defense; headquarters of the US Pacific Command are in Hawaii.

Background

The Northern Mariana Islands were discovered by Ferdinand Magellan in 1521 and colonized by Spain in 1668. Sold to Germany in 1899, they were occupied by Japan in 1914 and became a Japanese mandate from the League of Nations after 1919. They were the scene of fierce fighting in World War II; Tinian was the base for the US planes that dropped atomic bombs on Hiroshima and Nagasaki. They were granted to the US in 1947 as a UN trust territory, became self-governing in 1978, and became a commonwealth under US sovereignty in 1986, when its residents became US citizens. The UN trusteeship ended in 1986.

Recent Developments

US Pres. George W. Bush declared the Commonwealth of the Northern Mariana Islands (CNMI) and Guam disaster areas in July 2004 after Cyclone Tingting brought heavy rain, flooding, and mud slides. Under a new funding regime, the CNMI would receive some $12.4 million for capital projects in 2005, subject to an accountability protocol. The CNMI budget for 2004 was $226 million, with a heavy emphasis on health, education, and public safety.

Internet resources: <www.mymarianas.com>.

1 metric ton = about 1.1 short tons;   1 kilometer = 0.6 mi (statute);   1 metric ton-km cargo = about 0.68 short ton-mi cargo;   c.i.f.: cost, insurance, and freight;   f.o.b.: free on board

Norway

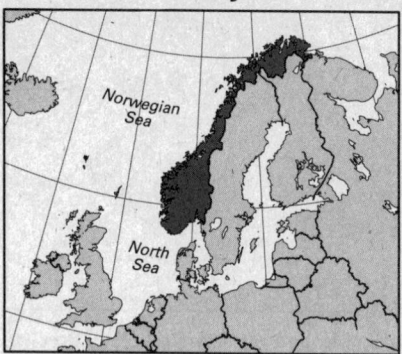

Official name: Kongeriket Norge (Kingdom of Norway). **Form of government:** constitutional monarchy with one legislative house (Parliament [165]). **Chief of state:** King Harald V (from 1991). **Head of government:** Prime Minister Kjell Magne Bondevik (from 2001). **Capital:** Oslo. **Official language:** Norwegian. **Official religion:** Evangelical Lutheran. **Monetary unit:** 1 Norwegian krone (NKr) = 100 øre; valuation (7 Jul 2005) $1 = NKr 6.63.

Demography

Area: 125,004 sq mi, 323,758 sq km. **Population** (2004): 4,591,000. **Density** (2004): persons per sq mi 36.7, persons per sq km 14.2. **Urban** (2003): 78.6%. **Sex distribution** (2003): male 49.56%; female 50.44%. **Age breakdown** (2003): under 15, 20.0%; 15–29, 18.7%; 30–44, 22.4%; 45–59, 19.7%; 60–74, 11.4%; 75 and over, 7.8%. **Ethnic composition** (2000): Norwegian 93.8%; Vietnamese 2.4%; Swedish 0.5%; Punjabi 0.4%; Urdu 0.3%; US white 0.3%; Lapp 0.3%; Danish 0.3%; other 1.7%. **Major cities** (2003): Oslo 517,401 (urban agglomeration [2003] 795,000); Bergen 235,423; Trondheim 152,699; Stavanger 111,007; Bærum 102,529. **Location:** northern Europe, bordering the Barents Sea, Russia, Finland, Sweden, the North Sea, and the Norwegian Sea.

Vital statistics

Birth rate per 1,000 population (2003): 12.4 (world avg. 21.3); legitimate 50.0%. **Death rate** per 1,000 population (2003): 9.3 (world avg. 9.1). **Natural increase rate** per 1,000 population (2003): 3.1 (world avg. 12.2). **Total fertility rate** (avg. births per childbearing woman; 2003): 1.8. **Marriage rate** per 1,000 population (2001): 5.1. **Divorce rate** per 1,000 population (2001): 2.3. **Life expectancy** at birth (2003): male 77.0 years; female 81.9 years.

National economy

Budget (2001). *Revenue:* NKr 829,345,000,000 (value-added taxes 30.7%, tax on income 28.6%, social security taxes 20.2%). *Expenditures:* NKr 617,372,000,000 (social security and welfare 37.8%, health 15.9%, education 13.6%, debt service 4.6%). **Public debt** (December 2002): $60,900,000,000. **Production** (metric tons except as noted). *Agriculture, forestry, fishing* (2002): barley 601,000, potatoes

389,000, oats 312,000; livestock (number of live animals) 2,396,000 sheep, 967,200 cattle; roundwood (2002) 8,649,000 cu m; fish catch (2003) 2,544,692, of which herring 561,858, capelin 249,124, cod 217,462, pollock 212,209. *Mining and quarrying* (2001): ilmenite concentrate 600,000, iron ore (metal content) 340,000, cobalt 3,134. *Manufacturing* (value added in $'000,000; 2001): food products 2,353; ship/boat construction and repair 1,543; nonelectrical machinery 1,257. *Energy production (consumption):* electricity (kW-hr; 2003) 107,268,000,000 ([2000] 123,985,000,000); coal (2000) 632,000 (1,035,000); crude petroleum (barrels; 2001) 1,275,000,000 ([2000] 119,000,000); petroleum products (2000) 17,338,000 (11,321,000); natural gas (cu m; 2001) 57,848,000,000 ([2000] 4,167,500). **Household income and expenditure.** Average household size (2001) 2.3; annual income (excluding taxes) per household (2002) NKr 333,500; expenditure (2001–03): housing 20.1%, transportation 17.3%, recreation and culture 12.6%, food 10.3%, household furnishings 7.0%. **Land use** as % of total land area (2000): in temporary crops 2.9%, in pasture 0.5%; overall forest area 28.9%. **Gross national product** (2003): $197,658,000,000 ($43,350 per capita). **Population economically active** (2001): total 2,362,000; activity rate of total population 52.3% (participation rates: ages 15–64, 80.3%; female 46.6%; unemployed [2003] 3.9%). **Tourism** (2002): receipts $2,738,000,000; expenditures $5,814,000,000.

Foreign trade

Imports (2001-c.i.f.): NKr 296,161,000,000 (machinery and transport equipment 42.1%, of which road vehicles 8.7%; ships 3.4%; chemicals and chemical products 9.5%; metals and metal products 7.7%; food products 6.7%; petroleum products 3.0%). *Major import sources:* Sweden 15.2%; Germany 12.6%; UK 7.9%; Denmark 7.1%; US 7.1%. **Exports** (2001-f.o.b.): NKr 529,966,000,000 (crude petroleum 44.3%; natural gas 11.5%; machinery and transport equipment 11.4%; metals and metal products 7.9%; fish 5.6%). *Major export destinations:* UK 19.6%; Germany 12.2%; The Netherlands 10.4%; France 9.4%; Sweden 8.0%.

Transport and communications

Transport. *Railroads* (2001): route length 4,178 km; passenger-km 2,536,000,000; metric ton-km cargo 2,451,000,000. *Roads* (2002): total length 91,545 km (paved [1998] 74%). *Vehicles* (2001): passenger cars 1,872,862; trucks and buses 444,626. *Air transport* (2002; principally SAS and Braathens ASA): passenger-km 11,549,000,000; metric ton-km cargo 190,500,000; airports (1996) 50. **Communications,** in total units (units per 1,000 persons). Daily newspaper circulation (2000): 2,620,000 (585); radios (2000): 4,110,000 (915); televisions (2000): 3,000,000 (669); telephone main lines (2002): 3,343,000 (734); cellular telephone subscribers (2003): 4,163,400 (909); personal computers (2002): 2,405,000 (528); Internet users (2002): 2,288,000 (503).

Education and health

Educational attainment (2000). Percentage of population age 16 and over having: primary and lower secondary education 21.5%; higher secondary 55.0%;

higher 21.3%; unknown 2.2%. **Literacy** (2000): virtually 100% literate. **Health:** physicians (2003) 12,322 (1 per 370 persons); hospital beds (2003) 22,662 (1 per 201 persons); infant mortality rate per 1,000 live births (2003) 3.4. **Food** (2001): daily per capita caloric intake 3,382 (vegetable products 67%, animal products 33%); 126% of FAO recommended minimum.

Military

Total active duty personnel (2003): 26,600 (army 58.3%, navy 22.9%, air force 18.8%). **Military expenditure as percentage of GNP** (1999): 2.2% (world avg. 2.4%); per capita expenditure $742.

Background

Several principalities were united into the kingdom of Norway in the 11th century. From 1380 it had the same king as Denmark until it was ceded to Sweden in 1814. The union with Sweden was dissolved in 1905, and Norway's economy grew rapidly. The country remained neutral during World War I, although its shipping industry played a vital role in the conflict. It declared its neutrality in World War II but was invaded and occupied by German troops. Norway is a member of NATO but turned down membership in the EU in 1994. Its economy grew consistently during the 1990s.

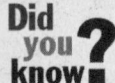 **Did you know?** Norway's capital, Oslo, was formerly Christiania (1624-1877) and Kristiania (1877-1925). The city was founded by King Harald Hardraade about 1050. After the city was destroyed by fire in 1624, Christian IV of Denmark-Norway built a new town and called it Christiania.

Recent Developments

Norway's favorable trade balance continued in 2004, thanks to strong oil and gas exports, and the Government Petroleum Fund continued to grow because of high oil prices. Despite these positive trends, Norwegians worried about the decrease in industrial employment. In 2004 this declining trend halted for a while as new investments in oil-related, metallurgical, and consumer-based industries had an effect, but many companies continued to move their production abroad to countries where costs were lower. Norwegian communities were often vulnerable because they were based on one factory, and many industrial workers had lost their jobs or had been handed early-retirement arrangements. The national average unemployment, however, remained stable at 4.5%.

Internet resources: <www.norway.org>.

Oman

Official name: Saltanat 'Uman (Sultanate of Oman). **Form of government:** monarchy with two advisory bodies (Council of State [57; all seats are nonelected]; Consultative Council [83]). **Head of state and government:** Sultan and Prime Minister Qabus ibn Sa'id (from 1970). **Capital:** Muscat. **Official language:** Arabic. Of-

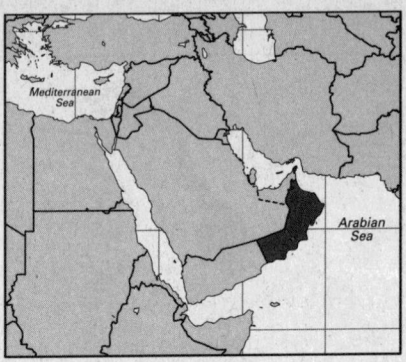

ficial religion: Islam. **Monetary unit:** 1 rial Omani (RO) = 1,000 baizas; valuation (7 Jul 2005) $1 = RO 0.38.

Demography

Area: 119,500 sq mi, 309,500 sq km. **Population** (2004): 2,350,000. **Density** (2004): persons per sq mi 19.7, persons per sq km 7.6. **Urban** (2001): 76.5%. **Sex distribution** (2002): male 56.9%; female 43.1%. **Age breakdown** (2002): under 15, 33.7%; 15-29, 32.3%; 30-44, 22.5%; 45-59, 7.7%; 60-74, 3.0%; 75 and over 0.8%. **Ethnic composition** (2000): Omani Arab 48.1%; Indo-Pakistani 31.7%, of which Balochi 15.0%, Bengali 4.4%, Tamil 2.5%; other Arab 7.2%; Persian 2.8%; Zanzibari (blacks originally from Zanzibar) 2.5%; other 7.7%. **Religious affiliation** (2000): Muslim 87.4%, of which Ibadiyah Muslim 75% (principal minorities are Sunni Muslim and Shi'i Muslim); Hindu 5.7%; Christian 4.9%; Buddhist 0.8%; other 1.2%. **Major cities** (2003): As-Sib 223,267 (within Muscat urban agglomeration); Salalah 156,587; Matrah 154,316 (within Muscat urban agglomeration); Bawshar 149,506 (within Muscat urban agglomeration); Suhar 104,057. **Location:** the Middle East, bordering the Gulf of Oman, the Arabian Sea, Yemen, Saudi Arabia, and the UAE; the Ru'us al-Jibal enclave occupies the northern tip of the Musandam Peninsula and borders the UAE, the Persian Gulf, and the Strait of Hormuz.

Vital statistics

Birth rate per 1,000 population (2003): 37.5 (world avg. 21.3). **Death rate** per 1,000 population (2003): 4.0 (world avg. 9.1). **Natural increase rate** per 1,000 population (2003): 33.5 (world avg. 12.2). **Total fertility rate** (avg. births per childbearing woman; 2003): 5.9. **Life expectancy** at birth (2003): male 70.4 years; female 74.9 years.

National economy

Budget (2004). *Revenue:* RO 2,925,000,000 (oil revenue 72.8%; other 27.2%). *Expenditures:* RO 3,425,000,000 (current expenditure 71.3%, of which civil ministries 36.7%, defense 28.4%, interest paid on loans 2.3%; capital expenditure 26.6%; other 2.1%). **Public debt** (external, outstanding; 2002) $1,979,-000,000. **Gross national product** (2003): $19,877,-000,000 ($7,830 per capita). **Tourism** (2002): receipts

1 metric ton = about 1.1 short tons;   1 kilometer = 0.6 mi (statute);   1 metric ton-km cargo = about 0.68 short ton-mi cargo;   c.i.f.: cost, insurance, and freight;   f.o.b.: free on board

$242,000,000; expenditures $771,000,000. **Households.** Average household size (2002) 6.7; expenditure (1995): housing and utilities 27.9%, food, beverages, and tobacco 26.4%, transportation 19.8%, clothing and shoes 7.9%, household goods and furniture 6.2%, education, health services, entertainment, and other 11.8%. **Production** (metric tons except as noted). *Agriculture and fishing* (2002): dates 248,458, bananas 33,680, watermelons 29,914; livestock (number of live animals) 998,000 goats, 354,000 sheep, 314,000 cattle; fish catch (2001) 128,544. *Mining and quarrying* (2002): marble 136,000; chromite (gross weight) 23,975; gold 301 kg. *Manufacturing* (value added in $'000,000; 2001): petroleum products 1,012; nonmetallic mineral products 124; food products 106. *Energy production (consumption):* electricity (kW-hr; 2002) 10,331,000,000 (10,331,000,000); crude petroleum (barrels; 2003) 299,000,000 (20,000,000); petroleum products (2000) 4,134,000 (3,176,000); natural gas (cu m; 2001) 9,100,000,000 (6,300,000,000). **Population economically active** (2003; employed only; includes 579,643 expatriate workers in private sector and 123,045 government employees, of which 80.5% are Omani): total 702,688; activity rate of total population 30.1% (participation rates: over age 15, 60.9%; female 9.7%; unemployed [1996] 20%). **Land use** as % of total land area (2000): in temporary crops 0.1%, in permanent crops 0.1%, in pasture 3.2%; overall forest area, negligible.

Foreign trade

Imports (2003-f.o.b. in balance of trade and c.i.f. for commodities and trading partners): RO 2,527,-000,000 (machinery and apparatus 28.4%; manufactured goods 15.4%; motor vehicles and parts 13.4%; food and live animals 11.4%; chemicals and chemical products 7.5%). *Major import sources:* UAE 21.6%; Japan 17.1%; US 6.2%; UK 5.7%; Germany 4.4%; India 4.4%. **Exports** (2003): RO 4,487,-000,000 (domestic exports 86.6%, of which crude and refined petroleum 66.5%, natural gas 13.3%, live animals and animal products 1.4%, base and fabricated [mostly copper] metals 0.9%; reexports 13.4%, of which motor vehicles and parts 7.5%, beverages and tobacco products 1.8%). *Major export destinations* (excludes petroleum and natural gas; includes reexports): UAE 32.7%; Iran 18.3%; Saudi Arabia 8.4%; US 3.6%; Yemen 2.6%.

Transport and communications

Transport. *Roads* (1999): total length 33,020 km (paved 24%). *Vehicles* (2001): passenger cars 309,217; trucks and buses 132,290. *Air transport* (2002; Oman Air only): passenger-km 1,189,-300,000; metric ton-km cargo 9,230,000; airports (1999) with scheduled flights 6. **Communications,** in total units (units per 1,000 persons). Daily newspaper circulation (1996): 63,000 (28); radios (2000): 1,490,000 (621); televisions (2002): 1,382,500 (553); telephone main lines (2002): 233,900 (92); cellular telephone subscribers (2002): 464,900 (183); personal computers (2002): 95,000 (37); Internet users (2002): 180,000 (71).

Education and health

Educational attainment (1993). Percentage of population age 15 and over having: no formal schooling

(illiterate) 41.2%; no formal schooling (literate) 14.9%; primary 18.9%; secondary 21.1%; higher technical 2.0%; higher undergraduate 1.5%; higher graduate 0.1%; other 0.3%. **Literacy** (2003): percentage of total population age 15 and over literate 75.8%; males literate 83.0%; females literate 67.2%. **Health** (2002): physicians 3,536 (1 per 713 persons); hospital beds 5,168 (1 per 488 persons); infant mortality rate per 1,000 live births (2003) 21.0.

Military

Total active duty personnel (2003): 41,700 (army 60.0%, navy 10.1%, air force 9.8%, royal household 20.1%). **Military expenditure as percentage of GNP** (1999): 15.3% (world 2.4%); per capita expenditure $726.

Background

Oman has been inhabited for at least 10,000 years. Arabs began migrating there in the 9th century BC. Tribal warfare was endemic until the conversion to Islam in the 7th century AD. It was ruled by Ibadi imams until 1154, when a royal dynasty was established. The Portuguese controlled the coastal areas from about 1507 to 1650, when they were expelled. The Al Bu Sa'id dynasty, founded in the mid-18th century, still rules Oman. Oil was discovered in 1964. In 1970 the sultan was deposed by his son, who began a policy of modernization, and under him the country joined the Arab League and the UN. In the Persian Gulf War, Oman cooperated with the allied forces against Iraq. In the 1990s it continued to expand its foreign relations.

Recent Developments

Oman continued on its path of incrementally privatizing sectors of its economy, replacing increasing numbers of foreign workers with citizens, and taking additional steps to further liberalize the climate for encouraging international investment. Dramatically higher oil prices in 2004 alleviated predictions of negative economic growth, and the accompanying spike in official revenues not only lessened earlier pressures to increase revenue by raising rates for water, electricity, and gasoline but also produced a surplus in the balance of trade.

Internet resources: <www.omantourism.gov.om>.

Pakistan

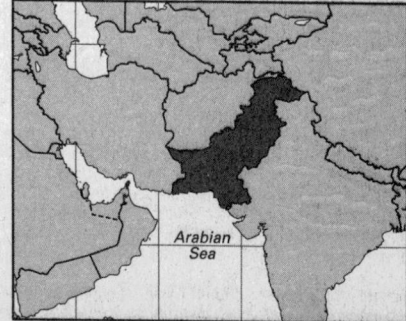

Arabian
Sea

Official name: Islam-i Jamhuriya-e Pakistan (Islamic Republic of Pakistan). **Form of government:** military-backed constitutional regime with two legislative houses (Senate [100]; National Assembly [342]). **Chiefs of state and government:** President Pervez Musharraf (from 2001), assisted by Prime Minister Shaukat Aziz (from 28 Aug 2004). **Capital:** Islamabad. **Official language:** Urdu. **Official religion:** Islam. **Monetary unit:** 1 Pakistan rupee (PRs) = 100 paisa; valuation (7 Jul 2005) $1 = PRs 59.76.

Demography

Demographic information, except ethnic and religious data, excludes Afghan refugees (2004; 1,100,000) and the 2004 populations of Azad Kashmir (3,175,000) and the Northern Areas (1,075,000); also excludes 32,494-sq-mi (84,159-sq-km) area of Pakistani-administered Jammu and Kashmir (comprising both Azad Kashmir and the Northern Areas). **Area:** 307,374 sq mi, 796,096 sq km. **Population** (2004): 151,600,000. **Density** (2003): persons per sq mi 493.2, persons per sq km 190.4. **Urban** (2002): 38.0%. **Sex distribution** (2002): male 51.92%; female 48.08%. **Age breakdown** (1998): under 15, 43.2%; 15–29, 26.9%; 30–44, 15.6%; 45–59, 8.8%; 60–74, 4.3%; 75 and over, 1.2%. **Ethnic composition** (2000): Punjabi 52.6%; Pashtun 13.2%; Sindhi 11.7%; Urdu-speaking muhajirs 7.5%; Balochi 4.3%; other 10.7%. **Religious affiliation** (2000): Muslim 96.1% (mostly Sunni, with Shi'i comprising about 17%); Christian 2.5%; Hindu 1.2%; others (including Ahmadiyah) 0.2%. **Major cities** (1998): Karachi 9,269,000; Lahore 5,063,000; Faisalabad 1,977,000; Rawalpindi 1,406,000; Multan 1,182,000. **Location:** southern Asia, bordering China, India, the Arabian Sea, Iran, and Afghanistan.

Vital statistics

Birth rate per 1,000 population (2003): 32.0 (world avg. 21.3). **Death rate** per 1,000 population (2003): 8.9 (world avg. 9.1). **Natural increase rate** per 1,000 population (2003): 23.1 (world avg. 12.2). **Total fertility rate** (avg. births per childbearing woman; 2003): 4.4. **Life expectancy** at birth (2003): male 61.3 years; female 63.1 years.

National economy

Budget (2001–02). *Revenue:* PRs 632,799,000,000 (sales tax 26.9%, nontax receipts 26.0%, income taxes 22.4%, customs duties 8.0%, excise taxes 7.4%). *Expenditures:* PRs 773,289,000,000 (public-debt service 41.4%, defense 19.6%, development 16.1%, general administration 6.6%, grants and subsidies 3.3%). **Public debt** (external, outstanding; 2002): $28,102,000,000. **Production** (metric tons except as noted). *Agriculture, forestry, fishing* (2002): sugarcane 48,041,600, wheat 18,226,100, rice 6,343,000; livestock (number of live animals) 50,900,000 goats, 24,398,000 sheep, 153,000,000 chickens; roundwood (2002) 27,691,679 cu m; fish catch (2001) 623,425. *Mining and quarrying* (2001–02): limestone 9,805,000; rock salt 1,359,000; gypsum 328,000. *Manufacturing* (2001–02): cement 9,935,000; urea 4,216,200; refined sugar 3,246,600. *Energy production (consumption):* electricity (kW-hr; 2001)

67,704,000,000 (67,704,000,000); coal (2000) 3,168,000 (4,125,000); crude petroleum (barrels; 2000–01) 21,100,000 ([2000] 51,188,000); petroleum products (2000) 6,123,000 (17,856,000); natural gas (cu m; 2000–01) 24,800,000,000 ([2000] 21,036,000,000). **Population economically active** (2002): total 41,540,000; activity rate of total population 28.5% (participation rates: ages 15–64 [1999] 43.1%; female [1996–97] 14.4%; unemployed 7.8%). **Gross national product** (2003): $69,236,000,000 ($470 per capita). **Household income and expenditure** (1998–99). Average household size 6.8; income per household PRs 81,444; sources of income: self-employment 40.9%, wages and salaries 32.3%, transfer payments 11.3%, other 15.5%; expenditure: food 49.1%, housing 20.9%, clothing and footwear 7.8%, education 3.6%, transportation and communications 3.3%, recreation 0.2%. **Tourism** (2002): receipts $105,000,000; expenditures $179,000,000. **Land use** as % of total land area (2000): in temporary crops 27.6%, in permanent crops 0.9%, in pasture 6.5%; overall forest area 3.1%.

Foreign trade

Imports (2001–02-f.o.b. in balance of trade and c.i.f. for commodities and trading partners): $10,339,000,000 (machinery and apparatus 15.6%; refined petroleum 15.2%; chemicals and chemical products 14.4%; crude petroleum 11.9%; food 8.0%; transport equipment 4.8%). *Major import sources* (2000–01): UAE 12.5%; Saudi Arabia 11.7%; Kuwait 8.9%; Japan 5.4%; US 5.2%; China 4.9%. **Exports** (2001–02): $9,135,000,000 (textiles 63.6%, of which cotton yarn and fabric 22.6%, bedding 10.1%, ready-made garments 9.6%, knitwear 9.3%; leather and leather products 7.4%; rice 4.9%; sporting goods 3.3%; carpets 2.7%). *Major export destinations:* EU 27.4%, of which UK 7.2%, Germany 4.9%; US 24.7%; UAE 7.9%; Hong Kong 4.8%.

Transport and communications

Transport. *Railroads* (2000–01): route length 7,791 km; passenger-km 19,590,000,000; metric ton-km cargo 4,520,000,000. *Roads* (2001–02): total length 251,661 km (paved 59%). *Vehicles* (2001): passenger cars 758,600; trucks and buses 253,100. *Air transport* (2000–01): passenger-km 9,739,000,000; (1999) metric ton-km cargo 329,832,000; airports (1997) 35. **Communications,** in total units (units per 1,000 persons). Daily newspaper circulation (2000): 4,190,000 (30); radios (2000): 14,700,000 (121); televisions (2000): 18,300,000 (131); telephone main lines (2003): 3,982,800 (27); cellular telephone subscribers (2003): 2,624,800 (18); personal computers (2001): 600,000 (4.1); Internet users (2002): 1,500,000 (10).

Education and health

Educational attainment (1990). Percentage of population age 25 and over having: no formal schooling 73.8%; some primary education 9.7%; secondary 14.0%; postsecondary 2.5%. **Literacy** (2000): total population age 15 and over literate 43.2%; males literate 57.5%; females literate 27.9%. **Health** (2001): physicians 96,248 (1 per 1,516 persons); hospital

---

1 metric ton = about 1.1 short tons;   1 kilometer = 0.6 mi (statute);   1 metric ton-km cargo = about 0.68 short ton-mi cargo;   c.i.f.: cost, insurance, and freight;   f.o.b.: free on board

beds 97,945 (1 per 1,490 persons); infant mortality rate per 1,000 live births (2003) 76.6. **Food** (2001): daily per capita caloric intake 2,457 (vegetable products 81%, animal products 19%); 106% of FAO recommended minimum.

Military

Total active duty personnel (2003): 620,000 (army 88.7%, navy 4.0%, air force 7.3%). **Military expenditure as percentage of GNP** (1999): 5.9% (world 2.4%); per capita expenditure $25.

Background

Pakistan has been inhabited since about 3500 BC. From the 3rd century BC to the 2nd century AD, it was part of the Mauryan and Kushan kingdoms. The first Muslim conquests were in the 8th century AD. The British East India Company subdued the reigning Mughal dynasty in 1757. During the period of British colonial rule, what is now Pakistan was part of India. When the British withdrew in 1947, the new state of Pakistan came into existence by act of the British Parliament. Kashmir remained a disputed territory between Pakistan and India, resulting in military clashes and full-scale war in 1965. Civil war between East Pakistan (now Bangladesh) and West Pakistan in 1971 resulted in independence for Bangladesh that same year. Many Afghan refugees migrated to Pakistan during the Soviet-Afghan War in the 1980s. Pakistan elected Benazir Bhutto, the first woman to head a modern Islamic state, in 1988. She was ousted in 1990 on charges of corruption and incompetence. During the 1990s conditions were volatile. Border flare-ups with India continued, and Pakistan conducted nuclear tests.

Recent Developments

Pakistan remained a troubled country in 2004, and terrorism remained the overriding concern. Sectarian and terrorist violence continued throughout the year, and the country suffered a series of mosque bombings and other Shi'ite-Sunni bloodletting. All religious gatherings were subsequently banned in the country. With young Pakistanis ever more drawn to militant religious organizations and amid reports that the police and army structures had been infiltrated by *jihadi* recruiters, on 27 June Prime Minister Mir Zafarullah Khan Jamali resigned. He was succeeded temporarily by the leader of the Pakistan Muslim League, Chaudry Shujaat Hussain, and a few weeks later by Finance Minister Shaukat Aziz. The civil terror continued, however, and in late July a suicide bomber exploded a device near Aziz's vehicle, killing the driver and several others. In August the government reported that it had foiled a terrorist plot to kill Pres. Pervez Musharraf and bomb the parliament and the US embassy. On 28 September the government announced the killing of Amjad Hussain Farooqui, the alleged mastermind of the plot. On 22 September Musharraf addressed the UN General Assembly, warning about an "iron curtain" descending between the Islamic world and the West. Musharraf accepted an arrangement to remain president until November 2007 but agreed to relinquish the post of chief of the army staff by 31 Dec 2004, but a bill that allowed Musharraf to keep both positions was signed into law on 1 December.

Internet resources: <www.infopak.gov.pk>.

Palau

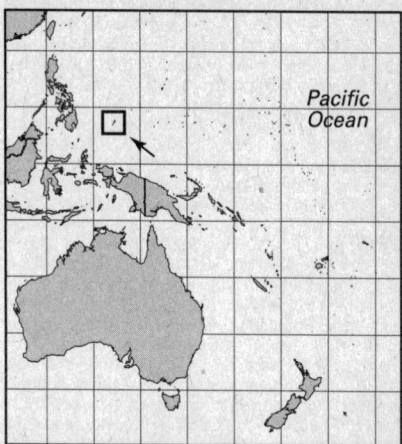

Pacific Ocean

Official name: Belu'u er a Belau (Palauan); Republic of Palau (English). **Form of government:** unitary republic with a national congress composed of two legislative houses (Senate [9]; House of Delegates [16]). **Head of state and government:** President Tommy Remengesau (from 2001). **Capital:** Koror; Melekeok on Babelthuap (the main island of Palau) is to be the eventual permanent capital. **Official languages:** Palauan; English; Sonsorolese-Tobian. **Official religion:** none. **Monetary unit:** 1 US dollar ($) = 100 cents.

Demography

Area: 188 sq mi, 488 sq km. **Population** (2004): 20,700. **Density** (2004): persons per sq mi 110.1, persons per sq km 42.4. **Urban** (2002): 73.0%. **Sex distribution** (2000): male 54.63%; female 45.37%. **Age breakdown** (2000): under 15, 23.9%; 15–29, 24.2%; 30–44, 29.9%; 45–59, 14.2%; 60–74, 5.5%; 75 and over 2.3%. **Ethnic composition** (2000): Palauan 69.9%; Asian 25.5%; other Micronesian 2.5%; other 2.1%. **Religious affiliation** (2000): Roman Catholic 41.6%; Protestant 23.3%; Modekngei (marginal Christian sect) 8.8%; other Christian 6.8%; other 19.5%. **Major city** (2000): Koror 13,303. **Location:** island group in the North Pacific Ocean, east of the Philippines.

Vital statistics

Birth rate per 1,000 population (2003): 19.0 (world avg. 21.3). **Death rate** per 1,000 population (2003): 7.0 (world avg. 9.1). **Natural increase rate** per 1,000 population (2003): 12.0 (world avg. 12.2). **Total fertility rate** (avg. births per childbearing woman; 2003): 2.5. **Life expectancy** at birth (2003): male 66.4 years; female 72.8 years.

National economy

Budget (2002). *Revenue:* $70,058,000 (grants from the US 49.4%; tax revenue 36.0%; nontax revenue 14.6%). *Expenditures:* $79,691,000 (current expenditure 74.6%, of which wages and salaries 38.1%; capital expenditure 25.4%). **Public debt** (external, outstanding; 2000): $20,000,000. **Production**. *Agriculture and fishing* (value of sales in $; 1998): eggs (1999) 609,626, fruit and vegetables 97,225, root crops (taro, cassava, sweet potatoes) 6,566; livestock (number of live animals; 2001) 702 pigs, 21,189 poultry; fish catch (2001; pounds) 593,473, of which sturgeon and unicorn fish 101,613, parrot fish 57,516, rabbit fish 25,613, groupers 23,835, emperor fish 20,586, crabs 17,347, wrasses 14,315, tuna and mackerel 13,366. *Manufacturing*: includes handicrafts and small items. *Energy production (consumption):* electricity (kW-hr; 2000) 210,000,000 (210,000,000); petroleum products (metric tons; 2000), none (79,000). **Tourism** (2002): receipts from visitors $59,000,000. **Land use** as % of total land area (2000): in temporary crops 9%, in permanent crops 4%, in pasture 7%; overall forest area 76%. **Population economically active** (2000): total 9,845; activity rate of total population 51.5% (participation rates: over age 15, 67.6%; female [1995] 39.6%; unemployed 2.3%), **Gross national product** (at current market prices; 2003): $150,000,000 ($7,500 per capita). **Household income and expenditure**. Average household size (2000) 5.7; income per household (1989) $8,882; sources of income (1989): wages 63.7%, social security 12.0%, self-employment 7.4%, retirement 5.5%, interest, dividend, or net rental 4.3%, remittance 4.1%, public assistance 1.0%, other 2.0%; expenditure (1997): food 42.2%, beverages and tobacco 14.8%, entertainment 13.1%, transportation 6.4%, clothing 5.7%, household goods 2.7%, other 15.1%.

Foreign trade

Imports (2001): $95,700,000 (machinery and transport equipment 24.2%; food and live animals 15.2%; mineral fuels and lubricants 10.4%; beverages and tobacco products 8.3%; chemicals and chemical products 7.4%). *Major import sources:* US 39.3%; Guam 14.0%; Japan 10.2%; Singapore 7.7%; South Korea 6.4%; Taiwan 5.3. **Exports** (2001): $9,000,000 (mostly high-grade tuna and garments). *Major export destinations:* mostly US, Japan, and Taiwan.

Transport and communications

Transport. *Roads* (1993): total length 64 km (paved 59%). *Vehicles* (2001): passenger cars and trucks 4,452. *Air transport* (2001): passenger arrivals 64,143, passenger departures 61,472; airports (1997) with scheduled flights 1. **Communications**, in total units (units per 1,000 persons). Radios (1997): 12,000 (663); televisions (1997): 11,000 (606); telephone main lines (1994): 2,615 (160).

Education and health

Educational attainment (2000). Percentage of population age 25 and over having: no formal schooling 3.1%; completed primary 11.5%; some secondary 7.9%; completed secondary 48.9%; some postsecondary 18.6%; higher 10.0%. **Literacy** (1997): total population age 15 and over literate 99.9%. **Health**: physicians (1998) 20 (1 per 906 persons); hospital beds (1990) 70 (1 per 200 persons); infant mortality rate per 1,000 live births (2003) 6.4.

Military

The US is responsible for the external security of Palau, as specified in the Compact of Free Association of 1 Oct 1994.

Background

Palau's inhabitants began arriving 3,000 years ago in successive waves from the Indonesian and Philippine archipelagos and from Polynesia. The islands had been under nominal Spanish ownership for more than three centuries when they were sold to Germany in 1899. They were seized by Japan in 1914 and taken by Allied forces in 1944 during World War II. Palau became part of the UN Trust Territory of the Pacific Islands in 1947 and became a sovereign state in 1994; the US provides economic assistance and maintains a military presence in the islands.

Recent Developments

Palau joined the "coalition of the willing" in March 2003 and supported the US-led war on Iraq, providing the use of Palau's facilities as an additional staging area for American military operations. Pres. Tommy Remengesau, Jr., won reelection in November 2004.

Internet resources: <www.visit-palau.com>.

Panama

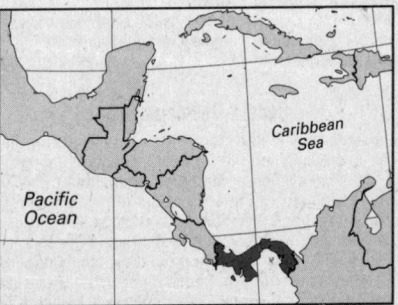

Caribbean Sea

Pacific Ocean

Official name: República de Panamá (Republic of Panama). **Form of government:** multiparty republic with one legislative house (Legislative Assembly [78]). **Head of state and government:** President Martín Torrijos (from 1 Sep 2004). **Capital:** Panama City. **Official language:** Spanish. **Official religion:** none. **Monetary unit:** 1 balboa (B) = 100 cents; valuation (7 Jul 2005) $1 = B 1.00.

Demography

Area: 28,973 sq mi, 75,040 sq km. **Population** (2004): 3,172,000. **Density** (2004): persons per sq mi 109.5, persons per sq km 42.3. **Urban** (2000): 56.3%. **Sex distribution** (2002): male 50.48%; female 49.52%. **Age breakdown** (2002): under 15, 31.3%; 15–29, 26.9%; 30–44, 21.4%; 45–59, 12.2%; 60–74, 6.1%; 75 and over, 2.1%. **Ethnic composition**

---

1 metric ton = about 1.1 short tons;   1 kilometer = 0.6 mi (statute);   1 metric ton-km cargo = about 0.68 short ton-mi cargo;   c.i.f.: cost, insurance, and freight;   f.o.b.: free on board

(2000): mestizo 58.1%; black and mulatto 14.0%; white 8.6%; Amerindian 6.7%; Asian 5.5%; other 7.1%. **Religious affiliation** (1995): Roman Catholic 82.2%; unaffiliated Christian 12.9%; other (mostly ethnoreligionist) 4.9%. **Major cities** (2000): Panama City 415,964 (urban agglomeration [2001] 1,202,000); San Miguelito 293,745 (district adjacent to Panama City within Panama City urban agglomeration); David 77,734 (pop. of *cabecera*); Arraiján 63,753 (pop. of *cabecera*); La Chorrera 55,871. **Location:** Central America, bordering the Caribbean Sea, Colombia, the North Pacific Ocean, and Costa Rica.

Vital statistics

Birth rate per 1,000 population (2003): 19.5 (world avg. 21.3); legitimate 19.7%. **Death rate** per 1,000 population (2003): 6.3 (world avg. 9.1). **Natural increase rate** per 1,000 population (2003): 13.2 (world avg. 12.2). **Total fertility rate** (avg. births per childbearing woman; 2003): 2.5. **Marriage rate** per 1,000 population (2001): 3.6. **Divorce rate** per 1,000 population (2001): 0.9. **Life expectancy** at birth (2003): male 70.0 years; female 74.8 years.

National economy

Budget (2000). *Revenue:* B 2,688,400,000 (tax revenue 62.6%, of which income taxes 12.6%, social security contributions 18.5%, corporate tax 5.8%; nontax revenue 37.4%, of which entrepreneurial and property income 21.1%). *Expenditures:* B 2,803,900,-000 (social security and welfare 20.9%; health 17.2%; education 16.6%; defense 7.1%; economic affairs 7.0%). **Public debt** (external, outstanding; 2002): $6,408,000,000. **Production** (metric tons except as noted). *Agriculture, forestry, fishing* (2002): sugarcane 1,441,000, bananas 600,000, rice 320,000; livestock (number of live animals) 1,533,000 cattle, 280,000 pigs, 170,000 horses; roundwood 1,321,-000 cu m; fish catch (2001) 237,394. *Mining and quarrying* (2001): limestone 270,000; gold 48,600 troy oz. *Manufacturing* (value of production in B '000,000; 1998): food products 1,203, of which meat 341, dairy products 144; refined petroleum 299; beverages 176. *Energy production (consumption):* electricity (kW-hr; 2001) 4,858,000,000 ([2000] 4,953,-000,000); coal (2000) none (70,000); crude petroleum (barrels; 2000) none (16,251,000); petroleum products (2000) 2,066,000 (2,258,000); natural gas (cu m; 2000) none (61,505,000). **Tourism** (2002): receipts from visitors $679,000,000; expenditures by nationals abroad $178,000,000. **Households.** Average household size (2000) 4.2; average annual income per household (1990) B 5,450 ($5,450). **Population economically active** (1998; excludes indigenous population): total 1,083,580; activity rate of total population 42.2% (participation rates: ages 15–69 [1997] 64.3%, female [1997] 35.6%, unemployed 13.6%). **Gross national product** (2003): $12,681,000,000 ($4,250 per capita). **Land use** as % of total land area (2000): in temporary crops 7.3%, in permanent crops 2.0%, in pasture 20.2%; overall forest area 38.6%.

Foreign trade

Data exclude Colón Free Zone. **Imports** (2001-c.i.f.): B 2,964,000,000 (mineral fuels 21.0%, of which crude petroleum 14.4%; machinery and apparatus 19.1%; chemicals and chemical products 11.2%; transport equipment 8.7%). *Major import sources:* US 32.5%; Colón Free Zone 11.9%; Ecuador 8.0%; Colombia 5.7%; Venezuela 5.2%. **Exports** (2001-f.o.b.): B 809,000,000 (bananas 15.1%; fish 11.9%; shrimps 8.7%; petroleum products 7.1%; unspecified 38.6%). *Major export destinations:* US 48.1%; Nicaragua 5.1%; Costa Rica 4.8%; Belgium 4.5%; Sweden 3.7%.

Transport and communications

Transport. *Railroads* (2000): route length 354 km. *Roads* (1997): total length 11,301 km (paved 33%). *Vehicles:* passenger cars (1998) 228,722; trucks and buses 84,020. Panama Canal traffic (2000–01): oceangoing transits 12,197; cargo 196,242,000 metric tons. *Air transport* (2001; COPA only): passenger-km 3,004,000,000; metric ton-km cargo 25,235,000; airports (1996) 10. **Communications,** in total units (units per 1,000 persons). Daily newspaper circulation (2000): 183,000 (62); radios (2000): 884,000 (300); televisions (2002): 553,900 (191); telephone main lines (2002): 386,900 (129); cellular telephone subscribers (2003): 834,000 (268); personal computers (2002): 115,000 (38); Internet users (2001): 120,000 (41).

Education and health

Educational attainment (1990). Percentage of population age 25 and over having: no formal schooling 11.6%; primary 41.6%; secondary 28.7%; undergraduate 12.4%; graduate 0.7%; other/unknown 5.0%. **Literacy** (2000): total population age 15 and over literate 91.3%; males 92.5%; females 91.3%. **Health** (2000): physicians 3,798 (1 per 776 persons); hospital beds 7,553 (1 per 390 persons); infant mortality rate per 1,000 live births (2003) 21.4. **Food** (2001): daily per capita caloric intake 2,386 (vegetable products 76%, animal products 24%); 103% of FAO recommended minimum.

Military

Total active duty personnel (2003): none; Panama has an 11,800-member national police force. **Military expenditure as percentage of GNP** (1999): 1.4% (world avg. 2.4%); per capita expenditure $45.

Background

Panama was inhabited by Native Americans when the Spanish arrived in 1501. The first successful Spanish settlement was founded by Vasco Núñez de Balboa in 1510. Panama was part of the viceroyalty of New Granada until it declared its independence from Spain in 1821 to join the Gran Colombia union. In 1903 it revolted against Colombia and was recognized by the US, to which it ceded the Canal Zone. The completed Panama Canal was opened in 1914; its jurisdiction reverted from the US to Panama in 1999. An invasion by US troops in 1989 overthrew the de facto ruler, Gen. Manuel Noriega.

Recent Developments

The national elections of 2 May 2004 and the transition from one administration to another dominated Panamanian politics. The outgoing administration of Pres. Mireya Moscoso had been accused of being one of the most corrupt in Panamanian history, with charges ranging from nepotism to the buying of votes in the Legislative Assembly. In the event, Martín Torrijos, son of former military strongman Gen. Omar Torrijos and candidate of the main opposition Democratic Revolutionary Party, easily defeated the second-place finisher, former president Guillermo Endara.

Internet resources: <www.visitpanama.com>.

Papua New Guinea

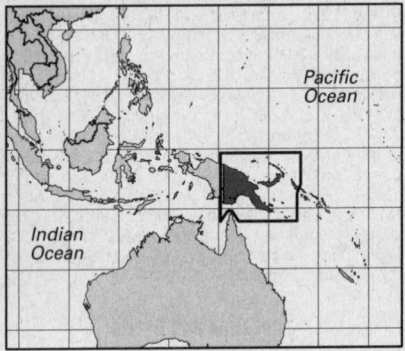

Pacific Ocean

Indian Ocean

Official name: Independent State of Papua New Guinea. **Form of government:** constitutional monarchy with one legislative house (National Parliament [109]). **Chief of state:** Queen Elizabeth II (from 1952), represented by Governor-General Sir Paulias Matane (from 29 Jun 2004). **Head of government:** Prime Minister Sir Michael Somare (from 2002). **Capital:** Port Moresby. **Official language:** English; English, Motu, and Tok Pisin (English Creole) are national languages. **Official religion:** none. **Monetary unit:** 1 Papua New Guinea kina (K) = 100 toea; valuation (7 Jul 2005) $1 = K 3.06.

Demography

Area: 178,704 sq mi, 462,840 sq km. **Population** (2004): 5,695,000. **Density** (2004): persons per sq mi 31.9, persons per sq km 12.3. **Urban** (2001): 17.6%. **Sex distribution** (2000): male 51.87%; female 48.13%. **Age breakdown** (2000): under 15, 38.8%; 15–29, 28.7%; 30–44, 17.1%; 45–59, 9.7%; 60–74, 4.7%; 75 and over, 1.0%. **Ethnic composition** (1983; PNG has several thousand separate communities, most with only a few hundred people): New Guinea Papuan 84.0%; New Guinea Melanesian 15.0%; other 1.0%. **Religious affiliation** (2000): Christian 95.1%, of which non-Anglican Protestant 56.6%, Roman Catholic 30.0%, Anglican 6.7%; traditional beliefs 3.6%; Baha'i 0.8%; other 0.5%. **Major cities** (2000): Port Moresby 254,158; Lae 78,038; Madang 27,394; Wewak 19,724; Goroka 18,618. **Location:** group of islands, including the eastern half of the island of New Guinea, in the South Pacific Ocean near the Equator, bordering Indonesia and to the north of Australia.

Vital statistics

Birth rate per 1,000 population (2003): 31.1 (world avg. 21.3). **Death rate** per 1,000 population (2003):

7.6 (world avg. 9.1). **Natural increase rate** per 1,000 population (2003): 23.5 (world avg. 12.2). **Total fertility rate** (avg. births per childbearing woman; 2003): 4.1. **Life expectancy** at birth (2003): male 62.1 years; female 66.4 years.

National economy

Budget (2001). *Revenue:* K 2,859,000,000 (tax revenue 86.6%, of which value-added tax 27.0%, corporate tax 24.2%, income tax 22.7%, excise tax 6.5%; nontax revenue 13.4%). Expenditures (2000): K 3,081,800,000 (current expenditure 70.8%, of which transfer to provincial governments 16.8%, interest payments 12.4%; development expenditure 29.2%). **Public debt** (external, outstanding; 2002): $1,488,000,000. **Production** (metric tons except as noted). *Agriculture, forestry, fishing* (2002): oil palm fruit 1,250,000, bananas 725,000, coconuts 513,000; livestock (number of live animals) 1,650,000 pigs, 3,800,000 chickens; roundwood (2002) 8,597,000 cu m; fish catch (2001) 53,763. *Mining and quarrying* (2000): copper (metal content) 200,900; gold 74,300 kg; silver 73,200 kg. *Manufacturing* (1998): palm oil 241,485; copra 124,349; wood products (excluding furniture) 3,054,000 cu m. *Energy production (consumption):* electricity (kW-hr; 2000) 2,180,000,000 (2,180,000,000); coal (2000) none (1,000); crude petroleum (barrels; 2000) 28,807,000 (513,100); natural gas (cu m; 2000) 83,544,000 (83,544,000); petroleum products (2000) 49,000 (717,000). **Land use** as % of total land area (2000): in temporary crops 0.5%, in permanent crops 1.4%, in pasture 0.4%; overall forest area 67.6%. **Gross national product** (2003): $2,823,000,000 ($510 per capita). **Population economically active** (1990; citizens of PNG over age 10 involved in "money-raising" activities only): total 1,715,330; activity rate 36.9% (participation rates: female 41.5%; unemployed 7.7%). **Tourism** (2001): receipts $101,000,000; expenditures $38,000,000.

Foreign trade

Imports (2000-c.i.f.): $1,035,000,000 (petroleum products 22%; food 16%; transport equipment 14%; nonelectrical machinery 12%; chemicals and chemical products 7%). *Major import sources* (2000): Australia 55.8%; Japan 11.3%; US 6.5%; Singapore 5.4%; New Zealand 3.5%. **Exports** (2002-f.o.b.): $1,638,000,000 (gold 36.0%; crude petroleum 22.5%; copper 16.0%; logs 5.7%; palm oil 5.1%). *Major export destinations* (2002): Australia 49.3%; Singapore 18.8%; New Zealand 4.4%; Japan 4.2%; Malaysia 2.8%.

Transport and communications

Transport. *Roads* (1996): total length 19,600 km (paved 4%). *Vehicles* (1998): passenger cars 21,700; trucks and buses 89,700. *Air transport* (1999): passenger-km 641,000,000; metric ton-km cargo 80,000,000; airports (1999) with scheduled flights 42. **Communications,** in total units (units per 1,000 persons). Daily newspaper circulation (2000): 72,600 (14); radios (2000): 446,000 (86); televisions (2000): 88,200 (17); telephone main lines (2002): 62,000 (11); cellular telephone subscribers

(2002): 15,000 (2.7); personal computers (2002): 321,000 (59); Internet users (2002): 75,000 (14).

Education and health

Educational attainment (1990). Percentage of population age 25 and over having: no formal schooling 82.6%; some primary education 8.2%; completed primary 5.0%; some secondary 4.2%. **Literacy** (2000): total population age 15 and over literate 63.9%; males literate 70.6%; females literate 56.8%. **Health:** physicians (1998) 342 (1 per 13,708 persons); hospital beds (1993) 14,119 (1 per 294 persons); infant mortality rate per 1,000 live births (2003) 54.8. **Food** (2001): daily per capita caloric intake 2,193 (vegetable products 91%, animal products 9%); 96% of FAO recommended minimum.

Military

Total active duty personnel (2004): 3,100 (army 80.6%, navy 12.9%, air force 6.5%). **Military expenditure as percentage of GNP** (1999): 1.1% (world 2.4%); per capita expenditure $7.

Background

Papua New Guinea has been inhabited since prehistoric times. The Portuguese sighted the coast in 1512, and in 1545 the Spanish claimed the island. The first colony was founded in 1793 by the British. In 1828 the Dutch claimed the western half as part of the Dutch East Indies. In 1884 Britain annexed the southeastern part and Germany took over the northeastern sector. The British part became the Territory of Papua in 1906 and passed to Australia, which also governed the German sector after World War I. After World War II, Australia governed both sectors as the Territory of Papua and New Guinea. Dutch New Guinea was annexed to Indonesia in 1969. Papua New Guinea achieved independence in 1975 and joined the British Commonwealth. It moved to resolve its war with Bougainville in 1997. The decade-long war on the island of Bougainville ended when final terms for peace were negotiated on 1 Jun 2001.

Recent Developments

On 29 Jun 2004 Papua New Guinea (PNG) and Australia formalized an Enhanced Cooperation Program worth $A 800 million (about US$550 million) over five years. Elections for the autonomy of Bougainville province were held in May 2005, but it was still not clear what the relationship between Bougainville and the PNG government would be.

Internet resources: <www.pngembassy.org>.

Paraguay

Official name: República del Paraguay (Spanish); Tetä Paraguáype (Guaraní) (Republic of Paraguay). **Form of government:** multiparty republic with two legislative houses (Senate [45]; Chamber of Deputies [80]). **Head of state and government:** President Nicanor Duarte Frutos (from 2003). **Capital:** Asunción. **Official languages:** Spanish; Guaraní. **Official religion:** none, although Roman Catholicism enjoys

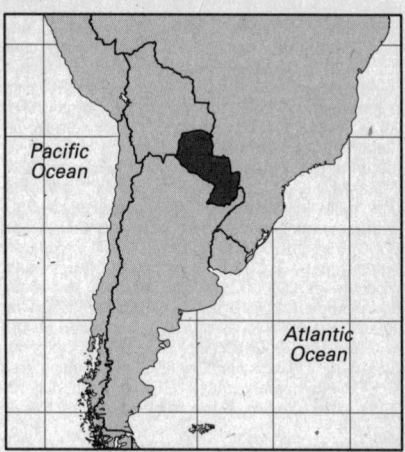

special recognition in the 1992 constitution. **Monetary unit:** 1 Paraguayan Guaraní (₲) = 100 céntimos; valuation (7 Jul 2005) $1 = ₲ 6,065.

Demography

Area: 157,048 sq mi, 406,752 sq km. **Population** (2004): 5,773,000. **Density** (2004): persons per sq mi 36.8, persons per sq km 14.2. **Urban** (2002): 56.7%. **Sex distribution** (2002): male 50.70%; female 49.30%. **Age breakdown** (2003): under 15, 38.4%; 15–29, 26.1%; 30–44, 17.8%; 45–59, 10.8%; 60–74, 5.2%; 75 and over, 1.7%. **Ethnic composition** (2000): mixed (white/Amerindian) 85.6%; white 9.3%, of which German 4.4%, Latin American 3.4%; Amerindian 1.8%; other 3.3%. **Religious affiliation** (2000): Roman Catholic 90.1%; Protestant 5.2%; nonreligious/atheist 1.3%; other 3.4%. **Major urban areas** (2002): Asunción 513,399 (2003 urban agglomeration population equals 1,639,000); Ciudad del Este 223,350; Encarnación 69,769; Pedro Juan Caballero 64,153; Caaguazú 50,329. **Location:** central South America, bordering Brazil, Argentina, and Bolivia.

Vital statistics

Birth rate per 1,000 population (2003): 30.1 (world avg. 21.3). **Death rate** per 1,000 population (2003): 4.6 (world avg. 9.1). **Natural increase rate** per 1,000 population (2003): 25.5 (world avg. 12.2). **Total fertility rate** (avg. births per childbearing woman; 2002): 4.1. **Marriage rate** per 1,000 population (2002; Civil Registry records only): 3.0. **Life expectancy** at birth (2003): male 71.9 years; female 77.0 years.

National economy

Budget (2002). *Revenue:* ₲5,048,300,000,000 (tax revenue 64.2%, of which taxes on goods and services 38.9%, customs duties 10.3%, income taxes 8.9%, social security 6.1%; nontax revenue including grants 35.8%). *Expenditures:* ₲6,072,900,000,000 (current expenditure 78.6%; capital expenditure 21.4%). **Public debt** (external, outstanding; 2002): $2,064,-000,000. **Population economically active** (2000): total 2,560,608; activity rate 48.5% (participation rates: ages 15 and over, 81.0%; female 38.6%; unemployed [2001] 15.3%). **Production** (metric tons except as noted). *Agriculture, forestry, fishing* (2002): cassava 4,142,000, soybeans 3,276,000, sugarcane 3,210,000; livestock (number of live animals) 9,900,000 cattle, 2,750,000 pigs, 15,500,000 chickens; roundwood 9,787,000 cu m; fish catch (2001) 25,000. *Mining and quarrying* (2002): hydraulic cement 650,000; kaolin 66,700; gypsum 4,300. *Manufacturing* (value added in constant prices of 1982, $'000,000; 2001): food products 61,056; wood products (excluding furniture) 21,695; beverages 18,589. *Energy production (consumption):* electricity (kW-hr; 2000) 53,521,000,000 (6,136,000,000); crude petroleum (barrels; 2000) none (777,000); petroleum products (2000) 102,000 (1,076,000). **Gross national product** (2003): $6,213,000,000 ($1,100 per capita). **Households.** Average household size (2000) 4.4. **Tourism** (2002): receipts $62,000,000; expenditures $65,000,000. **Land use** as % of total land area (2000): in temporary crops 7.2%, in permanent crops 0.2%, in pasture 54.6%; overall forest area 58.8%.

Foreign trade

Imports (2002-f.o.b. in balance of trade and c.i.f. in commodities and trading partners): $1,672,000,000 (machinery and apparatus 21.6%, chemicals and chemical products 17.4%, refined petroleum 14.3%, transport equipment 6.0%, food products 5.6%). *Major import sources:* Brazil 30.6%; Argentina 20.6%; China 12.6%; US 5.0%; Japan 4.0%. **Exports** (2002): $951,000,000 (excludes value of hydroelectricity exports to Brazil and Argentina; soybeans 35.8%, processed meats 7.6%, soybean oil 7.5%, leather and leather products 6.1%, wood manufactures 5.9%). *Major export destinations:* Brazil 37.1%; Uruguay 17.4%; Cayman Islands 8.2%; Chile 5.2%; US 3.9%.

Transport and communications

Transport. *Railroads* (1998): route length 441 km; passenger-km 3,000,000; metric ton-km cargo 5,500,000. *Roads* (1999): total length 29,500 km (paved 51%). *Vehicles* (2002): passenger cars 274,186; trucks 189,115. *Air transport* (2000): passenger-km 270,503,000; metric ton-km cargo 24,346,000; airports (1998) 5. **Communications,** in total units (units per 1,000 persons). Daily newspaper circulation (2000): 227,000 (43); radios (2000): 961,000 (182); televisions (2000): 1,150,000 (218); telephone main lines (2003): 273,200 (46); cellular telephone subscribers (2003): 1,770,300 (299); personal computers (2002): 200,000 (35); Internet users (2003): 120,000 (20).

Education and health

Educational attainment (2002). Percentage of population age 15 and over having: no formal schooling 5.0%; primary education 55.0%; secondary 33.5%; higher 5.3%; not stated 1.2%. **Literacy** (2002): percentage of total population age 15 and over literate 92.9%; males literate 93.9%; females literate 91.9%. **Health:** physicians (1995) 3,730 (1 per 1,294 persons); hospital beds (2002) 5,834 (1 per 945 persons); infant mortality rate per 1,000 live births (2003) 27.7. **Food** (2001): daily per capita caloric intake 2,576 (vegetable products 78%, animal products 22%); 112% of FAO recommended minimum.

Military

Total active duty personnel (2003): 18,600 (army 80.1%, navy 10.8%, air force 9.1%). **Military expenditure as percentage of GNP** (1999): 1.1% (world 2.4%); per capita expenditure $15.

 **Did you know?** Paraguay has a distinctive musical tradition, especially of songs and ballads. Typical music for dancing includes polkas and languid *guaranías,* played on the native harp. Perhaps the most famous dance is the *galopa,* a variant of which is the bottle dance, in which dancers balance bottles on their heads.

Background

Seminomadic tribes speaking Guaraní were in Paraguay long before it was settled by Spain in the 16th and 17th centuries. Paraguay was part of the viceroyalty of Río de la Plata until it became independent in 1811. It suffered from dictatorial governments in the 19th century and from the 1865 war with Brazil, Argentina, and Uruguay. The Chaco War with Bolivia over disputed territory was settled primarily in Paraguay's favor by the peace treaty of 1938. Military governments, including that of Alfredo Stroessner, predominated in the mid-20th century until the election of a civilian president, Juan Carlos Wasmosy, in 1993. Paraguay suffered a financial crisis in the late 1990s, and democratic government was in jeopardy.

Recent Developments

Pres. Nicanor Duarte Frutos's reputation as a reformer intent on cleaning up cronyism, corruption, and contraband in Paraguay was seriously put to the test in 2004. In early February Duarte's plans to purge and modernize Paraguay's national police force were stymied as state prosecutors charged that top police officers who were investigating the robbery of $500,000 from the state-owned National Development Bank had plotted to steal part of the recovered booty. In March Duarte's campaign to reform the judiciary by retiring six of the nine Supreme Court justices ended in a disappointing throwback to the old backroom practice of political-party quotas and a division of high-court seats. Gen. Lino Oviedo, who had been charged with having masterminded the 1999 assassination of Vice Pres. Luis María Argaña and had been convicted on charges surrounding an attempted coup in 1996, returned in June from exile in Brazil. He was greeted by a tumultuous welcome from party supporters. The government promptly clapped Oviedo in prison to serve out his 10-year sentence.

Internet resources: <www.senatur.gov.py>.

Peru

Official name: República del Perú (Spanish) (Republic of Peru). **Form of government:** unitary multiparty

---

1 metric ton = about 1.1 short tons;   1 kilometer = 0.6 mi (statute);   1 metric ton-km cargo = about 0.68 short ton-mi cargo;   c.i.f.: cost, insurance, and freight;   f.o.b.: free on board

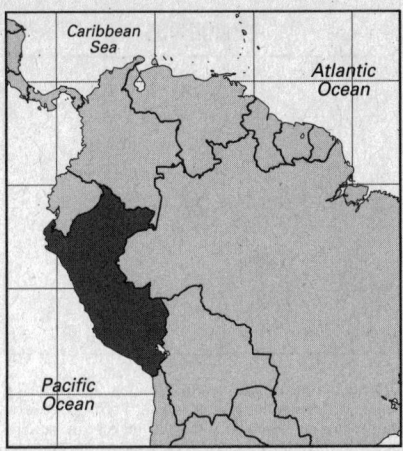

Caribbean Sea

Atlantic Ocean

Pacific Ocean

republic with one legislative house (Congress [120]). **Head of state and government:** President Alejandro Toledo (from 2001), assisted by Prime Minister Carlos Ferrero Costa (from 2003). **Capital:** Lima. **Official languages:** Spanish; Quechua; Aymara. **Official religion:** Roman Catholicism. **Monetary unit:** 1 nuevo sol (S/.) = 100 céntimos; valuation (7 Jul 2005) $1 = S/. 3.25.

Demography

Area: 496,234 sq mi, 1,285,216 sq km. **Population** (2004): 27,544,000. **Density** (2004): persons per sq mi 55.5, persons per sq km 21.4. **Urban** (2003): 73.5%. **Sex distribution** (2003): male 50.35%; female 49.65%. **Age breakdown** (2003): under 15, 32.6%; 15–29, 27.2%; 30–44, 20.8%; 45–59, 11.9%; 60–74, 6.0%; 75 and over, 1.5%. **Ethnic composition** (2000): Quechua 47.0%; mestizo 31.9%; white 12.0%; Aymara 5.4%; Japanese 0.5%; other 3.2%. **Religious affiliation** (2000): Roman Catholic 95.7%; other (of which mostly Protestant) 4.3%. **Major cities** (2000): metropolitan Lima 7,496,831; Arequipa 762,000; Trujillo 652,000; Chiclayo 517,000; Iquitos 367,000. **Location:** western South America, bordering Ecuador, Colombia, Brazil, Bolivia, Chile, and the South Pacific Ocean.

Vital statistics

Birth rate per 1,000 population (2003): 22.6 (world avg. 21.3). **Death rate** per 1,000 population (2003): 6.2 (world avg. 9.1). **Natural increase rate** per 1,000 population (2003): 16.4 (world avg. 12.2). **Total fertility rate** (avg. births per childbearing woman; 2003): 2.7. **Life expectancy** at birth (2003): male 67.2 years; female 70.7 years.

National economy

Budget (2001). *Revenue:* S/. 27,039,000,000 (VAT 43.7%, income taxes 20.8%, nontax revenue 15.1%, import duties 10.1%, payroll tax 3.1%), other taxes 7.2%. *Expenditures:* S/. 32,378,000,000 (current expenditure 73.7%, capital expenditure 13.8%, interest payments 12.5%). **Public debt** (external, outstanding; 2002): $20,477,000,000. **Production** (metric tons except as noted). *Agriculture, forestry, fishing* (2002): sugarcane 8,422,000, potatoes 3,299,000, rice

2,124,000; livestock (number of live animals) 14,300,000 sheep, 4,950,000 cattle, 90,000,000 chickens; roundwood 9,928,385 cu m; fish catch (2001) 7,995,500. *Mining and quarrying* (2003): iron ore 3,540,700 (metal content); zinc 1,171,000 (metal content); copper 625,300 (metal content). *Manufacturing* (value in S/. '000,000 [at market prices]; 1996): processed foods 275.1; base metal products 188.6; textiles and leather products 129.5. *Energy production (consumption):* electricity (kW-hr; 2000) 19,912,000,000 (19,912,000,000); coal (2000) 12,000 (528,000); crude petroleum (barrels; 2002) 35,661,000 ([2001] 70,800,000); petroleum products (2000) 7,503,000 (7,620,000); natural gas (cu m; 2000) 820,932,000 (820,932,000). **Population economically active** (1998): total 7,407,280; activity rate of total population 45.7% (participation rates: over age 15, 66.9%; female 43.8%; urban unemployed [2001] 7.9%). **Gross national product** (at current market prices; 2003): $58,458,000,000 ($2,150 per capita). **Household income and expenditure.** Average household size (2001) 4.5; income per household (1988) $2,173; sources of income (1991): self-employment 67.1%, wages 23.3%, transfers 7.6%; expenditure (1990): food 29.4%, recreation and education 13.2%, household durables 10.1%. **Tourism** (2002): receipts $801,000,000; expenditures $616,000,000. **Land use** as % of total land area (2000): in temporary crops 2.9%, in permanent crops 0.4%, in pasture 21.2%; overall forest area 50.9%.

Foreign trade

Imports (2001-f.o.b. in balance of trade and c.i.f. in commodities and trading partners): $7,316,000,000 (machinery and apparatus 25.0%, chemicals and chemical products 16.1%, crude and refined petroleum 11.9%, food 11.0%). *Major import sources:* US 23.1%; Argentina 6.2%; Japan 5.9%; Chile 5.9%; Colombia 5.2%. **Exports** (2001): $6,826,000,000 (gold 17.1%, fish foodstuffs for animals 12.3%, refined copper and copper products 11.7%, apparel and clothing accessories 7.4%, crude and refined petroleum 6.1%, zinc ores and concentrates 5.2%). *Major export destinations:* US 24.8%; UK 13.5%; China 6.2%; Japan 5.6%; Switzerland 4.5%.

Transport and communications

Transport. *Railroads* (2000): route length 1,608 km; (1999) passenger-km 144,000,000; metric ton-km cargo 891,000,000. *Roads* (1999): total length 78,128 km (paved 13%). *Vehicles* (1999): passenger cars 684,533; trucks and buses 403,652. *Air transport* (2002; Total for 5 national airlines): passenger-km 2,214,000,000; metric ton-km cargo 99,000,-000; airports (1996) 27. **Communications,** in total units (units per 1,000 persons). Daily newspaper circulation (1996): 2,000,000 (84); radios (1997): 7,080,000 (273); televisions (2002): 4,592,400 (172); telephone main lines (2003): 1,839,200 (67); cellular telephone subscribers (2003): 2,908,800 (106); personal computers (2002): 1,149,000 (43); Internet users (2003): 2,850,000 (104).

Education and health

Educational attainment (1993). Percentage of population age 15 and over having: no formal schooling 12.3%; less than primary education 0.3%; primary

31.5%; secondary 35.5%; higher 20.4%. **Literacy** (2000): total population age 15 and over literate 89.9%; males literate 94.7%; females literate 85.3%. **Health** (2002): physicians 32,619 (1 per 821 persons); hospital beds 43,074 (1 per 621 persons); infant mortality rate per 1,000 live births (2003) 34.0. **Food** (2001): daily per capita caloric intake 2,610 (vegetable products 87%, animal products 13%); 111% of FAO recommended minimum.

Military

Total active duty personnel (2003): 100,000 (army 60.0%, navy 25.0%, air force 15.0%). **Military expenditure as percentage of GNP** (1999): 2.4% (world 2.4%); per capita expenditure $45.

Background

Peru was the center of the Inca empire, which was established about 1230 with its capital at Cuzco. In 1533 it was conquered by Francisco Pizarro, and it was dominated by Spain for almost 300 years as the viceroyalty of Peru. It declared its independence in 1821, and freedom was achieved in 1824. Peru was defeated in the War of the Pacific with Chile (1879–83). A boundary dispute with Ecuador erupted into war in 1941 and gave Peru control over a larger part of the Amazon basin; further disputes ensued until the border was demarcated again in 1998. The government was overthrown by a military junta in 1968, and civilian rule was restored in 1980. The government of Alberto Fujimori dissolved the legislature in 1992 and promulgated a new constitution the following year. It later successfully combated the Shining Path and Tupac Amarú rebel movements. Fujimori won a second term in 1995 and a controversial third term in 2000, but he left office and the country late that year amid allegations of corruption.

Recent Developments

Peru exemplified a classic case of a less-developed country where the macro-level economic picture was bright but day-to-day political life posed enormous problems for its president, Alejandro Toledo. Most of Peru's economic indicators attested that the country was doing well. The GNP had been growing steadily between 3.5% and 4% annually for more than three years. Inflation was nowhere in sight, tax revenues were growing steadily, foreign reserves were at or near an all-time high, and as a general rule, foreign investors and international watchdogs, including the IMF, saw the country's prospects in a positive light overall. The long-awaited Camisea gas pipeline went online in August 2004, promising more revenues, and Peru was in the midst of multilateral discussions with the US for a free-trade pact. In political and social terms, however, the country was under considerable strain. President Toledo, whose term was due to expire in 2006, was surrounded by rumors and accusations of misconduct. Several of his siblings were also under investigation for a variety of alleged wrongdoings. Moreover, some high-ranking members of his party had either bolted from the party or were threatening to do so.

Internet resources: <www.peru.info>.

Philippines

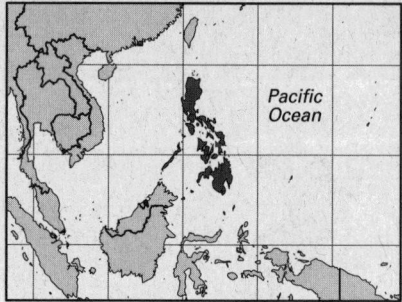

Official name: Republika ng Pilipinas (Pilipino); Republic of the Philippines (English). **Form of government:** unitary republic with two legislative houses (Senate [24]; House of Representatives [236]). **Chief of state and head of government:** President Gloria Macapagal Arroyo (from 2001). **Capital:** Quezon City/Manila; additional offices/ministries are located in other suburbs of Metro Manila. **Official languages:** Pilipino; English. **Official religion:** none. **Monetary unit:** 1 Philippine peso (P) = 100 centavos; valuation (7 Jul 2005) $1 = P 56.28.

Demography

Area: 122,121 sq mi, 316,294 sq km (sum of regional areas; actual total may be different). **Population** (2004): 82,670,000. **Density** (2004): persons per sq mi 677.0, persons per sq km 261.4. **Urban** (2003): 61.0%. **Sex distribution** (2002): male 50.37%; female 49.63%. **Age breakdown** (2002): under 15, 35.1%; 15–29, 28.1%; 30–44, 19.3%; 45–59, 11.2%; 60–74, 5.0%; 75 and over, 1.3%. **Ethnolinguistic composition** (by mother tongue of households; 1995): Pilipino (Tagalog) 29.3%; Cebuano 23.3%; Ilocano 9.3%; Hiligaynon Ilongo 9.1%; Bicol 5.7%; Waray 3.8%; Pampango 3.0%; Pangasinan 1.8%; other 14.7%. **Religious affiliation** (2000): Roman Catholic 81.0%; Protestant 6.6%; Muslim 5.1%; indigenous Christian 4.3%; other Christian 0.7%; traditional beliefs 0.2%; other/unknown 2.1%. **Major cities** (2000): Quezon City 2,173,831; Manila 1,581,082 (Metro Manila, 9,932,560); Caloocan 1,177,604; Davao 1,147,116; Cebu 718,821. **Location:** southeastern Asia, archipelago between the Philippine Sea and the South China Sea, east of Vietnam.

Vital statistics

Birth rate per 1,000 population (2003): 25.1 (world avg. 21.3). **Death rate** per 1,000 population (2003): 5.1 (world avg. 9.1). **Natural increase rate** per 1,000 population (2003): 20.0 (world avg. 12.2). **Total fertility rate** (avg. births per childbearing woman; 2003): 3.1. **Life expectancy** at birth (2003): male 67.2 years; female 72.5 years.

National economy

Budget (2001). *Revenue:* P 563,732,000,000 (income taxes 39.6%, international duties 17.1%, sales

---

1 metric ton = about 1.1 short tons; 1 kilometer = 0.6 mi (statute); 1 metric ton-km cargo = about 0.68 short ton-mi cargo; c.i.f.: cost, insurance, and freight; f.o.b.: free on board

tax 15.4%, nontax revenues 12.8%). *Expenditures:* P 706,327,000,000 (debt service 24.6%, education 17.2%, economic affairs 12.9%, public order 6.8%, defense 4.6%). **Public debt** (external, outstanding; 2002): $32,967,000,000. **Production** (metric tons except as noted). *Agriculture, forestry, fishing* (2002): sugarcane 25,835,000, coconuts 13,682,560, rice 13,270,653; livestock (number of live animals) 11,652,700 pigs, 6,250,000 goats, 125,730,000 chickens; roundwood (2001) 16,013,084 cu m; fish catch (2001) 2,280,512. *Mining and quarrying* (2002): nickel 26,532 (metal content); copper 18,364 (metal content); chromite 2,000. *Manufacturing* (gross value added in P '000,000; 2001): food products 361,217; electrical machinery 95,592; petroleum and coal products 73,280. *Energy production (consumption):* electricity (kW-hr; 2002) 48,180,000 ([2001] 47,049,000,000); hard coal (2002) 1,644,000 ([2000] 8,599,000); crude petroleum (barrels; 2000) 401,000 (117,700,000); petroleum products (2000) 13,913,000 (15,003,000); natural gas (cu m; 2000) 10,276,000 (10,276,000). **Household income and expenditure** (2000). Average household size (2002) 5.0; income per family P 144,506; sources of income: wages 52.1%, entrepreneurial income 25.1%, receipts from abroad 11.1%; expenditure: food, beverages, and tobacco 45.4%, housing 14.2%, transportation 6.8%. **Gross national product** (at current market prices; 2003): $87,771,000,000 ($1,080 per capita). **Population economically active** (2002): total 35,421,000; activity rate 42.8% (participation rates: ages 15 and over [2003] 67.1%; female [2001] 38.6%; unemployed [2003] 11.4%). **Tourism** (2002): receipts $1,741,000,000; expenditures $871,000,000. **Land use** as % of total land area (2000): in temporary crops 18.9%, in permanent crops 16.8%, in pasture 4.3%; overall forest area 19.4%.

Foreign trade

Imports (2001-c.i.f.): $29,551,000,000 (electronic components 16.0%, computer parts 9.3%, crude petroleum 9.0%, chemicals and chemical products 8.5%, food 7.4%, telecommunications equipment 5.8%). *Major import sources:* Japan 20.6%; US 16.9%; South Korea 6.6%; Singapore 6.1%; Taiwan 5.4%; Hong Kong 4.3%. **Exports** (2001-f.o.b.): $32,150,000,000 (electronic microcircuits 34.4%, computers and computer parts 21.9%, apparel and clothing accessories 7.5%, food 4.0%). *Major export destinations:* US 27.5%; Japan 15.7%; The Netherlands 9.3%; Singapore 7.2%; Taiwan 6.6%; Hong Kong 4.9%.

Transport and communications

Transport. *Railroads* (2000): route length 897 km; passenger-km 12,000,000; metric ton-km cargo 660,000,000. *Roads* (2000): total length 201,994 km (paved 39%). *Vehicles* (2001): passenger cars 729,350; trucks and buses 285,282. *Air transport* (2002; Philippines Airlines only): passenger-km 13,956,270,000; metric ton-km cargo 266,913,000; airports (1996) with scheduled flights 21. **Communications,** in total units (units per 1,000 persons). Daily newspaper circulation (2000): 6,300,000 (82); radios (2000): 12,400,000 (161); televisions (2002): 14,542,000 (182); telephone main lines (2002): 3,310,900 (42); cellular telephone subscribers (2002): 15,201,000 (191); personal computers (2002): 2,200,000 (28); Internet users (2002): 3,500,000 (44).

Education and health

Educational attainment (2000). Percentage of population age 25 and over having: no formal schooling 3.8%; primary education 38.5%; incomplete secondary 12.5%; complete secondary 17.2%; technical 5.9%; incomplete undergraduate 11.8%; complete undergraduate 7.3%; graduate 0.7%; unknown 2.3%. **Literacy** (2001): total population age 15 and over literate 95.1%. **Health** (2002): physicians 91,408 (1 per 872 persons); hospital beds 85,166 (1 per 936 persons); infant mortality rate per 1,000 live births (2003) 25.0. **Food** (2001): daily per capita caloric intake 2,372 (vegetable products 85%, animal products 15%); 105% of FAO recommended minimum.

Military

Total active duty personnel (2003): 106,000 (army 62.3%, navy 22.6%, air force 15.1%). **Military expenditure as percentage of GNP** (1999): 1.4% (world 2.4%); per capita expenditure $14.

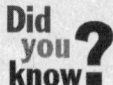 **Did you know?** Cadiz is a chartered city and port in northern Negros Island, Philippines. It is one of five chartered cities and one of the principal ports on the island, where most of the country's sugar is grown and refined and where fishing is a major industry.

Background

In ancient times, the inhabitants of the Philippines were a diverse agglomeration of peoples who arrived in various waves of immigrants from the Asian mainland. Ferdinand Magellan arrived in 1521. The islands were colonized by the Spanish, who retained control until the islands were ceded to the US in 1898 following the Spanish-American War. The Commonwealth of the Philippines was established in 1935 to prepare the country for political and economic independence, which was delayed by World War II and the Japanese invasion. The islands were liberated by US forces during 1944–45, and the Republic of the Philippines was proclaimed in 1946, with a government patterned on that of the US. In 1965 Ferdinand Marcos was elected president. He declared martial law in 1972, and it lasted until 1981. After 20 years of dictatorial rule, he was driven from power in 1986. Corazon Aquino became president and instituted a period of democratic rule that continued with the 1992 election of Fidel Ramos. Through the 1990s the government tried to come to terms with independence fighters in the southern islands.

Recent Developments

Gloria Macapagal Arroyo was sworn in 30 Jun 2004 as president for a full six-year term after she defeated Fernando Poe, Jr., by more than a million votes in the 10 May election. Arroyo campaigned on her record and on promises to improve the economy and reduce corruption. Poe, a movie star, was a high-school dropout with no political experience. He campaigned with other celebrities without offering a political program or being willing to debate issues. With politics in the Philippines widely being seen as show business, Arroyo chose a popular TV newsman as her vice presidential candidate. Arroyo's record as president was widely criticized as inadequate, but Poe was considered by many as a front man for ousted former president Joseph Estrada and for supporters of another ousted president, the late Ferdinand Marcos. Church groups and regional leaders rallied to Arroyo during a violent campaign in which 115 people died in election-related bombings, assassinations, and brawls. Poe was defeated, but he argued that vote rigging and other illegal methods had been used by Arroyo. Poe died of a stroke on 13 December.

Internet resources: <www.gov.ph>.

Poland

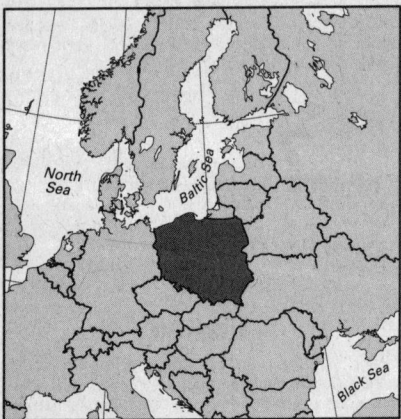

Official name: Rzeczpospolita Polska (Republic of Poland). **Form of government:** unitary multiparty republic with two legislative houses (Senate [100]; Diet [460]). **Chief of state:** President Aleksander Kwasniewski (from 1995). **Head of government:** Prime Minister Marek Belka (from 2 May 2004). **Capital:** Warsaw. **Official language:** Polish. **Official religion:** none (Roman Catholicism has special recognition per 1997 concordat with Vatican City). **Monetary unit:** 1 zloty (Zl) = 100 groszy; valuation (1 Jul 2005) $1 = Zl 3.34.

Demography

Area: 120,728 sq mi, 312,685 sq km. **Population** (2004): 38,176,000. **Density** (2004): persons per sq mi 316.2, persons per sq km 122.1. **Urban** (2002): 61.8%. **Sex distribution** (2002): male 48.43%; female 51.57%. **Age breakdown** (2002): under 15, 18.3%; 15–29, 24.6%; 30–44, 20.6%; 45–59, 20.1%; 60–74, 11.5%; 75 and over, 4.5%. **Ethnolinguistic composition** (1997): Polish 94.2%; Ukrainian 3.9%; German 1.3%; Belarusian 0.6%. **Religious affiliation** (1995): Roman Catholic 90.7%; Ukrainian Catholic 1.4%; Polish Orthodox 1.4%; Protestant 0.5%; Jehovah's Witness 0.5%;

other (mostly nonreligious) 5.5%. **Major cities** (2002): Warsaw 1,671,670 (urban agglomeration; 2001) 2,282,000; Lódz 789,318; Kraków 758,544; Wroclaw 640,367; Poznan 578,886. **Location:** central Europe, bordering the Baltic Sea, Russia (exclave of Kaliningrad), Lithuania, Belarus, Ukraine, Slovakia, Czech Republic, and Germany.

Vital statistics

Birth rate per 1,000 population (2003): 10.5 (world avg. 21.3); (2000) legitimate 87.9%. **Death rate** per 1,000 population (2003): 10.0 (world avg. 9.1). **Natural increase rate** per 1,000 population (2003): 0.5 (world avg. 12.2). **Total fertility rate** per births per childbearing woman; 2003): 1.4. **Marriage rate** per 1,000 population (2002): 5.0. **Divorce rate** per 1,000 population (2002): 1.2. **Life expectancy** at birth (2003): male 69.8 years; female 78.3 years.

National economy

Budget (2002). *Revenue:* Zl 143,022,000,000 (value-added tax 40.0%, income tax 27.3%, excise tax 21.9%, nontax revenue 10.8%). *Expenditures:* Zl 182,922,-000,000 (social security and welfare 25.2%, public debt 13.1%, education 12.2%, defense 5.1%). **Gross national product** (2003): $201,389,000,000 ($5,270 per capita). **Production** (metric tons except as noted). *Agriculture, forestry, fishing* (1999): (gross value of production in Zl '000,000) potatoes 4,066, wheat 3,747, fruit 3,578; livestock (number of live animals) 18,538,000 pigs, 6,555,000 cattle; roundwood (2001) 21,170,000 cu m; fish catch (2001) 261,376. *Mining and quarrying* (2000): sulfur 1,369,000; copper ore (metal content) 390,700; silver (recoverable metal content) 1,144. *Manufacturing* (value added in Zl '000,000; 1999): food products 13,764; beverages 13,582; transport equipment 10,596. *Energy production (consumption):* electricity ('000,000 kW-hr; 2002) 140,880 ([2000] 138,810); hard coal (2002) 104,112,000 ([2000] 83,390,000); lignite (2002) 58,212,000 ([2000] 59,500,000); crude petroleum (barrels; 2000) 4,844,000 (134,125,000); petroleum products (2000) 16,417,000 (16,668,000); natural gas (cu m; 2002) 5,255,000,000 ([2000] 14,760,-000,000). **Public debt** (external, outstanding; 2002): $29,374,000,000. **Population economically active** (2002): total 17,785,700; activity rate of total population 46.0% (participation rates: 15 and over, 55.0%; female 45.7%; unemployed 17.5%). **Household income and expenditure.** Average household size (2002) 2.9; average annual income (2002) Zl 25,600; sources of income (2001): wages 46.7%, transfers 33.8%, self-employment 13.9%; expenditure (2001): food, beverages, and tobacco 28.0%, housing and energy 25.6%, transportation and communications 14.6%, recreation 6.6%. **Tourism** (2002): receipts $4,500,-000,000; expenditures $3,200,000,000. **Land use** as % of total land area (2000): in temporary crops 46.0%, in permanent crops 1.1%, in pasture 13.4%; overall forest area 29.7%.

Foreign trade

Imports (2001-c.i.f.): Zl 206,253,000,000 (machinery and apparatus 26.1%, chemicals and chemical products 13.9%, road vehicles 7.8%, crude petroleum

---

1 metric ton = about 1.1 short tons;   1 kilometer = 0.6 mi (statute);   1 metric ton-km cargo = about 0.68 short ton-mi cargo;   c.i.f.: cost, insurance, and freight;   f.o.b.: free on board

5.7%, food 5.3%, textile yarn and fabrics 5.2%). *Major import sources:* Germany 24.0%; Russia 8.8%; Italy 8.3%; France 6.8%; UK 4.2%. **Exports** (2001-f.o.b.): Zl 148,115,000,000 (machinery and apparatus 20.4%, road vehicles 8.9%, food 7.1%, furniture and furniture parts 6.9%, chemicals and chemical products 5.9%, apparel and clothing accessories 5.4%, ships and boats 5.2%). *Major export destinations:* Germany 34.4%; Italy 5.4%; France 5.4%; UK 5.0%; The Netherlands 4.7%.

Transport and communications

Transport. *Railroads* (2002): length 22,981 km; passenger-km 20,809,000,000; metric ton-km cargo 47,756,000. *Roads* (1999): total length 381,046 km (paved 66%). *Vehicles* (2001): passenger cars 9,991,260; trucks and buses 1,783,008. *Air transport* (2002; LOT only): passenger-km 6,672,000,000; metric ton-km cargo 80,000,000; airports (1997) 8. **Communications**, in total units (units per 1,000 persons). Daily newspaper circulation (2000): 4,170,-000 (108); radios (2000): 20,200,000 (523); televisions (2000): 15,500,000 (400); telephone main lines (2003): 12,300,000 (319); cellular telephone subscribers (2003): 17,400,000 (451); personal computers (2002): 4,079,000 (106); Internet users (2003): 8,970,000 (232).

Education and health

Educational attainment (2002). Percentage of population age 13 and over having: no formal schooling/incomplete primary education 5.6%; complete primary 29.8%; secondary/vocational 51.5%; postsecondary 3.2%; university 9.9%, of which doctorate 0.3%. **Literacy** (2000): 99.8%. **Health** (2002): physicians 86,608 (1 per 446 persons); hospital beds 188,038 (1 per 205 persons); infant mortality rate per 1,000 live births (2003) 9.0. **Food** (2001): daily per capita caloric intake 3,397 (vegetable products 75%, animal products 25%); 130% of FAO recommended minimum.

Military

Total active duty personnel (2003): 163,000 (army 63.8%, navy 8.8%, air force 22.4%, other 5.0%). **Military expenditure as percentage of GNP** (1999): 2.1% (world 2.4%); per capita expenditure $173.

Background

Established as a kingdom in 922 under Mieszko I, Poland was united with Lithuania in 1386 under the Jagiellon Dynasty (1386–1572) to become the dominant power in east-central Europe. In 1466 it wrested western and eastern Prussia from the Teutonic Order, and its lands eventually stretched to the Black Sea. Wars with Sweden and Russia in the late 17th century led to the loss of considerable territory. In 1697 the electors of Saxony became kings of Poland, virtually ending Polish independence. In the late 18th century Poland was divided among Prussia, Russia, and Austria and ceased to exist. After 1815 the former Polish lands came under Russian domination, and from 1863 Poland was a Russian province. After World War I an independent Poland was established by the Allies. The invasion of Poland in 1939 by the USSR and Germany precipitated World War II, during which the Nazis sought to purge its culture and its large Jewish population. Reoccupied by Soviet forces

in 1945, it was controlled by a Soviet-dominated government from 1947. In the 1980s the Solidarity labor movement achieved major political reforms, and free elections were held in 1989. An economic austerity program instituted in 1990 sped the transition to a market economy.

Recent Developments

Public debate in Poland in early 2004 focused on the country's place in the European Union, which it joined on 1 May, and the new "double majority" voting system that would have reduced Poland's (and Spain's) voting powers in the EU. This issue united the political opposition against the ruling Democratic Left Alliance (SLD) for taking too soft a stance in the EU membership negotiations. SLD support had been declining anyway. Sleaze and political scandals had become hallmarks of Prime Minister Leszek Miller's government, which ironically had won office on an anticorruption platform. Miller stepped down, first as SLD chairman and later as prime minister, and former finance minister Marek Belka took over on 2 May. Many people, however, felt that the SLD had lost its legitimacy and that therefore no socialist government would be acceptable.

Internet resources: <www.polandtour.org>.

Portugal

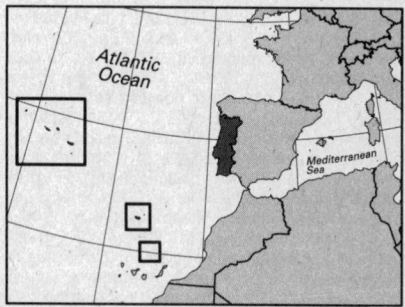

Official name: República Portuguesa (Portuguese Republic). **Form of government:** republic with one legislative house (Assembly of the Republic [230]). **Chief of state:** President Jorge Sampaio (from 1996). **Head of government:** Prime Minister José Sócrates (from 12 Mar 2005). **Capital:** Lisbon. **Official language:** Portuguese. **Official religion:** none. **Monetary unit:** 1 euro (€) = 100 cents; valuation (7 Jul 2005) $1 = €0.84; at conversion on 1 Jan 2002, € 1= 200.482 Portuguese escudos (Esc).

Demography

Area: 35,580 sq mi, 92,152 sq km. **Population** (2004): 10,524,000. **Density** (2004): persons per sq mi 295.8, persons per sq km 114.2. **Urban** (2001): 65.8%. **Sex distribution** (2001): male 48.34%; female 51.66%. **Age breakdown** (2000): under 15, 17.1%; 15–29, 23.0%; 30–44, 21.5%; 45–59, 17.8%; 60–74, 14.5%; 75 and over, 6.1%. **Ethnic composition** (2000): Portuguese 91.9%; mixed-race people from Angola, Mozambique, and Cape Verde 1.6%; Brazilian 1.4%; Marrano 1.2%; other European

1.2%; Han Chinese 0.9%; other 1.8%. **Religious affiliation** (2000): Christian 92.4%, of which Roman Catholic 87.4%, independent Christian 2.7%, Protestant 1.3%, other Christian 1.0%; nonreligious/atheist 6.5%; Buddhist 0.6%; other 0.5%. **Major cities** (2001): Lisbon 564,657 (urban agglomeration 3,447,173); Porto 263,131; Amadora 175,872; Braga 164,192; Coimbra 148,443. **Location:** southwestern Europe, bordering Spain and the North Atlantic Ocean.

Vital statistics

Birth rate per 1,000 population (2003): 11.0 (world avg. 21.3). **Death rate** per 1,000 population (2003): 10.3 (world avg. 9.1). **Natural increase rate** per 1,000 population (2003): 0.7 (world avg. 12.2). **Total fertility rate** (avg. births per childbearing woman; 2003): 1.5. **Marriage rate** per 1,000 population (2002): 5.4. **Divorce rate** per 1,000 population (2001): 1.8. **Life expectancy** at birth (2003): male 73.9 years; females 80.7 years.

National economy

Budget (2001). *Revenue:* Esc 5,793,400,000,000 (taxes on goods and services 52.0%, income taxes 39.5%). *Expenditures:* Esc 6,616,800,000,000 (current expenditure 89.2%, development expenditure 10.8%). **Public debt** (2001): $61,224,180,000. **Production** (metric tons except as noted). *Agriculture, forestry, fishing* (2002): potatoes 1,200,000, tomatoes 994,000, grapes 900,000; livestock (number of live animals) 5,478,000 sheep, 2,389,000 pigs, 1,399,000 cattle; roundwood (2002) 8,742,000 cu m; fish catch (2001) 199,000. *Mining and quarrying* (2001): marble 1,000,000; copper (metal content) 83,000; tin (metal content) 1,200. *Manufacturing* (value added in Esc '000,000; 1998): machinery and transport equipment 606,000, of which transport equipment 232,000; petroleum refining 517,000; wearing apparel and footwear 307,000. *Energy production (consumption):* electricity (kW-hr; 2000) 47,459,000,000 (48,390,000,000); coal (2000) negligible (6,154,000); crude petroleum (barrels; 2000) none (85,200,000); petroleum products (2000) 10,170,000 (12,200,000); natural gas (cu m; 2000) none (2,424,600,000). **Tourism** (2002): receipts $5,919,000,000; expenditures $2,276,000,000. **Population economically active** (2001): total 5,211,300; activity rate of total population 51.3% (participation rates: ages 15–64 [1997], 68.5%; female 45.6%; unemployed 4.1%). **Gross national product** (at current market prices; 2003): $123,664,000,000 ($12,130 per capita). **Household income and expenditure.** Average household size (1999) 3.1; sources of income (1995): wages and salaries 44.4%, self-employment 23.4%, transfers 22.2%; expenditure (1994–95): food 23.9%, housing 20.6%, transportation and communications 18.9%. **Land use** as % of total land area (2000): in temporary crops 21.7%, in permanent crops 7.8%, in pasture 15.7%; overall forest area 40.1%.

Foreign trade

Imports (2000-c.i.f.): €43,358,000,000 (road vehicles 14.1%; nonelectrical machinery and apparatus 11.4%; mineral fuels and lubricants 10.3%; electrical machinery and telecommunications equipment 9.9%; food products 9.3%; chemicals and chemical products 9.1%). *Major import sources* (2001): Spain 26.5%; Germany 13.9%; France 10.3%; Italy 6.7%; UK 5.0%. **Exports** (2000-f.o.b.): €26,446,000,000 (machinery and apparatus 19.7%, of which telecommunications equipment 4.2%; road vehicles 13.5%; apparel and clothing accessories 11.6%; footwear 5.7%; chemicals and chemical products 5.5%; fabrics 4.7%). *Major export destinations* (2001): Germany 19.2%; Spain 18.6%; France 12.6%; UK 10.3%; US 5.8%.

Transport and communications

Transport. *Railroads* (1999): route length 3,579 km; passenger-km 4,380,000,000; metric ton-km cargo 2,560,000,000. *Roads* (1999): total length 68,732 km (paved 86%). *Vehicles* (1998): passenger cars 3,200,000; trucks and buses 1,097,000. *Air transport* (2001): passenger-km 10,457,000,000; metric ton-km cargo 53,865,000,000; airports (2000) 16. **Communications,** in total units (units per 1,000 persons). Daily newspaper circulation (2000): 324,000 (32); radios (2000): 3,080,000 (304); televisions (2000): 6,380,000 (630); telephone main lines (2003): 4,279,000 (414); cellular telephone subscribers (2003): 9,341,000 (904); personal computers (2002): 1,394,000 (134); Internet users (2002): 2,000,000 (194).

Education and health

Educational attainment (1991). Percentage of population age 25 and over having: no formal schooling 16.1%; some primary education 61.5%; some secondary 10.6%; postsecondary 3.5%. **Literacy** (2000): total population age 15 and over literate 92.2%; males literate 94.8%; females literate 90.0%. **Health** (2001): physicians 33,536 (1 per 310 persons); hospital beds 38,802 (1 per 268 persons); infant mortality rate per 1,000 live births (2003) 5.2. **Food** (2002): daily per capita caloric intake 3,741 (vegetable products 71%, animal products 29%); 153% of FAO recommended minimum.

Military

Total active duty personnel (2003): 44,900 (army 59.5%, navy 24.4%, air force 16.1%). **Military expenditure as percentage of GNP** (1999): 2.1% (world 2.4%); per capita expenditure $240.

Did you know? Portugal is home to a third of the world's cork trees, which produce more than half of the world's annual supply of cork stoppers for wine.

Background

Celtic peoples settled the Iberian peninsula in the 1st millennium BC. They were conquered about 140 BC by the Romans, who ruled until the 5th century AD, when the area was invaded by Germanic tribes. A Muslim invasion in 711 left only the northern part of

---

1 metric ton = about 1.1 short tons;   1 kilometer = 0.6 mi (statute);   1 metric ton-km cargo = about 0.68 short ton-mi cargo;   c.i.f.: cost, insurance, and freight;   f.o.b.: free on board

Portugal in Christian hands. In 1139 it became the kingdom of Portugal and expanded as it reconquered the Muslim-held sectors. The boundaries of modern continental Portugal were completed in 1270 under King Afonso III. In the 15th and 16th centuries the monarchy encouraged exploration that took Portuguese navigators to Africa, India, Indonesia, China, the Middle East, and South America, where colonies were established. António de Oliveira Salazar ruled Portugal as a dictator in the mid-20th century; he died in office in 1970, and his successor was ousted in a coup in 1974. A new constitution was adopted in 1976 (revised 1982), and civilian rule resumed. Portugal was a charter member of NATO and is a member of the European Union.

Recent Developments

The selection of Portuguese Prime Minister José Manuel Durão Barroso as European Commission president set off a political crisis at home as his center-right coalition squabbled with the three main opposition parties over the rules of succession. Pres. Jorge Sampaio finally decided to let the ruling Social Democratic Party/Partido Popular coalition name a new government. Former Lisbon mayor Pedro Santana Lopes was tapped as prime minister, and he faced the difficult task of balancing the need to bolster the coalition's slipping popularity in the polls while keeping the fragile economy on a recovery path and trying to implement much-needed reforms, such as overhauls of the health care and social security systems. The opposition Socialist Party, meanwhile, was gaining electoral momentum, and in the February 2005 elections—held a year earlier than scheduled—they gained an absolute majority in the parliament for the first time. José Socrates Carvalho Pinto de Sousa became prime minister. The turnover was viewed as a popular vote against bad administration, poor management of the economy, and opposition to the pro-US stance of the previous government.

Internet resources: <www.portugal.org>.

Puerto Rico

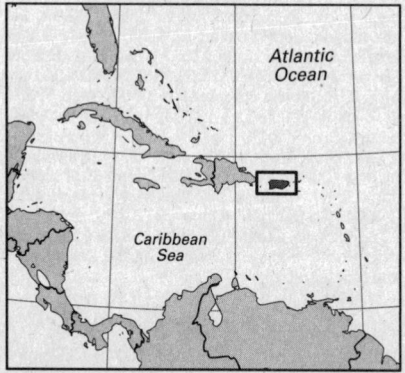

Atlantic Ocean

Caribbean Sea

Official name: Estado Libre Asociado de Puerto Rico; Commonwealth of Puerto Rico. **Political status:** self-governing commonwealth in association with the US, having two legislative houses (Senate [27]; House of Representatives [51]). **Chief of state:** President of the US George W. Bush (from 2001). **Head of government:** Governor Sila Maria Calderón (from 2001). **Capital:** San Juan. **Official languages:** Spanish; English. **Monetary unit:** 1 US dollar ($) = 100 cents.

Demography

Area: 3,515 sq mi, 9,104 sq km. **Population** (2004): 3,898,000. **Density** (2004): persons per sq mi 1,109, persons per sq km 428.2. **Urban** (2001): 75.6%. **Sex distribution** (2002): male 48.09%; female 51.91%. **Age breakdown** (2000): under 15, 23.8%; 15–29, 23.3%; 30–44, 20.4%; 45–59, 17.1%; 60–74, 10.6%; 75 and over, 4.8%. **Ethnic composition** (2000): local white 72.1%; black 15.0%; mulatto 10.0%; US white 2.2%; other 0.7%. **Religious affiliation** (2000): Roman Catholic 75.0%; Protestant 19.5%; other 5.5%. **Location:** island in the Caribbean Sea, east of Cuba.

Vital statistics

Birth rate per 1,000 population (2003): 14.3 (world avg. 21.3). **Death rate** per 1,000 population (2003): 7.7 (world avg. 9.1). **Natural increase rate** per 1,000 population (2003): 6.6 (world avg. 12.2). **Total fertility rate** (avg. births per childbearing woman; 2003): 1.9. **Marriage rate** per 1,000 population (2001): 6.9. **Divorce rate** per 1,000 population (2001): 3.8. **Life expectancy** at birth (2003): male 73.3 years; female 81.6 years.

National economy

Budget. Revenue (2002): $10,556,400,000 (tax revenue 62.6%, of which income taxes 46.5%, excise taxes 14.1%; federal grants 19.0%; nontax revenue 18.4%). *Expenditures:* $10,556,400,000 (2001; welfare 22.3%; education 22.3%; public safety and protection 15.7%; debt service 9.8%; health 9.2%). **Public debt** (outstanding; 1999): $22,678,200,000. **Production** (in metric tons except as noted). *Agriculture and fishing* (2002): sugarcane 320,000, plantains 82,000, bananas 50,000; livestock (number of live animals) 390,000 cattle, 118,000 pigs; fish catch (2001) 3,952. Mining (value of production in $'000; 2002): crushed stone 38. *Manufacturing* (value added in $'000,000; 2001): chemicals, pharmaceuticals, and allied products 17,365; nonelectrical machinery 3,320; professional and scientific equipment 1,874. *Energy production (consumption):* electricity (kW-hr; 2003) 23,700,000,000 (23,700,000,000); coal (2001) none (172,000); crude petroleum (barrels; 2001) none (58,400,000); petroleum products (2000) 2,478,000 (4,641,000). **Gross national product** (2003): $47,400,000,000 ($12,240 per capita). **Population economically active** (July 2004): total 1,400,400; activity rate 35.9% (participation rates: ages 16 and over, 46.3%; female (2002) 40.1%; unemployed 12.2%). **Household income and expenditure** (2002). Average family size 3.6; income per family $27,017; sources of income: wages and salaries 56.3%, transfers 29.5%, self-employment 6.4%, rent 5.2%, other 2.6%; expenditure (1999): food and beverages 18.8%, health care 17.8%, transportation 12.8%, housing 12.1%, household furnishings 11.6%, clothing 7.9%, recreation 7.7%. **Tourism** (2002): receipts $2,486,000,000; expenditures $928,000,000. **Land use** as % of total land area (2000): in temporary crops 3.9%, in permanent crops 5.5%, in pasture 23.7%; overall forest area 25.8%.

Foreign trade

Imports (2002–03): $33,800,000,000 (chemicals 44.8%, electronics 10.2%, transport equipment 7.0%, food and beverages 6.7%, refined petroleum 6.0%). *Major import sources:* US 48.9%; Ireland 20.7%; Japan 3.9%. **Exports** (2002–03): $55,200,000,000 (pharmaceutical and chemical products 71.8%, electronic and electrical products 12.5%). *Major export destinations:* US 86.4%; The Netherlands 2.1%; Belgium 2.0%.

Transport and communications

Transport. *Railroads* (2002; privately owned railway for sugarcane transport only): length 96 km. *Roads* (2003): total length 24,431 km (paved 94%). *Vehicles:* passenger cars (2001) 2,064,100; trucks and buses (1999) 306,600. *Air transport* (1998): passenger arrivals and departures 9,285,000; cargo loaded and unloaded 275,500 metric tons (handled by the Luis Muñoz Marín International Airport only); airports (1998) with scheduled flights 7. **Communications,** in total units (units per 1,000 persons). Daily newspaper circulation (2000): 481,000 (126); radios (2000): 2,830,000 (742); televisions (2000): 1,260,000 (330); telephone main lines (2001): 1,330,000 (336); cellular telephone subscribers (2001): 1,211,000 (307); Internet users (2001): 600,000 (152).

Education and health

Educational attainment (2000). Percentage of population age 25 and over having: no formal schooling to secondary education 25.4%; some upper secondary to some higher 56.3%; undergraduate or graduate degree 18.3%. **Literacy** (2001): total population age 15 and over literate 93.8%. **Health:** physicians (1999) 6,650 (1 per 571 persons); hospital beds (2001) 12,669 (1 per 303 persons); infant mortality rate (2003) 8.5.

Military

Total active duty personnel (2004): The US naval base at Ceiba was closed in March 2004.

Background

Puerto Rico was inhabited by Arawak Indians when it was settled by the Spanish in the early 16th century. It remained largely undeveloped economically until the late 18th century. After 1830 it gradually developed a plantation economy based on the export crops of sugarcane, coffee, and tobacco. The independence movement began in the late 19th century, and Spain ceded the island to the US in 1898, after the Spanish-American War. In 1917 Puerto Ricans were granted US citizenship, and in 1952 the island became a commonwealth with autonomy in internal affairs. The question of Puerto Rican statehood has been a political issue, with commonwealth status approved by voters in 1967, 1993, and 1998.

Recent Developments

After 60 years the US Navy officially closed Roosevelt Roads Naval Air Station in eastern Puerto Rico in March 2004, following the cessation of bombing practice on nearby Vieques Island in May 2003.

Internet resources: <www.gotopuertorico.com>.

Qatar

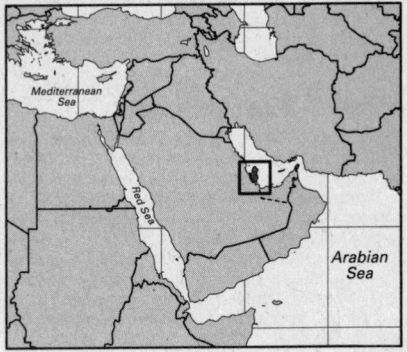

Official name: Dawlat Qatar (State of Qatar). **Form of government:** monarchy (emirate); Islamic law is the basis of legislation in the state. **Heads of state and government:** Emir Sheikh Hamad ibn Khalifah Al Thani (from 1995), assisted by Prime Minister Sheikh Abdullah ibn Khalifah Al Thani. **Capital:** Doha. **Official language:** Arabic. **Official religion:** Islam. **Monetary unit:** 1 riyal (QR) = 100 dirhams; valuation (7 Jul 2005) $1 = QR 3.64.

Demography

Area: 4,412 sq mi, 11,427 sq km (includes area of Hawar Island and adjacent islets, most of which were awarded to Bahrain in 2001). **Population** (2004): 754,000. **Density** (2004): persons per sq mi 170.9, persons per sq km 66.0. **Urban** (2001): 92.9%. **Sex distribution** (2003): male 65.5%; female 34.5%. **Age breakdown** (2003): under 15, 24.7%; 15–29, 23.5%; 30–44, 24.3%; 45–59, 21.8%; 60–74, 5.1%; 75 and over, 0.6%. **Ethnic composition** (2000): Arab 52.5%, of which Palestinian 13.4%, Qatari 13.3%, Lebanese 10.4%, Syrian 9.4%; Persian 16.5%; Indo-Pakistani 15.2%; black African 9.5%; other 6.3%. **Religious affiliation** (2000): Muslim (mostly Sunni) 82.7%; Christian 10.4%; Hindu 2.5%; other 4.4%. **Major cities** (2004): Ad-Dawhah (Doha) 338,760; Ar-Rayyan 272,583; Al-Wakrah 20,205; Umm Salal 15,935. **Location:** the Middle East, bordering the Persian Gulf and Saudi Arabia.

Vital statistics

Birth rate per 1,000 population (2004): 15.6 (world avg. 21.3). **Death rate** per 1,000 population (2004): 4.5 (world avg. 9.1). **Natural increase rate** per 1,000 population (2004): 11.1 (world avg. 12.2). **Total**

1 metric ton = about 1.1 short tons;   1 kilometer = 0.6 mi (statute);   1 metric ton-km cargo = about 0.68 short ton-mi cargo;   c.i.f.: cost, insurance, and freight;   f.o.b.: free on board

fertility rate (avg. births per childbearing woman; 2003): 3.1. **Marriage rate** per 1,000 population (2002): 3.9. **Divorce rate** per 1,000 population (2002): 1.2. **Life expectancy** at birth (2003): male 70.7 years; female 75.8 years.

National economy

Budget (2003–04). *Revenue:* QR 29,155,000,000 (oil and natural gas revenue 67.5%, investment income 23.5%, other 9.0%). *Expenditures:* QR 23,212,000,000 (current expenditure 73.6%, of which wages and salaries 26.0%; capital expenditure 26.4%). **Production** (metric tons except as noted). *Agriculture and fishing* (2002): dates 16,500, tomatoes 11,000, pumpkin and squash 8,500; livestock (number of live animals; 2002) 200,000 sheep, 179,000 goats, 50,000 camels; fish catch (2001) 7,142. *Mining and quarrying* (2002): limestone 900,000; sulfur 221,000; gypsum, sand and gravel, and clay are also produced. *Manufacturing* (value added in $'000,000; 2000): iron and steel 210; refined petroleum 144; industrial chemicals 133. *Energy production (consumption):* electricity (kW-hr; 2001) 9,951,100,000 (9,951,100,000); crude petroleum (barrels; 2001) 243,788,000 ([2000] 27,200,000); petroleum products (2000) 8,265,000 (1,974,000); natural gas (cu m; 2000) 29,558,-000,000 (15,993,000,000). **Population economically active** (2001): total 317,000; activity rate of total population 53.1% (participation rates [1997]: ages 15–64, 59.7%; female 21.0%). **Gross national product** (2001): $7,200,000,000 ($12,000 per capita). **Households.** Average household size (2002) 7.1; expenditure (2001): housing 17.8%, food 16.5%, transportation 15.8%, household furnishings 8.6%, clothing and footwear 7.1%, education 5.5%, communications 5.5%. **Tourism** (2002): total number of tourists staying in hotels 586,645. **Land use** as % of total land area (2000): in temporary crops 1.6%, in permanent crops 0.3%, in pasture 4.5%; overall forest area 0.1%.

Foreign trade

Imports (2002-c.i.f.): $4,052,000,000 (machinery and apparatus 30.7%, of which general industrial machinery 9.0%, specialized machinery 6.4%; road vehicles 13.3%; food and live animals 10.4%; chemicals and chemical products 6.8%). *Major import sources:* US 13.0%; Japan 10.5%; Italy 9.0%; UK 7.6%; Germany 7.0%; UAE 7.0%; Saudi Arabia 6.2%. **Exports** (2002-f.o.b.): $8,231,000,000 (liquefied natural gas 42.6%; crude petroleum 35.0%; refined petroleum 6.7%; iron and steel 2.8%). *Major export destinations:* Japan 28.9%; South Korea 21.1%; Singapore 12.4%; UAE 5.3%; Thailand 4.6%.

Transport and communications

Transport. *Roads* (1996): total length 1,230 km (paved 90%). *Vehicles* (2000): passenger cars 199,600; trucks and buses 92,900. *Air transport* (2002; Qatar Airways): passenger-km 5,664,301,000; metric ton-km cargo 178,710,000; airports (2002) with scheduled flights 1. **Communications,** in total units (units per 1,000 persons). Daily newspaper circulation (1995): 90,000 (161); radios (1997): 250,000 (432); televisions (1998): 490,000 (846); telephone main lines (2003): 184,500 (289); cellular telephone subscribers (2003): 376,500 (590); per-

sonal computers (2002): 110,000 (178); Internet users (2003): 126,000 (197).

Education and health

Educational attainment (1986). Percentage of population age 25 and over having: no formal education 53.3%, of which illiterate 24.3%; primary 9.8%; preparatory (lower secondary) 10.1%; secondary 13.3%; postsecondary 13.3%; other 0.2%. **Literacy** (2001): total population age 15 and over literate 81.7%; males literate 80.8%; females literate 83.7%. **Health** (2002): physicians 1,518 (1 per 399 persons); hospital beds 1,357 (1 per 447 persons); infant mortality rate per 1,000 live births (2002) 20.3.

Military

Total active duty personnel (2003): 12,400 (army 68.5%, navy 14.5%, air force 16.9%); US troops (August 2004) 3,400. **Military expenditure as percentage of GNP** (1999): 10.0% (world 2.4%); per capita expenditure $1,470.

Background

Qatar was partly controlled by Bahrain in the 18th and 19th centuries and was nominally part of the Ottoman Empire until World War I. In 1916 it became a British protectorate. Oil was discovered in 1939, and the country rapidly modernized. Qatar declared independence in 1971, when the British protectorate ended. In 1991 it served as a base for air strikes against Iraq in the Persian Gulf War.

Recent Developments

Achievements in 2004 underscored Qatar's continuing robust economic, social, and political development together with the further modernization of its system of governance. Qatar signed the Trade and Investment Framework Agreement with the US, an essential stepping-stone to a bilateral free-trade accord. The potential benefits—for the US an assured long-term supply of the world's most prodigious and least-expensive sources of natural gas and for Qatar a deepening strategic energy relationship with the world's largest economy—highlighted the growing depth and diversity of their bilateral cooperation.

Internet resources: <www.experienceqatar.com>.

Réunion

Official name: Département de la Réunion (Department of Réunion). **Political status:** overseas department (France) with two legislative houses (General Council [49]; Regional Council [45]). **Chief of state:** President of France Jacques Chirac (from 1995). **Head of government:** Prefect Dominique Vian (from 16 Aug 2004). **Capital:** Saint-Denis. **Official language:** French. **Official religion:** none. **Monetary unit:** 1 euro (€) = 100 cents; valuation (7 Jul 2005) $1 = €0.84 (1 French franc [F] = 100 centimes; at conversion on 1 Jan 2002, €1 = 6.56 French francs [F]).

Demography

Area: 968 sq mi, 2,507 sq km. **Population** (2004): 773,000. **Density** (2004): persons per sq mi 798.6,

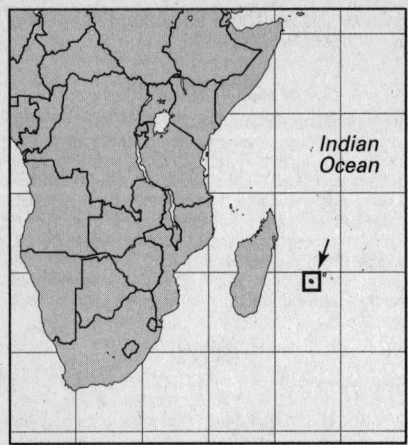

persons per sq km 308.3. **Urban** (1999): 82.7%. **Sex distribution** (1999): male 49.15%; female 50.85%. **Age breakdown** (1999): under 15, 27.0%; 15–29, 24.8%; 30–44, 24.4%; 45–59, 13.8%; 60–74, 7.2%; 75 and over, 2.8%. **Ethnic composition** (2000): mixed race (black-white-South Asian) 42.6%; local white 25.6%; South Asian 23.0%, of which Tamil 20.0%; Chinese 3.4%; East African 3.4%; Malagasy 1.4%; other 0.6%. **Religious affiliation** (1995): Roman Catholic 89.4%; Pentecostal 2.7%; other Christian 1.8%; other (mostly Muslim) 6.1%. **Major cities** (1999): Saint-Denis 131,557 (pop. of commune; agglomeration 158,139); Saint-Paul 87,712 (pop. of commune); Saint-Pierre 68,915 (pop. of commune); agglomeration 129,238); Le Tampon 60,323 (pop. of commune; within Saint-Pierre agglomeration); Saint-Louis 43,519 (pop. of commune). **Location:** island in the western Indian Ocean, east of Madagascar and near Mauritius.

Vital statistics

Birth rate per 1,000 population (2003): 20.2 (world avg. 21.3); (1997) legitimate 41.5%. **Death rate** per 1,000 population (2003): 5.5 (world avg. 9.1). **Natural increase rate** per 1,000 population (2003): 14.7 (world avg. 12.2). **Total fertility rate** (avg. births per childbearing woman; 2003): 2.5. **Marriage rate** per 1,000 population (1998): 4.8. **Divorce rate** per 1,000 population (1997): 1.3. **Life expectancy** at birth (2003): male 70.0 years; female 77.0 years.

National economy

Budget (1998). *Revenue:* F 4,624,000,000 (receipts from the French central government and local administrative bodies 52.7%, tax receipts 20.2%, loans 8.9%). *Expenditures:* F 4,300,000,000 (current expenditures 68.7%, development expenditures 31.3%). **Tourism** (2002): receipts $284,000,000. **Gross national product** (1998): $5,070,000,000 ($7,270 per capita). **Production** (metric tons except as noted). *Agriculture, forestry, fishing* (2001): sugarcane 1,850,000, corn (maize) 17,000, bananas 10,200; livestock (number of live animals) 78,000

pigs, 37,000 goats, 30,000 cattle; roundwood (2002) 36,100 cu m; fish catch (2002) 3,635. *Mining and quarrying:* gravel and sand for local use. *Manufacturing* (value added in F '000,000; 1997): food and beverages 1,019, of which meat and milk products 268; construction materials (mostly cement) 394; fabricated metals 258; printing and publishing 192. *Energy production (consumption):* electricity (kW-hr; 2000) 1,575,000,000 (1,575,000,000); petroleum products (2000) none (741,000). **Population economically active** (1998): total 288,760; activity rate of total population 41.2% (participation rates: ages 15–64, 57.5%; female 44.3%; unemployed [2000] 36.5%). **Household income and expenditure.** Average household size (1999) 3.3; average annual income per household (1997) F 136,800; sources of income (1997): wages and salaries and self-employment 41.8%, transfer payments 41.3%, other 16.9%; expenditure (1994–95): food and beverages 22.0%, transportation and communications 19.0%, housing and energy 10.0%, household furnishings 8.0%, recreation 6.0%. **Land use** as % of total land area (2000): in temporary crops 14%, in permanent crops 2%, in pasture 5%; overall forest area 28%.

Foreign trade

Imports (2002): €2,966,000,000 (food and agricultural products 18.2%, automobiles 12.9%, electrical machinery and electronics 9.0%, pharmaceuticals and medicines 8.4%, clothing and footwear 7.9%). *Major import sources* (1998): France 66.0%; EC 14.0%. **Exports** (1998): €185,700,000 (sugar 58.9%, machinery, apparatus, and transport equipment 17.5%, rum 2.5%, lobster 1.7%). *Major export destinations* (1998): France 70.0%; EC 9.0%; Madagascar 4.5%; Mauritius 2.3%.

Transport and communications

Transport. *Roads* (1994): total length 2,754 km (paved [1991] 79%). *Vehicles* (1999): passenger cars 190,300; trucks and buses 44,300. *Air transport* (2001; Saint-Denis airport only): passenger arrivals 747,044, passenger departures 744,788; cargo unloaded 17,945 metric tons, cargo loaded 8,881 metric tons; airports (2001) with scheduled flights 2. **Communications,** in total units (units per 1,000 persons). Daily newspaper circulation (1996): 83,000 (123); radios (1997): 173,000 (252); televisions (1998): 130,000 (186); telephone main lines (2001): 300,000 (410); cellular telephone subscribers (2002): 489,800 (659); personal computers (1999): 32,000 (45); Internet users (2002): 150,000 (202).

Education and health

Educational attainment (1986–87). Percentage of population age 25 and over having: no formal schooling 18.8%; primary education 44.3%; lower secondary 21.6%; upper secondary 11.0%; higher 4.3%. **Literacy** (1996): total population age 16–66 literate 373,487 (91.3%); males literate 179,154 (89.9%); females literate 194,333 (92.7%). **Health** (2002): physicians 1,137 (1 per 449 persons); hospital beds (2000) 2,124 (1 per 337 persons); infant mortality rate per 1,000 live births (2003) 8.3.

1 metric ton = about 1.1 short tons;   1 kilometer = 0.6 mi (statute);   1 metric ton-km cargo = about 0.68 short ton-mi cargo;   c.i.f.: cost, insurance, and freight;   f.o.b.: free on board

Military

Total active duty personnel (2003): 3,600 French troops (includes troops stationed on Mayotte).

Background

The island of Réunion was settled in the 17th century by the French, who brought slaves from eastern Africa to work on coffee and sugar plantations there. It was a French colony until 1946, when it became an overseas territory of France. Its economy is based almost entirely on the export of sugar.

Recent Developments

Elections held in Réunion during 2004 saw the country divided between radicals and conservatives. The Regional Council was won by a left-wing coalition headed by Paul Vergès of the Réunion Communist Party. The General Council, however, fell comfortably into the hands of the right.

Internet resources: <www.la-reunion-tourisme.com>.

Romania

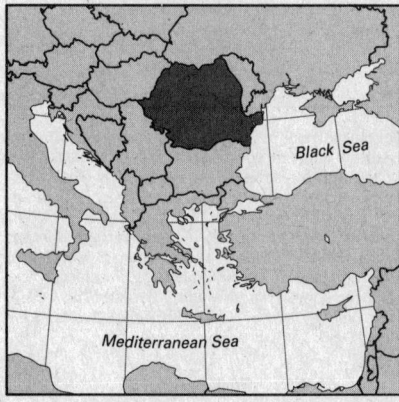

Official name: Romania. Form of government: unitary republic with two legislative houses (Senate [137]; Assembly of Deputies [332, including 18 non-elective seats]). Chief of state: President Traian Basescu (from 20 Dec 2004). Head of government: Prime Minister Calin Popescu-Tariceanu (from 29 Dec 2004). Capital: Bucharest. Official language: Romanian. Official religion: none. Monetary unit: 1 Romanian new leu (plural lei) = 100 bani; valuation (1 Jul 2005) $1 = 2.98 new lei.

Demography

Area: 92,043 sq mi, 238,391 sq km. Population (2004): 21,549,000. Density (2004): persons per sq mi 234.1, persons per sq km 90.4. Urban (2002): 52.7%. Sex distribution (2002): male 48.75%; female 51.25%. Age breakdown (2002): under 15, 17.6%; 15–29, 23.4%; 30–44, 21.0%; 45–59, 18.7%; 60–74, 14.4%; 75 and over, 4.9%. Ethnic composition (2002): Romanian 89.5%; Hungarian 6.6%; Roma (Gypsy) 2.5%; other 1.4%. Religious

affiliation (2002): Romanian Orthodox 86.7%; Protestant 6.4%; Roman Catholic 4.7%; Greek Orthodox 0.9%; Muslim 0.3%; other 1.0%. Major cities (2002): Bucharest 1,921,751; Iasi 321,580; Cluj-Napoca 318,027; Timisoara 317,651; Constanta 310,526. Location: southeastern Europe, bordering Ukraine, Moldova, the Black Sea, Bulgaria, Serbia and Montenegro, and Hungary.

Vital statistics

Birth rate per 1,000 population (2002): 9.7 (world avg. 21.3). Death rate per 1,000 population (2002): 12.4 (world avg. 9.1). Natural increase rate per 1,000 population (2002): -2.7 (world avg. 12.2). Total fertility rate (avg. births per childbearing woman; 2002): 1.3. Marriage rate per 1,000 population (1995): 6.8. Life expectancy at birth (2002): male 67.4 years; female 74.8 years.

National economy

Budget ('000,000 lei; 2000). Revenue: 119,763,500 (value-added tax 42.1%, excise tax 17.2%, personal income tax 16.6%, nontax revenue 4.5%). Expenditures: 105,923,100 (economic affairs 23.0%, education 19.0%, defense 13.3%, public order 13.2%). Public debt (external, outstanding; 2002): $8,112,000,000. Production (metric tons except as noted). Agriculture, forestry, and fishing (2002): corn (maize) 8,500,000, wheat 4,380,000, potatoes 4,000,000; livestock (number of live animals) 7,251,000 sheep, 4,446,-800 pigs, 2,799,800 cattle; roundwood (2002) 15,154,000 cu m; fish catch (2001) 18,455. Mining (2000): iron (metal content) 55,000; bauxite 135,000; zinc (metal content of concentrate) 27,455. Manufacturing (value-added in '000,000,000,000 lei; 1996): food products 5.8; beverages 3.0; iron and steel 1.6. Energy production (consumption): electricity (kW-hr; 2001) 53,640,000,000 ([2000] 51,241,-000,000); hard coal (2000) 281,000 (2,649,000); lignite (2001) 29,431,000 ([2000] 29,313,000); crude petroleum (barrels; 2001) 45,164,000 ([2000] 80,419,000); petroleum products (2000) 9,192,000 (8,230,000); natural gas (cu m; 2001) 12,172,-000,000 ([2000] 16,000,000,000). Population economically active (2001): total 11,446,900; activity rate 52.6% (participation rates: ages 15–64, 74.5%; female 46.2%; unemployed 6.6%). Households. Average household size (2000) 3.1. Gross national product (2003): $51,194,000,000 ($2,310 per capita). Tourism (2002): receipts $612,000,000; expenditures $396,000,000. Land use as % of total land area (2000): in temporary crops 40.7%, in permanent crops 2.3%, in pasture 21.5%; overall forest area 28.0%.

Foreign trade

Imports (2001-f.o.b. in balance of trade and c.i.f. in commodities and trading partners): $15,552,-000,000 (nonelectrical machinery and apparatus 11.9%, fabrics 11.6%, electrical machinery and telecommunications equipment 10.9%, chemicals and chemical products 9.3%, crude and refined petroleum 8.7%). Major import sources: Italy 20.0%; Germany 15.2%; Russia 7.6%; France 6.3%; Hungary 3.9%. Exports (2001): $11,385,000,000 (apparel and clothing accessories 24.4%, electrical machinery and telecommunications equipment 8.0%, iron and steel 7.2%, nonelectrical machinery and apparatus 6.7%, footwear 5.6%, refined petroleum 5.3%). Major *export destinations:* Italy 25.1%; Germany 15.6%; France 8.1%; UK 5.2%; Turkey 4.0%.

Transport and communications

Transport. *Railroads* (2000): length 11,385 km; passenger-km 11,632,000,000; metric ton-km cargo 17,982,000,000. *Roads* (2001): length 198,603 km (paved 64%). *Vehicles* (2000): cars 3,128,782; trucks and buses 461,635. *Air transport* (2002): passenger-km 1,908,000,000; metric ton-km cargo 8,664,000; airports (2001) 8. **Communications,** in total units (units per 1,000 persons). Daily newspaper circulation (2000): 6,560,000 (300); radios (2000): 7,310,000 (334); televisions (2000): 8,340,000 (381); telephone main lines (2003): 4,300,000 (205); cellular telephone subscribers (2003): 6,900,000 (329); personal computers (2002): 1,800,000 (83); Internet users (2003): 4,000,000 (191).

Education and health

Educational attainment (1992). Percentage of population age 25 and over having: no schooling 5.4%; some primary education 24.4%; some secondary 63.2%; postsecondary 6.9%. **Literacy** (2000): total population age 15 and over literate 98.1%; males literate 99.0%; females literate 97.3%. **Health:** physicians (2002) 41,300 (1 per 525 persons); hospital beds (2002) 161,500 (1 per 135 persons); infant mortality rate per 1,000 live births (2002) 17.3. **Food** (2001): daily per capita caloric intake 3,407 (vegetable products 80%, animal products 20%); 125% of FAO recommended minimum.

Military

Total active duty personnel (2004): 97,200 (army 67.9%, navy 7.4%, air force 14.4%, other 10.3%). **Military expenditure as percentage of GNP** (2001): 1.6% (world 2.4%); per capita expenditure $97.

Background

Romania was formed in 1862 by the unification of the principalities Moldavia and Walachia, which had once been part of the ancient country of Dacia. During World War I, Romania sided with the Allies and doubled its territory in 1918 with the addition of Transylvania, Bukovina, and Bessarabia. Allied with Germany in World War II, it was occupied by Soviet troops in 1944 and became a satellite country of the USSR in 1948. During the 1960s Romania's foreign policy was frequently independent of the Soviet Union's. The communist regime of Nicolae Ceausescu was overthrown in 1989, and free elections were held in 1990. Throughout the 1990s Romania struggled with rampant corruption and organized crime as it tried to stabilize its economy.

Recent Developments

Romania's ruling Social Democratic Party (PSD) suffered unexpected heavy losses in local elections held in June 2004. The winner by a narrow margin was the Truth and Justice Alliance, a centrist formation that appealed mainly to urban voters. In the 28 November and 12 December presidential and legislative elections, the Alliance nearly doubled its percentage of the vote for the Chamber of Deputies to 31.3%, while the PSD and a small ally obtained 36.6% of the vote. The presidential winner by the narrowest of margins was the Alliance's Traian Basescu, the mayor of Bucharest and a former sea captain. Calin Popescu-Tariceanu of the Alliance was asked to form a government on 21 December, and the new cabinet was approved by the parliament a week later. Top priorities included modernizing the country and reducing poverty.

Internet resources: <www.romaniatourism.com>.

Russia

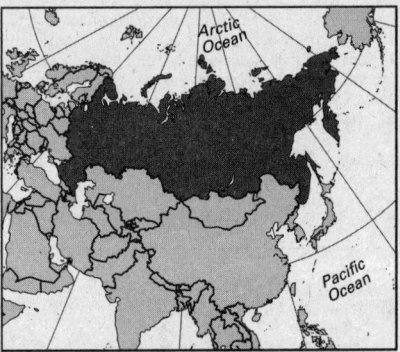

Official name: Rossiyskaya Federatsiya (Russian Federation). **Form of government:** federal multiparty republic with a bicameral legislative body (Federal Assembly comprising the Federation Council [178] and the State Duma [450]). **Head of state:** President Vladimir Putin (from 1999). **Head of government:** Prime Minister Mikhail Fradkov (from 5 Mar 2004). **Capital:** Moscow. **Official language:** Russian. **Official religion:** none. **Monetary unit:** 1 ruble (Rub) = 100 kopecks; valuation (7 Jul 2005) market rate, $1 = Rub 28.83.

Demography

Area: 6,592,800 sq mi, 17,075,400 sq km. **Population** (2004): 144,315,000. **Density** (2004): persons per sq mi 21.9, persons per sq km 8.5. **Urban** (2003): 73.3%. **Sex distribution** (2002): male 46.60%; female 53.40%. **Age breakdown** (2002): under 15, 16.7%; 15–29, 23.4%; 30–44, 22.4%; 45–59, 18.7%; 60–74, 14.0%; 75 and over, 4.8%. **Ethnic composition** (2002): Russian 79.82%; Tatar 3.83%; Ukrainian 2.03%; Bashkir 1.15%; Chuvash 1.13%; Chechen 0.94%; Armenian 0.78%; Mordvin 0.58%; Belarusian 0.56%; Avar 0.52%; Kazakh 0.45%; Udmurt 0.44%; Azerbaijani 0.43%; Mari 0.42%; German 0.41%; Kabardinian 0.36%; Ossetian 0.35%; other 5.80%. **Religious affiliation** (2000): Christian 57.4%, of which Orthodox 49.7%, Protestant 6.2%, Roman Catholic 1.0%, other Christian 0.5%; Muslim 7.6%; traditional beliefs 0.8%; Jewish 0.7%; Hindu 0.5%; Buddhist 0.4%; nonreligious 27.4%; atheist 5.2%. **Major cities** (2002): Moscow 10,101,500; St. Petersburg 4,669,400; Novosibirsk 1,425,600; Nizhny Nov-

---

1 metric ton = about 1.1 short tons;   1 kilometer = 0.6 mi (statute);   1 metric ton-km cargo = about 0.68 short ton-mi cargo;   c.i.f.: cost, insurance, and freight;   f.o.b.: free on board

gorod 1,311,200; Yekaterinburg 1,293,000; Samara 1,158,100; Omsk 1,133,900; Kazan 1,105,300; Chelyabinsk 1,078,300; Rostov-na-Donu 1,070,200; Ufa 1,042,400; Volgograd 1,012,800. **Location:** eastern Europe and northern Asia, bordering the Arctic Ocean, the Pacific Ocean, North Korea, China, Mongolia, Kazakhstan, the Caspian Sea, Azerbaijan, Georgia, the Black Sea, Ukraine, Belarus, Latvia, Estonia, Finland, and Norway; the exclave of Kaliningrad on the Baltic Sea borders Lithuania and Poland. **Migration** (2002): immigrants 184,612; emigrants 106,685. **Refugees** (2002): 828,784, of which from Kazakhstan 301,137, Uzbekistan 106,299, Tajikistan 86,041, Georgia 62,868. **Households** (1999). Total households 52,116,000; average household size 2.8; distribution by size (1995): 1 person 19.2%; 2 persons 26.2%; 3 persons 22.6%; 4 persons 20.5%; 5 persons or more 11.5%.

Vital statistics

Birth rate per 1,000 population (2002): 9.6 (world avg. 21.3); (2001) legitimate 70.5%; illegitimate 29.5%. **Death rate** per 1,000 population (2002): 16.3 (world avg. 9.1). **Natural increase rate** per 1,000 population (2002): –6.5 (world avg. 12.2). **Total fertility rate** (avg. births per childbearing woman; 2002): 1.3. **Marriage rate** per 1,000 population (2002): 7.1. **Divorce rate** per 1,000 population (2002): 6.0. **Life expectancy** at birth (2002): male 58.5 years; female 71.9 years.

Social indicators

Quality of working life (2002). Average workweek: 40 hours. Annual rate per 100,000 workers of: injury or accident 460; industrial illness 22.2; death 13.8. Average days lost to labor strikes per 1,000 employees (1999): 35.7. **Social participation.** Trade union membership in total workforce (2000; state enterprises only): 100%. **Social deviance.** Offense rate per 100,000 population (2002) for: murder 22.5; rape 5.6; serious injury 40.7; larceny-theft 761.5. Incidence per 100,000 population (2000) of: alcoholism (1992) 1,727.5; substance abuse 25.6; suicide 39.2. **Material well-being** (2002). Durable goods possessed per 100 households: automobiles 27; personal computers 7; televisions 126; refrigerators and freezers 113; washing machines 93; VCRs 50; motorcycles 26; bicycles 71.

National economy

Public debt (external, outstanding: 2002): $96,223,000,000. **Budget** (2001). *Revenue:* Rub 2,438,105,000,000 (tax revenue 83.3%, of which value-added tax 26.2%, social security tax 25.4%, individual income tax 9.0%, excise tax 8.5%; nontax revenue 16.7%). *Expenditures:* Rub 2,202,868,-000,000 (current expenditure 91.3%, of which social security 33.7%, defense 12.6%, public services 8.2%, law enforcement 5.9%; capital expenditure 8.7%). **Gross national product** (2003): $374,937,000,000 ($2,160 per capita). **Production** (metric tons except as noted). *Agriculture, forestry, fishing* (2002): wheat 50,557,000, potatoes 31,900,000, barley 18,688,-000, sugar beets 15,500,000, vegetables (other than potatoes) 13,800,000, rye 7,139,000, oats 5,700,000, sunflower seeds 3,600,000, apples 1,800,000, peas 1,578,000, corn (maize) 1,541,-000, rice 483,000, buckwheat 34,000; livestock

(number of live animals) 27,106,000 cattle, 16,048,000 pigs, 13,035,000 sheep; roundwood (2002) 176,900,000 cu m; fish catch (2001) 3,718,000. *Mining and quarrying* (2001): iron ore 82,800,000; copper (metal content) 600,000; nickel (metal content) 325,000; zinc (metal content) 124,000; chrome ore (marketable) 69,926; platinum 35,000; vanadium 9,000; antimony (metal content) 4,500; molybdenum 2,600; silver 380,000 kg; gold 152,500 kg; gem diamonds 11,600,000 carats. *Manufacturing* (value added in $'000,000; 2001): food products 5,090; nonferrous base metals 4,282; iron and steel 3,083; motor vehicles and parts 2,547; bricks, cement, ceramics 2,254; special purpose machinery 2,213; basic chemicals 2,037; general purpose machinery 2,024; fabricated metal products 1,794; beverages 1,780; refined petroleum products 1,761; paper and paper products 1,294; paints, soaps, pharmaceuticals 1,252; tobacco products 754; wood and wood products (excluding furniture) 753; electricity distribution and control apparatus 561. *Energy production (consumption):* electricity (kW-hr; 2003) 913,900,000,000 ([2000] 863,700,-000,000); hard coal (2003) 195,900,000 ([2000] 142,224,000); lignite (2003) 79,000,000 ([2000] 91,700,000); crude petroleum (barrels; 2003) 3,019,000,000 ([2000] 1,312,000,000); petroleum products (2001) 159,281,000 (96,990,000); natural gas (cu m; 2003) 526,000,000,000 ([2000] 318,-000,000,000). **Population economically active** (2002): total 71,919,000; activity rate of total population 50.0% (participation rates: ages over 15, 82.6%; female 48.6%; unemployed 8.6%). **Land use** as % of total land area (2000): in temporary crops 7.4%, in permanent crops 0.1%, in pasture 5.4%; overall forest area 50.4%. **Household income and expenditure.** Average household size (2002) 2.8; income per household: Rub 52,400; sources of income (2002): wages 66.2%, pensions and stipends 14.9%, income from entrepreneurial activities 12.0%, property income 4.9%, other 2.0%; expenditure (2002): food 41.7%, clothing 13.3%, housing 6.2%, furniture and household appliances 5.7%, alcohol and tobacco 3.2%, transportation 2.7%. **Tourism** (2002): receipts $4,188,000,000; expenditures $12,005,000,000.

Foreign trade

Imports (2001-c.i.f.): $41,528,000,000 (machinery and apparatus 21.8%, of which general industrial machinery 5.9%; food and live animals 16.1%; chemicals and chemical products 12.1%; road vehicles 4.5%; iron and steel 3.5%). *Major import sources* (2002): Germany 14.3%; Belarus 8.8%; Ukraine 7.0%; US 6.4%; China 5.2%; Italy 4.8%; Kazakhstan 4.2%; France 4.1%. **Exports** (2001-f.o.b.): $99,198,-000,000 (fuels and lubricants 53.9%, of which crude petroleum 24.8%, natural gas 18.0%, refined petroleum 9.5%; nonferrous metals 6.8%; iron and steel 5.6%; chemicals and chemical products 4.8%; machinery and apparatus 4.6%; special transactions 11.6%). *Major export destinations* (2002): Germany 7.6%; Italy 7.0%; The Netherlands 6.8%; China 6.4%; Belarus 5.5%; Ukraine 5.5%; Switzerland 5.1%; US 3.8%; UK 3.6%; Poland 3.5%.

Transport and communications

Transport. *Railroads* (2002): length 139,000 km; passenger-km 152,900,000,000; metric ton-km cargo 1,510,000,000. *Roads* (2002): total length

593,000 km (paved 91%). *Vehicles* (2000): passenger cars 20,247,800; trucks and buses (1999) 5,021,000. *Air transport* (2002): passenger-km 64,700,000,000; metric ton-km cargo 2,700,000,000; airports (1998) 75. **Communications**, in total units (units per 1,000 persons). Daily newspaper circulation (2000): 15,300,000 (105); radios (2000): 61,100,000 (418); televisions (2000): 61,500,000 (421); telephone main lines (2002): 35,500,000 (242); cellular telephone subscribers (2002): 17,608,800 (120); personal computers (2002): 13,000,000 (89); Internet users (2002): 6,000,000 (41).

Education and health

Educational attainment (2002). Percentage of population age 15 and over having: no formal schooling 2.1%; primary education 7.7%; some secondary 18.1%; complete secondary/basic vocational 53.0%; incomplete higher 3.1%; complete higher 16.0%, of which advanced degrees 0.3%. **Health** (2002): physicians 678,000 (1 per 212 persons); hospital beds 1,653,000 (1 per 87 persons); infant mortality rate per 1,000 live births (2002) 13.3. **Food** (2001): daily per capita caloric intake 3,014 (vegetable products 78%, animal products 22%); 115% of FAO recommended minimum.

Military

Total active duty personnel (2004): 1,212,700 (army 29.7%, navy 12.8%, air force 15.2%, strategic deterrent forces 8.2%, paramilitary [includes railway troops, special construction troops, federal border guards, interior troops, and other federal guard units] 34.1%). **Military expenditure as percentage of GNP** (1999): 5.6% (world 2.4%); per capita expenditure $239.

Background

The region between the Dniester and Volga rivers was inhabited from ancient times by various peoples, including the Slavs. The area was overrun from the 8th century BC to the 6th century AD by successive nomadic peoples, including the Sythians, Sarmatians, Goths, Huns, and Avars. Kievan Rus, a confederation of principalities ruled from Kiev, emerged c. 10th century. It lost supremacy in the 11th and 12th centuries to independent principalities, including Novgorod and Vladimir. Novgorod ascended in the north and was the only Russian principality to escape the domination of the Mongol Golden Horde in the 13th century. In the 14th–15th centuries the princes of Moscow gradually overthrew the Mongols. Under Ivan IV, Russia began to expand. The Romanov dynasty arose in 1613. Expansion continued under Peter I (the Great) and Catherine II (the Great). The area was invaded by Napoleon in 1812; after his defeat, Russia received most of the grand duchy of Warsaw (1815). Russia annexed Georgia, Armenia, and Caucasus territories in the 19th century. The Russian southward advance against the Ottoman empire was of key importance to Europe. Russia was defeated in the Crimean War. It sold Alaska to the US in 1867. Russia's defeat in the Russo-Japanese War led to an unsuccessful uprising in 1905. In

World War I it fought against the Central Powers. The Russian Revolution that overthrew the czarist regime in 1917 marked the beginning of a government of soviets ("councils"). The Bolsheviks brought the main part of the former empire under communist control and organized it as the Russian Soviet Federated Socialist Republic (RSFSR; coextensive with present-day Russia). The Russian SFSR joined other soviet republics in 1922 to form the USSR. Although it fought with the Allies in World War II, after the war tensions with the West led to the decades-long Cold War.

Upon the dissolution of the USSR in 1991, the Russian SFSR was renamed Russia and became the leading member of the Commonwealth of Independent States. It adopted a new constitution in 1993. During the 1990s it struggled on several fronts, beset with economic difficulties, political corruption, and independence movements. Vladimir Putin was elected president in 2000, with economic reform, governmental reorganization, cutbacks in the military, and rooting out corruption and favoritism as his chief goals.

Recent Developments

In March 2004 Vladimir Putin was elected to a second presidential term. Three weeks before the election, Putin sacked the entire government. He appointed as prime minister a little-known technocrat, Mikhail Fradkov. Putin's landslide victory put him in an extremely powerful position. In his annual address to the parliament on 26 May, Putin laid out his priorities for his second term and spoke of the importance of democracy, but at the same time he attacked human rights groups that had been critical of his record. Human rights activists and liberal journalists were particularly unhappy with what they saw as the Putin regime's efforts to control the country's mass media.

There was no letup in the separatist conflict in the North Caucasus republic of Chechnya. In May, Chechnya's pro-Moscow president, Akhmad Kadyrov, was assassinated by a bomb in the republic's capital, Grozny, while Chechen separatist leader Aslan Maskhadov was killed during a Russian special forces operation in March 2005. The summer of 2004 saw an escalation of terrorist attacks on Russian targets that included the midair explosions in August of two Russian commercial aircraft that killed all 90 people aboard, an August suicide bombing outside a Moscow subway station, and in September a siege at a provincial school in Beslan, North Ossetia, in which more than 1,000 people were held hostage and more than 330 died, nearly half of them children. Putin afterwards proposed a set of measures that would, he said, strengthen the Russian state against the terrorist threat, including a proposal that regional governors no longer be popularly elected but instead be appointed by the president, subject to endorsement by regional legislatures, which the president could dissolve if they rejected his nominations on two occasions. The legislation, which was approved by overwhelming majorities in both houses of the parliament, returned Russia to the unitary system of government that had existed prior to the collapse of the USSR in 1991.

Internet resources: <www.russiatourism.ru>.

---

1 metric ton = about 1.1 short tons;   1 kilometer = 0.6 mi (statute);   1 metric ton-km cargo = about 0.68 short ton-mi cargo;   c.i.f.: cost, insurance, and freight;   f.o.b.: free on board

Rwanda

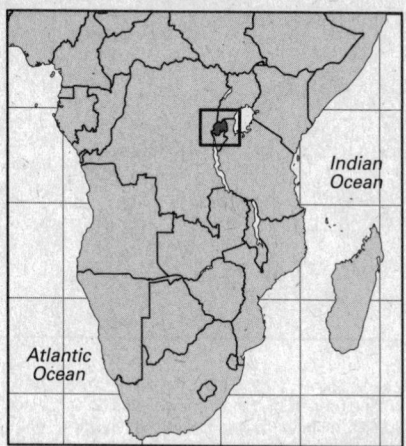

Indian Ocean

Atlantic Ocean

Official name: Republika y'u Rwanda (Rwanda); République Rwandaise (French); Republic of Rwanda (English). **Form of government:** multiparty republic with two legislative bodies (Senate [26]; Chamber of Deputies [80]). **Head of state and government:** President Maj. Gen. Paul Kagame (from 2000), assisted by Prime Minister Bernard Makuza (from 2000). **Capital:** Kigali. **Official languages:** Rwanda; French; English. **Official religion:** none. **Monetary unit:** 1 Rwanda franc (RF); valuation (21 Jul 2005) $1 = RF 541.65.

Demography

Area: 9,758 sq mi, 25,273 sq km (land area only). **Population** (2004): 8,380,000. **Density** (2004): persons per sq mi 858.7, persons per sq km 331.6. **Urban** (2002): 16.7%. **Sex distribution** (2002): male 47.71%; female 52.29%. **Age breakdown** (2002): under 15, 42.7%; 15–29, 30.7%; 30–44, 14.9%; 45–59, 7.6%; 60–74, 3.3%; 75 and over, 0.8%. **Ethnic composition** (2002): Hutu 85%; Tutsi 14%; Twa 1%. **Religious affiliation** (2000): Roman Catholic 51.0%; Protestant 28.8%; traditional beliefs 9.0%; Muslim 7.9%; independent Christian 2.1%; other 1.2%. **Major cities** (2002): Kigali 608,141; Gitarama 84,669; Butare 77,449; Ruhengeri 70,525; Gisenyi 67,192. **Location:** east-central Africa, bordering Uganda, Tanzania, Burundi, and the Democratic Republic of the Congo.

Vital statistics

Birth rate per 1,000 population (2003): 40.8 (world avg. 21.3). **Death rate** per 1,000 population (2003): 16.8 (world avg. 9.1). **Natural increase rate** per 1,000 population (2003): 24.0 (world avg. 12.2). **Total fertility rate** (avg. births per childbearing woman; 2003): 5.6. **Life expectancy** at birth (2003): male 45.3 years; female 47.4 years. **Adult population** (ages 15–49) **living with HIV** (2004): 5.1% (world avg. 1.1%).

National economy

Budget (2001). *Revenue:* RF 149,500,000,000 (grants 42.3%; taxes on goods and services 27.4%;

income tax 16.0%; import and export duties 7.4%; nontax revenue 6.9%). *Expenditures:* RF 189,200,000,000 (current expenditures 56.8%, of which wages 28.4%, education 15.8%, defense 15.1%, health 2.7%, debt payment 1.5%; capital expenditure 43.2%). **Production** (metric tons except as noted). *Agriculture, forestry, fishing* (2002): plantains 2,784,870, sweet potatoes 1,292,361, potatoes 1,038,931; livestock (number of live animals) 815,000 cattle, 760,000 goats, 260,000 sheep; roundwood (2002) 7,836,000 cu m; fish catch (2001) 7,263. *Mining and quarrying* (2002): cassiterite (tin content) 197; niobium 43; tantalum 24. *Manufacturing* (value added in RF '000,000; 2000): food and nonalcoholic beverages 37,981; nonmetallic products 3,109; metal products 1,087. *Energy production (consumption):* electricity (kW-hr; 2000) 169,000,000 (182,000,000); petroleum products (2000) none (174,000); natural gas (cu m; 2000) 250,300 (250,300). **Population economically active** (1996): total 3,021,000; activity rate of total population 50.8% (participation rates: ages 14 and over, 86.0%; female 49.0%). **Land use** as % of total land area (2000): in temporary crops 36.5%, in permanent crops 10.1%, in pasture 22.1%; overall forest area 12.4%. **Households.** Average household size (1991) 4.7. **Gross national product** (2002): $1,826,000,000 ($220 per capita). **Public debt** (external, outstanding; 2002): $1,305,000,000. **Tourism:** receipts (2002) $31,000,000; expenditures $24,000,000.

Foreign trade

Imports (2000): $239,800,000 (capital goods 22.1%, food 19.4%, energy products 18.7%, intermediate goods 18.1%). *Major import sources* (2002): Kenya 21.9%; Germany 8.4%; Belgium 7.9%; Israel 4.3%; US 3.5%. **Exports** (2001): $90,400,000 (niobium and tantalum 45.2%, tea 25.6%, coffee 20.1%). *Major export destinations* (2002): Indonesia 30.8%; Germany 14.6%; Hong Kong 8.9%; South Africa 5.5%.

Transport and communications

Transport. *Roads* (1999): total length 12,000 km (paved 8%). *Vehicles* (1996): passenger cars 13,000; trucks 17,100. *Air transport* (2000; Kigali airport only): passengers embarked and disembarked 101,000; cargo loaded and unloaded 4,300 metric tons; airports (2002) with scheduled flights 2. **Communications,** in total units (units per 1,000 persons). Daily newspaper circulation (1995): 500 (0.1); radios (1997): 601,000 (101); telephone main lines (2002): 23,200 (2.8); cellular telephone subscribers (2003): 134,000 (16); Internet users (2002): 25,000 (3).

Education and health

Literacy (2000): percentage of total population age 15 and over literate 66.8%; males literate 73.7%; females literate 60.2%. **Health:** physicians (1992) 150 (1 per 50,000 persons); hospital beds (1990) 12,152 (1 per 588 persons); infant mortality rate per 1,000 live births (2003) 94.3. **Food** (2001): daily per capita caloric intake 2,086 (vegetable products 97%, animal products 3%); 90% of FAO recommended minimum.

Military

Total active duty personnel (2003): 51,000 (army 78.4%, navy 2.0%, national police 19.6%). **Military**

expenditure as percentage of GNP (1999): 4.5% (world 2.4%); per capita expenditure $12.

Background

Originally inhabited by the Twa, a Pygmy people, Rwanda became home to the Hutu, who were well established there when the Tutsi appeared in the 14th century. The Tutsi conquered the Hutu and in the 15th century founded a kingdom near Kigali. The Belgians occupied Rwanda in 1916, and the League of Nations created Ruanda-Urundi as a Belgian mandate in 1923. The Tutsi retained their dominance until shortly before Rwanda reached independence in 1962, when the Hutu took control of the government and stripped the Tutsi of much of their land. Many Tutsi fled Rwanda, and the Hutu dominated the country's political system, waging sporadic civil wars until mid-1994, when the death of the country's leader in a plane crash—apparently shot down—led to massive violence. The Tutsi-led Rwandan Patriotic Front (RPF) took over the country by force after the massacre of almost 500,000 Tutsi by Hutu. Two million refugees, mostly Hutu, fled to neighboring countries after the RPF's victory.

Recent Developments

The year 2004 marked the 10th anniversary of the genocide in Rwanda that killed nearly a million Tutsi and moderate Hutu. Solemn commemorations attended by Rwandans and African leaders, with Europe and the US represented by junior officials, were held in locations throughout the country. Thirty thousand accused prisoners were granted amnesty. Rwanda came close to war with the Democratic Republic of the Congo (DRC) in June when Congolese rebels captured Bukavu, a DRC town near the Rwandan border. DRC Pres. Joseph Kabila accused Rwanda of backing the rebels, an accusation vigorously denied by the Rwandans. In December Rwanda made several invasion threats amid reports that its soldiers had already entered the DRC.

Internet resources: <www.rwandatourism.com>.

Saint Kitts and Nevis

Official name: Federation of Saint Kitts and Nevis. Form of government: constitutional monarchy with one legislative house (National Assembly [15, including 4 nonelective seats]). Chief of state: British Monarch Queen Elizabeth II (from 1952), represented by Governor-General Sir Cuthbert Sebastian (from 1996). Head of government: Prime Minister Denzil Douglas (from 1995). Capital: Basseterre. Official language: English. Official religion: none. Monetary unit: 1 Eastern Caribbean dollar (EC$) = 100 cents; valuation (7 Jul 2005) US$1 = EC$2.67.

Demography

Area: 104.0 sq mi, 269.4 sq km. Population (2004): 46,300. Density (2004): persons per sq mi 445.2, persons per sq km 172.1. Urban (2000): 34.2%. Sex distribution (2001): male 49.70%; female 50.30%. Age breakdown (2000): under 15, 30.3%; 15–29,

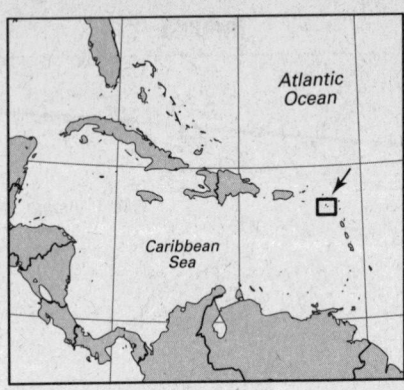

24.9%; 30–44, 22.2%; 45–59, 11.2%; 60–74, 7.1%; 75 and over, 4.3%. Ethnic composition (2000): black 90.4%; mulatto 5.0%; Indo-Pakistani 3.0%; white 1.0%; other/unspecified 0.6%. Religious affiliation (1995): Protestant 84.6%, of which Anglican 25.2%, Methodist 25.2%, Pentecostal 8.4%, Moravian 7.6%; Roman Catholic 6.7%; Hindu 1.5%; other 7.2%. Major towns (2001): Basseterre 13,033; Charlestown (1994) 1,411. Location: islands in the Caribbean Sea, between Puerto Rico and Trinidad and Tobago.

Vital statistics

Birth rate per 1,000 population (2003): 18.5 (world avg. 21.3); (1983) legitimate 19.2%. Death rate per 1,000 population (2003): 8.9 (world avg. 9.1). Natural increase rate per 1,000 population (2001): 9.6 (world avg. 12.2). Total fertility rate (avg. births per childbearing woman; 2003): 2.4. Marriage rate per 1,000 population (2001): 7.1. Divorce rate per 1,000 population (2002): 0.5. Life expectancy at birth (2003): male 68.8 years; female 74.6 years.

National economy

Budget (2001). Revenue: EC$270,100,000 (tax revenue 72.8%, of which import duties 34.0%, taxes on income and profits 21.4%, taxes on domestic goods and services 14.1%; nontax revenue 27.2%). Expenditures: EC$406,000,000 (current expenditure 75.6%; development expenditure 24.4%). Production (metric tons except as noted). Agriculture and fishing (2002): sugarcane 191,400, tropical fruit 1,300, coconuts 1,000; livestock (number of live animals) 14,400 goats, 14,000 sheep, 4,300 cattle; fish catch (2001) 291. Mining and quarrying: excavation of sand for local use. Manufacturing (2001): raw sugar 20,193; carbonated beverages (1995) 45,000 hectoliters; beer 20,000 hectoliters. Energy production (consumption): electricity (kW-hr; 2000) 100,000,-000 (100,000,000); petroleum products (2000) none (33,000). Gross national product (2003): US$321,000,000 (US$6,880 per capita). Household income and expenditure. Average household size (2001) 2.9; average annual income per wage earner (1994) EC$9,940; expenditure (1978): food, beverages, and tobacco 55.6%, household furnishings 9.4%, housing 7.6%, clothing and footwear 7.5%, fuel

1 metric ton = about 1.1 short tons;   1 kilometer = 0.6 mi (statute);   1 metric ton-km cargo = about 0.68 short ton-mi cargo;   c.i.f.: cost, insurance, and freight;   f.o.b.: free on board

and light 6.6%, transportation 4.3%, other 9.0%. **Public debt** (external, outstanding; 2002): US$252,-200,000. **Population economically active** (1980): total 17,125; activity rate of total population 39.5% (participation rates: ages 15–64, 69.5%; female 41.0%; unemployed [1997] 4.5%). **Land use** as % of total land area (2000): in temporary crops 19%, in permanent crops 3%, in pasture 6%; overall forest area 11%. **Tourism:** receipts from visitors (2002) US$57,000,000; expenditures by nationals abroad (2001) US$8,000,000.

Foreign trade

Imports (2001-c.i.f.): US$189,200,000 (machinery and apparatus 22.4%; food 14.4%; fabricated metals 7.9%; chemicals and chemical products 6.9%; refined petroleum 6.4%). *Major import sources* (2002): US 41.5%; Trinidad and Tobago 16.2%; Canada 9.8%; UK 6.9%; Japan 4.0%. **Exports** (2001-f.o.b.): US$31,-000,000 (electrical switches, relays, and fuses 56.1%; raw sugar 21.0%; telecommunications equipment [parts] 3.2%). *Major export destinations* (2002): US 66.6%; UK 7.6%; Canada 6.8%; Portugal 6.0%; Germany 2.9%.

Transport and communications

Transport. *Railroads* (2000; light railway serving the sugar industry on Saint Kitts): length 58 km. *Roads* (2001): total length 318 km (paved 44%). *Vehicles* (2001): passenger cars 5,826; trucks and buses 2,989. *Air transport* (2001; Saint Kitts airport only): passenger arrivals 135,237; passenger departures 134,937; cargo handled 1,802; airports (1998) with scheduled flights 2. **Communications,** in total units (units per 1,000 persons). Radios (1997): 28,000 (701); televisions (1997): 10,000 (264); telephone main lines (2002): 23,500 (500); cellular telephones (2002): 5,000 (106); personal computers (2002): 9,000 (191); Internet users (2002): 10,000 (213).

Education and health

Educational attainment (1991). Percentage of population age 25 and over having: no formal schooling 1.6%; primary education 45.9%; secondary 38.4%; higher 8.9%; other or not stated 5.2%. **Literacy** (1990): total population age 15 and over literate 25,500 (90.0%); males literate 13,100 (90.0%); females literate 12,400 (90.0%). **Health** (2001): physicians 49 (1 per 936 persons); hospital beds 178 (1 per 258 persons); infant mortality rate per 1,000 live births (2003) 15.4. **Food** (2001): daily per capita caloric intake 2,997 (vegetable products 74%, animal products 26%); 124% of FAO recommended minimum.

Military

Total active duty personnel: in July 1997 the National Assembly approved a bill creating a 50-member army. **Military expenditure as percentage of GNP** (1998; includes expenditure for police): 3.5%; per capita expenditure US$226.

Background

Saint Kitts became the first British colony in the West Indies in 1623. Anglo-French rivalry grew in the 17th century and lasted more than a century. In 1783, by the Treaty of Versailles, the islands became wholly British possessions. They were united with Anguilla from 1882 to 1980 but became an independent federation within the British Commonwealth in 1983. In 1997 Nevis considered becoming independent.

Recent Developments

In September 2004 Saint Kitts and Nevis accepted a $1.4 million check from Taiwan to help fund construction of a new world-class sports complex. The money was the first installment of a $12 million assistance package agreed to during Prime Minister Denzil Douglas's visit to Taiwan in November 2003.

Internet resources: <www.stkittsnevis.net>.

Saint Lucia

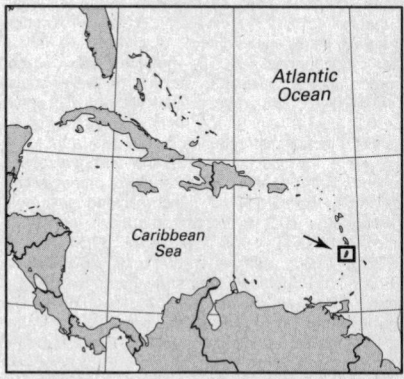

Official name: Saint Lucia. **Form of government:** constitutional monarchy with a parliament consisting of two legislative chambers (Senate [11]; House of Assembly [17 {elected seats only}]). **Chief of state:** Queen Elizabeth II (from 1952), represented by Governor-General Dame Pearlette Louisy (from 1997). **Head of government:** Prime Minister Kenny Anthony (from 1997). **Capital:** Castries. **Official language:** English. **Official religion:** none. **Monetary unit:** 1 Eastern Caribbean dollar (EC$) = 100 cents; valuation (7 Jul 2005) US$1 = EC$2.67.

Demography

Area: 238 sq mi, 617 sq km. **Population** (2004): 164,000. **Density** (2004): persons per sq mi 689.1, persons per sq km 265.8. **Urban** (2001): 38.0%. **Sex distribution** (2001): male 48.92%; female 51.08%. **Age breakdown** (2001): under 15, 31.2%; 15–29, 27.4%; 30–44, 20.6%; 45–59, 10.7%; 60 and over, 10.1%. **Ethnic composition** (2000): black 50%; mulatto 44%; East Indian 3%; white 1%; other 2%. **Religious affiliation** (2001): Roman Catholic 67.5%; Protestant 22.0%, of which Seventh-day Adventist 8.4%, Pentecostal 5.6%, Rastafarian 2.1%; nonreligious 4.5%; other/unknown 3.9%. **Major urban area** (2001): Castries 37,549. **Location:** island between the Caribbean Sea and North Atlantic Ocean, north of Trinidad and Tobago.

Vital statistics

Birth rate per 1,000 population (2003): 20.9 (world avg. 21.3); (2000) legitimate 14.3%. **Death rate** per 1,000 population (2003): 5.2 (world avg. 9.1). **Natural increase rate** per 1,000 population (2003): 15.7 (world avg. 12.2). **Total fertility rate** (avg. births per childbearing woman; 2003): 2.3. **Marriage rate** per 1,000 population (2001): 2.8. **Divorce rate** per 1,000 population (2001): 0.4. **Life expectancy** at birth (2003): male 69.5 years; female 76.9 years.

National economy

Budget (2002). *Revenue:* EC$505,700,000 (tax revenue 81.6%, of which consumption duties on imported goods 42.5%, taxes on income and profits 21.3%, goods and services 16.5%; nontax revenue 12.7%; grants 5.7%). *Expenditures:* EC$543,600,000 (current expenditures 74.6%; development expenditures and net lending 25.4%). **Public debt** (external, outstanding; 2002): US$210,700,000. **Production** (metric tons except as noted). *Agriculture and fishing* (2002): bananas 92,000, mangoes 28,000, coconuts 14,000; livestock (number of live animals) 14,950 pigs, 12,500 sheep, 12,400 cattle; fish catch (2001) 1,984. *Mining and quarrying:* excavation of sand for local construction and pumice. *Manufacturing* (value of production in EC$'000; 1998): alcoholic beverages and tobacco 31,120; paper products and cardboard boxes 28,747; electrical and electronic components 16,245. *Energy production (consumption):* electricity (kW-hr; 2000) 375,000,000 (375,000,000); petroleum products (2000) none (110,000). **Population economically active** (2002): total 74,949; activity rate of total population 47.0% (participation rates: ages 15 and over 66.8%; female [2000] 47.2%; unemployed 16.2%). **Gross national product** (at current market prices; 2003): US$650,000,000 (US$4,050 per capita). **Households.** Average household size (2001) 3.2. **Land use** as % of total land area (2000): in temporary crops 7%, in permanent crops 23%, in pasture 3%; overall forest area 15%. **Tourism:** receipts from visitors (2002) US$218,000,000; expenditures by nationals abroad (2001) US$32,000,000.

Foreign trade

Imports (2002): US$277,100,000 (food and beverages 26.2%; machinery and apparatus 23.5%; manufactured goods 17.3%; chemicals and chemical products 9.0%; refined petroleum 8.7%). *Major import sources:* US 38.0%; Trinidad and Tobago 14.6%; UK 9.5%; Japan 3.3%; Canada 3.1%. **Exports** (2002): US$54,900,000 (bananas 49.9%; beer and ale 15.9%; clothing 3.2%; electrical and electronic components 3.2%). *Major export destinations:* UK 37.6%; US 20.3%; Trinidad and Tobago 11.8%; Barbados 9.7%; Dominica 5.3%.

Transport and communications

Transport. *Roads* (1999): total length 1,210 km (paved 5%). *Vehicles* (2001): passenger cars 22,453; trucks and buses 8,972. *Air transport* (2001; combined data for both Castries and Vieux Fort airports):

passenger arrivals and departures 679,000; cargo unloaded and loaded 3,500 metric tons; airports (2000) with scheduled flights 2. **Communications,** in total units (units per 1,000 persons). Radios (1997): 100,000 (668); televisions (1997): 40,000 (267); telephone main lines (2002): 51,100 (320); cellular telephone subscribers (2002): 14,300 (90); personal computers (2002): 24,000 (150); Internet users (2001): 13,000 (82).

Education and health

Educational attainment (2000). Percentage of population age 15 over having: no formal schooling 6.5%; primary education 56.2%; secondary 27.5%; higher vocational 4.5%; university 2.7%; other/unknown 2.6%. **Literacy** (2000): 90.2%. **Health** (2002): physicians 92 (1 per 1,740 persons); hospital beds 285 (1 per 562 persons); infant mortality rate per 1,000 live births (2003) 15.4. **Food** (2001): daily per capita caloric intake 2,849 (vegetable products 72%, animal products 28%); 118% of FAO recommended minimum.

Military

Total active duty personnel (2000): the 300-member police force includes a specially trained paramilitary unit and a coast guard unit.

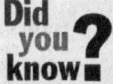

Did you know? The landmark twin mountain peaks of the Pitons on St. Lucia were added to the list of UNESCO World Heritage sites in 2004. The Pitons are volcanic spires rising to 2,526 ft. (770 m) and 2,438 ft. (743 m), and the site includes hot springs, a significant coral reef, and richly varied flora and fauna.

Background

Caribs replaced early Arawak inhabitants on the island c. AD 800–1300. Settled by the French in 1650, it was ceded to Great Britain in 1814 and became one of the Windward Islands in 1871. It became fully independent in 1979. The economy is based on agriculture and tourism.

Recent Developments

A sharp disagreement over the role of external institutions and governments in the financing of political parties in Saint Lucia arose in September 2004 when Prime Minister Kenny Anthony challenged Vaughan Lewis, leader of the opposition United Workers' Party, over a letter the latter had written to a political organization in the US, requesting support for the UWP. Anthony strongly cautioned against the practice.

Internet resources: <www.stlucia.org>.

Saint Vincent and the Grenadines

Official name: Saint Vincent and the Grenadines. **Form of government:** constitutional monarchy with one legislative house (House of Assembly [21, includ-

---

1 metric ton = about 1.1 short tons;   1 kilometer = 0.6 mi (statute);   1 metric ton-km cargo = about 0.68 short ton-mi cargo;   c.i.f.: cost, insurance, and freight;   f.o.b.: free on board

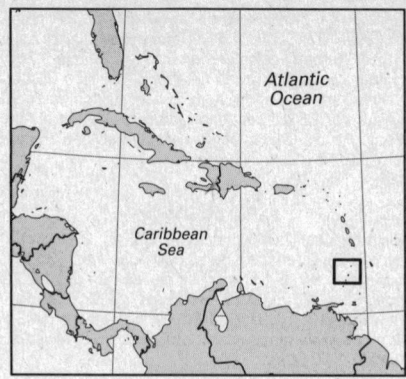

ing 6 nonelective seats and excluding speaker, who may be elected from within or from outside the House of Assembly membership]). **Chief of state:** British Monarch Queen Elizabeth II (from 1952), represented by Governor-General Sir Frederick Ballantyne (from 2002). **Head of government:** Prime Minister Ralph Gonsalves (from 2001). **Capital:** Kingstown. **Official language:** English. **Official religion:** none. **Monetary unit:** 1 Eastern Caribbean dollar (EC$) = 100 cents; valuation (7 Jul 2005) US$1 = EC$2.67.

Demography

Area: 150.3 sq mi, 389.3 sq km. **Population** (2004): 113,000. **Density** (2004): persons per sq mi 753.3, persons per sq km 290.5. **Urban** (2000): 54.4%. **Sex distribution** (2000): male 49.90%; female 50.10%. **Age breakdown** (1999): under 15, 31.3%; 15–29, 31.2%; 30–44, 19.6%; 45–59, 9.4%; 60–74, 5.9%; 75 and over, 2.6%. **Ethnic composition** (1999): black 65.5%; mulatto 23.5%; Indo-Pakistani 5.5%; white 3.5%; black-Amerindian 2.0%. **Religious affiliation** (1995): Protestant 57.6%; unaffiliated Christian 20.6%; Roman Catholic 10.7%; Hindu 3.3%; Muslim 1.5%; other/nonreligious 6.3%. **Major city** (2000): Kingstown 16,209. **Location:** islands in the Caribbean Sea, north of Trinidad and Tobago.

Vital statistics

Birth rate per 1,000 population (2002): 17.6 (world avg. 21.3); (1999) legitimate 17.9%. **Death rate** per 1,000 population (2002): 6.9 (world avg. 9.1). **Natural increase rate** per 1,000 population (2002): 10.7 (world avg. 12.2). **Total fertility rate** (avg. births per childbearing woman; 2003): 2.0. **Marriage rate** per 1,000 population (2002): 4.5. **Divorce rate** per 1,000 population (2002): 0.4. **Life expectancy** at birth (2003): male 71.3 years; female 74.9 years.

National economy

Budget (2002). *Revenue:* EC$312,000,000 (current revenue 80.8%, of which taxes on international trade and transactions 38.8%, income tax 25.6%, taxes on goods and services 15.7%; grants 5.1%; nontax revenue 13.8%; capital revenue 0.3%). *Expenditures:* EC$348,000,000 (current expenditure 81.3%, development expenditure 18.7%). **Public debt** (external, outstanding; 2002): US$173,-700,000. **Production** (metric tons except as noted).

Agriculture and fishing (2000): bananas 45,951, coconuts 23,700, eddoes and dasheens 4,400; livestock (number of live animals) 13,000 sheep, 9,500 pigs, 6,200 cattle; fish catch (2002) 643. *Mining and quarrying:* sand and gravel for local use. *Manufacturing* (value added in EC$'000,000; 2000): beverages and tobacco products 17.4; food 15.6; paper products and publishing 3.6. *Energy production (consumption):* electricity (kW-hr; 2000) 85,000,000 (85,000,000); petroleum products (2000) none (53,000). **Tourism:** receipts from visitors (2002) US$81,000,000; expenditures by nationals abroad (2001) US$10,000,000. **Land use** as % of total land area (2000): in temporary crops 18%, in permanent crops 18%, in pasture 5%; overall forest area 15%. **Gross national product** (2003): US$361,000,000 (US$3,300 per capita). **Population economically active** (1991): total 41,682; activity rate of total population 39.1% (participation rates: ages 15–64, 67.5%; female 35.9%; unemployed [1996] more than 30%). **Households.** Average household size (1991) 3.9; income per household (1988) EC$4,579.

Foreign trade

Imports (2001-c.i.f.): US$186,500,000 (food products 20.4%; machinery and transport equipment 19.0%; chemicals and chemical products 9.8%; fuels 9.0%). *Major import sources:* US 34.5%; Caricom countries 31.2%, of which Trinidad and Tobago 19.9%; UK 9.8%; Japan 3.5%. **Exports** (2001-f.o.b.): US$45,700,000 (domestic exports 86.9%, of which bananas 28.4%, packaged flour 13.2%, packaged rice 9.2%, eddoes and dasheens 3.4%; reexports 13.1%). *Major export destinations:* Caricom countries 53.7%, of which Trinidad and Tobago 17.0%, Barbados 9.8%, St. Lucia 7.9%; UK 36.8%.

Transport and communications

Transport. *Roads* (1999): total length 1,040 km (paved 31%). *Vehicles* (1999): passenger cars 7,989; trucks and buses 3,920. *Air transport* (2000): passenger arrivals 132,445; passenger departures 134,012; airports (1998) with scheduled flights 5. **Communications,** in total units (units per 1,000 persons). Radios (1995): 65,000 (591); televisions (1995): 17,700 (161); telephone main lines (2002): 27,300 (234); cellular telephone subscribers (2002): 10,000 (85); personal computers (2002): 14,000 (192); Internet users (2002): 7,000 (60).

Education and health

Educational attainment (1980). Percentage of population age 25 and over having: no formal schooling 2.4%; primary education 88.0%; secondary 8.2%; higher 1.4%. **Literacy** (1991): total population age 15 and over literate 64,000 (96.0%). **Health** (1998): physicians 59 (1 per 1,883 persons); hospital beds (2000) 209 (1 per 535 persons); infant mortality rate per 1,000 live births (2002) 18.1. **Food** (2001): daily per capita caloric intake 2,609 (vegetable products 83%, animal products 17%); 108% of FAO recommended minimum.

Military

Total active duty personnel (1992): 634-member police force includes a coast guard and paramilitary unit.

Background

The French and the British contested for control of Saint Vincent and the Grenadines until 1763, when it was ceded to England by the Treaty of Paris. The original inhabitants, the Caribs, recognized British sovereignty but revolted in 1795. Most of the Caribs were deported; many who remained were killed in volcanic eruptions in 1812 and 1902. In 1969 Saint Vincent and the Grenadines became a self-governing state in association with the United Kingdom, and in 1979 it achieved full independence.

Recent Developments

During 2004 Saint Vincent and the Grenadines continued to be an attractive location for international business companies, which operated under generous tax incentives. By the end of April, according to an official count, 357 new such companies had been registered in the country, compared with 194 in 2003.

Internet resources: <www.svgtourism.com>.

Samoa

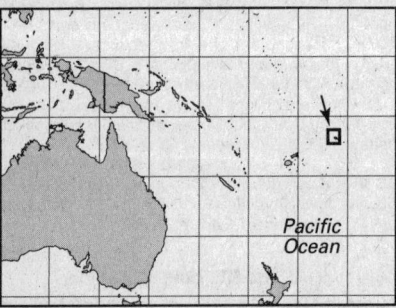

Pacific Ocean

Official name: Malo Sa'oloto Tuto'atasi o Samoa (Samoan); Independent State of Samoa (English). **Form of government:** constitutional monarchy with one legislative house (Legislative Assembly [49]). **Chief of state:** Head of State Malietoa Tanumafili II (from 1963). **Head of government:** Prime Minister Tuila'epa Sa'ilele Malielegaoi (from 1998). **Capital:** Apia. **Official languages:** Samoan; English. **Official religion:** none. **Monetary unit:** 1 tala (SA$ [WS$ prior to July 1997], plural tala) = 100 sene; valuation (7 Jul 2005) US$1 = SA$2.70.

Demography

Area: 1,093 sq mi, 2,831 sq km. **Population** (2004): 183,000. **Density** (2004): persons per sq mi 167.4, persons per sq km 64.6. **Urban** (2002): 22.0%. **Sex distribution** (2001): male 52.09%; female 47.91%. **Age breakdown** (2001): under 15, 40.8%; 15–29, 25.6%; 30–44, 17.9%; 45–59, 9.2%; 60–74, 5.0%; 75 and over, 1.5%. **Ethnic composition** (1997): Samoan (Polynesian) 92.6%; Euronesian (European and Polynesian) 7.0%; European 0.4%. **Religious affiliation** (1995): Mormon 25.8%; Congregational 24.6%; Roman Catholic 21.3%; Methodist 12.2%;

Pentecostal 8.0%; Seventh-day Adventist 3.9%; other Christian 1.7%; other 2.5%. **Major towns** (2001): Apia 38,836 (urban agglomeration 60,734); Vaitele 5,200 (within Apia urban agglomeration); Faleasi'u 3,209; Vailele 3,175 (within Apia urban agglomeration); Le'auva'a 2,828. **Location:** group of islands in the South Pacific Ocean, about halfway between Hawaii (US) and New Zealand.

Vital statistics

Birth rate per 1,000 population (2003): 28.6 (world avg. 21.3). **Death rate** per 1,000 population (2003): 5.5 (world avg. 9.1). **Natural increase rate** per 1,000 population (2003): 23.1 (world avg. 12.2). **Total fertility rate** (avg. births per childbearing woman; 2003): 4.1. **Life expectancy** at birth (2003): male 67.4 years; female 73.0 years.

National economy

Budget (2000–01). *Revenue:* SA$262,400,000 (tax revenue 66.6%, grants 24.8%, nontax revenue 8.6%). *Expenditures:* SA$281,700,000 (current expenditure 58.4%, development expenditure 36.6%, net lending 5.0%). **Public debt** (external, outstanding; 2002): US$156,800,000. **Production** (metric tons except as noted). *Agriculture, forestry, fishing* (2002): coconuts 140,000, bananas 21,500, taro 17,000; livestock (number of live animals) 201,000 pigs, 28,000 cattle, 450,000 chickens; roundwood (2001) 131,000 cu m; fish catch (2001) 12,966. *Manufacturing* (in WS$'000; 1990): beer 8,708; cigarettes 6,551; coconut cream 5,576. *Energy production (consumption):* electricity (kW-hr; 2000) 66,000,000 (66,000,000; petroleum products (2000) none (45,000). **Households.** Average household size (2001) 7.7. **Population economically active** (2001): total 50,000; activity rate of total population 28.3% (female [1991] 32.0%). **Gross national product** (at current market prices; 2003): US$284,000,000 (US$1,600 per capita). **Tourism:** receipts from visitors (2002) US$46,000,000; expenditures by nationals abroad (1999) US$4,000,000. **Land use** as % of total land area (2000): in temporary crops 20.8%, in permanent crops 24.0%, in pasture 0.7%; overall forest area 37.2%.

Foreign trade

Imports (2001–02-c.i.f.): SA$465,000,000 (petroleum products 10.2%, imports for government 5.2%, unspecified 84.6%). *Major import sources:* New Zealand 34.4%; Australia 26.6%; US 11.8%; Fiji 8.7%; Japan 6.6%. **Exports** (2001–02-f.o.b.): SA$49,500,000 (fresh fish 66.9%, garments 11.5%, beer 6.7%, coconut cream 6.6%). *Major export destinations:* American Samoa 52.3%; US 32.2%; New Zealand 6.8%; Germany 3.4%; Australia 2.7%.

Transport and communications

Transport. *Roads* (1996): total length 790 km (paved 42%). *Vehicles* (1995): passenger cars 1,068; trucks and buses 1,169. *Air transport* (1999): passenger-km 244,000,000; metric ton-km cargo 23,000,000; airports (1997) with scheduled flights 3. **Communications,** in total units (units per

---

1 metric ton = about 1.1 short tons;   1 kilometer = 0.6 mi (statute);   1 metric ton-km cargo = about 0.68 short ton-mi cargo;   c.i.f.: cost, insurance, and freight;   f.o.b.: free on board

1,000 persons). Radios (1997): 178,000 (1,035); televisions (1998): 9,000 (52); telephone main lines (2002): 11,800 (65); cellular telephone subscribers (2002): 2,700 (15); personal computers (2002): 1,000 (6.7); Internet users (2002): 4,000 (22).

Education and health

Literacy (2000): total population over age 15 literate 80.2%; males literate 81.2%; females literate 79.0%. **Health:** physicians (1996) 62 (1 per 2,919 persons); hospital beds (1991) 863 (1 per 255 persons); infant mortality rate per 1,000 live births (2003) 26.0. **Food** (1992): daily per capita caloric intake 2,828 (vegetable products 74%, animal products 26%); 124% of FAO recommended minimum.

Military

No military forces are maintained; New Zealand is responsible for defense.

Background

Polynesians inhabited the islands of the Samoan archipelago for thousands of years before they were visited by Europeans in the 18th century. Control of the islands was contested by the US, Britain, and Germany until 1899, when they were divided between the US and Germany. In 1914, Western Samoa was occupied by New Zealand, which received it as a League of Nations mandate in 1920. After World War II, it became a UN trust territory administered by New Zealand, and it achieved independence in 1962. In 1997, the word Western was dropped from the country's name.

Recent Developments

In January 2004 Cyclone Heta brushed Samoa; along with the severe drought conditions later in the year, it contributed to a continuing economic decline that had seen Samoan GDP growth fall from 6% to 2% over recent years. Exports had fallen by 10% in 2003 compared with 2002, with fishing and tourism most affected. Despite increased returns from the garment industry, the balance of trade declined. In August workers broke ground for a much-anticipated hotel complex on Taumeasina Island.

Internet resources: <www.visitsamoa.ws>.

San Marino

Official name: Serenissima Repubblica di San Marino (Most Serene Republic of San Marino). **Form of government:** unitary multiparty republic with one legislative house (Great and General Council [60]). **Heads of state and government:** two captains-regent who serve six-month terms beginning in April and October. **Capital:** San Marino. **Official language:** Italian. **Official religion:** none. **Monetary unit:** 1 euro (€) = 100 cents; valuation (7 Jul 2005) $1 = €0.84; at conversion on 1 Jan 2002, €1= 1,936.27 Italian lire (Lit).

Demography

Area: 23.63 sq mi, 61.20 sq km. **Population** (2004): 29,400. **Density** (2004): persons per sq mi 1,225, persons per sq km 482.0. **Urban** (2003): 88.7%. **Sex distribution** (2003): male 48.94%; female 51.06%.

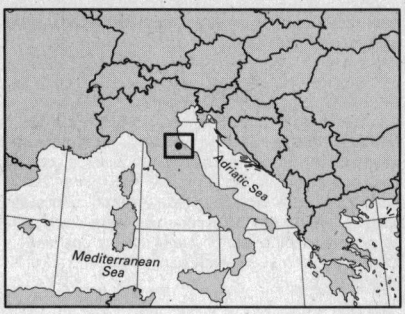

Age breakdown (2003): under 15, 14.1%; 15–29, 16.6%; 30–44, 27.3%; 45–59, 19.7%; 60–74, 14.2%; 75 and over, 8.1%. **Ethnic composition** (2003): Sammarinesi 85.7%; Italian 13.0%; other 1.3%. **Religious affiliation** (2000): Roman Catholic 88.7%; Pentecostal 1.8%; other 9.5%. **Major cities** (2000): Serravalle/Dogano 8,547; San Marino 4,439; Borgo Maggiore (1997) 2,394; Murata (1997) 1,549; Domagnano (1997) 1,048. **Location:** southern Europe, completely surrounded by Italy.

Vital statistics

Birth rate per 1,000 population (2002): 10.4 (world avg. 21.3). **Death rate** per 1,000 population (2002): 7.1 (world avg. 9.1). **Natural increase rate** per 1,000 population (2002): 3.3 (world avg. 12.2). **Total fertility rate** (avg. births per childbearing woman; 2002): 1.3. **Marriage rate** per 1,000 population (2002): 7.3. **Divorce rate** per 1,000 population (1998–2000): 1.6. **Life expectancy** at birth (2000): male 77.6 years; female 85.0 years.

National economy

Budget (2003). *Revenue:* €288,000,000 (direct taxes 34.7%; import taxes 33.0%; nontax revenue 22.0%). *Expenditures:* €272,400,000 (current expenditures 92.0%; capital expenditures 8.0%). **Public debt** (2003): $52,900,000. **Tourism:** number of tourist arrivals (2002) 3,102,453; receipts from visitors (1994) $252,500,000. **Population economically active** (2003): total 20,236; activity rate of total population 69.3% (participation rates: ages 15–64 [2002] 72.1%; female 41.5%; unemployed [2004] 3.9%). **Households.** Total number of households (2003) 11,723; average household size (2003) 2.5; expenditure (1991): food, beverages, and tobacco 22.1%, housing, fuel, and electrical energy 20.9%, transportation and communications 17.6%, clothing and footwear 8.0%, furniture, appliances, and goods and services for the home 7.2%, education 7.1%, health and sanitary services 2.6%, other goods and services 14.5%. **Production** (metric tons except as noted). *Agriculture* (early 1980s): wheat 4,400, grapes 700, barley 500; livestock (number of live animals; 1998) 831 cattle, 748 pigs. *Manufacturing* (1998): processed meats 324,073 kg, of which beef 226,570 kg, pork 87,764 kg, veal 7,803 kg; cheese 61,563 kg; butter 12,658 kg. *Energy production (consumption):* all electrical power is imported via electrical grid from Italy ([2001] 193,371,696); natural gas, none ([2001] 50,641,790). **Gross national product** (at current market prices; 2002): $836,000,000 ($29,360 per capita). **Land use** as % of total land area (2000): in temporary crops, permanent crops, pasture, or forest 65%.

Foreign trade

A customs union with Italy has existed since 1862. **Imports** (2002): $1,657,000,000 (manufactured goods of all kinds, petroleum products, electricity, and gold). *Major import source:* Italy. **Exports** (2002): $1,566,000,000 (goods include electronics, postage stamps, leather products, ceramics, wine, wood products, and building stone). *Major export destination:* Italy (in the late 1990s Italy accounted for 87% of all foreign trade).

Transport and communications

Transport. *Roads* (2001): total length 252 km. *Vehicles* (2002): passenger cars 28,470; trucks and buses 2,748. *Air transport:* airports with scheduled flights, none; there is, however, a heliport that provides passenger and cargo service between San Marino and Rimini, Italy, during the summer months. **Communications,** in total units (units per 1,000 persons). Daily newspaper circulation (1996): 2,000 (72); radios (1998): 16,000 (610); televisions (1998): 9,055 (358); telephone main lines (2002): 20,601 (716); cellular telephone subscribers (2002): 16,759 (583); Internet users (2002): 14,300 (531).

Education and health

Educational attainment (2003). Percentage of population age 14 and over having: basic literacy or primary education 41.0%; some secondary 25.0%; secondary 27.0%; higher degree 7.0%. **Literacy** (2001): total population age 15 and over literate 98.7%; males literate 98.9%; females literate 98.4%. **Health** (2002): physicians 117 (1 per 230 persons); hospital beds 134 (1 per 191 persons); infant mortality rate per 1,000 live births (2002) 6.8. **Food** (2000; figures are for Italy): daily per capita caloric intake 3,661 (vegetable products 74%, animal products 26%); 146% of FAO recommended minimum.

Military

Total active duty personnel (2003): none; defense is provided by a public security force of about 50. **Military expenditure as percentage of national budget** (1992): 1.0% (world 3.6%); per capita expenditure (1987) $155.

Did you know? Tourism is the sector of greatest expansion in San Marino, and it makes a major contribution to the inhabitants' income. Alongside traditional excursion tourism, a convention-type tourism, based on the development of modern hotel facilities, and residential tourism are growing.

Background

According to tradition, San Marino was founded in the early 4th century AD by St. Marinus. By the 12th century it had developed into a commune and remained independent despite challenges from neighboring rulers, including the Malatesta family in nearby Rimini, Italy. San Marino survived the Renaissance as a relic of the self-governing Italian city-state and remained an independent republic after the unification of Italy in 1861. It is one of the smallest republics in the world, and it may be the oldest one in Europe.

Recent Developments

San Marino continued to be an economic oasis in the turbulent Italian peninsula, although its unemployment rate, while still half the EU average, had increased since 2001. Part of this rise was ascribed to setbacks in the crucial banking sector, prompted by increasing competition and a recent tax amnesty that encouraged Italians to withdraw their savings from San Marino banks.

Internet resources:
<http://www.visitsanmarino.com>.

São Tomé and Príncipe

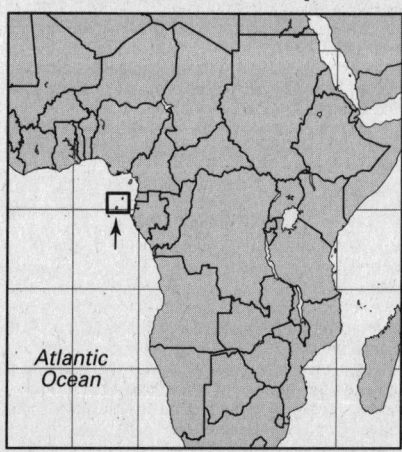

Atlantic Ocean

Official name: República democrática de São Tomé e Príncipe (Democratic Republic of São Tomé and Príncipe). **Form of government:** multiparty republic with one legislative house (National Assembly [55]). **Chief of state:** President Fradique de Menezes (from 2003). **Head of government:** Prime Minister Damião Vas d'Almeida (from 18 Sep 2004)). **Capital:** São Tomé. **Official language:** Portuguese. **Official religion:** none. **Monetary unit:** 1 dobra (Db) = 100 cêntimos; valuation (7 Jul 2005) $1 = Db 8,470.00.

Demography

Area: 386 sq mi, 1,001 sq km. **Population** (2004): 144,000. **Density** (2004): persons per sq mi 373.1, persons per sq km 143.9. **Urban** (2001): 47.7%. **Sex distribution** (2001): male 49.59%, female 50.41%.

---

1 metric ton = about 1.1 short tons;   1 kilometer = 0.6 mi (statute);   1 metric ton-km cargo = about 0.68 short ton-mi cargo;   c.i.f.: cost, insurance, and freight;   f.o.b.: free on board

Age breakdown (2001): under 15, 47.7%; 15–29, 27.5%; 30–44, 12.6%; 45–59, 6.3%; 60–74, 4.5%; 75 and over, 1.4%. **Ethnic composition** (2000): black-white admixture 79.5%; Fang 10.0%; angolares (descendants of former Angolan slaves) 7.6%; Portuguese 1.9%; other 1.0%. **Religious affiliation** (1995): Roman Catholic, about 89.5%; remainder mostly Protestant, predominantly Seventh-day Adventist and an indigenous Evangelical Church. **Major cities** (2001): São Tomé 51,886; Neves 6,700; Santana 6,300; Trindade 6,000; Santo António 1,040. **Location:** islands in the Gulf of Guinea, straddling the Equator west of Gabon.

Vital statistics

Birth rate per 1,000 population (2003): 41.9 (world avg. 21.3). **Death rate** per 1,000 population (2003): 7.1 (world avg. 9.1). **Natural increase rate** per 1,000 population (2003): 34.8 (world avg. 12.2). **Total fertility rate** (avg. births per childbearing woman; 2003): 5.8. **Life expectancy** at birth (2003): male 64.8 years; female 67.8 years.

National economy

Budget (2000). *Revenue:* Db 183,400,000,000 (grants 56.4%; taxes 32.4%, of which sales taxes 10.9%, import taxes 9.8%, income and profit taxes 9.1%; nontax revenue 11.2%). *Expenditures:* Db 244,400,000,000 (capital expenditure 63.3%; recurrent expenditure 36.7%, of which personnel costs 11.8%, debt service 10.0%, goods and services 6.2%, transfers 3.0%, defense 0.5%). **Public debt** (external, outstanding; 2002): $307,900,000. **Production** (metric tons except as noted). *Agriculture, forestry, fishing* (2002): oil palm fruit 40,000, bananas 35,000, coconuts 26,600; livestock (number of live animals) 4,800 goats, 4,100 cattle, 2,600 sheep; roundwood (2001) 9,000 cu m; fish catch (2001) 3,500, principally marine fish and shellfish. *Mining and quarrying:* some quarrying to support local construction industry. *Manufacturing* (value in Db; 1995): beer 880,000; clothing 679,000; lumber 369,000. *Energy production (consumption):* electricity (kW-hr; 2000) 18,000,000 (18,000,000); petroleum products (2000) none (29,000). **Households.** Average household size (1981) 4.0; expenditure (1995): food 71.9%, housing and energy 10.2%, transportation and communications 6.4%, clothing and other items 5.3%, household durable goods 2.8%, education and health 1.7%. **Tourism** (2002): receipts from visitors $10,000,000; expenditures by nationals abroad $1,000,000. **Population economically active** (1994): total 51,789; activity rate of total population 40.8% (participation rates: ages 15–64 [1981] 61.1%; female [1991] 32.4%; unemployed [1994] 29.0%). **Gross national product** (2003): $50,000,000 ($320 per capita). **Land use** as % of total land area (2000): in temporary crops 6.3%, in permanent crops 46.9%, in pasture 1.0%; overall forest area 28.3%.

Foreign trade

Imports (2002): $24,800,000 (investment goods 52.9%, food and other agricultural products 20.2%, petroleum products 17.9%). *Major import sources:* Portugal 38.9%; US 22.2%; UK 9.3%. **Exports** (2002): $5,500,000 (cocoa beans 80.0%; other exports include copra, coffee, and palm oil). *Major export des-*

tinations: The Netherlands 27.3%; Portugal 18.2%; Canada 9.1%.

Transport and communications

Transport. *Roads* (1999): total length 320 km (paved 68%). *Vehicles* (1996): passenger cars 4,040; trucks and buses 1,540. *Air transport* (1998): passenger-km 9,000,000; short ton-km cargo 1,000,000; airports (2000) 2. **Communications**, in total units (units per 1,000 persons). Radios (1997): 38,000 (272); televisions (1997): 23,000 (163); telephone main lines (2003): 7,000 (46); cellular telephone subscribers (2003): 4,800 (32); Internet users (2003): 15,000 (97).

Education and health

Literacy (1991): total population age 15 and over literate 73.0%; males literate 85.0%; females literate 62.0%. **Health:** physicians (1996) 61 (1 per 2,147 persons); hospital beds (1983) 640 (1 per 158 persons); infant mortality rate per 1,000 live births (2003) 46.0. **Food** (2001): daily per capita caloric intake 2,567 (vegetable products 96%, animal products 4%); 109% of FAO recommended minimum.

Military

Total active duty personnel (1995): 600 (a 5-member crew of the Portuguese air force is stationed in São Tomé and Príncipe to provide humanitarian assistance). **Military expenditure as percentage of GNP** (1999): 1.0% (world 2.4%); per capita expenditure $3.

 An Italian agronomist has revived production of cocoa from an ancient species on the island of Príncipe. Some of the plants date to 1820, when they were first introduced, and the flavor associated with chocolate produced from these plants is notably pure.

Background

First visited by European navigators in the 1470s, the islands of São Tomé and Príncipe were colonized by the Portuguese in the 16th century and were used in the trade and transshipment of slaves. Sugarcane and cacao were the main cash crops. The islands became an overseas province of Portugal in 1951 and achieved independence in 1975. During recent decades its economy was heavily dependent on international assistance.

Recent Developments

After a failed army coup in the summer of 2003, São Tomé and Príncipe Pres. Fradique de Menezes gradually reestablished his authority in the small, potentially oil-rich country. He entered into especially close relations with neighboring Nigeria, and the two countries set up an agency to administer the Joint Development Zone (JDZ) between them. In July 2004 de Menezes and Nigerian Pres. Olusegun Obasanjo signed a pact on governance in the JDZ that required all payments by oil companies to be made public.

Internet resources: <www.saotome.st>.

Saudi Arabia

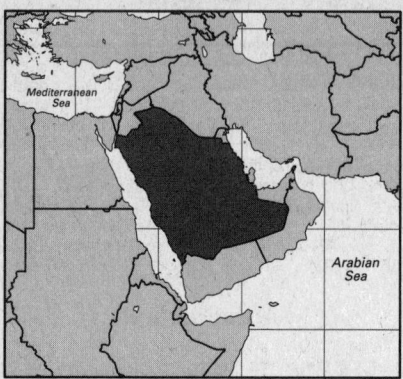

Official name: Al-Mamlakah al-ʿArabiyah al-Saʿudiyah (Kingdom of Saudi Arabia). **Form of government:** monarchy (assisted by the Consultative Council consisting of 120 appointed members). **Head of state and government:** King Abdullah (from 3 Aug 2005). **Capital:** Riyadh. **Official language:** Arabic. **Official religion:** Islam. **Monetary unit:** 1 Saudi riyal (SRls) = 100 halalah; valuation (7 Jul 2005) $1 = SRls 3.75.

Demography

Area: 830,000 sq mi, 2,149,690 sq km. **Population** (2004): 24,580,000. **Density** (2004): persons per sq mi 29.6, persons per sq km 11.4. **Urban** (2001): 86.7%. **Sex distribution** (2003): male 54.90%; female 45.10%. **Age breakdown** (2003): under 15, 39.7%; 15–29, 26.9%; 30–44, 21.7%; 45–59, 8.0%; 60–74, 2.9%; 75 and over, 0.8%. **Ethnic composition** (2000): Arab 88.1%, of which Saudi Arab 74.2%, Bedouin 3.9%, Gulf Arab 3.0%; Indo-Pakistani 5.5%; African black 1.5%; Filipino 1.0%; other 3.9%. **Religious affiliation** (2000): Muslim 94%, of which Sunni 84%, Shiʿi 10%; Christian 3.5%, of which Roman Catholic 3%; Hindu 1%; nonreligious/other 1.5%. **Major urban agglomerations** (2000): Riyadh 4,549,000; Jiddah 3,192,000; Mecca 1,335,000; Medina 891,000; Al-Dammam 764,000. **Location:** the Middle East, bordering Iraq, Kuwait, the Persian Gulf, Qatar, UAE, Oman, Yemen, the Red Sea, the Gulf of Aqaba, and Jordan.

Vital statistics

Birth rate per 1,000 population (2002): 37.3 (world avg. 21.3). **Death rate** per 1,000 population (2002): 5.9 (world avg. 9.1). **Natural increase rate** per 1,000 population (2002): 31.4 (world avg. 12.2). **Total fertility rate** (avg. births per childbearing woman; 2002): 6.2. **Life expectancy** at birth (2002): male 66.7 years; female 70.2 years.

National economy

Budget (2002). *Revenue:* SRls 157,000,000,000 (oil revenues 78.9%). *Expenditures:* SRls 202,000,000,-

000 (defense and security 34.3%, human resource development 23.3%, public administration, municipal transfers, and subsidies 22.4%, health and social development 9.4%). **Production** (metric tons except as noted). *Agriculture and fishing* (2002): alfalfa 2,000,000, wheat 1,800,000, dates 783,000; livestock (number of live animals) 8,000,000 sheep, 4,650,000 goats, 415,000 camels; fish catch (2001) 57,385. *Mining and quarrying* (2002): gypsum 450,000; silver 14,000 kg; gold 5,000 kg. *Manufacturing* (value added in $'000,000; 1998): industrial chemicals 3,349; refined petroleum 1,806; cement, bricks, and tiles 1,505. *Energy production (consumption):* electricity (kW-hr; 2002) 138,200,000,000 ([2000] 126,441,000,000); crude petroleum (barrels; 2002) 2,589,000,000 ([2000] 658,800,000); petroleum products (2000) 100,994,000 (52,045,000); natural gas (cu m; 2002) 62,014,000,000 ([2000] 49,808,300,000). **Population economically active** (2003): total 7,437,400, of which 3,833,000 foreign workers and 3,604,400 Saudi nationals; activity rate of total population 31.0% (participation rates: ages 15–64, 56.2%; unemployed [2002] 11.0%). **Gross national product** (2003): $186,776,000,000 ($8,530 per capita). **Households.** Average household size (2002) 6.1; expenditure (1998–99): food and nonalcoholic beverages 37.3%, transportation 18.9%, housing and energy 15.7%, household furnishings 9.7%. **Tourism** (in $'000,000; 2002): receipts 3,420; expenditures 7,356. **Land use** as % of total land area (2000): in temporary crops 1.7%, in permanent crops 0.1%, in pasture 79.1%; overall forest area 0.7%.

Foreign trade

Imports (2001-c.i.f.): SRls 116,930,000,000 (transport equipment 21.3%, of which road vehicles 16.5%; machinery and apparatus 20.6%, of which general industrial machinery 5.7%; food and live animals 13.5%; chemicals and chemical products 9.6%; iron and steel 4.0%). *Major import sources* (2003): US 15.0%; Japan 10.3%; Germany 8.9%; UK 5.9%; China 5.9%. **Exports** (2001-f.o.b.): SRls 274,085,000,000 (crude petroleum 72.8%; refined petroleum 16.0%; organic chemicals 3.6%; polyethylene 1.6%). *Major export destinations* (2002): US 19.7%; Japan 14.3%; South Korea 9.5%; Singapore 5.4%; India 5.1%.

Transport and communications

Transport. *Railroads* (2003): route length 1,392 km; (2001) passenger-km 222,000,000; (2001) metric ton-km cargo 856,000,000. *Roads* (2003): total length 167,857 km (paved 100%). *Vehicles* (1996): passenger cars 1,744,000; trucks and buses 1,192,000. *Air transport* (2003; Saudi Arabian Airlines only): passenger-km 23,372,000,000; metric ton-km cargo 85,451,000; airports (2002) with scheduled flights 25. **Communications**, in total units (units per 1,000 persons). Daily newspaper circulation (1996): 1,105,000 (59); radios (2000): 7,180,000 (326); televisions (2002): 5,803,500 (265); telephone main lines (2003): 3,502,600 (155); cellular telephone subscribers (2003): 7,238,200 (321); personal computers (2002): 3,003,000 (137); Internet users (2003): 1,500,000 (67).

1 metric ton = about 1.1 short tons;   1 kilometer = 0.6 mi (statute);   1 metric ton-km cargo = about 0.68 short ton-mi cargo;   c.i.f.: cost, insurance, and freight;   f.o.b.: free on board

Education and health

Educational attainment (2000). Percentage of Saudi (non-Saudi) population age 10 and over who: are illiterate 19.9% (12.1%), are literate/have primary education 39.5% (40.6%), have some/completed secondary education 34.2% (36.0%), have at least begun university education 6.4% (11.3%). **Health** (2001): physicians 31,983 (1 per 709 persons); hospital beds 46,622 (1 per 485 persons); infant mortality rate per 1,000 live births (2002) 49.6. **Food** (2001): daily per capita caloric intake 2,841 (vegetable products 85%, animal products 15%); 119% of FAO recommended minimum.

Military

Total active duty personnel (2003): 124,500 (army 60.2%, navy 12.4%, air force 27.4%); most US military withdrew in 2003. **Military expenditure as percentage of GNP** (1999): 14.9% (world 2.4%); per capita expenditure $996.

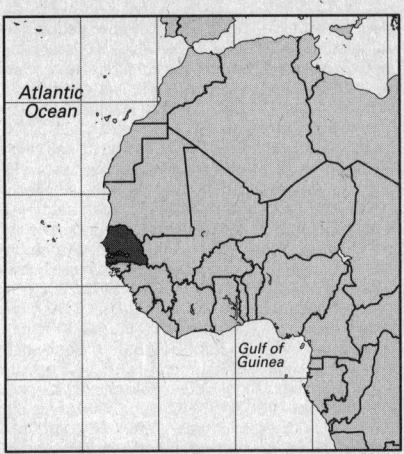

Background

Saudi Arabia is the historical home of Islam, founded by Muhammad in Medina in 622. During medieval times, local and foreign rulers fought for control of the Arabian Peninsula; in 1517 the Ottomans prevailed. In the 18th–19th centuries Islamic leaders supporting religious reform struggled to regain Saudi territory, all of which was restored by 1904. The British held Saudi lands as a protectorate from 1915 to 1927; then they acknowledged the sovereignty of the Kingdom of the Hejaz and Najd. The two kingdoms were unified as the Kingdom of Saudi Arabia in 1932. Since World War II, it has supported the Palestinian cause in the Middle East and maintained close ties with the US.

Recent Developments

The issue that dominated Saudi Arabian internal affairs in 2004 was the official campaign against anti-Western Islamist groups accused of carrying out acts of sabotage in the kingdom and abroad. The authorities even cracked down on charitable organizations accused of funding suspected radical groups. The al-Haramain Islamic Foundation, one of the largest non-governmental charitable organizations in Saudi Arabia, was disbanded in early October, and its 250 employees were sacked. Muslim militants stormed the US consulate in Jeddah on 6 December and killed five non-American staff members before Saudi forces shot dead three attackers and captured two to regain control. The government carried on with its program for internal reform in two ways. The first was to hold municipal elections, the first in decades, in various parts of the country in early 2005. Women, however, were still not allowed to vote. The second measure was to combat militant Islamism by making jobs in the private sector traditionally held by foreigners more available to Saudis. Only 13% of the private-sector workforce—800,000 people—was Saudi, far below the 45% goal of the government for 2004.

Internet resources: <www.sauditourism.gov.sa>.

Senegal

Official name: République du Sénégal (Republic of Senegal). **Form of government:** multiparty republic with one legislative house (National Assembly [120]). **Head of state and government:** President Abdoulaye Wade (from 2000), assisted by Prime Minister Macky Sall (from 21 Apr 2004). **Capital:** Dakar. **Official language:** French. **Official religion:** none. **Monetary unit:** 1 CFA franc (CFAF) = 100 centimes; valuation (7 Jul 2005) $1 = CFAF 549.50; the CFAF is pegged to the euro (€) at €1 = CFAF 656.96 from 1 Jan 2002.

Demography

Area: 75,955 sq mi, 196,722 sq km. **Population** (2004): 10,339,000. **Density** (2004): persons per sq mi 136.1, persons per sq km 52.6. **Urban** (2000): 47.4%. **Sex distribution** (2003): male 49.09%; female 50.91%. **Age breakdown** (2003): under 15, 43.7%; 15–29, 28.1%; 30–44, 15.7%; 45–59, 8.0%; 60–74, 3.6%; 75 and over, 0.9%. **Ethnic composition** (2000): Wolof 34.6%; Peul (Fulani) and Tukulor 27.1%; Serer 12.0%; Malinke (Mandingo) 9.7%; other 16.6%. **Religious affiliation** (2000): Muslim 87.6%; traditional beliefs 6.2%; Christian 5.5%, of which Roman Catholic 4.7%; other 0.7%. **Major cities** (2002): Dakar 1,983,093 (includes urban departments of Pikine [768,826] and Guédiawaye [pop. 258,370], adjacent to Dakar department [955,897]); Thiès 237,849; Kaolack 172,305; Saint-Louis 154,555; Mbour 153,503. **Location:** western Africa, bordering Mauritania, Mali, Guinea, Guinea-Bissau, the North Atlantic Ocean, and The Gambia.

Vital statistics

Birth rate per 1,000 population (2003): 36.2 (world avg. 21.3). **Death rate** per 1,000 population (2003): 11.0 (world avg. 9.1). **Natural increase rate** per 1,000 population (2003): 25.2 (world avg. 12.2). **Total fertility rate** (avg. births per childbearing woman; 2003): 4.9. **Life expectancy** at birth (2003): male 54.8 years; female 58.0 years.

National economy

Budget (2002). *Revenue:* CFAF 713,900,000,000 (tax revenue 85.7%; grants 9.6%; nontax revenue 4.7%). *Expenditures:* CFAF 738,100,000,000 (current expenditures 62.6%, of which wages 27.0%, education 21.2%, health 5.7%, interest payment 3.8%;

development expenditure 37.4%). **Public debt** (external, outstanding; 2002): $3,339,000,000. **Production** (metric tons except as noted). *Agriculture, forestry, fishing* (2002): sugarcane 890,000, peanuts (groundnuts) 501,298, millet 414,687; livestock (number of live animals) 4,900,000 sheep, 4,000,000 goats, 3,230,000 cattle; roundwood (2002) 5,971,559 cu m; fish catch (2001) 405,409, of which crustaceans and mollusks 22,288. *Mining and quarrying* (2003): phosphate 1,918,900; salt (2002) 141,000. *Manufacturing* ($'000,000; 2000): food products 81; transport equipment 74, of which ships and boats 39; printing and publishing 63. *Energy production (consumption):* electricity (kW-hr; 2001) 1,651,200,000 (1,651,200,000); crude petroleum (barrels; 2000) none (6,707,000); petroleum products (2000) 979,000 (1,243,000); natural gas (cu m; 2000) 538,000 (538,000). **Population economically active** (2001): total 4,294,000; activity rate of total population 44.6%. **Households.** Average household size (2002) 8.7. **Tourism** (2000): receipts $140,000,000; expenditures (1999) $54,000,000. **Gross national product** (at current market prices; 2003): $5,563,000,000 ($550 per capita). **Land use** as % of total land area (2000): in temporary crops 12.3%, in permanent crops 0.2%, in pasture 29.3%; overall forest area 32.2%.

Foreign trade

Imports (2001-f.o.b. in balance of trade and c.i.f. in commodities and trading partners): $1,730,000,000 (food and live animals 22.3%, of which cereals 13.2%, rice 8.2%; mineral fuels and lubricants 16.8%, of which crude petroleum 9.8%; machinery and apparatus 15.1%; chemicals and chemical products 11.1%). *Major import sources:* France 27.8%; Nigeria 9.8%; Thailand 7.7%; Germany 4.8%; US 4.2%. **Exports** (2001): $785,000,000 (fresh fish 16.1%; refined petroleum 15.5%; fresh crustaceans and mollusks 12.0%; bunkers and ships' stores 12.0%; phosphorous pentoxide and phosphoric acids 9.5%; peanut [groundnut] oil 9.1%). *Major export destinations:* France 16.7%; India 12.4%; Greece 7.3%; Mali 6.9%; Italy 6.0%.

Transport and communications

Transport. *Railroads* (2002): route length 906 km; passenger-km 105,000,000; metric ton-km cargo 345,000,000. *Roads* (1999): total length 14,576 km (paved 29%). *Vehicles* (2001): passenger cars 193,000; trucks and buses 79,000. *Air transport* (2001; Air Afrique, an airline jointly owned by 11 African countries [including Senegal], was declared bankrupt in February 2002): passenger-km 304,000,000; airports (1996) with scheduled flights 7. **Communications,** in total units (units per 1,000 persons). Daily newspaper circulation (2000): 47,000 (5); radios (2001): 1,254,400 (128); televisions (2000): 376,000 (40); telephone main lines (2003): 228,800 (22); cellular telephone subscribers (2003): 575,900 (56); personal computers (2003): 220,000 (21); Internet users (2003): 225,000 (22).

Education and health

Literacy (2000): percentage of total population age 15 and over literate 38.3%; males literate 48.1%;

females literate 28.7%. **Health:** physicians (1996) 649 (1 per 13,162 persons); hospital beds (1998) 3,582 (1 per 2,500 persons); infant mortality rate per 1,000 live births (2003): 57.6. **Food** (2001): daily per capita caloric intake 2,277 (vegetable products 91%, animal products 9%); 95% of FAO recommended minimum.

Military

Total active duty personnel (2004): 13,620 (army 87.4%, navy 7.0%, air force 5.6%); French troops (August 2004) 1,100. **Military expenditure as percentage of GNP** (1999): 1.7% (world 2.4%); per capita expenditure $8.

Background

Links between the peoples of Senegal and North Africa were established in the 10th century AD. Islam was introduced in the 11th century, although animism retained a hold on the country into the 19th century. The Portuguese explored the coast in 1445, and in 1638 the French established a trading post at the mouth of the Senegal River. Throughout the 17th and 18th centuries, Europeans exported slaves, ivory, and gold from Senegal. The French gained control over the coast in the early 19th century and moved inland, checking the expansion of the Tukulor empire; in 1895 Senegal became part of French West Africa. Its inhabitants were made French citizens in 1946, and it became an overseas territory of France. It became an autonomous republic in 1958 and was federated with Mali in 1959-60. It became an independent state in 1960. In 1982 it entered a confederation with The Gambia, called Senegambia, which was dissolved in 1989.

Recent Developments

Citing the need to restore unity in the government, Pres. Abdoulaye Wade sacked Prime Minister Idrissa Seck on 21 Apr 2004 and replaced him with former interior minister Macky Sall. Seck had been increasingly portrayed in the media as a possible challenger to Wade's leadership. In June President Wade announced that, effective 2005, he would introduce legislation provide public funding of political parties.

Internet resources: <www.senegal-tourism.com>.

Serbia and Montenegro

Official name: Srbija i Crna Gora (Serbia and Montenegro). **Form of government:** state union ("loose confederation") with one legislative house (Parliament [126]). **Head of state and government:** President Svetozar Marovic (from 2003). **Administrative centers:** principal executive and legislative bodies meet in Belgrade; the principal judicial body meets in Podgorica. **Official language:** none. **Official religion:** none. **Monetary unit:** 1 Serbian dinar = 100 paras; valuation (7 Jul 2005) $1 = 69.57 Serbian dinars; the Serbian dinar replaced Yugoslav new dinar on 4 Feb 2003, at rate of 1 to 1. Montenegro and Kosovo use the euro adopted on 1 Jan 2002; valuation (7 Jul 2005) $1 = €0.84.

1 metric ton = about 1.1 short tons; 1 kilometer = 0.6 mi (statute); 1 metric ton-km cargo = about 0.68 short ton-mi cargo; c.i.f.: cost, insurance, and freight; f.o.b.: free on board

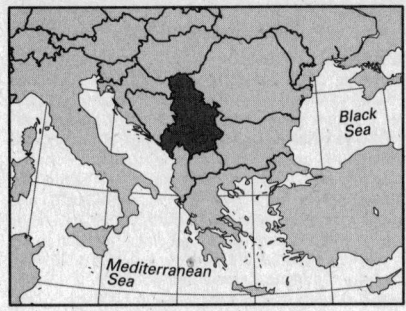

Black
Sea

Mediterranean
Sea

Demography

Area: 39,449 sq mi, 102,173 sq km. **Population** (2004): 10,826,000. **Density** (2004): persons per sq mi 274.4, persons per sq km 106.0. **Urban** (2002): 51.7%. **Sex distribution** (2003): male 49.19%; female 50.81%. **Age breakdown** (2003): under 15, 18.6%; 15–29, 22.5%; 30–44, 20.5%; 45–59, 19.0%; 60–74, 13.9%; 75 and over, 5.5%. **Ethnic composition** (2000): Serb 62.1%; Albanian 17.1%; Montenegrin 4.3%; Hungarian 4.3%; Croat 3.1%; Bosniac 1.8%; Rom (Gypsy) 1.4%; Slovak 0.9%; Romanian 0.8%; other 4.2%. **Religious affiliation** (1995): Serbian Orthodox 62.6%; Muslim 19.0%; Roman Catholic 5.8%; other, mostly nonreligious 12.6%. **Major cities** (2002): Belgrade 1,120,092; Novi Sad 191,405; Nis 173,724; Pristina (2003) 165,844; Kragujevac 146,373. **Location:** southeastern Europe, bordering Romania, Bulgaria, Macedonia, Albania, the Adriatic Sea, Bosnia and Herzegovina, Croatia, and Hungary.

Vital statistics

Birth rate per 1,000 population (2003): 12.1 (world avg. 21.3). **Death rate** per 1,000 population (2003): 10.6 (world avg. 9.1). **Natural increase rate** per 1,000 population (2003): 1.5 (world avg. 12.2). **Total fertility rate** (avg. births per childbearing woman; 2003): 1.7. **Life expectancy** at birth (2003): male 71.6 years; female 76.7 years.

National economy

Budget (2001). *Revenue:* 421,000,000,000 Yugoslav new dinars (tax revenue 91.5%, of which social security tax 26.8%, VAT 26.2%, income tax 12.5%, excise tax 11.9%; nontax revenue 8.5%). *Expenditure:* 477,000,000,000 Yugoslav new dinars (transfers 50.1%, wages 20.7%, other 29.2%). **Public debt** (external, outstanding; 2002): $8,514,-000,000. **Production** (metric tons except as noted; excludes Kosovo). *Agriculture, forestry, fishing* (2002): corn (maize) 5,597,207, wheat 2,245,030, sugar beets 2,098,080; livestock (number of live animals) 3,608,000 pigs, 1,691,000 sheep, 1,355,000 cattle; roundwood (2003) 3,155,000 cu m; fish catch (2001) 3,557. *Mining and quarrying* (2001): bauxite 610,000; copper (metal content of ore) 28,000; lead (metal content of ore) 19,000. *Manufacturing* (2000): cement 2,117,000; wheat flour 840,000; crude steel 682,000. *Energy production (consumption):* electricity (kW-hr; 2001) 34,594,000,000 (34,594,000,000); hard coal (2002) 70,000 ([2000] 137,000); lignite (2002)

31,789,000 ([2000] 34,343,000); crude petroleum (barrels; 2002) 5,534,000,000 ([2001] 5,534,-000,000); petroleum products (2000) 934,000 (2,538,000); natural gas (cu m; 2002) 111,-000,000 ([2000] 2,085,200,000). **Population economically active** (2001; excludes Kosovo): total 3,092,000; activity rate 37.1% (participation rates: over age 15 [1998] 58.3%; female [1995] 43.7%; [2003] unemployed 15.2%). **Household income and expenditure** (2002; excludes Kosovo). Average household size 2.9; income per household 206,267 Yugoslav new dinars; sources of income: wages and salaries 50.4%, transfers 27.3%, self-employment 8.8%; expenditure: food 46.2%, energy 11.9%, clothing and footwear 8.3%, transportation and communications 8.2%. **Gross national product** (2003; excludes Kosovo): $15,512,000,000 ($1,910 per capita). **Land use** as % of total land area (2000): in temporary crops 33.4%, in permanent crops 3.2%, in pasture 18.1%; overall forest area 28.3%. **Tourism** (2002): receipts from visitors $77,000,000.

Foreign trade

Imports (2002): $6,320,000,000 (machinery and transport equipment 25.8%; mineral fuels 16.9%, of which crude petroleum 7.6%; chemical products 11.0%; food 7.0%). *Major import sources:* Germany 13.1%; Russia 12.5%; Italy 10.3%; Hungary 4.4%; Slovenia 3.8%. **Exports** (2002): $2,275,000,000 (food 21.2%, of which refined sugar 4.0%; machinery and transport equipment 11.2%; chemical products 7.4%; aluminum 6.9%). *Major export destinations:* Bosnia and Herzegovina 14.6%; Italy 14.5%; Germany 10.7%; Macedonia 9.1%; Switzerland 7.5%.

Transport and communications

Transport. *Railroads* (2002): length 4,130 km; passenger-km (2001) 1,262,000,000 (excludes Kosovo); metric ton-km cargo (2001) 2,040,000,000 (excludes Kosovo). *Roads* (2000): total length 44,777 km (paved 63%). *Vehicles* (2001): passenger cars 1,481,400; trucks and buses 330,500. *Air transport* (2001; excludes Kosovo): passenger-km 1,003,000,-000; metric ton-km cargo 4,332,000; airports (2000) 5. **Communications,** in total units (units per 1,000 persons). Daily newspaper circulation (2000): 1,130,000 (107); radios (2000): 3,130,000 (297); televisions (2000): 2,980,000 (282); telephone main lines (2003): 2,611,700 (243); cellular telephone subscribers (2003): 3,634,600 (338); personal computers (2002): 290,000 (27); Internet users (2003): 847,000 (79).

Education and health

Educational attainment (1991). Percentage of population age 15 and over having: less than full primary education 33.5%; primary 25.0%; secondary 32.2%; postsecondary and higher 9.3%. **Literacy** (1991): total population age 10 and over literate 93.0%; males literate 97.2%; females literate 88.9%. **Health** (2001): physicians 27,769 (1 per 300 persons; excludes Kosovo); hospital beds 51,785 (1 per 161 persons; excludes Kosovo); infant mortality rate per 1,000 live births (2003) 14.0. **Food** (2001): daily per capita caloric intake 2,778 (vegetable products 65%, animal products 35%); 109% of FAO recommended minimum.

Military

Total active duty personnel (2003): 74,200 (army 84.1%, air force 10.8%, navy 5.1%); about 19,000 troops from many NATO and non-NATO countries were deployed in Kosovo in October 2004. **Military expenditure as percentage of government expenditure** (1991): 3.9% (world 4.0%); per capita expenditure $176.

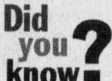

Did you know? The Adriatic Sea, like the Mediterranean in general, is deficient in life; nutrient content, as indicated by the amount of phosphates and nitrates, is extremely low. In the northern Adriatic area significant winter cooling and a lowered salinity further impoverish the typical Mediterranean marine life.

Background

The Kingdom of the Serbs, Croats, and Slovenes was created after the collapse of Austria-Hungary at the end of World War I. The country signed treaties with Czechoslovakia and Romania in 1920–21, marking the beginning of the Little Entente. In 1929 an absolute monarchy was established, the country's name was changed to Yugoslavia, and it was divided into regions without regard to ethnic boundaries. Axis powers invaded Yugoslavia in 1941, and German, Italian, Hungarian, and Bulgarian troops occupied it for the rest of World War II. In 1945 the Socialist Federal Republic of Yugoslavia was established; it included the republics of Bosnia and Herzegovina, Croatia, Macedonia, Montenegro, Serbia, and Slovenia. Its independent form of communism under Josip Broz Tito's leadership provoked the USSR. Internal ethnic tensions flared up in the 1980s, causing the country's ultimate collapse. In 1991–92 independence was declared by Croatia, Slovenia, Macedonia, and Bosnia and Herzegovina; the new Federal Republic of Yugoslavia (containing roughly 45% of the population and 40% of the area of its predecessor) was proclaimed by Serbia and Montenegro. Still fueled by long-standing ethnic tensions, hostilities continued into the 1990s. Despite the approval of the Dayton peace accord (1995), sporadic fighting continued and was followed in 1998–99 by Serbian repression and expulsion of ethnic populations in Kosovo. In September–October 2000, the battered nation of Yugoslavia ended the autocratic rule of Pres. Slobodan Milosevic. In April 2001 he was arrested and in June extradited to The Hague to stand trial for war crimes, genocide, and crimes against humanity committed during the fighting in Kosovo. On 4 Feb 2003 both houses of the Yugoslav federal legislature voted to accept a new state charter and change the name of the country from Yugoslavia to Serbia and Montenegro. Henceforth, defense, international political and economic relations, and human rights matters would be handled centrally, while all other functions would be run from the republican capitals, Belgrade and Podgorica, respectively. The move was seen as an acknowledgment that Serbia and Montenegro had little in common, and a provision was included for both states to vote on independence after three years.

Recent Developments

Some promising signs of political stability emerged in Serbia in 2004 amid the worst outbreak of inter-ethnic violence since 1999 in the predominantly ethnic Albanian Kosovo area. Major Serbian leaders continued to withhold cooperation with the war crimes tribunal in The Hague. A growing number of government officials, however, were eager to win Serbia and Montenegro's entry into the EU and NATO and pushed for cooperation with international investigators. In March formal talks took place between representatives of Serbia and Kosovo; the ethnic Albanian majority continued to insist on independence, while Serbia fiercely opposed the idea. In balloting for the Kosovo assembly, Pres. Ibrahim Rugova's party was not able to win a parliamentary majority. In December, Ramush Haradinaj, a former rebel commander, was named prime minister of Kosovo over the strong objections of the Serbian government. Haradinaj was indicted by the war crimes tribunal in February 2005, however, and was forced to resign.

Internet resources: <www.serbia-tourism.org>; <http://visit-montenegro.com>.

Seychelles

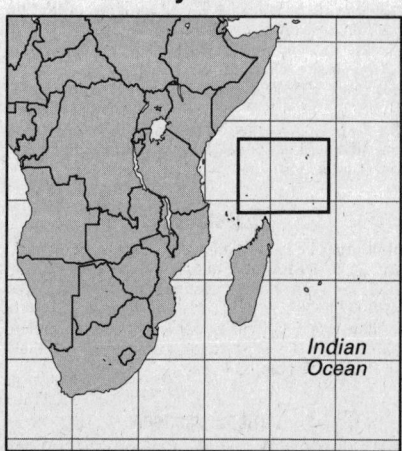

Indian Ocean

Official name: Repiblik Sesel (Creole); Republic of Seychelles (English); République des Seychelles (French). **Form of government:** multiparty republic with one legislative house (National Assembly [34]). **Head of state and government:** President James Michel (from 14 Apr 2004). **Capital:** Victoria. **Official languages:** none; Creole, English, and French are national languages. **Official religion:** none. **Monetary unit:** 1 Seychelles rupee (SR) = 100 cents; valuation (7 Jul 2005) $1 = SR 5.42.

Demography

Area: 176 sq mi, 455 sq km. **Population** (2004): 81,800. **Density** (2004): persons per sq mi 464.8, persons per sq km 179.8. **Urban** (2002): 64.6%. **Sex**

---

1 metric ton = about 1.1 short tons;   1 kilometer = 0.6 mi (statute);   1 metric ton-km cargo = about 0.68 short ton-mi cargo;   c.i.f.: cost, insurance, and freight;   f.o.b.: free on board

distribution (2002): male 49.81%; female 50.19%. **Age breakdown** (2003): under 15, 27.3%; 15–29, 28.2%; 30–44, 26.4%; 45–59, 9.9%; 60–74, 5.5%; 75 and over, 2.7%. **Ethnic composition** (2000): Seychellois Creole (mixture of Asian, African, and European) 93.2%; British 3.0%; French 1.8%; Chinese 0.5%; Indian 0.3%; other unspecified 1.2%. **Religious affiliation** (2000): Roman Catholic 90.4%; Anglican 6.7%; Hindu 0.6%; other (mostly nonreligious) 2.3%. **Major city** (2004): Victoria 25,500. **Location:** group of islands in the Indian Ocean, northeast of Madagascar.

Vital statistics

Birth rate per 1,000 population (2002): 18.3 (world avg. 21.3); (1998) legitimate 24.7%. **Death rate** per 1,000 population (2002): 8.0 (world avg. 9.1). **Natural increase rate** per 1,000 population (2002): 10.3 (world avg. 12.2). **Total fertility rate** (avg. births per childbearing woman; 2002): 2.0. **Marriage rate** per 1,000 population (2002): 5.3. **Divorce rate** per 1,000 population (2002): 1.4. **Life expectancy** at birth (2002): male 66.6 years; female 75.8 years.

National economy

Budget (2002). *Revenue:* SR 1,487,000,000 (tax revenue 70.0%, of which customs taxes and duties 23.7%, sales tax 18.9%, tax on income and profit 16.9%; nontax revenue 28.3%; grants 1.7%). *Expenditures:* SR 2,061,000,000 (current expenditure 82.0%, of which debt service 15.4%, education 7.6%, health 6.7%; capital expenditure 16.0%; net lending 2.0%). **Tourism** (2002): receipts from visitors $130,000,000; expenditures by nationals abroad $32,000,000. **Land use** as % of total land area (2000): in temporary crops 2%, in permanent crops 13%; overall forest area 67%. **Gross national product** (2003): $626,000,000 ($7,480 per capita). **Production** (metric tons except as noted). *Agriculture and fishing* (2003): coconuts 3,200, bananas 1,970, cinnamon 230; livestock (number of live animals) 18,500 pigs, 5,150 goats, 520,000 chickens; fish catch (2002) 48,960. *Mining and quarrying* (1998): guano 5,000. *Manufacturing* (2002): canned tuna 34,503; animal feed 18,565; copra 262. *Energy production (consumption):* electricity (kW-hr; 2002) 218,800,000 (182,400,000,000); petroleum products (2000) none (74,000). **Population economically active** (2002): total 34,017; activity rate of total population 41.9% (participation rates [2000]: ages 15–64, 81.5%; female [2000] 43.0%; unemployed [1999] 11.5%). **Public debt** (external, outstanding; 2002): $149,300,000. **Household income and expenditure.** Average household size (2002) 4.0; sources of income (1997): wages and salaries 77.2%, self-employment 3.8%, transfer payments 3.2%; expenditure (2001): food 25.5%, housing and energy 14.8%, beverages 13.3% (of which alcoholic 10.7%), clothing and footwear 6.7%, transportation 5.8%, recreation 5.5%.

Foreign trade

Imports (2003-c.i.f.): SR 2,231,000,000 (food and beverages 31.0%, of which fish, crustaceans, and mollusks 16.1%; mineral fuels 16.1%; machinery 12.3%; base and fabricated metals 8.1%; transport equipment 5.7%). *Major import sources:* Saudi Arabia 15.7%; South Africa 12.6%; Italy 10.6%; France 10.4%; Spain 10.4%; UK 7.7%. **Exports** (2003-f.o.b.): SR 1,484,000,000 (domestic exports 76.9%, of which canned tuna 69.0%, other processed fish 1.8%, fresh and frozen fish 1.9%; reexports 23.1%, of which petroleum products 19.8%). *Major export destinations* (2002): UK 39.2%; France 32.0%; Italy 14.5%; Germany 7.5%.

Transport and communications

Transport. *Roads* (2002): total length 456 km (paved 96%). *Vehicles* (2002): passenger cars 6,923; trucks and buses 2,551. *Air transport* (2002; Air Seychelles only): passenger-km 1,397,000,000; metric ton-km cargo 28,000,000; airports (2002) with scheduled flights 2. **Communications,** in total units (units per 1,000 persons). Daily newspaper circulation (1996): 3,000 (46); radios (1997): 42,000 (560); televisions (2000): 16,000 (203); telephone main lines (2002): 21,700 (269); cellular telephone subscribers (2003): 54,500 (682); personal computers (2002): 13,000 (157); Internet users (2002): 11,700 (145).

Education and health

Educational attainment (2003). Percentage of population age 12 and over having: less than primary or primary education 23.2%; secondary 73.4%; higher 3.4%. **Literacy** (2002): total population age 12 and over literate 91.0%; males literate 90.0%; females literate 92.0%. **Health** (2002): physicians 103 (1 per 792 persons); hospital beds 438 (1 per 185 persons); infant mortality rate per 1,000 live births (2002) 17.6. **Food** (2001): daily per capita caloric intake 2,461 (vegetable products 81%, animal products 19%; 105% of FAO recommended minimum.

Military

Total active-duty personnel (2003): 450. **Military expenditure as percentage of GNP** (1997): 3.8% (world 2.6%); per capita expenditure $194.

Did you know? The five rays on the Seychelles flag symbolize the sky and sea (blue); the life-giving sun (yellow); the people and their work for unity and love (red); social justice and harmony (white); and the land (green).

Background

The first recorded landing on the uninhabited Seychelles was made in 1609 by an expedition of the British East India Co. The archipelago was claimed by the French in 1756 and surrendered to the British in 1810. Seychelles became a British crown colony in 1903 and a republic within the Commonwealth in 1976. A one-party socialist state since 1979, Seychelles began moving toward democracy in the 1990s; it adopted a new constitution in 1993.

Recent Developments

France-Albert René, who had served as president of the Seychelles since he seized power in a coup in 1977, left his post on 14 Apr 2004 and turned over power to the vice president, James Michel, a close aide. The Indian Ocean tsunami in December caused some $30 million in damages in the Seychelles.

Internet resources: <www.seychelles.com>.

Sierra Leone

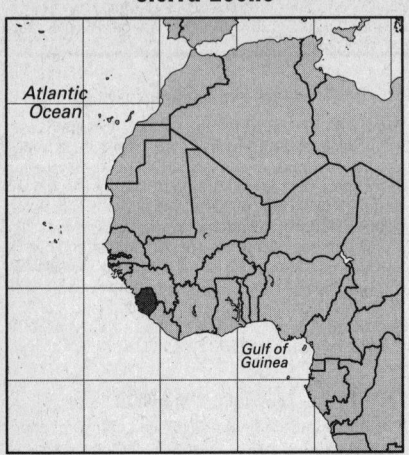

Official name: Republic of Sierra Leone. **Form of government:** republic with one legislative body (Parliament [124, including 12 paramount chiefs]). **Head of state and government:** President Ahmad Tejan Kabbah (from 1998). **Capital:** Freetown. **Official language:** English. **Official religion:** none. **Monetary unit:** 1 leone (Le) = 100 cents; valuation (7 Jul 2005) $1 = Le 2,355.00.

Demography

Area: 27,699 sq mi, 71,740 sq km. **Population** (2004): 5,168,000. **Density** (2004): persons per sq mi 186.6, persons per sq km 72.0. **Urban** (2000): 36.6%. **Sex distribution** (2003): màle 48.31%; female 51.69%. **Age breakdown** (2003): under 15, 44.8%; 15–29, 26.1%; 30–44, 15.3%; 45–59, 8.5%; 60–74, 4.4%; 75 and over, 0.8%. **Ethnic composition** (2000): Mende 26.0%; Temne 24.6%; Limba 7.1%; Kuranko 5.5%; Kono 4.2%; Fulani 3.8%; Bullom-Sherbro 3.5%; other 25.3%. **Religious affiliation** (2000): Sunni Muslim 45.9%; traditional beliefs 40.4%; Christian 11.4%; other 2.3%. **Major cities** (2003): Freetown (urban agglomeration; 2001) 837,000; Koidu 113,700; Makeni 110,700; Bo 82,400; Kenema 72,400. **Location:** western Africa, bordering Guinea, Liberia, and the North Atlantic Ocean.

Vital statistics

Birth rate per 1,000 population (2003): 43.9 (world avg. 21.3). **Death rate** per 1,000 population (2003): 20.7 (world avg. 9.1). **Natural increase rate** per 1,000 population (2003): 23.2 (world avg. 12.2). **Total fertility rate** (avg. births per childbearing woman; 2003): 5.9. **Life expectancy** at birth (2003): male 40.3 years; female 45.4 years.

National economy

Budget (2002). *Revenue:* Le 239,425,000,000 (customs duties and excise taxes 64.0%, income tax 25.1%, other 10.9%). *Expenditures:* Le 701,834,000,000 (re-current expenditures 65.1%, of which wages and salaries 18.8%, goods and services 12.9%, defense and security 12.9%, debt service 9.4%; capital expenditures 34.9%). **Gross national product** (2003): $808,000,000 ($150 per capita). **Production** (metric tons except as noted). *Agriculture, forestry, fishing* (2002): cassava 260,000, rice 250,000, oil palm fruit 180,000; livestock (number of live animals) 400,000 cattle, 370,000 sheep, 220,000 goats; roundwood (2002) 5,497,220 cu m; fish catch (2003) 82,923. *Mining and quarrying* (2002): rutile, none (production at world's richest deposit was halted between 1995 and August 2004 because of the civil war and its lasting effects); diamonds 351,860 carats (does not include smuggled artisanal production, which was estimated to be 600,000 carats between 1999 and 2001); gold 30 kg. *Manufacturing* (value added in Le '000,000; 1993): food 36,117; chemicals 10,560; earthenware 1,844. *Energy production (consumption):* electricity (kW-hr; 2000) 246,000,000 (246,000,000); crude petroleum (barrels; 2000) none (1,796,000); petroleum products (2000) 183,000 (145,000). **Households.** Average household size (2002) 6.6. **Public debt** (external, outstanding; 2002): $1,262,000,000. **Population economically active** (2002): total 1,771,000; activity rate of total population 36.7% (participation rates [1991]: ages 10–64, 53.3%; female [2001] 32.4%; unemployed [registered; 1992] 10.6%). **Tourism** (1999): receipts $8,000,000; expenditures $4,000,000. **Land use** as % of total land area (2000): in temporary crops 6.8%, in permanent crops 0.8%, in pasture 30.7%; overall forest area 14.7%.

Foreign trade

Imports (2002-c.i.f.): Le 554,837,500,000 (food and live animals 26.7%; fuels 19.6%; machinery and transport equipment 18.9%; chemicals and chemical products 6.9%). *Major import sources* (2001): UK 25.3%; The Netherlands 10.1%; US 7.9%; Germany 6.3%; Italy 5.6%. **Exports** (2002-f.o.b.): Le 102,011,900,000 (diamonds 85.7%; cacao 2.5%; rutile, none; reexports 4.8%). *Major export destinations* (2001): Belgium 40.6%; US 9.1%; UK 8.5%; Germany 7.8%; Japan 5.6%.

Transport and communications

Transport. *Railroads* (2002; Marampa Mineral Railway; there are no passenger railways): length 84 km. *Roads* (1999): total length 11,700 km (paved 11%). *Vehicles* (2003): passenger cars 17,439; trucks and buses 12,428. *Air transport* (2000): passenger-km 93,000,000; airports (2003) with scheduled flights 1. **Communications,** in total units (units per 1,000 persons). Daily newspaper circulation (2000): 17,700 (4); radios (2000): 1,140,000 (259); televisions (2000): 57,400 (13); telephone main lines (2002): 24,000 (4.8); cellular telephone subscribers (2002): 67,000 (14); personal computers (1999): 100 (n.a.); Internet users (2002): 8,000 (1.6).

Education and health

Educational attainment (1985). Percentage of population age 5 and over having: no formal schooling 64.1%; primary education 18.7%; secondary 9.7%; higher 1.5%. **Literacy** (1995): total population age 15

---

1 metric ton = about 1.1 short tons; 1 kilometer = 0.6 mi (statute); 1 metric ton-km cargo = about 0.68 short ton-mi cargo; c.i.f.: cost, insurance, and freight; f.o.b.: free on board

and over literate 791,000 (31.4%); males literate 555,000 (45.4%); females literate 236,000 (18.2%). **Health:** physicians (1996) 339 (1 per 13,696 persons); hospital beds (1998) 3,364 (1 per 1,250 persons); infant mortality rate per 1,000 live births (2003) 146.9. **Food** (2001): daily per capita caloric intake 1,874 (vegetable products 97%, animal products 3%); 81% of FAO recommended minimum.

Military

Total active duty personnel (2003): 14,000 (army 98.6%, navy 1.4%, air force, none); UN peacekeeping troops (September 2004) 8,500. **Military expenditure as percentage of GNP** (1999): 3.0% (world 2.4%); per capita expenditure $4.

Background

The earliest inhabitants of Sierra Leone were probably the Buloms; the Mende and Temne peoples arrived in the 15th century. The coastal region was visited by the Portuguese in the 15th century, and by 1495 there was a Portuguese fort on the site of modern Freetown. European ships visited the coast regularly to trade for slaves and ivory, and the English built trading posts on offshore islands in the 17th century. British abolitionists and philanthropists founded Freetown in 1787 as a private venture for freed and runaway slaves. In 1808 the coastal settlement became a British colony. The region became a British protectorate in 1896. It achieved independence in 1961 and became a republic in 1971. It was marked by political and economic turmoil in the late 20th century as successive military regimes tried to assume power. UN peacekeeping forces were stationed there but were ineffectual in preventing bloodletting and atrocities.

Recent Developments

During most of 2004 Sierra Leone, with the help of the UN, was preoccupied with the Special Court for Sierra Leone war crimes tribunal. A number of cases were heard involving the leading members of the rebel Revolutionary United Front and the government's Civil Defence Force—those most responsible for the atrocities that had been committed on civilians. The 11-year civil war, one of the worst in Africa's history, ended in 2002 after having claimed more than 50,000 lives and left 500,000 others directly affected by violence.

Internet resources: <www.sierra-leone.org>.

Singapore

Official name: Hsin-chia-p'o Kung-ho-kuo (Mandarin Chinese); Republik Singapura (Malay); Singapore Kudiyarasu (Tamil); Republic of Singapore (English). **Form of government:** unitary multiparty republic with one legislative house (Parliament [90, including 6 nonelective seats]). **Chief of state:** President Sellapan Rama (S.R.) Nathan (from 1999). **Head of state government:** Prime Minister Lee Hsien Loong (from 12 Aug 2004). **Capital:** Singapore. **Official languages:** Chinese; Malay; Tamil; English. **Official religion:** none. **Monetary unit:** 1 Singapore dollar (S$) = 100 cents; valuation (7 Jul 2005) US$1 = S$1.70.

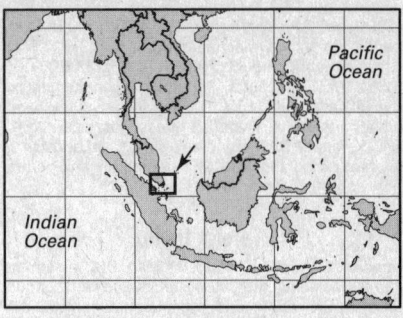

Demography

Area: 269.2 sq mi, 697.1 sq km. **Population** (2004): 4,229,000. **Density** (2004): persons per sq mi 15,710, persons per sq km 6,067. **Urban:** 100%. **Sex distribution** (2003): male 49.75%; female 50.25%. **Age breakdown** (2003): under 15, 20.8%; 15–29, 20.2%; 30–44, 27.4%; 45–59, 20.4%; 60–74, 8.5%; 75 and over, 2.7%. **Ethnic composition** (2003): Chinese 76.3%; Malay 13.8%; Indian 8.3%; other 1.6%. **Religious affiliation** (2000): Buddhist 42.5%; Muslim 14.9%; Christian 14.6%; Taoist 8.5%; Hindu 4.0%; traditional beliefs 0.6%; nonreligious 14.9%. **Location:** southeastern Asia, islands between Malaysia and Indonesia.

Vital statistics

Birth rate per 1,000 population (2003): 10.4 (world avg. 21.3). **Death rate** per 1,000 population (2003): 4.4 (world avg. 9.1). **Natural increase rate** per 1,000 population (2003): 6.0 (world avg. 12.2). **Total fertility rate** (avg. births per childbearing woman; 2003): 1.3. **Marriage rate** per 1,000 population (2003): 6.4. **Life expectancy** at birth (2003): male 76.9 years; female 80.9 years.

National economy

Budget (2003). *Revenue:* S$24,659,200,000 (income tax 42.2%, nontax revenue 14.6%, goods and services tax 11.0%, customs and excise duties 7.3%, motor vehicle taxes 5.3%). *Expenditures:* S$27,189,-300,000 (security 34.0%, development expenditure 29.3%, education 17.9%, health 6.1%, trade and industry 1.9%). **Production** (metric tons except as noted). *Agriculture and fishing* (2003): vegetables and fruits 5,010; livestock (number of live animals) 250,000 pigs, 2,000,000 chickens; fish catch (2001) 8,704. *Mining and quarrying* (value of output in S$; 1994): granite 75,800,000. *Manufacturing* (value added in US$'000,000; 2001): office, accounting, and computer equipment 5,576; electronic valves and tubes 4,829; chemicals and chemical products 4,209. *Energy production (consumption):* electricity (kW-hr; 2000) 31,665,000,000 (31,665,000,000); crude petroleum (barrels; 2000) none (306,629,000); petroleum products (2000) 27,613,000 (10,790,000); natural gas (cu m; 2000) none (1,411,000,000). **Household income and expenditure.** Average household size (2002) 4.2; income per household (2000) S$59,316; expenditure (1998): food 23.7%, transportation and communications 22.8%, housing costs and furnishings 21.6%, education 6.9%, clothing and footwear 4.1%, health 3.3%, other 17.6%. **Tourism**

(2002): receipts from visitors US$4,932,000,000; expenditures by nationals abroad US$5,213,000,000. **Gross national product** (2003): US$90,228,000,000 (US$21,230 per capita). **Population economically active** (2003): total 2,150,100; activity rate of total population 62.6% (participation rates: ages 15 and over, 64.2%; female 53.9%; unemployed 4.6%. **Land use** as % of total land area (2000): in temporary and permanent crops 1.4%; overall forest area 3.3%.

Foreign trade

Imports (2003-c.i.f.): S$222,811,000,000 (electronic valves [including integrated circuits and semiconductors] 21.7%; crude and refined petroleum 13.5%; computers and related parts 11.2%; chemicals and chemical products 6.7%; telecommunications equipment 4.0%). *Major import sources:* Malaysia 16.8%; US 13.9%; Japan 12.0%; China 8.7%; Taiwan 5.1%; Thailand 4.3%. **Exports** (2003-f.o.b.): S$251,096,000,000 (electronic valves 20.9%; computers and related parts 17.9%; chemicals and chemical products 11.8%, of which organic chemicals 6.4%; crude and refined petroleum 10.9%; telecommunications equipment 4.6%). *Major export destinations:* Malaysia 15.8%; US 13.3%; Hong Kong 10.0%; China 7.0%; Japan 6.7%; Taiwan 4.8%; Thailand 4.3%.

Transport and communications

Transport. *Railroads* (2003): length 131 km. *Roads* (2003): total length 3,144 km (paved 99%). *Vehicles* (2003): passenger cars 424,712; trucks and buses 138,538. *Air transport* (2003): passenger-km 65,376,000,000; metric ton-km cargo 6,683,000,000; airports (2003) 1. **Communications,** in total units (units per 1,000 persons). Daily newspaper circulation (2000): 1,197,301 (298); radios (2000): 2,700,000 (672); televisions (2000): 1,220,000 (304); telephone main lines (2002): 1,927,200 (463); cellular telephone subscribers (2002): 3,312,600 (795); personal computers (2002): 2,590,000 (622); Internet users (2002): 2,100,000 (504).

Education and health

Educational attainment (2000). Percentage of population age 15 and over having: no schooling 19.6%; primary education 23.1%; secondary 39.5%; postsecondary 17.8%. **Literacy** (2003): total population age 15 and over literate 94.2%. **Health** (2003): physicians 6,292 (1 per 670 persons); hospital beds 11,855 (1 per 290 persons); infant mortality rate per 1,000 live births 2.2. **Food** (1988–90): daily per capita caloric intake 3,121 (vegetable products 76%, animal products 24%); 136% of FAO recommended minimum.

Military

Total active duty personnel (2003): 72,500 (army 69.0%, navy 12.4%, air force 18.6%). **Military expenditure as percentage of GNP** (1999): 4.8% (world 2.4%); per capita expenditure US$1,100.

Background

Long inhabited by fishermen and pirates, Singapore was an outpost of the Sumatran empire of Srivijaya

until the 14th century, when it passed to Java and then Siam. It became part of the Malacca empire in the 15th century. In the 16th century the Portuguese controlled the area; they were followed by the Dutch in the 17th century. In 1819 Singapore was ceded to the British East India Co., becoming part of the Straits Settlements and the center of British colonial activity in southeast Asia. The Japanese occupied the islands in 1942–45. In 1946 it became a crown colony. It achieved full internal self-government in 1959, became a part of Malaysia in 1963, and gained independence in 1965. It is influential in the affairs of the Association of Southeast Asian Nations. The country's dominant voice in politics for 30 years after independence was Lee Kuan Yew.

Recent Developments

On 12 Aug 2004 Prime Minister Goh Chok Tong, who had held office since 1990, handed over power to Lee Hsien Loong, the deputy prime minister and son of Lee Kuan Yew, Singapore's first prime minister (1959–90). Goh remained in the cabinet, however, and assumed the position of senior minister, a post hitherto occupied by the elder Lee, who in turn became minister mentor—a new title created to reflect his role. In April 2005 it was announced that Singapore had legalized casinos and authorized the construction of two Las Vegas–style resorts.

Internet resources: <www.sg>.

Slovakia

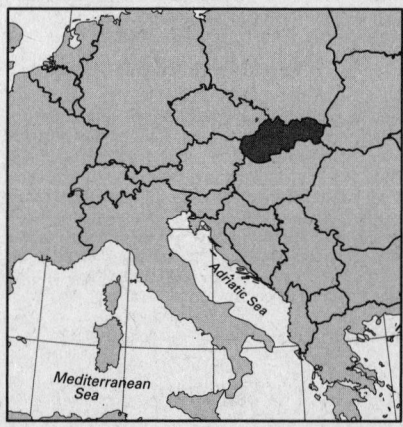

Official name: Slovenska Republika (Slovak Republic). **Form of government:** unitary multiparty republic with one legislative house (National Council [150]). **Chief of state:** President Ivan Gasparovic (from 15 Jun 2004). **Head of government:** Prime Minister Mikulas Dzurinda (from 1998). **Capital:** Bratislava. **Official language:** Slovak. **Official religion:** none. **Monetary unit:** 1 Slovak koruna (Sk) = 100 halura; valuation (7 Jul 2005) $1 = Sk 32.45.

---

1 metric ton = about 1.1 short tons;   1 kilometer = 0.6 mi (statute);   1 metric ton-km cargo = about 0.68 short ton-mi cargo;   c.i.f.: cost, insurance, and freight;   f.o.b.: free on board

Demography

Area: 18,933 sq mi, 49,035 sq km. **Population** (2004): 5,383,000. **Density** (2004): persons per sq mi 284.3, persons per sq km 109.8. **Urban** (2002): 57.6%. **Sex distribution** (2004): male 48.53%; female 51.47%. **Age breakdown** (2001): under 15, 18.9%; 15–29, 25.1%; 30–44, 21.5%; 45–59, 18.9%; 60–74, 11.0%; 75 and over, 4.6%. **Ethnic composition** (2001): Slovak 85.8%; Hungarian 9.7%; Rom (Gypsy) 1.7%; Czech 0.8%; Ruthenian and Ukrainian 0.7%; other 1.3%. **Religious affiliation** (2001): Roman Catholic 68.9%; Protestant 9.2%, of which Slovak Evangelical 6.9%, Reformed Christian 2.0%; Greek Catholic 4.1%; Eastern Orthodox 0.9%; nonreligious and other 16.9%. **Major cities** (2001): Bratislava 428,672; Kosice 236,093; Presov 92,786; Nitra 87,285; Zilina 85,400. **Location:** central Europe, bordering Poland, Ukraine, Hungary, Austria, and the Czech Republic.

Vital statistics

Birth rate per 1,000 population (2003): 9.6 (world avg. 21.3); (2001) legitimate 80.2%. **Death rate** per 1,000 population (2003): 9.7 (world avg. 9.1). **Natural increase rate** per 1,000 population (2003): –0.1 (world avg. 12.2). **Total fertility rate** (avg. births per childbearing woman; 2002): 1.3. **Marriage rate** per 1,000 population (2003): 4.8. **Divorce rate** per 1,000 population (2003): 2.0. **Life expectancy** at birth (2002): male 69.6 years; female 77.7 years.

National economy

Budget (2002). *Revenue:* Sk 391,800,000,000 (tax revenue 88.1%, of which social security contribution 35.6%, value-added tax 21.0%, income tax 11.9%; nontax revenue 11.9%). *Expenditures:* Sk 459,300,000,000 (current expenditures 88.9%, of which social welfare 26.5%, wages 14.4%, health 11.7%, debt service 8.3%; investment 11.1%). **Production** (metric tons except as noted). *Agriculture, forestry, fishing* (2002): wheat 1,554,000, sugar beets 1,340,000, corn (maize) 754,000; livestock (number of live animals) 1,554,000 pigs, 608,000 cattle, 316,000 sheep; roundwood (2002) 5,765,400 cu m; fish catch (2001) 3,142. *Mining and quarrying* (2001): iron ore (metal content) 300,000; gold 157 kg. *Manufacturing* (value added in $'000,000; 1998): food products 289; nonelectrical machinery 280; iron and steel 232. *Energy production (consumption):* electricity (kW-hr; 2002) 32,436,000,000 ([2000] 29,297,000,000); hard coal (2000) none (4,656,000); lignite (2001) 3,424,000 ([2000] 4,213,000); crude petroleum (barrels; 2001) 400,000 ([2000] 42,822,000); petroleum products (2000) 4,181,000 (1,777,000); natural gas (cu m; 2001) 212,000,000 ([2000] 6,886,000,000). **Population economically active** (2001): total 2,665,837; activity rate of total population 49.6% (participation rates: ages 15–64, 79.6%; female 47.7%; unemployed 18.0%). **Household income and expenditure.** Average household size (2002) 3.2; gross income per household (2001) Sk 89,352; sources of income (2001): wages and salaries 67.1%, transfer payments 15.8%; expenditure (2001): food, beverages, and tobacco 27.4%, housing and energy 17.2%, transportation and communications 13.7%, clothing and footwear 8.6%. **Public debt** (external, outstanding; 2002): $4,295,000,000. **Gross national product** (2003): $26,483,000,000 ($4,920 per capita). **Tourism:** receipts from visitors (2002) $724,000,000; expenditure by nationals abroad $442,000,000. **Land use** as % of total land area (2000): in temporary crops 30.2%, in permanent crops 2.6%, in pasture 18.0%; overall forest area 45.3%.

Foreign trade

Imports (2002): $16,502,000,000 (machinery and apparatus 25.6%, mineral fuels 14.6%, transport equipment 12.8%, base and fabricated metals 8.9%). *Major import sources:* Germany 22.6%; Czech Republic 15.2%; Russia 12.5%; Italy 6.9%; France 4.4%. **Exports** (2002): $14,385,000,000 (transport equipment [mostly road vehicles] 21.2%, machinery and apparatus 18.8%, base and fabricated metals [mostly iron and steel] 14.3%, mineral fuels 7.2%). *Major export destinations:* Germany 26.0%; Czech Republic 15.2%; Italy 10.7%; Austria 7.7%; Hungary 5.5%; Poland 5.3%.

Transport and communications

Transport. *Railroads* (2001): length 3,665 km; passenger-km 2,805,000,000; metric ton-km cargo 10,929,000,000. *Roads* (2001): total length 17,735 km. *Vehicles* (2003): passenger cars 1,327,000; trucks and buses 141,000. *Air transport* (2003: Slovak Airlines only): passenger-km 41,003,000; metric ton-km cargo 308,000; airports (2002) with scheduled flights 2. **Communications,** in total units (units per 1,000 persons). Daily newspaper circulation (2000): 938,000 (174); radios (2000): 5,200,000 (965); televisions (2000): 2,190,000 (407); telephone main lines (2002): 1,294,700 (241); cellular telephone subscribers (2003): 3,678,800 (684); personal computers (2002): 970,000 (180); Internet users (2003): 1,375,800 (256).

Education and health

Educational attainment (1991). Percentage of adult population having: incomplete primary education 0.7%; primary and incomplete secondary 37.9%; complete secondary 50.9%; higher 9.5%; unknown 1.0%. **Literacy** (2001): total population age 15 and over literate 100%. **Health** (2001): physicians 20,430 (1 per 263 persons); hospital beds 54,759 (1 per 98 persons); infant mortality rate per 1,000 live births (2002) 8.1. **Food** (2000): daily per capita caloric intake 3,133 (vegetable products 75%, animal products 25%); 127% of FAO recommended minimum.

Military

Total active duty personnel (2003): 22,000 (army 62.3%, air force 31.8%, headquarters staff 5.9%). **Military expenditure as percentage of GNP** (1999): 1.8% (world 2.4%); per capita expenditure $187.

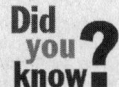

Did you know? The city of Bratislava is the capital of Zapadni Slovensko *kraj* (region) and the capital of Slovakia. It lies in the extreme southwestern part of the country, along the Danube. Vienna, Austria, is only 35 mi (56 km) to the west.

Background

Slovakia was inhabited in the first centuries AD by Illyrian, Celtic, and Germanic tribes. Slovaks settled there around the 6th century. It became part of Great Moravia in the 9th century but was conquered by the Magyars c. 907. It remained in the kingdom of Hungary until the end of World War I, when the Slovaks joined the Czechs to form the new state of Czechoslovakia in 1918. In 1938 Slovakia was declared an autonomous unit within Czechoslovakia; it was nominally independent under German protection in 1939–45. After the expulsion of the Germans, Slovakia joined a reconstituted Czechoslovakia, which came under Soviet domination in 1948. In 1969 a partnership between the Czechs and Slovaks established the Slovak Socialist Republic. The fall of the communist regime in 1989 led to a revival of interest in autonomy, and Slovakia became an independent nation in 1993.

Recent Developments

In 2004 Slovakia acceded to both NATO and the European Union and won international praise as a reform leader. Despite the political squabbling that had caused the ruling coalition to lose its parliamentary majority in late 2003, the cabinet managed to push through legislation on health care reform and fiscal decentralization and thereby wrapped up the key points of its program within the first two years of its term. Given the progress that Slovakia had made since 1998, the World Bank ranked the country as the world's top reformer and listed it as one of the top 20 economies in regard to "the ease of doing business." The reforms attracted new investment projects, including an automobile manufacturing plant by Hyundai affiliate Kia Motors, scheduled to open in 2006.

Internet resources: <www.slovakiatourism.sk>.

Slovenia

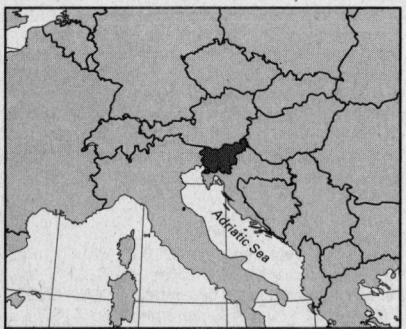

Official name: Republika Slovenija (Republic of Slovenia). Form of government: unitary multiparty republic with two legislative houses (National Council [40]; National Assembly [90]). Head of state: President Janez Drnovsek (from 2002). Head of government: Prime Minister Janez Jansa (from 9 Nov 2004). Capital: Ljubljana. Official language: Slovene. Official religion: none. Monetary unit: 1 Slovene tolar (SIT; plural tolarjev) = 100 stotin; valuation (7 Jul 2005) $1 = SIT 200.43.

Demography

Area: 7,827 sq mi, 20,273 sq km. Population (2004): 1,997,000. Density (2004): persons per sq mi 255.1, persons per sq km 98.5. Urban (2002): 50.8%. Sex distribution (2003): male 48.95%; female 51.05%. Age breakdown (2002): under 15, 15.3%; 15–29, 21.5%; 30–44, 22.7%; 45–59, 20.5%; 60–74, 14.4%; 75 and over, 5.6%. Ethnic composition (2002): Slovene 91.2%; Serb 2.2%; Croat 2.0%; Bosniac (ethnic Muslim) 1.8%; other 2.8%. Religious affiliation (2000): Christian 92.1%, of which Roman Catholic 83.5%, unaffiliated Christian 4.7%, Protestant 1.6%, Orthodox 0.6%; nonreligious/atheist 7.8%; other 0.1%. Major cities (2002): Ljubljana 258,873; Maribor 93,847; Celje 37,834; Kranj 35,587; Velenje 26,742. Location: southeastern Europe, bordering Austria, Hungary, Croatia, the Adriatic Sea, and Italy.

Vital statistics

Birth rate per 1,000 population (2002): 8.8 (world avg. 21.3); legitimate 59.8%. Death rate per 1,000 population (2002): 9.4 (world avg. 9.1). Natural increase rate per 1,000 population (2002): −0.6 (world avg. 12.2). Total fertility rate (avg. births per childbearing woman; 2002): 1.2. Marriage rate per 1,000 population (2002): 3.5. Divorce rate per 1,000 population (2002): 1.2. Life expectancy at birth (2002): male 72.3 years; female 79.9 years.

National economy

Budget (2003). Revenue: SIT 2,376,000,000,000 (2002; tax revenue 91.7%, of which social security contributions 32.7%, taxes on goods and services 32.3%, personal income tax 19.0%; nontax revenue 8.3%). Expenditures: SIT 2,454,000,000,000 (2002; current expenditures 90.8%, of which wages 45.9%, transfers 44.9%; development expenditures 9.2%). Public debt (external, outstanding; 2001): $2,700,-000,000. Production (metric tons except as noted). Agriculture, forestry, fishing (2002): silage 1,085,000, corn (maize) 255,000, sugar beets 190,000; livestock (number of live animals) 599,895 pigs, 477,075 cattle; roundwood (2001) 2,283,000 cu m; fish catch (2001) 3,040. Mining and quarrying (2002): dimension stone 105,000. Manufacturing (value added in $'000,000; 2001): base and fabricated metals 771; nonelectrical machinery and professional equipment 573; chemicals and chemical products 473. Energy production (consumption): electricity (kW-hr; 2003) 13,064,000,000 (12,588,000,000); hard coal (2000) none (446,000); lignite (2003) 4,854,000 (5,358,000); crude petroleum (barrels; 2000) 7,330 (1,165,000); petroleum products (2000) 133,000 (2,214,000); natural gas (cu m; 2003) 4,900,000 (1,114,000,000). Land use as % of total land area (2000): in temporary crops 8.6%, in permanent crops 1.5%, in pasture 15.6%; overall forest area 55.0%. Household income and expenditure (2001). Average

1 metric ton = about 1.1 short tons;   1 kilometer = 0.6 mi (statute);   1 metric ton-km cargo = about 0.68 short ton-mi cargo;   c.i.f.: cost, insurance, and freight;   f.o.b.: free on board

household size (2002) 2.8; income per household SIT 3,090,000; sources of income: wages 60.0%, transfers 26.6%; expenditure: transportation and communications 25.8%, food and beverages 17.8%, housing 10.4%, recreation 9.3%. **Gross national product** (at current market prices; 2003): $23,229,000,000 ($11,830 per capita). **Population economically active** (2003): total 959,000; activity rate 48.0% (participation rates: ages 15 and over 56.5%; female 45.9%; unemployed 10.9%). **Tourism** (2002): receipts from visitors $1,083,000,000; expenditures by nationals abroad $614,000,000.

Foreign trade

Imports (2003-c.i.f.): €12,237,000,000 (machinery and transport equipment 34.4%, of which road vehicles 11.1%; chemicals and chemical products 13.3%; mineral fuels 7.7%; food products 5.1%). *Major import sources:* Germany 19.3%; Italy 18.3%; France 10.1%; Austria 8.6%; Croatia 3.6%. **Exports** (2003-f.o.b.): €11,285,000,000 (machinery and transport equipment 36.5%, of which electrical machinery and apparatus 11.6%, road vehicles 11.4%; chemicals and chemical products 13.8%, of which medicines and pharmaceuticals 7.0%; furniture and parts 6.9%). *Major export destinations:* Germany 23.1%; Italy 13.1%; Croatia 8.9%; Austria 7.3%; France 5.7%.

Transport and communications

Transport. *Railroads* (2003): length 1,229 km; passenger-km 778,000,000; metric ton-km cargo 3,274,000,000. *Roads* (2003): total length 20,155 km (paved 81%). *Vehicles:* passenger cars (2003) 889,580; trucks and buses 69,363. *Air transport* (2003): passenger-km 837,000,000; metric ton-km cargo 3,538,000; airports (2003) with scheduled flights 3. **Communications**, in total units (units per 1,000 persons). Daily newspaper circulation (2000): 334,000 (171); radios (2000): 792,000 (405); televisions (2002): 732,000 (366); telephone main lines (2003): 812,300 (407); cellular telephone subscribers (2003): 1,739,100 (871); personal computers (2002): 600,000 (301); Internet users (2002): 750,000 (376).

Education and health

Educational attainment (2002). Percentage of population age 15 and over having: no formal schooling 0.7%; incomplete and complete primary education 32.2%; secondary 54.1%; some higher 5.1%; undergraduate 6.9%; advanced degree 1.0%. **Literacy** (2001): 99.6%. **Health** (2002): physicians 4,636 (1 per 430 persons); hospital beds 10,147 (1 per 197 persons); infant mortality rate per 1,000 live births 3.8.

Military

Total active duty personnel (2003): 6,550 (army 100%). **Military expenditure as percentage of GNP** (1999): 1.4% (world 2.4%); per capita expenditure $227.

Background

The Slovenes settled the region in the 6th century AD. In the 8th century it was incorporated into the Frankish empire of Charlemagne, and in the 10th century

it came under Germany as part of the Holy Roman Empire. Except for 1809–14, when Napoleon ruled the area, most of the lands belonged to Austria until the formation of the Kingdom of Serbs, Croats, and Slovenes in 1918. It became a constituent republic of Yugoslavia in 1946 and received a section of the former Italian Adriatic coastline in 1947. In 1990 Slovenia held the first contested multiparty elections in Yugoslavia since before World War II. In 1991 it seceded from Yugoslavia; its independence was internationally recognized in 1992.

Recent Developments

In 2004 Slovenia joined both NATO and the European Union; full membership in both organizations was the primary foreign-policy goal and was supported by all major political parties. Slovenia hosted the meeting of the NATO Parliamentary Assembly in late May 2005 and was scheduled to hold the presidency of the EU for the first half of 2008. In 2004 major strides were made in repairing somewhat tense relations with the Vatican, though Slovenia's relations with Croatia, its southern neighbor, remained strained, owing primarily to the still-unresolved demarcation of the sea and land border between them.

Internet resources: <www.slovenia-tourism.si>.

Solomon Islands

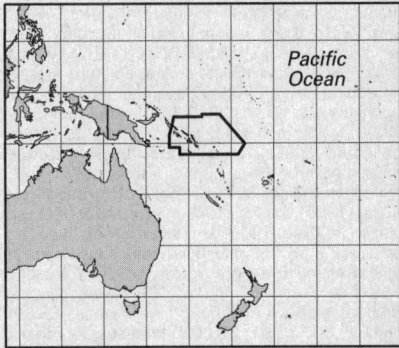

Pacific Ocean

Official name: Solomon Islands. **Form of government:** constitutional monarchy with one legislative house (National Parliament [50]). **Chief of state:** Queen Elizabeth II (from 1952), represented by Governor-General Sir Nathaniel Waena (from 7 Jul 2004). **Head of government:** Prime Minister Sir Allan Kemakeza (from 2001). **Capital:** Honiara. **Official language:** English. **Official religion:** none. **Monetary unit:** 1 Solomon Islands dollar (SI$) = 100 cents; valuation (7 Jul 2005) US$1 = SI$7.26.

Demography

Area: 10,954 sq mi, 28,370 sq km. **Population** (2004): 461,000. **Density** (2004): persons per sq mi 42.1, persons per sq km 16.2. **Urban** (2002): 21.0%. **Sex distribution** (2004): male 51.64%; female 48.36%. **Age breakdown** (2003): under 15, 42.9%; 15–29, 29.2%; 30–44, 15.5%; 45–59, 7.6%; 60–74, 3.8%; 75 and over, 1.0%. **Ethnic composition** (2002):

Melanesian 93.0%; Polynesian 4.0%; Micronesian 1.5%; other 1.5%. **Religious affiliation** (2000): Christian 90.8%, of which Protestant 74.0% (including Church of Melanesia [Anglican] 38.2%), Roman Catholic 10.8%; traditional beliefs 3.1%; other 6.1%. **Major cities** (1999): Honiara 49,107 (urban agglomeration [2001] 78,000); Noro 3,482; Gizo 2,960; Auki 1,606; Tulagi 1,333. **Location**: southwestern Pacific Ocean, east of Papua New Guinea.

Vital statistics

Birth rate per 1,000 population (2003): 32.5 (world avg. 21.3). **Death rate** per 1,000 population (2003): 4.1 (world avg. 9.1). **Natural increase rate** per 1,000 population (2003): 28.4 (world avg. 12.2). **Total fertility rate** (avg. births per childbearing woman; 2003): 4.5. **Life expectancy** at birth (2003): male 69.6 years; female 74.7 years.

National economy

Budget (2003). *Revenue:* SI$681,300,000 (tax revenue 48.9%, of which international trade tax 19.3%, sales tax 16.4%, income tax 13.2%; grants 45.4%; nontax revenue 5.7%). *Expenditures:* SI$670,900,-000 (current expenditure 60.2%, of which wages 24.4%, goods and services 13.2%, interest 7.4%; capital expenditure 39.8%). **Tourism** (2002): receipts from visitors US$1,000,000; expenditures by nationals abroad US$6,000,000. **Land use** as % of total land area (2000): in temporary crops 0.6%, in permanent crops 2.0%, in pasture 1.4%; overall forest area 88.8%. **Gross national product** (at current market prices; 2003): US$273,000,000 (US$600 per capita). **Household income and expenditure.** Average household size (2002) 6.6; average annual income per household (1991) US$2,387; sources of income (1983): wages and salaries 74.1%, other 25.9%; expenditure (1992): food 46.8%, housing 11.0%, household operations 10.9%, transportation 9.9%, recreation and health 7.9%. **Population economically active** (1999): total 85,124; activity rate of total population 21.0% (participation rates: female 32.2%; unemployed 32.5%). **Production** (metric tons except as noted). *Agriculture, forestry, fishing* (2002): coconuts 330,000, palm oil fruit 140,000, sweet potatoes 84,000; livestock (number of live animals) 68,000 pigs, 13,000 cattle, 220,000 chickens; roundwood (2002) 692,000 cu m; fish catch (2001) 30,075. *Manufacturing* (2002): vegetable oils and fats 50,000, palm oil 35,000, coconut oil 15,000. *Energy production (consumption):* electricity (kW-hr; 2002) 57,061,000 (57,061,000); petroleum products (2000) none (54,000). **Public debt** (external, outstanding; 2002): US$150,200,000.

Foreign trade

Imports (2003-c.i.f.): SI$639,500,000 (food, beverages, and tobacco 23.6%, crude petroleum 17.3%, machinery and transport equipment 12.7%, construction materials 10.7%, unspecified 32.9%). *Major import sources:* Australia 28.0%; Singapore 23.2%; New Zealand 5.2%; Fiji 4.6%; Papua New Guinea 4.4%. **Exports** (2003-f.o.b.): SI$557,000,000 (timber 66.6%, fish products 16.7%, cacao beans 9.6%). *Major export destinations:* China 25.8%;

Japan 17.9%; South Korea 15.2%; Philippines 9.9%; Thailand 6.2%; Singapore 5.6%.

Transport and communications

Transport. *Roads* (1996): total length 1,360 km (paved 2.5%). *Vehicles* (1993): passenger cars 2,052; trucks and buses 2,574. *Air transport* (1999): passenger-km 47,278,000; metric ton-km cargo 1,250,000; airports (1997) with scheduled flights 21. **Communications**, in total units (units per 1,000 persons). Radios (1997): 57,000 (141); televisions (2000): 9,570 (23); telephone main lines (2002): 6,600 (15); cellular telephone subscribers (2002): 1,000 (2.2); personal computers (2002): 18,000 (41); Internet users (2002): 2,200 (5).

Education and health

Educational attainment (1986; indigenous population only). Percentage of population age 25 and over having: no schooling 44.4%; primary education 46.2%; secondary 6.8%; higher 2.6%. **Literacy** (1999): total population age 15 and over literate 181,000 (76%); males literate 102,500 (83%); females literate 78,500 (68%). **Health:** physicians (2003) 53 (1 per 8,491 persons); hospital beds (1999) 881 (1 per 459 persons); infant mortality rate per 1,000 live births (2003) 22.9. **Food** (2001): daily per capita caloric intake 2,272 (vegetable products 92%, animal products 8%); 100% of FAO recommended minimum.

Military

Total active duty personnel (2003): none; multinational regional intervention force (from mid-2003; primarily Australian) for combating violence and lawlessness withdrew in 2004 except for police forces.

Background

The Solomon Islands were probably settled c. 2000 BC by Austronesian people. Visited by the Spanish in 1568, the islands were subsequently explored and charted by the Dutch, French, and British. They came under British protection in 1893 and became the British Solomon Islands. During World War II, the Japanese invasion of 1942 ignited three years of the most bitter fighting in the Pacific, particularly on Guadalcanal. The protectorate became self-governing in 1975 and fully independent in 1978. (Another island group named Solomon Islands, which includes Bougainville, is part of Papua New Guinea.)

Recent Developments

The Solomon Islands continued to make progress toward normalcy in 2004 after having endured civil disturbances over the previous few years. Peacekeepers were withdrawn from the Weather Coast of Guadalcanal beginning in February, but there were outbreaks of violence in the center of the island later in the year. One government minister was charged with having committed violent offenses in 2000 as a member of one of the warring militias.

Internet resources: <www.visitsolomons.com.sb>.

1 metric ton = about 1.1 short tons; 1 kilometer = 0.6 mi (statute); 1 metric ton-km cargo = about 0.68 short ton-mi cargo; c.i.f.: cost, insurance, and freight; f.o.b.: free on board

Somalia

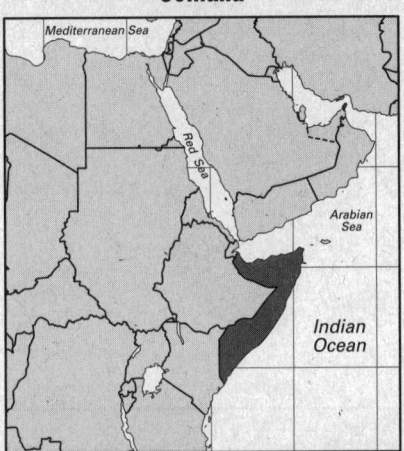

Official name: Soomaaliya (Somali); Al-Sumal (Arabic) (Somalia). **Form of government:** transitional regime (the "new transitional government" from October 2004 lacked effective control in December 2004) with one legislative body (Transitional Federal Assembly [216 planned; 194 members were sworn in on 22 Aug 2004]). At present Somalia is divided into three autonomous regions: Somaliland in the northwest, Puntland in the northeast, and Somalia in the south. **Head of state and government:** President Abdullahi Yusuf Ahmed (from 14 Oct 2004), assisted by Prime Minister Ali Muhammad Ghedi (from 3 Nov 2004). **Capital:** Mogadishu. **Official languages:** Somali; Arabic. **Official religion:** Islam. **Monetary unit:** 1 Somali shilling (So.Sh.) = 100 cents; valuation (7 Jul 2005) $1 = So.Sh. 2,750.00 (in the fall of 2003 the black-market value was about 18,000 So.Sh. = $1).

Demography

Area: 246,000 sq mi, 637,000 sq km. **Population** (2004): 8,305,000. **Density** (2004): persons per sq mi 33.8, persons per sq km 13.0. **Urban** (2002): 34%. **Sex distribution** (2002): male 51.47%; female 48.53%. **Age breakdown** (2002): under 15, 46.4%; 15–29, 26.4%; 30–44, 16.3%; 45–59, 8.1%; 60–74, 2.4%; 75 and over, 0.4%. **Ethnic composition** (2000): Somali 92.4%; Arab 2.2%; Afar 1.3%; other 4.1%. **Religious affiliation** (1995): Sunni Muslim 99.9%; other 0.1%. **Major cities** (1990): Mogadishu 1,212,000 (estimated urban agglomeration, 2003); Hargeysa 90,000; Kismaayo 90,000; Berbera 70,000; Marka 62,000. **Location:** eastern Africa, bordering Djibouti, the Gulf of Aden, the Indian Ocean, Kenya, and Ethiopia.

Vital statistics

Birth rate per 1,000 population (2003): 46.4 (world avg. 21.3). **Death rate** per 1,000 population (2003): 17.6 (world avg. 9.1). **Natural increase rate** per 1,000 population (2003): 28.8 (world avg. 12.2). **Total fertility rate** (avg. births per childbearing woman; 2003): 7.0. **Life expectancy** at birth (2003): male 45.7 years; female 49.1 years.

National economy

Budget (1991). *Revenue:* So.Sh. 151,453,000,000 (domestic revenue sources, principally indirect taxes and import duties 60.4%; external grants and transfers 39.6%). *Expenditures:* So.Sh. 141,141,000,000 (general services 46.9%; economic and social services 31.2%; debt service 7.0%). **Production** (metric tons except as noted). *Agriculture, forestry, fishing* (2002): fruits (excluding melons) 220,000, sugarcane 210,000, corn (maize) 210,000; livestock (number of live animals) 13,100,000 sheep, 12,700,000 goats, 6,200,000 camels; roundwood (2001) 9,936,520 cu m; fish catch (2001) 20,000. *Mining and quarrying* (2001): gypsum 1,500; salt 1,000. *Manufacturing* (value added in So.Sh. '000,000; 1988): food 794; cigarettes and matches 562; hides and skins 420. *Energy production (consumption):* electricity (kW-hr; 2000) 282,000,000 (282,000,000); crude petroleum (barrels; 1991) none (806,000); petroleum products (1991) none (59,000). **Household income and expenditure.** Average household size (2002) 5.2; income per household (2002): $226; sources of income (2002): self-employment 50%, remittances 22.5%, wages 14%, rent/aid 13.5%; expenditure (1983; Mogadishu only): food and tobacco 62.3%, housing 15.3%, clothing 5.6%, energy 4.3%, other 12.5%. **Population economically active** (2001): total 3,906,000; activity rate of total population 52.2% (participation rates: ages 15–64 [2002] 56.4%; unemployed [2002] 47.5%). **Gross domestic product** (2001): $1,000,-000,000 ($110 per capita). **Public debt** (external, outstanding; 2002): $1,860,000,000. **Land use** as % of total land area (2000): in temporary crops 1.7%, in permanent crops 0.04%, in pasture 68.5%; overall forest area 12.0%.

Foreign trade

Imports (2002-c.i.f.): $354,000,000 (agricultural products 32.9%, of which raw sugar 20.0%, cereals 5.1%; unspecified 67.1%). *Major import sources* (2003): Djibouti 32%; Kenya 15%; Brazil 11%; UAE 5%; Thailand 4%. **Exports** (2002-f.o.b.): $97,000,000 (agricultural products 85.4%, of which goats and sheep 56.9%, bovines 17.5%, camels 10.0%; unspecified 14.6%). *Major export destinations* (2003): UAE 39%; Yemen 24%; Oman 11%; China 6%; Kuwait 4%.

Transport and communications

Transport. *Roads* (1999): total length 22,100 km (paved 12%). *Vehicles* (1996): passenger cars 1,020; trucks and buses 6,440. *Air transport* (1991): passenger-km 131,000,000; metric ton-km cargo 5,000,000; airports (2002) with scheduled flights 1. **Communications,** in total units (units per 1,000 persons). Daily newspaper circulation (2000): 7,250 (1); radios (2002): 760,000 (98); televisions (2002): 28,700 (3.7); telephones (2002; includes cellular telephones): 116,000 (15); personal computers (2002): 6,200 (0.8).

Education and health

Literacy (2002): percentage of total population age 15 and over literate 19.2%; males literate 25.1%; females literate 13.1%. **Health** (1997): physicians 265 (1 per 25,032 persons); hospital beds 2,786 (1 per 2,381 persons); infant mortality rate per 1,000 live births (2003) 120.3. **Food** (2000): daily per capita caloric intake 1,628 (vegetable products 62%, animal products 38%); 70% of FAO recommended minimum.

Military

Total active duty personnel: no national army from 1991. **Military expenditure as percentage of GNP** (1990): 0.9% (world 4.3%); per capita expenditure $1.

Background

Muslim Arabs and Persians first established trading posts along the coasts of Somalia in the 7th–10th centuries. By the 10th century Somali nomads occupied the area inland from the Gulf of Aden, and the south and west were inhabited by various groups of pastoral Oromo peoples. Intensive European exploration began after the British occupation of Aden in 1839, and in the late 19th century Britain and Italy set up protectorates in the region. During World War II the Italians invaded British Somaliland (1940); a year later British troops retook the area, and Britain administered the region until 1950, when Italian Somaliland became a UN trust territory. In 1960 it was united with the former British Somaliland, and the two became the independent Republic of Somalia. Since then it has suffered political and civil strife, including military dictatorship, civil war, drought, and famine. In the 1990s no effective central government existed. In 1991 a proclamation of a Republic of Somaliland, on territory corresponding to the former British Somaliland, was issued by a breakaway group, but it did not receive international recognition. A multinational force intervened from 1992 to 1994 in an unsuccessful attempt to stabilize the region. The country remained in turmoil.

Recent Developments

The two-year peace and reconciliation conference between Somalia's warring factions culminated in January 2004 with the signing of a peace agreement in Nairobi, Kenya. In October a new transitional federal government was formed that was intended to bring to an end the 13 years of anarchy that had roiled the country since the fall of dictator Muhammad Siad Barre. The new government, however, was based outside Somalia in Nairobi and had yet to establish its power on the ground. By mid-2005 the seat of power had not yet been transferred to Somalia, though top officials visited the country in February. The dedication to the new government on the part of two secessionist regions in the north of Somalia—Somaliland and Puntland—remained tenuous.

Internet resources: <www.unsomalia.net>.

South Africa

Official name: Republic of South Africa. **Form of government:** multiparty republic with two legislative houses (National Council of Provinces [90]; National Assembly [400]). **Head of state and government:** President Thabo Mbeki (from 1999). **Capitals** (de facto): Pretoria/Tshwane (executive); Bloem-

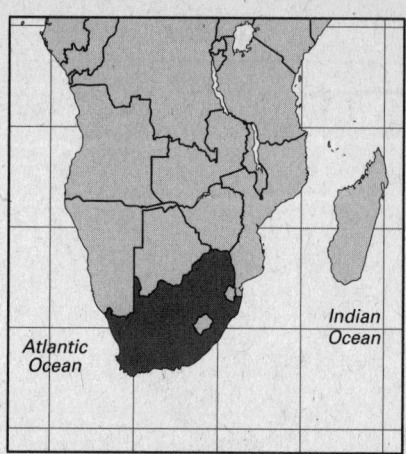

fontein/Mangaung (judicial); Cape Town (legislative). **Official languages:** Afrikaans; English; Ndebele; Pédi; Sotho; Swazi; Tsonga; Tswana; Venda; Xhosa; Zulu. **Official religion:** none. **Monetary unit:** 1 rand (R) = 100 cents; valuation (7 Jul 2005) $1 = R 6.83.

Demography

Area: 470,693 sq mi, 1,219,090 sq km. **Population** (2004): 46,587,000. **Density** (2004): persons per sq mi 99.0, persons per sq km 38.2. **Urban** (2002): 57.7%. **Sex distribution** (2001): male 47.82%; female 52.18%. **Age breakdown** (2001): under 15, 32.0%; 15–29, 29.5%; 30–44, 20.2%; 45–59, 11.0%; 60–74, 5.5%; 75 and over, 1.8%. **Ethnic composition** (2001): black 78.4%, of which Zulu 23.8%, Xhosa 17.6%, Pedi 9.4%, Tswana 8.2%, Sotho 7.9%, Tsonga 4.4%, Swazi 2.7%, other black 4.4%; white 9.6%; Coloured 8.9%; Asian 2.5%; other 0.6%. **Religious affiliation** (2000): Christian 83.1%, of which black independent churches 39.1%, Protestant 31.8%, Roman Catholic 7.1%; traditional beliefs 8.4%; Hindu 2.4%; Muslim 2.4%; nonreligious 2.4%; other 1.3%. **Major cities** (2003): Cape Town 2,733,000; Durban 2,396,100; Johannesburg 1,675,200; Pretoria 1,249,700; Port Elizabeth 848,400. **Location:** southern Africa, bordering Namibia, Botswana, Zimbabwe, Mozambique, Swaziland, and the southern Atlantic and western Indian Oceans; wholly contained within South Africa is the country of Lesotho.

Vital statistics

Birth rate per 1,000 population (2003): 19.7 (world avg. 21.3). **Death rate** per 1,000 population (2003): 19.3 (world avg. 9.1). **Natural increase rate** per 1,000 population (2003): 0.4 (world avg. 12.2). **Marriage rate** per 1,000 population (2000): 3.2. **Divorce rate** per 1,000 population (2000): 0.8. **Total fertility rate** (avg. births per childbearing woman; 2003): 2.4. **Life expectancy** at birth (2003): male 44.6 years; female 46.0 years. **Adult population** (ages 15–49) living with HIV (2004): 21.5% (world avg. 1.1%).

1 metric ton = about 1.1 short tons; 1 kilometer = 0.6 mi (statute); 1 metric ton-km cargo = about 0.68 short ton-mi cargo; c.i.f.: cost, insurance, and freight; f.o.b.: free on board

National economy

Budget (2001–02). *Revenue:* R 248,447,200,000 (personal income taxes 36.6%, value-added taxes 23.6%, company income taxes 17.7%, other 22.1%). *Expenditures:* R 262,589,800,000 (transfer to provinces 46.2%, interest on public debt 18.1%, police and prisons 9.2%, defense 6.1%). **Public debt** (external, outstanding; 2002): $9,427,000,000. **Production** (in R '000,000 except as noted). *Agriculture, forestry, fishing* (in value of production; 2000): poultry 8,270, corn (maize) 5,654, beef 3,904; roundwood (2001) 30,616,000 cu m; fish catch (2001) 760,000 metric tons. *Mining and quarrying* (in value of sales; 2002): gold 41,386; platinum-group metals 34,829; coal 31,140. *Manufacturing* (value added in $'000,000; 1999): food products 2,225; iron and steel 2,225; transport equipment 2,100. *Energy production (consumption):* electricity (kW-hr; 2002) 217,704,000,000 ([2001] 182,565,000,000); coal (metric tons; 2002) 222,456,000 ([2000] 156,-248,000); crude petroleum (barrels; 2000) 6,027,000 (193,255,000; includes Botswana, Lesotho, Namibia, and Swaziland); petroleum products (metric tons; 2000; includes Botswana, Lesotho, Namibia, and Swaziland) 24,653,000 (17,645,000); natural gas (cu m; 2000) 1,666,000,000 (1,666,-000,000). **Population economically active** (2001): total 15,358,000; activity rate of total population 34.5% (participation rates: over age 15, 50.7%; female 46.7%; unemployed [2001] 29.5%). **Household income and expenditure.** Average household size (2001) 3.8; average annual disposable income per household (1996) R 47,600; expenditure (1998): food, beverages, and tobacco 31.3%; transportation 14.3%; housing 9.3%; household furnishings and operation 8.9%. **Gross national product** (2003): $125,971,000,000 ($2,780 per capita). **Tourism** (2002): receipts $2,728,000,000; expenditures $1,804,000,000. **Land use** as % of total land area (2000): in temporary crops 12.1%, in permanent crops 0.8%, in pasture 68.7%; overall forest area 7.3%.

Foreign trade

Imports (2001): $24,188,000,000 (nonelectrical machinery 18.0%, crude petroleum 12.9%, chemicals and chemical products 11.9%, electrical machinery 11.5%). *Major import sources* (2001): US 11.0%; Germany 10.5%; UK 7.4%; Japan 5.5%; China 4.4%; unspecified 17.1%. **Exports** (2001): $27,928,000,000 (diamonds 18.6%, gold 12.6%, iron and steel 7.8%, food 6.5%, nonelectrical machinery 6.3%, industrial chemicals 6.2%, road vehicles 5.6%, coal 5.2%). *Major export destinations* (2002): UK 12.9%; US 12.8%; Germany 9.1%; Japan 8.9%; Italy 5.8%.

Transport and communications

Transport. *Railroads:* route length (2001) 20,384 km; passenger-km 3,930,000,000; metric ton-km cargo 106,786,000,000. *Roads* (1999): length 331,265 km (paved 41%). *Vehicles* (2002): passenger cars 4,135,037; trucks and buses 2,202,032. *Air transport* (2000; SAA only): passenger-km 19,320,-000,000; metric ton-km cargo 677,048,000; airports (1996) 24. **Communications,** in total units (units per 1,000 persons). Daily newspaper circulation (2000): 1,590,000 (32); radios (2000): 16,800,000 (338); televisions (2002): 8,018,000 (177); telephone main lines (2002): 4,844,000 (107); cellular telephone subscribers (2003): 16,860,000 (364); personal computers (2002): 3,300,000 (73); Internet users (2002): 3,100,000 (68).

Education and health

Educational attainment (2000). Percentage of population age 20 and over having: no formal schooling 17.9%; some primary education 16.0%; complete primary/some secondary 37.2%; complete secondary 20.4%; higher 8.5%. **Literacy** (2000): total population age 15 and over literate 85.3%; males literate 86.0%; females literate 84.6%. **Health:** physicians (2000) 29,788 (1 per 1,453 persons); hospital beds (1998) 144,363 (1 per 290 persons); infant mortality rate per 1,000 live births (2003) 63.7. **Food** (2001): daily per capita caloric intake 2,889 (vegetable products 87%, animal products 13%); 114% of FAO recommended minimum.

Military

Total active duty personnel (2003): 55,750 (army 64.6%, navy 8.1%, air force 16.6%, intraservice medical service 10.7%). **Military expenditure as percentage of GNP** (1999): 1.5% (world 2.4%); per capita expenditure $45.

 **Did you know?** The Cape of Good Hope is a rocky promontory at the southern end of the Cape Peninsula in South Africa. The Portuguese navigator Bartolomeu Dias first sighted it in 1488, and its discovery was considered a good omen that India could be reached by sea from Europe.

Background

San and Khoikhoi peoples roamed southern Africa as hunters and gatherers in the Stone Age, and the latter had developed a pastoralist culture by the time of European contact. By the 14th century, Bantu-speaking peoples had settled in the area and developed gold and copper mining and an active East African trade. In 1652 the Dutch established a colony at the Cape of Good Hope; the Dutch settlers became known as Boers and later as Afrikaners, after their Afrikaans language. In 1795 British forces captured the Cape, and in the 1830s, to escape British rule, Dutch settlers began the Great Trek northward and established the independent Boer republics of Orange Free State and the South African Republic (later the Transvaal region), which the British annexed as colonies by 1902 after the 30-month long Boer War. In 1910 the British colonies of Cape Colony, Transvaal, Natal, and Orange River were unified into the new Union of South Africa. It became independent and withdrew from the Commonwealth in 1961. Throughout the 20th century South African politics were dominated by the issue of maintaining white supremacy over the country's black majority, and in 1948 South Africa formally instituted apartheid. Faced by increasing worldwide condemnation, it began dismantling the policy in the 1980s and ended it in 1990. In free elections in 1994, Nelson Mandela became the country's first black president. South Africa also rejoined the Commonwealth in 1994.

Recent Developments

The African National Congress (ANC) was overwhelmingly returned to power in the national and provincial elections held on 14 Apr 2004, which led to the inauguration of Pres. Thabo Mbeki for a second term. For the first time, the ANC took office on its own, or as senior partner, in all nine provinces. Members of the Inkatha Freeedom Party, the New National Party, and the Azanian People's Organization were included in Mbeki's cabinet, which had 12 women. Though South Africa continued to be involved in peace-brokering exercises in Burundi and in Zimbabwe, no significant negotiations took place between the ruling Zimbabwe African National Union–Patriotic Front and the opposition Movement for Democratic Change.

Internet resources: <www.southafrica.net>.

Spain

Official name: Reino de España (Kingdom of Spain). **Form of government:** constitutional monarchy with two legislative houses (Senate [259, including 51 indirectly elected]; Congress of Deputies [350]). **Chief of state:** King Juan Carlos I (from 1975). **Head of government:** Prime Minister José Luis Rodríguez Zapatero (from 17 Apr 2004). **Capital:** Madrid. **Official language:** Castilian Spanish; per constitution, Euskera [Basque], Catalan, Galician, and all other Spanish languages are also official in their Autonomous Communities). **Official religion:** none. **Monetary unit:** 1 euro (€) = 100 céntimos; valuation (7 Jul 2005) $1 = €0.84; at conversion on 1 Jan 2002, €1 = 166.386 pesetas (Ptas).

Demography

Area: 195,363 sq mi, 505,988 sq km. **Population** (2004): 43,768,000. **Density** (2004): persons per sq mi 224.0, persons per sq km 86.5. **Urban** (2002): 77.8%. **Sex distribution** (2002): male 48.95%; female 51.05%. **Age breakdown** (2002): under 15, 14.6%; 15–29, 21.7%; 30–44, 24.0%; 45–59, 18.0%; 60–74, 14.2%; 75 and over, 7.5%. **Ethnic composition** (2000): Spaniard 44.9%; Catalonian 28.0%; Galician 8.2%; Basque 5.5%; Aragonese 5.0%; Rom (Gypsy) 2.0%; other 6.4%. **Religious affiliation** (2000): Roman Catholic 92.0%; Muslim 0.5%; Protestant 0.3%; other 7.2%. **Major cities** (2001): Madrid 2,938,723; Barcelona 1,503,884; Valencia

738,441; Seville 684,633; Zaragoza 614,905. **Location:** southwestern Europe, bordering France, Andorra, the Mediterranean Sea, Gibraltar, the Atlantic Ocean, and Portugal; the North African exclaves of Ceuta and Melilla border Morocco.

Vital statistics

Birth rate per 1,000 population (2003): 10.1 (world avg. 21.3). **Death rate** per 1,000 population (2003): 8.8 (world avg. 9.1). **Total fertility rate** (avg. births per childbearing woman; 2003): 1.3. **Life expectancy** at birth (2002): male 75.7 years; female 83.1 years.

National economy

Budget (2002). *Revenue:* €108,824,300,000 (direct taxes 46.6%, of which income tax 27.2%; indirect taxes 41.8%, of which value-added tax on products 27.8%; other taxes 11.6%). *Expenditures:* €112,586,900,000 (public debt 15.7%; health 9.8%; pensions 5.7%; defense 5.6%; public works 4.4%). **Tourism** (2002): receipts $33,609,000,000; expenditures $6,638,000,000. **Gross national product** (2003): $698,208,000,000 ($16,990 per capita). **Land use** as % of total land area (2000): in temporary crops 26.5%, in permanent crops 9.9%, in pasture 22.9%; overall forest area 28.8%. **Production** (metric tons except as noted). *Agriculture, forestry, fishing* (2002): barley 8,332,900, sugar beets 7,877,000, wheat 6,782,000; livestock (number of live animals) 24,300,624 sheep, 23,857,776 pigs, 6,411,000 cattle; roundwood (2001) 15,839,000 cu m; fish catch (2001) 1,289,081. *Mining and quarrying* (metal content in metric tons; 2001): zinc 164,900; lead 49,500. *Manufacturing* (value added in €'000,000; 2001): transport equipment 35,774; petroleum products 26,242; food products 14,771. *Energy production (consumption):* electricity (kW-hr; 2002) 229,000,000,000 (218,400,000,000); hard coal (2001) 10,491,000 ([2000] 32,804,000); lignite (2000) 12,154,000 (12,850,000); crude petroleum (barrels; 2003) 2,701,000 ([2000] 429,000,000); petroleum products (2000) 50,071,000 (50,840,000); natural gas (cu m; 2002) 509,700,000 ([2000] 17,752,000,000). **Public debt** (2001): $334,240,000,000. **Population economically active** (2001): total 17,814,600; activity rate of total population 43.7% (participation rates: ages [1995] 16–64, 60.7%; female 39.2%; unemployed 10.5%). **Household income and expenditure.** Average household size (2000) 3.2; income per household (2000) Ptas 3,205,693; expenditure (1995): housing 26.0%, food 24.0%, transportation 12.8%, clothing/footwear 7.4%.

Foreign trade

Imports (2001-f.o.b. in balance of trade): $154,993,000,000 (road vehicles 15.6%, nonelectrical machinery 13.3%, chemicals and chemical products 11.2%, electrical machinery 8.7%, crude and refined petroleum 8.6%). *Major import sources* (2002): France 16.9%; Germany 16.5%; Italy 8.6%; UK 6.4%; The Netherlands 4.8%. **Exports** (2001): $116,149,000,000 (road vehicles 23.0%; machinery 16.0%; food 12.0%, of which fruits and vegetables 6.3%; chemicals and chemical products 9.7%). *Major ex-*

---

1 metric ton = about 1.1 short tons;   1 kilometer = 0.6 mi (statute);   1 metric ton-km cargo = about 0.68 short ton-mi cargo;   c.i.f.: cost, insurance, and freight;   f.o.b.: free on board

port destinations (2002): France 18.9%; Germany 11.4%; Portugal 9.5%; UK 9.5%; Italy 9.3%.

Transport and communications

Transport. *Railroads* (2001): route length 13,832 km; passenger-km 19,190,000,000; metric ton-km cargo 12,216,000,000. *Roads* (1999): length 346,548 km (paved 99%). *Vehicles* (2001): cars 18,151,000; trucks and buses 4,005,000. *Air transport* (2003; combined total of Iberia, Air Europa, Air Nostrum, Binter Canarias, and Spanair): passenger-km 61,674,-000,000; metric ton-km cargo 820,963,000; airports (1997) with scheduled flights 25. **Communications,** in total units (units per 1,000 persons). Daily newspaper circulation (2000): 4,060,000 (100); radios (2000): 13,500,000 (333); televisions (2000): 24,000,000 (591); telephone main lines (2003): 17,567,500 (429); cellular telephone subscribers (2003): 37,507,000 (916); personal computers (2002): 7,972,000 (196); Internet users (2003): 9,789,000 (239).

Education and health

Educational attainment (2001). Percentage of population age 16 and over having: no formal schooling 15.4%; primary education 23.1%; secondary 48.0%; undergraduate degree 6.6%; graduate degree 6.9%. **Literacy** (2001): total population age 15 and over literate 97.7%; males literate 96.9%; females literate 98.6%. **Health:** physicians (2000) 179,033 (1 per 227 persons); hospital beds (2001) 160,815 (1 per 254 persons); infant mortality rate per 1,000 live births (2003) 3.6. **Food** (2000): daily per capita caloric intake 3,352 (vegetable products 73%, animal products 27%); 136% of FAO recommended minimum.

Military

Total active duty personnel (2003): 150,700 (army 63.4%, navy 15.2%, air force 15.1%, other 6.3%). **Military expenditure as percentage of GNP** (1999): 1.3% (world 2.4%); per capita expenditure $192.

Background

Remains of Stone Age populations dating back some 35,000 years have been found throughout Spain. Celtic peoples arrived in the 9th century BC, followed by the Romans, who dominated Spain from c. 200 BC until the Visigoth invasion in the early 5th century. In the early 8th century most of the peninsula fell to Muslims (Moors) from North Africa and remained under their control until it was gradually reconquered by the Christian kingdoms of Castile, Aragon, and Portugal. Spain was reunited in 1479 following the marriage of Ferdinand II (of Aragon) and Isabella I (of Castile). The last Muslim kingdom, Granada, was reconquered in 1492, and around this time Spain also established a colonial empire in the Americas. In 1516 the throne passed to the Habsburgs, whose rule ended in 1700 when Philip V became the first Bourbon king of Spain. His ascendancy caused the War of the Spanish Succession, which resulted in the loss of numerous European possessions and sparked revolution within most of Spain's American colonies. Spain lost its remaining overseas possessions to the US in the Spanish-American War (1898). It became a republic in 1931. The Spanish Civil War (1936–39) ended in victory for the Nationalists under Gen. Fran-

cisco Franco, who ruled as dictator until his death in 1975. His successor as head of state, King Juan Carlos I, restored the monarchy upon his accession to the throne; a new constitution in 1978 established a parliamentary monarchy. Spain joined NATO in 1982 and the European Community in 1986.

Recent Developments

High drama seized Spain in the spring of 2004. The climax was the explosion, during the morning rush hour on 11 March, of powerful bombs in three Madrid commuter railway stations that killed 190 people and injured an estimated 1,430 others. In terms of wanton destruction and trauma to the national psyche, the incident was likened to the 11 Sep 2001 terrorist attacks in the US. The bombings occurred just three days before parliamentary elections in Spain, and the government of Prime Minister José María Aznar, seeking to make political capital, precipitously accused ETA, the Basque terrorist organization, of the deeds. Many voters, however, apparently believed that the attacks were ordered not by ETA but by al-Qaeda terrorists in order to punish Aznar for his staunch support of the US-led invasion of Iraq (these suspicions later proved correct). On 14 March the voters unceremoniously dumped Aznar's center-right Popular Party and supported the Socialists. José Luis Rodríguez Zapatero was sworn in as prime minister and immediately fulfilled his perceived mandate from the electorate and announced the withdrawal of the 1,300 Spanish peacekeeping troops from Iraq. In two major controversial actions in 2005, the government in February announced an amnesty program that would grant civil rights to some 800,000 undocumented immigrants, and in April same-sex marriages were legalized.

Internet resources: <www.tourspain.es>.

Sri Lanka

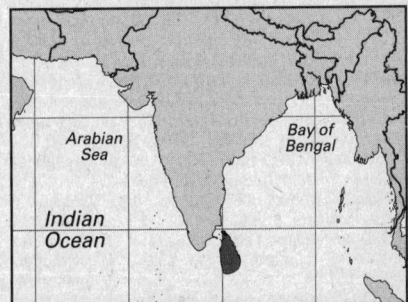

Arabian Sea

Bay of Bengal

Indian Ocean

Official name: Sri Lanka Prajatantrika Samajavadi Janarajaya (Sinhala); Ilangai Jananayaka Socialisa Kudiarasu (Tamil) (Democratic Socialist Republic of Sri Lanka). **Form of government:** unitary multiparty republic with one legislative house (Parliament [225]). **Head of state and government:** President Chandrika Kumaratunga (from 1994), assisted by Prime Minister Mahinda Rajapakse (from 6 Apr 2004). **Capitals:** Colombo (executive); Sri Jayewardenepura Kotte (Colombo suburb; legislative and judicial). **Official languages:** Sinhala; Tamil. **Official religion:** none. **Monetary unit:** 1 Sri Lanka rupee (SL Rs) = 100 cents; valuation (7 Jul 2005) $1 = SL Rs 100.05.

Demography

Area: 25,332 sq mi, 65,610 sq km. **Population** (2004): 19,218,000. **Density** (2004): persons per sq mi 758.6, persons per sq km 292.9. **Urban** (2002): 25.0%. **Sex distribution** (2001): male 49.47%; female 50.53%. **Age breakdown** (2001): under 15, 27.9%; 15–29, 27.1%; 30–44, 22.7%; 45–59, 13.6%; 60–74, 7.0%; 75 and over, 1.7%. **Ethnic composition** (2000): Sinhalese 72.4%; Tamil 17.8%; Sri Lankan Moor 7.4%; other 2.4%. **Religious affiliation** (2001): Buddhist 76.7%; Muslim 8.5%; Hindu 7.9%; Christian 6.8%; other 0.1%. **Major cities** (2001; provisional figures [except for 7 districts experiencing civil war]): Colombo 642,163; Dehiwala–Mount Lavinia 209,787; Moratuwa 177,190; Negombo 121,933; Sri Jayewardenepura Kotte 115,826. **Location:** island in the northern Indian Ocean, lying southeast of India.

Vital statistics

Birth rate per 1,000 population (2003): 16.1 (world avg. 21.3). **Death rate** per 1,000 population (2003): 6.5 (world avg. 9.1). **Natural increase rate** per 1,000 population (2003): 11.1 (world avg. 12.2). **Total fertility rate** (avg. births per childbearing woman; 2003): 1.9. **Marriage rate** per 1,000 population (1997): 8.9. **Life expectancy** at birth (2003): male 70.1 years; female 75.3 years.

National economy

Budget (2001). *Revenue:* SL Rs 231,463,000,000 (sales tax 19.7%, excise taxes 19.4%, income taxes 15.0%, nontax revenue 11.6%). *Expenditures:* SL Rs 383,686,000,000 (interest payments 24.6%, defense 17.8%, social welfare 13.4%). **Public debt** (external, outstanding; 2002): $8,455,000,000. **Production** (metric tons except as noted). *Agriculture, forestry, fishing* (2002): rice 2,794,000, coconuts 1,900,000, sugarcane 1,050,000; livestock (number of live animals) 1,565,000 cattle, 661,200 buffalo; roundwood (2001) 6,468,369 cu m; fish catch (2001) 288,010. *Mining and quarrying* (2001): graphite 6,585; sapphires 453,800 carats. *Manufacturing* (value added, in $'000,000; 1995): food, beverages, and tobacco 601; textiles and apparel 391; petrochemicals 116. *Energy production (consumption):* electricity (kW-hr; 2001) 6,520,000,000 (6,520,000,000); coal (2000) none (negligible); crude petroleum (barrels; 2000) none (16,712,000); petroleum products (2000) 2,062,000 (3,215,000). **Gross national product** (2003): $17,846,000,000 ($930 per capita). **Land use** as % of total land area (2000): in temporary crops 13.8%, in permanent crops 15.7%, in pasture 6.8%; overall forest area 30.0%. **Population economically active:** total (2001) 6,729,700 (excludes 7 districts experiencing civil war; activity rate 40% (participation rates: ages 10 and over, 48.3%; female 33.3%; unemployed 7.8%). **Household income and expenditure** (1992). Average household size (2000; excludes 7 districts experiencing civil war) 4.6; income per household SL Rs 116,100; sources of income: wages 48.5%, property income and self-employment 41.8%, transfers 9.7%; expenditure: food 58.6%, transportation 16.0%, clothing 8.4%. **Tourism** (2002): receipts $253,000,-000; expenditures $253,000,000.

Foreign trade

Imports (2002-c.i.f.): SL Rs 584,491,000,000 (textiles [mostly yarns and fabrics] 21.6%; petroleum and natural gas 12.9%; foods 11.4%; machinery and equipment 10.5%). *Major import sources:* India 13.9%; Hong Kong 8.2%; Singapore 7.2%; Japan 5.9%; South Korea 5.0%; Taiwan 4.8%. **Exports** (2002-f.o.b.): SL Rs 449,850,000,000 (clothing and accessories 51.6%; tea 13.5%; precious and semiprecious stones 5.9%; rubber products 3.9%). *Major export destinations:* US 38.9%; UK 13.0%; Belgium-Luxembourg 5.7%; Germany 4.4%; India 3.8%.

Transport and communications

Transport. *Railroads* (2001): route length 1,449 km; (1998) passenger-km 3,264,000,000; (1998) metric ton-km cargo 132,000,000. *Roads* (1996): total length 99,200 km (paved 40%). *Vehicles* (2001): passenger cars 353,701; trucks and buses 244,166. *Air transport* (2001): passenger-km 4,126,000,000; metric ton-km cargo 224,000,000; airports (2001) 1. **Communications,** in total units (units per 1,000 persons). Daily newspaper circulation (2000): 539,000 (29); radios (2000): 3,870,000 (208); televisions (2000): 2,060,000 (111); telephone main lines (2002): 881,400 (47); cellular telephone subscribers (2002): 931,600 (49); personal computers (2002): 250,000 (13); Internet users (2002): 200,000 (11).

Education and health

Literacy (2000): percentage of population age 15 and over literate 91.6%; males literate 94.4%; females literate 89.0%. **Health** (1999): physicians 6,938 (1 per 2,740 persons); hospital beds (2001) 57,946 (1 per 324 persons); infant mortality rate per 1,000 live births (2003) 15.2. **Food** (2001): daily per capita caloric intake 2,274 (vegetable products 93%, animal products 7%); 102% of FAO recommended minimum.

Military

Total active duty personnel (2003): 152,300 (army 77.5%, navy 9.8%, air force 12.7%). **Military expenditure as percentage of GNP** (1999): 4.7% (world 2.4%); per capita expenditure $38.

Background

The Sinhalese people of Sri Lanka (Ceylon) probably originated with the blending of aboriginal inhabitants and migrating Indo-Aryans from India c. 5th century BC. The Tamils were later immigrants from Dravidian India, migrating over a period from the early centuries AD to c. 1200. Buddhism was introduced during the 3rd century BC. As Buddhism spread, the Sinhalese kingdom extended its political control over Ceylon but lost it to invaders from southern India in the 10th century AD. Between 1200 and 1505 Sinhalese power gravitated to southwestern Ceylon, while a southern Indian dynasty seized power in the north and established the Tamil kingdom in the 14th century. Foreign invasions from India, China, and Malaya occurred in the 13th–15th centuries. In 1505 the Portuguese arrived, and by 1619 they controlled most of the island. The Sinhalese enlisted the Dutch to help oust the Por-

1 metric ton = about 1.1 short tons; 1 kilometer = 0.6 mi (statute); 1 metric ton-km cargo = about 0.68 short ton-mi cargo; c.i.f.: cost, insurance, and freight; f.o.b.: free on board

tuguese and eventually came under the control of the Dutch East India Co., which relinquished power in 1796 to the British. In 1802 Ceylon became a crown colony, gaining independence in 1948. It became the Republic of Sri Lanka in 1972 and was renamed the Democratic Socialist Republic of Sri Lanka in 1978. Civil strife between Tamil and Sinhalese groups has beset the country in recent years, with the Tamils demanding a separate autonomous state in northern Sri Lanka.

Recent Developments

In 2004 Sri Lanka experienced political turmoil, violence, and frustration over the seemingly endless complications of trying to arrange negotiations between the government and the Liberation Tigers of Tamil Eelam (LTTE) to end the conflict that had raged sporadically since 1983 and cost more than 60,000 lives. Then on 26 December coastal areas were swept by a tsunami that killed more than 30,000 Sri Lankans. The bitterly personal conflict between Pres. Chandrika Kumaratunga and Prime Minister Ranil Wickremesinghe, who uncomfortably shared power in Sri Lanka's complex political system, continued to dominate national politics until April 2004, when Mahinda Rajapakse became prime minister.

Internet resources: <www.priu.gov.lk>.

The Sudan

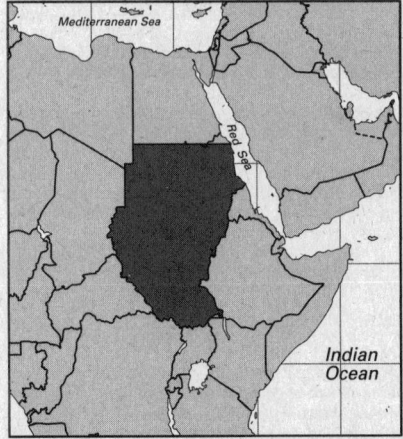

Official name: Jumhuriyat al-Sudan (Republic of the Sudan). **Form of government:** federal republic with one legislative body (National Assembly [360, including 90 seats not elected directly]). **Head of state and government:** President Omar Hassan Ahmad al-Bashir (from 1989). **Capitals:** Khartoum (executive); Omdurman (legislative). **Official language:** Arabic; English has been designated the "principal" language in southern Sudan. **Official religion:** Islamic law and custom are sources of national law per 1998 constitution. **Monetary unit:** 1 Sudanese dinar (Sd); valuation (7 Jul 2005) $1 = Sd 250.72 (the Sudanese dinar [Sd], introduced May 1992 at a value equal to 10 Sudanese pounds [LSd], officially replaced the Sudanese pound on March 1, 1999).

Demography

Area: 2,503,890 sq km (includes about 130,000 sq km of inland water). **Population** (2004): 39,148,000. **Density** (2004): persons per sq mi 40.5, persons per sq km 15.6. **Urban** (2002): 37.1%. **Sex distribution** (2001): male 50.64%; female 49.36%. **Age breakdown** (2001): under 15, 44.6%; 15–29, 27.6%; 30–44, 15.6%; 45–59, 8.4%; 60–74, 3.3%; 75 and over, 0.5%. **Ethnic composition** (1983): Sudanese Arab 49.1%; Dinka 11.5%; Nuba 8.1%; Beja 6.4%; Nuer 4.9%; Zande 2.7%; Bari 2.5%; Fur 2.1%; other 12.7%. **Religious affiliation** (2000): Sunni Muslim 70.3%; Christian 16.7%, of which Roman Catholic 8%, Anglican 6%; traditional beliefs 11.9%; other 1.1%. **Major cities** (1993): Omdurman 1,271,403; Khartoum 947,483; Khartoum North 700,887; Port Sudan 308,195; Kassala 234,622. **Location:** northeastern Africa, bordering Egypt, the Red Sea, Eritrea, Ethiopia, Kenya, Uganda, Democratic Republic of the Congo, Central African Republic, Chad, and Libya.

Vital statistics

Birth rate per 1,000 population (2003): 36.5 (world avg. 21.3). **Death rate** per 1,000 population (2003): 9.6 (world avg. 9.1). **Natural increase rate** per 1,000 population (2003): 26.9 (world avg. 12.2). **Total fertility rate** (avg. births per childbearing woman; 2003): 5.1. **Life expectancy** at birth (2003): male 56.6 years; female 58.9 years.

National economy

Budget (2001). *Revenue:* Sd 365,200,000,000 (tax revenue 51.5%, of which custom duties 21.3%, VAT 10.3%; nontax revenue 48.5%). *Expenditures:* Sd 418,800,000,000 (current expenditure 81.9%, of which wages 31.4%; development expenditure 18.1%). **Public debt** (external, outstanding; 2002): $9,043,000,000. **Production** (metric tons except as noted). *Agriculture, forestry, fishing* (2002): sugarcane 5,000,000, sorghum 2,800,000, peanuts (groundnuts) 945,000; livestock (number of live animals) 47,043,000 sheep, 40,000,000 goats, 38,325,000 cattle; roundwood (2002) 19,241,332 cu m; fish catch (2001) 59,000. *Mining and quarrying* (2001): salt 120,000; gold 6,800 kg. *Manufacturing* (2001): raw sugar 689,000; flour (2000) 600,000; cement 190,000. *Energy production (consumption):* electricity (kW-hr; 2000) 2,264,000,000 (2,264,000,000); crude petroleum (barrels; 2001) 145,100,000 ([2000] 14,609,000); petroleum products (2001) 2,674,700 ([2000] 1,876,000). **Gross national product** (2003): $15,372,000,000 ($460 per capita). **Population economically active** (2000): total 12,207,000; activity rate of total population 37.8% (female 29.9%). **Households.** Average household size (2000): 6.1. **Tourism** (2002): receipts from visitors $62,000,000; expenditures by nationals abroad $91,000,000. **Land use** as % of total land area (2000): in temporary crops 6.8%, in permanent crops 0.2%, in pasture 49.3%; overall forest area 25.9%.

Foreign trade

Imports (2001-c.i.f.): $1,586,000,000 (machinery and equipment 27.9%; foodstuffs 16.4%, of which wheat and wheat flour 8.7%; transport equipment 12.8%; chemicals and chemical products 7.8%). *Major import sources* (2002): China 19.8%; Saudi

Arabia 6.9%; India 5.5%; Germany 5.5%; UK 5.4%. **Exports** (2001-f.o.b.): $1,699,000,000 (crude petroleum 74.7%; refined petroleum 6.3%; sesame seeds 6.2%; gold 2.6%; cotton 2.6%). *Major export destinations* (2002): China 55.3%; Japan 13.9%; Saudi Arabia 5.4%; South Korea 3.8%; Egypt 3.3%.

 **Did you know?** The Nile, called "the father of African rivers," is the longest river in the world. The Nile River basin covers about one-tenth of the area of the African continent.

Transport and communications

Transport. *Railroads:* route length (2000) 5,901 km; (2001) passenger-km 78,000,000; metric ton-km cargo 1,250,000,000. *Roads* (1999): total length 11,900 km (paved 36%). *Vehicles* (1996): passenger cars 285,000; trucks and buses 53,000. *Air transport* (2001): passenger-km 803,000,000; metric ton-km cargo 54,542,000; airports (1997) with scheduled flights 3,300. **Communications,** in total units (units per 1,000 persons). Daily newspaper circulation (2000): 912,000 (26); radios (2001): 16,642,000 (461); televisions (2002): 12,661,000 (386); telephone main lines (2003): 900,000 (27); cellular telephone subscribers (2003): 650,000 (20); personal computers (2002): 200,000 (6.1); Internet users (2003): 300,000 (2.6).

Education and health

Literacy (2000): total population age 15 and over literate 55.8%; males literate 69.5%; females literate 46.3%. **Health:** physicians (1997) 3,423 (1 per 9,395 persons); hospital beds (1998) 36,419 (1 per 909 persons); infant mortality rate per 1,000 live births (2003) 65.6. **Food** (2001): daily per capita caloric intake 2,288 (vegetable products 80%, animal products 20%); 97% of FAO recommended minimum.

Military

Total active duty personnel (2004): 104,800 (army 95.4%, navy 1.7%, air force 2.9%); main opposition force in southern Sudan (Sudanese People's Liberation Army) between 20,000 and 30,000 (a permanent cease-fire between the central government and the main opposition force in southern Sudan was signed on 31 Dec 2004; a comprehensive peace plan was implemented in January 2005. African Union peacekeeping troops in Darfur (October 2004): 400; authorized 3,300. **Military expenditure as percentage of GNP** (1999): 4.8% (world 2.4%); per capita expenditure $33.

Background

From the end of the 4th millennium BC Nubia (now northern Sudan) periodically came under Egyptian rule, and it was part of the kingdom of Cush from the 11th century BC to the 4th century AD. Christian missionaries converted The Sudan's three principal kingdoms during the 6th century AD; these black Christian kingdoms coexisted with their Muslim Arab neighbors

in Egypt for centuries, until the influx of Arab immigrants brought about their collapse in the 13th–15th centuries. Egypt had conquered all of The Sudan by 1874 and encouraged British interference in the region; this aroused Muslim opposition and led to the revolt of al-Mahdi, who captured Khartoum in 1885 and established a Muslim theocracy in The Sudan that lasted until 1898, when his forces were defeated by the British. The British ruled the country, generally in partnership with Egypt, until The Sudan achieved independence in 1956. Since then the country has fluctuated between ineffective parliamentary government and unstable military rule. The non-Muslim population of the south has engaged in ongoing rebellion against the Muslim-controlled government of the north, leading to famines and the displacement of some four million people.

Recent Developments

In January 2005, one year after the Sudanese government and the rebels in the southern part of the country agreed on a plan for dividing oil revenues, the two parties signed a peace treaty ending one of the longest and most vicious civil wars in Africa's history, a conflict that resulted in the deaths of more than two million people. By April international donors had pledged some $4.5 billion in aid to rebuild the southern region. No such settlement or aid was at hand for the conflict in The Sudan's western Darfur region, however, where an estimated 180,000 people had died in the 18-month period ending with February 2005. With most of its troops engaged in the war in the south, the government had enlisted and armed Arab militias to quell the revolt of black subsistence farmers that had begun in February 2003. Aid agencies complained that obstacles were impeding their access to refugee camps, but the government insisted that it was committed to securing a just and peaceful settlement of the conflict. In March 2005 the UN Security Council voted to deploy a 10,000-strong force of peacekeepers in The Sudan as well as to send persons suspected of war crimes in Darfur to the International Criminal Court, a proposal the Sudanese government rejected.

Internet resources: <www.sudan.net>.

Suriname

Official name: Republiek Suriname (Republic of Suriname). **Form of government:** multiparty republic with one legislative house (National Assembly [51]). **Head of state and government:** President Ronald Venetiaan (from 2000), assisted by Vice President Jules Rattankoemar Ajodhia (from 2000). **Capital:** Paramaribo. **Official language:** Dutch. **Official religion:** none. **Monetary unit:** 1 Suriname dollar (SRD) = 100 cents; valuation (7 Jul 2005) $1 = SRD 2.74. In January 2004 the Suriname dollar (SRD) replaced the Suriname guilder (Sf); Sf 1,000 = SRD 1.

Demography

Area: 63,251 sq mi, 163,820 sq km. **Population** (2004): 437,000. **Density** (2004): persons per sq mi 6.9, persons per sq km 2.7. **Urban** (2001): 74.8%.

---

1 metric ton = about 1.1 short tons; 1 kilometer = 0.6 mi (statute); 1 metric ton-km cargo = about 0.68 short ton-mi cargo; c.i.f.: cost, insurance, and freight; f.o.b.: free on board

Caribbean Sea
Atlantic Ocean
Pacific Ocean

Sex distribution (2000): male 50.77%; female 49.23%. Age breakdown (2000): under 15, 32.1%; 15–29, 27.2%; 30–44, 22.7%; 45–59, 9.9%; 60–74, 6.4%; 75 and over, 1.7%. Ethnic composition (1999): Indo-Pakistani 37.0%; Suriname Creole 31.0%; Javanese 15.0%; Bush Negro 10.0%; Amerindian 2.5%; Chinese 2.0%; white 1.0%; other 1.5%. Religious affiliation (2000): Christian 50.4%, of which Roman Catholic 22.3%, Protestant (mostly Moravian) 17.1%, unaffiliated/other Christian 11.0%; Hindu 17.8%; Muslim 13.9%; nonreligious 4.8%; Spiritists (including followers of Voodoo) 3.5%; traditional beliefs 1.9%; other 7.7%. Major cities (1996/1997): Paramaribo 222,800 (urban agglomeration 289,000); Lelydorp 15,600; Nieuw Nickerie 11,100; Mungo (Moengo) 6,800; Meerzorg 6,600. Location: northern South America, bordering the North Atlantic Ocean, French Guiana, Brazil, and Guyana.

Vital statistics

Birth rate per 1,000 population (2003): 19.4 (world avg. 21.3). Death rate per 1,000 population (2003): 6.8 (world avg. 9.1). Natural increase rate per 1,000 population (2003): 12.6 (world avg. 12.2). Total fertility rate (avg. births per childbearing woman; 2003): 2.4. Marriage rate per 1,000 population (2000): 5.3. Divorce rate per 1,000 population (2000): 0.9. Life expectancy at birth (2003): male 66.8 years; female 71.8 years.

National economy

Budget (1998). Revenue: Sf 137,200,000,000 (indirect taxes 40.4%; direct taxes 36.2%; bauxite levy 10.9%; grants 12.5%). Expenditures: Sf 188,000,-000,000 (current expenditures 90.2%, of which wages and salaries 39.1%, transfers 11.7%, debt service 1.3%; capital expenditures 9.8%). Public debt (external, outstanding; 1996): $216,500,000. Production (metric tons except as noted). Agriculture, forestry, fishing (2002): rice 192,000, sugarcane 120,000, bananas 43,000; livestock (number of live animals) 136,000 cattle, 24,000 pigs, 2,200,000 chickens; roundwood (2002) 200,000 cu m; fish catch (2001) 18,915, of which shrimp 7,390. Mining and quarrying (2001): bauxite 4,512,000; alumina

1,900,000; gold 300 kg (recorded production; unrecorded production may be as high as 30,000 kg). Manufacturing (value of production at factor cost in Sf; 1993): food products 992,000,000; beverages 558,000,000; tobacco 369,000,000. Energy production (consumption): electricity (kW-hr; 2000) 1,648,000,000 (1,648,000,000); crude petroleum (barrels; 2001) 5,000,000 ([2000] 3,000,000); petroleum products (2000; production of petroleum products began in 2000; data not available) none (478,000). Population economically active (1999): total 84,646; activity rate of total population 19.8% (participation rates: [1992; districts of Wanica and Paramaribo only] ages 15–64, 56.0%; female 34.4%; unemployed 14.0%). Gross national product (2003): $841,000,000 ($1,940 per capita). Households. Average household size (1998) 4.8. Tourism (2002): receipts from visitors $3,000,000; expenditures by nationals abroad $10,000,000. Land use as % of total land area (2000): in temporary crops 0.4%, in permanent crops 0.06%, in pasture 0.1%; overall forest area 90.5%.

Foreign trade

Imports (2000-c.i.f.): $526,500,000 (nonelectrical machinery 22.5%, food products 13.4%, road vehicles 13.2%, chemicals and chemical products 10.2%, refined petroleum 5.8%). Major import sources (2001): US 34%; The Netherlands 17%; Trinidad and Tobago 13%; Netherlands Antilles 8%; Japan 5%. Exports (2000-f.o.b.): $514,000,000 (alumina 62.1%, gold 11.4%, crustaceans and mollusks 7.0%, crude petroleum 4.3%, refined petroleum 2.3%, rice 2.2%). Major export destinations (2001): US 26%; Norway 16%; France 10%; The Netherlands 9%; Canada 7%.

Transport and communications

Transport. Railroads (1997; all private): length 301 km; passengers, not applicable. Roads (1996): total length 4,530 km (paved 26%). Vehicles (2000): passenger cars 61,365; trucks and buses 23,220. Air transport (1998): passenger-km 1,072,000,000; metric ton-km cargo 127,000,000; airports with scheduled flights 1. Communications, in total units (units per 1,000 persons). Daily newspaper circulation (1996): 50,000 (122); radios (1997): 300,000 (728); televisions (2000): 109,000 (253); telephone main lines (2003): 79,800 (152); cellular telephone subscribers (2003): 168,100 (320); personal computers (2001): 20,000 (45); Internet users (2002): 20,000 (42).

Education and health

Literacy (2001): total population age 15 and over literate 92.2%; males literate 93.6%; females literate 90.7%. Health: physicians (1999) 213 (1 per 2,000 persons); hospital beds (1998) 1,449 (1 per 288 persons); infant mortality rate per 1,000 live births (2003) 24.7. Food (2001): daily per capita caloric intake 2,643 (vegetable products 86%, animal products 14%); 117% of FAO recommended minimum.

Military

Total active duty personnel (2003): 1,840 (army 76.1%, navy 13.0%, air force 10.9%). Military expenditure as percentage of GNP (1999): 1.8% (world 2.4%); per capita expenditure $33.

Background

Suriname was inhabited by various native peoples prior to European settlement. Spanish explorers claimed it in 1593, but the Dutch began to settle there in 1602, followed by the English in 1651. It was ceded to the Dutch in 1667, and in 1682 the Dutch West India Co. introduced coffee and sugarcane plantations and African slaves to cultivate them. Slavery was abolished in 1863, and indentured servants were brought from China, Java, and India to work the plantations, adding to the population mix. Except for brief interludes of British rule (1799–1802, 1804–15), it remained a Dutch colony. It gained internal autonomy in 1954 and independence in 1975. A military coup in 1980 ended civilian control until the electorate approved a new constitution in 1987. Military control resumed after a coup in 1990. Elections were held in 1991, followed by a resumption of democratic government.

Recent Developments

In 2004 Suriname enjoyed another good year, with growth near 5%. This was the second buoyant year in a row after prolonged periods of maladministration that had followed the civil conflict of the 1980s. A flourishing underground economy, a Chinese-backed palm-oil project, and a new gold mine, funded by Canadian entrepreneurs, fueled the economy, along with steady returns from the staple bauxite industry.

Internet resources: <www.parbo.com/tourism>.

Swaziland

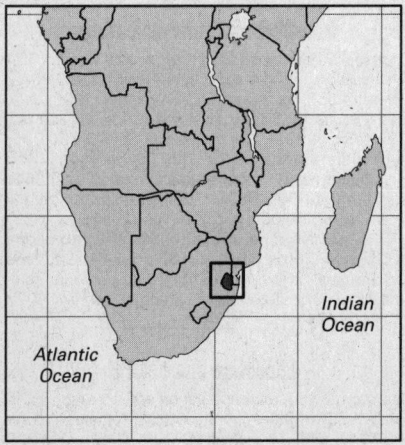

Indian Ocean

Atlantic Ocean

Official name: Umbuso weSwatini (Swazi); Kingdom of Swaziland (English). **Form of government:** constitutional monarchy with two legislative houses (Senate [30; includes 20 nonelective seats]; House of Assembly [65; includes 10 nonelective seats]). **Head of state and government:** King Mswati III (from 1986), assisted by Prime Minister Absalom Themba Dlamini (from 2003). **Capitals:** Mbabane (administrative and judicial); Lozitha and Ludzidzini (royal); Lobamba (legislative). **Official languages:** Swati (Swazi); English. **Official religion:** none. **Monetary unit:** 1 lilangeni (plural emalangeni [E]; at par with the South African rand) = 100 cents; valuation (7 Jul 2005) $1 = E 6.85.

Demography

Area: 6,704 sq mi, 17,364 sq km. **Population** (2004): 1,083,000. **Density** (2004): persons per sq mi 161.5; persons per sq km 62.4. **Urban** (2003): 23.5%. **Sex distribution** (2003): male 49.80%; female 50.20%. **Age breakdown** (2003): under 15, 41.4%; 15–29, 30.7%; 30–44, 14.7%; 45–59, 7.9%; 60–74, 4.3%; 75 and over, 1.0%. **Ethnic composition** (2000): Swazi 82.3%; Zulu 9.6%; Tsonga 2.3%; Afrikaner 1.4%; mixed (black-white) 1.0%; other 3.4%. **Religious affiliation** (2000): Christian 67.5%, of which African indigenous 45.6%, Protestant 15.2%, Roman Catholic 5.4%; traditional beliefs 12.2%; other (mostly unaffiliated Christian) 20.3%. **Major cities** (1997): Mbabane 57,992; Manzini 25,571 (urban agglomeration 78,734); Big Bend 9,374; Mhlume 7,661; Malkerns 7,400. **Location:** southern Africa, bordering South Africa and Mozambique.

Vital statistics

Birth rate per 1,000 population (2003): 28.6 (world avg. 21.3). **Death rate** per 1,000 population (2003): 23.1 (world avg. 9.1). **Natural increase rate** per 1,000 population (2003): 5.5 (world avg. 12.2). **Total fertility rate** (avg. births per childbearing woman; 2003): 3.8. **Life expectancy** at birth (2003): male 41.0 years; female 38.9 years. **Adult population** (ages 15–49) **living with HIV** (2004): 38.8% (world avg. 1.1%).

National economy

Budget (2001–02). *Revenue:* E 3,094,000,000 (receipts from Customs Union of Southern Africa 48.6%; tax on income and profits 23.4%; sales tax 13.2%; foreign-aid grants 3.9%). *Expenditures:* E 3,409,000,000 (current expenditure 74.4%; development expenditure 25.4%; net lending 0.2%). **Gross national product** (2003): $1,492,000,000 ($1,350 per capita). **Population economically active** (2001): total 392,000; activity rate of total population 39.3% (unemployed 31.6%). **Public debt** (external, outstanding; 2002): $273,700,000. **Land use** as % of total land area (2000): in temporary crops 10.3%, in permanent crops 0.7%, in pasture 69.8%; overall forest area 30.3%. **Production** (metric tons except as noted). *Agriculture, forestry, fishing* (2002): sugarcane 4,000,000, corn (maize) 85,000, grapefruit and pomelo 37,000; livestock (number of live animals) 615,000 cattle, 422,000 goats; roundwood (2002) 890,000 cu m; fish catch (2001) 142. *Mining and quarrying* (2001): stone 350,000 cu m. *Manufacturing* (value added in $'000; 1994): food and beverages 244,000, of which beverage processing 153,000; paper and paper products 35,000; textiles 19,000. *Energy production (consumption):* electricity (kW-hr; 2000) 265,000,000 (702,000,000); coal (2001) 380,000 (n.a.). **Household income and expenditure.** Average household size (1986) 5.7; annual income per household (1985) E 332; sources of income (1985): wages and salaries 44.4%, self-employment 22.2%, transfers 12.2%, other 21.2%; expenditure (1985): food and beverages 33.5%, rent and fuel 13.4%, household durable goods 12.8%, transportation and communications 8.8%, clothing and footwear 6.0%, recreation 3.3%. **Tourism** (2002): receipts $26,000,000; expenditures $33,000,000.

Foreign trade

Imports (2001-f.o.b. in balance of trade and c.i.f. in commodities and trading partners): $832,000,000 (food and live animals 15.6%; machinery and apparatus 13.6%; chemicals and chemical products 13.2%; road vehicles 9.5%; refined petroleum 9.2%). *Major import sources:* South Africa 94.5%; Hong Kong 1.0%; Japan 0.9%. **Exports** (2001): $678,000,-000 (soft drink [including sugar and fruit juice] concentrates 38%; sugar 14%; apparel and clothing accessories 12%; wood pulp 9%). *Major export destinations:* South Africa 78.0%; Mozambique 4.6%; US 4.0%.

Transport and communications

Transport. *Railroads* (2001; scheduled passenger train service was terminated in January 2001): route length 301 km; metric ton-km cargo 700,000,000. *Roads* (1996): total length 3,810 km (paved 29%). *Vehicles* (1998): passenger cars 34,064; trucks and buses 35,030. *Air transport:* (1998) passenger-km 43,000,000; (1995) metric ton-km cargo 127,000; airports (1997) with scheduled flights 1. **Communications,** in total units (units per 1,000 persons). Daily newspaper circulation (2000): 27,100 (26); radios (2000): 169,000 (162); televisions (2000): 124,000 (110); telephone main lines (2003): 46,200 (44); cellular telephone subscribers (2003): 88,000 (84); personal computers (2003): 30,000 (29); Internet users (2003): 27,000 (26).

Education and health

Educational attainment (1986). Percentage of population age 25 and over having: no formal schooling 42.1%; some primary education 23.9%; complete primary 10.5%; some secondary 19.2%; complete secondary and higher 4.3%. **Literacy** (2000): total population age 15 and over literate 79.6%; males literate 80.8%; females literate 78.6%. **Health:** physicians (1996) 148 (1 per 6,663 persons); hospital beds (2000; excludes National Psychiatric Hospital) 1,570 (1 per 665 persons); infant mortality rate per 1,000 live births (2003) 67.4. **Food** (2001): daily per capita caloric intake 2,593 (vegetable products 85%, animal products 15%); 112% of FAO recommended minimum.

Military

Total active duty personnel (2003): 3,500 troops. **Military expenditure as percentage of GNP** (1999): 1.5% (world 2.4%); per capita expenditure $20.

Background

Stone tools and rock paintings indicate prehistoric habitation in the region, but it was not settled until the Bantu-speaking Swazi people migrated there in the 18th century and established the nucleus of the Swazi nation. The British gained control in the 19th century after the Swazi king sought their aid against the Zulus. Following the South African War, the British governor of Transvaal administered Swaziland; his powers were transferred to the British high commissioner in 1906. In 1949 the British rejected the Union of South Africa's request to control Swaziland. The country gained limited self-government in 1963 and achieved independence in 1968. In the 1970s new constitutions were framed based on the supreme authority of the king and traditional tribal government. During the 1990s forces demanding democracy arose, but the kingdom remained in place.

Recent Developments

In 2004–05 local and international attention focused on the dreadful statistics that defined life for the people of Swaziland: 70% of the population living on an income of less than $1 a day; at almost 40%, the highest rate of HIV/AIDS infection in the world; and a continuing drought. Further, observers condemned the excessive lifestyle of the country's king, Mswati III, who in April 2004 arranged a birthday party for himself and 10,000 guests at the national football stadium at an estimated cost of $600,000. In late 2004 he bought himself a half-million-dollar car and then, two months later, 10 new BMW 5-Series autos for his wives.

Internet resources: <www.mintour.gov.sz>.

Sweden

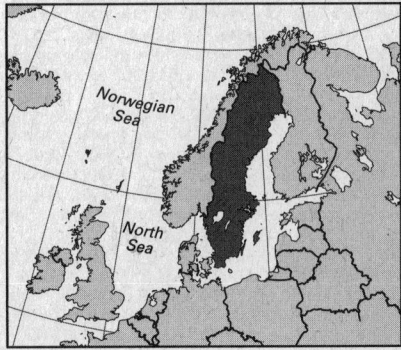

Official name: Konungariket Sverige (Kingdom of Sweden). **Form of government:** constitutional monarchy and parliamentary state with one legislative house (Parliament [349]). **Chief of state:** King Carl XVI Gustaf (from 1973). **Head of government:** Prime Minister Göran Persson (from 1996). **Capital:** Stockholm. **Official language:** Swedish. **Official religion:** none. **Monetary unit:** 1 Swedish krona (SKr) = 100 ore; valuation (7 Jul 2005) $1 = SKr 7.89.

Demography

Area: 173,860 sq mi, 450,295 sq km. **Population** (2004): 8,991,000. **Density** (2004): persons per sq mi 53.7, persons per sq km 20.4. **Urban** (2001): 81.2%. **Sex distribution** (2002): male 49.52%; female 50.48%. **Age breakdown** (2002): under 15, 18.2%; 15–29, 18.1%; 30–44, 20.8%; 45–59, 20.6%; 60–74, 13.4%; 75 and over, 8.9%. **Ethnic composition** (2002; by place of birth): Swedish

88.5%; other European 6.9%, of which Finnish 2.2%, Serb/Montenegrin 0.8%, Bosniac 0.6%; Asian 3.0%, of which Iranian 0.6%; African 0.6%; other 1.0%. **Religious affiliation** (1999): Church of Sweden 86.5% (about 30% nonpracticing); Muslim 2.3%; Roman Catholic 1.8%; Pentecostal 1.1%; other 8.3%. **Major cities** (2003): Stockholm 758,148; Göteborg 474,921; Malmö 265,481; Uppsala 179,673; Linköping 135,066. **Location:** northern Europe, bordering Finland, the Gulf of Bothnia, the Baltic Sea, and Norway.

Vital statistics

Birth rate per 1,000 population (2002): 10.7 (world avg. 21.3); legitimate (2001) 44.5%. **Death rate** per 1,000 population (2002): 10.6 (world avg. 9.1). **Natural increase rate** per 1,000 population (2002): 0.1 (world avg. 12.2). **Total fertility rate** (avg. births per childbearing woman; 2002): 1.6. **Marriage rate** per 1,000 population (2002): 4.3. **Divorce rate** per 1,000 population (2002): 2.4. **Life expectancy** at birth (2003): male 78.1 years; female 82.5 years.

National economy

Budget (2001). *Revenue:* SKr 755,126,000,000 (value-added and excise taxes 36.0%, social security 31.6%, income and capital gains taxes 17.9%, property taxes 5.3%). *Expenditures:* SKr 716,379,-000,000 (health and social affairs 30.6%, debt service 11.3%, defense 6.3%, education 5.7%). **Public debt** (2004): $170,915,000,000. **Production** (metric tons except as noted). *Agriculture, forestry, fishing* (2002): sugar beets 2,800,000, wheat 2,117,-000, barley 1,778,500; livestock (number of live animals) 1,882,000 pigs, 1,637,000 cattle, 427,-000 sheep; roundwood (2002) 67,500,000 cu m; fish catch (2001) 318,600. *Mining and quarrying* (2001): iron ore 19,486,000; zinc (metal content) 156,300; copper (metal content) 74,300. *Manufacturing* (value added in $'000,000; 1999): telecommunications equipment, electronics 9,200; nonelectrical machinery and apparatus 6,100; road vehicles 6,000. *Energy production (consumption):* electricity (kW-hr; 2002) 143,136,000,000 ([2000] 152,193,-000,000); coal (2000) none (3,057,000); crude petroleum (barrels; 2000) none (149,000,000); petroleum products (2000) 18,985,000 (12,227,000); natural gas (cu m; 2000) none (833,083,000). **Household income and expenditure.** Average household size (2000) 2.2; average annual disposable income per household (2000) SKr 239,000; sources of income (1996): wages and salaries 59.2%, transfer payments 26.1%, other 14.7%; expenditure (1996): housing 27.6%, transportation and communications 17.1%, food and beverages 16.5%, recreation 9.1%, energy 5.8%. **Tourism** (2002): receipts $4,233,000,000; expenditures $6,816,000,000. **Gross national product** (at current market prices; 2003): $258,319,000,000 ($28,840 per capita). **Population economically active** (2001): total 4,414,000; activity rate of total population 49.5% (participation rates: ages 16–64 [2000] 77.9%; female 47.8%; unemployed 4.0%). **Land use** as % of total land area (2000): in temporary crops 6.6%, in permanent crops 0.01%, in pasture 10.9%; overall forest area 65.9%.

Foreign trade

Imports (2001-c.i.f.): SKr 656,200,000,000 (nonelectrical machinery and apparatus 16.6%; electrical machinery and apparatus 14.0%; chemicals and chemical products 10.8%; road vehicles 9.3%; crude and refined petroleum 7.8%). *Major import sources* (2002): Germany 18.5%; Denmark 8.8%; UK 8.6%; Norway 8.2%; The Netherlands 6.7%. **Exports** (2001-f.o.b.): SKr 783,500,000,000 (nonelectrical machinery and apparatus 16.9%; road vehicles 12.1%; telecommunications equipment, electronics 9.3%; paper and paper products 8.5%; medicines and pharmaceuticals 5.5%; iron and steel 5.0%). *Major export destinations* (2002): US 11.6%; Germany 10.1%; Norway 9.0%; UK 8.2%; Denmark 5.9%.

Transport and communications

Transport. *Railroads* (2001): length 11,255 km; (2000) passenger-km 8,251,000,000; metric ton-km cargo 20,088,000,000. *Roads* (2002): total length 422,000 km (public 50.2%). *Vehicles* (2001): passenger cars 4,019,000; trucks and buses 410,000. *Air transport* (2002; includes SAS international and domestic traffic applicable to Sweden): passenger-km 10,896,000; metric ton-km cargo 266,676,000; airports (2001) 49. **Communications,** in total units (units per 1,000 persons). Daily newspaper circulation (2000): 3,830,000 (432); radios (2000): 8,270,000 (932); televisions (2000): 5,090,000 (574); telephone main lines (2002): 6,579,000 (736); cellular telephone subscribers (2002): 7,949,000 (889); personal computers (2002): 5,556,000 (621); Internet users (2002): 5,125,000 (573).

Education and health

Educational attainment (2002). Percentage of population age 16–74 having: lower secondary education 27%; incomplete or complete upper secondary education 45%; up to 3 years postsecondary 12%; 3 years or more postsecondary 14%; unknown 2%. **Literacy** (2002): virtually 100%. **Health** (2001): physicians 25,200 (1 per 354 persons); hospital beds 29,122 (1 per 306 persons); infant mortality rate per 1,000 live births (2002) 3.3. **Food** (2001): daily per capita caloric intake 3,164 (vegetable 70%, animal 30%); 118% of FAO recommended minimum.

Military

Total active duty personnel (2003): 27,600 (army 50.0%, navy 28.6%, air force 21.4%). **Military expenditure as percentage of GNP** (1999): 2.3% (world 2.4%); per capita expenditure $601.

Background

The first inhabitants of Sweden were apparently hunters who crossed the land bridge from Europe c. 9000 BC. During the Viking era (9th–10th centuries) the Swedes controlled river trade in eastern Europe between the Baltic Sea and the Black Sea and also raided western European lands. Sweden was loosely united and Christianized in the 11th–12th centuries. It conquered the Finns in the 12th century and in the

---

1 metric ton = about 1.1 short tons; 1 kilometer = 0.6 mi (statute); 1 metric ton-km cargo = about 0.68 short ton-mi cargo; c.i.f.: cost, insurance, and freight; f.o.b.: free on board

14th united with Norway and Denmark under a single monarchy. It broke away in 1523 under Gustav I Vasa. In the 17th century it emerged as a great European power in the Baltic region, but its dominance declined after its defeat in the Second Northern War (1700–21). Sweden became a constitutional monarchy in 1809 and united with Norway 1814–1905; it acknowledged Norwegian independence in 1905. It maintained its neutrality during both world wars. It was a charter member of the UN but abstained from membership in the European Union (EU) until the 1990s and in NATO altogether. A new constitution drafted in 1975 reduced the monarch's role to that of ceremonial head of state. In 1997 it decided to begin the controversial shutdown of its nuclear power industry.

Recent Developments

The Swedish economy performed well in 2004, but the Social Democratic government under Prime Minister Göran Persson failed to reap the political benefits as unemployment and problems in public services dominated the news. Sweden was severely affected by the December tsunami disaster in Southeast Asia. A large number of Swedes were vacationing in the area, and by mid-May 2005 the confirmed death toll had reached 428, with another 116 still missing.

Internet resources: <www.visit-sweden.com>.

Switzerland

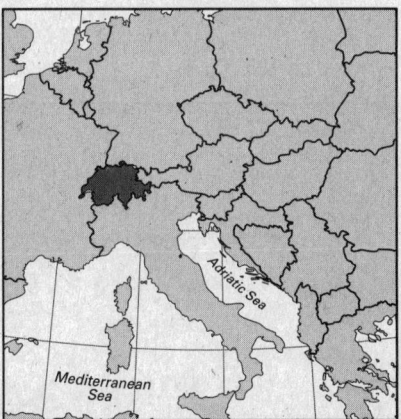

Official name: Confédération Suisse (French); Schweizerische Eidgenossenschaft (German); Confederazione Svizzera (Italian); Confederaziun Svizra (Romansh) (Swiss Confederation). Form of government: federal state with two legislative houses (Council of States [46]; National Council [200]). Head of state and government: President of the Federal Council Samuel Schmid (from 1 Jan 2005). Capitals: Bern (administrative); Lausanne (judicial). Official languages: French; German; Italian; Romansh (locally). Official religion: none. Monetary unit: 1 Swiss Franc (Sw F) = 100 centimes; valuation (7 Jul 2005) $1 = Sw F 1.30.

Demography

Area: 15,940 sq mi, 41,284 sq km. Population (2004): 7,392,000. Density (2004): persons per sq mi 463.7, persons per sq km 179.1. Urban (2002): 67.8%. Sex distribution (2003): male 48.90%; female 51.10%. Age breakdown (2003): under 15, 16.9%; 15–29, 18.0%; 30–44, 24.2%; 45–59, 20.2%; 60–74, 13.3%; 75 and over, 7.4%. National composition (2001): Swiss 80.2%; Yugoslav 4.8%; Italian 4.5%; Portuguese 1.9%; German 1.5%; Spanish 1.2%; other 5.9%. Religious affiliation (2000): Roman Catholic 41.8%; Protestant 35.2%; Muslim 4.3%; Orthodox 1.8%; Jewish 0.2%; nonreligious 11.1%; other 5.6%. Major urban agglomerations (2003): Zürich 978,300; Geneva 476,100; Basel 403,800; Bern 321,600; Lausanne 294,500. Location: central Europe, bordering Germany, Austria, Liechtenstein, Italy, and France.

Vital statistics

Birth rate per 1,000 population (2003): 9.8 (world avg. 21.3); legitimate 87.6%. Death rate per 1,000 population (2003): 8.6 (world avg. 9.1). Natural increase rate per 1,000 population (2003): 1.2 (world avg. 12.2). Total fertility rate (avg. births per childbearing woman; 2002): 1.4. Marriage rate per 1,000 population (2003): 5.5. Divorce rate per 1,000 population (2003): 2.2. Life expectancy at birth (2003): male 77.7 years; female 83.0 years.

National economy

Budget (2002). Revenue: Sw F 130,595,000,000 (1999; taxes on income and profits 51.1%, taxes on goods and services 20.1%, property taxes 1.5%). Expenditures: Sw F 132,989,000,000 (1999; social security 19.4%, education 18.4%, economic affairs 14.0%, health 12.6%, interest 8.4%, defense 4.5%). National debt (end of year; 2002): Sw F 122,366,000,000. Tourism (2002): receipts from visitors $7,628,000,000; expenditures by nationals abroad $6,427,000,000. Production (metric tons except as noted). Agriculture, forestry, fishing (2002): sugar beets 1,100,000; cow's milk (2001) 626,000; wheat 584,000; livestock (number of live animals) 1,593,000 cattle, 1,536,000 pigs; roundwood (2002) 4,344,000 cu m; fish catch (2001) 2,850. Mining (2003): salt 300,000; cut and polished diamond exports (1998): $1,340,000,000. Manufacturing (value added in $'000,000; 2001): chemicals and chemical products 7,363; nonelectrical machinery 7,067; professional and scientific equipment 6,233. Energy production (consumption): electricity (kW-hr; 2002) 65,011,000,000 (60,503,000,000); coal (2000) none (156,000); crude petroleum (barrels; 2000) none (33,900,000); petroleum products (2000) 4,861,000 (10,181,000); natural gas (cu m; 2000) negligible (2,971,000,000). Gross national product (2003): $292,892,000,000 ($39,880 per capita). Population economically active (2002): total 4,177,000 (includes 1,058,000 foreign workers); activity rate of total population 56.2% (participation rates: ages 15 and over, 68.7%; female 44.5%; unemployed 2.5%). Household income and expenditure (2000). Average household size 2.4; average gross income per household Sw F 104,352; sources of income (2000): work 72.4%, transfers 22.3%; expenditure (2001): housing and energy 27.5%, food and nonalcoholic beverages 13.5%, transportation

11.0%, recreation 10.5%, hotels and cafes 10.0%. **Land use** as % of total land area (2000): in temporary crops 10.4%, in permanent crops 0.6%, in pasture 28.9%; overall forest area 30.3%.

Foreign trade

Imports (2002-c.i.f.): Sw F 123,125,000,000 (chemical products 22.1%, machinery 21.1%, vehicles 10.4%, food products 8.0%). *Major import sources* (2003): Germany 33.3%; Italy 11.1%; France 11.1%; US 4.4%; UK 4.0%. **Exports** (2002-f.o.b.): Sw F 130,380,000,000 (chemicals and chemical products 34.4%, machinery 24.3%, precision instruments, watches, jewelry 17.3%, fabricated metals 7.5%). *Major export destinations* (2003): Germany 21.2%; US 10.6%; France 8.8%; Italy 8.4%; UK 4.8%; Japan 3.9%.

Transport and communications

Transport. *Railroads:* length (2000) 5,062 km; passenger-km 14,665,000,000; metric ton-km cargo 9,112,000,000. *Roads* (2002): total length 71,192 km. *Vehicles* (2003): passenger cars 3,753,890; trucks and buses 292,329. *Air transport* (2003; Swiss airlines only): passenger-km 24,083,000,000; metric ton-km cargo 1,305,000,000; airports (1996) with scheduled flights 5. **Communications**, in total units (units per 1,000 persons). Daily newspaper circulation (2000): 2,650,000 (369); radios (2000): 7,200,000 (1,002); televisions (2000): 3,940,000 (548); telephone main lines (2002): 5,419,000 (744); cellular telephone subscribers (2003): 6,172,000 (843); personal computers (2002): 5,160,000 (709); Internet users (2002): 2,556,000 (351).

Education and health

Educational attainment (2000). Percentage of resident Swiss and resident alien population age 25–64 having: compulsory education 19.0%; secondary 56.8%; higher 24.2%. **Health** (2002): physicians 25,921 (1 per 281 persons); hospital beds (2001) 44,316 (1 per 163 persons); infant mortality rate per 1,000 live births 4.5. **Food** (2001): daily per capita caloric intake 3,440 (vegetable products 66%, animal products 34%); 129% of FAO recommended minimum.

Military

Total active duty personnel (2003): 3,300 (excludes 351,000 reservists). **Military expenditure as percentage of GNP** (1999): 1.2% (world 2.4%); per capita expenditure $469.

Background

The original inhabitants of Switzerland were the Helvetians, who were conquered by the Romans in the 1st century BC. Germanic tribes penetrated the region from the 3rd to the 6th century AD, and Muslim and Magyar raiders ventured in during the 10th century. It came under the Holy Roman Empire in the 11th century. In 1291 three cantons formed an anti-Habsburg league that became the nucleus of the Swiss Confederation. It was a center of the Reformation, which divided the confederation and led to a period of polit-

ical and religious conflict. The French organized Switzerland as the Helvetic Republic in 1798. In 1815 the Congress of Vienna recognized Swiss independence and guaranteed its neutrality. A new federal state was formed in 1848 with Bern as the capital. It remained neutral in both world wars and continued to guard this stance. With the formation of the European Union (EU), it took steps toward provisional association with the European economic area.

Recent Developments

As 10 new members joined the European Union on 1 May 2004, Switzerland remained resolutely outside the organization and protective of its independence. The EU and Switzerland in March signed a bilateral package to make it harder for EU citizens to evade domestic taxes by having a Swiss bank account. Switzerland agreed to impose taxes on deposits of EU citizens and to transfer the revenue in lump sums to the respective European nations. In return, Swiss citizens won the right to travel more freely in the EU. Switzerland's new justice minister, Christoph Blocher, an outspoken critic of the EU and the UN, had been named to the seven-member federal executive in December 2003 after his nationalist Swiss People's Party (SVP) made sweeping gains in the October 2003 general elections. His ministerial responsibilities were expected to give Blocher a pivotal role in the June 2005 referendum on the so-called Schengen/Dublin agreements on border controls. The presence of Blocher—a combative billionaire industrialist—crippled the consensus politics that had shaped cabinet decisions since 1959.

Internet resources: <www.myswitzerland.com>.

Syria

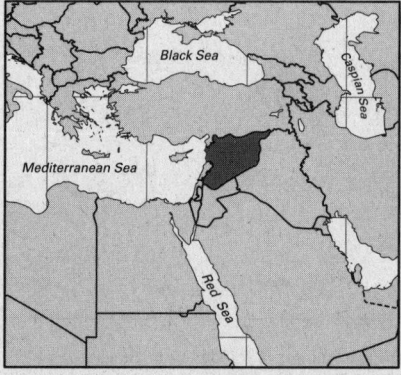

Official name: Al-Jumhuriyah al-‘Arabiyah al-Suriyah (Syrian Arab Republic). **Form of government:** unitary multiparty republic with one legislative house (People's Council [250]). **Head of state and government:** President Bashar al-Assad (from 2000), assisted by Prime Minister Muhammad Naji al-Otari (from 2003). **Capital:** Damascus. **Official language:** Arabic. **Official religion:** none, although Islam is the required religion

---

1 metric ton = about 1.1 short tons;　1 kilometer = 0.6 mi (statute);　1 metric ton-km cargo = about 0.68 short ton-mi cargo;　c.i.f.: cost, insurance, and freight;　f.o.b.: free on board

of the head of state and is the basis of the legal system. **Monetary unit:** 1 Syrian pound (LS) = 100 piastres; valuation (7 Jul 2005) $1 = LS 52.21.

Demography

Area (includes territory in the Golan Heights recognized internationally as part of Syria): 71,498 sq mi, 185,180 sq km. **Population** (2004): 18,017,000. **Density** (2004): persons per sq mi 252.0, persons per sq km 97.3. **Urban** (2001): 51.8%. **Sex distribution** (2001): male 51.15%; female 48.85%. **Age breakdown** (2001): under 15, 40.4%; 15–29, 30.1%; 30–44, 15.6%; 45–59, 8.8%; 60 and over, 5.1%. **Ethnic composition** (2000): Syrian Arab 74.9%; Bedouin Arab 7.4%; Kurd 7.3%; Palestinian Arab 3.9%; Armenian 2.7%; other 3.8%. **Religious affiliation** (1992): Muslim 86.0%, of which Sunni 74.0%, 'Alawite (Shi'i) 12.0%; Christian 5.5%; Druze 3.0%; other 5.5%. **Major cities:** Aleppo (2000) 2,229,000 (urban agglomeration); Damascus (2001) 2,195,000 (urban agglomeration); Homs (Hims) (2000) 811,000 (urban agglomeration); Latakia (1994) 306,535; Hamah (1994) 229,000. **Location:** the Middle East, bordering Turkey, Iraq, Jordan, Israel, Lebanon, and the Mediterranean Sea.

Vital statistics

Birth rate per 1,000 population (2003): 29.5 (world avg. 21.3). **Death rate** per 1,000 population (2003): 5.0 (world avg. 9.1). **Natural increase rate** per 1,000 population (2003): 24.5 (world avg. 12.2). **Total fertility rate** (avg. births per childbearing woman; 2003): 3.7. **Marriage rate** per 1,000 population (2000; Syrian Arabs only): 8.6. **Divorce rate** per 1,000 population (2000; Syrian Arabs only): 0.7. **Life expectancy** at birth (2003): male 68.2 years; female 70.7 years.

National economy

Budget (2000). *Revenue:* LS 275,400,000,000 (taxes 31.2%, revenue from loans 13.4%, transit duties 8.0%, other 47.4%). *Expenditures:* LS 275,400,-000,000 (current expenditures 52.1%, capital [development] expenditures 47.9%). **Public debt** (external, outstanding; 2002): $15,849,000,000. **Gross national product** (2003): $20,211,000,000 ($1,160 per capita). **Production** (metric tons except as noted). *Agriculture, forestry, fishing* (2002): wheat 4,755,000, sugar beets 1,481,000, olives 999,000; livestock (number of live animals) 13,497,000 sheep, 932,000 goats, 867,000 cattle; roundwood (2001) 50,400 cu m; fish catch (2001) 14,171. *Mining and quarrying* (2001): phosphate rock 2,043,000; gypsum 345,000; salt 106,000. *Manufacturing* (2000): cement 4,631,000; fertilizers 453,000; cottonseed cake 288,000. *Energy production (consumption):* electricity (kW-hr; 2000) 22,626,000,000 (23,946,-000,000); crude petroleum (barrels; 2002) 191,990,-000 ([2000] 88,342,000); petroleum products (2000) 11,351,000 (11,020,000); natural gas (cu m; 2001) 5,833,000,000 (5,833,000,000). **Population economically active** (2000): total 4,937,000; activity rate of total population 30.3% (participation rates: ages 15 and over, 50.9%; female 19.8%; unemployed 9.5%). **Households.** Average household size (2000): 6.0. **Tourism** (2002): receipts $1,366,000,000; expenditures (2001) $610,000,000. **Land use** as % of total land area (2000): in temporary crops 24.7%, in permanent crops 4.4%, in pasture 45.5%; overall forest area 2.5%.

Foreign trade

Imports (2000-c.i.f.): $3,815,000,000 (food 14.6%, of which cereals 4.9%; chemicals and chemical products 12.9%; nonelectrical machinery and equipment 10.9%; iron and steel 10.7%; textile yarn 7.5%). *Major import sources:* Germany 6.8%; US 6.8%; Italy 6.2%; Ukraine 6.2%; China 5.3%; Turkey 5.0%; South Korea 5.0%. **Exports** (2000-f.o.b.): $4,634,000,000 (crude petroleum 69.1%; refined petroleum 7.0%; raw cotton 4.1%; vegetables 2.9%; apparel and clothing accessories 2.8%). *Major export destinations:* Italy 32.0%; France 22.5%; Turkey 10.4%; Saudi Arabia 5.9%; Lebanon 4.1%.

Transport and communications

Transport. *Railroads* (2001; excludes length of Syrian part of railway opened in August 2000 linking Aleppo, Syria, and Mosul, Iraq): route length 2,676 km; passenger-km 304,000,000; metric ton-km cargo 1,491,000,000. *Roads* (2000): total length 44,575 km (paved 21%). *Vehicles* (2000): passenger cars 138,823; trucks and buses (1998) 282,664. *Air transport* (2001): passenger-km 1,626,950; metric ton-km cargo 15,357,000; airports with scheduled flights 5. **Communications,** in total units (units per 1,000 persons). Daily newspaper circulation (2000): 326,000 (20); radios (2000): 4,500,000 (276); televisions (2002): 3,094,000 (182); telephone main lines (2002): 2,099,300 (123); cellular telephone units (2002): 400,000 (24); personal computers (2002): 330,000 (19); Internet users (2002): 220,000 (13).

Education and health

Literacy (2000): percentage of population age 15 and over literate 74.4%; males literate 88.3%; females literate 60.5%. **Health** (2003): physicians 25,147 (1 per 699 persons); hospital beds 26,202 (1 per 671 persons); infant mortality rate per 1,000 live births (2003) 31.7. **Food** (2001): daily per capita caloric intake 3,038 (vegetable products 88%, animal products 12%); 123% of FAO recommended minimum.

Military

Total active duty personnel (2003): 319,000 (army 67.4%, navy 1.3%, air force 12.5%, air defense 18.8%); troops stationed in Lebanon (October 2003) 20,000. **Military expenditure as percentage of GNP** (1999): 7.0% (world 2.4%); per capita expenditure $280.

Did you know? Many scholars believe that Syria's capital, Damascus (colloquially al-Sham, "the northern" in relation to Arabia), may be the oldest continuously inhabited city in the world.

Background

Syria has been inhabited for several thousand years. From the 3rd millennium BC it was under the control variously of Sumerians, Akkadians, Amorites, Egyptians, Hittites, Assyrians, and Babylonians. In the 6th century BC it became part of the Persian Achaemenian dynasty, which fell to Alexander the Great in 330 BC. Seleucid rulers governed it from 301 BC to c. 164 BC; then Parthians and Nabataean Arabs divided the region. It flourished as a Roman province (64 BC–AD 300) and as part of the Byzantine Empire (300–634) until Muslims invaded and established control. It came under the Ottoman Empire in 1516, which held it, except for brief rules by Egypt, until the British invaded in World War I. After the war it became a French mandate; it achieved independence in 1945. It united with Egypt in the United Arab Republic (1958–61). During the Six-Day War (1967), it lost the Golan Heights to Israel. Syrian troops frequently clashed with Israeli troops in Lebanon during the 1980s and '90s. Hafez al-Assad's long and harsh regime was marked also by antagonism toward Syria's neighbors Turkey and Iraq.

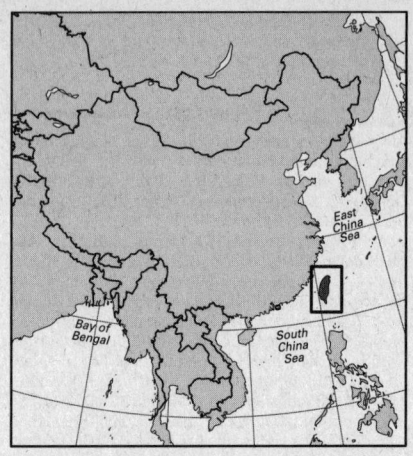

Recent Developments

The government of Syria, which had come under intense international scrutiny during 2003 for its close commercial and political relations with the Iraqi regime of Saddam Hussein, was feeling political pressure in early 2004 from a variety of directions. The international scrutiny, especially by the US, was seen to underlie the release in mid-February of 130 of the 3,000 political prisoners in Syrian prisons, but a month later the government broke up a human rights demonstration in front of the parliament building in Damascus and arrested at least seven activists. Also in mid-March, in cities in the north of the country, Syrian troops battled Kurdish protesters who apparently had drawn encouragement from the political successes of their kinsmen across the border in Iraq. A bomb attack and subsequent gunfight in the embassy district of Damascus on 27 April had the government at its wit's end. More international pressure on Syria followed the assassination of the former Lebanese prime minister in Beirut in February 2005, for which the Syrian regime was held at least indirectly responsible. Street demonstrations in Lebanon and diplomatic pressures convinced Pres. Bashar al-Assad that the time had come to withdraw some 10,000 Syrian troops that had been occupying Lebanon, and this was accomplished by May.

Internet resources: <www.syriatourism.org>.

Taiwan

Official name: Chung-hua Min-kuo (Republic of China) **Form of government:** multiparty republic with a Legislature (Legislative Yuan [225]). **Chief of state:** President Chen Shui-bian (from 2000). **Head of government:** Premier Frank Hsieh (from 1 Feb 2005). **Capital:** Taipei. **Official language:** Mandarin Chinese. **Official religion:** none. **Monetary unit:** 1 New Taiwan dollar (NT$) = 100 cents; valuation (7 Jul 2005) US$1 = NT$32.04.

Demography

Area: 13,972 sq mi, 36,188 sq km. **Population** (2004; includes Quemoy and Matsu groups): 22,640,000. **Density** (2004; includes Quemoy and Matsu groups): persons per sq mi 1,620.4, persons

per sq km 625.6. **Urban** (1991; excludes Quemoy and Matsu groups): 74.7%. **Sex distribution** (2003; includes Quemoy and Matsu groups): male 50.98%; female 49.02%. **Age breakdown** (2002; includes Quemoy and Matsu groups): under 15, 20.8%; 15–29, 24.9%; 30–44, 25.3%; 45–59, 16.7%; 60–74, 9.1%; 75 and over, 3.2%. **Ethnic composition** (1997): Han Chinese, Chinese mainland minorities, and others 98.2%; indigenous tribal peoples 1.8%, of which Ami 0.6%. **Religious affiliation** (1997): Buddhism 22.4%; Taoism 20.7%; I-kuan Tao 4.3%; Protestant 1.6%; Roman Catholic 1.4%; other Christian 0.3%; Muslim 0.2%; Baha'i 0.1%; other (mostly Christian folk-religionists) 49.0%. **Major cities** (2003): Taipei 2,638,065; Kao-hsiung 1,508,917; T'ai-chung 999,476; T'ai-nan 746,287; Chi-lung 391,657. **Location:** island between the East China Sea, the Philippine Sea, and the South China Sea north of the Philippines and southeast of mainland China.

Vital statistics

Birth rate per 1,000 population (2003): 10.1 (world avg. 21.3). **Death rate** per 1,000 population (2003): 5.8 (world avg. 9.1). **Natural increase rate** per 1,000 population (2003): 4.3 (world avg. 12.2). **Total fertility rate** (avg. births per childbearing woman; 2003): 1.2. **Marriage rate** per 1,000 population (2003): 7.6. **Divorce rate** per 1,000 population (2003): 2.9. **Life expectancy** at birth (2003): male 73.4 years; female 79.1 years.

National economy

Budget (1999). *Revenue:* NT$3,391,948,000,000 (income taxes 18.0%, business tax 9.1%, commodity tax 6.5%, land tax 6.4%, customs duties 4.6%). *Expenditures:* NT$3,371,702,000,000 (administration and defense 24.5%, education 19.4%). **Population economically active** (May 2003): total 10,022,000; activity rate of total population 44.4% (participation rates: over age 15 [December 2002], 57%; female [May 2003] 40.4%; unemployed [May 2003] 5.0%). **Production** (metric tons except as noted). *Agriculture,*

---

1 metric ton = about 1.1 short tons; 1 kilometer = 0.6 mi (statute); 1 metric ton-km cargo = about 0.68 short ton-mi cargo; c.i.f.: cost, insurance, and freight; f.o.b.: free on board

forestry, fishing (2000): sugarcane 2,894,000, rice 1,559,000, citrus fruits 440,382; livestock (number of live animals) 7,494,954 pigs, 202,491 goats, 161,700 cattle; timber 21,134 cu m; fish catch (2003) 1,498,983. *Mining and quarrying* (2000): marble 17,800,000. *Manufacturing* (2002): cement 19,228,026; steel ingots 18,240,256; paperboard 3,274,932. *Energy production (consumption):* electricity (kW-hr; 2002) 165,901,000,000 (151,193,-000,000); coal (2001) none (48,000,000); crude petroleum (barrels; 2002) 349,000 (360,000,000); natural gas (cu m; 2001) 918,000,000 (8,264,000,-000). **Tourism** (2002): receipts from visitors US$4,584,000,000; expenditures by nationals abroad US$6,956,000,000. **Gross national product** (2002): US$283,375,000,000 (US$12,570 per capita). **Household income and expenditure** (1999). Average household size (2003) 3.2; income per household NT$1,181,082; expenditure: food, beverages, and tobacco 25.1%, rent, fuel, and power 24.9%, education and recreation 13.0%, transportation 11.1%, health care 11.0%, clothing 4.1%. **Land use** as % of total land area (2001): in temporary crops 16.1%, in permanent crops 6.6%, in pasture 0.3%; overall forest area 58.1%.

Foreign trade

Imports (2002-c.i.f.): US$112,591,000,000 (electronic machinery 28.5%, nonelectrical machinery 16.0%, minerals 11.2%, chemicals 10.1%, metals and metal products 8.2%, precision instruments, clocks, watches, and musical instruments 5.8%). *Major import sources:* Japan 24.2%; US 16.1%; South Korea 6.8%; Germany 3.9%; Malaysia 3.7%. **Exports** (2002-f.o.b.): US$130,641,000,000 (nonelectrical machinery, electrical machinery, and electronics 57.4%, textile products 10.0%, plastic articles 5.9%, transportation equipment 3.7%). *Major export destinations:* Hong Kong 23.6%; US 20.5%; Japan 9.2%; Singapore 3.2%; Germany 2.9%.

Transport and communications

Transport. *Railroads* (2002; Taiwan Railway Administration only): route length 1,119 km; passenger-km 9,666,000,000, metric ton-km cargo 919,000,000. *Roads* (2002): total length 20,816 km (excludes urban). *Vehicles* (2002): passenger cars 4,989,000; trucks and buses 882,000. *Air transport* (1998): passenger-km 39,218,000,000; metric ton-km cargo 4,129,300,000; airports (1996) 13. **Communications**, in total units (units per 1,000 persons). Radios (1996): 8,620,000 (402); televisions (1999): 9,200,000 (418); telephone main lines (2003): 13,355,000 (590); cellular telephone subscribers (2003): 25,089,600 (1,108); personal computers (2002): 8,887,000 (396); Internet users (2003): 8,830,000 (390).

Education and health

Educational attainment (1999). Percentage of population age 25 and over having: no formal schooling 7.0%; less than complete primary education 6.3%; primary 21.3%; incomplete secondary 25.7%; secondary 21.8%; some college 10.4%; higher 7.5%. **Literacy** (1999): population age 15 and over literate 16,414,896 (94.6%); males literate 8,641,549 (97.6%); females literate 7,773,347 (91.4%). **Health** (2001): physicians 30,562 (1 per 731 persons); hospital beds 127,676 (1 per 175 persons); infant mortality rate per 1,000 live births (2003) 5.3.

Military

Total active duty personnel (2002): 290,000 (army 69.0%, navy 15.5%, air force 15.5%). **Military expenditure as percentage of GNP** (1999): 5.2% (world 2.4%); per capita expenditure US$690.

Background

Known to the Chinese as early as the 7th century, Taiwan was widely settled by them early in the 17th century. In 1646 the Dutch seized control of the island, only to be ousted in 1661 by a large influx of Chinese refugees from the Ming Dynasty. Taiwan fell to the Manchus in 1683 and was not open to Europeans again until 1858. In 1895 it was ceded to Japan following the Sino-Japanese War. A Japanese military center in World War II, it was frequently bombed by US planes. After Japan's defeat it was returned to China, which was then governed by the Nationalists. When the Communists took over mainland China in 1949, the Nationalist government fled to Taiwan and made it their seat of government, with Gen. Chiang Kai-shek as president. In 1954 he and the US signed a mutual defense treaty, and Taiwan received US support for almost three decades, developing its economy in spectacular fashion. It was recognized by many noncommunist countries as the representative of all China until 1971, when it was replaced in the UN by the People's Republic of China. Martial law was lifted in Taiwan in 1987 and travel restrictions with mainland China in 1988. In 1989 opposition parties were legalized. The relationship with the mainland became increasingly close in the 1990s.

Recent Developments

The campaign leading up to Taiwan's presidential election on 20 Mar 2004 turned out to be unexpectedly dramatic. The incumbent, Pres. Chen Shui-bian, who was running on a policy of emphasizing the country's separate Taiwanese identity, faced stiff opposition from the Nationalist Party, which advocated a more conciliatory policy toward mainland China. While Chen had retreated somewhat from a confrontational approach, urging China to remove missile batteries pointed at the island country and calling for a referendum on strengthening Taiwan's defenses, he still favored changing the constitution, possibly to eliminate mention of Taiwan's being a part of China. On 19 March, the day before the election, Chen and his vice presidential running mate, Annette Lu, were slightly wounded by a gunman while campaigning in the southern city of Tainan. The results of the election gave Chen a very slight margin. Huge demonstrations in the capital after the election turned violent and served as a reminder of the continuing volatility of Taiwan's political situation. In December parliamentary elections, Chen's government and the independence movement received an unexpected setback when the Democratic Progressive Party (DPP) and its allies failed to win a majority. Several days later Chen announced that he was stepping down as DPP chairman. Kaohsiung mayor Frank Hsieh was appointed prime minister on 25 Jan 2005. In March a delegation of the Nationalist Party was welcomed on a historic weeklong visit to mainland China.

Internet resources: <www.tbroc.gov.tw>.

Tajikistan

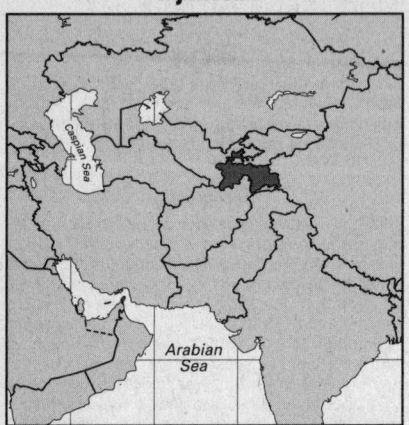

Official name: Jumhurii Tojikistan (Republic of Tajik-istan). **Form of government:** parliamentary republic with two legislative houses (National Assembly [33, including 8 members appointed by the president]; Assembly of Representatives [63]). **Chief of state:** President Imomali Rakhmonov (from 1994). **Head of government:** Prime Minister Akil Akilov (from 1999). **Capital:** Dushanbe. **Official language:** Tajik (Tojik). **Official religion:** none. **Monetary unit:** 1 somoni = 100 dinars; valuation (7 Jul 2005) $1 = 2.79 somoni. The somoni (equal to 1,000 Tajik rubles) was introduced on 30 Oct 2000.

Demography

Area: 55,300 sq mi, 143,100 sq km (includes c. 400 sq mi [c. 1,035 sq km] ceded to China in May 2002). **Population** (2004): 6,606,000. **Density** (2004): persons per sq mi 119.5, persons per sq km 46.2. **Urban** (2000): 26.6%. **Sex distribution** (2000): male 50.30%; female 49.70%. **Age breakdown** (2000): under 15, 39.4%; 15–29, 27.7%; 30–44, 18.4%; 45–59, 7.6%; 60–74, 5.4%; 75 and over, 1.5%. **Ethnic composition** (2000): Tajik 80.0%; Uzbek 15.3%; Russian 1.1%; Tatar 0.3%; other 3.3%. **Religious affiliation** (1995): Sunni Muslim 80.0%; Shi'i Muslim 5.0%; Russian Orthodox 1.5%; Jewish 0.1%; other (mostly nonreligious) 13.4%. **Major cities** (2002): Dushanbe 575,900; Khujand 147,400; Kulyab 79,500; Kurgan-Tyube 61,200; Ura-Tyube 51,700. **Location:** central Asia, bordering Kyrgyzstan, China, Afghanistan, and Uzbekistan.

Vital statistics

Birth rate per 1,000 population (2003): 24.3 (world avg. 21.3); (1994) legitimate 90.8%. **Death rate** per 1,000 population (2003): 6.0 (world avg. 9.1). **Natural increase rate** per 1,000 population (2003): 18.3 (world avg. 12.2). **Total fertility rate** (avg. births per childbearing woman; 2003): 3.0. **Marriage rate** per 1,000 population (2001): 4.6. **Divorce rate** per 1,000 population (1994): 0.8. **Life expectancy** at birth (2003): male 61.4 years; female 67.5 years.

National economy

Budget (2001). *Revenue:* 342,316,000 somoni (tax revenue 91.6%, of which value-added tax 25.1%, taxes on aluminum and cotton 18.3%, customs duties 15.1%, income and profit taxes 13.8%, excise taxes 4.5%; nontax revenue 8.4%). *Expenditures:* 338,-418,000 somoni (current expenditures 77.5%, of which state authorities 19.7%, education 18.9%, state bodies and administration 11.7%, defense 8.7%, health 7.3%, law enforcement 4.1%, debt payment 4.1%; capital expenditures 22.5%). **Production** (metric tons except as noted). *Agriculture, forestry, fishing* (2002): raw seed cotton 515,000, potatoes 400,000, wheat 361,000; livestock (number of live animals) 1,490,000 sheep, 1,091,000 cattle, 779,000 goats; fish catch (2001) 236. *Mining and quarrying* (2000): antimony (metal content) 2,000; gold 2,700 kg. *Manufacturing* (value of production in '000,000 somoni at 1998 constant prices; 2001): nonferrous metals 442,000 (aluminum production by weight in 2001 equaled 289,100 metric tons); food 138,000; textiles 104,000. *Energy production (consumption):* electricity (kW-hr; 2001) 14,400,000,000 (13,500,000,-000); coal (2001) 24,900 (122,000); crude petroleum (barrels; 2000) 132,000 (95,000); petroleum products (2000) none (753,000); natural gas (cu m; 2000) 38,594,000 (748,500,000). **Tourism** (2002): receipts from visitors $2,000,000; expenditures by nationals abroad $2,000,000. **Population economically active** (2002): total 1,829,000; activity rate of total population 29.6% (participation rates: ages 15–59 [male], 15–54 [female] 55.1%; female [1996] 46.5%; unemployed 2.3%). **Gross national product** (2003): $1,-221,000,000 ($190 per capita). **Public debt** (external, outstanding; 2002): $912,000,000. **Land use** as % of total land area (2000): in temporary crops 6.6%, in permanent crops 0.9%, in pasture 24.9%; overall forest area 2.8%. **Household income and expenditure.** Average household size (2000) 5.9; (1995) income per household 18,744 Tajik rubles; sources of income (1995): wages and salaries 34.5%, self-employment 34.0%, borrowing 2.4%, pension 2.0%, other 27.1%; expenditure: food 81.5%, clothing 10.2%, transport 2.5%, fuel 2.1%, other 3.7%.

Foreign trade

Imports (2001): $773,000,000 (alumina 23.9%, petroleum products and natural gas 12.9%, electricity 12.7%, grain and flour 8.0%). *Major import sources* (2000): Uzbekistan 28.8%; Russia 16.1%; Ukraine 13.1%; Kazakhstan 12.8%; Azerbaijan 9.8%. **Exports** (2001): $652,000,000 (aluminum 61.0%, electricity 12.1%, cotton fiber 10.9%). *Major export destinations* (2000): Russia 37.4%; The Netherlands 25.7%; Uzbekistan 14.1%; Switzerland 10.4%; Italy 2.8%.

Transport and communications

Transport. *Railroads* (2001): length 482 km; passenger-km 32,000,000; metric ton-km cargo 1,248,-000,000. *Roads* (1996): total length 13,747 km (paved 83%). *Vehicles* (1996): passenger cars 680,-000; trucks and buses 8,190. *Air transport* (2001; Tajikistan Airlines only): passenger-km 605,000,000; metric ton-km cargo 4,841,000; airports (2002) 2. **Communications,** in total units (units per 1,000 per-

1 metric ton = about 1.1 short tons;   1 kilometer = 0.6 mi (statute);   1 metric ton-km cargo = about 0.68 short ton-mi cargo;   c.i.f.: cost, insurance, and freight;   f.o.b.: free on board

sons). Daily newspaper circulation (2000): 123,000 (20); radios (2000): 870,000 (141); televisions (2000): 2,010,000 (326); telephone main lines (2003): 242,100 (37); cellular phone subscribers (2003): 47,600 (7.3); Internet users (2003): 4,100 (0.6).

Education and health

Educational attainment (1989). Percentage of population age 25 and over having: primary education or no formal schooling 16.3%; some secondary 21.1%; completed secondary and some postsecondary 55.1%; higher 7.5%. **Literacy** (2001): percentage of total population age 15 and over literate 99.3%; males literate 98.9%; females literate 99.6%. **Health** (2002): physicians 13,393 (1 per 472 persons); hospital beds 40,387 (1 per 157 persons); infant mortality rate per 1,000 live births (2003) 50.0. **Food** (2001): daily per capita caloric intake 1,662 (vegetable products 92%, animal products 8%); 65% of FAO recommended minimum.

Military

Total active duty personnel (2003): 6,000 (army 100%); Russian troops (2004) 20,000, including 9,-000 along the Tajik-Afghan border; US troops (2004) 3,000. **Military expenditure as percentage of GNP** (1999): 1.3% (world 2.4%); per capita expenditure $13.

Background

Settled by the Persians c. 6th century BC, Tajikistan was part of the empires of the Persians and of Alexander the Great and his successors. In the 7th–8th centuries AD it was conquered by the Arabs, who introduced Islam. The Uzbeks controlled the region in the 15th–18th centuries. In the 1860s Russia took over much of Tajikistan. In 1924 it became an autonomous republic under the administration of the Uzbek Soviet Socialist Republic, and it gained republic status in 1929. It achieved independence with the collapse of the Soviet Union in 1991. Civil war raged through much of the 1990s between government forces and an opposition of mostly Islamic forces. Peace was reached in 1997.

Recent Developments

In 2004 political life in Tajikistan was marked by growing tensions between Pres. Imomali Rakhmonov, his supporters, and opposition political parties, who accused the president of turning increasingly to authoritarian rule in the run-up to parliamentary elections scheduled for February 2005. In July Rakhmonov signed a controversial new election law, despite threats from four political parties to boycott the upcoming poll. Tajikistan's independent media also found it progressively more difficult to work as the election approached. In the event, the president's party won 80% of the vote with an official 92.6% voter turnout, although international observers were far from satisfied with the fairness of the process.

Internet resources: <www.tajiktour.tajnet.com>.

Tanzania

Official name: Jamhuri ya Muungano wa Tanzania (Swahili); United Republic of Tanzania (English). **Form**

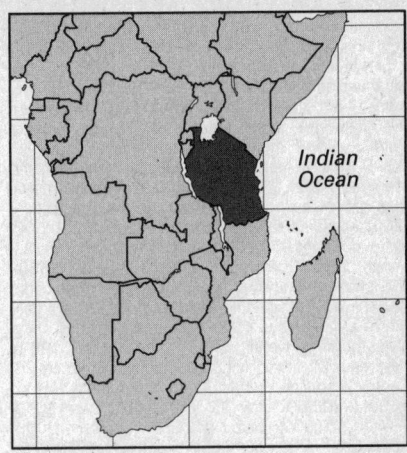

of government: unitary multiparty republic with one legislative house (National Assembly [274]). **Head of state and government:** President Benjamin William Mkapa (from 1995), assisted by Prime Minister Frederick Tulway Sumaye (from 1995). **Capital:** Dar es Salaam (capital designate, Dodoma). **Official languages:** Swahili; English. **Official religion:** none. **Monetary unit:** 1 Tanzania shilling (T Sh) = 100 cents; valuation (7 Jul 2005) $1 = T Sh 1,127.60.

Demography

Area: 364,901 sq mi, 945,090 sq km. **Population** (2004): 35,782,000. **Density** (2004): persons per sq mi 104.9, persons per sq km 40.5. **Urban** (2002): 23.0%. **Sex distribution** (2002): male 48.92%; female 51.08%. **Age breakdown** (2002): under 15, 44.3%; 15–29, 27.7%; 30–44, 15.3%; 45–59, 7.1%; 60–74, 4.1%; 75 and over, 1.5%. **Ethnolinguistic composition** (2000): Sukuma 9.5%; Hehet and Bena 4.5%; Gogo 4.4%; Haya 4.2%; Nyamwezi 3.6%; Makonde 3.3%; Chagga 3.0%; Ha 2.9%; other 64.6%. **Religious affiliation** (2000): Christian 46.9%; Muslim 31.8%; ethnoreligionist 16.1%. **Major urban areas** (2002): Dar es Salaam 2,336,055; Arusha 270,485; Mbeya 230,-318; Mwanza 209,806; Morogoro 206,868. **Location:** eastern Africa, bordering Kenya, the Indian Ocean, Mozambique, Malawi, Zambia, the Democratic Republic of the Congo, Burundi, Rwanda, and Uganda.

Vital statistics

Birth rate per 1,000 population (2003): 39.5 (world avg. 21.3). **Death rate** per 1,000 population (2003): 17.4 (world avg. 9.1). **Natural increase rate** per 1,000 population (2003): 22.1 (world avg. 12.2). **Total fertility rate** (avg. births per childbearing woman; 2003): 5.3. **Life expectancy** at birth (2003): male 43.3 years; female 45.8 years. **Adult population** (ages 15–49) **living with HIV** (2004): 8.8% (world avg. 1.1%).

National economy

Budget (2003–04). *Revenue:* T Sh 1,447,500,000,-000 (VAT 34.2%, income tax 24.9%, excise tax 15.0%, import duties 9.0%). *Expenditures:* T Sh 2,-531,500,000 (current expenditure 74.5%, of which wages 18.3%, education 17.7%, health 8.4%, interest payments on debt 4.8%; capital expenditure 25.5%). **Tourism** (2002): receipts from visitors $694,000,000; expenditures by nationals abroad $337,000,000. **Land use** as % of total land area (2000): in temporary crops 4.5%, in permanent crops 1.1%, in pasture 39.6%; overall forest area 43.9%. **Gross national product** (2002; mainland Tanzania only): $10,201,-000,000 ($290 per capita). **Public debt** (external, outstanding; 2002): $6,201,000,000. **Production** (metric tons except as noted). *Agriculture, forestry, fishing* (2002): cassava 6,880,000, corn (maize) 2,700,500, sweet potatoes 950,100; livestock (number of live animals) 17,700,000 cattle, 11,650,000 goats, 3,550,-000 sheep; roundwood 23,438,758 cu m; fish catch (2001) 336,200. *Mining and quarrying* (2002): gold 37,000 kg; garnets 23,000 kg; tanzanites 4,800 kg. *Manufacturing* (value added in $'000,000; 1999): beverages 39; food products 33; tobacco products 28. *Energy production (consumption):* electricity (kW-hr; 2000) 2,603,000,000 (2,548,000,000); coal (2000) 79,000 (79,000); crude petroleum (barrels; 2000) none (3,738,000); petroleum products (2000) 475,-000 (1,170,000). **Population economically active** (2002): total 18,525,000; activity rate 53.8% (participation rates [1991]: over age 10, 87.8%; female [1991] 40.0%). **Households.** Average household size (2002) 4.9; expenditure (1994): food 64.2%, clothing 9.9%, housing 8.3%, energy 7.6%, transportation 4.1%.

Foreign trade

Imports (2002-f.o.b. in balance of trade and c.i.f. in commodities and trading partners): T Sh 1,601,000,-000,000 (consumer goods 31.0%, of which food products 8.8%; machinery and apparatus 22.2%; transport equipment 13.2%; crude and refined petroleum 11.8%). *Major import sources:* South Africa 11.4%; Japan 8.4%; India 6.5%; Russia 6.1%; UAE 5.9%; UK 5.7%; Kenya 5.7%. **Exports** (2002): T Sh 846,000,000,000 (minerals [mostly gold, significantly diamonds and other gemstones] 42.4%; cashews 5.8%; tobacco 5.6%; coffee 4.0%; tea 3.4%; other [significantly fish products] 38.8%). *Major export destinations:* UK 18.5%; France 17.4%; Japan 11.0%; India 7.3%; The Netherlands 6.2%.

Transport and communications

Transport. *Railroads* (2001): length 3,690 km; passenger-km 471,000,000 (Tanzanian Railways only); metric ton-km cargo 1,380,000,000 (Tanzanian Railways only). *Roads* (1999): length 88,200 km (paved 4.2%). *Vehicles* (1999): passenger cars 33,900; trucks and buses 98,800. *Air transport* (2003; Air Tanzania only): passenger-km 151,332,000; metric ton-km 1,796,000; airports (1999) with scheduled flights 11. **Communications**, in total units (units per 1,000 persons). Daily newspaper circulation (2000): 130,000 (4); radios (2000): 9,130,000 (281); televisions (2000): 650,000 (20); telephone main lines (2003): 149,100 (4.2); cellular telephone subscribers (2003): 891,200 (25); personal computers (2003): 200,000 (5.7); Internet users (2003): 250,000 (7.1).

Education and health

Literacy (2001): percentage of population age 15 and over literate 76.0%; males literate 84.5%; fe-

males literate 67.9%. **Health:** physicians (1995) 1,-277 (1 per 22,030 persons); hospital beds (1993) 26,820 (1 per 1,000 persons); infant mortality rate (2003) 103.7. **Food** (2001): daily per capita caloric intake 1,997 (vegetable products 94%, animal products 6%); 86% of FAO recommended minimum.

Military

Total active duty personnel (2003): 27,000 (army 85.2%, navy 3.7%, air force 11.1%). **Military expenditure as percentage of GNP** (1999): 1.4% (world 2.4%); per capita expenditure $4.

Background

Inhabited from the 1st millennium BC, Tanzania was occupied by Arab and Indian traders and Bantu-speaking peoples by the 10th century AD. The Portuguese gained control of the coastline in the late 15th century, but they were driven out by the Arabs of Oman and Zanzibar in the late 18th century. German colonists entered the area in the 1880s, and in 1891 the Germans declared the region a protectorate as German East Africa. In World War I Britain captured the German holdings, which became a British mandate (1920) under the name Tanganyika. Britain retained control of the region after World War II when it became a UN trust territory (1947). Tanganyika gained independence in 1961 and became a republic in 1962. In 1964 it united with Zanzibar under the name Tanzania.

 Lake Victoria, also called Victoria Nyanza, having an area of 26,828 sq mi (69,484 sq km), is the largest lake in Africa and the chief reservoir of the Nile River.

Recent Developments

The most significant event in Tanzania in 2004 was the government's decision in February to launch a $27.6 million project to draw water from Lake Victoria to supply hundreds of villages in the western Shinyanga region. The announcement of a pipeline contract brought an immediate protest from Egypt, which claimed that Tanzania was in breach of a 1929 treaty that had determined the distribution of the water that flowed from the lake to Egypt through the Nile River to be in perpetuity. On 2 March the presidents of Tanzania, Kenya, and Uganda signed an agreement preparing the way for an East African customs union. The nearly 400,000 officially registered refugees from Burundi, along with another 400,000 who were undocumented and living in refugee circumstances, continued to impose a heavy financial and administrative burden on the country.

Internet resources: <www.tanzania.go.tz>.

Thailand

Official name: Muang Thai, or Prathet Thai (Kingdom of Thailand). **Form of government:** constitutional

---

1 metric ton = about 1.1 short tons;   1 kilometer = 0.6 mi (statute);   1 metric ton-km cargo = about 0.68 short ton-mi cargo;   c.i.f.: cost, insurance, and freight;   f.o.b.: free on board

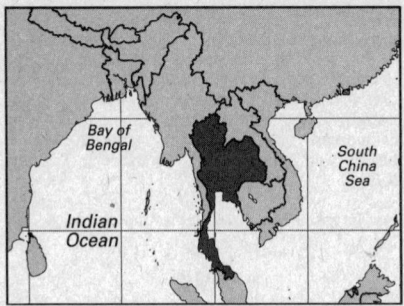

```
Bay of
Bengal                        South
                              China
                              Sea
Indian
Ocean
```

monarchy with two legislative houses (Senate [200]; House of Representatives [500]). **Chief of state:** King Bhumibol Adulyadej (from 1946). **Head of government:** Prime Minister Thaksin Shinawatra (from 2001). **Capital:** Bangkok. **Official language:** Thai. **Official religion:** Buddhism. **Monetary unit:** 1 Thai baht (B) = 100 stangs; valuation (7 Jul 2005) $1 = B 41.71.

Demography

Area: 198,117 sq mi, 513,120 sq km. **Population** (2004): 64,485,000. **Density** (2004): persons per sq mi 325.5, persons per sq km 125.7. **Urban** (2001): 28.6%. **Sex distribution** (2000): male 49.24%; female 50.76%. **Age breakdown** (2003): under 15, 24.5%; 15–29, 26.5%; 30–44, 23.7%; 45–59, 15.7%; 60–74, 7.8%; 75 and over, 1.8%. **Ethnic composition** (2000): Tai peoples 81.4%, of which Thai (Siamese) 34.9%, Lao 26.5%; Han Chinese 10.6%; Malay 3.7%; Khmer 1.9%; other 2.4%. **Religious affiliation** (2000): Buddhist 94.2%; Muslim 4.6%; Christian and other 1.2%. **Major cities** (2000): Bangkok 6,320,174; Samut Prakan 378,694; Nonthaburi 291,307; Udon Thani 220,493; Nakhon Ratchasima 204,391. **Location:** southeastern Asia, bordering Laos, Cambodia, the Gulf of Thailand, Malaysia, and Myanmar (Burma).

Vital statistics

Birth rate per 1,000 population (2002): 14.0 (world avg. 21.3). **Death rate** per 1,000 population (2002): 6.0 (world avg. 9.1). **Natural increase rate** per 1,000 population (2002): 8.0 (world avg. 12.2). **Total fertility rate** (avg. births per childbearing woman; 2002): 1.8. **Marriage rate** per 1,000 population (2000): 5.4. **Divorce rate** per 1,000 population (2000): 1.1. **Life expectancy** at birth (2002): male 69.9 years; female 74.9 years.

National economy

Budget (2001–02). *Revenue:* B 903,550,000,000 (tax revenue 90.3%, of which income taxes 28.7%, VAT 26.1%, taxes on international trade 11.5%, consumption tax 10.8%; nontax revenue 9.7%). *Expenditures:* B 1,023,000,000,000 (education 21.8%; defense 7.5%; agriculture 7.4%; health 7.1%; social security 6.9%; public order 5.5%). **Public debt** (external, outstanding; 2002): $22,628,000,000. **Production** (metric tons except as noted). *Agriculture, forestry, fishing* (2002): sugarcane 62,350,000, rice 25,945,000, cassava 16,870,000; livestock (number of live animals)

6,688,904 pigs, 4,640,355 cattle, 121,000,000 chickens; roundwood (2001) 27,351,000 cu m; fish catch (2001) 3,605,544, of which mollusks 224,222. *Mining and quarrying* (2001): gypsum 6,191,000; dolomite 871,300; feldspar 710,500. *Manufacturing* (2001): cement 27,913,000; refined sugar 4,865,000; crude steel 2,127,000. *Energy production (consumption):* electricity (kW-hr; 2002) 108,418,000,000 (105,182,000,000); hard coal (2000) negligible (4,098,000); lignite (2001) 19,619,000 ([2000] 17,586,000); crude petroleum (barrels; 2001) 22,600,000 ([2000] 252,000,000); petroleum products (2000) 34,968,000 (30,468,000); natural gas (cu m; 2001) 20,633,000,000 ([2000] 19,338,400,000). **Tourism** (2002): receipts from visitors $7,902,000,000; expenditures by nationals abroad $3,303,000,000. **Population economically active** (2001): total 33,920,000; activity rate of total population 53.9% (participation rates: over age 14, 72.1%; female [2000] 45.0%; unemployed 3.2%). **Gross national product** (2001): $136,063,000,000 ($2,190 per capita). **Household income and expenditure** (1998). Average household size (2000) 3.9; average annual income per household B 149,904; sources of income: wages and salaries 40.1%, self-employment 29.8%, transfer payments 7.9%, other 22.2%; expenditure: food, tobacco, and beverages 37.7%, housing 21.4%, transportation and communications 13.3%, medical and personal care 5.1%, clothing 3.5%, education 2.3%. **Land use** as % of total land area (2000): in temporary crops 29.4%, in permanent crops 6.5%, in pasture 1.6%; overall forest area 28.9%.

Foreign trade

Imports (2001-f.o.b. in balance of trade and c.i.f. for commodities and trading partners): $62,057,000,000 (electrical machinery 22.1%, of which electronic components and parts 10.9%; nonelectrical machinery 17.4%, of which computers and parts 6.3%; chemicals and chemical products 10.3%; crude petroleum 9.3%). *Major import sources* (2002): Japan 23.0%; US 9.6%; China 7.6%; Malaysia 5.6%; Singapore 4.5%. **Exports** (2001): $65,113,000,000 (food products 14.9%, of which fish, crustaceans, and mollusks 6.2%; computers and parts 12.3%; microcircuits and other electronics 7.2%; chemicals and chemical products 5.7%; garments and clothing accessories 5.6%). *Major export destinations* (2002): US 19.6%; Japan 14.5%; Singapore 8.1%; Hong Kong 5.4%; China 5.2%.

Transport and communications

Transport. *Railroads* (2000): route length 4,041 km; passenger-km 10,040,000,000; metric ton-km cargo 3,347,000,000. *Roads* (2001): total length 53,436 km (paved 98%). *Vehicles* (2002): passenger cars 2,281,000; trucks and buses 4,145,000. *Air transport* (1999): passenger-km 38,345,195,000; metric ton-km cargo 1,670,717,000; airports (1996) 25. **Communications,** in total units (units per 1,000 persons). Daily newspaper circulation (2000): 3,990,000 (64); radios (2000): 14,700,000 (235); televisions (2000): 17,700,000 (284); telephone main lines (2003): 6,600,000 (106); cellular telephone subscribers (2002): 16,117,000 (260); personal computers (2002): 2,461,000 (40); Internet users (2003): 6,031,300 (96).

Education and health

Educational attainment (2000). Percentage of population age 6 and over having: no formal schooling 8.5%; primary education 59.0%; lower secondary 12.5%; upper secondary 11.2%; some higher 2.2%; undergraduate 5.2%; advanced degree 0.4%; other/unknown 1.0%. Literacy (2000): 95.5%. Health (2001): physicians 18,531 (1 per 3,395 persons); hospital beds 141,380 (1 per 445 persons); infant mortality rate per 1,000 live births (2002) 20.0. Food (2001): daily per capita caloric intake 2,486 (vegetable products 88%, animal products 12%); 112% of FAO recommended minimum.

Military

Total active duty personnel (2003): 314,200 (army 60.5%, navy 25.2%, air force 14.3%). Military expenditure as percentage of GNP (1999): 1.7% (world 2.4%); per capita expenditure $34.

Background

The region of Thailand has been occupied continuously for 20,000 years. It was part of the Mon and Khmer kingdoms from the 9th century AD. Thai-speaking peoples emigrated from China c. the 10th century. During the 13th century two Thai states emerged: the Sukhothai kingdom, founded c. 1220 after a successful revolt against the Khmer, and Chiang Mai, founded in 1296 after the defeat of the Mon. In 1350 the Thai kingdom of Ayutthaya succeeded Sukhothai. The Burmese were its most powerful rivals, occupying it briefly in the 16th century and destroying the kingdom in 1767. The Chakri dynasty came to power in 1782, moving the capital to Bangkok and extending the empire along the Malay Peninsula and into Laos and Cambodia. The country was named Siam in 1856. Though Western influence increased during the 19th century, Siam's rulers avoided colonization by granting concessions to European countries; it was the only southeast Asian nation able to do so. In 1917 it entered World War I on the side of the Allies. It became a constitutional monarchy following a military coup in 1932 and was officially renamed Thailand in 1939. It was occupied by Japan in World War II. It participated in the Korean War as a UN forces member and was allied with South Vietnam in the Vietnam War. Along with other southeast Asian nations, it suffered from the 1990s regional financial crisis.

Recent Developments

In January 2004 a spate of violent incidents—arson attacks on schools, murders, and a militant assault on an arms depository—erupted in three southern provinces where 70–80% of the people were Muslims. On 28 April more Muslim-led attacks provoked the military into storming the famous Krue Se mosque in Pattani province, where the bandits took refuge. More than 100 people were killed. By October the number of casualties had exceeded 350. Then on 26 December Thailand was struck by a tsunami that severely damaged much of the south and caused the death of thousands of people, including many tourists. Another grave concern for Bangkok

was the outbreak of bird flu in January 2004. The government killed millions of infected chickens. During the year 12 people died of infection, and the damage to the poultry industry totaled an estimated several billion baht. Despite a number of serious problems, Prime Minister Thaksin Shinawatra's political position strengthened throughout 2004 such that he won reelection by a landslide in February 2005.

Internet resources: <www.tourismthailand.org>.

Togo

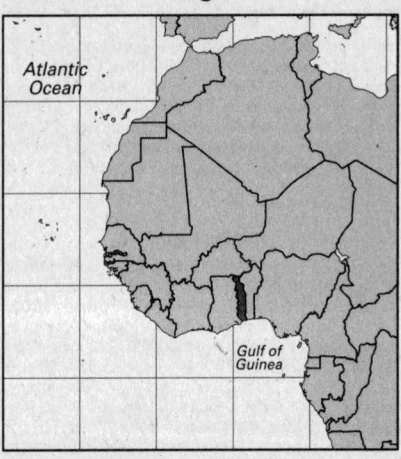

Official name: République Togolaise (Togolese Republic). Form of government: multiparty republic with one legislative body (National Assembly [81]). Chief of state: President Faure Gnassingbé (from 24 Apr 2005). Head of government: Prime Minister Koffi Sama (from 2002). Capital: Lomé. Official language: French. Official religion: none. Monetary unit: 1 CFA franc (CFAF) = 100 centimes; valuation (7 Jul 2005) $1 = CFAF 549.50; the CFAF is pegged to the euro (€) at €1 = CFAF 655.96 from 1 Jan 2002.

Demography

Area: 21,925 sq mi, 56,785 sq km. Population (2004): 5,557,000. Density (2004): persons per sq mi 253.5, persons per sq km 97.9. Urban (2002): 33.9%. Sex distribution (2004): male 49.55%; female 50.45%. Age breakdown (2001): under 15, 45.6%; 15–29, 28.1%; 30–44, 14.8%; 45–59, 7.5%; 60–74, 3.3%; 75 and over, 0.7%. Ethnic composition (2000): Ewe 22.2%; Kabre 13.4%; Wachi 10.0%; Mina 5.6%; Kotokoli 5.6%; Bimoba 5.2%; Losso 4.0%; Gurma 3.4%; Lamba 3.2%; Adja 3.0%; other 24.4%. Religious affiliation (2000): Christian 37.8%, of which Roman Catholic 24.3%; traditional beliefs 37.7%; Muslim 18.9%; other 5.6%. Major cities (2003): Lomé 676,400 (urban agglomeration 749,700); Sokodé 84,200; Kpalimé 75,200; Atakpamé 64,300; Kara 49,800. Location: western Africa, bordering Burkina Faso, Benin, the Bight of Benin, and Ghana.

---

1 metric ton = about 1.1 short tons;   1 kilometer = 0.6 mi (statute);   1 metric ton-km cargo = about 0.68 short ton-mi cargo;   c.i.f.: cost, insurance, and freight;   f.o.b.: free on board

Vital statistics

Birth rate per 1,000 population (2003): 35.2 (world avg. 21.3). **Death rate** per 1,000 population (2003): 11.5 (world avg. 9.1). **Natural increase rate** per 1,000 population (2003): 23.7 (world avg. 12.2). **Total fertility rate** (avg. births per childbearing woman; 2003): 5.0. **Life expectancy** at birth (2003): male 52.0 years; female 54.0 years. **Adult population** (ages 15–49) **living with HIV** (2004): 4.1% (world avg. 1.1%).

National economy

Budget (2002). *Revenue:* CFAF 128,300,000,000 (tax revenue 92.5%, nontax revenue 4.8%, grants 2.7%). *Expenditures:* CFAF 135,300,000,000 (current expenditure 89.4%, capital expenditure 10.6%). **Public debt** (external, outstanding; 2002): $1,337,000,000. **Production** (metric tons except as noted). *Agriculture, forestry, fishing* (2002): cassava 651,530, yams 549,070, corn (maize) 463,930; livestock (number of live animals) 1,700,000 sheep, 1,460,000 goats, 300,000 pigs; roundwood 5,-835,447 cu m; fish catch (2001) 23,283. *Mining and quarrying:* limestone (2001) 2,400,000; phosphate rock (2002) 1,380,000. *Manufacturing* (value added in CFAF '000,000; 1998): food products, beverages, and tobacco manufactures 41,400; metallic goods 12,000; nonmetallic manufactures 8,500. *Energy production (consumption):* electricity (kW-hr; 2000) 68,000,000 (580,000,000); petroleum products (2000) none (471,000). **Population economically active** (2000): total 1,913,000; activity rate of total population 38.1% (participation rates: over age 15, 70.7%; female 39.9%; unemployed [1994] 16–18%). **Gross national product** (at current market prices; 2003): $1,492,000,000 ($310 per capita). **Households.** Average household size (1999) 6.0; expenditure (1987): food and beverages 45.9%, services 20.5%, household durable goods 13.9%, clothing 11.4%, housing 5.9%. **Land use** as % of total land area (2000): in temporary crops 46.1%, in permanent crops 2.2%, in pasture 18.4%; overall forest area 9.4%. **Tourism** (2002): receipts $9,000,000; expenditures $4,000,000.

Foreign trade

Imports (2001-c.i.f. [except in 2002 balance of trade]): $355,000,000 (food 18.2%, of which cereals 9.4%; refined petroleum 15.7%; chemicals and chemical products 10.4%; machinery and apparatus 9.8%; cement 8.8%; iron and steel 8.8%). *Major import sources:* France 19.1%; Canada 6.5%; Italy 6.1%; Côte d'Ivoire 5.7%; Germany 4.5%. **Exports** (2001): $220,200,000 (cement 29.4%, phosphates 20.3%, cotton 10.1%, iron and steel 8.6%). *Major export destinations:* Ghana 22.4%; Benin 16.9%; Burkina Faso 10.4%; Philippines 6.3%; Niger 4.5%.

Transport and communications

Transport. *Railroads* (1999): route length 395 km; (1998) passenger-km 35,200,000; metric ton-km cargo 758,700,000. *Roads* (1999): total length 7,520 km (paved 32%). *Vehicles* (1996): passenger cars 79,200; trucks and buses 34,240. *Air transport* (Air Afrique, an airline jointly owned by 11 African countries [including Togo], was declared bankrupt in February 2002): airports (1998) 2. **Communications,** in total units (units per 1,000 persons). Daily newspaper circulation (2000): 20,100 (4); radios (2000): 1,330,000 (265); televisions (2002): 590,000 (123); telephone main lines (2003): 60,600 (12); cellular telephone subscribers (2003): 220,000 (44); personal computers (2003): 160,000 (32); Internet users (2003): 210,000 (42).

Education and health

Educational attainment (1981). Percentage of population age 25 and over having: no formal schooling 76.5%; primary education 13.5%; secondary 8.7%; higher 1.3%. **Literacy** (2000): total population age 15 and over literate 57.1%; males 72.4%; females 42.5%. **Health:** physicians (1995) 320 (1 per 13,158 persons); hospital beds (1990) 5,307 (1 per 694 persons); infant mortality rate per 1,000 live births (2003) 80.0. **Food** (2001): daily per capita caloric intake 2,287 (vegetable products 97%, animal products 3%); 99% of FAO recommended minimum.

Military

Total active duty personnel (2003): 8,550 (army 94.7%, navy 2.3%, air force 3.0%). **Military expenditure as percentage of GNP** (1999): 1.8% (world 2.4%); per capita expenditure $5.

Background

Until 1884 what is now Togo was an intermediate zone between the black African military states of Ashanti and Dahomey, and its various ethnic groups lived in general isolation from each other. In 1884 it became part of the Togoland German protectorate, which was occupied by British and French forces in 1914. In 1922 the League of Nations assigned eastern Togoland to France and the western portion to Britain. In 1946 the British and French governments placed the territories under UN trusteeship. Ten years later British Togoland was incorporated into the Gold Coast, and French Togoland became an autonomous republic within the French Union. Togo gained independence in 1960. It suspended its constitution 1967–80. A multiparty constitution was approved in 1992, but the political situation remained unstable.

Recent Developments

The death on 5 Feb 2005 of Gnassingbé Eyadéma, who had led Togo for 38 years, catalyzed a political crisis. Prompted by the military, the legislature hastily rewrote the constitution and installed in office Eyadéma's son, Faure Gnassingbé. This coup was loudly protested by Togolese and international observers alike. Weeks of demonstrations and a national strike ensued until, on 25 February, Gnassingbé stepped down and the deputy head of parliament took over as acting president, pending elections in 60 days' time. Gnassingbé, however, won the April elections (which international observers reported as flawed), setting off another round of violent protests; human rights organizations estimated that some 800 people had died in Togo since February. In April and May, Gnassingbé's party and the opposition met in Abuja, Nigeria, to discuss the possibility of a national-unity government.

Internet resources:
<www.republicoftogo.com/fr/home.asp>.

Tonga

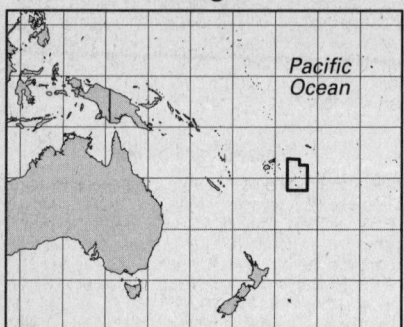

Pacific Ocean

Official name: Pule'anga Fakatu'i 'o Tonga (Tongan); Kingdom of Tonga (English). **Form of government:** constitutional monarchy with one legislative house (Legislative Assembly [30; includes 12 nonelective seats and 9 nobles elected by the 33 hereditary nobles of Tonga]). **Head of state and government:** King Taufa'ahau Tupou IV (from 1965), assisted by Prime Minister of the Privy Council Prince 'Ulukalala Lavaka Ata (from 2000). **Capital:** Nuku'alofa. **Official languages:** Tongan; English. **Official religion:** none. **Monetary unit:** 1 pa'anga (T$) = 100 seniti; valuation (7 Jul 2005) US$1 = T$1.98.

Demography

Area: 289.5 sq mi, 749.9 sq km, of which land area equals 278.1 sq mi, 720.3 sq km. **Population** (2004): 98,400. **Density** (2004; based on land area): persons per sq mi 353.8, persons per sq km 136.6. **Urban** (2002): 39.0%. **Sex distribution** (2002): male 50.93%; female 49.07%. **Age breakdown** (1996): under 15, 39.1%; 15–29, 28.0%; 30–44, 15.1%; 45–59, 10.0%; 60–74, 6.0%; 75 and over, 1.8%. **Ethnic composition** (1996): Tongan and part Tongan 98.2%; other 1.8%. **Religious affiliation** (1998): Free Wesleyan 41.2%; Roman Catholic 15.8%; Mormon 13.6%; other (mostly other Protestant) 29.4%. **Major cities** (1986): Nuku'alofa (1996) 22,400 (urban agglomeration [2001] 33,000); Neiafu 3,879; Haveluloto 3,070. **Location:** archipelago in the South Pacific Ocean between Hawaii and New Zealand.

Vital statistics

Birth rate per 1,000 population (2003): 24.5 (world avg. 21.3). **Death rate** per 1,000 population (2003): 5.5 (world avg. 9.1). **Natural increase rate** per 1,000 population (2003): 19.0 (world avg. 12.2). **Total fertility rate** (avg. births per childbearing woman; 2003): 3.0. **Marriage rate** per 1,000 population (1994): 7.7. **Divorce rate** per 1,000 population (1994): 0.8. **Life expectancy** at birth (2003): male 66.4 years; female 71.4 years.

National economy

Budget (2002). *Revenue:* T$93,200,000 (foreign-trade taxes 52.0%, government services revenue 13.7%, income tax 16.7%, sales taxes 8.2%). *Expenditures:*

T$99,400,000 (2001; general administration 20.9%, education 14.0%, health 10.2%, social security 6.7%, agriculture 6.5%, law and order 5.7%, defense 4.6%). **Public debt** (external, outstanding; 2002): US$72,600,000. **Production** (metric tons except as noted). *Agriculture, forestry, fishing* (2002): coconuts 57,700, pumpkins, squash, and gourds 17,000, cassava 9,000; livestock (number of live animals) 80,853 pigs, 12,500 goats, 300,000 chickens; roundwood 2,100 cu m; fish catch (2001) 4,673. *Mining and quarrying:* coral and sand for local use. *Manufacturing* (output in T$'000,000; 1996): food products and beverages 8,203; paper products 1,055; chemical products 964. *Energy production (consumption):* electricity (kW-hr; 2002) 36,176,000 (36,176,000); petroleum products (2000) n.a. (39,000). **Tourism:** receipts (2002) US$9,000,000; expenditures (2001) US$3,000,000. **Gross national product** (2003): US$152,000,000 (US$1,490 per capita). **Population economically active** (1996): total 33,908; activity rate 34.7% (participation rates: ages 15 and over 57.0%; female 36.0%; unemployed 13.3%). **Households.** Average household size (1996) 6.0; expenditure (1991–92): food 43.2%, transportation 15.5%, household 14.2%, housing 6.4%, tobacco and beverages 5.4%, clothing and footwear 4.2%. **Land use** as % of total land area (2000): in temporary crops 24%, in permanent crops 43%, in pasture 6%; overall forest area 5%.

Foreign trade

Imports (2000–01-f.o.b. in balance of trade and c.i.f. in commodities and trading partners): US$70,100,000 (food and live animals 32.3%, mineral fuels and chemical products 25.6%, machinery and transport equipment 11.2%). *Major import sources* (2002): New Zealand 30.8%; Fiji 20.7%; US 14.3%; Australia 13.2%; China 6.2%. **Exports** (2000–01): US$6,700,000 (squash 40.8%, fish 27.7%, root crops 15.4%, kava 2.3%, vanilla beans 2.3%). *Major export destinations* (2002): Japan 43.3%; US 41.0%; Greece 3.8%; New Zealand 3.6%; Taiwan 2.7%.

Transport and communications

Transport. *Roads* (1996): total length 680 km (paved 27%). *Vehicles* (1998): passenger cars 6,419, commercial vehicles 9,189. *Air transport* (1999): passenger-km 19,000,000; metric ton-km cargo 2,000,000; airports (1996) with scheduled flights 6. **Communications,** in total units (units per 1,000 persons). Daily newspaper circulation (2000): 12,300 (123); radios (1997): 61,000 (619); televisions (1997): 2,000 (21); telephone main lines (2002): 11,200 (113); cellular telephone subscribers (2002): 3,400 (34); personal computers (2002): 2,000 (20); Internet users (2002): 2,900 (29).

Education and health

Educational attainment (1996). Percentage of population age 25 and over having: primary education 26%; lower secondary 58%; upper secondary 8%; higher 6%; not stated 2%. **Literacy** (1996): 98.5%. **Health:** physicians (2002; government only) 32 (1 per 3,057 persons); hospital beds (1992) 307 (1 per 320 persons); infant mortality rate per 1,000 live births

1 metric ton = about 1.1 short tons;   1 kilometer = 0.6 mi (statute);   1 metric ton-km cargo = about 0.68 short ton-mi cargo;   c.i.f.: cost, insurance, and freight;   f.o.b.: free on board

(2003) 13.4. **Food** (1992): daily per capita caloric intake 2,946 (vegetable products 82%, animal products 18%); 129% of FAO recommended minimum.

Military

Total active duty personnel (1999): 125-member naval force; an air force was created in 1996.

Background

Tonga was inhabited at least 3,000 years ago by people of the Lapita culture. The Tongans developed a stratified social system headed by a paramount ruler whose dominion by the 13th century extended as far as the Hawaiian Islands. The Dutch visited the islands in the 17th century; in 1773 Capt. James Cook arrived and named the archipelago the Friendly Islands. The modern kingdom was established during the reign (1845–93) of King George Tupou I. It became a British protectorate in 1900. This was dissolved in 1970, when Tonga, the only ancient kingdom surviving from the pre-European period in Polynesia, achieved complete independence within the Commonwealth.

Recent Developments

The government-owned Royal Tongan Airlines collapsed after its sole aircraft used for international flights was repossessed in April 2004 and it lacked the funds to repair its sole domestic aircraft in May. The national economy suffered subsequently. With a narrow export base, high imports, and pressure on the currency because of high imported inflation, domestic inflation was running at 12% for the year.

Internet resources: <www.tongatapu.net.to>.

Trinidad and Tobago

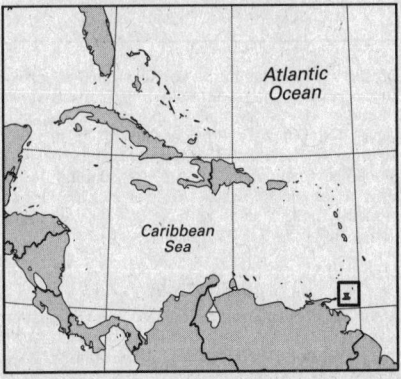

Atlantic Ocean

Caribbean Sea

Official name: Republic of Trinidad and Tobago. Form of government: multiparty republic with two legislative houses (Senate [31]; House of Representatives [36; excludes speaker]). Chief of state: President Maxwell Richards (from 2003). Head of government: Prime Minister Patrick Manning (from 2001). Capital: Port of Spain. Official language: English. Official religion: none. Monetary unit: 1 Trinidad and Tobago dollar (TT$) = 100 cents; valuation (7 Jul 2005) US$1 = TT$6.26.

Demography

Area: 1,980 sq mi, 5,127 sq km. **Population** (2004): 1,286,000. **Density** (2004): persons per sq mi 649.5, persons per sq km 250.8. **Urban** (2002): 74.5%. **Sex distribution** (2001): male 51.22%; female 48.78%. **Age breakdown** (2001): under 15, 24.3%; 15–29, 27.1%; 30–44, 22.5%; 45–59, 15.5%; 60–74, 7.7%; 75 and over, 2.9%. **Ethnic composition** (2000): black 39.2%; East Indian 38.6%; mixed 16.3%; Chinese 1.6%; white 1.0%; other/not stated 3.3%. **Religious affiliation** (1990): six largest Protestant bodies 29.7%; Roman Catholic 29.4%; Hindu 23.7%; Muslim 5.9%; other 11.3%. **Major cities** (2000): Chaguanas 67,433; San Fernando 55,149; Port of Spain 49,031; Arima 32,278; Point Fortin 19,056. **Location:** islands northeast of Venezuela between the North Atlantic Ocean and the Caribbean Sea.

Vital statistics

Birth rate per 1,000 population (2003): 12.7 (world avg. 21.3). **Death rate** per 1,000 population (2003): 8.7 (world avg. 9.1). **Natural increase rate** per 1,000 population (2003): 4.0 (world avg. 12.2). **Total fertility rate** (avg. births per childbearing woman; 2003): 1.8. **Marriage rate** per 1,000 population (1998): 6.2. **Divorce rate** per 1,000 population (1998): 1.1. **Life expectancy** at birth (2003): male 67.1 years; female 72.2 years.

National economy

Budget (2001–02). *Revenue:* TT$14,672,000,000 (income taxes 31.5%; petroleum sector 29.0%; sales tax 23.7%; taxes on international trade 5.7%; other 10.1%). *Expenditures:* TT$13,861,000,000 (current expenditures 90.4%, of which transfers and subsidies 33.9%, wages 30.9%, interest payment 16.8%, other 8.8%; development expenditures 9.6%). **Production** (metric tons except as noted). *Agriculture, forestry, fishing* (2002): sugarcane 1,050,000, coconuts 24,000, oranges 4,987; livestock (number of live animals) 60,500 goats, 31,600 cattle, 25,000,000 chickens; roundwood (2000) 116,500 cu m; fish catch (2001) 11,415. *Mining and quarrying* (2000): natural asphalt 9,900. *Manufacturing* (2000): anhydrous ammonia and urea 3,719,000; methanol 2,480,000; steel billets 744,000. *Energy production (consumption):* electricity (kW-hr; 2000) 5,460,-000,000 (5,460,000,000); crude petroleum (barrels; 2000) 43,786,000 (59,102,000); petroleum products (2000) 8,037,000 (1,055,000); natural gas (cu m; 2000) 10,448,000,000 (10,448,000,000). **Households.** Average household size (2000) 3.7; expenditure (1993): food, beverages, and tobacco 25.5%, housing 21.6%, transportation 15.2%, household furnishings 14.3%, clothing and footwear 10.4%. **Tourism** (2002): receipts from visitors US$224,-000,000; expenditures by nationals abroad (2001) US$151,000,000. **Land use** as % of total land area (2000): in temporary crops 14.6%, in permanent crops 9.2%, in pasture 2.1%; overall forest area 50.5%. **Gross national product** (at current market prices; 2003): US$9,538,000,000 (US$7,260 per capita). **Population economically active** (2001): total 576,900; activity rate of total population 45.5% (participation rates: ages 15 and over 60.7%; female 36.6%; unemployed 10.9%). **Public debt** (external, outstanding; 2002): US$1,697,000,000.

Foreign trade

Imports (2001-c.i.f.): TT$24,510,000,000 (crude petroleum 19.3%, general industrial machinery 16.1%, floating docks 9.3%, food products 7.5%, refined petroleum 4.1%). *Major import sources:* US 34.4%; Venezuela 11.1%; Brazil 5.1%; UK 4.9%; Panama 4.6%. **Exports** (2001-f.o.b.): TT$31,873,000,000 (refined petroleum 29.4%, floating docks 12.6%, crude petroleum 9.3%, anhydrous ammonia 8.5%, iron and steel 5.7%, methanol 5.0%). *Major export destinations:* US 42.3%; Mexico 7.4%; Jamaica 7.0%; Barbados 5.5%; France 3.9%.

Transport and communications

Transport. *Roads* (1999): total length 7,900 km (paved 51%). *Vehicles* (1996): passenger cars 122,000; trucks and buses 24,000. *Air transport* (2001; BWIA only): passenger-km 2,496,000,000; metric ton-km cargo 56,236,000; airports (2000) with scheduled flights 2. **Communications,** in total units (units per 1,000 persons). Daily newspaper circulation (2000): 155,000 (123); radios (2000): 672,000 (532); televisions (2000): 429,000 (340); telephone main lines (2002): 325,100 (250); cellular telephone subscribers (2002): 361,900 (278); personal computers (2002): 104,000 (80); Internet users (2002): 138,000 (106).

Education and health

Educational attainment (1990). Percentage of population age 25 and over having: no formal schooling 4.5%; primary education 56.4%; secondary 32.1%; higher 3.4%; other/not stated 3.6%. **Literacy** (2000): total population age 15 and over literate 93.8%; males literate 95.5%; females literate 92.1%. **Health:** physicians (1999) 1,171 (1 per 1,076 persons); hospital beds 4,384 (1 per 287 persons); infant mortality rate per 1,000 live births (2003) 25.0. **Food** (2001): daily per capita caloric intake 2,756 (vegetable products 84%, animal products 16%); 114% of FAO recommended minimum.

Military

Total active duty personnel (2003): 2,700 (army 74.1%, coast guard 25.9%). **Military expenditure as percentage of GNP** (1999): 1.4% (world 2.4%); per capita expenditure US$78.

Background

When Christopher Columbus visited Trinidad in 1498, it was inhabited by the Arawak Indians; Caribs inhabited Tobago. The islands were settled by the Spanish in the 16th century. In the 17th and 18th centuries African slaves were imported for plantation labor to replace the original Indian population, which had been worked to death by the Spanish. Trinidad was surrendered to the British in 1797. The British attempted to settle Tobago in 1721, but the French captured the island in 1781 and transformed it into a sugar-producing colony; the British acquired it in 1802. After slavery ended in the islands in 1834–38, immigrants from India were brought in to work the plantations. The islands of Trinidad and Tobago were administratively combined in 1889. Granted limited self-government in 1925, the islands became an independent state within the Commonwealth in 1962 and a republic in 1976. Political unrest was followed in 1990 by an attempted Muslim fundamentalist coup against the government.

Recent Developments

Trinidad and Tobago's rapid pace of heavy industrial development reached a milestone in May 2004 when the world's largest aluminum company, Alcoa Inc., announced that it would build a new smelter in the country. The complex, which was to include a power plant and downstream fabrication, would cost $1 billion to construct.

Internet resources: <www.visittnt.com>.

Tunisia

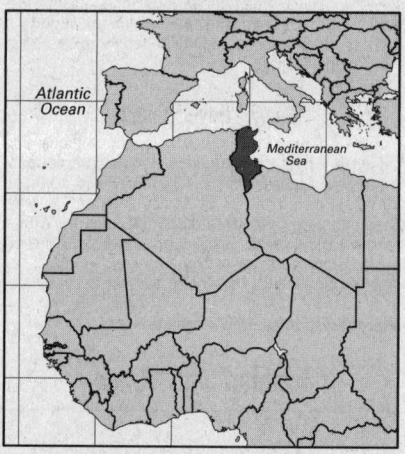

Official name: Al-Jumhuriyah al-Tunisiyah (Republic of Tunisia). **Form of government:** multiparty republic with one legislative house (Chamber of Deputies [189]). **Chief of state:** President Zine El Abidine Ben Ali (from 1987). **Head of government:** Prime Minister Mohamed Ghannouchi (from 1999). **Capital:** Tunis. **Official language:** Arabic. **Official religion:** Islam. **Monetary unit:** 1 dinar (D) = 1,000 millimes; valuation (7 Jul 2005) $1= D 1.34.

Demography

Area: 63,170 sq mi, 163,610 sq km. **Population** (2004): 9,975,000. **Density** (2004): persons per sq mi 157.9, persons per sq km 61.0. **Urban** (2002): 63.4%. **Sex distribution** (2002): male 50.30%; female 49.70%. **Age breakdown** (2002): under 15, 27.9%; 15–29, 30.6%; 30–44, 21.6%; 45–59, 10.8%; 60–74, 7.8%; 75 and over, 1.3%. **Ethnic composition** (2000): Tunisian Arab 67.2%; Bedouin Arab 26.6%; Algerian Arab 2.4%; Berber 1.4%; other 2.4%. **Religious affiliation** (2000): Sunni Muslim 98.9%; Christian 0.5%; other 0.6%. **Major cities** (2003): Tunis

699,700 (urban agglomeration [2001] 1,927,000); Safaqis 270,700; Al-Arianah 217,100 (within Tunis urban agglomeration); Ettadhamen 188,700 (within Tunis urban agglomeration); Susah 155,900. **Location:** northern Africa, bordering the Mediterranean Sea, Libya, and Algeria.

Vital statistics

Birth rate per 1,000 population (2003): 16.0 (world avg. 21.3). **Death rate** per 1,000 population (2003): 5.0 (world avg. 9.1). **Natural increase rate** per 1,000 population (2003): 11.0 (world avg. 12.2). **Total fertility rate:** avg. births per childbearing woman; 2003): 1.8. **Marriage rate** per 1,000 population (2001): 6.4. **Divorce rate** per 1,000 population (1999): 0.1. **Life expectancy** at birth (2003): male 72.8 years; female 76.2 years.

National economy

Budget (2002). *Revenue:* D 11,533,000,000 (tax revenue 91.5%, of which goods and services 34.4%, income tax 22.1%, social security 18.9%, import duties 9.9%; nontax revenue 8.5%). *Expenditures:* D 11,533,000,000 (current expenditure 79.8%, of which interest on public debt 8.5%; development expenditure 20.2%). **Public debt** (external, outstanding; 2002): $10,641,000,000. **Production** (metric tons except as noted). *Agriculture, forestry, fishing* (2002): olives 1,500,000, tomatoes 810,000, cereals 538,-000; livestock (number of live animals) 6,850,000 sheep, 1,450,000 goats, 760,000 cattle; roundwood (2002) 2,329,000 cu m; fish catch (2001) 100,000. *Mining and quarrying* (2002): phosphate rock 8,144,000; iron ore 198,000; zinc (metal content) 35,692. *Manufacturing* (2002): cement 6,022,000; phosphoric acid 1,219,000; lime 471,000. *Energy production (consumption):* electricity (kW-hr; 2001) 9,787,000,000 ([2000] 9,944,000,000); coal (2000) none (1,000); crude petroleum (barrels; 2001) 25,712,000 (13,625,000); petroleum products (2000) 1,889,000 (3,649,000); natural gas (cu m; 2001) 2,143,100,000 ([2000] 1,923,000,000). **Household income and expenditure.** Average household size (2000) 4.7; income per household D 6,450; expenditure (2000): food and beverages 38.0%, housing and energy 21.5%, household durables 11.1%, health and personal care 10.0%, transportation 9.7%, recreation 8.7%, other 1.0%. **Gross national product** (2003): $22,211,000,000 ($2,240 per capita). **Population economically active** (2002): total 3,375,700; activity rate of total population 34.5% (participation rates: age 15 and over 48.0%; female 24.3%; unemployed 14.9%). **Tourism** (2002): receipts $1,422,000,000; expenditures $260,000,-000. **Land use** as % of total land area (2000): in temporary crops 18.4%, in permanent crops 13.7%, in pasture 26.3%; overall forest area 3.1%.

Foreign trade

Imports (2002-c.i.f.): D 13,511,000,000 (nonelectrical machinery and equipment 19.6%, fabric 12.7%, food products 10.5%, electrical machinery and equipment 10.0%, crude and refined petroleum 8.3%). *Major import sources:* France 25.6%; Italy 19.5%; Germany 8.9%; Spain 5.0%; US 3.2%. **Exports** (2002-f.o.b.): D 9,749,000,000 (clothing 30.4%, knitwear 8.4%, crude petroleum 7.3%, phosphates and phosphate derivatives 6.8%, electrical cable and wire

4.7%). *Major export destinations:* France 31.3%; Italy 21.6%; Germany 11.5%; Spain 4.8%; Libya 4.6%.

Transport and communications

Transport. *Railroads* (2001): route length 2,169 km; passenger-km 1,283,500,000; metric ton-km cargo 2,286,100,000. *Roads* (1997): total length 23,100 km (paved 79%). *Vehicles* (2000): passenger cars 482,700; trucks and buses 250,300. *Air transport* (2001; Tunis Air only): passenger-km 2,696,313,000; metric ton-km cargo 20,104,000; airports (1998) 5. **Communications,** in total units (units per 1,000 persons). Daily newspaper circulation (1996): 280,000 (31); radios (1997): 2,060,000 (224); televisions (1999): 1,800,000 (190); telephone main lines (2003): 1,163,800 (118); cellular telephone subscribers (2003): 1,899,900 (192); personal computers (2003): 400,000 (41); Internet users (2003): 630,000 (64).

Education and health

Literacy (2000): total population age 10 and over literate 74.4%; males literate 83.5%; females literate 65.3%. **Health** (2002): physicians 8,463 (1 per 1,156 persons); hospital beds 16,682 (1 per 586 persons); infant mortality rate per 1,000 live births (2003) 26.8. **Food** (2001): daily per capita caloric intake 3,293 (vegetable products 89%, animal products 11%); 138% of FAO recommended minimum.

Military

Total active duty personnel (2003): 35,000 (army 77.1%, navy 12.9%, air force 10.0%). **Military expenditure as percentage of GNP** (1999): 1.8% (world 2.4%); per capita expenditure $38.

Background

From the 12th century BC the Phoenicians had a series of trading posts on the north African coast. By the 6th century BC the Carthaginian kingdom encompassed most of present-day Tunisia. The Romans ruled from 146 BC until the Muslim Arab invasions in the mid-7th century AD. The area was fought over, won, and lost by many, including the Abbasids, the Almohads, the Spanish, and the Ottoman Turks, who finally conquered it in 1574 and held it until the late 19th century. For a time it maintained autonomy as the French, British, and Italians contended for the region. In 1881 Tunisia became a French protectorate. In World War II US and British forces captured it (1943) to end a brief German occupation. In 1956 France granted it full independence; Habib Bourguiba assumed power and remained in office until 1987.

Recent Developments

On 24 Oct 2004, Tunisia held its simultaneous quinquennial presidential and legislative elections. A special constitutional amendment had been passed that allowed candidates to stand for reelection more than three times consecutively so that incumbent Pres. Gen. Zine al-Abidine Ben Ali could take part in the presidential election. As expected, he won a massive majority, capturing 94.49% of the vote. International concern about the nature of the electoral process in Tunisia reflected the wider disquiet over the state of human rights in the country. Both US Pres. George W.

Bush and Secretary of State Colin Powell brought the matter to President Ben Ali's attention during his visit to the US in February 2004. It was estimated that Tunisia still had about 500 political prisoners.

Internet resources: <www.tourismtunisia.com>.

population (2003): 13.9 (world avg. 12.2). **Total fertility rate** (avg. births per childbearing woman; 2003): 2.4. **Marriage rate** per 1,000 population (2000): 7.1. **Divorce rate** per 1,000 population (2000): 0.5. **Life expectancy** at birth (2003): male 66.4 years; female 71.0 years.

Turkey

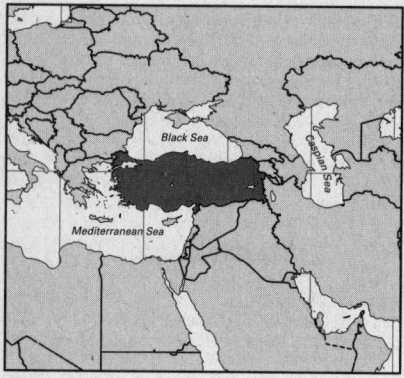

Official name: Turkiye Cumhuriyeti (Republic of Turkey). **Form of government:** multiparty republic with one legislative house (Turkish Grand National Assembly [550]). **Chief of state:** President Ahmet Necdet Sezer (from 2000). **Head of government:** Prime Minister Recep Tayyip Erdogan (from 2003). **Capital:** Ankara. **Official language:** Turkish. **Official religion:** none. **Monetary unit:** 1 Turkish lira (TL) = 100 kurush; valuation (7 Jul 2005) $1 = TL 1,356,000.01. (The New Lira, equal to 1,000 TL, is being phased in.)

Demography

Area: 299,158 sq mi, 774,815 sq km. **Population** (2004): 71,617,000. **Density** (2004): persons per sq mi 239.4, persons per sq km 92.4. **Urban** (2004): 61.2%. **Sex distribution** (2000): male 50.57%; female 49.43%. **Age breakdown** (2000): under 15, 29.1%; 15–29, 28.8%; 30–44, 21.5%; 45–59, 11.8%; 60–74, 6.8%; 75 and over, 2.0%. **Ethnic composition** (2000): Turk 65.1%; Kurd 18.9%; Crimean Tatar 7.2%; Arab 1.8%; Azerbaijani 1.0%; Yoruk 1.0%; other 5.0%. **Religious affiliation** (2000): Muslim 97.2%, of which Sunni 67%, Shi'i 30% (including nonorthodox Alevi 26%); Christian (mostly Eastern Orthodox) 0.6%; other 2.2%. **Major urban agglomerations** (2001): Istanbul 10,243,000; Ankara 4,611,000; Izmir 3,437,000; Bursa (2000) 1,166,000; Adana (2000) 1,091,000. **Location:** southwestern Asia and a small part in southeastern Europe, bordering the Black Sea, Georgia, Armenia, Azerbaijan, Iran, Iraq, Syria, the Mediterranean Sea, Greece, and Bulgaria.

Vital statistics

Birth rate per 1,000 population (2003): 20.9 (world avg. 21.3). **Death rate** per 1,000 population (2003): 7.0 (world avg. 9.1). **Natural increase rate** per 1,000

National economy

Budget (2003). *Revenue:* TL 100,238,122,000,000,-000 (tax revenue 84.1%, of which tax on income 27.7%; nontax revenue 14.0%; grants 1.9%). *Expenditures:* TL 140,053,981,000,000,000 (interest payments 41.8%; personnel 21.6%; investments 5.1%). **Public debt** (external, outstanding; 2002): $61,823,-000,000. **Production** (in '000 metric tons except as noted). *Agriculture, forestry, fishing* (2003): wheat 19,000, sugar beets 13,090, tomatoes 9,750; livestock (number of live animals) 27,000,000 sheep, 10,400,000 cattle, (2000) 373,000 angora goats; roundwood (2002) 18,465,000 cu m; fish catch (2001) 595,000. *Mining* (2002): refined borates 436,000; chromite 313,637; copper ore (metal content) 48,253. *Manufacturing* (value added in $'000,000; 2000): textiles 16,289; refined petroleum 4,839; food products 4,111. *Energy production (consumption):* electricity (kW-hr; 2003) 139,700,-000,000 ([2000] 117,709,000,000); hard coal (2003) 2,996,000 ([2000] 15,393,000); lignite (2003) 43,536,000 ([2000] 64,406,000); crude petroleum (barrels; 2003) 16,988,000 ([2000] 172,115,000); petroleum products (2000) 19,723,-000 (26,108,000); natural gas (cu m; 2000) 630,102,000 (15,762,000,000). **Tourism** (2002): receipts from visitors $11,901,000,000; expenditures by nationals abroad $1,880,000,000. **Population economically active** (2004): total 24,457,000; activity rate of total population 34.1% (participation rates: over age 14, 49.2%; female 26.6%; unemployed 9.3%). **Gross national product** (2003): $197,220,000,000 ($2,790 per capita). **Household income and expenditure** (1994). Average household size (2002) 4.5; income per household TL 165,089,000; expenditure: food, tobacco, and café expenditures 38.5%, housing 22.8%, clothing 9.0%. **Land use** as % of total land area (2000): in temporary crops 31.4%, in permanent crops 3.3%, in pasture 16.1%; overall forest area 13.3%.*

Foreign trade

Imports (2003-c.i.f.): $68,734,000,000 (chemicals and chemical products 16.2%; nonelectrical machinery 11.9%; crude petroleum and natural gas 11.3%; motor vehicles 9.3%; electrical machinery 9.1%; iron and steel 6.8%). *Major import sources:* Germany 13.7%; Italy 7.9%; Russia 7.9%; France 6.0%; US 5.0%; UK 5.0%. **Exports** (2003-f.o.b.): $46,878,-000,000 (textiles, apparel, and clothing accessories 20.3%; vehicles 11.2%; electrical and electronic machinery 7.4%; nonelectrical machinery 6.3%; iron and steel 6.2%; raw and prepared fruits and vegetables 5.3%). *Major export destinations:* Germany 15.9%; US 8.0%; UK 7.8%; Italy 6.8%; France 6.0%.

Transport and communications

Transport. *Railroads* (2003): length 8,671 km; passenger-km 5,893,000,000; metric ton-km cargo

---

1 metric ton = about 1.1 short tons;   1 kilometer = 0.6 mi (statute);   1 metric ton-km cargo = about 0.68 short ton-mi cargo;   c.i.f.: cost, insurance, and freight;   f.o.b.: free on board

8,271,000,000. *Roads* (2000): total length 383,636 km (paved [1997] 25%). *Vehicles* (2003): passenger cars 4,677,765; trucks and buses 1,713,605. *Air transport* (2003; Turkish Airlines only): passenger-km 16,113,000; metric ton-km cargo 369,199,000; airports (1996) 26. **Communications**, in total units (units per 1,000 persons). Daily newspaper circulation (2000): 7,480,000 (111); radios (2001): 32,195,000 (470); televisions (2002): 29,440,000 (423); telephone main lines (2003): 18,916,700 (277); cellular telephone subscribers (2003): 27,887,500 (408); personal computers (2002): 3,000,000 (45); Internet users (2003): 5,500,000 (81).

Education and health

Educational attainment (1993). Percentage of population age 25 and over having: no formal schooling 30.5%; incomplete primary education 6.6%; complete primary 40.4%; incomplete secondary 3.1%; complete secondary or higher 19.1%; unknown 0.3%. **Literacy** (2003): total population age 15 and over literate 88.3%; males literate 95.3%; females literate 79.9%. **Health:** physicians (2001) 82,920 (1 per 826 persons); hospital beds (2000) 156,549 (1 per 431 persons); infant mortality rate per 1,000 live births (2003) 38.3. **Food** (2000): daily per capita caloric intake 3,343 (vegetable products 90%, animal products 10%); 133% of FAO recommended minimum.

Military

Total active duty personnel (2003): 514,850 (army 78.1%, navy 10.2%, air force 11.7%). **Military expenditure as percentage of GNP** (1999): 5.3% (world 2.4%); per capita expenditure $154.

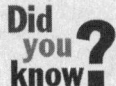

Did you know? The seaport city of Istanbul, originally Byzantium and later Constantinople, is the largest city in Turkey. It was formerly the capital of the Byzantine Empire, of the Ottoman Empire, and—until 1923—of the Turkish Republic. The old, walled city of Istanbul stands on a triangular peninsula between Europe and Asia.

Background

Turkey's early history corresponds to that of Asia Minor, the Byzantine Empire, and the Ottoman Empire. Byzantine rule emerged when Constantine the Great made Constantinople (now Istanbul) his capital. The Ottoman Empire, begun in the 12th century, dominated for more than 600 years; it ended in 1918 after the Young Turk revolt precipitated its demise. Under the leadership of Mustafa Kemal Ataturk, a republic was proclaimed in 1923, and the caliphate was abolished in 1924. Turkey remained neutral throughout most of World War II, siding with the Allies in 1945. Since the war it has alternated between civil and military governments and has had several conflicts with Greece over Cyprus. The 1990s saw political and civic turmoil between Islamists and secularists.

Recent Developments

The prospect of securing a firm date from the European Union for the opening of negotiations on Turkey's accession dominated domestic politics and foreign policy in 2004. Although a settlement of the Cyprus problem was not formally a precondition, Prime Minister Recep Tayyip Erdogan was active diplomatically in bringing about the referendum in Cyprus on 24 April and guaranteeing a positive attitude in Turkish Cyprus toward reunification of the island. Erdogan then concentrated on domestic reforms to satisfy the political criteria for Turkey's accession negotiations. In June the court of appeal in Ankara ordered the release, pending a retrial, of four Kurdish nationalist members of the parliament, including prominent writer Leyla Zana. Also in June, Turkish public-service television started broadcasting in minority languages, including two Kurdish dialects. The parliament in September amended the Turkish penal code in line with EU standards. At its meeting on 16–17 December, the European Council decided to begin EU membership talks for Turkey in 2005. The terrorist threat topped the agenda of the NATO summit meeting held in Istanbul on 28–29 Jun 2004. When US Pres. George W. Bush stopped over in Ankara on his way to Istanbul, the Turkish government pressed him once again to take action against People's Congress of Kurdistan terrorists based in northern Iraq.

Internet resources: <www.turizm.gov.tr>.

Turkmenistan

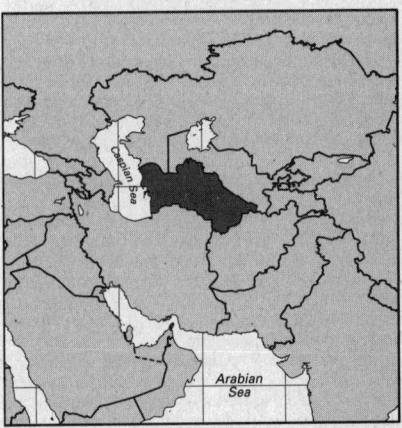

Official name: Turkmenistan. **Form of government:** unitary republic with one legislative body (Majlis [Parliament; 50]). **Head of state and government:** President Saparmurad Niyazov (from 1990). **Capital:** Ashgabat. **Official language:** Turkmen. **Official religion:** none. **Monetary unit:** manat; valuation (7 Jul 2005) $1 = 5,200.05 manat.

Demography

Area: 188,500 sq mi, 488,100 sq km. **Population** (2004): 4,940,000. **Density** (2004): persons per sq mi 26.2, persons per sq km 10.1. **Urban** (2002): 44.9%. **Sex distribution** (2001): male 49.44%; female 50.56%. **Age breakdown** (2001): under 15, 37.9%; 15–29, 27.9%; 30–44, 23.7%; 45–59, 6.5%; 60–74, 3.5%; 75 and over, 0.5%. **Ethnic composition** (1997): Turkmen 77.0%; Uzbek 9.2%; Russian 6.7%; Kazakh 2.0%; Tatar 0.8%; other 4.3%. **Religious affil-**

iation (1995): Muslim (mostly Sunni) 87.0%; Russian Orthodox 2.4%; other (mostly nonreligious) 10.6%. **Major cities** (1999): Ashgabat (2002) 743,000; Turkmenabat 203,000; Dasoguz 165,000; Mary 123,000; Balkanabat 108,000. **Location:** central Asia, bordering Kazakhstan, Uzbekistan, Afghanistan, Iran, and the Caspian Sea.

Vital statistics

Birth rate per 1,000 population (2003): 28.0 (world avg. 21.3); (1998) legitimate 96.2%. **Death rate** per 1,000 population (2003): 8.9 (world avg. 9.1). **Natural increase rate** per 1,000 population (2003): 19.1 (world avg. 12.2). **Total fertility rate** (avg. births per childbearing woman; 2003): 3.5. **Marriage rate** per 1,000 population (1998): 5.4. **Divorce rate** per 1,000 population (1994): 1.5. **Life expectancy** at birth (2003): male 57.7 years; female 64.8 years.

National economy

Budget (1999). *Revenue:* 3,693,100,000,000 manat (value-added tax 25.6%, pension and social security fund 22.5%, repayments of scheduled gas 13.0%, excise tax 10.2%, personal income tax 6.1%). *Expenditures:* 3,894,300,000,000 manat (education 26.9%, pension and social security 15.6%, defense and security 14.9%, health 14.1%, agriculture 5.7%). **Public debt** (external, outstanding; 2000): $1,731,000,000. **Production** (metric tons except as noted). *Agriculture, forestry, fishing* (2002): wheat 2,033,000, seed cotton 600,000, vegetables and melons 327,000; livestock (number of live animals) 6,375,000 sheep and goats, 860,000 cattle, 4,800,000 poultry; roundwood (2000) 2,000,000 cu m; fish catch (2001) 12,792. *Mining and quarrying* (2000): gypsum 100,000, sodium sulfate 60,000, sulfur 9,000. *Manufacturing* (value of production in '000,000 manat; 1994): ferrous and nonferrous metals 278; machinery and metalworks 223; food products 129. *Energy production (consumption):* electricity (kW-hr; 2000) 9,845,000,000 (8,777,000,000); crude petroleum (barrels; 2001) 58,000,000 (19,000,000); petroleum products (2000) 6,113,000 (2,354,000); natural gas (cu m; 2001) 46,439,000,000 (7,362,000,000). **Household income and expenditure.** Average household size (2000) 4.7; sources of income (1998): wages and salaries 70.6%, pensions and grants 20.9%, self-employment (mainly agricultural income) 2.3%, nonwage income of workers 1.1%; expenditure (1998): food 45.2%, clothing and footwear 16.8%, furniture 13.3%, transportation 7.6%, health 7.0%. **Population economically active** (2000): total 1,950,000; activity rate of total population 42.0% (participation rates [1996]: ages 16–59 [male], 16–54 [female] 73.0%; female 42.7%). **Gross national product** (2003): $5,400,000,000 ($1,120 per capita). **Tourism:** receipts from visitors (1998) $192,000,000; expenditures (1997) $125,000,000. **Land use** as % of total land area (2000): in temporary crops 3.7%, in permanent crops 0.1%, in pasture 65.3%; overall forest area 8.0%.

Foreign trade

Imports (2002 data in balance of trade is c.i.f.): $2,119,000,000 (machinery and transport equipment 40.5%, basic manufactures 18.6%, chemicals and chemical products 9.9%, food products 5.4%). *Major import sources* (2002): Ukraine 17.9%; Germany 12.1%; UAE 11.7%; Russia 10.6%; Turkey 8.8%; Iran 7.3%. **Exports** (2002): $2,856,000,000 (natural gas 57.5%, petrochemicals 14.2%, crude petroleum 11.9%, cotton yarn and fabrics 2.8%, raw cotton 1.7%). *Major export destinations* (2000): Russia 41.1%; Germany 16.2%; Iran 9.7%; Turkey 7.4%; Ukraine 6.6%.

Transport and communications

Transport. *Railroads* (1999): length 2,313 km; passenger-km 701,000,000; metric ton-km cargo 7,337,000,000. *Roads* (1999): total length 24,000 km (paved 81%). *Vehicles* (1995): passenger cars 220,000; trucks and buses 58,200. *Air transport* (2001; Turkmenavia only): passenger-km 1,631,000,000; metric ton-km cargo 35,000,000; airports (2002) with scheduled flights 1. **Communications,** in total units (units per 1,000 persons). Radios (2000): 1,190,000 (256); televisions (2000): 911,000 (196); telephone main lines (2002): 374,000 (77); cellular phone subscribers (2002): 8,200 (1.7); Internet users (2001): 8,000 (1.6).

Education and health

Literacy (1999): total population age 15 and over literate 98.0%. **Health** (1995): physicians 13,500 (1 per 330 persons); hospital beds 46,000 (1 per 97 persons); infant mortality rate per 1,000 live births (2003) 73.2. **Food** (2001): daily per capita caloric intake 2,738 (vegetable products 97%, animal products 3%); 107% of FAO recommended minimum.

Military

Total active duty personnel (2003): 29,000 (army 86.3%, navy 3.4%, air force 10.3%). **Military expenditure as percentage of GNP** (1999): 3.4% (world 2.4%); per capita expenditure $122.

Background

The earliest traces of human settlement in central Asia, dating back to Paleolithic times, have been found in Turkmenistan. The nomadic, tribal Turkmen probably entered the area in the 11th century AD. They were conquered by the Russians in the early 1880s, and the region became part of Russian Turkistan. It was organized as the Turkmen Soviet Socialist Republic in 1924 and became a constituent republic of the USSR in 1925. The country gained full independence from the USSR in 1991 under the name Turkmenistan. From 1990 the country was ruled by the ever more autocratic and mercurial strongman Saparmurad Niyazov.

Recent Developments

Pres. Saparmurad Niyazov continued to astonish the world with his erratic policies, which were intended to turn Turkmenistan into a great nation. In response to international ridicule of his all-pervasive personality cult, Niyazov had some portraits and statues of himself removed from public places, but the spirit of the cult remained. He continued his reorganization of the

1 metric ton = about 1.1 short tons;   1 kilometer = 0.6 mi (statute);   1 metric ton-km cargo = about 0.68 short ton-mi cargo;   c.i.f.: cost, insurance, and freight;   f.o.b.: free on board

educational system; according to official figures, fewer than 4,000 new students were admitted to higher education in 2004, and private study abroad became almost impossible after health officials were instructed not to provide health certificates to persons wishing to study outside Turkmenistan without official sponsorship. In February and March 2005 there were reports that Turkmenistan had closed all hospitals in the country except for those in the capital, Ashgabat, as well as all libraries except the National Library and those in educational institutions.

Internet resources:
<www.turkmenistanembassy.org>.

Tuvalu

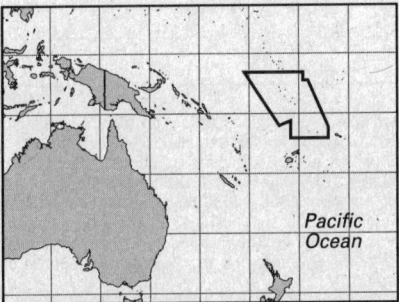

Pacific Ocean

Official name: Tuvalu. **Form of government:** constitutional monarchy with one legislative house (Parliament [12]). **Chief of state:** British Queen Elizabeth II (from 1952), represented by Governor-General Filoimea Telito (from 15 Apr 2005). **Head of government:** Prime Minister Maatia Toafa (from 27 Aug 2004). **Capital:** government offices are at Vaiaku, Fongafale islet, on Funafuti atoll. **Official language:** none. **Official religion:** none. **Monetary units:** 1 Tuvalu dollar = 1 Australian dollar ($T = $A) = 100 Tuvalu and Australian cents; valuation (7 Jul 2005) US$1 = $A 1.35.

Demography

Area: 9.90 sq mi, 25.63 sq km. **Population** (2004): 9,600. **Density** (2004): persons per sq mi 969.7, persons per sq km 374.6. **Urban** (2002): 47.0%. **Sex distribution** (2002): male 49.46%; female 50.54%. **Age breakdown** (2002): under 15, 36.2%; 15–29, 21.2%; 30–44, 20.2%; 45–59, 13.8%; 60–74, 6.8%; 75 and over, 1.8%. **Ethnic composition** (2000): Tuvaluan (Polynesian) 96.3%; mixed (Pacific Islander/European/Asian) 1.0%; Micronesian 1.0%; European 0.5%; other 1.2%. **Religious affiliation** (1995): Church of Tuvalu (Congregational) 85.4%; Seventh-day Adventist 3.6%; Roman Catholic 1.4%; Jehovah's Witness 1.1%; Baha'i 1.0%; other 7.5%. **Major locality** (2002): Fongafale, on Funafuti atoll, 4,492. **Location:** western Pacific Ocean, lying east of Papua New Guinea near the equator.

Vital statistics

Birth rate per 1,000 population (2002): 27.1 (world avg. 21.3). **Death rate** per 1,000 population (2002): 9.9 (world avg. 9.1). **Natural increase rate** per 1,000 population (2002): 17.2 (world avg. 12.2). **Total fertility rate** (avg. births per childbearing woman; 2002): 3.7. **Life expectancy** at birth (2002): male 61.7 years; female 65.1 years.

National economy

Budget (2001). *Revenue:* $A 33,519,000. *Expenditures:* $A 24,091,000. **Gross national product** (1998): US$14,700,000 (US$1,400 per capita). **Production** (metric tons except as noted). *Agriculture and fishing* (2002): coconuts 1,000, tropical fruit 400, vegetables 380,; livestock (number of live animals) 13,200 pigs, 10,000 ducks, 40,000 chickens; fish catch (2001) 500. *Manufacturing:* tiny amounts of copra, handicrafts, and garments. Overseas employment (2000) of Tuvaluan seafarers contributes about US$5,000,000 annually to the Tuvalu economy. *Energy production (consumption):* electricity (kW-hr; 1992) 1,300,000 (1,300,000). **Tourism** (1998): receipts from visitors US$200,000. **Population economically active** (1991): total 5,910; activity rate of total population 65.3% (participation rates: ages 15–64, 85.5%; female [1979] 51.3%; unemployed [1979] 4.0%). **Household income and expenditure.** Average household size (1994): Funafuti 7.0, other islands 5.8; average annual gross income per household (1994): Funafuti $A 12,012, other islands $A 3,536; sources of income (1987): agriculture and other 45.0%, cash economy only 38.0%, overseas remittances 17.0%; expenditure (1992): food 45.5%, housing and household operations 11.5%, transportation 10.5%, alcohol and tobacco 10.5%, clothing 7.5%, other 14.5%. **Land use** as % of total land area (2000): coconut trees occupy c. 77% of land area.

Foreign trade

Imports (2002): $A 20,362,000 (food products including live animals 23.5%, mineral fuels 13.8%, machinery and apparatus 12.4%, base and fabricated metals 8.8%, transport equipment 7.3%). *Major import sources:* Australia 34.7%; Fiji 29.4%; New Zealand 13.9%; Japan 10.3%; China 3.7%. **Exports** (2002): $A 252,000 (primarily copra, stamps, and handicrafts). *Major export destinations:* Fiji 58.9%; Australia 22.3%; New Zealand 11.4%; Japan 5.7%.

Transport and communications

Transport. *Roads* (2000): total length 28 km (paved, none). *Air transport:* airports (2001) 1. **Communications,** in total units (units per 1,000 persons). Radios (1997): 4,000 (384); televisions (1996): 100 (13); telephone main lines (2002): 1,300 (125).

Education and health

Educational attainment (mid-1990s). Percentage of population age 15 and over (on Funafuti) having: no formal schooling through completed primary education 31.9%; some secondary 46.6%; completed secondary to some higher 18.6%; completed higher 2.9%. **Literacy** (1990): total population literate in Tuvaluan 8,593 (95.0%); literacy in English estimated at 45.0%. **Health** (1999): physicians 8 (1 per 1,375 persons); hospital beds (1990) 30 (1 per 302 persons); infant mortality rate per 1,000 live births (2002): 35.0.

Military

Total active duty personnel: none; Tuvalu relies on Australian-trained volunteers from Fiji and Papua New Guinea.

Background

The original Polynesian settlers of Tuvalu probably came mainly from Samoa or Tonga. The islands were sighted by the Spanish in the 16th century. Europeans settled there in the 19th century and intermarried with Tuvaluans. During this period Peruvian slave traders, known as "blackbirders," decimated the population. In 1856 the US claimed the four southern islands for guano mining. Missionaries from Europe arrived in 1865 and rapidly converted the islanders to Christianity. In 1892 Tuvalu joined the British Gilbert Islands, a protectorate that became the Gilbert and Ellice Islands Colony in 1916. Tuvaluans voted in 1974 for separation from the Gilberts (now Kiribati), whose people are Micronesian. Tuvalu gained independence in 1978, and in 1979 the US relinquished its claims. Elections were held in 1981, and a revised constitution was adopted in 1986. In recent decades, the government has tried to find overseas job opportunities for its citizens.

Recent Developments

Tuvalu, comprising low coral atolls and reef islands vulnerable to rising sea levels, was a strong campaigner for the Kyoto Protocol on climate change and had regularly sought resettlement options for its people. In February 2004 unusually high "king tides" caused flooding on much of Funafuti Atoll. In July of that year Tuvalu joined the International Whaling Commission but denied that it had received additional aid from Japan as a consequence.

Internet resources: <www.timelesstuvalu.com>.

Uganda

Official name: Republic of Uganda. **Form of government:** nonparty republic with one legislative house (Parliament [305, including 10 nonelected members]). **Head of state and government:** President Yoweri Museveni (from 1986), assisted by Prime Minister Apolo Nsibambi (from 1999). **Capital:** Kampala. **Official language:** English. **Official religion:** none. **Monetary unit:** 1 Uganda shilling (U Sh) = 100 cents; valuation (7 Jul 2005) $1 = U Sh 1,732.

Demography

Area: 93,065 sq mi, 241,038 sq km (includes 16,984 sq mi [43,989 sq km] water area). **Population** (2004): 26,335,000. **Density** (2004; based on land area only): persons per sq mi 346.1, persons per sq km 133.6. **Urban** (2002): 12.2%. **Sex distribution** (2002): male 48.99%; female 51.01%. **Age breakdown** (2002): under 15, 50.9%; 15–29, 26.4%; 30–44, 13.4%; 45–59, 5.6%; 60–74, 3.0%; 75 and over, 0.7%. **Ethnolinguistic composition** (1991): Ganda 18.1%; Nkole 10.7%; Kiga 8.4%; Soga 8.2%; Lango 5.9%; Lugbara 4.7%; Gisu 4.5%;

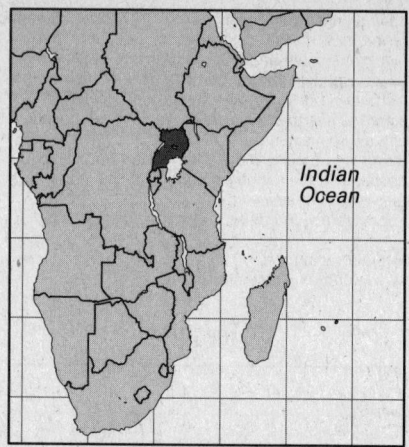

Acholi 4.4%. **Religious affiliation** (1995): Christian 66%, of which Roman Catholic 33%, Protestant 33% (of which mostly Anglican); traditional beliefs 18%; Muslim 16%. **Major cities** (2002): Kampala urban agglomeration 1,208,544; Gulu 113,144; Lira 89,871; Jinja 86,520; Mbale 70,437. **Location:** eastern Africa, bordering The Sudan, Kenya, Lake Victoria, Tanzania, Rwanda, and the Democratic Republic of the Congo.

Vital statistics

Birth rate per 1,000 population (2003): 46.6 (world avg. 21.3). **Death rate** per 1,000 population (2003): 17.0 (world avg. 9.1). **Natural increase rate** per 1,000 population (2003): 29.6 (world avg. 12.2). **Total fertility rate** (avg. births per childbearing woman; 2003): 6.7. **Life expectancy** at birth (2003): male 43.4 years; female 46.4 years. **Adult population** (ages 15–49) **living with HIV** (2004): 4.1% (world avg. 1.1%).

National economy

Budget (2001–02). *Revenue:* U Sh 1,977,500,000,-000 (tax revenue 58.4%, of which VAT 19.9%, excise taxes 18.3%, income taxes 14.4%, tax on international trade 5.9%; grants 36.6%; nontax revenue 5.0%). *Expenditures:* U Sh 2,565,000,000,000 (current expenditures 55.8%, of which public administration 14.3%, education 14.1%, defense 8.2%, health 6.4%, public order 4.5%; capital expenditures 44.2%). **Production** (metric tons except as noted). *Agriculture, forestry, fishing* (2002): plantains 9,600,000, cassava 5,300,000, sweet potatoes 2,515,000; livestock (number of live animals) 5,900,000 cattle, 5,600,000 goats, 25,500,000 chickens; roundwood 38,316,824 cu m; fish catch (2001) 356,032. *Mining and quarrying* (2002): cobalt 450; columbite-tantalite (ore and concentrate) 6,463 kg. *Manufacturing* (2001): cement 431,084; sugar 130,326; soap 90,807. *Energy production (consumption):* electricity (kW-hr; 2001) 1,534,-700,000 (1,534,700,000); petroleum products (2000) none (436,000). **Tourism** (2002): receipts

---

1 metric ton = about 1.1 short tons;   *1 kilometer = 0.6 mi (statute);*   *1 metric ton-km cargo = about 0.68 short ton-mi cargo;*   *c.i.f.: cost, insurance, and freight;*   *f.o.b.: free on board*

from visitors $185,000,000; expenditures by nationals abroad (1999) $141,000,000. **Gross national product** (2003): $6,173,000,000 ($240 per capita). **Population economically active** (2002): total 11,995,000; activity rate of total population 48.5% (participation rates [2001]: ages 15–64, 78.9%; female [2001] 35.2%). **Public debt** (external, outstanding; 2002): $3,690,000,000. **Household income and expenditure** (1999–2000). Average household size (2002) 4.7; income per household U Sh 141,000; sources of income: wages and self-employment 78.0%, transfers 13.0%, rent 9.0%; expenditure: food and beverages 51.0%, rent, energy, and services 17.0%, education 7.0%, household durable goods 6.0%, transportation 5.0%, health 4.0%. **Land use** as % of total land area (2000): in temporary crops 25.7%, in permanent crops 10.7%, in pasture 25.9%; overall forest area 21.0%.

Foreign trade

Imports (2001–02-c.i.f.): $1,084,900,000 (machinery and apparatus 28.3%, refined petroleum 16.1%, food and live animals 15.9%, road vehicles 15.8%, pharmaceuticals 4.9%). *Major import sources* (2002): Kenya 45.1%; South Africa 6.7%; India 5.6%; UK 5.5%; France 3.4%. **Exports** (2001–02-f.o.b.): $475,500,000 (unroasted coffee 21.6%, fish products 17.0%, tea 5.7%, cereal 2.8%, cotton 2.8%). *Major export destinations* (2002): Belgium 16.2%; The Netherlands 13.7%; Germany 7.5%; Spain 5.5%; Hong Kong 4.9%.

Transport and communications

Transport. *Railroads* (2000): route length 1,241 km; metric ton-km cargo (2001) 220,000,000. *Roads* (1996): total length 26,800 km (paved 7.7%). *Vehicles* (2000): passenger cars 49,016; trucks and buses 55,683. *Air transport* (2000): passenger-km 215,000,000; airports (2002) 1. **Communications**, in total units (units per 1,000 persons). Daily newspaper circulation (2000): 45,900 (2); radios (2000): 2,920,000 (127); televisions (2002): 442,800 (18); telephone main lines (2003): 61,000 (2.4); cellular telephone subscribers (2003): 776,200 (30); personal computers (2003): 103,000 (4); Internet users (2003): 125,000 (4.9).

Education and health

Educational attainment (1991). Percentage of population age 25 and over having: no formal schooling or less than one full year 46.9%; primary education 42.1%; secondary 10.5%; higher 0.5%. **Literacy** (2001): population age 10 and over literate 68.0%; males literate 78.1%; females literate 58.0%. **Health:** physicians (1993) 840 (1 per 22,399 persons); hospital beds (1996) 22,788 (1 per 880 persons); infant mortality rate per 1,000 live births (2003) 87.9. **Food** (2001): daily per capita caloric intake 2,398 (vegetable products 94%, animal products 6%); 103% of FAO recommended minimum.

Military

Total active duty personnel (2003): 60,000 (army 100%). **Military expenditure as percentage of GNP** (1999): 2.3% (world 2.4%); per capita military expenditure $6.

Background

By the 19th century the region around Uganda comprised several separate kingdoms inhabited by various peoples, including Bantu- and Nilotic-speaking tribes. Arab traders reached the area in the 1840s. The native kingdom of Buganda was visited by the first European explorers in 1862. Protestant and Roman Catholic missionaries arrived in the 1870s, and the development of religious factions led to persecution and civil strife. In 1894 Buganda was formally proclaimed a British protectorate. As Uganda, it gained its independence in 1962, and in 1967 it adopted a republican constitution. The civilian government was overthrown in 1971 and replaced by a military regime under Idi Amin. His invasion of Tanzania in late 1978 resulted in the collapse of his regime. In 1985 the civilian government was again deposed by the military, which in turn was overthrown in 1986. A constituent assembly enacted a new constitution in 1995.

Recent Developments

Operations by Joseph Kony's anarchic Lord's Resistance Army (LRA) in the northern quarter of Uganda, which had begun in 1994, caused grave concern and sapped state resources, but such military forces as were made available proved incapable of halting the devastation. In March 2003 the government launched Operation Iron Fist, aimed at putting an end to the rebellion. Little was accomplished, however, and, in a particularly ugly incident, in late April 2004, LRA fighters attacked a refugee camp in Lira district and massacred 190 internees. So long as the rebels remained at a distance from the more affluent south, however, international observers seemed prepared to turn a blind eye. Later in the year the army claimed successes against the LRA, killing a number of the rebels and inducing others to surrender. Kony narrowly escaped capture in July. Nevertheless, LRA attacks on unprotected civilians continued, and in August an advance team from the International Criminal Court arrived in the country to prepare for an investigation into crimes committed in the course of the conflict. A cease-fire in November in a restricted area did not last, and in December part of the Ugandan army was deployed once more on the border of the Democratic Republic of the Congo.

Internet resources: <www.visituganda.com>.

Ukraine

Official name: Ukrayina (Ukraine). **Form of government:** unitary multiparty republic with a single legislative body (Supreme Council [450]). **Head of state:** President Viktor Yushchenko (from 23 Jan 2005). **Head of government:** Prime Minister Yulia Tymoshenko (from 4 Feb 2005). **Capital:** Kiev (Kyyiv). **Official language:** Ukrainian. **Official religion:** none. **Monetary unit:** hryvnya (pl. hryvnyas); valuation (7 Jul 2005) $1 = 5.01 hryvnyas.

Demography

Area: 233,062 sq mi, 603,628 sq km. **Population** (2004): 47,470,000. **Density** (2004): persons per sq mi 203.7, persons per sq km 78.6. **Urban** (2004): 67.6%. **Sex distribution** (2004): male 46.22%; female

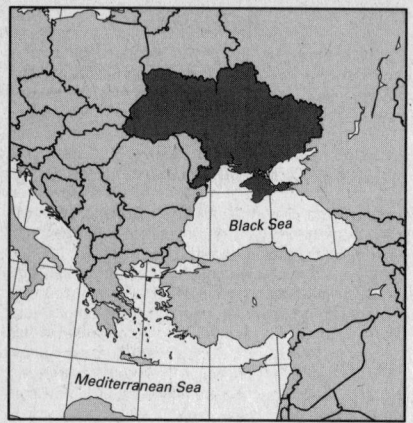

Black Sea

Mediterranean Sea

53.78%. **Age breakdown** (2003): under 15, 16.3%; 15–29, 22.6%; 30–44, 21.7%; 45–59, 18.7%; 60–74, 15.0%; 75 and over, 5.7%. **Ethnic composition** (2001): Ukrainian 77.8%; Russian 17.3%; Belarusian 0.6%; Moldovan 0.5%; Crimean Tatar 0.5%; other 3.3%. **Religious affiliation** (1995): Ukrainian Orthodox (Russian patriarchy) 19.5%; Ukrainian Orthodox (Kiev patriarchy) 9.7%; Ukrainian Catholic (Uniate) 7.0%; Protestant 3.6%; other Orthodox 1.6%; Roman Catholic 1.2%; Jewish 0.9%; other (mostly nonreligious) 56.5%. **Major cities** (2001): Kiev 2,621,700 (2003); Kharkiv 1,470,000; Dnipropetrovsk 1,064,000; Odessa 1,029,000; Donetsk 1,016,000. **Location:** eastern Europe, bordering Belarus, Russia, the Black Sea, Romania, Moldova, Hungary, Slovakia, and Poland.

Vital statistics

Birth rate per 1,000 population (2003): 8.6 (world avg. 21.3); legitimate 80.1%. **Death rate** per 1,000 population (2003): 16.1 (world avg. 9.1). **Natural increase rate** per 1,000 population (2003): –7.5 (world avg. 12.2). **Total fertility rate** (avg. births per childbearing woman; 2003): 1.3. **Life expectancy** at birth (2003): male 61.1 years; female 72.2 years.

National economy

Budget (2003). *Revenue:* 54,986,700,000 hryvnyas (tax revenue 64.9%, of which tax on profits of enterprises 23.8%, VAT 22.9%, excise tax 9.3%; nontax revenue 28.6%; other 6.5%). *Expenditures:* 56,010,-900,000 hryvnyas (2001; social security 43.2%; economy 8.2%; debt payment 6.7%; education 6.2%; public order 6.1%; defense 5.8%; health 1.9%). **Production** (metric tons except as noted). *Agriculture, forestry, fishing* (2002): wheat 20,550,000, potatoes 16,100,000, sugar beets 14,400,000; livestock (number of live animals) 9,421,000 cattle, 8,370,000 pigs, 1,875,000 sheep and goats; roundwood (2002) 9,859,300 cu m; fish catch (2001) 382,300. *Mining and quarrying* (2001): iron ore (2003) 62,952,000; manganese (metal content) 930,000; ilmenite concentrate 600,000. *Manufacturing* (value of production in '000,000 hryvnyas; 1998): iron and steel

14,525; food and beverages 12,974; nonelectrical machinery 3,838. *Energy production (consumption):* electricity (kW-hr; 2002) 172,800,000,000 ([2000] 167,596,000,000); hard coal (2003) 75,792,000 ([2000] 84,209,000); lignite (2003) 648,000 ([2000] 1,058,000); crude petroleum (barrels; 2003) 29,027,000 ([2000] 70,265,000); petroleum products (barrels; 2000) 8,822,000 (9,999,000); natural gas (cu m; 2003) 16,346,000,000 (76,089,-500,000). **Population economically active** (2002): total 22,701,700; activity rate of total population 47.2% (participation rates: ages 16–59 [male], 15–64 [female] 56.6%; female 48.9%; unemployed 10.1% [registered 5.8%]). **Public debt** (external; 2002): $8,349,000,000. **Gross national product** (2003): $46,739,000,000 ($970 per capita). **Tourism** (2002): receipts $2,992,000,000; expenditures $2,087,000,000. **Household income and expenditure.** Average household size (2002): 2.7; income per household (2003) 8,800 hryvnyas; sources of income (2003): wages and salaries 43.4%, subsidies and pensions 35.2%, profit and mixed income 16.4%, property income 5.0%; expenditures (2003): food and beverages 62.7%, consumer goods 30.6%, housing 6.7%. **Land use** as % of total land area (2000): in temporary crops 56.2%, in permanent crops 1.6%, in pasture 13.7%; overall forest area 16.5%.

Foreign trade

Imports (2002): $17,959,000,000 (machinery 22.4%, natural gas 19.6%, crude petroleum 13.5%, chemicals and chemical products 13.1%, food and raw materials 6.6%). *Major import sources* (2003): Russia 32.9%; Germany 13.5%; Turkmenistan 9.6%; Italy 4.6%; China 4.3%. **Exports** (2002): $18,669,000,000 (ferrous and nonferrous metals 39.3%, wood and wood products 14.5%, food and raw materials 13.2%, machinery 11.5%, chemicals and chemical products 10.0%). *Major export destinations* (2003): Russia 17.6%; Turkey 7.3%; Italy 6.0%; China 5.3%; Germany 3.6%.

Transport and communications

Transport. *Railroads* (2001): length 22,218 km; passenger-km 52,661,000,000; metric ton-km cargo 177,465,000,000. *Roads* (2003): total length 169,739 km (paved 97%). *Vehicles* (2001): passenger cars 5,313,000. *Air transport* (2003): passenger-km 2,352,000,000; metric ton-km cargo 13,536,000; airports (1999) with scheduled flights 12. **Communications,** in total units (units per 1,000 persons). Daily newspaper circulation (2000): 4,970,000 (101); radios (2000): 43,800,000 (889); televisions (2000): 22,500,000 (456); telephone main lines (2002): 10,833,200 (216); cellular telephone subscribers (2002): 4,200,000 (84); personal computers (2002): 951,000 (19); Internet users (2002): 900,000 (18).

Education and health

Literacy (1999): percentage of total population age 15 and over literate 99.6%; males literate 99.7%; females literate 99.5%. **Health** (2003): physicians 223,000 (1 per 214 persons); hospital beds 458,000 (1 per 104 persons); infant mortality rate

1 metric ton = about 1.1 short tons;   1 kilometer = 0.6 mi (statute);   1 metric ton-km cargo = about 0.68 short ton-mi cargo;   c.i.f.: cost, insurance, and freight;   f.o.b.: free on board

per 1,000 live births (2003) 20.8. **Food** (2001): daily per capita caloric intake 3,008 (vegetable products 80%, animal products 20%); 118% of FAO recommended minimum.

Military

Total active duty personnel (2003): 295,500 (army 50.1%, air force 16.6%, navy 4.6%, headquarters 14.2%, paramilitary 14.5%). **Military expenditure as percentage of GNP** (1999): 3.0% (world 2.4%); per capita expenditure $103.

Background

The area around Ukraine was invaded and occupied in the first millennium BC by the Cimmerians, Scythians, and Sarmatians, and in the first millennium AD by the Goths, Huns, Bulgars, Avars, Khazars, and Magyars. Slavic tribes settled there after the 4th century. Kiev was the chief town of Kievan Rus. The Mongol conquest in the mid-13th century decisively ended Kievan power. Ruled by Lithuania in the 14th century and Poland in the 16th century, it fell to Russian rule in the 18th century. The Ukrainian National Republic, established in 1917, declared its independence from Soviet Russia in 1918 but was reconquered in 1919; it was made the Ukrainian Soviet Socialist Republic of the USSR in 1922. The northwestern region was held by Poland from 1919 to 1939. Ukraine suffered a severe famine in 1932–33 under Soviet leader Joseph Stalin; over five million Ukrainians died of starvation in an unprecedented peacetime catastrophe. Overrun by Axis armies in 1941 in World War II, it was further devastated before being retaken by the Soviets in 1944. It was the site of the 1986 accident in Chernobyl, at a Soviet-built nuclear power plant. Ukraine declared independence in 1991. In recent years it has struggled economically as well as politically under Pres. Leonid Kuchma's regime.

Recent Developments

What was later called the "Orange Revolution" brought dramatic changes to Ukraine in 2004–05. Prime Minister Viktor Yanukovych and his major challenger, Our Ukraine party's Viktor Yushchenko, ran nearly neck and neck in the first round of presidential elections on 31 October, each drawing just under 40% of the vote. Though exit polls in the runoff round suggested that the opposition leader led by about nine points, the election commission announced that Yanukovych had won. Yushchenko's supporters maintained that the results were fabricated, and mass protests began in Kiev on 22 November. Several provinces recognized Yushchenko as the winner, and the candidate was sworn in as president in an informal session of the parliament. Gradually the television stations formerly controlled by Kuchma, as well as security and military leaders, switched support to the Yushchenko campaign. The impasse continued for two weeks. On 3 December the Supreme Court declared the election results to be invalid and ordered a rerun of the second round. Tensions rose again on 12 December when doctors in Vienna confirmed that Yushchenko's blood contained critically high levels of dioxin and concluded that he had been poisoned at the early stages of the election campaign. The runoff election was held on 26 December, and Yushchenko was eventually declared the winner.

He was sworn in as president on 23 Jan 2005, and he soon named the dynamic Yuliya Tymoshenko as prime minister.

Internet resources: <www.ukremb.com>.

United Arab Emirates

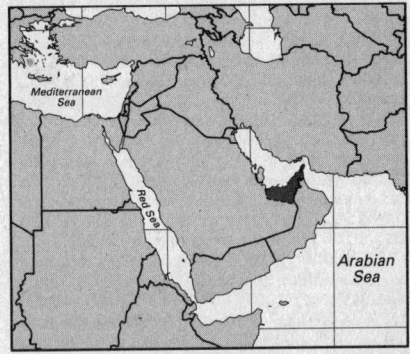

Official name: Al-Imarat al-'Arabiyah al-Muttahidah (United Arab Emirates). **Form of government:** federation of seven emirates with one advisory body (Federal National Council [40; all appointed seats]). **Chief of state:** President Sheikh Khalifah ibn Zayid Al Nahyan (from 3 Nov 2004). **Head of government:** Prime Minister Sheikh Maktum ibn Rashid al-Maktum (from 1990). **Capital:** Abu Dhabi. **Official language:** Arabic. **Official religion:** Islam. **Monetary unit:** 1 UAE dirham (Dh) = 100 fils; valuation (7 Jul 2005) $1 = Dh 3.67.

Demography

Area: 32,280 sq mi, 83,600 sq km. **Population** (2004): 4,298,000. **Density** (2004): persons per sq mi 133.1, persons per sq km 51.4. **Urban** (2001): 87.2%. **Sex distribution** (2001): male 67.63%; female 32.37%. **Age breakdown** (2001): under 15, 26.2%; 15–29, 29.2%; 30–44, 33.4%; 45–59, 9.6%; 60–74, 1.4%; 75 and over, 0.2%. **Ethnic composition** (2000): Arab 48.1%, of which UAE Arab 12.2%, UAE Bedouin 9.4%, Egyptian Arab 6.2%, Omani Arab 4.1%, Saudi Arab 4.0%; South Asian 35.7%, of which Pashtun 7.1%, Balochi 7.1%, Malayali 7.1%, Persian 5.0%; Filipino 3.4%; white 2.4%; other 5.4%. **Religious affiliation** (1995): Muslim 96.0% (Sunni 80.0%, Shi'i 16.0%); other (mostly Christian and Hindu) 4.0%. **Major cities** (2003): Dubai 1,171,000; Abu Dhabi 552,000; Sharjah 519,000; Al-'Ayn 348,000; 'Ajman 225,000. **Location:** the Middle East, bordering the Persian Gulf, the Gulf of Oman, Oman, and Saudi Arabia.

Vital statistics

Birth rate per 1,000 population (2003): 15.1 (world avg. 21.3). **Death rate** per 1,000 population (2003): 1.5 (world avg. 9.1). **Natural increase rate** per 1,000 population (2003): 13.6 (world avg. 12.2). **Total fertility rate** (avg. births per childbearing woman; 2003): 2.5. **Marriage rate** per 1,000 population (2003): 3.0. **Divorce rate** per 1,000 population (2003): 0.8. **Life expectancy** at birth (2003): male 72.3 years; female 77.4 years.

National economy

Budget (2001). *Revenue:* Dh 82,480,000,000 (oil revenue 58.5%, non-oil revenue 41.5%). *Expenditures:* Dh 96,083,000,000 (current expenditures 80.5%, capital [development] expenditure 19.5%). **Gross national product** (2001): $69,568,000,000 ($19,945 per capita). **Tourism** (2002): receipts $1,328,000,000. **Production** (metric tons except as noted). *Agriculture, forestry, fishing* (2002): dates 760,000, spinach 620,000, tomatoes 400,000; livestock (number of live animals) 1,300,000 goats, 510,000 sheep, 220,000 camels; fish catch (2001) 117,607. *Mining and quarrying* (2001): aluminum 500,000; gypsum 90,000; lime 50,000. *Manufacturing* (value of production in Dh '000,000; 1998): chemical products (including refined petroleum) 10,096; textiles and wearing apparel 2,397; fabricated metal products 1,999. *Energy production (consumption):* electricity (kW-hr; 2000) 31,890,000,000 (31,890,000,000); crude petroleum (barrels; 2001) 740,000,000 ([2000] 152,801,000); petroleum products (2000) 26,137,000 (6,028,000); natural gas (cu m; 2001) 41,300,000,000 ([2000] 16,469,000,000). **Population economically active** (2001): total 1,853,000; activity rate of total population 53.1% (participation rates [1995]: over age 15, 55.4%; female 11.7%; unemployed [2001] 1.8%). **Households.** Average household size (2000) 5.0; expenditure (1996): rent, fuel, and light 36.1%, transportation and communications 14.9%, food 14.4%, education, recreation, and entertainment 10.3%, durable household goods 7.4%, clothing 6.7%. **Land use** as % of total land area (2000): in temporary crops 0.7%, in permanent crops 2.2%, in pasture 3.6%; overall forest area 3.8%.

Foreign trade

Imports (2001): Dh 120,600,000,000 (for emirates of Abu Dhabi, Dubai, and Sharjah only; machinery and transport equipment 37.6%, food 23.2%, textiles 13.9%, basic manufactures 8.4%, chemicals 6.3%, optical and medical equipment 2.8%). *Major import sources:* Japan 10.2%; US 9.6%; UK 8.8%; China 8.6%; Germany 6.7%; India 6.7%; Italy 6.2%; South Korea 5.3%. **Exports** (2001): Dh 176,900,000,000 (domestic exports 71.1%, of which crude petroleum 36.7%, natural gas 7.1%, refined petroleum products 4.6%, nonmonetary gold 4.4%; reexports 28.9%). *Major export destinations:* Japan 36.4%; India 7.5%; South Korea 7.1%; Singapore 6.3%; Iran 3.8%; Oman 3.4%.

Transport and communications

Transport. *Roads* (1999): total length 3,791 km (paved 100%). *Vehicles* (1996): passenger cars 201,000; trucks and buses 56,950. *Air transport* (2002; Emirates Air only): passenger-km 30,170,000,000; metric ton-km cargo 1,960,764,000; airports (2001) with scheduled flights 6. **Communications,** in total units (units per 1,000 persons). Daily newspaper circulation (2000): 507,000 (156); radios (2000): 1,030,000 (318); televisions (2000): 948,000 (292); telephone main lines (2003): 1,135,800 (281); cellular telephone subscribers (2003): 2,972,300 (736); personal computers (2002): 450,000 (141); Internet users (2003): 1,110,200 (275).

Education and health

Educational attainment (1995). Percentage of population age 10 and over having: no formal schooling 47.6%; primary education 27.8%; secondary 16.0%; higher 8.6%. **Literacy** (2000): total population age 15 and over literate 76.3%; males literate 75.0%; females literate 79.3%. **Health** (1999): physicians 6,059 (1 per 485 persons); hospital beds 7,448 (1 per 394 persons); infant mortality rate per 1,000 live births (2003) 8.0. **Food** (2001): daily per capita caloric intake 3,192 (vegetable products 75%, animal products 25%); 132% of FAO recommended minimum.

Military

Total active duty personnel (2003): 50,500 (army 87.1%, navy 5.0%, air force 7.9%). **Military expenditure as percentage of GDP** (1999): 4.1% (world 2.4%); per capita expenditure $935.

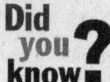 **Did you know?** For many centuries the oyster beds of the Persian Gulf produced some of the world's finest pearls, and pearling was once a thriving and profitable occupation. Since the Great Depression of the 1930s, however, the trade has declined continuously, mostly due to the competition of cheaper cultured pearls from Japan and elsewhere.

Background

The Persian Gulf was the location of important trading centers as early as Sumerian times. Its people converted to Islam in Muhammad's lifetime. The Portuguese entered the region in the early 16th century, and the British East India Company arrived about 100 years later. In 1820 the British exacted a peace treaty with local rulers along the coast of the eastern Arabian Peninsula. The area formerly called the Pirate Coast became known as the Trucial Coast. In 1892 the rulers agreed to restrict foreign relations to Britain. Though the British administered the region from 1853, they never assumed sovereignty; each state maintained full internal control. The states formed the Trucial States Council in 1960. In 1971 the sheiks terminated defense treaties with Britain and established the six-member federation. Ra's al-Khaymah joined it in 1972. The UAE aided coalition forces against Iraq in the Persian Gulf War (1991).

Recent Developments

In November 2004 Sheikh Zayid ibn Sultan Al Nahyan, the ruler of Abu Dhabi since 1966 and the president of the United Arab Emirates since it was founded in 1971, passed away. He was universally loved throughout the country and respected internationally. His eldest son, Sheikh Khalifah ibn Zayid, crown prince of Abu Dhabi, immediately became ruler of that emirate, and another son, Sheikh Muhammad ibn Zayid, became its crown prince. Sheikh Khalifah was also elected president of the UAE; he thus held the same two positions that his father had.

Internet resources: <www.uae.org.ae>.

---

1 metric ton = about 1.1 short tons;   1 kilometer = 0.6 mi (statute);   1 metric ton-km cargo = about 0.68 short ton-mi cargo;   c.i.f.: cost, insurance, and freight;   f.o.b.: free on board

United Kingdom

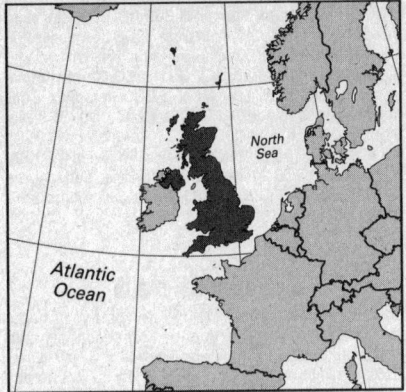

North Sea

Atlantic Ocean

Official name: United Kingdom of Great Britain and Northern Ireland. **Form of government:** constitutional monarchy with two legislative houses (House of Lords [688]; House of Commons [659]). **Chief of state:** Queen Elizabeth II (from 1952). **Head of government:** Prime Minister Anthony C.L. (Tony) Blair (from 1997). **Capital:** London. **Official language:** English. **Official religion:** Churches of England and Scotland "established" (protected by the state, but not "official") in their respective countries; no established church in Northern Ireland or Wales. **Monetary unit:** 1 pound sterling (£) = 100 new pence; valuation (7 Jul 2005) £1 = $0.57.

Demography

Area: 93,788 sq mi, 242,910 sq km, of which England 50,356 sq mi, 130,422 sq km; Wales 8,023 sq mi, 20,779 sq km; Scotland 30,167 sq mi, 78,133 sq km; Northern Ireland 5,242 sq mi, 13,576 sq km. **Population** (2004): 59,561,000. **Density** (2004): persons per sq mi 635.1, persons per sq km 245.2. **Urban** (2003): 89.1%. **Age breakdown** (2001): under 15, 18.9%; 15–29, 18.8%; 30–44, 22.6%; 45–59, 18.9%; 60–74, 13.3%; 75 and over, 7.5%. **Ethnic composition** (2001): white 92.1%; black 2.0%, of which Caribbean origin 1.0%, African origin 0.8%; Asian Indian 1.8%; Pakistani 1.3%; Bangladeshi 0.5%; Chinese 0.4%; other and not stated 1.9%. **Sex distribution** (2001): male 48.62%; female 51.38%. **Religious affiliation** (2001): Christian 71.6%, of which Anglican 29.0%, Roman Catholic 11.0%; Muslim 2.7%; Hindu 1.0%; Sikh 0.6%; Jewish 0.5%; nonreligious 15.5%; other 8.1%. **Major cities** (2001; urban agglomeration [2000]): Greater London 7,172,091; Manchester 392,819 ([2001] 2,482,328); Birmingham 977,087 (2,272,000); Leeds 715,402 (1,433,000); Newcastle 259,536 (1,026,000); Liverpool 439,473 (951,000); Glasgow 629,501; Sheffield 513,234; Bradford 467,665; Edinburgh 452,194; Bristol 380,615; Wakefield 315,172; Cardiff 305,353; Coventry 300,848; Doncaster 286,865; Sunderland 280,807; Belfast 277,391. **Location:** western Europe, bordering the North Sea, the English Channel, the Celtic Sea, the Irish Sea, and Ireland. **Dependencies:** Anguilla, Bermuda, British Virgin Islands, Cayman Islands, Falkland Islands, Gibraltar, Guernsey, Isle of Man, Jersey, Montserrat, Pitcairn Island, Saint Helena and Dependencies, and Turks and Caicos Islands. **Mobility** (1991; Great Britain only). Population living in the same residence as 1990: 90.1%; different residence, same country (of Great Britain) 8.1%; different residence, different country of Great Britain 1.2%; from outside Great Britain 0.6%. **Households** (2002; Great Britain only). Average household size 2.4; 1 person 29%, couple 29%, couple with 1–2 children 19%, couple with 3 or more children 10%, single parent with children 9%, other 4%. **Immigration** (2001): permanent residents 372,000, from Australia 13.4%, Bangladesh, India, and Sri Lanka 6.2%, South Africa 4.8%, New Zealand 4.3%, Pakistan 3.5%, US 3.2%, Canada 1.6%, other 63.0%, of which EU 22.3%.

Vital statistics

Birth rate per 1,000 population (2003): 11.7 (world avg. 21.3); (2002; Great Britain only) legitimate 59.4%. **Death rate** per 1,000 population (2003): 10.3 (world avg. 9.1). **Natural increase rate** per 1,000 population (2003): 1.4 (world avg. 12.2). **Total fertility rate** (avg. births per childbearing woman; 2003): 1.7. **Marriage rate** per 1,000 population (2001): 4.9. **Divorce rate** per 1,000 population (2002): 2.7. **Life expectancy** at birth (2002): male 75.7 years; female 80.4 years.

Social indicators

Quality of working life (2002). Average full-time workweek (hours): male 39.6, female 34.4. Annual rate per 100,000 workers for (2000–01; Great Britain only): injury or accident 2,778.6; death 5.0. Proportion of labor force (employed persons) insured for damages or income loss resulting from: injury 100%; permanent disability 100%; death 100%. Average days lost to labor stoppages per 1,000 employee workdays (2001): 20. **Access to services** (2000). Proportion of households having access to: bath or shower 100%; toilet 100%. **Social participation.** Eligible voters participating in last national election (June 2001): 59.4%. Population age 16 and over participating in voluntary work (2001; Great Britain only): 39%. Trade union membership in total workforce (2001) 29.1%. **Social deviance** (2001–02; England and Wales only). Offense rate per 100,000 population for: theft and handling stolen goods 3,856.2; vandalism 1,809.9; burglary 1,296.2; violence against the person 1,105.6; fraud and forgery 539.2; robbery 205.8; sexual offense 69.7. **Leisure** (1994). Favorite leisure activities (hours weekly): watching television 17.1; listening to radio 10.3; reading 8.8, of which books 3.8, newspapers 3.3; gardening 2.1. **Material well-being** (2001). Households possessing: automobile 74.0%, telephone 94.0%, television receiver (2000) 98.3%, refrigerator/freezer 95.0%, washing machine 93.0%, central heating 92.0%, video recorder 90.0%.

National economy

Budget (2001–02). *Revenue:* £388,357,000,000 (production and import taxes 35.5%, income tax 28.1%, social security contributions 16.3%). *Expenditures:* £380,367,000,000 (social protection 41.8%, health 16.1%, education 12.3%, defense 7.3%). **Gross national product** (2003): $1,680,300,000,000 ($28,350 per capita). **Total national debt** (31 Mar 2000): £426,239,200,000 ($679,894,200,000). **Land use** as % of total land area (2000): in temporary crops 24.4%, in permanent crops 0.2%, in pasture 45.8%; overall forest area 11.6%. **Tourism** (2002): receipts from visitors $17,591,000,000; expenditures by nationals abroad $40,409,000,000. **Production** (value of production in £'000,000). *Agriculture, forestry, fishing* (2001): wheat 1,322, vegetables 970, barley 726, potatoes 600, rapeseed 275, sugar beets 255, fruit 243, oats 64; livestock (number of live animals) 36,716,000 sheep, 10,602,000 cattle, 5,845,000 pigs; roundwood (2002) 7,577,000 cu m; fish catch (2001) 530,000 tons. *Mining and quarrying* (2000): limestone and dolomite 662; sand and gravel 619; china clay (kaolin) 234. *Manufacturing* (value added in £'000,000; 2000): electrical and optical equipment 21,137; food and beverages 20,628; paper, printing, and publishing 19,575; metal manufacturing 16,275; transport equipment 15,968; chemicals and chemical products 14,918; machinery and equipment 12,319; textiles and leather products 7,159. *Energy production (consumption):* electricity (kW-hr; 2001) 352,985,000,000 ([2000] 391,093,-000,000); hard coal (metric tons; 2000) 30,600,000 (58,440,000); crude petroleum (barrels; 2000) 880,107,000 (605,657,000); petroleum products (metric tons; 2000) 80,410,000 (72,458,000); natural gas (cu m; 2000) 127,197,000,000 (113,807,-600,000). **Population economically active** (2002): total 29,183,000; activity rate of total population 59.6% (participation rates: ages 16–64, 74.4%; female 45.9%; unemployed 5.2%). **Household income and expenditure** (2000–01). Average household size (2002) 2.4; average annual disposable income per household £21,242; sources of income: wages and salaries 67.0%, social security benefits 12.0%, income from self-employment 8.9%, dividends and interest 4.0%; expenditure: housing 16.6%, food and beverages 16.0%, transport and vehicles 14.3%, household goods 8.5%, clothing 5.7%.

Foreign trade

Imports (2002): £220,242,000,000 (machinery and apparatus 27.3%, of which radios, televisions, and electronics 6.7%, computers 6.1%; transport equipment 19.8%, of which motor vehicles and parts 13.7%, aircraft 5.4%; chemicals and chemical products 10.7%, of which pharmaceuticals 3.9%, basic chemicals 3.8%; food products 5.1%; wearing apparel 3.5%). *Major import sources:* Germany 13.7%; US 11.3%; France 8.5%; The Netherlands 6.8%; Belgium-Luxembourg 5.9%; Italy 4.7%; Ireland 4.2%; Japan 3.7%; Spain 3.7%; China 3.0%. **Exports** (2002): £185,848,000,000 (machinery and apparatus 32.5%, of which radios, televisions, and electronics 10.6%, nonelectrical machinery 8.5%, computers 5.6%; transport equipment 16.8%, of which motor vehicles and parts 10.1%, aircraft 6.2%; chemicals and chemical products 15.4%, of which pharmaceuticals 5.7%; crude petroleum and natural gas 5.8%; base metals 3.5%). *Major export destinations:* US 15.1%; Germany 11.8%; France 10.0%; Ireland 8.3%; The Netherlands 7.5%; Belgium-Luxembourg 5.7%; Italy 4.6%; Spain 4.5%; Sweden 2.1%; Japan 1.9%.

Transport and communications

Transport. *Railroads* (2001–02; Great Britain only): length 32,000 km; passenger-km 39,104,000,000;

metric ton-km cargo 19,700,000,000. *Roads* (2001): total length 392,408 km (paved 100%). *Vehicles* (2001): passenger cars 23,899,000, trucks and buses 2,544,000. *Air transport* (2001): passenger-km 249,000,000,000; metric ton-km cargo 5,196,000,000; airports (2001) 150. **Communications**, in total units (units per 1,000 persons). Daily newspaper circulation (2000): 19,300,000 (329); radios (2000): 84,500,000 (1,432); televisions (1999): 38,800,000 (652); telephone main lines (2002): 34,898,000 (591); cellular telephone subscribers (2002): 49,677,000 (841); personal computers (2002): 23,972,000 (406); Internet users (2002): 25,000,000 (423).

Education and health

Educational attainment (1999). Percentage of population age 25–64 having: up to lower secondary education only 38%; completed secondary 37%; higher 25%, of which at least some university 17%. **Literacy** (2002): total population literate, virtually 100%. **Health:** physicians (2001; Great Britain only) 71,107 (1 per 826 persons); hospital beds (2000) 242,671 (1 per 246 persons); infant mortality rate per 1,000 live births (2003) 4.7. **Food** (2001): daily per capita caloric intake 3,368 (vegetable products 70%, animal products 30%); 134% of FAO recommended minimum.

Military

Total active duty personnel (2003): 212,660 (army 54.9%, navy 19.9%, air force 25.2%); US troops (2004) 11,800. **Military expenditure as percentage of GNP** (1999): 2.5% (world 2.4%); per capita expenditure $615.

Background

The early pre-Roman inhabitants of Britain were Celtic-speaking peoples, including the Brythonic people of Wales, the Picts of Scotland, and the Britons of Britain. Celts also settled in Ireland c. 500 BC. Julius Caesar invaded and took control of the area in 55–54 BC. The Roman province of Britannia endured until the 5th century and included present-day England and Wales. In the 5th century Nordic tribes of Angles, Saxons, and Jutes invaded Britain. The invasions had little effect on the Celtic peoples of Wales and Scotland.

Christianity began to flourish in the 6th century. During the 8th–9th centuries, Vikings, particularly Danes, raided the coasts of Britain. In the late 9th century Alfred the Great repelled a Danish invasion, which helped bring about the unification of England under Athelstan. The Scots attained dominance in Scotland, which was finally unified under Malcolm II (1005–34).

William of Normandy took England in 1066. The Norman kings established a strong central government and feudal state. The French language of the Norman rulers eventually merged with the Anglo-Saxon of the common people to form the English language. From the 11th century, Scotland came under the influence of the English throne. Henry II conquered Ireland in the late 12th century. His sons, kings Richard I and John, had conflicts with the clergy and nobles, and eventually John was forced to grant the nobles concessions in Magna Carta (1215). The

1 metric ton = about 1.1 short tons;   1 kilometer = 0.6 mi (statute);   1 metric ton-km cargo = about 0.68 short ton-mi cargo;   c.i.f.: cost, insurance, and freight;   f.o.b.: free on board

concept of community of the realm developed during the 13th century, providing the foundation for parliamentary government. During the reign of Edward I, statute law developed to supplement English common law, and the first Parliament was convened. In 1314 Robert Bruce won independence for Scotland.

The Tudors became the ruling family of England following the Wars of the Roses (1455–85). Henry VIII established the Church of England and made Wales part of his realm. The reign of Elizabeth I began a period of colonial expansion; 1588 brought the defeat of the Spanish Armada. In 1603 James VI of Scotland ascended to the English throne, becoming James I, and established a personal union of the two kingdoms.

The English Civil Wars erupted in 1642 between Royalists and Parliamentarians, ending in the execution of Charles I (1649). After 11 years of Puritan rule under Oliver Cromwell and his son (1649–60), the monarchy was restored with Charles II. In 1707 England and Scotland assented to the Act of Union, forming the kingdom of Great Britain. The Hanoverians ascended to the English throne in 1714, when George Louis, elector of Hanover, became George I of Great Britain. During the reign of George III, Great Britain's American colonies won independence (1783). This was followed by a period of war with revolutionary France and later with the empire of Napoleon (1789–1815).

In 1801 legislation united Great Britain with Ireland to create the United Kingdom of Great Britain and Ireland. Britain was the birthplace of the Industrial Revolution in the late 18th century, and it remained the world's foremost economic power until the late 19th century. During the reign of Queen Victoria, Britain's colonial expansion reached its zenith, though the older dominions, including Canada and Australia, were granted independence (1867 and 1901, respectively).

The UK entered World War I allied with France and Russia in 1914. Following the war, revolutionary disorder erupted in Ireland, and in 1921 the Irish Free State was granted dominion status. The six counties of Ulster, however, remained in the UK as Northern Ireland. The UK entered World War II in 1939. Following the war the Irish Free State became the Irish Republic and left the Commonwealth. India gained independence from the UK in 1947.

Throughout the postwar period and into the 1970s, the UK continued to grant independence to its overseas colonies and dependencies. With UN forces, it participated in the Korean War (1950–53). In 1956 it intervened militarily in Egypt during the Suez Crisis. In 1982 it defeated Argentina in the Falkland Islands War. As a result of continuing social strife in Northern Ireland, it joined with Ireland in several peace initiatives, which eventually resulted in an agreement to establish an assembly in Northern Ireland. In 1997 referenda approved in Scotland and Wales devolved power to both countries, though both remained part of the UK.

Recent Developments

A general election in May 2005 returned Tony Blair to power for a third term, unprecedented for a Labour leader. Labour's majority in Parliament was drastically cut, however—from 166 to 67—with many of their former seats gone to the Liberal Democrats. Throughout 2004 UK domestic politics was overshadowed by disputes over Britain's involvement in Iraq. These disputes concerned both the deployment of British troops in Iraq and whether government ministers had told the truth when they said before the war that Pres. Saddam Hussein had weapons of mass destruction (WMD) at the time of the 2003 US-led invasion of Iraq. The report released in January 2004 by Lord Hutton on the circumstances that led to the suicide in July 2003 of a government expert on WMD exonerated ministers and criticized the BBC. Most Britons considered the Hutton report a whitewash and thought that ministers deserved far more criticism than the BBC. Prime Minister Blair established a fresh inquiry led by Lord Butler, a former cabinet secretary. He found that much of the intelligence was either wrong or greatly exaggerated. Blair endorsed Butler's conclusions and accepted responsibility for what had happened, but he was reluctant to apologize for anything, least of all for having taken Britain to war. On 13 October Blair issued a narrowly worded apology "for any information given in good faith that has subsequently turned out to be wrong." Blair's lack of penitence upset not only opponents of the war but also many voters. The prime minister was increasingly seen as arrogant and untrustworthy, and the Labour Party he headed suffered a series of electoral reverses.

Economic growth, which had started to accelerate in 2003, slowed in the second half of 2004. The chancellor of the Exchequer, however, was able to boast toward the end of the year that the economy had grown in each of the 30 quarters since Labour returned to power in May 1997. Both unemployment (at about 5%) and inflation (approximately 2%) remained low. Tax revenues proved to be less than forecast, with the result that the government had to borrow more than it had predicted.

Bombs detonated in the Underground and bus system in central London on 7 Jul 2005 killed dozens of people and injured many others, and a second incident two weeks later, although largely unsuccessful, had the potential to cause similar suffering. The incidents were quickly linked to British-born Muslim suicide bombers who probably had links to al-Qaeda terrorist organization.

On 9 Apr 2005 Charles, prince of Wales, married Camilla (Shand) Parker-Bowles. Camilla will in most situations bear the title of duchess of Cornwall and, should Charles become king, could choose to be known as either princess consort or queen.

Internet resources: <www.visitbritain.com>.

United States

Official name: United States of America. **Form of government:** federal republic with two legislative houses (Senate [100]; House of Representatives [435, excluding 4 nonvoting delegates from the District of Columbia, the US Virgin Islands, American Samoa, and Guam; a nonvoting resident commissioner from Puerto Rico; and a nonvoting resident representative from the Northern Mariana Islands]). **Head of state and government:** President George W. Bush (from 2001). **Capital:** Washington DC. **Official language:** none. **Official religion:** none. **Monetary unit:** 1 dollar ($) = 100 cents.

Demography

Area: 3,676,487 sq mi, 9,522,058 sq km (total area per 2000 computer-based survey equals 3,676,487

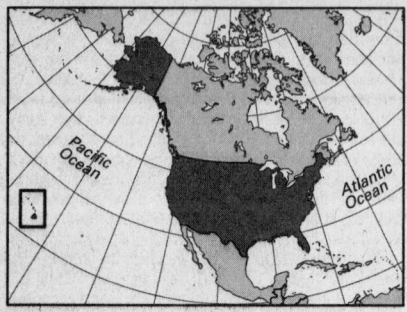

sq mi [9,522,058 sq km], of which land area equals 3,537,439 sq mi [9,161,926 sq km], inland water area equals 78,797 sq mi [204,083 sq km], and Great Lakes water area equals 60,251 sq mi [156,049 sq km]). **Population** (2004): 293,850,000. **Density** (2004; based on land area only): persons per sq mi 83.1, persons per sq km 32.1. **Urban** (2000): 79.0%. **Sex distribution** (2003): male 49.19%; female 50.81%. **Age breakdown** (2003): under 15, 20.9%; 15–29, 20.8%; 30–44, 22.4%; 45–59, 19.4%; 60–74, 10.5%; 75 and over, 6.0%. **Population by race and Hispanic origin** (2002; persons of Hispanic origin may be of any race): non-Hispanic white 68.5%; Hispanic 13.5%; non-Hispanic black 12.8%; Asian and Pacific Islander 4.2%; American Indian and Eskimo 1.0%. **Religious affiliation** (2000): Christian 84.7%, of which Protestant 45.7%, Roman Catholic 18.2%, un-affiliated Christian 15.8%, Orthodox 1.8%, other Christian (primarily Mormon and Jehovah's Witness) 3.2%; Jewish 2.0%; Muslim 1.5%; Buddhist 0.9%; Hindu 0.4%; nonreligious 9.0%; atheist 0.8%; other 0.7%. **Mobility** (2000). Population living in the same residence as in 1999: 84.0%; different residence, same county 9.0%; different county, same state 3.0%; different state 3.0%; moved from abroad 1.0%. **Households** (2002). Total households 109,297,000 (married-couple families 56,747,000 [51.9%]). Average household size (2002) 2.6; 1 person 26.4%, 2 persons 33.1%, 3 persons 16.2%, 4 persons 14.5%, 5 or more persons 9.8%. Family households: 74,329,000 (68.0%); nonfamily 34,968,000 (32.0%), of which 1-person 82.3%. **Place of birth** (2000): native-born 245,708,000 (89.6%); foreign-born 28,379,000 (10.4%), of which Mexico 7,841,000, the Philippines 1,222,000, China and Hong Kong 1,067,000, India 1,007,000, Cuba 952,000, Vietnam 863,000, El Salvador 765,000, South Korea 701,000. **Major cities** (2003): New York 8,085,742; Los Angeles 3,819,951; Chicago 2,869,121; Houston 2,009,690; Philadelphia 1,479,339; Phoenix 1,388,416; San Diego 1,266,753; San Antonio 1,214,725; Dallas 1,208,318; Detroit 911,402. **Location:** North America, bordering Canada, the Atlantic Ocean, the Gulf of Mexico, Mexico, and the Pacific Ocean. Outlying state of Alaska nearly touches eastern Russia and borders the Arctic Ocean and the Pacific Ocean; Hawaii is an island group in the Pacific Ocean. **Dependencies:** American Samoa, Guam, Northern Mariana Islands, Puerto Rico, and Virgin Islands (of the US). **Immigration** (2001): permanent immigrants admitted 1,064,318, from Mexico 19.2%, India 6.2%, former USSR 5.2%, China 4.8%, the Philippines 4.8%, Africa 4.7%, Viet-

nam 3.3%, El Salvador 2.9%, Canada 2.8%, Cuba 2.4%, Haiti 2.1%, Dominican Republic 2.0%, South Korea 1.9%, Jamaica 1.4%, other 36.3%. Refugees (end of 2003) 452,548. Asylum seekers (end of 2000) 386,330.

Vital statistics

Birth rate per 1,000 population (2001): 14.5 (world avg. 21.3); legitimate 66.5%; illegitimate 33.5%. **Death rate** per 1,000 population (2001): 8.5 (world avg. 9.1). **Natural increase rate** per 1,000 population (2001): 6.0 (world avg. 12.2). **Marriage rate** per 1,000 population (2001): 8.4; median age at first marriage (1991): men 26.3 years, women 24.1 years. **Divorce rate** per 1,000 population (2001): 4.0. **Total fertility rate** (avg. births per childbearing woman; 2001): 2.1. **Life expectancy** at birth (2001): white male 75.0 years, black and other male (1996) 68.9 years; white female 80.2 years, black and other female (1996) 76.1 years.

Social indicators

Quality of working life (2001). Average workweek: 39.2 hours. Annual death rate per 100,000 workers (2000): 4.5; leading causes of occupational deaths (1999): transportation incidents 43.4%, contact with objects/equipment 17.1%, assaults/violent acts 14.8%. Average days per 1,000 workdays lost to labor stoppages (2000): 1.8. Average duration of journey to work (2000): 20.7 minutes (private automobile 87.9%, of which drive alone 75.7%, carpool 12.2%; take public transportation 4.7%; walk 2.9%; work at home 3.3%; other 1.2%). Rate per 1,000 employed workers of discouraged workers (unemployed no longer seeking work; 2000): 1.8. **Access to services** (1995). Proportion of occupied dwellings having access to: electricity, virtually 100.0%; safe public water supply 99.4% (12.6% from wells); public sewage collection 77.0%; septic tanks 22.8%. **Social participation.** Eligible voters participating in last presidential election (2004): 60.7%. Population age 18 and over participating in voluntary work (1999): 66.0%. Trade-union membership in total workforce (2000): 14.9%. **Social deviance** (2002). Offense rate per 100,000 population for: murder 6.0; rape 33.9; robbery 158.6; aggravated assault 326.4; motor-vehicle theft 464.3; burglary and housebreaking 774.7; larceny-theft 2,540.1; drug-abuse violation 587.1; drunkenness 149.1. Estimated drug and substance users (population age 12 and over; 1999): cigarettes 57,296,000; binge alcohol 44,486,000; marijuana 11,476,000; other illicit drugs 6,645,000. Rate per 100,000 population of suicide (1999): 10.7. **Leisure** (2002). Favorite leisure activities (percentage of total population age 18 and over that undertook activity at least once in the previous year): movie 60.0%, exercise program 55.0%, gardening 47.0%, home improvement 42.0%, amusement park 42.0%, sports events 35.0%, playing sports 30.0%, charity work 29.0%. **Material well-being** (2001). Occupied dwellings with householder possessing: automobile 95.6%; telephone 94.6%; radio receiver 99.0%; television receiver 98.9%; videocassette recorder and DVD players 89.8%; washing machine 78.6%; air conditioner 75.5%; clothers dryer 73.6%; cable television

68.0%. **Recreational expenditures** (2001): $593,-900,000,000 (television and radio receivers, computers, and video equipment 17.8%; golfing, bowling, and other participatory activities 12.3%; nondurable toys and sports equipment 11.2%; sports supplies 10.2%; magazines and newspapers 5.9%; books and maps 5.9%; spectator amusements 4.9%, of which theater and opera 1.7%, spectator sports 1.7%, movies 1.5%; flowers, seeds, and potted plants 3.1%; other 28.7%).

National economy

Budget (2001). *Revenue:* $2,136,900,000,000 (individual income tax 48.8%, social-insurance taxes and contributions 36.4%, corporation income tax 10.4%, excise taxes 3.4%, customs duties 1.0%). *Expenditures:* $1,856,200,000,000 (social security and medicare 37.5%, defense 16.1%, interest on debt 11.1%, other 35.3%). **Total outstanding national debt** (mid-November 2004): $7,443,900,000,000. **Gross national product** (2003): $10,945,792,000,000 ($37,610 per capita). **Business activity** (1997): number of businesses 23,645,000 (sole proprietorships 72.6%, active corporations 19.9%, active partnerships 7.5%), of which services 10,114,000, wholesaling and retailing 4,455,000; business receipts $18,057,000,000,000 (active corporations 88.0%, sole proprietorships 4.8%, active partnerships 7.2%), of which wholesaling and retailing $5,136,000,-000,000, services $2,130,000,000,000; net profit $1,270,000,000,000 (active corporations 72.0%, sole proprietorships 14.7%, partnerships 13.3%), of which services $203,000,000,000, wholesaling and retailing $10,000,000,000. New business starts and business failures (1995): total number of new business starts 168,158; total failures 71,194, of which commercial service 21,850, retail trade 12,952; failure rate per 10,000 concerns 90.0; current liabilities of failed concerns $37,507,000,000; average liability $526,830. Business expenditures for new plant and equipment (1995): total $594,465,000,000, of which trade, services, and communications $244,-829,000,000, manufacturing businesses $172,-308,000,000 (durable goods 53.0%, nondurable goods 47.0%), public utilities $42,816,000,000, transportation $37,021,000,000, mining and construction $35,985,000. **Production.** *Agriculture, forestry, fishing* (value of production/catch in $'000,000 except as noted; 2002): corn (maize) 21,213, soybeans 14,755, wheat 5,863, cotton lint 3,394, potatoes 3,151, grapes 2,853, oranges 1,834, tobacco 1,726, apples 1,571, head lettuce 1,456, tomatoes 1,171, almonds 1,049, sorghum 884, rice 841, onions 716, cottonseed 638, barley 597, peanuts (groundnuts) 594, broccoli 551, carrots 551, sweet corn 531, dry beans 519, peaches 507, bell peppers 499, cantaloupes 404, avocados 362, lemons 341, watermelons 329, sunflower seeds 317, cabbage 301, pears 297, grapefruit 286, sweet cherries 274, cauliflower 241, pecans 169, strawberries 121; livestock (number of live animals) 97,277,000 cattle, 58,943,000 pigs, 6,685,000 sheep, 5,300,000 horses, 1,940,000 chickens; roundwood 500,434,000 cu m; fish and shellfish catch 3,467, of which fish 1,558 (including salmon 359, Alaska pollack 163), shellfish 1,909 (including shrimp 560, crabs 521). *Mining* (metal content in metric tons except as noted; 2001): iron 37,800,000; copper 1,340,000; zinc 830,000; lead 420,000; molybdenum 38,300; vanadium 2,700; mercury

550; silver 1,800,000 kg; gold 350,000 kg; helium 101,000,000 cu m. *Quarrying* (metric tons; 2000): crushed stone 1,300,000,000; sand and gravel 1,139,000,000; cement 75,000,000; common salt 45,000,000; clay 40,700,000; phosphate rock 34,200,000; lime 20,000,000; gypsum 18,800,000. *Manufacturing* (value added in $'000,000; 1999): transportation equipment 268,511, of which motor vehicle parts 86,310, motor vehicles 80,134, aerospace products and parts 73,897; computers and electronic products 265,442, of which semiconductors and related components 102,003; chemicals and chemical products 229,284, of which pharmaceuticals and medicine 74,108; food 177,659; fabricated metal products 142,451; nonelectrical machinery 138,798; paper and paper products 74,602; plastics 72,183; base metals 66,733; printing 62,428; electrical machinery 60,458. *Energy production (consumption):* electricity (kW-hr; 2001) 3,778,500,000,000 ([2000] 4,159,039,000); hard coal (metric tons; 2000) 895,189,000 (893,343,-000); lignite (metric tons; 2000) 80,505,000 (77,151,000); crude petroleum (barrels; 2001) 2,163,000,000 ([2000] 5,664,000,000); petroleum products (metric tons; 2000) 767,065,000 (767,-031,000); natural gas (cu m; 2001) 549,557,000,-000 ([2000] 660,039,000,000). Domestic production of energy by source (2001): coal 32.7%, natural gas 27.7%, crude petroleum 17.3%, nuclear power 11.2%, renewable energy 7.7%, other 3.4%. *Energy consumption by source* (2000): petroleum and petroleum products 40.5%, natural gas 24.2%, coal 23.8%, nuclear electric power 8.3%, hydroelectric and thermal 3.2%; by end use: industrial 38.9%, residential and commercial 33.7%, transportation 27.4%. **Household income and expenditure.** Average household size (2002) 2.6; median annual income per household (2001) $42,228, of which median Asian and Pacific Islander household $53,635, median white household $44,517, median non-Hispanic household $46,305, median Hispanic household $33,565, median black (including Hispanic) household $29,470; sources of personal income (2000): wages and salaries 57.6%, self-employment 8.6%, transfer payments 8.5%, other 25.3%; expenditure (1999): transportation 18.9%, housing 18.9%, food at home 7.9%, household furnishings 7.2%, fuel and utilities 6.4%, food away from home 5.7%, recreation 5.5%, health 5.3%, wearing apparel 4.7%, education 1.7%, other 17.8%. **Average annual expenditure** of "consumer units" (households, plus individuals sharing households or budgets; 2001): total $39,518, of which housing $13,011, transportation $7,633, food $5,321, pensions and social security $3,326, health care $2,182, clothing $1,743, other $6,302. **Selected household characteristics** (2002). Total number of households 109,297,000, of which (family households by race) white 83.0%, black 12.2%, other 4.8%; in central cities 31.4% (1994), in suburbs 46.3% (1994), outside metropolitan areas 22.3% (1994); (by tenure; 1994) owned 74,399,000 (68.1%), rented 34,897,000 (31.9%); family households 74,329,000, of which married couple 76.4%, female head with own children (includes adoptees and stepchildren) under age 18, 10.8%, female head without own children (includes adoptees and stepchildren) under 18, 6.9%; nonfamily households 34,969,000, of which female living alone 48.0%, male living alone 34.3%, other 17.7%. **Population economically active** (2002): total 144,863,000, activity rate of total population 50.1% (participation rates: age 16 and over 66.6%; female 46.5%; unemployed [October 2004] 5.5%). **Tourism** (2002): receipts from visitors $66,547,000,000; expenditures by nationals abroad $58,044,000,000; number of foreign visitors 41,892,000,000 ([2000] 14,594,000 from Canada, 10,322,000 from Mexico, 11,597,000 from Europe); number of nationals traveling abroad 56,359,000 ([2000] 18,849,000 to Mexico, 15,114,-000 to Canada). **Land use** as % of total land area (2000): in temporary crops 19.3%, in permanent crops 0.2%, in pasture 25.5%; overall forest area 24.7%.

Foreign trade

Imports (2002): $1,161,400,000,000 (motor vehicles and parts 14.5%, electrical machinery [excluding televisions and electronic components] 7.0%, crude petroleum 6.8%, computers and office equipment 6.6%, chemicals and chemical products 6.5%, televisions and electronic components 5.7%, wearing apparel 5.5%, general industrial machinery 3.0%, power generating machinery 2.9%). *Major import sources:* Canada 18.0%; Mexico 11.6%; China 10.8%; Japan 10.5%; Germany 5.4%; UK 3.5%; South Korea 3.1%; Taiwan 2.8%; France 2.4%; Italy 2.1%; Malaysia 2.1%; Ireland 1.9%. **Exports** (2002): $693,100,000,000 (electrical machinery [excluding televisions and electronic components] 9.7%, chemicals and related products 8.9%, motor vehicles 8.3%, agricultural commodities 7.7%, power generating machinery 4.7%, computers and office equipment 4.4%, general industrial machinery 4.3%, airplanes 3.9%, scientific and precision equipment 3.9%, specialized industrial machinery 3.4%). *Major export destinations:* Canada 23.2%; Mexico 14.1%; Japan 7.4%; UK 4.8%; Germany 3.8%; South Korea 3.3%; China 3.2%; Taiwan 2.7%; France 2.7%; The Netherlands 2.6%; Singapore 2.3%; Belgium 1.9%.

Transport and communications

Transport. *Railroads* (1998): length 212,433 km; (1999) passenger-km 21,568,000,000; metric ton-km cargo (1997) 2,075,000,000. *Roads* (2001): total length 6,354,231 km (paved 91%). *Vehicles* (2001): passenger cars 137,633,000; trucks and buses 92,795,000. *Air transport* (2002): passenger-km 1,598,000,000,000; metric ton-km cargo 87,390,000,000; localities (1996) with scheduled flights 834 (includes 292 localities in Alaska). Certified route passenger/cargo air carriers (1992) 77; operating revenue ($'000,000; 1991) 74,942, of which domestic 56,119, international 18,823; operating expenses 76,669, of which domestic 56,596, international 20,073. **Communications**, in total units (units per 1,000 persons). Daily newspaper circulation (2000): 55,773,000 (198); radios (2000): 598,000,000 (2,118); televisions (2000): 241,000,000 (854); telephone main lines (2003): 181,599,900 (621); cellular telephone subscribers (2003): 158,722,000 (543); personal computers (2002): 190,000,000 (659); Internet users (2002): 159,000,000 (551).

Education and health

Educational attainment (2000). Percentage of population age 25 and over having: primary and incomplete

secondary 15.9%; secondary 33.1%; some postsecondary 25.4%; 4-year higher degree 17.0%; advanced degree 8.6%. Number of earned degrees (2000): bachelor's degree 1,237,875; master's degree 457,056; doctor's degree 44,808; first-professional degrees (in fields such as medicine, theology, and law) 80,057. **Food** (2001): daily per capita caloric intake 3,776 (vegetable products 73%, animal products 27%); 143% of FAO recommended minimum. Per capita consumption of major food groups (kilograms annually; 2001): milk 256.6; fresh vegetables 124.5; cereal products 116.9; fresh fruits 113.4; red meat 72.5; potatoes 64.4; poultry products 47.8; sugar 32.6; fats and oils 32.5; fish and shellfish 21.2. **Health:** doctors of medicine (2001) 836,200 (1 per 346 persons), of which office-based practice 514,000 (including specialties in internal medicine 18.4%, general and family practice 13.6%, pediatrics 8.7%, other specialty 8.6%, obstetrics and gynecology 6.3%, anesthesiology 5.6%, psychiatry 5.0%, general surgery 5.0%, orthopedic surgery 3.5%, cardiovascular diseases 3.3%, ophthalmology 3.1%, emergency medicine 3.1%, diagnostic radiology 3.0%); doctors of osteopathy 47,000; nurses (2002) 2,311,000 (1 per 125 persons); dentists (2002) 180,000 (1 per 1,603 persons); hospital beds (2001) 987,000 (1 per 289 persons), of which nonfederal 94.7% (community hospitals 83.7%, psychiatric 9.0%, long-term general and special 1.9%), federal 5.3%; infant mortality rate per 1,000 live births (2001) 7.0.

Military

Total active duty personnel (2003): 1,427,000 (army 34.0%, navy 28.0%, air force 25.8%, marines 12.2%). **Military expenditure as percentage of GNP** (1999): 3.0% (world 2.4%); per capita expenditure $1,030. **Security assistance to the world** (2002): $7,209,-000,000, for underwriting the purchase of US weapons 50.6%, of which Israel 28.3%, Egypt 18.0%, Jordan 1.0%; for economic support 30.5%, of which Israel 10.0%, Egypt 9.1%, Jordan 2.1%; for the Andean Counterdrug Initiative 9.2%; for nonproliferation, antiterrorism, and de-mining 4.3%; for international narcotics and law enforcement 3.0%; for peacekeeping operations 1.9%.

Background

The territory that is now the US was originally inhabited for several thousand years by numerous American Indian peoples who had probably emigrated from Asia. European exploration and settlement from the 16th century began displacement of the Indians. The first permanent European settlement, by the Spanish, was at St. Augustine FL, in 1565; the British settled Jamestown VA (1607); Plymouth MA (1620); Maryland (1632); and Pennsylvania (1681). They took New York, New Jersey, and Delaware from the Dutch in 1664, a year after the Carolinas had been granted to British noblemen. The British defeat of the French in 1763 assured British political control over the 13 colonies.

Political unrest caused by British colonial policy culminated in the American Revolution (1775–83) and the Declaration of Independence (1776). The US was first organized under the Articles of Confederation

1 metric ton = about 1.1 short tons;   1 kilometer = 0.6 mi (statute);   1 metric ton-km cargo = about 0.68 short ton-mi cargo;   c.i.f.: cost, insurance, and freight;   f.o.b.: free on board

(1781), then finally under the Constitution (1787) as a federal republic. Boundaries extended west to the Mississippi River, excluding Spanish Florida. Land acquired from France by the Louisiana Purchase (1803) nearly doubled the country's territory. The US fought the War of 1812 with the British and acquired Florida from Spain in 1819. In 1830 it legalized removal of American Indians to lands west of the Mississippi River. Settlement expanded to the west coast in the mid-19th century, especially after the discovery of gold in California in 1848. Victory in the Mexican War (1846–48) brought the territory of seven more future states (including California and Texas) into US hands. The northwestern boundary was established by treaty with Great Britain in 1846. The US acquired southern Arizona by the Gadsden Purchase (1853). It suffered disunity during the conflict between the slavery-based plantation economy in the South and the free industrial and agricultural economy in the North, culminating in the American Civil War, and the abolition of slavery under the 13th Amendment.

After Reconstruction (1865–77), the US experienced rapid growth, urbanization, industrial development, and European immigration. In 1877 it authorized allotment of Indian reservation land to individual tribesmen, resulting in widespread loss of land to whites. By the beginning of the 20th century, it had acquired outlying territories, including Alaska, the Midway Islands, the Hawaiian Islands, the Philippines, Puerto Rico, Guam, Wake Island, American Samoa, the Panama Canal Zone, and the Virgin Islands.

The US participated in World War I during 1917–18. It granted suffrage to women in 1920 and citizenship to American Indians in 1924. The stock market crash of 1929 led to the Great Depression. The US entered World War II after the Japanese bombing of Pearl Harbor (7 Dec 1941). The explosion of the first atomic bomb on Hiroshima, Japan (6 Aug 1945), brought about the end of the war and set the US apart as a military power. After the war the US was involved in the reconstruction of Europe and Japan and embroiled in a rivalry with the Soviet Union that became known as the Cold War. It participated in the Korean War. In 1952 it granted autonomous commonwealth status to Puerto Rico.

Racial segregation in schools was declared unconstitutional in 1954. Alaska and Hawaii were made states in 1959, bringing the total to 50. In 1964 Congress passed the Civil Rights Act and authorized full-scale intervention in the Vietnam War. The mid- to late 1960s were marked by widespread civil disorder, including race riots and antiwar demonstrations. The US accomplished the first manned lunar landing in 1969. All US troops were withdrawn from Vietnam by 1973. The US led a coalition of forces against Iraq in the Persian Gulf War (1991), sent troops to Somalia (1992) to aid starving populations, and participated in NATO air strikes against Serb forces in the former Yugoslavia in 1995 and 1999. Administration of the Panama Canal was turned over to Panama in 1999.

Recent Developments

In the 2004 presidential elections incumbent Pres. George W. Bush won a second term over Sen. John F. Kerry of Massachusetts by 3.3 million votes, with the narrowest popular-ballot percentage of any incumbent since 1916, in an election that was remarkable for an extremely polarized electorate, unprecedented spending, and high voter turnout. As the year began, former Vermont governor Howard Dean was the front-runner for the Democratic nomination, but he faded rapidly. Kerry won all but three Democratic primaries, sewing up the nomination by mid-March. He eventually selected as his running mate a rival for the nomination, Sen. John Edwards, a former trial lawyer from North Carolina who had gained good reviews for his populist "two Americas" message. In his addresses Bush pointed to significant domestic accomplishments during his first term: a major tax reduction, prescription-drug assistance for seniors, an expansion of federal assistance to public schools, and a real if less-than-robust recovery from the 2001 recession. In contrast to Kerry, Bush also endorsed a constitutional amendment banning same-sex marriage, which energized religious and conservative voters. Kerry faulted the administration's health and education spending records as puny, vowed to raise taxes on the wealthiest Americans to finance a more muscular expansion, and taunted Bush repeatedly as the first president since Herbert Hoover to preside over a net loss of jobs during his term. The central campaign issue, however, was Bush's aggressive response to the 11 Sep 2001 terrorist attacks, a policy that split the country virtually down the middle. Both candidates spent the final campaign weeks fighting in 14 "battleground" states, with a dead heat and imperceptible movement in the polls. Ohio, ordinarily GOP-leaning but hard hit by manufacturing job losses, proved to be the decisive state, going to Bush after hours of anticipation on election night. Targeting infrequent voters in suburban, exurban, and rural areas, Bush attracted a total of 60.6 million votes, some 10.2 million more than he had earned in 2000, a 51% share of the electorate.

At year's end and through the spring of 2005 Bush reshuffled his top lieutenants, replacing 9 of 15 cabinet members, and again claimed a mandate for an activist agenda, including self-sustaining private accounts in Social Security, reform of the income-tax system, and staying the course in Iraq. Many of the personnel appointments seemed to point a direction for Bush's second term. Colin Powell, who was seen as a would-be foreign policy moderate, was replaced as secretary of state by National Security Advisor Condoleezza Rice, whose views were more congruent with those of the president. After a lengthy search John Negroponte, who had earlier served the administration as representative to the UN and ambassador to Iraq, was selected for the new job of director of national intelligence with a mandate to coordinate the activities of more than a dozen major intelligence organizations in Washington. In this role, Negroponte shouldered aside as "alpha intelligence officer" the director of central intelligence (CIA director), Porter Goss, who had been appointed to his post just a few months previously. The country's first director of homeland security, Tom Ridge, stepped down, and, after a false start with the nomination of Bernard B. Kerik, which was withdrawn under fire, was replaced by a former federal prosecutor, Michael Chertoff. Two controversial foreign-policy appointments were former Pentagon strategist Paul D. Wolfowitz as head of the World Bank and arms-control expert Paul Bolton as US representative to the UN. Hearings on Bolton's confirmation ran into tough opposition in the Senate and dragged on past midyear.

World turmoil affected the nation's domestic business climate but failed to stop a continued expansion of the resilient US economy. Dramatically higher oil prices put a damper on strong United States economic growth. The US, spending heavily at home and abroad, resumed its place as the world's main economic engine in 2004, at least temporarily shrugging off heavy costs associated with homeland security and the war on terrorism, and finally reversing a decline in employment that had started with the 2001 recession. Still the US trade deficit surged to a new record in 2004—to $617.7 billion, or more than 5% of the US economy. The president's budget for the new year, presented in early February 2005, was for $2.57 trillion and foresaw cuts in a number of domestic programs in order to reduce deficits and boost national security spending.

With maneuvering ability almost nonexistent, owing to the war in Iraq, and constricted by domestic political considerations, US diplomacy struggled through a dark 2004. Resentment toward perceived US unilateralism colored relationships with several countries, and despite earnest efforts, only marginal progress was recorded in expanding international participation in Iraq's security and reconstruction. The year saw some bright moments, particularly in nurturing democracy in Afghanistan, Indonesia, and Ukraine, but overall the year was replete with frustrations.

Internet resources: <www.seeamerica.org>.

Uruguay

Atlantic Ocean

Official name: República Oriental del Uruguay (Oriental Republic of Uruguay). **Form of government:** republic with two legislative houses (Senate [31, includes the vice president, who serves as ex officio presiding officer]; Chamber of Representatives [99]). **Head of state and government:** President Tabaré Vásquez (from 1 Mar 2005). **Capital:** Montevideo. **Official language:** Spanish. **Official religion:** none. **Monetary unit:** 1 peso uruguayo ($U) = 100 centesimos; valuation (7 Jul 2005) US$1 = $U 24.94.

Demography

Area: 68,037 sq mi, 176,215 sq km. **Population** (2004): 3,399,000. **Density** (2004): persons per sq mi 50.0, persons per sq km 19.3. **Urban** (2002): 92.5%. **Sex distribution** (2003): male 48.40%; female 51.60%. **Age breakdown** (2003): under 15, 24.2%; 15–29, 22.9%; 30–44, 19.7%; 45–59, 15.8%; 60–74, 11.6%; 75 and over, 5.8%. **Ethnic composition** (2000): white (mostly Spanish, Italian, or mixed Spanish-Italian) 94.5%; mestizo 3.1%; mulatto 2.0%; other 0.4%. **Religious affiliation** (2000): Roman Catholic 78.2% (about 30–40% of Roman Catholics are estimated to be nonreligious); Protestant 3.3%; other Christian 5.3%; Jewish 1.2%; atheist 6.3%; other 5.7%. **Major cities** (1996): Montevideo (2004) 1,383,416; Salto 93,113; Paysandú 74,568; Las Piedras 66,584; Rivera 62,859. **Location:** southern South America, bordering Brazil, the South Atlantic Ocean, and Argentina.

Vital statistics

Birth rate per 1,000 population (2003): 15.9 (world avg. 21.3). **Death rate** per 1,000 population (2003): 9.4 (world avg. 9.1). **Natural increase rate** per 1,000 population (2003): 6.5 (world avg. 12.2). **Total fertility rate** (avg. births per childbearing woman; 2003): 2.2. **Marriage rate** per 1,000 population (2003): 4.2. **Divorce rate** per 1,000 population (2003): 2.0. **Life expectancy** at birth (2003): male 71.3 years; female 79.2 years.

National economy

Budget (2002). *Revenue:* $U 55,949,000,000 (tax revenue 81.9%, of which taxes on goods and services 42.7%, income and profit taxes 20.7%, import tax 2.4%, nontax revenue 9.6%; grants 8.1%; other 0.4%). *Expenditures:* $U 68,851,000,000 (social security and welfare 42.2%, general public services 11.2%, education 8.9%, health 6.3%, defense 4.4%). **Public debt** (external, outstanding; 2002): US$6,-851,000,000. **Production** (metric tons except as noted). *Agriculture, forestry, fishing* (2002): rice 939,489, wheat 270,000, sugarcane 170,000; livestock (number of live animals) 11,667,000 cattle, 11,250,000 sheep; roundwood 5,674,646 cu m; fish catch (2001) 105,051. *Mining and quarrying* (2002): limestone 1,300,000; gypsum 183,000; gold 66,841 troy oz. *Manufacturing* (value added in US$'000,000; 2000): refined petroleum products 563; food products 505; chemicals and chemical products 186. *Energy production (consumption):* electricity (kW-hr; 2000) 7,588,000,000 (7,974,000,000); coal (2000) none (1,000); crude petroleum (barrels; 2000) none (14,088,000); petroleum products (2000) 1,793,-000 (1,640,000). **Households.** Avg. household size (2002) 3.4. **Population economically active** (2003): total 1,240,500 (from urban areas only); activity rate 48.3% (participation rates: ages 14 and over, 58.2%; female 45.0%; unemployed 16.8%). **Gross national product** (at current market prices; 2003): US$12,-904,000,000 (US$3,820 per capita). **Tourism** (2002): receipts US$318,000,000; expenditures US$178,000,000. **Land use** as % of total land area (2000): in temporary crops 7.4%, in permanent crops 0.2%, in pasture 77.4%; overall forest area 7.4%.

Foreign trade

Imports (2002-c.i.f.): US$1,964,000,000 (chemicals and chemical products 17.4%; machinery and

---

1 metric ton = about 1.1 short tons;   1 kilometer = 0.6 mi (statute);   1 metric ton-km cargo = about 0.68 short ton-mi cargo;   c.i.f.: cost, insurance, and freight;   f.o.b.: free on board

appliances 15.1%; crude and refined petroleum 15.0%; food, beverages, and tobacco 14.4%; plastic products 5.9%). *Major import sources:* Argentina 27.5%; Brazil 19.8%; US 8.4%; Russia 5.7%; Germany 4.1%. **Exports** (2002): US$1,861,000,000 (hides and leather goods 13.5%; beef 13.5%; textiles and wearing apparel 11.9%; dairy products and eggs 7.6%; rice 7.5%; fish and crustaceans 5.3%). *Major export destinations:* Brazil 23.2%; US 7.4%; Argentina 6.1%; Germany 5.8%; China 5.6%.

Transport and communications

Transport. *Railroads* (1998): track length 3,002 km; passenger-km 14,000,000; metric ton-km cargo 244,000,000. *Roads* (1997): length 8,683 km (excludes streets under local control; paved 30%). *Vehicles* (2002): passenger cars 617,028; trucks and buses 53,915. *Air transport* (2000): passenger-km 747,000,000; airports (1997) 1. **Communications,** in total units (units per 1,000 persons). Daily newspaper circulation (2000): 973,000 (293); radios (2000): 2,000,000 (603); televisions (2000): 1,760,000 (536); telephone main lines (2002): 946,500 (280); cellular telephone subscribers (2002): 652,000 (193); personal computers (2001): 370,000 (110); Internet users (2001): 400,000 (119).

Education and health

Educational attainment (2002). Percentage of population age 25 and over having: incomplete primary education 9.8%; primary 33.6%; some secondary 17.2%; complete secondary 22.2%; higher 17.2%. **Literacy** (2001 est.): population age 15 and over literate 97.6%; males 97.2%; females 98.1%. **Health** (2002): physicians 12,905 (1 per 261 persons); hospital beds 6,695 (1 per 502 persons); infant mortality rate per 1,000 live births (2002) 13.6. **Food** (2001): daily per capita. caloric intake 2,848 (vegetable products 65%, animal products 35%); 107% of FAO recommended minimum.

Military

Total active duty personnel (2003): 24,000 (army 63.3%, navy 23.8%, air force 12.9%). **Military expenditure as percentage of GNP** (1999): 1.3% (world 2.4%); per capita expenditure US$83.

Background

The Spanish navigator Juan Díaz de Solís sailed into the Río de la Plata in 1516. The Portuguese established Colonia in 1680. Subsequently, the Spanish established Montevideo in 1726, driving the Portuguese from their settlement; 50 years later Uruguay became part of the viceroyalty of Río de la Plata. It gained independence from Spain in 1811. The Portuguese regained it in 1821, incorporating it into Brazil as a province. A revolt against Brazil in 1825 led to its being recognized as an independent state in 1828. It battled Paraguay 1865–70. For much of World War II Uruguay remained neutral. The presidential office was abolished in 1951 and replaced with a nine-member council. The country adopted a new constitution and restored the presidential system in 1966. A military coup occurred in 1973, but the country returned to civilian rule in 1985. The 1990s brought a general upturn in the economy.

Recent Developments

After four years of sharply negative growth, the Uruguayan economy—aided by recovery in Argentina, strong growth in Brazil, and excellent commodity prices—grew by a robust 13.6% in the first half of 2004. Unfortunately, little of this positive macroeconomic performance filtered down to Uruguay's poor or to the middle class. Unemployment remained above 13%, and more than one-third of Uruguayans lived in poverty. In this context the presidential and congressional elections that took place on 31 October marked a sea change in Uruguayan politics. During the year the polls showed that the leftist coalition known as the Broad Front–Progressive Encounter was the largest party in the country. In the election, the left received just over 50% of the vote, and Tabaré Ramón Vázquez Rosas assumed office as president on 1 Mar 2005, at the head of the first leftist government in Uruguay's history.

Internet resources: <www.turismo.gub.uy>.

Uzbekistan

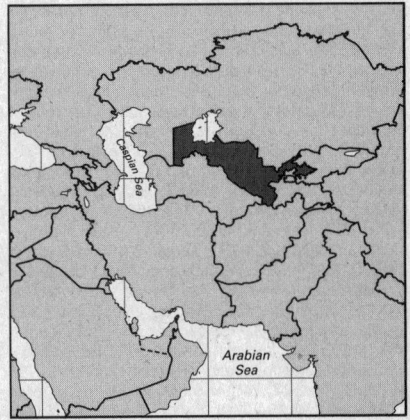

Official name: Uzbekiston Respublikasi (Republic of Uzbekistan). **Form of government:** multiparty republic with a single legislative body (Supreme Assembly [250]). **Heads of state and government:** President Islam Karimov (from 1990), assisted by Prime Minister Shavkat Mirziyayev (from 11 Dec 2003). **Capital:** Tashkent (Toshkent). **Official language:** Uzbek. **Official religion:** none. **Monetary unit:** sum (plural sumy); valuation (7 Jul 2005) $1 = 1,161.03 sumy.

Demography

Area: 172,700 sq mi, 447,400 sq km. **Population** (2004): 26,009,000. **Density** (2004): persons per sq mi 150.6, persons per sq km 58.1. **Urban** (2002): 36.6%. **Sex distribution** (2001): male 49.55%; female 50.45%. **Age breakdown** (2001): under 15, 36.4%; 15–29, 28.6%; 30–44, 19.6%; 45–59, 8.5%; 60–74, 5.4%; 75 and over, 1.5%. **Ethnic composition** (1998): Uzbek 75.8%; Russian 6.0%; Tajik 4.8%; Kazakh 4.1%; Tatar 1.6%; other 7.7%. **Religious affiliation** (2000): Muslim (mostly Sunni) 76.2%; nonreligious 18.1%; Russian Orthodox 0.8%; Jewish 0.2%;

other 4.7%. **Major cities** (1999): Tashkent 2,142,-700; Namangan 376,600; Samarkand 362,300; Andijon 323,900; Bukhara 237,900. **Location:** Central Asia, bordering Kazakhstan, Kyrgyzstan, Tajikistan, Afghanistan, and Turkmenistan.

Vital statistics

Birth rate per 1,000 population (2003): 21.6 (world avg. 21.3). **Death rate** per 1,000 population (2003): 5.8 (world avg. 9.1). **Natural increase rate** per 1,000 population (2003): 15.8 (world avg. 12.2). **Total fertility rate** (avg. births per childbearing woman; 2003): 2.4. **Marriage rate** per 1,000 population (1999): 7.1. **Life expectancy** at birth (2003): male 67.0 years; female 73.0 years.

National economy

Budget (1999). *Revenue:* 611,897,000,000 sumy (taxes on income and profits 30.5%, value-added tax 27.3%, excise taxes 22.8%, property and land taxes 12.1%, other 7.3%). *Expenditures:* 654,259,000,000 sumy (social and cultural affairs 36.7%, investments 18.7%, national economy 10.4%, transfers 10.4%, administration 2.2%, interest on debt 1.9%, other 19.2%). **Household income and expenditure** (1995). Average household size (2000) 5.5; income per household 35,165 sumy; sources of income: wages and salaries 63.0%, subsidies, grants, and nonwage income 34.9%, other 2.1%; expenditure: food and beverages 71%, clothing and footwear 14%, recreation 6%, household durables 4%, housing 3%. **Public debt** (external, outstanding; 2002): $3,901,000,000. **Tourism** (2002): receipts $68,000,000. **Production** (metric tons except as noted). *Agriculture, forestry, fishing* (2002): wheat 4,956,000, seed cotton 3,200,000, vegetables 2,300,000; livestock (number of live animals) 8,220,000 sheep, 5,400,000 cattle, 14,500,000 chickens; roundwood (2001) 24,980 cu m; fish catch (2001) 8,152. *Mining and quarrying* (2000): copper (metal content) 91,800; gold 62,276 kg. *Manufacturing* (1998): cement 3,358,000; cotton fiber 1,138,000; mineral fertilizer 897,000. *Energy production (consumption):* electricity (kW-hr; 2001) 47,961,000,000 (48,455,000,000); hard coal (2000) 69,000 (69,000); lignite (1999) 2,901,000 (2,829,000); crude petroleum (barrels; 2000) 30,412,000 (30,412,000); petroleum products (2000) 5,991,000 (5,695,000); natural gas (cu m; 2002) 58,429,000,000 (50,630,000,000). **Gross national product** (2003): $10,779,000,000 ($420 per capita). **Population economically active** (2001): total 9,136,000; activity rate of total population 36.5% (participation rates: ages 16–59 [male], 16–54 [female] 70.4%; female [1994] 43.0%; unemployed [official rate] 0.4%). **Land use** as % of total land area (2000): in temporary crops 10.8%, in permanent crops 0.8%, in pasture 55.0%; overall forest area 4.8%.

Foreign trade

Imports (2002-c.i.f.): $2,712,000,000 (machinery and metalworking products 48.9%, food products 21.3%, other 29.8%). *Major import sources:* Russia 20.5%; South Korea 17.4%; Germany 8.9%; Kazakhstan 7.5%; US 6.4%; Ukraine 6.3%. **Exports** (2002-f.o.b.): $2,988,400,000 ([2000] cotton fiber 27.5%,

energy products [including natural gas and crude petroleum] 10.3%, base metals [significantly] gold 6.6%, food products 5.4%). *Major export destinations* (2002): Russia 17.3%; Ukraine 10.2%; Italy 8.3%; Tajikistan 7.8%; South Korea 7.1%; Poland 4.7%.

Transport and communications

Transport. *Railroads* (2000): length 3,950 km; (1999) passenger-km 1,900,000,000; (1999) metric ton-km cargo 13,900,000,000. *Roads* (1997): total length 84,400 km (paved 87%). *Vehicles* (1994): passenger cars 865,300; buses 14,500. *Air transport* (2000; Uzbekistan Airways): passenger-km 3,732,-000,000; metric ton-km cargo 76,600,000; airports (1998) with scheduled flights 9. **Communications,** in total units (units per 1,000 persons). Daily newspaper circulation (2000): 74,200 (3); televisions (2000): 6,830,000 (276); telephone main lines (2003): 1,717,100 (67); cellular telephone subscribers (2003): 320,800 (13); Internet users (2003): 492,000 (19).

Education and health

Literacy (2000): percentage of total population age 15 and over literate 99.2%; males literate 99.6%; females literate 98.8%. **Health** (1995): physicians 76,200 (1 per 302 persons); hospital beds 192,000 (1 per 120 persons); infant mortality rate per 1,000 live births (2003) 36.0. **Food** (2001): daily per capita caloric intake 2,379 (vegetable products 82%, animal products 18%); 93% of FAO recommended minimum.

Military

Total active duty personnel (2003): 55,000 (army 72.7%, air force 27.3%). **Military expenditure as percentage of GNP** (1999): 1.7% (world 2.4%); per capita expenditure $38.

Background

Genghis Khan's grandson Shibaqan received the territory of Uzbekistan as his inheritance in the 13th century AD. His Mongols ruled over nearly 100 mainly Turkic tribes, who would eventually intermarry with the Mongols to form the Uzbeks and other Turkic peoples of central Asia. In the early 16th century, a federation of Mongol-Uzbeks invaded and occupied settled regions, including an area called Transoxania that would become the Uzbeks' permanent homeland. By the early 19th century the region was dominated by the khanates of Khiva, Bukhara, and Quqon, all of which eventually succumbed to Russian domination. The Uzbek Soviet Socialist Republic was created in 1924. In June 1990 Uzbekistan became the first central Asian republic to declare sovereignty. It achieved full independence from the USSR in 1991. During the 1990s its economy was considered the strongest in central Asia, though its political system was deemed harsh.

Recent Developments

A number of terrorist episodes in 2004 drew international attention to the unstable security situation in Uzbekistan. In late March and early April 2004, a series

---

1 metric ton = about 1.1 short tons;   1 kilometer = 0.6 mi (statute);   1 metric ton-km cargo = about 0.68 short ton-mi cargo;   c.i.f.: cost, insurance, and freight;   f.o.b.: free on board

of blasts in Tashkent and Bukhara were carried out by suicide bombers and resulted in the death of 28 persons. Pres. Islam Karimov, whose repressive policies almost certainly bore some responsibility for the disaffection of the terrorists, blamed international terrorists and the Muslim extremist group Hizb ut-Tahrir for having inspired the attacks. At the end of July, the US and Israeli embassies, along with the prosecutor-general's office, were targets of bomb attacks. Seven people were killed, including the three bombers themselves. An incident in early May 2005 in the eastern city of Andijon resulted in at least 169 people—and likely many hundreds more—being killed. Details were unclear, but the casualties seem to have resulted from attacks by government troops on demonstrators (whom the regime tagged as Muslim extremists) who had seized a government building and taken a number of hostages and were later joined by thousands of other demonstrators.

Internet resources: <www.uzbektourism.uz>.

Vanuatu

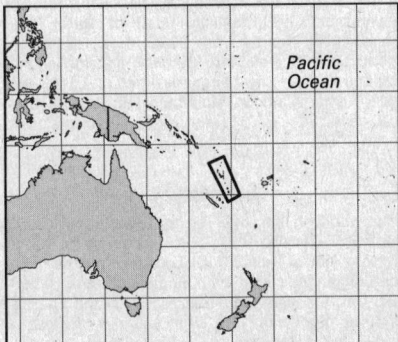

Pacific Ocean

Official name: Ripablik blong Vanuatu (Bislama); République de Vanuatu (French); Republic of Vanuatu (English). **Form of government:** republic with a single legislative house (Parliament [52]). **Chief of state:** President Kalcot Matas Kelekele (from 16 Aug 2004). **Head of government:** Prime Minister Ham Lini (from 11 Dec 2004). **Capital:** Vila. **Official languages:** Bislama; French; English. **Official religion:** none. **Monetary unit:** vatu (VT); valuation (7 Jul 2005) $1 = VT 110.98.

Demography

Area: 4,707 sq mi, 12,190 sq km. **Population** (2004): 216,000. **Density** (2004): persons per sq mi 45.9, persons per sq km 17.7. **Urban** (2002): 21.0%. **Sex distribution** (1999): male 51.46%; female 48.54%. **Age breakdown** (1999): under 15, 37.8%; 15–29, 29.4%; 30–44, 18.2%; 45–59, 9.7%; 60–74, 4.0%; 75 and over, 0.9%. **Ethnic composition** (1999): Ni-Vanuatu 98.7%; European and other Pacific Islanders 1.3%. **Religious affiliation** (2000): Christian 89.3%, of which Protestant 53.7%, Anglican 18.2%, Roman Catholic 15.5%; Custom (traditional beliefs) 3.5%; Baha'i 2.9%; other 4.3%. **Major towns** (1999): Vila (Port-Vila) 30,139; Luganville 11,360. **Location:** island group in Oceania, between the South Pacific Ocean and the Coral Sea.

Vital statistics

Birth rate per 1,000 population (2003): 24.3 (world avg. 21.3). **Death rate** per 1,000 population (2003): 8.1 (world avg. 9.1). **Natural increase rate** per 1,000 population (2003): 16.2 (world avg. 12.2). **Total fertility rate** (avg. births per childbearing woman; 2003): 3.0. **Life expectancy** at birth (2003): male 60.3 years; female 63.2 years.

National economy

Budget (2001). *Revenue:* VT 6,887,000,000 (tax revenue 84.0%, of which taxes on goods and services 48.4%, tax on import duties 33.2%; foreign grants 6.4%; nontax revenue 9.4%). *Expenditures:* VT 7,885,000,000 (wages and salary 47.4%; goods and services 23.3%; transfers 10.1%; interest payments 3.1%; other [including technical assistance] 16.0%). **Public debt** (external, outstanding; 2002): $69,700,000. **Production** (metric tons except as noted). *Agriculture, forestry, fishing* (2002): coconuts 200,000, roots and tubers 45,000, bananas 13,000; livestock (number of live animals) 151,000 cattle, 62,000 pigs, 340,000 chickens; roundwood 119,000 cu m; fish catch (2001) 26,690. *Mining and quarrying:* small quantities of coral-reef limestone, crushed stone, sand, and gravel. *Manufacturing* (value added in VT '000,000; 1995): food, beverages, and tobacco 645; wood products 423; fabricated metal products 377. *Energy production (consumption):* electricity (kW-hr; 2000) 38,000,000 (38,000,000); petroleum products (2000) none (26,000). **Land use** as % of total land area (2000): in temporary crops 2.5%, in permanent crops 7.4%, in pasture 3.4%; overall forest area 36.7%. **Population economically active** (1999): total 76,370; activity rate of total population 40.9% (participation rates: ages 15–64, 78.2%; female 49.6%). **Gross national product** (2003): $248,000,000 ($1,180 per capita). **Household income and expenditure** (1985; Vila and Luganville only). Average household size (1989) 5.1; income per household $11,299; sources of income: wages and salaries 59.0%, self-employment 33.7%; expenditure (1990; Vila and Luganville only): food and nonalcoholic beverages 30.5%, housing 20.7%, transportation 13.2%, health and recreation 12.3%, tobacco and alcohol 10.4%. **Tourism** (2001): receipts from visitors $46,000,000; expenditures by nationals abroad $8,000,000.

Foreign trade

Imports (2002-c.i.f.): VT 12,433,000,000 (machinery and transport equipment 22.9%, food and live animals 17.2%, chemicals and chemical products 12.1%, mineral fuels 11.2%). *Major import sources:* Australia 39.3%; New Zealand 17.6%; Fiji 8.3%; France 5.3%; New Caledonia 4.0%. **Exports** (2002-f.o.b.): VT 2,793,000,000 (domestic exports 76.3%, of which coconut oil 16.9%, kava 15.6%, timber 7.1%, beef 6.9%, copra 6.2%; reexports 23.7%). *Major export destinations* (domestic exports only): Australia 29.2%; EC 10.8%; Japan 10.7%; New Caledonia 9.0%; Bangladesh 4.9%.

Transport and communications

Transport. *Roads* (1996): total length 1,070 km (paved 24%). *Vehicles* (1996): passenger cars 4,000; trucks and buses 2,600. *Air transport* (2001;

Air Vanuatu only): passenger-km 212,039,000; metric ton-km 1,899,000; airports (1996) with scheduled flights 29. **Communications**, in total units (units per 1,000 persons). Radios (1997): 62,000 (350); televisions (2000): 2,280 (12); telephone main lines (2003): 6,500 (32); cellular telephone subscribers (2003): 7,800 (38); personal computers (2002): 3,000 (15); Internet users (2003): 7,500 (36).

Education and health

Educational attainment (1999). Percentage of population age 15 and over having: no formal schooling 18.0%; incomplete primary education 20.6%; completed primary 35.5%; some secondary 12.2%; completed secondary 8.5%; higher 5.2%, of which university 1.3%. **Literacy** (1998): total population age 15 and over literate 64%. **Health** (1997): physicians 21 (1 per 8,524 persons); hospital beds 573 (1 per 312 persons); infant mortality rate per 1,000 live births (2003) 58.1. **Food** (2001): daily per capita caloric intake 2,565 (vegetable products 87%, animal products 13%); 113% of FAO recommended minimum.

Military

Total active duty personnel: Vanuatu has a paramilitary force of about 300.

Background

The islands of Vanuatu were inhabited for at least 3,000 years by Melanesian peoples before being discovered in 1606 by the Portuguese. They were rediscovered by French navigator Louis-Antoine de Bougainville in 1768, then explored by English mariner Capt. James Cook in 1774 and named the New Hebrides. Sandalwood merchants and European missionaries arrived in the mid-19th century; they were followed by British and French cotton planters. Control of the islands was sought by both the French and British, who agreed in 1906 to form a condominium government. During World War II a major Allied naval base was on Espíritu Santo; the island group escaped Japanese invasion. The New Hebrides became the independent Republic of Vanuatu in 1980. Much of the nation's housing was ravaged by a hurricane in 1987.

Recent Developments

After a long period of instability in Vanuatu, during which the cabinet was reshuffled several times and the president dismissed because of his criminal record, Prime Minister Edward Natapei of the Vanua'aku Party called a snap election in July 2004 rather than face a no-confidence vote in Parliament. He was defeated at the polls, and former prime minister Serge Vohor of the Union of Moderate Parties joined with the National United Party, minor parties, and independents to form a coalition government. The new government was immediately tested by a vote of no confidence, which it won 31–21 in the 52-member house.

Internet resources: <www.vanuatutourism.com>.

Vatican City State

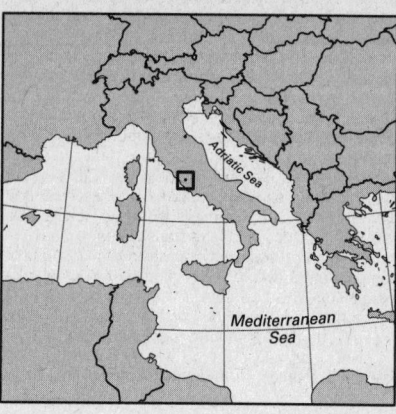

In full: State of the Vatican City (Holy See). **Form of government:** ecclesiastical. **Chief of state:** Pope Benedict XVI (from 19 Apr 2005). **Head of government:** Secretary of State Cardinal Angelo Sodano. **Capital:** Vatican City. **Languages:** Italian, Latin. **Religion:** Roman Catholic. **Monetary unit:** 1 euro (€) = 100 cents; $1 = €0.84 (7 Jul 2005); at conversion on 1 Jan 2002, €1 = 1,936.3 lira (Lit).

Demography

Area: 0.44 sq km, 0.17 sq mi. **Population:** (2002 est.): 900. **Density:** (2001): persons per sq mi 5,298, persons per sq km 2,045. **Location:** southern Europe, within the commune of Rome, Italy. **Annual budget:** $209 million. **Industries:** banking and finance; printing; production of a small amount of mosaics and uniforms; tourism.

Background

Vatican City, the independent papal state, is the smallest independent state in the world. Its medieval and Renaissance walls form its boundaries except on the southeast, at St. Peter's Square. Within the walls is a miniature nation, with its own diplomatic missions, newspaper, post office, radio station, banking system, army of more than 100 Swiss Guards, and publishing house. Extraterritoriality of the state extends to Castel Gandolfo, summer home of the Pope, and to several churches and palaces in Rome proper. Its independent sovereignty was recognized in the Lateran Treaty of 1929. The pope has absolute executive, legislative, and judicial powers within the city. He appoints the members of the Vatican's government organs, which are separate from those of the Holy See. Its many imposing buildings include St. Peter's Basilica, the Vatican Palace, and the Vatican Museums. Frescoes by Michelangelo and Pinturicchio in the Sistine Chapel and Raphael's Stanze are also there. The Vatican Library contains a priceless collection of manuscripts from the pre-Christian and Christian eras.

---

1 metric ton = about 1.1 short tons; 1 kilometer = 0.6 mi (statute); 1 metric ton-km cargo = about 0.68 short ton-mi cargo; c.i.f.: cost, insurance, and freight; f.o.b.: free on board

Recent Developments

On 2 Apr 2005 Pope John Paul II died in Vatican City. The beloved pope, the first ever from Poland, had been in office for 26 years, the third longest tenure of any pontiff. A German cardinal, Joseph Ratzinger, who chose the papal name Benedict XVI, was elected to succeed John Paul II. He had held the post of prefect of the Sacred Congregation for the Doctrine of Faith and had been the chief theological adviser to John Paul for two decades. Pope Benedict XVI was expected to continue the conservative doctrines of his predecessor.

Internet resources: <www.vatican.va>.

Venezuela

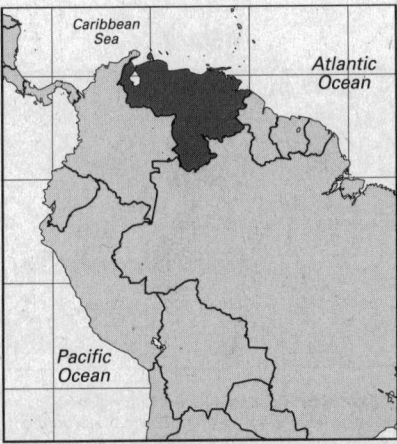

Official name: República Bolivariana de Venezuela (Bolivarian Republic of Venezuela). Form of government: federal multiparty republic with a unicameral legislature (National Assembly [165]). Head of state and government: President Hugo Chávez Frias (from 2002). Capital: Caracas. Official language: Spanish; 31 indigenous Indian languages were made official in May 2002. Official religion: none. Monetary unit: 1 bolívar (B, plural Bs) = 100 céntimos; valuation (7 Jul 2005) $1 = Bs 2,148.

Demography

Area: 353,841 sq mi, 916,445 sq km. Population (2004): 26,170,000. Density (2004): persons per sq mi 74.0, persons per sq km 28.6. Urban (2003 est.): 87.7%. Sex distribution (2001): male 49.56%; female 50.44%. Age breakdown (2001): under 15, 33.1%; 15–29, 27.5%; 30–44, 20.7%; 45–59, 11.7%; 60–74, 5.1%; 75 and over, 1.9%. Ethnic composition (1993): mestizo 67%; white 21%; black 10%; Indian 2%. Religious affiliation (2000): Roman Catholic 89.5%; Protestant 2.0%; other Christian 1.4%; Spiritist 1.1%; nonreligious/atheist 2.2%; other 3.8%. Major cities (2001; preliminary unadjusted census results): Caracas 1,836,000 (urban agglomeration 3,177,000); Maracaibo 1,609,000; Valencia 1,196,000; Barquisimeto 811,000; Ciudad Guayana 629,000. Location: northern South America, border-ing the Caribbean Sea, the North Atlantic Ocean, Guyana, Brazil, and Colombia.

Vital statistics

Birth rate per 1,000 population (2003): 22.6 (world avg. 21.3). Death rate per 1,000 population (2003): 5.1 (world avg. 9.1). Total fertility rate (avg. births per childbearing woman; 2003): 2.7. Marriage rate per 1,000 population (2003): 2.9. Life expectancy at birth (2002): male 70.8 years; female 76.6 years.

National economy

Budget (2000). Revenue: Bs 14,664,587,000,000 (oil revenues 59.2%, value-added tax 17.3%, income tax 9.0%, import duties 7.3%). Expenditures: Bs 17,238,854,000,000 (subsidies 50.5%, wages and salaries 19.1%, capital expenditure 14.5%, debt service 11.6%, goods and services 2.7%). Public debt (external, outstanding; 2002): $23,265,000,000. Production (metric tons except as noted). Agriculture, forestry, fishing (2002): sugarcane 6,909,000, corn (maize) 1,805,000, rice 790,000; livestock (number of live animals) 14,500,000 cattle, 5,655,000 pigs, 115,000,000 chickens; roundwood (2002) 4,667,-000 cu m; fish catch (2001) 435,000. Mining and quarrying (2001): iron ore 16,902,000; bauxite 4,526,000; gold 9,076 kg. Manufacturing (value added in 1984 Bs '000,000; 1997): ferrous and nonferrous metals 16,355; food products 13,277; chemicals 10,004. Energy production (consumption): electricity (kW-hr; 2000) 85,211,000,000 (85,211,000,000); coal (2000) 7,885,000 (180,000); crude petroleum (barrels; 2001) 972,000,000 ([2000] 382,000,000); petroleum products (2000) 53,937,000 (19,530,000); natural gas (cu m; 2000) 28,382,700,000 (28,382,-700,000). Tourism (2002): receipts $468,000,000; expenditures $1,041,000,000. Land use as % of total land area (2000): in temporary crops 2.9%, in permanent crops 0.9%, in pasture 20.7%; overall forest area 56.1%. Gross national product (2003): $89,150,-000,000 ($3,490 per capita). Population economically active (1997): total 9,507,125; activity rate 41.7% (participation rates: over age 15, 64.6%; female 35.9%; unemployed 10.6%). Household income and expenditure. Average household size (1990) 5.1; average annual income per household (1981) Bs 42,492; expenditure (1995): food 40.6%, housing 13.8%, transportation and communications 8.6%, clothing 5.3%, health 3.1%, education and recreation 2.9%.

Foreign trade

Imports (2001-f.o.b. in balance of trade): $16,435,-000,000 (nonelectrical machinery 16.5%, chemicals and chemical products 14.1%, road vehicles 14.0%, electrical machinery 9.8%). Major import sources: US 33.9%; Colombia 8.7%; Brazil 5.9%; Mexico 4.7%; Japan 4.6%. Exports (2001-f.o.b. in balance of trade): $25,304,000,000 (crude petroleum 58.3%, refined petroleum 23.6%, iron and steel 3.1%, aluminum 3.0%). Major export destinations (2002): US 56.4%; Netherlands Antilles 6.1%; Colombia 2.9%; Dominican Republic 2.8%; Brazil 2.7%.

Transport and communications

Transport. Railroads (1996): length (1994) 627 km; passenger-km 149,905; metric ton-km cargo 54,474,000. Roads (1999): total length 96,155 km (paved 34%). *Vehicles* (1997): passenger cars 1,505,000; trucks and buses 542,000. *Air transport* (1998): passenger-km 3,133,000,000; metric ton-km cargo 332,000,000; airports (1997) with scheduled flights 20. **Communications**, in total units (units per 1,000 persons). Daily newspaper circulation (2000): 5,000,000 (206); radios (2000): 7,140,000 (294); televisions (2000): 4,490,000 (185); telephone main lines (2002): 2,841,800 (112); cellular telephone subscribers (2002): 6,463,600 (256); personal computers (2002): 1,536,000 (61); Internet users (2002): 1,274,400 (51).

Education and health

Educational attainment (1993). Percentage of population age 25 and over having: no formal schooling 8.0%; primary education or less 43.7%; some secondary and secondary 38.3%; postsecondary 10.0%. **Literacy** (1995 est.): total population age 15 and over literate 91.1%; males 91.8%; females 90.3%. **Health** (1999): physicians 46,886 (1 per 508 persons); public hospital beds (2000) 40,675 (1 per 620 persons); infant mortality rate per 1,000 live births (2003) 17.2. **Food** (2002): daily per capita caloric intake 2,337 (vegetable products 83%, animal products 17%); 95% of FAO recommended minimum.

Military

Total active duty personnel (2003): 82,300 (army 69.3%, navy 22.2%, air force 8.5%). **Military expenditure as percentage of GNP** (1999): 1.4% (world 2.4%); per capita expenditure $61.

Background

In 1498 Christopher Columbus sighted Venezuela; in 1499 the navigators Alonso de Ojeda, Amerigo Vespucci, and Juan de la Cosa traced the coast. A Spanish missionary established the first European settlement at Cumaná c. 1520. In 1718 it was included in the viceroyalty of New Granada and was made a captaincy general in 1731. Venezuelan Creoles led by Francisco de Miranda and Simón Bolívar spearheaded the South American independence movement, and though Venezuela declared independence from Spain in 1811, that status was not assured until 1821. Military dictators generally ruled the country from 1830 until the overthrow of Marcos Pérez Jiménez in 1958. A new constitution adopted in 1961 marked the beginning of democracy. As a founding member of OPEC, it enjoyed relative economic prosperity from oil production during the 1970s, and its economy has remained dependent on the world petroleum market. The leftist president Hugo Chávez Frías promulgated a new constitution in 1999, and he was reelected in 2002; a period of great political and economic tumult ensued.

Recent Developments

The government's victory in the October 2004 regional and municipal elections flowed from the opposition's failure to oust Pres. Hugo Chávez Frías in the recall referendum on 15 August. This result shocked his opponents. By early November Venezuela's economy appeared on track to grow at an annual rate of 12%. Chávez continued his support for Cuban Pres. Fidel Castro, supplying petroleum to Cuba at cut-rate prices. In February 2005 he struck a "strategic alliance" with another leftist neighbor, Brazil's Pres. Luis Ignácio Lula da Silva. Chávez remained determined to reduce US economic influence in South America; he opposed the Free Trade Area of the Americas initiative and committed Venezuela to associate membership in the Southern Cone Common Market (Mercosur) in the summer of 2004. In mid-April 2005 Chávez signaled that he would limit American control of Venezuelan oil, in part by selling refineries and other facilities in the US, and increase state control over the industry by obliging private companies operating in Venezuela to accept joint-venture status with the government.

Internet resources: <www.venezuelatuya.com>.

Vietnam

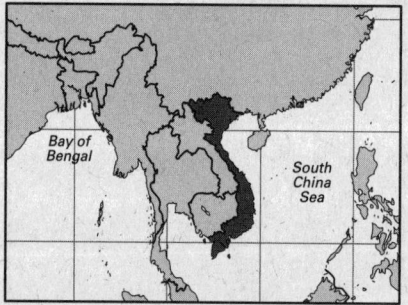

Bay of Bengal

South China Sea

Official name: Cong Hoa Xa Hoi Chu Nghia Viet Nam (Socialist Republic of Vietnam). **Form of government:** socialist republic with one legislative house (National Assembly [498]). **Head of state:** President Tran Duc Luong (from 1997). **Head of government:** Prime Minister Phan Van Khai (from 1997). **Capital:** Hanoi. **Official language:** Vietnamese. **Official religion:** none. **Monetary unit:** 1 dong (D) = 10 hao = 100 xu; valuation (7 Jul 2005) $1 = D 15,862.

Demography

Area: 128,379 sq mi, 332,501 sq km. **Population** (2004): 81,839,000. **Density** (2004): persons per sq mi 637.5, persons per sq km 246.1. **Urban** (2002): 25.1%. **Sex distribution** (2002): male 49.20%; female 50.80%. **Age breakdown** (2003): under 15, 30.2%; 15–29, 29.4%; 30–44, 21.8%; 45–59, 10.8%; 60–74, 5.7%; 75 and over, 2.0%. **Ethnic composition** (2000): Vietnamese 85.0%; Han Chinese 3.5%; Montagnards 1.9%; Tho (Tay) 1.6%; Tai 1.5%; Muong 1.4%; Khmer 1.2%; Nung 1.0%; other 2.9%. **Religious affiliation** (1995): Buddhist 66.7%; Christian 8.7%, of which Roman Catholic 7.7%, Protestant 1.0%; Cao Dai (a New-Religionist group) 3.5%; Hoa Hao (a New-Religionist group) 2.1%; other 19.0%. **Major cities** (1992): Ho Chi Minh City 5,479,000 (2002); Hanoi 2,931,400 (2002); Haiphong 783,133; Da Nang 382,674; Buon Ma Thuot 282,095. **Location:** southeastern Asia, bordering

China, the Gulf of Tonkin, the South China Sea, the Gulf of Thailand, Cambodia, and Laos.

Vital statistics

Birth rate per 1,000 population (2003): 20.1 (world avg. 21.3). **Death rate** per 1,000 population (2003): 6.4 (world avg. 9.1). **Natural increase rate** per 1,000 population (2003): 13.7 (world avg. 12.2). **Total fertility rate** (avg. births per childbearing woman; 2003): 2.3. **Life expectancy** at birth (2003): male 67.0 years; female 72.0 years.

National economy

Budget (2003). *Revenue:* D 123,700,000,000,000 (tax revenue 77.9%, of which corporate income taxes 24.6%, VAT 23.2%, taxes on trade 18.7%; nontax revenues 20.5%; grants 1.6%). *Expenditures:* D 148,400,000,000,000 (current expenditures 64.6%, of which social services 27.9%, economic services 5.3%, interest payment 4.5%; capital expenditures 35.4%). **Public debt** (external, outstanding; 2002): $12,181,000,000. **Gross national product** (2003): $38,786,000,000 ($480 per capita). **Tourism** (1998): receipts from visitors $86,000,000. **Production** (metric tons except as noted). *Agriculture, forestry, fishing* (2002): rice 34,064,000, sugarcane 16,824,000, cassava 4,158,000; livestock (number of live animals) 60,000,000 ducks, 23,170,000 pigs, 4,063,000 cattle; roundwood (2002) 30,730,000 cu m, of which fuelwood 26,547,000 cu m, industrial roundwood 4,183,000 cu m; fish catch (2001) 1,491,000, of which marine fish 1,321,000. *Mining and quarrying* (2002): phosphate rock (gross weight) 770,000; tin (metal content) 4,000. *Manufacturing* (gross value of production in $'000,000; 2000): food products 736; cement, bricks and pottery 418; wearing apparel 376. *Energy production (consumption):* electricity (kW-hr; 2001) 29,800,-000,000 ([2000] 26,594,000,000); coal (2002) 15,900,000 ([2000] 7,978,000); crude petroleum (barrels; 2002) 136,700,000 ([2000] negligible); petroleum products (2000) 154,000 (8,969,000); natural gas (cu m; 2002) 2,260,000,000 ([2000] 1,355,000,000). **Population economically active** (2002): total 38,715,000; activity rate 48.9% (participation rates [2001]: ages 15 and over 70.5%; unemployed 6.0%). **Household income and expenditure.** Average household size (2002) 5.0; income per household (1990; wage workers and government officials only) D 577,008; expenditure (1990): food 62.4%, clothing 5.0%, household goods 4.6%, education 2.9%, housing 2.5%. **Land use** as % of total land area (2000): in temporary crops 18.7%, in permanent crops 5.4%, in pasture 2.0%; overall forest area 30.2%.

Foreign trade

Imports (2002-f.o.b. in balance of trade and c.i.f. in commodities and trading partners): $19,733,-000,000 (machinery equipment [including aircraft] 19.2%; petroleum products 10.2%; garment material and leather 8.7%; iron and steel 6.8%; fertilizers 2.7%; motorcycles 2.1%). *Major import sources:* Taiwan 12.9%; Singapore 12.8%; Japan 12.7%; South Korea 11.6%; China 10.9%. **Exports** (2002): $16,706,000,000 (crude petroleum 19.6%; garments 16.5%; fish, crustaceans, and mollusks 12.1%; footwear 11.2%; rice 4.3%; electronic products 2.9%).

Major export destinations: Japan 14.6%; US 14.5%; China 9.0%; Australia 8.0%; Singapore 5.8%; Taiwan 4.9%.

Transport and communications

Transport. *Railroads* (2001): route length 3,142 km; passenger-km 3,428,000,000; metric ton-km cargo 2,054,400,000. *Roads* (1999): total length 93,300 km (paved 25%). *Vehicles* (2003): passenger cars, trucks, and buses 600,000. *Air transport* (2002; Vietnam Airlines only): passenger-km 2,963,000,000; metric ton-km cargo 81,000,000; airports (1997) with scheduled flights 12. **Communications,** in total units (units per 1,000 persons). Daily newspaper circulation (2000): 313,000 (4); radios (2000): 8,520,000 (109); televisions (2000): 14,500,000 (185); telephone main lines (2003): 4,402,000 (54); cellular telephone subscribers (2003): 2,742,000 (34); personal computers (2002): 800,000 (10); Internet users (2003): 3,500,000 (43).

Education and health

Educational attainment (1989). Percentage of population age 25 and over having: no formal education (illiterate) 16.6%; incomplete and complete primary 69.8%; incomplete and complete secondary 10.6%; higher 2.6%; unknown 0.4%. **Literacy** (2001): percentage of population age 15 and over literate 92.7%; males 94.5%; females 90.9%. **Health** (2002): physicians 45,073 (1 per 1,769 persons); hospital beds 178,385 (1 per 447 persons); infant mortality rate per 1,000 live births (2003) 30.8. **Food** (2001): daily per capita caloric intake 2,533 (vegetable products 89%, animal products 11%); 117% of FAO recommended minimum.

Military

Total active duty personnel (2003): 484,000 (army 85.1%, navy 8.7%, air force 6.2%). **Military expenditure as percentage of GNP** (1997): 2.4% (world 2.5%); per capita expenditure $44.

Background

A distinct Vietnamese group began to emerge c. 200 BC in the independent kingdom of Nam Viet, which was annexed to China in the 1st century BC. The Vietnamese were under continuous Chinese control until the 10th century AD. The southern region was gradually overrun by Vietnamese from the north in the late 15th century. The area was divided into two parts in the early 17th century, with the northern part known as Tonkin, and the southern part as Cochin China. In 1802 the northern and southern parts of Vietnam were unified under a single dynasty.

Following several years of attempted French colonial expansion in the region, the French captured Saigon in 1859 and later the rest of the area, controlling it until World War II. The Japanese occupied Vietnam 1940–45 and declared it independent at the end of World War II, a move the French opposed. The French and Vietnamese fought the First Indochina War until French forces with US financial backing were defeated at Dien Bien Phu in 1954; evacuation of French troops ensued.

Following an international conference at Geneva, Vietnam was partitioned along the 17th parallel, with the northern part under Ho Chi Minh and the southern part under Bao Dai; the partition was to be temporary, but the reunification elections scheduled for 1956 were never held. Bao Dai declared the independence of South Vietnam (Republic of Vietnam), while the Communists established North Vietnam (Democratic Republic of Vietnam). The activities of North Vietnamese guerrillas and pro-communist rebels in South Vietnam led to US intervention and the Vietnam War. A cease-fire agreement was signed in 1973, and US troops were withdrawn. The civil war soon resumed, and in 1975 North Vietnam invaded South Vietnam and the South Vietnamese government collapsed. In 1976 the two Vietnams were united as the Socialist Republic of Vietnam. From the mid-1980s, the government enacted a series of economic reforms and began to open up to Asian and western nations. During the 1990s the US moved to normalize relations with it.

Recent Developments

On 3 Feb 2004 the Vietnam Communist Party's Central Committee declared, "International reactionary forces are likely to intensify their schemes of using issues related to 'democracy,' 'human rights,' ethnicity, and religion while aiding and abetting reactionaries and extremists at home to cause sociopolitical instability as a pretext for intervention." This dire assessment was seemingly borne out on 10–11 April when a demonstration of more than 10,000 ethnic minorities in the Central Highlands turned violent. Western human rights organizations claimed that dozens of highlanders were killed and hundreds injured by security forces who reportedly responded in a heavy-handed fashion. Vietnamese authorities were quick to accuse the South Carolina–based Montagnard Foundation of having instigated unrest. On 15 June the National Assembly ratified the China-Vietnam agreement that had been signed in December 2000 on demarcation of the territorial sea, exclusive economic zones, and the continental shelf in the Gulf of Tonkin.

Internet resources: <www.vietnamtourism.com>.

Virgin Islands (US)

Official name: Virgin Islands of the United States. Political status: organized unincorporated territory of the US with one legislative house (Senate [15]). Chief of state: President of the US George W. Bush (from 2001). Head of government: Governor Charles Turnbull (from 1999). Capital: Charlotte Amalie. Official language: English. Official religion: none. Monetary unit: 1 US dollar ($) = 100 cents.

Demography

Area: 136 sq mi, 353 sq km. Population (2004): 109,000. Density (2004): persons per sq mi 801.5, persons per sq km 309.7. Urban (2000): 92.6%. Sex distribution (2000): male 47.75%; female 52.25%. Age breakdown (2000): under 15, 26.1%; 15–29, 19.4%; 30–44, 21.2%; 45–59, 20.5%; 60–74, 9.8%; 75 and over, 3.0%. Ethnic composition (2000): black 61.1%; US white 15.0%; Puerto Rican 12.0%; French Creole (from Martinique and Guadeloupe) 9.0%; British 1.0%; other 1.9%. Religious affiliation (2000):

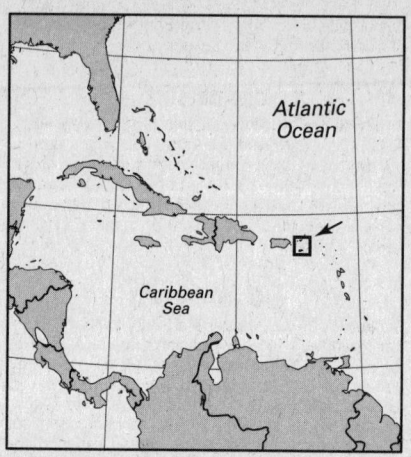

Christian 96.3%, of which Protestant 51.0% (including Anglican 13.0%), Roman Catholic 27.5%, independent Christian 12.2%; nonreligious 2.2%; other 1.5%. Major towns (2000): Charlotte Amalie 11,004 (urban agglomeration 18,914); Christiansted 2,637; Frederiksted 732. Location: northeastern Caribbean, islands between the Caribbean Sea and the North Atlantic Ocean.

Vital statistics

Birth rate per 1,000 population (2003): 15.0 (world avg. 21.3); (1998) legitimate 30.2%. Death rate per 1,000 population (2003): 5.7 (world avg. 9.1). Natural increase rate per 1,000 population (2003): 9.3 (world avg. 12.2). Total fertility rate (avg. births per childbearing woman; 2003): 2.2. Marriage rate per 1,000 population (1993): 35.1. Divorce rate per 1,000 population (1993): 4.5. Life expectancy at birth (2003): male 74.7 years; female 82.7 years.

National economy

Budget (2002). Revenue: $580,200,000 (personal income tax 54.7%, gross receipts tax 16.5%, property tax 7.9%). Expenditures: $573,000,000 (direct federal expenditures 100.0%). Production. Agriculture, forestry, fishing (value of sales in $'000; 1998): milk 1,263, livestock and livestock products 655 (of which cattle and calves 439, hogs and pigs 46), ornamental plants and other nursery products 364; livestock (number of live animals; 2002) 8,000 cattle, 4,000 goats, 3,500 chickens; fish catch (2001) 300 metric tons. Mining and quarrying: sand and crushed stone for local use. Manufacturing (value of sales in $'000; 1997): food and food products 31,949; stone, clay, and glass products 21,897; printing and publishing 21,127. Energy production (consumption): electricity (kW-hr; 2000) 1,090,000,000 (1,090,000,000); coal (metric tons; 2000) none (257,000); crude petroleum (barrels; 2000) none (124,700,000); petroleum products (metric tons; 2000) 15,385,000 (2,470,000). Tourism (2002): receipts from visitors

1 metric ton = about 1.1 short tons;   1 kilometer = 0.6 mi (statute);   1 metric ton-km cargo = about 0.68 short ton-mi cargo;   c.i.f.: cost, insurance, and freight;   f.o.b.: free on board

$1,240,000,000. **Household income and expenditure.** Average household size (2000) 2.6; average annual income per household (2000) $34,991; expenditures (2001): housing 38.8%, food and beverages 12.5%, transportation 11.1%, education and communications 7.1%, health 5.8%. **Population economically active** (2002; excludes armed forces): total 49,440; activity rate of total population 45.4% (participation rates: ages 16–64, 72.5% [1990]; female 47.8% [1990]; unemployed 8.7%). **Gross domestic product** (at current market prices; 2002): $2,479,000,000 ($22,530 per capita). **Public debt** (1999): $1,200,000,000. **Land use** as % of total land area (2000): in temporary crops 12%, in permanent crops 3%, in pasture 15%; overall forest area 41%.

Foreign trade

Imports (2002): $4,213,200,000 (foreign crude petroleum 75.8%, other [significantly manufactured goods] 24.2%). *Major import sources* (2001): US 13.8%; Puerto Rico 2.0%; other countries 84.2%. **Exports** (2002): $3,876,300,000 (refined petroleum 83.4%, unspecified 16.6%). *Major export destinations* (2001): US 74.8%; Puerto Rico 18.7%; other countries 6.5%.

Transport and communications

Transport. *Roads* (1996): total length 856 km. *Vehicles* (1993): passenger cars 51,000; trucks and buses 13,300. Cruise ships (2003): passenger arrivals 1,773,948. *Air transport* (2003; St. Croix and St. Thomas airports): passenger arrivals 598,907; airports (1999) with scheduled flights 2. **Communications,** in total units (units per 1,000 persons). Daily newspaper circulation (2000): 43,000 (364); radios (1996): 107,000 (927); televisions (2000): 64,700 (594); telephone main lines (2001): 69,400 (635); cellular telephone subscribers (2001): 41,000 (375); Internet users (2002): 30,000 (273).

Education and health

Educational attainment (2000). Percentage of population age 25 and over having: no formal schooling through lower secondary education 18.5%; incomplete upper secondary 21.0%; completed secondary 26.0%; incomplete undergraduate degree 17.8%; completed undergraduate degree 10.4%; graduate degree 6.3%. **Health** (2002): physicians 161 (1 per 675 persons); infant mortality rate per 1,000 live births (2003) 8.4.

Military

Total active duty personnel: no domestic military force is maintained; the US is responsible for defense and external security.

Background

The Virgin Islands of the US probably were originally settled by Arawak Indians, but they were inhabited by the Caribs when Christopher Columbus landed on St. Croix in 1493. St. Croix was occupied by the Dutch, English, French, and Spanish and was at one time owned by the Knights of Malta. Denmark occupied St. Thomas, St. John, and St. Croix and established them as a Danish colony in 1754. The US purchased the Danish West Indies in 1917 for $25 million and changed the name to the Virgin Islands. They were administered by the US Department of the Interior from 1931. In 1954 the Organic Act of the Virgin Islands created the current governmental structure, and in 1970 the first popularly elected governor took office. The area suffered extensive damage by hurricanes in 1995.

Recent Developments

Police violence was an issue of concern in the Virgin Islands, especially following a report by a local newspaper in December 2003 that found an unusually high incidence of deadly force being employed by law officers who were often insufficiently trained, underpaid, and badly supervised. The US Justice Department and local politicians became interested in the problem and began seeking solutions.

Internet resources: <www.usvitourism.vi>.

Yemen

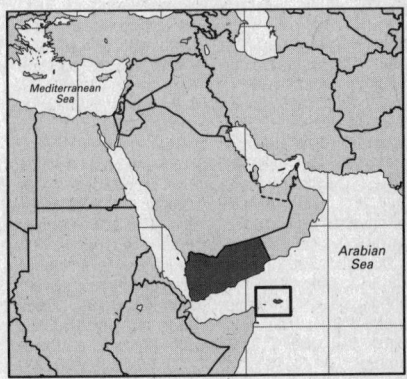

Official name: Al-Jumhuriyah al-Yamaniyah (Republic of Yemen). **Form of government:** multiparty republic with two legislative houses (Consultative Council [111 nonelected seats]; House of Representatives [301]). **Head of state:** President Major General 'Ali 'Abdallah Salih (from 1990). **Head of government:** Prime Minister 'Abd al-Qadir al-Ba Jamal (from 2001). **Capital:** Sanaa. **Official language:** Arabic. **Official religion:** Islam. **Monetary unit:** 1 Yemeni Rial (YRls) = 100 fils; valuation (7 Jul 2005): $1 = YRls 181.02.

Demography

Area: 214,300 sq mi, 555,000 sq km. **Population** (2004): 20,733,000. **Density** (2004): persons per sq mi 96.7, persons per sq km 37.4. **Urban** (2001): 25.0%. **Sex distribution** (2003): male 50.91%; female 49.09%. **Age breakdown** (2003): under 15, 46.8%; 15–29, 29.0%; 30–44, 12.8%; 45–59, 7.3%; 60–74, 3.1%; 75 and over, 1.0%. **Ethnic composition** (2000): Arab 92.8%; Somali 3.7%; black 1.1%; Indo-Pakistani 1.0%; other 1.4%. **Religious affiliation** (2000): Muslim 98.9%, of which Sunni 60%, Shi'i 40%; Hindu 0.7%; Christian 0.2%; other 0.2%. **Major cities** (2001): Sanaa 1,590,624; Aden 509,886;

Ta'izz 450,000; Al-Hudaydah 425,000; Al-Mukalla 165,000. **Location:** the Middle East, bordering Oman, the Arabian Sea, the Gulf of Aden, the Red Sea, and Saudi Arabia.

Vital statistics

Birth rate per 1,000 population (2003): 41.4 (world avg. 21.3). **Death rate** per 1,000 population (2003): 8.8 (world avg. 9.1). **Natural increase rate** per 1,000 population (2003): 32.6 (world avg. 12.2). **Total fertility rate** (avg. births per childbearing woman; 2003): 6.8. **Life expectancy** at birth (2003): male 59.2 years; female 62.9 years.

National economy

Budget (2002). *Revenue:* YRls 570,100,000,000 (tax revenue 91.9%, of which oil revenue 68.7%, indirect taxes 12.1%, direct taxes 11.1%; nontax revenue 6.5%; grants 1.6%). *Expenditures:* YRls 587,600,000,000 (wages and salaries 22.9%; defense 21.9%; transfers and subsidies 20.8%; economic development 18.1%; interest on debt 6.0%). **Public debt** (external, outstanding; 2002): $4,563,000,000. **Population economically active** (1999): total 4,090,680; activity rate of total population 23.5% (participation rates: age 15 and over, 45.9%; female 23.7%; unemployed 11.5%). **Production** (metric tons except as noted). *Agriculture, forestry, fishing* (2002): sorghum 360,000, tomatoes 261,692, potatoes 208,597; livestock (number of live animals) 5,028,968 sheep, 4,452,540 goats, 34,800,000 chickens; roundwood (2002) 326,262 cu m; fish catch (2001) 142,200. *Mining and quarrying* (2002): salt 150,000; gypsum 100,000. *Manufacturing* (value added in YRls '000,000; 2002): food, beverages, and tobacco 42,342; nonmetallic mineral products 13,209; chemicals and chemical products 9,884. *Energy production (consumption):* electricity (kW-hr; 2002) 3,100,000,000 (2,960,000,000); crude petroleum (barrels; 2003) 163,600,000 ([2000] 29,600,000); petroleum products (2000) 3,956,000 (2,635,000). **Gross national product** (2003): $9,894,000,000 ($520 per capita). **Households.** Average household size (2002) 7.1; income per household (1998) YRls 29,035. **Tourism** (2002): receipts $38,000,000; expenditures $78,000,000. **Land use** as % of total land area (2000): in temporary crops 2.9%, in permanent crops 0.2%, in pasture 30.4%; overall forest area 0.9%.

Foreign trade

Imports (2001-c.i.f. in balance of trade and f.o.b. in commodities and trading partners): $2,466,000,000 (food and live animals 29.0%, of which cereals and related products 13.3%; machinery and apparatus 15.6%; petroleum products 12.0%; chemicals and chemical products 9.2%). *Major import sources:* UAE 12.5%; Saudi Arabia 12.4%; India 5.5%; Kuwait 5.2%; US 4.9%. **Exports** (2001): $3,373,000,000 (crude petroleum 86.3%; refined petroleum 7.4%; fish and fish products 1.7%; vegetables and fruits 0.7%). *Major export destinations:* India 18.3%; Thailand 18.0%; South Korea 13.2%; China 9.6%; Singapore 9.4%.

Transport and communications

Transport. *Roads* (2001; excludes unimproved roads and all roads in 'Adan governorate): total length 17,973 km (paved 54%). *Vehicles* (2001): passenger cars 354,048; trucks and buses (2000) 454,584. *Air transport* (2000): passenger-km 1,574,000,000; metric ton-km cargo 32,000,000; airports (1998) with scheduled flights 12. **Communications,** in total units (units per 1,000 persons). Daily newspaper circulation (2000): 270,000 (15); radios (2000): 1,170,000 (65); televisions (2000): 5,100,000 (283); telephone main lines (2002): 542,200 (28); cellular telephone subscribers (2002): 411,100 (21); personal computers (2002): 145,000 (7.4); Internet users (2002): 100,000 (5.1).

Education and health

Educational attainment (1998). Percentage of population age 10 and over having: no formal schooling 49.5%; reading and writing ability 32.2%; primary education 11.0%; secondary education 4.6%; higher 2.7%. **Literacy** (2003): percentage of total population age 15 and over literate 50.3%; males literate 70.5%; females literate 30.1%. **Health:** physicians (2000) 3,491 (1 per 5,161 persons); hospital beds (2001) 9,802 (1 per 1,903 persons); infant mortality rate per 1,000 live births (2003) 65.0. **Food** (2001): daily per capita caloric intake 2,050 (vegetable products 94%, animal products 6%); 85% of FAO recommended minimum.

Military

Total active duty personnel (2003): 66,700 (army 90.0%, navy 2.5%, air force 7.5%). **Military expenditure as percentage of GNP** (1999): 6.1% (world 2.4%); per capita expenditure $22.

Background

Yemen was the home of ancient Minaean, Sabaean, and Himyarite kingdoms. The Romans invaded the region in the 1st century AD. In the 6th century it was conquered by Ethiopians and Persians. Following conversion to Islam in the 7th century, it was ruled nominally under a caliphate. The Egyptian Ayyubid dynasty ruled there from 1173 to 1229, after which the region passed to the Rasulids. From 1517 through 1918, the Ottoman Empire maintained varying degrees of control, especially in the northwestern section. A boundary agreement was reached in 1934 between the northwestern imam-controlled territory, which subsequently became the Yemen Arab Republic (North Yemen), and the southeastern British-controlled territory, which subsequently became the People's Democratic Republic of Yemen (South Yemen). Relations between the two Yemens remained tense and were marked by conflict throughout the 1970s and 1980s. Reaching an accord, the two officially united as the Republic of Yemen in 1990. Its 1993 elections were the first free, multiparty general elections held in the Arabian Peninsula, and they were the first in which women participated. In 1994, after a two-month civil war, a new constitution was approved.

---

1 metric ton = about 1.1 short tons;   1 kilometer = 0.6 mi (statute);   1 metric ton-km cargo = about 0.68 short ton-mi cargo;   c.i.f.: cost, insurance, and freight;   f.o.b.: free on board

Recent Developments

The Yemeni government continued to confront hostile elements that were using violence against the regime, but during 2004 progress was made in achieving greater internal security. The Yemeni military and law-enforcement authorities successfully shut down a number of small terrorist groups. In September a Yemeni judge sentenced two men to death and four others to terms of up to 10 years in prison for the 2000 bombing attack on the US destroyer *Cole*. After a five-month insurgency led by a royalist, Hussein al-Houthi, in October government forces found Houthi hiding in a cave and killed him. Health officials were alarmed when, in April and May 2005, more than 60 cases of polio—the first since 1999—were confirmed.

Internet resources: <www.yementourism.com>.

Zambia

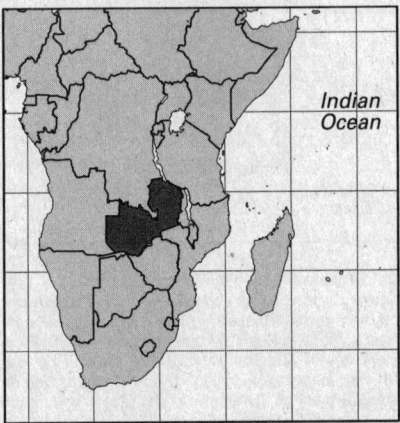

Indian Ocean

Official name: Republic of Zambia. Form of government: multiparty republic with one legislative house (National Assembly [158, including 8 nonelective seats]). Head of state and government: President Levy Mwanawasa (from 2002). Capital: Lusaka. Official language: English. Official religion: none; however, in 1996 Zambia was declared a Christian nation per the preamble of a constitutional amendment. Monetary unit: 1 Zambian kwacha (K) = 100 ngwee; valuation (7 Jul 2005) $1 = K 4,512.01.

Demography

Area: 290,585 sq mi, 752,612 sq km. Population (2004): 10,462,000. Density (2004): persons per sq mi 36.0, persons per sq km 13.9. Urban (2000): 34.7%. Sex distribution (2000): male 50.04%; female 49.96%. Age breakdown (2000): under 15, 47.0%; 15–29, 30.0%; 30–44, 12.9%; 45–59, 5.9%; 60–74, 3.4%; 75 and over, 0.8%. Ethnic composition (2000): Bemba 18.0%; Tonga 12.7%; Chewa 7.2%; Lozi 5.6%; Tumbuka 4.2%; other 52.3%. Religious affiliation (1995): Christian 47.8%, of which Protestant 22.9%, Roman Catholic 16.9%, African Christian 5.6%; traditional beliefs 27.0%; Muslim 1.0%; other 24.2%. Major cities (2000): Lusaka 1,084,703

(urban agglomeration [2003] 1,394,000); Ndola 374,757; Kitwe 363,734; Kabwe 176,758; Chingola 147,448. Location: southern Africa, bordering Tanzania, Malawi, Mozambique, Zimbabwe, Botswana, Namibia, Angola, and the Democratic Republic of the Congo.

Vital statistics

Birth rate per 1,000 population (2003): 39.5 (world avg. 21.3). Death rate per 1,000 population (2003): 24.3 (world avg. 9.1). Natural increase rate per 1,000 population (2003): 15.2 (world avg. 12.2). Total fertility rate (avg. births per childbearing woman; 2003): 5.2. Life expectancy at birth (2003): male 38.8 years; female 39.3 years. Adult population (ages 15–49) living with HIV (2004): 16.5% (world avg. 1.1%).

National economy

Budget (2003). *Revenue:* K 5,104,000,000,000 (tax revenue 69.5%, of which income tax 31.5%, value-added tax 28.3%, excise taxes 9.4%; grants 27.9%; nontax revenue 2.6%). *Expenditures:* K 6,338,000,-000,000 (current expenditures 63.2%, of which wages 27.3%, interest payment 12.5%, transfers 10.2%; capital expenditures 36.8%). Public debt (external, outstanding; 2002): $4,737,000,000. Production (metric tons except as noted). *Agriculture, forestry, fishing* (2002): sugarcane 1,800,000, cassava 950,000, corn (maize) 900,000; livestock (number of live animals) 2,600,000 cattle, 1,270,000 goats, 30,000,000 chickens; roundwood (2001) 8,053,000 cu m; fish catch (2001) 70,911. *Mining and quarrying* (2002): copper (metal content) 330,000; cobalt (metal content) 6,144; amethyst 1,065,000 kg. *Manufacturing* (value added in $'000,000; 1995): food products 86; beverages 77; paints, soaps, and pharmaceuticals 47. *Energy production (consumption):* electricity (kW-hr; 2000) 7,797,000,000 (6,023,000,000); coal (2000) 194,000 (128,000); crude petroleum (barrels; 2000) none (1,830,000); petroleum products (2000) 22,000 (438,000). Households. Average household size (2002) 5.1. Tourism (2002): receipts from visitors $134,000,000; expenditures by nationals abroad $67,000,000. Population economically active (1996): total 3,454,000; activity rate of total population 38.2% (participation rates [1991]: over age 10, 52.6%; female 29.6%). Gross national product (at current market prices; 2003): $3,946,000,000 ($520 per capita). Land use as % of total land area (2000): in temporary crops 7.1%, in permanent crops 0.03%, in pasture 40.4%; overall forest area 42.0%.

Foreign trade

Imports (2002): $1,253,000,000 (nonelectrical machinery and equipment 21.6%, chemicals and chemical products 14.9%, printed matter 11.3%, road vehicles 8.8%, cereals [all forms] 8.0%). *Major import sources:* South Africa 51.2%; UK 12.3%; Zimbabwe 7.8%; India 3.6%; Japan 3.2%. Exports (2002): $930,000,000 (refined copper 50.0%, other base metals [including cobalt] 8.9%, food and live animals 7.3%, manufactures of base metals 5.8%). *Major export destinations:* UK 42.3%; South Africa 23.0%; Tanzania 7.6%; Switzerland 6.1%; Democratic Republic of the Congo 4.3%.

Transport and communications

Transport. *Railroads* (2003; Zambia Railways Limited only): length 1,266 km; (1997) passenger-km 267,-000,000; (1998) metric ton-km cargo 702,000,000. *Roads* (1999): total length 38,898 km (paved 18%). *Vehicles* (1996): passenger cars 157,000; trucks and buses 81,000. *Air transport* (2003; Zambian Airways Limited only): passenger-km 14,217,000; airports (1998) 4. **Communications,** in total units (units per 1,000 persons). Daily newspaper circulation (2000): 125,000 (12); radios (2000): 1,510,000 (145); televisions (2000): 1,400,000 (134); telephone main lines (2003): 88,400 (7.9); cellular telephone subscribers (2003): 241,000 (22); personal computers (2003): 95,000 (8.5); Internet users (2003): 68,200 (6.1).

Education and health

Educational attainment (1993). Percentage of population age 14 and over having: no formal schooling 18.6%; some primary education 54.8%; some secondary 25.1%; higher 1.5%. **Literacy** (2000): population age 15 and over literate 78.1%; males literate 85.2%; females literate 71.5%. **Health:** physicians (1995) 647 (1 per 14,492 persons); hospital beds (1989) 22,461 (1 per 349 persons); infant mortality rate per 1,000 live births (2003) 99.3. **Food** (2001): daily per capita caloric intake 1,885 (vegetable products 95%, animal products 5%); 82% of FAO recommended minimum.

Military

Total active duty personnel (2003): 18,100 (army 91.2%; air force 8.8%). **Military expenditure as percentage of GNP** (1999): 1.0% (world 2.4%); per capita expenditure $3.

Background

Archaeological evidence suggests that early humans roamed present-day Zambia one to two million years ago. Ancestors of the modern Tonga tribe reached the region early in the 2nd millennium BC, but other modern peoples from Congo and Angola reached the country only in the 17th and 18th centuries. Portuguese trading missions were established early in the 18th century. Emissaries of Cecil Rhodes and the British South Africa Co. concluded treaties with most of the Zambian chiefs during the 1890s. The company administered the region known as Northern Rhodesia until 1924, when it became a British protectorate. It was part of the Central African Federation of Rhodesia and Nyasaland in 1953–63. In 1964 Northern Rhodesia became the independent republic of Zambia. A constitutional amendment was passed in 1990 allowing opposition parties; the following years were filled with political tension.

Recent Developments

The budget, which was presented in February 2004, provoked widespread but peaceful protest in Zambia; under pressure from the IMF to cut spending, the government proposed to freeze public-service salaries and to tax them at source. In August, as the impact of the measures became more apparent, the Civil Servants and Allied Workers Union threatened strike action unless the government agreed to increase the wages of lower-paid staff. On a more promising note, the corn (maize) harvest produced a generous surplus, but food aid was still required in some areas of the country because much of the surplus was produced by commercial farmers who sought to take advantage of the huge demand for their crop in Zimbabwe and other neighboring countries.

Internet resources: <www.zambia.co.zm>.

Zimbabwe

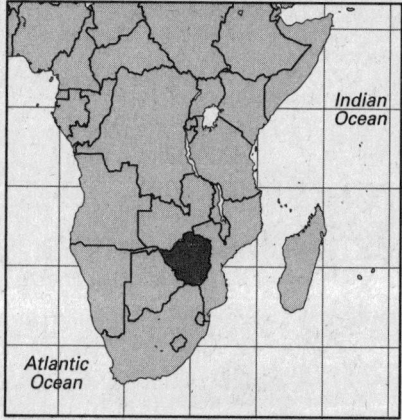

Official name: Republic of Zimbabwe. **Form of government:** multiparty republic with one legislative house (House of Assembly [150, including 30 nonelective seats]). **Head of state and government:** President Robert Mugabe (from 1987). **Capital:** Harare. **Official language:** English. **Official religion:** none. **Monetary unit:** 1 Zimbabwe dollar (Z$) = 100 cents; valuation (7 Jul 2005) US$1 = Z$9,994.

Demography

Area: 150,872 sq mi, 390,757 sq km. **Population** (2004): 11,821,000. **Density** (2004): persons per sq mi 78.4, persons per sq km 30.3. **Urban** (2001): 36.0%. **Sex distribution** (2003): male 49.57%; female 50.43%. **Age breakdown** (2003): under 15, 39.7%; 15–29, 32.6%; 30–44, 15.1%; 45–59, 7.3%; 60–74, 4.1%; 75 and over, 1.2%. **Ethnic composition** (2000): Shona 67.1%; Ndebele 13.0%; Chewa 4.9%; British 3.5%; other 11.5%. **Religious affiliation** (1995): Christian 45.4%, of which Protestant (including Anglican) 23.5%, African indigenous 13.5%, Roman Catholic 7.0%; animist 40.5%; other 14.1%. **Major cities** (2002): Harare 1,444,534; Bulawayo 676,787; Chitungwiza 321,-782; Mutare (1992) 131,808; Gweru (1992) 124,735. **Location:** southern Africa, bordering Mozambique, South Africa, Botswana, Namibia, and Zambia.

Vital statistics

Birth rate per 1,000 population (2003): 30.3 (world avg. 21.3). **Death rate** per 1,000 population (2003):

---

1 metric ton = about 1.1 short tons;   1 kilometer = 0.6 mi (statute);   1 metric ton-km cargo = about 0.68 short ton-mi cargo;   c.i.f.: cost, insurance, and freight;   f.o.b.: free on board

22.0 (world avg. 9.1). **Natural increase rate** per 1,000 population (2003): 8.3 (world avg. 12.2). **Total fertility rate** (avg. births per childbearing woman; 2003): 3.7. **Life expectancy** at birth (2002): male 41.6 years; female 38.8 years. **Adult population** (ages 15–49) **living with HIV** (2004): 24.6% (world avg. 1.1%).

National economy

Budget (2002). *Revenue:* Z$300,385,000,000 (tax revenue 93.5%, of which income tax 53.0%, sales tax 24.1%, customs duties 9.0%, excise tax 6.2%; nontax revenue 6.5%). *Expenditures:* Z$351,-321,000,000 (current expenditures 91.3%, of which goods and services 61.5%, transfer payments 15.7%, interest payments 14.1%; development expenditure 7.2%; net lending 1.5%). **Population economically active** (1992): total 3,600,000; activity rate of total population 34.6% (participation rates: over age 15, 63.4%; female 39.8%). **Production** (metric tons except as noted). *Agriculture, forestry, fishing* (2002): sugarcane 4,700,000, corn (maize) 499,000, seed cotton 200,400; livestock (number of live animals) 5,753,000 cattle, 2,970,000 goats, 605,000 pigs; roundwood 9,107,600 cu m; fish catch (2001) 13,200. *Mining and quarrying* (value of production in Z$'000,000; 2000): gold 8,521; asbestos 2,776; coal 2,690. *Manufacturing* (value added in US$'000,000; 1998): beverages 171; foodstuffs 148; textiles 99. *Energy production (consumption):* electricity (kW-hr; 2000) 6,996,000,000 ([2000] 12,110,000,000); coal (2000) 4,400,000 (4,437,000); petroleum products (2000) none (1,072,000). **Public debt** (external, outstanding; 2002): US$3,123,000,000. **Household income and expenditure.** Average household size (2002) 4.4; income per household (1992) Z$1,689; expenditure (1995): food 33.6%, housing 17.3%, beverages and tobacco 16.0%, household durable goods 7.5%, clothing and footwear 6.9%, transportation 6.6%, education 4.5%. **Gross national product** (2002): US$6,165,000,000 (US$480 per capita). **Tourism:** receipts (2002) US$76,000,000; expenditures (1998) US$131,000,000. **Land use** as % of total land area (2000): in temporary crops 8.3%, in permanent crops 0.3%, in pasture 44.5%; overall forest area 49.2%.

Foreign trade

Imports (2001): US$1,779,000,000 (machinery and transport equipment 28.1%, chemicals and chemical products 22.9%, petroleum products 15.7%, food 3.8%, electricity 3.1%). *Major import sources* (2002): South Africa 47.7%; Democratic Republic of the Congo 5.7%; Mozambique 5.3%; Germany 3.1%; UK 3.1%. **Exports** (2001): US$1,609,000,000 (tobacco 36.9%, gold 14.0%, horticultural products [including cut flowers] 7.4%, ferroalloys 5.1%, cotton lint 5.1%, sugar 4.4%). *Major export destinations* (2001): South Africa 17.7%; UK 12.6%; Germany 8.3%; China 7.1%; Japan 6.6%.

Transport and communications

Transport. *Railroads* (2001): route length 3,077 km; (1998) passenger-km 408,223,000; (2000) metric ton-km cargo 3,326,000. *Roads* (1996): total length 18,338 km (paved 47%). *Vehicles* (2000): passenger cars 573,000; trucks and

buses 39,000. *Air transport* (2003; Air Zimbabwe only): passenger-km 436,530,000; metric ton-km cargo 18,494,000; airports (1997) with scheduled flights 7. **Communications,** in total units (units per 1,000 persons). Daily newspaper circulation (2000): 205,000 (18); radios (2000): 4,110,000 (362); televisions (1999): 2,074,000 (183); telephone main lines (2003): 300,900 (26); cellular telephone subscribers (2003): 379,100 (32); personal computers (2003): 620,000 (53); Internet users (2002): 500,000 (43).

Education and health

Educational attainment (1992). Percentage of population age 25 and over having: no formal schooling 22.3%; primary 54.3%; secondary 13.1%; higher 3.4%. **Literacy** (2001): percentage of total population age 15 and over literate 89.3%; males literate 93.3%; females literate 85.5%. **Health:** physicians (1996) 1,603 (1 per 6,904 persons); hospital beds (1996) 22,975 (1 per 501 persons); infant mortality rate per 1,000 live births (2003) 65.5. **Food** (2001): daily per capita caloric intake 2,133 (vegetable products 92%, animal products 8%); 89% of FAO recommended minimum.

Military

Total active duty personnel (2003): 29,000 (army 86.2%, air force 13.8%). **Military expenditure as percentage of GNP** (1999): 5.0% (world 2.4%); per capita expenditure US$23.

Background

Remains of Stone Age cultures dating back 500,000 years have been found in the Zimbabwe area. The first Bantu-speaking peoples reached it during the 5th–10th centuries AD, driving the San (Bushmen) inhabitants into the desert. A second migration of Bantu-speakers began c. 1830. During this period the British and Afrikaners moved up from the south, and the area came under the administration of the British South Africa Co. 1889–1923. Called Southern Rhodesia (1911–64), it became a self-governing British colony in 1923. The colony united in 1953 with Nyasaland (Malawi) and Northern Rhodesia (Zambia) to form the Central African Federation of Rhodesia and Nyasaland. The federation dissolved in 1963, and Southern Rhodesia reverted to its former colonial status. In 1965 it issued a unilateral declaration of independence considered illegal by the British government, which led to economic sanctions against it. The country proclaimed itself a republic in 1970 and called itself Rhodesia 1964–79. In 1979 it instituted limited majority rule and changed its name to Zimbabwe Rhodesia. It was granted independence by Britain in 1980 and became Zimbabwe. Robert Mugabe, Zimbabwe's first prime minister, became president in 1987. Although a multiparty system was established in 1990, Mugabe's rule became more and more autocratic.

Recent Developments

Zimbabwe's international status remained controversial. Its withdrawal from the Commonwealth of Nations in December 2003 had won the sympathy of many African leaders who regarded Pres. Robert Mugabe's action as a justifiable response to the arrogance of the white members of the Commonwealth. Meanwhile, Mugabe continued to suppress dissent at home and to dismiss criticism from abroad. Early in June 2004 it was announced that all productive farmland would be nationalized, with title deeds replaced by 99-year leases. In November Mugabe suspended Zimbabwe's constitution and forced a number of repressive laws through the House of Assembly. For several weeks beginning in late May 2005 the government pursued "Operation Drive Out Trash" to uproot what it called illegal slums and black-market vendors by bulldozing the kiosks, homes, and subsistence gardens of the country's poorest. Hundreds of thousands of people were turned out into the winter cold and another 30,000 arrested as the campaign broadened from the capital, Harare, into the countryside.

Internet resources: <www.gta.gov.zw>.

Antarctica

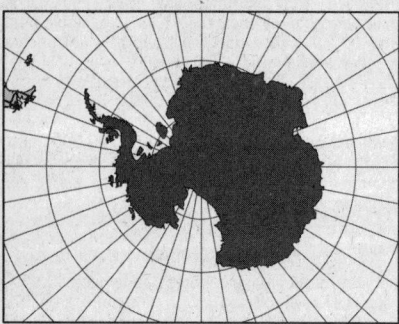

Background

The Russian F.G. von Bellingshausen (1778–1852), the Englishman Edward Bransfield (1795?–1852), and the American Nathaniel Palmer (1799–1877) all claimed first sightings of the continent in 1820. The period from the 1760s to c. 1900 was dominated by the exploration of Antarctic and subantarctic seas. In the early 20th century, the "heroic era" of Antarctic exploration, Robert Scott and later Ernest Shackleton made expeditions deep into the interior. Roald Amundsen reached the South Pole in December 1911, and Scott followed in 1912. The first half of the 20th century was also Antarctica's colonial period. Seven nations claimed sectors of the continent, while many other nations carried out explorations. In 1957–58, 12 nations established over 50 stations on the continent for cooperative study. In 1961 the Antarctic Treaty, which reserved Antarctica for free and nonpolitical scientific study, was enacted. A 1991 agreement imposed a permanent ban on mineral exploitation.

Recent Developments

The 45-member Antarctic Treaty system, after 43 years without an executive secretary, appointed its first, Jan Huber of The Netherlands, who in September

2004 took up his position in Buenos Aires, Argentina. Unprecedented construction and upgrading of research facilities in the heart of the Antarctic interior—on the vast East Antarctic Ice Sheet—was under way. China started on a year-round research station at Dome A, making a traverse there from the coast to take samples and set up a weather monitor. Dome A, at more than 4,000 m (13,000 ft), was the highest, driest, and coldest spot on the continent. The new station, which was scheduled to be completed by 2010, would support astrophysics, upper-atmosphere physics, ice coring, and drilling through the underlying ice sheet to study the Gamburtsev Mountains, the world's least-explored range.

Internet resources: <www.antarctica.org>.

Arctic Regions

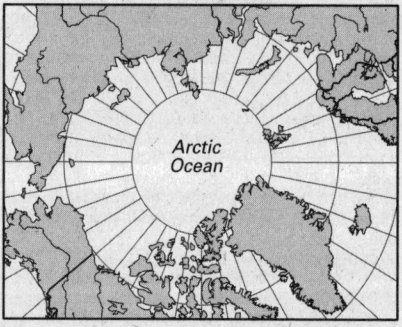

The Arctic regions may be defined in physical terms (astronomical [north of the Arctic Circle, latitude 66° 30' N], climatic [above the 10 °C (50 °F) July isotherm], or vegetational [above the northern limit of the tree line]) or in human terms (the territory inhabited by the circumpolar cultures—Inuit [Eskimo] and Aleut in North America and Russia, Sami [Lapp] in northern Scandinavia and Russia, and 29 other peoples of the Russian North, Siberia, and East Asia). No single national sovereignty or treaty regime governs the region, which includes portions of eight countries: Canada, the United States, Russia, Finland, Sweden, Norway, Iceland, and Greenland (part of Denmark). The Arctic Ocean, 14.09 million sq km (5.44 million sq mi) in area, constitutes about two-thirds of the region. The land area consists of permanent ice cap, tundra, or taiga. The population (2004 est.) of peoples belonging to the circumpolar cultures is nearly 450,000 (Aleuts [in Russia and Alaska], 3,000; Athabascans [North America], 32,000; Inuits [or Eskimos, in Russian Chukhotka, North America, and Greenland], 150,000; Sami [Northern Europe], 50,000; and 40 indigenous peoples of the Russian North, totaling more than 200,000). International organizations concerned with the Arctic include the Arctic Council, institutions of the Barents Region, the Inuit Circumpolar Conference, and the Indigenous Peoples' Secretariat. International scientific cooperation in the Arctic is the focus of the International Arctic Research Center of the University of Alaska at Fairbanks.

---

1 metric ton = about 1.1 short tons;   1 kilometer = 0.6 mi (statute);   1 metric ton-km cargo = about 0.68 short ton-mi cargo;   c.i.f.: cost, insurance, and freight;   f.o.b.: free on board

Membership in International Organizations

African Union (AU; formerly [until 2002] Organization for African Unity)
Founded: 1963. Members: 52 countries of Africa, excluding Morocco; Mauritania suspended in August 2005
Web site: <www.africa-union.org>.

Andean Community
Founded: 1969. Members: Bolivia, Colombia, Ecuador, Peru, Venezuela
Web site: <www.comunidadandina.org>.

Asia-Pacific Economic Cooperation (APEC)
Founded: 1989. Members: Australia, Brunei, Canada, Chile, China, Hong Kong, Indonesia, Japan, Malaysia, Mexico, New Zealand, Papua New Guinea, Peru, the Philippines, Russia, Singapore, South Korea, Taiwan, Thailand, US, Vietnam
Web site: <www.apec.org>.

Association of Southeast Asian Nations (ASEAN)
Founded: 1967. Members: Brunei, Cambodia, Indonesia, Laos, Malaysia, Myanmar (Burma), the Philippines, Singapore, Thailand, Vietnam
Web site: <www.aseansec.org>.

Caribbean Community and Common Market (CARICOM)
Founded: 1973. Members: Antigua and Barbuda, the Bahamas (Community member only), Barbados, Belize, Dominica, Grenada, Guyana, Haiti (suspended), Jamaica, Montserrat, St. Kitts and Nevis, St. Lucia, St. Vincent and the Grenadines, Suriname, Trinidad and Tobago; also 5 associate members
Web site: <www.caricom.org>.

Common Market for Eastern and Southern Africa (COMESA)
Founded: 1994. Members: Angola, Burundi, Comoros, Democratic Republic of the Congo, Djibouti, Egypt, Eritrea, Ethiopia, Kenya, Madagascar, Malawi, Mauritius, Namibia, Rwanda, Seychelles, The Sudan, Swaziland, Uganda, Zambia, Zimbabwe
Web site: <www.comesa.int>.

Commonwealth (also called Commonwealth of Nations)
Founded: 1931. Members: United Kingdom and 52 other countries, all of which were once under British rule or administratively connected to another member country
Web site: <www.thecommonwealth.org>.

Commonwealth of Independent States (CIS)
Founded: 1991. Members: Armenia, Azerbaijan, Belarus, Georgia, Kazakhstan, Kyrgyzstan, Moldova, Russia, Tajikistan, Turkmenistan, Uzbekistan, Ukraine
Web site: <www.cisstat.com>.

Community of Portuguese Language Countries (CPLP)
Founded: 1996. Members: Angola, Brazil, Cape Verde, East Timor, Guinea-Bissau, Mozambique, Portugal, São Tomé and Príncipe
Web site: <www.cplp.org>.

Council of Europe
Founded: 1949. Members: 46 European and former Soviet countries; 1 candidate for membership; 5 observer states
Web site: <www.coe.int>.

Economic Community of West African States (ECOWAS)
Founded: 1975. Members: Benin, Burkina Faso, Cape Verde, Côte d'Ivoire, The Gambia, Ghana, Guinea, Guinea-Bissau, Liberia, Mali, Niger, Nigeria, Senegal, Sierra Leone, Togo
Web site: <www.ecowas.int>.

European Free Trade Association (EFTA)
Founded: 1960. Members: Iceland, Liechtenstein, Norway, Switzerland
Web site: <www.efta.int>.

European Union (EU)
Founded: 1950. Members: Austria, Belgium, Cyprus, Czech Republic, Denmark, Estonia, Finland, France, Germany, Greece, Hungary, Ireland, Italy, Latvia, Lithuania, Luxembourg, Malta, The Netherlands, Poland, Portugal, Slovakia, Slovenia, Spain, Sweden, UK; in mid-2005, 4 additional countries in southeastern Europe were undergoing membership preparations
Web site: <www.europa.eu.int>.

Group of Eight (G-8)
Founded: 1975. Members: Canada, France, Germany, Italy, Japan, Russia, UK, US
Web site: <www.g8.utoronto.ca>.

Gulf Cooperation Council (GCC)
Founded: 1981. Members: Bahrain, Kuwait, Oman, Qatar, Saudi Arabia, United Arab Emirates
Web site: <www.gcc-sg.org/home_e.html>.

Latin American Integration Association (ALADI)
Founded: 1980. Members: Argentina, Bolivia, Brazil, Chile, Colombia, Cuba, Ecuador, Mexico, Paraguay, Peru, Uruguay, Venezuela
Web site: <www.aladi.org>.

League of Arab States (Arab League)
Founded: 1945. Members: Algeria, Bahrain, Comoros, Djibouti, Egypt, Iraq, Jordan, Kuwait, Lebanon, Libya, Mauritania, Morocco, Oman, Palestinian Authority, Qatar, Saudi Arabia, Somalia, The Sudan, Syria, Tunisia, United Arab Emirates, Yemen; Eritrea is an observer
Web site: <www.arableagueonline.org>.

Nordic Council of Ministers
Founded: 1971. Members: Denmark, Finland, Iceland, Norway, Sweden; autonomous regions of Greenland, Faroe Islands, Åland Islands
Web site: <www.norden.org>.

North Atlantic Treaty Organization (NATO)
Founded: 1949. Members: Belgium, Bulgaria, Canada, Czech Republic, Denmark, Estonia, France, Germany, Greece, Hungary, Iceland, Italy, Latvia, Lithuania, Luxembourg, The Netherlands, Norway, Poland, Portugal, Romania, Slovakia, Slovenia, Spain, Turkey, UK, US
Web site: <www.nato.int>.

Organisation for Economic Co-operation and Development (OECD)

Founded: 1961. **Members:** Australia, Austria, Belgium, Canada, Czech Republic, Denmark, Finland, France, Germany, Greece, Hungary, Iceland, Ireland, Italy, Japan, Luxembourg, Mexico, The Netherlands, New Zealand, Norway, Poland, Portugal, Slovak Republic, South Korea, Spain, Sweden, Switzerland, Turkey, UK, US
Web site: <www.oecd.org>.

Organization for Security and Co-operation in Europe (OSCE)

Founded: 1973. **Members:** 53 countries of Europe and Central Asia, plus Canada and the US
Web site: <www.osce.org>.

Organization of American States (OAS)

Founded: 1948. **Members:** all 35 independent countries of the Western Hemisphere (Cuba's participation has been denied since 1962)
Web site: <www.oas.org>.

Organization of the Petroleum Exporting Countries (OPEC)

Founded: 1960. **Members:** Algeria, Indonesia, Iran, Iraq, Kuwait, Libya, Nigeria, Qatar, Saudi Arabia, United Arab Emirates, Venezuela
Web site: <www.opec.org>.

Organization of the Islamic Conference (OIC)

Founded: 1969. **Members:** 56 Islamic countries, mainly in Africa and Asia, Palestinian Authority; 3 observer countries
Web site: <www.oic-oci.org>.

Pacific Islands Forum (PIF; formerly [until 2000] South Pacific Forum)

Founded: 1971. **Members:** Australia, Cook Islands, Fiji, Kiribati, Marshall Islands, Federated States of Micronesia, Nauru, New Zealand, Niue, Palau, Papua New Guinea, Samoa, Solomon Islands, Tonga, Tuvalu, Vanuatu
Web site: <www.forumsec.org.fj>.

Secretariat of the Pacific Community (SPC; formerly South Pacific Commission)

Founded: 1947. **Members:** American Samoa, Australia, Cook Islands, Fiji Islands, France, French Polynesia, Guam, Kiribati, Federated States of Micronesia, Marshall Islands, Nauru, New Caledonia, New Zealand, Niue, Northern Mariana Islands, Palau, Papua New Guinea (PNG), Pitcairn Islands, Samoa, Solomon Islands, Tokelau, Tonga, Tuvalu, US, Vanuatu, Wallis and Futuna
Web site: <www.spc.org.nc>.

South American Community of Nations (SACN)

Founded: 2004. **Members:** Argentina, Bolivia, Brazil, Chile, Colombia, Ecuador, Paraguay, Peru, Uruguay, Venezuela
Web site: <www.comunidadandina.org>.

South Asian Association for Regional Cooperation (SAARC)

Founded: 1985. **Members:** Bangladesh, Bhutan, India, Maldives, Nepal, Pakistan, Sri Lanka
Web site: <www.saarc-sec.org>.

Southern African Development Community (SADC)

Founded: 1980. **Members:** Angola, Botswana, Democratic Republic of the Congo, Lesotho, Malawi, Mauritius, Mozambique, Namibia, South Africa, Swaziland, Tanzania, Zambia, Zimbabwe
Web site: <www.sadc.int>.

Southern Common Market (MERCOSUL/MERCOSUR)

Founded: 1991. **Members:** Argentina, Brazil, Paraguay, Uruguay; associate members Chile, Bolivia, Mexico, Peru, Venezuela
Web site: <www.mercosur.org.uy>.

United Nations (UN)

Founded: 1945. **Members:** 191 countries (the Vatican and Taiwan are not members)
Web site: <www.un.org>.

World Trade Organization (WTO)

Founded: 1995. **Members:** 148 member countries worldwide; 33 observer states as of June 2005
Web site: <www.wto.org>.

Secretaries-General of the United Nations

The UN General Assembly appoints the Secretary-General to a five-year term on the recommendation of the 15-member Security Council; permanent members of the Security Council have veto power over nominees. The Secretary-General balances diverse and sometimes conflicting duties in the various roles of diplomat, advocate, administrator, and civil servant. The Secretary-General has a broad mandate, being able to marshal resources and advocacy on issues as various as peace efforts around the globe and disease prevention and treatment. Internet resource: <www.un.org>.

SECRETARY GENERAL	TERM	COMMENTS
Sir Gladwyn Jebb (acting) (UK)	1945–1946	
Trygve Lie (Norway)	1946–1952	resigned in November 1952
Dag Hammarskjöld (Sweden)	1953–1961	died in September 1961
U Thant (Burma, now Myanmar)	1961–1971	acting Secretary-General November 1961; elected 1962
Kurt Waldheim (Austria)	1972–1981	China vetoed a third term
Javier Pérez de Cuéllar (Peru)	1982–1991	
Boutros Boutros-Ghali (Egypt)	1992–1996	US vetoed a second term
Kofi Annan (Ghana)	1997–	

The International Criminal Court

The International Criminal Court (ICC) was established by the Rome Statute of the International Criminal Court on 17 Jul 1998. Although the ICC is not yet fully operational, the statute that created it went into force on 1 Jul 2002. As of May 2005, the ICC has 99 member countries.

President
Philippe Kirsch (Canada)

First Vice President
Akua Kuenyehia (Ghana)

Second Vice President
Elizabeth Odio Benito (Costa Rica)

Chief Prosecutor
Luis Moreno-Ocampo (Argentina)

Judges
List A—elected as experts in criminal law and procedure
Karl T. Hudson-Phillips (Trinidad and Tobago)
Claude Jorda (France)
Georghios M. Pikis (Cyprus)
Elizabeth Odio Benito (Costa Rica)
Tuiloma Neroni Slade (Samoa)

Judges (continued)
Song Sang-Hyun (Republic of Korea)
Maureen Harding Clark (Ireland)
Fatoumata Dembele Diarra (Mali)
Sir Adrian Fulford (United Kingdom)
Sylvia Steiner (Brazil)

List B—elected as experts in international law and human rights law
Navanethem Pillay (South Africa)
Hans-Peter Kaul (Germany)
Mauro Politi (Italy)
Akua Kuenyehia (Ghana)
Philippe Kirsch (Canada)
René Blattmann (Bolivia)
Erkki Kourula (Finland)
Anita Usacka (Latvia)

Registrar
Bruno Cathala (France)

United Nations Membership by Date of Admission

COUNTRY	DATE OF ADMISSION	COUNTRY	DATE OF ADMISSION	COUNTRY	DATE OF ADMISSION
Argentina	24 Oct 1945	Venezuela	15 Nov 1945	Malaysia	17 Sep 1957
Belarus	24 Oct 1945	Guatemala	21 Nov 1945	Guinea	12 Dec 1958
Brazil	24 Oct 1945	Norway	27 Nov 1945	Benin	20 Sep 1960
Chile	24 Oct 1945	The Netherlands	10 Dec 1945	Burkina Faso	20 Sep 1960
China[1]	24 Oct 1945	Honduras	17 Dec 1945	Cameroon	20 Sep 1960
Cuba	24 Oct 1945	Uruguay	18 Dec 1945	Central African Rep.	20 Sep 1960
Denmark	24 Oct 1945	Ecuador	21 Dec 1945	Chad	20 Sep 1960
Dominican Rep.	24 Oct 1945	Iraq	21 Dec 1945	Dem. Rep. of the	20 Sep 1960
Egypt	24 Oct 1945	Belgium	27 Dec 1945	Congo	
El Salvador	24 Oct 1945	Afghanistan	19 Nov 1946	Rep. of the Congo	20 Sep 1960
France	24 Oct 1945	Iceland	19 Nov 1946	Côte d'Ivoire	20 Sep 1960
Haiti	24 Oct 1945	Sweden	19 Nov 1946	Cyprus	20 Sep 1960
Iran	24 Oct 1945	Thailand	16 Dec 1946	Gabon	20 Sep 1960
Lebanon	24 Oct 1945	Pakistan	30 Sep 1947	Madagascar	20 Sep 1960
Luxembourg	24 Oct 1945	Yemen	30 Sep 1947	Niger	20 Sep 1960
New Zealand	24 Oct 1945	Myanmar	19 Apr 1948	Somalia	20 Sep 1960
Nicaragua	24 Oct 1945	Israel	11 May 1949	Togo	20 Sep 1960
Paraguay	24 Oct 1945	Indonesia	28 Sep 1950	Mali	28 Sep 1960
Philippines	24 Oct 1945	Albania	14 Dec 1955	Senegal	28 Sep 1960
Poland	24 Oct 1945	Austria	14 Dec 1955	Nigeria	7 Oct 1960
USSR (later Russia)	24 Oct 1945	Bulgaria	14 Dec 1955	Sierra Leone	27 Sep 1961
Saudi Arabia	24 Oct 1945	Cambodia	14 Dec 1955	Mauritania	27 Oct 1961
Syria	24 Oct 1945	Finland	14 Dec 1955	Mongolia	27 Oct 1961
Turkey	24 Oct 1945	Hungary	14 Dec 1955	Tanzania	14 Dec 1961
Ukraine	24 Oct 1945	Ireland	14 Dec 1955	Burundi	18 Sep 1962
UK	24 Oct 1945	Italy	14 Dec 1955	Jamaica	18 Sep 1962
US	24 Oct 1945	Jersey	14 Dec 1955	Rwanda	18 Sep 1962
Greece	25 Oct 1945	Jordan	14 Dec 1955	Trinidad and Tobago	18 Sep 1962
India	30 Oct 1945	Laos	14 Dec 1955	Algeria	8 Oct 1962
Peru	31 Oct 1945	Libya	14 Dec 1955	Uganda	25 Oct 1962
Australia	1 Nov 1945	Nepal	14 Dec 1955	Kuwait	14 May 1963
Costa Rica	2 Nov 1945	Portugal	14 Dec 1955	Kenya	16 Dec 1963
Liberia	2 Nov 1945	Romania	14 Dec 1955	Malawi	1 Dec 1964
Colombia	5 Nov 1945	Spain	14 Dec 1955	Malta	1 Dec 1964
Mexico	7 Nov 1945	Sri Lanka	14 Dec 1955	Zambia	1 Dec 1964
South Africa	7 Nov 1945	Morocco	12 Nov 1956	The Gambia	21 Sep 1965
Canada	9 Nov 1945	The Sudan	12 Nov 1956	Maldives	21 Sep 1965
Ethiopia	13 Nov 1945	Tunisia	12 Nov 1956	Singapore	21 Sep 1965
Panama	13 Nov 1945	Japan	18 Dec 1956	Guyana	20 Sep 1966
Bolivia	14 Nov 1945	Ghana	8 Mar 1957	Lesotho	17 Oct 1966

United Nations Membership by Date of Admission (continued)

COUNTRY	DATE OF ADMISSION	COUNTRY	DATE OF ADMISSION	COUNTRY	DATE OF ADMISSION
Botswana	17 Oct 1966	Djibouti	20 Sep 1977	Kyrgyzstan	2 Mar 1992
Barbados	9 Dec 1966	Vietnam	20 Sep 1977	Moldova	2 Mar 1992
Mauritius	24 Apr 1968	Solomon Islands	19 Sep 1978	San Marino	2 Mar 1992
Swaziland	24 Sep 1968	Dominica	18 Dec 1978	Tajikistan	2 Mar 1992
Equatorial Guinea	12 Nov 1968	St. Lucia	18 Sep 1979	Turkmenistan	2 Mar 1992
Fiji	13 Oct 1970	Zimbabwe	25 Aug 1980	Uzbekistan	2 Mar 1992
Bahrain	21 Sep 1971	St. Vincent and	16 Sep 1980	Bosnia and	22 May 1992
Bhutan	21 Sep 1971	the Grenadines		Herzegovina	
Qatar	21 Sep 1971	Vanuatu	15 Sep 1981	Croatia	22 May 1992
Oman	7 Oct 1971	Belize	25 Sep 1981	Slovenia	22 May 1992
United Arab	9 Dec 1971	Antigua and	11 Nov 1981	Georgia	31 Jul 1992
Emirates		Barbuda		Czech Republic	19 Jan 1993
The Bahamas	18 Sep 1973	St. Kitts and Nevis	23 Sep 1983	Slovakia	19 Jan 1993
Germany	18 Sep 1973	Brunei	21 Sep 1984	Macedonia[2]	8 Apr 1993
Bangladesh	17 Sep 1974	Namibia	23 Apr 1990	Eritrea	28 May 1993
Grenada	17 Sep 1974	Liechtenstein	18 Sep 1990	Monaco	28 May 1993
Guinea-Bissau	17 Sep 1974	Estonia	17 Sep 1991	Andorra	28 Jul 1993
Cape Verde	16 Sep 1975	North Korea	17 Sep 1991	Palau	15 Dec 1994
Mozambique	16 Sep 1975	South Korea	17 Sep 1991	Kiribati	14 Sep 1999
São Tomé	16 Sep 1975	Latvia	17 Sep 1991	Nauru	14 Sep 1999
and Príncipe		Lithuania	17 Sep 1991	Tonga	14 Sep 1999
Papua New Guinea	10 Oct 1975	Marshall Islands	17 Sep 1991	Tuvalu	5 Sep 2000
Comoros	12 Nov 1975	Federated States	17 Sep 1991	Serbia and	1 Nov 2000
Suriname	4 Dec 1975	of Micronesia		Montenegro	
Seychelles	21 Sep 1976	Armenia	2 Mar 1992	Switzerland	10 Sep 2002
Angola	1 Dec 1976	Azerbaijan	2 Mar 1992	East Timor	27 Sep 2002
Samoa	15 Dec 1976	Kazakhstan	2 Mar 1992	(Timor-Leste)	

[1]The Republic of China (Taiwan) held the seat until 25 Oct 1971, when UN Res. 2758 gave the membership and a seat on the Security Council to the People's Republic of China. [2]Macedonia is known in the UN as The Former Yugoslav Republic of Macedonia.

Rulers and Regimes

Europe

Roman Emperors

Overlapping reigns denote corulers. Diocletian (284–305) laid the foundation for the Byzantine Empire in the East when he appointed Maximian (286–305) to rule over the Western portion of the empire. Rome thus remained a unified state but was divided administratively. Theodosius I (379–395) was the last emperor to rule over a unified Roman Empire. When he died, Rome split into Eastern and Western empires. For a complete list of the Eastern emperors after the fall of Rome, see "Byzantine Empire."

REIGN	BYNAME	FULL NAME
27 BC–AD 14	Augustus	Caesar Augustus
14–37	Tiberius	Tiberius Caesar Augustus
37–41	Caligula	Gaius Caesar Augustus Germanicus
41–54	Claudius	Tiberius Claudius Caesar Augustus Germanicus
54–68	Nero	Nero Claudius Caesar Augustus Germanicus
68–69	Galba	Servius Galba Caesar Augustus
69	Otho	Marcus Otho Caesar Augustus
69	Vitellius	Aulus Vitellius Germanicus
69–79	Vespasian	Caesar Vespasianus Augustus
79–81	Titus	Titus Vespasianus Augustus
81–96	Domitian	Caesar Domitianus Augustus
96–98	Nerva	Nerva Caesar Augustus
98–117	Trajan	Caesar Nerva Traianus Augustus
117–138	Hadrian	Caesar Traianus Hadrianus Augustus
138–161	Antoninus Pius	Caesar Titus Aelius Hadrianus Antoninus Augustus Pius
161–180	Marcus Aurelius	Marcus Aurelius Antoninus
161–169	Lucius Verus	Lucius Aurelius Verus
177–192	Commodus	Lucius Aelius Aurelius Commodus
193	Pertinax	Publius Helvius Pertinax
193	Didius Julianus	Marcus Didius Severus Julianus

Roman Emperors (continued)

REIGN	BYNAME	FULL NAME
193–211	Septimius Severus	Lucius Septimius Severus Pertinax
198–217	Caracalla	Marcus Aurelius Severus Antoninus
209–212	Geta	Publius Septimius Geta
217–218	Macrinus	Marcus Opellius Severus Macrinus
218–222	Elagabalus	Sacerdos dei invicti solis Elagabali Marcus Aurelius Antoninus
222–235	Alexander Severus	Marcus Aurelius Severus Alexander
235–238	Maximin	Gaius Julius Verus Maximinus
238	Gordian I	Marcus Antonius Gordianus Sempronianus Romanus Africanus
238	Gordian II	Marcus Antonius Gordianus Sempronianus Romanus Africanus
238	Maximus	Marcus Clodius Pupienus Maximus
238	Balbinus	Decius Caelius Calvinus Balbinus
238–244	Gordian III	Marcus Antonius Gordianus
244–249	Philip	
249–251	Decius	Galus Messius Quintus Trianus Decius
251	Hostilian	Gaius Valens Hostilianus Messius Quintus
251–253	Gallus	Gaius Vibius Trebonianus Gallus
253	Aemilian	Marcus Aemilius Aemilianus
253–260	Valerian	Publius Licinius Valerianus
253–268	Gallienus	Publius Licinius Egnatius Gallienus
268–270	Claudius II Gothicus	Marcus Aurelius Valerius Claudius
269–270	Quintillus	Marcus Aurelius Claudius Quintillus
270–275	Aurelian	Lucius Domitius Aurelianus
275–276	Tacitus	Marcus Claudius Tacitus
276	Florian	Marcus Annius Florianus
276–282	Probus	Marcus Aurelius Probus
282–283	Carus	Marcus Aurelius Carus
283–285	Carinus	Marcus Aurelius Carinus
283–284	Numerian	Marcus Aurelius Numerius Numerianus
284–305[1]	Diocletian	Gaius Aurelius Valerius Diocletianus
286–305[2]	Maximian	Marcus Aurelius Valerius Maximianus Heraclius
305–311[1]	Galerius	Gaius Galerius Valerius Maximianus
305–306[2]	Constantius I Chlorus	Flavius Valerius Constantius
306–307[2]	Severus	Flavius Valerius Severus
306–312[2]	Maxentius	Marcus Aurelius Valerius Maxentius
308–324[1]	Licinius	Valerius Licinianus Licinius
312–337[2]	Constantine I	Flavius Valerius Constantinus
337–340[2]	Constantine II	Flavius Claudius [or Julius] Constantinus
337–350[2]	Constans I	Flavius Julius Constans
337–361[2]	Constantius II	Flavius Julius [or Valerius] Constantius
350–353[2]	Magnentius	Flavius Magnus Magnentius
361–363[2]	Julian	Flavius Claudius Julianus
363–364[2]	Jovian	Flavius Jovianus
364–375[2]	Valentinian I	Flavius Valentinianus
364–378[1]	Valens	Flavius Valens
365–366[1]	Procopius	
375–383[2]	Gratian	Flavius Gratianus Augustus
375–392[2]	Valentinian II	Flavius Valentinianus
379–395[2]	Theodosius I	Flavius Theodosius
395–408[1]	Arcadius	Flavius Arcadius
395–423[2]	Honorius	Flavius Honorius
408–450[1]	Theodosius II	
421[2]	Constantius III	
425–455[2]	Valentinian III	Flavius Placidius Valentinianus
450–457[1]	Marcian	Marcianus
455[2]	Petronius Maximus	Flavius Ancius Petronius Maximus
455–456[2]	Avitus	Flavius Maccilius Eparchus Avitus
457–474[1]	Leo I	Leo Thrax Magnus
457–461[2]	Majorian	Julius Valerius Majorianus
461–467[2]	Libius Severus	Libius Severianus Severus
467–472[2]	Anthemius	Procopius Anthemius
472[2]	Olybrius	Anicius Olybrius
473–474[2]	Glycerius	
474–475[2]	Julius Nepos	
474[1]	Leo II	
474–491[1]	Zeno	
475–476[2]	Romulus Augustulus	Flavius Momyllus Romulus Augustulus

[1]Ruled in the East only. [2]Ruled in the West only.

Sovereigns of Britain

SOVEREIGN	DYNASTY OR HOUSE	REIGN
Kings of Wessex (West Saxons)		
Egbert	Saxon	802–839
Aethelwulf (Ethelwulf)	Saxon	839–856/858
Aethelbald (Ethelbald)	Saxon	855/856–860
Aethelberht (Ethelbert)	Saxon	860–865/866
Aethelred I (Ethelred)	Saxon	865/866–871
Alfred the Great	Saxon	871–899
Edward the Elder	Saxon	899–924
Sovereigns of England		
Athelstan[1]	Saxon	925–939
Edmund I	Saxon	939–946
Eadred (Edred)	Saxon	946–955
Eadwig (Edwy)	Saxon	955–959
Edgar	Saxon	959–975
Edward the Martyr	Saxon	975–978
Ethelred II the Unready (Aethelred)	Saxon	978–1013
Sweyn Forkbeard	Danish	1013–14
Ethelred II the Unready (restored)	Saxon	1014–16
Edmund II Ironside	Saxon	1016
Canute	Danish	1016–35
Harold I Harefoot	Danish	1035–40
Hardecanute	Danish	1040–42
Edward the Confessor	Saxon	1042–66
Harold II	Saxon	1066
William I the Conqueror	Norman	1066–87
William II	Norman	1087–1100
Henry I	Norman	1100–35
Stephen	Blois	1135–54
Henry II	Plantagenet	1154–89
Richard I	Plantagenet	1189–99
John	Plantagenet	1199–1216
Henry III	Plantagenet	1216–72
Edward I	Plantagenet	1272–1307
Edward II	Plantagenet	1307–27
Edward III	Plantagenet	1327–77
Richard II	Plantagenet	1377–99
Henry IV	Plantagenet: Lancaster	1399–1413
Henry V	Plantagenet: Lancaster	1413–22
Henry VI	Plantagenet: Lancaster	1422–61
Edward IV	Plantagenet: York	1461–70

SOVEREIGN	DYNASTY OR HOUSE	REIGN
Sovereigns of England (continued)		
Henry VI (restored)	Plantagenet: Lancaster	1470–71
Edward IV (restored)	Plantagenet: York	1471–83
Edward V	Plantagenet: York	1483
Richard III	Plantagenet: York	1483–85
Henry VII	Tudor	1483–1509
Henry VIII	Tudor	1509–47
Edward VI	Tudor	1547–53
Mary I	Tudor	1553–58
Elizabeth I	Tudor	1558–1603
Sovereigns of Great Britain and the United Kingdom[2, 3]		
James I (VI of Scotland)[2]	Stuart	1603–25
Charles I	Stuart	1625–49
Commonwealth		
Oliver Cromwell, Lord Protector		1653–58
Richard Cromwell, Lord Protector		1658–59
Sovereigns of Great Britain and the United Kingdom (restored)		
Charles II	Stuart	1660–85
James II	Stuart	1685–88
William III and Mary II[4]	Orange/ Stuart	1689–1702
Anne	Stuart	1702–14
George I	Hanover	1714–27
George II	Hanover	1727–60
George III[3]	Hanover	1760–1820
George IV[5]	Hanover	1820–30
William IV	Hanover	1830–37
Victoria	Hanover	1837–1901
Edward VII	Saxe-Coburg-Gotha	1901–10
George V[6]	Windsor	1910–36
Edward VIII[7]	Windsor	1936
George VI	Windsor	1936–52
Elizabeth II	Windsor	1952–

[1]Athelstan was king of Wessex and the first king of all England.   [2]James VI of Scotland became also James I of England in 1603. Upon accession to the English throne he styled himself "King of Great Britain" and was so proclaimed. Legally, however, he and his successors held separate English and Scottish kingships until the Act of Union of 1707, when the two kingdoms were united as the Kingdom of Great Britain.   [3]The United Kingdom was formed on 1 Jan 1801, with the union of Great Britain and Ireland. After 1801 George III was styled "King of the United Kingdom of Great Britain and Ireland."   [4]William and Mary, as husband and wife, reigned jointly until Mary's death in 1694. William then reigned alone until his own death in 1702.   [5]George IV was regent from 5 Feb 1811.   [6]In 1917, during World War I, George V changed the name of his house from Saxe-Coburg-Gotha to Windsor.   [7]Edward VIII succeeded upon the death of his father, George V, on 20 Jan 1936, but abdicated on 11 Dec 1936, before coronation.

Rulers of Scotland

Knowledge about the early Scottish kings (until Malcolm II) is slim and is partly based on traditional lists. The dating of reigns is thus inexact.

RULER	REIGN	RULER	REIGN
Kenneth I MacAlpin	843–858	Aed (Aodh)	877–878
Donald I	858–862	Eochaid (Eocha) and Giric (Ciric)[1]	878–889
Constantine I	862–877	Donald II	889–900

Rulers of Scotland (continued)

RULER	REIGN	RULER	REIGN
Constantine II	900–943	Alexander III	1249–86
Malcolm I	943–954	Margaret, Maid of Norway	1286–90
Indulf	954–962		
Dub	962–966	**Interregnum**	1290–92
Culen	966–971		
Kenneth II	971–995	John de Balliol	1292–96
Constantine III	995–997		
Kenneth III	997–1005	**Interregnum**	1296–1306
Malcolm II	1005–34		
Duncan I	1034–40	Robert I the Bruce	1306–29
Macbeth	1040–57	David II	1329–71
Lulach	1057–58		
Malcolm III Canmore	1058–93	**House of Stewart (Stuart)[2]**	
Donald Bane (Donalbane)	1093–94	Robert II	1371–90
Duncan II	1093–94	Robert III	1390–1406
Donald Bane (restored)	1094–97	James I	1406–37
Edgar	1097–1107	James II	1437–60
Alexander I	1107–24	James III	1460–88
David I	1124–53	James IV	1488–1513
Malcolm IV	1153–65	James V	1513–42
William I the Lion	1165–1214	Mary, Queen of Scots	1542–67
Alexander II	1214–49	James VI[3]	1567–1625

[1]*Eochaid may have been a minor and Giric his guardian, or Giric may have been a usurper. Both appear in the lists of kings for the period.* [2]*"Stewart" was the original spelling for the Scottish family, but during the 16th century French influence led to the adoption of the spelling Stuart (or Steuart), owing to the absence of the letter "w" in the French alphabet.* [3]*James VI of Scotland became also James I of England in 1603. Upon accession to the English throne he styled himself "King of Great Britain" and was so proclaimed. Legally, however, he and his successors held separate English and Scottish kingships until the Act of Union of 1707, when the two kingdoms were united as the Kingdom of Great Britain.*

British Prime Ministers

The origin of the term prime minister and the question to whom it should originally be applied have long been issues of scholarly and political debate. Although the term was used as early as the reign of Queen Anne (1702–14), it acquired wider currency during the reign of George II (1727–60), when it began to be used as a term of reproach toward Robert Walpole. The title prime minister did not become official until 1905, to refer to the leader of a government.

Before the development of the Conservative and Liberal parties in the mid-19th century, parties in Britain were largely simply alliances of prominent groups or aristocratic families. The designations Whig and Tory tend often to be approximate. In all cases, the party designation is that of the prime minister; he might lead a coalition government, as did David Lloyd George and Winston Churchill (in his first term).

PRIME MINISTER	PARTY	TERM	PRIME MINISTER	PARTY	TERM
Robert Walpole	Whig	1721–42	William Henry Cavendish-Bentinck	Whig	1807–09
Spencer Compton	Whig	1742–43			
Henry Pelham	Whig	1743–54	Spencer Perceval	Tory	1809–12
Thomas Pelham-Holles	Whig	1754–56	Robert Banks Jenkinson	Tory	1812–27
William Cavendish	Whig	1756–57	George Canning	Tory	1827
Thomas Pelham-Holles	Whig	1757–62	Frederick John Robinson	Tory	1827–28
John Stuart		1762–63	Arthur Wellesley	Tory	1828–30
George Grenville		1763–65	Charles Grey	Whig	1830–34
Charles Watson Wentworth	Whig	1765–66	William Lamb	Whig	1834
			Arthur Wellesley	Tory	1834
William Pitt		1766–68	Robert Peel	Tory	1834–35
Augustus Henry Fitzroy		1768–70	William Lamb	Whig	1835–41
Frederick North		1770–82	Robert Peel	Conservative	1841–46
Charles Watson Wentworth	Whig	1782	John Russell	Whig-Liberal	1846–52
			Edward Geoffrey Stanley	Conservative	1852
William Petty-Fitzmaurice		1782–83	George Hamilton-Gordon		1852–55
William Henry Cavendish-Bentinck	Whig	1783	Henry John Temple	Liberal	1855–58
			Edward Geoffrey Stanley	Conservative	1858–59
William Pitt	Tory	1783–1801	Henry John Temple	Liberal	1859–65
Henry Addington	Tory	1801–04	John Russell	Liberal	1865–66
William Pitt	Tory	1804–06	Edward Geoffrey Stanley	Conservative	1866–68
William Wyndham Grenville		1806–07	Benjamin Disraeli	Conservative	1868
			William Ewart Gladstone	Liberal	1868–74

British Prime Ministers (continued)

PRIME MINISTER	PARTY	TERM
Benjamin Disraeli	Conservative	1874–80
William Ewart Gladstone	Liberal	1880–85
Robert Cecil	Conservative	1885–86
William Ewart Gladstone	Liberal	1886
Robert Cecil	Conservative	1886–92
William Ewart Gladstone	Liberal	1892–94
Archibald Philip Primrose	Liberal	1894–95
Robert Cecil	Conservative	1895–1902
Arthur James Balfour	Conservative	1902–05
Henry Campbell-Bannerman	Liberal	1905–08
H.H. Asquith	Liberal	1908–16
David Lloyd George	Liberal	1916–22
Bonar Law	Conservative	1922–23
Stanley Baldwin	Conservative	1923–24
Ramsay Macdonald	Labour	1924
Stanley Baldwin	Conservative	1924–29

PRIME MINISTER	PARTY	TERM
Ramsay Macdonald	Labour	1929–35
Stanley Baldwin	Conservative	1935–37
Neville Chamberlain	Conservative	1937–40
Winston Churchill	Conservative	1940–45
Clement Attlee	Labour	1945–51
Winston Churchill	Conservative	1951–55
Anthony Eden	Conservative	1955–57
Harold Macmillan	Conservative	1957–63
Alec Douglas-Home	Conservative	1963–64
Harold Wilson	Labour	1964–70
Edward Heath	Conservative	1970–74
Harold Wilson	Labour	1974–76
James Callaghan	Labour	1976–79
Margaret Thatcher	Conservative	1979–90
John Major	Conservative	1990–97
Tony Blair	Labour	1997–

Rulers of France

RULER	REIGN
Carolingian dynasty	
Pippin III the Short	751–768
Charles I (Charlemagne, Kingdom of the Franks)	768–814
Louis I (Kingdom of the Franks)	814–840
Civil War	840–843
Charles II (Kingdom of the West Franks)	843–877
Louis II (Kingdom of the West Franks)	877–879
Louis III (Kingdom of the West Franks)	879–882
Carloman (Kingdom of the West Franks)	879–884
Charles (III) (Charles III, Holy Roman Empire)	884–887
Robertian (Capetian) dynasty	
Eudes	888–898
Carolingian dynasty	
Charles III	893/898–923
Robertian (Capetian) dynasty	
Robert I	922–923
Rudolf (Raoul, or Rodolphe)	923–936
Carolingian dynasty	
Louis IV	936–954
Lothair (Lothaire)	954–986
Louis V	986–987
Capetian dynasty	
Hugh Capet (Hugues Capet)	987–996
Robert II	996–1031
Henry I (Henri)	1031–60
Philip I (Philippe)	1060–1108
Louis VI	1108–37
Louis VII	1137–80
Philip II (Philippe)	1180–1223
Louis VIII	1223–26
Louis IX (Saint Louis)	1226–70
Philip III (Philippe)	1270–85
Philip IV (Philippe)	1285–1314
Louis X	1314–16
John I (Jean)	1316
Philip V (Philippe)	1316–22
Charles IV	1322–28

RULER	REIGN
Valois dynasty	
Philip VI (Philippe)	1328–50
John II (Jean)	1350–64
Charles V	1364–80
Charles VI	1380–1422
Charles VII	1422–61
Louis XI	1461–83
Charles VIII	1483–98
Valois dynasty (Orléans branch)	
Louis XII	1498–1515
Valois dynasty (Angoulême branch)	
Francis I (François)	1515–47
Henry II (Henri)	1547–59
Francis II (François)	1559–60
Charles IX	1560–74
Henry III (Henri)	1574–89
House of Bourbon	
Henry IV (Henri)	1589–1610
Louis XIII	1610–43
Louis XIV	1643–1715
Louis XV	1715–74
Louis XVI	1774–92
Louis (XVII)	1793–95
First Republic	
National Convention	1792–95
Directorate	1795–99
Consulate (Napoléon Bonaparte)	1799–1804
First Empire (emperors)	
Napoleon I (Napoléon Bonaparte)	1804–14, 1815
Napoleon (II)	1815
House of Bourbon	
Louis XVIII	1814–24
Charles X	1824–30
House of Orléans	
Louis-Philippe	1830–48
Second Republic (president)	
Louis-Napoléon Bonaparte	1848–52

Rulers of France (continued)

RULER	REIGN
Second Empire (emperor)	
Napoleon III (Louis-Napoléon Bonaparte)	1852–70
Third Republic (presidents)	
Adolphe Thiers	1871–73
Marie-Edmé-Patrice-Maurice, comte de Mac-Mahon, duc de Magenta	1873–79
Jules Grévy	1879–87
Sadi Carnot	1887–94
Jean Casimir-Périer	1894–95
Félix Faure	1895–99
Émile Loubet	1899–1906
Armand Fallières	1906–13
Raymond Poincaré	1913–20
Paul Deschanel	1920
Alexandre Millerand	1920–24
Gaston Doumergue	1924–31
Paul Doumer	1931–32

RULER	REIGN
Third Republic (presidents) (continued)	
Albert Lebrun	1932–40
French State (État Français, or Vichy France)	
Philippe Pétain	1940–44
Provisional government	1944–47
Fourth Republic (presidents)	
Vincent Auriol	1947–54
René Coty	1954–59
Fifth Republic (presidents)	
Charles de Gaulle	1959–69
Georges Pompidou	1969–74
Valéry Giscard d'Estaing	1974–81
François Mitterrand	1981–95
Jacques Chirac	1995–

Rulers of Spain

RULER	REIGN
House of Habsburg	
Charles I (Carlos)	1516–56
Philip II (Felipe)	1556–98
Philip III (Felipe)	1598–1621
Philip IV (Felipe)	1621–65
Charles II (Carlos)	1665–1700
House of Bourbon (Borbón)	
Philip V (Felipe)	1700–24
Louis (Luis)	1724
Philip V (2nd time)	1724–46
Ferdinand VI (Fernando)	1746–59
Charles III (Carlos)	1759–88
Charles IV (Carlos)	1788–1808
Ferdinand VII (Fernando)	1808
House of Bonaparte	
Joseph (José)	1808–13
House of Bourbon (Borbón)	
Ferdinand VII (2nd time)	1814–33

RULER	REIGN
House of Bourbon (Borbón) continued	
Isabella II (Isabel)	1833–68
Interregnum	1868–70
House of Savoy	
Amadeus I (Amadeo)	1870–73
Republic	1873–74
House of Bourbon (Borbón)	
Alfonso XII	1874–85
Alfonso XIII	1886–1931
Republic	1931–39
Nationalist Regime	
Francisco Franco	1939–75
House of Bourbon (Borbón)	
Juan Carlos	1975–

Rulers of Germany

On 25 Jul 1806 the Confederation of the Rhine was founded, with Carl Theodor Reichsfreiherr von Dalberg as Prince-Primate (1806–13). After the dissolution of the Rhine Confederation, there was no true central power until 1815, when the German Confederation was founded. In 1867 the governing structure became the North German Confederation, and in 1871 the German Reich. For rulers of Germany before the Confederation of the Rhine, see "Holy Roman Emperors."

RULER	REIGN OR TERM
Emperors	
Hohenzollern dynasty	
Wilhelm I	1871–88
Friedrich III	1888
Wilhelm II	1888–1918
Presidents	
Richard Müller	1918
Robert Leinert	1918–19
Wilhelm Pfannkuch	1919
Eduard David	1919
Friedrich Ebert	1919–25
Hans Luther (acting)	1925

RULER	REIGN OR TERM
Presidents (continued)	
Walter Simons (acting)	1925
Paul von Hindenburg	1925–34
Adolf Hitler (Führer)	1934–45
Karl Dönitz	1945
Chancellors	
Otto Fürst von Bismarck	1871–90
Leo Graf von Caprivi	1890–94
Chlodwig Fürst zu Hohenlohe-Schillingsfürst	1894–1900
Bernhard Graf Fürst von Bülow	1900–09
Theobald von Bethmann Hollweg	1909–17

Rulers of Germany (continued)

RULER	REIGN OR TERM	RULER	REIGN OR TERM
Chancellors (continued)		**Chancellors (continued)**	
Georg Michaelis	1917	Wilhelm Marx	1923–24
Georg Graf von Hertling	1917–18	Hans Luther	1925–26
Maximilian Prinz von Baden	1918	Wilhelm Marx	1926–28
Friedrich Ebert	1918	Hermann Müller	1928–30
Philipp Scheidemann	1919	Heinrich Brüning	1930–32
Gustav Bauer	1919–20	Franz von Papen	1932
Wolfgang Kapp (in rebellion)	1920	Kurt von Schleicher	1932–33
Hermann Müller	1920	Adolf Hitler	1933–45
Konstantin Fehrenbach	1920–21	Joseph Goebbels	1945
Joseph Wirth	1921–22	Lutz Graf Schwerin von Krosigk	1945
Wilhelm Cuno	1922–23	(chairman of interim government)	
Gustav Stresemann	1923		
Allied occupation		1945–49	

German Democratic Republic (East Germany)[1]

Presidents		Chairmen of the Council of State (continued)	
Johannes Dieckmann (acting)	1949	Walter Ulbricht	1960–73
Wilhelm Pieck	1949–60	Friedrich Ebert (acting)	1973
Johannes Dieckmann (acting)	1960	Willi Stoph	1973–76
		Erich Honecker	1976–89
Chairmen of the Council of State		Egon Krenz	1989
Walter Ulbricht	1960–73	Manfred Gerlach (acting)	1989–90
Friedrich Ebert (acting)	1973	Sabine Bergmann–Pohl[2]	1990

Federal Republic of Germany (West Germany)[1]

Presidents		Chancellors	
Karl Arnold (acting)	1949	Konrad Adenauer	1949–63
Theodor Heuss	1949–59	Ludwig Erhard	1963–66
Heinrich Lübke	1959–69	Kurt Georg Kiesinger	1966–69
Gustav Heinemann	1969–74	Willy Brandt	1969–74
Walter Scheel	1974–79	Walter Scheel (acting)	1974
Karl Carstens	1979–84	Helmut Schmidt	1974–82
Richard von Weizsäcker	1984–94	Helmut Kohl	1982–98
Roman Herzog	1994–99	Gerhard Schröder	1998–
Johannes Rau	1999–		

[1]After WWII, Germany was split into four occupational zones, governed by the French, British, American, and Soviet powers. The Western zones were merged and, on 23 May 1949, became the independent Federal Republic of Germany. On 7 October of the same year, the Soviet zone was proclaimed the German Democratic Republic. On 3 Oct 1990, the latter was incorporated into the Federal Republic of Germany.
[2]Bergmann–Pohl was president of the People's Chamber.

Holy Roman Emperors

The Holy Roman Empire encompassed a varying complex of lands in Western and Central Europe. Ruled over by Frankish and then German kings, the empire officially dissolved on 6 Aug 1806, when Francis II resigned his title.

EMPEROR	REIGN	EMPEROR	REIGN
Carolingian dynasty		**House of Franconia**	
Charlemagne (Charles I)	800–814	Conrad I	911–918
Louis I	814–840		
Civil War	840–843	**Carolingian dynasty**	
Lothair I	843–855	Berengar	915–924
Louis II	855–875		
Charles II	875–877	**House of Saxony (Liudolfings)**	
Interregnum	877–881	Henry I	919–936
Charles III	881–887	Otto I	936–973
Interregnum	887–891	Otto II	973–983
		Otto III	983–1002
House of Spoleto		Henry II	1002–24
Guy	891–894		
Lambert	894–898	**Salian dynasty**	
		Conrad II	1024–39
Carolingian dynasty		Henry III	1039–56
Arnulf	896–899		
Louis III	901–905		

Holy Roman Emperors (continued)

EMPEROR	REIGN
Salian dynasty (continued)	
Henry IV	1056–1106
Rival claimants:	
Rudolf	1077–80
Hermann	1081–93
Conrad	1093–1101
Henry V	1105/06–25
House of Supplinburg	
Lothair II	1125–37
House of Hohenstaufen	
Conrad III	1138–52
Frederick I (Barbarossa)	1152–90
Henry VI	1190–97
Philip	1198–1208
Welf dynasty	
Otto IV	1198–1214
House of Hohenstaufen	
Frederick II	1215–50
Rival claimants:	
Henry (VII)	1220–35
Henry Raspe	1246–47
William of Holland	1247–56
Conrad IV	1250–54
Great Interregnum	1254–73
Richard	1257–72
Alfonso (Alfonso X of Castile)	1257–75
House of Habsburg	
Rudolf I	1273–91
House of Nassau	
Adolf	1292–98
House of Habsburg	
Albert I	1298–1308
House of Luxembourg	
Henry VII	1308–13

EMPEROR	REIGN
House of Habsburg	
Frederick (III)	1314–26
House of Wittelsbach	
Louis IV	1314–46
House of Luxembourg	
Charles IV	1346–78
Wenceslas	1378–1400
House of Wittelsbach	
Rupert	1400–10
House of Luxembourg	
Jobst	1410–11
Sigismund	1410–37
House of Habsburg	
Albert II	1438–39
Frederick III	1440–93
Maximilian I	1493–1519
Charles V	1519–56
Ferdinand I	1556–64
Maximilian II	1564–76
Rudolf II	1576–1612
Matthias	1612–19
Ferdinand II	1619–37
Ferdinand III	1637–57
Leopold I	1658–1705
Joseph I	1705–11
Charles VI	1711–40
House of Wittelsbach	
Charles VII	1742–45
House of Habsburg	
Francis I	1745–65
Joseph II	1765–90
Leopold II	1790–92
Francis II	1792–1806

Rulers of Russia[1]

RULER	REIGN
Princes and Grand Princes of Moscow	
(Muscovy): Danilovich dynasty[2]	
Daniel (son of Alexander Nevsky)	c. 1276–1303
Yury	1303–25
Ivan I	1325–40
Semyon (Simeon)	1340–53
Ivan II	1353–59
Dmitry Donskoy	1359–89
Vasily I	1389–1425
Vasily II	1425–62
Ivan III	1462–1505
Vasily III	1505–33
Ivan IV	1533–47
Tsars of Russia: Danilovich dynasty	
Ivan IV	1547–84
Fyodor I	1584–98
Tsars of Russia: Time of Troubles	
Boris Godunov	1598–1605
Fyodor II	1605

RULER	REIGN
Tsars of Russia: Time of Troubles (continued)	
False Dmitry	1605–06
Vasily (IV)	1606–10
Interregnum	1610–12
Tsars and Empresses of Russia and the	
Russian Empire: Romanov dynasty[3]	
Michael III	1613–45
Alexis	1645–76
Fyodor III	1676–82
Peter I (Ivan V coruler 1682–96)	1682–1725
Catherine I	1725–27
Peter II	1727–30
Anna	1730–40
Ivan VI	1740–41
Elizabeth	1741–61 (O.S.)
Peter III[4]	1761–62 (O.S.)
Catherine II	1762–96
Paul	1796–1801
Alexander I	1801–25

Rulers of Russia[1] (continued)

RULER	REIGN	RULER	REIGN
Tsars and Empresses of Russia and the Russian Empire: Romanov dynasty[3] (continued)		**Chairmen (or First Secretaries) of the Communist Party of the Soviet Union (continued)**	
Nicholas I	1825–55	Georgy Malenkov	1953
Alexander II	1855–81	Nikita Khrushchev	1953–64
Alexander III	1881–94	Leonid Brezhnev	1964–82
Nicholas II	1894–1917	Yury Andropov	1982–84
		Konstantin Chernenko	1984–85
Provisional government	1917	Mikhail Gorbachev	1985–91
Chairmen (or First Secretaries) of the Communist Party of the Soviet Union		**Presidents of Russia**	
		Boris Yeltsin	1990–99
Vladimir Lenin	1917–24	Vladimir Putin	2000–
Joseph Stalin	1924–53		

[1]*This table includes leaders of Muscovy, Russia, the Russian Empire, and the Soviet Union.* [2]*The Danilovich dynasty is a late branch of the Rurik dynasty, named after its progenitor, Daniel.* [3]*On 22 (O.S.) Oct 1721, Peter I the Great took the title of "emperor." However, despite the official titling, conventional usage took an odd turn. Every male sovereign continued usually to be called tsar, but every female sovereign was conventionally called empress.* [4]*The direct line of the Romanov dynasty came to an end in 1761 with the death of Elizabeth, daughter of Peter I, but subsequent rulers of the "Holstein-Gottorp dynasty" (the first, Peter III, was son of Charles Frederick, duke of Holstein-Gottorp, and Anna, daughter of Peter I) took the family name of Romanov.*

Middle East

Byzantine Emperors

The Byzantine Empire comprised what was previously the eastern half of the Roman Empire. It survived for nearly 1,000 years after the western half had crumbled into various feudal kingdoms; it finally fell to Ottoman Turkish onslaughts in 1453. For emperors of the Eastern Roman Empire (at Constantinople) before the fall of Rome, see "Roman Emperors."

EMPEROR	REIGN	EMPEROR	REIGN
Zeno	474–491	Alexander	912–913
Anastasius I	491–518	Constantine VII Porphyrogenitus	913–959
Justin I	518–527	Romanus I Lecapenus	920–944
Justinian I	527–565	Romanus II	959–963
Justin II	565–578	Nicephorus II Phocas	963–969
Tiberius II Constantine	578–582	John I Tzimisces	969–976
Maurice Tiberius	582–602	Basil II Bulgaroctonus	976–1025
Phocas	602–610	Constantine VIII	1025–28
Heraclius	610–641	Romanus III Argyrus	1028–34
Heraclius Constantine	641	Michael IV	1034–41
Heraclonas (or Heraclius)	641	Michael V Calaphates	1041–42
Constans II (Constantine Pogonatus)	641–668	Zoe (empress)	1042–56
Constantine IV	668–685	Constantine IX Monomachus	1042–55
Justinian II Rhinotmetus	685–695	Theodora (empress)	1055–56
Leontius	695–698	Michael VI Stratioticus	1056–57
Tiberius III	698–705	Isaac I Comnenus	1057–59
Justinian II Rhinotmetus (restored)	705–711	Constantine X Ducas	1059–67
Philippicus	711–713	Romanus IV Diogenes	1067–71
Anastasius II	713–715	Michael VII Ducas	1071–78
Theodosius III	715–717	Nicephorus III Botaniates	1078–81
Leo III	717–741	Alexius I Comnenus	1081–1118
Constantine V Copronymus	741–775	John II Comnenus	1118–43
Leo IV	775–780	Manuel I Comnenus	1143–80
Constantine VI	780–797	Alexius II Comnenus	1180–83
Irene (empress)	797–802	Andronicus I Comnenus	1183–85
Nicephorus I	802–811	Isaac II Angelus	1185–95
Stauracius	811	Alexius III Angelus	1195–1203
Michael I Rhangabe	811–813	Isaac II Angelus (restored) and Alexius IV Angelus (joint ruler)	1203–04
Leo V	813–820	Alexius V Ducas Murtzuphlus	1204
Michael II Balbus	820–829		
Theophilus	829–842	**Latin emperors**	
Michael III	842–867	Baldwin I	1204–06
Basil I	867–886	Henry	1206–16
Leo VI	886–912		

Byzantine Emperors (continued)

EMPEROR	REIGN	EMPEROR	REIGN
Latin emperors (continued)		**Greek emperors restored**	
Peter	1217	Michael VIII Palaeologus	1261–82
Yolande (empress)	1217–19	Andronicus II Palaeologus	1282–1328
Robert	1221–28	Andronicus III Palaeologus	1328–41
Baldwin II	1228–61	John V Palaeologus	1341–76
John	1231–37	John VI Cantacuzenus	1347–54
		Andronicus IV Palaeologus	1376–79
Nicaean emperors		John V Palaeologus (restored)	1379–90
Constantine (XI) Lascaris	1204–05?	John VII Palaeologus	1390
Theodore I Lascaris	1205?–22	John V Palaeologus (restored)	1390–91
John III Ducas Vatatzes	1222–54	Manuel II Palaeologus	1391–1425
Theodore II Lascaris	1254–58	John VIII Palaeologus	1421–48
John IV Lascaris	1258–61	Constantine XI Palaeologus	1449–53

Caliphs

When Muhammad died on 8 Jun 632, Abu Bakr, his father-in-law, succeeded to his political and administrative functions. He and his three immediate successors are known as the "perfect" or "rightly guided" caliphs. After them, the title was borne by the 14 Umayyad caliphs of Damascus (from 661–750) and subsequently by the 38 'Abbasid caliphs of Baghdad (both are named after their clans of origin). The empire of the caliphate grew rapidly through conquest during its first two centuries to include most of southwestern Asia, North Africa, and Spain. 'Abbasid power ended in 945, when the Buyids took Baghdad under their rule. They retained the 'Abbasid caliphs as figureheads; other dynasties in Central Asia and the Ganges River basin acknowledged the 'Abbasid caliphs as spiritual leaders. The Fatimids, however, proclaimed a new caliphate in 920 in their capital of al-Mahdiyah in Tunisia; it lasted until 1171, by which time opposition within the sect caused it to disintegrate. 'Abbasid authority was partially restored in the 12th century, but the caliphate ceased to exist with the Mongol destruction of Baghdad in 1258. Some principal caliphs are listed below.

CALIPH	REIGN	CALIPH	REIGN
"Perfect" caliphs		**Fatimid caliphs (al-Mahdiyah)**	
Abu Bakr	632–634	al-Mahdi	909–934
'Umar I	634–644	al-Qa'im	934–946
'Uthman ibn 'Affan	644–656	al-Mansur	946–953
'Ali	656–661	al-Mu'izz	953–975
		al-Hakim	996–1021
Umayyad caliphs (Damascus)		al-Mustansir	1036–94
Mu'awiyah I	661–680	al-Musta'li	1094–1101
Abd al-Malik	685–705		
al-Walid	705–715	**'Abbasid caliph (Baghdad)**	
Hisham	724–743	al-Nasir	1180–1225
Marwan II	744–750		
'Abbasid caliphs (Baghdad)			
as-Saffah	749–754		
Harun	786–809		
al-Ma'mun	813–833		

Sultans of the Ottoman Empire

One of the most powerful states in the world during the 15th and 16th centuries, the Ottoman empire was created by Turkish tribes in Anatolia and spanned more than 600 years. It came to an end in 1922, when it was replaced by the Turkish Republic and various successor states in southeastern Europe and the Middle East. At its height the empire included most of southeastern Europe, the Middle East as far east as Iraq, North Africa as far west as Algeria, and most of the Arabian Peninsula. The term Ottoman is a dynastic appellation derived from Osman (Arabic: 'Uthman), the nomadic Turkmen chief who founded both the dynasty and the empire.

SULTAN	REIGN	SULTAN	REIGN
Osman I	c. 1300–1324	Murad II (second reign)	1446–1451
Orhan	1324–1360	Mehmed II (second reign)	1451–1481
Murad I	1360–1389	Bayezid II	1481–1512
Bayezid I	1389–1402	Selim I	1512–1520
Mehmed I	1413–1421	Suleyman I	1520–1566
Murad II	1421–1444	Selim II	1566–1574
Mehmed II	1444–1446	Murad III	1574–1595

Sultans of the Ottoman Empire (continued)

SULTAN	REIGN	SULTAN	REIGN
Mehmed III	1595-1603	Osman III	1754-1757
Ahmed I	1603-1617	Mustafa III	1757-1774
Mustafa I	1617-1618	Abdulhamid I	1774-1789
Osman II	1618-1622	Selim III	1789-1807
Mustafa I (second reign)	1622-1623	Mustafa IV	1807-1808
Murad IV	1623-1640	Mahmud II	1808-1839
Ibrahim	1640-1648	Abdulmecid I	1839-1861
Mehmed IV	1648-1687	Abdulaziz	1861-1876
Suleyman II	1687-1691	Murad V	1876
Ahmed II	1691-1695	Abdulhamid II	1876-1909
Mustafa II	1695-1703	Mehmed V	1909-1918
Ahmed III	1703-1730	Mehmed VI	1918-1922
Mahmud I	1730-1754		

Persian Dynasties

Dates given are approximate and may overlap.

DYNASTY/KINGDOM	PERIOD	DYNASTY/KINGDOM	PERIOD
Median	728-550 BC	Seljuqs	1038-1157
Achaemenian	559-330 BC	Mongols[4]	1220-1335
Hellenistic period of Alexander and the Seleucids[1]	330 BC-247 BC	Timurids and Ottoman Turks	1380-1501
		Safavid	1502-1736
Parthian period (Arsacid dynasty)[2]	247 BC-AD 224	Afghan interlude	1723-36
Sasanian	224-651	Nader Shah	1736-47
Arab invasion and the advent of Islam	640-829	Zand	1750-79
		Qajars	1794-1925
Iranian intermezzo[3]	821-1055	Pahlavi	1925-79

[1]Dates from the death of Darius III, the last Achaemenian king, and the invasion of Alexander the Great.
[2]Dates from the year in which the Parnian chief Arsaces first battled the Seleucids.   [3]Includes the Tahirid, Samanid, Ghaznavids, and Buyid dynasties.   [4]Mainly the Il-Khanid dynasty (1256-1353).

Asia

Indian Dynasties

Dates given are approximations.

DYNASTY	LOCATION	DATES	DYNASTY	LOCATION	DATES
Nanda	Ganges Valley	400 BC	Pala	Bengal	800-1100
Maurya	India, barring the area south of Mysore (Karnataka)	400-200 BC	Pratihara	western India and upper Ganges Valley	900-1100
Indo-Greeks	northern India	200-100 BC	Rastrakuta	western and central Deccan	800-1100
Sunga	Ganges Valley and parts of central India	200-100 BC	Cola	Tamil Nadu	900-1300
			Candella	Bundelkhand	1000-1200
Satavahana	northern Deccan	100 BC-AD 300	Cauhan	Rajasthan	1000-1200
Saka	western India	100 BC-AD 400	Caulukya	Gujarat	1000-1300
Kusana	northern India and Central Asia	AD 100-300	Paramara	western and central India	1000-1100
Gupta	northern India	400-600	Later Calukya	western and central Deccan	1000-1200
Harsa	northern India	700			
Pallava	Tamil Nadu	400-900	Hoysala	central and southern Deccan	1200-1400
Calukya	western and central Deccan	600-800	Yadava	northern Deccan	1200-1300
			Pandya	Tamil Nadu	1300-1400

Japanese Historical Periods and Rulers

PERIOD	DATES	PERIOD	DATES
Asuka	552-710	Muromachi (or Ashikaga)	1338-1573
Nara	710-784	Azuchi-Momoyama	1574-1600
Heian	794-1185	Edo (or Tokugawa)	1603-1867
Kamakura	1192-1333	Meiji	1868-1912

Japanese Historical Periods and Rulers (continued)

Reign dates for the first 28 sovereigns (Jimmu through Senka) are taken from the *Nihon shoki* ("Chronicles of Japan"). The first 14 sovereigns are considered legendary, and while the next 14 are known to have existed, their exact reign dates have not been verified historically. When the year of actual accession and year of formal coronation are different, the latter is placed in parenthesis after the former. If the two events took place in the same year, no special notation is used. If only the coronation year is known, it is placed in parenthesis.

EMPEROR	REIGN
Jimmu	(660)–585 BC
Suizei	(581)–549 BC
Annei	549–511 BC
Itoku	(510)–477 BC
Kosho	(475)–393 BC
Koan	(392)–291 BC
Korei	(290)–215 BC
Kogen	(214)–158 BC
Kaika	158–98 BC
Sujin	(97)–30 BC
Suinin	(29 BC)–AD 70
Keiko	(71)–130
Seimu	(131)–190
Chuai	(192)–200
Jingu Kogo (regent)	201–269
Ojin	(270)–310
Nintoku	(313)–399
Richu	(400)–405
Hanzei	(406)–410
Ingyo	(412)–453
Anko	453–456
Yuryaku	456–479
Seinei	(480)–484
Kenzo	(485)–487
Ninken	(488)–498
Buretsu	498–506
Keitai	(507)–531
Ankan	531 (534)–535
Senka	535–539
Kimmei	539–571
Bidatsu	(572)–585
Yomei	585–587
Sushun	587–592
Suiko (empress regnant)	593–628
Jomei	(629)–641
Kogyoku (empress regnant)	(642)–645
Kotoku	645–654
Saimei (empress regnant: Kogyoku rethroned)	(655)–661
Tenji	661 (668)–672
Kobun	672
Temmu	672 (673)–686
Jito (empress regnant)	686 (690)–697
Mommu	697–707
Gemmei (empress regnant)	707–715
Gensho (empress regnant)	715–724
Shomu	724–749
Koken (empress regnant)	749–758
Junnin	758–764
Shotoku (empress regnant: Koken rethroned)	764 (765)–770
Konin	770–781
Kammu	781–806
Heizei	806–809
Saga	809–823
Junna	823–833
Nimmyo	833–850
Montoku	850–858
Seiwa	858–876
Yozei	876 (877)–884
Koko	884–887

EMPEROR	REIGN
Uda	887–897
Daigo	897–930
Suzaku	930–946
Murakami	946–967
Reizei	967–969
En'yu	969–984
Kazan	984–986
Ichijo	986–1011
Sanjo	1011–16
Go–Ichijo	1016–36
Go–Suzaku	1036–45
Go–Reizei	1045–68
Go–Sanjo	1068–72
Shirakawa	1072–86
Horikawa	1086–1107
Toba	1107–23
Sutoku	1123–41
Konoe	1141–55
Go–Shirakawa	1155–58
Nijo	1158–65
Rokujo	1165–68
Takakura	1168–80
Antoku	1180–85[1]
Go–Toba	1183 (1184)–98
Tsuchimikado	1198–1210
Juntoku	1210 (1211)–21
Chukyo	1221
Goshirakawa	1221 (1222)–32
Shijo	1232 (1233)–42
Go–Saga	1242–46
Go–Fukakusa	1246–59/60
Kameyama	1259/60–74
Gouda	1274–87
Fushimi	1287 (1288)–98
Go–Fushimi	1298–1301
Go–Nijo	1301–08
Hanazono	1308–18
Go–Daigo	1318–39
Go–Murakami	1339–68
Chokei	1368–83
Go–Kameyama	1383–92
The Northern court[2]	
Kogon	1331 (1332)–33
Komyo	1336 (1337/38)–48
Suko	1348 (1349/50)–51
Go–Kogon	1351 (1353/54)–71
Go–Enyu	1371 (1374/75)–82
Go–Komatsu	1382–92
Go–Komatsu	1392–1412
Shoko	1412 (1414)–28
Go–Hanazono	1428 (1429/30)–64
Go–Tsuchimikado	1464 (1465/66)–1500
Go–Kashiwabara	1500 (1521)–26
Go–Nara	1526 (1536)–57
Ogimachi	1557 (1560)–86
Go–Yozei	1586 (1587)–1611
Go–Mizunoo	1611–29
Meisho (empress regnant)	1629 (1630)–43
Go–Komyo	1643–54
Go–Sai	1654/55 (1656)–63

Japanese Historical Periods and Rulers (continued)

EMPEROR	REIGN	EMPEROR	REIGN
The Northern court[2] (continued)		**The Northern court[2] (continued)**	
Reigen	1663–87	Ninko	1817–46
Higashiyama	1687–1709	Komei	1846 (1847)–66
Nakamikado	1709 (1710)–35	Meiji (personal name:	1867 (1868)–1912
Sakuramachi	1735–47	Mutsuhito; era name: Meiji)	
Momozono	1747–62	Taisho (personal name:	1912 (1915)–26
Go–Sakuramachi	1762 (1763)–71	Yoshihito; era name: Taisho)	
(empress regnant)		Hirohito (era name: Showa)	1926 (1928)–1989
Go–Momozono	1771–79	Akihito (era name: Heisei)	1989 (1990)–
Kokaku	1780–1817		

[1]Antoku's reign overlaps that of Go-Toba. Go-Toba was placed on the throne by the Minamoto clan after the rival Taira clan had fled Kyoto with Antoku.   [2]From 1336 until 1392 Japan witnessed the spectacle of two contending Imperial courts—the Southern court of Go-Daigo and his descendants, whose sphere of influence was restricted to the immediate vicinity of the Yoshino Mountains, and the Northern court of Kogon and his descendants, which was under the domination of the Ashikaga family.

Chinese Dynasties

Dates given for early dynasties are approximate and may overlap.

DYNASTY	ALTERNATE NAME	DATES	DYNASTY	ALTERNATE NAME	DATES
Hsia[1]	Xia	c. 2205–1766 BC	Six Dynasties[2] (continued)		
Shang		c. 1760–1030 BC	Southern Qi		479–502
Western Zhou	Chou	c. 1050–771 BC	Southern Liang		502–57
Eastern Zhou	Chou	c. 771–255 BC	Southern Chen		557–89
Qin	Ch'in	221–206 BC	Sui		581–618
Han		206 BC–AD 220	T'ang	Tang	618–907
Western Jin	Chin	265–317	Five Dynasties[3]	Ten Kingdoms[3]	907–960
Eastern Jin[2]	Chin	317–420	Sung	Song	960–1279
Six Dynasties[2]		220–589	Yüan	Yuan, Mongol	1206–1368
Wu		222–80	Ming		1368–1644
Eastern Jin[2]		317–420	Ch'ing	Qing, Manchu	1644–1911/12
Liusong		420–79			

[1]The Hsia Dynasty is mentioned in legends but is of undetermined historicity.   [2]Between the fall of the Han and the establishment of the Sui, China was divided into two societies, northern and southern. The Six Dynasties had their capital at Nanjing in the south. The Eastern Jin is considered one of these six dynasties and so is listed twice.   [3]Period of time between the fall of the T'ang dynasty and the founding of the Sung dynasty, when five would-be dynasties followed one another in quick succession in North China. The era is also known as the period of the Ten Kingdoms because 10 regimes dominated separate regions of South China during the same period.

Leaders of the People's Republic of China Since 1949

Chinese Communist Party leaders

NAME	TITLE	DATES
Mao Zedong	CCP chairman	1949–1976
Hua Guofeng	CCP chairman	1976–1981
Hu Yaobang	CCP chairman; after September 1982, general secretary of the CCP	1981–1987
Zhao Ziyang	CCP general secretary	1987–1989
Jiang Zemin	CCP general secretary	1989–2002
Hu Jintao	CCP general secretary	2002–

premiers

NAME	DATES
Zhou Enlai	1949–1976
Hua Guofeng	1976–1980
Zhao Ziyang	1980–1987
Li Peng	1987–1998
Zhu Rongji	1998–2003
Wen Jiabao	2003–

Note: although he held no top party or state position, Deng Xiaoping was de facto leader of China from 1977 to 1997.

Dalai Lamas

The Dalai Lama is the head of the dominant Dge-lugs-pa (Yellow Hat) order of Tibetan Buddhists and, until 1959, was both spiritual and temporal ruler of Tibet. In accordance with the belief in reincarnation lamas, which began to develop in the 14th century, the successors of the first Dalai Lama were considered his rebirths and came to be regarded as physical manifestations of the compassionate bodhisattva ("buddha-to-be"), Avalokitesvara.

Dalai Lamas (continued)

DALAI LAMA	NAME	LIVED	DALAI LAMA	NAME	LIVED
first	Dge-'dun-grub-pa	1391–1475	eighth	'Jam-dpal-rgya-mtsho	1758–1804
second	Dge-'dun-rgya-mtsho	1475–1542	ninth	Lung-rtogs-rgya-mtsho	1806–1815[1]
third	Bsod-nams-rgya-mtsho	1543–1588	tenth	Tshul-khrims-rgya-mtsho	1816–1837[1]
fourth	Yon-tan-rgya-mtsho	1589–1617	eleventh	Mkhas-grub-rgya-mtsho	1838–1856[1]
fifth	Ngag-dbang-rgya-mtsho	1617–1682	twelfth	'Phrin-las-rgya-mtsho	1856–1875[1]
sixth	Tshangs-dbyangs-rgya-mtsho	1683–1706	thirteenth	Thub-bstan-rgya-mtsho	1875–1933[2]
seventh	Bskal-bzang-rgya-mtsho	1708–1757	fourteenth	Bstan-'dzin-rgya-mtsho	1935–[3]

[1]*Dalai Lamas 9–12 all died young, and the country was ruled by regencies.* [2]*Reigned as head of a sovereign state from 1912.* [3]*Ruled from exile in Dharmsala, India, from 1960.*

The Americas

Pre-Columbian Civilizations

Various aboriginal American Indian cultures evolved in Meso-America (part of Mexico and Central America) and the Andean region (western South America) prior to Spanish exploration and conquest in the 16th century. These pre-Columbian civilizations were extraordinary developments in human society and culture, characterized by kingdoms and empires, great monuments and cities, and refinements in the arts, metallurgy, and writing. Dates given below are approximations.

CULTURE	LOCATION	DATES
Meso-American civilizations		
Olmec	Gulf coast of southern Mexico	1150 BC–800 BC
Zapotec	Oaxaca, particularly Monte Albán	500 BC–AD 900
Totonac	east-central Mexico	500 BC–AD 900
Teotihuacán	Teotihuacán, in the Valley of Mexico	AD 400–600
Maya	southern Mexico and Guatemala	250–900
Toltec	central Mexico	900–1200
Aztec	central and southern Mexico	1400–early 1500s
Andean civilizations		
Nazca	southern coast of Peru	200 BC–AD 600
Recuay	northern highlands of Peru	200 BC–AD 600
Tiwanaku	Lake Titicaca, Bolivia	200 BC–AD 1000
Moche (Mochica)	northern coast of Peru	AD 1–700
Inca	Pacific coast of South America	1100–1532

Africa

Historic Sub-Saharan African States

STATE	LOCATION IN PRESENT-DAY COUNTRIES	FLOURISHED
Aksumite kingdom	Ethiopia, Sudan	1st–10th centuries
Asante empire	Ghana	18th–19th centuries
Basuto kingdom	Lesotho	19th century
Benin kingdom	Nigeria	12th–19th centuries
kingdom of Buganda	Uganda	14th–20th centuries
kingdom of Bunyoro	Uganda	15th–19th centuries
kingdom of Burundi	Burundi	17th–20th centuries
kingdom of Dahomey	Benin	17th–19th centuries
Darfur	Sudan	17th–19th centuries
kingdom of Dongola	Sudan	7th–14th centuries
Fulani empire	Cameroon, Niger, Nigeria	19th–20th centuries
Ghana empire	Mali, Mauritania	4th–13th centuries
Hausa states	Nigeria	14th–19th centuries
Kanem-Bornu	Nigeria, Chad, Cameroon, Niger, Libya	9th–19th centuries
Kongo kingdom	Angola, Dem. Rep. of Congo	14th–17th centuries
Kuba kingdom	Dem. Rep. of Congo	17th–19th centuries
kingdom of Kush	Egypt, Sudan	c. 850 BC–c. AD 325
Luba empire	Dem. Rep. of Congo	16th–19th centuries
Lunda empire	Dem. Rep. of Congo, Angola, Zambia	17th–19th centuries
Mali empire	Mali, Mauritania, Senegal, Gambia, Guinea-Bissau	13th–16th centuries

Historic Sub-Saharan African States (continued)

STATE	LOCATION IN PRESENT-DAY COUNTRIES	FLOURISHED
Ndongo kingdom	Angola	14th–17th centuries
kingdom of Nubia	Egypt, Sudan	4th–7th centuries
Oyo empire	Nigeria	16th–19th centuries
Rozwi empire	Zimbabwe, Botswana	17th–19th centuries
Shewa empire	Ethiopia	15th–19th centuries
Songhai empire	Nigeria, Niger	6th–17th centuries
Tukulor empire	Mali	19th century
Wolof empire	Senegal	14th–19th centuries
Zeng empire	Somalia, Kenya, Tanzania, Mozambique	10th–16th centuries
Zulu kingdom	South Africa	19th century

Did you know? According to a 2005 survey, the city of Luxembourg ranks as the world's best city for personal safety and security; Baghdad, Iraq, ranks worst because of civil unrest and the threat of attack.

Populations

Largest Urban Agglomerations

Agglomerations include a central city and associated neighboring communities.
Source: United Nations, World Urbanization Prospects, the 2003 Revision.

RANK	AGGLOMERATION	COUNTRY	POPULATION PROJECTION (2005)	RANK	AGGLOMERATION	COUNTRY	POPULATION PROJECTION (2005)
1	Tokyo	Japan	35,327,000	15	Osaka-Kobe	Japan	11,286,000
2	Mexico City	Mexico	19,013,000	16	Cairo	Egypt	11,146,000
3	New York City-Newark	US	18,498,000	17	Lagos	Nigeria	11,135,000
				18	Beijing	China	10,849,000
4	Mumbai	India	18,336,000	19	Manila	Philippines	10,677,000
5	São Paulo	Brazil	18,333,000	20	Moscow	Russia	10,672,000
6	Delhi	India	15,334,000	21	Paris	France	9,854,000
7	Calcutta	India	14,299,000	22	Istanbul	Turkey	9,760,000
8	Buenos Aires	Argentina	13,349,000	23	Seoul	Korea	9,592,000
9	Jakarta	Indonesia	13,194,000	24	Tianjin	China	9,346,000
10	Shanghai	China	12,665,000	25	Chicago	US	8,711,000
11	Dhaka	Bangladesh	12,560,000	26	Lima	Peru	8,180,000
12	Los Angeles-Long Beach-Santa Ana	US	12,146,000	27	London	UK	7,615,000
				28	Bogotá	Colombia	7,594,000
13	Karachi	Pakistan	11,819,000	29	Tehran	Iran	7,352,000
14	Rio de Janeiro	Brazil	11,469,000	30	Hong Kong	China	7,182,000

Migration of Foreigners into Selected Countries

Percentages of foreign or foreign-born populations in selected OECD countries. Source: <www.oecd.org>.

COUNTRY	FOREIGNERS AS % OF TOTAL POPULATION 1995[1]	2003[2]	COUNTRY	FOREIGNERS AS % OF TOTAL POPULATION 1995[1]	2003[2]
Luxembourg	33.4	32.6	Ireland	2.7	10.4
Australia	23.0	23.0	Greece	N/A	10.3
Switzerland	18.9	22.4	France	N/A	10.1
New Zealand	N/A	19.5	UK	3.4	8.3
Canada	17.4[3]	19.3	Denmark	4.2	6.8
Austria	9.0	12.5	Spain	1.3	5.3
Germany	8.8	12.5	Italy	1.7	N/A
US	8.8	12.3	Japan	1.1	1.0
Sweden	5.2	12.0	Mexico	0.5	0.5
Belgium	9.0	10.7	South Korea	0.2	0.3

N/A indicates data not available. [1]Indicates foreign except for Australia, Canada and the US, which specify foreign-born. [2]Indicates foreign-born except for Japan and South Korea, which specify foreign. [3]1996.

Persons of Concern Worldwide

The Office of the UN High Commissioner for Refugees (UNHCR) attempts to ease the plight of various "persons of concern," including refugees and asylum seekers. Sources: UNHCR Refugees by Numbers; UNHCR 2004 Global Refugee Trends, Global IDP Project.

Persons of Concern to UNHCR by Category (17 Jun 2005)

REGION	REFUGEES	ASYLUM SEEKERS	RETURNED REFUGEES	INTERNALLY DISPLACED PERSONS[1]	STATELESS AND OTHER	TOTAL
Asia and Pacific	836,725	20,247	10,263	386,104	341,414	1,594,753
Africa	2,748,365	198,848	329,710	1,233,927	34,758	4,548,308
Europe	2,317,817	285,030	18,971	1,767,199	1,152,899	5,541,916
North America	562,252	291,000	—	—	—	853,252
Latin America and Caribbean	36,190	8,109	89	2,000,000	26,350	2,070,738
Total	9,236,521	839,107	1,494,610	5,574,170	2,053,029	19,197,437

Total Number of Refugees (1 Jan of each year)

YEAR	REFUGEES	YEAR	REFUGEES
1996	14,860,600	2001	12,062,500
1997	13,317,400	2002	12,029,900
1998	11,966,200	2003	10,389,600
1999	11,429,700	2004	9,671,800
2000	11,625,700	2005	9,236,500

Origin of Major Refugee Populations[2] (1 Jan 2005)

COUNTRY OF ORIGIN	TOTAL	COUNTRY OF ORIGIN	TOTAL
Afghanistan	2,084,900	Vietnam	349,780
The Sudan	730,600	Iraq	311,800
Burundi	485,800	Azerbaijan	250,579
Dem. Rep. of the Congo	462,200	Serbia and Montenegro	236,999
Somalia	389,300	Bosnia and Herzegovina	229,339
Liberia	353,467	Angola	228,838

Destination of Major Refugee Populations[1] (estimates as of 1 Jan 2004)

COUNTRY OF ASYLUM	TOTAL	COUNTRY OF ASYLUM	TOTAL
Iran	1,045,976	China	299,375
Pakistan	960,617	United Kingdom	289,054
Germany	876,622	Serbia and Montenegro	276,683
Tanzania	602,088	Chad	259,880
United States	420,854	Uganda	250,482

Internally Displaced Persons (IDPs)

COUNTRY	TOTAL NUMBER	RECEIVING UNHCR ASSISTANCE
The Sudan	6,000,000	662,302
Colombia	1,580,396–3,410,041	2,000,000
Angola	40,000–340,000	—
Dem. Rep. of the Congo	2,330,000	—
Iraq	1,000,000+	—
Myanmar (Burma)	526,000	—
Indonesia	342,000–600,000	—
Turkey	350,000–1,000,000+	—
Afghanistan	167,000–200,000	159,549
Uganda	1,400,000	—
Côte d'Ivoire	500,000	38,039
India	600,000+	—
Azerbaijan	578,545	578,545
Sri Lanka	352,374	352,374
Burundi	170,000	—
Russia	339,000	334,796
Bosnia and Herzegovina	309,240	309,240

[1]Data include only those IDPs to whom UNHCR extends protection and/or assistance. [2]A separate mandate of the UN Relief and Works Agency for Palestine Refugees in the Near East (UNWRA) covers more than 4 million Palestinians. Palestinians outside of the UNWRA, such as those in Iraq and Libya, number 427,800.

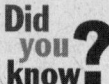

Languages of the World

Most Widely Spoken Languages

Listing the languages spoken by more than 1% of humankind, this table enumerates speakers of each tongue as a primary or secondary language. Figures based on data from Linguasphere 2000. For more information visit <www.linguasphere.org>.

LANGUAGE	NUMBER OF SPEAKERS (MILLIONS)	% OF WORLD POPULATION (APPROXIMATE)	LANGUAGE FAMILY
English	1,000	16	Indo-European (Germanic)
Mandarin	1,000	16	Sino-Tibetan (Chinese)
Hindi/Urdu[1]	900	15	Indo-European (Indo-Aryan)
Spanish	450	7	Indo-European (Romance)
Russian/Belarusian	320	5	Indo-European (Slavic)
Arabic	250	4	Afro-Asiatic (Semitic)
Bengali/Sylhetti	250	4	Indo-European (Indo-Aryan)
Malay/Indonesian	200	3	Austronesian (Malayo-Polynesian)
Portuguese	200	3	Indo-European (Romance)
Japanese	130	2	isolated language
French	125	2	Indo-European (Romance)
German	125	2	Indo-European (Germanic)
Thai/Lao	90	1	Tai
Punjabi	85	1	Indo-European (Indo-Aryan)
Wu	85	1	Sino-Tibetan (Chinese)
Javanese	80	1	Austronesian (Malayo-Polynesian)
Marathi	80	1	Indo-European (Indo-Aryan)
Turkish/Azeri/Turkmen	80	1	Altaic (Turkic)
Korean	75	1	isolated language
Vietnamese	75	1	Mon-Khmer (Vietic)
Cantonese	70	1	Sino-Tibetan (Chinese)
Italian	70	1	Indo-European (Romance)
Tamil	70	1	Dravidian
Telugu	70	1	Dravidian
Ukrainian	65	1	Indo-European (Slavic)
Bhojpuri/Maithili	60	1	Indo-European (Indo-Aryan)
Persian/Tajik	60	1	Indo-European (Iranian)
Swahili	60	1	Afro-Asiatic (Niger-Congo)
Tagalog	60	1	Austronesian (Malayo-Polynesian)

[1]*Although Hindi and Urdu use different writing systems, these languages are branches of Hindustani and are orally mutually intelligible.*

Foreign Words and Phrases

à droite [F] : to or on the right hand
à gauche [F] : to or on the left hand
aloha oe [Hawaiian] : love to you : greetings : farewell
amor patriae [L] : love of one's country
amor vincit omnia [L] : love conquers all things
aqua et igni interdictus [L] : forbidden to be furnished with water and fire : outlawed
ars longa, vita brevis [L] : art is long, life is short
à votre santé [F] : to your health—used as a toast
bella figura [It] : fine appearance or impression
bien entendu [F] : well understood : of course
bon appétit [F] : good appetite : enjoy your meal
bonjour [F] : good day : good morning
bonne foi [F] : good faith
bonsoir [F] : good evening
carte d'identité [F] : identity card
c'est la guerre [F] : that's war : it cannot be helped

c'est la vie [F] : that's life : that's how things happen
chacun à son goût [F] : everyone to his taste
cherchez la femme [F] : look for the woman
che sarà, sarà [It] : what will be, will be
cogito, ergo sum [L] : I think, therefore I exist
comédie humaine [F] : human comedy : the whole variety of human life
comme ci, comme ça [F] : so-so
compte rendu [F] : report (as of proceedings in an investigation)
cum grano salis [L] : with a grain of salt
d'accord [F] : in accord : agreed
de gustibus non est disputandum [L] : there is no disputing about tastes
Dei gratia [L] : by the grace of God
de integro [L] : anew : afresh
Deo gratias [L] : thanks (be) to God

Foreign Words and Phrases (continued)

de profundis [L] : out of the depths

dies irae [L] : day of wrath—used of the Judgment Day

Dieu et mon droit [F] : God and my right—motto on the British royal arms

Dominus vobiscum [L] : the Lord be with you

d'un certain âge [F] : of a certain age : no longer young

en famille [F] : in or with one's family : at home : informally

en garde [F] : on guard

en plein air [F] : in the open air

e pluribus unum [L] : one out of many—used on the Great Seal of the US and on several US coins

Erin go bragh [Ir *go brách* or *go bráth*, lit., till doomsday] : Ireland forever

errare humanum est [L] : to err is human

et tu Brute [L] : thou too, Brutus—exclamation attributed to Julius Caesar on seeing his friend Brutus among his assassins

eureka [Gk] : I have found it—motto of California

excelsior [L] : still higher—motto of New York

ex libris [L] : from the books of—used on bookplates

façon de parler [F] : manner of speaking : figurative or conventional expression

faire suivre [F] : have forwarded : please forward

fils [F] : son—used orig. after French and now also after other family names to distinguish a son from his father

force de frappe [F] : military striking force esp. with nuclear weapons

gardez la foi [F] : keep faith

guten Tag [G] : good day

hasta la vista [Sp] : good-bye

homme d'affaires [F] : man of business : business agent

hors commerce [F] : outside the trade : not offered through regular commercial channels

id est [L] : that is (*i.e.*)

ignorantia juris neminem excusat [L] : ignorance of the law excuses no one

in aeternum [L] : forever

inshallah [Ar] : if Allah wills : God willing

in vino veritas [L] : there is truth in wine

j'accuse [F] : I accuse : bitter denunciation

januis clausis [L] : behind closed doors

le roi est mort, vive le roi [F] : the king is dead, long live the king

l'état, c'est moi [F] : the state, it is I

mal vu [F] : badly regarded : disapproved of

mano a mano [Sp] : hand to hand : in direct competition or confrontation

mens sana in corpore sano [L] : a sound mind in a sound body

nolens volens [L] : unwilling (or) willing : willy-nilly

nuit blanche [F] : white night : a sleepless night

nyet [Russ] : no

omertà [It] : submission : code chiefly among members of the criminal underworld that enjoins private vengeance and the refusal to give information to outsiders (as the police)

ora pro nobis [L] : pray for us

outre-mer [F] : overseas : distant lands

par avion [F] : by airplane—used on airmail

pax vobiscum [L] : peace (be) with you

père [F] : father—used orig. after French and now also after other family names to distinguish a father from his son

pour rire [F] : for laughing : not to be taken seriously

pro bono publico [L] : for the public good

pro hac vice [L] : for this occasion

pro patria [L] : for one's country

quis custodiet ipsos custodes? [L] : who will keep the keepers themselves?

qui s'excuse s'accuse [F] : he who excuses himself accuses himself

quod vide [L] : which see (*q.v.*)

raison d'état [F] : reason of state

répondez s'il vous plaît [F] : reply, if you please (*RSVP*)

requiescat in pace [L] : may he or she rest in peace—used on tombstones (*RIP*)

sans souci [F] : without worry

sayonara [Jp] : good-bye

semper fidelis [L] : always faithful—motto of the US Marine Corps

s'il vous plaît [F] : if you please

tout à fait [F] : altogether : quite

tout de suite [F] : immediately *also* : all at once : consecutively

tout le monde [F] : all the world : everybody

tristesse [F] : melancholy

über alles [G] : above everything else

uebermensch [G] : superman

und so weiter [G] : and so on

urbi et orbi [L] : to the city (Rome) and the world : to everyone

veni, vidi, vici [L] : I came, I saw, I conquered

voilà tout [F] : that's all

wie geht's? [G] : how goes it?

English Neologisms

New entries from Merriam-Webster's Collegiate® Dictionary, Eleventh Edition (© 2005)

amuse-bouche (1984): a small complimentary appetizer offered at some restaurants

battle dress uniform (1982): a military uniform for field service

bikini wax (1985): a procedure for removing pubic hair from the skin near the edge of the bottom half of a bikini by applying hot wax, covering the wax with a cloth to which the wax and hair adhere, and then peeling it off quickly

brain freeze (1991): a sudden shooting pain in the head caused by ingesting very cold food (as ice cream) or drink

chick flick (1988): a motion picture intended to appeal especially to women

civil union (1992): the legal status that ensures to same-sex couples specified rights and responsibilities of married couples

cybrarian (1992): a person whose job is to find, collect, and manage information that is available on the World Wide Web

DHS (abbr): Department of Homeland Security

hazmat (1980): a material (as flammable or poisonous material) that would be a danger to life or to the environment if released without precautions

hospitalist (1996): a physician who specializes in treating hospitalized patients of other physicians in order to minimize the number of hospital visits by other physicians

metadata (1983): data that provides information about other data

English Neologisms (continued)

otology (1842): a science that deals with the ear and its diseases

retronym (1980): a term consisting of a noun and a modifier which specifies the original meaning of the noun ["film camera" is a *retronym*]

SARS (*severe acute respiratory syndrome*; 2003): a severe respiratory illness that is caused by a coronavirus (genus *Coronavirus*), is transmitted especially by contact with infectious material (as respiratory

droplets), and is marked by fever, headache, body aches, a dry cough, hypoxia, and usually pneumonia

steganography (1985): 1 *archaic*: cryptography 2: the art or practice of concealing a message, image, or file within another message, image, or file

Wi-Fi *certification mark*—used to certify the interoperability of wireless computer networking devices

zaibatsu (1947): a powerful financial and industrial conglomerate of Japan

Scholarship

National and Public Libraries of the World

The national and public libraries listed below are generally open to the public. National libraries are usually the primary repository for a nation's printed works. Sources: "National Libraries of the World: An Address List," IFLA Publications. *International Dictionary of Library Histories*, 2001, Fitzroy Dearborn Publishers. *The Bowker Annual Library and Book Trade Almanac 2004*, R.R. Bowker.

LIBRARY	LOCATION	YEAR FOUNDED	NUMBER OF VOLUMES (MILLIONS)	SPECIAL COLLECTIONS, ARCHIVES, PAPERS
national libraries				
Biblioteca Nacional Venezuela	Caracas	1833	1.2	politics and diplomacy, Simón Bolívar
Biblioteca Nazionale Centrale	Florence, Italy	1861	5.4	Reformation, Galileo Galilei
Biblioteca Nazionale Centrale di Roma	Rome, Italy	1876	6.0	Jesuit collections, Gabriele D'Annunzio
Bibliothèque Nationale de France	Paris	1461	14.0	Denis Diderot, Jean-Paul Sartre
National Library of Canada	Ottawa	1953	0.6	artists' books, musical scores
British Library[1]	London	1973	16.0	Charles Dickens, George B. Shaw
Deutsche Bibliothek	Frankfurt am Main, Germany	1947	6.3	bibliographies, exile literature (1933–45)
Deutsche Bücherei	Leipzig, Germany	1913	9.2	socialism, Anne-Frank-Shoah-Bibliothek
Jewish National and University Library[2]	Jerusalem	1892	5.0	world Jewish history, Albert Einstein
Library of Congress	Washington DC	1800	29.0	Americana, Irving Berlin, Walt Whitman
National Diet Library[3]	Tokyo, Japan	1948	7.9	Japanese culture, Allied occupation
National Library of China[4]	Beijing	1909	20.0	art, early communism
National Library of India	Calcutta	1903	2.3	rare journals of vernacular languages
National Library of Mexico	Mexico City	1867	1.2	Jesuit works, Mexican printing
National Library of Russia	St. Petersburg	1795	14.0	rare books, Russian history
public libraries				
Biblioteca Luis Ángel Arango	Bogotá, Colombia	1939	1.0	Spanish New World chroniclers
Bibliothèque Mazarine Institut de France	Paris	1643	0.6	French theology, Jansenist materials
Bibliothèque Municipale de Lyon	Lyon, France	1765	2.4	history of the book, occult studies
Bibliothèque Publique et Universitaire de Genéve	Switzerland	1562	2.0	Reformation, John Calvin, Voltaire
Birmingham Central Library	England	1865	0.7	Industrial Revolution, Shakespeare
Boston Public Library	Massachusetts	1848	8.0	music, fine arts, Emily Dickinson
Chetham's Library	Manchester, UK	1653	0.1	religious history, Robert Southey
Chicago Public Library	Illinois	1873	5.8	African American studies, blues music
Enoch Pratt Free Library	Baltimore MD	1886	2.4	H.L. Mencken, Edgar Allan Poe
Free Library of Philadelphia	Pennsylvania	1891	3.0	Oliver Goldsmith, Edgar Allan Poe
Los Angeles Public Library	California	1872	6.1	Calif. cookbooks, fairy tales, Mexicana
Manchester Central Library	UK	1852	2.1	music, commerce, Samuel T. Coleridge
Mitchell Library	Glasgow, Scotland	1877	1.2	angling, architecture, Robert Burns
New York Public Library	New York	1895	14	gay and lesbian works, theater and music
Öffentliche Bibliothek der Universität Basel	Switzerland	1470	3.1	Swiss Medical Academy, Friedrich Nietzsche

National and Public Libraries of the World (continued)

LIBRARY	LOCATION	YEAR FOUNDED	NUMBER OF VOLUMES (MILLIONS)	SPECIAL COLLECTIONS, ARCHIVES, PAPERS
public libraries (continued)				
Shanghai Library[6]	China	1952	18.7	chronicles, genealogies
Toronto Public Library[6]	Ontario, Canada	1884	1.4	science fiction, Arthur Conan Doyle

[1]Originally founded in 1753 as the British Museum Library.   [2]Bet Ha-Sefarim Ha-Leummi Weha-Universitai Giv'at Ram.   [3]Kokuritsu Kokkai Toshokan.   [4]Zhongguo Guojia Tushuguan.   [5]Shanghai Tushuguan.   [6]Metropolitan Toronto Library Board Reference Library.

World Education Profile

This table provides comparative data about the education systems in 30 selected countries. Definitions as well as information gathering and reporting methods vary widely from country to country, so the statistics presented here are not always exactly comparable.

Compulsory education = the number of years of education and ages of pupils required by the system; **net enrollment ratio** = the actual number of children attending primary school or secondary school as a percentage of all children in the primary school or secondary school age group as defined by the country (number may exceed 100%); **gross enrollment ratio** for higher education = total enrollment in higher education, regardless of age, as a percentage of all persons of school-leaving age to five years thereafter; **student/teacher ratio** = number of pupils or students per teacher at each level; **expenditure** = total public expenditure on education as a percentage of GDP.

Sources: Britannica World Data, 2004; UNESCO Statistical Yearbook, 2004.

COUNTRY	YEAR	% LITERACY RATE OF THOSE 15 AND OLDER			COMPULSORY EDUCATION		ENROLLMENT RATIO (2001–02)			STUDENT/TEACHER RATIO (2001–02)			EXPEN-DITURE
		TOTAL	M	F	# YEARS	AGES	NET PRI.	NET SEC.	GROSS HIGHER	PRI.	SEC.	HIGHER[1]	
Africa													
Egypt	2000	55.3	66.6	43.8	8	6-13	90	81	—	22	17	—	—
Kenya	1999	81.5	88.3	74.8	8	6-13	70	24	3	32	—	—	6.2
Senegal	2000	37.3	47.3	27.6	6	7-12	58	—	—	49	27	25.0[2]	3.2
South Africa	2000	85.3	86.0	84.6	9	7-15	90	62[4]	15	37	30	22.8[3]	—
Asia													
China	2000	90.9	95.1	86.5	9	6-14	93[4]	—	13[4]	20[4]	—	7.8	—
India	2000	57.2	68.4	45.4	9	6-14	83[4]	—	11[4]	40[4]	—	17.5	4.1
Indonesia	2000	86.9	91.8	82.0	9	7-15	92	—	15	21	14	15.0	1.3
Iran	2000	76.3	83.2	69.3	5	6-10	87	—	20	24	29	14.3	5.0
Israel	2000	96.7	—	—	11	5-15	100	89	58	12	8	19.0	7.3
Japan	2002	100.0	100.0	100.0	10	6-15	100	100	49	20	14	18.9	3.6
Philippines	2000	95.3	95.1	95.5	7	6-12	93	56	31	35	38	—	3.2
Saudi Arabia	2000	80.1[5]	84.1	67.2	6	6-11	59	53	22	12	13	18.4	—
Thailand	2000	95.5	—	—	9	6-14	86	—	37	19	—	19.1	5.0
Turkey	2000	85.1	93.5	76.5	9	6-14	88	—	25	—	—	22.7	3.7
Europe													
France	1995	98.8	98.9	98.7	11	6-16	100[4]	92[4]	54[4]	19[4]	—	39.6	5.8
Germany	1998	100.0	100.0	100.0	13	6-18	83	88	48	14	14	11.2	4.6
Greece	2000	97.2	98.6	96.0	10	6-15	95[4]	85[4]	61[4]	13[4]	—	22.6	3.8
Italy	2000	98.4	98.9	98.1	9	6-14	100[4]	—	50[4]	11[4]	—	32.0	4.7
Poland	2000	99.8	99.8	99.8	9	7-15	98	91	58	15	17	14.9	5.4
Russia	1999	99.4	—	—	10	6-15	—	—	70	17	—	12.7	3.1
Sweden	2000	100.0	100.0	100.0	10	7-16	100	99	76	11	13	8.2[1]	7.7
United Kingdom	1997	100.0[6]	100.0	100.0	12	5-16	100[4]	95[4]	59[4]	18[4]	—	20.4	—
Latin America													
Argentina	1999	96.7	96.8	96.7	10	5-14	100	81	56	20	12	—	4.6
Brazil	2000	86.7	85.5	85.3	8	7-14	97	72	18	23	19	11.2	4.0
Cuba	2000	96.4	96.9	96.8	9	6-14	96	83	27	14	12	5.3[6]	9.0
Mexico	2000	91.4	93.4	89.5	10	6-15	99	60	21	27	17	9.4	5.1
Peru	2000	89.9	94.7	85.3	11	6-16	100	66[4]	32	29	—	14.2	—
North America													
Canada	2002	100.0	—	—	11	6-16	100[4]	98[4]	59[4]	17[4]	—	14.4	5.2
United States	1998	95.5	95.7	95.3	12	6-17	93	85	81	15[4]	—	15.3	5.6
Oceania													
Australia	1998	99.5	—	—	10	6-15	96	88	65	—	—	20.6	4.6

[1]Latest data.   [2]Universities only.   [3]1994 data.   [4]2000–01.   [5]10 and over; non-Saudi population literate: 87.9%.   [6]Total population.

Selected World Universities and Colleges

Universities and colleges are selected based on enrollment, age of the institution, and prominence. Enrollment represents the latest available figures for all affiliated campuses and colleges and for all students, including correspondence and part-time students. Locations are included when the place is not mentioned in the name of the institution. Source: *The World of Learning 2005*. **Web site:** <www.unesco.org/iau>.

COUNTRY	INSTITUTION (LOCATION)	FOUNDING YEAR	ENROLLMENT
Afghanistan	Kabul University	1932	13,000
Albania	University of Tiranë	1957	8,755
Algeria	University of Algiers	1879	32,000
	Mentouri University (Constantine)	1969	27,995
Angola	Agostinho Neto University (Luanda)	1963	6,800
Argentina	University of Buenos Aires	1821	183,397
	National University of Córdoba	1613	114,918
	National Technical University (Buenos Aires)	1959	70,087
	National University of Rosario	1968	54,319
	National University of La Plata	1905	50,000
	National University of Tucumán (San Miguel de Tucumán)	1914	42,946
	National University of the Northeast (Corrientes)	1957	28,459
Armenia	Yerevan State University	1919	9,000
Aruba	University of Aruba (Oranjestad)	1988	300
Australia	Royal Melbourne Institute of Technology	1887	55,515
	Monash University (Clayton, VIC)	1958	48,246
	University of Sydney	1850	39,982
	Swinburne University of Technology (Hawthorn, VIC)	1908	38,000
	Queensland University of Technology (Brisbane)	1965	34,000
	University of Melbourne	1853	39,873
	Charles Sturt University (Bathurst, NSW)	1989	32,618
	University of Western Sydney (Penrith, NSW)	1989	32,000
	University of Queensland (Brisbane)	1910	33,345
	University of South Australia (Adelaide)	1991	27,263
Austria	Vienna University	1365	63,600
	Innsbruck University	1669	27,000
	Graz University	1585	24,059
Azerbaijan	Baku State University	1919	13,000
The Bahamas	College of the Bahamas (Nassau)	1974	3,463
Bahrain	University of Bahrain (Madinat ʿIsa)	1986	6,760
Bangladesh	University of Dhaka	1921	24,298
	University of Rajshahi	1953	24,032
	University of Chittagong	1966	10,273
Barbados	University of the West Indies at Cave Hill (Bridgetown)	1963	3,777
Belarus	Belarusian State University (Minsk)	1921	16,500
	Yanka Kupala State University of Grodno	1940	12,031
Belgium	Catholic University of Leuven (Louvain [Leuven])	1425	28,057
	Ghent University	1817	26,000
	Catholic University of Louvain (Louvain-la-Neuve)	1425	20,517
Belize	University of Belize (Belize City)	2000	2,300
Benin	University of Abomey-Calavi (Cotonou)	1970	18,533
Bermuda	Bermuda College (Paget)	1974	4,050
Bolivia	University of San Simón (Cochabamba)	1832	40,641
	University of San Andrés (La Paz)	1930	37,109
Bosnia and Herzegovina	University of Sarajevo	1949	40,919
Botswana	University of Botswana (Gaborone)	1976	15,405
Brazil	University of São Paulo	1934	69,123
	University of Brazil (Rio de Janeiro)	1920	40,000
	Federal University of Rio Grande do Sul (Pôrto Alegre)	1934	29,117
Brunei	University of Brunei Darussalam (Gadong)	1985	2,800
Bulgaria	St. Kliment Ohridsky University of Sofia	1888	25,454
Burkina Faso	University of Ouagadougou	1969	12,000
Burundi	University of Burundi (Bujumbura)	1960	2,749
Cambodia	Royal University of Phnom Penh	1960	6,500
Cameroon	University of Yaoundé I	1962	20,343
Cape Verde	Jean Piaget University of Cape Verde	2001	650
Central African Republic	University of Bangui	1969	6,474
Chad	University of N'Djamena	1971	5,600
Chile	University of Chile (Santiago)	1738	24,822
	Catholic University of Chile (Santiago)	1888	18,000
	University of Santiago de Chile	1947	17,691
China	Zhejiang University	1897	88,863

Selected World Universities and Colleges (continued)

COUNTRY	INSTITUTION (LOCATION)	FOUNDING YEAR	ENROLLMENT
China (continued)	Peking University (Beijing)	1898	55,000
	Wuhan University	1893	40,000
	Hunan University (Changsha)	976	34,000
	China University of Mining and Technology (Xuzhou City, Jiangsu)	1909	30,942
	Xian Jiaotong University (Sian [Xian], Shensi)	1896	26,410
	Harbin Engineering University	1953	23,000
	Nankai University (Tientsin)	1919	23,000
	Dalian University of Technology	1949	22,344
	Northeastern University (Shenyang, Liaoning)	1923	20,621
Colombia	National University of Colombia (Bogotá)	1867	28,000
	Xaverian Pontifical University (Bogotá)	1622	29,237
Comoros	University of the Comoros (Moroni)	2004	N/A
Democratic Republic of the Congo	University of Lubumbashi	1955	13,158
Republic of the Congo	Marien-Ngouabi University (Brazzaville)	1961	16,000
Costa Rica	University of Costa Rica (San Pedro de Montes de Oca)	1843	28,986
Côte d'Ivoire	University of Cocody (Abidjan)	1958	45,000
Croatia	University of Zagreb	1669	53,000
Cuba	University of Havana	1728	15,980
Cyprus	Eastern Mediterranean University (Gazi Magusa, Turkish Republic of Northern Cyprus)	1979	10,300
	University of Cyprus (Nicosia, Republic of Cyprus)	1989	2,234
Czech Republic	Charles (Karlova) University (Prague)	1348	42,475
	Czech Technical University in Prague	1707	21,282
	Masaryk University in Brno	1919	24,451
Denmark	University of Copenhagen	1479	35,000
	Aarhus University (Århus)	1928	22,000
	University of Southern Denmark (Odense)	1964	16,500
Djibouti	Pôle University of Djibouti	2000	728
Dominican Republic	Autonomous University of Santo Domingo	1538	26,040
Ecuador	University of Guayaquil	1867	60,000
	Central University of Ecuador (Quito)	1586	31,663
Egypt	Al-Azhar University (Cairo)	970	185,000
	Alexandria University	1942	144,707
	Ain Shams University (Cairo)	1950	163,326
	Zagazig University	1974	151,091
	Cairo University	1908	202,167
	Helwan University	1975	95,567
El Salvador	University of El Salvador (San Salvador)	1841	28,306
Eritrea	University of Asmara	1958	4,086
Estonia	University of Tartu	1632	17,653
Ethiopia	Addis Ababa University	1950	19,258
Faroe Islands	University of the Faroe Islands (Tórshavn)	1965	150
Fiji	University of the South Pacific (Suva)	1968	10,000
Finland	University of Helsinki	1640	34,843
	University of Turku	1920	18,150
France	University of Paris		
	I Panthéon-Sorbonne	1971	43,256
	IV Paris-Sorbonne	1970	30,898
	V René Descartes	1970	29,300
	VI Pierre and Marie Curie	1971	c. 30,000
	VII Denis Diderot	1970	26,000
	X Paris-Nanterre	1964	34,000
	XI Paris-Sud	1970	28,000
	University of Toulouse I, II, and III	1229	73,531
	University of Lille I, II, and III	1560	64,058
	University of Strasbourg I, II, and III	1538	40,042
	University of Nancy I and II	1572	38,764
	University of Nantes	1962	33,278
	University of Rouen (Mont-Saint-Aignan)	1966	30,000
	University of Burgundy (Dijon)	1722	24,879
	University of Caen	1432	26,667
	University of Grenoble I	1339	17,273
French Polynesia	University of French Polynesia (Tahiti)	1999	2,500
Gabon	Omar Bongo University (Libreville)	1970	2,400
The Gambia	University of The Gambia (Serrekunda)	1999	1,356

Selected World Universities and Colleges (continued)

COUNTRY	INSTITUTION (LOCATION)	FOUNDING YEAR	ENROLLMENT
Georgia	Georgian Technical University (Tbilisi)	1922	16,000
	Javakhishvili State University (Tbilisi)	1918	16,000
Germany	University of Cologne	1388	64,000
	Westphalian Wilhelm University of Münster	1780	44,688
	Free University of Berlin	1948	43,000
	Ludwig Maximilian University of Munich	1472	45,500
	University of Hamburg	1613	40,996
	Rhenish Friedrich Wilhelm University of Bonn	1786	30,000
	Johann Wolfgang Goethe University of Frankfurt (Frankfurt am Main)	1914	36,679
	Ruhr University (Bochum)	1961	35,126
	Humboldt University of Berlin	1810	33,740
	University of Hannover	1831	31,880
	Technical University of Berlin	1799	31,700
	Johannes Gutenberg University of Mainz	1477	30,000
	Rhenish-Westphalian Technical University (Aachen)	1870	30,000
	University of Leipzig	1409	28,000
	Ruprecht Karl University of Heidelberg	1386	24,290
	Georg August University of Göttingen	1737	23,000
	Eberhard-Karls University of Tübingen	1477	20,350
	Friedrich Alexander University of Erlangen-Nuremberg (Erlangen)	1743	19,623
	Martin Luther University of Halle-Wittenberg	1502	13,841
Ghana	Kwame Nkrumah University of Science and Technology (Kumasi)	1951	11,633
	University of Ghana (Accra)	1948	8,822
Greece	Aristotle University of Thessaloniki	1925	75,000
	National and Capodistrian University of Athens	1837	45,000
Greenland	University of Greenland (Nuuk)	1984	100
Grenada	St. George's University	1977	2,000
Guatemala	San Carlos University of Guatemala (Guatemala City)	1676	71,199
Guinea	Gamal Abdel Nasser University of Conakry	1962	5,000
Guyana	University of Guyana (Georgetown)	1963	5,330
Haiti	State University of Haiti (Port-au-Prince)	1920	10,446
Honduras	National Autonomous University of Honduras (Tegucigalpa)	1847	33,000
Hong Kong	Hong Kong Polytechnic University (Kowloon)	1937	23,218
Hungary	University of Pécs	1367	31,858
	Loránd Eötvös University (Budapest)	1635	24,427
	University of Debrecen	1538	25,888
Iceland	University of Iceland (Reykjavík)	1911	6,700
India	University of Kolkata (Calcutta [Kolkata])	1857	300,000
	University of Mumbai (Bombay [Mumbai])	1857	262,350
	Chhatrapati Shahuji Maharaj University (Kanpur)	1966	220,000
	Utkal University (Bhubaneswar)	1943	200,000
	University of Rajasthan (Gandhi Nagar)	1947	175,000
	Magadh University (Bodh Gaya)	1962	170,500
	Gujarat University (Ahmedabad)	1949	153,379
	Shivaji University (Kolhapur)	1962	149,427
	Bangalore University	1964	142,697
	Madurai-Kamaraj University (Madurai)	1966	133,100
	Meerut University	1966	125,365
	Mahatma Gandhi University (Kottayam)	1983	125,000
	University of Kerala (Thiruvananthapuram)	1937	123,310
	Deen Dayal Upadhyay Gorakhpur University	1957	115,000
	Lalit Narayan Mithila University (Darbhanga)	1972	110,355
	University of Madras	1857	107,518
	University of Delhi	1922	101,493
	Karnataka University (Dharwad)	1949	100,562
	Hemvati Nandan Bahuguna Garhwal University (Srinagar)	1973	100,000
Indonesia	Padjadjaran University (Bandung)	1957	40,482
	Gadjah Mada University (Yogyakarta)	1949	45,787
	Indonesia University (Jakarta)	1950	35,000
Iran	Islamic Azad University (Tehran)	1982	850,000
	University of Tehran	1934	32,000
Iraq	University of Baghdad	1957	85,000
	Al-Mustansiriya University (Baghdad)	1963	23,748

Selected World Universities and Colleges (continued)

COUNTRY	INSTITUTION (LOCATION)	FOUNDING YEAR	ENROLLMENT
Ireland	Unviersity College Dublin	1908	18,357
	University of Dublin Trinity College	1592	15,511
Israel	Tel Aviv University (Tel Aviv–Yafo)	1953	26,000
	Hebrew University of Jerusalem	1918	23,730
	Bar-Ilan University (Ramat-Gan)	1953	20,000
Italy	University of Rome "La Sapienza"	1303	189,000
	University of Bologna	1088	101,000
	University of Naples "Frederick II"	1224	83,975
	University of Padua	1222	65,579
	University of Turin	1404	65,000
	University of Milan	1923	60,158
	University of Florence	1321	59,847
	University of Catania	1434	53,674
	University of Pisa	1343	47,000
	University of Bari	1924	42,439
	Polytechnic of Milan	1863	42,402
	University of Messina	1548	42,300
	University of Genoa	1670	40,125
	Catholic University of the Sacred Heart (Milan)	1920	40,586
Jamaica	University of the West Indies at Mona (Kingston)	1948	9,073
Japan	Nihon University (Tokyo)	1889	82,677
	Waseda University (Tokyo)	1882	51,499
	Keio University (Tokyo)	1858	44,930
	Meiji University (Tokyo)	1880	35,000
	Ritsumeikan University (Kyoto)	1900	34,101
	Chuo University (Tokyo)	1885	29,573
	University of Tokyo	1877	28,350
	Doshisha University (Kyoto)	1875	24,166
	Kyoto University	1897	22,233
	Tohoku University (Sendai)	1907	17,247
Jordan	University of Jordan (Amman)	1962	23,623
Kazakhstan	Karaganda State University	1972	15,294
	Al-Farabi Kazakh National University (Almaty)	1934	14,500
Kenya	University of Nairobi	1956	22,000
North Korea	Kim Il-Sung University (Pyongyang)	1946	12,000
South Korea	Yonsei University (Seoul)	1885	52,410
	Seoul National University	1946	32,115
	Chosun University (Kwangju)	1946	26,164
	Pusan National University	1946	24,670
	Korea University (Seoul)	1905	21,685
	Pohang University of Science and Technology	1986	2,736
Kuwait	Kuwait University (Safat)	1962	18,168
Kyrgyzstan	Osh State University	1951	26,000
	Kyrgyz State National University (Frunze)	1932	22,000
Laos	National University of Laos (Vientiane)	1995	15,791
Latvia	University of Latvia (Riga)	1919	28,115
Lebanon	Lebanese University (Beirut)	1951	69,627
Lesotho	National University of Lesotho (Roma)	1945	1,800
Liberia	University of Liberia (Monrovia)	1862	5,056
Libya	Al-Fateh University (Tripoli)	1957	75,000
Lithuania	Vilnius University	1579	21,284
Luxembourg	University Center of Luxembourg	1969	1,600
Macau	University of Macau	1981	5,020
Macedonia	University of Skopje	1949	25,967
Madagascar	University of Antananarivo	1961	14,069
Malawi	University of Malawi (Zomba)	1964	4,000
Malaysia	Putra University (Serdang)	1971	33,566
	Malaysia University of Technology (Skudai)	1904	31,529
	University of Malaya (Kuala Lumpur)	1962	24,345
Malta	University of Malta (Msida)	1592	9,476
Mauritania	University of Nouakchott	1981	9,839
Mauritius	University of Mauritius (Réduit)	1965	5,760
Mexico	National Autonomous University of Mexico (Mexico City)	1551	269,000
	University of Guadalajara	1792	180,776
	National Polytechnic Institute (Mexico City)	1936	107,200
	Autonomous University of Nuevo León (San Nicolás de los Garza)	1933	104,300

Selected World Universities and Colleges (continued)

COUNTRY	INSTITUTION (LOCATION)	FOUNDING YEAR	ENROLLMENT
Mexico (continued)	Autonomous University of Guerrero (Chilpancingo)	1869	49,000
	Autonomous Metropolitan University (Mexico City)	1973	45,000
	University of Veracruz (Jalapa)	1944	44,903
	Benemérita Autonomous University of Puebla	1937	42,055
Moldova	Moldova State University (Chisinau)	1946	10,000
Mongolia	Mongolian University of Science and Technology (Ulaanbaatar)	1969	17,000
	National University of Mongolia (Ulaanbaatar)	1942	6,500
Morocco	Cadi Ayyad University (Marrakech)	1978	36,522
	Hassan II Aïn Chock University (Casablanca)	1975	33,213
	Mohammed V University—Agdal (Rabat)	1957	24,996
Mozambique	Eduardo Mondlane University (Maputo)	1962	7,000
Myanmar (Burma)	University of Yangon	1920	47,131
	University of Mandalay	1925	21,045
Namibia	University of Namibia (Windhoek)	1992	8,532
Nepal	Tribhuvan University (Kathmandu)	1959	166,058
The Netherlands	Utrecht University	1636	25,125
	University of Amsterdam	1632	24,000
	University of Groningen	1614	19,000
	Leiden University	1575	15,262
Netherlands Antilles	University of The Netherlands Antilles (Willemstad, Curaçao)	1970	600
New Caledonia	University of New Caledonia (Nouméa)	1999	2,200
New Zealand	University of Auckland	1882	33,000
	Massey University (Palmerston North)	1926	39,745
	Auckland University of Technology	1895	23,288
Nicaragua	National Autonomous University of Nicaragua (Managua)	1812	22,000
Niger	Abdou Moumouni University (Niamey)	1971	6,585
Nigeria	Lagos State University (Apapa)	1983	36,683
	University of Lagos	1962	35,083
	Ahmadu Bello University (Zaria)	1962	29,832
Norway	University of Oslo	1811	32,000
Oman	Sultan Qaboos University (Al-Khod)	1985	7,500
Pakistan	University of Peshawar	1950	17,000
	University of Sindh (Jamshoro)	1947	12,800
	University of Karachi	1951	12,500
Panama	University of Panamá (Panama City)	1935	65,225
Papua New Guinea	University of Papua New Guinea (Waigani)	1965	4,416
Paraguay	National University of Asunción	1889	19,898
Peru	National University of San Marcos (Lima)	1551	34,223
	Federico Villarreal National University (Lima)	1960	25,000
Philippines	University of the Philippines (Quezon City)	1908	48,090
	Polytechnic University of the Philippines (Manila)	1904	42,988
	University of Santo Tomás (Manila)	1611	32,061
Poland	University of Warsaw	1816	55,790
	Adam Mickiewicz University in Poznan	1919	51,677
	University of Silesia (Katowice)	1968	45,716
	University of Lodz	1945	42,027
	Jagiellonian University (Krakow)	1364	35,977
	University of Wroclaw	1702	42,868
Portugal	University of Porto	1911	27,050
	University of Coimbra	1290	21,165
	University of Lisbon	1288	19,917
Qatar	University of Qatar (Doha)	1973	8,235
Réunion	University of Réunion (Saint-Denis)	1970	11,196
Romania	Alexandru Ioan Cuza University (Iasi)	1860	40,000
	University of Oradea	1990	33,000
	University of Bucharest	1864	24,650
	Polytechnic University of Bucharest	1818	22,000
Russia	Moscow M.V. Lomonosov State University	1755	40,000
	Udmurt State University (Izhevsk)	1931	28,157
	St. Petersburg State University	1724	25,423
	Nizhny Novgorod N.I. Lobachevsky State University	1916	25,000
	Kuban State University (Krasnodar)	1924	23,000
	Mordovian N.P. Ogarev State University (Saransk)	1931	18,500
	Voronezh State University	1918	18,500
	Novgorod State University	1993	19,000
	Far Eastern State University (Vladivostok)	1899	16,000

Selected World Universities and Colleges (continued)

COUNTRY	INSTITUTION (LOCATION)	FOUNDING YEAR	ENROLLMENT
Russia (continued)	St. Petersburg State Technical University	1899	16,000
	People's Friendship University of Russia (Moscow)	1960	10,000
Rwanda	National University of Rwanda (Butare)	1963	7,240
Samoa	National University of Samoa (Apia)	1984	1,400
Saudi Arabia	Islamic University of Imam Muhammad ibn Saud (Riyadh)	1953	39,938
	King Saud University (Riyadh)	1957	37,324
Senegal	Cheikh Anta Diop University of Dakar	1949	20,000
Serbia and Montenegro	University of Belgrade	1863	92,652
	University of Novi Sad	1960	30,000
Sierra Leone	University of Sierra Leone (Freetown)	1967	4,310
Singapore	National University of Singapore	1980	30,698
Slovakia	Comenius University in Bratislava	1465	27,000
Slovenia	University of Ljubljana	1595	50,000
Solomon Islands	Solomon Islands College of Higher Education (Honiara)	1984	1,200
Somalia	Somali National University (Mogadishu)	1954	4,640
South Africa	University of South Africa (Unisa)	1873	200,000
	Rand Afrikaans University (Johannesburg)	1966	30,099
	University of Pretoria	1908	39,000
Spain	Complutensian University of Madrid	1508	98,142
	University of Seville	1505	75,000
	University of the Basque Country (Bilbao)	1968	50,222
	University of Barcelona	1450	76,000
	University of Granada	1526	85,124
	University of Valencia	1502	49,858
	University of Valladolid	13th c.	33,100
	University of Oviedo	1608	41,070
	University of Zaragoza	1542	38,071
	University of Santiago de Compostela	1495	35,000
Sri Lanka	University of Peradeniya	1942	9,500
	University of Sri Jayewardenepura (Gangodawila)	1959	8,400
	University of Colombo	1921	7,623
The Sudan	University of Khartoum	1956	14,000
Suriname	Anton de Kom University of Suriname (Paramaribo)	1968	3,400
Swaziland	University of Swaziland (Kwaluseni)	1964	4,198
Sweden	Göteborg University	1891	50,000
	Uppsala University	1477	36,000
	Lund University	1666	35,000
	Stockholm University	1877	32,000
Switzerland	University of Zürich	1833	22,362
	University of Geneva	1559	14,620
	University of Lausanne	1537	10,000
	University of Basel	1460	7,612
Syria	University of Damascus	1903	85,512
	University of Aleppo	1960	53,465
Taiwan	Tamkang University (Taipei)	1950	26,600
	National Taiwan University (Taipei)	1928	26,212
Tajikistan	Tajik State National University (Dushanbe)	1948	13,060
Tanzania	University of Dar es Salaam	1961	8,653
Thailand	Ramkhamhaeng University (Bangkok)	1971	340,231
	Kasetsart University (Bangkok)	1943	32,563
	Chiang Mai University	1964	24,053
Togo	University of Lomé	1965	14,168
Trinidad and Tobago	University of the West Indies (St. Augustine)	1948	6,641
Tunisia	University of Tunis I and II	1988	55,291
Turkey	Istanbul University	1453	49,000
	Gazi University (Ankara)	1982	61,447
	Selcuk University (Konya)	1975	60,000
	Ankara University	1946	42,438
	Hacettepe University (Ankara)	1206	24,415
Turkmenistan	Turkmen State University (Ashgabat)	1950	11,000
Uganda	Makerere University (Kampala)	1922	27,976
Ukraine	Ivan Franko National University of Lviv	1661	22,000
	Odessa I.I. Mechnikov National University	1865	18,200
	Taras Shevchenko University of Kiev	1834	18,000
United Arab Emirates	United Arab Emirates University (al-'Ayn)	1976	17,000
United Kingdom	University of London (England)	1836	116,288
	University of Wales (Cardiff)	1893	47,934

Selected World Universities and Colleges (continued)

COUNTRY	INSTITUTION (LOCATION)	FOUNDING YEAR	ENROLLMENT
United Kingdom	Manchester Metropolitan University (England)	1970	32,085
(continued)	University of Leeds (England)	1874	30,901
	De Montfort University (Leicester, England)	1969	27,500
	University of Nottingham (England)	1881	26,500
	Thames Valley University (London)	1991	25,741
	Sheffield Hallam University (England)	1969	24,396
	University of Plymouth (England)	1970	24,000
	Nottingham Trent University (England)	1970	24,376
	Queen's University Belfast (Northern Ireland)	1845	23,000
	Middlesex University (London, England)	1973	25,563
	University of Ulster (Coleraine, Northern Ireland)	1984	22,586
	University of Westminster (London, England)	1838	22,749
	University of Sheffield (England)	1897	23,273
	University of Edinburgh (Scotland)	1583	22,363
	University of Central England in Birmingham	1971	20,650
	University of Glasgow (Scotland)	1451	19,734
	University of Manchester (England)	1851	19,508
	University of Oxford (England)	12th c.	17,097
	University of Cambridge (England)	c. 1209	15,821
Uruguay	University of the Republic (Montevideo)	1849	59,436
Uzbekistan	Uzbeck National University (Tashkent)	1920	19,300
Vatican City	Pontifical Lateran University	1773	4,000
	Pontifical Gregorian University	1553	3,569
Venezuela	University of Zulia (Maracaibo)	1891	47,590
	Central University of Venezuela (Caracas)	1721	45,000
	University of Carabobo (Valencia)	1852	44,654
	University of the Andes (Mérida)	1785	34,294
	University of the East (Cumaná)	1958	23,084
Vietnam	University of Hue	1957	48,000
	Hanoi University of Technology	1956	31,000
	Vietnam National University (Hanoi)	1993	22,761
West Bank	Birzeit University	1924	6,317
Yemen	University of Aden	1975	22,538
Zambia	University of Zambia (Lusaka)	1965	3,464
Zimbabwe	University of Zimbabwe (Harare)	1955	8,784

Selected North American Universities and Colleges

Universities and colleges are selected based on enrollment, age of the institution, and prominence. Enrollment represents the latest available figures for all students, including correspondence and part-time students. Locations are included when the place is not mentioned in the name of the institution. Source: *The World of Learning 2005*. Web site: <www.unesco.org/iau>.

COUNTRY	STATE/PROVINCE	INSTITUTION (LOCATION)	FOUNDING YEAR	ENROLLMENT
United States	Alabama	University of Alabama		
		Tuscaloosa	1831	19,171
		Birmingham	1969	16,516
		Huntsville	1950	7,051
		Auburn University	1856	23,152
		Jacksonville State University	1883	8,478
		Alabama State University (Montgomery)	1867	5,608
		Troy State University	1887	5,100
		Tuskegee University	1881	3,000
	Alaska	University of Alaska		
		Anchorage	1954	17,512
		Fairbanks	1917	10,487
		Southeast (Juneau)	1972	2,700
	Arizona	Arizona State University (Tempe)	1885	43,000
		University of Arizona (Tucson)	1885	35,747
		Northern Arizona University (Flagstaff)	1899	19,907

Selected North American Universities and Colleges (continued)

COUNTRY	STATE/PROVINCE	INSTITUTION (LOCATION)	FOUNDING YEAR	ENROLLMENT
United States (continued)	Arkansas	University of Arkansas		
		Fayetteville	1871	16,499
		Little Rock	1927	10,889
		Pine Bluff	1873	3,710
		Arkansas State University (Jonesboro)	1909	16,653
		Arkansas Tech University (Russellville)	1909	5,855
		Harding University (Searcy)	1924	5,013
		Henderson State University (Arkadelphia)	1890	3,636
	California	California State University		
		Fullerton	1957	32,143
		Long Beach	1949	32,126
		Northridge	1958	29,066
		Sacramento	1947	28,558
		Fresno	1911	20,013
		Los Angeles	1947	18,000
		San Bernardino	1960	16,341
		Chico	1887	15,500
		Hayward	1957	13,240
		Dominguez Hills (Carson)	1960	10,400
		Stanislaus (Turlock)	1957	8,000
		Bakersfield	1965	6,210
		University of California		
		Los Angeles	1919	37,494
		Berkeley	1868	32,128
		Davis	1905	28,236
		Irvine	1965	22,000
		Santa Barbara	1909	20,559
		San Diego (La Jolla)	1912	18,324
		Riverside	1954	15,934
		Santa Cruz	1962	13,147
		San Francisco	1873	2,702
		San Diego State University	1897	34,319
		University of Southern California (Los Angeles)	1880	30,000
		San José State University	1857	28,007
		San Francisco State University	1899	26,866
		California Polytechnic State University (San Luis Obispo)	1901	18,453
		California State Polytechnic University (Pomona)	1938	18,424
		Stanford University	1885	14,454
		Loyola Marymount University (Los Angeles)	1911	8,215
		Pepperdine University (Malibu)	1937	8,000
		University of San Francisco	1855	7,662
		Humboldt State University (Arcata)	1913	7,611
		Sonoma State University (Rohnert Park)	1960	8,371
		Santa Clara University	1851	7,368
		University of San Diego	1949	6,880
		Alliant International University (San Diego)	2001	6,323
		Azusa Pacific University	1899	4,547
		University of the Pacific (Stockton)	1851	5,697
		St. Mary's College of California (Moraga)	1863	4,378
		Biola University (La Mirada)	1908	3,447
		University of La Verne	1891	3,004
	Colorado	University of Colorado		
		Boulder	1861	26,035
		Denver	1912	11,281
		Colorado Springs	1965	7,400
		Colorado State University		
		Fort Collins	1870	23,934
		Pueblo	1933	4,457
		University of Northern Colorado (Greeley)	1889	13,204
		University of Denver	1864	9,271
		US Air Force Academy (Colorado Springs)	1954	4,330
		Colorado School of Mines (Golden)	1874	3,200
	Connecticut	University of Connecticut (Storrs)	1881	24,842
		Central Connecticut State University (New Britain)	1849	12,131
		Southern Connecticut State University (New Haven)	1893	12,087

Selected North American Universities and Colleges (continued)

COUNTRY	STATE/PROVINCE	INSTITUTION (LOCATION)	FOUNDING YEAR	ENROLLMENT
United States (continued)	Connecticut (continued)	Yale University (New Haven)	1701	11,126
		University of Hartford (West Hartford)	1877	7,245
		Western Connecticut State University (Danbury)	1903	6,079
		Quinnipiac University (Hamden)	1929	5,434
		Eastern Connecticut State University (Willimantic)	1889	5,095
		Fairfield University	1942	5,053
		University of New Haven (West Haven)	1920	5,113
		Wesleyan University (Middletown)	1831	3,685
	Delaware	University of Delaware (Newark)	1765	21,289
		Delaware State University (Dover)	1891	3,343
	District of Columbia	George Washington University	1821	23,019
		Georgetown University	1789	12,629
		Howard University	1867	10,987
		American University	1893	10,914
		University of the District of Columbia	1851	9,660
		Catholic University of America	1887	5,510
	Florida	University of Florida (Gainesville)	1853	46,515
		University of South Florida (Tampa)	1956	39,262
		University of Central Florida (Orlando)	1963	38,598
		Florida State University (Tallahassee)	1851	36,683
		Florida International University (Miami)	1965	34,000
		Florida Atlantic University (Boca Raton)	1961	25,000
		Nova Southeastern University (Fort Lauderdale)	1964	21,619
		University of Miami (Coral Gables)	1925	14,436
		University of North Florida (South Jacksonville)	1972	13,160
		Florida Agricultural and Mechanical University (Tallahassee)	1887	12,161
		Saint Leo University	1889	12.000
		Barry University (Miami Shores)	1940	8,650
		Florida Institute of Technology (Melbourne)	1958	4,689
		Stetson University (DeLand)	1883	3,255
	Georgia	University of Georgia (Athens)	1785	33,878
		Georgia State University (Atlanta)	1913	28,042
		Georgia Institute of Technology (Atlanta)	1885	15,000
		Georgia Southern University (Statesboro)	1906	14,371
		Emory University (Atlanta)	1836	10,762
		Valdosta State University	1906	10,000
		State University of West Georgia (Carrollton)	1933	9,030
		Mercer University (Macon)	1833	7,300
		Georgia College and State University (Milledgeville)	1889	5,800
		Clark Atlanta University	1988	4,813
		North Georgia College and State University (Dahlonega)	1873	4,178
	Hawaii	University of Hawaii (Honolulu)	1907	45,994
		Hawaii Pacific University (Honolulu)	1965	7,900
	Idaho	Boise State University	1932	17,814
		Idaho State University (Pocatello)	1901	12,739
		University of Idaho (Moscow)	1889	11,027
	Illinois	University of Illinois		
		Urbana-Champaign	1867	37,743
		Chicago	1894	24,530
		Southern Illinois University		
		Carbondale	1869	21,387
		Edwardsville	1957	12,708
		Northern Illinois University (DeKalb)	1895	24,948
		DePaul University (Chicago)	1898	23,227
		Illinois State University (Normal)	1857	20,975
		Northwestern University (Evanston)	1851	13,460
		Loyola University Chicago	1870	13,759
		Western Illinois University (Macomb)	1899	13,206
		University of Chicago	1890	12,989
		Eastern Illinois University (Charleston)	1895	10,963
		Chicago State University	1867	9,500
		Columbia College (Chicago)	1890	8,848
		National-Louis University (Chicago)	1886	7,700
		Roosevelt University (Chicago)	1945	7,400
		Illinois Institute of Technology (Chicago)	1893	6,199

Selected North American Universities and Colleges (continued)

COUNTRY	STATE/PROVINCE	INSTITUTION (LOCATION)	FOUNDING YEAR	ENROLLMENT
United States (continued)	Illinois (continued)	Bradley University (Peoria)	1897	6,090
		Saint Xavier University (Chicago)	1846	5,281
		Lewis University (Romeoville)	1932	4,400
		School of the Art Institute of Chicago	1866	2,108
	Indiana	Indiana University		
		Bloomington	1820	38,903
		South Bend	1940	7,457
		Southeast (New Albany)	1941	6,716
		Northwest (Gary)	1963	5,149
		Purdue University		
		West Lafayette	1869	38,564
		Calumet (Hammond)	1943	8,863
		North Central (Westville)	1967	3,657
		Indiana University–Purdue University at Indianapolis	1969	29,025
		Ball State University (Muncie)	1918	18,000
		Indiana State University (Terre Haute)	1865	11,714
		University of Notre Dame	1842	11,311
		Indiana University–Purdue University at Fort Wayne	1964	6,463
		Butler University (Indianapolis)	1855	4,326
		University of Indianapolis	1902	4,300
		Valparaiso University	1859	3,603
		University of Evansville	1854	2,400
	Iowa	University of Iowa (Iowa City)	1847	29,745
		Iowa State University (Ames)	1858	27,898
		University of Northern Iowa (Cedar Falls)	1876	13,441
		Upper Iowa University (Fayette)	1857	5,428
		Drake University (Des Moines)	1881	5,150
	Kansas	University of Kansas (Lawrence)	1864	28,849
		Kansas State University (Manhattan)	1863	22,396
		Wichita State University	1894	15,000
		Washburn University of Topeka	1865	6,626
		Pittsburg State University	1903	6,500
		Emporia State University	1863	6,006
		Fort Hays State University (Hays)	1902	5,620
		Friends University (Wichita)	1898	2,887
	Kentucky	University of Kentucky (Lexington)	1865	25,397
		University of Louisville	1798	21,089
		Western Kentucky University (Bowling Green)	1906	16,579
		Eastern Kentucky University (Richmond)	1906	15,061
		Murray State University	1922	9,920
		Morehead State University	1922	8,171
	Louisiana	Louisiana State University		
		Baton Rouge	1860	30,000
		Shreveport	1965	4,100
		Eunice	1964	3,000
		University of Louisiana		
		Lafayette	1898	16,208
		Monroe	1931	9,400
		University of New Orleans	1956	16,262
		Southeastern Louisiana University (Hammond)	1925	15,662
		Tulane University (New Orleans)	1834	12,381
		Louisiana Tech University (Ruston)	1894	10,000
		Southern University and Agricultural and Mechanical College (Baton Rouge)	1880	9,172
		Northwestern State University of Louisiana (Natchitoches)	1884	8,600
		McNeese State University (Lake Charles)	1939	8,000
		Nicholls State University (Thibodaux)	1948	7,262
		Loyola University (New Orleans)	1905	5,500
		Grambling State University	1901	4,716
		Xavier University of Louisiana (New Orleans)	1915	3,994
	Maine	University of Maine		
		Orono	1865	9,213
		Augusta	1965	5,575
		University of Southern Maine (Portland)	1878	10,820

Selected North American Universities and Colleges (continued)

COUNTRY	STATE/PROVINCE	INSTITUTION (LOCATION)	FOUNDING YEAR	ENROLLMENT
United States (continued)	Maryland	University of Maryland System		
		University College (Adelphi)	1947	71,303
		College Park	1856	35,329
		Baltimore County	1963	10,265
		Baltimore (city)	1807	5,975
		Eastern Shore (Princess Anne)	1886	3,166
		Johns Hopkins University (Baltimore)	1876	17,967
		Towson University	1866	15,105
		Salisbury University	1925	6,816
		Frostburg State University	1898	5,295
		Morgan State University (Baltimore)	1867	5,034
		Bowie State University	1865	5,137
		University of Baltimore	1925	5,000
		US Naval Academy (Annapolis)	1845	4,265
		Coppin State College (Baltimore)	1900	3,749
		McDaniel College (Westminster)	1867	3,374
	Massachusetts	University of Massachusetts		
		Amherst	1863	24,884
		Boston	1964	12,142
		Lowell	1894	8,731
		Dartmouth (North Dartmouth)	1895	8,284
		Boston University	1839	29,544
		Northeastern University (Boston)	1898	24,009
		Harvard University (Cambridge)	1636	19,638
		Boston College (Chestnut Hill)	1863	14,297
		Massachusetts Institute of Technology (Cambridge)	1861	10,340
		Tufts University (Medford)	1852	9,400
		Bridgewater State College	1840	8,400
		Fitchburg State College	1894	7,000
		Suffolk University (Boston)	1906	6,203
		Bentley College (Waltham)	1917	6,169
		Framingham State College	1839	6,093
		Salem State College	1854	5,400
		Worcester State College	1874	5,369
		Springfield College	1885	5,090
		Brandeis University (Waltham)	1948	4,985
		Western New England College (Springfield)	1919	4,732
		Worcester Polytechnic Institute	1865	4,000
		Babson College (Wellesley)	1919	3,342
		Simmons College (Boston)	1899	3,334
		Westfield State College	1838	3,200
		Smith College (Northampton)	1871	2,781
		Wellesley College	1870	2,136
		Amherst College	1821	1,668
	Michigan	University of Michigan		
		Ann Arbor	1817	37,197
		Dearborn	1959	8,215
		Flint	1956	6,488
		Michigan State University (East Lansing)	1855	43,038
		Wayne State University (Detroit)	1868	33,091
		Western Michigan University (Kalamazoo)	1903	29,732
		Central Michigan University (Mount Pleasant)	1892	28,159
		Eastern Michigan University (Ypsilanti)	1849	25,000
		Oakland University (Rochester)	1957	16,576
		Ferris State University (Big Rapids)	1884	11,074
		Marygrove College (Detroit)	1905	8,942
		Northern Michigan University (Marquette)	1899	8,577
		University of Detroit Mercy	1877	5,600
		Michigan Technological University (Houghton)	1885	6,630
		Calvin College (Grand Rapids)	1876	4,162
		Madonna University (Livonia)	1947	4,000
	Minnesota	Minnesota State University System		
		St. Cloud State University	1869	16,000
		Minnesota State University (Mankato)	1868	12,316
		Metropolitan State University (St. Paul)	1971	8,600
		Winona State University	1858	7,925

Selected North American Universities and Colleges (continued)

COUNTRY	STATE/PROVINCE	INSTITUTION (LOCATION)	FOUNDING YEAR	ENROLLMENT
United States	Minnesota	Minnesota State University (Moorhead)	1887	7,400
(continued)	(continued)	Southwest Minnesota State University (Marshall)	1963	5,500
		Bemidji State University	1919	4,991
		University of Minnesota		
		Twin Cities (Minneapolis)	1851	49,474
		Duluth	1895	10,114
		University of St. Thomas (St. Paul)	1885	11,473
		Saint Mary's University (Winona)	1912	8,000
		St. Olaf College (Northfield)	1874	3,041
		Augsburg College (Minneapolis)	1869	3,023
	Mississippi	Mississippi State University	1878	14,831
		University of Southern Mississippi (Hattiesburg)	1910	15,919
		University of Mississippi (University)	1844	11,000
		Jackson State University	1877	6,224
		Delta State University (Cleveland)	1924	4,000
		Mississippi College (Clinton)	1826	3,400
		Mississippi University for Women (Columbus)	1884	3,314
		Alcorn State University	1871	3,309
	Missouri	University of Missouri		
		Columbia	1839	23,667
		St. Louis	1963	15,599
		Kansas City	1929	12,000
		Rolla	1870	5,504
		Webster University (St. Louis)	1915	19,823
		Southwest Missouri State University (Springfield)	1905	16,439
		Washington University in Saint Louis	1853	12,367
		Central Missouri State University (Warrensburg)	1871	11,300
		Saint Louis University	1818	11,112
		Southeast Missouri State University (Cape Girardeau)	1873	9,534
		Northwest Missouri State University (Maryville)	1905	6,280
		Truman State University (Kirksville)	1867	5,712
		Lindenwood University (St. Charles)	1827	5,000
		Lincoln University (Jefferson City)	1866	3,347
		Maryville University of Saint Louis	1872	3,055
	Montana	Montana State University		
		Bozeman	1893	10,700
		Billings	1927	4,300
		University of Montana (Missoula)	1893	10,953
	Nebraska	University of Nebraska		
		Lincoln	1869	24,491
		Omaha	1908	15,899
		Kearney	1903	8,045
		Creighton University (Omaha)	1878	6,537
		Wayne State College	1910	4,000
		Chadron State College	1911	3,206
	Nevada	University of Nevada		
		Las Vegas	1957	21,820
		Reno	1874	15,534
	New Hampshire	University of New Hampshire (Durham)	1866	14,431
		Dartmouth College (Hanover)	1769	5,683
		Keene State College	1909	4,839
		Plymouth State College	1871	4,629
	New Jersey	Rutgers, the State University of New Jersey		
		New Brunswick	1766	34,696
		Newark	1936	10,293
		Camden	1926	5,563
		Montclair State University (Upper Montclair)	1908	13,502
		Kean University (Union)	1855	12,779
		Fairleigh Dickinson University (Teaneck)	1942	11,000
		William Paterson University (Wayne)	1855	9,945
		Seton Hall University (South Orange)	1856	9,920
		Rowan University (Glassboro)	1923	9,368
		New Jersey Institute of Technology (Newark)	1881	7,837
		Jersey City State College	1927	7,000
		College of New Jersey (Ewing)	1855	6,706

Selected North American Universities and Colleges (continued)

COUNTRY	STATE/PROVINCE	INSTITUTION (LOCATION)	FOUNDING YEAR	ENROLLMENT
United States (continued)	New Jersey (continued)	Princeton University	1746	6,610
		Rider University (Lawrenceville)	1865	5,519
		Monmouth University (West Long Branch)	1933	5,311
		Saint Peter's College (Jersey City)	1872	4,698
	New Mexico	University of New Mexico (Albuquerque)	1889	25,009
		New Mexico State University (Las Cruces)	1888	15,409
		Eastern New Mexico University (Portales)	1934	3,632
	New York	City University of New York		
		Hunter College (New York)	1870	19,689
		Queens College (Flushing)	1937	16,381
		Baruch College (New York)	1919	15,071
		Brooklyn College	1930	14,964
		City College (New York)	1847	12,083
		College of Staten Island	1976	12,023
		New York City Technical College (Brooklyn)	1881	11,124
		John Jay College of Criminal Justice (New York)	1964	10,834
		Lehman College (Bronx)	1931	9,283
		York College (Jamaica)	1966	6,030
		Medgar Evers College (Brooklyn)	1969	5,063
		Graduate School and University Center (New York)	1961	3,813
		Colleges of the State University of New York		
		Empire State College (Saratoga Springs)	1971	17,000
		Buffalo State	1871	11,072
		Brockport	1841	8,742
		Oswego	1861	8,716
		New Paltz	1828	7,908
		College of Technology (Farmingdale)	1912	5,400
		Cortland	1868	7,500
		Plattsburgh	1889	6,100
		Oneonta	1889	5,700
		Fredonia	1826	5,359
		Geneseo	1867	5,000
		Potsdam	1816	4,327
		Purchase	1967	4,078
		Old Westbury	1965	3,000
		State University of New York		
		Buffalo	1846	24,830
		Stony Brook	1957	19,924
		Albany	1844	16,751
		Binghamton	1946	12,473
		New York University	1831	38,188
		Long Island University	1926	23,540
		Columbia University (New York)	1754	20,504
		Cornell University (Ithaca)	1865	19,000
		Syracuse University	1870	18,600
		St. John's University (Jamaica)	1870	18,478
		Rochester Institute of Technology	1829	15,300
		Pace University (New York)	1906	15,000
		Fordham University (Bronx)	1841	14,000
		Hofstra University (Hempstead)	1935	12,439
		University of Rochester	1850	7,885
		Iona College (New Rochelle)	1940	7,466
		Rensselaer Polytechnic Institute (Troy)	1824	6,509
		College of New Rochelle	1904	6,475
		Adelphi University (Garden City)	1896	6,349
		Yeshiva University (New York)	1886	6,335
		Dowling College (Oakdale)	1968	6,000
		Ithaca College	1892	5,897
		Canisius College (Buffalo)	1870	4,944
		Pratt Institute (Brooklyn)	1887	4,280
		College of Saint Rose (Albany)	1920	4,167
		US Military Academy (West Point)	1802	4,112
		Marist College (Poughkeepsie)	1929	4,025
		Siena College (Loudonville)	1937	3,436
		Polytechnic University (Brooklyn)	1854	3,282
		Niagara University	1856	3,548
		Le Moyne College (Syracuse)	1946	3,130

Selected North American Universities and Colleges (continued)

COUNTRY	STATE/PROVINCE	INSTITUTION (LOCATION)	FOUNDING YEAR	ENROLLMENT
United States	New York	Manhattan College (Riverdale)	1853	3,070
(continued)	(continued)	Colgate University (Hamilton)	1819	2,675
		Vassar College (Poughkeepsie)	1861	2,444
		Juilliard School (New York)	1905	1,425
		Sarah Lawrence College (Bronxville)	1926	1,111
	North Carolina	University of North Carolina		
		Chapel Hill	1789	24,189
		Charlotte	1946	18,308
		Greensboro	1891	12,731
		Wilmington	1947	10,929
		Asheville	1927	3,179
		Pembroke	1887	4,722
		North Carolina State University (Raleigh)	1887	29,637
		East Carolina University (Greenville)	1907	21,756
		Appalachian State University (Boone)	1899	14,178
		Duke University (Durham)	1838	12,192
		Campbell University (Buie's Creek)	1887	9,220
		North Carolina Agricultural and Technical State University (Greensboro)	1891	7,533
		Western Carolina University (Cullowhee)	1889	6,619
		North Carolina Central University (Durham)	1910	6,521
		Wake Forest University (Winston-Salem)	1834	5,841
		Elon University	1889	4,138
	North Dakota	University of North Dakota (Grand Forks)	1883	13,034
		North Dakota State University (Fargo)	1890	10,000
	Ohio	Ohio State University (Columbus)	1870	54,781
		University of Cincinnati	1819	33,823
		Kent State University	1910	36,000
		Ohio University (Athens)	1804	27,386
		University of Akron	1870	24,000
		Miami University (Oxford)	1809	20,517
		University of Toledo	1872	20,307
		Bowling Green State University	1910	18,200
		Cleveland State University	1964	17,137
		Youngstown State University	1908	12,222
		Wright State University (Dayton)	1967	11,878
		University of Dayton	1850	9,906
		Case Western Reserve University (Cleveland)	1826	9,534
		Xavier University (Cincinnati)	1831	6,523
		Ashland University	1878	6,105
		John Carroll University (University Heights)	1886	4,300
		Capital University (Columbus)	1850	4,047
		University of Findlay	1882	4,018
		Antioch University (Yellow Springs)	1852	3,250
		Oberlin College	1833	2,900
	Oklahoma	University of Oklahoma (Norman)	1890	24,887
		Oklahoma State University (Stillwater)	1890	23,571
		University of Central Oklahoma (Edmond)	1890	15,400
		Northeastern State University (Tahlequah)	1851	8,750
		Southwestern Oklahoma State University (Weatherford)	1901	5,226
		Oral Roberts University (Tulsa)	1965	5,000
		Oklahoma City University	1904	4,400
		East Central University (Ada)	1909	4,378
		University of Tulsa	1894	4,072
		Southeastern Oklahoma State University (Durant)	1909	4,000
		Langston University	1897	3,482
	Oregon	Portland State University	1946	24,193
		University of Oregon (Eugene)	1872	17,207
		Oregon State University (Corvallis)	1858	16,061
		Southern Oregon University (Ashland)	1926	5,478
		Lewis and Clark College (Portland)	1867	3,076
	Pennsylvania	Pennsylvania State University		
		Pennsylvania State University (University Park)	1855	75,489
		Erie, The Behrend College	1948	3,700
		Harrisburg, The Capital College (Middletown)	1966	3,729

Selected North American Universities and Colleges (continued)

COUNTRY	STATE/PROVINCE	INSTITUTION (LOCATION)	FOUNDING YEAR	ENROLLMENT
United States (continued)	Pennsylvania (continued)	Temple University (Philadelphia)	1884	31,001
		University of Pittsburgh	1787	26,795
		University of Pennsylvania (Philadelphia)	1740	22,769
		Drexel University (Philadelphia)	1891	17,000
		Indiana University of Pennsylvania	1875	13,410
		West Chester University	1871	11,344
		Villanova University	1842	9,833
		Duquesne University (Pittsburgh)	1878	9,701
		Carnegie Mellon University (Pittsburgh)	1900	8,514
		Kutztown University of Pennsylvania	1866	9,100
		Edinboro University of Pennsylvania	1857	8,045
		Millersville University of Pennsylvania	1855	7,861
		Slippery Rock University of Pennsylvania	1889	7,789
		Bloomsburg University	1839	7,500
		Shippensburg University of Pennsylvania	1871	7,607
		Widener University (Chester)	1821	7,355
		Saint Joseph's University (Philadelphia)	1851	7,027
		Lehigh University (Bethlehem)	1865	6,479
		Clarion University of Pennsylvania	1867	6,300
		La Salle University (Philadelphia)	1863	6,300
		California University of Pennsylvania	1852	5,850
		University of Scranton	1888	4,615
		Gannon University (Erie)	1925	4,491
		Lock Haven University of Pennsylvania	1870	3,945
		Philadelphia University	1884	3,600
		Bucknell University (Lewisburg)	1846	3,491
		Mansfield University	1857	3,500
		Bryn Mawr College	1885	1,701
	Rhode Island	University of Rhode Island (Kingston)	1892	13,698
		Rhode Island College (Providence)	1854	9,066
		Brown University (Providence)	1764	7,333
		Providence College	1917	3,597
		Bryant College (Smithfield)	1863	3,332
		Rhode Island School of Design (Providence)	1877	2,294
	South Carolina	University of South Carolina		
		Columbia	1801	25,288
		Upstate (Spartanburg)	1967	4,500
		Aiken	1961	3,350
		Clemson University	1889	16,980
		College of Charleston	1770	11,356
		The Citadel (Charleston)	1842	7,500
		Winthrop University (Rock Hill)	1886	5,107
		South Carolina State University (Orangeburg)	1896	4,500
	South Dakota	South Dakota State University (Brookings)	1881	10,561
		University of South Dakota (Vermillion)	1862	7,317
		Black Hills State University (Spearfish)	1883	3,873
		Northern State University (Aberdeen)	1901	3,315
	Tennessee	University of Tennessee System		
		Knoxville	1794	25,650
		Chattanooga	1886	8,689
		Martin	1900	6,098
		University of Memphis	1912	20,100
		Middle Tennessee State University (Murfreesboro)	1911	17,000
		East Tennessee State University (Johnson City)	1911	12,000
		Vanderbilt University (Nashville)	1873	11,092
		Tennessee State University (Nashville)	1912	8,625
		Tennessee Technological University (Cookeville)	1915	9,107
		Austin Peay State University (Clarksville)	1927	7,033
	Texas	University of Texas System		
		Austin	1883	51,426
		Arlington	1895	21,200
		San Antonio	1969	18,606
		El Paso	1913	16,220
		Pan American (Edinburg)	1927	14,399
		Dallas (Richardson)	1969	13,718
		Tyler	1971	4,760

Selected North American Universities and Colleges (continued)

COUNTRY	STATE/PROVINCE	INSTITUTION (LOCATION)	FOUNDING YEAR	ENROLLMENT
United States	Texas	Texas A & M University System		
(continued)	(continued)	College Station	1876	41,461
		Tarleton State University (Stephenville)	1899	8,845
		Corpus Christi	1947	8,227
		Commerce	1889	7,260
		West Texas A & M (Canyon)	1910	6,775
		Kingsville	1917	5,876
		Prairie View A & M	1876	5,600
		University of Houston		
		University of Houston	1927	35,066
		University of Houston—Downtown	1974	10,528
		University of Houston—Clear Lake	1974	7,753
		Texas State University—San Marcos	1899	26,827
		University of North Texas (Denton)	1890	25,605
		Texas Tech University (Lubbock)	1923	24,007
		Sam Houston State University (Huntsville)	1879	13,091
		Stephen F. Austin State University (Nacogdoches)	1923	12,500
		Baylor University (Waco)	1845	14,000
		Southern Methodist University (Dallas)	1911	10,266
		Texas Woman's University (Denton)	1901	8,690
		Lamar University (Beaumont)	1923	8,235
		Texas Southern University (Houston)	1947	10,567
		Texas Christian University (Fort Worth)	1873	8,275
		Angelo State University (San Angelo)	1928	6,234
		Midwestern State University (Wichita Falls)	1922	6,500
		Abilene Christian University	1906	4,648
		Rice University (Houston)	1891	4,274
		St. Edwards University (Austin)	1885	4,443
		University of Dallas (Irving)	1956	3,008
	Utah	Brigham Young University (Provo)	1875	30,465
		University of Utah (Salt Lake City)	1850	28,369
		Utah State University (Logan)	1888	23,474
		Weber State University (Ogden)	1889	14,000
	Vermont	University of Vermont (Burlington)	1791	10,967
		Bennington College	1925	400
	Virginia	Virginia Polytechnic Institute and State University (Blacksburg)	1872	25,912
		Virginia Commonwealth University (Richmond)	1838	25,001
		George Mason University (Fairfax)	1957	24,897
		University of Virginia (Charlottesville)	1819	23,077
		Old Dominion University (Norfolk)	1930	20,656
		James Madison University (Harrisonburg)	1908	15,000
		Radford University	1910	9,142
		College of William and Mary (Williamsburg)	1693	7,749
		Hampton University	1868	5,305
		University of Richmond	1830	4,705
		Virginia State University (Petersburg)	1882	4,007
		Longwood College (Farmville)	1839	3,558
		Virginia Military Institute (Lexington)	1839	1,300
	Washington	University of Washington (Seattle)	1861	39,136
		Washington State University (Pullman)	1890	21,073
		Western Washington University (Bellingham)	1893	11,708
		Eastern Washington University (Cheney)	1882	8,000
		Central Washington University (Ellensburg)	1891	7,471
		Seattle University	1891	6,337
		Gonzaga University (Spokane)	1887	5,572
		Evergreen State College (Olympia)	1971	4,410
		Seattle Pacific University	1891	3,615
	West Virginia	West Virginia University (Morgantown)	1867	22,774
		Marshall University (Huntington)	1837	16,551
		Fairmont State College	1867	6,500
		West Virginia State College (Institute)	1891	4,545
		Shepherd College (Shepherdstown)	1871	4,000
	Wisconsin	University of Wisconsin System		
		Madison	1848	41,507
		Milwaukee	1885	23,000
		Oshkosh	1871	10,619

Selected North American Universities and Colleges (continued)

COUNTRY	STATE/PROVINCE	INSTITUTION (LOCATION)	FOUNDING YEAR	ENROLLMENT
United States (continued)	Wisconsin (continued)	Whitewater	1868	10,800
		Eau Claire	1916	10,500
		La Crosse	1909	8,500
		Stevens Point	1894	8,500
		Stout (Menomonie)	1891	7,702
		River Falls	1874	5,849
		Green Bay	1965	5,300
		Platteville	1866	5,100
		Parkside (Kenosha)	1968	5,000
		Marquette University (Milwaukee)	1881	10,892
		Cardinal Stritch University (Milwaukee)	1937	5,600
	Wyoming	University of Wyoming (Laramie)	1886	12,402
	Guam	University of Guam (Mangilao)	1952	3,200
	Puerto Rico	University of Puerto Rico (San Juan)	1903	69,567
		Inter-American University of Puerto Rico (San Juan)	1912	39,000
	US Virgin Islands	University of the Virgin Islands (St. Thomas)	1962	2,610
Canada	Alberta	University of Alberta (Edmonton)	1908	37,000
		University of Calgary	1945	27,448
		University of Lethbridge	1967	5,361
	British Columbia	University of British Columbia (Vancouver)	1908	31,331
		Simon Fraser University (Burnaby)	1963	25,248
		University of Victoria	1963	18,415
	Manitoba	University of Manitoba (Winnipeg)	1877	24,981
		University of Winnipeg	1871	6,152
	New Brunswick	University of New Brunswick (Fredericton)	1785	12,315
		University of Moncton	1864	6,492
	Newfoundland and Labrador	Memorial University of Newfoundland (St. John's)	1925	16,000
	Nova Scotia	Dalhousie University (Halifax)	1818	15,528
		Saint Mary's University (Halifax)	1802	7,109
		St. Francis Xavier University (Antigonish)	1853	5,200
		Acadia University (Wolfville)	1838	3,894
		University College of Cape Breton (Sydney)	1974	3,600
	Ontario	University of Toronto	1827	55,024
		York University (Toronto)	1959	33,749
		University of Western Ontario (London)	1878	30,080
		University of Ottawa	1848	27,462
		University of Waterloo	1957	22,677
		Carleton University (Ottawa)	1942	22,535
		McMaster University (Hamilton)	1887	17,775
		Queens University at Kingston	1841	17,510
		University of Windsor	1857	16,266
		Brock University (St. Catharines)	1964	15,500
		Ryerson University (Toronto)	1948	15,287
		University of Guelph	1964	14,000
		Wilfrid Laurier University (Waterloo)	1911	12,296
		Lakehead University (Thunder Bay)	1965	6,585
		Laurentian University of Sudbury	1960	5,873
		Trent University (Peterborough)	1963	5,564
		Nipissing University (North Bay)	1967	5,556
	Prince Edward Island	University of Prince Edward Island (Charlottetown)	1969	2,800
	Quebec	University of Quebec		
		Montreal	1969	37,395
		Trois-Rivières	1969	9,647
		Chicoutimi	1969	6,500
		Hull	1970	4,766
		Rimouski	1969	4,400
		University of Montreal	1878	54,465
		Laval University (Quebec City)	1852	38,181
		McGill University (Montreal)	1821	30,580
		Concordia University (Montreal)	1974	30,824
		University of Sherbrooke	1954	22,272
	Saskatchewan	University of Saskatchewan (Saskatoon)	1907	20,113
		University of Regina	1974	11,593

Religion

World Religions

At the beginning of the 21st century, one-third of the world's population is Christian, another one-fifth is Muslim, about one-eighth is Hindu, and one-eighth is nonreligious. Most people living in Europe and the Americas are Christian, while the vast majority of Muslims and Hindus are found in Asia. The plurality of Christians are Roman Catholics, of Muslims are Sunni, and of Hindus are Vaishnavites. Africa hosts slightly more Christians than Muslims, with much of the rest of the population listed as ethnic religionists, which describes followers of local, tribal, animistic, or shamanistic religions.

In addition to the predominant world religions (Christianity, Islam, Hinduism), there are small but noticeable percentages of Chinese folk religionists, Buddhists, other ethnic religionists, atheists, and new-religionists. Among the remaining distinct religions, Sikhs, Spiritists, Jews, Baha'is, Confucianists, Jains, Shintoists, Taoists, and Zoroastrians each make up less than one-half of one percent of religious adherents.

Christianity

Christianity traces its origins to the 1st century AD and to Jesus of Nazareth, whom it affirms to be the chosen one (Christ) of God. Geographically the most widely diffused of all faiths, it has a constituency of more than two billion people. Its largest groups are the Roman Catholic Church, the Eastern Orthodox churches, and the Protestant churches; in addition, there are several independent churches of Eastern Christianity as well as numerous sects throughout the world.

Christianity's sacred scripture is the Bible, particularly the New Testament. Its principal tenets are that Jesus is the son of God (the second person of the Holy Trinity), that God's love for the world is the essential component of his being, and that Jesus died to redeem humankind.

Christianity was originally a movement of Jews who accepted Jesus as the messiah, but the movement quickly became predominantly Gentile. Nearly all Christian churches have an ordained clergy, which lead group worship services and are viewed as intermediaries between the laity and the divine in some churches. Most Christian churches administer at least two sacraments: baptism and the Lord's Supper.

Islam

Islam is a religion that originated in the Middle East and was promulgated by the Prophet Muhammad in Arabia in the 7th century AD. The Arabic term *islam*, literally "surrender," illuminates the fundamental religious idea of Islam—that the believer (called a Muslim, from the active particle of *islam*) accepts "surrender to the will of Allah (Arabic: God)." Allah's will is made known through the sacred scriptures, the Qur'an (Koran), which Allah revealed to his messenger, Muhammad. In Islam, Muhammad is considered the last of a series of prophets (including Adam, Noah, Jesus, and others), and his message simultaneously consummates and abrogates the "revelations" attributed to earlier prophets.

The religious obligations of all Muslims are summed up in the Five Pillars of Islam. The fundamental concept in Islam is the Shari'ah, or Law, which embraces the total way of life commanded by God. Observant Muslims pray five times a day and join in community worship on Fridays at the mosque, where worship is led by an imam. Every believer is required to make a pilgrimage to Mecca, the holiest city, at least once in a lifetime, barring poverty or physical incapacity. The month of Ramadan is set aside for fasting. Jihad, considered a sixth pillar by some sects, is not accepted by most of the Islamic community as a call to wage physical war against unbelievers.

Divisions occurred early in Islam, brought about by disputes over the succession to the caliphate, resulting in various sects (Sunni, Shi'ite, Ismaili, Sufi). From the 19th century, the concept of the Islamic community inspired Muslim peoples to cast off Western colonial rule, and in the late 20th century fundamentalist movements toppled a number of secular Middle Eastern governments. A movement of African American Muslims emerged in the 20th century in the US.

Hinduism

Hinduism is the oldest of the world's major religions, dating back more than 3,000 years, though its present forms are of more recent origin. It evolved from Vedism, the religion of the Indo-European peoples who settled in India at the end of the 2nd millennium BC. The vast majority of the world's Hindus live in India, though significant minorities may be found in Pakistan and Sri Lanka, and smaller numbers live in Myanmar, South Africa, Trinidad, Europe, and the US.

Though the various Hindu sects each rely on their own set of scriptures, they all revere the ancient Vedas, which were brought to India by Aryan invaders after 1200 BC. The philosophical Vedic texts called the Upanishads explored the search for knowledge that would allow mankind to escape the cycle of reincarnation. Fundamental to Hinduism is the belief in a cosmic principle of ultimate reality called brahman, and its identity with the individual soul, or atman. All creatures go through a cycle of rebirth, or samsara, which can be broken only by spiritual self-realization, after which liberation, or moksha, is attained. The principle of karma determines a being's status within the cycle of rebirth.

The greatest Hindu deities are Brahma, Vishnu, and Shiva. The major sources of classical mythology are the Mahabharata (which includes the Bhagavad-gita, the most important religious text of Hinduism), the Ramayana, and the Puranas. The hierarchical social structure of the caste system is important in Hinduism; it is supported by the principle of dharma. During the 20th century Hinduism was blended with Indian nationalism to become a potent political force.

Other major religions

Buddhism, a religion concentrated in Asia with some representation in North America, was founded by the Buddha (Siddhartha Gautama, or Gotama) in northeast India in the 5th century BC. By adhering to the Buddha's teachings, the believer can alleviate suffering through an understanding of the transitory nature of existence, in the hopes of achieving enlightenment. Distinct from Buddhism, **Shinto** is the
(continued on page 673)

The 2005 Annual Megacensus of Religions

David B. Barrett, Todd M. Johnson, and Peter F. Crossing

Statistical data about religions and churches has been generated from various sources at least since 1750, and the amount of data available has been growing quickly. In addition to the religious groups' own statistics, much data comes from decennial governmental censuses: about half the countries of the world ask their populations to state their religions, if any. The United States has never asked a religious question in the federal censuses. In its 2000 census the British government introduced a religion question for the first time since 1851, acknowledging that the information is valuable

Worldwide Adherents of All Religions, mid-2005

	AFRICA	ASIA	EUROPE	LATIN AMERICA
Christians	410,973,000	350,633,000	553,271,000	517,107,000
Affiliated Christians	389,304,000	344,834,000	530,967,000	511,908,000
Roman Catholics	147,123,000	123,781,000	276,559,000	483,033,000
Independents	90,262,000	181,645,000	24,696,000	46,311,000
Protestants	118,513,000	57,641,000	70,760,000	55,141,000
Orthodox	38,865,000	13,244,000	159,042,000	886,000
Anglicans	44,480,000	743,000	25,656,000	914,000
Marginal Christians	3,395,000	3,183,000	4,551,000	10,812,000
Multiple affiliation	−53,334,000	−35,403,000	−30,297,000	−85,189,000
Unaffiliated Christians	21,669,000	5,799,000	22,304,000	5,199,000
Muslims	357,846,000	910,375,000	33,303,800	1,745,000
Hindus	2,637,000	853,371,000	1,465,000	770,000
Chinese universists	35,900	403,564,000	266,000	203,000
Buddhists	150,000	372,698,000	1,643,000	709,000
Ethnoreligionists	107,162,000	143,174,000	1,233,000	3,159,000
Neoreligionists	114,000	105,197,000	382,000	774,000
Sikhs	58,700	24,457,000	239,000	0
Jews	226,000	5,327,000	2,015,000	1,221,000
Spiritists	3,100	2,000	135,000	12,721,000
Baha'is	1,964,000	3,730,000	146,000	827,000
Confucianists	300	6,402,000	16,700	800
Jains	76,100	4,505,000	0	0
Shintoists	0	2,721,000	0	7,200
Taoists	0	2,722,000	0	0
Zoroastrians	900	2,471,000	90,500	0
Other religionists	80,000	70,000	260,000	110,000
Nonreligious	6,042,000	602,308,000	108,304,000	16,139,000
Atheists	595,000	123,781,000	21,952,000	2,787,000
Global population	**887,964,000**	**3,917,508,000**	**724,722,000**	**558,280,000**

Continents. These follow current UN demographic terminology, which now divides the world into the six major areas shown above. *See* United Nations, *World Population Prospects: The 2002 Revision* (New York: UN, 2003), with populations of all continents, regions, and countries covering the period 1950–2050, with 100 variables for every country each year. Note that "Asia" includes the former Soviet Central Asian states, and "Europe" includes all of Russia eastward to the Pacific.

Countries. The last column enumerates sovereign and nonsovereign countries in which each religion or religious grouping has a numerically significant and organized following.

Adherents. As defined in the 1948 Universal Declaration of Human Rights, a person's religion is what he or she professes, confesses, or states that it is. Totals are enumerated for each of the world's 238 countries following the methodology of the *World Christian Encyclopedia*, 2nd ed. (2001), and *World Christian Trends* (2001), using recent censuses, polls, surveys, yearbooks, reports, Web sites, literature, and other data. *See* the World Christian Database <www.worldchristiandatabase.org> for more detail. Religions are ranked in order of worldwide size in mid-2005.

Christians. Followers of Jesus Christ, enumerated here under **Affiliated Christians**, those affiliated with churches (church members, with names written on church rolls, usually total number of baptized persons including children baptized, dedicated, or undedicated): total in 2005 is 2,020,184,000, shown above divided among the six standardized ecclesiastical blocs and with (negative and italicized) figures for those persons with **Multiple affiliation** (all who are baptized members of more than one denomination); and **Unaffiliated Christians**, who are persons professing or confessing in censuses or polls to be Christians though not so affiliated.

Independents. This term here denotes members of Christian churches and networks who regard themselves as postdenominationalist and neo-apostolic and thus independent of historic, mainstream, organized, institutionalized, confessional, denominationalist Christianity.

Marginal Christians. Members of denominations who define themselves as Christians but who are on the

for enumerating and serving the social needs of ethnic minorities. Developing countries began to drop religion questions owing to the high cost of including them, but this trend seems to have been reversing in recent years.

A second major source of church membership data is the decentralized censuses taken by many religious headquarters. Almost all 37,000 Christian denominations ask statistical questions each year on at least some of 180 major religious subjects. All Roman Catholic bishops, for instance, are required to answer 141 statistical questions about their activities over the previous 12 months.

Each year about 27,000 new books on the religious situation in a single country, as well as some 9,000 printed annual yearbooks or official handbooks, appear in print. Although not centralized or coordinated, these publications are the third significant source of data for the megacensus of world religion.

The two tables below are the result of a combination and synthesis of these data around the major characteristic, namely individuals' religious profession and/or affiliation. The first table summarizes worldwide adherents by the 19 major or largest religions. The second goes into more detail for the United States.

NORTHERN AMERICA	OCEANIA	WORLD	%	NUMBER OF COUNTRIES
275,364,000	26,458,000	2,133,806,000	33.1	238
220,913,000	22,258,000	2,020,184,000	31.3	238
79,915,000	8,580,000	1,118,991,000	17.3	235
80,484,000	1,772,000	425,170,000	6.6	221
65,990,000	7,770,000	375,815,000	5.8	232
6,684,000	780,000	219,501,000	3.4	134
2,950,000	4,975,000	79,718,000	1.2	163
11,561,000	649,000	34,151,000	0.5	215
-26,671,000	-2,268,000	-233,162,000	-3.6	163
54,451,000	4,200,000	113,622,000	1.8	232
5,259,600	412,400	1,308,941,800	20.3	206
1,469,000	421,000	860,133,000	13.3	116
719,000	134,000	404,921,900	6.3	94
3,110,000	498,000	378,808,000	5.9	130
1,279,000	325,000	256,332,000	4.0	144
1,578,000	86,200	108,131,200	1.7	107
598,000	25,000	25,377,700	0.4	34
6,179,000	105,000	15,073,000	0.2	134
162,000	7,400	13,030,500	0.2	56
859,000	124,000	7,650,000	0.1	218
0	51,100	6,470,900	0.1	16
8,000	700	4,589,800	0.1	11
61,000	0	2,789,200	0.0	8
12,000	0	2,734,000	0.0	5
82,400	3,200	2,648,000	0.0	23
670,000	10,000	1,200,000	0.0	78
32,656,000	3,930,000	769,379,000	11.9	237
2,090,000	407,000	151,612,000	2.3	219
332,156,000	32,998,000	6,453,628,000	100.0	238

margins of organized mainstream Christianity (e.g. Unitarians, Mormons, Jehovah's Witnesses, Christian Scientists, and Religious Scientists).

Muslims. 84% Sunnites, 14% Shi'ites, 2% other schools.

Hindus. 68% Vaishnavites, 27% Shaivites, 2% neo-Hindus and reform Hindus.

Chinese universists. Followers of a unique complex of beliefs and practices that may include: universism (yin/yang cosmology, with dualities earth/heaven, evil/good, darkness/light), ancestor cult, Confucian ethics, divination, festivals, folk religion, goddess worship, household gods, local deities, mediums, metaphysics, monasteries, neo-Confucianism, popular religion, sacrifices, shamans, spirit writing, and Taoist and Buddhist elements.

Buddhists. 56% Mahayana, 38% Theravada (Hinayana), 6% Tantrayana (Lamaism).

Ethnoreligionists. Followers of local, tribal, animistic, or shamanistic religions, with members restricted to one ethnic group.

Neoreligionists. Followers of Asian 20th-century neoreligions, neoreligious movements, radical new crisis religions, and non-Christian syncretistic mass religions.

Jews. Adherents of Judaism. For detailed data on "core" Jewish population, see the annual "World Jewish Populations" article in the American Jewish Committee's *American Jewish Year Book.*

Confucianists. Non-Chinese followers of Confucius and Confucianism, mostly Koreans in Korea.

Other religionists. Including a handful of religions, quasi-religions, pseudoreligions, parareligions, religious or mystic systems, and religious and semireligious brotherhoods of numerous varieties.

Atheists. Persons professing atheism, skepticism, disbelief, or irreligion, including the militantly antireligious (opposed to all religion).

Nonreligious. Persons professing no religion, nonbelievers, agnostics, freethinkers, uninterested, or dereligionized secularists indifferent to all religion but not militantly so.

Total population. UN medium variant figures for mid-2005, as given in *World Population Prospects: The 2002 Revision.*

Religious Adherents in the United States of America, 1900–2005

For categories not described below, see notes to "Worldwide Adherents of All Religions," pp. 670–671.

	1900	%	MID-1970	%	MID-1990	%
Christians	73,260,000	96.4	190,732,000	90.8	218,335,000	85.4
Affiliated Christians	54,425,000	71.6	152,874,000	72.8	175,500,000	68.6
Independents	5,850,000	7.7	35,666,000	17.0	66,900,000	26.2
Roman Catholics	10,775,000	14.2	48,305,000	23.0	56,500,000	22.1
Protestants	35,000,000	46.1	58,568,000	27.9	60,216,000	23.5
Marginal Christians	800,000	1.1	6,126,000	2.9	8,940,000	3.5
Orthodox	400,000	0.5	4,189,000	2.0	5,150,000	2.0
Anglicans	1,600,000	2.1	3,196,000	1.5	2,450,000	1.0
Multiple affiliation	*0*	*0.0*	*-3,176,000*	*-1.5*	*-24,656,000*	*-9.6*
Evangelicals	*32,068,000*	*42.2*	*35,248,000*	*16.8*	*38,400,000*	*15.0*
evangelicals	*11,000,000*	*14.5*	*45,500,000*	*21.7*	*88,449,000*	*34.6*
Unaffiliated Christians	18,835,000	24.8	37,858,000	18.0	42,835,000	16.8
Nonreligious	1,000,000	1.3	10,070,000	4.8	21,442,000	8.4
Jews	1,500,000	2.0	6,700,000	3.2	5,535,000	2.2
Muslims	10,000	0.0	800,000	0.4	3,471,600	1.4
Black Muslims	0		200,000	0.1	1,250,000	0.5
Buddhists	30,000	0.0	200,000	0.1	1,880,000	0.7
Neoreligionists	10,000	0.0	560,000	0.3	1,155,000	0.5
Atheists	1,000	0.0	200,000	0.1	770,000	0.3
Ethnoreligionists	100,000	0.1	70,000	0.0	780,000	0.3
Hindus	1,000	0.0	100,000	0.0	750,000	0.3
Baha'is	2,800	0.0	138,000	0.1	600,000	0.2
Sikhs	0	0.0	1,000	0.0	160,000	0.1
Spiritists	0	0.0	0	0.0	120,000	0.0
Chinese universists	70,000	0.1	90,000	0.0	76,000	0.0
Shintoists	0	0.0	0	0.0	50,000	0.0
Zoroastrians	0	0.0	0	0.0	42,400	0.0
Taoists	0	0.0	0	0.0	10,000	0.0
Jains	0	0.0	0	0.0	5,000	0.0
Other religionists	10,200	0.0	450,000	0.2	530,000	0.2
US population	**75,995,000**	**100.0**	**210,111,000**	**100.0**	**255,712,000**	**100.0**

Methodology. This table extracts and analyzes a microcosm of the world religion table. It depicts the United States, the country with the largest number of adherents to Christianity, the world's largest religion. Statistics at five points in time from 1900 to 2005 are presented. Each religion's **Annual Change** for 1990–2000 is also analyzed by **Natural** increase (births minus deaths, plus immigrants minus emigrants) per year and **Conversion** increase (new converts minus new defectors) per year, which together constitute the **Total** increase per year. **Rate** increase is then computed as a percentage per year.

Structure. Vertically the table lists 30 major religious categories. The major categories (including nonreligious) in the US are listed with the largest (Christians) first. Indented names of groups in the "Adherents" column are subcategories of the groups above them and are also counted in these unindented totals, so they should not be added twice into the column total. Figures in italics draw adherents from all categories of Christians above and so cannot be added together with them. Figures for Christians are built upon detailed head counts by churches, often to the last digit. Totals are then rounded to the nearest 1,000. Because of rounding, the corresponding percentage figures may sometimes not total exactly 100%. Religions are ranked in order of size in 2005.

Christians. This means all persons who profess publicly to follow Jesus Christ as God and Savior. This category is subdivided into **Affiliated Christians** (church members) and **Unaffiliated** (nominal) **Christians** (professing Christians not affiliated with any church). *See also* the note on Christians at the world religion table. The first six lines under "Affiliated Christians" are ranked by size in 2005 of megabloc (Anglican, Independent, Marginal Christian, Orthodox, Protestant, and Roman Catholic).

Evangelicals/evangelicals. These two designations—italicized and enumerated separately here—cut across all of the six Christian traditions or ecclesiastical blocs listed above and should be considered separately from them. The **Evangelicals** (capital "E") are mainly Protestant churches, agencies, and individuals that call themselves by this term (for example, members of the National Association of Evangelicals); they usually emphasize 5 or more of 7, 9, or 21 fundamental doctrines (salvation by faith, personal acceptance, verbal inspiration of Scripture, depravity of man, Virgin Birth, miracles of Christ, atonement, evangelism, Second Advent, et al.). The **evangelicals** (lowercase "e") are Christians of evangelical conviction from all traditions who are committed to the evangel (gospel) and involved in personal witness and mission in the world.

Jews. Core Jewish population relating to Judaism, excluding Jewish persons professing a different religion.

Other categories. Definitions are as given under the world religion table.

MID-2000	%	MID-2005	%	ANNUAL CHANGE, 1990-2000 NATURAL	CONVERSION	TOTAL	RATE (%)
239,575,000	84.1	250,042,000	83.3	2,501,000	-377,000	2,124,000	0.93
194,498,000	68.2	200,614,000	66.9	2,010,000	-110,000	1,900,000	1.03
75,218,000	26.4	78,786,000	26.3	766,000	66,000	832,000	1.18
62,970,000	22.1	65,900,000	22.0	647,200	-200	647,000	1.09
60,497,000	21.2	61,295,000	20.4	690,000	-662,000	28,000	0.05
10,188,000	3.6	11,018,000	3.7	102,000	23,000	125,000	1.32
5,733,000	2.0	5,992,000	2.0	59,000	-700	58,300	1.08
2,325,00	0.8	2,206,000	0.7	28,100	-40,600	-12,500	-0.52
-22,433,000	7.9	-24,583,000	-8.2	-282,000	504,000	222,000	-0.94
42,600,000	14.9	44,800,000	14.9	440,000	-20,000	420,000	1.04
98,326,000	34.5	103,500,000	34.5	1,013,000	-25,000	988,000	1.06
45,077,000	15.8	49,428,000	16.5	491,000	-267,000	224,000	0.51
26,123,000	9.2	29,390,000	9.8	246,000	222,000	468,000	1.99
5,659,000	2.0	5,764,000	1.9	63,400	-51,000	12,400	0.22
4,291,000	1.5	4,745,200	1.6	39,800	42,100	81,900	2.14
1,650,000	0.6	1,850	0.6	12,700	17,300	30,000	2.29
2,517,000	0.9	2,721,000	0.9	21,500	42,200	63,700	2.96
1,428,000	0.5	1,509,000	0.5	13,200	14,100	27,300	2.14
1,328,000	0.5	1,493,000	0.5	8,800	47,000	55,800	5.60
1,083,000	0.4	1,158,000	0.4	8,900	21,400	30,300	3.34
1,056,000	0.4	1,144,000	0.4	8,600	22,000	30,600	3.48
774,000	0.3	829,000	0.3	6,900	10,500	17,400	2.58
239,000	0.1	270,000	0.1	1,800	6,100	7,900	4.09
142,000	0.0	149,000	0.0	1,400	800	2,200	1.70
80,900	0.0	86,700	0.0	870	-370	500	0.63
57,600	0.0	60,600	0.0	570	190	760	1.43
54,000	0.0	56,800	0.0	490	670	1,160	2.45
11,400	0.0	12,000	0.0	110	30	140	1.32
7,100	0.0	7,700	0.0	60	140	200	3.57
577,000	0.2	600,000	0.2	6,100	-1,400	4,700	0.85
285,003,000	**100.0**	**300,038,000**	**100.0**	**2,929,000**	**0**	**2,929,000**	**1.09**

World Religions (continued)

(continued from page 669)
indigenous religion of Japan and has no founder, sacred scriptures, or fixed dogmas. Also based in Asia, **Chinese folk religionists** are followers of local deities and engage in ancestor worship and divination. They also adhere to Confucian ethics, though statistically **Confucianists** are categorized as non-Chinese (mostly Korean) followers of Confucius, a Chinese philosopher of the 6th century BC. Confucianism is not an organized religion as much as it is a political and social ideology. Also in the Confucian tradition, a **Taoist** seeks the correct path of human conduct and an understanding of the Absolute Tao.

Zoroastrianism is an ancient pre-Islamic religion of Iran that survives there and in India. It was founded by the Iranian prophet Zoroaster in the 6th century BC and has both monotheistic and dualistic features. Also founded in Iran is the **Baha'i** faith, created as a universal religion in the mid-19th century AD for the worship of Baha' Ullah and his forerunner, the Bab; it has no priesthood or formal sacraments and is chiefly concerned with social ethics.

Jainism was founded in India in the 6th century BC by Vardhamana, or Mahavira, a monastic reformer in the Vedic, or early Hindu, tradition. Jainism emphasizes a path to spiritual purity and enlightenment through a disciplined mode of life founded upon the tradition of ahimsa, nonviolence to all living creatures.

Sikhism is a monotheistic religion founded in the late 15th century AD in India, historically associated with the Punjab region, though it includes representation in Europe and North America.

Judaism, like Christianity and Islam, is monotheistic and maintains the manifestation of God in human events, particularly through Moses in the Torah at Mount Sinai in the 13th century BCE. Jews, who come together in both religious and ethnic communities, have worldwide representation, with the greatest concentration in North America and the Middle East.

New-Religionists are followers of New Religious movements and non-Christian syncretistic mass religions.

Chronological List of Popes

According to Roman Catholic doctrine, the pope is the successor of **St. Peter**, who was head of the Apostles. The pope thus is seen to have full and supreme power of jurisdiction over the universal church in matters of faith and morals, as well as in church discipline and government. Until the 4th century, the popes were usually known only as bishops of Rome. From 1309–77, the popes' seat was at Avignon, France. In the table, **antipopes**, who opposed the legitimately elected bishop of Rome and endeavored to secure the papal throne, are listed in italics. The elections of several antipopes are greatly obscured by incomplete or biased records, and at times even their contemporaries could not decide who was the true pope. It is impossible, therefore, to establish an absolutely definitive list of antipopes.

POPE	REIGN	POPE	REIGN	POPE	REIGN
Peter	?–c. 64	Anastasius II	496–498	Valentine	827
Linus	c. 67–76/79	Symmachus	498–514	Gregory IV	827–844
Anacletus	76–88 or	*Laurentius*	498, 501–	*John*	844
	79–91		c. 505/507	Sergius II	844–847
Clement I	88–97 or	Hormisdas	514–523	Leo IV	847–855
	92–101	John I	523–526	Benedict III	855–858
Evaristus	c. 97–c. 107	Felix IV (or III)[1]	526–530	*Anastasius*	855
Alexander I	105–115 or	*Dioscorus*	530	*(Anastasius*	
	109–119	Boniface II	530–532	*the Librarian)*	
Sixtus I	c. 115–c. 125	John II	533–535	Nicholas I	858–867
Telesphorus	c. 125–c. 136	Agapetus I	535–536	Adrian II	867–872
Hyginus	c. 136–c. 140	Silverius	536–537	John VIII	872–882
Pius I	c. 140–155	Vigilius	537–555	Marinus I	882–884
Anicetus	c. 155–c. 166	Pelagius I	556–561	Adrian III	884–885
Soter	c. 166–c. 175	John III	561–574	Stephen V (or VI)[2]	885–891
Eleutherius	c. 175–189	Benedict I	575–579	Formosus	891–896
Victor I	c. 189–199	Pelagius II	579–590	Boniface VI	896
Zephyrinus	c. 199–217	Gregory I	590–604	Stephen VI (or VII)[2]	896
Calixtus I	217?–222	Sabinian	604–606	Romanus	897
(Callistus)		Boniface III	604	Theodore II	897
Hippolytus	217, 218–235	Boniface IV	608–615	John IX	898–900
Urban I	222–230	Deusdedit	615–618	Benedict IV	900
Pontian	230–235	(Adeodatus I)		Leo V	903
Anterus	235–236	Boniface V	619–625	*Christopher*	903–904
Fabian	236–250	Honorius I	625–638	Sergius III	904–911
Cornelius	251–253	Severinus	640	Anastasius III	911–913
Novatian	251	John IV	640–642	Lando	913–914
Lucius I	253–254	Theodore I	642–649	John X	914–928
Stephen I	254–257	Martin I	649–655	Leo VI	928
Sixtus II	257–258	Eugenius I	654–657	Stephen VII (or VIII)[2]	929–931
Dionysius	259–268	Vitalian	657–672	John XI	931–935
Felix I	269–274	Adeodatus II	672–676	Leo VII	936–939
Eutychian	275–283	Donus	676–678	Stephen VIII (or IX)[2]	939–942
Gaius	283–296	Agatho	678–681	Marinus II	942–946
Marcellinus	291/296–304	Leo II	682–683	Agapetus II	946–955
Marcellus I	308–309	Benedict II	684–685	John XII	955–964
Eusebius	309/310	John V	685–686	Leo VIII[3]	963–965
Miltiades	311–314	Conon	686–687	Benedict V[3]	964–966?
(Melchiades)		Sergius I	687–701	John XIII	965–972
Sylvester I	314–335	*Theodore*	687	Benedict VI	973–974
Mark	336	*Paschal*	687	*Boniface VII*	974
Julius I	337–352	John VI	701–705	*(1st time)*	
Liberius	352–366	John VII	705–707	Benedict VII	974–983
Felix (II)	355–358	Sisinnius	708	John XIV	983–984
Damasus I	366–384	Constantine	708–715	*Boniface VII*	984–985
Ursinus	366–367	Gregory II	715–731	*(2nd time)*	
Siricius	384–399	Gregory III	731–741	John XV (or XVI)[4]	985–996
Anastasius I	399–401	Zacharias (Zachary)	741–752	Gregory V	996–999
Innocent I	401–417	Stephen (II)[2]	752	*John XVI (or XVII)[4]*	997–998
Zosimus	417–418	Stephen II (or III)[2]	752–757	Sylvester II	999–1003
Boniface I	418–422	Paul I	757–767	John XVII (or XVIII)[4]	1003
Eulalius	418–419	Constantine (II)	767–768	John XVIII (or XIX)[4]	1004–09
Celestine I	422–432	*Philip*	768	Sergius IV	1009–12
Sixtus III	432–440	Stephen III (or IV)[2]	768–772	*Gregory (VI)*	1012
Leo I	440–461	Adrian I	772–795	Benedict VIII	1012–24
Hilary	461–468	Leo III	795–816	John XIX (or XX)[4]	1024–32
Simplicius	468–483	Stephen IV (or V)[2]	816–817	Benedict IX	1032–44
Felix III (or II)[1]	483–492	Paschal I	817–824	*(1st time)*	
Gelasius I	492–496	Eugenius II	824–827	Sylvester III	1045

Chronological List of Popes (continued)

POPE	REIGN	POPE	REIGN	POPE	REIGN
Benedict IX	1045	Clement IV	1265–68	Innocent VIII	1484–92
(2nd time)		Gregory X	1271–76	Alexander VI	1492–1503
Gregory VI	1045–46	Innocent V	1276	Pius III	1503
Clement II	1046–47	Adrian V	1276	Julius II	1503–13
Benedict IX	1047–48	John XXI[4]	1276–77	Leo X	1513–21
(3rd time)		Nicholas III	1277–80	Adrian VI	1522–23
Damasus II	1048	Martin IV[5]	1281–85	Clement VII	1523–34
Leo IX	1049–54	Honorius IV	1285–87	Paul III	1534–49
Victor II	1055–57	Nicholas IV	1288–92	Julius III	1550–55
Stephen IX (or X)[2]	1057–58	Celestine V	1294	Marcellus II	1555
Benedict X	1058–59	Boniface VIII	1294–1303	Paul IV	1555–59
Nicholas II	1059–61	Benedict XI	1303–04	Pius IV	1559–65
Alexander II	1061–73	Clement V (at	1305–14	Pius V	1566–72
Honorius (II)	1061–72	Avignon from		Gregory XIII	1572–85
Gregory VII	1073–85	1309)		Sixtus V	1585–90
Clement (III)	1080–1100	John XXII[4]	1316–34	Urban VII	1590
Victor III	1086–87	(at Avignon)		Gregory XIV	1590–91
Urban II	1088–99	*Nicholas (V)*	1328–30	Innocent IX	1591
Paschal II	1099–1118	*(at Rome)*		Clement VIII	1592–1605
Theodoric	1100–02	Benedict XII	1334–42	Leo XI	1605
Albert (Aleric)	1102	(at Avignon)		Paul V	1605–21
Sylvester (IV)	1105–11	Clement VI	1342–52	Gregory XV	1621–23
Gelasius II	1118–19	(at Avignon)		Urban VIII	1623–44
Gregory (VIII)	1118–21	Innocent VI	1352–62	Innocent X	1644–55
Calixtus II	1119–24	(at Avignon)		Alexander VII	1655–67
(Callistus)		Urban V	1362–70	Clement IX	1667–69
Honorius II	1124–30	(at Avignon)		Clement X	1670–76
Celestine (II)	1124	Gregory XI	1370–78	Innocent XI	1676–89
Innocent II	1130–43	(at Avignon, then		Alexander VIII	1689–91
Anacletus (II)	1130–38	Rome from 1377)		Innocent XII	1691–1700
Victor (IV)	1138	Urban VI	1378–89	Clement XI	1700–21
Celestine II	1143–44	*Clement (VII)*	1378–94	Innocent XIII	1721–24
Lucius II	1144–45	*(at Avignon)*		Benedict XIII	1724–30
Eugenius III	1145–53	Boniface IX	1389–1404	Clement XII	1730–40
Anastasius IV	1153–54	*Benedict (XIII)*	1394–1423	Benedict XIV	1740–58
Adrian IV	1154–59	*(at Avignon)*		Clement XIII	1758–69
Alexander III	1159–81	Innocent VII	1404–06	Clement XIV	1769–74
Victor (IV)	1159–64	Gregory XII	1406–15	Pius VI	1775–99
Paschal (III)	1164–68	*Alexander (V)*	1409–10	Pius VII	1800–23
Calixtus (III)	1168–78	*(at Bologna)*		Leo XII	1823–29
Innocent (III)	1179–80	*John (XXIII)*	1410–15	Pius VIII	1829–30
Lucius III	1181–85	*(at Bologna)*		Gregory XVI	1831–46
Urban III	1185–87	Martin V[5]	1417–31	Pius IX	1846–78
Gregory VIII	1187	Clement (VIII)	1423–29	Leo XIII	1878–1903
Clement III	1187–91	Eugenius IV	1431–47	Pius X	1903–14
Celestine III	1191–98	*Felix (V) (Amadeus*	1439–49	Benedict XV	1914–22
Innocent III	1198–1216	*VIII of Savoy)*		Pius XI	1922–39
Honorius III	1216–27	Nicholas V	1447–55	Pius XII	1939–58
Gregory IX	1227–41	Calixtus III	1455–58	John XXIII	1958–63
Celestine IV	1241	(Callistus)		Paul VI	1963–78
Innocent IV	1243–54	Pius II	1458–64	John Paul I	1978
Alexander IV	1254–61	Paul II	1464–71	John Paul II	1978–2005
Urban IV	1261–64	Sixtus IV	1471–84	Benedict XVI	2005–

[1]*The higher number is used if Felix (II), who reigned from 355 to 358 and is ordinarily classed as an antipope, is counted as a pope.* [2]*Though elected on 23 Mar 752, Stephen (II) died two days later before he could be consecrated and thus is ordinarily not counted. The issue has made the numbering of subsequent Stephens somewhat irregular.* [3]*Either Leo VIII or Benedict V may be considered an antipope.* [4]*A confusion in the numbering of popes named John after John XIV (reigned 983–984) resulted because some 11th-century historians mistakenly believed that there had been a pope named John between antipope Boniface VII and the true John XV (reigned 985–996). Therefore they mistakenly numbered the real popes John XV to XIX as John XVI to XX. These popes have since customarily been renumbered XV to XIX, but John XXI and John XXII continue to bear numbers that they themselves formally adopted on the assumption that there had indeed been 20 Johns before them. In current numbering there thus exists no pope by the name of John XX.* [5]*In the 13th century the papal chancery misread the names of the two popes Marinus as Martin, and as a result of this error Simon de Brie in 1281 assumed the name of Pope Martin IV instead of Martin II. The enumeration has not been corrected, and thus there exist no Martin II and Martin III.*

Roman Catholic Cardinals

Members of the **Sacred College of Cardinals** elect the pope, act as his principal counselors, and aid in the government of the Roman Catholic church throughout the world. Cardinals serve as chief officials of the **Roman Curia** (the papal administration), as bishops of major dioceses, and often as papal envoys. New cardinals are appointed only by the pope. He calls a secret **consistory** (meeting) of the cardinals and announces to them the names of the new cardinals. The newly named cardinals then receive the red biretta and the ring symbolic of the office in a public consistory. There are three orders of cardinals: bishops, priests, and deacons. These ranks correspond not to a cardinal's rank of ordination but to his position within the College of Cardinals. These distinctions are not made in the table below. The total **number of cardinals** was fixed at 70 by Sixtus V in 1586. John XXIII eliminated that restriction in 1959. The number of papal electors was later set at 120 by Paul VI, but that number was exceeded by John Paul II. Those aged over 80 no longer serve as papal electors.

The following cardinals hold specific offices within the college. **Dean:** Angelo Sodano; **Sub-Dean:** Roger Etchegaray; **Senior Deacon:** Jorge Arturo Medina Estévez; **Camerlengo of the Holy Roman Church:** Eduardo Martínez Somalo; **Emeritus Dean:** Bernardin Gantin.

APPOINTED CARDINAL ON 28 Apr 1969
Eugênio de Araújo Sales (Brazil [b. 1920]); Stephen Sou Hwan Kim (Korea [b. 1922]); Johannes Willebrands (The Netherlands [b. 1909])

APPOINTED CARDINAL ON 5 Mar 1973
Luis Aponte Martínez (Puerto Rico [b. 1922]); Paulo Evaristo Arns (Brazil [b. 1921]); Salvatore Pappalardo (Italy [b. 1918]); Raúl Francisco Primatesta (Argentina [b. 1919]); Pio Taofinu'u (Samoa [b. 1923])

APPOINTED CARDINAL ON 24 May 1976
William Wakefield Baum (US [b. 1926]); Aloísio Lorscheider (Brazil [b. 1924])

APPOINTED CARDINAL ON 27 Jun 1977
Bernardin Gantin (Benin [b. 1922])

APPOINTED CARDINAL ON 30 Jun 1979
Giuseppe Caprio (Italy [b. 1914]); Marco Cé (Italy [b. 1925]); Ernesto Corripio Ahumada (Mexico [b. 1919]); Roger Etchegaray (France [b. 1922]); Franciszek Macharski (Poland [b. 1927])

APPOINTED CARDINAL ON 2 Feb 1983
Godfried Danneels (Belgium [b. 1933]); Alexandre do Nascimento (Angola [b. 1925]); Józef Glemp (Poland [b. 1929]); Michael Michai Kitbunchu (Thailand [b. 1929]); Alfonso López Trujillo (Colombia [b. 1935]); Jean-Marie Lustiger (France [b. 1926]); Carlo Maria Martini (Italy [b. 1927]); Joachim Meisner (Poland [b. 1933]); Thomas Stafford Williams (New Zealand [b. 1930])

APPOINTED CARDINAL ON 25 May 1985
Francis Arinze (Nigeria [b. 1932]); Giacomo Biffi (Italy [b. 1928]); Rosalio José Castillo Lara (Venezuela [b. 1922]); Andrzej Maria Deskur (Poland [b. 1924]); Edouard Gagnon (Canada [b. 1918]); Henryk Roman Gulbinowicz (Poland [b. 1923]); Antonio Innocenti (Italy [b. 1915]); Bernard Francis Law (US [b. 1931]); D. Simon Lourdusamy (India [b. 1924]); Paul Augustin Mayer (Germany [b. 1911]); Miguel Obando Bravo (Nicaragua [b. 1926]); Silvano Piovanelli (Italy [b. 1924]); Paul Poupard (France [b. 1930]); Adrianus Johannes Simonis (The Netherlands [b. 1931]); Alfons Maria Stickler (Austria [b. 1910]); Angel Suquía Goicoechea (Spain [b. 1916]); Jozef Tomko (Slovakia [b. 1924]); Louis-Albert Vachon (Canada [b. 1912]); Ricardo Vidal (Philippines [b. 1931]); Friedrich Wetter (Germany [b. 1928])

APPOINTED CARDINAL ON 28 Jun 1988
Giovanni Canestri (Italy [b. 1918]); Edward Bede Clancy (Australia [b. 1923]); José Freire Falcão (Brazil [b. 1925]); Angelo Felici (Italy [b. 1919]); Michele Giordano (Italy [b. 1930]); Antonio María Javierre Ortas (Spain [b. 1921]); Jean Margéot (Mauritius [b. 1916]); Eduardo Martínez Somalo (Spain [b. 1927]); László Paskai (Hungary [b. 1927]); Simon Ignatius Pimenta (India [b. 1920]); Alexandre José Maria dos Santos (Mozambique [b. 1924]); Achille Silvestrini (Italy [b. 1923]); Edmund Casimir Szoka (US [b. 1927]); Christian Wiyghan Tumi (Cameroon [b. 1930])

APPOINTED CARDINAL ON 28 Jun 1991
Fiorenzo Angelini (Italy [b. 1916]); Anthony Joseph Bevilacqua (US [b. 1923]); Edward Idris Cassidy (Australia [b. 1924]); Cahal Brendan Daly (Ireland [b. 1917]); Frédéric Etsou-Nzabi-Bamungwabi (Dem. Rep. of the Congo [b. 1930]); Ján Chryzostom Korec (Slovakia [b. 1924]); Pio Laghi (Italy [b. 1922]); Nicolás de Jesús López Rodríguez (Dominican Rep. [b. 1936]); Roger Michael Mahony (US [b. 1936]); Virgilio Noè (Italy [b. 1922]); Camillo Ruini (Italy [b. 1931]); Giovanni Saldarini (Italy [b. 1924]); José T. Sánchez (Philippines [b. 1920]); Henri Schwery (Switzerland [b. 1932]); Angelo Sodano (Italy [b. 1927]); Georg Maximilian Sterzinsky (Germany [b. 1936])

Roman Catholic Cardinals (continued)

APPOINTED CARDINAL ON 26 Nov 1994
Gilberto Agustoni (Switzerland [b. 1922]); Ricardo María Carles Gordó (Spain [b. 1926]); Julius Riyadi Darmaatmadja (Indonesia [b. 1934]); Carlo Furno (Italy [b. 1921]); William Henry Keeler (US [b. 1931]); Adam Joseph Maida (US [b. 1930]); Jaime Lucas Ortega y Alamino (Cuba [b. 1936]); Paul Joseph Pham Dình Tung (Vietnam [b. 1919]); Luigi Poggi (Italy [b. 1917]); Vinko Puljic (Bosnia-Herzegovina [b. 1945]); Armand Gaétan Razafindratandra (Madagascar [b. 1925]); Juan Sandoval Iñiguez (Mexico [b. 1933]); Nasrallah Pierre Sfeir (Lebanon [b. 1920]); Peter Seiichi Shirayanagi (Japan [b. 1928]); Adolfo Antonio Suárez Rivera (Mexico [b. 1927]); Kazimierz Swiatek (Estonia [b. 1914]); Ersilio Tonini (Italy [b. 1914]); Jean-Claude Turcotte (Canada [b. 1936]); Miloslav Vlk (Czech Rep. [b. 1932]); Emmanuel Wamala (Uganda [b. 1926])

APPOINTED CARDINAL ON 21 Feb 1998
Aloysius Matthew Ambrozic (Slovenia [b. 1930]); Lorenzo Antonetti (Italy [b. 1922]); Serafim Fernandes de Araújo (Brazil [b. 1924]); Darío Castrillón Hoyos (Colombia [b. 1929]); Giovanni Cheli (Italy [b. 1918]); Salvatore de Giorgi (Italy [b. 1930]); Francis Eugene George (US [b. 1937]); Adam Kozlowiecki (Poland [b. 1911]); Jorge Arturo Medina Estévez (Chile [b. 1926]); Dino Monduzzi (Italy [b. 1922]); Polycarp Pengo (Tanzania [b. 1944]); Norberto Rivera Carrera (Mexico [b. 1942]); Antonio María Rouco Varela (Spain [b. 1936]); Christoph Schönborn (Bohemia [present-day Czech Rep.] [b. 1945]); Paul Shan Kuo-Hsi (China [b. 1923]); James Francis Stafford (US [b. 1932]); Dionigi Tettamanzi (Italy [b. 1934])

APPOINTED CARDINAL ON 21 Feb 2001
Geraldo Majella Agnelo (Brazil [b. 1933]); Bernard Agré (Côte d'Ivoire [b. 1926]); Francisco Álvarez Martínez (Spain [b. 1925]); Audrys Juozas Backis (Lithuania [b. 1937]); Jorge Mario Bergoglio (Argentina [b. 1936]); Agostino Cacciavillan (Italy [b. 1926]); Juan Luis Cipriani Thorne (Peru [b. 1943]); Desmond Connell (Ireland [b. 1926]); José da Cruz Policarpo (Portugal [b. 1936]); Ignace Moussa I Daoud (Syria [b. 1930]); Ivan Dias (India [b. 1936]); Avery Dulles (US [b. 1918]); Edward Michael Egan (US [b. 1932]); Francisco Javier Errázuriz Ossa (Chile [b. 1933]); Stéphanos II Ghattas (Egypt [b. 1920]); Antonio José González Zumárraga (Ecuador [b. 1925]); Zenon Grocholewski (Poland [b. 1939]); Jean Honoré (France [b. 1920]); Cláudio Hummes (Brazil [b. 1934]); Lubomyr Husar (Ukraine [b. 1933]); Marian Jaworski[1] (Ukraine [b. 1926]); Walter Kasper (Germany [b. 1933]); Karl Lehmann (Germany [b. 1936]); Theodore Edgar McCarrick (US [b. 1930]); Jorge María Mejía (Argentina [b. 1923]); Cormac Murphy-O'Connor (UK [b. 1932]); Wilfrid Fox Napier (South Africa [b. 1941]); Severino Poletto (Italy [b. 1933]); Mario Francesco Pompedda (Italy [b. 1929]); Janis Pujats[1] (Latvia [b. 1930]); Giovanni Battista Re (Italy [b. 1934]); Oscar Andrés Rodríguez Maradiaga (Honduras [b. 1942]); Pedro Rubiano Sáenz (Colombia [b. 1932]); José Saraiva Martins (Portugal [b. 1932]); Leo Scheffczyk (Germany [b. 1920]); Sergio Sebastiani (Italy [b. 1931]); Crescenzio Sepe (Italy [b. 1943]); Julio Terrazas Sandoval (Bolivia [b. 1936]); Roberto Tucci (Italy [b. 1921]); Varkey Vithayathil (India [b. 1927])

APPOINTED CARDINAL ON 21 Oct 2003
Carlos Amigo Vallejo (Spain [b. 1934]); Ennio Antonelli (Italy [b. 1936]); Philippe Barbarin (France [b. 1950]); Tarcisio Bertone (Italy [b. 1934]); Josip Bozanic (Croatia [b. 1949]); George Marie Martin Cottier (Switzerland [b. 1922]); Peter Erdö (Hungary [b. 1952]); Stephen Fumio Hamao (Japan [b. 1930]); Julian Herranz (Spain [b. 1930]); Javier Lozano Barragán (Mexico [b. 1933]); Francesco Marchisano (Italy [b. 1929]); Renato Raffaele Martino (Italy [b. 1932]); Stanislaw Kazimierz Nagy (Poland [b. 1921]); Attilio Nicora (Italy [b. 1937]); Keith Michael Patrick O'Brien (Scotland [b. 1938]); Anthony Olubumni Okogie (Nigeria [b. 1936]); Marc Ouellet (Canada [b. 1944]); Bernard Panafieu (France [b. 1931]); George Pell (Australia [b. 1941]); Jean-Baptiste Pham Minh Man (Vietnam [b. 1934]); Rodolfo Quezada Toruño (Guatemala [b. 1932]); Justin Francis Rigali (USA [b. 1935]); Eusebio Oscar Scheid (Brazil [b. 1932]); Angelo Scola (Italy [b. 1941]); Tomas Spidlik (Czech Republic [b. 1919]); Jean-Louis Tauran (France [b. 1943]); Telesphore Placidus Toppo (India b. 1939]); Peter Kodwo Appiah Turkson (Ghana [b. 1948]); Gabriel Zubeir Wako (Sudan [b. 1941])

[1]Held in pectore *(in secret)* from the consistory of 21 Feb 1998; officially announced 28 Jan 2001.

Did you know? The *miter* is a liturgical headdress worn by Roman Catholic bishops and abbots and some Anglican and Lutheran bishops. It has two shield-shaped stiffened halves that face the front and back. Two fringed streamers, known as lappets, hang from the back. It developed from the papal tiara and came into use in the 11th century. Three types of miters are worn in the Roman Catholic Church. The *simplex* is made of undecorated white linen or silk and is worn at funeral, Good Friday, and some other services. The *auriphrygiata* is made of plain gold cloth or white silk with gold or silver embroidered bands and is worn during penitential seasons and at some other times. The *pretiosa* is decorated with precious stones and gold and worn on Sundays and feast days.

Archbishops of Canterbury

The Archbishop of Canterbury has served as the diocesan Bishop of Canterbury since AD 597, when Augustine (Austin) founded the Christian church in England. The archbishop also serves as the Metropolitan for the Southern Province of the Church of England and as the Primate of All England, which recognizes the seat's lead ecclesiastical role in England. Until the middle of the 16th century, the English church was part of the Roman Catholic Church. In the early 1530s King Henry VIII established the Church of England as a separate faith, subject not to the authority of Rome but to that of the English monarch.

ARCHBISHOP	TERM	ARCHBISHOP	TERM	ARCHBISHOP	TERM
Augustine (Austin)	597–604	Thomas Becket	1162–1170	William Sancroft	1677–1690
Laurentius (Lawrence)	604–619	Richard of Dover	1174–1184	John Tillotson	1691–1694
Mellitus	619–624	Baldwin	1184–1190	Thomas Tenison	1694–1715
Justus	624–627	Hubert Walter	1193–1205	William Wake	1715–1737
Honorius	627–653	Stephen Langton	1206–1228	John Potter	1737–1747
Deusdedit	655–664	Richard le Grant	1229–1231	Thomas Herring	1747–1757
Theodore (Theodorus)	668–690	Edmund Rich	1233–1240	Matthew Hutton	1757–1758
Berhtwald (Beorht-weald)	693–731	Boniface of Savoy	1241–1270	Thomas Secker	1758–1768
		Robert Kilwardby	1272–1278	Frederick Cornwallis	1768–1783
Tatwine	731–734	John Pecham	1279–1292		
Nothelm	735–739	Robert Winchelsey	1293–1313	John Moore	1783–1805
Cuthbert (Cuthbeorht)	740–760	Walter Reynolds	1313–1327	Charles Manners Sutton	1805–1828
Bregowine (Bregu-wine)	761–764	Simon Mepham	1327–1333		
		John Stratford	1333–1348	William Howley	1828–1848
Jaenberht (Jaen-beorht)	765–792	Thomas Bradwardine	1348–1349	John Bird Sumner	1848–1862
Aethelheard	793–805	Simon Islip	1349–1366	Charles Thomas Longley	1862–1868
Wulfred	805–832	Simon Langham	1366–1368		
Feologild	832	William Whittlesey	1368–1374	Archibald Campbell Tait	1868–1882
Ceolnoth	833–870	Simon Sudbury	1375–1381		
Aethelred	870–889	William Courtenay	1381–1396	Edward White Benson	1883–1896
Plegmund	890–914	Thomas Arundel	1396–1397		
Aethelhelm	914–923	Roger Walden	1397–1399	Frederick Temple	1896–1902
Wulfhelm	923–942	Thomas Arundel (restored)	1399–1414	Randall Thomas Davidson	1903–1928
Oda	942–958				
Aelfsige	959	Henry Chichele	1414–1443	Cosmo Gordon Lang (from 1942, Baron Lang of Lambeth)	1928–1942
Beorhthelm	959	John Stafford	1443–1452		
Dunstan	960–988	John Kempe	1452–1454		
Aethelgar	988–990	Thomas Bourgchier	1454–1486		
Sigeric Serio	990–994	John Morton	1486–1500	William Temple	1942–1944
Aelfric	995–1005	Henry Deane	1501–1503	Geoffrey Francis Fisher (from 1961, Baron Fisher of Lambeth)	1945–1961
Aelfheah	1005–1012	William Warham	1504–1532		
Lyfing	1013–1020	Thomas Cranmer	1533–1556		
Aethelnoth	1020–1038	Reginald Pole	1556–1558	Arthur Michael Ramsey	1961–1974
Eadsige	1038–1050	Matthew Parker	1559–1575		
Robert of Jumièges	1051–1052	Edmund Grindal	1575–1583	Frederick Donald Coggan	1974–1980
Stigand	1052–1070	John Whitgift	1583–1604		
Lanfranc	1070–1089	Richard Bancroft	1604–1610	Robert A.K. Runcie	1980–1991
Anselm	1093–1109	George Abbot	1611–1633	George Carey	1991–2002
Ralph d'Escures	1114–1122	William Laud	1633–1645	Rowan Williams	2002–
William of Corbeil	1123–1136	William Juxon	1660–1663		
Theobald	1138–1161	Gilbert Sheldon	1663–1677		

Did you know? According to tradition, the first Christian church in Scotland was founded about 400 by St. Ninian. In the 6th century, Irish missionaries included St. Columba, who settled at Iona about 563. In 1192 the Scottish church was declared "a special daughter" of the Roman see, subject only to the pope. St. Andrews became an archiepiscopal see in 1472, followed by Glasgow in 1492. After King Henry VIII's break with the Roman Catholic Church, a long and complicated struggle took place over the issue of whether the church in Scotland would be episcopal or presbyterian in government, but, when William and Mary became the English monarchs in 1689, Presbyterianism was permanently established in Scotland by constitutional act.

Law & Crime

International Terrorist Organizations

"Terrorism" is a subjective term. The list of organizations included here is that of the US Department of State, issued on 23 Mar 2005. The list is updated periodically.

Abu Nidal Organization (ANO) (Fatah Revolutionary Council, Arab Revolutionary Brigades, Black September, Revolutionary Organization of Socialist Muslims)
Founded in 1974 as splinter group from PLO; led by Sabri al-Banna.
country or region of operation: Middle East, primarily Iraq and Lebanon; has also operated in Asia and Europe
primary goals: elimination of Israel, establishment of Palestinian state

Abu Sayyaf Group (ASG)
Founded in early 1990s as splinter group from Moro National Liberation Front by Abdurajak Abubakar Janjalani; mainly made up of semiautonomous factions.
country or region of operation: the Philippines, Malaysia
primary goals: establishment of independent Islamic state in southern Philippines

al-Aqsa Martyrs Brigades
Founded in 2000 as an offshoot of Fatah; diffuse cell-based leadership structure.
country or region of operation: Gaza Strip, West Bank, Israel
primary goals: drive Israeli forces out of the West Bank and Gaza Strip, establish a Palestinian state with Jerusalem as its capital

Ansar al-Islam (Partisans of Islam)
Founded in 2001, an offshoot of the Islamic Movement in Iraqi Kurdistan; led by Najmeddin Faraj Ahmed, aka Mullah Krekar (currently in custody in Norway awaiting deportation to Iraq).
country or region of operation: Iraq
primary goals: establishment of an Islamic state in the Kurdish areas of northern Iraq, expulsion of Operation Iraqi Freedom (OIF) coalition from Iraq

Armed Islamic Group (GIA)
Founded in 1992; leadership uncertain; fewer than 50 active members thought to be at large.
country or region of operation: Algeria
primary goals: replacement of secular Algerian government with an Islamic state

Asbat al-Ansar
Founded in the late 1980s, a splinter faction of Muslim fighters in Lebanon's civil war; led by Abou Mahjan, aka Abdel Karim as-Saadi.
country or region of operation: Lebanon
primary goals: replacement of secular Lebanese government with an Islamic state based on the ancient caliphate system of government

Aum Shinrikyo (Aum Supreme Truth, Aleph)
Founded in 1987 by Shoko Asahara; led by Fumihiro Joyu.
country or region of operation: Japan
primary goals: takeover of Japan and the world

Basque Fatherland and Liberty (ETA) (Euzkadi Ta Askatasuna)
Founded in 1959; allegedly led by Mikel Albizu Iriarte, aka Mikel Antza.
country or region of operation: Basque autonomous regions of northern Spain and southwestern France
primary goals: establishment of independent Basque state based on Marxism

Communist Party of the Philippines/New People's Army (CPP/NPA)
Founded in 1969 as a Maoist successor to the pro-Soviet Partido Komunista Pilipinas; led from exile by José María Sisón.
country or region of operation: the Philippines
primary goals: overthrow of the Philippine government

Continuity Irish Republican Army (CIRA)
Founded in 1994 as a splinter group of Irish Republican Army (IRA) after the latter declared its first cease-fire.
country or region of operation: Northern Ireland, Irish Republic.
primary goals: removal of British forces from Northern Ireland

al-Gamaa al-Islamiyya (Islamic Group, IG)
Founded late 1970s; loosely organized in two factions led by Mustafa Hamza (currently in custody in Egypt) and Rifai Taha Musa; spiritual leader Sheikh Umar Abd al-Rahman.
country or region of operation: Egypt; also operates in several countries worldwide
primary goals: replacement of Egyptian government with an Islamic state

Hamas (Islamic Resistance Movement)
Founded in 1987 by Sheikh Ahmed Yasin as offshoot of Muslim Brotherhood; led by Khalid Meshal.
country or region of operation: Gaza Strip, West Bank, Israel; also present throughout Middle East
primary goals: elimination of Israel, establishment of Islamic Palestinian state

Harakat ul-Mujahidin (HUM) (Movement of Holy Warriors)
Founded in mid-1980s or early 1990s; led by Farooq Kashmiri.
country or region of operation: the Kashmir region of Pakistan and India
primary goals: to make Kashmir part of an Islamic state

International Terrorist Organizations (continued)

Hezbollah (Party of God) (Islamic Jihad, Revolutionary Justice Organization, Organization of the Oppressed on Earth, Islamic Jihad for the Liberation of Palestine)
> Founded in 1982; governed by the Majlis al-Shura (Consultative Council) led by Hassan Nasrallah; spiritual leader Sheikh Muhammad Hussein Fadlallah.
> **country or region of operation:** Lebanon; also has cells worldwide
> **primary goals:** establishment of Islamic rule in Lebanon, elimination of Israel, liberation of occupied Arab lands

Islamic Jihad Group (IJG)
> Founded in 2004; offshoot of Islamic Movement of Uzbekistan (IMU).
> **country or region of operation:** Central Asia
> **primary goals:** replacement of secular Uzbekistan government with an Islamic state

Islamic Movement of Uzbekistan (IMU)
> Founded in 1996; led by Tohir Yoldashev.
> **country or region of operation:** Central and South Asia, primarily Uzbekistan, Tajikistan, Kyrgyzstan, Afghanistan, Iran, and Pakistan
> **primary goals:** replacement of secular Uzbekistan government with an Islamic state

Jaish-e-Mohammed
> Founded in 2000 as a spin-off from Harakat ul-Mujahidin; led by Maulana Masood Azhar.
> **country or region of operation:** South Asia, primarily Pakistan and India
> **primary goals:** establishment of Pakistani control over India-administered Kashmir

Jemaah Islamiya (JI)
> Founded in the mid-1990s as a successor to Darul Islam; led by Abu Bakar Baasyir.
> **country or region of operation:** Southeast Asia, particularly Indonesia, Singapore, and Malaysia
> **primary goals:** establishment of a pan-Islamic state in Southeast Asia

al-Jihad (Egyptian Islamic Jihad, Jihad Group, Islamic Jihad)
> Founded late 1970s by Ayman al-Zawahiri; merged with al-Qaeda in 2001.
> **country or region of operation:** Egypt and other countries, including Yemen, Afghanistan, Pakistan, Lebanon, and Great Britain; activities now centered mainly outside Egypt
> **primary goals:** replacement of Egyptian government with an Islamic state, attacks on US and Israeli interests

Kahane Chai (Kach)
> Kach founded in 1971 by Meir Kahane; Kahane Chai founded as follow-up group by Binyamin Kahane after Meir's assassination in 1990; Binyamin Kahane assassinated in 2000.
> **country or region of operation:** Israel, West Bank
> **primary goals:** expansion of Israel, removal of Palestinians

Kongra-Gel (KGK, formerly Kurdistan Workers Party, PKK)
> Founded in 1974; led by Abdullah Ocalan (imprisoned since 1999).
> **country or region of operation:** Turkey; also operates in Europe and the Middle East
> **primary goals:** establishment of independent Kurdish state

Ashkar-e Tayyiba (LT, Army of the Righteous)
> Founded in 1990 as the military arm of Markaz-ud-Dawa-wal-Irshad (MDI), a Pakistani-based Islamic fundamentalist organization; led by Abdul Wahid Kashmiri.
> **country or region of operation:** South Asia, primarily Pakistan and India
> **primary goals:** establishment of Pakistani control over India-administered Kashmir, creation of a pan-Islamic state in Central Asia

Lashkar I Jhangvi
> Founded in 1996 as an offshoot of the Sipah-e Sahaba (the Army of Mohamed's Companions); decentralized leadership structure.
> **country or region of operation:** Pakistan
> **primary goals:** replacement of the Pakistani government with an Islamic state

Liberation Tigers of Tamil Eelam (LTTE)
> Founded in 1976; led by Velupillai Prabhakaran.
> **country or region of operation:** Sri Lanka
> **primary goals:** establishment of an independent Tamil state

Libyan Islamic Fighting Group (LIFG)
> Founded in 1995 among Libyans who had fought against Soviet forces in Afghanistan; led by Anas Sebai.
> **country or region of operation:** Libya, various Middle Eastern and European countries
> **primary goals:** overthrow of the government of Libyan leader Muammar Qadhafi

Mujahedin-e Khalq Organization (MEK) (National Liberation Army of Iran [NLA, the militant wing], People's Mujahidin of Iran [PMOI], National Council of Resistance [NCR], Muslim Iranian Student's Society [front organization to garner financial support])
> Founded 1960s; led by Maryam and Masud Rajavi.
> **country or region of operation:** Iran, Iraq
> **primary goals:** establishment of secular government in Iran

National Liberation Army (ELN)
> Founded in 1965; led by Nicolas Rodríguez Bautista.
> **country or region of operation:** Colombia
> **primary goals:** replacement of ruling Colombian government with Marxist state

International Terrorist Organizations (continued)

Palestine Islamic Jihad (PIJ)
Founded in 1970s; most active faction led by Ramadan Shallah.
country or region of operation: Israel, West Bank, Gaza Strip; also elsewhere in Middle East, primarily Lebanon and Syria
primary goals: elimination of Israel, establishment of Islamic Palestinian state

Palestine Liberation Front (PLF)
Founded in mid-1970s as splinter group from PFLP–GC.
country or region of operation: Israel, Iraq
primary goals: elimination of Israel, establishment of Palestinian state

Popular Front for the Liberation of Palestine (PFLP)
Founded as part of PLO in 1967 by George Habash (discontinued PLO participation in 1993); led by Ahmed Sadat (imprisoned by the Palestinian Authority since 2002).
country or region of operation: Syria, Lebanon, Israel, West Bank, Gaza Strip
primary goals: promotion of national unity and revitalization of PLO, opposition to peace negotiations with Israel

Popular Front for the Liberation of Palestine–General Command (PFLP– GC)
Founded in 1968 as splinter group from PFLP; led by Ahmad Jabril.
country or region of operation: Syria, Lebanon, Israel, West Bank, Gaza Strip
primary goals: opposition to PLO and to peace negotiations with Israel

al-Qaeda
Founded in late 1980s; established and led by Osama bin Laden.
country or region of operation: worldwide
primary goals: establishment of worldwide Islamic rule, overthrow of non-Islamic governments, expulsion of Western influences from Muslim states, killing of US citizens

Real IRA (True IRA)
Founded in 1998 as splinter group of Irish Republican Army (IRA); led by Michael "Mickey" McKevitt (imprisoned since 2001).
country or region of operation: Northern Ireland; also elsewhere in Great Britain and in Ireland
primary goals: removal of British forces from Northern Ireland, unification of Ireland

Revolutionary Armed Forces of Colombia (FARC)
Founded in 1964 as military branch of Colombian Communist Party; governed by group led by Manuel Marulanda and including Jorge Briceno and five others.
country or region of operation: Colombia; also some operations in Venezuela, Ecuador, and Panama
primary goals: replacement of ruling Colombian government with Marxist state

Revolutionary Nuclei (Revolutionary Cells)
Founded in 1995 as offshoot of or successor to Revolutionary People's Struggle (ELA).
country or region of operation: Greece, primarily Athens
primary goals: elimination of US military bases in Greece, opposition to capitalism and NATO/EU membership

Revolutionary Organization 17 November
Founded in 1975; relatively small group operating secretly, allegedly led by Alexandros Giotopoulos (imprisoned in Greece since 2002).
country or region of operation: Greece, primarily Athens
primary goals: elimination of US military bases in Greece, removal of Turkish forces from Cyprus, opposition to capitalism and NATO/EU membership

Revolutionary People's Liberation Party/Front (DHKP/C) (Devrimci Sol, Revolutionary Left, Dev Sol)
Founded in 1978 as splinter group from Turkish People's Liberation Party/Front; led by Dursun Karatas.
country or region of operation: Turkey, primarily Istanbul
primary goals: promotion of Marxism, opposition to US and NATO

Salafist Group for Call and Combat (GSPC)
Founded in 1996 as a splinter of the Armed Islamic Group; led by Abou Mossaab Abdelouadoud.
country or region of operation: primarily Algeria, with significant activity elsewhere in North Africa and in Europe
primary goals: replacement of the Algerian government with an Islamic state

Shining Path (Sendero Luminoso, SL)
Founded late 1960s by Abimael Guzman; led by Macario Ala.
country or region of operation: Peru, primarily rural areas
primary goals: replacement of Peruvian government with communist state, opposition to influence by foreign governments

Tanzim Qaidat al-Jihad fi Bilad al-Rafidayn (QJBR) (al-Qaeda in Iraq) (formerly Jamaat al-Tawhid waal-Jihad, JTJ, al-Zarqawi Network)
Founded April 2004 by Abu Mus'ab al-Zarqawi shortly after the commencement of OIF; adopted current name October 2004 after merging with Osama bin Laden's al-Qaeda.
country or region of operation: Iraq
primary goals: expulsion of OIF coalition from Iraq, establishment of Islamic state in Iraq

United Self-Defense Forces of Colombia (Autodefensas Unidas de Colombia, AUC)
Founded in 1997 as umbrella organization of paramilitary groups; led by Carlos Castaño.
country or region of operation: Colombia
primary goals: opposition to and defense against leftist guerrilla groups

Universal Declaration of Human Rights

Completed by the UN Commission on Human Rights in June 1948, the Declaration was adopted by the General Assembly on 10 Dec 1948 by unanimous vote (with the six members of the Soviet bloc, Saudi Arabia, and the Union of South Africa abstaining). The declaration contained general definitions not only of those principal civil and political rights recognized in democratic constitutions but also of several so-called economic, social, and cultural rights.

Preamble

Whereas recognition of the inherent dignity and of the equal and inalienable rights of all members of the human family is the foundation of freedom, justice and peace in the world,

Whereas disregard and contempt for human rights have resulted in barbarous acts which have outraged the conscience of mankind, and the advent of a world in which human beings shall enjoy freedom of speech and belief and freedom from fear and want has been proclaimed as the highest aspiration of the common people,

Whereas it is essential, if man is not to be compelled to have recourse, as a last resort, to rebellion against tyranny and oppression, that human rights should be protected by the rule of law,

Whereas it is essential to promote the development of friendly relations between nations,

Whereas the peoples of the United Nations have in the Charter reaffirmed their faith in fundamental human rights, in the dignity and worth of the human person and in the equal rights of men and women and have determined to promote social progress and better standards of life in larger freedom,

Whereas Member States have pledged themselves to achieve, in co-operation with the United Nations, the promotion of universal respect for and observance of human rights and fundamental freedoms,

Whereas a common understanding of these rights and freedoms is of the greatest importance for the full realization of this pledge,

Now, therefore,
The General Assembly
Proclaims this Universal Declaration of Human Rights as a common standard of achievement for all peoples and all nations, to the end that every individual and every organ of society, keeping this Declaration constantly in mind, shall strive by teaching and education to promote respect for these rights and freedoms and by progressive measures, national and international, to secure their universal and effective recognition and observance, both among the peoples of Member States themselves and among the peoples of territories under their jurisdiction.

Article 1

All human beings are born free and equal in dignity and rights. They are endowed with reason and conscience and should act towards one another in a spirit of brotherhood.

Article 2

Everyone is entitled to all the rights and freedoms set forth in this Declaration, without distinction of any kind, such as race, colour, sex, language, religion, political or other opinion, national or social origin, property, birth or other status.

Furthermore, no distinction shall be made on the basis of the political, jurisdictional or international status of the country or territory to which a person belongs, whether it be independent, trust, non-self-governing or under any other limitation of sovereignty.

Article 3

Everyone has the right to life, liberty and the security of person.

Article 4

No one shall be held in slavery or servitude; slavery and the slave trade shall be prohibited in all their forms.

Article 5

No one shall be subjected to torture or to cruel, inhuman or degrading treatment or punishment.

Article 6

Everyone has the right to recognition everywhere as a person before the law.

Article 7

All are equal before the law and are entitled without any discrimination to equal protection of the law. All are entitled to equal protection against any discrimination in violation of this Declaration and against any incitement to such discrimination.

Article 8

Everyone has the right to an effective remedy by the competent national tribunals for acts violating the fundamental rights granted him by the constitution or by law.

Article 9

No one shall be subjected to arbitrary arrest, detention or exile.

Article 10

Everyone is entitled in full equality to a fair and public hearing by an independent and impartial tribunal, in the determination of his rights and obligations and of any criminal charge against him.

Article 11

1. Everyone charged with a penal offence has the right to be presumed innocent until proved guilty according to law in a public trial at which he has had all the guarantees necessary for his defence.
2. No one shall be held guilty of any penal offence on account of any act or omission which did not constitute a penal offence, under national or international law, at the time when it was committed. Nor shall a heavier penalty be imposed than the one that was applicable at the time the penal offence was committed.

Article 12

No one shall be subjected to arbitrary interference with his privacy, family, home or correspondence, nor to attacks upon his honour and reputation. Everyone has the right to the protection of the law against such interference or attacks.

Article 13

1. Everyone has the right to freedom of movement and residence within the borders of each state.
2. Everyone has the right to leave any country, including his own, and to return to his country.

Article 14
1. Everyone has the right to seek and to enjoy in other countries asylum from persecution.
2. This right may not be invoked in the case of prosecutions genuinely arising from non-political crimes or from acts contrary to the purposes and principles of the United Nations.

Article 15
1. Everyone has the right to a nationality.
2. No one shall be arbitrarily deprived of his nationality nor denied the right to change his nationality.

Article 16
1. Men and women of full age, without any limitation due to race, nationality or religion, have the right to marry and to found a family. They are entitled to equal rights as to marriage, during marriage and at its dissolution.
2. Marriage shall be entered into only with the free and full consent of the intending spouses.
3. The family is the natural and fundamental group unit of society and is entitled to protection by society and the State.

Article 17
1. Everyone has the right to own property alone as well as in association with others.
2. No one shall be arbitrarily deprived of his property.

Article 18
Everyone has the right to freedom of thought, conscience and religion; this right includes freedom to change his religion or belief, and freedom, either alone or in community with others and in public or private, to manifest his religion or belief in teaching, practice, worship and observance.

Article 19
Everyone has the right to freedom of opinion and expression; this right includes freedom to hold opinions without interference and to seek, receive and impart information and ideas through any media and regardless of frontiers.

Article 20
1. Everyone has the right to freedom of peaceful assembly and association.
2. No one may be compelled to belong to an association.

Article 21
1. Everyone has the right to take part in the government of his country, directly or through freely chosen representatives.
2. Everyone has the right of equal access to public service in his country.
3. The will of the people shall be the basis of the authority of government; this will shall be expressed in periodic and genuine elections which shall be by universal and equal suffrage and shall be held by secret vote or by equivalent free voting procedures.

Article 22
Everyone, as a member of society, has the right to social security and is entitled to realization, through national effort and international co-operation and in accordance with the organization and resources of each State, of the economic, social and cultural rights indispensable for his dignity and the free development of his personality.

Article 23
1. Everyone has the right to work, to free choice of employment, to just and favourable conditions of work and to protection against unemployment.
2. Everyone, without any discrimination, has the right to equal pay for equal work.
3. Everyone who works has the right to just and favourable remuneration ensuring for himself and his family an existence worthy of human dignity, and supplemented, if necessary, by other means of social protection.
4. Everyone has the right to form and to join trade unions for the protection of his interests.

Article 24
Everyone has the right to rest and leisure, including reasonable limitation of working hours and periodic holidays with pay.

Article 25
1. Everyone has the right to a standard of living adequate for the health and well-being of himself and of his family, including food, clothing, housing and medical care and necessary social services, and the right to security in the event of unemployment, sickness, disability, widowhood, old age or other lack of livelihood in circumstances beyond his control.
2. Motherhood and childhood are entitled to special care and assistance. All children, whether born in or out of wedlock, shall enjoy the same social protection.

Article 26
1. Everyone has the right to education. Education shall be free, at least in the elementary and fundamental stages. Elementary education shall be compulsory. Technical and professional education shall be made generally available and higher education shall be equally accessible to all on the basis of merit.
2. Education shall be directed to the full development of the human personality and to the strengthening of respect for human rights and fundamental freedoms. It shall promote understanding, tolerance and friendship among all nations, racial or religious groups, and shall further the activities of the United Nations for the maintenance of peace.
3. Parents have a prior right to choose the kind of education that shall be given to their children.

Article 27
1. Everyone has the right freely to participate in the cultural life of the community, to enjoy the arts and to share in scientific advancement and its benefits.
2. Everyone has the right to the protection of the moral and material interests resulting from any scientific, literary or artistic production of which he is the author.

Article 28
Everyone is entitled to a social and international order in which the rights and freedoms set forth in this Declaration can be fully realized.

Article 29
1. Everyone has duties to the community in which alone the free and full development of his personality is possible.
2. In the exercise of his rights and freedoms, everyone shall be subject only to such limitations as are determined by law solely for the purpose of securing due recognition and respect for the rights

and freedoms of others and of meeting the just requirements of morality, public order and the general welfare in a democratic society.
3. These rights and freedoms may in no case be exercised contrary to the purposes and principles of the United Nations.

Article 30
Nothing in this Declaration may be interpreted as implying for any State, group or person any right to engage in any activity or to perform any act aimed at the destruction of any of the rights and freedoms set forth herein.

The International Court of Justice

The International Court of Justice is the principal judicial organ of the United Nations. Its seat is at the Peace Palace in The Hague (The Netherlands). It began work in 1946, when it replaced the Permanent Court of International Justice which had functioned in the Peace Palace since 1922. It operates under a Statute largely similar to that of its predecessor, which is an integral part of the Charter of the United Nations.

Functions of the Court
The Court has a dual role: to settle in accordance with international law the legal disputes submitted to it by States, and to give advisory opinions on legal questions referred to it by duly authorized international organs and agencies.

Composition
The Court is composed of 15 judges elected to nine-year terms of office by the United Nations General Assembly and Security Council sitting independently of each other. It may not include more than one judge of any nationality. Elections are held every three years for one-third of the seats, and retiring judges may be re-elected. The Members of the Court do not represent their governments but are independent magistrates.

The judges must possess the qualifications required in their respective countries for appointment to the highest judicial offices, or be jurists of recognized competence in international law. The composition of the Court has also to reflect the main forms of civilization and the principal legal systems of the world.

When the Court does not include a judge possessing the nationality of a State party to a case, that State may appoint a person to sit as a judge ad hoc for the purpose of the case.

The present composition of the Court is as follows: President Gilbert Guillaume (France), Vice-President Shi Jiuyong (China), Judges Shigeru Oda (Japan), Raymond Ranjeva (Madagascar), Géza Herczegh (Hungary), Carl-August Fleischhauer (Germany), Abdul G. Koroma (Sierra Leone), Vladlen S. Vereshchetin (Russian Federation), Rosalyn Higgins (United Kingdom), Gonzalo Parra-Aranguren (Venezuela), Pieter H. Kooijmans (Netherlands), Francisco Rezek (Brazil), Awn Shawkat Al-Khasawneh (Jordan), Thomas Buergenthal (United States of America) and Nabil Elaraby (Egypt).

The Registrar of the Court is Mr. Philippe Couvreur (Belgium) and Deputy-Registrar of the Court is Mr. Jean-Jacques Arnaldez (France).

Cases between States
The Parties: Only States may apply to and appear before the Court. The States Members of the United Nations (at present numbering 189), and one State which is not a Member of the United Nations but which has become party to the Court's Statute (Switzerland), are so entitled.

Jurisdiction: The Court is competent to entertain a dispute only if the States concerned have accepted its jurisdiction in one or more of the following ways:
1. by the conclusion between them of a special agreement to submit the dispute to the Court;

2. by virtue of a jurisdictional clause, i.e., typically, when they are parties to a treaty containing a provision whereby, in the event of a disagreement over its interpretation or application, one of them may refer the dispute to the Court. Several hundred treaties or conventions contain a clause to such effect;
3. through the reciprocal effect of declarations made by them under the Statute whereby each has accepted the jurisdiction of the Court as compulsory in the event of a dispute with another State having made a similar declaration. The declarations of 64 States are at present in force, a number of them having been made subject to the exclusion of certain categories of dispute.

In cases of doubt as to whether the Court has jurisdiction, it is the Court itself which decides.

Procedure: The procedure followed by the Court in contentious cases is defined in its Statute, and in the Rules of Court adopted by it under the Statute. The latest version of the Rules dates from 5 December 2000. The proceedings include a written phase, in which the parties file and exchange pleadings, and an oral phase consisting of public hearings at which agents and counsel address the Court. As the Court has two official languages (English and French) everything written or said in one is translated into the other.

After the oral proceedings the Court deliberates in camera and then delivers its judgment at a public sitting. The judgment is final and without appeal. Should one of the States involved fail to comply with it, the other party may have recourse to the Security Council of the United Nations.

The Court discharges its duties as a full court but, at the request of the parties, it may also establish a special chamber. The Court constituted such a chamber in 1982 for the first time, formed a second one in 1985 and constituted two more in 1987. A Chamber of Summary Procedure is elected every year by the Court in accordance with its Statute. In July 1993 the Court has also established a seven-member Chamber to deal with any environmental cases falling within its jurisdiction.

Since 1946 the Court has delivered 74 Judgments on disputes concerning inter alia land frontiers and maritime boundaries, territorial sovereignty, the non-use of force, non-interference in the internal affairs of States, diplomatic relations, hostage-taking, the right of asylum, nationality, guardianship, rights of passage and economic rights.

Sources of applicable law: The Court decides in accordance with international treaties and conventions

The International Court of Justice (continued)

in force, international custom, the general principles of law and, as subsidiary means, judicial decisions and the teachings of the most highly qualified publicists.

Advisory Opinions

The advisory procedure of the Court is open solely to international organizations. The only bodies at present authorized to request advisory opinions of the Court are five organs of the United Nations and 16 specialized agencies of the United Nations family.

On receiving a request, the Court decides which States and organizations might provide useful information and gives them an opportunity of presenting written or oral statements. The Court's advisory procedure is otherwise modelled on that for contentious proceedings, and the sources of applicable law are the same.

In principle the Court's advisory opinions are consultative in character and are therefore not binding as such on the requesting bodies. Certain instruments or regulations can, however, provide in advance that the advisory opinion shall be binding.

Since 1946 the Court has given 24 Advisory Opinions, concerning inter alia admission to United Nations membership, reparation for injuries suffered in the service of the United Nations, territorial status of South-West Africa (Namibia) and Western Sahara, judgments rendered by international administrative tribunals, expenses of certain United Nations operations, applicability of the United Nations Headquarters Agreement, the status of human rights rapporteurs, and the legality of the threat or use of nuclear weapons.

Internet resources: <www.icj-cij.org>.

Military Affairs

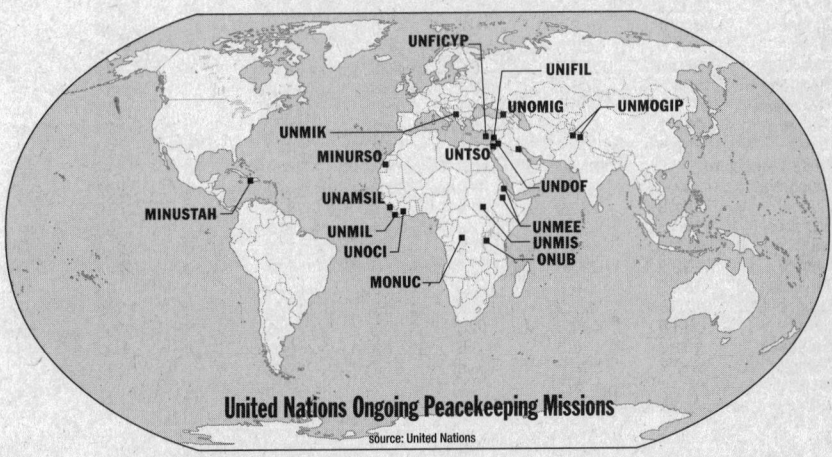

United Nations Ongoing Peacekeeping Missions

source: United Nations

MINURSO	United Nations Mission for the Referendum in Western Sahara – since April 1991 (231)	**UNMEE**	United Nations Mission in Ethiopia and Eritrea – since July 2000 (3,330)
MINUSTAH	United Nations Stabilization Mission in Haiti – since June 2004 (6,700)[1, 2, 4]	**UNMIK**	United Nations Interim Administration Mission in Kosovo – since June 1999 (37)[3]
MONUC	United Nations Organization Mission in the Democratic Republic of the Congo – since November 1999 (16,511)	**UNMIL**	United Nations Mission in Liberia – since September 2003 (15,786)
ONUB	United Nations Operation in Burundi – since June 2004 (5,650)[1]	**UNMIS**	United Nations Mission in Sudan – since March 2005 (10,007)[1, 2, 5]
UNAMSIL	United Nations Mission in Sierra Leone – since October 1999 (3,451)	**UNMOGIP**	United Nations Military Observer Group in India and Pakistan – since January 1949 (44)
UNDOF	United Nations Disengagement Observer Force (in the Golan Heights) – since May 1974 (1,028)	**UNOCI**	United Nations Operation in Côte d'Ivoire – since April 2004 (6,240)[1]
UNFICYP	United Nations Peacekeeping Force in Cyprus – since March 1964 (920)	**UNOMIG**	United Nations Observer Mission in Georgia – since August 1993 (130)
UNIFIL	United Nations Interim Force in Lebanon – since March 1978 (1,996)	**UNTSO**	United Nations Truce Supervision Organization (in Jerusalem) – since May 1948 (150)

Parenthetical figures indicate military personnel as of 30 Apr 2005. [1]*Authorized strength.* [2]*1,288 civilian police are also assigned to MINUSTAH.* [3]*3,500 civilian police are also assigned to UNMIK.* [4]*Current strength: 6,207.* [5]*Current strength: 69.*

Nations with Largest Armed Forces

Countries with a military strength of at least 150,000 active personnel. Personnel numbers are in thousands ('000) and reflect 2004–05 data; spending totals are from 2003–04. Dollars refer to US currency. Source: The International Institute of Strategic Studies, The Military Balance, 2004–05.

COUNTRY	MILITARY PERSONNEL ACTIVE	RESERVES	DEFENSE SPENDING ($ BILLIONS)	ARMY MAIN BATTLE TANKS	NAVY MAJOR WARSHIPS/ CARRIERS	SUB- MARINES	AIR FORCE COMBAT AIRCRAFT	STRATEGIC NUCLEAR WEAPONS
China	2,255.0	800.0	55.9	7,580	63/0	69	1,900	yes
United States	1,433.6	1,162.3	404.9	7,620	118/12	72	3,716	yes
India	1,325.0	535.0	15.5	3,898	25/1	16	679	yes
Russia	1,212.7	20,000.0	65.2	22,800	27/1	51	3,444	yes
Korea, North	1,106.0	4,700.0	5.5	3,500	3/0	92	584	yes
Korea, South	687.7	4,500.0	14.6	2,330	39/0	20	538	
Pakistan	619.0	513.0	3.1	2,461	7/0	11	374	yes
Iran	540.0	350.0	3.1[1]	1,613	3/0	3	306	
Turkey	514.9	378.7	11.7	4,205	19/0	13	480	
Myanmar (Burma)	485.0	0.0	6.2[1]	150	0/0	0	125	
Vietnam	484.0	3,000.0	2.9[1]	1,315	6/0	2	195	
Egypt	450.0	410.0	2.7	3,755	11/0	4	571	
Thailand	306.6	200.0	1.9[1]	333	13/1	0	190	
Brazil	302.9	1,115.0	9.3	178	16/1	4	254	
Indonesia	302.0	400.0	6.4	0	16/0	2	94	
Syria	296.8	354.0	1.5[1]	4,600	2/0	0	520	
Taiwan	290.0	1,657.5	6.6[1]	926	32/0	4	479	
Germany	284.5	358.7	35.1	2,398	13/0	12	384	
Ukraine	272.5	1,000.0	5.5	3,784	3/0	1	499	
France	259.1	100.0	45.7	614	34/1	10	478	yes
Japan	239.9	44.4	42.8[1]	980	54/0	16	280	
United Kingdom	207.6	272.6	42.8	543	34/3	15	426	yes
Colombia	207.0	60.7	3.2	0	4/0	4	57	
Eritrea	201.8	120.0	0.1[1]	150	0/0	0	18	
Morocco	196.3	150.0	1.8[1]	544	2/0	0	95	
Italy	194.0	63.2	27.8	1,293	17/1	6	220	
Mexico	192.8	300.0	2.9[1]	0	11/0	0	107	
Ethiopia	182.5	0.0	0.3[1]	250	0/0	0	48	
Greece	170.8	291.0	7.2	1,723	14/0	8	389	
Israel	168.0	408.0	10.8	3,090	0/0	3	399	yes
Sri Lanka	151.0	5.5	0.5[1]	62	0/0	0	22	
Spain	150.7	328.5	9.9	552	17/1	6	177	

[1]Spending estimate based on 2003–04 budget.

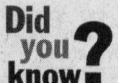

Did you know? Papua New Guinea has the greatest linguistic diversity of any country in the world; 820 languages are spoken as mother tongues there. By contrast, in North Korea, only Korean is spoken as a first language.

United States

United States History

United States Chronology

1492 Christopher Columbus, sailing under the Spanish flag, discovers America, 12 October.

1497 John Cabot, representing England, explores Atlantic coast of what is now Canada.

1513 Ponce de León of Spain lands in Florida and gives that region its name.

1519–22 Magellan's Spanish ship—the *Vittoria*—is the first to sail around the world.

1534 France sends out Jacques Cartier to find a route to the Far East; he explores along the St. Lawrence River, and France then lays claim to part of North America.

1541 Hernando de Soto of Spain discovers Mississippi River near site of Memphis.

1565 St. Augustine, oldest permanent settlement in the US, founded by Spaniards.

1587 A party under John White lands at Roanoke Island (now North Carolina); when White returns three years later, entire settlement has disappeared.

1607 English make first permanent settlement in New World at Jamestown; Virginia becomes first of 13 English colonies.

1619 First representative assembly in America, the House of Burgesses, meets in Virginia; first blacks land in Virginia.

1620 Pilgrims from ship *Mayflower* found settlement at Plymouth.

1649 Act Concerning Religion passed by Maryland legislature is first law of religious toleration in English colonies.

1682 La Salle explores lower Mississippi Valley and claims entire region for France.

1733 Georgia, 13th and last of English colonies in America, is founded.

1754 Both England and the colonies reject Albany Plan of Union to unite colonies. Decisive French and Indian War between France and England begins in America.

1763 Treaty of Paris ends French and Indian War; Britain wins control of New World; Louisiana ceded to Spain; Florida, to Britain.

1765 Quartering Act and Stamp Act anger Americans; nine colonies represented at Stamp Act Congress.

1770 British troops fire on a crowd, killing five people in the so-called Boston Massacre.

1772 Committees of Correspondence organized in almost all colonies.

1773 Boston Tea Party is first action in chain leading to war with Britain.

1774 First Continental Congress meets at Philadelphia; protests Five Intolerable Acts.

1775 Battles of Lexington and Concord, Bunker Hill; Second Continental Congress meets.

1776 Declaration of Independence is adopted. Washington crosses the Delaware to fight at Trenton.

1777 Americans capture General Burgoyne and large British force at Saratoga, New York.

1778–79 Gen. George Rogers Clark leads victorious expedition into Northwest Territory.

1781 Washington accepts surrender of Cornwallis at Yorktown, Virginia. Articles of Confederation become government of the US.

1783 Treaty of peace with Great Britain signed at Paris, formally ending Revolutionary War.

1786–87 Shays's Rebellion in Massachusetts shows weaknesses of Confederation government.

1787 Northwest Territory organized by Congress. Convention meets to draft new constitution.

1788 US Constitution is ratified by necessary nine states to ensure adoption.

1789 New US government goes into effect; Washington inaugurated president; first Congress meets in New York City.

1791 Bill of Rights added to Constitution. Vermont is first new state admitted to Union.

1793 Eli Whitney invents cotton gin, which leads to large-scale cotton growing in the South.

1800 National capital moved from Philadelphia PA to Washington DC.

1803 Louisiana purchased from France. Supreme Court makes *Marbury* v. *Madison* decision; Congress halts the importation of slaves into the US after 1807.

1804–06 Lewis and Clark blaze overland trail to the Pacific and return.

1807 Robert Fulton's steamboat makes successful journey from New York City to Albany NY.

1812–14 US maintains its independence in conflict with Britain, War of 1812.

1818 US and Canada settle boundary dispute, agree on open border between countries.

1820 Missouri Compromise settles problem of slavery in new states for next 30 years.

1823 Monroe Doctrine warns European nations that US will protect the Americas.

1825 Erie Canal, from Hudson River to Great Lakes, becomes great water highway to Middle West.

1829 Inauguration of Pres. Andrew Jackson introduces era of Jacksonian Democracy.

1836 Texas wins its independence from Mexico.

1843 First great migration begins on Oregon Trail.

1845 Texas annexed and admitted as a state.

1846 Oregon boundary dispute settled with Britain. Mexican War begins.

1847 Brigham Young leads party of Mormons into Salt Lake Valley UT.

1848 Mexican War ends; US gains possession of California and New Mexico regions.

1849 Gold rush to California begins.

1850 Compromise of 1850 admits California as free state; postpones war between North and South.

1853 Gadsden Purchase adds 117,935 sq km (45,535 sq mi) to what is now southern Arizona and New Mexico.

1854 Kansas-Nebraska Act reopens slavery issue, leads to organization of Republican party.

1857 Dred Scott Decision of Supreme Court declares Missouri Compromise illegal.

1860 Lincoln elected president; South Carolina secedes from the Union.

1861 Confederate States of America formed; Civil War begins; Union forces routed at Bull Run VA. Telegraph links New York City with San Francisco CA.

1862 Grant launches Union attack in the West; Confederate invasion of Maryland halted at Antietam. Homestead Act grants 160 acres to each settler.

1863 Federal forces win decisive battles at Gettysburg, Vicksburg, and Chattanooga. Emancipation Proclamation takes effect.

1864 Sherman captures Atlanta and marches across Georgia. Grant closes in on Richmond VA.

1865 Lee surrenders to Grant at Appomattox Court House VA, ending Civil War. Lincoln is assassinated.

1867 Reconstruction acts impose military rule on South. Alaska purchased from Russia.

1869 First transcontinental railroad completed as two lines meet at Promontory UT.

1876 Telephone is invented. Centennial Exposition in Philadelphia PA celebrates 100th birthday of the US.

1877 Withdrawal of last federal troops from South ends Reconstruction period. Railroad workers begin first nationwide strike.

1879 First practical electric light is invented by Thomas A. Edison.

1883 Pendleton Civil Service Act provides for examinations as basis of appointment to some government positions.

1884-85 First skyscraper, the Home Insurance Building, is erected in Chicago.

1886 American Federation of Labor is organized; first president is Samuel Gompers.

1887 Interstate Commerce Act adopted to control railroads that cross state lines.

1889-90 First Pan American Conference is held in Washington DC.

1890 Sherman Anti-Trust Act is passed in effort to curb growth of monopolies.

1896 Henry Ford's first car is driven on streets of Detroit MI.

1898 US wins Spanish-American War; gains Philippines, Puerto Rico, and Guam.

1903 Air age begins with successful airplane flight by Wright brothers.

1906 Federal Food and Drug Act passed to protect public from impure food and drugs.

1912 New Mexico and Arizona, 47th and 48th states, admitted to the Union.

1913 Federal income tax authorized by 16th Amendment; 17th Amendment provides for popular election of US senators.

1914 Panama Canal opened. World War I breaks out in Europe; Pres. Woodrow Wilson appeals for neutrality in the US.

1915 German submarine sinks *Lusitania* with loss of 124 American lives. Telephone line established coast to coast.

1917 Germany begins open submarine warfare; US declares war against Germany.

1918 Pres. Wilson proposes "Fourteen Points" as basis for peace. Americans fight at Chateau-Thierry, Belleau Wood, St-Mihiel, Argonne Forest. Armistice ends war.

1918-19 Pres. Wilson attends Paris Peace Conference of victorious nations.

1919 US Senate rejects League of Nations. Navy pilots make first flight across Atlantic. Prohibition established by 18th Amendment.

1920 Right to vote given women by 19th Amendment. Pittsburgh PA radio station, KDKA, begins broadcasting.

1921 Immigration restricted according to national quotas.

1921-22 Washington Conference restricts warship construction among chief naval powers.

1924 Army plane *Chicago* makes first flight around the world.

1927 Charles A. Lindbergh makes first nonstop solo flight across Atlantic.

1928 US signs Kellogg-Briand Pact to outlaw war.

1929 Stock market reaches new high, then crashes. Panic marks beginning of Great Depression; millions of workers are unemployed.

1932 Franklin Delano Roosevelt elected president.

1933 New Deal launched; gold standard suspended; National Recovery Act passed; bank deposits insured; Tennessee Valley Authority organized. 21st Amendment repeals prohibition.

1934 Congress tightens control over securities; passes first Reciprocal Trade Agreement Act; launches federal housing program.

1935 National Labor Relations (Wagner) Act guarantees collective bargaining to labor. Social Security Act passed. CIO founded.

1936 Hoover Dam (Boulder Dam) completed across Colorado River.

1938 Fair Labor Standards Act provides federal yardstick for wages and hours of workers.

1939 Germany invades Poland to start World War II. US declares neutrality.

1940 US begins huge rearmament program; first peacetime draft takes effect. Roosevelt defies tradition and accepts presidential nomination for a third term.

1941 Lend-Lease Act passed. Atlantic Charter signed. Japanese attack on Pearl Harbor brings US into World War II.

1942 Americans launch counteroffensive in Pacific. Allies invade North Africa.

1943 Allied invasion of Italy is first landing on European continent.

1944 Allies launch greatest sea-to-land assault in history in invasion of France. Allies invade Philippines. "GI Bill of Rights" passed.

1945 Germany surrenders, 8 May; atomic bomb dropped on Hiroshima, 6 August; Japan surrenders, 2 September. Cold War begins between US and Soviet Union. United Nations (UN) formally launched on 24 October.

1946 Philippines granted independence by US. Atomic Energy Commission created.

1947 Senate passes Truman Doctrine. Taft-Hartley labor law enacted. Department of Defense consolidates Army, Navy, and Air Force.

1948 European Recovery Program enacted. Truman elected president.

1949 Fair Deal program announced. US and its allies force Soviet Union to lift Berlin blockade. North Atlantic Treaty Organization (NATO) founded.

1950 US and several other members of UN send military forces to aid of Republic of Korea; bitter war develops.

1951 Two-term limit put on presidency by ratification of 22nd Amendment to Constitution.

1952 US and allies end occupation of West Germany. Election of Eisenhower ends 20 years of Democratic governance.

1953 Korean War ends. Department of Health, Education, and Welfare becomes 10th Cabinet post.

1954 Racial segregation of public schools declared illegal by Supreme Court. Southeast Asia Treaty Organization (SEATO) founded.

1955 Two largest labor organizations merge into one group—the AFL-CIO. Salk poliomyelitis vaccine is proved successful.

1956 Eisenhower reelected president. Democrats win control of Congress.

1957 Eisenhower Doctrine to strengthen US position in Middle East adopted.

1958 First US artificial Earth satellite launched. US joins the International Atomic Energy Agency.

1959 Alaska becomes 49th state, Hawaii the 50th.

1960 US reconnaissance plane shot down over Soviet Union.

1961 CIA is involved in unsuccessful invasion of Cuba at Bay of Pigs. 23rd Amendment to Constitution gives Washington DC residents right to vote in presidential elections. First American makes spaceflight. American troops sent to defend West Berlin.

1962 Cuban missile crisis erupts; Soviets remove missiles from Cuba on US urging.

1963 March on Washington for Jobs and Freedom takes place. Pres. John F. Kennedy assassinated in Dallas TX. Nuclear test-ban treaty signed.

1964 24th Amendment to Constitution bans poll taxes in federal elections. Civil rights bill passed. Supreme Court makes possible reapportionment.

1965 US combat forces fight in Vietnam. Voting-rights bill and Medicare act signed. Department of Housing and Urban Development becomes 11th Cabinet post.

1966 Department of Transportation becomes 12th Cabinet post.

1967 25th Amendment to Constitution provides for presidential succession.

1968 Assassinations of Martin Luther King, Jr., and Robert F. Kennedy provoke race riots.

1969 US astronauts become the first men to land on the moon.

1970 Four students at Kent State University in Ohio killed by National Guard during anti-Vietnam War protest.

1971 26th Amendment to Constitution gives 18-year-olds right to vote in all elections.

1972 Pres. Richard M. Nixon visits China and Soviet Union.

1973 US withdraws troops from Vietnam. Vice-Pres. Spiro T. Agnew resigns. OPEC raises price of petroleum 400%.

1974 Watergate scandal and threat of impeachment force Nixon to resign.

1977 Department of Energy becomes new Cabinet post. Treaty altered to return Panama Canal to Panama by year 2000.

1978 Pres. Jimmy Carter hosts Camp David talks between Israel's Menachem Begin and Egypt's Anwar el-Sadat.

1979 Strategic Arms Limitation Talks (SALT II) signed by US and Soviet Union. Militants seize 66 American hostages in takeover of US embassy in Iran.

1980 Department of Health, Education, and Welfare is separated into Department of Health and Human Services and Department of Education.

1981 Pres. Ronald Reagan wounded in assassination attempt. Major tax cut and increased defense spending pass Congress. Sandra Day O'Connor appointed first woman Supreme Court justice.

1983 Reagan announces Star Wars missile-defense program. US invades Grenada.

1985 Summit conference between Reagan and Soviet leader Mikhail Gorbachev held in Geneva, Switzerland.

1986 Space shuttle *Challenger* explodes shortly after liftoff. US bombs targets in Libya. Summit conference in Iceland fails. Iran-contra affair revealed.

1987 Iran-contra hearings held. Stock market collapses. Reagan and Gorbachev sign Intermediate-Range Nuclear Forces (INF) treaty.

1988 Fourth Reagan-Gorbachev summit held in Moscow. Department of Veterans Affairs approved as Cabinet post.

1989 *Exxon Valdez* supertanker spills 10 million gallons of crude oil off Alaskan coast. US invades Panama. Berlin Wall ceases to divide the two Germanys, signaling the end of the Cold War.

1990 Troops sent to Saudi Arabia in response to Iraq's invasion of Kuwait.

1991 Air and ground war leads to Iraqi surrender and withdrawal from Kuwait. Soviet Union comes apart.

1992 27th Amendment to Constitution bars Congress from giving itself a midterm pay raise. Riots erupt in Los Angeles CA after jury fails to convict white policemen accused of beating African American Rodney King. North American Free Trade Agreement (NAFTA) signed by US, Canada, and Mexico.

1993 Janet Reno becomes the first woman attorney general. World Trade Center in New York City bombed.

1995 Timothy McVeigh detonates a bomb in a terrorist attack on the Alfred P. Murrah Federal Building in Oklahoma City OK, killing 168 people.

1998 Pres. Clinton impeached for perjury and obstruction of justice; he is acquitted by the Senate the following year.

2000 The results of the presidential election are challenged by Vice Pres. Al Gore; US Supreme Court overrules Florida Supreme Court's order for a statewide manual recount of ballots; George W. Bush wins the presidency.

2001 On 11 September, two hijacked airplanes demolish the World Trade Center in New York City; another crashes into the Pentagon outside Washington DC; and a fourth crashes in the southern Pennsylvania countryside. Pres. Bush calls for a global war on terrorism and sends US troops into Afghanistan, eventually helping to displace the Taliban regime.

2002 Republicans take control of both houses of Congress, holding both the legislative and the executive branches of government for the first time since 1952.

2003 The US launches a war to depose the Saddam Hussein regime in Iraq and takes control of the country after just weeks of fighting. Congress passes a $350 billion tax cut.

2004 Scandal erupts with the publication of photos of prisoner abuse at Abu Ghraib prison in Iraq. The independent 9/11 Commission finds no credible evidence of a connection between Iraq and al-Qaeda's attacks of 11 Sep 2001. Pres. Bush is reelected president.

2005 The US lags among donor nations in debt forgiveness for developing nations and disaster aid. A group of 14 moderate senators from both parties brokers an agreement to preserve the filibuster and end a conflict over judicial nominees.

Important Documents in US History

Mayflower Compact

On 21 Nov 1620 (11 November, Old Style), 41 male passengers on the Mayflower signed the following compact prior to their landing at Plymouth (now Massachusetts). The compact resulted from the fear that some members of the company might leave the group and settle on their own. The Mayflower Compact bound the signers into a body politic for the purpose of forming a government and pledged them to abide by any laws and regulations that would later by established. The document was not a constitution but rather an adaptation of the usual church covenant to a civil situation. It became the foundation of Plymouth's government.

In the name of God, Amen.

We whose names are underwritten, the loyal subjects of our dread sovereign Lord, King James, by the grace of God, of Great Britain, France and Ireland king, defender of the faith, etc., having undertaken, for the glory of God, and advancement of the Christian faith, and honor of our king and country, a voyage to plant the first colony in the Northern parts of Virginia, do by these presents solemnly and mutually in the presence of God, and one of another, covenant and combine ourselves together into a civil body politic, for our better ordering and preservation and furtherance of the ends aforesaid; and by virtue hereof to enact, constitute, and frame such just and equal laws, ordinances, acts, constitutions, and offices, from time to time, as shall be thought most meet and convenient for the general good of the colony, unto which we promise all due submission and obedience.

In witness whereof we have hereunder subscribed our names at Cape-Cod the 11 of November, in the year of the reign of our sovereign lord, King James, of England, France, and Ireland the eighteenth, and of Scotland the fifty-fourth. Anno Domine 1620.

Declaration of Independence

On 4 Jul 1776 the Continental Congress officially adopted the Declaration of Independence. Two days before, the Congress had "unanimously" voted (with New York abstaining) to be free and independent from Britain. The Declaration of Independence was written largely by Thomas Jefferson. After modifications by the Congress, the document was prepared and voted upon. New York delegates voted to accept it on 15 July, and on 19 July the Congress ordered the document to be engrossed as "The Unanimous Declaration of the Thirteen United States of America." It was accordingly put on parchment, and members of the Congress present on 2 August affixed their signatures to this parchment copy on that day, and others later. The last signer was Thomas McKean of Delaware, whose name was not placed on the document before 1777.

The Unanimous Declaration of the Thirteen United States of America

When in the Course of human events, it becomes necessary for one people to dissolve the political bands which have connected them with another, and to assume among the powers of the earth, the separate and equal station to which the Laws of Nature and of Nature's God entitle them, a decent respect to the opinions of mankind requires that they should declare the causes which impel them to the separation.—We hold these truths to be self-evident, that all men are created equal, that they are endowed by their Creator with certain unalienable Rights, that among these are Life, Liberty and the pursuit of Happiness.—That to secure these rights, Governments are instituted among Men, deriving their just powers from the consent of the governed,—That whenever any Form of Government becomes destructive of these ends, it is the Right of the People to alter or to abolish it, and to institute new Government, laying its foundation on such principles and organizing its powers in such form, as to them shall seem most likely to effect their Safety and Happiness.

Prudence, indeed, will dictate that Governments long established should not be changed for light and transient causes; and accordingly all experience hath shown, that mankind are more disposed to suffer, while evils are sufferable, than to right themselves by abolishing the forms to which they are accustomed. But when a long train of abuses and usurpations, pursuing invariably the same Object evinces a design to reduce them under absolute Despotism, it is their right, it is their duty, to throw off such Government, and to provide new Guards for their future security.—Such has been the patient sufferance of these Colonies; and such is now the necessity which constrains them to alter their former Systems of Government. The history of the present King of Great Britain is a history of repeated injuries and usurpations, all having in direct object the establishment of an absolute Tyranny over these States.

To prove this, let Facts be submitted to a candid world.—He has refused his Assent to Laws, the most wholesome and necessary for the public good.—He has forbidden his Governors to pass Laws of immediate and pressing importance, unless suspended in their operation till his Assent should be obtained; and when so suspended, he has utterly neglected to attend to them.—He has refused to pass other Laws for the accommodation of large districts of people, unless those people would relinquish the right of Representation in the Legislature, a right inestimable to them and formidable to tyrants only.—He has called together legislative bodies at places unusual, uncomfortable, and distant from the depository of their public Records, for the sole purpose of fatiguing them into compliance with his measures.—He has dissolved Representative Houses repeatedly, for opposing with manly firmness his invasions on the rights of the people.—He has refused for a long time, after such dissolutions, to cause others to be elected; whereby the Legislative powers, incapable of Annihilation, have returned to the People at large for their exercise; the State remaining in the mean time exposed to all the dangers of invasion from without, and convulsions within.—He has endeavoured to prevent the population of these States; for that purpose obstructing the Laws for Naturalization of Foreigners; refusing to pass others to encourage their migration hither, and raising the conditions of new Appropriations of Lands.—He has obstructed the Administration of Justice, by refusing his Assent to Laws for establishing Judiciary powers.—He has made judges dependent on his Will alone, for the tenure of their offices, and the amount and payment of their salaries.—He has erected a multitude of New Offices, and sent hither swarms of Officers to harrass our people, and eat out their substance.—He has kept among us, in times of peace, Standing Armies, without the Consent of our legislatures.—He has affected to render the Military independent of and superior to the Civil power.—He has combined with others to subject us to a jurisdiction foreign to our constitution, and unacknowledged by our laws; giving his Assent to their Acts of pretended Legislation:—For quartering large bodies of armed troops among us:—For protecting them, by a mock Trial, from punishment for any Murders which they should commit on the Inhabitants of these States:—For cutting off our Trade with all parts of the world:—For imposing Taxes on us without our Consent:—For depriving us in many cases, of the benefits of Trial by Jury:—For transporting us beyond Seas to be tried for pretended offences:—For abolishing the free System of English Laws in a neighbouring Province, establishing therein an Arbitrary government, and enlarging its Boundaries so as to render it at once an example and fit instrument for introducing the same absolute rule into these Colonies:—For taking away our Charters, abolishing our most valuable Laws, and altering fundamentally the Forms of our Governments:—For suspending our own Legislatures, and declaring themselves invested with power to legislate for us in all cases whatsoever.—He has abdicated Government here, by declaring us out of his Protection and waging War against us.—He has plundered our seas, ravaged our Coasts, burnt our towns, and destroyed the lives of our people.—He is at this time transporting large Armies of foreign Mercenaries to compleat the works of death, desolation and tyranny, already begun with circumstances of Cruelty & perfidy scarcely paralleled in the most barbarous ages, and totally unworthy the Head of a civilized nation.—He has constrained our fellow Citizens taken Captive on the high Seas to bear Arms against their Country, to become the executioners of their friends and Brethren, or to fall themselves by their Hands.—He has excited domestic insurrections amongst us, and has endeavoured to bring on the inhabitants of our frontiers, the merciless Indian Savages, whose known rule of warfare, is an undistinguished destruction of all ages, sexes and conditions. In every stage of these Oppressions We have Petitioned for Redress in the most humble terms: Our repeated Petitions have been answered only by repeated injury. A Prince, whose character is thus marked by every act which may define a Tyrant, is unfit to be the ruler of a free people. Nor have We been wanting in attentions to our Brittish brethren. We have warned them from time to time of attempts by their legislature to extend an unwarrantable jurisdiction over us. We have reminded them of the circumstances of our emigration and settlement here. We have appealed to their native justice and magnanimity, and we have conjured them by the ties of our common kindred to disavow these usurpations, which, would inevitably interrupt our connections and correspondence. They too have been deaf to the voice of justice and of consanguinity. We must, therefore, acquiesce in the necessity, which denounces our Separation, and hold them, as we hold the rest of mankind. Enemies in War, in Peace Friends.—

We, therefore, the Representatives of the United States of America, in General Congress, Assembled, appealing to the Supreme Judge of the world for the rectitude of our intentions, do, in the Name, and by Authority of the good People of these Colonies, solemnly publish and declare, That these United Colonies are, and of Right ought to be Free and Independent States; that they are Absolved from all Allegiance to the British Crown, and that all political connection between them and the State of Great Britain, is and ought to be totally dissolved; and that as Free and Independent States, they have full Power to levy War, conclude Peace, contract Alliances, establish Commerce, and to do all other Acts and Things which Independent States may of right do.—And for the support of this Declaration, with a firm reliance on the protection of Divine Providence, we mutually pledge to each other our Lives, our Fortunes and our sacred Honor.

Signers of the Declaration of Independence

	BIRTHPLACE	OCCUPATION
Connecticut		
Samuel Huntington (1731–1796)	Windham CT	lawyer, judge
Roger Sherman (1721–1793)	Newton MA	cobbler, surveyor, lawyer, judge
William Williams (1731–1811)	Lebanon CT	merchant, judge
Oliver Wolcott (1726–1797)	Windsor CT	soldier, sheriff, judge
Delaware		
Thomas McKean (1734–1817)	New London PA	lawyer, judge
George Read (1733–1798)	North East MD	lawyer, judge
Caesar Rodney (1728–1784)	Dover DE	judge
Georgia		
Button Gwinnett (c. 1735–1777)	bapt. Gloucester, England	merchant
Lyman Hall (1724–1790)	Wallingford CT	physician
George Walton (c. 1741–1804)	Farmville VA	lawyer, judge

Signers of the Declaration of Independence (continued)

	BIRTHPLACE	OCCUPATION
Maryland		
Charles Carroll of Carrollton (1737–1832)	Annapolis MD	lawyer
Samuel Chase (1741–1811)	Somerset county MD	lawyer, judge
William Paca (1740–1799)	Abingdon MD	lawyer, judge
Thomas Stone (1743–1787)	Charles county MD	lawyer
Massachusetts		
John Adams (1735–1826)	Braintree (Quincy) MA	lawyer
Samuel Adams (1722–1803)	Boston MA	politician
Elbridge Gerry (1744–1814)	Marblehead MA	merchant
John Hancock (1737–1793)	Braintree (Quincy) MA	merchant
Robert Treat Paine (1731–1814)	Boston MA	lawyer, judge
New Hampshire		
Josiah Bartlett (1729–1795)	Amesbury MA	physician, judge
Matthew Thornton (c. 1714–1803)	Ireland	physician
William Whipple (1730–1785)	Kittery ME	merchant, soldier, judge
New Jersey		
Abraham Clark (1726–1794)	Elizabethtown NJ	surveyor, lawyer, sheriff
John Hart (c. 1711–1779)	Stonington CT	farmer, judge
Francis Hopkinson (1737–1791)	Philadelphia PA	lawyer, judge, author
Richard Stockton (1730–1781)	near Princeton NJ	lawyer
John Witherspoon (1723–1794)	Gifford, Scotland	clergyman, author, educator
New York		
William Floyd (1734–1821)	Brookhaven NY	soldier
Francis Lewis (1713–1802)	Llandaff, Wales	merchant
Philip Livingston (1716–1778)	Albany NY	merchant
Lewis Morris (1726–1798)	Morrisania (Bronx county) NY	farmer, soldier, judge
North Carolina		
Joseph Hewes (1730–1779)	Kingston NJ	merchant
William Hooper (1742–1790)	Boston MA	lawyer, judge
John Penn (1741–1788)	near Port Royal VA	lawyer
Pennsylvania		
George Clymer (1739–1813)	Philadelphia PA	merchant
Benjamin Franklin (1706–1790)	Boston MA	printer, publisher, author, scientist
Robert Morris (1734–1806)	Lancashire, England	merchant
John Morton (1724–1777)	Ridley PA	judge
George Ross (1730–1779)	New Castle DE	lawyer, judge
Benjamin Rush (1746–1813)	Byberry PA	physician
James Smith (c. 1719–1806)	Dublin, Ireland	lawyer
George Taylor (1716–1781)	Ireland	ironmaster
James Wilson (1742–1798)	Fife, Scotland	lawyer, judge
Rhode Island		
William Ellery (1727–1820)	Newport RI	lawyer, judge
Stephen Hopkins (1707–1785)	Providence RI	judge, educator
South Carolina		
Thomas Heyward, Jr. (1746–1809)	St. Helena's (now St. Luke's) parish SC	lawyer, judge
Thomas Lynch, Jr. (1749–1779)	Winyah SC	lawyer
Arthur Middleton (1742–1787)	near Charleston SC	planter, legislator
Edward Rutledge (1749–1800)	Charleston SC	lawyer
Virginia		
Carter Braxton (1736–1797)	Newington Plantation VA	planter
Thomas Jefferson (1743–1826)	Shadwell VA	lawyer, author, educator
Benjamin Harrison (c. 1726–1791)	Berkeley VA	planter, politician
Francis Lightfoot Lee (1734–1797)	Westmoreland county VA	farmer
Richard Henry Lee (1732–1794)	Westmoreland county VA	planter, judge
Thomas Nelson, Jr. (1738–1789)	Yorktown VA	planter
George Wythe (1726–1806)	Elizabeth City county (Hampton) VA	lawyer, educator

The Constitution of the United States

The Constitution was written during the summer of 1787 in Philadelphia by 55 delegates to a Constitutional Convention that was called ostensibly to amend the Articles of Confederation. It was submitted for ratification to the 13 states on 28 Sep 1787. In June 1788, after the Constitution had been ratified by nine states (as required by Article VII), Congress set 4 Mar 1789 as the date for the new government to commence proceedings.

Preamble

We the People of the United States, in Order to form a more perfect Union, establish Justice, insure domestic Tranquility, provide for common defence, promote the general Welfare, and secure the Blessings of Liberty to ourselves and our Posterity, do ordain and establish this Constitution for the United States of America.

Article I

Section 1—

All legislative Powers herein granted shall be vested in a Congress of the United States, which shall consist of a Senate and House of Representatives.

Section 2—

The House of Representatives shall be composed of Members chosen every second Year by the People of the several States, and the Electors in each State shall have the Qualifications requisite for Electors of the most numerous Branch of the State Legislature.

No Person shall be a Representative who shall not have attained to the Age of twenty five Years, and been seven Years a Citizen of the United States, and who shall not, when elected, be an Inhabitant of that State in which he shall be chosen.

Representatives and direct Taxes shall be apportioned among the several States which may be included within this Union, according to their respective Numbers, which shall be determined by adding to the whole Number of free Persons, including those bound to Service for a Term of Years, and excluding Indians not taxed, three fifths of all other Persons. The actual Enumeration shall be made within three Years after the first Meeting of the Congress of the United States, and within every subsequent Term of ten Years, in such Manner as they shall by Law direct. The Number of Representatives shall not exceed one for every thirty Thousand, but each State shall have at Least one Representative; and until such enumeration shall be made, the State of New Hampshire shall be entitled to chuse three, Massachusetts eight, Rhode-Island and Providence Plantations one, Connecticut five, New-York six, New Jersey four, Pennsylvania eight, Delaware one, Maryland six, Virginia ten, North Carolina five, South Carolina five, and Georgia three.

When vacancies happen in the Representation from any State, the Executive Authority thereof shall issue Writs of Election to fill such Vacancies.

The House of Representatives shall chuse their speaker and other Officers; and shall have the sole Power of Impeachment.

Section 3—

The Senate of the United States shall be composed of two Senators from each State, chosen by the Legislature thereof for six Years; and each Senator shall have one Vote.

Immediately after they shall be assembled in Consequence of the first Election, they shall be divided as equally as may be into three Classes. The Seats of the Senators of the first Class shall be vacated at the Expiration of the second Year, of the second Class at the Expiration of the fourth Year, and of the third Class at the Expiration of the sixth Year, so that one third may be chosen every second Year; and if Vacancies happen by Resignation, or otherwise, during the Recess of the Legislature of any State, the Executive thereof may make temporary Appointments until the next Meeting of the Legislature, which shall then fill such Vacancies.

No Person shall be a Senator who shall not have attained to the Age of thirty Years, and been nine Years a Citizen of the United States, and who shall not, when elected, be an Inhabitant of that State for which he shall be chosen.

The Vice President of the United States shall be President of the Senate, but shall have no Vote, unless they be equally divided.

The Senate shall chuse their other Officers, and also a President pro tempore, in the Absence of the Vice President, or when he shall exercise the Office of President of the United States.

The Senate shall have the sole Power to try all Impeachments. When sitting for that Purpose, they shall be on Oath or Affirmation. When the President of the United States is tried, the Chief Justice shall preside: And no Person shall be convicted without the concurrence of two thirds of the Members present. Judgment in Cases of Impeachment shall not extend further than to removal from Office, and disqualification to hold and enjoy any Office of honor, Trust or Profit under the United States: but the Party convicted shall nevertheless be liable and subject to Indictment, Trial, Judgment and Punishment, according to law.

Section 4—

The Times, Places and Manner of holding Elections for Senators and Representatives, shall be prescribed in each State by the Legislature thereof; but the Congress may at any time by Law make or alter such Regulations, except as to the Places of chusing Senators.

The Congress shall assemble at least once in every Year, and such Meeting shall be on the first Monday in December, unless they shall by Law appoint a different Day.

Section 5—

Each House shall be the Judge of the Elections, Returns and Qualifications of its own Members, and a Majority of each shall constitute a Quorum to do business; but a smaller Number may adjourn from day to day, and may be authorized to compel the Attendance of absent Members, in such Manner, and under such Penalties as each House may provide.

Each House may determine the Rules of its Proceedings, punish its Members for disorderly Behaviour, and, with the Concurrence of two thirds, expel a Member.

Each House shall keep a journal of its Proceedings, and from time to time publish the same, excepting such Parts as may in their Judgment require Secrecy; and the yeas and Nays of the Members of either House on any question shall, at the Desire of one fifth of those Present, be entered on the journal.

Neither House, during the Session of Congress, shall, without the Consent of the other, adjourn for more than three days, nor to any other place than that in which the two Houses shall be sitting.

Section 6—

The Senators and Representatives shall receive a Compensation for their Services, to be ascertained by Law, and paid out of the Treasury of the United States. They shall in all Cases, except Treason, Felony and Breach of the Peace, be privileged from Arrest during their Attendance at the Session of their respective Houses, and in going to and returning from the same; and for any Speech or Debate in either House, they shall not be questioned in any other Place.

No Senator or Representative shall, during the Time for which he was elected, be appointed to any civil Office under the Authority of the United States, which shall have been created, or the Emoluments whereof shall have been encreased during such time; and no Person holding any Office under the United States, shall be a Member of either House during his Continuance in Office.

Section 7—

All Bills for raising Revenue shall originate in the House of Representatives; but the Senate may propose or concur with Amendments as on other Bills.

Every Bill which shall have passed the House of Representatives and the Senate, shall, before it become a Law, be presented to the President of the United States; If he approve he shall sign it, but if not he shall return it, with his Objections to that House in which it shall have originated, who shall enter the Objections at large on their Journal, and proceed to reconsider it. If after such Reconsideration two thirds of that House shall agree to pass the Bill, it shall be sent, together with the Objections, to the other House, by which it shall likewise be reconsidered, and if approved by two thirds of that House, it shall become a Law. But in all such Cases the Votes of both Houses shall be determined by yeas and Nays, and the Names of the Persons voting for and against the Bill shall be entered on the Journal of each House respectively. If any Bill shall not be returned by the President within ten Days (Sundays excepted) after it shall have been presented to him, the Same shall be a Law, in like Manner as if he had signed it, unless the Congress by their Adjournment prevent its Return, in which Case it shall not be a Law.

Every Order, Resolution, or Vote to which the Concurrence of the Senate and House of Representatives may be necessary (except on a question of Adjournment) shall be presented to the President of the United States; and before the Same shall take Effect, shall be approved by him, or being disapproved by him, shall be repassed by two thirds of the Senate and House of Representatives, according to the Rules and Limitations prescribed in the Case of a Bill.

Section 8—

The Congress shall have Power To lay and collect Taxes, Duties, Imposts and Excises, to pay the Debts and provide for the common Defence and general Welfare of the United States; but all Duties, Imposts and Excises shall be uniform throughout the United States;

To borrow Money on the credit of the United States;

To regulate Commerce with foreign Nations, and among the several States, and with the Indian Tribes;

To establish an uniform Rule of Naturalization, and uniform Laws on the subject of Bankruptcies throughout the United States;

To coin Money, regulate the Value thereof, and of foreign Coin, and fix the Standard of Weights and Measures;

To provide for the Punishment of counterfeiting the Securities and current Coin of the United States;

To establish Post Offices and post Roads;

To promote the Progress of Science and useful Arts, by securing for limited Times to Authors and Inventors the exclusive Right to their respective Writings and Discoveries;

To constitute Tribunals inferior to the supreme Court;

To define and punish Piracies and Felonies committed on the high Seas, and Offences against the Law of Nations;

To declare War, grant Letters of Marque and Reprisal, and make rules concerning Captures on Land and Water;

To raise and support Armies, but no Appropriation of Money to that Use shall be for a longer Term than two Years;

To provide and maintain a Navy;

To make Rules for the Government and Regulation of the land and naval Forces;

To provide for calling forth the Militia to execute the Laws of the Union, suppress Insurrections and repel Invasions;

To provide for organizing, arming, and disciplining, the Militia, and for governing such Part of them as may be employed in the Service of the United States, reserving to the States respectively, the Appointment of the Officers, and the Authority of training the Militia according to the discipline prescribed by Congress;

To exercise exclusive Legislation in all Cases whatsoever, over such District (not exceeding ten Miles square), as may, by Cession of particular States, and the Acceptance of Congress, become the Seat of the Government of the United States, and to exercise like Authority over all Places purchased by the Consent of the Legislature of the State in which the Same shall be for the Erection of Forts, Magazines, Arsenals, dock-Yards, and other needful Buildings; — And

To make all Laws which shall be necessary and proper for carying into Execution the foregoing Powers, and all other Powers vested by this Constitution in the Government of the United States, or in any Department or Officer thereof.

Section 9—

The Migration or Importation of such Persons as any of the States now existing shall think proper to admit, shall not be prohibited by the Congress prior to the Year one thousand eight hundred and eight, but a Tax or duty may be imposed on such Importation, not exceeding ten dollars for each Person.

The Privilege of the Writ of Habeas Corpus shall not be suspended, unless when in Cases of Rebellion or Invasion the public Safety may require it.

No Bill of Attainder or ex post facto Law shall be passed.

No Capitation, or other direct, Tax shall be laid, unless in Proportion to the Census or Enumeration herein before directed to be taken.

No Tax or Duty shall be laid on Articles exported from any State.

No Preference shall be given by any Regulation of Commerce or Revenue to the Ports of one State over those of another; nor shall Vessels bound to, or from, one State, be obliged to enter, clear or pay Duties in another.

No money shall be drawn from the Treasury, but in Consequence of Appropriations made by Law; and a regular Statement and Account of the Receipts and Expenditures of all public Money shall be published from time to time.

No Title of Nobility shall be granted by the United States: And no Person holding any Office of Profit or Trust under them, shall, without the Consent of the Congress, accept of any present, Emolument, Office, or Title, of any kind whatever, from any King, Prince, or foreign State.

Section 10—

No State shall enter into any Treaty, Alliance, or Confederation; grant Letters of Marque and Reprisal; coin Money; emit Bills of Credit; make any Thing but gold and silver Coin a Tender in Payment of Debts; pass any Bill of Attainder, ex post facto Law, or Law impairing the Obligation of Contracts, or grant any Title of Nobility.

No State shall, without the Consent of the Congress, lay any Imposts or Duties on Imports or Exports, except what may be absolutely necessary for executing it's inspection Laws: and the net Produce of all Duties and Imposts, laid by any State on Imports or Exports, shall be for the Use of the Treasury of the United States; and all such Laws shall be subject to the Revision and Controul of the Congress.

No State shall, without the Consent of Congress, lay any Duty of Tonnage, keep Troops, or Ships of War in time of Peace, enter into any Agreement or Compact with another State, or with a foreign Power, or engage in War, unless actually invaded, or in such imminent Danger as will not admit of delay.

Article II

Section 1—

The executive Power shall be vested in a President of the United States of America. He shall hold his Office during the Term of four Years, and, together with the Vice President, chosen for the same Term, be elected, as follows

Each State shall appoint, in such Manner as the Legislature thereof may direct, a Number of Electors, equal to the whole Number of Senators and Representatives to which the State may be entitled in the Congress: but no Senator or Representative, or Person holding an Office of Trust or Profit under the United States, shall be appointed an Elector.

The Electors shall meet in their respective States, and vote by Ballot for two Persons, of whom one at least shall not be an Inhabitant of the same State with themselves. And they shall make a List of all the Persons voted for, and of the Number of Votes for each; which List they shall sign and certify, and transmit sealed to the Seat of the Government of the United States, directed to the President of the Senate. The President of the Senate shall, in the Presence of the Senate and House of Representatives, open all the Certificates, and the Votes shall then be counted. The Person having the greatest Number of Votes shall be the President, if such Number be a Majority of the whole Number of Electors appointed; and if there be more than one who have such Majority, and have an equal Number of Votes, then the House of Representatives shall immediately chuse by Ballot one of them for President: and if no Person have a Majority, then from the five

highest on the List the said House shall in like Manner chuse the President. But in chusing the President, the Votes shall be taken by States, the Representation from each State having one Vote; A quorum for this Purpose shall consist of a Member or Members from two thirds of the States, and a Majority of all the States shall be necessary to a Choice. In every Case, after the Choice of the President, the Person having the greatest Number of Votes of the Electors shall be the Vice President. But if there should remain two or more who have equal Votes, the Senate shall chuse from them by Ballot the Vice President.

The Congress may determine the Time of chusing the Electors, and the Day on which they shall give their Votes; which Day shall be the same throughout the United States.

No Person except a natural born Citizen, or a Citizen of the United States, at the time of the Adoption of this Constitution, shall be eligible to the Office of President; neither shall any Person be eligible to that Office who shall not have attained to the Age of thirty five Years, and been fourteen Years a Resident within the United States.

In Case of the Removal of the President from Office, or of his Death, Resignation, or Inability to discharge the Powers and Duties of the said Office, the Same shall devolve on the Vice President, and the Congress may by Law provide for the Case of Removal, Death, Resignation or Inability, both of the President and Vice President, declaring what Officer shall then act as President, and such Officer shall act accordingly, until the Disability be removed, or a President shall be elected.

The President shall, at stated Times, receive for his Services, a Compensation, which shall neither be encreased nor diminished during the Period for which he shall have been elected, and he shall not receive within that Period any other Emolument from the United States, or any of them.

Before he enter on the Execution of his Office, he shall take the following Oath or Affirmation: "I do solemnly swear (or affirm) that I will faithfully execute the Office of President of the United States, and will to the best of my Ability, preserve, protect and defend the Constitution of the United States."

Section 2—

The President shall be Commander in Chief of the Army and Navy of the United States, and of the Militia of the several States, when called into the actual Service of the United States; he may require the Opinion, in writing, of the principal Officer in each of the executive Departments, upon any Subject relating to the Duties of their respective Offices, and he shall have Power to grant Reprieves and Pardons for Offences against the United States, except in Cases of Impeachment.

He shall have Power, by and with the Advice and Consent of the Senate, to make Treaties, provided two thirds of the Senators present concur; and he shall nominate, and by and with the Advice and Consent of the Senate, shall appoint Ambassadors, other public Ministers and Consuls, Judges of the supreme Court, and all other Officers of the United States, whose Appointments are not herein otherwise provided for, and which shall be established by Law: but the Congress may by Law vest the Appointment of such inferior Officers, as they think proper, in the President alone, in the Courts of Law, or in the Heads of Departments.

The President shall have Power to fill up all Vacancies that may happen during the Recess of the Senate, by granting Commissions which shall expire at the End of their next Session.

Section 3—
He shall from time to time give to the Congress Information of the State of the Union, and recommend to their Consideration such Measures as he shall judge necessary and expedient; he may, on extraordinary Occasions, convene both Houses, or either of them, and in Case of Disagreement between them, with Respect to the Time of Adjournment, he may adjourn them to such Time as he shall think proper; he shall receive Ambassadors and other public Ministers; he shall take Care that the Laws be faithfully executed, and shall Commission all the Officers of the United States.

Section 4—
The President, Vice President and all civil Officers of the United States, shall be removed from Office on Impeachment for, and Conviction of, Treason, Bribery, or other High Crimes and Misdemeanors.

Article III
Section 1—
The judicial Power of the United States, shall be vested in one supreme Court, and in such inferior Courts as the Congress may from time to time ordain and establish. The Judges, both of the supreme and inferior Courts, shall hold their Offices during good Behaviour, and shall, at stated Times, receive for their Services, a Compensation, which shall not be diminished during their Continuance in Office.

Section 2—
The judicial Power shall extend to all Cases, in Law and Equity, arising under this Constitution, the Laws of the United States, and Treaties made, or which shall be made, under their Authority; — to all Cases affecting Ambassadors, other public Ministers and Consuls; — to all Cases of admiralty and maritime jurisdiction; — to Controversies to which the United States shall be a Party; — to Controversies between two or more States;-between a State and Citizens of another State; — between Citizens of different States; — between Citizens of the same State claiming Lands under Grants of different States, and between a State, or the Citizens thereof, and foreign States, Citizens or Subjects.

In all Cases affecting Ambassadors, other public Ministers and Consuls, and those in which a State shall be Party, the supreme Court shall have original Jurisdiction. In all the other Cases before mentioned, the supreme Court shall have appellate Jurisdiction, both as to Law and Fact, with such Exceptions, and under such Regulations as the Congress shall make.

The Trial of all Crimes, except in Cases of Impeachment, shall be by Jury; and such Trial shall be held in the State where the said Crimes shall have been committed; but when not committed within any State, the Trial shall be at such Place or Places as the Congress may by Law have directed.

Section 3—
Treason against the United States, shall consist only in levying War against them, or in adhering to their Enemies, giving them Aid and Comfort. No Person shall be convicted of Treason unless on the Testimony of two Witnesses to the same overt Act, or on Confession in open Court.

The Congress shall have Power to declare the Punishment of Treason, but no Attainder of Treason shall work Corruption of Blood, or Forfeiture except during the Life of the Person attainted.

Article IV
Section 1—
Full Faith and Credit shall be given in each State to the public Acts, Records, and judicial Proceedings of every other State. And the Congress may by general Laws prescribe the Manner in which such Acts, Records and Proceedings shall be proved, and the Effect thereof.

Section 2—
The Citizens of each State shall be entitled to all Privileges and Immunities of Citizens in the several States.

A person charged in any State with Treason, Felony, or other Crime, who shall flee from Justice, and be found in another State, shall on Demand of the executive Authority of the State from which he fled, be delivered up, to be removed to the State having Jurisdiction of the Crime.

No Person held to Service or Labour in one State, under the Laws thereof, escaping into another, shall in Consequence of any Law or Regulation therein, be discharged from such Service or Labour, but shall be delivered upon on Claim of the Party to whom such Service or Labour may be due.

Section 3—
New States may be admitted by the Congress into this Union; but no new State shall be formed or erected within the Jurisdiction of any other State; nor any State be formed by the Junction of two or more States, or Parts of States, without the Consent of the Legislatures of the States concerned as well as of the Congress.

The Congress shall have Power to dispose of and make all needful Rules and Regulations respecting the Territory or other Property belonging to the United States; and nothing in this Constitution shall be so construed as to Prejudice any Claims of the United States, or of any particular State.

Section 4—
The United States shall guarantee to every State in this Union a Republican Form of Government, and shall protect each of them against Invasion; and on Application of the Legislature, or of the Executive (when the Legislature cannot be convened) against domestic Violence.

Article V
The Congress, whenever two thirds of both Houses shall deem it necessary, shall propose Amendments to this Constitution, or, on the Application of the Legislatures of two thirds of the several States, shall call a Convention for proposing Amendments, which, in either Case, shall be valid to all Intents and Purposes, as Part of this Constitution, when ratified by the Legislatures of three fourths of the several States, or by Conventions in three fourths thereof, as the one or the other Mode of Ratification may be proposed by the Congress; Provided that no Amendment which may be made prior to the Year One thousand eight hundred and eight shall in any Manner affect the first and fourth Clauses in the Ninth Section of the first

Article; and that no State, without its Consent, shall be deprived of its equal Suffrage in the Senate.

Article VI

All Debts contracted and Engagements entered into, before the Adoption of this Constitution, shall be as valid against the United States under this Constitution, as under the Confederation.

This Constitution, and the Laws of the United States which shall be made in Pursuance thereof; and all Treaties made, or which shall be made, under the Authority of the United States, shall be the supreme Law of the Land; and the Judges in every State shall be bound thereby, any Thing in the Constitution or Laws of any State to the Contrary notwithstanding.

The Senators and Representatives before mentioned, and the Members of the several State Legislatures, and all executive and judicial Officers, both of the United States and of the several States, shall be bound by Oath or Affirmation, to support this Constitution; but no religious Test shall ever be required as a Qualification to any Office or public Trust under the United States.

Article VII

The Ratification of the Conventions of nine States, shall be sufficient for the Establishment of this Constitution between the States so ratifying the Same.

Done in Convention by the Unanimous Consent of the States present the Seventeenth Day of September in the Year of our Lord one thousand seven hundred and Eighty seven and of the Independence of the United States of America the Twelfth IN WITNESS whereof We have hereunto subscribed our Names,

G⁰. Washington—
Presid'. and deputy from Virginia

New Hampshire
John Langdon
Nicholas Gilman

Massachusetts
Nathaniel Gorham
Rufus King

Connecticut
Wm. Saml. Johnson
Roger Sherman

New York
Alexander Hamilton

New Jersey
Wil: Livingston
David Brearley
Wm. Paterson
Jona: Dayton

Pennsylvania
B. Franklin
Thomas Mifflin
Rob'. Morris
Geo. Clymer
Thos. FitzSimons
Jared Ingersoll
James Wilson
Gouv Morris

Delaware
Geo: Read
Gunning Bedford jun
John Dickinson
Richard Bassett
Jaco: Broom

Maryland
James McHenry
Dan of S'. Thos. Jenifer
Dan'. Carroll

Virginia
John Blair—
James Madison Jr.

North Carolina
Wm. Blount
Rich'd Dobbs Spaight
Hu Williamson

South Carolina
J. Rutledge
Charles Cotesworth Pinckney
Charles Pinckney
Pierce Butler

Georgia
William Few
Abr Baldwin

Attest:
William Jackson, *Secretary*

[Rhode Island and the Providence Plantations Rhode Island did not send delegates to the Constitutional Convention.]

Bill of Rights

The first 10 amendments to the Constitution were adopted as a single unit on 15 Dec 1791. Together, they constitute a collection of mutually reinforcing guarantees of individual rights and of limitations on federal and state governments.

Amendment I

Congress shall make no law respecting an establishment of religion, or prohibiting the free exercise thereof; or abridging the freedom of speech, or of the press; or the right of the people peaceably to assemble, and to petition the Government for a redress of grievances.

Amendment II

A well regulated Militia, being necessary to the secu-

rity of a free State, the right of the people to keep and bear Arms, shall not be infringed.

Amendment III

No Soldier shall, in time of peace be quartered in any house, without the consent of the Owner, nor in time of war, but in a manner to be prescribed by law.

Amendment IV

The right of the People to be secure in their persons,

houses, papers, and effects, against unreasonable searches and seizures, shall not be violated, and no Warrants shall issue, but upon probable cause, supported by Oath or affirmation, and particularity describing the place to be searched, and the persons or things to be seized.

Amendment V

No person shall be held to answer for a capital, or otherwise infamous crime, unless on a presentment or indictment of a Grand Jury, except in cases arising in the land or naval forces, or in the Militia, when in actual service in time of War or public danger; nor shall any person be subject for the same offence to be twice put in jeopardy of life or limb; nor shall be compelled in any criminal case to be a witness against himself, nor be deprived of life, liberty, or property, without due process of law; nor shall private property be taken for public use, without just compensation.

Amendment VI

In all criminal prosecutions, the accused shall enjoy the right to a speedy and public trial, by an impartial jury of the State and district wherein the crime shall have been committed, which district shall have been previously ascertained by law, and to be informed of the nature and cause of the accusation; to be confronted with the witnesses against him; to have compulsory process for obtaining witnesses in his favor, and to have Assistance of Counsel for his defence.

Amendment VII

In Suits at common law, where the value in controversy shall exceed twenty dollars, the right of trial by jury shall be preserved, and no fact tried by a jury, shall be otherwise re-examined in any Court of the United States, than according to the rules of the common law.

Amendment VIII

Excessive bail shall not be required, nor excessive fines imposed, nor cruel and unusual punishments inflicted.

Amendment IX

The enumeration in the Constitution, of certain rights, shall not be construed to deny or disparage others retained by the people.

Amendment X

The powers not delegated to the United States by the Constitution, nor prohibited by it to the States, are reserved to the States respectively, or to the people.

Further Amendments

Amendment XI
(ratified 7 Feb 1795)

The Judicial power of the United States shall not be construed to extend to any suit in law or equity, commenced or prosecuted against one of the United States by Citizens of another State, or by Citizens or Subjects of any Foreign State.

Amendment XII
(ratified 15 Jun 1804)

The Electors shall meet in their respective states and vote by ballot for President and Vice-President, one of whom, at least, shall not be an inhabitant of the same state with themselves; they shall name in their ballots the person voted for as President, and in distinct ballots the person voted for as Vice-President, and they shall make distinct lists of all persons voted for as President, and of all persons voted for as Vice-President, and of the number of votes for each, which lists they shall sign and certify, and transmit sealed to the seat of the government of the United States, directed to the President of the Senate; — The President of the Senate shall, in the presence of the Senate and House of Representatives, open all the certificates and the votes shall then be counted; — The person having the greatest number of votes for President, shall be the President, if such number be a majority of the whole number of Electors appointed; and if no person have such majority, then from the persons having the highest numbers not exceeding three on the list of those voted for as President, the House of Representatives shall choose immediately, by ballot, the President. But in choosing the President, the votes shall be taken by states, the representation from each state having one vote; a quorum for this purpose shall consist of a member or members from two-thirds of the states, and a majority of all the states shall be necessary to a choice. And if the House of Representatives shall not choose a President whenever the right of choice shall devolve upon then, before the fourth day of March next following, then the Vice-President shall act as President, as in the case of the death or other constitutional disability of the President. — The person having the greatest number of votes as Vice-President, shall be the Vice-President, if such number be a majority of the whole number of Electors appointed, and if no person have a majority, then from the two highest numbers on the list, the Senate shall choose the Vice-President; a quorum for the purpose shall consist of two-thirds of the whole number of Senators, and a majority of the whole number shall be necessary to a choice. But no person constitutionally ineligible to the office of President shall be eligible to that of Vice-President of the United States.

Amendment XIII
(ratified 6 Dec 1865)

Section 1—

Neither slavery nor involuntary servitude, except as a punishment for crime whereof the party shall have been duly convicted, shall exist within the United States, or any place subject to their jurisdiction.

Section 2—

Congress shall have power to enforce this article by appropriate legislation.

Amendment XIV
(ratified 9 Jul 1868)

Section 1—

All persons born or naturalized in the United States, and subject to the jurisdiction thereof, are citizens of the United States and of the State wherein they reside. No State shall make or enforce any law which shall abridge the privileges or immunities of citizens of the United States; nor shall any State deprive any person of life, liberty, or property, without due process of law; nor deny to any person within its jurisdiction the equal protection of the laws.

Section 2—

Representatives shall be apportioned among the several States according to their respective numbers, counting the whole number of persons in each State, excluding Indians not taxed. But when the right to vote at any election for the choice of electors for President and Vice President of the United States, Representatives in Congress, the Executive and Judicial officers of a State, or the members of the Legislature thereof, is denied to any of the male inhabitants of such State, being twenty-one years of age, and citizens of the United States, or in any way abridged, except for participation in rebellion, or other crime, the basis of representation therein shall be reduced in the proportion which the number of such male citizens shall bear to the whole number of male citizens twenty-one years of age in such State.

Section 3—

No person shall be a Senator or Representative in Congress, or elector of President and Vice President, or hold any office, civil or military, under the United States, or under any State, who, having previously taken an oath, as a member of Congress, or as an officer of the United States, or as a member of any State legislature, or as an executive or judicial officer of any State, to support the Constitution of the United States, shall have engaged in insurrection or rebellion against the same, or given aid or comfort to the enemies thereof. But Congress may by a vote of two-thirds of each House, remove such disability.

Section 4—

The validity of the public debt of the United States, authorized by law, including debts incurred for payment of pensions and bounties for services in suppressing insurrection or rebellion, shall not be questioned. But neither the United States nor any State shall assume or pay any debt or obligation incurred in aid of insurrection or rebellion against the United States, or any claim for the loss or emancipation of any slave; but all such debts, obligations and claims shall be held illegal and void.

Section 5—

The Congress shall have power to enforce, by appropriate legislation, the provisions of this article.

Amendment XV
(ratified 8 Feb 1870)

Section 1—

The right of citizens of the United States to vote shall not be denied or abridged by the United States or by any State on account of race, color, or previous condition of servitude.

Section 2—

The Congress shall have power to enforce this article by appropriate legislation.

Amendment XVI
(ratified 3 Feb 1913)

The Congress shall have power to lay and collect taxes on incomes, from whatever source derived, without apportionment among the several States, and without regard to any census or enumeration.

Amendment XVII
(ratified 13 Feb 1913)

The Senate of the United States shall be composed of two Senators from each State, elected by the people thereof for six years; and each Senator shall have one vote. The electors in each State shall have the qualifications requisite for electors of the most numerous branch of the State legislatures.

When vacancies happen in the representation of any State in the Senate, the executive authority of such State shall issue writs of election to fill such vacancies: Provided, That the legislature of any State may empower the executive thereof to make temporary appointments until the people fill the vacancies by election as the legislature may direct.

This amendment shall not be so construed as to affect the election or term of any Senator chosen before it becomes valid as part of the Constitution.

Amendment XVIII
(ratified 16 Jan 1919; repealed 5 Dec 1933
by Amendment XXI)

Section 1—

After one year from the ratification of this article the manufacture, sale, or transportation of intoxicating liquors within, the importation thereof into, or the exportation thereof from the United States and all territory subject to the jurisdiction thereof for beverage purposes is hereby prohibited.

Section 2—

The Congress and the several States shall have concurrent power to enforce this article by appropriate legislation.

Section 3—

This article shall be inoperative unless it shall have been ratified as an amendment to the Constitution by the legislatures of the several States as provided in the Constitution, within seven years from the date of the submission hereof to the States by the Congress.

Amendment XIX
(ratified 18 Aug 1920)

The right of citizens of the United States to vote shall not be denied or abridged by the United States or by any State on account of sex.

Congress shall have power to enforce this article by appropriate legislation.

Amendment XX
(ratified 23 Jan 1933)

Section 1—

The terms of the President and Vice President shall end at noon on the 20th day of January, and the terms of Senators and Representatives at noon on the 3d day of January, of the years in which such terms would have ended if this article had not been ratified; and the terms of their successors shall then begin.

Section 2—

The Congress shall assemble at least once in every year, and such meeting shall begin at noon on the 3d day of January, unless they shall by law appoint a different day.

Section 3—

If, at the time fixed for the beginning of the term of the President, the President elect shall have died, the Vice President elect shall become President. If a President shall not have been chosen before the time fixed for the beginning of his term, or if the President elect shall have failed to qualify, then the Vice President elect shall act as President until a President shall have qualified; and the Congress may by law provide for the case wherein neither a President elect nor a Vice President elect shall have qualified, declaring who shall then act as President, or the manner in which one who is to act shall be selected, and such person shall act accordingly until a President or Vice President shall have qualified.

Section 4—
The Congress may by law provide for the case of the death of any of the persons from whom the House of Representatives may choose a President whenever the right of choice shall have devolved upon them, and for the case of the death of any of the persons from whom the Senate may choose a Vice President whenever the right of choice shall have devolved upon them.

Section 5—
Sections 1 and 2 shall take effect on the 15th day of October following the ratification of this article.

Section 6—
This article shall be inoperative unless it shall have been ratified as an amendment to the Constitution by the legislatures of three-fourths of the several States within seven years from the date of its submission.

Amendment XXI
(ratified 5 Dec 1933)

Section 1—
The eighteenth article of amendment to the Constitution of the United States is hereby repealed.

Section 2—
The transportation or importation into any State, Territory, or possession of the United States for delivery or use therein of intoxicating liquors, in violation of the laws thereof, is hereby prohibited.

Section 3—
This article shall be inoperative unless it shall have been ratified as an amendment to the Constitution by conventions in the several States, as provided in the Constitution, within seven years from the date of the submission hereof to the States by the Congress.

Amendment XXII
(ratified 27 Feb 1951)

Section 1—
No person shall be elected to the office of the President more than twice, and no person who has held the office of President, or acted as President, for more than two years of a term to which some other person was elected President shall be elected to the office of the President more than once. But this Article shall not apply to any person holding the office of President when this Article was proposed by the Congress, and shall not prevent any person who may be holding the office of President, or acting as President, during the term within which this Article becomes operative from holding the office of President or acting as President during the remainder of such term.

Section 2—
This Article shall be inoperative unless it shall have been ratified as an amendment to the Constitution by the legislatures of three-fourths of the several States within seven years from the date of its submission to the States by the Congress.

Amendment XXIII
(ratified 29 Mar 1961)

Section 1—
The District constituting the seat of Government of the United States shall appoint in such manner as the Congress may direct:
A number of electors of President and Vice President equal to the whole number of Senators and Representatives in Congress to which the District would be entitled if it were a State, but in no event more than the least populous State; they shall be in addition to those appointed by the States, but they shall be considered, for the purposes of the election of President and Vice President, to be electors appointed by a State; and they shall meet in the District and perform such duties as provided by the twelfth article of amendment.

Section 2—
The Congress shall have power to enforce this article by appropriate legislation.

Amendment XXIV
(ratified 23 Jan 1964)

Section 1—
The right of citizens of the United States to vote in any primary or other election for President or Vice President, for electors for President or Vice President, or for Senator or Representative in Congress, shall not be denied or abridged by the United States or any State by reason of failure to pay any poll tax or other tax.

Section 2—
The Congress shall have power to enforce this article by appropriate legislation.

Amendment XXV
(ratified 23 Jan 1967)

Section 1—
In case of the removal of the President from office or of his death or resignation, the Vice President shall become President.

Section 2—
Whenever there is a vacancy in the office of the Vice President, the President shall nominate a Vice President who shall take office upon confirmation by a majority vote of both Houses of Congress.

Section 3—
Whenever the President transmits to the President pro tempore of the Senate and the Speaker of the House of Representatives his written declaration that he is unable to discharge the powers and duties of his office, and until he transmits to them a written declaration to the contrary, such powers and duties shall be discharged by the Vice President as Acting President.

Section 4—
Whenever the Vice president and a majority of either the principal officers of the executive departments or of such other body as Congress may by law provide, transmit to the President pro tempore of the Senate and the Speaker of the House of Representatives their written declaration that the President is unable to discharge the powers and duties of his office, the Vice President shall immediately assume the powers and duties of the office as Acting President.

Thereafter, when the President transmits to the President pro tempore of the Senate and the Speaker of the House of Representatives his written declaration that no inability exists, he shall resume the powers and duties of his office unless the Vice President and a majority of either the principal officers of the executive department or of such other body as Congress may by law provide, transmit within four days to the President pro tempore of the Senate and the Speaker of the House of Representatives their written declaration that the President is unable to discharge the powers and duties of his office. Thereupon Congress shall decide the issue, assembling within forty-eight hours for that purpose if not in session. If the Congress, within twenty-one days after receipt of the latter written declaration, or, if Congress is not in session, within twenty-one days after Congress is required to assemble, determines by two-thirds vote of both Houses that the President is unable to discharge the powers and duties of his office, the Vice President shall continue to discharge the same as Acting President; otherwise, the President shall resume the powers and duties of his office.

Amendment XXVI
(ratified 1 Jul 1971)

Section 1—
The right of citizens of the United States, who are eighteen years of age or older, to vote shall not be denied or abridged by the United States or by any State on account of age.

Section 2—
The Congress shall have power to enforce this article by appropriate legislation.

Amendment XXVII
(ratified 7 May 1992)

No law, varying the compensation for the services of the Senators and Representatives, shall take effect, until an election of representatives shall have intervened.

Confederate States and Secession Dates

In the months following Abraham Lincoln's election as president in 1860, seven states of the Deep South held conventions and approved secession, thus precipitating the Civil War. After the attack on Fort Sumter SC on 12 Apr 1861, Virginia, Arkansas, North Carolina, and Tennessee also seceded (Tennessee was the only state to hold a popular referendum without a convention on secession). The Confederacy operated as a separate government, with Jefferson Davis as president and Alexander H. Stephens as vice president. Its principal goals were the preservation of states' rights and the institution of slavery. Although it enjoyed a series of military victories in the first two years of fighting, the surrender at Appomattox VA by Gen. Robert E. Lee on 9 Apr 1865 signaled its dissolution.

STATE	DATE	STATE	DATE	STATE	DATE
South Carolina	20 Dec 1860	Georgia	19 Jan 1861	Arkansas	6 May 1861
Mississippi	9 Jan 1861	Louisiana	26 Jan 1861	North Carolina	20 May 1861
Florida	10 Jan 1861	Texas	1 Feb 1861	Tennessee	8 Jun 1861
Alabama	11 Jan 1861	Virginia	17 Apr 1861		

Emancipation Proclamation

The Emancipation Proclamation was issued by Pres. Abraham Lincoln and freed the slaves of the Confederate states in rebellion against the Union. After the Battle of Antietam (17 Sep 1862), Lincoln issued his proclamation calling on the revolted states to return to their allegiance before the next year, otherwise their slaves would be declared free men. No state returned, and the threatened declaration was issued on 1 Jan 1863.

By the President of the United States of America:

A Proclamation.

Whereas, on the twenty-second day of September, in the year of our Lord one thousand eight hundred and sixty-two, a proclamation was issued by the President of the United States, containing, among other things, the following, to wit:

"That on the first day of January, in the year of our Lord one thousand eight hundred and sixty-three, all persons held as slaves within any State or designated part of a State, the people whereof shall then be in rebellion against the United States, shall be then, thenceforward, and forever free; and the Executive Government of the United States, including the military and naval authority thereof, will recognize and maintain the freedom of such persons, and will do no act or acts to repress such persons, or any of them, in any efforts they may make for their actual freedom.

"That the Executive will, on the first day of January aforesaid, by proclamation, designate the States and parts of States, if any, in which the people thereof, respectively, shall then be in rebellion against the United States; and the fact that any State, or the people thereof, shall on that day be, in good faith, represented in the Congress of the United States by members chosen thereto at elections wherein a majority of the qualified voters of such State shall have participated, shall, in the absence of strong countervailing testimony, be deemed conclusive evidence that such State, and the people thereof, are not then in rebellion against the United States."

Now, therefore I, Abraham Lincoln, President of the United States, by virtue of the power in me vested as Commander-in-Chief, of the Army and Navy of the United States in time of actual armed rebellion against the authority and government of the United States, and as a fit and necessary war measure for suppressing said rebellion, do, on this first day of January, in the year of our Lord one thousand eight hundred and sixty-three, and in accordance with my purpose so to do publicly proclaimed for the full period of one hundred days, from the day first above mentioned, order and designate as the States and parts of States wherein the people thereof respectively, are this day in rebellion against the United States, the following, to wit:

Arkansas, Texas, Louisiana, (except the Parishes of St. Bernard, Plaquemines, Jefferson, St. John, St. Charles, St. James Ascension, Assumption, Terrebonne, Lafourche, St. Mary, St. Martin, and Orleans, including the City of New Orleans) Mississippi, Alabama, Florida, Georgia, South Carolina, North Carolina, and Virginia, (except the forty-eight counties designated as West Virginia, and also the counties of Berkley, Accomac, Northampton, Elizabeth City, York, Princess Ann, and Norfolk, including the cities of Norfolk and Portsmouth[)], and which excepted parts, are for the present, left precisely as if this proclamation were not issued.

And by virtue of the power, and for the purpose aforesaid, I do order and declare that all persons held as slaves within said designated States, and parts of States, are, and henceforward shall be free; and that the Executive government of the United States, including the military and naval authorities thereof, will recognize and maintain the freedom of said persons.

And I hereby enjoin upon the people so declared to be free to abstain from all violence, unless in necessary self-defence; and I recommend to them that, in all cases when allowed, they labor faithfully for reasonable wages.

And I further declare and make known, that such persons of suitable condition, will be received into the armed service of the United States to garrison forts, positions, stations, and other places, and to man vessels of all sorts in said service.

And upon this act, sincerely believed to be an act of justice, warranted by the Constitution, upon military necessity, I invoke the considerate judgment of mankind, and the gracious favor of Almighty God.

In witness whereof, I have hereunto set my hand and caused the seal of the United States to be affixed.

Done at the City of Washington, this first day of January, in the year of our Lord one thousand eight hundred and sixty three, and of the Independence of the United States of America the eighty-seventh.

By the President: Abraham Lincoln.
William H. Seward, Secretary of State.

Gettysburg Address

On 19 Nov 1863 Pres. Abraham Lincoln delivered this speech at the consecration of the National Cemetery at Gettysburg PA, the site of one of the most decisive battles of the American Civil War. The main address at the dedication ceremony was one of two hours, delivered by Edward Everett, the best-known orator of the time. It is Lincoln's short speech, however, which is remembered, not only as a memorial to those who gave their lives on the battlefield, but as a statement of the ideals on which the nation was founded.

Four score and seven years ago our fathers brought forth on this continent a new nation, conceived in Liberty, and dedicated to the proposition that all men are created equal. Now we are engaged in a great civil war, testing whether that nation or any nation so conceived and so dedicated, can long endure. We are met on a great battle-field of that war. We have come to dedicate a portion of that field, as a final resting place for those who here gave their lives that that nation might live. It is altogether fitting and proper that we should do this. But, in a larger sense, we can not dedicate—we can not consecrate—we can not hallow—this ground. The brave men, living and dead, who struggled here, have consecrated it, far above our poor power to add or detract. The world will little note, nor long remember what we say here, but it can never forget what they did here. It is for us the living, rather, to be dedicated here to the unfinished work which they who fought here have thus far so nobly advanced. It is rather for us to be here dedicated to the great task remaining before us—that from these honored dead we take increased devotion to that cause for which they gave the last full measure of devotion—that we here highly resolve that these dead shall not have died in vain—that this nation, under God, shall have a new birth of freedom—and that government of the people, by the people, for the people, shall not perish from the earth.

United States Government

The Presidency at a Glance

	PRESIDENCY	POLITICAL PARTY	TIME IN OFFICE	VICE PRESIDENT
1	George Washington	Federalist	1789–1797	John Adams
2	John Adams	Federalist	1797–1801	Thomas Jefferson
3	Thomas Jefferson	Jeffersonian Republican	1801–1809	Aaron Burr
				George Clinton
4	James Madison	Jeffersonian Republican	1809–1817	George Clinton
				Elbridge Gerry
5	James Monroe	Jeffersonian Republican	1817–1825	Daniel D. Tompkins

The Presidency at a Glance (continued)

	PRESIDENCY	POLITICAL PARTY	TIME IN OFFICE	VICE PRESIDENT
6	John Quincy Adams	National Republican	1825–1829	John C. Calhoun
7	Andrew Jackson	Democratic	1829–1837	John C. Calhoun
				Martin Van Buren
8	Martin Van Buren	Democratic	1837–1841	Richard M. Johnson
9	William Henry Harrison*	Whig	4 Mar–4 Apr 1841	John Tyler
10	John Tyler	Whig	1841–1845	none
11	James K. Polk	Democratic	1845–1849	George Mifflin Dallas
12	Zachary Taylor*	Whig	1849–1850	Millard Fillmore
13	Millard Fillmore	Whig	1850–1853	none
14	Franklin Pierce	Democratic	1853–1857	William Rufus de Vane King
15	James Buchanan	Democratic	1857–1861	John C. Breckinridge
16	Abraham Lincoln*†	Republican	1861–1865	Hannibal Hamlin
				Andrew Johnson
17	Andrew Johnson	Democratic (Union)	1865–1869	none
18	Ulysses S. Grant	Republican	1869–1877	Schuyler Colfax
				Henry Wilson
19	Rutherford B. Hayes	Republican	1877–1881	William A. Wheeler
20	James A. Garfield*†	Republican	4 Mar–19 Sep 1881	Chester A. Arthur
21	Chester A. Arthur	Republican	1881–1885	none
22	Grover Cleveland	Democratic	1885–1889	Thomas A. Hendricks
23	Benjamin Harrison	Republican	1889–1893	Levi Parons Morton
24	Grover Cleveland	Democratic	1893–1897	Adlai E. Stevenson
25	William McKinley*†	Republican	1897–1901	Garret A. Hobart
				Theodore Roosevelt
26	Theodore Roosevelt	Republican	1901–1909	Charles Warren Fairbanks
27	William Howard Taft	Republican	1909–1913	James Schoolcraft Sherman
28	Woodrow Wilson	Democratic	1913–1921	Thomas R. Marshall
29	Warren G. Harding*	Republican	1921–1923	Calvin Coolidge
30	Calvin Coolidge	Republican	1923–1929	Charles G. Dawes
31	Herbert Hoover	Republican	1929–1933	Charles Curtis
32	Franklin D. Roosevelt*	Democratic	1933–1945	John Nance Garner
				Henry A. Wallace
				Harry S. Truman
33	Harry S. Truman	Democratic	1945–1953	Alben W. Barkley
34	Dwight D. Eisenhower	Republican	1953–1961	Richard M. Nixon
35	John F. Kennedy*†	Democratic	1961–1963	Lyndon B. Johnson
36	Lyndon B. Johnson	Democratic	1963–1969	Hubert H. Humphrey
37	Richard M. Nixon**	Republican	1969–1974	Spiro T. Agnew
				Gerald R. Ford
38	Gerald R. Ford	Republican	1974–1977	Nelson A. Rockefeller
39	Jimmy Carter	Democratic	1977–1981	Walter F. Mondale
40	Ronald Reagan	Republican	1981–1989	George H.W. Bush
41	George H.W. Bush	Republican	1989–1993	Dan Quayle
42	William J. Clinton	Democratic	1993–2001	Albert Gore
43	George W. Bush	Republican	2001–	Richard B. Cheney

*Died in office.   **Resigned from office.   †Assassinated.

Presidential Biographies

George Washington (22 Feb [11 Feb, Old Style] 1732, Westmoreland county VA—14 Dec 1799, Mt. Vernon, in Fairfax county VA), American Revolutionary commander-in-chief (1775–83) and first president of the US (1789–97). Born into a wealthy family, he was educated privately and worked as a surveyor from age 14. In 1752 he inherited his brother's estate at Mount Vernon, including 18 slaves whose ranks grew to 49 by 1760, though he disapproved of slavery. In the French and Indian War he was commissioned a colonel and sent to the Ohio Territory. After Edward Braddock was killed, Washington became commander of all Virginia forces, entrusted with defending the western frontier (1755–58). He resigned to manage his es-

tate and in 1759 married Martha Dandridge Custis (1731–1802), a widow. He served in the House of Burgesses 1759–74, where he supported the colonists' cause, and in the Continental Congress 1774–75. In 1775 he was elected to command the Continental Army. In the ensuing American Revolution, he proved a brilliant commander and stalwart leader despite several defeats. With the war effectively ended by the capture of Yorktown (1781), he resigned his commission and returned to Mount Vernon (1783). He was a delegate to and presiding officer of the Constitutional Convention (1787) and helped secure ratification of the Constitution in Virginia. When the state electors met to select the first president (1789), Washington was the unanimous choice. He formed a cabinet to balance sectional and political differences but was committed to a strong central government. Elected to a second term, he followed a middle course between the political factions that became the Federalist Party and Democratic Party. He proclaimed a policy of neutrality in the war between Britain and France (1793) and sent troops to suppress the Whiskey Rebellion (1794). He declined to serve a third term, setting a 144-year precedent, and retired in 1797 after delivering his "Farewell Address." Known as the "father of his country," he is regarded as one of the greatest figures in US history.

John Adams (30 Oct [19 Oct, Old Style] 1735, Braintree [now in Quincy] MA—4 Jul 1826, Quincy MA), first vice president (1789–97) and second president (1797–1801) of the US. He practiced law in Boston and in 1764 married Abigail Smith. Active in the American independence movement, he was elected to the Massachusetts legislature and served as a delegate to the Continental Congress (1774–78), where he was appointed to several committees, including one with Thomas Jefferson and others to draft the Declaration of Independence. He served as a diplomat in France, The Netherlands, and England (1778–88). In the first US presidential election, he received the second-largest number of votes and became vice president under George Washington. Adams's term as president was marked by controversy over his signing the Alien and Sedition Acts in 1798 and by his alliance with the conservative Federalist Party. In 1800 he was defeated for reelection by Jefferson and retired to live a secluded life in Massachusetts. In 1812 he was reconciled with Jefferson, with whom he began an illuminating correspondence. Both men died on 4 Jul 1826, the Declaration's 50th anniversary. Pres. John Quincy Adams was his son.

Thomas Jefferson (13 Apr [2 Apr, Old Style] 1743, Shadwell VA—4 Jul 1826, Monticello VA), third president of the US (1801–9). He was a planter and lawyer from 1767, as well as a slaveholder who opposed slavery. While a member of the House of Burgesses (1769–75), he initiated the Committee of Correspondence (1773) with Richard Henry Lee and Patrick Henry. In 1774 he wrote the influential *Summary View of the Rights of British America*, stating that the British Parliament had no authority to legislate for the colonies. A delegate to the second Continental Congress, he was appointed to the committee to draft the Declaration of Independence and became its primary author. He was elected governor of Virginia (1779–81) but was unable to organize effective opposition when British forces invaded the colony (1780–81). Criticized for his conduct, he retired, vowing to remain a private citizen. Again a member of the Continental Congress (1783–85), he proposed territorial provisions later incorporated in the Northwest Ordinances. He traveled in Europe on diplomatic missions and became minister to France (1785–89). George Washington made him secretary of state (1790–93). He soon became embroiled in conflict with Alexander Hamilton over their opposing interpretations of the Constitution. This led to the rise of factions and political parties, with Jefferson representing the Democratic-Republicans. He served as vice president (1797–1801) but opposed the Alien and Sedition Acts enacted under Pres. John Adams. As part of this opposition, Jefferson drafted one of the Virginia and Kentucky Resolutions. In 1801

he became president after an electoral-vote tie with Aaron Burr was settled by the House of Representatives. Jefferson initiated frugal fiscal policies and simplicity in the ceremonial role of the president. He oversaw the Louisiana Purchase and authorized the Lewis and Clark Expedition. He sought to avoid involvement in the Napoleonic Wars by signing the Embargo Act. He retired to his plantation, Monticello, where he pursued his many interests in science, philosophy, and architecture. He served as president of the American Philosophical Society 1797–1815, and in 1819 founded and designed the University of Virginia. In January 2000, the Thomas Jefferson Memorial Foundation accepted the conclusion, supported by DNA evidence, that Jefferson had fathered at least one, and perhaps as many as six, children with Sally Hemings, one of his house slaves. After a long estrangement, he and Adams became reconciled in 1813 and exchanged views on national issues. They both died on July 4, 1826, the 50th anniversary of the signing of the Declaration of Independence.

James Madison (16 Mar [5 Mar, Old Style] 1751, Port Conway VA—28 Jun 1836, Montpelier VA), fourth president of the US (1809–17). He served in the state legislature (1776–80, 1784–86). At the Constitutional Convention (1787), his active participation and his careful notes on the debates earned him the title "father of the Constitution." To promote ratification, he collaborated with Alexander Hamilton and John Jay on *The Federalist*. In the House of Representatives (1789–97), he sponsored the Bill of Rights, was a leading Jeffersonian Republican, and split with Hamilton over funding state war debts. In reaction to the Alien and Sedition Acts, he drafted one of the Virginia and Kentucky Resolutions (1798). He was appointed secretary of state (1801–9) by Thomas Jefferson, with whom he developed US foreign policy. Elected president in 1808, he was occupied by the trade and shipping embargo problems caused by France and Britain that led to the War of 1812. He was reelected in 1812; his second term was marked principally by the war, during which he reinvigorated the Army, and also saw approval of the charter of the Second Bank of the US and the first US protective tariff. He retired to his Virginia estate, Montpelier, with his wife, Dolley (1768–1849), whose political acumen he had long prized. He continued to write articles and letters and served as rector of the University of Virginia (1826–36).

James Monroe (28 Apr 1758, Westmoreland county VA—4 Jul 1831, New York NY), fifth president of the US (1817–25). He fought in the American Revolution and studied law under Thomas Jefferson. He served in the Congress (1783–86) and Senate (1790–94), where he opposed George Washington's administration. He nevertheless became minister to France (1794–96), where he misled the French about US politics and was recalled. He served as governor of Virginia 1799–1802. Pres. Jefferson sent him to France, where he helped negotiate the Louisiana Purchase (1803), then named him minister to Britain (1803–7). He returned to Virginia and became governor (1811), but resigned to become US secretary of state (1811–17) and secretary of war (1814–15). He served two terms as president, presiding in a period that became known as the Era of Good Feelings. He oversaw the Seminole War (1817–18) and the acquisition of the Floridas (1819–21), and signed the Missouri Compromise (1820). With secretary of state John Quincy Adams, he developed the principles of US foreign policy later called the Monroe Doctrine.

John Quincy Adams (11 Jul 1767, Braintree [now in Quincy] MA–23 Feb 1848, Washington DC), sixth president of the US (1825–29). He was the eldest son of Pres. John Adams and Abigail. He accompanied his father to Europe on diplomatic missions (1778–80) and was later appointed minister to The Netherlands (1794) and Prussia (1797). In 1801 he returned to Massachusetts and served in the Senate (1803–8). Resuming his diplomatic service, he became minister to Russia (1809–11) and Britain (1815–17). Appointed secretary of state (1817–24), he was instrumental in acquiring Florida from Spain and in drafting the Monroe Doctrine. He was one of three candidates in the 1824 presidential election, in which none received a majority of the electoral votes, though Andrew Jackson received a plurality. The decision went to the House of Representatives, where Adams received crucial support from Henry Clay and the electoral votes necessary to elect him president. He appointed Clay secretary of state, which further angered Jackson. Adams's presidency was unsuccessful; when he ran for reelection, Jackson defeated him. In 1830 he was elected to the House of Representatives, where he served until his death. He was outspoken in his opposition to slavery and in 1839 proposed a constitutional amendment forbidding slavery in any new state admitted to the Union. Southern congressmen prevented discussion of antislavery petitions by passing gag rules (repealed in 1844 as a result of Adams's persistence). In 1841 he successfully defended the slaves in the Amistad Mutiny case.

Andrew Jackson (15 Mar 1767, Waxhaws region SC—8 Jun 1845, the Hermitage, near Nashville TN), seventh president of the US (1829–37). He fought briefly in the American Revolution near his frontier home, where his family was killed. He studied law and in 1788 was appointed prosecuting attorney for western North Carolina. When the region became the state of Tennessee, he was elected to the House of Representatives (1796–97) and Senate (1797–98). He served on the state supreme court (1798–1804) and in 1802 was elected major general of the Tennessee militia. When the War of 1812 began, he offered the US the services of his 50,000-volunteer militia. He was sent to fight the Creek Indians allied with the British in Mississippi Territory. After a lengthy battle (1813–14), he defeated them at the Battle of Horseshoe Bend. After capturing Pensacola FL from the British-allied Spanish, he marched overland to engage the British in Louisiana. A decisive victory at the Battle of New Orleans made him a national hero, dubbed "Old Hickory" by the press. After US acquisition of Florida, he was named governor of the territory (1821). One of four candidates in the 1824 presidential election, he won an electoral-votes plurality but the House gave the election to John Quincy Adams. In 1828 Jackson defeated Adams after a fierce campaign and became the first president elected from west of the Appalachian Mountains. His election was considered a triumph of political democracy. He replaced many federal officeholders with his supporters, a process that became known as the spoils system. He pursued a policy of moving

Native Americans westward with the Indian Removal Acts. He split with his vice president, John C. Calhoun, over the nullification movement. His reelection in 1832 was due in part to support for his anticapitalistic fiscal policies and a controversial veto that affected the Bank of the US. His popularity continued to build throughout his presidency. During his tenure a strong Democratic Party developed that led to a vigorous two-party system.

Martin Van Buren (5 Dec 1782, Kinderhook NY–24 Jul 1862, Kinderhook NY), eighth president of the US (1837–41). He practiced law and served in the NY state senate (1812–20) and as state attorney general (1816–19). He became the leader of an informal group of political supporters, called the Albany Regency because they dominated state politics even while Van Buren was in Washington. He was elected to the US Senate (1821–28), where he supported states' rights and opposed a strong central government. After John Quincy Adams became president, he joined with Andrew Jackson and others to form a group that later became the Democratic Party. He was elected governor of New York (1828) but resigned to become US secretary of state (1829–31). He was nominated for vice president at the first Democratic Party convention (1832) and served under Jackson (1833–37). As Jackson's chosen successor, he defeated William H. Harrison to win the 1836 election. His presidency was marked by an economic depression, the Maine–Canada border dispute, the Seminole War in Florida, and debate over the annexation of Texas. He was defeated in his bid for reelection and failed to win the Democratic nomination in 1844 because of his antislavery views. In 1848 he was nominated for president by the Free Soil Party but failed to win the election and retired.

William Henry Harrison (9 Feb 1773, Charles City county VA–4 Apr 1841, Washington DC), ninth president of the US (1841). Born into a political family, he enlisted in the army at 18 and served under Anthony Wayne at the Battle of Fallen Timbers. In 1798 he became secretary of the Northwest Territories, and in 1800 governor of the new Indiana Territory. In response to pressure from white settlers, he negotiated treaties with the Native Americans that ceded millions of acres of additional land to the US When Tecumseh organized an uprising in 1811, Harrison led a US force to defeat the Indians at the Battle of Tippecanoe, a victory that largely established his reputation in the public mind. In the War of 1812 he was made a brigadier general and defeated the British and their Indian allies at the Battle of the Thames in Ontario. After the war he moved to Ohio, where he became prominent in the Whig Party. He served in the House of Representatives (1816–19) and Senate (1825–28). As the Whig candidate in the 1836 presidential election, he lost narrowly. In 1840 he and his running mate, John Tyler, won election with a slogan emphasizing Harrison's frontier triumph: "Tippecanoe and Tyler too." The 68-year-old Harrison delivered his inaugural speech without a hat or overcoat in a cold drizzle, contracted pneumonia, and died one month later, the first president to die in office.

John Tyler (29 Mar 1790, Charles City county VA–18 Jan 1862, Richmond VA), 10th president of the US (1841–45). He practiced law before serving in the state legislature (1811–16, 1823–25, 1839) and as governor of Virginia (1825–27). In the House of

Representatives (1817–21) and Senate (1827–36), he was a states-rights supporter. Though a slaveholder, he sought to prohibit the slave trade in the District of Columbia, provided Maryland and Virginia concurred. He resigned from the Senate rather than acquiesce to state instructions to change his vote on a censure of Pres. Andrew Jackson. After breaking with the Democratic Party, he was nominated by the Whig Party for vice president under William H. Harrison. They won the 1840 election, carefully avoiding the issues and stressing party loyalty and the slogan "Tippecanoe and Tyler too!" Harrison died a month after taking office, and Tyler became the first to attain the presidency "by accident." He vetoed a national bank bill supported by the Whigs, and all but one member of the cabinet resigned, leaving him without party support. Nonetheless, he reorganized the navy, settled the second of the Seminole Wars in Florida, and oversaw the annexation of Texas. He was nominated for reelection but withdrew in favor of James Polk and retired to his Virginia plantation. Committed to states' rights but opposed to secession, he organized the Washington Peace Conference (1861) to resolve sectional differences. When the Senate rejected a proposed compromise, Tyler urged Virginia to secede.

James Knox Polk (2 Nov 1795, Mecklenburg county NC–15 Jun 1849, Nashville TN), 11th president of the US (1845–49). He became a lawyer in Tennessee and a friend and supporter of Andrew Jackson, who helped Polk win election to the House of Representatives (1825–39). He left the House to become governor of Tennessee (1839–41). At the deadlocked 1844 Democratic convention Polk was nominated as the compromise candidate; he is considered the first dark-horse presidential candidate. A proponent of western expansion, he campaigned with the slogan "Fifty-four Forty or Fight," to bring a solution to the Oregon Question. Elected at 49, the youngest president to that time, he successfully concluded the Oregon border dispute with Britain (1846) and secured passage of the Walker Tariff Act (1846), which lowered import duties and helped foreign trade. He led the prosecution of the Mexican War, which resulted in large territorial gains but reopened the debate over the extension of slavery. His administration also established the Department of the Interior, the US Naval Academy, and the Smithsonian Institution, oversaw revision of the treasury system, and proclaimed the validity of the Monroe Doctrine. Though an efficient and competent president, deft in his handling of Congress, he was exhausted by his efforts and did not seek reelection; he died three months after leaving office.

Zachary Taylor (24 Nov 1784, Montebello VA–9 Jul 1850, Washington DC), 12th president of the US (1849–50). Born in Virginia, he grew up on the Kentucky frontier. He fought in the War of 1812, the Black Hawk War (1832), and the Seminole War in Florida (1835–42), earning the nickname "Old Rough-and-Ready" for his indifference to hardship. Sent to Texas in anticipation of war with Mexico, he defeated the Mexican invaders at the battles of Palo Alto and Resaca de la Palma (1846). After the Mexican War formally began, he captured Monterrey and granted the Mexican army an eight-week armistice. Displeased, Pres. James Polk moved Taylor's best troops to serve under Winfield Scott in the invasion of Veracruz. Taylor ignored orders to remain in Monterrey and marched south to defeat a large Mexican force at the Battle of Buena Vista (1847). He became a national hero and was nominated as the Whig candidate for president (1848). He defeated Lewis Cass to win the election. His brief term was marked by a controversy over the new territories that produced the Compromise of 1850 as well as by a scandal involving members of his cabinet. He died, probably of cholera, after only 16 months in office and was succeeded by Millard Fillmore.

Millard Fillmore (7 Jan 1800, Locke Township, NY–8 Mar 1874, Buffalo NY), 13th president of the US (1850–53). Born into poverty, he became an indentured apprentice at 15. He studied law with a local judge and began to practice in Buffalo in 1823. Initially identified with the Anti-Masonic Party (1828–34), he followed his political mentor, Thurlow Weed, to the Whigs and was soon a leader of the party's northern wing. He served in the House of Representatives (1833–35, 1837–43), where he became a follower of Henry Clay. In 1848 the Whigs nominated Fillmore as vice president, and he was elected with Zachary Taylor. He became president on Taylor's death in 1850. Though he abhorred slavery, he supported the Compromise of 1850 and insisted on federal enforcement of the Fugitive Slave Act. His stand, which alienated the North, led to his defeat by Winfield Scott at the Whigs' nominating convention in 1852 and effectively led to the death of the party. Throughout his career he advocated US internal development and was an early champion of expansion in the Pacific. In 1853 he sent Matthew Perry with a US fleet to Japan, forcing its isolationist government to enter into trade and diplomatic relations. He returned to Buffalo and was nominated for president by the third-party Know-Nothing Party in 1856, won by Democrat James Buchanan.

Franklin Pierce (23 Nov 1804, Hillsboro NH–8 Oct 1869, Concord NH), 14th president of the US (1853–57). He practiced law and served in the House of Representatives (1833–37) and Senate (1837–42). He returned to his law practice, serving briefly in the Mexican War. At the deadlocked Democratic convention of 1852, he was nominated as the compromise candidate; though largely unknown nationally, he unexpectedly trounced Winfield Scott in the general election. For the sake of harmony and business prosperity, he was inclined to oppose antislavery agitation so as to placate Southern opinion. He promoted US territorial expansion, resulting in the diplomatic controversy of the Ostend Manifesto. He reorganized the diplomatic and consular service and created the Court of Claims. He encouraged plans for a transcontinental railroad and approved the Gadsden Purchase. To promote northwestern migration and conciliate sectional demands, he approved the Kansas-Nebraska Act but was unable to settle the resultant problems. Defeated for renomination by James Buchanan in 1856, he retired from politics.

James Buchanan (23 Apr 1791, near Mercersburg PA–1 Jun 1868, near Lancaster PA), 15th president of the US (1857–61). He became a lawyer and member of the Pennsylvania legislature before serving in the House of Representatives (1821–31), as minister to Russia (1832–34), and in the Senate (1834–45). He was secretary of state in James Polk's cabinet (1845–49). As minister to Britain (1853–56), he helped draft the Ostend Manifesto. In 1856 he secured the Democratic nomination and election as president, defeating John C. Fremont. Though experienced in government and law, he lacked the moral courage to deal effectively with the slavery crisis and equivocated on the question of Kansas's status as a slaveholding state. The ensuing split within his party allowed Abraham Lincoln to win the election of 1860. He denounced the secession of South Carolina following the election and sent reinforcements to Fort Sumter, but failed to respond further to the mounting crisis.

Abraham Lincoln (12 Feb 1809, near Hodgenville KY—15 Apr 1865, Washington DC), 16th president of the US (1861–65). Born in a Kentucky log cabin, he moved to Indiana in 1816 and to Illinois in 1830. He worked as a storekeeper, rail-splitter, postmaster, and surveyor, then enlisted as a volunteer in the Black Hawk War and became a captain. Though largely self-taught, he practiced law in Springfield IL and served in the state legislature (1834–40). He was elected as a Whig to the House of Representatives (1847–49). As a circuit-riding lawyer from 1849, he became one of the state's most successful lawyers, noted for his shrewdness, common sense, and honesty (earning the nickname "Honest Abe"). In 1856 he joined the Republican Party, which nominated him as its candidate in the 1858 Senate election. In a series of seven debates with Stephen A. Douglas (the Lincoln-Douglas Debates), he argued against the extension of slavery into the territories, though not against slavery itself. Although morally opposed to slavery, he was not an abolitionist. During the campaign, he attempted to rebut Douglas' charge that he was a dangerous radical by reassuring audiences that he did not favor political equality for blacks. Despite his loss in the election, the debates brought him national attention. He again ran against Douglas in the 1860 presidential election, which he won by a large margin. But the South opposed his position on slavery in the territories, and before his inauguration seven Southern states had seceeded from the Union. The ensuing American Civil War completely consumed Lincoln's administration. He excelled as a wartime leader, creating a high command for directing all the country's energies and resources toward the war effort and combining statecraft and overall command of the armies with what some have called military genius. However, his abrogation of some civil liberties, especially the writ of habeas corpus, and the closing of several newspapers by his generals disturbed both Democrats and Republicans, including some members of his own cabinet. To unite the North and influence foreign opinion, he issued the Emancipation Proclamation (1863); his Gettysburg Address (1863) further ennobled the war's purpose. The continuing war affected some Northerners' resolve and his reelection was not assured, but strategic battle victories turned the tide and he easily defeated George B. McClellan in 1864. His platform included passage of the 13th Amendment outlawing slavery (ratified 1865). At his second inaugural, with victory in sight, he spoke of moderation in reconstructing the South and building a harmonious Union. On 14 Apr, five days after the war ended, he was shot by John Wilkes Booth and soon after died.

Andrew Johnson (29 Dec 1808, Raleigh NC—31 Jul 1875, near Carter Station TN), 17th president of the US (1865–69). Born in North Carolina and reared in Tennessee, he was self-educated and initially worked as a tailor. He organized a workingman's party and was elected to the state legislature (1835–43), where he became a spokesman for small farmers. He served in the House of Representatives (1843–53) and as governor of Tennessee (1853–57). Elected to the Senate (1857–62), he opposed antislavery agitation, but in 1860 he opposed Southern secession, even after Tennessee seceded in 1861, and during the Civil War he was the only Southern senator who refused to join the Confederacy. In 1862 he was appointed military governor of Tennessee, then under Union control. In 1864 he was selected to run for vice president with Pres. Abraham Lincoln; he assumed the presidency after Lincoln's assassination. During Reconstruction he favored a moderate policy that readmitted former Confederate states to the Union with few provisions for reform or civil rights for freedmen. In 1867 the Radical Republicans in Congress passed civil rights legislation and established the Freedmen's Bureau. His veto angered Congress, which passed the Tenure of Office Act. In 1868 in defiance of the act, Johnson dismissed secretary of war Edwin M. Stanton, an ally of the Radicals. The House responded by impeaching the president for the first time in US history. In the subsequent Senate trial, the charges proved weak and the necessary two-thirds vote needed for conviction failed by one vote. Johnson remained in office until 1869, but his effectiveness had ended. He returned to Tennessee, where he won reelection to the Senate shortly before he died.

Ulysses S. Grant (Hiram Ulysses Grant) (27 Apr 1822, Point Pleasant OH—23 Jul 1885, Mount McGregor NY), 18th president of the US (1869–77). He served in the Mexican War under Zachary Taylor; he resigned his commission in 1854 when he could not afford to bring his family west. Allegations that he became a drunkard in the lonely years in the West and in later life, though never proved, would affect his reputation. He worked unsuccessfully at farming in Missouri and at his family's leather business in Illinois. When the Civil War began (1861), he was appointed brigadier general; his 1862 attack on Fort Donelson TN, produced the first major Union victory. He drove off a Confederate attack at Shiloh but was criticized for heavy Union losses. He devised the campaign to take the stronghold of Vicksburg MS, in 1863, cutting the Confederacy in half from east to west. Following his victory at the Battle of Chattanooga in 1864, he was appointed commander of the Union army. While William T. Sherman made his famous march across Georgia, Grant attacked Robert E. Lee's forces in Virginia, bringing the war to an end in 1865. Grant's administrative ability and innovative strategies were largely responsible for the Union victory. His successful Republican presidential campaign made him, at 46, the youngest man yet elected president. His two terms were marred by administrative inaction and political scandal involving members of his cabinet, including the Crédit Mobilier scandal and the Whiskey Ring operation. He was more successful in foreign affairs, in which he was aided by his secretary of state, Hamilton Fish. He supported amnesty for Confederate leaders and protection for black civil rights. His veto of a bill to increase the amount of legal tender (1874) diminished the currency crisis in the next 25 years. In 1881 he moved to New York; when a partner defrauded an investment firm co-owned by his son, the family was impoverished. His memoirs were published by his friend Mark Twain.

Rutherford Birchard Hayes (4 Oct 1822, Delaware OH—17 Jan 1893, Fremont OH), 19th president of the US (1877–81). He practiced law in Cincinnati, representing defendants in several fugitive-slave cases and becoming associated with the new Republican Party. After fighting in the Union army, he served in the House of Representatives (1865–67). As governor of Ohio (1868–72, 1875–76), he advocated a sound currency backed by gold. In 1876 he won the Republican nomination for president. His opponent, Samuel Tilden, won a larger popular vote, but Hayes's managers contested the electoral-vote returns in four states, and a special Electoral Commission awarded the election to Hayes. As part of a secret compromise reached with Southerners, he withdrew the remaining federal troops from the South, ending Reconstruction, and promised not to interfere with elections there, ensuring the return of white Democratic supremacy. He introduced civil-service reform based on merit, incurring a dispute with Roscoe Conkling and the conservative "stalwart" Republicans. At the request of state governors, he used federal troops against strikers in the railroad strikes of 1877. Declining to run for a second term, he retired to work for humanitarian causes.

James Abram Garfield (19 Nov 1831, near Orange [in Cuyahoga county] OH—19 Sep 1881, Elberon [now in Long Branch] NJ), 20th president of the US (1881). He graduated from Williams College, then returned to Ohio to teach and head an academy that became Hiram College. In the Civil War he led the 42nd Ohio Volunteers and fought at Shiloh and Chickamauga. He resigned as a major general to serve in the House of Representatives (1863–80). A Radical Republican during Reconstruction, he served on the Electoral Commission in the 1876 election, and was the House Republican leader from 1876 to 1880, when he was elected to the Senate. At the 1880 Republican nominating convention, the delegates supporting Ulysses S. Grant and James Blaine became deadlocked. On the 36th ballot Garfield was nominated as a compromise presidential candidate, with Chester Arthur as vice president, and won by a narrow margin. His brief term, less than 150 days, was marked by a dispute with Sen. Roscoe Conkling over patronage. On July 2 he was shot at Washington's railroad station by Charles J. Guiteau, an Arthur supporter. He died on September 19 after 11 weeks of public debate over the ambiguous constitutional conditions for presidential succession (later clarified by the 20th and 25th Amendments).

Chester Alan Arthur (5 Oct 1829, North Fairfield VT—18 Nov 1886, New York NY), 21st president of the US (1881–85). He practiced law in New York City from 1854. He became active in local Republican politics and a close associate of party leader Roscoe Conkling, and was appointed customs collector for the port of New York (1871–78), an office long known for its employment of the spoils system. He conducted the business of the office with integrity but continued to pad its payroll with Conkling loyalists. At the Republican national convention in 1880, Arthur became the compromise choice for vice president on the ticket with James Garfield, and he became president upon Garfield's assassination. As president, Arthur displayed unexpected independence by vetoing measures that rewarded

political patronage. He also signed the Pendleton Act, which created a civil-service system based on merit. He recommended the appropriations that initiated the rebuilding of the Navy toward the strength it later achieved in the Spanish-American War (1898). He failed to win his party's nomination for a second term.

(Stephen) Grover Cleveland (18 Mar 1837, Caldwell NJ—24 Jun 1908, Princeton NJ), 22nd and 24th president of the US (1885–89, 1893–97). He practiced law in Buffalo NY from 1859, where he entered Democratic Party politics. As mayor of Buffalo (1881–82), he was known as a foe of corruption. As governor of New York (1883–85), he earned the hostility of Tammany Hall with his independence, but in 1884 he won the Democratic nomination for president. The first Democratic president since 1856, he supported civil-service reform and opposed high protective tariffs, which became an issue in the 1888 election, when he was narrowly defeated by Benjamin Harrison. In 1892 he was re-elected by a huge popular plurality. In 1893 he attributed the US's severe economic depression to the Sherman Silver Purchase Act of 1890 and strongly urged Congress to repeal the act. The economic unrest resulted in the Pullman Strike in 1894. An isolationist, he opposed territorial expansion. In 1895 he invoked the Monroe Doctrine in the border dispute between Britain and Venezuela. By 1896 supporters of the Free Silver Movement controlled the Democratic Party, which nominated William Jennings Bryan instead of Cleveland for president. He retired to New Jersey, where he lectured at Princeton University.

Benjamin Harrison (20 Aug 1833, North Bend OH—13 Mar 1901, Indianapolis IN), 23rd president of the US (1889–93). The grandson of Pres. William H. Harrison, he practiced law in Indianapolis from the mid-1850s. He served in the Union army in the Civil War, rising to brigadier general. He served a term in the Senate (1881–87) and, even though he lost reelection, was nominated for president by the Republicans. He went on to defeat the incumbent, Grover Cleveland, who lost despite winning more of the popular vote. As president, his domestic policy was marked by passage of the Sherman Antitrust Act. His foreign policy expanded US influence abroad. His secretary of state, James Blaine, presided at the conference that led to the establishment of the Pan-American Union, resisted pressure to abandon US interests in the Samoan Islands (1889), and negotiated a treaty with Britain in the Bering Sea Dispute (1891). Defeated for reelection by Cleveland in 1892, he returned to Indianapolis to practice law. In 1898–99 he was the leading counsel for Venezuela in its boundary dispute with Britain.

William McKinley (29 Jan 1843, Niles OH—14 Sep 1901, Buffalo NY), 25th president of the US (1897–1901). He served in the Civil War as an aide to Col. Rutherford B. Hayes, who later encouraged his political career. He was elected to the House of Representatives (1877–91), where he favored protective tariffs and sponsored the McKinley Tariff of 1890. With the support of Mark Hanna, he was elected governor (1892–96). In 1896 he won the Republican presidential nomination and the general election, defeating William Jennings Bryan. He called a special session of Congress to increase customs duties, but was soon embroiled in events in Cuba and responses to the sinking of the USS

Maine, which led to the Spanish-American War. At the war's end, he advocated US dependency status for the Philippines, Puerto Rico, and other former Spanish territories. He again defeated Bryan by a large majority in 1900, and began a tour to urge control of trusts and commercial reciprocity to boost foreign trade, issues neglected during the war. In Buffalo NY on 6 Sep 1901, he was fatally shot by an anarchist, Leon Czolgosz. He was succeeded by Theodore Roosevelt.

Theodore Roosevelt (27 Oct 1858, New York NY—6 Jan 1919, Oyster Bay NY), 26th president of the US (1901–9). He was elected to the New York legislature in 1882, where he became a Republican leader opposed to the Democratic political machine. After political defeats and the death of his wife, he went to the Dakota Territory to ranch. He returned to New York to serve on the US Civil Service Commission (1889–95) and as head of the city's board of police commissioners (1895–97). A supporter of William McKinley, he served as assistant secretary of the navy (1897–98). When the Spanish–American War was declared, he resigned to organize a cavalry unit, the Rough Riders. He returned to New York a hero and was elected governor in 1899. As the Republican vice-presidential nominee, he took office when McKinley was reelected, and he became president on McKinley's assassination in 1901. One of his early initiatives was to urge enforcement of the Sherman Antitrust Act against business monopolies. He won election in his own right in 1904, defeating Alton Parker. At his urging, Congress regulated railroad rates and passed the Pure Food and Drug Act and Meat Inspection Act (1906) to provide new consumer protections. He set aside national forests, parks, and mineral, oil, and coal lands for conservation. He and secretary of state Elihu Root announced the Roosevelt corollary to the Monroe Doctrine, which reinforced the US position as defender of the Western Hemisphere. For mediating an end to the Russo–Japanese War, he received the 1906 Nobel Peace Prize. He secured a treaty with Panama for construction of a trans-isthmus canal. Declining to seek reelection, he secured the nomination for William H. Taft. After traveling in Africa and Europe, he tried to win the Republican presidential nomination in 1912; when he was rejected, he organized the Bull Moose Party and ran on a policy of New Nationalism, but failed to win the election. Throughout his life he continued to write, publishing extensively on history, politics, travel, and nature.

William Howard Taft (15 Sep 1857, Cincinnati OH—8 Mar 1930, Washington DC), 27th president of the US (1909–13). He served on the state superior court (1887–90), as US solicitor general (1890–92), and as US appellate judge (1892–1900). He was appointed head of the Philippine Commission to set up a civilian government in the islands and was its first civilian governor (1901–4). He served as US secretary of war (1904–8) under Pres. Theodore Roosevelt, who supported Taft's nomination for president in 1908. He won the election but became allied with the conservative Republicans, causing a rift with party progressives. He was again the nominee in 1912, but the split with Roosevelt and the Bull Moose Party resulted in the electoral victory of Woodrow Wilson. Taft later taught law at Yale University (1913–21), served on the National War Labor Board (1918), and was a supporter of the League of Nations. As chief justice of the Supreme Court (1921–30), he introduced reforms that made it more efficient. He secured passage of the Judges Act of 1925, which gave the Court wider discretion in accepting cases. His important opinion in *Myers* v *US* (1926) upheld the president's authority to remove federal officials. In poor health, he resigned in 1930.

(Thomas) Woodrow Wilson (28 Dec 1856, Staunton VA—3 Feb 1924, Washington DC), 28th president of the US (1913–21). He earned a law degree and later received his doctorate from Johns Hopkins University. He taught political science at Princeton University (1890–1902), and as its president (1902–10), he introduced various reforms. With the support of progressives, he was elected governor of New Jersey. His reform measures attracted national attention, and he became the Democratic presidential nominee in 1912. His campaign emphasized the progressive measures of his New Freedom policy, and he defeated Theodore Roosevelt and William H. Taft to win the presidency. As president, he approved legislation that lowered tariffs, created the Federal Reserve System, established the Federal Trade Commission, and strengthened labor unions. In foreign affairs he promoted self-government for the Philippines and sought to contain the Mexican civil war. From 1914 he maintained US neutrality in World War I, offering to mediate a settlement and initiate peace negotiations. After the sinking of the *Lusitania* (1915) and other unarmed ships, he obtained a pledge from Germany to stop its submarine campaign. Campaigning on the theme that he had "kept us out of war," he was narrowly reelected in 1916, defeating Charles Evans Hughes. Germany's renewed submarine attacks on unarmed passenger ships caused Wilson to ask for a declaration of war in April 1917. In a continuing effort to negotiate a peace agreement, he presented the Fourteen Points (1918). He led the US delegation to the Paris Peace Conference, where he attempted to stand on his original principles but was forced to compromise by the demands of various countries. The Treaty of Versailles faced opposition in the Senate from the Republican majority led by Henry C. Lodge. In search of popular support for the treaty and its League of Nations, Wilson began a cross-country speaking tour, but he collapsed and returned to Washington DC (Sep 1919), where a stroke left him partially paralyzed. He rejected any attempts to compromise his version of the League of Nations and urged his Senate followers to vote against ratification of the treaty, which was defeated in 1920. He was awarded the 1919 Nobel Peace Prize for his work on the League of Nations.

Warren Gamaliel Harding (2 Nov 1865, Caledonia (now Blooming Grove) OH—2 Aug 1923, San Francisco CA), 29th president of the US (1921–23). He became a newspaper publisher in Marion OH, where he was allied with the Republican Party's political machine. He served successively as state senator (1899–1902), lieutenant governor (1903–4), and US senator (1915–21), supporting conservative policies. At the deadlocked 1920 Republican presidential convention, he was chosen as the compromise candidate. Pledging a "return to normalcy" after World War I, he defeated James Cox with over 60% of the popular vote, the largest margin to that time. On his recommendation, Congress established a budget system for the federal government, passed a high protective tariff, revised wartime taxes, and restricted immigration. His administration convened the Washington Conference (1921–22). His ill-advised cabinet and patronage appointments, including Albert Fall, led to the Teapot Dome scandal and characterized his administration as corrupt. While in Alaska, he received word of the corruption about to be exposed and headed back. He arrived in San Francisco exhausted, reportedly suffering from food poisoning and other ills, and died there under unclear circumstances. He was succeeded by his vice president, Calvin Coolidge.

(John) Calvin Coolidge (4 Jul 1872, Plymouth VT–5 Jan 1933, Northampton MA), 30th president of the US (1923–29). He practiced law in Massachusetts from 1897 and served as lieutenant governor before being elected governor in 1918. He gained national attention by calling out the state guard during the Boston police strike in 1919. At the 1920 Republican convention, "Silent Cal" was nominated for vice president on Warren G. Harding's winning ticket. When Harding died in office in 1923, Coolidge became president. He restored confidence in an administration discredited by scandals and won the presidential election in 1924, defeating Robert La Follette. He vetoed measures to provide farm relief and bonuses to World War I veterans. His presidency was marked by apparent prosperity. Congress maintained a high protective tariff and instituted tax reductions that favored capital. Coolidge declined to run for a second term. His conservative policies of domestic and international inaction have come to symbolize the era between World War I and the Great Depression.

Herbert Clark Hoover (10 Aug 1874, West Branch IA–20 Oct 1964, New York NY), 31st president of the US (1929–33). As a mining engineer, he administered engineering projects on four continents (1895–1913). He then headed Allied relief operations in England and Belgium prior to World War I, at which time he was appointed national food administrator (1917–19) and instituted programs that furnished food to the Allies and famine-stricken areas of Europe. Appointed secretary of commerce (1921–27), he reorganized the department, creating divisions to regulate broadcasting and aviation. He oversaw commissions to build Boulder (later Hoover) Dam and the St. Lawrence Seaway. In 1928, as the Republican presidential candidate, he soundly defeated Alfred E. Smith. His hopes for a "New Day" program were quickly overwhelmed by the Great Depression. As a believer in individual freedom, he vetoed bills to create a federal unemployment agency and to fund public-works projects, instead favoring private charity. In 1932 he finally allowed relief to farmers through the Reconstruction Finance Corp. He was overwhelmingly defeated in 1932 by Franklin Roosevelt. He continued to speak out against relief measures and criticized New Deal programs. After World War II he participated in famine-relief work in Europe and was appointed head of the Hoover Commission.

Franklin Delano Roosevelt (30 Jan 1882, Hyde Park NY–12 Apr 1945, Warm Springs GA), 32nd president of the US (1933–45). He was attracted to politics as an admirer of his cousin Pres. Theodore Roosevelt and became active in the Democratic Party. In 1905 he married distant cousin Eleanor Roosevelt, who would become a valued adviser in future years. He served in the state senate (1910–13) and as assistant secretary of the navy (1913–20). In 1920 he was nominated for vice president. The next year he was stricken with polio; though unable to walk, he remained active in politics. As governor of New York (1929–33), he set up the first state relief agency in the US In 1932 he won the Democratic presidential nomination with the help of James Farley and easily defeated Pres. Herbert Hoover. In his inaugural address to a nation of more than 13 million unemployed, he pronounced that "the only thing we have to fear is fear itself." Congress passed most of the changes he sought in his New Deal program in the first hundred days of his term. He was overwhelmingly reelected in 1936 over Alf Landon. To solve legal challenges to the New Deal, he proposed enlarging the Supreme Court, but his "court-packing" plan aroused strong opposition and had to be abandoned. By the late 1930s economic recovery had slowed, but Roosevelt was more concerned with the growing threat of war. In 1940 he was reelected to an unprecedented third term, defeating Wendell Willkie. He maintained US neutrality toward the war in Europe, but approved the principle of lend-lease and in 1941 met with Winston Churchill to draft the Atlantic Charter. With US entry into World War II, he mobilized industry for military production and formed an alliance with Britain and the Soviet Union; he met with Churchill and Joseph Stalin to form war policy at Tehran (1943) and Yalta (1945). Despite declining health, he won reelection for a fourth term against Thomas Dewey (1944) but served only briefly before his death. His presidency is well regarded in US history.

Harry S. Truman (8 May 1884, Lamar MO–26 Dec 1972, Kansas City MO), 33rd president of the US (1945–53). He worked at various jobs before serving with distinction in World War I. He became a partner in a Kansas City haberdashery; when the business failed, he entered Democratic Party politics with the help of Thomas Pendergast. He was elected county judge (1922–24), and later became presiding judge of the county court (1926–34). His reputation for honesty and good management gained him bipartisan support. In the Senate (1935–45), he led a committee that exposed fraud in defense production. In 1944 he was chosen to replace the incumbent Henry Wallace as vice-presidential nominee and was elected with Pres. Franklin Roosevelt. After only 82 days as vice president, he became president on Roosevelt's death (April 1945). He quickly made final arrangements for the San Francisco charter-writing meeting of the UN, helped arrange Germany's unconditional surrender on 8 May, which ended World War II in Europe, and in July attended the Potsdam Conference. The Pacific war ended officially on 2 Sep, after he ordered atomic bombs dropped on Hiroshima and Nagasaki; his justification was a report that 500,000 US troops would be lost in a conventional invasion of Japan. He announced the Truman Doctrine to aid Greece and Turkey (1947), established the Central Intelligence Agency, and pressed for passage of the Marshall Plan to aid European countries. In 1948 he defeated Thomas Dewey despite widespread expectation of his own defeat. He initiated a foreign policy of containment to restrict the Soviet Union's sphere of influence, pursued his Point Four Program, and initiated the Berlin airlift and the NATO pact of 1949. In the Korean War he sent troops under Gen. Douglas MacArthur to head the United Nations forces.

Problems of pursuing the war occupied his administration until he retired. Though he was often criticized during his presidency, Truman's reputation grew steadily in later years.

Dwight David Eisenhower (14 Oct 1890, Denison TX — 28 Mar 1969, Washington DC), 34th president of the US (1953–61). He graduated from West Point (1915), then served in the Panama Canal Zone (1922–24) and in the Philippines under Douglas MacArthur (1935–39). In World War II Gen. George Marshall appointed him to the army's war-plans division (1941), then chose him to command US forces in Europe (1942). After planning the invasions of North Africa, Sicily, and Italy, he was appointed supreme commander of Allied forces (1943). He planned the Normandy Campaign (1944) and the conduct of the war in Europe until the German surrender (1945). He was promoted to five-star general (1944) and was named army chief of staff in 1945. He served as president of Columbia University from 1948 until being appointed supreme commander of NATO in 1951. Both Democrats and Republicans courted Eisenhower as a presidential candidate; in 1952, as the Republican candidate, he defeated Adlai Stevenson with the largest popular vote up to that time. He defeated Stevenson again in 1956 in an even larger landslide. His achievements included efforts to contain Communism with the Eisenhower Doctrine. He sent federal troops to Little Rock AR to enforce integration of a city high school (1957). When the Soviet Union launched Sputnik I (1957), he was criticized for failing to develop the US space program and responded by creating NASA (1958). In his last weeks in office the US broke diplomatic relations with Cuba.

John Fitzgerald Kennedy (29 May 1917, Brookline MA—22 Nov 1963, Dallas TX), 35th president of the US (1961–63). The son of Joseph P. Kennedy, he graduated from Harvard University and joined the Navy in World War II, where he earned medals for heroism. Elected to the House of Representatives (1947–53) and the Senate (1953–60), he supported social legislation and became increasingly committed to civil rights legislation. He supported the policies of Harry Truman but accused the State Department of trying to force Chiang Kai-shek into a coalition with Mao Zedong. In 1960 he won the Democratic nomination for president; after a vigorous campaign, managed by his brother Robert F. Kennedy and aided financially by his father, he narrowly defeated Richard Nixon. He was the youngest person and the first Roman Catholic elected president. In his inaugural address he called on Americans to "ask not what your country can do for you, ask what you can do for your country." He proposed tax-reform and civil rights legislation but received little congressional support. He established the Peace Corps and the Alliance for Progress. His foreign policy began with the abortive Bay of Pigs invasion (1961), which emboldened the Soviet Union to move missiles to Cuba, sparking the Cuban missile crisis. In 1963 he successfully concluded the Nuclear Test-Ban Treaty. In November 1963 he was assassinated while riding in a motorcade in Dallas by a sniper, allegedly Lee Harvey Oswald. The killing is considered the most notorious political murder of the 20th century. Kennedy's youth, energy, and charming family brought him world adulation and sparked the idealism of a generation, for whom the Kennedy White House became known as

"Camelot." Details about his powerful family and personal life, especially concerning his extramarital affairs, tainted his image in later years.

Lyndon Baines Johnson (27 Aug 1908, Gillespie county TX—22 Jan 1973, San Antonio TX), 36th president of the US (1963–69). He taught school in Houston before going to Washington DC in 1932 as a congressional aide. There he was befriended by Sam Rayburn and his political career blossomed. He won a seat in the House of Representatives (1937–49) as the New Deal was under conservative attack. His loyalty impressed Pres. Franklin Roosevelt, who made Johnson a protégé. He won election to the Senate in 1949 in a vicious campaign that saw fraud on both sides. As Democratic whip (1951–55) and majority leader (1955–61), he developed a talent for consensus building among dissident factions with methods both tactful and ruthless. He was largely responsible for passage of the civil rights bills of 1957 and 1960, the first in the 20th century. In 1960 he was elected vice president; he became president after the assassination of John F. Kennedy. In his first few months in office he won from Congress passage of a huge quantity of important civil rights, tax-reduction, antipoverty, and conservation legislation. He defeated Barry Goldwater in the 1964 election by the largest popular majority to that time and announced his Great Society program. He was diverted from overseeing its enactment by the escalation of US involvement in the Vietnam War, beginning with the Gulf of Tonkin Resolution. His approval ratings diminished markedly and led to his decision not to seek reelection in 1968. He retired to his Texas ranch.

Richard Milhous Nixon (9 Jan 1913, Yorba Linda CA—22 Apr 1994, New York NY), 37th president of the US (1969–74). He studied law at Duke University and practiced in California 1937–42. After serving in World War II, he was elected to the House of Representatives in 1947, employing harsh campaign tactics. He came to national attention with the Alger Hiss case, and was elected to the Senate in 1951, again following a bitter campaign. He won the vice presidency in 1952 on a ticket with Dwight D. Eisenhower; they were reelected easily in 1956. As presidential candidate in 1960, he lost narrowly to John F. Kennedy. After failing to win the 1962 California gubernatorial race, he retired from politics and moved to New York to practice law. He reentered politics by running for president in 1968, and he defeated Hubert H. Humphrey with his "southern strategy" of seeking votes from southern and western conservatives in both parties. As president, he began to gradually withdraw US military forces in an effort to end the Vietnam War while ordering the secret bombing of North Vietnamese military centers in Laos and Cambodia. Attacks on North Vietnamese sanctuaries in Cambodia drew widespread protest. Economic problems caused by inflation made the US budget deficit the largest to date, and in 1971 Nixon established unprecedented peacetime controls on wages and prices. He won reelection in 1972 with a landslide victory over George McGovern. Assisted by Henry A. Kissinger, he concluded the Vietnam War. He reopened communications with Communist China and made a state visit there. On his visit to the Soviet Union, the first by a US president, he signed the bilateral SALT agreements. The Watergate scandal overshadowed his second term; his complicity in efforts to cover up his involvement and the likelihood of impeachment led to his becoming, in August 1974, the first president to resign from office. Though never convicted of wrongdoing, he was pardoned by his successor, Gerald Ford. He retired to write his memoirs and books on foreign policy.

Gerald Rudolph Ford, Jr. (Leslie Lynch King, Jr.; 14 Jul 1913, Omaha NE), 38th president of the US (1974–77). He was an infant when his parents divorced, and his mother later married Gerald R. Ford. He attended the University of Michigan and Yale Law School, and practiced law in Michigan after World War II. He served in the House of Representative 1948–73, becoming minority leader in 1965. After Spiro Agnew resigned as vice president in 1973, Richard Nixon nominated Ford to fill the vacant post. When the Watergate scandal forced Nixon's departure, Ford became the first president who had not been elected to either the vice presidency or the presidency. A month later he pardoned Nixon; to counter widespread outrage, he voluntarily appeared before a House subcommittee to explain his action. His administration gradually lowered the high inflation rate it inherited. Ford's relations with the Democratic-controlled Congress were typified by his more than 50 vetoes, of which more than 40 were sustained. In the final days of the Vietnam War in 1975, he ordered an airlift of 237,000 anti-Communist Vietnamese refugees, most of whom came to the US. Reaction against Watergate contributed to his defeat by James Earl Carter, Jr., in 1976.

James Earl Carter, Jr. (1 Oct 1924, Plains GA), 39th president of the US (1977–81). He graduated from the US Naval Academy and served in the navy until 1953, when he left to manage the family peanut business. He served in the state senate 1962–66. Elected governor (1971–75), he opened Georgia's government offices to blacks and women and introduced stricter budgeting procedures for state agencies. In 1976, though lacking a national political base or major backing, he won the Democratic nomination and the presidency, defeating the sitting president, Gerald Ford. As president, Carter helped negotiate a peace treaty between Egypt and Israel, signed a treaty with Panama to make the Panama Canal a neutral zone after 1999, and established full diplomatic relations with China. In 1979–80 the Iran hostage crisis became a major political liability. He responded more forcefully to the USSR's invasion of Afghanistan in 1979, embargoing the shipment of US grain to that country and leading a boycott of the 1980 Summer Olympics in Moscow. Hampered by high inflation and a recession engineered to tame it, he lost his bid for reelection to Ronald Reagan. He subsequently became involved in international diplomatic negotiations and helped oversee elections in countries with insecure democratic traditions. Carter was awarded the Nobel Peace Prize in 2002.

Ronald Wilson Reagan (6 Feb 1911, Tampico IL–5 Jun 2004, Bel Air CA), 40th president of the US (1981–89). He attended Eureka College and worked as a radio sports announcer before going to Hollywood in 1937. In his career as a movie actor, he had roles in 50 films and was twice president of the Screen Actors Guild (1947–52, 1959–60). Reagan became a spokesman for the General Electric Co. and hosted its television theater program 1954–62. Having gradually changed his political affiliation from liberal Democrat to conservative Republican, he was elected governor of California and

served 1967–74. In 1980 he defeated incumbent Pres. James Earl Carter, Jr., to become president. Shortly after taking office, he was wounded in an assassination attempt. Reagan adopted supply-side economics to promote rapid economic growth and reduce the federal deficit. Congress approved most of his proposals (1981), which succeeded in lowering inflation but doubled the national debt by 1986. He began the largest peacetime military buildup in US history and in 1983 proposed construction of the Strategic Defense Initiative. His foreign policy included the INF Treaty to restrict intermediate-range nuclear weapons and the invasion of Grenada. In 1984 Reagan defeated Walter Mondale in a landslide for reelection. Details of his administration's involvement in the Iran-Contra Affair emerged in 1986 and significantly weakened his popularity and authority. Though his intellectual capacity for governing was often disparaged, his artful communication skills enabled him to pursue numerous conservative policies with conspicuous success. In 1994 he revealed that he had Alzheimer disease.

George Herbert Walker Bush (12 Jun 1924, Milton MA), 41st president of the US (1989–93). The son of Prescott Bush, later a Connecticut senator, he served in World War II, graduated from Yale University, and started an oil business in Texas. He served in the House of Representatives 1966–70 as a Republican. He then served as ambassador to the UN (1971–72), chief of liaison to China (1974–76), and head of the CIA (1976–77). In 1980 he ran for president but lost the nomination to Ronald Reagan. Bush served as vice president with Reagan (1981–88), whom he succeeded as president, defeating Michael Dukakis. He made no dramatic departures from Reagan's policies. In 1989 he ordered a brief military invasion of Panama, which toppled that country's leader, Gen. Manuel Noriega. He helped impose a UN-approved embargo against Iraq in 1990 to force its withdrawal from Kuwait. When Iraq refused, he authorized a US-led air offensive that began the Persian Gulf War. Despite general approval of his foreign policy, an economic recession led to his defeat by William Jefferson Clinton in 1992. His son George W. Bush was elected president in 2000 and reelected in 2004. In the aftermath of the 26 Dec 2004 tsunami, Bush joined fellow former president Bill Clinton as leader of a fundraising effort to aid victims of the disaster.

William Jefferson Clinton (William Jefferson Blythe III; 19 Aug 1946, Hope AR), 42nd president of the US (1993–2001). He was adopted, after his father's death in a car crash, by his mother's second husband, Roger Clinton. He attended Georgetown University, Oxford University (as a Rhodes Scholar), and Yale Law School, then taught at the University of Arkansas School of Law. He served as state attorney general (1977–79) and served several terms as governor (1979–81, 1983–92), during which he reformed Arkansas's educational system and encouraged the growth of industry through favorable tax policies. He won the Democratic presidential nomination in 1992 after withstanding charges of personal impropriety, and defeated the incumbent, George H.W. Bush. As president, he obtained approval of the North American Free Trade Agreement in 1993. He and his wife, Hillary Rodham Clinton, strongly advocated their plan to overhaul the US health care system, but Congress rejected it. He committed US forces to a peacekeeping initiative in Bosnia and Herzegovina. In 1994 the Democrats lost control of Congress for the first time since 1954. Clinton defeated Robert Dole to win reelection in 1996. He faced renewed charges of personal impropriety, this time involving Monica Lewinsky, and as a result, in 1998 he became the second president in history to be impeached. Charged with perjury and obstruction of justice, he was acquitted at his Senate trial in 1999. His two terms saw sustained economic growth and successive budget surpluses, the first in three decades. In the aftermath of the 26 Dec 2004 tsunami, Clinton joined fellow former president George H. W. Bush as leader of a fundraising effort to aid victims of the disaster.

George Walker Bush (6 Jul 1946, New Haven CT), 43rd president of the US (from 2001). The eldest child of Pres. George H.W. Bush, he attended Yale University and Harvard Business School. After spending a decade in the oil business with mixed success, he served as managing general partner of the Texas Rangers baseball franchise. In 1994 he was elected governor of Texas (1995–2000). Despite losing the national popular vote to Vice President Al Gore by more than 500,000 votes, he gained the presidency when a Supreme Court ruling effectively ended a recount of ballots in Florida. His commitment to lower taxes, the unilateralist tendencies of his policies, and his response to the terrorist attacks on 11 Sep 2001, which included military retaliation in Afghanistan, gave shape to his administration. The invasion of Iraq by American-led forces in March 2003 was followed by a problematic occupation during which a burgeoning insurgency threatened Iraqi efforts to stabilize a democratically elected government. Bush won reelection in 2004 with themes centering on national security and forthright conservatism, and in 2005 he made the privatization of Social Security a centerpiece of his administration's policy endeavors.

Presidents' Wives and Children

Maiden names of the presidents' wives appear in small capital letters.

DATE OF MARRIAGE	PRESIDENTS, WIVES, AND CHILDREN
	George Washington
6 Jan 1759	**Martha DANDRIDGE Custis** (2 Jun 1731–22 May 1802) no children
	John Adams
25 Oct 1764	**Abigail SMITH** (22 Nov 1744–28 Oct 1818) ▸ Abigail Amelia Adams (1765–1813), ▸ John Quincy Adams (1767–1848), ▸ Susanna Adams (1768–1770), ▸ Charles Adams (1770–1800), ▸ Thomas Boylston Adams (1772–1832)
	Thomas Jefferson
1 Jan 1772	**Martha WAYLES Skelton** (30 Oct 1748–6 Sep 1782) ▸ Martha Washington Jefferson (1772–1836), ▸ Jane Randolph Jefferson (1774–1775), ▸ infant son (1777–1777), ▸ Mary Jefferson (1778–1804), ▸ Lucy Elizabeth Jefferson (1780–1781), ▸ Lucy Elizabeth Jefferson (1782–1785)
	James Madison
15 Sep 1794	**Dolley Dandridge PAYNE Todd** (20 May 1768–12 Jul 1849) no children
	James Monroe
16 Feb 1786	**Elizabeth KORTRIGHT** (30 Jun 1768–23 Sep 1830) ▸ Eliza Kortright Monroe (1786–1835?), ▸ James Spence Monroe (1799–1800), ▸ Maria Hester Monroe (1803–1850)
	John Quincy Adams
26 Jul 1797	**Louisa Catherine JOHNSON** (12 Feb 1775–15 May 1852) ▸ George Washington Adams (1801–1829), ▸ John Adams (1803–1834), ▸ Charles Francis Adams (1807–1886), ▸ Louisa Catherine Adams (1811–1812)
	Andrew Jackson
Aug 1791	**Rachel DONELSON Robards** (15? Jun 1767–22 Dec 1828) no children
	Martin Van Buren
21 Feb 1807	**Hannah HOES** (8 Mar 1783–5 Feb 1819) ▸ Abraham Van Buren (1807–1873), ▸ John Van Buren (1810–1866), ▸ Martin Van Buren (1812–1855), ▸ Smith Thompson Van Buren (1817–1876)
	William Henry Harrison
25 Nov 1795	**Anna Tuthill SYMMES** (25 Jul 1775–25 Feb 1864) ▸ Elizabeth Bassett Harrison (1796–1846), ▸ John Cleves Symmes Harrison (1798–1830), ▸ Lucy Singleton Harrison (1800–1826), ▸ William Henry Harrison (1802–1838), ▸ John Scott Harrison (1804–1878), ▸ Benjamin Harrison (1806–1840), ▸ Mary Symmes Harrison (1809–1842), ▸ Carter Bassett Harrison (1811–1839), ▸ Anna Tuthill Harrison (1813–1865), ▸ James Findlay Harrison (1814–1817)

Presidents' Wives and Children (continued)

DATE OF MARRIAGE	PRESIDENTS, WIVES, AND CHILDREN

John Tyler

29 Mar 1813   **Letitia** CHRISTIAN (12 Nov 1790–10 Sep 1842)
▶ Mary Tyler (1815–1848), ▶ Robert Tyler (1816–1877), ▶ John Tyler (1819–1896), ▶ Letitia Tyler (1821–1907), ▶ Anne Contesse Tyler (1825–1825), ▶ Alice Tyler (1827–1854), ▶ Tazewell Tyler (1830–1874)

26 Jun 1844   **Julia** GARDINER (4 May 1820–10 Jul 1889)
▶ David Gardiner Tyler (1846–1927), ▶ John Alexander Tyler (1848–1883), ▶ Julia Gardiner Tyler (1849?–1871), ▶ Lachlan Tyler (1851–1902), ▶ Lyon Gardiner Tyler (1853–1935), ▶ Robert Fitzwalter Tyler (1856–1927), ▶ Pearl Tyler (1860–1947)

James K. Polk

1 Jan 1824   **Sarah** CHILDRESS (4 Sep 1803–14 Aug 1891)
no children

Zachary Taylor

21 Jun 1810   **Margaret Mackall** SMITH (21 Sep 1788–14 Aug 1852)
▶ Anne Margaret Mackall Taylor (1811–1875), ▶ Sarah Knox Taylor (1814–1835), ▶ Octavia Pannel Taylor (1816–1820), ▶ Margaret Smith Taylor (1819–1820), ▶ Mary Elizabeth Taylor (1824–1909), ▶ Richard Taylor (1826–1879)

Millard Fillmore

5 Feb 1826   **Abigail** POWERS (13 Mar 1798–30 Mar 1853)
▶ Millard Powers Fillmore (1828–1889), ▶ Mary Abigail Fillmore (1832–1854)

10 Feb 1858   **Caroline** CARMICHAEL McIntosh (21 Oct 1813–11 Aug 1881)
no children

Franklin Pierce

10 Nov 1834   **Jane Means** APPLETON (12 Mar 1806–2 Dec 1863)
▶ Franklin Pierce (1836–1836), ▶ Frank Robert Pierce (1839–1843), ▶ Benjamin Pierce (1841–1853)

James Buchanan
never married

Abraham Lincoln

4 Nov 1842   **Mary Ann** TODD (13 Dec 1818–16 Jul 1882)
▶ Robert Todd Lincoln (1843–1926), ▶ Edward Baker Lincoln (1846–1850), ▶ William Wallace Lincoln (1850–1862), ▶ Thomas Lincoln (1853–1871)

Andrew Johnson

17 May 1827   **Eliza** McCARDLE (4 Oct 1810–15 Jan 1876)
▶ Martha Johnson (1828–1901), ▶ Charles Johnson (1830–1863), ▶ Mary Johnson (1832–1883), ▶ Robert Johnson (1834–1869), ▶ Andrew Johnson (1852–1879)

Ulysses S. Grant

22 Aug 1848   **Julia Boggs** DENT (26 Jan 1826–14 Dec 1902)
▶ Frederick Dent Grant (1850–1912), ▶ Ulysses Simpson Grant (1852–1929), ▶ Ellen Wrenshall Grant (1855–1922), ▶ Jesse Root Grant (1858–1934)

Rutherford B. Hayes

30 Dec 1852   **Lucy Ware** WEBB (28 Aug 1831–25 Jun 1889)
▶ Birchard Austin Hayes (1853–1926), ▶ James Webb Cook Hayes (1856–1934), ▶ Rutherford Platt Hayes (1858–1927), ▶ Joseph Thompson Hayes (1861–1863), ▶ George Crook Hayes (1864–1866), ▶ Fanny Hayes (1867–1950), ▶ Scott Russell Hayes (1871–1923), ▶ Manning Force Hayes (1873–1874)

James A. Garfield

11 Nov 1858   **Lucretia** RUDOLPH (19 Apr 1832–13 Mar 1918)
▶ Eliza Arabella Garfield (1860–1863), ▶ Harry Augustus Garfield (1863–1942), ▶ James Rudolph Garfield (1865–1950), ▶ Mary Garfield (1867–1947), ▶ Irvin McDowell Garfield (1870–1951), ▶ Abram Garfield (1872–1958), ▶ Edward Garfield (1874–1876)

Chester A. Arthur

25 Oct 1859   **Ellen Lewis** HERNDON (30 Aug 1837–12 Jan 1880)
▶ William Lewis Herndon Arthur (1860–1863), ▶ Chester Alan Arthur (1864–1937), ▶ Ellen Herndon Arthur (1871–1915)

Presidents' Wives and Children (continued)

| DATE OF MARRIAGE | PRESIDENTS, WIVES, AND CHILDREN |

Grover Cleveland

2 Jun 1886 — Frances FOLSOM (21 Jul 1864–29 Oct 1947)
▶ Ruth Cleveland (1891–1904), ▶ Esther Cleveland (1893–1980), ▶ Marion Cleveland (1895–1977), ▶ Richard Folsom Cleveland (1897–1974), ▶ Francis Grover Cleveland (1903–1995)

Benjamin Harrison

20 Oct 1853 — Caroline Lavinia SCOTT (1 Oct 1832–25 Oct 1892)
▶ Russell Benjamin Harrison (1854–1936), ▶ Mary Scott Harrison (1858–1930)

6 Apr 1896 — Mary Scott LORD Dimmick (30 Apr 1858–5 Jan 1948)
▶ Elizabeth Harrison (1897–1955)

William McKinley

25 Jan 1871 — Ida SAXTON (8 Jun 1847–26 May 1907)
▶ Katherine McKinley (1871–1875), ▶ Ida McKinley (1873–1873)

Theodore Roosevelt

27 Oct 1880 — Alice Hathaway LEE (29 Jul 1861–14 Feb 1884)
▶ Alice Lee Roosevelt (1884–1980)

2 Dec 1886 — Edith Kermit CAROW (6 Aug 1861–30 Sep 1948)
▶ Theodore Roosevelt (1887–1944), ▶ Kermit Roosevelt (1889–1943), ▶ Ethel Carow Roosevelt (1891–1977), ▶ Archibald Bulloch Roosevelt (1894–1979), ▶ Quentin Roosevelt (1897–1918)

William Howard Taft

19 Jun 1886 — Helen HERRON (2 Jun 1861–22 May 1943)
▶ Robert Alphonso Taft (1889–1953), ▶ Helen Herron Taft (1891–1987), ▶ Charles Phelps Taft (1897–1983)

Woodrow Wilson

24 Jun 1885 — Ellen Louise AXSON (15 May 1860–6 Aug 1914)
▶ Margaret Woodrow Wilson (1886–1944), ▶ Jessie Woodrow Wilson (1887–1933), ▶ Eleanor Randolph Wilson (1889–1967)

18 Dec 1915 — Edith BOLLING Galt (15 Oct 1872–28 Dec 1961)
no children

Warren G. Harding

8 Jul 1891 — Florence Mabel KLING De Wolf (15 Aug 1860–21 Nov 1924)
no children

Calvin Coolidge

4 Oct 1905 — Grace Anna GOODHUE (3 Jan 1879–8 Jul 1957)
▶ John Coolidge (1906–2000), ▶ Calvin Coolidge (1908–1924)

Herbert Hoover

10 Feb 1899 — Lou HENRY (29 Mar 1874–7 Jan 1944)
▶ Herbert Clark Hoover (1903–1969), ▶ Allan Henry Hoover (1907–1993)

Franklin D. Roosevelt

17 Mar 1905 — (Anna) Eleanor ROOSEVELT (11 Oct 1884–7 Nov 1962)
▶ Anna Eleanor Roosevelt (1906–1975), ▶ James Roosevelt (1907–1991), ▶ Franklin Roosevelt (1909–1909), ▶ Elliott Roosevelt (1910–1990), ▶ Franklin Delano Roosevelt (1914–1988), ▶ John Aspinwall Roosevelt (1916–1981)

Harry S. Truman

28 Jun 1919 — Elizabeth Virginia (Bess) WALLACE (13 Feb 1885–18 Oct 1982)
▶ Margaret (Mary) Truman (1924–)

Dwight D. Eisenhower

1 Jul 1916 — Marie (Mamie) Geneva DOUD (14 Nov 1896–1 Nov 1979)
▶ Doud Dwight Eisenhower (1917–1921), ▶ John Sheldon Doud Eisenhower (1922–)

John F. Kennedy

12 Sep 1953 — Jacqueline Lee BOUVIER (28 Jul 1929–19 May 1994)
▶ Caroline Bouvier Kennedy (1957–), ▶ John Fitzgerald Kennedy (1960–1999), Patrick Bouvier Kennedy (1963–1963)

Presidents' Wives and Children (continued)

DATE OF MARRIAGE   PRESIDENTS, WIVES, AND CHILDREN
Lyndon B. Johnson
17 Nov 1934   **Claudia Alta (Lady Bird)** TAYLOR (22 Dec 1912–)
▸ Lynda Bird Johnson (1944–), ▸ Luci Baines Johnson (1947–)

Richard M. Nixon
21 Jun 1940   **Thelma Catherine (Patricia)** RYAN (16 Mar 1912–22 Jun 1993)
▸ Patricia Nixon (1946–), ▸ Julie Nixon (1948–)

Gerald R. Ford
15 Oct 1948   **Elizabeth Ann (Betty)** BLOOMER **Warren** (8 Apr 1918–)
▸ Michael Gerald Ford (1950–), ▸ John Gardner Ford (1952–), ▸ Steven Meigs
Ford (1956–), ▸ Susan Elizabeth Ford (1957–)

Jimmy Carter
7 Jul 1946   **(Eleanor) Rosalynn** SMITH (18 Aug 1927–)
▸ John William Carter (1947–), ▸ James Earl Carter (1950–), ▸ Donnel Jeffrey
Carter (1952–), ▸ Amy Lynn Carter (1967–)

Ronald Reagan
24 Jan 1940   **Jane Wyman (née Sarah Jane** FULKS) (4 Jan 1914–)
▸ Maureen Elizabeth Reagan (1941–2001), ▸ Michael Edward Reagan (1945–)
4 Mar 1952   **Nancy Davis (née Anne Frances** ROBBINS) (6 Jul 1921–)
▸ Patricia Ann Reagan (1952–), ▸ Ronald Prescott Reagan (1958–)

George H.W. Bush
6 Jan 1945   **Barbara** PIERCE (8 Jun 1925–)
▸ George Walker Bush (1946–), ▸ Robin Bush (1949–1953), ▸ John Ellis (Jeb)
Bush (1953–), ▸ Neil Mallon Bush (1955–), ▸ Marvin Pierce Bush (1956–),
▸ Dorothy Walker Bush (1959–)

William J. Clinton
11 Oct 1975   **Hillary Diane** RODHAM (26 Oct 1947–)
▸ Chelsea Clinton (1980–)

George W. Bush
5 Nov 1977   **Laura Lane** WELCH (4 Nov 1946–)
▸ Barbara Bush (1981–), ▸ Jenna Bush (1981–)

Presidential Succession

The president is the chief executive of the US. In contrast to the parliamentary form of government, under which the head of state is mainly ceremonial, the presidential system, such as that in the US, vests the president with great authority. The role of the president—including the process of presidential succession—is outlined in Article II of the Constitution of 1787, the fundamental law of the US federal system of government. Presidential nomination procedures are often recognized as constitutional elements, though they are outside the letter of the Constitution.

The Presidential Succession Act of 1792 established the stages of succession: from the president to the vice president, then to the Senate president pro tempore and next to the speaker of the House of Representatives. In 1886 new legislation removed the latter two from succession, replacing them with cabinet officers. The pattern of presidential succession was again changed in 1947, when the speaker of the House was placed next in line after the vice president, followed by the Senate president pro tempore, the secretary of state, and finally, the remaining cabinet officers in the order that their departments were first formed.

History

The administration of the first president, George Washington, set the customary precedent of serving only two terms, a tradition maintained until Pres. Franklin D. Roosevelt was elected to a third and fourth term in the 1940s. Congress adopted the 22nd Amendment in 1951, which limits presidents to two terms in office.

In 1841 William Henry Harrison became the first president to die in office and was succeeded by his vice president, John Tyler. In 1850, when Zachary Taylor died after only 16 months in office, he was succeeded by Millard Fillmore. In the same manner, vice president Andrew Johnson assumed the presidency after Pres. Abraham Lincoln's assassination.

When Pres. James Garfield was shot on 2 Jul 1881, he became incapacitated, raising serious constitutional questions over who should perform the functions of the presidency. For 80 days the president lay ill, and it was generally agreed that, in such cases, the vice president (Chester Arthur) was empowered by the Constitution to assume the powers and duties of the office of president. But should Arthur be only acting president until Garfield recovered, or would he receive the office itself and thus displace his predecessor?

Because of an ambiguity in the Constitution, opinion was divided, and, because Congress was not in session, the problem could not be debated there. No further action was taken before the death of the president, the result of slow blood poisoning, on 19 September. This ambiguity over succession was later clarified by the 20th (1933) and 25th (1967) Amendments. Other vice presidents who succeeded upon the death of presidents included Theodore Roosevelt in 1901; Calvin Coolidge in 1923; Harry S. Truman in 1945; and Lyndon B. Johnson in 1963.

In the 2000 presidential election, Republican George W. Bush lost the popular vote but narrowly defeated Democratic Vice President Al Gore after a divided Supreme Court intervened to halt the manual recounting of disputed ballots in Florida, thereby giving Bush enough electoral votes to capture the presidency.

Please visit <www.britannica.com/presidents> for information about the 2004 US presidential election and all previous presidential elections.

Vice Presidents

	NAME	DATES OF BIRTH/DEATH	BIRTHPLACE	TIME IN OFFICE	PRESIDENT
1	John Adams	30 Oct 1735–4 Jul 1826	Braintree (now Quincy) MA	1789–97	George Washington
2	Thomas Jefferson	13 Apr 1743–4 Jul 1826	Shadwell VA	1797–1801	John Adams
3	Aaron Burr	6 Feb 1756–14 Sep 1836	Newark NJ	1801–05	Thomas Jefferson
4	George Clinton[1]	26 Jul 1739–20 Apr 1812	Little Britain NY	1805–09 1809–12	Thomas Jefferson James Madison
5	Elbridge Gerry	17 Jul 1744–23 Nov 1814	Marblehead MA	1813–14	James Madison
6	Daniel D. Tompkins	21 Jun 1774–11 Jun 1825	Scarsdale NY	1817–25	James Monroe
7	John C. Calhoun[2]	18 Mar 1782–31 Mar 1850	Abbeville district SC	1825–29 1829–32	John Quincy Adams Andrew Jackson
8	Martin Van Buren	5 Dec 1782–24 Jul 1862	Kinderhook NY	1833–37	Andrew Jackson
9	Richard M. Johnson	17 Oct 1781–19 Nov 1850	Beargrass VA (now Louisville KY)	1837–41	Martin Van Buren
10	John Tyler	29 Mar 1790–18 Jan 1862	Charles City county VA	1841	William Henry Harrison[1]
11	George Mifflin Dallas	10 Jul 1792–31 Dec 1864	Philadelphia PA	1845–49	James K. Polk
12	Millard Fillmore	7 Jan 1800–8 Mar 1874	Locke township NY	1849–50	Zachary Taylor[1]
13	William Rufus de Vane King[1]	7 Apr 1786–18 Apr 1853	Sampson county NC	4 Mar– 18 Apr 1853	Franklin Pierce
14	John C. Breckinridge	21 Jan 1821–17 May 1875	near Lexington KY	1857–61	James Buchanan
15	Hannibal Hamlin	27 Aug 1809–4 Jul 1891	Paris Hill ME	1861–65	Abraham Lincoln[1]
16	Andrew Johnson	29 Dec 1808–31 Jul 1875	Raleigh NC	1865	
17	Schuyler Colfax	23 Mar 1823–13 Jan 1885	New York NY	1869–73	Ulysses S. Grant
18	Henry Wilson[1]	16 Feb 1812–22 Nov 1875	Farmington NH	1873–75	Ulysses S. Grant
19	William A. Wheeler	30 Jun 1819–4 Jun 1887	Malone NY	1877–81	Rutherford B. Hayes
20	Chester A. Arthur	5 Oct 1829–18 Nov 1886	North Fairfield VT	1881	James A. Garfield[1]
21	Thomas A. Hendricks[1]	7 Sep 1819–25 Nov 1885	Zanesville OH	4 Mar– 25 Nov 1885	Grover Cleveland
22	Levi Parsons Morton	16 May 1824–16 May 1920	Shoreham VT	1889–93	Benjamin Harrison
23	Adlai E. Stevenson	23 Oct 1835–14 Jun 1914	Christian county KY	1893–97	Grover Cleveland
24	Garret A. Hobart[1]	3 Jun 1844–21 Nov 1899	Long Branch NJ	1897–99	William McKinley
25	Theodore Roosevelt	27 Oct 1858–6 Jan 1919	New York NY	1901	William McKinley[1]
26	Charles Warren Fairbanks	11 May 1852–4 Jun 1918	Union county OH	1905–09	Theodore Roosevelt
27	James Schoolcraft Sherman[1]	24 Oct 1855–30 Oct 1912	Utica NY	1909–12	William Howard Taft
28	Thomas R. Marshall	14 Mar 1854–1 Jun 1925	North Manchester IN	1913–21	Woodrow Wilson
29	Calvin Coolidge	4 Jul 1872–5 Jan 1933	Plymouth VT	1921–23	Warren G. Harding[1]
30	Charles G. Dawes	27 Aug 1865–23 Apr 1851	Marietta OH	1925–29	Calvin Coolidge
31	Charles Curtis	25 Jan 1860–8 Feb 1936	Kansas Territory	1929–33	Herbert Hoover

Vice Presidents (continued)

NAME	DATES OF BIRTH/DEATH	BIRTHPLACE	TIME IN OFFICE	PRESIDENT
32 John Nance Garner	22 Nov 1868–7 Nov 1967	Red River county TX	1933–41	Franklin D. Roosevelt
33 Henry A. Wallace	7 Oct 1888–18 Nov 1965	Adair county IA	1941–45	Franklin D. Roosevelt
34 Harry S. Truman	8 May 1884–26 Dec 1972	Lamar MO	1945	Franklin D. Roosevelt[1]
35 Alben W. Barkley	24 Nov 1877–30 Apr 1956	Graves county KY	1949–53	Harry S. Truman
36 Richard M. Nixon	9 Jan 1913–22 Apr 1994	Yorba Linda CA	1953–61	Dwight D. Eisenhower
37 Lyndon B. Johnson	27 Aug 1908–22 Jan 1973	Gillespie county TX	1961–63	John F. Kennedy[1]
38 Hubert H. Humphrey	27 May 1911–13 Jan 1978	Wallace SD	1965–69	Lyndon B. Johnson
39 Spiro T. Agnew[2]	9 Nov 1918–17 Sep 1996	Baltimore MD	1969–73	Richard M. Nixon
40 Gerald R. Ford	14 Jul 1913	Omaha NE	1973–74	Richard M. Nixon[2]
41 Nelson A. Rockefeller	8 Jul 1908–26 Jan 1979	Bar Harbor ME	1974–77	Gerald R. Ford
42 Walter F. Mondale	5 Jan 1928	Ceylon MN	1977–81	Jimmy Carter
43 George H.W. Bush	12 Jun 1924	Milton MA	1981–89	Ronald Reagan
44 Dan Quayle	4 Feb 1947	Indianapolis IN	1989–93	George H.W. Bush
45 Albert Gore	31 Mar 1948	Washington DC	1993–2001	William J. Clinton
46 Richard B. Cheney	30 Jan 1941	Lincoln NE	2001–	George W. Bush

[1]Died in office.
[2]Resigned from office.

US Presidential Cabinets

The cabinet is composed of the heads of executive departments chosen by the president with the consent of the Senate. Cabinet officials do not hold seats in Congress and are not regulated by the US Constitution, which makes no mention of such a body. The existence of the cabinet is a matter of custom dating back to George Washington, who consulted regularly with his department heads as a group. Original dates of service are given for officials appointed midterm and for newly created posts. Ad interim officials are not listed. Presidencies and new positions are indicated in bold.

George Washington

30 APR 1789–3 MARCH 1793 (TERM 1)

State	Thomas Jefferson
Treasury	Alexander Hamilton
War	Henry Knox
Attorney General	Edmund Randolph

4 MAR 1793–3 MAR 1797 (TERM 2)

State	Thomas Jefferson; Edmund Randolph (2 Jan 1794); Timothy Pickering (20 Aug 1795)
Treasury	Alexander Hamilton; Oliver Wolcott, Jr. (2 Feb 1795)
War	Henry Knox; Timothy Pickering (2 Jan 1795); James McHenry (6 Feb 1796)
Attorney General	Edmund Randolph; William Bradford (29 Jan 1794); Charles Lee (10 Dec 1795)

John Adams

4 MAR 1797–3 MAR 1801

State	Timothy Pickering; John Marshall (6 Jun 1800)
Treasury	Oliver Wolcott, Jr.; Samuel Dexter (1 Jan 1801)
War	James McHenry; Samuel Dexter (12 Jun 1800)
Navy	Benjamin Stoddert (18 Jun 1798)
Attorney General	Charles Lee

Thomas Jefferson

4 MAR 1801–3 MAR 1805 (TERM 1)

State	James Madison
Treasury	Samuel Dexter; Albert Gallatin (14 May 1801)
War	Henry Dearborn
Navy	Benjamin Stoddert; Robert Smith (27 Jul 1801)
Attorney General	Levi Lincoln

US Presidential Cabinets (continued)

Thomas Jefferson (continued)

4 MAR 1805–3 MAR 1809 (TERM 2)

State	James Madison
Treasury	Albert Gallatin
War	Henry Dearborn
Navy	Robert Smith
Attorney General	John Breckenridge; Caesar Augustus Rodney (20 Jan 1807)

James Madison

4 MAR 1809–3 MAR 1813 (TERM 1)

State	Robert Smith
Treasury	Albert Gallatin
War	John Smith; William Eustis (8 Apr 1809); John Armstrong (5 Feb 1813)
Navy	Robert Smith; Paul Hamilton (15 May 1809); William Jones (19 Jan 1813)
Attorney General	Caesar Augustus Rodney; William Pinkney (6 Jan 1812)

4 MAR 1813–3 MAR 1817 (TERM 2)

State	James Monroe
Treasury	Albert Gallatin; George Washington Campbell (9 Feb 1814); Alexander James Dallas (14 Oct 1814); William Harris Crawford (22 Oct 1816)
War	John Armstrong; James Monroe (1 Oct 1814); William Harris Crawford (8 Aug 1815)
Navy	William Jones; Benjamin Williams Crowninshield (16 Jan 1815)
Attorney General	William Pinkney; Richard Rush (11 Feb 1814)

James Monroe

4 MAR 1817–3 MAR 1821 (TERM 1)

State	John Quincy Adams
Treasury	William Harris Crawford
War	John C. Calhoun
Navy	Benjamin Williams Crowninshield; Smith Thompson (1 Jan 1819)
Attorney General	Richard Rush; William Wirt (15 Nov 1817)

4 MAR 1821–3 MAR 1825 (TERM 2)

State	John Quincy Adams
Treasury	William Harris Crawford
War	John C. Calhoun
Navy	Smith Thompson; Samuel Lewis Southard (16 Sep 1823)
Attorney General	William Wirt

John Quincy Adams

4 MAR 1825–3 MAR 1829

State	Henry Clay
Treasury	Richard Rush
War	James Barbour; Peter Buell Porter (21 Jun 1828)
Navy	Samuel Lewis Southard
Attorney General	William Wirt

Andrew Jackson

4 MAR 1829–3 MAR 1833 (TERM 1)

State	Martin Van Buren; Edward Livingston (24 May 1831)
Treasury	Samuel Delucenna Ingham; Louis McLane (8 Aug 1831)
War	John Henry Eaton; Lewis Cass (8 Aug 1831)
Navy	John Branch; Levi Woodbury (23 May 1831)
Attorney General	John Macpherson Berrien; Roger Brooke Taney (20 Jul 1831)

4 MAR 1833–3 MAR 1837 (TERM 2)

State	Edward Livingston; Louis McLane (29 May 1833); John Forsyth (1 Jul 1834)
Treasury	Louis McLane; William John Duane (1 Jun 1833); Roger Brooke Taney (23 Sep 1833); Levi Woodbury (1 Jul 1834)
War	Lewis Cass
Navy	Levi Woodbury; Mahlon Dickerson (30 Jun 1834)
Attorney General	Roger Brooke Taney; Benjamin Franklin Butler (18 Nov 1833)

US Presidential Cabinets (continued)

Martin Van Buren

4 MAR 1837–3 MAR 1841

State	John Forsyth
Treasury	Levi Woodbury
War	Joel Roberts Poinsett
Navy	Mahlon Dickerson; James Kirke Paulding (1 Jul 1838)
Attorney General	Benjamin Franklin Butler; Felix Grundy (1 Sep 1838); Henry Dilworth Gilpin (11 Jan 1840)

William Henry Harrison

4 MAR 1841–4 APR 1841

State	Daniel Webster
Treasury	Thomas Ewing
War	John Bell
Navy	George Edmund Badger
Attorney General	John Jordan Crittenden

John Tyler

6 APR 1841–3 MAR 1845

State	Daniel Webster; Abel Parker Upshur (24 Jul 1843); John C. Calhoun (1 Apr 1844)
Treasury	Thomas Ewing; Walter Forward (13 Sep 1841); John Canfield Spencer (8 Mar 1843); George Mortimer Bibb (4 Jul 1844)
War	John Bell; John Canfield Spencer (12 Oct 1841); James Madison Porter (8 Mar 1843); William Wilkins (20 Feb 1844)
Navy	George Edmund Badger; Abel Parker Upshur (11 Oct 1841); David Henshaw (24 Jul 1843); Thomas Walker Gilmer (19 Feb 1844); John Young Mason (26 Mar 1844)
Attorney General	John Jordan Crittenden; Hugh Swinton Legaré (20 Sep 1841); John Nelson (1 Jul 1843)

James K. Polk

4 MAR 1845–3 MAR 1849

State	James Buchanan
Treasury	Robert James Walker
War	William Learned Marcy
Navy	George Bancroft; John Young Mason (9 Sep 1846)
Attorney General	John Young Mason; Nathan Clifford (17 Oct 1846); Isaac Toucey (29 Jun 1848)

Zachary Taylor

4 MAR 1849–9 JUL 1850

State	John Middleton Clayton
Treasury	William Morris Meredith
War	George Washington Crawford
Navy	William Ballard Preston
Attorney General	Reverdy Johnson
Interior	Thomas Ewing (8 Mar 1849)

Millard Fillmore

10 JUL 1850–3 MAR 1853

State	Daniel Webster; Edward Everett (6 Nov 1852)
Treasury	Thomas Corwin
War	George Washington Crawford; Charles Magill Conrad (15 Aug 1850)
Navy	William Alexander Graham; John Pendleton Kennedy (26 Jul 1852)
Attorney General	Reverdy Johnson; John Jordan Crittenden (14 Aug 1850)
Interior	Thomas Ewing; Thomas McKean Thompson McKennan (15 Aug 1850); Alexander Hugh Holmes Stuart (16 Sep 1850)

Franklin Pierce

4 MAR 1853–3 MAR 1857

State	William Learned Marcy
Treasury	James Guthrie
War	Jefferson Davis
Navy	James Cochran Dobbin
Attorney General	Caleb Cushing
Interior	Robert McClelland

US Presidential Cabinets (continued)

James Buchanan

4 MAR 1857–3 MAR 1861

State	Lewis Cass; Jeremiah Sullivan Black (17 Dec 1860)
Treasury	Howell Cobb; Philip Francis Thomas (12 Dec 1860); John Adams Dix (15 Jan 1861)
War	John Buchanan Floyd
Navy	Isaac Toucey
Attorney General	Jeremiah Sullivan Black; Edwin McMasters Stanton (22 Dec 1860)
Interior	Jacob Thompson

Abraham Lincoln

4 MAR 1861–3 MAR 1865 (TERM 1)

State	William Henry Seward
Treasury	Salmon Portland Chase; William Pitt Fessenden (5 Jul 1864)
War	Simon Cameron; Edwin McMasters Stanton (20 Jun 1862)
Navy	Gideon Welles
Attorney General	Edward Bates; James Speed (5 Dec 1864)
Interior	Caleb Blood Smith; John Palmer Usher (8 Jan 1863)

4 MAR 1865–15 APR 1865 (TERM 2)

State	William Henry Seward
Treasury	Hugh McCulloch
War	Edwin McMasters Stanton
Navy	Gideon Welles
Attorney General	James Speed
Interior	John Palmer Usher

Andrew Johnson

15 APR 1865–3 MAR 1869

State	William Henry Seward
Treasury	Hugh McCulloch
War	Edwin McMasters Stanton; John McAllister Schofield (1 Jun 1868)
Navy	Gideon Welles
Attorney General	James Speed; Henry Stanbery (23 Jul 1866); William Maxwell Evarts (20 Jul 1868)
Interior	John Palmer Usher; James Harlan (15 May 1865); Orville Hickman Browning (1 Sep 1866)

Ulysses S. Grant

4 MAR 1869–3 MAR 1873 (TERM 1)

State	Elihu Benjamin Washburne; Hamilton Fish (17 Mar 1869)
Treasury	George Sewall Boutwell
War	John Aaron Rawlins; William Tecumseh Sherman (11 Sep 1869); William Worth Belknap (1 Nov 1869)
Navy	Adolph Edward Borie; George Maxwell Robeson (25 Jun 1869)
Attorney General	Ebenezer Rockwood Hoar; Amos Tappan Akerman (8 Jul 1870); George Henry Williams (10 Jan 1872)
Interior	Jacob Dolson Cox; Columbus Delano (1 Nov 1870)

4 MAR 1873–3 MAR 1877 (TERM 2)

State	Hamilton Fish
Treasury	William Adams Richardson; Benjamin Helm Bristow (4 Jun 1874); Lot Myrick Morrill (7 Jul 1876)
War	William Worth Belknap; Alphonso Taft (11 Mar 1876); James Donald Cameron (1 Jun 1876)
Navy	George Maxwell Robeson
Attorney General	George Henry Williams; Edward Pierrepont (15 May 1875); Alphonso Taft (1 Jun 1876)
Interior	Columbus Delano; Zachariah Chandler (19 Oct 1875)

Rutherford B. Hayes

4 MAR 1877–3 MAR 1881

State	William Maxwell Evarts
Treasury	John Sherman
War	George Washington McCrary; Alexander Ramsey (12 Dec 1879)
Navy	Richard Wigginton Thompson; Nathan Goff, Jr. (6 Jan 1881)
Attorney General	Charles Devens
Interior	Carl Schurz

US Presidential Cabinets (continued)

James A. Garfield

4 MAR 1881–19 SEP 1881

State	James Gillespie Blaine
Treasury	William Windom
War	Robert Todd Lincoln
Attorney General	(Isaac) Wayne MacVeagh
Navy	William Henry Hunt
Interior	Samuel Jordan Kirkwood

Chester A. Arthur

20 SEP 1881–3 MAR 1885

State	James Gillespie Blaine; Frederick Theodore Frelinghuysen (19 Dec 1881)
Treasury	William Windom; Charles James Folger (14 Nov 1881); Walter Quintin Gresham (24 Sep 1884); Hugh McCulloch (31 Oct 1884)
War	Robert Todd Lincoln
Navy	William Henry Hunt; William Eaton Chandler (17 Apr 1882)
Attorney General	(Isaac) Wayne MacVeagh; Benjamin Harris Brewster (3 Jan 1882)
Interior	Samuel Jordan Kirkwood; Henry Moore Teller (17 Apr 1882)

Grover Cleveland

4 MAR 1885–3 MAR 1889

State	Thomas Francis Bayard
Treasury	Daniel Manning; Charles Stebbins Fairchild (1 Apr 1887)
War	William Crowninshield Endicott
Navy	William Collins Whitney
Attorney General	Augustus Hill Garland
Interior	Lucius Quintus Cincinnatus Lamar; William Freeman Vilas (16 Jan 1888)
Agriculture	Norman Jay Colman (13 Feb 1889)

Benjamin Harrison

4 MAR 1889–3 MAR 1893

State	James Gillespie Blaine; John Watson Foster (29 Jun 1892)
Treasury	William Windom; Charles Foster (24 Feb 1891)
War	Redfield Proctor; Stephen Benton Elkins (24 Dec 1891)
Navy	Benjamin Franklin Tracy
Attorney General	William Henry Harrison Miller
Interior	John Willock Noble
Agriculture	Jeremiah McLain Rusk

Grover Cleveland

4 MAR 1893–3 MAR 1897

State	Walter Quintin Gresham; Richard Olney (10 Jun 1895)
Treasury	John Griffin Carlisle
War	Daniel Scott Lamont
Navy	Hilary Abner Herbert
Attorney General	Richard Olney; Judson Harmon (11 Jun 1895)
Interior	Hoke Smith; David Rowland Francis (4 Sep 1896)
Agriculture	Julius Sterling Morton

William McKinley

4 MAR 1897–3 MAR 1901 (TERM 1)

State	John Sherman; William Rufus Day (28 Apr 1898); John Hay (30 Sep 1898)
Treasury	Lyman Judson
War	Russell Alexander Alger; Elihu Root (1 Aug 1899)
Navy	John Davis Long
Attorney General	Joseph McKenna; John William Griggs (1 Feb 1898)
Interior	Cornelius Newton Bliss; Ethan Allen Hitchcock (20 Feb 1899)
Agriculture	James Wilson

4 MAR 1901–14 SEP 1901 (TERM 2)

State	John Hay
Treasury	Lyman Judson Gage
War	Elihu Root
Navy	John Davis Long
Attorney General	John William Griggs; Philander Chase Knox (10 Apr 1901)
Interior	Ethan Allen Hitchcock
Agriculture	James Wilson

US Presidential Cabinets (continued)

Theodore Roosevelt

14 SEP 1901–3 MAR 1905 (TERM 1)

State	John Hay
Treasury	Lyman Judson Gage; Leslie Mortier Shaw (1 Feb 1902)
War	Elihu Root; William Howard Taft (1 Feb 1904)
Navy	John Davis Long; William Henry Moody (1 May 1902); Paul Morton (1 Jul 1904)
Attorney General	Philander Chase Knox; William Henry Moody (1 Jul 1904)
Interior	Ethan Allen Hitchcock
Agriculture	James Wilson
Commerce and Labor	George Bruce Cortelyou (16 Feb 1903); Victor Howard Metcalf (1 Jul 1904)

4 MAR 1905–3 MAR 1909 (TERM 2)

State	John Hay; Elihu Root (19 Jul 1905); Robert Bacon (27 Jan 1909)
Treasury	Leslie Mortier Shaw; George Bruce Cortelyou (4 Mar 1907)
War	William Howard Taft; Luke Edward Wright (1 Jul 1908)
Navy	Paul Morton; Charles Joseph Bonaparte (1 Jul 1905); Victor Howard Metcalf (17 Dec 1906); Truman Handy Newberry (1 Dec 1908)
Attorney General	William Henry Moody; Charles Joseph Bonaparte (17 Dec 1906)
Interior	Ethan Allen Hitchcock; James Rudolph Garfield (4 Mar 1907)
Agriculture	James Wilson
Commerce and Labor	Victor Howard Metcalf; Oscar Solomon Straus (17 Dec 1906)

William Howard Taft

4 MAR 1909–3 MAR 1913

State	Philander Chase Knox
Treasury	Franklin MacVeagh
War	Jacob McGavock Dickinson; Henry Lewis Stimson (22 May 1911)
Navy	George von Lengerke Meyer
Attorney General	George Woodward Wickersham
Interior	Richard Achilles Ballinger; Walter Lowrie Fisher (7 Mar 1911)
Agriculture	James Wilson
Commerce and Labor	Charles Nagel

Woodrow Wilson

4 MAR 1913–3 MAR 1917 (TERM 1)

State	William Jennings Bryan; Robert Lansing (23 Jun 1915)
Treasury	William Gibbs McAdoo
War	Lindley Miller Garrison; Newton Diehl Baker (9 Mar 1916)
Navy	Josephus Daniels
Attorney General	James Clark McReynolds; Thomas Watt Gregory (3 Sep 1914)
Interior	Franklin Knight Lane
Agriculture	David Franklin Houston
Commerce	William Cox Redfield (5 Mar 1913)
Labor	William Bauchop Wilson (5 Mar 1913)

4 MAR 1917–3 MAR 1921 (TERM 2)

State	Robert Lansing; Bainbridge Colby (23 Mar 1920)
Treasury	William Gibbs McAdoo; Carter Glass (16 Dec 1918); David Franklin Houston (2 Feb 1920)
War	Newton Diehl Baker
Navy	Josephus Daniels
Attorney General	Thomas Watt Gregory; Alexander Mitchell Palmer (5 Mar 1919)
Interior	Franklin Knight Lane; John Barton Payne (13 Mar 1920)
Agriculture	David Franklin Houston; Edwin Thomas Meredith (2 Feb 1920)
Commerce	William Cox Redfield; Joshua Willis Alexander (16 Dec 1919)
Labor	William Bauchop Wilson

Warren G. Harding

4 MAR 1921–2 AUG 1923

State	Charles Evans Hughes
Treasury	Andrew William Mellon
War	John Wingate Weeks
Navy	Edwin Denby
Attorney General	Harry Micajah Daugherty

US Presidential Cabinets (continued)

Warren G. Harding (continued)

4 MAR 1921–2 AUG 1923 (CONTINUED)

Interior	Albert Bacon Fall; Hubert Work (5 Mar 1923)
Agriculture	Henry Cantwell Wallace
Commerce	Herbert Hoover
Labor	James John Davis

Calvin Coolidge

3 AUG 1923–3 MAR 1925 (TERM 1)

State	Charles Evans Hughes
Treasury	Andrew William Mellon
War	John Wingate Weeks
Navy	Edwin Denby; Curtis Dwight Wilbur (18 Mar 1924)
Attorney General	Harry Micajah Daugherty; Harlan Fiske Stone (9 Apr 1924)
Interior	Hubert Work
Agriculture	Henry Cantwell Wallace; Howard Mason Gore (21 Nov 1924)
Commerce	Herbert Hoover
Labor	James John Davis

4 MAR 1925–3 MAR 1929 (TERM 2)

State	Frank Billings Kellogg
Treasury	Andrew William Mellon
War	John Wingate Weeks; Dwight Filley Davis (14 Oct 1925)
Navy	Curtis Dwight Wilbur
Attorney General	John Garibaldi Sargent
Interior	Hubert Work; Roy Owen West (21 Jan 1929)
Agriculture	William Marion Jardine
Commerce	Herbert Hoover; William Fairfield Whiting (11 Dec 1928)
Labor	James John Davis

Herbert Hoover

4 MAR 1929–3 MAR 1933

State	Henry Lewis Stimson
Treasury	Andrew William Mellon; Ogden Livingston Mills (13 Feb 1932)
War	James William Good; Patrick Jay Hurley (9 Dec 1929)
Navy	Charles Francis Adams
Attorney General	William De Witt Mitchell
Interior	Ray Lyman Wilbur
Agriculture	Arthur Mastick Hyde
Commerce	Robert Patterson Lamont; Roy Dikeman Chapin (14 Dec 1932)
Labor	James John Davis; William Nuckles Doak (9 Dec 1930)

Franklin D. Roosevelt

4 MAR 1933–20 JAN 1937 (TERM 1)

State	Cordell Hull
Treasury	William Hartman Woodin; Henry Morgenthau, Jr. (8 Jan 1934)
War	George Henry Dern
Navy	Claude Augustus Swanson
Attorney General	Homer Stille Cummings
Interior	Harold Le Claire Ickes
Agriculture	Henry Agard Wallace
Commerce	Daniel Calhoun Roper
Labor	Frances Perkins

20 JAN 1937–20 JAN 1941 (TERM 2)

State	Cordell Hull
Treasury	Henry Morgenthau, Jr.
War	Harry Hines Woodring; Henry Lewis Stimson (10 Jul 1940)
Attorney General	Homer Stille Cummings; Frank Murphy (17 Jan 1939); Robert Houghwout Jackson (18 Jan 1940)
Navy	Claude Augustus Swanson; Charles Edison (11 Jan 1940); Frank Knox (10 Jul 1940)
Interior	Harold Le Claire Ickes
Agriculture	Henry Agard Wallace; Claude Raymond Wickard (5 Sep 1940)
Commerce	Daniel Calhoun Roper; Harry Lloyd Hopkins (23 Jan 1939); Jesse Holman Jones (19 Sep 1940)
Labor	Frances Perkins

US Presidential Cabinets (continued)

Franklin D. Roosevelt (continued)

20 JAN 1941–20 JAN 1945 (TERM 3)

State	Cordell Hull; Edward Reilly Stettinius (1 Dec 1944)
Treasury	Henry Morgenthau, Jr.
War	Henry Lewis Stimson
Navy	Frank Knox; James Vincent Forrestal (18 May 1944)
Attorney General	Robert Houghwout Jackson; Francis Biddle (5 Sep 1941)
Interior	Harold Le Claire Ickes
Agriculture	Claude Raymond Wickard
Commerce	Jesse Holman Jones
Labor	Frances Perkins

20 JAN 1945–12 APR 1945 (TERM 4)

State	Edward Reilly Stettinius
Treasury	Henry Morgenthau, Jr.
War	Henry Lewis Stimson
Navy	James Vincent Forrestal
Attorney General	Francis Biddle
Interior	Harold Le Claire Ickes
Agriculture	Claude Raymond Wickard
Commerce	Jesse Holman Jones; Henry Agard Wallace (2 Mar 1945)
Labor	Frances Perkins

Harry S. Truman

12 APR 1945–20 JAN 1949 (TERM 1)

State	Edward Reilly Stettinius; James Francis Byrnes (3 Jul 1945); George Catlett Marshall (21 Jan 1947)
Treasury	Henry Morgenthau, Jr.; Frederick Moore (23 Jul 1945); John Wesley Snyder (25 Jun 1946)
War	Henry Lewis Stimson; Robert Porter Patterson (27 Sep 1945); Kenneth Clairborne Royall (25 Jul 1947)
Defense	James Vincent Forrestal (17 Sep 1947)
Navy	James Vincent Forrestal
Attorney General	Francis Biddle; Thomas Campbell Clark (1 Jul 1945)
Interior	Harold Le Claire Ickes; Julius Albert Krug (18 Mar 1946)
Agriculture	Claude Raymond Wickard; Clinton Presba Anderson (30 Jun 1945); Charles Franklin Brannan (2 Jun 1948)
Commerce	Henry Agard Wallace; William Averell Harriman (28 Jan 1947); Charles Sawyer (6 May 1948)
Labor	Frances Perkins; Lewis Baxter Schwellenbach (1 Jul 1945)

20 JAN 1949–20 JAN 1953 (TERM 2)

State	Dean Gooderham Acheson
Treasury	John Wesley Snyder
Defense	James Vincent Forrestal; Louis Arthur Johnson (28 Mar 1949); George Catlett Marshall (21 Sep 1950); Robert Abercrombie Lovett (17 Sep 1951)
Attorney General	Thomas Campbell Clark; James Howard McGrath (24 Aug 1949)
Interior	Julius Albert Krug; Oscar Littleton Chapman (19 Jan 1950)
Agriculture	Charles Franklin Brannan
Commerce	Charles Sawyer
Labor	Maurice Joseph Tobin

Dwight D. Eisenhower

20 JAN 1953–20 JAN 1957 (TERM 1)

State	John Foster Dulles
Treasury	George Magoffin Humphrey
Defense	Charles Erwin Wilson
Attorney General	Herbert Brownell
Interior	Douglas McKay; Frederick Andrew Seaton (8 Jun 1956)
Agriculture	Ezra Taft Benson
Commerce	Sinclair Weeks
Labor	Martin Patrick Durkin; James Paul Mitchell (9 Oct 1953)
Health, Education, and Welfare	Oveta Culp Hobby (11 Apr 1953); Marion Bayard Folson (1 Aug 1955)

20 JAN 1957–20 JAN 1961 (TERM 2)

State	John Foster Dulles; Christian Archibald Herter (22 Apr 1959)
Treasury	George Magoffin Humphrey; Robert Bernerd Anderson (29 Jul 1957)

US Presidential Cabinets (continued)

Dwight D. Eisenhower (continued)

20 JAN 1957–20 JAN 1961 (TERM 2) (CONTINUED)

Defense	Charles Erwin Wilson; Neil Hosler McElroy (9 Oct 1957); Thomas Sovereign Gates, Jr. (2 Dec 1959)
Attorney General	Herbert Brownell, Jr.; William Pierce Rogers (27 Jan 1958)
Interior	Frederick Andrew Seaton
Agriculture	Ezra Taft Benson
Commerce	Sinclair Weeks; Frederick Henry Mueller (10 Aug 1959)
Labor	James Paul Mitchell
Health, Education, and Welfare	Marion Bayard Folsom; Arthur Sherwood Flemming (1 Aug 1958)

John F. Kennedy

20 JAN 1961–22 NOV 1963

State	(David) Dean Rusk
Treasury	C. (Clarence) Douglas Dillon
Defense	Robert Strange McNamara
Attorney General	Robert F. Kennedy
Interior	Stewart Lee Udall
Agriculture	Orville Lothrop Freeman
Commerce	Luther Hartwell Hodges
Labor	Arthur Joseph Goldberg; W. (William) Willard Wirtz (25 Sep 1962)
Health, Education, and Welfare	Abraham Alexander Ribicoff; Anthony Joseph Celebrezze (31 Jul 1962)

Lyndon B. Johnson

22 NOV 1963–20 JAN 1965 (TERM 1)

State	(David) Dean Rusk
Treasury	C. (Clarence) Douglas Dillon
Defense	Robert Strange McNamara
Attorney General	Robert F. Kennedy
Interior	Stewart Lee Udall
Agriculture	Orville Lothrop Freeman
Commerce	Luther Hartwell Hodges
Labor	W. (William) Willard Wirtz
Health, Education, and Welfare	Anthony Joseph Celebrezze

20 JAN 1965–20 JAN 1969 (TERM 2)

State	(David) Dean Rusk
Treasury	C. (Clarence) Douglas Dillon; Henry Hamill Fowler (1 Apr 1965); Joseph Walker Barr (23 Dec 1968)
Defense	Robert Strange McNamara; Clark McAdams Clifford (1 Mar 1968)
Attorney General	Nicholas deBelleville Katzenbach; William Ramsey Clark (10 Mar 1967)
Interior	Stewart Lee Udall
Agriculture	Orville Lothrop Freeman
Commerce	John Thomas Connor; Alexander Buel Trowbridge (14 Jun 1967); Cyrus Rowlett Smith (6 Mar 1968)
Labor	W. William Willard Wirtz
Health, Education, and Welfare	Anthony Joseph Celebrezze; John William Gardner (18 Aug 1965); Wilbur Joseph Cohen (9 May 1968)
Housing and Urban Development	Robert Clifton Weaver (18 Jan 1966); Robert Coldwell Wood (7 Jan 1969)
Transportation	Alan Stephenson Boyd (16 Jan 1967)

Richard Nixon

20 JAN 1969–20 JAN 1973 (TERM 1)

State	William Pierce Rogers
Treasury	David Matthew Kennedy; John Bowden Connally, Jr. (11 Feb 1971); George Pratt Shultz (12 Jun 1972)
Defense	Melvin Robert Laird
Attorney General	John Newton Mitchell; Richard Gordon Kleindienst (12 Jun 1972)
Interior	Walter Joseph Hickel; Rogers Clark Ballard Morton (29 Jan 1971)
Agriculture	Clifford Morris Hardin; Earl Lauer Butz (2 Dec 1971)
Commerce	Maurice Hubert Stans; Peter George Peterson (21 Feb 1972)
Labor	George Pratt Shultz; James Day Hodgson (2 Jul 1970)
Health, Education, and Welfare	Robert Hutchinson Finch; Elliot Lee Richardson (24 Jun 1970)
Housing and Urban Development	George Wilcken Romney
Transportation	John Anthony Volpe

20 JAN 1973–9 AUG 1974 (TERM 2)

State	William Pierce Rogers; Henry Alfred Kissinger (22 Sep 1973)
Treasury	George Pratt Shultz; William Edward Simon (8 May 1974)

US Presidential Cabinets (continued)

Richard Nixon (continued)

20 JAN 1973–9 AUG 1974 (TERM 2) (CONTINUED)

Defense	Elliot Lee Richardson; James Rodney Schlesinger (2 Jul 1973)
Attorney General	Richard Gordon Kleindienst; Elliot Lee Richardson (25 May 1973); William Bart Saxbe (4 Jan 1974)
Interior	Rogers Clark Ballard Morton
Agriculture	Earl Lauer Butz
Commerce	Frederick Baily Dent
Labor	Peter Joseph Brennan
Health, Education, and Welfare	Caspar Willard Weinberger
Housing and Urban Development	James Thomas Lynn
Transportation	Claude Stout Brinegar

Gerald Ford

9 AUG 1974–20 JAN 1977

State	Henry Alfred Kissinger
Treasury	William Edward Simon
Defense	James Rodney Schlesinger; Donald Henry Rumsfeld (20 Nov 1975)
Attorney General	William Bart Saxbe; Edward Hirsch Levi (7 Feb 1975)
Interior	Rogers Clark Ballard Morton, Jr.; Stanley Knapp Hathaway (13 Jun 1975); Thomas Savig Kleppe (17 Oct 1975)
Agriculture	Earl Lauer Butz; John Albert Knebel (4 Nov 1976)
Commerce	Frederick Baily Dent; Rogers Clark Ballard Morton, Jr. (1 May 1975); Elliot Lee Richardson (2 Feb 1976)
Labor	Peter Joseph Brennan; John Thomas Dunlop (18 Mar 1975); Willie Julian Usery, Jr. (10 Feb 1976)
Health, Education, and Welfare	Caspar Willard Weinberger; Forrest David Matthews (8 Aug 1975)
Housing and Urban Development	James Thomas Lynn; Carla Anderson Hills (10 Mar 1975)
Transportation	Claude Stout Brinegar; William Thaddeus Coleman, Jr. (7 Mar 1975)

Jimmy Carter

20 JAN 1977–20 JAN 1981

State	Cyrus Vance; Edmund Sixtus Muskie (8 May 1980)
Treasury	Werner Michael Blumenthal; George William Miller (6 Aug 1979)
Defense	Harold Brown
Attorney General	Griffin Boyette Bell; Benjamin Richard Civiletti (16 Aug 1979)
Interior	Cecil Dale Andrus
Agriculture	Robert Selmer Bergland
Commerce	Juanita Morris Kreps; Philip Morris Klutznick (9 Jan 1980)
Labor	Fred Ray Marshall
Health, Education, and Welfare	Joseph Anthony Califano, Jr.; Patricia Roberts Harris (3 Aug 1979)
Health and Human Services	Patricia Roberts Harris (27 Sep 1979)
Housing and Urban Development	Patricia Roberts Harris; Moon Landrieu (24 Sep 1979)
Transportation	Brockman Adams; Neil Edward Goldschmidt (24 Sep 1979)
Energy	James Rodney Schlesinger (1 Oct 1977); Charles William Duncan, Jr. (24 Aug 1979)
Education	Shirley Mount Hufstedler (6 Dec 1979)

Ronald Reagan

20 JAN 1981–20 JAN 1985 (TERM 1)

State	Alexander Meigs Haig, Jr.; George Pratt Shultz (16 Jul 1982)
Treasury	Donald Thomas Regan
Defense	Caspar Willard Weinberger
Attorney General	William French Smith
Interior	James Gaius Watt; William Patrick Clark (21 Nov 1983)
Agriculture	John Rusling Block
Commerce	Malcolm Baldrige
Labor	Raymond Joseph Donovan
Health and Human Services	Richard Schultz Schweiker; Margaret Mary O'Shaughnessy Heckler (9 Mar 1983)
Housing and Urban Development	Samuel Riley Pierce, Jr.
Transportation	Drew (Andrew) Lindsay Lewis, Jr.; Elizabeth Hanford Dole (7 Feb 1983)
Energy	James Burrows Edwards; Donald Paul Hodel (8 Dec 1982)
Education	Terrel Howard Bell

20 JAN 1985–20 JAN 1989 (TERM 2)

State	George Pratt Shultz
Treasury	Donald Thomas Regan; James Addison Baker III (25 Feb 1985); Nicholas Frederick Brady (18 Aug 1988)

US Presidential Cabinets (continued)

Ronald Reagan (continued)

20 JAN 1985-20 JAN 1989 (TERM 2) (CONTINUED)

Defense	Caspar Willard Weinberger; Frank Charles Carlucci III (21 Nov 1987)
Attorney General	William French Smith; Edwin Meese III (25 Feb 1985); Richard Lewis (Dick) Thornburgh (11 Aug 1988)
Interior	Donald Paul Hodel
Agriculture	John Rusling Block; Richard Edmund Lyng (7 Mar 1986)
Commerce	Malcolm Baldrige; Calvin William Verity, Jr. (19 Oct 1987)
Labor	Raymond James Donovan; William Emerson (Bill) Brock III (29 Apr 1985); Ann Dore McLaughlin (17 Dec 1987)
Health and Human Services	Margaret Mary O'Shaughnessy Heckler; Otis Ray Bowen (13 Dec 1985)
Housing and Urban Development	Samuel Riley Pierce, Jr.
Transportation	Elizabeth Hanford Dole; James Horace Burnley IV (3 Dec 1987)
Energy	John Stewart Herrington
Education	Terrel Howard Bell; William John Bennett (7 Feb 1985); Lauro Fred Cavazos, Jr. (20 Sep 1988)

George H.W. Bush

20 JAN 1989-20 JAN 1993

State	James Addison Baker III
Treasury	Nicholas Frederick Brady
Attorney General	Richard Lewis (Dick) Thornburgh; William P. Barr (20 Nov 1991)
Interior	Manuel Lujan, Jr.
Agriculture	Clayton Keith Yeutter; Edward Madigan (7 Mar 1991)
Commerce	Robert Adam Mosbacher
Labor	Elizabeth Hanford Dole
Defense	Richard (Dick) Cheney
Health and Human Services	Louis Wade Sullivan
Housing and Urban Development	Jack F. Kemp
Transportation	Samuel K. Skinner; Andrew H. Card (22 Jan 1992)
Energy	James David Watkins
Education	Lauro Fred Cavazos, Jr.; Lamar Alexander (14 Mar 1991)
Veterans Affairs	Edward Joseph Derwinski (15 Mar 1989)

William J. Clinton

20 JAN 1993-20 JAN 1997 (TERM 1)

State	Warren M. Christopher
Treasury	Lloyd Bentsen, Jr.; Robert E. Rubin (10 Jan 1995)
Attorney General	Janet Reno
Interior	Bruce Babbitt
Agriculture	Mike Espy; Dan Glickman (30 Mar 1995)
Commerce	Ronald H. Brown; Mickey Kantor (12 Apr 1996)
Labor	Robert B. Reich
Defense	Les Aspin; William J. Perry (3 Feb 1994)
Health and Human Services	Donna E. Shalala
Housing and Urban Development	Henry G. Cisneros
Transportation	Federico Peña
Energy	Hazel R. O'Leary
Education	Richard W. Riley
Veterans Affairs	Jesse Brown

20 JAN 1997-20 JAN 2001 (TERM 2)

State	Madeleine Albright
Treasury	Robert E. Rubin; Lawrence H. Summers (2 Jul 1999)
Attorney General	Janet Reno
Interior	Bruce Babbitt
Agriculture	Dan Glickman
Commerce	William M. Daley; Norman Mineta (21 Jul 2000)
Labor	Alexis M. Herman
Defense	William Cohen
Health and Human Services	Donna E. Shalala
Housing and Urban Development	Andrew M. Cuomo
Transportation	Rodney Slater
Energy	Federico Peña; Bill Richardson (18 Aug 1998)
Education	Richard W. Riley
Veterans Affairs	Togo D. West, Jr.; Hershel W. Gober (25 Jul 2000)

US Presidential Cabinets (continued)

George W. Bush

(20 JAN 2001–20 JAN 2005) (TERM 1)

State	Colin Powell
Treasury	Paul O'Neill; John Snow (7 Feb 2003)
Attorney General	John Ashcroft
Interior	Gale Norton
Agriculture	Ann M. Veneman
Commerce	Don Evans
Labor	Elaine Chao
Defense	Donald Rumsfeld
Health and Human Services	Tommy Thompson
Housing and Urban Development	Mel Martinez; Alphonso Jackson (31 Mar 2004)
Transportation	Norman Mineta
Energy	Spencer Abraham
Education	Rod Paige
Veterans Affairs	Anthony Principi
Homeland Security	Tom Ridge (8 Oct 2001)

(20 JAN 2005–   ) (TERM 2)

State	Condoleezza Rice
Treasury	John Snow
Attorney General	Alberto Gonzales
Interior	Gale Norton
Agriculture	Mike Johanns
Commerce	Carlos Gutierrez
Labor	Elaine Chao
Defense	Donald Rumsfeld
Health and Human Services	Michael O. Leavitt
Housing and Urban Development	Alphonso Jackson
Transportation	Norman Mineta
Energy	Samuel W. Bodman
Education	Margaret Spellings
Veterans Affairs	Jim Nicholson
Homeland Security	Michael Chertoff

Additionally, the White House lists the following as cabinet-rank members: Vice President Richard (Dick) B. Cheney, Chief of Staff Andrew H. Card, Jr., Environmental Protection Agency Administrator Stephen Johnson, US Trade Representative Ambassador Rob Portman, Office of Management and Budget Director Joshua B. Bolten, and Office of National Drug Control Policy Director John Walters.

Presidential Libraries

The presidential libraries serve as repositories for the papers, records, and materials of the US presidents since Herbert Hoover. Each of the 12 libraries contains a museum and conducts public programs. The network is administered by the Office of Presidential Libraries, which is itself a division of the US National Archives and Records Administration (NARA). The system also includes the Nixon Presidential Materials Staff.

NAME, ADDRESS, & CONTACT INFORMATION
Herbert Hoover Library
210 Parkside Drive
P.O. Box 488
West Branch IA 52358-0488
Web site: <http://hoover.archives.gov>

Franklin D. Roosevelt Library
4079 Albany Post Road
Hyde Park NY 12538-1999
Web site: <www.fdrlibrary.marist.edu>

Harry S. Truman Library
500 West US Highway 24
Independence MO 64050-1798
Web site: <www.trumanlibrary.org>

NAME, ADDRESS, & CONTACT INFORMATION
Dwight D. Eisenhower Library
200 SE 4th Street
Abilene KS 67410-2900
Web site: <http://eisenhower.archives.gov>

John F. Kennedy Library
Columbia Point
Boston MA 02125-3398
Web site: <www.jfklibrary.org>

Lyndon B. Johnson Library
2313 Red River Street
Austin TX 78705-5702
Web site: <www.lbjlib.utexas.edu>

Presidential Libraries (continued)

NAME, ADDRESS, & CONTACT INFORMATION
Richard Nixon Library and Birthplace
18001 Yorba Linda Boulevard
Yorba Linda CA 92886-3903
Web site: <www.nixonlibrary.org>

Nixon Presidential Materials Staff
National Archives at College Park
8601 Adelphi Road
College Park MD 20740-6001
Web site: <http://nixon.archives.gov>

Gerald R. Ford Library
1000 Beal Avenue
Ann Arbor MI 48109-2114
Web site: <www.fordlibrarymuseum.gov>

Jimmy Carter Library
441 Freedom Parkway
Atlanta GA 30307-1498
Web site: <www.jimmycarterlibrary.gov>

NAME, ADDRESS, & CONTACT INFORMATION
Ronald Reagan Library
40 Presidential Drive
Simi Valley CA 93065-0600
Web site: <www.reagan.utexas.edu>

George Bush Library
1000 George Bush Drive West
College Station TX 77845
Web site: <http://bushlibrary.tamu.edu>

William J. Clinton Library
1200 President Clinton Avenue
Little Rock AR 72201
Web site: <www.clintonlibrary.gov>

Office of Presidential Libraries
National Archives and Records Administration
8601 Adelphi Road
College Park MD 20740-6001
Web site: <www.archives.gov/presidential_libraries>

Impeachment

The American federal impeachment process is rooted in Article II, Section 4, of the US Constitution. Impeachment has rarely been employed, largely because it is such a cumbersome process. It can occupy Congress for a lengthy period of time, fill thousands of pages of testimony, and involve conflicting and troublesome political pressures. Repeated attempts in the US Congress to amend the procedure, however, have been unsuccessful, partly because impeachment is regarded as an integral part of the system of checks and balances in the US government.

Andrew Johnson was the first US president ever impeached. In 1868 he was charged with attempting to remove, contrary to statute, the secretary of war, Edwin M. Stanton, with inducing a general of the army to violate an act of Congress, and with contempt of Congress. Johnson was acquitted by a margin of a single vote. In 1974 the Judiciary Committee of the House of Representatives voted three articles of impeachment against Pres. Richard M. Nixon, but he resigned before impeachment proceedings in the full House could begin. In December 1998 the House of Representatives voted to impeach Pres. William J. Clinton, charging him with perjury and obstruction of justice in investigations of his relationship with a White House intern, Monica Lewinsky. In the trial, the Senate voted not guilty on the perjury charge (55–45) and not guilty on the obstruction of justice charge (50–50); since 67 guilty votes are needed for a conviction, President Clinton was acquitted.

Every US state except Oregon provides for the removal of executive and judicial officers by impeachment. Exact procedures vary somewhat from state to state, but they are all similar to federal impeachment.

Executive Departments

Department of Agriculture
Secretary: Mike Johanns
Deputy secretary: Chuck Conner
Web site: <www.usda.gov>.
Mission: To "provide leadership on food, agriculture, natural resources, and related issues based on sound public policy, the best available science, and efficient management."
Selected divisions and agencies:
  Farm and Foreign Agricultural Service
    Farm Service Agency
    Foreign Agricultural Service
    Risk Management Agency
  Food Safety
    Food Safety and Inspection Service
  Natural Resources and Environment
    Forest Service
    Natural Resources Conservation Service
  Rural Development
  Food, Nutrition, and Consumer Services
    Food and Nutrition Service
    Center for Nutrition Policy and Promotion
  Marketing and Regulatory Programs

  Agricultural Marketing Service
  Animal and Plant Health Inspection Service
  Grain Inspection, Packers and Stockyards
    Administration
  Research, Education, and Economics
    Agricultural Research Service
    Cooperative State Research, Education, and
      Extension Service
    Economic Research Service
    National Agricultural Statistics Service

Department of Commerce
Secretary: Carlos M. Gutierrez
Deputy secretary: David A. Sampson (acting)
Web site: <www.commerce.gov>.
Mission: To "promote job creation, economic growth, sustainable development, and improved living standards for all Americans by working in partnership with businesses, universities, communities, and workers."
Selected divisions and agencies:
  Economics and Statistics Administration
    Bureau of Economic Analysis

Bureau of the Census
National Oceanic and Atmospheric Administration
National Weather Service
Technology Administration
National Institute of Standards and Technology
National Technical Information Service
Office of Technology Policy
Economic Development Administration
Bureau of Industry and Security
International Trade Administration
Minority Business Development Agency
National Telecommunications and Information Administration
Patent and Trademark Office

Department of Defense
Secretary: Donald H. Rumsfeld
Deputy secretary: Gordon England (acting)
Web site: <www.defenselink.mil>.
Mission: To "provide the military forces needed to deter war and to protect the security of the US."
Selected divisions and agencies:
Army Department
Navy Department
Marine Corps
Air Force Department
Defense Advanced Research Projects Agency
Defense Commissary Agency
Defense Contract Audit Agency
Defense Contract Management Agency
Defense Finance and Accounting Service
Defense Information Systems Agency
Defense Intelligence Agency
Defense Legal Services Agency
Defense Logistics Agency
Defense Security Cooperation Agency
Defense Security Service
Defense Threat Reduction Agency
Missile Defense Agency
National Imagery and Mapping Agency
National Security Agency
Pentagon Force Protection Agency

Department of Education
Secretary: Margaret Spellings
Deputy secretary: Raymond Simon
Web site: <www.ed.gov>.
Mission: To strengthen the federal commitment to assuring access to equal educational opportunity for every individual; to supplement and complement the efforts of states, the local school systems and other instrumentalities of the states, the private sector, public and private nonprofit educational research institutions, community-based organizations, parents, and students to improve the quality of education; to encourage the increased involvement of the public, parents, and students in federal education programs; to promote improvements in the quality and usefulness of education through federally supported research, evaluation, and sharing of information; to improve the coordination of federal education programs; to improve the management of federal education activities; and to increase the accountability of federal education programs to the President, the Congress, and the public.
Selected divisions and agencies:
White House Initiatives
Center for Faith-Based and Community Initiatives
Historically Black Colleges and Universities

Educational Excellence for Hispanic Americans
Tribal Colleges and Universities
Institute of Education Sciences
Office of Elementary and Secondary Education
Office of Postsecondary Education
Office of Innovation and Improvement
Office of Safe and Drug-Free Schools
Office of Special Education and Rehabilitative Services
Office of Federal Student Aid
Office of Vocational and Adult Education
Office for Civil Rights
Office of English Language Acquisition
Office of Educational Technology

Department of Energy
Secretary: Samuel W. Bodman
Deputy secretary: Clay Sell
Web site: <www.energy.gov>.
Mission: To "advance the national, economic and energy security of the United States; to promote scientific and technological innovation in support of that mission; and to ensure the environmental cleanup of the national nuclear weapons complex."
Selected divisions and agencies:
National Nuclear Security Administration
Defense Programs
Defense Nuclear Nonproliferation
Naval Reactors
Emergency Operations
Infrastructure and Environment
Defense Nuclear Security
Management and Administration
Energy, Science, and Environment
Office of Science
Office of Civilian Radioactive Waste Management
Office of Nuclear Energy, Science, and Technology
Office of Counterintelligence
Office of Intelligence
Office of Security
Office of the Inspector General
Office of Independent Oversight and Performance Assurance
Office of Hearings and Appeals
Office of Energy Assurance
Office of Management, Budget, and Evaluation/CFO
Energy Information Administration
Office of Economic Impact and Diversity
Office of Public Affairs

Department of Health and Human Services
Secretary: Mike Leavitt
Deputy secretary: Alex Azar (acting)
Web site: <www.hhs.gov>.
Mission: To "protect the health of all Americans and provide essential human services, especially for those who are least able to help themselves."
Selected divisions and agencies:
Administration for Children and Families
Administration on Aging
Centers for Medicare and Medicaid Services
Agency for Healthcare Research and Quality
Centers for Disease Control and Prevention
Agency for Toxic Substances and Disease Registry
Food and Drug Administration
Health Resources and Services Administration
Indian Health Service
National Institutes of Health
Substance Abuse and Mental Health Services Administration
Program Support Center

Office of Public Health Emergency Preparedness
Office for Civil Rights
Departmental Appeals Board

Department of Homeland Security

Secretary: Michael Chertoff
Deputy Secretary: Michael P. Jackson
Web site: <www.dhs.gov>.
Mission: To "prevent terrorist attacks within the United States, reduce America's vulnerability to terrorism, and minimize the damage from potential attacks and natural disasters."
Selected divisions and agencies:
Directorate of Border and Transportation Security
  Bureau of US Immigration and Customs Enforcement
    Office of Detention and Removal
    Office of Federal Air Marshal Service
  Federal Law Enforcement Training Center
  Transportation Security Administration
Directorate of Emergency Preparedness and Response
  Federal Emergency Management Agency
  National Disaster Medical System
Directorate of Science & Technology
Directorate of Information Analysis and Infrastructure Protection
  National Cyber Security Division
Directorate of Management
Coast Guard
Secret Service
Bureau of US Citizenship and Immigration Services
Office of the Inspector General

Department of Housing and Urban Development

Secretary: Alphonso R. Jackson
Deputy secretary: Roy A. Bernardi
Web site: <www.hud.gov>.
Mission: To "increase home ownership, support community development and increase access to affordable housing free from discrimination."
Selected divisions and agencies:
Office of Housing
  Office of Multifamily Housing Assistance Restructuring
Office of Community Planning and Development
Office of Fair Housing and Equal Opportunity
Office of Congressional and Intergovernmental Relations
Government National Mortgage Association (Ginnie Mae)
Office of Public and Indian Housing
Office Healthy Homes and Lead Hazard Control
Center for Faith-Based and Community Initiatives

Department of the Interior

Secretary: Gale A. Norton
Deputy secretary: *vacant*
Web site: <www.doi.gov>.
Mission: To "protect and provide access to the nation's natural and cultural heritage, and to honor responsibilities to Indian tribes and commitments to island communities."
Selected divisions and agencies:
National Park Service
US Fish and Wildlife Service
Bureau of Indian Affairs
Bureau of Land Management
Minerals Management Service
Office of Surface Mining

US Geological Survey
Bureau of Reclamation

Department of Justice

Attorney General: Alberto Gonzales
Deputy Attorney General: James Comey
Web site: <www.usdoj.gov>.
Mission: To "enforce the law and defend the interests of the US according to the law; to ensure public safety against threats foreign and domestic; to provide federal leadership in preventing and controlling crime; to seek just punishment for those guilty of unlawful behavior; to administer and enforce the nation's immigration laws fairly and effectively; and to ensure fair and impartial administration of justice for all Americans."
Selected divisions and agencies:
Office of Legal Policy
Office of Legislative Affairs
Office of Intergovernmental and Public Liaison
Office of Public Affairs
Office of Legal Counsel
Office of the Solicitor General
Office of Justice Programs
Office of Community Oriented Policing Services
Bureau of Alcohol, Tobacco, Firearms, and Explosives
Executive Office for United States Trustees
Office of Dispute Resolution
Office of Information and Privacy
Foreign Claims Settlement Commission
Civil Rights Division
Civil Division
Antitrust Division
Environment and Natural Resources Division
Tax Division
Community Relations Service
Federal Bureau of Investigation
Drug Enforcement Administration
Executive Office for United States Attorneys
Criminal Division
Federal Bureau of Prisons
United States Marshals Service
US National Central Bureau—Interpol
Office of the Federal Detention Trustee
Office of the Inspector General
Office of Intelligence Policy and Review
Justice Management Division
Executive Office for Immigration Review
Professional Responsibility Advisory Office
Office of the Pardon Attorney
United States Parole Commission
National Drug Intelligence Center
Professional Responsibility Advisory Office
Office on Violence Against Women

Department of Labor

Secretary: Elaine L. Chao
Deputy secretary: Steven J. Law
Web site: <www.dol.gov>.
Mission: To "foster and promote the welfare of the job seekers, wage earners, and retirees of the US by improving their working conditions, advancing their opportunities for profitable employment, protecting their retirement and health care benefits, helping employers find workers, strengthening free collective bargaining, and tracking changes in employment, prices, and other national economic measurements."

Selected divisions and agencies:
Office of Disability Employment Policy
Occupational Safety and Health Administration
Mine Safety and Health Administration
Employee Benefits Security Administration
Bureau of Labor Statistics
Pension Benefit Guaranty Corporation
Employment and Training Administration
Women's Bureau
Office of the Solicitor
Veterans' Employment and Training Service
Bureau of International Labor Affairs
Office of the Assistant Secretary for Policy
Employment Standards Administration
Office of Small Business Programs
Office of the 21st Century Workforce
Office of Congressional and Inter-Governmental Affairs

Department of State
Secretary: Condoleezza Rice
Deputy secretary: Robert B. Zoellick
Web site: <www.state.gov>.
Mission: To "create a more secure, democratic, and prosperous world for the benefit of the American people and the international community."
Selected divisions, agencies, and bureaus:
Political Affairs
  African Affairs
  East Asian and Pacific Affairs
  European and Eurasian Affairs
  Near Eastern Affairs
  South Asian Affairs
  Western Hemisphere Affairs
  International Organization Affairs
Economic, Business, and Agricultural Affairs
Arms Control and International Security
  Arms Control
  Nonproliferation
  Political-Military Affairs
  Verification and Compliance
Public Diplomacy and Public Affairs
  Educational and Cultural Affairs
  Public Affairs
  International Information Programs
Management
  Consular Affairs
  Diplomatic Security
  Foreign Service Institute
  Information Resource Management
  Office of White House Liaison
  Overseas Buildings Operations
Global Affairs
  Democracy, Human Rights, and Labor
  International Narcotics and Law Enforcement Affairs
  Oceans and International Environmental and Scientific Affairs
  Population, Refugees, and Migration
  Office to Monitor and Combat Trafficking in Persons
Policy Planning Staff
Office of Civil Rights
Intelligence and Research
Office of Protocol
Counterterrorism Office
Office of War Crimes Issues

Department of Transportation
Secretary: Norman Y. Mineta
Deputy secretary: Maria Cino
Web site: <www.dot.gov>.
Mission: To "serve the US by ensuring a fast, safe, efficient, accessible, and convenient transportation system that meets vital national interests and enhances the quality of life of the American people."
Selected divisions and agencies:
Federal Aviation Administration
Federal Highway Administration
Federal Railroad Administration
National Highway Traffic Safety Administration
Federal Transit Administration
Saint Lawrence Seaway Development Corporation
Maritime Administration
Pipeline and Hazardous Materials Safety Administration
Surface Transportation Board
Research and Innovative Technology Administration
Federal Motor Carrier Safety Administration

Department of the Treasury
Secretary: John W. Snow
Deputy secretary: Arnold I. Havens (acting)
Web site: <www.treas.gov>.
Mission: To "promote the conditions for prosperity and stability in the United States and encourage prosperity and stability in the rest of the world."
Selected divisions and agencies:
Treasurer of the United States
Alcohol and Tobacco Tax and Trade Bureau
Bureau of Engraving and Printing
Bureau of the Public Debt
Community Development Financial Institution
Financial Crimes Enforcement Network
Financial Management Service
Internal Revenue Service
Office of the Comptroller of the Currency
Office of Thrift Supervision
US Mint
Office of Terrorism and Financial Intelligence

Department of Veterans Affairs
Secretary: R. James Nicholson
Deputy secretary: Gordon H. Mansfield
Web site: <www.va.gov>.
Mission: To serve US veterans and their families with dignity and compassion and be their principal advocate in ensuring that they receive medical care, benefits, social support, and lasting memorials promoting the health, welfare, and dignity of all veterans in recognition of their service.
Selected divisions and agencies:
Veterans Health Administration
Veterans Benefits Administration
National Cemetery Administration
Board of Contract Appeals
Board of Veterans' Appeals
Office of Small and Disadvantaged Business Adjudication
Center for Minority Veterans
Center for Women Veterans
Office of Employment Discrimination Complaint Adjudication

United States Congress

The Senate, 109th Congress

According to Article I, Section 3, of the US Constitution, a US senator must be at least 30 years old, must reside in the state he or she represents at the time of the election, and must have been a citizen of the United States for 9 years. Voters elect two senators from each state; terms are for 6 years and begin on 3 January. Senators originally made $6.00 per day; each current senator's salary is $162,100 per year. The majority and minority leaders and the president pro tempore receive $180,100 per year.

US Senate Web site: <www.senate.gov>.

Senate leadership

president:	Richard Cheney
president pro tempore:	Ted Stevens
majority leader:	Bill Frist
minority leader:	Harry Reid
asst. majority leader (majority whip):	Mitch McConnell
asst. minority leader (minority whip):	Dick Durbin

STATE	NAME AND PARTY	SERVICE BEGAN	TERM ENDS
Alabama	Richard C. Shelby (R)	1987	2011
	Jeff Sessions (R)	1997	2009
Alaska	Ted Stevens (R)	1968[1]	2009
	Lisa Murkowski (R)	2002	2011
Arizona	John McCain (R)	1987	2011
	Jon Kyl (R)	1995	2007
Arkansas	Blanche Lincoln (D)	1999	2011
	Mark Pryor (D)	2003	2009
California	Dianne Feinstein (D)	1992[2]	2007
	Barbara Boxer (D)	1993	2011
Colorado	Wayne Allard (R)	1997	2009
	Ken Salazar (D)	2005	2011
Connecticut	Chris Dodd (D)	1981	2011
	Joe Lieberman (D)	1989	2007
Delaware	Joseph R. Biden, Jr. (D)	1973	2009
	Tom Carper (D)	2001	2007
Florida	Bill Nelson (D)	2001	2007
	Mel Martinez (R)	2005	2011
Georgia	Saxby Chambliss (R)	2003	2009
	Johnny Isakson (R)	2005	2011
Hawaii	Daniel K. Inouye (D)	1963	2011
	Daniel Kahikina Akaka (D)	1990[3]	2007
Idaho	Larry Craig (R)	1991	2009
	Mike Crapo (R)	1999	2011
Illinois	Dick Durbin (D)	1997	2009
	Barack Obama (D)	2005	2011
Indiana	Richard G. Lugar (R)	1977	2007
	Evan Bayh (D)	1999	2011
Iowa	Chuck Grassley (R)	1981	2011
	Tom Harkin (D)	1985	2009
Kansas	Sam Brownback (R)	1996[4]	2011
	Pat Roberts (R)	1997	2009
Kentucky	Mitch McConnell (R)	1985	2009
	Jim Bunning (R)	1999	2011
Louisiana	Mary L. Landrieu (D)	1997	2009
	David Vitter (R)	2005	2011
Maine	Olympia J. Snowe (R)	1995	2007
	Susan Collins (R)	1997	2009
Maryland	Paul S. Sarbanes (D)	1977	2007
	Barbara Mikulski (D)	1987	2011
Massachusetts	Edward M. Kennedy (D)	1963	2007
	John Kerry (D)	1985	2009
Michigan	Carl Levin (D)	1979	2009
	Debbie Stabenow (D)	2001	2007
Minnesota	Mark Dayton (D)	2001	2007
	Norm Coleman (R)	2003	2009
Mississippi	Thad Cochran (R)	1979	2009
	Trent Lott (R)	1989	2007
Missouri	Kit Bond (R)	1987	2011
	Jim Talent (R)	2002	2007

The Senate, 109th Congress (continued)

STATE	NAME AND PARTY	SERVICE BEGAN	TERM ENDS
Montana	Max Baucus (D)	1979	2009
	Conrad Burns (R)	1989	2007
Nebraska	Chuck Hagel (R)	1997	2009
	Ben Nelson (D)	2001	2007
Nevada	Harry Reid (D)	1987	2011
	John Ensign (R)	2001	2007
New Hampshire	Judd Gregg (R)	1993	2011
	John E. Sununu (R)	2003	2009
New Jersey	Jon S. Corzine (D)	2001	2007
	Frank R. Lautenberg (D)	2003	2009
New Mexico	Pete V. Domenici (R)	1973	2009
	Jeff Bingaman (D)	1983	2007
New York	Charles E. Schumer (D)	1999	2011
	Hillary Rodham Clinton (D)	2001	2007
North Carolina	Elizabeth Dole (R)	2003	2009
	Richard Burr (R)	2005	2011
North Dakota	Kent Conrad (D)	1987	2007
	Byron L. Dorgan (D)	1993	2011
Ohio	Mike DeWine (R)	1995	2007
	George V. Voinovich (R)	1999	2011
Oklahoma	James M. Inhofe (R)	1994[5]	2009
	Tom Coburn (R)	2005	2011
Oregon	Ron Wyden (D)	1996[6]	2011
	Gordon H. Smith (R)	1997	2009
Pennsylvania	Arlen Specter (R)	1981	2011
	Rick Santorum (R)	1995	2007
Rhode Island	Jack Reed (D)	1997	2009
	Lincoln Chafee (R)	1999[7]	2007
South Carolina	Lindsey Graham (R)	2003	2009
	Jim DeMint (R)	2005	2011
South Dakota	Tim Johnson (D)	1997	2009
	John Thune (R)	2005	2011
Tennessee	Bill Frist (R)	1995	2007
	Lamar Alexander (R)	2003	2009
Texas	Kay Bailey Hutchison (R)	1993[8]	2007
	John Cornyn (R)	2002	2009
Utah	Orrin G. Hatch (R)	1977	2007
	Bob Bennett (R)	1993	2011
Vermont	Patrick Leahy (D)	1975	2011
	Jim Jeffords (I)	1989	2007
Virginia	John Warner (R)	1979	2009
	George Allen (R)	2001	2007
Washington	Patty Murray (D)	1993	2011
	Maria Cantwell (D)	2001	2007
West Virginia	Robert C. Byrd (D)	1959	2007
	Jay Rockefeller (D)	1985	2009
Wisconsin	Herb Kohl (D)	1989	2007
	Russ Feingold (D)	1993	2011
Wyoming	Craig Thomas (R)	1995	2007
	Mike Enzi (R)	1997	2009

Republicans: 55; Democrats: 44; Independents: 1

[1]Ted Stevens was appointed in December 1968 to fill the vacancy caused by the death of Edward Lewis (Bob) Bartlett. [2]Dianne Feinstein was elected in November 1992 to complete the term of Pete Wilson, who resigned in 1991 to become California's governor. [3]Daniel Kahikina Akaka was appointed in April 1990 after winning a special election to fill the vacancy caused by the death of Spark M. Matsunaga. [4]Sam Brownback was elected in November 1996 to complete the term of Bob Dole, who resigned to campaign for the presidency. [5]James M. Inhofe was elected in November 1994 to complete the term of David Boren, who resigned to become president of the University of Oklahoma. [6]Ron Wyden was elected in January 1996 to complete the term of Bob Packwood, who resigned in 1995. [7]Lincoln Chafee was appointed in November 1999 to fill the vacancy caused by the death of his father, John H. Chafee. [8]Kay Bailey Hutchison was elected in June 1993 to fill the vacancy left by the retirement of Lloyd Bentsen, Jr.

Senate Standing Committees

COMMITTEE	CHAIRMAN (PARTY–STATE)	RANKING MINORITY MEMBER (PARTY–STATE)	NUMBER OF MEMBERS: MAJORITY	MINORITY	NUMBER OF SUBCOM-MITTEES
Agriculture, Nutrition, and Forestry	Saxby Chambliss (R-GA)	Tom Harkin (D-IA)	11	9	4
Appropriations	Thad Cochran (R-MS)	Robert C. Byrd (D-WV)	15	13	12
Armed Services	John Warner (R-VA)	Carl Levin (D-MI)	13	11	6
Banking, Housing, and Urban Affairs	Richard C. Shelby (R-AL)	Paul S. Sarbanes (D-MD)	11	9	5
Budget	Judd Gregg (R-NH)	Kent Conrad (D-ND)	12	10	none
Commerce, Science, and Transportation	Ted Stevens (R-AK)	Daniel Inouye (D-HI)	12	10	10
Energy and Natural Resources	Pete V. Domenici (R-NM)	Jeff Bingaman (D-NM)	12	10	4
Environment and Public Works	James M. Inhofe (R-OK)	James M. Jeffords (I-VT)	10	8	4
Finance	Chuck Grassley (R-IA)	Max Baucus (D-MT)	11	9	5
Foreign Relations	Richard G. Lugar (R-IN)	Joseph R. Biden, Jr. (D-DE)	10	8	7
Health, Education, Labor, and Pensions	Mike Enzi (R-WY)	Edward M. Kennedy (D-MA)	11	9	4
Homeland Security and Governmental Affairs	Susan Collins (R-ME)	Joseph Lieberman (D-CT)	9	7	3
Judiciary	Arlen Specter (R-PA)	Patrick Leahy (D-VT)	10	8	6
Rules and Administration	Trent Lott (R-MS)	Christopher Dodd (D-CT)	10	8	none
Small Business and Entrepreneurship	Olympia J. Snowe (R-ME)	John F. Kerry (D-MA)	10	8	none
Veterans Affairs	Larry Craig (R-ID)	Daniel Akaka (D-HI)	8	6	none

Senate Special, Select, and Other Committees

COMMITTEE	CHAIRMAN (PARTY–STATE)	RANKING MINORITY MEMBER (PARTY–STATE)	NUMBER OF MEMBERS: MAJORITY	MINORITY
Special Committee on Aging	Gordon Smith (R-OR)	Herb Kohl (D-WI)	11	9
Select Committee on Ethics	George V. Voinovich (R-OH)	Tim Johnson (D-SD)	3	3
Committee on Indian Affairs	John McCain (R-AZ)	Bryan Dorgan (D-ND)	8	6
Select Committee on Intelligence	Pat Roberts (R-KS)	John D. Rockefeller IV (D-WV)	8	7

Joint Committees of Congress

The joint committees of Congress include members from the Senate and the House of Representatives. They function as overseeing entities but do not have the power to approve appropriations or legislation. Chairmanship of the Joint Economic Committee is determined by seniority and alternates between the Senate and the House every Congress. The Joint Committee on the Library of Congress is evenly made up of members from the House Administration Committee and the Senate Rules and Administration committees. Chairmanship and vice chairmanship of the Joint Committee on Printing alternates between the House and the Senate every Congress. The Joint Committee on Taxation is composed of five members from the Senate Committee on Finance and five members from the House Committee on Ways and Means (three majority and two minority members from each).

COMMITTEE	CHAIRMAN (PARTY-STATE)	VICE CHAIRMAN (PARTY-STATE)	NUMBER OF MEMBERS: REPUBLICANS	DEMOCRATS
Economic	Rep. Jim Saxton (R-NJ)	Sen. Robert F. Bennett (R-UT)	12	8
Library	Sen. Ted Stevens (R-AK)	Rep. Vernon J. Ehlers (R-MI)	6	4
Printing	Rep. Robert W. Ney (R-OH)	Sen. Saxby Chambliss (R-GA)	6	4
Taxation	Rep. William M. Thomas (R-CA)	Sen. Charles E. Grassley (R-IA)	6	4

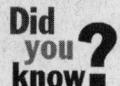

Did you know? Strom Thurmond of South Carolina (1902–2003) was the oldest person (101) to serve in the Senate, the longest-serving senator (49 years, 1954–2003), and the first person elected to the Senate as a write-in candidate.

The House of Representatives, 109th Congress

Parties: Democrat (D); Republican (R); Independent (I).
*Party totals: **Republicans** 232; **Democrats** 202; **Independents** 1.*

According to Article I, Section 2, of the US Constitution, a US representative must be at least 25 years old, must reside in the state he or she represents at the time of the election, and must have been a citizen of the United States for 7 years. Each state is entitled to at least one representative, with additional seats apportioned based on population. Each congressperson originally represented 30,000 people; the current range is from 495,304 (Wyoming) to 905,316 (Montana) persons per representative. Terms are for 2 years and begin on 3 January (unless otherwise noted). The current representative's salary is $162,100 per year. The majority and minority leaders receive $180,100 per year; the speaker of the house receives $208,100 per year.

American Samoa, the District of Columbia, Guam, and the Virgin Islands elect delegates; Puerto Rico elects a resident commissioner. Their formal duties are the same, but the resident commissioner serves a 4-year term. They may participate in debate and serve on committees but are not permitted to vote. US House Web site: <www.house.gov>.

Numbers preceding the names refer to districts. Certain states gained (+) or lost (–) districts by reapportionment since the 107th Congress.

House leadership

Speaker of the house:	J. Dennis Hastert (R-IL)
Majority leader:	Tom DeLay (R-TX)
Minority leader:	Nancy Pelosi (D-CA)
Republican whip:	Roy Blunt (MO)
Democratic whip:	Steny H. Hoyer (MD)

STATE	REPRESENTATIVES	SERVICE BEGAN
Alabama	1. Jo Bonner (R)	Jan 2003
	2. Terry Everett (R)	Jan 1993
	3. Mike Rogers (R)	Jan 2003
	4. Robert B. Aderholt (R)	Jan 1997
	5. Robert E. (Bud) Cramer, Jr. (D)	Jan 1991
	6. Spencer Bachus (R)	Jan 1993
	7. Artur Davis (D)	Jan 2003
Alaska	Don Young (R)	Mar 1973
Arizona (+2)	1. Rick Renzi (R)	Jan 2003
	2. Trent Franks (R)	Jan 2003
	3. John B. Shadegg (R)	Jan 1995
	4. Ed Pastor (D)	Sep 1991
	5. J.D. Hayworth (R)	Jan 1995
	6. Jeff Flake (R)	Jan 2001
	7. Raúl M. Grijalva (D)	Jan 2003
	8. Jim Kolbe (R)	Jan 1985
Arkansas	1. Marion Berry (D)	Jan 1997
	2. Vic Snyder (D)	Jan 1997
	3. John Boozman (R)[1]	Nov 2001
	4. Mike Ross (D)	Jan 2001
California (+1)	1. Mike Thompson (D)	Jan 1999
	2. Wally Herger (R)	Jan 1987
	3. Daniel E. Lungren (R)	Jan 2005
	4. John T. Doolittle (R)	Jan 1991
	5. Doris O. Matsui (D)[2]	Mar 2005
	6. Lynn C. Woolsey (D)	Jan 1993
	7. George Miller (D)	Jan 1975
	8. Nancy Pelosi (D)	Jun 1987
	9. Barbara Lee (D)	Apr 1998
	10. Ellen O. Tauscher (D)	Jan 1997
	11. Richard W. Pombo (R)	Jan 1993
	12. Tom Lantos (D)	Jan 1981
	13. Fortney "Pete" Stark (D)	Jan 1973
	14. Anna G. Eshoo (D)	Jan 1993
	15. Michael M. Honda (D)	Jan 2001
	16. Zoe Lofgren (D)	Jan 1995
	17. Sam Farr (D)	Jun 1993
	18. Dennis A. Cardoza (D)	Jan 2003
	19. George Radanovich (R)	Jan 1995
	20. Jim Costa (D)	Jan 2005
	21. Devin Nunes (R)	Jan 2003
	22. William M. Thomas (R)	Jan 1979

STATE	REPRESENTATIVES	SERVICE BEGAN
California (continued)	23. Lois Capps (D)	Mar 1998
	24. Elton Gallegly (R)	Jan 1987
	25. Howard P. "Buck" McKeon (R)	Jan 1993
	26. David Dreier (R)	Jan 1981
	27. Brad Sherman (D)	Jan 1997
	28. Howard L. Berman (D)	Jan 1983
	29. Adam B. Schiff (D)	Jan 2001
	30. Henry A. Waxman (D)	Jan 1975
	31. Xavier Becerra (D)	Jan 1993
	32. Hilda L. Solis (D)	Jan 2001
	33. Diane E. Watson (D)[3]	Jun 2001
	34. Lucille Roybal-Allard (D)	Jan 1993
	35. Maxine Waters (D)	Jan 1991
	36. Jane F. Harman (D)[4]	Jan 1993
	37. Juanita Millender-McDonald (D)	Mar 1996
	38. Grace F. Napolitano (D)	Jan 1999
	39. Linda T. Sánchez (D)	Jan 2003
	40. Edward R. Royce (R)	Jan 1993
	41. Jerry Lewis (R)	Jan 1979
	42. Gary G. Miller (R)	Jan 1999
	43. Joe Baca (D)	Nov 1999
	44. Ken Calvert (R)	Jan 1993
	45. Mary Bono (R)	Apr 1998
	46. Dana Rohrabacher (R)	Jan 1989
	47. Loretta Sanchez (D)	Jan 1997
	48. Christopher Cox (R)	Jan 1989
	49. Darrell E. Issa (R)	Jan 2001
	50. Randy "Duke" Cunningham (R)	Jan 1991
	51. Bob Filner (D)	Jan 1993
	52. Duncan Hunter (R)	Jan 1981
	53. Susan A. Davis (D)	Jan 2001
Colorado (+1)	1. Diana DeGette (D)	Jan 1997
	2. Mark Udall (D)	Jan 1999
	3. John T. Salazar (D)	Jan 2005
	4. Marilyn N. Musgrave (R)	Jan 2003
	5. Joel Hefley (R)	Jan 1987
	6. Thomas G. Tancredo (R)	Jan 1999
	7. Bob Beauprez (R)	Jan 2003
Connecticut (–1)	1. John B. Larson (D)	Jan 1999
	2. Rob Simmons (R)	Jan 2001
	3. Rosa L. DeLauro (D)	Jan 1991
	4. Christopher Shays (R)	Aug 1987

The House of Representatives, 109th Congress (continued)

STATE	REPRESENTATIVES	SERVICE BEGAN
Connecticut (continued)	5. Nancy L. Johnson (R)	Jan 1983
Delaware	Michael N. Castle (R)	Jan 1993
Florida (+2)	1. Jeff Miller (R)[5]	Oct 2001
	2. Allen Boyd (D)	Jan 1997
	3. Corrine Brown (D)	Jan 1993
	4. Ander Crenshaw (R)	Jan 2001
	5. Ginny Brown-Waite (R)	Jan 2003
	6. Cliff Stearns (R)	Jan 1989
	7. John L. Mica (R)	Jan 1993
	8. Ric Keller (R)	Jan 2001
	9. Michael Bilirakis (R)	Jan 1983
	10. C.W. Bill Young (R)	Jan 1971
	11. Jim Davis (D)	Jan 1997
	12. Adam H. Putnam (R)	Jan 2001
	13. Katherine Harris (R)	Jan 2003
	14. Connie Mack (R)	Jan 2005
	15. Dave Weldon (R)	Jan 1995
	16. Mark Foley (R)	Jan 1995
	17. Kendrick B. Meek (D)	Jan 2003
	18. Ileana Ros-Lehtinen (R)	Aug 1989
	19. Robert Wexler (D)	Jan 1997
	20. Debbie Wasserman Schultz (D)	Jan 2005
	21. Lincoln Diaz-Balart (R)	Jan 1993
	22. E. Clay Shaw, Jr. (R)	Jan 1981
	23. Alcee L. Hastings (D)	Jan 1993
	24. Tom Feeney (R)	Jan 2003
	25. Mario Diaz-Balart (R)	Jan 2003
Georgia (+2)	1. Jack Kingston (R)	Jan 1993
	2. Sanford D. Bishop, Jr. (D)	Jan 1993
	3. Jim Marshall (D)	Jan 2003
	4. Cynthia McKinney (D)	Jan 2005
	5. John Lewis (D)	Jan 1987
	6. Tom Price (R)	Feb 2005
	7. John Linder (R)	Jan 1993
	8. Lynn A. Westmoreland (R)	Jan 2005
	9. Charlie Norwood (R)	Jan 1995
	10. Nathan Deal (R)	Jan 1993
	11. Phil Gingrey (R)	Jan 2003
	12. John Barrow (D)	Jan 2005
	13. David Scott (D)	Jan 2003
Hawaii	1. Neil Abercrombie (D)[6]	Sep 1986
	2. Ed Case (D)[7]	Jan 2003
Idaho	1. C.L. "Butch" Otter (R)	Jan 2001
	2. Michael K. Simpson (R)	Jan 1999
Illinois (−1)	1. Bobby L. Rush (D)	Jan 1993
	2. Jesse L. Jackson, Jr. (D)	Dec 1995
	3. Daniel Lipinski (D)	Jan 2005
	4. Luis V. Gutierrez (D)	Jan 1993
	5. Rahm Emanuel (D)	Jan 2003
	6. Henry J. Hyde (R)	Jan 1975
	7. Danny K. Davis (D)	Jan 1997
	8. Melissa L. Bean (D)	Jan 2005
	9. Janice D. Schakowsky (D)	Jan 1999
	10. Mark Steven Kirk (R)	Jan 2001
	11. Jerry Weller (R)	Jan 1995
	12. Jerry F. Costello (D)	Aug 1988
	13. Judy Biggert (R)	Jan 1999
	14. J. Dennis Hastert (R)	Jan 1987
	15. Timothy V. Johnson (R)	Jan 2001
	16. Donald A. Manzullo (R)	Jan 1993

STATE	REPRESENTATIVES	SERVICE BEGAN
Illinois (continued)	17. Lane Evans (D)	Jan 1983
	18. Ray LaHood (R)	Jan 1995
	19. John Shimkus (R)	Jan 1997
Indiana (−1)	1. Peter J. Visclosky (D)	Jan 1985
	2. Chris Chocola (R)	Jan 2003
	3. Mark E. Souder (R)	Jan 1995
	4. Steve Buyer (R)	Jan 1993
	5. Dan Burton (R)	Jan 1983
	6. Mike Pence (R)	Jan 2001
	7. Julia Carson (D)	Jan 1997
	8. John N. Hostettler (R)	Jan 1995
	9. Michael E. Sodrel (R)	Jan 2005
Iowa	1. Jim Nussle (R)	Jan 1991
	2. James A. Leach (R)	Jan 1977
	3. Leonard L. Boswell (D)	Jan 1997
	4. Tom Latham (R)	Jan 1995
	5. Steve King (R)	Jan 2003
Kansas	1. Jerry Moran (R)	Jan 1997
	2. Jim Ryun (R)	Nov 1996
	3. Dennis Moore (D)	Jan 1999
	4. Todd Tiahrt (R)	Jan 1995
Kentucky	1. Ed Whitfield (R)	Jan 1995
	2. Ron Lewis (R)	May 1994
	3. Anne M. Northup (R)	Jan 1997
	4. Geoff Davis (R)	Jan 2005
	5. Harold Rogers (R)	Jan 1981
	6. Ben Chandler (D)[8]	Feb 2004
Louisiana	1. Bobby Jindal (R)	Jan 2005
	2. William J. Jefferson (D)	Jan 1991
	3. Charlie Melancon (D)	Jan 2005
	4. Jim McCrery (R)	Apr 1988
	5. Rodney Alexander (R)	Jan 2003
	6. Richard H. Baker (R)	Jan 1987
	7. Charles W. Boustany, Jr. (R)	Jan 2005
Maine	1. Thomas H. Allen (D)	Jan 1997
	2. Michael H. Michaud (D)	Jan 2003
Maryland	1. Wayne T. Gilchrest (R)	Jan 1991
	2. C.A. Dutch Ruppersberger (D)	Jan 2003
	3. Benjamin L. Cardin (D)	Jan 1987
	4. Albert Russell Wynn (D)	Jan 1993
	5. Steny H. Hoyer (D)	May 1981
	6. Roscoe G. Bartlett (R)	Jan 1993
	7. Elijah E. Cummings (D)	Apr 1996
	8. Chris Van Hollen (D)	Jan 2003
Massachusetts	1. John W. Olver (D)	Jun 1991
	2. Richard E. Neal (D)	Jan 1989
	3. James P. McGovern (D)	Jan 1997
	4. Barney Frank (D)	Jan 1981
	5. Martin T. Meehan (D)	Jan 1993
	6. John F. Tierney (D)	Jan 1997
	7. Edward J. Markey (D)	Nov 1976
	8. Michael E. Capuano (D)	Jan 1999
	9. Stephen F. Lynch (D)[9]	Oct 2001
	10. William D. Delahunt (D)	Jan 1997
Michigan (−1)	1. Bart Stupak (D)	Jan 1993
	2. Peter Hoekstra (R)	Jan 1993
	3. Vernon J. Ehlers (R)	Dec 1993

The House of Representatives, 109th Congress (continued)

STATE	REPRESENTATIVES	SERVICE BEGAN	STATE	REPRESENTATIVES	SERVICE BEGAN
Michigan (continued)	4. Dave Camp (R)	Jan 1991	New Mexico	1. Heather Wilson (R)	Jun 1998
	5. Dale E. Kildee (D)	Jan 1977		2. Steve Pearce (R)	Jan 2003
	6. Fred Upton (R)	Jan 1987		3. Tom Udall (D)	Jan 1999
	7. John J.H. "Joe" Schwarz (R)	Jan 2005	New York (–2)	1. Timothy H. Bishop (D)	Jan 2003
	8. Mike Rogers (R)	Jan 2001		2. Steve Israel (D)	Jan 2001
	9. Joe Knollenberg (R)	Jan 1993		3. Peter T. King (R)	Jan 1993
	10. Candice S. Miller (R)	Jan 2003		4. Carolyn McCarthy (D)	Jan 1997
	11. Thaddeus G. McCotter (R)	Jan 2003		5. Gary L. Ackerman (D)	Mar 1983
	12. Sander M. Levin (D)	Jan 1983		6. Gregory W. Meeks (D)	Feb 1998
	13. Carolyn C. Kilpatrick (D)	Jan 1997		7. Joseph Crowley (D)	Jan 1999
	14. John Conyers, Jr. (D)	Jan 1965		8. Jerrold Nadler (D)	Nov 1992
	15. John D. Dingell (D)	Dec 1955		9. Anthony D. Weiner (D)	Jan 1999
				10. Edolphus Towns (D)	Jan 1983
Minnesota	1. Gil Gutknecht (R)	Jan 1995		11. Major R. Owens (D)	Jan 1983
	2. John Kline (R)	Jan 2003		12. Nydia M. Velázquez (D)	Jan 1993
	3. Jim Ramstad (R)	Jan 1991		13. Vito Fossella (R)	Nov 1997
	4. Betty McCollum (D)	Jan 2001		14. Carolyn B. Maloney (D)	Jan 1993
	5. Martin Olav Sabo (D)	Jan 1979		15. Charles B. Rangel (D)	Jan 1971
	6. Mark R. Kennedy (R)	Jan 2001		16. José E. Serrano (D)	Mar 1990
	7. Collin C. Peterson (D)	Jan 1991		17. Eliot L. Engel (D)	Jan 1989
	8. James L. Oberstar (D)	Jan 1975		18. Nita M. Lowey (D)	Jan 1989
				19. Sue W. Kelly (R)	Jan 1995
Mississippi (–1)	1. Roger F. Wicker (R)	Jan 1995		20. John E. Sweeney (R)	Jan 1999
	2. Bennie G. Thompson (D)	Apr 1993		21. Michael R. McNulty (D)	Jan 1989
	3. Charles W. "Chip" Pickering (R)	Jan 1997		22. Maurice D. Hinchey (D)	Jan 1993
	4. Gene Taylor (D)	Oct 1989		23. John M. McHugh (R)	Jan 1993
				24. Sherwood L. Boehlert (R)	Jan 1983
Missouri	1. William Lacy Clay (D)	Jan 2001		25. James T. Walsh (R)	Jan 1989
	2. W. Todd Akin (R)	Jan 2001		26. Thomas M. Reynolds (R)	Jan 1999
	3. Russ Carnahan (D)	Jan 2005		27. Brian Higgins (D)	Jan 2005
	4. Ike Skelton (D)	Jan 1977		28. Louise McIntosh Slaughter (D)	Jan 1987
	5. Emanuel Cleaver (D)	Jan 2005		29. John R. "Randy" Kuhl, Jr. (R)	Jan 2005
	6. Sam Graves (R)	Jan 2001			
	7. Roy Blunt (R)	Jan 1997	North Carolina (+1)	1. G.K. Butterfield (D)	Jan 2005
	8. Jo Ann Emerson (R)	Nov 1996		2. Bob Etheridge (D)	Jan 1997
	9. Kenny C. Hulshof (R)	Jan 1997		3. Walter B. Jones (R)	Jan 1995
				4. David E. Price (D)	Jan 1997
Montana	Dennis R. Rehberg (R)	Jan 2001		5. Virginia Foxx (R)	Jan 2005
				6. Howard Coble (R)	Jan 1985
Nebraska	1. Jeff Fortenberry (R)	Jan 2005		7. Mike McIntyre (D)	Jan 1997
	2. Lee Terry (R)	Jan 1999		8. Robin Hayes (R)	Jan 1999
	3. Tom Osborne (R)	Jan 2001		9. Sue Wilkins Myrick (R)	Jan 1995
				10. Patrick T. McHenry (R)	Jan 2005
Nevada (+1)	1. Shelley Berkley (D)	Jan 1999		11. Charles H. Taylor (R)	Jan 1991
	2. Jim Gibbons (R)	Jan 1997		12. Melvin L. Watt (D)	Jan 1993
	3. Jon C. Porter (R)	Jan 2003		13. Brad Miller (D)	Jan 2003
New Hampshire	1. Jeb Bradley (R)	Jan 2003	North Dakota	Earl Pomeroy (D)	Jan 1993
	2. Charles F. Bass (R)	Jan 1995			
			Ohio (–1)	1. Steve Chabot (R)	Jan 1995
New Jersey	1. Robert E. Andrews (D)	Nov 1990		2. Jean Schmidt (R)	Jul 2005
	2. Frank A. LoBiondo (R)	Jan 1995		3. Michael R. Turner (R)	Jan 2003
	3. Jim Saxton (R)	Nov 1984		4. Michael G. Oxley (R)	Jun 1981
	4. Christopher H. Smith (R)	Jan 1981		5. Paul E. Gillmor (R)	Jan 1989
	5. Scott Garrett (R)	Jan 2003		6. Ted Strickland (D)	Jan 1997
	6. Frank Pallone, Jr. (D)	Nov 1988		7. David L. Hobson (R)	Jan 1991
	7. Mike Ferguson (R)	Jan 2001		8. John A. Boehner (R)	Jan 1991
	8. Bill Pascrell, Jr. (D)	Jan 1997		9. Marcy Kaptur (D)	Jan 1983
	9. Steven R. Rothman (D)	Jan 1997		10. Dennis J. Kucinich (D)	Jan 1997
	10. Donald M. Payne (D)	Jan 1989		11. Stephanie Tubbs Jones (D)	Jan 1999
	11. Rodney P. Frelinghuysen (R)	Jan 1995		12. Patrick J. Tiberi (R)	Jan 2001
	12. Rush D. Holt (D)	Jan 1999		13. Sherrod Brown (D)	Jan 1993
	13. Robert Menendez (D)	Jan 1993			

The House of Representatives, 109th Congress (continued)

STATE	REPRESENTATIVES	SERVICE BEGAN
Ohio (continued)	14. Steven C. LaTourette (R)	Jan 1995
	15. Deborah Pryce (R)	Jan 1993
	16. Ralph Regula (R)	Jan 1973
	17. Tim Ryan (D)	Jan 2003
	18. Robert W. Ney (R)	Jan 1995
Oklahoma (−1)	1. John Sullivan (R)[10]	Feb 2002
	2. Dan Boren (D)	Jan 2005
	3. Frank D. Lucas (R)	May 1994
	4. Tom Cole (R)	Jan 2003
	5. Ernest J. Istook, Jr. (R)	Jan 1993
Oregon	1. David Wu (D)	Jan 1999
	2. Greg Walden (R)	Jan 1999
	3. Earl Blumenauer (D)	May 1996
	4. Peter A. DeFazio (D)	Jan 1987
	5. Darlene Hooley (D)	Jan 1997
Pennsylvania (−2)	1. Robert A. Brady (D)	May 1998
	2. Chaka Fattah (D)	Jan 1995
	3. Phil English (R)	Jan 1995
	4. Melissa A. Hart (R)	Jan 2001
	5. John E. Peterson (R)	Jan 1997
	6. Jim Gerlach (R)	Jan 2003
	7. Curt Weldon (R)	Jan 1987
	8. Michael G. Fitzpatrick (R)	Jan 2005
	9. Bill Shuster (R)	May 2001
	10. Don Sherwood (R)	Jan 1999
	11. Paul E. Kanjorski (D)	Jan 1985
	12. John P. Murtha (D)	Feb 1974
	13. Allyson Y. Schwartz (D)	Jan 2005
	14. Michael F. Doyle (D)	Jan 1995
	15. Charles W. Dent (R)	Jan 2005
	16. Joseph R. Pitts (R)	Jan 1997
	17. Tim Holden (D)	Jan 1993
	18. Tim Murphy (R)	Jan 2003
	19. Todd Russell Platts (R)	Jan 2001
Rhode Island	1. Patrick J. Kennedy (D)	Jan 1995
	2. James R. Langevin (D)	Jan 2001
South Carolina	1. Henry E. Brown, Jr. (R)	Jan 2001
	2. Joe Wilson (R)[11]	Dec 2001
	3. J. Gresham Barrett (R)	Jan 2003
	4. Bob Inglis (R)	Jan 2005
	5. John M. Spratt, Jr. (D)	Jan 1983
	6. James E. Clyburn (D)	Jan 1993
South Dakota	Stephanie Herseth (D)[12]	Jun 2004
Tennessee	1. William L. Jenkins (R)	Jan 1997
	2. John J. Duncan, Jr. (R)	Nov 1988
	3. Zach Wamp (R)	Jan 1995
	4. Lincoln Davis (D)	Jan 2003
	5. Jim Cooper (D)[13]	Jan 1983
	6. Bart Gordon (D)	Jan 1985
	7. Marsha Blackburn (R)	Jan 2003
	8. John S. Tanner (D)	Jan 1989
	9. Harold E. Ford, Jr. (D)	Jan 1997
Texas (+2)	1. Louie Gohmert (R)	Jan 2005
	2. Ted Poe (R)	Jan 2005
	3. Sam Johnson (R)	May 1991
	4. Ralph M. Hall (R)[14]	Jan 1981

STATE	REPRESENTATIVES	SERVICE BEGAN
Texas (continued)	5. Jeb Hensarling (R)	Jan 2003
	6. Joe Barton (R)	Jan 1985
	7. John Abney Culberson (R)	Jan 2001
	8. Kevin Brady (R)	Jan 1997
	9. Al Green (D)	Jan 2005
	10. Michael T. McCaul (R)	Jan 2005
	11. K. Michael Conaway (R)	Jan 2005
	12. Kay Granger (R)	Jan 1997
	13. Mac Thornberry (R)	Jan 1995
	14. Ron Paul (R)	Jan 1997
	15. Rubén Hinojosa (D)	Jan 1997
	16. Silvestre Reyes (D)	Jan 1997
	17. Chet Edwards (D)	Jan 2005
	18. Sheila Jackson-Lee (D)	Jan 1995
	19. Randy Neugebauer (R)[15]	Jun 2003
	20. Charles A. Gonzalez (D)	Jan 1999
	21. Lamar S. Smith (R)	Jan 1987
	22. Tom DeLay (R)	Jan 1985
	23. Henry Bonilla (R)	Jan 1993
	24. Kenny Marchant (R)	Jan 2005
	25. Lloyd Doggett (D)	Jan 1995
	26. Michael C. Burgess (R)	Jan 2003
	27. Solomon P. Ortiz (D)	Jan 1983
	28. Henry Cuellar (D)	Jan 2005
	29. Gene Green (D)	Jan 1993
	30. Eddie Bernice Johnson (D)	Jan 1993
	31. John R. Carter (R)	Jan 2003
	32. Pete Sessions (R)	Jan 1997
Utah	1. Rob Bishop (R)	Jan 2003
	2. Jim Matheson (D)	Jan 2001
	3. Chris Cannon (R)	Jan 1997
Vermont	Bernard Sanders (I)	Jan 1991
Virginia	1. Jo Ann Davis (R)	Jan 2001
	2. Thelma D. Drake (R)	Jan 2005
	3. Robert C. Scott (D)	Jan 1993
	4. J. Randy Forbes (R)[16]	Jun 2001
	5. Virgil H. Goode, Jr. (R)	Jan 1997
	6. Bob Goodlatte (R)	Jan 1993
	7. Eric Cantor (R)	Jan 2001
	8. James P. Moran (D)	Jan 1991
	9. Rick Boucher (D)	Jan 1983
	10. Frank R. Wolf (R)	Jan 1981
	11. Tom Davis (R)	Jan 1995
Washington	1. Jay Inslee (D)[17]	Jan 1993
	2. Rick Larsen (D)	Jan 2001
	3. Brian Baird (D)	Jan 1999
	4. Doc Hastings (R)	Jan 1995
	5. Cathy McMorris (R)	Jan 2005
	6. Norman D. Dicks (D)	Jan 1977
	7. Jim McDermott (D)	Jan 1989
	8. David G. Reichert (R)	Jan 2005
	9. Adam Smith (D)	Jan 1997
West Virginia	1. Alan B. Mollohan (D)	Jan 1983
	2. Shelley Moore Capito (R)	Jan 2001
	3. Nick J. Rahall II (D)	Jan 1977

The House of Representatives, 109th Congress (continued)

STATE	REPRESENTATIVES	SERVICE BEGAN	STATE	REPRESENTATIVES	SERVICE BEGAN
Wisconsin	1. Paul Ryan (R)	Jan 1999	Wisconsin	6. Thomas E. Petri (R)	Apr 1979
(-1)	2. Tammy Baldwin (D)	Jan 1999	(continued)	7. David R. Obey (D)	Apr 1969
	3. Ron Kind (D)	Jan 1997		8. Mark Green (R)	Jan 1999
	4. Gwen Moore (D)	Jan 2005			
	5. F. James Sensen-	Jan 1979	Wyoming	Barbara Cubin (R)	Jan 1995
	brenner, Jr. (R)				

JURISDICTION	REPRESENTATIVES	SERVICE BEGAN
American Samoa	(Delegate) Eni F.H. Faleomavaega (D)	Jan 1989
District of Columbia	(Delegate) Eleanor Holmes Norton (D)	Jan 1991
Guam	(Delegate) Madeleine Bordallo (D)	Jan 2003
Puerto Rico	(Resident Commissioner) Luis G. Fortuño (R)	Jan 2005
Virgin Islands	(Delegate) Donna M. Christensen (D)	Jan 1997

[1]John Boozman was elected 20 Nov 2001 following the resignation of Asa Hutchinson. [2]Doris O. Matsui was elected 8 Mar 2005 following the death of Robert T. Matsui. [3]Diane E. Watson was elected 5 Jun 2001 to complete the term of the late Julian C. Dixon. [4]Jane F. Harman did not serve 3 Jan 1999–3 Jan 2001. [5]Jeff Miller was elected 16 Oct 2001 following the resignation of Joe Scarborough. [6]Neil Abercrombie did not serve 3 Jan 1987–3 Jan 1991. [7]Ed Case was elected 4 Jan 2003 following the death of Patsy Mink. [8]Ben Chandler was elected 17 Feb 2004 following the resignation of Ernie Fletcher. [9]Stephen F. Lynch was elected 16 Oct 2001 to complete the term of the late John Joseph Moakley. [10]John Sullivan was elected 8 Jan 2002 following the resignation of Steve Largent. [11]Joe Wilson was elected 18 Dec 2001 to complete the term of the late Floyd Spence. [12]Stephanie Herseth was elected 1 Jun 2004 following the resignation of William Janklow. [13]Jim Cooper did not serve 3 Jan 1995–3 Jan 2003. [14]Ralph M. Hall defected to the Republican Party on 5 Jan 2004. [15]Randy Neugebauer was elected 3 June 2003 following the resignation of Larry Combest. [16]J. Randy Forbes was elected 19 Jun 2001 to complete the term of the late Norman Sisisky. [17]Jay Inslee did not serve 3 Jan 1995–3 Jan 1999.

House of Representatives Standing Committees

COMMITTEE	CHAIRMAN (PARTY-STATE)	RANKING MINORITY MEMBER (PARTY-STATE)	NUMBER OF MEMBERS: MAJORITY	MINORITY	NUMBER OF SUBCOM- MITTEES
Agriculture	Bob Goodlatte (R-VA)	Collin C. Peterson (D-MN)	25	21	5
Appropriations	Jerry Lewis (R-CA)	David Obey (D-WI)	37	29	10
Armed Services	Duncan Hunter (R-CA)	Ike Skelton (D-MO)	34	28	6
Budget	Jim Nussle (R-IA)	John Spratt (D-SC)	22	17	none
Education and the Workforce	John A. Boehner (R-OH)	George Miller (D-CA)	27	22	5
Energy and Commerce	Joe Barton (R-TX)	John D. Dingell (D-MI)	31	26	6
Financial Services	Michael G. Oxley (R-OH)	Barney Frank (D-MA)	37	32[1]	5
Government Reform	Tom Davis (R-VA)	Henry A. Waxman (D-CA)	23	17[1]	7
Homeland Security	Christopher Cox (R-CA)	Bennie G. Thompson (D-MS)	19	15	5
House Administration	Robert W. Ney (R-OH)	Juanita Millender-McDonald (D-CA)	6	3	none
International Relations	Henry J. Hyde (R-IL)	Tom Lantos (D-CA)	27	23	7
Judiciary	F. James Sensenbrenner, Jr. (R-WI)	John Conyers, Jr. (D-MI)	23	17	5
Resources	Richard W. Pombo (R-CA)	Nick J. Rahall II (D-WV)	27	22	5
Rules	David Dreier (R-CA)	Louise McIntosh Slaughter (D-NY)	9	4	2
Science	Sherwood L. Boehlert (R-NY)	Bart Gordon (D-TN)	24	20	4
Small Business	Donald Manzullo (R-IL)	Nydia M. Velázquez (D-NY)	18	15	4
Standards of Official Conduct	Doc Hastings (R-WA)	Alan B. Mollohan (D-WV)	5	5	none
Transportation and Infrastructure	Don Young (R-AK)	James L. Oberstar (D-MN)	41	34	6
Veterans' Affairs	Steve Buyer (R-IN)	Lane Evans (D-IL)	16	13	4
Ways and Means	William M. Thomas (R-CA)	Charles B. Rangel (D-NY)	24	17	6
Permanent Select Committee on Intelligence	Peter Hoekstra (R-MI)	Jane Harman (D-CA)	12	9	4

[1]Bernard Sanders (VT) is an independent but caucuses with the Democratic Party.

Congressional Apportionment

The US Constitution requires a decennial census to determine the apportionment of representatives for each state in the House of Representatives. There was no reapportionment based on 1920 census figures.

	representatives										
STATE	1790	1800	1810	1820	1830	1840	1850	1860	1870	1880	1890
Alabama	NA	NA	1[1]	3	5	7	7	6	8	8	9
Alaska	NA	NA	NA	NA	NA	NA	NA	NA	NA	NA	NA
Arizona	NA	NA	NA	NA	NA	NA	NA	NA	NA	NA	NA
Arkansas	NA	NA	NA	NA	1[1]	1	2	3	4	5	6
California	NA	NA	NA	NA	NA	2[1]	2	3	4	6	7
Colorado	NA	NA	NA	NA	NA	NA	NA	NA	1[1]	1	2
Connecticut	7	7	7	6	6	4	4	4	4	4	4
Delaware	1	1	2	1	1	1	1	1	1	1	1
Florida	NA	NA	NA	NA	NA	1[1]	1	1	2	2	2
Georgia	2	4	6	7	9	8	8	7	9	10	11
Hawaii	NA	NA	NA	NA	NA	NA	NA	NA	NA	NA	NA
Idaho	NA	NA	NA	NA	NA	NA	NA	NA	NA	1[1]	1
Illinois	NA	NA	1[1]	1	3	7	9	14	19	20	22
Indiana	NA	NA	1[1]	3	7	10	11	11	13	13	13
Iowa	NA	NA	NA	NA	NA	2[1]	2	6	9	11	11
Kansas	NA	NA	NA	NA	NA	NA	NA	1	3	7	8
Kentucky	2	6	10	12	13	10	10	9	10	11	11
Louisiana	NA	NA	1[1]	3	3	4	4	5	6	6	6
Maine	NA	NA	NA	7	8	7	6	5	5	4	4
Maryland	8	9	9	9	8	6	6	5	6	6	6
Massachusetts	14	17	20	13	12	10	11	10	11	12	13
Michigan	NA	NA	NA	NA	1[1]	3	4	6	9	11	12
Minnesota	NA	NA	NA	NA	NA	NA	2[1]	2	3	5	7
Mississippi	NA	NA	1[1]	1	2	4	5	5	6	7	7
Missouri	NA	NA	NA	1	2	5	7	9	13	14	15
Montana	NA	NA	NA	NA	NA	NA	NA	NA	NA	1[1]	1
Nebraska	NA	NA	NA	NA	NA	NA	NA	1[1]	1	3	6
Nevada	NA	NA	NA	NA	NA	NA	NA	1[1]	1	1	1
New Hampshire	4	5	6	6	5	4	3	3	3	2	2
New Jersey	5	6	6	6	6	5	5	5	7	7	8
New Mexico	NA	NA	NA	NA	NA	NA	NA	NA	NA	NA	NA
New York	10	17	27	34	40	34	33	31	33	34	34
North Carolina	10	12	13	13	13	9	8	7	8	9	9
North Dakota	NA	NA	NA	NA	NA	NA	NA	NA	NA	1[1]	1
Ohio	NA	1[1]	6	14	19	21	21	19	20	21	21
Oklahoma	NA	NA	NA	NA	NA	NA	NA	NA	NA	NA	NA
Oregon	NA	NA	NA	NA	NA	NA	1[1]	1	1	1	2
Pennsylvania	13	18	23	26	28	24	25	24	27	28	30
Rhode Island	2	2	2	2	2	2	2	2	2	2	2
South Carolina	6	8	9	9	9	7	6	4	5	7	7
South Dakota	NA	NA	NA	NA	NA	NA	NA	NA	NA	2[1]	2
Tennessee	1[1]	3	6	9	13	11	10	8	10	10	10
Texas	NA	NA	NA	NA	NA	2[1]	2	4	6	11	13
Utah	NA	NA	NA	NA	NA	NA	NA	NA	NA	NA	1[1]
Vermont	2	4	6	5	5	4	3	3	3	2	2
Virginia	19	22	23	22	21	15	13	11	9	10	10
Washington	NA	NA	NA	NA	NA	NA	NA	NA	NA	1[1]	2
West Virginia	NA	NA	NA	NA	NA	NA	NA	NA	3	4	4
Wisconsin	NA	NA	NA	NA	NA	2[1]	3	6	8	9	10
Wyoming	NA	NA	NA	NA	NA	NA	NA	NA	NA	1[1]	1
Total	106	142	186	213	242	232	237	243	293	332	357

Congressional Apportionment (continued)

STATE	representatives									
	1900	1910	1930	1940	1950	1960	1970	1980	1990	2000
Alabama	9	10	9	9	9	8	7	7	7	7
Alaska	NA	NA	NA	NA	1[1]	1	1	1	1	1
Arizona	NA	1[2]	1	2	2	3	4	5	6	8
Arkansas	7	7	7	7	6	4	4	4	4	4
California	8	11	20	23	30	38	43	45	52	53
Colorado	3	4	4	4	4	4	5	6	6	7
Connecticut	5	5	6	6	6	6	6	6	6	5
Delaware	1	1	1	1	1	1	1	1	1	1
Florida	3	4	5	6	8	12	15	19	23	25
Georgia	11	12	10	10	10	10	10	10	11	13
Hawaii	NA	NA	NA	NA	1[1]	2	2	2	2	2
Idaho	1	2	2	2	2	2	2	2	2	2
Illinois	25	27	27	26	25	24	24	22	20	19
Indiana	13	13	12	11	11	11	11	10	10	9
Iowa	11	11	9	8	8	7	6	6	5	5
Kansas	8	8	7	6	6	5	5	5	4	4
Kentucky	11	11	9	9	8	7	7	7	6	6
Louisiana	7	8	8	8	8	8	8	8	7	7
Maine	4	4	3	3	3	2	2	2	2	2
Maryland	6	6	6	6	7	8	8	8	8	8
Massachusetts	14	16	15	14	14	12	12	11	10	10
Michigan	12	13	17	17	18	19	19	18	16	15
Minnesota	9	10	9	9	9	8	8	8	8	8
Mississippi	8	8	7	7	6	5	5	5	5	4
Missouri	16	16	13	13	11	10	10	9	9	9
Montana	1	2	2	2	2	2	2	2	1	1
Nebraska	6	6	5	4	4	3	3	3	3	3
Nevada	1	1	1	1	1	1	1	2	2	3
New Hampshire	2	2	2	2	2	2	2	2	2	2
New Jersey	10	12	14	14	14	15	15	14	13	13
New Mexico	NA	1[2]	1	2	2	2	2	3	3	3
New York	37	43	45	45	43	41	39	34	31	29
North Carolina	10	10	11	12	12	11	11	11	12	13
North Dakota	2	3	2	2	2	2	1	1	1	1
Ohio	21	22	24	23	23	24	23	21	19	18
Oklahoma	5[1]	8	9	8	6	6	6	6	6	5
Oregon	2	3	3	4	4	4	4	5	5	5
Pennsylvania	32	36	34	33	30	27	25	23	21	19
Rhode Island	2	3	2	2	2	2	2	2	2	2
South Carolina	7	7	6	6	6	6	6	6	6	6
South Dakota	2	3	2	2	2	2	2	1	1	1
Tennessee	10	10	9	10	9	9	8	9	9	9
Texas	16	18	21	21	22	23	24	27	30	32
Utah	1	2	2	2	2	2	2	3	3	3
Vermont	2	2	1	1	1	1	1	1	1	1
Virginia	10	10	9	9	10	10	10	10	11	11
Washington	3	5	6	6	7	7	7	8	9	9
West Virginia	5	6	6	6	6	5	4	4	3	3
Wisconsin	11	11	10	10	10	10	9	9	9	8
Wyoming	1	1	1	1	1	1	1	1	1	1
Total	391	435	435	435	437	435	435	435	435	435

NA: Not applicable.   [1]Number assigned after apportionment.   [2]Included in anticipation of statehood.

Electoral Votes by State

Each state receives one electoral vote for each of its representatives and one for each of its two senators, ensuring at least three votes for each state, as the Constitution guarantees at least one representative regardless of population. Allocations are based on the 2000 census and applicable for the 2004 presidential election.

Total: 538; Majority needed to elect president and vice president: 270

STATE	NUMBER OF VOTES	STATE	NUMBER OF VOTES	STATE	NUMBER OF VOTES
Alabama	9	Kentucky	8	North Dakota	3
Alaska	3	Louisiana	9	Ohio	20
Arizona	10	Maine	4	Oklahoma	7
Arkansas	6	Maryland	10	Oregon	7
California	55	Massachusetts	12	Pennsylvania	21
Colorado	9	Michigan	17	Rhode Island	4
Connecticut	7	Minnesota	10	South Carolina	8
Delaware	3	Mississippi	6	South Dakota	3
District of Columbia	3	Missouri	11	Tennessee	11
Florida	27	Montana	3	Texas	34
Georgia	15	Nebraska	5	Utah	5
Hawaii	4	Nevada	5	Vermont	3
Idaho	4	New Hampshire	4	Virginia	13
Illinois	21	New Jersey	15	Washington	11
Indiana	11	New Mexico	5	West Virginia	5
Iowa	7	New York	31	Wisconsin	10
Kansas	6	North Carolina	15	Wyoming	3

Supreme Court

Justices of the Supreme Court of the United States

Listed under presidents who made appointments (bold). Chief justices' names appear in italics.

NAME	TERM OF SERVICE[1]	NAME	TERM OF SERVICE[1]	NAME	TERM OF SERVICE[1]
George Washington		**Martin Van Buren**		**James Garfield**	
John Jay	1789–95	John Catron	1837–65	Stanley Matthews	1881–89
James Wilson	1789–98	John McKinley	1838–52	**Chester A. Arthur**	
John Rutledge	1790–91	Peter V. Daniel	1842–60	Horace Gray	1882–1902
William Cushing	1790–1810	**John Tyler**		Samuel Blatchford	1882–93
John Blair	1790–96	Samuel Nelson	1845–72	**Grover Cleveland**	
James Iredell	1790–99	**James Polk**		Lucius Q.C. Lamar	1888–93
Thomas Johnson	1792–93	Levi Woodbury	1845–51	*Melville Weston Fuller*	1888–1910
William Paterson	1793–1806	Robert C. Grier	1846–70	**Benjamin Harrison**	
John Rutledge[2]	1795	**Millard Fillmore**		David J. Brewer	1890–1910
Samuel Chase	1796–1811	Benjamin R. Curtis	1851–57	Henry B. Brown	1891–1906
Oliver Ellsworth	1796–1800	**Franklin Pierce**		George Shiras, Jr.	1892–1903
John Adams		John Archibald Campbell	1853–61	Howell E. Jackson	1893–95
Bushrod Washington	1799–1829	**James Buchanan**		**Grover Cleveland**	
Alfred Moore	1800–04	Nathan Clifford	1858–81	Edward Douglass White	1894–1910
John Marshall	1801–35	**Abraham Lincoln**		Rufus Wheeler Peckham	1896–1909
Thomas Jefferson		Noah H. Swayne	1862–81	**William McKinley**	
William Johnson	1804–34	Samuel Freeman Miller	1862–90	Joseph McKenna	1898–1925
Brockholst Livingston	1807–23	David Davis	1862–77	**Theodore Roosevelt**	
Thomas Todd	1807–26	Stephen Johnson Field	1863–97	Oliver Wendell Holmes	1902–32
James Madison		*Salmon P. Chase*	1864–73	William R. Day	1903–22
Gabriel Duvall	1811–35	**Ulysses S. Grant**		William H. Moody	1906–10
Joseph Story	1812–45	William Strong	1870–80	**William H. Taft**	
James Monroe		Joseph P. Bradley	1870–92	Horace H. Lurton	1910–14
Smith Thompson	1823–43	Ward Hunt	1873–82	Charles Evans Hughes	1910–16
John Quincy Adams		*Morrison Remick Waite*	1874–88	Willis Van Devanter	1911–37
Robert Trimble	1826–28	**Rutherford B. Hayes**		Joseph R. Lamar	1911–16
Andrew Jackson		John Marshall Harlan	1877–1911	*Edward Douglass White*	1910–21
John McLean	1830–61	William B. Woods	1881–87	Mahlon Pitney	1912–22
Henry Baldwin	1830–44				
James M. Wayne	1835–67				
Roger Brooke Taney	1836–64				
Philip P. Barbour	1836–41				

Justices of the Supreme Court of the United States (continued)

NAME	TERM OF SERVICE[1]	NAME	TERM OF SERVICE[1]	NAME	TERM OF SERVICE[1]
Woodrow Wilson		*Harlan Fiske Stone*	1941–46	**Richard M. Nixon**	
James C. McReynolds	1914–41	James F. Byrnes	1941–42	*Warren E. Burger*	1969–86
Louis Brandeis	1916–39	Robert H. Jackson	1941–54	Harry A. Blackmun	1970–94
John H. Clarke	1916–22	Wiley B. Rutledge	1943–49	Lewis F. Powell, Jr.	1972–87
Warren G. Harding		**Harry S. Truman**		William H. Rehnquist	1972–86
William Howard Taft	1921–30	Harold H. Burton	1945–58	**Gerald Ford**	
George Sutherland	1922–38	*Fred M. Vinson*	1946–53	John Paul Stevens	1975–
Pierce Butler	1923–39	Tom C. Clark	1949–67	**Ronald Reagan**	
Edward T. Sanford	1923–30	Sherman Minton	1949–56	Sandra Day	1981–2005
Calvin Coolidge		**Dwight D. Eisenhower**		O'Connor	
Harlan Fiske Stone	1925–41	*Earl Warren*	1953–69	*William H. Rehnquist*	1986–
Herbert Hoover		John Marshall Harlan	1955–71	Antonin Scalia	1986–
Charles Evans Hughes	1930–41	William J. Brennan, Jr.	1956–90	Anthony M. Kennedy	1988–
Owen Roberts	1930–45	Charles E. Whittaker	1957–62	**George H.W. Bush**	
Benjamin N. Cardozo	1932–38	Potter Stewart	1958–81	David H. Souter	1990–
Franklin D. Roosevelt		**John F. Kennedy**		Clarence Thomas	1991–
Hugo L. Black	1937–71	Byron R. White	1962–93	**Bill Clinton**	
Stanley F. Reed	1938–57	Arthur J. Goldberg	1962–65	Ruth Bader Ginsburg	1993–
Felix Frankfurter	1939–62	**Lyndon B. Johnson**		Stephen G. Breyer	1994–
William O. Douglas	1939–75	Abe Fortas	1965–69		
Frank Murphy	1940–49	Thurgood Marshall	1967–91		

[1]*The year the justice took the judicial oath is here used as the beginning date of service, for until that oath is taken the justice is not vested with the prerogatives of the office. Justices, however, receive their commissions ("letters patent") before taking their oaths—in some instances, in the preceding year.* [2]*John Rutledge was acting chief justice; the US Senate refused to confirm him.*

Milestones of US Supreme Court Jurisprudence

Information includes cases' short names, year of release, citation, and a short description of the Supreme Court's findings and importance for US law.

Marbury v. Madison, 5 U.S. 137 (1803): the first instance in which the high court declared an act of Congress (the Judiciary Act of 1789, which in part authorized the court to compel action by the executive branch) to be unconstitutional, thus establishing the doctrine of judicial review.

Martin v. Hunter's Lessee, 14 U.S. 304 (1816): asserted the US Supreme Court's power of appellate review of state supreme court decisions.

McCulloch v. Maryland, 17 U.S. 316 (1819): affirmed the constitutional doctrine of the "implied powers" of Congress, determining that Congress had not only the powers expressly conferred upon it by the Constitution but also all authority "appropriate" to carry out such powers.

Dred Scott v. Sandford, 60 U.S. 393 (1857): ruled that blacks, free or enslaved, were not citizens under the Constitution, and further determined that only states, and not Congress or territorial governments, had the power to prohibit slavery, thus overturning the Missouri Compromise of 1820 and legalizing slavery in all US territories. The citizenship of all races was affirmed with the ratification of the Fourteenth Amendment in 1868.

Santa Clara County v. Southern Pacific Railroad Co., 118 U.S. 394 (1886): established that corporations are "persons" within the meaning of the Fourteenth Amendment, extending to them the rights of due process and equal protection.

Plessy v. Ferguson, 163 U.S. 537 (1896): permitted racial segregation in "separate but equal" public facilities.

Lochner v. New York, 198 U.S. 45 (1905): found that a state labor law limiting the number of hours in the work week violated due process because the "right of contract between the employer and employees" is protected under the Fourteenth Amendment.

Standard Oil Co. of New Jersey et al. v. United States, 221 U.S. 1 (1911): ruled that the activities of the Standard Oil Company of New Jersey, a holding company that through its subsidiaries controlled most of the US petroleum industry, constituted an undue restraint of trade, and ordered the company's dissolution under the Sherman Antitrust Act.

Schenck v. United States, 249 U.S. 47 (1919): found, in the case of an American socialist convicted of espionage for distributing antidraft leaflets during wartime, that First Amendment freedom of expression is limited when there exists a "clear and present danger that [the speech] will bring about the substantive evils that Congress has a right to prevent."

Brown v. Board of Education of Topeka, 349 U.S. 294 (1954): ruled that racial segregation in public schools violated the Fourteenth Amendment, overturning the doctrine of "separate but equal" facilities reached in Plessy v. Ferguson.

Mapp v. Ohio, 367 U.S. 643 (1961): found that the Fourth Amendment prohibition of unreasonable search and seizure, and the inadmissibility of evidence obtained in violation of it, applied to state as well as to federal government.

Baker v. Carr, 369 U.S. 186 (1962): ruled that, under the equal protection clause of the Fourteenth Amendment, issues relating to the apportionment of congressional districts could be resolved in federal courts.

Gideon v. Wainwright, 372 U.S. 335 (1963): declared that the Sixth Amendment right to counsel applies to defendants in state as well as federal courts.

New York Times Co. v. *Sullivan,* 376 U.S. 254 (1964): protected the press from the prospects of large damage awards in libel cases by requiring that "actual malice" be demonstrated; public officials who sue for damages must prove that a falsehood had been issued with knowledge that it was false or in reckless disregard of whether it was false or not.

Heart of Atlanta Motel v. *United States,* 379 U.S. 241; *Katzenbach* v. *McClung,* 379 U.S. 294 (1964): upheld Title II of the Civil Rights Act of 1964 (which prohibits segregation or discrimination in places of public accommodation involved in interstate commerce) in the cases of an Atlanta motel and a Birmingham AL restaurant, both of which discriminated against blacks. The court ruled that both engaged in transactions affecting interstate commerce and thus were within the purview of congressional regulation, and that the Civil Rights Act itself was constitutional.

Griswold v. *Connecticut,* 381 U.S. 479 (1965): ruled that a state law prohibiting the use of contraceptives (including providing information, advice, or prescriptions for them) violated "the right of marital privacy" implied within the Bill of Rights.

Miranda v. *Arizona,* 384 U.S. 436 (1966): ruled that the prosecution may not use statements made by a person in police custody unless minimum procedural safeguards were followed and established guidelines to guarantee arrested persons' Fifth Amendment right not to be compelled to incriminate themselves. These guidelines included informing arrestees prior to questioning that they have the right to remain silent, that anything they say may be used against them as evidence, and that they have the right to the counsel of an attorney.

Loving v. *Virginia,* 388 U.S. 1 (1967): declared that antimiscegenation laws (prohibitions of interracial marriage) have no legitimate purpose outside of racial discrimination, and thus violate the Fourteenth Amendment.

New York Times Co. v. *United States,* 403 U.S. 713 (1971): in what was known as the "Pentagon Papers" case, the court vacated a US Justice Department injunction that restrained the *New York Times* and *Washington Post* from publishing excerpts of a top-secret report on the Vietnam War, ruling that such prior restraint of the press was subject to a "heavy burden of . . . justification" which the government failed to meet.

Wisconsin v. *Yoder,* 406 U.S. 205 (1972): in the case of members of an Old Order Amish community who refused on religious grounds to keep their children in school past the eighth grade, found that the right to free exercise of religion outweighed the state's interest in universal education.

Roe v. *Wade,* 410 U.S. 113 (1973): held that overly restrictive state regulation of abortion is unconstitutional. In balancing the "compelling state interest[s]" in protecting the health of pregnant women and the potential life of fetuses, the court ruled that regulation of abortion could begin no sooner than about the end of the first trimester, with increasing regulation permissible in the second and third trimesters; the state's interest in protecting the fetus was found to increase with the fetus's "capability for meaningful life outside the mother's womb."

Gregg v. *Georgia,* 428 U.S. 153; *Proffitt* v. *Florida,* 428 U.S. 242; *Jurek* v. *Texas,* 428 U.S. 262 (1976): ruled that the death penalty, in and of itself, does not violate the Eighth Amendment if applied under certain guidelines in first-degree murder cases.

Cruzan by Cruzan v. *Director, Missouri Department of Health,* 497 U.S. 261 (1990): found that, in the absence of "clear and convincing evidence" of a person's desire to refuse medical treatment or not to live on life support, a state could require that such treatment continue. When such evidence exists, however, a patient's wishes must be respected.

Rust v. *Sullivan,* 500 U.S. 173 (1991): ruled that Congress could prohibit recipients of family-planning funds from providing or discussing abortion as a family planning option. The court held that this did not violate the First Amendment because clinics were still free to provide such counseling as a "financially and physically" separate activity.

Planned Parenthood of Southeastern Pennsylvania v. *Casey,* 505 U.S. 833 (1992): softened the ruling in *Roe* v. *Wade* by finding that some state regulation of abortion prior to fetal viability, including a 24-hour waiting period, mandatory counseling, and a parental-consent requirement for minors, is permissible as long as the regulations do not place an "undue burden" on the woman.

Romer v. *Evans,* 517 U.S. 620 (1996): invalidated a Colorado referendum passed by popular vote that prohibited conferral of protected status on the basis of sexual orientation; the court ruled that the referendum was overbroad, bore little relationship to legitimate state interests, and violated the Fourteenth Amendment of the US Constitution.

Oncale v. *Sundowner Offshore Services, Inc., et al.,* 523 U.S. 75 (1998): found that Title VII's prohibition of workplace sexual discrimination applied equally in cases when the harasser and victim are of the same sex.

Boy Scouts of America v. *Dale,* 530 U.S. 640 (2000): ruled that the Boy Scouts, because it is a private organization, was within its rights when it dismissed a scoutmaster expressly because of his avowed homosexuality. The court reasoned that a state statute banning discrimination on the basis of sexual orientation in places of public accommodation was outweighed by the Scouts' First Amendment right to freedom of association.

Stenberg v. *Carhart,* 530 U.S. 914 (2000): ruled that a state law criminalizing the performance of dilation and extraction—or late-term—abortions violated the Constitution (following the same reasoning as in *Roe* v. *Wade*) because it allowed no consideration of the health of the woman in choosing the procedure.

Bush v. *Gore,* 531 U.S. 98 (2000): stopped the manual recounts, then underway in certain Florida counties at the demand of Al Gore, of disputed ballots from the November 2000 presidential election on the grounds that inconsistent vote-counting standards among the several counties involved amounted to a violation of the Fourteenth Amendment's equal protection clause. Because George W. Bush at the time led Al Gore in the number of officially recognized Florida votes, the decision meant that he would win the state and thus the general election, despite having lost the popular vote.

Atkins v. *Virginia,* 536 U.S. 304 (2002): ruled that the death penalty, when applied to mentally retarded individuals, constitutes a "cruel and unusual punishment" prohibited by the Eighth Amendment.

Eldred v. *Ashcroft,* 537 U.S. 186 (2003): upheld a 1998 federal statute that granted a 20-year extension to all existing copyrights.

Lockyer v. *Andrade*, 538 U.S. 63; *Ewing* v. *California*, 538 U.S. 11 (2003): upheld a "three-strikes" law that imposes long prison sentences for a third offense, even nonviolent crimes.

State Farm Mutual Auto Insurance Co. v. *Campbell*, 538 U.S. 408 (2003): placed limits on "irrational and arbitrary" punitive damages and established new guidelines that generally bar consideration of a defendant's wealth or conduct outside the state's borders and lower the ratio of punitive to compensatory damages.

Brown v. *Legal Foundation of Washington*, 538 U.S. 216 (2003): held that channeling interest on short-term deposits by lawyers on accounts held in trust for their clients to legal assistance programs for the poor is not an unconstitutional taking of property.

Nevada Department of Human Resources v. *Hibbs*, 538 U.S. 721 (2003): held that state governments may be sued by their employees for failing to honor the federally guaranteed right to take time off from work for family emergencies.

United States v. *American Library Association*, 539 U.S. 194 (2003): upheld the Children's Internet Protection Act, which conditions access to federal grants and subsidies upon the installation of antipornography filters on all Internet-connected computers.

Grutter v. *Bollinger*, 539 U.S. 306 (2003); *Gratz* v. *Bollinger*, 539 U.S. 244 (2003): in a pair of decisions addressing affirmative action in admissions at the University of Michigan, the court endorsed *Regents of the University of California* v. *Bakke*'s articulation of diversity as a compelling interest, so long as the admissions program's operation is "holistic" and "individualized," and upheld Michigan's law school admissions program. In *Gratz*, the court struck down Michigan's undergraduate admissions program because reserving spaces for underrepresented minorities was the "functional equivalent of a quota."

Georgia v. *Ashcroft*, 539 U.S. 461 (2003): ruled that race-sensitive redistricting could consider more general minority influence in the political process when drawing particular district lines rather than addressing only the actual number of minority voters present.

Lawrence v. *Texas*, 539 U.S. 558 (2003): explicitly overruling *Bowers* v. *Hardwick*, 478 U.S. 186 (1986), the court declared that gay men and lesbians are "entitled to respect for their private lives" under the Due Process Clause of the Fourteenth Amendment and rendered unconstitutional state statutes outlawing sex between adults of the same gender.

Elk Grove Unified School District v. *Newdow*, 542 U.S. 1 (2004): sidestepping the question whether the inclusion of the phrase "under God" was an un-constitutional endorsement by a public school of a religious viewpoint, the court ruled that Michael Newdow, who filed suit on behalf of his daughter, lacked standing to file on her behalf because he was not the custodial parent.

Blakely v. *Washington*, 542 U.S. 296 (2004): held that the Washington state system permitting judges to make independent findings that increase a convicted defendant's sentence beyond the ordinary range for the crime violated the Sixth Amendment guarantee of a right to trial by jury and to a higher standard of proof.

Cheney v. *US District Court*, 542 U.S. 367 (2004): sent the Sierra Club and Judicial Watch back to the lower court in a dispute over the level of executive privilege the vice president's energy policy task force exercises in the face of discovery orders. The court held that "[s]pecial considerations control when the Executive's interests in maintaining its autonomy and safeguarding its communications' confidentiality are implicated."

Hamdi v. *Rumsfeld*, 542 U.S. 507; *Rasul* v. *Bush*, 542 U.S. 466 (2004): ruled that while the Congress may empower the executive branch to detain even US citizens as enemy combatants, any enemy combatant in US custody may challenge detention as illegal in federal court with the assistance of counsel. The court declared that "a state of war is not a blank check for the president when it comes to the rights of the nation's citizens."

United States v. *Booker* and *United States* v. *Fanfan*, 543 U.S. ___ (2005): ruled that that mandatory federal sentencing guidelines violated defendants' Sixth Amendment right to jury trials because the guidelines require judges to make decisions of fact affecting prison time.

Roper v. *Simmons*, 543 U.S. ___ (2005): held that the execution of a felon who had committed a capital crime while a juvenile violates the Eighth Amendment prohibition of cruel and unusual punishment, that "the State cannot extinguish [the juvenile defendant's] life and his potential to attain a mature understanding of his own humanity."

Gonzales v. *Raich* 545 U.S. ___ (2005): ruled that doctors may not prescribe marijuana to ease the symtoms patients and sufferers of other serious illnesses experience. The Court held that the federal Controlled Substances Act, which bars medical use of marijuana, overrides state legislation allowing such use.

Kelo v. *City of New London* 545 U.S. ___ (2005): found that governmental entities may exercise the power of eminent domain over private property and cede the property to private developers to promote economic growth, so long as a carefully formulated plan to provide significant benefits to the community provides a rational basis for the taking.

Military Affairs

US Military Leadership

President, Commander in Chief:	George W. Bush (20 Jan 2001)
Secretary of Defense:	Donald Rumsfeld (20 Jan 2001)
Chairman, Joint Chiefs of Staff:	Richard B. Myers (1 Oct 2001)
Vice Chairman, Joint Chiefs of Staff:	Peter Pace (1 Oct 2001)

RANK/POSITION	NAME (DATE ASSUMED POST)	RANK/POSITION	NAME (DATE ASSUMED POST)
Army		**Army (continued)**	
Chief of Staff	Peter J. Schoomaker (1 Aug 2003)	Vice Chief of Staff	Richard A. Cody (24 Jun 2004)

US Military Leadership (continued)

RANK/POSITION	NAME (DATE ASSUMED POST)
Army (continued)	
Sergeant Major	Kenneth O. Preston (15 Jan 2004)
Sec. of the Army	Francis J. Harvey (19 Nov 2004)
Under Sec. of the Army	Raymond F. DuBois (8 Mar 2005)
Navy	
Chief of Naval Operations	Michael Mullen (July 2005)
Vice Chief of Naval Operations	Robert F. Willard (17 Feb 2005)
Master Chief Petty Officer	Terry D. Scott (22 Apr 2002)
Sec. of the Navy	Gordon England (1 Oct 2003)
Under Sec. of the Navy	Dionel M. Aviles (8 Oct 2004)
Air Force	
Chief of Staff	John P. Jumper (6 Sep 2001)
Vice Chief of Staff	T. Michael Moseley (14 Aug 2003)

RANK/POSITION	NAME (DATE ASSUMED POST)
Air Force (continued)	
Chief Master Sergeant	Gerald R. Murray (1 Jul 2002)
Sec. of the Air Force (acting)	Michael L. Dominguez (28 Mar 2005)
Under Sec. of the Air Force	*vacant*
Marine Corps	
Commandant	Michael W. Hagee (13 Jan 2003)
Asst. Commandant	William L. Nyland (10 Sep 2002)
Sergeant Major	John L. Estrada (27 Jun 2003)
Coast Guard	
Commandant	Thomas H. Collins (30 May 2002)
Vice Commandant	Terry M. Cross (July 2004)
Chief of Staff	Thad W. Allen (14 May 2002)
Master Chief Petty Officer	Franklin A. Welch (10 Oct 2002)

Unified Combatant Commands

The Unified Combatant Commands provide operational control of US combat forces and are organized geographically to a significant extent. Unified Commanders receive orders through the chairman of the Joint Chiefs of Staff. Its structure is flexible, changing to accommodate evolving US security needs. Although the number of commands may vary, each command must be composed of forces from at least two of the armed services. Information is current as of June 2005.

COMMAND	HEADQUARTERS	COMMANDER IN CHIEF
US European Command	Stuttgart-Vaihingen, Germany	Gen. James L. Jones, USMC
US Pacific Command	Honolulu HI	Adm. William J. Fallon, USN
US Joint Forces Command	Norfolk VA	Adm. E.P. Giambastiani, USN
US Southern Command	Miami FL	Gen. Bantz J. Craddock, USA
US Central Command	MacDill Air Force Base, Florida	Gen. John Abizaid, USA
US Northern Command	Peterson Air Force Base, Colorado	Adm. Timothy J. Keating, USN
US Special Operations Command	MacDill Air Force Base, Florida	Gen. Bryan D. Brown, USA
US Transportation Command	Scott Air Force Base, Illinois	Gen. John W. Handy, USAF
US Strategic Command	Offutt Air Force Base, Nebraska	Adm. James O. Ellis, Jr., USN

North Atlantic Treaty Organization (NATO) International Commands

The NATO military command structure comprises two main strategic commands, Allied Command for Operations (ACO) and Allied Command Transformation (ACT, which works closely with the US Joint Forces Command). Their subordinate commands, also listed, change as their security measures evolve.

ALLIED COMMAND FOR OPERATIONS (ACO)
Headquarters (SHAPE) Casteau, Belgium
Supreme Allied Commander Europe (SACEUR)
  Gen. James L. Jones (USMC) (Jan 2003–)

SUBORDINATE REGIONAL COMMANDS
Joint Forces Command Headquarters North
  (JFC HQ North), Brunssum, The Netherlands
Commander-in-Chief: Gen. Gerhard W. Back
  (Air Force, Germany) (15 Jan 2004–)

Joint Forces Command Headquarters South
  (JFC HQ South), Naples, Italy
Commander-in-Chief: Adm. H.G. Ulrich III (USN) (23
  May 2005–)

ALLIED COMMAND TRANSFORMATION (ACT)
Headquarters Norfolk VA
Supreme Allied Commander Transformation: Adm.
  Edmund P. Giambastiani, Jr. (USN) (19 Jun 2003–)

SUBORDINATE COMMANDS
Joint Warfare Centre (JWC), Stavanger, Norway
Director: Air Marshall Peter B. Walker (Royal Air
  Force, UK) (4 Feb 2005–)

NATO Undersea Research Centre (NURC)[1]
  La Spezia, Italy
Director: Dr. Steven E. Ramberg

NATO School (SHAPE), Oberammergau, Germany
Commandant: Col. Mark P. Sullivan (USAF) (27 Jun
  2003–)

[1]*Formerly SACLANT.*

Chairmen of the Joint Chiefs of Staff, 1949–2005

The 1949 Amendments to the National Security Act of 1947 created the position of chairman of the Joint Chiefs of Staff, the principal military adviser to the president, the secretary of defense, and the NSC. The president appoints the chairman for a two-year term with the advice and consent of the Senate. In 1986 the chairman's eligibility for service increased from two to three reappointments (there is no limit on reappointment during wartime). The Joint Chiefs of Staff consist of the chairman, a vice chairman, the chiefs of staff of the Army and of the Air Force, the chief of naval operations, and the commandant of the Marine Corps.

NAME	MILITARY BRANCH	DATES OF SERVICE
Gen. of the Army Omar N. Bradley	US Army	16 Aug 1949–15 Aug 1953
Adm. Arthur W. Radford	US Navy	15 Aug 1953–15 Aug 1957
Gen. Nathan F. Twining	US Air Force	15 Aug 1957–30 Sep 1960
Gen. Lyman L. Lemnitzer	US Army	1 Oct 1960–30 Sep 1962
Gen. Maxwell D. Taylor	US Army	1 Oct 1962–1 Jul 1964
Gen. Earle G. Wheeler	US Army	3 Jul 1964–2 Jul 1970
Adm. Thomas H. Moorer	US Navy	2 Jul 1970–1 Jul 1974
Gen. George S. Brown	US Air Force	1 Jul 1974–20 Jun 1978
Gen. David C. Jones	US Air Force	21 Jun 1978–18 Jun 1982
Gen. John W. Vessey, Jr.	US Army	18 Jun 1982–30 Sep 1985
Adm. William J. Crowe, Jr.	US Navy	1 Oct 1985–30 Sep 1989
Gen. Colin L. Powell	US Army	1 Oct 1989–30 Sep 1993
Adm. David E. Jeremiah (acting)	US Navy	1 Oct 1993–24 Oct 1993
Gen. John M. Shalikashvili	US Army	25 Oct 1993–30 Sep 1997
Gen. Harry Shelton	US Army	1 Oct 1997–1 Oct 2001
Gen. Richard B. Myers	US Air Force	1 Oct 2001–

Worldwide Deployment of the US Military

Deployments of 1,000 or more active duty military personnel as of 31 Dec 2004. Regional totals include countries and areas not shown in the table. N/A means not available. Source: US Department of Defense.

COUNTRY/REGIONAL AREA	TOTAL	ARMY	NAVY	MARINE CORPS	AIR FORCE
US and territories					
continental US[1]	913,259	366,731	170,394	106,143	269,991
Alaska	17,395	7,619	94	19	9,663
Hawaii[1]	34,658	16,996	7,361	5,540	4,761
Guam[1]	3,237	40	1,334	5	1,858
Puerto Rico[1]	282	163	71	21	27
transients	47,391	7,309	10,847	24,021	5,214
afloat	114,584	0	114,584	0	0
total ashore and afloat	1,130,835	398,882	304,688	135,749	291,516
Europe					
Belgium	1,451	834	82	38	497
Bosnia and Herzegovina	894	872	0	16	6
Germany[1]	74,745	58,075	266	258	16,146
Greece	444	13	363	11	57
Iceland	1,408	1	741	1	665
Italy[1]	12,493	3,353	4,384	63	4,693
The Netherlands	688	345	25	15	303
Portugal	1,016	16	40	8	952
Serbia (including Kosovo)	1,773	1,770	0	3	0
Spain	1,835	67	1,262	201	305
Turkey[1]	1,722	61	30	18	1,613
United Kingdom[1]	11,341	401	1,009	92	9,839
afloat	2,431	0	2,431	0	0
total ashore and afloat	112,823	65,881	10,672	931	35,339
East Asia and Pacific					
Japan[1]	36,036	1,789	4,634	15,544	14,069
South Korea[1]	36,050	26,309	340	385	9,016
afloat	13,931	0	11,904	2,027	0
total ashore and afloat	86,730	28,226	17,080	18,164	23,260
North Africa, Near East, and South Asia					
Afghanistan[2]	19,200	14,000	400	2,000	2,800
Iraq (Operation Iraqi Freedom)[2]	202,100	135,700	17,300	30,500	18,600
Bahrain	1,770	21	1,567	159	23
Qatar	272	148	5	39	80

Worldwide Deployment of the US Military (continued)

COUNTRY/REGIONAL AREA	TOTAL	ARMY	NAVY	MARINE CORPS	AIR FORCE
North Africa, Near East, and South Asia (continued)					
afloat	603	0	372	231	0
total ashore and afloat (excludes Iraq and Afghanistan)	4,479	610	2,334	606	929
Western Hemisphere					
total ashore and afloat	1,861	413	639	437	372
all foreign countries (excluding Iraq and Afghanistan)					
ashore	257,668	95,230	45,231	39,200	78,007
afloat	22,784	0	20,526	2,258	0
total ashore and afloat	280,452	95,230	65,757	41,458	78,007
worldwide (excluding Iraq and Afghanistan)					
ashore	1,273,919	494,112	235,335	174,949	369,523
afloat	137,368	0	135,110	2,258	0
total ashore and afloat	1,411,287	494,112	370,445	177,207	369,523

[1]Service members deployed to Operation Iraqi Freedom are included in these country figures.
[2]Includes deployed Reserve/National Guard.

Military Ranks and Monthly Pay

Pay given in dollars as of 1 Jan 2005.

Enlisted personnel

	E-1	E-2	E-3	E-4	E-5
Army	private	private	private first class	corporal	sergeant
Navy	seaman recruit	seaman apprentice	seaman	petty officer third class	petty officer second class
Air Force	airman basic	airman	airman first class	senior airman	staff sergeant
Marine Corps	private	private first class	lance corporal	corporal	sergeant
0–6 years	1,143–1,235	1,385	1,456–1,641	1,613–1,878	1,760–2,061
6–12 years				1,958	2,205–2,422
12–18 years					2,451
18–24 years					
24 years and over					

	E-6	E-7	E-8	E-9
Army	staff sergeant	sergeant first class	master sergeant, first sergeant	sergeant major
Navy	petty officer first class	chief petty officer	senior chief petty officer	master chief petty officer
Air Force	technical sergeant	master sergeant, first sergeant	senior master sergeant, first sergeant	chief master sergeant
Marine Corps	staff sergeant	gunnery sergeant	master sergeant, first sergeant	master gunnery sergeant, sergeant major
0–6 years	1,920–2,297	2,220–2,639		
6–12 years	2,391–2,687	2,735–2,992	3,194–3,335	3,901
12–18 years	2,779–2,889	3,085–3,332	3,422–3,641	3,990–4,232
18–24 years	2,908	3,411–3,620	3,845–4,126	4,364–4,755
over 24 years		3,725–3,990	4,224–4,465	4,944–5,232

Warrant officers

	W-1	W-2	W-3	W-4	W-5
Army	warrant officer	chief warrant officer	chief warrant officer	chief warrant officer	chief warrant officer
Navy	"	"	"	"	
Marine Corps	"	"	"	"	
0–6 years	2,290–2,684	2,594–2,966	2,948–3,239	3,229–3,671	
6–12 years	2,900–3,146	3,046–3,438	3,371–3,722	3,840–4,176	
12–18 years	3,275–3,438	3,564–3,771	3,919–4,286	4,341–4,779	
18–24 years	3,564–3,660	3,842–4,112	4,442–4,579	4,950–5,291	5,548–5,738
over 24 years		4,247	4,730–4,881	5,462–5,636	5,929–6,121

Military Ranks and Monthly Pay (continued)

Officers (with more than 4 years served as an enlisted or warrant member of the armed services)

	O-1E	O-2E	O-3E
Army	second lieutenant	first lieutenant	captain
Navy	ensign	lieutenant, jr. grade	lieutenant
Air Force	second lieutenant	first lieutenant	captain
Marine Corps	second lieutenant	first lieutenant	captain
0–6 years	2,948	3,661	4,168
6–12 years	3,149–3,384	3,736–4,056	4,368–4,729
12–18 years	3,501–3,661	4,211–4,327	4,962–5,271
18–24 years		4,327	5,425
over 24 years			

Officers

	O-1	O-2	O-3	O-4	O-5
Army	second lieutenant	first lieutenant	captain	major	lieutenant colonel
Navy	ensign	lieutenant, jr. grade	lieutenant	lieutenant commander	commander
Air Force	second lieutenant	first lieutenant	captain	major	lieutenant colonel
Marine Corps	second lieutenant	first lieutenant	captain	major	lieutenant colonel
0–6 years	2,344–2,948	2,699–3,661	3,125–4,168	3,554–4,450	4,119–5,021
6–12 years		3,736	4,368–4,729	4,704–5,318	5,222–5,606
12–18 years			4,962–5,083	5,583–5,872	5,799–6,431
18–24 years				5,934	6,613–6,998
over 24 years					

	O-6	O-7	O-8	O-9	O-10
Army	colonel	brigadier general	major general	lieutenant general	general
Navy	captain	rear admiral (lower half)	rear admiral (upper half)	vice admiral	admiral
Air Force	colonel	brigadier general	major general	lieutenant general	general
Marine Corps	colonel	brigadier general	major general	lieutenant general	general
0–6 years	4,941–5,784	6,666–7,233	8,022–8,508		
6–12 years	5,806–6,088	7,439–7,878	8,726–9,174		
12–18 years	6,088–7,046	8,114–9,089	9,519–9,915		
18–24 years	7,405–7,968	9,715	10,346–11,008	11,338–11,501	12,963–13,027
over 24 years	8,174–8,576	9,715–9,764	11,008	11,737–12,149	13,298–13,769

Women in the US Armed Forces

Few early American women were soldiers. With the rise of the women's movement in the late 19th century, women gradually made inroads into the US military, most often in auxiliary roles. It was not until the late 20th century that they achieved regular combat status in the armed forces. By the 21st century, women continued to demand full equality across all branches of the military, especially in terms of combat duty.

During World War I many women had enlisted as volunteers in the military services; they usually served in clerical roles. When the war ended, they were released from their duties. The same was true during World War II, when an even greater number of women volunteers served in the armed forces. The war opened other employment opportunities for women—as factory workers ("Rosie the Riveter" became an American icon), nurses, and journalists—but these doors of opportunity were largely closed after the war, when women routinely lost their jobs to men discharged from military service.

During World War II several gender-specific military organizations were formed. Never before had women,

with the exception of nurses, served within the ranks of the US Army until the advent of the **Women's Army Corps** (WAC), which placed more than 150,000 women in noncombat positions. In anticipation of the expiration of the WAC law in 1948, the leaders of the Army in 1946 requested that the WACs be made a permanent part of its personnel. Following two years of legislative debate, the bill was passed by Congress and signed into law by Pres. Harry S. Truman on 12 Jun 1948, as the **Women's Armed Services Integration Act.** It enabled women to serve as permanent, regular members of not only the Army but also the Navy, the Marine Corps, and the recently formed Air Force. The law limited the number of women who could serve in the military to 2% of the total forces in each branch. The WAC remained a separate unit of the Army until 1978, when male and female forces were integrated.

Another group formed during World War II was the **Coast Guard Women's Reserve,** founded in 1942 for the purpose of making more men available to serve at sea by assigning women to onshore duties. Also established in 1942, the military unit **Women Accepted** for Volunteer Emergency Service (WAVES) was the Navy's corps of female members. During the war some 100,000 WAVES served in a wide variety of capacities, ranging from performing essential clerical duties to serving as instructors for male pilots-in-training. Several thousand WAVES later participated in the Korean War. Unlike the WAC, the WAVES was not an auxiliary and its members were accorded a status comparable to that of male members of the reserve. The Navy, however, did come under fire for excluding African American women from the ranks until the final months of the war, when Pres. Franklin D. Roosevelt ordered racial integration. The corps continued its separate existence until 1978.

At the advent of the 21st century, about 200,000 women were listed as active members of the US armed forces, comprising about 15% of the total military balance. The largest representation of women was in the Air Force, where nearly one-fifth were female, though a larger gross number of women were active in the Army. The smallest number and smallest female-to-male proportion were found in the Marine Corps. Women served in a number of combat and combat-support roles in Operation Iraqi Freedom in 2005. Of the 1,752 service members who had died in Iraq up to 8 Jul 2005, 43 were women. In June 2005 Sgt. Leigh Ann Hester, a military police officer in the Kentucky National Guard became the first female soldier to receive the Silver Star since World War II. Sgt Hester received the honor for bravery during a firefight her unit engaged in with heavily armed insurgents.

Military education

In the late 20th century women made advances in military education. In 1976 they were first admitted to the US Military Academy, US Naval Academy, and US Air Force Academy; the previous year they had been admitted to the US Coast Guard Academy. In 1990 the Justice Department ruled that the Virginia Military Institute's male-only admissions policy was unconstitutional. In response, the institute established an associated military program for women at Mary Baldwin College in Staunton VA in 1995. Nonetheless, the Supreme Court ruled in 1996 that the admissions policy was unconstitutional, and the school admitted its first women cadets in 1997.

Military figures

Deborah Sampson of Massachusetts assumed a male identity to serve for the Continental Army in the American Revolutionary War in 1782 until her true identity was discovered and she was discharged; her heirs received a full military pension in 1838. Sarah Emma Evelyn Edmonds enlisted as a man in the American Civil War and saw military action as a Union soldier and a spy until she deserted in April 1863; she later received a veteran's pension. According to legend, Lucy Brewer was the first woman marine, who, perhaps inspired by the story of Deborah Sampson, disguised herself as a man to serve on the USS *Constitution* during the War of 1812. Officially, however, Opha Mae Johnson is credited as the first female in the Marine Corps, enrolling in 1918.

Among the female leaders of military outfits during and after World War II were Florence A. Blanchfield (Army Nurse Corps), Sue Sophia Dauser (Navy Nurse Corps), Joy Bright Hancock (WAVES), Oveta Culp Hobby and Mary Agnes Hallaren (WAC), Dorothy Constance Stratton (Coast Guard Women's Reserve), and Katherine Amelia Towle, who was director of the women's reserve of the Marine Corps from 1948 to 1953.

Did you know? The highest-ranking woman in US Army history, Lt. Gen. Claudia J. Kennedy, served for 31 years prior to her retirement in 2000. Kennedy was the first woman to become a three-star general.

African American Service in US Wars

During the American Civil War the Union Army enlisted some 179,000 soldiers in 166 all-black regiments, but the first official group of African American professional soldiers was not recognized until the war had ended and the US was re-unified. A 1866 law authorized the creation of African American cavalry regiments in the Army; though it required their officers to be white. The resulting units were the 9th and 10th cavalries and the 38th through 41st infantries. These buffalo soldiers, as they came to be known, patrolled the Western frontier in the late 19th century, helping to pacify Native Americans.

The 9th and 10th cavalries later distinguished themselves by their fighting in the Spanish-American War and in the 1916 Mexican campaign. One of the 10th Cavalry's officers was John J. Pershing, afterwards a World War I general, whose nickname "Black Jack" reflected his advocacy of black troops.

The Medal of Honor, which became a permanent military decoration in 1863, was bestowed upon African Americans in the Civil War, Indian campaigns, Spanish-American War, both World Wars, the Korean conflict, and the Vietnam War. The seven Medals of Honor awarded to black soldiers in World War II were not granted until 1997, after a study revealed there was racial disparity in the awarding process.

More than 1.2 million African Americans served during World War II. Mostly restricted to segregated units, black soldiers not only fought for the Army but first saw combat duty in the Navy, Marines, and Army Air Corps (later Air Force). The Tuskegee Airmen of the all-black 99th Pursuit Squadron of the Air Corps were commanded by Lt. Col. Benjamin Oliver Davis, Jr., whose father, Benjamin O. Davis, Sr., was the first African American to become a US general (Army).

In 1948 President Truman integrated all branches of the military, and all-black units were phased out by 1954. In the decades following, the Civil Rights Movement continued to erode public racial segregation, and African Americans continued to figure prominently in the military. Colin Powell became the the first black officer to hold the highest military post in the US when Pres. George Bush nominated him chairman of the Joint Chiefs of Staff in 1989.

Number of Living Veterans[1]

Source: Statistical Abstract of the US.

AGE IN YEARS	KOREAN CONFLICT	VIETNAM ERA	GULF WAR (1ST)	TOTAL WARTIME[2]	TOTAL PEACETIME	TOTAL VETERANS[3]
Under 35	—	—	2,032,000	2,032,000	280,000	2,116,000
35-39	—	—	672,000	672,000	733,000	1,405,000
40-44	—	—	415,000	415,000	1,379,000	1,794,000
45-49	—	705,000	307,000	951,000	1,071,000	2,021,000
50-54	—	2,111,000	223,000	2,173,000	171,000	2,344,000
55-59	—	3,301,000	101,000	3,314,000	121,000	3,435,000
60-64	—	1,390,000	28,000	1,394,000	1,012,000	2,406,000
65 and over	3,580,000	703,000	6,000	7,840,000	1,819,000	9,659,000
Female, total	84,000	265,000	594,000	1,106,000	568,000	1,675,000
Total	3,580,000	8,211,000	3,783,000	18,791,000	6,389,000	25,179,000

[1]As of 30 Sep 2003. Includes those living outside of the US. Estimated. [2]Veterans who served in more than one wartime period are counted only once. The total does not reflect the current situation in Iraq and Afghanistan. [3]Includes an estimate of 4,370,000 veterans of World War II, all 65 or over.

Disabled Veterans Receiving Compensation

Numbers of veterans receiving compensation for service-related disabilities.

TIME OF SERVICE	1980	1990	1998	1999	2000	2001	2002	2003
World War I[1]	30,000	3,000	—[2]	—[2]	—[2]	—[2]	—[2]	—[2]
World War II	1,193,000	876,000	578,000	541,000	505,000	470,000	440,000	414,000
Korean Conflict	236,000	209,000	179,000	175,000	171,000	166,000	165,000	164,000
Vietnam War	553,000	652,000	729,000	736,000	741,000	750,000	799,000	848,000
Gulf War (1st)	N/A	N/A	241,000	282,000	325,000	366,000	419,000	476,000
Peacetime	262,000	444,000	550,000	561,000	567,000	569,000	575,000	583,000
Total	2,274,000	2,184,000	2,277,000	2,294,000	2,308,000	2,321,000	2,398,000	2,485,000

[1]Includes Spanish-American War and Mexican Border service. [2]Fewer than 500. N/A means not applicable.

US Casualties of War

Data prior to World War I are based on incomplete records. Casualty data exclude personnel captured or missing in action. N/A means not available or unknown. Sources: US Department of Defense and US Coast Guard.

WAR	SERVICE BRANCH	NUMBER OF COMBATANTS	WOUNDED[1]	CASUALTIES BATTLE DEATHS	OTHER DEATHS	TOTAL DEATHS
Revolutionary War	Army	N/A	6,004	4,044	N/A	N/A
(1775–1783)	Navy	N/A	114	342	N/A	N/A
	Marines	N/A	70	49	N/A	N/A
	total	184,000–250,000[2]	6,188	4,435	20,000[2]	24,435
War of 1812	Army	N/A	4,000	1,950	N/A	N/A
(1812–1815)	Navy	N/A	439	265	N/A	N/A
	Marines	N/A	66	45	N/A	N/A
	Coast Guard	100	N/A	0	N/A	N/A
	total	286,830	4,505	2,260	N/A	N/A
Indian Wars (about 1817–1898)	total	106,000[2]	N/A	1,000[2]	N/A	N/A
Mexican War	Army	N/A	4,102	1,721	11,550	13,271
(1846–1848)	Navy	N/A	3	1	N/A	N/A
	Marines	N/A	47	11	N/A	N/A
	Coast Guard	71	N/A	N/A	N/A	N/A
	total	78,789	4,152[4]	1,733[4]	N/A	N/A
Civil War (1861–1865)						
Union	Army	2,128,948	280,040	138,154	221,374	359,528
	Navy	N/A	1,710	2,112	2,411	4,523
	Marines	84,415	131	148	312	460
	Coast Guard	219	N/A	1	N/A	N/A
	total	N/A	281,881[4]	140,415	224,097[4]	364,512[4]
Confederate[3]	total	600,000–1,500,000	137,000[2]	74,524	124,000[2]	198,524

US Casualties of War (continued)

WAR	SERVICE BRANCH	NUMBER OF COMBATANTS	WOUNDED[1]	CASUALTIES BATTLE DEATHS	CASUALTIES OTHER DEATHS	CASUALTIES TOTAL DEATHS
Spanish-American War	Army	280,564	1,594	369	2,061	2,430
(1898)	Navy	22,875	47	10	N/A	N/A
	Marines	3,321	21	6	N/A	N/A
	Coast Guard	660	N/A	0	N/A	0
	total	307,420	1,662	385	2,061	N/A
World War I	Army[4]	4,057,101	193,663	50,510	55,868	106,378
(1917–1918)	Navy	599,051	819	431	6,856	7,287
	Marines	78,839	9,520	2,461	390	2,851
	Coast Guard	8,835	N/A	111	81	192
	total	4,743,826	204,002[4]	53,513	63,195	116,708
World War II	Army[4]	11,260,000	565,861	234,874	83,400	318,274
(1941–1946)	Navy	4,183,466	37,778	36,950	25,664	62,614
	Marines	669,100	68,207	19,733	4,778	24,511
	Coast Guard	241,093	N/A	574	1,343	1,917
	total	16,353,659	671,846[4]	292,131	115,185	407,316
Korean War	Army	2,834,000	77,596	27,731	2,125	29,856
(1950–1953)	Navy	1,177,000	1,576	506	154	660
	Marines	424,000	23,744	4,266	242	4,508
	Air Force	1,285,000	368	1,238	314	1,552
	Coast Guard	8,500[5]	0	0	0	0
	total	5,764,143	103,284	33,741	2,835	36,576
Vietnam War[5]	Army	4,368,000	96,802	30,952	7,261	38,213
(1964–1973)	Navy	1,842,000	4,178	1,628	934	2,562
	Marines	794,000	51,392	13,091	1,749	14,840
	Air Force	1,740,000	931	1,744	841	2,585
	Coast Guard	8,000	60	7	N/A	7
	total	8,752,000	153,363[6]	47,422[4]	10,785[4]	58,207[4]
1st Persian Gulf War[7]	Army	338,636	354	98	126	224
(1990–1991)	Navy	152,419	12[8]	5[8]	50[8]	55[8]
	Marines	97,878	92	24	44	68
	Air Force	76,543	9	20	15	35
	Coast Guard	400	N/A	N/A	N/A	N/A
	total	665,876	467	147	235	382
War on Terrorism[9]	Army	N/A	394	58	76	134
(2001–)	Navy	N/A	4	4	11	15
	Marines	N/A	44	6	14	20
	Air Force	N/A	34	8	12	20
	Coast Guard	N/A	N/A	N/A	N/A	N/A
	total	N/A	476	76	113	189
2nd Persian	Army	N/A	8,284	845	279	1,124
Gulf War[10]	Navy	N/A	274	20	11	31
(2003–)	Marines	N/A	4,138	396	94	490
	Air Force	N/A	165	8	11	19
	Coast Guard	N/A	N/A	1	0	1
	total	N/A	12,861	1,270	395	1,665

other[11]

[1]Data in this column account for the total number of wounds. Marine Corps data for World War II, the Spanish-American War, and earlier wars represent the number of combatants wounded. [2]Estimate. [3]US service members only. [4]Excluding unavailable Coast Guard data. [5]Number eligible for Korean Service Medal. [6]Excludes 150,332 wounded that did not require hospital care. [7]Data for military personnel serving in the theater of operation. [8]Includes Coast Guard. [9]Data for 7 Oct 2001–4 Jun 2005. [10]Data through 4 Jun 2005. [11]US casualties of other recent military operations: in Grenada (1983) 119 wounded, 19 battle deaths; in Panama (1989) 324 wounded, 23 battle deaths; in Somalia (1992–1994) 153 wounded, 43 battle deaths.

Weapons of Mass Destruction (WMD)

Following the explosion of the first atomic bombs in 1945 over Hiroshima and Nagasaki, Japan, by the US at the end of World War II, critics were less concerned about the economic and military inefficacies of an arms buildup than about the danger that nuclear weapons threatened the continued existence of civilization itself. During the Cold War the world's two superpowers, the US and the USSR, each developed large arsenals of nuclear weapons. The possibility of both nations' mutual destruction in an intercontinental exchange of nuclear-armed missiles prompted them to undertake increasingly serious efforts to limit first the testing, then the deployment, and finally the possession of these weapons. Often negotiations were facilitated by the UN. The US and the USSR sponsored several international agreements of a limited-risk form.

The first agreement was the Nuclear Test-Ban Treaty (1963), which banned tests of nuclear weapons in the atmosphere, in outer space, and underwater, thus effectively confining nuclear explosions to underground sites. With the Treaty on the Non-proliferation of Nuclear Weapons (1968), the two superpowers agreed not to promote the spread of nuclear weapons to countries that did not already possess them. Per other treaties, nuclear weapons could not be orbited around the Earth (the Outer Space Treaty of 1967) or placed on the seabed (the Seabed Treaty of 1971).

Substantial advances in limiting the nuclear arms race in the 1970s came out of the Strategic Arms Limitation Talks (SALT), which were intended to restrain the continuing buildup in nuclear-armed intercontinental (long-range or strategic) ballistic missiles (ICBMs). Part of SALT, the Anti-Ballistic Missile Treaty (1972), severely limited each nation's future deployment of antiballistic missiles, which could be used to destroy incoming ICBMs; the agreement thus kept both sides subject to the deterrent effect of the other's strategic offensive forces. The SALT II agreement of 1979 set limits on each side's store of multiple independent reentry vehicles (MIRVs), which are strategic missiles equipped with multiple nuclear warheads capable of hitting different targets on the ground.

Arms-control efforts between the two superpowers were facilitated in 1985 by the more liberal Soviet regime under Mikhail Gorbachev and bore fruit in the Intermediate-Range Nuclear Forces Treaty (1987), in which the US and the USSR agreed to eliminate their stocks of intermediate- and medium-range land-based missiles. Also in the 1980s, the nations decided to reduce rather than merely limit their arsenals of nuclear warheads and launch platforms (missiles and bombers), during the Strategic Arms Reduction Treaty (START), signed in 1991.

Following the breakup of the USSR in late 1991, a followup agreement, START II (1993), further reduced each nation's strategic nuclear forces. Both START II and the Comprehensive Test Ban Treaty (1996) were ratified by Russia in 2000. The following year, however, the US announced its intention to withdraw from the 1972 Anti-Ballistic Missile Treaty because it presented an obstacle to its proposed National Missile Defense.

There have also been attempts to eliminate other WMD. In 1971 the UN General Assembly approved a convention (in effect in 1975) prohibiting the manufacture, stockpiling, and use of biological weapons, although many states have never acceded to it. In 1993 the Chemical Weapons Convention, prohibiting the development, production, stockpiling, and use of chemical weapons and providing for their destruction, was opened for signature.

WMD have reemerged as a key political topic in recent years. The alleged existence of programs for the development of WMD in Iraq was a primary impetus for the US-led invasion in 2003, though no evidence for such programs has yet been found. Iran's nuclear power development program is under the scrutiny of the International Atomic Energy Agency for having potentially lethal goals. India and Pakistan have both developed nuclear arsenals, and Dr. Abdul Qadeer Khan, the "father" of Pakistan's nuclear program, has admitted passing nuclear secrets to Libya, North Korea, and Iran.

Leading Department of Defense Contractors

Top 100 Department of Defense contractors listed according to net value of prime contract awards, fiscal year 2004. Source: <www.defenselink.mil/pubs>.

RANK	CONTRACTOR	AMOUNT, IN '000 (US$)	RANK	CONTRACTOR	AMOUNT, IN '000 (US$)
1	Lockheed Martin	20,690,912	29	Titan	933,554
2	Boeing	17,066,413	30	Boeing Sikorsky Comanche Team	929,238
3	Northrop Grumman	11,894,090	31	Booz Allen & Hamilton	909,663
4	General Dynamics	9,563,280	32	Veritas Capital Management	863,011
5	Raytheon	8,472,814	33	GM GDLS Defense Group	811,807
6	Halliburton	7,996,794	34	Parsons Corporation	809,150
7	United Technologies	5,056,938	35	Public Warehousing	804,820
8	Science Applications International	2,450,781	36	URS	803,827
			37	Government of Canada	751,147
9	Computer Sciences	2,390,806	38	Anteon International	700,777
10	Humana	2,372,078	39	Johnson Controls	696,616
11	L-3 Communications Holding	2,260,293	40	Engineered Support Systems	693,854
12	BAE Systems	2,192,647			
13	Health Net	1,899,825	41	Dell Computer	642,979
14	General Electric	1,822,720	42	A.P. Møller Gruppen	638,728
15	Bechtel Group	1,742,470	43	McKesson	627,637
16	Bell Boeing Joint Program	1,539,815	44	Massachusetts Institute of Technology	607,115
17	ITT Industries	1,539,742			
18	Electronic Data Systems	1,538,272	45	Harris	605,789
19	Honeywell International	1,462,915	46	BP	597,674
20	Carlyle Group	1,442,680	47	Alliant Techsystems	592,439
21	Triwest Healthcare Alliance	1,279,718	48	Rockwell Collins	588,368
22	Renco Group	1,107,715	49	American Body Armor and Equipment	579,264
23	N.V. Koninklijke Nederlandsche	1,070,123			
			50	Cardinal Health	575,550
24	Oshkosh Truck	1,024,394	51	Mitre	555,180
25	Government of the US	1,005,126	52	Fluor	549,931
26	North American Airlines	961,601	53	Aerospace	545,619
27	FedEx	953,938	54	CACI International	530,858
28	Textron	940,267	55	Chugach Alaska Corporation	524,060

Leading Department of Defense Contractors (continued)

RANK	CONTRACTOR	AMOUNT, IN '000 (US$)	RANK	CONTRACTOR	AMOUNT, IN '000 (US$)
56	Shaw Group	499,388	78	Motorola	307,816
57	Amerisourcebergen	495,976	79	DRS Technologies	305,782
58	Morrison Knudsen	458,405	80	Raytheon/Lockheed Martin Javelin	300,796
59	Pernini Corporation	444,586	81	Battelle Memorial Institute	298,573
60	Alliant Lake City Small Caliber Ammunition	428,534	82	Exxon Mobil	283,999
			83	Abu Dhabi National Oil	276,572
61	Sierra Health Services	427,762	84	Environmental Chemical Corporation	272,592
62	Rolls-Royce Group	417,259	85	Cubic Defense Systems	267,744
63	Arinc	392,104	86	Combat Support Associates	265,499
64	Jacobs Engineering Group	391,401	87	Tetra Tech	261,787
65	IBM	386,288	88	Parker Hannifin	261,182
66	Johns Hopkins University	377,339	89	Atlantic Diving Supply	256,921
67	Stewart & Stevenson Services	375,815	90	Anham Joint Venture	256,370
68	General Atomic Technologies	357,069	91	Team Apache Systems	253,488
69	Goodyear	356,817	92	Tyco International	252,526
70	Goodrich	351,560	93	CH2M Hill Companies	244,492
71	Valero Energy	349,714	94	Charles Stark Draper Laboratories	240,280
72	Unicor/Federal Prison Industries	348,762	95	Smith Industries	236,159
73	Mantech International	344,465	96	Army Fleet Support	234,587
74	Thales	339,054	97	Ssangyong (USA)	233,382
75	GTSI	335,068	98	Procter & Gamble	233,221
76	United Industrial Corp.	330,750	99	DHB Industries	232,252
77	Contrack	329,301	100	VSE Corporation	231,733

The Central Intelligence Agency (CIA)

The CIA is the principal intelligence and counter-intelligence agency of the US government. Formally created in 1947, the agency grew out of the World War II Office of Strategic Services (OSS). Previous US intelligence and counterintelligence efforts had been conducted by the Army and Navy and by the Federal Bureau of Investigation (FBI) and suffered from duplication, competition, and lack of coordination. US allies had criticized the lack of any central intelligence function.

In June 1942 Pres. Franklin D. Roosevelt created the OSS so that the fragmented and uncoordinated strands of US intelligence-gathering would be brought together under a single organization. William J. ("Wild Bill") Donovan became head of the OSS upon its founding and was largely responsible for building that organization. During World War II the OSS collected and analyzed foreign intelligence concerning areas where US military forces operated. The OSS obtained intelligence through secret agents in enemy territory, it carried out counterpropaganda and disinformation activities, and it staged special operations behind enemy lines involving sabotage, demolition, and the supplying and direction of resistance fighters. Under Donovan, the OSS was remarkably effective despite the initial inexperience of most of its personnel.

The OSS was dismantled in October 1945, but the administration of Pres. Harry S. Truman recognized the need for a coordinated postwar intelligence establishment. In 1946 the president established by executive order a Central Intelligence Group and a National Intelligence Authority. These bodies selected key personnel from the group assembled under wartime pressures by the OSS and tried to impose some central direction on postwar intelligence operations, although the armed forces maintained their own independent intelligence services.

In 1947 Congress created the National Security Council (NSC) and, under its direction, the Central Intelligence Agency, which was to advise the NSC on intelligence matters bearing on national security, make recommendations on coordinating intelligence activities of government agencies generally, correlate and evaluate intelligence and see to its proper communication within government, and carry out such other national-security intelligence functions as the NSC might direct.

The CIA is organized into four major groups. The Directorate of Intelligence analyzes intelligence that is gathered overtly from available sources and obtained covertly through espionage, aerial and satellite photography, and interception of radio, telephone, and other forms of communication. Its analyses are distributed variously as bulletins, reports, and exhaustive surveys. It also monitors foreign radio broadcasts. The Directorate of Operations is responsible for covert operations, including clandestine collection of intelligence (i.e., espionage) and special covert activities. The Directorate of Science and Technology is charged with keeping the agency abreast of scientific and technological advances, and it develops technical devices useful to the agency and supplies technical and scientific support to agency operations. The Directorate of Support not only administers but also contains the Office of Security, which is responsible for the security of personnel, facilities, information, and information sources such as defectors from other governments.

Clandestine activities are carried on under various guises—including the diplomatic cloak used by virtually every intelligence service, as well as fronts such as corporations that the CIA creates or acquires. The agency also "debriefs" business travelers, journalists willing to be so interviewed, and others returning to the US from a sensitive or professionally interesting place.

Among the CIA's major covert operations were the expulsion of Mohammad Mosaddeq as premier and the restoration of the shah of Iran in 1953, and the following year the toppling of an unfriendly leftist government in Guatemala. The attempted Bay of Pigs invasion of

Cuba (1961) by CIA-supported Cuban dissidents was a fiasco. In 1973 and 1974 the agency was damaged by the revelation that former CIA operatives had repeatedly played illegal roles in the Watergate affair.

The CIA came under intense scrutiny in the wake of the attacks of 11 Sep 2001, and efforts to improve the coordination and sharing of intelligence, particularly with the FBI, were undertaken. In June 2004,

George Tenet resigned as director of the CIA after revelations of intelligence lapses in the run-up to the Second Persian Gulf War and of prisoner abuse at Abu Ghraib prison in Iraq. Reorganization of the CIA, partly in response to the findings of the 9/11 Commission, have been ongoing and include interagency data sharing and integration of technological and personnel functions.

CIA Directors

The National Security Act of 26 Jul 1947 established the CIA on 18 Sep 1947. By authority of a presidential directive of 22 Jan 1946, the director of central intelligence serves as a member of the National In-

telligence Authority and as head of the Central Intelligence Group. The director coordinates the nation's intelligence activities and informs the president on issues of national security.

NAME	DATES OF SERVICE	NAME	DATES OF SERVICE
Rear Adm. Sidney W. Souers, USNR	23 Jan 1946–10 Jun 1946	James R. Schlesinger	2 Feb 1973–2 Jul 1973
Lt. Gen. Hoyt S. Vandenberg, USA	10 Jun 1946–1 May 1947	William E. Colby	4 Sep 1973–30 Jan 1976
		George H.W. Bush	30 Jan 1976–20 Jan 1977
Rear Adm. Roscoe H. Hillenkoetter, USN	1 May 1947–7 Oct 1950	Adm. Stansfield Turner, USN (Ret)	9 Mar 1977–20 Jan 1981
Gen. Walter Bedell Smith, USA	7 Oct 1950–9 Feb 1953	William J. Casey	28 Jan 1981–29 Jan 1987
		William H. Webster	26 May 1987–31 Aug 1991
Allen W. Dulles	26 Feb 1953–29 Nov 1961	Robert M. Gates	6 Nov 1991–20 Jan 1993
John A. McCone	29 Nov 1961–28 Apr 1965	R. James Woolsey	5 Feb 1993–10 Jan 1995
Vice Adm. William F. Raborn, Jr., USN (Ret)	28 Apr 1965–30 Jun 1966	John M. Deutch	10 May 1995–15 Dec 1996
		George J. Tenet	11 Jul 1997–11 Jul 2004
Richard M. Helms	30 Jun 1966–2 Feb 1973	John E. McLaughlin	12 Jul 2004–20 Apr 2005
		Porter J. Goss	21 Apr 2005–

The National Security Council (NSC)

The National Security Act of 1947 established the NSC to advise the president on policies relating to national security. In addition to regular attendees, the chief of staff to the president, counsel to the presi-

dent, and assistant to the president for economic policy are invited to attend all meetings. The attorney general and the director of the office of management and budget are also invited to attend when needed.

chair	George W. Bush (president)
regular attendees	Richard B. Cheney (vice president)
	Condoleezza Rice (secretary of state)
	John Snow (secretary of the treasury)
	Donald H. Rumsfeld (secretary of defense)
	Stephen Hadley (assistant to the president for national security affairs)
military adviser	Richard B. Myers (chairman of the joint chiefs of staff)
intelligence adviser	Porter J. Goss (director of the CIA)
additional participants	Andrew H. Card, Jr. (chief of staff)
	Harriet Miers (counsel to the president)
	Allan Hubbard (assistant to the president for economic policy)
	Alberto Gonzales (attorney general)
	Joshua B. Bolten (director of the Office of Management and Budget)

On 23 Mar 1953 Pres. Dwight D. Eisenhower established the office of assistant to the president for national security affairs (commonly referred to as the

national security advisor). Holders of this office are listed below.

NAME	DATES OF SERVICE	NAME	DATES OF SERVICE
Robert Cutler	23 Mar 1953–2 Apr 1955	William P. Clark	4 Jan 1982–17 Oct 1983
Dillon Anderson	2 Apr 1955–1 Sep 1956	Robert C. McFarlane	17 Oct 1983–4 Dec 1985
Robert Cutler	7 Jan 1957–24 Jun 1958	John M. Poindexter	4 Dec 1985– 25 Nov 1986
Gordon Gray	24 Jun 1958–13 Jan 1961	Frank C. Carlucci	2 Dec 1986–23 Nov 1987
McGeorge Bundy	20 Jan 1961–28 Feb 1966	Colin L. Powell	23 Nov 1987–20 Jan 1989
Walt W. Rostow	1 Apr 1966–2 Dec 1968	Brent Scowcroft	20 Jan 1989–20 Jan 1993
Henry A. Kissinger	2 Dec 1968–3 Nov 1975[1]	W. Anthony Lake	20 Jan 1993–14 Mar 1997
Brent Scowcroft	3 Nov 1975–20 Jan 1977	Samuel R. Berger	14 Mar 1997–20 Jan 2001
Zbigniew Brzezinski	20 Jan 1977–21 Jan 1981	Condoleezza Rice	26 Jan 2001–26 Jan 2005
Richard V. Allen	21 Jan 1981–4 Jan 1982	Stephen Hadley	26 Jan 2005–

[1]Henry A. Kissinger served concurrently as secretary of state from 21 Sep 1973.

United States Population

The Census, History and Gathering

A census enumerates people, houses, firms, or other important items in a country or region at a particular time. Used alone, the term usually refers to a population census and considers population size and density, distribution, and vital statistics. National population censuses, being expensive, are taken only at infrequent intervals: every 10 years in many countries, every 5 years or at irregular intervals in other countries. Specialists such as demographers interpret the statistical results, which are useful to policymakers and businessmen.

Census, a Latin word, was first used by the ancient Romans to describe the counting of the citizenry in order to value their estates for the purpose of taxation. The Domesday Book was an inquest of England in 1086 that was made to acquaint William the Conqueror with the landholders and holdings of his new domain. In 1449, under the threat of siege, the German city of Nürnberg made an almost complete count of its people.

Strictly speaking, though, the modern population census as a complete enumeration of all the people and their characteristics began to evolve only in the 17th century. The United States was the first modern nation to adopt a legal provision for taking a census at regular intervals, which it began in 1790 to establish a basis for representation in Congress. Censuses were taken in England, France, and Canada in 1801, 1836, and 1871, respectively. China was the last major country to report a census, in 1953.

Over time, improvements were made in the administration of census taking and in the compilation of its data. Census information is obtained by using a fixed questionnaire covering such topics as place of residence, sex, age, marital status, occupation, citizenship, language, ethnicity, religious affiliation, and education. From the responses demographers derive data on population distribution, household and family composition, internal migration, labor-force participation, and other topics.

A "de jure" census tallies people according to their regular or legal residence, whereas a "de facto" census allocates them to the place where enumerated—normally where they spend the night of the day enumerated. By either method, the reported territorial distribution is according to where people sleep (nighttime population) rather than where they work (daytime population).

Census 2000—Interpreting the Numbers

The undertaking of a national census every 10 years was mandated in the Constitution of 1787. Since the first census in 1790, each census counts the population of the states, and that population total determines each state's congressional representation. In general, the results of Census 2000 showed states in the Northeast and Midwest losing representatives to states in the West and South.

Twelve seats in the 435-member House of Representatives shifted with the changes in population. Arizona, Florida, Georgia, and Texas each gained two representatives, while California, Colorado, Nevada, and North Carolina each gained one. New York and Pennsylvania each lost two representatives. Connecticut, Illinois, Indiana, Michigan, Mississippi, Ohio, Oklahoma, and Wisconsin all lost one congressional seat.

The Changing Face of America

The population of the United States increased by 32.7 million people between the censuses of 1990 and 2000. That increase represented the largest population growth in census history. Census 2000 revealed a nation with more ethnic and racial diversity. During the 1990s the Hispanic population (Hispanics may be of any race) increased by 58%, the Asian population by 48%. The immigration of these and other groups accounted for about 13.3 million of the country's total population—a number not equaled in United States history. The second largest number of immigrants recorded—10.1 million people—occurred between 1905 and 1914. Of the 281.4 million people residing in the United States on census day, non-Hispanic whites accounted for 69.1% of the population; Hispanics, 12.5%; blacks, 12.3%; and Asians, 3.6%.

The changing face of the United States was reflected in cities, suburbs, and rural areas. For the first time, nearly half of the nation's 100 largest cities were home to more African Americans, Hispanics, Asians, and other minorities than to non-Hispanic whites. While the population of the country's fastest-growing cities, such as Las Vegas and Phoenix, increased in all racial and ethnic categories, the vast majority of cities—71 of the top 100—lost non-Hispanic white residents to the suburbs and beyond. The nation's largest cities gained 3.8 million Hispanic residents, a 43% increase from a decade ago. Many cities, including Boston, Los Angeles, and Dallas, would have lost population in the 1990s were it not for large gains in the number of Hispanics.

Even with the arrival of a record number of immigrants (who tend to be relatively young), the United States continued to age as a nation. The median age of the country's population in 2000 was 35.3—five years older than the median age in 1950. (The median age splits the population in half, 50% are over the median age, 50% under it.) This increase in median age was tied to the graying of the post-World War II "Baby Boom" generation. Born from 1946 through 1964, Baby Boomers between 36 and 54 years of age represented 28% of the country's total population. The median age for non-Hispanic whites was 38.6, for Asians 32.7, blacks 30.2, and Hispanics 25.8. Census 2000 revealed that the country's population was 50.9% female and 49.1% male. There were 37.1 million males under the age of 18 as compared to 35.2 million females. By the age of 36, however, there were more females than males. Female senior citizens 65 years and older outnumbered males 20.6 million to 14.4 million.

Although they were not totally comprised of Baby Boomers and their parents, the Northeast and

Midwest regions had the country's oldest populations. Median ages for those regions were 36.8 and 35.6, respectively. Interestingly, the Northeast was the only region in the country where all of its states had median ages above the national level. In contrast, the West had the population with the youngest median age, 33.8.

Total US Population and Area, 1790–2000

The total land/water area numbers from 1790 to 1970 were recalculated for the 1980 census. Information for Alaska and Hawaii is included in all censuses after 1940. Source: US Census Bureau.

CENSUS	POPULATION	POPULATION GROWTH (%)	TOTAL LAND/WATER AREA (SQ MI)	LAND AREA (SQ MI)	PEOPLE/ SQ MI OF LAND AREA
1790	3,929,214	—	891,364	864,746	4.5
1800	5,308,483	35.1	891,364	864,746	6.1
1810	7,239,881	36.4	1,722,685	1,681,828	4.3
1820	9,638,453	33.1	1,792,552	1,749,462	5.5
1830	12,866,020	33.5	1,792,552	1,749,462	7.4
1840	17,069,453	32.7	1,792,552	1,749,462	9.8
1850	23,191,876	35.9	2,991,655	2,940,042	7.9
1860	31,443,321	35.6	3,021,295	2,969,640	10.6
1870	39,818,449	26.6	3,612,299	3,540,705	11.2
1880	50,189,209	26.0	3,612,299	3,540,705	14.2
1890	62,979,766	25.5	3,612,299	3,540,705	17.8
1900	76,212,168	21.0	3,618,770	3,547,314	21.5
1910	92,228,496	21.0	3,618,770	3,547,045	26.0
1920	106,021,537	15.0	3,618,770	3,546,931	29.9
1930	123,202,624	16.2	3,618,770	3,551,608	34.7
1940	132,164,569	7.3	3,618,770	3,551,608	37.2
1950	151,325,798	14.5	3,618,770	3,552,206	42.6
1960	179,323,175	18.5	3,618,770	3,540,911	50.6
1970	203,302,031	13.4	3,618,770	3,536,855	57.5
1980	226,542,199	11.4	3,618,770	3,539,289	64.0
1990	248,718,302	9.8	3,717,796	3,536,278	70.3
2000	281,422,509	13.1	3,794,083	3,537,439	79.6

US Population by Race, Sex, Median Age, and Residence

Numbers are in thousands ('000) except for the median age figures and the residency percentages. N/A means not available. Source: US Census Bureau.

YEAR	RACE			SEX		MEDIAN AGE	RESIDENCE[2]	
	WHITE	BLACK	OTHER[1]	MALE	FEMALE		URBAN (%)	RURAL (%)
1790	3,172	757	N/A	N/A	N/A	N/A	5.1	94.9
1800	4,306	1,002	N/A	N/A	N/A	N/A	6.1	93.9
1810	5,862	1,378	N/A	N/A	N/A	N/A	7.3	92.7
1820	7,867	1,772	N/A	4,897	4,742	16.7	7.2	92.8
1830	10,537	2,329	N/A	6,532	6,334	17.2	8.8	91.2
1840	14,196	2,874	N/A	8,689	8,381	17.8	10.8	89.2
1850	19,553	3,639	N/A	11,838	11,354	18.9	15.4	84.6
1860	26,923	4,442	79	16,085	15,358	19.4	19.8	80.2
1870	34,337	5,392	89	19,494	19,065	20.2	25.7	74.3
1880	43,403	6,581	172	25,519	24,637	20.9	28.2	71.8
1890	55,101	7,489	358	32,237	30,711	22.0	35.1	64.9
1900	66,809	8,834	351	38,816	37,178	22.9	39.6	60.4
1910	81,732	9,828	413	47,332	44,640	24.1	45.6	54.4
1920	94,821	10,463	427	53,900	51,810	25.3	51.2	48.8
1930	110,287	11,891	597	62,137	60,638	26.4	56.1	43.9
1940	118,215	12,866	589	66,062	65,608	29.0	56.5	43.5
1950	134,942	15,042	713	74,833	75,864	30.2	64.0	36.0
1960	158,832	18,872	1,620	88,331	90,992	29.5	69.9	30.1
1970	178,098	22,581	2,557	98,926	104,309	28.0	73.6	26.3
1980	194,713	26,683	5,150	110,053	116,493	30.0	73.7	26.3
1990	199,686	29,986	9,233	121,271	127,494	32.8	78.0	22.0
2000	211,461	34,658	13,118	138,054	143,368	35.3	79.0	21.0
2003	234,196	37,099	19,515	143,037	147,773	35.9	N/A	N/A

[1]"Other" refers to Asians, Pacific Islanders, American Indians, Alaska Natives, and those belonging to two or more races. Alaska and Hawaii are excluded from the population numbers until 1960, the first census after they became states in 1959.   [2]The census definitions for urban and rural areas have changed through the decades.

State Populations, 1790–2004

Resident population of the states and the District of Columbia. Numbers are in thousands ('000).
Source: US Census Bureau.

STATE	1790	1800	1810	1820	1830	1840	1850	1860	1870	1880	1890	1900
AL		1	9	128	310	591	772	964	997	1,263	1,513	1,829
AK										33	32	64
AZ									10	40	88	123
AR			1	14	30	98	210	435	484	803	1,128	1,312
CA							93	380	560	865	1,213	1,485
CO								34	40	194	413	540
CT	238	251	262	275	298	310	371	460	537	623	746	908
DE	59	64	73	73	77	78	92	112	125	147	168	185
DC		8	15	23	30	34	52	75	132	178	230	279
FL					35	54	87	140	188	269	391	529
GA	83	163	252	341	517	691	906	1,057	1,184	1,542	1,837	2,216
HI												154
ID									15	33	89	162
IL			12	55	157	476	851	1,712	2,540	3,078	3,826	4,822
IN		6	25	147	343	686	988	1,350	1,681	1,978	2,192	2,516
IA						43	192	675	1,194	1,625	1,912	2,232
KS								107	364	996	1,428	1,470
KY	74	221	407	564	688	780	982	1,156	1,321	1,649	1,859	2,147
LA			77	153	216	352	518	708	727	940	1,119	1,382
ME	97	152	229	298	399	502	583	628	627	649	661	694
MD	320	342	381	407	447	470	583	687	781	935	1,042	1,188
MA	379	423	472	523	610	738	995	1,231	1,457	1,783	2,239	2,805
MI			5	9	32	212	398	749	1,184	1,637	2,094	2,421
MN							6	172	440	781	1,310	1,751
MS		8	31	75	137	376	607	791	828	1,132	1,290	1,551
MO			20	67	140	384	682	1,182	1,721	2,168	2,679	3,107
MT									21	39	143	243
NE								29	123	452	1,063	1,066
NV								7	42	62	47	42
NH	142	184	214	244	269	285	318	326	318	347	377	412
NJ	184	211	246	278	321	373	490	672	906	1,131	1,445	1,884
NM								62	94	92	120	160	195
NY	340	589	959	1,373	1,919	2,429	3,097	3,881	4,383	5,083	6,003	7,269
NC	394	478	556	639	738	753	869	993	1,071	1,400	1,618	1,894
ND								5	2	37	191	319
OH		45	231	581	938	1,519	1,980	2,340	2,665	3,198	3,672	4,158
OK											259	790
OR							12	52	91	175	318	414
PA	434	602	810	1,049	1,348	1,724	2,312	2,906	3,522	4,283	5,258	6,302
RI	69	69	77	83	97	109	148	175	217	277	346	429
SC	249	346	415	503	581	594	669	704	706	996	1,151	1,340
SD									12	98	349	402
TN	36	106	262	423	682	829	1,003	1,110	1,259	1,542	1,768	2,021
TX							213	604	819	1,592	2,236	3,049
UT							11	40	87	144	211	277
VT	85	154	218	236	281	292	314	315	331	332	332	344
VA	692	808	878	938	1,044	1,025	1,119	1,220	1,225	1,513	1,656	1,854
WA							1	12	24	75	357	518
WV	56	79	105	137	177	225	302	377	442	618	763	959
WI						31	305	776	1,055	1,315	1,693	2,069
WY									9	21	63	93
US total[1]	3,929	5,308	7,240	9,638	12,866	17,069	23,192	31,443	39,818[2]	50,156	62,948	75,995

[1]Alaska and Hawaii are not included in the US total until 1960, the year after both achieved statehood.

State Populations, 1790–2004 (continued)

1910	1920	1930	1940	1950	1960	1970	1980	1990	2000	2004 EST.
2,138	2,348	2,646	2,833	3,062	3,267	3,444	3,894	4,040	4,447	4,530
64	55	59	73	129	226	300	402	550	627	655
204	334	436	499	750	1,302	1,771	2,718	3,665	5,131	5,744
1,574	1,752	1,854	1,949	1,910	1,786	1,923	2,286	2,351	2,673	2,753
2,378	3,427	5,677	6,907	10,586	15,717	19,953	23,668	29,811	33,872	35,894
799	940	1,036	1,123	1,325	1,754	2,207	2,890	3,294	4,301	4,601
1,115	1,381	1,607	1,709	2,007	2,535	3,032	3,108	3,287	3,406	3,504
202	223	238	267	318	446	548	594	666	784	830
331	438	487	663	802	764	757	638	607	572	554
753	968	1,468	1,897	2,771	4,952	6,789	9,746	12,938	15,982	17,397
2,609	2,896	2,909	3,124	3,445	3,943	4,590	5,463	6,478	8,186	8,829
192	256	368	423	500	633	769	965	1,108	1,212	1,263
326	432	445	525	589	667	713	944	1,007	1,294	1,393
5,639	6,485	7,631	7,897	8,712	10,081	11,114	11,427	11,431	12,419	12,714
2,701	2,930	3,239	3,428	3,934	4,662	5,194	5,490	5,544	6,080	6,238
2,225	2,404	2,471	2,538	2,621	2,758	2,824	2,914	2,777	2,926	2,954
1,691	1,769	1,881	1,801	1,905	2,179	2,247	2,364	2,478	2,688	2,736
2,290	2,417	2,615	2,846	2,945	3,038	3,219	3,661	3,687	4,042	4,146
1,656	1,799	2,102	2,364	2,684	3,257	3,641	4,206	4,222	4,469	4,516
742	768	797	847	914	969	992	1,125	1,228	1,275	1,317
1,295	1,450	1,632	1,821	2,343	3,101	3,922	4,217	4,781	5,296	5,558
3,366	3,852	4,250	4,317	4,691	5,149	5,689	5,737	6,016	6,349	6,417
2,810	3,668	4,842	5,256	6,372	7,823	8,875	9,262	9,295	9,938	10,113
2,076	2,387	2,564	2,792	2,982	3,414	3,805	4,076	4,376	4,919	5,101
1,797	1,791	2,010	2,184	2,179	2,178	2,217	2,521	2,575	2,845	2,903
3,293	3,404	3,629	3,785	3,955	4,320	4,677	4,917	5,117	5,595	5,755
376	549	538	559	591	675	694	787	799	902	927
1,192	1,296	1,378	1,316	1,326	1,411	1,483	1,570	1,578	1,711	1,747
82	77	91	110	160	285	489	800	1,202	1,998	2,335
431	443	465	492	533	607	738	921	1,109	1,236	1,300
2,537	3,156	4,041	4,160	4,835	6,067	7,168	7,365	7,748	8,414	8,699
327	360	423	532	681	951	1,016	1,303	1,515	1,819	1,903
9,114	10,385	12,588	13,479	14,830	16,782	18,237	17,558	17,991	18,976	19,227
2,206	2,559	3,170	3,572	4,062	4,556	5,082	5,882	6,632	8,049	8,541
577	647	681	642	620	632	618	653	639	642	634
4,767	5,759	6,647	6,908	7,947	9,706	10,652	10,798	10,847	11,353	11,459
1,657	2,028	2,396	2,336	2,233	2,328	2,559	3,025	3,146	3,451	3,524
673	783	954	1,090	1,521	1,769	2,091	2,633	2,842	3,421	3,595
7,665	8,720	9,631	9,900	10,498	11,319	11,794	11,864	11,883	12,281	12,406
543	604	687	713	792	859	947	947	1,003	1,048	1,081
1,515	1,684	1,739	1,900	2,117	2,383	2,591	3,122	3,486	4,012	4,198
584	637	693	643	653	681	666	691	696	755	771
2,185	2,338	2,617	2,916	3,292	3,567	3,924	4,591	4,877	5,689	5,901
3,897	4,663	5,825	6,415	7,711	9,580	11,197	14,229	16,986	20,852	22,490
373	449	508	550	689	891	1,059	1,461	1,723	2,233	2,389
356	352	360	359	378	390	444	511	563	609	621
2,062	2,309	2,422	2,678	3,319	3,967	4,648	5,347	6,189	7,079	7,460
1,142	1,357	1,563	1,736	2,379	2,853	3,409	4,132	4,867	5,894	6,204
1,221	1,464	1,729	1,902	2,006	1,860	1,744	1,950	1,793	1,808	1,815
2,334	2,632	2,939	3,138	3,435	3,952	4,418	4,706	4,892	5,364	5,509
146	194	226	251	291	330	332	470	454	494	507
91,972	105,711	122,775	131,669	150,697	179,323	203,302[2]	226,546[2]	248,791[2]	281,422	293,655

[2]Figures were revised by the Census Bureau after the census.

US Population by Race and Hispanic Origin

Census 2000 was the first US census in which individuals could report themselves as being of more than one race. For the comparison with the 1990 census results, this table uses the 2000 census information for the population indicating one race. Hispanic or Latino people may be of any race.

Source: US Census Bureau.

RACE	1990 CENSUS NUMBER	%	2000 CENSUS NUMBER	%	% INCREASE FROM 1990 TO 2000
White	199,686,070	80.3	211,460,626	75.1	+5.9
Black or African American	29,986,060	12.1	34,658,190	12.3	+15.6
American Indian or Alaska Native	1,959,234	0.8	2,475,956	0.9	+26.4
Asian	6,908,638	2.8	10,242,998	3.6	+48.3
Native Hawaiian/other Pacific Islander	365,024	0.1	398,835	0.1	+9.3
Some other race	9,804,847	3.9	15,359,073	5.5	+56.6
Two or more races	N/A[1]	N/A	6,826,228	2.4	N/A
Total population	**248,709,873**	**100.0**	**281,421,906**	**100.0[2]**	**+13.2**

HISPANIC OR LATINO POPULATION	1990 CENSUS NUMBER	%	2000 CENSUS NUMBER	%	% DIFFERENCE 1990/2000
Hispanic or Latino (of any race)	22,354,059	9.0	35,305,818	12.5	+57.9
Not Hispanic or Latino	226,355,814	91.0	246,116,088	87.5	+8.7
Total population	**248,709,873**	**100.0**	**281,421,906**	**100.0**	**+13.2**

[1]N/A: not available.   [2]Totals may not equal 100% due to rounding.

Foreign-Born Population in the US, 1850–2004

The foreign-born population consists of persons born outside the United States to parents who were not US citizens. Information from 1950 to 1990 was taken from sample data. Year 2000 information was an estimate derived before the decennial census was conducted. Populations of Alaska and Hawaii were included starting in 1960. In 1850 and 1860, information on nativity was not collected for slaves. The data in the table includes the slave population as part of the native-born population.

Source: US Census Bureau.

YEAR	POPULATION TOTAL	FOREIGN-BORN	% OF TOTAL	YEAR	POPULATION TOTAL	FOREIGN-BORN	% OF TOTAL
1850	23,191,876	2,244,602	9.7	1940	131,669,275	11,594,896	8.8
1860	31,443,321	4,138,697	13.2	1950	150,216,110	10,347,395	6.9
1870	38,558,371	5,567,229	14.4	1960	179,325,671	9,738,091	5.4
1880	50,155,783	6,679,943	13.3	1970	203,210,158	9,619,302	4.7
1890	62,622,250	9,249,547	14.8	1980	226,545,805	14,079,906	6.2
1900	75,994,575	10,341,276	13.6	1990	248,709,873	19,767,316	7.9
1910	91,972,266	13,515,886	14.7	2000	274,087,000	28,379,000	10.4
1920	105,710,620	13,920,692	13.2	2002	287,033,000	32,453,000	11.3
1930	122,775,046	14,204,149	11.6	2004	288,280,000	34,244,000	11.9

Total Immigrants Admitted to the US, 1901–2002

Numbers shown include only immigrant aliens admitted for permanent residence and are for fiscal years. Currently the fiscal year begins 1 October and ends 30 September. Prior to 1976, the fiscal year began 1 July and ended 30 June.

YEAR	NUMBER	YEAR	NUMBER	YEAR	NUMBER	YEAR	NUMBER
1901	487,918	1911	878,587	1921	805,228	1931	97,139
1902	648,743	1912	838,172	1922	309,556	1932	35,576
1903	857,046	1913	1,197,892	1923	522,919	1933	23,068
1904	812,870	1914	1,218,480	1924	706,896	1934	29,470
1905	1,026,499	1915	326,700	1925	294,314	1935	34,956
1906	1,100,735	1916	298,826	1926	304,488	1936	36,329
1907	1,285,349	1917	295,403	1927	335,175	1937	50,244
1908	782,870	1918	110,618	1928	307,255	1938	67,895
1909	751,786	1919	141,132	1929	279,678	1939	82,998
1910	1,041,570	1920	430,001	1930	241,700	1940	70,756
Totals 1901–10	8,795,386	1911–20	5,735,811	1921–30	4,107,209	1931–40	528,431

Total Immigrants Admitted to the US, 1901–2002 (continued)

YEAR	NUMBER	YEAR	NUMBER	YEAR	NUMBER	YEAR	NUMBER
1941	51,776	1951	205,717	1961	271,344	1971	370,478
1942	28,781	1952	265,520	1962	283,763	1972	384,685
1943	23,725	1953	170,434	1963	306,260	1973	400,063
1944	28,551	1954	208,177	1964	292,248	1974	394,861
1945	38,119	1955	237,790	1965	296,697	1975	386,194
1946	108,721	1956	321,625	1966	323,040	1976	398,613
1947	147,292	1957	326,867	1967	361,972	1976 (TQ)[1]	103,676
1948	170,570	1958	253,265	1968	454,448	1977	462,315
1949	188,317	1959	260,686	1969	358,579	1978	601,442
1950	249,187	1960	265,398	1970	373,326	1979	460,348
Totals 1941–50	**1,035,039**	**1951–60**	**2,515,479**	**1961–70**	**3,321,677**	1980	530,639
						1971–80	**4,493,314**

YEAR	NUMBER	YEAR	NUMBER	YEAR	NUMBER
1981	596,600	1991	1,827,167	2001	1,064,300
1982	594,131	1992	973,977	2002	1,063,732
1983	559,763	1993	904,292		
1984	543,903	1994	804,416		
1985	570,009	1995	720,461		
1986	601,708	1996	915,900		
1987	601,516	1997	798,378		
1988	643,025	1998	654,451		
1989	1,090,924	1999	646,568		
1990	1,536,483	2000	849,807		
Totals 1981–90	**7,338,062**	**1991–2000**	**9,095,417**	**2001–02**	**2,128,032**

Totals 1901–2002: 49,093,857

[1]*Transition quarter (TQ) to new fiscal year, 1 July through 30 September 1976.*

Immigrants Admitted to the US by Selected Country of Birth and State of Intended Residence

Fiscal Year 2003. Source: <www.uscis.gov>.

STATE OF INTENDED RESIDENCE	TOTAL IMMIGRANTS	TOP FIVE COUNTRIES OF BIRTH (NUMBER OF IMMIGRANTS)
Alabama	1,689	Mexico (250), India (114), China (113), Russia (87), Philippines (77)
Alaska	1,188	Philippines (405), Russia (92), Mexico (69), Korea (59), Canada (49)
Arizona	10,955	Mexico (5,722), Philippines (433), India (322), Canada (316), China (299)
Arkansas	1,903	Mexico (688), El Salvador (351), India (84), Vietnam (74), Philippines (72)
California	175,579	Mexico (51,269), Philippines (18,134), El Salvador (13,683), China (11,573), India (9,508)
Colorado	10,661	Mexico (3,275), China (632), India (468), Vietnam (418), Canada (362)
Connecticut	8,274	Jamaica (740), India (722), Poland (561), China (403), Colombia (399)
Delaware	1,487	India (244), Korea (101), Mexico (101), China (99), Haiti (99)
District of Columbia	2,491	El Salvador (416), Philippines (215), Ethiopia (185), China (132), Nigeria (101)
Florida	52,770	Cuba (6,303), Haiti (5,472), Colombia (4,983), Jamaica (3,842), Peru (2,290)
Georgia	10,794	Mexico (1,482), India (1,023), Vietnam (447), Nigeria (426), China (387), Ethiopia (387)
Hawaii	4,899	Philippines (3,050), China (397), Japan (380), Vietnam (175), Korea (111)
Idaho	1,686	Mexico (586), Bosnia and Herzegovina (145), China (107), Canada (91), Philippines (56)
Illinois	32,413	Mexico (6,044), India (4,536), Poland (4,117), Philippines (2,116), China (1,609)
Indiana	5,241	Mexico (901), India (437), China (346), Russia (252), Philippines (230)
Iowa	3,419	Mexico (693), Bosnia and Herzegovina (429), China (307), India (215), Vietnam (190)
Kansas	3,804	Mexico (883), India (415), Vietnam (240), China (212), Kenya (155)
Kentucky	3,038	Cuba (331), India (248), Mexico (232), China (194), Bosnia and Herzegovina (191)
Louisiana	2,214	Vietnam (225), India (171), Honduras (153), Mexico (133), China (118)
Maine	992	Canada (128), China (95), Philippines (84), United Kingdom (58), Vietnam (37)

Immigrants Admitted to the US by Selected Country of Birth and State of Intended Residence (continued)

STATE OF INTENDED RESIDENCE	TOTAL IMMIGRANTS	TOP FIVE COUNTRIES OF BIRTH (NUMBER OF IMMIGRANTS)
Maryland	17,770	El Salvador (1,440), India (1,339), Philippines (1,284), Nigeria (1,118), China (1,071)
Massachusetts	20,127	Dominican Republic (1,958), China (1,718), India (1,463), Haiti (1,211), Brazil (1,025)
Michigan	13,515	India (1,864), Iraq (809), China (762), Mexico (625), Lebanon (585)
Minnesota	8,406	Somalia (786), India (651), Ethiopia (627), Philippines (419), Mexico (398)
Mississippi	729	Mexico (77), India (74), Vietnam (57), Philippines (49), Russia (48)
Missouri	6,160	Bosnia and Herzegovina (661), India (449), Mexico (439), China (379), Russia (269)
Montana	453	Canada (104), Philippines (30), China (28), Russia (27), United Kingdom (26)
Nebraska	2,827	Mexico (882), Vietnam (212), Guatemala (171), India (119), China (108)
Nevada	6,336	Mexico (1,730), Philippines (1,159), El Salvador (420), Cuba (263), China (232)
New Hampshire	1,868	India (206), China (174), Bosnia and Herzegovina (131), Canada (122), Philippines (101)
New Jersey	40,699	India (7,442), Dominican Republic (3,956), Philippines (2,639), Colombia (1,922), China (1,688)
New Mexico	2,336	Mexico (1,256), Vietnam (84), India (77), Philippines (65), Cuba (61)
New York	89,538	Dominican Republic (13,335), China (8,356), Jamaica (4,840), Guyana (4,693), India (4,138)
North Carolina	9,451	Mexico (1,175), India (868), China (749), Philippines (419), Canada (381)
North Dakota	331	Canada (46), Bosnia and Herzegovina (40), Sudan (28), Germany (14), India (14), Philippines (14)
Ohio	9,787	India (1,743), China (767), Somalia (448), Philippines (417), Russia (371)
Oklahoma	2,385	Mexico (543), Vietnam (191), India (175), Philippines (107), China (91)
Oregon	6,946	Mexico (1,487), China (503), Ukraine (478), Vietnam (430), India (336)
Pennsylvania	14,606	India (1,964), China (1,314), Vietnam (567), Dominican Republic (551), Russia (550)
Rhode Island	2,492	Dominican Republic (621), Guatemala (233), Colombia (160), Cape Verde (135), China (94)
South Carolina	1,942	Philippines (209), India (198), Mexico (186), Russia (130), China (105)
South Dakota	487	Ethiopia (45), Bosnia and Herzegovina (43), Ukraine (39), Mexico (33), Sudan (30)
Tennessee	3,367	India (308), Mexico (281), Philippines (221), China (203), Russia (151)
Texas	53, 412	Mexico (25,342), India (2,770), El Salvador (2,369), Vietnam (2,201), Philippines (1,995)
Utah	3,159	Mexico (755), China (166), Vietnam (129), Canada (121), Peru (115)
Vermont	550	Canada (56), Bosnia and Herzegovina (45), China (38), India (30), Russia (24)
Virginia	19,726	India (2,036), El Salvador (1,581), Philippines (1,154), China (1,000), Pakistan (824)
Washington	17,935	Mexico (1,965), Ukraine (1,680), Philippines (1,626), India (1,231), Vietnam (1,076)
West Virginia	483	India (87), China (32), Philippines (32), Russia (28), United Kingdom (18)
Wisconsin	4,357	Mexico (603), India (453), China (345), Russia (237), Philippines (228)
Wyoming	253	Mexico (75), China (21), Russia (20), Philippines (17), Canada (15)

Americans 65 and Older, 1900–2004

Data for Hawaii and Alaska are included after 1950. Source: US Census Bureau.

CENSUS YEAR	NUMBER OF PEOPLE 65 AND OLDER	% OF TOTAL POPULATION	CENSUS YEAR	NUMBER OF PEOPLE 65 AND OLDER	% OF TOTAL POPULATION
1900	3,080,498	4.1	1960	16,559,580	9.2
1910	3,949,524	4.3	1970	20,065,502	9.8
1920	4,933,215	4.7	1980	25,549,427	11.3
1930	6,633,805	5.4	1990	31,241,831	12.6
1940	9,019,314	6.8	2000	34,991,753	12.4
1950	12,269,537	8.1	2004	36,293,985	12.4

Poverty Level by State

Source: US Census Bureau. Totals may vary due to rounding.

STATE	% OF PEOPLE IN POVERTY			NUMBER OF PEOPLE IN POVERTY ('000)		
	1980	1990	2003	1980	1990	2003
Alabama	21.2	19.2	15.0	810	779	663
Alaska	9.6	11.4	9.6	36	57	62
Arizona	12.8	13.7	13.5	354	484	749
Arkansas	21.5	19.6	17.8	484	472	474
California	11	13.9	13.1	2,619	4,128	4,634
Colorado	8.6	13.7	9.7	247	461	436
Connecticut	8.3	6	8.1	255	196	278
Delaware	11.8	6.9	7.3	68	48	60
District of Columbia	20.9	21.1	16.8	131	120	92
Florida	16.7	14.4	12.7	1,692	1,896	2,148
Georgia	13.9	15.8	11.9	727	1,001	1,014
Hawaii	8.5	11	9.3	81	121	117
Idaho	14.7	14.9	10.2	138	157	138
Illinois	12.3	13.7	12.6	1,386	1,606	1,592
Indiana	11.8	13	9.9	645	714	610
Iowa	10.8	10.4	8.9	311	289	260
Kansas	9.4	10.3	10.8	215	259	288
Kentucky	19.3	17.3	14.4	701	628	589
Louisiana	20.3	23.6	17.0	868	952	750
Maine	14.6	13.1	11.6	158	162	149
Maryland	9.5	9.9	8.6	389	468	472
Massachusetts	9.5	10.7	10.3	542	626	652
Michigan	12.9	14.3	11.4	1,194	1,315	1,125
Minnesota	8.7	12	7.4	342	524	376
Mississippi	24.3	25.7	16.0	591	684	456
Missouri	13	13.4	10.7	625	700	602
Montana	13.2	16.3	15.1	102	134	139
Nebraska	13	10.3	9.8	199	167	168
Nevada	8.3	9.8	10.9	70	119	244
New Hampshire	7	6.3	5.8	63	68	73
New Jersey	9	9.2	8.6	659	711	741
New Mexico	20.6	20.9	18.1	268	319	338
New York	13.8	14.3	14.3	2,391	2,571	2,707
North Carolina	15	13	15.7	877	829	1,289
North Dakota	15.5	13.7	9.7	99	87	61
Ohio	9.8	11.5	10.9	1,046	1,256	1,226
Oklahoma	13.9	15.6	12.8	406	481	440
Oregon	11.5	9.2	12.5	309	267	446
Pennsylvania	9.8	11	10.5	1,142	1,328	1,279
Rhode Island	10.7	7.5	11.5	97	71	121
South Carolina	16.8	16.2	12.7	534	548	516
South Dakota	18.8	13.3	12.7	127	93	95
Tennessee	19.6	16.9	14.0	884	833	829
Texas	15.7	15.9	17.0	2,247	2,684	3,705
Utah	10	8.2	9.1	148	143	213
Vermont	12	10.9	8.5	62	61	52
Virginia	12.4	11.1	10.0	647	705	740
Washington	12.7	8.9	12.6	538	434	766
West Virginia	15.2	18.1	17.4	297	328	310
Wisconsin	8.5	9.3	9.8	403	448	528
Wyoming	10.4	11	9.8	49	51	48
All US	13.0	13.5	11.9	29,272	33,585	35,860

Population of US Territories

Total midyear population. Source: US Census Bureau.

YEAR	PUERTO RICO	GUAM	VIRGIN ISLANDS	AMERICAN SAMOA	NORTHERN MARIANA ISLANDS
1970	2,721,754	86,470	63,476	27,267	12,359
1975	2,935,124	102,110	94,484	29,640	14,938
1980	3,209,648	106,869	99,636	32,418	16,890
1985	3,382,106	120,615	100,760	38,633	21,386
1990	3,536,910	134,110	104,235	47,199	44,037
1995	3,731,006	143,856	113,896	56,911	58,128
2000	3,915,798	154,623	120,917	65,446	71,912
2004	3,895,000	166,090	108,775	57,902	78,252

States and Other Areas of the United States

Alabama

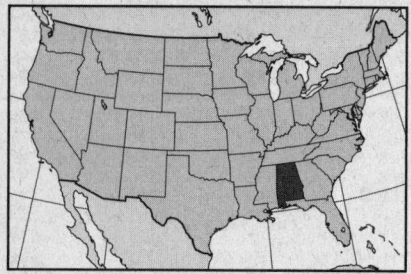

Name: Alabama, from the Choctaw language, meaning "thicket clearers." **Nickname:** Heart of Dixie. **Capital:** Montgomery. **Rank:** population: 23rd; area: 28th; pop. density: 26th. **Motto:** *Audemus Jura Nostra Defendere* (We Dare Defend Our Rights). **Song:** "Alabama," words by Julia S. Tutwiler and music by Edna Gockel Gussen. **Amphibian:** Red Hills salamander. **Bird:** yellowhammer. **Fish:** largemouth bass (freshwater); tarpon (saltwater). **Flower:** camellia. **Fossil:** *Basilosaurus cetoides.* **Gemstone:** star blue quartz. **Insect:** monarch butterfly. **Mineral:** hematite. **Reptile:** Alabama red-bellied turtle. **Rock:** marble. **Tree:** southern longleaf pine.

Natural features

Area: 52,419 sq mi, 135,765 sq km. **Mountain ranges:** Appalachians, Raccoon, Lookout. **Highest point:** Cheaha Mountain, 2,407 ft (734 m). **Largest lake:** Lake Guntersville. **Major rivers:** Mobile, Alabama, Tombigbee, Tennessee, Chattahoochee, Conecuh, Pea, Tensaw, Tallapoosa. **Natural regions:** the Appalachian Plateaus, extending across the north central region; interior low plateaus, far north; valley and ridge province and small portion of the Piedmont Province, covering the east; coastal plain, covering the southern half of the state. **Location:** South, bordering Tennessee, Georgia, Florida, Mississippi. **Climate:** temperate, with mild winters and hot, humid summers; temperatures mellowed by altitude in the northern counties and relatively higher in the southern counties; summer heat is often alleviated by winds blowing in from the Gulf of Mexico. **Land use:** forested, 67.5%; agricultural, 13.8%; pasture, 5.7%; other, 13.0%.

People

Population (2003): 4,501,000; 88.7 persons per sq mi (34.2 persons per sq km) (land area only). **Vital statistics** (2001; per 1,000 population): birth rate, 13.7; death rate, 10.1; marriage rate, 9.6; divorce rate, 5.3. **Major cities:** Birmingham, 239,000; Montgomery, 201,000; Mobile, 195,000; Huntsville, 163,000.

Government

Statehood: entered the Union on 14 Dec 1819 as the 22nd state. **State constitution:** adopted 1901. **Representation in US Congress:** 2 senators; 7 representatives. **Electoral college:** 9 votes (in the 2004 general elections based on the 2000 census). **Political divisions:** 67 counties.

Economy

Employment: services, 25.2%; trade, 21.6%; manufacturing, 16.9%; government, 16.4%; construction, 6.2%; finance, insurance, real estate, 4.9%; transportation, public utilities, 4.6%; agriculture, forestry, fishing, 3.5%; mining, 0.5%. **Production:** manufacturing, 19.0%; services, 16.9%; trade, 16.9%; government, 15.8%; finance, insurance, real estate, 14.7%; transportation, utilities, 8.7%; construction, 4.7%; agriculture, forestry, fisheries, 2.0%; mining, 1.3%. **Chief agricultural products:** *Crops:* cotton, corn, soybeans, peanuts (groundnuts), potatoes, sweet potatoes, peaches, pecans, fruits and vegetables, winter wheat, hay, honey. *Livestock:* cattle, poultry, hogs. *Fish catch:* marine fish, including red snapper; freshwater fish, including catfish; marine crustaceans, including shrimp, crab; marine mollusks, including mussels, oysters. **Chief manufactured products:** food products, meat products, poultry processing, textiles, apparel, wood products, mobile homes, paper and paperboard, petroleum products, plastics and rubber products, iron and steel, aluminum products, semiconductors, electronic components, motor vehicle parts.

Internet resources: <www.touralabama.org>; <www.alabama.gov>.

Alaska

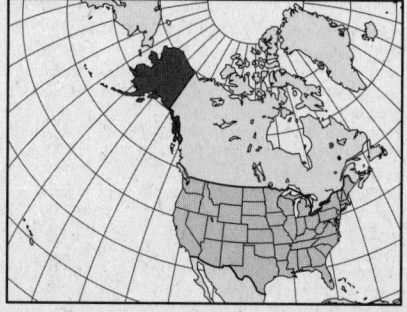

Name: Alaska, from the Aleut word *Alyeska,* meaning "great land." **Nickname:** The Last Frontier. **Capital:** Juneau. **Rank:** population: 47th; area: 1st; pop. density: 50th. **Motto:** North to the Future. **Song:** "Alaska's Flag," words by Marie Drake and music by Elinor Dusenbury. **Bird:** willow ptarmigan. **Fish:** giant king salmon. **Flower:** forget-me-not. **Fossil:** *Mammuthus primigenius* (woolly mammoth). **Gemstone:** jade. **Insect:** four spot skimmer dragonfly. **Mammal:** moose. **Marine mammal:** bowhead whale. **Mineral:** gold. **Tree:** sitka spruce.

Natural features

Area: 663,267 sq mi, 1,717,854 sq km. **Mountain ranges:** Wrangell, Chugach, Alaska, Brooks, Aleutian,

Boundary. **Highest point:** Mount McKinley (Denali), 20,320 ft (6,194 m). **Largest lake:** Iliamna. **Major rivers:** Yukon, Porcupine, Tanana, Koyukuk, Noatak, Kuskokwim, Susitna, Copper. **Natural regions:** panhandle, a narrow strip of land that includes portions of the Coast Mountains; coastal archipelago and the Gulf of Alaska islands; the Alaska Peninsula and Aleutian island chain that separates the North Pacific from the Bering Sea; the Alaska Range, extending across the south-central region; the Interior Plateau, including the basin of the Yukon River, and the central plains and tablelands of the interior, the Seward Peninsula to the west, and the Brooks Range, sometimes called the North Slope, to the north; the Arctic Coastal Plain, a treeless region of tundra lying at the northernmost edge of the state; tundra-covered islands of the Bering Sea. **Location:** bordered by Canada. **Climate:** temperate with much regional variation in temperature and precipitation; *southern coastal and southeastern region, Gulf of Alaska and Aleutian islands:* cool summers and moderate winters, with high precipitation; *interior basin:* moderate summers and very cold winters, with low to moderate precipitation; *islands and coast of the Bering Sea:* cool summers and very cold winters; *central plains and uplands:* moderate summers and frigid winters; *North Slope:* moderate summers and frigid winters, though not as severe as interior regions. **Land use:** forested, 24.1 (24)%; pasture, 0.0%; other, 75.6 (76)%.

People

Population (2003): 649,000; 1.1 persons per sq mi (0.4 person per sq km) (land area only). **Vital statistics** (2001; per 1,000 population): birth rate, 16.0; death rate, 4.7; marriage rate, 8.2; divorce rate, 4.1. **Major cities:** Anchorage, 269,000; Juneau (metropolitan area; 2001 est.), 30,558; College, 11,402 (2000); Sitka, 8,716 (2001 est.).

Government

Statehood: entered the Union on 3 Jan 1959 as the 49th state. **State constitution:** adopted 1956. **Representation in US Congress:** 2 senators; 1 representative. **Electoral college:** 3 votes. **Political divisions:** 16 boroughs.

Economy

Employment: services, 26.9%; government, 24.4%; trade, 18.7%; transportation, public utilities, 7.7%; finance, insurance, real estate, 5.3%; construction, 5.1%; manufacturing, 4.8%; agriculture, forestry, fishing, 4.1%; mining, 3.0%. **Production:** mining, 20.1%; government, 19.4%; transportation, utilities, 16.7%; services, 13.0%; trade, 10.1%; finance, insurance, real estate, 10.1%; construction, 4.6%; manufacturing, 4.2%; agriculture, forestry, fishing, 1.7%. **Chief agricultural products:** *Crops:* hay, milk, potatoes, timber. *Livestock:* cattle, pigs. *Fish catch:* marine fish, salmon, herring, groundfish, shellfish, crab, shrimp. **Chief manufactured products:** processed fish and seafood (fresh, frozen, canned, and cured), lumber and wood products, paper products, transportation products.

Internet resources: <www.travelalaska.com>; <www.alaska.gov>.

Arizona

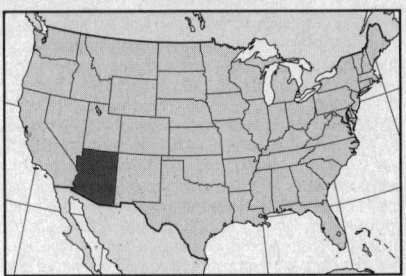

Name: Arizona, from *arizonac,* derived from two Papago Indian words meaning "place of the young spring." **Nickname:** Grand Canyon State. **Capital:** Phoenix. **Rank:** population: 18th; area: 6th; pop. density: 36th. **Motto:** *Ditat Deus* (God Enriches). **Song:** "Arizona March Song," words by Margaret Rowe Clifford and music by Maurice Blumenthal. **Amphibian:** Arizona treefrog. **Bird:** cactus wren. **Fish:** Arizona trout. **Flower:** saguaro blossom. **Fossil:** petrified wood. **Gemstone:** turquoise. **Mammal:** ringtail. **Reptile:** Arizona ridgenose rattlesnake. **Tree:** palo verde.

Natural features

Area: 113,998 sq mi, 295,254 sq km. **Mountain ranges:** Black, Gila Bend, Chuska, Hualapai, San Francisco, White. **Highest point:** Humphreys Peak, 12,633 ft (3,851 m). **Largest lake:** Lake Roosevelt. **Major rivers:** Colorado, Little Colorado, Verde, Salt, Gila. **Natural regions:** the Colorado Plateaus, northeast third of the state, include Grand Canyon and Painted Desert; the basin and range province, south, east, central, and northwest, includes Sonoran Desert in the southwest corner and part of the Great Basin Desert to the northwest. **Location:** Southwest, bordering Utah, Colorado, New Mexico, California, and Nevada; international border with Mexico. **Climate:** varies with location; half of Arizona is semiarid, one-third is arid, and the remainder is humid; *basin and range region:* arid and semiarid to subtropical climate; *Colorado Plateaus:* cool to cold winters and a semiarid climate; *Transition Zone:* climate ranges widely, from arid to humid. **Land use:** pasture, 55.7%; forested, 22.4%; agricultural, 1.7%; other, 20.2%.

People

Population (2003): 5,581,000; 49.1 persons per sq mi (19.0 persons per sq km) (land area only). **Vital statistics** (2001; per 1,000 population): birth rate, 17.1; death rate, 7.7; marriage rate, 8.0; divorce rate, 4.2. **Major cities:** Phoenix, 1,372,000; Tucson, 503,000; Mesa, 427,000; Glendale, 231,000; Scottsdale, 216,000; Chandler, 202,000; Tempe, 160,000.

Government

Statehood: entered the Union on 14 Feb 1912 as the 48th state. **State constitution:** adopted 1911. **Representation in US Congress:** 2 senators; 6 representatives. **Electoral college:** 10 votes (in the 2004 general elections based on the 2000 census). **Political divisions:** 15 counties.

Economy

Employment: services, 32.5%; trade, 22.7%; government, 13.4%; manufacturing, 8.8%; finance, insurance, real estate, 8.3%; construction, 6.6%; transportation, public utilities, 4.5%; agriculture, forestry, fishing, 2.6%; mining, 0.6%. **Production:** services, 22.0%; finance, insurance, real estate, 18.7%; trade, 17.4%; manufacturing, 14.4%; government, 12.1%; transportation, public utilities, 7.3%; construction, 5.8%; agriculture, forestry, fishing, 1.5%; mining, 0.8%. **Chief agricultural products:** *Crops:* cotton and cottonseed, wheat, sorghum, hay, barley, corn (maize), potatoes, grapes, apples, vegetables and melons, dairy products, lettuce. *Livestock:* cattle and calves, hogs and pigs, sheep and lambs, angora goats. **Chief manufactured products:** semiconductors, communications equipment, electric and electronic equipment, transportation equipment, soap products, nonferrous metal products.

Internet resources: <www.arizonaguide.com>; <www.az.gov>.

 **Did you know?** Thought extinct since the 1940s, the ivory-billed woodpecker was spotted in Arkansas in early 2004 and confirmed alive in 2005.

Arkansas

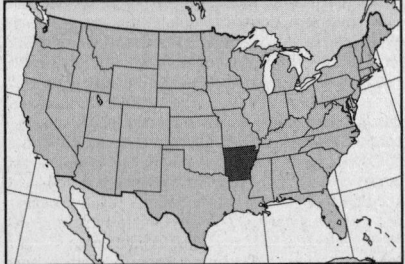

Name: Arkansas, from an unknown Native American word describing the Quapaw tribe (also known as the Arkansaw), meaning "people who live downstream." **Nickname:** The Natural State. **Capital:** Little Rock. **Rank:** population: 32nd; area: 27th; pop. density: 34th. **Motto:** *Regnat Populus* (The People Rule). **Song:** "Arkansas," words and music by Eva Ware Barnett. **Bird:** mockingbird. **Flower:** apple blossom. **Gemstone:** diamond. **Insect:** honeybee. **Mammal:** white-tailed deer. **Mineral:** quartz crystal. **Rock:** bauxite. **Tree:** pine tree.

Natural features

Area: 53,179 sq mi, 137,732 sq km. **Mountain ranges:** Ozark, Ouachita. **Highest point:** Mount Magazine, 2,753 ft (839 m). **Largest lake:** Lake Chicot. **Major rivers:** Arkansas, Red, Ouachita, White. **Natural regions:** the Ozark Plateaus, including the Boston Mountains, north and northwest regions; the Ouachita Province, including the Arkansas valley and the

Ouachita Mountains, central region; Coastal Plain, extends from southwest to northeast. **Location:** South, bordering Missouri, Tennessee, Mississippi, Louisiana, Texas, and Oklahoma. **Climate:** temperate, with mild winters and hot summers. **Land use:** forested, 55.2%; agricultural, 30.3%; pasture, 6.0%; other, 8.5%.

People

Population (2003): 2,726,000; 52.4 persons per sq mi (20.2 persons per sq km) (land area only). **Vital statistics** (2001; per 1,000 population): birth rate, 14.3; death rate, 10.3; marriage rate, 14.8; divorce rate, 6.6. **Major cities** (2000): Little Rock, 184,000 (2002); Fort Smith, 80,268; North Little Rock, 60,433; Fayetteville, 58,047; Jonesboro, 55,515.

Government

Statehood: entered the Union on 15 Jun 1836 as the 25th state. **State constitution:** adopted 1874. **Representation in US Congress:** 2 senators; 4 representatives. **Electoral college:** 6 votes (in the 2004 general elections based on the 2000 census). **Political divisions:** 75 counties.

Economy

Employment: services, 24.4%; trade, 21.3%; manufacturing, 18.3%; government, 13.9%; agriculture, forestry, fishing, 6.6%; construction, 5.8%; transportation, public utilities, 5.5%; finance, insurance, real estate, 4.8%; mining, 0.4%. **Production:** manufacturing, 22.5%; trade, 18.4%; services, 15.6%; government, 12.3%; finance, insurance, real estate, 11.6%; transportation, public utilities, 10.5%; construction, 4.6%; agriculture, forestry, fisheries, 3.7%; mining, 0.8%. **Chief agricultural products:** *Crops:* corn (maize), cotton, hay, rice, sorghum, soybeans, wheat, apples, blueberries, grapes, peaches, pecans, strawberries, tomatoes, watermelon. *Livestock:* cattle and calves, hogs and pigs, poultry. *Aquaculture:* catfish. **Chief manufactured products:** food products, meatpacking, poultry processing, lumber, paper and paper products, refined petroleum, chemical products, plastic and rubber products, iron and steel manufacturing, fabricated metal products, machinery, transportation products.

Internet resources: <www.arkansas.com>; <www.arkansas.gov>.

California

Nickname: Golden State. **Capital:** Sacramento. **Rank:** population: 1st; area: 3rd; pop. density: 12th. **Motto:** *Eureka* (I Have Found It). **Song:** "I Love You, California," words by F.B. Silverwood and music by A.F. Frankenstein. **Bird:** California quail. **Fish:** golden trout (freshwater); garibaldi (saltwater). **Flower:** California poppy. **Fossil:** saber-tooth cat. **Gemstone:** benitoite. **Insect:** California dogface butterfly. **Mammal:** California grizzly bear. **Marine mammal:** California gray whale. **Mineral:** gold. **Reptile:** desert tortoise. **Rock:** serpentine. **Tree:** California redwood.

For details about state governments, see pages 800–805; for energy data, see pages 830–832.

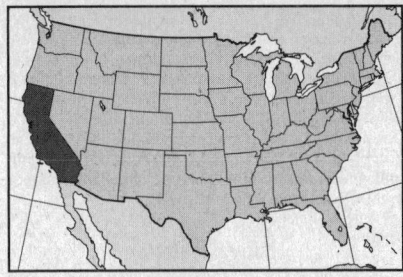

Natural features

Area: 163,696 sq mi, 423,970 sq km. **Mountain ranges:** Coast Range, Sierra Nevada, Santa Lucia, Cascade Range, Klamath Mountains, Tehachapi Mountains, San Gabriel Mountains, San Bernardino Mountains. **Highest point:** Mount Whitney, 14,494 ft (4,417 m). **Largest lake:** Lake Tahoe. **Major rivers:** Colorado, Sacramento, Pit, San Joaquin. **Natural regions:** Basin and Range Province, northeast corner, also eastern border with Arizona and southern Nevada; Cascade-Sierra Mountains, running from north to south along the east-central region; Pacific Border Province, west, including the Coast Ranges to the west, the Klamath Mountains to the north, the Los Angeles Ranges to the south, and the California Trough (commonly referred to as the Central Valley) to the east; Lower Californian Province, southwest tip. **Location:** West, bordering Oregon, Nevada, and Arizona; international border with Mexico. **Climate:** Mediterranean climate, with moderate temperatures, warm, dry summers, and cool, rainy winters. **Land use:** forested, 32.6%; pasture, 22.4%; agricultural, 10.6%; other, 34.4%.

People

Population (2003): 35,484,000; 227.5 persons per sq mi (87.8 persons per sq km) (land area only). **Vital statistics** (2001; per 1,000 population): birth rate, 15.5; death rate, 6.8; marriage rate, 6.6; divorce rate, 6.6. **Major cities:** Los Angeles, 3,799,000; San Diego, 1,260,000; San Jose, 900,000; San Francisco, 764,000; Long Beach, 472,000; Fresno, 445,000; Sacramento, 435,000; Oakland, 403,000.

Government

Statehood: entered the Union on 9 Sep 1850 as the 31st state. **State constitution:** adopted 1879. **Representation in US Congress:** 2 senators; 52 representatives. **Electoral college:** 55 votes (in the 2004 general elections based on the 2000 census). **Political divisions:** 58 counties.

Economy

Employment: services, 33.8%; trade, 20.7%; government, 13.3%; manufacturing, 11.2%; finance, insurance, real estate, 8.0%; construction, 4.6%; transportation, public utilities, 4.5%; agriculture, forestry, fishing, 3.7%; mining, 0.2%. **Production:** services, 23.4%; finance, insurance, real estate, 21.7%; trade, 15.9%; manufacturing, 14.6%; government, 10.7%; transportation, utilities, 7.3%; construction, 3.8%; agriculture, forestry, fishing, 1.9%; mining, 0.6%. **Chief agricultural products:** *Crops:* wheat, oats, rice, grains, apples, apricots, cherries, grapes, olives, peaches, pears, citrus fruits, strawberries, onions, lima beans, artichokes, broccoli, snap beans, vegetables, dairy products, eggs. *Livestock:* cattle and calves, sheep and lambs. *Fish catch:* bonito, halibut, mackerel, groundfish, rockfish (commonly called Pacific red snapper), sablefish (also called black cod), soles and sanddabs, sardines, white seabass, shark, swordfish, tuna, crab, California spiny lobster, Pacific Ocean (pink) shrimp, prawns, squid. *Extractive products:* timber. **Chief manufactured products:** food products, meat and poultry processing, soft drink products, beer and wine, textiles, apparel, lumber and wood products, paper and paper products, printing, refined petroleum, asphalt, chemical products, pharmaceuticals, plastic and rubber products, glass and glass products, construction materials, steel products, metal products, machinery, communications equipment, semiconductors and computers, electronics, transportation equipment, furniture, medical equipment, sporting goods.

Internet resources: <www.gocalif.com>; <www.ca.gov>.

Colorado

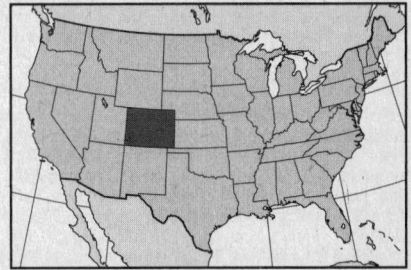

Name: Colorado, from a Spanish word meaning "red." **Nickname:** Centennial State. **Capital:** Denver. **Rank:** population: 22nd; area: 8th; pop. density: 37th. **Motto:** *Nil Sine Numine* (Nothing Without Providence). **Song:** "Where the Columbines Grow," words and music by A.J. Flynn. **Bird:** lark bunting. **Fish:** greenback cutthroat trout. **Flower:** white and lavender columbine. **Fossil:** stegosaurus. **Gemstone:** aquamarine. **Insect:** Colorado hairstreak butterfly. **Mammal:** Rocky Mountain bighorn sheep. **Tree:** Colorado blue spruce.

Natural features

Area: 104,094 sq mi, 269,601 sq km. **Mountain ranges:** Rocky Mountains, Front, Medicine Bow, Park, Rabbit Ears, San Juan Mountains, Sangre de Cristo Range, Sawatch. **Highest point:** Mount Elbert, 14,433 ft (4,399 m). **Largest lakes:** Blue Mesa Reservoir (man-made); Grand Lake (natural). **Major rivers:** Colorado, Arkansas, South Platte, Rio Grande. **Natural regions:** the Great Plains Province, eastern half of state, includes the High Plains to the east, Colorado Piedmont to the west, and Raton Section to the south; Southern Rocky Mountains, running down the middle of the state; Middle Rocky Mountains and Wyoming Basin, northwest corner; Colorado Plateaus, western and southwestern border, include the Uinta Basin to the north, the Canyon Lands in the middle, and the Navajo Section to the south. **Location:** West, bordering Wyoming, Nebraska, Kansas, Oklahoma, New Mexico, and Utah. **Climate:** *Eastern* *plains:* with hot summers and dry, cold, windy, and generally harsh winters; *piedmont:* similar to eastern plains, also experiences the Chinook wind, a dry, descending winter airstream from the high mountains that is warmed by compression as it descends; *mountains and high plateaus:* cool summers, cold winters and much increased precipitation; snow may fall during any month of the year, with amounts ranging from about 20 to 50 inches. **Land use:** pasture, 42.0%; forest, 28.3%; agricultural, 17.2%; other, 12.5%.

People

Population (2003): 4,551,000; 43.9 persons per sq mi (16.9 persons per sq km) (land area only). **Vital statistics** (2001; per 1,000 population): birth rate, 15.9; death rate, 6.4; marriage rate, 8.7; divorce rate, N/A. **Major cities:** Denver, 560,000; Colorado Springs, 371,000; Aurora, 286,000; Lakewood, 144,000; Fort Collins, 125,000.

Government

Statehood: entered the Union on 1 Aug 1876 as the 38th state. **State constitution:** adopted 1876. **Representation in US Congress:** 2 senators; 6 representatives. **Electoral college:** 9 votes (in the 2004 general elections based on the 2000 census). **Political divisions:** 63 counties.

Economy

Employment: services, 32.3%; trade, 22.0%; government, 13.5%; finance, insurance, real estate, 8.4%; manufacturing, 8.2%; construction, 6.5%; transportation, public utilities, 5.4%; agriculture, forestry, fishing, 2.8%; mining, 0.9%. **Production:** services, 23.1%; finance, insurance, real estate, 17.5%; trade, 16.1%; transportation, utilities, 12.2%; government, 11.9%; manufacturing, 10.2%; construction, 6.0%; mining, 1.6%; agriculture, 1.5%. **Chief agricultural products:** *Crops:* millet, corn (maize), hay, potatoes, onions, sugar beets, sunflowers, wheat, dairy products, eggs, greenhouse products. *Livestock:* cattle and calves, hogs and pigs, sheep and lambs. **Chief manufactured products:** meat products, beverages, printing, semiconductors, computer and electronic products.

Internet resources: <www.colorado.com>; <www.colorado.gov>.

Connecticut

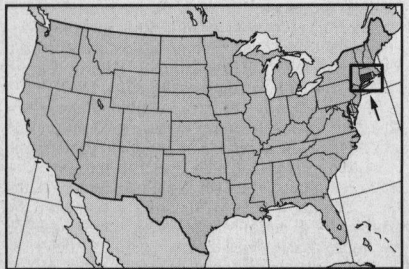

Name: Connecticut, from the Mohegan word *Quinnehtukqut,* meaning "long river place" or "beside the long tidal river." **Nickname:** Constitution State. **Capital:** Hartford. **Rank:** population: 29th; area: 48th; pop. density: 4th. **Motto:** *Qui Transtulit Sustinet* (He Who Transplanted Still Sustains). **Song:** "Yankee Doodle," words from folk tradition, melody from an English tune, "The World Turned Upside Down." **Bird:** robin. **Flower:** mountain laurel. **Fossil:** *Eubrontes giganteus.* **Insect:** praying mantis. **Mammal:** sperm whale. **Mineral:** garnet. **Shellfish:** eastern oyster. **Tree:** white oak.

Natural features

Area: 5,543 sq mi, 14,357 sq km. **Mountain range:** Berkshire Hills. **Highest point:** Mount Frissell, 2,380 ft (725 m). **Largest lake:** Candlewood Lake. **Major rivers:** Connecticut, Housatonic, Thames. **Natural regions:** the New England Province covers the state, divided into the Western Upland, Central Lowland (Connecticut Valley), and Eastern Upland. **Location:** New England, bordering Massachusetts, Rhode Island, and New York. **Climate:** moderate temperate climate; coastal portions have somewhat warmer winters and cooler summers than does the interior; northwestern uplands have cooler and longer winters with heavier falls of snow; occasional hurricanes cause flooding and damage, particularly along the coastline. **Land use:** forest, 54.2%; agricultural, 5.4%; pasture, 1.0%; other, 39.4%.

People

Population (2003): 3,483,000; 718.9 persons per sq mi (277.6 persons per sq km) (land area only). **Vital statistics** (2001; per 1,000 population): birth rate, 12.9; death rate, 8.7; marriage rate, 5.6; divorce rate, 2.9. **Major cities:** Bridgeport, 140,000; Hartford, 125,000; New Haven, 124,000; Stamford, 120,000.

Government

Statehood: entered the Union on 9 Jan 1788 as the 5th state. **State constitution:** adopted 1965. **Representation in US Congress:** 2 senators; 6 representatives. **Electoral college:** 7 votes (in the 2004 general elections based on the 2000 census). **Political divisions:** 8 counties.

Economy

Employment: services, 34.3%; trade, 20.2%; manufacturing, 14.0%; government, 11.2%; finance, insurance, real estate, 9.5%; construction, 4.8%; transportation, public utilities, 4.2%; agriculture, forestry, fishing, 1.5%; mining, 0.1%. **Production:** finance, insurance, real estate, 28.7%; services, 22.0%; manufacturing, 16.5%; trade, 14.5%; government, 8.3%; transportation, utilities, 5.9%; construction, 3.3%; agriculture, 0.7%; mining, 0.1%. **Chief agricultural products:** *Crops:* corn (maize), silage, hay, tobacco, apples, pears, dairy products, eggs. *Livestock:* poultry, cattle, sheep, horses. *Fish catch:* lobster, clams, oysters, shad, marine fish. **Chief manufactured products:** printing, pharmaceutical products, soap and cleaning products, plastics, metal products, machinery, communications equipment, electronics, aerospace products, aircraft engines.

Internet resources: <www.ctbound.org>; <www.ct.gov>.

For details about state governments, see pages 800–805; for energy data, see pages 830–832.

Delaware

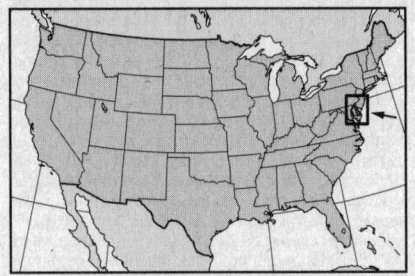

Name: Delaware, from Delaware River and Bay; named in turn for Sir Thomas West, Baron De La Warr. **Nickname:** First State. **Capital:** Dover. **Rank:** population: 45th; area: 49th; pop. density: 6th. **Motto:** Liberty and Independence. **Song:** "Our Delaware," words by George B. Hynson and music by Will M.S. Brown. **Bird:** Blue Hen Chicken. **Fish:** weakfish. **Flower:** peach blossom. **Insect:** ladybug. **Mineral:** sillimanite. **Tree:** American holly.

Natural features

Area: 2,489 sq mi, 6,447 sq km. **Highest point:** Ebright Road, New Castle County, 442 ft (135 m). **Largest lake:** Red Mill Pond. **Major rivers:** Delaware, Nanticoke, Pocomoke. **Natural regions:** the Piedmont Province, including the Piedmont Upland, covers the northernmost tip of the state; the remainder consists of the Coastal Plain. **Location:** East Coast, bordering Pennsylvania, New Jersey, and Maryland. **Climate:** temperate, with high humidity, hot summers and cold winters. **Land use:** agricultural, 36.1%; forest, 30.1%; pasture, 0.6%; other, 33.3%.

People

Population (2003): 817,000; 418.1 persons per sq mi (161.5 persons per sq km) (land area only). **Vital statistics** (2001; per 1,000 population): birth rate, 13.9; death rate, 8.9; marriage rate, 6.7; divorce rate, 4.0. **Major cities** (2000): Wilmington, 72,664; Dover, 32,135; Newark, 28,547.

Government

Statehood: entered the Union on 7 Dec 1787 as the 1st state. **State constitution:** adopted 1897. **Representation in US Congress:** 2 senators; 1 representative. **Electoral college:** 3 votes. **Political divisions:** 3 counties.

Economy

Employment: services, 28.6%; trade, 20.6%; government, 13.5%; finance, insurance, real estate, 12.8%; manufacturing, 12.6%; construction, 6.1%; transportation, public utilities, 3.8%; agriculture, forestry, fishing, 1.9%. **Production:** finance, insurance, real estate, 39.8%; services, 15.5%; manufacturing, 14.2%; trade, 11.1%; government, 9.2%; transportation, utilities, 5.1%; construction, 4.3%; agriculture, 0.8%. **Chief agricultural products:** *Crops:* corn, soybeans, wheat, barley, peas, vegetables, dairy products. *Livestock:* poultry, cattle, hogs. *Fish catch:* crustaceans, crab, clams. **Chief manufactured products:** chem-

icals, food products, paper products, rubber and plastics products, metal products, printed materials.

Internet resources: <www.visitdelaware.net>; <www.delaware.gov>.

District of Columbia

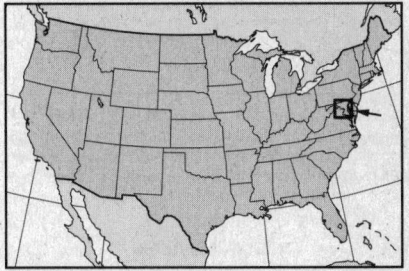

Motto: *Justitia Omnibus* (Justice for All). **Bird:** woodthrush. **Flower:** American Beauty rose. **Tree:** scarlet oak.

Natural features

Area: 68 sq mi, 177 sq km. **Major river:** Potomac. **Location:** Atlantic seaboard, bordered by Maryland and Virginia. **Climate:** humid, subtropical climate.

People

Population (2003): 563,000; 9,229.5 persons per sq mi (3,540.9 persons per sq km) (land area only). **Vital statistics** (2001; per 1,000 population): birth rate, 14.8; death rate, 10.4; marriage rate, 6.8; divorce rate, 2.3.

Government

Representation in US Congress: 1 congressional delegate. **Political divisions:** 8 wards.

Economy

Employment (1997): services, 43.5%; government, 36.0%; trade, 7.3%; finance, insurance, real estate, 5.2%; transportation, public utilities, 3.0%; manufacturing, 1.9%; construction, 1.5%; agricultural service, forestry, fishing, 1.4%. **Production** (2000): services, 38.3%; government, 36.6%; finance, insurance, real estate, 13.5%; transportation, utilities, 5.0%; trade, 4.0%; manufacturing, 1.4%; construction, 1.0%; others, 0.2%. **Chief manufactured products:** printing and publishing products.

Internet resources: <www.dc.gov>.

Florida

Name: Florida, in honor of *Pascua florida* ("feast of the flowers"), Spain's Easter celebration. **Nickname:** Sunshine State. **Capital:** Tallahassee. **Rank:** population: 4th; area: 26th; pop. density: 8th. **Motto:** In God We Trust. **Song:** "Old Folks at Home" ("Swanee River"), words and music by Stephen Foster. **Bird:** mockingbird. **Butterfly:** zebra longwing. **Fish:** sailfish

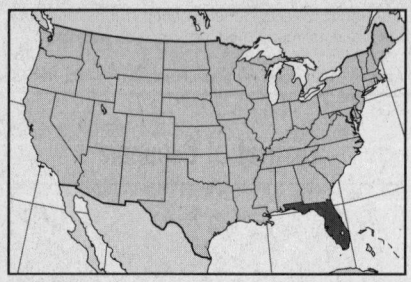

(saltwater); largemouth bass (freshwater). **Flower:** orange blossom. **Gemstone:** moonstone. **Mammal:** Florida panther. **Marine mammal:** manatee. **Saltwater mammal:** porpoise. **Reptile:** alligator. **Rock:** agatized coral. **Tree:** sabal palm.

Natural features

Area: 65,755 sq mi, 170,304 sq km. **Highest point:** 345 ft (105 m), in Walton County. **Largest lake:** Lake Okeechobee. **Major rivers:** Kissimmee, Suwannee, St. Johns, Caloosahatchee, Indian, Withlacoochee, Apalachicola, Perdido, St. Marys. **Natural regions:** Western Highlands, a region at the westernmost end of the panhandle; Marianna Lowlands, east of the Western Highlands; Tallahassee Hills, covering the northern border with Georgia; Central Highlands, extending down the middle two-thirds of the peninsula; Coastal Lowlands, curving along the east, south, and west coasts of the peninsula; the Everglades, far southern quarter of the peninsula. **Location:** Southeast, bordering Georgia and Alabama. **Climate:** tropical south of a west–east line drawn from Bradenton along the south shore of Lake Okeechobee to Vero Beach, and subtropical north of this line; hot, humid summers and mild, pleasant winters; hurricane season from June to November. **Land use:** forest, 42.3%; pasture, 15.8%; agricultural, 10.6%; other, 31.4%.

People

Population (2003): 17,019,000; 315.6 persons per sq mi (121.9 persons per sq km) (land area only). **Vital statistics** (2001; per 1,000 population): birth rate, 13.2; death rate, 10.2; marriage rate, 9.7; divorce rate, 5.4. **Major cities:** Jacksonville, 762,000; Miami, 375,000; Tampa, 315,000; St. Petersburg, 249,000; Hialeah, 228,000; Orlando, 194,000; Fort Lauderdale, 158,000; Tallahassee, 155,000.

Government

Statehood: entered the Union on 3 Mar 1845 as the 27th state. **State constitution:** adopted 1968. **Representation in US Congress:** 2 senators; 23 representatives. **Electoral college:** 27 votes (in the 2004 general elections based on the 2000 census). **Political divisions:** 67 counties.

Economy

Employment: services, 35.3%; trade, 23.2%; government, 13.1%; finance, insurance, real estate, 8.2%; manufacturing, 6.4%; construction, 5.7%; transportation, public utilities, 4.8%; agriculture, forestry,

fishing, 3.0%; mining, 0.1%. **Production:** services, 24.4%; finance, insurance, real estate, 21.5%; trade, 19.1%; government, 12.2%; transportation, utilities, 8.6%; manufacturing, 7.2%; construction, 5.1%; agriculture, 1.8%; mining, 0.2%. **Chief agricultural products:** *Crops:* citrus fruit, fruits and vegetables, corn (maize), cotton, peanuts (groundnuts), soybeans, sugarcane, tobacco, honey, dairy products, eggs, nursery plants and flowers. *Livestock:* cattle and calves, poultry, hogs and pigs. *Aquaculture:* catfish. *Fish catch:* marine fish, crab, shrimp, oyster. **Chief manufactured products:** food products, meatpacking, soft drinks, apparel, paper products, pesticides and fertilizers, agricultural chemicals, plastics, construction materials, fabricated metal products, machinery, communications equipment, semiconductors, electronics, aerospace products, airplane engines, ships and boats, medical and surgical equipment.

Internet resources: <www.flausa.com>; <www.myflorida.com>.

Georgia

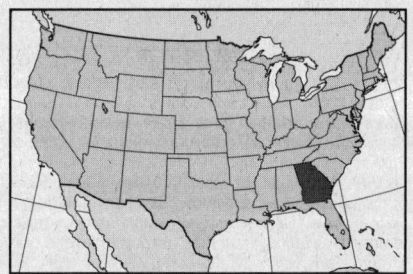

Name: Georgia, named for George II, king of England at the time the colony of Georgia was founded. **Nickname:** Empire State of the South; Peach State. **Capital:** Atlanta. **Rank:** population: 9th; area: 21st; pop. density: 18th. **Mottos:** Wisdom, Justice, and Moderation; Agriculture and Commerce, 1776. **Song:** "Georgia on My Mind," words by Stuart Gorrell and music by Hoagy Carmichael. **Bird:** brown thrasher. **Fish:** largemouth bass. **Flower:** cherokee rose. **Fossil:** shark tooth. **Gemstone:** quartz. **Insect:** honeybee. **Marine mammal:** right whale. **Mineral:** staurolite. **Reptile:** gopher tortoise. **Tree:** live oak.

Natural features

Area: 59,425 sq mi, 153,909 sq km. **Mountain range:** Blue Ridge Mountains. **Highest point:** Brasstown Bald, 4,784 ft (1,458 m). **Largest lake:** Lanier. **Major rivers:** Chattahoochee, Flint, Apalachicola, Ocmulgee, Oconee, Altamaha, Savannah. **Natural regions:** Blue Ridge Province, north-central edge; Valley and Ridge Province, northwest corner; Piedmont Province, northern half of state; Coastal Plain, southern half of state, divided into the Sea Island Section (southeast) and the East Gulf Coastal Plain (southwest). **Location:** South, bordering North Carolina, South Carolina, Florida, Alabama, and Tennessee. **Climate:** temperate, though maritime tropical air masses dominate the climate in summer; generally hot summers and cool winters; precipitation somewhat evenly distributed throughout the

For details about state governments, see pages 800–805; for energy data, see pages 830–832.

seasons in the north, whereas the southern and coastal areas have more summer rains; snow seldom occurs outside the mountainous northern counties. **Land use:** forest, 62.1%; agricultural, 19.8%; pasture, 3.6%; other, 14.6%.

People

Population (2003): 8,685,000; 150.0 persons per sq mi (57.9 persons per sq km) (land area only). **Vital statistics** (2001; per 1,000 population): birth rate, 16.5; death rate, 7.7; marriage rate, 6.3; divorce rate, 3.8. **Major cities:** Atlanta, 425,000; Columbus, 186,000; Savannah, 128,000.

Government

Statehood: entered the Union on 2 Jan 1788 as the 4th state. **State constitution:** adopted 1982. **Representation in US Congress:** 2 senators; 11 representatives. **Electoral college:** 15 votes (in the 2004 general elections based on the 2000 census). **Political divisions:** 159 counties.

Economy

Employment: services, 27.7%; trade, 23.1%; government, 14.9%; manufacturing, 13.5%; finance, insurance, real estate, 6.7%; transportation, public utilities, 5.8%; construction, 5.7%; agriculture, forestry, fishing, 2.5%; mining, 0.2%. **Production:** services, 19.2%; trade, 18.4%; manufacturing, 17.0%; finance, insurance, real estate, 15.3%; government, 11.9%; transportation, utilities, 11.4%; construction, 5.0%; agriculture, 1.3%; mining, 0.5%. **Chief agricultural products:** *Crops:* peanuts (groundnuts), pecans, rye, corn (maize), cotton, cottonseed, hay, oats, sorghum, soybeans, tobacco, wheat, peaches, apples, onions, watermelon, snap beans, cabbage, cucumbers, blueberries, grapes, honey, dairy products. *Livestock:* poultry, pigs, cattle. *Aquaculture:* catfish, trout. *Extractive products:* timber. **Chief manufactured products:** food products, soft drinks, textiles, wood products, paper products, chemical products, transportation equipment.

Internet resources: <www.georgia.org>; <www.georgia.gov>.

Hawaii

Nickname: Aloha State. **Capital:** Honolulu. **Rank:** population: 42nd; area: 47th; pop. density: 13th. **Motto:** *Ua Mau ke Ea o ka Aina i ka Pono* (The Life of the Land Is Perpetuated in Righteousness). **Song:** *"Hawaii Ponoi"* ("Our Hawaii"). **Bird:** nene, or Hawaiian goose. **Fish:** rectangular triggerfish (in Hawaiian, *humuhumunukunuku apua'a*). **Flower:** yellow hibiscus (in Hawaiian, *pua ma'o hau hele*). **Gemstone:** black coral. **Marine mammal:** humpback whale. **Tree:** kukui, or candlenut.

Natural features

Area: Total area,10,931 sq mi, 29,311 sq km; the eight largest islands are: *Hawaii:* 4,028 sq mi, 10,433 sq km; *Maui:* 728 sq mi, 1,886 sq km; *Oahu:* 607 sq mi, 1,574 sq km; *Kauai:* 552 sq mi, 1,430 sq km; *Molokai:* 280 sq mi, 725 sq km; *Lanai:* 140 sq mi, 363 sq km; *Niihau:* 72 sq mi, 186 sq km; *Kahoolawe:* 45 sq mi, 117 sq km. **Highest point:** Mauna Kea, Hawaii, 13,796 ft (4,205 m). **Major rivers:** *Hawaii:* Wailuku; *Kauai:* Waimea, Hanalei. **Natural regions:** The eight major islands at the eastern end of the 1,500-mile-long chain of islands are, from west to east, Niihau, Kauai, Oahu, Molokai, Lanai, Kahoolawe, Maui, and Hawaii; each island contains regions of mountains, deeps, ridges, and wide beaches; active volcanoes are found on the island of Hawaii. **Location:** islands surrounded by the Pacific Ocean. **Climate:** tropical; rainfall variations throughout the state are dramatic, ranging from 8.7 inches (220 mm) a year at Kawaihae on the island of Hawaii, to roughly 444 inches (11,280 mm) at Mount Waialeale on the island of Kauai. **Land use:** forest, 28.9%; pasture, 23.4%; agricultural, 7.1%; other, 40.6%.

People

Population (2003): Total, 1,258,000; 195.9 persons per sq mi (75.6 persons per sq km) (land area only). Populations by county (2001 estimates): *Kaui County:* 59,223; *Honolulu County:* 881,295; *Maui County:* 131,662; *Hawaii County:* 152,083. **Vital statistics** (2001; per 1,000 population): birth rate, 14.5; death rate, 6.8; marriage rate, 20.4; divorce rate, 3.8. **Major cities** (2000): Honolulu, 378,000 (2002); Hilo, 40,759; Kailua, 36,513; Kaneohe, 34,970; Waipahu, 33,108.

Government

Statehood: entered the Union on 21 Aug 1959 as the 50th state. **State constitution:** adopted 1950. **Representation in US Congress:** 2 senators; 2 representatives. **Electoral college:** 4 votes. **Political divisions:** 5 counties.

Economy

Employment: services, 31.3%; government, 22.3%; trade, 22.0%; finance, insurance, real estate, 8.4%; transportation, public utilities, 6.3%; construction, 4.2%; agriculture, forestry, fishing, 2.8%; manufacturing, 2.7%; mining, 0.1%. **Production:** finance, insurance, real estate, 23.2%; services, 22.1%; government, 21.8%; trade, 14.7%; transportation, utilities, 10.4%; construction, 4.0%; manufacturing, 2.5%; agriculture, 1.2%; mining, 0.1%. **Chief agricultural products:** *Crops:* pineapples, sugarcane, flowers, macadamia nuts, coffee, milk, eggs. *Livestock:* cattle. *Aquaculture:* fish, shellfish. **Chief manufactured products:** food products, processed sugar, canned pineapple, preserved fruits and vegetables, apparel and textile products, printing and publishing.

Internet resources: <www.gohawaii.com>; <www. hawaii.gov>.

Idaho

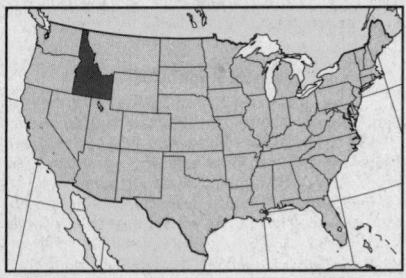

Nickname: Gem State. **Capital:** Boise. **Rank:** population: 39th; area: 11th; pop. density: 44th. **Motto:** *Esto Perpetua* (It Is Forever). **Song:** "Here We Have Idaho," words by McKinley Helm and Albert J. Tompkins, music by Sallie Hume Douglas. **Bird:** mountain bluebird. **Fish:** cutthroat trout. **Flower:** syringa. **Fossil:** Hagerman horse fossil (*Equus simplicidens*). **Gemstone:** star garnet. **Horse:** Appaloosa. **Insect:** monarch butterfly. **Tree:** western white pine.

Natural features

Area: 83,570 sq mi, 216,446 sq km. **Mountain ranges:** Northern Rocky Mountains, Middle Rocky Mountains, Sawtooth, Pioneer, Continental Divide, Beaverhead, Clearwater, Bitterroot, Salmon River, Lost River Range, Lemhi Range. **Highest point:** Borah Peak, 12,662 ft (3,859 m). **Largest lake:** Lake Pend Oreille. **Major rivers:** Snake, Salmon. **Natural regions:** Northern Rocky Mountains, covering most of the northern half of the state; Columbia Plateaus, extending across the south-central and southwestern regions; Great Basin region of the Basin and Range Province, southeast; Middle Rocky Mountains, extreme southeast tip. **Location:** Northwest, bordering Montana, Wyoming, Utah, Nevada, Oregon, and Washington; international border with Canada. **Climate:** continental, with warm wet summers and cold dry winters, but regionally diverse: in general, precipitation increases and mean temperatures drop with increases in altitude. **Land use:** pasture, 40.0%; forest, 32.3%; agricultural, 10.9%; other, 16.8%.

People

Population (2003): 1,366,000; 16.5 persons per sq mi (6.4 persons per sq km) (land area only). **Vital statistics** (2001; per 1,000 population): birth rate, 16.0; death rate, 7.4; marriage rate, 11.4; divorce rate, 5.6. **Major cities** (2000): Boise, 190,000 (2002); Nampa, 51,867; Pocatello, 51,466; Idaho Falls, 50,730; Meridian, 34,919.

Government

Statehood: entered the Union on 3 Jul 1890 as the 43rd state. **State constitution:** adopted 1889. **Representation in US Congress:** 2 senators; 2 representatives. **Electoral college:** 4 votes. **Political divisions:** 44 counties.

Economy

Employment: services, 26.1%; trade, 22.7%; government, 15.0%; manufacturing, 11.4%; agriculture, forestry, fishing, 7.5%; construction, 7.1%; finance, insurance, real estate, 5.4%; transportation, public utilities, 4.4%; mining, 0.5%. **Production:** manufacturing, 21.6%; trade, 16.6%; services, 16.3%; government, 13.4%; finance, insurance, real estate, 11.8%; transportation, utilities, 7.8%; construction, 6.6%; agriculture, 5.2%; mining, 0.6%. **Chief agricultural products:** *Crops:* potatoes, wheat, hay, sugar beets, barley, alfalfa seed, Kentucky Blue Grass seed, hops, beans, onions, lentils, peas, honey, dairy products. *Livestock:* cattle, calves, sheep, lambs. *Extractive products:* timber, trout. **Chief manufactured products:** food processing, lumber and wood products, paper, printing, chemicals, plastics and rubber products, nonmetallic mineral products, fabricated metal products, machinery, computers and electronic products, transportation equipment, furniture.

Internet resources: <www.visitid.org>; <www. idaho.gov>.

Illinois

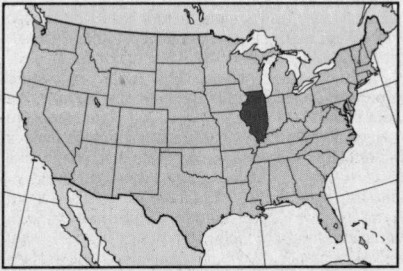

Name: Illinois, from a Native American word meaning "tribe of superior men." **Nickname:** Prairie State. **Capital:** Springfield. **Rank:** population: 5th; area: 24th; pop. density: 11th. **Motto:** State Sovereignty, National Union. **Slogan:** Land of Lincoln. **Song:** "Illinois," words by Charles H. Chamberlain and music by Archibald Johnston. **Bird:** cardinal. **Fish:** bluegill. **Flower:** violet. **Fossil:** tully monster. **Insect:** monarch butterfly. **Mammal:** white-tailed deer. **Mineral:** fluorite. **Tree:** white oak.

Natural features

Area: 57,914 sq mi, 149,998 sq km. **Highest point:** Charles Mound, 1,235 ft (376 m). **Largest lake:** Carlyle Lake. **Major rivers:** Mississippi, Ohio, Wabash. **Natural regions:** central Lowland, a region of sloping hills and broad, shallow river valleys covering almost the entire state; Ozark Plateaus, extreme southwest; Interior Low Plateaus and Coastal Plain, extreme southeastern tip. **Location:** Midwest, bordering Wisconsin, Indiana, Kentucky, Missouri, and Iowa. **Climate:** continental, with hot summers and cold, snowy winters; wide seasonal and regional variations.

For details about state governments, see pages 800–805; for energy data, see pages 830–832.

Land use: agricultural, 70.1%; forest, 11.4%; pasture, 4.4%; other, 14.2%.

People

Population (2003): 12,654,000; 227.7 persons per sq mi (87.9 persons per sq km) (land area only). **Vital statistics** (2001; per 1,000 population): birth rate, 15.0; death rate, 8.4; marriage rate, 7.3; divorce rate, 3.2. **Major cities:** Chicago, 2,886,000; Aurora, 157,000; Rockford, 151,000; Naperville, 135,000; Joliet, 118,000; Peoria, 113,000; Springfield, 112,000.

Government

Statehood: entered the Union on 3 Dec 1818 as the 21st state. **State constitution:** adopted 1970. **Representation in US Congress:** 2 senators; 20 representatives. **Electoral college:** 21 votes (in the 2004 general elections based on the 2000 census). **Political divisions:** 102 counties.

Economy

Employment: services, 30.9%; trade, 21.2%; manufacturing, 14.0%; government, 12.2%; finance, insurance, real estate, 9.0%; transportation, public utilities, 5.5%; construction, 4.7%; agriculture, forestry, fishing, 2.3%; mining, 0.3%. **Production:** services, 22.6%; finance, insurance, real estate, 20.4%; manufacturing, 16.3%; trade, 16.2%; government, 9.9%; transportation, utilities, 9.2%; construction, 4.5%; agriculture, 0.8%; mining, 0.3%. **Chief agricultural products:** *Crops:* corn (maize), soybeans, wheat, hay, oats, sorghum, apples, peaches, snap beans, sweet corn, potatoes, cabbage, dairy products, eggs. *Livestock:* pigs, cattle, calves, horses, poultry. **Chief manufactured products:** food products, beverages, textiles, leather goods, apparel, wood products, paper products, printing, petroleum and coal products, asphalt paving, chemicals, pharmaceuticals, plastics and rubber products, nonmetallic mineral products, iron and steel products, fabricated metals, machinery, computers and electronics, appliances, and transportation equipment.

Internet resources: <www.enjoyillinois.com>; <www.illinois.gov>.

Indiana

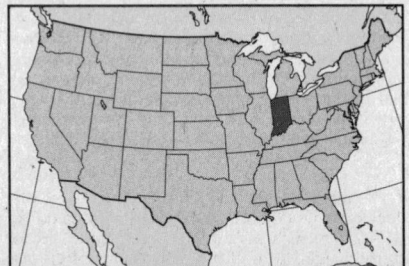

Name: Indiana, generally thought to mean "land of the Indians." **Nickname:** Hoosier State. **Capital:** Indianapolis. **Rank:** population: 14th; area: 38th; pop. density: 16th. **Motto:** The Crossroads of America. **Song:** "On the Banks of the Wabash, Far Away,"

words and music by Paul Dresser. **Bird:** cardinal. **Flower:** peony. **Rock:** limestone. **Tree:** tulip tree (yellow poplar).

Natural features

Area: 36,418 sq mi, 94,321 sq km. **Highest point:** 1,257 ft (383 m), near Fountain City. **Largest lake:** Lake Monroe. **Major rivers:** Wabash, Ohio. **Natural regions:** Central Lowland comprises most of the state and includes the Eastern Lake section to the north, and the Till Plains in the center; Interior Low Plateaus, including the Highland Rim section, cover the southern quarter of the state. **Location:** Midwest, bordering Michigan, Ohio, Kentucky, and Illinois. **Climate:** continental, with four distinct seasons; hot summers, cold winters, mild spring and fall, with increased risk of tornadoes in spring. **Land use:** agricultural, 59.6%; forest, 18.9%; pasture, 5.0%; other, 16.4%.

People

Population (2003): 6,196,000; 172.7 persons per sq mi (66.7 persons per sq km) (land area only). **Vital statistics** (2001; per 1,000 population): birth rate, 14.4; death rate, 9.0; marriage rate, 5.7; divorce rate, N/A. **Major cities:** Indianapolis, 784,000; Fort Wayne, 210,000; Evansville, 119,000; South Bend, 107,000; Gary, 101,000.

Government

Statehood: entered the Union on 11 Dec 1816 as the 19th state. **State constitution:** adopted 1851. **Representation in US Congress:** 2 senators; 10 representatives. **Electoral college:** 11 votes (in the 2004 general elections based on the 2000 census). **Political divisions:** 92 counties.

Economy

Employment: services, 26.2%; trade, 22.7%; manufacturing, 19.7%; government, 11.7%; finance, insurance, real estate, 6.0%; construction, 5.8%; transportation, public utilities, 4.8%; agriculture, forestry, fishing, 3.0%; mining, 0.3%. **Production:** manufacturing, 30.9%; services, 16.6%; trade, 15.4%; finance, insurance, real estate, 13.0%; government, 10.0%; transportation, utilities, 7.6%; construction, 5.1%; agriculture, 1.0%; mining, 0.4%. **Chief agricultural products:** *Crops:* corn (maize), soybeans, wheat, hay, popcorn, tobacco, tomatoes, peppermint, spearmint, watermelon, blueberries, snap beans, cucumbers, apples, milk, eggs. *Livestock:* pigs, cattle, calves, poultry. **Chief manufactured products:** iron and steel, metal products, motor vehicle parts, machinery, food products, dairy products, soft drinks, wood products, paper products, mobile homes, asphalt.

Internet resources: <www.enjoyindiana.com>; <www.in.gov>.

Iowa

Name: Iowa, named for the Iowa (or Ioway) Indians who once inhabited the area. **Nickname:** Hawkeye State. **Capital:** Des Moines. **Rank:** population: 30th; area: 23rd; pop. density: 33rd. **Motto:** Our Liberties We Prize and Our Rights We Will Maintain. **Song:** "The Song of Iowa," words by S.H.M. Byers, to the tune of

"O Tannenbaum." **Bird:** eastern goldfinch. **Flower:** wild rose. **Rock:** geode. **Tree:** oak.

Internet resources: <www.traveliowa.com>; <www.iowa.gov>.

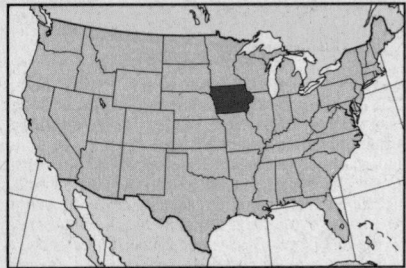

Did you know? The first woman elected mayor in the US was Susanna Madora Salter. She was voted into office in Argonia KS in 1887.

Natural features

Area: 56,272 sq mi, 145,743 sq km. **Highest point:** near Sibley, 1,670 ft (509 m). **Largest lake:** Spirit Lake. **Major rivers:** Des Moines, Mississippi, Missouri, Big Sioux. **Natural regions:** overall, Central Lowland, including the Western Lake section, north and central regions; Dissected Till Plains, south; Wisconsin Driftless Section, northeast corner. **Location:** Midwest, bordering Minnesota, Wisconsin, Illinois, Missouri, Nebraska, and South Dakota. **Climate:** continental, with hot summers and cold, snowy winters. **Land use:** agricultural, 78.1%; forest, 5.4%; pasture, 4.1%; other, 12.4%.

People

Population (2003): 2,944,000; 52.7 persons per sq mi (20.3 persons per sq km) (land area only). **Vital statistics** (2001; per 1,000 population): birth rate, 13.0; death rate, 9.5; marriage rate, 7.2; divorce rate, 3.2. **Major cities:** Des Moines, 198,000; Cedar Rapids, 123,000; Davenport, 98,359 (2000); Sioux City, 85,013 (2000); Waterloo, 68,747 (2000).

Government

Statehood: entered the Union on 28 Dec 1846 as the 29th state. **State constitution:** adopted 1857. **Representation in US Congress:** 2 senators, 5 representatives. **Electoral college:** 7 votes. **Political divisions:** 99 counties.

Economy

Employment: services, 26.8%; trade, 22.4%; manufacturing, 14.0%; government, 13.2%; agriculture, forestry, fishing, 7.7%; finance, insurance, real estate, 6.2%; construction, 5.1%; transportation, public utilities, 4.4%; mining, 0.1%. **Production:** manufacturing, 22.4%; services, 17.0%; trade, 16.9%; finance, insurance, real estate, 15.1%; government, 12.0%; transportation, utilities, 8.5%; construction, 4.4%; agriculture, 3.5%; mining, 0.3%. **Chief agricultural products:** *Crops:* corn (maize), soybeans, hay, oats, grain, milk, eggs, butter, honey, popcorn, sorghum. *Livestock:* poultry, hogs and pigs, beef cattle, sheep. **Chief manufactured products:** food products, dairy products, meatpacking, pesticide, fertilizer, and other agricultural chemicals, farm machinery, construction machinery, household appliances, motor vehicle parts.

Kansas

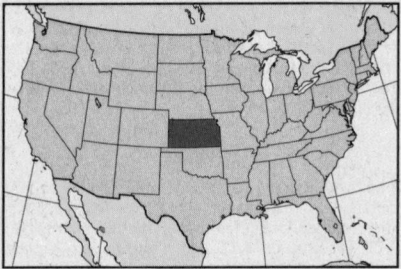

Name: Kansas, from the Sioux word *kansa* ("people of the south wind") for the Native Americans who lived in the region. **Nickname:** Sunflower State. **Capital:** Topeka. **Rank:** population: 33rd; area: 13th; pop. density: 40th. **Motto:** *Ad Astra Per Aspera* (To the Stars Through Difficulties). **Song:** "Home on the Range," words by Brewster Higley and music by Dan Kelly. **Amphibian:** barred tiger salamander. **Bird:** western meadowlark. **Flower:** wild native sunflower. **Insect:** honeybee. **Mammal:** American buffalo. **Reptile:** ornate box turtle. **Tree:** cottonwood.

Natural features

Area: 82,277 sq mi, 213,096 sq km. **Highest point:** Mount Sunflower, 4,039 ft (1,231 m). **Largest lake:** Milford Lake. **Major rivers:** Kansas, Arkansas, Big Blue, Republican, Solomon, Saline, Smoky Hill, Cimarron, Verdigris, Neosho (Grand). **Natural regions:** the Great Plains Province, covering the western half of the state, consists of the High Plains to the west and the Plains Border to the east; the Central Lowland covers the eastern half of the state and consists of the Dissected Till Plains to the north and the Osage Plains to the south. **Location:** Midwest, bordering Nebraska, Missouri, Oklahoma, and Colorado. **Climate:** temperate but continental, with great extremes between summer and winter temperatures but few long periods of extreme hot or cold. **Land use:** agricultural, 64.4%; pasture, 24.0%; forest, 2.8%; other, 8.8%.

People

Population (2003): 2,724,000; 33.3 persons per sq mi (12.9 persons per sq km) (land area only). **Vital statistics** (2001; per 1,000 population): birth rate, 14.5; death rate, 9.1; marriage rate, 7.6; divorce rate, 3.2. **Major cities:** Wichita, 355,000; Overland Park, 158,000; Kansas City, 147,000; Topeka, 122,000; Olathe, 101,000.

For details about state governments, see pages 800–805; for energy data, see pages 830–832.

Government

Statehood: entered the Union on 29 Jan 1861 as the 34th state. **State constitution:** adopted 1859. **Representation in US Congress:** 2 senators; 4 representatives. **Electoral college:** 6 votes. **Political divisions:** 105 counties.

Economy

Employment: services, 26.5%; trade, 22.2%; government, 16.0%; manufacturing, 12.6%; agriculture, forestry, fishing, 5.9%; finance, insurance, real estate, 5.7%; construction, 5.2%; transportation, public utilities, 4.9%; mining, 1.2%. **Production:** trade, 18.2%; services, 17.4%; manufacturing, 16.8%; government, 13.5%; finance, insurance, real estate, 12.9%; transportation, utilities, 12.5%; construction, 4.6%; agriculture, 2.9%; mining, 1.3%. **Chief agricultural products:** *Crops:* wheat, corn (maize), sorghum, hay, soybeans, sunflower seed and oil, apples, peaches, pecans. *Livestock:* beef cattle and calves, hogs, lambs, sheep, dairy cows, horses and other equines. **Chief manufactured products:** food products, grain and oilseed milling, meat products, printing, refined petroleum, soap and cleaning products, plastic products, aerospace products and parts, aircraft.

Internet resources: <www.travelks.com>; <www.accesskansas.org>.

Kentucky

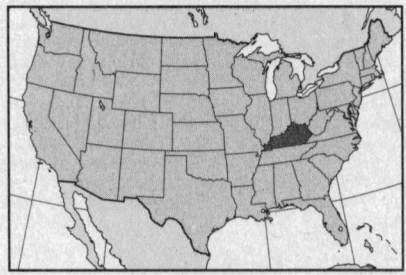

Name: Kentucky, possibly from the Iroquois word for "prairie." **Nickname:** Bluegrass State. **Capital:** Frankfort. **Rank:** population: 26th; area: 36th; pop. density: 22nd. **Motto:** United We Stand, Divided We Fall. **Song:** "My Old Kentucky Home," words and music by Stephen Foster. **Bird:** cardinal. **Butterfly:** viceroy butterfly. **Fish:** Kentucky bass. **Flower:** goldenrod. **Horse:** Thoroughbred. **Tree:** tulip poplar. **Wild animal:** gray squirrel.

Natural features

Area: 40,409 sq mi, 104,659 sq km. **Mountain ranges:** Cumberland, Pine. **Highest point:** Black Mountain, 4,145 ft (1,263 m). **Largest lake:** Kentucky Lake. **Major rivers:** Mississippi, Ohio, Big Sandy, Licking, Kentucky, Salt, Green, Tradewater, Cumberland, Tennessee. **Natural regions:** Appalachian Plateaus, eastern third of the state; Interior Low Plateaus, including the Highland Rim section and the Lexington Plain, cover the remainder, with the exception of the Coastal Plain, which covers the extreme southwest tip. **Location:** Midwest, bordering Indiana, Ohio, West Virginia, Virginia, Tennessee, Missouri, and Illinois. **Climate:** temperate continental climate, with hot, humid summers and cold winters. **Land use:** forest, 48.6%; agricultural, 34.8%; pasture, 5.9%; other, 10.7%.

People

Population (2003): 4,118,000; 103.7 persons per sq mi (40.0 persons per sq km) (land area only). **Vital statistics** (2001; per 1,000 population): birth rate, 13.6; death rate, 9.8; marriage rate, 9.1; divorce rate, 5.5. **Major cities** (2000): Lexington-Fayette, 264,000 (2002); Louisville, 251,000 (2002); Owensboro, 54,067; Bowling Green, 49,296; Covington, 43,370.

Government

Statehood: entered the Union on 1 Jun 1792 as the 15th state. **State constitution:** adopted 1891. **Representation in US Congress:** 2 senators; 6 representatives. **Electoral college:** 8 votes. **Political divisions:** 120 counties.

Economy

Employment: services, 25.4%; trade, 21.7%; government, 14.9%; manufacturing, 14.9%; agriculture, forestry, fishing, 6.4%; construction, 5.8%; transportation, public utilities, 5.2%; finance, insurance, real estate, 4.5%; mining, 1.2%. **Production:** manufacturing, 27.5%; services, 16.0%; trade, 15.7%; government, 13.5%; finance, insurance, real estate, 10.9%; transportation, utilities, 8.0%; construction, 4.5%; mining, 2.1%; agriculture, 1.8%. **Chief agricultural products:** *Crops:* tobacco, soybeans, corn (maize), wheat, hay, sorghum, eggs, dairy products. *Livestock:* racing and show horses, beef and dairy cattle, hogs, poultry, sheep. **Chief manufactured products:** food products, meat packing, beverages, tobacco, apparel, paper products, printing, chemical products, paint, resin and synthetic rubber products, plastic products, iron and steel, aluminum, fabricated metal products, machinery, appliances, motor vehicles.

Internet resources: <www.kentuckytourism.com>; <www.kentucky.gov>.

Louisiana

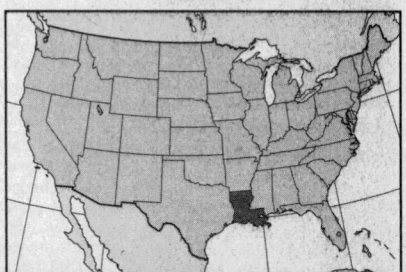

Name: Louisiana, named for Louis XIV, king of France. **Nickname:** Pelican State. **Capital:** Baton Rouge. **Rank:** population: 24th; area: 33rd; pop. density: 23rd. **Motto:** Union, Justice and Confidence. **Songs:** "Give Me Louisiana," words and music by Doralice Fontane, arranged by John W. Schaum; "You Are My Sunshine,"

words and music by Jimmy H. Davis and Charles Mitchell. **Amphibian:** green tree frog. **Bird:** brown pelican. **Crustacean:** crawfish. **Freshwater fish:** white perch. **Flower:** magnolia. **Fossil:** petrified palmwood. **Gemstone:** agate. **Insect:** honeybee. **Mammal:** black bear. **Reptile:** alligator. **Tree:** bald cypress.

Natural features

Area: 51,840 sq mi, 134,264 sq km. **Highest point:** Driskill Mountain, 535 ft (163 m). **Largest lake:** Lake Ponchartrain. **Major rivers:** Mississippi, Red, Sabine. **Natural regions:** the entire state consists of the Coastal Plain and is divided into the West Gulf Coastal Plain to the west, the Mississippi Alluvial Plain to the northeast, and the East Gulf Coastal Plain in the southeast. **Location:** South, bordering Arkansas, Mississippi, and Texas. **Climate:** subtropical, with hot, humid summers, tempered by frequent afternoon thunder showers, alternating with mild winters; subject to tropical storms: the hurricane season extends for six months, from June through November. **Land use:** forest, 49.1%; agricultural, 19.7%; pasture, 5.7%; other, 25.6%.

People

Population (2003): 4,496,000; 103.2 persons per sq mi (39.8 persons per sq km) (land area only). **Vital statistics** (2001; per 1,000 population): birth rate, 14.9; death rate, 9.3; marriage rate, 8.6; divorce rate, N/A. **Major cities:** New Orleans, 474,000; Baton Rouge, 226,000; Shreveport, 199,000; Lafayette, 111,000.

Government

Statehood: entered the Union on 30 Apr 1812 as the 18th state. **State constitution:** adopted 1974. **Representation in US Congress:** 2 senators; 7 representatives. **Electoral college:** 9 votes. **Political divisions:** 64 parishes.

Economy

Employment: services, 29.2%; trade, 21.6%; government, 17.4%; manufacturing, 8.7%; construction, 6.8%; transportation, public utilities, 5.6%; finance, insurance, real estate, 5.3%; agriculture, forestry, fishing, 2.8%; mining, 2.7%. **Production:** services, 17.6%; manufacturing, 15.2%; trade, 15.1%; finance, insurance, real estate, 13.0%; government, 12.3%; mining, 11.7%; transportation, utilities, 9.2%; construction, 4.9%; agriculture, 1.0%. **Chief agricultural products:** *Crops:* soybeans, cotton, corn (maize), sorghum, hay, sugarcane, rice, wheat, sweet potatoes, pecans, strawberries, peaches, milk, eggs. *Livestock:* cattle, chickens, hogs. *Aquaculture:* catfish, crawfish. *Fish catch:* shrimp, oysters, marine fish, freshwater fish. *Extractive products:* timber. **Chief manufactured products:** industrial chemicals, agricultural chemicals, plastics materials and resins, petroleum refining, cane sugar products, beverages, food products, paper, metal products, wood products, communications equipment, ships and boats.

Internet resources: <www.louisianatravel.com>; <www.louisiana.gov>.

Maine

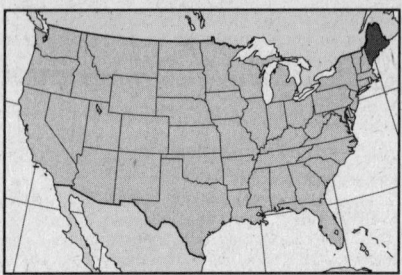

Name: Maine, possibly named for the former French province of Maine, or used to distinguish the mainland portion of the territory from offshore islands. **Nickname:** Pine Tree State. **Capital:** Augusta. **Rank:** population: 40th; area: 39th; pop. density: 38th. **Motto:** *Dirigo* (I Direct). **Song:** "State of Maine Song," words and music by Roger Vinton Snow. **Bird:** chickadee. **Fish:** landlocked salmon. **Flower:** white pine cone and tassel. **Fossil:** *Pertica quadrifaria*. **Gemstone:** tourmaline. **Insect:** honeybee. **Mammal:** moose. **Tree:** white pine.

Natural features

Area: 35,385 sq mi, 91,646 sq km. **Mountain ranges:** Appalachians, Longfellow. **Highest point:** Mount Katahdin, 5,268 ft (1,606 m). **Largest lake:** Moosehead Lake. **Major rivers:** Saco, Androscoggin, Kennebec, Penobscot, St. John's, St. Croix, Allagash. **Natural regions:** entire state is part of the larger New England Province, subdivided into the White Mountain section (southwest), Seaboard Lowland Section (southeast coastline), and New England Upland Section (north and central regions). **Location:** New England, bordering New Hampshire; international border with Canada. **Climate:** cool maritime climate, with coldest temperatures and greatest snowfall occurring in northern regions. **Land use:** forest, 85.8%; agricultural, 2.4%; pasture, 0.2%; other, 11.6%.

People

Population (2003): 1,306,000; 42.3 persons per sq mi (16.3 persons per sq km) (land area only). **Vital statistics** (2001; per 1,000 population): birth rate, 10.9; death rate, 9.7; marriage rate, 9.0; divorce rate, 3.9. **Major cities** (2000): Portland, 64,249; Lewiston, 35,690; Bangor, 31,473; South Portland, 23,324; Auburn, 23,203.

Government

Statehood: entered the Union on 15 Mar 1820 as the 23rd state. **State constitution:** adopted 1819. **Representation in US Congress:** 2 senators; 2 representatives. **Electoral college:** 4 votes. **Political divisions:** 16 counties.

Economy

Employment: services, 30.2%; trade, 23.0%; government, 13.7%; manufacturing, 13.1%; construction,

For details about state governments, see pages 800–805; for energy data, see pages 830–832.

6.3%; finance, insurance, real estate, 5.9%; transportation, public utilities, 4.1%; agriculture, forestry, fishing, 3.7%. **Production:** services, 20.1%; finance, insurance, real estate, 18.8%; trade, 18.0%; manufacturing, 15.4%; government, 14.0%; transportation, utilities, 7.0%; construction, 4.6%; agriculture, forestry, fishing 2.0%. **Chief agricultural products:** *Crops:* potatoes, blueberries, hay, apples, cranberries, oats, honey, corn (maize), dairy products, eggs. *Livestock:* poultry, cattle, sheep. *Aquaculture:* salmon, rainbow trout. *Fish catch:* marine fish, lobster, shrimp, crab, clams, haddock, cod, mackerel. *Extractive industries:* timber. **Chief manufactured products:** paper, leather, lumber and wood products, food products, semiconductors, apparel, printing and publishing, plastic products, ships and boats.

Internet resources: <www.visitmaine.com>; <www.maine.gov>.

Maryland

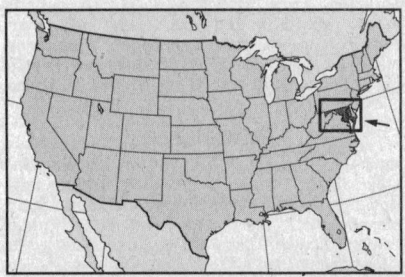

Name: Maryland, in honor of Henrietta Maria (queen of Charles I of England). **Nickname:** Old Line State. **Capital:** Annapolis. **Rank:** population: 19th; area: 42nd; pop. density: 5th. **Motto:** *Fatti Maschii, Parole Femine* (Manly Deeds, Womanly Words). **Song:** "Maryland, My Maryland," words by James Ryder Randall, to the tune of "Lauriger Horatius." **Bird:** Baltimore oriole. **Crustacean:** Maryland blue crab. **Dinosaur:** *Astrodon johnstoni*. **Fish:** rockfish (striped bass). **Flower:** black-eyed Susan. **Insect:** Baltimore checkerspot. **Reptile:** diamondback terrapin. **Tree:** white oak.

Natural features

Area: 12,407 sq mi, 32,133 sq km. **Mountain ranges:** Allegheny Mountains, Appalachians. **Highest point:** Backbone Mountain, 3,360 ft (1,024 m). **Largest lake:** Deep Creek Lake. **Major rivers:** Potomac, Patuxent, Susquehanna. **Natural regions:** Coastal Plain, eastern half of the state, includes the Embayed Section near the southwest corner of the peninsula; Piedmont Province, central, and including the Piedmont Upland to the north and the Piedmont Lowlands to the west; Blue Ridge Province, northwest; Valley and Ridge Province, part of western neck; Appalachian Plateau, extreme western neck. **Location:** East coast, bordering Pennsylvania, Delaware, District of Columbia, Virginia, and West Virginia. **Climate:** continental in the west, but a humid, subtropical climate prevails in the east; hurricanes often bring much rain to eastern regions. **Land use:** forest, 38.7%; agricultural, 24.9%; pasture, 3.3%; other, 33.1%.

People

Population (2003): 5,509,000; 563.6 persons per sq mi (217.6 persons per sq km) (land area only). **Vital statistics** (2001; per 1,000 population): birth rate, 13.9; death rate, 8.1; marriage rate, 7.1; divorce rate, 3.0. **Major cities** (2000): Baltimore, 639,000 (2002); Frederick, 52,767; Gaithersburg, 52,613; Bowie, 50,269; Rockville, 47,388.

Government

Statehood: entered the Union on 28 Apr 1788 as the 7th state. **State constitution:** adopted 1867. **Representation in US Congress:** 2 senators; 8 representatives. **Electoral college:** 10 votes. **Political divisions:** 23 counties.

Economy

Employment: services, 34.4%; trade, 21.1%; government, 17.3%; finance, insurance, real estate, 8.3%; manufacturing, 6.4%; construction, 6.3%; transportation, public utilities, 4.4%; agriculture, forestry, fishing, 1.8%; mining, 0.1%. **Production:** services, 24.2%; finance, insurance, real estate, 21.3%; government, 17.5%; trade, 15.2%; manufacturing, 8.1%; transportation, utilities, 7.5%; construction, 5.4%; agriculture, 0.8%; mining, 0.1%. **Chief agricultural products:** *Crops:* corn (maize), soybeans, wheat, vegetables, potatoes, tobacco, dairy products, eggs. *Livestock:* cattle, pigs, poultry. *Aquaculture:* hybrid striped bass, catfish, tilapia, trout, oysters. *Fish catch:* blue crab, other crustaceans, oysters, mollusks, marine fish. **Chief manufactured products:** primary metals, ships and boats, food products, motor vehicles, chemical products, paper and printing, plastics and rubber, fabricated metal products, machinery, computers and electronics, transportation equipment.

Internet resources: <www.mdisfun.org>; <www.maryland.gov>.

Massachusetts

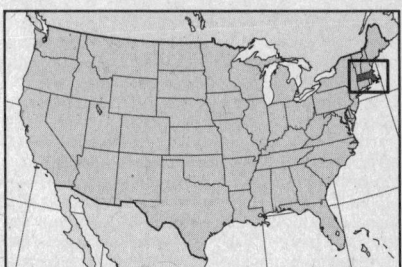

Name: Massachusetts, named for the Massachusett tribe of Native Americans who lived in the Great Blue Hill region south of Boston; the word *Massachusett* means "at or about the great hill." **Nickname:** Bay State. **Capital:** Boston. **Rank:** population: 13th; area: 45th; pop. density: 3rd. **Motto:** *Ense Petit Placidam Sub Libertate Quietem* (By the Sword We Seek Peace, but Peace Only Under Liberty). **Song:** "All Hail to Massachusetts," words and music by Arthur J. Marsh. **Bird:** black-capped chickadee. **Fish:** cod. **Flower:** mayflower. **Fossil:** theropod dinosaur tracks.

Gemstone: rhodonite. Insect: ladybug. Marine mammal: right whale. Mineral: babingtonite. Rock: Roxbury puddingstone. Tree: American elm.

Natural features

Area: 10,555 sq mi, 27,336 sq km. Mountain ranges: Berkshire Mountains, Hoosac Range, Taconic Range. Highest point: Mount Greylock, 3,491 ft (1,064 m). Largest lake: Webster Lake. Major rivers: Connecticut, Charles, Merrimack, Housatonic, Taunton. Natural regions: the New England Province, comprising most of the state, subdivided into the Taconic Section along the west, the New England Upland Section in the central region, and the Seaboard Lowland Section covering the eastern third of the state; Coastal Plain, comprising the peninsula region. Location: New England, bordering New Hampshire, Rhode Island, Connecticut, New York, and Vermont. Climate: temperate continental climate, with cold snowy winters and warm, humid summers; climate is colder but drier in western Massachusetts, although its winter snowfalls may be more severe. Land use: forest, 53.3%; agricultural, 4.2%; pasture, 0.7%; other, 41.8%.

People

Population (2003): 6,433,000; 820.5 persons per sq mi (316.8 persons per sq km) (land area only). Vital statistics (2001; per 1,000 population): birth rate, 13.0; death rate, 8.9; marriage rate, 6.4; divorce rate, 2.4. Major cities: Boston, 589,000; Worcester, 175,000; Springfield, 152,000; Lowell, 105,000; Cambridge, 102,000.

Government

Statehood: entered the Union on 6 Feb 1788 as the 6th state. State constitution: adopted 1780. Representation in US Congress: 2 senators; 10 representatives. Electoral college: 12 votes. Political divisions: 14 counties.

Economy

Employment: services, 38.2%; trade, 20.6%; manufacturing, 11.9%; government, 11.2%; finance, insurance, real estate, 8.2%; construction, 4.6%; transportation, public utilities, 4.1%; agriculture, forestry, fishing, 1.3%; mining, 0.1%. Production: services, 26.8%; finance, insurance, real estate, 24.5%; trade, 15.3%; manufacturing, 13.9%; government, 9.1%; transportation, utilities, 5.6%; construction, 4.1%; agriculture, 0.5%. Chief agricultural products: Crops: tobacco, cranberries, hay, potatoes, sweet corn, dairy products, eggs. Livestock: cattle, poultry. Fish catch: marine fish, lobster, crab, mollusks. Aquaculture: oysters, quahogs, soft-shelled clams, scallops. Chief manufactured products: Food products, dairy products, soft drinks, textiles, paper products, printing, pharmaceuticals, plastic products, nonferrous metal products, fabricated metal products, machinery, communications equipment, semiconductors and electronics, electrical equipment, software, aerospace equipment, aircraft engines, surgical and medical equipment.

Internet resources: <www.mass-vacation.com>; <www.mass.gov>.

Michigan

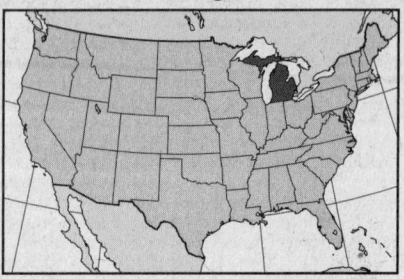

Name: Michigan, from Native American word Michigana meaning "great, or, large lake." Nicknames: Wolverine State and Great Lake State. Capital: Lansing. Rank: population: 8th; area: 22nd; pop. density: 15th. Motto: Si Quaeris Peninsulam Amoenam, Circumspice (If You Seek a Pleasant Peninsula, Look Around You). Song: "Michigan, My Michigan," words by Giles Kavanagh and music by H.J. O'Reilly Clint. Bird: robin. Fish: brook trout. Flower: apple blossom. Gemstone: chlorastrolite. Mammal: white-tailed deer (game mammal). Reptile: painted turtle. Rock: Petoskey stone. Tree: white pine.

Natural features

Area: 96,716 sq mi, 250,494 sq km. Highest point: Mount Arvon, 1,980 ft (604 m). Largest lake: Houghton Lake. Major rivers: Montreal, Brule, Menominee, St. Clair. Natural regions: the Central Lowland, Eastern Lake Section, covers all of Lower Michigan and part of the Upper Peninsula region; the western half of the Upper Peninsula consists of Superior Upland, as do two small areas at the eastern end. Location: Midwest, bordering Ohio, Indiana, and Wisconsin; international border with Canada. Climate: continental; the Great Lakes cool the hot winds of summer and warm the cold winds of winter, giving Michigan a milder climate than some other north-central states, although the Upper Peninsula is relatively cooler; very high snowfall along the coast of Lake Michigan. Land use: forest, 51.3%; agricultural, 22.8%; pasture, 4.4%; other, 21.4%.

People

Population (2003): 10,080,000; 177.5 persons per sq mi (68.5 persons per sq km) (land area only). Vital statistics (2001; per 1,000 population): birth rate, 13.4; death rate, 8.6; marriage rate, 6.7; divorce rate, 3.9. Major cities: Detroit, 925,000; Grand Rapids, 197,000; Warren, 138,000; Flint, 122,000; Sterling Heights, 126,000; Lansing, 119,000; Ann Arbor, 115,000; Livonia, 100,000.

Government

Statehood: entered the Union on 26 Jan 1837 as the 26th state. State constitution: adopted 1963. Representation in US Congress: 2 senators; 16 representatives. Electoral college: 17 votes (in the 2004 general elections based on the 2000 census). Political divisions: 83 counties.

For details about state governments, see pages 800–805; for energy data, see pages 830–832.

Economy

Employment: services, 29.2%; trade, 22.2%; manufacturing, 18.4%; government, 12.1%; finance, insurance, real estate, 6.9%; construction, 4.9%; transportation, public utilities, 3.8%; agriculture, forestry, fishing, 2.3%; mining, 0.2%. **Production:** manufacturing, 26.2%; services, 19.6%; trade, 17.1%; finance, insurance, real estate, 14.1%; government, 10.3%; transportation, utilities, 6.6%; construction, 4.8%; agriculture, 0.9%; mining, 0.3%. **Chief agricultural products:** *Crops:* apples, asparagus, beans, blueberries, carrots, celery, cherries, corn (maize), flowers, grapes and wine, honey, wool, maple syrup, mint, onions, peaches, plums, potatoes, dairy products, eggs, strawberries, sugar, soybeans. *Livestock:* beef and dairy cattle and calves, pigs, poultry, sheep and lambs. *Aquaculture:* Rainbow, brook and brown trout, yellow perch, catfish. *Extractive industries:* Christmas trees. **Chief manufactured products:** Motor vehicles, salt, plastics, pharmaceuticals, soaps and cleansers, milled grain, dry cereals, agricultural machinery, office furniture, dairy products, preserved fruits and vegetables, printed matter, electrical equipment, construction materials, measuring and control devices.

Internet resources: <www.michigan.org>; <www.michigan.gov>.

Minnesota

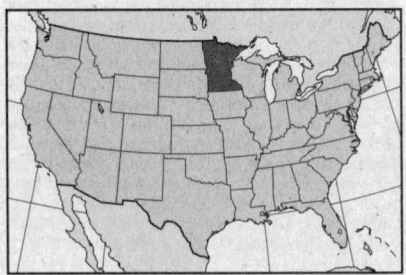

Name: Minnesota, from a Dakota word meaning "sky-tinted water." **Nickname:** North Star State. **Capital:** St. Paul. **Rank:** population: 21st; area: 14th; pop. density: 31st. **Motto:** *L'Étoile du Nord* (The Star of the North). **Song:** "Hail! Minnesota," first verse and music by Truman E. Rickard, second verse by Arthur E. Upson. **Bird:** common loon. **Fish:** walleye pike. **Flower:** pink and white lady slipper. **Gemstone:** Lake Superior agate. **Insect:** monarch butterfly. **Tree:** Norway pine.

Natural features

Area: 86,939 sq mi, 225,171 sq km. **Mountain ranges:** Mesabi, Vermillion, Cuyuna. **Highest point:** Eagle Mountain, 2,301 ft (701 m). **Largest lake:** Red Lake. **Major rivers:** Minnesota, St. Croix, Mississippi. **Natural regions:** Superior Upland, northeast corner; Central Lowland, covering most of the state; Western Lake Section, center; Dissected Till Plains, extreme southwest corner and south-central edge; Wisconsin Driftless Section, extreme southeast. **Location:** North central, bordering Wisconsin, Iowa, South Dakota, and North Dakota; international border with Canada. **Climate:** continental, with very cold winters and warm summers. **Land use:** agricultural, 44.8 (45)%; forest, 29.1 (29)%; pasture, 3.0%; other, 23.1 (23)%.

People

Population (2003): 5,059,000; 63.5 persons per sq mi (24.5 persons per sq km) (land area only). **Vital statistics** (2001; per 1,000 population): birth rate, 13.8; death rate, 7.6; marriage rate, 6.8; divorce rate, 3.3 **Major cities** (2000) Minneapolis, 376,000 (2002); St. Paul, 284,000 (2002); Duluth, 86,918; Rochester, 85,806; Bloomington, 85,172.

Government

Statehood: entered the Union on 11 May 1858 as the 32nd state. **State constitution:** adopted 1857. **Representation in US Congress:** 2 senators; 8 representatives. **Electoral college:** 10 votes. **Political divisions:** 87 counties.

Economy

Employment: services, 30.3%; trade, 22.0%; manufacturing, 14.3%; government, 12.0%; finance, insurance, real estate, 7.6%; transportation, public utilities, 4.7%; construction, 4.6%; agriculture, forestry, fishing, 4.2%; mining, 0.3%. **Production:** services, 20.8%; finance, insurance, real estate, 18.5%; manufacturing, 18.1%; trade, 17.6%; government, 10.2%; transportation, utilities, 7.6%; construction, 5.0%; agriculture, 1.7%; mining, 0.5%. **Chief agricultural products:** *Crops:* corn (maize), green peas, dry beans, onions, carrots, apples, oats, hay, spring wheat, barley, soybeans, potatoes, sugar beets, flaxseed, dairy products, eggs. *Livestock:* pigs, cattle and calves, poultry, sheep and lambs. **Chief manufactured products:** food processing, beer and malt beverages, dairy products, meatpacking, industrial machinery, computers and office machines, electronics and electric equipment, precision instruments, printing and publishing, call centers and communications, information technology, forest products, medical manufacturing, plastics manufacturing.

Internet resources: <www.exploreminnesota.com>; <www.state.mn.us>.

Mississippi

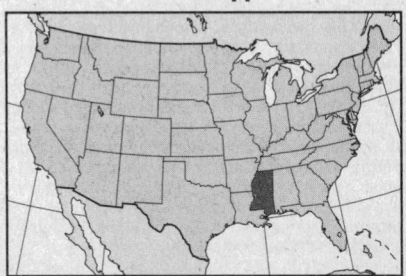

Name: Mississippi, from a Native American word meaning "great waters" or "father of waters." **Nickname:** Magnolia State. **Capital:** Jackson. **Rank:** population: 31st; area: 31st; pop. density: 32nd. **Motto:** *Virtute et Armis* (By Valor and Arms). **Song:** "Go, Mississippi," words and music by Houston Davis. **Bird:**

mockingbird. **Fish:** largemouth bass. **Flower:** magnolia. **Fossil:** prehistoric whale. **Insect:** honeybee. **Mammal:** white-tailed deer. **Marine mammal:** bottle-nosed dolphin (porpoise). **Rock:** petrified wood. **Tree:** magnolia tree.

Natural features

Area: 48,430 sq mi, 125,434 sq km. **Highest point:** Woodall Mountain, 806 ft (246 m). **Major rivers:** Mississippi, Pearl, Big Black, Yazoo, Tombigbee, Pascagoula, Tennessee. **Natural regions:** the entire state consists of the Coastal Plain, subdivided into the Mississippi Alluvial Plain in the west, and the East Gulf Coastal Plain comprising the central and eastern regions. **Location:** South, bordering Tennessee, Alabama, Louisiana, and Arkansas. **Climate:** mild, with hot, humid summers and mild winters; coastal area is subject to hurricanes from June to October. **Land use:** forest, 61.9%; agricultural, 21.5%; pasture, 6.5%; other, 10.1%.

People

Population (2003): 2,881,000; 61.4 persons per sq mi (23.7 persons per sq km) (land area only). **Vital statistics** (2001; per 1,000 population): birth rate, 15.1; death rate, 9.9; marriage rate, 6.7; divorce rate, 5.4. **Major cities** (2000): Jackson, 181,000 (2002); Gulfport, 71,127; Biloxi, 50,644; Hattiesburg, 44,779; Greenville, 41,633.

Government

Statehood: entered the Union on 10 Dec 1817 as the 20th state. **State constitution:** adopted 1890. **Representation in US Congress:** 2 senators; 5 representatives. **Electoral college:** 6 votes (in the 2004 general elections based on the 2000 census). **Political divisions:** 82 counties.

Economy

Employment: services, 24.5%; trade, 19.7%; government, 17.8%; manufacturing, 17.5%; construction, 5.5%; agriculture, forestry, fishing, 5.2%; finance, insurance, real estate, 4.7%; transportation, public utilities, 4.5%; mining, 0.6%. **Production:** manufacturing, 20.6%; services, 17.4%; trade, 16.8%; government, 16.0%; finance, insurance, real estate, 11.4%; transportation, utilities, 9.5%; construction, 4.7%; agriculture, 2.6%; mining, 1.0%. **Chief agricultural products:** Crops: cotton, soybeans, rice, wheat, corn, greenhouse and nursery plants, sweet potatoes, pecans, eggs. Livestock: poultry, cattle. Aquaculture: catfish, pearl farming. Fish catch: marine fish, freshwater fish, shrimp, oysters, crustaceans. Extractive industries: timber. **Chief manufactured products:** food products, transportation equipment, apparel, textiles, paper, electrical equipment, rubber products, primary metal products.

Internet resources: <www.visitmississippi.org>; <www.mississippi.gov>.

Missouri

Name: Missouri, named for Native American tribe that lived in the region; the name means "town of the

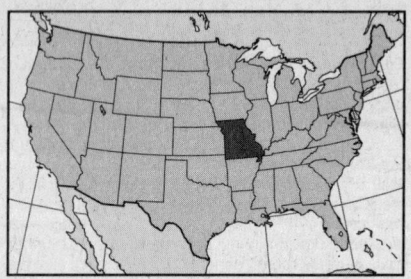

large canoes." **Nickname:** Show Me State. **Capital:** Jefferson City. **Rank:** population: 17th; area: 18th; pop. density: 28th. **Motto:** Salus Populi Suprema Lex Esto (The Welfare of the People Shall Be the Supreme Law). **Song:** "Missouri Waltz," words by J.R. Shannon and music by John Valentine Eppel, arrangement by Frederick Knight Logan. **Aquatic animal:** paddlefish. **Bird:** bluebird. **Fish:** channel catfish. **Flower:** white hawthorn blossom. **Fossil:** crinoid. **Insect:** honeybee. **Mammal:** Missouri mule. **Mineral:** galena. **Rock:** mozarkite. **Tree:** flowering dogwood.

Natural features

Area: 69,704 sq mi, 180,533 sq km. **Mountain ranges:** Ozark Plateau, St. Francois Mountains. **Highest point:** Taum Sauk Mountain, 1,772 ft (540 m). **Largest lake:** Truman Lake. **Major rivers:** Missouri, Mississippi, Des Plaines. **Natural regions:** the Central Lowland, northwestern, subdivided into the Dissected Till Plains to the north and the Osage Plains to the west; Ozark Plateaus, including the Springfield-Salem Plateaus, southeast; Coastal Plain, including the Mississippi Alluvial Plain, extreme southeast tip. **Location:** Midwest, bordering Iowa, Illinois, Kentucky, Tennessee, Arkansas, Oklahoma, Kansas, and Nebraska. **Climate:** continental, with hot, humid summers and cold winters; lies in "Tornado Alley," the zone of maximum tornado occurrence, and has an average of 27 tornadoes annually. **Land use:** agricultural, 45.4%; forest, 30.4%; pasture, 13.6%; other, 10.6%.

People

Population (2003): 5,704,000; 82.8 persons per sq mi (32.0 persons per sq km) (land area only). **Vital statistics** (2001; per 1,000 population): birth rate, 13.6; death rate, 9.8; marriage rate, 7.6; divorce rate, 4.3. **Major cities:** Kansas City, 443,000; St. Louis, 338,000; Springfield, 152,000; Independence, 113,000.

Government

Statehood: entered the Union on 10 Aug 1821 as the 24th state. **State constitution:** adopted 1945. **Representation in US Congress:** 2 senators; 9 representatives. **Electoral college:** 11 votes. **Political divisions:** 114 counties.

Economy

Employment: services, 29.3%; trade, 21.8%; government, 13.3%; manufacturing, 12.9%; finance, insurance, real estate, 6.8%; transportation, public

For details about state governments, see pages 800–805; for energy data, see pages 830–832.

utilities, 5.8%; construction, 5.5%; agriculture, forestry, fishing, 4.5%; mining, 0.2%. **Production:** services, 20.5%; manufacturing, 19.3%; trade, 17.1%; finance, insurance, real estate, 15.3%; government, 11.4%; transportation, utilities, 10.1%; construction, 4.9%; agriculture, 1.1%; mining, 0.3%. **Chief agricultural products:** *Crops:* soybeans, corn (maize), cotton, rice, grain sorghum, hay, wheat, fruits and vegetables, dairy products. *Livestock:* cattle, pigs, sheep, poultry. *Extractive industries:* timber. **Chief manufactured products:** industrial machinery, transportation equipment, food processing, malt beverages, soft drinks, meat and poultry products, preserved fruits and vegetables, soaps and detergents, agricultural chemicals, pharmaceuticals, printing and publishing, primary metals, nonelectrical machinery, fabricated metals, petroleum and coal products, electrical equipment, stone, clay and glass products.

Internet resources: <www.missouritourism.org>; <www.missouri.gov>.

Montana

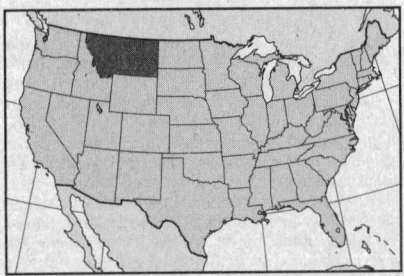

Name: Montana, from the Spanish word *montaña* ("mountain," or "mountainous region"). **Nickname:** Treasure State. **Capital:** Helena. **Rank:** population: 44th; area: 4th; pop. density: 48th. **Motto:** *Oro y Plata* (Gold and Silver). **Song:** "Montana," words by Charles C. Cohan and music by Joseph E. Howard. **Bird:** western meadowlark. **Fish:** cutthroat trout. **Flower:** bitterroot. **Fossil:** *Maiasaura.* **Gemstones:** agate and sapphire. **Mammal:** grizzly bear. **Tree:** ponderosa pine.

Natural features

Area: 147,042 sq mi, 380,838 sq km. **Mountain ranges:** Rocky Mountains, Grand Tetons. **Highest point:** Granite Peak, 12,799 ft (3,901 m). **Largest lake:** Flathead Lake. **Major rivers:** Kootenai, Clark Fork, Flathead, Missouri, Yellowstone. **Natural regions:** Northern Rocky Mountains, western two-fifths of the state; Middle Rocky Mountains, small area along the south-central border; Missouri Plateau region of the Great Plains Province, eastern three-fifths of the state. **Location:** Northwest, bordering North Dakota, South Dakota, Wyoming, and Idaho; international border with Canada. **Climate:** continental; most of Great Plains region is semiarid, with warm summers and cold winters; west of the Rocky Mountains the climate is milder. **Land use:** pasture, 49.4%; forest, 20.6%; agricultural, 19.9%; other, 10.1%.

People

Population (2003): 918,000; 6.3 persons per sq mi (2.4 persons per sq km) (land area only). **Vital statistics** (2001; per 1,000 population): birth rate, 12.3; death rate, 9.1; marriage rate, 7.2; divorce rate, 2.6. **Major cities** (2000): Billings, 89,847; Missoula, 57,053; Great Falls, 56,690; Butte-Silver Bow, 34,606; Bozeman, 27,509; Helena, 25,780.

Government

Statehood: entered the Union on 8 Nov 1889 as the 41st state. **State constitution:** adopted 1972. **Representation in US Congress:** 2 senators; 1 representative. **Electoral college:** 3 votes. **Political divisions:** 56 counties.

Economy

Employment: services, 30.4%; trade, 23.4%; government, 15.5%; agriculture, forestry, fishing, 6.7%; finance, insurance, real estate, 6.1%; construction, 6.1%; manufacturing, 5.6%; transportation, public utilities, 5.0%; mining, 1.3%. **Production:** services, 20.3%; trade, 16.9%; government, 16.4%; finance, insurance, real estate, 13.7%; transportation, utilities, 11.9%; manufacturing, 7.5%; construction, 5.6%; agriculture, 4.0%; mining, 3.7%. **Chief agricultural products:** *Crops:* wheat, barley, hay, oats, safflowers, sunflowers, mustard, sugar beets, dry beans, grapes, garlic, oil seeds, corn (maize), potatoes, honey, cherries, dairy products. *Livestock:* beef and dairy cattle and calves, sheep and lambs, poultry, horses, llamas. *Extractive industries:* timber, Christmas trees. **Chief manufactured products:** food processing, lumber and wood products, metal processing, petroleum products, chemical manufacturing, cement and concrete products, fabricated metal products, machinery.

Internet resources: <www.visitmt.com>; <www.mt.gov>.

Nebraska

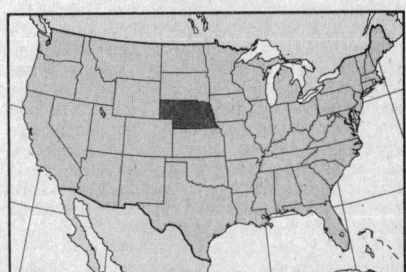

Name: Nebraska, from a Native American word meaning "flat water," a reference to the Platte River. **Nickname:** Cornhusker State. **Capital:** Lincoln. **Rank:** population: 38th; area: 15th; pop. density: 42nd. **Motto:** Equality Before the Law. **Song:** "Beautiful Nebraska," words and music by Jim Fras. **Bird:** western meadowlark. **Fish:** channel catfish. **Flower:** goldenrod. **Fossil:** mammoth. **Gemstone:** blue agate. **Insect:** honeybee. **Mammal:** white-tailed deer. **Rock:** prairie agate. **Tree:** cottonwood.

Natural features

Area: 77,354 sq mi, 200,345 sq km. **Highest point:** 5,424 ft (1,653 m), in Johnson Township, southwestern part of Kimball County. **Largest lake:** Lake McConaughy. **Major rivers:** Missouri, Platte, Elkhorn, Loup, Republican, Big Blue, Niobrara. **Natural regions:** Great Plains Province, western three-quarters of the state; Missouri Plateau at the northern corners; High Plains, central and north central; Plains Border, south border; Central Lowland, including the Dissected Till Plains, eastern quarter of the state. **Location:** Central, bordering South Dakota, Iowa, Missouri, Kansas, Colorado, and Wyoming. **Climate:** continental, with hot summers and very cold winters; blizzards are not uncommon in winter; western half of state is semiarid. **Land use:** agricultural, 47.9%; pasture, 44.4%; forest, 1.6%; other, 6.1%.

People

Population (2003): 1,739,000; 22.6 persons per sq mi (8.7 persons per sq km) (land area only). **Vital statistics** (2001; per 1,000 population): birth rate, 14.8; death rate, 8.8; marriage rate, 8.1; divorce rate, 3.7. **Major cities** (2000): Omaha, 399,000 (2002); Lincoln, 232,000 (2002); Bellevue, 44,382; Grand Island, 42,940; Kearney, 27,431.

Government

Statehood: entered the Union on 1 Mar 1867 as the 37th state. **State constitution:** adopted 1875. **Representation in US Congress:** 2 senators; 3 representatives. **Electoral college:** 5 votes. **Political divisions:** 93 counties.

Economy

Employment: services, 28.1%; trade, 22.2%; government, 14.1%; manufacturing, 10.4%; agriculture, forestry, fishing, 7.3%; finance, insurance, real estate, 7.2%; transportation, public utilities, 5.5%; construction, 5.0%; mining, 0.2%. **Production:** services, 19.1%; trade, 16.7%; finance, insurance, real estate, 15.5%; government, 14.1%; manufacturing, 14.0%; transportation, utilities, 10.8%; agriculture, 4.8%; construction, 4.8%; mining, 0.1%. **Chief agricultural products:** *Crops:* corn (maize), soybeans, hay, wheat, sorghum, dry edible beans, sugar beets. *Livestock:* beef and dairy cattle, pigs, sheep, poultry. **Chief manufactured products:** meatpacking, canned and frozen fruits and vegetables, flour, cereal, grain products, beverages, dairy products, livestock feeds, transportation equipment, motorcycles, small commercial vehicles, printing and publishing, rubber and plastic goods, fabricated metals, primary metals.

Internet resources: <www.visitnebraska.org>; <www.nebraska.gov>.

Nevada

Name: Nevada, from the Spanish *nevada* ("snow clad"), a reference to the high mountain scenery of the Sierra Nevada on the southwestern border with California. **Nicknames:** Sagebrush State and Silver State. **Capital:** Carson City. **Rank:** population: 35th; area:

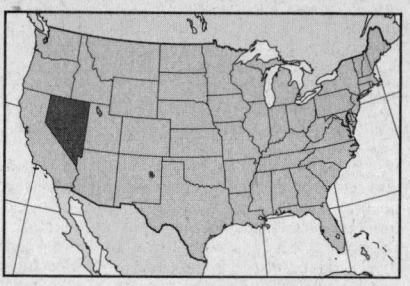

7th; pop. density: 43rd. **Motto:** All for Our Country. **Song:** "Home Means Nevada," words and music by Bertha Raffeto. **Bird:** mountain bluebird. **Fish:** Lahontan cutthroat trout. **Flower:** sagebrush. **Fossil:** ichthyosaur. **Gemstones:** fire opal, turquoise. **Mammal:** desert bighorn sheep. **Metal:** silver. **Reptile:** desert tortoise. **Rock:** sandstone. **Trees:** single-leaf piñon and bristlecone pine.

Natural features

Area: 110,561 sq mi, 286,351 sq km. **Mountain ranges:** Snake, Schell Creek, Monitor, Toiyabe, Shoshone, Humboldt, Santa Rosa. **Highest point:** Boundary Peak, 13,140 ft (4,005 m). **Largest lakes:** Pyramid Lake (natural), Lake Mead (artificial). **Major rivers:** Humboldt, Truckee, Carson, Walker, Muddy, Virgin. **Natural regions:** Basin and Range Province covers all of the state, except for the southwestern corner, which consists of the Cascade-Sierra Mountains, and the northeastern corner, which comprises part of the Columbia Plateau. **Location:** West, bordering Idaho, Utah, Arizona, California, and Oregon. **Climate:** semiarid but with regional variation: northern and eastern areas have long, cold winters and short, relatively hot summers, whereas in southern Nevada the summers are long and hot and the winters brief and mild. **Land use:** pasture, 65.9%; forest, 11.7%; agricultural, 1.2%; other, 21.2%.

People

Population (2003): 2,241,000; 20.4 persons per sq mi (7.9 persons per sq km) (land area only). **Vital statistics** (2001; per 1,000 population): birth rate, 16.1; death rate, 7.8; marriage rate, 75.0; divorce rate, 6.8. **Major cities:** Las Vegas, 509,000; Reno, 190,000; Henderson, 206,000; North Las Vegas, 136,000; Sparks, 66,346 (2000).

Government

Statehood: entered the Union on 31 Oct 1864 as the 36th state. **State constitution:** adopted 1864. **Representation in US Congress:** 2 senators; 2 representatives. **Electoral college:** 5 votes (in the 2004 general elections based on the 2000 census). **Political divisions:** 16 counties; 1 independent city.

Economy

Employment: services, 42.2%; trade, 19.5%; government, 10.7%; construction, 8.9%; finance, insurance, real estate, 7.0%; transportation, public utilities, 4.7%; manufacturing, 4.1%; agriculture, forestry, fishing, 1.5%; mining, 1.5%. **Production:** services, 32.5%; finance, insurance, real estate, 16.9%; trade, 15.0%; government, 10.3%; construction, 10.2%; transportation, utilities, 8.0%; manufacturing, 4.1%; mining, 2.2%; agriculture, 0.7%. **Chief agricultural products:** *Crops:* hay, wheat, corn (maize), potatoes, rye, oats, alfalfa, barley, vegetables, dairy products, some fruits. *Livestock:* cattle, horses, sheep, hogs, poultry. **Chief manufactured products:** food processing, candy, frozen desserts, dairy products, soft drinks, paper products, chemical products, plastics, construction materials, industrial machinery, printing and publishing.

Internet resources: <www.travelnevada.com>; <www.nevada.gov>.

New Hampshire

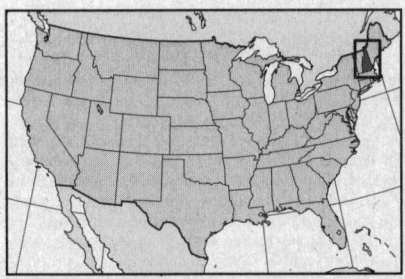

Name: New Hampshire, named for Hampshire, England, by Captain John Mason. **Nickname:** Granite State. **Capital:** Concord. **Rank:** population: 41st; area: 44th; pop. density: 19th. **Motto:** Live Free or Die. **Songs:** "Old New Hampshire," words by John F. Holmes and music by Maurice Hoffmann; "New Hampshire, My New Hampshire," words by Julius Richelson and music by Walter P. Smith. **Amphibian:** red-spotted newt. **Bird:** purple finch. **Fish:** brook trout (freshwater); striped bass (saltwater). **Flower:** purple lilac. **Gemstone:** smokey quartz. **Insect:** ladybug. **Mammal:** white-tailed deer. **Mineral:** beryl. **Rock:** granite. **Tree:** white birch.

Natural features

Area: 9,350 sq mi, 24,216 sq km. **Mountain ranges:** White Mountains, Ossipee, Sandwich Range, Presidential Range. **Highest point:** Mount Washington, 6,288 ft (1,917 m). **Largest lake:** Lake Winnipesaukee. **Major rivers:** Merrimack, Salmon Falls, Connecticut, Saco, Piscataqua, Androscoggin. **Natural regions:** the New England Province covers the entire state, and is subdivided into the White Mountain Section occupying the northern third, the New England Upland Section in the south-central region, and the Seaboard Lowland Section in the southeast corner. **Location:** New England, bordering Maine, Massachusetts, and Vermont; international border with Canada. **Climate:** temperate, but highly varied: winter temperatures may drop below 0 °F (–18 °C) for days at a time; summers are relatively cool, and precipitation is rather evenly distributed over the four seasons. **Land use:** forest, 79.3%; agricultural, 2.0%; pasture, 0.7%; other, 18.1%.

People

Population (2003): 1,288,000; 143.6 persons per sq mi (55.5 persons per sq km) (land area only). **Vital statistics** (2001; per 1,000 population): birth rate, 11.9; death rate, 7.8; marriage rate, 8.6; divorce rate, 5.0. **Major cities** (2000): Manchester, 108,000 (2002); Nashua, 86,605; Concord, 40,687; Derry, 34,021; Rochester, 28,461.

Government

Statehood: entered the Union on 21 Jun 1788 as the 9th state. **State constitution:** adopted 1784. **Representation in US Congress:** 2 senators; 2 representatives. **Electoral college:** 4 votes. **Political divisions:** 10 counties.

Economy

Employment: services, 31.5%; trade, 24.0%; manufacturing, 15.5%; government, 10.9%; finance, insurance, real estate, 6.9%; construction, 6.0%; transportation, public utilities, 3.5%; agriculture, forestry, fishing, 1.6%; mining, 0.1%. **Production:** finance, insurance, real estate, 23.2%; manufacturing, 22.1%; services, 19.6%; trade, 16.5%; government, 7.8%; transportation, utilities, 5.8%; construction, 4.1%; agriculture, 0.7%; mining, 0.1%. **Chief agricultural products:** *Crops:* apples, honey, fruits and vegetables, ornamental horticulture, Christmas trees, dairy products, eggs, herbs, maple syrup, wool. *Livestock:* horses, dairy cattle, sheep. *Fish catch:* marine fish, seafood. *Extractive products:* timber. **Chief manufactured products:** industrial machinery, computers and software, electrical equipment, semiconductors, processed foods, precision instruments, medical and surgical instruments, fabricated metal products, rubber and plastic products, printing and publishing, paper products.

Internet resources: <www.visitnh.gov>; <www.state.nh.us>.

New Jersey

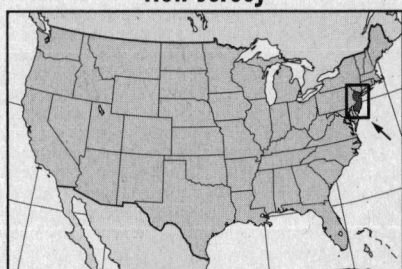

Name: New Jersey, named for the island of Jersey in the English Channel. **Nickname:** Garden State. **Capital:** Trenton. **Rank:** population: 10th; area: 46th; pop. density: 1st. **Motto:** Liberty and Prosperity. **Bird:** eastern goldfinch. **Fish:** brook trout. **Flower:** violet. **Fossil:** *Hadrosaurus foulkii.* **Insect:** honeybee. **Mammal:** horse. **Tree:** red oak.

Natural features

Area: 8,721 sq mi, 21,588 sq km. **Mountain range:** Appalachians. **Highest point:** Kittatinny Mountain,

1,803 ft (550 m). **Largest lake:** Lake Hopatcong. **Major rivers:** Delaware, Hudson, Passaic, Hackensack, Raritan. **Natural regions:** the Valley and Ridge Province, Middle Section, northwest corner; the New England Province, consisting of the New England Upland Section, located east of the Valley and Ridge area; Piedmont Province, including the Piedmont Lowlands, extending from the northeast corner to part of the border with Pennsylvania; the southern half of the state consists of the Coastal Plain, Embayed Section. **Location:** Northeast, bordering New York, Delaware, and Pennsylvania. **Climate:** continental; relatively colder winters in northwest, milder conditions in the south, and hot summers throughout the state. **Land use:** forest, 31.7%; agricultural, 13.4%; pasture, 0.6%; other, 54.3%.

People

Population (2003): 8,638,000; 1,164.6 persons per sq mi (449.6 persons per sq km) (land area only). **Vital statistics** (2001; per 1,000 population): birth rate, 14.0; death rate, 8.8; marriage rate, 6.6; divorce rate, 3.5. **Major cities:** Newark, 277,000; Jersey City, 240,000; Paterson, 151,000; Elizabeth, 123,000; Trenton, 85,403 (2000).

Government

Statehood: entered the Union on 18 Dec 1787 as the 3rd state. **State constitution:** adopted 1947. **Representation in US Congress:** 2 senators; 13 representatives. **Electoral college:** 15 votes. **Political divisions:** 21 counties.

Economy

Employment: services, 32.8%; trade, 21.6%; government, 13.0%; manufacturing, 11.0%; finance, insurance, real estate, 9.7%; transportation, public utilities, 6.3%; construction, 4.3%; agriculture, forestry, fishing, 1.2%; mining, 0.1%. **Production:** finance, insurance, real estate, 23.7%; services, 23.5%; trade, 17.0%; manufacturing, 11.9%; government, 10.1%; transportation, utilities, 9.5%; construction, 3.8%; agriculture, 0.5%; mining, 0.1%. **Chief agricultural products:** *Crops:* cranberries, blueberries, peaches, asparagus, bell peppers, spinach, lettuce, cucumbers, sweet corn, tomatoes, snap beans, cabbage, escarole and endive, eggplants, nursery and greenhouse products, dairy products, eggs. *Livestock:* horses, cattle, poultry. *Fish catch:* bluefish, tilefish, flounder, hake, shellfish. **Chief manufactured products:** chemical products, pharmaceuticals, electronic and electrical equipment, communications equipment, semiconductors, industrial equipment, petroleum products, fabricated metal products, clay products, food products.

Internet resources: <www.visitnj.org>; <www.newjersey.gov>.

New Mexico

Name: New Mexico, named for the country of Mexico. **Nickname:** Land of Enchantment. **Capital:** Santa Fe. **Rank:** population: 36th; area: 5th; pop. density: 45th. **Motto:** *Crescit Eundo* (It Grows as It Goes). **Songs:** "O,

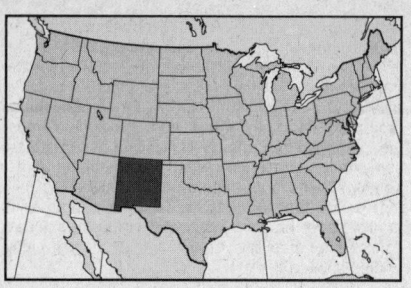

Fair New Mexico," words and music by Elizabeth Garrett; *"Así es Nuevo Mexico,"* words and music by Amadeo Lucero. **Bird:** roadrunner. **Fish:** New Mexico cutthroat trout. **Flower:** yucca. **Fossil:** coelophysis. **Gemstone:** turquoise. **Insect:** tarahtula hawk wasp. **Tree:** piñon pine.

Natural features

Area: 121,590 sq mi, 314,915 sq km. **Mountain ranges:** Rocky Mountains, Sangre de Cristo Range. **Highest point:** Wheeler Peak, 13,160 ft (4,011 m). **Largest lake:** Elephant Butte Reservoir. **Major rivers:** Rio Grande, Pecos, Canadian, San Juan, Gila. **Natural regions:** eastern third of the state consists of the Great Plains Province, subdivided into the Raton Section to the north, the High Plains along the eastern edge, and the Pecos Valley to the west; Southern Rocky Mountains, north-central region; Colorado Plateau, including the Navajo Section and Datil Section, northwest corner; Basin and Range Province, central region and southwest corner, with the Sacramento Section to the east and the Mexican Highland to the south. **Location:** Southwest, bordering Colorado, Oklahoma, Texas, and Arizona; international border with Mexico. **Climate:** arid; moderate temperatures but great variation by altitude; temperatures drop dramatically after dark. **Land use:** pasture, 67.2%; forest, 18.1%; agricultural, 3.1%; other, 11.6%.

People

Population (2003): 1,875,000; 15.5 persons per sq mi (6.0 persons per sq km). **Vital statistics** (2001; per 1,000 population). Birth rate, 15.4; death rate, 7.7; marriage rate, 7.9; divorce rate, 5.1. **Major cities** (2000): Albuquerque, 464,000 (2002); Las Cruces, 74,267; Santa Fe, 62,203; Rio Rancho, 51,765; Roswell, 45,293.

Government

Statehood: entered the Union on 6 Jan 1912 as the 47th state. **State constitution:** adopted 1911. **Representation in US Congress:** 2 senators; 3 representatives. **Electoral college:** 5 votes. **Political divisions:** 33 counties.

Economy

Employment: services, 29.7%; trade, 21.9%; government, 20.4%; construction, 6.4%; finance, insurance, real estate, 6.0%; manufacturing, 5.7%; transportation, public utilities, 4.2%; agriculture, forestry, fishing, 3.6%; mining, 2.1%. **Production:** services, 18.0%;

For details about state governments, see pages 800–805; for energy data, see pages 830–832.

government, 16.8%; manufacturing, 16.7%; trade, 13.6%; finance, insurance, real estate, 13.1%; mining, 8.4%; transportation, utilities, 7.4%; construction, 4.0%; agriculture, 2.1%. **Chief agricultural products:** *Crops:* pecans, apples, potatoes, onions, dry beans, chile, peanuts (groundnuts), hay, sorghum, corn (maize), wheat, eggs, dairy products, wool. *Livestock:* dairy and beef cattle, poultry, sheep and lambs. *Extractive industries:* timber. **Chief manufactured products:** electronic equipment, semiconductors, printing and publishing, processed foods.

Internet resources: <www.newmexico.org>; <www.state.nm.us>.

New York

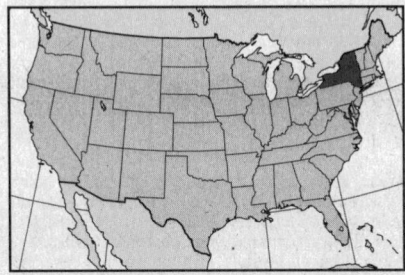

Name: New York, named in honor of the English Duke of York. **Nickname:** Empire State. **Capital:** Albany. **Rank:** population: 3rd; area: 30th; pop. density: 7th. **Motto:** *Excelsior* (Ever Upward). **Song:** "I Love New York," words and music by Steve Karmen. **Bird:** bluebird. **Fish:** brook trout. **Flower:** rose. **Fossil:** *Eurypterus remipes.* **Gemstone:** garnet. **Mammal:** beaver. **Tree:** sugar maple.

Natural features

Area: 54,556 sq mi, 141,299 sq km. **Mountain ranges:** Adirondack, Catskill, Shawangunk, Taconic. **Highest point:** Mount Marcy, 5,344 ft (1,629 m). **Largest lake:** Oneida Lake. **Major rivers:** Hudson, Mohawk, Genesee, Oswego, Delaware, Susquehanna, Allegheny. **Natural regions:** the Central Lowland, Eastern Lake Section, extends along the northern coast of Lake Ontario; St. Lawrence Valley, Northern Section, extends along the northern border with Canada; Adirondack Province, northeast; Appalachian Plateaus, including the Mohawks, Southern New York, and Catskill Sections, extend along southern border with Pennsylvania and up halfway through the state; Valley and Ridge Province, southeastern edge bordering Connecticut and Massachusetts; Coastal Plain, Embayed Section, covering the islands of Manhattan and Long Island. **Location:** Northeast, bordering Vermont, Massachusetts, Connecticut, New Jersey, and Pennsylvania; international border with Canada. **Climate:** temperate continental, with hot, humid summers and cold, dry, snowy winters. **Land use:** forest, 56.4%; agricultural, 17.4%; pasture, 8.7%; other, 17.5%.

People

Population (2003): 19,190,000; 406.4 persons per sq mi (156.9 persons per sq km) (land area only). **Vital statistics** (1999; per 1,000 population): birth rate, 13.9; death rate, 8.3; marriage rate, 7.9; divorce

rate, 3.0. **Major cities:** New York, 8,084,000; Buffalo, 288,000; Rochester, 217,000; Yonkers, 197,000; Syracuse, 145,000; Albany, 95,658 (2000).

Government

Statehood: entered the Union on 26 Jul 1788 as the 11th state. **State constitution:** adopted 1894. **Representation in US Congress:** 2 senators; 31 representatives. **Electoral college:** 31 votes (in the 2004 general elections based on the 2000 census). **Political divisions:** 62 counties.

Economy

Employment: services, 35.9%; trade, 19.0%; government, 14.1%; finance, insurance, real estate, 11.1%; manufacturing, 9.7%; transportation, public utilities, 4.9%; construction, 3.9%; agriculture, forestry, fishing, 1.3%; mining, 0.1%. **Production:** finance, insurance, real estate, 32.8%; services, 23.0%; trade, 12.9%; manufacturing, 10.3%; government, 10.2%; transportation, utilities, 7.3%; construction, 3.0%; agriculture, 0.4%; mining, 0.1%. **Chief agricultural products:** *Crops:* apples, cabbage, corn (maize), potatoes, onions, grapes, snap beans, dry beans, grain, hay, cherries, strawberries, maple syrup, horticulture products, milk, eggs, dairy products. *Livestock:* cattle and calves, chickens. **Chief manufactured products:** food processing, chemical products, apparel, primary metals, industrial machinery, computers and software, scientific and measuring instruments, transportation equipment, electric and electronic equipment, industrial machinery, printing and publishing, biotechnology.

Internet resources: <www.iloveny.com>; <www.state.ny.us>.

North Carolina

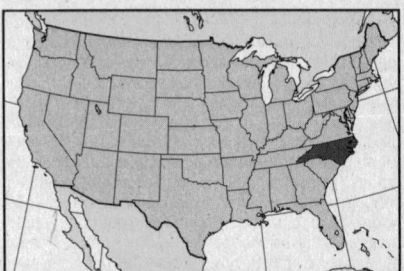

Name: North Carolina, named in honor of Charles I of England. **Nickname:** The Old North State. **Capital:** Raleigh. **Rank:** population: 11th; area: 29th; pop. density: 17th. **Motto:** *Esse Quam Videri* (To Be Rather Than to Seem). **Song:** "The Old North State," words by William Gaston to a German tune. **Bird:** cardinal. **Fish:** channel bass. **Flower:** dogwood. **Gemstone:** emerald. **Insect:** honeybee. **Mammal:** gray squirrel. **Reptile:** eastern box turtle. **Rock:** granite. **Tree:** pine.

Natural features

Area: 53,819 sq mi, 139,389 sq km. **Mountain ranges:** Appalachian, Great Smoky, Blue Ridge. **Highest point:** Mount Mitchell, 6,684 ft (2,037 m).

Largest lake: Lake Mattamuskeet. **Major rivers:** Roanoke, Yadkin, Pee Dee. **Natural regions:** Valley and Ridge Province, far western edge; Piedmont Province, consisting of the Piedmont Upland, extends in a southwest to northeast direction through the center of the state; Coastal Plain comprises the eastern third, divided into the Sea Island Section to the south and the Embayed Section to the north. **Location:** East coast, bordering Virginia, South Carolina, Georgia, and Tennessee. **Climate:** ranges from medium continental conditions in the mountain region (though summers are cooler and rainfall heavier) to the subtropical conditions of the state's southeastern corner; hurricanes occasionally occur along the coast, and there have been tornadoes inland. **Land use:** forest, 60%; agricultural, 19%; pasture, 3%; other, 19%.

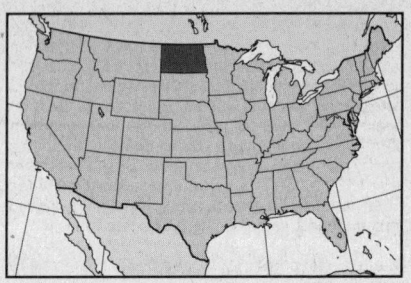

People

Population (2003): 8,407,000; 172.6 persons per sq mi (66.6 persons per sq km) (land area only). **Vital statistics** (2001; per 1,000 population): birth rate, 15.1; death rate, 8.6; marriage rate, 7.8; divorce rate, 4.5. **Major cities:** Charlotte, 581,000; Raleigh, 307,000; Greensboro, 228,000; Durham, 196,000; Winston-Salem, 189,000; Fayetteville, 124,000.

Government

Statehood: entered the Union on 21 Nov 1789 as the 12th state. **State constitution:** adopted 1970. **Representation in US Congress:** 2 senators, 12 representatives. **Electoral college:** 15 votes (in the 2004 general elections based on the 2000 census). **Political divisions:** 100 counties.

Economy

Employment: services, 25.1%; trade, 21.2%; manufacturing, 18.5%; government, 15.2%; construction, 6.6%; finance, insurance, real estate, 5.9%; transportation, public utilities, 4.3%; agriculture, forestry, fishing, 3.1%; mining, 0.1%. **Production:** manufacturing, 24.1%; finance, insurance, real estate, 18.3%; services, 16.4%; trade, 15.0%; government, 12.5%; transportation, utilities, 7.1%; construction, 4.9%; agriculture, 1.5%; mining, 0.2%. **Chief agricultural products:** *Crops:* tobacco, corn (maize), barley, potatoes, peanuts (groundnuts), apples, blueberries, grapes, peaches, pecans, strawberries, tomatoes, cabbages, watermelons, cucumbers, sweet potatoes, horticultural products, Christmas trees, dairy products, eggs. *Livestock:* cattle, chickens, pigs, horses. *Aquaculture:* catfish, trout. *Extractive industries:* timber. **Chief manufactured products:** textiles, cotton and synthetic fibers, yarns, threads, knitted goods, cigarettes and tobacco products, chemical products, pharmaceuticals, electronic and electrical equipment, furniture, lumber, paper products, processed foods.

Internet resources: <www.visitnc.com>; <www.northcarolina.gov>.

North Dakota

Name: North Dakota, from the Dakota division of the Sioux, the Native American tribe that inhabited the plains before the arrival of Europeans; *dakota* is the Sioux word for "friend." **Nickname:** Peace Garden State. **Capital:** Bismarck. **Rank:** population: 48th; area: 17th; pop. density: 47th. **Motto:** Liberty and Union Now and Forever, One and Inseparable. **Song:** "North Dakota Hymn," words by James W. Foley and music by C.S. Putnam. **Bird:** western meadowlark. **Fish:** northern pike. **Flower:** wild prairie rose. **Fossil:** teredo petrified wood. **Tree:** American elm.

Natural features

Area: 70,700 sq mi, 183,112 sq km. **Highest point:** White Butte, 3,506 ft (1,069 m). **Largest lake:** Devils Lake. **Major rivers:** Red, Souris, Missouri, Little Missouri, James. **Natural regions:** central Lowland covers eastern half of the state, with the Western Lake Section lying in the east-central region; Great Plains Province, western half of the state, includes sections of the Missouri Plateau to the north and south. **Location:** North central, bordering Minnesota, South Dakota, and Montana; international border with Canada. **Climate:** continental, with hot summers and cold winters, warm days and cool nights in summer, low humidity and low precipitation, and much wind and sunshine. **Land use:** agricultural, 65.3%; pasture, 25.7%; forest, 1.0%; other, 8.1%.

People

Population (2003): 634,000; 9.2 persons per sq mi (3.5 persons per sq km) (land area only). **Vital statistics** (2001; per 1,000 population): birth rate, 12.2; death rate, 9.5; marriage rate, 6.6; divorce rate, 2.7. **Major cities** (2000) Fargo, 90,599; Bismarck, 55,532; Grand Forks, 49,321; Minot, 36,567.

Government

Statehood: entered the Union on 2 Nov 1889 as the 39th state. **State constitution:** adopted 1889. **Representation in US Congress:** 2 senators; 1 representative. **Electoral college:** 3 votes. **Political divisions:** 53 counties.

Economy

Employment: services, 28.5%; trade, 22.5%; government, 16.4%; agriculture, forestry, fishing, 9.7%; manufacturing, 5.7%; finance, insurance, real estate, 5.6%; transportation, public utilities, 5.3%; construction, 5.2%; mining, 1.1%. **Production:** trade, 19.5%; services, 19.4%; government, 14.4%; finance, insurance, real estate, 14.1%; transportation, utilities, 10.3%; manufacturing, 9.0%; construction, 5.5%;

For details about state governments, see pages 800–805; for energy data, see pages 830–832.

agriculture, 4.1%; mining, 3.6%. **Chief agricultural products:** *Crops:* hard red spring wheat, durum wheat, flaxseed, canola, dry beans, sunflowers, barley, honey, potatoes, dairy products, wool. *Livestock:* cattle, sheep, pigs. *Extractive industries:* timber. **Chief manufactured products:** food processing, wood products, petroleum products, transportation equipment, machinery.

Internet resources: <www.ndtourism.com>; <www.northdakota.gov>.

Ohio

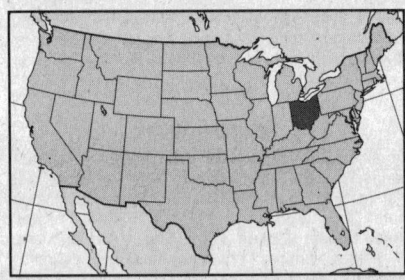

Name: Ohio, from an Iroquois word meaning "great river." **Nickname:** Buckeye State. **Capital:** Columbus. **Rank:** population: 7th; area: 35th; pop. density: 9th. **Motto:** With God, All Things Are Possible. **Song:** "Beautiful Ohio," words by Ballad MacDonald and music by Mary Earl. **Bird:** cardinal. **Flower:** red carnation. **Fossil:** *Trilobite isotelus.* **Gemstone:** flint. **Insect:** ladybug. **Mammal:** white-tailed deer. **Reptile:** black racer snake. **Tree:** Ohio buckeye.

Natural features

Area: 44,825 sq mi, 116,096 sq km. **Highest point:** Campbell Hill, 1,550 ft (472 m). **Largest lake:** Grand Lake St. Marys. **Major rivers:** Ohio, Maumee, Cuyahoga, Miami, Scioto, Muskingum. **Natural regions:** the Appalachian Plateau, eastern half of the state, includes the Southern New York Section to the north, and the Kanawha Section to the east; the Central Lowlands, western half of the state, includes the Eastern Lake Section in the northwest corner, the Till Plains in the central region, and the Lexington Plain in the southwest. **Location:** Midwest, bordering Michigan, Pennsylvania, West Virginia, Kentucky, and Indiana. **Climate:** continental, with hot, humid summers and cold, dry winters. **Land use:** agricultural, 45.9%; forest, 28.9%; pasture, 5.3%; other, 20.0%.

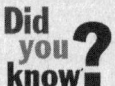

Did you know? Ohio is the only state in the US in which the three largest cities start with the same letter—Columbus, Cleveland, and Cincinnati.

People

Population (2003): 11,436,000; 279.3 persons per sq mi (107.8 persons per sq km) (land area only). **Vital statistics** (2001; per 1,000 population): birth rate, 13.4; death rate, 9.5; marriage rate, 7.3; divorce

rate, 4.0. **Major cities:** Columbus, 725,000; Cleveland, 468,000; Cincinnati, 324,000; Toledo, 309,000; Akron, 214,000; Dayton, 163,000.

Government

Statehood: entered the Union on 1 Mar 1803 as the 17th state. **State constitution:** adopted 1851. **Representation in US Congress:** 2 senators; 19 representatives. **Electoral college:** 20 votes (in the 2004 general elections based on the 2000 census). **Political divisions:** 88 counties.

Economy

Employment: services, 29.0%; trade, 22.8%; manufacturing, 17.0%; government, 12.1%; finance, insurance, real estate, 7.2%; construction, 5.1%; transportation, public utilities, 4.3%; agriculture, forestry, fishing, 2.3%; mining, 0.3%. **Production:** manufacturing, 25.8%; services, 18.2%; trade, 16.8%; finance, insurance, real estate, 15.5%; government, 10.7%; transportation, utilities, 7.4%; construction, 4.3%; agriculture, 0.8%; mining, 0.4%. **Chief agricultural products:** *Crops:* corn (maize), soybeans, grapes, apples, vegetables, tobacco, winter wheat, dairy products, eggs, greenhouse and nursery products. *Livestock:* cattle, hogs, poultry, goats. *Extractive industries:* timber. **Chief manufactured products:** industrial machinery, non-electrical machinery, food processing, transportation equipment, fabricated metals, iron and steel, chemical products and pharmaceuticals, rubber products.

Internet resources: <www.discoverohio.com>; <www.ohio.gov>.

Oklahoma

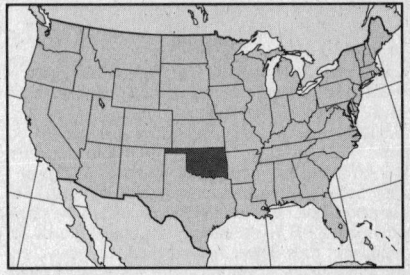

Name: Oklahoma, from two Choctaw words: *okla* meaning "people" and *humma* meaning "red." **Nickname:** Sooner State. **Capital:** Oklahoma City. **Rank:** population: 28th; area: 19th; pop. density: 35th. **Motto:** *Labor Omnia Vincit* (Labor Conquers All Things). **Song:** "Oklahoma," words by Richard Rodgers and music by Oscar Hammerstein. **Bird:** scissor-tailed flycatcher. **Fish:** white, or sand, bass. **Flower:** mistletoe. **Insect:** honeybee. **Mammal:** bison. **Reptile:** collared lizard (also know as the mountain boomer). **Rock:** rose rock. **Tree:** redbud.

Natural features

Area: 69,898 sq mi, 181,036 sq km. **Mountain ranges:** Ouachita, Arbuckle, Wichita, Sandstone Hills. **Highest point:** Black Mesa, 4,978 ft (1,517 m).

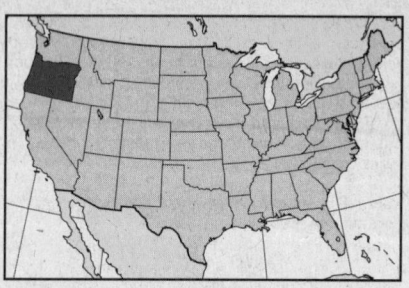

Largest lake: Lake Eufaula. Major rivers: Arkansas, Red, Canadian. Natural regions: Great Plains Province, panhandle region, includes the High Plains to the west and the Plains Border to the east; Central Lowland, covers most of the state, includes the Osage Plains in the central region; West Gulf Coastal Plain, southeastern corner; Ouachita Province, east-central region, includes the Arkansas Valley in the center and the Ouachita Mountains to the south; Ozark Plateaus, northeast corner, includes the Boston Mountains and Springfield-Salem Plateaus. Location: South central, bordering Kansas, Missouri, Arkansas, Texas, New Mexico, and Colorado. Climate: variable by region: the southern humid belt merges with a colder northern continental one and humid eastern and dry western zones that cut through the state; no region is free from heavy wind; typical sudden rises and falls in temperature cause many heavy thunderstorms, blizzards, and tornadoes. Land use: pasture, 39.4%; agricultural, 37.2%; forest, 14.2%; other, 9.3%.

People

Population (2003); 3,512,000; 51.1 persons per sq mi (19.7 persons per sq km) (land area only). Vital statistics (2001; per 1,000 population): birth rate, 14.8; death rate, 10.0; marriage rate, 4.9; divorce rate, 3.4. Major cities (2000): Oklahoma City, 519,000 (2002); Tulsa, 392,000 (2002); Norman, 95,694; Lawton, 92,757; Broken Arrow, 74,859.

Government

Statehood: entered the Union on 16 Nov 1907 as the 46th state. State constitution: adopted 1907. Representation in US Congress: 2 senators; 6 representatives. Electoral college: 7 votes (in the 2004 general elections based on the 2000 census). Political divisions: 77 counties.

Economy

Employment: services, 28.3%; trade, 20.9%; government, 16.6%; manufacturing, 10.0%; finance, insurance, real estate, 5.8%; agriculture, forestry, fishing, 5.6%; transportation, public utilities, 5.1%; construction, 4.8%; mining, 3.0%. Production: services, 18.2%; manufacturing, 16.9%; trade, 16.5%; government, 15.9%; finance, insurance, real estate, 12.2%; transportation, utilities, 9.2%; mining, 4.9%; construction, 3.8%; agriculture, 2.3%. Chief agricultural products: Crops: wheat, hay, sorghum, soybeans, cotton, dairy products. Livestock: cattle and calves, poultry, hogs and pigs. Chief manufactured products: electronics and electrical equipment, communications equipment, transportation equipment, food processing, petroleum products.

Internet resources: <www.travelok.com>; <www.ok.gov>.

Oregon

Nickname: Beaver State. Capital: Salem. Rank: population: 27th; area: 10th; pop. density: 39th. Motto: Alis Volat Propiis (She Flies with Her Own Wings). Song: "Oregon, My Oregon," words by J.A. Buchanan

and music by Henry B. Murtagh. Bird: western meadowlark. Fish: Chinook salmon. Flower: Oregon grape. Gemstone: Oregon sunstone. Insect: Oregon swallowtail. Mammal: beaver. Rock: thunderegg. Tree: Douglas fir.

Natural features

Area: 98,381 sq mi, 254,805 sq km. Mountain ranges: Coast Range, Klamath Mountains, Cascade Range, Blue Mountains, Wallowa Mountains. Highest point: Mount Hood, 11,235 ft (3,424 m). Largest lake: Upper Klamath Lake. Major rivers: Snake, Owyhee, Columbia, Coquille. Natural regions: northern Rocky Mountains, northeastern corner, includes the Blue Mountain Section; Columbia Plateaus, north and north-central region, includes the Walla Walla Plateau in the central section, Harney Section to the south, and Payette Section to the southeast; Basin and Range Province, south-central border, includes the Great Basin; Cascade Sierra Mountains, includes the Middle and Southern Cascades, west central; Pacific Border Province, western coast, with the Klamath Mountains to the south, the Oregon Coast Range in the center and north, and the Puget Trough to the east. Location: Northwest, bordering Washington, Idaho, Nevada, and California. Climate: ranges from equable, mild, marine conditions on the coast to continental conditions of dryness and extreme temperature in the interior. Land use: forest, 43.4%; pasture, 36.4%; agricultural, 8.7%; other, 11.5%.

People

Population (2003): 3,560,000; 37.1 persons per sq mi (14.3 persons per sq km) (land area only). Vital statistics (2001; per 1,000 population): birth rate, 13.5; death rate, 8.7; marriage rate, 7.7; divorce rate, 4.9. Major cities: Portland, 539,000; Eugene, 140,000; Salem, 141,000; Gresham, 90,205 (2000); Beaverton, 76,129 (2000).

Government

Statehood: entered the Union on 14 Feb 1859 as the 33rd state. State constitution: adopted 1857. Representation in US Congress: 2 senators; 5 representatives. Electoral college: 7 votes. Political divisions: 36 counties.

Economy

Employment: services, 29.4%; trade, 22.8%; manufacturing, 13.1%; government, 12.6%; finance, insurance, real estate, 6.6%; construction, 5.7%;

For details about state governments, see pages 800–805; for energy data, see pages 830–832.

agriculture, forestry, fishing, 5.1%; transportation, public utilities, 4.5%; mining, 0.2%. **Production:** manufacturing, 24.8%; services, 17.6%; trade, 16.1%; finance, insurance, real estate, 14.4%; government, 11.8%; transportation, utilities, 7.1%; construction, 5.3%; agriculture, 2.8%; mining, 0.1%. **Chief agricultural products:** *Crops:* horticulture and nursery products, Christmas trees, berries, pears, cherries, apples, hazelnuts, snap beans, peas, onions, carrots, wheat, hay, potatoes, barley, dry beans, mint, hops, corn (maize), sugar beets, dairy products. *Livestock:* cattle and calves, horses, mink, poultry, sheep and lambs. *Fish catch:* marine fish, tuna, salmon, shellfish, crab, shrimp. *Extractive industries:* timber. **Chief manufactured products:** lumber and wood products, food processing, aircraft and spacecraft, electronics, semiconductors, computers.

Internet resources: <www.traveloregon.com>; <www.oregon.gov>.

Pennsylvania

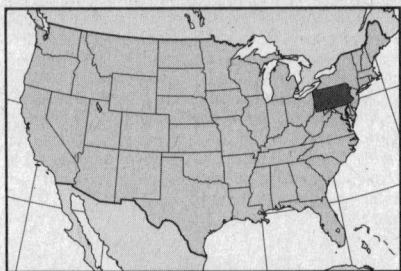

Name: Pennsylvania, named for Admiral Sir William Penn, father of the territory's founder, William Penn, and including also the term *sylvania* ("woodlands"). **Nickname:** Keystone State. **Capital:** Harrisburg. **Rank:** population: 6th; area: 32nd; pop. density: 10th. **Motto:** Virtue, Liberty, and Independence. **Song:** "Pennsylvania," written and composed by Eddie Khoury and Ronnie Bonner. **Bird:** ruffled grouse. **Fish:** brook trout. **Flower:** mountain laurel. **Fossil:** *Phacops rana.* **Insect:** firefly. **Mammal:** white-tailed deer. **Tree:** hemlock.

Natural features

Area: 46,055 sq mi, 119,283 sq km. **Mountain ranges:** Appalachian, Allegheny. **Highest point:** Mount Davis, 3,213 ft (979 m). **Largest lake:** Raystown Lake. **Major rivers:** Delaware, Lehigh, Schuylkill, Susquehanna, Ohio. **Natural regions:** central Lowland, Eastern Lake Section, extreme northwestern edge; Appalachian Plateaus, including the Southern New York, Allegheny Mountain, and Kanawha Sections, western half of state; Valley and Ridge Province, central region, includes portions of the Appalachian Mountains; Piedmont Province, comprising the Piedmont Lowlands and Upland, southeast corner; Coastal Plain, extreme southeast edge; New England Province, with the New England Upland Section, east-central border. **Location:** Northeast, bordering New York, New Jersey, Delaware, Maryland, West Virginia, Ohio. **Climate:** continental, with warm humid summers and cold snowy winters in general, but with wide fluctuations in seasonal temperatures. **Land use:** forest, 55.3%; agricultural, 18.1%; pasture, 3.2%; other, 23.5%.

People

Population (2003): 12,365,000; 275.9 persons per sq mi (106.5 persons per sq km) (land area only). **Vital statistics** (2001; per 1,000 population): birth rate, 12.0; death rate, 10.5; marriage rate, 6.0; divorce rate, 3.2. **Major cities:** Philadelphia, 1,492,000; Pittsburgh, 328,000; Allentown, 106,000; Erie, 102,000; Reading, 81,207 (2000).

Government

Statehood: entered the Union on 12 Dec 1787 as the 2nd state. **State constitution:** adopted 1968. **Representation in US Congress:** 2 senators, 21 representatives. **Electoral college:** 21 votes (in the 2004 general elections based on the 2000 census). **Political divisions:** 67 counties.

Economy

Employment: services, 32.7%; trade, 21.5%; manufacturing, 14.5%; government, 11.4%; finance, insurance, real estate, 7.7%; construction, 5.0%; transportation, public utilities, 4.9%; agriculture, forestry, fishing, 2.0%; mining, 0.4%. **Production:** services, 22.4%; manufacturing, 19.4%; finance, insurance, real estate, 18.4%; trade, 15.2%; government, 10.2%; transportation, utilities, 8.6%; construction, 4.2%; agriculture, 0.9%; mining, 0.7%. **Chief agricultural products:** *Crops:* mushrooms, apples, tobacco, grapes, peaches, cut flowers, dairy products. *Livestock:* cattle, poultry, pigs, horses. **Chief manufactured products:** electronic equipment, communications systems, semiconductors, chemical and pharmaceutical products, food processing, iron and steel, industrial machinery, transportation equipment, paper products, printing and publishing.

Internet resources: <www.visitpa.com>; <www.state.pa.us>.

Rhode Island

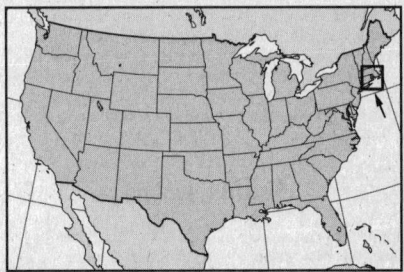

Name: Rhode Island, from the Greek island of Rhodes. **Nicknames:** Little Rhody and Ocean State. **Capital:** Providence. **Rank:** population: 43rd; area: 50th; pop. density: 2nd. **Motto:** Hope. **Song:** "Rhode Island," words and music by T. Clarke Brown. **Bird:** Rhode Island red. **Flower:** violet. **Mineral:** bowenite. **Rock:** cumberlandite.

Natural features

Area: 1,545 sq mi, 4,002 sq km, including 168 sq mi, 435 sq km of water surface. **Highest point:** Jerimoth Hill, 812 ft (247 m). **Largest lake:** Scituate Reservoir.

Major rivers: Blackstone, Pawtuxet, Pawcatuck. **Natural regions:** the entire state is part of the New England Province, subdivided into the New England Upland (western two-thirds) and the Seaboard Lowland (eastern third). **Location:** New England, bordering Connecticut and Massachusetts. **Climate:** humid continental climate; marine influences are discernible in differences between coastal and inland location; extreme weather conditions including tropical storms, ice storms, and heavy snow. **Land use:** forest, 53.2%; agricultural, 4.5%; pasture, 0.4%; other, 41.9%.

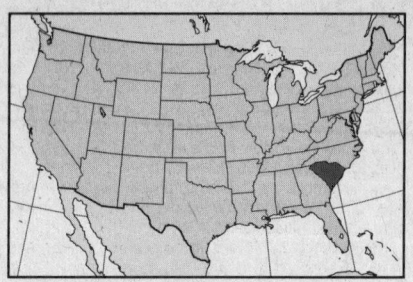

People

Population (2003): 1,076,000; 1,029.7 persons per sq mi (397.6 persons per sq km) (land area only). **Vital statistics** (2001; per 1,000 population): birth rate, 12.7; death rate, 9.5; marriage rate, 8.6; divorce rate, 3.3. **Major cities** (2000) Providence, 176,000 (2002); Warwick, 85,808; Cranston, 79,269; Pawtucket, 72,958; East Providence, 48,688.

Government

Statehood: entered the Union on 29 May 1790 as the 13th state. **State constitution:** adopted 1986. **Representation in US Congress:** 2 senators; 2 representatives. **Electoral college:** 4 votes. **Political divisions:** 5 counties.

Economy

Employment: services, 34.7%; trade, 20.3%; manufacturing, 14.8%; government, 13.4%; finance, insurance, real estate, 7.6%; construction, 4.4%; transportation, public utilities, 3.4%; agriculture, forestry, fishing, 1.3%; mining, 0.1%. **Production:** finance, insurance, real estate, 26.7%; services, 21.7%; trade, 14.3%; manufacturing, 12.6%; government, 12.0%; transportation, utilities, 6.7%; construction, 5.3%; agriculture, 0.7%. **Chief agricultural products:** *Crops:* hay, corn (maize), apples, peaches, dairy products, eggs, potatoes. *Livestock:* poultry, cattle, sheep. *Fish catch:* marine fish, shellfish. **Chief manufactured products:** jewelry, silverware, textiles, fabricated metal products, electrical equipment, machinery, surgical and navigation instruments, plastic goods, printing and publishing, primary metals, food processing.

Internet resources: <www.visitrhodeisland.com>; <www.ri.gov>.

South Carolina

Name: South Carolina, named in honor of Charles I of England. **Nickname:** Palmetto State. **Capital:** Columbia. **Rank:** population: 25th; area: 40th; pop. density: 21st. **Mottoes:** *Animis Opibusque Parati* (Prepared in Mind and Resources); *Dum Spiro Spero* (While I Breathe, I Hope). **Songs:** "Carolina," words by Henry Timrod and music by Anne Custis Burgess; "South Carolina on My Mind," words and music by Hank Martin and Buzz Arledge. **Amphibian:** spotted salamander. **Bird:** Carolina wren. **Fish:** striped bass. **Flower:** Carolina jessamine. **Gemstone:** amethyst. **Insect:** Carolina mantid. **Mammal:** white-tailed deer. **Reptile:** loggerhead turtle. **Rock:** blue granite. **Tree:** palmetto.

Natural features

Area: 32,020 sq mi, 82,932 sq km. **Mountain range:** Blue Ridge Mountains. **Highest point:** Sassafras Mountain, 3,560 ft (1,085 m). **Largest lake:** Lake Marion. **Major rivers:** Pee Dee, Savannah, Ashley, Combahee, Edisto. **Natural regions:** Coastal Plain covers the eastern two-thirds of the state and includes the Sea Island Section in the central region; Piedmont Province extends across the central and western region, includes the Piedmont Upland; Blue Ridge Province, Southern Section, far northwestern corner. **Location:** Southeast, bordering North Carolina and Georgia. **Climate:** subtropical, with hot, humid summers and generally mild winters; an average of 10 tornadoes a year, usually occurring during the spring; hurricanes are less frequent, but they do in some years cause damage to the coast. **Land use:** forest, 64.4%; agricultural, 13.1%; pasture, 2.4%; other, 20.0%.

People

Population (2003): 4,147,000; 137.7 persons per sq mi (53.2 persons per sq km) (land area only). **Vital statistics** (2001; per 1,000 population): birth rate, 14.1; death rate, 9.0; marriage rate, 9.3; divorce rate, 3.5. **Major cities** (2000): Columbia, 117,000 (2002); Charleston, 96,650; North Charleston, 79,641; Greenville, 56,002; Rock Hill, 49,765.

Government

Statehood: entered the Union on 23 May 1788 as the 8th state. **State constitution:** adopted 1895. **Representation in US Congress:** 2 senators; 6 representatives. **Electoral college:** 8 votes. **Political divisions:** 46 counties.

Economy

Employment: services, 24.7%; trade, 22.4%; manufacturing, 17.3%; government, 16.7%; construction, 6.4%; finance, insurance, real estate, 5.9%; transportation, public utilities, 4.1%; agriculture, forestry, fishing, 2.4%; mining, 0.1%. **Production:** manufacturing, 21.4%; trade, 17.4%; services, 16.4%; government, 15.1%; finance, insurance, real estate, 13.7%; transportation, utilities, 8.9%; construction, 5.9%; agriculture, 1.1%; mining, 0.2%. **Chief agricultural products:** *Crops:* tobacco, cotton, barley, corn (maize), peanuts, oats, grains, peaches, apples, pecans, watermelons, sweet potatoes, tomatoes, snap beans, cucumbers, dairy products, eggs. *Livestock:* cattle

For details about state governments, see pages 800–805; for energy data, see pages 830–832.

and calves, chickens, pigs. **Chief extractive products:** timber, marine fish, oysters, clams, shrimp. **Chief manufactured products:** Chemical products, industrial chemicals, pharmaceuticals, and agricultural fertilizers, textiles, apparel, industrial machinery, plastic and rubber products, paper and paperboard, electronics and electrical equipment, motor vehicle parts and accessories, lumber.

Internet resources: <www.discoversouthcarolina.com>; <www.myscgov.com>.

South Dakota

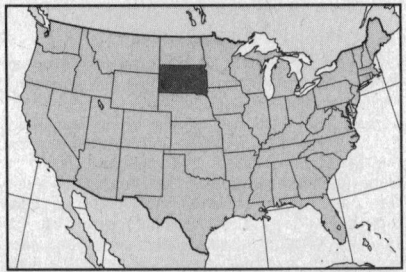

Name: South Dakota, from the Dakota division of the Sioux, the Native American tribe that inhabited the plains before the arrival of Europeans; *dakota* is the Sioux word for "friend." **Nickname:** Mount Rushmore State. **Capital:** Pierre. **Rank:** population: 46th; area: 16th; pop. density: 46th. **Motto:** Under God the People Rule. **Song:** "Hail! South Dakota," words and music by Deecort Hammitt. **Bird:** Chinese ring-necked pheasant. **Fish:** walleye. **Flower:** pasque. **Fossil:** triceratops. **Gemstone:** Fairburn agate. **Insect:** honeybee. **Mammal:** coyote. **Mineral:** rose quartz. **Tree:** Black Hills spruce.

Natural features

Area: 77,117 sq mi, 199,731 sq km. **Mountain range:** Black Hills. **Highest point:** Harney Peak, 7,242 ft (2,207 m). **Largest lake:** Lake Thompson. **Major rivers:** Big Sioux, Vermillion, James, Grand, Moreau, Cheyenne, Bad, White. **Natural regions:** the Central Lowland, eastern third of the state, includes the Dissected Till Plains along the eastern edge and the Western Lake Section at the center; the Great Plains Province, western two-thirds of the state; Black Hills, far west; High Plains, southern border; Missouri Plateau, west. **Location:** North central, bordering North Dakota, Minnesota, Iowa, Nebraska, Wyoming, and Montana. **Climate:** characterized by extremes in temperature, low precipitation, and relatively low humidity; cyclonic storms occur frequently in the east-river section during the spring and summer. **Land use:** pasture, 46.5%; agricultural, 44.8%; forest, 3.3%; other, 5.4%.

People

Population (2003): 764,000; 10.1 persons per sq mi (3.9 persons per sq km) (land area only). **Vital statistics** (2001; per 1,000 population): birth rate, 14.1; death rate, 9.1; marriage rate, 9.1; divorce rate, 3.4. **Major cities** (2000): Sioux Falls, 130,000 (2002); Rapid City, 59,607; Aberdeen, 24,658.

Government

Statehood: entered the Union on 2 Nov 1889 as the 40th state. **State constitution:** adopted 1889. **Representation in US Congress:** 2 senators; 1 representative. **Electoral college:** 3 votes. **Political divisions:** 66 counties.

Economy

Employment: services, 27.5%; trade, 22.3%; government, 13.7%; manufacturing, 10.3%; agriculture, forestry, fishing, 9.1%; finance, insurance, real estate, 7.2%; construction, 5.0%; transportation, public utilities, 4.5%; mining, 0.5%. **Production:** finance, insurance, real estate, 18.1%; trade, 17.7%; services, 17.6%; manufacturing, 14.0%; government, 12.6%; transportation, utilities, 8.2%; agriculture, 6.9%; construction, 4.1%; mining, 0.6%. **Chief agricultural products:** *Crops:* corn (maize), hay, wheat, sunflowers, dairy products, eggs, flaxseed, barley, wool, rye, sorghum, soybeans. *Livestock:* cattle and calves, pigs, sheep. **Chief manufactured products:** industrial machinery, office machines, computers, food products, electronics, printing and publishing, lumber mills, fabricated metal products, medical instruments, truck-trailer manufactures, jewelry.

Internet resources: <www.travelsd.com>; <www.state. sd.us>.

Tennessee

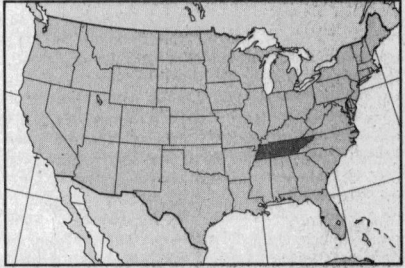

Name: Tennessee, from Cherokee village name. **Nickname:** Volunteer State. **Capital:** Nashville. **Rank:** population: 16th; area: 34th; pop. density: 20th. **Motto:** Agriculture and Commerce. **Songs:** "My Homeland, Tennessee," by Nell Grayson Taylor and Roy Lamont Smith; "When It's Iris Time in Tennessee," by Willa Mae Waid; "My Tennessee," by Francis Hannah Tranum; "The Tennessee Waltz," by Redd Stewart and Pee Wee King; "Rocky Top," by Boudleaux and Felice Bryant. **Amphibian:** cave salamander. **Bird:** mockingbird. **Fish:** largemouth bass, channel catfish. **Flower:** iris. **Gemstone:** river pearl. **Insects:** firefly, ladybug. **Mammal:** raccoon. **Reptile:** box turtle. **Rocks:** limestone, agate. **Tree:** tulip poplar.

Natural features

Area: 42,143 sq mi, 109,151 sq km. **Mountain ranges:** Unaka Mountains, Great Smoky Mountains. **Highest point:** Clingmans Dome, 6,642 ft (2,024 m). **Largest lake:** Reelfoot. **Major rivers:** Tennessee, Cumberland, Mississippi. **Natural regions:** Blue Ridge Province, eastern border; Valley and Ridge Province, extends from southwest to northeast; Appalachian Plateau, central, running from south to north, includes the Cumberland Plateau Section in the center and the Cumberland Mountain Section at the northern end; Interior Low Plateau, west central, includes the Nashville Basin and Highland Rim Section. **Location:** South, bordering Kentucky, Virginia, North Carolina, Georgia, Alabama, Mississippi, Arkansas, and Missouri. **Climate:** moderate continental climate, with cool, but not cold, winters and warm summers. **Land use:** forest, 50.3%; agricultural, 28.4%; pasture, 4.3%; other, 17.1%.

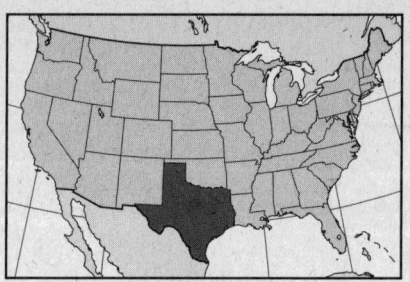

People

Population (2003): 5,842,000; 141.7 persons per sq mi (54.7 persons per sq km) (land area only). **Vital statistics** (2001; per 1,000 population): birth rate, 14.0; death rate, 9.6; marriage rate, 13.9; divorce rate, 5.2. **Major cities:** Memphis, 649,000; Nashville-Davidson, 546,000; Knoxville, 174,000; Chattanooga, 155,000; Clarksville, 106,000.

Government

Statehood: entered the Union on 1 Jun 1796 as the 16th state. **State constitution:** adopted 1870. **Representation in US Congress:** 2 senators; 9 representatives. **Electoral college:** 11 votes. **Political divisions:** 95 counties.

Economy

Employment: services, 27.8%; trade, 21.8%; manufacturing, 16.2%; government, 12.1%; finance, insurance, real estate, 6.7%; construction, 5.9%; transportation, public utilities, 5.4%; agriculture, forestry, fishing, 3.8%; mining, 0.2%. **Production:** manufacturing, 20.8%; services, 20.6%; trade, 19.1%; finance, insurance, real estate, 14.1%; government, 11.5%; transportation, utilities, 8.3%; construction, 4.4%; agriculture, 0.9%; mining, 0.3%. **Chief agricultural products:** *Crops:* cotton, tobacco, peaches, apples, tomatoes, snap beans, honey, dairy products, eggs, wool, hay, corn (maize), wheat, sorghum. *Livestock:* cattle, poultry, hogs, sheep. *Aquaculture:* catfish, trout. *Extractive products:* timber. **Chief manufactured products:** transportation equipment, motor vehicles, aircraft parts, boats, chemical and pharmaceutical products, printing and publishing, electronics, lumber, paper, apparel, surgical appliances and supplies.

Internet resources: <www.tennessee.gov>.

Texas

Name: Texas, from the Caddo Indian word *teysha*, or *tejas*, which means "hello friend." **Nickname:** Lone Star State. **Capital:** Austin. **Rank:** population: 2nd; area: 2nd; pop. density: 27th. **Motto:** Friendship. **Song:** "Texas, Our Texas," by William J. Marsh and Gladys Yoakum Wright. **Bird:** mockingbird. **Fish:** Guadalupe bass. **Flower:** bluebonnet. **Fossil:** pleurocoelus. **Gemstone:** Texas blue topaz. **Insect:** monarch butterfly. **Mammal:** Mexican free-tailed bat (flying); longhorn (large); armadillo (small). **Reptile:** horned lizard. **Rock:** petrified palmwood. **Tree:** pecan.

Natural features

Area: 268,581 sq mi, 695,621 sq km. **Mountain ranges:** Rocky Mountains, Guadalupe Mountains. **Highest point:** Guadalupe Peak, 8,751 ft (2,667 m). **Largest lake:** Caddo Lake. **Major rivers:** Red, Trinity, Brazos, Colorado, Rio Grande. **Natural regions:** Coastal Plain, southern and eastern regions, includes the West Gulf Coastal Plain near the east-central coast; Central Lowland, north central, includes the Osage Plains; Great Plains Province, extends from the panhandle across most of central and western Texas, includes the Edwards Plateau to the south, Pecos Valley to the west, High Plains to the north, and Central Texas Section; Basin and Range Province, extreme western region, comprising the Mexican Highland to the south and the Sacramento Section to the north. **Location:** Southwest, bordering Oklahoma, Arkansas, Louisiana, and New Mexico; international border with Mexico. **Climate:** varies by region, though summers are generally very hot and winters are somewhat mild; East Texas is considerably wetter than the very dry West Texas region; tornadoes are a frequent threat between April and November. **Land use:** pasture, 58.5%; agricultural, 23.9%; forest, 7.0%; other, 10.6%.

People

Population (2003): 22,119,000; 84.5 persons per sq mi (32.6 persons per sq km) (land area only). **Vital statistics** (2001; per 1,000 population): birth rate, 17.6; death rate, 7.1; marriage rate, 9.4; divorce rate, 4.1. **Major cities:** Houston, 2,010,000; Dallas, 1,211,000; San Antonio, 1,194,000; Austin, 672,000; El Paso, 577,000; Fort Worth, 568,000; Arlington, 350,000; Corpus Christi, 279,000; Plano, 238,000; Garland, 220,000.

Government

Statehood: entered the Union on 29 Dec 1845 as the 28th state. **State constitution:** adopted 1876. **Representation in US Congress:** 2 senators; 30 representatives. **Electoral college:** 34 votes (in the 2004 general elections based on the 2000 census). **Political divisions:** 254 counties.

Economy

Employment: services, 29.1%; trade, 21.6%; government, 14.5%; manufacturing, 10.1%; finance, insurance, real estate, 7.5%; construction, 6.1%; transportation, public utilities, 5.4%; agriculture, forestry,

For details about state governments, see pages 800–805; for energy data, see pages 830–832.

fishing, 3.5%; mining, 2.2%. **Production:** services, 19.9%; trade, 17.6%; finance, insurance, real estate, 14.7%; manufacturing, 14.0%; government, 11.2%; transportation, utilities, 10.9%; mining, 5.7%; construction, 4.7%; agriculture, 1.3%. **Chief agricultural products:** *Crops:* cotton, apples, greenhouse and nursery products, corn (maize), sorghum, wheat, dairy products, eggs, rice. *Livestock:* cattle, pigs, chickens. *Extractive products:* timber, shrimp. **Chief manufactured products:** Refined petroleum, petroleum products, food products, computers and electronics, chemicals and plastics, apparel, wood and paper products, nonelectrical machinery, fabricated metal products, aerospace products and parts, aircraft parts, motor vehicle parts.

Internet resources: <www.traveltex.com>; <www.texas.gov>.

Utah

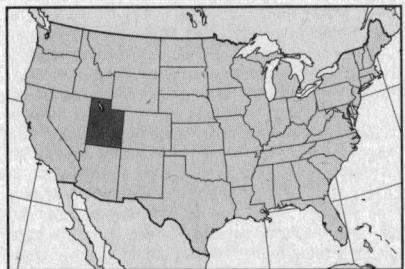

Name: Utah, named for the Ute tribe; the word *ute* means "people of the mountains." **Nickname:** Beehive State. **Capital:** Salt Lake City. **Rank:** population: 34th; area: 12th; pop. density: 41st. **Motto:** Industry. **Song:** "Utah, We Love Thee," by Evan Stephens. **Bird:** California seagull. **Fish:** Bonneville cutthroat trout. **Flower:** sego lily. **Fossil:** allosaurus. **Gemstone:** topaz. **Insect:** honeybee. **Mammal:** Rocky Mountain elk. **Mineral:** copper. **Rock:** coal. **Tree:** blue spruce.

Natural features

Area: 84,899 sq mi, 219,887 sq km. **Mountain ranges:** Uinta Mountains, Wasatch Range, Rocky Mountains. **Highest point:** Kings Peak, 13,528 ft (4,123 m). **Largest lake:** Great Salt Lake. **Major rivers:** Colorado, Green, Sevier. **Natural regions:** Basin and Range Province, western half of the state, includes the Great Salt Lake Desert and Bonneville Salt Flats to the north and the Great Basin to the south; Middle Rocky Mountains, northeast; Colorado Plateaus, east-central and southeast regions, includes the Grand Canyon Section to the south, the High Plateaus of Utah and Canyon Lands in the center, the Navajo Section in the extreme southeast corner, and the Uinta Basin to the north. **Location:** West, bordering Idaho, Wyoming, Colorado, Arizona, and Nevada. **Climate:** primarily arid; southwest has a warm, almost dry, subtropical climate, while the southern part of the Colorado Plateau has cool, dry winters and wet summers. **Land use:** pasture, 45.1%; forest, 26.3%; agricultural, 3.9%; other, 24.7%.

People

Population (2003): 2,351,000; 28.6 persons per sq mi (11.0 persons per sq km) (land area only). **Vital statistics** (2001; per 1,000 population): birth rate, 21.8; death rate, 5.6; marriage rate, 10.6; divorce rate, 4.4. **Major cities:** Salt Lake City, 181,000; West Valley City, 111,000; Provo, 105,000; Sandy, 88,418 (2000); Orem, 84,324 (2000).

Government

Statehood: entered the Union on 4 Jan 1896 as the 45th state. **State constitution:** adopted 1895. **Representation in US Congress:** 2 senators; 3 representatives. **Electoral college:** 5 votes. **Political divisions:** 29 counties.

Economy

Employment: services, 29.7%; trade, 22.0%; government, 14.6%; manufacturing, 10.9%; finance, insurance, real estate, 7.8%; construction, 7.0%; transportation, public utilities, 4.9%; agriculture, forestry, fishing, 2.4%; mining, 0.7%. **Production:** services, 20.6%; trade, 16.9%; finance, insurance, real estate, 16.4%; government, 14.4%; manufacturing, 13.3%; transportation, utilities, 8.8%; construction, 6.5%; mining, 1.8%; agriculture, 1.1%. **Chief agricultural products:** *Crops:* hay, grains, peaches, cherries, onions, dairy products. *Livestock:* cattle, sheep, mink, poultry. *Aquaculture:* trout. **Chief manufactured products:** industrial machinery, computers, office equipment, transportation equipment, aerospace products, missile parts, motor vehicle parts, surgical tools, electromedical equipment, food processing.

Internet resources: <www.utah.com>; <www.utah.gov>.

Vermont

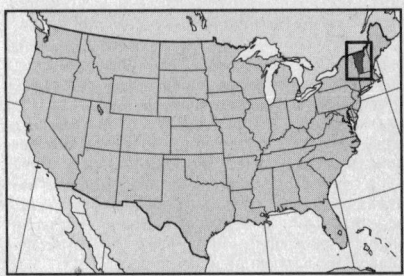

Name: Vermont, from the French *vert mont,* meaning "green mountain." **Nickname:** Green Mountain State. **Capital:** Montpelier. **Rank:** population: 49th; area: 43rd; pop. density: 30th. **Motto:** Freedom and Unity. **Song:** "These Green Mountains," by Diane Martin and Rita Burgess Gluck. **Bird:** hermit thrush. **Flower:** red clover. **Insect:** honeybee. **Mammal:** Morgan horse. **Tree:** sugar maple.

Natural features

Area: 9,614 sq mi, 24,901 sq km. **Mountain ranges:** Green Mountains, Appalachian Mountains, Hoosac Range, Taconic Range. **Highest point:** Mount Mansfield, 4,393 ft (1,339 m). **Largest lake:** Lake Champlain. **Major rivers:** Lamoille, Winooski, Otter Creek, Poultney, White, Missisquoi. **Natural regions:** the New England Province, eastern two-thirds of the state, includes the Taconic Section to the south, the Green Mountain Section in the center, New England Upland Section along the east-central edge, and the White Mountain Section in the far northeast corner; the St. Lawrence Valley, western edge of the state, with the Champlain Section in the central portion; the Valley and Ridge Province, with the Hudson Valley, small section along the west-central edge. **Location:** New England, bordering New Hampshire, Massachusetts, and New York; international border with Canada. **Climate:** cool continental, with very cold, snowy winters and warm, mild summers. **Land use:** forest, 75.4%; agricultural, 8.2%; pasture, 3.6%; other, 12.9%.

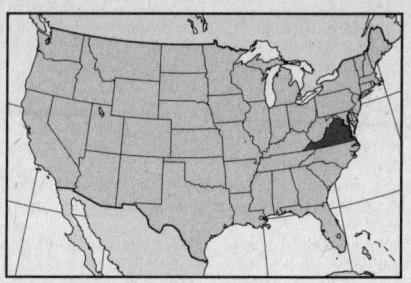

People

Population (2003): 619,000; 66.9 persons per sq mi (25.8 persons per sq km) (land area only). **Vital statistics** (2001; per 1,000 population): birth rate, 10.6; death rate, 8.5; marriage rate, 9.9; divorce rate, 4.0. **Major city:** Burlington, 38,889 (2000).

Government

Statehood: entered the Union on 4 Mar 1791 as the 14th state. **State constitution:** adopted 1793. **Representation in US Congress:** 2 senators; 1 representative. **Electoral college:** 3 votes. **Political divisions:** 14 counties.

Economy

Employment: services, 32.4%; trade, 21.0%; manufacturing, 13.7%; government, 12.8%; construction, 6.5%; finance, insurance, real estate, 5.7%; transportation, public utilities, 4.0%; agriculture, forestry, fishing, 3.7%; mining, 0.2%. **Production:** services, 22.3%; finance, insurance, real estate, 17.7%; manufacturing, 17.5%; trade, 15.7%; government, 12.4%; transportation, utilities, 7.6%; construction, 4.4%; agriculture, 2.2%; mining, 0.3%. **Chief agricultural products:** *Crops:* apples, honey, corn (maize), hay, greenhouse and nursery products, Christmas trees, maple syrup, fruits and vegetables, dairy products, eggs, wool. *Livestock:* cattle and calves, chickens, turkeys, sheep, horses. *Extractive products:* timber. **Chief manufactured products:** electrical and electronic equipment, fabricated metal products, nonelectrical machinery, paper and allied products, printing and publishing, food products, transportation equipment, lumber and wood products.

Internet resources: <www.travel-vermont.com>; <www.vermont.gov>.

Virginia

Name: Virginia, named in honor of Elizabeth I of England, known as the "Virgin Queen." **Nickname:** Old Dominion. **Capital:** Richmond. **Rank:** population: 12th; area: 37th; pop. density: 14th. **Motto:** *Sic Semper Tyrannis* (Thus Ever to Tyrants). **Song:** "Carry Me Back to Old Virginia," words and music by James B.

Bland. **Bird:** cardinal. **Fish:** brook trout. **Flower:** dogwood. **Fossil:** *Chesapecten jeffersonius.* **Insect:** tiger swallowtail butterfly. **Tree:** dogwood.

Natural features

Area: 42,774 sq mi, 109,151 sq km. **Mountain ranges:** Blue Ridge, Appalachian Mountains. **Highest point:** Mount Rogers, 5,729 ft (1,746 m). **Largest lake:** Smith Mountain Lake. **Major rivers:** Potomac, Shenandoah, James, Roanoke. **Natural regions:** Coastal Plain, eastern region below the Potomac River; Piedmont Province extends from the south-central border up to the border with Maryland, includes the Piedmont Upland and Piedmont Lowlands; Blue Ridge Province, west of the Piedmont Province; Valley and Ridge region, covers most of western Virginia, includes the Shenandoah Valley and Allegheny, Shenandoah, and Appalachian Mountains; Appalachian Plateau, extreme western tip of the state, includes the Cumberland Mountain and Kanawha Sections. **Location:** East coast, bordering Maryland, North Carolina, Tennessee, Kentucky, and West Virginia. **Climate:** generally mild and equable but varies according to elevation and proximity to Chesapeake Bay and the Atlantic. **Land use:** forest, 60.5%; agricultural, 17.1%; pasture, 6.0%; other, 16.3%.

People

Population (2003): 7,386,000; 186.5 persons per sq mi (72.0 persons per sq km) (land area only). **Vital statistics** (2001; per 1,000 population): birth rate, 14.0; death rate, 7.8; marriage rate, 9.0; divorce rate, 4.3. **Major cities:** Virginia Beach, 434,000; Norfolk, 239,000; Chesapeake, 207,000; Richmond, 197,000; Newport News, 180,000; Hampton, 146,000; Alexandria, 131,000; Portsmouth, 100,565 (2000); Roanoke, 94,911 (2000).

Government

Statehood: entered the Union on 26 Jun 1788 as the 10th state. **State constitution:** adopted 1970. **Representation in US Congress:** 2 senators; 11 representatives. **Electoral college:** 13 votes. **Political divisions:** 95 counties.

Economy

Employment: services, 30.1%; trade, 20.1%; government, 18.9%; manufacturing, 10.2%; finance, insurance, real estate, 6.9%; construction, 6.2%; transportation, public utilities, 4.7%; agriculture, forestry, fishing, 2.5%; mining, 0.3%. **Production:** services,

For details about state governments, see pages 800–805; for energy data, see pages 830–832.

22.6%; government, 17.8%; finance, insurance, real estate, 17.3%; trade, 14.4%; manufacturing, 13.1%; transportation, utilities, 9.0%; construction, 4.6%; agriculture, 0.8%; mining, 0.4%. **Chief agricultural products:** *Crops:* tobacco, soybeans, corn (maize), peanuts (groundnuts), cotton, apples, tomatoes, wheat, hay, potatoes, honey. *Livestock:* chickens, turkeys, pigs, cattle, sheep. *Aquaculture:* clams, soft-shell crabs, oysters, trout, catfish, hybrid striped bass. *Extractive products:* timber, blue crab. **Chief manufactured products:** electronics and electrical equipment, paper products, tobacco products, plastic materials, pharmaceutical and chemical products, food products, printing and publishing.

Internet resources: <www.virginia.org>; <www.virginia.gov>.

Washington

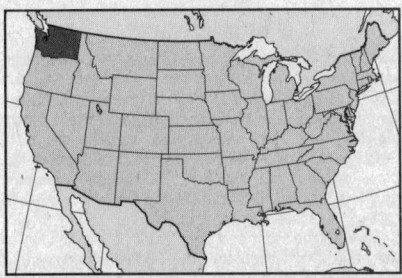

Name: Washington, named in honor of George Washington. **Nickname:** Evergreen State. **Capital:** Olympia. **Rank:** population: 15th; area: 20th; pop. density: 25th. **Motto:** *Alki* (By and By). **Song:** "Washington My Home," words and music by Helen Davis. **Bird:** willow goldfinch. **Fish:** steelhead trout. **Flower:** coast rhododendron. **Fossil:** Columbian mammoth. **Gemstone:** petrified wood. **Insect:** green darner dragonfly. **Tree:** western hemlock.

Natural features

Area: 71,300 sq mi, 184,665 sq km. **Mountain ranges:** Olympic Mountains, Cascade Range, Blue Mountains. **Highest point:** Mount Rainier, 14,410 ft (4,392 m). **Largest lake:** Moses Lake. **Major rivers:** Columbia, Pend Oreille, Snake, Yakima. **Natural regions:** Pacific Border Province, western quarter of the state, includes the Olympic Mountains to the west and the Puget Trough to the east; Cascade-Sierra Mountains, running north to south down center of state, include the Northern and Middle Cascades; Northern Rocky Mountains, northeast corner; Columbia Plateaus, eastern, central, and southern regions, include the Walla Walla Plateau in the center and the Blue Mountain Section in the southeast corner. **Location:** Northwest, bordering Idaho and Oregon; international border with Canada. **Climate:** moderate winters and cool summers west of the Cascades; east of the Cascade Range seasonal temperature variations are greater, with cold winters and warm, mild summers; throughout the state precipitation is greatest in the cooler months, with frequent cyclonic storms, some with gale-force winds. **Land use:** forest, 40.9%; agricultural, 19.7%; pasture, 17.4%; other, 22.0%.

People

Population (2003): 6,131,000; 92.1 persons per sq mi (35.6 persons per sq km) (land area only). **Vital statistics** (2001; per 1,000 population): birth rate, 13.6; death rate, 7.4; marriage rate, 7.2; divorce rate, 4.5. **Major cities:** Seattle, 570,000; Spokane, 196,000; Tacoma, 198,000; Vancouver, 150,000; Bellevue, 113,000; Everett, 91,488 (2000).

Government

Statehood: entered the Union on 11 Nov 1889 as the 42nd state. **State constitution:** adopted 1889. **Representation in US Congress:** 2 senators; 9 representatives. **Electoral college:** 11 votes. **Political divisions:** 39 counties.

Economy

Employment: services, 28.7%; trade, 21.9%; government, 15.7%; manufacturing, 11.8%; finance, insurance, real estate, 7.3%; construction, 5.6%; transportation, public utilities, 4.6%; agriculture, forestry, fishing, 4.2%; mining, 0.2%. **Production:** services, 25.0%; finance, insurance, real estate, 17.4%; trade, 16.8%; government, 13.2%; manufacturing, 12.6%; transportation, utilities, 7.9%; construction, 4.9%; agriculture, 2.1%; mining, 0.2%. **Chief agricultural products:** *Crops:* apples, peaches, pears, cherries, grapes, apricots, raspberries, dried peas, lentils, asparagus, carrots, sweet corn, green peas, potatoes, mint oil, hops, wheat, hay. *Livestock:* cattle and calves, poultry, horses. *Extractive products:* oysters, clams, mussels, crab, shrimp, geoduck, sea cucumbers, marine fish, salmon, timber. **Chief manufactured products:** aerospace equipment, food processing, forest products, advanced medical and technology products, aluminum products, fish processing.

Internet resources: <www.experiencewashington.com>; <www.access.wa.gov>.

West Virginia

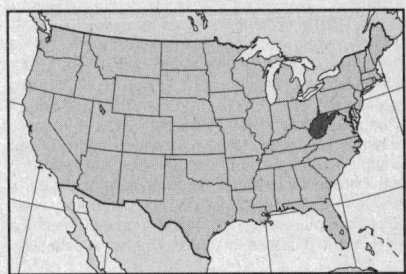

Name: West Virginia, named in honor of Elizabeth I of England, who was also known as the "Virgin Queen." **Nickname:** Mountain State. **Capital:** Charleston. **Rank:** population: 37th; area: 41st; pop. density: 29th. **Motto:** *Montani Semper Liberi* (Mountaineers Are Always Free). **Song:** "This Is My West Virginia," words and music by Iris Bell; "West Virginia, My Home Sweet Home," words and music by Julian G. Hearne, Jr.; "The West Virginia Hills," words by David King and music by H.E. Engle. **Bird:** cardinal. **Fish:** brook trout.

Flower: rhododendron. **Gemstone:** West Virginia fossil coral. **Insect:** monarch butterfly. **Mammal:** black bear. **Tree:** sugar maple.

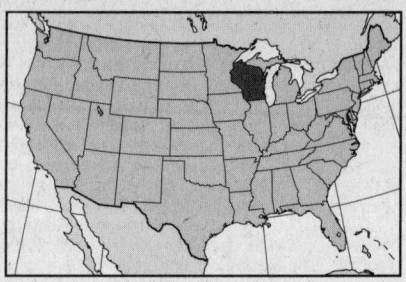

Natural features

Area: 24,230 sq mi, 62,755 sq km. **Mountain ranges:** Appalachian Mountains, Allegheny Mountains. **Highest point:** Spruce Knob, 4,862 ft (1,482 m). **Largest lake:** Summersville Lake. **Major rivers:** Ohio, Big Sandy, Guyandotte, Great Kanawha, Little Kanawha, Monongahela, Potomac. **Natural regions:** Valley and Ridge Province, eastern edge of the state, includes portions of the Shenandoah Mountains; the remainder of the state consists of the Appalachian Plateaus and includes the Kanawha Section to the south, the Allegheny Mountains, and the Allegheny Mountains in the northeast. **Location:** East, bordering Pennsylvania, Maryland, Virginia, Kentucky, and Ohio. **Climate:** humid continental, except for a marine modification in the lower panhandle. **Land use:** forest, 77.2%; agricultural, 9.2%; pasture, 3.1%; other, 10.5%.

People

Population (2003): 1,810,000; 75.2 persons per sq mi (29.0 persons per sq km) (land area only). **Vital statistics** (2001; per 1,000 population): birth rate, 11.4; death rate, 11.6; marriage rate, 7.9; divorce rate, 5.2. **Major cities** (2000): Charleston, 53,421; Huntington, 51,475; Parkersburg, 33,099; Wheeling, 31,419; Morgantown, 26,809.

Government

Statehood: entered the Union on 20 Jun 1863 as the 35th state. **State constitution:** adopted 1872. **Representation in US Congress:** 2 senators; 3 representatives. **Electoral college:** 5 votes. **Political divisions:** 55 counties.

Economy

Employment: services, 28.1%; trade, 22.2%; government, 17.1%; manufacturing, 9.9%; construction, 5.9%; transportation, public utilities, 5.2%; finance, insurance, real estate, 4.8%; agriculture, forestry, fishing, 3.3%; mining, 3.3%. **Production:** services, 17.9%; manufacturing, 16.0%; government, 15.5%; trade, 15.5%; finance, insurance, real estate, 11.3%; transportation, utilities, 11.3%; mining, 7.3%; construction, 4.6%; agriculture, 0.6%. **Chief agricultural products:** *Crops:* hay, apples, corn (maize), tobacco, peaches, dairy products. *Livestock:* cattle, sheep, poultry. *Extractive products:* timber. **Chief manufactured products:** chemical products, automobile parts, primary metal and fabricated metal products, glassware, computer software, wood products, electrical equipment, industrial machinery, pharmaceuticals.

Internet resources: <www.wvtourism.com>; <www.wv.gov>.

Wisconsin

Name: Wisconsin, an anglicized version of a French rendering of a Native American name said to mean "the place where we live." **Nickname:** Badger State.

Capital: Madison. **Rank:** population: 20th; area: 25th; pop. density: 24th. **Motto:** Forward. **Song:** "On, Wisconsin," words and music by William T. Purdy. **Bird:** robin. **Fish:** muskellunge (muskie). **Flower:** wood violet. **Fossil:** trilobite. **Insect:** honeybee. **Mammal:** badger. **Mineral:** galena. **Rock:** red granite. **Tree:** sugar maple.

Natural features

Area: 65,498 sq mi, 169,639 sq km. **Mountain ranges:** Baraboo Range, Rib Mountain, Gogebic Range. **Highest point:** Timms Hill, 1,953 ft (595 m). **Largest lake:** Lake Winnebago. **Major rivers:** Wisconsin, St. Croix, Rock, Mississippi, Namekagon, Wolf, Pine-Popple, Brule, Pike. **Natural regions:** Superior Upland, divided into highland and lowland sections, northern half of the state; Central Lowland, southern half of the state, divided into the Wisconsin Driftless Section to the west and the Eastern Lake Section to the east, with a section of the Till Plains occupying a small area at the southern border. **Location:** Midwest, bordering Michigan, Illinois, Iowa, and Minnesota. **Climate:** continental, with long, cold winters and warm, but relatively short, summers. **Land use:** forest, 45.2%; agricultural, 27.5%; pasture, 5.3%; other, 22.0%.

People

Population (2003): 5,472,000; 100.8 persons per sq mi (38.9 persons per sq km). **Vital statistics** (2001; per 1,000 population): birth rate, 12.9; death rate, 8.6; marriage rate, 6.5; divorce rate, 3.2. **Major cities:** Milwaukee, 591,000; Madison, 215,000; Green Bay, 102,000; Kenosha, 90,352 (2000); Racine, 81,855 (2000).

Government

Statehood: entered the Union on 29 May 1848 as the 30th state. **State constitution:** adopted 1848. **Representation in US Congress:** 2 senators; 9 representatives. **Electoral college:** 10 votes (in the 2004 general elections based on the 2000 census). **Political divisions:** 72 counties.

Economy

Employment: services, 26.7%; trade, 21.8%; manufacturing, 19.2%; government, 11.9%; finance, insurance, real estate, 6.8%; construction, 4.8%; transportation, public utilities, 4.4%; agriculture, forestry, fishing, 4.2%; mining, 0.1%. **Production:** manufacturing, 26.3%; services, 17.8%; trade, 15.8%; finance, insurance, real estate, 15.6%; government, 10.6%; transportation, utilities, 7.1%; construction, 4.7%;

For details about state governments, see pages 800–805; for energy data, see pages 830–832.

agriculture, 1.9%; mining, 0.1%. **Chief agricultural products:** *Crops:* Dairy products, corn (maize), honey, maple syrup, oats, hay, snap and green beans, potatoes, strawberries, tart cherries, cranberries, Christmas trees, mint for oil, beets, cabbage, carrots, green peas, cucumbers. *Livestock:* cattle and calves, hogs, mink. *Extractive products:* freshwater fish. **Chief manufactured products:** processed foods, beer, industrial machinery, paper and paper products, fabricated metal products, transportation equipment, household appliances.

Internet resources: <www.travelwisconsin.com>; <www.wisconsin.gov>.

Wyoming

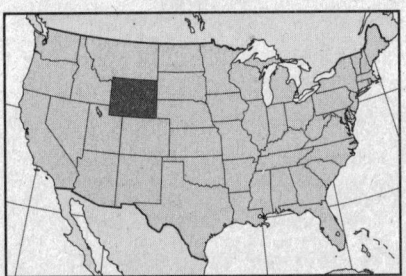

Name: Wyoming, from the Delaware Indian word, meaning "mountains and valleys alternating." **Nicknames:** Equality State and Cowboy State. **Capital:** Cheyenne. **Rank:** population: 50th; area: 9th; pop. density: 49th. **Motto:** Equal Rights. **Song:** "Wyoming," words by Charles E. Winter and music by George E. Knapp. **Bird:** meadowlark. **Fish:** cutthroat trout. **Flower:** Indian paintbrush. **Fossil:** knightia. **Gemstone:** jade. **Mammal:** bison. **Reptile:** horned toad. **Tree:** plains cottonwood.

Natural features

Area: 97,814 sq mi, 253,336 sq km. **Mountain ranges:** Rocky Mountains, Big Horn, Grand Tetons, Wind River Range, Continental Divide, Sierra Madre Range, Washakie Mountains. **Highest point:** Gannett Peak, 13,804 ft (4,207 m). **Largest lake:** Yellowstone Lake. **Major rivers:** Snake, Colorado, Green,

Columbia. **Natural regions:** Great Plains Province, eastern third of the state, includes the Black Hills in the northeast corner, the High Plains in the southwest corner, and the Missouri Plateau in the center; Wyoming Basin, central and southern regions; Southern Rocky Mountains, southern border; the Middle Rocky Mountains, northwest third of the state, also cover a small area on the southern border; Northern Rocky Mountains, extreme northwest tip of the state. **Location:** West, bordering Montana, South Dakota, Nebraska, Colorado, Utah, and Idaho. **Climate:** semiarid continental, with long, cold winters and relatively short, warm summers. **Land use:** pasture, 72.2%; forest, 8.2%; agricultural, 5.0%; other, 14.7%.

People

Population (2003): 501,000; 5.2 persons per sq mi (2.0 persons per sq km) (land area only). **Vital statistics** (2001; per 1,000 population): birth rate, 12.7; death rate, 8.2; marriage rate, 10.3; divorce rate, 6.1. **Major cities** (2000): Cheyenne, 53,011; Casper, 49,644; Laramie, 27,204.

Government

Statehood: entered the Union on 10 Jul 1890 as the 44th state. **State constitution:** adopted 1889. **Representation in US Congress:** 2 senators; 1 representative. **Electoral college:** 3 votes. **Political divisions:** 23 counties.

Economy

Employment: services, 25.0%; trade, 21.3%; government, 19.5%; construction, 6.9%; finance, insurance, real estate, 6.6%; mining, 5.9%; transportation, public utilities, 5.4%; agriculture, forestry, fishing, 5.3%; manufacturing, 4.1%. **Production:** mining, 22.0%; transportation, utilities, 14.8%; government, 14.1%; trade, 11.8%; services, 11.6%; finance, insurance, real estate, 11.3%; manufacturing, 6.6%; construction, 5.4%; agriculture, 2.5%. **Chief agricultural products:** *Crops:* hay, wheat, barley, sugar beets and sugar, corn (maize), wool. *Livestock:* cattle and calves, sheep and lambs. **Chief manufactured products:** refined petroleum, lumber and wood products, food products, fabricated metal products.

Internet resources: <www.wyomingtourism.org>; <www.wyoming.gov>.

Famous People from the 50 States, DC, and Puerto Rico

Alabama
Charles Barkley
Mia Hamm
Condoleezza Rice
Lionel Richie
Alaska
Irene Bedard
Ray Mala
Lisa Murkowski
Virgil Partch
Arizona
Barbara Eden
R.C. Gorman
Ty Murray
Linda Ronstadt

Arkansas
Helen Gurley Brown
Bear Bryant
Iris Dement
John Grisham
California
Tyra Banks
Daniel Handler
Rick Warren
Venus Williams
Colorado
India.Arie
John F. Kerry
Karl Rove
Barbara Rush

Connecticut
Porter J. Goss
Michiko Kakutani
Liz Phair
Lawrence H. Summers
District of Columbia
Connie Chung
Al Gore
William Hurt
Queen Noor al-Hussein
Delaware
Valerie Bertinelli
Susan Stroman
G. Richard Wagoner
Jamie Wyeth

Florida
Patricia Cornwell
Faye Dunaway
Brad Mehldau
Wesley Snipes
Georgia
Hulk Hogan
Holly Hunter
Jessye Norman
Steven Soderbergh
Hawaii
Steve Case
Kimberly Dozier
Nicole Kidman
Barack Obama

Famous People from the 50 States, DC, and Puerto Rico (continued)

Idaho
Larry E. Craig
Harmon Killebrew
Picabo Street
Lana Turner
Illinois
Dennis Franz
Alison Krauss
Suze Orman
Gil Shaham
Indiana
Gary Burton
Janet Jackson
Twyla Tharp
Kurt Vonnegut
Iowa
Lara Flynn Boyle
Bill Bryson
Ted Kooser
Sara Paretsky
Kansas
Kirstie Alley
Melissa Etheridge
Jim Lehrer
Jim Ryun
Kentucky
Johnny Depp
Wynonna Judd
Diane Sawyer
George M. Whitesides
Louisiana
Karl Malone
Paul Prudhomme
Anne Rice
Lucinda Williams
Maine
David E. Kelley
Linda Lavin
George Mitchell
Liv Tyler
Maryland
Ira Glass
Philip Glass
Nancy Pelosi
Nora Roberts
Massachusetts
King Bhumibol
Adulyadej
Emeril Lagasse
Donna Summer
Uma Thurman

Michigan
James P. Hoffa
Julie Krone
Anna Sui
Stevie Wonder
Minnesota
Merrill Ashley
Tammy Faye Messner
Prince
Anne Tyler
Mississippi
Brandy
Faith Hill
Tavis Smiley
Richard H. Truly
Missouri
Sheryl Crow
Julia "Butterfly" Hill
Rush Limbaugh
Dick Van Dyke
Montana
Judith Blegen
Missy Gold
Phil Jackson
Evel Knievel
Nebraska
Gerald R. Ford
Andy Roddick
Paula Zahn
Mary
Zimmerman
Nevada
Andre Agassi
Mädchen Amick
Jack Kramer
Dawn Wells
New Hampshire
Brooke Astor
Dan Brown
Bode Miller
Mandy Moore
New Jersey
Savion Glover
Robert Pinsky
Patricia F. Russo
Cindy Sherman
New Mexico
Rudolfo Anaya
Jeffrey P. Bezos
Dolores Huerta
Demi Moore

New York
Scott Adams
Tommy Hilfiger
Paris Hilton
Meg Whitman
North Carolina
Dale Earnhardt, Jr.
Roberta Flack
Julianne Moore
Charlie Rose
North Dakota
Phyllis Bryn-Julson
Warren Christopher
Leonard Peltier
Bobby Vee
Ohio
Elizabeth George
Arsenio Hall
Maya Lin
Marilyn Manson
Oklahoma
Rick Bayless
Joy Harjo
Jennifer Jones
Cornel West
Oregon
Dick Fosbury
Matt Groening
Patricia Schroeder
Sally Struthers
Pennsylvania
Arden L. Bement
Kobe Bryant
Judith Jamison
Pink
Puerto Rico
Sila María Calderón
Benicio Del Toro
Gigi Fernandez
Antonia Novello
Rhode Island
Wendy Carlos
Van Johnson
Galway Kinnell
Sylvia Poggioli
South Carolina
Joe Frazier
Charlayne
Hunter-Gault
Andie MacDowell
Charles H. Townes

South Dakota
Tom Brokaw
Shawn Colvin
Mary Hart
Russell Means
Tennessee
Morgan Freeman
Nikki Giovanni
Justin Timberlake
Dawn Upshaw
Texas
Jerry D. Bailey
Beyoncé
Michael S. Dell
Heloise
Utah
Jewel
Brent Scowcroft
J. Craig Venter
Loretta Young
Vermont
Carlton Fisk
Kevin McKenzie
Patty Sheehan
Jody Williams
Virginia
Hilary Hahn
Laura
Hillenbrand
Tim Koogle
Cy Twombly
Washington
Jim Caviezel
Chuck Close
Gail Devers
Carolyn Kizer
West Virginia
Phyllis Curtin
John F. Nash
Mary Lou Retton
Cecil E. Roberts
Wisconsin
William Rehnquist
Gena Rowlands
Alice Sebold
Tony Shalhoub
Wyoming
Lynne Cheney
Dave Freudenthal
Rulon Gardner
Curt Gowdy

State Government

Governors of US States and Territories

Governors of New Hampshire and Vermont serve two-year terms; all others serve four-year terms. Parties: Democrat (D); Republican (R); Popular Democrat (PD). Source: National Governors Association.

STATE	GOVERNOR	IN OFFICE SINCE	PRESENT TERM EXPIRES
Alabama	Bob Riley (R)	January 2003	January 2007*
Alaska	Frank Murkowski (R)	December 2002	December 2006*
Arizona	Janet Napolitano (D)	January 2003	January 2007*
Arkansas	Mike Huckabee (R)[1]	July 1996	January 2007
California	Arnold Schwarzenegger (R)[2]	November 2003	January 2007*
Colorado	Bill Owens (R)	January 1999	January 2007
Connecticut	M. Jodi Rell (R)[3]	July 2004	January 2007*

Governors of US States and Territories (continued)

STATE	GOVERNOR	IN OFFICE SINCE	PRESENT TERM EXPIRES
Delaware[4]	Ruth Ann Minner (D)	January 2001	January 2009
Florida	Jeb Bush (R)	January 1999	January 2007
Georgia	Sonny Perdue (R)	January 2003	January 2007*
Hawaii	Linda Lingle (R)	December 2002	December 2006*
Idaho	Dirk Kempthorne (R)	January 1999	January 2007
Illinois	Rod Blagojevich (D)	January 2003	January 2007*
Indiana	Mitch Daniels (R)	January 2005	January 2009*
Iowa	Tom Vilsack (D)	January 1999	January 2007*
Kansas	Kathleen Sebelius (D)	January 2003	January 2007*
Kentucky	Ernie Fletcher (R)	December 2003	December 2007*
Louisiana	Kathleen Blanco (D)	January 2004	January 2008*
Maine	John Baldacci (D)	January 2003	January 2007*
Maryland	Robert Ehrlich (R)	January 2003	January 2007*
Massachusetts	Mitt Romney (R)	January 2003	January 2007*
Michigan	Jennifer Granholm (D)	January 2003	January 2007*
Minnesota	Tim Pawlenty (R)	January 2003	January 2007*
Mississippi	Haley Barbour (R)	January 2004	January 2008*
Missouri	Matt Blunt (R)	January 2005	January 2009*
Montana[5]	Brian Schweitzer (D)	January 2005	January 2009*
Nebraska[6]	Dave Heineman (R)[7]	January 2005	January 2007*
Nevada	Kenny C. Guinn (R)	January 1999	January 2007
New Hampshire	John Lynch (D)	January 2005	January 2007*
New Jersey	Richard Codey (D)[8]	November 2004	January 2006*
New Mexico	Bill Richardson (D)	January 2003	January 2007*
New York	George E. Pataki (R)	January 1995	January 2007*
North Carolina	Michael F. Easley (D)	January 2001	January 2009
North Dakota	John Hoeven (R)	December 2000	December 2008*
Ohio	Bob Taft (R)	January 1999	January 2007
Oklahoma	Brad Henry (D)	January 2003	January 2007*
Oregon	Ted Kulongoski (D)	January 2003	January 2007*
Pennsylvania	Edward G. Rendell (D)	January 2003	January 2007*
Rhode Island	Don Carcieri (R)	January 2003	January 2007*
South Carolina	Mark Sanford (R)	January 2003	January 2007*
South Dakota	Michael Rounds (R)	January 2003	January 2007*
Tennessee	Phil Bredesen (D)	January 2003	January 2007*
Texas	Rick Perry (R)[9]	December 2000	January 2007*
Utah	Jon Huntsman, Jr. (R)	January 2005	January 2009*
Vermont	Jim Douglas (R)	January 2005	January 2007*
Virginia[10]	Mark R. Warner (D)	January 2002	January 2006
Washington	Christine Gregoire (D)	January 2005	January 2009*
West Virginia	Joe Manchin III (D)	January 2005	January 2009*
Wisconsin	Jim Doyle (D)	January 2003	January 2007*
Wyoming	David Freudenthal (D)	January 2003	January 2007*

TERRITORY	GOVERNOR	IN OFFICE SINCE	PRESENT TERM EXPIRES
American Samoa	Togiola T.A. Tulafono (D)[11]	April 2003	January 2009
Guam	Felix Perez Camacho (R)	January 2003	January 2007*
Northern Mariana Islands	Juan N. Babauta (R)	January 2002	January 2006*
Puerto Rico	Aníbal Acevedo Vilá (PD)	January 2005	January 2009*
Virgin Islands	Charles W. Turnbull (D)	January 1999	January 2007

Present governor is eligible for reelection. [1]*Lt. Gov. Mike Huckabee became governor in July 1996 following Jim Guy Tucker's resignation. He was elected to full four-year terms in November 1998 and November 2002.* [2]*Arnold Schwarzenegger was elected in October 2003 following the recall of former Governor Gray Davis.* [3] *Lt. Gov. M. Jodi Rell became governor on 1 Jul 2004 following John G. Rowland's resignation.* [4]*Delaware allows two terms, but these need not be served consecutively.* [5]*Montana allows no more than 8 years of service every 16 years.* [6]*Nebraska allows the governor to serve two consecutive terms, but the candidate must wait four years before running for a third term.* [7]*Lt. Gov. Dave Heineman became governor on 21 Jan 2005 following Mike Johanns's appointment to the office of US secretary of agriculture.* [8]*New Jersey Senate President Richard Codey became acting governor on 15 Nov 2004 following James E. McGreevey's resignation.* [9]*Lt. Gov. Rick Perry became governor in December 2000 following George W. Bush's election as president of the United States. Gov. Perry was elected to a full term in November 2002.* [10]*In Virginia the governor cannot serve successive terms.* [11]*Lt. Gov. Togiola T.A. Tulafono became governor in April 2003 following the death of Gov. Tauese Sunia.*

State Officers and Legislatures

Sources: Web sites from the individual states, The Book of the States, vol. 37, and the CSG State Directory, *published by The Council of State Governments.*

STATE/OFFICE	OFFICEHOLDER	PAY[1]
Alabama		
Governor	Bob Riley (R)	$96,361
Lt. Gov.	Lucy Baxley (D)	$45,360
Sec. of State	Nancy Worley (D)	$71,500
Atty. Gen.	Troy King (R)	$163,429
Treasurer	Kay Ivey (R)	$71,500
Legislature		
Senate	Dem: 25; Rep: 10	
House	Dem: 63; Rep: 42	
Alaska		
Governor	Frank H. Murkowski (R)	$85,766
Lt. Gov.	Loren Leman (R)	$80,040
Sec. of State[2]		
Atty. Gen.	David W. Márquez (R)	$91,200
Treasurer	Tom Boutin	$91,200
Legislature		
Senate	Dem: 8; Rep: 12	
House	Dem: 14; Rep: 26	
Arizona		
Governor	Janet Napolitano (D)	$95,000
Lt. Gov.[3]		
Sec. of State	Jan Brewer (R)	$70,000
Atty. Gen.	Terry Goddard (D)	$90,000
Treasurer	David A. Petersen (R)	$70,000
Legislature		
Senate	Dem: 12; Rep: 18	
House	Dem: 22; Rep: 38	
Arkansas		
Governor	Mike Huckabee (R)	$75,296
Lt. Gov.	Winthrop Rockefeller (R)	$37,229
Sec. of State	Charlie Daniels (D)	$48,182
Atty. Gen.	Mike Beebe (D)	$64,189
Treasurer	Gus Wingfield (D)	$48,182
General Assembly		
Senate	Dem: 27; Rep: 8	
House	Dem: 72; Rep: 28	
California		
Governor	Arnold Schwarzenegger (R)	$175,000
Lt. Gov.	Cruz M. Bustamante (D)	$131,250
Sec. of State	Bruce McPherson (R)	$131,250
Atty. Gen.	Bill Lockyer (D)	$148,750
Treasurer	Philip Angelides (D)	$140,000
Legislature		
Senate	Dem: 25; Rep: 15	
Assembly	Dem: 48; Rep: 32	
Colorado		
Governor	Bill Owens (R)	$90,000
Lt. Gov.	Jane Norton (R)	$68,500
Sec. of State	Donetta Davidson (R)	$68,500
Atty. Gen.	John W. Suthers (R)	$80,000
Treasurer	Mark Hillman (acting)	$68,500
General Assembly		
Senate	Dem: 18; Rep: 17	
House	Dem: 35; Rep: 30	
Connecticut		
Governor	M. Jodi Rell (R)	$150,000
Lt. Gov.	Kevin B. Sullivan (D)	$110,000
Sec. of State	Susan Bysiewicz (D)	$110,000
Atty. Gen.	Richard Blumenthal (D)	$110,000

STATE/OFFICE	OFFICEHOLDER	PAY[1]
Connecticut (continued)		
Treasurer	Denise L. Nappier (D)	$110,000
General Assembly		
Senate	Dem: 24; Rep: 12	
House	Dem: 99; Rep: 52	
Delaware		
Governor	Ruth Ann Minner (D)	$132,500
Lt. Gov.	John Carney (D)	$64,900
Sec. of State	Harriet Smith Windsor (D)	$109,800
Atty. Gen.	M. Jane Brady (R)	$120,800
Treasurer	Jack Markell (D)	$97,400
General Assembly		
Senate	Dem: 13; Rep: 8	
House	Dem: 15; Rep: 25; Ind: 1	
Florida		
Governor	Jeb Bush (R)	$120,171
Lt. Gov.	Toni Jennings (R)	$119,390
Sec. of State	Glenda Hood (R)	$118,400
Atty. Gen.	Charlie Crist (R)	$123,331
Treasurer	Tom Gallagher (R)	$123,331
Legislature		
Senate	Dem: 14; Rep: 26	
House	Dem: 36; Rep: 84	
Georgia		
Governor	Sonny Perdue (R)	$127,303
Lt. Gov.	Mark Taylor (D)	$83,148
Sec. of State	Cathy Cox (D)	$112,776
Atty. Gen.	Thurbert E. Baker (D)	$125,871
Treasurer	W. Daniel Ebersole	$117,893
General Assembly		
Senate	Dem: 22; Rep: 34	
House	Dem: 80; Rep: 99; Ind: 1	
Hawaii		
Governor	Linda Lingle (R)	$94,780
Lt. Gov.	James Aiona (R)	$90,041
Sec. of State[2]		
Atty. Gen.	Mark J. Bennett (R)	$105,000
Treasurer[4]	Georgina K. Kawamura (Director of Finance)	$100,000
Legislature		
Senate	Dem: 20; Rep: 5	
House	Dem: 41; Rep: 10	
Idaho		
Governor	Dirk Kempthorne (R)	$98,500
Lt. Gov.	Jim Risch (R)	$26,750
Sec. of State	Ben Ysursa (R)	$82,500
Atty. Gen.	Lawrence Wasden (R)	$91,500
Treasurer	Ron G. Crane (R)	$82,500
Legislature		
Senate	Dem: 7; Rep: 28	
House	Dem: 13; Rep: 57	
Illinois		
Governor	Rod R. Blagojevich (D)	$150,691
Lt. Gov.	Pat Quinn (D)	$118,400
Sec. of State	Jesse White (D)	$136,600
Atty. Gen.	Lisa Madigan (D)	$136,600
Treasurer	Judy Baar Topinka (R)	$118,400
General Assembly		
Senate	Dem: 31; Rep: 27; Ind: 1	
House	Dem: 65; Rep: 53	

State Officers and Legislatures (continued)

STATE/OFFICE	OFFICEHOLDER	PAY[1]
Indiana		
Governor	Mitch Daniels (R)	$95,000
Lt. Gov.	Becky Skillman (R)	$76,000
Sec. of State	Todd Rokita (R)	$66,000
Atty. Gen.	Steve Carter (R)	$79,400
Treasurer	Tim Berry (R)	$66,000
General Assembly		
Senate	Dem: 17; Rep: 33	
House	Dem: 48; Rep: 52	
Iowa		
Governor	Tom Vilsack (D)	$107,482
Lt. Gov.	Sally Pederson (D)	$76,698
Sec. of State	Chet Culver (D)	$87,990
Atty. Gen.	Tom Miller (D)	$105,430
Treasurer	Michael L. Fitzgerald (D)	$87,990
General Assembly		
Senate	Dem: 25; Rep: 25	
House	Dem: 49; Rep: 51	
Kansas		
Governor	Kathleen Sebelius (D)	$98,331
Lt. Gov.	John Moore (D)	$111,523
Sec. of State	Ron Thornburgh (R)	$76,389
Atty. Gen.	Phill Kline (R)	$76,389
Treasurer	Lynn Jenkins (R)	$76,389
Legislature		
Senate	Dem: 10; Rep: 30	
House	Dem: 42; Rep: 83	
Kentucky		
Governor	Ernie Fletcher (R)	$127,146
Lt. Gov.	Steve Pence (R)	$91,075
Sec. of State	Trey Grayson (R)	$91,075
Atty. Gen.	Greg Stumbo (D)	$91,075
Treasurer	Jonathan Miller (D)	$91,075
General Assembly		
Senate	Dem: 15; Rep: 22; Ind: 1	
House	Dem: 57; Rep: 43	
Louisiana		
Governor	Kathleen Babineaux Blanco (D)	$94,532
Lt. Gov.	Mitch Landrieu (D)	$85,000
Sec. of State	W. Fox McKeithen (R)	$85,000
Atty. Gen.	Charles C. Foti, Jr. (D)	$85,000
Treasurer	John Kennedy (D)	$85,000
Legislature		
Senate	Dem: 24; Rep: 15	
House	Dem: 67; Rep: 37; Ind: 1	
Maine		
Governor	John Baldacci (D)	$70,000
Lt. Gov.[3]		
Sec. of State	Matthew Dunlap (D)	N/A
Atty. Gen.	G. Steven Rowe (D)	$78,062
Treasurer	David Lemoine (D)	$71,032
Legislature		
Senate	Dem: 19; Rep: 16	
House	Dem: 76; Rep: 73; Unenrolled: 2; Green Independent Party: 1	
Maryland		
Governor	Robert L. Ehrlich, Jr. (R)	$135,000
Lt. Gov.	Michael Steele (R)	$120,833
Sec. of State	R. Karl Aumann (R)	$84,583
Atty. Gen.	J. Joseph Curran, Jr. (D)	$120,833
Treasurer	Nancy Kopp (D)	$120,833

STATE/OFFICE	OFFICEHOLDER	PAY[1]
Maryland (continued)		
General Assembly		
Senate	Dem: 33; Rep: 14	
House	Dem: 98; Rep: 43	
Massachusetts		
Governor	Mitt Romney (R)[5]	$135,000
Lt. Gov.	Kerry Healey (R)[5]	$120,000
Sec. of State	William Francis Galvin (D)	$120,000
Atty. Gen.	Tom Reilly (D)	$122,500
Treasurer	Timothy Cahill (D)	$120,000
General Court (legislature)		
Senate	Dem: 34; Rep: 6	
House	Dem: 136; Rep: 21; Vacant: 3	
Michigan		
Governor	Jennifer Granholm (D)	$177,000
Lt. Gov.	John Cherry (D)	$123,900
Sec. of State	Terri Lynn Land (R)	$124,900
Atty. Gen.	Mike Cox (R)	$124,900
Treasurer	Jay Rising	$167,504
Legislature		
Senate	Dem: 16; Rep: 22	
House	Dem: 52; Rep: 58	
Minnesota		
Governor	Tim Pawlenty (R)	$120,311
Lt. Gov.	Carol Molnau (R)	$78,197
Sec. of State	Mary Kiffmeyer (R)	$90,227
Atty. Gen.	Mike Hatch (D)	$114,288
Treasurer[4]	Peggy Ingison (Commissioner of Finance)	$108,388
Legislature		
Senate	Dem: 35; Rep: 31; Ind: 1	
House	Dem: 66; Rep: 68	
Mississippi		
Governor	Haley Barbour (R)	$122,160
Lt. Gov.	Amy Tuck (R)	$60,000
Sec. of State	Eric Clark (D)	$90,000
Atty. Gen.	Jim Hood (D)	$108,960
Treasurer	Tate Reeves (R)	$90,000
Legislature		
Senate	Dem: 28; Rep: 24	
House	Dem: 75; Rep: 47	
Missouri		
Governor	Matt Blunt (R)	$120,087
Lt. Gov.	Peter Kinder (R)	$77,184
Sec. of State	Robin Carnahan (D)	$96,455
Atty. Gen.	Jeremiah W. Nixon (D)	$104,332
Treasurer	Sarah Steelman (R)	$96,455
General Assembly		
Senate	Dem: 11; Rep: 23	
House	Dem: 66; Rep: 97	
Montana		
Governor	Brian Schweitzer (D)	$93,089
Lt. Gov.	John Bohlinger (R)	$66,724
Sec. of State	Brad Johnson (R)	$72,085
Atty. Gen.	Mike McGrath (D)	$82,233
Treasurer[4]	Janet Kelly (Dept. of Administration)	$83,932
Legislature		
Senate	Dem: 27; Rep: 23	
House	Dem: 49; Rep: 50; Constitution: 1	

State Officers and Legislatures (continued)

STATE/OFFICE	OFFICEHOLDER	PAY[1]
Nebraska		
Governor	Dave Heineman (R)	$85,000
Lt. Gov.	Rick Sheehy (R)	$60,000
Sec. of State	John A. Gale (R)	$65,000
Atty. Gen.	Jon Bruning (R)	$75,000
Treasurer	Ron Ross	$60,000
Legislature (unicameral)		
Senate	49 nonpartisan members	
Nevada		
Governor	Kenny C. Guinn (R)	$117,000
Lt. Gov.	Lorraine Hunt (R)	$50,000
Sec. of State	Dean Heller (R)	$80,000
Atty. Gen.	Brian Sandoval (R)	$110,000
Treasurer	Brian K. Krolicki (R)	$80,000
Legislature		
Senate	Dem: 9; Rep: 12	
Assembly	Dem: 26; Rep: 16	
New Hampshire		
Governor	John Lynch (D)	$96,060
Lt. Gov.[6]		
Sec. of State	William Gardner (D)	$89,128
Atty. Gen.	Kelly Ayotte (R)	$99,317
Treasurer	Michael A. Ablowich	$89,128
General Court (legislature)		
Senate	Dem: 8; Rep: 16	
House	Dem: 147; Rep: 250; Vacant: 3	
New Jersey		
Governor	Richard Codey (D)	$157,000
Lt. Gov.[6]		
Sec. of State	Regena L. Thomas (D)	$141,000
Atty. Gen.	Peter C. Harvey (D)	$141,000
Treasurer	John E. McCormac	$141,000
Legislature		
Senate	Dem: 22; Rep: 18	
General Assembly	Dem: 47; Rep: 33	
New Mexico		
Governor	Bill Richardson (D)	$110,000
Lt. Gov.	Diane Denish (D)	$85,000
Sec. of State	Rebecca Vigil-Giron (D)	$85,000
Atty. Gen.	Patricia A. Madrid (D)	$95,000
Treasurer	Robert E. Vigil (D)	$85,000
Legislature		
Senate	Dem: 24; Rep: 18	
House	Dem: 42; Rep: 28	
New York		
Governor	George E. Pataki (R)	$179,000
Lt. Gov.	Mary O. Donohue (R)	$151,500
Sec. of State	Randy Daniels (R)	$120,800
Atty. Gen.	Eliot Spitzer (D)	$151,500
Treasurer	Aida Brewer	$109,190
Legislature		
Senate	Dem: 28; Rep: 34	
Assembly	Dem: 104; Rep: 46	
North Carolina		
Governor	Michael F. Easley (D)	$121,391
Lt. Gov.	Beverly Perdue (D)	$107,136
Sec. of State	Elaine Marshall (D)	$107,136
Atty. Gen.	Roy Cooper (D)	$107,136
Treasurer	Richard H. Moore (D)	$107,136

STATE/OFFICE	OFFICEHOLDER	PAY[1]
North Carolina (continued)		
General Assembly		
Senate	Dem: 29; Rep: 21	
House	Dem: 63; Rep: 57	
North Dakota		
Governor	John Hoeven (R)	$85,506
Lt. Gov.	Jack Dalrymple (R)	$66,380
Sec. of State	Alvin A. Jaeger (R)	$68,018
Atty. Gen.	Wayne Stenehjem (R)	$74,668
Treasurer	Kelly Schmidt (R)	$64,236
Legislative Assembly		
Senate	Dem: 15; Rep: 32	
House	Dem: 27; Rep: 67	
Ohio		
Governor	Bob Taft (R)	$126,485
Lt. Gov.	Bruce Johnson (R)	$73,715
Sec. of State	J. Kenneth Blackwell (R)	$90,725
Atty. Gen.	Jim Petro (R)	$93,434
Treasurer	Jeanette Bradley (R)	$93,434
General Assembly		
Senate	Dem: 11; Rep: 22	
House	Dem: 40; Rep: 59	
Oklahoma		
Governor	Brad Henry (D)	$110,298
Lt. Gov.	Mary Fallin (R)	$85,500
Sec. of State	M. Susan Savage (D)	$90,000
Atty. Gen.	W.A. Drew Edmondson (D)	$103,109
Treasurer	Scott Meacham (D)	$87,875
Legislature		
Senate	Dem: 26; Rep: 22	
House	Dem: 44; Rep: 57	
Oregon		
Governor	Ted Kulongoski (D)	$93,600
Lt. Gov.[3]		
Sec. of State	Bill Bradbury (D)	$72,000
Atty. Gen.	Hardy Myers (D)	$77,200
Treasurer	Randall Edwards (D)	$72,000
Legislative Assembly		
Senate	Dem: 18; Rep: 12	
House	Dem: 27; Rep: 33	
Pennsylvania		
Governor	Edward G. Rendell (D)	$155,753
Lt. Gov.	Catherine Baker Knoll (D)	$121,309
Sec. of State	Pedro A. Cortés (D)	$103,980
Atty. Gen.	Tom Corbett (R)	$120,154
Treasurer	Robert Casey, Jr. (D)	$120,154
General Assembly		
Senate	Dem: 20; Rep: 30	
House	Dem: 93; Rep: 110	
Rhode Island		
Governor	Don Carcieri (R)	$105,194
Lt. Gov.	Charles J. Fogarty (D)	$88,584
Sec. of State	Matthew Brown (D)	$88,584
Atty. Gen.	Patrick Lynch (D)	$94,121
Treasurer	Paul J. Tavares (D)	$88,584
General Assembly		
Senate	Dem: 33; Rep: 5	
House	Dem: 60; Rep: 15	

State Officers and Legislatures (continued)

STATE/OFFICE	OFFICEHOLDER	PAY[1]
South Carolina		
Governor	Mark Sanford (R)	$106,078
Lt. Gov.	André Bauer (R)	$46,545
Sec. of State	Mark Hammond (R)	$92,007
Atty. Gen.	Henry McMaster (R)	$92,007
Treasurer	Grady L. Patterson, Jr. (D)	$92,007
General Assembly		
Senate	Dem: 20; Rep: 26	
House	Dem: 50; Rep: 74	
South Dakota		
Governor	Mike Rounds (R)	$103,222
Lt. Gov.	Dennis Daugaard (R)	$12,635
Sec. of State	Chris Nelson (R)	$64,812
Atty. Gen.	Larry Long (R)	$80,995
Treasurer	Vernon L. Larson (R)	$64,813
Legislature		
Senate	Dem: 10; Rep: 25	
House	Dem: 19; Rep: 51	
Tennessee		
Governor	Phil Bredesen (D)	$85,000
Lt. Gov.	John S. Wilder (D)	$49,500
Sec. of State	Riley Darnell (D)	$135,060
Atty. Gen.	Paul G. Summers (D)	$126,528
Treasurer	Dale Sims	$131,060
General Assembly		
Senate	Dem: 16; Rep: 17	
House	Dem: 53; Rep: 46	
Texas		
Governor	Rick Perry (R)	$115,345
Lt. Gov.	David Dewhurst (R)	$97,200
Sec. of State	Roger Williams (R)	$117,546
Atty. Gen.	Greg Abbott (R)	$92,217
Treasurer[4]	Carole Keeton Strayhorn (Comptroller) (R)	$92,217
Legislature		
Senate	Dem: 12; Rep: 19	
House	Dem: 63; Rep: 87	
Utah		
Governor	Jon M. Huntsman, Jr. (R)	$101,600
Lt. Gov.	Gary Herbert (R)	$78,200
Sec. of State[2]		
Atty. Gen.	Mark Shurtleff (R)	$84,600
Treasurer	Edward T. Alter (R)	$78,200
Legislature		
Senate	Dem: 8; Rep: 21	
House	Dem: 19; Rep: 56	
Vermont		
Governor	Jim Douglas (R)	$133,162
Lt. Gov.	Brian Dubie (R)	$56,514
Sec. of State	Deborah Markowitz (D)	$84,427
Atty. Gen.	William H. Sorrell (D)	$101,067
Treasurer	Jeb Spaulding (D)	$84,427

STATE/OFFICE	OFFICEHOLDER	PAY[1]
Vermont (continued)		
General Assembly		
Senate	Dem: 21; Rep: 9	
House	Dem: 83; Rep: 60; Ind: 1; Progressive: 6	
Virginia		
Governor	Mark R. Warner (D)	$124,855
Lt. Gov.	Tim Kaine (D)	$36,321
Sec. of State	Anita A. Rimler (D)	$135,311
Atty. Gen.	Judith W. Jagdmann (R)	$110,667
Treasurer	Jody M. Wagner	$118,644
General Assembly		
Senate	Dem: 16; Rep: 24	
House	Dem: 38; Rep: 60; Ind: 2	
Washington		
Governor	Christine Gregoire (D)	$139,087
Lt. Gov.	Brad Owen (D)	$75,865
Sec. of State	Sam Reed (R)	$101,702
Atty. Gen.	Rob McKenna (R)	$131,938
Treasurer	Michael J. Murphy (D)	$101,702
Legislature		
Senate	Dem: 26; Rep: 23	
House	Dem: 55; Rep: 43	
West Virginia		
Governor	Joe Manchin III (D)	$90,000
Lt. Gov.[7]	Earl Ray Tomblin (D)	—
Sec. of State	Betty Ireland (R)	$70,000
Atty. Gen.	Darrell Vivian (D) McGraw, Jr.	$85,000
Treasurer	John D. Perdue (D)	$75,000
Legislature		
Senate	Dem: 21; Rep: 13	
House	Dem: 68; Rep: 32	
Wisconsin		
Governor	Jim Doyle (D)[8]	$131,768
Lt. Gov.	Barbara Lawton (D)	$69,579
Sec. of State	Douglas LaFollette (D)	$62,549
Atty. Gen.	Peg Lautenschlager (D)	$127,868
Treasurer	Jack C. Voight (R)	$62,549
Legislature		
Senate	Dem: 14; Rep: 19	
Assembly	Dem: 39; Rep: 60	
Wyoming		
Governor	Dave Freudenthal (D)	$130,000
Lt. Gov.[3]		
Sec. of State	Joe Meyer (R)	$92,000
Atty. Gen.	Patrick J. Crank (D)	$97,843
Treasurer	Cynthia Lummis (R)	$92,000
Legislature		
Senate	Dem: 7; Rep: 23	
House	Dem: 14; Rep: 46	

[1]In most cases, the salary rates are from January 2004. [2]Lieutenant governor serves as secretary of state. [3]Secretary of state assumes duties of lieutenant governor. [4]No official state treasurer; official in charge of general treasury performs duties. [5]Gov. Mitt Romney and Lt. Gov. Kerry Healey plan to forfeit their salaries during their terms. [6]No official lieutenant governor; president of the senate succeeds the governor. [7]In West Virginia president of the Senate and lieutenant governor are one and the same. [8]Gov. Jim Doyle remits a portion of his salary to the state.

Area and Zip Codes Web Sites

US telephone area codes and postal codes change frequently to accommodate telecommunications user patterns and expansions and shifts in patterns of business and residential development. With regard to telephone area codes, in some cases, an area receives an entirely new area code; in others, a new area code "overlays" the preceding one. Check local

listings to determine whether to dial "1" before dialing outside of the area code or to dial the area code as well as the telephone number when dialing within the area code.

Area codes: <www.nanpa.com>.
Zip codes: <www.usps.com/zip4/welcome.htm>.

Cities of the United States

US Urban Growth, 1850–2004

Source: US Census Bureau.

RANK	CITY	1850	1900	1950	1980	1990	2004
1	New York NY[1]	515,547	3,437,202	7,891,957	7,071,639	7,322,564	8,104,079
2	Los Angeles CA	1,610	102,479	1,970,358	2,966,850	3,485,398	3,845,541
3	Chicago IL	29,963	1,698,575	3,620,962	3,005,072	2,783,726	2,862,244
4	Houston TX	2,396	44,633	596,163	1,595,138	1,630,553	2,012,626
5	Philadelphia PA[1]	121,376	1,293,697	2,071,605	1,688,210	1,585,577	1,470,151
6	Phoenix AZ		5,544	106,818	789,704	983,403	1,418,041
7	San Diego CA		17,700	334,387	875,538	1,110,549	1,263,756
8	San Antonio TX	3,488	53,321	408,442	785,880	935,933	1,236,249
9	Dallas TX		42,638	434,462	904,078	1,006,877	1,210,393
10	San Jose CA		21,500	95,280	629,442	782,248	904,522
11	Detroit MI	21,019	285,704	1,849,568	1,203,339	1,027,974	900,198
12	Indianapolis IN	8,091	169,164	427,173	700,807	741,952	784,242
13	Jacksonville FL	1,045	28,429	204,517	540,920	635,230	777,704
14	San Francisco CA[1]	34,776	342,782	775,357	678,974	723,959	744,230
15	Columbus OH	17,882	125,560	375,901	564,871	632,910	730,008
16	Austin TX	629	22,258	132,459	345,496	465,622	681,804
17	Memphis TN	8,841	102,320	396,000	646,356	610,337	671,929
18	Baltimore MD	169,054	508,957	949,708	786,775	736,014	636,251
19	Fort Worth TX		26,688	278,778	385,164	447,619	603,337
20	Charlotte NC	1,065	18,091	134,042	314,447	395,934	594,359
21	El Paso TX		15,906	130,485	425,259	515,342	592,099
22	Milwaukee WI	20,061	285,315	637,392	636,212	628,088	583,624
23	Seattle WA		80,671	467,591	493,846	516,259	571,480
24	Boston MA	136,881	560,892	801,444	562,994	574,283	569,165
25	Denver CO[1]		133,859	415,786	492,365	467,610	556,835
26	Louisville KY[1]	43,194	204,731	369,129	298,451	269,063	556,332
27	Washington DC[1]	40,001	278,718	802,178	638,333	606,900	553,523
28	Nashville TN[1]	10,165	80,865	174,307	455,651	510,784	546,719
29	Las Vegas NV			24,624	164,674	258,295	534,847
30	Portland OR		90,426	373,628	366,383	437,319	533,492
31	Oklahoma City OK		10,037	243,504	403,213	444,719	528,042
32	Tucson AZ		7,531	45,454	330,537	405,390	512,023
33	Albuquerque NM		6,238	96,815	331,767	384,736	484,246
34	Long Beach CA		2,252	250,767	361,334	429,433	476,564
35	New Orleans LA	116,375	287,104	570,445	557,515	496,938	462,269
36	Cleveland OH	17,034	381,768	914,808	573,822	505,616	458,684
37	Fresno CA		12,470	91,669	218,202	354,202	457,719
38	Sacramento CA	6,820	29,282	137,572	275,741	369,365	454,330
39	Kansas City MO		163,752	456,622	448,159	435,146	444,387
40	Virginia Beach VA			5,390	262,199	393,069	440,098
41	Mesa AZ		722	16,790	152,453	288,091	437,454
42	Atlanta GA	2,572	89,872	331,314	425,022	394,017	419,122
43	Omaha NE		102,555	251,117	314,255	335,795	409,416
44	Oakland CA		66,960	384,575	339,337	372,242	397,976
45	Tulsa OK			182,740	360,919	367,302	383,764
46	Miami FL		1,681	249,276	346,865	358,548	379,724
47	Honolulu HI[1]		39,306	248,034	365,048	365,272	377,260
48	Minneapolis MN		202,718	521,718	370,951	368,383	373,943
49	Colorado Springs CO		21,085	45,472	215,150	281,140	369,363
50	Arlington TX		1,079	7,692	160,113	261,721	359,467
51	Wichita KS		24,671	168,279	279,272	304,011	353,823
52	St. Louis MO	77,860	575,238	856,796	453,085	396,685	343,279
53	Santa Ana CA		4,933	45,533	203,713	293,742	342,715

US Urban Growth, 1850–2004 (continued)

RANK	CITY	1850	1900	1950	1980	1990	2004
54	Anaheim CA		1,456	14,556	219,311	266,406	333,776
55	Raleigh NC	4,518	13,643	65,679	150,255	207,951	326,653
56	Pittsburgh PA	46,601	321,616	676,806	423,938	369,879	322,450
57	Tampa FL		15,839	124,681	271,523	280,015	321,772
58	Cincinnati OH	115,435	325,902	503,998	385,457	364,040	314,154
59	Toledo OH	3,829	131,822	303,616	354,635	332,943	304,973
60	Aurora CO		202	11,421	158,588	222,103	291,843
61	Riverside CA		7,973	46,764	170,876	226,505	288,384
62	Bakersfield CA		4,836	34,784	105,611	174,820	283,936
63	Buffalo NY	42,261	352,387	580,132	357,870	328,123	282,864
64	Corpus Christi TX		4,703	108,287	231,999	257,453	281,196
65	Newark NJ	38,894	246,070	438,776	329,248	275,221	280,451
66	Stockton CA		17,506	70,853	149,779	210,943	279,888
67	St. Paul MN	1,112	163,065	311,349	270,230	272,235	276,963
68	Anchorage AK[1]			11,254	174,431	226,338	272,687
69	Lexington KY[1]	8,159	26,369	55,534	204,165	225,366	266,358
70	St. Petersburg FL		1,575	96,738	238,647	238,629	249,090
71	Plano TX				72,331	128,713	245,411
72	Jersey City NJ	6,856	206,433	299,017	223,532	228,537	239,079
73	Norfolk VA	14,326	46,624	213,513	266,979	261,229	237,835
74	Lincoln NE		40,169	98,884	171,932	191,972	236,146
75	Glendale AZ				97,172	148,134	235,591
76	Birmingham AL		38,415	326,037	284,413	265,968	233,149
77	Greensboro NC		10,035	74,389	155,642	183,521	231,543
78	Henderson NV				24,363	64,942	224,829
79	Hialeah FL			19,676	145,254	188,004	224,522
80	Baton Rouge LA	3,905	11,269	125,629	219,419	219,531	224,097
81	Chandler AZ			3,800	30,000	90,533	223,991
82	Scottsdale AZ				88,412	130,069	221,792
83	Madison WI	1,525	19,164	96,056	170,616	191,262	220,332
84	Fort Wayne IN	4,282	45,115	133,607	172,196	173,072	219,351
85	Garland TX		819	10,571	138,857	180,650	217,176
86	Chesapeake VA				114,486	151,976	214,725
87	Rochester NY	36,403	162,608	332,488	241,741	231,636	212,481
88	Akron OH	3,266	42,728	274,605	237,177	223,019	212,179
89	Lubbock TX			71,747	173,979	186,206	207,852
90	Modesto CA			17,389	106,602	164,730	206,769
91	Orlando FL		2,481	52,367	128,291	164,693	205,648
92	Chula Vista CA			15,927	83,927	135,163	204,879
93	Laredo TX		13,429	51,910	91,449	122,899	203,212
94	Fremont CA				131,945	173,339	202,373
95	Durham NC		6,679	71,311	100,831	136,611	201,726
96	Glendale CA			95,702	139,060	180,038	201,326
97	Montgomery AL	8,728	30,346	106,525	177,857	187,106	200,983
98	Shreveport LA	1,728	16,013	127,206	205,820	198,525	198,675
99	San Bernardino CA		6,150	63,058	117,490	164,164	198,406
100	Reno NV		4,500	32,497	100,756	133,850	197,963

[1] Cities with boundaries contiguous with their respective counties: New York, Philadelphia, San Francisco, Denver, Louisville (Jefferson county), Washington (District of Columbia), Nashville (Davidson county), Honolulu, Anchorage, and Lexington (Fayette county).

Ten Fastest-Growing Cities in the US

Based on a population of 250,000 or more. Source: US Census Bureau.

CITY	POPULATION		CHANGE (%)
	1 APR 1990	1 APR 2000	
Las Vegas NV	258,295	478,434	+85.2
Austin TX	465,622	656,562	+41.0
Mesa AZ	288,091	396,375	+37.6
Charlotte NC	395,934	540,828	+36.6
Phoenix AZ	983,403	1,321,045	+34.3
Raleigh NC	207,951	276,093	+32.8
Colorado Springs CO	281,140	360,890	+28.4
Arlington TX	261,721	332,969	+27.2
Aurora CO	222,103	276,393	+24.4
Anaheim CA	266,406	328,014	+23.1

Ten Cities with the Greatest Population Losses in the US

Based on a population of 250,000 or more. Source: US Census Bureau.

CITY	CHANGE (%)	POPULATION 1 APR 1990	POPULATION 1 APR 2000	CITY	CHANGE (%)	POPULATION 1 APR 1990	POPULATION 1 APR 2000
St. Louis MO	−12.2	396,685	348,189	Detroit MI	−7.5	1,027,974	951,270
Baltimore MD	−11.5	736,014	651,154	Toledo OH	−5.8	332,943	313,619
Buffalo NY	−10.8	328,123	292,648	Washington DC	−5.7	606,900	572,059
Pittsburgh PA	−9.5	369,879	334,563	Cleveland OH	−5.4	505,616	478,403
Cincinnati OH	−9.0	364,040	331,285	Milwaukee WI	−5.0	628,088	596,974

Racial Makeup of the Ten Largest US Cities

Information is given in percent of the total population. The Hispanic or Latino category is listed for comparative purposes even though Hispanic or Latino people may be of any race; thus, the rows of racial percentages will not add up to 100 if the Hispanic or Latino entries are included. Source: *American Community Survey*, 2003 Data Profiles, US Census Bureau.

CITY	WHITE	BLACK OR AFRICAN AMERICAN	AMERICAN INDIAN AND ALASKA NATIVE	ASIAN	NATIVE HAWAIIAN AND OTHER PACIFIC ISLANDER	SOME OTHER RACE	TWO OR MORE RACES	HISPANIC OR LATINO	TOTAL POPULATION
New York NY	46.1	26.2	0.2	11.3	7.3	12.9	3.1	28.4	7,902,897
Los Angeles CA	55.7	10.4	0.5	10.9	0.2	20.5	1.8	48.1	3,719,310
Chicago IL	46.9	36.1	0.2	4.4	0.1	10.9	1.3	27.4	2,722,562
Houston TX	61.0	24.5	0.3	5.3	0.1	7.5	1.2	40.1	1,938,502
Philadelphia PA	42.2	44.1	−	5.1	−	7.0	2.4	9.3	1,423,538
Phoenix AZ	78.7	5.2	2.0	2.0	0.3	10.2	1.6	39.2	1,319,037
San Diego CA	68.9	7.2	0.4	14.4	0.4	6.1	2.6	26.4	1,220,734
Dallas TX	56.5	20.2	0.4	4.2	−	16.5	2.0	34.7	2,247,812
San Antonio TX	69.2	6.1	0.7	1.6	0.1	20.3	2.0	61.5	1,193,652
Detroit MI	12.1	80.9	0.2	0.1	−	4.0	2.4	5.7	879,575

− Percent rounds to 0.0.

Law and Crime

US Crime Trends, 2004

The crime trends shown below represent the percent change in crimes reported to police for the year 2004 as compared to the same time period in the year 2003. A negative number indicates that crime has declined. Figures may not add up to totals due to rounding.
Source: Federal Bureau of Investigation, *Uniform Crime Reports, January–December 2004.*

POPULATION GROUP AND AREA	NUMBER OF AGENCIES[1]	POPULATION ('000)	VIOLENT CRIME[2]	PROPERTY CRIME[3]	MURDER
cities					
1,000,000 and over	10	24,790	−5.4	−2.6	−7.1
500,000 to 999,999	22	14,643	−3.4	−3.5	−2.3
250,000 to 499,999	37	13,146	+1.3	−4.2	−1.8
100,000 to 249,999	175	26,249	−1.3	−2.4	−8.4
50,000 to 99,999	388	26,749	+0.3	−0.5	−4.9
25,000 to 49,999	707	24,566	+1.1	−1.0	+1.7
10,000 to 24,999	1,566	24,753	−1.3	−0.3	+0.8
under 10,000	6,126	19,895	+0.3	−0.9	−12.2
counties					
metropolitan[4]	1,528	59,778	−2.1	−1.5	+2.2
nonmetropolitan[5]	2,156	23,433	+0.7	−1.5	−3.1
total	**12,715**	**258,001**	**−1.7**	**−1.8**	**−3.6**

US Crime Trends, 2004 (continued)

POPULATION GROUP AND AREA	FORCIBLE RAPE	ROBBERY	AGGRAVATED ASSAULT	BURGLARY	LARCENY/ THEFT	CAR THEFT	ARSON
cities							
1,000,000 and over	+0.2	−6.7	−4.7	−1.5	−2.3	−4.4	−11.8
500,000 to 999,999	−3.9	−5.7	−1.8	−2.9	−3.8	−2.9	−2.7
250,000 to 499,999	−1.1	−2.9	+4.5	−2.0	−4.2	−6.6	−8.5
100,000 to 249,999	+1.1	−2.0	−1.0	−1.3	−2.6	−2.7	−11.8
50,000 to 99,999	−0.2	+0.5	+0.3	+2.0	−1.1	−1.5	−6.1
25,000 to 49,999	+1.4	−0.1	+1.5	−0.4	−1.1	−0.9	−4.2
10,000 to 24,999	+2.1	−3.1	−1.1	+0.2	−0.2	−1.6	−5.6
under 10,000	−0.2	−1.0	+0.8	−1.1	−0.8	−1.9	−1.4
counties							
metropolitan[4]	−1.8	−3.1	−1.9	−2.8	−1.3	−0.1	−6.1
nonmetropolitan[5]	+0.3	−7.5	+1.6	−3.0	−0.9	+0.6	−4.7
total	**−0.3**	**−3.6**	**−0.8**	**−1.4**	**−1.8**	**−2.6**	**−6.8**

[1]Law enforcement agencies.   [2]Includes murder, forcible rape, robbery, and aggravated assault.   [3]Includes burglary, larceny/theft, and car theft, but excludes data for arson.   [4]Includes crimes reported to sheriffs' departments, county police departments, and state police within Metropolitan Statistical Areas.   [5]Includes crimes reported to sheriffs' departments, county police departments, and state police outside Metropolitan Statistical Areas.

Did you know? In 1908, Attorney General Charles J. Bonaparte appointed a force of special agents to be the investigative force of the Department of Justice. The Federal Bureau of Investigation (FBI) evolved from this small group. In 2005 the FBI is one of 32 federal agencies responsible for law enforcement, employing 12,406 special agents.

State Crime Rates, 2000–2002

Crimes reported to the police per 100,000 population. Source: US Federal Bureau of Investigation.

STATE	2000 TOTAL	2001[1] TOTAL	2002 TOTAL	STATE	2000 TOTAL	2001[1] TOTAL	2002 TOTAL
AL	4,546	4,319	4,465	NE	4,096	4,330	4,257
AK	4,249	4,236	4,310	NV	4,269	4,266	4,498
AZ	5,830	6,077	6,386	NH	2,433	2,322	2,220
AR	4,115	4,134	4,158	NJ	3,161	3,225	3,024
CA	3,740	3,903	3,944	NM	5,519	5,324	5,078
CO	3,983	4,219	4,348	NY	3,100	2,925	2,804
CT	3,233	3,118	2,997	NC	4,919	4,938	4,721
DE[2]	4,478	4,053	3,939	ND	2,288	2,418	2,406
DC[3]	7,277	7,710	8,022	OH	4,042	4,178	4,107
FL	5,695	5,570	5,421	OK	4,559	4,607	4,743
GA	4,751	4,646	4,507	OR	4,845	5,044	4,868
HI	5,199	5,386	6,044	PA	2,995	2,961	2,841
ID	3,186	3,133	3,173	RI	3,476	3,685	3,589
IL[4]	4,286	4,098	4,016	SC	5,221	4,753	5,297
IN	3,752	3,831	3,750	SD	2,320	2,332	2,279
IA	3,234	3,301	3,448	TN	4,890	5,153	5,019
KS[5]	4,409	4,321	4,087	TX	4,956	5,153	5,190
KY[4]	2,960	2,938	2,903	UT	4,476	4,243	4,452
LA	5,423	5,338	5,098	VT	2,987	2,769	2,530
ME	2,620	2,688	2,656	VA	3,028	3,178	3,140
MD	4,816	4,867	4,747	WA	5,106	5,152	5,107
MA	3,026	3,099	3,094	WV	2,603	2,560	2,515
MI	4,110	4,082	3,874	WI	3,209	3,321	3,253
MN	3,488	3,584	3,535	WY	3,298	3,518	3,581
MS	4,004	4,185	4,159				
MO	4,528	4,776	4,602	**US crime rate**	**4,125**	**4,161**	**4,119**
MT[5]	3,533	3,689	3,513				

State Crime Rates, 2000–2002 (continued)

2002 CRIME RATES IN DETAIL

	VIOLENT CRIMES					PROPERTY CRIMES			
STATE	MURDER[6]	FORCIBLE RAPE	AGGRAVATED ASSAULT	ROBBERY	TOTAL[7]	BURGLARY	LARCENY/ THEFT	MOTOR VEHICLE THEFT	TOTAL[7]
AL	6.8	37.1	268	133	444	949	2,762	310	4021
AK	5.1	79.4	403	76	564	607	2,755	384	3,746
AZ	7.1	29.5	370	147	553	1,083	3,694	1,057	5,833
AR	5.2	27.8	298	93.1	424	857	2,625	251	3,733
CA	6.8	29.0	373	185	593	679	2,038	633	3,350
CO	4.0	45.8	223	79.4	352	703	2,778	514	3,995
CT	2.3	21.1	170	117	311	494	1,858	334	2,686
DE	3.2	44.3	409	143	599	663	2,298	379	3,340
DC[3]	46.2	45.9	869	672	1,633	906	3,802	1,681	6,389
FL	5.5	40.4	529	195	770	1,061	3,060	530	4,650
GA	7.1	24.6	270	157	459	864	2,740	444	4,048
HI	1.9	29.9	133	97.2	262	1,022	3,964	796	5,782
ID	2.7	37.1	197	17.9	255	555	2,167	196	2,918
IL[4]	7.5	34.1	379	201	621	644	2,396	356	3,396
IN	5.9	29.9	214	107	357	692	2,372	329	3,393
IA	1.5	27.1	217	39.8	286	635	2,330	198	3,163
KS	2.9	38.1	256	80	377	725	2,720	266	3,710
KY[4]	4.5	26.6	173	74.8	279	681	1,729	214	2,624
LA	13.2	34.1	456	159	662	1,012	2,974	450	4,436
ME	1.1	29.1	56.8	20.9	108	538	1,900	110	2,548
MD	9.4	25.1	490	246	770	729	2,626	623	3,978
MA	2.7	27.6	343	112	484	517	1,679	414	2,610
MI	6.7	53.4	362	118	540	706	2,133	495	3,334
MN	2.2	45.3	142	78.4	268	559	2,433	276	3,268
MS	9.2	39.2	178	117	343	1,031	2,454	332	3,816
MO	5.8	25.8	383	124	539	753	2,819	492	4,064
MT	1.8	26.1	293	31.1	352	362	2,604	196	3,161
NE	2.8	26.8	206	78.6	314	597	2,975	371	3,943
NV	8.3	42.7	351	236	638	872	2,184	805	3,860
NH	0.9	35.0	93	32.4	161	379	1,527	153	2,059
NJ	3.9	15.7	193	162	375	511	1,723	416	2,650
NM	8.2	55.4	557	119	740	1,058	2,879	401	4,338
NY	4.7	20.3	280	191	496	400	1,660	247	2,308
NC	6.6	26.4	291	147	470	1,196	2,756	299	4,251
ND	0.8	25.7	42.6	9.1	78.2	354	1,814	161	2,328
OH	4.6	42.1	148	157	351	868	2,513	375	3,756
OK	4.7	45.0	369	84.9	503	1,007	2,868	366	4,240
OR	2.0	35.2	177	77.9	292	730	3,377	469	4,576
PA	5.1	30.2	228	139	402	451	1,722	266	2,439
RI	3.8	36.9	159	85.6	285	600	2,248	456	3,304
SC	7.3	47.7	627	141	822	1,065	3,000	411	4,475
SD	1.4	47.4	113	15.4	177	399	1,595	108	2,101
TN	7.2	39.5	508	162	717	1,057	2,788	458	4,302
TX	6.0	39.1	361	173	579	976	3,163	471	4,611
UT	2.0	40.7	145	49.2	237	653	3,229	333	4,216
VT	2.1	20.4	71.7	12.5	107	566	1,733	125	2,423
VA	5.3	25.2	166	95.4	291	435	2,160	253	2,849
WA	3.0	45.0	202	95.5	345	905	3,189	667	4,761
WV	3.2	18.2	176	36.5	234	537	1,528	216	2,281
WI	2.8	22.7	113	86.6	225	513	2,267	247	3,028
WY	3.0	29.7	222	18.6	274	491	2,668	149	3,307
Total US	**5.6**	**33.0**	**310**	**146**	**495**	**746**	**2,446**	**432**	**3,624**

[1]This table does not include the murder and nonnegligent homicides that occurred because of the terrorist attacks of 11 Sep 2001. [2]Forcible rape count estimated for 2000. [3]Includes offenses at the National Zoo. [4]Crime counts estimated for 2000 and 2001; limited data for 2002 were available. [5]Crime counts estimated for 2000. [6]Includes nonnegligent manslaughter. [7]Totals may not add due to rounding.

Crime in the US, 1981–2003

This table presents the number of crimes reported in the seven categories that make up the FBI's Crime Index. The FBI's Crime Index trends reflect the per- cent change in the offenses reported to law enforcement for the calendar years indicated. Source: Federal Bureau of Investigation.

YEAR	CRIME INDEX TOTAL	VIOLENT CRIME				PROPERTY CRIME		
		MURDER[1]	FORCIBLE RAPE	ROBBERY	AGGRA- VATED ASSAULT	BURGLARY	LARCENY/ THEFT	MOTOR VEHICLE THEFT
1981	13,423,800	22,520	82,500	592,910	663,900	3,779,700	7,194,400	1,087,800
1982	12,974,400	21,010	78,770	553,130	669,480	3,447,100	7,142,500	1,062,400
1983	12,108,630	19,308	78,918	506,567	653,294	3,129,851	6,712,759	1,007,933
1984	11,881,755	18,692	84,233	485,008	685,349	2,984,434	6,591,874	1,032,165
1985	12,430,357	18,976	87,671	497,874	723,246	3,073,348	6,926,380	1,102,862
1986	13,211,869	20,613	91,459	542,775	834,322	3,241,410	7,257,153	1,224,137
1987	13,508,708	20,096	91,111	517,704	855,088	3,236,184	7,499,851	1,288,674
1988	13,923,086	20,675	92,486	542,968	910,092	3,218,077	7,705,872	1,432,916
1989	14,251,449	21,500	94,504	578,326	951,707	3,168,170	7,872,442	1,564,800
1990	14,475,613	23,438	102,555	639,271	1,054,863	3,073,909	7,945,670	1,635,907
1991	14,872,883	24,703	106,593	687,732	1,092,739	3,157,150	8,142,228	1,661,738
1992	14,438,191	23,760	109,062	672,478	1,126,974	2,979,884	7,915,199	1,610,834
1993	14,144,794	24,526	106,014	659,870	1,135,607	2,834,808	7,820,909	1,563,060
1994	13,989,543	23,326	102,216	618,949	1,113,179	2,712,774	7,879,812	1,539,287
1995	13,862,727	21,606	97,470	580,509	1,099,207	2,593,784	7,997,710	1,472,441
1996	13,493,863	19,645	96,252	535,594	1,037,049	2,506,400	7,904,685	1,394,238
1997	13,194,571	18,208	96,153	498,534	1,023,201	2,460,526	7,743,760	1,354,189
1998	12,485,714	16,974	93,144	447,186	976,583	2,332,735	7,376,311	1,242,781
1999	11,634,378	15,522	89,411	409,371	911,740	2,100,739	6,955,520	1,152,075
2000	11,608,070	15,586	90,178	408,016	911,706	2,050,992	6,971,590	1,160,002
2001	11,876,669	16,037	90,863	423,557	909,023	2,116,531	7,092,267	1,228,391
2002	11,877,218	16,204	95,136	420,637	894,348	2,151,875	7,052,922	1,246,096
2003	11,816,782	16,503	93,433	413,402	857,921	2,153,464	7,021,588	1,260,471

Crime Index trends: percent change in number of offenses[2]

YEARS COMPARED	CRIME INDEX TOTAL	VIOLENT CRIME				PROPERTY CRIME		
		MURDER	FORCIBLE RAPE	ROBBERY	AGGRA- VATED ASSAULT	BURGLARY	LARCENY/ THEFT	MOTOR VEHICLE THEFT
2003/2002	-3.0	+1.7	-1.9	-1.8	-3.8	+0.1	-0.5	+1.1
2003/1999	-3.1	+6.3	+4.5	+1.0	-5.9	+2.5	+0.9	+9.4
2003/1994	-25.6	-29.3	-8.6	-33.2	-22.9	-20.6	-10.9	-18.1

[1]Includes the crime of nonnegligent manslaughter.   [2]A minus sign indicates a decrease in crime; a plus sign indicates an increase.   [3]Less than one-tenth of 1 percent.

US Cities with Highest and Lowest Crime Rates

This table ranks cities by the number of violent and property crimes—the crime index total—reported during 2003. All cities listed have a population of 100,000 or more. The information in the table is derived from preliminary data provided by the Federal Bureau of Investigation.

CITIES	CRIME INDEX TOTAL[1]	MURDER	FORCIBLE RAPE	ROBBERY	AGGRAVATED ASSAULT	BURGLARY	LARCENY/ THEFT	CAR THEFT
Highest Crime Rates								
New York NY	236,215	597	1,609	25,989	31,253	28,293	124,846	23,628
Los Angeles CA	184,605	515	1,226	16,577	30,506	25,115	77,111	33,555
Chicago IL[2]	182,306	598	N/A	17,302	19,784	25,064	96,779	22,779
Houston TX	143,993	278	768	10,985	11,957	26,522	72,032	21,451
Dallas TX	114,765	226	601	7,963	8,075	21,927	58,554	17,419
Phoenix AZ	107,545	241	526	3,676	5,279	17,104	55,068	25,651
San Antonio TX	90,252	85	537	2,060	4,570	14,619	62,179	6,202
Philadelphia PA	83,074	348	1,004	9,617	9,651	10,656	37,864	13,934
Detroit MI	83,533	366	814	5,817	11,727	14,100	25,353	25,356
Memphis TN	65,853	126	449	4,299	5,438	16,908	30,099	8,534

US Cities with Highest and Lowest Crime Rates (continued)

CITIES	CRIME INDEX TOTAL[1]	MURDER	FORCIBLE RAPE	ROBBERY	AGGRAVATED ASSAULT	BURGLARY	LARCENY/ THEFT	CAR THEFT
Lowest Crime Rates								
Thousand Oaks CA	1,986	1	12	38	150	332	1,311	142
Simi Valley CA	2,046	2	16	45	101	466	1,211	205
Amherst Town NY	2,097	1	5	40	74	176	1,735	66
Cary NC	2,353	0	17	36	56	397	1,717	130
Stamford CT	2,438	2	11	135	123	319	1,595	253
Centennial CO	2,502	1	28	22	133	415	1,693	210
Daly City CA	2,516	0	24	154	166	242	1,490	440
Naperville IL[2]	2,555	0	N/A	23	61	291	2,096	84
Livonia MI	2,691	0	13	56	116	389	1,846	271
Edison Township NJ	2,918	1	11	115	158	465	1,755	413

N/A stands for not available.   [1]Includes murder, forcible rape, robbery, aggravated assault, burglary, larceny/theft, and car theft.   [2]Total excludes the crime of forcible rape.

US Crime Rates by Type of Victim

This table shows rates of violent crime, personal theft, and property crime for the year 2003. The crime rates are based on the reports of victims; thus, the table does not include rates for murder and manslaughter. For violent crime and personal theft, each crime rate represents victimizations per 1,000 people of age 12 or older. Property crime rates are related in victimizations per 1,000 households.

Source: US Bureau of Justice Statistics.

PROFILE OF VICTIM	VIOLENT CRIME RATES					PERSONAL THEFT RATES
	ALL VIOLENT CRIME	RAPE/ SEXUAL ASSAULT	ROBBERY	ASSAULT		
				AGGRAVATED	SIMPLE	
sex						
male	26.3	0.2[1]	3.2	5.9	17.1	0.4
female	19.0	1.5	1.9	3.3	12.4	1.1
age						
12–15	51.6	1.2[1]	5.2	8.9	36.4	1.5[1]
16–19	53.0	1.3[1]	5.1	11.9	34.7	1.4[1]
20–24	43.3	1.7	6.4	9.8	25.5	1.6
25–34	26.4	1.6	2.5	6.0	16.3	1.0[1]
35–49	18.5	0.6	1.7	3.8	12.3	0.5
50–64	10.3	0.4[1]	1.4	1.6	7.0	0.3[1]
65 or older	2.0	0.1[1]	0.7[1]	0.1[1]	1.1	0.5[1]
race/ethnicity						
white	21.5	0.8	1.9	4.2	14.7	0.6
black	29.1	0.8[1]	5.9	6.0	16.3	0.7
other race[2]	16.0	0.2[1]	3.4[1]	5.4[1]	7.0	0.9[1]
Hispanic[3]	24.2	0.4[1]	3.1	4.6	16.1	1.11
Non-Hispanic[3]	22.3	0.9	2.4	4.6	14.4	0.7
household income						
less than $7,500	49.9	1.6[1]	9.0	10.8	28.5	1.2[1]
$7,500–$14,999	30.8	1.8[1]	4.0	7.9	17.0	1.1[1]
$15,000–$24,999	26.3	0.8[1]	4.0	4.5	17.0	0.7[1]
$25,000–$34,999	24.9	0.9[1]	2.2	5.0	16.9	0.8[1]
$35,000–$49,999	21.4	0.9[1]	2.1	4.8	13.5	0.7[1]
$50,000–$74,999	22.9	0.5[1]	2.0	5.2	15.2	0.5[1]
$75,000 or more	17.5	0.5[1]	1.7	2.7	12.6	1.0

PROFILE OF VICTIM	PROPERTY CRIME RATES			
	ALL PROPERTY CRIME	BURGLARY	CAR THEFT	THEFT
region				
Northeast	122.1	20.5	7.2	94.4
Midwest	160.2	32.5	6.9	120.9
South	160.5	32.2	7.8	120.4
West	207.4	30.6	15.2	161.6

US Crime Rates by Type of Victim (continued)

PROFILE OF VICTIM	PROPERTY CRIME RATES (CONTINUED)			
	ALL PROPERTY CRIME	BURGLARY	CAR THEFT	THEFT
household income				
less than $7,500	204.6	58.0	6.3	140.3
$7,500–$14,999	167.7	42.2	7.3	118.3
$15,000–$24,999	179.2	38.4	8.9	131.9
$25,000–$34,999	180.7	35.3	12.3	133.1
$35,000–$49,999	177.1	27.6	9.5	140.0
$50,000–$74,999	168.1	24.9	8.4	134.7
$75,000 or more	176.4	20.8	11.9	143.7

[1]Based on 10 or fewer sample cases.   [2]Asians, Native Hawaiians, other Pacific Islanders, Alaska Natives, and American Indians.   [3]Hispanics may be of any race.

Total Arrests in the US

Estimates for the year 2003. Numbers may not add up to totals because of rounding. Source: Federal Bureau of Investigation, Crime in the United States, 2003.

TYPE OF CRIME	NUMBER OF ARRESTS	TYPE OF CRIME	NUMBER OF ARRESTS
violent crime		other crime types (continued)	
aggravated assault	449,933	liquor laws	612,079
robbery	107,553	fraud	229,138
forcible rape	26,350	vandalism	273,431
murder and nonnegligent manslaughter	13,190	weapons (carrying, possessing, etc.)	167,972
violent crime total	597,026	offenses against the family and children	136,034
		curfew and loitering law violations	136,461
property crime		runaways	123,581
larceny/theft	1,145,074	stolen property (buying, receiving, possessing)	126,775
burglary	290,956	forgery and counterfeiting	111,823
motor vehicle theft	152,934	sex offenses (except forcible rape and prostitution)	91,546
arson	16,163	prostitution and commercialized vice	75,190
property crime total	1,605,127	vagrancy	28,948
		embezzlement	16,826
other crime types		gambling	10,954
drug abuse violations	1,678,192	suspicion (not included in total)	7,163
driving under the influence	1,448,148	all other offenses	3,665,543
other assaults	1,246,698	total arrests	13,639,479
disorderly conduct	636,371		
drunkenness	548,616		

US State and Federal Prison Population

Source: US Bureau of Justice Statistics.

STATE	NUMBER OF PRISONERS				% CHANGE (31 DEC 2002 TO 31 DEC 2003)
	31 DEC 1980	31 DEC 1990	31 DEC 2002	31 DEC 2003	
Alabama	6,543	15,665	27,947	29,253	+4.7
Alaska[1]	822	2,622	4,398	4,527	+2.9
Arizona[2]	4,372	14,261	29,359	31,170	+6.2
Arkansas	2,911	7,322	13,091	13,084	-0.1
California	24,569	97,309	161,361	164,487	+1.9
Colorado	2,629	7,671	18,833	19,671	+4.4
Connecticut[1]	4,308	10,500	20,720	19,846	+7.9
Delaware[1]	1,474	3,471	6,778	6,794	+0.2
Florida[2]	20,735	44,387	75,210	79,594	+5.8
Georgia[2]	12,178	22,411	47,445	47,208	-0.5
Hawaii[1]	985	2,533	5,423	5,828	+7.5
Idaho	817	1,961	5,746	5,887	+2.5
Illinois	11,899	27,516	42,693	43,418	+1.7
Indiana	6,683	12,736	21,611	23,069	+6.7
Iowa[2]	2,481	3,967	8,398	8,546	+1.8
Kansas	2,494	5,775	8,935	9,132	+2.2
Kentucky	3,588	9,023	15,820	16,622	+5.1
Louisiana	8,889	18,599	36,032	36,047	0.0

US State and Federal Prison Population (continued)

STATE	NUMBER OF PRISONERS				% CHANGE (31 DEC 2002 TO 31 DEC 2003)
	31 DEC 1980	31 DEC 1990	31 DEC 2002	31 DEC 2003	
Maine	814	1,523	1,900	2,013	+5.9
Maryland	7,731	17,848	24,162	23,791	-1.5
Massachusetts	3,185	8,345	10,329	10,232	-0.9
Michigan	15,124	34,267	50,591	49,358	-2.4
Minnesota	2,001	3,176	7,129	7,865	+10.3
Mississippi	3,902	8,375	22,705	23,182	+2.1
Missouri	5,726	14,943	30,099	30,303	+0.7
Montana	739	1,425	3,323	3,620	+8.9
Nebraska	1,446	2,403	4,058	4,040	-0.4
Nevada	1,839	5,322	10,478	10,543	+0.6
New Hampshire	326	1,342	2,451	2,434	-0.7
New Jersey	5,884	21,128	27,891	27,246	-2.3
New Mexico	1,279	3,187	5,991	6,223	+3.9
New York	21,815	54,895	67,065	65,198	-2.8
North Carolina	15,513	18,411	32,832	33,560	+2.2
North Dakota	253	483	1,112	1,239	+11.4
Ohio	13,489	31,822	45,646	44,778	-1.9
Oklahoma	4,796	12,285	22,802	22,821	+0.1
Oregon	3,177	6,492	12,085	12,715	+5.2
Pennsylvania	8,171	22,290	40,168	40,890	+1.8
Rhode Island[1]	813	2,392	3,520	3,527	+0.2
South Carolina	7,862	17,319	23,715	23,719	0.0
South Dakota	635	1,341	2,918	3,026	+3.7
Tennessee	7,022	10,388	24,989	25,403	+1.7
Texas	29,892	50,042	162,003	166,911	+3.0
Utah	932	2,496	5,562	5,763	+3.6
Vermont[1]	480	1,049	1,863	1,944	+4.3
Virginia	8,920	17,593	34,973	35,067	+0.3
Washington	4,399	7,995	16,062	16,148	+0.5
West Virginia	1,257	1,565	4,544	4,758	+4.7
Wisconsin	3,980	7,465	22,113	22,614	+2.3
Wyoming	534	1,110	1,737	1,872	+7.8
state	305,458	708,393	1,276,616	1,296,986	+1.6
federal[3]	24,363	65,526	163,528	173,059	+5.8
US total	**329,821**	**773,919**	**1,440,655**	**1,470,045**	**+2.1**

[1]*Jails and prisons are part of an integrated system. Data include total jail and prison population.* [2]*Population figures are based on custody counts.* [3]*As of 31 Dec 2001, the transfer of responsibility for sentenced felons from the District of Columbia to the Federal Bureau of Prisons was completed, so the District of Columbia no longer operates a prison system and has been excluded from National Prisoner Statistics.*

Death Penalty Sentences in the US

This table excludes military and federal sentences and executions. Sources: US Bureau of Justice Statistics; Death Penalty Information Center; NAACP Legal Defense and Educational Fund, Inc.

STATE	EXECUTIONS		PRISONERS UNDER DEATH SENTENCE (AS OF 1 JAN 2005)[2]	SOME DEATH-PENALTY CRIMES
	1976–PRESENT[1]	2004		
Alabama	32	2	196	intentional murder[3]
Alaska	—	—	—	no death penalty
Arizona	22	0	131	1st-degree murder[3]
Arkansas	26	1	38	capital murder[3]; treason
California	11	0	639	1st-degree murder[3]; treason; train wrecking
Colorado	1	0	3	1st-degree murder[3]; treason
Connecticut	1	0	8	capital felony (8 types of aggravated murder)
Delaware	13	0	19	1st-degree murder[3]
District of Columbia	—	—	—	no death penalty
Florida	60	2	382	1st-degree murder; felonious murder; capital drug trafficking; capital sexual battery
Georgia	38	2	113	murder; treason; aircraft hijacking; kidnapping[4]
Hawaii	—	—	—	no death penalty
Idaho	1	0	20	1st-degree murder[3]; aggravated kidnapping
Illinois	12	0	9	1st-degree murder[3]
Indiana	14	0	35	murder[3]

Death Penalty Sentences in the US (continued)

STATE	EXECUTIONS 1976–PRESENT[1]	2004	PRISONERS UNDER DEATH SENTENCE (AS OF 1 JAN 2005)[2]	SOME DEATH-PENALTY CRIMES
Iowa	—	—	—	no death penalty
Kansas	0	0	7	capital murder[3]
Kentucky	2	0	36	murder[3]; aggravated kidnapping
Louisiana	27	0	94	1st-degree murder; treason; rape[5]
Maine	—	—	—	no death penalty
Maryland	4	1	9	1st-degree murder[6]
Massachusetts	—	—	—	no death penalty
Michigan	—	—	—	no death penalty
Minnesota	—	—	—	no death penalty
Mississippi	6	0	70	capital murder; aircraft hijacking
Missouri	64	0	57	1st-degree murder
Montana	2	0	4	capital murder[3]; capital sexual assault
Nebraska	3	0	8	1st-degree murder[3]
Nevada	11	2	86	1st-degree murder[3]
New Hampshire	0	0	0	capital murder (6 types)
New Jersey	0	0	15	murder by one's own conduct; contract murder; solicitation[7]
New Mexico	1	0	2	1st-degree murder[3]
New York	0	0	2	1st-degree murder[3]
North Carolina	36	4	197	1st-degree murder
North Dakota	—	—	—	no death penalty
Ohio	16	7	202	murder[3]
Oklahoma	77	6	98	1st-degree murder[3]
Oregon	2	0	32	murder[3]
Pennsylvania	3	0	231	1st-degree murder[3]
Rhode Island	—	—	—	no death penalty
South Carolina	33	4	74	murder[3]
South Dakota	0	0	4	1st-degree murder[3]; aggravated kidnapping
Tennessee	1	0	106	1st-degree murder[3]
Texas	345	23	447	criminal homicide[3]
Utah	6	0	10	murder[3]
Vermont	—	—	—	no death penalty
Virginia	94	5	23	1st-degree murder[3]
Washington	4	0	11	1st-degree murder[3]
West Virginia	—	—	—	no death penalty
Wisconsin	—	—	—	no death penalty
Wyoming	1	0	2	1st-degree murder
totals	970	59	3,420	

[1]In 1976 the US Supreme Court ruled that capital punishment was not unconstitutional. [2]In mid-2002 the Supreme Court ruled that juries, not judges, must make decisions determining death penalty cases and that it was unconstitutional to execute mentally retarded offenders. These two decisions could reduce the number of people sentenced to death. [3]With aggravating factors or circumstances. [4]With bodily injury or ransom when the victim dies. [5]Aggravated rape of a victim under 12. [6]Premeditated or committed during the act of a felony and meeting certain death penalty requirements. [7]By command or threat in the act of a narcotics conspiracy.

Directors of the Federal Bureau of Investigation (FBI)

The FBI evolved from an unnamed force appointed by Attorney General Charles J. Bonaparte on 26 Jul 1908. It is the unit of the Department of Justice responsible for investigating foreign intelligence and terrorist activities and violations of federal criminal law. The president appoints the director of the FBI with confirmation from the Senate. Since Hoover's tenure, a director's term may not exceed 10 years.

NAME	DATES OF SERVICE
Stanley Finch	26 Jul 1908–30 Apr 1912
Alexander Bruce Bielaski	30 Apr 1912–10 Feb 1919
William E. Allen (acting)	10 Feb 1919–30 Jun 1919
William J. Flynn	1 Jul 1919–21 Aug 1921
William J. Burns	22 Aug 1921–14 Jun 1924
J. Edgar Hoover	10 May 1924–2 May 1972
L. Patrick Gray (acting)	3 May 1972–27 Apr 1973
William D. Ruckelshaus (acting)	30 Apr 1973–9 Jul 1973
Clarence M. Kelley	9 Jul 1973–15 Feb 1978
William H. Webster	23 Feb 1978–25 May 1987
John Otto (acting)	26 May 1987–2 Nov 1987
William S. Sessions	2 Nov 1987–19 Jul 1993
Floyd I. Clarke (acting)	19 Jul 1993–1 Sep 1993
Louis J. Freeh	1 Sep 1993–25 Jun 2001
Thomas J. Pickard (acting)	25 Jun 2001–4 Sep 2001
Robert S. Mueller, III	4 Sep 2001–

Society

Family

Average Family Size, 1950–2003

Source: US Census Bureau.

YEAR	NUMBER OF FAMILIES ('000)	PEOPLE PER FAMILY (AVERAGE)	YEAR	NUMBER OF FAMILIES ('000)	PEOPLE PER FAMILY (AVERAGE)	YEAR	NUMBER OF FAMILIES ('000)	PEOPLE PER FAMILY (AVERAGE)
1950	39,303	3.54	1970	51,586	3.58	1990	66,090	3.17
1955	41,951	3.59	1975	55,712	3.42	1995	69,305	3.19
1960	45,111	3.67	1980	59,550	3.29	2000	72,025	3.17
1965	47,956	3.70	1985	62,706	3.23	2003	75,596	3.13

US Population by Age

Numbers are in thousands ('000). Source: US Census Bureau estimate of 1 Jul 2004.

AGE	POPULATION NUMBER	(%)	AGE	POPULATION NUMBER	(%)
under 5 years	20,071	6.8	60 to 64 years	12,589	4.3
5 to 9 years	19,606	6.7	65 to 74 years	18,463	6.3
10 to 14 years	21,145	7.2	75 to 84 years	12,971	4.4
15 to 19 years	20,730	7.1	85 years and over	4,860	1.7
20 to 24 years	20,971	7.1	total population	293,655	100.0
25 to 34 years	40,032	13.6			
35 to 44 years	44,109	15.0	under 18 years	73,278	25.0
45 to 54 years	41,619	14.2	18 years and over	220,377	75.0
55 to 59 years	16,490	5.6	65 years and over	36,294	12.4

Living Arrangements of Children Under 18 in the US

Children under 18 years of age, 2004. Numbers in thousands ('000). Source: US Census Bureau.

LIVING IN HOUSEHOLD WITH:	YEARS OF AGE UNDER 6	6–11	12–17	UNDER 18
both parents	16,110	16,136	16,436	48,682
mother only	4,036	4,802	5,339	14,176
father only	939	914	1,097	2,950
neither parent	3	18	38	60
totals	23,793	24,106	25,307	73,205

Children Living Below the Poverty Level

This table covers children under the age of 18 (as of March of the following year). Hispanics may be of any race. All numbers are in thousands ('000). Statistics that are not available are noted N/A. Source: US Census Bureau. For the definition of the poverty level, see <www.census.gov/hhes/poverty/povdef.html>.

	% OF CHILDREN BELOW THE POVERTY LEVEL					NUMBER OF CHILDREN BELOW THE POVERTY LEVEL				
YEAR	ALL[1]	WHITE[2]	BLACK	ASIAN/ PACIFIC ISLANDER	HISPANIC	ALL[1]	WHITE[2]	BLACK	ASIAN/ PACIFIC ISLANDER	HISPANIC
1980	18.3	11.8	42.3	N/A	33.2	11,543	5,510	3,961	N/A	1,749
1981	20.0	12.9	45.2	N/A	35.9	12,505	5,946	4,237	N/A	1,925
1982	21.9	14.4	47.6	N/A	39.5	13,647	6,566	4,472	N/A	2,181
1983	22.3	14.8	46.7	N/A	38.1	13,911	6,649	4,398	N/A	2,312
1984	21.5	13.7	46.6	N/A	39.2	13,420	6,156	4,413	N/A	2,376
1985	20.7	13.0	43.6	N/A	40.3	13,010	5,745	4,157	N/A	2,606
1986	20.5	13.0	43.1	N/A	37.7	12,876	5,789	4,148	N/A	2,507
1987	20.3	11.8	45.1	23.5	39.3	12,843	5,230	4,385	455	2,670
1988	19.5	11.0	43.5	24.1	37.6	12,455	4,888	4,296	474	2,631
1989	19.6	11.5	43.7	19.8	36.2	12,590	5,110	4,375	392	2,603
1990	20.6	12.3	44.8	17.6	38.4	13,431	5,532	4,550	374	2,865
1991	21.8	13.1	45.9	17.5	40.4	14,341	5,918	4,755	360	3,094
1992	22.3	13.2	46.6	16.4	40.0	15,294	6,017	5,106	363	3,637
1993	22.7	13.6	46.1	18.2	40.9	15,727	6,255	5,125	375	3,873
1994	21.8	12.5	43.8	18.3	41.5	15,289	5,823	4,906	318	4,075

Children Living Below the Poverty Level (continued)

	% OF CHILDREN BELOW THE POVERTY LEVEL					NUMBER OF CHILDREN BELOW THE POVERTY LEVEL				
YEAR	ALL[1]	WHITE[2]	BLACK	ASIAN/ PACIFIC ISLANDER	HISPANIC	ALL[1]	WHITE[2]	BLACK	ASIAN/ PACIFIC ISLANDER	HISPANIC
1995	20.8	11.2	41.9	19.5	40.0	14,665	5,115	4,761	564	4,080
1996	20.5	11.1	39.9	19.5	40.3	14,463	5,072	4,519	571	4,237
1997	19.9	11.4	37.2	20.3	36.8	14,113	5,204	4,225	628	3,972
1998	18.9	10.6	36.7	18.0	34.4	13,467	4,822	4,151	564	3,837
1999	16.9	9.4	33.2	11.9	30.3	12,280	4,155	3,813	381	3,693
2000	16.2	9.1	31.2	12.7	28.4	11,587	4,018	3,581	420	3,522
2001	16.3	9.5	30.2	11.5	28.0	11,733	4,194	3,492	369	3,570
2002	16.7	9.4	32.3	11.7[3]	28.6	12,133	4,090	3,645	315[3]	3,782
2003	17.6	9.8	34.1	12.5[3]	29.7	12,866	4,233	3,877	344[3]	4,077

[1]Includes other and unclassified. [2]Excludes Hispanic population. [3]Excludes Pacific Islanders.

Child Care Arrangements in the US

This table is based on sample surveys of households with children 3–5 years old who were not yet in kindergarten. Day care centers, Head Start programs, preschools, prekindergarten, and nursery schools were included as center-based programs. The columns do not add to 100% because some children participated in more than one type of nonparental arrangement. Detail may not add to totals due to rounding. Although complete statistics from the 2001 survey were not available before press time, 56.4% of children ages 3–5 were enrolled in center-based programs in 2001, down 3.3% from 1999. Source: US National Center for Education Statistics.

YEAR OF SURVEY	CHILDREN NUMBER	(%)	UNDER PARENTAL CARE (%)	UNDER A RELATIVE'S CARE (%)	UNDER A NONRELATIVE'S CARE (%)	IN A CENTER-BASED PROGRAM (%)
1991	8,428,000	100.0	31.0	16.9	14.8	52.8
1995	9,232,000	100.0	25.9	19.4	16.9	55.1
1999	8,525,000	100.0	23.1	22.8	16.1	59.7

details from the 1999 survey

FEATURE	CHILDREN NUMBER	(%)	UNDER PARENTAL CARE (%)	UNDER A RELATIVE'S CARE (%)	UNDER A NONRELATIVE'S CARE (%)	IN A CENTER-BASED PROGRAM (%)
age						
3 years old	3,814,000	44.7	30.8	24.4	16.2	45.7
4 years old	3,705,000	43.5	17.7	22.0	15.9	69.6
5 years old	1,006,000	11.8	13.5	20.2	16.1	76.5
race/ethnic group						
white, non-Hispanic	5,389,000	63.2	23.2	18.8	19.4	60.0
black, non-Hispanic	1,214,000	14.2	13.7	33.4	7.4	73.2
Hispanic	1,376,000	16.1	33.4	26.5	12.7	44.2
other	547,000	6.4	16.6	30.2	10.4	66.1
household income						
less than $10,001	1,064,000	12.5	27.5	27.5	13.2	55.9
$10,001–20,000	1,342,000	15.7	27.7	29.4	13.7	51.1
$20,001–30,000	1,333,000	15.6	29.8	27.1	12.5	51.4
$30,001–40,000	1,098,000	12.9	24.8	22.5	14.7	55.4
$40,001–50,000	848,000	9.9	23.1	21.3	13.6	60.2
$50,001–75,000	1,397,000	16.4	17.8	17.3	21.0	66.6
more than $75,000	1,443,000	16.9	13.1	15.9	21.3	74.6

Children in the US Living with Nonparents

Children under 18 years of age, March 2002. Numbers in thousands ('000). Source: US Census Bureau.

LIVING ARRANGEMENT	YEARS OF AGE			
	UNDER 6	6–11	12–17	UNDER 18
with grandparent	635	462	476	1,273
with other relative	192	224	386	802
in foster home	62	81	92	235
with other nonrelative	137	171	268	575
with opposite-sex unmarried adults (children under 15 only)	62	83	40	186

US Adoptions of Foreign-Born Children

Adoptions of foreign children by US citizens are tracked by the number of immigrant visas issued to orphans entering the US. Source: US Department of State.

TOP 10 COUNTRIES OF ORIGIN	ADOPTIONS FISCAL YEAR		TOP 10 COUNTRIES OF ORIGIN	ADOPTIONS FISCAL YEAR		TOTAL FOREIGN ADOPTIONS CALENDAR YEAR	
	2003	2004		2003	2004	1998	15,774
1. China	6,859	7,044	6. Ukraine	702	723	1999	16,363
2. Russia	5,209	5,865	7. India	472	406	2000	17,718
3. Guatemala	2,328	3,264	8. Haiti	250	356	2001	19,237
4. South Korea	1,790	1,716	9. Ethiopia	135	289	2002	20,099
5. Kazakhstan	825	826	10. Colombia	272	287	2003	21,616
						2004	22,884

US Nursing Home Population

The data in this table were gathered in 1999 through interviews conducted by the National Nursing Home Survey. Residents of more than one race were recorded in the "black and other" category. Numbers may not add to totals because of rounding. N/A indicates that reliable numbers were not available.

Source: US National Center for Health Statistics.

AGE AT INTERVIEW	TOTAL RESIDENTS	%	GENDER MALE	%	FEMALE	%
under 65	158,700	9.8	80,000	17.5	78,700	6.7
65–74	194,800	12.0	84,100	18.4	110,700	9.5
75–84	517,600	31.8	149,500	32.7	368,100	31.5
85 and older	757,100	46.5	144,200	31.5	612,900	52.4
total	1,628,300	100.0	457,900	100.0	1,170,400	100.0

	WHITE	%	RACE BLACK AND OTHER	%	BLACK	%	UNKNOWN
under 65	115,400	8.3	39,300	18.2	32,800	18.4	N/A
65–74	157,300	11.3	35,800	16.6	30,300	17.0	N/A
75–84	440,600	31.6	71,100	32.9	58,700	32.8	N/A
85 and older	681,700	48.9	69,700	32.3	56,900	31.8	N/A
total	1,394,400	100.0	215,900	100.0	178,700	100.0	17,400

	NORTHWEST	%	RESIDENT LOCATION MIDWEST	%	SOUTH	%	WEST	%
under 65	34,200	8.9	45,000	9.0	51,300	9.7	28,200	13.1
65–74	46,400	12.1	58,900	11.8	63,400	11.9	26,100	12.1
75–84	118,500	30.9	153,200	30.8	179,100	33.7	66,800	31.1
85 and older	184,300	48.1	241,100	48.4	237,700	44.7	94,000	43.7
total	383,400	100.0	498,200	100.0	531,500	100.0	215,200	100.0

Unmarried-Couple Households in the US

Data based on Current Population Survey except for census years of 1960 and 1970. Census 2000 data shown separately. Numbers in thousands ('000). Source: US Census Bureau.

YEAR	TOTAL US HOUSEHOLDS	UNMARRIED-COUPLE HOUSEHOLDS (OPPOSITE SEX)	% OF TOTAL HOUSEHOLDS	NO CHILDREN UNDER 15	WITH CHILDREN UNDER 15
1960 census	52,799	439	0.8	242	197
1970 census	63,401	523	0.8	327	196
1980	80,776	1,589	2.0	1,159	431
1985	86,789	1,983	2.3	1,380	603
1990	93,347	2,856	3.1	1,966	891
1995	98,990	3,668	3.7	2,349	1,319
1996	99,627	3,958	3.9	2,516	1,442
1997	101,018	4,130	4.0	2,660	1,470
1998	102,528	4,236	4.1	2,716	1,520
1999	103,874	4,486	4.3	2,981	1,505
2000	104,705	4,736	4.5	3,061	1,675

Unmarried-Couple Households in the US (continued)

UNMARRIED-COUPLE HOUSEHOLDS	2000 CENSUS
male householder/female partner	2,615
male householder/male partner	301
female householder/female partner	293
female householder/male partner	2,266
unmarried-couple households	**5,475**
total households	**105,480**

Marital Status of Population by Sex, 1950–2003

The data in this table are taken from surveys of individuals 18 or over conducted by the US Census Bureau and exclude members of the armed forces except those living off post or with their families on post. Data exclude Alaska and Hawaii prior to 1960. Source: US Census Bureau.

	TOTAL						
	1950	1960	1970	1980	1990	2000	2003
Total individuals surveyed in hundred thousands ('000,000)	111.7	125.5	132.5	159.5	181.8	201.8	212.4
Percentage of individuals never married	22.8	22.0	16.2	20.3	22.2	23.9	24.4
Percentage of individuals married	67.0	67.3	71.7	65.5	61.9	59.5	56.6
Percentage of individuals widowed	8.3	8.4	8.9	8.0	7.6	6.8	6.6
Percentage of individuals divorced	1.9	2.3	3.2	6.2	8.3	9.8	10.2
Percentage of males never married	26.2	25.3	18.9	23.8	25.8	27.0	27.9
Percentage of males married	68.0	69.1	75.3	68.4	64.3	61.5	58.9
Percentage of males widowed	4.2	3.7	3.3	2.6	2.7	2.7	2.6
Percentage of males divorced	1.7	1.9	2.5	5.2	7.2	8.8	8.8
Percentage of females never married	11.1	12.3	13.7	17.1	18.9	21.1	21.2
Percentage of females married	37.6	42.6	68.5	63.0	59.7	57.6	54.5
Percentage of females widowed	7.0	8.3	13.9	12.8	12.1	10.5	10.3
Percentage of females divorced	1.2	1.7	3.9	7.1	9.3	10.8	11.5

Did you know? Polygamy, or marriage to more than one spouse at a time, appears once to have been common in most of the world. Nowhere, however, has it been the exclusive form of marriage. Among most peoples who permit or prefer it, the large majority of men live in monogamy either because of a limited number of eligible women or because only the well-to-do can afford to support several wives and households. In the US polygyny (one husband with multiple wives) was historically associated with the Church of Latter-day Saints (Mormons) and the state of Utah. Congress passed a law in 1862 outlawing polygamy throughout the country, specifically mentioning the Territory of Utah.

United States Education

Educational Attainment by Gender and Race

For people 25 years old and older. Percentage rates for 1960, 1970, and 1980 are based on sample data from the decennial censuses. Rates for 1990, 2000, and 2002 are based on the Current Population Survey. Source: US Census Bureau.

Percentage who had graduated from high school[1]

	ALL RACES[2]		WHITE		BLACK		HISPANIC[3]		ASIAN/PACIFIC ISLANDER	
CENSUS	MALE	FEMALE	MALE	FEMALE	MALE	FEMALE	MALE	FEMALE	MALE	FEMALE
1960	39.5	42.5	41.6	44.7	18.2	21.8	N/A	N/A	N/A	N/A
1970	51.9	52.8	54.0	55.0	30.1	32.5	37.9	34.2	N/A	N/A
1980	67.3	65.8	69.6	68.1	50.8	51.5	67.3	65.8	N/A	N/A
1990	77.7	77.5	79.1	79.0	65.8	66.5	50.3	51.3	84.0	77.2
2000	84.2	84.0	84.8	85.0	78.7	78.3	56.6	57.5	88.2	83.4
2002	83.8	84.4	84.3	85.2	78.5	78.9	56.1	57.9	89.5	85.5

Educational Attainment by Gender and Race (continued)

Percentage who had graduated from college[4]

	ALL RACES[2]		WHITE		BLACK		HISPANIC[3]		ASIAN/PACIFIC ISLANDER	
CENSUS	MALE	FEMALE	MALE	FEMALE	MALE	FEMALE	MALE	FEMALE	MALE	FEMALE
1960	9.7	5.8	10.3	6.0	2.8	3.3	N/A	N/A	N/A	N/A
1970	13.5	8.1	14.4	8.4	4.2	4.6	7.8	4.3	N/A	N/A
1980	20.1	12.8	21.3	13.3	8.4	8.3	9.4	6.0	N/A	N/A
1990	24.4	18.4	25.3	19.0	11.9	10.8	9.8	8.7	44.9	35.4
2000	27.8	23.6	28.5	23.9	16.3	16.7	10.7	10.6	47.6	40.7
2002	28.5	25.1	29.1	25.4	16.4	17.5	11.0	11.2	50.9	43.8

N/A means not available. [1]Through 1990, finished four years or more of high school. [2]Includes races not shown separately in the table. [3]Hispanics may be of any race. [4]Through 1990, finished four years or more of college.

Libraries and Museums

Public Libraries in the US

Information from public libraries reporting for fiscal year 2002. The number of libraries includes central and branch libraries. 7,358 of the 9,137 libraries in the 50 states and DC were single-outlet libraries, and 1,779 were multiple-outlet libraries. A single-outlet library may be a bookmobile or a books-by-mail only outlet. Multiple-outlet libraries may refer to branches only, bookmobiles only, or branches and bookmobiles only.

Data for operating income and the number of books and serial volumes are given in thousands ('000). The circulation percentages for children's materials are given as a percentage of total circulation. The totals used at the bottom of the table were those provided by the source.

Source: National Center for Education Statistics.

STATE	NUMBER OF LIBRARIES	OPERATING INCOME ($)	TOTAL NUMBER OF BOOKS AND SERIAL VOLUMES	AVERAGE NUMBER OF INTERNET TERMINALS PER STATIONARY OUTLET	CIRCULATION OF CHILDREN'S MATERIALS (%)
Alabama	207	71,059	8,913	6.04	33.5
Alaska	85	24,139	2,272	4.5	34.7
Arizona	35	122,036	9,109	12.75	34.6
Arkansas	47	40,042	5,357	4.83	27.7
California	179	959,701	68,291	10.6	40.2
Colorado	115	181,392	11,469	9.57	33.2
Connecticut	194	151,858	14,336	6.78	36.4
Delaware	21	17,553	1,488	5.55	35.8
District of Columbia	1	28,413	2,650	8.37	32.2
Florida	72	422,470	30,775	13.9	29.6
Georgia	58	155,492	14,869	11.8	39.7
Hawaii	1	25,414	3,052	13.76	36.5
Idaho	106	27,048	3,636	5.3	40.4
Illinois	627	581,222	42,390	7.24	41.3
Indiana	239	258,505	23,667	10.26	33
Iowa	538	77,008	11,494	3.52	36.4
Kansas	323	83,344	10,691	5.37	40.2
Kentucky	116	87,316	8,154	11.01	30.4
Louisiana	65	122,029	11,092	6.75	27.7
Maine	274	29,586	6,016	3.76	38
Maryland	24	192,316	15,389	14.85	39.6
Massachusetts	370	238,952	30,795	7.33	39.1
Michigan	383	335,297	31,695	8.77	37.3
Minnesota	142	161,240	16,115	7.88	41.1
Mississippi	49	37,985	5,712	5.75	26.6
Missouri	148	159,964	18,204	9.85	38.8
Montana	79	18,831	2,652	4.4	33.2
Nebraska	275	39,232	6,152	3.9	44.7
Nevada	22	62,644	4,137	7.65	34.3
New Hampshire	230	37,743	5,725	2.96	41.7
New Jersey	309	335,803	31,203	8.74	37.4
New Mexico	89	29,070	4,098	6.48	33.4

Public Libraries in the US (continued)

STATE	NUMBER OF LIBRARIES	OPERATING INCOME ($)	TOTAL NUMBER OF BOOKS AND SERIAL VOLUMES	AVERAGE NUMBER OF INTERNET TERMINALS PER STATIONARY OUTLET	CIRCULATION OF CHILDREN'S MATERIALS (%)
New York	751	884,665	79,003	9.3	33.7
North Carolina	76	155,205	16,243	9.85	34.9
North Dakota	82	9,173	2,246	3.92	40.2
Ohio	250	645,383	48,075	11.45	31.7
Oklahoma	110	66,313	6,345	7.62	34.7
Oregon	124	120,079	8,811	7.7	32.2
Pennsylvania	451	292,397	28,548	10.25	37.3
Rhode Island	48	39,904	4,109	8.99	34.6
South Carolina	41	79,675	8,379	10.39	37.9
South Dakota	125	17,194	2,837	4.62	32.7
Tennessee	184	81,765	10,376	8.66	37.1
Texas	557	337,926	36,890	12.07	37.6
Utah	72	62,314	6,063	9.24	42
Vermont	189	13,702	2,739	3.22	43.5
Virginia	90	203,157	19,385	9.76	35.3
Washington	64	241,379	17,133	9.78	30.5
West Virginia	97	27,259	5,010	5.11	31.7
Wisconsin	380	176,262	18,864	7.24	37.9
Wyoming	23	17,279	2,420	4.46	33
total	9,137	8,585,738	785,075	8.56	36

Selected Specialized Libraries in the United States

NAME	LOCATION	TYPE OF COLLECTION	WEB SITE
American Antiquarian Society	Worcester MA	American history	<www.americanantiquarian.org>
American Philosophical Society	Philadelphia PA	history of science, medicine, and technology	<www.amphilsoc.org>
The Athenaeum of Philadelphia	Philadelphia PA	architecture, interior design	<www.philaathenaeum.org>
Boston Athenaeum	Boston MA	history, art, literature	<www.bostonathenaeum.org>
Dumbarton Oaks Research Library	Washington DC	Byzantine and pre-Columbian art, gardening	<www.doaks.org>
Folger Shakespeare Library	Washington DC	Shakespeare	<www.folger.edu>
Frick Art Reference Library	New York NY	Western art	<www.frick.org>
Hagley Museum and Library	Wilmington DE	American business and technology history	<www.hagley.lib.de.us>
The Huntington Library, Art Collections, and Botanical Gardens	San Marino CA	history, literature, science	<www.huntington.org>
John Carter Brown Library	Providence RI	history, humanities	<www.brown.edu/Facilities/John_Carter_Brown_Library>
The Library Company of Philadelphia	Philadelphia PA	American history and culture through the end of 19th century	<www.librarycompany.org>
Library of Congress	Washington DC	diverse knowledge	<www.loc.gov>
Linda Hall Library	Kansas City MO	science, engineering, technology	<www.lindahall.org>
The Morgan Library	New York NY	rare manuscripts, books, and prints	<www.morganlibrary.org>
National Agricultural Library	Beltsville MD	agriculture	<www.nal.usda.gov>
National Archives	College Park MD	American history	<www.archives.gov>
National Library of Education	Washington DC	education	<www.ed.gov/about/offices/list/ies/ncee/nle.html>
National Library of Medicine	Bethesda MD	medical science	<www.nlm.nih.gov>
New York Academy of Medicine	New York NY	medical science	<www.nyam.org/library>
The Newberry Library	Chicago IL	humanities	<www.newberry.org>
Smithsonian Institution Libraries	Washington DC	science, history, art, culture	<www.sil.si.edu>
US Geological Survey Library	Reston VA	earth sciences	<http://library.usgs.gov>
Winterthur Museum, Garden, and Library	Winterthur DE	art, design, American material culture	<www.winterthur.org/about/library.asp>
YIVO Institute for Jewish Research	New York NY	Jewish history and culture	<www.yivoinstitute.org>

National Spelling Bee

A spelling bee is a contest or game in which players attempt to spell correctly and aloud words assigned them by an impartial judge. Competition may be individual, with players eliminated when they misspell a word and the last remaining player being the winner, or between teams, the winner being the team with the most players remaining at the close of the contest. The spelling bee is an old custom that was revived in schools in the United States in the late 19th century and enjoyed a great vogue there and in Great Britain. In the US, local, regional, and national competitions continue to be held annually. The US National Spelling Bee was begun by the *Louisville Courier-Journal* newspaper in 1925, and it was taken over by Scripps Howard, Inc., in 1941. The National Spelling Bee was not held in 1943–45. To qualify, spellers must meet nine requirements, including that they have neither reached their 16th birthday nor passed beyond the eighth grade. National Spelling Bee Web site: <www.spellingbee.com>.

YEAR	CHAMPION & SPONSOR	WINNING WORD
1951	Irving Belz, *Memphis Press-Scimitar* (Tennessee)	insouciant
1952	Doris Ann Hall, *Winston-Salem Journal,* (North Carolina)	vignette
1953	Elizabeth Hess, *Arizona Republic* (Phoenix AZ)	soubrette
1954	William Cashore, *Norristown Times Herald* (Pennsylvania)	transept
1955	Sandra Sloss, *St. Louis Globe-Democrat* (Missouri)	crustaceology
1956	Melody Sachko, *Pittsburgh Press* (Pennsylvania)	condominium
1957	Sandra Owen, *Canton Repository* (Ohio)	
	Dana Bennett, *Rocky Mountain News* (Denver CO)	schappe
1958	Jolitta Schlehuber, *Topeka Daily Capital* (Kansas)	syllepsis
1959	Joel Montgomery, *Rocky Mountain News* (Denver CO)	catamaran
1960	Henry Feldman, *Knoxville News-Sentinel* (Tennessee)	eudaemonic
1961	John Capehart, *Tulsa Tribune* (Oklahoma)	smaragdine
1962	Nettie Crawford, *El Paso Herald-Post* (Texas)	
	Michael Day, *St. Louis Globe-Democrat* (Missouri)	esquamulose
1963	Glen Van Slyke III, *Knoxville News-Sentinel* (Tennessee)	equipage
1964	William Kerek, *Akron Beacon Journal* (Ohio)	sycophant
1965	Michael Kerpan, Jr., *Tulsa Tribune* (Oklahoma)	eczema
1966	Robert A. Wake, *Houston Chronicle* (Texas)	ratoon
1967	Jennifer Reinke, *Omaha World-Herald* (Nebraska)	chihuahua
1968	Robert L. Walters, *Topeka Daily Capital* (Kansas)	abalone
1969	Susan Yoachum, *Dallas Morning News* (Texas)	interlocutory
1970	Libby Childress, *Winston-Salem Journal & Sentinel* (North Carolina)	croissant
1971	Jonathan Knisely, *Philadelphia Bulletin* (Pennsylvania)	shalloon
1972	Robin Kral, *Lubbock Avalanche-Journal* (Texas)	macerate
1973	Barrie Trinkle, *Fort Worth Press* (Texas)	vouchsafe
1974	Julie Ann Junkin, *Birmingham Post-Herald* (Alabama)	hydrophyte
1975	Hugh Tosteson, *San Juan Star* (Puerto Rico)	incisor
1976	Tim Kneale, *Syracuse Herald Journal-American* (New York)	narcolepsy
1977	John Paola, *Pittsburgh Press* (Pennsylvania)	cambist
1978	Peg McCarthy, *Topeka Capital-Journal* (Kansas)	deification
1979	Katie Kerwin, *Rocky Mountain News* (Denver CO)	maculature
1980	Jacques Bailly, *Rocky Mountain News* (Denver CO)	elucubrate
1981	Paige Pipkin, *El Paso Herald-Post* (Texas)	sarcophagus
1982	Molly Dieveney, *Rocky Mountain News* (Denver CO)	psoriasis
1983	Blake Giddens, *El Paso Herald-Post* (Texas)	purim
1984	Daniel Greenblatt, *Loudoun Times-Mirror* (Virginia)	luge
1985	Balu Natarajan, *Chicago Tribune* (Illinois)	milieu
1986	Jon Pennington, *Patriot News* (Harrisburg PA)	odontalgia
1987	Stephanie Petit, *Pittsburgh Press* (Pennsylvania)	staphylococci
1988	Rageshree Ramachandran, *Sacramento Bee* (California)	elegiacal
1989	Scott Isaacs, *Rocky Mountain News* (Denver CO)	spoliator
1990	Amy Marie Dimak, *Seattle Times* (Washington)	fibranne
1991	Joanne Lagatta, *Wisconsin State Journal* (Madison WI)	antipyretic
1992	Amanda Goad, *Richmond News Leader* (Virginia)	lyceum
1993	Geoff Hooper, *Commercial Appeal* (Memphis TN)	kamikaze
1994	Ned G. Andrews, *Knoxville News-Sentinel* (Tennessee)	antediluvian
1995	Justin Tyler Carroll, *Commercial Appeal* (Memphis TN)	xanthosis
1996	Wendy Guey, *Palm Beach Post* (Florida)	vivisepulture
1997	Rebecca Sealfon, *Daily News* (New York NY)	euonym
1998	Jody-Anne Maxwell, Phillips & Phillips Stationery Suppliers, Ltd., (Kingston, Jamaica)	chiaroscurist
1999	Nupur Lala, *Tampa Tribune* (Florida)	logorrhea
2000	George Abraham Thampy, *St. Louis Post-Dispatch* (Missouri)	demarche
2001	Sean Conley, *Aitkin Independent Age* (Minnesota)	succedaneum
2002	Pratyush Buddiga, *Rocky Mountain News* (Denver CO)	prospicience
2003	Sai Gunturi, *Dallas Morning News* (Texas)	pococurante
2004	David Tidmarsh, *South Bend Tribune* (Indiana)	autochthonous
2005	Anurag Kashyap, *San Diego Union-Tribune* (California)	appoggiatura

Economics & Business

World Economy
Banking

History of Banking

Functions performed by banks today have been carried out by individuals, families, or state officials for at least 4,000 years. Clay tablets dating from about 2000 BC indicate that the Babylonians deposited personal valuables for a service charge of one 60th of their worth. Interest charges on loans ran as high as one-third.

The widespread commerce of Rome required a well-developed banking system. Roman authorities set aside the Street of Janus in the Forum for money changers. These traders not only bought and sold foreign coins, they accepted deposits, made loans, issued bills of exchange and bills of credit (similar to today's checks), and bought mortgages. The Justinian Code of the 6th century AD included laws that governed lending and trading in money. During the Middle Ages banking activities were curbed by usury laws, which imposed severe restrictions on lending practices or forbade the collection of interest on loans. During the early Renaissance, however, as international trade revived, money changers once again flourished in Italy, conducting business in the streets from a bench (*banca* in Italian; hence the word bank). Florence, Italy, became a great banking center, dominated by the Medici family.

Banking as it is now practiced dates from the Banco di Rialto, founded in Venice in 1587. It accepted demand deposits and permitted depositors to transfer their credits by checks. It could not make loans, however, or pay interest on deposits. Its services were free since its expenses were paid by the city. The Banco Giro was formed in Venice in 1619. The two banks merged in 1637 and continued to operate under the name Banco Giro until Napoleon liquidated it in 1806.

The development of banking accompanied the growth of commerce and trade in northern Europe. The Netherlands became an international financial center, especially after the establishment of the Bank of Amsterdam (1609). The bank played a crucial part in Dutch economic growth by bringing order to the currency and facilitating transfers. A chartered public bank was opened in Sweden in 1656. It was probably the first financial institution in the world to issue standard-size payable-on-demand bank bills, which eliminated the handling of coins.

Organized banking did not spread to England until the end of the 17th century. Up to that time, England's goldsmiths were its first bankers. They kept money and other valuables in safe custody for their customers. They also dealt in gold bullion and foreign exchange, profiting from acquiring and sorting coins of all kinds. The smiths offered to pay interest to attract coins. The goldsmiths observed that deposits remained at a fairly steady level over long periods of time, that deposits and withdrawals tended to balance each other because customers wanted only enough money on hand to meet everyday needs. This allowed the smiths to lend at interest cash that would otherwise stand idle. From this practice emerged the modern customs of banking: keeping deposits, making loans, and maintaining reserves. Another practice of the goldsmiths, by which a customer could arrange to transfer part of his balance to another party by written order, developed into the modern check-writing system. These customs eventually changed with the establishment of the Bank of England in 1694. Modeled after the Bank of Hamburg and the Bank of Amsterdam, it was founded as a private company and was soon to have a relationship of mutual dependence with the state. The Bank of France was not created until 1800.

Banking in the US

The first bank in the US was the Bank of North America, which was founded in Philadelphia by Robert Morris in 1782. In 1784 it was followed by the Bank of Massachusetts and the Bank of New York. Alexander Hamilton, the first secretary of the treasury, was largely responsible for founding the first Bank of the United States. It was chartered by Congress on 25 Feb 1791, for 20 years. Opposition by the nation's other banks led Congress to refuse renewal of the charter in 1811, but the country's finances were in such a critical condition after the War of 1812 that Congress again chartered a strong central bank in 1816.

The second Bank of the US prospered until its officers mixed business with national politics. Pres. Andrew Jackson took issue with what he considered a concentration of economic power in the hands of a small monied elite beyond the public's control and vetoed the bill that would have renewed the bank's charter. Although Jackson ordered that no more government funds be deposited in the bank, it continued under a Pennsylvania state charter until it failed in 1841 in the aftermath of national financial troubles.

The present system of national banks grew out of the government's need for credit during the American Civil War. The National Bank Act of 1863 permitted banks to organize under national charters and to issue notes up to the amount of their capital, secured by government bonds deposited with the treasury. In 1864 the law was modified to establish a bureau in the Department of the Treasury, with a comptroller of the currency in charge.

Disarray stemming from periodic financial panics and depressions after 1837 caused considerable uncertainty among Americans. This, combined with hostility toward great concentrations of banking power, led to the founding of the Federal Reserve System in 1913. It performs a wide array of financial and economic tasks that include guiding national monetary policy. The agency also supervises and examines the activities and policies of all member banks. It, too, must approve branch banking, bank mergers, and bank holding companies (corporations that own the stock of one or more banks). It oversees foreign banking operations in the US and American international banking operations.

Modern Bank Regulation in the US

The three federal agencies for overseeing the national banks are—in order of their creation—the Comptroller of the Currency, the Federal Reserve System, and the Federal Deposit Insurance Corporation (FDIC). Under a provision of the federal McFadden Act of 1927, the decision on whether or not to allow branch banking was left entirely up to each state.

The severe banking crisis of 1933, when thousands of banks failed, prompted Congress to enact further legislation to safeguard the monies deposited in banks. No bank was allowed to reopen until it had been examined and found to be in good condition. Roughly 4,500 banks failed to reopen, indicating the magnitude of losses suffered by average Americans in the Great Depression. The Banking Act of 1933 established the FDIC as a means of insuring money (up to $100,000) deposited in bank accounts. Also known as the Glass-Steagall Act, this was the law that took away from commercial banks the right to operate as investment banks in the securities industry, but these limitations were loosened toward the end of the 20th century.

Most states did not permit branch banking until after World War II. By 1945 there were only 4,168 branch banks. In 1994, the Riegle-Neal Interstate Banking and Branching Efficiency Act lifted restrictions on interstate banking, thereby making it possible for banks to operate branches across the country.

Later Developments in American Banking

In 1956 Congress passed the Bank Holding Company Act. Holding companies with 25 percent or more of the stock in two or more banks were required to register with the Federal Reserve Board. An amendment to the act in 1970 required that all bank holding companies register with the Federal Reserve and obtain federal approval before buying any nonbank business. Holding companies multiplied during the decades that followed.

In the late 1980s, a considerable number of savings and loan associations (S&Ls) failed because inadequate regulation had allowed risky investments and fraud to flourish. The government was obliged to cover vast losses in excess of $200 billion, causing the Federal Savings and Loan Insurance Corp. (FSLIC) to become insolvent in 1989. Its insurance functions were taken over by a new organization supervised by the Federal Deposit Insurance Corp., and the Resolution Trust Corp. (dissolved in December 1995) was established to handle the bailout of the failed S&Ls.

Banking in the UK

British banking developed through a system of branch banking, in which one or a few leading banks operate branches throughout the country. Its development was linked to the growth of transportation and communications, for otherwise banks cannot clear checks drawn on other banks and effect remittances speedily and efficiently. The Scots also favored branch banking (the Bank of Scotland was founded in 1695), although they were early hampered by poor communications and inadequate coinage.

As the Industrial Revolution progressed and as the size of businesses increased, the structure of English banking underwent a corresponding change. The growth in size of banks stemmed from legislation that encouraged joint-stock ownership, beginning in 1826. The banking system in England and Wales evolved into its modern form before World War I, albeit with further concentration in the years after World War II. By these means, British banks were able to attract deposits from all parts of the country and to spread the banking risk over a wide range of industries and areas. The financial deregulation of 1986, nicknamed the Big Bang, paved the way for increased competition and efficiency in the banking industry. In 2002 the UK was one of three countries opting out of the euro currency adoption. (Denmark and Sweden also voted to retain their national currencies.)

Canadian Banking

During the first decades of Canada's Confederation period, beginning in 1867, Canada demonstrated little interest in establishing its own bank independent of British banks. Given the relative sparseness of the population and the adequacy of branch banking within the British model, no urgent need for a central bank presented itself. However, in response to changes in the economy and the political climate, the Bank of Canada opened in 1935, and it was nationalized in 1938.

Like other central banks, the Bank of Canada controls monetary policy, oversees the production of currency, regulates Canada's financial system, and provides funds management. Canada has maintained a flexible exchange rate system for the Canadian dollar over most of the past century, a choice which rests on three key elements of the Canadian economy: the country's role as a major commodity producer and exporter; the extensive nature of capital mobility, particularly between Canada and the US; and efforts to direct policy toward achieving objectives supporting stable growth. Privately controlled Canadian banks, such as RBC Financial Group, ScotiaBank, and the Bank of Montreal, compete successfully in a number of sectors in the US and elsewhere.

Banking in France

In the years following World War II, banking activities in France were tightly controlled by the government through the Banque de France. However, deregulation in the last four decades of the century gradually reduced federal controls and led to a substantial increase in branch banking and bank account holders. The advent of the EU in the 1990s allowed the free movement of capital across country borders. In 1993 the Banque de France was granted independent status, which freed it from state control. It joined the European System of Banks in June 1998. These trends contributed to consolidation among French banks, making the industry more competitive with its global counterparts.

Banking in Germany

In Germany, modern banking developed in the latter part of the 19th century and eventually became concentrated in Berlin. The Berlin banks built up a widespread network of branch offices, which were also used to establish and maintain industrial contacts throughout the country. Each of the big Berlin banks came to be associated with a group of provincial banks more or less under its control. At the same time, all of the banks, Berlin and provincial alike, expanded their business by opening branches.

During World War I the degree of centralization increased, and this trend continued during the financial crisis of 1931, resulting in further consolidation until the German banking system was dominated by three giants. Among the countervailing forces were the establishment of publicly owned banking institutions, such as the communal savings banks and their central institutions, the Girozentralen, which became of increasing importance after World War II.

German savings banks offer a wide range of services, especially to lower-income groups and smaller businesses, and now compete in wholesale banking as well. The large commercial banks have concerned themselves more with business finance and wealth management. Leading banks such as Bayerische Hypo- und Vereinsbank AG (HVB), Deutsche Bank, Dresdner (a subsidiary of Allianz Group), and Commerzbank remain unchallenged in stock exchange and foreign banking business.

Banking in the Euro Zone

European economic integration has always influenced the nature of trade in what came to be the euro zone, bringing about steady changes in banking practices and the relationships between banks. In 1930 the Bank for International Settlements (BIS) was founded in Basel, Switzerland, to foster coordination between international central banks. As the BIS worked toward building financial and monetary stability, it sponsored the Basel Capital Accord in 1988. Known as the Basel Accord, the agreement established guidelines for assessing credit risk and was accepted by the central banks of the Group of Ten nations (comprising 11 industrial countries). The accord's guidelines were eventually followed by roughly 100 countries. Weaknesses in the original accord, however, led to the development of Basel 2, which was accepted by the Group of Ten member countries on 26 Jun 2004. The new accord establishes three pillars of sound international banking practice: (1) minimum capital requirements keyed to each particular bank's risk profile; (2) involvement of national regulators in the supervision of a bank's risk assessment; and (3) disclosure of policies and financial practices that inform the public of a bank's fiscal health. Implementation of Basel 2 will be spotty: it is expected to be applied to all European banks in the coming year, but in the US Basel 2 will apply only to the country's largest international banks.

The European Central Bank (ECB) was set up in 1998 to oversee the introduction and maintenance of the euro, a unified currency intended for use in the EU. The ECB works with the national central banks of EU member countries to manage price stability and maintain the value of the euro, which became the currency of 12 EU member countries as of 1 Jan 2002. A number of EU members that joined in 2004 are considering adopting the euro in coming years. To date, the UK, Denmark, and Sweden have declined to adopt the euro, though their national central banks do participate in the interdependent consortium of central banks and the ECB, a structure called the Eurosystem.

Banking in Japan

Banking business in Japan is largely concentrated in the hands of the big banks (some of which are specialized), though a number of small banks still survive. The principal classes of banks are city banks and regional banks, but it should be noted that the distinction has no legal basis, though they are separately supervised. Both belong to the Japanese Bankers Association.

Between World War II and the 1990s, Japanese banking enjoyed notable stability. The decline in overall economic performance of the past decade, exacerbated by burdensome bad loans and a persistent lack of profitability, led to changes in the Japanese banking system including financial deregulation, increased competition, and greater governmental intervention.

Banking in India

Until the 1950s banking in India was carried on by a large number of banks, many of them quite small. India remains agricultural in parts, with an economic and social structure based on the village, and so banking and credit was handled by the so-called indigenous banker and the village moneylender. Although their influence has been greatly reduced in recent years, the indigenous bankers offer genuine banking services: accepting deposits and remitting funds; making loans quickly and with a minimum of formality; and making use of the *hundi*, a credit instrument in the form of a bill of exchange.

Banking in India has developed through the expansion of bank branches into the underserved rural areas. Efforts to eliminate local moneylenders caused many smaller banks to close down by the turn of the 21st century, leaving a few dozen large national and commercial banks as well as multinational banks such as HSBC and ABN AMRO.

Banking services are also provided by chit funds, which accept and pay interest on monthly deposits against which it is possible to draw only by way of loan, and by Nidhis, mutual loan societies that have developed into semibanking institutions but deal only with their member shareholders. Many such banks offering microcredit follow the model established in 1976 by Grameen Bank of Bangladesh.

Islamic Banking

Under a strict interpretation of Islamic canon law, such standard Western banking practices as giving or receiving interest on loans and speculating on futures are forbidden. The proscription on charging interest is based on the Muslim revulsion—based in the Qu'ran and Sunnah—to the practice of usury (*riba*). Speculating on futures, in the traditional view, violates the principle that an item should not be paid for sight-unseen. A number of Muslim countries, such as Saudi Arabia, enforce Islamic norms in banking, and Islamic style banks have appeared even in countries that have been integrated into the world banking system, including some countries in Europe and the Americas. Rather than charging interest, such banks generally charge a service fee for loans, though institutions have differed on what types of speculation are permissible. Although not properly considered a type of Islamic banking, many people in Muslim countries manage their finances through a system of money changing known as *hawala* (similar to the *hundi* of India), in which capital is moved about through a trust-based system of personal contacts. Without governmental or institutional oversight, this system has been, at times, viewed as part of the black market.

Global Trends in Banking

For two decades after World War II the US—nearly alone among the industrial nations—prospered in an unprecedented way. Its banks had become the largest and most powerful in the world, in part because they continued developing new ways of serving their customers. One innovation came about in the 1960s, when many banks began issuing their own credit cards. These permitted the cardholders to purchase goods and services on credit from retailers that honored the cards. Once the bank cards became nationally recognized, most were consolidated as either Visa or MasterCard—both of which are accepted around the world. Comparable bank cards issued in other countries include JCB (in Japan), Eurocard-MasterCard (sponsored by Europay in Europe and Eurasia), and Barclaycard (in Great Britain, Europe, and the Caribbean).

By 1990 the pressures of international competition challenged the limits imposed by American banking regulations. US banks no longer dominated the global banking business. In fact, ranked by assets, not one of the world's 20 largest banks was in the US. Thirteen were in Japan and seven in Europe—a change that reflected shifts in world economic power.

coupled with the benefits of international trade and development that many economies experienced in the decades after 1945. By the end of the 20th century, changes in US banking laws soon led to the creation of American banks that competed with the largest banks of Europe and Asia.

At the start of the 21st century, an increasing number of bank mergers occurred across national borders. Banks within the Nordic region merged, while BNP Paribas of France increased its presence in the US market by purchasing a majority share of BancWest in early 2001 and then acquiring United California Bank from UFJ Holdings, Inc., of Japan. Several countries, notably Israel and Poland, took measures to promote an expanded foreign bank presence in their domestic markets, while in Japan such actions focused on the rescue of failed domestic institutions. Still, just as technology made global transactions more efficient, concerns about money laundering and illegal funding of terrorist organizations forced banks to offer greater transparency in their dealings.

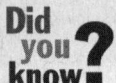

Did you know? The colorful chief of the Metro-Goldwyn-Mayer movie studios, Louis B. Mayer, was heard to say about his film *Gone With the Wind* before its release, "You can never make a nickel on a Civil War picture."

Economic Performance
Real Gross Domestic Products of Selected Developed Countries
% annual change. Source: OECD; IMF World Economic Outlook, September 2004.

COUNTRY	1999	2000	2001	2002	2003	2004[1]
US	4.4	3.7	0.8	1.9	3.0	4.3
Japan	0.2	2.8	0.4	-0.3	2.5	4.4
Germany	2.0	2.9	0.8	0.1	-0.1	2.0
France	3.2	4.2	2.1	1.1	0.5	2.6
Italy	1.7	3.0	1.8	0.4	0.3	1.4
UK	2.9	3.9	2.3	1.8	2.2	3.4
Canada	5.5	5.2	1.8	3.4	2.0	2.9
EU	2.8	3.7	1.8	1.2	1.1	2.6
Seven major countries above	3.0	3.5	1.0	2.2	2.2	3.7
All developed countries	3.1	3.9	1.2	1.6	2.1	3.6

[1]Estimated.   Note: Seasonally adjusted at annual rates.

Standardized Unemployment Rates in Selected Developed Countries
% of total labor force. Source: OECD, Economic Outlook, November 2003 and November 2004.

COUNTRY	1999	2000	2001	2002	2003	2004[1]
US	4.2	4.0	4.8	5.8	6.0	5.5
Japan	4.7	4.7	5.0	5.4	5.3	4.8
Germany	8.0	7.3	7.4	8.2	9.1	9.2
France	10.7	9.4	8.7	9.0	9.7	9.8
Italy	11.5	10.7	9.6	9.1	8.8	8.1
UK	6.0	5.5	5.1	5.2	5.0	4.7
Canada	7.6	6.8	7.2	7.6	7.6	7.2
Euro zone[2]	8.7	8.4	8.0	8.4	8.8	8.8
Seven major countries above	6.1	5.7	5.9	6.5	6.7	6.4
All developed countries	6.6	5.9	6.2	6.7	6.9	6.9

[1]Projected.   [2]Austria, Belgium, France, Germany, Greece, Ireland, Italy, Luxembourg, The Netherlands, Norway, Portugal, and Spain.

Consumer Price Change in Selected Countries

This table shows the change in consumer prices from the year previous, expressed in percent. The change in consumer prices is used as an indicator of inflation. An increase in percent from one year to the next indicates an increase in the overall price of certain goods and services purchased by the average consumer. A negative number indicates a decrease in consumer prices. N/A means data were not available. Source: International Monetary Fund, *International Financial Statistics*, April 2005.

COUNTRY	2001	2002	2003	2004	COUNTRY	2001	2002	2003	2004
Argentina	-1.1	25.9	13.4	4.4	The Netherlands	4.5	3.5	2.1	1.3
Australia	4.4	3.1	3.0	2.6					
Austria	2.7	1.8	1.4	2.1	Nigeria	13.0	12.9	14	0.1
Bangladesh	1.9	3.4	4.6	N/A	Norway	3.0	1.3	2.5	4.7
Belgium	2.5	1.6	1.6	2.1	Pakistan	3.1	3.3	2.9	7.5
Bolivia	1.6	0.9	3.3	4.4	Peru	2.0	0.2	2.3	3.6
Brazil	6.8	8.4	14.7	6.6	Philippines	6.1	2.9	3.1	6.0
Canada	2.5	2.2	2.8	2.7					
Chile	3.6	2.5	2.8	1.1	Portugal	4.4	3.7	3.5	2.7
Colombia	8.0	6.3	7.1	5.9	Romania	34.5	22.5	15.3	0.1
Egypt	2.3	2.7	4.2	11.3	Russia	21.5	15.8	13.7	0.1
France	1.7	1.9	2.1	2.4	South Africa	4.8	8.9	6.0	1.4
Germany	2.5	1.3	1.0	1.6					
Ghana	32.9	14.8	N/A	0.1	South Korea	4.1	2.7	3.6	3.6
Greece	3.4	3.7	3.8	3.2					
Guatemala	7.6	8.0	5.5	7.5	Spain	3.6	3.1	3.0	0.0
India	3.7	4.5	4.2	4.2	Sri Lanka	14.2	9.6	6.3	7.5
Indonesia	12	11.5	5.8	6.2	Sweden	2.4	2.2	1.9	3.8
Iran	11.3	15.9	21.0	N/A	Switzerland	1.0	0.6	0.6	N/A
Israel	1.1	5.6	-0.6	-4.6					
Italy	2.8	2.5	2.8	2.4	Thailand	1.7	0.6	1.8	2.8
Japan	-0.7	-0.9	-0.3	0	Turkey	54.4	45.0	25.3	8.6
Kenya	5.7	2.0	9.8	0.1	UK	1.8	1.6	2.9	3.0
Malaysia	1.4	1.8	1.1	1.5	US	2.8	1.6	2.3	2.7
Mexico	6.4	5.0	4.5	4.7	Venezuela	12.5	22.4	31.1	0.2

Changes in Consumer Prices in Less-Developed Countries

% change from preceding year. Source: IMF, World Economic Outlook, *September 2004.*

AREA	1999	2000	2001	2002	2003	2004[1]
All less-developed countries	6.5	7.3	6.8	6.0	6.1	6.0
Regional groups						
Africa	12.2	13.1	12.0	9.7	10.3	8.4
Asia	2.5	1.9	2.7	2.1	2.6	4.5
Middle East, Europe, Malta, & Turkey	23.6	8.5	7.1	7.5	8.0	9.2
Western Hemisphere	7.4	6.7	6.0	9.0	10.6	6.5

[1]Projected.

Changes in Output in Less-Developed Countries

% annual change in real gross domestic product. Source: IMF, World Economic Outlook, *September 2004.*

AREA	2000	2001	2002	2003	2004[1]
All less-developed countries	5.9	4.0	4.8	6.1	6.6
Regional groups					
Africa	2.9	4.0	3.5	4.3	4.5
Asia	6.7	5.5	6.6	7.7	7.6
Middle East	5.5	3.6	4.3	6.0	5.1
Western Hemisphere	3.9	0.5	-0.1	1.8	4.6
Central and Eastern Europe	4.9	0.2	4.4	4.5	5.5
Commonwealth of Independent States	9.1	6.4	5.4	7.8	8.0

[1]Projected.

US Economy
Banking
The Federal Reserve System

The Federal Reserve System is the central banking authority of the United States. It acts as a fiscal agent for the US government, is custodian of the reserve accounts of commercial banks, makes loans to commercial banks, and issues paper currency. It protects the stability of the nation's financial system by regulating and supervising banking institutions and containing risk in financial markets. Created on 23 Dec 1913, it consists of the Board of Governors, the 12 Federal Reserve districts, and the Federal Open Market Committee. There are also several thousand member banks.

The Board of Governors determines the reserve requirements of the member banks, reviews and determines, with the Federal Reserve Banks, the discount rates established by the reserve banks, and reviews reserve bank budgets. It has seven members who each serve a single 14-year term (a member who finishes an incomplete term may be reappointed). The chairman and vice chairman are chosen for four-year terms. In mid-2005, the Federal Reserve Board consisted of Alan Greenspan (chairman), Roger W. Ferguson, Jr. (vice chairman), Edward M. Gramlich, Susan Schmidt Bies, Mark W. Olson, and Donald L. Kohn, with one vacancy.

Each Federal Reserve bank is governed by nine directors. The banks are located in Boston, New York, Philadelphia PA, Chicago IL, San Francisco CA, Cleveland OH, Richmond VA, Atlanta GA, St. Louis MO, Minneapolis MN, Kansas City MO, and Dallas TX. The Federal Open Market Committee determines reserve bank policy for securities transactions on the open market. It consists of the Board of Governors, the president of the Federal Reserve Bank of New York, and four other bank presidents serving rotating one-year terms. All national banks are members of the Federal Reserve System, and state banks may qualify to become members. The Federal Advisory Council operates as a general advisory group. The Consumer Advisory Council addresses consumer finance and credit issues. The Thrift Institutions Advisory Council offers input on issues relating to banks, credit unions, and savings and loans.

The Federal Reserve System exercises its regulatory powers in several ways. One method is to adjust the legal reserve ratio (the proportion of deposits a member bank must hold in its reserve account), thus increasing or reducing the amount of new loans a bank can make. Because loans create new deposits, the money supply is expanded or reduced. The money supply is also influenced by manipulating the discount rate (the rate of interest charged by reserve banks on short-term secured loans to member banks). Since these loans are typically sought to maintain reserves at their required level, an increase in the cost of such loans has an effect similar to that of increasing the reserve requirement. Open-market operations may be employed to make small adjustments in the market. Reserve bank sales or purchases of securities on the open market tend to reduce or increase the size of commercial-bank reserves. The board can also change the margin requirements involved in the purchase of securities.

The US Mint

The US Mint, the world's largest producer of coins and medals, was established by Congress on 2 Apr 1792. It is a bureau of the US Department of the Treasury. The mint manufactures and distributes coins, protects the country's gold and silver assets, and creates medals, commemorative coins, and coin proof sets for purchase by the public. In 2004 it produced 13.5 billion pennies, nickels, dimes, quarters, half dollars, and golden dollars. The director of the mint is appointed by the president and serves a five-year term; in mid-2005 the director was Henrietta Holsman Fore.

From its Washington DC headquarters, the mint operates facilities in Philadelphia PA, Denver CO, San Francisco CA, and West Point NY. All engraving of coins is done at the Philadelphia site (established 1792), where general circulation coins, medals, and coin dies are also produced. Denver (1863) manufactures general circulation coins and coin dies and provides storage for gold and silver bullion. San Francisco (1854) produces only commemorative coins and proof sets; West Point (1937) manufactures uncirculated and proof sets of gold, silver, and platinum coins and stores these metals. The mint is also responsible for the storage and protection of more than 145 million ounces of gold bullion at Fort Knox KY.

Although general circulation coins were once made from gold, silver, and copper, this is no longer the case. Gold coin production was discontinued in 1933, and in 1966 silver ceased to be used in dimes and quarters. Currently, pennies are composed of copper-plated zinc, golden dollar coins of manganese brass, and all other general circulation coins of cupronickel, an alloy of copper and nickel. In early 2000 the mint began circulating the golden dollar coin, intended to replace the older Susan B. Anthony dollar coin. The new coin featured the image of Sacagawea, the Shoshone Indian woman who traveled as a guide with the Lewis and Clark Expedition in 1804–06. In 1999 the mint began issuing a series of quarters featuring the 50 states. Five quarters were to be issued annually, about 10 weeks apart, each featuring one state's design. State quarters were released in order of the states' ratification of the US Constitution. Introduced in 2005 were California, Kansas, Minnesota, Oregon, and West Virginia; scheduled for 2006 are Nevada, Nebraska, Colorado, North Dakota, and South Dakota. Nickels commemorating the Lewis and Clark Expedition were released in 2004 and 2005; those issued in 2005 featured a slightly different portrait of Thomas Jefferson.

US Bureau of Engraving and Printing

The US Bureau of Engraving and Printing is responsible for the printing of paper money and is a part of the US Department of the Treasury. In addition to Federal Reserve Notes (paper currency), the bureau produces other government security documents and creates postage stamps for the United States Postal Service. Each year it prints billions of bills at a rate of some 37 million per day (valued at nearly $700 million). The bureau operates facilities in Washington DC and Fort Worth TX. A director is appointed by the secretary of the treasury; in mid-2005 the director was Thomas A. Ferguson.

The vast majority of bills are printed to replace those already in circulation. Currency is printed on paper made of cotton and linen with red and blue fibers throughout and is produced in denominations of $1, $5, $10, $20, $50, $100, and, occasionally, $2. No currency has been printed in denominations of $500, $1,000, $5,000, or $10,000 since 1946. The greatest number of bills printed are the $1 denomination.

The bureau was established in 1862 and by 1877 was the only producer of US paper money; previously, private companies had printed currency. In 1894 the bureau began producing postage stamps. By the mid-1980s it was recognized that a western office was needed, and the Fort Worth facility opened in April 1991. To protect against technologically advanced counterfeiting techniques, new currency designs began circulating in 1996 that incorporated enhanced deterrence measures. Since 1990 all paper money except $1 bills has included a security thread and microprinting, components that were improved for later print series. New anticounterfeiting features included watermarks, color-shifting inks, fine-line printing patterns, and enlarged, off-center portraits; elements were also added to help the blind and those with poor vision identify different denominations. Counterfeiting crimes are handled by the US Secret Service. A newly redesigned $10 note is expected to enter circulation in early 2006.

Denominations of US Currency

A new $20 bill appeared in autumn 2003. In addition to the watermark, color-shifting ink, security thread, and microprinting that are present in the current $5–$100 bills, the new bill has multicolored printing, a blue eagle in the background, a metallic green eagle and shield, and other anti-counterfeiting features. A new $50 note, with tones of red, blue, and yellow, released in autumn 2004 marked the first time US cash prominently included colors other than black and green.

PAPER MONEY			
VALUE	PORTRAIT ON FRONT	DESIGN ON BACK	WHEN CIRCULATED
$1	George Washington	Great Seal of US	1929–
$2	Thomas Jefferson	Monticello	1929–75
$2	Thomas Jefferson	John Trumbull's *Signing of the Declaration of Independence*	1976–
$5[1]	Abraham Lincoln	Lincoln Memorial	2000–
$10[1]	Alexander Hamilton	US Treasury	2000–
$20[1]	Andrew Jackson	White House	1998–
$50[1]	Ulysses S. Grant	US Capitol	1997–
$100[1]	Benjamin Franklin	Independence Hall	1996–
$500[2]	William McKinley	ornate figure of value	1929–69
$1,000[2]	Grover Cleveland	ornate figure of value	1929–69
$5,000[2]	James Madison	ornate figure of value	1929–69
$10,000[2]	Salmon P. Chase	ornate figure of value	1929–69
$100,000[3]	Woodrow Wilson	ornate figure of value	—

[1]*Earlier versions issued starting 1929 had same subjects front and back.* [2]*Last printed in 1945.* [3]*Printed 1934–35 but never issued to public.*

COINS			
VALUE	PORTRAIT ON FRONT	DESIGN ON BACK	WHEN CIRCULATED
1¢	Abraham Lincoln	"one cent" and wheat	1909–58
1¢	Abraham Lincoln	Lincoln Memorial	1959–
5¢	Thomas Jefferson	Monticello	1938–2003; 2006–
5¢	Thomas Jefferson	"Westward Journey" designs	2004–05
10¢	Franklin D. Roosevelt	torch	1946–
25¢	George Washington	eagle	1932–74; 1977–98
25¢	George Washington	colonial drummer	1975/76[1]
25¢	George Washington	50 state designs	1999–2008
50¢	John F. Kennedy	presidential seal	1964–74; 1977–
50¢	John F. Kennedy	Independence Hall	1975/76[1]
$1	Dwight D. Eisenhower	eagle	1971–74; 1977–78
$1	Dwight D. Eisenhower	Liberty Bell and Moon	1975/76[1]
$1	Susan B. Anthony	eagle	1979–80; 1999
$1	Sacagawea	eagle	2000–

[1]*All 25¢, 50¢, and $1 coins issued in 1975 and 1976 carried the double date 1776–1976.*

Denominations of US Currency (continued)

50 STATE QUARTERS PROGRAM

STATE	WHEN ISSUED	STATE	WHEN ISSUED	STATE	WHEN ISSUED
Alabama	March 2003	Louisiana	May 2002	Ohio	March 2002
Alaska	2008	Maine	June 2003	Oklahoma	2008
Arizona	2008	Maryland	March 2000	Oregon	2005
Arkansas	October 2003	Massachusetts	January 2000	Pennsylvania	March 1999
California	2005	Michigan	January 2004	Rhode Island	May 2001
Colorado	2006	Minnesota	2005	South Carolina	May 2000
Connecticut	October 1999	Mississippi	October 2002	South Dakota	2006
Delaware	January 1999	Missouri	August 2003	Tennessee	January 2002
Florida	March 2004	Montana	2007	Texas	June 2004
Georgia	July 1999	Nebraska	2006	Utah	2007
Hawaii	2008	Nevada	2006	Vermont	August 2001
Idaho	2007	New Hampshire	August 2000	Virginia	October 2000
Illinois	January 2003	New Jersey	May 1999	Washington	2007
Indiana	August 2002	New Mexico	2008	West Virginia	2005
Iowa	2004	New York	January 2001	Wisconsin	2004
Kansas	2005	North Carolina	March 2001	Wyoming	2007
Kentucky	October 2001	North Dakota	2006		

US Currency and Coins in Circulation

Currency and coins outstanding and currency in circulation by denomination,
31 Mar 2005. Source: Treasury Bulletin, June 2005.

	TOTAL CURRENCY AND COINS	CURRENCY	COINS[1]
amounts in circulation	$754,625,192,930	$719,575,433,933	$35,049,758,997
less amounts held by:			
US Treasury	292,046,769	21,410,225	270,636,544
Federal Reserve Banks	135,962,131,601	135,242,395,284	719,736,317
total amounts outstanding	**890,879,371,300**	**854,839,239,442**	**36,040,131,858**

DENOMINATION	TOTAL CURRENCY IN CIRCULATION	FEDERAL RESERVE NOTES[2]	US NOTES	CURRENCY NO LONGER ISSUED
$1	$ 8,192,667,246	$ 8,047,982,182	$ 143,503	$144,541,561
$2	1,416,209,502	1,283,952,008	132,244,918	12,576
$5	9,580,590,715	9,442,759,825	109,299,310	28,531,580
$10	14,652,042,640	14,630,588,370	6,300	21,447,970
$20	106,192,515,780	106,172,407,660	3,840	20,104,280
$50	59,775,821,750	59,764,323,200	500	11,498,050
$100	519,452,026,200	519,415,479,500	14,556,000	21,990,700
$500	142,516,500	142,321,500	5,500	189,500
$1,000	165,818,000	165,606,000	5,000	207,000
$5,000	1,765,000	1,710,000	—	55,000
$10,000	3,460,000	3,360,000	—	100,000
fractional notes[3]	600	—	90	510
total currency	**719,575,433,933**	**719,070,490,245**	**256,264,961**	**248,678,727**

[1]*Excludes coins sold to collectors at premium prices.*   [2]*Issued on or after 1 Jul 1929.*   [3]*Represents value of certain partial denominations not presented for redemption.*

Energy

Energy Consumption by State and Sector

Figures represent '000,000,000,000 Btu for the year 2001. Source: Energy Information Administration www.eia.doe.gov, US Census Bureau..

	TOTAL	RESIDENTIAL	COMMERCIAL	INDUSTRIAL	TRANS-PORTATION	PER CAPITA ('000,000 BTU)
Alabama	1,943	380	254	863	446	435
Alaska	737	53	65	413	206	1,165
Arizona	1,353	344	312	221	476	255
Arkansas	1,106	219	148	462	278	411
California	7,853	1,446	1,509	1,928	2,971	227
Colorado	1,270	303	287	294	386	287
Connecticut	853	267	215	134	238	248
Delaware	293	62	52	113	66	368

Energy Consumption by State and Sector (continued)

	TOTAL	RESIDENTIAL	COMMERCIAL	INDUSTRIAL	TRANS-PORTATION	PER CAPITA ('000,000 BTU)
District of Columbia	168	34	104	4	26	295
Florida	4,135	1,193	958	598	1,386	253
Georgia	2,881	642	503	876	860	343
Hawaii	282	35	39	77	132	231
Idaho	501	105	95	180	122	379
Illinois	3,870	928	829	1,173	939	309
Indiana	2,881	504	397	1,296	604	457
Iowa	1,151	229	179	472	270.	393
Kansas	1,044	215	192	385	252	386
Kentucky	1,880	339	246	846	449	462
Louisiana	3,500	348	264	2,135	753	783
Maine	491	111	74	199	107	381
Maryland	1,420	391	372	252	405	264
Massachusetts	1,549	461	379	261	447	242
Michigan	3,120	790	598	928	804	312
Minnesota	1,745	381	336	526	502	350
Mississippi	1,173	234	163	427	349	410
Missouri	1,815	496	389	374	559	322
Montana	366	70	60	128	108	403
Nebraska	627	152	130	182	163	365
Nevada	629	147	108	169	205	300
New Hampshire	322	87	65	68	102	256
New Jersey	2,500	573	554	491	882	294
New Mexico	679	107	122	220	230	371
New York	4,135	1,194	1,303	667	970	217
North Carolina	2,591	641	513	743	694	316
North Dakota	407	61	56	203	88	639
Ohio	3,982	892	682	1,429	979	350
Oklahoma	1,540	298	233	544	466	444
Oregon	1,064	252	208	298	307	306
Pennsylvania	3,923	931	709	1,286	997	319
Rhode Island	227	73	63	26	66	215
South Carolina	1,549	322	235	609	383	381
South Dakota	248	60	50	54	83	327
Tennessee	2,195	500	369	746	581	382
Texas	12,029	1,570	1,356	6,426	2,677	564
Utah	725	140	140	233	213	318
Vermont	164	48	33	31	52	267
Virginia	2,315	549	534	547	685	322
Washington	2,034	471	377	586	600	339
West Virginia	762	157	111	311	183	423
Wisconsin	1,863	401	313	729	422	345
Wyoming	439	39	51	238	111	889
total	96,275	20,241	17,332	32,431	26,272	338

Energy Consumption by Source

Figures represent '000,000,000,000 Btu. Source: US Energy Information Administration <www.eia.doe.gov>.

	PETROLEUM	NATURAL GAS	COAL	HYDROELECTRIC POWER	NUCLEAR ELECTRIC POWER
Alabama	539.6	342.3	845.6	85.0	317.2
Alaska	292.2	413.1	15.9	13.7	0.0
Arizona	524.2	245.2	424.1	80.4	300.1
Arkansas	378.6	231.6	274.0	25.9	154.4
California	3,604.4	2,513.9	67.9	256.3	347.1
Colorado	461.8	385.0	400.3	12.7	0.0
Conneticut	438.7	149.4	40.0	2.9	161.2
Delaware	146.5	51.8	38.3	0.0	0.0
District of Columbia	33.5	30.6	0.7	0.0	0.0
Florida	1,989.7	569.8	726.1	1.5	330.0
Georgia	1,034.0	362.7	772.0	20.6	351.9
Hawaii	239.8	2.9	17.6	1.0	0.0
Idaho	155.3	81.8	11.2	73.5	0.0
Illinois	1,304.1	970.7	993.6	1.5	965.0
Indiana	837.3	513.7	1,567.1	5.8	0.0

Energy Consumption by Source (continued)

	PETROLEUM	NATURAL GAS	COAL	HYDROELECTRIC POWER	NUCLEAR ELECTRIC POWER
Iowa	400.9	225.2	444.9	8.6	40.3
Kansas	391.0	273.8	354.6	0.3	108.1
Kentucky	704.3	216.7	1,010.7	39.2	0.0
Louisiana	1,491.4	1,339.5	240.0	7.4	181.1[1]
Maine	233.4	101.2	7.9	26.9	0.0
Maryland	568.1	191.4	317.3	12.0	142.7
Massachusetts	762.4	364.1	109.0	−0.1[1]	53.7
Michigan	1,041.7	928.7	796.5	4.4	279.1
Minnesota	673.5	345.0	353.1	8.5	123.2
Mississippi	485.5	340.8	198.3	0.0	103.7
Missouri	718.8	288.6	716.1	8.5	87.6
Montana	168.0	66.5	184.3	67.3	0.0
Nebraska	217.8	124.1	227.5	11.4	91.2
Nevada	250.2	181.3	188.6	25.6	0.0
New Hampshire	178.3	24.8	40.1	10.1	90.8
New Jersey	1,246.3	585.8	112.2	−1.3[1]	318.3
New Mexico	251.0	262.1	297.1	2.4	0.0
New York	1,712.5	1,205.9	315.0	225.4	422.0
North Carolina	949.6	215.6	756.5	26.4	394.7
North Dakota	138.0	62.6	419.8	13.6	0.0
Ohio	1,305.2	835.7	1,343.0	5.2	161.6
Oklahoma	588.4	548.4	376.8	22.5	0.0
Oregon	368.2	235.5	43.4	291.4	0.0
Pennsylvania	1,454.4	669.1	1,378.5	10.5	770.3
Rhode Island	99.8	98.6	0.1	<0.05	0.0
South Carolina	469.5	147.2	414.4	1.9	521.0
South Dakota	111.9	37.0	44.3	34.9	0.0
Tennessee	708.2	265.4	688.0	63.2	298.6
Texas	5,521.0	4,434.6	1,493.4	12.2	398.7
Utah	261.4	168.1	398.6	5.2	0.0
Vermont	88.9	8.0	0.1	9.0	43.6
Virginia	911.2	246.7	482.4	−12.5[1]	269.1
Washington	842.5	323.1	99.5	556.9	86.2
West Virginia	215.0	152.2	872.3	9.7	0.0
Wisconsin	668.4	363.0	494.7	20.9	120.2
Wyoming	157.0	104.0	500.2	8.9	0.0
total	**38,333.3**	**22,844.5**	**21,904.7**	**2,117.6**	**8,032.7**

[1]Results from pumped storage expending more electricity to meet demand during peak periods than is created.

Travel and Tourism
Passports, Visas, and Immunizations

With certain exceptions, a passport is required by law for all US citizens, including infants, to travel outside the United States and its territories. Exceptions include travel to Canada and Mexico; these usually require a birth certificate or other proof of US citizenship for entry. Passports can be applied for at 7,000 passport acceptance facilities nationwide, including most government facilities. State Department passport agencies generally accept applications only by appointment, usually from those in need of expedited service (two weeks or less). Passport agencies are located in Boston MA, Chicago IL, Norwalk CT, Honolulu HI, Houston TX, Los Angeles CA, Miami FL, New Orleans LA, New York City NY, Philadelphia PA, San Francisco CA, Seattle WA, and Washington DC. Everyone must apply in person for new passports; those issued to persons aged 16 and up may be renewed by mail. Applicants should submit the appropriate paperwork several months in advance of planned travel to allow for processing. New passport fees total $97 for persons age 16 and up ($55 passport fee, $30 execution fee, $12 security surcharge) and $82 for those under 16 ($40 passport fee, $30 execution fee, $12 security surcharge); expedited service is an additional $60. Renewal fees are $67 for all ages. Passports are mailed to applicants in about six weeks, or about two weeks for rush service. The status of a passport application may be checked by contacting the National Passport Information Center at 1-877-487-2778 (toll-free; automated information; representatives available weekdays 8 am to 8 pm EST, except federal holidays).

To apply in person for a passport requires submission of an application form; proof of US citizenship, such as a certified birth certificate; proof of identity, such as a driver's license; two identical recent 2×2-inch photographs; a social security number; and all applicable fees. Options for proving identity or citizenship are listed on the State Department Web site. A passport is valid for 10 years, or 5 years if issued to a person age 15 or younger. Passports can be renewed by mail if the applicant has an undamaged passport, has received a passport within the past 15 years, was over age 16 when the passport was issued, and has legal documentation to verify any name changes (such as a marriage certificate or divorce decree). To renew by mail requires submission of an application form, the most recent passport, two identical photographs, and applicable fees. Frequent travelers may request a passport with extra pages. A passport that is lost or stolen in a foreign country must be immediately reported to local police and the nearest US embassy or consulate to allow for the citizen's reentry into the US. Replacing a lost or stolen passport requires completion of a form reporting the loss or theft and an application for a new passport, as well as the usual documentation, photographs, and fees.

Visas. A visa is usually a stamp placed on a US passport by a foreign country's officials allowing the passport owner to visit that country. It is the traveler's responsibility to check visa regulations and obtain visas where necessary before traveling to a foreign country. Visas may be acquired from the embassy or consulate of the intended destination, and can be applied for by mail. Processing fees vary among countries.

Immunizations. Under regulations adopted by the World Health Organization, some countries require International Certificates of Vaccination against yellow fever. Other immunizations, such as those for tetanus and polio, should also be up-to-date. Preventive measures for malaria are recommended for some destinations. There are no immunization requirements for returning to the United States. Many countries require HIV/AIDS testing for work, study, or residence permits or for long-term stays.

For passport information, forms, and office locations, access the State Department Web site at <http://travel.state.gov/passport>.

Entry requirements for foreign countries, including necessity of visas, immunizations, and HIV testing, are available at <http://travel.state.gov/foreignentry reqs.html>. Additional information on required or recommended health-care measures can be obtained from the Centers for Disease Control and Prevention at <www.cdc.gov/travel> or by calling 1-877-FYI-TRIP; also helpful are local health departments and the Government Printing Office publication Health Information for International Travel, available for $20 at <http://travel.state.gov/foreignentry reqs.html>.

Travelers to and from the US

Data for 2002 showed that overseas travel to the US dropped significantly during 2002, primarily as a response to the terrorist attacks of 11 Sep 2001. Since then, however, travel has rebounded at varying levels. 2004 data for US resident travel to specific overseas countries are not yet available, but 2003 data for air travel to the various regions, as well as Mexico and Canada, are presented below. Source: US Department of Commerce, International Trade Administration.

TOP COUNTRIES OF ORIGIN FOR VISITORS TO THE US (2004)

		% CHANGE FROM 2003
UK	4,302,737	+9
Japan	3,747,620	+18
Germany	1,319,904	+12
France	775,274	+13
South Korea	626,595	+1
Australia	519,955	+28
Italy	470,805	+15
The Netherlands	424,872	+14
Brazil	384,734	+10
Ireland	345,119	+36
total overseas	20,322,257	+13
Canada	13,849,000	+9
Mexico	11,906,000	+13
total worldwide	46,077,257	+12

REGIONAL DESTINATION OF US TRAVELERS ABROAD (2003)

		% CHANGE FROM 2002
Europe	10,992,891	+3
Caribbean	4,941,373	+14
Asia	3,502,203	−11
South America	1,845,248	+10
Central America	1,834,248	+17
Oceania	760,566	+2
Middle East	366,190	+18
Africa	209,088	+17
total overseas	24,451,807	+5
Mexico	4,562,351	+9
Canada	3,530,508	−7
total worldwide	32,544,666	+4

Top 10 States and Cities Visited by Overseas Visitors in 2004[1]

STATE	VISITORS/ IN THOUSANDS ('000)	% CHANGE FROM 2003	CITY	VISITORS/ IN THOUSANDS ('000)	% CHANGE FROM 2003
New York	5,426	+29	New York NY	5,162	+30
Florida	4,430	+5	Los Angeles CA	2,276	+7
California	4,207	+6	Miami FL	2,195	+6
Hawaii	2,215	+14	Orlando FL	1,951	+10
Nevada	1,626	+19	Oahu/Honolulu HI	1,870	+15
Guam[2]	1,036	+22	San Francisco CA	1,870	+10
Illinois	975	+18	Las Vegas NV	1,565	+21
Massachusetts	935	+13	Washington DC	1,057	+22
Texas	874	+5	Chicago IL	935	+21
New Jersey	833	+22	Boston MA	833	+10

[1]Excludes Canadian and Mexican visitors to the US.   [2]Guam is a US territory. If Guam were excluded, Pennsylvania would rank 10th on the list with about 691,000 overseas visitors.

Customs Exemptions

Upon returning to the US from a foreign country, travelers must pay duty on items acquired outside the US. If the value of the items is greater than the allowable exemption, duty must be paid on the excess amount. The general exemption is $800 per person, but it can also be $200 or $1,600 in certain situations. Exemptions apply if the items are in the traveler's possession, are for the traveler's own use, and are declared to Customs. The traveler must also have been out of the country for at least 48 hours (unless returning from Mexico or the US Virgin Islands) and must not have used any part of the exemption within the past 30 days; if one or both of these requirements does not apply, the allowable exemption drops to $200 per person and includes additional restrictions. The general exemption of $800 applies to travelers returning from any country except several in the Caribbean Sea region and from US island possessions. This exemption includes no more than 200 previously exported cigarettes, 100 cigars, and no more than one liter of alcoholic beverages. Cuban tobacco products are prohibited. Family members may combine their total exemptions in a joint declaration. The $800 exemption applies to travelers returning from any of 30 countries in the Caribbean Basin or Andean Region and may include two liters of alcoholic beverages, as long as one of the liters was produced in one of those countries. The 30 countries are Antigua and Barbuda, Aruba, The Bahamas, Barbados, Belize, Bolivia, the British Virgin Islands, Colombia, Costa Rica, Dominica, the Dominican Republic, Ecuador, El Salvador, Grenada, Guatemala, Guyana, Haiti, Honduras, Jamaica, Montserrat, the Netherlands Antilles, Nicaragua, Panama, Peru, St. Kitts and Nevis, St. Lucia, St. Vincent and the Grenadines, and Trinidad and Tobago. A $1,600 exemption applies to travelers returning from a trip that included the US Virgin Islands, American Samoa, or Guam. This exemption includes 1,000 cigarettes and five liters of alcoholic beverages; of this amount, 800 cigarettes and one liter of alcohol must be from one of the US islands. The $1,600 exemption also applies to multi-country travel (such as a cruise) to a US possession and any of the 30 Caribbean and Andean region countries, as long as no more than $800 worth of goods was purchased in the Caribbean and Andean countries.

Gifts valued at $100 or less may be sent to the US without duty as long as no single person receives more than this value within a single day; the exempt value increases to $200 for gifts sent from American Samoa, Guam, or the US Virgin Islands. Alcoholic beverages may not be sent by mail; tobacco and alcohol-based perfumes worth more than $5 are not included in the exemption. Travelers may ship goods home for personal use without duty if the value of the goods is $200 or less and no single person receives more than this value within a single day. This personal exemption increases to $1,600 for goods purchased and shipped from American Samoa, Guam, or the US Virgin Islands.

Customs information is available from the Customs and Border Protection Web site at <www.cbp.gov/xp/cgov/travel>. The general-information brochure "Know Before You Go" and other Customs publications can be viewed or ordered online.

US State Department Travel Warnings

The State Department issues Travel Warnings when it is believed best for Americans to avoid certain countries in the interests of safety. It also releases Public Announcements of more short-term hazards, such as terrorist threats or political coups, that may endanger American travelers; these include an expiration date when the announcement need no longer be heeded. The department also makes available Consular Information Sheets for all countries, which may discuss safety conditions in that country not severe enough to require a travel warning. Current information can be found at <http://travel.state.gov/travel/cis_pa_tw/tw/tw_17 64.html> or by phone at 1-202-647-5225.

Travel Warnings were in effect on 1 Jul 2005 for the following: Afghanistan, Algeria, Bosnia and Herzegovina, Burundi, the Central African Republic, Colombia, the Democratic Republic of the Congo, Côte d'Ivoire, Haiti, Indonesia, Iran, Iraq, Israel (including the West Bank and Gaza Strip), Kenya, Kyrgyzstan, Lebanon, Liberia, Libya, Nepal, Nigeria, Pakistan, the Philippines, Saudi Arabia, Somalia, The Sudan, Uzbekistan, Yemen, and Zimbabwe.

Public Announcements in effect on the same day and set to expire on various dates in July–December included advisories for Central Asia, Chad, East Africa, Egypt, Ethiopia, Guatemala, Kuwait, Laos, Libya, Malaysia, Mexico, the Middle East and North Africa, Myanmar, Russia, Tajikistan, and Tunisia, as well as a worldwide caution.

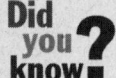

Did you know? According to the US mint, the only US coin that is identified by reference to its metal content is the nickel. The nickel coin, however, contains only 25% nickel; the rest is made up of copper.

Employment

US Employment by Gender and Occupation

Numbers may not add up to totals due to rounding. Source: US Bureau of Labor Statistics.

OCCUPATION	WORKERS 16 YEARS AND OLDER (NUMBERS IN '000)					
	TOTAL		MEN		WOMEN	
	2003	2004	2003	2004	2003	2004
management, professional, and related occupations	47,929	48,532	23,735	24,136	24,194	24,396
management, business, and financial operations occupations	19,934	20,235	11,534	11,718	8,400	8,517
management occupations	14,468	14,555	9,094	9,210	5,374	5,344
business and financial operations occupations	5,465	5,680	2,440	2,508	3,026	3,172
professional and related occupations	27,995	28,297	12,201	12,418	15,794	15,879
computer and mathematical occupations	3,122	3,140	2,223	2,292	900	848
architecture and engineering occupations	2,727	2,760	2,343	2,380	384	380
life, physical, and social science occupations	1,375	1,365	783	777	592	588
community and social services occupations	2,184	2,170	862	845	1,323	1,325
legal occupations	1,508	1,554	811	795	697	759
education, training, and library occupations	7,768	7,900	2,038	2,104	5,730	5,796
arts, design, entertainment, sports, and media occupations	2,663	2,687	1,395	1,425	1,267	1,262
health care practitioner and technical occupations	6,648	6,721	1,746	1,799	4,902	4,922
service occupations	22,086	22,720	9,460	9,826	12,626	12,894
health care support occupations	2,926	2,921	311	311	2,616	2,609
protective service occupations	2,727	2,847	2,164	2,230	563	616
food preparation and serving-related occupations	7,254	7,279	3,151	3,196	4,104	4,084
building and grounds cleaning and maintenance occupations	4,947	5,185	2,920	3,085	2,027	2,100
personal care and service occupations	4,232	4,488	915	1,004	3,316	3,484
sales and office occupations	35,496	35,464	12,851	12,805	22,645	22,660
sales and related occupations	15,960	15,983	8,137	8,105	7,823	7,878
office and administrative support occupations	19,536	19,481	4,714	4,700	14,823	14,781
natural resources, construction, and maintenance occupations	14,205	14,582	13,541	13,930	665	652
farming, fishing, and forestry occupations	1,050	991	819	786	231	204
construction and extraction occupations	8,114	8,522	7,891	8,306	223	216
installation, maintenance, and repair occupations	5,041	5,069	4,830	4,838	211	231
production, transportation, and material moving occupations	18,020	17,954	13,745	13,827	4,274	4,126
production occupations	9,700	9,462	6,696	6,587	3,004	2,875
transportation and material moving occupations	8,320	8,491	7,049	7,240	1,270	1,251
total	137,736	139,252	73,332	74,524	64,404	64,728

US Workers Earning the Minimum Wage

This table refers to wage and salary workers who are paid hourly rates. It excludes the incorporated self-employed. The prevailing federal minimum wage was $5.15/hour in 2004. Workers earning less than $5.15/hour may be working in jobs that are exempted from the minimum wage provision of the Fair Labor Standards Act. Numbers in thousands ('000). Source: US Bureau of Labor Statistics.

WORKER CHARACTERISTICS	TOTAL NUMBER OF WORKERS	BELOW $5.15/HR	AT $5.15/HR	TOTAL NUMBER OF WORKERS AT OR BELOW $5.15/HR NUMBER	%
age					
16–24 years	16,174	750	272	1,021	6.3
25 years and over	57,765	733	249	982	1.7
total (16 years and over)	73,939	1,483	520	2,003	2.7
men					
16–24 years	8,305	239	127	366	4.4
25 years and over	28,500	231	83	314	1.1
16 years and over	36,806	470	210	680	1.8
women					
16–24 years	7,869	510	145	655	8.3
25 years and over	29,265	502	166	668	2.3
16 years and over	37,133	1,013	310	1,323	3.6
race and Hispanic or Latino ethnicity					
white (16 years and over)[1]	59,877	1,286	395	1,681	2.8
black (16 years and over)[1]	9,417	128	99	228	2.4
Asian (16 years and over)[1]	2,672	30	8	38	1.4
Hispanic or Latino (16 years and over)	12,073	168	82	250	2.1
full- and part-time workers[2]					
full-time	55,739	583	177	760	1.4
part-time	18,046	897	343	1,240	6.9

[1]Data for racial groups other than those listed are not included. Hispanics may be of any race and are included in both white and black population groups. For these reasons, data for the race/ethnic group category will not add up to total. [2]Full- and part-time workers are distinguished by the number of hours worked. These data do not add up to total because of a small number of multiple jobholders whose status on the principal job is unknown.

Comparative Hourly Compensation Costs

The table shows private-industry employer compensation costs per hour worked by an employee in March 2005. Sums may not add to totals due to rounding. Source: US Bureau of Labor Statistics.

COMPENSATION	ALL WORKERS COST ($)	(%)	GOODS-PRODUCING WORKERS[1] COST ($)	(%)	SERVICE WORKERS[2] COST ($)	(%)
wages and salaries	17.15	71	18.66	65.5	16.78	72.6
paid leave	1.54	6.4	1.72	6.0	1.5	6.5
vacation	0.76	3.2	0.89	3.1	0.73	3.2
holiday	0.53	2.2	0.63	2.2	0.51	2.2
sick	0.19	0.8	0.13	0.5	0.2	0.9
other	0.06	0.3	0.07	0.3	0.06	0.3
supplemental pay	0.68	2.8	1.24	4.4	0.54	2.3
premium[3]	0.24	1.0	0.59	2.1	0.16	0.7
shift differentials	0.06	0.2	0.08	0.3	0.05	0.2
nonproduction bonuses	0.38	1.6	0.57	2.0	0.33	1.4
insurance	1.76	7.3	2.45	8.6	1.59	6.9
life	0.04	0.2	0.06	0.2	0.04	0.2
health	1.64	6.8	2.28	8.0	1.48	6.4
short-term disability	0.05	0.2	0.08	0.3	0.04	0.2
long-term disability	0.03	0.1	0.03	0.1	0.03	0.1
retirement and savings	0.9	3.7	1.59	5.6	0.73	3.1
defined benefit	0.45	1.9	1.08	3.8	0.3	1.3
defined contribution	0.45	1.8	0.51	1.8	0.43	1.9

Comparative Hourly Compensation Costs (continued)

COMPENSATION	ALL WORKERS		GOODS-PRODUCING WORKERS[1]		SERVICE WORKERS[2]	
	COST ($)	(%)	COST ($)	(%)	COST ($)	(%)
legally required benefits	2.10	8.7	2.73	9.6	1.95	8.4
Social Security[4]	1.43	5.9	1.61	5.6	1.39	6.0
Old-Age, Survivors, and Disability Insurance (OASDI)	1.15	4.8	1.29	4.5	1.12	4.8
Medicare	0.28	1.2	0.31	1.1	0.28	1.2
federal unemployment insurance	0.03	0.1	0.03	0.1	0.03	0.1
state unemployment insurance	0.16	0.7	0.2	0.7	0.15	0.6
workers' compensation	0.48	2.0	0.89	3.1	0.37	1.6
other benefits[5]	0.04	0.2	0.08	0.3	0.03	0.1
total benefits	7.02	29.0	9.82	34.5	6.34	27.4
total compensation	24.17	100	28.48	100	23.11	100

[1]Includes mining, construction, and manufacturing. [2]Includes transportation, communication, and public utilities; wholesale and retail trade; finance, insurance, and real estate; and service industries. [3]Pay for overtime, weekends, and holidays. [4]The total employer cost for Social Security comprises an OASDI portion and a Medicare portion. [5]Includes severance pay and supplemental unemployment benefits.

Median Income by Educational and Social Variables

Table refers to people who worked full-time throughout the year and are 15 years and over as of March of the following year. Median income dollar amounts are not adjusted for inflation. N/A means not available.
Source: US Census Bureau.

	median income ($) males				median income ($) females			
	1980	1990	2000	2003	1980	1990	2000	2003
full-time workers	19,173	28,979	38,891	41,503	11,591	20,591	29,123	31,653
educational level[1]								
less than 9th grade	N/A	10,319	14,131	15,461	N/A	6,268	8,546	9,296
9th to 12th grade (no diploma)	N/A	14,736	18,915	18,990	N/A	7,055	10,063	10,786
high school graduate	N/A	21,546	27,480	28,763	N/A	10,818	15,153	15,962
some college, no degree	N/A	26,591	33,319	35,073	N/A	13,963	20,166	21,007
associate degree	N/A	29,358	38,026	39,015	N/A	17,364	23,124	24,808
bachelor's degree	N/A	36,067	49,080	50,916	N/A	20,967	30,418	31,309
master's degree	N/A	43,125	59,732	61,698	N/A	29,747	40,619	41,334
professional degree	N/A	63,741	83,701	88,530	N/A	34,064	46,084	48,536
doctorate degree	N/A	51,845	71,271	73,853	N/A	37,242	51,460	53,003
race and origin[2,3]								
white	13,328	21,170	29,797	30,732	4,947	10,317	16,079	17,422
white (non-Hispanic)	13,681	21,958	31,508	32,331	4,980	10,581	16,665	18,301
black	8,009	12,868	21,343	21,986	4,580	8,328	15,881	16,581
Hispanic origin	9,659	13,470	19,498	21,053	4,405	7,532	12,248	13,642
age[2]								
15 to 24 years	4,597	6,319	9,546	9,961	3,124	4,902	7,360	7,435
25 to 34 years	15,580	21,393	30,254	30,562	6,973	12,589	21,049	21,992
35 to 44 years	20,037	29,773	37,922	39,195	6,465	14,504	22,077	23,472
45 to 54 years	19,974	31,007	41,039	42,079	6,403	14,230	23,732	25,866
55 to 64 years	15,914	24,804	34,189	38,915	4,926	9,400	16,920	20,368
65 years and over	7,339	14,183	19,411	20,363	4,226	8,044	11,023	11,845
all workers over age 14	12,530	20,293	28,343	29,931	4,920	10,070	16,063	17,259

[1]The income figures for the various educational levels are for workers 25 years old and over. Before 1991, the level of education categories used by the US Census Bureau differed from the categories presented in this table. Because of this, the 1980 figures for the median income by educational level are not completely comparable with the figures for later years. The figures presented in the 1990 column for educational levels are actually for 1991, the first year the educational categories listed in this table were used by the US Census Bureau. [2]Figures for the 1980 sections covering "race and origin" and "age" are for civilian workers only. [3]Hispanic people may be of any race.

The 20 US Metropolitan Areas with the Highest Average Annual Salaries

Includes workers covered by two programs, Unemployment Insurance and Unemployment Compensation for Federal Employees. A minus sign indicates a decrease in the average annual salary. Source: US Bureau of Labor Statistics.

METROPOLITAN AREA	ANNUAL SALARY ($) 2001	ANNUAL SALARY ($) 2002	SALARY CHANGE (%)	METROPOLITAN AREA	ANNUAL SALARY ($) 2001	ANNUAL SALARY ($) 2002	SALARY CHANGE (%)
San Jose, CA	65,931	63,056	-4.4	Seattle-Bellevue-Everett, WA	45,299	46,093	1.8
New York, NY	59,097	57,708	-2.4	Boston, MA[4]	45,766	45,685	-0.2
San Francisco, CA	59,654	56,602	-5.1	Bergen-Passaic, NJ	44,701	45,185	1.1
New Haven, CT[1]	52,198	51,170	-2.0	Hartford, CT	43,880	44,387	1.2
Middlesex, NJ[2]	49,950	50,457	1.0	Boulder-Longmont, CO	44,310	44,037	-0.6
Jersey City, NJ	47,638	49,562	4.0	Wilmington-Newark, DE-MD[5]	42,177	43,401	2.9
Newark, NJ	47,715	48,781	2.2	Chicago, IL	42,685	43,239	1.3
Washington, DC[3]	47,589	48,430	1.8	Detroit, MI	42,704	43,224	1.2
Trenton, NJ	46,831	47,969	2.4	Dallas, TX	42,706	43,000	0.7
Oakland, CA	45,920	46,877	2.1	Houston, TX	42,784	42,712	-0.2

[1]New Haven area includes Bridgeport, Stamford, Waterbury, and Danbury. [2]Middlesex area includes Somerset and Hunterdon. [3]Washington DC area includes areas in Maryland, Virginia, and West Virginia. [4]Boston area includes Worcester, Lawrence, Lowell, and Brockton. [5]Wilmington-Newark area includes parts of Maryland.

US Federal Minimum Wage Rates

The table shows the actual minimum wage for the year in question (since 1950) and the value of that minimum wage adjusted for inflation in the year 2005. Source: US Bureau of Labor Statistics.

YEAR	minimum wage DOLLARS	minimum wage 2005 DOLLARS	YEAR	minimum wage DOLLARS	minimum wage 2005 DOLLARS	YEAR	minimum wage DOLLARS	minimum wage 2005 DOLLARS
1950	0.75	6.05	1969	1.60	8.48	1988	3.35	5.50
1951	0.75	5.61	1970	1.60	8.02	1989	3.35	5.25
1952	0.75	5.50	1971	1.60	7.68	1990	3.80	5.65
1953	0.75	5.46	1972	1.60	7.44	1991	4.25	6.07
1954	0.75	5.42	1973	1.60	7.01	1992	4.25	5.89
1955	0.75	5.44	1974	2.00	7.89	1993	4.25	5.72
1956	1.00	7.15	1975	2.10	7.59	1994	4.25	5.57
1957	1.00	6.92	1976	2.30	7.86	1995	4.25	5.42
1958	1.00	6.73	1977	2.30	7.38	1996	4.75	5.89
1959	1.00	6.68	1978	2.65	7.90	1997	5.15	6.24
1960	1.00	6.57	1979	2.90	7.77	1998	5.15	6.14
1961	1.15	7.48	1980	3.10	7.31	1999	5.15	6.01
1962	1.15	7.40	1981	3.35	7.16	2000	5.15	5.81
1963	1.25	7.94	1982	3.35	6.75	2001	5.15	5.65
1964	1.25	7.84	1983	3.35	6.54	2002	5.15	5.57
1965	1.25	7.71	1984	3.35	6.27	2003	5.15	5.44
1966	1.25	7.50	1985	3.35	6.05	2004	5.15	5.30
1967	1.40	8.15	1986	3.35	5.94	2005	5.15	5.15
1968	1.60	8.94	1987	3.35	5.73			

US Civilian Federal Employment

Sources: US Office of Personnel Management; Statistical Abstract of the United States (2004–2005).

AGENCIES[1]	1970	1980	1990	2000	2003
legislative branch	29,939	39,710	37,495	31,157	31,297
judicial branch	6,879	15,178	23,605	32,186	34,472
departments of the executive branch	1,772,363	1,716,970	2,065,542	1,592,200	1,687,158
State	40,042	23,497	25,288	27,983	31,402
Treasury	90,683	124,663	158,655	143,508	134,302
Defense	1,169,173	960,116	1,034,152	676,268	669,096
Justice	40,075	56,327	83,932	125,970	115,259
Interior	71,671	77,357	77,679	73,818	74,818
Agriculture	114,309	129,139	122,594	104,466	107,204
Commerce	36,124	48,563	69,920	47,652	37,330
Labor	10,928	23,400	17,727	16,040	16,296
Health & Human Services (HHS)	110,186	155,662	123,959	62,605	67,240
Housing & Urban Development	15,046	16,964	13,596	10,319	10,660
Transportation	66,970	72,361	67,364	63,598	89,262
Energy	7,156	21,557	17,731	15,692	15,823
Education	0	7,364	4,771	4,734	4,593

US Civilian Federal Employment (continued)

AGENCIES[1]	1970	1980	1990	2000	2003
departments of the executive branch (continued)					
Veterans Affairs	169,241	228,285	248,174	219,547	226,171
independent agencies[2]	N/A	N/A	999,894	1,050,900	988,434
Board of Governors of the Federal Reserve System	N/A	N/A	1,525	1,644	1,761
Commodity Futures Trading Commission	N/A	N/A	542	574	534
Consumer Product Safety Commission	N/A	N/A	520	479	482
Environmental Protection Agency	0	14,715	17,123	18,036	18,126
Equal Employment Opportunity Commission	797	3,515	2,880	2,780	2,669
Federal Communications Commission	N/A	N/A	1,778	1,965	2,058
Federal Deposit Insurance Corporation	2,462	3,520	17,641	6,958	5,502
Federal Emergency Management Agency (FEMA)	0	3,427	3,137	4,813	6,191
Federal Trade Commission	N/A	N/A	988	1,019	1,076
General Services Administration[3]	37,661	37,654	20,277	14,334	13,615
National Aeronautics & Space Administration	30,674	23,714	24,872	18,819	18,908
National Archives & Records Administration	N/A	N/A	3,120	2,702	3,027
National Labor Relations Board	N/A	N/A	2,263	2,054	1,932
National Science Foundation	N/A	N/A	1,318	1,247	1,327
Nuclear Regulatory Commission	0	3,283	3,353	2,858	3,034
Office of Personnel Management	5,513	8,280	6,636	3,780	3,410
Peace Corps	N/A	N/A	1,178	1,065	1,118
Securities & Exchange Commission	N/A	N/A	2,302	2,955	3,132
Small Business Administration	4,397	5,804	5,128	4,150	3,824
Smithsonian Institution	2,547	4,403	5,092	5,065	5,133
Social Security Administration	N/A	N/A	N/A4	64,474	64,414
Tennessee Valley Authority	23,785	51,714	28,392	13,145	13,379
US Information Agency	10,156	8,138	8,555	2,436	2,362
US Postal Service	721,183	660,014	816,886	860,726	801,552
total, all agencies	**2,866,313**	**2,875,866**	**3,128,267**	**2,798,101**	**2,743,063**

N/A means not available. [1]*Includes other branches or agencies not shown separately. The Office of Homeland Security was created by an executive order of Pres. George W. Bush after the terrorist attacks of 11 Sep 2001. On 24 Jan 2003 the Department of Homeland Security, a cabinet-level agency within the executive branch of government, replaced the Office of Homeland Security. In the largest US governmental reorganization since World War II, the new department acquired 22 security-related agencies. Prior to this reorganization, the agencies had been administered by other governmental entities or, in FEMA's case, had been an independent agency.* [2]*The Defense Intelligence Agency was excluded as of November 1984, the National Imagery and Mapping Agency as of October 1996. Entries for 1990, 2000, and 2001 exclude the Central Intelligence Agency and the National Security Agency.* [3]*Entry for 1980 includes the National Archives and Records Administration, which became an independent agency in 1985.*

Older Americans in the Workforce

All numbers are in thousands ('000). Figures are from March 2002 and may not add up to totals due to rounding. Source: US Census Bureau.

	WORKFORCE BY AGE							
	55 AND OVER		55–59		60–64		65 AND OLDER	
GENDER AND OCCUPATION TYPE	NUMBER	%	NUMBER	%	NUMBER	%	NUMBER	%
men and women								
managerial and professional	6,561	33.4	3,590	36.3	1,731	32	1,241	28.6
technical, sales, and administrative support	5,668	28.9	2,720	27.5	1,608	29.7	1,340	30.9
service occupations	2,525	12.9	1,130	11.4	733	13.6	662	15.3
precision production, craft, and repair	1,820	9.3	1,044	10.6	488	9	288	6.6
operators, fabricators, and laborers	2,344	11.9	1,163	11.8	680	12.6	501	11.6
farming, forestry, and fishing	700	3.6	233	2.4	169	3.1	299	6.9
total	**19,618**	**100**	**9,878**	**100**	**5,408**	**100**	**4,331**	**100**
men								
managerial and professional	3,701	34.9	1,868	35.7	1,025	35.8	808	32.3
technical, sales, and administrative support	2,072	19.5	984	18.8	541	18.9	546	21.9
service occupations	938	8.9	387	7.4	273	9.5	278	11.1

Older Americans in the Workforce (continued)

GENDER AND OCCUPATION TYPE	WORKFORCE BY AGE							
	55 AND OVER		55–59		60–64		65 AND OLDER	
	NUMBER	%	NUMBER	%	NUMBER	%	NUMBER	%
men (continued)								
precision production, craft, and repair	1,633	15.4	956	18.3	427	14.9	250	10
operators, fabricators, and laborers	1,731	16.3	859	16.4	477	16.7	395	15.8
farming, forestry, and fishing	523	4.9	183	3.5	118	4.1	221	8.9
total	10,598	100	5,237	100	2,861	100	2,499	100
women								
managerial and professional	2,860	31.7	1,722	37.1	705	27.7	432	23.6
technical, sales, and administrative support	3,596	39.9	1,736	37.4	1,066	41.9	794	43.3
service occupations	1,587	17.6	743	16	461	18.1	384	20.9
precision production, craft, and repair	187	2.1	87	1.9	61	2.4	38	2.1
operators, fabricators, and laborers	613	6.8	304	6.5	203	8	107	5.8
farming, forestry, and fishing	177	2	49	1.1	51	2	78	4.2
total	9,020	100	4,641	100	2,547	100	1,832	100

Strikes and Lockouts in the US

Strikes and lockouts are referred to as work stoppages by the Bureau of Labor Statistics. This table covers work stoppages since 1950 involving 1,000 workers or more. The number of workers and stoppages are for stoppages begun during that year. The number of days out from work pertains to all strikes or lockouts in effect during the year, whether they began in that year or not. The heading for estimated working time includes all workers except those employed in private households, forestry, or fisheries. Source: US Bureau of Labor Statistics.

	strikes and lockouts		work time lost			strikes and lockouts		work time lost	
YEAR	NUMBER	WORKERS INVOLVED ('000)	DAYS LOST ('000)	% OF WORKING TIME	YEAR	NUMBER	WORKERS INVOLVED ('000)	DAYS LOST ('000)	% OF WORKING TIME
1950	424	1,698	30,390	0.26	1978	219	1,006	23,774	0.11
1951	415	1,462	15,070	0.12	1979	235	1,021	20,409	0.09
1952	470	2,746	48,820	0.38	1980	187	795	20,844	0.09
1953	437	1,623	18,130	0.14	1981	145	729	16,908	0.07
1954	265	1,075	16,630	0.13	1982	96	656	9,061	0.04
1955	363	2,055	21,180	0.16	1983	81	909	17,461	0.08
1956	287	1,370	26,840	0.20	1984	62	376	8,499	0.04
1957	279	887	10,340	0.07	1985	54	324	7,079	0.03
1958	332	1,587	17,900	0.13	1986	69	533	11,861	0.05
1959	245	1,381	60,850	0.43	1987	46	174	4,481	0.02
1960	222	896	13,260	0.09	1988	40	118	4,381	0.02
1961	195	1,031	10,140	0.07	1989	51	452	16,996	0.07
1962	211	793	11,760	0.08	1990	44	185	5,926	0.02
1963	181	512	10,020	0.07	1991	40	392	4,584	0.02
1964	246	1,183	16,220	0.11	1992	35	364	3,989	0.01
1965	268	999	15,140	0.10	1993	35	182	3,981	0.01
1966	321	1,300	16,000	0.10	1994	45	322	5,021	0.02
1967	381	2,192	31,320	0.18	1995	31	192	5,771	0.02
1968	392	1,855	35,367	0.20	1996	37	273	4,889	0.02
1969	412	1,576	29,397	0.16	1997	29	339	4,497	0.01
1970	381	2,468	52,761	0.29	1998	34	387	5,116	0.02
1971	298	2,516	35,538	0.19	1999	17	73	1,996	0.01
1972	250	975	16,764	0.09	2000	39	394	20,419	0.06
1973	317	1,400	16,260	0.08	2001	29	99	1,151	0.00
1974	424	1,796	31,809	0.16	2002	19	46	660	0.00
1975	235	965	17,563	0.09	2003	14	129	4,091	0.01
1976	231	1,519	23,962	0.12	2004	17	171	3,344	0.01
1977	298	1,212	21,258	0.10					

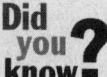

Did you know? In the Great Depression, during the decade of the 1930's, unemployment in the US averaged over 18%, and in the worst year, 1933, it topped 25%. Only in 1941 did the rate fall to 10%, and the US has not had double-digit unemployment in any year since.

US Trade Union Membership

Numbers are in thousands ('000). N/A means not available. Source: US Bureau of Labor Statistics.

YEAR	NUMBER OF UNION MEMBERS	% OF TOTAL LABOR FORCE	YEAR	NUMBER OF UNION MEMBERS	% OF TOTAL LABOR FORCE	YEAR	NUMBER OF UNION MEMBERS	% OF TOTAL LABOR FORCE
1900[1]	791	N/A	1940	8,717	26.9	1980	20,095	23.0
1905	1,918	N/A	1945	14,322	35.5	1985	16,996	18.0
1910	2,116	N/A	1950	14,300[3]	31.5	1990	16,740	16.1
1915	2,560	N/A	1955	16,802	33.2	1995	16,360	14.9
1920	5,034	N/A	1960	17,049	31.4	2000	16,258	13.5
1925	3,566	N/A	1965	17,299	28.4	2002	16,145	13.3
1930[2]	3,401	11.6	1970	19,381	27.4	2003	15,776	12.9
1935	3,584	13.2	1977[4]	19,335	23.8	2004	15,472	12.5

[1]Data from 1900 to 1925 include Canadian members whose union headquarters were in the US.   [2]Agricultural workers were not included as part of the total labor force for the years from 1930 to 1970.   [3]Rounded to nearest hundred thousand.   [4]Data for 1975 were not available. Data for 1977 on include only employed union members.

US Unemployment Rates

Unemployment rates of the civilian labor force 16 years and older. Source: US Bureau of Labor Statistics.

YEAR	UNEMPLOYMENT RATE (%)	YEAR	UNEMPLOYMENT RATE (%)	YEAR	UNEMPLOYMENT RATE (%)	YEAR	UNEMPLOYMENT RATE (%)
1947	3.9	1962	5.5	1977	7.1	1992	7.5
1948	3.8	1963	5.7	1978	6.1	1993	6.9
1949	5.9	1964	5.2	1979	5.8	1994	6.1
1950	5.3	1965	4.5	1980	7.1	1995	5.6
1951	3.3	1966	3.8	1981	7.6	1996	5.4
1952	3.0	1967	3.8	1982	9.7	1997	4.9
1953	2.9	1968	3.6	1983	9.6	1998	4.5
1954	5.5	1969	3.5	1984	7.5	1999	4.2
1955	4.4	1970	4.9	1985	7.2	2000	4.0
1956	4.1	1971	5.9	1986	7.0	2001	4.7
1957	4.3	1972	5.6	1987	6.2	2002	5.8
1958	6.8	1973	4.9	1988	5.5	2003	6.0
1959	5.5	1974	5.6	1989	5.3	2004	5.5
1960	5.5	1975	8.5	1990	5.6		
1961	6.7	1976	7.7	1991	6.8		

Social Characteristics of the Unemployed in the US

Unemployment as a % of the civilian labor force. N/A means not available. Source: US Bureau of Labor Statistics.

SOCIAL CHARACTERISTICS	UNEMPLOYMENT RATES BY YEAR (%)									
	1975	1980	1985	1990	1995	2000	2001	2002	2003	2004
age (both sexes)										
16–19[3]	19.9	17.8	18.6	15.5	17.3	13.1	14.7	16.5	17.4	17.0
25 and over	6.0	5.1	5.6	4.4	4.3	3.0	3.7	4.6	5.0	4.3
sex (20 years and older)										
men[3]	6.8	5.9	6.2	5.0	4.8	3.3	4.2	5.3	5.7	5.0
women[3]	8.0	6.4	6.6	4.9	4.9	3.6	4.1	5.1	5.1	4.9
race/ethnicity										
white[3]	7.8	6.3	6.2	4.8	4.9	3.5	4.2	5.1	5.2	4.8
black[3]	14.8	14.3	15.1	11.4	10.4	7.6	8.6	10.2	10.8	10.4
Hispanic[1, 3]	12.2	10.1	10.5	8.2	9.3	5.7	6.6	7.5	7.7	7.0
family										
women maintaining families	10.0	9.2	10.4	8.3	8.0	5.9	6.6	N/A	N/A	N/A
married men, spouse present	5.1	4.2	4.3	3.4	3.3	2.0	2.7	3.6	3.8	3.1[4]
overall unemployment[3]	8.5	7.1	7.2	5.6	5.6	4.0	4.7	5.8	6.0	5.5

[1]Hispanics may be of any race and are included in both the white and black racial categories in this table.   [2]25 and over (2004): quarterly average.   [3]2003 and 2004 figures are averages of monthly figures of the given year.   [4]Average of June–December 2004 figures.

US Unemployment by Occupation

Unemployment rates are for the civilian noninstitutional population aged 16 years and older. Rates represent unemployment as a percent of the labor force for each occupational group. The unemployment rate totals include people without previous work experience and those whose last job was in the military. 2004 data reflect revised population controls used in the survey. Source: US Bureau of Labor Statistics.

	THOUSANDS OF PERSONS		TOTAL (%)	
OCCUPATION	2003	2004	2003	2004
Management, professional, and related occupations	**1,556**	**1,346**	**3.1**	**2.7**
Management, business, and financial operations occupations	627	544	3.1	2.6
Management occupations	430	369	2.9	2.5
Business and financial operations occupations	198	175	3.5	3.0
Professional and related occupations	929	801	3.2	2.8
Computer and mathematical occupations	181	136	5.5	4.2
Architecture and engineering occupations	124	80	4.4	2.8
Life, physical, and social science occupations	48	35	3.3	2.5
Community and social services occupations	57	65	2.5	2.9
Legal occupations	35	31	2.3	1.9
Education, training, and library occupations	225	207	2.8	2.5
Arts, design, entertainment, sports, and media occupations	171	157	6.0	5.5
Health care practitioner and technical occupations	88	90	1.3	1.3
Service occupations	**1,681**	**1,617**	**7.1**	**6.6**
Health care support occupations	171	169	5.5	5.5
Protective service occupations	129	113	4.5	3.8
Food preparation and serving related occupations	683	656	8.6	8.3
Building and grounds cleaning and maintenance occupations	447	421	8.3	7.5
Personal care and service occupations	250	257	5.6	5.4
Sales and office occupations	**2,070**	**1,937**	**5.5**	**5.2**
Sales and related occupations	995	912	5.9	5.4
Office and administrative support occupations	1,076	1,025	5.2	5.0
Natural resources, construction, and maintenance occupations	**1,244**	**1,440**	**8.1**	**7.3**
Farming, fishing, and forestry occupations	136	132	11.4	11.8
Construction and extraction occupations	814	786	9.1	8.4
Installation, maintenance, and repair occupations	295	222	5.5	4.2
Production, transportation, and material moving occupations	**1,555**	**1,393**	**7.9**	**7.2**
Production occupations	807	714	7.7	7.0
Transportation and material moving occupations	748	679	8.2	7.4
Total, 16 years and over	**8,774**	**8,149**	**6.0**	**5.5**

Occupational Illnesses and Injuries in the US

This table displays the number of nonfatal work injuries and illnesses recorded in 2002. The injuries and illnesses resulted in days away from work in the private industries listed. Numbers may not add to totals because of rounding and nonclassifiable responses. Numbers are in thousands ('000). N/A means not available. Source: US Bureau of Labor Statistics.

		GOODS-PRODUCING INDUSTRIES			
CHARACTERISTIC	PRIVATE INDUSTRY[1]	AGRICULTURE, FORESTRY, FISHING[1]	MINING[2]	CONSTRUCTION	MANU-FACTURING
injury or illness					
sprains, strains	617.2	10.5	4.5	60.3	105.5
bruises, contusions	127	2.4	1.2	11.3	23.5
cuts, lacerations	110.2	2.9	0.7	17.7	25.1
fractures	99.2	2.9	1.8	17.4	19.6
heat burns	21.5	0.1	0.1	1.7	4.8
carpal tunnel syndrome	22.6	0.2	—[3]	0.9	9
tendinitis	9.3	0.3	—[3]	0.8	3
chemical burns	8.3	0.3	0.1	0.6	2.6
amputations	8.8	0.4	0.2	0.9	4.2
multiple traumatic injuries	52.5	1.5	0.5	6.5	10.2
body part affected by injury or illness					
head	90.2	2.8	0.7	11.3	20.3
eye	42.3	1.6	0.3	6.3	12.4
neck	22.9	0.5	0.2	2.2	3.7
trunk	522.1	10	4.1	54.3	94.7
shoulder	83.9	1.7	0.6	7.9	18.6
back	345.3	6.2	2.5	34.7	55.7

Occupational Illnesses and Injuries in the US (continued)

CHARACTERISTIC	PRIVATE INDUSTRY[1]	GOODS-PRODUCING INDUSTRIES			
		AGRICULTURE, FORESTRY, FISHING[1]	MINING[2]	CONSTRUCTION	MANU-FACTURING
body part affected by injury or illness (continued)					
upper extremities	328.3	7.2	2.5	40	88.5
wrist	69.2	1.1	0.5	5.8	19
hand, except finger	55.9	1.5	0.3	7.7	14.6
finger	121.6	2.6	1.3	16.7	36.5
lower extremities	304.5	7	2.8	39.5	49.4
knee	113	2.2	1	14.9	18.7
foot, except toe	46.2	1.1	0.4	6.2	8.2
toe	14.5	0.3	—[3]	2.2	2.7
body systems	19.9	0.7	0.1	1.3	3.2
multiple parts	139.4	2.8	1	13.8	18.5
source of injury or illness					
chemicals and chemical products	20.7	0.8	0.8	1.2	5.6
containers	193.1	2.8	0.6	8.6	35
furniture and fixtures	52.4	0.3	—[3]	2.7	7.7
machinery	92.6	1.9	1.4	10.2	34.3
parts and materials	147.6	2.2	2.3	37.5	49.1
worker motion or position	220.8	4.4	0.6	20.7	54
floors, walkways, ground surfaces	255.5	5.4	1.9	33.6	32
tools, instruments, and equipment	93.2	2.5	0.9	18.1	19.2
vehicles	118.6	3.1	0.6	9.8	13.6
health care patient	70	N/A	N/A	N/A	N/A
exposure or event leading to injury or illness					
contact with objects and equipment	380.5	9.5	4.8	57.4	95.5
struck by object	191.6	5.2	2.8	32.3	41.1
struck against object	99.9	2	0.8	12.3	20.8
caught in equipment or object	62.6	1.8	1.1	7	26.2
fall to lower level	86.9	2.4	0.9	22.4	10
fall on same level	176	2.9	1	12.3	23.9
slip, trip, loss of balance—without fall	48.1	0.8	0.2	4.7	7.7
overexertion	381	5	3.1	33.8	68.8
overexertion in lifting	208.3	2.7	1.1	17.9	35.6
repetitive motion	58.6	0.7	—[3]	2.9	23.6
exposure to harmful substances	60	1.9	0.4	4.3	14
transportation accidents	63	1.8	0.3	6.7	5.8
fires and explosions	2.7	0.1	0.1	0.4	0.6
assaults and violent acts by person	18.1	0.1	N/A	0.2	0.4
total cases	**1,436.2**	**31.5**	**11.4**	**163.6**	**280.0**

CHARACTERISTIC	SERVICE-PRODUCING INDUSTRIES				
	TRANSPORTATION AND PUBLIC UTILITIES[2]	WHOLE-SALE TRADE	RETAIL TRADE	FINANCE, INSURANCE, REAL ESTATE	SERVICES
injury or illness					
sprains, strains	81.9	51.4	108.4	13.3	181.3
bruises, contusions	15.7	10.2	27.4	2.8	32.4
cuts, lacerations	6.6	7.6	30.9	2	16.8
fractures	10.5	7.7	16.5	3	19.9
heat burns	0.7	0.7	8.2	0.2	4.9
carpal tunnel syndrome	1.8	1.2	3	1.9	4.6
tendinitis	0.8	0.5	1.2	0.5	2.1
chemical burns	0.6	0.5	1.2	0.2	2.2
amputations	0.8	0.7	0.7	0.1	0.7
multiple traumatic injuries	7.2	4.3	7.4	1.4	13.5
body part affected by injury or illness					
head	9.2	6	16.3	1.6	22
eye	3.5	2.6	6.8	0.5	8.4
neck	3.3	2.4	3.7	0.4	6.4
trunk	67.1	42.2	93.8	11.1	144.7
shoulder	12.4	6.4	13.3	1.5	21.5
back	42.6	28.3	64.1	7.7	103.6

Occupational Illnesses and Injuries in the US (continued)

| | SERVICE-PRODUCING INDUSTRIES | | | | |
CHARACTERISTIC	TRANSPORTATION AND PUBLIC UTILITIES[2]	WHOLE-SALE TRADE	RETAIL TRADE	FINANCE, INSURANCE, REAL ESTATE	SERVICES
body part affected by injury or illness (continued)					
upper extremities	27.3	21.1	66	8.6	67
wrist	6.4	4	12	3.3	17.1
hand, except finger	4.8	3.6	11.4	1.1	10.9
finger	7.9	8.3	26.9	2.1	19.2
lower extremities	39.8	25.2	55.6	8.1	77.2
knee	14.7	8.3	18.8	3	31.4
foot, except toe	6.1	4.3	9.6	1.1	9.2
toe	1.3	1.2	3.9	0.3	2.5
body systems	2.1	0.7	2.8	1.7	7.3
multiple parts	19	10.3	23.5	5	45
source of injury or illness					
chemicals and chemical products	1.4	1.1	3.3	0.5	5.8
containers	30.4	24.9	59.5	3.3	28
furniture and fixtures	3.4	3	15	2	18.3
machinery	3.9	6.7	17.4	1.8	14.9
parts and materials	14.6	12.4	15.4	1.7	12.4
worker motion or position	26.9	14.4	35.7	8.4	55.7
floors, walkways, ground surfaces	30	17.4	51.4	9	74.9
tools, instruments, and equipment	7.7	4.9	18.4	2	19.4
vehicles	31.3	15.5	16.6	2.8	25.2
health care patient	1.4	0.1	N/A	0.2	68.2
exposure or event leading to injury or illness					
contact with objects and equipment	35.7	29.4	74.6	6.3	67.3
struck by object	17.1	14.6	41.5	3	34
struck against object	11.3	7.6	20.6	2.6	21.9
caught in equipment or object	4.2	5.5	8.8	0.5	7.7
fall to lower level	13.1	6.8	11.8	2.8	16.8
fall on same level	17.4	10.9	42.5	6.3	58.9
slip, trip, loss of balance—without fall	6.4	3.2	9.9	1.3	13.9
overexertion	46.2	32.5	69.7	7.3	114.7
overexertion in lifting	23.3	19.8	45.8	4.2	57.8
repetitive motion	5	2.6	8.4	3.6	11.8
exposure to harmful substances	4.9	2.4	13	1.4	17.7
transportation accidents	16.2	8.7	6.6	2	14.8
fires and explosions	0.2	0.2	0.8	N/A	0.3
assaults and violent acts by person	0.7	0.3	2.4	0.4	13.6
total cases	**168.6**	**108.8**	**263.4**	**36.7**	**372.2**

[1]Excludes farms with fewer than 11 employees. [2]The Mine Safety and Health Administration provided data for mining; the Federal Railroad Administration provided railroad transportation data. The mining category excludes independent mining contractors. [3]Fewer than 50 cases.

US Work-Related Fatalities by Cause

Totals for major categories may include some smaller categories not listed in the table. Percentages may not add up to totals because of rounding. Source: US Bureau of Labor Statistics.

| | 1998–2002 | 2003 | |
CAUSE OF FATALITY	NUMBER (AVG.)	NUMBER	(%)
transportation incidents	**2,549**	**2,357**	**42**
highway	1,417	1,350	24
collision between vehicles, mobile equipment	696	648	12
moving in same direction	136	135	2
moving in opposite directions, oncoming	249	269	5
moving in intersection	148	123	2
vehicle struck stationary object or equipment	308	341	6
noncollision	367	321	6
jackknifed or overturned—no collision	303	252	5
nonhighway (farm, industrial premises)	358	347	6
overturned	192	186	3

US Work-Related Fatalities by Cause (continued)

CAUSE OF FATALITY	1998–2002 NUMBER (AVG.)	2003 NUMBER	(%)
transportation incidents (continued)			
aircraft	235	208	4
worker struck by a vehicle	380	336	6
water vehicle	92	68	1
rail vehicle	63	43	1
assaults and violent acts	910	901	16
homicides	659	631	11
shooting	519	487	9
stabbing	61	58	1
other, including bombing	N/A	N/A	N/A
self-inflicted injury	218	218	4
contact with objects and equipment	963	911	16
struck by object	547	530	10
struck by falling object	336	322	6
struck by flying object	55	58	1
caught in or compressed by equipment or objects	272	237	4
caught in running equipment or machinery	141	121	2
caught in or crushed in collapsing materials	126	126	2
falls	738	691	12
fall to lower level	651	601	11
fall from ladder	113	113	2
fall from roof	152	127	2
fall from scaffold, staging	91	85	2
fall on same level	65	69	1
exposure to harmful substances or environments	526	485	9
contact with electric current	289	246	4
contact with overhead power lines	130	107	2
contact with temperature extremes	45	42	1
exposure to caustic, noxious, or allergenic substances	102	121	2
inhalation of substance	50	65	1
oxygen deficiency	89	73	1
drowning, submersion	69	52	1
fires and explosions	190	198	4
total	5,896	5,559	100

Consumer Prices

US Consumer Price Index, 1913–2004

This table presents the annual change in the Consumer Price Index (CPI) since 1913. The CPI is used as an indicator of price changes in the goods and services purchased by US consumers. The information provided is based on the purchases of a specific group of urban consumers who serve as a sample population representing more than 80% of the total US population. Each annual CPI is compared with the average index level of 100, which is a base number that represents the average price level for the 36-month period covering the years 1982, 1983, and 1984. A minus sign indicates a decrease. Source: US Bureau of Labor Statistics.

YEAR	ANNUAL CPI	% ANNUAL CHANGE IN CPI	YEAR	ANNUAL CPI	% ANNUAL CHANGE IN CPI	YEAR	ANNUAL CPI	% ANNUAL CHANGE IN CPI
1913	9.9		1920	20.0	15.6	1927	17.4	-1.7
1914	10.0	1.0	1921	17.9	-10.5	1928	17.1	-1.7
1915	10.1	1.0	1922	16.8	-6.1	1929	17.1	0.0
1916	10.9	7.9	1923	17.1	1.8	1930	16.7	-2.3
1917	12.8	17.4	1924	17.1	0.0	1931	15.2	-9.0
1918	15.1	18.0	1925	17.5	2.3	1932	13.7	-9.9
1919	17.3	14.6	1926	17.7	1.1	1933	13.0	-5.1

US Consumer Price Index, 1913–2004 (continued)

YEAR	ANNUAL CPI	% ANNUAL CHANGE IN CPI	YEAR	ANNUAL CPI	% ANNUAL CHANGE IN CPI	YEAR	ANNUAL CPI	% ANNUAL CHANGE IN CPI
1934	13.4	3.1	1958	28.9	2.8	1982	96.5	6.2
1935	13.7	2.2	1959	29.1	0.7	1983	99.6	3.2
1936	13.9	1.5	1960	29.6	1.7	1984	103.9	4.3
1937	14.4	3.6	1961	29.9	1.0	1985	107.6	3.6
1939	13.9	-1.4	1962	30.2	1.0	1986	109.6	1.9
1938	14.1	-2.1	1963	30.6	1.3	1987	113.6	3.6
1940	14.0	0.7	1964	31.0	1.3	1988	118.3	4.1
1941	14.7	5.0	1965	31.5	1.6	1989	124.0	4.8
1942	16.3	10.9	1966	32.4	2.9	1990	130.7	5.4
1943	17.3	6.1	1967	33.4	3.1	1991	136.2	4.2
1944	17.6	1.7	1968	34.8	4.2	1992	140.3	3.0
1945	18.0	2.3	1969	36.7	5.5	1993	144.5	3.0
1946	19.5	8.3	1970	38.8	5.7	1994	148.2	2.6
1947	22.3	14.4	1971	40.5	4.4	1995	152.4	2.8
1948	24.1	8.1	1972	41.8	3.2	1996	156.9	3.0
1949	23.8	-1.2	1973	44.4	6.2	1997	160.5	2.3
1950	24.1	1.3	1974	49.3	11.0	1998	163.0	1.6
1951	26.0	7.9	1975	53.8	9.1	1999	166.6	2.2
1952	26.5	1.9	1976	56.9	5.8	2000	172.2	3.4
1953	26.7	0.8	1977	60.6	6.5	2001	177.1	2.8
1954	26.9	0.7	1978	65.2	7.6	2002	179.9	1.6
1955	26.8	-0.4	1979	72.6	11.3	2003	184.0	2.3
1956	27.2	1.5	1980	82.4	13.5	2004	188.9	2.7
1957	28.1	3.3	1981	90.9	10.3			

US Consumer Price Indexes by Item Group, 1975–2004

The information provided is based on the purchases of a specific group of urban consumers who serve as a sample population representing more than 80% of the total US population. Each annual CPI is compared with the average index level of 100, which is a base number that represents the average price level for the 36-month period covering the years 1982, 1983, and 1984. Source: US Bureau of Labor Statistics.

ITEM GROUP	CONSUMER PRICE INDEX								
	1975	1980	1985	1990	1995	2000	2002	2003	2004
all items	53.8	82.4	107.6	130.7	152.4	172.2	179.9	184.0	188.9
commodities	58.2	86.0	105.4	122.8	136.4	149.2	149.7	151.2	154.7
energy	42.1	86.0	101.6	102.1	105.2	124.6	121.7	136.5	151.4
food	59.8	86.8	105.6	132.4	148.4	167.8	176.2	180.0	186.2
shelter	48.8	81.0	109.8	140.0	165.7	193.4	208.1	213.1	218.8
transportation	50.1	83.1	106.4	120.5	139.1	153.3	152.9	157.6	163.1
medical care	47.5	74.9	113.5	162.8	220.5	260.8	285.6	297.1	310.1
apparel	72.5	90.9	105.0	124.1	132.0	129.6	124.0	120.9	120.4

ITEM GROUP	% CHANGE IN CPI[1]								
	1975	1980	1985	1990	1995	2000	2002	2003	2004
all items	9.1	13.5	3.6	5.4	2.8	3.4	2.4	2.3	2.7
commodities	8.8	12.3	2.1	5.2	1.9	3.3	-0.7	1.0	2.3
energy	10.5	30.9	0.7	8.3	0.6	16.9	-5.9	12.2	10.9
food	8.5	8.6	2.3	5.8	2.8	2.3	1.8	2.2	3.4
shelter	9.9	17.6	5.6	5.4	3.2	3.3	3.7	2.4	2.7
transportation	9.4	17.9	2.6	5.6	3.6	6.2	-0.9	3.1	3.5
medical care	12.0	11.0	6.3	9.0	4.5	4.1	4.7	4.0	4.4
apparel	4.5	7.1	2.8	4.6	-1.0	-1.3	-2.6	-2.5	-0.4

[1]Annual percent change from the preceding year.

Sample US Consumer Price Indexes by Region, 2003–2004

This table presents the regional annual averages of the Consumer Price Index (CPI) for 2004 and the percent change of those averages from 2003 to 2004. The information provided is based on the purchases of a specific group of urban consumers who serve as a sample population representing more than 80% of the total US population. Each annual CPI is compared with the average index level of 100, which is a base number that represents the average price level for the 36-month period covering the years 1982, 1983, and 1984. A minus sign indicates a decrease in price from 2003. Source: US Bureau of Labor Statistics.

Sample US Consumer Price Indexes by Region, 2003–2004 (continued)

	NORTHEAST		MIDWEST		SOUTH		WEST	
ITEM GROUP	2004 CPI	% CHANGE FROM 2003	2004 CPI	% CHANGE FROM 2003	2004 CPI	% CHANGE FROM 2003	2004 CPI	% CHANGE FROM 2003
all items	200.2	3.5	182.6	2.4	181.8	2.5	193.0	2.3
commodities	157.5	3.0	150.7	1.8	155.3	2.6	155.6	2.0
energy	150.3	11.1	150.3	11.3	144.2	11.5	167.9	9.4
food	188.4	3.6	180.1	2.9	184.2	3.6	192.1	3.5
shelter	251.5	4.1	209.0	2.1	193.2	2.4	222.6	2.2
transportation	163.9	3.7	162.8	3.5	160.1	3.9	166.3	3.0
medical care	329.9	4.5	306.9	5.2	299.9	3.9	309.8	4.3
apparel	120.9	1.6	114.8	-0.3	131.4	-1.6	111.7	-0.4

US Budget

US Governmental Spending, 1800–2004

Entries for the years prior to 1933 are based on the administrative budget concept rather than on the unified budget concept. For a discussion of the unified budget concept see <www.whitehouse.gov/omb/budget/fy2005/histint.html>. The figures are in thousands ('000). A minus sign indicates a deficit.

Source: US Office of Management and Budget.

YEAR[1]	FEDERAL INCOME	FEDERAL SPENDING	SURPLUS OR DEFICIT	YEAR[1]	FEDERAL INCOME	FEDERAL SPENDING	SURPLUS OR DEFICIT
1800	10,849	10,786	63	1842	19,976	25,206	-5,230
1801	12,935	9,395	3,541	1843	8,303	11,858	-3,555
1802	14,996	7,862	7,134	1844	29,321	22,338	6,984
1803	11,064	7,852	3,212	1845	29,970	22,937	7,033
1804	11,826	8,719	3,107	1846	29,700	27,767	1,933
1805	13,561	10,506	3,054	1847	26,496	57,281	-30,786
1806	15,560	9,804	5,756	1848	35,736	45,377	-9,641
1807	16,398	8,354	8,044	1849	31,208	45,052	-13,844
1808	17,061	9,932	7,128	1850	43,603	39,543	4,060
1809	7,773	10,281	-2,507	1851	52,559	47,709	4,850
1810	9,384	8,157	1,228	1852	49,847	44,195	5,652
1811	14,424	8,058	6,365	1853	61,587	48,184	13,403
1812	9,801	20,281	-10,480	1854	73,800	58,045	15,755
1813	14,340	31,682	-17,341	1855	65,351	59,743	5,608
1814	11,182	34,721	-23,539	1856	74,057	69,571	4,486
1815	15,729	32,708	-16,979	1857	68,965	67,796	1,170
1816	47,678	30,587	17,091	1858	46,655	74,185	-27,530
1817	33,099	21,844	11,255	1859	53,486	69,071	-15,585
1818	21,585	19,825	1,760	1860	56,065	63,131	-7,066
1819	24,603	21,464	3,140	1861	41,510	66,547	-25,037
1820	17,881	18,261	-380	1862	51,987	474,762	-422,774
1821	14,573	15,811	-1,237	1863	112,697	714,741	-602,043
1822	20,232	15,000	5,232	1864	264,627	865,323	-600,696
1823	20,541	14,707	5,834	1865	333,715	1,297,555	-963,841
1824	19,381	20,327	-945	1866	558,033	520,809	37,223
1825	21,841	15,857	5,984	1867	490,634	357,543	133,091
1826	25,260	17,036	8,225	1868	405,638	377,340	28,298
1827	22,966	16,139	6,827	1869	370,944	322,865	48,078
1828	24,764	16,395	8,369	1870	411,255	309,654	101,602
1829	24,828	15,203	9,624	1871	383,324	292,177	91,147
1830	24,844	15,143	9,701	1872	374,107	277,518	96,589
1831	28,527	15,248	13,279	1873	333,738	290,345	43,393
1832	31,866	17,289	14,577	1874	304,979	302,634	2,345
1833	33,948	23,018	10,931	1875	288,000	274,623	13,377
1834	21,792	18,628	3,164	1876	294,096	265,101	28,995
1835	35,430	17,573	17,857	1877	281,406	241,334	40,072
1836	50,827	30,868	19,959	1878	257,764	236,964	20,800
1837	24,954	37,243	-12,289	1879	273,827	266,948	6,879
1838	26,303	33,865	-7,562	1880	333,527	267,643	65,884
1839	31,483	26,899	4,584	1881	360,782	260,713	100,069
1840	19,480	24,318	-4,837	1882	403,525	257,981	145,544
1841	16,860	26,566	-9,706	1883	398,288	265,408	132,879

US Governmental Spending, 1800–2004 (continued)

YEAR[1]	FEDERAL INCOME	FEDERAL SPENDING	SURPLUS OR DEFICIT	YEAR[1]	FEDERAL INCOME	FEDERAL SPENDING	SURPLUS OR DEFICIT
1884	348,520	244,126	104,394	1945	45,159,000	92,712,000	-47,553,000
1885	323,691	260,227	63,464	1946	39,296,000	55,232,000	-15,936,000
1886	336,440	242,483	93,957	1947	38,514,000	34,496,000	4,018,000
1887	371,403	267,932	103,471	1948	41,560,000	29,764,000	11,796,000
1888	379,266	267,925	111,341	1949	39,415,000	38,835,000	580,000
1889	387,050	299,289	87,761	1950	39,443,000	42,562,000	-3,119,000
1890	403,081	318,041	85,040	1951	51,616,000	45,514,000	6,102,000
1891	392,612	365,774	26,839	1952	66,167,000	67,686,000	-1,519,000
1892	354,938	345,023	9,914	1953	69,608,000	76,101,000	-6,493,000
1893	385,820	383,478	2,342	1954	69,701,000	70,855,000	-1,154,000
1894	306,355	367,525	-61,170	1955	65,451,000	68,444,000	-2,993,000
1895	324,729	356,195	-31,466	1956	74,587,000	70,640,000	3,947,000
1896	338,142	352,179	-14,037	1957	79,990,000	76,578,000	3,412,000
1897	347,722	365,774	-18,052	1958	79,636,000	82,405,000	-2,769,000
1898	405,321	443,369	-38,047	1959	79,249,000	92,098,000	-12,849,000
1899	515,961	605,072	-89,112	1960	92,492,000	92,191,000	301,000
1900	567,241	520,861	46,380	1961	94,388,000	97,723,000	-3,335,000
1901	587,685	524,617	63,068	1962	99,676,000	106,821,000	-7,146,000
1902	562,478	485,234	77,244	1963	106,560,000	111,316,000	-4,756,000
1903	561,881	517,006	44,875	1964	112,613,000	118,528,000	-5,915,000
1904	541,087	583,660	-42,573	1965	116,817,000	118,228,000	-1,411,000
1905	544,275	567,279	-23,004	1966	130,835,000	134,532,000	-3,698,000
1906	594,984	570,202	24,782	1967	148,822,000	157,464,000	-8,643,000
1907	665,860	579,129	86,732	1968	152,973,000	178,134,000	-25,161,000
1908	601,862	659,196	-57,334	1969	186,882,000	183,640,000	3,242,000
1909	604,320	693,744	-89,423	1970	192,807,000	195,649,000	-2,842,000
1910	675,512	693,617	-18,105	1971	187,139,000	210,172,000	-23,033,000
1911	701,833	691,202	10,631	1972	207,309,000	230,681,000	-23,373,000
1912	692,609	689,881	2,728	1973	230,799,000	245,707,000	-14,908,000
1913	714,463	714,864	-401	1974	263,224,000	269,359,000	-6,135,000
1914	725,117	725,525	-408	1975	279,090,000	332,332,000	-53,242,000
1915	683,417	746,093	-62,676	1976	298,060,000	371,792,000	-73,732,000
1916	761,445	712,967	48,478	TQ	81,232,000	95,975,000	-14,744,000
1917	1,100,500	1,953,857	-853,357	1977	355,559,000	409,218,000	-53,659,000
1918	3,645,240	12,677,359	-9,032,120	1978	399,561,000	458,746,000	-59,185,000
1919	5,130,042	18,492,665	-13,362,623	1979	463,302,000	504,028,000	-40,726,000
1920	6,648,898	6,357,677	291,222	1980	517,112,000	590,941,000	-73,830,000
1921	5,570,790	5,061,785	509,005	1981	599,272,000	678,241,000	-78,968,000
1922	4,025,901	3,289,404	736,496	1982	617,766,000	745,743,000	-127,977,000
1923	3,852,795	3,140,287	712,508	1983	600,562,000	808,364,000	-207,802,000
1924	3,871,214	2,907,847	963,367	1984	666,486,000	851,853,000	-185,367,000
1925	3,640,805	2,923,762	717,043	1985	734,088,000	946,396,000	-212,308,000
1926	3,795,108	2,929,964	865,144	1986	769,215,000	990,430,000	-221,215,000
1927	4,012,794	2,857,429	1,155,365	1987	854,353,000	1,004,082,000	-149,728,000
1928	3,900,329	2,961,245	939,083	1988	909,303,000	1,064,455,000	-155,152,000
1929	3,861,589	3,127,199	734,391	1989	991,190,000	1,143,646,000	-152,456,000
1930	4,057,884	3,320,211	737,673	1990	1,031,969,000	1,253,165,000	-221,195,000
1931	3,115,557	3,577,434	-461,877	1991	1,055,041,000	1,324,369,000	-269,328,000
1932	1,923,892	4,659,182	-2,735,290	1992	1,091,279,000	1,381,655,000	-290,376,000
1933	1,996,844	4,598,496	-2,601,652	1993	1,154,401,000	1,409,489,000	-255,087,000
1934	2,955,000	6,541,000	-3,586,000	1994	1,258,627,000	1,461,877,000	-203,250,000
1935	3,609,000	6,412,000	-2,803,000	1995	1,351,830,000	1,515,802,000	-163,972,000
1936	3,923,000	8,228,000	-4,304,000	1996	1,453,062,000	1,560,535,000	-107,473,000
1937	5,387,000	7,580,000	-2,193,000	1997	1,579,292,000	1,601,250,000	-21,958,000
1938	6,751,000	6,840,000	-89,000	1998	1,721,798,000	1,652,585,000	69,213,000
1939	6,295,000	9,141,000	-2,846,000	1999	1,827,454,000	1,701,891,000	125,563,000
1940	6,548,000	9,468,000	-2,920,000	2000	2,025,218,000	1,788,773,000	236,445,000
1941	8,712,000	13,653,000	-4,941,000	2001	1,991,194,000	1,863,770,000	127,424,000
1942	14,634,000	35,137,000	-20,503,000	2002	1,853,173,000	2,010,970,000	-157,797,000
1943	24,001,000	78,555,000	-54,554,000	2003	1,782,342,000	2,157,637,000	-375,295,000
1944	43,747,000	91,304,000	-47,557,000	2004	1,880,071,000	2,292,215,000	-412,144,000

[1]The fiscal year ended on 31 December for the budgets from 1800 to 1842. It ended on 30 June for the budgets from 1844 through 1976 and on 30 September from fiscal year 1977. The budget figures for 1843 are for the period from 1 January to 30 June. The third quarter of 1976 was budgeted separately because of the change in the fiscal year calendar. It is referred to as the Transition Quarter (TQ).

US Public Debt

In order to fund governmental operations while the federal budget is running at a deficit, the Department of the Treasury borrows money by selling Treasury bills, US savings bonds, and other securities to the public. The money borrowed by the Treasury is re-ferred to as the public debt. A broader measure of the federal debt is known as the gross federal debt. It consists of the public debt plus money borrowed by federal agencies. The GDP is the gross domestic product. Source: US Office of Management and Budget.

END OF FISCAL YEAR	PUBLIC DEBT (IN $ MILLIONS)	% OF GDP	GROSS FEDERAL DEBT (IN $ MILLIONS)	% OF GDP	END OF FISCAL YEAR	PUBLIC DEBT (IN $ MILLIONS)	% OF GDP	GROSS FEDERAL DEBT (IN $ MILLIONS)	% OF GDP
1940	42,772	44.2	50,696	52.4	1980	711,923	26.1	909,041	33.3
1945	235,182	106.3	260,123	117.5	1985	1,507,260	36.4	1,817,423	43.9
1950	219,023	80.1	256,853	93.9	1990	2,411,558	42.0	3,206,290	55.9
1955	226,616	57.3	274,366	69.4	1995	3,604,378	49.2	4,920,586	67.2
1960	236,840	45.6	290,525	56.0	2000	3,409,804	35.1	5,628,700	58.0
1965	260,778	37.9	322,318	46.9	2002	3,540,395	34.1	6,198,401	59.8
1970	283,198	28.0	380,921	37.6	2003	3,913,607	36.1	6,760,014	62.4
1975	394,700	25.3	541,925	34.7	2004	4,295,544	37.2	7,354,673	63.7

Annual National Average Terms on Conventional Single-Family Mortgages, 1965–2004

Source: Federal Housing Finance Board Monthly Interest Rate Survey.

YEAR	CONTRACT INTEREST RATE (%)	INITIAL FEES AND CHARGES (%)	EFFECTIVE INTEREST RATE (%)	TERM TO MATURITY (YEARS)	MORTGAGE AMOUNT ($'000)	PURCHASE PRICE ($'000)	LOAN TO PRICE RATIO (%)
1965	5.83	0.53	5.92	22.6	16.4	22.5	73.0
1966	6.26	0.71	6.37	22.5	16.9	23.3	72.3
1967	6.38	0.77	6.50	23.1	18.3	25.1	72.9
1968	6.88	0.84	7.02	23.4	19.7	26.9	73.2
1969	7.67	0.89	7.82	23.5	21.5	29.9	71.9
1970	8.22	0.95	8.38	23.5	22.5	31.5	71.3
1971	7.56	0.80	7.69	24.7	24.2	32.8	74.0
1972	7.40	0.83	7.53	26.1	26.1	34.3	76.2
1973	7.80	1.01	7.97	24.0	24.6	33.7	74.8
1974	8.76	1.18	8.96	24.1	26.8	37.6	72.9
1975	8.92	1.28	9.13	24.9	29.7	41.2	73.7
1976	8.87	1.22	9.07	25.2	31.9	44.3	73.9
1977	8.82	1.22	9.02	26.3	36.3	49.6	75.0
1978	9.37	1.30	9.59	26.7	41.4	57.1	74.6
1979	10.59	1.50	10.85	27.4	48.2	67.7	73.5
1980	12.46	1.97	12.84	27.2	51.7	73.4	72.9
1981	14.39	2.39	14.91	26.4	53.7	76.3	73.1
1982	14.73	2.65	15.31	25.6	55.0	78.4	72.9
1983	12.26	2.39	12.73	26.0	59.9	83.1	74.5
1984	11.99	2.57	12.48	26.8	64.5	86.6	77.0
1985	11.17	2.51	11.64	25.9	70.2	96.1	75.8
1986	9.79	2.21	10.18	25.6	79.3	110.6	74.1
1987	8.95	2.08	9.30	26.8	89.1	121.8	75.2
1988	8.98	1.96	9.30	27.7	97.4	131.6	76.0
1989	9.81	1.87	10.13	27.7	104.5	142.8	74.8
1990	9.74	1.79	10.05	27.0	104.0	142.6	74.7
1991	9.07	1.58	9.34	26.5	106.3	146.7	74.4
1992	7.83	1.58	8.11	25.4	108.7	146.4	76.6
1993	6.93	1.20	7.13	25.5	107.0	143.1	77.2
1994	7.31	1.10	7.49	27.1	109.9	142.0	79.9
1995	7.69	0.97	7.85	27.4	110.4	142.8	79.9
1996	7.58	0.97	7.74	26.9	118.7	155.1	79.0
1997	7.52	0.98	7.68	27.5	126.6	164.5	79.4
1998	6.97	0.85	7.10	27.8	131.8	173.4	78.9
1999	7.14	0.74	7.25	28.2	139.3	184.2	78.5
2000	7.86	0.67	7.96	28.7	148.3	198.9	77.8
2001	6.94	0.53	7.03	27.6	155.7	215.5	76.2
2002	6.44	0.46	6.51	27.3	163.4	231.2	75.1
2003	5.67	0.37	5.73	26.8	167.9	243.4	73.5
2004	5.68	0.40	5.74	27.9	185.5	262.0	74.9

US Bankruptcy Filings, 1980–2004

This table shows the number of business and nonbusiness (consumer) bankruptcy filings in the US since 1980. Bankruptcy is intended give debtors a fresh start in managing their resources by cancelling many of their debts through a court order called a "discharge." It is also meant to give creditors a fair share of the money that the debtors can afford to pay back.

Businesses may file for bankruptcy under chapter 11 of the IRS Code. Chapter 11 offers protection from creditor demands to a business in debt so that its officers and managers have time to reorganize in

order to fulfill obligations to creditors. In some instances, creditors may receive dollar-for-dollar what the business owes them, plus interest. In others, the creditor may only receive pennies on the owed dollar.

Individuals may file for bankruptcy under either chapter 7 of the IRS Code (under which debtors may liquidate assets with the supervision of a trustee in order to receive a nearly immediate discharge of debts) or chapter 13 (under which the debtor enters into a payment plan to repay debt out of future earnings over a three-to-five-year period, with the oversight of a trustee). Source: American Bankruptcy Institute.

YEAR	TOTAL FILINGS	BUSINESS FILINGS	NONBUSINESS FILINGS	CONSUMER FILINGS AS A PERCENTAGE OF TOTAL FILINGS
1980	331,264	43,694	287,570	86.81%
1981	363,943	48,125	315,818	86.78%
1982	380,251	69,300	310,951	81.78%
1983	348,880	62,436	286,444	82.10%
1984	348,521	64,004	284,517	81.64%
1985	412,510	71,277	341,233	82.72%
1986	530,438	81,235	449,203	84.69%
1987	577,999	82,446	495,553	85.74%
1988	613,465	63,853	549,612	89.59%
1989	679,461	63,235	616,226	90.69%
1990	782,960	64,853	718,107	91.72%
1991	943,987	71,549	872,438	92.42%
1992	971,517	70,643	900,874	92.73%
1993	875,202	62,304	812,898	92.88%
1994	832,829	52,374	780,455	93.71%
1995	926,601	51,959	874,642	94.39%
1996	1,178,555	53,549	1,125,006	95.46%
1997	1,404,145	54,027	1,350,118	96.15%
1998	1,442,549	44,367	1,398,182	96.92%
1999	1,319,465	37,884	1,281,581	97.12%
2000	1,253,444	35,472	1,217,972	97.17%
2001	1,492,129	40,099	1,452,030	97.31%
2002	1,577,651	38,540	1,539,111	97.56%
2003	1,660,245	35,037	1,625,208	97.89%
2004	1,597,462	34,317	1,563,145	97.85%

US Taxes

US Federal Taxation Structure

This table shows the range of income taxes for various types of households in each tax bracket. In 2005 the standard deductions are $5,000 for those submitting returns under status "single" and status "married filing separately"; $7,300 for those filing

under status "head of household"; and $10,000 for those submitting returns under status "married filing jointly" or "qualifying widows and widowers with a dependent child". Source: US Department of the Treasury, Internal Revenue Service.

Single — Schedule X

IF TAXABLE INCOME IS OVER	BUT NOT OVER	THEN THE TAX IS	PLUS	OF THE AMOUNT OVER
$0	$7,300	-	10%	$0
$7,300	$29,700	$730.00	15%	$7,300
$29,700	$71,950	$4,090.00	25%	$29,700
$71,950	$150,150	$14,652.50	28%	$71,950
$150,150	$326,450	$36,548.50	33%	$150,150
$326,450	-	$94,727.50	35%	$326,450

US Federal Taxation Structure (continued)

Married Filing Jointly or Qualifying Widow(er) — Schedule Y-1
IF TAXABLE INCOME

IS OVER	BUT NOT OVER	THEN THE TAX IS	PLUS	OF THE AMOUNT OVER
$0	$14,600	-	10%	$0
$14,600	$59,400	$1,460.00	15%	$14,600
$59,400	$119,950	$8,180.00	25%	$59,400
$119,950	$182,800	$23,317.50	28%	$119,950
$182,800	$326,450	$40,915.50	33%	$182,800
$326,450	–	$88,320.00	35%	$326,450

Married Filing Separately — Schedule Y-2
IF TAXABLE INCOME

IS OVER	BUT NOT OVER	THEN THE TAX IS	PLUS	OF THE AMOUNT OVER
$0	$7,300	-	10%	$0
$7,300	$29,700	$730.00	15%	$7,300
$29,700	$59,975	$4,090.00	25%	$29,700
$59,975	$91,400	$11,658.75	28%	$59,975
$91,400	$163,225	$20,457.75	33%	$91,400
$163,225	–	$44,160.00	35%	$163,225

Head of Household — Schedule Z
IF TAXABLE INCOME

IS OVER	BUT NOT OVER	THEN THE TAX IS	PLUS	OF THE AMOUNT OVER
$0	$10,450	-	10%	$0
$10,450	$39,800	$1,045.00	15%	$10,450
$39,800	$102,800	$5,447.50	25%	$39,800
$102,800	$166,450	$21,197.50	28%	$102,800
$166,450	$326,450	$39,019.50	33%	$166,450
$326,450	–	$91,819.50	35%	$326,450

Individual Income Taxes by State

This table shows tax rates as of 1 Jan 2005 for tax year 2005. Source: The Federation of Tax Administrators (from various sources). <www.taxadmin.org/fta/rate/ind_inc.html>.

STATE	TAX RATES LOW	TAX RATES HIGH	NUMBER OF BRACKETS	INCOME BRACKETS LOW	INCOME BRACKETS HIGH	PERSONAL EXEMPTION SINGLE	PERSONAL EXEMPTION MARRIED	PERSONAL EXEMPTION CHILDREN	FEDERAL TAX DEDUCTIBLE
AL	2	5	3	500[2]	3,000[2]	1,500	3,000	300	Yes
AK	No state income tax								
AZ	2.87	5.04	5	10,000[2]	150,000[2]	2,100	4,200	2,300	
AR[1]	1	7[5]	6	3,999	28,500	20[3]	40[3]	20[3]	
CA[1]	1	9.3	6	6,147[2]	40,346[2]	85[3]	170[3]	265[3]	
CO	4.63		1	Flat rate		None			
CT	3	5	2	10,000[2]	10,000[2]	12,750[6]	24,500[6]	0	
DE	2.2	5.95	6	5,000	60,000	110[3]	220[3]	110[3]	
DC	5	9[7]	3	10,000	30,000	1,370	2,740	1,370	
FL	No state income tax								
GA	1	6	6	750[8]	7,000[8]	2,700	5,400	2,700	
HI	1.4	8.25	9	2,000[2]	40,000[2]	1,040	2,080	1,040	
ID[1]	1.6	7.8	8	1,129[9]	22,577[9]	3,200[4]	6,400[4]	3,200[4]	
IL	3		1	Flat rate		2,000	4,000	2,000	
IN	3.4		1	Flat rate		1,000	2,000	1,000	
IA[1]	0.36	8.98	9	1,242	55,890	40[3]	80[3]	40[3]	Yes
KS	3.5	6.45	3	15,000[2]	30,000[2]	2,250	4,500	2,250	
KY	2	6	5	3,000	8,000	20[3]	40[3]	20[3]	
LA	2	6	3	12,500[2]	25,000[2]	4,500[10]	9,000[10]	1,000[10]	Yes
ME[1]	2	8.5	4	4,350[2]	17,350[2]	2,850	5,700	2,850	
MD	2	4.75	4	1,000	3,000	2,400	4,800	2,400	
MA	5.3		1	Flat rate		3,575	7,150	1,000	
MI[1]	3.9		1	Flat rate		3,100	6,200	3,100	
MN[1]	5.35	7.85	3	19,890[11]	65,350[11]	3,200[4]	6,400[4]	3,200[4]	
MS	3	5	3	5,000	10,000	6,000	12,000	1,500	
MO	1.5	6	10	1,000	9,000	2,100	4,200	2,100	Yes[20]

Individual Income Taxes by State (continued)

STATE	TAX RATES LOW	TAX RATES HIGH	NUMBER OF BRACKETS	INCOME BRACKETS LOW	INCOME BRACKETS HIGH	PERSONAL EXEMPTION SINGLE	PERSONAL EXEMPTION MARRIED	PERSONAL EXEMPTION CHILDREN	FEDERAL TAX DEDUCTIBLE
MT[1]	2	6.9	7	2,300	13,900	1,900	3,800	1,900	Yes
NE[1]	2.56	6.84	4	2,400[12]	26,500[12]	101[3]	202[3]	101[3]	
NV	No state income tax								
NH	State income tax is limited to dividends and interest income only								
NJ	1.4	8.97	6	20,000[13]	500,000[13]	1,000	2,000	1,500	
NM	1.7	6	4	5,500[14]	16,000[14]	3,200[4]	6,400[4]	3,200[4]	
NY	4	7.7	7	8,000[15]	500,000[15]	0	0	1,000	
NC[16]	6	8.25	4	12,750[16]	120,000[16]	3,200[4]	6,400[4]	3,200[4]	
ND	2.1	5.54[17]	5	29,050[17]	319,100[17]	3,200[4]	6,400[4]	3,200[4]	
OH[1]	0.743	7.5	9	5,000	200,000	1,300[18]	2,600[18]	1,300[18]	
OK	0.5	6.65[19]	8	1,000[2]	10,000[2]	1,000	2,000	1,000	Yes[19]
OR[1]	5	9	3	2,650[2]	6,550[2]	154[3]	308[3]	154[3]	Yes[20]
PA	3.07		1	—Flat rate—		—None—			
RI	25.0% Federal tax liability[21]								
SC[1]	2.5	7	6	2,460	12,300	3,200[4]	6,400[4]	3,200[4]	
SD	No state income tax								
TN	State income tax is limited to dividends and interest income only								
TX	No state income tax								
UT	2.3	7	6	863[2]	4,313[2]	2,400[4]	4,800[4]	2,400[4]	Yes[22]
VT[1]	3.6	9.5	5	29,900[23]	326,450[23]	3,200[4]	6,400[4]	3,200[4]	
VA	2	5.75	4	3,000	17,000	800	1,600	800	
WA	No state income tax								
WV	3	6.5	5	10,000	60,000	2,000	4,000	2,000	
WI	4.6	6.75	4	8,840[24]	132,580[24]	700	1,400	400	
WY	No state income tax								

[1]Fifteen states have statutory provision for automatic adjustment of tax brackets, personal exemption, or standard deductions to the rate of inflation. Massachusetts, Michigan, Nebraska, and Ohio index the personal exemption amounts only.   [2]For joint returns, the taxes are twice the tax imposed on half the income.   [3]Tax credits.   [4]These states allow personal exemption or standard deductions as provided in the Internal Revenue Code. Utah allows a personal exemption equal to three-fourths the federal exemptions.   [5]A special tax table is available for low-income taxpayers reducing their tax payments.   [6]Combined personal exemptions and standard deduction. An additional tax credit is allowed ranging from 75% to 0% based on state adjusted gross income. Exemption amounts are phased out for higher-income taxpayers until they are eliminated for households earning over $55,500.   [7]Tax rate decreases are scheduled for tax years after 2005.   [8]The tax brackets reported are for single individuals. For married households filing separately, the same rates apply to income brackets ranging from $500 to $5,000; the income brackets range from $1,000 to $10,000 for joint filers.   [9]For joint returns, the tax is twice the tax imposed on half the income. A $10 filing tax is charge for each return, and a $15 credit is allowed for each exemption.   [10]Combined personal exemption and standard deduction.   [11]The tax brackets reported are for single individuals. For married couples filing jointly, the same rates apply for income under $29,070 to over $115,510.   [12]The tax brackets reported are for single individuals. For married couples filing jointly, the same rates apply for income under $4,000 to over $46,750.   [13]The tax brackets reported are for single individuals. For married couples filing jointly, the same rates apply for income under $20,000 to over $500,000.   [14]The tax brackets reported are for single individuals. For married couples filing jointly, the same rates apply for income under $8,000 to over $24,000. Married households filing separately pay the tax imposed on half the income.   [15]The tax brackets reported are for single individuals. For married taxpayers, the same rates apply for income brackets ranging from $16,000 to $500,000.   [16]The tax brackets reported are for single individuals. For married taxpayers, the same rates apply to income brackets ranging from $21,250 to $200,000. Lower exemption amounts allowed for high income taxpayers. Tax rate scheduled to decrease after tax year 2005.   [17]Brackets reported are for single individuals. For married taxpayers, the same rates apply to income brackets ranging from $48,500 to $319,100. An additional $300 personal exemption is allowed for joint returns or unmarried heads of households.   [18]Plus an additional $20 per exemption tax credit.   [19]The rate range reported is for single persons not deducting federal income tax. For married persons filing jointly, the same rates apply to income brackets that are twice the dollar amounts. Separate schedules, with rates ranging from 0.5% to 10%, apply to taxpayers deducting federal income taxes.   [20]Deduction is limited to $10,000 for joint returns, $5,000 for individuals in Missouri, and $5,000 in Oregon.   [21]Federal tax liability prior to the enactment of Economic Growth and Tax Relief Act of 2001.   [22]One-half of the federal income taxes are deductible.   [23]The tax brackets reported are for single individuals. For married couples filing jointly, the same rates apply for income under $49,650 to over $326,450.   [24]The tax brackets reported are for single individuals. For married taxpayers, the same rates apply to income brackets ranging from $11,780 to $176,770. An additional $250 exemption is provided for each taxpayer or spouse aged 65 or over.

Arts, Entertainment, & Leisure

Encyclopædia Britannica's 50 Great Museums of the World

A select list, alphabetical by country.

National Museum of Australia, Canberra, Australia: The National Museum of Australia houses unique exhibitions that explore all aspects of Australian history and culture. Historical artifacts and interactive exhibits tell the story of the people, land, and symbols of the island nation.

Kunsthistorisches Museum, Vienna, Austria: The Museum of Art History's Picture Gallery was built around the collection of Archduke Leopold Wilhelm, who in the mid-17th century acquired some 1,400 paintings of the Venetian Renaissance (including works by Titian, Veronese, Tintoretto) and of Flemish masters from the 15th–17th century (van Eyck, Rubens, van Dyck). The museum's extensive collections also include ancient Egyptian and Near Eastern art and artifacts, Greek and Roman antiquities, more than 700,000 examples of historical currency, ancient musical instruments, arms and armor, and historical carriages and court uniforms.

Liechtenstein Museum, Vienna, Austria: Opened in March 2004, it houses the Princely Collection of Hans-Adam II, Prince of Liechtenstein, most of which has not been seen publicly since 1938. Its wide range of baroque art forms includes paintings by Raphael, Rembrandt, Rubens, and van Dyck, as well as sculpture and important collections of decorative arts.

The Bahrain National Museum, Manama, Bahrain: The museum houses a large collection of documents, artifacts, and craftwork relating to Arabic history and Islamic studies.

Museum of Art, São Paulo, Brazil: Known as "MASP" (Museu de Arte de São Paulo), the museum owns one of the world's most prestigious collections of works by European masters, including pieces from the 13th century through the present, with a strong emphasis on Impressionists.

Museum of Art and History, Shanghai, China: Also known as the Shanghai Museum, the institution is primarily devoted to ancient Chinese art. It has more than 120,000 relics on permanent display and is especially renowned for its collections of bronzes, ceramics, paintings, and calligraphy.

Egyptian Museum, Cairo, Egypt: Established by the Egyptian government in 1835, the Egyptian Museum houses more than 120,000 objects from prehistoric civilizations to the Greco-Roman period. Much of the museum is devoted to ancient Egyptian history; permanent exhibits explore the Pharaonic era.

The British Museum, London, England: The British Museum explores the histories of virtually all world cultures, from ancient to contemporary. Nations and their civilizations are represented by displays of art, sciences, cultural and historical artifacts, clothing, and currency.

The National Gallery, London, England: On permanent display at the National Gallery is one of the world's greatest collections of Western European painting, with more than 2,300 works from the 13th–20th century.

Tate Britain (formerly the Tate Gallery), London, England: One of the world's most prestigious art institutions, Tate Britain houses the world's most extensive collection of British art from the 16th century to the present. Branches of the Tate in Liverpool, St. Ives, and Bankside are devoted to modern British and world art.

Victoria and Albert Museum, London, England: Although it boasts a wide array of fine arts and cultural artifacts, the Victoria and Albert Museum is especially devoted to applied and decorative arts. Examples of fashion, sculpture, ceramics, glass, metalwork, jewelry, furniture, photography, and paintings from various nations are on permanent display.

La Cité des Sciences et d'Industrie, Paris, France: The museum is devoted primarily to popular science. It houses its own planetarium as well as permanent exhibits on space, information technology, medicine, mathematics, the ocean, and numerous other topics. Also on display is a French navy submarine.

Musée d'Orsay, Paris, France: The Musée d'Orsay acquired a reputation as a world-class museum soon after it opened in 1986. It is devoted to art of the Western world from 1848 to 1914, and its collection is drawn from three art institutions: the Louvre Museum, the Musée du Jeu de Paume, and France's National Museum of Modern Art.

The Louvre Museum, Paris, France: The Louvre is the most famous and revered museum in the world. The main building served as a medieval fortress and as a palace for the kings of France and has been used as a museum since 1793. The Louvre's collections are divided into seven departments: paintings; sculptures; prints and drawings; objets d'art; Oriental antiquities and Islamic art; Egyptian antiquities; and Greek, Etruscan, and Roman antiquities.

Château de Versailles, Versailles, France: The original château of the Palace of Versailles was built in 1623 as a hunting lodge and retreat for King Louis XIII. The palace was expanded throughout the 17th century, and in 1682 it became the official residence of the king and the Court of France. It is still used as an official national palace when both houses of parliament are convened, although much of the palace—including its many rooms of artistic and architectural masterpieces—is open to the public.

Deutsches Historisches Museum, Berlin, Germany: The German Historical Museum chronicles German history through its vast collection of artwork, historical documents, militaria, and artifacts of German culture.

Gemäldegalerie Alte Meister, Dresden, Germany: Located in historic Zwinger Castle, the Old Masters Picture Gallery houses a large collection of Italian Renaissance, Baroque, and 17th-century Flemish and Dutch paintings, including works by such masters as Rembrandt, Rubens, and Raphael.

Alte Pinakothek, Munich, Germany: The Old Pinakothek is home to one of the world's premier collections of 14th–18th-century European paintings, including works by Rembrandt, da Vinci, and Raphael.

The Acropolis Museum, Athens, Greece: Located near the ruins of the Acropolis, the museum is the world's main repository of masterpieces of ancient Greek civilization, especially those of the Archaic period.

National Archaeological Museum, Athens, Greece: Considered the most important archaeological museum in Greece, the National Archaeological Museum is home to exhibits representative of all aspects of Greek cultural history. The museum houses one of the largest collections of ancient Greek art in the world.

National Museum, New Delhi, India: The National Museum houses a vast collection of art objects from India and the world. Its major holdings include archaeological objects, jewelry, paintings, decorative arts, and arms and armor.

National Museum of Ireland, Dublin, Ireland: The museum merged several major collections of Irish art and artifacts when it opened in 1890. Its archaeological and artistic exhibits include masterworks from 2000 BC to the 20th century.

Galleria dell'Accademia, Florence, Italy: The Gallery of the Academy houses a collection of 15th- and 16th-century paintings and many Tuscan paintings from the 13th–16th century. The museum is best known, however, for its sculptures by Michelangelo, notably his *David*.

Galleria degli Uffizi, Florence, Italy: The Uffizi is renowned for its world's finest collection of Italian Renaissance painting, particularly of the Florentine school. The gallery was established in the 16th century to house the many art treasures of the Medici family.

Pinacoteca di Brera, Milan, Italy: One of Italy's largest art galleries, founded in 1809 by Napoleon I, the Brera Picture Gallery is especially renowned for its paintings by the Venetian school.

The Vatican Museums, Rome, Italy: The Vatican Museums have housed the art collections of the Roman Catholic popes since the beginning of the 15th century. The various galleries contain ancient sculptures and epigraphy, Etruscan and Egyptian artifacts, an outstanding collection of Italian religious paintings, and Russian and Byzantine paintings. A modern art collection was initiated in 1956, and the Vatican's first museum of contemporary art, housed in 65 galleries in the Vatican palace, opened in 1973.

Gallerie dell'Accademia di Venezia, Venice, Italy: The Galleries of the Academy of Venice house an unrivaled collection of paintings from the Venetian masters of the 13th–18th century, including outstanding works by Giovanni Bellini, Giorgione, Titian, Tintoretto, and Canaletto.

Tokugawa Art Museum, Nagoya, Japan: The Tokugawa Art Museum holds a vast collection of objects belonging to the descendants of the Tokugawa family, including weapons and furniture used by the family's feudal lords. One section of the museum is dedicated to the 12th-century picture scrolls of the Tale of Genji.

Tokyo National Museum, Tokyo, Japan: The TNM's collection includes major exhibits of Asian painting, sculpture, calligraphy, decorative art, rare books, photographs, metalwork, lacquerware, ceramics, textiles, and antiquities.

Museo Nacional de Antropología, Mexico City, Mexico: The collection of the National Museum of Anthropology includes anthropological, ethnological, and archaeological materials from Mexico's pre-Hispanic past, including treasures of the Aztecs, Mayas, Zapotecs, Mixtec, Purépechas, and Olmecs.

Rijksmuseum, Amsterdam, The Netherlands: With nearly one million objects, the Rijksmuseum is the largest museum of art and history in The Netherlands. It is perhaps best known for its collection of 17th-century Dutch paintings, including works by Rembrandt, Vermeer, and Jan Steen.

Muzeum Narodowe w Warszawie, Warsaw, Poland: The National Museum in Warsaw houses 780,000 items in its permanent galleries, including one of the richest and most diverse collections of European art in Poland. It is also home to the largest Polish scholarly library of books and documents related to art and world culture.

The Catherine Palace, Moscow, Russia: The immense Catherine Palace, with its extravagantly gilded interior, was originally built in the early 18th century for Catherine I. Visitors have access to several of the palace's suites, the Cameron Gallery, and the rooms of the Agate Pavilion.

The State Hermitage Museum, St. Petersburg, Russia: Occupying six buildings in the heart of St. Petersburg, the Hermitage was founded in 1764 as a private gallery for the art amassed by Empress Catherine the Great. In addition to its many Russian masterpieces, the museum houses works by Renaissance Italian and Baroque Dutch, Flemish, and French painters. Also noteworthy is its collection of Central Asian art.

The State Russian Museum, St. Petersburg, Russia: Housed in the buildings of the former Mikhailovsky Palace, the State Russian Museum is the central museum of Russian art and culture. The main building houses art from the 10th century through the revolution, including a comprehensive collection of painting and sculpture from the 18th and 19th centuries and an excellent collection of early Russian art, with fine icons from the 12th–14th century. In addition, there are collections of late 19th- and early 20th-century paintings and applied arts.

Asian Civilisations Museum, Singapore: The Asian Civilisations Museum traces the cultural history of China, Southeast Asia, India, and West Asia through its vast collection of ceramics, sculptures, and other artifacts.

South African Museum, Cape Town, South Africa: The South African Museum documents the natural history and anthropology of southern Africa. Objects dating to the origins of the region's indigenous populations are featured in the collection. The museum also houses a planetarium.

Museo del Prado, Madrid, Spain: The Prado Museum houses the world's richest and most comprehensive collection of Spanish painting, as well as masterpieces of other schools of European painting, especially Italian and Flemish art. The museum contains the world's most complete collections of the works of El Greco, Diego Velázquez, and Francisco de Goya.

Swedish Museum of Natural History, Stockholm, Sweden: Dedicated to the history of natural sciences, the Swedish Museum of Natural History houses millions of specimens within its four main divisions of botany, geology, paleontology, and zoology.

National Palace Museum, Taipei, Taiwan: The National Palace Museum houses several international art masterpieces but is especially known for its collections of porcelain, jade, silk paintings, calligraphy, and other arts of ancient China.

The National Museum, Bangkok, Thailand: In 1874 King Rama V established this first public museum in Bangkok to display the royal art collection. The museum today houses objects of art, archaeology, and culture from prehistoric to modern times. Among the major permanent exhibits are the Gallery of Thai History and the Gallery of Prehistory.

Boston Museum of Fine Arts, Boston MA: One of the world's most comprehensive art museums, the MFA was founded in 1870 with the art holdings of the Boston Athenaeum library as the nucleus of its collection. The museum has a major collection of Asian art from the 3rd millennium BC to modern times. It also has the largest collection outside France of paintings by Claude Monet, the world's foremost collection of 19th-century American art, and one of the world's finest collections of Egyptian Old Kingdom objects.

The Art Institute of Chicago, Chicago IL: The Art Institute's permanent exhibits include European, American, and Oriental sculpture, paintings, prints and drawings, and decorative arts, as well as photography and African and pre-Columbian American art. The museum is noted for its extensive collections of 19th-century French painting (Impressionist works in particular) and of 20th-century painting.

Field Museum of Natural History, Chicago IL: The Field Museum was established in 1893 to display the biological and anthropological artifacts gathered for the World's Columbian Exposition. Permanent exhibits explore the Earth's cultural history and biological and geologic development. A major addition to the museum in 2000 was "Sue," the largest, most complete, and best-preserved *Tyrannosaurus rex* fossil ever discovered.

Los Angeles County Museum of Art, Los Angeles CA: The museum's permanent collections emphasize Asian, Islamic, European, and American art from ancient times to the present. Also important are the exhibits of costumes and textiles, decorative arts, and photography that represent various cultures from around the world.

Guggenheim Museum, New York NY: The museum's permanent collections emphasize modern art, including Impressionist, nonobjective, abstract, surrealist, minimalist, and avant-garde works.

Metropolitan Museum of Art, New York NY: The most prestigious art institution in the United States, the museum houses more than 3,000,000 objects representing virtually all nations and all periods of human history.

Museum of Modern Art, New York NY: The collection at "MoMA" includes more than 100,000 paintings, sculptures, drawings, prints, photographs, architectural models and drawings, and design objects. Also housed in the museum are more than 14,000 films, 4,000,000 film stills, and an extensive library of books and periodicals.

The National Gallery of Art, Washington DC: The National Gallery, founded by Andrew Mellon in the 1930s, houses many of the world's most renowned examples of European and American painting, sculpture, and graphic arts from the 14th century to the present.

The Smithsonian Institution, Washington DC: One of the world's leading museums and research institutions, the Smithsonian comprises 16 museums (which house more than 140 million artifacts) and several research facilities throughout the world. The museums include the National Museum of American History, the National Zoological Park, the National Air and Space Museum, the Anacostia Museum and Center for African American History and Culture, the National Museum of the American Indian, and the National Portrait Gallery.

United States Holocaust Memorial Museum, Washington DC: The United States' national institution for studying the Holocaust, the museum also serves as a memorial to the millions who died in the Holocaust. Located near the National Mall in Washington DC, the museum uses exhibitions, publications, and public programs to promote awareness of the issues related to the Holocaust.

Motion Pictures

Academy Awards (Oscars), 2004

The Academy of Motion Picture Arts and Sciences was formed in 1927 and first awarded the Academy Awards of Merit in May 1929. The honored categories have varied over the years, but best picture, actor, actress, and director have been awarded since the beginning. Awards for supporting actor and actress were added for the films of 1936 and best foreign-language film for 1947. The ceremony is generally held in the early spring of the year following the release of films under consideration; the latest Oscars were awarded 27 Feb 2005 in Los Angeles. Award: gold-plated statuette of a man with a sword.

Academy of Motion Picture Arts and Sciences Web site: <www.oscars.org>.

CATEGORY	WINNER
Motion picture of the year	*Million Dollar Baby* (US; Clint Eastwood, Albert S. Ruddy and Tom Rosenberg, producers)
Director	Clint Eastwood (*Million Dollar Baby*, US)
Actor	Jamie Foxx (*Ray*, US)
Actress	Hilary Swank (*Million Dollar Baby*, US)
Supporting actor	Morgan Freeman (*Million Dollar Baby*, US)
Supporting actress	Cate Blanchett (*The Aviator*, US/Japan/Germany)
Foreign language film	*The Sea Inside* (Spain/France/Italy; Alejandro Amenábar, director)
Animated feature	*The Incredibles* (US; Brad Bird, director)
Animated short	*Ryan* (Canada; Chris Landreth, director)
Live-action short	*Wasp* (UK; Andrea Arnold, director)

Academy Awards (Oscars), 2004 (continued)

CATEGORY	WINNER
Documentary feature	*Born into Brothels* (India/US; Ross Kauffman and Zana Briski, directors)
Documentary short	*Mighty Times: The Children's March* (US; Robert Hudson and Bobby Houston, directors)
Cinematography	Robert Richardson (*The Aviator,* US/Japan/Germany)
Art direction	Dante Ferretti, art direction; Francesca Lo Schiavo, set decoration (*The Aviator,* US/Japan/Germany)
Film editing	Thelma Schoonmaker (*The Aviator,* US/Japan/Germany)
Costume design	Sandy Powell (*The Aviator,* US/Japan/Germany)
Makeup	Valli O'Reilly and Bill Corso (*Lemony Snicket's A Series of Unfortunate Events,* US)
Original score	Jan A.P. Kaczmarek (*Finding Neverland,* UK/US)
Original song	"Al otro lado del río," Jorge Drexler (*Motorcycle Diaries,* US/Germany/UK/Argentina/Chile/Peru/France)
Sound mixing	Scott Millan, Greg Orloff, Bob Beemer, and Steve Cantamessa (*Ray,* US)
Sound editing	Michael Silvers and Randy Thom (*The Incredibles,* US)
Visual effects	John Dykstra, Scott Stokdyk, Anthony LaMolinara, and John Frazier (*Spider-Man 2,* US)
Screenplay, adaptation	Alexander Payne and Jim Taylor (*Sideways,* US)
Screenplay, original	Charlie Kaufman (*Eternal Sunshine of the Spotless Mind,* US)

Academy Awards (Oscars), 1928–2004

2005 awards ceremony scheduled to be held 5 Mar 2006 in Los Angeles.

BEST PICTURE

1928	*Wings*
1929	*The Broadway Melody*
1930	*All Quiet on the Western Front*
1931	*Cimarron*
1932	*Grand Hotel*
1933	*Cavalcade*
1934	*It Happened One Night*
1935	*Mutiny on the Bounty*
1936	*The Great Ziegfeld*
1937	*The Life of Emile Zola*
1938	*You Can't Take It with You*
1939	*Gone with the Wind*
1940	*Rebecca*
1941	*How Green Was My Valley*
1942	*Mrs. Miniver*
1943	*Casablanca*
1944	*Going My Way*
1945	*The Lost Weekend*
1946	*The Best Years of Our Lives*
1947	*Gentleman's Agreement*
1948	*Hamlet*
1949	*All the King's Men*
1950	*All About Eve*
1951	*An American in Paris*
1952	*The Greatest Show on Earth*
1953	*From Here to Eternity*

BEST PICTURE (CONTINUED)

1954	*On the Waterfront*
1955	*Marty*
1956	*Around the World in 80 Days*
1957	*The Bridge on the River Kwai*
1958	*Gigi*
1959	*Ben-Hur*
1960	*The Apartment*
1961	*West Side Story*
1962	*Lawrence of Arabia*
1963	*Tom Jones*
1964	*My Fair Lady*
1965	*The Sound of Music*
1966	*A Man for All Seasons*
1967	*In the Heat of the Night*
1968	*Oliver!*
1969	*Midnight Cowboy*
1970	*Patton*
1971	*The French Connection*
1972	*The Godfather*
1973	*The Sting*
1974	*The Godfather Part II*
1975	*One Flew Over the Cuckoo's Nest*
1976	*Rocky*
1977	*Annie Hall*
1978	*The Deer Hunter*

BEST PICTURE (CONTINUED)

1979	*Kramer vs. Kramer*
1980	*Ordinary People*
1981	*Chariots of Fire*
1982	*Gandhi*
1983	*Terms of Endearment*
1984	*Amadeus*
1985	*Out of Africa*
1986	*Platoon*
1987	*The Last Emperor*
1988	*Rain Man*
1989	*Driving Miss Daisy*
1990	*Dances with Wolves*
1991	*The Silence of the Lambs*
1992	*Unforgiven*
1993	*Schindler's List*
1994	*Forrest Gump*
1995	*Braveheart*
1996	*The English Patient*
1997	*Titanic*
1998	*Shakespeare in Love*
1999	*American Beauty*
2000	*Gladiator*
2001	*A Beautiful Mind*
2002	*Chicago*
2003	*The Lord of the Rings: The Return of the King*
2004	*Million Dollar Baby*

BEST ACTOR

1928	Emil Jannings (*The Last Command; The Way of All Flesh*)
1929	Warner Baxter (*In Old Arizona*)
1930	George Arliss (*Disraeli*)
1931	Lionel Barrymore (*A Free Soul*)
1932	Wallace Beery (*The Champ*), Fredric March (*Dr. Jekyll and Mr. Hyde*)
1933	Charles Laughton (*The Private Life of Henry VIII*)
1934	Clark Gable (*It Happened One Night*)

BEST ACTOR (CONTINUED)

1935	Victor McLaglen (*The Informer*)
1936	Paul Muni (*The Story of Louis Pasteur*)
1937	Spencer Tracy (*Captains Courageous*)
1938	Spencer Tracy (*Boys Town*)
1939	Robert Donat (*Goodbye, Mr. Chips*)
1940	James Stewart (*The Philadelphia Story*)
1941	Gary Cooper (*Sergeant York*)
1942	James Cagney (*Yankee Doodle Dandy*)
1943	Paul Lukas (*Watch on the Rhine*)
1944	Bing Crosby (*Going My Way*)

Academy Awards (Oscars), 1928–2004 (continued)

BEST ACTOR (CONTINUED)

1945 Ray Milland (The Lost Weekend)
1946 Fredric March (The Best Years of Our Lives)
1947 Ronald Colman (A Double Life)
1948 Laurence Olivier (Hamlet)
1949 Broderick Crawford (All the King's Men)
1950 José Ferrer (Cyrano de Bergerac)
1951 Humphrey Bogart (The African Queen)
1952 Gary Cooper (High Noon)
1953 William Holden (Stalag 17)
1954 Marlon Brando (On the Waterfront)
1955 Ernest Borgnine (Marty)
1956 Yul Brynner (The King and I)
1957 Alec Guinness (The Bridge on the River Kwai)
1958 David Niven (Separate Tables)
1959 Charlton Heston (Ben-Hur)
1960 Burt Lancaster (Elmer Gantry)
1961 Maximilian Schell (Judgment at Nuremberg)
1962 Gregory Peck (To Kill a Mockingbird)
1963 Sidney Poitier (Lilies of the Field)
1964 Rex Harrison (My Fair Lady)
1965 Lee Marvin (Cat Ballou)
1966 Paul Scofield (A Man for All Seasons)
1967 Rod Steiger (In the Heat of the Night)
1968 Cliff Robertson (Charly)
1969 John Wayne (True Grit)
1970 George C. Scott (Patton) (refused)
1971 Gene Hackman (The French Connection)
1972 Marlon Brando (The Godfather)
1973 Jack Lemmon (Save the Tiger)
1974 Art Carney (Harry and Tonto)
1975 Jack Nicholson (One Flew Over the Cuckoo's Nest)
1976 Peter Finch (Network) (posthumous)
1977 Richard Dreyfuss (The Goodbye Girl)
1978 Jon Voight (Coming Home)
1979 Dustin Hoffman (Kramer vs. Kramer)
1980 Robert De Niro (Raging Bull)
1981 Henry Fonda (On Golden Pond)
1982 Ben Kingsley (Gandhi)
1983 Robert Duvall (Tender Mercies)
1984 F. Murray Abraham (Amadeus)
1985 William Hurt (Kiss of the Spider Woman)
1986 Paul Newman (The Color of Money)
1987 Michael Douglas (Wall Street)
1988 Dustin Hoffman (Rain Man)
1989 Daniel Day-Lewis (My Left Foot)
1990 Jeremy Irons (Reversal of Fortune)
1991 Anthony Hopkins (The Silence of the Lambs)
1992 Al Pacino (Scent of a Woman)
1993 Tom Hanks (Philadelphia)
1994 Tom Hanks (Forrest Gump)
1995 Nicolas Cage (Leaving Las Vegas)
1996 Geoffrey Rush (Shine)
1997 Jack Nicholson (As Good as It Gets)
1998 Roberto Benigni (Life Is Beautiful)
1999 Kevin Spacey (American Beauty)
2000 Russell Crowe (Gladiator)
2001 Denzel Washington (Training Day)
2002 Adrien Brody (The Pianist)
2003 Sean Penn (Mystic River)
2004 Jamie Foxx (Ray)

BEST ACTRESS

1928 Janet Gaynor (7th Heaven; Street Angel; Sunrise)
1929 Mary Pickford (Coquette)
1930 Norma Shearer (The Divorcee)
1931 Marie Dressler (Min and Bill)

BEST ACTRESS (CONTINUED)

1932 Helen Hayes (The Sin of Madelon Claudet)
1933 Katharine Hepburn (Morning Glory)
1934 Claudette Colbert (It Happened One Night)
1935 Bette Davis (Dangerous)
1936 Luise Rainer (The Great Ziegfeld)
1937 Luise Rainer (The Good Earth)
1938 Bette Davis (Jezebel)
1939 Vivien Leigh (Gone with the Wind)
1940 Ginger Rogers (Kitty Foyle)
1941 Joan Fontaine (Suspicion)
1942 Greer Garson (Mrs. Miniver)
1943 Jennifer Jones (The Song of Bernadette)
1944 Ingrid Bergman (Gaslight)
1945 Joan Crawford (Mildred Pierce)
1946 Olivia de Havilland (To Each His Own)
1947 Loretta Young (The Farmer's Daughter)
1948 Jane Wyman (Johnny Belinda)
1949 Olivia de Havilland (The Heiress)
1950 Judy Holliday (Born Yesterday)
1951 Vivien Leigh (A Streetcar Named Desire)
1952 Shirley Booth (Come Back, Little Sheba)
1953 Audrey Hepburn (Roman Holiday)
1954 Grace Kelly (The Country Girl)
1955 Anna Magnani (The Rose Tattoo)
1956 Ingrid Bergman (Anastasia)
1957 Joanne Woodward (The Three Faces of Eve)
1958 Susan Hayward (I Want to Live!)
1959 Simone Signoret (Room at the Top)
1960 Elizabeth Taylor (Butterfield 8)
1961 Sophia Loren (Two Women)
1962 Anne Bancroft (The Miracle Worker)
1963 Patricia Neal (Hud)
1964 Julie Andrews (Mary Poppins)
1965 Julie Christie (Darling)
1966 Elizabeth Taylor (Who's Afraid of Virginia Woolf?)
1967 Katharine Hepburn (Guess Who's Coming to Dinner)
1968 Katharine Hepburn (The Lion in Winter), Barbra Streisand (Funny Girl)
1969 Maggie Smith (The Prime of Miss Jean Brodie)
1970 Glenda Jackson (Women in Love)
1971 Jane Fonda (Klute)
1972 Liza Minnelli (Cabaret)
1973 Glenda Jackson (A Touch of Class)
1974 Ellen Burstyn (Alice Doesn't Live Here Anymore)
1975 Louise Fletcher (One Flew Over the Cuckoo's Nest)
1976 Faye Dunaway (Network)
1977 Diane Keaton (Annie Hall)
1978 Jane Fonda (Coming Home)
1979 Sally Field (Norma Rae)
1980 Sissy Spacek (Coal Miner's Daughter)
1981 Katharine Hepburn (On Golden Pond)
1982 Meryl Streep (Sophie's Choice)
1983 Shirley MacLaine (Terms of Endearment)
1984 Sally Field (Places in the Heart)
1985 Geraldine Page (The Trip to Bountiful)
1986 Marlee Matlin (Children of a Lesser God)
1987 Cher (Moonstruck)
1988 Jodie Foster (The Accused)
1989 Jessica Tandy (Driving Miss Daisy)
1990 Kathy Bates (Misery)
1991 Jodie Foster (The Silence of the Lambs)
1992 Emma Thompson (Howards End)
1993 Holly Hunter (The Piano)

Academy Awards (Oscars), 1928–2004 (continued)

BEST ACTRESS (CONTINUED)

1994 Jessica Lange (Blue Sky)
1995 Susan Sarandon (Dead Man Walking)
1996 Frances McDormand (Fargo)
1997 Helen Hunt (As Good as It Gets)
1998 Gwyneth Paltrow (Shakespeare in Love)
1999 Hilary Swank (Boys Don't Cry)
2000 Julia Roberts (Erin Brockovich)
2001 Halle Berry (Monster's Ball)
2002 Nicole Kidman (The Hours)
2003 Charlize Theron (Monster)
2004 Hilary Swank (Million Dollar Baby)

BEST SUPPORTING ACTOR

1936 Walter Brennan (Come and Get It)
1937 Joseph Schildkraut (The Life of Emile Zola)
1938 Walter Brennan (Kentucky)
1939 Thomas Mitchell (Stagecoach)
1940 Walter Brennan (The Westerner)
1941 Donald Crisp (How Green Was My Valley)
1942 Van Heflin (Johnny Eager)
1943 Charles Coburn (The More the Merrier)
1944 Barry Fitzgerald (Going My Way)
1945 James Dunn (A Tree Grows in Brooklyn)
1946 Harold Russell (The Best Years of Our Lives)
1947 Edmund Gwenn (Miracle on 34th Street)
1948 Walter Huston (The Treasure of the Sierra Madre)
1949 Dean Jagger (Twelve O'Clock High)
1950 George Sanders (All About Eve)
1951 Karl Malden (A Streetcar Named Desire)
1952 Anthony Quinn (Viva Zapata!)
1953 Frank Sinatra (From Here to Eternity)
1954 Edmond O'Brien (The Barefoot Contessa)
1955 Jack Lemmon (Mister Roberts)
1956 Anthony Quinn (Lust for Life)
1957 Red Buttons (Sayonara)
1958 Burl Ives (The Big Country)
1959 Hugh Griffith (Ben-Hur)
1960 Peter Ustinov (Spartacus)
1961 George Chakiris (West Side Story)
1962 Ed Begley (Sweet Bird of Youth)
1963 Melvyn Douglas (Hud)
1964 Peter Ustinov (Topkapi)
1965 Martin Balsam (A Thousand Clowns)
1966 Walter Matthau (The Fortune Cookie)
1967 George Kennedy (Cool Hand Luke)
1968 Jack Albertson (The Subject Was Roses)
1969 Gig Young (They Shoot Horses, Don't They?)
1970 John Mills (Ryan's Daughter)
1971 Ben Johnson (The Last Picture Show)
1972 Joel Grey (Cabaret)
1973 John Houseman (The Paper Chase)
1974 Robert De Niro (The Godfather Part II)
1975 George Burns (The Sunshine Boys)
1976 Jason Robards (All the President's Men)
1977 Jason Robards (Julia)
1978 Christopher Walken (The Deer Hunter)
1979 Melvyn Douglas (Being There)
1980 Timothy Hutton (Ordinary People)
1981 John Gielgud (Arthur)
1982 Louis Gossett, Jr. (An Officer and a Gentleman)
1983 Jack Nicholson (Terms of Endearment)
1984 Haing S. Ngor (The Killing Fields)
1985 Don Ameche (Cocoon)
1986 Michael Caine (Hannah and Her Sisters)
1987 Sean Connery (The Untouchables)
1988 Kevin Kline (A Fish Called Wanda)

BEST SUPPORTING ACTOR (CONTINUED)

1989 Denzel Washington (Glory)
1990 Joe Pesci (Goodfellas)
1991 Jack Palance (City Slickers)
1992 Gene Hackman (Unforgiven)
1993 Tommy Lee Jones (The Fugitive)
1994 Martin Landau (Ed Wood)
1995 Kevin Spacey (The Usual Suspects)
1996 Cuba Gooding, Jr. (Jerry Maguire)
1997 Robin Williams (Good Will Hunting)
1998 James Coburn (Affliction)
1999 Michael Caine (The Cider House Rules)
2000 Benicio Del Toro (Traffic)
2001 Jim Broadbent (Iris)
2002 Chris Cooper (Adaptation)
2003 Tim Robbins (Mystic River)
2004 Morgan Freeman (Million Dollar Baby)

BEST SUPPORTING ACTRESS

1936 Gale Sondergaard (Anthony Adverse)
1937 Alice Brady (In Old Chicago)
1938 Fay Bainter (Jezebel)
1939 Hattie McDaniel (Gone with the Wind)
1940 Jane Darwell (The Grapes of Wrath)
1941 Mary Astor (The Great Lie)
1942 Teresa Wright (Mrs. Miniver)
1943 Katina Paxinou (For Whom the Bell Tolls)
1944 Ethel Barrymore (None but the Lonely Heart)
1945 Anne Revere (National Velvet)
1946 Anne Baxter (The Razor's Edge)
1947 Celeste Holm (Gentleman's Agreement)
1948 Claire Trevor (Key Largo)
1949 Mercedes McCambridge (All the King's Men)
1950 Josephine Hull (Harvey)
1951 Kim Hunter (A Streetcar Named Desire)
1952 Gloria Grahame (The Bad and the Beautiful)
1953 Donna Reed (From Here to Eternity)
1954 Eva Marie Saint (On the Waterfront)
1955 Jo Van Fleet (East of Eden)
1956 Dorothy Malone (Written on the Wind)
1957 Miyoshi Umeki (Sayonara)
1958 Wendy Hiller (Separate Tables)
1959 Shelley Winters (The Diary of Anne Frank)
1960 Shirley Jones (Elmer Gantry)
1961 Rita Moreno (West Side Story)
1962 Patty Duke (The Miracle Worker)
1963 Margaret Rutherford (The V.I.P.s)
1964 Lila Kedrova (Zorba the Greek)
1965 Shelley Winters (A Patch of Blue)
1966 Sandy Dennis (Who's Afraid of Virginia Woolf?)
1967 Estelle Parsons (Bonnie and Clyde)
1968 Ruth Gordon (Rosemary's Baby)
1969 Goldie Hawn (Cactus Flower)
1970 Helen Hayes (Airport)
1971 Cloris Leachman (The Last Picture Show)
1972 Eileen Heckart (Butterflies Are Free)
1973 Tatum O'Neal (Paper Moon)
1974 Ingrid Bergman (Murder on the Orient Express)
1975 Lee Grant (Shampoo)
1976 Beatrice Straight (Network)
1977 Vanessa Redgrave (Julia)
1978 Maggie Smith (California Suite)
1979 Meryl Streep (Kramer vs. Kramer)
1980 Mary Steenburgen (Melvin and Howard)
1981 Maureen Stapleton (Reds)
1982 Jessica Lange (Tootsie)
1983 Linda Hunt (The Year of Living Dangerously)
1984 Peggy Ashcroft (A Passage to India)

Academy Awards (Oscars), 1928–2004 (continued)

BEST SUPPORTING ACTRESS (CONTINUED)

1985 Anjelica Huston (Prizzi's Honor)
1986 Dianne Wiest (Hannah and Her Sisters)
1987 Olympia Dukakis (Moonstruck)
1988 Geena Davis (The Accidental Tourist)
1989 Brenda Fricker (My Left Foot)
1990 Whoopi Goldberg (Ghost)
1991 Mercedes Ruehl (The Fisher King)
1992 Marisa Tomei (My Cousin Vinny)
1993 Anna Paquin (The Piano)
1994 Dianne Wiest (Bullets over Broadway)
1995 Mira Sorvino (Mighty Aphrodite)
1996 Juliette Binoche (The English Patient)
1997 Kim Basinger (L.A. Confidential)
1998 Judi Dench (Shakespeare in Love)
1999 Angelina Jolie (Girl, Interrupted)
2000 Marcia Gay Harden (Pollock)
2001 Jennifer Connelly (A Beautiful Mind)
2002 Catherine Zeta-Jones (Chicago)
2003 Renée Zellweger (Cold Mountain)
2004 Cate Blanchett (The Aviator)

FOREIGN LANGUAGE FILM (AMERICAN TITLES)

1947 Shoe-Shine (Italy)
1948 Monsieur Vincent (France)
1949 The Bicycle Thief (Italy)
1950 The Walls of Malapaga (France/Italy)
1951 Rashomon (Japan)
1952 Forbidden Games (France)
1953 not awarded
1954 Gate of Hell (Japan)
1955 Samurai, the Legend of Musashi (Japan)
1956 La Strada (Italy)
1957 The Nights of Cabiria (Italy)
1958 My Uncle (France)
1959 Black Orpheus (France)
1960 The Virgin Spring (Sweden)
1961 Through a Glass Darkly (Sweden)
1962 Sundays and Cybele (France)
1963 8½ (Italy)
1964 Yesterday, Today and Tomorrow (Italy)
1965 The Shop on Main Street (Czechoslovakia)
1966 A Man and a Woman (France)
1967 Closely Watched Trains (Czechoslovakia)
1968 War and Peace (USSR)
1969 Z (Algeria)
1970 Investigation of a Citizen Above Suspicion (Italy)
1971 The Garden of the Finzi Continis (Italy)
1972 The Discreet Charm of the Bourgeoisie (France)
1973 Day for Night (France)
1974 Amarcord (France)
1975 Dersu Uzala (USSR)
1976 Black and White in Color (Ivory Coast)
1977 Madame Rosa (France)
1978 Get Out Your Handkerchiefs (France)
1979 The Tin Drum (West Germany)
1980 Moscow Does Not Believe in Tears (USSR)
1981 Mephisto (Hungary)
1982 To Begin Again (Spain)
1983 Fanny & Alexander (Sweden)
1984 Dangerous Moves (Switzerland)
1985 The Official Story (Argentina)
1986 The Assault (The Netherlands)
1987 Babette's Feast (Denmark)
1988 Pelle the Conqueror (Denmark)
1989 Cinema Paradiso (Italy)
1990 Journey of Hope (Switzerland)

FOREIGN LANGUAGE FILM (AMERICAN TITLES) (CONTINUED)

1991 Mediterraneo (Italy)
1992 Indochine (France)
1993 Belle Epoque (Spain)
1994 Burnt by the Sun (Russia)
1995 Antonia's Line (The Netherlands)
1996 Kolya (Czech Republic)
1997 Character (The Netherlands)
1998 Life Is Beautiful (Italy)
1999 All About My Mother (Spain)
2000 Crouching Tiger, Hidden Dragon (Taiwan)
2001 No Man's Land (Belgium/Bosnia and Herzegovina/France/Italy/Slovenia/UK)
2002 Nowhere in Africa (Germany)
2003 The Barbarian Invasions (Canada)
2004 The Sea Inside (Spain)

DIRECTING

1928 Lewis Milestone (Two Arabian Knights), Frank Borzage (7th Heaven)
1929 Frank Lloyd (The Divine Lady)
1930 Lewis Milestone (All Quiet on the Western Front)
1931 Norman Taurog (Skippy)
1932 Frank Borzage (Bad Girl)
1933 Frank Lloyd (Cavalcade)
1934 Frank Capra (It Happened One Night)
1935 John Ford (The Informer)
1936 Frank Capra (Mr. Deeds Goes to Town)
1937 Leo McCarey (The Awful Truth)
1938 Frank Capra (You Can't Take It with You)
1939 Victor Fleming (Gone with the Wind)
1940 John Ford (The Grapes of Wrath)
1941 John Ford (How Green Was My Valley)
1942 William Wyler (Mrs. Miniver)
1943 Michael Curtiz (Casablanca)
1944 Leo McCarey (Going My Way)
1945 Billy Wilder (The Lost Weekend)
1946 William Wyler (The Best Years of Our Lives)
1947 Elia Kazan (Gentleman's Agreement)
1948 John Huston (The Treasure of the Sierra Madre)
1949 Joseph L. Mankiewicz (A Letter to Three Wives)
1950 Joseph L. Mankiewicz (All About Eve)
1951 George Stevens (A Place in the Sun)
1952 John Ford (The Quiet Man)
1953 Fred Zinnemann (From Here to Eternity)
1954 Elia Kazan (On the Waterfront)
1955 Delbert Mann (Marty)
1956 George Stevens (Giant)
1957 David Lean (The Bridge on the River Kwai)
1958 Vincente Minnelli (Gigi)
1959 William Wyler (Ben-Hur)
1960 Billy Wilder (The Apartment)
1961 Robert Wise, Jerome Robbins (West Side Story)
1962 David Lean (Lawrence of Arabia)
1963 Tony Richardson (Tom Jones)
1964 George Cukor (My Fair Lady)
1965 Robert Wise (The Sound of Music)
1966 Fred Zinnemann (A Man for All Seasons)
1967 Mike Nichols (The Graduate)
1968 Carol Reed (Oliver!)
1969 John Schlesinger (Midnight Cowboy)
1970 Franklin J. Schaffner (Patton)
1971 William Friedkin (The French Connection)
1972 Bob Fosse (Cabaret)
1973 George Roy Hill (The Sting)

Academy Awards (Oscars), 1928–2004 (continued)

DIRECTING (CONTINUED)

1974 Francis Ford Coppola (The Godfather Part II)
1975 Milos Forman (One Flew Over the Cuckoo's Nest)
1976 John G. Avildsen (Rocky)
1977 Woody Allen (Annie Hall)
1978 Michael Cimino (The Deer Hunter)
1979 Robert Benton (Kramer vs. Kramer)
1980 Robert Redford (Ordinary People)
1981 Warren Beatty (Reds)
1982 Richard Attenborough (Gandhi)
1983 James L. Brooks (Terms of Endearment)
1984 Milos Forman (Amadeus)
1985 Sydney Pollack (Out of Africa)
1986 Oliver Stone (Platoon)
1987 Bernardo Bertolucci (The Last Emperor)
1988 Barry Levinson (Rain Man)
1989 Oliver Stone (Born on the Fourth of July)
1990 Kevin Costner (Dances with Wolves)
1991 Jonathan Demme (The Silence of the Lambs)
1992 Clint Eastwood (Unforgiven)
1993 Steven Spielberg (Schindler's List)
1994 Robert Zemeckis (Forrest Gump)
1995 Mel Gibson (Braveheart)
1996 Anthony Minghella (The English Patient)
1997 James Cameron (Titanic)
1998 Steven Spielberg (Saving Private Ryan)
1999 Sam Mendes (American Beauty)
2000 Steven Soderbergh (Traffic)
2001 Ron Howard (A Beautiful Mind)
2002 Roman Polanski (The Pianist)
2003 Peter Jackson (The Lord of the Rings: The Return of the King)
2004 Clint Eastwood (Million Dollar Baby)

SCREENPLAY, ADAPTATION[1]

1928 Benjamin Glazer (7th Heaven)
1931 Howard Estabrook (Cimarron)
1932 Edwin Burke (Bad Girl)
1933 Victor Heerman, Sarah Y. Mason (Little Women)
1934 Robert Riskin (It Happened One Night)
1935 Dudley Nichols (The Informer)[2]
1936 Pierre Collings, Sheridan Gibney (The Story of Louis Pasteur)[2]
1937 Norman Reilly Raine, Heinz Herald, Geza Herczeg (The Life of Emile Zola)[2]
1938 George Bernard Shaw, W.P. Lipscomb, Cecil Lewis, Ian Dalrymple (Pygmalion)[2]
1939 Sidney Howard (Gone with the Wind)[2]
1940 Donald Ogden Stewart (The Philadelphia Story)[2]
1941 Sidney Buchman, Seton I. Miller (Here Comes Mr. Jordan)[2]
1942 George Froeschel, James Hilton, Claudine West, Arthur Wimperis (Mrs. Miniver)[2]
1943 Julius J. Epstein, Philip G. Epstein, Howard Koch (Casablanca)[2]
1944 Frank Butler, Frank Cavett (Going My Way)[2]
1945 Charles Brackett, Billy Wilder (The Lost Weekend)[2]
1946 Robert E. Sherwood (The Best Years of Our Lives)[2]
1947 George Seaton (Miracle on 34th Street)[2]
1948 John Huston (The Treasure of the Sierra Madre)[2]
1949 Joseph L. Mankiewicz (A Letter to Three Wives)[2]

SCREENPLAY, ADAPTATION[1] (CONTINUED)

1950 Joseph L. Mankiewicz (All About Eve)[2]
1951 Michael Wilson, Harry Brown (A Place in the Sun)[2]
1952 Charles Schnee (The Bad and the Beautiful)[2]
1953 Daniel Taradash (From Here to Eternity)[2]
1954 George Seaton (The Country Girl)[2]
1955 Paddy Chayefsky (Marty)[2]
1956 James Poe, John Farrow, S.J. Perelman (Around the World in 80 Days)
1957 Pierre Boulle, Michael Wilson, Carl Foreman (The Bridge on the River Kwai)
1958 Alan Jay Lerner (Gigi)
1959 Neil Paterson (Room at the Top)
1960 Richard Brooks (Elmer Gantry)
1961 Abby Mann (Judgment at Nuremberg)
1962 Horton Foote (To Kill a Mockingbird)
1963 John Osborne (Tom Jones)
1964 Edward Anhalt (Becket)
1965 Robert Bolt (Doctor Zhivago)
1966 Robert Bolt (A Man for All Seasons)
1967 Stirling Silliphant (In the Heat of the Night)
1968 James Goldman (The Lion in Winter)
1969 Waldo Salt (Midnight Cowboy)
1970 Ring Lardner, Jr. (M*A*S*H)
1971 Ernest Tidyman (The French Connection)
1972 Mario Puzo, Francis Ford Coppola (The Godfather)
1973 William Peter Blatty (The Exorcist)
1974 Francis Ford Coppola, Mario Puzo (The Godfather Part II)
1975 Lawrence Hauben, Bo Goldman (One Flew Over the Cuckoo's Nest)
1976 William Goldman (All the President's Men)
1977 Alvin Sargent (Julia)
1978 Oliver Stone (Midnight Express)
1979 Robert Benton (Kramer vs. Kramer)
1980 Alvin Sargent (Ordinary People)
1981 Ernest Thompson (On Golden Pond)
1982 Costa-Gavras, Donald Stewart (Missing)
1983 James L. Brooks (Terms of Endearment)
1984 Peter Shaffer (Amadeus)
1985 Kurt Luedtke (Out of Africa)
1986 Ruth Prawer Jhabvala (A Room with a View)
1987 Mark Peploe, Bernardo Bertolucci (The Last Emperor)
1988 Christopher Hampton (Dangerous Liaisons)
1989 Alfred Uhry (Driving Miss Daisy)
1990 Michael Blake (Dances with Wolves)
1991 Ted Tally (The Silence of the Lambs)
1992 Ruth Prawer Jhabvala (Howards End)
1993 Steven Zaillian (Schindler's List)
1994 Eric Roth (Forrest Gump)
1995 Emma Thompson (Sense and Sensibility)
1996 Billy Bob Thornton (Sling Blade)
1997 Brian Helgeland, Curtis Hanson (L.A. Confidential)
1998 Bill Condon (Gods and Monsters)
1999 John Irving (The Cider House Rules)
2000 Stephen Gaghan (Traffic)
2001 Akiva Goldsman (A Beautiful Mind)
2002 Ronald Harwood (The Pianist)
2003 Fran Walsh, Philippa Boyens, Peter Jackson (The Lord of the Rings: The Return of the King)
2004 Alexander Payne, Jim Taylor (Sideways)

Academy Awards (Oscars), 1928–2004 (continued)

SCREENPLAY, ORIGINAL[1]

1928 Ben Hecht (Underworld),[4] Joseph Farnham (The Fair Co-Ed; Laugh, Clown, Laugh; Telling the World [titles])
1929 Hans Kraly (The Patriot)
1930 Frances Marion (The Big House)
1931 John Monk Saunders (The Dawn Patrol)[4]
1932 Frances Marion (The Champ)[4]
1933 Robert Lord (One Way Passage)[4]
1934 Arthur Caesar (Manhattan Melodrama)[4]
1935 Ben Hecht, Charles MacArthur (The Scoundrel)[4]
1936 Pierre Collings, Sheridan Gibney (The Story of Louis Pasteur)[4]
1937 William A. Wellman, Robert Carson (A Star Is Born)[4]
1938 Eleanore Griffin, Dore Schary (Boys Town)[4]
1939 Lewis R. Foster (Mr. Smith Goes to Washington)[4]
1940 Preston Sturges (The Great McGinty),[3] Benjamin Glazer, John S. Toldy (Arise, My Love)[4]
1941 Herman J. Mankiewicz, Orson Welles (Citizen Kane),[3] Harry Segall (Here Comes Mr. Jordan)[4]
1942 Michael Kanin, Ring Lardner, Jr. (Woman of the Year),[3] Emeric Pressburger (Forty-Ninth Parallel)[4]
1943 Norman Krasna (Princess O'Rourke),[3] William Saroyan (The Human Comedy)[4]
1944 Lamar Trotti (Wilson),[3] Leo McCarey (Going My Way)[4]
1945 Richard Schweizer (Marie-Louise),[3] Charles G. Booth (The House on 92nd Street)[4]
1946 Muriel Box, Sydney Box (The Seventh Veil),[3] Clemence Dane (Vacation from Marriage)[4]
1947 Sidney Sheldon (The Bachelor and the Bobby-Soxer),[3] Valentine Davies (Miracle on 34th Street)[4]
1948 Richard Schweizer, David Wechsler (The Search)[4]
1949 Robert Pirosh (Battleground),[3] Douglas Morrow (The Stratton Story)[4]
1950 Charles Brackett, Billy Wilder, D.M. Marshman, Jr. (Sunset Boulevard),[3] Edna Anhalt, Edward Anhalt (Panic in the Streets)[4]
1951 Alan Jay Lerner (An American in Paris),[3] Paul Dehn, James Bernard (Seven Days to Noon)[4]
1952 T.E.B. Clarke (The Lavender Hill Mob),[3] Fredric M. Frank, Theodore St. John, Frank Cavett (The Greatest Show on Earth)[4]
1953 Charles Brackett, Walter Reisch, Richard L. Breen (Titanic),[3] Dalton Trumbo[5] (as Ian McLellan Hunter, Roman Holiday)[4]
1954 Budd Schulberg (On the Waterfront),[3] Philip Yordan (Broken Lance)[4]
1955 William Ludwig, Sonya Levien (Interrupted Melody),[3] Daniel Fuchs (Love Me or Leave Me)[4]
1956 Albert Lamorisse (The Red Balloon),[3] Dalton Trumbo[5] (as Robert Rich, The Brave One)[4]
1957 George Wells (Designing Woman)
1958 Nedrick Young[5] (as Nathan E. Douglas), Harold Jacob Smith (The Defiant Ones)
1959 Russell Rouse, Clarence Greene, Stanley Shapiro, Maurice Richlin (Pillow Talk)
1960 Billy Wilder, I.A.L. Diamond (The Apartment)
1961 William Inge (Splendor in the Grass)

SCREENPLAY, ORIGINAL[1] (CONTINUED)

1962 Ennio de Concini, Alfredo Giannetti, Pietro Germi (Divorce—Italian Style)
1963 James R. Webb (How the West Was Won)
1964 S.H. Barnett, Peter Stone, Frank Tarloff (Father Goose)
1965 Frederic Raphael (Darling)
1966 Claude Lelouch, Pierre Uytterhoeven (A Man and a Woman)
1967 William Rose (Guess Who's Coming to Dinner)
1968 Mel Brooks (The Producers)
1969 William Goldman (Butch Cassidy and the Sundance Kid)
1970 Francis Ford Coppola, Edmund H. North (Patton)
1971 Paddy Chayefsky (The Hospital)
1972 Jeremy Larner (The Candidate)
1973 David S. Ward (The Sting)
1974 Robert Towne (Chinatown)
1975 Frank Pierson (Dog Day Afternoon)
1976 Paddy Chayefsky (Network)
1977 Woody Allen, Marshall Brickman (Annie Hall)
1978 Nancy Dowd, Waldo Salt, Robert C. Jones (Coming Home)
1979 Steve Tesich (Breaking Away)
1980 Bo Goldman (Melvin and Howard)
1981 Colin Welland (Chariots of Fire)
1982 John Briley (Gandhi)
1983 Horton Foote (Tender Mercies)
1984 Robert Benton (Places in the Heart)
1985 Earl W. Wallace, William Kelley, Pamela Wallace (Witness)
1986 Woody Allen (Hannah and Her Sisters)
1987 John Patrick Shanley (Moonstruck)
1988 Ronald Bass, Barry Morrow (Rain Man)
1989 Tom Schulman (Dead Poets Society)
1990 Bruce Joel Rubin (Ghost)
1991 Callie Khouri (Thelma & Louise)
1992 Neil Jordan (The Crying Game)
1993 Jane Campion (The Piano)
1994 Quentin Tarantino, Roger Avary (Pulp Fiction)
1995 Christopher McQuarrie (The Usual Suspects)
1996 Joel Coen, Ethan Coen (Fargo)
1997 Ben Affleck, Matt Damon (Good Will Hunting)
1998 Marc Norman, Tom Stoppard (Shakespeare in Love)
1999 Alan Ball (American Beauty)
2000 Cameron Crowe (Almost Famous)
2001 Julian Fellowes (Gosford Park)
2002 Pedro Almodóvar (Talk to Her)
2003 Sofia Coppola (Lost in Translation)
2004 Charlie Kaufman (Eternal Sunshine of the Spotless Mind)

CINEMATOGRAPHY

1928 Charles Rosher, Karl Struss (Sunrise)
1929 Clyde De Vinna (White Shadows in the South Seas)
1930 Joseph T. Rucker, Willard Van Der Veer (With Byrd at the South Pole)
1931 Floyd Crosby (Tabu)
1932 Lee Garmes (Shanghai Express)
1933 Charles Bryant Lang, Jr. (A Farewell to Arms)
1934 Victor Milner (Cleopatra)
1935 Hal Mohr (A Midsummer Night's Dream)
1936 Gaetano Gaudio (Anthony Adverse)
1937 Karl Freund (The Good Earth)

Academy Awards (Oscars), 1928–2004 (continued)

CINEMATOGRAPHY (CONTINUED)

1938   Joseph Ruttenberg *(The Great Waltz)*
1939   Gregg Toland *(Wuthering Heights)*,[6] Ernest Haller, Ray Rennahan *(Gone with the Wind)*[7]
1940   George Barnes *(Rebecca)*,[6] Georges Perinal *(The Thief of Bagdad)*[7]
1941   Arthur Miller *(How Green Was My Valley)*,[6] Ernest Palmer, Ray Rennahan *(Blood and Sand)*[7]
1942   Joseph Ruttenberg *(Mrs. Miniver)*,[6] Leon Shamroy *(The Black Swan)*[7]
1943   Arthur Miller *(The Song of Bernadette)*,[6] Hal Mohr, W. Howard Greene *(The Phantom of the Opera)*[7]
1944   Joseph LaShelle *(Laura)*,[6] Leon Shamroy *(Wilson)*[7]
1945   Harry Stradling *(The Picture of Dorian Gray)*,[6] Leon Shamroy *(Leave Her to Heaven)*[7]
1946   Arthur Miller *(Anna and the King of Siam)*,[6] Charles Rosher, Leonard Smith, Arthur Arling *(The Yearling)*[7]
1947   Guy Green *(Great Expectations)*,[6] Jack Cardiff *(Black Narcissus)*[7]
1948   William Daniels *(The Naked City)*,[6] Joseph Valentine, William V. Skall, Winton Hoch *(Joan of Arc)*[7]
1949   Paul C. Vogel *(Battleground)*,[6] Winton Hoch *(She Wore a Yellow Ribbon)*[7]
1950   Robert Krasker *(The Third Man)*,[6] Robert Surtees *(King Solomon's Mines)*[7]
1951   William C. Mellor *(A Place in the Sun)*,[6] Alfred Gilks, John Alton *(An American in Paris)*[7]
1952   Robert Surtees *(The Bad and the Beautiful)*,[6] Winton C. Hoch, Archie Stout *(The Quiet Man)*[7]
1953   Burnett Guffey *(From Here to Eternity)*,[6] Loyal Griggs *(Shane)*[7]
1954   Boris Kaufman *(On the Waterfront)*,[6] Milton Krasner *(Three Coins in the Fountain)*[7]
1955   James Wong Howe *(The Rose Tattoo)*,[6] Robert Burks *(To Catch a Thief)*[7]
1956   Joseph Ruttenberg *(Somebody Up There Likes Me)*,[6] Lionel Lindon *(Around the World in 80 Days)*[7]
1957   Jack Hildyard *(The Bridge on the River Kwai)*
1958   Sam Leavitt *(The Defiant Ones)*,[6] Joseph Ruttenberg *(Gigi)*[7]
1959   William C. Mellor *(The Diary of Anne Frank)*,[6] Robert L. Surtees *(Ben-Hur)*[7]
1960   Freddie Francis *(Sons and Lovers)*,[6] Russell Metty *(Spartacus)*[7]
1961   Eugen Shuftan *(The Hustler)*,[6] Daniel L. Fapp *(West Side Story)*[7]
1962   Jean Bourgoin, Walter Wottitz *(The Longest Day)*,[6] Fred A. Young *(Lawrence of Arabia)*[7]
1963   James Wong Howe *(Hud)*,[6] Leon Shamroy *(Cleopatra)*[7]
1964   Walter Lassally *(Zorba the Greek)*,[6] Harry Stradling *(My Fair Lady)*[7]
1965   Ernest Laszlo *(Ship of Fools)*,[6] Freddie Young *(Doctor Zhivago)*[7]
1966   Haskell Wexler *(Who's Afraid of Virginia Woolf?)*,[6] Ted Moore *(A Man for All Seasons)*[7]
1967   Burnett Guffey *(Bonnie and Clyde)*
1968   Pasqualino De Santis *(Romeo and Juliet)*
1969   Conrad Hall *(Butch Cassidy and the Sundance Kid)*
1970   Freddie Young *(Ryan's Daughter)*

CINEMATOGRAPHY (CONTINUED)

1971   Oswald Morris *(Fiddler on the Roof)*
1972   Geoffrey Unsworth *(Cabaret)*
1973   Sven Nykvist *(Cries and Whispers)*
1974   Fred Koenekamp, Joseph Biroc *(The Towering Inferno)*
1975   John Alcott *(Barry Lyndon)*
1976   Haskell Wexler *(Bound for Glory)*
1977   Vilmos Zsigmond *(Close Encounters of the Third Kind)*
1978   Nestor Almendros *(Days of Heaven)*
1979   Vittorio Storaro *(Apocalypse Now)*
1980   Geoffrey Unsworth, Ghislain Cloquet *(Tess)*
1981   Vittorio Storaro *(Reds)*
1982   Billy Williams, Ronnie Taylor *(Gandhi)*
1983   Sven Nykvist *(Fanny & Alexander)*
1984   Chris Menges *(The Killing Fields)*
1985   David Watkin *(Out of Africa)*
1986   Chris Menges *(The Mission)*
1987   Vittorio Storaro *(The Last Emperor)*
1988   Peter Biziou *(Mississippi Burning)*
1989   Freddie Francis *(Glory)*
1990   Dean Semler *(Dances with Wolves)*
1991   Robert Richardson *(JFK)*
1992   Philippe Rousselot *(A River Runs Through It)*
1993   Janusz Kaminski *(Schindler's List)*
1994   John Toll *(Legends of the Fall)*
1995   John Toll *(Braveheart)*
1996   John Seale *(The English Patient)*
1997   Russell Carpenter *(Titanic)*
1998   Janusz Kaminski *(Saving Private Ryan)*
1999   Conrad L. Hall *(American Beauty)*
2000   Peter Pau *(Crouching Tiger, Hidden Dragon)*
2001   Andrew Lesnie *(The Lord of the Rings: The Fellowship of the Ring)*
2002   Conrad L. Hall *(Road to Perdition)*
2003   Russell Boyd *(Master and Commander: The Far Side of the World)*
2004   Robert Richardson *(The Aviator)*

VISUAL EFFECTS[8]

1939   E.H. Hansen *(The Rains Came)*
1940   Lawrence Butler *(The Thief of Bagdad)*
1941   Farciot Edouart, Gordon Jennings *(I Wanted Wings)*
1942   Farciot Edouart, Gordon Jennings, William L. Pereira *(Reap the Wild Wind)*
1943   Fred Sersen *(Crash Dive)*
1944   A. Arnold Gillespie, Donald Jahraus, Warren Newcombe *(Thirty Seconds Over Tokyo)*
1945   John P. Fulton *(Wonder Man)*
1946   Thomas Howard *(Blithe Spirit)*
1947   A. Arnold Gillespie, Warren Newcombe *(Green Dolphin Street)*
1948   Paul Eagler, J. McMillan Johnson, Russell Shearman, Clarence Slifer *(Portrait of Jennie)*
1949   *Mighty Joe Young*
1950   *Destination Moon*
1951   *When Worlds Collide*
1952   *Plymouth Adventure*
1953   *The War of the Worlds*
1954   *20,000 Leagues Under the Sea*
1955   *The Bridges at Toko-Ri*
1956   John Fulton *(The Ten Commandments)*
1958   Tom Howard *(tom thumb)*
1959   A. Arnold Gillespie, Robert MacDonald *(Ben-Hur)*

Academy Awards (Oscars), 1928–2004 (continued)

VISUAL EFFECTS[a] (CONTINUED)

1960 Gene Warren, Tim Baar (The Time Machine)
1961 Bill Warrington (The Guns of Navarone)
1962 Robert MacDonald (The Longest Day)
1963 Emil Kosa, Jr. (Cleopatra)
1964 Peter Ellenshaw, Hamilton Luske, Eustace Lycett (Mary Poppins)
1965 John Stears (Thunderball)
1966 Art Cruickshank (Fantastic Voyage)
1967 L.B. Abbott (Doctor Dolittle)
1968 Stanley Kubrick (2001: A Space Odyssey)
1969 Robbie Robertson (Marooned)
1970 A.D. Flowers, L.B. Abbott (Tora! Tora! Tora!)
1971 Alan Maley, Eustace Lycett, Danny Lee (Bedknobs and Broomsticks)
1972 L.B. Abbott, A.D. Flowers (The Poseidon Adventure)
1974 Frank Brendel, Glen Robinson, Albert Whitlock (Earthquake)
1975 Albert Whitlock, Glen Robinson (The Hindenburg)
1976 Carlo Rambaldi, Glen Robinson, Frank Van der Veer (King Kong), L.B. Abbott, Glen Robinson, Matthew Yuricich (Logan's Run)
1977 John Stears, John Dykstra, Richard Edlund, Grant McCune, Robert Blalack (Star Wars)
1978 Les Bowie, Colin Chilvers, Denys Coop, Roy Field, Derek Meddings, Zoran Perisic (Superman)
1979 H.R. Giger, Carlo Rambaldi, Brian Johnson, Nick Allder, Denys Ayling (Alien)
1980 Brian Johnson, Richard Edlund, Dennis Muren, Bruce Nicholson (The Empire Strikes Back)
1981 Richard Edlund, Kit West, Bruce Nicholson, Joe Johnston (Raiders of the Lost Ark)
1982 Carlo Rambaldi, Dennis Muren, Kenneth F. Smith (E.T. the Extra-Terrestrial)
1983 Richard Edlund, Dennis Muren, Ken Ralston, Phil Tippet (Return of the Jedi)
1984 Dennis Muren, Michael McAlister, Lorne Peterson, George Gibbs (Indiana Jones and the Temple of Doom)
1985 Ken Ralston, Ralph McQuarrie, Scott Farrar, David Berry (Cocoon)
1986 Robert Skotak, Stan Winston, John Richardson, Suzanne Benson (Aliens)
1987 Dennis Muren, William George, Harley Jessup, Kenneth Smith (Innerspace)
1988 Ken Ralston, Richard Williams, Edward Jones, George Gibbs (Who Framed Roger Rabbit)
1989 John Bruno, Dennis Muren, Hoyt Yeatman, Dennis Skotak (The Abyss)
1990 Eric Brevig, Rob Bottin, Tim McGovern, Alex Funke (Total Recall)
1991 Robert Skotak (Terminator 2: Judgment Day)
1992 Ken Ralston, Doug Chiang, Doug Smythe, Tom Woodruff, Jr. (Death Becomes Her)
1993 Dennis Muren, Stan Winston, Phil Tippett, Michael Lantieri (Jurassic Park)
1994 Ken Ralston, George Murphy, Stephen Rosenbaum, Allen Hall (Forrest Gump)
1995 Scott E. Anderson, Charles Gibson, Neal Scanlan, John Cox (Babe)
1996 Volker Engel, Douglas Smith, Clay Pinney, Joseph Viskocil (Independence Day)

VISUAL EFFECTS[a] (CONTINUED)

1997 Robert Legato, Mark Lasoff, Thomas L. Fisher, Michael Kanfer (Titanic)
1998 Joel Hynek, Nicholas Brooks, Stuart Robertson, Kevin Mack (What Dreams May Come)
1999 John Gaeta, Janek Sirrs, Steve Courtley, Jon Thum (The Matrix)
2000 John Nelson, Neil Corbould, Tim Burke, Rob Harvey (Gladiator)
2001 Jim Rygiel, Randall William Cook, Richard Taylor, Mark Stetson (The Lord of the Rings: The Fellowship of the Ring)
2002 Jim Rygiel, Joe Letteri, Randall William Cook, Alex Funke (The Lord of the Rings: The Two Towers)
2003 Jim Rygiel, Joe Letteri, Randall William Cook, Alex Funke (The Lord of the Rings: The Return of the King)
2004 John Dykstra, Scott Stokdyk, Anthony LaMolinara, John Frazier (Spider-Man 2)

MAKEUP

1981 Rick Baker (An American Werewolf in London)
1982 Sarah Monzani, Michele Burke (Quest for Fire)
1984 Paul LeBlanc, Dick Smith (Amadeus)
1985 Michael Westmore, Zoltan Elek (Mask)
1986 Chris Walas, Stephan Dupuis (The Fly)
1987 Rick Baker (Harry and the Hendersons)
1988 Ve Neill, Steve La Porte, Robert Short (Beetlejuice)
1989 Manlio Rocchetti, Lynn Barber, Kevin Haney (Driving Miss Daisy)
1990 John Caglione, Jr., Doug Drexler (Dick Tracy)
1991 Stan Winston, Jeff Dawn (Terminator 2: Judgment Day)
1992 Greg Cannom, Michele Burke, Matthew W. Mungle (Bram Stoker's Dracula)
1993 Greg Cannom, Ve Neill, Yolanda Toussieng (Mrs. Doubtfire)
1994 Rick Baker, Ve Neill, Yolanda Toussieng (Ed Wood)
1995 Peter Frampton, Paul Pattison, Lois Burwell (Braveheart)
1996 Rick Baker, David LeRoy Anderson (The Nutty Professor)
1997 Rick Baker, David LeRoy Anderson (Men in Black)
1998 Jenny Shircore (Elizabeth)
1999 Christine Blundell, Trefor Proud (Topsy-Turvy)
2000 Rick Baker, Gail Ryan (Dr. Seuss' How the Grinch Stole Christmas)
2001 Peter Owen, Richard Taylor (The Lord of the Rings: The Fellowship of the Ring)
2002 John Jackson, Beatrice Alba (Frida)
2003 Richard Taylor, Peter King (The Lord of the Rings: The Return of the King)
2004 Valli O'Reilly, Bill Corso (Lemony Snicket's A Series of Unfortunate Events)

ORIGINAL SCORE

1938 Erich Wolfgang Korngold (The Adventures of Robin Hood)
1939 Herbert Stothart (The Wizard of Oz)
1940 Leigh Harline, Paul J. Smith, Ned Washington (Pinocchio)

Academy Awards (Oscars), 1928–2004 (continued)

ORIGINAL SCORE (CONTINUED)

1941 Bernard Herrmann (*All That Money Can Buy*)
1942 Max Steiner (*Now, Voyager*)
1943 Alfred Newman (*The Song of Bernadette*)
1944 Max Steiner (*Since You Went Away*)
1945 Miklos Rozsa (*Spellbound*)
1946 Hugo Friedhofer (*The Best Years of Our Lives*)
1947 Dr. Miklos Rozsa (*A Double Life*)
1948 Brian Easdale (*The Red Shoes*)
1949 Aaron Copland (*The Heiress*)
1950 Franz Waxman (*Sunset Blvd.*)
1951 Franz Waxman (*A Place in the Sun*)
1952 Dimitri Tiomkin (*High Noon*)
1953 Bronislau Kaper (*Lili*)
1954 Dimitri Tiomkin (*The High and Mighty*)
1955 Alfred Newman (*Love Is a Many-Splendored Thing*)
1956 Victor Young (*Around the World in 80 Days*)
1957 Scoring Malcolm Arnold (*The Bridge on the River Kwai[9]*)
1958 Dimitri Tiomkin (*The Old Man and The Sea*)
1959 Miklos Rozsa (*Ben-Hur*)
1960 Ernest Gold (*Exodus*)
1961 Henry Mancini (*Breakfast at Tiffany's*)
1962 Maurice Jarre (*Lawrence of Arabia*)
1963 John Addison (*Tom Jones*)
1964 Richard M. Sherman, Robert B. Sherman (*Mary Poppins*)
1965 Maurice Jarre (*Doctor Zhivago*)
1966 John Barry (*Born Free*)
1967 Elmer Bernstein (*Thoroughly Modern Millie*)
1968 John Barry (*The Lion in Winter[10]*); John Green (*Oliver![11]*)
1969 Burt Bacharach (*Butch Cassidy and the Sundance Kid[10]*); Lennie Hayton, Lionel Newman (*Hello, Dolly![11]*)
1970 Francis Lai (*Love Story*); The Beatles (*Let It Be[12]*)
1971 Michel Legrand (*Summer of '42*)
1972 Charles Chaplin, Raymond Rasch, Larry Russell (*Limelight*)
1973 Marvin Hamlisch (*The Way We Were*)
1974 Nino Rota, Carmine Coppola (*The Godfather Part II*)
1975 John Williams (*Jaws*); Leonard Rosenman (*Barry Lyndon[12]*)
1976 Jerry Goldsmith (*The Omen*); Leonard Rosenman (*Bound for Glory[12]*)
1977 John Williams (*Star Wars*); Jonathan Tunick (*A Little Night Music[12]*)
1978 Giorgio Moroder (*Midnight Express*)
1979 Georges Delerue (*A Little Romance*); Ralph Burns (*All That Jazz[12]*)
1980 Michael Gore (*Fame*)
1981 Vangelis (*Chariots of Fire*)
1982 John Williams (*E.T. The Extra-Terrestrial*); Henry Mancini, Leslie Bricusse (*Victor/Victoria[12]*)
1983 Bill Conti (*The Right Stuff*); Michel Legrand, Alan Bergman, Marilyn Bergman (*Yentl[12]*)
1984 Maurice Jarre (*A Passage to India*); Prince (*Purple Rain[12]*)
1985 John Barry (*Out of Africa*)
1986 Herbie Hancock (*'Round Midnight*)
1987 Ryuichi Sakamoto, David Byrne, Cong Su (*The Last Emperor*)
1988 Dave Grusin (*The Milagro Beanfield War*)
1989 Alan Menken (*The Little Mermaid*)
1990 John Barry (*Dances with Wolves*)

ORIGINAL SCORE (CONTINUED)

1991 Alan Menken (*Beauty and the Beast*)
1992 Alan Menken (*Aladdin*)
1993 John Williams (*Schindler's List*)
1994 Hans Zimmer (*The Lion King*)
1995 Luis Enrique Bacalov (*The Postman [Il. Postino][10]*); Alan Menken, Stephen Schwartz (*Pocahontas[13]*)
1996 Gabriel Yared (*The English Patient[10]*); Rachel Portman (*Emma[13]*)
1997 James Horner (*Titanic[10]*); Anne Dudley (*The Full Monty[13]*)
1998 Nicola Piovani (*Life Is Beautiful[10]*); Stephen Warbeck (*Shakespeare in Love[13]*)
1999 John Corigliano (*The Red Violin*)
2000 Tan Dun (*Crouching Tiger, Hidden Dragon*)
2001 Howard Shore (*The Lord of the Rings: The Fellowship of the Ring*)
2002 Elliot Goldenthal (*Frida*)
2003 Howard Shore (*The Lord of the Rings: The Return of the King*)
2004 Jan A.P. Kaczmarek (*Finding Neverland*)

ORIGINAL SONG

1934 Con Conrad, Herb Magidson, "The Continental" from *The Gay Divorcee*
1935 Harry Warren, Al Dubin, "Lullaby of Broadway" from *Gold Diggers of 1935*
1936 Jerome Kern, Dorothy Fields, "The Way You Look Tonight" from *Swing Time*
1937 Harry Owens, "Sweet Leilani" from *Waikiki Wedding*
1938 Ralph Rainger, Leo Robin, "Thanks for the Memory" from *The Big Broadcast of 1938*
1939 Harold Arlen, E. Y. Harburg, "Over the Rainbow" from *The Wizard of Oz*
1940 Leigh Harline, Ned Washington, "When You Wish Upon a Star" from *Pinocchio*
1941 Jerome Kern, Oscar Hammerstein II, "The Last Time I Saw Paris" from *Lady Be Good*
1942 Irving Berlin, "White Christmas" from *Holiday Inn*
1943 Harry Warren, Mack Gordon, "You'll Never Know" from *Hello, Frisco, Hello*
1944 James Van Heusen, Johnny Burke, "Swinging on a Star" from *Going My Way*
1945 Richard Rodgers, Oscar Hammerstein, "It Might As Well Be Spring" from *State Fair*
1946 Harry Warren, Johnny Mercer, "On the Atchison, Topeka and the Santa Fe" from *The Harvey Girls*
1947 Allie Wrubel, Ray Gilbert, "Zip-a-dee-doo-dah" from *Song of the South*
1948 Jay Livingston, Ray Evans, "Buttons and Bows" from *The Paleface*
1949 Frank Loesser, "Baby, It's Cold Outside" from *Neptune's Daughter*
1950 Ray Evans, Jay Livingston, "Mona Lisa" from *Captain Carey, U.S.A.*
1951 Hoagy Carmichael, Johnny Mercer, "In The Cool, Cool, Cool of the Evening" from *Here Comes the Groom*
1952 Dimitri Tiomkin, Ned Washington, "High Noon (Do Not Forsake Me, Oh My Darlin')" from *High Noon*
1953 Sammy Fain, Paul Francis Webster, "Secret Love" from *Calamity Jane*
1954 Jule Styne, Sammy Cahn, "Three Coins in the Fountain" from *Three Coins in the Fountain*

Academy Awards (Oscars), 1928–2004 (continued)

ORIGINAL SONG (CONTINUED)

1955 Sammy Fain, Paul Francis Webster, "Love Is a Many-Splendored Thing" from *Love Is a Many-Splendored Thing*

1956 Jay Livingston, Ray Evans, "Whatever Will Be, Will Be (Que Sera, Sera)" from *The Man Who Knew Too Much*

1957 James Van Heusen, Sammy Cahn, "All the Way" from *The Joker is Wild*

1958 Frederick Loewe, Alan Jay Lerner, "Gigi" from *Gigi*

1959 James Van Heusen, Sammy Cahn, "High Hopes" from *A Hole in the Head*

1960 Manos Hadjidakis, "Never on Sunday" from *Never on Sunday*

1961 Henry Mancini, Johnny Mercer, "Moon River" from *Breakfast at Tiffany's*

1962 Henry Mancini, Johnny Mercer, "Days of Wine and Roses" from *Days of Wine and Roses*

1963 James Van Heusen, Sammy Cahn, "Call Me Irresponsible" from *Papa's Delicate Condition*

1964 Richard M. Sherman, Robert B. Sherman, "Chim Chim Cher-ee" from *Mary Poppins*

1965 Johnny Mandel, Paul Francis Webster, "The Shadow of Your Smile" from *The Sandpiper*

1966 John Barry, Don Black, "Born Free" from *Born Free*

1967 Leslie Bricusse, "Talk to the Animals" from *Doctor Doolittle*

1968 Michel Legrand, Alan Bergman, Marilyn Bergman, "The Windmills of Your Mind" from *The Thomas Crown Affair*

1969 Burt Bacharach, Hal David, "Raindrops Keep Fallin' On My Head" from *Butch Cassidy and the Sundance Kid*

1970 Fred Karlin, Robb Royer [aka Robb Wilson], James Griffin [aka Arthur James], "For All We Know" from *Lovers and Other Strangers*

1971 Isaac Hayes, "Theme from Shaft" from *Shaft*

1972 Al Kasha, Joel Hirschhorn, "The Morning After" from *The Poseidon Adventure*

1973 Marvin Hamlisch, Alan Bergman, Marilyn Bergman, "The Way We Were" from *The Way We Were*

1974 Al Kasha, Joel Hirschhorn, "We May Never Love Like This Again" from *The Towering Inferno*

1975 Keith Carradine, "I'm Easy" from *Nashville*

1976 Barbra Streisand, Paul Williams, "Evergreen (Love Theme from A Star is Born)" from *A Star is Born*

1977 Joseph Brooks, "You Light Up My Life" from *You Light Up My Life*

1978 Paul Jabara, "Last Dance" from *Thank God It's Friday*

ORIGINAL SONG (CONTINUED)

1979 David Shire, Norman Gimbel, "It Goes Like It Goes" from *Norma Rae*

1980 Michael Gore, Dean Pitchford, "Fame" from *Fame*

1981 Burt Bacharach, Carole Bayer Sager, Christopher Cross, Peter Allen, "Arthur's Theme (Best That You Can Do)" from *Arthur*

1982 Jack Nitzsche, Buffy Sainte-Marie, Will Jennings, "Up Where We Belong" from *An Officer and a Gentleman*

1983 Giorgio Moroder, Keith Forsey, Irene Cara, "Flashdance...What a Feeling" from *Flashdance*

1984 Stevie Wonder, "I Just Called to Say I Love You" from *The Woman in Red*

1985 Lionel Richie, "Say You, Say Me" from *White Nights*

1986 Giorgio Moroder, Tom Whitlock, "Take My Breath Away" from *Top Gun*

1987 Franke Previte, John DeNicola, Donald Markowitz, "(I've Had) The Time of My Life" from *Dirty Dancing*

1988 Carly Simon, "Let the River Run" from *Working Girl*

1989 Alan Menken, Howard Ashman, "Under the Sea" from *The Little Mermaid*

1990 Stephen Sondheim, "Sooner or Later (I Always Get My Man)" from *Dick Tracy*

1991 Alan Menken, Howard Ashman, "Beauty and the Beast" from *Beauty and the Beast*

1992 Alan Menken, Tim Rice, "A Whole New World" from *Aladdin*

1993 Bruce Springsteen, "Streets of Philadelphia" from *Philadelphia*

1994 Elton John, Tim Rice, "Can You Feel the Love Tonight" from *The Lion King*

1995 Alan Menken, Stephen Schwartz, "Colors of the Wind" from *Pocahontas*

1996 Andrew Lloyd Webber, Tim Rice, "You Must Love Me" from *Evita*

1997 James Horner, Will Jennings, "My Heart Will Go On" from *Titanic*

1998 Stephen Schwartz, "When You Believe" from *The Prince of Egypt*

1999 Phil Collins, "You'll be in My Heart" from *Tarzan*

2000 Bob Dylan, "Things Have Changed" from *Wonder Boys*

2001 Randy Newman, "If I Didn't Have You" from *Monsters, Inc.*

2002 Eminem, Jeff Bass, Luis Resto, "Lose Yourself" from *8 Mile*

2003 Fran Walsh, Howard Shore, Annie Lennox, "Into the West," from *The Lord of the Rings: The Return of the King*

2004 Jorge Drexler, "Al otro lado del río," from *The Motorcycle Diaries*

---

[1]The current screenplay categories were adopted for the 1957 awards. Until then, various separate writing awards were given for silent-film title writing, screenplay, story and screenplay, and motion picture story. [2]Screenplay (for script only). [3]Story and screenplay (for narrative and script; also called original screenplay). [4]Motion picture story (for narrative only; also called original story). [5]Actual winner was blacklisted at the time of the award and the honored work was attributed to another name or person; pseudonym or nominal winner listed in parentheses. [6]Black and white. [7]Color. [8]Until 1963, both visual and sound effects were honored as special effects. Only those awards for visual effects are listed here. [9]Scoring. [10]Drama or not a musical. [11]Musical [12]Song score. [13]Musical or comedy.

Encyclopædia Britannica's Best Love Stories in Cinema

Encyclopædia Britannica's editors have created this list of the best stories about love on film from around the world and from all across cinema history. Each entry includes the movie's leading performers.

An Affair to Remember (Deborah Kerr and Cary Grant; 1957)

The African Queen (Humphrey Bogart and Katharine Hepburn; 1951)

The Age of Innocence (Daniel Day-Lewis, Michelle Pfeiffer, and Winona Ryder; 1993)

Ali: Fear Eats the Soul (*Angst essen Seele auf;* Brigitte Mira and El Hedi ben Salem; 1974)

All That Heaven Allows (Rock Hudson and Jane Wyman; 1955)

Amélie (*Le Fabuleux destin d'Amélie Poulain;* Audrey Tautou and Mathieu Kassovitz; 2001)

The American President (Michael Douglas and Annette Bening; 1995)

An American in Paris (Gene Kelly and Leslie Caron; 1951)

Anna Karenina (Greta Garbo and Fredric March; 1935)

Annie Hall (Woody Allen and Diane Keaton; 1977)

Antonia's Line (ensemble cast; 1995)

The Apartment (Jack Lemmon and Shirley MacLaine; 1960)

The Awful Truth (Irene Dunne and Cary Grant; 1937)

Ballad of a Soldier (*Ballada o soldate;* Vladimir Ivashov and Zhanna Prokhorenko; 1959)

Barefoot in the Park (Jane Fonda and Robert Redford; 1967)

Beauty and the Beast (*La Belle et la bête;* Josette Day and Jean Marais; 1946)

Before Sunrise (Ethan Hawke and Julie Delpy; 1995)

Before Sunset (Ethan Hawke and Julie Delpy; 2004)

The Best Years of Our Lives (Myrna Loy and Fredric March; 1946)

Black Orpheus (*Orfeu negro;* Breno Mello and Marpessa Dawn; 1959)

Bonnie and Clyde (Warren Beatty and Faye Dunaway; 1967)

Breakfast at Tiffany's (Audrey Hepburn and George Peppard; 1961)

The Bridges of Madison County (Meryl Streep and Clint Eastwood; 1995)

Brief Encounter (Trevor Howard and Celia Johnson; 1945)

Bringing Up Baby (Katharine Hepburn and Cary Grant; 1938)

Camille (Greta Garbo and Robert Taylor; 1936)

The Captive (*La Captive;* Stanislas Merhar and Sylvie Testud; 2000)

Carmen (Laura del Sol and Antonio Gades; 1983)

Casablanca (Humphrey Bogart and Ingrid Bergman; 1942)

Charade (Audrey Hepburn and Cary Grant; 1963)

Chungking Express (*Chong qing sen lin;* Takeshi Kaneshiro and Tony Leung Chiu Wai; 1994)

Chunhyang (Lee Hyo-jeong and Cho Seung-woo; 2000)

Cinema Paradiso (*Nuovo Cinema Paradiso;* Enzo Cannavale; 1989)

City Lights (Virginia Cherrill and Charlie Chaplin; 1931)

The Color Purple (Whoopi Goldberg; 1985)

Coming Home (Jon Voigt and Jane Fonda; 1978)

Crouching Tiger, Hidden Dragon (*Wo hu cang long;* Chow Yun-Fat and Michelle Yeoh; 2000)

The Crying Game (Jaye Davidson and Stephen Rea; 1992)

Dark Victory (Bette Davis and George Brent; 1939)

Days of Heaven (Richard Gere and Brooke Adams; 1978)

Dirty Dancing (Patrick Swayze and Jennifer Grey; 1987)

Doctor Zhivago (Omar Sharif and Julie Christie; 1965)

Dodsworth (Walter Huston, Ruth Chatterton, and Mary Astor; 1936)

Double Indemnity (Barbara Stanwyck and Fred MacMurray; 1944)

Eat Drink Man Woman (*Yin shi nan nu;* Lung Sihung, Wang Yu-Wen, Wu Chien-lien, and Yang Kuei-Mei; 1994)

Elvira Madigan (Pia Degermark and Thommy Berggren; 1967)

Enemies: A Love Story (Ron Silver, Anjelica Huston, Lena Olin, and Margaret Sophie Stein; 1989)

Les Enfants du paradis (Arletty and Jean-Louis Barrault; 1945)

The English Patient (Kristin Scott Thomas, Ralph Fiennes, Naveen Andrews, and Juliette Binoche; 1996)

Entre Nous (*Coup de foudre;* Isabelle Huppert and Miou-Miou; 1983)

Eternal Sunshine of the Spotless Mind (Jim Carrey and Kate Winslet; 2004)

Farewell My Concubine (*Ba wang bie ji;* Leslie Cheung, Zhang Fengyi, and Li Gong; 1993)

Fire (Shabana Azmi and Nandita Das; 1996)

For Whom the Bell Tolls (Ingrid Bergman and Gary Cooper; 1943)

The French Lieutenant's Woman (Meryl Streep and Jeremy Irons; 1981)

From Here to Eternity (Burt Lancaster, Deborah Kerr, Donna Reed, and Montgomery Clift; 1953)

Funny Girl (Barbra Streisand and Omar Sharif; 1968)

Gabbeh (Shaghayeh Djodat, Hossein Moharami, and Rogheih Moharami; 1996)

The General (Buster Keaton and Marion Mack; 1927)

Ghost (Patrick Swayze and Demi Moore; 1990)

The Ghost and Mrs. Muir (Gene Tierney and Rex Harrison; 1947)

Gigi (Leslie Caron and Maurice Chevalier; 1958)

The Gold Rush (Charlie Chaplin and Georgia Hale; 1925)

Gone with the Wind (Vivien Leigh and Clark Gable; 1939)

The Goodbye Girl (Marsha Mason and Richard Dreyfuss; 1977)

Goodbye, Mr. Chips (Robert Donat and Greer Garson; 1939)

The Graduate (Dustin Hoffman and Anne Bancroft; 1967)

Grease (John Travolta and Olivia Newton-John; 1978)

Guess Who's Coming to Dinner (Katharine Hepburn, Spencer Tracy, Sidney Poitier, and Katharine Houghton; 1967)

Happy Together (*Cheun gwong tsa sit;* Leslie Cheung, Tony Leung Chiu Wai, and Chang Chen; 1997)

Harold and Maude (Bud Cort and Ruth Gordon; 1971)

His Girl Friday (Rosalind Russell and Cary Grant; 1940)

The Hunchback of Notre Dame (Charles Laughton and Maureen O'Hara; 1939)

In America (Paddy Considine and Samantha Morton; 2002)

Indochine (Catherine Deneuve, Vincent Perez, and Linh Dan Pham; 1992)

It Happened One Night (Clark Gable and Claudette Colbert; 1934)

It's a Wonderful Life (James Stewart and Donna Reed; 1946)

Jane Eyre (Orson Welles and Joan Fontaine; 1944)

Jezebel (Bette Davis and Henry Fonda; 1939)

Ju Dou (Li Gong and Li Bao-tian; 1990)

Encyclopædia Britannica's Best Love Stories in Cinema (continued)

Jules and Jim (*Jules et Jim;* Jeanne Moreau, Oscar Werner, and Henri Serre; 1962)

Juliet of the Spirits (*Giulietta degli spiriti;* Giulietta Masina; 1965)

The King and I (Yul Brynner and Deborah Kerr; 1956)

The Lady and the Duke (*L'Anglaise et le duc;* Lucy Russell and Jean-Claude Dreyfus; 2001)

Lady and the Tramp (voices by Barbara Luddy and Larry Roberts; 1955)

The Lady Eve (Barbara Sanwyck and Henry Fonda; 1941)

Laura (Gene Tierney and Dana Andrews; 1944)

Life Is Beautiful (*La vita è bella;* Roberto Benigni and Nicoletta Braschi; 1997)

Like Water for Chocolate (*Como agua para chocolate;* Marco Leonardi and Lumi Cavazos; 1992)

A Little Romance (Diane Lane and Thelonious Bernard; 1979)

Lost in Translation (Bill Murray and Scarlett Johansson; 2003)

Love Is a Many-Splendored Thing (William Holden and Jennifer Jones; 1955)

The Love of Actress Sumako (*Joyu Sumako-no-koi;* Kinuyo Tanaka and So Yamamura; 1947)

Love Story (Ali MacGraw and Ryan O'Neal; 1970)

Mädchen in Uniform (*Girls in Uniform;* Hertha Thiele and Dorothea Wieck; 1931)

A Man and a Woman (*Un Homme et une femme;* Anouk Aimée and Jean-Louis Trintingnant; 1966)

The Man Who Copied (*O homem que copiava;* Lázaro Ramos and Leandra Leal; 2003)

Marty (Ernest Borgnine and Betsy Blair; 1955)

Midnight (Claudette Colbert and Don Ameche; 1939)

Midnight Cowboy (Dustin Hoffman and Jon Voigt; 1969)

Modern Times (Charlie Chaplin and Paulette Goddard; 1936)

Monsoon Wedding (Vasundhara Das, Parvin Dabas, Sameer Arya, Vijay Raaz, and Tilotama Shome; 2001)

Moonstruck (Cher and Nicolas Cage; 1987)

Morocco (Gary Cooper and Marlene Dietrich; 1930)

My Beautiful Laundrette (Daniel Day-Lewis and Gordon Warnecke; 1985)

My Fair Lady (Audrey Hepburn and Rex Harrison; 1964)

My Sassy Girl (*Yeopgijeogin geunyeo;* Cha Tae-hyun and Jun Ji-hyun; 2001)

Ninotchka (Greta Garbo and Melvyn Douglas; 1939)

Notorious (Cary Grant and Ingrid Bergman; 1946)

Now, Voyager (Bette Davis and Paul Henreid; 1942)

Oasis (Sol Kyung-gu and Moon So-ri; 2002)

An Officer and a Gentleman (Richard Gere and Debra Winger; 1982)

Old Yeller (Tommy Kirk; 1957)

On Golden Pond (Katharine Hepburn, Henry Fonda, and Jane Fonda; 1981)

Out of Africa (Meryl Streep and Robert Redford; 1985)

Personal Best (Mariel Hemingway, Patrice Donnelly, and Kenny Moore; 1982)

The Phantom of the Opera (Lon Chaney and Mary Philbin; 1925)

The Philadelphia Story (Cary Grant and Katharine Hepburn; 1940)

Picnic (William Holden and Kim Novak; 1955)

Pillow Talk (Doris Day and Rock Hudson; 1959)

A Place in the Sun (Elizabeth Taylor and Montgomery Clift; 1951)

Porgy and Bess (Sidney Poitier and Dorothy Dandridge; 1959)

Pretty Woman (Julia Roberts and Richard Gere; 1990)

Pride and Prejudice (Laurence Olivier and Greer Garson; 1940)

The Princess Bride (Robin Wright and Cary Elwes; 1987)

The Quiet Man (John Wayne and Maureen O'Hara; 1952)

Random Harvest (Ronald Colman and Greer Garson; 1942)

Rebecca (Joan Fontaine and Laurence Olivier; 1940)

The Red Shoes (Moira Shearer and Marius Goring; 1948)

Reds (Warren Beatty and Diane Keaton; 1981)

Roman Holiday (Gregory Peck and Audrey Hepburn; 1953)

Roxanne (Daryl Hannah and Steve Martin; 1987)

Run Lola Run (*Lola rennt;* Franka Potente and Moritz Bleibtreu; 1998)

Sabrina (Audrey Hepburn and Humphrey Bogart; 1954)

Sense and Sensibility (Emma Thompson, Hugh Grant, Alan Rickman, and Kate Winslet; 1995)

Separate Tables (ensemble cast; 1958)

Shakespeare in Love (Joseph Fiennes and Gwyneth Paltrow; 1998)

The Sheik (Rudolph Valentino and Agnes Ayres; 1921)

The Shop Around the Corner (James Stewart and Margaret Sullavan; 1940)

Singin' in the Rain (Gene Kelly and Debbie Reynolds; 1952)

Sleepless in Seattle (Tom Hanks and Meg Ryan; 1993)

Some Like It Hot (Tony Curtis, Jack Lemmon, Marilyn Monroe, and Joe E. Brown; 1959)

The Sound of Music (Julie Andrews and Christopher Plummer; 1965)

Splendor in the Grass (Warren Beatty and Natalie Wood; 1961)

Stairway to Heaven (also called *A Matter of Life and Death;* David Niven and Kim Hunter; 1946)

A Star Is Born (Judy Garland and James Mason; 1954)

A Streetcar Named Desire (Marlon Brando, Vivien Leigh, Kim Hunter, and Karl Malden; 1951)

Swing Time (Fred Astaire and Ginger Rogers; 1936)

Talk to Her (*Hable con ella;* Javier Cámara, Darío Grandinetti, Leonor Watling, and Rosario Flores; 2002)

Tango (*Tango, no me dejes nunca;* ensemble cast; 1998)

Tea over Rice (*Ochazuke no aji;* Shin Saburi and Michiyo Kogure; 1952)

Titanic (Kate Winslet and Leonardo DiCaprio; 1997)

To Catch a Thief (Cary Grant and Grace Kelly; 1955)

To Have and Have Not (Humphrey Bogart and Lauren Bacall; 1944)

Tortilla Soup (Hector Elizondo, Elizabeth Peña, Jacqueline Obrados, and Tamara Mello; 2001)

Two for the Road (Albert Finney and Audrey Hepburn; 1967)

The Umbrellas of Cherbourg (*Les Parapluies de Cherbourg;* Catherine Deneuve, Nino Castelnuovo, and Marc Michel; 1964)

The Unbearable Lightness of Being (Lena Olin, Daniel Day-Lewis, and Juliette Binoche; 1988)

Vertigo (James Stewart and Kim Novak; 1958)

Victor/Victoria (Julie Andrews, James Garner, Robert Preston, and Malcolm Jamieson; 1982)

War and Peace (*Voyna i mir;* Lyudmila Savelyeva and Vyacheslav Tikhonov; 1968)

Way Down East (Lillian Gish; 1920)

Encyclopædia Britannica's Best Love Stories in Cinema (continued)

The Way We Were (Barbra Streisand and Robert Redford; 1973)
West Side Story (Natalie Wood and Richard Beymer; 1961)
What's Up, Doc? (Barbra Streisand and Ryan O'Neal; 1972)
When Harry Met Sally... (Billy Crystal and Meg Ryan; 1989)
When Night Is Falling (Pascale Bussières and Rachel Crawford; 1995)

While You Were Sleeping (Sandra Bullock and Bill Pullman; 1995)
Wings of Desire (*Der Himmel über Berlin*; Bruno Ganz; 1987)
Witness (Harrison Ford and Kelly McGillis; 1985)
Woman of the Year (Spencer Tracy and Katharine Hepburn; 1942)
Women in Love (Glenda Jackson, Alan Bates, Oliver Reed, and Jennie Linden; 1969)

Working Girl (Harrison Ford and Melanie Griffith; 1988)
Wuthering Heights (Merle Oberon and Laurence Olivier; 1939)
Yentl (Barbra Streisand and Mandy Patinkin; 1983)
Yesterday, Today and Tomorrow (*Ieri, oggi, domani*; Sophia Loren and Marcello Mastroianni; 1963)

Golden Globes, 2005

The Hollywood Foreign Press Association, a group of non-US film critics working in Hollywood, began awarding prizes for outstanding American motion pictures and acting in 1944 and created the Golden Globe Award in 1945. Over the years the prizes have expanded from recognizing only motion pictures and actors and actresses to include direction (1946), screenwriting and film music (1947), foreign-language film (1950), and television (1955) as well as a number of other categories of achievement. Prize: globe encircled by a strip of motion picture film, in gold.

Golden Globes/Hollywood Foreign Press Association Web site: <www.hfpa.org>.

Film
Drama	*The Aviator* (director, Martin Scorsese)
Musical/comedy	*Sideways* (director, Alexander Payne)
Director	Clint Eastwood (*Million Dollar Baby*)
Actress, drama	Hilary Swank (*Million Dollar Baby*)
Actor, drama	Leonardo DiCaprio (*The Aviator*)
Actress, musical/comedy	Annette Bening (*Being Julia*)
Actor, musical/comedy	Jamie Foxx (*Ray*)
Best foreign language film	*The Sea Inside* (Spain; director, Alejandro Amenábar)
Supporting actress	Natalie Portman (*Closer*)
Supporting actor	Clive Owen (*Closer*)
Screenplay	Alexander Payne and Jim Taylor (*Sideways*)
Original score	Howard Shore (*The Aviator*)
Original song	"Old Habits Die Hard" (*Sideways*), music and lyrics, Mick Jagger and David A. Stewart

Television
Drama series	*Nip/Tuck*, Shephard-Robin Company/Warner Bros. Television Productions
Actress, drama series	Mariska Hargitay (*Law and Order: Special Victims Unit*)
Actor, drama series	Ian McShane (*Deadwood*)
Musical/comedy series	*Desperate Housewives*; Touchstone Television
Actress, musical/comedy series	Teri Hatcher (*Desperate Housewives*)
Actor, musical/comedy series	Jason Bateman (*Arrested Development*)
Miniseries/movie for TV	*The Life and Death of Peter Sellers*, DeMann Entertainment/ Company Pictures/BBC Films/HBO Films
Actress, miniseries/movie for TV	Glenn Close (*The Lion in Winter*)
Actor, miniseries/movie for TV	Geoffrey Rush (*The Life and Death of Peter Sellers*)
Supporting actress, series/miniseries/movie	Angelica Huston (*Iron Jawed Angels*)
Supporting actor, series/miniseries/movie	William Shatner (*Boston Legal*)

Sundance Film Festival, 2005

Founded as the Utah/US Film Festival in Salt Lake City in 1978, the exhibition has traditionally focused on documentary and dramatic works from outside the Hollywood mainstream. It came under the auspices of actor Robert Redford's Sundance Institute in 1985 and is held every January in Park City UT.

Sundance Institute Web site: <www.sundance.org>.

American Grand Jury Prize, drama	*Forty Shades of Blue* (US; director, Ira Sachs)
American Grand Jury Prize, documentary	*Why We Fight* (US; director, Eugene Jarecki)
World Grand Jury Prize, drama	*The Hero* (Angola/Portugal/France; director, Zézé Gamboa)
World Grand Jury Prize, documentary	*Shape of the Moon* (The Netherlands; director, Leonard Retel Helmrich)
Audience Award, drama	*Hustle & Flow* (US; director, Craig Brewer)
Audience Award, documentary	*Murderball* (US; directors, Henry-Alex Rubin and Dana Adam Shapiro)
Audience Award, world cinema, drama	*Brothers* (Denmark; director, Susanne Bier)

Sundance Film Festival, 2005 (continued)

Audience Award, world cinema, documentary	*Shake Hands with the Devil: The Journey of Roméo Dallaire* (Canada; director, Peter Raymont)
Best director, drama	Noah Baumbach (*The Squid and the Whale*, US)
Best director, documentary	Jeff Feuerzeig (*The Devil and Daniel Johnston*, US)
Cinematography, drama	Amelia Vincent (*Hustle & Flow*, US)
Cinematography, documentary	Gary Griffin (*The Education of Shelby Knox*, US)
Waldo Salt Screenwriting Award	Noah Baumbach (*The Squid and the Whale*, US)
Special Jury Prize, documentary	*Murderball* (US; editors, Geoffrey Richman and Conor O'Neill)
Special Jury Prize, documentary	*After Innocence* (US; director, Jessica Sanders)
Special Jury Prize, world cinema, documentary	*The Liberace of Baghdad* (UK; director, Sean McAllister); *Wall* (France/Israel; director, Simone Bitton)
Special Jury Prize, drama (acting)	Amy Adams (*Junebug*, US); Lou Pucci (*Thumbsucker*, US)
Special Jury Prize, drama (originality of vision)	Miranda July (*Me and You and Everyone We Know*, US); Rian Johnson (*Brick*, US)
Special Jury Prize, world cinema, drama	*The Forest for the Trees* (Germany; director, Maren Ade); *Live-In Maid* (Argentina/Spain; director, Jorge Gaggero)
Jury Prize, short filmmaking	*Family Portrait* (US; director, Patricia Riggen); *WASP*, (UK; director, Andrea Arnold)
Sundance/NHK International Filmmakers Award	*How I Spent the End of the World* (Europe; director, Catalin Mitulescu); *The Minder* (Latin America; director, Rodrigo Moreno); *Virtual Love* (US; director, Richard Press); *Yomoyama Blues* (Japan; director, Mipo Oh)
Alfred P. Sloan Prize	*Grizzly Man* (US/Canada; director, Werner Herzog)

Toronto International Film Festival, 2004

Founded in 1976, the Toronto International Film Festival is one of North America's best-attended exhibitions and a frequent forum for the premiere of major feature films. The festival, held in September, awards six prizes, three of which are for Canadian films.

Toronto International Film Festival Web site: <www.e.bell.ca/filmfest>.

Canadian feature film	*It's All Gone to Pete Tong* (director, Michael Dowse)
Canadian first feature	*La Peau blanche* (*White Skin*) (director, Daniel Roby)
Canadian short	*Man Feel Pain* (director, Dylan Akio Smith)
FIPRESCI Prize	*In My Father's Den* (New Zealand/UK; director, Brad McGann)
People's Choice Award	*Hotel Rwanda* (UK/South Africa/Italy; director, Terry George)
Discovery Award	*Omagh* (Ireland/UK; director, Peter Travis)

Cannes International Film Festival, 2005

Established in 1946, the Cannes International Film Festival is among the best known and most influential film exhibitions in the world. Some 50 feature films and 30 short films are chosen for several categories of the Official Selection each year, with a majority of those competing for the festival's various prizes. A nine-member feature film jury and a four-member short film and Cinéfondation jury give awards to the best film (Palme d'Or) and other outstanding films (special jury prizes) in their respective categories. The Grand Prix goes to the feature film judged the most original, and the feature jury also chooses the winners of the performance, direction, and screenplay awards. The Caméra d'Or, for best first film, draws on feature films from the Official Selection and from two parallel exhibitions, the Directors' Fortnight and the International Critics' Week, and is awarded by a jury comprising film industry professionals and members of the moviegoing public. The Cinéfondation awards are for works of one hour or less by film-school students.

Cannes International Film Festival Web site: <www.festival-cannes.com>.

feature films ▶ **Palme d'Or:** *L'Enfant* (*The Child*) (Belgium; directors, Jean-Pierre and Luc Dardenne); ▶ **Grand Prix:** *Broken Flowers* (US; director, Jim Jarmusch); ▶ **Best actress:** Hanna Laslo (*Free Zone*, Israel/Belgium); ▶ **Best actor:** Tommy Lee Jones (*The Three Burials of Melquiades Estrada*, US/France); ▶ **Best direction:** Michael Haneke *Caché* (*Hidden*) (France); ▶ **Best screenplay:** Guillermo Arriaga (*The Three Burials of Melquiades Estrada*, US/France); ▶ **Special jury award:** Wang Xiaoshuai (*Shanghai Dreams*, China); ▶ **Caméra d'Or:** *Sulanga Enu Pinisa* (*The Forsaken Land*) (France; director, Vimukthi Jayasundara) and *Me and You and Everyone We Know* (US; director, Miranda July)

short films ▶ **Palme d'Or:** *Podorozhni* (*Wayfarers*) (Ukraine; director, Igor Strembitsky); ▶ **Special jury award:** *Moartea domnului Lazarescu* (*The Death of Mr. Lazarescu*) (Romania; director, Cristi Puiu)

Cinéfondation ▶ **1st prize:** *Buy It Now* (US; director, Antonio Campos); ▶ **2nd prize:** *Vdvoyom* (*For Two*) (France; director, Nikolai Khomeriki) and *Bikur holim* (*Visiting Hours*) (Israel; director, Maya Dreifuss); ▶ **3rd prize:** *Be Quiet* (US; director, Sameh Zoabi) and *La Plaine* (*The Plain*) (France; director, Roland Edzard)

Berlin International Film Festival, 2005

The Berlin International Film Festival (Internationale Filmfestspiele Berlin), held annually since its founding in West Berlin in 1951, comprises some 20 separate competitions and juries emphasizing aspects of both worldwide and German cinema, each with their own prizes. The International Jury, made up of film-industry figures from across the globe, selects the winners of the Golden and Silver Berlin Bears, the festival's top awards.

Berlin International Film Festival Web site: <www.berlinale.de>.

Golden Berlin Bear	*U-Carmen e-Khayelitsha* (South Africa; director, Mark Dornford-May)
Jury Grand Prize (Silver Bear)	*Kong que* (*Peacock*) (China; director, Gu Changwei)
Silver Berlin Bear, director	Marc Rothemund (*Sophie Scholl – Die letzten Tage* [*Sophie Scholl – The Final Days*], Germany)
Silver Berlin Bear, actress	Julia Jentsch (*Sophie Scholl – Die letzten Tage* [*Sophie Scholl – The Final Days*], Germany)
Silver Berlin Bear, actor	Lou Taylor Pucci (*Thumbsucker*, US)
Silver Berlin Bear, artistic contribution	Tsai Ming Liang, screenwriter (*Tian bian yi duo yun* [*The Wayward Cloud*], China/France/Taiwan)
Silver Berlin Bear, film music	Alexandre Desplat (*De battre mon coeur s'est arrêté* [*The Beat That My Heart Skipped*], France)
Ecumenical Jury Prizes	Competition: *Sophie Scholl – Die letzten Tage* ([*Sophie Scholl – The Final Days*]; Germany; director, Marc Rothemund); Panorama: *Va, vis et deviens* ([*Live and Become*]; France; director, Radu Mihaileanu); Forum: *Ratziti lihiyot gibor* ([*On the Objection Front*]; Israel; director, Shiri Tsur)
FIPRESCI Awards	Competition: *Tian bian yi duo yun* ([*The Wayward Cloud*]; China/France/Taiwan; director, Tsai Ming Liang); Panorama: *Massaker* ([*Massacre*]; Germany; directors, Monika Borgmann, Lokman Slim, Hermann Theissen); Forum: *Niu pi* ([*Oxhide*]; China; director, Liu Jiayin)

US National Film Registry

The US Library of Congress established the National Film Preservation Board in 1988 with the goal of identifying "culturally, historically, or esthetically important" American films. The board selects 25 films to add to the National Film Registry every year.

National Film Registry Web site: <www.loc.gov/film/>.

Abbott and Costello Meet Frankenstein (1948)
Adam's Rib (1949)
The Adventures of Robin Hood (1938)
The African Queen (1951)
Alien (1979)
All About Eve (1950)
All My Babies (1953)
All Quiet on the Western Front (1930)
All That Heaven Allows (1955)
All That Jazz (1979)
All the King's Men (1949)
America, America (1963)
American Graffiti (1973)
An American in Paris (1951)
Annie Hall (1977)
Antonia: A Portrait of the Woman (1974)
The Apartment (1960)
Apocalypse Now (1979)
Atlantic City (1980)
The Awful Truth (1937)
The Bad and the Beautiful (1953)
Badlands (1973)
The Band Wagon (1953)
The Bank Dick (1940)
The Battle of San Pietro (1945)
Beauty and the Beast (1991)
Ben-Hur (1926)
Ben-Hur (1959)
The Best Years of Our Lives (1946)

Big Business (1929)
The Big Parade (1925)
The Big Sleep (1946)
The Birth of a Nation (1915)
The Black Pirate (1926)
The Black Stallion (1979)
Blacksmith Scene (1893)
Blade Runner (1982)
The Blood of Jesus (1941)
The Blue Bird (1918)
Bonnie and Clyde (1967)
Boyz N the Hood (1991)
Bride of Frankenstein (1935)
The Bridge on the River Kwai (1957)
Bringing Up Baby (1938)
Broken Blossoms (1919)
A Bronx Morning (1931)
Butch Cassidy and the Sundance Kid (1969)
Cabaret (1972)
Carmen Jones (1954)
Casablanca (1942)
Castro Street (1966)
Cat People (1942)
Chan Is Missing (1982)
The Cheat (1915)
The Chechahcos (1924)
Chinatown (1974)
Chulas Fronteras (1976)
Citizen Kane (1941)
The City (1939)
City Lights (1931)

Civilization (1916)
Clash of the Wolves (1925)
Cologne: From the Diary of Ray and Esther (1939)
The Conversation (1974)
The Cool World (1963)
Cops (1922)
A Corner in Wheat (1909)
The Court Jester.(1956)
The Crowd (1928)
Czechoslovakia 1968 (1969)
Daughters of the Dust (1991)
David Holzman's Diary (1968)
The Day the Earth Stood Still (1951)
Dead Birds (1964)
The Deer Hunter (1978)
Destry Rides Again (1939)
Detour (1946)
Dickson Experimental Sound Film (1894–95)
D.O.A. (1950)
Do the Right Thing (1989)
The Docks of New York (1928)
Dodsworth (1936)
Dog Star Man: Part IV (1964)
Don't Look Back (1967)
Double Indemnity (1944)
Dr. Strangelove or: How I Learned to Stop Worrying and Love the Bomb (1964)
Dracula (1931)
Duck Amuck (1953)

US National Film Registry (continued)

Duck and Cover (1951)
Duck Soup (1933)
E.T. The Extra-Terrestrial (1982)
Easy Rider (1969)
Eaux d'Artifice (1953)
El Norte (1983)
Empire (1964)
The Emperor Jones (1933)
The Endless Summer (1966)
Enter the Dragon (1973)
Eraserhead (1977)
Evidence of the Film (1913)
The Exploits of Elaine (1914)
The Fall of the House of
  Usher (1928)
Fantasia (1940)
Fatty's Tintype Tangle (1915)
Film Portrait (1970)
Five Easy Pieces (1970)
Flash Gordon (series) (1936)
Footlight Parade (1933)
Force of Evil (1948)
The Forgotten Frontier (1931)
42nd Street (1933)
The Four Horsemen of
  the Apocalypse (1921)
Fox Movietone News: Jenkins
  Orphanage Band (1928)
Frank Film (1973)
Frankenstein (1931)
Freaks (1932)
The Freshman (1925)
From Here to Eternity (1953)
From Stump to Ship (1930)
From the Manger to the
  Cross (1912)
Fuji (1974)
Fury (1936)
Garlic Is As Good As Ten
  Mothers (1980)
The General (1927)
Gerald McBoing-Boing (1950)
Gertie the Dinosaur (1914)
Gigi (1958)
The Godfather (1972)
The Godfather, Part II (1974)
Going My Way (1944)
Gold Diggers of 1933 (1933)
The Gold Rush (1925)
Gone with the Wind (1939)
Goodfellas (1990)
The Graduate (1967)
The Grapes of Wrath (1940)
Grass: A Nation's Battle for
  Life (1925)
The Great Dictator (1940)
The Great Train Robbery (1903)
Greed (1924)
Gun Crazy (1949)
Gunga Din (1939)
Harlan County, U.S.A. (1976)
Harold and Maude (1971)
The Heiress (1949)
Hell's Hinges (1916)
High Noon (1952)
High School (1968)
Hindenburg disaster newsreel
  footage (1937)
His Girl Friday (1940)

The Hitch-Hiker (1953)
Hoosiers (1986)
Hospital (1970)
The Hospital (1971)
The House in the Middle (1954)
How Green Was My Valley (1941)
How the West Was Won (1962)
The Hunters (1957)
The Hustler (1961)
I Am a Fugitive from a Chain
  Gang (1932)
The Immigrant (1917)
In the Heat of the Night (1967)
In the Land of the Head
  Hunters (1914)
Intolerance (1916)
Invasion of the Body
  Snatchers (1956)
It (1927)
It Happened One Night (1934)
The Italian (1915)
It's a Wonderful Life (1946)
Jailhouse Rock (1957)
Jam Session (1942)
Jammin' the Blues (1944)
Jaws (1975)
Jazz on a Summer's Day (1959)
The Jazz Singer (1927)
Kannapolis, NC (1941)
Killer of Sheep (1977)
King: A Filmed Record ...
  Montgomery to Memphis (1970)
King Kong (1933)
The Kiss (1896)
Kiss Me Deadly (1955)
Knute Rockne, All American
  (1940)
Koyaanisqatsi (1983)
The Lady Eve (1941)
Lady Helen's Escapade (1909)
Lady Windermere's Fan (1925)
Lambchops (1929)
The Land Beyond the
  Sunset (1912)
Lassie Come Home (1943)
The Last of the Mohicans (1920)
The Last Picture Show (1971)
Laura (1944)
Lawrence of Arabia (1962)
The Learning Tree (1969)
Let's All Go to the Lobby (1957)
Letter from an Unknown
  Woman (1948)
The Life and Death of 9413: A
  Hollywood Extra (1928)
Life and Times of Rosie the
  Riveter (1980)
The Life of Emile Zola (1937)
Little Caesar (1930)
Little Fugitive (1953)
Little Miss Marker (1934)
The Living Desert (1953)
The Lost World (1925)
Louisiana Story (1948)
Love Finds Andy Hardy (1938)
Love Me Tonight (1932)
Magical Maestro (1952)
The Magnificent
  Ambersons (1942)

The Maltese Falcon (1941)
The Manchurian Candidate (1962)
Manhatta (1921)
Manhattan (1979)
March of Time: Inside Nazi
  Germany (1938)
Marian Anderson: The Lincoln
  Memorial Concert (1939)
Marty (1955)
M*A*S*H (1970)
Master Hands (1936)
Matrimony's Speed Limit (1913)
Mean Streets (1973)
Medium Cool (1969)
Meet Me in St. Louis (1944)
Melody Ranch (1940)
The Memphis Belle: A Story of a
  Flying Fortress (1944)
Meshes of the Afternoon (1943)
Midnight Cowboy (1969)
Mildred Pierce (1945)
The Miracle of Morgan's
  Creek (1944)
Miss Lulu Bett (1921)
Modern Times (1936)
Modesta (1956)
Morocco (1930)
Motion Painting No. 1 (1947)
A Movie (1958)
Mr. Smith Goes to
  Washington (1939)
Multiple Sidosis (1970)
The Music Box (1932)
My Darling Clementine (1946)
My Man Godfrey (1936)
The Naked Spur (1953)
Nanook of the North (1922)
Nashville (1975)
National Lampoon's
  Animal House (1978)
National Velvet (1944)
Naughty Marietta (1935)
Network (1976)
A Night at the Opera (1935)
The Night of the Hunter (1955)
Night of the Living Dead (1968)
Ninotchka (1939)
North by Northwest (1959)
Nostalgia (1971)
Nothing but a Man (1964)
The Nutty Professor (1963)
OffOn (1968)
On the Waterfront (1954)
One Flew Over the Cuckoo's
  Nest (1975)
One Froggy Evening (1955)
Out of the Past (1947)
The Outlaw Josey Wales (1976)
The Ox-Bow Incident (1943)
Pass the Gravy (1928)
Paths of Glory (1957)
Patton (1970)
The Pearl (1948)
Peter Pan (1924)
The Phantom of the Opera (1925)
The Philadelphia Story (1940)
Pinocchio (1940)
A Place in the Sun (1951)
Planet of the Apes (1968)

US National Film Registry (continued)

The Plow That Broke the Plains (1936)
Point of Order (1964)
The Poor Little Rich Girl (1917)
Popeye the Sailor Meets Sindbad the Sailor (1936)
Porky in Wackyland (1938)
Powers of Ten (1978)
President McKinley inauguration footage (1901)
Primary (1960)
Princess Nicotine; or, The Smoke Fairy (1909)
The Prisoner of Zenda (1937)
The Producers (1968)
Psycho (1960)
The Public Enemy (1931)
Pull My Daisy (1958)
Punch Drunks (1934)
Pups Is Pups (Our Gang) (1930)
Raging Bull (1980)
Raiders of the Lost Ark (1981)
Rear Window (1954)
Rebel Without a Cause (1955)
Red River (1948)
Regeneration (1915)
Republic Steel strike riots newsreel footage (1937)
Return of the Secaucus 7 (1980)
Ride the High Country (1962)
Rip Van Winkle (1896)
The River (1937)
Road to Morocco (1942)
Roman Holiday (1953)
Rose Hobart (1936)
Sabrina (1954)
Safety Last (1923)
Salesman (1969)
Salome (1922)
Salt of the Earth (1954)
Scarface (1932)
Schindler's List (1993)
The Searchers (1956)
Serene Velocity (1970)
Seven Brides for Seven Brothers (1954)
Seventh Heaven (1927)
Shadow of a Doubt (1943)
Shadows (1959)

Shaft (1971)
Shane (1953)
She Done Him Wrong (1933)
Sherlock, Jr. (1924)
Sherman's March (1986)
Shock Corridor (1963)
The Shop Around the Corner (1940)
Show Boat (1936)
Show People (1928)
Singin' in the Rain (1952)
Sky High (1922)
Snow White (1933)
Snow White and the Seven Dwarfs (1937)
Some Like It Hot (1959)
The Son of the Sheik (1926)
The Sound of Music (1965)
Stagecoach (1939)
A Star Is Born (1954)
Star Theatre (1901)
Star Wars (1977)
Steamboat Willie (1928)
Stormy Weather (1943)
Stranger Than Paradise (1984)
A Streetcar Named Desire (1951)
Sullivan's Travels (1941)
Sunrise (1927)
Sunset Boulevard (1950)
Sweet Smell of Success (1957)
Swing Time (1936)
Tabu (1931)
Tacoma Narrows Bridge Collapse (1940)
The Tall T (1957)
Tarzan and His Mate (1934)
Taxi Driver (1976)
The Tell-Tale Heart (1953)
The Ten Commandments (1956)
Tevye (1939)
Theodore Case Sound Test: Gus Visser and his Singing Duck (1925)
There It Is (1928)
The Thief of Bagdad (1924)
The Thin Blue Line (1988)
The Thin Man (1934)
The Thing From Another World (1951)

This Is Cinerama (1952)
This Is Spinal Tap (1984)
Through Navajo Eyes (series) (1966)
Tin Toy (1988)
To Be or Not To Be (1942)
To Fly (1976)
To Kill a Mockingbird (1962)
Tootsie (1982)
Top Hat (1935)
Topaz (1945)
Touch of Evil (1958)
Trance and Dance in Bali (1952)
The Treasure of the Sierra Madre (1948)
Trouble in Paradise (1932)
Tulips Shall Grow (1942)
Twelve O'Clock High (1949)
2001: A Space Odyssey (1968)
Unforgiven (1992)
Verbena Tragica (1939)
Vertigo (1958)
The Wedding March (1928)
West Side Story (1961)
Westinghouse Works (1904)
What's Opera, Doc? (1957)
Where Are My Children? (1916)
White Heat (1949)
Why Man Creates (1968)
Why We Fight (series) (1943-45)
Wild and Woolly (1917)
The Wild Bunch (1969)
Wild River (1960)
Will Success Spoil Rock Hunter? (1957)
The Wind (1928)
Wings (1927)
Within Our Gates (1920)
The Wizard of Oz (1939)
Woman of the Year (1942)
A Woman Under the Influence (1974)
Woodstock (1970)
Yankee Doodle Dandy (1942)
Young Frankenstein (1974)
Young Mr. Lincoln (1939)
Zapruder film of Kennedy assassination (1963)

25 Top-Grossing Films (Actual Dollars)

As of 5 Jul 2005. Source: The Internet Movie Database, <http://imdb.com>.

1	Titanic	1997
2	The Lord of the Rings: The Return of the King	2003
3	Harry Potter and the Sorcerer's Stone	2001
4	Star Wars: The Phantom Menace	1999
5	The Lord of the Rings: The Two Towers	2002
6	Jurassic Park	1993
7	Shrek 2	2004
8	Harry Potter and the Chamber of Secrets	2002
9	Finding Nemo	2003
10	The Lord of the Rings: The Fellowship of the Ring	2001
11	Independence Day	1996
12	Spider-Man	2002
13	Star Wars	1977
14	Harry Potter and the Prisoner of Azkaban	2004
15	Spider-Man 2	2004
16	The Lion King	1994
17	E.T. the Extra-Terrestrial	1982
18	Star Wars: Revenge of the Sith	2005
19	The Matrix Reloaded	2003
20	Forrest Gump	1994
21	The Sixth Sense	1999
22	Pirates of the Caribbean: The Curse of the Black Pearl	2003
23	Star Wars: Attack of the Clones	2002
24	The Incredibles	2004
25	The Lost World: Jurassic Park	1997

US Top-Grossing Films in Constant Dollars (Estimated)

Admissions—the number of tickets sold to a movie—tell a different story from the raw dollars earned. While recent films have made hundreds of millions of dollars, only seven of the top 20 films in terms of attendance were released after 1980. Source: Exhibitor Relations Co., Inc.

		ADMISSIONS	2005 DOLLARS	ACTUAL DOLLARS
1	Gone with the Wind (1939)[1]	202,044,569	1,299,538,040	198,655,278
2	Star Wars (1977)[1]	178,119,595	1,145,654,103	460,998,007
3	The Sound of Music (1965)[1]	142,415,376	916,006,797	158,671,368
4	E.T. The Extra-Terrestrial (1982)[1]	141,925,359	912,855,039	434,538,449
5	The Ten Commandments (1956)	131,000,000	842,583,813	65,500,000
6	Titanic (1997)	129,201,761	831,017,650	600,788,188
7	Jaws (1975)[1]	128,078,818	823,794,951	260,000,000
8	Birth of a Nation (1915)	123,333,333	793,272,291	18,500,000
9	Snow White (1937)[1]	109,000,000	701,081,188	184,925,486
10	101 Dalmatians (1961)[1]	99,917,251	642,661,514	144,880,014
11	Star Wars: The Empire Strikes Back (1980)[1]	98,106,044	631,011,943	290,266,497
12	Ben-Hur (1959)[1]	98,000,000	630,329,875	74,000,000
13	The Exorcist (1973)	94,285,714	606,439,821	165,000,000
14	Star Wars: Return of the Jedi (1983)[1]	94,026,245	604,770,931	309,153,948
15	The Sting (1973)	89,142,857	573,361,286	156,000,000
16	Raiders of the Lost Ark (1981)[1]	88,141,855	566,922,905	245,034,358
17	Jurassic Park (1993)	86,248,296	554,743,651	357,067,947
18	Star Wars: Episode I—The Phantom Menace (1999)	84,859,901	545,813,577	431,088,295
19	Fantasia (1940)	83,043,478	534,130,462	76,400,000
20	The Godfather (1972)[1]	79,392,006	510,644,423	134,996,411

[1]Includes reissues.

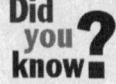

Film labs processed over a million feet (more than 300,000 meters) of film during the shooting of Michael Cimino's epic *Heaven's Gate*, the biggest flop in Hollywood history at the time of its release in 1980.

Top US Video Rentals and Sales, 2004

Data reflect combined VHS and DVD numbers.
Source: Video Business. Web site: <www.videobusiness.com>.

	RENTALS	SALES
1	The Day After Tomorrow	Shrek 2
2	Mystic River	The Lord of the Rings: The Return of the King
3	Man on Fire	The Passion of the Christ
4	50 First Dates	Star Wars Trilogy
5	The Butterfly Effect	Harry Potter and the Prisoner of Azkaban
6	The Last Samurai	Spider-Man 2
7	Radio	The Lion King 1½
8	Out of Time	Brother Bear
9	Along Came Polly	Elf
10	Something's Gotta Give	The Matrix Revolutions
11	Cold Mountain	The Day After Tomorrow
12	Cheaper by the Dozen	American Wedding
13	The Rundown	The Bourne Supremacy
14	Gothika	The Last Samurai
15	Secret Window	Cheaper by the Dozen
16	School of Rock	Van Helsing
17	Open Range	Seinfeld Seasons 1 & 2

Television

Emmy Award-winning Television Series, 1948–2004

1948
Most popular program: *Pantomime Quiz*, KTLA
TV film: "The Necklace," *Your Show Time*

1949
Live show: *The Ed Wynn Show*, KTTV
Kinescope show: *The Texaco Star Theater*, KNBH (NBC)
TV film: *The Life of Riley*, KNBH
Pub. svc./cultural/educ.: *Crusade in Europe*, KECA-TV/KTTV (ABC)
Children's: *Time for Beany*, KTLA

1950
Variety: *The Alan Young Show*, KTTV (CBS)
Drama: *Pulitzer Prize Playhouse*, KECA-TV (ABC)
Game/audience particip.: *Truth or Consequences*, KTTV (CBS)
Children's: *Time for Beany*, KTLA
Educational: *KFI-TV University*, KFI-TV
Cultural: *Campus Chorus and Orchestra*, KTSL

1951
Variety: *Your Show of Shows* (NBC)
Comedy: *The Red Skelton Show* (NBC)
Drama: *Studio One* (CBS)

1952
Variety: *Your Show of Shows* (NBC)
Comedy: *I Love Lucy* (CBS)
Drama: *Robert Montgomery Presents* (NBC)
Mystery/action/adventure: *Dragnet* (NBC)
Public affairs: *See It Now* (CBS)
Aud. particip./quiz/panel: *What's My Line?* (CBS)
Children's: *Time for Beany* (syndicated)

1953
Variety: *Omnibus* (CBS)
Comedy: *I Love Lucy* (CBS)
Drama: *The U.S. Steel Hour* (ABC)
Mystery/action/adventure: *Dragnet* (NBC)
Public affairs: *Victory at Sea* (NBC)
Aud. particip./quiz/panel: *This Is Your Life* (NBC); *What's My Line?* (CBS)
Children's: *Kukla, Fran and Ollie* (NBC)

1954
Variety: *Disneyland* (ABC)
Comedy: *Make Room for Daddy* (ABC)
Drama: *The United States Steel Hour* (ABC)
Mystery/intrigue: *Dragnet* (NBC)
Western/adventure: *Stories of the Century* (syndicated)
Cultural/relig./educ.: *Omnibus* (CBS)
Aud. particip./quiz/panel: *This Is Your Life* (NBC)
Children's: *Lassie* (CBS)

1955
Variety: *The Ed Sullivan Show* (CBS)
Comedy: *The Phil Silvers Show: You'll Never Get Rich* (CBS)
Drama: *Producers' Showcase* (NBC)
Action/adventure: *Disneyland* (ABC)
Music: *Your Hit Parade* (NBC)
Documentary: *Omnibus* (CBS)
Aud. particip. *The $64,000 Question* (CBS)
Children's: *Lassie* (CBS)

1956
Series (½ hr. or less): *The Phil Silvers Show: You'll Never Get Rich* (CBS)
Series (1 hr. or more): *Caesar's Hour* (NBC)
New series: *Playhouse 90* (CBS)

1957
Mus./var./aud.par./quiz: *The Dinah Shore Chevy Show* (NBC)
Comedy: *The Phil Silvers Show: You'll Never Get Rich* (CBS)
Drama, continuing: *Gunsmoke* (CBS)
Drama, anthology: *Playhouse 90* (CBS)
New series: *The Seven Lively Arts* (CBS)
Public service: *Omnibus* (ABC/NBC)

1959[1]
Musical/variety: *The Dinah Shore Chevy Show* (NBC)
Comedy: *The Jack Benny Show* (CBS)
Drama (<1 hr.): *Alcoa-Goodyear Playhouse* (NBC)
Drama (1 hr.+): *Playhouse 90* (CBS)
Western: *Maverick* (ABC)
News reporting: *The Huntley-Brinkley Report* (NBC)
Public service: *Omnibus* (NBC)
Panel/quiz/aud. particip.: *What's My Line?* (CBS)

1960
Variety: "The Fabulous Fifties" (CBS)
Humor: "Art Carney Special" (NBC)
Drama: *Playhouse 90* (CBS)
News: *The Huntley-Brinkley Report* (NBC)
Public affairs/education: *The Twentieth Century* (CBS)
Children's: *Huckleberry Hound* (syndicated)

1961
Variety: *Astaire Time* (NBC)
Humor: *The Jack Benny Show* (CBS)
Drama: "Macbeth," *Hallmark Hall of Fame* (NBC)
News: *The Huntley-Brinkley Report* (NBC)
Public affairs/education: *The Twentieth Century* (CBS)
Children's: "Aaron Copland's Birthday Party," *Young People's Concert* (CBS)
Program of the year: "Macbeth," *Hallmark Hall of Fame* (NBC)

1962
Variety: *The Garry Moore Show* (CBS)
Humor: *The Bob Newhart Show* (NBC)
Drama: *The Defenders* (CBS)
News: *The Huntley-Brinkley Report* (NBC)
Educational/public affairs: *David Brinkley's Journal* (NBC)
Children's: "New York Philharmonic Young People's Concert with Leonard Bernstein" (CBS)
Program of the year: "Victoria Regina," *Hallmark Hall of Fame* (NBC)

1963
Variety: *The Andy Williams Show* (NBC)
Humor: *The Dick Van Dyke Show* (CBS)
Drama: *The Defenders* (CBS)
News: *The Huntley-Brinkley Report* (NBC)
Commentary/public affairs: *David Brinkley's Journal* (NBC)
Documentary: "The Tunnel" (NBC)
Panel/quiz/aud. particip.: *G-E College Bowl* (CBS)

Emmy Award-winning Television Series, 1948–2004 (continued)

1963 (continued)
Children's: *Walt Disney's Wonderful World of Color* (NBC)
Program of the year: "The Tunnel" (NBC)

1964
Variety: *The Danny Kaye Show* (CBS)
Comedy: *The Dick Van Dyke Show* (CBS)
Drama: *The Defenders* (CBS)
News reports: *The Huntley-Brinkley Report* (NBC)
Commentary/public affairs: "Cuba—Part I: The Bay of Pigs," "Cuba—Part II: The Missile Crisis," *NBC White Paper* (NBC)
Documentary: "The Making of the President 1960" (ABC)
Children's: *Discovery '63–'64* (ABC)
Program of the year: "The Making of the President 1960" (ABC)

1965[2]
Entertainment: *The Dick Van Dyke Show* (CBS); "The Magnificent Yankee," *Hallmark Hall of Fame* (NBC); "My Name Is Barbra" (CBS); "What Is Sonata Form?," *New York Philharmonic Young People's Concerts with Leonard Bernstein* (CBS)
News/docu./info./sports: "I, Leonardo da Vinci," *Saga of Western Man* (ABC); "The Louvre" (NBC)

1966
Variety: *The Andy Williams Show* (NBC)
Comedy: *The Dick Van Dyke Show* (CBS)
Drama: *The Fugitive* (ABC)

1967
Variety: *The Andy Williams Show* (NBC)
Comedy: *The Monkees* (NBC)
Drama: *Mission: Impossible* (CBS)

1968
Musical/variety: *Rowan and Martin's Laugh-In* (NBC)
Comedy: *Get Smart* (NBC)
Drama: *Mission: Impossible* (CBS)

1969
Musical/variety: *Rowan and Martin's Laugh-In* (NBC)
Comedy: *Get Smart* (NBC)
Drama: *NET Playhouse* (NET)

1970
Variety/musical: *The David Frost Show* (syndicated)
Comedy: *My World and Welcome to It* (NBC)
Drama: *Marcus Welby, M.D.* (ABC)

1971
Comedy: *All in the Family* (CBS)
Drama: *The Senator* (segment), *The Bold Ones* (NBC)
Variety, musical: *The Flip Wilson Show* (NBC)
Variety, talk: *The David Frost Show* (syndicated)
New series: *All in the Family* (CBS)

1972
Comedy: *All in the Family* (CBS)
Drama: "Elizabeth R," *Masterpiece Theatre* (PBS)
Variety, musical: *The Carol Burnett Show* (CBS)
Variety, talk: *The Dick Cavett Show* (ABC)
New series: "Elizabeth R," *Masterpiece Theatre* (PBS)

1973
Comedy: *All in the Family* (CBS)
Drama (continuing): *The Waltons* (CBS)
Drama/comedy (limited): "Tom Brown's Schooldays," *Masterpiece Theatre* (PBS)
Variety, musical: *The Julie Andrews Hour* (ABC)
New series: *America* (NBC)

1974
Comedy: *M*A*S*H* (CBS)
Drama: "Upstairs, Downstairs," *Masterpiece Theatre* (PBS)
Limited series: *Columbo* (NBC)
Music/variety: *The Carol Burnett Show* (CBS)

1975
Comedy: *The Mary Tyler Moore Show* (CBS)
Drama: "Upstairs, Downstairs," *Masterpiece Theatre* (PBS)
Limited series: "Benjamin Franklin" (CBS)
Comedy-variety/music: *The Carol Burnett Show* (CBS)

1976
Comedy: *The Mary Tyler Moore Show* (CBS)
Drama: *Police Story* (NBC)
Limited series: "Upstairs, Downstairs," *Masterpiece Theatre* (PBS)
Comedy-variety/music: *NBC's Saturday Night* (NBC)

1977
Comedy: *The Mary Tyler Moore Show* (CBS)
Drama: "Upstairs, Downstairs," *Masterpiece Theatre* (PBS)
Limited series: *Roots* (ABC)
Comedy-variety/music: *Van Dyke and Company* (NBC)

1978
Comedy: *All in the Family* (CBS)
Drama: *The Rockford Files* (NBC)
Limited series: *Holocaust* (NBC)
Comedy-variety/music: *The Muppet Show* (syndicated)
Informational: *The Body Human* (CBS)

1979
Comedy: *Taxi* (ABC)
Drama: *Lou Grant* (CBS)
Limited series: *Roots: The Next Generations* (ABC)
Comedy-variety/music: "Steve & Eydie Celebrate Irving Berlin" (NBC)

1980
Comedy: *Taxi* (ABC)
Drama: *Lou Grant* (CBS)
Limited series: *Edward & Mrs. Simpson* (syndicated)
Variety/music: *IBM Presents Baryshnikov on Broadway* (ABC)

1981
Comedy: *Taxi* (ABC)
Drama: *Hill Street Blues* (NBC)
Limited series: *Shogun* (NBC)
Informational: *Steve Allen's Meeting of Minds* (PBS)

Emmy Award-winning Television Series, 1948–2004 (continued)

1982
Comedy: *Barney Miller* (ABC)
Drama: *Hill Street Blues* (NBC)
Limited series: *Marco Polo* (NBC)
Informational: *Creativity with Bill Moyers* (PBS)

1983
Comedy: *Cheers* (NBC)
Drama: *Hill Street Blues* (NBC)
Limited series: *Nicholas Nickleby* (syndicated)
Informational: *The Barbara Walters Specials* (ABC)

1984
Comedy: *Cheers* (NBC)
Drama: *Hill Street Blues* (NBC)
Limited series: "Concealed Enemies," *American Playhouse* (PBS)
Informational: *A Walk Through the 20th Century with Bill Moyers* (PBS)

1985
Comedy: *The Cosby Show* (NBC)
Drama: *Cagney & Lacey* (CBS)
Limited series: "The Jewel in the Crown," *Masterpiece Theatre* (PBS)
Informational: *The Living Planet: A Portrait of the Earth* (PBS)

1986
Comedy: *The Golden Girls* (NBC)
Drama: *Cagney & Lacey* (CBS)
Miniseries: *Peter the Great* (NBC)
Informational: "Laurence Olivier—A Life," *Great Performances* (PBS); *Planet Earth* (PBS)

1987
Comedy: *The Golden Girls* (NBC)
Drama: *L.A. Law* (NBC)
Miniseries: *A Year in the Life* (NBC)
Informational: *Smithsonian World* (PBS); "Unknown Chaplin," *American Masters* (PBS)

1988
Comedy: *The Wonder Years* (ABC)
Drama: *thirtysomething* (ABC)
Miniseries: *The Murder of Mary Phagan* (NBC)
Informational: "Buster Keaton: A Hard Act to Follow," *American Masters* (PBS); *Nature* (PBS)

1989
Comedy: *Cheers* (NBC)
Drama: *L.A. Law* (NBC)
Miniseries: *War and Remembrance* (ABC)
Variety/music/comedy: *The Tracy Ullman Show* (Fox)
Informational: *Nature* (PBS)

1990
Comedy: *Murphy Brown* (CBS)
Drama: *L.A. Law* (NBC)
Miniseries: *Drug Wars: The Camarena Story* (NBC)
Variety/music/comedy: *In Living Color* (Fox)
Informational: *Smithsonian World* (PBS)

1991
Comedy: *Cheers* (NBC)
Drama: *L.A. Law* (NBC)
Miniseries: *Separate But Equal* (ABC)
Informational: *The Civil War* (PBS)

1992
Comedy: *Murphy Brown* (CBS)
Drama: *Northern Exposure* (CBS)
Miniseries: *A Woman Named Jackie* (NBC)
Variety/music/comedy: *The Tonight Show Starring Johnny Carson* (NBC)
Informational: *MGM: When the Lion Roars* (TNT)

1993
Comedy: *Seinfeld* (NBC)
Drama: *Picket Fences* (CBS)
Miniseries: *Prime Suspect 2* (PBS)
Variety/music/comedy: *Saturday Night Live* (NBC)
Informational: *Healing and the Mind with Bill Moyers* (PBS)

1994
Comedy: *Frasier* (NBC)
Drama: *Picket Fences* (CBS)
Miniseries: *Prime Suspect 3* (PBS)
Variety/music/comedy: *Late Show with David Letterman* (CBS)
Informational: *Later with Bob Costas* (NBC)

1995
Comedy: *Frasier* (NBC)
Drama: *NYPD Blue* (ABC)
Miniseries: *Joseph* (TNT)
Variety/music/comedy: *The Tonight Show with Jay Leno* (NBC)
Informational: *Baseball* (PBS); *TV Nation* (NBC)

1996
Comedy: *Frasier* (NBC)
Drama: *ER* (NBC)
Miniseries: *Gulliver's Travels* (NBC)
Variety/music/comedy: *Dennis Miller Live* (HBO)
Informational: *Lost Civilizations* (NBC)

1997
Comedy: *Frasier* (NBC)
Drama: *Law & Order* (NBC)
Miniseries: *Prime Suspect 5: Errors of Judgment* (PBS)
Variety/music/comedy: *Tracey Takes On . . .* (HBO)
Informational: *Biography* (A&E); *The Great War and the Shaping of the 20th Century* (PBS)

1998
Comedy: *Frasier* (NBC)
Drama: *The Practice* (ABC)
Miniseries: *From the Earth to the Moon* (HBO)
Variety/music/comedy: *Late Show with David Letterman* (CBS)
Non-fiction: *The American Experience* (PBS)

1999
Comedy: *Ally McBeal* (Fox)
Drama: *The Practice* (ABC)
Miniseries: *Horatio Hornblower: The Even Chance* (A&E)
Variety/music/comedy: *Late Show with David Letterman* (CBS)
Non-fiction: *The American Experience* (PBS); *American Masters* (PBS)

2000
Comedy: *Will & Grace* (NBC)
Drama: *The West Wing* (NBC)
Miniseries: *The Corner* (HBO)

Emmy Award-winning Television Series, 1948–2004 (continued)

2000 (continued)
Variety/music/comedy: *Late Show with David Letterman* (CBS)
Non-fiction: "Hitchcock, Selznick and the End of Hollywood," *American Masters* (PBS)

2001
Comedy: *Sex and the City* (HBO)
Drama: *The West Wing* (NBC)
Miniseries: *Anne Frank* (ABC)
Variety/music/comedy: *Late Show with David Letterman* (CBS)
Non-fiction: "Lucille Ball: Finding Lucy," *American Masters* (PBS)

2002
Comedy: *Friends* (NBC)
Drama: *The West Wing* (NBC)
Miniseries: *Band of Brothers* (HBO)
Variety/music/comedy: *Late Show with David Letterman* (CBS)
Non-fiction special: *9/11* (CBS)

2003
Comedy: *Everybody Loves Raymond* (CBS)
Drama: *The West Wing* (NBC)
Miniseries: *Steven Spielberg Presents Taken* (Sci Fi)
Variety/music/comedy: *The Daily Show with Jon Stewart* (Comedy Central)
Non-fiction special: *Benjamin Franklin* (PBS); *American Masters* (PBS)

2004
Comedy: *Arrested Development* (Fox)
Drama: *The Sopranos* (HBO)
Miniseries: *Angels in America* (HBO)
Variety/music/comedy: *The Daily Show with Jon Stewart* (Comedy Central)
Non-fiction special: *The Forgetting: A Portrait of Alzheimer's* (PBS)

[1]Because of a change in the eligibility period, no awards were given in 1958; the 1959 awards included all of calendar year 1958 and part of 1959.   [2]Programs this year were classified only so far as "Entertainment" and "News, Documentaries, Information and Sports," with several winners in each classification.

Did you know? *The West Wing* won a record nine Emmy awards in 2000, the most awards for any season of a television series; the show was also only in its first season.

Theater

Tony Award Winners, 2005

The American Theatre Wing, a philanthropic and educational organization established in 1939, created the Tony Awards in 1947 to recognize distinguished achievement in the theater arts as presented on Broadway. The award is named for Antoinette Perry, a former director of the American Theatre Wing; since 1967 it has been presented in conjunction with the League of American Theatres and Producers, a Broadway trade association. A 15–30-member nominating committee selects nominees each May from among the year's new or newly revived Broadway shows; a body of some 750 current and former theater professionals, critics, and agents votes for the winners. The awards are presented in New York City in early June. Prize: silver medallion, set in a base, depicting on one face the masks of tragedy and comedy and on the other the profile of Antoinette Perry.

Tony Awards Web site: <www.tonyawards.com>.

musical: *Monty Python's Spamalot* (book, Eric Idle; music and lyrics, John Du Prez and Eric Idle); ▶ **play:** *Doubt* (playwright, John Patrick Shanley); ▶ **revival of a musical:** *La Cage aux Folles* (book, Harvey Fierstein; music and lyrics, Jerry Herman); ▶ **revival of a play:** *Glengarry Glen Ross* (playwright, David Mamet); ▶ **book, musical:** Rachel Sheinkin (*The 25th Annual Putnam County Spelling Bee*); ▶ **score:** Adam Guettel (*The Light in the Piazza*); ▶ **leading actress, musical:** Victoria Clark (*The Light in the Piazza*); ▶ **leading actor, musical:** Norbert Leo Butz (*Dirty Rotten Scoundrels*); ▶ **leading actress, play:** Cherry Jones (*Doubt*); ▶ **leading actor, play:** Bill Irwin (*Who's Afraid of Virginia Woolf?*); ▶ **featured actress, musical:** Sara Ramirez (*Monty Python's Spamalot*); ▶ **featured actor, musical:** Dan Fogler (*The 25th Annual Putnam County Spelling Bee*); ▶ **featured actress, play:** Adriane Lenox (*Doubt*); ▶ **featured actor, play:** Liev Schreiber (*Glengarry Glen Ross*); ▶ **direction, musical:** Mike Nichols (*Monty Python's Spamalot*); ▶ **direction, play:** Doug Hughes (*Doubt*); ▶ **costume design, play:** Jess Goldstein (*The Rivals*); ▶ **costume design, musical:** Catherine Zuber (*The Light in the Piazza*); ▶ **lighting design, play:** Brian MacDevitt (*The Pillowman*); ▶ **lighting design, musical:** Christopher Akerlind (*The Light in the Piazza*); ▶ **scenic design, play:** Scott Pask (*The Pillowman*); ▶ **scenic design, musical:** Michael Yeargan (*The Light in the Piazza*); ▶ **orchestrations:** Ted Sperling, Adam Guettel, and Bruce Coughlin (*The Light in the Piazza*); ▶ **choreography:** Jerry Mitchell (*La Cage aux Folles*); ▶ **special award for lifetime achievement in the theater:** Edward Albee; ▶ **regional theater award:** Theatre de la Jeune Lune, Minneapolis MN.

Tony Awards, 1947–2005

YEAR	BEST MUSICAL	BEST PLAY
1947	*not awarded*	*All My Sons* (Arthur Miller)[1]
1948	*not awarded*	*Mister Roberts* (Thomas Heggen, Joshua Logan)
1949	*Kiss Me, Kate* (book, Bella and Samuel Spewack; music and lyrics, Cole Porter)	*Death of a Salesman* (Arthur Miller)
1950	*South Pacific* (book, Oscar Hammerstein II, Joshua Logan; music, Richard Rodgers; lyrics, Oscar Hammerstein II)	*The Cocktail Party* (T.S. Eliot)
1951	*Guys and Dolls* (book, Jo Swerling, Abe Burrows; music and lyrics, Frank Loesser)	*The Rose Tattoo* (Tennessee Williams)
1952	*The King and I* (book and lyrics, Oscar Hammerstein II; music, Richard Rodgers)	*The Fourposter* (Jan de Hartog)
1953	*Wonderful Town* (book, Joseph Fields, Jerome Chodorov; music, Leonard Bernstein; lyrics, Betty Comden, Adolph Green)	*The Crucible* (Arthur Miller)
1954	*Kismet* (book, Charles Lederer, Luther Davis; music, Alexander Borodin; adaptation and lyrics, Robert Wright, George Forrest)	*The Teahouse of the August Moon* (John Patrick)
1955	*The Pajama Game* (book, George Abbott, Richard Bissell; music and lyrics, Richard Adler, Jerry Ross)	*The Desperate Hours* (Joseph Hayes)
1956	*Damn Yankees* (book and lyrics, George Abbott, Douglass Wallop; music, Richard Adler, Jerry Ross)	*The Diary of Anne Frank* (Frances Goodrich, Albert Hackett)
1957	*My Fair Lady* (book and lyrics, Alan Jay Lerner; music, Frederick Loewe)	*Long Day's Journey into Night* (Eugene O'Neill)
1958	*The Music Man* (book, Meredith Willson, Franklin Lacey; music and lyrics, Meredith Willson)	*Sunrise at Campobello* (Dore Schary)
1959	*Redhead* (book, Herbert and Dorothy Fields, Sidney Sheldon, David Shaw; music, Albert Hague; lyrics, Dorothy Fields)	*J.B.* (Archibald MacLeish)
1960 (tie)	*The Sound of Music* (book, Howard Lindsay, Russel Crouse; music, Richard Rodgers; lyrics, Oscar Hammerstein II); *Fiorello!* (book, Jerome Weidman, George Abbott; music, Jerry Brock; lyrics, Sheldon Harnick)	*The Miracle Worker* (William Gibson)
1961	*Bye, Bye Birdie* (book, Michael Stewart; music, Charles Strouse; lyrics, Lee Adams)	*Beckett* (Jean Anouilh, translated by Lucienne Hill)
1962	*How to Succeed in Business Without Really Trying* (book, Abe Burrows, Jack Weinstock, Willie Gilbert; music and lyrics, Frank Loesser)	*A Man for All Seasons* (Robert Bolt)
1963	*A Funny Thing Happened on the Way to the Forum* (book, Burt Shevelove, Larry Gelbart; music and lyrics, Stephen Sondheim)	*Who's Afraid of Virginia Woolf?* (Edward Albee)
1964	*Hello, Dolly!* (book, Michael Stewart; music and lyrics, Jerry Herman)	*Luther* (John Osborne)
1965	*Fiddler on the Roof* (book, Joseph Stein; music, Jerry Bock; lyrics, Sheldon Harnick)	*The Subject Was Roses* (Frank Gilroy)
1966	*Man of La Mancha* (book, Dale Wasserman; music; Mitch Leigh; lyrics, Joe Darion)	*Marat/Sade* (Peter Weiss, translated by Geoffrey Skelton)
1967	*Cabaret* (book, Joe Masteroff; music, John Kander; lyrics, Fred Ebb)	*The Homecoming* (Harold Pinter)
1968	*Hallelujah, Baby!* (book, Arthur Laurents; music, Jule Styne; lyrics, Betty Comden, Adolph Green)	*Rosencrantz and Guildenstern Are Dead* (Tom Stoppard)
1969	*1776* (book, Peter Stone; music and lyrics, Sherman Edwards)	*The Great White Hope* (Howard Sackler)
1970	*Applause* (book, Betty Comden, Adolph Greene; music, Charles Strouse; lyrics, Lee Adams)	*Borstal Boy* (Frank McMahon)
1971	*Company* (book, George Furth; music and lyrics, Stephen Sondheim)	*Sleuth* (Anthony Shaffer)
1972	*Two Gentlemen of Verona* (book, John Guare, Mel Shapiro; music, Galt MacDermot; lyrics, John Guare)	*Sticks and Bones* (David Rabe)
1973	*A Little Night Music* (book, Hugh Wheeler; music and lyrics, Stephen Sondheim)	*That Championship Season* (Jason Miller)
1974	*Raisin* (book, Robert Nemiroff, Charlotte Zaltzberg; music, Judd Woldin; lyrics, Robert Brittan)	*The River Niger* (Joseph A. Walker)
1975	*The Wiz* (book, William F. Brown; music and lyrics, Charlie Smalls)	*Equus* (Peter Shaffer)
1976	*A Chorus Line* (book, James Kirkwood, Nicholas Dante; music, Marvin Hamlisch; lyrics, Edward Kleban)	*Travesties* (Tom Stoppard)
1977	*Annie* (book, Thomas Meehan; music, Charles Strouse; lyrics, Martin Charnin)	*The Shadow Box* (Michael Christofer)
1978	*Ain't Misbehavin'* (book, Murray Horwitz, Richard Maltby, Jr.; music, Fats Waller; lyrics, Fats Waller and many others)	*Da* (Hugh Leonard)
1979	*Sweeney Todd* (book, Hugh Wheeler; music and lyrics, Stephen Sondheim)	*The Elephant Man* (Bernard Pomerance)
1980	*Evita* (book and lyrics, Tim Rice; music, Andrew Lloyd Webber)	*Children of a Lesser God* (Mark Medoff)
1981	*42nd Street* (book, Michael Stewart, Mark Bramble; music, Harry Warren; lyrics, Al Dubin)	*Amadeus* (Peter Shaffer)

Tony Awards, 1947–2005 (continued)

YEAR	BEST MUSICAL	BEST PLAY
1982	*Nine* (book, Arthur Kopit; music and lyrics, Maury Yeston)	*The Life and Adventures of Nicholas Nickleby* (David Edgar)
1983	*Cats* (book and lyrics, T.S. Eliot; music, Andrew Lloyd Webber)	*Torch Song Trilogy* (Harvey Fierstein)
1984	*La Cage aux Folles* (book, Harvey Fierstein; music and lyrics, Jerry Herman)	*The Real Thing* (Tom Stoppard)
1985	*Big River* (book, William Hauptman; music and lyrics, Roger Miller)	*Biloxi Blues* (Neil Simon)
1986	*The Mystery of Edwin Drood* (book, music, lyrics, Rupert Holmes)	*I'm Not Rappaport* (Herb Gardner)
1987	*Les Misérables* (book, Alain Boublil, Claude-Michel Schönberg; music, Claude-Michel Schönberg; lyrics, Herbert Kretzmer, Alain Boublil)	*Fences* (August Wilson)
1988	*The Phantom of the Opera* (book, Richard Stilgoe, Andrew Lloyd Webber; music, Andrew Lloyd Webber; lyrics, Charles Hart, Richard Stilgoe)	*M. Butterfly* (David Henry Hwang)
1989	*Jerome Robbins' Broadway* (compilation)	*The Heidi Chronicles* (Wendy Wasserstein)
1990	*City of Angels* (book, Larry Gelbart; music, Cy Coleman; lyrics, David Zippel)	*The Grapes of Wrath* (Frank Galati)
1991	*The Will Rogers Follies* (book, Peter Stone; music, Cy Coleman; lyrics, Betty Comden, Adolph Green)	*Lost in Yonkers* (Neil Simon)
1992	*Crazy for You* (book, Ken Ludwig; music and lyrics, George and Ira Gershwin)	*Dancing at Lughnasa* (Brian Friel)
1993	*Kiss of the Spider Woman—The Musical* (book, Terrence McNally; music, John Kander; lyrics, Fred Ebb)	*Angels in America: Millennium Approaches* (Tony Kushner)
1994	*Passion* (book, James Lapine; music and lyrics, Stephen Sondheim)	*Angels in America: Perestroika* (Tony Kushner)
1995	*Sunset Boulevard* (book and lyrics, Don Black, Christopher Hampton; music, Andrew Lloyd Webber)	*Love! Valour! Compassion!* (Terrence McNally)
1996	*Rent* (book, music, lyrics, Jonathan Larson)	*Master Class* (Terrence McNally)
1997	*Titanic* (book, Peter Stone; music and lyrics, Maury Yeston)	*The Last Night of Ballyhoo* (Alfred Uhry)
1998	*The Lion King* (book, Roger Allers, Irene Mecchi; music and lyrics, Elton John, Tim Rice, and others)	*Art* (Yasmina Reza)
1999	*Fosse* (compilation)	*Side Man* (Warren Leight)
2000	*Contact* (book, John Weidman; music and lyrics, various artists)	*Copenhagen* (Michael Frayn)
2001	*The Producers, the New Mel Brooks Musical* (book, Mel Brooks, Thomas Meehan; music and lyrics, Mel Brooks)	*Proof* (David Auburn)
2002	*Thoroughly Modern Millie* (book, Richard Morris, Dick Scanlan; music, Jeanine Tesori; lyrics, Dick Scanlan)	*The Goat or Who Is Sylvia?* (Edward Albee)
2003	*Hairspray* (book, Mark O'Donnell and Thomas Meehan; music, Marc Shaiman; lyrics, Scott Wittman and Marc Shaiman)	*Take Me Out* (Richard Greenberg)
2004	*Avenue Q* (book, Jeff Whitty; music and lyrics, Robert Lopez and Jeff Marx)	*I Am My Own Wife* (Doug Wright)
2005	*Monty Python's Spamalot* (book, Eric Idle; music and lyrics, John Du Prez and Eric Idle)	*Doubt* (John Patrick Shanley)

[1]Awarded to author.

Longest-Running Broadway Shows

As of 6 Jul 2005. Source: Internet Broadway Database, <www.ibdb.com>.

	SHOW	RUN	TOTAL PERFORMANCES		SHOW	RUN	TOTAL PERFORMANCES
1	Cats	1982–2000	7,485	12	Fiddler on the Roof	1964–1972	3,242
2	The Phantom of the Opera	1988–	7,261	13	Life with Father	1939–1947	3,224
				14	Tobacco Road	1933–1941	3,182
3	Les Misérables	1987–2003	6,680	15	The Lion King	1997–	3,179
4	A Chorus Line	1975–1990	6,137	16	Hello, Dolly!	1964–1970	2,844
5	Oh! Calcutta! [revival]	1976–1989	5,959	17	My Fair Lady	1956–1962	2,717
				18	Annie	1977–1983	2,377
6	Beauty and the Beast	1994–	4,588	19	Cabaret [revival]	1998–2004	2,377
				20	Man of La Mancha	1965–1971	2,328
7	Miss Saigon	1991–2001	4,092	21	Abie's Irish Rose	1922–1927	2,327
8	Rent	1996–	3,816	22	Oklahoma!	1943–1948	2,212
9	Chicago [revival]	1996–	3,587	23	Smokey Joe's Cafe	1995–2000	2,036
10	42nd Street	1980–1989	3,486	24	Pippin	1972–1977	1,944
11	Grease	1972–1980	3,388	25	South Pacific	1949–1954	1,925

Did you know? Among the performers who studied with legendary acting coach Lee Strasberg are Marilyn Monroe, Al Pacino, Jane Fonda, James Dean, Dustin Hoffman, Paul Newman, Robert DeNiro, Jack Nicholson, Ellen Burstyn, Steve McQueen, Martin Landau, and Sally Field.

Encyclopædia Britannica's 25 Notable US Theater Companies

COMPANY	LOCATION	ARTISTIC DIRECTOR (2005)
The Acting Company	New York NY	Margot Harley
Actors Theatre of Louisville	Louisville KY	Marc Masterson
Alley Theatre	Houston TX	Gregory Boyd
American Conservatory Theater	San Francisco CA	Carey Perloff
American Repertory Theatre	Cambridge MA	Robert Woodruff
Arena Stage	Washington DC	Molly Smith
Black Ensemble Theater	Chicago IL	Jackie Taylor
Center Theatre Group	Los Angeles CA	Gordon Davidson
Circle in the Square	New York NY	Theodore Mann
Cincinnati Playhouse in the Park	Cincinnati OH	Edward Stern
Cleveland Public Theatre	Cleveland OH	Randy Rollison
Colony Theatre Company	Burbank CA	Barbara Beckley
El Teatro Campesino	San Juan Bautista CA	Luis Valdez
Ford's Theatre	Washington DC	Paul R. Tetreault
Goodman Theatre	Chicago IL	Robert Falls
Guthrie Theater	Minneapolis MN	Joe Dowling
La Jolla Playhouse	La Jolla CA	Des McAnuff
Long Wharf Theatre	New Haven CT	Gordon Edelstein
Pasadena Playhouse	Pasadena CA	Sheldon Epps
The Public Theater	New York NY	Oskar Eustis
Seattle Repertory Theatre	Seattle WA	Sharon Ott
Steppenwolf Theatre Company	Chicago IL	Martha Lavey
Studio Arena Theatre	Buffalo NY	Gavin Cameron-Webb
Victory Gardens Theater	Chicago IL	Dennis Zacek
Yale Repertory Theatre	New Haven CT	James Bundy

Music

Grammy Awards 2004

The National Academy of Recording Arts and Sciences was established in 1957 as a professional organization for musicians, producers, technicians, and executives in the US recording industry. The Grammys, first awarded in 1958, recognize excellence in the recording industry without regard to record sales or chart position. Nominees and winners are selected by the Academy's individual members according to the members' areas of expertise. In addition to the four general categories (record, album, and song of the year, and best new artist) for which all members are eligible to vote, for 2004 there were 107 categories in 31 fields, of which Academy members were permitted to vote in no more than 8 fields. Prizes for works released 1 Oct 2003–30 Sep 2004 were awarded in Los Angeles on 13 Feb 2005; the ceremony for 2004–05 works is scheduled for late February 2005 in New York City. Prize: gold miniature phonograph.

Grammy Award Web site: <www.grammy.com>.

category: winner (performer in parentheses for songwriting/production awards)

record (single) of the year: "Here We Go Again," Ray Charles and Norah Jones; ▶ album of the year: Genius Loves Company, Ray Charles and various artists; ▶ song of the year: "Daughters," John Mayer; ▶ new artist: Maroon5; ▶ pop vocal performance, female: "Sunrise," Norah Jones; ▶ pop vocal performance, male: "Daughters," John Mayer; ▶ pop vocal performance, duo/group: "Heaven," Los Lonely Boys; ▶ pop vocal album: Genius Loves Company, Ray Charles and various artists; ▶ pop vocal album, traditional: Stardust...The Great American Songbook Volume III, Rod Stewart; ▶ rock vocal solo performance: "Code of Silence," Bruce Springsteen; ▶ rock vocal performance, duo/group: "Vertigo," U2; ▶ hard rock performance: "Slither," Velvet Revolver; ▶ metal performance: "Whiplash," Motörhead; ▶ rock song: "Vertigo," Bono, Adam Clayton, The Edge and Larry Mullen, songwriters (U2); ▶ rock album: American Idiot, Green Day; ▶ alternative album: A Ghost is Born, Wilco; ▶ R&B vocal performance, female: "If I Ain't Got You," Alicia Keys; ▶ R&B vocal performance, male: "Call My Name," Prince; ▶ R&B vocal performance, duo/group: "My Boo," Usher and Alicia Keys; ▶ R&B song: "You Don't Know My Name," Alicia Keys, Harold Lilly & Kanye West, songwriters (Alicia Keys); ▶ R&B album: The Diary of Alicia Keys, Alicia Keys;

Grammy Awards 2004 (continued)

‣ **contemporary R&B album:** *Confessions,* Usher; ‣ **rap solo performance:** "99 Problems," Jay-Z; ‣ **rap performance, duo/group:** "Let's Get It Started," The Black Eyed Peas; ‣ **rap song:** *Jesus Walks,* Miri Ben Ari, C. Smith, & Kanye West, songwriters (Kanye West); ‣ **rap album:** *The College Dropout,* Kanye West; ‣ **country vocal performance, female:** "Redneck Woman," Gretchen Wilson; ‣ **country vocal performance, male:** "Live Like You Were Dying," Tim McGraw; ‣ **country vocal performance, duo/group:** "Top of the World," Dixie Chicks; ‣ **country song:** "Live Like You Were Dying," Tim Nichols & Craig Wiseman, songwriters (Tim McGraw); ‣ **country album:** *Van Lear Rose,* Loretta Lynn; ‣ **bluegrass album:** *Brand New Strings,* Ricky Skaggs & Kentucky Thunder; ‣ **new age album:** *Returning,* Will Ackerman; ‣ **jazz album, contemporary:** *Unspeakable,* Bill Frisell; ‣ **jazz album, vocal:** *R.S.V.P. (Rare Songs, Very Personal),* Nancy Wilson; ‣ **jazz album, instrumental solo:** *Speak Like a Child,* Herbie Hancock; ‣ **jazz album, instrumental:** *Illuminations,* McCoy Tyner with Gary Bartz, Terence Blanchard, Christian McBride & Lewis Nash; ‣ **jazz album, large ensemble:** *Concert in the Garden,* Maria Schneider Orchestra; ‣ **Latin jazz album:** *Land of the Sun,* Charlie Haden; ‣ **gospel album, rock:** *Wire,* Third Day; ‣ **gospel album, pop/contemporary:** *All Things New,* Steven Curtis Chapman; ‣ **gospel album, southern/country/bluegrass:** *Worship & Faith,* Randy Travis; ‣ **gospel album, soul, traditional:** *There Will Be a Light,* Ben Harper & The Blind Boys of Alabama; ‣ **gospel album, soul, contemporary:** *Nothing Without You,* Smokie Norful; ‣ **gospel album, choir/chorus:** *Live...This is Your House,* Carol Cymbala, choir director; The Brooklyn Tabernacle Choir; ‣ **Latin album, pop:** *Amar Sin Mentiras,* Marc Anthony; ‣ **Latin album, rock/alternative:** *Street Signs,* Ozomatli; ‣ **Latin album, traditional tropical:** *¡Ahora Sí!,* Israel López "Cachao"; ‣ **salsa/merengue album:** *Across 110th Street,* Spanish Harlem Orchestra featuring Rubén Blades; ‣ **Mexican/Mexican-American album:** *Intimamente,* Intocable; ‣ **Tejano album:** *Polkas, Gritos y Acordeónes,* David Lee Garza, Joel Guzman & Sunny Sauceda; ‣ **traditional blues album:** *Blues to the Bone,* Etta James; ‣ **contemporary blues album:** *Keep it Simple,* Keb' Mo'; ‣ **traditional folk album:** *Beautiful Dreamer: The Songs of Stephen Foster,* various artists; ‣ **contemporary folk album:** *The Revolution Starts...Now,* Steve Earle; ‣ **Native American album:** *Cedar Dream Songs,* Bill Miller; ‣ **Hawaiian music album:** *Slack Key Guitar Volume 2,* various artists; ‣ **reggae album:** *True Love,* Toots & the Maytalls; ‣ **traditional world music album:** *Raise Your Spirit Higher,* Ladysmith Black Mambazo; ‣ **contemporary world music album:** *Egypt,* Youssou N'Dour; ‣ **polka album:** *Let's Kiss,* Brave Combo; ‣ **spoken word album:** *My Life,* Bill Clinton; ‣ **spoken comedy album:** *The Daily Show with Jon Stewart Presents...America: A Citizen's Guide to Democracy Inaction,* Jon Stewart and the cast of *The Daily Show;* ‣ **producer, non-classical:** John Shanks; ‣ **producer, classical:** David Frost; ‣ **classical album:** *Adams: On the Transmigration of Souls;* Lorin Maazel, conductor; John Adams and Lawrence Rock, producers (Brooklyn Youth Chorus and New York Choral Artists; New York Philharmonic); ‣ **orchestral performance:** *Adams: On the Transmigration of Souls;* Lorin Maazel, conductor (Brooklyn Youth Chorus and New York Choral Artists; New York Philharmonic); ‣ **opera recording:** *Mozart: Le nozze di Figaro,* René Jacobs, conductor; Patrizia Ciofi, Véronique Gens, Simon Keenlyside, Angelika Kirchschlager and Lorenzo Regazzo; Martin Sauer, producer (various artists, Concerto Köln); ‣ **chamber music performance:** *Prokofiev: Cinderella-Suite for Two Pianos/Ravel: Ma mère l'oye,* Martha Argerich, piano, and Mikhail Pletnev, piano; ‣ **classical vocal performance:** *Ives: Songs (The Things Our Fathers Loved; The Housatonic at Stockbridge, etc.),* Susan Graham, mezzo soprano (Pierre-Laurent Aimard, piano); ‣ **contemporary classical composition:** *Adams: On the Transmigration of Souls,* Lorin Maazel, conductor (Brooklyn Youth Chorus and New York Choral Artists; New York Philharmonic); ‣ **short form music video:** "Vertigo," Alex & Martin, directors; Grace Bodie, producer (U2)

Grammy Awards Top Winners, 1958–2004

The year denotes the period for which the winning work or artist was recognized; the prizes were generally awarded during the following year.

YEAR	RECORD (SINGLE) OF THE YEAR	ALBUM OF THE YEAR	BEST NEW ARTIST
1958	"Nel Blu Dipinto Di Blu (Volare)," Domenico Modugno	*The Music from Peter Gunn,* Henry Mancini	*not awarded*
1959	"Mack the Knife," Bobby Darin	*Come Dance with Me,* Frank Sinatra	Bobby Darin
1960	"Theme from A Summer Place," Percy Faith	*The Button-down Mind of Bob Newhart,* Bob Newhart	Bob Newhart
1961	"Moon River," Henry Mancini	*Judy at Carnegie Hall,* Judy Garland	Peter Nero
1962	"I Left My Heart in San Francisco," Tony Bennett	*The First Family,* Vaughn Meader	Robert Goulet
1963	"The Days of Wine and Roses," Henry Mancini	*The Barbra Streisand Album,* Barbra Streisand	Ward Swingle (The Swingle Singers)
1964	"The Girl from Ipanema," Stan Getz & Astrud Gilberto	*Getz/Gilberto,* Stan Getz & João Gilberto	The Beatles
1965	"A Taste of Honey," Herb Alpert	*September of My Years,* Frank Sinatra	Tom Jones

Grammy Awards Top Winners, 1958–2004 (continued)

YEAR	RECORD (SINGLE) OF THE YEAR	ALBUM OF THE YEAR	BEST NEW ARTIST
1966	"Strangers in the Night," Frank Sinatra	A Man and His Music, Frank Sinatra	not awarded
1967	"Up, Up and Away," The 5th Dimension	Sgt. Pepper's Lonely Hearts Club Band, The Beatles	Bobbie Gentry
1968	"Mrs. Robinson," Simon & Garfunkel	By the Time I Get to Phoenix, Glen Campbell	José Feliciano
1969	"Aquarius/Let the Sunshine In," The 5th Dimension	Blood, Sweat & Tears, Blood, Sweat & Tears	Crosby, Stills & Nash
1970	"Bridge over Troubled Water," Simon & Garfunkel	Bridge over Troubled Water, Simon & Garfunkel	Carpenters
1971	"It's Too Late," Carole King	Tapestry, Carole King	Carly Simon
1972	"The First Time Ever I Saw Your Face," Roberta Flack	The Concert for Bangla Desh, George Harrison & Friends	America
1973	"Killing Me Softly with His Song," Roberta Flack	Innervisions, Stevie Wonder	Bette Midler
1974	"I Honestly Love You," Olivia Newton-John	Fulfillingness' First Finale, Stevie Wonder	Marvin Hamlisch
1975	"Love Will Keep Us Together," Captain & Tennille	Still Crazy After All These Years, Paul Simon	Natalie Cole
1976	"This Masquerade," George Benson	Songs in the Key of Life, Stevie Wonder	Starland Vocal Band
1977	"Hotel California," The Eagles	Rumours, Fleetwood Mac	Debby Boone
1978	"Just the Way You Are," Billy Joel	Saturday Night Fever, The Bee Gees	A Taste of Honey
1979	"What a Fool Believes," The Doobie Brothers	52nd Steet, Billy Joel	Rickie Lee Jones
1980	"Sailing," Christopher Cross	Christopher Cross, Christopher Cross	Christopher Cross
1981	"Bette Davis Eyes," Kim Carnes	Double Fantasy, John Lennon & Yoko Ono	Sheena Easton
1982	"Rosanna," Toto	Toto IV, Toto	Men at Work
1983	"Beat It," Michael Jackson	Thriller, Michael Jackson	Culture Club
1984	"What's Love Got to Do with It," Tina Turner	Can't Slow Down, Lionel Richie	Cyndi Lauper
1985	"We Are the World," USA for Africa	No Jacket Required, Phil Collins	Sade
1986	"Higher Love," Steve Winwood	Graceland, Paul Simon	Bruce Hornsby and the Range
1987	"Graceland," Paul Simon	The Joshua Tree, U2	Jody Watley
1988	"Don't Worry, Be Happy," Bobby McFerrin	Faith, George Michael	Tracy Chapman
1989	"Wind Beneath My Wings," Bette Midler	Nick of Time, Bonnie Raitt	Milli Vanilli [revoked]
1990	"Another Day in Paradise," Phil Collins	Back on the Block, Quincy Jones	Mariah Carey
1991	"Unforgettable," Natalie Cole w/ Nat "King" Cole	Unforgettable, Natalie Cole w/ Nat "King" Cole	Marc Cohn
1992	"Tears in Heaven," Eric Clapton	Unplugged, Eric Clapton	Arrested Development
1993	"I Will Always Love You," Whitney Houston	The Bodyguard, Whitney Houston	Toni Braxton
1994	"All I Wanna Do," Sheryl Crow	MTV Unplugged, Tony Bennett	Sheryl Crow
1995	"Kiss from a Rose," Seal	Jagged Little Pill, Alanis Morissette	Hootie and the Blowfish
1996	"Change the World," Eric Clapton	Falling into You, Celine Dion	LeAnn Rimes
1997	"Sunny Came Home," Shawn Colvin	Time Out of Mind, Bob Dylan	Paula Cole
1998	"My Heart Will Go On," Celine Dion	The Miseducation of Lauryn Hill, Lauryn Hill	Lauryn Hill
1999	"Smooth," Santana feat. Rob Thomas	Supernatural, Santana	Christina Aguilera
2000	"Beautiful Day," U2	Two Against Nature, Steely Dan	Shelby Lynne
2001	"Walk On," U2	O Brother, Where Art Thou?, various artists	Alicia Keys
2002	"Don't Know Why," Norah Jones	Come Away with Me, Norah Jones	Norah Jones
2003	"Clocks," Coldplay	Speakerboxxx/The Love Below, OutKast	Evanescence
2004	"Here We Go Again," Ray Charles and Norah Jones	Genius Loves Company, Ray Charles and various artists	Maroon5
2005	to be held in February 2006		

Eurovision Song Contest, 1956–2005

The European Broadcasting Union (EBU), an association of national television and radio companies from Europe and the Mediterranean, began the Eurovision Song Contest in 1956 to promote European pop-music composers and performers. Each EBU member country, along with several provisional partici-pants, can nominate one original song per year, in any language, with a maximum length of three min-utes. The overall winner is selected through a point scheme based on call-in votes from viewers and juries in each participating country. Eurovision Song Contest Web site: <www.eurosong.net>.

YEAR   SONG, SONGWRITER(S) (PERFORMER, COUNTRY)

1956   "Refrain," Emile Gardaz, Géo Voumard (Lys Assia, Switzerland)
1957   "Net als toen," Willy van Hemert, Guus Jansen (Corry Brokken, The Netherlands)
1958   "Dors mon amour," Pierre Delanoe, Hubert Giraud (André Claveau, France)
1959   "Een beetje," Willy van Hemert, Dick Schallies (Teddy Scholten, The Netherlands)
1960   "Tom Pillibi," Pierre Cour, André Popp (Jacqueline Boyer, France)
1961   "Nous les amoureux," Jacques Datin, Maurice Vidalin (Jean-Claude Pascal, Luxembourg)
1962   "Un Premier amour," Rolande Valade, Claude Henri Vic (Isabelle Aubret, France)
1963   "Dansevise," Sejr Volmer Sorensen, Otto Francker (Grethe and Jorgen Ingmann, Denmark)
1964   "Non ho l'étà," Nicola Salerno (Gigliola Cinquetti, Italy)
1965   "Poupée de cire, poupée de son," Serge Gainsbourg (France Gall, Luxembourg)
1966   "Merci chérie," Udo Jürgens, Thomas Horbiger (Udo Jürgens, Austria)
1967   "Puppet on a String," Bill Martin, Phil Coulter (Sandie Shaw, United Kingdom)
1968   "La, la, la . . ." Ramon Arcusa, Manuel de la Calva (Massiel, Spain)
1969   "Vivo cantando," A. Alcaide, Maria José de Cerato (Salomé, Spain); "Boom Bang-a-Bang," Peter Warne, Alan Moorhouse (Lulu, United Kingdom); "De Troubadour," Lennie Kuhr, David Hartsena (Lennie Kuhr, The Netherlands); "Un Jour, un enfant," Eddy Marnay, Emile Stern (Frida Boccara, France) (four-way tie)
1970   "All Kinds of Everything," Derry Lindsay, Jackie Smith (Dana, Ireland)
1971   "Un Banc, un arbre, une rue," Yves Dessca, Jean-Pierre Bourtayre (Séverine, Monaco)
1972   "Après toi," Klaus Munro, Yves Dessca, Mario Panas (Vicky Leandros, Luxembourg)
1973   "Tu te reconnaîtras," Vline Buggy, Claude Morgan (Anne-Marie David, Luxembourg)
1974   "Waterloo," Stikkan Anderson, Benny Andersson, Björn Ulvaeus (Abba, Sweden)
1975   "Ding dinge dong," Wil Luikinga, Eddy Owens, Dick Bakker (Teach-In, The Netherlands)
1976   "Save Your Kisses for Me," Tony Hiller, Lee Sheriden, Martin Lee (Brotherhood of Man, United Kingdom)
1977   "L'Oiseau et l'enfant," José Gracy, Jean-Paul Cara (Marie Myriam, France)
1978   "A-Ba-Ni-Bi," Ehud Manor, Nurit Hirsh (Izhar Cohen and the Alphabeta, Israel)
1979   "Hallelujah," Shimrit Orr, Kobi Oshrat (Gali Atari and Milk and Honey, Israel)
1980   "What's Another Year," Shay Healy (Johnny Logan, Ireland)
1981   "Making Your Mind Up," Andy Hill, John Danter (Bucks Fizz, United Kingdom)
1982   "Ein bisschen Frieden," Bernd Meinunger, Ralph Siegel (Nicole, West Germany)
1983   "Si la vie est cadeau," Alain Garcia, Jean-Pierre Millers (Corinne Hermes, Luxembourg)
1984   "Diggi-loo-diggi-ley," Britt Lindeborg, Torgny Soederberg (Herrey's, Sweden)
1985   "La det swinge," Rolg Loevland (Bobbysocks, Norway)
1986   "J'aime la vie," Marino Atria, J.P. Furnemont, A. Crisci (Sandra Kim, Belgium)
1987   "Hold Me Now," Sean Sherrard (Johnny Logan, Ireland)
1988   "Ne partez pas sans moi," Nella Martinetti, Atilla Sereftug (Céline Dion, Switzerland)
1989   "Rock Me," Stevo Cvikich, Rajko Dujmich (Riva, Yugoslavia)
1990   "Insieme: 1992," Toto Cutugno (Toto Cutugno, Italy)
1991   "Fångad av en stormvind," Stephan Berg (Carola, Sweden)
1992   "Why Me," Sean Sherrard (Linda Martin, Ireland)
1993   "In Your Eyes," Jimmy Walsh (Niamh Kavanagh, Ireland)
1994   "Rock'n Roll Kids," Brendan Graham (Paul Harrington and Charlie McGettigan, Ireland)
1995   "Nocturne," Petter Skavlan, Rolf Lovland (Secret Garden, Norway)
1996   "The Voice," Brendan Graham (Eimear Quinn, Ireland)
1997   "Love Shine a Light," Kimberley Rew (Katrina and the Waves, United Kingdom)
1998   "Diva," Yoav Ginay (Dana International, Israel)
1999   "Take Me to Your Heaven," Gert Lengstrand (Charlotte Nilsson, Sweden)
2000   "Fly on the Wings of Love," Jørgen Olsen (Olsen Brothers, Denmark)
2001   "Everybody," Maian-Anna Käarmas, Ivar Must (Tanel Padar, Dave Benton, and 2XL, Estonia)
2002   "I Wanna," Marija Naumova, Marats Samauskis (Marie N, Latvia)
2003   "Every Way That I Can," Demir Demirkan, Sertab Erener (Sertab Erener, Turkey)
2004   "Wild Dances," Ruslana Lyzhichko, Aleksandr Ksenofontov (Ruslana, Ukraine)
2005   "My Number One," Christos Dantis, Natalia Germanou (Elena Paparizou, Greece)

Did you know? Dean Reed was an American-born pop star and self-described Marxist who enjoyed popularity in the former Soviet bloc, beginning with his first tour of the USSR in 1966. Reed signed a record deal in Hollywood in 1958, but his political commitments led overseas. Reed moved to East Germany in 1973, where he lived until his death by drowning in 1986.

Brit Awards, 2005

The British Phonographic Industry, a trade association of record companies, established the Brit Awards in 1977 to recognize pop acts from Great Britain and abroad. Prize: statuette. Web site: <www.brits.co.uk>.

BRITISH CATEGORIES
Male solo artist: The Streets
Female solo artist: Joss Stone
Group: Franz Ferdinand
Album: Keane, *Hopes and Fears*
Breakthrough artist: Keane
Single: Will Young, "Your Game"
Rock act: Franz Ferdinand
Urban act: Joss Stone
Best song: Robbie Williams, "Angels"

INTERNATIONAL CATEGORIES
Male solo artist: Eminem
Female solo artist: Gwen Stefani
Group: Scissor Sisters
Album: Scissor Sisters, *Scissor Sisters*
Breakthrough artist: Scissor Sisters

ADDITIONAL CATEGORIES
Pop act: McFly
Outstanding contribution: Sir Bob Geldof

Country Music Association Awards, 2004

The Country Music Association, founded in 1958 as a trade organization for the country and western music industry, began its annual awards ceremony in 1967 and made it the first nationally televised music awards show the following year. Ceremonies are held in November. Prize: hand-blown crystal statuette. Country Music Association Web site: <www.cmaworld.com>

▸ **entertainer of the year:** Kenny Chesney; ▸ **female vocalist of the year:** Martina McBride; ▸ **male vocalist of the year:** Keith Urban; ▸ **Horizon Award:** Gretchen Wilson; ▸ **vocal duo of the year:** Brooks & Dunn; ▸ **vocal group of the year:** Rascal Flatts; ▸ **album of the year:** *When the Sun Goes Down*, Kenny Chesney; Buddy Cannon, Kenny Chesney, prod.; ▸ **song of the year:** "Live Like You Were Dying" Tim Nichols, Craig Wiseman, songwriters; ▸ **single of the year:** "Live Like You Were Dying," Tim McGraw; Byron Gallimore, Tim McGraw, Darran Smith, prod.; ▸ **music video of the year:** "Whiskey Lullaby," Rick Schroeder, dir. (Brad Paisley with Alison Krauss); ▸ **musical event of the year:** "Whiskey Lullaby," Brad Paisley with Alison Krauss; ▸ **musician of the year:** Dann Huff (guitar)

The All-Time Top 50 Best-Selling Albums

As of June 2005. Source: Recording Industry Association of America (RIAA), <www.riaa.com>.

	ALBUM	ARTIST	YEAR		ALBUM	ARTIST	YEAR
1	Their Greatest Hits (1971–1975)	The Eagles	1976	26	Backstreet Boys	Backstreet Boys	1997
				27	Ropin' the Wind	Garth Brooks	1991
2	Thriller	Michael Jackson	1982	28	Bat out of Hell	Meat Loaf	1977
3	The Wall	Pink Floyd	1979	29	Metallica	Metallica	1991
4	Untitled ("Led Zeppelin IV")	Led Zeppelin	1971	30	Simon & Garfunkel's Greatest Hits	Simon & Garfunkel	1972
5	Back in Black	AC/DC	1980	31	...Baby One More Time	Britney Spears	1999
6	Greatest Hits, Vols. 1 & 2 (1973–1985)	Billy Joel	1985	32	Millennium	Backstreet Boys	1999
7	Come on Over	Shania Twain	1997	33	Whitney Houston	Whitney Houston	1985
8	The Beatles ("The White Album")	The Beatles	1968	34	Greatest Hits 1974–1978	Steve Miller Band	1978
9	Rumours	Fleetwood Mac	1977	35	Purple Rain Soundtrack	Prince & the Revolution	1984
10	Boston	Boston	1976	36	Live 1975–85	Bruce Springsteen and the E Street Band	1986
11	The Bodyguard Soundtrack	Whitney Houston & various artists	1992				
12	1967–70	The Beatles	1973	37	Abbey Road	The Beatles	1969
13	No Fences	Garth Brooks	1990	38	Slippery When Wet	Bon Jovi	1986
14	Hotel California	The Eagles	1976	39	II	Boyz II Men	1994
15	Cracked Rear View	Hootie & the Blowfish	1994	40	No Jacket Required	Phil Collins	1985
				41	Hysteria	Def Leppard	1987
16	Greatest Hits	Elton John	1974	42	Wide Open Spaces	Dixie Chicks	1998
17	Jagged Little Pill	Alanis Morissette	1995	43	Breathless	Kenny G	1992
18	1962–66	The Beatles	1973	44	Led Zeppelin II	Led Zeppelin	1969
19	Saturday Night Fever Soundtrack	The Bee Gees & various artists	1977	45	Yourself or Someone Like You	matchbox twenty	1996
20	Double Live	Garth Brooks	1998	46	Ten	Pearl Jam	1991
21	Appetite for Destruction	Guns 'n' Roses	1987	47	Kenny Rogers' Greatest Hits	Kenny Rogers	1980
22	Physical Graffiti	Led Zeppelin	1975	48	Hot Rocks, 1964–1971	The Rolling Stones	1972
23	Dark Side of the Moon	Pink Floyd	1973	49	Forrest Gump Soundtrack	various artists	1994
24	Supernatural	Santana	1999				
25	Born in the U.S.A.	Bruce Springsteen	1984	50	The Woman in Me	Shania Twain	1995

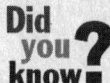

Did you know? The legendary folk-blues singer, songwriter, and guitarist Leadbelly was born Huddie William Ledbetter. Musical from childhood, he played accordion, 6- and 12-string guitar, bass, and harmonica. In 1918 he was imprisoned for murder; after serving six years, he was pardoned by the governor of Texas, who had visited the prison and heard him sing.

Rock and Roll Hall of Fame Inductees

Music-industry professionals established the Rock and Roll Hall of Fame Foundation in 1983 in order to "recognize the contributions of those who have had a significant impact on the evolution, development and perpetuation of rock and roll." Performers are eligible for induction 25 years after the release of their first record. The foundation's nominating committee compiles an annual list of eligible artists and distributes this list to about 1,000 rock experts throughout the world. Those performers receiving the highest number of votes, as well as at least 50% of the vote, are inducted. Special committees select inductees in other categories. Those elected to membership receive a statuette depicting an abstract human figure holding aloft a gold record. 2005 inductees appear in **boldface**.
Web site: <www.rockhall.com>.

NAME (YEAR OF INDUCTION)

AC/DC (2003)
Paul Ackerman[1] (1995)
Aerosmith (2001)
The Allman Brothers Band (1995)
The Animals (1994)
Louis Armstrong[2] (1990)
Chet Atkins[3] (2002)
LaVern Baker (1991)
Hank Ballard (1990)
The Band (1994)
Dave Bartholomew[1] (1991)
Frank Barsalona[4] (2005)
Ralph Bass[1] (1991)
The Beach Boys (1988)
The Beatles (1988)
The Bee Gees (1997)
Benny Benjamin[3] (2003)
Chuck Berry (1986)
Chris Blackwell[1] (2001)
Hal Blaine[3] (2000)
Bob Wills and His Texas Playboys[2] (1999)
Bobby "Blue" Bland (1992)
Booker T. and the M.G.'s (1992)
David Bowie (1996)
Charles Brown[2] (1999)
James Brown (1986)
Ruth Brown (1993)
Jackson Browne (2004)
Buffalo Springfield (1997)
Solomon Burke (2001)
James Burton[3] (2001)
The Byrds (1991)
Johnny Cash (1992)
Ray Charles (1986)
Leonard Chess[1] (1987)
Charlie Christian[2] (1990)
Eric Clapton (2000)
Dick Clark[1] (1993)
The Clash (2003)
The Coasters (1987)
Eddie Cochran (1987)
Nat "King" Cole[2] (2000)

Sam Cooke (1986)
Elvis Costello & the Attractions (2003)
Floyd Cramer[3] (2003)
Cream (1993)
Creedence Clearwater Revival (1993)
Crosby, Stills & Nash (1997)
King Curtis[3] (2000)
Bobby Darin (1990)
Clive Davis[1] (2000)
The Dells (2004)
Bo Diddley (1987)
Dion (1989)
Willie Dixon[2] (1994)
Fats Domino (1986)
Tom Donahue[1] (1996)
The Doors (1993)
Steve Douglas[3] (2003)
The Drifters (1988)
Bob Dylan (1988)
The Eagles (1998)
Earth, Wind & Fire (2000)
Duane Eddy (1994)
Ahmet Ertegun[1] (1987)
Nesuhi Ertegun[4] (1991)
The Everly Brothers (1986)
Leo Fender[1] (1992)
The Flamingos (2001)
Fleetwood Mac (1998)
The Four Seasons (1990)
The Four Tops (1990)
Frankie Lymon and the Teenagers (1993)
Aretha Franklin (1987)
Alan Freed[1] (1986)
Milt Gabler[1] (1993)
Marvin Gaye (1987)
Gladys Knight and the Pips (1996)
Gerry Goffin and Carole King[1] (1990)
Berry Gordy, Jr.[1] (1988)

Bill Graham[1] (1992)
The Grateful Dead (1994)
Al Green (1995)
Woody Guthrie[2] (1988)
Buddy Guy (2005)
Bill Haley (1987)
John Hammond[4] (1986)
George Harrison (2004)
Isaac Hayes (2002)
Billie Holiday[2] (2000)
Holland, Dozier, and Holland[1] (1990)
Buddy Holly (1986)
John Lee Hooker (1991)
The Impressions (1991)
The Inkspots[2] (1989)
The Isley Brothers (1992)
The Jackson Five (1997)
Mahalia Jackson[2] (1997)
Michael Jackson (2001)
James Jamerson[3] (2000)
Elmore James[2] (1992)
Etta James (1993)
Jefferson Airplane (1996)
The Jimi Hendrix Experience (1992)
Billy Joel (1999)
Elton John (1994)
Little Willie John (1996)
Johnnie Johnson[3] (2001)
Robert Johnson[2] (1986)
Janis Joplin (1995)
Louis Jordan[2] (1987)
B.B. King (1987)
The Kinks (1990)
Leadbelly[2] (1988)
Led Zeppelin (1995)
Brenda Lee (2002)
Jerry Leiber and Mike Stoller[1] (1987)
John Lennon (1994)
Jerry Lee Lewis (1986)
Professor Longhair[2] (1992)

Rock and Roll Hall of Fame Inductees (continued)

NAME (YEAR OF INDUCTION)	NAME (YEAR OF INDUCTION)	NAME (YEAR OF INDUCTION)
The Lovin' Spoonful (2000)	Elvis Presley (1986)	Jim Stewart[1] (2002)
The Mamas and the Papas (1998)	**The Pretenders (2005)**	Rod Stewart (1994)
Bob Marley (1994)	Lloyd Price (1998)	The Supremes (1988)
Martha and the Vandellas (1995)	Prince (2004)	Talking Heads (2002)
George Martin[1] (1999)	Queen (2001)	James Taylor (2000)
Curtis Mayfield (1999)	Ma Rainey[2] (1990)	The Temptations (1989)
Paul McCartney (1999)	Bonnie Raitt (2000)	Tom Petty and the Heartbreakers (2002)
Clyde McPhatter (1987)	Ramones (2002)	Allen Toussaint[1] (1998)
Joni Mitchell (1997)	Otis Redding (1989)	Traffic (2004)
Bill Monroe[2] (1997)	Jimmy Reed (1991)	Big Joe Turner (1987)
The Moonglows (2000)	Little Richard (1986)	Ike and Tina Turner (1991)
Scotty Moore[3] (2000)	The Righteous Brothers (2003)	**U2 (2005)**
Van Morrison (1993)	Smokey Robinson (1987)	Ritchie Valens (2001)
Jelly Roll Morton[2] (1998)	Jimmie Rodgers[2] (1986)	The Velvet Underground (1996)
Syd Nathan[1] (1997)	The Rolling Stones (1989)	Gene Vincent (1998)
Ricky Nelson (1987)	Sam and Dave (1992)	T-Bone Walker[2] (1987)
The O'Jays (2005)	Santana (1998)	Dinah Washington[2] (1993)
Roy Orbison (1987)	Pete Seeger[2] (1996)	Muddy Waters (1987)
The Orioles[2] (1995)	Bob Seger (2004)	Jann S. Wenner[4] (2004)
Mo Ostin[1] (2003)	Del Shannon (1999)	Jerry Wexler[1] (1987)
Johnny Otis[1] (1994)	The Shirelles (1996)	The Who (1990)
Earl Palmer[3] (2000)	Simon and Garfunkel (1990)	Hank Williams[2] (1987)
Parliament-Funkadelic (1997)	Paul Simon (2001)	Jackie Wilson (1987)
Les Paul[2] (1988)	**Percy Sledge (2005)**	Howlin' Wolf[2] (1991)
Carl Perkins (1987)	Sly and the Family Stone (1993)	Stevie Wonder (1989)
Sam Phillips[1] (1986)	Bessie Smith[2] (1989)	Jimmy Yancey[2] (1986)
Wilson Pickett (1991)	The Soul Stirrers[2] (1989)	The Yardbirds (1992)
Pink Floyd (1996)	Phil Spector[1] (1989)	Neil Young (1995)
Gene Pitney (2002)	Dusty Springfield (1999)	The (Young) Rascals (1997)
The Platters (1990)	Bruce Springsteen (1999)	Frank Zappa (1995)
The Police (2003)	The Staple Singers (1999)	ZZ Top (2004)
Doc Pomus[1] (1992)	Steely Dan (2001)	
	Seymour Stein[4] (2005)	

[1]*Non-performers.*   [2]*Early Influences.*   [3]*Sidemen.*   [4]*Lifetime Achievement.*

Encyclopædia Britannica's 25 World-Class Orchestras

ORCHESTRA	LOCATION	FOUNDED	CONDUCTOR (2005)
Berlin Philharmonic Orchestra	Berlin, Germany	1882	Sir Simon Rattle
Boston Symphony Orchestra	Boston MA	1881	James Levine
Chicago Symphony Orchestra	Chicago IL	1891	Daniel Barenboim
Cleveland Orchestra	Cleveland OH	1918	Franz Welser-Möst
Gewandhaus Orchestra	Leipzig, Germany	1743	Riccardo Chailly
Israel Philharmonic Orchestra	Tel Aviv, Israel	1936	Zubin Mehta
London Philharmonic Orchestra	London, England	1932	Kurt Masur
London Symphony Orchestra	London, England	1904	Sir Colin Davis
Los Angeles Philharmonic	Los Angeles CA	1919	Esa-Pekka Salonen
Montreal Symphony Orchestra	Montreal, Quebec	1934	Kent Nagano[1]
New York Philharmonic	New York NY	1842	Lorin Maazel
NHK Symphony Orchestra	Tokyo, Japan	1926	Vladimir Ashkenazy
Orchestre de la Suisse Romande	Geneva, Switzerland	1918	Pinchas Steinberg
Orchestre de Paris	Paris, France	1967	Christoph Eschenbach
Orchestre National de France	Paris, France	1934	Kurt Masur
Oslo Philharmonic Orchestra	Oslo, Norway	1919	André Previn[2]
Philadelphia Orchestra	Philadelphia PA	1900	Christoph Eschenbach
Philharmonia Orchestra	London, England	1945	Christoph von Dohnányi
Pittsburgh Symphony Orchestra	Pittsburgh PA	1896	Mariss Jansons
Royal Concertgebouw Orchestra	Amsterdam, The Netherlands	1888	Mariss Jansons
Royal Philharmonic Orchestra	London, England	1946	Daniele Gatti
Saint Louis Symphony Orchestra	St. Louis MO	1880	David Robertson
St. Petersburg State Symphony Orchestra	St. Petersburg, Russia	1988	Aleksandr Kantorov
San Francisco Symphony	San Francisco CA	1911	Michael Tilson Thomas
Vienna Philharmonic Orchestra	Vienna, Austria	1842	*guest conductors*

[1]*Nagano will assume the musical directorship of the Montreal Symphony Orchestra in 2006.*   [2]*Jukka-Pekka Saraste will assume the musical directorship of the Oslo Philharmonic Orchestra in the fall of 2006.*

Encyclopædia Britannica's Top 25 Opera Companies

COMPANY	LOCATION	FOUNDED	GENERAL OR ARTISTIC DIRECTOR (2005)
Arena di Verona[1]	Verona, Italy	1913	Claudio Orazi
Bayerische Staatsoper (Bavarian State Opera)	Munich, Germany	1653	Sir Peter Jonas
Bolshoi Opera	Moscow, Russia	1776	Aleksandr Vedernikov
Canadian Opera Company	Toronto, ON, Canada	1950	Richard Bradshaw
Cleveland Opera	Cleveland OH	1976	Robert Chumbley
Grand Théâtre de Genève	Geneva, Switzerland	1962	Jean-Marie Blanchard
Los Angeles Opera	Los Angeles CA	1986	Plácido Domingo
Lyric Opera of Chicago	Chicago IL	1954	William Mason
Magyar Allami Opera (Hungarian State Opera)	Budapest, Hungary	1884	to be replaced 15 July
Mariinsky Opera Company	St. Petersburg, Russia	1783	Valery Gergiev
Metropolitan Opera	New York NY	1883	James Levine
Opera Australia	Sydney and Melbourne, Australia	1956	Richard Hickox
Opéra National de Paris	Paris, France	1669	Gerard Mortier
Royal Opera	London, England	1732	Antonio Pappano
San Francisco Opera	San Francisco CA	1923	Pamela Rosenberg
Staatsoper Unter den Linden (Unter den Linden State Opera)	Berlin, Germany	1742	Peter Mussbach
Suomen Kansallisooppera (Finnish National Opera)	Helsinki, Finland	1873	Erkki Korhonen
Teatro alla Scala (La Scala)	Milan, Italy	1778	Stéphane Lissner
Teatro dell'Opera di Roma	Rome, Italy	1880	Mauro Trombetta
Teatro di San Carlo	Naples, Italy	1737	Giandomenico Vaccari
Teatro Massimo	Palermo, Italy	1897	Lorenzo Mariani
Théâtre du Châtelet	Paris, France	1862	Jean-Pierre Brossmann
Vancouver Opera	Vancouver, BC, Canada	1958	James W. Wright
Washington National Opera	Washington DC	1956	Plácido Domingo
Wiener Staatsoper (Vienna State Opera)	Vienna, Austria	1869	Ioan Holender

[1]The Arena di Verona was built in the first century AD; it has been primarily an opera venue since 1913.

Did you know? ■ Philip Glass's opera *Satyagraha* (1980) is a portrayal of incidents from the early life of Mohandas K. Gandhi. The dronelike repetition of symmetrical sequences of chords in this work attains a haunting and hypnotic power well attuned to the spiritual themes of the libretto, which is adapted from the Hindu scripture, the *Bhagavadgita*.

Pageants

Miss America Winners, 1921–2005

The Miss America Pageant was founded in 1921 as an Atlantic City NJ tourist attraction. Purely a beauty contest in its early years, the competition added a talent category in 1935 and began awarding scholarships a decade later. After 1989 the pageant required evidence of community service, and by 2001 contestants were judged on the basis of talent, community service, leadership, knowledge and understanding, and appearance in swimsuits and eveningwear. Prize: $50,000 college scholarship. Miss America Contest Web site: <www.missamerica.org>.

YEAR	WINNER (HOMETOWN)	YEAR	WINNER (HOMETOWN)
1921	Margaret Gorman (Washington DC)	1927	Lois Delander (Joliet IL)
1922	Mary Katherine Campbell (Columbus OH)	1928–32	not held
1923	Mary Katherine Campbell (Columbus OH)	1933	Marian Bergeron (West Haven CT)
1924	Ruth Malcomson (Philadelphia PA)	1934	not held
1925	Fay Lanphier (Oakland CA)	1935	Henrietta Leaver (Pittsburgh PA)
1926	Norma Smallwood (Tulsa OK)	1936	Rose Coyle (Philadelphia PA)

Miss America Winners, 1921–2005 (continued)

YEAR	WINNER (HOMETOWN)	YEAR	WINNER (HOMETOWN)
1937	Bette Cooper (Bertrand Island NJ)	1972	Laurel Schaefer (Bexley OH)
1938	Marilyn Meseke (Marion OH)	1973	Terry Meeuwsen (De Pere WI)
1939	Patricia Donnelly (Detroit MI)	1974	Rebecca King (Denver CO)
1940	Frances Burke (Philadelphia PA)	1975	Shirley Cothran (Denton TX)
1941	Rosemary LaPlanche (Los Angeles CA)	1976	Tawny Godin (Saratoga Springs NY)
1942	Jo-Carroll Dennison (Tyler TX)	1977	Dorothy Benham (Edina MN)
1943	Jean Bartel (Los Angeles CA)	1978	Susan Perkins (Columbus OH)
1944	Venus Ramey (Washington DC)	1979	Kylene Barker (Roanoke VA)
1945	Bess Myerson (New York NY)	1980	Cheryl Prewitt (Ackerman MS)
1946	Marilyn Buferd (Los Angeles CA)	1981	Susan Powell (Elk City OK)
1947	Barbara Walker (Memphis TN)	1982	Elizabeth Ward (Russellville AR)
1948	BeBe Shopp (Hopkins MN)	1983	Debra Maffett (Anaheim CA)
1949	Jacque Mercer (Litchfield AZ)	1984	Suzette Charles (Mays Landing NJ)[2]
1950[1]		1985	Sharlene Wells (Salt Lake City UT)
1951	Yolande Betbeze (Mobile AL)	1986	Susan Akin (Meridian MS)
1952	Colleen Hutchins (Salt Lake City UT)	1987	Kellye Cash (Memphis TN)
1953	Neva Langley (Macon GA)	1988	Kaye Lani Rae Rafko (Monroe MI)
1954	Evelyn Ay (Ephrata PA)	1989	Gretchen Carlson (Anoka MN)
1955	Lee Meriwether (San Francisco CA)	1990	Debbye Turner (Columbia MO)
1956	Sharon Ritchie (Denver CO)	1991	Marjorie Vincent (Oak Park IL)
1957	Marian McKnight (Manning SC)	1992	Carolyn Sapp (Honolulu HI)
1958	Marilyn Van Derbur (Denver CO)	1993	Leanza Cornett (Jacksonville FL)
1959	Mary Ann Mobley (Brandon MS)	1994	Kimberly Aiken (Columbia SC)
1960	Lynda Mead (Natchez MS)	1995	Heather Whitestone (Birmingham AL)
1961	Nancy Fleming (Montague MI)	1996	Shawntel Smith (Muldrow OK)
1962	Maria Fletcher (Asheville NC)	1997	Tara Dawn Holland (Overland Park KS)
1963	Jacquelyn Mayer (Sandusky OH)	1998	Kate Shindle (Evanston IL)
1964	Donna Axum (El Dorado AR)	1999	Nicole Johnson (Virginia Beach VA)
1965	Vonda Van Dyke (Phoenix AZ)	2000	Heather French (Maysville KY)
1966	Deborah Bryant (Overland Park KS)	2001	Angela Perez Baraquio (Honolulu HI)
1967	Jane Jayroe (Laverne OK)	2002	Katie Harman (Gresham OR)
1968	Debra Barnes (Pittsburg KS)	2003	Erika Harold (Urbana IL)
1969	Judith Ford (Belvidere IL)	2004	Ericka Dunlap (Orlando FL)
1970	Pam Eldred (Bloomfield MI)	2005	Deirdre Downs (Birmingham AL)
1971	Phyllis George (Denton TX)		

[1]Until the 1950 competition, winners were given the title for the year in which they won; thereafter, they were given the title for the following year, during which most of their reign took place. As a result no Miss America 1950 was named. [2]Runner-up, crowned after resignation of Vanessa Williams (Millwood NY).

Miss Universe Winners, 1952–2005

The Miss Universe contest originated in 1952 as a swimwear competition in Long Beach CA in conjunction with the Miss USA pageant. The two pageants were held concurrently until 1965. Women aged 18–27 from some 80 countries and dependencies participate in the competition annually, and the contest is broadcast across the globe. Judging is based on an interview and appearances in swimwear and evening wear. Though it remains primarily a beauty contest, the competition's organizers emphasize a message of cross-cultural harmony and opportunity for women, and winners work with the UN and other organizations to promote HIV/AIDS awareness and women's health and reproductive initiatives. Prize: one-year employment contract, cash, products, and services.

Miss Universe Contest Web site: <www.missuniverse.com>.

YEAR	WINNER (COUNTRY)	YEAR	WINNER (COUNTRY)
1952	Armi Kuusela (Finland)	1965	Apasra Hongsakula (Thailand)
1953	Christiane Martel (France)	1966	Margareta Arvidsson (Sweden)
1954	Miriam Stevenson (US)	1967	Sylvia Louise Hitchcock (US)
1955	Hillevi Rombin (Sweden)	1968	Martha Vasconcellos (Brazil)
1956	Carol Morris (US)	1969	Gloria Diaz (Philippines)
1957	Gladys Zender (Peru)	1970	Marisol Malaret (Puerto Rico)
1958	Luz Marina Zuluaga (Colombia)	1971	Georgina Rizk (Lebanon)
1959	Akiko Kojima (Japan)	1972	Kerry Anne Wells (Australia)
1960	Linda Bement (US)	1973	Margarita Moran (Philippines)
1961	Marlene Schmidt (West Germany)	1974	Amparo Muñoz (Spain)
1962	Norma Nolan (Argentina)	1975	Anne Marie Pohtamo (Finland)
1963	Ieda Maria Vargas (Brazil)	1976	Rina Messinger (Israel)
1964	Kiriaki Corinna Tsopei (Greece)	1977	Janelle Commissiong (Trinidad and Tobago)

Miss Universe Winners, 1952–2005 (continued)

YEAR	WINNER (COUNTRY)	YEAR	WINNER (COUNTRY)
1978	Margaret Gardiner (South Africa)	1992	Michelle McLean (Namibia)
1979	Maritza Sayalero (Venezuela)	1993	Dayanara Torres (Puerto Rico)
1980	Shawn Nichols Weatherly (US)	1994	Sushmita Sen (India)
1981	Mona Irene Lailan Sáez Conde (Venezuela)	1995	Chelsi Smith (US)
1982	Karen Diane Baldwin (Canada)	1996	Joseph Alicia Machado Fajardo (Venezuela)
1983	Lorraine Downes (New Zealand)	1997	Brook Antoinette Mahealani Lee (US)
1984	Yvonne Ryding (Sweden)	1998	Wendy Fitzwilliam (Trinidad and Tobago)
1985	Deborah Carthy-Deu (Puerto Rico)	1999	Mpule Kwelagobe (Botswana)
1986	Bárbara Palacios Teyde (Venezuela)	2000	Lara Dutta (India)
1987	Cecilia Carolina Bolocco Fonck (Chile)	2001	Denise M. Quiñones August (Puerto Rico)
1988	Porntip Nakhirunkanok (Thailand)	2002	Justine Pasek (Panama)[1]
1989	Angela Visser (The Netherlands)	2003	Amelia Vega (Dominican Republic)
1990	Mona Grudt (Norway)	2004	Jennifer Hawkins (Australia)
1991	Lupita Jones (Mexico)	2005	Natalie Glebova (Canada)

[1]Oksana Fyodorova (Russia) was dismissed for breach of contract on 23 Sep 2002.

Arts and Letters Awards

Pulitzer Prizes, 2005

The Pulitzer Prizes are awarded annually by Columbia University, New York City, based on recommendations from the Pulitzer Prize Board. The prizes, originally endowed by newspaper editor Joseph Pulitzer, were first awarded in 1917. Over the years categories have been added, and 21 prizes are now presented. All prizes include a $10,000 cash award; the exception is the prize for public service in journalism, which is a gold medal.

Pulitzer Prize Web site: <www.pulitzer.org>.

Journalism

CATEGORY AND DESCRIPTION	WINNER	PUBLICATION	SUBJECT
Public Service: awarded to a newspaper for notable public service	Tracy Weber, Charles Ornstein, Steve Hymon, and Mitchell Landsberg	Los Angeles Times	coverage of deadly medical problems and racial injustice at a major public hospital
Breaking News Reporting: awarded for local reporting of breaking news	staff	Star-Ledger, Newark NJ	coverage of the resignation and acknowledgment of marital infidelity of the governor
Investigative Reporting: awarded to an individual or team for an investigative article or series	Nigel Jaquiss	Willamette Week, Portland OR	investigation exposing the sexual misconduct of a former governor with a 14-year-old girl
Explanatory Reporting: awarded for clarification of a difficult subject through clear communication of in-depth knowledge	Gareth Cook	Boston Globe	scientific and ethical complexities surrounding stem cell research
Beat Reporting: awarded for consistent, intelligent coverage of a particular topic	Amy Dockser Marcus	The Wall Street Journal	illumination of the experiences of cancer survivors through stories about doctors, patients, and their families
National Reporting: awarded for coverage of national news	Walt Bogdanich	New York Times	corporate cover-ups of responsibility for fatal accidents at railway crossings
International Reporting: awarded for coverage of international news	Kim Murphy	Los Angeles Times	coverage of Russia's struggle with terrorism, democracy, and economic development
	Dele Olojede	Newsday, Long Island NY	Rwanda's Tutsi 10 years after the genocide of 1994
Feature Writing	Julia Keller	Chicago Tribune	deadly tornado that hit Utica IL
Commentary	Connie Schultz	Plain Dealer, Cleveland OH	giving voice to underdogs and the underprivileged
Criticism	Joe Morgenstern	The Wall Street Journal	film reviews

Journalism (continued)

CATEGORY AND DESCRIPTION	WINNER	PUBLICATION	SUBJECT
Editorial Writing: awarded for ability to sway public opinion through solid reasoning, clear style, and "moral purpose"	Tom Philp	*Sacramento Bee*	reclamation of California's flooded Hetch Hetchy Valley
Editorial Cartooning: awarded for a cartoon or group of cartoons displaying creativity, superior drawing, and editorial effectiveness	Nick Anderson	*Courier-Journal,* Louisville KY	
Breaking News Photography: awarded for color or black-and-white photographs of breaking news, individually or as a group	Associated Press staff		coverage of the war in Iraq
Feature Photography: awarded for color or black-and-white feature photographs, individually or as a group	Deanne Fitzmaurice	*San Francisco Chronicle*	photo essay on an Oakland hospital's rehabilitation of an Iraqi boy nearly killed in an explosion

Letters, Drama, and Music

Fiction
Awarded for a work of fiction, preferably about American life, by an American author.

YEAR	TITLE	AUTHOR	YEAR	TITLE	AUTHOR
1917	no award		1949	*Guard of Honor*	James Gould Cozzens
1918	*His Family*	Ernest Poole	1950	*The Way West*	A.B. Guthrie, Jr.
1919	*The Magnificent Ambersons*	Booth Tarkington	1951	*The Town*	Conrad Richter
1920	no award		1952	*The Caine Mutiny*	Herman Wouk
1921	*The Age of Innocence*	Edith Wharton	1953	*The Old Man and the Sea*	Ernest Hemingway
1922	*Alice Adams*	Booth Tarkington			
1923	*One of Ours*	Willa Cather	1954	no award	
1924	*The Able McLaughlins*	Margaret Wilson	1955	*A Fable*	William Faulkner
1925	*So Big*	Edna Ferber	1956	*Andersonville*	MacKinlay Kantor
1926	*Arrowsmith*	Sinclair Lewis	1957	no award	
1927	*Early Autumn*	Louis Bromfield	1958	*A Death In The Family*[1]	James Agee
1928	*The Bridge of San Luis Rey*	Thornton Wilder	1959	*The Travels of Jaimie McPheeters*	Robert Lewis Taylor
1929	*Scarlet Sister Mary*	Julia Peterkin	1960	*Advise and Consent*	Allen Drury
1930	*Laughing Boy*	Oliver Lafarge	1961	*To Kill A Mockingbird*	Harper Lee
1931	*Years of Grace*	Margaret Ayer Barnes	1962	*The Edge of Sadness*	Edwin O'Connor
			1963	*The Reivers*	William Faulkner
1932	*The Good Earth*	Pearl S. Buck	1964	no award	
1933	*The Store*	T.S. Stribling	1965	*The Keepers Of The House*	Shirley Ann Grau
1934	*Lamb in His Bosom*	Caroline Miller			
1935	*Now in November*	Josephine Winslow Johnson	1966	*Collected Stories*	Katherine Anne Porter
1936	*Honey in the Horn*	Harold L. Davis	1967	*The Fixer*	Bernard Malamud
1937	*Gone With the Wind*	Margaret Mitchell	1968	*The Confessions of Nat Turner*	William Styron
1938	*The Late George Apley*	John Phillips Marquand	1969	*House Made of Dawn*	N. Scott Momaday
1939	*The Yearling*	Marjorie Kinnan Rawlings	1970	*Collected Stories*	Jean Stafford
			1971	no award	
1940	*The Grapes of Wrath*	John Steinbeck	1972	*Angle of Repose*	Wallace Stegner
1941	no award		1973	*The Optimist's Daughter*	Eudora Welty
1942	*In This Our Life*	Ellen Glasgow	1974	no award	
1943	*Dragon's Teeth*	Upton Sinclair	1975	*The Killer Angels*	Michael Shaara
1944	*Journey in the Dark*	Martin Flavin	1976	*Humboldt's Gift*	Saul Bellow
1945	*A Bell for Adano*	John Hersey	1977	no award	
1946	no award		1978	*Elbow Room*	James Alan McPherson
1947	*All the King's Men*	Robert Penn Warren	1979	*The Stories of John Cheever*	John Cheever
1948	*Tales of the South Pacific*	James A. Michener	1980	*The Executioner's Song*	Norman Mailer

Letters, Drama, and Music (continued)

Fiction (continued)

YEAR	TITLE	AUTHOR	YEAR	TITLE	AUTHOR
1981	A Confederacy of Dunces[1]	John Kennedy Toole	1994	The Shipping News	E. Annie Proulx
1982	Rabbit Is Rich	John Updike	1995	The Stone Diaries	Carol Shields
1983	The Color Purple	Alice Walker	1996	Independence Day	Richard Ford
1984	Ironweed	William Kennedy	1997	Martin Dressler: The Tale of an American Dreamer	Steven Millhauser
1985	Foreign Affairs	Alison Lurie			
1986	Lonesome Dove	Larry McMurtry	1998	American Pastoral	Philip Roth
1987	A Summons to Memphis	Peter Taylor	1999	The Hours	Michael Cunningham
1988	Beloved	Toni Morrison			
1989	Breathing Lessons	Anne Tyler	2000	Interpreter of Maladies	Jhumpa Lahiri
1990	The Mambo Kings Play Songs of Love	Oscar Hijuelos	2001	The Amazing Adventures of Kavalier and Clay	Michael Chabon
1991	Rabbit At Rest	John Updike	2002	Empire Falls	Richard Russo
1992	A Thousand Acres	Jane Smiley	2003	Middlesex	Jeffrey Eugenides
1993	A Good Scent from a Strange Mountain	Robert Olen Butler	2004	The Known World	Edward P. Jones
			2005	Gilead	Marilynne Robinson

[1]Work published and prize awarded posthumously.

Drama
Awarded for a play, preferably about American life, by an American author.

YEAR	TITLE	AUTHOR	YEAR	TITLE	AUTHOR
1917	no award		1950	South Pacific	Richard Rodgers, Oscar Hammerstein II, Joshua Logan
1918	Why Marry?	Jesse Lynch Williams			
1919	no award		1951	no award	
1920	Beyond the Horizon	Eugene O'Neill	1952	The Shrike	Joseph Kramm
1921	Miss Lulu Bett	Zona Gale	1953	Picnic	William Inge
1922	Anna Christie	Eugene O'Neill	1954	The Teahouse of the August Moon	John Patrick
1923	Icebound	Owen Davis			
1924	Hell-Bent Fer Heaven	Hatcher Hughes	1955	Cat on a Hot Tin Roof	Tennessee Williams
1925	They Knew What They Wanted	Sidney Howard	1956	Diary of Anne Frank	Albert Hackett, Frances Goodrich
1926	Craig's Wife	George Kelly			
1927	In Abraham's Bosom	Paul Green	1957	Long Day's Journey Into Night	Eugene O'Neill
1928	Strange Interlude	Eugene O'Neill			
1929	Street Scene	Elmer L. Rice	1958	Look Homeward, Angel	Ketti Frings
1930	The Green Pastures	Marc Connelly	1959	J.B.	Archibald MacLeish
1931	Alison's House	Susan Glaspell	1960	Fiorello!	Jerome Weidman, George Abbott, Jerry Bock, Sheldon Harnick
1932	Of Thee I Sing	George S. Kaufman, Morrie Ryskind, Ira Gershwin			
1933	Both Your Houses	Maxwell Anderson	1961	All The Way Home	Tad Mosel
1934	Men in White	Sidney Kingsley	1962	How To Succeed In Business Without Really Trying	Frank Loesser, Abe Burrows
1935	The Old Maid	Zoe Akins			
1936	Idiots Delight	Robert E. Sherwood			
1937	You Can't Take It With You	Moss Hart, George S. Kaufman	1963	no award	
			1964	no award	
1938	Our Town	Thornton Wilder	1965	The Subject Was Roses	Frank D. Gilroy
1939	Abe Lincoln in Illinois	Robert E. Sherwood	1966	no award	
1940	The Time of Your Life	William Saroyan	1967	A Delicate Balance	Edward Albee
1941	There Shall Be No Night	Robert E. Sherwood	1968	no award	
			1969	The Great White Hope	Howard Sackler
1942	no award		1970	No Place To Be Somebody	Charles Gordone
1943	The Skin of Our Teeth	Thornton Wilder			
1944	no award		1971	The Effect of Gamma Rays on Man-in-the-Moon Marigolds	Paul Zindel
1945	Harvey	Mary Chase			
1946	State of the Union	Russel Crouse, Howard Lindsay	1972	no award	
			1973	That Championship Season	Jason Miller
1947	no award		1974	no award	
1948	A Streetcar Named Desire	Tennessee Williams	1975	Seascape	Edward Albee
1949	Death of a Salesman	Arthur Miller			

Letters, Drama, and Music (continued)

Drama (continued)

YEAR	TITLE	AUTHOR	YEAR	TITLE	AUTHOR
1976	A Chorus Line	Michael Bennett, James Kirkwood, Nicholas Dante, Marvin Hamlisch, Edward Kleban	1990	The Piano Lesson	August Wilson
			1991	Lost in Yonkers	Neil Simon
			1992	The Kentucky Cycle	Robert Schenkkan
			1993	Angels in America: Millennium Approaches	Tony Kushner
1977	The Shadow Box	Michael Cristofer	1994	Three Tall Women	Edward Albee
1978	The Gin Game	Donald L. Coburn	1995	The Young Man From Atlanta	Horton Foote
1979	Buried Child	Sam Shepard			
1980	Talley's Folly	Lanford Wilson	1996	Rent[1]	Jonathan Larson
1981	Crimes of the Heart	Beth Henley	1997	no award	
1982	A Soldier's Play	Charles Fuller	1998	How I Learned to Drive	Paula Vogel
1983	'Night, Mother	Marsha Norman	1999	Wit	Margaret Edson
1984	Glengarry Glen Ross	David Mamet	2000	Dinner With Friends	Donald Margulies
1985	Sunday in the Park With George	Stephen Sondheim, James Lapine	2001	Proof	David Auburn
			2002	Topdog/Underdog	Suzan-Lori Parks
			2003	Anna in the Tropics	Nilo Cruz
1986	no award		2004	I Am My Own Wife	Doug Wright
1987	Fences	August Wilson	2005	Doubt, a Parable	John Patrick Shanley
1988	Driving Miss Daisy	Alfred Uhry			
1989	The Heidi Chronicles	Wendy Wasserstein			

[1]Awarded posthumously.

History

Awarded for a work on the subject of American history.

YEAR	TITLE	AUTHOR	YEAR	TITLE	AUTHOR
1917	With Americans of Past and Present Days	J.J. Jusserand	1933	The Significance of Sections in American History	Frederick J. Turner
1918	A History of the Civil War, 1861–1865	James Ford Rhodes	1934	The People's Choice	Herbert Agar
1919	no award		1935	The Colonial Period of American History	Charles McLean Andrews
1920	The War with Mexico, 2 vols.	Justin H. Smith	1936	A Constitutional History of the United States	Andrew C. McLaughlin
1921	The Victory at Sea	William Sowden Sims, Burton Jesse Hendrick	1937	The Flowering of New England, 1815–1865	Van Wyck Brooks
1922	The Founding of New England	James Truslow Adams	1938	The Road to Reunion, 1865–1900	Paul Herman Buck
1923	The Supreme Court in United States History	Charles Warren	1939	A History of American Magazines	Frank Luther Mott
1924	The American Revolution: A Constitutional Interpretation	Charles Howard McIlwain	1940	Abraham Lincoln: The War Years	Carl Sandburg
			1941	The Atlantic Migration, 1607–1860	Marcus Lee Hansen
1925	History of the American Frontier	Frederic L. Paxson	1942	Reveille in Washington, 1860–1865	Margaret Leech
1926	A History of the United States	Edward Channing	1943	Paul Revere and the World He Lived In	Esther Forbes
1927	Pinckney's Treaty	Samuel Flagg Bemis	1944	The Growth of American Thought	Merle Curti
1928	Main Currents in American Thought, 2 vols.	Vernon Louis Parrington	1945	Unfinished Business	Stephen Bonsal
			1946	The Age of Jackson	Arthur M. Schlesinger, Jr.
1929	The Organization and Administration of the Union Army, 1861–1865	Fred Albert Shannon	1947	Scientists Against Time	James Phinney Baxter III
			1948	Across the Wide Missouri	Bernard De Voto
1930	The War of Independence	Claude H. Van Tyne	1949	The Disruption of American Democracy	Roy Franklin Nichols
1931	The Coming of the War, 1914	Bernadotte E. Schmitt	1950	Art and Life in America	Oliver W. Larkin
1932	My Experiences in the World War	John J. Pershing	1951	The Old Northwest: Pioneer Period, 1815–1840	R. Carlyle Buley

Letters, Drama, and Music (continued)

History (continued)

YEAR	TITLE	AUTHOR
1952	The Uprooted	Oscar Handlin
1953	The Era of Good Feelings	George Dangerfield
1954	A Stillness at Appomattox	Bruce Catton
1955	Great River: The Rio Grande in North American History	Paul Horgan
1956	The Age of Reform	Richard Hofstadter
1957	Russia Leaves the War: Soviet-American Relations, 1917–1920	George F. Kennan
1958	Banks and Politics in America	Bray Hammond
1959	The Republican Era: 1869–1901	Leonard D. White, Jean Schneider
1960	In the Days of McKinley	Margaret Leech
1961	Between War and Peace: The Potsdam Conference	Herbert Feis
1962	The Triumphant Empire: Thunder-Clouds Gather in the West, 1763–1766	Lawrence H. Gipson
1963	Washington, Village and Capital, 1800–1878	Constance McLaughlin Green
1964	Puritan Village: The Formation of a New England Town	Sumner Chilton Powell
1965	The Greenback Era	Irwin Unger
1966	The Life of the Mind in America[1]	Perry Miller
1967	Exploration and Empire: The Explorer and the Scientist in the Winning of the American West	William H. Goetzmann
1968	The Ideological Origins of the American Revolution	Bernard Bailyn
1969	Origins of the Fifth Amendment	Leonard W. Levy
1970	Present At The Creation: My Years In The State Department	Dean Acheson
1971	Roosevelt: The Soldier Of Freedom	James MacGregor Burns
1972	Neither Black Nor White	Carl N. Degler
1973	People of Paradox: An Inquiry Concerning the Origins of American Civilization	Michael Kammen
1974	The Americans: The Democratic Experience	Daniel J. Boorstin
1975	Jefferson and His Time, Vols. I–V	Dumas Malone
1976	Lamy of Santa Fe	Paul Horgan
1977	The Impending Crisis, 1841–1867[2]	David M. Potter, Don E. Fehrenbacher
1978	The Visible Hand: The Managerial Revolution in American Business	Alfred D. Chandler, Jr.
1979	The Dred Scott Case	Don E. Fehrenbacher
1980	Been in the Storm So Long	Leon F. Litwack
1981	American Education: The National Experience, 1783–1876	Lawrence A. Cremin
1982	Mary Chesnut's Civil War[3]	C. Vann Woodward
1983	The Transformation of Virginia, 1740–1790	Rhys L. Isaac
1984	no award	
1985	Prophets of Regulation	Thomas K. McCraw
1986	...the Heavens and the Earth: A Political History of the Space Age	Walter A. McDougall
1987	Voyagers to the West: A Passage in the Peopling of America on the Eve of the Revolution	Bernard Bailyn
1988	The Launching of Modern American Science, 1846–1876	Robert V. Bruce
1989	Battle Cry of Freedom: The Civil War Era	James M. McPherson
1989	Parting the Waters: America in the King Years, 1954–1963	Taylor Branch
1990	In Our Image: America's Empire in the Philippines	Stanley Karnow
1991	A Midwife's Tale	Laurel Thatcher Ulrich
1992	The Fate of Liberty: Abraham Lincoln and Civil Liberties	Mark E. Neely, Jr.
1993	The Radicalism of the American Revolution	Gordon S. Wood
1994	no award	
1995	No Ordinary Time: Franklin and Eleanor Roosevelt: The Home Front in World War II	Doris Kearns Goodwin
1996	William Cooper's Town: Power and Persuasion on the Frontier of the Early American Republic	Alan Taylor
1997	Original Meanings: Politics and Ideas in the Making of the Constitution	Jack N. Rakove
1998	Summer for the Gods: The Scopes Trial and America's Continuing Debate Over Science and Religion	Edward J. Larson
1999	Gotham: A History of New York City to 1898	Edwin G. Burrows, Mike Wallace
2000	Freedom From Fear: The American People in Depression and War, 1929–1945	David M. Kennedy
2001	Founding Brothers: The Revolutionary Generation	Joseph J. Ellis

Letters, Drama, and Music (continued)

History (continued)

YEAR	TITLE	AUTHOR	YEAR	TITLE	AUTHOR
2002	The Metaphysical Club: A Story of Ideas in America	Louis Menand	2005	Washington's Crossing	David Hackett Fischer
2003	An Army at Dawn: The War in North Africa, 1942–1943	Rick Atkinson			
2004	A Nation Under Our Feet: Black Political Struggles in the Rural South from Slavery to the Great Migration	Steven Hahn			

[1]Awarded posthumously.   [2]Potter died before completing the work; Fehrenbacher wrote the final chapters and edited it.   [3]Edited by Woodward.

Biography or Autobiography
Awarded for a biography or autobiography by an American author.

YEAR	TITLE	AUTHOR	YEAR	TITLE	AUTHOR
1917	Julia Ward Howe	Laura Elizabeth Howe Richards, Maude Howe Elliott; assisted by Florence Howe Hall	1938	Andrew Jackson, 2 vols.	Marquis James
			1938	Pedlar's Progress	Odell Shepard
			1939	Benjamin Franklin	Carl Van Doren
			1940	Woodrow Wilson, Life and Letters, Vols. VII and VIII	Ray Stannard Baker
1918	Benjamin Franklin, Self-Revealed	William Cabell Bruce	1941	Jonathan Edward	Ola Elizabeth Winslow
1919	The Education of Henry Adams	Henry Adams	1942	Crusader in Crinoline	Forrest Wilson
1920	The Life of John Marshall, 4 vols.	Albert J. Beveridge	1943	Admiral of the Ocean Sea	Samuel Eliot Morison
1921	The Americanization of Edward Bok	Edward Bok	1944	The American Leonardo: The Life of Samuel F.B. Morse	Carleton Mabee
1922	A Daughter of the Middle Border	Hamlin Garland	1945	George Bancroft: Brahmin Rebel	Russell Blaine Nye
1923	The Life and Letters of Walter H. Page	Burton J. Hendrick	1946	Son of the Wilderness	Linnie Marsh Wolfe
1924	From Immigrant to Inventor	Michael Idvorsky Pupin	1947	The Autobiography of William Allen White	William Allen White
1925	Barrett Wendell and His Letters	M.A. De Wolfe Howe	1948	Forgotten First Citizen: John Bigelow	Margaret Clapp
1926	The Life of Sir William Osler, 2 vols.	Harvey Cushing	1949	Roosevelt and Hopkins	Robert E. Sherwood
1927	Whitman	Emory Holloway	1950	John Quincy Adams and the Foundations of American Foreign Policy	Samuel Flagg Bemis
1928	The American Orchestra and Theodore Thomas	Charles Edward Russell			
1929	The Training of an American: The Earlier Life and Letters of Walter H. Page	Burton J. Hendrick	1951	John C. Calhoun: American Portrait	Margaret Louise Coit
			1952	Charles Evans Hughes	Merlo J. Pusey
1930	The Raven	Marquis James	1953	Edmund Pendleton, 1721–1803	David J. Mays
1931	Charles W. Eliot	Henry James			
1932	Theodore Roosevelt	Henry F. Pringle	1954	The Spirit of St. Louis	Charles A. Lindbergh
1933	Grover Cleveland	Allan Nevins			
1934	John Hay	Tyler Dennett	1955	The Taft Story	William S. White
1935	R.E. Lee	Douglas S. Freeman	1956	Benjamin Henry Latrobe	Talbot Faulkner Hamlin
1936	The Thought and Character of William James	Ralph Barton Perry	1957	Profiles in Courage	John F. Kennedy
			1958	George Washington, Volumes I–VI and Volume VII[1]	Douglas Southall Freeman, John Alexander Carroll, Mary Wells Ashworth
1937	Hamilton Fish	Allan Nevins			

Letters, Drama, and Music (continued)

Biography or Autobiography (continued)

YEAR	TITLE	AUTHOR
1959	Woodrow Wilson, American Prophet	Arthur Walworth
1960	John Paul Jones	Samuel Eliot Morison
1961	Charles Sumner and the Coming of the Civil War	David Donald
1962	no award	
1963	Henry James	Leon Edel
1964	John Keats	Walter Jackson Bate
1965	Henry Adams, three volumes	Ernest Samuels
1966	A Thousand Days	Arthur M. Schlesinger, Jr.
1967	Mr. Clemens and Mark Twain	Justin Kaplan
1968	Memoirs	George E. Kennan
1969	The Man From New York: John Quinn and His Friends	Benjamin Lawrence Reid
1970	Huey Long	T. Harry Williams
1971	Robert Frost: The Years of Triumph, 1915–1938	Lawrance Thompson
1972	Eleanor and Franklin	Joseph P. Lash
1973	Luce and His Empire	W.A. Swanberg
1974	O'Neill, Son and Artist	Louis Sheaffer
1975	The Power Broker: Robert Moses and the Fall of New York	Robert Caro
1976	Edith Wharton: A Biography	R.W.B. Lewis
1977	A Prince of Our Disorder: The Life of T.E. Lawrence	John E. Mack
1978	Samuel Johnson	Walter Jackson Bate
1979	Days of Sorrow and Pain: Leo Baeck and the Berlin Jews	Leonard Baker
1980	The Rise of Theodore Roosevelt	Edmund Morris
1981	Peter the Great: His Life and World	Robert K. Massie
1982	Grant: A Biography	William McFeely
1983	Growing Up	Russell Baker
1984	Booker T. Washington: The Wizard of Tuskegee, 1901–1915	Louis R. Harlan
1985	The Life and Times of Cotton Mather	Kenneth Silverman
1986	Louise Bogan: A Portrait	Elizabeth Frank
1987	Bearing the Cross: Martin Luther King Jr. and the Southern Christian Leadership Conference	David J. Garrow
1988	Look Homeward: A Life of Thomas Wolfe	David Herbert Donald
1989	Oscar Wilde[2]	Richard Ellmann
1990	Machiavelli in Hell	Sebastian de Grazia
1991	Jackson Pollock	Steven Naifeh, Gregory White Smith
1992	Fortunate Son: The Healing of a Vietnam Vet	Lewis B. Puller, Jr.
1993	Truman	David McCullough
1994	W.E.B. Du Bois: Biography of a Race 1868–1919	David Levering Lewis
1995	Harriet Beecher Stowe: A Life	Joan D. Hedrick
1996	God: A Biography	Jack Miles
1997	Angela's Ashes: A Memoir	Frank McCourt
1998	Personal History	Katharine Graham
1999	Lindbergh	A. Scott Berg
2000	Vera (Mrs. Vladimir Nabokov)	Stacy Schiff
2001	W.E.B. Du Bois: The Fight for Equality and the American Century, 1919–1963	David Levering Lewis
2002	John Adams	David McCullough
2003	Master of the Senate	Robert A. Caro
2004	Khrushchev: The Man and His Era	William Taubman
2005	De Kooning: An American Master	Mark Stevens and Annalyn Swan

[1]Freeman died in 1953 after completing Volumes I–VI; Carroll and Ashworth continued his work with Volume VII.   [2]Awarded posthumously.

Poetry
Awarded for a collection of original verse by an American author.

YEAR	TITLE	AUTHOR
1922	Collected Poems	Edwin Arlington Robinson
1923	The Ballad of the Harp-Weaver: A Few Figs from Thistles: Eight Sonnets in American Poetry, 1922. A Miscellany	Edna St. Vincent Millay
1924	New Hampshire: A Poem with Notes and Grace Notes	Robert Frost
1925	The Man Who Died Twice	Edwin Arlington Robinson
1926	What's O'Clock[1]	Amy Lowell
1927	Fiddler's Farewell	Leonora Speyer

Letters, Drama, and Music (continued)

Poetry (continued)

YEAR	TITLE	AUTHOR	YEAR	TITLE	AUTHOR
1928	Tristram	Edwin Arlington Robinson	1965	77 Dream Songs	John Berryman
1929	John Brown's Body	Stephen Vincent Benét	1966	Selected Poems	Richard Eberhart
1930	Selected Poems	Conrad Aiken	1967	Live or Die	Anne Sexton
1931	Collected Poems	Robert Frost	1968	The Hard Hours	Anthony Hecht
1932	The Flowering Stone	George Dillon	1969	Of Being Numerous	George Oppen
1933	Conquistador	Archibald MacLeish	1970	Untitled Subjects	Richard Howard
			1971	The Carrier of Ladders	William S. Merwin
1934	Collected Verse	Robert Hillyer	1972	Collected Poems	James Wright
1935	Bright Ambush	Audrey Wurdemann	1973	Up Country	Maxine Kumin
1936	Strange Holiness	Robert P. Tristram Coffin	1974	The Dolphin	Robert Lowell
			1975	Turtle Island	Gary Snyder
1937	A Further Range	Robert Frost	1976	Self-Portrait in a Convex Mirror	John Ashbery
1938	Cold Morning Sky	Marya Zaturenska	1977	Divine Comedies	James Merrill
1939	Selected Poems	John Gould Fletcher	1978	Collected Poems	Howard Nemerov
			1979	Now and Then	Robert Penn Warren
1940	Collected Poems	Mark Van Doren			
1941	Sunderland Capture	Leonard Bacon	1980	Selected Poems	Donald Justice
1942	The Dust Which Is God	William Rose Benét	1981	The Morning of the Poem	James Schuyler
1943	A Witness Tree	Robert Frost	1982	The Collected Poems[2]	Sylvia Plath
1944	Western Star[1]	Stephen Vincent Benét	1983	Selected Poems	Galway Kinnell
			1984	American Primitive	Mary Oliver
1945	V-Letter and Other Poems	Karl Shapiro	1985	Yin	Carolyn Kizer
			1986	The Flying Change	Henry Taylor
1946	no award		1987	Thomas and Beulah	Rita Dove
1947	Lord Weary's Castle	Robert Lowell	1988	Partial Accounts: New and Selected Poems	William Meredith
1948	The Age of Anxiety	W.H. Auden			
1949	Terror and Decorum	Peter Viereck	1989	New and Collected Poems	Richard Wilbur
1950	Annie Allen	Gwendolyn Brooks			
1951	Complete Poems	Carl Sandburg	1990	The World Doesn't End	Charles Simic
1952	Collected Poems	Marianne Moore	1991	Near Changes	Mona Van Duyn
1953	Collected Poems, 1917–1952	Archibald MacLeish	1992	Selected Poems	James Tate
			1993	The Wild Iris	Louise Gluck
1954	The Waking	Theodore Roethke	1994	Neon Vernacular: New and Selected Poems	Yusef Komunyakaa
1955	Collected Poems	Wallace Stevens			
1956	Poems: North & South	Elizabeth Bishop	1995	The Simple Truth	Philip Levine
1957	Things of This World	Richard Wilbur	1996	The Dream of the Unified Field	Jorie Graham
1958	Promises: Poems 1954–1956	Robert Penn Warren			
			1997	Alive Together: New and Selected Poems	Lisel Mueller
1959	Selected Poems 1928–1958	Stanley Kunitz			
			1998	Black Zodiac	Charles Wright
1960	Heart's Needle	W.D. Snodgrass	1999	Blizzard of One	Mark Strand
1961	Times Three: Selected Verse from Three Decades	Phyllis McGinley	2000	Repair	C.K. Williams
			2001	Different Hours	Stephen Dunn
			2002	Practical Gods	Carl Dennis
			2003	Moy Sand and Gravel	Paul Muldoon
1962	Poems	Alan Dugan	2004	Walking to Martha's Vineyard	Franz Wright
1963	Pictures from Breughel[1]	William Carlos Williams	2005	Delights & Shadows	Ted Kooser
1964	At The End Of The Open Road	Louis Simpson			

[1]Awarded posthumously.   [2]Work published and prize awarded posthumously.

General Nonfiction
Awarded for a work of nonfiction, ineligible for any other category, by an American author.

YEAR	TITLE	AUTHOR	YEAR	TITLE	AUTHOR
1962	The Making of the President, 1960	Theodore H. White	1965	O Strange New World	Howard Mumford Jones
1963	The Guns of August	Barbara W. Tuchman	1966	Wandering Through Winter	Edwin Way Teale
1964	Anti-Intellectualism in American Life	Richard Hofstadter	1967	The Problem of Slavery in Western Culture	David Brion Davis

Letters, Drama, and Music (continued)

<u>General nonfiction (continued)</u>

YEAR	TITLE	AUTHOR
1968	Rousseau and Revolution: A History of Civilization in France, England, and Germany from 1756, and in the Remainder of Europe from 1715 to 1789	Will and Ariel Durant
1969	The Armies of the Night	Norman Mailer
1969	So Human an Animal	Rene Jules Dubos
1970	Gandhi's Truth	Erik H. Erikson
1971	The Rising Sun	John Toland
1972	Stilwell and the American Experience in China, 1911–1945	Barbara W. Tuchman
1973	Fire in the Lake: The Vietnamese and the Americans in Vietnam	Frances Fitzgerald
1973	Children of Crisis, Vols. II and III	Robert Coles
1974	The Denial of Death[1]	Ernest Becker
1975	Pilgrim at Tinker Creek	Annie Dillard
1976	Why Survive? Being Old In America	Robert N. Butler
1977	Beautiful Swimmers	William W. Warner
1978	The Dragons of Eden	Carl Sagan
1979	On Human Nature	Edward O. Wilson
1980	Gödel, Escher, Bach: An Eternal Golden Braid	Douglas R. Hofstadter
1981	Fin-de-Siècle Vienna: Politics and Culture	Carl E. Schorske
1982	The Soul of a New Machine	Tracy Kidder
1983	Is There No Place On Earth For Me?	Susan Sheehan
1984	The Social Transformation of American Medicine	Paul Starr
1985	The Good War: An Oral History of World War Two	Studs Terkel
1986	Common Ground: A Turbulent Decade in the Lives of Three American Families	J. Anthony Lukas
1986	Move Your Shadow: South Africa, Black and White	Joseph Lelyveld
1987	Arab and Jew: Wounded Spirits in a Promised Land	David K. Shipler

YEAR	TITLE	AUTHOR
1988	The Making of the Atomic Bomb	Richard Rhodes
1989	A Bright Shining Lie: John Paul Vann and America in Vietnam	Neil Sheehan
1990	And Their Children After Them	Dale Maharidge, Michael Williamson
1991	The Ants	Bert Holldobler, Edward O. Wilson
1992	The Prize: The Epic Quest For Oil, Money, and Power	Daniel Yergin
1993	Lincoln at Gettysburg: The Words That Remade America	Garry Wills
1994	Lenin's Tomb: The Last Days Of The Soviet Empire	David Remnick
1995	The Beak Of The Finch: A Story Of Evolution In Our Time	Jonathan Weiner
1996	The Haunted Land: Facing Europe's Ghosts After Communism	Tina Rosenberg
1997	Ashes to Ashes: America's Hundred-Year Cigarette War, the Public Health, and the Unabashed Triumph of Philip Morris	Richard Kluger
1998	Guns, Germs and Steel: The Fates of Human Societies	Jared Diamond
1999	Annals of the Former World	John McPhee
2000	Embracing Defeat: Japan in the Wake of World War II	John W. Dower
2001	Hirohito and the Making of Modern Japan	Herbert P. Bix
2002	Carry Me Home: Birmingham, Alabama, the Climactic Battle of the Civil Rights Revolution	Diane McWhorter
2003	"A Problem from Hell": America and the Age of Genocide	Samantha Power
2004	Gulag: A History	Anne Applebaum
2005	Ghost Wars	Steve Coll

[1]Awarded posthumously.

Music
Awarded for a musical piece of "significant dimension" composed by an American and first performed or recorded in the United States during the year.

YEAR	TITLE	COMPOSER
1943	Secular Cantata No. 2. A Free Song	William Schuman
1944	Symphony No. 4. Opus 34	Howard Hanson
1945	Appalachian Spring	Aaron Copland

YEAR	TITLE	COMPOSER
1946	The Canticle of the Sun	Leo Sowerby
1947	Symphony No. 3	Charles Ives
1948	Symphony No. 3	Walter Piston
1949	Music for the film Louisiana Story	Virgil Thomson

Letters, Drama, and Music (continued)

Music (continued)

YEAR	TITLE	COMPOSER	YEAR	TITLE	COMPOSER
1950	The Consul	Gian Carlo Menotti	1982	Concerto for Orchestra	Roger Sessions
1951	Giants in the Earth	Douglas S. Moore	1983	Symphony No. 1 (Three Movements for Orchestra)	Ellen Taaffe Zwilich
1952	Symphony Concertante	Gail Kubik			
1953	no award				
1954	Concerto For Two Pianos and Orchestra	Quincy Porter	1984	"Canti del Sole" for Tenor and Orchestra	Bernard Rands
1955	The Saint of Bleecker Street	Gian Carlo Menotti	1985	Symphony, RiverRun	Stephen Albert
			1986	Wind Quintet IV	George Perle
1956	Symphony No. 3	Ernst Toch	1987	The Flight Into Egypt	John Harbison
1957	Meditation on Ecclesiastics	Norman Dello Joio	1988	12 New Etudes for Piano	William Bolcom
1958	Vanessa	Samuel Barber	1989	Whispers Out of Time	Roger Reynolds
1959	Concerto for Piano and Orchestra	John LaMontaine	1990	"Duplicates": A Concerto for Two Pianos and Orchestra	Mel Powell
1960	Second String Quartet	Elliott Carter			
1961	Symphony No. 7	Walter Piston	1991	Symphony	Shulamit Ran
1962	The Crucible	Robert Ward	1992	The Face of the Night, The Heart of the Dark	Wayne Peterson
1963	Piano Concerto No. 1	Samuel Barber			
1964	no award				
1965	no award		1993	Trombone Concerto	Christopher Rouse
1966	Variations for Orchestra	Leslie Bassett			
1967	Quartet No. 3	Leon Kirchner	1994	Of Reminiscences and Reflections	Gunther Schuller
1968	Echoes of Time and the River	George Crumb			
			1995	Stringmusic	Morton Gould
1969	String Quartet No. 3	Karel Husa	1996	Lilacs, for voice and orchestra	George Walker
1970	Time's Encomium	Charles Wuorinen			
1971	Synchronisms No. 6 for Piano and Electronic Sound (1970)	Mario Davidovsky	1997	Blood on the Fields	Wynton Marsalis
			1998	String Quartet #2 (musica instrumentalis)	Aaron Jay Kernis
1972	Windows	Jacob Druckman			
1973	String Quartet No. 3	Elliott Carter	1999	Concerto for Flute, Strings and Percussion	Melinda Wagner
1974	Notturno	Donald Martino			
1975	From the Diary of Virginia Woolf	Dominick Argento			
1976	Air Music	Ned Rorem	2000	Life is a Dream, Opera in Three Acts: Act II, Concert Version	Lewis Spratlan
1977	Visions of Terror and Wonder	Richard Wernick			
1978	Deja Vu for Percussion Quartet and Orchestra	Michael Colgrass	2001	Symphony No. 2 for String Orchestra	John Corigliano
1979	Aftertones of Infinity	Joseph Schwantner	2002	Ice Field	Henry Brant
			2003	On the Transmigration of Souls	John Adams
1980	In Memory of a Summer Day	David Del Tredici	2004	Tempest Fantasy	Paul Moravec
1981	no award		2005	Second Concerto for Orchestra	Steven Stucky

Special Awards

YEAR	RECIPIENT	FOR	YEAR	RECIPIENT	FOR
1944	Richard Rodgers, Oscar Hammerstein II	theatrical musical Oklahoma!	1982	Milton Babbitt	life's work in music
			1984	Theodor Seuss Geisel	Dr. Seuss children's books
1957	Kenneth Roberts	historical novels	1985	William Schuman	life's work in composition and music education
1960	Garrett Mattingly	nonfiction work The Armada			
			1992	Art Spiegelman	graphic novel Maus
1961	American Heritage Picture History of the Civil War	"a distinguished example of American book publishing"	1998	George Gershwin[1]	centennial commemoration of his birth, celebrating his life's work in music
1973	James Thomas Flexner	nonfiction work George Washington, Vols. I–IV			
1974	Roger Sessions	life's work in music	1999	Duke Ellington[1]	centennial commemoration of his birth, celebrating his life's work in music
1976	Scott Joplin[1]	contributions to American music			
1977	Alex Haley	novel Roots			
1978	E.B. White	full body of his work			

[1]Awarded posthumously.

National Book Awards

In 1950 a consortium of publishing groups established the National Book Awards. The goals were to bring exceptional books written by Americans to the public's attention and to encourage reading in general. Award categories have varied from the inaugural 3 to as many as 28 in 1980. Today, the awards recognize achievements in 4 genres: fiction, nonfiction, poetry, and young people's literature. A five-member, independent judging panel chooses a winner for each genre. Award: $10,000 cash and a bronze sculpture.

Fiction

YEAR	TITLE	AUTHOR
1950	The Man with the Golden Arm	Nelson Algren
1951	The Collected Stories of William Faulkner	William Faulkner
1952	From Here to Eternity	James Jones
1953	Invisible Man	Ralph Ellison
1954	The Adventures of Augie March	Saul Bellow
1955	A Fable	William Faulkner
1956	Ten North Frederick	John O'Hara
1957	The Field of Vision	Wright Morris
1958	The Wapshot Chronicle	John Cheever
1959	The Magic Barrel	Bernard Malamud
1960	Goodbye, Columbus	Philip Roth
1961	The Waters of Kronos	Conrad Richter
1962	The Moviegoer	Walker Percy
1963	Morte d'Urban	J.F. Powers
1964	The Centaur	John Updike
1965	Herzog	Saul Bellow
1966	The Collected Stories of Katherine Anne Porter	Katherine Anne Porter
1967	The Fixer	Bernard Malamud
1968	The Eighth Day	Thornton Wilder
1969	Steps	Jerzy Kosinski
1970	Them	Joyce Carol Oates
1971	Mr. Sammler's Planet	Saul Bellow
1972	The Complete Stories	Flannery O'Connor
1973	Augustus	John Williams
1973	Chimera	John Barth
1974	A Crown of Feathers and Other Stories	Isaac Bashevis Singer
1974	Gravity's Rainbow	Thomas Pynchon

Fiction (continued)

YEAR	TITLE	AUTHOR
1975	Dog Soldiers: A Novel	Robert Stone
1975	The Hair of Harold Roux	Thomas Williams
1976	J.R.	William Gaddis
1977	The Spectator Bird	Wallace Stegner
1978	Blood Tie	Mary Lee Settle
1979	Going After Cacciato	Tim O'Brien
1980	Sophie's Choice[1]	William Styron
1981	Plains Song[1]	Wright Morris
1982	Rabbit Is Rich[1]	John Updike
1983	The Color Purple[1]	Alice Walker
1984	Victory over Japan: A Book of Stories	Ellen Gilchrist
1985	White Noise	Don DeLillo
1986	World's Fair	E.L. Doctorow
1987	Paco's Story	Larry Heinemann
1988	Paris Trout	Pete Dexter
1989	Spartina	John Casey
1990	Middle Passage	Charles Johnson
1991	Mating	Norman Rush
1992	All the Pretty Horses	Cormac McCarthy
1993	The Shipping News	E. Annie Proulx
1994	A Frolic of His Own	William Gaddis
1995	Sabbath's Theater	Philip Roth
1996	Ship Fever	Andrea Barrett
1997	Cold Mountain	Charles Frazier
1998	Charming Billy	Alice McDermott
1999	Waiting	Ha Jin
2000	In America	Susan Sontag
2001	The Corrections	Jonathan Franzen
2002	Three Junes	Julia Glass
2003	The Great Fire	Shirley Hazzard
2004	The News From Paraguay	Lily Tuck

Nonfiction

YEAR	TITLE	AUTHOR
1950	The Life of Ralph Waldo Emerson	Ralph L. Rusk
1951	Herman Melville	Newton Arvin
1952	The Sea Around Us	Rachel Carson
1953	The Course of Empire	Bernard A. De Voto
1954	A Stillness at Appomattox	Bruce Catton
1955	The Measure of Man: On Freedom, Human Values, Survival, and the Modern Temper	Joseph Wood Krutch
1956	American in Italy	Herbert Kubly
1957	Russia Leaves the War	George F. Kennan
1958	The Lion and the Throne: The Life and Times of Sir Edward Coke (1552–1634)	Catherine Drinker Bowen
1959	Mistress to an Age: A Life of Madame de Staël	J. Christopher Herold
1960	James Joyce	Richard Ellmann
1961	The Rise and Fall of the Third Reich: A History of Nazi Germany	William L. Shirer
1962	The City in History: Its Origins, Its Transformations, and Its Prospects	Lewis Mumford
1963	Henry James, Vol. II: The Conquest of London (1870–1881); Vol. III: The Middle Years (1882–1895)	Leon Edel
1964	The Rise of the West: A History of the Human Community[2]	William H. McNeill
1965	The Life of Lenin[2]	Louis Fischer
1966	A Thousand Days: John F. Kennedy in the White House[2]	Arthur M. Schlesinger, Jr.
1967	The Enlightenment: An Interpretation, Vol. I[2]	Peter Gay
1968	Memoirs: 1925–1950[2]	George F. Kennan
1969	White over Black: American Attitudes Toward the Negro, 1550–1812[2]	Winthrop D. Jordan

National Book Awards (continued)

Nonfiction (continued)

YEAR	TITLE	AUTHOR
1970	Huey Long[2]	T. Harry Williams
1971	Roosevelt: The Soldier of Freedom[2]	James MacGregor Burns
1972	Eleanor and Franklin: The Story of Their Relationship, Based on Eleanor Roosevelt's Private Papers[3]	Joseph P. Lash
1973	George Washington, Vol. IV: Anguish and Farewell, 1793–1799[3]	James Thomas Flexner
1974	Macaulay: The Shaping of the Historian[4]	John Clive
1975	The Life of Emily Dickinson[3]	Richard B. Sewall
1976	The Problem of Slavery in the Age of Revolution, 1770–1823[2]	David Brion Davis
1977	Norman Thomas: The Last Idealist[5]	W.A. Swanberg
1978	Samuel Johnson[5]	W. Jackson Bate
1979	Robert Kennedy and His Times[5]	Arthur M. Schlesinger, Jr.
1980	The Right Stuff[6]	Tom Wolfe
1981	China Men[6]	Maxine Hong Kingston
1982	The Soul of a New Machine[6]	Tracy Kidder
1983	China: Alive in the Bitter Sea[6]	Fox Butterfield
1984	Andrew Jackson and the Course of American Democracy, 1833–1845	Robert V. Remini
1985	Common Ground: A Turbulent Decade in the Lives of Three American Families	J. Anthony Lukas
1986	Arctic Dreams	Barry Lopez
1987	The Making of the Atomic Bomb	Richard Rhodes
1988	A Bright Shining Lie: John Paul Vann and America in Vietnam	Neil Sheehan
1989	From Beirut to Jerusalem	Thomas L. Friedman
1990	The House of Morgan: An American Banking Dynasty and the Rise of Modern Finance	Ron Chernow
1991	Freedom	Orlando Patterson
1992	Becoming a Man: Half a Life Story	Paul Monette
1993	United States: Essays, 1952–1992	Gore Vidal
1994	How We Die: Reflections on Life's Final Chapter	Sherwin B. Nuland
1995	The Haunted Land: Facing Europe's Ghosts After Communism	Tina Rosenberg
1996	An American Requiem: God, My Father, and the War That Came Between Us	James Carroll
1997	American Sphinx: The Character of Thomas Jefferson	Joseph J. Ellis
1998	Slaves in the Family	Edward Ball
1999	Embracing Defeat: Japan in the Wake of World War II	John W. Dower
2000	In the Heart of the Sea: The Tragedy of the Whaleship Essex	Nathaniel Philbrick
2001	The Noonday Demon: An Atlas of Depression	Andrew Solomon
2002	Master of the Senate: The Years of Lyndon Johnson	Robert A. Caro
2003	Waiting for Snow in Havana	Carlos Eire
2004	Arc of Justice: A Saga of Race, Civil Rights, and Murder in the Jazz Age	Kevin Boyle

Poetry

YEAR	TITLE	AUTHOR
1950	Paterson: Book III and Selected Poems	William Carlos Williams
1951	The Auroras of Autumn	Wallace Stevens
1952	Collected Poems	Marianne Moore
1953	Collected Poems, 1917–1952	Archibald MacLeish
1954	Collected Poems	Conrad Aiken
1955	The Collected Poems of Wallace Stevens	Wallace Stevens
1956	The Shield of Achilles	W.H. Auden
1957	Things of This World: Poems	Richard Wilbur
1958	Promises: Poems, 1954–1956	Robert Penn Warren
1959	Words for the Wind: The Collected Verse of Theodore Roethke	Theodore Roethke
1960	Life Studies	Robert Lowell
1961	The Woman at the Washington Zoo	Randall Jarrell
1962	Poems	Alan Dugan
1963	Traveling Through the Dark	William Stafford
1964	Selected Poems	John Crowe Ransom
1965	The Far Field	Theodore Roethke
1966	Buckdancer's Choice: Poems	James Dickey
1967	Nights and Days	James Merrill
1968	The Light Around the Body: Poems	Robert Bly
1969	His Toy, His Dream, His Rest: 308 Dream Songs	John Berryman
1970	The Complete Poems	Elizabeth Bishop
1971	To See, To Take: Poems	Mona Van Duyn
1972	The Collected Poems of Frank O'Hara	Frank O'Hara
1972	Selected Poems	Howard Moss

National Book Awards (continued)

Poetry (continued)

YEAR	TITLE	AUTHOR
1973	Collected Poems, 1951–1971	A.R. Ammons
1974	Diving into the Wreck: Poems, 1971–1972	Adrienne Rich
1974	The Fall of America: Poems of These States	Allen Ginsberg
1975	Presentation Piece	Marilyn Hacker
1976	Self-Portrait in a Convex Mirror: Poems	John Ashbery
1977	Collected Poems, 1930–1976	Richard Eberhart
1978	The Collected Poems of Howard Nemerov	Howard Nemerov
1979	Mirabell: Books of Number	James Merrill
1980	Ashes: Poems New & Old	Philip Levine
1981	The Need to Hold Still	Lisel Mueller
1982	Life Supports: New and Collected Poems	William Bronk
1983	Country Music: Selected Early Poems	Charles Wright
1984	Selected Poems	Galway Kinnell
1985	Yin	Carolyn Kizer
1986	The Flying Change	Henry Taylor
1987	Thomas and Beulah	Rita Dove
1988	Partial Accounts: New and Selected Poems	William Meredith
1989	New and Collected Poems	Richard Wilbur
1990	The World Doesn't End	Charles Simic
1991	What Work Is: Poems	Philip Levine
1992	New and Selected Poems	Mary Oliver
1993	Garbage	A.R. Ammons
1994	Worshipful Company of Fletchers: Poems	James Tate
1995	Passing Through: The Later Poems, New and Selected	Stanley Kunitz
1996	Scrambled Eggs & Whiskey: Poems, 1991–1995	Hayden Carruth
1997	Effort at Speech: New and Selected Poems	William Meredith
1998	This Time: New and Selected Poems	Gerald Stern
1999	Vice: New and Selected Poems	Ai
2000	Blessing the Boats: New and Selected Poems, 1988–2000	Lucille Clifton
2001	Poems Seven: New and Complete Poetry	Alan Dugan
2002	In the Next Galaxy	Ruth Stone
2003	The Singing	C.K. Williams
2004	Door in the Mountain: New and Collected Poems, 1965–2003	Jean Valentine

Young People's Literature

YEAR	TITLE	AUTHOR
1969	Journey from Peppermint Street	Meindert De Jong
1970	A Day of Pleasure: Stories of a Boy Growing Up in Warsaw[7]	Isaac Bashevis Singer
1971	The Marvelous Misadventures of Sebastian[7]	Lloyd Alexander
1972	The Slightly Irregular Fire Engine; or, The Hithering Thithering Djinn[7]	Donald Barthelme
1973	The Farthest Shore[7]	Ursula Le Guin
1974	The Court of the Stone Children[7]	Eleanor Cameron
1975	M.C. Higgins, the Great[7]	Virginia Hamilton
1976	Bert Breen's Barn	Walter D. Edmonds
1977	The Master Puppeteer	Katherine Paterson
1978	The View from the Oak: The Private Worlds of Other Creatures	Judith Kohl & Herbert Kohl
1979	The Great Gilly Hopkins	Katherine Paterson
1980	A Gathering of Days: A New England Girl's Journal, 1830–32[8]	Joan Blos
1981	The Night Swimmers[9]	Betsy Byars
1982	Westmark[9]	Lloyd Alexander
1983	Homesick: My Own Story[9]	Jean Fritz
1996	Parrot in the Oven: Mi Vida[10]	Victor Martinez
1997	Dancing on the Edge[10]	Han Nolan
1998	Holes[10]	Louis Sachar
1999	When Zachary Beaver Came to Town[10]	Kimberly Willis Holt
2000	Homeless Bird[10]	Gloria Whelan
2001	True Believer[10]	Virginia Euwer Wolff
2002	The House of the Scorpion[10]	Nancy Farmer
2003	The Canning Season	Polly Horvath
2004	The Godless	Pete Hautman

[1]Fiction (Hardcover). [2]History and Biography (Nonfiction). [3]Biography. [4]History. [5]Biography and Autobiography. [6]General Nonfiction (Hardcover). [7]Children's Books. [8]Children's Books (Hardcover). [9]Children's Books, Fiction (Hardcover). [10]Young People's Literature.

The PEN/Faulkner Award for Fiction

Named for William Faulkner and affiliated with the international writers' organization Poets, Playwrights, Editors, Essayists and Novelists (PEN), the PEN/Faulkner Award was founded by writers in 1980 to honor their peers. A panel of fiction writers selects a winning novel or short-story collection and four runners-up. The winning author receives $15,000, and each of the others receives $5,000.

PEN/Faulkner Web site: <www.penfaulkner.org>.

YEAR	TITLE	AUTHOR
1981	How German Is It?	Walter Abish
1982	The Chaneysville Incident	David Bradley
1983	Seaview	Toby Olson
1984	Sent for You Yesterday	John Edgar Wideman
1985	The Barracks Thief	Tobias Wolff
1986	The Old Forest and Other Stories	Peter Taylor
1987	Soldiers in Hiding	Richard Wiley
1988	World's End	T. Coraghessan Boyle
1989	Dusk and Other Stories	James Salter
1990	Billy Bathgate	E.L. Doctorow
1991	Philadelphia Fire	John Edgar Wideman
1992	Mao II	Don Delillo
1993	Postcards	E. Annie Proulx
1994	Operation Shylock	Philip Roth
1995	Snow Falling on Cedars	David Guterson
1996	Independence Day	Richard Ford
1997	Women in Their Beds	Gina Berriault
1998	The Bear Comes Home	Rafi Zabor
1999	The Hours	Michael Cunningham
2000	Waiting	Ha Jin
2001	The Human Stain	Philip Roth
2002	Bel Canto	Ann Patchett
2003	The Caprices	Sabina Murray
2004	The Early Stories	John Updike
2005	War Trash	Ha Jin
2006	scheduled to be announced in March	

Did you know?  Not only did Dr. Seuss (Theodore Geisel) write award-winning children's books, he also made documentary films; *Hitler Lives* (1946) and *Design for Death* (1947, with his wife Helen Palmer Geisel [d. 1967]), which both won Academy Awards, as did his animated cartoon *Gerald McBoing Boing* (1951). He also designed and produced animated cartoons for television, many of them based on his books.

Newbery Medal Winners, 1922–2005

The American Library Association (ALA) began awarding the John Newbery Medal in 1922 to the author of the most distinguished American children's book of the previous year, as judged by the ALA's Children's Librarians' Section (now called the Association for Library Service to Children). Established at the suggestion of Frederic G. Melcher of the R.R. Bowker Publishing Company, the award is named for John Newbery, the 18th-century English publisher who was among the first to publish books exclusively for children. Prize: inscribed bronze medal.

ALA Newbery Medal Web site: <www.ala.org/alsc/newbery.html>.

YEAR	TITLE	AUTHOR
1922	The Story of Mankind	Hendrik Willem van Loon
1923	The Voyages of Doctor Dolittle	Hugh Lofting
1924	The Dark Frigate	Charles Hawes
1925	Tales from Silver Lands	Charles Finger
1926	Shen of the Sea	Arthur Bowie Chrisman
1927	Smoky, the Cowhorse	Will James
1928	Gay Neck, the Story of a Pigeon	Dhan Gopal Mukerji
1929	The Trumpeter of Krakow	Eric P. Kelly
1930	Hitty, Her First Hundred Years	Rachel Field
1931	The Cat Who Went to Heaven	Elizabeth Coatsworth
1932	Waterless Mountain	Laura Adams Armer
1933	Young Fu of the Upper Yangtze	Elizabeth Lewis
1934	Invincible Louisa: The Story of the Author of Little Women	Cornelia Meigs
1935	Dobry	Monica Shannon
1936	Caddie Woodlawn	Carol Ryrie Brink
1937	Roller Skates	Ruth Sawyer
1938	The White Stag	Kate Seredy
1939	Thimble Summer	Elizabeth Enright
1940	Daniel Boone	James Daugherty
1941	Call It Courage	Armstrong Sperry
1942	The Matchlock Gun	Walter Edmonds
1943	Adam of the Road	Elizabeth Janet Gray
1944	Johnny Tremain	Esther Forbes
1945	Rabbit Hill	Robert Lawson
1946	Strawberry Girl	Lois Lenski
1947	Miss Hickory	Carolyn Sherwin Bailey
1948	The Twenty-One Balloons	William Pène du Bois
1949	King of the Wind	Marguerite Henry
1950	The Door in the Wall	Marguerite de Angeli
1951	Amos Fortune, Free Man	Elizabeth Yates
1952	Ginger Pye	Eleanor Estes
1953	Secret of the Andes	Ann Nolan Clark
1954	...And Now Miguel	Joseph Krumgold

Newbery Medal Winners, 1922–2005 (continued)

YEAR	TITLE	AUTHOR
1955	The Wheel on the School	Meindert DeJong
1956	Carry On, Mr. Bowditch	Jean Lee Latham
1957	Miracles on Maple Hill	Virginia Sorenson
1958	Rifles for Watie	Harold Keith
1959	The Witch of Blackbird Pond	Elizabeth George Speare
1960	Onion John	Joseph Krumgold
1961	Island of the Blue Dolphins	Scott O'Dell
1962	The Bronze Bow	Elizabeth George Speare
1963	A Wrinkle in Time	Madeleine L'Engle
1964	It's Like This, Cat	Emily Neville
1965	Shadow of a Bull	Maia Wojciechowska
1966	I, Juan de Pareja	Elizabeth Borton de Trevino
1967	Up a Road Slowly	Irene Hunt
1968	From the Mixed-Up Files of Mrs. Basil E. Frankweiler	E.L. Konigsburg
1969	The High King	Lloyd Alexander
1970	Sounder	William H. Armstrong
1971	Summer of the Swans	Betsy Byars
1972	Mrs. Frisby and the Rats of NIMH	Robert C. O'Brien
1973	Julie of the Wolves	Jean Craighead George
1974	The Slave Dancer	Paula Fox
1975	M. C. Higgins, the Great	Virginia Hamilton
1976	The Grey King	Susan Cooper
1977	Roll of Thunder, Hear My Cry	Mildred D. Taylor
1978	Bridge to Terabithia	Katherine Paterson
1979	The Westing Game	Ellen Raskin
1980	A Gathering of Days: A New England Girl's Journal, 1830–1832	Joan W. Blos
1981	Jacob Have I Loved	Katherine Paterson
1982	A Visit to William Blake's Inn: Poems for Innocent and Experienced Travelers	Nancy Willard
1983	Dicey's Song	Cynthia Voigt
1984	Dear Mr. Henshaw	Beverly Cleary
1985	The Hero and the Crown	Robin McKinley
1986	Sarah, Plain and Tall	Patricia MacLachlan
1987	The Whipping Boy	Sid Fleischman
1988	Lincoln: A Photo-biography	Russell Freedman
1989	Joyful Noise: Poems for Two Voices	Paul Fleischman
1990	Number the Stars	Lois Lowry
1991	Maniac Magee	Jerry Spinelli
1992	Shiloh	Phyllis Reynolds Naylor
1993	Missing May	Cynthia Rylant
1994	The Giver	Lois Lowry
1995	Walk Two Moons	Sharon Creech
1996	The Midwife's Apprentice	Karen Cushman
1997	The View from Saturday	E.L. Konigsburg
1998	Out of the Dust	Karen Hesse
1999	Holes	Louis Sachar
2000	Bud, Not Buddy	Christopher Paul Curtis
2001	A Year Down Yonder	Richard Peck
2002	A Single Shard	Linda Sue Park
2003	Crispin: The Cross of Lead	Avi
2004	The Tale of Despereaux: Being the Story of a Mouse, a Princess, Some Soup, and a Spool of Thread	Kate DiCamillo
2005	Kira-Kira	Cynthia Kadohata

Caldecott Medal Winners, 1938–2005

The American Library Association (ALA) awards the Caldecott Medal annually to "the artist of the most distinguished American picture book for children." It was established by the ALA in 1938 on the suggestion of Frederic G. Melcher, chairman of the board of the R.R. Bowker Publishing Company, and named for the 19th-century English illustrator Randolph Calde-cott. If the author/reteller/translator/editor is other than the illustrator, that person's name appears in parentheses after that of the illustrator. Prize: inscribed bronze medal.

ALA Caldecott Medal Web site: <www.ala.org/alsc/caldecott.html>.

EAR	TITLE	ILLUSTRATOR
1938	Animals of the Bible: A Picture Book	Dorothy P. Lathrop (Helen Dean Fish)
1939	Mei Li	Thomas Handforth
1940	Abraham Lincoln	Ingri and Edgar Parin d'Aulaire
1941	They Were Strong and Good	Robert Lawson
1942	Make Way for Ducklings	Robert McCloskey
1943	The Little House	Virginia Lee Burton
1944	Many Moons	Louis Slobodkin (James Thurber)
1945	Prayer for a Child	Elizabeth Orton Jones (Rachel Field)
1946	The Rooster Crows	Maude and Miska Petersham

Caldecott Medal Winners, 1938–2005 (continued)

YEAR	TITLE	ILLUSTRATOR
1947	The Little Island	Leonard Weisgard (Golden MacDonald, pseud. [Margaret Wise Brown])
1948	White Snow, Bright Snow	Roger Duvoisin (Alvin Tresselt)
1949	The Big Snow	Berta and Elmer Hader
1950	Song of the Swallows	Leo Politi
1951	The Egg Tree	Katherine Milhous
1952	Finders Keepers	Nicolas, pseud.; Nicholas Mordvinoff (Will, pseud. [William Lipkind])
1953	The Biggest Bear	Lynd Ward
1954	Madeline's Rescue	Ludwig Bemelmans
1955	Cinderella, or the Little Glass Slipper	Marcia Brown (translated from Charles Perrault by Marcia Brown)
1956	Frog Went A-Courtin'	Feodor Rojankovsky (John Langstaff)
1957	A Tree Is Nice	Marc Simont (Janice Udry)
1958	Time of Wonder	Robert McCloskey
1959	Chanticleer and the Fox	Barbara Cooney (adapted from Chaucer's Canterbury Tales by Barbara Cooney)
1960	Nine Days to Christmas	Marie Hall Ets (Marie Hall Ets and Aurora Labastida)
1961	Baboushka and the Three Kings	Nicolas Sidjakov (Ruth Robbins)
1962	Once a Mouse	Marcia Brown
1963	The Snowy Day	Ezra Jack Keats
1964	Where the Wild Things Are	Maurice Sendak
1965	May I Bring a Friend?	Beni Montresor (Beatrice Schenk de Regniers)
1966	Always Room for One More	Nonny Hogrogian (Sorche Nic Leodhas, pseud. [Leclair Alger])
1967	Sam, Bangs & Moonshine	Evaline Ness
1968	Drummer Hoff	Ed Emberley (Barbara Emberley)
1969	The Fool of the World and the Flying Ship	Uri Shulevitz (Arthur Ransome)
1970	Sylvester and the Magic Pebble	William Steig
1971	A Story A Story	Gail E. Haley
1972	One Fine Day	Nonny Hogrogian
1973	The Funny Little Woman	Blair Lent (Arlene Mosel)
1974	Duffy and the Devil	Margot Zemach (Harve Zemach)
1975	Arrow to the Sun	Gerald McDermott
1976	Why Mosquitoes Buzz in People's Ears	Leo and Diane Dillon (Verna Aardema)
1977	Ashanti to Zulu: African Traditions	Leo and Diane Dillon (Margaret Musgrove)
1978	Noah's Ark	Peter Spier
1979	The Girl Who Loved Wild Horses	Paul Goble
1980	Ox-Cart Man	Barbara Cooney (Donald Hall)
1981	Fables	Arnold Lobel
1982	Jumanji	Chris Van Allsburg
1983	Shadow	Marcia Brown (also translator of original French text by Blaise Cendrars)
1984	The Glorious Flight: Across the Channel with Louis Blériot	Alice and Martin Provensen
1985	Saint George and the Dragon	Trina Schart Hyman (Margaret Hodges)
1986	The Polar Express	Chris Van Allsburg
1987	Hey, Al	Richard Egielski (Arthur Yorinks)
1988	Owl Moon	John Schoenherr (Jane Yolen)
1989	Song and Dance Man	Stephen Gammell (Karen Ackerman)
1990	Lon Po Po: A Red-Riding Hood Story from China	Ed Young
1991	Black and White	David Macaulay
1992	Tuesday	David Wiesner
1993	Mirette on the High Wire	Emily Arnold McCully
1994	Grandfather's Journey	Allen Say (Walter Lorraine)
1995	Smoky Night	David Diaz (Eve Bunting)
1996	Officer Buckle and Gloria	Peggy Rathmann
1997	Golem	David Wisniewski
1998	Rapunzel	Paul O. Zelinsky
1999	Snowflake Bentley	Mary Azarian (Jacqueline Briggs Martin)
2000	Joseph Had a Little Overcoat	Simms Taback
2001	So You Want to Be President?	David Small (Judith St. George)
2002	The Three Pigs	David Wiesner
2003	My Friend Rabbit	Eric Rohmann
2004	The Man Who Walked Between the Towers	Mordicai Gerstein
2005	Kitten's First Full Moon	Kevin Henkes

Coretta Scott King Award

Established in 1970, the Coretta Scott King Award honors outstanding African American authors and illustrators of books for young people. The books, which may be fiction or nonfiction, must be original works that portray some aspect of the black experience. In 1982 the award came under the aegis of the American Library Association. Only authors were eligible for the award until 1974, and no illustrator awards were given in 1975–1977. Prize: citation, honorarium, and encyclopedia set.

Coretta Scott King Award Web site:
<www.ala.org/ala/emiert/corettascottking
  bookawards/corettascott.htm>.

1970	Lillie Patterson, *Martin Luther King, Jr.: Man of Peace*
1971	Charlemae Rollins, *Black Troubador: Langston Hughes*
1972	Elton C. Fax, *17 Black Artists*
1973	*I Never Had It Made: The Autobiography of Jackie Robinson,* as told to Alfred Duckett
1974	author: Sharon Bell Mathis, *Ray Charles;* illustrator: George Ford, *Ray Charles*
1975	author: Dorothy Robinson, *The Legend of Africana*
1976	author: Pearl Bailey, *Duey's Tale*
1977	author: James Haskins, *The Story of Stevie Wonder*
1978	author: Eloise Greenfield, *Africa Dream;* illustrator: Carole Bayard, *Africa Dream*
1979	author: Ossie Davis, *Escape to Freedom;* illustrator: Tom Feelings, *Something on My Mind*
1980	author: Walter Dean Myers, *The Young Landlords;* illustrator: Carole Byard, *Cornrows*
1981	author: Sidney Poitier, *This Life;* illustrator: Ashley Bryan, *Beat the Story Drum, Pum-Pum*
1982	author: Mildred D. Taylor, *Let the Circle Be Unbroken;* illustrator: John Steptoe, *Mother Crocodile*
1983	author: Virginia Hamilton, *Sweet Whispers, Brother Rush;* illustrator: Peter Mugabane, *Black Child*
1984	author: Lucille Clifton, *Everett Anderson's Good-bye;* illustrator: Pat Cummings, *My Mama Needs Me*
1985	author: Walter Dean Myers, *Motown and Didi;* no illustrator award
1986	author: Virginia Hamilton, *The People Could Fly: American Black Folktales;* illustrator: Jerry Pinkney, *The Patchwork Quilt*
1987	author: Mildred Pitts Walter, *Justin and the Best Biscuits in the World;* illustrator: Jerry Pinkney, *Half a Moon and One Whole Star*
1988	author: Mildred L. Taylor, *The Friendship;* illustrator: John Steptoe, *Mufaro's Beautiful Daughters: An African Tale*
1989	author: Walter Dean Myers, *Fallen Angels;* illustrator: Jerry Pinkney, *Mirandy and Brother Wind*
1990	author: Patricia C. & Frederick L. McKissack, *A Long Hard Journey: The Story of the Pullman Porter;* illustrator: Jan Spivey Gilchrist, *Nathaniel Talking*
1991	author: Mildred D. Taylor, *The Road to Memphis;* illustrator: Leo and Diane Dillon, *Aida*
1992	author: Walter Dean Myers, *Now Is Your Time: The African American Struggle for Freedom;* illustrator: Faith Ringgold, *Tar Beach*
1993	author: Patricia A. McKissack, *Dark Thirty: Southern Tales of the Supernatural;* illustrator: Kathleen Atkins Wilson, *The Origin of Life on Earth: An African Creation Myth*
1994	author: Angela Johnson, *Toning the Sweep;* illustrator: Tom Feelings, *Soul Looks Back in Wonder*
1995	author: Patricia C. & Frederick L. McKissack, *Christmas in the Big House, Christmas in the Quarters;* illustrator: James Ransome, *The Creation*
1996	author: Virginia Hamilton, *Her Stories;* illustrator: Tom Feelings, *The Middle Passage: White Ships Black Cargo*
1997	author: Walter Dean Myers, *Slam;* illustrator: Jerry Pinkney, *Minty: A Story of Young Harriet Tubman*
1998	author: Sharon M. Draper, *Forged by Fire;* illustrator: Javaka Steptoe, *In Daddy's Arms I am Tall: African Americans Celebrating Fathers*
1999	author: Angela Johnson, *Heaven;* illustrator: Michele Wood, *i see the rhythm*
2000	author: Christopher Paul Curtis, *Bud, Not Buddy;* illustrator: Brian Pinkney, *In the Time of the Drums*
2001	author: Jacqueline Woodson, *Miracle's Boys;* illustrator: Bryan Collier, *Uptown*
2002	author: Mildred Taylor, *The Land;* illustrator: Jerry Pinkney, *Goin' Someplace Special*
2003	author: Nikki Grimes, *Bronx Masquerade;* illustrator: E.B. Lewis, *Talkin' About Bessie: The Story of Aviator Elizabeth Coleman*
2004	author: Angela Johnson, *The First Part Last;* illustrator: Ashley Bryan, *Beautiful Blackbird*
2005	author: Toni Morrison, *Remember: The Journey to School Integration;* illustrator: Kadir Nelson, *Ellington Was Not a Street*
2006	*prizes scheduled to be awarded in January*

Did you know? Friends who had searched the Frank family's hiding place after their capture later gave Otto Frank the papers left behind by the Gestapo. Among them he found Anne's diary, which was published as *The Diary of a Young Girl* (originally in Dutch, 1947). Precocious in style and insight, it traces her emotional growth amid adversity. In it she wrote, "In spite of everything I still believe that people are really good at heart." The diary has been translated into more than 50 languages and is the most widely read diary of the Holocaust.

The Man Booker Prize

Awarded to the best full-length novel of the year written by a citizen of the Commonwealth or the Republic of Ireland and published in the UK between 1 October and 30 September. Prize: £20,000 (about $37,000); each shortlisted author receives £1000 (about $1,850). In 1993, Salman Rushdie was awarded the Booker of Bookers, a special award to mark 25 years of the Booker Prize, for *Midnight's Children*. In 2005, the Man Booker International Prize was created, to be awarded biennially to a living writer for outstanding lifetime achievement. Prize: £60,000 (about $105,000).

Albanian novelist Ismail Kadare won the first Man Booker International Prize in 2005.

Booker Prize Web site: <www.bookerprize.co.uk>.

YEAR	TITLE	AUTHOR
1969	Something to Answer For	P. H. Newby
1970	The Elected Member	Bernice Rubens
1971	In a Free State	V. S. Naipaul
1972	G.	John Berger
1973	The Siege of Krishnapur	J. G. Farrell
1974	The Conservationist	Nadine Gordimer
1974	Holiday	Stanley Middleton
1975	Heat and Dust	Ruth Prawer Jhabvala
1976	Saville	David Storey
1977	Staying On	Paul Scott
1978	The Sea, The Sea	Iris Murdoch
1979	Offshore	Penelope Fitzgerald
1980	Rites of Passage	William Golding
1981	Midnight's Children	Salman Rushdie
1982	Schindler's Ark	Thomas Keneally
1983	Life and Times of Michael K	J. M. Coetzee
1984	Hotel du Lac	Anita Brookner
1985	The Bone People	Keri Hulme
1986	The Old Devils	Kingsley Amis

YEAR	TITLE	AUTHOR
1987	Moon Tiger	Penelope Lively
1988	Oscar and Lucinda	Peter Carey
1989	The Remains of the Day	Kazuo Ishiguro
1990	Possession	A. S. Byatt
1991	The Famished Road	Ben Okri
1992	The English Patient	Michael Ondaatje
1992	Sacred Hunger	Barry Unsworth
1993	Paddy Clarke Ha Ha Ha	Roddy Doyle
1994	How Late It Was, How Late	James Kelman
1995	The Ghost Road	Pat Barker
1996	Last Orders	Graham Swift
1997	The God of Small Things	Arundhati Roy
1998	Amsterdam	Ian McEwan
1999	Disgrace	J. M. Coetzee
2000	The Blind Assassin	Margaret Atwood
2001	True History of the Kelly Gang	Peter Carey
2002	Life of Pi	Yann Martel
2003	Vernon God Little	DBC Pierre
2004	The Line of Beauty	Alan Hollinghurst
2005	scheduled to be awarded 10 October	

The Whitbread Book Awards

The Whitbread Book Awards were inaugurated in 1971. Since 1985, Whitbread Book Awards have been given in five categories: Novel, First Novel, Biography, Poetry, and Children's. From these a panel of judges chooses one overall winner—the Whitbread Book of the Year. The total prize fund is £50,000 (about $88,000): each of the category award winners receives £5,000 (about $9,000), and the Book of the Year winner receives an additional £25,000 (about $44,000).

This list includes Novel award winners from 1971 to 1984 and Book of the Year winners from 1985 to 2004.

Whitbread Book Awards Web site: <www.whitbread-bookawards.co.uk>.

YEAR	TITLE	AUTHOR
1971	The Destiny Waltz	Gerda Charles
1972	The Bird of Night	Susan Hill
1973	The Chip-Chip Gatherers	Shiva Naipaul
1974	The Sacred and Profane Love Machine	Iris Murdoch
1975	Docherty	William McIlvanney
1976	The Children of Dynmouth	William Trevor
1977	Injury Time	Beryl Bainbridge
1978	Picture Palace	Paul Theroux
1979	The Old Jest	Jennifer Johnston
1980	How Far Can You Go?	David Lodge
1981	Silver's City	Maurice Leitch
1982	Young Shoulders	John Wain
1983	Fools of Fortune	William Trevor
1984	Kruger's Alp	Christopher Hope
1985	Elegies	Douglas Dunn
1986	An Artist of the Floating World	Kazuo Ishiguro
1987	Under the Eye of the Clock	Christopher Nolan

YEAR	TITLE	AUTHOR
1988	The Comforts of Madness	Paul Sayer
1989	Coleridge: Early Visions	Richard Holmes
1990	Hopeful Monsters	Nicholas Mosley
1991	A Life of Picasso	John Richardson
1992	Swing Hammer Swing!	Jeff Torrington
1993	Theory of War	Joan Brady
1994	Felicia's Journey	William Trevor
1995	Behind the Scenes at the Museum	Kate Atkinson
1996	The Spirit Level	Seamus Heaney
1997	Tales from Ovid	Ted Hughes
1998	Birthday Letters	Ted Hughes
1999	Beowulf	Seamus Heaney
2000	English Passengers	Matthew Kneale
2001	The Amber Spyglass	Philip Pullman
2002	Samuel Pepys: The Unequalled Self	Claire Tomalin
2003	The Curious Incident of the Dog in the Night-Time	Mark Haddon
2004	Small Island	Andrea Levy

The Orange Prize

Awarded to a work of published fiction written in English by a woman and published in the United Kingdom between 1 April and 31 March. Prize: £30,000 (about $53,000) and a bronze figurine called "The Bessie."

Orange Prize Web site: <www.orangeprize.co.uk>.

YEAR	TITLE	AUTHOR	YEAR	TITLE	AUTHOR
1996	A Spell of Winter	Helen Dunmore	2001	The Idea of Perfection	Kate Grenville
1997	Fugitive Pieces	Anne Michaels	2002	Bel Canto	Ann Patchett
1998	Larry's Party	Carol Shields	2003	Property	Valerie Martin
1999	A Crime in the Neighbourhood	Suzanne Berne	2004	Small Island	Andrea Levy
2000	When I Lived in Modern Times	Linda Grant	2005	We Need to Talk About Kevin	Lionel Shriver

Prix Goncourt

The Prix de l'Académie Goncourt was first awarded in 1903 from the estate of the brothers and French literary figures Edmond Huot de Goncourt (1822–1896) and Jules Huot de Goncourt (1830–1870) for a work of contemporary prose in French. Prize: €10 (about $12.00). An additional prize is awarded for the best work of new fiction.

YEAR	TITLE	AUTHOR	YEAR	TITLE	AUTHOR
1903	Force ennemie	John Antoine Nau	1940	Les Grandes Vacances	Francis Ambrière
1904	La Maternelle	Léon Frapié	1941	Le Vent de mars	Henri Pourrat
1905	Les Civilisés	Claude Farrère	1942	Pareil à des enfants	Bernard Marc
1906	Dingley, l'illustre écrivain	Jérôme and Jean Tharaud	1943	Passage de l'homme	Marius Grout
1907	Le Rouet d'ivoire	Emile Moselly	1944	Le Premier Accroc coûte 200 francs	Elsa Triolet
1908	Ecrit sur l'eau	Francis de Miomandre	1945	Mon village à l'heure allemande	Jean-Louis Bory
1909	En France	Marius & Ary Leblond	1946	Histoire d'un fait divers	Jean-Jacques Gautier
1910	De Goupil à Margot	Louis Pergaud	1947	Les Forêts de la nuit	Jean-Louis Curtis
1911	Monsieur des Lourdines	Alphonse de Chateaubriant	1948	Les Grandes Familles	Maurice Druon
1912	Les Filles de la pluie	André Savignon	1949	Week-end à Zuydcoote	Robert Merle
1913	Le Peuple de la mer	Marc Elder	1950	Les Jeux sauvages	Paul Colin
1914	L'Appel du sol	Adrien Bertrand	1951	Le Rivage des Syrtes	Julien Gracq
1915	Gaspard	René Benjamin	1952	Léon Morin, prêtre	Béatrice Beck
1916	Le Feu	Henri Barbusse	1953	Les Bêtes	Pierre Gascar
1917	La Flamme au poing	Henri Malherbe	1954	Mandarins	Simone de Beauvoir
1918	Civilisation	Georges Duhamel	1955	Les Eaux mêlées	Roger Ikor
1919	A l'ombre des jeunes filles en fleur	Marcel Proust	1956	Les Racines du ciel	Romain Gary
1920	Nene	Ernest Perochon	1957	La Loi	Roger Vailland
1921	Batouala	René Maran	1958	Saint Germain; ou, la négociation	Francis Walder
1922	Le Vitriol de la lune	Henry Béraud	1959	Le Dernier des justes	André Schwartz-Bart
1922	Le Martyre de l'obèse	Henry Béraud	1960	Dieu est né en exil	Vintila Horia
1923	Rabevel; ou, le mal des ardents	Lucien Fabré	1961	La Pitié de Dieu	Jean Cau
1924	Le Chèvrefeuille, le Purgatoire, le Chapitre XIII	Thierry Sandre	1962	Les Bagages de sable	Anna Langfus
			1963	Quand la mer se retire	Armand Lanoux
1925	Raboliot	Maurice Genevoix	1964	L'État sauvage	Georges Conchon
1926	Le Supplice de Phèdre	Henry Deberly	1965	L'Adoration	Jacques Borel
1927	Latitude nord	Maurice Bedel	1966	Oublier Palerme	Edmonde Charles-Roux
1928	Un Homme se penche sur son passé	Maurice Constantin Weyer	1967	La Marge	André-Pierre de Mandiargues
1929	L'Ordre	Marcel Arland	1968	Les Fruits de l'hiver	Bernard Clavel
1930	Malaisie	Henri Fauconnier	1969	Creezy	Félicien Marceau
1931	Mal d'amour	Jean Fayard	1970	Le Roi des Aulnes	Michel Tournier
1932	Les Loups	Guy Mazeline	1971	Les Bêtises	Jacques Laurent
1933	La Condition humaine	André Malraux	1972	L'Épervier de Maheux	Jean Carrière
1934	Capitaine Conan	Roger Vercel	1973	L'Ogre	Jacques Chessex
1935	Sang et lumières	Joseph Peyré	1974	La Dentellière	Pascal Lainé
1936	L'Empreinte de Dieu	Maxence Van Der Meersch	1975	La Vie devant soi	Emile Ajar
			1976	Les Flamboyants	Patrick Grainville
1937	Faux passeports	Charles Plisnier	1977	John l'enfer	Didier Decoin
1938	L'Araignée	Henri Troyat	1978	Rue des boutiques obscures	Patrick Modiano
1939	Les Enfants gâtés	Philippe Hériat			

Prix Goncourt (continued)

YEAR	TITLE	AUTHOR
1979	*Pélagie la charrette*	Antonine Maillet
1980	*Le Jardin d'acclimatation*	Yves Navarre
1981	*Anne Marie*	Lucien Bodard
1982	*Dans la main de l'ange*	Dominique Fernandez
1983	*Les Égarés*	Frédérick Tristan
1984	*L'Amant*	Marguerite Duras
1985	*Les Noces barbares*	Yann Queffélec
1986	*Valet de nuit*	Michel Host
1987	*La Nuit sacrée*	Tahar Ben Jelloun
1988	*L'Exposition coloniale*	Erik Orsenna
1989	*Un Grand Pas vers le Bon Dieu*	Jean Vautrin
1990	*Les Champs d'honneur*	Jean Rouaud
1991	*Les Filles du calvaire*	Pierre Combescot
1992	*Texaco*	Patrick Chamoiseau
1993	*La Rocher de Tanios*	Amin Maalouf
1994	*Un Aller simple*	Didier Van Cauwelaert
1995	*Le Testament français*	Andreï Makine
1996	*Le Chasseur zéro*	Pascale Roze
1997	*La Bataille*	Patrick Rambaud
1998	*Confidence pour confidence*	Paule Constant
1999	*Je m'en vais*	Jean Echenoz
2000	*Ingrid Caven*	Jean-Jacques Schuhl
2001	*Rouge Brésil*	Jean-Christophe Rufin
2002	*Les Ombres errantes*	Pascal Quignard
2003	*La Maîtresse de Brecht*	Jacques-Pierre Amette
2004	*Le Soleil des Scorta*	Laurent Gaudé
2005	*scheduled to be announced in November*	

Premio Cervantes, the Cervantes Prize for Hispanic Literature

The Spanish Ministry of Culture sponsors the annual prize, which carries an award of €100,000 (about $125,000). Cervantes Prize Web site: <http://agora.mcu.es/libro/p_cervantes_f.asp>.

YEAR	AUTHOR
1976	Jorge Guillén
1977	Alejo Carpentier
1978	Dámaso Alonso
1979	Jorge Luis Borges and Gerardo Diego
1980	Juan Carlos Onetti
1981	Octavio Paz
1982	Luis Rosales
1983	Rafael Alberti
1984	Ernesto Sábato
1985	Juan Rulfo
1986	Antonio Buero Vallejo
1987	Carlos Fuentes
1988	María Zambrano
1989	Augusto Roa Bastos
1990	Adolfo Bioy Casares
1991	Francisco Ayala
1992	Dulce María Loynaz
1993	Miguel Delibes
1994	Mario Vargas Llosa
1995	Camilo José Cela
1996	José García Nieto
1997	Guillermo Cabrera Infante
1998	José Hierro
1999	Jorge Edwards
2000	Francisco Umbral
2001	Álvaro Mutis
2002	José Jiménez Lozano
2003	Gonzalo Rojas
2004	Rafael Sánchez Ferlosio
2005	*scheduled to be awarded in April 2006*

The Jerusalem Prize

The municipality of Jerusalem awards this prize at the biennial Jerusalem International Book Fair to a writer whose work explores the freedom of the individual in society. Prize: $10,000.
Jerusalem Prize Web site: <www.jerusalembookfair.com>.

YEAR	AUTHOR	COUNTRY
1963	Bertrand Russell	United Kingdom
1965	Max Frisch	Switzerland
1967	André Schwarz-Bart	France
1969	Ignazio Silone	Italy
1971	Jorge Luis Borges	Argentina
1973	Eugène Ionesco	France
1975	Simone de Beauvoir	France
1977	Octavio Paz	Mexico
1979	Sir Isaiah Berlin	United Kingdom
1981	Graham Greene	United Kingdom
1983	V.S. Naipaul	United Kingdom
1985	Milan Kundera	France
1987	J.M. Coetzee	South Africa
1989	Ernesto Sábato	Argentina
1991	Zbigniew Herbert	France
1993	Stefan Heym	Germany
1995	Mario Vargas Llosa	Peru
1997	Jorge Semprun	Spain
1999	Don DeLillo	United States
2001	Susan Sontag	United States
2003	Arthur Miller	United States
2005	António Lobo Antunes	Portugal

Did you know? Miguel de Cervantes, the creator of *Don Quixote* (1605), by 1570 had enlisted as a soldier in Naples, then a possession of the Spanish crown. On a voyage he undertook in 1575, his ship was attacked and captured by Barbary corsairs, and Cervantes was sold into slavery in Algiers, the center of the Christian slave traffic in the Muslim world. He was released in September 1580.

T.S. Eliot Prize

Great Britain's Poetry Book Society awards the T.S. Eliot Prize to the best new collection of poetry published in the UK or the Republic of Ireland during the preceding year. The prize is £10,500 (about $18,500).

YEAR	WORK	AUTHOR	COUNTRY
1993	*First Language*	Ciaran Carson	Ireland
1994	*The Annals of Chile*	Paul Muldoon	Northern Ireland
1995	*My Alexandria*	Mark Doty	United States
1996	*Sub-Human Redneck Poems*	Les Murray	Australia
1997	*God's Gift to Women*	Don Paterson	United Kingdom
1998	*Birthday Letters*	Ted Hughes	United Kingdom
1999	*Billy's Rain*	Hugo Williams	United Kingdom
2000	*The Weather in Japan*	Michael Longley	Northern Ireland
2001	*The Beauty of the Husband*	Anne Carson	Canada
2002	*Dart*	Alice Oswald	United Kingdom
2003	*Landing Light*	Don Paterson	United Kingdom
2004	*Reel*	George Szirtes	United Kingdom
2005	to be awarded in January 2006		

The Bollingen Prize in Poetry

The Bollingen Prize in Poetry is awarded biennially to "the American poet whose work, in the opinion of the Committee of Award, represents the highest achievement in the field of American poetry during the preceding two year period." The committee considers published work, particularly work published during the preceding two year period, although the Committee may consider prior achievement. Former winners of the prize are not eligible. Award amount: $75,000.

YEAR	POET	YEAR	POET	YEAR	POET
1949	Wallace Stevens	1961	Richard Eberhart	1983	Anthony Hecht
1950	John Crowe Ransom		John Hall Wheelock		John Hollander
1951	Marianne Moore	1963	Robert Frost	1985	John Ashbery
1952	Archibald MacLeish	1965	Horace Gregory		Fred Chappell
	William Carlos Williams	1967	Robert Penn Warren	1987	Stanley Kunitz
1953	W.H. Auden	1969	John Berryman	1989	Edgar Bowers
1954	Léonie Adams		Karl Shapiro	1991	Laura (Riding) Jackson
	Louise Bogan	1971	Richard Wilbur		Donald Justice
1955	Conrad Aiken		Mona Van Duyn	1993	Mark Strand
1956	Allen Tate	1973	James Merrill	1995	Kenneth Koch
1957	E.E. Cummings	1975	A.R. Ammons	1997	Gary Snyder
1958	Theodore Roethke	1977	David Ignatow	1999	Robert Creeley
1959	Delmore Schwartz	1979	W.S. Merwin	2001	Louise Glück
1960	Yvor Winters	1981	May Swenson	2003	Adrienne Rich
			Howard Nemerov	2005	Jay Wright

Architecture

Pritzker Architecture Prize

The Pritzker Prize, awarded by the Hyatt Foundation since 1979, is given to an outstanding living architect for built work. Prize: $100,000 and a bronze medallion. Web site: <www.pritzkerprize.com>.

YEAR	NAME	COUNTRY	YEAR	NAME	COUNTRY
1979	Philip Johnson	United States	1993	Fumihiko Maki	Japan
1980	Luis Barragán	Mexico	1994	Christian de Portzamparc	France
1981	James Stirling	Great Britain			
1982	Kevin Roche	United States	1995	Tadao Ando	Japan
1983	Ieoh Ming Pei	United States	1996	Rafael Moneo	Spain
1984	Richard Meier	United States	1997	Sverre Fehn	Norway
1985	Hans Hollein	Austria	1998	Renzo Piano	Italy
1986	Gottfried Boehm	West Germany	1999	Sir Norman Foster	Great Britain
1987	Kenzo Tange	Japan	2000	Rem Koolhaas	The Netherlands
1988	Gordon Bunshaft	United States	2001	Jacques Herzog	Switzerland
	Oscar Niemeyer	Brazil		Pierre de Meuron	Switzerland
1989	Frank O. Gehry	United States	2002	Glenn Murcutt	Australia
1990	Aldo Rossi	Italy	2003	Jørn Utzon	Denmark
1991	Robert Venturi	United States	2004	Zaha Hadid	Great Britain
1992	Alvaro Siza	Portugal	2005	Thom Mayne	United States

AIA Gold Medal

The American Institute of Architects awards the gold medal for an outstanding body of work.

YEAR	NAME	YEAR	NAME	YEAR	NAME
1907	Sir Aston Webb	1956	Clarence S. Stein	1981	José Luis Sert
1909	Charles Follen McKim	1957	Ralph Walker	1982	Romaldo Giurgola
1911	George Browne Post		Louis Skidmore	1983	Nathaniel A. Owings
1914	Jean Louis Pascal	1958	John Wellborn Root[1]	1985	William Wayne Caudill[1]
1922	Victor Laloux	1959	Walter Gropius	1986	Arthur Erickson
1923	Henry Bacon	1960	Ludwig Mies van der Rohe	1989	Joseph Esherick
1925	Sir Edwin L. Lutyens	1961	Le Corbusier (Charles-	1990	E. Fay Jones
	Bertram Grosvenor		Édouard Jeanneret)	1991	Charles W. Moore
	Goodhue[1]	1962	Eero Saarinen[1]	1992	Benjamin Thompson
1927	Howard Van Doren Shaw	1963	Alvar Aalto	1993	Thomas Jefferson[1]
1929	Milton Bennett Medary	1964	Pier Luigi Nervi		Kevin Roche
1933	Ragnar Ostberg	1966	Kenzo Tange	1994	Sir Norman Foster
1938	Paul Philippe Cret	1967	Wallace K. Harrison	1995	César Pelli
1944	Louis Henry Sullivan[1]	1968	Marcel Breuer	1997	Richard Meier
1947	Eliel Saarinen	1969	William Wilson Wurster	1999	Frank O. Gehry
1948	Charles Donagh Maginnis	1970	Richard Buckminster	2000	Ricardo Legorreta
1949	Frank Lloyd Wright		Fuller	2001	Michael Graves
1950	Sir Patrick Abercrombie	1971	Louis I. Kahn	2002	Tadao Ando
1951	Bernard Ralph Maybeck	1972	Pietro Belluschi	2004	Samuel Mockbee[1]
1952	Auguste Perret	1977	Richard Joseph Neutra[1]	2005	Santiago Calatrava
1953	William Adams Delano	1978	Philip C. Johnson		
1955	Willem Marinus Dudok	1979	Ieoh Ming Pei		

[1]*Awarded posthumously.*

Special Honors

Hasty Pudding Theatricals Woman of the Year and Man of the Year

The Hasty Pudding Theatricals of Harvard University, an organization of undergraduates, has presented the Woman of the Year award since 1951 and the Man of the Year award since 1967 to performers who have made a "lasting and impressive contribution to the world of entertainment."

YEAR	NAME	YEAR	NAME
1951	Gertrude Lawrence	1979	Candice Bergen and Robert De Niro
1952	Barbara Bel Geddes	1980	Meryl Streep and Alan Alda
1953	Mamie Eisenhower	1981	Mary Tyler Moore and John Travolta
1954	Shirley Booth	1982	Ella Fitzgerald and James Cagney
1955	Debbie Reynolds	1983	Julie Andrews and Steven Spielberg
1956	Peggy Ann Garner	1984	Joan Rivers and Sean Connery
1957	Carroll Baker	1985	Cher and Bill Murray
1958	Katharine Hepburn	1986	Sally Field and Sylvester Stallone
1959	Joanne Woodward	1987	Bernadette Peters and Mikhail Baryshnikov
1960	Carol Lawrence	1988	Lucille Ball and Steve Martin
1961	Jane Fonda	1989	Kathleen Turner and Robin Williams
1962	Piper Laurie	1990	Glenn Close and Kevin Costner
1963	Shirley MacLaine	1991	Diane Keaton and Clint Eastwood
1964	Rosalind Russell	1992	Jodie Foster and Michael Douglas
1965	Lee Remick	1993	Whoopi Goldberg and Chevy Chase
1966	Ethel Merman	1994	Meg Ryan and Tom Cruise
1967	Lauren Bacall and Bob Hope	1995	Michelle Pfeiffer and Tom Hanks
1968	Angela Lansbury and Paul Newman	1996	Susan Sarandon and Harrison Ford
1969	Carol Burnett and Bill Cosby	1997	Julia Roberts and Mel Gibson
1970	Dionne Warwick and Robert Redford	1998	Sigourney Weaver and Kevin Kline
1971	Carol Channing and James Stewart	1999	Goldie Hawn and Samuel L. Jackson
1972	Ruby Keeler and Dustin Hoffman	2000	Jamie Lee Curtis and Billy Crystal
1973	Liza Minnelli and Jack Lemmon	2001	Drew Barrymore and Anthony Hopkins
1974	Faye Dunaway and Peter Falk	2002	Sarah Jessica Parker and Bruce Willis
1975	Valerie Harper and Warren Beatty	2003	Anjelica Huston and Martin Scorsese
1976	Bette Midler and Robert Blake	2004	Sandra Bullock and Robert Downey, Jr.
1977	Elizabeth Taylor and Johnny Carson	2005	Catherine Zeta-Jones and Tim Robbins
1978	Beverly Sills and Richard Dreyfuss	2006	*scheduled to be awarded in February*

Sports

The tables that follow contain the significant information about the top contests of all the major sports that are international in character, as well as some professional and amateur sports that attract a huge national following—such as baseball in the United States and cricket in the United Kingdom, Australia, India, and the other Test Match countries—and some sports, such as rowing, in which national competition overshadows international events. In many sports the Olympic Games held every four years constitute the world championships; they are included in the listings below.

Sporting Codes for Countries

These codes are used to identify countries in the Sports section of the Britannica Almanac.

Codes of the International Olympic Committee (IOC)

AFG	Afghanistan	CZE	Czech Rep.	KOR	Korea, Rep. of (South Korea)
AHO	Netherlands Antilles	DEN	Denmark		
		DJI	Djibouti	KSA	Saudi Arabia
ALB	Albania	DMA	Dominica	KUW	Kuwait
ALG	Algeria	DOM	Dominican Rep.	LAO	Laos
AND	Andorra	ECU	Ecuador	LAT	Latvia
ANG	Angola	EGY	Egypt	LBA	Libya
ANT	Antigua and Barbuda	ERI	Eritrea	LBR	Liberia
ARG	Argentina	ESA	El Salvador	LCA	St. Lucia
ARM	Armenia	ESP	Spain	LES	Lesotho
ARU	Aruba	EST	Estonia	LIB	Lebanon
ASA	American Samoa	ETH	Ethiopia	LIE	Liechtenstein
AUS	Australia	FIJ	Fiji	LTU	Lithuania
AUT	Austria	FIN	Finland	LUX	Luxembourg
AZE	Azerbaijan	FRA	France	MAD	Madagascar
BAH	Bahamas	FSM	Micronesia, Fed. States of	MAR	Morocco
BAN	Bangladesh			MAS	Malaysia
BAR	Barbados	GAB	Gabon	MAW	Malawi
BDI	Burundi	GAM	Gambia	MDA	Moldova
BEL	Belgium	GBR	Great Britain	MDV	Maldives
BEN	Benin	GBS	Guinea-Bissau	MEX	Mexico
BER	Bermuda	GEO	Georgia	MGL	Mongolia
BHU	Bhutan	GEQ	Equatorial Guinea	MKD	Macedonia
BIH	Bosnia and Herzegovina	GER	Germany	MLI	Mali
BIZ	Belize	GHA	Ghana	MLT	Malta
BLR	Belarus	GRE	Greece	MON	Monaco
BOL	Bolivia	GRN	Grenada	MOZ	Mozambique
BOT	Botswana	GUA	Guatemala	MRI	Mauritius
BRA	Brazil	GUI	Guinea	MTN	Mauritania
BRN	Bahrain	GUM	Guam	MYA	Myanmar (Burma)
BRU	Brunei Darussalam	GUY	Guyana	NAM	Namibia
BUL	Bulgaria	HAI	Haiti	NCA	Nicaragua
BUR	Burkina Faso	HKG	Hong Kong	NED	Netherlands, The
CAF	Central African Rep.	HON	Honduras	NEP	Nepal
CAM	Cambodia	HUN	Hungary	NGR	Nigeria
CAN	Canada	INA	Indonesia	NIG	Niger
CAY	Cayman Islands	IND	India	NOR	Norway
CGO	Congo, Rep. of the	IRI	Iran	NRU	Nauru
CHA	Chad	IRL	Ireland	NZL	New Zealand
CHI	Chile	IRQ	Iraq	OMA	Oman
CHN	China, People's Rep. of	ISL	Iceland	PAK	Pakistan
CIV	Côte d'Ivoire	ISR	Israel	PAN	Panama
CMR	Cameroon	ISV	US Virgin Islands	PAR	Paraguay
COD	Congo, Dem. Rep. of the	ITA	Italy	PER	Peru
COK	Cook Islands	IVB	British Virgin Islands	PHI	Philippines
COL	Colombia	JAM	Jamaica	PLE	Palestine
COM	Comoros	JOR	Jordan	PLW	Palau
CPV	Cape Verde	JPN	Japan	PNG	Papua New Guinea
CRC	Costa Rica	KAZ	Kazakhstan	POL	Poland
CRO	Croatia	KEN	Kenya	POR	Portugal
CUB	Cuba	KGZ	Kyrgyzstan	PRK	Korea, Dem. People's Rep. of (North Korea)
CYP	Cyprus	KIR	Kiribati		

Sporting Codes for Countries (continued)

Codes of the International Olympic Committee (IOC) (continued)

PUR	Puerto Rico	SRI	Sri Lanka	TRI	Trinidad and Tobago
QAT	Qatar	STP	São Tomé and Príncipe	TUN	Tunisia
ROM	Romania	SUD	Sudan	TUR	Turkey
RSA	South Africa	SUI	Switzerland	UAE	United Arab Emirates
RUS	Russia	SUR	Suriname	UGA	Uganda
RWA	Rwanda	SVK	Slovakia	UKR	Ukraine
SAM	Samoa	SWE	Sweden	URU	Uruguay
SCG	Serbia and Montenegro	SWZ	Swaziland	USA	United States
SEN	Senegal	SYR	Syria	UZB	Uzbekistan
SEY	Seychelles	TAN	Tanzania	VAN	Vanuatu
SIN	Singapore	TGA	Tonga	VEN	Venezuela
SKN	St. Kitts and Nevis	THA	Thailand	VIE	Vietnam
SLE	Sierra Leone	TJK	Tajikistan	VIN	St. Vincent and
SLO	Slovenia	TKM	Turkmenistan		the Grenadines
SMR	San Marino	TLS	East Timor (Timor Leste)	YEM	Yemen
SOL	Solomon Islands	TOG	Togo	ZAM	Zambia
SOM	Somalia	TPE	Taiwan	ZIM	Zimbabwe

Continental, Historical, and Other Country Codes

AFR	Africa	DMN	Dominica	KZK	Kazakhstan	SAA	Saarland
AIA	Anguilla	ENG	England	LIT	Lithuania	SCO	Scotland
AME	The Americas	EUR	Europe	MAC	Macao	SKR	Korea, Rep. of
ARS	Saudi Arabia	FRG	Germany, Federal	MAU	Mauritius		(South Korea)
ASI	Asia		Rep. of (West	MOL	Moldova	SPA	Spain
BIR	Burma (Myanmar)		Germany)	MOR	Morocco	SWZ	Switzerland
BLS	Belarus	FRO	Faroe Islands	MSR	Montserrat	TAH	Tahiti
BOH	Bohemia	GDR	German Demo-	NIC	Nicaragua	TAI	Taiwan
BOS	Bosnia and		cratic Rep. (East	NIR	Northern Ireland	TCA	Turks and Caicos
	Herzegovina		Germany)	NKO	Korea, Dem.		Islands
BUR	Burma	HBR	British Honduras		People's Rep. of	TCH	Czechoslovakia
BWI	British West	HEB	New Hebrides		(North Korea)	UAR	United Arab Rep.
	Indies	HOL	Holland/The	OCE	Oceania	UCS	Union of the
CAM	Cameroon		Netherlands	PAL	Palestine		Czech Rep. and
CEY	Ceylon	IOA	International	PDR	Korea, Dem.		Slovakia
CIS	Commonwealth of		Olympic Athlete		People's Rep. of	UNT	Unified Team
	Indep. States	ICE	Iceland		(North Korea)	UPV	Upper Volta
CKN	Congo-Kinshasa	IHO	Netherlands India	PNG	Papua New	URS	USSR
COB	Congo-Brazzaville	IRE	Ireland		Guinea	UVI	US Virgin Islands
CSV	Czechoslovakia	IVC	Côte d'Ivoire/Ivory	RHO	Rhodesia	WAL	Wales
CUR	Curaçao		Coast	ROC	China, People's	YUG	Yugoslavia
DAH	Dahomey	JAP	Japan		Rep. of	ZAI	Zaire

The James E. Sullivan Memorial Trophy

The trophy is awarded by the Amateur Athletic Union (AAU) since 1930 to honor an athlete who, "by his or her performance, example and influence as an amateur, has done the most during the year to advance the cause of sportsmanship." The award, named for a past president of the AAU, is usually announced in April of the year after that for which the award is given. Winners receive a replica in bronze of the original trophy.

Web site: <www.aausports.org>.

YEAR	WINNER	SPORT	YEAR	WINNER	SPORT
1930	Bobby Jones	golf	1941	Leslie MacMitchell	track (middle distance running)
1931	Barney Berlinger	track (decathlon)			
1932	Jim Bausch	track (decathlon)	1942	Cornelius "Dutch" Warmerdam	track (pole vault)
1933	Glenn Cunningham	track (distance running)			
1934	Bill Bonthron	track (middle distance running)	1943	Gilbert Dodds	track (middle distance running)
1935	Lawson Little	golf	1944	Ann Curtis	swimming
1936	Glenn Morris	track (decathlon)	1945	Doc Blanchard	football
1937	Don Budge	tennis	1946	Arnold Tucker	football
1938	Don Lash	track (distance running)	1947	John B. Kelly, Jr.	rowing
1939	Joe Burk	rowing	1948	Bob Mathias	track (decathlon)
1940	Greg Rice	track (distance running)	1949	Dick Button	figure skating

The James E. Sullivan Memorial Trophy (continued)

YEAR	WINNER	SPORT	YEAR	WINNER	SPORT
1950	Fred Wilt	track (distance running)	1979	Kurt Thomas	gymnastics
1951	Bob Richards	track (pole vault/decathlon)	1980	Eric Heiden	speed skating
1952	Horace Ashenfelter	track (distance running)	1981	Carl Lewis	track (sprints/long jump)
1953	Sammy Lee	diving	1982	Mary Decker	track (distance running)
1954	Mal Whitfield	track (middle distance running)	1983	Edwin Moses	track (hurdles)
1955	Harrison Dillard	track (sprints/hurdles)	1984	Greg Louganis	diving
1956	Pat McCormick	diving	1985	Joan Benoit Samuelson	track (marathon)
1957	Bobby Morrow	track (sprints)	1986	Jackie Joyner-Kersee	track (heptathlon)
1958	Glenn Davis	track (hurdles)	1987	Jim Abbott	baseball (pitcher)
1959	Parry O'Brien	track (shot put)	1988	Florence Griffith Joyner	track (sprints)
1960	Rafer Johnson	track (decathlon)	1989	Janet Evans	swimming
1961	Wilma Rudolph	track (sprints)	1990	John Smith	freestyle wrestling
1962	Jim Beatty	track (distance running)	1991	Mike Powell	track (long jump)
1963	John Pennel	track (pole vault)	1992	Bonnie Blair	speed skating
1964	Don Schollander	swimming	1993	Charlie Ward	football
1965	Bill Bradley	basketball	1994	Dan Jansen	speed skating
1966	Jim Ryun	track (middle distance running)	1995	Bruce Baumgartner	freestyle wrestling
1967	Randy Matson	track (shot put/discus)	1996	Michael Johnson	track (middle distance running)
1968	Debbie Meyer	swimming	1997	Peyton Manning	football
1969	Bill Toomey	track (decathlon)	1998	Chamique Holdsclaw	basketball
1970	John Kinsella	swimming	1999	Coco and Kelly Miller	basketball
1971	Mark Spitz	swimming	2000	Rulon Gardner	Greco-Roman wrestling
1972	Frank Shorter	track (distance running)	2001	Michelle Kwan	figure skating
1973	Bill Walton	basketball	2002	Sarah Hughes	figure skating
1974	Rick Wohlhuter	track (middle distance running)	2003	Michael Phelps	swimming
1975	Tim Shaw	swimming	2004	Paul Hamm	gymnastics
1976	Bruce Jenner	track (decathlon)			
1977	John Naber	swimming			
1978	Tracy Caulkins	swimming			

The Olympic Games

By the 6th century BC several sporting festivals had achieved cultural importance in the Greek world. The most prominent among them were the Olympic Games at the city of Olympia, first recorded in 776 BC and held at four-year intervals thereafter. Those games, comprising many of the sports now included in the Summer Games, were abolished in AD 393 by the Roman emperor Theodosius I, probably because of their pagan associations.

In 1887 the 24-year-old French aristocrat and educator Pierre, baron de Coubertin, conceived the idea of reviving the Olympic Games and spent seven years gathering support for his plan. At a international congress in 1894, his plan was accepted and the International Olympic Committee (IOC) was founded. The first modern Olympic Games were held in Athens in April 1896, with some 300 representatives from 13 nations competing. The revival led to the formation of international amateur sports organizations and national Olympic committees throughout the world.

The IOC is responsible for maintaining the regular celebration of the games, seeing that the games are carried out in a spirit of peace and intercultural communication, and promoting amateur sport throughout the world. IOC members may not accept from the government of their country, or from any other entity, instructions that compromise their independence.

The Olympic Games have come to be regarded as the world's foremost sports competition. Before the 1970s the Games were officially limited to amateurs, but since that time many events have been opened to professional athletes. In 1924 the Winter Games were created, and in 1986 the IOC voted to alternate the Winter and Summer Games every two years, beginning in 1994.

The games were canceled during the two world wars (1916, 1940, and 1944) and have frequently served as venues for the expression of political dissent. China refused to participate in the Summer Games from 1956 until 1984 because of Taiwan's participation; 26 nations boycotted the games in 1976 over the participation of New Zealand, some of whose athletes had competed in apartheid-era South Africa; the United States and some 60 other countries boycotted the 1980 games in Moscow to protest the Soviet invasion of Afghanistan, and the Communist bloc and Cuba in turn boycotted the 1984 Los Angeles games.

In light of the IOC's declared independence from political and financial interests, in 1998 the world was shocked by allegations of widespread corruption within the committee. Several committee members, it was found, had accepted bribes to approve the bid of Salt Lake City UT as the site for the 2002 Winter Games. Impropriety was also alleged for several previous bid committees. The IOC responded by expelling six members and in 1999 announced a number of wide-ranging reforms.

IOC Web site: <www.olympic.org>.

Sites of the Modern Olympic Games

Summer Games

YEAR	LOCATION	YEAR	LOCATION	YEAR	LOCATION
1896	Athens, Greece	1940–44	*not held*	1992	Barcelona, Spain
1900	Paris, France	1948	London, England	1996	Atlanta GA
1904	St. Louis MO	1952	Helsinki, Finland	2000	Sydney, Australia
1908	London, England	1956	Melbourne, Australia	2004	Athens, Greece
1912	Stockholm, Sweden	1960	Rome, Italy	2008	*scheduled to be held*
1916	*not held*	1964	Tokyo, Japan		*8–24 August, Beijing,*
1920	Antwerp, Belgium	1968	Mexico City, Mexico		*China*
1924	Paris, France	1972	Munich, West Germany	2012	*scheduled to be held in*
1928	Amsterdam, The Nether-	1976	Montreal, Quebec		*London, England*
	lands	1980	Moscow, USSR		
1932	Los Angeles CA	1984	Los Angeles CA		
1936	Berlin, Germany	1988	Seoul, South Korea		

Winter Games

YEAR	LOCATION	YEAR	LOCATION	YEAR	LOCATION
1924	Chamonix, France	1960	Squaw Valley CA	1994	Lillehammer, Norway
1928	St. Moritz, Switzerland	1964	Innsbruck, Austria	1998	Nagano, Japan
1932	Lake Placid NY	1968	Grenoble, France	2002	Salt Lake City UT
1936	Garmisch-Partenkirchen,	1972	Sapporo, Japan	2006	*scheduled to be held*
	Germany	1976	Innsbruck, Austria		*10–26 February, Turin,*
1940–44	*not held*	1980	Lake Placid NY		*Italy*
1948	St. Moritz, Switzerland	1984	Sarajevo, Yugoslavia	2010	*scheduled to be held*
1952	Oslo, Norway	1988	Calgary, Alberta		*12–26 February,*
1956	Cortina d'Ampezzo, Italy	1992	Albertville, France		*Vancouver BC*

Summer Olympic Games Champions

Gold-medal winners in all Summer Olympic contests since 1896. Note: East and West Germany fielded a joint all-Germany team in 1956, 1960, and 1964, abbreviated here as GER. The Unified Team in 1992 consisted of the Commonwealth of Independent States plus Georgia, and is abbreviated here as UNT.

Archery

MEN'S INDIVIDUAL
1972　John Williams (USA)
1976　Darrell Pace (USA)
1980　Tomi Poikolainen (FIN)
1984　Darrell Pace (USA)
1988　Jay Barrs (USA)
1992　Sebastien Flute (FRA)
1996　Justin Huish (USA)
2000　Simon Fairweather (AUS)
2004　Marco Galiazzo (ITA)

AU CORDON DORÉ (50 METERS)
1900　Henri Herouin (FRA)

AU CORDON DORÉ (33 METERS)
1900　Hubert van Innis (BEL)

AU CHAPELET (50 METERS)
1900　Eugène Mougin (FRA)

SUR LA PERCHE À LA HERSE
1900　Emmanuel Foulon (FRA)

AU CHAPELET (33 METERS)
1900　Hubert van Innis (BEL)

SUR LA PERCHE À LA PYRAMIDE
1900　Émile Grumiaux (FRA)

Archery (continued)

DOUBLE AMERICAN ROUND
1904　George Philipp Bryant (USA)

(DOUBLE) YORK ROUND
1904　George Philipp Bryant (USA)
1908　William Dod (GBR)

CONTINENTAL STYLE
1908　Eugène G. Grizot (FRA)

FIXED BIRD TARGET (SMALL)
1920　Edmond van Moer (BEL)

FIXED BIRD TARGET (LARGE)
1920　Édouard Cloetens (BEL)

MOVING BIRD TARGET (28 M)
1920　Hubert van Innis (BEL)

MOVING BIRD TARGET (33 M)
1920　Hubert van Innis (BEL)

MOVING BIRD TARGET (50 M)
1920　Julien Brulé (FRA)

WOMEN'S INDIVIDUAL
1972　Doreen Wilber (USA)
1976　Luann Ryon (USA)
1980　Ketevan Losaberidze (URS)

Summer Olympic Games Champions (continued)

Archery (continued)

WOMEN'S INDIVIDUAL
1984 Seo Hyang Soon (KOR)
1988 Kim Soo Nyung (KOR)
1992 Cho Youn Jeong (KOR)
1996 Kim Kyung-Wook (KOR)
2000 Yun Mi-Jin (KOR)
2004 Park Sung Hyun (KOR)

DOUBLE COLUMBIA ROUND
1904 Matilda Scott Howell (USA)

(DOUBLE) NATIONAL ROUND
1904 Matilda Scott Howell (USA)
1908 Sybil Fenton "Queenie" Newall (GBR)

MEN'S TEAM
1904 United States
1988 South Korea
1992 Spain
1996 United States
2000 South Korea
2004 South Korea

WOMEN'S TEAM
1904 United States
1988 South Korea
1992 South Korea
1996 South Korea
2000 South Korea
2004 South Korea

FIXED TARGET (2 EVENTS)
1920 Belgium

MOVING TARGET (28 M)
1920 The Netherlands

MOVING TARGET (33 M)
1920 Belgium

MOVING TARGET (50 M)
1920 Belgium

Association football (soccer)[1]

MEN
1900 Great Britain
1904 Canada
1908 Great Britain
1912 Great Britain
1920 Belgium
1924 Uruguay
1928 Uruguay
1936 Italy
1948 Sweden
1952 Hungary
1956 USSR
1960 Yugoslavia
1964 Hungary
1968 Hungary
1972 Poland
1976 East Germany
1980 Czechoslovakia
1984 France
1988 USSR
1992 Spain
1996 Nigeria

Association football (soccer)[1] (continued)
2000 Cameroon
2004 Argentina

WOMEN
1996 United States
2000 Norway
2004 United States

Athletics (track-and-field) (men)

60 METERS		SEC
1900	Alvin Kraenzlein (USA)	7
1904	Archie Hahn (USA)	7

100 METERS		SEC
1896	Thomas Burke (USA)	12.0
1900	Francis Jarvis (USA)	11.0
1904	Archie Hahn (USA)	11.0
1908	Reginald Walker (RSA)	10.8
1912	Ralph Craig (USA)	10.8
1920	Charles Paddock (USA)	10.8
1924	Harold Abrahams (GBR)	10.6
1928	Percy Williams (CAN)	10.8
1932	Eddie Tolan (USA)	10.3
1936	Jesse Owens (USA)	10.3
1948	Harrison Dillard (USA)	10.3
1952	Lindy Remigino (USA)	10.4
1956	Robert Morrow (USA)	10.5
1960	Armin Hary (GER)	10.2
1964	Robert Hayes (USA)	10.0
1968	James Hines (USA)	9.9
1972	Valery Borzov (URS)	10.14
1976	Hasely Crawford (TRI)	10.06
1980	Allan Wells (GBR)	10.25
1984	Carl Lewis (USA)	9.99
1988	Carl Lewis (USA)	9.92
1992	Linford Christie (GBR)	9.96
1996	Donovan Bailey (CAN)	9.84
2000	Maurice Greene (USA)	9.87
2004	Justin Gatlin (USA)	9.85

200 METERS		SEC
1900	Walter Tewksbury (USA)	22.2
1904	Archie Hahn (USA)	21.6
1908	Robert Kerr (CAN)	22.6
1912	Ralph Craig (USA)	21.7
1920	Allen Woodring (USA)	22.0
1924	Jackson Scholz (USA)	21.6
1928	Percy Williams (CAN)	21.8
1932	Eddie Tolan (USA)	21.2
1936	Jesse Owens (USA)	20.7
1948	Melvin Patton (USA)	21.1
1952	Andy Stanfield (USA)	20.7
1956	Robert Morrow (USA)	20.6
1960	Livio Berruti (ITA)	20.5
1964	Henry Carr (USA)	20.3
1968	Tommie Smith (USA)	19.8
1972	Valery Borzov (URS)	20.00
1976	Donald Quarrie (JAM)	20.23
1980	Pietro Mennea (ITA)	20.19
1984	Carl Lewis (USA)	19.80
1988	Joe DeLoach (USA)	19.75
1992	Mike Marsh (USA)	20.01
1996	Michael Johnson (USA)	19.32
2000	Konstantinos Kenteris (GRE)	20.09
2004	Shawn Crawford (USA)	19.79

Summer Olympic Games Champions (continued)

Athletics (track-and-field) (men) (continued)

400 METERS — SEC
1896	Thomas Burke (USA)	54.2
1900	Maxwell Long (USA)	49.4
1904	Harry Hillman (USA)	49.2
1908	Wyndham Halswelle (GBR)	50.0
1912	Charles Reidpath (USA)	48.2
1920	Bevil Rudd (RSA)	49.6
1924	Eric Liddell (GBR)	47.6
1928	Raymond Barbuti (USA)	47.8
1932	William Carr (USA)	46.2
1936	Archie Williams (USA)	46.5
1948	Arthur Wint (JAM)	46.2
1952	Vincent George Rhoden (JAM)	45.9
1956	Charles Jenkins (USA)	46.7
1960	Otis Davis (USA)	44.9
1964	Michael Larrabee (USA)	45.1
1968	Lee Evans (USA)	43.8
1972	Vincent Matthews (USA)	44.66
1976	Alberto Juantorena (CUB)	44.26
1980	Viktor Markin (URS)	44.60
1984	Alonzo Babers (USA)	44.27
1988	Steven Lewis (USA)	43.87
1992	Quincy Watts (USA)	43.50
1996	Michael Johnson (USA)	43.49
2000	Michael Johnson (USA)	43.84
2004	Jeremy Wariner (USA)	44.00

800 METERS — MIN:SEC
1896	Edwin Flack (AUS)	2:11.0
1900	Alfred Tysoe (GBR)	2:01.2
1904	James Lightbody (USA)	1:56.0
1908	Melvin Sheppard (USA)	1:52.8
1912	James Edward Meredith (USA)	1:51.9
1920	Albert Hill (GBR)	1:53.4
1924	Douglas Lowe (GBR)	1:52.4
1928	Douglas Lowe (GBR)	1:51.8
1932	Thomas Hampson (GBR)	1:49.7
1936	John Woodruff (USA)	1:52.9
1948	Malvin Whitfield (USA)	1:49.2
1952	Malvin Whitfield (USA)	1:49.2
1956	Thomas Courtney (USA)	1:47.7
1960	Peter Snell (NZL)	1:46.3
1964	Peter Snell (NZL)	1:45.1
1968	Ralph Doubell (AUS)	1:44.3
1972	David Wottle (USA)	1:45.9
1976	Alberto Juantorena (CUB)	1:43.50
1980	Steven Ovett (GBR)	1:45.40
1984	Joaquim Cruz (BRA)	1:43.00
1988	Paul Ereng (KEN)	1:43.45
1992	William Tanui (KEN)	1:43.66
1996	Vebjoern Rodal (NOR)	1:42.58
2000	Nils Schumann (GER)	1:45.08
2004	Yury Borzakovsky (RUS)	1:44.45

1,500 METERS — MIN:SEC
1896	Edwin Flack (AUS)	4:33.2
1900	Charles Bennett (GBR)	4:06.2
1904	James Lightbody (USA)	4:05.4
1908	Melvin Sheppard (USA)	4:03.4
1912	Arnold Jackson (GBR)	3:56.8
1920	Albert Hill (GBR)	4:01.8
1924	Paavo Nurmi (FIN)	3:53.6
1928	Harry Larva (FIN)	3:53.2
1932	Luigi Beccali (ITA)	3:51.2
1936	John Lovelock (NZL)	3:47.8
1948	Henry Eriksson (SWE)	3:49.8

Athletics (track-and-field) (men) (continued)

1,500 METERS — MIN:SEC
1952	Joseph Barthel (LUX)	3:45.1
1956	Ronald Delany (IRE)	3:41.2
1960	Herbert Elliott (AUS)	3:35.6
1964	Peter Snell (NZL)	3:38.1
1968	Hezekiah Kipchoge ("Kip") Keino (KEN)	3:34.9
1972	Pekka Vasala (FIN)	3:36.3
1976	John Walker (NZL)	3:39.17
1980	Sebastian Coe (GBR)	3:38.40
1984	Sebastian Coe (GBR)	3:32.53
1988	Peter Rono (KEN)	3:35.96
1992	Fermin Cacho Ruiz (ESP)	3:40.12
1996	Noureddine Morceli (ALG)	3:35.78
2000	Noah Ngeny (KEN)	3:32.07
2004	Hicham El Guerrouj (MAR)	3:34.18

5,000 METERS — MIN:SEC
1912	Hannes Kolehmainen (FIN)	14:36.6
1920	Joseph Guillemot (FRA)	14:55.6
1924	Paavo Nurmi (FIN)	14:31.2
1928	Vilho Ritola (FIN)	14:38.0
1932	Lauri Lehtinen (FIN)	14:30.0
1936	Gunnar Höckert (FIN)	14:22.2
1948	Gaston Reiff (BEL)	14:17.6
1952	Emil Zatopek (TCH)	14:06.6
1956	Vladimir Kuts (URS)	13:39.6
1960	Murray Halberg (NZL)	13:43.4
1964	Robert Keyser Schul (USA)	13:48.8
1968	Mohamed Gammoudi (TUN)	14:05.0
1972	Lasse Viren (FIN)	13:26.4
1976	Lasse Viren (FIN)	13:24.76
1980	Miruts Yifter (ETH)	13:21.00
1984	Said Aouita (MAR)	13:05.59
1988	John Ngugi (KEN)	13:11.70
1992	Dieter Baumann (GER)	13:12.52
1996	Venuste Niyongabo (BDI)	13:07.97
2000	Million Wolde (ETH)	13:35.49
2004	Hicham El Guerrouj (MAR)	13:14.39

5 MILES — MIN:SEC
1908	Emil Voigt (GBR)	25:11.2

10,000 METERS — MIN:SEC
1912	Hannes Kolehmainen (FIN)	31:20.8
1920	Paavo Nurmi (FIN)	31:45.8
1924	Vilho Ritola (FIN)	30:23.2
1928	Paavo Nurmi (FIN)	30:18.8
1932	Janusz Kusocinski (POL)	30:11.4
1936	Ilmari Salminen (FIN)	30:15.4
1948	Emil Zatopek (TCH)	29:59.6
1952	Emil Zatopek (TCH)	29:17.0
1956	Vladimir Kuts (URS)	28:45.6
1960	Pyotr Bolotnikov (URS)	28:32.2
1964	William Mills (USA)	28:24.4
1968	Nabiba Temu (KEN)	29:27.4
1972	Lasse Viren (FIN)	27:38.4
1976	Lasse Viren (FIN)	27:40.38
1980	Miruts Yifter (ETH)	27:42.70
1984	Alberto Cova (ITA)	27:47.54
1988	Brahim Boutaib (MAR)	27:21.46
1992	Khalid Skah (MAR)	27:46.70
1996	Haile Gebrselassie (ETH)	27:07.34
2000	Haile Gebrselassie (ETH)	27:18.20
2004	Kenenisa Bekele (ETH)	27:05.10

Summer Olympic Games Champions (continued)

Athletics (track-and-field) (men) (continued)

MARATHON

Year	Champion	HR:MIN:SEC
1896	Spiridon Louis (GRE)	2:58:50.0
1900	Michel Theato (FRA)	2:59:45.0
1904	Thomas Hicks (USA)	3:28:53.0
1908	John Hayes (USA)	2:55:18.4
1912	Kenneth McArthur (RSA)	2:36:54.8
1920	Hannes Kolehmainen (FIN)	2:32:35.8
1924	Albin Stenroos (FIN)	2:41:22.6
1928	Boughèra El Ouafi (FRA)	2:32:57.0
1932	Juan Carlos Zabala (ARG)	2:31:36.0
1936	Kitei Son (JPN)	2:29:19.2
1948	Delfo Cabrera (ARG)	2:34:51.6
1952	Emil Zatopek (TCH)	2:23:03.2
1956	Alain Mimoun-O-Kacha (FRA)	2:25:00.0
1960	Abebe Bikila (ETH)	2:15:16.2
1964	Abebe Bikila (ETH)	2:12:11.2
1968	Mamo Wolde (ETH)	2:20:26.4
1972	Frank Shorter (USA)	2:12:19.8
1976	Waldemar Cierpinski (GDR)	2:09:55.0
1980	Waldemar Cierpinski (GDR)	2:11:03.0
1984	Carlos Lopes (POR)	2:09:21.0
1988	Gelindo Bordin (ITA)	2:10:32.0
1992	Hwang Young-Cho (KOR)	2:13:23.0
1996	Josia Thugwane (RSA)	2:12:36.0
2000	Gezahgne Abera (ETH)	2:10:11.0
2004	Stefano Baldini (ITA)	2:10.55.0

110-METER HURDLES

Year	Champion	SEC
1896[2]	Thomas Curtis (USA)	17.6
1900	Alvin Kraenzlein (USA)	15.4
1904	Frederick Schule (USA)	16.0
1908	Forrest Smithson (USA)	15.0
1912	Frederick Kelly (USA)	15.1
1920	Earl Thomson (CAN)	14.8
1924	Daniel Kinsey (USA)	15.0
1928	Sydney Atkinson (RSA)	14.8
1932	George Saling (USA)	14.6
1936	Forrest Towns (USA)	14.2
1948	William Porter (USA)	13.9
1952	Harrison Dillard (USA)	13.7
1956	Lee Calhoun (USA)	13.5
1960	Lee Calhoun (USA)	13.8
1964	Hayes Wendell Jones (USA)	13.6
1968	Willie Davenport (USA)	13.3
1972	Rodney Milburn (USA)	13.24
1976	Guy Drut (FRA)	13.30
1980	Thomas Munkelt (GDR)	13.39
1984	Roger Kingdom (USA)	13.20
1988	Roger Kingdom (USA)	12.98
1992	Mark McKoy (CAN)	13.12
1996	Allen Johnson (USA)	12.95
2000	Anier Garcia (CUB)	13.00
2004	Liu Xiang (CHN)	12.91

200-METER HURDLES

Year	Champion	SEC
1900	Alvin Kraenzlein (USA)	25.4
1904	Harry Hillman (USA)	24.6

400-METER HURDLES

Year	Champion	SEC
1900	Walter Tewksbury (USA)	57.6
1904[3]	Harry Hillman (USA)	53.0
1908	Charles Bacon (USA)	55.0
1920	Frank Loomis (USA)	54.0
1924	Frederick Morgan Taylor (USA)	52.6
1928	David George Burghley (GBR)	53.4
1932	Robert Tisdall (IRE)	51.7
1936	Glenn Hardin (USA)	52.4
1948	Roy Cochran (USA)	51.1

Athletics (track-and-field) (men) (continued)

400-METER HURDLES

Year	Champion	SEC
1952	Charles Moore (USA)	50.8
1956	Glenn Davis (USA)	50.1
1960	Glenn Davis (USA)	49.3
1964	Warren Cawley (USA)	49.6
1968	David Hemery (GBR)	48.1
1972	John Akii-Bua (UGA)	47.82
1976	Edwin Moses (USA)	47.64
1980	Volker Beck (GDR)	48.70
1984	Edwin Moses (USA)	47.75
1988	Andre Phillips (USA)	47.19
1992	Kevin Young (USA)	46.78
1996	Derrick Adkins (USA)	47.54
2000	Angelo Taylor (USA)	47.50
2004	Felix Sánchez (DOM)	47.63

2,500-METER STEEPLECHASE

Year	Champion	MIN:SEC
1900	George Orton (USA)	7:34.4

2,590-METER STEEPLECHASE

Year	Champion	MIN:SEC
1904	James Lightbody (USA)	7:39.6

3,000-METER STEEPLECHASE

Year	Champion	MIN:SEC
1920	Percy Hodge (GBR)	10:00.4
1924	Vilho Ritola (FIN)	9:33.6
1928	Toivo Loukola (FIN)	9:21.8
1932	Volmari Iso-Hollo (FIN)	10:33.4[4]
1936	Volmari Iso-Hollo (FIN)	9:03.8
1948	Thore Sjöstrand (SWE)	9:04.6
1952	Horace Ashenfelter (USA)	8:45.4
1956	Christopher Brasher (GBR)	8:41.2
1960	Zdislaw Krzyszkowiak (POL)	8:34.2
1964	Gaston Roelants (BEL)	8:30.8
1968	Amos Biwott (KEN)	8:51.0
1972	Kipchoge Keino (KEN)	8:23.6
1976	Anders Gärderud (SWE)	8:08.02
1980	Bronislaw Malinowski (POL)	8:09.70
1984	Julius Korir (KEN)	8:11.80
1988	Julius Kariuki (KEN)	8:05.51
1992	Mathew Birir (KEN)	8:08.84
1996	Joseph Keter (KEN)	8:07.12
2000	Reuben Kosgei (KEN)	8:21.43
2004	Ezekiel Kemboi (KEN)	8:05.81

3,200-METER STEEPLECHASE

Year	Champion	MIN:SEC
1908	Arthur Russell (GBR)	10:47.8

3,000 METERS (TEAM) (TEAM/INDIVIDUAL WINNER)

Year	Champion	MIN:SEC
1912	United States/Tell Berna	8:44.6
1920	United States/Horace Brown	8:45.4
1924	Finland/Paavo Nurmi	8:32

3 MILES (TEAM) (TEAM/INDIVIDUAL WINNER)

Year	Champion	MIN:SEC
1908	Great Britain/Joseph Deakin	14:39.6

5,000 METERS (TEAM) (TEAM/INDIVIDUAL WINNER)

Year	Champion	MIN:SEC
1900	Great Britain-Australia/Charles Bennett	15:20

Summer Olympic Games Champions (continued)

Athletics (track-and-field) (men) (continued)

4 MILES (TEAM) (TEAM/INDIVIDUAL WINNER)		MIN:SEC
1904	United States/Arthur Newton (USA)	21:17.8

4 × 100 METER RELAY		SEC
1912	Great Britain	42.4
1920	United States	42.2
1924	United States	41.0
1928	United States	41.0
1932	United States	40.0
1936	United States	39.8
1948	United States	40.6
1952	United States	40.1
1956	United States	39.5
1960	Germany	39.5
1964	United States	39.0
1968	United States	38.2
1972	United States	38.19
1976	United States	38.33
1980	USSR	38.26
1984	United States	37.83
1988	USSR	38.19
1992	United States	37.40
1996	Canada	37.69
2000	United States	37.61
2004	Great Britain	38.07

4 × 400 METER RELAY		MIN:SEC
1912	United States	3:16.6
1920	Great Britain	3:22.2
1924	United States	3:16.0
1928	United States	3:14.2
1932	United States	3:08.2
1936	Great Britain	3:09.0
1948	United States	3:10.4
1952	Jamaica	3:03.9
1956	United States	3:04.8
1960	United States	3:02.2
1964	United States	3:00.7
1968	United States	2:56.1
1972	Kenya	2:59.8
1976	United States	2:58.65
1980	USSR	3:01.1
1984	United States	2:57.91
1988	United States	2:56.16
1992	United States	2:55.74
1996	United States	2:55.99
2000	United States	2:56.35
2004	United States	2:55.91

1,600-METER RELAY (200 × 200 × 400 × 800 METERS)		MIN:SEC
1908	United States	3:29.4

8,000 M CROSS-COUNTRY		MIN:SEC
1920	Paavo Nurmi (FIN)	27:15

10,000 M CROSS-COUNTRY		MIN:SEC
1924	Paavo Nurmi (FIN)	32:54.8

12,000 M CROSS-COUNTRY		MIN:SEC
1912	Hannes Kolehmainen (FIN)	45:11.6

3,000-METER WALK		MIN:SEC
1920	Ugo Frigerio (ITA)	13:14.2

3,500-METER WALK		MIN:SEC
1908	George Larner (GBR)	14:55

Athletics (track-and-field) (men) (continued)

10,000-METER WALK		MIN:SEC
1912	George Goulding (CAN)	46:28.4
1920	Ugo Frigerio (ITA)	48:06.2
1924	Ugo Frigerio (ITA)	47:49
1948	John Mikaelsson (SWE)	45:13.2
1952	John Mikaelsson (SWE)	45:02.8

10-MILE WALK		HR:MIN:SEC
1908	George Larner (GBR)	1:15:57.4

20,000-METER WALK		HR:MIN:SEC
1956	Leonid Spirin (URS)	1:31:27.4
1960	Vladimir Golubnichy (URS)	1:34:07.2
1964	Kenneth Matthews (GBR)	1:29:34.0
1968	Vladimir Golubnichy (URS)	1:33:58.4
1972	Peter Frenkel (GDR)	1:26:42.6
1976	Daniel Bautista (MEX)	1:24:40.6
1980	Maurizio Damilano (ITA)	1:23:35.5
1984	Ernesto Canto (MEX)	1:23:13.0
1988	Jozef Pribilinec (TCH)	1:19:57.0
1992	Daniel Plaza Montero (ESP)	1:21:45.0
1996	Jefferson Pérez (ECU)	1:20:07.0
2000	Robert Korzeniowski (POL)	1:18:59.0
2004	Ivano Brugnetti (ITA)	1:19.40.0

50,000-METER WALK		HR:MIN:SEC
1932	Thomas Green (GBR)	4:50:10.0
1936	Harold Whitlock (GBR)	4:30:41.4
1948	John Ljunggren (SWE)	4:41:52.0
1952	Giuseppe Dordoni (ITA)	4:28:07.8
1956	Norman Read (NZL)	4:30:42.8
1960	Donald Thompson (GBR)	4:25:30.0
1964	Abdon Pamich (ITA)	4:11:12.4
1968	Christophe Höhne (GDR)	4:20:13.6
1972	Bernd Kannenberg (FRG)	3:56:11.6
1980	Hartwig Gauder (GDR)	3:49:24.0
1984	Raúl Gonzáles (MEX)	3:47:26.0
1988	Vyacheslav Ivanenko (URS)	3:38:29.0
1992	Andrey Perlov (UNT)	3:50:13.0
1996	Robert Korzeniowski (POL)	3:43:03.0
2000	Robert Korzeniowski (POL)	3:42:22.0
2004	Robert Korzeniowski (POL)	3:38:46.0

HIGH JUMP		METERS
1896	Ellery Clark (USA)	1.81
1900	Irving Baxter (USA)	1.90
1904	Samuel Jones (USA)	1.80
1908	Harry Porter (USA)	1.90
1912	Alma Richards (USA)	1.93
1920	Richmond Landon (USA)	1.93
1924	Harold Osborn (USA)	1.98
1928	Robert King (USA)	1.94
1932	Duncan McNaughton (CAN)	1.97
1936	Cornelius Johnson (USA)	2.03
1948	John Winter (AUS)	1.98
1952	Walter Davis (USA)	2.04
1956	Charles Dumas (USA)	2.12
1960	Robert Shavlakadze (URS)	2.16
1964	Valery Brumel (URS)	2.18
1968	Richard Fosbury (USA)	2.24
1972	Yury Tarmak (URS)	2.23
1976	Jacek Wszola (POL)	2.25
1980	Gerd Wessig (GDR)	2.36
1984	Dietmar Mögenburg (FRG)	2.35
1988	Gennady Avdeyenko (URS)	2.38
1992	Javier Sotomayor (CUB)	2.34

Summer Olympic Games Champions (continued)

Athletics (track-and-field) (men) (continued)

HIGH JUMP		METERS
1996	Charles Austin (USA)	2.39
2000	Sergey Klyugin (RUS)	2.35
2004	Stefan Holm (SWE)	2.36

STANDING HIGH JUMP		METERS
1900	Ray Ewry (USA)	1.65
1904	Ray Ewry (USA)	1.6
1908	Ray Ewry (USA)	1.57
1912	Platt Adams (USA)	1.63

POLE VAULT		METERS
1896	William Welles Hoyt (USA)	3.30
1900	Irving Baxter (USA)	3.30
1904	Charles Dvorak (USA)	3.50
1908	Edward Cooke (USA); Alfred Gilbert (USA) (tied)	3.71
1912	Harry Babcock (USA)	3.95
1920	Frank Foss (USA)	4.09
1924	Lee Barnes (USA)	3.95
1928	Sabin Carr (USA)	4.20
1932	William Miller (USA)	4.31
1936	Earle Meadows (USA)	4.35
1948	Owen Guinn Smith (USA)	4.30
1952	Robert Richards (USA)	4.55
1956	Robert Richards (USA)	4.56
1960	Donald Bragg (USA)	4.70
1964	Fred Hansen (USA)	5.10
1968	Robert Seagren (USA)	5.40
1972	Wolfgang Nordwig (GDR)	5.50
1976	Tadeusz Slusarski (POL)	5.50
1980	Wladyslaw Kozakiewicz (POL)	5.78
1984	Pierre Quinon (FRA)	5.75
1988	Sergey Bubka (URS)	5.90
1992	Maksim Tarasov (UNT)	5.80
1996	Jean Galfione (FRA)	5.92
2000	Nick Hysong (USA)	5.90
2004	Timothy Mack (USA)	5.95

LONG JUMP		METERS
1896	Ellery Clark (USA)	6.35
1900	Alvin Kraenzlein (USA)	7.18
1904	Meyer Prinstein (USA)	7.34
1908	Francis Irons (USA)	7.48
1912	Albert Gutterson (USA)	7.60
1920	William Pettersson (SWE)	7.15
1924	William de Hart-Hubbard (USA)	7.44
1928	Edward Hamm (USA)	7.73
1932	Edward Gordon (USA)	7.64
1936	Jesse Owens (USA)	8.06
1948	Willie Steele (USA)	7.82
1952	Jerome Biffle (USA)	7.57
1956	Gregory Bell (USA)	7.83
1960	Ralph Boston (USA)	8.12
1964	Lynn Davies (GBR)	8.07
1968	Robert Beamon (USA)	8.90
1972	Randy Williams (USA)	8.24
1976	Arnie Robinson (USA)	8.35
1980	Lutz Dombrowski (GDR)	8.54
1984	Carl Lewis (USA)	8.54
1988	Carl Lewis (USA)	8.72
1992	Carl Lewis (USA)	8.67
1996	Carl Lewis (USA)	8.50
2000	Ivan Pedroso (CUB)	8.55
2004	Dwight Phillips (USA)	8.59

Athletics (track-and-field) (men) (continued)

STANDING LONG JUMP		METERS
1900	Ray Ewry (USA)	3.21
1904	Ray Ewry (USA)	3.47
1908	Ray Ewry (USA)	3.33
1912	Constantinos Tsiklitiras (GRE)	3.37

TRIPLE JUMP		METERS
1896	James Connolly (USA)	13.71
1900	Myer Prinstein (USA)	14.47
1904	Myer Prinstein (USA)	14.35
1908	Timothy Ahearne (GBR)	14.91
1912	Gustaf Lindblom (SWE)	14.76
1920	Vilho Tuulos (FIN)	14.50
1924	Anthony Winter (AUS)	15.53
1928	Mikio Oda (JPN)	15.21
1932	Chuhei Nambu (JPN)	15.72
1936	Naoto Tajima (JPN)	16.00
1948	Arne Åhman (SWE)	15.40
1952	Adhemar Ferreira da Silva (BRA)	16.22
1956	Adhemar Ferreira da Silva (BRA)	16.35
1960	Josef Szmidt (POL)	16.81
1964	Josef Szmidt (POL)	16.85
1968	Viktor Saneyev (URS)	17.39
1972	Viktor Saneyev (URS)	17.35
1976	Viktor Saneyev (URS)	17.29
1980	Jaak Uudmae (URS)	17.35
1984	Al Joyner (USA)	17.26
1988	Khristo Markov (BUL)	17.61
1992	Michael Conley (USA)	17.63
1996	Kenny Harrison (USA)	18.09
2000	Jonathan Edwards (GBR)	17.71
2004	Christian Olsson (SWE)	17.79

STANDING TRIPLE JUMP		METERS
1900	Ray Ewry (USA)	10.58
1904	Ray Ewry (USA)	10.54

SHOT PUT		METERS
1896	Robert Garrett (USA)	11.22
1900	Richard Sheldon (USA)	14.10
1904	Ralph Rose (USA)	14.81
1908	Ralph Rose (USA)	14.21
1912	Patrick McDonald (USA)	15.34
1920	Frans Pörhölä (FIN)	14.81
1924	Lemuel Clarence Houser (USA)	14.99
1928	John Kuck (USA)	15.87
1932	Leo Sexton (USA)	16.00
1936	Hans Woellke (GER)	16.20
1948	Wilbur Thompson (USA)	17.12
1952	William Parry O'Brien (USA)	17.41
1956	William Parry O'Brien (USA)	18.57
1960	William Nieder (USA)	19.68
1964	Dallas Long (USA)	20.33
1968	Randy Matson (USA)	20.54
1972	Wladislaw Komar (POL)	21.18
1976	Udo Beyer (GDR)	21.05
1980	Vladimir Kiselyov (URS)	21.35
1984	Alessandro Andrei (ITA)	21.26
1988	Ulf Timmermann (GDR)	22.47
1992	Michael Stulce (USA)	21.70
1996	Randy Barnes (USA)	21.62
2000	Arsi Harju (FIN)	21.29
2004	Yury Bilonog (UKR)	21.16

SHOT PUT (TWO HANDS)		METERS
1912	Ralph Rose (USA)	27.7

Summer Olympic Games Champions (continued)

Athletics (track-and-field) (men) (continued)

DISCUS THROW		METERS
1896	Robert Garrett (USA)	29.15
1900	Rezso Bauer (HUN)	36.04
1904	Martin Sheridan (USA)	39.28
1908	Martin Sheridan (USA)	40.89
1912	Armas Taipale (FIN)	45.21
1920	Elmer Niklander (FIN)	44.68
1924	Lemuel Clarence Houser (USA)	46.15
1928	Lemuel Clarence Houser (USA)	47.32
1932	John Anderson (USA)	49.49
1936	Kenneth Carpenter (USA)	50.48
1948	Adolfo Consolini (ITA)	52.78
1952	Sim Iness (USA)	55.03
1956	Alfred Oerter (USA)	56.36
1960	Alfred Oerter (USA)	59.18
1964	Alfred Oerter (USA)	61.00
1968	Alfred Oerter (USA)	64.78
1972	Ludvig Danek (TCH)	64.40
1976	Mac Wilkins (USA)	67.50
1980	Viktor Rashchupkin (URS)	66.64
1984	Rolf Danneberg (FRG)	66.60
1988	Jürgen Schult (GDR)	68.82
1992	Romas Ubartas (LTU)	65.12
1996	Lars Riedel (GER)	69.40
2000	Virgilijus Alekna (LTU)	69.30
2004	Virgilijus Alekna (LTU)	69.89

DISCUS (GREEK STYLE)		METERS
1908	Martin Sheridan (USA)	37.99

DISCUS (TWO HANDS)		METERS
1912	Armas Taipale (FIN)	82.86

HAMMER THROW		METERS
1900	John Flanagan (USA)	49.73
1904	John Flanagan (USA)	51.23
1908	John Flanagan (USA)	51.92
1912	Matthew McGrath (USA)	54.74
1920	Patrick Ryan (USA)	52.87
1924	Frederick Tootell (USA)	53.30
1928	Patrick O'Callaghan (IRE)	51.39
1932	Patrick O'Callaghan (IRE)	53.92
1936	Karl Hein (GER)	56.49
1948	Imre Nemeth (HUN)	56.07
1952	Jozsef Csermak (HUN)	60.34
1956	Harold Connolly (USA)	63.19
1960	Vasily Rudenkov (URS)	67.10
1964	Romuald Klim (URS)	69.74
1968	Gyula Zsivotzky (HUN)	73.36
1972	Anatoly Bondarchuk (URS)	75.50
1976	Yury Sedykh (URS)	77.52
1980	Yury Sedykh (URS)	81.80
1984	Juha Tiainen (FIN)	78.08
1988	Sergey Litvinov (URS)	84.80
1992	Andrey Abduvaliyev (UNT)	82.53
1996	Balazs Kiss (HUN)	81.24
2000	Szymon Ziolkowski (POL)	80.02
2004	Koji Murofushi (JPN)	82.91

JAVELIN THROW		METERS
1908	Eric Lemming (SWE)	54.83
1912	Eric Lemming (SWE)	60.64
1920	Jonni Myyrä (FIN)	65.78
1924	Jonni Myyrä (FIN)	62.96
1928	Erik Lundkvist (SWE)	66.60
1932	Matti Järvinen (FIN)	72.71
1936	Gerhard Stöck (GER)	71.84
1948	Kai Rautavaara (FIN)	69.77

Athletics (track-and-field) (men) (continued)

JAVELIN THROW		METERS
1952	Cy Young (USA)	73.78
1956	Egil Danielson (NOR)	85.71
1960	Viktor Tsybulenko (URS)	84.64
1964	Pauli Nevala (FIN)	82.66
1968	Janis Lusis (URS)	90.10
1972	Klaus Wolfermann (FRG)	90.48
1976	Miklos Nemeth (HUN)	94.58
1980	Dainis Kula (URS)	91.20
1984	Arto Härkönen (FIN)	86.76
1988	Tapio Korjus (FIN)	84.28
1992	Jan Zelezny (TCH)	89.66
1996	Jan Zelezny (CZE)	88.16
2000	Jan Zelezny (CZE)	90.17
2004	Andreas Thorkildsen (NOR)	86.50

JAVELIN (FREESTYLE)		METERS
1908	Eric Lemming (SWE)	54.45

JAVELIN (TWO HANDS)		METERS
1912	Juho Saaristo (FIN)	109.42

THROWING THE 56 LB WEIGHT		METERS
1904	Étienne Desmarteau (CAN)	10.46
1920	Patrick McDonald (USA)	11.26

TUG-OF-WAR

1900	Sweden-Denmark
1904	United States
1908	Great Britain
1912	Sweden
1920	Great Britain

TRIATHLON (LONG JUMP/SHOT PUT/100 YARDS)

1904	Max Emmerich (USA)

PENTATHLON

1912	Jim Thorpe (USA)[5]; Ferdinand Bie (NOR) (cowinners)
1920	Eero Lehtonen (FIN)
1924	Eero Lehtonen (FIN)

DECATHLON

1904	Thomas Kiely (IRL)
1912	Jim Thorpe (USA)[5]; Hugo Wieslander (SWE) (cowinners)
1920	Helge Lövland (NOR)
1924	Harold Osborn (USA)
1928	Paavo Yrjölä (FIN)
1932	James Bausch (USA)
1936	Glenn Morris (USA)
1948	Robert Mathias (USA)
1952	Robert Mathias (USA)
1956	Milton Campbell (USA)
1960	Rafer Johnson (USA)
1964	Willi Holdorf (GER)
1968	William Toomey (USA)
1972	Nikolay Avilov (URS)
1976	Bruce Jenner (USA)
1980	Daley Thompson (GBR)
1984	Daley Thompson (GBR)
1988	Christian Schenk (GDR)
1992	Robert Zmelik (TCH)
1996	Dan O'Brien (USA)
2000	Erki Nool (EST)
2004	Roman Sebrle (CZE)

Summer Olympic Games Champions (continued)

Athletics (track-and-field) (women)

100 METERS		SEC
1928	Elizabeth Robinson (USA)	12.2
1932	Stanislawa Walasiewicz (POL)	11.9
1936	Helen Stephens (USA)	11.5
1948	Francina Blankers-Koen (NED)	11.9
1952	Marjorie Jackson (AUS)	11.5
1956	Elizabeth Cuthbert (AUS)	11.5
1960	Wilma Rudolph (USA)	11.0
1964	Wyomia Tyus (USA)	11.4
1968	Wyomia Tyus (USA)	11.0
1972	Renate Stecher (GDR)	11.07
1976	Annegret Richter (FRG)	11.08
1980	Lyudmila Kondratyeva (URS)	11.06
1984	Evelyn Ashford (USA)	10.97
1988	Florence Griffith Joyner (USA)	10.54
1992	Gail Devers (USA)	10.82
1996	Gail Devers (USA)	10.94
2000	Marion Jones (USA)	10.75
2004	Yuliya Nesterenko (BLR)	10.93

200 METERS		SEC
1948	Francina Blankers-Koen (NED)	24.4
1952	Marjorie Jackson (AUS)	23.7
1956	Elizabeth Cuthbert (AUS)	23.4
1960	Wilma Rudolph (USA)	24.0
1964	Edith Marie McGuire (USA)	23.0
1968	Irena Szewinska (POL)	22.5
1972	Renate Stecher (GDR)	22.40
1976	Bärbel Eckert (GDR)	22.37
1980	Bärbel Eckert-Wöckel (GDR)	22.03
1984	Valerie Brisco-Hooks (USA)	21.81
1988	Florence Griffith Joyner (USA)	21.34
1992	Gwen Torrence (USA)	21.81
1996	Marie-Jose Perec (FRA)	22.12
2000	Marion Jones (USA)	21.84
2004	Veronica Campbell (JAM)	22.05

400 METERS		SEC
1964	Elizabeth Cuthbert (AUS)	52.0
1968	Colette Besson (FRA)	52.0
1972	Monika Zehrt (GDR)	51.08
1976	Irena Szewinska (POL)	49.29
1980	Marita Koch (GDR)	48.88
1984	Valerie Brisco-Hooks (USA)	48.83
1988	Olga Bryzgina (URS)	48.65
1992	Marie-Jose Perec (FRA)	48.83
1996	Marie-Jose Perec (FRA)	48.25
2000	Cathy Freeman (AUS)	49.11
2004	Tonique Williams-Darling (BAH)	49.41

800 METERS		MIN:SEC
1928	Lina Radke-Batschauer (GER)	2:16.8
1960	Lyudmila Lysenko-Shevtsova (URS)	2:04.3
1964	Ann Packer (GBR)	2:01.1
1968	Madeline Manning (USA)	2:00.9
1972	Hildegard Falck (FRG)	1:58.6
1976	Tatyana Kazankina (URS)	1:54.94
1980	Nadezhda Olizarenko (URS)	1:53.50
1984	Doina Melinte (ROM)	1:57.6
1988	Sigrun Wodars (GDR)	1:56.10
1992	Ellen van Langen (NED)	1:55.54
1996	Svetlana Masterkova (RUS)	1:57.73
2000	Maria Mutola (MOZ)	1:56.15
2004	Kelly Holmes (GBR)	1:56.38

Athletics (track-and-field) (women) (continued)

1,500 METERS		MIN:SEC
1972	Lyudmila Bragina (URS)	4:01.4
1976	Tatyana Kazankina (URS)	4:05.48
1980	Tatyana Kazankina (URS)	3:56.6
1984	Gabriella Dorio (ITA)	4:03.25
1988	Paula Ivan (ROM)	3:53.96
1992	Hassiba Boulmerka (ALG)	3:55.30
1996	Svetlana Masterkova (RUS)	4:00.83
2000	Nouria Merah-Benida (ALG)	4:05.10
2004	Kelly Holmes (GBR)	3:57.90

3,000 METERS		MIN:SEC
1984	Maricica Puica (ROM)	8:35.96
1988	Tatyana Samolenko (URS)	8:26.53
1992	Yelena Romanova (UNT)	8:46.04

5,000 METERS		MIN:SEC
1996	Wang Jungxia (CHN)	14:59.88
2000	Gabriela Szabo (ROM)	14:40.79
2004	Meseret Defar (ETH)	14:45.65

10,000 METERS		MIN:SEC
1988	Olga Bondarenko (URS)	31:05.21
1992	Derartu Tulu (ETH)	31:06.02
1996	Fernanda Ribeiro (POR)	31:01.63
2000	Derartu Tulu (ETH)	30:17.49
2004	Xing Huina (CHN)	30:24.36

MARATHON		HR:MIN:SEC
1984	Joan Benoit (USA)	2:24:52
1988	Rosa Mota (POR)	2:25:40
1992	Valentina Yegorova (UNT)	2:32:41
1996	Fatuma Roba (ETH)	2:26:05
2000	Naoko Takahashi (JPN)	2:23:14
2004	Mizuki Noguchi (JPN)	2:26:20

80-METER HURDLES (100 METERS FROM 1972)		SEC
1932	Mildred "Babe" Didrikson (USA)	11.7
1936	Trebisonda Valla (ITA)	11.7
1948	Francina Blankers-Koen (NED)	11.2
1952	Shirley Strickland de La Hunty (AUS)	10.9
1956	Shirley Strickland de La Hunty (AUS)	10.7
1960	Irina Press (URS)	10.8
1964	Karin Balzer (GER)	10.5
1968	Maureen Caird (AUS)	10.3
1972	Annelie Ehrhardt (GDR)	12.59
1976	Johanna Schaller (GDR)	12.77
1980	Vera Komisova (URS)	12.56
1984	Benita Fitzgerald-Brown (USA)	12.84
1988	Iordanka Donkova (BUL)	12.38
1992	Paraskevi Patoulidou (GRE)	12.64
1996	Ludmila Engquist (SWE)	12.58
2000	Olga Shishigina (KAZ)	12.65
2004	Joanna Hayes (USA)	12.37

400-METER HURDLES		SEC
1984	Nawal el Moutawakel (MAR)	54.61
1988	Debra Flintoff-King (AUS)	53.17
1992	Sally Gunnell (GBR)	53.23
1996	Deon Hemmings (JAM)	52.82
2000	Irina Privalova (RUS)	53.02
2004	Fani Halkia (GRE)	52.82

Summer Olympic Games Champions (continued)

Athletics (track-and-field) (women) (continued)

4 × 100-METER RELAY		SEC
1928	Canada	48.4
1932	United States	47.0
1936	United States	46.9
1948	The Netherlands	47.5
1952	United States	45.9
1956	Australia	44.5
1960	United States	44.5
1964	Poland	43.6
1968	United States	42.8
1972	West Germany	42.81
1976	East Germany	42.55
1980	East Germany	41.60
1984	United States	41.65
1988	United States	41.98
1992	United States	42.11
1996	United States	41.95
2000	The Bahamas	41.95
2004	Jamaica	41.73

4 × 400-METER RELAY		MIN:SEC
1972	East Germany	3:23.0
1976	East Germany	3:19.23
1980	USSR	3:20.2
1984	United States	3:18.29
1988	USSR	3:15.18
1992	Unified Team	3:20.20
1996	United States	3:20.91
2000	United States	3:22.62
2004	United States	3:19.01

10,000-METER WALK		MIN:SEC
1992	Chen Yueling (CHN)	44:32
1996	Yelena Nikolayeva (RUS)	41:49

20,000-METER WALK		MIN:SEC
2000	Wang Liping (CHN)	1:29.05
2004	Athanasia Tsoumeleka (GRE)	1:29:12

HIGH JUMP		METERS
1928	Ethel Catherwood (CAN)	1.59
1932	Jean Shiley (USA)	1.66
1936	Ibolya Csak (HUN)	1.60
1948	Alice Coachman (USA)	1.68
1952	Esther Brand (RSA)	1.67
1956	Mildred Louise McDaniel (USA)	1.76
1960	Iolanda Balas (ROM)	1.85
1964	Iolanda Balas (ROM)	1.90
1968	Miloslava Rezkova (TCH)	1.82
1972	Ulrike Meyfarth (FRG)	1.92
1976	Rosemarie Ackermann (GDR)	1.93
1980	Sara Simeoni (ITA)	1.97
1984	Ulrike Meyfarth (FRG)	2.02
1988	Louise Ritter (USA)	2.03
1992	Heike Henkel (GER)	2.02
1996	Stefka Kostadinova (BUL)	2.05
2000	Yelena Yelesina (RUS)	2.01
2004	Yelena Slesarenko (RUS)	2.06

POLE VAULT		METERS
2000	Stacy Dragila (USA)	4.60
2004	Yelena Isinbayeva (RUS)	4.91

Athletics (track-and-field) (women) (continued)

LONG JUMP		METERS
1948	Olga Gyarmati (HUN)	5.69
1952	Yvette Williams (NZL)	6.24
1956	Elzbieta Krzesinska (POL)	6.35
1960	Vera Krepkina (URS)	6.37
1964	Mary Rand (GBR)	6.76
1968	Viorica Viscopoleanu (ROM)	6.82
1972	Heidemarie Rosendahl (FRG)	6.78
1976	Angela Voigt (GDR)	6.72
1980	Tatyana Kolpakova (URS)	7.06
1984	Anisoara Stanciu (ROM)	6.96
1988	Jackie Joyner-Kersee (USA)	7.40
1992	Heike Drechsler (GER)	7.14
1996	Chioma Ajunwa (NGR)	7.12
2000	Heike Drechsler (GER)	6.99
2004	Tatyana Lebedeva (RUS)	7.07

TRIPLE JUMP		METERS
1996	Inessa Kravets (UKR)	15.33
2000	Tereza Marinova (BUL)	15.20
2004	Françoise Mbango Etone (CMR)	15.30

SHOT PUT		METERS
1948	Micheline Ostermeyer (FRA)	13.75
1952	Galina Zybina (URS)	15.28
1956	Tamara Tyshkevich (URS)	16.59
1960	Tamara Press (URS)	17.32
1964	Tamara Press (URS)	18.14
1968	Margitta Gummel (GDR)	19.61
1972	Nadezhda Chizhova (URS)	21.03
1976	Ivanka Khristova (BUL)	21.16
1980	Ilona Slupianek (GDR)	22.41
1984	Claudia Losch (FRG)	20.48
1988	Natalya Lisovskaya (URS)	22.24
1992	Svetlana Krivalyova (UNT)	21.06
1996	Astrid Kumbernuss (GER)	20.56
2000	Yanina Korolchik (BLR)	20.56
2004	Yumileidi Cumba (CUB)	19.59

DISCUS THROW		METERS
1928	Halina Konopacka (POL)	39.62
1932	Lillian Copeland (USA)	40.58
1936	Gisela Mauermayer (GER)	47.63
1948	Micheline Ostermeyer (FRA)	41.92
1952	Nina Romashkova (URS)	51.42
1956	Olga Fikotova (TCH)	53.69
1960	Nina Ponomaryova-Romashkova (URS)	55.10
1964	Tamara Press (URS)	57.27
1968	Lia Manoliu (ROM)	58.28
1972	Faina Melnik (URS)	66.62
1976	Evelin Schlaak (GDR)	69.00
1980	Evelin Schlaak Jahl (GDR)	69.96
1984	Ria Stalman (NED)	65.36
1988	Martina Hellmann (GDR)	72.30
1992	Maritza Marten (CUB)	70.06
1996	Ilke Wyludda (GER)	69.66
2000	Ellina Zvereva (BLR)	68.40
2004	Natalya Sadova (RUS)	67.02

HAMMER THROW		METERS
2000	Kamila Skolimowska (POL)	71.16
2004	Olga Kuzenkova (RUS)	75.02

Summer Olympic Games Champions (continued)

Athletics (track-and-field) (women) (continued)

JAVELIN THROW — METERS

Year	Champion	Meters
1932	Mildred "Babe" Didrikson (USA)	43.68
1936	Tilly Fleischer (GER)	45.18
1948	Hermine Bauma (AUT)	45.57
1952	Dana Zatopkova (TCH)	50.47
1956	Inese Jaunzeme (URS)	53.86
1960	Elvira Ozolina (URS)	55.98
1964	Mihaela Penes (ROM)	60.54
1968	Angela Nemeth (HUN)	60.36
1972	Ruth Fuchs (GDR)	63.88
1976	Ruth Fuchs (GDR)	65.94
1980	María Colón (CUB)	68.40
1984	Tessa Sanderson (GBR)	69.56
1988	Petra Felke (GDR)	74.68
1992	Silke Renk (GER)	68.34
1996	Heli Rantanen (FIN)	67.94
2000	Trine Hattestad (NOR)	68.91
2004	*Osleidys Menéndez (CUB)	71.53

PENTATHLON (HEPTATHLON FROM 1984)

1964	Irina Press (URS)
1968	Ingrid Becker (FRG)
1972	Mary Peters (GBR)
1976	Siegrun Siegl (GDR)
1980	Nadezhda Tkachenko (URS)
1984	Glynis Nunn (AUS)
1988	Jackie Joyner-Kersee (USA)
1992	Jackie Joyner-Kersee (USA)
1996	Ghada Shouaa (SYR)
2000	Denise Lewis (GBR)
2004	Carolina Klüft (SWE)

Badminton

MEN'S SINGLES

1992	Allan Budi Kusuma (INA)
1996	Poul-Erik Hoyer-Larsen (DEN)
2000	Ji Xinpeng (CHN)
2004	Taufik Hidayat (INA)

MEN'S DOUBLES

1992	South Korea
1996	Indonesia
2000	Indonesia
2004	South Korea

WOMEN'S SINGLES

1992	Susi Susanti (INA)
1996	Bang Soo-Hyun (KOR)
2000	Gong Zhichao (CHN)
2004	Zhang Ning (CHN)

WOMEN'S DOUBLES

1992	South Korea
1996	China
2000	China
2004	China

MIXED DOUBLES

1996	South Korea
2000	China
2004	China

Baseball

1992	Cuba
1996	Cuba
2000	United States
2004	Cuba

Basketball

MEN

1936	United States
1948	United States
1952	United States
1956	United States
1960	United States
1964	United States
1968	United States
1972	USSR
1976	United States
1980	Yugoslavia
1984	United States
1988	USSR
1992	United States
1996	United States
2000	United States
2004	Argentina

WOMEN

1976	USSR
1980	USSR
1984	United States
1988	United States
1992	Unified Team
1996	United States
2000	United States
2004	United States

Boxing

48 KG (105.6 LB)

1968	Francisco Rodríguez (VEN)
1972	Gyorgy Gedo (HUN)
1976	Jorge Hernández (CUB)
1980	Shamil Sabyrov (URS)
1984	Paul Gonzales (USA)
1988	Ivailo Khristov (BUL)
1992	Rogelio Marcelo (CUB)
1996	Daniel Petrov Bojilov (BUL)
2000	Brahim Asloum (FRA)
2004	Yan Bhartelemy Varela (CUB)

51 KG (112 LB)

1904	George Finnegan (USA)
1920	Frank di Genaro (USA)
1924	Fidel La Barba (USA)
1928	Antal Kocsis (HUN)
1932	Istvan Enekes (HUN)
1936	Willi Kaiser (GER)
1948	Pascual Pérez (ARG)
1952	Nate Brooks (USA)
1956	Terence Spinks (GBR)
1960	Gyula Torok (HUN)
1964	Fernando Atzori (ITA)
1968	Ricardo Delgado (MEX)
1972	Georgi Kostadinov (BUL)
1976	Leo Randolph (USA)
1980	Petar Lesov (BUL)
1984	Steven McCrory (USA)
1988	Kim Kwang Sun (KOR)
1992	Chol Choi Su (PRK)
1996	Maikro Romero (CUB)
2000	Wijan Ponlid (THA)
2004	Yuriorkis Gamboa Toledano (CUB)

Summer Olympic Games Champions (continued)

Boxing (continued)

54 KG (118.8 LB)

1904	Oliver Kirk (USA)
1908	Henry Thomas (GBR)
1920	Clarence Walker (RSA)
1924	William Smith (RSA)
1928	Vittorio Tamagnini (ITA)
1932	Horace Gwynne (CAN)
1936	Ulderico Sergo (ITA)
1948	Tibor Csik (HUN)
1952	Pentti Hämäläinen (FIN)
1956	Wolfgang Behrendt (GER)
1960	Oleg Grigoryev (URS)
1964	Takao Sakurai (JPN)
1968	Valery Sokolov (URS)
1972	Orlando Martínez (CUB)
1976	Gu Yong Jo (PRK)
1980	Juan Hernández (CUB)
1984	Maurizio Stecca (ITA)
1988	Kennedy McKinney (USA)
1992	Joel Casamayor (CUB)
1996	Istvan Kovacs (HUN)
2000	Guillermo Rigondeaux Ortiz (CUB)
2004	Guillermo Rigondeaux Ortiz (CUB)

57 KG (125.4 LB)

1904	Oliver Kirk (USA)
1908	Richard Gunn (GBR)
1920	Paul Fritsch (FRA)
1924	John Fields (USA)
1928	Lambertus van Kleveren (NED)
1932	Carmelo Robledo (ARG)
1936	Oscar Casanovas (ARG)
1948	Ernesto Formenti (ITA)
1952	Jan Zachara (TCH)
1956	Vladimir Safronov (URS)
1960	Francesco Musso (ITA)
1964	Stanislav Stepashkin (URS)
1968	Antonio Roldan (MEX)
1972	Boris Kuznetsov (URS)
1976	Angel Herrera (CUB)
1980	Rudi Fink (GDR)
1984	Meldrick Taylor (USA)
1988	Giovanni Parisi (ITA)
1992	Andreas Tews (GER)
1996	Somluck Kamsing (THA)
2000	Bekzat Sattarkhanov (KAZ)
2004	Aleksey Tishchenko (RUS)

60 KG (132 LB)

1904	Harry Spanger (USA)
1908	Frederick Grace (GBR)
1920	Samuel Mosberg (USA)
1924	Hans Nielsen (DEN)
1928	Carlo Orlandi (ITA)
1932	Lawrence Stevens (RSA)
1936	Imre Harangi (HUN)
1948	Gerald Dreyer (RSA)
1952	Aureliano Bolognesi (ITA)
1956	Richard McTaggart (GBR)
1960	Kazimierz Pazdzior (POL)
1964	Jozef Grudzien (POL)
1968	Ronnie Harris (USA)
1972	Jan Szczepanski (POL)
1976	Howard Davis (USA)
1980	Angel Herrera (CUB)
1984	Pernell Whitaker (USA)
1988	Andreas Zuelow (GDR)
1992	Oscar De La Hoya (USA)

Boxing (continued)

60 KG (132 LB)

1996	Hocine Soltani (ALG)
2000	Mario Kindelan (CUB)
2004	Mario César Kindelan Mesa (CUB)

64 KG (140.8 LB)

1952	Charles Adkins (USA)
1956	Vladimir Engibaryan (URS)
1960	Bohumil Nemecek (TCH)
1964	Jerzy Kulej (POL)
1968	Jerzy Kulej (POL)
1972	Ray Seales (USA)
1976	Ray Leonard (USA)
1980	Patrizio Oliva (ITA)
1984	Jerry Page (USA)
1988	Vyacheslav Yanovsky (URS)
1992	Héctor Vinent (CUB)
1996	Héctor Vinent (CUB)
2000	Mahamadkadyz Abdullayev (UZB)
2004	Manus Boonjumnong (THA)

69 KG (151.8 LB)

1904	Albert Young (USA)
1920	Julius Schneider (CAN)
1924	Jean Delarge (BEL)
1928	Edward Morgan (NZL)
1932	Edward Flynn (USA)
1936	Sten Suvio (FIN)
1948	Julius Torma (TCH)
1952	Zygmunt Chychla (POL)
1956	Nicolae Linca (ROM)
1960	Giovanni Benvenuti (ITA)
1964	Marian Kasprzyk (POL)
1968	Manfred Wolke (GDR)
1972	Emilio Correa (CUB)
1976	Jochen Bachfeld (GDR)
1980	Andres Aldama (CUB)
1984	Mark Breland (USA)
1988	Robert Wangila (KEN)
1992	Michael Carruth (IRL)
1996	Oleg Saytov (RUS)
2000	Oleg Saytov (RUS)
2004	Bakhtiyar Artayev (KAZ)

71 KG (156.2 LB)

1952	Laszlo Papp (HUN)
1956	Laszlo Papp (HUN)
1960	Wilbert McClure (USA)
1964	Boris Lagutin (URS)
1968	Boris Lagutin (URS)
1972	Dieter Kottysch (FRG)
1976	Jerzy Rybicki (POL)
1980	Armando Martínez (CUB)
1984	Frank Tate (USA)
1988	Park Si Hun (KOR)
1992	Juan Lemus (CUB)
1996	David Reid (USA)
2000	Yermakhan Ibraimov (KAZ)

75 KG (165 LB)

1904	Charles Mayer (USA)
1908	John Douglas (GBR)
1920	Harry Mallin (GBR)
1924	Harry Mallin (GBR)
1928	Piero Toscani (ITA)
1932	Carmen Barth (USA)
1936	Jean Despeaux (FRA)
1948	Laszlo Papp (HUN)

Summer Olympic Games Champions (continued)

Boxing (continued)

75 KG (165 LB)
1952 Floyd Patterson (USA)
1956 Gennady Shatkov (URS)
1960 Edward Crook (USA)
1964 Valery Popenchenko (URS)
1968 Christopher Finnegan (GBR)
1972 Vyatcheslav Lemeshev (URS)
1976 Michael Spinks (USA)
1980 Jose Gómez (CUB)
1984 Shin Joon Sup (KOR)
1988 Henry Maske (GDR)
1992 Ariel Hernández (CUB)
1996 Ariel Hernández (CUB)
2000 Jorge Gutiérrez (CUB)
2004 Gaydarbek Gaydarbekov (RUS)

81 KG (178.2 LB)
1920 Edward Eagan (USA)
1924 Harry Mitchell (GBR)
1928 Viktor Avendano (ARG)
1932 David Carstens (RSA)
1936 Roger Michelot (FRA)
1948 George Hunter (RSA)
1952 Norvel Lee (USA)
1956 James Boyd (USA)
1960 Cassius Clay (USA)
1964 Cosimo Pinto (ITA)
1968 Dan Poznyak (URS)
1972 Mate Parlov (YUG)
1976 Leon Spinks (USA)
1980 Slobodan Kacar (YUG)
1984 Anton Josipovic (YUG)
1988 Andrew Maynard (USA)
1992 Torsten May (GER)
1996 Vasily Zhirov (KAZ)
2000 Aleksandr Lebzyak (RUS)
2004 Andre Ward (USA)

OVER 81 KG (178.2 LB) (91 KG; 200.2 LB FROM 1984)
1904 Samuel Berger (USA)
1908 Albert Oldman (GBR)
1920 Ronald Rawson (GBR)
1924 Otto Von Porat (NOR)
1928 Arturo Rodriguez (ARG)
1932 Alberto Santiago Lovell (ARG)
1936 Herbert Runge (GER)
1948 Rafael Iglesias (ARG)
1952 Edward Sanders (USA)
1956 Peter Rademacher (USA)
1960 Franco de Piccoli (ITA)
1964 Joseph Frazier (USA)
1968 George Foreman (USA)
1972 Teofilo Stevenson (CUB)
1976 Teofilo Stevenson (CUB)
1980 Teofilo Stevenson (CUB)
1984 Henry Tillman (USA)
1988 Ray Mercer (USA)
1992 Félix Savon (CUB)
1996 Félix Savon (CUB)
2000 Félix Savon (CUB)
2004 Odlanier Solis Fonte (CUB)

OVER 91 KG (200.2 LB)
1984 Tyrell Biggs (USA)
1988 Lennox Lewis (CAN)
1992 Roberto Balado (CUB)
1996 Vladimir Klichko (UKR)

Boxing (continued)

OVER 91 KG (200.2 LB)
2000 Audley Harrison (GBR)
2004 Aleksandr Povetkin (RUS)

Canoeing (men)

KAYAK SINGLES (500 METERS)	MIN:SEC
1976 Vasile Diba (ROM)	1:46.41
1980 Vladimir Parfenovich (URS)	1:43.43
1984 Ian Ferguson (NZL)	1:47.84
1988 Zsolt Gyulay (HUN)	1:44.82
1992 Mikko Kolehmainen (FIN)	1:40.34
1996 Antonio Rossi (ITA)	1:37.423
2000 Knut Holmann (NOR)	1:57.84
2004 Adam van Koeverden (CAN)	1:37.919

KAYAK PAIRS (500 METERS)	MIN:SEC
1976 East Germany	1:35.87
1980 USSR	1:32.38
1984 New Zealand	1:34.21
1988 New Zealand	1:33.98
1992 Germany	1:29.84
1996 Germany	1:28.697
2000 Hungary	1:47.05
2004 Germany	1:27.040

KAYAK SINGLES (1,000 METERS)	MIN:SEC
1936 Gregor Hradetzky (AUT)	4:22.90
1948 Gert Fredriksson (SWE)	4:33.20
1952 Gert Fredriksson (SWE)	4:07.90
1956 Gert Fredriksson (SWE)	4:12.80
1960 Erik Hansen (DEN)	3:53.00
1964 Rolf Peterson (SWE)	3:57.13
1968 Mihaly Hesz (HUN)	4:03.58
1972 Aleksandr Shaparenko (URS)	3:48.06
1976 Rüdiger Helm (GDR)	3:48.20
1980 Rüdiger Helm (GDR)	3:48.77
1984 Alan Thompson (NZL)	3:45.73
1988 Gregory Barton (USA)	3:55.27
1992 Clint Robinson (AUS)	3:37.26
1996 Knut Holmann (NOR)	3:25.785
2000 Knut Holmann (NOR)	3:33.26
2004 Eirik Veraas Larsen (NOR)	3:25.897

KAYAK PAIRS (1,000 METERS)	MIN:SEC
1936 Austria	4:03.80
1948 Sweden	4:07.30
1952 Finland	3:51.10
1956 Germany	3:49.60
1960 Sweden	3:34.70
1964 Sweden	3:38.54
1968 USSR	3:37.54
1972 USSR	3:31.23
1976 USSR	3:29.01
1980 USSR	3:26.72
1984 Canada	3:24.22
1988 United States	3:32.42
1992 Germany	3:16.10
1996 Italy	3:09.190
2000 Italy	3:14.46
2004 Sweden	3:18.420

KAYAK FOURS (1,000 METERS)	MIN:SEC
1964 USSR	3:14.67
1968 Norway	3:14.38
1972 USSR	3:14.02
1976 USSR	3:08.69
1980 East Germany	3:13.76

Summer Olympic Games Champions (continued)

Canoeing (men) (continued)

KAYAK FOURS (1,000 METERS) — MIN:SEC

1984	New Zealand	3:02.28
1988	Hungary	3:00.20
1992	Germany	2:54.18
1996	Germany	2:51.528
2000	Hungary	2:55.18
2004	Hungary	2:56.919

KAYAK SINGLES (10,000 METERS) — MIN:SEC

1936	Ernst Krebs (GER)	46:01.6
1948	Gert Fredriksson (SWE)	50:47.7
1952	Thorvald Strömberg (FIN)	47:22.8
1956	Gert Fredriksson (SWE)	47:43.4

KAYAK PAIRS (10,000 METERS) — MIN:SEC

1936	Germany	41:45
1948	Sweden	46:09.4
1952	Finland	44:21.3
1956	Hungary	43:37

COLLAPSIBLE KAYAK SINGLES (10,000 METERS) — MIN:SEC

1936	Gregor Hradetzky (AUT)	50:01.2

COLLAPSIBLE KAYAK PAIRS (10,000 METERS) — MIN:SEC

1936	Sweden	45:48.9

KAYAK SINGLES RELAY (1,500 METERS) — MIN:SEC

1960	Germany	7:39.43

SLALOM KAYAK SINGLES

1972	Siegbert Horn (GDR)
1992	Pierpaolo Ferrazzi (ITA)
1996	Oliver Fix (GER)
2000	Thomas Schmidt (GER)
2004	Benoit Peschier (FRA)

CANADIAN SINGLES (500 METERS) — MIN:SEC

1976	Aleksandr Rogov (URS)	1:59.23
1980	Sergey Postrekin (URS)	1:53.37
1984	Larry Cain (CAN)	1:57.01
1988	Olaf Heukrodt (GDR)	1:56.42
1992	Nikolay Bukhalov (BUL)	1:51.15
1996	Martin Doktor (CZE)	1:49.934
2000	Gyorgy Kolonics (HUN)	2:24.81
2004	Andreas Dittmer (GER)	1:46.383

CANADIAN PAIRS (500 METERS) — MIN:SEC

1976	USSR	1:45.81
1980	Hungary	1:43.39
1984	Yugoslavia	1:43.67
1988	USSR	1:41.77
1992	Unified Team	1:41.54
1996	Hungary	1:40.420
2000	Hungary	1:51.28
2004	China	1:40.278

CANADIAN SINGLES (1,000 METERS) — MIN:SEC

1936	Francis Amyot (CAN)	5:32.10
1948	Josef Holecek (TCH)	5:42.00
1952	Josef Holecek (TCH)	4:56.30
1956	Leon Rottman (ROM)	5:05.30
1960	Janos Parti (HUN)	4:33.03
1964	Jürgen Eschert (GER)	4:35.14
1968	Tibor Tatai (HUN)	4:36.14
1972	Ivan Patzaichin (ROM)	4:08.94
1976	Matija Ljubek (YUG)	4:09.51
1980	Lyubomir Lyubenov (BUL)	4:12.38
1984	Ulrich Eicke (FRG)	4:06.32

Canoeing (men) (continued)

CANADIAN SINGLES (1,000 METERS) — MIN:SEC

1988	Ivans Klementyev (URS)	4:12.78
1992	Nikolay Bukhalov (BUL)	4:05.92
1996	Martin Doktor (CZE)	3:54.418
2000	Andreas Dittmer (GER)	3:54.37
2004	David Cal (ESP)	3:46.201

CANADIAN PAIRS (1,000 METERS) — MIN:SEC

1936	Czechoslovakia	4:50.10
1948	Czechoslovakia	5:07.10
1952	Denmark	4:38.30
1956	Romania	4:47.40
1960	USSR	4:17.04
1964	USSR	4:04.65
1968	Romania	4:07.18
1972	USSR	3:52.60
1976	USSR	3:52.76
1980	Romania	3:47.65
1984	Romania	3:40.60
1988	USSR	3:48.36
1992	Germany	3:37.42
1996	Germany	3:31.870
2000	Romania	3:37.35
2004	Germany	3:41.802

CANADIAN SINGLES (10,000 METERS) — MIN:SEC

1948	Frantisek Capek (TCH)	62:05.2
1952	Frank Havens (USA)	57:41.1
1956	Leon Rottman (ROM)	56:41.0

CANADIAN PAIRS (10,000 METERS) — MIN:SEC

1936	Czechoslovakia	50:35.5
1948	United States	55:55.4
1952	France	54:08.3
1956	USSR	54:02.4

SLALOM CANADIAN SINGLES

1972	Reinhard Eiben (GDR)
1992	Lukas Pollert (TCH)
1996	Michal Martikan (SVK)
2000	Tony Estanguet (FRA)
2004	Tony Estanguet (FRA)

SLALOM CANADIAN PAIRS

1972	East Germany
1992	United States
1996	France
2000	Slovakia
2004	Slovakia

Canoeing (women)

KAYAK SINGLES (500 METERS) — MIN:SEC

1948	Karen Hoff (DEN)	2:31.90
1952	Sylvi Saimo (FIN)	2:18.40
1956	Yelizaveta Dementyeva (URS)	2:18.90
1960	Antonina Seredina (URS)	2:08.08
1964	Lyudmila Khvedosyuk (URS)	2:12.87
1968	Lyudmila Pinayeva-Khvedosyuk (URS)	2:11.09
1972	Yuliya Ryabchinskaya (URS)	2:03.17
1976	Carola Zirzow (GDR)	2:01.05
1980	Birgit Fischer (GDR)	1:57.96
1984	Agneta Andersson (SWE)	1:58.72
1988	Vanya Gecheva (BUL)	1:55.19
1992	Birgit Fischer Schmidt (GER)	1:51.60
1996	Rita Koban (HUN)	1:47.655
2000	Josefa Idem Guerrini (ITA)	2:13.84
2004	Natasa Janics (HUN)	1:47.741

Summer Olympic Games Champions (continued)

Canoeing (women) (continued)

KAYAK PAIRS (500 METERS)

		MIN:SEC
1960	USSR	1:54.76
1964	Germany	1:56.95
1968	West Germany	1:56.44
1972	USSR	1:53.50
1976	USSR	1:51.15
1980	East Germany	1:43.88
1984	Sweden	1:45.25
1988	East Germany	1:43.46
1992	Germany	1:40.29
1996	Sweden	1:39.329
2000	Germany	1:56.99
2004	Hungary	1:38.101

KAYAK FOURS (500 METERS)

		MIN:SEC
1984	Romania	1:38.34
1988	East Germany	1:40.78
1992	Hungary	1:38.32
1996	Germany	1:31.077
2000	Germany	1:34.53
2004	Germany	1:34.340

SLALOM KAYAK SINGLES

1972	Angelika Bahmann (GDR)
1992	Elisabeth Micheler (GER)
1996	Stepanka Hilgertova (CZE)
2000	Stepanka Hilgertova (CZE)
2004	Elena Kaliska (SVK)

Cricket

1900	Great Britain

Croquet

SINGLES (ONE BALL)

1900	Aumoitte (FRA)

SINGLES (TWO BALLS)

1900	Waydelick (FRA)

DOUBLES

1900	France

Cycling (men)

1,000-METER SPRINT

1896[6]	Paul Masson (FRA)
1900[6]	Georges Taillandier (FRA)
1920	Mauritius Peeters (NED)
1924	Lucien Michard (FRA)
1928	Roger Beaufrand (FRA)
1932	Jacobus Van Egmond (NED)
1936	Toni Merkens (GER)
1948	Mario Ghella (ITA)
1952	Enzo Sacchi (ITA)
1956	Michel Rousseau (FRA)
1960	Sante Gaiardoni (ITA)
1964	Giovanni Pettenella (ITA)
1968	Daniel Morelon (FRA)
1972	Daniel Morelon (FRA)
1976	Anton Tkac (TCH)
1980	Lutz Hesslich (GDR)
1984	Mark Gorski (USA)
1988	Lutz Hesslich (GDR)
1992	Jens Fiedler (GER)
1996	Jens Fiedler (GER)
2000	Marty Nothstein (USA)
2004	Ryan Bayley (AUS)

Cycling (men) (continued)

1,000-METER TIME TRIAL

		MIN:SEC
1896[7]	Paul Masson (FRA)	24.0
1928	Willy Falck-Hansen (DEN)	1:14.4
1932	Edgar Gray (AUS)	1:13.0
1936	Arie van Vliet (NED)	1:12.0
1948	Jacques Dupont (FRA)	1:13.5
1952	Russell Mockridge (AUS)	1:11.1
1956	Leandro Faggin (ITA)	1:09.8
1960	Sante Gaiardoni (ITA)	1:07.27
1964	Patrick Sercu (BEL)	1:09.59
1968	Pierre Trentin (FRA)	1:03.91
1972	Niels Fredborg (DEN)	1:06.44
1976	Klaus-Jürgen Grünke (GDR)	1:05.927
1980	Lothar Thoms (GDR)	1:02.955
1984	Fredy Schmidtke (FRG)	1:06.104
1988	Aleksandr Kirichenko (URS)	1:04.499
1992	José Moreno (ESP)	1:03.342
1996	Florian Rousseau (FRA)	1:02.712
2000	Jason Queally (GBR)	1:01.609
2004	Chris Hoy (GBR)	1:00.711

1,500-METER TEAM PURSUIT

1900	United States

2,000 METERS

1904	Marcus Hurley (USA)

2,000-METER TANDEM

1908	France
1920	Great Britain
1924	France
1928	The Netherlands
1932	France
1936	Germany
1948	Italy
1952	Australia
1956	Australia
1960	Italy
1964	Italy
1968	France
1972	USSR

4,000-METER INDIVIDUAL PURSUIT

1964	Jiri Daler (TCH)
1968	Daniel Rebillard (FRA)
1972	Knut Knudsen (NOR)
1976	Gregor Braun (FRG)
1980	Robert Dill-Bondi (SUI)
1984	Steve Hegg (USA)
1988	Gintautas Umaras (URS)
1992	Christopher Boardman (GBR)
1996	Andrea Collinelli (ITA)
2000	Robert Bartko (GER)
2004	Bradley Wiggins (GBR)

4,000-METER TEAM PURSUIT

1908	Great Britain
1920	Italy
1924	Italy
1928	Italy
1932	Italy
1936	France
1948	France
1952	Italy
1956	Italy
1960	Italy
1964	Germany
1968	Denmark

Summer Olympic Games Champions (continued)

Cycling (men) (continued)

4,000-METER TEAM PURSUIT
1972	West Germany
1976	West Germany
1980	USSR
1984	Australia
1988	USSR
1992	Germany
1996	France
2000	Germany
2004	Australia

5,000 METERS — MIN:SEC
| 1908 | Benjamin Jones (GBR) | 8:36.2 |

10,000 METERS — MIN:SEC
| 1896 | Paul Masson (FRA) | 17:54.2 |

20,000 METERS — MIN:SEC
| 1908 | Charles Kingsbury (GBR) | 34:13.6 |

50,000 METERS — HR:MIN:SEC
| 1920 | Henry George (BEL) | 1:16:43.2 |
| 1924 | Jacobus Willems (NED) | 1:18:24.0 |

100,000 METERS — HR:MIN:SEC
| 1896 | Léon Flameng (FRA) | 3:08:19.2 |
| 1908 | Charles Bartlett (GBR) | 2:41:48.6 |

ONE-QUARTER MILE (440 YARDS) — SEC
| 1904 | Marcus Hurley (USA) | 31.8 |

ONE-THIRD MILE (586⅔ YARDS) — SEC
| 1904 | Marcus Hurley (USA) | 43.8 |

ONE-LAP TIME TRIAL (660 YARDS) — SEC
| 1908 | Victor Johnson (GBR) | 51.2 |

ONE-HALF MILE (880 YARDS) — MIN:SEC
| 1904 | Marcus Hurley (USA) | 1:09.0 |

1 MILE — MIN:SEC
| 1904 | Marcus Hurley (USA) | 2:41.6 |

1 MILE 1 FURLONG (1,980 YARDS) TEAM PURSUIT
| 1908 | Great Britain |

2 MILES — MIN:SEC
| 1904 | Burton Downing (USA) | 4:58.0 |

5 MILES — MIN:SEC
| 1904 | Charles Schlee (USA) | 13:08.2 |

25 MILES
| 1904 | Burton Downing (USA) |

12 HOURS
| 1896 | Adolf Schmal (AUT) |

INDIVIDUAL POINTS RACE
1984	Roger Ilegems (BEL)
1988	Dan Frost (DEN)
1992	Giovanni Lombardi (ITA)
1996	Silvio Martinello (ITA)
2000	Juan Llaneras (ESP)
2004	Mikhail Ignatyev (RUS)

Cycling (men) (continued)

KEIRIN — SEC
| 2000 | Florian Rousseau (FRA) | 11.020 |
| 2004 | Ryan Bayley (AUS) | 10.601 |

MADISON
| 2000 | Australia |
| 2004 | Australia |

TEAM SPRINT — SEC
| 2000 | France | 44.233 |
| 2004 | Germany | 43.980 |

ROAD RACE (INDIVIDUAL)[8] — HR:MIN:SEC
1896	Aristidis Konstantinidis (GRE)	3:22:31.0
1912	Rudolph Lewis (RSA)	10:42:39.0
1920	Harry Stenqvist (SWE)	4:40:01.8
1924	Armand Blanchonnet (FRA)	6:20:48.0
1928	Henry Hansen (DEN)	4:47:18.0
1932	Attilio Pavesi (ITA)	2:28:05.6
1936	Robert Charpentier (FRA)	2:33:05.0
1948	Jose Beyaert (FRA)	5:18:12.6
1952	Andre Noyelle (BEL)	5:06:03.4
1956	Ercole Baldini (ITA)	5:21:17.0
1960	Viktor Kapitonov (URS)	4:20:37.0
1964	Mario Zanin (ITA)	4:39:51.63
1968	Pierfranco Vianelli (ITA)	4:41:25.24
1972	Hennie Kuiper (NED)	4:14:37.0
1976	Bernt Johansson (SWE)	4:46:52.0
1980	Sergey Sukhoruchenkov (URS)	4:48:28.90
1984	Alexei Grewal (USA)	4:59:57.0
1988	Olaf Ludwig (GDR)	4:32:22.0
1992	Fabio Casartelli (ITA)	4:35:21.0
1996	Pascal Richard (SUI)	4:53:56.0
2000	Jan Ullrich (GER)	5:29:08.0
2004	Paolo Bettini (ITA)	5:41:44:0

ROAD RACE (TEAM) — HR:MIN:SEC
1912	Sweden	44:35:33.6
1920	France	19:16:43.2
1924	France	19:30:14
1928	Denmark	15:09:14
1932	Italy	7:27:15.2
1936	France	7:39:16.2
1948	Belgium	15:58:17.4
1952	Belgium	15:20:46.6
1956	France	5:21:17

ROAD TIME TRIAL (INDIVIDUAL) — HR:MIN:SEC
1996	Miguel Indurain (ESP)	1:04:05
2000	Vyacheslav Yekimov (RUS)	57:40.42
2004	Tyler Hamilton (USA)	57.31.74

ROAD TIME TRIAL (TEAM) — HR:MIN:SEC
1960	Italy	2:14:33.53
1964	The Netherlands	2:26:31.19
1968	The Netherlands	2:07:49.06
1972	USSR	2:11:17.8
1976	USSR	2:08:53
1980	USSR	2:01:21.7
1984	Italy	1:58:28
1988	East Germany	1:57:47.7
1992	Germany	2:01:39

CROSS COUNTRY (MOUNTAIN BIKE) — HR:MIN:SEC
1996	Bart Jan Brentjens (NED)	2:17:38
2000	Miguel Martinez (FRA)	2:09:2.50
2004	Julien Absalon (FRA)	2:15.02

Summer Olympic Games Champions (continued)

Cycling (women)

500-METER TIME TRIAL   HR:MIN:SEC
2000   Felicia Ballanger (FRA)   34.140
2004   Anna Meares (AUS)   53.016

INDIVIDUAL SPRINT
1988   Erika Salumae (URS)
1992   Erika Salumae (EST)
1996   Felicia Ballanger (FRA)
2000   Felicia Ballanger (FRA)
2004   Lori-Ann Muenzer (CAN)

3,000-METER INDIVIDUAL PURSUIT
1992   Petra Rossner (GER)
1996   Antonella Bellutti (ITA)
2000   Leontien Zijlaard–van Moorsel
        (NED)
2004   Sarah Ulmer (NZL)

POINTS RACE
1996   Nathalie Lancien (FRA)
2000   Antonella Bellutti (ITA)
2004   Olga Slyusareva (RUS)

ROAD RACE (INDIVIDUAL)   HR:MIN:SEC
1984   Connie Carpenter-Phinney (USA) 2:11:14.0
1988   Monique Knol (NED)   2:00:52.0
1992   Kathryn Watt (AUS)   2:04:42.0
1996   Jeannie Longo-Ciprelli (FRA)   2:36:13.0
2000   Leontien Zijlaard–van Moorsel   3:06:31
        (NED)
2004   Sara Carrigan (AUS)   3:24:24

ROAD TIME TRIAL (INDIVIDUAL)   MIN:SEC
1996   Zulfiya Zabirova (RUS)   36:40
2000   Leontien Zijlaard–van Moorsel   42:00.781
        (NED)
2004   Leontien Zijlaard–van   31:11.53
        Moorsel (NED)

CROSS COUNTRY (MOUNTAIN BIKE)   HR:MIN:SEC
1996   Paola Pezzo (ITA)   1:50:51
2000   Paola Pezzo (ITA)   1:49:24.38
2004   Gunn-Rita Dahle (NOR)   1:56:51

Diving (men)

3-METER SPRINGBOARD DIVING
1908   Albert Zürner (GER)
1912   Paul Günther (GER)
1920   Louis Kuehn (USA)
1924   Albert White (USA)
1928   Peter Desjardins (USA)
1932   Michael Galitzen (USA)
1936   Richard Degener (USA)
1948   Bruce Harlan (USA)
1952   David Browning (USA)
1956   Robert Clotworthy (USA)
1960   Gary Tobian (USA)
1964   Kenneth Sitzberger (USA)
1968   Bernie Wrightson (USA)
1972   Vladimir Vasin (URS)
1976   Philip Boggs (USA)
1980   Aleksandr Portnov (URS)
1984   Gregory Louganis (USA)
1988   Gregory Louganis (USA)
1992   Mark Edward Lenzi (USA)
1996   Xiong Ni (CHN)
2000   Xiong Ni (CHN)
2004   Peng Bo (CHN)

Diving (men) (continued)

10-METER PLATFORM (HIGH) DIVING
1904   George Sheldon (USA)
1908   Hjalmar Johansson (SWE)
1912   Erik Adlerz (SWE)
1920   Clarence Pinkston (USA)
1924   Albert White (USA)
1928   Peter Desjardins (USA)
1932   Harold Smith (USA)
1936   Marshall Wayne (USA)
1948   Samuel Lee (USA)
1952   Samuel Lee (USA)
1956   Joaquin Capilla Perez (MEX)
1960   Robert Webster (USA)
1964   Robert Webster (USA)
1968   Klaus DiBiasi (ITA)
1972   Klaus DiBiasi (ITA)
1976   Klaus DiBiasi (ITA)
1980   Falk Hoffman (GDR)
1984   Gregory Louganis (USA)
1988   Gregory Louganis (USA)
1992   Sun Shuwei (CHN)
1996   Dmitry Sautin (RUS)
2000   Tian Liang (CHN)
2004   Hu Jia (CHN)

3-METER SYNCHRONIZED SPRINGBOARD DIVING
2000   China
2004   Greece

10-METER SYNCHRONIZED PLATFORM (HIGH) DIVING
2000   Russia
2004   China

PLUNGE FOR DISTANCE
1904   William Paul Dickey (USA)

PLAIN HIGH DIVING
1912   Erik Adlerz (SWE)
1920   Arvid Wallman (SWE)
1924   Richmond Eve (AUS)

Diving (women)

3-METER SPRINGBOARD DIVING
1920   Aileen Riggin (USA)
1924   Elizabeth Becker-Pinkton (USA)
1928   Helen Meany (USA)
1932   Georgia Coleman (USA)
1936   Marjorie Gestring (USA)
1948   Victoria Draves (USA)
1952   Patricia McCormick (USA)
1956   Patricia McCormick (USA)
1960   Ingrid Krämer-Engel-Gulbin (GER)
1964   Ingrid Krämer-Engel-Gulbin (GER)
1968   Sue Gossick (USA)
1972   Micki King (USA)
1976   Jennifer Chandler (USA)
1980   Irina Kalinina (URS)
1984   Sylvie Bernier (CAN)
1988   Gao Min (CHN)
1992   Gao Min (CHN)
1996   Fu Mingxia (CHN)
2000   Fu Mingxia (CHN)
2004   Guo Jingjing (CHN)

10-METER PLATFORM (HIGH) DIVING
1912   Greta Johansson (SWE)

Summer Olympic Games Champions (continued)

Diving (women) (continued)

10-METER PLATFORM (HIGH) DIVING

1920	Stefani Fryland Clausen (DEN)
1924	Caroline Smith (USA)
1928	Elizabeth Anna Becker-Pinkston (USA)
1932	Dorothy Poynton (USA)
1936	Dorothy Poynton-Hill (USA)
1948	Victoria Draves (USA)
1952	Patricia McCormick (USA)
1956	Patricia McCormick (USA)
1960	Ingrid Krämer-Engel-Gulbin (GER)
1964	Lesley Leigh Bush (USA)
1968	Milena Duchkova (TCH)
1972	Ulrika Knape (SWE)
1976	Yelena Vaytsekhovskaya (URS)
1980	Martina Jäschke (GDR)
1984	Zhou Ji-Hong (CHN)
1988	Xu Yan-Mei (CHN)
1992	Fu Mingxia (CHN)
1996	Fu Mingxia (CHN)
2000	Laura Wilkinson (USA)
2004	Chantelle Newbery (AUS)

3-METER SYNCHRONIZED SPRINGBOARD DIVING

2000	Russia
2004	China

10-METER SYNCHRONIZED PLATFORM (HIGH) DIVING

2000	China
2004	China

Equestrian sports

GRAND PRIX (DRESSAGE) INDIVIDUAL — MOUNT

1912	Carl Bonde (SWE)	Emperor
1920	Janne Lundblad (SWE)	Uno
1924	Ernst Linder (SWE)	Piccolomini
1928	Carl Friedrich Freiherr von Langen-Parow (GER)	Draufgänger
1932	Xavier Lesage (FRA)	Taine
1936	Heinz Pollay (GER)	Kronos
1948	Hans Moser (SUI)	Hummer
1952	Henri St. Cyr (SWE)	Master Rufus
1956	Henri St. Cyr (SWE)	Juli
1960	Sergey Filatov (URS)	Absent
1964	Henri Chammartin (SUI)	Woermann
1968	Ivan Kizimov (URS)	Ikhor
1972	Liselott Linsenhoff (FRG)	Piaff
1976	Christine Stückelberger (SUI)	Granat
1980	Elisabeth Theurer (AUT)	Mon Cherie
1984	Reiner Klimke (FRG)	Ahlerich
1988	Nicole Uphoff (FRG)	Rembrandt 24
1992	Nicole Uphoff (GER)	Rembrandt 24
1996	Isabell Werth (GER)	Gigolo
2000	Anky van Grunsven (NED)	Bonfire
2004	Anky van Grunsven (NED)	Salinero

GRAND PRIX (DRESSAGE) TEAM

1928	Germany
1932	France
1936	Germany
1948	France
1952	Sweden
1956	Sweden
1964	Germany
1968	West Germany
1972	USSR
1976	West Germany
1980	USSR
1984	West Germany

Equestrian sports (continued)

GRAND PRIX (DRESSAGE) TEAM

1988	West Germany
1992	Germany
1996	Germany
2000	Germany
2004	Germany

GRAND PRIX (JUMPING) INDIVIDUAL — MOUNT

1900	Aimé Haegeman (BEL)	Benton II
1912	Jean Cariou (FRA)	Mignon
1920	Tommaso Lequio di Assaba (ITA)	Trebecco
1924	Alphonse Gemuseus (SUI)	Lucette
1928	Frantisek Ventura (TCH)	Eliot
1932	Takeichi Nishi (JPN)	Uranus
1936	Kurt Hasse (GER)	Tora
1948	Humberto Mariles Cortés (MEX)	Arete
1952	Pierre Jonquères d'Oriola (FRA)	Ali Baba
1956	Hans-Günter Winkler (GER)	Halla
1960	Raimondo d'Inzeo (ITA)	Posillipo
1964	Pierre Jonquères d'Oriola (FRA)	Lutteur
1968	William Steinkraus (USA)	Snowbound
1972	Graziano Mancinelli (ITA)	Ambassador
1976	Alwin Schockemöhle (FRG)	Warwick Rex
1980	Jan Kowalczyk (POL)	Artemor
1984	Joe Fargis (USA)	Touch of Class
1988	Pierre Durand (FRA)	Jappeloup
1992	Ludger Beerbaum (GER)	Classic Touch
1996	Ulrich Kirchhoff (GER)	Jus des Pommes
2000	Jeroen Dubbeldam (NED)	Sjiem
2004	Rodrigo Pessoa (BRA)	Baloubet du Rouet

GRAND PRIX (JUMPING) TEAM

1912	Sweden
1920	Sweden
1924	Sweden
1928	Spain
1936	Germany
1948	Mexico
1952	Great Britain
1956	Germany
1960	Germany
1964	Germany
1968	Canada
1972	West Germany
1976	France
1980	USSR
1984	United States
1988	West Germany
1992	The Netherlands
1996	Germany
2000	Germany
2004	Germany

THREE-DAY EVENT (INDIVIDUAL) — MOUNT

1912	Axel Nordlander (SWE)	Lady Artist
1920	Helmer Mörner (SWE)	Germania
1924	Adolph van der Voort van Zijp (NED)	Silver Piece
1928	Charles Pahud de Mortanges (NED)	Marcroix
1932	Charles Pahud de Mortanges (NED)	Marcroix
1936	Ludwig Stubbendorff (GER)	Nurmi
1948	Bernard Chevallier (FRA)	Aiglonne
1952	Hans von Blixen-Finecke, Jr. (SWE)	Jubal
1956	Petrus Kastenman (SWE)	Iluster
1960	Lawrence Morgan (AUS)	Salad Days

Summer Olympic Games Champions (continued)

Equestrian sports (continued)

THREE-DAY EVENT (INDIVIDUAL)

		MOUNT
1964	Mauro Checcoli (ITA)	Surbean
1968	Jean-Jacques Goyon (FRA)	Pitou
1972	Richard Meade (GBR)	Laurieston
1976	Edmund Coffin (USA)	Bally-Cor
1980	Federico Euro Roman (ITA)	Rossinan
1984	Mark Todd (NZL)	Charisma
1988	Mark Todd (NZL)	Charisma
1992	Matthew Ryan (AUS)	Kibah Tic Toc
1996	Robert Blyth Tait (NZL)	Ready Teddy
2000	David O'Connor (USA)	Custom Made
2004	Leslie Law (GBR)	Shear L'Eau

THREE-DAY EVENT (TEAM)

1912	Sweden
1920	Sweden
1924	The Netherlands
1928	The Netherlands
1932	United States
1936	Germany
1948	United States
1952	Sweden
1956	Great Britain
1960	Australia
1964	Italy
1968	Great Britain
1972	Great Britain
1976	United States
1980	USSR
1984	United States
1988	West Germany
1992	Australia
1996	Australia
2000	Australia
2004	France

HIGH JUMP

		MOUNT
1900	Dominique Maximien Gardéres (FRA); Gian Giorgio Trissino (ITA) (tied)	Canela; Oreste

LONG JUMP

		MOUNT
1900	Constant van Langhendonck (BEL)	Extra Dry

FIGURE RIDING (INDIVIDUAL)

1920	T. Bouckaert (BEL)

FIGURE RIDING (TEAM)

1920	Belgium

Fencing (men)

FOIL (INDIVIDUAL)

1896	Eugène-Henri Gravelotte (FRA)
1900	Émile Coste (FRA)
1904	Ramón Fonst (CUB)
1912	Nedo Nadi (ITA)
1920	Nedo Nadi (ITA)
1924	Roger Ducret (FRA)
1928	Lucien Gaudin (FRA)
1932	Gustavo Marzi (ITA)
1936	Giulio Gaudini (ITA)
1948	Jehan Buhan (FRA)
1952	Christian d'Oriola (FRA)
1956	Christian d'Oriola (FRA)
1960	Viktor Zhdanovich (URS)
1964	Egon Franke (POL)

Fencing (men) (continued)

FOIL (INDIVIDUAL)

1968	Ion Drimba (ROM)
1972	Witold Woyda (POL)
1976	Fabio dal Zotto (ITA)
1980	Vladimir Smirnov (URS)
1984	Mauro Numa (ITA)
1988	Stefano Cerioni (ITA)
1992	Philippe Omnes (FRA)
1996	Alessandro Puccini (ITA)
2000	Kim Young Ho (KOR)
2004	Brice Guyart (FRA)

FOIL (TEAM)

1904	Cuba
1920	Italy
1924	France
1928	Italy
1932	France
1936	Italy
1948	France
1952	France
1956	Italy
1960	USSR
1964	USSR
1968	France
1972	Poland
1976	West Germany
1980	France
1984	Italy
1988	USSR
1992	Germany
1996	Russia
2000	France
2004	Italy

INDIVIDUAL FOIL, PROFESSIONAL (MASTERS)

1896	Leon Pyrgos (GRE)
1900	Lucien Mérignac (FRA)

INDIVIDUAL FOIL, JUNIOR

1904	Arthur Fox (USA)

ÉPÉE (INDIVIDUAL)

1900	Ramón Fonst (CUB)
1904	Ramón Fonst (CUB)
1908	Gaston Alibert (FRA)
1912	Paul Anspach (BEL)
1920	Armand Massard (FRA)
1924	Charles Delporte (BEL)
1928	Lucien Gaudin (FRA)
1932	Giancarlo Cornaggia-Medici (ITA)
1936	Franco Riccardi (ITA)
1948	Luigi Cantone (ITA)
1952	Edoardo Mangiarotti (ITA)
1956	Carlo Pavesi (ITA)
1960	Giuseppe Delfino (ITA)
1964	Grigory Kriss (URS)
1968	Gyoso Kulcsar (HUN)
1972	Csaba Fenyvesi (HUN)
1976	Alexander Pusch (FRG)
1980	Johan Harmenberg (SWE)
1984	Philippe Boisse (FRA)
1988	Arnd Schmitt (FRG)
1992	Eric Srecki (FRA)
1996	Aleksandr Beketov (RUS)
2000	Pavel Kolobkov (RUS)
2004	Marcel Fischer (SUI)

Summer Olympic Games Champions (continued)

Fencing (men) (continued)

ÉPÉE (TEAM)

1908	France
1912	Belgium
1920	Italy
1924	France
1928	Italy
1932	France
1936	Italy
1948	France
1952	Italy
1956	Italy
1960	Italy
1964	Hungary
1968	Hungary
1972	Hungary
1976	Sweden
1980	France
1984	West Germany
1988	France
1992	Germany
1996	Italy
2000	Italy
2004	France

INDIVIDUAL ÉPÉE, PROFESSIONAL (MASTERS)

1900	Albert Ayat (FRA)

INDIVIDUAL ÉPÉE, OPEN (AMATEUR AND MASTERS)

1900	Albert Ayat (FRA)

SABRE (INDIVIDUAL)

1896	Ioannis Georgiadis (GRE)
1900	Georges de la Falaise (FRA)
1904	Manuel Díaz (CUB)
1908	Jeno Fuchs (HUN)
1912	Jeno Fuchs (HUN)
1920	Nedo Nadi (ITA)
1924	Sandor Posta (HUN)
1928	Odon Vitez Tersztyanszky (HUN)
1932	Gyorgy Piller (HUN)
1936	Endre Kabos (HUN)
1948	Aladar Gerevich (HUN)
1952	Pal Kovacs (HUN)
1956	Rudolph Karpati (HUN)
1960	Rudolph Karpati (HUN)
1964	Tibor Pezsa (HUN)
1968	Jerzy Pawlowski (POL)
1972	Viktor Sidyak (URS)
1976	Viktor Krovopuskov (URS)
1980	Viktor Krovopuskov (URS)
1984	Jean-François Lamour (FRA)
1988	Jean-François Lamour (FRA)
1992	Bence Szabo (HUN)
1996	Stanislav Pozdnyakov (RUS)
2000	Mihai Claudiu Covaliu (ROM)
2004	Aldo Montano (ITA)

SABRE (TEAM)

1908	Hungary
1912	Hungary
1920	Italy
1924	Italy
1928	Hungary
1932	Hungary
1936	Hungary
1948	Hungary
1952	Hungary
1956	Hungary

Fencing (men) (continued)

SABRE (TEAM)

1960	Hungary
1964	USSR
1968	USSR
1972	Italy
1976	USSR
1980	USSR
1984	Italy
1988	Hungary
1992	Unified Team
1996	Russia
2000	Russia
2004	France

INDIVIDUAL SABRE, PROFESSIONAL (MASTERS)

1900	Antonio Conte (ITA)

THREE-CORNERED SABRE

1906	Gustav Casmir (GER)

SINGLE STICK

1904	Albertson Van Zo Post (CUB)

Fencing (women)

FOIL (INDIVIDUAL)

1924	Ellen Osiier (DEN)
1928	Helene Mayer (GER)
1932	Ellen Preis (AUT)
1936	Ilona Schacherer-Elek (HUN)
1948	Ilona Elek (HUN)
1952	Irene Camber (ITA)
1956	Gillian Sheen (GBR)
1960	Adelheid Schmid (GER)
1964	Ildiko Ujlaki-Rejto (HUN)
1968	Yelena Novikova (URS)
1972	Antonella Ragno Lonzi (ITA)
1976	Ildiko Schwarczenberger (HUN)
1980	Pascale Trinquet (FRA)
1984	Jujie Luan (CHN)
1988	Anja Fichtel (FRG)
1992	Giovanna Trillini (ITA)
1996	Laura Gabriela Badea (ROM)
2000	Valentina Vezzali (ITA)
2004	Valentina Vezzali (ITA)

FOIL (TEAM)

1960	USSR
1964	Hungary
1968	USSR
1972	USSR
1976	USSR
1980	France
1984	West Germany
1988	West Germany
1992	Italy
1996	Italy
2000	Italy

ÉPÉE (INDIVIDUAL)

1996	Laura Flessel (FRA)
2000	Timea Nagy (HUN)
2004	Timea Nagy (HUN)

ÉPÉE (TEAM)

1996	France
2000	Russia
2004	Russia

Summer Olympic Games Champions (continued)

Fencing (women) (continued)

SABRE (INDIVIDUAL)

2004 Mariel Zagunis (USA)

Field hockey

MEN

1908	Great Britain
1920	Great Britain
1928	India
1932	India
1936	India
1948	India
1952	India
1956	India
1960	Pakistan
1964	India
1968	Pakistan
1972	West Germany
1976	New Zealand
1980	India
1984	Pakistan
1988	Great Britain
1992	Germany
1996	The Netherlands
2000	The Netherlands
2004	Australia

WOMEN

1980	Zimbabwe
1984	The Netherlands
1988	Australia
1992	Spain
1996	Australia
2000	Australia
2004	Germany

Golf

MEN, INDIVIDUAL

1900	Charles Sands (USA)
1904	George Lyon (CAN)

MEN, TEAM

1904 United States

WOMEN

1900 Margaret Abbott (USA)

Gymnastics (men)

COMBINED, OR ALL-AROUND (INDIVIDUAL)

1900	Gustave Sandras (FRA)
1904	Julius Lenhardt (USA)
1908	G. Alberto Braglia (ITA)
1912	G. Alberto Braglia (ITA)
1920	Giorgio Zampori (ITA)
1924	Leon Stukelj (YUG)
1928	Georges Miez (SUI)
1932	Romeo Neri (ITA)
1936	Karl-Alfred Schwarzmann (GER)
1948	Veikko Huhtanen (FIN)
1952	Viktor Chukarin (URS)
1956	Viktor Chukarin (URS)
1960	Boris Shakhlin (URS)
1964	Yukio Endo (JPN)
1968	Sawao Kato (JPN)
1972	Sawao Kato (JPN)

Gymnastics (men) (continued)

COMBINED, OR ALL-AROUND (INDIVIDUAL)

1976	Nikolay Andrianov (URS)
1980	Aleksandr Dityatin (URS)
1984	Koji Gushiken (JPN)
1988	Vladimir Artyomov (URS)
1992	Vitaly Shcherbo (UNT)
1996	Li Xiaosahuang (CHN)
2000	Aleksey Nemov (RUS)
2004	Paul Hamm (USA)

COMBINED, OR ALL-AROUND (TEAM)

1920	Italy
1924	Italy
1928	Switzerland
1932	Italy
1936	Germany
1948	Finland
1952	USSR
1956	USSR
1960	Japan
1964	Japan
1968	Japan
1972	Japan
1976	Japan
1980	USSR
1984	United States
1988	USSR
1992	Unified Team
1996	Russia
2000	China
2004	Japan

FLOOR EXERCISE

1932	Istvan Pelle (HUN)
1936	Georges Miez (SUI)
1948	Ferenc Pataki (HUN)
1952	William Thoresson (SWE)
1956	Valentin Muratov (URS)
1960	Nobuyuki Aihara (JPN)
1964	Franco Menichelli (ITA)
1968	Sawao Kato (JPN)
1972	Nikolay Andrianov (URS)
1976	Nikolay Andrianov (URS)
1980	Roland Brückner (GDR)
1984	Li Ning (CHN)
1988	Sergey Kharikov (URS)
1992	Li Xiaosahuang (CHN)
1996	Ioannis Melissanidis (GRE)
2000	Igors Vihrovs (LAT)
2004	Kyle Shewfelt (CAN)

HIGH BAR

1896	Hermann Weingärtner (GER)
1904	Anton Heida (USA); Edward Henning (USA) (tied)
1924	Leon Stukelj (YUG)
1928	Georges Miez (SUI)
1932	Dallas Bixler (USA)
1936	Aleksanteri Saarvala (FIN)
1948	Josef Stalder (SUI)
1952	Jack Günthard (SUI)
1956	Takashi Ono (JPN)
1960	Takashi Ono (JPN)
1964	Boris Shakhlin (URS)
1968	Mikhail Voronin (URS); Akinori Nakayama (JPN) (tied)

Summer Olympic Games Champions (continued)

Gymnastics (men) (continued)

HIGH BAR

1972   Mitsuo Tsukahara (JPN)
1976   Mitsuo Tsukahara (JPN)
1980   Stoyan Delchev (BUL)
1984   Shinji Morisue (JPN)
1988   Vladimir Artyomov (URS); Valery Lyukin (URS)
      (*tied*)
1992   Trent Dimas (USA)
1996   Andreas Wecker (GER)
2000   Aleksey Nemov (RUS)
2004   Igor Cassina (ITA)

PARALLEL BARS

1896   Alfred Flatow (GER)
1904   George Eyser (USA)
1924   August Güttinger (SUI)
1928   Ladislav Vacha (TCH)
1932   Romeo Neri (ITA)
1936   Konrad Frey (GER)
1948   Michael Reusch (SUI)
1952   Hans Eugster (SUI)
1956   Viktor Chukarin (URS)
1960   Boris Shakhlin (URS)
1964   Yukio Endo (JPN)
1968   Akinori Nakayama (JPN)
1972   Sawao Kato (JPN)
1976   Sawao Kato (JPN)
1980   Aleksandr Tkachyov (URS)
1984   Bart Conner (USA)
1988   Vladimir Artyomov (URS)
1992   Vitaly Shcherbo (UNT)
1996   Rustam Sharipov (UKR)
2000   Li Xiaopeng (CHN)
2004   Valery Goncharov (UKR)

SIDE, OR POMMEL, HORSE

1896   Louis Zutter (SUI)
1904   Anton Heida (USA)
1924   Josef Wilhelm (SUI)
1928   Hermann Hänggi (SUI)
1932   Istvan Pelle (HUN)
1936   Konrad Frey (GER)
1948   Paavo Aaltonen (FIN); Veikko Huhtanen (FIN);
      Heikki Savolainen (FIN) (*tied*)
1952   Viktor Chukarin (URS)
1956   Boris Shakhlin (URS)
1960   Boris Shakhlin (URS); Eugen Ekman (FIN)
      (*tied*)
1964   Miroslav Cerar (YUG)
1968   Miroslav Cerar (YUG)
1972   Viktor Klimenko (URS)
1976   Zoltan Magyar (HUN)
1980   Zoltan Magyar (HUN)
1984   Li Ning (CHN); Peter Vidmar (USA) (*tied*)
1988   Lyubomir Geraskov (BUL); Zsolt Borkai (HUN);
      Dmitry Bilozerchev (URS) (*tied*)
1992   Vitaly Shcherbo (UNT); Pae Gil-su (PRK) (*tied*)
1996   Li Donghua (SUI)
2000   Marius Urzica (ROM)
2004   Teng Haibin (CHN)

LONG, OR VAULTING, HORSE

1896   Karl Schuhmann (GER)
1904   Anton Heida (USA); George Eyser (USA) (*tied*)
1924   Frank Kriz (USA)
1928   Eugen Mack (SUI)
1932   Savino Guglielmetti (ITA)
1936   Karl-Alfred Schnorzmann (GER)

Gymnastics (men) (continued)

LONG, OR VAULTING, HORSE

1948   Paavo Johannes Aaltonen (FIN)
1952   Viktor Chukarin (URS)
1956   Valentin Muratov (URS); Helmut Bantz (GER)
      (*tied*)
1960   Takashi Ono (JPN); Boris Shakhlin (URS)
      (*tied*)
1964   Haruhiro Yamashita (JPN)
1968   Mikhail Voronin (URS)
1972   Klaus Köste (GDR)
1976   Nikolay Andrianov (URS)
1980   Nikolay Andrianov (URS)
1984   Lou Yun (CHN)
1988   Lou Yun (CHN)
1992   Vitaly Shcherbo (UNT)
1996   Aleksey Nemov (RUS)
2000   Gervasio Deferr (ESP)
2004   Gervasio Deferr (ESP)

RINGS

1896   Ioannis Mitropoulos (GRE)
1904   Hermann Glass (USA)
1924   Francesco Martino (ITA)
1928   Leon Stukelj (YUG)
1932   George Gulack (USA)
1936   Alois Hudec (TCH)
1948   Karl Frei (SUI)
1952   Grant Shaginyan (URS)
1956   Albert Azaryan (URS)
1960   Albert Azaryan (URS)
1964   Takuji Hayata (JPN)
1968   Akinori Nakayama (JPN)
1972   Akinori Nakayama (JPN)
1976   Nikolay Andrianov (URS)
1980   Aleksandr Dityatin (URS)
1984   Li Ning (CHN); Koji Gushiken (JPN) (*tied*)
1988   Holger Behrendt (GDR); Dmitry Bilozerchev
      (URS) (*tied*)
1992   Vitaly Shcherbo (UNT)
1996   Yury Chechi (ITA)
2000   Szilveszter Csollany (HUN)
2004   Dimosthenis Tampakos (GRE)

TRAMPOLINE

2000   Aleksandr Moskalenko (RUS)
2004   Yury Nikitin (UKR)

ROPE CLIMBING

1896   Nicolaos Andriakopoulos (GRE)
1904   George Eyser (USA)
1924   Bedrich Supcik (TCH)
1932   Raymond Bass (USA)

SWEDISH EXERCISES (TEAM)

1912   Sweden
1920   Sweden

OPTIONAL EXERCISES (TEAM)

1912   Norway
1920   Denmark
1932   United States

PARALLEL BARS (TEAM)

1896   Germany

HORIZONTAL BARS (TEAM)

1896   Germany

Summer Olympic Games Champions (continued)

Gymnastics (men) (continued)

CLUB SWINGING
1904 Edward Hennig (USA)
1932 George Roth (USA)

TUMBLING
1932 Rowland Wolfe (USA)

COMBINED COMPETITION (7 APPARATUS)
1904 Anton Heida (USA)

COMBINED COMPETITION (9 EVENTS)
1904 Adolf Spinnler (SUI)

PRESCRIBED APPARATUS (TEAM)
1904 United States
1908 Sweden
1912 Italy
1952 Sweden
1956 Hungary

MASS EXERCISES (TEAM)
1952 Finland

SIDE HORSE (VAULTS)
1924 Albert Séguin (FRA)

Gymnastics (women)

COMBINED, OR ALL-AROUND (INDIVIDUAL)
1952 Mariya Gorokhovskaya (URS)
1956 Larisa Latynina (URS)
1960 Larisa Latynina (URS)
1964 Vera Caslavska (TCH)
1968 Vera Caslavska (TCH)
1972 Lyudmila Turishcheva (URS)
1976 Nadia Comaneci (ROM)
1980 Yelena Davydova (URS)
1984 Mary-Lou Retton (USA)
1988 Yelena Shushunova (URS)
1992 Tatyana Gutsu (UNT)
1996 Liliya Podkopayeva (UKR)
2000 Simona Amanar (ROM)
2004 Carly Patterson (USA)

COMBINED, OR ALL-AROUND (TEAM)
1928 The Netherlands
1936 Germany
1948 Czechoslovakia
1952 USSR
1956 USSR
1960 USSR
1964 USSR
1968 USSR
1972 USSR
1976 USSR
1980 USSR
1984 Romania
1988 USSR
1992 Unified Team
1996 United States
2000 Romania
2004 Romania

BALANCE BEAM
1952 Nina Bocharova (URS)
1956 Agnes Keleti (HUN)
1960 Eva Bosakova (TCH)

Gymnastics (women) (continued)

BALANCE BEAM
1964 Vera Caslavska (TCH)
1968 Natalya Kuchinskaya (URS)
1972 Olga Korbut (URS)
1976 Nadia Comaneci (ROM)
1980 Nadia Comaneci (ROM)
1984 Ecaterina Szabo (ROM); Simona Pauca
       (ROM) (tied)
1988 Daniela Silivas (ROM)
1992 Tatyana Lysenko (UNT)
1996 Shannon Miller (USA)
2000 Liu Xuan (CHN)
2004 Catalina Ponor (ROM)

UNEVEN PARALLEL BARS
1952 Margit Korondi (HUN)
1956 Agnes Keleti (HUN)
1960 Polina Astakhova (URS)
1964 Polina Astakhova (URS)
1968 Vera Caslavska (TCH)
1972 Karin Janz (GDR)
1976 Nadia Comaneci (ROM)
1980 Maxi Gnauck (GDR)
1984 Julianne McNamara (USA); Ma Yanhong
       (CHN) (tied)
1988 Daniela Silivas (ROM)
1992 Li Lu (CHN)
1996 Svetlana Khorkina (RUS)
2000 Svetlana Khorkina (RUS)
2004 Emilie Lepennec (FRA)

VAULT
1952 Yekaterina Kalinchuk (URS)
1956 Larisa Latynina (URS)
1960 Margarita Nikolayeva (URS)
1964 Vera Caslavska (TCH)
1968 Vera Caslavska (TCH)
1972 Karin Janz (GDR)
1976 Nelli Kim (URS)
1980 Natalya Shaposhnikova (URS)
1984 Ecaterina Szabo (ROM)
1988 Svetlana Boginskaya (URS)
1992 Henrietta Onodi (HUN); Lavinia Milosovici
       (ROM) (tied)
1996 Simona Amanar (ROM)
2000 Yelena Zamolodchikova (RUS)
2004 Monica Rosu (ROM)

FLOOR EXERCISE
1952 Agnes Keleti (HUN)
1956 Larisa Latynina (URS); Agnes Keleti (HUN)
       (tied)
1960 Larisa Latynina (URS)
1964 Larisa Latynina (URS)
1968 Vera Caslavska (TCH); Larissa Petrik (URS)
       (tied)
1972 Olga Korbut (URS)
1976 Nelli Kim (URS)
1980 Nadia Comaneci (ROM); Nelli Kim (URS) (tied)
1984 Ecaterina Szabo (ROM)
1988 Daniela Silivas (ROM)
1992 Lavinia Milosovici (ROM)
1996 Liliya Podkopayeva (UKR)
2000 Yelena Zamolodchikova (RUS)
2004 Catalina Ponor (ROM)

Summer Olympic Games Champions (continued)

Gymnastics (women) (continued)

RHYTHMIC GYMNASTICS (INDIVIDUAL)
1984   Lori Fung (CAN)
1988   Marina Lobatch (URS)
1992   Aleksandra Timoshenko (UNT)
1996   Yekaterina Serebryanskaya (UKR)
2000   Yuliya Barsukova (RUS)
2004   Alina Kabayeva (RUS)

RHYTHMIC GYMNASTICS (TEAM)
1996   Spain
2000   Russia
2004   Russia

TRAMPOLINE
2000   Irina Karavayeva (RUS)
2004   Anna Dogonadze (GER)

HAND APPARATUS (TEAM)
1952   Sweden
1956   Hungary

Handball (team) (outdoors to 1972)

MEN
1936   Germany
1952   Sweden (demonstration)
1972   Yugoslavia
1976   USSR
1980   East Germany
1984   Yugoslavia
1988   USSR
1992   Unified Team
1996   Croatia
2000   Russia
2004   Croatia

WOMEN
1976   USSR
1980   USSR
1984   Yugoslavia
1988   South Korea
1992   South Korea
1996   Denmark
2000   Denmark
2004   Denmark

JEU DE PAUME (ROYAL TENNIS)
1908   Jay Gould (USA)

Judo (men)[9]

60 KG; (132 LB)
1964   Takehide Nakatani (JPN)
1972   Takao Kawaguchi (JPN)
1976   Héctor Rodríguez (CUB)
1980   Thierry Rey (FRA)
1984   Shinji Hosokawa (JPN)
1988   Kim Jae-Yup (KOR)
1992   Nazim Guseynov (UNT)
1996   Tadahiro Nomura (JPN)
2000   Tadahiro Nomura (JPN)
2004   Tadahiro Nomura (JPN)

66 KG (145.2 LB)
1980   Nikolay Solodukhin (URS)
1984   Yoshiyuki Matsuoka (JPN)
1988   Lee Kyung Ken (KOR)
1992   Rogerio Sampaio Cardoso (BRA)
1996   Udo Quellmalz (GER)
2000   Huseyin Ozkan (TUR)

Judo (men)[9] (continued)

66 KG (145.2 LB)
2004   Masato Uchishiba (JPN)

73 KG (160.6 LB)
1972   Takao Kawaguchi (JPN)
1976   Héctor Rodríguez Torres (CUB)
1980   Ezio Gamba (ITA)
1984   Ahn Byeong Keun (KOR)
1988   Marc Alexandre (FRA)
1992   Toshihiko Koga (JPN)
1996   Kenzo Nakamura (JPN)
2000   Giuseppe Maddaloni (ITA)
2004   Lee Won Hee (KOR)

81 KG (178.2 LB)
1972   Toyojazu Nomura (JPN)
1976   Vladimir Nevzorov (URS)
1980   Shota Khabareli (URS)
1984   Frank Wieneke (FRG)
1988   Waldemar Legien (POL)
1992   Hidehiko Yoshida (JPN)
1996   Djamel Bouras (FRA)
2000   Makoto Takimoto (JPN)
2004   Ilias Iliadis (GRE)

90 KG (198 LB)
1964   Isao Okano (JPN)
1972   Shinobu Sekine (JPN)
1976   Isamu Sonoda (JPN)
1980   Jürg Röthlisberger (SUI)
1984   Peter Seisenbacher (AUT)
1988   Peter Seisenbacher (AUT)
1992   Waldemar Legien (POL)
1996   Jeon Ki-Young (KOR)
2000   Mark Huizinga (NED)
2004   Zurab Zviadauri (GEO)

100 KG (220 LB)
1972   Shota Chochoshvili (URS)
1976   Kazuhiro Ninomiya (JPN)
1980   Robert van de Walle (BEL)
1984   Ha Young Zoo (KOR)
1988   Aurelio Miguel (BRA)
1992   Antal Kovacs (HUN)
1996   Pawel Nastula (POL)
2000   Kosei Inoue (JPN)
2004   Ihar Makarau (BLR)

OVER 100 KG (220+ LB)
1964   Isao Inokuma (JPN)
1972   Willem Ruska (NED)
1976   Sergey Novikov (URS)
1980   Angelo Parisi (FRA)
1984   Hitoshi Saito (JPN)
1988   Hitoshi Saito (JPN)
1992   David Khakhaleishvili (UNT)
1996   David Douillet (FRA)
2000   David Douillet (FRA)
2004   Keiji Suzuki (JPN)

OPEN (NO WEIGHT LIMIT)
1964   Antonius Johannes Geesink (NED)
1972   Willem Ruska (NED)
1976   Haruki Uemura (JPN)
1980   Dietmar Lorenz (GDR)
1984   Yasuhiro Yamashita (JPN)

Summer Olympic Games Champions (continued)

Judo (women)[10]

48 KG (105.6 LB)
1992 Cecile Nowak (FRA)
1996 Kye Sun-Hi (PRK)
2000 Ryoko Tamura (JPN)
2004 Ryoko Tani (JPN)

52 KG (114.4 LB)
1992 Almudena Muñoz Martínez (ESP)
1996 Marie-Claire Restoux (FRA)
2000 Legna Verdecia (CUB)
2004 Xian Dongmei (CHN)

57 KG (125.4 LB)
1992 Miriam Blasco Soto (ESP)
1996 Driulis González Morales (CUB)
2000 Isabel Fernández (ESP)
2004 Yvonne Bönisch (GER)

63 KG (138.6 LB)
1992 Catherine Fleury-Vachon (FRA)
1996 Yuko Emoto (JPN)
2000 Severine Vandenhende (FRA)
2004 Ayumi Tanimoto (JPN)

70 KG (154 LB)
1992 Odalis Reve Jiménez (CUB)
1996 Cho Min-Sun (KOR)
2000 Sibelis Veranes (CUB)
2004 Masae Ueno (JPN)

78 KG (171.6 LB)
1992 Kim Mi-Jung (KOR)
1996 Ulla Werbrouck (BEL)
2000 Tang Lin (CHN)
2004 Noriko Anno (JPN)

OVER 78 KG (171.6+ LB)
1992 Zhuang Xiaoyan (CHN)
1996 Sun Fuming (CHN)
2000 Yuan Hua (CHN)
2004 Maki Tsukada (JPN)

Lacrosse
1904 Canada
1908 Canada

Modern pentathlon

INDIVIDUAL (MEN)
1912 Gösta Lilliehöök (SWE)
1920 Gustaf Dyrssen (SWE)
1924 Bo Lindman (SWE)
1928 Sven Thofelt (SWE)
1932 Johan Oxenstierna (SWE)
1936 Gotthardt Handrick (GER)
1948 William Grut (SWE)
1952 Lars-Goran Hall (SWE)
1956 Lars-Goran Hall (SWE)
1960 Ferenc Nemeth (HUN)
1964 Ferenc Torok (HUN)
1968 Björn Ferm (SWE)
1972 Andras Balczo (HUN)
1976 Janusz Pyciak-Peciak (POL)
1980 Anatoly Starostin (URS)
1984 Daniele Masala (ITA)
1988 Janos Martinek (HUN)
1992 Arkadiusz Skrzypaszek (POL)

Modern pentathlon (continued)

INDIVIDUAL (MEN)
1996 Aleksandr Parygin (KAZ)
2000 Dmitry Svatkovsky (RUS)
2004 Andrey Moiseyev (RUS)

INDIVIDUAL (WOMEN)
2000 Stephanie Cook (GBR)
2004 Zsuzsanna Voros (HUN)

TEAM (MEN)
1952 Hungary
1956 USSR
1960 Hungary
1964 USSR
1968 Hungary
1972 USSR
1976 Great Britain
1980 USSR
1984 Italy
1988 Hungary
1992 Poland

Motorboat racing

OPEN CLASS, 40 NAUTICAL MILES		BOAT
1908	Émile Thubron (FRA)	*Camille*

8-METER CLASS, 40 NAUTICAL MILES		
1908	Thomas Thornycroft, Bernard Redwood (GBR)	*Cyrinus*

UNDER 60-FOOT CLASS, 40 NAUTICAL MILES		
1908	Thomas Thornycroft, Bernard Redwood (GBR)	*Cyrinus*

Polo
1900 team comprising members from Great Britain and the United States
1908 Great Britain
1920 Great Britain
1924 Argentina
1936 Argentina

Rackets

SINGLES
1908 Evan Noel (GBR)

DOUBLES
1908 Vane Pennell, John Jacob Astor (GBR)

Roque
1904 Charles Jacobus (USA)

Rowing (men)[11]

SINGLE SCULLS		MIN:SEC
1900	Henri Barrelet (FRA)	7:35.6
1904	Frank Greer (USA)	10:08.5
1908	Harry Blackstaffe (GBR)	9:26.0
1912	William Kinnear (GBR)	7:47.6
1920	John Kelly, Sr. (USA)	7:35.0
1924	Jack Beresford (GBR)	7:49.2
1928	Henry Pearce (AUS)	7:11.0
1932	Henry Pearce (AUS)	7:44.4
1936	Gustav Schäfer (GER)	8:21.5
1948	Mervyn Wood (AUS)	7:24.4
1952	Yury Tyukalov (URS)	8:12.8
1956	Vyacheslav Ivanov (URS)	8:02.5

Summer Olympic Games Champions (continued)

Rowing (men)[11] (continued)

SINGLE SCULLS

		MIN:SEC
1960	Vyacheslav Ivanov (URS)	7:13.96
1964	Vyacheslav Ivanov (URS)	8:22.51
1968	Henri-Jan Wienese (NED)	7:47.80
1972	Yury Malyshev (URS)	7:10.12
1976	Pertti Karppinen (FIN)	7:29.03
1980	Pertti Karppinen (FIN)	7:09.61
1984	Pertti Karppinen (FIN)	7:00.24
1988	Thomas Lange (GDR)	6:49.86
1992	Thomas Lange (GER)	6:51.40
1996	Xeno Mueller (SUI)	6:44.85
2000	Robert Waddell (NZL)	6:48.90
2004	Olaf Tufte (NOR)	6:49.30

DOUBLE SCULLS

		MIN:SEC
1904	United States	10:03.2
1920	United States	7:09.0
1924	United States	6:34.0
1928	United States	6:41.4
1932	United States	7:17.4
1936	Great Britain	7:20.8
1948	Great Britain	6:51.3
1952	Argentina	7:32.2
1956	USSR	7:24.0
1960	Czechoslovakia	6:47.50
1964	USSR	7:10.66
1968	USSR	6:51.82
1972	USSR	7:01.77
1976	Norway	7:13.20
1980	East Germany	6:24.33
1984	United States	6:36.87
1988	The Netherlands	6:21.13
1992	Australia	6:17.32
1996	Italy	6:16.98
2000	Slovenia	6:16.63
2004	France	6:29.00

FOUR SCULLS

		MIN:SEC
1976	East Germany	6:18.65
1980	East Germany	5:49.81
1984	West Germany	5:57.55
1988	Italy	5:53.37
1992	Germany	5:45.17
1996	Germany	5:56.93
2000	Italy	5:45.56
2004	Russia	5:56.85

LIGHTWEIGHT DOUBLE SCULLS

		MIN:SEC
1996	Switzerland	6:23.47
2000	Poland	6:21.75
2004	Poland	6:20.93

PAIRS (WITHOUT COXSWAIN)

		MIN:SEC
1904	United States	10:57.0
1908	Great Britain	9:41.0
1924	The Netherlands	8:19.4
1928	Germany	7:06.4
1932	Great Britain	8:00.0
1936	Germany	8:16.1
1948	Great Britain	7:21.1
1952	United States	8:20.7
1956	United States	7:55.4
1960	USSR	7:02.01
1964	Canada	7:32.94
1968	East Germany	7:26.56
1972	East Germany	6:53.16

Rowing (men)[11] (continued)

PAIRS (WITHOUT COXSWAIN)

		MIN:SEC
1976	East Germany	7:23.31
1980	East Germany	6:48.01
1984	Romania	6:45.39
1988	Great Britain	6:36.84
1992	Great Britain	6:27.72
1996	Great Britain	6:20.09
2000	France	6:32.97
2004	Australia	6:30.76

PAIRS (WITH COXSWAIN)

		MIN:SEC
1900	The Netherlands/France	7:34.2
1920	Italy	7:56.0
1924	Switzerland	8:39.0
1928	Switzerland	7:42.6
1932	United States	8:25.8
1936	Germany	8:36.9
1948	Denmark	8:00.5
1952	France	8:28.6
1956	United States	8:26.1
1960	Germany	7:29.14
1964	United States	8:21.23
1968	Italy	8:04.81
1972	East Germany	7:17.25
1976	East Germany	7:58.99
1980	East Germany	7:02.54
1984	Italy	7:05.99
1988	Italy	6:58.79
1992	Great Britain	6:49.83

LIGHTWEIGHT FOURS (WITHOUT COXSWAIN)

		MIN:SEC
1996	Denmark	6:09.58
2000	France	6:01.68
2004	Denmark	6:01.39

FOURS (WITHOUT COXSWAIN)

		MIN:SEC
1900	France	7:11.0
1904	United States	9:53.8
1908	Great Britain	8:34.0
1920	Great Britain	7:08.6
1928	Great Britain	6:36.0
1932	Great Britain	6:58.2
1936	Germany	7:01.8
1948	Italy	6:39.0
1952	Yugoslavia	7:16.0
1956	Canada	7:08.8
1960	United States	6:26.26
1964	Denmark	6:59.30
1968	East Germany	6:39.18
1972	East Germany	6:24.27
1976	East Germany	6:37.42
1980	East Germany	6:08.17
1984	New Zealand	6:03.48
1988	East Germany	6:03.11
1992	Australia	5:55.04
1996	Australia	6:06.37
2000	Great Britain	5:56.24
2004	Great Britain	6:06.98

FOURS (WITH COXSWAIN)

		MIN:SEC
1900	Germany	5:59.0
1912	Germany	6:59.4
1920	Switzerland	6:54.0
1924	Switzerland	7:18.4
1928	Italy	6:47.8
1932	Germany	7:19.0

Summer Olympic Games Champions (continued)

Rowing (men)[11] (continued)

FOURS (WITH COXSWAIN)

		MIN:SEC
1936	Germany	7:16.2
1948	United States	6:50.3
1952	Czechoslovakia	7:33.4
1956	Italy	7:19.4
1960	Germany	6:39.12
1964	Germany	7:00.44
1968	New Zealand	6:45.62
1972	West Germany	6:31.85
1976	USSR	6:40.22
1980	East Germany	6:14.51
1984	Great Britain	6:18.64
1988	East Germany	6:10.74
1992	Romania	5:59.37

FOURS, INRIGGERS (WITH COXSWAIN)

		MIN:SEC
1912	Denmark	7:47.0

EIGHTS (WITH COXSWAIN)

		MIN:SEC
1900	United States	6:09.8
1904	United States	7:50.0
1908	Great Britain	7:52.0
1912	Great Britain	6:15.0
1920	United States	6:02.6
1924	United States	6:33.4
1928	United States	6:03.2
1932	United States	6:37.6
1936	United States	6:25.4
1948	United States	5:56.7
1952	United States	6:25.9
1956	United States	6:35.2
1960	Germany	5:57.18
1964	United States	6:18.23
1968	West Germany	6:07.00
1972	New Zealand	6:08.94
1976	East Germany	5:58.29
1980	East Germany	5:49.05
1984	Canada	5:41.32
1988	West Germany	5:46.05
1992	Canada	5:29.53
1996	The Netherlands	5:42.74
2000	Great Britain	5:33.08
2004	United States	5:42.48

SIX-MAN NAVAL ROWING BOATS (2,000 METERS)

		MIN:SEC
1906	Italy	10:45.0

SIXTEEN-MAN NAVAL ROWING BOATS (3,000 METERS)

		MIN:SEC
1906	Greece	16:35.0

Rowing (women)[12]

SINGLE SCULLS

		MIN:SEC
1976	Christine Scheiblich (GDR)	4:05.56
1980	Sanda Toma (ROM)	3:40.69
1984	Valeria Racila (ROM)	3:40.68
1988	Jutta Behrendt (GDR)	7:47.19
1992	Elisabeta Lipa (ROM)	7:25.54
1996	Yekaterina Khodotovich (BLR)	7:32.21
2000	Yekaterina Khodotovich Karsten (BLR)	7:28.14
2004	Katrin Rutschow-Stomporowski (GER)	7:18.12

DOUBLE SCULLS

		MIN:SEC
1976	Bulgaria	3:44.36
1980	USSR	3:16.27

Rowing (women)[12] (continued)

DOUBLE SCULLS

		MIN:SEC
1984	Romania	3:26.75
1988	East Germany	7:00.48
1992	Germany	6:49.00
1996	Canada	6:56.84
2000	Germany	6:55.44
2004	New Zealand	7:01.79

LIGHTWEIGHT DOUBLE SCULLS

		MIN:SEC
1996	Romania	7:12.78
2000	Romania	7:02.64
2004	Romania	6:56.05

FOUR SCULLS

		MIN:SEC
1976	East Germany	3:29.99
1980	East Germany	3:15.32
1984	Romania	3:14.11
1988	East Germany	6:21.06
1992	Germany	6:20.18
1996	Germany	6:27.44
2000	Germany	6:19.58
2004	Germany	6:29.29

PAIRS (WITHOUT COXSWAIN)

		MIN:SEC
1976	Bulgaria	4:01.22
1980	East Germany	3:30.49
1984	Romania	3:32.60
1988	Romania	7:28.13
1992	Canada	7:06.22
1996	Australia	7:01.39
2000	Romania	7:11.00
2004	Romania	7:06.55

FOURS (WITH COXSWAIN [WITHOUT IN 1992])

		MIN:SEC
1976	East Germany	3:45.08
1980	East Germany	3:19.27
1984	Romania	3:19.3
1988	East Germany	6:56.0
1992	Canada	6:30.85

EIGHTS (WITH COXSWAIN)

		MIN:SEC
1976	East Germany	3:33.32
1980	East Germany	3:03.32
1984	United States	2:59.80
1988	East Germany	6:15.17
1992	Canada	6:02.62
1996	Romania	6:19.73
2000	Romania	6:06.44
2004	Romania	6:17.70

Rugby football

1900	France
1908	Australia
1920	United States
1924	United States

Sailing (yachting)

BOARDSAILING (WINDGLIDER/DIVISION II) (OPEN)

1984	Stephan van den Berg (NED)
1988	Anthony Bruce Kendall (NZL)

BOARDSAILING (MISTRAL FROM 1996) (MEN)

1992	Franck David (FRA)
1996	Nikolaos Kaklamanakis (GRE)
2000	Christoph Sieber (AUT)
2004	Gal Fridman (ISR)

Summer Olympic Games Champions (continued)

Sailing (yachting) (continued)

BOARDSAILING (MISTRAL FROM 1996) (WOMEN)
1992　Barbara Anne Kendall (NZL)
1996　Lee Lai Shan (HKG)
2000　Alessandra Sensini (ITA)
2004　Faustine Merret (FRA)

SINGLE-HANDED DINGHY (EUROPE) (WOMEN)
1992　Linda Andersen (NOR)
1996　Kristine Roug (DEN)
2000　Shirley Anne Robertson (GBR)
2004　Siren Sundby (NOR)

SINGLE-HANDED DINGHY (LASER) (OPEN)
1996　Robert Scheidt (BRA)
2000　Ben Ainslie (GBR)
2004　Robert Scheidt (BRA)

SINGLE-HANDED DINGHY (FINN FROM 1952)
(MEN; OPEN UNTIL 1992)
1924　Léon Huybrechts (BEL)
1928　Sven Thorell (SWE)
1932　Jacques Lebrun (FRA)
1936　Daniel Kagchelland (NED)
1948　Paul Elvström (DEN)
1952　Paul Elvström (DEN)
1956　Paul Elvström (DEN)
1960　Paul Elvström (DEN)
1964　Wilhelm Kuhweide (GER)
1968　Valentin Mankin (URS)
1972　Serge Maury (FRA)
1976　Jochen Schümann (GDR)
1980　Esko Rechardt (FIN)
1984　Russell Coutts (NZL)
1988　José Luis Doreste (ESP)
1992　José van der Ploeg (ESP)
1996　Mateusz Kusznierewicz (POL)
2000　Iain Percy (GBR)
2004　Ben Ainslie (GBR)

DOUBLE-HANDED DINGHY (470) (MEN)
1976　West Germany
1980　Brazil
1984　Spain
1988　France
1992　Spain
1996　Ukraine
2000　Australia
2004　United States

DOUBLE-HANDED DINGHY (470) (WOMEN)
1988　United States
1992　Spain
1996　Spain
2000　Australia
2004　Greece

YNGLING (WOMEN)
2004　Great Britain

HIGH-PERFORMANCE DINGHY (49ER) (OPEN)
2000　Finland
2004　Spain

MULTIHULL (TORNADO) (OPEN)
1976　Great Britain
1980　Brazil

Sailing (yachting) (continued)

MULTIHULL (TORNADO) (OPEN)
1984　New Zealand
1988　France
1992　France
1996　Spain
2000　Austria
2004　Austria

FLEET/MATCH RACE KEELBOAT (SOLING) (OPEN)
1972　United States
1976　Denmark
1980　Denmark
1984　United States
1988　East Germany
1992　Denmark
1996　Germany
2000　Denmark

TWO-PERSON KEELBOAT (STAR) (OPEN)
1932　United States
1936　Germany
1948　United States
1952　Italy
1956　United States
1960　USSR
1964　The Bahamas
1968　United States
1972　Australia
1980　USSR
1984　United States
1988　Great Britain
1992　United States
1996　Brazil
2000　United States
2004　Brazil

40-METER CLASS
1920　Sweden

30-METER CLASS
1920　Sweden

12-METER CLASS
1920 (old)　Norway
1920 (new)　Norway

OVER-10-METER CLASS
1900　France
1908　Great Britain
1912　Norway

10-METER CLASS
1900　Germany
1912　Sweden
1920 (old)　Norway
1920 (new)　Norway

8-METER CLASS
1900　Great Britain
1908　Great Britain
1912　Norway
1920 (old)　Norway
1920 (new)　Norway
1924　Norway
1928　France

Summer Olympic Games Champions (continued)

Sailing (yachting) (continued)

8-METER CLASS

1932	United States
1936	Italy

7-METER CLASS

1908	Great Britain
1920 (old)	Great Britain

6.5-METER CLASS

1920 (new)	The Netherlands

6-METER CLASS

1900	Switzerland
1908	Great Britain
1912	France
1920 (old)	Belgium
1920 (new)	Norway
1924	Norway
1928	Norway
1932	Sweden
1936	Great Britain
1948	United States
1952	United States

5.5-METER CLASS

1952	United States
1956	Sweden
1960	United States
1964	Australia
1968	Sweden

18-FOOT CENTERBOARD BOAT

1920	Great Britain

12-FOOT CENTERBOARD BOAT

1920	The Netherlands
1924	Belgium

12-FOOT DINGHY

1928	Sweden

MONOTYPE CLASS

1932	France

MONOTYPE CLASS "NÜRNBERG"

1936	The Netherlands

SWALLOW

1948	Great Britain

FIREFLY

1948	Denmark

SHARPIE

1956	New Zealand

DRAGON

1948	Norway
1952	Norway
1956	Sweden
1960	Greece
1964	Denmark
1968	United States
1972	Australia

Sailing (yachting) (continued)

TEMPEST

1972	USSR
1976	Sweden

FLYING DUTCHMAN

1960	Norway
1964	New Zealand
1968	Great Britain
1972	Great Britain
1976	West Germany
1980	Spain
1984	United States
1988	Denmark
1992	Spain

Shooting (men)

individual

TRAP (CLAY PIGEON) (OPEN 1968–92)

1900	Roger de Barbarin (FRA)
1908	Walter Ewing (CAN)
1912	James Graham (USA)
1920	Mark Arie (USA)
1924	Gyula Halasy (HUN)
1952	George Généreux (CAN)
1956	Galliano Rossini (ITA)
1960	Ion Dumitrescu (ROM)
1964	Ennio Mattarelli (ITA)
1968	John Braithwaite (GBR)
1972	Angelo Scalzone (ITA)
1976	Donald Haldeman (USA)
1980	Luciano Giovannetti (ITA)
1984	Luciano Giovannetti (ITA)
1988	Donald Monakov (URS)
1992	Petr Hrdlicka (TCH)
1996	Michael Constantine Diamond (AUS)
2000	Michael Constantine Diamond (AUS)
2004	Aleksey Alipov (RUS)

DOUBLE TRAP

1996	Russell Andrew Mark (AUS)
2000	Richard Faulds (GBR)
2004	Ahmed Almaktoum (UAE)

SKEET (OPEN UNTIL 1996)

1968	Yevgeny Petrov (URS)
1972	Konrad Wirnhier (FRG)
1976	Josef Panacek (TCH)
1980	Hans Kjeld Rasmussen (DEN)
1984	Matthew Dryke (USA)
1988	Axel Wegner (GDR)
1992	Zhang Shan (CHN)
1996	Ennio Falco (ITA)
2000	Mykola Milchev (UKR)
2004	Andrea Benelli (ITA)

FREE PISTOL

1896	Sumner Paine (USA)
1900	Karl Konrad Röderer (SUI)
1912	Alfred Lane (USA)
1920	Carl Frederick (USA)
1936	Torsten Ullmann (SWE)
1948	Edwin Vásquez Cam (PER)
1952	Huelet Benner (USA)
1956	Pentti Tapio Linnosvuo (FIN)
1960	Aleksey Gushchin (URS)
1964	Väinö Johannes Markkanen (FIN)
1968	Grigory Kosykh (URS)
1976	Uwe Potteck (GDR)

Summer Olympic Games Champions (continued)

Shooting (men) (continued)
individual (continued)

FREE PISTOL

1980	Aleksandr Melentev (URS)
1984	Xu Haifeng (CHN)
1988	Sorin Babii (ROM)
1992	Konstantin Lukachik (UNT)
1996	Boris Kokorev (RUS)
2000	Tanyu Kiryakov (BUL)
2004	Mikhail Nestruyev (RUS)

RAPID-FIRE PISTOL

1896	Joannis Phrangudis (GRE)
1900	Maurice Larrouy (FRA)
1908	Paul van Asbrock (BEL)
1912	Alfred Lane (USA)
1920	Guilherme Paraense (BRA)
1924	Henry Bailey (USA)
1932	Renzo Morigi (ITA)
1936	Cornelius van Oyen (GER)
1948	Karoly Takacs (HUN)
1952	Karoly Takacs (HUN)
1956	Stefan Petrescu (ROM)
1960	William McMillan (USA)
1964	Pentti Tapio Linnosvuo (FIN)
1968	Jozef Zapedzki (POL)
1972	Jozef Zapedzki (POL)
1976	Norbert Klaar (GDR)
1980	Corneliu Ion (ROM)
1984	Takeo Kamachi (JPN)
1988	Afanasy Kuzmin (URS)
1992	Ralf Schumann (GER)
1996	Ralf Schumann (GER)
2000	Sergey Alifirenko (RUS)
2004	Ralf Schumann (GER)

SMALL-BORE RIFLE (PRONE)

1908	Arthur Ashton Carnell (GBR)
1912	Frederick Hird (USA)
1920	Lawrence Nuesslein (USA)
1924	Pierre Coquelin de Lisle (FRA)
1932	Bertil Rönnmark (SWE)
1936	Willy Røgeberg (NOR)
1948	Arthur Cook (USA)
1952	Iosif Sarbu (ROM)
1956	Gerald Ouellette (CAN)
1960	Peter Kohnke (GER)
1964	Laszlo Hammerl (HUN)
1968	Jan Kurka (TCH)
1972	Ho Jun Li (PRK)
1976	Karlheinz Smieszek (FRG)
1980	Karoly Varga (HUN)
1984	Edward Etzel (USA)
1988	Miroslav Varga (TCH)
1992	Lee Eun Chul (KOR)
1996	Christian Klees (GER)
2000	Jonas Edman (SWE)
2004	Matthew Emmons (USA)

SMALL-BORE RIFLE (3 POSITIONS)

1952	Erling Kongshaug (NOR)
1956	Anatoly Bogdanov (URS)
1960	Viktor Shamburkin (URS)
1964	Lones Wesley Wigger (USA)
1968	Bernd Klingner (FRG)
1972	John Writer (USA)
1976	Lanny Bassham (USA)

Shooting (men) (continued)
individual (continued)

SMALL-BORE RIFLE (3 POSITIONS)

1980	Viktor Vlasov (URS)
1984	Malcolm Cooper (GBR)
1988	Malcolm Cooper (GBR)
1992	Gratchia Petikian (UNT)
1996	Jean-Pierre Amat (FRA)
2000	Rajmond Debevec (SLO)
2004	Jia Zhanbo (CHN)

10-METER RUNNING (GAME) TARGET

1900	Louis Debray (FRA)
1972	Yakov Zheleznyak (URS)
1976	Aleksandr Gazov (URS)
1980	Igor Sokolov (URS)
1984	Li Yuwei (CHN)
1988	Tor Heiestad (NOR)
1992	Michael Jakosits (GER)
1996	Yang Ling (CHN)
2000	Yang Ling (CHN)
2004	Manfred Kurzer (GER)

AIR RIFLE

1984	Philippe Heberle (FRA)
1988	Goran Maksimovic (YUG)
1992	Yury Fedkin (UNT)
1996	Artyom Khadzhibekov (RUS)
2000	Cai Yalin (CHN)
2004	Zhu Quinan (CHN)

AIR PISTOL

1988	Tanyu Kiryakov (BUL)
1992	Wang Yifu (CHN)
1996	Roberto di Donna (ITA)
2000	Franck Dumoulin (FRA)
2004	Wang Yifu (CHN)

FREE RIFLE (300 M, 3 POSITIONS)

1908	Albert Helgerud (NOR)
1912	Paul René Colas (FRA)
1920	Morris Fisher (USA)
1924	Morris Fisher (USA)
1948	Emil Grünig (SUI)
1952	Anatoly Bogdanov (URS)
1956	Vasily Borisov (URS)
1960	Hubert Hammerer (AUT)
1964	Gary Lee Anderson (USA)
1968	Gary Lee Anderson (USA)
1972	Lones Wesley Wigger (USA)

ARMY RIFLE (300 M, 3 POSITIONS)

1896	Georgios Orphanidis (GRE)
1900	Emil Kellenberger (SUI)
1912	Sandor Prokop (HUN)

ARMY RIFLE (200 M)

1896	Pantelis Karasevdas (GRE)

FREE RIFLE (1,000 YD PRONE)

1908	Joshua Millner (GBR)

FULL-BORE RIFLE (300 M STANDING)

1900	Lars Madsen (DEN)

FULL-BORE RIFLE (300 M KNEELING)

1900	Konrad Staeheli (SUI)

Summer Olympic Games Champions (continued)

Shooting (men) (continued)

individual (continued)

FULL-BORE RIFLE (300 M PRONE)
1900   Achille Paroche (FRA)

FULL-BORE RIFLE (300 M)
1900   Emil Kellenberger (SUI)

RIFLE (300 M, 2 POSITIONS)
1920   Morris Fisher (USA)

RIFLE (300 M STANDING)
1920   Carl Osburn (USA)

RIFLE (300 M PRONE)
1920   Otto Olsen (NOR)

RIFLE (600 M PRONE)
1920   Hugo Johansson (SWE)

6-MILLIMETER SMALL GUN (OPEN REAR SIGHT)
1900   C. Grosett (FRA)

SMALL-BORE RIFLE (VANISHING TARGET)
1908   William Styles (GBR)
1912   Wilhelm Carlberg (SWE)

SMALL-BORE RIFLE (MOVING TARGET)
1908   John Francis Fleming (GBR)

RUNNING DEER (100 M SINGLE SHOT)
1908   Oscar Swahn (SWE)
1912   Alfred Swahn (SWE)
1920   Otto Olsen (NOR)
1924   John Boles (USA)

RUNNING DEER (100 M DOUBLE SHOT)
1908   Walter Winans (USA)
1912   Ake Lundeberg (SWE)
1920   Ole Andreas Lilloe-Olsen (NOR)
1924   Ole Andreas Lilloe-Olsen (NOR)

RUNNING DEER (100 M SINGLE AND DOUBLE SHOT)
1952   John Larsen (NOR)
1956   Vitaly Romanenko (URS)

LIVE PIGEON
1900   Léon de Lunden (BEL)

GAME SHOOTING
1900   Donald Mackintosh (AUS)

MILITARY REVOLVER (25 M)
1896   John Paine (USA)

MILITARY REVOLVER (20 M)
1906   Louis Richardet (SUI)
1906 (model 1873–74)   Jean Fouconnier (FRA)

REVOLVER AND PISTOL
1900   Paul van Asbrock (BEL)
1908   Paul van Asbrock (BEL)
1912   Alfred Lane (USA)

DUELING PISTOL
1906 (20 m)   Léon Moreaux (FRA)
1906 (25 m)   Konstantinos Skarlatos (GRE)
1912   Alfred Lane (USA)

Shooting (men) (continued)

team

FREE RIFLE (300 M)
1908   Norway
1912   Sweden

ARMY RIFLE (300 M)
1900   Norway

ARMY RIFLE (ALL-AROUND)
1900   United States
1908   United States
1912   United States

FULL-BORE RIFLE (300 M)
1900   Switzerland

SMALL-BORE RIFLE
1900   Great Britain
1908   Great Britain
1920   United States
1924   France

SMALL-BORE RIFLE (VANISHING TARGET)
1912   Sweden

RIFLE (600 M PRONE)
1920   United States

RIFLE (300 M, 2 POSITIONS)
1920   United States

RIFLE (300 M STANDING)
1920   Denmark

RIFLE (300 M PRONE)
1920   United States

RIFLE (ALL-AROUND)
1920   United States
1924   United States

RUNNING DEER (SINGLE SHOT)
1908   Sweden
1912   Sweden
1920   Norway
1924   Norway

RUNNING DEER (DOUBLE SHOT)
1920   Norway
1924   Great Britain

CLAY PIGEON
1900   Great Britain
1908   Great Britain
1912   United States
1920   United States
1924   United States

REVOLVER
1900   Switzerland

PISTOL
1920   United States
1924   United States

REVOLVER AND PISTOL
1900   United States
1908   United States

Summer Olympic Games Champions (continued)

Shooting (men) (continued)

team (continued)

REVOLVER AND PISTOL
1912   United States
1920   United States

DUELING PISTOL
1912   Sweden

Shooting (women)

TRAP (CLAY PIGEON)
2000   Daina Gudzineviciute (LTU)
2004   Suzanne Balogh (AUS)

DOUBLE TRAP
1996   Kim Rhode (USA)
2000   Pia Hansen (SWE)
2004   Kimberly Rhode (USA)

SKEET
2000   Zemfira Meftakhetdinova (AZE)
2004   Diana Igaly (HUN)

SPORT PISTOL
1984   Linda Thom (CAN)
1988   Nino Salukvadze (URS)
1992   Marina Logvinenko (UNT)
1996   Li Duihong (CHN)
2000   Mariya Zdravkova Grozdeva (BUL)
2004   Mariya Zdravkova Grozdeva (BUL)

SMALL-BORE RIFLE (3 POSITIONS)
1984   Wu Xiao-Xuan (CHN)
1988   Silvia Sperber (FRG)
1992   Launi Meili (USA)
1996   Aleksandra Ivosev (YUG)
2000   Renata Mauer (POL)
2004   Lyubov Galkina (RUS)

AIR RIFLE
1984   Pat Spurgin (USA)
1988   Irina Chilova (URS)
1992   Yeo Kab Soon (KOR)
1996   Renata Mauer (POL)
2000   Nancy Johnson (USA)
2004   Du Li (CHN)

AIR PISTOL
1988   Jasna Sekaric (YUG)
1992   Marina Logvinenko (UNT)
1996   Olga Klochneva (RUS)
2000   Tao Luna (CHN)
2004   Olena Kostevych (UKR)

Softball

1996   United States
2000   United States
2004   United States

Swimming (men)

50-METER FREESTYLE		SEC
1988	Matthew Biondi (USA)	22.14
1992	Aleksandr Popov (UNT)	21.91
1996	Aleksandr Popov (RUS)	22.13
2000	Anthony Ervin (USA); Gary Hall, Jr.	21.98
	(USA) (*tied*)	
2004	Gary Hall (USA)	21.93

Swimming (men) (continued)

100-METER FREESTYLE		MIN:SEC
1896	Alfred Hajos (HUN)	1:22.2
1904	Zoltan Halmay (HUN)	1:02.8[13]
1908	Charles Daniels (USA)	1:05.6
1912	Duke Paoa Kahanamoku (USA)	1:03.4
1920	Duke Paoa Kahanamoku (USA)	1:00.4
1924	Johnny Weissmuller (USA)	59.0
1928	Johnny Weissmuller (USA)	58.6
1932	Yasuji Miyazaki (JPN)	58.2
1936	Ferenc Csik (HUN)	57.6
1948	Walter Ris (USA)	57.3
1952	Clark Scholes (USA)	57.4
1956	Jon Henricks (AUS)	55.4
1960	John Devitt (AUS)	55.2
1964	Donald Schollander (USA)	53.4
1968	Michael Wenden (AUS)	52.2
1972	Mark Spitz (USA)	51.22
1976	Jim Montgomery (USA)	49.99
1980	Jörg Wöithe (GDR)	50.40
1984	Ambrose Gaines (USA)	49.80
1988	Matthew Biondi (USA)	48.63
1992	Aleksandr Popov (UNT)	49.02
1996	Aleksandr Popov (RUS)	48.74
2000	Pieter Van den Hoogenband (NED)	48.30
2004	Pieter Van den Hoogenband (NED)	48.17

100 METER FREESTYLE FOR SAILORS		MIN:SEC
1896	Ioannis Malokinis (GRE)	2:20.4

200-METER FREESTYLE		MIN:SEC
1900	Fred Lane (AUS)	2:25.2
1904	Charles Daniels (USA)	2:44.2[14]
1968	Michael Wenden (AUS)	1:55.2
1972	Mark Spitz (USA)	1:52.78
1976	Bruce Furniss (USA)	1:50.29
1980	Sergey Koplyakov (URS)	1:49.81
1984	Michael Gross (FRG)	1:47.44
1988	Duncan Armstrong (AUS)	1:47.25
1992	Yevgeny Sadovy (UNT)	1:46.70
1996	Danyon Loader (NZL)	1:47.63
2000	Pieter Van den Hoogenband (NED)	1:45.35
2004	Ian Thorpe (AUS)	1:44.71

400-METER FREESTYLE		MIN:SEC
1896	Paul Neumann (AUT)	8:12.6[15]
1904	Charles Daniels (USA)	6:16.2[16]
1908	Henry Taylor (GBR)	5:36.8
1912	George Hodgson (CAN)	5:24.4
1920	Norman Ross (USA)	5:26.8
1924	Johnny Weissmuller (USA)	5:04.2
1928	Victoriano Zorilla (ARG)	5:01.6
1932	Clarence Crabbe (USA)	4:48.4
1936	Jack Medica (USA)	4:44.5
1948	William Smith (USA)	4:41.0
1952	Jean Boiteux (FRA)	4:30.7
1956	Murray Rose (AUS)	4:27.3
1960	Murray Rose (AUS)	4:18.3
1964	Donald Schollander (USA)	4:12.2
1968	Michael Burton (USA)	4:09.0
1972	Bradford Cooper (AUS)	4:00.27
1976	Brian Goodell (USA)	3:51.93
1980	Vladimir Salnikov (URS)	3:51.31
1984	George DiCarlo (USA)	3:51.23
1988	Uwe Dassler (GDR)	3:46.95
1992	Yevgeny Sadovy (UNT)	3:45.00

Summer Olympic Games Champions (continued)

Swimming (men) (continued)

400-METER FREESTYLE		MIN:SEC
1996	Danyon Loader (NZL)	3:47.97
2000	Ian Thorpe (AUS)	3:40.59
2004	Ian Thorpe (AUS)	3:43.10

1,500-METER FREESTYLE		MIN:SEC
1896	Alfred Hajos (HUN)	18:22.2[17]
1900	Johnny Arthur Jarvis (GBR)	13:40.2[18]
1904	Emil Rausch (GER)	27:18.2[19]
1908	Henry Taylor (GBR)	22:48.4
1912	George Hodgson (CAN)	22:00.0
1920	Norman Ross (USA)	22:23.2
1924	Andrew Charlton (AUS)	20:06.6
1928	Arne Borg (SWE)	19:51.8
1932	Kusuo Kitamura (JPN)	19:12.4
1936	Noboru Terada (JPN)	19:13.7
1948	James McLane (USA)	19:18.5
1952	Ford Konno (USA)	18:30:0
1956	Murray Rose (AUS)	17:58.9
1960	John Konrads (AUS)	17:19.6
1964	Robert Windle (AUS)	17:01.7
1968	Michael Burton (USA)	16:38.9
1972	Michael Burton (USA)	15:52.58
1976	Brian Goodell (USA)	15:02.40
1980	Vladimir Salnikov (URS)	14:58.27
1984	Michael O'Brien (USA)	15:05.20
1988	Vladimir Salnikov (URS)	15:00.40
1992	Kieren Perkins (AUS)	14:43.48
1996	Kieren Perkins (AUS)	14:56.40
2000	Grant Hackett (AUS)	14:48.33
2004	Grant Hackett (AUS)	14:43.40

4,000-METER FREESTYLE		MIN:SEC
1900	Johnny Arthur Jarvis (GBR)	58:24

880-YARD FREESTYLE		MIN:SEC
1904	Emil Rausch (GER)	13:11.4

1-MILE FREESTYLE		MIN:SEC
1904	Emil Rausch (GER)	27:18.2

100-METER BUTTERFLY		SEC
1968	Douglas Russell (USA)	55.9
1972	Mark Spitz (USA)	54.27
1976	Matt Vogel (USA)	54.35
1980	Pär Arvidsson (SWE)	54.92
1984	Michael Gross (FRG)	53.08
1988	Anthony Nesty (SUR)	53.00
1992	Pablo Morales (USA)	53.32
1996	Denis Pankratov (RUS)	52.27
2000	Lars Frölander (SWE)	52.00
2004	Michael Phelps (USA)	51.25

200-METER BUTTERFLY		MIN
1956	William Yorzyk (USA)	2:19.3
1960	Michael Troy (USA)	2:12.8
1964	Kevin Berry (AUS)	2:06.6
1968	Carl Robie (USA)	2:08.7
1972	Mark Spitz (USA)	2:00.70
1976	Mike Bruner (USA)	1:59.23
1980	Sergey Fesenko (URS)	1:59.76
1984	Jonathan Sieben (AUS)	1:57.04
1988	Michael Gross (FRG)	1:56.94
1992	Mel Stewart (USA)	1:56.26
1996	Denis Pankratov (RUS)	1:56.51
2000	Tom Malchow (USA)	1:55.35
2004	Michael Phelps (USA)	1:54.04

Swimming (men) (continued)

100-METER BACKSTROKE		MIN:SEC
1904	Walter Brack (GER)	1:16.8[20]
1908	Arno Bieberstein (GER)	1:24.6
1912	Harry Hebner (USA)	1:21.2
1920	Warren Paoa Kealoha (USA)	1:15.2
1924	Warren Paoa Kealoha (USA)	1:13.2
1928	George Kojac (USA)	1:08.2
1932	Masaji Kiyokawa (JPN)	1:08.6
1936	Adolph Kiefer (USA)	1:05.9
1948	Allen Stack (USA)	1:06.4
1952	Yoshinobu Oyakawa (JPN)	1:05.4
1956	David Theile (AUS)	1:02.2
1960	David Theile (AUS)	1:01.9
1968	Roland Matthes (GDR)	58.7
1972	Roland Matthes (GDR)	56.58
1976	John Naber (USA)	55.49
1980	Bengt Baron (SWE)	56.53
1984	Richard Carey (USA)	55.79
1988	Daichi Suzuki (JPN)	55.05
1992	Mark Tewksbury (CAN)	53.98
1996	Jeff Rouse (USA)	54.10
2000	Lenny Krayzelburg (USA)	53.72
2004	Aaron Peirsol (USA)	54.06

200-METER BACKSTROKE		MIN:SEC
1900	Ernst Hoppenberg (GER)	2:47.0
1964	Jed Graef (USA)	2:10.3
1968	Roland Matthes (GDR)	2:09.6
1972	Roland Matthes (GDR)	2:02.82
1976	John Naber (USA)	1:59.19
1980	Sandor Wladar (HUN)	2:01.93
1984	Richard Carey (USA)	2:00.23
1988	Igor Polyansky (URS)	1:59.37
1992	Martin López-Zubero (ESP)	1:58.47
1996	Brad Bridgewater (USA)	1:58.54
2000	Lenny Krayzelburg (USA)	1:56.76
2004	Aaron Peirsol (USA)	1:54.95

100-METER BREASTSTROKE		MIN:SEC
1968	Donald McKenzie (USA)	1:07.7
1972	Nobutaka Tagushi (JPN)	1:04.94
1976	John Hencken (USA)	1:03.11
1980	Duncan Goodhew (GBR)	1:03.34
1984	Steve Lundquist (USA)	1:01.65
1988	Adrian Moorhouse (GBR)	1:02.04
1992	Nelson Diebel (USA)	1:01.50
1996	Frederick Deburghgraeve (BEL)	1:00.65
2000	Domenico Fioravanti (ITA)	1:00.46
2004	Kosuke Kitajima (JPN)	1:00.08

200-METER BREASTSTROKE		MIN:SEC
1908	Frederick Holman (GBR)	3:09.2
1912	Walter Bathe (GER)	3:01.8
1920	Hakan Malmroth (SWE)	3:04.4
1924	Robert Skelton (USA)	2:56.6
1928	Yoshiyuki Tsuruta (JPN)	2:48.8
1932	Yoshiyuki Tsuruta (JPN)	2:45.4
1936	Tetsuo Hamuro (JPN)	2:42.5
1948	Joseph Verdeur (USA)	2:39.3
1952	John Davies (AUS)	2:34.4
1956	Masaru Furukawa (JPN)	2:34.7
1960	William Mulliken (USA)	2:37.4
1964	Ian O'Brien (AUS)	2:27.8
1968	Felipe Muñoz (MEX)	2:28.7
1972	John Hencken (USA)	2:21.55
1976	David Wilkie (GBR)	2:15.11
1980	Robertas Zulpa (URS)	2:15.85
1984	Victor Davis (CAN)	2:13.34

Summer Olympic Games Champions (continued)

Swimming (men) (continued)

200-METER BREASTSTROKE — MIN:SEC
1988	Jozsef Szabo (HUN)	2:13.52
1992	Mike Barrowman (USA)	2:10.16
1996	Norbert Rozsa (HUN)	2:12.57
2000	Domenico Fioravanti (ITA)	2:10.87
2004	Kosuke Kitajima (JPN)	2:09.44

400-METER BREASTSTROKE — MIN:SEC
1904	Georg Zacharias (GER)	7:23.6[21]
1912	Walter Bathe (GER)	6:29.6
1920	Hakan Malmroth (SWE)	6:31.8

200-YARD RELAY — MIN:SEC
1904	United States	2:04.6

200-METER MEDLEY — MIN:SEC
1968	Charles Hickcox (USA)	2:12.0
1972	Gunnar Larsson (SWE)	2:07.17
1984	Alex Baumann (CAN)	2:01.42
1988	Tamas Darnyi (HUN)	2:00.17
1992	Tamas Darnyi (HUN)	2:00.76
1996	Attila Czene (HUN)	1:59.91
2000	Massimiliano Rosolino (ITA)	1:58.98
2004	Michael Phelps (USA)	1:57.14

400-METER MEDLEY — MIN:SEC
1964	Richard William Roth (USA)	4:45.4
1968	Charles Hickcox (USA)	4:48.4
1972	Gunnar Larsson (SWE)	4:31.98
1976	Rod Strachan (USA)	4:23.68
1980	Aleksandr Sidorenko (URS)	4:22.89
1984	Alex Baumann (CAN)	4:17.41
1988	Tamas Darnyi (HUN)	4:14.75
1992	Tamas Darnyi (HUN)	4:14.23
1996	Tom Dolan (USA)	4:14.90
2000	Tom Dolan (USA)	4:11.76
2004	Michael Phelps (USA)	4:08.26

4 × 100-METER MEDLEY RELAY — MIN:SEC
1960	United States	4:05.4
1964	United States	3:58.4
1968	United States	3:54.9
1972	United States	3:48.16
1976	United States	3:42.22
1980	Australia	3:45.70
1984	United States	3:39.30
1988	United States	3:36.93
1992	United States	3:36.93
1996	United States	3:34.84
2000	United States	3:33.73
2004	United States	3:30.68

4 × 100-METER FREESTYLE RELAY — MIN:SEC
1964	United States	3:33.2
1968	United States	3:31.7
1972	United States	3:26.42
1984	United States	3:19.03
1988	United States	3:16.53
1992	United States	3:16.74
1996	United States	3:15.41
2000	Australia	3:13.67
2004	South Africa	3:13.17

4 × 200-METER FREESTYLE RELAY — MIN:SEC
1908	Great Britain	10:55.6
1912	Australia	10:11.2
1920	United States	10:04.4
1924	United States	9:53.4

Swimming (men) (continued)

4 × 200-METER FREESTYLE RELAY — MIN:SEC
1928	United States	9:36.2
1932	Japan	8:58.4
1936	Japan	8:51.5
1948	United States	8:46.0
1952	United States	8:31.1
1956	Australia	8:23.6
1960	United States	8:10.2
1964	United States	7:52.1
1968	United States	7:52.3
1972	United States	7:35.78
1976	United States	7:23.22
1980	USSR	7:23.50
1984	United States	7:15.69
1988	United States	7:12.51
1992	Unified Team	7:11.95
1996	United States	7:14.84
2000	Australia	7:07.05
2004	United States	7:07.33

60-METER UNDERWATER — MIN:SEC (UNDERWATER)
1900	Charles de Vendeville (FRA)	1:08.4

200-METER OBSTACLE — MIN:SEC
1900	Frederick Lane (AUS)	2:38.4

Swimming (women)

50-METER FREESTYLE — SEC
1988	Kristin Otto (GDR)	25.49
1992	Yang Wenyi (CHN)	24.79
1996	Amy Van Dyken (USA)	24.87
2000	Inge de Bruijn (NED)	24.32
2004	Inge de Bruijn (NED)	24.58

100-METER FREESTYLE — MIN:SEC
1912	Fanny Durack (AUS)	1:22.2
1920	Ethelda Bleibtrey (USA)	1:13.6
1924	Ethel Lackie (USA)	1:12.4
1928	Albina Osipowich (USA)	1:11.0
1932	Helene Madison (USA)	1:06.8
1936	Hendrika Mastenbroek (NED)	1:05.9
1948	Greta Andersen (DEN)	1:06.3
1952	Katalin Szoke (HUN)	1:06.8
1956	Dawn Fraser (AUS)	1:02.0
1960	Dawn Fraser (AUS)	1:01.2
1964	Dawn Fraser (AUS)	59.5
1968	Jan Henne (USA)	1:00.0
1972	Sandra Neilson (USA)	58.59
1976	Kornelia Ender (GDR)	55.65
1980	Barbara Krause (GDR)	54.79
1984	Carrie Steinseifer (USA); Nancy Hogshead (USA) (tied)	55.92
1988	Kristin Otto (GDR)	54.93
1992	Zhuang Yong (CHN)	54.64
1996	Le Jingyi (CHN)	54.50
2000	Inge de Bruijn (NED)	53.83
2004	Jodie Henry (AUS)	53.84

200-METER FREESTYLE — MIN:SEC
1968	Debbie Meyer (USA)	2:10.5
1972	Shane Gould (AUS)	2:03.56
1976	Kornelia Ender (GDR)	1:59.26
1980	Barbara Krause (GDR)	1:58.33
1984	Mary Wayte (USA)	1:59.23
1988	Heike Friedrich (GDR)	1:57.65
1992	Nicole Haislett (USA)	1:57.90
1996	Claudia Poll (CRC)	1:58.16

Summer Olympic Games Champions (continued)

Swimming (women) (continued)

200-METER FREESTYLE		MIN:SEC
2000	Susie O'Neill (AUS)	1:58.24
2004	Camelia Potec (ROM)	1:58.03

400-METER FREESTYLE		MIN:SEC
1920	Ethelda Bleibtrey (USA)	4:34.0[22]
1924	Martha Norelius (USA)	6:02.2
1928	Martha Norelius (USA)	5:42.8
1932	Helene Madison (USA)	5:28.5
1936	Hendrika Mastenbroek (NED)	5:26.4
1948	Ann Curtis (USA)	5:17.8
1952	Valeria Gyenge (HUN)	5:12.1
1956	Lorraine Crapp (AUS)	4:54.6
1960	Susan Christina von Saltza (USA)	4:50.6
1964	Virginia Duenkel (USA)	4:43.3
1968	Debbie Meyer (USA)	4:31.8
1972	Shane Gould (AUS)	4:19.04
1976	Petra Thümer (GDR)	4:09.89
1980	Ines Diers (GDR)	4:08.76
1984	Tiffany Cohen (USA)	4:07.10
1988	Janet Evans (USA)	4:03.85
1992	Dagmar Hase (GER)	4:07.18
1996	Michelle Smith (IRE)	4:07.25
2000	Brooke Bennett (USA)	4:05.80
2004	Laure Manaudou (FRA)	4:05.34

800-METER FREESTYLE		MIN:SEC
1968	Debbie Meyer (USA)	9:24.0
1972	Keena Rothhammer (USA)	8:53.68
1976	Petra Thümer (GDR)	8:37.14
1980	Michelle Ford (AUS)	8:28.90
1984	Tiffany Cohen (USA)	8:24.95
1988	Janet Evans (USA)	8:20.20
1992	Janet Evans (USA)	8:25.52
1996	Brooke Bennett (USA)	8:27.89
2000	Brooke Bennett (USA)	8:19.67
2004	Ai Shibata (JPN)	8:24.54

100-METER BUTTERFLY		MIN:SEC
1956	Shelley Mann (USA)	1:11.0
1960	Carolyn Schuler (USA)	1:09.5
1964	Sharon Stouder (USA)	1:04.7
1968	Lynette McClements (AUS)	1:05.5
1972	Mayumi Aoki (JPN)	1:03.34
1976	Kornelia Ender (GDR)	1:00.13
1980	Caren Metschuck (GDR)	1:00.42
1984	Mary Meagher (USA)	59.26
1988	Kristin Otto (GDR)	59.00
1992	Qian Hong (CHN)	58.62
1996	Amy Van Dyken (USA)	59.13
2000	Inge de Bruijn (NED)	56.61
2004	Petria Thomas (AUS)	57.72

200-METER BUTTERFLY		MIN:SEC
1968	Aagje Kok (NED)	2:24.7
1972	Karen Moe (USA)	2:15.57
1976	Andrea Pollack (GDR)	2:11.41
1980	Ines Geissler (GDR)	2:10.44
1984	Mary Meagher (USA)	2:06.90
1988	Kathleen Nord (GDR)	2:09.51
1992	Summer Sanders (USA)	2:08.67
1996	Susie O'Neill (AUS)	2:07.76
2000	Misty Hyman (USA)	2:05.88
2004	Otylia Jedrzejczak (POL)	2:06.05

Swimming (women) (continued)

100-METER BACKSTROKE		MIN:SEC
1924	Sybil Bauer (USA)	1:23.2
1928	Maria Braun (NED)	1:22.0
1932	Eleanor Holm (USA)	1:19.4
1936	Dina Senff (NED)	1:18.9
1948	Karen-Margrete Harup (DEN)	1:14.4
1952	Joan Harrison (RSA)	1:14.3
1956	Judith Grinham (GBR)	1:12.9
1960	Lynn Burke (USA)	1:09.3
1964	Cathy Ferguson (USA)	1:07.7
1968	Kaye Hall (USA)	1:06.2
1972	Melissa Belote (USA)	1:05.78
1976	Urike Richter (GDR)	1:01.83
1980	Rica Reinisch (GDR)	1:00.86
1984	Theresa Andrews (USA)	1:02.55
1988	Kristin Otto (GDR)	1:00.89
1992	Krisztina Egerszegi (HUN)	1:00.68
1996	Beth Botsford (USA)	1:01.19
2000	Diana Mocanu (ROM)	1:00.21
2004	Natalie Coughlin (USA)	1:00.37

200-METER BACKSTROKE		MIN:SEC
1968	Pokey Watson (USA)	2:24.8
1972	Melissa Belote (USA)	2:19.19
1976	Ulrike Richter (GDR)	2:13.43
1980	Rica Reinisch (GDR)	2:11.77
1984	Jolanda De Rover (NED)	2:12.38
1988	Krisztina Egerszegi (HUN)	2:09.29
1992	Krisztina Egerszegi (HUN)	2:07.06
1996	Krisztina Egerszegi (HUN)	2:07.83
2000	Diana Mocanu (ROM)	2:08.16
2004	Kirsty Coventry (ZIM)	2:09.19

100-METER BREASTSTROKE		MIN:SEC
1968	Djurdjica Bjedov (YUG)	1:15.8
1972	Cathy Carr (USA)	1:13.58
1976	Hannelore Anke (GDR)	1:11.16
1980	Ute Geveniger (GDR)	1:10.22
1984	Petra van Staveren (NED)	1:09.88
1988	Tanya Dangalakova (BUL)	1:07.95
1992	Yelena Rudkovskaya (UNT)	1:08.00
1996	Penelope Heyns (RSA)	1:07.73
2000	Megan Quann (USA)	1:07.05
2004	Luo Xuejuan (CHN)	1:06.64

200-METER BREASTSTROKE		MIN:SEC
1924	Lucy Morton (GBR)	3:33.2
1928	Hilde Schrader (GER)	3:12.6
1932	Claire Dennis (AUS)	3:06.3
1936	Hideko Maehata (JPN)	3:03.6
1948	Petronella van Vliet (NED)	2:57.2
1952	Eva Szekely (HUN)	2:51.7
1956	Ursula Happe (GER)	2:53.1
1960	Anita Lonsbrough (GBR)	2:49.5
1964	Galina Prozumenshchikova-Stepanova (URS)	2:46.4
1968	Sharon Wichman (USA)	2:44.4
1972	Beverley Whitfield (AUS)	2:41.71
1976	Marina Koshevaya (URS)	2:33.35
1980	Lina Kachushite (URS)	2:29.54
1984	Anne Ottenbrite (CAN)	2:30.38
1988	Silke Hörner (GDR)	2:26.71
1992	Kyoko Iwasaki (JPN)	2:26.65
1996	Penelope Heyns (RSA)	2:25.41
2000	Agnes Kovacs (HUN)	2:24.35
2004	Amanda Beard (USA)	2:23.37

Summer Olympic Games Champions (continued)

Swimming (women) (continued)

200-METER MEDLEY   MIN:SEC
1968	Claudia Kolb (USA)	2:24.7
1972	Shane Gould (AUS)	2:23.07
1984	Tracy Caulkins (USA)	2:12.64
1988	Daniela Hunger (GDR)	2:12.59
1992	Li Lin (CHN)	2:11.65
1996	Michelle Smith (IRE)	2:13.93
2000	Yana Klochkova (UKR)	2:10.68
2004	Yana Klochkova (UKR)	2:11.14

400-METER MEDLEY   MIN:SEC
1964	Donna De Varona (USA)	5:18.7
1968	Claudia Kolb (USA)	5:08.5
1972	Gail Neall (AUS)	5:02.97
1976	Ulrike Tauber (GDR)	4:42.77
1980	Petra Schneider (GDR)	4:36.29
1984	Tracy Caulkins (USA)	4:39.24
1988	Janet Evans (USA)	4:37.76
1992	Krisztina Egerszegi (HUN)	4:36.54
1996	Michelle Smith (IRE)	4:39.18
2000	Yana Klochkova (UKR)	4:33.59
2004	Yana Klochkova (UKR)	4:34.83

4 × 100-METER MEDLEY RELAY   MIN:SEC
1960	United States	4:41.1
1964	United States	4:33.9
1968	United States	4:28.3
1972	United States	4:20.75
1976	East Germany	4:07.95
1980	East Germany	4:06.67
1984	United States	4:08.34
1988	East Germany	4:03.74
1992	United States	4:02.54
1996	United States	4:02.88
2000	United States	3:58.30
2004	Australia	3:57.32

4 × 100-METER FREESTYLE RELAY   MIN:SEC
1912	Great Britain	5:52.8
1920	United States	5:11.6
1924	United States	4:58.8
1928	United States	4:47.6
1932	United States	4:38.0
1936	The Netherlands	4:36.0
1948	United States	4:29.2
1952	Hungary	4:24.4
1956	Australia	4:17.1
1960	United States	4:08.9
1964	United States	4:03.8
1968	United States	4:02.5
1972	United States	3:55.19
1976	United States	3:44.82
1980	East Germany	3:42.71
1984	United States	3:43.43
1988	East Germany	3:40.63
1992	United States	3:39.46
1996	United States	3:39.29
2000	United States	3:36.61
2004	Australia	3:35.94

4 × 200-METER FREESTYLE RELAY   MIN:SEC
1996	United States	7:59.87
2000	United States	7:57.80
2004	United States	7:53.42

Swimming (women) (continued)

SYNCHRONIZED SWIMMING (INDIVIDUAL)
1984	Tracie Ruiz (USA)
1988	Carolyn Waldo (CAN)
1992	Kristen Babb-Sprague (USA); Sylvie Fréchette (CAN)[23]

SYNCHRONIZED SWIMMING (DUET)
1984	United States
1988	Canada
1992	United States
2000	Russia
2004	Russia

SYNCHRONIZED SWIMMING (TEAM)
1996	United States
2000	Russia
2004	Russia

Table tennis (men)

SINGLES
1988	Yoo Nam Kyu (KOR)
1992	Jan-Ove Waldner (SWE)
1996	Liu Guoliang (CHN)
2000	Kong Linghui (CHN)
2004	Ryu Seung Min (KOR)

DOUBLES
1988	China
1992	China
1996	China
2000	China
2004	China

Table tennis (women)

SINGLES
1988	Chen Jing (CHN)
1992	Deng Yaping (CHN)
1996	Deng Yaping (CHN)
2000	Wang Nan (CHN)
2004	Zhang Yining (CHN)

DOUBLES
1988	South Korea
1992	China
1996	China
2000	China
2004	China

Taekwondo (men)

58 KG (127.6 LB)
2000	Michail Mouroutsos (GRE)
2004	Chu Mu Yen (TPE)

68 KG (149.6 LB)
2000	Steven Lopez (USA)
2004	Hadi Saei Bonehkohal (IRI)

80 KG (176 LB)
2000	Angel Valodia Matos (CUB)
2004	Steven Lopez (USA)

OVER 80 KG (176+ LB)
2000	Kim Kyong-Hun (KOR)
2004	Moon Sung Dae (KOR)

Summer Olympic Games Champions (continued)

Taekwondo (women)

49 KG (107.8 LB)
2000 Lauren Burns (AUS)
2004 Chen Shih Hsin (TPE)

57 KG (125.4 LB)
2000 Jung Jae-Eun (KOR)
2004 Jang Ji Won (KOR)

67 KG (147.4 LB)
2000 Lee Sun-Hee (KOR)
2004 Luo Wei (CHN)

OVER 67 KG (147.4+ LB)
2000 Chen Zhong (CHN)
2004 Chen Zhong (CHN)

Tennis (men)

SINGLES
1896 John Pius Boland (GBR)
1900 Hugh (Laurie) Doherty (GBR)
1904 Beals Wright (USA)
1908 Josiah Ritchie (GBR)
1912 Charles Winslow (RSA)
1920 Louis Raymond (RSA)
1924 Vincent Richards (USA)
1988 Miloslav Mecir (TCH)
1992 Marc Rosset (SUI)
1996 Andre Agassi (USA)
2000 Yevgeny Kafelnikov (RUS)
2004 Nicolas Massu (CHI)

DOUBLES
1896 John Pius Boland (GBR), Friedrich Thraun (GER)
1900 Hugh (Laurie) Doherty, Reginald Doherty (GBR)
1904 Edgar Leonard, Beals Wright (USA)
1908 George Hillyard, Reginald Doherty (GBR)
1912 Harold Kitson, Charles Winslow (RSA)
1920 Oswald Noel Turnbull, Maxwell Woosnam (GBR)
1924 Francis Hunter, Vincent Richards (USA)
1988 Kenneth Flach, Robert Seguso (USA)
1992 Boris Becker, Michael Stich (GER)
1996 Todd Woodbridge, Mark Woodforde (AUS)
2000 Sebastien Lareau, Daniel Nestor (CAN)
2004 Fernando Gonzalez, Nicolas Massu (CHI)

MIXED DOUBLES
1900 Charlotte Cooper, Reginald Doherty (GBR)
1912 Dora Köring, Heinrich Schomburgk (GER)
1920 Suzanne Lenglen, Max Décugis (FRA)
1924 Hazel Wightman, R. Norris Williams (USA)

Tennis (women)

SINGLES
1900 Charlotte Cooper (GBR)
1908 Dorothy Chambers-Lambert (GBR)
1912 Marguerite Broquedis (FRA)
1920 Suzanne Lenglen (FRA)
1924 Helen Wills-Moody (USA)
1988 Steffi Graf (FRG)
1992 Jennifer Capriati (USA)
1996 Lindsay Davenport (USA)
2000 Venus Williams (USA)
2004 Justine Henin-Hardenne (BEL)

Tennis (women) (continued)

DOUBLES
1920 Winifred Margaret McNair, Kathleen McKane (GBR)
1924 Helen Wills-Moody, Hazel Wightman (USA)
1988 Zina Garrison, Pamela Shriver (USA)
1992 Gigi Fernandez, Mary Joe Fernandez (USA)
1996 Gigi Fernandez, Mary Joe Fernandez (USA)
2000 Serena Williams, Venus Williams (USA)
2004 Li Ting, Sun Tian Tian (CHN)

Tennis—Covered Courts (indoor tennis)

MEN'S SINGLES
1908 Arthur Gore (GBR)
1912 André Gobert (FRA)

MEN'S DOUBLES
1908 Arthur Gore, Herbert Roper-Barrett (GBR)
1912 Maurice Germot, André Gobert (FRA)

WOMEN'S SINGLES
1908 Gladys Eastlake-Smith (GBR)
1912 Edith Hannam (GBR)

MIXED DOUBLES
1912 Edith Hannam, Charles Dixon (GBR)

Triathlon (swim/bike/run) (men)
2000 Simon Whitfield (CAN)
2004 Hamish Carter (NZL)

Triathlon (swim/bike/run) (women)
2000 Brigitte McMahon (SUI)
2004 Kate Allen (AUT)

Volleyball (men)

INDOOR
1964 USSR
1968 USSR
1972 Japan
1976 Poland
1980 USSR
1984 United States
1988 United States
1992 Brazil
1996 The Netherlands
2000 Yugoslavia
2004 Brazil

BEACH
1996 United States
2000 United States
2004 Brazil

Volleyball (women)

INDOOR
1964 Japan
1968 USSR
1972 USSR
1976 Japan
1980 USSR
1984 China
1988 USSR
1992 Cuba
1996 Cuba
2000 Cuba
2004 China

Summer Olympic Games Champions (continued)

Volleyball (women) (continued)

BEACH

1996	Brazil
2000	Australia
2004	United States

Water polo (men)

1900	Great Britain
1904	United States
1908	Great Britain
1912	Great Britain
1920	Great Britain
1924	France
1928	Germany
1932	Hungary
1936	Hungary
1948	Italy
1952	Hungary
1956	Hungary
1960	Italy
1964	Hungary
1968	Yugoslavia
1972	USSR
1976	Hungary
1980	USSR
1984	Yugoslavia
1988	Yugoslavia
1992	Italy
1996	Spain
2000	Hungary
2004	Hungary

Water polo (women)

2000	Australia
2004	Italy

Weight lifting (men)[24, 25]

56 KG (123.2 LB)		KG
1972	Zygmunt Smalcerz (POL)	337.5
1976	Aleksandr Voronin (URS)	242.5
1980	Kanybek Osmanaliyev (URS)	245.0
1984	Zeng Guoqiang (CHN)	235.0
1988	Sevdalin Marinov (BUL)	270.0
1992	Ivan Ivanov (BUL)	265.0
1996	Halil Mutlu (TUR)	287.5
2000	Halil Mutlu (TUR)	305.0
2004	Halil Mutlu (TUR)	295.0

62 KG (136.4 LB)		KG
1948	Joseph de Pietro (USA)	307.5
1952	Ivan Udodov (URS)	315.0
1956	Charles Vinci (USA)	342.5
1960	Charles Vinci (USA)	345.0
1964	Aleksey Vakhonin (URS)	357.5
1968	Mohammad Nassiri (IRI)	367.5
1972	Imre Foldi (HUN)	377.5
1976	Norair Nurikian (BUL)	262.5
1980	Daniel Núñez (CUB)	275.0
1984	Wu Shude (CHN)	267.5
1988	Oksen Mirzoyan (URS)	292.5
1992	Chun Byung Kwan (KOR)	287.5
1996	Tang Ningsheng (CHN)	307.5
2000	Nikolay Pechalov (CRO)	325.0
2004	Shi Zhiyong (CHN)	325.0

Weight lifting (men)[24, 25] (continued)

69 KG (151.8 LB)		KG
1920	Frans de Haes (BEL)	220.0
1924	Pierino Gabetti (ITA)	402.5[26]
1928	Franz Andrysek (AUT)	287.5
1932	Raymond Suvigny (FRA)	287.5
1936	Anthony Terlazzo (USA)	312.5
1948	Mahmoud Fayad (EGY)	332.5
1952	Rafael Chimishkyan (URS)	337.5
1956	Isaac Berger (USA)	352.5
1960	Yevgeny Minayev (URS)	372.5
1964	Yoshinobu Miyake (JPN)	397.5
1968	Yoshinobu Miyake (JPN)	392.5
1972	Norair Nurikian (BUL)	402.5
1976	Nikolay Kolesnikov (URS)	285.0
1980	Viktor Mazin (URS)	290.0
1984	Chen Weiqiang (CHN)	282.5
1988	Naim Suleymanoglu (TUR)	342.5
1992	Naim Suleymanoglu (TUR)	320.0
1996	Naim Suleymanoglu (TUR)	335.0
2000	Galabin Boevski (BUL)	357.5
2004	Zhang Guozheng (CHN)	347.5

70 KG (154 LB)		KG
1920	Alfred Neyland (EST)	257.5
1924	Edmond Décottignies (FRA)	440.0[26]
1928	Kurt Helbig (GER); Hans Haas (AUT) (tied)	322.5
1932	René Duverger (FRA)	325.0
1936	Mohamed Ahmed Mesbah (EGY); Robert Fein (AUT) (tied)	342.5
1948	Ibrahim Shams (EGY)	360.0
1952	Tommy Kono (USA)	362.5
1956	Igor Rybak (URS)	380.0
1960	Viktor Bushuyev (URS)	397.5
1964	Waldemar Baszanowski (POL)	432.5
1968	Waldemar Baszanowski (POL)	437.5
1972	Mukharbi Kirzhinov (URS)	460.0
1976	Pyotr Korol (URS)	305.0
1980	Yanko Rusev (BUL)	342.5
1984	Yao Jingyuan (CHN)	320.0
1988	Joachim Kunz (GDR)	340.0
1992	Israil Militosyan (UNT)	337.5
1996	Zhan Xugang (CHN)	357.5

77 KG (169.4 LB)		KG
1920	Henri Gance (FRA)	245.0
1924	Carlo Galimberti (ITA)	492.5[26]
1928	François Roger (FRA)	335.0
1932	Rudolf Ismayr (GER)	345.0
1936	Khadr el Thouni (EGY)	387.5
1948	Frank Spellman (USA)	390.0
1952	Peter George (USA)	400.0
1956	Fyodor Bogdanovsky (URS)	420.0
1960	Aleksandr Kurynov (URS)	437.5
1964	Hans Zdrazila (TCH)	445.0
1968	Viktor Kurentsov (URS)	475.0
1972	Iordan Bikov (BUL)	485.0
1976	Iordan Mitkov (BUL)	335.0
1980	Asen Zlatev (BUL)	360.0
1984	Karl-Heinz Radschinsky (FRG)	340.0
1988	Borislav Gidikov (BUL)	375.0
1992	Fyodor Kassapu (UNT)	357.5
1996	Pablo Lara (CUB)	367.5
2000	Zhan Xugang (CHN)	367.5
2004	Taner Sagir (TUR)	375.0

Summer Olympic Games Champions (continued)

Weight lifting (men)[24, 25] (continued)

85 KG (187 LB)

		KG
1920	Ernest Cadine (FRA)	290.0
1924	Charles Rigoulot (FRA)	502.5[26]
1928	El Sayed Nosseir (EGY)	355.0
1932	Louis Hostin (FRA)	365.0
1936	Louis Hostin (FRA)	372.5
1948	Stanley Stanczyk (USA)	417.5
1952	Trofim Lomakin (URS)	417.5
1956	Tommy Kono (USA)	447.5
1960	Ireneusz Palinski (POL)	442.5
1964	Rudolph Plyukfelder (URS)	475.0
1968	Boris Selitsky (URS)	485.0
1972	Leif Jenssen (NOR)	507.5
1976	Valery Shary (URS)	365.0
1980	Yury Vardanyan (URS)	400.0
1984	Petre Becheru (ROM)	355.0
1988	Israil Arsamakov (URS)	377.5
1992	Pyrros Dimas (GRE)	370.0
1996	Pyrros Dimas (GRE)	392.5
2000	Pyrros Dimas (GRE)	390.0
2004	George Asanidze (GEO)	382.5

94 KG (206.8 LB)

		KG
1952	Norbert Schemansky (USA)	445.0
1956	Arkady Vorobyev (URS)	462.5
1960	Arkady Vorobyev (URS)	472.5
1964	Vladimir Golovanov (URS)	487.5
1968	Kaarlo Kangasniemi (FIN)	517.5
1972	Andon Nikolov (BUL)	525.0
1976	David Rigert (URS)	382.5
1980	Peter Baczako (HUN)	377.5
1984	Nicu Vlad (ROM)	392.5
1988	Anatoly Khrapaty (URS)	412.5
1992	Kakhi Kakhiashvili (UNT)	412.5
1996	Aleksey Petrov (RUS)	402.5
2000	Akakios Kakhiashvilis (GRE)	405.0
2004	Milen Dobrev (BUL)	407.5

99 KG (217.8 LB)

		KG
1980	Ota Zaremba (TCH)	395.0
1984	Rolf Milser (FRG)	385.0
1988	Pavel Kuznetsov (URS)	425.0
1992	Viktor Tregubov (UNT)	410.0
1996	Akakios Kakhiashvilis (GRE)	420.0

105 KG (231 LB)

		KG
1972	Jan Talts (URS)	580.0
1976	Yury Zaytsev (URS)	385.0
1980	Leonid Taranenko (URS)	422.5
1984	Norberto Oberburger (ITA)	390.0
1988	Yury Zakharevitch (URS)	455.0
1992	Ronny Weller (GER)	432.5
1996	Timur Taymazov (UKR)	430.0
2000	Hossein Tavakoli (IRI)	425.0
2004	Dmitry Berestov (RUS)	425.0

OVER 105 KG (231+ LB)

		KG
1920	Filippo Bottino (ITA)	265.5
1924	Giuseppe Tonani (ITA)	517.5[26]
1928	Josef Strassberger (GER)	372.5
1932	Jaroslav Skobla (TCH)	380.0
1936	Josef Manger (GER)	410.0
1948	John Davis (USA)	452.5
1952	John Davis (USA)	460.0
1956	Paul Anderson (USA)	500.0

Weight lifting (men)[24, 25] (continued)

OVER 105 KG (231 LB)

		KG
1960	Yury Vlasov (URS)	537.5
1964	Leonid Zhabotinsky (URS)	572.5
1968	Leonid Zhabotinsky (URS)	572.5
1972	Vasily Alekseyev (URS)	640.0
1976	Vasily Alekseyev (URS)	440.0
1980	Sultan Rakhmanov (URS)	440.0
1984	Dinko Lukin (AUS)	412.5
1988	Aleksandr Kurlovich (URS)	462.5
1992	Aleksandr Kurlovich (UNT)	450.0
1996	Andrey Chemerkin (RUS)	457.5
2000	Hossein Reza Zadeh (IRI)	472.5
2004	Hossein Reza Zadeh (IRI)	472.5

ONE-HAND LIFT (UNLIMITED CLASS)

		KG
1896	Launceston Elliot (GBR)	71.0
1906	Josef Steinbach (AUT)	76.55

TWO-HAND LIFT (UNLIMITED CLASS)

		KG
1896	Viggo Jensen (DEN)	111.5
1904	Perikles Kakousis (GRE)	111.7
1906	Dimitrios Tofalos (GRE)	142.4

ALL-AROUND DUMBBELLS (UNLIMITED CLASS)

1904	Oscar Osthoff (USA)

Weight lifting (women)

48 KG (105.6 LB)

		KG
2000	Tara Nott (USA)	185.0
2004	Nurcan Taylan (TUR)	210.0

53 KG (116.6 LB)

		KG
2000	Yang Xia (CHN)	225.0
2004	Udomporn Polsak (THA)	222.5

58 KG (127.6 LB)

		KG
2000	Soraya Jiménez Mendívil (MEX)	222.5
2004	Chen Yanqing (CHN)	237.5

63 KG (138.6 LB)

		KG
2000	Chen Xiaomin (CHN)	242.5
2004	Natalya Skakun (UKR)	242.5

69 KG (151.8 LB)

		KG
2000	Lin Weining (CHN)	242.5
2004	Liu Chunhong (CHN)	275.0

75 KG (165 LB)

		KG
2000	Maria Isabel Urrutia (COL)	245.0
2004	Pawina Thongsuk (THA)	272.5

OVER 75 KG (165+ LB)

		KG
2000	Ding Meiyuan (CHN)	300.0
2004	Tang Gonghong (CHN)	305.0

Wrestling—Freestyle (men)[24]

48 KG (105.6 LB)

1904	Robert Curry (USA)
1972	Roman Dmitriyev (URS)
1976	Khassan Issaev (BUL)
1980	Claudio Pollio (ITA)
1984	Robert Weaver (USA)
1988	Takashi Kobayashi (JPN)
1992	Kim Il (PRK)
1996	Kim Il (PRK)

Summer Olympic Games Champions (continued)

Wrestling—Freestyle (men)[24] (continued)

55 KG (121 LB)
1904	George Mehnert (USA)
1948	Lennart Viitala (FIN)
1952	Hasan Gemici (TUR)
1956	Mirian Tsalkalamanidze (URS)
1960	Ahmet Bilek (TUR)
1964	Yoshikatsu Yoshida (JPN)
1968	Shigeo Nakata (JPN)
1972	Kiyomi Kato (JPN)
1976	Yuji Takada (JPN)
1980	Anatoly Beloglazov (URS)
1984	Saban Trstena (YUG)
1988	Mitsuru Sato (JPN)
1992	Li Hak-son (PRK)
1996	Valentin Iordanov (BUL)
2000	Namig Amdullayev (AZE)
2004	Mavlet Batirov (RUS)

60 KG (132 LB)
1904	Isidor "Jack" Niflot (USA)
1908	George Mehnert (USA)
1924	Kustaa Pihlajamäki (FIN)
1928	Kaarlo Maakinen (FIN)
1932	Robert Pearce (USA)
1936	Odon Zombory (HUN)
1948	Nasuh Akar (TUR)
1952	Shohachi Ishii (JPN)
1956	Mustafa Dagistanli (TUR)
1960	Terence McCann (USA)
1964	Yojiro Uetake (JPN)
1968	Yojiro Uetake (JPN)
1972	Hideaki Yanagida (JPN)
1976	Vladimir Yumin (URS)
1980	Sergey Beloglazov (URS)
1984	Hideaki Tomiyama (JPN)
1988	Sergey Beloglazov (URS)
1992	Alejandro Puerto Diaz (CUB)
1996	Kendall Cross (USA)
2000	Alireza Dabir (IRI)
2004	Yandro Miguel Quintana (CUB)

63 KG (138.6 LB)
1904	Benjamin Bradshaw (USA)
1908	George Dole (USA)
1920	Charles Ackerly (USA)
1924	Robin Reed (USA)
1928	Allie Morrison (USA)
1932	Hermanni Pihlajamäki (FIN)
1936	Kustaa Pihlajamäki (FIN)
1948	Gazanfer Bilge (TUR)
1952	Bayram Sit (TUR)
1956	Shozo Sasahara (JPN)
1960	Mustafa Dagistanli (TUR)
1964	Osamu Watanabe (JPN)
1968	Masaaki Kaneko (JPN)
1972	Zagalav Abdulbekov (URS)
1976	Yang Jung Mo (KOR)
1980	Magomedgasan Abushev (URS)
1984	Randy Lewis (USA)
1988	John Smith (USA)
1992	John Smith (USA)
1996	Tom Brands (USA)
2000	Murad Umakhanov (RUS)

Wrestling—Freestyle (men)[24] (continued)

66 KG (145.2 LB)
1904	Otto Roehm (USA)
1908	George de Relwyskow (GBR)
1920	Kaarlo "Kalle" Anttila (FIN)
1924	Russell Vis (USA)
1928	Osvald Käpp (EST)
1932	Charles Pacome (FRA)
1936	Karoly Karpati (HUN)
1948	Celal Atik (TUR)
1952	Olle Anderberg (SWE)
1956	Emamali Habibi (IRI)
1960	Shelby Wilson (USA)
1964	Enio Valchev Dimov (BUL)
1968	Abdollah Movahed (IRI)
1972	Dan Gable (USA)
1976	Pavel Pinigin (URS)
1980	Saipulla Absaidov (URS)
1984	You In Tak (KOR)
1988	Arsen Fadzayev (URS)
1992	Arsen Fadzayev (UNT)
1996	Vadim Bogiyev (RUS)
2000	Daniel Igali (CAN)
2004	Elbrus Tedeyev (UKR)

74 KG (162.8 LB)
1904	Charles Eriksen (USA)
1924	Hermann Gehri (SUI)
1928	Arvo Haavisto (FIN)
1932	Jack van Bebber (USA)
1936	Frank Lewis (USA)
1948	Yasar Dogu (TUR)
1952	William Smith (USA)
1956	Mitsuo Ikeda (JPN)
1960	Douglas Blubaugh (USA)
1964	Ismail Ogan (TUR)
1968	Mahmut Atalay (TUR)
1972	Wayne Wells (USA)
1976	Jiichiro Date (JPN)
1980	Valentin Raychev (BUL)
1984	David Schultz (USA)
1988	Kenneth Monday (USA)
1992	Park Jang Soon (KOR)
1996	Buvaysa Saytyev (RUS)
2000	Brandon Slay (USA)
2004	Buvaysa Saytyev (RUS)

84 KG (184.8 LB)
1908	Stanley Bacon (GBR)
1920	Eino Leino (FIN)
1924	Fritz Haggmann (SUI)
1928	Ernst Kyburz (SUI)
1932	Ivar Johansson (SWE)
1936	Émile Poilvé (FRA)
1948	Glen Brand (USA)
1952	David Tsimakurdze (URS)
1956	Nikola Stanchev (BUL)
1960	Hasan Gungor (TUR)
1964	Prodan Stoyanov Gardchev (BUL)
1968	Boris Gurevich (URS)
1972	Levan Tediashvili (URS)
1976	John Peterson (USA)
1980	Ismail Abilov (BUL)
1984	Mark Schultz (USA)
1988	Han Myung Woo (KOR)
1992	Kevin Jackson (USA)
1996	Khadshimurad Magomedov (RUS)

Summer Olympic Games Champions (continued)

Wrestling—Freestyle (men)[24] (continued)

84 KG (184.8 LB)
2000   Adam Saytev (RUS)
2004   Cael Sanderson (USA)

90 KG (198.5 LB)
1920   Anders Larsson (SWE)
1924   John Franklin Spellman (USA)
1928   Thure Sjöstedt (SWE)
1932   Peter Mehringer (USA)
1936   Knut Fridell (SWE)
1948   Henry Wittenberg (USA)
1952   Bror Wiking Palm (SWE)
1956   Gholam-Reza Takhti (IRI)
1960   Ismet Atli (TUR)
1964   Aleksandr Medved (URS)
1968   Ahmet Ayuk (TUR)
1972   Ben Peterson (USA)
1976   Levan Tediashvili (URS)
1980   Sanasar Oganesyan (URS)
1984   Ed Banach (USA)
1988   Macharbek Khadartsev (URS)
1992   Macharbek Khadartsev (UNT)
1996   Rasul Khadem Azghadi (IRI)

96 KG (211.2 LB)
1896   Karl Schumann (GER)
1904   Bernhuff Hansen (USA)
1908   George O'Kelly (GBR)
1920   Robert Rothe (SUI)
1924   Harry Steele (USA)
1928   Johan Richthoff (SWE)
1932   Johan Richthoff (SWE)
1936   Kristjan Palusalu (EST)
1948   Gyula Bobis (HUN)
1952   Arsen Mekokishvili (URS)
1956   Hamit Kaplan (TUR)
1960   Wilfried Dietrich (GER)
1964   Aleksandr Ivanitsky (URS)
1968   Aleksandr Medved (URS)
1972   Ivan Yarygin (URS)
1976   Ivan Yarygin (URS)
1980   Ilya Mate (URS)
1984   Lou Banach (USA)
1988   Vasile Puscasu (ROM)
1992   Leri Khabelov (UNT)
1996   Kurt Angle (USA)
2000   Sagid Murtasaliyev (RUS)
2004   Khajimurat Gatsalov (RUS)

120 KG (264 LB)
1972   Aleksandr Medved (URS)
1976   Soslan Andiyev (URS)
1980   Soslan Andiyev (URS)
1984   Bruce Baumgartner (USA)
1988   David Gobedishvili (URS)
1992   Bruce Baumgartner (USA)
1996   Mahmut Demir (TUR)
2000   David Musulbes (RUS)
2004   Artur Taymazov (UZB)

Wrestling—Freestyle (women)

48 KG (105.6 LB)
2004   Irini Merleni (UKR)

55 KG (121 LB)
2004   Saori Yoshida (JPN)

Wrestling—Freestyle (women) (continued)

63 KG (138.6 LB)
2004   Kaori Icho (JPN)

72 KG (158 LB)
2004   Wang Xu (CHN)

Wrestling—Greco-Roman (men)[24]

48 KG (105.6 LB)
1972   Gheorghe Berceanu (ROM)
1976   Aleksey Shumakov (URS)
1980   Zhaksylyk Ushkempirov (URS)
1984   Vincenzo Maenza (ITA)
1988   Vincenzo Maenza (ITA)
1992   Oleg Kucherenko (UNT)
1996   Sim Kwon-Ho (KOR)

55 KG (121 LB)
1948   Pietro Lombardi (ITA)
1952   Boris Gurevich (URS)
1956   Nikolay Solovyev (URS)
1960   Dumitru Pirvulescu (ROM)
1964   Tsutomu Hanahara (JPN)
1968   Petar Kirov (BUL)
1972   Petar Kirov (BUL)
1976   Vitaly Konstantinov (URS)
1980   Vakhtang Blagidze (URS)
1984   Atsuji Miyahara (JPN)
1988   Jon Ronningen (NOR)
1992   Jon Ronningen (NOR)
1996   Armen Nazaryan (ARM)
2000   Sim Kwon-Ho (KOR)
2004   Istvan Majoros (HUN)

60 KG (132 LB)
1924   Eduard Pütsep (EST)
1928   Kurt Leucht (GER)
1932   Jakob Brendel (GER)
1936   Marton Lorincz (HUN)
1948   Kurt Pettersen (SWE)
1952   Imre Hodos (HUN)
1956   Konstantin Vyrupayev (URS)
1960   Oleg Karavayev (URS)
1964   Masamitsu Ichiguchi (JPN)
1968   Janos Varga (HUN)
1972   Rustem Kazakov (URS)
1976   Pertti Ukkola (FIN)
1980   Shamil Serikov (URS)
1984   Pasquale Passarelli (FRG)
1988   Andras Sike (HUN)
1992   An Han Bong (KOR)
1996   Yury Melnichenko (KAZ)
2000   Armen Nazarian (BUL)
2004   Jung Ji Hyun (KOR)

63 KG (138.6 LB)
1912   Kaarlo Koskelo (FIN)
1920   Oskar Friman (FIN)
1924   Kalle Anttila (FIN)
1928   Voldemar Väli (EST)
1932   Giovanni Gozzi (ITA)
1936   Yasar Erkan (TUR)
1948   Mehmet Oktav (TUR)
1952   Yakov Punkin (URS)
1956   Rauno Leonard Mäkinen (FIN)
1960   Muzahir Sille (TUR)
1964   Imre Polyak (HUN)
1968   Roman Rurua (URS)
1972   Georgi Markov (BUL)

Summer Olympic Games Champions (continued)

Wrestling—Greco-Roman (men)[24] (continued)

63 KG (138.6 LB)
1976 Kazimierz Lipien (POL)
1980 Stilianos Migiakis (GRE)
1984 Kim Weon Kee (KOR)
1988 Kamandar Madzhidov (URS)
1992 Akif Pirim (TUR)
1996 Wlodzimierz Zawadzki (POL)
2000 Varteres Samurgashev (RUS)

66 KG (145.2 LB)
1908 Enrico Porro (ITA)
1912 Eemil Väre (FIN)
1920 Eemil Väre (FIN)
1924 Oskar Friman (FIN)
1928 Lajos Keresztes (HUN)
1932 Erik Malmberg (SWE)
1936 Lauri Koskela (FIN)
1948 Karl Freij (SWE)
1952 Shazam Safin (URS)
1956 Kyösti Emil Lehtonen (FIN)
1960 Avtandil Koridze (URS)
1964 Kazim Ayvaz (TUR)
1968 Munji Mumemura (JPN)
1972 Shamil Khisamutdinov (URS)
1976 Suren Nalbandyan (URS)
1980 Stefan Rusu (ROM)
1984 Vlado Lisjak (YUG)
1988 Levon Dzhulfalakyan (URS)
1992 Attila Repka (HUN)
1996 Ryszard Wolny (POL)
2000 Filiberto Ascuy Aguilera (CUB)
2004 Farid Mansurov (AZE)

74 KG (162.8 LB)
1932 Ivar Johansson (SWE)
1936 Rudolf Svedberg (SWE)
1948 Erik Gösta Andersson (SWE)
1952 Miklos Szilvasi (HUN)
1956 Mithat Bayrak (TUR)
1960 Mithat Bayrak (TUR)
1964 Anatoly Kolesov (URS)
1968 Rudolf Vesper (GDR)
1972 Viteslav Macha (TCH)
1976 Anatoly Bykov (URS)
1980 Ferenc Kocsis (HUN)
1984 Jouko Salomaki (FIN)
1988 Kim Young Nam (KOR)
1992 Mnatsakan Iskandaryan (UNT)
1996 Filiberto Ascuy Aguilera (CUB)
2000 Murat Kardanov (URS)
2004 Aleksandr Dokturishivili (UZB)

84 KG (184.8 LB)
1908 Frithiof Martenson (SWE)
1912 Claes Johansson (SWE)
1920 Carl Westergren (SWE)
1924 Edward Westerlund (FIN)
1928 Väinö Kokkinen (FIN)
1932 Väinö Kokkinen (FIN)
1936 Ivar Johansson (SWE)
1948 Axel Grönberg (SWE)
1952 Axel Grönberg (SWE)
1956 Givi Kartoziya (URS)
1960 Dimitar Dobrev (BUL)
1964 Branislav Simic (YUG)

Wrestling—Greco-Roman (men)[24] (continued)

84 KG (184.8 LB)
1968 Lothar Metz (GDR)
1972 Csaba Hegedus (HUN)
1976 Momir Petkovic (YUG)
1980 Gennady Korban (URS)
1984 Ion Draica (ROM)
1988 Mikhail Mamiashvili (URS)
1992 Peter Farkas (HUN)
1996 Hamza Yerlikaya (TUR)
2000 Hamza Yerlikaya (TUR)
2004 Aleksey Mishin (RUS)

90 KG (198.5 LB)
1908 Verner Weckman (FIN)
1912 Anders Ahlgren (SWE)
1920 Claes Johansson (SWE)
1924 Carl Westergren (SWE)
1928 Ibrahim Moustafa (EGY)
1932 Rudolf Svensson (SWE)
1936 Axel Cadier (SWE)
1948 Karl-Erik Nilsson (SWE)
1952 Kelpo Olavi Gröndahl (FIN)
1956 Valentin Nikolayev (URS)
1960 Tevfik Kis (TUR)
1964 Boyan Radev (BUL)
1968 Boyan Radev (BUL)
1972 Valery Rezantsev (URS)
1976 Valery Rezantsev (URS)
1980 Norbert Nottny (HUN)
1984 Steven Fraser (USA)
1988 Atanas Komchev (BUL)
1992 Maik Bullmann (GER)
1996 Vyacheslav Oleynyk (UKR)

96 KG (211.2 LB)
1896 Karl Schumann (GER)
1908 Richard Weisz (HUN)
1912 Yrjö Saarela (FIN)
1920 Adolf Lindfors (FIN)
1924 Henri Deglane (FRA)
1928 Rudolf Svensson (SWE)
1932 Carl Westergren (SWE)
1936 Kristjan Palusalu (EST)
1948 Ahmet Kirecci (TUR)
1952 Johannes Kotkas (URS)
1956 Anatoly Parfenov (URS)
1960 Ivan Bogdan (URS)
1964 Istvan Kozma (HUN)
1968 Istvan Kozma (HUN)
1972 Nicolae Martinescu (ROM)
1976 Nikolay Balboshin (URS)
1980 Georgi Raikov-Petkov (BUL)
1984 Vasile Andrei (ROM)
1988 Andrzej Wronski (POL)
1992 Héctor Milian (CUB)
1996 Andrzej Wronski (POL)
2000 Mikael Ljungberg (SWE)
2004 Karam Ibrahim (EGY)

120 KG (264 LB)
1972 Anatoly Roshchin (URS)
1976 Aleksandr Kolchinsky (URS)
1980 Aleksandr Kolchinsky (URS)
1984 Jeffrey Blatnick (USA)
1988 Aleksandr Karelin (URS)
1992 Aleksandr Karelin (UNT)

Summer Olympic Games Champions (continued)

Wrestling—Greco-Roman (men)[24] (continued)

120 KG (264 LB)
1996   Aleksandr Karelin (RUS)
2000   Rulon Gardner (USA)
2004   Khasan Baroyev (RUS)

[1]*The competitions in 1900 and 1904 are said to be unofficial.*   [2]*100-meter event.*   [3]*Hurdles were 2′ 6″ high, not 3′.*   [4]*An extra lap of 460 meters was run in error.*   [5]*Jim Thorpe was stripped of his gold medals in 1913 when it was discovered he had briefly competed as a professional athlete; in 1982 his gold medals were restored, and he was declared "cowinner" of the events.*   [6]*2,000-meter event.*   [7]*333.3-meter event.*   [8]*Distance varied from 87 to 320 km.*   [9]*Weight classifications were changed in 1980 and 1996.*   [10]*Weight classifications were changed in 2000.*   [11]*The distances in men's rowing events have varied from time to time. In 1904 it was 2 miles; in 1908, 1.5 miles; from 1912 to 1936, 2,000 m; in 1948, 1 mile 350 yards; and since 1952, 2,000 m (1 mile 427 yards).*   [12]*The distance in women's rowing events was 1,000 m until 1988, at which time it became 2,000, m.*   [13]*100 yards.*   [14]*220 yards.*   [15]*500 meters.*   [16]*440 yards.*   [17]*1,200 meters.*   [18]*1,000 meters.*   [19]*One mile.*   [20]*100 yards.*   [21]*440 yards.*   [22]*300 meters.*   [23]*Fréchette's gold medal awarded in 1993 on basis of error in scoring.*   [24]*Weight classifications have been revised numerous times, most recently after the 1996 Games.*   [25]*In 1976 the press lift was removed, weights given thereafter being the total for the clean and jerk and the snatch.*   [26]*Total of five lifts.*

How a Sport Becomes a Competing Olympic Event

The Olympic Games' return to Athens in 2004 came with great fanfare. The Games have expanded from 241 to 10,500 competitors since their original reestablishment in Athens with the 1896 Games. Dozens of additions and changes have been made in the Olympic program since 1896, with almost 100 events being added since 1980 alone. Although enthusiasts of many activities hope to see their avocations become Olympic sports, only a few receive one of the coveted slots in the Olympic program.

The first step in the process of becoming an Olympic sport is recognition as a sport from the International Olympic Committee (IOC). The IOC requires that the activity have administration by an international non-governmental organization that oversees at least one sport. Once a sport is recognized, it then moves to International Sports Federation (IF) status. At that point, the international organization administering the sport must enforce the Olympic Movement Anti-Doping Code, including conducting effective out-of-competition tests on the sport's competitors, while maintaining rules set forth by the Olympic Charter.

A sport may gain IOC recognition but not become a competing event at the Olympic Games. Bowling, rugby, and chess are recognized sports, but they do not compete at the Games. To become a part of the Games the sport's IF must apply for admittance by filing a petition establishing its criteria of eligibility to the IOC. The IOC may then admit an activity into the Olympic program in one of three different ways: as a sport, a discipline, which is a branch of a sport, or an event, which is a competition within a discipline. For instance, triathlon was admitted as a sport, debuting at the 2000 Games in Sydney. Women's wrestling was a new discipline in the sport of wrestling at the Athens Games, and women's pole vaulting was the most recently added track and field event. Rules for admittance vary slightly between a new sport, a discipline, and an event, but the intent is the same.

Once an IF has presented its petition, many rules and regulations control whether the sport will become part of the Olympic Games. The Olympic Charter indicates that to be accepted, a sport must be widely practiced by men in at least 75 countries and on four continents, and by women in no fewer than 40 countries and on three continents. The sport must also increase the "value and appeal" of the Olympic Games and retain and reflect its modern traditions. There are numerous other rules, including bans on purely "mind sports" and sports dependent on mechanical propulsion. These rules have kept chess, automobile racing, and other recognized sports out of the Olympic Games.

In recent years the IOC has worked to manage the scope of the Olympics by permitting new sports only in conjunction with the simultaneous discontinuation of others. Sports that have already been part of the Games are periodically reviewed to determine whether they should be retained. The Olympic Program Commission notes that problems have arisen when trying to find venues to accommodate some sports' specific needs, such as baseball and softball, which will be discontinued from Olympic programming starting with the London Games in 2012. When choosing sports to include in the program the IOC must take into consideration media and public interest, since these are a key drive behind the Olympic Games, but must simultaneously manage costs.

While a number of events have been added to the Games since their resumption in 1896, a good number have been sidelined. Tug-of-war, for example, was once a respected Olympic sport. Cricket, golf, lacrosse, polo, power boating, rackets, rink-hockey, roque, rugby, and water skiing were all once part of the Olympic Games but have been discontinued over the years.

Winter Olympic Games Champions

Gold medalists in all events, 1908–2002 (separate Winter Games were not held until 1924).
Since the Salt Lake City games, several athletes have been stripped of medals for having
failed drug tests. New medalists are shown in this table.

Biathlon

MEN

10 KILOMETER		MIN:SEC
1980	Frank Ullrich (GDR)	32:10.69
1984	Eirik Kvalfoss (NOR)	30:53.8
1988	Frank-Peter Rötsch (GDR)	25:08.1
1992	Mark Kirchner (GER)	26:02.3
1994	Sergey Chepikov (RUS)	28:07.0
1998	Ole Einar Bjørndalen (NOR)	27:16.2
2002	Ole Einar Bjørndalen (NOR)	24:51.3

12.5 KILOMETER PURSUIT		MIN:SEC
2002	Ole Einar Bjørndalen (NOR)	32:34.6

20 KILOMETER		HR:MIN:SEC
1960	Klas Lestander (SWE)	1:33:21.6
1964	Vladimir Melanin (URS)	1:20:26.8
1968	Magnar Solberg (NOR)	1:13:45.9
1972	Magnar Solberg (NOR)	1:15:55.50[1]
1976	Nikolay Kruglov (URS)	1:14:12.26
1980	Anatoly Alyabyev (URS)	1:08:16.31
1984	Peter Angerer (FRG)	1:11:52.70
1988	Frank-Peter Rötsch (GDR)	56:33.3
1992	Yevgeny Redkin (UNT)[2]	57:34.4
1994	Sergey Tarasov (RUS)	57:25.3
1998	Halvard Hanevold (NOR)	56:16.4
2002	Ole Einar Bjørndalen (NOR)	51:03.3

4 × 7.5-KILOMETER RELAY		HR:MIN:SEC
1968	USSR	2:13:02.4
1972	USSR	1:51:44.92[1]
1976	USSR	1:57:55.64
1980	USSR	1:34:03.27
1984	USSR	1:38:51.70
1988	USSR	1:22:30.00
1992	Germany	1:24:43.5
1994	Germany	1:30:22.1
1998	Germany	1:19:43.3
2002	Norway	1:23:42.3

MILITARY SKI PATROL	
1924	Switzerland
1928	Norway
1936	Italy
1948	Switzerland

DISTANCE SHOOTING	
1936	Georg Edenhauser (AUT)

ICE SHOOTING (TEAM)	
1936	Austria

TARGET SHOOTING	
1936	Ignaz Reiterer (AUT)

WOMEN

7.5 KILOMETER		MIN:SEC
1992	Anfisa Restsova (UNT)[2]	24:29.2
1994	Myriam Bédard (CAN)	26:08.8
1998	Galina Kukleva (RUS)	23:08.0
2002	Kati Wilhelm (GER)	20:41.4

10 KILOMETER PURSUIT		MIN:SEC
2002	Olga Pyleva (RUS)	31:07.7

Biathlon (continued)

15 KILOMETER		MIN:SEC
1992	Antje Misersky (GER)	51:47.2
1994	Myriam Bédard (CAN)	52:06.6
1998	Ekaterina Dafovska (BUL)	54:52.0
2002	Andrea Henkel (GER)	47:29.1

4 × 7.5-KILOMETER RELAY		HR:MIN:SEC
1992	France (3 × 7.5-meter event)	1:15:55.6
1994	Russia	1:47:19.5
1998	Germany	1:40:13.6
2002	Germany	1:27:55.0

Bobsled

TWO-MAN BOBSLED		MIN:SEC
1932	United States	8:14.74
1936	United States	5:29.29
1948	Switzerland	5:29.2
1952	West Germany	5:24.54
1956	Italy	5:30.14
1964	Great Britain	4:21.90
1968	Italy	4:41.54
1972	West Germany	4:57.07
1976	East Germany	3:44.42
1980	Switzerland	4:09.36
1984	East Germany	3:25.56
1988	USSR	3:53.48
1992	Switzerland	4:03.26
1994	Switzerland	3:30.81
1998	Canada, Italy (tied)	3:37.24
2002	Germany	3:10.11

FOUR-MAN BOBSLED		MIN:SEC
1924	Switzerland	5:45.54
1928	United States	3:20.5[3]
1932	United States	7:53.68
1936	Switzerland	5:19.85
1948	United States	5:20.1
1952	West Germany	5:07.84
1956	Switzerland	5:10.44
1964	Canada	4:14.46
1968	Italy	2:17.39
1972	Switzerland	4:43.07
1976	East Germany	3:40.43
1980	East Germany	3:59.92
1984	East Germany	3:20.22
1988	Switzerland	3:47.51
1992	Austria	3:53.90
1994	Germany	3:27.78
1998	Germany	2:39.41
2002	Germany	3:07.51

TWO-WOMAN BOBSLED		MIN:SEC
2002	United States	1:37.76

Curling

MEN

1924	Great Britain
1998	Switzerland
2002	Norway

WOMEN

1998	Canada
2002	Great Britain

Winter Olympic Games Champions (continued)

Figure Skating

MEN'S SINGLES

1908	Ulrich Salchow (SWE)
1920	Gillis Gräfström (SWE)
1924	Gillis Gräfström (SWE)
1928	Gillis Gräfström (SWE)
1932	Karl Schäfer (AUT)
1936	Karl Schäfer (AUT)
1948	Richard Button (USA)
1952	Richard Button (USA)
1956	Hayes Alan Jenkins (USA)
1960	David Jenkins (USA)
1964	Manfred Schnelldorfer (GER)[4]
1968	Wolfgang Schwarz (AUT)
1972	Ondrej Nepela (TCH)
1976	John Curry (GBR)
1980	Robin Cousins (GBR)
1984	Scott Hamilton (USA)
1988	Brian Boitano (USA)
1992	Viktor Petrenko (UNT)[2]
1994	Aleksey Urmanov (RUS)
1998	Ilia Kulik (RUS)
2002	Aleksey Yagudin (RUS)

WOMEN'S SINGLES

1908	Madge Syers (GBR)
1920	Magda Julin-Mauroy (SWE)
1924	Herma Planck-Szabo (AUT)
1928	Sonja Henie (NOR)
1932	Sonja Henie (NOR)
1936	Sonja Henie (NOR)
1948	Barbara Ann Scott (CAN)
1952	Jeanette Altwegg (GBR)
1956	Tenley Albright (USA)
1964	Sjoukje Dijkstra (NED)
1968	Peggy Fleming (USA)
1972	Beatrix Schuba (AUT)
1976	Dorothy Hamill (USA)
1980	Annett Potzsch (GDR)
1984	Katarina Witt (GDR)
1988	Katarina Witt (GDR)
1992	Kristi Yamaguchi (USA)
1994	Oksana Bayul (UKR)
1998	Tara Lipinski (USA)
2002	Sarah Hughes (USA)

PAIRS

1908	Anna Hübler, Heinrich Burger (GER)
1920	Ludoviga Jakobsson-Eilers, Walter Jakobsson (FIN)
1924	Helene Engelmann, Alfred Berger (AUT)
1928	Andrée Joly, Pierre Brunet (FRA)
1932	Andrée Brunet-Joly, Pierre Brunet (FRA)
1936	Maxi Herber, Ernst Baier (GER)
1948	Micheline Lannoy, Pierre Baugniet (BEL)
1952	Ria Falk, Paul Falk (FRG)
1956	Elisabeth Schwarz, Kurt Oppelt (AUT)
1960	Barbara Wagner, Robert Paul (CAN)
1964	Lyudmila Belousova, Oleg Protopopov (URS)
1968	Lyudmila Belousova, Oleg Protopopov (URS)
1972	Irina Rodnina, Aleksey Ulanov (URS)
1976	Irina Rodnina, Aleksandr Zaytsev (URS)
1980	Irina Rodnina, Aleksandr Zaytsev (URS)
1984	Yelena Valova, Oleg Vasilyev (URS)

PAIRS

1988	Yekaterina Gordeyeva, Sergey Grinkov (URS)
1992	Natalya Mishkutyonok, Artur Dmitriyev (UNT)[2]
1994	Yekaterina Gordeyeva, Sergey Grinkov (RUS)

Figure Skating (continued)

PAIRS

1998	Oksana Kazakova, Artur Dmitriyev (RUS)
2002	Yelena Berezhnaya, Anton Sikharulidze (RUS); Jamie Sale, David Pelletier (CAN) (shared)

ICE DANCING

1976	Lyudmila Pakhomova, Aleksandr Gorshkov (URS)
1980	Natalya Linichuk, Gennady Karponosov (URS)
1984	Jayne Torvill, Christopher Dean (GBR)
1988	Natalya Bestemyanova, Andrey Bukin (URS)
1992	Marina Klimova, Sergey Ponomarenko (UNT)[2]
1994	Oksana Grishchuk, Yevgeny Platov (RUS)
1998	Oksana Grishchuk, Yevgeny Platov (RUS)
2002	Marina Anissina, Gwendal Peizerat (FRA)

Ice Hockey

MEN

1920	Canada
1924	Canada
1928	Canada
1932	Canada
1936	Great Britain
1948	Canada
1952	Canada
1956	USSR
1960	United States
1964	USSR
1968	USSR
1972	USSR
1976	USSR
1980	United States
1984	USSR
1988	USSR
1992	Unified Team[2]
1994	Sweden
1998	Czech Republic
2002	Canada

WOMEN

1998	United States
2002	Canada

Luge

MEN'S SINGLES		**MIN:SEC**
1964	Thomas Köhler (GER)[4]	3:26.77
1968	Manfred Schmid (AUT)	2:52.48
1972	Wolfgang Schneidel (GDR)	3:27.58
1976	Detlef Guenther (GDR)	3:27.688[5]
1980	Bernhard Glass (GDR)	2:54.796
1984	Paul Hildgartner (ITA)	3:04.258
1988	Jens Müller (GDR)	3:05.548
1992	Georg Hackl (GER)	3:02.363
1994	Georg Hackl (GER)	3:21.571
1998	Georg Hackl (GER)	3:18.436
2002	Armin Zöggeler (ITA)	2:57.941

MEN'S PAIRS		**MIN:SEC**
1964	Austria	1:41.62
1968	East Germany	1:35.85
1972	Italy; East Germany (tied)	1:28.35
1976	East Germany	1:25.604[5]
1980	East Germany	1:19.331
1984	West Germany	1:23.620
1988	East Germany	1:31.940

Winter Olympic Games Champions (continued)

Luge (continued)

MEN'S PAIRS — MIN:SEC

		MIN:SEC
1992	Germany	1:32.053
1994	Italy	1:36.720
1998	Germany	1:41.105
2002	Germany	1:26.082

WOMEN'S SINGLES

		MIN:SEC
1964	Ortrun Enderlein (GER)[4]	3:24.67
1968	Erica Lechner (ITA)	2:29.37
1972	Anna-Maria Müller (GDR)	2:59.18
1976	Margit Schumann (GDR)	2:50.621[5]
1980	Vera Zozulya (URS)	2:36.537
1984	Steffi Martin (GDR)	2:46.570
1988	Steffi Walter-Martin (GDR)	3:03.973
1992	Doris Neuner (AUT)	3:06.696
1994	Gerda Weissensteiner (ITA)	3:15.517
1998	Silke Kraushaar (GER)	3:23.779
2002	Sylke Otto (GER)	2:52.464

Skeleton

MEN

		MIN:SEC
1928	Jennison Heaton (USA)	3:01.8
1948	Nino Bibbia (ITA)	5:23.2
2002	Jim Shea (USA)	1:41.96

WOMEN

		MIN:SEC
2002	Tristan Gale (USA)	1:45.11

Alpine Skiing (men)

DOWNHILL

		MIN:SEC
1948	Henri Oreiller (FRA)	2:55.0
1952	Zeno Colò (ITA)	2:30.8
1956	Toni Sailer (AUT)	2:52.2
1960	Jean Vuarnet (FRA)	2:06.0
1964	Egon Zimmermann (AUT)	2:18.16[1]
1968	Jean-Claude Killy (FRA)	1:59.85
1972	Bernhard Russi (SUI)	1:51.43
1976	Franz Klammer (AUT)	1:45.73
1980	Leonhard Stock (AUT)	1:45.50
1984	Bill Johnson (USA)	1:45.59
1988	Pirmin Zurbriggen (SUI)	1:59.63
1992	Patrick Ortlieb (AUT)	1:50.37
1994	Tommy Moe (USA)	1:45.75
1998	Jean-Luc Cretier (FRA)	1:50.11
2002	Fritz Strobl (AUT)	1:39.13

SLALOM

		MIN:SEC
1948	Edy Reinalter (SUI)	2:10.3
1952	Othmar Schneider (AUT)	2:00.0
1956	Toni Sailer (AUT)	3:14.7
1960	Ernst Hinterseer (AUT)	2:08.9
1964	Josef Stiegler (AUT)	2:21.13[1]
1968	Jean-Claude Killy (FRA)	1:39.73
1972	Francisco Ochoa (ESP)	1:49.27
1976	Piero Gros (ITA)	2:03.29
1980	Ingemar Stenmark (SWE)	1:44.26
1984	Phil Mahre (USA)	1:39.41
1988	Alberto Tomba (ITA)	1:39.47
1992	Finn Christian Jagge (NOR)	1:44.39
1994	Thomas Stangassinger (AUT)	2:02.02
1998	Hans-Petter Buraas (NOR)	1:49.31
2002	Jean-Pierre Vidal (FRA)	1:41.06

GIANT SLALOM

		MIN:SEC
1952	Stein Eriksen (NOR)	2:25.0
1956	Toni Sailer (AUT)	3:00.1
1960	Roger Staub (SUI)	1:48.3
1964	François Bonlieu (FRA)	1:46.71[1]

Alpine Skiing (men) (continued)

GIANT SLALOM

		MIN:SEC
1968	Jean-Claude Killy (FRA)	3:29.28
1972	Gustavo Thöni (ITA)	3:09.62
1976	Heini Hemmi (SUI)	3:26.97
1980	Ingemar Stenmark (SWE)	2:40.74
1984	Max Julen (SUI)	2:41.18
1988	Alberto Tomba (ITA)	2:06.37
1992	Alberto Tomba (ITA)	2:06.98
1994	Markus Wasmeier (GER)	2:52.46
1998	Hermann Maier (AUT)	2:38.51
2002	Stephan Eberharter (AUT)	2:23.28

SUPERGIANT SLALOM

		MIN:SEC
1988	Franck Piccard (FRA)	1:39.66
1992	Kjetil Andre Aamodt (NOR)	1:13.04
1994	Markus Wasmeier (GER)	1:32.53
1998	Hermann Maier (AUT)	1:34.82
2002	Kjetil Andre Aamodt (NOR)	1:21.58

ALPINE COMBINED

		MIN:SEC
1936	Franz Pfnür (GER)	
1948	Henri Oreiller (FRA)	
1972	Gustavo Thoeni (ITA)	
1976	Gustavo Thoeni (ITA)	
1988	Hubert Strolz (AUT)	
1992	Josef Polig (ITA)	
1994	Lasse Kjus (NOR)	3:17.53[6]
1998	Mario Reiter (AUT)	3:08.06
2002	Kjetil Andre Aamodt (NOR)	3:17.56

Alpine Skiing (women)

DOWNHILL

		MIN:SEC
1948	Hedy Schlunegger (SUI)	2:28.3
1952	Trude Jochom-Beiser (AUT)	1:47.1
1956	Madeleine Berthod (SUI)	1:40.7
1960	Heidi Beibl (GER)[4]	1:37.6
1964	Christl Haas (AUT)	1:55.39[1]
1968	Olga Pall (AUT)	1:40.87
1972	Marie-Therèse Nadig (SUI)	1:36.68
1976	Rosi Mittermaier (FRG)	1:46.16
1980	Annemarie Moser-Pröll (AUT)	1:37.52
1984	Michael Figini (SUI)	1:13.36
1988	Marina Kiehl (FRG)	1:25.86
1992	Kerrin Lee-Gartner (CAN)	1:52.55
1994	Katja Seizinger (GER)	1:35.93
1998	Katja Seizinger (GER)	1:28.29
2002	Carole Montillet (FRA)	1:39.56

SLALOM

		MIN:SEC
1948	Gretchen Fraser (USA)	1:57.2
1952	Andrea Lawrence-Mead (USA)	2:10.6
1956	Renée Colliard (SUI)	1:52.3
1960	Anne Heggtveit (CAN)	1:49.6
1964	Christine Goitschel (FRA)	1:29.86[1]
1968	Marielle Goitschel (FRA)	1:59.85
1972	Barbara Cochran (USA)	1:31.24
1976	Rosi Mittermaier (FRG)	1:30.54
1980	Hanni Wenzel (LIE)	1:25.09
1984	Paoletta Magoni (ITA)	1:36.47
1988	Vreni Schneider (SUI)	1:36.69
1992	Petra Kronberger (AUT)	1:32.68
1994	Vreni Schneider (SUI)	1:56.01
1998	Hilde Gerg (GER)	1:32.40
2002	Janica Kostelic (CRO)	1:46.10

GIANT SLALOM

		MIN:SEC
1952	Andrea Lawrence-Mead (USA)	2:06.8
1956	Ossi Reichert (GER)[4]	1:56.5

Winter Olympic Games Champions (continued)

Alpine Skiing (women) (continued)

GIANT SLALOM

		MIN:SEC
1960	Yvonne Rüegg (SUI)	1:39.9
1964	Marielle Goitschel (FRA)	1:52.24[1]
1968	Nancy Greene (CAN)	1:51.97
1972	Marie-Therèse Nadig (SUI)	1:29.90
1976	Kathy Kreiner (CAN)	1:29.13
1980	Hanni Wenzel (LIE)	2:41.66
1984	Debbie Armstrong (USA)	2:20.98
1988	Vreni Schneider (SUI)	2:06.49
1992	Pernilla Wiberg (SWE)	2:12.74
1994	Deborah Compagnoni (ITA)	2:30.97
1998	Deborah Compagnoni (ITA)	2:50.59
2002	Janica Kostelic (CRO)	2:30.01

SUPERGIANT SLALOM

		MIN:SEC
1988	Sigrid Wolf (AUT)	1:19.03
1992	Deborah Compagnoni (ITA)	1:21.22
1994	Diann Roffe-Steinrotter (USA)	1:22.15
1998	Picabo Street (USA)	1:18.02
2002	Daniela Ceccarelli (ITA)	1:13.59

ALPINE COMBINED

		MIN:SEC
1936	Chrislt Cranz (GER)	
1948	Trude Beiser (AUT)	
1972	Annemarie Pröll (AUT)	
1976	Rosi Mittermaier (FRG)	
1988	Anita Wachter (AUT)	
1992	Petra Kronberger (AUT)	
1994	Pernilla Wiberg (SWE)	3:05.16[6]
1998	Katja Seizinger (GER)	2:40.74
2002	Janica Kostelic (CRO)	2:43.28

Freestyle Skiing

MEN'S MOGULS

1992	Edgar Grospiron (FRA)
1994	Jean-Luc Brassard (CAN)
1998	Jonny Moseley (USA)
2002	Janne Lahtela (FIN)

MEN'S AERIALS

1994	Andreas Schönbächler (SUI)
1998	Eric Bergoust (USA)
2002	Ales Valenta (CZE)

WOMEN'S MOGULS

1992	Donna Weinbrecht (USA)
1994	Stine Lise Hattestad (NOR)
1998	Tae Satoya (JPN)
2002	Kari Traa (NOR)

WOMEN'S AERIALS

1994	Lina Cheryazova (UZB)
1998	Nikki Stone (USA)
2002	Alisa Camplin (AUS)

Nordic Skiing (men)

1.5-KILOMETER CROSS-COUNTRY SPRINT

		MIN:SEC
2002	Tor Arne Hetland (NOR)	2:56.9

10-KILOMETER CROSS-COUNTRY

		MIN:SEC
1992	Vegard Ulvang (NOR)	27:36.0
1994	Bjørn Daehlie (NOR)	24:20.1
1998	Bjørn Daehlie (NOR)	27:24.5

15-KILOMETER CROSS-COUNTRY[7]

		HR:MIN:SEC
1924	Thorleif Haug (NOR)	1:14:31.0
1928	Johan Gröttumsbraaten (NOR)	1:37:01.0
1932	Sven Utterström (SWE)	1:23:07.0

Nordic Skiing (men) (continued)

15-KILOMETER CROSS-COUNTRY[7]

		HR:MIN:SEC
1936	Erik-August Larsson (SWE)	1:14:38.0
1948	Martin Lundström (SWE)	1:13:50.0
1952	Hallgeir Brenden (NOR)	1:01:34.0
1956	Hallgeir Brenden (NOR)	49:39.0
1960	Hakkon Brusveen (NOR)	51:55.5
1964	Eero Mäntyranta (FIN)	50:54.1
1968	Harald Grönningen (NOR)	47:54.2
1972	Sven-Ake Lundbäck (SWE)	45:28.24[1]
1976	Nikolay Bazhukov (URS)	43:58.47
1980	Thomas Wassberg (SWE)	41:57.63
1984	Gunde Svan (SWE)	41:25.60
1988	Mikhail Devyatyarov (URS)	41:18.9
1998	Thomas Alsgaard (NOR)	39:13.7
2002	Andrus Veerpalu (EST)	37:07.4

COMBINED PURSUIT[8]

		HR:MIN:SEC
1992	Bjørn Daehlie (NOR)	1:05:37.9
1994	Bjørn Daehlie (NOR)	1:00:08.8
1998	Thomas Alsgaard (NOR)	1:07:01.7
2002	Thomas Alsgaard, Frode Estil (NOR)	49:48.9

30-KILOMETER CROSS-COUNTRY

		HR:MIN:SEC
1956	Veikko Hakulinen (FIN)	1:44:06.0
1960	Sixten Jernberg (SWE)	1:51:03.9
1964	Eero Mäntyranta (FIN)	1:30:50.7
1968	Franco Nones (ITA)	1:35:39.2
1972	Vyacheslav Vedenin (URS)	1:36:31.15[1]
1976	Sergey Savelyev (URS)	1:30:29.38
1980	Nikolay Zimyatov (URS)	1:27:02.80
1984	Nikolay Zimyatov (URS)	1:28:56.30
1988	Aleksey Prokourorov (URS)	1:24:26.3
1992	Vegard Ulvang (NOR)	1:22:27.8
1994	Thomas Alsgaard (NOR)	1:12:26.4
1998	Mika Myllylä (FIN)	1:33:56.0
2002	Christian Hoffmann (AUT)	1:11:31.0

50-KILOMETER CROSS-COUNTRY

		HR:MIN:SEC
1924	Thorleif Haug (NOR)	3:44:32.0
1928	Per Erik Hedlund (SWE)	4:52:03.3
1932	Veli Saarinen (FIN)	4:28:00.0
1936	Elis Viklund (SWE)	3:30:11.0
1948	Nils Karlsson (SWE)	3:47:48.0
1952	Veikko Hakulinen (FIN)	3:33:33.0
1956	Sixten Jernberg (SWE)	2:50:27.0
1960	Kalevi Hämäläinen (FIN)	2:59:06.3
1964	Sixten Jernberg (SWE)	2:43:52.6
1968	Olle Ellefsäter (NOR)	2:28:45.8
1972	Pål Tyldum (NOR)	2:43:14.75[1]
1976	Ivar Formo (NOR)	2:37:30.05
1980	Nikolay Zimyatov (URS)	2:27:24.60
1984	Thomas Wassberg (SWE)	2:15:55.80
1988	Gunde Svan (SWE)	2:04:30.9
1992	Bjørn Daehlie (NOR)	2:03:41.5
1994	Vladimir Smirnov (KAZ)	2:07:20.3
1998	Bjørn Daehlie (NOR)	2:05:08.2
2002	Mikhail Ivanov (RUS)[9]	2:06:20.8

4 × 10-KILOMETER RELAY

		HR:MIN:SEC
1936	Finland	2:41:33.0
1948	Sweden	2:32:08.0
1952	Finland	2:20:16.0
1956	USSR	2:15:30.0
1960	Finland	2:18:45.6
1964	Sweden	2:18:34.6
1968	Norway	2:08:33.5
1972	USSR	2:04:47.94[1]
1976	Finland	2:07:59.72

Winter Olympic Games Champions (continued)

Nordic Skiing (men) (continued)

4 × 10-KILOMETER RELAY		HR:MIN:SEC
1980	USSR	1:57:03.46
1984	Sweden	1:55:06.30
1988	Sweden	1:43:58.6
1992	Norway	1:39:26.0
1994	Italy	1:41:15.0
1998	Norway	1:40:55.7
2002	Norway	1:32:45.5

SKI JUMPING (70 M)[10]
1924 Jacob Tullin Thams (NOR)
1928 Alf Andersen (NOR)
1932 Birger Ruud (NOR)
1936 Birger Ruud (NOR)
1948 Petter Hugsted (NOR)
1952 Arnfinn Bergmann (NOR)
1956 Antti Hyvärinen (FIN)
1960 Helmut Recknagel (GER)[4]
1964 Veikko Kankkonen (FIN)
1968 Jiri Raska (TCH)
1972 Yukio Kasaya (JPN)
1976 Hans-Georg Aschenbach (GDR)
1980 Toni Innauer (AUT)
1984 Jens Weissflog (GDR)
1988 Matti Nykänen (FIN)

SKI JUMPING (90 M)[10]
1964 Toralf Engan (NOR)
1968 Vladimir Belousov (URS)
1972 Wojciech Fortuna (POL)
1976 Karl Schnabl (AUT)
1980 Jens Tormanen (FIN)
1984 Matti Nykänen (FIN)
1988 Matti Nykänen (FIN)
1992 Ernst Vettori (AUT)
1994 Espen Bredesen (NOR)
1998 Jani Soininen (FIN)
2002 Simon Ammann (SUI)

SKI JUMPING (120 M)[10]
1992 Toni Nieminen (FIN)
1994 Jens Weissflog (GER)
1998 Kazuyoshi Funaki (JPN)
2002 Simon Ammann (SUI)

NORDIC COMBINED SPRINT (7.5 KILOMETERS)
2002 Samppa Lajunen (FIN)

NORDIC COMBINED 15 KILOMETERS
1924 Thorleif Haug (NOR)
1928 Johan Gröttumsbraaten (NOR)
1932 Johan Gröttumsbraaten (NOR)
1936 Oddbjörn Hagen (NOR)
1948 Heikki Hasu (NOR)
1952 Simon Slåttvik (NOR)
1956 Sverre Stenersen (NOR)
1960 Georg Thoma (GER)[4]
1964 Tormod Knutsen (NOR)
1968 Franz Keller (FRG)
1972 Ulrich Wehling (GDR)
1976 Ulrich Wehling (GDR)
1980 Ulrich Wehling (GDR)
1984 Tom Sandberg (NOR)
1988 Hippolyt Kempf (SUI)
1992 Fabrice Guy (FRA)
1994 Fred Börre Lundberg (NOR)
1998 Bjarte Engen Vik (NOR)
2002 Samppa Lajunen (FIN)

Nordic Skiing (men) (continued)

TEAM SKI JUMPING (120 M)
1988 Finland (90-m event)
1992 Finland
1994 Germany
1998 Japan
2002 Germany

NORDIC COMBINED TEAM RELAY
1988 West Germany
1992 Japan
1994 Japan
1998 Norway
2002 Finland

Nordic Skiing (women)

1.5-KILOMETER CROSS-COUNTRY SPRINT		MIN:SEC
2002	Yuliya Chepalova (RUS)	3:10.6

5-KILOMETER CROSS-COUNTRY		MIN:SEC
1964	Klavdiya Boyarskikh (URS)	17:50.5
1968	Toini Gustafsson (SWE)	16:45.2
1972	Galina Kulakova (URS)	17:00.50[1]
1976	Helena Takalo (FIN)	15:48.69
1980	Raisa Smetanina (URS)	15:06.92
1984	Marja-Liisa Hämäläinen (FIN)	17:04.00
1988	Marjo Matikainen (FIN)	15:04.00
1992	Marjut Lukkarinen (FIN)	14:13.8
1994	Lyubov Yegorova (RUS)	14:08.8
1998	Larisa Lazutina (RUS)	17:39.9

10-KILOMETER CROSS-COUNTRY		MIN:SEC
1952	Lydia Wideman (FIN)	41:40.0
1956	Lyubov Kozyreva (URS)	38:11.0
1960	Mariya Gusakova (URS)	39:46.6
1964	Klavdiya Boyarskikh (URS)	40:24.3
1968	Toini Gustafsson (SWE)	36:46.5
1972	Galina Kulakova (URS)	34:17.82[1]
1976	Raisa Smetanina (URS)	30:13.41
1980	Barbara Petzold (GDR)	30:31.54
1984	Marja-Liisa Hämäläinen (FIN)	31:44.20
1988	Vida Ventsene (URS)	30:08.30
1998	Larisa Lazutina (RUS)	46:06.9
2002	Bente Skari (NOR)	28:05.6

COMBINED PURSUIT[11]		MIN:SEC
1992	Lyubov Yegorova (UNT)[2]	40:08.4
1994	Lyubov Yegorova (RUS)	41:38.1
1998	Larisa Lazutina (RUS)	46:06.9
2002	Beckie Scott (CAN)	25.09:9

15-KILOMETER CROSS-COUNTRY		MIN:SEC
1992	Lyubov Yegorova (UNT)[2]	42:20.8
1994	Manuela di Centa (ITA)	39:44.5
1998	Olga Danilova (RUS)	46:55.40
2002	Stefania Belmondo (ITA)	39:54.4

20-KILOMETER CROSS-COUNTRY		HR:MIN:SEC
1984	Marja-Liisa Hämäläinen (FIN)	1:01:45.0
1988	Tamara Tikhonova (URS)	55:53.6

30-KILOMETER CROSS-COUNTRY		HR:MIN:SEC
1992	Stefania Belmondo (ITA)	1:22:30.1
1994	Manuela di Centa (ITA)	1:25:41.6
1998	Yuliya Chepalova (RUS)	1:22:01.5
2002	Gabriella Paruzzi (ITA)[9]	1:30:57.1

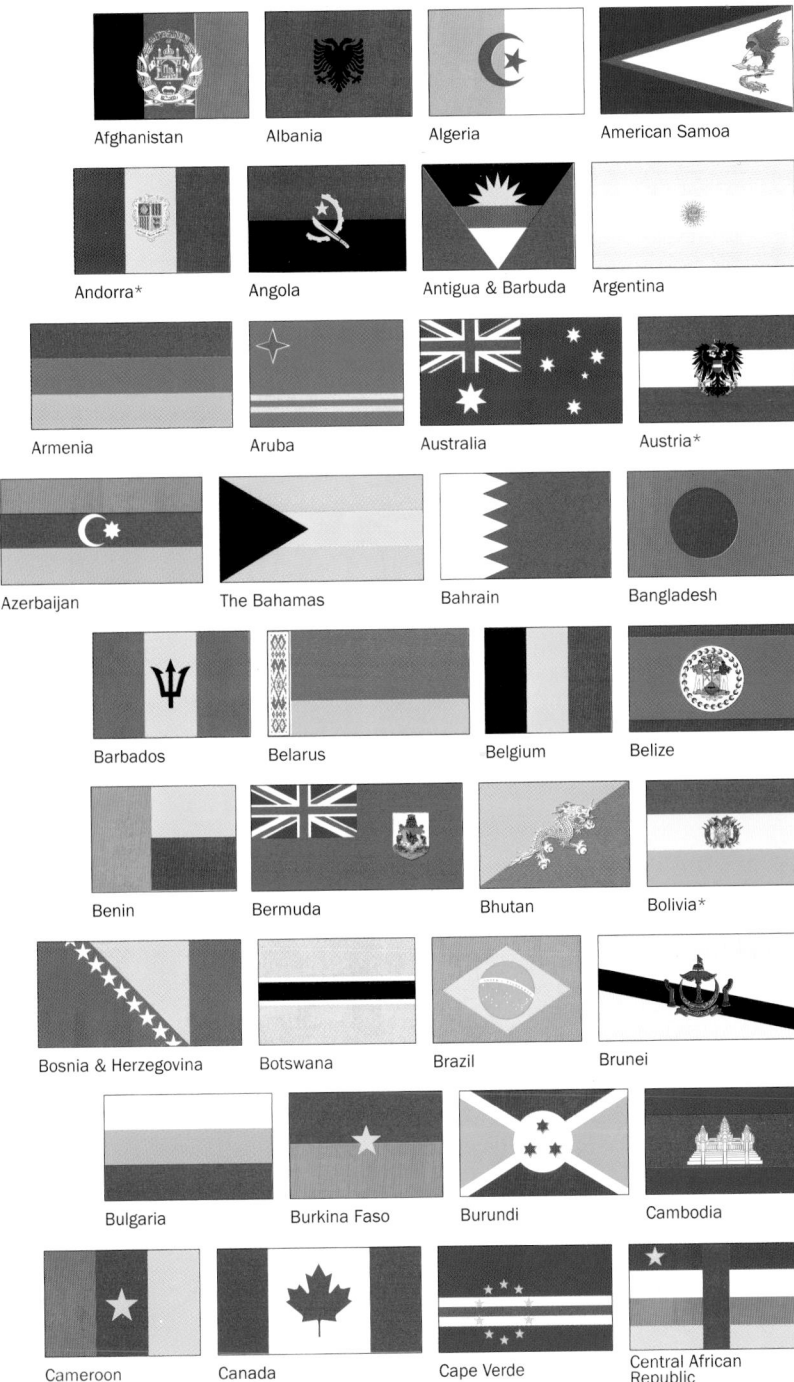

Afghanistan

Albania

Algeria

American Samoa

Andorra*

Angola

Antigua & Barbuda

Argentina

Armenia

Aruba

Australia

Austria*

Azerbaijan

The Bahamas

Bahrain

Bangladesh

Barbados

Belarus

Belgium

Belize

Benin

Bermuda

Bhutan

Bolivia*

Bosnia & Herzegovina

Botswana

Brazil

Brunei

Bulgaria

Burkina Faso

Burundi

Cambodia

Cameroon

Canada

Cape Verde

Central African Republic

Civil flags are shown except where marked thus (*); in these cases, government flags are shown in order to illustrate emblems. Both styles are official national flags.

Plate 2   **FLAGS OF THE WORLD**

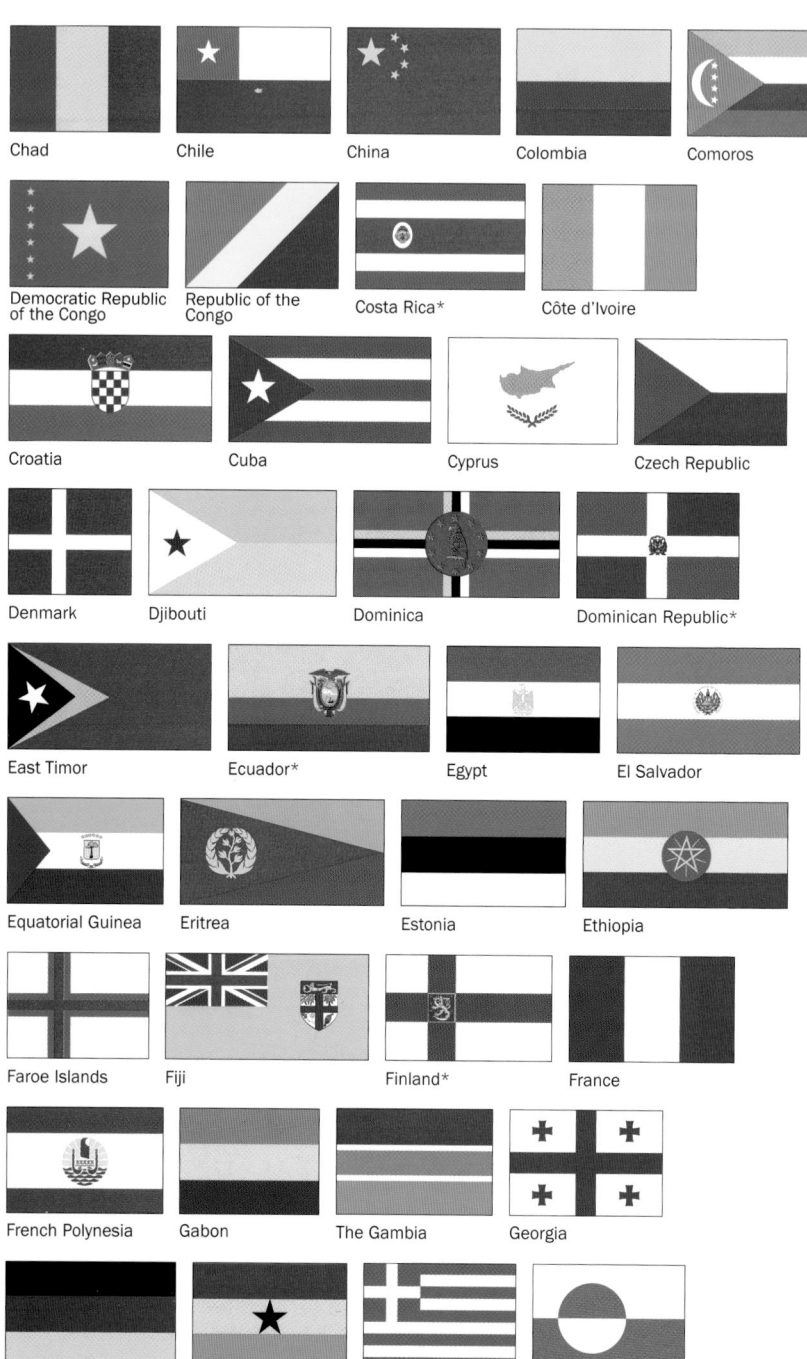

Chad   Chile   China   Colombia   Comoros

Democratic Republic of the Congo   Republic of the Congo   Costa Rica*   Côte d'Ivoire

Croatia   Cuba   Cyprus   Czech Republic

Denmark   Djibouti   Dominica   Dominican Republic*

East Timor   Ecuador*   Egypt   El Salvador

Equatorial Guinea   Eritrea   Estonia   Ethiopia

Faroe Islands   Fiji   Finland*   France

French Polynesia   Gabon   The Gambia   Georgia

Germany   Ghana   Greece   Greenland

Civil flags are shown except where marked thus (*); in these cases, government flags are shown in order to illustrate emblems. Both styles are official national flags.

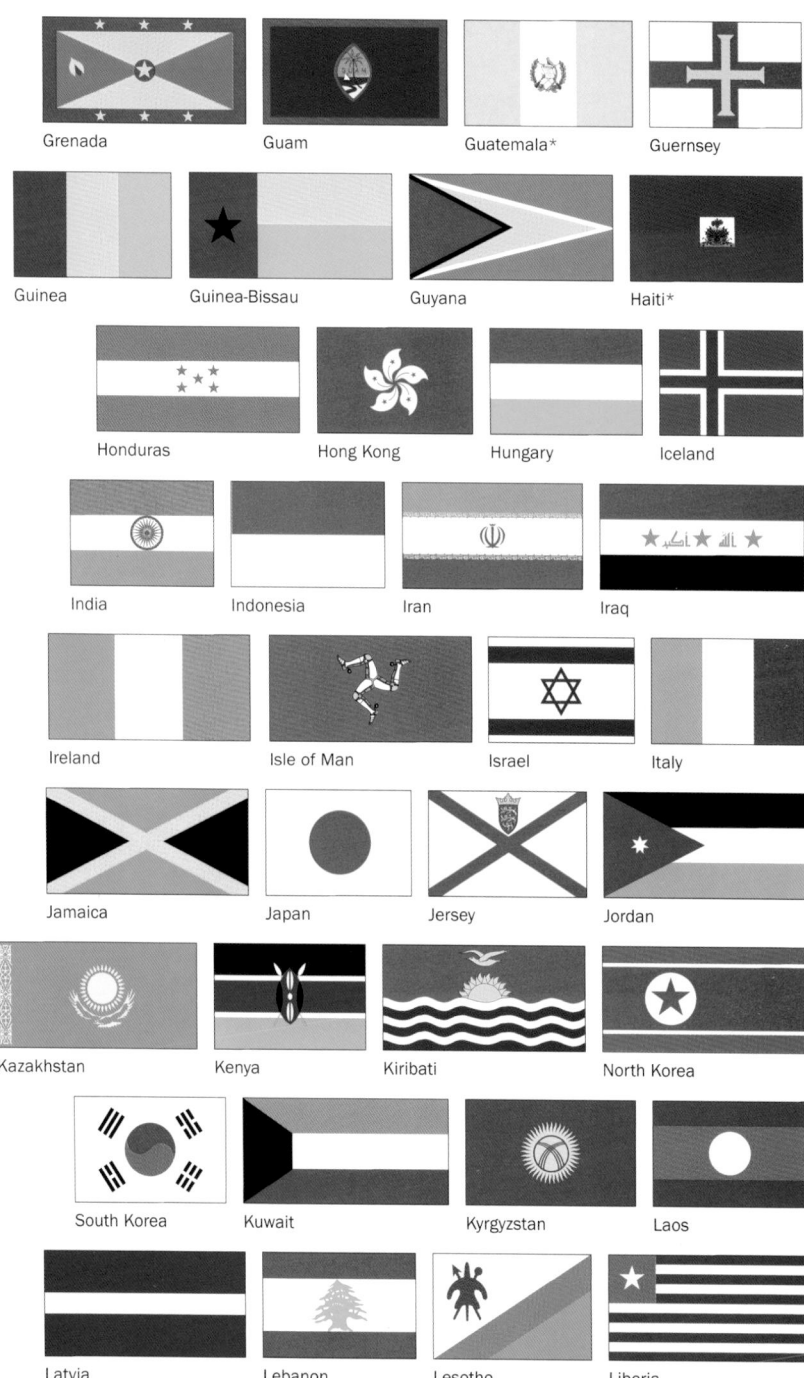

Grenada

Guam

Guatemala*

Guernsey

Guinea

Guinea-Bissau

Guyana

Haiti*

Honduras

Hong Kong

Hungary

Iceland

India

Indonesia

Iran

Iraq

Ireland

Isle of Man

Israel

Italy

Jamaica

Japan

Jersey

Jordan

Kazakhstan

Kenya

Kiribati

North Korea

South Korea

Kuwait

Kyrgyzstan

Laos

Latvia

Lebanon

Lesotho

Liberia

Civil flags are shown except where marked thus (*); in these cases, government flags are shown in order to illustrate emblems. Both styles are official national flags.

Plate 4 FLAGS OF THE WORLD

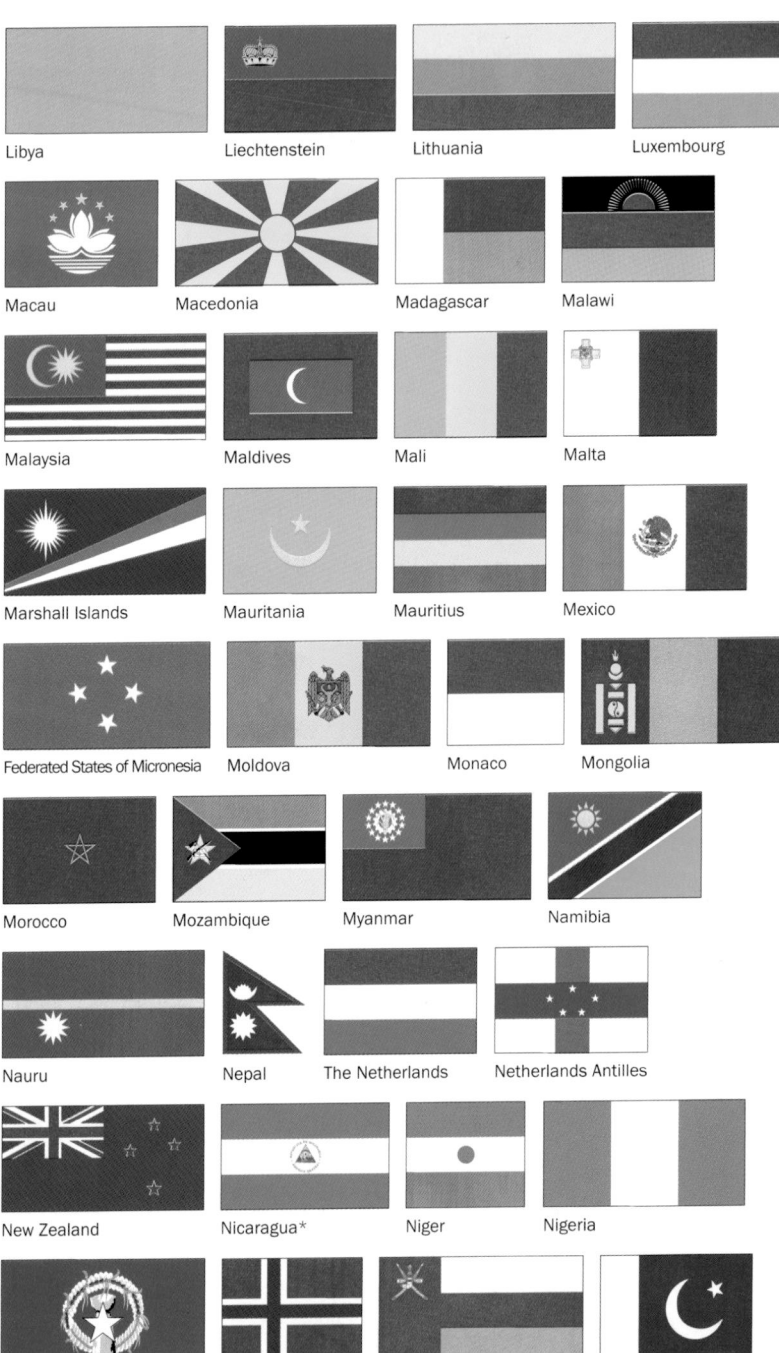

Libya

Liechtenstein

Lithuania

Luxembourg

Macau

Macedonia

Madagascar

Malawi

Malaysia

Maldives

Mali

Malta

Marshall Islands

Mauritania

Mauritius

Mexico

Federated States of Micronesia

Moldova

Monaco

Mongolia

Morocco

Mozambique

Myanmar

Namibia

Nauru

Nepal

The Netherlands

Netherlands Antilles

New Zealand

Nicaragua*

Niger

Nigeria

Northern Mariana Islands

Norway

Oman

Pakistan

Civil flags are shown except where marked thus (*); in these cases, government flags are shown in order to illustrate emblems. Both styles are official national flags.

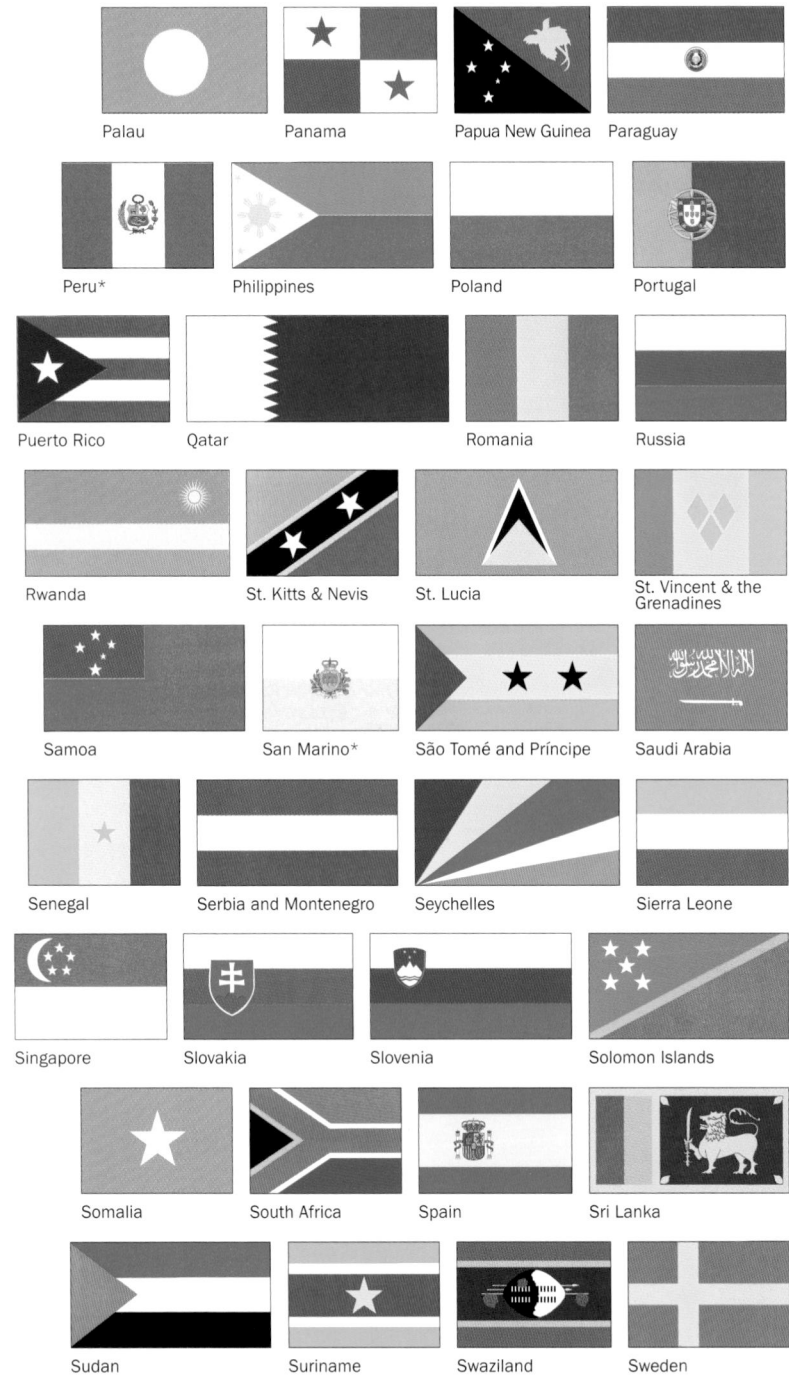

Palau Panama Papua New Guinea Paraguay

Peru* Philippines Poland Portugal

Puerto Rico Qatar Romania Russia

Rwanda St. Kitts & Nevis St. Lucia St. Vincent & the Grenadines

Samoa San Marino* São Tomé and Príncipe Saudi Arabia

Senegal Serbia and Montenegro Seychelles Sierra Leone

Singapore Slovakia Slovenia Solomon Islands

Somalia South Africa Spain Sri Lanka

Sudan Suriname Swaziland Sweden

Civil flags are shown except where marked thus (*); in these cases, government flags are shown in order to illustrate emblems. Both styles are official national flags.

Plate 6   FLAGS OF THE WORLD

Switzerland    Syria    Taiwan    Tajikistan

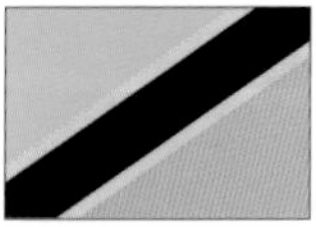

Tanzania    Thailand    Togo    Tonga

Trinidad & Tobago    Tunisia    Turkey    Turkmenistan

Tuvalu    Uganda   Ukraine    United Arab Emirates

United Kingdom 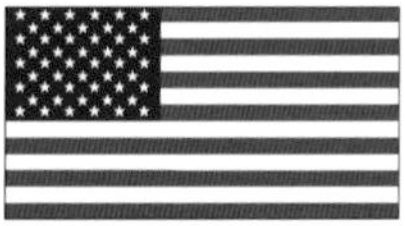   United States 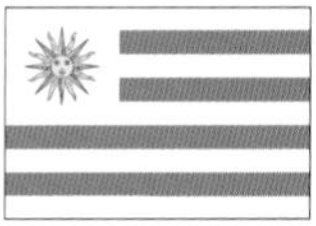   Uruguay

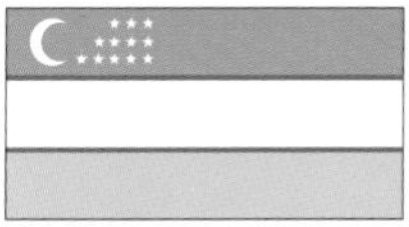

Uzbekistan 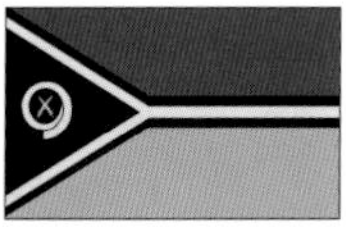   Vanuatu    Vatican City    Venezuela*

Vietnam    Virgin Islands (US)   Yemen 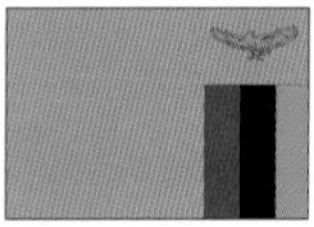   Zambia

Zimbabwe

Civil flags are shown except where marked thus (*); in these cases, government flags are shown in order to illustrate emblems. Both styles are official national flags.

World Religions

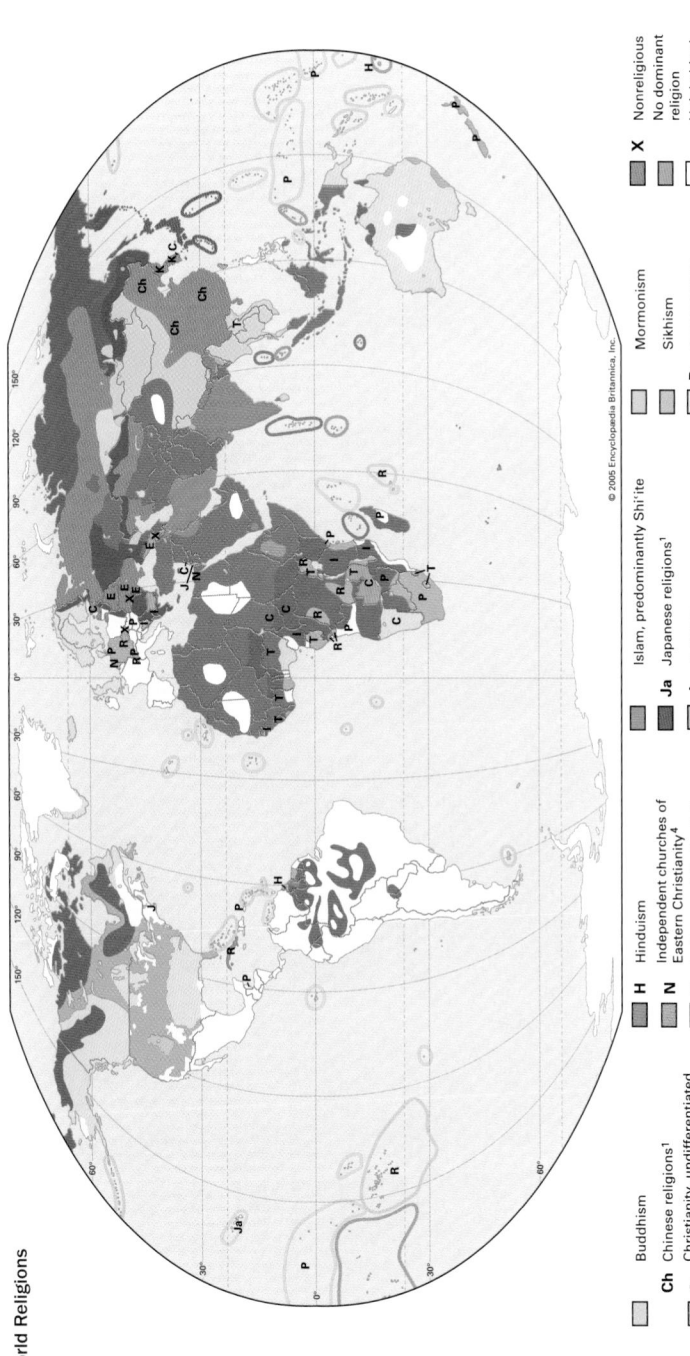

© 2005 Encyclopædia Britannica, Inc.

Legend:

- Buddhism
- **Ch** Chinese religions[1]
- **C** Christianity, undifferentiated by branch[2]
- **E** Eastern Orthodoxy[3]
- **H** Hinduism
- **N** Independent churches of Eastern Christianity[4]
- **T** Indigenous (tribal) religions
- **I** Islam, predominantly Sunni
- Islam, predominantly Shi'ite
- **Ja** Japanese religions[1]
- **J** Judaism
- **K** Korean religions[1]
- Mormonism
- Sikhism
- **P** Protestantism
- **R** Roman Catholicism
- **X** Nonreligious
- No dominant religion
- Uninhabited

Note:
The majority of the inhabitants in each of the areas colored on the map share the religious tradition indicated. Letter symbols show religious traditions shared by at least 25 percent of the inhabitants within areas no smaller than 1,000 square miles. Therefore minority religions of city dwellers have generally not been represented.

Footnotes:
[1] In certain eastern Asian areas, many of the people have plural religious affiliations. Religions in China and Korea include Buddhism, Taoism, Confucianism, and folk cults. The Japanese religions include Shinto and Buddhism.
[2] Chiefly mingled Protestantism and Roman Catholicism; neither predominant.
[3] Including Greek and Russian Orthodox Christianity.
[4] Including Armenian, Coptic, Ethiopian, East and West Syrian.

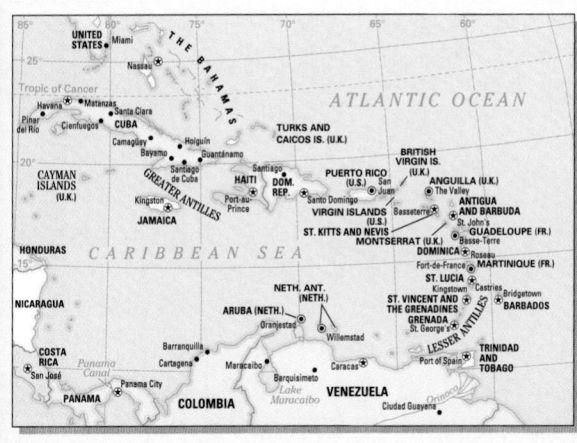
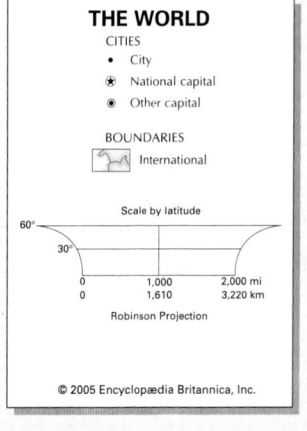

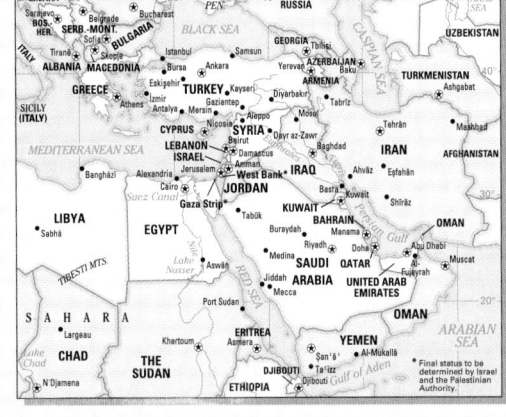

Plate 10

WORLD MAPS

Africa

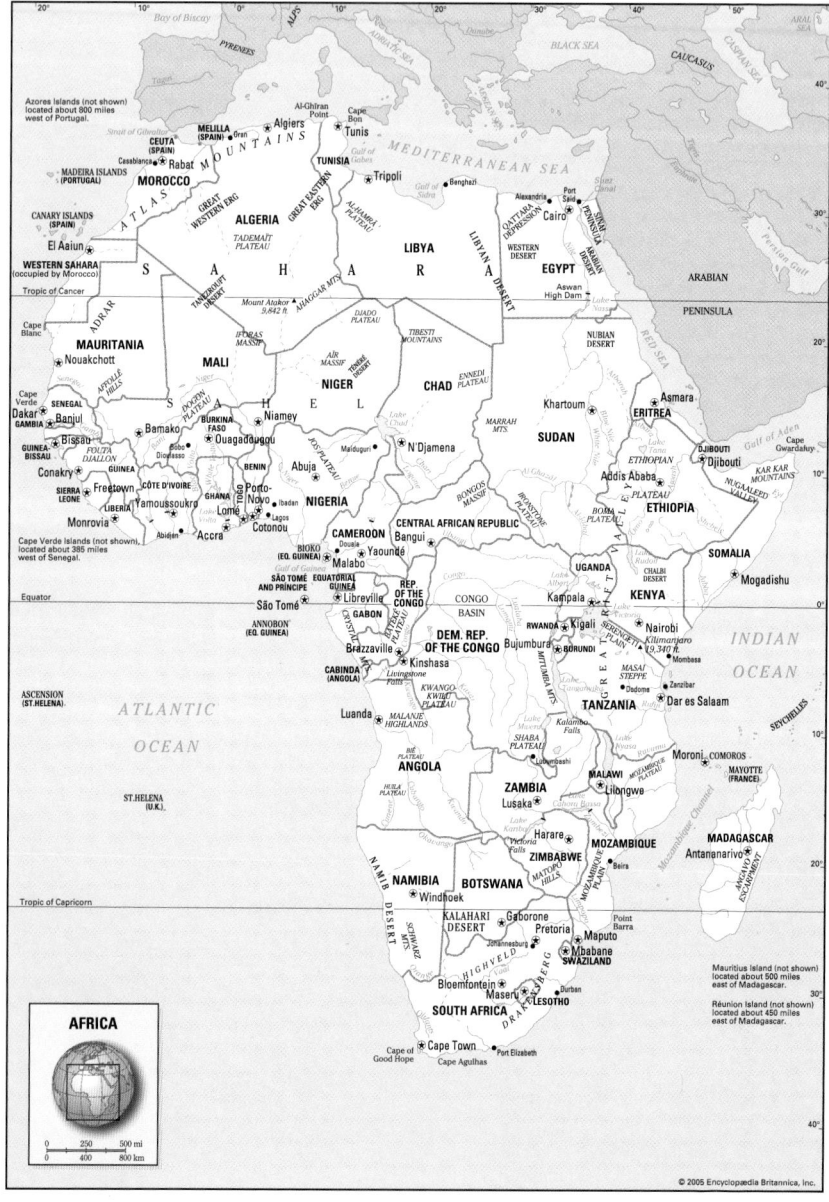

Asia

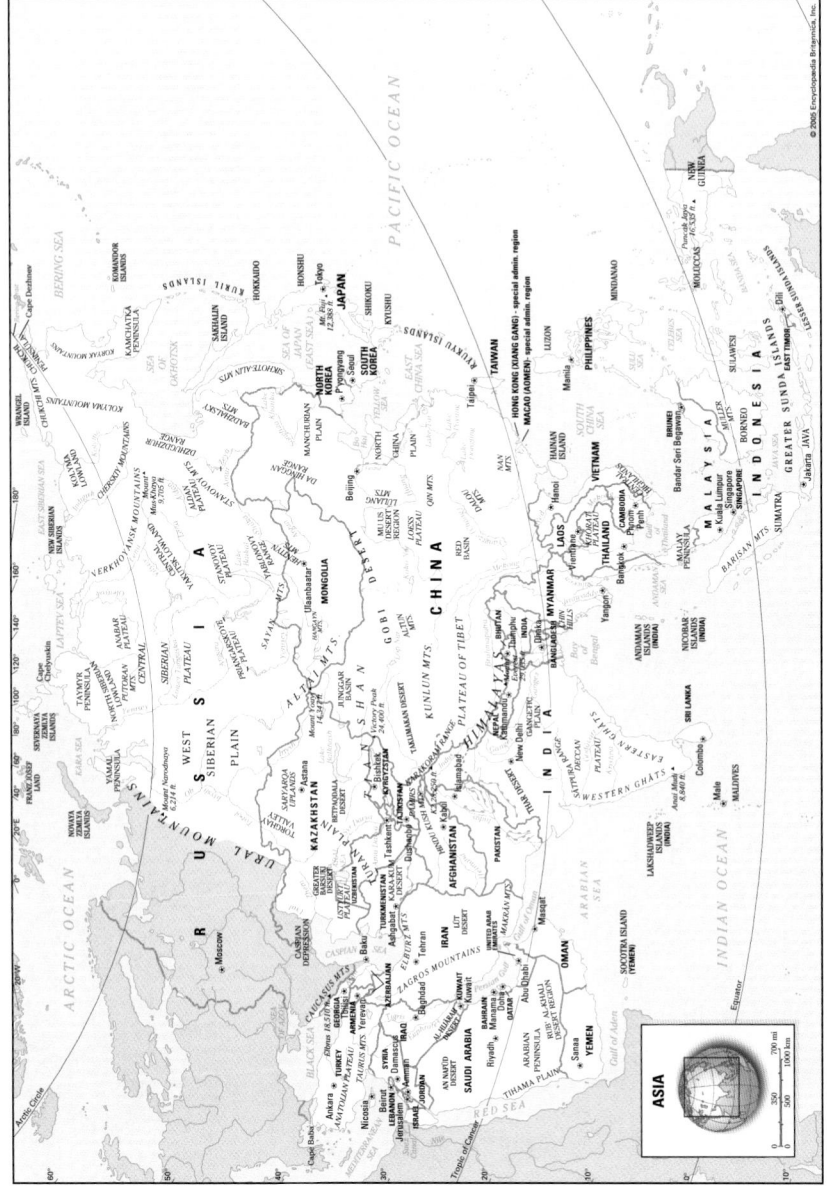

© 2005 Encyclopædia Britannica, Inc.

Plate 12

WORLD MAPS

Europe

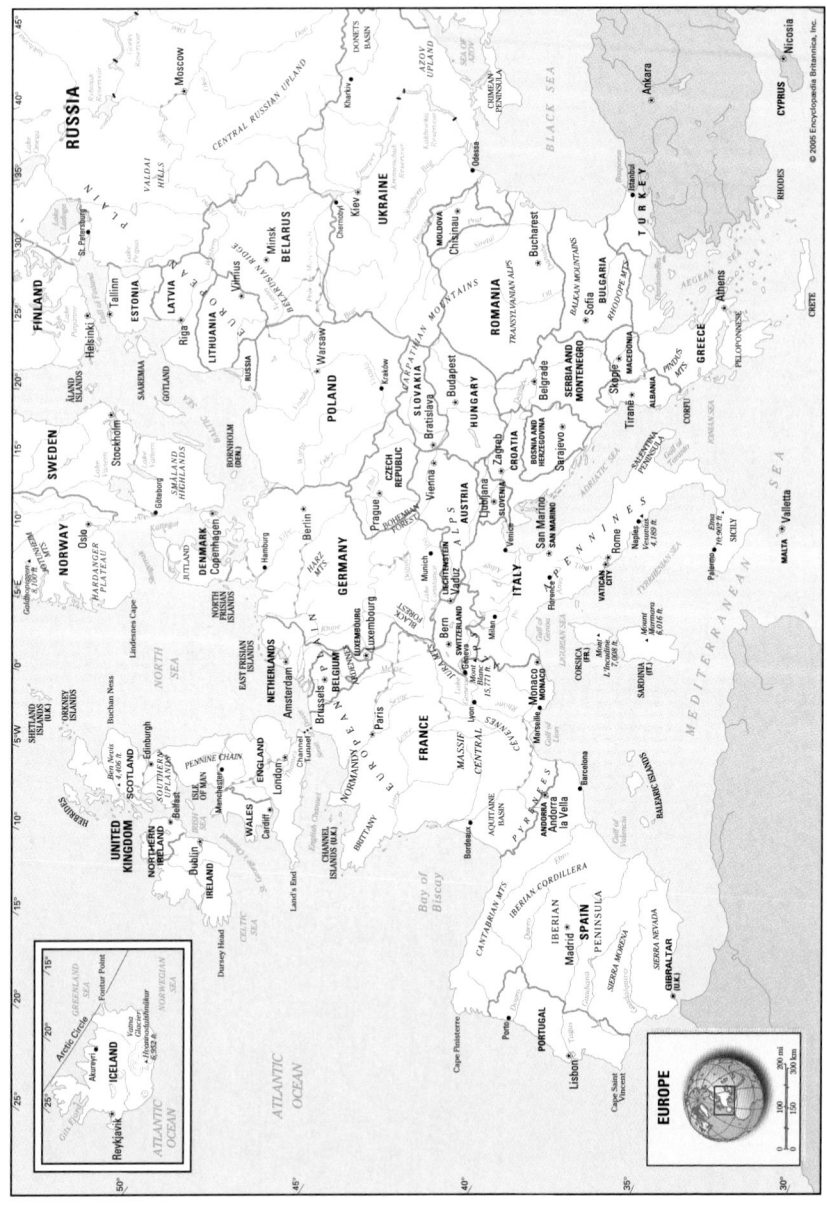

EUROPE

North America

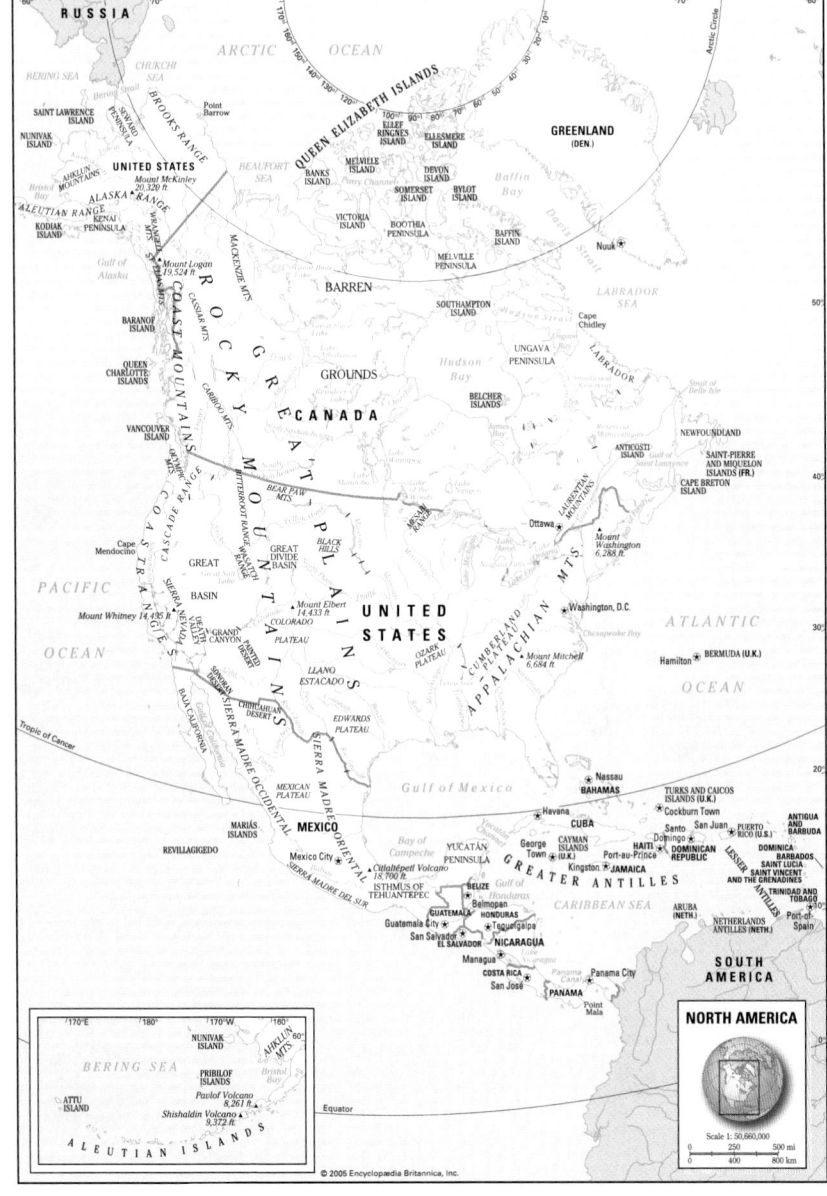

Plate 14 | WORLD MAPS

South America

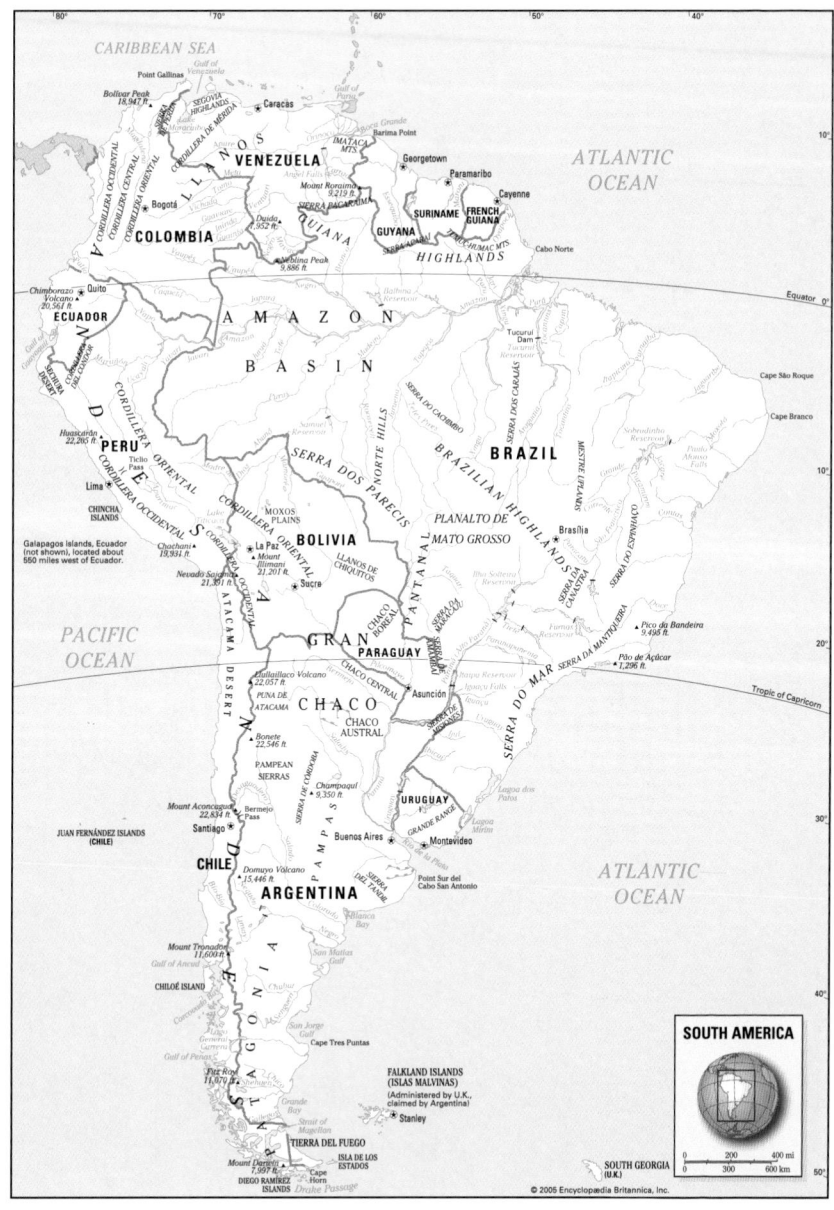

Australia

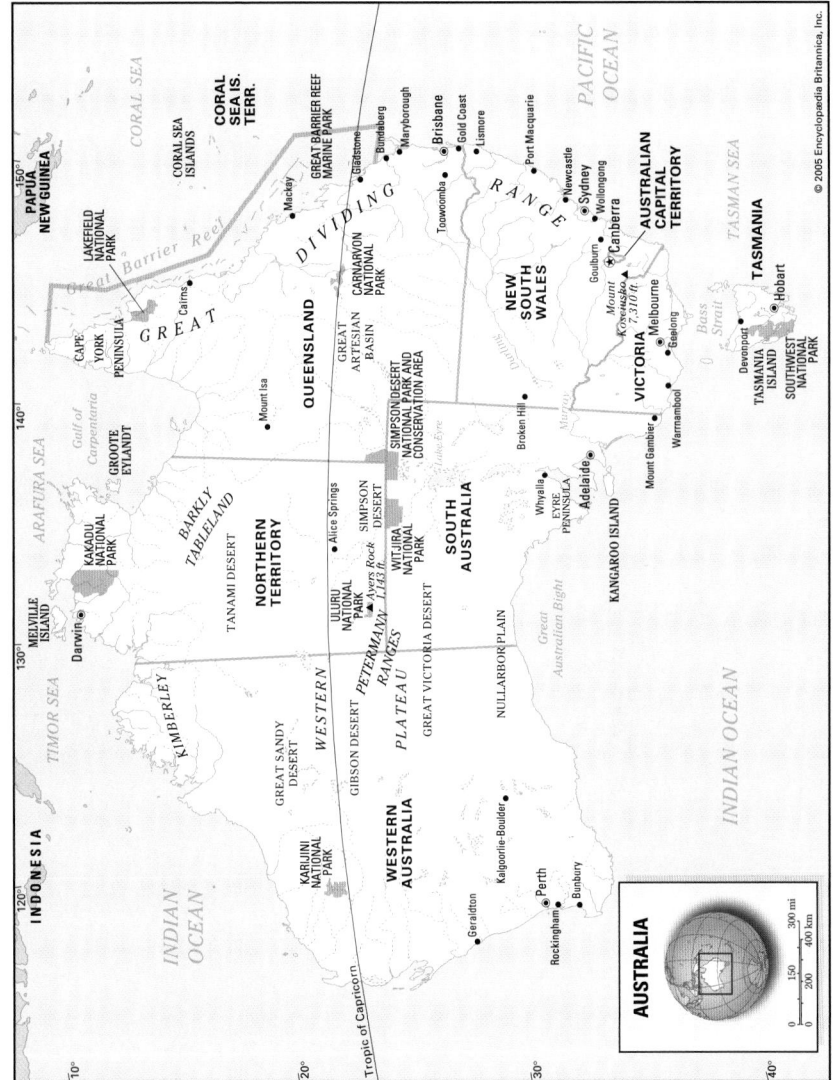

© 2005 Encyclopædia Britannica, Inc.

Plate 16 WORLD MAPS

Oceania/Pacific Islands

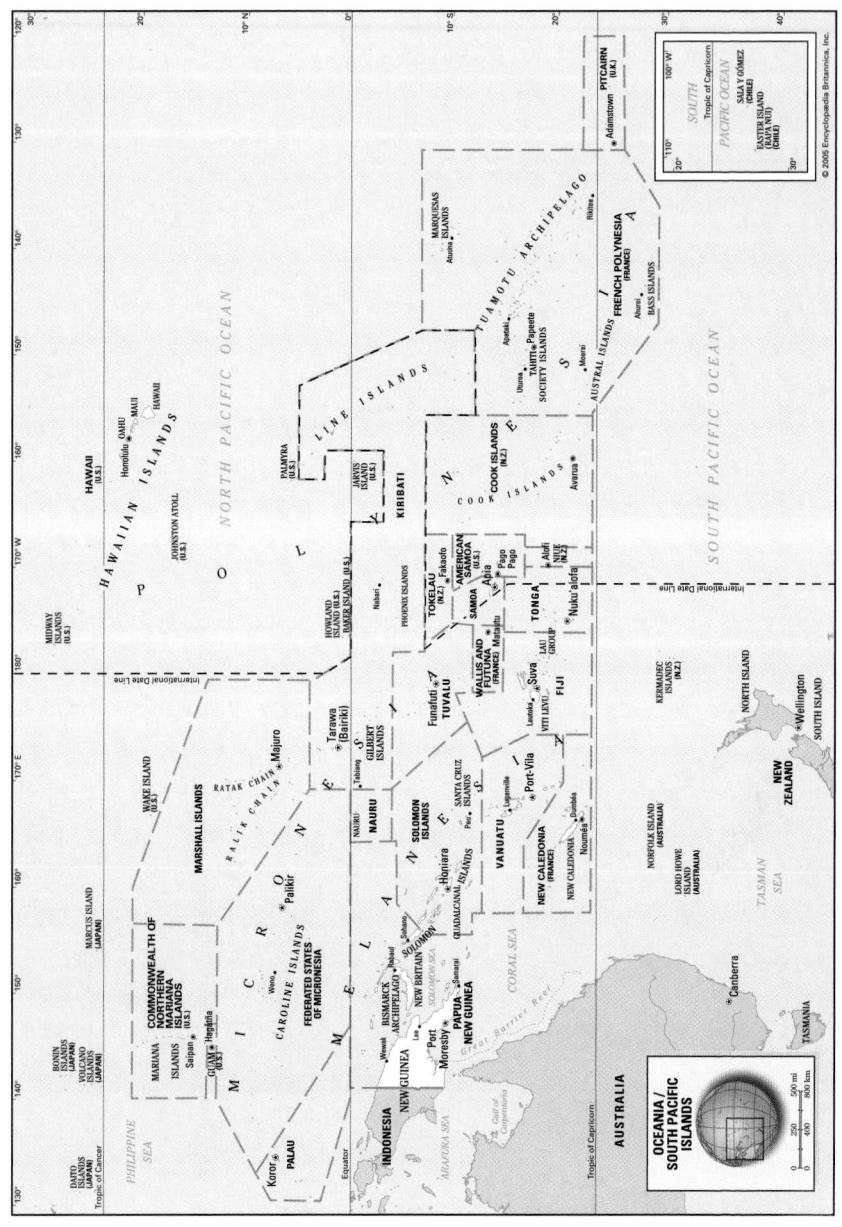

Winter Olympic Games Champions (continued)

Nordic Skiing (women) (continued)

4 × 5-KILOMETER RELAY HR:MIN:SEC
2002   Germany   49:30.6

Sled-dog Race

1932   Emile St.Goddard (CAN)

Snowboarding

GIANT SLALOM—MEN
1998   Ross Rebagliati (CAN)
2002   Philipp Schoch (SUI)

GIANT SLALOM—WOMEN
1998   Karine Ruby (FRA)
2002   Isabelle Blanc (FRA)

HALFPIPE—MEN
1998   Gian Simmen (SUI)
2002   Ross Powers (USA)

HALFPIPE—WOMEN
1998   Nicola Thost (GER)
2002   Kelly Clark (USA)

Speed Skating (men)

4 × 5-KILOMETER RELAY[12]   HR:MIN:SEC
1956   Finland   1:09:01.0
1960   Sweden   1:04:21.4
1964   USSR   59:20.2
1968   Norway   57:30.0
1972   USSR   48:46.15[1]
1976   USSR   1:07:49.75
1980   East Germany   1:02:11.10
1984   Norway   1:06:49.70
1988   USSR   59:51.10
1992   Unified Team[2]   59:34.8
1994   Russia   57:12.5

500 METERS   SEC
1924   Charles Jewtraw (USA)   44.0
1928   Clas Thunberg; Bernt Evensen 43.4
       (tied) (FIN; NOR)
1932   John Shea (USA)   43.4
1936   Ivar Ballangrud (NOR)   43.4
1948   Finn Helgesen (NOR)   43.1
1952   Kenneth Henry (USA)   43.2
1956   Yevgeny Grishin (URS)   40.2
1960   Yevgeny Grishin (URS)   40.2
1964   Richard McDermott (USA)   40.1
1968   Erhard Keller (FRG)   40.3
1972   Erhard Keller (FRG)   39.44[1]
1976   Yevgeny Kulikov (URS)   39.17
1980   Eric Heiden (USA)   38.03
1984   Sergey Fokichev (URS)   38.19
1988   Uew-Jens Mey (GDR)   36.45
1992   Uew-Jens Mey (GER)   37.14
1994   Aleksandr Golubyov (RUS)   36.33
1998   Hiroyasu Shimizu (JPN)   71.35[13]
2002   Casey Fitzrandolph (USA)   69.23[13]

1,000 METERS   MIN:SEC
1976   Peter Mueller (USA)   1:19.32[1]
1980   Eric Heiden (USA)   1:15.18
1984   Gaetan Boucher (CAN)   1:15.80
1988   Nikolay Gulyayev (URS)   1:13.03
1992   Olaf Zinke (GER)   1:14.85
1994   Dan Jansen (USA)   1:12.43
1998   Ids Postma (NED)   1:10.71
2002   Gerard van Velde (NED)   1:07.18

Speed Skating (men) (continued)

1,500 METERS   MIN:SEC
1924   Clas Thunberg (FIN)   2:20.8
1928   Clas Thunberg (FIN)   2:21.1
1932   John Shea (USA)   2:57.5
1936   Charles Mathisen (NOR)   2:19.2
1948   Sverre Farstad (NOR)   2:17.6
1952   Hjalmar Andersen (NOR)   2:20.4
1956   Yury Mikhaylov;   2:08.6
       Yevgeny Grishin (tied)
       (URS; URS)
1960   Yevegeny Grishin;   2:10.4
       Roald Aas (tied)
       (URS; NOR)
1964   Ants Antson (URS)   2:10.3
1968   Cornelis Verkerk (NED)   2:03.4
1972   Ard Schenk (NED)   2:02.96[1]
1976   Jan Egil Storholt (NOR)   1:59.38
1980   Eric Heiden (USA)   1:55.44
1984   Gaetan Boucher (CAN)   1:58.36
1988   André Hoffmann (GDR)   1:52.06
1992   Johann Olav Koss (NOR)   1:54.81
1994   Johann Olav Koss (NOR)   1:51.29
1998   Aadne Sondral (NOR)   1:47.87
2002   Derek Parra (USA)   1:43.95

5,000 METERS   MIN:SEC
1924   Clas Thunberg (FIN)   8:39.0
1928   Ivar Ballangrud (NOR)   8:50.5
1932   Irving Jaffee (USA)   9:40.8
1936   Ivar Ballangrud (NOR)   8:19.6
1948   Reidar Liaklev (NOR)   8:29.4
1952   Hjalmar Andersen (NOR)   8:10.6
1956   Boris Shilkov (URS)   7:48.7
1960   Viktor Kosichkin (URS)   7:51.3
1964   Knut Johannesen (NOR)   7:38.4
1968   Fred Anton Maier (NOR)   7:22.4
1972   Ard Schenk (NED)   7:23.61[1]
1976   Sten Stensen (NOR)   7:24.48
1980   Eric Heiden (USA)   7:02.29
1984   Thomas Gustafson (SWE)   7:12.28
1988   Thomas Gustafson (SWE)   6:44.63
1992   Geir Karlstad (NOR)   6:59.97
1994   Johann Olav Koss (NOR)   6:34.96
1998   Gianni Romme (NED)   6:22.20
2002   Jochem Uytdehaage (NED)   6:14.66

10,000 METERS   MIN:SEC
1924   Julius Skutnabb (FIN)   18:04.8
1932   Irving Jaffee (USA)   19:13.6
1936   Ivar Ballangrud (NOR)   17:24.3
1948   Ake Seyffarth (SWE)   17:26.3
1952   Hjalmar Andersen (NOR)   16:45.8
1956   Sigvard Ericsson (SWE)   16:35.9
1960   Knut Johannesen (NOR)   15:46.6
1964   Jonny Nilsson (SWE)   15:50.1
1968   Johnny Höglin (SWE)   15:23.6
1972   Ard Schenk (NED)   15:01.35[1]
1976   Piet Kleine (NED)   14:50.59
1980   Eric Heiden (USA)   14:28.13
1984   Igor Malkov (URS)   14:39.90
1988   Thomas Gustafson (SWE)   13:48.20
1992   Bart Veldkamp (NED)   14:12.12
1994   Johann Olav Koss (NOR)   13:30.55
1998   Gianni Romme (NED)   13:15.33
2002   Jochem Uytdehaage (NED)   12:58.92

COMBINED SPEED SKATING (MEN)
1922   Clas Thunberg (FIN)

Winter Olympic Games Champions (continued)

Speed Skating (women)

500 METERS		SEC
1960	Helga Haase (GER)[4]	45.9
1964	Lidiya Skoblikova (URS)	45.0
1968	Lyudmila Titova (URS)	46.1
1972	Anne Henning (USA)	43.33[1]
1976	Sheila Young (USA)	42.76
1980	Karin Enke (GDR)	41.78
1984	Christa Rothenburger (GDR)	41.02
1988	Bonnie Blair (USA)	39.10
1992	Bonnie Blair (USA)	40.33
1994	Bonnie Blair (USA)	39.25
1998	Catriona LeMay Doan (CAN)	76.60[13]
2002	Catriona LeMay Doan (CAN)	74.75[13]

1,000 METERS		MIN:SEC
1960	Klara Guseva (URS)	1:34.1
1964	Lidiya Skoblikova (URS)	1:32.6
1968	Carolina Geijssen (NED)	1:32.6
1972	Monika Pflug (FRG)	1:31.40[1]
1976	Tatyana Averina (URS)	1:28.43
1980	Natalya Petruseva (URS)	1:24.10
1984	Karin Enke (GDR)	1:21.61
1988	Christa Rothenburger (GDR)	1:17.65
1992	Bonnie Blair (USA)	1:21.90
1994	Bonnie Blair (USA)	1:18.74
1998	Marianne Timmer (NED)	1:16.51
2002	Chris Witty (USA)	1:13.83

1,500 METERS		MIN:SEC
1960	Lidiya Skoblikova (URS)	2:25.2
1964	Lidiya Skoblikova (URS)	2:22.6
1968	Kaija Mustonen (FIN)	2:22.4
1972	Dianne Holum (USA)	2:20.85[1]
1976	Galina Stepanskaya (URS)	2:16.58
1980	Annie Borckink (NED)	2:10.95
1984	Karin Enke (GDR)	2:03.42
1988	Yvonne van Gennip (NED)	2:00.68
1992	Jacqueline Börner (GER)	2:05.87
1994	Emese Hunyady (AUT)	2:02.19
1998	Marianne Timmer (NED)	1:57.58
2002	Anni Friesinger (GER)	1:54.02

3,000 METERS		MIN:SEC
1960	Lidiya Skoblikova (URS)	5:14.3
1964	Lidiya Skoblikova (URS)	5:14.9
1968	Johanna Schut (NED)	4:56.2
1972	Christina Baas-Kaiser (NED)	4:52.14[1]
1976	Tatyana Averina (URS)	4:45.19
1980	Björg Eva Jensen (NOR)	4:32.13
1984	Andrea Schöne (GDR)	4:24.79
1988	Yvonne van Gennip (NED)	4:11.94
1992	Gunda Niemann (GER)	4:19.90
1994	Svetlana Bazhanova (RUS)	4:17.43
1998	Gunda Niemann-Stirnemann (GER)	4:07.29
2002	Claudia Pechstein (GER)	3:57.70

Speed Skating (women) (continued)

5,000 METERS		MIN:SEC
1988	Yvonne van Gennip (NED)	7:14.13
1992	Gunda Niemann (GER)	7:31.57
1994	Claudia Pechstein (GER)	7:14.37
1998	Claudia Pechstein (GER)	6:59.61
2002	Claudia Pechstein (GER)	6:46.91

Short-track Speed Skating (men)

500 METERS		SEC
1994	Chae Ji-Hoon (KOR)	43.45
1998	Takafumi Nishitani (JPN)	42.862[5]
2002	Marc Gagnon (CAN)	41.802

1,000 METERS		MIN:SEC
1992	Kim Ki-Hoon (KOR)	1:30.76
1994	Kim Ki-Hoon (KOR)	1:34.57
1998	Kim Dong Sung (KOR)	1:32.428[9]
2002	Steven Bradbury (AUS)	1:29.109

1,500 METERS		MIN:SEC
2002	Apolo Anton Ohno (USA)	2:18.541

5000-METER RELAY		MIN:SEC
1992	South Korea	7:14.02
1994	Italy	7:11.74
1998	Canada	7:06.075[5]
2002	Canada	6:51.579

Short-track Speed Skating (women)

500 METERS		SEC
1992	Cathy Turner (USA)	47.04
1994	Cathy Turner (USA)	45.98
1998	Annie Perreault (CAN)	46.568[5]
2002	Yang Yang (A) (CHN)	44.187

1,000 METERS		MIN:SEC
1994	Chun Lee-Kyung (KOR)	1:36.87
1998	Chun Lee-Kyung (KOR)	1:42.776[5]
2002	Yang Yang (A) (CHN)	1:36.391

1,500 METERS		MIN:SEC
2002	Ko Gi-Hyun (KOR)	2:31.581

3000-METER RELAY		MIN:SEC
1992	Canada	4:36.62
1994	South Korea	4:26.64
1998	South Korea	4:16.260[5]
2002	South Korea	4:12.793

Winter Pentathlon[14]

1948	Gustav Lindh (SWE)	

[1]Race first timed in hundredths of a second.   [2]Unified Team, consisting of athletes from the Commonwealth of Independent States plus Georgia.   [3]Five men.   [4]Joint East-West German team.   [5]Race first timed in thousandths of a second.   [6]Competition scored on points until 1994.   [7]1924–52, 18 km.   [8]Results of a 10-km classical leg determine the starting order of a 10- or 15-km freestyle leg, the first finisher of which is the overall winner; the freestyle leg was shortened from 15 to 10 km in the 2002 games.   [9]Winner after disqualification of top finisher for drug use.   [10]From 1924 to 1960 the jumping was held on one hill. In 1964 there were two events, one on a 70-m and the other on an 80-m hill; from 1968 to 1988 there were 70-m and 90-m events. From 1992 there were 90-m and 120-m events.   [11]Results of a 5-km classical leg determine the starting order of a 5- or 10-km freestyle leg, the first finisher of which is the overall winner; the freestyle leg was shortened from 10 to 5 km in the 2002 games.   [12]3 × 5-km relay until 1976.   [13]Combined time for two runs.   [14]Includes elements of cross-country skiing, downhill skiing, shooting, fencing, and horse riding.

Olympic Medal Winners—XXVIII Summer Games (2004)

The XXVIII Summer Games were held in Athens, Greece, 13–29 Aug 2004.

EVENT	GOLD MEDALIST	PERFORMANCE	SILVER MEDALIST	BRONZE MEDALIST
Archery				
Men's individual	Marco Galiazzo (ITA)	111–109	Hiroshi Yamamoto (JPN)	Tim Cuddihy (AUS)
Men's team	South Korea	251–245	Taiwan	Ukraine
Women's individual	Park Sung Hyun (KOR)	110–108	Lee Sung Jin (KOR)	Alison Williamson (GBR)
Women's team	South Korea	241–240	China	Taiwan
Badminton				
Men's singles	Taufik Hidayat (INA)	15–8, 15–7	Shon Seung Mo (KOR)	Soni Dwi Kuncoro (INA)
Men's doubles	South Korea	15–11, 15–4	South Korea	Indonesia
Women's singles	Zhang Ning (CHN)	11–8, 6–11, 7–11	Mia Audina (NED)	Zhou Mi (CHN)
Women's doubles	China	7–15, 15–4, 15–8	China	South Korea
Mixed doubles	China	1–15, 15–12, 12–15	Great Britain	Denmark
Baseball				
	Cuba	6–2	Australia	Japan
Basketball				
Men	Argentina	84–69	Italy	United States
Women	United States	74–63	Australia	Russia
Boxing[1]				
48 kg (105.6 lb)	Yan Bhartelemy Varela (CUB)		Atagun Yalcinkaya (TUR)	Zou Shiming (CHN); Sergey Kazakov (RUS)
51 kg (112.2 lb)	Yuriorkis Gamboa Toledano (CUB)		Jerome Thomas (FRA)	Rustamhodza Rahimov (GER); Fuad Aslanov (AZE)
54 kg (118.8 lb)	Guillermo Rigondeaux Ortiz (CUB)		Worapoj Petchkoom (THA)	Bahodirjon Sooltonov (UZB); Aghasi Mammadov (AZE)
57 kg (125.4 lb)	Aleksey Tishchenko (RUS)		Kim Song Guk (PRK)	Jo Seok Hwan (KOR); Vitali Tajbert (GER)
60 kg (132 lb)	Mario César Kindelan Mesa (CUB)		Amir Khan (GBR)	Murat Khrachev (RUS); Serik Yeleuov (KAZ)
64 kg (140.8)	Manus Boonjumnong (THA)		Yudel Johnson Cedeno (CUB)	Ionut Gheorghe (ROM); Boris Georgiev (BUL)
69 kg (151.8 lb)	Bakhtiyar Artayev (KAZ)		Lorenzo Aragon Armenteros (CUB)	Oleg Saytov (RUS); Kim Jung Joo (KOR)
75 kg (165 lb)	Gaydarbek Gaydarbekov (RUS)		Gennady Golovkin (KAZ)	Suriya Prasathinphimai (THA); Andre Dirrell (USA)
81 kg (178.2 lb	Andre Ward (USA)		Magomed Aripgadzhiyev (BLR)	Utkirbek Haydarov (UZB); Ahmed Ismail (EGY)
91 kg (200.2 lb)	Odlanier Solis Fonte (CUB)		Viktar Zuyev (BLR)	Naser Al-Shami (SYR); Mohamed Elsayed (EGY)
91+ kg (200.2+ lb)	Aleksandr Povetkin (RUS)		Mohamed Aly (EGY)	Roberto Cammarelle (ITA); Michel López Nuñez (CUB)
Canoeing				
Men				
500-m kayak singles	Adam van Koeverden (CAN)	1 min 37.919 sec	Nathan Baggaley (AUS)	Ian Wynne (GBR)
1,000-m kayak singles	Eirik Veraas Larsen (NOR)	3 min 25.897sec	Ben Fouhy (NZL)	Adam van Koeverden (CAN)
500-m kayak pairs	Germany	1 min 27.040 sec	Australia	Belarus
1,000-m kayak pairs	Sweden	3 min 18.420 sec	Italy	Norway
1,000-m kayak fours	Hungary	2 min 56.919 sec	Germany	Slovakia
Slalom kayak singles	Benoit Peschier (FRA)	187.96 pt	Campbell Walsh (GBR)	Fabien Lefevre (FRA)

Olympic Medal Winners—XXVIII Summer Games (2004) (continued)

EVENT	GOLD MEDALIST	PERFORMANCE	SILVER MEDALIST	BRONZE MEDALIST
Canoeing (continued)				
Men				
500-m Canadian singles	Andreas Dittmer (GER)	1 min 46.383 sec	David Cal (ESP)	Maksim Opalev (RUS)
1,000-m Canadian singles	David Cal (ESP)	3 min 46.201 sec	Andreas Dittmer (GER)	Attila Vajda (HUN)
500-m Canadian pairs	China	1 min 40.278 sec	Cuba	Russia
1,000-m Canadian pairs	Germany	3 min 41.802 sec	Russia	Hungary
Slalom Canadian singles	Tony Estanguet (FRA)	189.16 pt	Michal Martikan (SVK)	Stefan Pfannmöller (GER)
Slalom Canadian pairs	Slovakia	207.16 pt	Germany	Czech Rep.
Women				
500-m kayak singles	Natasa Janics (HUN)	1 min 47.741 sec	Josefa Idem (ITA)	Caroline Brunet (CAN)
500-m kayak pairs	Hungary	1 min 38.101 sec	Germany	Poland
500-m kayak fours	Germany	1 min 34.340 sec	Hungary	Ukraine
Slalom kayak singles	Elena Kaliska (SVK)	210.03 pt	Rebecca Giddens (USA)	Helen Reeves (GBR)
Cycling				
Men				
Road race	Paolo Bettini (ITA)	5 hr 41 min 44 sec	Sergio Paulinho (POR)	Axel Merckx (BEL)
Individual road time trial	Tyler Hamilton (USA)	57 min 31.74 sec	Vyacheslav Yekimov (RUS)	Bobby Julich (USA)
1-km time trial	Chris Hoy (GBR)	1 min 0.711 sec	Arnaud Tournant (FRA)	Stefan Nimke (GER)
4,000-m individual pursuit	Bradley Wiggins (GBR)	4 min 16.304 sec	Brad McGee (AUS)	Sergi Escobar (ESP)
4,000-m team pursuit	Australia	3 min 58.223 sec	Great Britain	Spain
Individual sprint	Ryan Bayley (AUS)		Theo Bos (NED)	Rene Wolff (GER)
Team sprint	Germany	43.980 sec	Japan	France
Individual points race	Mikhail Ignatyev (RUS)	93 pt	Joan Llaneras (ESP)	Guido Fulst (GER)
Madison	Australia		Switzerland	Great Britain
Keirin	Ryan Bayley (AUS)		José Escuredo (ESP)	Shane Kelly (AUS)
Mountain bike	Julien Absalon (FRA)	2 hr 15 min 2 sec	José Antonio Hermida (ESP)	Bart Brentjens (NED)
Women				
Road race	Sara Carrigan (AUS)	3 hr 24 min 24 sec	Judith Arndt (GER)	Olga Slyusareva (RUS)
Individual road time trial	Leontien Zijlaard–van Moorsel (NED)	31 min 11.53 sec	Deirdre Demet-Barry (USA)	Karin Thürig (SUI)
500-m time trial	Anna Meares (AUS)	33.952 sec[3]	Jiang Yonghua (CHN)	Natalya Tsylinskaya (BLR)
Individual pursuit	Sarah Ulmer (NZL)	3 min 24.357 sec	Katie Mactier (AUS)	Leontien Zijlaard-van Moorsel (NED)
Individual sprint	Lori-Ann Muenzer (CAN)		Tamilla Abasova (RUS)	Anna Meares (AUS)
Individual points race	Olga Slyusareva (RUS)	20 pt	Bélem Guerrero Méndez (MEX)	Maria Luisa Calle Williams (COL)
Mountain bike	Gunn-Rita Dahle (NOR)	1 hr 56 min 51 sec	Marie-Helene Premont (CAN)	Sabine Spitz (GER)
Diving				
Men				
3-m springboard	Peng Bo (CHN)	787.38 pt	Alexandre Despatie (CAN)	Dmitry Sautin (RUS)
10-m platform	Hu Jia (CHN)	748.08 pt	Mathew Helm (AUS)	Tian Liang (CHN)
3-m synchronized springboard	Greece	353.34 pt	Germany	Australia

Olympic Medal Winners—XXVIII Summer Games (2004) (continued)

EVENT	GOLD MEDALIST	PERFORMANCE	SILVER MEDALIST	BRONZE MEDALIST
Diving (continued)				
Men				
10-m synchronized platform	China	383.88 pt	Great Britain	Australia
Women				
3-m springboard	Guo Jingjing (CHN)	633.15 pt	Wu Minxia (CHN)	Yuliya Pakhalina (RUS)
10-m platform	Chantelle Newbery (AUS)	590.31 pt	Lao Lishi (CHN)	Loudy Tourky (AUS)
3-m synchronized springboard	China	336.90 pt	Russia	Australia
10-m synchronized platform	China	352.14 pt	Russia	Canada
Equestrian				
Individual 3-day event	Leslie Law (GBR)		Kimberly Severson (USA)	Philippa Funnell (GBR)
Team 3-day event	France		Great Britain	United States
Individual dressage	Anky van Grunsven (NED)		Ulla Salzgeber (GER)	Beatriz Ferrer-Salat (ESP)
Team dressage	Germany		Spain	United States
Individual jumping	Rodrigo Pessoa (BRA)		Chris Kappler (USA)	Marco Kutscher (GER)
Team jumping	Germany		United States	Sweden
Fencing				
Men				
Individual foil	Brice Guyart (FRA)		Salvatore Sanzo (ITA)	Andrea Cassara (ITA)
Team foil	Italy		China	Russia
Individual épée	Marcel Fischer (SUI)		Wang Lei (CHN)	Pavel Kolobkov (RUS)
Team épée	France		Hungary	Germany
Individual sabre	Aldo Montano (ITA)		Zsolt Nemcsik (HUN)	Vladislav Tretiyak (UKR)
Team sabre	France		Italy	Russia
Women				
Individual foil	Valentina Vezzali (ITA)		Giovanna Trillini (ITA)	Sylwia Gruchala (POL)
Individual épée	Timea Nagy (HUN)		Laura Flessel-Colovic (FRA)	Maureen Nisima (FRA)
Team épée	Russia		Germany	France
Individual sabre	Mariel Zagunis (USA)		Tan Xue (CHN)	Sada Jacobson (USA)
Field Hockey				
Men	Australia	2–1	The Netherlands	Germany
Women	Germany	2–1	The Netherlands	Argentina
Gymnastics				
Men				
Team	Japan	173.821 pt	United States	Romania
All-around	Paul Hamm (USA)	57.823 pt	Kim Dae Eun (KOR)	Yang Tae Young (KOR)
Floor exercise	Kyle Shewfelt (CAN)	9.787 pt	Marian Dragulescu (ROM)	Iordan Iovtchev (BUL)
Vault	Gervasio Deferr (ESP)	9.737 pt	Evkeni Sapronenko (LAT)	Marian Dragulescu (ROM)
Pommel horse	Teng Haibin (CHN)	9.837pt	Marius Daniel Urzica (ROM)	Takehiro Kashima (JPN)
Rings	Dimosthenis Tampakos (GRE)	9.862 pt	Iordan Iovtchev (BUL)	Yuri Chechi (ITA)
Parallel bars	Valery Goncharov (UKR)	9.787 pt	Hiroyuki Tomita (JPN)	Li Xiaopeng (CHN)
High bar	Igor Cassina (ITA)	9.812 pt	Paul Hamm (USA)	Isao Yoneda (JPN)
Trampoline	Yury Nikitin (UKR)	41.50 pt	Aleksandr Moskalenko (RUS)	Henrik Stehlik (GER)
Women				
Team	Romania	114.283 pt	United States	Russia
All-around	Carly Patterson (USA)	38.387 pt	Svetlana Khorkina (RUS)	Zhang Nan (CHN)

Olympic Medal Winners—XXVIII Summer Games (2004) (continued)

EVENT	GOLD MEDALIST	PERFORMANCE	SILVER MEDALIST	BRONZE MEDALIST
Gymnastics (continued)				
Women				
Floor exercise	Catalina Ponor (ROM)	9.750 pt	Nicoleta Daniela Sofronie (ROM)	Patricia Moreno (ESP)
Vault	Monica Rosu (ROM)	9.656 pt	Annia Hatch (USA)	Anna Pavlova (RUS)
Uneven bars	Emilie Lepennec (FRA)	9.687 pt	Terin Humphrey (USA)	Courtney Kupets (USA)
Balance beam	Catalina Ponor (ROM)	9.787 pt	Carly Patterson (USA)	Alexandra Georgiana Eremia (ROM)
Trampoline	Anna Dogonadze (GER)	39.60 pt	Karen Cockburn (CAN)	Huang Shanshan (CHN)
Individual rhythmic	Alina Kabayeva (RUS)	108.400 pt	Irina Chashchina (RUS)	Anna Bessonova (UKR)
Team rhythmic	Russia	51.100 pt	Italy	Bulgaria
Handball (Team)				
Men	Croatia	26–24	Germany	Russia
Women	Denmark	38–36	South Korea	Ukraine
Judo[1,4]				
Men				
60 kg (132 lb)	Tadahiro Nomura (JPN)		Nestor Khergiani (GEO)	Khashbaatar Tsagaanbaatar (MGL); Choi Min Ho (KOR)
66 kg (145.2 lb)	Masato Uchishiba (JPN)		Jozef Krnac (SVK)	Georgi Georgiev (BUL); Yordanis Arencibia (CUB)
73 kg (160.6 lb)	Lee Won Hee (KOR)		Vitaly Makarov (RUS)	Leandro Guilheiro (BRA); James Pedro (USA)
81 kg (178.2 lb)	Ilias Iliadis (GRE)		Roman Gontyuk (UKR)	Dmitry Nosov (RUS); Flavio Canto (BRA)
90 kg (198 lb)	Zurab Zviadauri (GEO)		Hiroshi Izumi (JPN)	Khasanbi Taov (RUS); Mark Huizinga (NED)
100 kg (220 lb)	Ihar Makarau (BLR)		Jang Sung Ho (KOR)	Michael Jurack (GER); Ariel Zeevi (ISR)
100+ kg (220+ lb)	Keiji Suzuki (JPN)		Tamerlan Tmenov (RUS)	Dennis van der Geest (NED); Indrek Pertelson (EST)
Women				
48 kg (105.6 lb)	Ryoko Tani (JPN)		Frederique Jossinet (FRA)	Julia Matijass (GER); Gao Feng (CHN)
52 kg (114.4 lb)	Xian Dongmei (CHN)		Yuki Yokosawa (JPN)	Amarilys Savon (CUB); Ilse Heylen (BEL)
57 kg (125.4 lb)	Yvonne Bönisch (GER)		Kye Sun Hui (PRK)	Deborah Gravenstijn (NED); Yurisleidy Lupetey (CUB)
63 kg (138.6 lb)	Ayumi Tanimoto (JPN)		Claudia Heill (AUT)	Urska Zolnir (SLO); (KOR); Driulys Gonzales (CUB)
70 kg (154 lb)	Masae Ueno (JPN)		Edith Bosch (NED)	Qin Dongya (CHN); Annett Böhm (GER)
78 kg (171.6 lb)	Noriko Anno (JPN)		Liu Xia (CHN)	Lucia Morico (ITA); Yurisel Laborde (CUB)
78+ kg (171.6 lb)	Maki Tsukada (JPN)		Dayma Beltran (CUB)	Tea Donguzashvili (RUS); Sun Fuming (CHN)
Modern Pentathlon				
Men	Andrey Moiseyev (RUS)		Andrejus Zadneprovskis (LTU)	Libor Capalini (CZE)
Women	Zsuzsanna Voros (HUN)		Jelena Rublevska (LAT)	Georgina Harland (GBR)

Olympic Medal Winners—XXVIII Summer Games (2004) (continued)

EVENT	GOLD MEDALIST	PERFORMANCE	SILVER MEDALIST	BRONZE MEDALIST
Rowing				
Men				
Single sculls	Olaf Tufte (NOR)	6 min 49.30 sec	Jueri Jaanson (EST)	Ivo Yanakiev (BUL)
Double sculls	France	6 min 29.00 sec	Slovenia	Italy
Quadruple sculls	Russia	5 min 56.85 sec	Czech Rep.	Ukraine
Coxless pairs (oars)	Australia	6 min 30.76 sec	Croatia	South Africa
Coxless fours (oars)	Great Britain	6 min 6.98 sec	Canada	Italy
Eights	United States	5 min 42.48 sec	The Netherlands	Australia
Lightweight double sculls	Poland	6 min 20.93 sec	France	Greece
Lightweight fours	Denmark	6 min 1.39 sec	Australia	Italy
Women				
Single sculls	Katrin Rutschow-Stomporowski (GER)	7 min 18.12 sec	Yekaterina Karsten-Khodotovitch (BLR)	Rumyana Neykova (BUL)
Double sculls	New Zealand	7 min 1.79 sec	Germany	Great Britain
Quadruple sculls	Germany	6 min 29.29 sec	Great Britain	Australia
Coxless pairs (oars)	Romania	7 min 6.55 sec	Great Britain	Belarus
Eights	Romania	6 min 17.70 sec	United States	The Netherlands
Lightweight double sculls	Romania	6 min 56.05 sec	Germany	The Netherlands
Sailing				
Men's 470	United States		Great Britain	Japan
Women's 470	Greece		Spain	Sweden
Men's Mistral	Gal Fridman (ISR)		Nikolaos Kaklamanakis (GRE)	Nick Dempsey (GBR)
Women's Mistral	Faustine Merret (FRA)		Yin Jian (CHN)	Alessandra Sensini (ITA)
Men's Finn	Ben Ainslie (GBR)		Rafael Trujillo (ESP)	Mateusz Kusznierewicz (POL)
Women's Europe	Siren Sundby (NOR)		Lenka Smidova (CZE)	Signe Livbjerg (DEN)
Women's Yngling	Great Britain		Ukraine	Denmark
Mixed 49er	Spain		Ukraine	Great Britain
Mixed Laser	Robert Scheidt (BRA)		Andreas Geritzer (AUT)	Vasilij Zbogar (SLO)
Mixed Star	Brazil		Canada	France
Mixed Tornado	Austria		United States	Argentina
Shooting				
Men				
Rapid-fire pistol	Ralf Schumann (GER)	694.9 pt	Sergey Poliakov (RUS)	Sergey Aliferenko (RUS)
Free pistol	Mikhail Nestruyev (RUS)	663.3 pt	Jin Jong Oh (KOR)	Kim Jong Su (PRK)
Air pistol	Wang Yifu (CHN)	690.0pt[2]	Mikhail Nestruyev (RUS)	Vladimir Isakov (RUS)
10-m running (game) target	Manfred Kurzer (GER)	682.4 pt[3]	Aleksandr Blinov (RUS)	Dmitry Lykin (RUS)
Small-bore (sport) rifle, 3 positions	Jia Zhanbo (CHN)	1264.5 pt	Michael Anti (USA)	Christian Planer (AUT)
Small-bore (sport) rifle, prone	Matthew Emmons (USA)	599.0 pt	Christian Lusch (GER)	Sergey Martynov (BLR)
Air rifle	Zhu Quinan (CHN)	702.7 pt[3]	Li Jie (CHN)	Jozef Gonci (SVK)
Trap	Aleksey Alipov (RUS)	149.0 pt	Giovanni Pellielo (ITA)	Adam Vella (AUS)
Double trap	Ahmed Almaktoum (UAE)	189.0 pt	Rajyavardhan Rathore (IND)	Wang Zheng (CHN)
Skeet	Andrea Benelli (ITA)	149.0 pt	Marko Kemppainen (FIN)	Juan Miguel Rodríguez (CUB)
Women				
Sport pistol	Mariya Grozdeva (BUL)	688.2 pt	Lenka Hykova (CZE)	Irada Ashumova (AZE)
Air pistol	Olena Kostevych (UKR)	483.3 pt	Jasna Sekaric (SCG)	Mariya Grozdeva (BUL)
Small-bore (sport) rifle	Lyubov Galkina (RUS)	688.4 pt	Valentina Turisini (ITA)	Wang Chengyi (CHN)
Air rifle	Du Li (CHN)	502.0 pt[2]	Lyubov Galkina (RUS)	Katerina Kurkova (CZE)

Olympic Medal Winners—XXVIII Summer Games (2004) (continued)

EVENT	GOLD MEDALIST	PERFORMANCE	SILVER MEDALIST	BRONZE MEDALIST
Shooting (continued)				
Women				
Trap	Suzanne Balogh (AUS)	88.0 pt	Maria Quintanal (ESP)	Lee Bo Na (KOR)
Double trap	Kimberly Rhode (USA)	146.0 pt	Lee Bo Na (KOR)	Gao E (CHN)
Skeet	Diana Igaly (HUN)	97.0	Wei Ning (CHN)	Zemfira Meftakhet-dinova (AZE)
Soccer (Association Football)				
Men	Argentina	1–0	Paraguay	Italy
Women	United States	2–1 (overtime)	Brazil	Germany
Softball				
	United States	5–1	Australia	Japan
Swimming				
Men				
50-m freestyle	Gary Hall, Jr. (USA)	21.93 sec	Duje Draganja (CRO)	Roland Mark Schoeman (RSA)
100-m freestyle	Pieter van den Hoogenband (NED)	48.17 sec	Roland Mark Schoeman (RSA)	Ian Thorpe (AUS)
200-m freestyle	Ian Thorpe (AUS)	1 min 44.71 sec[2]	Pieter van den Hoogenband (NED)	Michael Phelps (USA)
400-m freestyle	Ian Thorpe (AUS)	3 min 43.10 sec	Grant Hackett (AUS)	Klete Keller (USA)
1,500-m freestyle	Grant Hackett (AUS)	14 min 43.40 sec[2]	Larsen Jensen (USA)	David Davies (GBR)
100-m backstroke	Aaron Peirsol (USA)	54.06 sec	Markus Rogan (AUT)	Tomomi Morita (JPN)
200-m backstroke	Aaron Peirsol (USA)	1 min 54.95 sec[2]	Markus Rogan (AUT)	Razvan Florea (ROM)
100-m breaststroke	Kosuke Kitajima (JPN)	1 min 0.08 sec	Brendan Hansen (USA)	Hugues Duboscq (FRA)
200-m breaststroke	Kosuke Kitajima (JPN)	2 min 9.44 sec[2]	Daniel Gyurta (HUN)	Brendan Hansen (USA)
100-m butterfly	Michael Phelps (USA)	51.25 sec[2]	Ian Crocker (USA)	Andriy Serdinov (UKR)
200-m butterfly	Michael Phelps (USA)	1 min 54.04 sec[2]	Takashi Yamamoto (JPN)	Stephen Parry (GBR)
200-m individual medley	Michael Phelps (USA)	1 min 57.14 sec[2]	Ryan Lochte (USA)	George Bovell (TRI)
400-m individual medley	Michael Phelps (USA)	4 min 8.26 sec[3]	Erik Vendt (USA)	Laszlo Cseh (HUN)
4 x 100-m freestyle relay	South Africa	3 min 13.17 sec[3]	The Netherlands	United States
4 x 200-m freestyle relay	United States	7 min 7.33 sec	Australia	Italy
4 x 100-m medley relay	United States	3 min 30.68 sec[3]	Germany	Japan
Women				
50-m freestyle	Inge de Bruijn (NED)	24.58 sec	Malia Metella (FRA)	Lisbeth Lenton (AUS)
100-m freestyle	Jodie Henry (AUS)	53.84 sec	Inge de Bruijn (NED)	Natalie Coughlin (USA)
200-m freestyle	Camelia Potec (ROM)	1 min 58.03 sec	Federica Pellegrini (ITA)	Solenne Figues (FRA)
400-m freestyle	Laure Manaudou (FRA)	4 min 05.34 sec	Otylia Jedrzejczak (POL)	Kaitlin Sandeno (USA)
800-m freestyle	Ai Shibata (JPN)	8 min 24.54 sec	Laure Manaudou (FRA)	Diana Munz (USA)
100-m backstroke	Natalie Coughlin (USA)	1 min 0.37 sec	Kirsty Coventry (ZIM)	Laure Manaudou (FRA)
200-m backstroke	Kirsty Coventry (ZIM)	2 min 9.19 sec	Stanislava Komarova (RUS)	Reiko Nakamura (JPN)
100-m breaststroke	Luo Xuejuan (CHN)	1 min 6.64 sec[2]	Brooke Hanson (AUS)	Leisel Jones (AUS)
200-m breaststroke	Amanda Beard (USA)	2 min 23.37 sec[2]	Leisel Jones (AUS)	Anne Poleska (GER)
100-m butterfly	Petria Thomas (AUS)	57.72 sec	Otylia Jedrzejczak (POL)	Inge de Bruijn (NED)
200-m butterfly	Otylia Jedrzejczak (POL)	2 min 6.05 sec	Petria Thomas (AUS)	Yuko Nakanishi (JPN)
200-m individual medley	Yana Klochkova (UKR)	2 min 11.14 sec	Amanda Beard (USA)	Kirsty Coventry (ZIM)
400-m individual	Yana Klochkova (UKR)	4 min 34.83 sec	Kaitlin Sandeno (USA)	Georgina Bardach (ARG)

Olympic Medal Winners—XXVIII Summer Games (2004) (continued)

EVENT	GOLD MEDALIST	PERFORMANCE	SILVER MEDALIST	BRONZE MEDALIST
Swimming (continued)				
Women				
4 x 100-m freestyle relay	Australia	3 min 35.94 sec[3]	United States	The Netherlands
4 x 200-m freestyle relay	United States	7 min 53.42 sec[3]	China	Germany
4 x 100-m medley relay	Australia	3 min 57.32 sec[3]	United States	Germany
Synchronized Swimming				
Duet	Russia	99.833 pt	Japan	United States
Team	Russia	99.667 pt	Japan	United States
Table Tennis				
Men's singles	Ryu Seung Min (KOR)	11–3, 9–11, 11–9, 11–9, 11–13, 11–9	Wang Hao (CHN)	Wang Liqin (CHN)
Men's doubles	China	11–6, 11–9, 7–11, 11–8, 8–11, 11–5	Hong Kong	Denmark
Women's singles	Zhang Yining (CHN)	11–8, 11–7, 11–2, 11–2	Kim Hyang Mi (PRK)	Kim Kyung Ah (KOR)
Women's doubles	China	11–9, 11–7, 11–6, 11–6	South Korea	China
Taekwondo				
Men				
58 kg (127.6 lb)	Chu Mu Yen (TPE)		Oscar Francisco Salazar Blanco (MEX)	Tamer Bayoumi (EGY)
68 kg (149.6 lb)	Hadi Saei Bonehkohal (IRI)		Huang Hsiung Chih (TPE)	Song Seob Myeong (KOR)
80 kg (176 lb)	Steven Lopez (USA)		Bahri Tanrikulu (TUR)	Yossef Karami (IRI)
80+ kg (176+ lb)	Moon Dae Sung (KOR)		Alexandros Nikolaidis (GRE)	Pascal Gentil (FRA)
Women				
49 kg (107.8 lb)	Chen Shih Hsin (TPE)		Yanelis Yuliet Labrada Diaz (CUB)	Yaowapa Boorapolchai (THA)
57 kg (125.4 lb)	Jang Ji Won (KOR)		Nia Abdallah (USA)	Iridia Salazar Blanco (MEX)
67 kg (147.4 lb)	Luo Wei (CHN)		Elisavet Mystakidou (GRE)	Hwang Kyung Sun (KOR)
67+ kg (147.4+ lb)	Chen Zhong (CHN)		Myriam Baverel (FRA)	Adriana Carmona (VEN)
Tennis				
Men's singles	Nicolas Massu (CHI)	6–3, 3–6, 2–6, 6–3, 6–4	Mardy Fish (USA)	Fernando González (CHI)
Men's doubles	Chile	6–2, 4–6 3–6, 7–6, 6–4	Germany	Croatia
Women's singles	Justine Henin-Hardenne (BEL)	6–3, 6–3	Amelie Mauresmo (FRA)	Alicia Molik (AUS)
Women's doubles	China	6–3, 6–3	Spain	Argentina
Track and Field (Athletics)				
Men				
100 m	Justin Gatlin (USA)	9.85 sec	Francis Obikwelu (POR)	Maurice Greene (USA)
200 m	Shawn Crawford (USA)	19.79 sec	Bernard Williams (USA)	Justin Gatlin (USA)
400 m	Jeremy Wariner (USA)	44.00 sec	Otis Harris (USA)	Derrick Brew (USA)
4 x 100-m relay	Great Britain	38.07 sec	United States	Nigeria
4 x 400-m relay	United States	2 min 55.91 sec	Australia	Nigeria
800 m	Yury Borzakovsky (RUS)	1 min 44.45 sec	Mbulaeni Mulaudzi (RSA)	Wilson Kipketer (DEN)
1,500 m	Hicham El Guerrouj (MAR)	3 min 34.18 sec	Bernard Lagat (KEN)	Rui Silva (POR)
5,000 m	Hicham El Guerrouj (MAR)	13 min 14.39 sec	Kenenisa Bekele (ETH)	Eliud Kipchoge (KEN)
10,000 m	Kenenisa Bekele (ETH)	27 min 05.10 sec[2]	Sileshi Sihine (ETH)	Zersenay Tadesse (ERI)

Olympic Medal Winners—XXVIII Summer Games (2004) (continued)

EVENT	GOLD MEDALIST	PERFORMANCE	SILVER MEDALIST	BRONZE MEDALIST
Track and Field (Athletics) (continued)				
Men				
Marathon	Stefano Baldini (ITA)	2 hr 10 min 55 sec	Mebrahtom Keflezighi (USA)	Vanderlei Lima (BRA)
110-m hurdles	Liu Xiang (CHN)	12.91 sec^2	Terrence Trammell (USA)	Anier Garcia (CUB)
400-m hurdles	Felix Sánchez (DOM)	47.63 sec	Danny McFarlane (JAM)	Naman Keita (FRA)
3,000-m steeple-chase	Ezekiel Kemboi (KEN)	8 min 5.81sec	Brimin Kipruto (KEN)	Paul Kipsiele Koech (KEN)
20-km walk	Ivano Brugnetti (ITA)	1 hour 19.40 sec	Francisco Javier Fernández (ESP)	Nathan Deakes (AUS)
50-km walk	Robert Korzeniowski (POL)	3 hr 38 min 46 sec	Denis Nizhegorodov (RUS)	Aleksey Voyevodin (RUS)
High jump	Stefan Holm (SWE)	2.36 m	Matt Hemingway (USA)	Jaroslav Baba (CZE)
Long jump	Dwight Phillips (USA)	8.59 m	John Moffitt (USA)	Joan Lino Martínez (ESP)
Triple jump	Christian Olsson (SWE)	17.79 m	Marian Oprea (ROM)	Danila Burkenya (RUS)
Pole vault	Timothy Mack (USA)	5.95 sec^2	Toby Stevenson (USA)	Giuseppe Gibilisco (ITA)
Shot put	Yury Bilonog (UKR)	21.16 m	Adam Nelson (USA)	Joachim Olsen (DEN)
Discus throw	Virgilijus Alekna (LTU)	69.89 m^2	Zoltan Kovago (HUN)	Aleksander Tammert (EST)
Javelin throw	Andreas Thorkildsen (NOR)	86.50 m	Vadims Vasilevskis (LAT)	Sergey Makarov (RUS)
Hammer throw	Adrian Annus (HUN)	83.19 m	Koji Murofushi (JPN)	Ivan Tikhon (BLR)
Decathlon	Roman Sebrele (CZE)		Bryan Clay (USA)	Dmitry Karpov (KAZ)
Women				
100 m	Yuliya Nesterenko (BLR)	10.93 sec	Lauryn Williams (USA)	Veronica Campbell (JAM)
200 m	Veronica Campbell (JAM)	22.05 sec	Allyson Felix (USA)	Debbie Ferguson (BAH)
400 m	Tonique Williams-Darling (BAH)	49.41 sec	Ana Guevara (MEX)	Natalya Antyukh (RUS)
4 x 100-m relay	Jamaica	41.73 sec	Russia	France
4 x 400-m relay	United States	3 min 19.01 sec	Russia	Jamaica
800 m	Kelly Holmes (GBR)	1 min 56.38 sec	Hasna Benhassi (MAR)	Jolanda Ceplak (SLO)
1,500 m	Kelly Holmes (GBR)	3 min 57.90 sec	Tatyana Tomashova (RUS)	Maria Cioncan (ROM)
5,000 m	Meseret Defar (ETH)	14 min 45.65 sec	Isabella Ochichi (KEN)	Tirunesh Dibaba (ETH)
10,000 m	Xing Huina (CHN)	30 min 24.36 sec	Ejegayehu Dibaba (ETH)	Derartu Tulu (ETH)
Marathon	Mizuki Noguchi (JPN)	2 hr 26 min 20 sec	Catherine Ndereba (KEN)	Deena Kastor (USA)
100-m hurdles	Joanna Hayes (USA)	12.37 sec^2	Olena Krasovska (UKR)	Melissa Morrison (USA)
400-m hurdles	Fani Halkia (GRE)	52.82 sec	Ionela Tirlea-Manolache (ROM)	Tetyana Tereshchuk-Antipova (UKR)
20-km walk	Athanasia Tsoumeleka (GRE)	1 hr 29 min 12 sec	Olimpiada Ivanova (RUS)	Jane Saville (AUS)
High jump	Yelena Slesarenko (RUS)	2.06 m^2	Hestrie Cloete (RSA)	Viktoriya Styopina (UKR)
Long jump	Tatyana Lebedeva (RUS)	7.07 m	Irina Simagina (RUS)	Tatyana Kotova (RUS)
Triple jump	Françoise Mbango Etone (CMR)	15.30 m	Hrysopiyi Devetzi (GRE)	Tatyana Lebedeva (RUS)
Pole vault	Yelena Isinbayeva (RUS)	4.91 m^3	Svetlana Feofanova (RUS)	Anna Rogowska (POL)
Shot put	Irina Korzhanenko (RUS)	21.06 m	Yumileidi Cumba (CUB)	Nadine Kleinert (GER)
Discus throw	Natalya Sadova (RUS)	67.02 m	Anastasia Kelesidou (GRE)	Irina Yachenko (BLR)
Javelin throw	Osleidys Menéndez (CUB)	71.53 m^2	Steffi Nerius (GER)	Mirela Manjani (GRE)
Hammer throw	Olga Kuzenkova (RUS)	75.02 m^2	Yipsi Moreno (CUB)	Yunaika Crawford (CUB)
Heptathlon	Carolina Klüft (SWE)		Austra Skujyte (LTU)	Kelly Sotherton (GBR)

Olympic Medal Winners—XXVIII Summer Games (2004) (continued)

EVENT	GOLD MEDALIST	PERFORMANCE	SILVER MEDALIST	BRONZE MEDALIST
Triathlon				
Men	Hamish Carter (NZL)	1 hr 51 min 7.73 sec	Bevan Docherty (NZL)	Sven Reiderer (SUI)
Women	Kate Allen (AUT)	2 hrs 4 min 43.45 sec	Loretta Harrop (AUS)	Susan Williams (USA)
Volleyball				
Men's 12-team tournament	Brazil	25-15, 24-26, 25-20, 25-22	Italy	Russia
Women's 12-team tournament	China	28-30, 25-27, 25-20, 25-23, 15-12	Russia	Cuba
Men's beach	Brazil	21-16, 21-15	Spain	Switzerland
Women's beach	United States	21-17, 21-11	Brazil	United States
Water Polo				
Men	Hungary	8-7	Serbia and Montenegro	Russia
Women	Italy	10-9	Greece	United States
Weightlifting[4]				
Men				
56 kg (123.2 lb)	Halil Mutlu (TUR)	295.0	Wu Meijin (CHN)	Sedat Artuc (TUR)
62 kg (136.4 lb)	Shi Zhiyong (CHN)	325.0 kg	Le Maosheng (CHN)	Israel José Rubio (VEN)
69 kg (151.8 lb)	Zhang Guozheng (CHN)	347.5 kg	Lee Bae Young (KOR)	Nikolay Pechalov (CRO)
77 kg (169.4 lb)	Taner Sagir (TUR)	375.0 kg	Sergey Filimonov (KAZ)	Oleg Perepechenov (RUS)
85 kg (187 lb)	George Asanidze (GEO)	382.5 kg	Andrey Rybakou (BLR)	Pyrros Dimas (GRE)
94 kg (206.8 lb)	Milen Dobrev (BUL)	407.5 kg	Khajimurad Akkayev (RUS)	Eduard Tyukin (RUS)
105 kg (231 lb)	Dimitry Berestov (RUS)	425.0	Igor Razoronov (UKR)	Gleb Pisarevsky (RUS)
105+ kg (231+ lb)	Hossein Reza Zadeh (IRI)	472.5 kg	Viktors Scerbatihs (LAT)	Velichko Cholakov (BUL)
Women				
48 kg (105.6 lb)	Nurcan Taylan (TUR)	210.0 kg	Li Zhuo (CHN)	Aree Wiratthaworn (THA)
53 kg (116.6 lb)	Udomporn Polsak (THA)	222.5 kg	Raema Lisa Rumbewas (INA)	Mabel Mosquera (COL)
58 kg (127.6 lb)	Chen Yanqing (CHN)	237.5 kg	Ri Song Hui (PRK)	Wandee Kameaim (THA)
63 kg (138.6 lb)	Natalya Skakun (UKR)	242.5 kg	Hanna Batsyushka (BLR)	Tatsyana Stukalava (BLR)
69 kg (151.8 lb)	Liu Chunhong (CHN)	275.0	Eszter Krutzler (HUN)	Zarema Kasayeva (RUS)
75 kg (165 lb)	Pawina Thongsuk (THA)	272.5 kg	Nataliya Zabolotnaya (RUS)	Valentina Popova (RUS)
75+ kg (165 lb)	Tang Gonghong (CHN)	305.0 kg	Jang Mi Ran (KOR)	Agata Wrobel (POL)
Wrestling[4]				
Freestyle				
Men				
55 kg (121 lb)	Mavlet Batirov (RUS)		Stephen Abas (USA)	Chikara Tanabe (JPN)
60 kg (132 lb)	Yandro Miguel Quintana (CUB)		Masuod Jokar (IRI)	Kenji Inoue (JPN)
66 kg (145.2 lb)	Elbrus Tedeyev (UKR)		Jamill Kelly (USA)	Makhach Murtazaliyev (RUS)
74 kg (162.8 lb)	Buvaysa Saytyev (RUS)		Gennadiy Laliev (KAZ)	Ivan Fundora (CUB)
84 kg (184.8 lb)	Cael Sanderson (USA)		Moon Eui Jae (KOR)	Sazhid Sazhidov (RUS)

Olympic Medal Winners—XXVIII Summer Games (2004) (continued)

EVENT	GOLD MEDALIST	PERFORMANCE	SILVER MEDALIST	BRONZE MEDALIST
Wrestling (continued)				
Freestyle				
96 kg (211.2 lb)	Khajimurat Gatsalov (RUS)		Magomed Ibragimov (UZB)	Alireza Heidari (IRI)
120+ kg (264 lb)	Artur Taymazov (UZB)		Alireza Rezaei (IRI)	Aydin Polatci (TUR)
Women				
48-kg (105.6 lb)	Irini Merleni (UKR)		Chiharu Icho (JPN)	Patricia Miranda (USA)
55-kg (121 lb)	Saori Yoshida (JPN)		Tonya Verbeek (CAN)	Anna Gomis (FRA)
63-kg (138.6 lb)	Kaori Icho (JPN)		Sara McMann (USA)	Lise Legrand (FRA)
72-kg (158.4 lb)	Wang Xu (CHN)		Guzel Manyurova (RUS)	Kyoko Hamaguchi (JPN)
Greco-Roman				
Men				
55 kg (121 lb)	Istvan Majoros (HUN)		Geidar Mamedaliyev (RUS)	Artiom Kiouregkian (GRE)
60 kg (132 lb)	Jung Ji Hyun (KOR)		Roberto Monzón (CUB)	Armen Nazarian (BUL)
66 kg (145.2 lb)	Farid Mansurov (AZE)		Seref Eroglu (TUR)	Mkkhitar Manukyan (KAZ)
74 kg (162.8 lb)	Aleksandr Dokturishivili (UZB)		Marko Yli-Hannuksela (FIN)	Varteres Samurgachev (RUS)
84 kg (184.8 lb)	Alexey Mishin (RUS)		Ara Abrahamian (SWE)	Vyachaslau Makaranka (BLR)
96 kg (211.2 lb)	Karam Ibrahim (EGY)		Ramaz Nozadze (GEO)	Mehmet Ozal (TUR)
120+ kg (264 lb)	Khasan Baroyev (RUS)		Georgy Tsurtsumiya (KAZ)	Rulon Gardner (USA)

[1]Two bronze medals awarded in each weight division.   [2]Olympic record.   [3]World record.   [4]New weight classes introduced for 2000 games.   [5]Tie.

Olympic Medal Winners—XIX Winter Games (2002)

The XIX Winter Games were held in Salt Lake City UT, 8–24 Feb 2002. Since the games, several athletes have been stripped of medals for having failed drug tests. New medalists are shown in this table.

EVENT	GOLD MEDALIST	PERFORMANCE	SILVER MEDALIST	BRONZE MEDALIST
Alpine Skiing				
Men				
Downhill	Fritz Strobl (AUT)	1 min 39.13 sec	Lasse Kjus (NOR)	Stephan Eberharter (AUT)
Slalom	Jean-Pierre Vidal (FRA)	1 min 41.06 sec	Sebastien Amiez (FRA)	Benjamin Raich (AUT)
Giant slalom	Stephan Eberharter (AUT)	2 min 23.28 sec	Bode Miller (USA)	Lasse Kjus (NOR)
Super G	Kjetil Andre Aamodt (NOR)	1 min 21.58 sec	Stephan Eberharter (AUT)	Andreas Schifferer (AUT)
Combined event	Kjetil Andre Aamodt (NOR)	3 min 17.56 sec	Bode Miller (USA)	Benjamin Raich (AUT)
Women				
Downhill	Carole Montillet (FRA)	1 min 39.56 sec	Isolde Kostner (ITA)	Renate Götschl (AUT)
Slalom	Janica Kostelic (CRO)	1 min 46.10 sec	Laure Pequegnot (FRA)	Anja Pärson (SWE)
Giant slalom	Janica Kostelic (CRO)	2 min 30.01 sec	Anja Pärson (SWE)	Sonja Nef (SUI)
Super G	Daniela Ceccarelli (ITA)	1 min 13.59 sec	Janica Kostelic (CRO)	Karen Putzer (ITA)
Combined event	Janica Kostelic (CRO)	2 min 43.28 sec	Renate Götschl (AUT)	Martina Ertl (GER)

Olympic Medal Winners—XIX Winter Games (2002) (continued)

EVENT	GOLD MEDALIST	PERFORMANCE	SILVER MEDALIST	BRONZE MEDALIST
Nordic Skiing				
Men				
1.5-km sprint	Tor Arne Hetland (NOR)	2 min 56.9 sec	Peter Schlickenrieder (GER)	Cristian Zorzi (ITA)
10-km freestyle pursuit	Thomas Alsgaard (NOR) Frode Estil (NOR)	49 min 48.9 sec		
15-km classical	Andrus Veerpalu (EST)	37 min 7.4 sec	Frode Estil (NOR)	Jaak Mae (EST)
30-km freestyle mass start	Christian Hoffmann (AUT)	1 hr 11 min 31 sec	Mikhail Botvinov (AUT)	
50-km classical	Mikhail Ivanov (RUS)	2 hr 6 min 20.8 sec	Andrus Veerpalu (EST)	Odd-Björn Hjelmeset (NOR)
4 x 10-km relay	Norway	1 hr 32 min 45.5 sec	Italy	Germany
90-m ski jump	Simon Ammann (SUI)	269.0 pt	Sven Hannawald (GER)	Adam Malysz (POL)
120-m ski jump	Simon Ammann (SUI)	281.4 pt	Adam Malysz (POL)	Matti Hautamäki (FIN)
120-m team ski jump	Germany	974.1 pt	Finland	Slovenia
Nordic combined sprint (7.5-km)	Samppa Lajunen (FIN)	16 min 40.1 sec	Ronny Ackermann (GER)	Felix Gottwald (AUT)
Nordic combined 15-km	Samppa Lajunen (FIN)	39 min 11.7sec	Jaakko Tallus (FIN)	Felix Gottwald (AUT)
Nordic combined team relay	Finland	48 min 42.2 sec	Germany	Austria
Women				
1.5-km sprint	Yuliya Chepalova (RUS)	3 min 10.6 sec	Evi Sachenbacher (GER)	Anita Moen (NOR)
5-km freestyle pursuit	Beckie Scott (CAN)	25 min 09.9 sec		
10-km classical	Bente Skari (NOR)	28 min 5.6 sec	Olga Danilova (RUS)	Yuliya Chepalova (RUS)
15-km freestyle mass start	Stefania Belmondo (ITA)	39 min 54.4 sec	Larisa Lazutina (RUS)	Katerina Neumannova (CZE)
30-km classical	Gabriella Paruzzi (ITA)	1 hr 30 min 57.1 sec	Stefania Belmondo (ITA)	Bente Skari (NOR)
4 x 5-km relay	Germany	49 min 30.6 sec	Norway	Switzerland
Biathlon				
Men				
10-km sprint	Ole Einar Björndalen (NOR)	24 min 51.3 sec	Sven Fischer (GER)	Wolfgang Perner (AUT)
12.5-km pursuit	Ole Einar Björndalen (NOR)	32 min 34.6 sec	Raphael Poiree (FRA)	Ricco Gross (GER)
20 km	Ole Einar Björndalen (NOR)	51 min 3.3 sec	Frank Luck (GER)	Viktor Maygurov (RUS)
4 x 7.5-km relay	Norway	1 hr 23 min 42.3 sec	Germany	France
Women				
7.5-km sprint	Kati Wilhelm (GER)	20 min 41.4 sec	Uschi Disl (GER)	Magdalena Forsberg (SWE)
10-km pursuit	Olga Pyleva (RUS)	31 min 7.7 sec	Kati Wilhelm (GER)	Irina Nikulchina (RUS)
15 km	Andrea Henkel (GER)	47 min 29.1 sec	Liv Grete Poiree (NOR)	Magdalena Forsberg (SWE)
4 x 7.5-km relay	Germany	1 hr 27 min 55.0 sec	Norway	Russia
Freestyle Skiing				
Men				
Moguls	Janne Lahtela (FIN)	27.97 pt	Travis Mayer (USA)	Richard Gay (FRA)
Aerials	Ales Valenta (CZE)	257.02 pt	Joe Pack (USA)	Aleksey Grishin (BLR)
Women				
Moguls	Kari Traa (NOR)	25.94 pt	Shannon Bahrke (USA)	Tae Satoya (JPN)
Aerials	Alisa Camplin (AUS)	193.47 pt	Veronica Brenner (CAN)	Deidra Dionne (CAN)

Olympic Medal Winners—XIX Winter Games (2002) (continued)

EVENT	GOLD MEDALIST	PERFORMANCE	SILVER MEDALIST	BRONZE MEDALIST
Snowboarding				
Men				
Parallel giant slalom	Philipp Schoch (SUI)		Richard Richardsson (SWE)	Chris Klug (USA)
Halfpipe	Ross Powers (USA)	46.1 pt	Danny Kass (USA)	Jarret Thomas (USA)
Women				
Parallel giant slalom	Isabelle Blanc (FRA)		Karine Ruby (FRA)	Lidia Trettel (ITA)
Halfpipe	Kelly Clark (USA)	47.9 pt	Doriane Vidal (FRA)	Fabienne Reuteler (SUI)
Figure skating				
Men	Aleksey Yagudin (RUS)	1.5 pt	Yevgeny Plushchenko (RUS)	Timothy Goebel (USA)
Women	Sarah Hughes (USA)	3.0 pt	Irina Slutskaya (RUS)	Michelle Kwan (USA)
Pairs	Yelena Berezhnaya, Anton Sikharulidze (RUS)[1]; Jamie Salé, David Pelletier (CAN)[1]			Shen Xue, Zhao Hongbo (CHN)
Ice dancing	Marina Anissina, Gwendal Peizerat (FRA)	2.0 pt	Irina Lobacheva, Ilya Averbukh (RUS)	Barbara Fusar Poli, Maurizio Margaglio (ITA)
Speed Skating				
Men				
500 m	Casey FitzRandolph (USA)	1 min 9.23 sec	Hiroyasu Shimizu (JPN)	Kip Carpenter (USA)
1,000 m	Gerard van Velde (NED)	1 min 7.18 sec[2]	Jan Bos (NED)	Joey Cheek (USA)
1,500 m	Derek Parra (USA)	1 min 43.95 sec[2]	Jochem Uytdehaage (NED)	Adne Sondral (NOR)
5,000 m	Jochem Uytdehaage (NED)	6 min 14.66 sec[2]	Derek Parra (USA)	Jens Boden (GER)
10,000 m	Jochem Uytdehaage (NED)	12 min 58.92 sec[2]	Gianni Romme (NED)	Lasse Saetre (NOR)
Women				
500 m	Catriona LeMay Doan (CAN)	1 min 14.75 sec	Monique Garbrecht-Enfeldt (GER)	Sabine Völker (GER)
1,000 m	Chris Witty (USA)	1 min 13.83 sec[2]	Sabine Völker (GER)	Jennifer Rodriguez (USA)
1,500 m	Anni Friesinger (GER)	1 min 54.02 sec[2]	Sabine Völker (GER)	Jennifer Rodriguez (USA)
3,000 m	Claudia Pechstein (GER)	3 min 57.70 sec[2]	Renate Groenewold (NED)	Cindy Klassen (CAN)
5,000 m	Claudia Pechstein (GER)	6 min 46.91 sec[2]	Gretha Smit (NED)	Clara Hughes (CAN)
Short-Track Speed Skating				
Men				
500 m	Marc Gagnon (CAN)	41.802 sec[3]	Jonathan Guilmette (CAN)	Rusty Smith (USA)
1,000 m	Steven Bradbury (AUS)	1 min 29.109 sec	Apolo Anton Ohno (USA)	Mathieu Turcotte (CAN)
1,500 m	Apolo Anton Ohno (USA)	2 min 18.541 sec	Li Jiajun (CHN)	Marc Gagnon (CAN)
5,000-m relay	Canada	6 min 51.579 sec	Italy	China
Women				
500 m	Yang Yang (A) (CHN)	44.187 sec	Evgeniya Radanova (BUL)	Wang Chunlu (CHN)
1,000 m	Yang Yang (A) (CHN)	1 min 36.391 sec	Ko Gi Hyun (KOR)	Yang Yang (S) (CHN)
1,500 m	Ko Gi Hyun (KOR)	2 min 31.581 sec	Choi Eun Kyung (KOR)	Evgeniya Radanova (BUL)
3,000-m relay	South Korea	4 min 12.793 sec[2]	China	Canada
Ice Hockey				
Men (winning team)	Canada	4-1-1	United States	Russia
Women (winning team)	Canada	5-0-0	United States	Sweden

Olympic Medal Winners—XIX Winter Games (2002) (continued)

EVENT	GOLD MEDALIST	PERFORMANCE	SILVER MEDALIST	BRONZE MEDALIST
Curling				
Men (winning team)	Norway	9-2-0	Canada	Switzerland
Women (winning team)	Great Britain	9-4-0	Switzerland	Canada
Bobsleigh (Bobsled)				
Two man	Christoph Langen, Markus Zimmermann (GER 1)	3 min 10.11 sec	Steve Anderhub, Christian Reich (SUI 1)	Martin Annen, Beat Hefti (SUI 2)
Four man	Germany 2	3 min 7.51 sec	United States 1	United States 2
Women	Jill Bakken, Vonetta Flowers (USA 2)	1 min 37.76 sec	Sandra Prokoff, Ulrike Holzner (GER 1)	Susi-Lisa Erdmann, Nicole Herschmann (GER 2)
Luge				
Men (singles)	Armin Zöggeler (ITA)	2 min 57.941 sec	Georg Hackl (GER)	Markus Prock (AUT)
Men (doubles)	Patric-Fritz Leitner, Alexander Resch (GER)	1 min 26.082 sec	Brian Martin, Mark Grimmette (USA)	Chris Thorpe, Clay Ives (USA)
Women (singles)	Sylke Otto (GER)	2 min 52.464 sec	Barbara Niedernhuber (GER)	Silke Kraushaar (GER)
Skeleton				
Men	Jim Shea (USA)	1 min 41.96 sec	Martin Rettl (AUT)	Gregor Staehli (SUI)
Women	Tristan Gale (USA)	1 min 45.11 sec	Lea Ann Parsley (USA)	Alex Coomber (GBR)

[1]Two medals awarded. [2]World record. [3]Olympic record.

Special Olympics

The Special Olympics is an international program to provide individuals with intellectual disabilities who are eight years of age or older with year-round sports training and athletic competition in a variety of Olympic-type summer and winter sports. Inaugurated in 1968, the Special Olympics was officially recognized by the International Olympic Committee on 15 Feb 1988. **International headquarters** are in Washington DC.

In June 1963, with support from the Joseph P. Kennedy, Jr., Foundation, **Eunice Kennedy Shriver** (sister of Pres. John F. Kennedy) started a summer day-camp for retarded children at her home in Rockville MD. Between 1963 and 1968, the Kennedy Foundation promoted the creation of dozens of similar camps in the United States and Canada. Special awards were developed for physical achievements, and by 1968 Shriver had persuaded the Chicago Park District to join with the Kennedy Foundation in sponsoring a "Special Olympics," held at Soldier Field on 20 July. About 1,000 athletes from 26 US states and Canada participated. The games were such a success that, in December, Special Olympics, Inc. (now **Special Olympics International**), was founded, with chapters in the United States, Canada, and France. The first International Winter Special Olympics Games were held on **5–11 Feb 1977** (in Steamboat Springs CO). The number of participating countries proliferated so that by the early 21st century, there were chapters in some 150 countries. Over 20,000 meets and tournaments are held worldwide each year, culminating in the International Special Olympics Games every two years, alternating between winter and summer sports and each lasting for eight or nine days.

Special Olympics Web site:
<www.specialolympics. org>.

Archery

The international governing body for archery, the **Fédération Internationale de Tir à l'Arc (FITA)**, instituted world championships in 1931. Between 1931 and 1957 a variety of scoring rounds were used. In 1957, however, FITA established its own competition standard—two FITA rounds shot over four days. A single FITA **round** consists of 36 arrows shot from each of four distances; different distances are used for men's and women's competition. From 1987 to 1991 the grand FITA round was used. The Olympic round was used for the 1992 Olympic Games and the 1993 world championships; under this system the highest possible individual score in the finals round was 120. Since 1959 championships have been held biennially. Olympic competition is held with the **recurve style** of bow in which the limbs of the bow curve in one direction, then "recurve" in the other.

FITA Web site: <www.archery.org>.

FITA Outdoor World Target Archery Championships

Competition dates from 1931. Table includes data from 1987 in the Olympic (recurve) division only.

	men's				women's			
YEAR	INDIVIDUAL	POINTS	TEAM	POINTS	INDIVIDUAL	POINTS	TEAM	POINTS
1987	Vladimir Yesheyev (URS)	329	FRG	891	Ma Xiangjun (CHN)	330	URS	884
1989	Stanislav Zabrodsky (URS)	332	URS	985	Kim Soo Nyung (KOR)	338	KOR	995
1991	Simon Fairweather (AUS)	334	KOR	998	Kim Soo Nyung (KOR)	333	KOR	1,030
1993	Park Kyung Mo (KOR)	113	FRA	249	Kim Soo Nyung (KOR)	104	KOR	236
1995	Lee Kyung Chul (KOR)	109	KOR	255	Natalya Valeyeva (MDA)	113	KOR	247
1997	Kim Kyung Ho (KOR)	108	KOR	254	Kim Du Ri (KOR)	105	KOR	242
1999	Hong Sung Chil (KOR)	115	ITA	252	Lee Eun Kyung (KOR)	115	ITA	240
2001	Yeon Jung Ki (KOR)	115	KOR	247	Park Sung Hyun (KOR)	111	CHN	232
2003	Michele Frangilli (ITA)	113	KOR	238	Mi-Jin Yun (KOR)	116	KOR	252
2005	Chung Jae Hun (KOR)	102	KOR	244	Lee Sung Jin (KOR)	111	KOR	251

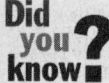

Did you know? *Kyudo*, meaning "way of the bow" in Japanese, is a traditional form of archery, closely associated with Zen Buddhism. When firearms supplanted the bow and arrow in warfare, the art of archery was retained by Zen monks and some members of the Japanese upper class as a mental and physical discipline. In *kyudo* the primary aim is not to hit the target, as in Western archery, but to achieve through spiritual and physical training an intense concentration on the act of shooting and a style expressing perfect serenity.

Automobile Racing

Of the various types of automobile races, the closed-circuit, or speedway, course was developed largely in the United States. The Indianapolis 500—now the premier Indy car event—was first run in 1911. A low-slung, fenderless (open-wheel) car—called an Indy car—is essential for this race; its suspension (i.e., its ability to hold the track) is as important to a car's performance as its turbocharged engine. Often the chassis manufacturer is different from the engine manufacturer, resulting in cars identified, for example, as a Brabham/Repco. In such cases the chassis-maker is listed first, and the chassis-maker receives any money or awards that the car may win.

Indy car racing began in 1909, when the American Automobile Association (AAA) began sponsoring a 24-race championship series, including three races at the newly opened Indianapolis Motor Speedway (IMS). In 1956 the AAA gave up its involvement with auto racing, and the United States Auto Club (**USAC**) was organized as the sport's governing body. In 1978 two race-car owners broke away from USAC to form a new organization, Championship Auto Racing Teams, Inc. (**CART**), which sponsored its own series of races. In 1980 CART and USAC joined to form the Championship Racing League, which dissolved after five races. In 1994 the IMS announced a new Indy Racing League (IRL) to oversee the Indianapolis 500 beginning in 1996 and a new series of IRL races (leading to an annual drivers' championship separate from those sponsored by CART.

The standard cars used for Grand Prix road (i.e., closed highway) racing are known as Formula One (or F-1) cars because they are built according to an evolving formula that was established after World War I by the Fédération Internationale de l'Automobile (**FIA**). Like the Indy car, the Formula One racer is open-wheeled and low-slung, but the F-1 is slightly smaller and more maneuverable.

There are approximately 17 Grand Prix events held worldwide throughout the year. Drivers compete for the **World Championship of Drivers** (inaugurated in 1950), receiving a total number of points based on their placement in each of the official Grand Prix events.

Many Grand Prix drivers participate in various endurance races, the most famous of which is the **Le Mans Grand Prix d'Endurance**, held on the 13.4-km (8.3-mi) Sarthe circuit, Le Mans, France.

Another type of popular racing event is the rally, which was established in 1907. More than 35 such competitions, raced over a specified route on public roads, take place yearly throughout the world. The classic occasion for rally racing is the **Rallye Automobile Monte-Carlo**, now started in various European cities with Monaco as its terminal point.

Stock car racing, which began in the United States in the first half of the 20th century, involves the racing of commercial cars that have been altered to increase their speed and maneuverability. The National Association for Stock Car Auto Racing (**NASCAR**) was founded in 1947 and awards the Winston Cup to the driver who has achieved the greatest number of points earned in a series of official NASCAR Winston Cup events over the stock car racing season. The **Daytona 500** is the premiere stock car event.

Related Internet sites: Champ Car: <www.champcar worldseries.com>; USAC: <www.usacracing.com>; IRL: <www.indycar.com>; FIA: <www.fia.com>; Automobile Club de Monaco <www.acm.mc>; NASCAR: <www.nascar.com>.

Formula One Grand Prix Race Results, 2004–05

The following 18 races constitute the Formula One circuit. The season is March–October.
The United States Grand Prix, held at the Indianapolis Motor Speedway, was added in 2000.

RACE	DATE	LOCALE	DRIVER (COUNTRY)	WINNER'S TIME (HR:MIN:SEC)
Hungarian GP	15 Aug 2004	Budapest	Michael Schumacher (GER)	1:35:26.131
Belgian GP	29 Aug 2004	Spa-Francorchamps	Kimi Räikkönen (FIN)	1:32:35.274
Italian GP	12 Sep 2004	Monza	Rubens Barrichello (BRA)	1:15:18.448
Chinese GP	26 Sep 2004	Shanghai	Rubens Barrichello (BRA)	1:29:12.420
Japanese GP	10 Oct 2004	Suzuka	Michael Schumacher (GER)	1:24:26.985
Brazilian GP	24 Oct 2004	São Paulo	Juan Pablo Montoya (COL)	1:28:01.451
Australian GP	6 Mar 2005	Melbourne	Giancarlo Fisichella (ITA)	1:24:17.336
Malaysian GP	20 Mar 2005	Kuala Lumpur	Fernando Alonso (ESP)	1:31:33.736
Bahrain GP	3 Apr 2005	Bahrain	Fernando Alonso (ESP)	1:29:18.531
San Marino GP	24 Apr 2005	Imola	Fernando Alonso (ESP)	1:27:41.921
Spanish GP	8 May 2005	Catalonia	Kimi Räikkönen (FIN)	1:27:16.830
Monaco GP	22 May 2005	Monte Carlo	Kimi Räikkönen (FIN)	1:45:15.556
European GP	29 May 2005	Nürburgring	Fernando Alonso (ESP)	1:31:46.648
Canadian GP	12 Jun 2005	Montreal	Kimi Räikkönen (FIN)	1:32:09.290
United States GP	19 Jun 2005	Indianapolis	Michael Schumacher (GER)	1:29:43.181
French GP	3 Jul 2005	Magny-Cours	Fernando Alonso (ESP)	1:31:22.233
British GP	10 Jul 2005	Silverstone	Juan Pablo Montoya (COL)	1:24:29.588
German GP	24 Jul 2005	Hockenheim	Fernando Alonso (ESP)	1:26:28.599

World Championship of Drivers

Points are awarded to the top-finishing drivers in each race on the Grand Prix circuit and totaled at the end of the season to determine the championship. In 2004 the top three were: Michael Schumacher (GER), 148 points, Rubens Barrichello (BRA), 114 points, and Jenson Button (GBR), 85 points. Where chassis and engine are made by different manufacturers, the chassis is given first and separated from the engine name by a slash.

YEAR	DRIVER (NATIONALITY)	CONSTRUCTOR
1950	Giuseppe Farina (ITA)	Alfa Romeo
1951	Juan Manuel Fangio (ARG)	Alfa Romeo
1952	Alberto Ascari (ITA)	Ferrari
1953	Alberto Ascari (ITA)	Ferrari
1954	Juan Manuel Fangio (ARG)	Mercedes & Maserati
1955	Juan Manuel Fangio (ARG)	Mercedes
1956	Juan Manuel Fangio (ARG)	Lancia/Ferrari
1957	Juan Manuel Fangio (ARG)	Maserati
1958	Mike Hawthorn (GBR)	Ferrari
1959	Jack Brabham (AUS)	Cooper/Climax
1960	Jack Brabham (AUS)	Cooper/Climax
1961	Phil Hill (USA)	Ferrari
1962	Graham Hill (GBR)	BRM
1963	Jim Clark (GBR)	Lotus/Climax
1964	John Surtees (GBR)	Ferrari
1965	Jim Clark (GBR)	Lotus/Climax
1966	Jack Brabham (AUS)	Brabham/Repco
1967	Denny Hulme (NZL)	Brabham/Repco
1968	Graham Hill (GBR)	Lotus/Ford
1969	Jackie Stewart (GBR)	Matra/Ford
1970	Jochen Rindt (AUT)	Lotus/Ford
1971	Jackie Stewart (GBR)	Tyrrell/Ford
1972	Emerson Fittipaldi (BRA)	John Player Special/Ford
1973	Jackie Stewart (GBR)	Tyrrell/Ford
1974	Emerson Fittipaldi (BRA)	McLaren/Ford
1975	Niki Lauda (AUT)	Ferrari
1976	James Hunt (GBR)	McLaren/Ford
1977	Niki Lauda (AUT)	Ferrari
1978	Mario Andretti (USA)	Lotus
1979	Jody Scheckter (RSA)	Ferrari
1980	Alan Jones (AUS)	Williams
1981	Nelson Piquet (BRA)	Brabham
1982	Keke Rosberg (FIN)	Williams
1983	Nelson Piquet (BRA)	Brabham
1984	Niki Lauda (AUT)	McLaren/Porsche-TAG
1985	Alain Prost (FRA)	McLaren/Porsche-TAG
1986	Alain Prost (FRA)	McLaren/Porsche-TAG
1987	Nelson Piquet (BRA)	Williams/Honda
1988	Ayrton Senna (BRA)	McLaren/Honda
1989	Alain Prost (FRA)	McLaren/Honda
1990	Ayrton Senna (BRA)	McLaren/Honda
1991	Ayrton Senna (BRA)	McLaren/Honda
1992	Nigel Mansell (GBR)	Williams/Renault
1993	Alain Prost (FRA)	Williams/Renault
1994	Michael Schumacher (GER)	Benetton/Ford
1995	Michael Schumacher (GER)	Benetton/Renault
1996	Damon Hill (GBR)	Williams/Renault
1997	Jacques Villeneuve (CAN)	Williams/Renault
1998	Mika Häkkinen (FIN)	McLaren/Mercedes
1999	Mika Häkkinen (FIN)	McLaren/Mercedes
2000	Michael Schumacher (GER)	Ferrari
2001	Michael Schumacher (GER)	Ferrari
2002	Michael Schumacher (GER)	Ferrari
2003	Michael Schumacher (GER)	Ferrari
2004	Michael Schumacher (GER)	Ferrari

Constructors' Championship

Points are awarded to the constructors of the top-finishing autos in each race on the Grand Prix circuit and are totaled at the end of the season to determine the Constructors' Championship. In 2004 the top three were: Ferrari 262 points, BAR/Honda 119 points, Renault 105 points.

YEAR	CONSTRUCTOR	YEAR	CONSTRUCTOR	YEAR	CONSTRUCTOR	YEAR	CONSTRUCTOR
1958	Vanwall	1970	Lotus	1982	Ferrari	1994	Williams/Renault
1959	Cooper	1971	Tyrrell	1983	Ferrari	1995	Benetton/Renault
1960	Cooper	1972	Lotus	1984	McLaren	1996	Williams/Renault
1961	Ferrari	1973	Lotus	1985	McLaren	1997	Williams/Renault
1962	BRM	1974	McLaren	1986	Williams/Honda	1998	McLaren/Mercedes
1963	Lotus	1975	Ferrari	1987	Williams/Honda	1999	Ferrari
1964	Ferrari	1976	Ferrari	1988	McLaren/Honda	2000	Ferrari
1965	Lotus	1977	Ferrari	1989	McLaren/Honda	2001	Ferrari
1966	Brabham	1978	Lotus	1990	McLaren/Honda	2002	Ferrari
1967	Brabham	1979	Ferrari	1991	McLaren/Honda	2003	Ferrari
1968	Lotus	1980	Williams	1992	Williams/Renault	2004	Ferrari
1969	Matra	1981	Williams	1993	Williams/Renault		

Champ Car Champions

Between 1909 and 1955 called the AAA National Champions; called the USAC National Champions from 1956 to 1978 and Indy Car champions until 2003. There was no competition 1942–45. Until 1989 the title was won by an American racer. Web site: <www.champcarworldseries.com>.

YEAR	DRIVER	YEAR	DRIVER	YEAR	DRIVER
1909	George Robertson	1941	Rex Mays	1977	Tom Sneva
1910	Ray Harroun	1946	Ted Horn	1978	Tom Sneva
1911	Ralph Mulford	1947	Ted Horn	1979	A.J. Foyt, Jr.[1]; Rick
1912	Ralph DePalma	1948	Ted Horn		Mears[2]
1913	Earl Cooper	1949	Johnnie Parsons	1980	Johnny Rutherford
1914	Ralph DePalma	1950	Henry Banks	1981	Rick Mears
1915	Earl Cooper	1951	Tony Bettenhausen, Sr.	1982	Rick Mears
1916	Dario Resta (FRA)	1952	Chuck Stevenson	1983	Al Unser
1917	Earl Cooper	1953	Sam Hanks	1984	Mario Andretti
1918	Ralph Mulford	1954	Jimmy Bryan	1985	Al Unser
1919	Howard ("Howdy") Wilcox	1955	Robert Sweikert	1986	Bobby Rahal
1920	Tommy Milton	1956	Jimmy Bryan	1987	Bobby Rahal
1921	Tommy Milton	1957	Jimmy Bryan	1988	Danny Sullivan
1922	Jimmy Murphy	1958	Tony Bettenhausen, Sr.	1989	Emerson Fittipaldi (BRA)
1923	Eddie Hearne	1959	Rodger Ward	1990	Al Unser, Jr. (USA)
1924	Jimmy Murphy	1960	A.J. Foyt, Jr.	1991	Michael Andretti (USA)
1925	Peter DePaolo	1961	A.J. Foyt, Jr.	1992	Bobby Rahal (USA)
1926	Harry Hartz	1962	Rodger Ward	1993	Nigel Mansell (GBR)
1927	Peter DePaolo	1963	A.J. Foyt, Jr.	1994	Al Unser, Jr. (USA)
1928	Louie Meyer	1964	A.J. Foyt, Jr.	1995	Jacques Villeneuve (CAN)
1929	Louie Meyer	1965	Mario Andretti	1996	Jimmy Vasser (USA)
1930	Billy Arnold	1966	Mario Andretti	1997	Alessandro (Alex) Zanardi (ITA)
1931	Louis Schneider	1967	A.J. Foyt, Jr.		
1932	Bob Carey	1968	Bobby Unser	1998	Alessandro (Alex) Zanardi (ITA)
1933	Louie Meyer	1969	Mario Andretti		
1934	Bill Cummings	1970	Al Unser	1999	Juan Montoya (COL)
1935	Kelly Petillo	1971	Joe Leonard	2000	Gil de Ferran (BRA)
1936	Mauri Rose	1972	Joe Leonard	2001	Gil de Ferran (BRA)
1937	Wilbur Shaw	1973	Roger McCluskey	2002	Cristiano da Matta (BRA)
1938	Floyd Roberts	1974	Bobby Unser	2003	Paul Tracy (CAN)
1939	Wilbur Shaw	1975	A.J. Foyt, Jr.	2004	Sebastien Bourdais (FRA)
1940	Rex Mays	1976	Gordon Johncock		

[1]USAC champion.   [2]CART/Champ Car champion from 1980.

Indianapolis 500

There was no competition in 1917–18 and 1942–45. An American racer won the race unless otherwise noted.

YEAR	WINNER	AVG. SPEED (MPH)	YEAR	WINNER	AVG. SPEED (MPH)	YEAR	WINNER	AVG. SPEED (MPH)
1911	Ray Harroun	74.602	1913	Jules Goux (FRA)	75.933	1915	Ralph DePalma	89.840
1912	Joe Dawson	78.719	1914	René Thomas (FRA)	82.474	1916[1]	Dario Resta (FRA)	84.001

Indianapolis 500 (continued)

YEAR	WINNER	AVG. SPEED (MPH)	YEAR	WINNER	AVG. SPEED (MPH)	YEAR	WINNER	AVG. SPEED (MPH)
1919	Howdy Wilcox	88.050	1956	Pat Flaherty	128.490	1985	Danny Sullivan	152.982
1920	Gaston Chevrolet	88.618	1957	Sam Hanks	135.601	1986	Bobby Rahal	170.722
1921	Tommy Milton	89.621	1958	Jimmy Bryan	133.791	1987	Al Unser	162.175
1922	Jimmy Murphy	94.484	1959	Rodger Ward	135.857	1988	Rick Mears	144.809
1923	Tommy Milton	90.954	1960	Jim Rathmann	138.767	1989	Emerson Fittipaldi (BRA)	167.581
1924	L.L. Corum, Joe Boyer	98.234	1961	A.J. Foyt, Jr.	139.131			
			1962	Rodger Ward	140.293	1990	Arie Luyendyk (NED)	185.984
1925	Peter DePaolo	101.127	1963	Parnelli Jones	143.137			
1926[2]	Frank Lockhart	95.904	1964	A.J. Foyt, Jr.	147.350	1991	Rick Mears	176.457
1927	George Souders	97.545	1965	Jim Clark (GBR)	150.686	1992	Al Unser, Jr.	134.479
1928	Louie Meyer	99.482	1966	Graham Hill (GBR)	144.317	1993	Emerson Fittipaldi (BRA)	157.207
1929	Ray Keech	97.585						
1930	Billy Arnold	100.448	1967	A.J. Foyt, Jr.	151.207	1994	Al Unser, Jr.	160.872
1931	Louis Schneider	96.629	1968	Bobby Unser	152.882	1995	Jacques Villeneuve (CAN)	153.616
1932	Fred Frame	104.144	1969	Mario Andretti	156.867			
1933	Louie Meyer	104.162	1970	Al Unser	155.749	1996	Buddy Lazier	147.956
1934	Bill Cummings	104.863	1971	Al Unser	157.735	1997	Arie Luyendyk (NED)	145.827
1935	Kelly Petillo	106.240	1972	Mark Donohue	162.962			
1936	Louie Meyer	109.069	1973[2]	Gordon Johncock	159.036	1998	Eddie Cheever, Jr.	145.155
1937	Wilbur Shaw	113.580						
1938	Floyd Roberts	117.200	1974	Johnny Rutherford	158.589	1999	Kenny Brack (SWE)	153.176
1939	Wilbur Shaw	115.035						
1940	Wilbur Shaw	114.277	1975[2]	Bobby Unser	149.213	2000	Juan Montoya (COL)	167.607
1941	Floyd Davis, Mauri Rose	115.117	1976[2]	Johnny Rutherford	148.725			
						2001	Helio Castroneves (BRA)	153.601
1946	George Robson	114.820	1977	A.J. Foyt, Jr.	161.331			
1947	Mauri Rose	116.338	1978	Al Unser	161.363	2002	Helio Castroneves (BRA)	166.499
1948	Mauri Rose	119.814	1979	Rick Mears	158.899			
1949	Bill Holland	121.327	1980	Johnny Rutherford	142.862	2003	Gil de Ferran (BRA)	156.291
1950[2]	Johnnie Parsons	124.002						
1951	Lee Wallard	126.244	1981	Bobby Unser	139.084	2004[2]	Buddy Rice	138.518
1952	Troy Ruttman	128.922	1982	Gordon Johncock	162.029	2005	Dan Wheldon (GBR)	157.603
1953	Bill Vukovich	128.740						
1954	Bill Vukovich	130.840	1983	Tom Sneva	162.117			
1955	Robert Sweikert	128.209	1984	Rick Mears	163.612			

[1]Scheduled 300-mile race.   [2]Race stopped because of rain (in 1926 after 400 miles, in 1950 after 345 miles, in 1973 after 332.5 miles, in 1975 after 435 miles, in 1976 after 255 miles, in 2004 after 450 miles).

Le Mans Grand Prix d'Endurance
Also called Le Mans 24-hour Race.

YEAR	CAR	DRIVERS
1923	Chenard & Walcker	André Lagache, René Léonard
1924	Bentley	John Duff, Frank Clément
1925	Lorraine-Dietrich	Gérard de Courcelles, André Rossignol
1926	Lorraine-Dietrich	Robert Bloch, André Rossignol
1927	Bentley	John Benjafield, Sammy Davis
1928	Bentley	Woolf Barnato, Bernard Rubin
1929	Bentley	Woolf Barnato, Henry Birkin
1930	Bentley	Woolf Barnato, Glen Kidston
1931	Alfa Romeo	Lord Howe, Henry Birkin
1932	Alfa Romeo	Raymond Sommer, Luigi Chinetti
1933	Alfa Romeo	Raymond Sommer, Tazio Nuvolari
1934	Alfa Romeo	Luigi Chinetti, Philippe Etancelin
1935	Lagonda	John Hindmarsh, Luis Fontés
1936	no competition	
1937	Bugatti	Jean-Pierre Wimille, Robert Benoist
1938	Delahaye	Eugene Chaboud, Jean Tremoulet
1939	Bugatti	Jean-Pierre Wimille, Pierre Veyron
1940–48	no competition	
1949	Ferrari	Luigi Chinetti, Lord Selsdon
1950	Talbot	Louis Rosier, Jean-Louis Rosier
1951	Jaguar	Peter Walker, Peter Whitehead
1952	Mercedes-Benz	Hermann Lang, Fritz Riess
1953	Jaguar C-type	Tony Rolt, Duncan Hamilton

Le Mans Grand Prix d'Endurance (continued)

YEAR	CAR	DRIVERS
1954	Ferrari 375	Froilan Gonzalez, Maurice Trintignant
1955	Jaguar D-type	Mike Hawthorn, Ivor Bueb
1956	Jaguar D-type	Ron Flockhart, Ninian Sanderson
1957	Jaguar D-type	Ivor Bueb, Ron Flockhart
1958	Ferrari	Phil Hill, Olivier Gendebien
1959	Aston Martin	Roy Salvadori, Carroll Shelby
1960	Ferrari	Paul Frère, Olivier Gendebien
1961	Ferrari	Phil Hill, Olivier Gendebien
1962	Ferrari	Phil Hill, Olivier Gendebien
1963	Ferrari	Lodovico Scarfiotti, Lorenzo Bandini
1964	Ferrari	Jean Guichet, Nino Vaccarella
1965	Ferrari	Masten Gregory, Jochen Rindt
1966	Ford Mk II	Bruce McLaren, Chris Amon
1967	Ford Mk IV	A.J. Foyt, Dan Gurney
1968	Ford G.T. 40	Pedro Rodriguez, Lucien Bianchi
1969	Ford G.T. 40	Jacky Ickx, Jackie Oliver
1970	Porsche	Richard Attwood, Hans Hermann
1971	Porsche	Helmut Marko, Gijs van Lennep
1972	Matra-Simca	Henri Pescarolo, Graham Hill
1973	Matra-Simca	Henri Pescarolo, Gérard Larrousse
1974	Matra-Simca	Henri Pescarolo, Gérard Larrousse
1975	Gulf-Ford	Jacky Ickx, Derek Bell
1976	Porsche	Jacky Ickx, Gijs van Lennep
1977	Porsche	Jacky Ickx, Jurgen Barth, Hurley Haywood
1978	Renault-Alpine	Jean-Pierre Jaussaud, Didier Pironi
1979	Porsche	Klaus Ludwig, Don Whittington, Bill Whittington
1980	Porsche	Jean Rondeau, Jean-Pierre Jaussaud
1981	Porsche	Derek Bell, Jacky Ickx
1982	Porsche 956	Derek Bell, Jacky Ickx
1983	Porsche 956	Al Holbert, Hurley Hayward, Vern Schuppan
1984	Porsche 956	Henri Pescarolo, Klaus Ludwig
1985	Porsche 956	Klaus Ludwig, John Winter, Paulo Barilla
1986	Porsche 962 C	Derek Bell, Hans Stuck, Al Holbert
1987	Porsche 962 C	Hans Stuck, Derek Bell, Al Holbert
1988	Jaguar XJR 9 LM	Jan Lammers, Johnny Dumfries, Andy Wallace
1989	Sauber Mercedes-Benz C9	Jochen Mass, Manuel Reuter, Stanley Dickens
1990	Jaguar XJR 12	John Nielsen, Price Cobb, Martin Brundle
1991	Mazda 787 B	Volker Weidler, Johnny Herbert, Bertrand Gachot
1992	Peugeot 905	Yannick Dalmas, Mark Blundell, Derek Warwick
1993	Peugeot 905	Geoff Brabham, Christophe Bouchut, Eric Helary
1994	Dauer Porsche 962 LM	Yannick Dalmas, Hurley Haywood, Mauro Baldi
1995	McLaren F1 GTR	Yannick Dalmas, J.J. Lehto, Masanori Sekiya
1996	TWR-Porsche WSC 95	Manuel Reuter, Davy Jones, Alex Wurz
1997	TWR-Porsche WSC 95	Michele Alboreto, Stefan Johansson, Tom Kristensen
1998	Porsche 911 GT1	Alan McNish, Laurent Aiello, Stephane Ortelli
1999	BMW V12 LMR	Yannick Dalmas, Pierluigi Martini, Joachim Winkelhock
2000	Audi R8	Frank Biela, Tom Kristensen, Emanuele Pirro
2001	Audi 3596 T	Frank Biela, Tom Kristensen, Emanuele Pirro
2002	Audi R8 2002	Frank Biela, Tom Kristensen, Emanuele Pirro
2003	Bentley	Tom Kristensen, Rinaldo Capello, Guy Smith
2004	Audi R8	Tom Kristensen, Rinaldo Capello, Seiji Ara
2005	Audi R8	Tom Kristensen, J.J. Lehto, Marcus Werner

Monte-Carlo Rally
There was no competition in 1913–23, 1940–48, 1957, and 1974.

YEAR	CAR	DRIVER, CODRIVER
1911	Turcat Méry	Henri Rougier (FRA)
1912	Berliet	Julius Beutler (GER)
1924	Bignan	Jean Ledure (FRA)
1925	Renault 40CV	François Repusseau (FRA)
1926	A.C. Bristol	Victor Bruce (GBR)
1927	Amilcar	Lefèbvre (FRA), Despeaux (FRA)
1928	Fiat	Jacques Bignan (FRA)
1929	Graham-Paige	Sprenger van Eijk (NED)
1930	Licorne	Hector Petit (FRA)
1931	Invicta	Donald Healey (GBR)

Monte-Carlo Rally (continued)

YEAR	CAR	DRIVER, CODRIVER
1932	Hotchkiss	Maurice Vasselle (FRA)
	Peugeot	G. de Lavallette, Charles de Cortanze
1933	Hotchkiss	Maurice Vasselle (FRA)
1934	Hotchkiss	Gas (FRA), Jean Trévoux (FRA)
1935	Renault Nervasport	Christian Lahaye (FRA), R. Quatresous (FRA)
1936	Ford	Lionel Samfirescu (ROM), Petre Cristea (ROM)
1937	Delahaye	René Lebègue (FRA), Julio Quinlin (FRA)
1938	Ford	G. Baker Schut (NED), Karelton (NED)
1939	Hotchkiss	Jean Trévoux (FRA), Marcel Lesurque (FRA)
	Delahaye	Joseph Paul, Marcel Contet (FRA)
1949	Hotchkiss	Jean Trévoux (FRA), Marcel Lesurque (FRA)
1950	Hotchkiss	Marcel Becquart (FRA), H. Secret (FRA)
1951	Delahaye	Jean Trévoux (FRA), Roger Crovetto (FRA)
1952	Allard P-1	Sydney Allard (GBR), Guy Warburton (GBR), Tom Lush (GBR)
1953	Ford Zephyr	Maurice Gatsonides (NED), P. Worledge (GBR)
1954	Lancia Aurelia	Louis Chiron (FRA), Giro Basadonna (SPA)
1955	Sunbeam Talbot	Per Malling (NOR), Gunnar Fadum (NOR)
1956	Jaguar Mk VII	Ronnie Adams (GBR), Frank Bigger (GBR)
1958	Renault Dauphine	Guy Monraisse (FRA), Jacques Feret (FRA)
1959	Citroën ID19	Paul Coltelloni (FRA), Pierre Alexandre (FRA)
1960	Mercedes 220SE	Walter Schock (FRG), Rolf Moll (FRG)
1961	Panhard PL17	M. Martin (FRA), Roger Bateau (FRA)
1962	Saab 96	Erik Carlsson (SWE), Gunnar Häggbom (SWE)
1963	Saab 96	Erik Carlsson (SWE), Gunnar Palm (SWE)
1964	Mini-Cooper S	Paddy Hopkirk (GBR), Henry Liddon (GBR)
1965	Mini-Cooper S	Timo Makinen (FIN), Paul Easter (GBR)
1966	Citroën ID19	Pauli Toivonen (FIN), Ensio Mikkander (FIN)
1967	Mini-Cooper S	Rauno Aaltonen (FIN), Henry Liddon (GBR)
1968	Porsche 911T	Vic Elford (GBR), David Stone (GBR)
1969	Porsche 911S	Bjorn Waldegaard (SWE), Lars Helmer (SWE)
1970	Porsche 911S	Bjorn Waldegaard (SWE), Lars Helmer (SWE)
1971	Alpine-Renault A110	Ove Andersson (SWE), David Stone (GBR)
1972	Lancia Fulvia 1.6HF	Sandro Munari (ITA), Mario Mannucci (ITA)
1973	Alpine-Renault A110	Jean-Claude Andruet (FRA), Michèle "Biche" Petit (FRA)
1975	Lancia Stratos HF	Sandro Munari (ITA), Mario Mannucci (ITA)
1976	Lancia Stratos HF	Sandro Munari (ITA), Mario Mannucci (ITA)
1977	Lancia Stratos HF	Sandro Munari (ITA), Silvio Maiga (ITA)
1978	Porsche 911 Carrera	Jean-Pierre Nicolas (FRA), Vincent Laverne (FRA)
1979	Lancia Stratos HF	Bernard Darniche (FRA), Alain Mahé (FRA)
1980	Fiat 131 Abarth	Walter Röhrl (FRG), Christian Geistdorfer (FRG)
1981	Renault 5 Turbo	Jean Ragnotti (FRA), Jean-Marc Andrie (FRA)
1982	Opel Ascona 400	Walter Röhrl (FRG), Christian Geistdorfer (FRG)
1983	Lancia Rally 037	Walter Röhrl (FRG), Christian Geistdorfer (FRG)
1984	Audi Quattro	Walter Röhrl (FRG), Christian Geistdorfer (FRG)
1985	Peugeot 205 Turbo	Ari Vatanen (FIN), Terry Harryman (GBR)
1986	Lancia Delta S4	Henri Toivonen (FIN), Sergio Cresto (USA)
1987	Lancia Delta HF 4WD	Mickey Biasion (ITA), Tiziano Siviero (ITA)
1988	Lancia Delta HF 4WD	Bruno Saby (FRA), Jean-François Fauchille (FRA)
1989	Lancia Delta HF Integrale	Mickey Biasion (ITA), Tiziano Siviero (ITA)
1990	Lancia Delta HF Integrale	Didier Auriol (FRA), Bernard Occelli (FRA)
1991	Toyota Celica GT4	Carlos Sainz (ESP), Luis Moya (ESP)
1992	Lancia Delta HF Integrale	Didier Auriol (FRA), Bernard Occelli (FRA)
1993	Toyota Celica Turbo 4WD	Didier Auriol (FRA), Bernard Occelli (FRA)
1994	Ford Escort RS Cosworth	François Delecour (FRA), Daniel Grataloup (FRA)
1995	Subaru Impreza 555	Carlos Sainz (ESP), Luis Moya (ESP)
1996	Ford Escort RS Cosworth	Patrick Bernardini (FRA), Bernard Occelli (FRA)
1997	Subaru Impreza WRC97	Piero Liatti (ITA), Fabrizia Pons (ITA)
1998	Toyota Corolla WRC	Carlos Sainz (ESP), Luis Moya (ESP)
1999	Mitsubishi Lancer Evo VI	Tommi Mäkinen (FIN), Risto Mannisenmaki (FIN)
2000	Mitsubishi Lancer Evo VI	Tommi Mäkinen (FIN), Risto Mannisenmaki (FIN)
2001	Mitsubishi Lancer Evo VI	Tommi Mäkinen (FIN), Risto Mannisenmaki (FIN)
2002	Subaru Impreza	Tommi Mäkinen (FIN), Kaj Lindstrom (FIN)
2003	Citroën	Sébastien Loeb (FRA), Daniel Elena (MON)
2004	Citroën	Sébastien Loeb (FRA), Daniel Elena (MON)
2005	Citroën	Sébastien Loeb (FRA), Daniel Elena (MON)
2006	*to be held 22–25 January*	

NASCAR Nextel Cup Champions

YEAR	WINNER	YEAR	WINNER	YEAR	WINNER	YEAR	WINNER
1949	Red Byron	1964	Richard Petty	1979	Richard Petty	1994	Dale Earnhardt
1950	Bill Rexford	1965	Ned Jarrett	1980	Dale Earnhardt	1995	Jeff Gordon
1951	Herb Thomas	1966	David Pearson	1981	Darrell Waltrip	1996	Terry Labonte
1952	Tim Flock	1967	Richard Petty	1982	Darrell Waltrip	1997	Jeff Gordon
1953	Herb Thomas	1968	David Pearson	1983	Bobby Allison	1998	Jeff Gordon
1954	Lee Petty	1969	David Pearson	1984	Terry Labonte	1999	Dale Jarrett
1955	Tim Flock	1970	Bobby Isaac	1985	Darrell Waltrip	2000	Bobby Labonte
1956	Buck Baker	1971	Richard Petty	1986	Dale Earnhardt	2001	Jeff Gordon
1957	Buck Baker	1972	Richard Petty	1987	Dale Earnhardt	2002	Tony Stewart
1958	Lee Petty	1973	Benny Parsons	1988	Bill Elliott	2003	Matt Kenseth
1959	Lee Petty	1974	Richard Petty	1989	Rusty Wallace	2004	Kurt Busch
1960	Rex White	1975	Richard Petty	1990	Dale Earnhardt	2005	*season ends*
1961	Ned Jarrett	1976	Cale Yarborough	1991	Dale Earnhardt		*20 November in*
1962	Joe Weatherly	1977	Cale Yarborough	1992	Alan Kulwicki		*Homestead FL*
1963	Joe Weatherly	1978	Cale Yarborough	1993	Dale Earnhardt		

Daytona 500 Winners, 1959–2005

The most recent race was held at Daytona International Speedway, Daytona Beach FL, 20 Feb 2005.
Daytona 500 Web site: <www.daytona500.com>.

YEAR	WINNER	YEAR	WINNER	YEAR	WINNER
1959	Lee Petty	1973	Richard Petty	1990	Derrike Cope
1960	Junior Johnson	1974	Richard Petty	1991	Ernie Irvan
1961	Marvin Panch	1975	Benny Parsons	1992	David Carl ("Davey")
1962	Edward Glen ("Fireball")	1976	David Pearson		Allison
	Roberts	1977	Cale Yarborough	1993	Dale Jarrett
1963	DeWayne Louis ("Tiny")	1978	Bobby Allison	1994	Sterling Marlin
	Lund	1979	Richard Petty	1995	Sterling Marlin
1964	Richard Petty	1980	Wylie ("Buddy") Baker, Jr.	1996	Dale Jarrett
1965	Fred Lorenzen	1981	Richard Petty	1997	Jeff Gordon
1966	Richard Petty	1982	Bobby Allison	1998	Dale Earnhardt, Sr.
1967	Mario Andretti	1983	Cale Yarborough	1999	Jeff Gordon
1968	William Caleb ("Cale")	1984	Cale Yarborough	2000	Dale Jarrett
	Yarborough	1985	Bill Elliott	2001	Michael Waltrip
1969	Lee Roy Yarbrough	1986	Geoff Bodine	2002	Ward Burton
1970	Pete Hamilton	1987	Bill Elliott	2003	Michael Waltrip
1971	Richard Petty	1988	Bobby Allison	2004	Dale Earnhardt, Jr.
1972	A.J. Foyt	1989	Darrell Waltrip	2005	Jeff Gordon

Badminton

The oldest, and still the classic, tournament for badminton is the All-England Badminton Championships, which have been held annually since 1900. A governing body, the International Badminton Federation (**IBF**), was established in 1934. It first proposed international team badminton for men in 1939, but actual tournament play for the **Thomas Cup** did not begin until 1948–49. A similar contest for women's teams, the **Uber Cup**, was inaugurated in 1956–57. Competition for the biennial team championships (held in even years since 1982) consists of three singles matches and two doubles matches.

Official **world badminton championships** were first held in 1977. The program for this biennial event (held in odd years) includes mixed doubles and individual and doubles competition for men and for women.

International Badminton Federation Web site: <www.worldbadminton.net>.

Uber Cup

YEAR	WINNER	RUNNER-UP	YEAR	WINNER	RUNNER-UP
1956–57	United States	Denmark	1985–86	China	Indonesia
1959–60	United States	Denmark	1987–88	China	South Korea
1962–63	United States	England	1989–90	China	South Korea
1965–66	Japan	United States	1991–92	China	South Korea
1968–69	Japan	Indonesia	1993–94	Indonesia	China
1971–72	Japan	Indonesia	1995–96	Indonesia	China
1974–75	Indonesia	Japan	1997–98	China	Indonesia
1977–78	Japan	Indonesia	1999–2000	China	Denmark
1980–81	Japan	Indonesia	2001–02	China	South Korea
1983–84	China	England	2003–04	China	South Korea

All-England Championships—Singles

Held since 1900. No competition 1915–19 or 1940–46. Table shows results for past 20 years.

YEAR	MEN	WOMEN	YEAR	MEN	WOMEN
1986	Morten Frost (DEN)	Kim Yun Ja (KOR)	1997	Dong Jiong (CHN)	Ye Zhaoying (CHN)
1987	Morten Frost (DEN)	Kirsten Larsen (DEN)	1998	Sun Jun (CHN)	Ye Zhaoying (CHN)
1988	Ib Frederiksen (DEN)	Gu Jiaming (CHN)	1999	Peter Gade Christen-sen (DEN)	Ye Zhaoying (CHN)
1989	Yang Yang (CHN)	Li Lingwei (CHN)			
1990	Zhao Jianhua (CHN)	Susi Susanti (INA)	2000	Xia Xuanze (CHN)	Gong Zhichao (CHN)
1991	Ardy Wiranata (INA)	Susi Susanti (INA)	2001	Pulella Gopichand (IND)	Gong Zhichao (CHN)
1992	Liu Jun (CHN)	Tang Jiuhong (CHN)			
1993	Heryanto Arbi (INA)	Susi Susanti (INA)	2002	Chen Hong (CHN)	Camilla Martin (DEN)
1994	Heryanto Arbi (INA)	Susi Susanti (INA)	2003	Muhammad Hafiz Hashim (MAS)	Zhou Mi (CHN)
1995	Poul-Erik Hoyer-Larsen (DEN)	Lim Xiao Qing (SWE)	2004	Lin Dan (CHN)	Gong Ruina (CHN)
1996	Poul-Erik Hoyer-Larsen (DEN)	Bang Soo Hyun (KOR)	2005	Chen Hong (CHN)	Xie Xingfang (CHN)

Thomas Cup

YEAR	WINNER	RUNNER-UP	YEAR	WINNER	RUNNER-UP
1948–49	Malaya	Denmark	1981–82	China	Indonesia
1951–52	Malaya	United States	1983–84	Indonesia	China
1954–55	Malaya	Denmark	1985–86	China	Indonesia
1957–58	Indonesia	Malaya	1987–88	China	Malaysia
1960–61	Indonesia	Thailand	1989–90	China	Malaysia
1963–64	Indonesia	Denmark	1991–92	Malaysia	Indonesia
1966–67	Malaysia (by default)	Indonesia	1993–94	Indonesia	Malaysia
			1995–96	Indonesia	Denmark
1969–70	Indonesia	Malaysia	1997–98	Indonesia	Malaysia
1972–73	Indonesia	Denmark	1999–2000	Indonesia	China
1975–76	Indonesia	Malaysia	2001–02	Indonesia	Malaysia
1978–79	Indonesia	Denmark	2003–04	China	Denmark

World Badminton Championships

YEAR	MEN'S SINGLES	WOMEN'S SINGLES	MEN'S DOUBLES
1977	Flemming Delfs (DEN)	Lene Köppen (DEN)	Tjun Tjun, Johan Wahjudi (INA)
1980	Rudy Hartono (INA)	Verawaty Wiharjo (INA)	Ade Chandra, Christian Hadinata (INA)
1983	Icuk Sugiarto (INA)	Li Lingwei (CHN)	Steen Fladberg, Jasper Helledie (DEN)
1985	Han Jian (CHN)	Han Aiping (CHN)	Park Joo Bong, Kim Moon Soo (KOR)
1987	Yang Yang (CHN)	Han Aiping (CHN)	Li Yongbo, Tian Bingyi (CHN)
1989	Yang Yang (CHN)	Li Lingwei (CHN)	Li Yongbo, Tian Bingyi (CHN)
1991	Zhao Jianhua (CHN)	Tang Jiuhong (CHN)	Park Joo Bong, Kim Moon Soo (KOR)
1993	Joko Suprianto (INA)	Susi Susanti (INA)	Ricky Subagja, Rudy Gunawan (INA)
1995	Heryanto Arbi (INA)	Ye Zhaoying (CHN)	Ricky Subagja, Rexy Mainaky (INA)
1997	Peter Rasmussen (DEN)	Ye Zhaoying (CHN)	Budiarto Sigit, Candra Wijaya (INA)
1999	Sun Jun (CHN)	Camilla Martin (DEN)	Kim Dong Moon, Ha Tae Kwon (KOR)
2001	Hendrawan (INA)	Gong Ruina (CHN)	Tony Gunawan, Halim Haryanto (INA)
2003	Xia Huanze (CHN)	Zhang Ning (CHN)	Lars Paaske, Jonas Rasmussen (DEN)
2005	Taufik Hidayat (INA)	Xie Xingfang (CHN)	Tony Gunawan, Howard Bach (USA)

YEAR	WOMEN'S DOUBLES	MIXED DOUBLES
1977	Etsuko Toganu, Erniko Ueno (JPN)	Steen Skovgaard, Lene Köppen (DEN)
1980	Nora Perry, Jane Webster (ENG)	Christian Hadinata, Imelda Wiguno (INA)
1983	Lin Ying, Wu Dixi (CHN)	Thomas Kihlström, Nora Perry (SWE, ENG)
1985	Han Aiping, Li Lingwei (CHN)	Park Joo Bong, Yoo Sang Hee (KOR)
1987	Lin Ying, Guan Weizhen (CHN)	Wang Pengren, Shi Fangjing (CHN)
1989	Lin Ying, Guan Weizhen (CHN)	Park Joo Bong, Chung Myung Hee (KOR)
1991	Guan Weizhen, Nong Qunhua (CHN)	Park Joo Bong, Chung Myung Hee (KOR)
1993	Nong Qunhua, Zhou Lei (CHN)	Thomas Lund, Catrine Bengtsson (DEN, SWE)
1995	Gil Young Ah, Jang Hye Ock (KOR)	Thomas Lund, Marlene Thomsen (DEN)
1997	Ge Fei, Gu Jun (CHN)	Liu Yong, Ge Fei (CHN)
1999	Ge Fei, Gu Jun (CHN)	Kim Dong Moon, Ra Kyung Min (KOR)
2001	Gao Ling, Huang Sui (CHN)	Zhang Jun, Gao Ling (CHN)
2003	Gao Ling, Huang Sui (CHN)	Kim Dong Moon, Ra Kyung Min (KOR)
2005	Yang Wei, Zhang Jiewen (CHN)	Nova Widianto, Lilyana Natsir (INA)

Baseball

The sport of baseball—given its definitive form in the United States in the late 19th century—is popular throughout the world, though it is not organized internationally except for **Little League** players (children ages 5–18). Little League Baseball was founded in Pennsylvania in 1939. The first Little League World Series was in 1947, and the first Little League outside the US was organized in British Columbia in 1951. Baseball is especially popular in Japan and Latin America; it is also one of the national sports of the US.

On a **professional** level, the premier event of baseball in the US is the **World Series** of **Major League Baseball**, in which the first team to win four games wins the Series. In fact, the Series is not contested on an international level, but rather it is played between the leading team of the **National League** (NL; formed 1876) and the leading team of the **American League** (AL; formed 1900 and including, from 1977, one Canadian team).

Professional baseball began in Japan in 1936. Teams are organized into two leagues of six teams each. The seven-game **Japan Series**, first played in 1950, is contested between the leading team of the Central League (CL) and the leading team of the Pacific League (PL). The modern **Caribbean Series** began in 1970 with the winning team from each league in the Dominican Republic, Mexico, Puerto Rico, and Venezuela.

Related Web sites: Major League: <www.mlb.com>; Little League: <www.littleleague.org>.

Final Major League Standings, 2004

American League

East Division				Central Division				West Division			
CLUB	WON	LOST	GAMES BACK	CLUB	WON	LOST	GAMES BACK	CLUB	WON	LOST	GAMES BACK
New York[1]	101	61	—	Minnesota[1]	92	70	—	Anaheim[1]	92	70	—
Boston[1]	98	64	3	Chicago	83	79	9	Oakland	91	71	1
Baltimore	78	84	23	Cleveland	80	82	12	Texas	89	73	3
Tampa Bay	70	91	30½	Detroit	72	90	20	Seattle	63	99	29
Toronto	67	94	33½	Kansas City	58	104	34				

National League

East Division				Central Division				West Division			
CLUB	WON	LOST	GAMES BACK	CLUB	WON	LOST	GAMES BACK	CLUB	WON	LOST	GAMES BACK
Atlanta[1]	96	66	—	St. Louis[1]	105	57	—	Los Angeles[1]	93	69	—
Philadelphia	86	76	10	Houston[1]	92	70	13	San Francisco	91	71	2
Florida	83	79	13	Chicago	89	73	16	San Diego	87	75	6
New York	71	91	25	Cincinnati	76	86	29	Colorado	68	94	25
Montreal	67	95	29	Pittsburgh	72	89	32½	Arizona	51	111	42
				Milwaukee	67	94	37½				

[1]Gained play-off berth.

World Series

AL—American League; NL—National League.

YEAR	WINNING TEAM	LOSING TEAM	RESULTS
1903	Boston Pilgrims (AL)	Pittsburgh Pirates (NL)	5–3
1904	not held		
1905	New York Giants (NL)	Philadelphia Athletics (AL)	4–1
1906	Chicago White Sox (AL)	Chicago Cubs (NL)	4–2
1907[1]	Chicago Cubs (NL)	Detroit Tigers (AL)	4–0
1908	Chicago Cubs (NL)	Detroit Tigers (AL)	4–1
1909	Pittsburgh Pirates (NL)	Detroit Tigers (AL)	4–3
1910	Philadelphia Athletics (AL)	Chicago Cubs (NL)	4–1
1911	Philadelphia Athletics (AL)	New York Giants (NL)	4–2
1912[1]	Boston Red Sox (AL)	New York Giants (NL)	4–3
1913	Philadelphia Athletics (AL)	New York Giants (NL)	4–1
1914	Boston Braves (NL)	Philadelphia Athletics (AL)	4–0
1915	Boston Red Sox (AL)	Philadelphia Phillies (NL)	4–1
1916	Boston Red Sox (AL)	Brooklyn Robins (NL)	4–1
1917	Chicago White Sox (AL)	New York Giants (NL)	4–2
1918	Boston Red Sox (AL)	Chicago Cubs (NL)	4–2
1919	Cincinnati Reds (NL)	Chicago White Sox (AL)	5–3
1920	Cleveland Indians (AL)	Brooklyn Robins (NL)	5–2
1921	New York Giants (NL)	New York Yankees (AL)	5–3
1922[1]	New York Giants (NL)	New York Yankees (AL)	4–0

World Series (continued)

YEAR	WINNING TEAM	LOSING TEAM	RESULTS
1923	New York Yankees (AL)	New York Giants (NL)	4-2
1924	Washington Senators (AL)	New York Giants (NL)	4-3
1925	Pittsburgh Pirates (NL)	Washington Senators (AL)	4-3
1926	St. Louis Cardinals (NL)	New York Yankees (AL)	4-3
1927	New York Yankees (AL)	Pittsburgh Pirates (NL)	4-0
1928	New York Yankees (AL)	St. Louis Cardinals (NL)	4-0
1929	Philadelphia Athletics (AL)	Chicago Cubs (NL)	4-1
1930	Philadelphia Athletics (AL)	St. Louis Cardinals (NL)	4-2
1931	St. Louis Cardinals (NL)	Philadelphia Athletics (AL)	4-3
1932	New York Yankees (AL)	Chicago Cubs (NL)	4-0
1933	New York Giants (NL)	Washington Senators (AL)	4-1
1934	St. Louis Cardinals (NL)	Detroit Tigers (AL)	4-3
1935	Detroit Tigers (AL)	Chicago Cubs (NL)	4-2
1936	New York Yankees (AL)	New York Giants (NL)	4-2
1937	New York Yankees (AL)	New York Giants (NL)	4-1
1938	New York Yankees (AL)	Chicago Cubs (NL)	4-0
1939	New York Yankees (AL)	Cincinnati Reds (NL)	4-0
1940	Cincinnati Reds (NL)	Detroit Tigers (AL)	4-3
1941	New York Yankees (AL)	Brooklyn Dodgers (NL)	4-1
1942	St. Louis Cardinals (NL)	New York Yankees (AL)	4-1
1943	New York Yankees (AL)	St. Louis Cardinals (NL)	4-1
1944	St. Louis Cardinals (NL)	St. Louis Browns (AL)	4-2
1945	Detroit Tigers (AL)	Chicago Cubs (NL)	4-3
1946	St. Louis Cardinals (NL)	Boston Red Sox (AL)	4-3
1947	New York Yankees (AL)	Brooklyn Dodgers (NL)	4-3
1948	Cleveland Indians (AL)	Boston Braves (NL)	4-2
1949	New York Yankees (AL)	Brooklyn Dodgers (NL)	4-1
1950	New York Yankees (AL)	Philadelphia Phillies (NL)	4-0
1951	New York Yankees (AL)	New York Giants (NL)	4-2
1952	New York Yankees (AL)	Brooklyn Dodgers (NL)	4-3
1953	New York Yankees (AL)	Brooklyn Dodgers (NL)	4-2
1954	New York Giants (NL)	Cleveland Indians (AL)	4-0
1955	Brooklyn Dodgers (NL)	New York Yankees (AL)	4-3
1956	New York Yankees (AL)	Brooklyn Dodgers (NL)	4-3
1957	Milwaukee Braves (NL)	New York Yankees (AL)	4-3
1958	New York Yankees (AL)	Milwaukee Braves (NL)	4-3
1959	Los Angeles Dodgers (NL)	Chicago White Sox (AL)	4-2
1960	Pittsburgh Pirates (NL)	New York Yankees (AL)	4-3
1961	New York Yankees (AL)	Cincinnati Reds (NL)	4-1
1962	New York Yankees (AL)	San Francisco Giants (NL)	4-3
1963	Los Angeles Dodgers (NL)	New York Yankees (AL)	4-0
1964	St. Louis Cardinals (NL)	New York Yankees (AL)	4-3
1965	Los Angeles Dodgers (NL)	Minnesota Twins (AL)	4-3
1966	Baltimore Orioles (AL)	Los Angeles Dodgers (NL)	4-0
1967	St. Louis Cardinals (NL)	Boston Red Sox (AL)	4-3
1968	Detroit Tigers (AL)	St. Louis Cardinals (NL)	4-3
1969	New York Mets (NL)	Baltimore Orioles (AL)	4-1
1970	Baltimore Orioles (AL)	Cincinnati Reds (NL)	4-1
1971	Pittsburgh Pirates (NL)	Baltimore Orioles (AL)	4-3
1972	Oakland Athletics (AL)	Cincinnati Reds (NL)	4-3
1973	Oakland Athletics (AL)	New York Mets (NL)	4-3
1974	Oakland Athletics (AL)	Los Angeles Dodgers (NL)	4-1
1975	Cincinnati Reds (NL)	Boston Red Sox (AL)	4-3
1976	Cincinnati Reds (NL)	New York Yankees (AL)	4-0
1977	New York Yankees (AL)	Los Angeles Dodgers (NL)	4-2
1978	New York Yankees (AL)	Los Angeles Dodgers (NL)	4-2
1979	Pittsburgh Pirates (NL)	Baltimore Orioles (AL)	4-3
1980	Philadelphia Phillies (NL)	Kansas City Royals (AL)	4-2
1981	Los Angeles Dodgers (NL)	New York Yankees (AL)	4-2
1982	St. Louis Cardinals (NL)	Milwaukee Brewers (AL)	4-3
1983	Baltimore Orioles (AL)	Philadelphia Phillies (NL)	4-1
1984	Detroit Tigers (AL)	San Diego Padres (NL)	4-1
1985	Kansas City Royals (AL)	St. Louis Cardinals (NL)	4-3
1986	New York Mets (NL)	Boston Red Sox (AL)	4-3
1987	Minnesota Twins (AL)	St. Louis Cardinals (NL)	4-3
1988	Los Angeles Dodgers (NL)	Oakland Athletics (AL)	4-1
1989	Oakland Athletics (AL)	San Francisco Giants (NL)	4-0
1990	Cincinnati Reds (NL)	Oakland Athletics (AL)	4-0

World Series (continued)

YEAR	WINNING TEAM	LOSING TEAM	RESULTS
1991	Minnesota Twins (AL)	Atlanta Braves (NL)	4–3
1992	Toronto Blue Jays (AL)	Atlanta Braves (NL)	4–2
1993	Toronto Blue Jays (AL)	Philadelphia Phillies (NL)	4–2
1994	*not held*		
1995	Atlanta Braves (NL)	Cleveland Indians (AL)	4–2
1996	New York Yankees (AL)	Atlanta Braves (NL)	4–2
1997	Florida Marlins (NL)	Cleveland Indians (AL)	4–3
1998	New York Yankees (AL)	San Diego Padres (NL)	4–0
1999	New York Yankees (AL)	Atlanta Braves (NL)	4–0
2000	New York Yankees (AL)	New York Mets (NL)	4–1
2001	Arizona Diamondbacks (NL)	New York Yankees (AL)	4–3
2002	Anaheim Angels (AL)	San Francisco Giants (NL)	4–3
2003	Florida Marlins (NL)	New York Yankees (AL)	4–2
2004	Boston Red Sox (AL)	St. Louis Cardinals (NL)	4–0

[1]*One tied game.*

Major League Baseball All-Time Records[1]

	PLAYERS/TEAMS	NUMBER	SEASON/DATE
Individual career records			
Games played	Pete Rose	3,562	1963–86
Consecutive games played	Cal Ripken, Jr.	2,632	1982–98
Batting average[2]	Ty Cobb	.366	1905–28
Hits	Pete Rose	4,256	1963–86
Doubles	Tris Speaker	792	1907–28
Triples	Sam Crawford	309	1899–17
Home runs	Hank Aaron	755	1954–76
Runs	Rickey Henderson	2,295	1979–2003
Runs batted in	Hank Aaron	2,297	1954–76
Walks (batting)	Barry Bonds[3]	2,302	1986–2004
Stolen bases (batting)	Rickey Henderson	1,406	1979–2003
Wins	Cy Young	511	1890–1911
Earned run average[4]	Ed Walsh	1.82	1904–17
Strikeouts (pitching)	Nolan Ryan	5,714	1966–93
Saves	Lee Smith	478	1980–97
No-hitters	Nolan Ryan	7	1966–93
Shutouts	Walter Johnson	110	1907–27
Coaching, total wins	Connie Mack	3,731	1894–96; 1901–50
Individual season records			
Batting average[5]	Hugh Duffy	.440	1894
Hits	Ichiro Suzuki	262	2004
Doubles	Earl Webb	67	1931
Triples	Chief Wilson	36	1912
Home runs	Barry Bonds	73	2001
Runs	Billy Hamilton	198	1894
Runs batted in	Hack Wilson	191	1930
Walks (batting)	Barry Bonds	232	2004
Stolen bases (batting)	Hugh Nicol	138	1887
Wins	Charley Radbourn	59	1884
Earned run average[6]	Tim Keefe	0.86	1880
Strikeouts (pitching)	Matt Kilroy	513	1886
No-hitters	*4 players hold record*	2	N/A
Saves	Bobby Thigpen	57	1990
Shutouts	George Bradley; Grover Alexander	16	1876; 1916
Individual game records[7]			
Hits	Wilbert Robinson; Rennie Stinnett	7	10 Jun 1892; 16 Sep 1975
Doubles	*too numerous to list*	4	N/A
Triples	George Strief; Bill Joyce	4	25 Jun 1885; 18 May 1897
Home runs	*12 players hold record*	4	N/A
Runs	Guy Hecker	7	15 Aug 1886
Runs batted in	Jim Bottomley; Mark Whiten	12	16 Sep 1924; 7 Sep 1993

Major League Baseball All-Time Records[1] (continued)

PLAYERS/TEAMS		NUMBER	SEASON/DATE
Individual game records[7] (cont.)			
Walks (batting)	Walt Wilmot; Jimmie Foxx	6	22 Aug 1891; 16 Jun 1938
Stolen bases (batting)	George Gore; Billy Hamilton	7	25 Jun 1881; 31 Aug 1894
Strikeouts (pitching)	Roger Clemens (twice); Kerry Wood	20	29 Apr 1986 and 18 Sep 1996; 6 May 1998
Team season records			
World Series titles	New York Yankees	26	
Consecutive World Series titles	New York Yankees	5	1949–53
Games won (percentage)	Chicago Cubs	116–36 (.763)	1906
Batting average	Philadelphia Phillies	.349	1894
Doubles	St. Louis Cardinals; Boston Red Sox	373	1930; 1997
Triples	Baltimore Orioles	153	1894
Home runs	Seattle Mariners	264	1997
Runs	Boston Braves	1,220	1894
Runs batted in	Boston Braves	1,043	1894
Walks (batting)	Boston Red Sox	835	1949
Stolen bases (batting)	New York Giants	347	1911
Strikeouts (pitching)	Chicago Cubs	1,404	2003
Game season records			
Highest total score	Chicago Cubs versus Philadelphia Phillies	26 to 23 (total 49)	25 Aug 1922
Longest nine-inning game	Los Angeles Dodgers versus San Francisco Giants	4 hr 27 min	5 Oct 2001
Longest extra-innings game (time)	Chicago White Sox versus Milwaukee Brewers	8 hr 6 min	9 May 1984
Longest extra-innings game (innings)	Brooklyn Dodgers versus Boston Braves	26 innings	1 May 1920

[1]*Through 2004 season.* [2]*Minimum of 5,000 at-bats.* [3]*Active in 2005.* [4]*Minimum of 1,500 innings pitched.*
[5]*Minimum of 3.1 plate appearances per game played.* [6]*Minimum of one inning pitched per game played.*
[7]*Nine-inning games only.*

Caribbean Series

YEAR	WINNING TEAM	COUNTRY	YEAR	WINNING TEAM	COUNTRY
1970	Magallanes Navigators	VEN	1988	Escogido Lions	DOM
1971	Licey Tigers	DOM	1989	Zulia Eagles	VEN
1972	Ponce Lions	PUR	1990	Escogido Lions	DOM
1973	Licey Tigers	DOM	1991	Licey Tigers	DOM
1974	Caguas Creoles	PUR	1992	Mayagüez Indians	PUR
1975	Bayamon Cowboys	PUR	1993	Santurce Crabbers	PUR
1976	Hermosillo Orange Growers	MEX	1994	Licey Tigers	DOM
1977	Licey Tigers	DOM	1995	San Juan Senators	PUR
1978	Mayagüez Indians	PUR	1996	Culiacán Tomato Growers	MEX
1979	Magallanes Navigators	VEN	1997	Northern Eagles	DOM
1980	Licey Tigers	DOM	1998	Northern Eagles	DOM
1981	*not held*		1999	Licey Tigers	DOM
1982	Caracas Lions	VEN	2000	Santurce Crabbers	PUR
1983	Arecibo Wolves	PUR	2001	Cibao Eagles	DOM
1984	Zulia Eagles	VEN	2002	Culiacán Tomato Growers	MEX
1985	Licey Tigers	DOM	2003	Cibao Eagles	DOM
1986	Mexicali Eagles	MEX	2004	Licey Tigers	DOM
1987	Caguas Creoles	PUR	2005	Mazatlán Venados	MEX

Japan Series

CL—Central League; PL—Pacific League.

YEAR	WINNING TEAM	LOSING TEAM	RESULTS
1995	Yakult Swallows (CL)	Orix BlueWave (PL)	4–1
1996	Orix BlueWave (PL)	Yomiuri Giants (CL)	4–1
1997	Yakult Swallows (CL)	Seibu Lions (PL)	4–1
1998	Yokohama BayStars (CL)	Seibu Lions (PL)	4–2
1999	Fukuoka Daiei Hawks (PL)	Chunichi Dragons (CL)	4–1
2000	Yomiuri Giants (CL)	Fukuoka Daiei Hawks (PL)	4–2
2001	Yakult Swallows (CL)	Osaka Kintetsu Buffaloes (PL)	4–1
2002	Yomiuri Giants (CL)	Seibu Lions (PL)	4–0
2003	Fukuoka Daiei Hawks (PL)	Hanshin Tigers (CL)	4–3
2004	Seibu Lions (PL)	Chunichi Dragons (CL)	4–3
2005	*to be held in October*		

Little League World Series

The Little League World Series, first called the National Little League Tournament, was established in 1947. The table shows the Series winners for the past 10 years.

YEAR	WINNING TEAM/HOME	RUNNER-UP	SCORE
1996	Fu-Hsing/Kao-Hsuing (TAI)	Cranston/Cranston RI	13–3
1997	Linda Vista/Guadalupe (MEX)	South Mission Viejo/Mission Viejo CA	5–4
1998	Toms River/Toms River NJ	Kashima/Ibaraki (JPN)	12–9
1999	Hirakata/Osaka (JPN)	Phenix City National/Phenix City AL	5–0
2000	Sierra Maestra/Maracaibo (VEN)	Bellaire/Bellaire TX	3–2
2001	Kitasuna/Tokyo (JPN)	Apopka National/Apopka FL	2–1
2002	Valley Sports American/Louisville KY	Sendai Higashi/Sendai (JPN)	1–0
2003	Musashi-Fuchu/Tokyo (JPN)	East Boynton Beach/Boynton Beach FL	10–1
2004	Pabao/Willemstad (AHO)	Conejo Valley/Thousand Oaks CA	5–2
2005	*to be held in August*		

Basketball

American professional basketball is directed by the **National Basketball Association** (NBA; formed 1949). The NBA is divided into two conferences, the top-ranking teams of which compete yearly for the championship. The NBA began a **women's professional league**, known as the WNBA, in 1997.

As an **amateur** sport, basketball is organized on an international level. Since the inclusion of basketball as an **Olympic sport** in 1936, the winners of the Olympic tournament have been considered the world champions. The **Fédération Internationale de Basketball** (FIBA; founded 1932) instituted separate world championships in 1950 for men and in 1953 for women. (Women's basketball was not admitted to the Olympics until 1976.) Amateur basketball in the United States is most closely followed at the **collegiate** level, where the most important event of the season is the **National Collegiate Athletic Association (NCAA) Championship.** The NCAA tournament was first contested in 1939 (by men's teams only). Women's college basketball was first played on a national level in 1972, under the auspices of the Association for Intercollegiate Athletics for Women (AIAW), which gave way in 1982 to the NCAA's first tournament for women.

Related Web sites: NBA: <www.nba.com>; WNBA: <www.wnba.com>; NCAA: <www.ncaa.org>; FIBA: <www.fiba.com>.

National Basketball Association Final Standings, 2004–05

EASTERN CONFERENCE

Atlantic Division				Central Division				Southeast Division			
TEAM	WON	LOST	GAMES BACK	TEAM	WON	LOST	GAMES BACK	TEAM	WON	LOST	GAMES BACK
Boston[1]	45	37	—	Detroit[1]	54	28	—	Miami[1]	59	23	—
Philadelphia[1]	43	39	2	Chicago[1]	47	35	7	Washington[1]	45	37	14
New Jersey[1]	42	40	3	Indiana[1]	44	38	10	Orlando	36	46	23
Toronto	33	49	12	Cleveland	42	40	12	Charlotte	18	64	41
New York	33	49	12	Milwaukee	30	52	24	Atlanta	13	69	46

National Basketball Association Final Standings, 2004–05 (continued)

WESTERN CONFERENCE

Northwest Division				Pacific Division				Southwest Division			
TEAM	WON	LOST	GAMES BACK	TEAM	WON	LOST	GAMES BACK	TEAM	WON	LOST	GAMES BACK
Seattle[1]	52	30	—	Phoenix[1]	62	20	—	San Antonio[1]	59	23	—
Denver[1]	49	33	3	Sacramento[1]	50	32	12	Dallas[1]	58	24	1
Minnesota	44	38	8	L.A. Clippers	37	45	25	Houston[1]	51	31	8
Portland	27	55	25	L.A. Lakers	34	48	28	Memphis[1]	45	37	14
Utah	26	56	26	Golden State	34	48	28	New Orleans	18	64	41

[1]Gained play-off berth.

National Basketball Association All-Time Records

Source: <www.nba.com>.

	PLAYERS/TEAMS	NUMBER	SEASON/DATE
Individual career records			
Games played	Robert Parish	1,611	1976-77—1996-97
Points scored	Kareem Abdul-Jabbar	38,387	1969-70—1988-89
Field goals attempted	Kareem Abdul-Jabbar	28,307	1969-70—1988-89
Field goals made	Kareem Abdul-Jabbar	15,837	1969-70—1988-89
Field-goal percentage[1]	Artis Gilmore	.599	1976-77—1987-88
Three-point field goals attempted	Reggie Miller	6,486	1987-88—2004-05
Three-point field goals made	Reggie Miller	2,560	1987-88—2004-05
Three-point field-goal percentage[2]	Steve Kerr	.454	1988-89—2002-03
Free throws attempted	Karl Malone	13,188	1985-86—2003-04
Free throws made	Karl Malone	9,787	1985-86—2003-04
Free-throw percentage[3]	Mark Price	.904	1986-87—1997-98
Assists	John Stockton	15,806	1984-85—2002-03
Rebounds	Wilt Chamberlain	23,924	1959-60—1972-73
Coaching, total wins	Lenny Wilkens	1,332	1969-70—2004-05
Individual season records			
Points scored	Wilt Chamberlain (Philadelphia Warriors)	4,029	1961-62
Field goals attempted	Wilt Chamberlain (Philadelphia Warriors)	3,159	1961-62
Field goals made	Wilt Chamberlain (Philadelphia Warriors)	1,597	1961-62
Field-goal percentage	Wilt Chamberlain (Los Angeles Lakers)	.727	1972-73
Three-point field goals attempted	George McCloud (Dallas Mavericks)	678	1995-96
Three-point field goals made	Dennis Scott (Orlando Magic)	267	1995-96
Three-point field-goal percentage	Steve Kerr (Chicago Bulls)	.524	1994-95
Free throws attempted	Wilt Chamberlain (Philadelphia Warriors)	1,363	1961-62
Free throws made	Jerry West (Los Angeles Lakers)	840	1965-66
Free-throw percentage	Calvin Murphy (Houston Rockets)	.958	1980-81
Assists	John Stockton (Utah Jazz)	1,164	1990-91
Rebounds	Wilt Chamberlain (Philadelphia Warriors)	2,149	1960-61
Individual game records			
Points scored	Wilt Chamberlain (Philadelphia Warriors)	100	2 Mar 1962
Field goals attempted	Wilt Chamberlain (Philadelphia Warriors)	63	2 Mar 1962
Field goals made	Wilt Chamberlain (Philadelphia Warriors)	36	2 Mar 1962
Three-point field goals attempted	Michael Adams (Denver Nuggets); George McCloud (Dallas Mavericks)	20	12 Apr 1991; 5 Mar 1996
Three-point field goals made	Kobe Bryant (Los Angeles Lakers)	12	7 Jan 2003
Free throws attempted	Wilt Chamberlain (Philadelphia Warriors)	34	22 Feb 1962
Free throws made	Wilt Chamberlain (Philadelphia Warriors); Adrian Dantley (Utah Jazz)	28	2 Mar 1962; 4 Jan 1984

National Basketball Association All-Time Records (continued)

	PLAYERS/TEAMS	NUMBER	SEASON/DATE
Individual game records (cont.)			
Assists	Scott Skiles (Orlando Magic)	30	30 Dec 1990
Rebounds	Wilt Chamberlain (Philadelphia Warriors)	55	24 Nov 1960
Team records			
Games won (percentage), single season	Chicago Bulls	72–10 (.878)	1995–96
Championships	Boston Celtics	16	
Consecutive championships	Boston Celtics	8	1959–66
Game records			
Highest combined score	Detroit Pistons v. Denver Nuggets	370 (186–184)	13 Dec 1983
Longest game (overtime periods)	Indianapolis Olympians v. Rochester Royals	6	6 Jan 1951

[1]Minimum 2,000 made. [2]Minimum 250 made. [3]Minimum 1,200 made.

Did you know? Basketball was invented by James Naismith in 1891 in Springfield MA, where Naismith was a physical education instructor at the YMCA Training School. For the first game of basketball in 1891, Naismith used as goals two half-bushel peach baskets, which gave the sport its name.

National Basketball Association (NBA) Championship

SEASON	WINNER	RUNNER-UP	RESULTS
1946–47	Philadelphia Warriors	Chicago Stags	4–1
1947–48	Baltimore Bullets	Philadelphia Warriors	4–2
1948–49	Minneapolis Lakers	Washington Capitols	4–2
1949–50	Minneapolis Lakers	Syracuse Nationals	4–2
1950–51	Rochester Royals	New York Knickerbockers	4–3
1951–52	Minneapolis Lakers	New York Knickerbockers	4–3
1952–53	Minneapolis Lakers	New York Knickerbockers	4–1
1953–54	Minneapolis Lakers	Syracuse Nationals	4–3
1954–55	Syracuse Nationals	Fort Wayne Pistons	4–3
1955–56	Philadelphia Warriors	Fort Wayne Pistons	4–1
1956–57	Boston Celtics	St. Louis Hawks	4–3
1957–58	St. Louis Hawks	Boston Celtics	4–2
1958–59	Boston Celtics	Minneapolis Lakers	4–0
1959–60	Boston Celtics	St. Louis Hawks	4–3
1960–61	Boston Celtics	St. Louis Hawks	4–1
1961–62	Boston Celtics	Los Angeles Lakers	4–3
1962–63	Boston Celtics	Los Angeles Lakers	4–2
1963–64	Boston Celtics	San Francisco Warriors	4–1
1964–65	Boston Celtics	Los Angeles Lakers	4–1
1965–66	Boston Celtics	Los Angeles Lakers	4–3
1966–67	Philadelphia 76ers	San Francisco Warriors	4–2
1967–68	Boston Celtics	Los Angeles Lakers	4–2
1968–69	Boston Celtics	Los Angeles Lakers	4–3
1969–70	New York Knickerbockers	Los Angeles Lakers	4–3
1970–71	Milwaukee Bucks	Baltimore Bullets	4–0
1971–72	Los Angeles Lakers	New York Knickerbockers	4–1
1972–73	New York Knickerbockers	Los Angeles Lakers	4–1
1973–74	Boston Celtics	Milwaukee Bucks	4–3
1974–75	Golden State Warriors	Washington Bullets	4–0
1975–76	Boston Celtics	Phoenix Suns	4–2
1976–77	Portland Trail Blazers	Philadelphia 76ers	4–2
1977–78	Washington Bullets	Seattle SuperSonics	4–3
1978–79	Seattle SuperSonics	Washington Bullets	4–1
1979–80	Los Angeles Lakers	Philadelphia 76ers	4–2
1980–81	Boston Celtics	Houston Rockets	4–2
1981–82	Los Angeles Lakers	Philadelphia 76ers	4–2
1982–83	Philadelphia 76ers	Los Angeles Lakers	4–0

National Basketball Association (NBA) Championship (continued)

SEASON	WINNER	RUNNER-UP	RESULTS
1983–84	Boston Celtics	Los Angeles Lakers	4–3
1984–85	Los Angeles Lakers	Boston Celtics	4–2
1985–86	Boston Celtics	Houston Rockets	4–2
1986–87	Los Angeles Lakers	Boston Celtics	4–2
1987–88	Los Angeles Lakers	Detroit Pistons	4–3
1988–89	Detroit Pistons	Los Angeles Lakers	4–0
1989–90	Detroit Pistons	Portland Trail Blazers	4–1
1990–91	Chicago Bulls	Los Angeles Lakers	4–1
1991–92	Chicago Bulls	Portland Trail Blazers	4–2
1992–93	Chicago Bulls	Phoenix Suns	4–2
1993–94	Houston Rockets	New York Knickerbockers	4–3
1994–95	Houston Rockets	Orlando Magic	4–0
1995–96	Chicago Bulls	Seattle SuperSonics	4–2
1996–97	Chicago Bulls	Utah Jazz	4–2
1997–98	Chicago Bulls	Utah Jazz	4–2
1998–99	San Antonio Spurs	New York Knickerbockers	4–1
1999–2000	Los Angeles Lakers	Indiana Pacers	4–2
2000–01	Los Angeles Lakers	Philadelphia 76ers	4–1
2001–02	Los Angeles Lakers	New Jersey Nets	4–0
2002–03	San Antonio Spurs	New Jersey Nets	4–2
2003–04	Detroit Pistons	Los Angeles Lakers	4–1
2004–05	San Antonio Spurs	Detroit Pistons	4–3

Women's National Basketball Association (WNBA) Championship

SEASON	WINNER	RUNNER-UP	RESULTS
1997	Houston Comets	New York Liberty	1–0
1998	Houston Comets	Phoenix Mercury	2–1
1999	Houston Comets	New York Liberty	2–1
2000	Houston Comets	New York Liberty	2–0
2001	Los Angeles Sparks	Charlotte Sting	2–0
2002	Los Angeles Sparks	New York Liberty	2–0
2003	Detroit Shock	Los Angeles Sparks	2–1
2004	Seattle Storm	Connecticut Sun	2–1
2005	*to be held in September*		

Division I National Collegiate Athletic Association (NCAA) Championship—Men

YEAR	WINNER	RUNNER-UP	SCORE	YEAR	WINNER	RUNNER-UP	SCORE
1939	Oregon	Ohio State	46–43	1964	UCLA	Duke	98–83
1940	Indiana	Kansas	60–42	1965	UCLA	Michigan	91–80
1941	Wisconsin	Washington State	39–34	1966	Texas Western	Kentucky	72–65
1942	Stanford	Dartmouth	53–38	1967	UCLA	Dayton	79–64
1943	Wyoming	Georgetown	46–34	1968	UCLA	North Carolina	78–55
1944	Utah	Dartmouth	42–40	1969	UCLA	Purdue	92–72
1945	Oklahoma A & M	New York	49–45	1970	UCLA	Jacksonville	80–69
1946	Oklahoma A & M	North Carolina	43–40	1971	UCLA	Villanova	68–62
1947	Holy Cross	Oklahoma	58–47	1972	UCLA	Florida State	81–76
1948	Kentucky	Baylor	58–42	1973	UCLA	Memphis State	87–66
1949	Kentucky	Oklahoma State	46–36	1974	North Carolina State	Marquette	76–64
1950	CCNY	Bradley	71–68				
1951	Kentucky	Kansas State	68–58	1975	UCLA	Kentucky	92–85
1952	Kansas	St. John's (NY)	80–63	1976	Indiana	Michigan	86–68
1953	Indiana	Kansas	69–68	1977	Marquette	North Carolina	67–59
1954	La Salle	Bradley	92–76	1978	Kentucky	Duke	94–88
1955	San Francisco	La Salle	77–63	1979	Michigan State	Indiana State	75–64
1956	San Francisco	Iowa	83–71	1980	Louisville	UCLA	59–54
1957	North Carolina	Kansas	54–53	1981	Indiana	North Carolina	63–50
1958	Kentucky	Seattle	84–72	1982	North Carolina	Georgetown	63–62
1959	California (Berkeley)	West Virginia	71–70	1983	North Carolina State	Houston	54–52
1960	Ohio State	California (Berkeley)	75–55	1984	Georgetown	Houston	84–75
				1985	Villanova	Georgetown	66–64
1961	Cincinnati	Ohio State	70–65	1986	Louisville	Duke	72–69
1962	Cincinnati	Ohio State	71–59	1987	Indiana	Syracuse	74–73
1963	Loyola (IL)	Cincinnati	60–58	1988	Kansas	Oklahoma	83–79

Division I National Collegiate Athletic Association (NCAA) Championship—Men (continued)

YEAR	WINNER	RUNNER-UP	SCORE	YEAR	WINNER	RUNNER-UP	SCORE
1989	Michigan	Seton Hall	80–79	1998	Kentucky	Utah	78–69
1990	UNLV	Duke	103–73	1999	Connecticut	Duke	77–74
1991	Duke	Kansas	72–65	2000	Michigan State	Florida	89–76
1992	Duke	Michigan	71–51	2001	Duke	Arizona	82–72
1993	North Carolina	Michigan	77–71	2002	Maryland	Indiana	64–52
1994	Arkansas	Duke	76–72	2003	Syracuse	Kansas	81–78
1995	UCLA	Arkansas	89–78	2004	Connecticut	Georgia Tech	82–73
1996	Kentucky	Syracuse	76–67	2005	North Carolina	Illinois	75–70
1997	Arizona	Kentucky	84–79				

Division I National Collegiate Athletic Association (NCAA) Championship—Women

YEAR	WINNER	RUNNER-UP	SCORE	YEAR	WINNER	RUNNER-UP	SCORE
1982	Louisiana Tech	Cheyney (PA)	76–62	1994	North Carolina	Louisiana Tech	60–59
1983	Southern California	Louisiana Tech	69–67	1995	Connecticut	Tennessee	70–64
1984	Southern California	Tennessee	72–61	1996	Tennessee	Georgia	83–65
1985	Old Dominion	Georgia	70–65	1997	Tennessee	Old Dominion	68–59
1986	Texas	Southern California	97–81	1998	Tennessee	Louisiana Tech	93–75
1987	Tennessee	Louisiana Tech	67–44	1999	Purdue	Duke	62–45
1988	Louisiana Tech	Auburn	56–54	2000	Connecticut	Tennessee	71–52
1989	Tennessee	Auburn	76–60	2001	Notre Dame	Purdue	68–66
1990	Stanford	Auburn	88–81	2002	Connecticut	Oklahoma	82–70
1991	Tennessee	Virginia	70–67	2003	Connecticut	Tennessee	73–68
1992	Stanford	Western Kentucky	78–62	2004	Connecticut	Tennessee	70–61
1993	Texas Tech	Ohio State	84–82	2005	Baylor	Michigan State	84–62

World Amateur Basketball Championship—Men

YEAR	WINNER	RUNNER-UP	YEAR	WINNER	RUNNER-UP
1936[1]	United States	Canada	1976[1]	United States	Yugoslavia
1948[1]	United States	France	1978	Yugoslavia	USSR
1950	Argentina	United States	1980[1]	Yugoslavia	Italy
1952[1]	United States	USSR	1982	USSR	United States
1954	United States	Brazil	1984[1]	United States	Spain
1956[1]	United States	USSR	1986	United States	USSR
1959	Brazil[2]	United States	1988[1]	USSR	Yugoslavia
1960[1]	United States	USSR	1990	Yugoslavia	USSR
1963	Brazil	Yugoslavia	1992[1]	United States	Croatia
1964[1]	United States	USSR	1994	United States	Russia
1967	USSR	Yugoslavia	1996[1]	United States	Yugoslavia
1968[1]	United States	Yugoslavia	1998	Yugoslavia	Russia
1970	Yugoslavia	Brazil	2000[1]	United States	France
1972[1]	USSR	United States	2002	Yugoslavia	Argentina
1974	USSR	Yugoslavia	2004[1]	Argentina	Italy

[1]Olympic championships, recognized as world championships.　　[2]By default.

World Amateur Basketball Championship—Women

YEAR	WINNER	RUNNER-UP	YEAR	WINNER	RUNNER-UP
1953	United States	Chile	1984[1]	United States	South Korea
1957	United States	USSR	1986	United States	USSR
1959	USSR	Bulgaria	1988[1]	United States	Yugoslavia
1964	USSR	Czechoslovakia	1990	United States	Yugoslavia
1967	USSR	South Korea	1992[1]	Unified Team[2]	China
1971	USSR	Czechoslovakia	1994	Brazil	China
1975	USSR	Japan	1996[1]	United States	Brazil
1976[1]	USSR	United States	1998	United States	Russia
1979	United States	South Korea	2000[1]	United States	Australia
1980[1]	USSR	Bulgaria	2002	United States	Russia
1983	USSR	United States	2004[1]	United States	Australia

[1]Olympic championships, recognized as world championships.　　[2]Athletes from the Commonwealth of Independent States plus Georgia.

Billiard Games

The game of billiards has a surprising number of **varieties** throughout the world. Factors in that variety include the number and appearance of the billiard balls, the size of the table, the existence of side and corner pockets, and the object of play. The classic form of the game—**three-cushion billiards**—is played on a pocketless table with one red ball and two white balls, one of which is marked with a spot; it is often known as French billiards, carom billiards, or (simply) billiards.

Pocket billiards, which embraces both **snooker** and the game sometimes known (for the sake of clarity) as **English billiards,** is the prevalent form of billiards in the United Kingdom. The world professional snooker championship was first held in 1927; until 1947 it was won every year by Joe Davis (championships were not held during World War II). The championship was discontinued during the 1950s, was revived during the 1960s, and became a knockout event in 1969. The results that are given in the table below begin with that year.

The American form of pocket billiards, usually known as **pool,** differs markedly from the British game. Its most popular variations are **eight-ball, nine-ball,** and **straight (or 14.1) pool.** Though earlier straight pool tournaments were held with regularity, the game is now not often played in national competition. Since the 1970s nine-ball and eight-ball pool have surpassed straight pool in popularity in the United States, and nine-ball has gained some prominence internationally. In 1990 the **World Pool-Billiard Association** (WPA; founded 1987) inaugurated the nine-ball world championship.

WPA Web site: <www.wpa-pool.com>.

World Three-Cushion Championship

Competition has been held since 1928; table shows champions for the past 20 years.

YEAR	WINNER	YEAR	WINNER	YEAR	WINNER
1986	Avelino Rico (SPA)	1994	Torbjörn Blomdahl (SWE)	2002	Marco Zanetti (ITA)
1987	Torbjörn Blomdahl (SWE)	1995	Torbjörn Blomdahl (SWE)	2003	Semih Sayginer (TUR)
1988	Torbjörn Blomdahl (SWE)	1996	Torbjörn Blomdahl (SWE)	2004	Dick Jaspers (NED)
1989	Ludo Dielis (BEL)	1997	Dick Jaspers (NED)	2005	Daniel Sánchez (ESP)
1990	Raymond Ceulemans (BEL)	1998	Torbjörn Blomdahl (SWE)	2006	*to be held 20–24 September, St. Wendel, Germany*
1991	Torbjörn Blomdahl (SWE)	1999	Dick Jaspers (NED)		
1992	Torbjörn Blomdahl (SWE)	2000	Dick Jaspers (NED)		
1993	Sang Chun Lee (USA)	2001	Raymond Ceulemans (BEL)		

World Professional Snooker Championship

Won by a British player unless otherwise noted.

YEAR	WINNER	YEAR	WINNER	YEAR	WINNER	YEAR	WINNER
1969	John Spencer	1979	Terry Griffiths	1989	Steve Davis	1998	John Higgins
1970	Ray Reardon	1980	Cliff Thorburn (CAN)	1990	Stephen Hendry	1999	Stephen Hendry
1971	John Spencer	1981	Steve Davis	1991	John Parrott	2000	Mark Williams
1972	Alex Higgins	1982	Alex Higgins	1992	Stephen Hendry	2001	Ronnie O'Sullivan
1973	Ray Reardon	1983	Steve Davis	1993	Stephen Hendry	2002	Peter Ebdon
1974	Ray Reardon	1984	Steve Davis	1994	Stephen Hendry	2003	Mark Williams
1975	Ray Reardon	1985	Dennis Taylor	1995	Stephen Hendry	2004	Ronnie O'Sullivan
1976	Ray Reardon	1986	Joe Johnson	1996	Stephen Hendry	2005	Shaun Murphy
1977	John Spencer	1987	Steve Davis	1997	Ken Doherty (IRE)		
1978	Ray Reardon	1988	Steve Davis				

WPA World Nine-Ball Championships

YEAR	MEN'S CHAMPION	WOMEN'S CHAMPION	YEAR	MEN'S CHAMPION	WOMEN'S CHAMPION
1990	Earl Strickland (USA)	Robin Bell (USA)	1998	Kunihiko Takahashi (JPN)	Allison Fisher (GBR)
1991	Earl Strickland (USA)	Robin Bell (USA)	1999	Nick Varner (USA)	Liu Shin-Mei (TPE)
1992	Johnny Archer (USA)	Franziska Stark (FRG)	2000	Chao Fong-Pang (TPE)	Julie Kelly (IRE)
1993	Chao Fong-Pang (TPE)	Loree Jon Jones (USA)	2001	Mika Immonen (FIN)	Allison Fisher (GBR)
1994	Takeshi Okumura (JPN)	Ewa Mataya-Laurance (USA)	2002	Earl Strickland (USA)	Liu Shin-Mei (TPE)
1995	Oliver Ortmann (GER)	Gerda Hofstatter (AUT)	2003	Thorsten Hohmann (GER)	*canceled*
1996	Ralf Souquet (GER)	Allison Fisher (GBR)	2004	Alex Pagulayan (CAN)	Kim Ga Young (KOR)
1997	Johnny Archer (USA)	Allison Fisher (GBR)	2005	Wu Chia-Ching (TPE)	

Bowling

The world governing body for bowling is the **Fédération Internationale des Quilleurs (FIQ)**. Since 1954 it has sponsored world bowling championships. In 1979 the FIQ discontinued the eights for men and fours for women and introduced the triples competition for men and for women.

In the **United States** men's bowling is governed by the **American Bowling Congress (ABC)**, which was founded in 1895, but became a constituent of the **United States Bowling Congress (USBC)** in 2004. In 1901 the first national championship was organized; in 1961 the yearly competition was split into two divisions—regular (for those with a combined average score of 851 or higher) and classic for professionals. The classic division was discontinued in 1980. The

Women's International Bowling Congress (WIBC) was organized in 1916 and sponsored an annual women's championship until 2004, when organizational mergers created the USBC. Competition takes place between teams, doubles, and singles. The all-events category is won by the individual who has the best score of nine games—three team, three doubles, and three singles scores. The **Professional Bowlers Association (PBA)** was established in 1958. One of its major tournaments is the annual Tournament of Champions.

Related Web sites: FIQ: <www.fiq.org>; USBC: <www.bowl.com>; PBA: <www.pba.com>.

Professional Bowlers Association (PBA) Tournament of Champions

YEAR	CHAMPION	YEAR	CHAMPION	YEAR	CHAMPION
1965	Billy Hardwick	1979	George Pappas	1993	George Branham III
1966	Wayne Zahn	1980	Wayne Webb	1994	Norm Duke
1967	Jim Stefanich	1981	Steve Cook	1995	Mike Aulby
1968	Dave Davis	1982	Mike Durbin	1996	Dave D'Entremont
1969	Jim Godman	1983	Joe Berardi	1997	John Gant
1970	Don Johnson	1984	Mike Durbin	1998	Bryan Goebel
1971	Johnny Petraglia	1985	Mark Williams	1999	Jason Couch
1972	Mike Durbin	1986	Marshall Holman	2000	Jason Couch
1973	Jim Godman	1987	Pete Weber	2001–02	*not held*
1974	Earl Anthony	1988	Mark Williams	2002–03	Jason Couch
1975	Dave Davis	1989	Del Ballard, Jr.	2003–04	Patrick Healey, Jr.
1976	Marshall Holman	1990	Dave Ferraro	2004–05	Steve Jaros
1977	Mike Berlin	1991	David Ozio		
1978	Earl Anthony	1992	Marc McDowell		

American Bowling Congress (ABC) Bowling Championships—Regular Division

The championships have been held since 1901. This table shows results for the past 20 years.

YEAR	SINGLES	SCORE	ALL-EVENTS	SCORE
1986	Jeff Mackey	774	Ed Marzka	2,116
1987	Terry Taylor	749	Ryan Shafer	2,044
1988	Steve Hutkowski	774	Rick Steelsmith	2,053
1989	Paul Tetreault	813	George Hall	2,227
1990	Robert Hochrein	791	Mike Neumann	2,168
1991	Ed Deines	826	Tom Howery	2,216
1992	Gary Blatchford & Bob Youker, Jr. (tied)	801	Mike Tucker	2,158
1993	Dan Bock	798	Jeff Nimke	2,254
1994	John Weltzien	810	Thomas Holt	2,190
1995	Matt Surina	826	Jeff Kwiatkowski	2,191
1996	Don Scudder, Jr.	823	Scott Kurtz	2,224
1997	John Socha	847	Jeff Richgels	2,241
1998	John Gaines	814	Chris Barnes	2,151
1999	Dan Winter	825	Thomas Jones	2,158
2000	Garran Hein	811	Roy Daniels	2,181
2001	Nicholas Hoagland	798	D.J. Archer	2,219
2002	Mark Millsap	823	Stephen A. Hardy	2,279
2003	Ron Bahr	837	Steve Kloempken	2,215
2004	John Janawicz	858	John Janawicz	2,224
2005	David Adam	791	Scott Craddock	2,131

Women's International Bowling Congress (WIBC) Bowling Championships—Classic Division

The championships have been held since 1916. The table shows results for the past 20 years.

YEAR	SINGLES	SCORE	ALL-EVENTS	SCORE
1986	Dana Stewart	698	Robin Romeo & Maria Lewis (tied)	1,877
1987	Regi Jonak	728	Leanne Barrette	1,972
1988	Michelle Meyer-Welty	690	Lisa Wagner	1,988

Women's International Bowling Congress (WIBC) Bowling Championships—Classic Division (continued)

YEAR	SINGLES	SCORE	ALL-EVENTS	SCORE
1989	Laura Anderson	683	Nancy Fehr	1,911
1990	Paula Carter & Dana Miller-Mackie (tied)	705	Carol Norman	1,984
1991	Debbie Kuhn	773	Debbie Kuhn	2,036
1992	Patty Ann	680	Mitsuko Tokimoto (JPN)	1,928
1993	Karen Collura (CAN) & Kari Murph (tied)	747	Anne Marie Duggan	1,990
1994	Vicki Fifield	716	Wendy Macpherson-Papanos	1,940
1995	Beth Owen	749	Beth Owen	1,983
1996	Cindy Berlanga	723	Lorrie Nichols	1,985
1997	Jan Schmidt	765	Kendra Cameron	2,039
1998	Nellie Glandon	714	Liz Johnson	1,989
1999	Nikki Gianulias	746	Hidemi Mizobuchi	2,065
2000	Cathy Krasner	729	Carolyn Dorin-Ballard	2,147
2001	Lisa Wagner	756	Jonquay Armon	2,044
2002	Theresa Smith	752	Cara Honeychurch	2,150
2003	Michelle Feldman	764	Michelle Feldman	2,048
2004	Sharon Smith	754	Kim Adler	2,133
2005	Leanne Barrette	774	Leanne Barrette	2,231

World Tenpin Bowling Championships—Men

In 1979 the singles category was added; previously, the masters had been the only individual event. Also in that year, eights were discontinued and triples were introduced.

YEAR	SINGLES	MASTERS	PAIRS	TRIPLES	FIVES	EIGHTS
1954		Gösta Algeskog (SWE)	FIN		SWE	SWE
1955		Nisse Backstrom (SWE)	SWE		FRG	FIN
1958		Kalle Asukas (FIN)	SWE		FIN	SWE
1960		Tito Reynolds (MEX)	MEX		VEN	MEX
1963		Les Zikes (USA)	USA		USA	USA
1967		David Pond (GBR)	GBR		FIN	USA
1971		Ed Luther (USA)	PUR		USA	USA
1975		Bud Stoudt (USA)	GBR		FIN	FRG
1979	Ollie Ongtawco (PHI)	Gary Bugden (GBR)	AUS	MAS	AUS	
1983	Armando Marino (COL)	Tony Cariello (USA)	AUS	SWE	FIN	
1987	Patrick Rolland (FRA)	Roger Pieters (BEL)	SWE	USA	SWE	
1991	Ying Chieh Ma (TAI)	Mika Koivuniemi (FIN)	USA	USA	TAI	
1995	Marc Doi (CAN)	Chen-Min Yang (TPE)	SWE	NED	NED	
1999	Gery Verbruggen (BEL)	Ahmed Shaheen (QAT)	SWE	FIN	SWE	
2003	Mika Luoto (FIN)	Michael Little (AUS)	SWE	USA	SWE	

World Tenpin Bowling Championships—Women

In 1963 fives was played as a four-woman team, European style (either the entire game on one lane or half of game on one lane, balance on accompanying lane). In 1979 fours were discontinued altogether and triples were introduced. Also in that year, the singles category was added; previously, the masters had been the only individual event.

YEAR	SINGLES	MASTERS	PAIRS	TRIPLES	FOURS	FIVES
1963		Helen Shablis (USA)	USA		MEX	USA
1967		Helen Weston (USA)	MEX		FIN	FIN
1971		Ashie Gonzalez (PUR)	JPN		USA	USA
1975		Anne Haefker (FRG)	SWE		JPN	JPN
1979	Lita de la Rosa (PHI)	Lita de la Rosa (PHI)	PHI	USA		USA
1983	Lena Sulkanen (SWE)	Lena Sulkanen (SWE)	DEN	FRG		SWE
1987	Edda Piccini (MEX)	Annette Hägre (SWE)	USA	USA		USA
1991	Martina Beckel (GER)	Catherine Willis (CAN)	JPN	CAN		KOR
1995	Debby Ship (CAN)	Celia Flores (MEX)	THA	AUS		FIN
1999	Kelly Kulick (USA)	Ann-Maree Putney (AUS)	AUS	KOR		KOR
2003	Zara Glover (GBR)	Diandra Hyman (USA)	GBR	PHI		MAS

Boxing

Modern boxing is dated to about the 1880s, when the **Marquess of Queensberry**'s rules (or rules derived from them) became more or less standard. John L. Sullivan (USA) was the last of the **bare-knuckles** heavyweight champions and one of the first recognized champions to fight by the "new" rules. Despite an early trend toward some kind of organization, there is no single recognized world governing body in professional boxing. Europe, the Commonwealth, and Great Britain—not to mention a number of Asian boxing federations—all have championships. The **World Boxing Association (WBA)**, formed under a different name in 1920, is basically an American organization, though its headquarters are currently in Venezuela. It was once the largely undisputed governing body for the Americas. Since 1963 it has had some competition from the **World Boxing Council (WBC)**, which includes British and European countries as well as Latin American and Asian countries. In 1983 another organization, the **International Boxing Federation** (IBF; called the United States Boxing Association International from 1983 to 1984), was born of dissatisfaction with the WBA and the WBC. Other federations, such as the World Boxing Organization (WBO; formed in 1988), have not received international recognition.

The tables below contain the names of the **undisputed champions** in each weight class, their nationalities, and the dates of title bouts when titles changed hands, followed by the champions recognized by the three sanctioning bodies. Each organization (or sanctioning body) ranks boxers according to its own criteria and sanctions fights according to its own rules. Only a ranked boxer who wins a sanctioned fight is recognized as champion. Unless otherwise indicated, a champion retains his title until he is defeated. In the early 1990s the WBA, WBC, and IBF all recognized 17 weight divisions. In the tables below, the primary name given for each division is that used by the WBA. If a different name is used by the WBC or the IBF, or by both, that name is given as an alternate.

Related Web sites: WBA: <www.wbaonline.com>; WBC: <www.wbcboxing.com>; IBF-USBA: <www.ibf-usba-boxing.com>.

World Heavyweight Champions
No weight limit.

CHAMPION (NATIONALITY)	DATE OF TITLE
Undisputed champions	
John L. Sullivan (USA)	29 Aug 1885
James J. Corbett (USA)	7 Sep 1892
Bob Fitzsimmons (USA—formerly a British subject)	17 Mar 1897
James J. Jeffries (USA) retired in 1905	9 Jun 1899
Marvin Hart (USA)	3 Jul 1905
Tommy Burns (CAN)	23 Feb 1906
Jack Johnson (USA)	26 Dec 1908
Jess Willard (USA)	5 Apr 1915
Jack Dempsey (USA)	4 Jul 1919
Gene Tunney (USA) retired in 1928	23 Sep 1926
Max Schmeling (GER)	12 Jun 1930
Jack Sharkey (USA)	21 Jun 1932
Primo Carnera (ITA)	29 Jun 1933
Max Baer (USA)	14 Jun 1934
James J. Braddock (USA)	13 Jun 1935
Joe Louis (USA) retired in 1949	22 Jun 1937
Ezzard Charles (USA)	27 Sep 1950
Jersey Joe Walcott (USA)	18 Jul 1951
Rocky Marciano (USA)	23 Sep 1952
Floyd Patterson (USA)	30 Nov 1956
Ingemar Johansson (SWE)	26 Jun 1959
Floyd Patterson (USA)	20 Jun 1960
Sonny Liston (USA)	25 Sep 1962
Cassius Clay (later Muhammad Ali) (USA) stripped of WBA title in 1965; stripped of WBC title in 1967; title in dispute	25 Feb 1964
WBA	
Ernest Terrell (USA) defeated by Ali 6 Feb 1967; gave up title	5 Mar 1965
Jimmy Ellis (USA)	27 Apr 1968
Joe Frazier (USA)	16 Feb 1970
George Foreman (USA)	22 Jan 1973

CHAMPION (NATIONALITY)	DATE OF TITLE
WBA (continued)	
Muhammad Ali (USA)	30 Oct 1974
Leon Spinks (USA)	15 Feb 1978
Muhammad Ali (USA) retired in 1979	15 Sep 1978
John Tate (USA)	20 Oct 1979
Mike Weaver (USA)	21 Mar 1980
Michael Dokes (USA)	10 Dec 1982
Gerrie Coetzee (RSA)	23 Sep 1983
Greg Page (USA)	1 Dec 1984
Tony Tubbs (USA)	29 Apr 1985
Tim Witherspoon (USA)	17 Jan 1986
James Smith (USA)	12 Dec 1986
Mike Tyson (USA)	7 Mar 1987
James Douglas (USA)	11 Feb 1990
Evander Holyfield (USA)	26 Oct 1990
Riddick Bowe (USA)	13 Nov 1992
Evander Holyfield (USA)	6 Nov 1993
Michael Moorer (USA)	22 Apr 1994
George Foreman (USA) stripped of title in 1995	5 Nov 1994
Bruce Seldon (USA)	8 Apr 1995
Mike Tyson (USA)	7 Sep 1996
Evander Holyfield (USA)	9 Nov 1996
Lennox Lewis (GBR) stripped of title in 2000	13 Nov 1999
Evander Holyfield (USA)	12 Aug 2000
John Ruiz (PUR)	3 Mar 2001
Roy Jones, Jr. (USA)	1 Mar 2003
John Ruiz (USA)	13 Dec 2003
WBC	
Joe Frazier (USA)	16 Feb 1970
George Foreman (USA)	22 Jan 1973
Muhammad Ali (USA) stripped of title in 1978	30 Oct 1974
Ken Norton (USA)	18 Mar 1978
Larry Holmes (USA) gave up title in 1983	9 Jun 1978
Tim Witherspoon (USA)	9 Mar 1984

World Heavyweight Champions (continued)

CHAMPION (NATIONALITY)	DATE OF TITLE	CHAMPION (NATIONALITY)	DATE OF TITLE
WBC (continued)		**IBF (continued)**	
Pinklon Thomas (USA)	31 Aug 1984	Michael Spinks (USA)	21 Sep 1985
Trevor Berbick (CAN)	22 Mar 1986	stripped of title in 1987	
Mike Tyson (USA)	22 Nov 1986	Tony Tucker (USA)	30 May 1987
James Douglas (USA)	11 Feb 1990	Mike Tyson (USA)	1 Aug 1987
Evander Holyfield (USA)	26 Oct 1990	James Douglas (USA)	11 Feb 1990
Riddick Bowe (USA)	13 Nov 1992	Evander Holyfield (USA)	25 Oct 1990
stripped of title in 1992		Riddick Bowe (USA)	13 Nov 1992
Lennox Lewis (GBR)	14 Dec 1992	Evander Holyfield (USA)	6 Nov 1993
Oliver McCall (USA)	24 Sep 1994	Michael Moorer (USA)	22 Apr 1994
Frank Bruno (GBR)	2 Sep 1995	George Foreman (USA)	5 Nov 1994
Mike Tyson (USA)	16 Mar 1996	gave up title in 1995	
gave up title in 1996		François Botha (RSA)	9 Dec 1995
Lennox Lewis (GBR)	7 Feb 1997	stripped of title in 1996	
Hasim Rahman (USA)	22 Apr 2001	Michael Moorer (USA)	22 Jun 1996
Lennox Lewis (GBR)	17 Nov 2001	Evander Holyfield (USA)	8 Nov 1997
gave up title in 2004		Lennox Lewis (GBR)	13 Nov 1999
Vitali Klitschko (UKR)	24 Apr 2004	Hasim Rahman (USA)	22 Apr 2001
		Lennox Lewis (GBR)	17 Nov 2001
IBF		gave up title in 2002	
Larry Holmes (USA)	25 Nov 1983	Chris Byrd (USA)	14 Dec 2002
recognized as champion in 1983			

World Cruiserweight Champions

Top weight 195 pounds; until 1982 not over 182 pounds. Division first recognized by WBA in 1982.

CHAMPION (NATIONALITY)	DATE OF TITLE	CHAMPION (NATIONALITY)	DATE OF TITLE
WBA		**WBC (continued)**	
Ossie Ocasio (PUR)	13 Feb 1982	Anaclet Wamba (FRA)	20 Jul 1991
Piet Crous (RSA)	1 Dec 1984	Marcelo Domínguez (ARG)	19 Apr 1996
Dwight Muhammad Qawi (USA)	27 Jul 1985	Juan Carlos Gómez (GER—formerly	21 Feb 1998
Evander Holyfield (USA)	12 Jul 1986	a Cuban citizen)	
gave up title in 1988		gave up title in 2000	
Taoufik Belbouli (FRA)	25 Mar 1989	Wayne Braithwaite (GUY)	11 Oct 2002
declared vacant in 1989		Jean-Marc Mormeck (FRA)	2 Apr 2005
Robert Daniels (USA)	28 Nov 1989		
Bobby Czyz (USA)	8 Mar 1991	**IBF**	
vacant		Marvin Camel (USA)	13 Dec 1983
Orlin Norris (USA)	6 Nov 1993	Lee Roy Murphy (USA)	6 Oct 1984
Nate Miller (USA)	22 Jul 1995	Rickey Parkey (USA)	25 Oct 1986
Fabrice Tiozzo (FRA)	8 Nov 1997	Evander Holyfield (USA)	15 May 1987
Virgil Hill (USA)	9 Dec 2000	Glenn McCrory (GBR)	3 Jun 1989
Jean-Marc Mormeck (FRA)	22 Feb 2002	Jeff Lampkin (USA)	22 Mar 1990
		gave up title in 1991	
WBC		James Warring (USA)	7 Sep 1991
Marvin Camel (USA)	31 Mar 1980	Alfred Cole (USA)	30 Jul 1992
Carlos de León (PUR)	25 Nov 1980	gave up title in 1996	
S.T. Gordon (USA)	27 Jun 1982	Adolpho Washington (USA)	31 Aug 1996
Carlos de León (PUR)	17 Jul 1983	Uriah Grant (USA)	21 Jun 1997
Alfonso Ratliff (USA)	6 Jun 1985	Imamu Mayfield (USA)	8 Nov 1997
Bernard Benton (USA)	21 Sep 1985	Arthur Williams (USA)	30 Oct 1998
Carlos de León (PUR)	22 Mar 1986	Vassily Jirov (KAZ)	5 Jun 1999
Evander Holyfield (USA)	9 Apr 1988	James Toney (USA)	26 Apr 2003
gave up title in 1988		Kelvin Davis (USA)	1 May 2004
Carlos de León (PUR)	17 May 1989	stripped of title in 2005	
Massimiliano Duran (ITA)	27 Jul 1990	O'Neil Bell (USA)	20 May 2005

World Light Heavyweight Champions

Top weight 175 pounds.

CHAMPION (NATIONALITY)	DATE OF TITLE	CHAMPION (NATIONALITY)	DATE OF TITLE
Undisputed champions		**Undisputed champions (continued)**	
Jack Root (AUT)	22 Apr 1903	Philadelphia Jack O'Brien (USA)	20 Dec 1905
George Gardner (IRE)	4 Jul 1903	retired in 1912	
Bob Fitzsimmons (USA—formerly a	25 Nov 1903	Jack Dillon (USA)	28 Apr 1914
British subject)		Battling Levinsky (USA)	24 Oct 1916

World Light Heavyweight Champions (continued)

Top weight 175 pounds.

CHAMPION (NATIONALITY)	DATE OF TITLE	CHAMPION (NATIONALITY)	DATE OF TITLE
Undisputed champions (continued)		**WBC**	
Georges Carpentier (FRA)	12 Oct 1920	Bob Foster (USA)	24 May 1968
Battling Siki (Louis Phal) (SEN)	24 Sep 1922	retired in 1974	
Mike McTigue (IRE)	17 Mar 1923	John Conteh (GBR)	1 Oct 1974
Paul Berlenbach (USA)	30 May 1925	stripped of title in 1977	
Jack Delaney (CAN)	16 Jul 1926	Miguel Cuello (ARG)	21 May 1977
gave up title in 1927		Mate Parlov (YUG)	7 Jan 1978
Tommy Loughran (USA)	12 Dec 1927	Marvin Johnson (USA)	2 Dec 1978
gave up title in 1929		Matthew Franklin (later Matthew	22 Apr 1979
Maxie Rosenbloom (USA)	14 Jul 1932	Saad Muhammad) (USA)	
Bob Olin (USA)	16 Nov 1934	Dwight Braxton (later Dwight	19 Dec 1981
John Henry Lewis (USA)	31 Oct 1935	Muhammad Qawi) (USA)	
retired in 1939		Michael Spinks (USA)	18 Mar 1983
Melio Bettina (USA)	3 Feb 1939	gave up title in 1985	
Billy Conn (USA)	13 Jul 1939	J.B. Williamson (USA)	10 Dec 1985
gave up title in 1941		Dennis Andries (GBR)	30 Apr 1986
Gus Lesnevich (USA)	14 May 1946	Thomas Hearns (USA)	7 Mar 1987
Freddie Mills (GBR)	26 Jul 1948	gave up title in 1987	
Joey Maxim (CAN)	24 Jan 1950	Don Lalonde (CAN)	27 Nov 1987
Archie Moore (USA)	17 Dec 1952	Sugar Ray Leonard (USA)	7 Nov 1988
stripped of title in 1962		gave up title in 1988	
Harold Johnson (USA)	12 May 1962	Dennis Andries (GBR)	2 Feb 1989
Willie Pastrano (USA)	1 Jun 1963	Jeff Harding (AUS)	24 Jun 1989
José Torres (PUR)	30 Mar 1965	Dennis Andries (GBR)	28 Jul 1990
Dick Tiger (NGR)	16 Dec 1966	Jeff Harding (AUS)	11 Sep 1991
Bob Foster (USA)	24 May 1968	Mike McCallum (JAM)	23 Jul 1994
stripped of WBA title in 1970		Fabrice Tiozzo (FRA)	16 Jun 1995
		Roy Jones, Jr. (USA)	23 Nov 1996
WBA		Montell Griffin (USA)	21 Mar 1997
Vicente Rondon (VEN)	27 Feb 1971	Roy Jones, Jr. (USA)	7 Aug 1997
Bob Foster (USA)	7 Apr 1972	gave up title in 2003	
retired in 1974		Antonio Tarver (USA)	26 Apr 2003
Víctor Galíndez (ARG)	7 Dec 1974	Roy Jones, Jr. (USA)	8 Nov 2003
Mike Rossman (USA)	15 Sep 1978	Antonio Tarver (USA)	15 May 2004
Víctor Galíndez (ARG)	14 Apr 1979	gave up title in 2004	
Marvin Johnson (USA)	30 Nov 1979	Tomasz Adamek (POL)	21 May 2005
Eddie Gregory (later Eddie	31 Mar 1980		
Mustafa Muhammad) (USA)		**IBF**	
Michael Spinks (USA)	18 Jul 1981	Slobodan Kacar (YUG)	21 Dec 1985
gave up title in 1985		Bobby Czyz (USA)	6 Sep 1986
Marvin Johnson (USA)	9 Feb 1986	Charles Williams (USA)	29 Oct 1987
Leslie Stewart (TRI)	23 May 1987	Henry Maske (GER)	20 Mar 1993
Virgil Hill (USA)	5 Sep 1987	Virgil Hill (USA)	23 Nov 1996
Thomas Hearns (USA)	3 Jun 1991	Dariusz Michalczewski (GER)	13 Jun 1997
Iran Barkley (USA)	21 Mar 1992	gave up title in 1997	
gave up title in 1992		William Guthrie (USA)	19 Jul 1997
Virgil Hill (USA)	29 Sep 1992	Reggie Johnson (USA)	6 Feb 1998
Dariusz Michalczewski (GER)	13 Jun 1997	Roy Jones, Jr. (USA)	5 Jun 1999
stripped of title in 1997		stripped of title in 2002	
Lou Del Valle (USA)	20 Sep 1997	Antonio Tarver (USA)	26 Apr 2003
Roy Jones, Jr. (USA)	18 Jul 1998	Glencoffe Johnson (USA)	6 Feb 2004
gave up title in 2002		gave up title in 2004	
Mehdi Sahnoune (FRA)	8 Mar 2003	Clinton Woods (GBR)	4 Mar 2005
Silvio Branco (ITA)	10 Oct 2003		
Fabrice Tiozzo (FRA)	20 Mar 2004		

World Super Middleweight Champions

Top weight 168 pounds. Super middleweight division first recognized by WBA in 1987 and by WBC in 1988.

CHAMPION (NATIONALITY)	DATE OF TITLE	CHAMPION (NATIONALITY)	DATE OF TITLE
WBA		**WBA (continued)**	
Park Chong-Pal (KOR)	6 Dec 1987	Christophe Tiozzo (FRA)	30 Mar 1990
Fulgencio Obelmejias (VEN)	23 May 1988	Víctor Córdoba (PAN)	5 Apr 1991
Baek In-chul (KOR)	27 May 1989	Michael Nunn (USA)	12 Sep 1992

World Super Middleweight Champions (continued)

CHAMPION (NATIONALITY)	DATE OF TITLE	CHAMPION (NATIONALITY)	DATE OF TITLE
WBA (continued)		**WBC (continued)**	
Steve Little (USA)	26 Feb 1994	Dingaan Thobela (RSA)	1 Sep 2000
Frank Liles (USA)	12 Aug 1994	Davey Hilton (CAN)	15 Dec 2000
Byron Mitchell (USA)	12 Jun 1999	stripped of title in 2001	
Bruno Girard (FRA)	8 Apr 2000	Eric Lucas (CAN)	10 Jul 2001
stripped of title in 2001		Markus Beyer (GER)	5 Apr 2003
Byron Mitchell (USA)	3 Mar 2001	Cristian Sanavia (ITA)	5 Jun 2004
Sven Ottke (GER)	15 Mar 2003	Markus Beyer (GER)	9 Oct 2004
gave up title in 2004			
Anthony Mundine (AUS)	3 Sep 2003	**IBF**	
Manny Siaca (PUR)	5 May 2004	Murray Sutherland (GBR)	28 Mar 1984
Mikkel Kessler (DEN)	12 Nov 2004	Park Chong-Pal (KOR)	22 Jul 1984
		gave up title in 1987	
WBC		Graciano Rocchigiani (GER)	12 Mar 1988
Sugar Ray Leonard (USA)	7 Nov 1988	gave up title in 1989	
gave up title in 1990		Lindell Holmes (USA)	27 Jan 1990
Mauro Galvano (ITA)	15 Dec 1990	Darrin Van Horn (USA)	18 May 1991
Nigel Benn (GBR)	3 Oct 1992	Iran Barkley (USA)	10 Jan 1992
Thulane Malinga (RSA)	2 Mar 1996	James Toney (USA)	13 Feb 1993
Vincenzo Nardiello (ITA)	6 Jul 1996	Roy Jones, Jr. (USA)	18 Nov 1994
Robin Reid (GBR)	12 Oct 1996	gave up title in 1997	
Thulane Malinga (RSA)	19 Dec 1997	Charles Brewer (USA)	21 Jun 1997
Richie Woodhall (GBR)	27 Mar 1998	Sven Ottke (GER)	24 Oct 1998
Markus Beyer (GER)	23 Oct 1999	gave up title in 2004	
Glenn Catley (GBR)	6 May 2000	Jeff Lacy (USA)	2 Oct 2004

World Middleweight Champions

Top weight 160 pounds; until 1915 not over 158 pounds.

CHAMPION (NATIONALITY)	DATE OF TITLE	CHAMPION (NATIONALITY)	DATE OF TITLE
Undisputed champions		**Undisputed champions (continued)**	
Jack ("the Nonpareil") Dempsey (USA)	30 Jul 1884	Dick Tiger (Richard Ihetu) (NGR)	10 Aug 1963
Bob Fitzsimmons (GBR—later	14 Jan 1891	Joey Giardello (USA)	7 Dec 1963
became US citizen)		Dick Tiger (NGR)	21 Oct 1965
gave up title in 1895		Emile Griffith (USA)	25 Apr 1966
Tommy Ryan (USA)	24 Oct 1898	Nino Benvenuti (ITA)	17 Apr 1967
retired in 1907		Emile Griffith (USA)	29 Sep 1967
Stanley Ketchel (USA)	9 May 1908	Nino Benvenuti (ITA)	4 Mar 1968
Billy Papke (USA)	7 Sep 1908	Carlos Monzón (ARG)	7 Nov 1970
Stanley Ketchel (USA)	26 Nov 1908	stripped of WBC title in 1974	
died in 1910			
George Chip (USA)	11 Oct 1913	**WBA**	
Al McCoy (USA)	6 Apr 1914	Carlos Monzón (ARG)	5 Oct 1974
Mike O'Dowd (USA)	14 Nov 1917	gave up title in 1977	
Johnny Wilson (USA)	6 May 1920	Rodrigo Valdés (COL)	5 Nov 1977
Harry Greb (USA)	31 Aug 1923	Hugo Corro (ARG)	22 Apr 1978
Tiger Flowers (USA)	26 Feb 1926	Vito Antuofermo (ITA)	30 Jun 1979
Mickey Walker (USA)	3 Dec 1926	Alan Minter (GBR)	16 Mar 1980
gave up title in 1931;		Marvin Hagler (USA)	27 Sep 1980
title in dispute		stripped of title in 1987	
Tony Zale (USA)	28 Nov 1941	Sumbu Kalambay (ITA)	23 Oct 1987
Rocky Graziano (USA)	16 Jul 1947	stripped of title in 1989	
Tony Zale (USA)	10 Jun 1948	Mike McCallum (JAM)	13 May 1989
Marcel Cerdan (FRA)	21 Sep 1948	stripped of title in 1991	
Jake La Motta (USA)	16 Jun 1949	Reggie Johnson (USA)	22 Apr 1992
Sugar Ray Robinson (USA)	14 Feb 1951	John David Jackson (USA)	2 Oct 1993
Randy Turpin (GBR)	10 Jul 1951	stripped of title in 1994	
Sugar Ray Robinson (USA)	12 Sep 1951	Jorge Castro (ARG)	12 Aug 1994
retired 1952–54		Shinji Takehara (JPN)	19 Dec 1995
Carl Olson (USA)	21 Oct 1953	William Joppy (USA)	24 Jun 1996
Sugar Ray Robinson (USA)	9 Dec 1955	Julio César Green (DOM)	23 Aug 1997
Gene Fullmer (USA)	2 Jan 1957	William Joppy (USA)	31 Jan 1998
Sugar Ray Robinson (USA)	1 May 1957	Félix Trinidad (PUR)	12 May 2001
Carmen Basilio (USA)	23 Sep 1957	Bernard Hopkins (USA)	29 Sep 2001
Sugar Ray Robinson (USA)	25 Mar 1958	William Joppy (USA)	17 Nov 2001
stripped of National Boxing Association		Bernard Hopkins (USA)	13 Dec 2003
(later WBA) title in 1959		declared undisputed champion	

World Middleweight Champions (continued)

CHAMPION (NATIONALITY)	DATE OF TITLE
WBA (continued)	
Maselino Masoe (NZL)	1 May 2004
Jermain Taylor (USA)	16 Jul 2005
declared undisputed champion	
WBC	
Rodrigo Valdés (COL)	24 May 1974
Carlos Monzón (ARG)	26 Jun 1976
gave up title in 1977	
Rodrigo Valdés (COL)	5 Nov 1977
Hugo Corro (ARG)	22 Apr 1978
Vito Antuofermo (ITA)	30 Jun 1979
Alan Minter (GBR)	16 Mar 1980
Marvin Hagler (USA)	27 Sep 1980
Sugar Ray Leonard (USA)	6 Apr 1987
gave up title in 1987	
Thomas Hearns (USA)	29 Oct 1987
Iran Barkley (USA)	6 Jun 1988
Roberto Durán (PAN)	24 Feb 1989
stripped of title in 1990	
Julian Jackson (USA)	24 Nov 1990
Gerald McClellan (USA)	8 May 1993

CHAMPION (NATIONALITY)	DATE OF TITLE
WBC (continued)	
vacant	
Julian Jackson (USA)	17 Mar 1995
Quincy Taylor (USA)	19 Aug 1995
Keith Holmes (USA)	16 Mar 1996
Hassine Cherifi (FRA)	2 May 1998
Keith Holmes (USA)	24 Apr 1999
Bernard Hopkins (USA)	14 Apr 2001
Jermain Taylor (USA)	16 Jul 2005
IBF	
Marvin Hagler (USA)	27 May 1983
relinquished title in 1987	
Frank Tate (USA)	10 Oct 1987
Michael Nunn (USA)	28 Jul 1988
James Toney (USA)	10 May 1991
gave up title in 1993	
Roy Jones, Jr. (USA)	22 May 1993
gave up title in 1994	
Bernard Hopkins (USA)	29 Apr 1995
Jermain Taylor (USA)	16 Jul 2005

World Super Welterweight Champions

Top weight 154 pounds. Also called junior middleweight.

CHAMPION (NATIONALITY)	DATE OF TITLE
WBA	
Dennis Moyer (USA)	20 Oct 1962
Ralph Dupas (USA)	29 Apr 1963
Sandro Mazzinghi (ITA)	7 Sep 1963
Nino Benvenuti (ITA)	18 Jun 1965
Kim Ki Soo (KOR)	25 Jun 1966
Sandro Mazzinghi (ITA)	25 May 1968
stripped of title in 1969	
Freddie Little (USA)	17 Mar 1969
Carmelo Bossi (ITA)	9 Jul 1970
Koichi Wajima (JPN)	31 Oct 1971
Oscar Albarado (USA)	3 Jun 1974
Koichi Wajima (JPN)	21 Jan 1975
Yuh Jae Do (KOR)	7 Jun 1975
Koichi Wajima (JPN)	17 Feb 1976
José Durán (ESP)	18 May 1976
Miguel Castellini (ARG)	8 Oct 1976
Eddie Gazo (NCA)	5 Mar 1977
Kudo Masashi (JPN)	9 Aug 1978
Ayub Kalule (DEN)	24 Oct 1979
Sugar Ray Leonard (USA)	25 Jun 1981
gave up title in 1981	
Tadashi Mihara (JPN)	7 Nov 1981
Davey Moore (USA)	2 Feb 1982
Roberto Durán (PAN)	16 Jun 1983
gave up title in 1984	
Mike McCallum (JAM)	19 Oct 1984
gave up title in 1987	
Julian Jackson (USA)	21 Nov 1987
gave up title in 1990	
Gilbert Dele (FRA)	23 Feb 1991
Vinny Pazienza (USA)	11 Oct 1991
gave up title in 1992	
Julio César Vásquez (ARG)	22 Dec 1992
Pernell Whitaker (USA)	4 Mar 1995
gave up title in 1995	
Carl Daniels (USA)	16 Jun 1995
Julio César Vásquez (ARG)	16 Dec 1995
Laurent Boudouani (FRA)	21 Aug 1996
David Reid (USA)	6 Mar 1999

CHAMPION (NATIONALITY)	DATE OF TITLE
WBA (continued)	
Félix Trinidad (PUR)	3 Mar 2000
gave up title in 2001	
Fernando Vargas (USA)	22 Sep 2001
Oscar de la Hoya (USA)	14 Sep 2002
Shane Mosley (USA)	13 Sep 2003
Travis Simms (USA)	13 Dec 2003
Ronald ("Winky") Wright (USA)	13 Mar 2004
gave up title in 2004	
Alejandro ("Terra") García (MEX)	21 May 2005
WBC	
Miguel de Oliveira (BRA)	7 May 1975
Elisha Obed (BAH)	13 Nov 1975
Eckhard Dagge (FRG)	18 Jun 1976
Rocco Mattioli (ITA)	6 Aug 1977
Maurice Hope (GBR)	4 Mar 1979
Wilfred Benítez (PUR)	3 May 1981
Thomas Hearns (USA)	3 Dec 1982
gave up title in 1986	
Duane Thomas (USA)	5 Dec 1986
Lupe Aquino (MEX)	12 Jul 1987
Gianfranco Rosi (ITA)	2 Oct 1987
Donald Curry (USA)	8 Jul 1988
René Jacquot (FRA)	11 Feb 1989
John Mugabi (UGA)	8 Jul 1989
Terry Norris (USA)	31 Mar 1990
Simon Brown (USA)	18 Dec 1993
Terry Norris (USA)	7 May 1994
Luis Santana (DOM)	12 Nov 1994
Terry Norris (USA)	19 Aug 1995
Keith Mullings (USA)	6 Dec 1997
Javier Castillejo (ESP)	29 Jan 1999
Oscar de la Hoya (USA)	23 Jun 2001
Shane Mosley (USA)	13 Sep 2003
Ronald ("Winky") Wright (USA)	13 Mar 2004
gave up title in 2004	
IBF	
Mark Medal (USA)	11 Mar 1984

World Super Welterweight Champions (continued)

CHAMPION (NATIONALITY)	DATE OF TITLE	CHAMPION (NATIONALITY)	DATE OF TITLE
IBF (continued)		**IBF (continued)**	
Carlos Santos (PUR)	2 Nov 1984	Raul Marquez (USA)	12 Apr 1997
Buster Drayton (USA)	4 Jun 1986	Yory Boy Campas (MEX)	6 Dec 1997
Matthew Hilton (CAN)	27 Jun 1987	Fernando Vargas (USA)	12 Dec 1998
Robert Hines (USA)	4 Nov 1988	Félix Trinidad (PUR)	2 Dec 2000
Darrin Van Horn (USA)	4 Feb 1989	gave up title in 2001	
Gianfranco Rosi (ITA)	16 Jul 1989	Ronald ("Winky") Wright (USA)	12 Oct 2001
Vincent Pettway (USA)	17 Sep 1994	stripped of title in 2004	
Paul Vaden (USA)	12 Aug 1995	Verno Phillips (USA)	5 Jun 2004
Terry Norris (USA)	16 Dec 1995	Kasim Ouma (USA)	2 Oct 2004
gave up title in 1997		Roman Karmazin (RUS)	14 Jul 2005

World Welterweight Champions

Top weight 147 pounds; until about 1909 not over 145 pounds.

CHAMPION (NATIONALITY)	DATE OF TITLE	CHAMPION (NATIONALITY)	DATE OF TITLE
Undisputed champions		**Undisputed champions (continued)**	
Paddy Duffy (USA)	30 Oct 1888	Benny ("Kid") Paret (CUB)	3 Sep 1961
died in 1890		Emile Griffith (USA)	24 Mar 1962
Mysterious Billy Smith (USA)	14 Dec 1892	Luis Rodríguez (CUB)	21 Mar 1963
Tommy Ryan (USA)	26 Jul 1894	Emile Griffith (USA)	8 Jun 1963
gave up title in 1898		gave up title in 1966	
Mysterious Billy Smith (USA)	25 Aug 1898	Curtis Cokes (USA)	28 Nov 1966
Jim ("Rube") Ferns (USA)	15 Jan 1900	José Nápoles (MEX)	18 Apr 1969
Matty Matthews (USA)	16 Oct 1900	Billy Backus (USA)	3 Dec 1970
Jim ("Rube") Ferns (USA)	24 May 1901	José Nápoles (MEX)	4 Jun 1971
Joe Walcott (BAR)	18 Dec 1901	stripped of WBA title in 1975	
title in dispute from 1904		Cory Spinks (USA)	13 Dec 2003
Ted ("Kid") Lewis (GBR)	31 Aug 1915	Zab Judah (USA)	5 Feb 2005
Jack Britton (USA)	24 Apr 1916		
Ted ("Kid") Lewis (GBR)	25 Jun 1917	**WBA**	
Jack Britton (USA)	17 Mar 1919	Ángel Espada (PUR)	28 Jun 1975
Mickey Walker (USA)	1 Nov 1922	Pipino Cuevas (MEX)	17 Jul 1976
Pete Latzo (USA)	20 May 1926	Thomas Hearns (USA)	2 Aug 1980
Joe Dundee (USA)	3 Jun 1927	Sugar Ray Leonard (USA)	16 Sep 1981
stripped of National Boxing Association		retired in 1982	
(later WBA) title in 1928		Donald Curry (USA)	13 Feb 1983
Jackie Fields (USA)	25 Jul 1929	Lloyd Honeyghan (GBR)	27 Sep 1986
Young Jack Thompson (USA)	9 May 1930	gave up title in 1986	
Tommy Freeman (USA)	5 Sep 1930	Mark Breland (USA)	6 Feb 1987
Young Jack Thompson (USA)	14 Apr 1931	Marlon Starling (USA)	22 Aug 1987
Lou Brouillard (CAN)	23 Oct 1931	Tomás Molinares (COL)	29 Jul 1988
Jackie Fields (USA)	28 Jan 1932	gave up title in 1988	
Young Corbett III (Rafelle Giordano)	22 Feb 1933	Mark Breland (USA)	4 Feb 1989
(USA)		Aaron Davis (USA)	8 Jul 1990
Jimmy McLarnin (CAN)	29 May 1933	Meldrick Taylor (USA)	19 Jan 1991
Barney Ross (USA)	28 May 1934	Crisanto España (VEN)	31 Oct 1992
Jimmy McLarnin (CAN)	17 Sep 1934	Ike Quartey (GHA)	4 Jun 1994
Barney Ross (USA)	28 May 1935	stripped of title in 1998	
Henry Armstrong (USA)	31 May 1938	James Page (USA)	10 Oct 1998
Fritzie Zivic (USA)	4 Oct 1940	stripped of title in 2000	
Freddie ("Red") Cochrane (USA)	29 Jul 1941	Andrew Lewis (GUY)	17 Feb 2001
Marty Servo (USA)	1 Feb 1946	Ricardo Mayorga (NCA)	28 Jul 2001
retired in 1946		Cory Spinks (USA)	13 Dec 2003
Sugar Ray Robinson (USA)	20 Dec 1946	Zab Judah (USA)	5 Feb 2005
gave up title in 1951		declared undisputed champion in 2005	
Kid Gavilan (CUB)	18 May 1951	Luis Collazo (USA)	2 Apr 2005
Johnny Saxton (USA)	20 Oct 1954		
Tony DeMarco (USA)	1 Apr 1955	**WBC**	
Carmen Basilio (USA)	10 Jun 1955	John Stracey (GBR)	6 Dec 1975
Johnny Saxton (USA)	14 Mar 1956	Carlos Palomino (USA)	22 Jun 1976
Carmen Basilio (USA)	12 Sep 1956	Wilfred Benítez (PUR)	14 Jan 1979
gave up title in 1957		Sugar Ray Leonard (USA)	30 Nov 1979
Virgil Akins (USA)	6 Jun 1958	Roberto Durán (PAN)	20 Jun 1980
Don Jordan (USA)	5 Dec 1958	Sugar Ray Leonard (USA)	25 Nov 1980
Benny ("Kid") Paret (CUB)	27 May 1960	retired in 1982	
Emile Griffith (USA)	1 Apr 1961	Milton McCrory (USA)	13 Aug 1983

World Welterweight Champions (continued)

CHAMPION (NATIONALITY)	DATE OF TITLE
WBC (continued)	
Donald Curry (USA)	6 Dec 1985
Lloyd Honeyghan (GBR)	27 Sep 1986
Jorge Vaca (MEX)	28 Oct 1987
Lloyd Honeyghan (GBR)	29 Mar 1988
Marlon Starling (USA)	4 Feb 1989
Maurice Blocker (USA)	19 Aug 1990
Simon Brown (JAM)	18 Mar 1991
James McGirt (USA)	29 Nov 1991
Pernell Whitaker (USA)	6 Mar 1993
Oscar de la Hoya (USA)	12 Apr 1997
Félix Trinidad (PUR)	18 Sep 1999
gave up title in 2000	
Oscar de la Hoya (USA)	20 Mar 2000
Shane Mosley (USA)	17 Jun 2000
Ricardo Mayorga (NCA)	25 Jan 2003
Cory Spinks (USA)	13 Dec 2003

CHAMPION (NATIONALITY)	DATE OF TITLE
WBC (continued)	
Zab Judah (USA)	5 Feb 2005
IBF	
Donald Curry (USA)	4 Feb 1984
Lloyd Honeyghan (GBR)	27 Sep 1986
stripped of title in 1987	
Simon Brown (JAM)	23 Apr 1988
gave up title in 1991	
Maurice Blocker (USA)	4 Oct 1991
Félix Trinidad (PUR)	19 Jun 1993
gave up title in 2000	
Vernon Forrest (USA)	12 May 2001
stripped of title in 2001	
Michele Piccirillo (ITA)	13 Apr 2002
Cory Spinks (USA)	22 Mar 2003
Zab Judah (USA)	5 Feb 2005

World Super Lightweight Champions

Top weight 140 pounds. Also called junior welterweight.

CHAMPION (NATIONALITY)	DATE OF TITLE
Undisputed champions	
Myron Mitchell (USA)	15 Nov 1922
proclaimed champion as the result	
of a poll taken by *The Boxing Blade*	
Mushy Callahan (USA)	21 Sep 1926
Jack ("Kid") Berg (GBR)	18 Feb 1930
Tony Canzoneri (USA)	24 Apr 1931
Johnny Jadick (USA)	18 Jan 1932
Battling Shaw (MEX)	20 Feb 1933
Tony Canzoneri (USA)	21 May 1933
Barney Ross (USA)	23 Jun 1933
gave up title in 1935; title vacant	
Tippy Larkin (USA)	29 Apr 1946
title vacant from 1946	
Carlos Ortíz (PUR)	12 Jun 1959
Duilio Loi (ITA)	1 Sep 1960
Eddie Perkins (USA)	14 Sep 1962
Duilio Loi (ITA)	15 Dec 1962
retired in 1963	
Eddie Perkins (USA)	15 Jun 1963
Carlos Hernández (VEN)	18 Jan 1965
Sandro Lopopolo (ITA)	29 Apr 1966
Paul Takeshi Fujii (USA)	30 Apr 1967
Kostya Tszyu (AUS)	3 Nov 2001
stripped of WBC title in 2004	
WBA	
Nicolino Loche (ARG)	12 Dec 1968
Alfonso Frazer (PAN)	10 Mar 1972
Antonio Cervantes (COL)	28 Oct 1972
Wilfred Benítez (PUR)	6 Mar 1976
stripped of title in 1976	
Antonio Cervantes (COL)	25 Jun 1977
Aaron Pryor (USA)	2 Aug 1980
retired in 1983	
Johnny Bumphus (USA)	22 Jan 1984
Gene Hatcher (USA)	1 Jun 1984
Ubaldo Sacco (ARG)	21 Jul 1985
Patrizio Oliva (ITA)	15 Mar 1986
Juan Martín Coggi (ARG)	4 Jul 1987
Loreto Garza (USA)	17 Aug 1990
Edwin Rosario (PUR)	15 Jun 1991
Akinobu Hiranaka (JPN)	10 Apr 1992
Morris East (PHI)	9 Sep 1992
Juan Martín Coggi (ARG)	12 Jan 1993

CHAMPION (NATIONALITY)	DATE OF TITLE
WBA (continued)	
Frankie Randall (USA)	17 Sep 1994
Juan Martín Coggi (ARG)	13 Jan 1996
Frankie Randall (USA)	16 Aug 1996
Khalid Rahilou (FRA)	11 Jan 1997
Sharmba Mitchell (USA)	10 Oct 1998
Kostya Tszyu (AUS)	3 Feb 2001
stripped of title in 2004	
Diobelys Hurtado (CUB)	11 May 2002
Vivian Harris (GUY)	19 Oct 2002
Carlos Maussa (COL)	25 Jun 2005
WBC	
Pedro Adigue (PHI)	14 Dec 1968
Bruno Arcari (ITA)	31 Jan 1970
gave up title in 1974	
Perico Fernández (ESP)	21 Sep 1974
Saensak Muangsurin (THA)	15 Jul 1975
Miguel Velásquez (ESP)	30 Jun 1976
Saensak Muangsurin (THA)	29 Oct 1976
Kim Sang Hyun (KOR)	30 Dec 1978
Saoul Mamby (USA)	23 Feb 1980
Leroy Haley (USA)	26 Jun 1982
Bruce Curry (USA)	18 May 1983
Bill Costello (USA)	29 Jan 1984
Lonnie Smith (USA)	21 Aug 1985
René Arredondo (MEX)	6 May 1986
Tsuyoshi Hamada (JPN)	24 Jul 1986
René Arredondo (MEX)	22 Jul 1987
Roger Mayweather (USA)	12 Nov 1987
Julio César Chávez (MEX)	13 May 1989
Frankie Randall (USA)	29 Jan 1994
Julio César Chávez (MEX)	7 May 1994
Oscar de la Hoya (USA)	7 Jun 1996
gave up title in 1997	
Kostya Tszyu (AUS)	21 Aug 1999
Arturo Gatti (CAN)	24 Jan 2004
Floyd Mayweather (USA)	25 Jun 2005
IBF	
Aaron Pryor (USA)	December 1984
recognized as champion by	
the IBF; stripped of title in 1985	
Gary Hinton (USA)	26 Apr 1986
Joe Louis Manley (USA)	30 Oct 1986

World Super Lightweight Champions (continued)

CHAMPION (NATIONALITY)	DATE OF TITLE	CHAMPION (NATIONALITY)	DATE OF TITLE
IBF (continued)		**IBF (continued)**	
Terry Marsh (GBR)	4 Mar 1987	Charles Murray (USA)	15 May 1993
gave up title in 1987		Jake Rodriguez (PUR)	13 Feb 1994
James McGirt (USA)	14 Feb 1988	Kostya Tszyu (AUS)	28 Jan 1995
Meldrick Taylor (USA)	3 Sep 1988	Vince Phillips (USA)	31 May 1997
Julio César Chávez (MEX)	17 Mar 1990	Terronn Millett (USA)	20 Feb 1999
gave up title in 1991		stripped of title in 2000	
Rafael Pineda (COL)	7 Dec 1991	Zab Judah (USA)	12 Feb 2000
Pernell Whitaker (USA)	18 Jul 1992	Kostya Tszyu (AUS)	3 Nov 2001
gave up title in 1993		Ricky Hatton (GBR)	4 Jun 2005

World Lightweight Champions

Top weight 135 pounds; until 1912 usually 133 pounds, but sometimes as high as 140 pounds.

CHAMPION (NATIONALITY)	DATE OF TITLE	CHAMPION (NATIONALITY)	DATE OF TITLE
Undisputed champions		**WBA (continued)**	
George ("Kid") Lavigne (USA)	1 Jun 1896	Edwin Rosario (PUR)	26 Sep 1986
Frank Erne (USA)	3 Jul 1899	Julio César Chávez (MEX)	21 Nov 1987
Joe Gans (USA)	12 May 1902	gave up title in 1989	
Battling Nelson (USA)	4 Jul 1908	Edwin Rosario (PUR)	9 Jul 1989
Ad Wolgast (USA)	22 Feb 1910	Juan Nazario (PUR)	4 Apr 1990
Willie Ritchie (USA)	28 Nov 1912	Pernell Whitaker (USA)	11 Aug 1990
Freddie Welsh (GBR)	7 Jul 1914	gave up title in 1992	
Benny Leonard (USA)	28 May 1917	Joey Gamache (USA)	13 Jun 1992
retired in 1925		Tony Lopez (USA)	24 Oct 1992
Jimmy Goodrich (USA)	13 Jul 1925	Dingaan Thobela (RSA)	26 Jun 1993
Rocky Kansas (USA)	7 Dec 1925	Olzubek Nazarov (RUS)	30 Oct 1993
Sammy Mandell (USA)	3 Jul 1926	Jean-Baptiste Mendy (FRA)	16 May 1998
Al Singer (USA)	17 Jul 1930	Julien Lorcy (FRA)	10 Apr 1999
Tony Canzoneri (USA)	14 Nov 1930	Stefano Zoff (ITA)	7 Aug 1999
Barney Ross (USA)	23 Jun 1933	Gilberto Serrano (VEN)	13 Nov 1999
gave up title in 1933		Takanori Hatakeyama (JPN)	11 Jun 2000
Tony Canzoneri (USA)	10 May 1935	Julien Lorcy (FRA)	1 Jul 2001
Lou Ambers (USA)	3 Sep 1936	Raul Balbi (ARG)	8 Oct 2001
Henry Armstrong (USA)	17 Aug 1938	Leonard Dorin (ROM)	5 Jan 2002
Lou Ambers (USA)	22 Aug 1939	stripped of title in 2004	
Lew Jenkins (USA)	10 May 1940	Lakva Sim (MON)	10 Apr 2004
Sammy Angott (USA)	19 Dec 1941	Juan Diaz (USA)	17 Jul 2004
retired in 1942			
Ike Williams (USA)	4 Aug 1947	**WBC**	
Jimmy Carter (USA)	25 May 1951	Rodolfo Gonzáles (MEX)	10 Nov 1972
Lauro Salas (MEX)	14 May 1952	Ishimatsu Suzuki (JPN)	11 Apr 1974
Jimmy Carter (USA)	15 Oct 1952	Esteban de Jesus (PUR)	8 May 1976
Paddy DeMarco (USA)	5 Mar 1954	Roberto Durán (PAN)	21 Jan 1978
Jimmy Carter (USA)	17 Nov 1954	gave up title in 1979	
Wallace ("Bud") Smith (USA)	29 Jun 1955	Jim Watt (GBR)	17 Apr 1979
Joe Brown (USA)	24 Aug 1956	Alexis Argüello (NCA)	20 Jun 1981
Carlos Ortíz (PUR)	21 Apr 1962	gave up title in 1983	
Ismael Laguna (PAN)	10 Apr 1965	Edwin Rosario (PUR)	1 May 1983
Carlos Ortíz (PUR)	13 Nov 1965	José Luis Ramírez (MEX)	3 Nov 1984
Carlos Teo Cruz (DOM)	29 Jun 1968	Hector Camacho (PUR)	10 Aug 1985
Armando Ramos (USA)	18 Feb 1969	stripped of title in 1987	
Ismael Laguna (PAN)	3 Mar 1970	José Luis Ramírez (MEX)	19 Jul 1987
stripped of WBC title in 1970		Julio César Chávez (MEX)	29 Oct 1988
		gave up title in 1989	
WBA		Pernell Whitaker (USA)	20 Aug 1989
Ken Buchanan (GBR)	26 Sep 1970	gave up title in 1992	
Roberto Durán (PAN)	26 Jun 1972	Miguel González (MEX)	24 Aug 1992
gave up title in 1979		gave up title in 1996	
Ernesto España (VEN)	16 Jun 1979	Jean-Baptiste Mendy (FRA)	20 Apr 1996
Hilmer Kenty (USA)	2 Mar 1980	Steve Johnston (USA)	1 Mar 1997
Sean O'Grady (USA)	12 Apr 1981	César Bazan (MEX)	13 Jun 1998
stripped of title in 1981		Steve Johnston (USA)	27 Feb 1999
Claude Noel (TRI)	12 Sep 1981	José Luis Castillo (MEX)	17 Jun 2000
Arturo Frias (USA)	5 Dec 1981	Floyd Mayweather, Jr. (USA)	20 Apr 2002
Ray Mancini (USA)	8 May 1982	gave up title in 2004	
Livingstone Bramble (ISV)	1 Jun 1984	José Luis Castillo (MEX)	5 Jun 2004

World Lightweight Champions (continued)

CHAMPION (NATIONALITY)	DATE OF TITLE	CHAMPION (NATIONALITY)	DATE OF TITLE
WBC (continued)		**IBF (continued)**	
Diego Corrales (USA)	7 May 2005	Rafael Ruelas (USA)	19 Feb 1994
		Oscar de la Hoya (USA)	6 May 1995
IBF		gave up title in 1995	
Charlie Brown (USA)	30 Jan 1984	Philip Holiday (RSA)	19 Aug 1995
Harry Arroyo (USA)	15 Apr 1984	Shane Mosley (USA)	2 Aug 1997
Jimmy Paul (USA)	6 Apr 1985	gave up title in 1999	
Greg Haugen (USA)	6 Dec 1986	Paul Spadafora (USA)	20 Aug 1999
Vinny Pazienza (USA)	7 Jun 1987	gave up title in 2003	
Greg Haugen (USA)	6 Feb 1988	Javier Jauregui (MEX)	22 Nov 2003
Pernell Whitaker (USA)	20 Feb 1989	Julio Díaz (MEX)	13 May 2004
gave up title in 1992		gave up title in 2005	
Fred Pendleton (USA)	10 Jan 1993	Leavander Johnson (USA)	17 June 2005

World Super Featherweight Champions
Top weight 130 pounds. Also called junior lightweight.

CHAMPION (NATIONALITY)	DATE OF TITLE	CHAMPION (NATIONALITY)	DATE OF TITLE
Undisputed champions		**WBC**	
Johnny Dundee (USA)	18 Nov 1921	Rene Barrientos (PHI)	15 Feb 1969
Jack Bernstein (USA)	30 May 1923	Yoshiaki Numata (JPN)	5 Apr 1970
Johnny Dundee (USA)	17 Dec 1923	Ricardo Arredondo (MEX)	10 Oct 1971
Steve ("Kid") Sullivan (USA)	20 Jun 1924	Kuniaki Shibata (JPN)	28 Feb 1974
Mike Ballerino (USA)	1 Apr 1925	Alfredo Escalera (PUR)	5 Jul 1975
Tod Morgan (USA)	2 Dec 1925	Alexis Argüello (NCA)	28 Jan 1978
Benny Bass (USA)	20 Dec 1929	gave up title in 1980	
Kid Chocolate (Eligio Sardinias)	15 Jul 1931	Rafael Limón (MEX)	11 Dec 1980
(CUB)		Cornelius Boza-Edwards (UGA)	8 Mar 1981
Frankie Klick (USA)	25 Dec 1933	Rolando Navarette (PHI)	29 Aug 1981
title vacant from 1934		Rafael Limón (MEX)	29 May 1982
Sandy Saddler (USA)	6 Dec 1949	Bobby Chacon (USA)	11 Dec 1982
title vacant from 1951		stripped of title in 1983	
Harold Gomes (USA)	20 Jul 1959	Hector Camacho (USA)	7 Aug 1983
Gabriel ("Flash") Elorde (PHI)	16 Mar 1960	gave up title in 1984	
Yoshiaki Numata (JPN)	15 Jun 1967	Julio César Chávez (MEX)	13 Sep 1984
Hiroshi Kobayashi (JPN)	14 Dec 1967	*vacant*	
stripped of WBC title in 1969		Azumah Nelson (GHA)	29 Feb 1988
		Jesse James Leija (USA)	7 May 1994
WBA		Gabriel Ruelas (USA)	17 Sep 1994
Alfredo Marcano (VEN)	29 Jul 1971	Azumah Nelson (GHA)	1 Dec 1995
Ben Villaflor (PHI)	25 Apr 1972	Genaro Hernandez (USA)	22 Mar 1997
Kuniaki Shibata (JPN)	12 Mar 1973	Floyd Mayweather, Jr. (USA)	3 Oct 1998
Ben Villaflor (PHI)	17 Oct 1973	gave up title in 2002	
Samuel Serrano (PUR)	16 Oct 1976	Sirimongkol Singmanassuk (THA)	24 Aug 2002
Yasutsune Uehara (JPN)	2 Aug 1980	Jesús Chávez (MEX)	15 Aug 2003
Samuel Serrano (PUR)	9 Apr 1981	Erik Morales (MEX)	28 Feb 2004
Roger Mayweather (USA)	19 Jan 1983	Marco Antonio Barrera (MEX)	27 Feb 2004
Rocky Lockridge (USA)	26 Feb 1984		
Wilfredo Gómez (PUR)	19 May 1985	**IBF**	
Alfredo Layne (PAN)	24 May 1986	Yuh Hwan-Kil (KOR)	2 Apr 1984
Brian Mitchell (RSA)	27 Sep 1986	Lester Ellis (AUS)	15 Feb 1985
gave up title in 1991		Barry Michael (AUS)	12 Jul 1985
Joey Gamache (USA)	28 Jun 1991	Rocky Lockridge (USA)	9 Aug 1987
gave up title in 1991		Tony Lopez (USA)	27 Jul 1988
Genaro Hernandez (USA)	22 Nov 1991	Juan Molina (PUR)	7 Oct 1989
gave up title in 1995		Tony Lopez (USA)	20 May 1990
Choi Yong Soo (KOR)	21 Oct 1995	Brian Mitchell (RSA)	13 Sep 1991
Takanori Hatakeyama (JPN)	5 Sep 1998	gave up title in 1992	
Lakva Sim (MGL)	27 Jun 1999	Juan Molina (PUR)	22 Feb 1992
Jong Kwon Baek (KOR)	31 Oct 1999	*vacant*	
Joel Casamayor (CUB)	21 May 2000	Eddie Hopson (USA)	22 Apr 1995
Acelino Freitas (BRA)	12 Jan 2002	Tracy Patterson (USA)	9 Jul 1995
gave up title in 2002		Arturo Gatti (USA)	15 Dec 1995
Yodsanan Nanthachai (THA)	13 Apr 2002	gave up title in 1998	
Vicente Mosquera (PAN)	30 Apr 2005	Roberto Garcia (USA)	13 Mar 1998
		Diego Corrales (USA)	23 Oct 1999
		gave up title in 2000	

World Super Featherweight Champions (continued)
Top weight 130 pounds. Also called junior lightweight.

CHAMPION (NATIONALITY) IBF (continued)	DATE OF TITLE	CHAMPION (NATIONALITY) IBF (continued)	DATE OF TITLE
Steve Forbes (USA)	3 Dec 2000	Erik Morales (MEX)	31 Jul 2004
stripped of title in 2002		stripped of title in 2004	
Carlos Hernández (ESA)	1 Feb 2003	Robbie Peden (AUS)	23 Feb 2005

World Featherweight Champions
Top weight 126 pounds; until 1901 weight varied between 115 and 122 pounds.

CHAMPION (NATIONALITY) Undisputed champions	DATE OF TITLE	CHAMPION (NATIONALITY) WBA (continued)	DATE OF TITLE
Billy Murphy (NZL)	13 Jan 1890	Park Yung Kyun (KOR)	30 Mar 1991
Young Griffo (AUS)	2 Feb 1890	Eloy Rojas (VEN)	4 Dec 1993
vacant		Wilfredo Vásquez (PUR)	18 May 1996
George Dixon (CAN)	27 Jun 1892	gave up title in 1998	
Solly Smith (USA)	4 Oct 1897	Freddie Norwood (USA)	3 Apr 1998
Dave Sullivan (GBR)	26 Sep 1898	stripped of title in 1998	
George Dixon (CAN)	11 Nov 1898	Antonio Cermeño (VEN)	3 Oct 1998
Terry McGovern (USA)	19 Jan 1900	Freddie Norwood (USA)	29 May 1999
Young Corbett (USA)	28 Nov 1901	Derrick Gainer (USA)	9 Sep 2000
Jimmy Britt (USA)	25 Mar 1904	Juan Manuel Márquez (MEX)	1 Nov 2003
title vacant in 1904			
Tommy Sullivan (USA)	13 Oct 1904	CHAMPION (NATIONALITY) WBC	DATE OF TITLE
title vacant from 1905			
Abe Atell (USA)	22 Feb 1906	José Legra (CUB)	24 Jul 1968
Johnny Kilbane (USA)	22 Feb 1912	Johnny Famechon (AUS)	21 Jan 1969
Eugène Criqui (FRA)	2 Jun 1923	Vicente Saldivar (MEX)	9 May 1970
Johnny Dundee (USA)	26 Jul 1923	Kuniaki Shibata (JPN)	11 Dec 1970
gave up title in 1924		Clemente Sánchez (MEX)	19 May 1972
Louis ("Kid") Kaplan (USA)	2 Jan 1925	José Legra (ESP)	16 Dec 1972
gave up title in 1926		Eder Jofre (BRA)	5 May 1973
Tony Canzoneri (USA)	24 Oct 1927	stripped of title in 1974	
André Routis (FRA)	28 Sep 1928	Bobby Chacon (USA)	7 Sep 1974
Battling Battalino (USA)	23 Sep 1929	Rubén Olivares (MEX)	20 Jun 1975
gave up title in 1932		David Kotey (GHA)	20 Sep 1975
Henry Armstrong (USA)	29 Oct 1937	Danny López (USA)	5 Nov 1976
gave up title in 1938		Salvador Sánchez (MEX)	2 Feb 1980
Joey Archibald (USA)	18 Apr 1939	died in 1982	
Harry Jeffra (USA)	20 May 1940	Juan LaPorte (PUR)	15 Sep 1982
Joey Archibald (USA)	12 May 1941	Wilfredo Gómez (PUR)	31 Mar 1984
Chalky Wright (USA)	11 Sep 1941	Azumah Nelson (GHA)	8 Dec 1984
Willie Pep (USA)	20 Nov 1942	gave up title in 1988	
Sandy Saddler (USA)	29 Oct 1948	Jeff Fenech (AUS)	7 Mar 1988
Willie Pep (USA)	11 Feb 1949	gave up title in 1990	
Sandy Saddler (USA)	8 Sep 1950	Marcos Villasana (MEX)	2 Jun 1990
retired in 1957		Paul Hodkinson (GBR)	13 Nov 1991
Hogan Bassey (NGR)	24 Jun 1957	Gregorio Vargas (MEX)	28 Apr 1993
Davey Moore (USA)	18 Mar 1959	Kevin Kelley (USA)	4 Dec 1993
Sugar Ramos (CUB)	21 Mar 1963	Alejandro González (MEX)	7 Jan 1995
Vicente Saldivar (MEX)	26 Sep 1964	Manuel Medina (MEX)	23 Sep 1995
retired 1967–70		Luisito Espinosa (PHI)	11 Dec 1995
		César Soto (MEX)	15 May 1999
WBA		Naseem Hamed (GBR)	22 Oct 1999
Raoul Rojas (USA)	28 Mar 1968	stripped of title in 1999	
Shozo Saijo (JPN)	28 Sep 1968	Gustavo Espadas (MEX)	14 Apr 2000
Antonio Gómez (VEN)	2 Sep 1971	Erik Morales (MEX)	17 Feb 2001
Ernesto Marcel (PAN)	19 Aug 1972	Marco Antonio Barrera (MEX)	22 Jun 2002
retired in 1974		declined title; declared vacant	
Rubén Olivares (MEX)	9 Jul 1974	Erik Morales (MEX)	16 Nov 2002
Alexis Argüello (NCA)	23 Nov 1974	gave up title in 2004	
gave up title in 1976		Chi In-Jin (KOR)	10 Apr 2004
Rafael Ortega (PAN)	15 Jan 1977		
Cecilio Lastra (ESP)	17 Dec 1977	IBF	
Eusebio Pedroza (PAN)	15 Apr 1978	Oh Min-kuem (KOR)	4 Mar 1984
Barry McGuigan (NIR)	8 Jun 1985	Chung Ki-yung (KOR)	29 Nov 1985
Steve Cruz (USA)	23 Jun 1986	Antonio Rivera (PUR)	30 Aug 1986
Antonio Esparragoza (VEN)	6 Mar 1987	Calvin Grove (USA)	23 Jan 1988

World Featherweight Champions (continued)

CHAMPION (NATIONALITY)	DATE OF TITLE	CHAMPION (NATIONALITY)	DATE OF TITLE
IBF (continued)		**IBF (continued)**	
Jorge Paez (MEX)	4 Aug 1988	Manuel Medina (MEX)	24 Apr 1998
gave up title in 1991		Paul Ingle (GBR)	13 Nov 1999
Troy Dorsey (USA)	3 Jun 1991	Mbulelo Botile (RSA)	16 Dec 2000
Manuel Medina (MEX)	12 Aug 1991	Frankie Toledo (USA)	6 Apr 2001
Tom Johnson (USA)	26 Feb 1993	Manuel Medina (MEX)	16 Nov 2001
Naseem Hamed (GBR)	8 Feb 1997	Johnny Tapia (USA)	27 Apr 2002
gave up title in 1997		stripped of title in 2002	
Hector Lizarraga (USA)	13 Dec 1997	Juan Manuel Márquez (MEX)	1 Feb 2003

World Super Bantamweight Champions

Top weight 122 pounds. Also called junior featherweight. Weight division at first recognized only by WBC.

CHAMPION (NATIONALITY)	DATE OF TITLE	CHAMPION (NATIONALITY)	DATE OF TITLE
WBA		**WBC (continued)**	
Hong Soo Hwan (KOR)	26 Nov 1977	Juan Meza (MEX)	3 Nov 1984
Ricardo Cardona (COL)	7 May 1978	Guadalupe Pintor (MEX)	18 Aug 1985
Leo Randolph (USA)	4 May 1980	Samart Payakaroon (THA)	18 Jan 1986
Sergio Palma (ARG)	9 Aug 1980	Jeff Fenech (AUS)	8 May 1987
Leonardo Cruz (DOM)	12 Jun 1982	gave up title in 1990	
Loris Stecca (ITA)	22 Feb 1984	Daniel Zaragoza (MEX)	29 Feb 1988
Víctor Callejas (PUR)	26 May 1984	Paul Banke (USA)	23 Apr 1990
stripped of title in 1986		Pedro Decima (ARG)	5 Nov 1990
Louie Espinoza (USA)	16 Jan 1987	Kiyoshi Hatanaka (JPN)	3 Feb 1991
Julio Gervacio (DOM)	28 Nov 1987	Daniel Zaragoza (MEX)	14 Jun 1991
Bernardo Pinango (VEN)	5 Mar 1988	Thierry Jacob (FRA)	20 Mar 1992
Juan José Estrada (MEX)	28 May 1988	Tracy Patterson (USA)	23 Jun 1992
Jesus Salud (USA)	11 Dec 1989	Hector Acero-Sánchez (USA)	26 Aug 1994
stripped of title in 1990		Daniel Zaragoza (MEX)	6 Nov 1995
Luís Mendoza (COL)	11 Sep 1990	Erik Morales (MEX)	6 Sep 1997
Raul Pérez (MEX)	7 Oct 1991	gave up title in 2000	
Wilfredo Vásquez (PUR)	27 Mar 1992	Willie Jorrin (USA)	9 Sep 2000
Antonio Cermeño (VEN)	13 May 1995	Oscar Larios (MEX)	1 Nov 2002
gave up title in 1997			
Enrique Sanchez (MEX)	8 Feb 1998	**IBF**	
vacant		Bobby Berna (PHI)	4 Dec 1983
Néstor Garza (MEX)	12 Dec 1998	Suh Seung-il (KOR)	15 Apr 1984
Clarence Adams (USA)	4 Mar 2000	Kim Ji-won (KOR)	3 Jan 1985
stripped of title in 2001		*vacant*	
Yober Ortega (VEN)	17 Nov 2001	Lee Seung-hoon (KOR)	18 Jan 1987
Yoddamrong Sithyodthong (THA)	21 Feb 2002	gave up title in 1988	
Osamu Sato (JPN)	18 May 2002	José Sanabria (VEN)	21 May 1988
Salim Medjkoune (FRA)	9 Oct 2002	Fabrice Benichou (FRA)	10 Mar 1989
Mahyar Monshipour (FRA)	4 Jul 2003	Welcome Ncita (RSA)	10 Mar 1990
		Kennedy McKinney (USA)	2 Dec 1992
WBC		Vuyani Bungu (RSA)	20 Aug 1994
Rigoberto Riasco (PAN)	3 Apr 1976	gave up title in 1999	
Kazuo Kobayashi (JPN)	10 Oct 1976	Lehlohonolo Ledwaba (RSA)	29 May 1999
Yum Dong Kyun (KOR)	24 Nov 1976	Manny Pacquiao (PHI)	23 Jun 2001
Wilfredo Gómez (PUR)	21 May 1977	gave up title in 2004	
gave up title in 1983		Israel Vásquez (MEX)	25 Mar 2004
Jaime Garza (USA)	15 Jun 1983		

World Bantamweight Champions

Top weight 118 pounds; until 1920 weight limits varied between 105 and 116 pounds.

CHAMPION (NATIONALITY)	DATE OF TITLE	CHAMPION (NATIONALITY)	DATE OF TITLE
Undisputed champions		**Undisputed champions**	
Terry McGovern (USA)	12 Sep 1899	Kid Williams (USA)	9 Jun 1914
gave up title in 1900		Pete Herman (USA)	9 Jan 1917
Harry Harris (USA)	18 Mar 1901	Joe Lynch (USA)	22 Dec 1920
gave up title in 1901		Pete Herman (USA)	25 Jul 1921
Harry Forbes (USA)	2 Apr 1901	Johnny Buff (USA)	23 Sep 1921
Frankie Neil (USA)	13 Aug 1903	Joe Lynch (USA)	10 Jul 1922
Joe Bowker (GBR)	17 Oct 1904	Abe Goldstein (USA)	21 Mar 1924
gave up title in 1905; title in dispute		Eddie Martin (USA)	19 Dec 1924

World Bantamweight Champions (continued)

CHAMPION (NATIONALITY)	DATE OF TITLE
Undisputed champions (continued)	
Charlie Rosenberg (USA)	20 Mar 1925
stripped of title in 1927;	
title in dispute	
Panama Al Brown (PAN)	18 Jun 1929
stripped of NBA (later WBA) title	
in 1934; title in dispute	
Sixto Escobar (PUR)	31 Aug 1936
Harry Jeffra (USA)	23 Sep 1937
Sixto Escobar (PUR)	20 Feb 1938
gave up title in 1939	
Lou Salica (USA)	13 Jan 1941
Manuel Ortiz (USA)	7 Aug 1942
Harold Dade (USA)	6 Jan 1947
Manuel Ortiz (USA)	11 Mar 1947
Vic Toweel (RSA)	31 May 1950
Jimmy Carruthers (AUS)	15 Nov 1952
retired in 1954; title in dispute	
Alphonse Halimi (ALG)	6 Nov 1957
José Becerra (MEX)	8 Jul 1959
retired in 1961	
Eder Jofre (BRA)	18 Jan 1962
Masahiko Harada (JPN)	17 May 1965
Lionel Rose (AUS)	26 Feb 1968
Rubén Olivares (MEX)	22 Aug 1969
Chucho Castillo (MEX)	16 Oct 1970
Rubén Olivares (MEX)	3 Apr 1971
Rafael Herrera (MEX)	19 Mar 1972
Enrique Pinder (PAN)	30 Jul 1972
stripped of WBC title in 1972	
WBA	
Romeo Anaya (MEX)	20 Jan 1973
Arnold Taylor (RSA)	3 Nov 1973
Hong Soo Hwan (KOR)	3 Jul 1974
Alfonso Zamora (MEX)	14 Mar 1975
Jorge Luján (PAN)	19 Nov 1977
Julian Solís (PUR)	29 Aug 1980
Jeff Chandler (USA)	14 Nov 1980
Richie Sandoval (USA)	7 Apr 1984
Gaby Canizales (USA)	10 Mar 1986
Bernardo Pinango (VEN)	4 Jun 1986
gave up title in 1987	
Takuyama Muguruma (JPN)	29 Mar 1987
Park Chang Young (KOR)	24 May 1987
Wilfredo Vásquez (PUR)	4 Oct 1987
Khaokor Galaxy (THA)	9 May 1988
Moon Sung Kil (KOR)	14 Aug 1988
Khaokor Galaxy (THA)	9 Jul 1989
Luisito Espinosa (PHI)	18 Oct 1989
Israel Contreras (VEN)	19 Oct 1991
Eddie Cook (USA)	15 Mar 1992

CHAMPION (NATIONALITY)	DATE OF TITLE
WBA (continued)	
Eliecer Julio (COL)	10 Oct 1992
Junior Jones (USA)	23 Oct 1993
John Michael Johnson (USA)	22 Apr 1994
Daorung Chuvatana Siriwat (THA)	16 Jul 1994
Veeraphol Sahaprom (THA)	17 Sep 1995
Nana Konadu (GHA)	28 Jan 1996
Daorung Chuvatana Siriwat (THA)	26 Oct 1996
Nana Konadu (GHA)	21 Jun 1997
Johnny Tapia (USA)	6 Dec 1998
Paulie Ayala (USA)	26 Jun 1999
stripped of title in 2001	
Eidy Moya (VEN)	14 Oct 2001
Johnny Bredahl (DEN)	19 Apr 2002
retired in 2004	
Wladimir Sidorenko (UKR)	26 Apr 2005
WBC	
Rafael Herrera (MEX)	15 Apr 1973
Rudolfo Martínez (MEX)	7 Dec 1974
Carlos Zárate (MEX)	8 May 1976
Guadalupe Pintor (MEX)	3 Jun 1979
stripped of title in 1983	
Alberto Davila (USA)	1 Sep 1983
stripped of title in 1985	
Daniel Zaragoza (MEX)	4 May 1985
Miguel Lora (COL)	9 Aug 1985
Raul Pérez (MEX)	29 Oct 1988
Greg Richardson (USA)	25 Feb 1991
Joichiro Tatsuyoshi (JPN)	19 Sep 1991
vacant	
Victor Rabañales (MEX)	30 Mar 1992
Byun Jong-il (KOR)	28 Mar 1993
Yasuei Yakushiji (JPN)	22 Dec 1993
Wayne McCullough (NIR)	30 Jul 1995
Sirimongkol Singmanassuk (THA)	10 Aug 1996
Joichiro Tatsuyoshi (JPN)	22 Nov 1997
Veeraphol Sahaprom (THA)	29 Dec 1998
Hozumi Hasegawa (JPN)	16 Apr 2005
IBF	
Satoshi Shingaki (JPN)	15 Apr 1984
Jeff Fenech (AUS)	26 Apr 1985
vacant	
Kelvin Seabrooks (USA)	16 May 1987
Orlando Canizales (USA)	9 Jul 1988
gave up title in 1994	
Harold Mestre (COL)	21 Jan 1995
Mbulelo Botile (RSA)	29 Apr 1995
Tim Austin (USA)	19 Jul 1997
Rafael Márquez (MEX)	15 Feb 2003

World Super Flyweight Champions

Top weight 115 pounds. Also called junior bantamweight.

CHAMPION (NATIONALITY)	DATE OF TITLE
WBA	
Gustavo Ballas (ARG)	12 Sep 1981
Rafael Pedroza (PAN)	5 Dec 1981
Watanabe Jiro (JPN)	8 Apr 1982
stripped of title in 1984	
Khaosai Galaxy (THA)	21 Nov 1984
gave up title in 1991	
Katsuya Onizuka (JPN)	10 Apr 1992
Lee Hyung Chul (KOR)	18 Sep 1994
Alima Goitia (VEN)	22 Jul 1995

CHAMPION (NATIONALITY)	DATE OF TITLE
WBA (continued)	
Yokthai Sithoar (THA)	24 Aug 1996
Satoshi Iida (JPN)	23 Dec 1997
Jesús Rojas (VEN)	23 Dec 1998
Hideki Todaka (JPN)	31 Jul 1999
Leo Gámez (VEN)	9 Oct 2000
Shoji Kobayashi (JPN)	11 Mar 2001
Alexander Muñoz (VEN)	9 Mar 2002
Martin Castillo (MEX)	3 Dec 2004

World Super Flyweight Champions (continued)

CHAMPION (NATIONALITY)	DATE OF TITLE
WBC	
Rafael Oroño (VEN)	1 Feb 1980
Kim Chul Ho (KOR)	24 Jan 1981
Rafael Oroño (VEN)	28 Nov 1982
Payao Poontarat (THA)	27 Nov 1983
Watanabe Jiro (JPN)	5 Jul 1984
Gilberto Román (MEX)	30 Mar 1986
Santos Laciar (ARG)	16 May 1987
Jesús Rojas (COL)	9 Aug 1987
Gilberto Román (MEX)	8 Apr 1988
Nana Konadu (GHA)	7 Nov 1989
Moon Sung Kil (KOR)	20 Jan 1990
José Luis Bueno (MEX)	13 Nov 1993
Hiroshi Kawashima (JPN)	4 May 1994
Gerry Peñalosa (PHI)	20 Feb 1997
Cho In Joo (KOR)	29 Aug 1998
Masamori Tokuyama (JPN)	27 Aug 2000
Katsushige Kawashima (JPN)	28 Jun 2004
Masamori Tokuyama (JPN)	18 Jul 2005

CHAMPION (NATIONALITY)	DATE OF TITLE
IBF	
Chun Joo-do (KOR)	10 Dec 1983
Ellyas Pical (INA)	3 May 1985
César Polanco (DOM)	15 Feb 1986
Ellyas Pical (INA)	6 Jul 1986
vacant	
Chang Tae-il (KOR)	17 May 1987
Ellyas Pical (INA)	17 Oct 1987
Juan Polo Pérez (COL)	14 Oct 1989
Robert Quiroga (USA)	21 Apr 1990
Julio Borboa (MEX)	16 Jan 1993
Harold Grey (COL)	29 Aug 1994
Carlos Salazar (ARG)	7 Oct 1995
Harold Grey (COL)	27 Apr 1996
Danny Romero (USA)	24 Aug 1996
Johnny Tapia (USA)	18 Jul 1997
gave up title in 1998	
Mark Johnson (USA)	24 Apr 1999
stripped of title in 2000	
Félix Machado (VEN)	22 Jul 2000
Luis Pérez (NCA)	4 Jan 2003

World Flyweight Champions

Top weight 112 pounds.

CHAMPION (NATIONALITY)	DATE OF TITLE
Undisputed champions	
Jimmy Wilde (GBR)	18 Dec 1916
Pancho Villa (Francisco Guilledo) (PHI)	18 Jun 1923
died in 1925	
Fidel La Barba (USA)	21 Jan 1927
retired in 1927; title in dispute	
Benny Lynch (GBR)	19 Jan 1937
gave up title in 1938	
Peter Kane (GBR)	22 Sep 1938
Jackie Paterson (GBR)	19 Jun 1943
title in dispute from 1947	
Rinty Monaghan (IRE)	23 Mar 1948
retired in 1950	
Terry Allen (GBR)	25 Apr 1950
Dado Marino (Hawaii)	1 Aug 1950
Yoshio Shirai (JPN)	19 May 1952
Pascual Pérez (ARG)	26 Nov 1954
Pone Kingpetch (THA)	16 Apr 1960
Masahiko Harada (JPN)	10 Oct 1962
Pone Kingpetch (THA)	12 Jan 1963
Hiroyuki Ebihara (JPN)	18 Sep 1963
Pone Kingpetch (THA)	23 Jan 1964
Salvatore Burruni (ITA)	23 Apr 1965
title in dispute from 1965	
WBA	
Horacio Accavallo (ARG)	1 Mar 1966
retired in 1968	
Hiroyuki Ebihara (JPN)	30 Mar 1969
Bernabe Villacampo (PHI)	19 Oct 1969
Berkrerk Chartvanchai (THA)	14 Apr 1970
Ohba Masao (JPN)	22 Oct 1970
died in 1973	
Chartchai Chionoi (THA)	17 May 1973
Susumu Hanagata (JPN)	18 Oct 1974
Erbito Salavarria (PHI)	1 Apr 1975
Alfonso López (PAN)	27 Feb 1976
Gustavo Espadas (MEX)	2 Oct 1976
Betulio González (VEN)	12 Aug 1978
Luis Ibarra (PAN)	17 Nov 1979
Kim Tae Shik (KOR)	16 Feb 1980

CHAMPION (NATIONALITY)	DATE OF TITLE
WBA (continued)	
Peter Mathebula (RSA)	13 Dec 1980
Santos Laciar (ARG)	28 Mar 1981
Luis Ibarra (PAN)	6 Jun 1981
Juan Herrera (MEX)	26 Sep 1981
Santos Laciar (ARG)	1 May 1982
gave up title in 1985	
Hilario Zapata (PAN)	5 Oct 1985
Fidel Bassa (COL)	13 Feb 1987
Jesús Rojas (VEN)	30 Sep 1989
Lee Yul Woo (KOR)	10 Mar 1990
Leopard Tamakuma (JPN)	29 Jul 1990
Elvis Álvarez (COL)	14 Mar 1991
Kim Yong Kang (KOR)	1 Jun 1991
Aquiles Guzmán (VEN)	26 Sep 1992
David Griman (VEN)	15 Dec 1992
San Sow Ploenchit (THA)	13 Feb 1994
José Bonilla (VEN)	14 Nov 1996
Hugo Soto (ARG)	29 May 1998
Leo Gámez (VEN)	13 Mar 1999
Sornpichai Kratchingdaeng (THA)	3 Sep 1999
Eric Morel (PUR)	5 Aug 2000
Lorenzo Parra (VEN)	6 Dec 2003
WBC	
Walter McGowan (GBR)	14 Jun 1966
Chartchai Chionoi (THA)	30 Dec 1966
Efren Torres (MEX)	23 Feb 1969
Chartchai Chionoi (THA)	20 Mar 1970
Erbito Salavarria (PHI)	7 Dec 1970
stripped of title in 1971	
Betulio González (VEN)	20 Nov 1971
Venice Borkorsor (THA)	29 Sep 1972
gave up title in 1973	
Betulio González (VEN)	4 Aug 1973
Shoji Oguma (JPN)	1 Oct 1974
Miguel Canto (MEX)	8 Jan 1975
Park Chan Hee (KOR)	18 Mar 1979
Shoji Oguma (JPN)	18 May 1980
Antonio Avelar (MEX)	12 May 1981
Prudencio Cardona (COL)	20 Mar 1982

World Flyweight (continued)

CHAMPION (NATIONALITY)	DATE OF TITLE	CHAMPION (NATIONALITY)	DATE OF TITLE
WBC (continued)		**IBF**	
Freddie Castillo (MEX)	24 Jul 1982	Kwon Soon Chun (KOR)	24 Dec 1983
Eleoncio Mercedes (DOM)	6 Nov 1982	Chung Chong Kwan (KOR)	20 Dec 1985
Charlie Magri (GBR)	15 Mar 1983	Chung Bi Won (KOR)	27 Apr 1986
Frank Cedeno (PHI)	27 Sep 1983	Shin Hi Sup (KOR)	2 Aug 1986
Koji Kobayashi (JPN)	18 Jan 1984	Dodie Penalosa (PHI)	22 Feb 1987
Gabriel Bernal (MEX)	9 Apr 1984	Choi Chang Ho (KOR)	5 Sep 1987
Sot Chitalada (THA)	8 Oct 1984	Rolando Bohol (PHI)	16 Jan 1988
Kim Yong Kang (KOR)	24 Jul 1988	Duke McKenzie (GBR)	5 Oct 1988
Sot Chitalada (THA)	3 Jun 1989	Dave McAuley (GBR)	7 Jun 1989
Muangchai Kittikasem (THA)	15 Feb 1991	Rodolfo Blanco (COL)	11 Jun 1992
Yury Arbachakov (RUS)	23 Jun 1992	Phichit Sithbangprachan (THA)	29 Nov 1992
Chatchai Dutchboygym (Sasakul) (THA)	9 May 1997	vacant	
Manny Pacquiao (PHI)	4 Dec 1998	Francisco Tejedor (COL)	18 Feb 1995
stripped of title in 1999		Danny Romero (USA)	22 Apr 1995
Medgeon Singsurat (THA)	17 Sep 1999	gave up title in 1996	
Malcolm Tunacao (PHI)	19 May 2000	Mark Johnson (USA)	4 May 1996
Pongsaklek Wonjongkam (THA)	2 Mar 2001	gave up title in 1999	
		Irene Pacheco (COL)	10 Apr 1999
		Vic Darchinyan (AUS)	16 Dec 2004

World Light Flyweight Champions

Top weight 108 pounds. Also called junior flyweight.

CHAMPION (NATIONALITY)	DATE OF TITLE	CHAMPION (NATIONALITY)	DATE OF TITLE
WBA		**WBC (continued)**	
Jaime Ríos (PAN)	23 Aug 1975	Chang Jung Koo (KOR)	26 Mar 1983
Juan Guzmán (DOM)	1 Jul 1976	gave up title in 1988	
Yoko Gushiken (JPN)	10 Oct 1976	German Torres (MEX)	11 Dec 1988
Pedro Flores (MEX)	8 Mar 1981	Lee Yul Woo (KOR)	19 Mar 1989
Kim Hwan Jin (KOR)	19 Jul 1981	Humberto González (MEX)	25 Jun 1989
Katsuo Tokashiki (JPN)	16 Dec 1981	Rolando Pascua (PHI)	19 Dec 1990
Lupe Madera (MEX)	10 Jul 1983	Melchor Cob Castro (MEX)	25 Mar 1991
Francisco Quiroz (DOM)	19 May 1984	Humberto González (MEX)	4 Jun 1991
Joey Olivo (USA)	29 Mar 1985	Michael Carbajal (USA)	13 Mar 1993
Yuh Myung Woo (KOR)	8 Dec 1985	Chiquita González (MEX)	19 Feb 1994
Hiroki Ioka (JPN)	17 Dec 1991	Saman Sorjaturong (THA)	15 Jul 1995
Yuh Myung Woo (KOR)	18 Nov 1992	Choi Yo Sam (KOR)	17 Oct 1999
gave up title in 1993		Jorge Arce (MEX)	6 Jul 2002
Leo Gámez (VEN)	21 Oct 1993	gave up title in 2005	
Choi Hi Yong (KOR)	4 Feb 1995	Eric Ortiz (MEX)	11 Mar 2005
Carlos Murillo (PAN)	13 Jan 1996		
Keiji Yamaguchi (JPN)	21 May 1996	**IBF**	
Pichitnoi Siriwat (THA)	3 Dec 1996	Dodie Penalosa (PHI)	10 Dec 1983
vacant		stripped of title in 1986	
Bebis Mendoza (COL)	12 Aug 2000	Choi Chong Hwon (KOR)	7 Dec 1986
Rosendo Álvarez (NCA)	3 Mar 2001	Tacy Macalos (PHI)	6 Nov 1988
stripped of title in 2004		Muangchai Kittikasem (THA)	2 May 1989
Roberto Vásquez (PAN)	29 Apr 2005	Michael Carbajal (USA)	29 Jul 1990
		Chiquita González (MEX)	19 Feb 1994
WBC		Saman Sorjaturong (THA)	15 Jul 1995
Franco Udella (ITA)	4 Apr 1975	vacant	
stripped of title in 1975		Michael Carbajal (USA)	16 Mar 1996
Luis Alberto Estaba (VEN)	13 Sep 1975	Mauricio Pastrana (COL)	18 Jan 1997
Freddie Castillo (MEX)	19 Feb 1978	stripped of title in 1997	
Netrnoi Sor Vorasingh (THA)	6 May 1978	Mauricio Pastrana (COL)	13 Dec 1997
Kim Sung Jun (KOR)	30 Sep 1978	stripped of title in 1998	
Shigeo Nakajima (JPN)	3 Jan 1980	Will Grigsby (USA)	18 Dec 1998
Hilario Zapata (PAN)	24 Mar 1980	Ricardo López (MEX)	2 Oct 1999
Amado Ursua (MEX)	6 Feb 1982	gave up title in 2003	
Tadashi Tomori (JPN)	13 Apr 1982	Victor Burgos (MEX)	15 Feb 2003
Hilario Zapata (PAN)	20 Jul 1982	Will Grigsby (USA)	14 May 2005

World Miniflyweight Champions

Top weight 105 pounds. Also called strawweight. Division first recognized by WBA in 1988 and by WBC and IBF in 1987.

CHAMPION (NATIONALITY)	DATE OF TITLE	CHAMPION (NATIONALITY)	DATE OF TITLE
WBA		**WBC (continued)**	
Leo Gámez (VEN)	10 Jan 1988	Wande Chareon (THA)	4 May 1999
vacant		José Antonio Aguirre (MEX)	11 Feb 2000
Kim Bong Jun (KOR)	16 Apr 1989	Eagle Akakura (later Eagle Kyowa)	
Choi Hi Yong (KOR)	2 Feb 1991	(JPN)	10 Jan 2004
Hideyuki Ohashi (JPN)	14 Oct 1992	Isaac Bustos (MEX)	18 Dec 2004
Chana Porpaoin (THA)	10 Feb 1993	Katsunari Takayama (JPN)	4 Apr 2005
Rosendo Álvarez (NCA)	2 Dec 1995		
Ricardo López (MEX)	13 Nov 1998	**IBF**	
gave up title in 1999		Lee Kyung Yun (KOR)	14 Jun 1987
Noel Arambulet (VEN)	9 Oct 1999	vacant	
stripped of title in 2000		Samuth Sithnaruepol (THA)	24 Mar 1988
Joma Gamboa (PHI)	20 Aug 2000	Nico Thomas (INA)	17 Jun 1989
Hoshino Keitaro (JPN)	6 Dec 2000	Eric Chávez (PHI)	21 Sep 1989
Chana Porpaoin (THA)	16 Apr 2001	Falan Lookmingkwan (THA)	21 Feb 1990
Yutaka Niida (JPN)	25 Aug 2001	Manny Melchor (PHI)	6 Sep 1992
gave up title in 2001		Ratanapol Vorapin (THA)	10 Dec 1992
Hoshino Keitaro (JPN)	29 Jan 2002	stripped of title in 1996	
Noel Arambulet (VEN)	29 Jul 2002	Ratanapol Vorapin (THA)	16 May 1996
stripped of title in 2004		Zolani Petelo (RSA)	27 Dec 1997
Yutaka Niida (JPN)	3 Jul 2004	gave up title in 2000	
		Roberto Leyva (MEX)	29 Apr 2001
WBC		Miguel Barrera (COL)	9 Aug 2002
Ioka Hiroki (JPN)	18 Oct 1987	Edgar Cárdenas (MEX)	31 May 2003
Napa Kiatwanchai (THA)	13 Nov 1988	Daniel Reyes (COL)	4 Oct 2003
Choi Jum Hwan (KOR)	12 Nov 1989	Muhammad Rachman (INA)	14 Sep 2004
Hideyuki Ohashi (JPN)	7 Feb 1990		
Ricardo López (MEX)	25 Oct 1990		
gave up title in 1999			

Chess

William Steinitz is generally recognized as the first official chess world champion, although dates for his 19th-century reign vary. With a few notable exceptions, each successive champion defeated his predecessor in match play. The first exception followed the death of the incumbent **Alexander Alekhine** in 1946. The **Fédération Internationale des Échecs** (FIDE; founded 1924) stepped in and arranged a tournament among leading contenders to determine a new champion in 1948. FIDE continued to oversee regular tournaments and matches to determine challengers—although another exception occurred in 1975, when **Robert (Bobby) Fischer** refused to defend his crown and retired. In 1993 **Garry Kasparov** pulled out of FIDE to defend his title under rival organizations (Professional Chess Association and later Braingames). Without a universally recognized champion, FIDE struggled to obtain funding for its multiyear system of tournaments and matches leading to a title match. So, in 1999 FIDE began to hold annual "**knockout**" **tournaments**, with very fast game play, to determine their champion. Few chess players recognize the FIDE champion as legitimate, however.

FIDE began organizing the **women's chess championship** in 1953. Controversy has also afflicted this title, with **Zsuzsa Polgar** refusing to accept FIDE's terms for her title defense in 1999. In 2000, FIDE adopted a knockout tournament format for the women's championship similar to that of the open tournament.

The **Olympiads** are held biennially. Competition is open to both men and women, but since 1957 there has been a separate Olympiad that is restricted to women.

FIDE Web site: <www.fide.com>.

World Chess Champions—Men

Generally recognized (see "Chess" above)

REIGN	NAME	NATIONALITY	REIGN	NAME	NATIONALITY
1866–94	Wilhelm Steinitz	Austrian American	1948–57	Mikhail Botvinnik	Soviet Russian
1894–1921	Emanuel Lasker	German	1957–58	Vasily Smyslov	Soviet Russian
1921–27	José Raúl Capablanca	Cuban	1958–60	Mikhail Botvinnik	Soviet Russian
			1960–61	Mikhail Tal	Soviet Russian
1927–35	Alexander Alekhine	Russian-born French	1961–63	Mikhail Botvinnik	Soviet Russian
			1963–69	Tigran Petrosyan	Soviet Georgian-born Armenian
1935–37	Max Euwe	Dutch			
1937–46	Alexander Alekhine	Russian-born French	1969–72	Boris Spassky	Soviet Russian

World Chess Champions—Men (continued)

REIGN	NAME	NATIONALITY	REIGN	NAME	NATIONALITY
1972–75	Robert (Bobby) Fischer	American	1985–2000	Garry Kasparov	Azerbaijani-born Russian
1975–85	Anatoly Karpov	Soviet Russian	2000–	Vladimir Kramnik	Russian

World Chess Champions—Women

REIGN	NAME	NATIONALITY	REIGN	NAME	NATIONALITY
1927–44	Vera Menchik[1]	Soviet Russian	1978–91	Maya Chiburdanidze	Soviet Georgian
1949–53	Lyudmila Rudenko	Soviet Russian	1991–96	Xie Jun	Chinese
1953–56	Yelizaveta Bykova	Soviet Russian	1996–99	Zsuzsa Polgar[2]	Hungarian
1956–58	Olga Rubtsova	Soviet Russian	1999–2001	Xie Jun	Chinese
1958–62	Yelizaveta Bykova	Soviet Russian	2001–04	Zhu Chen	Chinese
1962–78	Nona Gaprindashvili	Soviet Georgian	2004–	Antoaneta Stefanova	Bulgarian

[1]Killed in an air raid on London in 1944; title left vacant.   [2]Rejected conditions for title defense; title regained by Xie.

Chess Olympiads

The table lists the competitions for the past 20 years only.
The 2004 Olympiads took place 14–31 October in Calviá, Spain.

	Open		Women			Open		Women	
YEAR	WINNER	RUNNER-UP	WINNER	RUNNER-UP	YEAR	WINNER	RUNNER-UP	WINNER	RUNNER-UP
1986	USSR	Great Britain	USSR	Hungary	1996	Russia	Ukraine	Georgia	China
1988	USSR	Great Britain	Hungary	USSR	1998	Russia	United States	China	Russia
1990	USSR	US	Hungary	USSR	2000	Russia	Germany	China	Georgia
1992	Russia	Uzbekistan	Georgia	Ukraine	2002	Russia	Hungary	China	Russia
1994	Russia	Bosnia	Georgia	Hungary	2004	Ukraine	Russia	China	US

Contract Bridge

The world team contract bridge championships were instituted in 1950 with what was then an annual and zonal competition called the **Bermuda Bowl**. When the **World Team Olympiad**, held quadrennially, was instituted in 1960, it represented the world team championship. The only exception to this rule occurred in 1976, when both events were held. The Bermuda Bowl is organized by the **World Bridge Federation** (WBF; founded 1958), and since 1977 it has been held in odd-numbered years (the 1999 competition took place in January 2000). Among women's teams the major competition is the World Team Olympiad, although another team competition, the **Venice Cup**, was inaugurated in 1974. In pairs competition the quadrennial **World Bridge Championships** (inaugurated in 1962, it features open and women's sections) is the premiere international event.

WBF Web site: <www.worldbridge.org>.

Bermuda Bowl

YEAR	WINNER	RUNNER-UP	YEAR	WINNER	RUNNER-UP
1950	United States	United Kingdom	1968	*not held*[1]	
1951	United States	Italy	1969	Italy	Taiwan
1952	*postponed*		1970	North America	Taiwan
1953	United States	Sweden	1971	United States	France
1954	United States	France	1972	*not held*[1]	
1955	United Kingdom	United States	1973	Italy	North America
1956	France	United States	1974	Italy	North America
1957	Italy	United States	1975	Italy	North America
1958	Italy	United States	1976	North America	Italy
1959	Italy	United States	1977	North American Defenders	North American Challengers
1960	*not held*[1]		1979	North America	Italy
1961	Italy	North America	1981	United States	Pakistan
1962	Italy	North America	1983	United States	Italy
1963	Italy	North America	1985	United States	Austria
1964	not held[1]		1987	United States	United Kingdom
1965	Italy	United States	1989	Brazil	United States
1966	Italy	North America	1991	Iceland	Poland
1967	Italy	North America			

Bermuda Bowl (continued)

YEAR	WINNER	RUNNER-UP	YEAR	WINNER	RUNNER-UP
1993	The Netherlands	Norway	2000	United States	Brazil
1995	United States	Canada	2001	United States II	Norway
1997	France	United States	2003	United States I	Italy

[1]Not held because of World Team Olympiad.

World Contract Bridge Team Olympiad

YEAR	open		women	
	WINNER	RUNNER-UP	WINNER	RUNNER-UP
1960	France	United Kingdom	United Arab Republic	France
1964	Italy	United States	Great Britain	United States
1968	Italy	United States	Sweden	South Africa
1972	Italy	United States	Italy	South Africa
1976	Brazil	Italy	Italy	United Kingdom
1980	France	United States	United States	Italy
1984	Poland	France	United States	United Kingdom
1988	United States	Austria	Denmark	United Kingdom
1992	France	United States	Austria	United Kingdom
1996	France	Indonesia	United States	China
2000	Italy	Poland	United States	Canada
2004	Italy	The Netherlands	Russia	United States

World Contract Bridge Pair Championships

YEAR	OPEN WINNERS	WOMEN'S WINNERS	MIXED WINNERS
1962	Pierre Jais, Roger Trézel (FRA)	Rixi Markus, Fritzi Gordon (GBR)	[1]
1966	Bob Slavenburg, Hans Kreyns (NED)	Joan Durran, Jane Juan (GBR)	Mary Jane Ferell, Ivan Erdos (USA)
1970	Fritz Babsch, Peter Manhardt (AUT)	Mary Jane Farell, Marilyn Johnson (USA)	Barbara Brier, Waldemar von Zedtwitz (USA)
1974	Robert Hamman, Bobby Wolff (USA)	Fritzi Gordon, Rixi Markus (GBR)	Loula Gordon, Tony Trad (SUI)
1978	Marcelo Branco, Gabino Cintra (BRA)	Kathie Wei, Judi Radin (USA)	Barry Crane, Kerri Shuman (USA)
1982	Chip Martel, Lew Stansby (USA)	Carol Saders, Betty Ann Kennedy (USA)	Dianna Gordon, George Mittelman (CAN)
1986	Jeff Mecksroth, Eric Rodwell (USA)	Jacqui Mitchell, Amalya Kearse (USA)	Pam Wittes, John Wittes (USA)
1990	Marcelo Branco, Gabriel Chagas (BRA)	Kerri Shuman, Karen McCallum (USA)	Peter Wechsel, Juanita Chambers (USA)
1994	Martin Lesniewski, Marek Szymanowski (POL)	Carla Arnolds, Bep Vriend (NED)	Danuta Hocheker, Apolinare Kowalski (POL)
1998	Michal Kwiecien, Jacek Pszczola (POL)	Jill Meyers, Shawn Quinn (USA)	Enza Rossano, Antonio Vivaldi (ITA)
2002	Fulvio Fantoni, Claudio Nunes (ITA)	Karen McCallum, Debbie Rosenberg (USA)	Becky Rogers, Jeff Meckstroth (USA)

[1]A mixed team competition, won by a team from the United Kingdom, was held in 1962.

Cricket

Cricket is one of the **national sports** of England, and consequently it is played in nearly all the countries with which England has been associated. The world governing body is the **International Cricket Council** (ICC; founded as the Imperial Cricket Conference in 1909). The most important international cricket matches are the **Test matches**, which have been played since 1877. The Test-playing countries are England, Australia, South Africa (banned from international competition between about 1970 and 1992), West Indies (representing Barbados, Guyana, Jamaica, Trinidad and Tobago, and the Leeward and Windward islands), New Zealand, India, Pakistan, Sri Lanka, Zimbabwe (since 1992), and Bangladesh (since 2000).

The Test table is designed to be read from left to right across the columns. This will indicate, for example, that in Test match play against England, South Africa has won 25 games, has had 48 drawn matches, and has lost 52 games.

The **World Cup** is a quadrennial series of one-day, limited-overs competitions. It was first held in 1975.

Related Web sites: <www.icc-cricket.com>.

All-Time First-Class Test Cricket Standings (as of 30 Sep 2004)

	England			Australia			South Africa			West Indies			New Zealand		
	WINS	DRAWS	LOSSES	W	D	L	W	D	L	W	D	L	W	D	L
England v.	—	—	—	95	86	125	52	48	25	38	44*	52	41	40	7
Australia v.	125	86	95	—	—	—	39	17	15	45	22†	32	18	15	7
South Africa v.	25	48	52	15	17	39	—	—	—	10	3	2	16	10	4
West Indies v.	52	44*	38	32	22†	45	2	3	10	—	—	—	10	15	7
New Zealand v.	7	40	41	7	15	18	4	10	16	7	15	10	—	—	—
India v.	16	42	33	14	20†	30	2	5	7	10	38	30	14	22*	9
Pakistan v.	10	34	16	11	17	21	2	2	4	12	14	13	21	18	6
Sri Lanka v.	4	4	7	1	6	11	2	5	8	3	3	2	4	9	7
Zimbabwe v.	0	3	3	0	0	3	0	1	4	0	2	4	0	6	5
Bangladesh v.	0	0	2	0	0	2	0	0	4	0	1	3	0	0	2

	India			Pakistan			Sri Lanka			Zimbabwe			Bangladesh		
	WINS	DRAWS	LOSSES	W	D	L	W	D	L	W	D	L	W	D	L
England v.	33	42	16	16	34	10	7	4	4	3	3	0	2	0	0
Australia v.	30	20†	14	21	17	11	11	6	1	3	0	0	2	0	0
South Africa v.	7	5	4	2	2	2	8	5	2	4	1	0	4	0	0
West Indies v.	30	38	10	13	14	12	2	3	3	4	2	0	3	1	0
New Zealand v.	9	22*	14	6	18	21	7	9	4	5	6	0	2	0	0
India v.	—	—	—	7	33	10	8	12	3	5	2	2	1	0	0
Pakistan v.	10	33	7	—	—	—	13	9*	6	8	5*	2	6	0	0
Sri Lanka v.	3	12	8	6	9*	13	—	—	—	10	5	0	3	0	0
Zimbabwe v.	2	2	5	2	5*	8	0	5	10	—	—	—	4	2	0
Bangladesh v.	0	0	1	0	0	6	0	0	3	0	2	4	—	—	—

*Including one match abandoned.   †Including one tie.

Cricket World Cup

YEAR	RESULT				YEAR	RESULT			
1975	West Indies	291–8	Australia	274	1992	Pakistan	249–6	England	227
1979	West Indies	286–9	England	194	1996	Sri Lanka	245–3	Australia	241
1983	India	183	West Indies	140	1999	Australia	133–2	Pakistan	132
1987	Australia	253–5	England	246–8	2003	Australia	359–2	India	234

Curling

The game of curling, played on ice and somewhat akin to bowls or shuffleboard, varies little from country to country. The maximum permitted weight of the curling stones is 44 lb (19.96 kg). The top international **men's competition** was instituted in 1959 (called the Scotch Whisky Cup from 1959 to 1967; the Silver Broom from 1968 to 1985; and the World Curling Championship since 1986). Although curling has been played among women of many countries since at least the mid-20th century, the first **women's world curling championship** was not held until 1979.

World Curling Federation Web site:
<www.worldcurling.org>.

World Curling Championships—Men

YEAR	WINNER	RUNNER-UP	YEAR	WINNER	RUNNER-UP
1959	Canada	Scotland	1975	Switzerland	Canada
1960	Canada	Scotland	1976	United States	Scotland
1961	Canada	Scotland	1977	Sweden	Canada
1962	Canada	Scotland	1978	United States	Canada
1963	Canada	Scotland	1979	Norway	Switzerland
1964	Canada	Scotland	1980	Canada	Norway
1965	United States	Canada	1981	Switzerland	United States
1966	Canada	Scotland	1982	Canada	Switzerland
1967	Scotland	Canada	1983	Canada	West Germany
1968	Canada	Scotland	1984	Norway	Switzerland
1969	Canada	Scotland	1985	Canada	Sweden
1970	Canada	Scotland	1986	Canada	Scotland
1971	Canada	Scotland	1987	Canada	West Germany
1972	Canada	United States	1988	Norway	Canada
1973	Sweden	Canada	1989	Canada	Switzerland
1974	United States	Canada	1990	Canada	Scotland

World Curling Championships—Men (continued)

YEAR	WINNER	RUNNER-UP	YEAR	WINNER	RUNNER-UP
1991	Scotland	Canada	1999	Scotland	Canada
1991	Scotland	Canada	2000	Canada	Sweden
1992	Switzerland	Scotland	2001	Sweden	Switzerland
1993	Canada	Scotland	2002	Canada	Norway
1994	Canada	Sweden	2003	Canada	Switzerland
1995	Canada	Scotland	2004	Sweden	Germany
1996	Canada	Scotland	2005	Canada	Scotland
1997	Sweden	Germany	2006	*to be held 1–9 April in Lowell MA*	
1998	Canada	Sweden			

World Curling Championships—Women

YEAR	WINNER	RUNNER-UP	YEAR	WINNER	RUNNER-UP
1979	Switzerland	Sweden	1994	Canada	Scotland
1980	Canada	Sweden	1995	Sweden	Canada
1981	Sweden	Canada	1996	Canada	United States
1982	Denmark	Sweden	1997	Canada	Norway
1983	Switzerland	Norway	1998	Sweden	Denmark
1984	Canada	Switzerland	1999	Sweden	United States
1985	Canada	Scotland	2000	Canada	Switzerland
1986	Canada	West Germany	2001	Canada	Sweden
1987	Canada	West Germany	2002	Scotland	Sweden
1988	West Germany	Canada	2003	United States	Canada
1989	Canada	Norway	2004	Canada	Norway
1990	Norway	Scotland	2005	Sweden	United States
1991	Norway	Canada	2006	*to be held 18–26 March*	
1992	Sweden	United States		*in Grand Prairie, AB, Canada*	
1993	Canada	Germany			

Did you know? Crossword puzzles were first printed in 19th-century England in books of general puzzles for children. Later these became very popular with adults in the US. The first modern crossword puzzle appeared in a New York newspaper on Sunday, 21 Dec 1913. By the early 1920s most leading newspapers in the US had at least one crossword.

Cycling

By all accounts, the greatest cycling event of all is the annual **Tour de France** road race (founded 1903). It is raced in several stages over a distance usually exceeding 3,500 km (2,175 mi). From 1911 to 1929 distances exceeded 5,300 km. A Tour de France for women was first held in 1984, over an 18-stage course of 991 km. In addition to this and a great number of other road races held yearly, there are yearly **road racing world championships.**

Track racing championships are also held. The oldest events of track racing are the **sprint** (in which only the last part of the race can actually be considered sprinting) and the **pursuit** (both a team and an individual event in which contestants start the race on opposite sides of the track and attempt to catch each other). **Mountain bike racing** and **cyclo-cross**, a cross-country bicycle race that requires cyclists to carry their bikes over parts of the course, developed in the latter part of the 20th century. World championships were established for these sports in 1997.

International Cycling Union (Union Cycliste Internationale—UCI) Web site: <www.uci.ch>.

Cycling Champions, 2004–05

In the case of multiday events, the concluding date is given.

EVENT	WINNER (COUNTRY)	DATE
world champions—mountain bikes		**12 Sep 2004**
men		
Cross-country	Julien Absalon (FRA)	
Downhill	Fabien Barel (FRA)	
women		
Cross-country	Gunn-Rita Dahle (NOR)	
Downhill	Jana Horakova (CZE)	

Cycling Champions, 2004–05 (continued)

EVENT	WINNER (COUNTRY)	DATE
world champions—road		
men		
Individual road race	Oscar Freire Gomez (ESP)	3 Oct 2004
Individual time trial	Michael Rogers (AUS)	29 Sep 2004
women		
Individual road race	Judith Arndt (GER)	2 Oct 2004
Individual time trial	Karin Thürig (SUI)	28 Sep 2004
world champions—cyclo-cross		**30 Jan 2005**
Men	Sven Nijs (BEL)	
Women	Hanka Kupfernagel (GER)	
world champions—track		**27 Mar 2005**
men		
Individual pursuit	Robert Bartko (GER)	
Individual sprint	René Wolff (GER)	
Kilometer time trial	Theo Bos (NED)	
Points	Volodymyr Rybin (UKR)	
Team pursuit	Great Britain	
Keirin	Teun Mulder (NED)	
Team sprint	Great Britain	
Madison	M. Cavendish, R. Hayles (GBR)	
Scratch	Alex Rasmussen (DEN)	
women		
Sprint	Victoria Pendleton (GBR)	
Individual pursuit	Katie Mactier (AUS)	
500-m time trial	Natallia Tsylinskaya (BLR)	
Points	Vera Carrara (ITA)	
Scratch	Olga Slyusareva (RUS)	
Keirin	Clara Sanchez (FRA)	
major elite road-race winners (starred races comprise the World Cup)		
*HEW–Cyclassics Cup–Hamburg	Stuart O'Grady (AUS)	1 Aug 2004
*San Sebastian Classic (Clasica Ciclista San Sebastian)	Miguel Martín Perdiguero (ESP)	7 Aug 2004
*Zürich Championship (Züri-Metzgete)	Juan Antonio Flecha Giannoni (ESP)	22 Aug 2004
Tour of Spain (Vúelta a España)	Roberto Heras Hernandez (ESP)	26 Sep 2004
*Paris–Tours	Erik Dekker (NED)	10 Oct 2004
*Tour of Lombardy (Giro di Lombardia)	Damiano Cunego (ITA)	16 Oct 2004
Paris–Nice	Bobby Julich (USA)	13 Mar 2005
Tirreno–Adriatico	Oscar Freire Gomez (ESP)	15 Mar 2005
Milan–San Remo	Alessandro Petacchi (ITA)	19 Mar 2005
*Tour of Flanders (Ronde van Vlaanderen)	Tom Boonen (BEL)	3 Apr 2005
Ghent–Wevelgem	Nico Mattan (BEL)	6 Apr 2005
Paris–Roubaix	Tom Boonen (BEL)	10 Apr 2005
Amstel Gold	Danilo Di Luca (ITA)	17 Apr 2005
*La Flèche Wallonne	Danilo Di Luca (ITA)	20 Apr 2005
Liège–Bastogne–Liège	Aleksandr Vinokurov (KAZ)	24 Apr 2005
Tour of Romandie (Tour de Romandie)	Santigo Botero Echeverry (COL)	1 May 2005
Tour of Italy (Giro d'Italia)	Paolo Savoldelli (ITA)	29 May 2005
Critérium du Dauphiné Libéré	Inigo Landaluze Intxaurraga (ESP)	12 Jun 2005
Tour of Switzerland (Tour de Suisse)	Aitor Gonzalez Jimenez (ESP)	19 Jun 2005
Tour de France	Lance Armstrong (USA)	24 Jul 2005

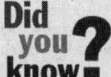

Did you know? In 1865 the rich young Olivier brothers, René and Aimé, pedaled velocipedes (early bicycles) more than 800 km (500 miles) from Paris to Marseille, and their subsequent enthusiasm for the new sport helped it to become a worldwide craze for the young, fit, and well-to-do.

Tour de France

YEAR	WINNER (COUNTRY)	LENGTH OF ROUTE (KM)	YEAR	WINNER (COUNTRY)	LENGTH OF ROUTE (KM)
1903	Maurice Garin (FRA)	2,428	1959	Federico Bahamontes (ESP)	4,355
1904	Henri Cornet (FRA)	2,388	1960	Gastone Nencini (ITA)	4,173
1905	Louis Trousselier (FRA)	2,975	1961	Jacques Anquetil (FRA)	4,397
1906	René Pottier (FRA)	4,637	1962	Jacques Anquetil (FRA)	4,274
1907	Lucien Petit-Breton (FRA)	4,488	1963	Jacques Anquetil (FRA)	4,137
1908	Lucien Petit-Breton (FRA)	4,487	1964	Jacques Anquetil (FRA)	4,504
1909	François Faber (LUX)	4,507	1965	Felice Gimondi (ITA)	4,183
1910	Octave Lapize (FRA)	4,474	1966	Lucien Aimar (FRA)	4,303
1911	Gustave Garrigou (FRA)	5,344	1967	Roger Pingeon (FRA)	4,780
1912	Odile Defraye (BEL)	5,319	1968	Jan Janssen (NED)	4,662
1913	Philippe Thys (BEL)	5,387	1969	Eddy Merckx (BEL)	4,110
1914	Philippe Thys (BEL)	5,405	1970	Eddy Merckx (BEL)	4,366
1915–18	not held		1971	Eddy Merckx (BEL)	3,689
1919	Firmin Lambot (BEL)	5,560	1972	Eddy Merckx (BEL)	3,846
1920	Philippe Thys (BEL)	5,519	1973	Luis Ocaña (ESP)	4,140
1921	Léon Scieur (BEL)	5,484	1974	Eddy Merckx (BEL)	4,098
1922	Firmin Lambot (BEL)	5,375	1975	Bernard Thévenet (FRA)	4,000
1923	Henri Pélissier (FRA)	5,386	1976	Lucien Van Impe (BEL)	4,050
1924	Ottavio Bottecchia (ITA)	5,425	1977	Bernard Thévenet (FRA)	4,098
1925	Ottavio Bottecchia (ITA)	5,430	1978	Bernard Hinault (FRA)	3,920
1926	Lucien Buysse (BEL)	5,745	1979	Bernard Hinault (FRA)	3,719
1927	Nicolas Frantz (LUX)	5,341	1980	Joop Zoetemelk (NED)	3,948
1928	Nicolas Frantz (LUX)	5,377	1981	Bernard Hinault (FRA)	3,765
1929	Maurice De Waele (BEL)	5,286	1982	Bernard Hinault (FRA)	3,489
1930	André Leducq (FRA)	4,818	1983	Laurent Fignon (FRA)	3,568
1931	Antonin Magne (FRA)	5,095	1984	Laurent Fignon (FRA)	3,880
1932	André Leducq (FRA)	4,520	1985	Bernard Hinault (FRA)	4,100
1933	Georges Speicher (FRA)	4,395	1986	Greg LeMond (USA)	4,091
1934	Antonin Magne (FRA)	4,363	1987	Stephen Roche (IRL)	4,100
1935	Romain Maes (BEL)	4,338	1988	Pedro Delgado (ESP)	3,300
1936	Romain Maes (BEL)	4,442	1989	Greg LeMond (USA)	3,215
1937	Roger Lapébie (FRA)	4,415	1990	Greg LeMond (USA)	3,399
1938	Gino Bartali (ITA)	4,694	1991	Miguel Indurain (ESP)	3,935
1939	Sylvere Maes (BEL)	4,224	1992	Miguel Indurain (ESP)	3,983
1940–46	not held		1993	Miguel Indurain (ESP)	3,700
1947	Jean Robic (FRA)	4,640	1994	Miguel Indurain (ESP)	3,978
1948	Gino Bartali (ITA)	4,922	1995	Miguel Indurain (ESP)	3,635
1949	Fausto Coppi (ITA)	4,808	1996	Bjarne Riis (DEN)	3,764
1950	Ferdi Kubler (SUI)	4,775	1997	Jan Ullrich (GER)	3,944
1951	Hugo Koblet (SUI)	4,697	1998	Marco Pantani (ITA)	3,831
1952	Fausto Coppi (ITA)	4,807	1999	Lance Armstrong (USA)	3,687
1953	Louison Bobet (FRA)	4,479	2000	Lance Armstrong (USA)	3,663
1954	Louison Bobet (FRA)	4,469	2001	Lance Armstrong (USA)	3,454
1955	Louison Bobet (FRA)	4,855	2002	Lance Armstrong (USA)	3,272
1956	Roger Walkowiak (FRA)	4,496	2003	Lance Armstrong (USA)	3,428
1957	Jacques Anquetil (FRA)	4,686	2004	Lance Armstrong (USA)	3,391
1958	Charly Gaul (LUX)	4,319	2005	Lance Armstrong (USA)	3,608

Fencing

What had been the European fencing championship from 1921 to 1935 was officially recognized as the **world fencing** championship at the Olympic Games of 1936. The only event that does not reflect Olympic winners in the designated years is the women's team foil competition, which was not an Olympic event until 1960. Traditionally **women** competed only in the foil; women's épée competition has been part of the world championships since 1989 and women's sabre since 1999.

Men's fencing bouts last about six minutes, and the first man to score five hits with the designated portion of the weapon (for foil and épée, only hits made with the point of the weapon are scored) is the winner. Women's bouts last about five minutes, and only four hits must be scored.

Each **weapon** has a different target area: for the **foil**, it is the torso; for the **épée**, the entire body; and for the **sabre**, roughly the upper half of the body (including the head and arms).

Related Web sites: Fédération Internationale d'Escrime (FIE): <www.fie.ch>; US Fencing Association (USFA): <www.usfencing.org>.

World Fencing Championships—Men

Competition has been held since 1936. Table shows results for the past 20 years.
The 2005 championships are scheduled to conclude 15 October in Leipzig, Germany.

Foil / Épée

YEAR	INDIVIDUAL	TEAM	YEAR	INDIVIDUAL	TEAM
1985	Mauro Numa (ITA)	Italy	1985	Philippe Boisse (FRA)	West Germany
1986	Andrea Borella (ITA)	Italy	1986	Philippe Riboud (FRA)	West Germany
1987	Mathias Gey (FRG)	West Germany	1987	Volker Fischer (FRG)	USSR
1988[1]	Stefano Cerioni (ITA)	USSR	1988[1]	Arnd Schmitt (FRG)	France
1989	Alexander Koch (FRG)	USSR	1989	Manuel Pereira (SPA)	Italy
1990	Philippe Omnès (FRA)	Italy	1990	Thomas Gerull (FRG)	Italy
1991	Ingo Weissenborn (GER)	Cuba	1991	Andrey Shuvalov (URS)	USSR
1992[1]	Philippe Omnès (FRA)	Germany	1992[1]	Eric Srecki (FRA)	Germany
1993	Alexander Koch (GER)	Germany	1993	Pavel Kolobkov (RUS)	Italy
1994	Rolando Tucker (CUB)	Germany	1994	Pavel Kolobkov (RUS)	France
1995	Dmitry Shevchenko (RUS)	Cuba	1995	Eric Srecki (FRA)	Germany
1996[1]	Alessandro Puccini (ITA)	Russia	1996[1]	Aleksandr Beketov (RUS)	Italy
1997	Sergey Golubitsky (UKR)	France	1997	Eric Srecki (FRA)	Cuba
1998	Sergey Golubitsky (UKR)	Poland	1998	Hugues Obry (FRA)	Hungary
1999	Sergey Golubitsky (UKR)	France	1999	Arnd Schmitt (GER)	France
2000[1]	Kim Young Ho (KOR)	France	2000[1]	Pavel Kolobkov (RUS)	Italy
2001	Salvatore Sanzo (ITA)	France	2001	Paolo Milanoli (ITA)	Hungary
2002	Simone Vanni (ITA)	Germany	2002	Pavel Kolobkov (RUS)	France
2003	Peter Joppich (GER)	Italy	2003	Fabrice Jeannet (FRA)	Russia
2004[1]	Brice Guyart (FRA)	Italy	2004[1]	Marcel Fischer (SUI)	France

Sabre / Sabre

YEAR	INDIVIDUAL	TEAM	YEAR	INDIVIDUAL	TEAM
1985	Gyorgy Nebald (HUN)	USSR	1995	Grigory Kiriyenko (URS)	Italy
1986	Sergey Mindirgasov (URS)	USSR	1996[1]	Stanislav Pozdnyakov (RUS)	Russia
1987	Jean-François Lamour (FRA)	USSR	1997	Stanislav Pozdnyakov (RUS)	France
1988[1]	Jean-François Lamour (FRA)	Hungary	1998	Luigi Tarantino (ITA)	Hungary
1989	Grigory Kiriyenko (URS)	USSR	1999	Damien Touya (FRA)	France
1990	Gyorgy Nebald (HUN)	USSR	2000[1]	Mihai Claudiu Covaliu (ROM)	Russia
1991	Grigory Kiriyenko (URS)	Hungary	2001	Stanislav Pozdnyakov (RUS)	Russia
1992[1]	Bence Szabo (HUN)	Unified Team[2]	2002	Stanislav Pozdnyakov (RUS)	Russia
1993	Grigory Kiriyenko (URS)	Hungary	2003	Vladimir Lukashenko (UKR)	Russia
1994	Felix Becker (GER)	Russia	2004[1]	Aldo Montano (ITA)	France

[1]Olympic titles are recognized as world championships. [2]Consisting of athletes from the Commonwealth of Independent States and Georgia.

World Fencing Championships—Women

Foil competition has been held since 1936. Table shows results for the past 20 years.
The 2005 championships are scheduled to conclude 15 October in Leipzig, Germany.

Foil / Foil (continued)

YEAR	INDIVIDUAL	TEAM	YEAR	INDIVIDUAL	TEAM
1985	Cornelia Hanisch (FRG)	West Germany	2004	Valentina Vezzali (ITA)[1]	Italy
1986	Anja Fichtel (FRG)	USSR			
1987	Elisabeta Tufan (ROM)	Hungary		**Épée**	
1988[1]	Anja Fichtel (FRG)	West Germany	YEAR	INDIVIDUAL	TEAM
1989	Olga Velichko (URS)	West Germany	1989	Anja Straub (SUI)	Hungary
1990	Anja Fichtel (FRG)	Italy	1990	Taymi Chappe (CUB)	West Germany
1991	Giovanna Trillini (ITA)	Italy	1991	Mariann Horvath (HUN)	Hungary
1992[1]	Giovanna Trillini (ITA)	Italy	1992	not held	
1993	Francesca Bortolozzi (ITA)	Germany	1993	Oksana Jermakova (EST)	Hungary
			1994	Laura Chiesa (ITA)	Spain
1994	Reka Szabo (ROM)	Romania	1995	Joanna Jakimiuk (POL)	Hungary
1995	Laura Badea (ROM)	Italy	1996[1]	Laura Flessel (FRA)	France
1996[1]	Laura Badea (ROM)	Italy	1997	Mirayda Garcia-Soto (CUB)	Hungary
1997	Giovanna Trillini (ITA)	Italy	1998	Laura Flessel (FRA)	France
1998	Sabine Bau (GER)	Italy	1999	Laura Flessel-Colovic (FRA)	Hungary
1999	Valentina Vezzali (ITA)	Germany	2000[1]	Timea Nagy (HUN)	Russia
2000[1]	Valentina Vezzali (ITA)	Italy	2001	Claudia Bokel (GER)	Russia
2001	Valentina Vezzali (ITA)	Italy	2002	Hyun Hee (KOR)	Hungary
2002	Svetlana Boyko (RUS)	Russia	2003	Natalya Conrad (UKR)	Russia
2003	Valentina Vezzali (ITA)	Poland	2004[1]	Timea Nagy (HUN)	Russia

World Fencing Championships—Women (continued)

Sabre

YEAR	INDIVIDUAL	TEAM
1999	Yelena Yemayeva (AZE)	Italy
2000[1]	Yelena Yemayeva (AZE)	United States
2001	Anne-Lise Touya (FRA)	Russia
2002	Tan Xue (CHN)	Russia
2003	Dorina Mihai (ROM)	Italy
2004	Mariel Zagunis (USA)[1]	Russia

[1]Olympic titles are recognized as world championships.

Field Hockey

The sport of **field hockey** is quite popular with both men and women in the United Kingdom, India, Pakistan, and much of Europe. Curiously, the sport was not seriously promoted among American men, so in the United States field hockey has been largely regarded as a sport for women. Despite its recognizable origins in the mid-19th century, the game was not organized on an **international** level until the mid-20th century. One of a number of international tournaments is the **World Cup**, which is organized by the **International Hockey Federation** (Fédération Internationale de Hockey, FIH; founded 1924).

FIH Web site: <www.fihockey.org>.

World Cup Field Hockey Championship

	men			women	
YEAR	WINNER	RUNNER-UP	YEAR	WINNER	RUNNER-UP
1971	Pakistan	India	1974	The Netherlands	Argentina
1973	The Netherlands	India	1976	West Germany	Argentina
1975	India	Pakistan	1978	The Netherlands	West Germany
1978	Pakistan	The Netherlands	1981	West Germany	The Netherlands
1982	Pakistan	West Germany	1983	The Netherlands	Canada
1986	Australia	England	1986	The Netherlands	West Germany
1990	The Netherlands	Pakistan	1990	The Netherlands	Australia
1994	Pakistan	The Netherlands	1994	Australia	Argentina
1998	The Netherlands	Spain	1998	Australia	The Netherlands
2002	Germany	Australia	2002	Argentina	The Netherlands

Football

Many types of games are known as football, among them association football (also called soccer), gridiron football (also called American football and known in the United States as, simply, football), Canadian football (also called rugby football), Australian Rules Football (also called footy), and Rugby Union and Rugby League football (also known as rugby, or rugger). Each of these games is unique, although some—such as US football and Canadian football—bear more than a little resemblance, and each has its own distinct following.

American football—professional. The National Football League (NFL) championship play-offs were organized in 1933. The American Football League (founded 1959) was a rival organization until 1970, when it merged with the NFL. The resulting reorganization added a few new teams (1976) and divided the reconstituted NFL into two conferences, the American Football Conference and the National Football Conference. The play-off winner in each conference becomes that conference's representative in the Super Bowl, the final game of the professional football season.

American football—college. Historically the national champion of college football has been informally selected by two rival opinion polls—one based on a survey of collegiate football coaches (currently conducted by *USA Today*/ESPN) and the other on a survey of sportswriters (conducted by the Associated Press [AP]). The AP sportswriters' poll began in 1936. The coaches' poll was begun in 1950 by the United Press (now United Press International [UPI]). Where polls designated different teams, both are listed. Desire for a clear-cut national champion led to the creation of the Bowl Championship Series (BCS) in 1999. The BCS uses a formula involving team records, strength of schedule, and rankings to determine the top two teams, who then meet in a national championship game. The site of the game annually shifts between the four major Bowls—Fiesta, Orange, Rose, and Sugar. The first of the Bowl games, the Rose Bowl, had its inaugural game in 1902 during the 12th annual Tournament of Roses festival in Pasadena CA. In 1935 the Sugar Bowl (played in New Orleans LA) and the Orange Bowl (played in Miami FL) were inaugurated. The Fiesta Bowl (played in Phoenix AZ) began play in 1971.

Canadian football—professional. The rules and organization of professional football in Canada have evolved gradually for well over 100 years based on the Canadian Rugby Union (formed in 1891). Until 1936 the game included intercollegiate teams. Since 1959 the Canadian Football League has been divided into two conferences, Eastern and Western. The two teams that win the division championships meet for the championship of the League, the Grey Cup (instituted in 1909). The intercollegiate teams withdrew from the Grey Cup competition in 1936, but the league did not become strictly professional until the mid-1950s.

Australian football—professional. Australian Rules Football, originally called Melbourne Rules Football, emerged in the state of Victoria in the late 1850s as a sporting alternative during the southern winter, when cricket was not played. The Victorian Football Association (formed in 1877) was supplanted by the Victorian Football League (formed in 1896), which was renamed the Australian Football League (AFL) in 1990 after two teams from outside Victoria were admitted in 1987. Currently, the eight AFL teams with the best records at the end of a 22-week season qualify for the play-offs. The first premiership Grand Final was played in 1886.

Association football. The game of association football is governed by the Fédération Internationale de Football Association (FIFA; founded 1904). The quadrennial FIFA World Cup (organized as the World Cup in 1930) was the first official internationally contested association football match. The popularity of the World Cup and even earlier the Copa América (1916) in South America led to the development of several regional cup competitions, including the European Champion Clubs' Cup (1955; discontinued after the 1992–93 season and superseded by the UEFA Champions League), the Asian Cup (1956), the African Cup of Nations (1957), and the Libertadores de América Cup (1960). Competition for the FIFA Women's World Cup began in 1991. The Major League Soccer Cup in the US was launched in 1996.

Rugby Union football. Rugby Union football was open to amateurs only until 1995. The Six Nations Championship was first played in 1882 (as the Four Nations) and is now contested by England, Scotland, Wales, Ireland, France (since 1910), and Italy (since 2000). The international Test matches further include South Africa, New Zealand, and Australia. The International Rugby Football League (FIRA; now FIRA-AER) oversees rugby in 39 other (i.e., non-Test) countries. The chief international competition between Rugby Union clubs in the southern hemisphere is the tri-nation Super 12 (Super 10 from 1993 until 1996). Teams from Australia (three), South Africa (four), and New Zealand (five) play in a round-robin tournament; the four teams with the best records qualify for the semifinals. The World Cup, sponsored by the International Rugby Board (IRB; founded 1886), was inaugurated in 1987. The competition is held every four years.

Rugby League football. Rugby League World Cup competition began in 1954 between professionals from Australia, France, Great Britain, and New Zealand. In 1975 it was renamed the International Championship. Competition was discontinued after 1977 but revived during the 1980s. The match has been held irregularly every few years.

Related Web sites: National Football League (NFL): <www.nfl.com>; Canadian Football League (CFL): <www.cfl.ca>; Australian Football League (AFL): <www.afl.com.au>; Fédération Internationale de Football Association (FIFA): <www.fifa.com>; Union of European Football Associations (UEFA): <www.uefa.com>; Major League Soccer (MLS): <www.majorleaguesoccer.com>; International Rugby Board (Rugby Union): <www.irb.com>; International Rugby League: <http://world.rleague.com>, (Super 12) <www.super12.rugby. com.au>.

National Football League (NFL) Final Standings, 2004—05

American Football Conference

TEAM	WON	LOST	TIED	TEAM	WON	LOST	TIED
East Division				**South Division**			
New England[1]	14	2	0	Indianapolis[1]	12	4	0
New York Jets[1]	10	6	0	Jacksonville	9	7	0
Buffalo	9	7	0	Houston	7	9	0
Miami	4	12	0	Tennessee	5	11	0
North Division				**West Division**			
Pittsburgh[1]	15	1	0	San Diego[1]	12	4	0
Baltimore	9	7	0	Denver[1]	10	6	0
Cincinnati	8	8	0	Kansas City	7	9	0
Cleveland	4	12	0	Oakland	5	11	0

National Football Conference

TEAM	WON	LOST	TIED	TEAM	WON	LOST	TIED
East Division				**South Division**			
Philadelphia[1]	13	3	0	Atlanta[1]	11	5	0
New York Giants	6	10	0	New Orleans	8	8	0
Dallas	6	10	0	Carolina	7	9	0
Washington	6	10	0	Tampa Bay	5	11	0
North Division				**West Division**			
Green Bay[1]	10	6	0	Seattle[1]	9	7	0
Minnesota	8	8	0	St. Louis[1]	8	8	0
Detroit	6	10	0	Arizona	6	10	0
Chicago	5	11	0	San Francisco	2	14	0

[1]Gained play-off berth.

American Pro Football All-Time Records

Source: <www.nfl.com>.

PLAYERS/TEAMS		NUMBER	SEASON/DATE
Individual career records			
Total appearances	Morten Andersen[1]	354	1982–2004
Total points	Gary Anderson[1]	2,434	1982–2004
Touchdowns, total	Jerry Rice[1]	207	1985–2004
Touchdowns, passing	Dan Marino	420	1983–99
Touchdowns, receiving	Jerry Rice[1]	197	1985–2004
Touchdowns, rushing	Emmitt Smith	155	1990–2004
Field goals made	Gary Anderson[1]	538	1982–2004
Extra points made (kicked)	George Blanda	943	1949–75, except 1959
Passing yardage	Dan Marino	61,361	1983–99
Passing completions	Dan Marino	4,967	1983–99
Receiving yardage	Jerry Rice[1]	22,895	1985–2004
Rushing yardage	Emmitt Smith	17,418	1990–2004
Interceptions (defense)	Paul Krause	81	1964–79
Sacks (defense)[2]	Bruce Smith	200	1985–2003
Coaching, total wins	Don Shula	328	1963–95
Individual season records			
Total points	Paul Hornung (Green Bay Packers)	176	1960
Touchdowns, total	Priest Holmes (Kansas City Chiefs)	27	2003
Touchdowns, passing	Peyton Manning (Indianapolis Colts)	49	2004
Touchdowns, receiving	Jerry Rice (San Francisco 49ers)	22	1987
Touchdowns, rushing	Priest Holmes (Kansas City Chiefs)	27	2003
Field goals made	Olindo Mare (Miami Dolphins); Jeff Wilkins (St. Louis Rams)	39	1999; 2003
Extra points made (kicked)	Uwe von Schamann (Miami Dolphins)	66	1984
Passing yardage	Dan Marino (Miami Dolphins)	5,084	1984
Passing completions	Rich Gannon (Oakland Raiders)	418	2002
Receiving yardage	Jerry Rice (San Francisco 49ers)	1,848	1995
Rushing yardage	Eric Dickerson (Los Angeles Rams)	2,105	1984
Interceptions (defense)	Dick "Night Train" Lane (Los Angeles Rams)	14	1952
Sacks (defense)[2]	Michael Strahan (New York Giants)	22.5	2001
Individual game records			
Total points	Ernie Nevers (Chicago Cardinals)	40	28 Nov 1929
Touchdowns, total	Ernie Nevers (Chicago Cardinals); Dub Jones (Cleveland Browns); Gale Sayers (Chicago Bears)	6	28 Nov 1929; 25 Nov 1951; 12 Dec 1965
Touchdowns, passing	Sid Luckman (Chicago Bears); Adrian Burk (Philadelphia Eagles); George Blanda (Houston Oilers); Y.A. Tittle (New York Giants); Joe Kapp (Minnesota Vikings)	7	14 Nov 1943; 17 Oct 1954; 19 Nov 1961; 28 Oct 1962; 28 Sep 1969
Touchdowns, receiving	Bob Shaw (Chicago Cardinals); Kellen Winslow (San Diego Chargers); Jerry Rice (San Francisco 49ers)	5	2 Oct 1950; 22 Nov 1981; 14 Oct 1990
Touchdowns, rushing	Ernie Nevers (Chicago Cardinals)	6	28 Nov 1929
Field goals made	Jim Bakken (St. Louis Cardinals); Rich Karlis (Minnesota Vikings); Chris Boniol (Dallas Cowboys)	7	24 Sep 1967; 5 Nov 1989 (OT); 18 Nov 1996
Longest field goal	Tom Dempsey (New Orleans Saints); Jason Elam (Denver Broncos)	63 yd	8 Nov 1970; 25 Oct 1998
Extra points scored (kicked)	Pat Harder (Chicago Cardinals); Bob Waterfield (Los Angeles Rams); Charlie Gogolack (Washington Redskins)	9	17 Oct 1948; 22 Oct 1950; 27 Nov 1966
Passing yardage	Norm Van Brocklin (Los Angeles Rams)	554	28 Sep 1951
Passing completions	Drew Bledsoe (New England Patriots)	45	13 Nov 1994
Receiving yardage	Willie Anderson (Los Angeles Rams)	336	11 Nov 1989
Rushing yardage	Jamal Lewis (Baltimore Ravens)	295	14 Sep 2003
Longest run from scrimmage	Tony Dorsett (Dallas Cowboys)	99 yd	3 Jan 1983
Interceptions (defense)	*too numerous to list*	4	
Sacks (defense)[2]	Derrick Thomas (Kansas City Chiefs)	7	11 Nov 1990

American Pro Football All-Time Records (continued)

	PLAYERS/TEAMS	NUMBER	SEASON/DATE
Team season records			
Super Bowl titles	Dallas Cowboys; San Francisco 49ers	5	
Consecutive Super Bowl titles	seven teams	2	
Total points scored	Minnesota Vikings	556	1998
Touchdowns, total	Miami Dolphins	70	1984
Touchdowns, passing	Indianapolis Colts	51	2004
Touchdowns, rushing	Green Bay Packers	36	1962
Field goals made	Miami Dolphins; St. Louis Rams	39	1999; 2003
Passing yardage	St. Louis Rams	5,492	2000
Passing completions	San Francisco 49ers	432	1995
Rushing yardage	New England Patriots	3,165	1978
Game records			
Highest total score	Washington Redskins v. New York Giants	113 (72–41)	27 Nov 1966
Longest game	Miami Dolphins v. Kansas City Chiefs	82:40 (two overtimes)	25 Dec 1971

[1]Active in 2005. [2]Since 1982; before that year sacks were not officially recorded by the NFL.

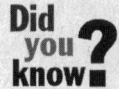

Did you know? Archie Griffin is the only two-time winner of the Heisman Trophy, awarded annually to the best player in college football. He won the award in 1974 and 1975 while playing for Ohio State.

Super Bowl

NFL-AFL championship 1966–70; NFL championship from 1971–72 season.

	SEASON	WINNER	RUNNER-UP	SCORE
I	1966–67	Green Bay Packers (NFL)	Kansas City Chiefs (AFL)	35–10
II	1967–68	Green Bay Packers (NFL)	Oakland Raiders (AFL)	33–14
III	1968–69	New York Jets (AFL)	Baltimore Colts (NFL)	16–7
IV	1969–70	Kansas City Chiefs (AFL)	Minnesota Vikings (NFL)	23–7
V	1970–71	Baltimore Colts (AFC)	Dallas Cowboys (NFC)	16–13
VI	1971–72	Dallas Cowboys (NFC)	Miami Dolphins (AFC)	24–3
VII	1972–73	Miami Dolphins (AFC)	Washington Redskins (NFC)	14–7
VIII	1973–74	Miami Dolphins (AFC)	Minnesota Vikings (NFC)	24–7
IX	1974–75	Pittsburgh Steelers (AFC)	Minnesota Vikings (NFC)	16–6
X	1975–76	Pittsburgh Steelers (AFC)	Dallas Cowboys (NFC)	21–17
XI	1976–77	Oakland Raiders (AFC)	Minnesota Vikings (NFC)	32–14
XII	1977–78	Dallas Cowboys (NFC)	Denver Broncos (AFC)	27–10
XIII	1978–79	Pittsburgh Steelers (AFC)	Dallas Cowboys (NFC)	35–31
XIV	1979–80	Pittsburgh Steelers (AFC)	Los Angeles Rams (NFC)	31–19
XV	1980–81	Oakland Raiders (AFC)	Philadelphia Eagles (NFC)	27–10
XVI	1981–82	San Francisco 49ers (NFC)	Cincinnati Bengals (AFC)	26–21
XVII	1982–83	Washington Redskins (NFC)	Miami Dolphins (AFC)	27–17
XVIII	1983–84	Los Angeles Raiders (AFC)	Washington Redskins (NFC)	38–9
XIX	1984–85	San Francisco 49ers (NFC)	Miami Dolphins (AFC)	38–16
XX	1985–86	Chicago Bears (NFC)	New England Patriots (AFC)	46–10
XXI	1986–87	New York Giants (NFC)	Denver Broncos (AFC)	39–20
XXII	1987–88	Washington Redskins (NFC)	Denver Broncos (AFC)	42–10
XXIII	1988–89	San Francisco 49ers (NFC)	Cincinnati Bengals (AFC)	20–16
XXIV	1989–90	San Francisco 49ers (NFC)	Denver Broncos (AFC)	55–10
XXV	1990–91	New York Giants (NFC)	Buffalo Bills (AFC)	20–19
XXVI	1991–92	Washington Redskins (NFC)	Buffalo Bills (AFC)	37–24
XXVII	1992–93	Dallas Cowboys (NFC)	Buffalo Bills (AFC)	52–17
XXVIII	1993–94	Dallas Cowboys (NFC)	Buffalo Bills (AFC)	30–13
XXIX	1994–95	San Francisco 49ers (NFC)	San Diego Chargers (AFC)	49–26
XXX	1995–96	Dallas Cowboys (NFC)	Pittsburgh Steelers (AFC)	27–17
XXXI	1996–97	Green Bay Packers (NFC)	New England Patriots (AFC)	35–21
XXXII	1997–98	Denver Broncos (AFC)	Green Bay Packers (NFC)	31–24
XXXIII	1998–99	Denver Broncos (AFC)	Atlanta Falcons (NFC)	34–19

Super Bowl (continued)

	SEASON	WINNER	RUNNER-UP	SCORE
XXXIV	1999–2000	St. Louis Rams (NFC)	Tennessee Titans (AFC)	23–16
XXXV	2000–01	Baltimore Ravens (AFC)	New York Giants (NFC)	34–7
XXXVI	2001–02	New England Patriots (AFC)	St. Louis Rams (NFC)	20–17
XXXVII	2002–03	Tampa Bay Buccaneers (NFC)	Oakland Raiders (AFC)	48–21
XXXVIII	2003–04	New England Patriots (AFC)	Carolina Panthers (NFC)	32–29
XXXIX	2004–05	New England Patriots (AFC)	Philadelphia Eagles (NFC)	24–21

College Football National Champions

SEASON	CHAMPION	SEASON	CHAMPION	SEASON	CHAMPION
1924	Notre Dame	1955	Oklahoma	1983	Miami (FL)
1925	Dartmouth	1956	Oklahoma	1984	Brigham Young
1926	Stanford	1957	Auburn (AP), Ohio State (UP)	1985	Oklahoma
1927	Illinois	1958	Louisiana State	1986	Penn State
1928	Southern California	1959	Syracuse	1987	Miami (FL)
1929	Notre Dame	1960	Minnesota	1988	Notre Dame
1930	Notre Dame	1961	Alabama	1989	Miami (FL)
1931	Southern California	1962	Southern California	1990	Colorado (AP),
1932	Michigan	1963	Texas		Georgia Tech (UPI)
1933	Michigan	1964	Alabama	1991	Miami (FL; AP),
1934	Minnesota	1965	Alabama (AP), Michigan		Washington (UPI)
1935	Southern Methodist		State (UPI)	1992	Alabama
1936	Minnesota	1966	Notre Dame	1993–94	Florida State
1937	Pittsburgh	1967	Southern California	1994–95	Nebraska
1938	Texas Christian	1968	Ohio State	1995–96	Nebraska
1939	Texas A&M	1969	Texas	1996–97	Florida
1940	Minnesota	1970	Nebraska (AP), Texas (UPI)	1997–98	Michigan (AP),
1941	Minnesota	1971	Nebraska		Nebraska (USA
1942	Ohio State	1972	Southern California		Today/ESPN)
1943	Notre Dame	1973	Notre Dame (AP), Alabama	1998–99	Tennessee
1944	Army		(UPI)	1999–2000	Florida State
1945	Army	1974	Oklahoma (AP), Southern	2000–01	Oklahoma
1946	Notre Dame		California (UPI)	2001–02	Miami (FL)
1947	Notre Dame	1975	Oklahoma	2002–03	Ohio State
1948	Michigan	1976	Pittsburgh	2003–04	Louisiana State
1949	Notre Dame	1977	Notre Dame		(BCS), Southern
1950	Oklahoma	1978	Alabama (AP),		California (AP)
1951	Tennessee		Southern California (UPI)	2004–05	Southern California
1952	Michigan State	1979	Alabama		
1953	Maryland	1980	Georgia		
1954	Ohio State (AP),	1981	Clemson		
	UCLA (UP)	1982	Penn State		

Rose Bowl

SEASON	WINNER	RUNNER-UP	SCORE	SEASON	WINNER	RUNNER-UP	SCORE
1901–02	Michigan	Stanford	49–0	1927–28	Stanford	Pittsburgh	7–6
1915–16	Washington State	Brown	14–0	1928–29	Georgia Tech	California	8–7
1916–17	Oregon	Pennsylvania	14–0	1929–30	Southern California	Pittsburgh	47–14
1917–18	Mare Island	Camp Lewis	19–7	1930–31	Alabama	Washington State	24–0
1918–19	Great Lakes	Mare Island	17–0				
1919–20	Harvard	Oregon	7–6	1931–32	Southern California	Tulane	21–12
1920–21	California	Ohio State	28–0				
1921–22	California	Washington & Jefferson	0–0	1932–33	Southern California	Pittsburgh	35–0
1922–23	Southern California	Penn State	14–3	1933–34	Columbia	Stanford	7–0
				1934–35	Alabama	Stanford	29–13
1923–24	Washington	Navy	14–14	1935–36	Stanford	Southern Methodist	7–0
1924–25	Notre Dame	Stanford	27–10				
1925–26	Alabama	Washington	20–19	1936–37	Pittsburgh	Washington	21–0
1926–27	Alabama	Stanford	7–7	1937–38	California	Alabama	13–0

Rose Bowl (continued)

SEASON	WINNER	RUNNER-UP	SCORE
1938-39	Southern California	Duke	7-3
1939-40	Southern California	Tennessee	14-0
1940-41	Stanford	Nebraska	21-13
1941-42	Oregon State	Duke	20-16
1942-43	Georgia	UCLA	9-0
1943-44	Southern California	Washington	29-0
1944-45	Southern California	Tennessee	25-0
1945-46	Alabama	Southern California	34-14
1946-47	Illinois	UCLA	45-14
1947-48	Michigan	Southern California	49-0
1948-49	Northwestern	California	20-14
1949-50	Ohio State	California	17-14
1950-51	Michigan	California	14-6
1951-52	Illinois	Stanford	40-7
1952-53	Southern California	Wisconsin	7-0
1953-54	Michigan State	UCLA	28-20
1954-55	Ohio State	Southern California	20-7
1955-56	Michigan State	UCLA	17-14
1956-57	Iowa	Oregon State	35-19
1957-58	Ohio State	Oregon	10-7
1958-59	Iowa	California	38-12
1959-60	Washington	Wisconsin	44-8
1960-61	Washington	Minnesota	17-7
1961-62	Minnesota	UCLA	21-3
1962-63	Southern California	Wisconsin	42-37
1963-64	Illinois	Washington	17-7
1964-65	Michigan	Oregon State	34-7
1965-66	UCLA	Michigan State	14-12
1966-67	Purdue	Southern California	14-13
1967-68	Southern California	Indiana	14-3
1967-68	Southern California	Indiana	14-3
1968-69	Ohio State	Southern California	27-16
1969-70	Southern California	Michigan	10-3
1970-71	Stanford	Ohio State	27-17
1971-72	Stanford	Michigan	13-12
1972-73	Southern California	Ohio State	42-17
1973-74	Ohio State	Southern California	42-21
1974-75	Southern California	Ohio State	18-17
1975-76	UCLA	Ohio State	23-10
1976-77	Southern California	Michigan	14-6
1977-78	Washington	Michigan	27-20
1978-79	Southern California	Michigan	17-10
1979-80	Southern California	Ohio State	17-16
1980-81	Michigan	Washington	23-6
1981-82	Washington	Iowa	28-0
1982-83	UCLA	Michigan	24-14
1983-84	UCLA	Illinois	45-9
1984-85	Southern California	Ohio State	20-17
1985-86	UCLA	Iowa	45-28
1986-87	Arizona State	Michigan	22-15
1987-88	Michigan State	Southern California	20-17
1988-89	Michigan	Southern California	22-14
1989-90	Southern California	Michigan	17-10
1990-91	Washington	Iowa	46-34
1991-92	Washington	Michigan	34-14
1992-93	Michigan	Washington	38-31
1993-94	Wisconsin	UCLA	21-16
1994-95	Penn State	Oregon	38-20
1995-96	Southern California	Northwestern	41-32
1996-97	Ohio State	Arizona State	20-17
1997-98	Michigan	Washington State	21-16
1998-99	Wisconsin	UCLA	38-31
1999-2000	Wisconsin	Stanford	17-9
2000-01	Washington	Purdue	34-24
2001-02	Miami (FL)	Nebraska	37-14
2002-03	Oklahoma	Washington State	34-14
2003-04	Southern California	Michigan	28-14
2004-05	Texas	Michigan	38-37

Orange Bowl

SEASON	WINNER	RUNNER-UP	SCORE
1934-35	Bucknell	Miami (FL)	26-0
1935-36	Catholic	Mississippi	20-19
1936-37	Duquesne	Mississippi State	13-12
1937-38	Auburn	Michigan State	6-0
1938-39	Tennessee	Oklahoma	17-0
1939-40	Georgia Tech	Missouri	21-7
1940-41	Mississippi State	Georgetown	14-7
1941-42	Georgia	Texas Christian	40-26
1942-43	Alabama	Boston College	37-21
1943-44	Louisiana State	Texas A&M	19-14
1944-45	Tulsa	Georgia Tech	26-12
1945-46	Miami (FL)	Holy Cross	13-6
1946-47	Rice	Tennessee	8-0
1947-48	Georgia Tech	Kansas	20-14
1948-49	Texas	Georgia	41-28
1949-50	Santa Clara	Kentucky	21-13
1950-51	Clemson	Miami (FL)	15-14
1951-52	Georgia Tech	Baylor	17-14
1952-53	Alabama	Syracuse	61-6
1953-54	Oklahoma	Maryland	7-0
1954-55	Duke	Nebraska	34-7
1955-56	Oklahoma	Maryland	20-6
1956-57	Colorado	Clemson	27-21
1957-58	Oklahoma	Duke	48-21
1958-59	Oklahoma	Syracuse	21-6
1959-60	Georgia	Missouri	14-0

Orange Bowl (continued)

SEASON	WINNER	RUNNER-UP	SCORE	SEASON	WINNER	RUNNER-UP	SCORE
1960-61	Missouri	Navy	21-14	1983-84	Miami (FL)	Nebraska	31-30
1961-62	Louisiana State	Colorado	25-7	1984-85	Washington	Oklahoma	28-17
1962-63	Alabama	Oklahoma	17-0	1985-86	Oklahoma	Penn State	25-10
1963-64	Nebraska	Auburn	13-7	1986-87	Oklahoma	Arkansas	42-8
1964-65	Texas	Alabama	21-17	1987-88	Miami (FL)	Oklahoma	20-14
1965-66	Alabama	Nebraska	39-28	1988-89	Miami (FL)	Nebraska	23-3
1966-67	Florida	Georgia Tech	27-12	1989-90	Notre Dame	Colorado	21-6
1967-68	Oklahoma	Tennessee	26-24	1990-91	Colorado	Notre Dame	10-9
1968-69	Penn State	Kansas	15-14	1991-92	Miami (FL)	Nebraska	22-0
1969-70	Penn State	Missouri	10-3	1992-93	Florida State	Nebraska	27-14
1970-71	Nebraska	Louisiana State	17-12	1993-94	Florida State	Nebraska	18-16
1971-72	Nebraska	Alabama	38-6	1994-95	Nebraska	Miami	24-17
1972-73	Nebraska	Notre Dame	40-6	1995-96	Florida State	Notre Dame	31-26
1973-74	Penn State	Louisiana State	16-9	1996-97	Nebraska	Virginia Tech	41-21
1974-75	Notre Dame	Alabama	13-11	1997-98	Nebraska	Tennessee	42-17
1975-76	Oklahoma	Michigan	14-6	1998-99	Florida	Syracuse	31-10
1976-77	Ohio State	Colorado	27-10	1999-2000	Michigan	Alabama	35-34
1977-78	Arkansas	Oklahoma	31-6	2000-01	Oklahoma	Florida State	13-2
1978-79	Oklahoma	Nebraska	31-24	2001-02	Florida	Maryland	56-23
1979-80	Oklahoma	Florida State	24-7	2002-03	Southern	Iowa	38-17
1980-81	Oklahoma	Florida State	18-17			California	
1981-82	Clemson	Nebraska	22-15	2003-04	Miami (FL)	Florida State	16-14
1982-83	Nebraska	Louisiana State	21-20	2004-05	USC	Oklahoma	55-19

Sugar Bowl

SEASON	WINNER	RUNNER-UP	SCORE	SEASON	WINNER	RUNNER-UP	SCORE
1934-35	Tulane	Temple	20-14	1970-71	Tennessee	Air Force	34-13
1935-36	Texas Christian	Louisiana State	3-2	1971-72	Oklahoma	Auburn	40-22
1936-37	Santa Clara	Louisiana State	21-14	1972-73	Oklahoma	Penn State	14-0
1937-38	Santa Clara	Louisiana State	6-0	1973-74	Notre Dame	Alabama	24-23
1938-39	Texas Christian	Carnegie Tech	15-7	1974-75	Nebraska	Florida	13-10
1939-40	Texas A&M	Tulane	14-13	1975-76	Alabama	Penn State	13-6
1940-41	Boston College	Tennessee	19-13	1976-77	Pittsburgh	Georgia	27-3
1941-42	Fordham	Missouri	2-0	1977-78	Alabama	Ohio State	35-6
1942-43	Tennessee	Tulsa	14-7	1978-79	Alabama	Penn State	14-7
1943-44	Georgia Tech	Tulsa	20-18	1979-80	Alabama	Arkansas	24-9
1944-45	Duke	Alabama	29-26	1980-81	Georgia	Notre Dame	17-10
1945-46	Oklahoma A&M	St. Mary's	33-13	1981-82	Pittsburgh	Georgia	24-20
1946-47	Georgia	North Carolina	20-10	1982-83	Penn State	Georgia	27-23
1947-48	Texas	Alabama	27-7	1983-84	Auburn	Michigan	9-7
1948-49	Oklahoma	North Carolina	14-6	1984-85	Nebraska	Louisiana State	28-10
1949-50	Oklahoma	Louisiana State	35-0	1985-86	Tennessee	Miami (FL)	35-7
1950-51	Kentucky	Oklahoma	13-7	1986-87	Nebraska	Louisiana State	30-15
1951-52	Maryland	Tennessee	28-13	1987-88	Auburn	Syracuse	16-16
1952-53	Georgia Tech	Mississippi	24-7	1988-89	Florida State	Auburn	13-7
1953-54	Georgia Tech	West Virginia	42-19	1989-90	Miami (FL)	Alabama	33-25
1954-55	Navy	Mississippi	21-0	1990-91	Tennessee	Virginia	23-22
1955-56	Georgia Tech	Pittsburgh	7-0	1991-92	Notre Dame	Florida	39-28
1956-57	Baylor	Tennessee	13-7	1992-93	Alabama	Miami (FL)	34-13
1957-58	Mississippi	Texas	39-7	1993-94	Florida	West Virginia	41-7
1958-59	Louisiana State	Clemson	7-0	1994-95	Florida State	Florida	23-17
1959-60	Mississippi	Louisiana State	21-0	1995-96	Virginia Tech	Texas	28-10
1960-61	Mississippi	Rice	14-6	1996-97	Florida	Florida State	52-20
1961-62	Alabama	Arkansas	10-3	1997-98	Florida State	Ohio State	31-14
1962-63	Mississippi	Arkansas	17-13	1998-99	Ohio State	Texas A&M	24-14
1963-64	Alabama	Mississippi	12-7	1999-2000	Florida State	Virginia Tech	46-29
1964-65	Louisiana	Syracuse	13-10	2000-01	Miami (FL)	Florida	37-20
	State			2001-02	Louisiana	Illinois	47-34
1965-66	Missouri	Florida	20-18			State	
1966-67	Alabama	Nebraska	34-7	2002-03	Georgia	Florida State	26-13
1967-68	Louisiana	Wyoming	20-13	2003-04	Louisiana	Oklahoma	21-14
	State				State		
1968-69	Arkansas	Georgia	16-2	2004-05	Auburn	Virginia Tech	16-13
1969-70	Mississippi	Arkansas	27-22				

Fiesta Bowl

SEASON	WINNER	RUNNER-UP	SCORE	SEASON	WINNER	RUNNER-UP	SCORE
1971–72	Arizona State	Florida State	45–38	1988–89	Notre Dame	West Virginia	34–21
1972–73	Arizona State	Missouri	49–35	1989–90	Florida State	Nebraska	41–17
1973–74	Arizona State	Pittsburgh	28–7	1990–91	Louisville	Alabama	34–7
1974–75	Oklahoma State	Brigham Young	16–6	1991–92	Penn State	Tennessee	42–17
1975–76	Arizona State	Nebraska	17–14	1992–93	Syracuse	Colorado	26–22
1976–77	Oklahoma	Wyoming	41–7	1993–94	Arizona	Miami (FL)	29–0
1977–78	Penn State	Arizona State	42–30	1994–95	Colorado	Notre Dame	41–24
1978–79	Arkansas	UCLA	10–10	1995–96	Nebraska	Florida	62–24
1979–80	Pittsburgh	Arizona	16–10	1996–97	Penn State	Texas	38–15
1980–81	Penn State	Ohio State	31–19	1997–98	Kansas State	Syracuse	35–18
1981–82	Penn State	Southern California	26–10	1998–99	Tennessee	Florida State	23–16
				1999–2000	Nebraska	Tennessee	31–21
1982–83	Arizona State	Oklahoma	32–21	2000–01	Oregon State	Notre Dame	41–9
1983–84	Ohio State	Pittsburgh	28–23	2001–02	Oregon	Colorado	38–16
1984–85	UCLA	Miami (FL)	39–37	2002–03	Ohio State	Miami (FL)	31–24
1985–86	Michigan	Nebraska	27–23	2003–04	Ohio State	Kansas State	35–28
1986–87	Penn State	Miami (FL)	14–10	2004–05	Utah	Pittsburgh	35–7
1987–88	Florida State	Nebraska	31–28				

Heisman Trophy Winners

The Heisman Trophy is named for John Heisman, a director of the Downtown Athletic Club (DAC) in New York City who died in 1936. The trophy goes to an outstanding college football player at the end of the football season each year. A committee comprised of DAC members, members of the media, and representatives from each of the 50 states cast ballots to determine the winner. Web site: <www.heisman.com>.

YEAR	WINNER	COLLEGE	POSITION	YEAR	WINNER	COLLEGE	POSITION
1935	Jay Berwanger	University of Chicago	HB	1970	Jim Plunkett	Stanford	QB
1936	Larry Kelley	Yale	E	1971	Pat Sullivan	Auburn	QB
1937	Clint Frank	Yale	HB	1972	Johnny Rodgers	Nebraska	WR
1938	Davey O'Brien	TCU	QB	1973	John Cappelletti	Penn State	HB
1939	Nile Kinnick	Iowa	HB	1974	Archie Griffin	Ohio State	HB
1940	Tom Harmon	Michigan	HB	1975	Archie Griffin	Ohio State	HB
1941	Bruce Smith	Minnesota	HB	1976	Tony Dorsett	Pittsburgh	HB
1942	Frank Sinkwich	Georgia	HB	1977	Earl Campbell	Texas	HB
1943	Angelo Bertelli	Notre Dame	HB	1978	Billy Sims	Oklahoma	HB
1944	Les Horvath	Ohio State	QB	1979	Charles White	USC	HB
1945	Felix Blanchard	Army	FB	1980	George Rogers	South Carolina	HB
1946	Glenn Davis	Army	HB	1981	Marcus Allen	USC	HB
1947	John Lujack	Notre Dame	QB	1982	Herschel Walker	Georgia	HB
1948	Doak Walker	SMU	HB	1983	Mike Rozier	Nebraska	HB
1949	Leon Hart	Notre Dame	DE	1984	Doug Flutie	Boston College	QB
1950	Vic Janowicz	Ohio State	HB	1985	Bo Jackson	Auburn	HB
1951	Dick Kazmaier	Princeton	HB	1986	Vinny Testaverde	Miami	QB
1952	Billy Vessels	Oklahoma	HB	1987	Tim Brown	Notre Dame	WR
1953	John Lattner	Notre Dame	HB	1988	Barry Sanders	Oklahoma State	RB
1954	Alan Ameche	Wisconsin	FB	1989	Andre Ware	Houston	QB
1955	Howard Cassady	Ohio State	HB	1990	Ty Detmer	BYU	QB
1956	Paul Hornung	Notre Dame	QB	1991	Desmond Howard	Michigan	WR
1957	John David Crow	Texas A&M	HB	1992	Gino Torretta	Miami	QB
1958	Pete Dawkins	Army	HB	1993	Charlie Ward	Florida State	QB
1959	Billy Cannon	LSU	HB	1994	Rashaan Salaam	Colorado	TB
1960	Joe Bellino	Navy	HB	1995	Eddie George	Ohio State	RB
1961	Ernie Davis	Syracuse	HB	1996	Danny Wuerffel	Florida	QB
1962	Terry Baker	Oregon State	QB	1997	Charles Woodson	Michigan	DB
1963	Roger Staubach	Navy	QB	1998	Ricky Williams	Texas	RB
1964	John Huarte	Notre Dame	QB	1999	Ron Dayne	Wisconsin	RB
1965	Mike Garrett	USC	HB	2000	Chris Weinke	Florida State	QB
1966	Steve Spurrier	Florida	QB	2001	Eric Crouch	Nebraska	QB
1967	Gary Beban	UCLA	QB	2002	Carson Palmer	USC	QB
1968	O.J. Simpson	USC	HB	2003	Jason White	Oklahoma	QB
1969	Steve Owens	Oklahoma	HB	2004	Matt Leinart	USC	QB

Canadian Football League Grey Cup

Held since 1909. Table shows results for past 20 years.

YEAR	WINNER	RUNNER-UP	SCORE
1985	British Columbia Lions (WFC)	Hamilton Tiger-Cats (EFC)	37–24
1986	Hamilton Tiger-Cats (EFC)	Edmonton Eskimos (WFC)	39–15
1987	Edmonton Eskimos (WFC)	Toronto Argonauts (EFC)	38–36
1988	Winnipeg Blue Bombers (EFC)	British Columbia Lions (WFC)	22–21
1989	Saskatchewan Roughriders (WFC)	Hamilton Tiger-Cats (EFC)	43–40
1990	Winnipeg Blue Bombers (EFC)	Edmonton Eskimos (WFC)	50–11
1991	Toronto Argonauts (EFC)	Calgary Stampeders (WFC)	36–21
1992	Calgary Stampeders (WFC)	Winnipeg Blue Bombers (EFC)	24–10
1993	Edmonton Eskimos (WFC)	Winnipeg Blue Bombers (EFC)	33–23
1994	British Columbia Lions (WFC)	Baltimore Stallions (EFC)	26–23
1995	Baltimore Stallions (SD)	Calgary Stampeders (ND)	37–20
1996	Toronto Argonauts (ED)	Edmonton Eskimos (WD)	43–37
1997	Toronto Argonauts (ED)	Saskatchewan Roughriders (WD)	47–23
1998	Calgary Stampeders (WD)	Hamilton Tiger-Cats (ED)	26–24
1999	Hamilton Tiger-Cats (ED)	Calgary Stampeders (WD)	32–21
2000	British Columbia Lions (WD)	Montreal Alouettes (ED)	28–26
2001	Calgary Stampeders (WD)	Winnipeg Blue Bombers (EFC)	27–19
2002	Montreal Alouettes (ED)	Edmonton Eskimos (WD)	25–16
2003	Edmonton Eskimos (WD)	Montreal Alouettes (ED)	34–22
2004	Toronto Argonauts (ED)	British Columbia Lions (WD)	27–19

Australian Football League Final Standings, 2004

League ladder after round 22; teams that qualified for play-offs only.

TEAM	WON	LOST	TIED	POINTS	TEAM	WON	LOST	TIED	POINTS
Port Adelaide Power	17	5	0	68	Melbourne Demons	14	8	0	56
Brisbane Lions	16	6	0	64	Sydney Swans	13	9	0	52
St. Kilda Saints	16	6	0	64	West Coast Eagles	13	9	0	52
Geelong Cats	15	7	0	60	Essendon Bombers	12	10	0	48

Super 12 Rugby Championship

Four points are awarded for a win and two for a draw; one bonus point is given for a loss by seven points or fewer and one for a team that scores four or more tries. Final match held 28 May 2005, Christchurch, New Zealand.

TEAMS (COUNTRY)	POINTS	W	L	D	BONUS	TEAMS (COUNTRY)	POINTS	W	L	D	BONUS
Canterbury Crusaders (NZL)	44	9	2	0	8	Auckland Blues (NZL)	27	6	5	0	3
NSW Waratahs (AUS)	44	9	2	0	8	Otago Highlanders (NZL)	27	6	4	1	1
Northern Bulls (RSA)	34	7	4	0	5	Stormers (RSA)	18	3	7	1	4
Wellington Hurricanes (NZL)	34	8	3	0	5	QLD Reds (AUS)	17	3	8	0	5
ACT Brumbies (AUS)	29	5	5	1	7	Cats (RSA)	13	1	9	1	7
Waikato Chiefs (NZL)	28	5	5	1	6	Sharks (RSA)	11	1	9	1	5

Six Nations Championship

Five Nations until 2000. Round-robin tournament, usually ending in April.

YEAR	WINNER	YEAR	WINNER	YEAR	WINNER
1947	England, Wales[1]	1962	France	1977	France[4, 5]
1948	Ireland[2]	1963	England	1978	Wales[2]
1949	Ireland[3]	1964	Scotland, Wales[1]	1979	Wales[3]
1950	Wales[2]	1965	Wales[3]	1980	England[2]
1951	Ireland	1966	Wales	1981	France[4]
1952	Wales[2]	1967	France	1982	Ireland[3]
1953	England	1968	France[4]	1983	France, Ireland[1]
1954	England[3], France, Wales[1]	1969	Wales[3]	1984	Scotland[2]
1955	France, Wales[1]	1970	France, Wales[1]	1985	Ireland[2]
1956	Wales	1971	Wales[2]	1986	France, Scotland[1]
1957	England[2]	1972	not completed	1987	France[4]
1958	England	1973	quintuple tie	1988	Wales[2]
1959	France	1974	Ireland	1989	France
1960	England[3], France[1]	1975	Wales	1990	Scotland[4]
1961	France	1976	Wales[2]	1991	England[4]

Six Nations Championship (continued)

YEAR	WINNER	YEAR	WINNER	YEAR	WINNER
1992	England[4]	1998	France[4]	2004	France
1993	France	1999	Scotland	2005	Wales[4]
1994	Wales	2000	England		
1995	England[4]	2001	England		
1996	England	2002	France[4]		
1997	France[4]	2003	England[4]		

[1]Tied.   [2]Triple Crown (all three matches, excluding France) and Grand Slam (all four matches) winner.
[3]Triple Crown winner.   [4]Grand Slam winner.   [5]Triple Crown won by Wales.

Rugby World Cup

YEAR	WINNER	RUNNER-UP	SCORE	YEAR	WINNER	RUNNER-UP	SCORE
1987	New Zealand	France	29–9	1999	Australia	France	35–12
1991	Australia	England	12–6	2003	England	Australia	20–17
1995	South Africa	New Zealand	15–12				

Rugby League World Cup

YEAR	WINNER	RUNNER-UP	SCORE	YEAR	WINNER	RUNNER-UP	SCORE
1954	Great Britain	France	16–12	1977[2]	Australia	Great Britain	13–12
1957	Australia	Great Britain	29–21	1988	Australia	New Zealand	25–12
1960	Great Britain	Australia	66–37	1992	Australia	Great Britain	10–6
1968	Australia	France	20–2	1995	Australia	England	16–8
1970	Australia	Great Britain	12–7	2000	Australia	New Zealand	40–12
1972	Great Britain	Australia	10–10[1]	2008	scheduled to be held in Australia		
1975[2]	Australia[3]						

[1]Great Britain won on match points.   [2]Called International Championship from 1975 to 1977.   [3]Championships played without a grand final match; England was the runner-up.

FIFA World Cup—Men

YEAR	WINNER	RUNNER-UP	SCORE	YEAR	WINNER	RUNNER-UP	SCORE
1930	Uruguay	Argentina	4–2	1974	West Germany	The Netherlands	2–1
1934	Italy	Czechoslovakia	2–1	1978	Argentina	The Netherlands	3–1
1938	Italy	Hungary	4–2	1982	Italy	West Germany	3–1
1950	Uruguay	Brazil	2–1	1986	Argentina	West Germany	3–2
1954	West Germany	Hungary	3–2	1990	West Germany	Argentina	1–0
1958	Brazil	Sweden	5–2	1994	Brazil	Italy	0–0 (3–2[1])
1962	Brazil	Czechoslovakia	3–1	1998	France	Brazil	3–0
1966	England	West Germany	4–2	2002	Brazil	Germany	2–0
1970	Brazil	Italy	4–1				

[1]Penalty kick shoot-out.

FIFA World Cup—Women

YEAR	WINNER	RUNNER-UP	SCORE	YEAR	WINNER	RUNNER-UP	SCORE
1991	United States	Norway	2–1	2003	Germany	Sweden	2–1
1995	Norway	Germany	2–0	2007	to be held September–October 2007 in China		
1999	United States[1]	China	0–0				

[1]Won on penalty kicks.

Association Football (Soccer) National Champions

List reflects the reigning champions of selected countries as of 30 Jun 2005.

COUNTRY	LEAGUE CHAMPION	CUP WINNER	COUNTRY	LEAGUE CHAMPION	CUP WINNER
Albania	Sportklub Tirana	Teuta Durrës	Israel	Maccabi Haifa	Maccabi Tel
Andorra	Sant Julia	Santa Coloma			Aviv
Argentina	Newell's Old Boys (opening)		Italy	Juventus	Internazionale
			Japan	Yokohama	Tokyo Verdy
	Vélez Sarsfield (closing)			F. Marinos	1969
Australia	N/A		Luxembourg	Dudelange	Pétange
Austria	Rapid	Austria	Mexico	Pumas (opening)	
Belgium	Club Brugge	Germinal Beerschot		América (closing)	
Bolivia	Bolívar (opening) Oriente Petrolero (closing)		Morocco	FAR Rabat	Raja Casablanca
			Netherlands	PSV Eindhoven	PSV Eindhoven
Bosnia and Herzegovina	Zrinjski	Sarajevo	Nigeria	Dolphin	Dolphin
			Northern Ireland	Glentoran	Portadown
Brazil	Santos	Paulista			
Bulgaria	CSKA	Levski	Norway	Rosenborg	Brann
Cameroon	Cotonsport	Cotonsport	Peru	Alianza Lima	Sport Ancash
Chile	Universidad de Chile (opening)		Poland	Wisla Krakow	Dyskobolia Groclin
	Cobreloa (closing)		Portugal	Benfica	Vitória
China	Shenzhen Jianlibao	Shandong Lu-neng Taishan	Romania	Steaua	Dinamo
			Russia	Lokomotiv Moscow	CSKA Moscow
Colombia	Independiente Medellín (opening)		Saudi Arabia	Al-Shabab	Al-Hilal
	Atlético Junior (closing)		Scotland	Rangers	Celtic
			Senegal	Diaraf	Douanes
Costa Rica	Alajuelense		Serbia & Montenegro	Partizan	Zeleznik
Croatia	Hajduk	Rijeka			
Cyprus	Anorthosis Famagusta	Omonia Nicosia	Slovakia	Artmedia Petrzalka	Banská Bystrica
Czech Rep.	Sparta Praha	Baník Ostrava	Slovenia	ND Gorica	Publikum Celje
Denmark	Brøndby	Brøndby	South Africa	Kaizer Chiefs	SuperSport United
Ecuador	Deportivo Cuenca		South Korea	Suwon Samsung Bluewings	Pusan Icons
England	Chelsea	Arsenal			
Finland	Haka Valkeakoski	MyPa Anjalankoski	Spain	Barcelona	Real Betis
			Sweden	Malmö	Djurgårdens
France	Lyon	Auxerre	Switzerland	Basel	Zurich
Georgia	Dinamo Tbilisi	Lokomotiv Tblisi	Tunisia	Sfaxien	Zarzis
			Turkey	Fenerbahce	Galatasaray
Germany	Bayern Munich	Bayern Munich	Ukraine	Shakhtar Donetsk	Dinamo Kiev
Greece	Olympiakos	Olympiakos	United States	D.C. United	Kansas City Wizards
Hungary	Debreceni VSC	FC Sopron			
Ireland	Shelbourne	Longford Town	Uruguay	Nacional	
			Wales	Llansantffraid	Llansantffraid

UEFA European Championship

YEAR	WINNING TEAM	RUNNER–UP	SCORE
1960	Soviet Union	Yugoslavia	2–1
1964	Spain	Soviet Union	2–1
1968	Italy	Yugoslavia	2–0
1972	West Germany	Soviet Union	3–0
1976	Czechoslovakia	West Germany	2–2
1980	West Germany	Belgium	2–1
1984	France	Spain	2–0
1988	Holland	Soviet Union	2–0
1992	Denmark	Germany	2–0
1996	Germany	Czech Republic	2–1
2000	France	Italy	2–1
2004	Greece	Portugal	1–0
2008	*to be hosted jointly by Austria and Switzerland*		

UEFA Champions League

Known until 1992–93 as the European Champion Clubs' Cup; played on a knockout basis until 1992–93 and a combination of group, knockout, and quarterfinals, semifinals, and finals since then. Table shows results for the past 20 years.

SEASON	WINNING TEAM (COUNTRY)	RUNNER-UP (COUNTRY)	SCORE
1985–86	FC Steaua Bucuresti (ROM)	FC Barcelona (ESP)	0–0[1]
1986–87	FC Porto (POR)	Bayern München (FRG)	2–1
1987–88	PSV Eindhoven (NED)	SL Benfica (POR)	0–0[1]
1988–89	AC Milan (ITA)	FC Steaua Bucuresti (ROM)	4–0
1989–90	AC Milan (ITA)	SL Benfica (POR)	1–0
1990–91	FK Crvena Zvezda Beograd (YUG)	Olympique de Marseille (FRA)	0–0[1]
1991–92	FC Barcelona (ESP)	Sampdoria UC (ITA)	1–0
1992–93	Olympique de Marseille (FRA)	AC Milan (ITA)	1–0
1993–94	AC Milan (ITA)	FC Barcelona (ESP)	4–0
1994–95	AFC Ajax (NED)	AC Milan (ITA)	1–0
1995–96	Juventus FC (ITA)	AFC Ajax (NED)	1–1[1]
1996–97	BV Borussia Dortmund (GER)	Juventus FC (ITA)	3–1
1997–98	Real Madrid CF (ESP)	Juventus FC (ITA)	1–0
1998–99	Manchester United (ENG)	Bayern München (GER)	2–1
1999–2000	Real Madrid CF (ESP)	Valencia CF (ESP)	3–0
2000–01	Bayern München (GER)	Valencia CF (ESP)	1–1[1]
2001–02	Real Madrid CF (ESP)	Bayer 04 Leverkusen (GER)	2–1
2002–03	AC Milan (ITA)	Juventus FC (ITA)	0–0[1]
2003–04	FC Porto (POR)	AS Monaco (FRA)	3–0
2004–05	Liverpool FC (ENG)	AC Milan (ITA)	3–3[1]

[1]Won on penalty kicks.

UEFA Cup

The UEFA Cup is considered Europe's second most important football competition. Established in the 1971–72 season, the Cup was restructured after the UEFA Cup Winners' Cup was abolished in 1998–99. Originally played on a knockout basis, since 1998 the competition has concluded with a single match. The Cup competition is open to top- and second-ranked teams in each country's league as well as winners of domestic cups.

SEASON	WINNING TEAM (COUNTRY)	RUNNER-UP (COUNTRY)	SCORE
1971–72	Tottenham Hotspur FC (ENG)	Wolverhampton Wanderers FC (ENG)	2–1; 1–1
1972–73	Liverpool FC (ENG)	VfL Borussia Mönchengladbach (FRG)	3–0; 0–2
1973–74	Feyenoord (NED)	Tottenham Hotspur FC (ENG)	2–2; 2–0
1974–75	VfL Borussia Mönchengladbach (FRG)	FC Twente (NED)	0–0; 5–1
1975–76	Liverpool FC (ENG)	Club Brugge KV (BEL)	3–2; 1–1
1976–77	Juventus FC (ITA)	Athletic Club Bilbao (ESP)	1–0; 1–2
1977–78	PSV Eindhoven (NED)	SC Bastia (FRA)	0–0; 3–0
1978–79	VfL Borussia Mönchengladbach (FRG)	FK Crvena Zvezda Beograd (YUG)	1–1; 1–0
1979–80	Eintracht Frankfurt (FRG)	VfL Borussia Mönchengladbach (FRG)	2–3; 1–0
1980–81	Ipswich Town FC (ENG)	AZ Alkmaar (NED)	3–0; 2–4
1981–82	IFK Göteborg (SWE)	Hamburger SV (FRG)	1–0; 3–0
1982–83	RSC Anderlecht (BEL)	SL Benfica (POR)	1–0; 1–1
1983–84	Tottenham Hotspur FC (ENG)[1]	RSC Anderlecht (BEL)	1–1; 1–1
1984–85	Real Madrid CF (ESP)	Videoton FCF (HUN)	3–0; 0–1
1985–86	Real Madrid CF (ESP)	1. FC Köln (FRG)	5–1; 0–2
1986–87	IFK Göteborg (SWE)	Dundee United FC (SCO)	1–0; 1–1
1987–88	Bayer 04 Leverkusen (FRG)[1]	RCD Espanyol (ESP)	0–3; 3–0
1988–89	SSC Napoli (ITA)	VfB Stuttgart (FRG)	2–1; 3–3
1989–90	Juventus FC (ITA)	AC Fiorentina (ITA)	3–1; 0–0
1990–91	Internazionale FC (ITA)	AS Roma (ITA)	2–0; 0–1
1991–92	AFC Ajax (NED)	Torino Calcio (ITA)	2–2; 0–0
1992–93	Juventus FC (ITA)	BV Borussia Dortmund (FRG)	3–1; 3–0
1993–94	Internazionale FC (ITA)	SV Austria Salzburg (AUT)	1–0; 1–0
1994–95	Parma AC (ITA)	Juventus FC (ITA)	1–0; 1–1
1995–96	FC Bayern München (GER)	FC Girondins de Bordeaux (FRA)	2–0; 3–1
1996–97	FC Schalke 04 (GER)[1]	Internazionale FC (ITA)	1–0; 0–1
1997–98	Internazionale FC (ITA)	S.S. Lazio (ITA)	3–0
1998–99	Parma AC (ITA)	Olympique de Marseille (FRA)	3–0

UEFA Cup (continued)

SEASON	WINNING TEAM (COUNTRY)	RUNNER-UP (COUNTRY)	SCORE
1999–2000	Galatasaray SK (TUR)[1]	Arsenal FC (ENG)	0–0
2000–01	Liverpool FC (ENG)	Deportivo Alavés (ESP)	5–4
2001–02	Feyenoord (NED)	BV Borussia Dortmund (GER)	3–2
2002–03	FC Porto (POR)[2]	Celtic FC (SCO)	3–2[2]
2003–04	Valencia CF (ESP)	Olympique de Marseille (FRA)	2–0
2004–05	CSKA Moscow (RUS)	Sporting (POR)	3–1

[1]Won on penalty kicks.   [2]Won on "Silver Goal" in overtime.

Libertadores de América Cup

Contested since 1960. Table shows results for the past 20 years.

YEAR	WINNER (COUNTRY)	RUNNER-UP (COUNTRY)	SCORES
1986	River Plate (ARG)	América de Cali (COL)	2–1, 1–0
1987	Peñarol (URU)	América de Cali (COL)	0–2, 2–1, 1–0[1]
1988	Nacional (URU)	Newell's Old Boys (ARG)	0–1, 3–0
1989	Atlético Nacional (COL)	Olímpia (PAR)	0–2, 2–0, 5–4[1]
1990	Olímpia (PAR)	Barcelona (ECU)	2–0, 1–1
1991	Colo Colo (CHI)	Olímpia (PAR)	0–0, 3–0
1992	São Paulo (BRA)	Newell's Old Boys (ARG)	0–1, 1–0, 3–2[1]
1993	São Paulo (BRA)	Universidad Católica (CHI)	5–1, 0–2
1994	Vélez Sarsfield (ARG)	São Paulo (BRA)	1–0, 0–1, 5–4[1]
1995	Grêmio (BRA)	Atlético Nacional (COL)	3–1, 1–1
1996	River Plate (ARG)	América de Cali (COL)	0–1, 2–0
1997	Cruzeiro (BRA)	Sporting Cristal (PER)	0–0, 1–0
1998	Vasco da Gama (BRA)	Barcelona (ECU)	2–0, 2–1
1999	Palmeiras (BRA)	Deportiva Cali (COL)	0–1, 2–1, 4–3[1]
2000	Boca Juniors (ARG)	Palmeiras (BRA)	2–2, 0–0, 4–2[1]
2001	Boca Juniors (ARG)	Cruz Azul (MEX)	1–0, 0–1, 3–1[1]
2002	Olímpia (PAR)	São Caetano (BRA)	0–1, 2–1, 4–2[1]
2003	Boca Juniors (ARG)	Santos (BRA)	2–0, 3–1
2004	Once Caldas (COL)	Boca Juniors (ARG)	0–0, 1–1, 2–0[1]
2005	São Paulo (BRA)	Atlético Paranaense (BRA)	1–1, 4–0

[1]Winner determined in penalty shoot-out after tie-breaking game.

Copa América

Held since 1916. Table shows results for past 20 years. The cup was contested by a best-of-series in 1983, by rounds in 1989 and 1991 (scores are shown here as winner's wins/losses/draws in final round), and by a final championship match in 1987 and from 1993.

YEAR	WINNER	RUNNER-UP	SCORE	YEAR	WINNER	RUNNER-UP	SCORE
1987	Uruguay	Chile	1–0	1999	Brazil	Uruguay	3–0
1989	Brazil	Uruguay	3/0/0	2001	Colombia	Mexico	1–0
1991	Argentina	Brazil	4/0/0	2003	postponed until 2004		
1993	Argentina	Mexico	2–1	2004	Brazil	Argentina	4–2
1995	Uruguay[1]	Brazil	1–1	2006	to be held in Venezuela		
1997	Brazil	Bolivia	3–1				

[1]Uruguay won penalty shoot-out 5–3.

Asian Cup

Scored on a points (percentage of wins) system until 1972.

YEAR	WINNER	RUNNER-UP	SCORE	YEAR	WINNER	RUNNER-UP	SCORE
1956	South Korea	Israel	83.3	1984	Saudi Arabia	China	2–0
1960	South Korea	Israel	100	1988	Saudi Arabia	South Korea	0–0 (4–3[1])
1964	Israel	India	100	1992	Japan	Saudi Arabia	1–0
1968	Iran	Burma	100	1996	Saudi Arabia	United Arab Emirates	0–0 (4–2[1])
1972	Iran	South Korea	2–1	2000	Japan	Saudi Arabia	1–0
1976	Iran	Kuwait	1–0	2004	Japan	China	3–1
1980	Kuwait	South Korea	3–0	2005			

[1]Penalty kick shoot-out.

African Cup of Nations

YEAR	WINNER	RUNNER-UP	SCORE	YEAR	WINNER	RUNNER-UP	SCORE
1957	Egypt	Ethiopia	4–0	1982	Ghana	Libya	1–1 (7–6[3])
1959	Egypt	The Sudan	2–1	1984	Cameroon	Nigeria	3–1
1962	Ethiopia	Egypt	4–2	1986	Egypt	Cameroon	0–0 (5–4[3])
1963	Ghana	The Sudan	3–0	1988	Cameroon	Nigeria	1–0
1965	Ghana	Tunisia	3–2	1990	Algeria	Nigeria	1–0
1968	Congo (Kinshasa)	Ghana	1–0	1992	Côte d'Ivoire	Ghana	0–0 (11–10[3])
1970	The Sudan	Ghana	1–0	1994	Nigeria	Zambia	2–1
1972	Congo (Brazzaville)	Mali	3–2	1996	South Africa	Tunisia	2–0
1974	Zaire	Zambia	2–2, 2–0[1]	1998	Egypt	South Africa	2–0
1976	Morocco	Guinea	1–1[2]	2000	Cameroon	Nigeria	2–2 (4–3[3])
1978	Ghana	Uganda	2–0	2002	Cameroon	Senegal	0–0 (3–2[3])
1980	Nigeria	Algeria	3–0	2004	Tunisia	Morocco	2–1

[1]Game replayed.   [2]Group format.   [3]Penalty kick shoot-out.

Major League Soccer Cup

YEAR	WINNER	RUNNER-UP	SCORE	YEAR	WINNER	RUNNER-UP	SCORE
1996	DC United	Los Angeles Galaxy	3–2 (OT)	2002	Los Angeles Galaxy	New England Revolution	1–0
1997	DC United	Colorado Rapids	2–1	2003	San Jose Earthquakes	Chicago Fire	4–2
1998	Chicago Fire	DC United	2–0	2004	DC United	Kansas City Wizards	3–2
1999	DC United	Los Angeles Galaxy	2–0	2005	final match to be held 13 November, Frisco TX		
2000	Kansas City Wizards	Chicago Fire	1–0				
2001	San Jose Earthquakes	Los Angeles Galaxy	2–1 (OT)				

Golf

In **individual events**, two of the major men's golf championships, the **British and US Open tournaments**, are played annually at a variety of golf courses in their respective countries. Each is played over 72 holes, and each is preceded by qualifying rounds. The **Professional Golfers' Association Championship** and the invitational **Masters Tournament** (which is held annually at the Augusta [GA] National Golf Course) are also top tournaments. Events for amateurs include the **US and British Amateur championships.**

Women's golf has been around nearly as long as men's golf, but until the late 1940s, it was limited to amateurs. Thus, for women, the **British and US Amateur championships** were the major tournaments. The **US Women's Open Championship** was started in 1946, and the **Ladies Professional Golf Association** (LPGA) was formed in 1950. Since that time, women's professional golf has flourished. In 1976 the **Women's British Open Championship** was added to the golf calendar.

In **team events**, the **Ryder Cup** was originally a biennial match between the US and Great Britain, but beginning in 1979, it was expanded into a biennial match between the United States and Europe. The **World Cup**, formerly known as the Canada Cup, is a men's tournament for two-man professional teams. Teams of British and US women golfers compete every two years for the **Curtis Cup**, which since 1964 has involved two days' play of three 18-hole foursomes and six 18-hole singles. The **Solheim Cup**, the women's professional team tournament, had been played in even-numbered years since 1990 but was moved to odd-numbered years (beginning in 2003) following the rescheduling of the Ryder Cup because of the events of 11 Sep 2001.

Related Web sites: United States Golf Association: <www.usga.org>; Professional Golf Association: <www.pgatour.com>; Ladies Professional Golf Association: <www.lpga.com>.

Masters Tournament
Won by an American golfer except as indicated.

YEAR	WINNER	YEAR	WINNER	YEAR	WINNER
1934	Horton Smith	1948	Claude Harmon	1960	Arnold Palmer
1935	Gene Sarazen	1949	Sam Snead	1961	Gary Player (RSA)
1936	Horton Smith	1950	Jimmy Demaret	1962	Arnold Palmer
1937	Byron Nelson	1951	Ben Hogan	1963	Jack Nicklaus
1938	Henry Picard	1952	Sam Snead	1964	Arnold Palmer
1939	Ralph Guldahl	1953	Ben Hogan	1965	Jack Nicklaus
1940	Jimmy Demaret	1954	Sam Snead	1966	Jack Nicklaus
1941	Craig Wood	1955	Cary Middlecoff	1967	Gay Brewer
1942	Byron Nelson	1956	Jack Burke	1968	Bob Goalby[1]
1943–45	*not held*	1957	Doug Ford	1969	George Archer
1946	Herman Keiser	1958	Arnold Palmer	1970	Billy Casper
1947	Jimmy Demaret	1959	Art Wall	1971	Charles Coody

Masters Tournament (continued)

YEAR	WINNER	YEAR	WINNER	YEAR	WINNER
1972	Jack Nicklaus	1985	Bernhard Langer (FRG)	1998	Mark O'Meara
1973	Tommy Aaron	1986	Jack Nicklaus	1999	José María Olazábal (ESP)
1974	Gary Player (RSA)	1987	Larry Mize	2000	Vijay Singh (FIJ)
1975	Jack Nicklaus	1988	Sandy Lyle (SCO)	2001	Tiger Woods
1976	Raymond Floyd	1989	Nick Faldo (GBR)	2002	Tiger Woods
1977	Tom Watson	1990	Nick Faldo (GBR)	2003	Mike Weir (CAN)
1978	Gary Player (RSA)	1991	Ian Woosnam (GBR)	2004	Phil Mickelson
1979	Fuzzy Zoeller[2]	1992	Fred Couples	2005	Tiger Woods
1980	Seve Ballesteros (ESP)	1993	Bernhard Langer (GER)	2006	*to be held*
1981	Tom Watson	1994	José María Olazábal (ESP)		*3–9 April,*
1982	Craig Stadler[3]	1995	Ben Crenshaw		*Augusta GA*
1983	Seve Ballesteros (ESP)	1996	Nick Faldo (GBR)		
1984	Ben Crenshaw	1997	Tiger Woods		

[1]*Play-off averted when R. de Vicenzo was penalized for signing an incorrect scorecard.*   [2]*Sudden-death play-off against T. Watson and E. Sneed.*   [3]*Won on the first hole of a play-off against D. Pohl.*

United States Open Championship—Men

Won by an American golfer except as indicated.

YEAR	WINNER	YEAR	WINNER	YEAR	WINNER
1895	Horace Rawlins	1933	John Goodman	1973	Johnny Miller
1896	James Foulis	1934	Olin Dutra	1974	Hale Irwin
1897	Joe Lloyd	1935	Sam Parks, Jr.	1975	Lou Graham
1898	Fred Herd	1936	Tony Manero	1976	Jerry Pate
1899	Willie Smith	1937	Ralph Guldahl	1977	Hubert Green
1900	Harry Vardon (GBR)	1938	Ralph Guldahl	1978	Andy North
1901	Willie Anderson	1939	Byron Nelson	1979	Hale Irwin
1902	Laurence Auchterlonie	1940	Lawson Little	1980	Jack Nicklaus
1903	Willie Anderson	1941	Craig Wood	1981	David Graham (AUS)
1904	Willie Anderson	1942–45 *not held*		1982	Tom Watson
1905	Willie Anderson	1946	Lloyd Mangrum	1983	Larry Nelson
1906	Alex Smith	1947	Lew Worsham	1984	Fuzzy Zoeller
1907	Alex Ross	1948	Ben Hogan	1985	Andy North
1908	Fred McLeod	1949	Cary Middlecoff	1986	Raymond Floyd
1909	George Sargent	1950	Ben Hogan	1987	Scott Simpson
1910	Alex Smith	1951	Ben Hogan	1988	Curtis Strange
1911	John J. McDermott	1952	Julius Boros	1989	Curtis Strange
1912	John J. McDermott	1953	Ben Hogan	1990	Hale Irwin
1913	Francis Ouimet	1954	Ed Furgol	1991	Payne Stewart
1914	Walter Hagen	1955	Jack Fleck	1992	Tom Kite
1915	Jerome D. Travers	1956	Cary Middlecoff	1993	Lee Janzen
1916	Chick Evans	1957	Dick Mayer	1994	Ernie Els (RSA)
1917–18 *not held*		1958	Tommy Bolt	1995	Corey Pavin
1919	Walter Hagen	1959	Billy Casper	1996	Steve Jones
1920	Edward Ray (GBR)	1960	Arnold Palmer	1997	Ernie Els (RSA)
1921	James M. Barnes	1961	Gene Littler	1998	Lee Janzen
1922	Gene Sarazen	1962	Jack Nicklaus	1999	Payne Stewart
1923	Bobby Jones	1963	Julius Boros	2000	Tiger Woods
1924	Cyril Walker	1964	Ken Venturi	2001	Retief Goosen (RSA)
1925	Willie MacFarlane, Jr.	1965	Gary Player (RSA)	2002	Tiger Woods
1926	Bobby Jones	1966	Billy Casper	2003	Jim Furyk
1927	Tommy Armour	1967	Jack Nicklaus	2004	Retief Goosen (RSA)
1928	Johnny Farrell	1968	Lee Trevino	2005	Michael Campbell (NZL)
1929	Bobby Jones	1969	Orville Moody	2006	*to be held 15–18 June,*
1930	Bobby Jones	1970	Tony Jacklin (GBR)		*Winged Foot Golf*
1931	Billy Burke	1971	Lee Trevino		*Club, Mamaroneck NY*
1932	Gene Sarazen	1972	Jack Nicklaus		

British Open Tournament—Men

Won by a British golfer unless otherwise indicated.

YEAR	WINNER	YEAR	WINNER	YEAR	WINNER
1860	Willie Park, Sr.	1863	Willie Park, Sr.	1866	Willie Park, Sr.
1861	Tom Morris, Sr.	1864	Tom Morris, Sr.	1867	Tom Morris, Sr.
1862	Tom Morris, Sr.	1865	Andrew Strath	1868	Tom Morris, Jr.

British Open Tournament—Men (continued)

YEAR	WINNER	YEAR	WINNER	YEAR	WINNER
1869	Tom Morris, Jr.	1913	John H. Taylor	1966	Jack Nicklaus (USA)
1870	Tom Morris, Jr.	1914	Harry Vardon	1967	Roberto de Vicenzo (ARG)
1871	*not held*	1915–19	*not held*	1968	Gary Player (RSA)
1872	Tom Morris, Jr.	1920	George Duncan	1969	Tony Jacklin
1873	Tom Kidd	1921	Jock Hutchison (USA)	1970	Jack Nicklaus (USA)
1874	Mungo Park	1922	Walter Hagen (USA)	1971	Lee Trevino (USA)
1875	Willie Park, Jr.	1923	Arthur Havers	1972	Lee Trevino (USA)
1876	Bob Martin	1924	Walter Hagen (USA)	1973	Tom Weiskopf (USA)
1877	Jamie Anderson	1925	James Barnes (USA)	1974	Gary Player (RSA)
1878	Jamie Anderson	1926	Bobby Jones (USA)	1975	Tom Watson (USA)
1879	Jamie Anderson	1927	Bobby Jones (USA)	1976	Johnny Miller (USA)
1880	Robert Ferguson	1928	Walter Hagen (USA)	1977	Tom Watson (USA)
1881	Robert Ferguson	1929	Walter Hagen (USA)	1978	Jack Nicklaus (USA)
1882	Robert Ferguson	1930	Bobby Jones (USA)	1979	Seve Ballesteros (ESP)
1883	Willie Fernie	1931	Tommy Armour (USA)	1980	Tom Watson (USA)
1884	Jack Simpson	1932	Gene Sarazen (USA)	1981	Bill Rogers (USA)
1885	Bob Martin	1933	Denny Shute (USA)	1982	Tom Watson (USA)
1886	David Brown	1934	Henry Cotton	1983	Tom Watson (USA)
1887	Willie Park, Jr.	1935	Alfred Perry	1984	Seve Ballesteros (ESP)
1888	Jack Burns	1936	Alfred Padgham	1985	Sandy Lyle (SCO)
1889	Willie Park, Jr.	1937	Henry Cotton	1986	Greg Norman (AUS)
1890	John Ball	1938	Reg A. Whitcombe	1987	Nick Faldo
1891	Hugh Kirkaldy	1939	Richard Burton	1988	Seve Ballesteros (ESP)
1892	Harold Hilton	1940–45	*not held*	1989	Mark Calcavecchia (USA)
1893	William Auchterlonie	1946	Sam Snead (USA)	1990	Nick Faldo
1894	John H. Taylor	1947	Fred Daly (IRE)	1991	Ian Baker-Finch (AUS)
1895	John H. Taylor	1948	Henry Cotton	1992	Nick Faldo
1896	Harry Vardon	1949	Bobby Locke (RSA)	1993	Greg Norman (AUS)
1897	Harold Hilton	1950	Bobby Locke (RSA)	1994	Nick Price (ZIM)
1898	Harry Vardon	1951	Max Faulkner	1995	John Daly (USA)
1899	Harry Vardon	1952	Bobby Locke (RSA)	1996	Tom Lehman (USA)
1900	John H. Taylor	1953	Ben Hogan (USA)	1997	Justin Leonard (USA)
1901	James Braid	1954	Peter Thomson (AUS)	1998	Mark O'Meara (USA)
1902	Sandy Herd	1955	Peter Thomson (AUS)	1999	Paul Lawrie (SCO)
1903	Harry Vardon	1956	Peter Thomson (AUS)	2000	Tiger Woods (USA)
1904	Jack White	1957	Bobby Locke (RSA)	2001	David Duval (USA)
1905	James Braid	1958	Peter Thomson (AUS)	2002	Ernie Els (RSA)
1906	James Braid	1959	Gary Player (RSA)	2003	Ben Curtis (USA)
1907	Arnaud Massy (FRA)	1960	Kel Nagle (AUS)	2004	Todd Hamilton (USA)
1908	James Braid	1961	Arnold Palmer (USA)	2005	Tiger Woods (USA)
1909	John H. Taylor	1962	Arnold Palmer (USA)	2006	*to be held 20–23 July,*
1910	James Braid	1963	Bob Charles (NZL)		*Royal Liverpool Golf*
1911	Harry Vardon	1964	Tony Lema (USA)		*Club, Liverpool, England*
1912	Ted Ray	1965	Peter Thomson (AUS)		

US Professional Golfers' Association (PGA) Championship

Won by an American golfer except as indicated.

YEAR	WINNER	YEAR	WINNER	YEAR	WINNER
1916	James M. Barnes	1935	Johnny Revolta	1953	Walter Burkemo
1917–18	*not held*	1936	Denny Shute	1954	Chick Harbert
1919	James M. Barnes	1937	Denny Shute	1955	Doug Ford
1920	Jock Hutchison	1938	Paul Runyan	1956	Jack Burke
1921	Walter Hagen	1939	Henry Picard	1957	Lionel Hebert
1922	Gene Sarazen	1940	Byron Nelson	1958	Dow Finsterwald
1923	Gene Sarazen	1941	Vic Ghezzi	1959	Bob Rosburg
1924	Walter Hagen	1942	Sam Snead	1960	Jay Hebert
1925	Walter Hagen	1943	*not held*	1961	Jerry Barber[1]
1926	Walter Hagen	1944	Bob Hamilton	1962	Gary Player (RSA)
1927	Walter Hagen	1945	Byron Nelson	1963	Jack Nicklaus
1928	Leo Diegel	1946	Ben Hogan	1964	Bobby Nichols
1929	Leo Diegel	1947	Jim Ferrier	1965	Dave Marr
1930	Tommy Armour	1948	Ben Hogan	1966	Al Geiberger
1931	Tom Creavy	1949	Sam Snead	1967	Don January[1]
1932	Olin Dutra	1950	Chandler Harper	1968	Julius Boros
1933	Gene Sarazen	1951	Sam Snead	1969	Raymond Floyd
1934	Paul Runyan	1952	Jim Turnesa	1970	Dave Stockton

US Professional Golfers' Association (PGA) Championship (continued)

YEAR	WINNER	YEAR	WINNER	YEAR	WINNER
1971	Jack Nicklaus	1984	Lee Trevino	1997	Davis Love III
1972	Gary Player (RSA)	1985	Hubert Green	1998	Vijay Singh (FIJ)
1973	Jack Nicklaus	1986	Bob Tway	1999	Tiger Woods
1974	Lee Trevino	1987	Larry Nelson	2000	Tiger Woods
1975	Jack Nicklaus	1988	Jeff Sluman	2001	David Toms
1976	Dave Stockton	1989	Payne Stewart	2002	Rich Beems
1977	Lanny Wadkins	1990	Wayne Grady (AUS)	2003	Shaun Micheel
1978	John Mahaffey[1]	1991	John Daly	2004	Vijay Singh (FIJ)
1979	David Graham (AUS)[1]	1992	Nick Price (ZIM)	2005	Phil Mickelson
1980	Jack Nicklaus	1993	Paul Azinger	2006	to be held 14–20 August,
1981	Larry Nelson	1994	Nick Price (ZIM)		Medina Country Club,
1982	Raymond Floyd	1995	Steve Elkington (AUS)		Medina IL
1983	Hal Sutton	1996	Mark Brooks		

[1]Winner by play-off.

Ladies Professional Golf Association (LPGA) Champions

Won by an American golfer except as indicated.

YEAR	WINNER	YEAR	WINNER	YEAR	WINNER
1955	Beverly Hanson	1972	Kathy Ahern	1989	Nancy Lopez
1956	Marlene Hagge	1973	Mary Mills	1990	Beth Daniel
1957	Louise Suggs	1974	Sandra Haynie	1991	Meg Mallon
1958	Mickey Wright	1975	Kathy Whitworth	1992	Betsy King
1959	Betsy Rawls	1976	Betty Burfeindt	1993	Patty Sheehan
1960	Mickey Wright	1977	Chako Higuchi	1994	Laura Davies (GBR)
1961	Mickey Wright	1978	Nancy Lopez	1995	Kelly Robbins
1962	Judy Kimball	1979	Donna Caponi	1996	Laura Davies (GBR)
1963	Mickey Wright	1980	Sally Little	1997	Chris Johnson
1964	Mary Mills	1981	Donna Caponi	1998	Se Ri Pak (KOR)
1965	Sandra Haynie	1982	Jan Stephenson (AUS)	1999	Juli Inkster
1966	Gloria Ehret	1983	Patty Sheehan	2000	Juli Inkster
1967	Kathy Whitworth	1984	Patty Sheehan	2001	Karrie Webb (AUS)
1968	Sandra Post	1985	Nancy Lopez	2002	Se Ri Pak (KOR)
1969	Betsy Rawls	1986	Pat Bradley	2003	Annika Sörenstam (SWE)
1970	Shirley Englehorn	1987	Jane Geddes	2004	Annika Sörenstam (SWE)
1971	Kathy Whitworth	1988	Sherri Turner	2005	Annika Sörenstam (SWE)

United States Women's Open Champions

Won by an American golfer except as indicated.

YEAR	WINNER	YEAR	WINNER	YEAR	WINNER
1946	Patty Berg	1968	Susie Berning	1990	Betsy King
1947	Betty Jameson	1969	Donna Caponi	1991	Meg Mallon
1948	Babe Didrikson Zaharias	1970	Donna Caponi	1992	Patty Sheehan
1949	Louise Suggs	1971	JoAnne Carner	1993	Lauri Merten
1950	Babe Didrikson Zaharias	1972	Susie Berning	1994	Patty Sheehan
1951	Betsy Rawls	1973	Susie Berning	1995	Annika Sörenstam (SWE)
1952	Louise Suggs	1974	Sandra Haynie	1996	Annika Sörenstam (SWE)
1953	Betsy Rawls	1975	Sandra Palmer	1997	Alison Nicholas (GBR)
1954	Babe Didrikson Zaharias	1976	JoAnne Carner	1998	Se Ri Pak (KOR)
1955	Fay Crocker	1977	Hollis Stacy	1999	Juli Inkster
1956	Kathy Cornelius	1978	Hollis Stacy	2000	Karrie Webb (AUS)
1957	Betsy Rawls	1979	Jerilyn Britz	2001	Karrie Webb (AUS)
1958	Mickey Wright	1980	Amy Alcott	2002	Juli Inkster
1959	Mickey Wright	1981	Pat Bradley	2003	Hilary Lunke
1960	Betsy Rawls	1982	Janet Anderson	2004	Meg Mallon
1961	Mickey Wright	1983	Jan Stephenson (AUS)	2005	Birdie Kim (KOR)
1962	Murle Breer	1984	Hollis Stacy	2006	to be held 26 June–
1963	Mary Mills	1985	Kathy Baker		2 July, Newport Country
1964	Mickey Wright	1986	Jane Geddes		Club, Newport RI
1965	Carol Mann	1987	Laura Davies (GBR)		
1966	Sandra Spuzich	1988	Liselotte Neumann (SWE)		
1967	Catherine Lacoste (FRA)[1]	1989	Betsy King		

[1]Amateur.

Ryder Cup

YEAR	RESULT
1927	United States 9½, Great Britain 2½
1929	Great Britain 7, United States 5
1931	United States 9, Great Britain 3
1933	Great Britain 6½, United States 5½
1935	United States 9, Great Britain 3
1937	United States 8, Great Britain 4
1939–45	not held
1947	United States 11, Great Britain 1
1949	United States 7, Great Britain 5
1951	United States 9½, Great Britain 2½
1953	United States 6½, Great Britain 5½
1955	United States 8, Great Britain 4
1957	Great Britain 7½, United States 4½
1959	United States 8½, Great Britain 3½
1961	United States 14½, Great Britain 9½
1963	United States 23, Great Britain 9
1965	United States 19½, Great Britain 12½
1967	United States 23½, Great Britain 8½
1969	United States 16, Great Britain 16
1971	United States 18½, Great Britain 13½

YEAR	RESULT
1973	United States 19, Great Britain 13
1975	United States 21, Great Britain 11
1977	United States 12½, Great Britain 7½
1979	United States 17, Europe 11
1981	United States 18½, Europe 9½
1983	United States 14½, Europe 13½
1985	Europe 16½, United States 11½
1987	Europe 15, United States 13
1989	Europe 14, United States 14
1991	United States 14½, Europe 13½
1993	United States 15, Europe 13
1995	Europe 14½, United States 13½
1997	Europe 14½, United States 13½
1999	United States 14½, Europe 13½
2001	postponed until 2002
2002	Europe 15½, United States 12½
2004	Europe 18½, United States 9½
2006	to be held 22–24 September, K Club, Straffan, Ireland

British Amateur Championship—Men

Won by a British golfer except as indicated.

YEAR	WINNER
1885	Allen MacFie
1886	Horace Hutchinson
1887	Horace Hutchinson
1888	John Ball
1889	Johnny Laidlay
1890	John Ball
1891	Johnny Laidlay
1892	John Ball
1893	Peter Anderson
1894	John Ball
1895	Leslie Balfour-Melville
1896	Freddie Tait
1897	Jack Allan
1898	Freddie Tait
1899	John Ball
1900	Harold Hilton
1901	Harold Hilton
1902	Charles Hutchings
1903	Robert Maxwell
1904	Walter Travis (USA)
1905	Arthur Barry
1906	James Robb
1907	John Ball
1908	E.A. Lassen
1909	Robert Maxwell
1910	John Ball
1911	Harold Hilton
1912	John Ball
1913	Harold Hilton
1914	J.L.C. Jenkins
1915–19	not held
1920	Cyril Tolley
1921	William Hunter
1922	Ernest Holderness
1923	Roger Wethered
1924	Ernest Holderness
1925	Robert Harris
1926	Jesse Sweetser (USA)

YEAR	WINNER
1927	William Tweddell
1928	Thomas Perkins
1929	Cyril Tolley
1930	Bobby Jones (USA)
1931	Eric Smith
1932	John de Forest
1933	Michael Scott
1934	Lawson Little (USA)
1935	Lawson Little (USA)
1936	Hector Thomson
1937	Robert Sweeny, Jr. (USA)
1938	Charles Yates (USA)
1939	Alexander Kyle
1940–45	not held
1946	James Bruen
1947	William Turnesa
1948	Frank Stranahan (USA)
1949	Samuel McCready
1950	Frank Stranahan (USA)
1951	Richard Chapman (USA)
1952	Harvie Ward (USA)
1953	Joe Carr (IRL)
1954	Douglas Bachli
1955	Joe Conrad (USA)
1956	John Beharrell
1957	Reid Jack
1958	Joe Carr (IRL)
1959	Deane Beman (USA)
1960	Joe Carr (IRL)
1961	Michael Bonallack
1962	Richard Davies (USA)
1963	Michael Lunt
1964	Gordon Clark
1965	Michael Bonallack
1966	Bobby Cole (RSA)
1967	Bob Dickson (USA)
1968	Michael Bonallack
1969	Michael Bonallack

YEAR	WINNER
1970	Michael Bonallack
1971	Steve Melnyk (USA)
1972	Trevor Homer
1973	Richard Siderowf (USA)
1974	Trevor Homer
1975	Vinny Giles (USA)
1976	Richard Siderowf (USA)
1977	Peter McEvoy
1978	Peter McEvoy
1979	Jay Sigel (USA)
1980	Duncan Evans
1981	Phillipe Ploujoux (FRA)
1982	Martin Thompson
1983	Philip Parkin
1984	José María Olazábal (ESP)
1985	Garth McGimpsey (IRL)
1986	David Curry
1987	Paul Mayo
1988	Christian Hardin (SWE)
1989	Stephen Dodd
1990	Rolf Muntz (NED)
1991	Gary Wolstenholme
1992	Stephen Dundas
1993	Ian Pyman
1994	Lee James
1995	Gordon Sherry
1996	Warren Bledon
1997	Craig Watson
1998	Sergio Garcia (ESP)
1999	Graeme Storm
2000	Mikko Ilonen (FIN)
2001	Michael Hoey (IRL)
2002	Alejandro Larrazabal (ESP)
2003	Gary Wolstenholme
2004	Stuart Wilson
2005	Brian McElhinney (IRL)

United States Amateur Championship—Men

Won by an American golfer except as indicated.

YEAR	WINNER	YEAR	WINNER	YEAR	WINNER
1895	Charles Macdonald	1932	Ross Somerville	1971	Gary Cowan (CAN)
1896	H.J. Whigham	1933	George Dunlap	1972	Vinny Giles
1897	H.J. Whigham	1934	Lawson Little	1973	Craig Stadler
1898	Findlay Douglas	1935	Lawson Little	1974	Jerry Pate
1899	H.M. Harriman	1936	John Fischer	1975	Fred Ridley
1900	Walter Travis	1937	John Goodman	1976	Bill Sander
1901	Walter Travis	1938	William Turnesa	1977	John Fought
1902	Louis James	1939	Bud Ward	1978	John Cook
1903	Walter Travis	1940	Richard Chapman	1979	Mark O'Meara
1904	H. Chandler Egan	1941	Bud Ward	1980	Hal Sutton
1905	H. Chandler Egan	1942–45	not held	1981	Nathaniel Crosby
1906	Eben Byers	1946	Ted Bishop	1982	Jay Sigel
1907	Jerry Travers	1947	Skee Riegel	1983	Jay Sigel
1908	Jerry Travers	1948	William Turnesa	1984	Scott Verplank
1909	Robert Gardner	1949	Charles Coe	1985	Sam Randolph
1910	W.C. Fownes, Jr.	1950	Sam Urzetta	1986	Buddy Alexander
1911	Harold Hilton	1951	Billy Maxwell	1987	Billy Mayfair
1912	Jerry Travers	1952	Jack Westland	1988	Eric Meeks
1913	Jerry Travers	1953	Gene Littler	1989	Chris Patton
1914	Francis Ouimet	1954	Arnold Palmer	1990	Phil Mickelson
1915	Robert Gardner	1955	Harvie Ward	1991	Mitch Voges
1916	Chick Evans	1956	Harvie Ward	1992	Justin Leonard
1917–18	not held	1957	Hillman Robbins	1993	John Harris
1919	Davidson Herron	1958	Charles Coe	1994	Tiger Woods
1920	Chick Evans	1959	Jack Nicklaus	1995	Tiger Woods
1921	Jesse Guildford	1960	Deane Beman	1996	Tiger Woods
1922	Jess Sweetser	1961	Jack Nicklaus	1997	Matt Kuchar
1923	Max Marston	1962	Labron Harris, Jr.	1998	Hank Kuehne
1924	Bobby Jones	1963	Deane Beman	1999	David Gossett
1925	Bobby Jones	1964	Bill Campbell	2000	Jeff Quinney
1926	George von Elm	1965	Bob Murphy	2001	Ben Dickerson
1927	Bobby Jones	1966	Gary Cowan (CAN)	2002	Ricky Barnes
1928	Bobby Jones	1967	Bob Dickson	2003	Nick Flanagan (AUS)
1929	Harrison Johnston	1968	Bruce Fleisher	2004	Ryan Moore
1930	Bobby Jones	1969	Steve Melnyk		
1931	Francis Ouimet	1970	Lanny Wadkins		

Women's British Open Championship

YEAR	WINNER	YEAR	WINNER	YEAR	WINNER
1976	J. Lee Smith (GBR)	1986	Laura Davies (GBR)	1996	Emilee Klein (USA)
1977	Vivien Saunders (GBR)	1987	Alison Nicholas (GBR)	1997	Karrie Webb (AUS)
1978	Janet Melville (GBR)	1988	Corinne Dibnah (AUS)	1998	Sherri Steinhauer (USA)
1979	Alison Sheard (RSA)	1989	Jane Geddes (USA)	1999	Sherri Steinhauer (USA)
1980	Debbie Massey (USA)	1990	Helen Alfredsson (SWE)	2000	Sophie Gustafson (SWE)
1981	Debbie Massey (USA)	1991	Penny Grice-Whittaker (GBR)	2001	Pak Se Ri (KOR)
1982	Marta Figueras-Dotti (SPA)	1992	Patty Sheehan (USA)	2002	Karrie Webb (AUS)
1983	not held	1993	Mardi Lunn (AUS)	2003	Annika Sörenstam (SWE)
1984	Okamoto Ayako (JAP)	1994	Liselotte Neumann (SWE)	2004	Karen Stupples (GBR)
1985	Betsy King (USA)	1995	Karrie Webb (AUS)	2005	Jang Jeong (KOR)

Ladies' British Amateur Championship

Won by a British golfer except as indicated.

YEAR	WINNER	YEAR	WINNER	YEAR	WINNER
1893	Lady Margaret Scott	1903	Rhona Adair	1913	Muriel Dodd
1894	Lady Margaret Scott	1904	Lottie Dod	1914	Cecil Leitch
1895	Lady Margaret Scott	1905	Bertha Thompson	1915–19	not held
1896	Amy Pascoe	1906	Mrs. W. Kennion	1920	Cecil Leitch
1897	Edith Orr	1907	May Hezlet	1921	Cecil Leitch
1898	Lena Thomson	1908	Maud Titterton	1922	Joyce Wethered
1899	May Hezlet	1909	Dorothy Campbell	1923	Doris Chambers
1900	Rhona Adair	1910	Elsie Grant-Suttie	1924	Joyce Wethered
1901	Mary Graham	1911	Dorothy Campbell	1925	Joyce Wethered
1902	May Hezlet	1912	Gladys Ravenscroft	1926	Cecil Leitch

Ladies' British Amateur Championship (continued)

YEAR	WINNER	YEAR	WINNER	YEAR	WINNER
1927	Simone de la Chaume (FRA)	1956	Wiffi Smith (USA)	1981	Belle Robertson
1928	Nanette le Blan (FRA)	1957	Philomena Garvey	1982	Kitrina Douglas
1929	Joyce Wethered	1958	Jessie Valentine	1983	Jill Thornhill
1930	Diana Fishwick	1959	Elizabeth Price	1984	Jody Rosenthal (USA)
1931	Enid Wilson	1960	Barbara McIntire (USA)	1985	Lillian Behan (IRE)
1932	Enid Wilson	1961	Marley Spearman	1986	Marnie McGuire
1933	Enid Wilson	1962	Marley Spearman	1987	Janet Collingham
1934	Helen Holm	1963	Brigitte Varangot (FRA)	1988	Joanne Furby
1935	Wanda Morgan	1964	Carol Sorenson (USA)	1989	Helen Dobson
1936	Pam Barton	1965	Brigitte Varangot (FRA)	1990	Julie Wade Hall
1937	Jessie Anderson	1966	Elizabeth Chadwick	1991	Valerie Michaud
1938	Helen Holm	1967	Elizabeth Chadwick	1992	Bernille Pedersen (DEN)
1939	Pam Barton	1968	Brigitte Varangot (FRA)	1993	Catriona Lambert
1940–45	*not held*	1969	Catherine Lacoste (FRA)	1994	Emma Duggleby
1946	Jean Hetherington	1970	Dinah Oxley	1995	Julie Wade Hall
1947	Babe Didrikson Zaharias	1971	Michelle Walker	1996	Kelli Kuehne (USA)
	(USA)	1972	Michelle Walker	1997	Alison Rose
1948	Louise Suggs (USA)	1973	Ann Irvin	1998	Kim Rostron
1949	Frances Stephens	1974	Carol Semple (USA)	1999	Marine Monnet (FRA)
1950	Lally de Saint Sauveur (FRA)	1975	Nancy Roth Syms (USA)	2000	Rebecca Hudson
1951	Catherine MacCann	1976	Cathy Panton	2001	Marta Prieto (ESP)
1952	Moira Paterson	1977	Angela Uzielli	2002	Rebecca Hudson
1953	Marlene Stewart (CAN)	1978	Edwina Kennedy (AUS)	2003	Elisa Serramia (ESP)
1954	Frances Stephens	1979	Maureen Madill	2004	Louise Stahle (SWE)
1955	Jessie Valentine	1980	Anne Quast Sander (USA)	2005	Louise Stahle (SWE)

United States Women's Amateur Championship

Won by an American golfer except as indicated.

YEAR	WINNER	YEAR	WINNER	YEAR	WINNER
1895	Mrs. C.S. Brown	1933	Virginia Van Wie	1973	Carol Semple
1896	Beatrix Hoyt	1934	Virginia Van Wie	1974	Cynthia Hill
1897	Beatrix Hoyt	1935	Glenna Collett Vare	1975	Beth Daniel
1898	Beatrix Hoyt	1936	Pamela Barton (GBR)	1976	Donna Horton
1899	Ruth Underhill	1937	Estelle Lawson Page	1977	Beth Daniel
1900	Frances C. Griscom	1938	Patty Berg	1978	Cathy Sherk (CAN)
1901	Genevieve Hecker	1939	Betty Jameson	1979	Cynthia Hill
1902	Genevieve Hecker	1940	Betty Jameson	1980	Juli Inkster
1903	Bessie Anthony	1941	Elizabeth Hicks	1981	Juli Inkster
1904	Georgianna M. Bishop	1942–45	*not held*	1982	Juli Inkster
1905	Pauline Mackay	1946	Babe Didrikson Zaharias	1983	Joanne Pacillo
1906	Harriot S. Curtis	1947	Louise Suggs	1984	Deb Richard
1907	Margaret Curtis	1948	Grace Lenczyk	1985	Michiko Hattori (JPN)
1908	Katherine Harley	1949	Dorothy Porter	1986	Kay Cockerill
1909	Dorothy I. Campbell (GBR)	1950	Beverly Hanson	1987	Kay Cockerill
1910	Dorothy I. Campbell (GBR)	1951	Dorothy Kirby	1988	Pearl Sinn
1911	Margaret Curtis	1952	Jacqueline Pung	1989	Vicki Goetze
1912	Margaret Curtis	1953	Mary Lena Faulk	1990	Pat Hurst
1913	Gladys Ravenscroft (GBR)	1954	Barbara Romack	1991	Amy Fruhwirth
1914	Katherine Harley Jackson	1955	Patricia Lesser	1992	Vicki Goetze
1915	Florence Vanderbeck	1956	Marlene Stewart (CAN)	1993	Jill McGill
1916	Alexa Stirling	1957	JoAnne Gunderson	1994	Wendy Ward
1917–18	*not held*	1958	Anne Quast	1995	Kelli Kuehne
1919	Alexa Stirling	1959	Barbara McIntire	1996	Kelli Kuehne
1920	Alexa Stirling	1960	JoAnne Gunderson	1997	Silvia Cavalleri (ITA)
1921	Marion Hollins	1961	Anne Quast Sander	1998	Grace Park
1922	Glenna Collett	1962	JoAnne Gunderson	1999	Dorothy Delasin
1923	Edith Cummings	1963	Anne Quast Sander	2000	Marcy Newton
1924	Dorothy Campbell Hurd	1964	Barbara McIntire	2001	Meredith Duncan
1925	Glenna Collett	1965	Jean Ashley	2002	Becky Lucidi
1926	Helen Stetson	1966	JoAnne Gunderson Carner	2003	Virada Nirapath-
1927	Miriam Burns Horn	1967	Mary Lou Dill		pongporn (THA)
1928	Glenna Collett	1968	JoAnne Gunderson Carner	2004	Jane Park
1929	Glenna Collett	1969	Catherine Lacoste (FRA)	2005	Morgan Pressel
1930	Glenna Collett	1970	Martha Wilkinson	2006	*to be held 7–13 August,*
1931	Helen Hicks	1971	Laura Baugh		*Pumpkin Ridge Golf*
1932	Virginia Van Wie	1972	Mary Budke		*Club, North Plains OR*

World Cup

YEAR	WINNER
1953	Argentina (Antonio Cerda and Roberto de Vicenzo)
1954	Australia (Peter Thomson and Kel Nagle)
1955	United States (Chick Harbert and Ed Furgol)
1956	United States (Ben Hogan and Sam Snead)
1957	Japan (Torakichi Nakamura and Koichi Ono)
1958	Ireland (Harry Bradshaw and Christy O'Connor)
1959	Australia (Peter Thomson and Kel Nagle)
1960	United States (Sam Snead and Arnold Palmer)
1961	United States (Sam Snead and Jimmy Demaret)
1962	United States (Sam Snead and Arnold Palmer)
1963	United States (Arnold Palmer and Jack Nicklaus)
1964	United States (Arnold Palmer and Jack Nicklaus)
1965	South Africa (Gary Player and Harold Henning)
1966	United States (Arnold Palmer and Jack Nicklaus)
1967	United States (Arnold Palmer and Jack Nicklaus)
1968	Canada (Al Balding and George Knudson)
1969	United States (Orville Moody and Lee Trevino)
1970	Australia (David Graham and Bruce Devlin)
1971	United States (Jack Nicklaus and Lee Trevino)
1972	Taiwan (Hsieh Min-nan and Lu Liang-huan)
1973	United States (Johnny Miller and Jack Nicklaus)
1974	South Africa (Bobby Cole and Dale Hayes)
1975	United States (Johnny Miller and Lou Graham)
1976	Spain (Seve Ballesteros and Manuel Piñero)
1977	Spain (Seve Ballesteros and Antonio Garrido)
1978	United States (John Mahaffey and Andy North)
1979	United States (Hale Irwin and John Mahaffey)
1980	Canada (Dan Halldorson and Jim Nelford)
1981	*not held*
1982	Spain (Manuel Piñero and Jose-Maria Cañizares)
1983	United States (Rex Caldwell and John Cook)
1984	Spain (Jose-Maria Cañizares and Jose Rivero)
1985	Canada (Dan Halldorson and Dave Barr)
1986	*not held*
1987	Wales (Ian Woosnam and David Llewellyn)
1988	United States (Ben Crenshaw and Mark McCumber)
1989	Australia (Peter Fowler and Wayne Grady)
1990	Germany (Bernhard Langer and Torsten Giedeon)
1991	Sweden (Anders Forsbrand and Per-Ulrik Johansson)
1992	United States (Fred Couples and Davis Love III)
1993	United States (Fred Couples and Davis Love III)
1994	United States (Fred Couples and Davis Love III)
1995	United States (Fred Couples and Davis Love III)
1996	South Africa (Ernie Els and Wayne Westner)
1997	Ireland (Padraig Harrington and Paul McGinley)
1998	England (Nick Faldo and David Carter)
1999	United States (Tiger Woods and Mark O'Meara)
2000	United States (Tiger Woods and David Duval)
2001	South Africa (Ernie Els and Retief Goosen)
2002	Japan (Shigeki Maruyama and Toshi Izawa)
2003	South Africa (Trevor Immelman and Rory Sabbatini)
2004	England (Paul Casey and Luke Donald)
2005	*to be held 17–20 November, Victoria Clube de Golfe Course, Algarve, Portugal*

Curtis Cup

YEAR	RESULT
1932	United States 5½, Britain 3½
1934	United States 6½, Britain and Ireland 2½
1936	United States[1] 4½, Britain and Ireland 4½
1938	United States 5½, Britain and Ireland 3½
1940–46	not held
1948	United States 6½, Britain and Ireland 2½
1950	United States 7½, Britain and Ireland 2½
1952	Britain and Ireland 5, United States 4
1954	United States 6, Britain and Ireland 3
1956	Britain and Ireland 5, United States 4
1958	Britain and Ireland[1] 4½, United States 4½
1960	United States 6½, Britain and Ireland 2½
1962	United States 8, Britain and Ireland 1
1964	United States 10½, Britain and Ireland 7½
1966	United States 13, Britain and Ireland 5
1968	United States 10½, Britain and Ireland 7½
1970	United States 11½, Britain and Ireland 6½
1972	United States 10, Britain and Ireland 8
1974	United States 13, Britain and Ireland 5
1976	United States 11½, Britain and Ireland 6½
1978	United States 12, Britain and Ireland 6
1980	United States 13, Britain and Ireland 5
1982	United States 14½, Britain and Ireland 3½
1984	United States 9½, Britain and Ireland 8½
1986	Britain and Ireland 13, United States 5
1988	Britain and Ireland 11, United States 7
1990	United States 14, Britain and Ireland 4
1992	Britain and Ireland 10, United States 8
1994	Britain and Ireland[1] 9, United States 9
1996	Britain and Ireland 11½, United States 6½
1998	United States 10, Britain and Ireland 8
2000	United States 10, Britain and Ireland 8
2002	United States 11, Britain and Ireland 7
2004	United States 10, Britain and Ireland 8
2006	*to be held 29–30 July, Bandon Dunes Golf Resort, Bandon OR*

[1]*In case of a tie the defenders retain the cup.*

Gymnastics

Aside from the gymnastics events in **Olympic Games,** the most popular venue for gymnastics competition is that of the **world championship games.** Men's events are six in number with all-around individual and all-around team awards in addition. The latter two awards are given on the basis of cumulative points. Women also have all-around team and individual awards, determined by their performance in four individual events.

Fédération Internationale de Gymnastique Web site: <www.fig-gymnastics.com>.

World Gymnastics Championships—Men

YEAR	ALL-AROUND TEAM	ALL-AROUND INDIVIDUAL	HORIZONTAL BAR	PARALLEL BARS
1950	Switzerland	Walter Lehmann (SUI)	Paavo Aaltonen (FIN)	Hans Eugster (SUI)
1952[1]	USSR	Viktor Chukarin (URS)	Jack Günthard (SUI)	Hans Eugster (SUI)
1954	USSR	Valentin Muratov (URS)	Valentin Muratov (URS)	Viktor Chukarin (URS)
1956[1]	USSR	Viktor Chukarin (URS)	Takashi Ono (JPN)	Viktor Chukarin (URS)
1958	USSR	Boris Shakhlin (URS)	Boris Shakhlin (URS)	Boris Shakhlin (URS)
1960[1]	Japan	Boris Shakhlin (URS)	Takashi Ono (JPN)	Boris Shakhlin (URS)
1962	Japan	Yury Titov (URS)	Takashi Ono (JPN)	Miroslav Cerar (YUG)
1964[1]	Japan	Yukio Endo (JPN)	Boris Shakhlin (URS)	Yukio Endo (JPN)
1966	Japan	Mikhail Voronin (URS)	Akinori Nakayama (JPN)	Sergey Diomidov (URS)
1968[1]	Japan	Sawao Kato (JPN)	Mikhail Voronin (URS), Akinori Nakayama (JPN)[2]	Akinori Nakayama (JPN)
1970	Japan	Eizo Kenmotsu (JPN)	Eizo Kenmotsu (JPN)	Akinori Nakayama (JPN)
1972[1]	Japan	Sawao Kato (JPN)	Mitsuo Tsukahara (JPN)	Sawao Kato (JPN)
1974	Japan	Shigeru Kasamatsu (JPN)	Eberhard Gienger (FRG)	Eizo Kenmotsu (JPN)
1976[1]	Japan	Nikolay Andrianov (URS)	Mitsuo Tsukahara (JPN)	Sawao Kato (JPN)
1978	Japan	Nikolay Andrianov (URS)	Shigeru Kasamatsu (JPN)	Eizo Kenmotsu (JPN)
1979	USSR	Aleksandr Dityatin (URS)	Kurt Thomas (USA)	Bart Conner (USA)
1980[1]	USSR	Aleksandr Dityatin (URS)	Stoyan Delchev (BUL)	Aleksandr Tkachyov (URS)
1981	USSR	Yury Korolyov (URS)	Aleksandr Tkachyov (URS)	Aleksandr Dityatin (URS), Koji Gushiken (JPN)[2]
1983	China	Dmitry Bilozerchev (URS)	Dmitry Bilozerchev (URS)	Lou Yun (CHN), Vladimir Artyomov (URS)[2]
1984[1]	United States	Koji Gushiken (JPN)	Shinji Morisue (JPN)	Bart Conner (USA)
1985	USSR	Yury Korolyov (URS)	Tong Fei (CHN)	Sylvio Kroll (GDR), Valentin Mogilny (URS)[2]
1987	USSR	Dmitry Bilozerchev (URS)	Dmitry Bilozerchev (URS)	Vladimir Artyomov (URS)
1988[1]	USSR	Vladimir Artyomov (URS)	Vladimir Artyomov (URS), Valery Lyukin (URS)[2]	Vladimir Artyomov (URS)
1989	USSR	Igor Korobchinsky (URS)	Li Chunyang (CHN)	Vladimir Artyomov (URS), Li Jing (CHN)[2]
1991	USSR	Grigory Misutin (URS)	Ralf Buechner (GER), Li Chunyang (CHN)[2]	Li Jing (CHN)
1992	[3]	[3]	Grigory Misutin (CIS)	Li Jing (CHN), Aleksey Voropayev (CIS)[2]
1993	[3]	Vitaly Sherbo (BLR)	Sergey Charkov (RUS)	Vitaly Sherbo (BLR)
1994	China	Ivan Ivankov (BLR)	Vitaly Sherbo (BLR)	Liping Huang (CHN)
1995	China	Li Xiaoshuang (CHN)	Andreas Wecker (GER)	Vitaly Sherbo (BLR)
1996	[3]	[3]	Jesús Carballo (ESP)	Rustam Charipov (UKR)
1997	China	Ivan Ivankov (BLR)	Jani Tanskanen (FIN)	Zhang Jinjing (CHN)
1999	China	Nikolay Krukov (RUS)	Jesús Carballo (ESP)	Lee Joo Hyung (KOR)
2000[1]	China	Aleksey Nemov (RUS)	Aleksey Nemov (RUS)	Li Xiaopeng (CHN)
2001	Belarus	Feng Jing (CHN)	Vlasios Maras (GRE)	Sean Townsend (USA)
2002	[3]	[3]	Vlasios Maras (GRE)	Li Xiaopeng (CHN)
2003	China	Paul Hamm (USA)	Takehiro Kashima (JPN)	Li Xiaopeng (CHN)
2004[1]	Japan	Paul Hamm (USA)	Igor Cassina (ITA)	Valery Goncharov (UKR)
2005	*Competition scheduled to be held 21–27 November in Melbourne, VIC, Australia.*			

YEAR	POMMEL HORSE	RINGS	VAULT	FLOOR EXERCISE
1950	Josef Stalder (SUI)	Walter Lehmann (SUI)	Ernst Gebendinger (SUI)	Josef Stalder (SUI)
1952[1]	Viktor Chukarin (URS)	Grant Shaginyan (URS)	Viktor Chukarin (URS)	Karl Thoresson (SWE)
1954	Grant Shaginyan (URS)	Albert Azaryan (URS)	Leo Sotornik (TCH)	Valetin Muratov (URS), Masao Takemoto (JPN)[2]
1956[1]	Boris Shakhlin (URS)	Albert Azaryan (URS)	Valentin Muratov (URS), Helmut Bantz (FRG)[2]	Valentin Muratov (URS)
1958	Boris Shakhlin (URS)	Albert Azaryan (URS)	Yury Titov (URS)	Masao Takemoto (JPN)

World Gymnastics Championships—Men (continued)

YEAR	POMMEL HORSE	RINGS	VAULT	FLOOR EXERCISE
1960[1]	Boris Shakhlin (URS), Eugen Ekman (FIN)[2]	Albert Azaryan (URS)	Takashi Ono (JPN), Boris Shakhlin (URS)[2]	Nobuyuki Aihara (JPN)
1962	Miroslav Cerar (YUG)	Yury Titov (URS)	Premysel Krbec (TCH)	Nobuyuki Aihara (JPN), Yukio Endo (JPN)[2]
1964[1]	Miroslav Cerar (YUG)	Takuji Hayata (JPN)	Haruhiro Yamasita (JPN)	Franco Menichelli (ITA)
1966	Miroslav Cerar (YUG)	Mikhail Voronin (URS)	Haruhiro Matsuda (JPN)	Akinori Nakayama (JPN)
1968[1]	Miroslav Cerar (YUG)	Akinori Nakayama (JPN)	Mikhail Voronin (URS)	Sawao Kato (JPN)
1970	Miroslav Cerar (YUG)	Akinori Nakayama (JPN)	Mitsuo Tsukahara (JPN)	Akinori Nakayama (JPN)
1972[1]	Viktor Klimenko (URS)	Akinori Nakayama (JPN)	Klaus Koeste (GDR)	Nikolay Andrianov (URS)
1974	Zoltan Magyar (HUN)	Danut Grecu (ROM), Nikolay Andrianov (URS)[2]	Shigeru Kasamatsu (JPN)	Shigeru Kasamatsu (JPN)
1976[1]	Zoltan Magyar (HUN)	Nikolay Andrianov (URS)	Nikolay Andrianov (URS)	Nikolay Andrianov (URS)
1978	Zoltan Magyar (HUN)	Nikolay Andrianov (URS)	Junichi Shimizu (JPN)	Kurt Thomas (USA)
1979	Zoltan Magyar (HUN)	Aleksandr Dityatin (URS)	Alexandr Dityatin (URS)	Kurt Thomas (USA), Roland Bruckner (GDR)[2]
1980[1]	Zoltan Magyar (HUN)	Aleksandr Dityatin (URS)	Nikolay Andrianov (URS)	Roland Bruckner (GDR)
1981	Li Xiaoping (CHN), Michael Nikolay (GDR)[2]	Aleksandr Dityatin (URS)	Ralf-Peter Hemmann (GDR)	Li Yuijiu (CHN), Yury Korolyov (URS)[2]
1983	Dmitry Bilozerchev (URS)	Dmitry Bilozerchev (URS), Koji Gushiken (JPN)[2]	Arthur Akopyan (URS)	Tong Fei (CHN)
1984[1]	Li Ning (CHN), Peter Vidmar (USA)[2]	Koji Gushiken (JPN), Li Ning (CHN)[2]	Lou Yun (CHN)	Li Ning (CHN)
1985	Valentin Mogilny (URS)	Li Ning (CHN), Yury Korolyov (URS)[2]	Yury Korolyov (URS)	Tong Fei (CHN)
1987	Dmitry Bilozerchev (URS), Zsolt Borkai (HUN)[2]	Yury Korolyov (URS)	Sylvio Kroll (GDR), Lou Yun (CHN)[2]	Lou Yun (CHN)
1988[1]	Dmitry Bilozerchev (URS), Zsolt Borkai (HUN), Lyubomir Geraskov (BUL)[2]	Holger Behrendt (GDR), Dmitry Bilozerchev (URS)[2]	Lou Yun (CHN)	Sergey Kharkov (URS)
1989	Valentin Mogilny (URS)	Andreas Aguilar (FRG)	Joerg Behrend (GDR)	Igor Korobchinsky (URS)
1991	Valery Belenky (URS)	Grigory Misutin (URS)	You Ok Youl (KOR)	Igor Korobchinsky (URS)
1992	Pae Gil Su (PRK), Vitaly Sherbo (CIS), Li Jing (CHN)[2]	Vitaly Sherbo (CIS)	You Ok Youl (KOR)	Igor Korobchinsky (CIS)
1993	Pae Gil Su (PRK)	Yury Chechi (ITA)	Vitaly Sherbo (BLR)	Grigory Misutin (UKR)
1994	Marius Urzica (ROM)	Yury Chechi (ITA)	Vitaly Sherbo (BLR)	Vitaly Sherbo (BLR)
1995	Li Donghua (SUI)	Yury Chechi (ITA)	Aleksey Nemov (RUS), Grigory Misutin (UKR)[2]	Vitaly Sherbo (BLR)
1996	Pae Gil Su (PRK)	Yury Chechi (ITA)	Aleksey Nemov (RUS)	Vitaly Sherbo (BLR)
1997	Valery Belenki (GER)	Yury Chechi (ITA)	Sergey Fedorchenko (KAZ)	Aleksey Nemov (RUS)
1999	Aleksey Nemov (RUS)	Dong Zhen (CHN)	Li Xiaopeng (CHN)	Aleksey Nemov (RUS)
2000[1]	Marius Urzica (ROM)	Szilveszter Csollany (HUN)	Gervasio Deferr (ESP)	Igor Vihrons (LAT)
2001	Marius Urzica (ROM)	Jordan Jovtchev (BUL)	Marian Dragulescu (ROM)	Iordan Iovtchev (BUL), Marian Dragulescu (ROM)[2]
2002	Marius Urzica (ROM)	Szilveszter Csollany (HUN)	Li Xiaopeng (CHN)	Marian Dragulescu (ROM)
2003	Teng Haibin (CHN), Takehiro Kashima (JPN)[2]	Iordan Iovtchev (BUL), Dimosthenis Tampakos (GRE)[2]	Li Xiaopeng (CHN)	Paul Hamm (USA), Iordan Iovtchev (BUL)[2]
2004[1]	Teng Haibin (CHN)	Dimosthenis Tampakos (GRE)	Gervasio Deferr (ESP)	Kyle Shewfelt (CAN)
2005	*Competition scheduled to be held 21–27 November in Melbourne, VIC, Australia.*			

[1]*Olympic championships, recognized as world championships (for Olympic results 1896–1948, and from 1992, see Olympic Games).* [2]*Tied.* [3]*Not held.*

World Gymnastics Championships—Women

YEAR	ALL-AROUND TEAM	ALL-AROUND INDIVIDUAL	BALANCE BEAM	UNEVEN PARALLEL BARS
1950	Sweden	Helena Rakoczy (POL)	Helena Rakoczy (POL)	Gertchen Kolar (AUT), Anna Pettersson (SWE)[1]
1952[2]	USSR	Mariya Gorokhovskaya (URS)	Nina Bocharova (URS)	Margit Korondi (HUN)
1954	USSR	Galina Rudiko (URS)	Keiko Tanaka (JPN)	Agnes Keleti (HUN)
1956[2]	USSR	Larisa Latynina (URS)	Agnes Keleti (HUN)	Agnes Keleti (HUN)
1958	USSR	Larisa Latynina (URS)	Larisa Latynina (URS)	Larisa Latynina (URS)
1960[2]	USSR	Larisa Latynina (URS)	Eva Bosakova (TCH)	Polina Astakhova (URS)
1962	USSR	Larisa Latynina (URS)	Eva Bosakova (TCH)	Irina Pervushina (URS)
1964[2]	USSR	Vera Caslavska (TCH)	Vera Caslavska (TCH)	Polina Astakhova (URS)
1966	Czechoslovakia	Vera Caslavska (TCH)	Natalya Kuchinskaya (URS)	Natalya Kuchinskaya (URS)
1968[2]	USSR	Vera Caslavska (TCH)	Natalya Kuchinskaya (URS)	Vera Caslavska (TCH)
1970	USSR	Lyudmila Turishcheva (URS)	Erika Zuchold (GDR)	Karin Janz (GDR)
1972[2]	USSR	Lyudmila Turishcheva (URS)	Olga Korbut (URS)	Karin Janz (GDR)
1974	USSR	Lyudmila Turishcheva (URS)	Lyudmila Turishcheva (URS)	Annelore Zinke (GDR)
1976[2]	USSR	Nadia Comaneci (ROM)	Nadia Comaneci (ROM)	Nadia Comaneci (ROM)
1978	USSR	Yelena Mukhina (URS)	Nadia Comaneci (ROM)	Marcia Frederick (USA)
1979	Romania	Nelli Kim (URS)	Vera Cerna (TCH)	Ma Yanhong (CHN), Maxi Gnauck (GDR)[1]
1980[2]	USSR	Yelena Davydova (URS)	Nadia Comaneci (ROM)	Maxi Gnauck (GDR)
1981	USSR	Olga Bicherova (URS)	Maxi Gnauck (GDR)	Maxi Gnauck (GDR)
1983	USSR	Natalya Yurchenko (URS)	Olga Mostepanova (URS)	Maxi Gnauck (GDR)
1984[2]	Romania	Mary Lou Retton (USA)	Ecaterina Szabo (ROM), Simona Pauca (ROM)[1]	Julianne McNamara (USA), Ma Yanhong (CHN)[1]
1985	USSR	Yelena Shushunova (URS), Oksana Omelyanchik (URS)[1]	Daniela Silivas (ROM)	Gabriele Fahnrich (GDR)
1987	Romania	Aurelia Dobre (ROM)	Aurelia Dobre (ROM)	Daniela Silivas (ROM), Doerte Thuemmler (GDR)[1]
1988[2]	USSR	Yelena Shushunova (URS)	Daniela Silivas (ROM)	Daniela Silivas (ROM)
1989	USSR	Svetlana Boginskaya (URS)	Daniela Silivas (ROM)	Fan Di (CHN), Daniela Silivas (ROM)[1]
1991	USSR	Kim Zmeskal (USA)	Svetlana Boginskaya (URS)	Kim Gwang Suk (PRK)
1992	[3]	[3]	Kim Zmeskal (USA)	Lavinia Milosovici (ROM)
1993	[3]	Shannon Miller (USA)	Lavinia Milosovici (ROM)	Shannon Miller (USA)
1994	Romania	Shannon Miller (USA)	Shannon Miller (USA)	Li Luo (CHN)
1995	Romania	Liliya Podkopayeva (UKR)	Mo Huilan (CHN)	Svetlana Khorkina (RUS)
1996	[3]	[3]	Dina Kochetkova (RUS)	Svetlana Khorkina (RUS), Yelena Piskun (BLR)[1]
1997	Romania	Svetlana Khorkina (RUS)	Gina Gogean (ROM)	Svetlana Khorkina (RUS)
1999	Romania	Maria Olaru (ROM)	Ling Jie (CHN)	Svetlana Khorkina (RUS)
2000[2]	Romania	Simona Amanar (ROM)	Liu Xuan (CHN)	Svetlana Khorkina (RUS)
2001	Romania	Svetlana Khorkina (RUS)	Andreea Raducan (ROM)	Svetlana Khorkina (RUS)
2002	[3]	[3]	Ashley Postell (USA)	Courtney Kupets (USA)
2003	United States	Svetlana Khorkina (RUS)	Fan Ye (CHN)	Chellsie Memmel (USA), Hollie Vise (USA)[1]
2004[2]	Romania	Carly Patterson (USA)	Catalina Ponor (ROM)	Emilie Lepennec (FRA)
2005	*Competition scheduled to be held 21–27 November in Melbourne, VIC, Australia.*			

YEAR	VAULT	FLOOR EXERCISE
1950	Helena Rakoczy (POL)	Helena Rakoczy (POL)
1952[2]	Yekaterina Kalinchuk (URS)	Agnes Keleti (HUN)
1954	Anna Pettersson (SWE), Tamara Manina (URS)[1]	Tamara Manina (URS)
1956[2]	Larisa Latynina (URS)	Larissa Latynina (URS), Agnes Keleti (HUN)[1]
1958	Larisa Latynina (URS)	Eva Bosakova (TCH)
1960[2]	Margarita Nikolayeva (URS)	Larisa Latynina (URS)
1962	Vera Caslavska (TCH)	Larisa Latynina (URS)
1964[2]	Vera Caslavska (TCH)	Larisa Latynina (URS)
1966	Vera Caslavska (TCH)	Natalya Kuchinskaya (URS)
1968[2]	Vera Caslavska (TCH)	Vera Caslavska (TCH), Larisa Petrik (URS)[1]

World Gymnastics Championships—Women (continued)

YEAR	VAULT	FLOOR EXERCISE
1970	Erika Zuchold (GDR)	Lyudmila Turishcheva (URS)
1972[2]	Karin Janz (GDR)	Olga Korbut (URS)
1974	Olga Korbut (URS)	Lyudmila Turishcheva (URS)
1976[2]	Nelli Kim (URS)	Nelli Kim (URS)
1978	Nelli Kim (URS)	Yelena Mukhina (URS), Nelli Kim (URS)[1]
1979	Dumitrita Turner (ROM)	Emilia Eberle (ROM)
1980[2]	Natalya Shaposhnikova (URS)	Nadia Comaneci (ROM), Nelli Kim (URS)[1]
1981	Maxi Gnauck (GDR)	Natalya Ilenko (URS)
1983	Boriana Stoyanova (BUL)	Ecaterina Szabo (ROM)
1984[2]	Ecaterina Szabo (ROM)	Ecaterina Szabo (ROM)
1985	Yelena Shushunova (URS)	Oksana Omelyanchik (URS)
1987	Yelena Shushunova (URS)	Yelena Shushunova (URS), Daniela Silivas (ROM)[1]
1988[2]	Svetlana Boginskaya (URS)	Daniela Silivas (ROM)
1989	Olesia Dudnik (URS)	Svetlana Boginskaya (URS), Daniela Silivas (ROM)[1]
1991	Lavinia Milosovici (ROM)	Cristina Bontas (ROM), Oksana Chusovitina (URS)[1]
1992	Henrietta Onodi (HUN)	Kim Zmeskal (USA)
1993	Yelena Piskun (BLR)	Shannon Miller (USA)
1994	Gina Gogean (ROM)	Dina Kochetkova (RUS)
1995	Simona Amanar (ROM), Liliya Podkopayeva (UKR)[1]	Gina Gogean (ROM)
1996	Gina Gogean (ROM)	Gina Gogean (ROM), Kui Yuanyuan (CHN)[1]
1997	Simona Amanar (ROM)	Gina Gogean (ROM)
1999	Yelena Zamolodchikova (RUS)	Andreea Raducan (ROM)
2000[2]	Yelena Zamolodchikova (RUS)	Yelena Zamolodchikova (RUS)
2001	Svetlana Khorkina (RUS)	Andreea Raducan (ROM)
2002	Yelena Zamolodchikova (RUS)	Elena Gómez (ESP)
2003	Oksana Chusovitina (UZB)	Daiane Dos Santos (BRA)
2004[2]	Monica Rosu (ROM)	Catalina Ponor (ROM)
2005	Competition scheduled to be held 21–27 November in Melbourne, VIC, Australia.	

[1]Tied.   [2]Olympic championships, recognized as world championships (for 1896–1952 Olympics, and from 1992, see Olympic Games).   [3]Not held.

Horse Racing

In the **oldest type** of horse racing, the rider sits astride the horse; in the other type of race, best known as **harness racing**, the driver sits in a sulky— a two-wheeled vehicle attached by shafts and traces to the horse. In the former type, a **Thoroughbred** horse is raced over either a track or a course of jumps and turns (**steeplechase**). Harness horses can be trotters or pacers and are Standardbred horses raced on a track.

The English Thoroughbred classics. The races are run by 3-year-old colts and fillies. **The Derby**, first run in 1780, is run at Epsom Downs, Surrey, over 1½ miles. **The Oaks** (for fillies only), also run at Epsom Downs, was first run in 1779; the oldest of the English races, however, is the **St. Leger** (1776). It is run over 1 mile 6½ furlongs at Doncaster, South Yorkshire. The **2,000 Guineas** (1809) is run over 1 mile at Newmarket, Suffolk. A horse that wins the 2,000 Guineas, the Derby, and the St. Leger all in one year is said to have won the **British Triple Crown.**

The American Thoroughbred classics. The Kentucky Derby, a **Triple Crown** event first run in 1875 and perhaps the best known of American horse races, is raced at Churchill Downs in Louisville KY, over a 10-furlong (1¼-mile) track. Another of the Triple Crown classics, the **Preakness Stakes**, was instituted in 1873; it is run over 9½ furlongs (1³⁄₁₆ miles) at Pimlico Race Track in Baltimore MD. The third Triple Crown event is the 12-furlong (1½-mile)

Belmont Stakes, established in 1867. It is run at Belmont Park Race Track, Long Island NY. All three events are for 3-year-old horses.

Australian Thoroughbred racing. The Victoria Racing Club's **Melbourne Cup**, first run in 1861, is one of the world's great handicap races. The day on which it is held (the first Tuesday in November) is a public holiday in Melbourne, Victoria.

Dubai World Cup, first run in 1996, is the world's richest horse race ($6 million in 2004). The 2,000-m (about 1¼-mi) race is held on the dirt track at the Nad Al Sheba Racecourse in Dubai, United Arab Emirates, and is open to four-year-old and older Thoroughbred horses.

The **Grand National**, the world's most significant and widely followed **steeplechase** race, has been run annually at Aintree Racecourse near Liverpool, England, since 1839. The race includes 30 jumps over a traditional distance of 4 miles 4 furlongs.

Harness racing. In the United States, the **Hambletonian Trot** is probably the most prestigious of harness races. It was established in 1926, was raced in New York, Kentucky, and Illinois, and is now run at The Meadowlands in New Jersey.

Related Web sites: US National Thoroughbred Racing Association: <www.ntra.com>; Fédération Equestre Internationale: <www.horsesport.org>; the magazine *Thoroughbred Times:* <www.thoroughbredtimes. com>; and <www.racingpost.co.uk>.

Major Thoroughbred Race Winners 2004–05

United States

DATE	RACE	WINNER	JOCKEY
8 Aug 2004	Haskell Invitational Handicap	Lion Heart	Joe Bravo
14 Aug 2004	Sword Dancer Invitational Handicap	Better Talk Now	Ramon Dominguez
14 Aug 2004	Secretariat Stakes	Kitten's Joy	Jerry Bailey
14 Aug 2004	Arlington Million Stakes[1]	Kicken Kris	Kent Desormeaux
14 Aug 2004	Beverly D. Stakes	Crimson Palace	Frankie Dettori
20 Aug 2004	Spinaway Stakes	Sense of Style	Edgar Prado
21 Aug 2004	Alabama Stakes	Society Selection	Cornelio Velasquez
21 Aug 2004	Hopeful Stakes	Afleet Alex	Jeremy Rose
22 Aug 2004	Pacific Classic Stakes	Pleasantly Perfect	Jerry Bailey
27 Aug 2004	Personal Ensign Handicap	Storm Flag Flying	John Velazquez
28 Aug 2004	Del Mar Debutante Stakes	Sweet Catomine	Victor Espinoza
28 Aug 2004	King's Bishop Stakes	Pomeroy	Edgar Prado
28 Aug 2004	Travers Stakes	Birdstone	Edgar Prado
29 Aug 2004	Ballerina Handicap	Lady Tak	Jerry Bailey
4 Sep 2004	Forego Handicap	Midas Eyes	Edgar Prado
11 Sep 2004	Gazelle Handicap	Stellar Jayne	Robby Albarado
11 Sep 2004	Man o' War Stakes	Magistretti	Edgar Prado
11 Sep 2004	Woodward Stakes	Ghostzapper	Javier Castellano
18 Sep 2004	Kentucky Cup Classic Handicap	Roses in May	John Velazquez
19 Sep 2004	Ruffian Handicap	Sightseek	John Velazquez
19 Sep 2004	Matron Stakes	Sense of Style	Edgar Prado
19 Sep 2004	Futurity Stakes	Park Avenue Ball	Javier Castellano
25 Sep 2004	Super Derby XXV	Fantasticat	Gerard Melancon
2 Oct 2004	Vosburgh Stakes	Pico Central	Victor Espinoza
2 Oct 2004	Jockey Club Gold Cup Stakes	Funny Cide	José Santos
2 Oct 2004	Flower Bowl Invitational Handicap	Riskaverse	Cornelio Velasquez
2 Oct 2004	Turf Classic Invitational Stakes	Kitten's Joy	John Velazquez
2 Oct 2004	Yellow Ribbon Stakes	Light Jig	Rene Douglas
2 Oct 2003	Oak Leaf Stakes	Sweet Catomine	Corey Nakatani
3 Oct 2004	Clement L. Hirsch Memorial Turf Championship Stakes	Star Over the Bay	Tyler Baze
9 Oct 2004	Frizette Stakes	Balletto	Corey Nakatani
9 Oct 2004	Champagne Stakes	Proud Accolade	John Velazquez
9 Oct 2004	Beldame Stakes	Sightseek	Javier Castellano
10 Oct 2004	Ancient Title Breeders' Cup Handicap	PT's Grey Eagle	Alex Bisono
10 Oct 2004	Overbrook Spinster Stakes	Azeri	Pat Day
16 Oct 2004	Queen Elizabeth II Challenge Cup Stakes	Ticker Tape	Kent Desormeaux
30 Oct 2004	Breeders' Cup Juvenile Fillies	Sweet Catomine	Corey Nakatani
30 Oct 2004	Breeders' Cup Sprint	Speightstown	John Velazquez
30 Oct 2004	Breeders' Cup Juvenile	Wilko	Frankie Dettori
30 Oct 2004	Breeders' Cup Mile	Singletary	David Romero Flores
30 Oct 2004	Breeders' Cup Filly and Mare Turf	Ouija Board	Kieren Fallon
30 Oct 2004	Breeders' Cup Turf[1]	Better Talk Now	Ramon Dominguez
30 Oct 2004	Breeders' Cup Distaff	Ashado	John Velazquez
30 Oct 2004	Breeders' Cup Classic[1]	Ghostzapper	Javier Castellano
20 Nov 2004	Frank J. De Francis Memorial Dash Stakes	Wildcat Heir	Stewart Elliott
27 Nov 2004	Cigar Mile Handicap	Lion Tamer	José Santos
28 Nov 2004	Hollywood Derby	Good Reward	Jerry Bailey
28 Nov 2004	Matriarch Stakes	Intercontinental	Jerry Bailey
4 Dec 2004	Hollywood Turf Cup Handicap	Pellegrino	Gary Stevens
18 Dec 2004	Hollywood Futurity	Declan's Moon	Victor Espinoza
5 Feb 2005	Charles H. Strub Stakes	Rock Hard Ten	Gary Stevens
5 Feb 2005	Donn Handicap	Saint Liam	Edgar Prado
5 Mar 2005	Fountain of Youth Stakes	High Fly	Jerry Bailey
5 Mar 2005	Gulfstream Park Handicap	Eddington	Eibar Coa
5 Mar 2005	Santa Anita Handicap	Rock Hard Ten	Gary Stevens
12 Mar 2005	Louisiana Derby	High Limit	Ramon Dominguez
13 Mar 2005	Santa Anita Oaks	Sweet Catomine	Corey Nakatani
26 Mar 2005	Lane's End Stakes	Flower Alley	Jorge Chavez
2 Apr 2005	Florida Derby	High Fly	Jerry Bailey
9 Apr 2005	Santa Anita Derby	Buzzards Bay	Mark Guidry
9 Apr 2005	Ashland Stakes	Sis City	Edgar Prado
9 Apr 2005	Illinois Derby	Greeley's Galaxy	Kent Desormeaux
9 Apr 2005	Oaklawn Handicap	Grand Reward	John McKee
9 Apr 2005	Apple Blossom Handicap	Dream of Summer	Patrick Valenzuela
16 Apr 2005	Blue Grass Stakes	Bandini	John Velazquez

Major Thoroughbred Race Winners 2004–2005 (continued)

United States (continued)

DATE	RACE	WINNER	JOCKEY
16 Apr 2005	Arkansas Derby	Afleet Alex	Jeremy Rose
9 Apr 2005	Wood Memorial Stakes	Bellamy Road	Javier Castellano
16 Apr 2005	San Juan Capistrano Invitational Handicap	T.H. Approval	Rene Douglas
6 May 2005	Kentucky Oaks	Summerly	Jerry Bailey
7 May 2005	Kentucky Derby[2]	Giacomo	Mike Smith
21 May 2005	Preakness Stakes[2]	Afleet Alex	Jeremy Rose
30 May 2005	Gamely Breeders' Cup Handicap	Mea Domina	Tyler Baze
30 May 2005	Metropolitan Mile Handicap	Ghostzapper	Javier Castellano
30 May 2005	Shoemaker Breeders' Cup Mile Stakes	Castledale	Rene Douglas
4 Jun 2005	Acorn Stakes	Round Pond	Stewart Elliott
11 Jun 2005	Belmont Stakes[2]	Afleet Alex	Jeremy Rose
11 Jun 2005	Charles Whittingham Memorial Handicap	Sweet Return	Alex Solis
18 Jun 2005	Californian Stakes	Lava Man	Patrick Valenzuela
25 Jun 2005	Mother Goose Stakes	Smuggler	Edgar Prado
2 Jul 2005	United Nations Handicap	Better Talk Now	Ramon Dominguez
2 Jul 2005	Suburban Handicap	Offlee Wild	Edgar Prado
9 Jul 2005	Hollywood Gold Cup	Lava Man	Patrick Valenzuela
23 Jul 2005	Coaching Club American Oaks	Smuggler	Edgar Prado
24 Jul 2005	Eddie Read Handicap	Sweet Return	Alex Solis
30 Jul 2005	Diana Stakes	Sand Springs	John Velazquez
30 Jul 2005	Jim Dandy Stakes	Flower Alley	John Velazquez
6 Aug 2005	Test Stakes	Leave Me Alone	Kent Desormeaux

Canada

8 Aug 2004	Breeders' Stakes[3]	A Bit O'Gold	Jono Jones
19 Sep 2004	Atto Mile Stakes	Soaring Free	Todd Kabel
3 Oct 2004	Mazarine Breeders' Cup Stakes	Higher World	Patrick Husbands
24 Oct 2004	Canadian International Stakes[1]	Sulamani	Frankie Dettori
26 Jun 2005	Queen's Plate Stakes[3]	Wild Desert	Patrick Valenzuela
17 Jul 2005	Prince of Wales Stakes[3]	Ablo	Gerry Olguin

England

17 Aug 2004	Juddmonte International Stakes	Sulamani	Frankie Dettori
19 Aug 2004	Nunthorpe Stakes	Bahamian Pirate	David Nicholls
11 Sep 2004	St. Leger	Rule of Law	Kerrin McEvoy
25 Sep 2004	Queen Elizabeth II Stakes	Rakti	Philip Robinson
30 April 2005	2,000 Guineas	Footstepsinthesand	Kieren Fallon
1 May 2005	1,000 Guineas	Virginia Waters	Kieren Fallon
4 Jun 2005	The Derby	Motivator	Johnny Murtagh
16 Jun 2005	Ascot Gold Cup	Westerner	Olivier Peslier
2 Jul 2005	Coral-Eclipse Stakes	Oratorio	Kieren Fallon
23 Jul 2005	King George VI and Queen Elizabeth Diamond Stakes[1]	Azamour	Mick Kinane
27 Jul 2005	Sussex Stakes	Proclamation	Mick Kinane

Ireland

11 Sep 2004	Irish Champion Stakes[1]	Azamour	Michael Kinane
18 Sep 2004	Irish St. Leger	Vinnie Roe	Patrick Smullen
21 May 2005	Irish 2,000 Guineas	Dubawi	Frankie Dettori
22 May 2005	Irish 1,000 Guineas	Saoire	Michael Kinane
26 Jun 2005	Irish Derby	Hurricane	Andre Fabre
17 Jul 2005	Irish Oaks	Shawanda	Christophe Soumillon

France

15 Aug 2004	Prix du Haras de Fresnay-le-Buffard	Whipper	Christophe Soumillon
12 Sep 2004	Prix Niel	Valixir	Eric Legrix
3 Oct 2004	Prix de l'Arc de Triomphe[1]	Bago	Thierry Gillet
3 Oct 2004	Grand Criterium	Oratorio	Jamie Spencer
24 Oct 2004	Prix Royal-Oak	Westerner	Stephane Pasquier
24 Apr 2005	Prix Ganay	Bago	Thierry Gillet
15 May 2005	Poule d'Essai des Pouliches	Divine Proportions	Christophe-Patrice Lemaire
15 May 2005	Poule d'Essai des Poulains	Shamardal	Frankie Dettori
5 Jun 2005	Prix du Jockey Club	Shamardal	Frankie Dettori
12 Jun 2005	Prix de Diane	Divine Proportions	Christophe-Patrice Lemaire

Major Thoroughbred Race Winners 2004—05 (continued)

DATE	RACE	WINNER	JOCKEY
	France (continued)		
26 Jun 2005	Grand Prix de Saint-Cloud	Alkaased	Frankie Dettori
14 Jul 2005	Grand Prix de Paris	Scorpion	Kieren Fallon
	Germany		
4 Jul 2004	Deutsches Derby	Shirocco	Andreas Suborics
5 Sep 2004	Grosser Preis von Baden[1]	Warrsan	Kerrin McEvoy
26 Sep 2004	Preis von Europa	Albanova	Seb Sanders
3 Jul 2005	Deutsches Derby	Nicaron	Davy Bonilla
	Italy		
17 Oct 2004	Gran Premio del Jockey Club	Shirocco	Andreas Suborics
22 May 2005	Derby Italiano	De Sica	Marco Monteriso
	Australia		
16 Oct 2004	Caulfield Cup	Elvstroem	Nash Rawiller
23 Oct 2004	Cox Plate[1]	Savabeel	Chris Munce
1 Nov 2004	Melbourne Cup	Makybe Diva	Glen Boss
	United Arab Emirates		
26 Mar 2005	Godolphin Mile	Grand Emporium	Weichong Marwing
26 Mar 2005	UAE Derby	Blues and Royals	Kerrin McEvoy
26 Mar 2005	Dubai Sheema Classic	Phoenix Reach	Martin Dwyer
26 Mar 2005	Dubai Golden Shaheen	Saratoga County	Javier Castellano
26 Mar 2005	Dubai Duty Free	Elvstroem	Nash Rawiller
26 Mar 2005	Dubai World Cup	Roses in May	John Velazquez
	Japan		
28 Nov 2004	Japan Cup[1]	Zenno Rob Roy	Olivier Peslier
	Hong Kong		
12 Dec 2004	Hong Kong Cup[1]	Alexander Goldrun	Kevin Manning
20 Feb 2005	Hong Kong Gold Cup	Perfect Partner	Christophe Soumillon
24 Apr 2005	Queen Elizabeth II Cup[1]	Vengeance of Rain	Anthony Delpech
	Singapore		
15 May 2005	International Cup[1]	Mummify	Danny Nikolic

[1]World Series race (13 races in 10 countries). [2]American Triple Crown race. [3]Canadian Triple Crown race.

Triple Crown Champions—United States

YEAR	HORSE	YEAR	HORSE	YEAR	HORSE	YEAR	HORSE
1919	Sir Barton	1937	War Admiral	1946	Assault	1977	Seattle Slew
1930	Gallant Fox	1941	Whirlaway	1948	Citation	1978	Affirmed
1935	Omaha	1943	Count Fleet	1973	Secretariat		

The Kentucky Derby

YEAR	HORSE	JOCKEY	YEAR	HORSE	JOCKEY
1875	Aristides	Oliver Lewis	1888	Macbeth II	George Covington
1876	Vagrant	Bobby Swim	1889	Spokane	Thomas Kiley
1877	Baden-Baden	William Walker	1890	Riley	Isaac Murphy
1878	Day Star	Jimmy Carter	1891	Kingman	Isaac Murphy
1879	Lord Murphy	Charlie Shauer	1892	Azra	Alonzo Clayton
1880	Fonso	George Garret Lewis	1893	Lookout	Eddie Kunze
1881	Hindoo	James McLaughlin	1894	Chant	Frank Goodale
1882	Apollo	Babe Hurd	1895	Halma	James Perkins
1883	Leonatus	William Donohue	1896	Ben Brush	Willie Simms
1884	Buchanan	Isaac Murphy	1897	Typhoon II	Fred Garner
1885	Joe Cotton	Erskine Henderson	1898	Plaudit	Willie Simms
1886	Ben Ali	Paul Duffy	1899	Manuel	Fred Taral
1887	Montrose	Isaac Lewis	1900	Lieut. Gibson	Jimmy Boland

The Kentucky Derby (continued)

YEAR	HORSE	JOCKEY	YEAR	HORSE	JOCKEY
1901	His Eminence	James Winkfield	1954	Determine	Raymond York
1902	Alan-a-Dale	James Winkfield	1955	Swaps	William Shoemaker
1903	Judge Himes	Harold Booker	1956	Needles	David Erb
1904	Elwood	Frank Prior	1957	Iron Liege	William Hartack
1905	Agile	Jack Martin	1958	Tim Tam	Ismael Valenzuela
1906	Sir Huon	Roscoe Troxler	1959	Tomy Lee	William Shoemaker
1907	Pink Star	Andy Minder	1960	Venetian Way	William Hartack
1908	Stone Street	Arthur Pickens	1961	Carry Back	John Sellers
1909	Wintergreen	Vincent Powers	1962	Decidedly	William Hartack
1910	Donau	Fred Herbert	1963	Chateaugay	Braulio Baeza
1911	Meridian	George Archibald	1964	Northern Dancer	William Hartack
1912	Worth	Carroll Hugh Shilling	1965	Lucky Debonair	William Shoemaker
1913	Donerail	Roscoe Goose	1966	Kauai King	Don Brumfield
1914	Old Rosebud	John McCabe	1967	Proud Clarion	Robert Ussery
1915	Regret	Joe Notter	1968	Forward Pass	Ismael Valenzuela
1916	George Smith	John Loftus	1969	Majestic Prince	William Hartack
1917	Omar Khayyam	Charles Borel	1970	Dust Commander	Mike Manganello
1918	Exterminator	William Knapp	1971	Canonero II	Gustavo Avila
1919	Sir Barton	John Loftus	1972	Riva Ridge	Ron Turcotte
1920	Paul Jones	Ted Rice	1973	Secretariat[1]	Ron Turcotte
1921	Behave Yourself	Charles Thompson	1974	Cannonade	Angel Cordero, Jr.
1922	Morvich	Albert Johnson	1975	Foolish Pleasure	Jacinto Vasquez
1923	Zev	Earl Sande	1976	Bold Forbes	Angel Cordero, Jr.
1924	Black Gold	John D. Mooney	1977	Seattle Slew	Jean Cruguet
1925	Flying Ebony	Earl Sande	1978	Affirmed	Steve Cauthen
1926	Bubbling Over	Albert Johnson	1979	Spectacular Bid	Ronnie Franklin
1927	Whiskery	Linus McAtee	1980	Genuine Risk	Jacinto Vasquez
1928	Reigh Count	Charles Lang	1981	Pleasant Colony	Jorge Velasquez
1929	Clyde Van Dusen	Linus McAtee	1982	Gato del Sol	Eddie Delahoussaye
1930	Gallant Fox	Earl Sande	1983	Sunny's Halo	Eddie Delahoussaye
1931	Twenty Grand	Charles Kurtsinger	1984	Swale	Laffit Pincay, Jr.
1932	Burgoo King	Eugene James	1985	Spend a Buck	Angel Cordero, Jr.
1933	Brokers Tip	Don Meade	1986	Ferdinand	William Shoemaker
1934	Cavalcade	Mack Garner	1987	Alysheba	Chris McCarron
1935	Omaha	William Saunders	1988	Winning Colors	Gary Stevens
1936	Bold Venture	Ira Hanford	1989	Sunday Silence	Patrick Valenzuela
1937	War Admiral	Charles Kurtsinger	1990	Unbridled	Craig Perret
1938	Lawrin	Eddie Arcaro	1991	Strike the Gold	Chris Antley
1939	Johnstown	James Stout	1992	Lil E. Tee	Pat Day
1940	Gallahadion	Carroll Bierman	1993	Sea Hero	Jerry Bailey
1941	Whirlaway	Eddie Arcaro	1994	Go for Gin	Chris McCarron
1942	Shut Out	Wayne D. Wright	1995	Thunder Gulch	Gary Stevens
1943	Count Fleet	John Longden	1996	Grindstone	Jerry Bailey
1944	Pensive	Conn McCreary	1997	Silver Charm	Gary Stevens
1945	Hoop Jr.	Eddie Arcaro	1998	Real Quiet	Kent Desormeaux
1946	Assault	Warren Mehrtens	1999	Charismatic	Chris Antley
1947	Jet Pilot	Eric Guerin	2000	Fusaichi Pegasus	Kent Desormeaux
1948	Citation	Eddie Arcaro	2001	Monarchos	Jorge Chávez
1949	Ponder	Steve Brooks	2002	War Emblem	Victor Espinoza
1950	Middleground	William Boland	2003	Funny Cide	José Santos
1951	Count Turf	Conn McCreary	2004	Smarty Jones	Stewart Elliott
1952	Hill Gail	Eddie Arcaro	2005	Giacomo	Mike Smith
1953	Dark Star	Henry Moreno			

[1]*Fastest time—1 min 59⅖ sec.*

The Preakness Stakes

YEAR	HORSE	JOCKEY	YEAR	HORSE	JOCKEY
1873	Survivor	George Barbee	1880	Grenada	Lloyd Hughes
1874	Culpepper	William Donohue	1881	Saunterer	T. Costello
1875	Tom Ochiltree	Lloyd Hughes	1882	Vanguard	T. Costello
1876	Shirley	George Barbee	1883	Jacobus	George Barbee
1877	Cloverbrook	Cyrus Holloway	1884	Knight of Ellerslie	S. Fisher
1878	Duke of Magenta	Cyrus Holloway	1885	Tecumseh	James McLaughlin
1879	Harold	Lloyd Hughes	1886	The Bard	S. Fisher

The Preakness Stakes (continued)

YEAR	HORSE	JOCKEY	YEAR	HORSE	JOCKEY
1887	Dunboyne	William Donohue	1948	Citation	Eddie Arcaro
1888	Refund	F. Littlefield	1949	Capot	Ted Atkinson
1889	Buddhist	George Anderson	1950	Hill Prince	Eddie Arcaro
1890	Montague	W. Martin	1951	Bold	Eddie Arcaro
1894[1]	Assignee	Fred Taral	1952	Blue Man	Conn McCreary
1895	Belmar	Fred Taral	1953	Native Dancer	Eric Guerin
1896	Margrave	Henry Griffin	1954	Hasty Road	Johnny Adams
1897	Paul Kauvar	T. Thorpe	1955	Nashua	Eddie Arcaro
1898	Sly Fox	Willie Simms	1956	Fabius	William Hartack
1899	Half Time	R. Clawson	1957	Bold Ruler	Eddie Arcaro
1900	Hindus	H. Spencer	1958	Tim Tam	Ismael Valenzuela
1901	The Parader	Fred Landry	1959	Royal Orbit	William Harmatz
1902	Old England	L. Jackson	1960	Bally Ache	Robert Ussery
1903	Flocarline	W. Gannon	1961	Carry Back	John Sellers
1904	Bryn Mawr	Eugene Hildebrand	1962	Greek Money	John L. Rotz
1905	Cairngorm	W. Davis	1963	Candy Spots	William Shoemaker
1906	Whimsical	Walter Miller	1964	Northern Dancer	William Hartack
1907	Don Enrique	G. Mountain	1965	Tom Rolfe	Ron Turcotte
1908	Royal Tourist	Eddie Dugan	1966	Kauai King	Don Brumfield
1909	Effendi	Willie Doyle	1967	Damascus	William Shoemaker
1910	Layminster	R. Estep	1968	Forward Pass	Ismael Valenzuela
1911	Watervale	Eddie Dugan	1969	Majestic Prince	William Hartack
1912	Colonel Holloway	C. Turner	1970	Personality	Eddie Belmonte
1913	Buskin	James Butwell	1971	Canonero II	Gustavo Avila
1914	Holiday	Andy Schuttinger	1972	Bee Bee Bee	Eldon Nelson
1915	Rhine Maiden	Douglas Hoffman	1973	Secretariat	Ron Turcotte
1916	Damrosch	Linus McAtee	1974	Little Current	Miguel Rivera
1917	Kalitan	E. Haynes	1975	Master Derby	Darrel McHargue
1918[2]	War Cloud	John Loftus	1976	Elocutionist	John Lively
	Jack Hare, Jr.	Charles Peak	1977	Seattle Slew	Jean Cruguet
1919	Sir Barton	John Loftus	1978	Affirmed	Steve Cauthen
1920	Man o' War	Clarence Kummer	1979	Spectacular Bid	Ron Franklin
1921	Broomspun	Frank Coltiletti	1980	Codex	Angel Cordero, Jr.
1922	Pillory	L. Morris	1981	Pleasant Colony	Jorge Velasquez
1923	Vigil	Benny Marinelli	1982	Aloma's Ruler	Jack Kaenel
1924	Nellie Morse	John Merimee	1983	Deputed Testamony	Donald Miller
1925	Coventry	Clarence Kummer	1984	Gate Dancer	Angel Cordero, Jr.
1926	Display	John Maiben	1985	Tank's Prospect[3]	Pat Day
1927	Bostonian	A. Abel	1986	Snow Chief	Alex Solis
1928	Victorian	Raymond Workman	1987	Alysheba	Chris McCarron
1929	Dr. Freeland	Louis Schaefer	1988	Risen Star	Eddie Delahoussaye
1930	Gallant Fox	Earl Sande	1989	Sunday Silence	Patrick Valenzuela
1931	Mate	George Ellis	1990	Summer Squall	Pat Day
1932	Burgoo King	Eugene James	1991	Hansel	Jerry Bailey
1933	Head Play	Charles Kurtsinger	1992	Pine Bluff	Chris McCarron
1934	High Quest	Robert Jones	1993	Prairie Bayou	Mike Smith
1935	Omaha	Willie Saunders	1994	Tabasco Cat	Pat Day
1936	Bold Venture	George Woolf	1995	Timber Country	Pat Day
1937	War Admiral	Charles Kurtsinger	1996	Louis Quatorze	Pat Day
1938	Dauber	Maurice Peters	1997	Silver Charm	Gary Stevens
1939	Challedon	George Seabo	1998	Real Quiet	Kent Desormeaux
1940	Bimelech	Fred A. Smith	1999	Charismatic	Chris Antley
1941	Whirlaway	Eddie Arcaro	2000	Red Bullet	Jerry Bailey
1942	Alsab	Basil James	2001	Point Given	Gary Stevens
1943	Count Fleet	John Longden	2002	War Emblem	Victor Espinoza
1944	Pensive	Conn McCreary	2003	Funny Cide	José Santos
1945	Polynesian	Wayne D. Wright	2004	Smarty Jones	Stewart Elliott
1946	Assault	Warren Mehrtens	2005	Afleet Alex	Jeremy Rose
1947	Faultless	Doug Dodson			

[1]*No competition 1891–93.* [2]*Run in two divisions in 1918 because of the large number of starters.*
[3]*Fastest time—1 min 53⅖ sec.*

The Belmont Stakes

YEAR	HORSE	JOCKEY	YEAR	HORSE	JOCKEY
1867	Ruthless	Gilbert Patrick	1935	Omaha	Willie Saunders
1868	General Duke	Bobby Swim	1936	Granville	James Stout
1869	Fenian	Charley Miller	1937	War Admiral	Charles Kurtsinger
1870	Kingfisher	Edward Brown	1938	Pasteurized	James Stout
1871	Harry Bassett	W. Miller	1939	Johnstown	James Stout
1872	Joe Daniels	James Rowe	1940	Bimelech	Fred A. Smith
1873	Springbok	James Rowe	1941	Whirlaway	Eddie Arcaro
1874	Saxon	George Barbee	1942	Shut Out	Eddie Arcaro
1875	Calvin	Bobby Swim	1943	Count Fleet	John Longden
1876	Algerine	Billy Donohue	1944	Bounding Home	Gayle L. Smith
1877	Cloverbrook	Cyrus Holloway	1945	Pavot	Eddie Arcaro
1878	Duke of Magenta	Lloyd Hughes	1946	Assault	Warren Mehrtens
1879	Spendthrift	George Evans	1947	Phalanx	Ruperto Donoso
1880	Grenada	Lloyd Hughes	1948	Citation	Eddie Arcaro
1881	Saunterer	T. Costello	1949	Capot	Ted Atkinson
1882	Forester	James McLaughlin	1950	Middleground	William Boland
1883	George Kinney	James McLaughlin	1951	Counterpoint	David Gorman
1884	Panique	James McLaughlin	1952	One Count	Eddie Arcaro
1885	Tyrant	Paul Duffy	1953	Native Dancer	Eric Guerin
1886	Inspector B	James McLaughlin	1954	High Gun	Eric Guerin
1887	Hanover	James McLaughlin	1955	Nashua	Eddie Arcaro
1888	Sir Dixon	James McLaughlin	1956	Needles	David Erb
1889	Eric	W. Hayward	1957	Gallant Man	William Shoemaker
1890	Burlington	Shelby Barnes	1958	Cavan	Pete Anderson
1891	Foxford	Edward Garrison	1959	Sword Dancer	William Shoemaker
1892	Patron	W. Hayward	1960	Celtic Ash	William Hartack
1893	Comanche	Willie Simms	1961	Sherluck	Braulio Baeza
1894	Henry of Navarre	Willie Simms	1962	Jaipur	William Shoemaker
1895	Belmar	Fred Taral	1963	Chateaugay	Braulio Baeza
1896	Hastings	Henry Griffin	1964	Quadrangle	Manuel Ycaza
1897	Scottish Chieftain	J. Scherrer	1965	Hail to All	John Sellers
1898	Bowling Brook	F. Littlefield	1966	Amberoid	William Boland
1899	Jean Bereaud	R. Clawson	1967	Damascus	William Shoemaker
1900	Ildrim	Nash Turner	1968	Stage Door Johnny	Heliodoro Gustines
1901	Commando	H. Spencer	1969	Arts and Letters	Braulio Baeza
1902	Masterman	John Bullman	1970	High Echelon	John Rotz
1903	Africander	John Bullman	1971	Pass Catcher	Walter Blum
1904	Delhi	George Odom	1972	Riva Ridge	Ron Turcotte
1905	Tanya	Eugene Hildebrand	1973²	Secretariat	Ron Turcotte
1906	Burgomaster	Lucien Lyne	1974	Little Current	Miguel Rivera
1907	Peter Pan	G. Mountain	1975	Avatar	William Shoemaker
1908	Colin	Joe Notter	1976	Bold Forbes	Angel Cordero, Jr.
1909	Joe Madden	Eddie Dugan	1977	Seattle Slew	Jean Cruguet
1910	Sweep	James Butwell	1978	Affirmed	Steve Cauthen
1913¹	Prince Eugene	Roscoe Troxler	1979	Coastal	Ruben Hernandez
1914	Luke McLuke	Merritt Buxton	1980	Temperence Hill	Eddie Maple
1915	The Finn	George Byrne	1981	Summing	George Martens
1916	Friar Rock	E. Haynes	1982	Conquistador Cielo	Laffit Pincay, Jr.
1917	Hourless	James Butwell	1983	Caveat	Laffit Pincay, Jr.
1918	Johren	Frank Robinson	1984	Swale	Laffit Pincay, Jr.
1919	Sir Barton	John Loftus	1985	Creme Fraiche	Eddie Maple
1920	Man o' War	Clarence Kummer	1986	Danzig Connection	Chris McCarron
1921	Grey Lag	Earl Sande	1987	Bet Twice	Craig Perret
1922	Pillory	C.H. Miller	1988	Risen Star	Eddie Delahoussaye
1923	Zev	Earl Sande	1989	Easy Goer	Pat Day
1924	Mad Play	Earl Sande	1990	Go and Go	Michael Kinane
1925	American Flag	Albert Johnson	1991	Hansel	Jerry Bailey
1926	Crusader	Albert Johnson	1992	A.P. Indy	Eddie Delahoussaye
1927	Chance Shot	Earl Sande	1993	Colonial Affair	Julie Krone
1928	Vito	Clarence Kummer	1994	Tabasco Cat	Pat Day
1929	Blue Larkspur	Mack Garner	1995	Thunder Gulch	Gary Stevens
1930	Gallant Fox	Earl Sande	1996	Editor's Note	Rene Douglas
1931	Twenty Grand	Charles Kurtsinger	1997	Touch Gold	Chris McCarron
1932	Faireno	Tom Malley	1998	Victory Gallop	Gary Stevens
1933	Hurryoff	Mack Garner	1999	Lemon Drop Kid	José Santos
1934	Peace Chance	Wayne D. Wright			

The Belmont Stakes (continued)

YEAR	HORSE	JOCKEY	YEAR	HORSE	JOCKEY
2000	Commendable	Pat Day	2003	Empire Maker	Jerry Bailey
2001	Point Given	Gary Stevens	2004	Birdstone	Edgar Prado
2002	Sarava	Edgar S. Prado	2005	Afleet Alex	Jeremy Rose

[1]No competition 1911–1912.   [2]Fastest time—2 min 24 sec.

Horse of the Year

A Horse of the Year was selected by the *Daily Racing Form* from 1936 to 1970 and independently by the Thoroughbred Racing Association beginning in 1950. From 1971 these two organizations, plus the National Turf Writers Association, founded the Eclipse Awards, of which the Horse of the Year is the top among the 22 American prizes.

YEAR	HORSE	YEAR	HORSE	YEAR	HORSE	YEAR	HORSE
1936	Granville	1953	Tom Fool	1970	Fort Marcy;[1] Personality[2]	1987	Ferdinand
1937	War Admiral	1954	Native Dancer			1988	Alysheba
1938	Seabiscuit	1955	Nashua	1971	Ack Ack	1989	Sunday Silence
1939	Challedon	1956	Swaps	1972	Secretariat	1990	Criminal Type
1940	Challedon	1957	Bold Ruler;[1] Dedicate[2]	1973	Secretariat	1991	Black Tie Affair
1941	Whirlaway			1974	Forego	1992	A.P. Indy
1942	Whirlaway	1958	Round Table	1975	Forego	1993	Kotashaan
1943	Count Fleet	1959	Sword Dancer	1976	Forego	1994	Holy Bull
1944	Twilight Tear	1960	Kelso	1977	Seattle Slew	1995	Cigar
1945	Busher	1961	Kelso	1978	Affirmed	1996	Cigar
1946	Assault	1962	Kelso	1979	Affirmed	1997	Favorite Trick
1947	Armed	1963	Kelso	1980	Spectacular Bid	1998	Skip Away
1948	Citation	1964	Kelso	1981	John Henry	1999	Charismatic
1949	Capot;[1] Coaltown[2]	1965	Roman Brother;[1] Moccasin[2]	1982	Conquistador Cielo	2000	Tiznow
						2001	Point Given
1950	Hill Prince	1966	Buckpasser	1983	All Along	2002	Azeri
1951	Counterpoint	1967	Damascus	1984	John Henry	2003	Mineshaft
1952	One Count;[1] Native Dancer[2]	1968	Dr. Fager	1985	Spend a Buck	2004	Ghostzapper
		1969	Arts and Letters	1986	Lady's Secret		

[1]Daily Racing Form.   [2]Thoroughbred Racing Association.

2,000 Guineas

England's 2,000 Guineas race has been run since 1809. The table shows the winners for the past 20 years.

YEAR	HORSE	JOCKEY	YEAR	HORSE	JOCKEY
1986	Dancing Brave	Greville Starkey	1996	Mark of Esteem	Frankie Dettori
1987	Don't Forget Me	Willie Carson	1997	Entrepreneur	Michael Kinane
1988	Doyoun	Walter R. Swinburn	1998	King of Kings	Michael Kinane
1989	Nashwan	Willie Carson	1999	Island Sands	Frankie Dettori
1990	Tirol	Michael Kinane	2000	King's Best	Kieren Fallon
1991	Mystiko	Michael Roberts	2001	Golan	Kieren Fallon
1992	Rodrigo de Triano	Lester Piggot	2002	Rock of Gibraltar	Johnny Murtagh
1993	Zafonic	Pat Eddery	2003	Refuse To Bend	Pat Smullen
1994	Mister Baileys	Jason Weaver	2004	Haafhd	Richard Hills
1995	Pennekamp	Thierry Jarnet	2005	Footstepsinthesand	Kieren Fallon

The Derby

The Derby has been run since 1780. The table shows the winners for the past 20 years.

YEAR	HORSE	JOCKEY	YEAR	HORSE	JOCKEY
1986	Shahrastani	Walter R. Swinburn	1996	Shaamit	Michael Hills
1987	Reference Point	Steve Cauthen	1997	Benny the Dip	Willie Ryan
1988	Kahyasi	Ray Cochrane	1998	High Rise	Olivier Peslier
1989	Nashwan	Willie Carson	1999	Oath	Kieren Fallon
1990	Quest for Fame	Pat Eddery	2000	Sinndar	Johnny Murtagh
1991	Generous	Alan Munro	2001	Galileo	Michael Kinane
1992	Dr Devious	John Reid	2002	High Chaparral	Johnny Murtagh
1993	Commander in Chief	Michael Kinane	2003	Kris Kin	Kieren Fallon
1994	Erhaab	Willie Carson	2004	North Light	Kieren Fallon
1995	Lammtarra	Walter R. Swinburn	2005	Motivator	Johnny Murtagh

The St. Leger

The St. Leger has been run since 1776. The table shows the winners for the past 20 years.

YEAR	HORSE	JOCKEY	YEAR	HORSE	JOCKEY
1985	Oh So Sharp	Steve Cauthen	1996	Shantou	Frankie Dettori
1986	Moon Madness	Pat Eddery	1997	Silver Patriarch	Pat Eddery
1987	Reference Point	Steve Cauthen	1998	Nedawi	John Reid
1988	Minster Son	Willie Carson	1999	Mutafaweq	Richard Hills
1989	Michelozzo	Steve Cauthen	2000	Millenary	Richard Quinn
1990	Snurge	Richard Quinn	2001	Milan	Michael Kinane
1991	Toulon	Pat Eddery	2002	Bollin Eric	Kevin Darley
1992	User Friendly	George Duffield	2003	Brian Boru	Jamie Spencer
1993	Bob's Return	Philip Robinson	2004	Monsoon Rain	Frankie Dettori
1994	Moonax	Pat Eddery	2005	to be held 10 September, Doncaster, England	
1995	Classic Cliché	Frankie Dettori			

Triple Crown Champions—British

YEAR	WINNER	YEAR	WINNER	YEAR	WINNER	YEAR	WINNER
1853	West Australian	1891	Common	1900	Diamond Jubilee	1918	Gainsborough
1865	Gladiateur	1893	Isinglass	1903	Rock Sand	1935	Bahram
1866	Lord Lyon	1897	Galtee More	1915	Pommern	1970	Nijinsky
1886	Ormonde	1899	Flying Fox	1917	Gay Crusader		

Melbourne Cup

The Melbourne Cup race has been run since 1861. The table shows the winners for the past 20 years.

YEAR	HORSE	JOCKEY	YEAR	HORSE	JOCKEY
1985	What a Nuisance	Pat Hyland	1996	Saintly	Darren Beadman
1986	At Talaq	Michael Clarke	1997	Might and Power	Jim Cassidy
1987	Kensei	Larry Olsen	1998	Jezabeel	Chris Munce
1988	Empire Rose	Tony Allan	1999	Rogan Josh	John Marshall
1989	Tawrrific	Shane Dye	2000	Brew	Kerrin McEvoy
1990	Kingston Rule	Darren Beadman	2001	Ethereal	Scott Seamer
1991	Let's Elope	Steven King	2002	Media Puzzle	Damien Oliver
1992	Subzero	Greg Hall	2003	Makybe Diva	Glen Boss
1993	Vintage Crop	Michael Kinane	2004	Makybe Diva	Glen Boss
1994	Jeune	Wayne Harris	2005	to be held 1 November, Flemington, Australia·	
1995	Doriemus	Damien Oliver			

The Dubai World Cup

YEAR	HORSE	JOCKEY	YEAR	HORSE	JOCKEY
1996	Cigar	Jerry Bailey	2002	Street Cry	Jerry Bailey
1997	Singspiel	Jerry Bailey	2003	Moon Ballad	Frankie Dettori
1998	Silver Charm	Gary Stevens	2004	Pleasantly Perfect	Alex Solis
1999	Almutawakel	Richard Hills	2005	Roses in May	John Velazquez
2000	Dubai Millennium	Frankie Dettori	2006	to be held 24 March, Dubai, UAE	
2001	Captain Steve	Jerry Bailey			

The Hambletonian Trot

YEAR	HORSE	DRIVER	YEAR	HORSE	DRIVER
1926	Guy McKinney	Nat Ray	1940	Spencer Scott	Fred Egan
1927	Iosola's Worthy	Marvin Childs	1941	Bill Gallon	Lee Smith
1928	Spencer	William H. Leese	1942	The Ambassador	Ben White
1929	Walter Dear	Walter Cox	1943	Volo Song	Ben White
1930	Hanover's Bertha	Thomas Berry	1944	Yankee Maid	Henry Thomas
1931	Calumet Butler	Richard D. McMahon	1945	Titan Hanover	Harry Pownall, Sr.
1932	The Marchioness	William Caton	1946	Chestertown	Thomas Berry
1933	Mary Reynolds	Ben White	1947	Hoot Mon	Scepter F. Palin
1934	Lord Jim	Hugh M. Parshall	1948	Demon Hanover	Harrison Hoyt
1935	Greyhound	Scepter F. Palin	1949	Miss Tilly	Fred Egan
1936	Rosalind	Ben White	1950	Lusty Song	Delvin Miller
1937	Shirley Hanover	Henry Thomas	1951	Mainliner	Guy Crippen
1938	McLin Hanover	Henry Thomas	1952	Sharp Note	Bion Shively
1939	Peter Astra	Hugh M. Parshall	1953	Helicopter	Harry Harvey

The Hambletonian Trot (continued)

YEAR	HORSE	DRIVER	YEAR	HORSE	DRIVER
1954	Newport Dream	Adelbert Cameron	1981	Shiaway St. Pat	Ray Remmen
1955	Scott Frost	Joseph O'Brien	1982	Speed Bowl	Tom Haughton
1956	The Intruder	Ned Bower	1983	Duenna	Stanley Dancer
1957	Hickory Smoke	John Simpson, Sr.	1984	Historic Freight	Ben Webster
1958	Emily's Pride	Flave Nipe	1985	Prakas	William O'Donnell
1959	Diller Hanover	Frank Ervin	1986	Nuclear Kosmos	Ulf Thoresen
1960	Blaze Hanover	Joseph O'Brien	1987	Mack Lobell	John Campbell
1961	Harlan Dean	James Arthur	1988	Armbro Goal	John Campbell
1962	A.C.'s Viking	Sanders Russell	1989[1]	Park Avenue Joe	Ronald Waples
1963	Speedy Scot	Ralph Baldwin		Probe	William Fahy
1964	Ayres	John Simpson, Sr.	1990	Harmonious	John Campbell
1965	Egyptian Candor	Adelbert Cameron	1991	Giant Victory	Jack Moiseyev
1966	Kerry Way	Frank Ervin	1992	Alf Palema	Mickey McNichol
1967	Speedy Streak	Adelbert Cameron	1993	American Winner	Ron Pierce
1968	Nevele Pride	Stanley Dancer	1994	Victory Dream	Michel Lachance
1969	Lindy's Pride	Howard Beissinger	1995	Tagliabue	John Campbell
1970	Timothy T.	John Simpson, Sr.	1996	Continentalvictory	Michel Lachance
1971	Speedy Crown	Howard Beissinger	1997	Malabar Man	Malvern Burroughs
1972	Super Bowl	Stanley Dancer	1998	Muscles Yankee	John Campbell
1973	Flirth	Ralph Baldwin	1999	Self Possessed	Michel Lachance
1974	Christopher T.	William Haughton	2000	Yankee Paco	Trevor Ritchie
1975	Bonefish	Stanley Dancer	2001	Scarlet Knight	Stefan Melander
1976	Steve Lobell	William Haughton	2002	Chip Chip Hooray	Eric Ledford
1977	Green Speed	William Haughton	2003	Amigo Hall	Michel Lachance
1978	Speedy Somolli	Howard Beissinger	2004	Windsong's Legacy	Trond Smedshammer
1979	Legend Hanover	George Sholty	2005	Vivid Photo	Roger Hammer
1980	Burgomeister	William Haughton			

[1]Tied.

Ice Hockey

The **National Hockey League** (NHL), which was organized in Canada in 1917 with five professional teams, welcomed the first US team, the Boston Bruins, in 1924. Since 1926 the symbol of supremacy in professional hockey has been the **Stanley Cup**, which is awarded to the winner of a play-off that concludes the season of the National Hockey League. The Stanley Cup was presented to amateur champions from 1893 to 1925. The **World Hockey Championships**, contested by national teams and sponsored by the **International Ice Hockey Federation** (IIHF; founded 1908), have been held since 1930 for men and since 1990 for women.

Related Web sites: National Hockey League: <www.nhl.com>; International Ice Hockey Federation: <www.iihf.com>.

World Hockey Championship—Men

YEAR	WINNER	YEAR	WINNER	YEAR	WINNER	YEAR	WINNER
1930	Canada	1954	USSR	1972[2]	Czechoslovakia	1990	Sweden
1931	Canada	1955	Canada	1973	USSR	1991	Sweden
1932[1]	Canada	1956[1]	USSR	1974	USSR	1992	Sweden
1933	United States	1957	Sweden	1975	USSR	1993	Russia
1934	Canada	1958	Canada	1976	Czechoslovakia	1994	Canada
1935	Canada	1959	Canada	1977	Czechoslovakia	1995	Finland
1936[1]	Great Britain	1960[1]	United States	1978	USSR	1996	Czech Republic
1937	Canada	1961	Canada	1979	USSR	1997	Canada
1938	Canada	1962	Sweden	1980[1]	United States	1998	Sweden
1939	Canada	1963	USSR	1981	USSR	1999	Czech Republic
1940–46	not held	1964[1]	USSR	1982	USSR	2000	Czech Republic
1947	Czechoslovakia	1965	USSR	1983	USSR	2001	Czech Republic
1948[1]	Canada	1966	USSR	1984[1]	USSR	2002	Slovakia
1949	Czechoslovakia	1967	USSR	1985	Czechoslovakia	2003	Canada
1950	Canada	1968[1]	USSR	1986	USSR	2004	Canada
1951	Canada	1969	USSR	1987	Sweden	2005	Czech Republic
1952[1]	Canada	1970	USSR	1988	USSR	2006	to be held in Latvia
1953	Sweden	1971	USSR	1989	USSR		

[1]Olympic champions, recognized as world champions (for earlier Olympics, see Olympic Games).
[2]In 1972 a separate world championship was held for the first time.

World Hockey Championship—Women

YEAR	WINNER	YEAR	WINNER	YEAR	WINNER
1990	Canada	1999	Canada	2004	Canada
1992	Canada	2000	Canada	2005	United States
1994	Canada	2001	Canada	2006	*to be held in Turin, Italy*
1997	Canada	2002[1]	Canada		
1998[1]	United States	2003	*canceled*		

[1]*Olympic champion; separate world championships have not been held in Olympic years. Olympic gold medalists are sometimes considered world champions.*

National Hockey League (NHL) Final Standings, 2004

The 2004–05 NHL season was canceled.

EASTERN CONFERENCE

Northeast Division	W	L	T	OTL[1]	Atlantic Division	W	L	T	OTL[1]	Southeast Division	W	L	T	OTL[1]
Boston Bruins[2]	41	19	15	7	Philadelphia Flyers[2]	40	21	15	6	Tampa Bay Lightning[2]	46	22	8	6
Toronto Maple Leafs[2]	45	24	10	3	New Jersey Devils[2]	43	25	12	2	Atlanta Thrashers	33	37	8	4
Ottawa Senators[2]	43	23	10	6	New York Islanders[2]	38	29	11	4	Carolina Hurricanes	28	34	14	6
Montreal Canadiens[2]	41	30	7	4	New York Rangers	27	40	7	8	Florida Panthers	28	35	15	4
Buffalo Sabres	37	34	7	4	Pittsburgh Penguins	23	47	8	4	Washington Capitals	23	46	10	3

WESTERN CONFERENCE

Central Division	W	L	T	OTL[1]	Northwest Division	W	L	T	OTL[1]	Pacific Division	W	L	T	OTL[1]
Detroit Red Wings[2]	48	21	11	2	Vancouver Canucks[2]	43	24	10	5	San Jose Sharks[2]	43	21	12	6
St. Louis Blues[2]	39	30	11	2	Colorado Avalanche[2]	40	22	13	7	Dallas Stars[2]	41	26	13	2
Nashville Predators[2]	38	29	11	4	Calgary Flames[2]	42	30	7	3	Los Angeles Kings	28	29	16	9
Columbus Blue Jackets	25	45	8	4	Edmonton Oilers	36	29	12	5	Anaheim Mighty Ducks	29	35	10	8
Chicago Blackhawks	20	43	11	8	Minnesota Wild	30	29	20	3	Phoenix Coyotes	22	36	18	6

[1]*Overtime losses, worth one point.*   [2]*Qualified for play-offs.*

The Stanley Cup

SEASON	WINNER	RUNNER-UP	GAMES
1892–93	Montreal Amateur Athletic Association	*no challengers*	
1893–94	Montreal Amateur Athletic Association	Ottawa Generals	2–0
1894–95	Montreal Victorias	*no challengers*	
1895–96	Winnipeg Victorias (Feb.), Montreal Victorias (Dec.)	Montreal Victorias (Feb.), Winnipeg Victorias (Dec.)	1–0, 1–0
1896–97	Montreal Victorias	Ottawa Capitals	1–0
1897–98	Montreal Victorias	*no challengers*	
1898–99	Montreal Victorias (Feb.), Montreal Shamrocks (March)	Winnipeg Victorias (Feb.), Queen's University (March)	2–0, 1–0
1899–1900	Montreal Shamrocks	Winnipeg Victorias, Halifax Crescents	2–1, 2–0
1900–01	Winnipeg Victorias	Montreal Shamrocks	2–0
1901–02	Winnipeg Victorias (Jan.), Montreal Amateur Athletic Association (March)	Toronto Wellingtons (Jan.), Winnipeg Victorias (March)	2–0, 2–1
1902–03	Montreal Amateur Athletic Association (Feb.), Ottawa Silver Seven (March)	Winnipeg Victorias (Feb.), Montreal Victorias (March), Rat Portage Thistles (March)	2–1, 1–0, 2–0
1903–04	Ottawa Silver Seven	Winnipeg Rowing Club, Toronto Marlboros, Montreal Wanderers, Brandon Wheat Kings	2–1, 2–0, tie, 2–0
1904–05	Ottawa Silver Seven	Dawson City Nuggets, Rat Portage Thistles	2–0, 2–1

The Stanley Cup (continued)

SEASON	WINNER	RUNNER-UP	GAMES
1905–06	Ottawa Silver Seven (Feb.), Montreal Wanderers (March, Dec.)	Queen's University (Feb.), Smiths Falls (Feb.), Ottawa Silver Seven (March), New Glasgow Cubs (Dec.)	2–0, 2–0, 1–1, 2–0
1906–07	Kenora Thistles (Jan.), Montreal Wanderers (March)	Montreal Wanderers (Jan.), Kenora Thistles (March)	2–0, 1–1
1907–08	Montreal Wanderers	Ottawa Victorias, Winnipeg Maple Leafs, Toronto Trolley Leaguers, Edmonton Eskimos	2–0, 2–0, 1–0, 1–1
1908–09	Ottawa Senators	no challengers	
1909–10	Montreal Wanderers, Ottawa Senators	Berlin Union Jacks, Edmonton Eskimos, Galt	1–0, 2–0, 2–0
1910–11	Ottawa Senators	Port Arthur Bearcats, Galt	1–0, 1–0
1911–12	Quebec Bulldogs	Moncton Victories	2–0
1912–13[1]	Quebec Bulldogs	Sydney Miners	2–0
1913–14	Toronto Blueshirts	Victoria Cougars, Montreal Canadiens	3–0, 1–1
1914–15	Vancouver Millionaires	Ottawa Senators	3–0
1915–16	Montreal Canadiens	Portland Rosebuds	3–2
1916–17	Seattle Metropolitans	Montreal Canadiens	3–1
1917–18	Toronto Arenas	Vancouver Millionaires	3–2
1918–19	no decision[2]		
1919–20	Ottawa Senators	Seattle Metropolitans	3–2
1920–21	Ottawa Senators	Vancouver Millionaires	3–2
1921–22	Toronto St. Pats	Vancouver Millionaires	3–2
1922–23	Ottawa Senators	Edmonton Eskimos, Vancouver Maroons	2–0, 3–1
1923–24	Montreal Canadiens	Calgary Tigers, Vancouver Maroons	2–0, 2–0
1924–25	Victoria Cougars	Montreal Canadiens	3–1
1925–26	Montreal Maroons	Victoria Cougars	3–1
1926–27	Ottawa Senators	Boston Bruins	2–0
1927–28	New York Rangers	Montreal Maroons	3–2
1928–29	Boston Bruins	New York Rangers	2–0
1929–30	Montreal Canadiens	Boston Bruins	2–0
1930–31	Montreal Canadiens	Chicago Black Hawks	3–2
1931–32	Toronto Maple Leafs	New York Rangers	3–0
1932–33	New York Rangers	Toronto Maple Leafs	3–1
1933–34	Chicago Black Hawks	Detroit Red Wings	3–1
1934–35	Montreal Maroons	Toronto Maple Leafs	3–0
1935–36	Detroit Red Wings	Toronto Maple Leafs	3–1
1936–37	Detroit Red Wings	New York Rangers	3–2
1937–38	Chicago Black Hawks	Toronto Maple Leafs	3–1
1938–39	Boston Bruins	Toronto Maple Leafs	4–1
1939–40	New York Rangers	Toronto Maple Leafs	4–2
1940–41	Boston Bruins	Detroit Red Wings	4–0
1941–42	Toronto Maple Leafs	Detroit Red Wings	4–3
1942–43	Detroit Red Wings	Boston Bruins	4–0
1943–44	Montreal Canadiens	Chicago Black Hawks	4–0
1944–45	Toronto Maple Leafs	Detroit Red Wings	4–3
1945–46	Montreal Canadiens	Boston Bruins	4–1
1946–47	Toronto Maple Leafs	Montreal Canadiens	4–2
1947–48	Toronto Maple Leafs	Detroit Red Wings	4–0
1948–49	Toronto Maple Leafs	Detroit Red Wings	4–0
1949–50	Detroit Red Wings	New York Rangers	4–3
1950–51	Toronto Maple Leafs	Montreal Canadiens	4–1
1951–52	Detroit Red Wings	Montreal Canadiens	4–0
1952–53	Montreal Canadiens	Boston Bruins	4–1
1953–54	Detroit Red Wings	Montreal Canadiens	4–3
1954–55	Detroit Red Wings	Montreal Canadiens	4–3
1955–56	Montreal Canadiens	Detroit Red Wings	4–1
1956–57	Montreal Canadiens	Boston Bruins	4–1
1957–58	Montreal Canadiens	Boston Bruins	4–2
1958–59	Montreal Canadiens	Toronto Maple Leafs	4–1
1959–60	Montreal Canadiens	Toronto Maple Leafs	4–0
1960–61	Chicago Black Hawks	Detroit Red Wings	4–2
1961–62	Toronto Maple Leafs	Chicago Black Hawks	4–2
1962–63	Toronto Maple Leafs	Detroit Red Wings	4–1
1963–64	Toronto Maple Leafs	Detroit Red Wings	4–3
1964–65	Montreal Canadiens	Chicago Black Hawks	4–3
1965–66	Montreal Canadiens	Detroit Red Wings	4–2
1966–67	Toronto Maple Leafs	Montreal Canadiens	4–2

The Stanley Cup (continued)

SEASON	WINNER	RUNNER-UP	GAMES
1967–68	Montreal Canadiens	St. Louis Blues	4–0
1968–69	Montreal Canadiens	St. Louis Blues	4–0
1969–70	Boston Bruins	St. Louis Blues	4–0
1970–71	Montreal Canadiens	Chicago Black Hawks	4–3
1971–72	Boston Bruins	New York Rangers	4–2
1972–73	Montreal Canadiens	Chicago Black Hawks	4–2
1973–74	Philadelphia Flyers	Boston Bruins	4–2
1974–75	Philadelphia Flyers	Buffalo Sabres	4–2
1975–76	Montreal Canadiens	Philadelphia Flyers	4–0
1976–77	Montreal Canadiens	Boston Bruins	4–0
1977–78	Montreal Canadiens	Boston Bruins	4–2
1978–79	Montreal Canadiens	New York Rangers	4–1
1979–80	New York Islanders	Philadelphia Flyers	4–2
1980–81	New York Islanders	Minnesota North Stars	4–1
1981–82	New York Islanders	Vancouver Canucks	4–0
1982–83	New York Islanders	Edmonton Oilers	4–0
1983–84	Edmonton Oilers	New York Islanders	4–1
1984–85	Edmonton Oilers	Philadelphia Flyers	4–1
1985–86	Montreal Canadiens	Calgary Flames	4–1
1986–87	Edmonton Oilers	Philadelphia Flyers	4–3
1987–88	Edmonton Oilers	Boston Bruins	4–0
1988–89	Calgary Flames	Montreal Canadiens	4–2
1989–90	Edmonton Oilers	Boston Bruins	4–1
1990–91	Pittsburgh Penguins	Minnesota North Stars	4–2
1991–92	Pittsburgh Penguins	Chicago Black Hawks	4–0
1992–93	Montreal Canadiens	Los Angeles Kings	4–1
1993–94	New York Rangers	Vancouver Canucks	4–3
1994–95	New Jersey Devils	Detroit Red Wings	4–0
1995–96	Colorado Avalanche	Florida Panthers	4–0
1996–97	Detroit Red Wings	Philadelphia Flyers	4–0
1997–98	Detroit Red Wings	Washington Capitals	4–0
1998–99	Dallas Stars	Buffalo Sabres	4–2
1999–2000	New Jersey Devils	Dallas Stars	4–2
2000–01	Colorado Avalanche	New Jersey Devils	4–3
2001–02	Detroit Red Wings	Carolina Hurricanes	4–1
2002–03	New Jersey Devils	Mighty Ducks of Anaheim	4–3
2003–04	Tampa Bay Lightning	Calgary Flames	4–3
2004–05	not held due to players' strike and season cancellation		
2005–06	to be held in May or June 2006		

[1]Though Victoria defeated Quebec in challenge games, Victoria's win was not officially recognized.
[2]Series called because of flu epidemic.

Ice Skating

The world governing body for ice skating, the International Skating Union (ISU; founded 1892), held the first world figure skating competition in 1896. Women's figure skating was not a separate event until 1906, and pairs championships were first held in 1908. Until 1991 individual competitors were judged on a set of compulsory figures as well as programs of freestyle moves. In 1991 the compulsory figures portion of the competition was eliminated, and judging was based on a short technical program and a long freestyle program. In 2004 the ISU issued new guidelines for scoring that promoted more consistency among judges and preserved judges' anonymity. Ice dancing, officially introduced in 1950, is based on compulsory and freestyle movements—in this case, dances.

In contrast to figure skating and ice dancing, speed skating involves only two factors—speed and endurance. Men compete over distances of 500 m, 1,000 m, 1,500 m, 5,000 m, and 10,000 m. Women, who entered the sport several decades after men, compete over 500 m, 1,000 m, 1,500 m, 3,000 m, and 5,000 m. World speed-skating sprint championships for both men and women were inaugurated in 1972. Short-track speed skating—very different from distance skating in strategy and skill—is held indoors over distances of 500 m, 1,000 m, 1,500 m, and 3,000 m. The skater having the best combined results is the overall winner. Championships have been held annually since 1978 but have been recognized by only the ISU since 1981.

International Skating Union Web site: <www.isu.org>.

World Figure Skating Championship—Men

YEAR	WINNER	YEAR	WINNER	YEAR	WINNER
1896	Gilbert Fuchs (GER)	1936	Karl Schäfer (AUT)	1976	John Curry (GBR)
1897	Gustav Hügel (AUT)	1937	Felix Kaspar (AUT)	1977	Vladimir Kovalyov (URS)
1898	Henning Grenander (SWE)	1938	Felix Kaspar (AUT)	1978	Charles Tickner (USA)
1899	Gustav Hügel (AUT)	1939	Graham Sharp (GBR)	1979	Vladimir Kovalyov (URS)
1900	Gustav Hügel (AUT)	1940–46	not held	1980	Jan Hoffmann (GDR)
1901	Ulrich Salchow (SWE)	1947	Hans Gerschwiler (SUI)	1981	Scott Hamilton (USA)
1902	Ulrich Salchow (SWE)	1948	Richard Button (USA)	1982	Scott Hamilton (USA)
1903	Ulrich Salchow (SWE)	1949	Richard Button (USA)	1983	Scott Hamilton (USA)
1904	Ulrich Salchow (SWE)	1950	Richard Button (USA)	1984	Scott Hamilton (USA)
1905	Ulrich Salchow (SWE)	1951	Richard Button (USA)	1985	Aleksandr Fadeyev (URS)
1906	Gilbert Fuchs (GER)	1952	Richard Button (USA)	1986	Brian Boitano (USA)
1907	Ulrich Salchow (SWE)	1953	Hayes Alan Jenkins (USA)	1987	Brian Orser (CAN)
1908	Ulrich Salchow (SWE)	1954	Hayes Alan Jenkins (USA)	1988	Brian Boitano (USA)
1909	Ulrich Salchow (SWE)	1955	Hayes Alan Jenkins (USA)	1989	Kurt Browning (CAN)
1910	Ulrich Salchow (SWE)	1956	Hayes Alan Jenkins (USA)	1990	Kurt Browning (CAN)
1911	Ulrich Salchow (SWE)	1957	David Jenkins (USA)	1991	Kurt Browning (CAN)
1912	Fritz Kachler (AUT)	1958	David Jenkins (USA)	1992	Viktor Petrenko (UNT[2])
1913	Fritz Kachler (AUT)	1959	David Jenkins (USA)	1993	Kurt Browning (CAN)
1914	Gösta Sandahl (SWE)	1960	Alain Giletti (FRA)	1994	Elvis Stojko (CAN)
1915–21	not held	1961	not held[1]	1995	Elvis Stojko (CAN)
1922	Gillis Grafström (SWE)	1962	Donald Jackson (CAN)	1996	Todd Eldredge (USA)
1923	Fritz Kachler (AUT)	1963	Donald McPherson (CAN)	1997	Elvis Stojko (CAN)
1924	Gillis Grafström (SWE)	1964	Manfred Schnelldorfer (FRG)	1998	Aleksey Yagudin (RUS)
1925	Willy Böckl (AUT)	1965	Alain Calmat (FRA)	1999	Aleksey Yagudin (RUS)
1926	Willy Böckl (AUT)	1966	Emmerich Danzer (AUT)	2000	Aleksey Yagudin (RUS)
1927	Willy Böckl (AUT)	1967	Emmerich Danzer (AUT)	2001	Yevgeny Plushchenko (RUS)
1928	Willy Böckl (AUT)	1968	Emmerich Danzer (AUT)	2002	Aleksey Yagudin (RUS)
1929	Gillis Grafström (SWE)	1969	Tim Wood (USA)	2003	Yevgeny Plushchenko (RUS)
1930	Karl Schäfer (AUT)	1970	Tim Wood (USA)	2004	Yevgeny Plushchenko (RUS)
1931	Karl Schäfer (AUT)	1971	Ondrej Nepela (TCH)	2005	Stephane Lambiel (SUI)
1932	Karl Schäfer (AUT)	1972	Ondrej Nepela (TCH)	2006	to be held 20–26
1933	Karl Schäfer (AUT)	1973	Ondrej Nepela (TCH)		March, Calgary, AB,
1934	Karl Schäfer (AUT)	1974	Jan Hoffmann (GDR)		Canada
1935	Karl Schäfer (AUT)	1975	Sergey Volkov (URS)		

[1]The entire US team died in an airplane crash, and the championships were canceled.
[2]Unified Team, consisting of athletes from the Commonwealth of Independent States plus Georgia.

World Figure Skating Championship—Women

YEAR	WINNER	YEAR	WINNER	YEAR	WINNER
1906	Madge Syers (GBR)	1937	Cecilia Colledge (GBR)	1969	Gabriele Seyfert (GDR)
1907	Madge Syers (GBR)	1938	Megan Taylor (GBR)	1970	Gabriele Seyfert (GDR)
1908	Lily Kronberger (HUN)	1939	Megan Taylor (GBR)	1971	Beatrix Schuba (AUT)
1909	Lily Kronberger (HUN)	1940–46	not held	1972	Beatrix Schuba (AUT)
1910	Lily Kronberger (HUN)	1947	Barbara Ann Scott (CAN)	1973	Karen Magnussen (CAN)
1911	Lily Kronberger (HUN)	1948	Barbara Ann Scott (CAN)	1974	Christine Errath (GDR)
1912	Opika von Meray Horvath (HUN)	1949	Alena Vrzanova (TCH)	1975	Dianne de Leeuw (NED)
1913	Opika von M. Horvath (HUN)	1950	Alena Vrzanova (TCH)	1976	Dorothy Hamill (USA)
1914	Opika von M. Horvath (HUN)	1951	Jeannette Altwegg (GBR)	1977	Linda Fratianne (USA)
1915–21	not held	1952	Jacqueline du Bief (FRA)	1978	Anett Pötzsch (GDR)
1922	Herma Planck-Szabo (AUT)	1953	Tenley Albright (USA)	1979	Linda Fratianne (USA)
1923	Herma Planck-Szabo (AUT)	1954	Gundi Busch (GER)	1980	Anett Pötzsch (GDR)
1924	Herma Planck-Szabo (AUT)	1955	Tenley Albright (USA)	1981	Denise Biellmann (SUI)
1925	Herma Planck-Szabo (AUT)	1956	Carol Heiss (USA)	1982	Elaine Zayak (USA)
1926	Herma Planck-Szabo (AUT)	1957	Carol Heiss (USA)	1983	Rosalynn Sumners (USA)
1927	Sonja Henie (NOR)	1958	Carol Heiss (USA)	1984	Katarina Witt (GDR)
1928	Sonja Henie (NOR)	1959	Carol Heiss (USA)	1985	Katarina Witt (GDR)
1929	Sonja Henie (NOR)	1960	Carol Heiss (USA)	1986	Debi Thomas (USA)
1930	Sonja Henie (NOR)	1961	not held[1]	1987	Katarina Witt (GDR)
1931	Sonja Henie (NOR)	1962	Sjoukje Dijkstra (NED)	1988	Katarina Witt (GDR)
1932	Sonja Henie (NOR)	1963	Sjoukje Dijkstra (NED)	1989	Midori Ito (JPN)
1933	Sonja Henie (NOR)	1964	Sjoukje Dijkstra (NED)	1990	Jill Trenary (USA)
1934	Sonja Henie (NOR)	1965	Petra Burka (CAN)	1991	Kristi Yamaguchi (USA)
1935	Sonja Henie (NOR)	1966	Peggy Fleming (USA)	1992	Kristi Yamaguchi (USA)
1936	Sonja Henie (NOR)	1967	Peggy Fleming (USA)	1993	Oksana Baiul (UKR)
		1968	Peggy Fleming (USA)	1994	Yuka Sato (JPN)

World Figure Skating Championship—Women (continued)

YEAR	WINNER	YEAR	WINNER	YEAR	WINNER
1995	Chen Lu (CHN)	2000	Michelle Kwan (USA)	2004	Shizuka Arakawa (JPN)
1996	Michelle Kwan (USA)	2001	Michelle Kwan (USA)	2005	Irina Slutskaya (RUS)
1997	Tara Lipinski (USA)	2002	Irina Slutskaya (RUS)	2006	to be held 20–26
1998	Michelle Kwan (USA)	2003	Michelle Kwan (USA)		March, Calgary, AB,
1999	Maria Butyrskaya (RUS)				Canada

[1]The entire US team died in an airplane crash, and the championships were canceled.

World Figure Skating Championship—Pairs

YEAR	WINNERS	YEAR	WINNERS
1908	Anna Hübler, Heinrich Burger (GER)	1963	Marika Kilius, Hans-Jürgen Bäumler (FRG)
1909	Phyllis Johnson, James Johnson (GBR)	1964	Marika Kilius, Hans-Jürgen Bäumler (FRG)
1910	Anna Hübler, Heinrich Burger (GER)	1965	Lyudmila Belousova, Oleg Protopopov (URS)
1911	Ludowika Eilers, Walter Jakobsson (FIN)	1966	Lyudmila Belousova, Oleg Protopopov (URS)
1912	Phyllis Johnson, James Johnson (GBR)	1967	Lyudmila Belousova, Oleg Protopopov (URS)
1913	Helene Engelmann, Karl Mejstrik (AUT)	1968	Lyudmila Belousova, Oleg Protopopov (URS)
1914	Ludowika Jakobsson, Walter Jakobsson (FIN)	1969	Irina Rodnina, Aleksey Ulanov (URS)
1915–21	not held	1970	Irina Rodnina, Aleksey Ulanov (URS)
1922	Helene Engelmann, Alfred Berger (AUT)	1971	Irina Rodnina, Aleksey Ulanov (URS)
1923	Ludowika Jakobsson, Walter Jakobsson (FIN)	1972	Irina Rodnina, Aleksey Ulanov (URS)
1924	Helene Engelmann, Alfred Berger (AUT)	1973	Irina Rodnina, Aleksandr Zaytsev (URS)
1925	Herma Planck-Szabo, Ludwig Wrede (AUT)	1974	Irina Rodnina, Aleksandr Zaytsev (URS)
1926	Andrée Joly, Pierre Brunet (FRA)	1975	Irina Rodnina, Aleksandr Zaytsev (URS)
1927	Herma Planck-Szabo, Ludwig Wrede (AUT)	1976	Irina Rodnina, Aleksandr Zaytsev (URS)
1928	Andrée Joly, Pierre Brunet (FRA)	1977	Irina Rodnina, Aleksandr Zaytsev (URS)
1929	Lily Scholz, Otto Kaiser (AUT)	1978	Irina Rodnina, Aleksandr Zaytsev (URS)
1930	Andrée Brunet, Pierre Brunet (FRA)	1979	Tai Babilonia, Randy Gardner (USA)
1931	Emilia Rotter, Laszlo Szollas (HUN)	1980	Marina Cherkasova, Sergey Shakhray (URS)
1932	Andrée Brunet, Pierre Brunet (FRA)	1981	Irina Vorobyova, Igor Lisovsky (URS)
1933	Emilia Rotter, Laszlo Szollas (HUN)	1982	Sabine Baess, Tassilo Thierbach (GDR)
1934	Emilia Rotter, Laszlo Szollas (HUN)	1983	Yelena Valova, Oleg Vasilyev (URS)
1935	Emilia Rotter, Laszlo Szollas (HUN)	1984	Barbara Underhill, Paul Martini (CAN)
1936	Maxi Herber, Ernst Baier (GER)	1985	Yelena Valova, Oleg Vasilyev (URS)
1937	Maxi Herber, Ernst Baier (GER)	1986	Yekaterina Gordeyeva, Sergey Grinkov (URS)
1938	Maxi Herber, Ernst Baier (GER)	1987	Yekaterina Gordeyeva, Sergey Grinkov (URS)
1939	Maxi Herber, Ernst Baier (GER)	1988	Yelena Valova, Oleg Vasilyev (URS)
1940–46	not held	1989	Yekaterina Gordeyeva, Sergey Grinkov (URS)
1947	Micheline Lannoy, Pierre Baugniet (BEL)	1990	Yekaterina Gordeyeva, Sergey Grinkov (URS)
1948	Micheline Lannoy, Pierre Baugniet (BEL)	1991	Natalya Mishkutyonok, Artur Dmitriyev (URS)
1949	Andrea Kekessy, Ede Kiraly (HUN)	1992	Natalya Mishkutyonok, Artur Dmitriyev (UNT[2])
1950	Karol Kennedy, Peter Kennedy (USA)	1993	Isabelle Brasseur, Lloyd Eisler (CAN)
1951	Ria Baran, Paul Falk (FRG)	1994	Yevgeniya Shishkova, Vadim Naumov (RUS)
1952	Ria Falk, Paul Falk (FRG)	1995	Radka Kovarikova, René Novotny (CZE)
1953	Jennifer Nicks, John Nicks (GBR)	1996	Marina Yeltsova, Andrey Bushkov (RUS)
1954	Frances Dafoe, Norris Bowden (CAN)	1997	Mandy Wötzel, Ingo Steur (GER)
1955	Frances Dafoe, Norris Bowden (CAN)	1998	Yelena Berezhnaya, Anton Sikharulidze (RUS)
1956	Elisabeth Schwarz, Kurt Oppelt (AUT)	1999	Yelena Berezhnaya, Anton Sikharulidze (RUS)
1957	Barbara Wagner, Robert Paul (CAN)	2000	Mariya Petrova, Aleksey Tikhonov (RUS)
1958	Barbara Wagner, Robert Paul (CAN)	2001	Jamie Sale, David Pelletier (CAN)
1959	Barbara Wagner, Robert Paul (CAN)	2002	Xue Shen, Hongbo Zhao (CHN)
1960	Barbara Wagner, Robert Paul (CAN)	2003	Xue Shen, Hongbo Zhao (CHN)
1961	not held[1]	2004	Tatyana Totmyanina, Maksim Marinin (RUS)
1962	Maria Jelinek, Otto Jelinek (CAN)	2005	Tatyana Totmyanina, Maksim Marinin (RUS)
		2006	to be held 20–26 March, Calgary, AB

[1]The entire US team died in an airplane crash, and the championships were canceled.   [2]Unified Team, consisting of athletes from the Commonwealth of Independent States plus Georgia.

World Ice Dancing Championships

YEAR	WINNERS	YEAR	WINNERS
1950	Lois Waring, Michael McGean (USA)	1953	Jean Westwood, Lawrence Demmy (GBR)
1951	Jean Westwood, Lawrence Demmy (GBR)	1954	Jean Westwood, Lawrence Demmy (GBR)
1952	Jean Westwood, Lawrence Demmy (GBR)	1955	Jean Westwood, Lawrence Demmy (GBR)

World Ice Dancing Championships (continued)

YEAR	WINNERS	YEAR	WINNERS
1956	Pamela Weight, Paul Thomas (GBR)	1981	Jayne Torvill, Christopher Dean (GBR)
1957	June Markham, Courtney Jones (GBR)	1982	Jayne Torvill, Christopher Dean (GBR)
1958	June Markham, Courtney Jones (GBR)	1983	Jayne Torvill, Christopher Dean (GBR)
1959	Doreen Denny, Courtney Jones (GBR)	1984	Jayne Torvill, Christopher Dean (GBR)
1960	Doreen Denny, Courtney Jones (GBR)	1985	Natalya Bestemyanova, Andrey Bukin (URS)
1961	not held[1]	1986	Natalya Bestemyanova, Andrey Bukin (URS)
1962	Eve Romanova, Pavel Roman (TCH)	1987	Natalya Bestemyanova, Andrey Bukin (URS)
1963	Eve Romanova, Pavel Roman (TCH)	1988	Natalya Bestemyanova, Andrey Bukin (URS)
1964	Eve Romanova, Pavel Roman (TCH)	1989	Marina Klimova, Sergey Ponomarenko (URS)
1965	Eve Romanova, Pavel Roman (TCH)	1990	Marina Klimova, Sergey Ponomarenko (URS)
1966	Diane Towler, Bernard Ford (GBR)	1991	Isabelle Duchesnay, Paul Duchesnay (FRA)
1967	Diane Towler, Bernard Ford (GBR)	1992	Marina Klimova, Sergey Ponomarenko (UNT[2])
1968	Diane Towler, Bernard Ford (GBR)	1993	Maya Usova, Aleksandr Zhulin (RUS)
1969	Diane Towler, Bernard Ford (GBR)	1994	Oksana Grichuk, Yevgeny Platov (RUS)
1970	Lyudmila Pakhomova, Aleksandr Gorshkov (URS)	1995	Oksana Grichuk, Yevgeny Platov (RUS)
1971	L. Pakhomova, A. Gorshkov (URS)	1996	Oksana Grichuk, Yevgeny Platov (RUS)
1972	L. Pakhomova, A. Gorshkov (URS)	1997	Oksana Grichuk, Yevgeny Platov (RUS)
1973	L. Pakhomova, A. Gorshkov (URS)	1998	Angelika Krylova, Oleg Ovsyannikov (RUS)
1974	L. Pakhomova, A. Gorshkov (URS)	1999	Angelika Krylova, Oleg Ovsyannikov (RUS)
1975	Irina Moiseyeva, Andrey Minenkov (URS)	2000	Marina Anissina, Gwendal Peizarat (FRA)
1976	L. Pakhomova, A. Gorshkov (URS)	2001	Barbara Fusar-Poli, Maurizio Margaglio (ITA)
1977	Irina Moiseyeva, Andrey Minenkov (URS)	2002	Irina Lobachyova, Ilya Averbukh (RUS)
1978	Natalya Linichuk, Gennady Karponosov (URS)	2003	Shae-Lynn Bourne, Victor Kraatz (CAN)
1979	N. Linichuk, G. Karponosov (URS)	2004	Tatyana Navka, Roman Kostomarov (RUS)
1980	Krisztina Regoczy, Andras Sallay (HUN)	2005	Tatyana Navka, Roman Kostomarov (RUS)
		2006	to be held 20–26 March, Calgary, AB, Canada

[1]The entire US team died in an airplane crash, and the championships were canceled.
[2]Unified Team, consisting of athletes from the Commonwealth of Independent States plus Georgia.

Speed Skating World Records (Major Tracks)

men

EVENT	RECORD HOLDER (NATIONALITY)	PERFORMANCE	DATE
500 m	Hiroyasu Shimizu (JPN)	34.32 sec	10 Mar 2001
2 × 500 m	Hiroyasu Shimizu (JPN)	68.96 sec	10 Mar 2001
1,000 m	Gerard van Velde (NED)	1 min 7.18 sec	16 Feb 2002
1,500 m	Shani Davis (USA)	1 min 43.33 sec	9 Jan 2005
3,000 m	Chad Hendrick (USA)	3 min 39.02 sec	10 Mar 2005
5,000 m	Jochem Uytdehaage (NED)	6 min 14.66 sec	9 Feb 2002
10,000 m	Jochem Uytdehaage (NED)	12 min 58.92 sec	22 Feb 2002

women

EVENT	RECORD HOLDER (NATIONALITY)	PERFORMANCE	DATE
500 m	Catriona LeMay Doan (CAN)	37.22 sec	9 Dec 2001
2 × 500 m	Catriona LeMay Doan (CAN)	74.72 sec	9 Mar 2001
1,000 m	Christine Witty (USA)	1 min 13.83 sec	17 Feb 2002
1,500 m	Cindy Klassen (CAN)	1 min 53.87 sec	9 Jan 2005
3,000 m	Claudia Pechstein (GER)	3 min 57.70 sec	10 Feb 2002
5,000 m	Claudia Pechstein (GER)	6 min 46.91 sec	23 Feb 2002

Speed Skating World Records (Short Tracks)

men

EVENT	RECORD HOLDER (NATIONALITY)	PERFORMANCE	DATE
500 m	Jeff Scholten (CAN)	41.289 sec	8 Mar 2003
1,000 m	Jean-François Monette (CAN)	1 min 25.662 sec	9 Mar 2003
1,500 m	Steve Robillard (CAN)	2 min 12.234 sec	11 Oct 2002
3,000 m	Steve Robillard (CAN)	4 min 38.061 sec	13 Oct 2002
5,000-m relay	Canada National Team	6 min 43.730 sec	14 Oct 2001

women

EVENT	RECORD HOLDER (NATIONALITY)	PERFORMANCE	DATE
500 m	Evgeniya Radanova (BUL)	43.671 sec	19 Oct 2001
1,000 m	Chun-Sa Byun (KOR)	1 min 30.483 sec	12 Jan 2003
1,500 m	Choi Eun Kyung (KOR)	2 min 21.069 sec	13 Feb 2002
3,000 m	Choi Eun Kyung (KOR)	5 min 01.976 sec	22 Oct 2000
3,000-m relay	South Korea National Team	4 min 12.793 sec	20 Feb 2002

World All-Around Speed-Skating Championship—Men

There was no winner in 1894, 1902, 1903, 1906, and 1907. Before the points system was established, only a contestant who had won at least three of the four events was considered the all-around champion.

YEAR	WINNER	YEAR	WINNER	YEAR	WINNER
1893	Jaap Eden (NED)	1937	Michael Staksrud (NOR)	1977	Eric Heiden (USA)
1895	Jaap Eden (NED)	1938	Ivar Ballangrud (NOR)	1978	Eric Heiden (USA)
1896	Jaap Eden (NED)	1939	Birger Wasenius (FIN)	1979	Eric Heiden (USA)
1897	Jack K. McCullock (CAN)	1940–	*no competition*	1980	Hilbert van der Duim
1898	Peder Østlund (NOR)	46			(NED)
1899	Peder Østlund (NOR)	1947	Lassi Parkkinen (FIN)	1981	Amund Sjøbrend (NOR)
1900	Edvard Engelsaas (NOR)	1948	Odd Lundberg (NOR)	1982	Hilbert van der Duim
1901	Franz Wathen (FIN)	1949	Kornel Pajor (HUN)		(NED)
1904	Sigurd Mathisen (NOR)	1950	Hjalmar Andersen (NOR)	1983	Rolf Falk-Larssen (NOR)
1905	C. Coen de Koning (NED)	1951	Hjalmar Andersen (NOR)	1984	Oleg Bozhyev (URS)
1908	Oscar Mathisen (NOR)	1952	Hjalmar Andersen (NOR)	1985	Hein Vergeer (NED)
1909	Oscar Mathisen (NOR)	1953	Oleg Goncharenko (URS)	1986	Hein Vergeer (NED)
1910	Nikolay Strunnikov (RUS)	1954	Boris Shilkov (URS)	1987	Nikolai Gulyaev (URS)
1911	Nikolay Strunnikov (RUS)	1955	Sigvard Ericsson (SWE)	1988	Eric Flaim (USA)
1912	Oscar Mathisen (NOR)	1956	Oleg Goncharenko (URS)	1989	Leo Visser (NED)
1913	Oscar Mathisen (NOR)	1957	Knut Johannesen (NOR)	1990	Johann Olav Koss (NOR)
1914	Oscar Mathisen (NOR)	1958	Oleg Goncharenko (URS)	1991	Johann Olav Koss (NOR)
1915–	*no competition*	1959	Juhani Jäevinen (FIN)	1992	Roberto Sighel (ITA)
21		1960	Boris Stenin (URS)	1993	Falko Zandstra (NED)
1922	Harald Strom (NOR)	1961	Henk van der Grift (NED)	1994	Johann Olav Koss (NOR)
1923	Clas Thunberg (FIN)	1962	Viktor Kosichkin (URS)	1995	Rintje Ritsma (NED)
1924	Roald Larsen (NOR)	1963	Jonny Nilsson (SWE)	1996	Rintje Ritsma (NED)
1925	Clas Thunberg (FIN)	1964	Knut Johannesen (NOR)	1997	Ids Postma (NED)
1926	Ivar Ballangrud (NOR)	1965	Per Ivar Moe (NOR)	1998	Ids Postma (NED)
1927	Bernt Evensen (NOR)	1966	Kees Verkerk (NED)	1999	Rintje Ritsma (NED)
1928	Clas Thunberg (FIN)	1967	Kees Verkerk (NED)	2000	Gianni Romme (NED)
1929	Clas Thunberg (FIN)	1968	Fred Anton Maier (NOR)	2001	Rintje Ritsma (NED)
1930	Michael Staksrud (NOR)	1969	Dag Fornaess (NOR)	2002	Jochem Uytdehaage (NED)
1931	Clas Thunberg (FIN)	1970	Ard Schenk (NED)	2003	Gianni Romme (NED)
1932	Ivar Ballangrud (NOR)	1971	Ard Schenk (NED)	2004	Chad Hedrick (USA)
1933	Hans Engnestangen	1972	Ard Schenk (NED)	2005	Shani Davis (USA)
	(NOR)	1973	Göran Claeson (SWE)	2006	*to be held 18–19 March,*
1934	Bernt Evensen (NOR)	1974	Sten Stensen (NOR)		*Calgary, AB, Canada*
1935	Michael Staksrud (NOR)	1975	Harm Kuipers (NED)		
1936	Ivar Ballangrud (NOR)	1976	Piet Kleine (NED)		

World All-Around Speed-Skating Championship—Women

YEAR	WINNER	YEAR	WINNER	YEAR	WINNER
1936	Kit Klein (USA)	1967	Stien Kaiser (NED)	1989	Constanze Moser (GDR)
1937	Laila Schou Nilsen (NOR)	1968	Stien Kaiser (NED)	1990	Jacqueline Börner (GDR)
1938	Laila Schou Nilsen (NOR)	1969	Lasma Kauniste (URS)	1991	Gunda Kleeman (GER)
1939	Verné Lesche (FIN)	1970	Atje Keulen-Deelstra	1992	Gunda Kleeman (GER)
1940–46	*not held*		(NED)	1993	Gunda Kleeman (GER)
1947	Verné Lesche (FIN)	1971	Nina Statkevich (URS)	1994	Emese Hunyady (AUT)
1948	Mariya Isakova (URS)	1972	Atje Keulen-Deelstra	1995	Gunda Niemann (GER)
1949	Mariya Isakova (URS)		(NED)	1996	Gunda Niemann (GER)
1950	Mariya Isakova (URS)	1973	Atje Keulen-Deelstra	1997	Gunda Niemann (GER)
1951	Eevi Huttunen (FIN)		(NED)	1998	Gunda Niemann-
1952	Lidiya Selikhova (URS)	1974	Atje Keulen-Deelstra		Stirnemann (GER)
1953	Khalida Shchegoleva		(NED)	1999	Gunda Niemann-
	(URS)	1975	Karin Kessow (GDR)		Stirnemann (GER)
1954	Lidiya Selikhova (URS)	1976	Sylvia Burka (CAN)	2000	Claudia Pechstein (GER)
1955	Rimma Zhukova (URS)	1977	Vera Bryndzey (URS)	2001	Anni Friesinger (GER)
1956	Sofiya Kondakova (URS)	1978	Tatyana Averina (URS)	2002	Anni Friesinger (GER)
1957	Inga Artamonova (URS)	1979	Beth Heiden (USA)	2003	Cindy Klassen (CAN)
1958	Inga Artamonova (URS)	1980	Natalya Petruseva (URS)	2004	Renate Groenewold (NED)
1959	Tamara Rylova (URS)	1981	Natalya Petruseva (URS)	2005	Anni Friesinger (GER)
1960	Valentina Stenina (URS)	1982	Karin Busch (GDR)	2006	*to be held 18–19 March,*
1961	Valentina Stenina (URS)	1983	Andrea Schöne (GDR)		*Calgary, AB, Canada*
1962	Inga Artamonova (URS)	1984	Karin Enke (GDR)		
1963	Lidiya Skoblikova (URS)	1985	Andrea Schöne (GDR)		
1964	Lidiya Skoblikova (URS)	1986	Karin Kania (GDR)		
1965	Inga Artamonova (URS)	1987	Karin Kania (GDR)		
1966	Valentina Stenina (URS)	1988	Karin Kania (GDR)		

World Speed-Skating Sprint Championships

YEAR	MEN	WOMEN	YEAR	MEN	WOMEN
1970	Valery Muratov (URS)	Lyudmila Titova (URS)	1990	Ki-Tae Bae (KOR)	Angela Hauck (GDR)
1971	Erhard Keller (FRG)	Ruth Schleiermacher (GDR)	1991	Igor Zhelezovsky (URS)	Monique Garbrecht (GER)
1972	Leo Linkovesi (FIN)	Monica Pflug (FRG)	1992	Igor Zhelezovsky (UNT[1])	Ye Qiaobo (CHN)
1973	Valery Muratov (URS)	Sheila Young (USA)	1993	Igor Zhelezovsky (URS)	Ye Qiaobo (CHN)
1974	Per Bjørang (NOR)	Leah Poulos (USA)	1994	Dan Jansen (USA)	Bonnie Blair (USA)
1975	Aleksandr Safronov (URS)	Sheila Young (USA)	1995	Kim Yoon Man (KOR)	Bonnie Blair (USA)
1976	Johan Granath (SWE)	Sheila Young (USA)	1996	Sergey Klevchenya (RUS)	Christine Witty (USA)
1977	Eric Heiden (USA)	Sylvia Burka (CAN)	1997	Sergey Klevchenya (RUS)	Franziska Schenk (GER)
1978	Eric Heiden (USA)	Lyubov Sadchikova (URS)	1998	Jan Bos (NED)	Catriona LeMay Doan (CAN)
1979	Eric Heiden (USA)	Leah Poulos-Mueller (USA)	1999	Jeremy Wotherspoon (CAN)	Monique Garbrecht (GER)
1980	Eric Heiden (USA)	Karin Enke (GDR)	2000	Jeremy Wotherspoon (CAN)	Monique Garbrecht (GER)
1981	Frode Ronning (NOR)	Karin Enke (GDR)	2001	Michael Ireland (CAN)	Monique Garbrecht-Enfeldt (GER)
1982	Sergey Khlebnikov (URS)	Natalya Petruseva (URS)	2002	Jeremy Wotherspoon (CAN)	Catriona LeMay Doan (CAN)
1983	Akira Kuroiwa (JPN)	Karin Enke (GDR)	2003	Jeremy Wotherspoon (CAN)	Monique Garbrecht-Enfeldt (GER)
1984	Gaetan Boucher (CAN)	Karin Enke (GDR)	2004	Erben Wennemars (NED)	Marianne Timmer (NED)
1985	Igor Zhelezovsky (URS)	Christa Rothenburger (GDR)	2005	Erben Wennemars (NED)	Jennifer Rodriguez (USA)
1986	Igor Zhelezovsky (URS)	Karin Kania (GDR)	2006	to be held 21–22 January, Heerenveen, Netherlands	
1987	Akira Kuroiwa (JPN)	Karin Kania (GDR)			
1988	Dan Jansen (USA)	Christa Rothenburger (GDR)			
1989	Igor Zhelezovsky (URS)	Bonnie Blair (USA)			

[1]Unified Team, consisting of athletes from the Commonwealth of Independent States plus Georgia.

World Short-Track Speed-Skating Championships—Overall Winners

YEAR	MEN	WOMEN	YEAR	MEN	WOMEN
1976	Alan Rattray (USA)	Celeste Chlapaty (USA)	1989	Michel Daignault (CAN)	Sylvie Daigle (CAN)
1977	Gaetan Boucher (CAN)	Brenda Webster (CAN)	1990	Joon-ho Lee (KOR)	Sylvie Daigle (CAN)
1978	James Lynch (AUS)	Sarah Docter (CAN)	1991	Wilfred O'Reilly (GBR)	Nathalie Lambert (CAN)
1979	Hiroshi Toda (JPN)	Sylvie Daigle (CAN)	1992	Ki Hoon Kim (KOR)	So He Kim (KOR)
1980	Gaetan Boucher (CAN)	Miyoshi Kato (JPN)	1993	Marc Gagnon (CAN)	Nathalie Lambert (CAN)
1981	Benoît Baril (CAN)	Miyoshi Kato (JPN)	1994	Marc Gagnon (CAN)	Nathalie Lambert (CAN)
1982	Guy Daigneault (CAN)	Maryse Perreault (CAN)	1995	Chae Ji Hoon (KOR)	Chun Lee Kyung (KOR)
1983	Louis Grenier (CAN)	Sylvie Daigle (CAN)	1996	Marc Gagnon (CAN)	Chun Lee Kyung (KOR)
1984	Guy Daigneault (CAN)	Mariko Kinoshita (JPN)	1997	Kim Dong Sung (KOR)	Chun Lee Kyung (KOR), Yang Yang (A) (CHN)[1]
1985	Toshinobu Kawai (JPN)	Eiko Shishii (JPN)	1998	Marc Gagnon (CAN)	Yang Yang (A) (CHN)
1986	Tatsuyoshi Isihara (JPN)	Bonnie Blair (USA)	1999	Li Jianjun (CHN)	Yang Yang (A) (CHN)
1987	Michel Daignault (CAN), Toshinobu Kawai (JPN)[1]	Eiko Shishii (JPN)	2000	Min Ryung (KOR)	Yang Yang (A) (CHN)
			2001	Li Jianjun (CHN)	Yang Yang (A) (CHN)
1988	Peter van der Velde (NED)	Sylvie Daigle (CAN)	2002	Kim Dong Sung (KOR)	Yang Yang (A) (CHN)
			2003	Ahn Hyun Soo (KOR)	Choi Eun Kyung (KOR)
			2004	Ahn Hyun Soo (KOR)	Choi Eun Kyung (KOR)
			2005	Ahn Hyun Soo (KOR)	Jin Sun Yu (KOR)
			2006	to be held 31 March–2 April, Minneapolis MN	

[1]Tied.

Judo

World championships for judo were first held in 1956 under the auspices of the International Judo Federation (IJF; founded 1951). At that time all contestants participated on an equal basis. At the fourth world championship match, 65 kg, 78 kg, and 95 kg classes were added to the open weight division; at the next championship match, two more weight classes were added; and in 1979 two of the classes were divided once more and assigned weight values. World championships for women were first held in 1980; they are contested biennially in eight weight classes. New weight classes were established in 1999. The 2005 World Judo Championships are scheduled to be held 8–11 Sep in Cairo, Egypt.

International Judo Federation Web site: <www.ijf.org>.

World Judo Championships—Men

Figures in parentheses represent weight classes before 1999.

YEAR	OPEN WEIGHTS
1956[1]	Shokichi Natsui (JPN)
1958[1]	Koji Sone (JPN)
1961[1]	Anton Geesink (NED)
1965[2]	Isao Inokuma (JPN)
1967[3]	Mitsuo Matsunaga (JPN)
1969[3]	Masatoshi Shinomaki (JPN)
1971[3]	Masatoshi Shinomaki (JPN)
1973[3]	Kasuhiro Ninomiya (JPN)
1975[3]	Haruki Uemura (JPN)
1979	Sumio Endo (JPN)
1981	Yasuhiro Yamashita (JPN)
1983	Hitoshi Saito (JPN)
1985	Y. Masaki (JPN)
1987	Naoya Ogawa (JPN)
1989	Naoya Ogawa (JPN)
1991	Naoya Ogawa (JPN)
1993	Rafael Kubacki (POL)
1995	David Douillet (FRA)
1997	Rafael Kubacki (POL)
1999	Shinichi Shinohara (JPN)
2001	Aleksandr Mikhaylin (RUS)
2003	Keiji Suzuki (JPN)

YEAR	60 KG
1979	Thierry Rey (FRA)
1981	Yasuhiro Moriwaki (JPN)
1983	Khazret Tletseri (URS)
1985	Shinji Hosokawa (JPN)
1987	Kim Jae Yup (KOR)
1989	Amiran Totikashvili (URS)
1991	Tadanori Koshino (JPN)
1993	Ryoji Sonada (JPN)
1995	Nikolay Ozhegin (RUS)
1997	Tadahiro Nomura (JPN)
1999	Manuelo Poulot (CUB)
2001	Anis Lounifi (TUN)
2003	Choi Min Ho (KOR)

YEAR	66 KG (65 KG)
1965[2]	Hirofumi Matsuda (JPN)
1967[3]	Takafumi Shigeoka (JPN)
1969[3]	Yoshio Sonoda (JPN)
1971[3]	Takao Kawaguchi (JPN)
1973[3]	Yoshiharu Minami (JPN)
1975[3]	Yoshiharu Minami (JPN)
1979	Nikolay Solodukhin (URS)
1981	Katsuhito Kashiwazaki (JPN)
1983	Nicolay Solodukhin (URS)
1985	Yuri Sokolov (URS)
1987	Yosuke Yamamoto (JPN)

YEAR	66 KG (65 KG) (CONTINUED)
1989	Dragomir Becanovic (YUG)
1991	Udo Quellmalz (GER)
1993	Yukimasa Nakamura (JPN)
1995	Udo Quellmalz (GER)
1997	Kim Hyuk (KOR)
1999	Larbi Benboudaoud (FRA)
2001	Arash Miresmaeili (IRI)
2003	Arash Miresmaeili (IRI)

YEAR	73 KG (71 KG)
1967[3]	Hiroshi Minatoya (JPN)
1969[3]	Hiroshi Minatoya (JPN)
1971[3]	Hisashi Tsuzawa (JPN)
1973[3]	Toyokazu Nomura (JPN)
1975[3]	Vladimir Nevzorov (URS)
1979	Kyoto Katsuki (JPN)
1981	Park Chong Hak (KOR)
1983	Hidetoshi Nakanishi (JPN)
1985	Keun Ahn Byung (KOR)
1987	Mike Swain (USA)
1989	Toshihigo Koga (JPN)
1991	Toshihigo Koga (JPN)
1993	Yung Chung Hoon (KOR)
1995	Daisuke Hideshima (JPN)
1997	Kenzo Nakamura (JPN)
1999	Jimmy Pedro (USA)
2001	Vitaly Makarov (RUS)
2003	Lee Won Hee (KOR)

YEAR	81 KG (78 KG)
1965[2]	Isao Okano (JPN)
1967[3]	Eijii Maruki (JPN)
1969[3]	Isamu Sonoda (JPN)
1971[3]	Shozo Fujii (JPN)
1973[3]	Shozo Fujii (JPN)
1975[3]	Shozo Fujii (JPN)
1979	Shozo Fujii (JPN)
1981	Neil Adams (GBR)
1983	Nobutoshi Hikage (JPN)
1985	Nobutoshi Hikage (JPN)
1987	Hirotaka Okada (JPN)
1989	Kim Bying Ju (KOR)
1991	Daniel Lascau (GER)
1993	Chun Ki Young (KOR)
1995	Toshihigo Koga (JPN)
1997	Cho In Chul (KOR)
1999	Graeme Randall (GBR)
2001	Cho In Chul (KOR)
2003	Florian Wanner (GER)

YEAR	90 KG (86 KG)
1967[3]	Nobuyuki Sato (JPN)
1969[3]	Fumio Sasahara (JPN)

YEAR	90 KG (86 KG) (CONTINUED)
1971[3]	Fumio Sasahara (JPN)
1973[3]	Nobuyuki Sato (JPN)
1975[3]	Jean-Louc Rouge (FRA)
1979	Detlef Ultsch (GDR)
1981	Bernard Tchoullouyan (FRA)
1983	Detlef Ultsch (GDR)
1985	Peter Seisenbacher (AUT)
1987	Fabien Canu (FRA)
1989	Fabien Canu (FRA)
1991	Hirotaka Okada (JPN)
1993	Yoshio Nakamura (JPN)
1995	Chun Ki Young (KOR)
1997	Jeon Ki Young (KOR)
1999	Hidehiko Yoshida (JPN)
2001	Frédéric Demontfaucon (FRA)
2003	Hwang Hee Tae (KOR)

YEAR	100 KG (95 KG)
1965[2]	Anton Geesink (NED)
1967[3]	Wilhem Ruska (NED)
1969[3]	Shuji Suma (JPN)
1971[3]	Wilhem Ruska (NED)
1973[3]	Chonosuke Takagi (JPN)
1975[3]	Sumio Endo (JPN)
1979	Tengiz Khubuluri (URS)
1981	Tengiz Khubuluri (URS)
1983	Andreas Preschel (GDR)
1985	Hitoshi Sugai (JPN)
1987	Hitoshi Sugai (JPN)
1989	Koba Kurtanidze (URS)
1991	Stéphane Traineau (FRA)
1993	Antal Kovacs (HUN)
1995	Pawel Nastula (POL)
1997	Pawel Nastula (POL)
1999	Kosei Inoue (JPN)
2001	Kosei Inoue (JPN)
2003	Kosei Inoue (JPN)

YEAR	+100 KG (+95 KG)
1979	Yasuhiro Yamashita (JPN)
1981	Yasuhiro Yamashita (JPN)
1983	Yasuhiro Yamashita (JPN)
1985	Chul Cho Yong (KOR)
1987	Grigory Verichev (URS)
1989	Naoya Ogawa (JPN)
1991	Sergey Kosorotov (URS)
1993	David Douillet (FRA)
1995	David Douillet (FRA)
1997	David Douillet (FRA)
1999	Shinichi Shinohara (JPN)
2001	Aleksandr Mikhaylin (RUS)
2003	Yasuyuki Muneta (JPN)

[1]Weight classes not held—open weight division only. [2]Divisions called lightweight, middleweight, heavyweight. [3]Divisions called lightweight, light-middleweight, middleweight, light-heavyweight, and heavyweight.

World Judo Championships—Women

Figures in parentheses represent weight classes before 1999.

YEAR	OPEN WEIGHTS	YEAR	52 KG (CONTINUED)	YEAR	70 KG (66 KG) (CONTINUED)
1980	Ingrid Berghmans (BEL)	1997	Marie-Claire Restoux (FRA)	1987	Alexandra Schreiber (FRG)
1982	Ingrid Berghmans (BEL)	1999	Noriko Narasaki (JPN)	1989	Emanuela Pierantozzi (ITA)
1984	Ingrid Berghmans (BEL)	2001	Kye Sun Hui (PRK)	1991	Emanuela Pierantozzi (ITA)
1986	Ingrid Berghmans (BEL)	2003	Amarilis Savon (CUB)		
1987	Fengliang Gao (CHN)			1993	Cho Min Sun (KOR)
1989	Estela Rodriguez (CUB)	YEAR	57 KG (56 KG)	1995	Cho Min Sun (KOR)
1991	Zhuang Xiaoyan (CHN)	1980	Gerda Winklbauer (AUT)	1997	Kate Howey (GBR)
1993	Beata Maksymow (POL)	1982	Béatrice Rodriguez (FRA)	1999	Sibelis Veranes (CUB)
1995	Monique van der Lee (NED)	1984	Anne-Marie Burns (USA)	2001	Masae Ueno (JPN)
1997	Daina Beltran (CUB)	1986	Ann Hughes (GBR)	2003	Masae Ueno (JPN)
1999	Daina Beltran (CUB)	1987	Catherine Arnaud (FRA)		
2001	Celine Lebrun (FRA)	1989	Catherine Arnaud (FRA)	YEAR	78 KG (72 KG)
2003	Tong Wen (CHN)	1991	Miriam Blasco (ESP)	1980	Jocelyne Triadou (FRA)
		1993	Nicola Fairbrother (GBR)	1982	Barbara Classen (FRG)
YEAR	48 KG	1995	Driulis González (CUB)	1984	Ingrid Berghmans (BEL)
1980	Jane Bridge (GBR)	1997	Isabel Fernández (ESP)	1986	Irene de Kok (NED)
1982	Karen Briggs (GBR)	1999	Driulis González (CUB)	1987	Irene de Kok (NED)
1984	Karen Briggs (GBR)	2001	Yurisleidis Lupetey (CUB)	1989	Ingrid Berghmans (BEL)
1986	Karen Briggs (GBR)	2003	Kye Sun Hui (PRK)	1991	Kim Mi Jong (KOR)
1987	Zhang Yun Li (CHN)			1993	Leng Chin Hui (CHN)
1989	Karen Briggs (GBR)	YEAR	63 KG (61 KG)	1995	Castellano Diaz Luna (CUB)
1991	Cecile Nowak (FRA)	1980	Anita Staps (NED)		
1993	Ryoko Tamura (JPN)	1982	Martine Rottier (FRA)	1997	Noriko Anno (JPN)
1995	Ryoko Tamura (JPN)	1984	Natasha Hernández (VEN)	1999	Noriko Anno (JPN)
1997	Ryoko Tamura (JPN)	1986	Diane Bell (GBR)	2001	Noriko Anno (JPN)
1999	Ryoko Tamura (JPN)	1987	Diane Bell (GBR)	2003	Noriko Anno (JPN)
2001	Ryoko Tamura (JPN)	1989	Catherine Fleury (FRA)		
2003	Ryoko Tamura (JPN)	1991	Frauke Eickoff (GER)	YEAR	+78 KG (+72 KG)
		1993	Gella van de Cavaye (BEL)	1980	Margerita de Cal (ITA)
YEAR	52 KG	1995	Jung Sung Sook (KOR)	1982	Natalina Lupino (FRA)
1980	Edith Hrovat (AUT)	1997	Severin Vandenhende (FRA)	1984	Maria-Theresa Motta (ITA)
1982	Loretta Doyle (GBR)	1999	Keiko Maeda (JPN)	1986	Fengliang Gao (CHN)
1984	Kaori Yamaguchi (JPN)	2001	Gella van de Cavaye (BEL)	1987	Fengliang Gao (CHN)
1986	Dominique Brun (FRA)	2003	Daniela Krukower (ARG)	1989	Fengliang Gao (CHN)
1987	Sharon Rendle (GBR)			1991	Moon Ji Yoon (KOR)
1989	Sharon Rendle (GBR)	YEAR	70 KG (66 KG)	1993	Johanna Hagn (GER)
1991	Alessandra Giungi (ITA)	1980	Edith Simon (AUT)	1995	Angelique Seriese (NED)
1993	Legna Verdecia Rodríguez (CUB)	1982	Brigitte Deydier (FRA)	1997	Christine Cicot (FRA)
1995	Marie-Claire Restoux (FRA)	1984	Brigitte Deydier (FRA)	1999	Beata Maksymow (POL)
		1986	Brigitte Deydier (FRA)	2001	Yuan Hua (CHN)
				2003	Sun Fuming (CHN)

Marathon

The marathon is a long-distance footrace first held at the revival of the Olympic Games at Athens in 1896. It commemorates the legendary feat of a Greek soldier who, in 490 BC, is supposed to have run from Marathon to Athens, a distance of about 40 km (25 mi), to bring news of the Athenian victory over the Persians. Appropriately, the first modern marathon winner in 1896 was a Greek, Spyridon Louis. In 1924 the **Olympic marathon distance** was standardized at 42,195 m, or 26 mi 385 yd. This was based on a decision of the British Olympic Committee to start the 1908 Olympic race from Windsor Castle and finish it in front of the royal box in the stadium at London. The marathon was added to the **women's Olympic program** in 1984. Because marathon courses are not of equal difficulty, the International Association of Athletics Federations, does not list a world record for the event. After the Olympic Games championship, one of the most coveted honors in marathon running is victory in the **Boston Marathon**, held annually since 1897. It draws athletes from all parts of the world and in 1972 became the first marathon officially to allow women to compete. The **New York Marathon** also attracts participants from many countries. Other popular marathons are held in London, Berlin, Rotterdam (The Netherlands), Dublin, and Chicago.

Related Web sites: Boston Marathon: <www.boston marathon.org>; New York City Marathon: <www.nyrrc.org>.

Boston Marathon

Won by an American runner except as indicated. Times are given in hours:minutes:seconds.

men

YEAR	WINNER	TIME	YEAR	WINNER	TIME
1897	John J. McDermott	2:55:10	1952	Doroteo Flores (GUA)	2:31:53
1898	Ronald J. McDonald (CAN)	2:42:00	1953	Yamada Keizo (JPN)	2:18:51
1899	Lawrence J. Brignoli	2:54:38	1954	Veikko L. Karanen (FIN)	2:20:39
1900	John J. Caffrey (CAN)	2:39:44	1955	Hamamura Hideo (JPN)	2:18:22
1901	John J. Caffrey (CAN)	2:29:23	1956	Antti Viskari (FIN)	2:14:14
1902	Sammy A. Mellor	2:43:12	1957	John J. Kelley	2:20:05
1903	John C. Lorden	2:41:29	1958	Franjo Mihalic (YUG)	2:25:54
1904	Michael Spring	2:39:04	1959	Eino Oksanen (FIN)	2:22:42
1905	Frederick Lorz	2:38:25	1960	Paavo Kotila (FIN)	2:20:54
1906	Tim Ford	2:45:45	1961	Eino Oksanen (FIN)	2:23:39
1907	Thomas Longboat (CAN)	2:24:24	1962	Eino Oksanen (FIN)	2:23:48
1908	Thomas P. Morrissey	2:25:43	1963	Aurele Vandendriessche (BEL)	2:18:58
1909	Henri Renaud	2:53:36	1964	Aurele Vandendriessche (BEL)	2:19:59
1910	Fred L. Cameron (CAN)	2:28:52	1965	Shigematsu Morio (JPN)	2:16:33
1911	Clarence H. DeMar	2:21:39	1966	Kimihara Kenji (JPN)	2:17:11
1912	Michael J. Ryan	2:21:18	1967	David McKenzie (NZL)	2:15:45
1913	Fritz Carlson	2:25:14	1968	Amby Burfoot	2:22:17
1914	James Duffy (CAN)	2:25:01	1969	Unetani Yoshiaki (JPN)	2:13:49
1915	Edouard Fabre (CAN)	2:31:41	1970	Ron Hill (ENG)	2:10:30
1916	Arthur V. Roth	2:27:16	1971	Alvaro Mejia (COL)	2:18:45
1917	William K. Kennedy	2:28:37	1972	Olavi Suomalainen (FIN)	2:15:30
1918	*no regular competition*		1973	Jon Anderson	2:16:03
1919	Carl W.A. Linder	2:29:13	1974	Neil Cusack	2:13:39
1920	Peter Trivoulides (GRE)	2:29:31	1975	Bill Rodgers	2:09:55
1921	Frank Zuna	2:18:57	1976	Jack Fultz	2:20:19
1922	Clarence H. DeMar	2:18:10	1977	Jerome Drayton (CAN)	2:14:46
1923	Clarence H. DeMar	2:23:47	1978	Bill Rodgers	2:10:13
1924	Clarence H. DeMar	2:29:40	1979	Bill Rodgers	2:09:27
1925	Charles L. Mellor	2:33:06	1980	Bill Rodgers	2:12:11
1926	John C. Miles (CAN)	2:25:40	1981	Seko Toshihiko (JPN)	2:09:26
1927	Clarence H. DeMar	2:40:22	1982	Alberto Salazar	2:08:51
1928	Clarence H. DeMar	2:37:07	1983	Greg A. Meyer	2:09:00
1929	John C. Miles (CAN)	2:33:08	1984	Geoff Smith (ENG)	2:10:34
1930	Clarence H. DeMar	2:34:48	1985	Geoff Smith (ENG)	2:14:05
1931	James P. Hennigan	2:46:45	1986	Robert de Castella (AUS)	2:07:51
1932	Paul deBruyn	2:33:36	1987	Seko Toshihiko (JPN)	2:11:50
1933	Leslie S. Pawson	2:31:01	1988	Ibrahim Hussein (KEN)	2:08:43
1934	Dave Komonen (CAN)	2:32:53	1989	Abebe Mekonnen (ETH)	2:09:06
1935	John A. Kelley	2:32:07	1990	Gelindo Bordin (ITA)	2:08:19
1936	Ellison M. Brown	2:33:40	1991	Ibrahim Hussein (KEN)	2:11:06
1937	Walter Young (CAN)	2:33:20	1992	Ibrahim Hussein (KEN)	2:08:14
1938	Leslie S. Pawson	2:35:34	1993	Cosmas N'Deti (KEN)	2:09:33
1939	Ellison M. Brown	2:28:51	1994	Cosmas N'Deti (KEN)	2:07:15
1940	Gerard Cote (CAN)	2:28:28	1995	Cosmas N'Deti (KEN)	2:09:22
1941	Leslie S. Pawson	2:30:38	1996	Moses Tanui (KEN)	2:09:16
1942	Joe Smith	2:26:51	1997	Lameck Aguta (KEN)	2:10:34
1943	Gerard Cote (CAN)	2:28:25	1998	Moses Tanui (KEN)	2:07:34
1944	Gerard Cote (CAN)	2:31:50	1999	Joseph Chebet (KEN)	2:09:52
1945	John A. Kelley	2:30:40	2000	Elijah Lagat (KEN)	2:09:47
1946	Stylianos Kyriakides (GRE)	2:29:27	2001	Bong-Ju Lee (KOR)	2:09:43
1947	Suh Yun Bok (KOR)	2:25:39	2002	Rodgers Rop (KEN)	2:09:02
1948	Gerard Cote (CAN)	2:31:02	2003	Robert Kipkoech Cheruiyot (KEN)	2:10:11
1949	Karl G. Leandersson (SWE)	2:31:50	2004	Timothy Cherigat (KEN)	2:10:37
1950	Ham Kee Yong (KOR)	2:32:39	2005	Hailu Negussie (ETH)	2:11:45
1951	Tanaka Shigeki (JPN)	2:27:45	2006	*to be run April 17*	

women

YEAR	WINNER	TIME	YEAR	WINNER	TIME
1972	Nina Kuscsik	3:10:26	1980	Jacqueline Gareau (CAN)	2:34:28
1973	Jacqueline Hansen	3:05:59	1981	Allison Roe (NZL)	2:26:46
1974	Michiko Gorman	2:47:11	1982	Charlotte Teske (FRG)	2:29:33
1975	Liane Winter (FRG)	2:42:24	1983	Joan Benoit	2:22:42
1976	Kim Merritt	2:47:10	1984	Lorraine Moller (NZL)	2:29:28
1977	Michiko Gorman	2:46:22	1985	Lisa Larsen	2:34:06
1978	Gayle S. Barron	2:44:52	1986	Ingrid Kristiansen (NOR)	2:24:55
1979	Joan Benoit	2:35:15	1987	Rosa Mota (POR)	2:25:21

Boston Marathon (continued)

women (continued)

YEAR	WINNER	TIME	YEAR	WINNER	TIME
1988	Rosa Mota (POR)	2:24:30	1998	Fatuma Roba (ETH)	2:23:21
1989	Ingrid Kristiansen (NOR)	2:24:33	1999	Fatuma Roba (ETH)	2:23:25
1990	Rosa Mota (POR)	2:25:23	2000	Catherine Ndereba (KEN)	2:26:11
1991	Wanda Panfil (POL)	2:24:18	2001	Catherine Ndereba (KEN)	2:23:53
1992	Olga Markova (RUS)	2:23:43	2002	Margaret Okayo (KEN)	2:20:43
1993	Olga Markova (RUS)	2:25:27	2003	Svetlana Zakharova (RUS)	2:25:20
1994	Uta Pippig (GER)	2:21:45	2004	Catherine Ndereba (KEN)	2:24:27
1995	Uta Pippig (GER)	2:25:11	2005	Catherine Ndereba (KEN)	2:25:13
1996	Uta Pippig (GER)	2:27:12	2006	*to be run April 17*	
1997	Fatuma Roba (ETH)	2:26:23			

New York City Marathon

Won by an American runner except as indicated. Times are given in hours:minutes:seconds.

YEAR	MEN	TIME	WOMEN	TIME
1970	Gary Muhrcke	2:31:38	*no finisher*	
1971	Norm Higgins	2:22:54	Beth Bonner	2:55:22
1972	Robert Karlin	2:27:52	Nina Kuscsik	3:08:41
1973	Tom Fleming	2:21:54	Nina Kuscsik	2:57:07
1974	Norbert Sander	2:26:30	Katherine Switzer	3:07:29
1975	Tom Fleming	2:19:27	Kim Merritt	2:46:14
1976	Bill Rodgers	2:10:09	Michiko Gorman	2:39:11
1977	Bill Rodgers	2:11:28	Michiko Gorman	2:43:10
1978	Bill Rodgers	2:12:12	Grete Waitz (NOR)	2:32:30
1979	Bill Rodgers	2:11:42	Grete Waitz (NOR)	2:27:33
1980	Alberto Salazar	2:09:41	Grete Waitz (NOR)	2:25:41
1981	Alberto Salazar	2:08:13	Allison Roe (NZL)	2:25:29
1982	Alberto Salazar	2:09:29	Grete Waitz (NOR)	2:27:14
1983	Rod Dixon	2:08:59	Grete Waitz (NOR)	2:27:00
1984	Orlando Pizzolato	2:14:53	Grete Waitz (NOR)	2:29:30
1985	Orlando Pizzolato	2:11:34	Grete Waitz (NOR)	2:28:34
1986	Gianni Poli (ITA)	2:11:06	Grete Waitz (NOR)	2:28:06
1987	Ibrahim Hussein (KEN)	2:11:01	Priscilla Welch (GBR)	2:30:17
1988	Steve Jones (WAL)	2:08:20	Grete Waitz (NOR)	2:28:07
1989	Juma Ikangaa (TAN)	2:08:01	Ingrid Kristiansen (NOR)	2:25:30
1990	Douglas Wakiihuri (KEN)	2:12:39	Wanda Panfil (POL)	2:30:45
1991	Salvador Garcia (MEX)	2:09:28	Liz McColgan (SCO)	2:27:23
1992	Willie Mtolo (RSA)	2:09:29	Lisa Ondieki (AUS)	2:24:40
1993	Andres Espinosa (MEX)	2:10:04	Uta Pippig (GER)	2:26:24
1994	German Silva (MEX)	2:11:21	Tegla Loroupe (KEN)	2:27:37
1995	German Silva (MEX)	2:11:00	Tegla Loroupe (KEN)	2:28:06
1996	Giacomo Leone (ITA)	2:09:54	Anuta Catuna (ROM)	2:28:18
1997	John Kagwe (KEN)	2:08:12	Franziska Rochat-Moser (SUI)	2:28:43
1998	John Kagwe (KEN)	2:08:45	Franca Fiacconi (ITA)	2:25:17
1999	Joseph Chebet (KEN)	2:09:14	Adriana Fernández (MEX)	2:25:06
2000	Abdelkhader El Mouaziz (MAR)	2:10:09	Lyudmila Petrova (RUS)	2:25:45
2001	Tesfaye Jifar (ETH)	2:07:43	Margaret Okayo (KEN)	2:24:21
2002	Rodgers Rop (KEN)	2:08:07	Joyce Chepchumba (KEN)	2:25:56
2003	Martin Lel (KEN)	2:10:30	Margaret Okayo (KEN)	2:22:31
2004	Hendrik Ramaala (RSA)	2:09:28	Paula Radcliffe (GBR)	2:23:10
2005	*to be run 6 November*			

Rodeo

A uniquely North American competition, the rodeo has been held on a more-or-less formal basis since the late 1920s. From 1929 to 1944 the **men's world all-around rodeo champion** was named by the **Rodeo Association of America**. Since 1944 the all-around champion has been the leading money winner of the year—with the exception of the years 1976-78, when the champion was the cowboy who won the most money at the National Finals Rodeo. The Rodeo Association of America changed its name several times, but has been known as the **Professional Rodeo Cowboys Association** (PRCA) since 1975. Among other rodeo sanctioning activities, the PRCA qualifies cowboys for the **National Finals Rodeo**, a contest held in early December in Las Vegas NV among the top competitors in each of several events, including bronc riding (bareback and saddle), bull riding, calf roping, and steer wrestling (individual and team). Women compete in one event only, barrel racing.

Professional Rodeo Cowboys Association Web site: <http://prorodeo.org>.

Men's World All-Around Rodeo Champions

Awarded since 1929. Table shows champions for the past 20 years.

YEAR	WINNER	YEAR	WINNER	YEAR	WINNER	YEAR	WINNER
1985	Lewis Feild	1990	Ty Murray	1995	Joe Beaver	2000	Joe Beaver
1986	Lewis Feild	1991	Ty Murray	1996	Joe Beaver	2001	Cody Ohl
1987	Lewis Feild	1992	Ty Murray	1997	Dan Mortensen	2002	Trevor Brazile
1988	Dave Appleton	1993	Ty Murray	1998	Ty Murray	2003	Trevor Brazile
1989	Ty Murray	1994	Ty Murray	1999	Fred Whitfield	2004	Trevor Brazile

Rowing

World championship rowing was established in 1962 by the **Fédération Internationale des Sociétés d'Aviron** (FISA; International Federation of Rowing Associations; founded 1892). Events are contested over a 2,000-m (6,560-ft) course and include single, double, and quadruple sculls; pairs (with and without coxswain); fours (with and without coxswain); and eights (with coxswain). **Women's world championships,** held since 1974, include single, double, and quadruple sculls; coxless pairs; fours; and eights, and were raced over a 1,000-m (3,280-ft) course until 1985 (2,000-m course thereafter).

The most famous and historic of rowing courses is the 2,112-m (1 mi 550-yd) course at Henley-on-Thames, Oxfordshire, England. Some events of the **Henley Regatta** are open to the world; these include the **Diamond Challenge Sculls** for single sculls and the **Grand Challenge Cup** for eights. Unless otherwise mentioned, the clubs listed in the Henley Regatta events are English.

Another historic event is the annual University Boat Race between eights from Oxford and Cambridge universities, which was instituted on 10 Jun 1829. The record time for the course of 6,779 m (4 mi 374 yd) from Putney to Mortlake on the River Thames is 16 min 19 sec by Cambridge in 1998.

FISA Web site: <www.worldrowing.com>.

World Rowing Championships—Men

The competition has been held since 1962. The table shows only the past 20 years. Results are for heavyweight events only. Times are given in minutes:seconds. The next championship is scheduled to be held 3 Aug 2005 in Brandenburg, Germany.

YEAR	SINGLE SCULLS	TIME	DOUBLE SCULLS	TIME
1985	Pertti Karppinen (FIN)	6:48.08	Uwe Heppner, Thomas Lange (GDR)	6:15.49
1986	Peter-Michael Kolbe (FRG)	6:54.09	Alberto Belgeri, Igor Pescialli (ITA)	6:33.64
1987	Thomas Lange (GDR)	7:36.41	D. Iordanov, V. Dadev (BUL)	7:03.33
1988[1]	Thomas Lange (GDR)	6:49.86	Ronald Florijan, Nicolaas Rienks (NED)	6:21.13
1989	Thomas Lange (GDR)	6:58.14	Rolf Thorsen, Lars Bjoenness (NOR)	6:23.40
1990	Yury Jensen (URS)	7:22.15	Christoph Zerbst, Arnold Jonke (AUT)	6:56.37
1991	Thomas Lange (GDR)	6:41.29	Henk-Jan Zwolle, Nicolaas Rienks (NED)	6:06.14
1992[1]	Thomas Lange (GDR)	6:51.40	Stephen Hawkins, Peter Antonie (AUT)	6:17.32
1993	Derek Porter (CAN)	6:59.03	Yves Lamarque, Samuel Barathay (FRA)	6:24.69
1994	André Willims (GER)	6:46.33	Rolf Thorsen, Lars Bjoenness (NOR)	6:08.33
1995	Iztok Cop (SLO)	6:52.93	Lars Christensen, Martin Haldbo-Hansen (DEN)	6:17.01
1996	Xeno Müller (SUI)	6:44.85	Davide Tizzano, Agostino Abbagnale (ITA)	6:16.90
1997	James Koven (USA)	6:44.86	Stephan Volkert, Andreas Hajek (GER)	6:13.35
1998	Robert Waddell (NZL)	6:39.65	Stephan Volkert, Andreas Hajek (GER)	6:13.20
1999	Robert Waddell (NZL)	6:36.68	Luka Spik, Iztok Cop (SLO)	6:04.37
2000[1]	Robert Waddell (NZL)	6:48.90	Luka Spik, Iztok Cop (SLO)	6:16.63
2001	Olaf Tufte (NOR)	6:43.04	Akos Haller, Tibor Peto (HUN)	6:14.16
2002	Marcel Hacker (GER)	6:36.33	Akos Haller, Tibor Peto (HUN)	6:05.74
2003	Olaf Tufte (NOR)	6:46.15	Sebastien Vieilledent, Adrien Hardy (FRA)	6:13.93
2004[1]	Olaf Tufte (NOR)	6:49.30	Sebastien Vieilledent, Adrien Hardy (FRA)	6:29.00

YEAR	COXED PAIRS	TIME	COXLESS PAIRS	TIME
1985	G. Abbagnale, C. Abbagnale (ITA)	6:53.40	Nikolay Pimenov, Yury Pimenov (URS)	6:38.39
1986	Andy Holmes, Steve Redgrave (GBR)	6:51.66	Nikolay Pimenov, Yury Pimenov (URS)	6:42.37
1987	G. Abbagnale, C. Abbagnale (ITA)	7:40.81	Steve Redgrave, Andrew Holmes (GBR)	7:11.20
1988[1]	G. Abbagnale, C. Abbagnale (ITA)	6:58.79	Steve Redgrave, Andrew Holmes (GBR)	6:36.84
1989	G. Abbagnale, C. Abbagnale (ITA)	6:54.81	Thomas Jung, Uwe Kellner (GDR)	6:39.95
1990	G. Abbagnale, C. Abbagnale (ITA)	6:48.30	Thomas Jung, Uwe Kellner (GDR)	7:07.91
1991	G. Abbagnale, C. Abbagnale (ITA)	7:34.49	Steve Redgrave, Matthew Pinsent (GBR)	6:21.35
1992[1]	Jonny Searle, Greg Searle (GBR)	6:49.83	Steve Redgrave, Matthew Pinsent (GBR)	6:27.72
1993	Jonny Searle, Greg Searle (GBR)	7:01.50	Steve Redgrave, Matthew Pinsent (GBR)	6:37.11
1994	Tihomir Frankovic, Igor Boraska (CRO)	6:42.16	Steve Redgrave, Matthew Pinsent (GBR)	6:18.65
1995	Luca Sartori, Giuliano DeStabile (ITA)	7:35.11	Steve Redgrave, Matthew Pinsent (GBR)	6:28.11
1996[1]	Yannick Schulte, Luc Prevot (FRA)	7:18.26	Steve Redgrave, Matthew Pinsent (GBR)	6:20.09
1997	Scott Fentress, Jordan Irving (USA)	6:56.30	Michel Andrieux, Jean-Christophe Rolland (FRA)	6:27.69

World Rowing Championships—Men (continued)

YEAR	COXED PAIRS	TIME	COXLESS PAIRS	TIME
1998	Nick Green, James Tomkins (AUS)	6:45.01	Robert Sens, Detlef Kirchhoff (GER)	6:22.32
1999	James Neil, Phil Henry (USA)	6:48.56	Drew Ginn, James Tomkins (AUS)	6:19.00
2000	Kurt Borcherding, Matt Guerrieri (USA)	7:07.15	Michel Andrieux, Jean-Christophe Rolland (FRA)[1]	6:32.97
2001	James Cracknell, Matthew Pinsent (GBR)	6:49.33	James Cracknell, Matthew Pinsent (GBR)	6:27.57
2002	Lars Krisch, Andreas Werner (GER)	6:47.93	James Cracknell, Matthew Pinsent (GBR)	6:14.27
2003	Daniel Berry, Matthew Rich (USA)	7:10.11	Drew Ginn, James Tomkins (AUS)	6:19.31
2004	Mario Palmisano, Mattia Trombetta (ITA)	6:54.46	Drew Ginn, James Tomkins (AUS)[1]	6:30.76

YEAR	COXED FOURS	TIME	YEAR	COXLESS FOURS	TIME	YEAR	EIGHTS	TIME
1985	USSR	6:07.23	1985	West Germany	6:00.19	1985	USSR	5:33.71
1986	East Germany	6:03.81	1986	United States	6:03.53	1986	Australia	5:33.54
1987	East Germany	6:41.74	1987	East Germany	6:39.70	1987	United States	5:58.83
1988[1]	East Germany	6:10.74	1988[1]	East Germany	6:03.11	1988[1]	West Germany	5:46.05
1989	Romania	6:14.90	1989	East Germany	6:06.94	1989	West Germany	5:43.88
1990	East Germany	6:46.73	1990	Australia	5:52.20	1990	West Germany	5:26.62
1991	Germany	5:58.96	1991	Australia	6:29.69	1991	Germany	5:50.98
1992[1]	Romania	5:59.37	1992[1]	Australia	5:55.04	1992[1]	Canada	5:29.53
1993	Romania	6:14.64	1993	France	6:04.54	1993	Germany	5:37.08
1994	Romania	6:06.69	1994	Italy	5:48.44	1994	United States	5:24.50
1995	United States	6:37.50	1995	Italy	5:58.28	1995	Germany	5:53.40
1996	Romania	6:25.74	1996	Australia	6:06.37	1996	Netherlands	5:42.74
1997	France	6:04.17	1997	Great Britain	5:52.40	1997	United States	5:27.20
1998	Australia	6:09.43	1998	Great Britain	5:48.06	1998	United States	5:38.78
1999	United States	6:38.31	1999	Great Britain	5:48.57	1999	United States	6:01.58
2000	Great Britain	6:16.82	2000	Great Britain	5:56.24	2000	Great Britain	5:33.08
2001	France	6:08.25	2001	Great Britain	5:48.98	2001	Romania	5:27.48
2002	Great Britain	6:06.70	2002	Germany	5:41.35	2002	Canada	5:26.92
2003	United States	6:04.68	2003	Canada	5:52.91	2003	Canada	6:00.44
2004	Italy	6:11.53	2004	Great Britain	6:06.98	2004	United States	5:42.48

[1]Olympic champions, recognized as world champions.

World Rowing Championships—Women

The competition has been held since 1974. The table shows only the past 20 years. Results are for heavyweight events only. Times are given in minutes:seconds.

YEAR	SINGLE SCULLS	TIME	DOUBLE SCULLS	TIME
1986	Jutta Behrendt-Hampe (GDR)	7:29.60	Sylvia Schwabe, Martina Schröter (GDR)	6:57.71
1987	Magdalena Georgieva (BUL)	8:59.26	Stefka Madina, Violeta Ninova (BUL)	7:47.89
1988[1]	Jutta Behrendt-Hampe (GDR)	7:47.19	Birgit Peter, Martina Schröter (GDR)	7:00.48
1989	Elisabeth Lipa (ROM)	7:27.96	Jana Sorges, Beate Schramm (GDR)	7:01.71
1990	Birgit Peter (GDR)	7:24.10	Kathrin Boron, Beate Schramm (GDR)	8:18.63
1991	Silken Laumann (CAN)	8:17.58	Kathrin Boron, Beate Schramm (GER)	6:44.71
1992[1]	Elisabeth Lipa (ROM)	7:25.54	Kathrin Boron, Kerstin Köppen (GER)	6:49.00
1993	Jana Thieme (GER)	7:26.00	Philippa Baker, Brenda Lawson (NZL)	7:03.42
1994	Trine Hansen (DEN)	7:23.96	Philippa Baker, Brenda Lawson (NZL)	6:45.30
1995	Maria Brandin (SWE)	7:26.00	Marnie McBean, Kathleen Heddle (CAN)	6:55.76
1996	Yekaterina Khodotovich (BLR)	7:32.21	Marnie McBean, Kathleen Heddle (CAN)	6:56.84
1997	Yekaterina Khodotovich (BLR)	7:29.30	Meike Evers, Kathrin Boron (GER)	6:51.07
1998	Irina Fedotova (RUS)	7:25.09	Miriam Batten, Gillian Lindsay (GBR)	6:48.85
1999	Yekaterina Khodotovich-Karsten (BLR)	7:11.68	Jana Thieme, Kathrin Boron (GER)	6:41.98
2000	Yekaterina Khodotovich-Karsten (BLR)	7:28.14	Jana Thieme, Kathrin Boron (GER)	6:55.44
2001	Katrin Rutschow-Stomporowski (GER)	7:19.25	Kathrin Boron, Kerstin Kowalski (GER)	6:50.20
2002	Rumyana Neykova (BUL)	7:07.71	Georgina Evers-Swindell, Caroline Evers-Swindell (NZL)	6:38.78
2003	Rumyana Neykova (BUL)	7:18.12	Georgina Evers-Swindell, Caroline Evers-Swindell (NZL)	6:45.79
2004[1]	Katrin Rutschow-Stomporowski (GER)	7:18.12	Georgina Evers-Swindell, Caroline Evers-Swindell (NZL)	7:01.79

World Rowing Championships—Women (continued)

YEAR	QUADRUPLE SCULLS	TIME		YEAR	QUADRUPLE SCULLS	TIME
1986	East Germany	6:13.91		1996	Germany	6:27.44
1987	East Germany	6:58.42		1997	Germany	6:16.15
1988[1]	East Germany	6:21.06		1998	Germany	6:24.38
1989	East Germany	6:16.62		1999	Germany	7:06.53
1990	East Germany	6:14.08		2000	Germany	6:19.58
1991	Germany	6:55.85		2001	Germany	6:12.95
1992[1]	Germany	6:20.18		2002	Germany	6:15.66
1993	China	6:21.07		2003	Australia	6:46.52
1994	Germany	6:11,73		2004[1]	Germany	6:29.29
1995	Germany	6:40.80				

YEAR	COXLESS PAIRS	TIME		YEAR	COXLESS PAIRS	TIME
1986	Rodica Arba, Olga Homeghi (ROM)	7:12.2		1996	Megan Still, Kate Slatter (AUS)	7:01.4
1987	Rodica Arba, Olga Homeghi (ROM)	8:00.7		1997	Emma Robinson, Alison Korn (CAN)	7:08.1
1988[1]	Rodica Arba, Olga Homeghi (ROM)	7:28.1		1998	Emma Robinson, Alison Korn (CAN)	7:05.2
1989	K. Haaker, Judith Zeidler (GDR)	7:27.0		1999	Emma Robinson, Theresa Luke (CAN)	7:00.9
1990	Stefani Werremeier, Ingeburg Althoff (FRG)	8:28.4		2000	Georgeta Damian, Doina Ignat (ROM)	7:11.0
1991	Marnie McBean, Kathleen Heddle (CAN)	6:57.4		2001	Georgeta Damian, Viorica Susanu (ROM)	7:01.2
1992[1]	Marnie McBean, K. Heddle (CAN)	7:06.2		2002	Georgeta Andrunache, Viorica Susanu (ROM)	6:53.8
1993	Christine Gosse, Helene Cortin (FRA)	7:24.7		2003	Catherine Bishop, Katherine Grainger (GBR)	7:04.88
1994	Christine Gosse, Helene Cortin (FRA)	7:01.8		2004[1]	Georgeta Andrunache-Damian, Viorica Susanu (ROM)	7:06.55
1995	Megan Still, Kate Slatter (AUS)	7:12.7				

YEAR	FOURS[2]	TIME		YEAR	FOURS[2]	TIME		YEAR	EIGHTS	TIME
1986	Romania	6:43.86		2001	Australia	6:27.23		1994	Germany	6:07.42
1987	Romania	7:30.12		2002	Australia	6:26.11		1995	United States	6:50.73
1988[1]	East Germany	6:56.00		2003	United States	6:53.08		1996[1]	Romania	6:19.73
1989	East Germany	6:45.81		2004	France	6:36.28		1997	Romania	6:02.40
1990	Romania	7:51.68						1998	Romania	6:14.62
1991	Canada	6:25.43		YEAR	EIGHTS	TIME		1999	Romania	6:47.66
1992[1]	Canada	6:30.85		1986	USSR	6:08.76		2000[1]	Romania	6:44.00
1993	China	6:42.06		1987	Romania	6:55.61		2001	Australia	6:03.66
1994	Netherlands	6:30.76		1988[1]	East Germany	6:15.17		2002	United States	6:04.25
1995	United States	7:03.53		1989	Romania	6:07.92		2003	Germany	6:41.23
1996	United States	6:49.48		1990	Romania	5:59.26		2004[1]	Romania	6:17.70
1997	Great Britain	6:40.30		1991	Canada	6:28.20				
1998	Ukraine	6:30.63		1992[1]	Canada	6:02.62				
1999	Belarus	6:26.25		1993	Romania	6:18.88				
2000	Belarus	6:44.90								

[1]Olympic champions, recognized as world champions.   [2]With coxswain until 1989; coxless since then.

Grand Challenge Cup

Cup has been contested since 1839. Table shows results for the past 20 years. Winners are British except as indicated. Times are given in minutes:seconds.

YEAR	WINNER	TIME		YEAR	WINNER	TIME
1986	Nautilus R.C.[1]	6:18		1997	Institutes of Sport (AUS)	6:03
1987	Soviet Army (URS)	6:11		1998	Hansa Dortmund and Berlin (GER)	6:18
1988	Leander-University of London	6:17		1999	Hansa Dortmund and Berlin (GER)	6:15
1989	Hansa Dortmund (FRG)	5:58		2000	Institutes of Sport (AUS)	6:19
1990	Hansa Dortmund (FRG)	6:36		2001	H.A.V.K. Mladost and V.K. Croatia (CRO)	6:29
1991	Leander and Star R.C.[1]	6:22		2002	Victoria City R.C.[1] and University of Victoria (CAN)	6:20
1992	University of London	6:04				
1993	Dortmund (GER)	6:11		2003	Victoria City R.C.[1] (CAN)	6:12
1994	Charles River and San Diego (USA)	6:13		2004	Hollandia Roeiclub (NED)	6:17
1995	San Diego Training Center (USA)	5:59		2005	Dortmund Rowing Center (GER)	6:19
1996	Imperial College & Queens Tower	6:11		2006	to be held in July	

[1]R.C.—Rowing Club.

The Diamond Challenge Sculls

The race has been rowed since 1844. The table shows the winners for the past 20 years. Winners are British except as indicated. Times are given in minutes:seconds.

YEAR	WINNER (CLUB, COUNTRY)	TIME	YEAR	WINNER (CLUB, COUNTRY)	TIME
1986	B. Eltang (DEN)	8:08[1]	1996	Merlin Vervoorn (Delft, NED)	7:42
1987	Peter-Michael Kolbe (Ruder-Club Hamburg, FRG)	7:52	1997	Greg Searle (Molesey Boating Club)	7:38
			1998	James Koven (USA)	7:56
1988	Hamish McGlashan (Melbourne University, AUS)	7:43	1999	Marcel Hacker (GER)	7:59
			2000	Aquil Abdullah (Princeton T.C.,[3] USA)	8:12
1989	Vaclav Chalupa (Dukla Praha, TCH)	7:23[2]	2001	Duncan Free (AUS)	8:18
1990	Eric Verdonk (Koru, NZL)	8:21	2002	P.J.C. Wells (Univ. of London)	8:30
1991	W. Van Belleghem (BEL)	8:14[1]	2003	Alan Campbell (The Tideway Scullers' School)	8:03
1992	R.G.F. Henderson (Leander Club)	7:44			
1993	Tomas Lange (GER)	7:39	2004	Marcel Hacker (Casseler Frauen, GER)	7:44
1994	Xeno Müller (Grasshopper, SUI)	7:35			
1995	Juri Jaanson (Parnu, EST)	7:24	2005	Wyatt Allen (Princeton T.C.,[3] USA)	8:23
			2006	*to be held in July*	

[1]*Not rowed out.*   [2]*Record.*   [3]*Training Center.*

Sailing (Yachting)

One of the classic sailing events is the race that was first proposed by the Royal Yacht Squadron (RYS), best known as the **America's Cup**. This cup, open to challenge since 1870, was originally the Hundred-Guinea Cup, presented by the RYS for a race around the Isle of Wight, UK, and won handily by the American yacht *America*. The most graceful of the yachts entered for the America's Cup are generally considered to have been the J-class yachts raced between 1930 and 1937. The cost of maintenance, however, was prohibitive, and since 1958, both winning and challenging vessels have been 12-m (39-ft).

The **Transpacific Race** was inaugurated in 1906 and usually was raced over 3,580 km (2,225 mi) between San Pedro CA, and Diamond Head Light, Oahu, HI. It was made biennial in 1939, alternating with the Bermuda Race.

The **Bermuda Race**, from 1906 to 1910, was an annual race between Gravesend Bay NY (in 1908 the starting point was Marblehead MA), and Bermuda. Six races from New London CT, and one from Montauk Point NY (1932), were held in 1923–34. Since 1936 it has been raced biennially from Newport RI over a 1,022-km (635-mi) course. In 1982 it was divided into two classes—one for cruiser/racers and one for grand prix racers—with the craft winning its race by the greatest margin as overall winner. Since 1986 two equal awards have been offered.

The **Admiral's Cup** is awarded biennially to the national team accumulating the most total points in a series of six races (five until 1987) held off the southern coast of England.

Related Internet resources: America's Cup: <www.americascup.com>; Transpacific Race: <www.transpacificyc.org>; Newport Bermuda Race: <www.bermudarace.com>; Admiral's Cup (Royal Ocean Racing Club Web site): <www.rorc.org>.

World-Class Boat Champions, 2004

CLASS	WINNER	CLASS	WINNER
Europe	Siren Sundby (NOR)	Mistral (men)	Julien Bontemps (FRA)
Finn	Ben Ainslie (GBR)	Mistral (women)	Alessandra Sensini (ITA)
470 (men)	Nathan Wilmot/Malcolm Page (AUS)	Star	Fredrik Loof/Anders Ekstrom (SWE)
470 (women)	Therese Torgersson/Vendela Zachrisson (SWE)	Tornado	Santiago Lange/Carlos Espínola (ARG)
49er	Iker Martinez/Xavier Fernandez (ESP)	Yngling	Shirley Robertson/Sarah Webb/Sarah Ayton (GBR)
Laser	Robert Scheidt (BRA)		

America's Cup

YEAR	WINNING YACHT	OWNER	SKIPPER	LOSING YACHT	OWNER
1851	*America* (USA)	John Cox Stevens	Richard Brown	*Aurora* (GBR)	Thomas Le Marchant
1870	*Magic* (USA)	Franklin Osgood	Andrew Comstock	*Cambria* (GBR)	James Ashbury
1871	*Columbia* (USA)	Franklin Osgood	Nelson Comstock	*Livonia* (GBR)	James Ashbury
	Sappho (USA)	William P. Douglas	Sam Greenwood		
1876	*Madeleine* (USA)	John S. Dickerson	Josephus Williams	*Countess of Dufferin* (CAN)	Charles Gifford and syndicate
1881	*Mischief* (USA)	Joseph R. Busk	Nathaniel Clock	*Atalanta* (CAN)	Alexander Cuthbert
1885	*Puritan* (USA)	J. Malcolm Forbes, Charles J. Paine and syndicate	Aubrey Crocker	*Genesta* (GBR)	Sir Richard Sutton

America's Cup (continued)

YEAR	WINNING YACHT	OWNER	SKIPPER	LOSING YACHT	OWNER
1886	Mayflower (USA)	Charles J. Paine	Martin V.B. Stone	Galatea (GBR)	William Henn
1887	Volunteer (USA)	Charles J. Paine	Henry C. Haff	Thistle (GBR)	James Bell and syndicate
1893	Vigilant (USA)	C. Oliver Iselin and syndicate	William Hansen	Valkyrie II (GBR)	Lord Dunraven
1895	Defender (USA)	William K. Vanderbilt, C. Oliver Iselin, Edwin D. Morgan	Henry C. Haff	Valkyrie III (GBR)	Lord Dunraven, Lord Lonsdale, Lord Wolverton, H. McCalmont
1899	Columbia (USA)	J.P. Morgan, C. Oliver Iselin, Edwin D. Morgan	Charles Barr	Shamrock (GBR)	Sir Thomas Lipton
1901	Columbia (USA)	J.P. Morgan, Edwin D. Morgan	Charles Barr	Shamrock II (GBR)	Sir Thomas Lipton
1903	Reliance (USA)	C. Oliver Iselin and syndicate	Charles Barr	Shamrock III (GBR)	Sir Thomas Lipton
1920	Resolute (USA)	Henry Walters and syndicate	Charles Francis Adams II	Shamrock IV (GBR)	Sir Thomas Lipton
1930	Enterprise (USA)	Winthrop Aldrich and syndicate	Harold S. Vanderbilt	Shamrock V (GBR)	Sir Thomas Lipton
1934	Rainbow (USA)	Harold S. Vanderbilt and syndicate	Harold S. Vanderbilt	Endeavour (GBR)	Thomas Octave Murdoch Sopwith
1937	Ranger (USA)	Harold S. Vanderbilt	Harold S. Vanderbilt	Endeavour II (GBR)	Thomas Octave Murdoch Sopwith
1958	Columbia (USA)	Henry Sears and syndicate	Briggs S. Cunningham	Sceptre (GBR)	Hugh L. Goodson and syndicate
1962	Weatherly (USA)	Henry D. Mercer, Arnold D. Frese, Cornelius S. Walsh	Emil Mosbacher, Jr.	Gretel (AUS)	Sir Frank Packer and syndicate
1964	Constellation (USA)	Walter S. Gubelmann, Eric Ridder and syndicate	Robert N. Bavier, Jr., Eric Ridder	Sovereign (GBR)	J. Anthony Boyden
1967	Intrepid (USA)	Intrepid syndicate	Emil Mosbacher, Jr.	Dame Pattie (GBR)	Emil Christensen and 15 commercial firms
1970	Intrepid (USA)	Intrepid syndicate	William Ficker	Gretel II (AUS)	Sir Frank Packer and syndicate
1974	Courageous (USA)	Courageous syndicate	Ted Hood	Southern Cross (AUS)	Alan Bond
1977	Courageous (USA)	Courageous syndicate	Ted Turner	Australia (AUS)	Alan Bond and syndicate
1980	Freedom (USA)	Maritime College at Ft. Schuyler Foundation, Inc.	Dennis Conner	Australia (AUS)	Alan Bond and syndicate
1983	Australia II (AUS)	Alan Bond and syndicate	John Bertrand	Liberty (USA)	Maritime Col. at Ft. Schuyler Foundation, Inc.
1987	Stars & Stripes (USA)	Sail America syndicate	Dennis Conner	Kookaburra III (AUS)	Kevin Parry and syndicate
1988	Stars & Stripes (USA)	Sail America syndicate	Dennis Conner	New Zealand (NZL)	Michael Fay
1992	America[3] (USA)	America[3] Foundation	William Koch	Il Moro di Venezia (ITA)	Compagnia della Vela di Venezia
1995	Black Magic (NZL)	Peter Blake and Team New Zealand	Russell Coutts	Young America (USA)	Pact 95 syndicate
2000	Black Magic (NZL)	Team New Zealand	Russell Coutts	Luna Rossa (ITA)	Prada Challenge
2003	Alinghi (SUI)	Alinghi Swiss Challenge	Russell Coutts	New Zealand (NZL)	Team New Zealand

Transpacific Race

YEAR	WINNING YACHT	OWNER	YEAR	WINNING YACHT	OWNER
1906	Lurline	Harold H. Sinclair	1963	Islander	Earl Corkett
1908	Lurline	Harold H. Sinclair	1965	Psyche	Don Salisbury
1910	Hawaii	Honolulu Yachting Club	1967	Holiday Too	Robert Allan
1912	Lurline	A.E. Davis	1969	Argonaut	Jon Andron
1923	Diablo	A.R. Pedder	1971	Windward Passage	Robert Johnson
1925	Mariner	L.A. Norris	1973	Chutzpah	Stuart Cowan
1926	Invader	Don M. Lee	1975	Chutzpah	Stuart Cowan
1928	Teva	Clem W. Stose	1977	Merlin	Bill Lee
1930	Enchantress	Morgan Adams	1979	Arriba	Dennis Choate
1932	Fayth	William S. McNutt	1981	Sweet Okole	Dean Treadway
1934	Manulwa	Harold Dillingham	1983	Bravura	Irving Loube
1936	Dorade	James Flood	1985	Montgomery Street	James Denning
1939	Blitzen	T.J. Reynolds	1987	Merlin	Don Campion
1941	Escapade	D.W. Elliott	1989	Silver Bullet	John DeLaura
1943–45	not held		1991	Chance	Robert McNulty
1947	Dolphin	Frank Morgan	1993	Silver Bullet	John DeLaura
1949	Kitten	Fred W. Lyon	1995	Merlin	Dan Sinclair
1951	Sea Witch	A.L. McCormick	1997	Ralphie	Jerry Montgomery
1953	Staghound	Ira P. Fulmor	1999	Grand Illusion	James McDowell
1955	Staghound	Ira P. Fulmor	2001	Bull	Seth Radow
1957	Legend	Charles Ullman	2003	Alta Vita	Bill Turpin
1959	Nalu II	Peter Grant	2005	Rosebud	Roger Sturgeon
1961	Nam Sang	A.B. Robbs, Jr.	2007	to be held in July, Los Angeles to Hawaii	

Bermuda Race[1]

YEAR	WINNING YACHT	OWNER	YEAR	WINNING YACHT	OWNER
1906	Tamerlane	Frank Maier	1964	Burgoo	Milton Ernstof
1907	Dervish	Henry A. Morss	1966	Thunderbird	T.V. Learson
1908	Venona	Elmer J. Bliss	1968	Robin	Ted Hood
1909	Margaret	George S. Runk	1970	Carina	Richard S. Nye
1910	Vagrant	Harold S. Vanderbilt	1972	Noryema	Ron Amey
1923[2]	Malabar IV	John G. Alden	1974	Scaramouche	Charles Kirsch
1924	Memory	Robert N. Bavier	1976	Running Tide	Al Van Metre
1926	Malabar VII	John G. Alden	1978	Babe	Arnie Gay
1928	Rugosa II	Russell Grinnell	1980	Holger Danske	Rich Wilson
1930	Malay	Raymond W. Ferris	1982[3]	Brigadoon III	Robert Morton
1932	Malabar X	John G. Alden and R.I. Gale	1984	Pamir	Francis H. Curren, Jr.
1934	Edlu	Rudolph J. Schaefer	1986[4]	Silver Star	David H. Clarke
1936	Kirawan	Robert P. Baruch		Puritan	Donald P. Robinson
1938	Baruna	Henry C. Taylor	1988	Congere	Bevin Koeppel
1946[2]	Gesture	Howard Fuller	1990	Denali	Lawrence S. Huntington
1948	Baruna	Henry C. Taylor	1992	Constellation	US Naval Academy
1950	Argyll	William T. Moore	1994	Gaylark	Kaighn Smith
1952	Carina	Richard S. Nye	1996	Boomerang	George Coumantaros
1954	Malay	D.D. Strohmeier	1998	Kodiak	Llwyd Ecclestone
1956	Finisterre	Carleton Mitchell	2000	Restless	Eric Crawford
1958	Finisterre	Carleton Mitchell	2002	Zaraffa	Huntington Sheldon, M.D.
1960	Finisterre	Carleton Mitchell	2004	Alliance	Dominick Porco
1962	Nina	DeCoursey Fales			

[1]St. David's Lighthouse Trophy winner from 2002.   [2]No competition 1911–22; 1940–44.   [3]Overall winner under new measurement rules.   [4]First listed is IOR (International Offshore Rule) winner; second is IMS (International Measurement System) winner.

Admiral's Cup

YEAR	WINNING TEAM	YEAR	WINNING TEAM	YEAR	WINNING TEAM	YEAR	WINNING TEAM
1957	United Kingdom	1971	United Kingdom	1985	West Germany	1999	The Netherlands
1959	United Kingdom	1973	West Germany	1987	New Zealand	2001	canceled
1961	United States	1975	United Kingdom	1989	United Kingdom	2003	Australia
1963	United Kingdom	1977	United Kingdom	1991	France	2005	canceled
1965	United Kingdom	1979	Australia	1993	Germany		
1967	Australia	1981	United Kingdom	1995	Italy		
1969	United States	1983	West Germany	1997	United States		

Skiing

Although most of the events had been contested at the regional level since the mid-19th century, the first internationally organized **skiing championships** did not take place until 1924. From 1924 to 1931 only **Nordic** competition was involved; **Alpine** championship events were added to world competition in 1931 and to the Olympics in 1936. Except in Olympic years, the Nordic and Alpine championships are held separately and at different locations. **Events** include cross-country races, ski jumping, biathlon, and relay races (Nordic) and downhill and slalom skiing (Alpine). Since 1967, an **Alpine World Cup** has been presented to the competitor with the best combined downhill, slalom, supergiant slalom (super-G), and giant slalom performance over a series of major contests. A **Nordic World Cup** for cross-country events has been awarded since 1979.

International Ski Federation Web site:
<www.fis-ski.com>.

Alpine Skiing World Championships—Men

The next championships are scheduled to be held in 2006 in Turin, Italy.

DOWNHILL

1931	Walter Prager (SUI)
1932	not held
1933	Walter Prager (SUI), Hans Hauser (AUT)[1]
1934	David Zogg (SUI)
1935	Franz Zingerle (AUT)
1936[2]	not held
1937	Emile Allais (FRA)
1938	James Couttet (FRA)
1939	Hermuth Lantschner (GER)
1940–47	not held
1948[2]	Henri Oreiller (FRA)
1950	Zeno Colo (ITA)
1952[2]	Zeno Colo (ITA)
1954	Christian Pravda (AUT)
1956[2]	Anton (Toni) Sailer (AUT)
1958	Anton (Toni) Sailer (AUT)
1960[2]	Jean Vuarnet (FRA)
1962	Karl Schranz (AUT)
1964[2]	Egon Zimmermann (AUT)
1966	Jean-Claude Killy (FRA)
1968[2]	Jean-Claude Killy (FRA)
1970	Bernhard Russi (SUI)
1972[2]	Bernhard Russi (SUI)
1974	David Zwilling (AUT)
1976[2]	Franz Klammer (AUT)
1978	Josef Walcher (AUT)
1980[2]	Leonhard Stock (AUT)
1982	Harti Weirather (AUT)
1984[2]	Bill Johnson (USA)
1985	Permin Zurbriggen (SUI)
1987	Peter Müller (SUI)
1988[2]	Permin Zurbriggen (SUI)
1989	Hansjorg Tauscher (FRG)
1991	Franz Heinzer (SUI)
1992[2]	Patrick Ortlieb (AUS)
1993	Urs Lehmann (SUI)
1994[2]	Tommy Moe (USA)
1995	not held
1996	Patrick Ortlieb (AUS)
1997	Bruno Kernen (SUI)
1998[2]	Jean-Luc Cretier (FRA)
1999	Hermann Maier (AUT)
2000	not held
2001	Hannes Trinkl (AUT)
2002[2]	Fritz Strobl (AUT)
2003	Michael Walchhofer (AUT)
2005	Bode Miller (USA)

COMBINED

1933	Anton Seelos (AUT)
1934	David Zogg (SUI)

COMBINED (CONTINUED)

1935	Anton Seelos (AUT)
1936[2]	Franz Pfnür (GER)
1937	Emile Allais (FRA)
1938	Emile Allais (FRA)
1939	Josef Jennewein (GER)
1940–47	not held
1948[2]	Henri Oreiller (FRA)
1950	not held
1952[2]	not held
1954	Stein Eriksen (NOR)
1956[2]	not held
1958	Anton (Toni) Sailer (AUT)
1960[2]	not held
1962	Karl Schranz (AUT)
1964[2]	not held
1966	Jean-Claude Killy (FRA)
1968[2]	not held
1970	Bill Kidd (USA)
1972[2]	Gustavo Thoeni (ITA)
1974	Franz Klammer (AUT)
1976[2]	Gustavo Thoeni (ITA)
1978	Andreas Wenzel (LIE)
1980[2]	not held
1982	Michel Vion (FRA)
1984[2]	not held
1985	Pirmin Zurbriggen (SUI)
1986	not held
1987	Marc Girardelli (LUX)
1988[2]	Hubert Strolz (AUT)
1989	Marc Girardelli (LUX)
1991	Stefan Eberharter (AUT)
1992[2]	Josef Polig (ITA)
1993	Lasse Kjus (NOR)
1994[2]	Lasse Kjus (NOR)
1995	not held
1996	Marc Girardelli (LUX)
1997	Kjetil Andre Aamodt (NOR)
1998[2]	Mario Reiter (AUT)
1999	Kjetil Andre Aamodt (NOR)
2000	not held
2001	Kjetil Andre Aamodt (NOR)
2002[2]	Kjetil Andre Aamodt (NOR)
2003	Bode Miller (USA)
2005	Benjamin Raich (AUT)

SLALOM

1931	David Zogg (SUI)
1932	not held
1933	Anton Seelos (AUT)
1934	Franz Pfnür (GER)
1935	Anton Seelos (AUT)
1936[2]	not held
1937	Emile Allais (FRA)

SLALOM (CONTINUED)

1938	Rudi Rominger (SUI)
1939	Rudi Rominger (SUI)
1940–47	not held
1948[2]	Edi Reinalter (SUI)
1950	Georges Schneider (SUI)
1952[2]	Othmar Schneider (AUT)
1954	Stein Eriksen (NOR)
1956[2]	Anton (Toni) Sailer (AUT)
1958	Josi Rieder (AUT)
1960[2]	Ernst Hinterseer (AUT)
1962	Charles Bozon (FRA)[3]
1964[2]	Josef Stiegler (AUT)
1966	Carlo Senoner (ITA)[3]
1968[2]	Jean-Claude Killy (FRA)
1970	Jean-Noël Augert (FRA)
1972[2]	Francisco Ochoa (ESP)
1974	Gustavo Thoeni (ITA)
1976[2]	Piero Gros (ITA)
1978	Ingemar Stenmark (SWE)
1980[2]	Ingemar Stenmark (SWE)
1982	Ingemar Stenmark (SWE)
1984[2]	Phil Mahre (USA)
1985	Jonas Nilsson (SWE)
1987	Frank Woerndl (FRG)
1988[2]	Alberto Tomba (ITA)
1989	Rudolf Nierlich (AUT)
1991	Marc Girardelli (LUX)
1992[2]	Finn Christian Jagge (NOR)
1993	Kjetil Andre Aamodt (NOR)
1994[2]	Thomas Stangassinger (AUT)
1995	not held
1996	Alberto Tomba (ITA)
1997	Tom Stiansen (NOR)
1998[2]	Hans-Petter Buraas (NOR)
1999	Kalle Palander (FIN)
2000	not held
2001	Mario Matt (AUT)
2002[2]	Jean-Pierre Vidal (FRA)
2003	Ivica Kostelic (CRO)
2005	Benjamin Raich (AUT)

GIANT SLALOM

1950	Zeno Colo (ITA)
1952[2]	Stein Eriksen (NOR)
1954	Stein Eriksen (NOR)
1956[2]	Anton (Toni) Sailer (AUT)
1958	Anton (Toni) Sailer (AUT)
1960[2]	Roger Staub (SUI)
1962	Egon Zimmermann (AUT)
1964[2]	François Bonlieu (FRA)

Alpine Skiing World Championships—Men (continued)

GIANT SLALOM (CONTINUED)

1966	Guy Perillat (FRA)
1968[2]	Jean-Claude Killy (FRA)
1970	Karl Schranz (AUT)
1972[2]	Gustavo Thoeni (ITA)
1974	Gustavo Thoeni (ITA)
1976[2]	Heini Hemmi (SUI)
1978	Ingemar Stenmark (SWE)
1980[2]	Ingemar Stenmark (SWE)
1982	Steve Mahre (USA)
1984[2]	Max Julen (SUI)
1985	Markus Wasmeier (FRG)
1987	Pirmin Zurbriggen (SUI)
1988[2]	Alberto Tomba (ITA)
1989	Rudolf Nierlich (AUT)
1991	Rudolf Nierlich (AUT)
1992[2]	Alberto Tomba (ITA)
1993	Kjetil Andre Aamodt (NOR)

GIANT SLALOM (CONTINUED)

1994[2]	Markus Wasmeier (GER)
1995	not held
1996	Alberto Tomba (ITA)
1997	Michael von Grünigen (SUI)
1998[2]	Hermann Maier (AUT)
1999	Lasse Kjus (NOR)
2000	not held
2001	Michael von Grünigen (SUI)
2002[2]	Stephan Eberharter (AUT)
2003	Bode Miller (USA)
2005	Hermann Maier (AUT)

SUPERGIANT SLALOM

1987	Pirmin Zurbriggen (SUI)
1988[2]	Franck Piccard (FRA)

SUPERGIANT SLALOM (CONTINUED)

1989	Martin Hangl (SUI)
1991	Stephan Eberharter (AUT)
1992[2]	Kjetil Andre Aamodt (NOR)
1993	not held
1994[2]	Markus Wasmeier (GER)
1995	not held
1996	Atle Skaardal (NOR)
1997	Atle Skaardal (NOR)
1998[2]	Hermann Maier (AUT)
1999	Lasse Kjus (NOR), Hermann Maier (AUT)[4]
2000	not held
2001	Daron Rahlves (USA)
2002[2]	Kjetil Andre Aamodt (NOR)
2003	Stephan Eberharter (AUT)
2005	Bode Miller (USA)

[1]Special downhill champion. [2]Olympic champions, recognized as world champions. [3]Special slalom. [4]Tie.

Alpine Skiing World Championships—Women

The next championships are scheduled to be held in 2006 in Turin, Italy.

DOWNHILL

1931	Esme Mackinnon (GBR)
1932	Paula Wiesinger (ITA)
1933	Inge Wersin-Lantschner (AUT)
1934	Anny Rüegg (SUI)
1935	Christl Cranz (GER)
1936	Evelyn Pinching (GBR)
1937	Christl Cranz (GER)
1938	Lisa Resch (GER)
1939	Christl Cranz (GER)
1940–47	not held
1948[1]	Hedy Schlunegger (SUI)
1950	Trude Jochum-Beiser (AUT)
1952[1]	Trude Jochum-Beiser (AUT)
1954	Ida Schöpfer (SUI)
1956[1]	Madeleine Berthod (SUI)
1958	Lucille Wheeler (CAN)
1960[1]	Heidi Beibl (GER[2])
1962	Christl Hass (AUT)
1964[1]	Christl Hass (AUT)
1966	Marielle Goitschel (FRA)[3]
1968[1]	Olga Pall (AUT)
1970	Annerösli Zryd (SUI)
1972[1]	Marie-Thérèse Nadig (SUI)
1974	Annemarie Moser-Pröll (AUT)
1976[1]	Rosi Mittermaier (FRG)
1978	Annemarie Moser-Pröll (AUT)
1980[1]	Annemarie Moser-Pröll (AUT)
1982	Gerry Sorensen (CAN)
1984[1]	Michela Figini (SUI)
1985	Michela Figini (SUI)
1987	Maria Walliser (SUI)
1988[1]	Marina Kiehl (FRG)
1989	Maria Walliser (SUI)
1991	Petra Kronberger (AUT)
1992[1]	Kerrin Lee-Gartner (CAN)

DOWNHILL (CONTINUED)

1993	Kate Pace (CAN)
1994[1]	Katja Seizinger (GER)
1995	not held
1996	Picabo Street (USA)
1997	Hilary Lindh (USA)
1998[1]	Katja Seizinger (GER)
1999	Renate Götschl (AUT)
2000	not held
2001	Michaela Dorfmeister (AUT)
2002[1]	Carole Montillet (FRA)
2003	Mélanie Turgeon (CAN)
2005	Janica Kostelic (CRO)

COMBINED

1932	Rösli Streiff (SUI)
1933	Inge Wersin-Lantschner (AUT)
1934	Christl Cranz (GER)
1935	Christl Cranz (GER)
1936	Evelyn Pinching (GBR)
1937	Christl Cranz (GER)
1938	Christl Cranz (GER)
1939	Christl Cranz (GER)
1940–47	not held
1948[1]	Trude Beiser (AUT)
1950	not held
1952	not held
1954	Ida Schöpfer (SUI)
1956	Madeleine Berthod (SUI)
1958	Frida Dänzer (SUI)
1960	Anne Heggveit (CAN)
1962	Marielle Goitschel (FRA)
1964	Marielle Goitschel (FRA)
1966	Marielle Goitschel (FRA)
1968	Nancy Greene (CAN)
1970	Michèle Jacot (FRA)
1972	Toril Forland (NOR)
1974	Fabienne Serrat (FRA)
1976	Rosi Mittermaier (FRG)
1978	Annemarie Moser-Pröll (AUT)

COMBINED (CONTINUED)

1980	Hanni Wenzel (LIE)
1982	Erika Hess (SUI)
1984[1]	not held
1985	Erika Hess (SUI)
1987	Erika Hess (SUI)
1988[1]	Anita Wachter (AUT)
1989	Tamara McKinney (USA)
1991	Chantal Bournissen (SUI)
1992[1]	Petra Kronberger (AUT)
1993	Miriam Vogt (GER)
1994[1]	Pernilla Wiberg (SWE)
1995	not held
1996	Pernilla Wiberg (SWE)
1997	Renate Götschl (AUT)
1998[1]	Katja Seizinger (GER)
1999	Pernilla Wiberg (SWE)
2000	not held
2001	Martina Ertl (GER)
2002[1]	Janica Kostelic (CRO)
2003	Janica Kostelic (CRO)
2005	Janica Kostelic (CRO)

SLALOM

1931	Esme Mackinnon (GBR)
1932	Rösli Streiff (SUI)
1933	Inge Wersin-Lantschner (AUT)
1934	Christl Cranz (GER)
1935	Anny Rüegg (SUI)
1936	Gerda Paumgarten (AUT)
1937	Christl Cranz (GER)
1938	Christl Cranz (GER)
1939	Christl Cranz (GER)
1940–47	not held
1948[1]	Gretchen Fraser (USA)
1950	Dagmar Rom (AUT)
1952[1]	Andrea Mead Lawrence (USA)
1954	Trude Klecker (AUT)
1956[1]	Renée Colliard (SUI)
1958	Inge Björnbakken (NOR)
1960[1]	Anne Heggtveit (CAN)

Alpine Skiing World Championships—Women (continued)

SLALOM (CONTINUED)		GIANT SLALOM		GIANT SLALOM (CONTINUED)	
1962	Marianne Jahn (Austria)[4]	1950	Dagmar Rom (AUT)	1999	Alexandra Meissnitzer (AUT)
1964[1]	Christine Goitschel (FRA)	1952[1]	Andrea M. Lawrence (USA)	2000	not held
1966	Annie Famose (FRA)[3]	1954	Lucienne Schmidt-Couttet (FRA)	2001	Sonja Nef (SUI)
1968[1]	Marielle Goitschel (FRA)			2002[1]	Janica Kostelic (CRO)
1970	Ingrid Lafforgue (FRA)	1956[1]	Ossi Reichert (FRG)	2003	Anja Pärson (SWE)
1972[1]	Barbara Cochran (USA)	1958	Lucille Wheeler (CAN)	2005	Anja Pärson (SWE)
1974	Hanni Wenzel (LIE)	1960[1]	Yvonne Rüegg (SUI)		
1976[1]	Rosi Mittermaier (FRG)	1962	Marianne Jahn (AUT)	SUPERGIANT SLALOM	
1978	Lea Sölkner (AUT)	1964[1]	Marielle Goitschel (FRA)	1987	Maria Walliser (SUI)
1980[1]	Hanni Wenzel (LIE)	1966	Marielle Goitschel (FRA)	1988[1]	Sigrid Wolf (AUT)
1982	Erika Hess (SUI)	1968[1]	Nancy Greene (CAN)	1989	Ulrike Maier (AUT)
1984[1]	Paoletta Magoni (ITA)	1970	Betsy Clifford (CAN)	1991	Ulrike Maier (AUT)
1985	Perrine Pelen (FRA)	1972[1]	Marie-Therese Nadig (SUI)	1992[1]	Deborah Compagnoni (ITA)
1987	Erika Hess (SUI)	1974	Fabienne Serrat (FRA)		
1988[1]	Vreni Schneider (SUI)	1976[1]	Kathy Kreiner (CAN)	1993	Katja Seizinger (GER)
1989	Mateja Svet (YUG)	1978	Maria Epple (FRG)	1994[1]	Diann Roffe-Steinrotter (USA)
1991	Vreni Schneider (SUI)	1980[1]	Hanni Wenzel (LIE)		
1992[1]	Petra Kronberger (AUT)	1982	Erika Hess (SUI)	1995	not held
1993	Karin Buder (AUT)	1984[1]	Debbie Armstrong (USA)	1996	Isolde Kostner (ITA)
1994[1]	Vreni Schneider (SUI)	1985	Diann Roffe (USA)	1997	Isolde Kostner (ITA)
1995	not held	1987	Vreni Schneider (SUI)	1998[1]	Picabo Street (USA)
1996	Pernilla Wiberg (SWE)	1988[1]	Vreni Schneider (SUI)	1999	Alexandra Meissnitzer (AUT)
1997	Deborah Compagnoni (ITA)	1989	Vreni Schneider (SUI)		
1998[1]	Hilde Gerg (GER)	1991	Pernilla Wiberg (SWE)	2000	not held
1999	Zali Steggall (AUS)	1992[1]	Pernilla Wiberg (SWE)	2001	Régine Cavagnoud (FRA)
2000	not held	1993	Carole Merle (FRA)	2002[1]	Daniela Ceccarelli (ITA)
2001	Anja Paerson (SWE)	1994[1]	Deborah Compagnoni (ITA)	2003	Michaela Dorfmeister (AUT)
2002[1]	Janica Kostelic (CRO)	1995	not held		
2003	Janica Kostelic (CRO)	1996	Deborah Compagnoni (ITA)	2005	Anja Pärson (SWE)
2005	Janica Kostelic (CRO)	1997	Deborah Compagnoni (ITA)		
		1998[1]	Deborah Compagnoni (ITA)		

[1]Olympic champions, recognized as world champions.   [2]Joint East-West German team.   [3]Originally won by Erika Schinegger (AUT), who renounced the medal after a sex test performed for a later Olympic game determined she was actually a man.   [4]Special slalom.

Alpine World Cup

The winner is determined by the number of points awarded for various wins during the season.

YEAR	MEN	WOMEN	YEAR	MEN	WOMEN
1967	Jean-Claude Killy (FRA)	Nancy Greene (CAN)	1986	Marc Girardelli (LUX)	Maria Walliser (SUI)
1968	Jean-Claude Killy (FRA)	Nancy Greene (CAN)	1987	Pirmin Zurbriggen (SUI)	Maria Walliser (SUI)
1969	Karl Schranz (AUT)	Gertrude Gabl (AUT)	1988	Pirmin Zurbriggen (SUI)	Michela Figini (SUI)
1970	Karl Schranz (AUT)	Michele Jacot (FRA)	1989	Marc Girardelli (LUX)	Vreni Schneider (SUI)
1971	Gustavo Thoeni (ITA)	Annemarie Pröll (AUT)	1990	Pirmin Zurbriggen (SUI)	Petra Kronberger (AUT)
1972	Gustavo Thoeni (ITA)	Annemarie Pröll (AUT)			
1973	Gustavo Thoeni (ITA)	Annemarie Pröll (AUT)	1991	Marc Girardelli (LUX)	Petra Kronberger (AUT)
1974	Piero Gros (ITA)	Annemarie Moser-Pröll (AUT)			
			1992	Paul Accola (SUI)	Petra Kronberger (AUT)
1975	Gustavo Thoeni (ITA)	Annemarie Moser-Pröll (AUT)			
			1993	Marc Girardelli (LUX)	Anita Wachter (AUT)
1976	Ingemar Stenmark (SWE)	Rosi Mittermaier (FRG)	1994	Kjetil Andre Aamodt (NOR)	Vreni Schneider (SUI)
1977	Ingemar Stenmark (SWE)	Lise-Marie Morerod (SUI)	1995	Alberto Tomba (ITA)	Vreni Schneider (SUI)
1978	Ingemar Stenmark (SWE)	Hanni Wenzel (LIE)	1996	Lasse Kjus (NOR)	Katja Seizinger (GER)
1979	Peter Luescher (SUI)	Annemarie Moser-Pröll (AUT)	1997	Luc Alphand (FRA)	Pernilla Wiberg (SWE)
			1998	Hermann Maier (AUT)	Katja Seizinger (GER)
1980	Andreas Wenzel (LIE)	Hanni Wenzel (LIE)	1999	Lasse Kjus (NOR)	Alexandra Meissnitzer (AUT)
1981	Phil Mahre (USA)	Marie-Therese Nadig (SUI)			
			2000	Hermann Maier (AUT)	Renate Götschl (AUT)
1982	Phil Mahre (USA)	Erika Hess (SUI)	2001	Hermann Maier (AUT)	Janica Kostelic (CRO)
1983	Phil Mahre (USA)	Tamara McKinney (USA)	2002	Stephan Eberharter (AUT)	Michaela Dorfmeister (AUT)
1984	Pirmin Zurbriggen (SUI)	Erika Hess (SUI)	2003	Stephan Eberharter (AUT)	Janica Kostelic (CRO)
1985	Marc Girardelli (LUX)	Michela Figini (SUI)	2004	Hermann Maier (AUT)	Anja Pärson (SWE)
			2005	Bode Miller (USA)	Anja Pärson (SWE)

Nordic Skiing World Championships—Men

Championships in some events have been held since 1924. The table shows results for the past 20 years. The next championships are scheduled to be held in 2006 in Turin, Italy.

SPRINT

2001	Tor Arne Hetland (NOR)
2002[1]	Samppa Lajunen (FIN)
2003	Thobias Fredriksson (SWE)
2005	Vassily Rotchev (RUS)

10-KM CROSS-COUNTRY

1991	Terje Langli (NOR)
1992[1]	Vegard Ulvang (NOR)
1993	Sture Sivertsen (NOR)
1994[1]	Bjørn Daehlie (NOR)
1995	Vladimir Smirnov (KAZ)
1996	*not held*
1997	Bjørn Daehlie (NOR)
1998[1]	Bjørn Daehlie (NOR)
1999	Mika Myllyla (FIN)
2000	*not held*
2001[2]	Per Elofsson (SWE)
2002[1, 2]	Johann Mühlegg (ESP)
2003	*discontinued*

15-KM CROSS-COUNTRY[3]

1984[1]	Gunde Svan (SWE)
1985	Kari Härkönen (FIN)
1987	Marco Albarello (ITA)
1988[1]	Mikhail Devyatyarov (URS)
1989	Gunde Svan (SWE)
1991	Bjørn Daehlie (NOR)
1992[1]	Bjørn Daehlie (NOR)
1993	Bjørn Daehlie (NOR)
1994[1]	Bjørn Daehlie (NOR)
1995	Vladimir Smirnov (KAZ)
1996	*not held*
1997	Bjørn Daehlie (NOR)

15-KM CROSS-COUNTRY[3] (CONTINUED)

1998[1]	Thomas Alsgaard (NOR)
1999	Thomas Alsgaard (NOR)
2000	*not held*
2001[2]	Per Elofsson (SWE)
2002[1, 2]	Andrus Veerpalu (EST)
2003	Axel Teichmann (GER)
2005	Pietro Piller Cottrer (ITA)

30-KM CROSS-COUNTRY

1984[1]	Nikolay Zimyatov (URS)
1985	Gunde Svan (SWE)
1987	Thomas Wassberg (SWE)
1988[1]	Aleksey Prokurorov (URS)
1989	Vladimir Smirnov (URS)
1991	Gunde Svan (SWE)
1992[1]	Vegard Ulvang (NOR)
1993	Bjørn Daehlie (NOR)
1994[1]	Thomas Alsgaard (NOR)
1995	Vladimir Smirnov (KAZ)
1996	*not held*
1997	Aleksey Prokurorov (RUS)
1998[1]	Mika Myllyla (FIN)
1999	Mika Myllyla (FIN)
2000	*not held*
2001	Andrus Veerpalu (EST)
2002[1]	Johann Mühlegg (ESP)
2003	Thomas Alsgaard (NOR)
2005	*not held*

50-KM CROSS-COUNTRY

1984[1]	Thomas Wassberg (SWE)
1985	Gunde Svan (SWE)
1987	Maurilio DeZolt (ITA)
1988[1]	Gunde Svan (SWE)
1989	Gunde Svan (SWE)

50-KM CROSS-COUNTRY (CONTINUED)

1991	Torgny Mogren (SWE)
1992[1]	Bjørn Daehlie (NOR)
1993	Torgny Mogren (SWE)
1994	Vladimir Smirnov (KAZ)
1995	Silvio Fauner (ITA)
1996	*not held*
1997	Mika Myllyla (FIN)
1998[1]	Bjørn Daehlie (NOR)
1999	Mika Myllyla (FIN)
2000	*not held*
2001	Johann Mühlegg (ESP)
2002[1]	Mikhail Ivanov (RUS)
2003	Martin Koukal (CZE)
2005	Frode Estil (NOR)

RELAY[4]

1984[1]	Sweden
1985	Norway
1987	Sweden
1988[1]	Sweden
1989	Sweden
1991	Norway
1992[1]	Norway
1993	Norway
1994[1]	Italy
1995	Norway
1996	*not held*
1997	Norway
1998[1]	Norway
1999	Austria
2001	Norway
2002[1]	Norway
2003	Norway
2005	Norway

[1]*Olympic champions, recognized as world champions.* [2]*From 1991 to 2000, the 10-km event was held in tandem with the 15-km event; one event featured classical and the other freestyle technique. Medals were awarded for both races. Beginning in 2001 this pursuit race (skiers competing directly against each other rather than against the clock) led to one medal being awarded upon winning. In 2002 the pursuit race featured two 10-km races and the 15-km was a stand-alone event featuring classical technique.* [3]*18-km cross-country until 1952; 15-km in 1954 and thereafter.* [4]*Military relay until 1939; 40-km relay in 1948 and thereafter.*

Nordic Skiing World Championships—Nordic Combined

The Nordic combined involves a 15-km cross-country race and ski jumping; the sprint is a 7.5-km race plus ski jumping. The next championships are scheduled to be held in 2006 in Turin, Italy.

YEAR	COMBINED	YEAR	COMBINED (CONTINUED)	YEAR	COMBINED (CONTINUED)
1924[1]	Thorleif Haug (NOR)	1937	Sigurd Røen (NOR)	1972[1]	Ulrich Wehling (GDR)
1925	Ottokar Nemecky (TCH)	1938	Olaf Hoffsbakken (NOR)	1974	Ulrich Wehling (GDR)
1926	Johan Gröttumsbraaten (NOR)	1939	Gustl Berauer (TCH)	1976[1]	Ulrich Wehling (GDR)
1927	Rudolf Purkert (TCH)	1940–47	*not held*	1978	Konrad Winkler (GDR)
1928[1]	Johan Gröttumsbraaten (NOR)	1948[1]	Heikki Hasu (FIN)	1980[1]	Ulrich Wehling (GDR)
1929	Hans Vinjarengen (NOR)	1950	Heikki Hasu (FIN)	1982	Tom Sandberg (NOR)
1930	Hans Vinjarengen (NOR)	1952[1]	Simon Slåttvik (NOR)	1984[1]	Tom Sandberg (NOR)
1931	Johan Gröttumsbraaten (NOR)	1954	Sverre Stenersen (NOR)	1985	Herman Weinbach (FRG)
1932[1]	Johan Gröttumsbraaten (NOR)	1956[1]	Sverre Stenersen (NOR)	1987	Torbjøm Løkken (NOR)
1933	Sven Eriksson (SWE)	1958	Paavo Korhonen (FIN)	1988[1]	Hippolyt Kempf (SUI)
1934	Oddbjørn Hagen (NOR)	1960[1]	Georg Thoma (GER[2])	1989	Trond Einar Elden (NOR)
1935	Oddbjørn Hagen (NOR)	1962	Arne Larsen (NOR)	1991	Fred Børre Lundberg (NOR)
1936[1]	Oddbjørn Hagen (NOR)	1964[1]	Tormod Knutsen (NOR)	1992[1]	Fabrice Guy (FRA)
		1966	Georg Thoma (FRG)	1993	Kenji Ogiwara (JPN)
		1968[1]	Franz Keller (FRG)	1994[1]	Fred Børre Lundberg (NOR)
		1970	Ladislav Rygl (TCH)	1995	Fred Børre Lundberg (NOR)
				1996	*not held*

Nordic Skiing World Championships—Nordic Combined (continued)

YEAR	COMBINED (CONTINUED)	YEAR	TEAM	YEAR	TEAM (CONTINUED)
1997	Kenji Ogiwara (JPN)	1982	East Germany	1999	Finland
1998[1]	Bjarte Engen Vik (NOR)	1984[1]	Norway	2001	Norway
1999	Bjarte Engen Vik (NOR)	1985	West Germany	2002[1]	Finland
2001	Bjarte Engen Vik (NOR)	1987	West Germany	2003	Austria
2002[1]	Samppa Lajunen (FIN)	1988[1]	West Germany	2005	Norway
2003	Ronny Ackermann (GER)	1989	Norway		
2005	Ronny Ackermann (GER)	1991	Austria		
		1992[1]	Japan		
YEAR	SPRINT	1993	Japan		
1999	Bjarte Engen Vik (NOR)	1994[1]	Japan		
2001	Marco Baacke (GER)	1995	Japan		
2002[1]	Samppa Lajunen (FIN)	1996	*not held*		
2003	Johnny Spillane (USA)	1997	Norway		
2005	Ronny Ackermann (GER)	1998[1]	Norway		

[1]*Olympic champions, recognized as world champions.*   [2]*Combined East and West German team.*

Nordic Skiing World Championships—Ski Jump
The next championships are scheduled to be held in February 2006 in Turin, Italy.

YEAR	NORMAL HILL[1]	YEAR	NORMAL HILL[1] (CONTINUED)	YEAR	LARGE HILL[4] (CONTINUED)
1924[2]	Jacob Tullin-Thams (NOR)	1991	Heinz Kuttin (AUT)		
1925	Willen Dick (TCH)	1992[2]	Ernst Vettori (AUT)	2001	Martin Schmitt (GER)
1926	Jacob Tullin-Thams (NOR)	1993	Masahiko Harada (JPN)	2002[2]	Simon Ammann (SUI)
1927	Tore Edman (SWE)	1994[2]	Espen Bredesen (NOR)	2003	Adam Malysz (POL)
1928[2]	Alf Gunnar Andersen (NOR)	1995	Takanobu Okabe (JPN)	2005	Janne Ahonen
1929	Sigmund Ruud (NOR)	1996	*not held*		
1930	Gunnar Andersen (NOR)	1997	Janne Ahonen (FIN)	YEAR	TEAM JUMP (NORMAL
1931	Birger Ruud (NOR)	1998[2]	Jani Soininen (FIN)		HILL)
1932[2]	Birger Ruud (NOR)	1999	Kazuyoshi Funaki (JPN)	2001	Austria
1933	Marcel Reymond (SUI)	2001	Adam Malysz (POL)	2002[2]	*not held*
1934	Kristian Johansson (NOR)	2002[2]	Simon Ammann (SUI)	2003	*not held*
1935	Birger Ruud (NOR)	2003	Adam Malysz (POL)	2005	Austria
1936[2]	Birger Ruud (NOR)	2005	Rok Benkovic (SLO)		
1937	Birger Ruud (NOR)			YEAR	TEAM JUMP (LARGE HILL)
1938	Asbjørn Ruud (NOR)	YEAR	LARGE HILL[4]	1982	Norway
1939	Josef Bradl (AUS)	1962	Helmut Recknagel (GDR)	1984[2]	*not held*
1940–47	*not held*	1964[2]	Toralf Engan (NOR)	1985	Finland
1948[2]	Petter Hugsted (NOR)	1966	Bjørn Wirkola (NOR)	1987	Finland
1950	Hans Bjørnstad (NOR)	1968[2]	Vladimir Belousov (URS)	1988[2]	Finland
1952[2]	Arnfinn Bergmann (NOR)	1970	Gary Napalkov (URS)	1989	Finland
1954	Matti Pietikäinen (FIN)	1972[2]	Wojciech Fortuna (POL)	1991	Austria
1956[2]	Antti Hyvärinen (FIN)	1974	Hans-Georg Aschenbach	1992[2]	Finland
1958	Juhani Kärkinen (FIN)		(GDR)	1993	Norway
1960[2]	Helmut Recknagel (GER[3])	1976[2]	Karl Schnabl (AUT)	1994[2]	Germany
1962	Toralf Engan (NOR)	1978	Tapio Räisänen (FIN)	1995	Finland
1964[2]	Veikko Kankkonen (FIN)	1980[2]	Jouko Törmänen (FIN)	1996	*not held*
1966	Bjørn Wirkola (NOR)	1982	Matti Nykänen (FIN)	1997	Finland
1968[2]	Jiri Raška (TCH)	1984[2]	Matti Nykänen (FIN)	1998[2]	Japan
1970	Gary Napalkov (URS)	1985	Per Bergerud (NOR)	1999	Germany
1972[2]	Yukio Kasaya (JPN)	1987	Andreas Felder (AUT)	2001	Germany
1974	Hans-Georg Aschenbach	1988[2]	Matti Nykänen (FIN)	2002[2]	Germany
	(GDR)	1989	Jari Puikkonen (FIN)	2003	Finland
1976[2]	Hans-Georg Aschenbach	1991	Franci Petek (YUG)	2005	Austria
	(GDR)	1992[2]	Toni Nieminen (FIN)		
1978	Mathias Buse (GDR)	1993	Espen Bredesen (NOR)		
1980[2]	Toni Innauer (AUT)	1994[2]	Jens Weissflog (GER)		
1982	Armin Kogler (AUT)	1995	Tommy Ingebrigtsen		
1984[2]	Jens Weissflog (GDR)		(NOR)		
1985	Jens Weissflog (GDR)	1996	*not held*		
1987	Jiri Parma (TCH)	1997	Masahiko Harada (JPN)		
1988[2]	Matti Nykänen (FIN)	1998[2]	Kazuyoshi Funaki (JPN)		
1989	Jens Weissflog (GDR)	1999	Martin Schmitt (GER)		

[1]*The distance of the jump in the normal hill competition has varied over time; as of 1992 it was set at 90 meters.* [2]*Olympic champions, recognized as world champions.* [3]*Combined East and West German team.* [4]*The distance of the jump in the large hill competition has varied over time; it was set at 120 meters in 1992.*

Nordic Skiing World Championships—Women

Championships in some events have been held since 1952. The table shows results for the past 20 years. The next championships are scheduled to be held in 2007.

SPRINT

2001	Pirjo Manninen (FIN)
2002[1]	Yuliya Chepalova (RUS)
2003	Marit Bjørgen (NOR)
2005	Emilie Öhrstig (SWE)

5-KM CROSS-COUNTRY[2]

1984[1]	Marja-Liisa Hämäläinen (FIN)
1985	*not held*
1987	Marjo Matikainen (FIN)
1988[1]	Marjo Matikainen (FIN)
1989	*not held*
1991	Trude Dybendahl (NOR)
1992[1]	Marjut Lukkarinen (FIN)
1993	Larisa Lazutina (RUS)
1994[1]	Lyubov Yegorova (RUS)
1995	Larisa Lazutina (RUS)
1997	Yelena Vyalbe (RUS)
1998[1]	Larisa Lazutina (RUS)
1999	Bente Martinsen (NOR)
2001	Virpi Kuitunen (FIN)
2002[1]	Olga Danilova (RUS)
2003	*not held*
2005	*not held*

10-KM CROSS-COUNTRY[2]

1984[1]	Marja-Liisa Hämäläinen (FIN)
1985	Anette Böe (NOR)
1987	Anne Jahren (NOR)
1988[1]	Vida Ventsene (URS)
1989	Marja-Liisa Kirvesniemi (FIN–classical); Yelena Vyalbe (URS–freestyle)
1991	Yelena Vyalbe (URS)

10-KM CROSS-COUNTRY[2] (CONT.)

1992[1]	Lyubov Yegorova (UNT[3])
1993	Stefania Belmondo (ITA)
1994[1]	Lyubov Yegorova (RUS)
1995	Larisa Lazutina (RUS)
1997	Stefania Belmondo (ITA)
1998[1]	Larisa Lazutina (RUS)
1999	Stefania Belmondo (ITA)
2001	Bente Skari-Martinsen (NOR)
2002[1]	Bente Skari (NOR)
2003	Bente Skari (NOR)
2005	Katerina Neumannova (CZE)

15-KM CROSS-COUNTRY

1989	Marjo Matikainen (FIN)
1991	Yelena Vyalbe (URS)
1992[1]	Lyubov Yegorova (URS)
1993	Yelena Vyalbe (RUS)
1994[1]	Manuela Di Centa (ITA)
1995	Larissa Lazutina (RUS)
1997	Yelena Vyalbe (RUS)
1998[1]	Olga Danilova (RUS)
1999	Stefania Belmondo (ITA)
2001	Bente Skari-Martinsen (NOR)
2002[1]	Stefania Belmondo (ITA)
2003	Bente Skari (NOR)
2005	*not held*

20-KM CROSS-COUNTRY

1984[1]	Marja-Liisa Hämäläinen (FIN)
1985	Grete Nykelmo (NOR)
1987	Marie H. Oestlund (SWE)
1988[1]	Tamara Tikhonova (URS)
1989	*discontinued*

30-KM CROSS-COUNTRY

1989	Yelena Vyalbe (URS)
1991	Lyubov Yegorova (URS)
1992[1]	Stefania Belmondo (ITA)
1993	Stefania Belmondo (ITA)
1994[1]	Manuela Di Centa (ITA)
1995	Yelena Vyalbe (RUS)
1997	Yelena Vyalbe (RUS)
1998[1]	Yulia Chepalova (RUS)
1999	Larisa Lazutina (RUS)
2001	*canceled*
2002[1]	Gabriella Paruzzi (ITA)
2003	Olga Savyalova (RUS)
2005	Marit Bjørgen (NOR)

RELAY[4]

1984[1]	Norway
1985	USSR
1987	USSR
1988[1]	USSR
1989	Finland
1991	USSR
1992[1]	Unified Team
1993	Russia
1994[1]	Russia
1995	Russia
1997	Russia
1998[1]	Russia
1999	Russia
2001	Russia
2002[1]	Germany
2003	Germany
2005	Norway

[1]*Olympic champions, recognized as world champions.* [2]*From 1991 to 2001, the 5-km event was held in tandem with the 10-km event; one event would feature classical and the other freestyle technique. Medals were awarded for both races. Beginning in 2001 this pursuit race instead led to one medal being awarded upon winning. In 2001 and 2002 the pursuit race featured two 5-km races and the 10-km was a stand-alone event featuring classical technique.* [3]*Unified Team, consisting of athletes from the Commonwealth of Independent States plus Georgia.* [4]*15-km relay until 1974; 20-km in 1976 and thereafter.*

Nordic World Cup

YEAR	MEN	WOMEN	YEAR	MEN	WOMEN
1979	Oddvar Braa (NOR)	Galina Kulakova (URS)	1994	Vladimir Smirnov (KAZ)	Manuela Di Centa (ITA)
1981	Aleksandr Zavyalov (URS)	Raisa Smetanina (URS)			
1982	Bill Koch (USA)	Berit Aunli (NOR)	1995	Bjørn Daehlie (NOR)	Yelena Vyalbe (RUS)
1983	Aleksandr Zavyalov (URS)	Marja-Liisa Hämäläinen (FIN)	1996	Bjørn Daehlie (NOR)	Manuela Di Centa (ITA)
			1997	Bjørn Daehlie (NOR)	Yelena Vyalbe (RUS)
1984	Gunde Svan (SWE)	Marja-Liisa Hämäläinen (FIN)	1998	Thomas Alsgaard (NOR)	Larisa Lazutina (RUS)
1985	Gunde Svan (SWE)	Anette Boe (NOR)	1999	Bjørn Daehlie (NOR)	Bente Martinsen (NOR)
1986	Gunde Svan (SWE)	Marjo Matikainen (FIN)	2000	Johann Mühlegg (ESP)	Bente Skari-Martinsen (NOR)
1987	Torgny Mogren (SWE)	Marjo Matikainen (FIN)	2001	Per Elofsson (SWE)	Yuliya Chepalova (RUS)
1988	Gunde Svan (SWE)	Marjo Matikainen (FIN)	2002	Per Elofsson (SWE)	Bente Skari (NOR)
1989	Gunde Svan (SWE)	Yelena Vyalbe (URS)	2003	Mathias Fredriksson (SWE)	Bente Skari (NOR)
1990	Vegard Ulvang (NOR)	Larisa Lazutina (URS)	2004	Rene Sommerfeldt (GER)	Gabriella Paruzzi (ITA)
1991	Vladimir Smirnov (URS)	Yelena Vyalbe (URS)	2005	Axel Teichmann (GER)	Marit Bjørgen (NOR)
1992	Bjørn Daehlie (NOR)	Yelena Vyalbe (URS)			
1993	Bjørn Daehlie (NOR)	Lyudmila Yegorova (RUS)			

Sled Dog Racing

Sled dog racing (or dogsled racing) is the sport of racing sleds pulled by sled dogs over snow-covered cross-country courses; it was developed from a principal Eskimo method of transportation. Dogsleds are still used for transportation and working purposes in some northern areas, although they largely have been replaced by aircraft and snowmobiles. The modern, lightweight racing sled weighs about 30 lb (13.5 kg). Its ash frame is lashed together with leather and its runners sheathed with steel or aluminum. Dogs usually are specially bred and trained Eskimo dogs, Siberian huskies, Samoyeds, or Alaskan Malamutes. The teams typically consist of 4–10 dogs, with more being used for longer races. They are driven in pairs in a gang hitch.

Control of the team is by voice, although drivers may carry whips of limited length. In open country, point-to-point races are held. In more populated areas, back roads form the course, with races usually varying in length from 12–30 mi (19–48 km). A team of 6–8 dogs can pull the sled and its driver, called a musher, at speeds of more than 20 mph (32 km/hr). Teams start at intervals and race for time. Usually, all dogs must finish in the order they start, and an injured dog must be carried on the sled.

A dogsled-racing event was included in the 1932 Winter Olympics program. The sport is popular in Norway, Canada, Alaska, and the northern states of the contiguous United States. The Iditarod Trail Sled Dog Race has been held in Alaska since 1973.

Iditarod Trail Sled Dog Race

Men and women compete together in this annual race held in March between Anchorage and Nome AK. A short race of 56 mi (90 km) organized in 1967 evolved in 1973 into the current race. The course, roughly 1,100 mi (1,770 km) long, partially follows the old Iditarod Trail dogsled mail route blazed from Knik to Nome in 1910. The course length and route vary slightly from year to year, and the middle third takes alternate routes in odd and even years. In 1976 the US Congress designated the original Iditarod Trail as a National Historic Trail.

Iditarod Web site: <www.iditarod.com>.

YEAR	WINNER	TIME	YEAR	WINNER	TIME
1973	Dick Wilmarth	20 days 49 min 41 sec	1990	Susan Butcher	11 days 1 hr 53 min 23 sec
1974	Carl Huntington	20 days 15 hr 2 min 7 sec	1991	Rick Swenson	12 days 16 hr 34 min 39 sec
1975	Emmitt Peters	14 days 14 hr 43 min 45 sec	1992	Martin Buser	10 days 19 hr 17 min 15 sec
1976	Gerald Riley	18 days 22 hr 58 min 17 sec	1993	Jeff King	10 days 15 hr 38 min 15 sec
1977	Rick Swenson	16 days 16 hr 27 min 13 sec	1994	Martin Buser	10 days 13 hr 5 min 39 sec
1978	Dick Mackey	14 days 18 hr 52 min 24 sec	1995	Doug Swingley	10 days 13 hr 2 min 39 sec
1979	Rick Swenson	15 days 10 hr 37 min 47 sec	1996	Jeff King	9 days 5 hr 43 min 13 sec
1980	Joe May	14 days 7 hr 11 min 51 sec	1997	Martin Buser	9 days 8 hr 30 min 45 sec
1981	Rick Swenson	12 days 8 hr 45 min 2 sec	1998	Jeff King	9 days 5 hr 52 min 26 sec
1982	Rick Swenson	16 days 4 hr 40 min 10 sec	1999	Doug Swingley	9 days 14 hr 31 min 7 sec
1983	Rick Mackey	12 days 14 hr 10 min 44 sec	2000	Doug Swingley	9 days 58 min 6 sec
1984	Dean Osmar	12 days 15 hr 7 min 33 sec	2001	Doug Swingley	9 days 19 hr 55 min 50 sec
1985	Libby Riddles	18 days 20 hr 17 min	2002	Martin Buser	8 days 22 hr 46 min 2 sec
1986	Susan Butcher	11 days 15 hr 6 min 0 sec	2003	Robert Sørlie	9 days 15 hr 47 min 36 sec
1987	Susan Butcher	11 days 2 hr 5 min 13 sec	2004	Mitch Seavey	9 days 12 hr 20 min 22 sec
1988	Susan Butcher	11 days 11 hr 41 min 40 sec	2005	Robert Sørlie	9 days 18 hr 39 min 31 sec
1989	Joe Runyan	11 days 5 hr 24 min 34 sec			

Squash

The oldest professional squash rackets tournament recognized as such is the British Open, inaugurated in 1930. Both men's amateur and women's squash rackets championships had been held since 1922. The International Squash Rackets Federation (ISRF; founded 1967) instituted world open championships in 1974 (men) and 1976 (women). The game as played in Great Britain and the rest of the world is quite different in a number of ways from that played in the United States, Canada, and Mexico.

World Squash Federation Web site: <www.worldsquash.org>.

World Open Championship

	men					
YEAR	WINNER (NATIONALITY)	YEAR	WINNER (NATIONALITY)	YEAR	WINNER (NATIONALITY)	
1975	Geoff B. Hunt (AUS)	1984	Jahangir Khan (PAK)	1991	Rodney Martin (AUS)	
1977	Geoff B. Hunt (AUS)	1985	Jahangir Khan (PAK)	1992	Jansher Khan (PAK)	
1979	Geoff B. Hunt (AUS)	1986	Ross Norman (NZL)	1993	Jansher Khan (PAK)	
1980	Geoff B. Hunt (AUS)	1987	Jansher Khan (PAK)	1994	Jansher Khan (PAK)	
1981	Jahangir Khan (PAK)	1988	Jahangir Khan (PAK)	1995	Jansher Khan (PAK)	
1982	Jahangir Khan (PAK)	1989	Jansher Khan (PAK)	1996	Jansher Khan (PAK)	
1983	Jahangir Khan (PAK)	1990	Jansher Khan (PAK)	1997	Rodney Eyles (AUS)	

World Open Championship (continued)

men (continued)

YEAR	WINNER (NATIONALITY)	YEAR	WINNER (NATIONALITY)	YEAR	WINNER (NATIONALITY)
1998	Jonathon Power (CAN)	2001	canceled	2003	Amr Shabana (EGY)
1999	Peter Nicol (SCO)	2002	David Palmer (AUS)	2004	Thierry Lincou (FRA)
2000	not held				

women

YEAR	WINNER (NATIONALITY)	YEAR	WINNER (NATIONALITY)	YEAR	WINNER (NATIONALITY)
1976	Heather P. Blundell McKay (AUS)	1990	Susan Devoy (NZL)	1999	Cassie Campion (ENG)
		1991	not held	2000	Carol Owens (AUS)
1979	Heather McKay (AUS)	1992	Susan Devoy (NZL)	2001	Sarah Fitz-Gerald (AUS)
1981	Rhonda Thorne (AUS)	1993	Michelle Martin (AUS)	2002	Sarah Fitz-Gerald (AUS)
1983	Vicki Hoffman Cardwell (AUS)	1994	Michelle Martin (AUS)	2003	Carol Owens (NZL)
		1995	Michelle Martin (AUS)	2004	Vanessa Atkinson (NED)
1985	Susan Devoy (NZL)	1996	Sarah Fitz-Gerald (AUS)		
1987	Susan Devoy (NZL)	1997	Sarah Fitz-Gerald (AUS)		
1989	Martine LeMoignan (GBR)	1998	Sarah Fitz-Gerald (AUS)		

British Open Championship

The championships have been held since 1921–22 (women's) and 1930–31 (men's). The table shows the results for the past 20 years.

men		women	
SEASON	WINNER (NATIONALITY)	SEASON	WINNER (NATIONALITY)
1984–85 through 1990–91	Jahangir Khan (PAK)	1984–85 through 1989–90	Susan Devoy (NZL)
1991–92 through 1996–97	Jansher Khan (PAK)	1990–91	Liz Opie (GBR)
		1991–92	Susan Devoy (NZL)
1997–98	Peter Nicol (SCO)	1992–93 through 1997–98	Michelle Martin (AUS)
1998–99	Jonathon Power (CAN)		
1999–2000	David Evans (WAL)	1998–99	Leilani Joyce (NZL)
2000–01	David Palmer (AUS)	1999–2000	Leilani Joyce (NZL)
2001–02	Peter Nicol (GBR)	2000–01	Sarah Fitz-Gerald (AUS)
2002–03	David Palmer (AUS)	2001–02	Sarah Fitz-Gerald (AUS)
2003–04	David Palmer (AUS)	2002–03	Rachael Grinham (AUS)
		2003–04	Rachael Grinham (AUS)

Swimming

The **Fédération Internationale de Natation** (International Swimming Federation, still known by its French acronym that includes an "a" for "Amateur," FINA; founded 1908) is the world governing body for amateur swimming. It held the first world swimming championships in 1973. After 1975 the FINA championships were held in non-Olympic, even-numbered years. (An exception was the 1991 championship that took place in Australia during the summer month of January.) Diving, synchronized (or synchro) swimming, and water polo events are included in the competition.

A distinction is made between **long-course** (50-m) and **short-course** (25-m) pools for purposes of record-setting; world championships and other major contests were long held in 50-m pools, but now a separate World Championship and World Cup take place for 25-m pools.
International Swimming Federation Web site: <www.fina.org>.

World Swimming & Diving Championships—Men

The next competition is scheduled to be held in 2007 in Melbourne, VIC, Australia.

swimming

50-M FREESTYLE		50-M FREESTYLE (CONT.)		100-M FREESTYLE	
1986	Tom Jager (USA)	2001	Anthony Ervin (USA)	1973	Jim Montgomery (USA)
1991	Tom Jager (USA)	2003	Aleksandr Popov (RUS)	1975	Andy Coan (USA)
1994	Aleksandr Popov (RUS)	2005	Roland Schoeman (RSA)	1978	David McCagg (USA)
1998	Bill Pilczuk (USA)			1982	Jorg Woithe (GDR)

World Swimming & Diving Championships—Men (continued)

100-M FREESTYLE (CONT.)
1986 Matt Biondi (USA)
1991 Matt Biondi (USA)
1994 Aleksandr Popov (RUS)
1998 Aleksandr Popov (RUS)
2001 Anthony Ervin (USA)
2003 Aleksandr Popov (RUS)
2005 Filippo Magnini (ITA)

200-M FREESTYLE
1973 Jim Montgomery (USA)
1975 Tim Shaw (USA)
1978 Bill Forrester (USA)
1982 Michael Gross (FRG)
1986 Michael Gross (FRG)
1991 Giorgio Lamberti (ITA)
1994 Antti Kasvio (FIN)
1998 Michael Klim (AUS)
2001 Ian Thorpe (AUS)
2003 Ian Thorpe (AUS)
2005 Michael Phelps (USA)

400-M FREESTYLE
1973 Rick DeMont (USA)
1975 Tim Shaw (USA)
1978 Vladimir Salnikov (URS)
1982 Vladimir Salnikov (URS)
1986 Rainer Henkel (FRG)
1991 Jörg Hoffmann (GER)
1994 Kieren Perkins (AUS)
1998 Ian Thorpe (AUS)
2001 Ian Thorpe (AUS)
2003 Ian Thorpe (AUS)
2005 Grant Hackett (AUS)

800-M FREESTYLE
2001 Ian Thorpe (AUS)
2003 Grant Hackett (AUS)
2005 Grant Hackett (AUS)

1,500-M FREESTYLE
1973 Steve Holland (AUS)
1975 Tim Shaw (USA)
1978 Vladimir Salnikov (URS)
1982 Vladimir Salnikov (URS)
1986 Rainer Henkel (FRG)
1991 Jörg Hoffmann (GER)
1994 Kieren Perkins (AUS)
1998 Grant Hackett (AUS)
2001 Grant Hackett (AUS)
2003 Grant Hackett (AUS)
2005 Grant Hackett (AUS)

50-M BACKSTROKE
2001 Randall Bal (USA)
2003 Thomas Rupprath (GER)
2005 Aristeidis Grigoriadis (GRE)

100-M BACKSTROKE
1973 Roland Matthes (GDR)
1975 Roland Matthes (GDR)
1978 Bob Jackson (USA)
1982 Dirk Richter (GDR)
1986 Igor Polyansky (URS)
1991 Jeff Rouse (USA)
1994 Martín Lopez-Zubero (ESP)
1998 Lenny Krayzelburg (USA)
2001 Matt Welsh (AUS)
2003 Aaron Peirsol (USA)

100-M BACKSTROKE (CONT.)
2005 Aaron Peirsol (USA)

200-M BACKSTROKE
1973 Roland Matthes (GDR)
1975 Zoltan Verraszto (HUN)
1978 Jesse Vassallo (USA)
1982 Rick Carey (USA)
1986 Igor Polyansky (URS)
1991 Martín Lopez-Zubero (ESP)
1994 Vladimir Selkov (RUS)
1998 Lenny Krayzelburg (USA)
2001 Aaron Peirsol (USA)
2003 Aaron Peirsol (USA)
2005 Aaron Peirsol (USA)

50-M BREASTSTROKE
2001 Oleg Lisogor (UKR)
2003 James Gibson (GBR)
2005 Mark Warnecke (GER)

100-M BREASTSTROKE
1973 John Hencken (USA)
1975 David Wilkie (GBR)
1978 Walter Kusch (FRG)
1982 Steve Lundquist (USA)
1986 Victor Davis (CAN)
1991 Norbert Rozsa (HUN)
1994 Norbert Rozsa (HUN)
1998 Fred De Burghgraeve (BEL)
2001 Roman Sloudnov (RUS)
2003 Kosuke Kitajima (JPN)
2005 Brendan Hansen (USA)

200-M BREASTSTROKE
1973 David Wilkie (GBR)
1975 David Wilkie (GBR)
1978 Nick Nevid (USA)
1982 Victor Davis (CAN)
1986 Joszef Szabo (HUN)
1991 Mike Barrowman (USA)
1994 Norbert Rozsa (HUN)
1998 Kurt Grote (USA)
2001 Brendan Hansen (USA)
2003 Kosuke Kitajima (JPN)
2005 Brendan Hansen (USA)

50-M BUTTERFLY
2001 Geoff Huegill (AUS)
2003 Matt Welsh (AUS)
2005 Roland Schoeman (RSA)

100-M BUTTERFLY
1973 Bruce Robertson (CAN)
1975 Greg Jagenburg (USA)
1978 Joseph Bottom (USA)
1982 Matt Gribble (USA)
1986 Pablo Morales (USA)
1991 Anthony Nesty (SUR)
1994 Rafal Szukala (POL)
1998 Michael Klim (AUS)
2001 Lars Frolander (SWE)
2003 Ian Crocker (USA)
2005 Ian Crocker (USA)

200-M BUTTERFLY
1973 Robin Backhaus (USA)
1975 Bill Forrester (USA)
1978 Mike Bruner (USA)

200-M BUTTERFLY (CONT.)
1982 Michael Gross (FRG)
1986 Michael Gross (FRG)
1991 Melvin Stewart (USA)
1994 Denis Pankratov (RUS)
1998 Denys Silantyev (UKR)
2001 Michael Phelps (USA)
2003 Michael Phelps (USA)
2005 Pawel Korzeniowski (POL)

200-M INDIVIDUAL MEDLEY
1973 Gunnar Larsson (SWE)
1975 Andras Hargitay (HUN)
1978 Graham Smith (CAN)
1982 Aleksandr Sidorenko (URS)
1986 Tamas Darnyi (HUN)
1991 Tamas Darnyi (HUN)
1994 Jani Sievinen (FIN)
1998 Marcel Wouda (NED)
2001 Massimiliano Rosolino (ITA)
2003 Michael Phelps (USA)
2005 Michael Phelps (USA)

400-M INDIVIDUAL MEDLEY
1973 Andras Hargitay (HUN)
1975 Andras Hargitay (HUN)
1978 Jesse Vassallo (USA)
1982 Ricardo Prado (BRA)
1986 Tamas Darnyi (HUN)
1991 Tamas Darnyi (HUN)
1994 Tom Dolan (USA)
1998 Tom Dolan (USA)
2001 Alessio Boggiatto (ITA)
2003 Michael Phelps (USA)
2005 Laszlo Cseh (HUN)

4 X 100-M FREESTYLE RELAY
1973 United States
1975 United States
1978 United States
1982 United States
1986 United States
1991 United States
1994 United States
1998 United States
2001 Australia
2003 Russia
2005 United States

4 X 200-M FREESTYLE RELAY
1973 United States
1975 West Germany
1978 United States
1982 United States
1986 East Germany
1991 Germany
1994 Sweden
1998 Australia
2001 Australia
2003 Australia
2005 United States

4 X 100-M MEDLEY RELAY
1973 United States
1975 United States
1978 United States
1982 United States

World Swimming & Diving Championships—Men (continued)

4 X 100-M MEDLEY RELAY (CONT.)	4 X 100-M MEDLEY RELAY (CONT.)	4 X 100-M MEDLEY RELAY (CONT.)
1986 United States	1994 United States	2001 Australia
1991 United States	1998 Australia	2003 United States
		2005 United States

diving

1-M SPRINGBOARD
1991 Edwin Jongejans (NED)
1994 Evan Stewart (ZIM)
1998 Yu Zhuocheng (CHN)
2001 Wang Feng (CHN)
2003 Xu Xiang (CHN)
2005 Alexandre Despatie (CAN)

3-M SPRINGBOARD
1973 Phil Boggs (USA)
1975 Phil Boggs (USA)

3-M SPRINGBOARD (CONT.)
1978 Phil Boggs (USA)
1982 Greg Louganis (USA)
1986 Greg Louganis (USA)
1991 Kent Ferguson (USA)
1994 Yu Zhuocheng (CHN)
1998 Dmitry Sautin (RUS)
2001 Dmitry Sautin (RUS)
2003 Aleksandr Dobrosok (RUS)
2005 Alexandre Despatie (CAN)

PLATFORM
1973 Klaus Dibiasi (ITA)
1975 Klaus Dibiasi (ITA)
1978 Greg Louganis (USA)
1982 Greg Louganis (USA)
1986 Greg Louganis (USA)
1991 Sun Shuwei (CHN)
1994 Dmitry Sautin (RUS)
1998 Dmitry Sautin (RUS)
2001 Tian Liang (CHN)
2003 Alexandre Despatie (CAN)
2005 Hu Jia (CHN)

World Swimming & Diving Championships—Women

The next competition is scheduled to be held in 2007 in Melbourne, VIC, Australia.

swimming

50-M FREESTYLE
1986 Tamara Costache (ROM)
1991 Zhuang Yong (CHN)
1994 Le Jingyi (CHN)
1998 Amy Van Dyken (USA)
2001 Inge De Bruijn (NED)
2003 Inge De Bruijn (NED)
2005 Lisbeth Lenton (AUS)

100-M FREESTYLE
1973 Kornelia Ender (GDR)
1975 Kornelia Ender (GDR)
1978 Barbara Krause (GDR)
1982 Birgit Meineke (GDR)
1986 Kristin Otto (GDR)
1991 Nicole Haislett (USA)
1994 Le Jingyi (CHN)
1998 Jenny Thompson (USA)
2001 Inge De Bruijn (NED)
2003 Hanna-Maria Seppälä (FIN)
2005 Jodie Henry (AUS)

200-M FREESTYLE
1973 Keena Rothhammer (USA)
1975 Shirley Babashoff (USA)
1978 Cynthia Woodhead (USA)
1982 Annemarie Verstappen (NED)
1986 Heike Friedrich (GDR)
1991 Hayley Lewis (AUS)
1994 Franziska van Almsick (GER)
1998 Claudia Poll (CRC)
2001 Giaan Rooney (AUS)
2003 Alena Popchanka (BLR)
2005 Solenne Figues (FRA)

400-M FREESTYLE
1973 Heather Greenwood (USA)
1975 Shirley Babashoff (USA)
1978 Tracey Wickham (AUS)
1982 Carmela Schmidt (GDR)

400-M FREESTYLE (CONT.)
1986 Heike Friedrich (GDR)
1991 Janet Evans (USA)
1994 Yang Aihua (CHN)
1998 Chen Yan (CHN)
2001 Yana Klochkova (UKR)
2003 Hannah Stockbauer (GER)
2005 Laure Manaudou (FRA)

800-M FREESTYLE
1973 Novella Calligaris (ITA)
1975 Jenny Turrall (AUS)
1978 Tracey Wickham (AUS)
1982 Kim Linehan (USA)
1986 Astrid Strauss (GDR)
1991 Janet Evans (USA)
1994 Janet Evans (USA)
1998 Brooke Bennett (USA)
2001 Hannah Stockbauer (GER)
2003 Hannah Stockbauer (GER)
2005 Kate Ziegler (USA)

1,500-M FREESTYLE
2001 Hannah Stockbauer (GER)
2003 Hannah Stockbauer (GER)
2005 Kate Ziegler (USA)

50-M BREASTSTROKE
2001 Luo Xuejuan (CHN)
2003 Luo Xuejuan (CHN)
2005 Jade Edmistone (AUS)

100-M BREASTSTROKE
1973 Renate Vogel (GDR)
1975 Hannelore Anke (GDR)
1978 Yuliya Bogdanova (URS)
1982 Ute Geweniger (GDR)
1986 Sylvia Gerasch (GDR)
1991 Linley Frame (AUS)
1994 Samantha Riley (AUS)
1998 Kristy Kowal (USA)
2001 Luo Xuejuan (CHN)

100-M BREASTSTROKE (CONT.)
2003 Luo Xuejuan (CHN)
2005 Leisel Jones (AUS)

200-M BREASTSTROKE
1973 Renate Vogel (GDR)
1975 Hannelore Anke (GDR)
1978 Lina Kachushite (URS)
1982 Svetlana Varganova (URS)
1986 Silke Hörner (GDR)
1991 Yelena Volkova (URS)
1994 Samantha Riley (AUS)
1998 Agnes Kovacs (HUN)
2001 Agnes Kovacs (HUN)
2003 Amanda Beard (USA)
2005 Leisel Jones (AUS)

50-M BUTTERFLY
2001 Inge De Bruijn (NED)
2003 Inge De Bruijn (NED)
2005 Danni Miatke (AUS)

100-M BUTTERFLY
1973 Kornelia Ender (GDR)
1975 Kornelia Ender (GDR)
1978 Joan Pennington (USA)
1982 Mary T. Meagher (USA)
1986 Kornelia Gressler (GDR)
1991 Qian Hong (CHN)
1994 Liu Limin (CHN)
1998 Jenny Thompson (USA)
2001 Petria Thomas (AUS)
2003 Jenny Thompson (USA)
2005 Jessicah Schipper (AUS)

200-M BUTTERFLY
1973 Rosemarie Kother (GDR)
1975 Rosemarie Kother (GDR)
1978 Tracy Caulkins (USA)
1982 Ines Geissler (GDR)
1986 Mary T. Meagher (USA)
1991 Summer Sanders (USA)

World Swimming & Diving Championships—Women (continued)

200-M BUTTERFLY (CONT.)

1994	Liu Limin (CHN)
1998	Susie O'Neill (AUS)
2001	Petria Thomas (AUS)
2003	Otylia Jedrzejczak (POL)
2005	Otylia Jedrzejczak (POL)

50-M BACKSTROKE

2001	Haley Cope (USA)
2003	Nina Zhivanevskaya (ESP)
2005	Giaan Rooney (AUS)

100-M BACKSTROKE

1973	Ulrike Richter (GDR)
1975	Ulrike Richter (GDR)
1978	Linda Jezek (USA)
1982	Kristin Otto (GDR)
1986	Betsy Mitchell (USA)
1991	Krisztina Egerszegi (HUN)
1994	He Cihong (CHN)
1998	Lea Maurer (USA)
2001	Natalie Coughlin (USA)
2003	Antje Buschschulte (GER)
2005	Kirsty Coventry (ZIM)

200-M BACKSTROKE

1973	Melissa Belote (USA)
1975	Birgit Treiber (GDR)
1978	Linda Jezek (USA)
1982	Cornelia Sirch (GDR)
1986	Cornelia Sirch (GDR)
1991	Krisztina Egerszegi (HUN)
1994	He Cihong (CHN)

200-M BACKSTROKE (CONT.)

1998	Roxanna Maracineanu (FRA)
2001	Diana Mocanu (ROM)
2003	Katy Sexton (GBR)
2005	Kirsty Coventry (ZIM)

200-M INDIVIDUAL MEDLEY

1973	Andrea Hubner (GDR)
1975	Kathy Heddy (USA)
1978	Tracy Caulkins (USA)
1982	Petra Schneider (GDR)
1986	Kristin Otto (GDR)
1991	Lin Li (CHN)
1994	Lu Bin (CHN)
1998	Wu Yanyan (CHN)
2001	Martha Bowen (USA)
2003	Yana Klochkova (UKR)
2005	Katie Hoff (USA)

400-M INDIVIDUAL MEDLEY

1973	Gudrun Wegner (GDR)
1975	Ulrika Tauber (GDR)
1978	Tracy Caulkins (USA)
1982	Petra Schneider (GDR)
1986	Kathleen Nord (GDR)
1991	Lin Li (CHN)
1994	Dai Guohong (CHN)
1998	Chen Yan (CHN)
2001	Yana Klochkova (UKR)
2003	Yana Klochkova (UKR)
2005	Katie Hoff (USA)

4 X 100-M FREESTYLE RELAY

1973	East Germany
1975	East Germany
1978	United States
1982	East Germany
1986	East Germany
1991	United States
1994	China
1998	United States
2001	Germany
2003	United States
2005	Australia

4 X 200-M FREESTYLE RELAY

1986	East Germany
1991	Germany
1994	China
1998	Germany
2001	Great Britain
2003	United States
2005	United States

4 X 100-M MEDLEY RELAY

1973	East Germany
1975	East Germany
1978	United States
1982	East Germany
1986	East Germany
1991	United States
1994	China
1998	United States
2001	Australia
2003	China
2005	Australia

diving

1-M SPRINGBOARD

1991	Gao Min (CHN)
1994	Chen Lixia (CHN)
1998	Irina Lashko (RUS)
2001	Blythe Hartley (CAN)
2003	Irina Lashko (AUS)
2005	Blythe Hartley (CAN)

3-M SPRINGBOARD

1973	Christa Kohler (GDR)
1975	Irina Kalinina (URS)

3-M SPRINGBOARD (CONT.)

1978	Irina Kalinina (URS)
1982	Megan Neyer (USA)
1986	Gao Min (CHN)
1991	Gao Min (CHN)
1994	Tan Shuping (CHN)
1998	Yulia Pakhalina (RUS)
2001	Guo Jingjing (CHN)
2003	Guo Jingjing (CHN)
2005	Guo Jingjing (CHN)

PLATFORM

1973	Ulrika Knape (SWE)
1975	Janet Ely (USA)
1978	Irina Kalinina (URS)
1982	Wendy Wyland (USA)
1986	Chen Lin (CHN)
1991	Fu Mingxia (CHN)
1994	Fu Mingxia (CHN)
1998	Olena Zhupina (UKR)
2001	Xu Mian (CHN)
2003	Emilie Heymans (CAN)
2005	Laura Wilkinson (USA)

Swimming World Records—Long Course (50-m)

men

EVENT	RECORD HOLDER (NATIONALITY)	PERFORMANCE	DATE
50-m freestyle	Aleksandr Popov (RUS)	21.64 sec	16 Jun 2000
100-m freestyle	Pieter van den Hoogenband (NED)	47.84 sec	19 Sep 2000
200-m freestyle	Ian Thorpe (AUS)	1 min 44.06 sec	25 Jul 2001
400-m freestyle	Ian Thorpe (AUS)	3 min 40.08 sec	30 Jul 2002
800-m freestyle	Grant Hackett (AUS)	7 min 38.65 sec	27 Jul 2005
1,500-m freestyle	Grant Hackett (AUS)	14 min 34.56 sec	29 Jul 2001
50-m backstroke	Thomas Rupprath (GER)	24.80 sec	27 Jul 2003
100-m backstroke	Aaron Peirsol (USA)	53.17 sec	2 Apr 2005
200-m backstroke	Aaron Peirsol (USA)	1 min 54.66 sec	29 Jul 2005
50-m breaststroke	Oleg Lisogor (UKR)	27.18 sec	2 Aug 2002
100-m breaststroke	Brendan Hansen (USA)	59.30 sec	8 Jul 2004
200-m breaststroke	Brendan Hansen (USA)	2 min 9.04 sec	11 Jul 2004
50-m butterfly	Roland Schoeman (RSA)	22.96 sec	25 Jul 2005
100-m butterfly	Ian Crocker (USA)	50.40 sec	30 Jul 2005

Swimming World Records—Long Course (50-m) (continued)

men (continued)

EVENT	RECORD HOLDER (NATIONALITY)	PERFORMANCE	DATE
200-m butterfly	Michael Phelps (USA)	1 min 53.93 sec	22 Jul 2003
200-m individual medley	Michael Phelps (USA)	1 min 55.94 sec	9 Aug 2003
400-m individual medley	Michael Phelps (USA)	4 min 8.26 sec	14 Aug 2004
4 × 100-m free relay	South Africa (Roland Schoeman, Lyndon Ferns, Darian Townsend, Ryk Neethling)	3 min 13.17 sec	15 Aug 2004
4 × 200-m free relay	Australia (Grant Hackett, Michael Klim, William Kirby, Ian Thorpe)	7 min 4.66 sec	27 Jul 2001
4 × 100-m medley relay	United States (Aaron Peirsol, Brendan Hansen, Ian Crocker, Jason Lezak)	3 min 30.68 sec	21 Aug 2004

women

EVENT	RECORD HOLDER (NATIONALITY)	PERFORMANCE	DATE
50-m freestyle	Inge de Bruijn (NED)	24.13 sec	22 Sep 2000
100-m freestyle	Jodie Henry (AUS)	53.52 sec	18 Aug 2004
200-m freestyle	Franziska Van Almsick (GER)	1 min 56.64 sec	3 Aug 2002
400-m freestyle	Janet Evans (USA)	4 min 3.85 sec	22 Sep 1988
800-m freestyle	Janet Evans (USA)	8 min 16.22 sec	20 Aug 1989
1,500-m freestyle	Janet Evans (USA)	15 min 52.10 sec	26 Mar 1988
50-m backstroke	Janine Pietsch (GER)	28.19 sec	25 May 2005
100-m backstroke	Natalie Coughlin (USA)	59.58 sec	13 Aug 2002
200-m backstroke	Kristina Egerszegi (HUN)	2 min 6.62 sec	25 Aug 1991
50-m breaststroke	Jade Edmistone (AUS)	30.45 sec	31 Jul 2005
100-m breaststroke	Jessica Hardy (USA)	1 min 6.20 sec	25 Jul 2005
200-m breaststroke	Leisel Jones (AUS)	2 min 21.72 sec	29 Jul 2005
50-m butterfly	Anna-Karin Kammerling (SWE)	25.57 sec	20 Jul 2000
100-m butterfly	Inge de Bruijn (NED)	56.61 sec	17 Sep 2000
200-m butterfly	Otylia Jedrzejczak (POL)	2 min 5.61 sec	28 Jul 2005
200-m individual medley	Wu Yanyan (CHN)	2 min 9.72 sec	17 Oct 1997
400-m individual medley	Yana Klochkova (UKR)	4 min 33.59 sec	16 Sep 2000
4 × 100-m free relay	Australia (Alice Mills, Lisbeth Lenton Petria Thomas, Jodie Henry)	3 min 35.94 sec	14 Aug 2004
4 × 200-m free relay	United States (Natalie Coughlin, Carly Piper, Dana Vollmer, Kaitlin Sandeno)	7 min 53.42 sec	18 Aug 2004
4 × 100-m medley relay	Australia (Giaan Rooney, Leisel Jones, Petria Thomas, Jodie Henry)	3 min 57.32 sec	21 Aug 2004

Swimming World Records—Short Course (25-m)

men

EVENT	RECORD HOLDER (NATIONALITY)	PERFORMANCE	DATE
50-m freestyle	Fred Bousquet (FRA)	21.10 sec	25 Mar 2004
100-m freestyle	Roland Schoeman (RSA)	46.25 sec	22 Jan 2005
200-m freestyle	Ian Thorpe (AUS)	1 min 41.10 sec	6 Feb 2000
400-m freestyle	Grant Hackett (AUS)	3 min 34.58 sec	18 Jul 2002
800-m freestyle	Grant Hackett (AUS)	7 min 25.28 sec	3 Aug 2001
1,500-m freestyle	Grant Hackett (AUS)	14 min 10.10 sec	7 Aug 2001
50-m backstroke	Thomas Rupprath (GER)	23.27 sec	10 Dec 2004
100-m backstroke	Peter Marshall (USA)	50.32 sec	26 Mar 2004
200-m backstroke	Aaron Peirsol (USA)	1 min 50.52 sec	11 Oct 2004
50-m breaststroke	Oleg Lisogor (UKR)	26.20 sec	26 Jan 2002
100-m breaststroke	Ed Moses (USA)	57.47 sec	23 Jan 2002
200-m breaststroke	Ed Moses (USA)	2 min 2.92 sec	17 Jan 2004
50-m butterfly	Ian Crocker (USA)	22.71 sec	10 Oct 2004
100-m butterfly	Ian Crocker (USA)	49.07 sec	26 Mar 2004
200-m butterfly	Frank Esposito (FRA)	1 min 50.73 sec	8 Dec 2002
100-m individual medley	Ryk Neethling (RSA)	51.52 sec	11 Feb 2005
200-m individual medley	George Bovell (TRI)	1 min 53.93 sec	25 Mar 2004
400-m individual medley	Brian Johns (CAN)	4 min 2.72 sec	21 Feb 2003
4 × 100-m free relay	Sweden (Johan Nystrom, Lars Frölander, Mattias Ohlin, Stefan Nystrand)	3 min 9.57 sec	16 Mar 2000
4 × 200-m free relay	Australia (William Kirby, Ian Thorpe, Michael Klim, Grant Hackett)	6 min 56.41 sec	7 Aug 2001
4 × 100-m medley relay	United States (Aaron Peirsol, Brendan Hansen, Ian Crocker, Jason Lezak)	3 min 25.09 sec	11 Oct 2004

Swimming World Records—Short Course (25-m) (continued)

women

EVENT	RECORD HOLDER (NATIONALITY)	PERFORMANCE	DATE
50-m freestyle	Therese Alshammar (SWE)	23.59 sec	18 Mar 2000
100-m freestyle	Therese Alshammar (SWE)	52.17 sec	17 Mar 2000
200-m freestyle	Lindsay Benko (USA)	1 min 54.04 sec	7 Apr 2002
400-m freestyle	Lindsay Benko (USA)	3 min 59.53 sec	26 Jan 2003
800-m freestyle	Sachiko Yamada (JPN)	8 min 13.35 sec	24 Jan 2004
50-m backstroke	Li Hui (CHN)	26.83 sec	2 Dec 2001
100-m backstroke	Natalie Coughlin (USA)	56.71 sec	23 Nov 2002
200-m backstroke	Natalie Coughlin (USA)	2 min 3.62 sec	27 Nov 2001
50-m breaststroke	Jade Edmistone (AUS)	29.90 sec	26 Sep 2004
100-m breaststroke	Tara Kirk (USA)	1 min 4.79 sec	19 Mar 2004
200-m breaststroke	Liesel Jones (AUS)	2 min 17.75 sec	29 Nov 2003
50-m butterfly	Anna-Karin Kammerling (SWE)	25.36 sec	25 Jan 2001
100-m butterfly	Natalie Coughlin (USA)	56.34 sec	22 Nov 2002
200-m butterfly	Yang Yu (CHN)	2 min 4.04 sec	18 Jan 2004
100-m individual medley	Natalie Coughlin (USA)	58.80 sec	23 Nov 2002
200-m individual medley	Allison Wagner (USA)	2 min 7.79 sec	5 Dec 1993
400-m individual medley	Yana Klochkova (UKR)	4 min 27.83 sec	19 Jan 2002
4 × 100-m free relay	China (Le Jingyi, Na Chao, Shang Ying, Nian Yin)	3 min 34.55 sec	19 Apr 1997
4 × 200-m free relay	China (Xu Yanvei, Zhu Yingven, Tang Jingzhi, Yang Yu)	7 min 46.30 sec	3 Apr 2002
4 × 100-m medley relay	Australia (Sophie Edington, Brooke Hanson, Jessicah Schipper, Lisbeth Lenton)	3 min 54.95 sec	9 Oct 2004

Table Tennis

Official **world table tennis championships** were first held in 1927 under the auspices of the **International Table Tennis Federation** (ITTF; founded 1926). **Women's doubles** competition was added in 1928 and women's team competition in 1934. In 1980 the ITTF first sponsored a men's **World Cup** competition for the top 16 ranking players; it has been held annually since then.

At world championships, held biennially since 1957, players compete for: the **Swaythling Cup** (men's team event); the **Marcel Corbillon Cup** (women's team event); the **St. Bride Vase** (men's singles); the **G. Geist Prize** (women's singles); the **Iran Cup** (men's doubles championships); the **W.J. Pope Trophy** (women's doubles championships); and the **Heydusek Prize** (mixed doubles championships).

International Table Tennis Federation Web site: <www.ittf.com>.

Table Tennis World Rankings
ITTF rankings as of 3 Aug 2005.

	MEN (NATIONALITY)		WOMEN (NATIONALITY)
1	Wang Liqin (CHN)	1	Zhang Yining (CHN)
2	Ma Lin (CHN)	2	Niu Jianfeng (CHN)
3	Timo Boll (GER)	3	Wang Nan (CHN)
4	Wang Hao (CHN)	4	Li Jia Wei (SIN)
5	Vladimir Samsonov (BLR)	5	Guo Yue (CHN)

World Table Tennis Championships—Men
Competition was held annually beginning in 1927 and usually every other year since 1957.
Table shows results for the past 20 years.

YEAR	ST. BRIDE VASE	IRAN CUP	YEAR	SWAYTHLING CUP
1985	Jiang Jialiang (CHN)	Mikael Appelgren, Ulf Carlsson (SWE)	1985	China
1987	Jiang Jialiang (CHN)	Chen Longcan, Wei Qingguang (CHN)	1987	China
1989	Jan-Ove Waldner (SWE)	Jorg Rosskopf, Steffen Fetzner (FRG)	1989	Sweden
1991	Jorgen Persson (SWE)	Peter Karlsson, Thomas Von Scheele (SWE)	1991	Sweden
1993	Jean-Philippe Gatien (FRA)	Wang Tao, Lu Lin (CHN)	1993	Sweden
1995	Kong Linghui (CHN)	Wang Tao, Lu Lin (CHN)	1995	China
1997	Jan-Ove Waldner (SWE)	Kong Linghui, Liu Guoliang (CHN)	1997	China
1999	Liu Guoliang (CHN)	Kong Linghui, Liu Guoliang (CHN)	2000	Sweden
2001	Wang Liqin (CHN)	Wang Liqin, Yan Sen (CHN)	2001	China
2003	Werner Schlager (AUT)	Wang Liqin, Yan Sen (CHN)	2004	China
2005	Wang Liqin (CHN)	Kong Linghui, Wang Hao (CHN)		

World Table Tennis Championships—Women

Competition was held annually beginning in 1927 (Geist Prize), 1928 (Pope Trophy), and 1934 (Corbillon Cup) and usually every other year since 1957. Table shows the results for the past 20 years.

YEAR	G. GEIST PRIZE	W.J. POPE TROPHY	YEAR	CORBILLON CUP
1983	Cao Yanhua (CHN)	Shen Jianping, Dai Lili (CHN)	1983	China
1985	Cao Yanhua (CHN)	Dai Lili, Geng Lijuan (CHN)	1985	China
1987	He Zhili (CHN)	Hyun Jung Hwa, Yang Young Ja (KOR)	1987	China
1989	Qiao Hong (CHN)	Qiao Hong, Deng Yaping (CHN)	1989	China
1991	Deng Yaping (CHN)	Gao Jun, Chen Zihe (CHN)	1991	Korea
1993	Hyun Jung Hwa (KOR)	Liu Wei, Qiao Yunping (CHN)	1993	China
1995	Deng Yaping (CHN)	Deng Yaping, Qiao Hong (CHN)	1995	China
1997	Deng Yaping (CHN)	Deng Yaping, Yang Ying (CHN)	1997	China
1999	Wang Nan (CHN)	Wang Nan, Li Ju (CHN)	2000	China
2001	Wang Nan (CHN)	Wang Nan, Li Ju (CHN)	2001	China
2003	Wang Nan (CHN)	Wang Nan, Zhang Yining (CHN)	2004	China
2005	Zhang Yining (CHN)	Wang Nan, Zhang Yining (CHN)		

World Table Tennis Championships—Mixed

Competition has been held since 1927–28. Table shows results for the past 20 years.

YEAR	HEYDUSEK PRIZE	YEAR	HEYDUSEK PRIZE
1987	Hui Jun, Geng Lijuan (CHN)	1997	Liu Guoliang, Wu Na (CHN)
1989	Yoo Nam Kyu, Hyung Jung Hwa (KOR)	1999	Ma Lin, Zhang Yingying (CHN)
1991	Wang Tao, Liu Wei (CHN)	2001	Qin Zhijian, Yang Ying (CHN)
1993	Wang Tao, Liu Wei (CHN)	2003	Ma Lin, Wang Nan (CHN)
1995	Wang Tao, Liu Wei (CHN)	2005	Guo Yue, Wang Liqin (CHN)

Table Tennis World Cup

	men				women	
YEAR	WINNER	YEAR	WINNER	YEAR	WINNER	
1980	Guo Yuehua (CHN)	1993	Zoran Primorac (CRO)	1996	Deng Yaping (CHN)	
1981	Tibor Klampar (HUN)	1994	Jean-Philippe Gatien (FRA)	1997	Wang Nan (CHN)	
1982	Guo Yuehua (CHN)	1995	Kong Linghui (CHN)	1998	Wang Nan (CHN)	
1983	Mikael Appelgren (SWE)	1996	Liu Guoliang (CHN)	1999	Wang Nan (CHN)	
1984	Jiang Jialiang (CHN)	1997	Zoran Primorac (CRO)	2000	Li Ju (CHN)	
1985	Chen Xinhua (CHN)	1998	Jorg Rosskopf (GER)	2001	Zhang Yining (CHN)	
1986	Chen Longcan (CHN)	1999	Vladimir Samsonov (BLR)	2002	Zhang Yining (CHN)	
1987	Teng Yi (CHN)	2000	Ma Lin (CHN)	2003	Wang Nan (CHN)	
1988	Andrzej Grubba (POL)	2001	Vladimir Samsonov (BLR)	2004	Zhang Yining (CHN)	
1989	Ma Wenge (CHN)	2002	Timo Boll (GER)	2005	*to be held 9–11 September*	
1990	Jan-Ove Waldner (SWE)	2003	Ma Lin (CHN)			
1991	Jörgen Persson (SWE)	2004	Ma Lin (CHN)			
1992	Ma Wenge (CHN)	2005	*to be held 27–30 October*			

Tennis

Four events dominate world championship tennis. The first of the traditional "Big Four," or "Grand Slam," events was the **All-England Lawn Tennis Championships** (better known as the Wimbledon Championships), founded in 1877. Its only event the first year was the men's singles championships; women first competed in 1884. Major tennis tournaments also sprang up in the **United States** (1881 for men; women's singles competition first contested 1887, added officially 1889), **France** (1891 for men; women's singles competition added 1897), and **Australia** (1905 for men; women's singles competition added 1922). Open tennis (open, that is, to both professionals and amateurs) became the rule in the Big Four tournaments in 1968. International team tennis was organized in 1900 with the institution of the

Davis Cup. Competing men's teams play four singles matches and one doubles match for the trophy. The **Wightman Cup** was contested yearly between British and American women's teams from 1923 to 1989. The **International Tennis Federation** (ITF, formerly the International Lawn Tennis Federation; founded 1913) established the **Federation Cup** in 1963 (called the Fed Cup since 1994) for international women's team competition. It is decided by elimination rounds of two singles and one doubles contest.

Related Web sites: International Tennis Federation: <www.itftennis.com>; ATP (formerly Association of Tennis Professionals): <www.atptennis.com>; Women's Tennis Association: <www.wtatour.com>.

Australian Open Tennis Championships—Singles

YEAR	MEN	WOMEN
1905	Rodney Heath (AUS)	
1906	Tony Wilding (NZL)	
1907	Horace Rice (AUS)	
1908	Fred Alexander (USA)	
1909	Tony Wilding (NZL)	
1910	Rodney Heath (AUS)	
1911	Norman Brookes (AUS)	
1912	J. Cecil Parke (GBR)	
1913	E.F. Parker (AUS)	
1914	Pat O'Hara Wood (AUS)	
1915	Francis Lowe (GBR)	
1916–18	*not held*	
1919	A.R.F. Kingscote (GBR)	
1920	Pat O'Hara Wood (AUS)	
1921	Rhys Gemmell (AUS)	
1922	James Anderson (AUS)	Margaret Molesworth (AUS)
1923	Pat O'Hara Wood (AUS)	Margaret Molesworth (AUS)
1924	James Anderson (AUS)	Sylvia Lance (AUS)
1925	James Anderson (AUS)	Daphne Akhurst (AUS)
1926	John Hawkes (AUS)	Daphne Akhurst (AUS)
1927	Gerald Patterson (AUS)	Esna Boyd (AUS)
1928	Jean Borotra (FRA)	Daphne Akhurst (AUS)
1929	John Gregory (GBR)	Daphne Akhurst (AUS)
1930	Gar Moon (AUS)	Daphne Akhurst (AUS)
1931	Jack Crawford (AUS)	Coral Buttsworth (AUS)
1932	Jack Crawford (AUS)	Coral Buttsworth (AUS)
1933	Jack Crawford (AUS)	Joan Hartigan (AUS)
1934	Fred Perry (GBR)	Joan Hartigan (AUS)
1935	Jack Crawford (AUS)	Dorothy Round (GBR)
1936	Adrian Quist (AUS)	Joan Hartigan (AUS)
1937	Vivian McGrath (AUS)	Nancye Wynne (AUS)
1938	Don Budge (USA)	Dorothy Bundy (USA)
1939	John Bromwich (AUS)	Emily Westacott (AUS)
1940	Adrian Quist (AUS)	Nancye Wynne (AUS)
1941–45	*not held*	
1946	John Bromwich (AUS)	Nancye Wynne Bolton (AUS)
1947	Dinny Pails (AUS)	Nancye Wynne Bolton (AUS)
1948	Adrian Quist (AUS)	Nancye Wynne Bolton (AUS)
1949	Frank Sedgman (AUS)	Doris Hart (USA)
1950	Frank Sedgman (AUS)	Louise Brough (USA)
1951	Dick Savitt (USA)	Nancye Wynne Bolton (AUS)
1952	Ken McGregor (AUS)	Thelma Long (AUS)
1953	Ken Rosewall (AUS)	Maureen Connolly (USA)
1954	Mervyn Rose (AUS)	Thelma Long (AUS)
1955	Ken Rosewall (AUS)	Beryl Penrose (AUS)
1956	Lew Hoad (AUS)	Mary Carter (AUS)
1957	Ashley Cooper (AUS)	Shirley Fry (USA)
1958	Ashley Cooper (AUS)	Angela Mortimer (GBR)
1959	Alex Olmedo (PER)	Mary Carter-Reitano (AUS)
1960	Rod Laver (AUS)	Margaret Smith (AUS)
1961	Roy Emerson (AUS)	Margaret Smith (AUS)
1962	Rod Laver (AUS)	Margaret Smith (AUS)
1963	Roy Emerson (AUS)	Margaret Smith (AUS)
1964	Roy Emerson (AUS)	Margaret Smith (AUS)
1965	Roy Emerson (AUS)	Margaret Smith (AUS)
1966	Roy Emerson (AUS)	Margaret Smith (AUS)
1967	Roy Emerson (AUS)	Nancy Richey (USA)
1968	Bill Bowrey (AUS)	Billie Jean King (USA)
1969	Rod Laver (AUS)	Margaret Smith Court (AUS)
1970	Arthur Ashe (USA)	Margaret Smith Court (AUS)
1971	Ken Rosewall (AUS)	Margaret Smith Court (AUS)
1972	Ken Rosewall (AUS)	Virginia Wade (GBR)
1973	John Newcombe (AUS)	Margaret Smith Court (AUS)
1974	Jimmy Connors (USA)	Evonne Goolagong (AUS)
1975	John Newcombe (AUS)	Evonne Goolagong (AUS)
1976	Mark Edmondson (AUS)	Evonne Goolagong Cawley (AUS)
1977	Roscoe Tanner (USA)	Kerry Reid (AUS)
1978[1]	Vitas Gerulaitis (USA)	Evonne Goolagong Cawley (AUS)

Australian Open Tennis Championships—Singles (continued)

YEAR	MEN	WOMEN
1979	Guillermo Vilas (ARG)	Chris O'Neill (AUS)
1980	Guillermo Vilas (ARG)	Barbara Jordan (USA)
1981	Brian Teacher (USA)	Hana Mandlikova (TCH)
1982	Johan Kriek (RSA)	Martina Navratilova (USA)
1983	Johan Kriek (RSA)	Chris Evert Lloyd (USA)
1984	Mats Wilander (SWE)	Martina Navratilova (USA)
1985	Mats Wilander (SWE)	Chris Evert Lloyd (USA)
1986	Stefan Edberg (SWE)	Martina Navratilova (USA)
1987	Stefan Edberg (SWE)	Hana Mandlikova (TCH)
1988	Mats Wilander (SWE)	Steffi Graf (FRG)
1989	Ivan Lendl (TCH)	Steffi Graf (FRG)
1990	Ivan Lendl (TCH)	Steffi Graf (FRG)
1991	Boris Becker (GER)	Monica Seles (YUG)
1992	Jim Courier (USA)	Monica Seles (YUG)
1993	Jim Courier (USA)	Monica Seles (YUG)
1994	Pete Sampras (USA)	Steffi Graf (GER)
1995	Andre Agassi (USA)	Mary Pierce (FRA)
1996	Boris Becker (GER)	Monica Seles (YUG)
1997	Pete Sampras (USA)	Martina Hingis (SUI)
1998	Petr Korda (TCH)	Martina Hingis (SUI)
1999	Yevgeny Kafelnikov (RUS)	Martina Hingis (SUI)
2000	Andre Agassi (USA)	Lindsay Davenport (USA)
2001	Andre Agassi (USA)	Jennifer Capriati (USA)
2002	Thomas Johansson (SWE)	Jennifer Capriati (USA)
2003	Andre Agassi (USA)	Serena Williams (USA)
2004	Roger Federer (SUI)	Justine Henin-Hardenne (BEL)
2005	Marat Safin (RUS)	Serena Williams (USA)
2006	*to be held 16–29 January*	

[1]*Tournaments since December 1977 held in December rather than January.*

Australian Open Tennis Championships—Doubles

YEAR	MEN	WOMEN
1905	Tom Tachell, Randolph Lycett	
1906	Tony Wilding, Rodney Heath	
1907	Harry Parker, William Gregg	
1908	Fred Alexander, Alfred Dunlop	
1909	Ernie F. Parker, J.P. Keane	
1910	Horace Rice, Ashley Campbell	
1911	Rodney Heath, Randolph Lycett	
1912	J. Cecil Parke, Charles Dixon	
1913	Ernie F. Parker, Alf Hedemann	
1914	Ashley Campbell, Gerald Patterson	
1915	Horace Rice, Clarrie Todd	
1916–18	*not held*	
1919	Pat O'Hara Wood, Ron Thomas	
1920	Pat O'Hara Wood, Ron Thomas	
1921	S.H. Eaton-Rice, Rhys Gemmell	
1922	Gerald Patterson, John Hawkes	Esne Boyd, Marjorie Mountain
1923	Pat O'Hara Wood, Bert St. John	Esne Boyd, Sylvia Lance
1924	Norman Brookes, James Anderson	Daphne Akhurst, Sylvia Lance
1925	Gerald Patterson, Pat O'Hara Wood	Daphne Akhurst, Sylvia Lance Harper
1926	Gerald Patterson, John Hawkes	Meryl O'Hara Wood, Esne Boyd
1927	Gerald Patterson, John Hawkes	Meryl O'Hara Wood, Louise Bickerton
1928	Jean Borotra, Jacques Brugnon	Daphne Akhurst, Esne Boyd
1929	Jack Crawford, Harry Hopman	Daphne Akhurst, Louise Bickerton
1930	Jack Crawford, Harry Hopman	Margaret Molesworth, Emily Hood
1931	Charles Donohoe, Ray Dunlop	Daphne Akhurst Cozens, Louise Bickerton
1932	Jack Crawford, Gar Moon	Coral Buttsworth, Marjorie Cox Crawford
1933	Ellsworth Vines, Keith Gledhill	Margaret Molesworth, Emily Hood Westacott
1934	Fred Perry, George Hughes	Margaret Molesworth, Emily Hood Westacott
1935	Jack Crawford, Vivian McGrath	Evelyn Dearman, Nancye Wynne Lyle
1936	Adrian Quist, D.P. Turnbull	Thelma Coyne, Nancye Wynne
1937	Adrian Quist, D.P. Turnbull	Thelma Coyne, Nancye Wynne
1938	Adrian Quist, John Bromwich	Thelma Coyne, Nancye Wynne
1939	Adrian Quist, John Bromwich	Thelma Coyne, Nancye Wynne

Australian Open Tennis Championships—Doubles (continued)

YEAR	MEN	WOMEN
1940	Adrian Quist, John Bromwich	Thelma Coyne, Nancye Wynne Bolton
1941–45	*not held*	
1946	Adrian Quist, John Bromwich	Joyce Fitch, Mary Bevis
1947	Adrian Quist, John Bromwich	Thelma Coyne Long, Nancye Wynne Bolton
1948	Adrian Quist, John Bromwich	Thelma Coyne Long, Nancye Wynne Bolton
1949	Adrian Quist, John Bromwich	Thelma Coyne Long, Nancye Wynne Bolton
1950	Adrian Quist, John Bromwich	Louise Brough, Doris Hart
1951	Frank Sedgman, Ken McGregor	Thelma Coyne Long, Nancye Wynne Bolton
1952	Frank Sedgman, Ken McGregor	Thelma Coyne Long, Nancye Wynne Bolton
1953	Lew Hoad, Ken Rosewall	Marueen Connolly, Julia Sampson
1954	Rex Hartwig, Mervyn Rose	Mary Bevis Hawton, Beryl Penrose
1955	Vic Seixas, Tony Trabert	Mary Bevis Hawton, Beryl Penrose
1956	Lew Hoad, Ken Rosewall	Mary Bevis Hawton, Thelma Coyne Long
1957	Lew Hoad, Neale Fraser	Althea Gibson, Shirley Fry
1958	Ashley Cooper, Neale Fraser	Mary Bevis Hawton, Thelma Coyne Long
1959	Rod Laver, Robert Mark	Renee Schuurman, Sandra Reynolds
1960	Rod Laver, Robert Mark	Maria Bueno, Christine Truman
1961	Rod Laver, Robert Mark	Mary Reitano, Margaret Smith
1962	Roy Emerson, Neale Fraser	Margaret Smith, Robyn Ebbern
1963	Bob Hewitt, Fred Stolle	Margaret Smith, Robyn Ebbern
1964	Bob Hewitt, Fred Stolle	Judy Tegart, Lesley Turner
1965	John Newcombe, Tony Roche	Margaret Smith, Lesley Turner
1966	Roy Emerson, Fred Stolle	Carole Graebner, Nancy Richey
1967	John Newcombe, Tony Roche	Judy Tegart, Lesley Turner
1968	Dick Crealy, Allan Stone	Karen Krantzcke, Karrie Melville
1969	Roy Emerson, Rod Laver	Margaret Smith Court, Judy Tegart
1970	Bob Lutz, Stan Smith	Margaret Smith Court, Judy Tegart Dalton
1971	John Newcombe, Tony Roche	Margaret Smith Court, Evonne Goolagong
1972	Owen Davidson, Ken Rosewall	Kerry Harris, Helen Gourlay
1973	Mal Anderson, John Newcombe	Margaret Smith Court, Virginia Wade
1974	Ross Case, Geoff Masters	Evonne Goolagong, Peggy Michel
1975	John Alexander, Phil Dent	Evonne Goolagong, Peggy Michel
1976	John Newcombe, Tony Roche	Evonne Goolagong Cawley, Helen Gourlay
1977	Arthur Ashe, Tony Roche	Dianne Fromholtz, Helen Gourlay
1978[1]	Allan Stone, Ray Ruffels	Evonne Goolagong Cawley, Helen Gourlay Cawley; Mona Guerrant, Kerry Reid[2]
1979	Wojtek Fibak, Kim Warwick	Renata Tomanova, Betsy Nagelsen
1980	Peter McNamara, Paul McNamee	Judy Chaloner, Dianne Evers
1981	Kim Warwick, Mark Edmondson	Martina Navratilova, Betsy Nagelsen
1982	Kim Warwick, Mark Edmondson	Kathy Jordan, Anne Smith
1983	John Alexander, John Fitzgerald	Martina Navratilova, Pam Shriver
1984	Mark Edmondson, Paul McNamee	Martina Navratilova, Pam Shriver
1985	Mark Edmondson, Sherwood Stewart	Martina Navratilova, Pam Shriver
1986	Paul Annacone, Christo van Rensburg	Martina Navratilova, Pam Shriver
1987	Stefan Edberg, Anders Jarryd	Martina Navratilova, Pam Shriver
1988	Rick Leach, Jim Pugh	Martina Navratilova, Pam Shriver
1989	Rick Leach, Jim Pugh	Martina Navratilova, Pam Shriver
1990	Pieter Aldrich, Danie Visser	Jana Novotna, Helena Sukova
1991	Scott Davis, David Pate	Patty Fendick, Mary Joe Fernandez
1992	Todd Woodbridge, Mark Woodforde	Arantxa Sánchez Vicario, Helena Sukova
1993	Danie Visser, Laurie Warder	Gigi Fernandez, Natasha Zvereva
1994	Paul Haarhuis, Jacco Eltingh	Gigi Fernandez, Natasha Zvereva
1995	Jared Palmer, Richey Reneberg	Arantxa Sánchez Vicario, Jana Novotna
1996	Stefan Edberg, Petr Korda	Arantxa Sánchez Vicario, Chanda Rubin
1997	Todd Woodbridge, Mark Woodforde	Martina Hingis, Natasha Zvereva
1998	Jonas Bjorkman, Jacco Eltingh	Martina Hingis, Mirjana Lucic
1999	Jonas Bjorkman, Patrick Rafter	Martina Hingis, Anna Kournikova
2000	Ellis Ferreira, Rick Leach	Lisa Raymond, Rennae Stubbs
2001	Jonas Bjorkman, Todd Woodbridge	Serena Williams, Venus Williams
2002	Mark Knowles, Daniel Nestor	Martina Hingis, Anna Kournikova
2003	Michael Llodra, Fabrice Santoro	Serena Williams, Venus Williams
2004	Michael Llodra, Fabrice Santoro	Virginia Ruano Pascual, Paola Suárez
2005	Wayne Black, Kevin Ullyett	Alicia Molik, Svetlana Kuznetsova
2006	*to be held 16–29 January*	

[1]*Tournaments since December 1977 held in December rather than January.*   [2]*Tie; finals rained out.*

French Open Tennis Championships—Singles

From 1891 to 1924, only members of French tennis clubs were eligible to play in the French Open. The table shows the winners only since 1925, when the tournament was opened to international competition.

YEAR	MEN	WOMEN
1925	René Lacoste (FRA)	Suzanne Lenglen (FRA)
1926	Henri Cochet (FRA)	Suzanne Lenglen (FRA)
1927	René Lacoste (FRA)	Kornelia Bouman (NED)
1928	Henri Cochet (FRA)	Helen Wills (USA)
1929	René Lacoste (FRA)	Helen Wills (USA)
1930	Henri Cochet (FRA)	Helen Wills Moody (USA)
1931	Jean Borotra (FRA)	Cilly Aussem (GER)
1932	Henri Cochet (FRA)	Helen Wills Moody (USA)
1933	John Crawford (AUS)	Margaret Scriven (GBR)
1934	Gottfried von Cramm (GER)	Margaret Scriven (GBR)
1935	Fred Perry (GBR)	Hilde Sperling (DEN)
1936	Gottfried von Cramm (GER)	Hilde Sperling (DEN)
1937	Henner Henkel (GER)	Hilde Sperling (DEN)
1938	Don Budge (USA)	Simone Mathieu (FRA)
1939	Don McNeill (USA)	Simone Mathieu (FRA)
1940	*not held*	*not held*
1941	Bernard Destremau (FRA)	*not held*
1942	Bernard Destremau (FRA)	*not held*
1943	Yvon Petra (FRA)	*not held*
1944	Yvon Petra (FRA)	*not held*
1945	Yvon Petra (FRA)	*not held*
1946	Marcel Bernard (FRA)	Margaret Osborne (USA)
1947	Joseph Asboth (HUN)	Patricia Todd (USA)
1948	Frank Parker (USA)	Nelly Landry (BEL)
1949	Frank Parker (USA)	Margaret Osborne du Pont (USA)
1950	Budge Patty (USA)	Doris Hart (USA)
1951	Jaroslav Drobny (TCH)	Shirley Fry (USA)
1952	Jaroslav Drobny (TCH)	Doris Hart (USA)
1953	Ken Rosewall (AUS)	Maureen Connolly (USA)
1954	Tony Trabert (USA)	Maureen Connolly (USA)
1955	Tony Trabert (USA)	Angela Mortimer (GBR)
1956	Lew Hoad (AUS)	Althea Gibson (USA)
1957	Sven Davidson (SWE)	Shirley Bloomer (GBR)
1958	Mervyn Rose (AUS)	Zsuzsi Kormoczi (HUN)
1959	Nicola Pietrangeli (ITA)	Christine Truman (GBR)
1960	Nicola Pietrangeli (ITA)	Darlene Hard (USA)
1961	Manuel Santana (ESP)	Ann Haydon (GBR)
1962	Rod Laver (AUS)	Margaret Smith (AUS)
1963	Roy Emerson (AUS)	Lesley Turner (AUS)
1964	Manuel Santana (ESP)	Margaret Smith (AUS)
1965	Fred Stolle (AUS)	Lesley Turner (AUS)
1966	Tony Roche (AUS)	Ann Haydon Jones (GBR)
1967	Roy Emerson (AUS)	Françoise Durr (FRA)
1968	Ken Rosewall (AUS)	Nancy Richey (USA)
1969	Rod Laver (AUS)	Margaret Smith Court (AUS)
1970	Jan Kodes (TCH)	Margaret Smith Court (AUS)
1971	Jan Kodes (TCH)	Evonne Goolagong (AUS)
1972	Andres Gimeno (ESP)	Billie Jean King (USA)
1973	Ilie Nastase (ROM)	Margaret Smith Court (AUS)
1974	Bjorn Borg (SWE)	Chris Evert (USA)
1975	Bjorn Borg (SWE)	Chris Evert (USA)
1976	Adriano Panatta (ITA)	Sue Barker (USA)
1977	Guillermo Vilas (ARG)	Mima Jausovec (YUG)
1978	Bjorn Borg (SWE)	Virginia Ruzici (ROM)
1979	Bjorn Borg (SWE)	Chris Evert Lloyd (USA)
1980	Bjorn Borg (SWE)	Chris Evert Lloyd (USA)
1981	Bjorn Borg (SWE)	Hana Mandlikova (TCH)
1982	Mats Wilander (SWE)	Martina Navratilova (USA)
1983	Yannick Noah (FRA)	Chris Evert Lloyd (USA)
1984	Ivan Lendl (TCH)	Martina Navratilova (USA)
1985	Mats Wilander (SWE)	Chris Evert Lloyd (USA)
1986	Ivan Lendl (TCH)	Chris Evert Lloyd (USA)
1987	Ivan Lendl (TCH)	Steffi Graf (FRG)
1988	Mats Wilander (SWE)	Steffi Graf (FRG)
1989	Michael Chang (USA)	Arantxa Sánchez Vicario (ESP)
1990	Andres Gómez (ECU)	Monica Seles (YUG)

French Open Tennis Championships—Singles (continued)

YEAR	MEN	WOMEN
1991	Jim Courier (USA)	Monica Seles (YUG)
1992	Jim Courier (USA)	Monica Seles (YUG)
1993	Sergi Bruguera (ESP)	Steffi Graf (GER)
1994	Sergi Bruguera (ESP)	Arantxa Sánchez Vicario (ESP)
1995	Thomas Muster (AUT)	Steffi Graf (GER)
1996	Yevgeny Kafelnikov (RUS)	Steffi Graf (GER)
1997	Gustavo Kuerten (BRA)	Iva Majoli (CRO)
1998	Carlos Moya (ESP)	Arantxa Sánchez Vicario (ESP)
1999	Andre Agassi (USA)	Steffi Graf (GER)
2000	Gustavo Kuerten (BRA)	Mary Pierce (FRA)
2001	Gustavo Kuerten (BRA)	Jennifer Capriati (USA)
2002	Albert Costa (ESP)	Serena Williams (USA)
2003	Juan Carlos Ferrero (ESP)	Justine Henin-Hardenne (BEL)
2004	Gastón Gaudio (ARG)	Anastasya Myskina (RUS)
2005	Rafael Nadal (ESP)	Justine Henin-Hardenne (BEL)

French Open Tennis Championships—Doubles

YEAR	MEN	WOMEN
1925	Jean Borotra, René Lacoste	Suzanne Lenglen, Didi Vlasto
1926	Vinnie Richards, Howard Kinsey	Suzanne Lenglen, Didi Vlasto
1927	Henri Cochet, Jacques Brugnon	Irene Peacock, Bobby Heine
1928	Jean Borotra, Jacques Brugnon	Phoebe Watson, Eileen Bennett
1929	Jean Borotra, René Lacoste	Lili de Alvarez, Kea Bouman
1930	Henri Cochet, Jacques Brugnon	Helen Wills Moody, Elizabeth Ryan
1931	George Lott, John Van Ryn	Eileen Whittingstall, Betty Nuthall
1932	Henri Cochet, Jacques Brugnon	Helen Wills Moody, Elizabeth Ryan
1933	Pat Hughes, Fred Perry	Simone Mathieu, Elizabeth Ryan
1934	Jean Borotra, Jacques Brugnon	Simone Mathieu, Elizabeth Ryan
1935	Jack Crawford, Adrian Quist	Margaret Scriven, Kay Stammers
1936	Jean Borotra, Marcel Bernard	Simone Mathieu, Billy Yorke
1937	Gottfried von Cramm, Henner Henkel	Simone Mathieu, Billy Yorke
1938	Bernard Destremau, Yvon Petra	Simone Mathieu, Billy Yorke
1939	Don McNeill, Charles Harris	Simone Mathieu, Jadwiga Jedrzejowska
1940–45	not held	
1946	Marcel Bernard, Yvon Petra	Louise Brough, Margaret Osborne
1947	Eustace Fannin, Eric Sturgess	Louise Brough, Margaret Osborne
1948	Lennart Bergelin, Jaroslav Drobny	Doris Hart, Patricia Todd
1949	Pancho Gonzales, Frank Parker	Louise Brough, Margaret Osborne du Pont
1950	Billy Talbert, Tony Trabert	Doris Hart, Shirley Fry
1951	Ken McGregor, Frank Sedgman	Doris Hart, Shirley Fry
1952	Ken McGregor, Frank Sedgman	Doris Hart, Shirley Fry
1953	Lew Hoad, Ken Rosewall	Doris Hart, Shirley Fry
1954	Vic Seixas, Tony Trabert	Maureen Connolly, Nell Hopman
1955	Vic Seixas, Tony Trabert	Beverly Fleitz, Darlene Hard
1956	Don Candy, Robert Perry	Angela Buxton, Althea Gibson
1957	Mal Anderson, Ashley Cooper	Shirley Bloomer, Darlene Hard
1958	Ashley Cooper, Neale Fraser	Rosie Reyes, Yola Ramirez
1959	Nicola Pietrangeli, Orlando Sirola	Sandra Reynolds, Renee Schuurman
1960	Roy Emerson, Neale Fraser	Maria Bueno, Darlene Hard
1961	Roy Emerson, Rod Laver	Sandra Reynolds, Renee Schuurman
1962	Roy Emerson, Neale Fraser	Sandra Reynolds Price, Renee Schuurman
1963	Roy Emerson, Manuel Santana	Ann Haydon Jones, Renee Schuurman
1964	Roy Emerson, Ken Fletcher	Margaret Smith, Leslie Turner
1965	Roy Emerson, Fred Stolle	Margaret Smith, Leslie Turner
1966	Clark Graebner, Dennis Ralston	Margaret Smith, Judy Tegart
1967	John Newcombe, Tony Roche	Françoise Durr, Gail Sheriff
1968	Ken Rosewall, Fred Stolle	Françoise Durr, Ann Haydon Jones
1969	John Newcombe, Tony Roche	Françoise Durr, Ann Haydon Jones
1970	Ilie Nastase, Ion Tiriac	Françoise Durr, Gail Chanfreau
1971	Arthur Ashe, Marty Riessen	Françoise Durr, Gail Chanfreau
1972	Bob Hewitt, Frew McMillan	Billie Jean King, Betty Stove
1973	John Newcombe, Tom Okker	Margaret Smith Court, Virginia Wade
1974	Dick Crealy, Onny Parun	Chris Evert, Olga Morozova
1975	Brian Gottfried, Raul Ramirez	Chris Evert, Martina Navratilova
1976	Fred McNair, Sherwood Stewart	Fiorella Bonicelli, Gail Chanfreau Lovera
1977	Brian Gottfried, Raul Ramirez	Regina Marsikova, Pam Teeguarden

French Open Tennis Championships—Doubles (continued)

YEAR	MEN	WOMEN
1978	Hank Pfister, Gene Mayer	Mimi Jausovec, Virginia Ruzici
1979	Sandy Mayer, Gene Mayer	Betty Stove, Wendy Turnbull
1980	Victor Amaya, Hank Pfister	Kathy Jordan, Anne Smith
1981	Heinz Gunthardt, Balazs Taroczy	Rosalyn Fairbank, Tanya Harford
1982	Sherwood Stewart, Ferdi Taygan	Martina Navratilova, Anne Smith
1983	Anders Jarryd, Hans Simonsson	Rosalyn Fairbank, Candy Reynolds
1984	Henri Leconte, Yannick Noah	Martina Navratilova, Pam Shriver
1985	Mark Edmondson, Kim Warwick	Martina Navratilova, Pam Shriver
1986	John Fitzgerald, Tomas Smid	Martina Navratilova, Andrea Temesvari
1987	Robert Seguso, Anders Jarryd	Martina Navratilova, Pam Shriver
1988	Emilio Sánchez, Andres Gomez	Martina Navratilova, Pam Shriver
1989	Jim Grabb, Patrick McEnroe	Larisa Savchenko, Natasha Zvereva
1990	Sergio Casal, Emilio Sánchez	Jana Novotna, Helena Sukova
1991	John Fitzgerald, Anders Jarryd	Gigi Fernandez, Jana Novotna
1992	Jacob Hlasek, Marc Rosset	Gigi Fernandez, Natasha Zvereva
1993	Luke Jensen, Murphy Jensen	Gigi Fernandez, Natasha Zvereva
1994	Byron Black, Jonathan Stark	Gigi Fernandez, Natasha Zvereva
1995	Jacco Eltingh, Paul Haarhuis	Gigi Fernandez, Natasha Zvereva
1996	Yevgeny Kafelnikov, Daniel Vacek	Lindsay Davenport, Mary Joe Fernandez
1997	Yevgeny Kafelnikov, Daniel Vacek	Gigi Fernandez, Natasha Zvereva
1998	Jacco Eltingh, Paul Haarhuis	Martina Hingis, Jana Novotna
1999	Mahesh Bhupathi, Leander Paes	Serena Williams, Venus Williams
2000	Todd Woodbridge, Mark Woodforde	Martina Hingis, Mary Pierce
2001	Mahesh Bhupathi, Leander Paes	Virginia Ruano Pascual, Paola Suárez
2002	Yevgeny Kafelnikov, Paul Haarhuis	Virginia Ruano Pascual, Paola Suárez
2003	Bob Bryan, Mike Bryan	Kim Clijsters, Ai Sugiyama
2004	Xavier Malisse, Olivier Rochus	Virginia Ruano Pascual, Paola Suárez
2005	Jonas Bjorkman, Max Mirnyi	Virginia Ruano Pascual, Paola Suárez

All-England (Wimbledon) Tennis Championships—Singles

YEAR	MEN	WOMEN
1877	Spencer Gore (GBR)	
1878	Frank Hadow (GBR)	
1879	John Hartley (GBR)	
1880	John Hartley (GBR)	
1881	Willie Renshaw (GBR)	
1882	Willie Renshaw (GBR)	
1883	Willie Renshaw (GBR)	
1884	Willie Renshaw (GBR)	Maud Watson (GBR)
1885	Willie Renshaw (GBR)	Maud Watson (GBR)
1886	Willie Renshaw (GBR)	Blanche Bingley (GBR)
1887	Herbert Lawford (GBR)	Lottie Dod (GBR)
1888	Ernest Renshaw (GBR)	Lottie Dod (GBR)
1889	Willie Renshaw (GBR)	Blanche Bingley Hillyard (GBR)
1890	William Hamilton (GBR)	Lena Rice (GBR)
1891	Wilfred Baddeley (GBR)	Lottie Dod (GBR)
1892	Wilfred Baddeley (GBR)	Lottie Dod (GBR)
1893	Joshua Pim (GBR)	Lottie Dod (GBR)
1894	Joshua Pim (GBR)	Blanche Bingley Hillyard (GBR)
1895	Wilfred Baddeley (GBR)	Charlotte Cooper (GBR)
1896	Harold Mahony (GBR)	Charlotte Cooper (GBR)
1897	Reggie Doherty (GBR)	Blanche Bingley Hillyard (GBR)
1898	Reggie Doherty (GBR)	Charlotte Cooper (GBR)
1899	Reggie Doherty (GBR)	Blanche Bingley Hillyard (GBR)
1900	Reggie Doherty (GBR)	Blanche Bingley Hillyard (GBR)
1901	Arthur Gore (GBR)	Charlotte Cooper Sterry (GBR)
1902	Laurie Doherty (GBR)	Muriel Robb (GBR)
1903	Laurie Doherty (GBR)	Dorothea Douglass (GBR)
1904	Laurie Doherty (GBR)	Dorothea Douglass (GBR)
1905	Laurie Doherty (GBR)	May Sutton (USA)
1906	Laurie Doherty (GBR)	Dorothea Douglass (GBR)
1907	Norman Brookes (AUS)	May Sutton (USA)
1908	Arthur Gore (GBR)	Charlotte Cooper Sterry (GBR)
1909	Arthur Gore (GBR)	Dora Boothby (GBR)
1910	Tony Wilding (NZL)	Dorothea Douglass Lambert Chambers (GBR)

All-England (Wimbledon) Tennis Championships—Singles (continued)

YEAR	MEN	WOMEN
1911	Tony Wilding (NZL)	Dorothea Douglass Lambert Chambers (GBR)
1912	Tony Wilding (NZL)	Ethel Larcombe (GBR)
1913	Tony Wilding (NZL)	Dorothea Douglass Lambert Chambers (GBR)
1914	Norman Brookes (AUS)	Dorothea Douglass Lambert Chambers (GBR)
1915–18	*not held*	
1919	Gerald Patterson (AUS)	Suzanne Lenglen (FRA)
1920	Bill Tilden (USA)	Suzanne Lenglen (FRA)
1921	Bill Tilden (USA)	Suzanne Lenglen (FRA)
1922	Gerald Patterson (AUS)	Suzanne Lenglen (FRA)
1923	Bill Johnston (USA)	Suzanne Lenglen (FRA)
1924	Jean Borotra (FRA)	Kathleen McKane (GBR)
1925	René Lacoste (FRA)	Suzanne Lenglen (FRA)
1926	Jean Borotra (FRA)	Kathleen McKane Godfree (GBR)
1927	Henri Cochet (FRA)	Helen Wills (USA)
1928	René Lacoste (FRA)	Helen Wills (USA)
1929	Henri Cochet (FRA)	Helen Wills (USA)
1930	Bill Tilden (USA)	Helen Wills Moody (USA)
1931	Sidney Wood (USA)	Cilly Aussem (GER)
1932	Ellsworth Vines (USA)	Helen Wills Moody (USA)
1933	Jack Crawford (AUS)	Helen Wills Moody (USA)
1934	Fred Perry (GBR)	Dorothy Round (GBR)
1935	Fred Perry (GBR)	Helen Wills Moody (USA)
1936	Fred Perry (GBR)	Helen Jacobs (USA)
1937	Don Budge (USA)	Dorothy Round (GBR)
1938	Don Budge (USA)	Helen Wills Moody (USA)
1939	Bobby Riggs (USA)	Alice Marble (USA)
1940–45	*not held*	
1946	Yvon Petra (FRA)	Pauline Betz (USA)
1947	Jack Kramer (USA)	Margaret Osborne (USA)
1948	Bob Falkenburg (USA)	Louise Brough (USA)
1949	Ted Schroeder (USA)	Louise Brough (USA)
1950	Budge Patty (USA)	Louise Brough (USA)
1951	Dick Savitt (USA)	Doris Hart (USA)
1952	Frank Sedgman (AUS)	Maureen Connolly (USA)
1953	Vic Seixas (USA)	Maureen Connolly (USA)
1954	Jaroslav Drobny (TCH)	Maureen Connolly (USA)
1955	Tony Trabert (USA)	Louise Brough (USA)
1956	Lew Hoad (AUS)	Shirley Fry (USA)
1957	Lew Hoad (AUS)	Althea Gibson (USA)
1958	Ashley Cooper (AUS)	Althea Gibson (USA)
1959	Alex Olmedo (PER)	Maria Bueno (BRA)
1960	Neale Fraser (AUS)	Maria Bueno (BRA)
1961	Rod Laver (AUS)	Angela Mortimer (GBR)
1962	Rod Laver (AUS)	Karen Susman (USA)
1963	Chuck McKinley (USA)	Margaret Smith (AUS)
1964	Roy Emerson (AUS)	Maria Bueno (BRA)
1965	Roy Emerson (AUS)	Margaret Smith (AUS)
1966	Manuel Santana (ESP)	Billie Jean King (USA)
1967	John Newcombe (AUS)	Billie Jean King (USA)
1968[1]	Rod Laver (AUS)	Billie Jean King (USA)
1969	Rod Laver (AUS)	Ann Jones (GBR)
1970	John Newcombe (AUS)	Margaret Smith Court (AUS)
1971	John Newcombe (AUS)	Evonne Goolagong (AUS)
1972	Stan Smith (USA)	Billie Jean King (USA)
1973	Jan Kodes (TCH)	Billie Jean King (USA)
1974	Jimmy Connors (USA)	Chris Evert (USA)
1975	Arthur Ashe (USA)	Billie Jean King (USA)
1976	Björn Borg (SWE)	Chris Evert (USA)
1977	Björn Borg (SWE)	Virginia Wade (GBR)
1978	Björn Borg (SWE)	Martina Navratilova (TCH)
1979	Björn Borg (SWE)	Martina Navratilova (USA)
1980	Björn Borg (SWE)	Evonne Goolagong Cawley (AUS)
1981	John McEnroe (USA)	Chris Evert Lloyd (USA)
1982	Jimmy Connors (USA)	Martina Navratilova (USA)
1983	John McEnroe (USA)	Martina Navratilova (USA)
1984	John McEnroe (USA)	Martina Navratilova (USA)
1985	Boris Becker (FRG)	Martina Navratilova (USA)
1986	Boris Becker (FRG)	Martina Navratilova (USA)

All-England (Wimbledon) Tennis Championships—Singles (continued)

YEAR	MEN	WOMEN
1987	Pat Cash (AUS)	Martina Navratilova (USA)
1988	Stefan Edberg (SWE)	Steffi Graf (GDR)
1989	Boris Becker (FRG)	Steffi Graf (GDR)
1990	Stefan Edberg (SWE)	Martina Navratilova (USA)
1991	Michael Stich (GER)	Steffi Graf (GER)
1992	Andre Agassi (USA)	Steffi Graf (GER)
1993	Pete Sampras (USA)	Steffi Graf (GER)
1994	Pete Sampras (USA)	Conchita Martínez (ESP)
1995	Pete Sampras (USA)	Steffi Graf (GER)
1996	Richard Krajicek (NED)	Steffi Graf (GER)
1997	Pete Sampras (USA)	Martina Hingis (SUI)
1998	Pete Sampras (USA)	Jana Novotna (CZE)
1999	Pete Sampras (USA)	Lindsay Davenport (USA)
2000	Pete Sampras (USA)	Venus Williams (USA)
2001	Goran Ivanisevic (CRO)	Venus Williams (USA)
2002	Lleyton Hewitt (AUS)	Serena Williams (USA)
2003	Roger Federer (SUI)	Serena Williams (USA)
2004	Roger Federer (SUI)	Mariya Sharapova (RUS)
2005	Roger Federer (SUI)	Venus Williams (USA)

[1]Open since 1968.

All-England (Wimbledon) Tennis Championships—Doubles

YEAR	MEN	WOMEN
1879	L.R. Erskine, H. Lawford	
1880	William Renshaw, Ernest Renshaw	
1881	William Renshaw, Ernest Renshaw	
1882	J.T. Hartley, R.T. Richardson	
1883	C.W. Grinstead, C.E. Welldon	
1884	William Renshaw, Ernest Renshaw	
1885	William Renshaw, Ernest Renshaw	
1886	William Renshaw, Ernest Renshaw	
1887	Herbert Wilberforce, P.B. Lyon	
1888	William Renshaw, Ernest Renshaw	
1889	William Renshaw, Ernest Renshaw	
1890	Joshua Pim, F.O. Stoker	
1891	Wilfred Baddeley, Herbert Baddeley	
1892	E.W. Lewis, H.S. Barlow	
1893	Joshua Pim, F.O. Stoker	
1894	Wilfred Baddeley, Herbert Baddeley	
1895	Wilfred Baddeley, Herbert Baddeley	
1896	Wilfred Baddeley, Herbert Baddeley	
1897	Reggie Doherty, Laurie Doherty	
1898	Reggie Doherty, Laurie Doherty	
1899	Reggie Doherty, Laurie Doherty	
1900	Reggie Doherty, Laurie Doherty	
1901	Reggie Doherty, Laurie Doherty	
1902	Sidney Smith, Frank Riseley	
1903	Reggie Doherty, Laurie Doherty	
1904	Reggie Doherty, Laurie Doherty	
1905	Reggie Doherty, Laurie Doherty	
1906	Sidney Smith, Frank Riseley	
1907	Norman Brookes, Anthony Wilding	
1908	Anthony Wilding, M.J.G. Ritchie	
1909	Arthur Gore, H. Roper Barrett	
1910	Anthony Wilding, M.J.G. Ritchie	
1911	Andre Gobert, Max Decugis	
1912	H. Roper Barrett, Charles Dixon	
1913	H. Roper Barrett, Charles Dixon	Winifred McNair, Dora Boothby
1914	Norman Brookes, Anthony Wilding	Elizabeth Ryan, Agatha Morton
1915–18	not held	
1919	R.V. Thomas, Pat O'Hara Wood	Suzanne Lenglen, Elizabeth Ryan
1920	Richard Williams, Chuck Garland	Suzanne Lenglen, Elizabeth Ryan
1921	Randolph Lycett, Max Woosnam	Suzanne Lenglen, Elizabeth Ryan
1922	James Anderson, Randolph Lycett	Suzanne Lenglen, Elizabeth Ryan

All-England (Wimbledon) Tennis Championships—Doubles (continued)

YEAR	MEN	WOMEN
1923	Leslie Godfree, Randolph Lycett	Suzanne Lenglen, Elizabeth Ryan
1924	Frank Hunter, Vincent Richards	Hazel Wightman, Helen Wills
1925	Jean Borotra, René Lacoste	Suzanne Lenglen, Elizabeth Ryan
1926	Jacques Brugnon, Henri Cochet	Mary Browne, Elizabeth Ryan
1927	Bill Tilden, Frank Hunter	Helen Wills, Elizabeth Ryan
1928	Jacques Brugnon, Henri Cochet	Peggy Saunders, Phoebe Watson
1929	Wilmer Allison, John Van Ryn	Peggy Saunders Michell, Phoebe Watson
1930	Wilmer Allison, John Van Ryn	Helen Wills Moody, Elizabeth Ryan
1931	George Lott, John Van Ryn	Phyllis Mudford, Dorothy Barron
1932	Jean Borotra, Jacques Brugnon	Doris Metaxa, Josane Sigart
1933	Jean Borotra, Jacques Brugnon	Elizabeth Ryan, Simone Mathieu
1934	George Lott, Lester Stoefen	Elizabeth Ryan, Simone Mathieu
1935	Jack Crawford, Adrian Quist	Freda James, Kay Stammers
1936	Pat Hughes, Raymond Tuckey	Freda James, Kay Stammers
1937	Don Budge, Gene Mako	Simone Mathieu, Billie Yorke
1938	Don Budge, Gene Mako	Sarah Palfrey Fabyan, Alice Marble
1939	Bobby Riggs, Elwood Cooke	Sarah Palfrey Fabyan, Alice Marble
1940–45	*not held*	
1946	Jack Kramer, Tom Brown	Louise Brough, Margaret Osborne
1947	Jack Kramer, Bob Falkenburg	Patricia Todd, Doris Hart
1948	John Bromwich, Frank Sedgman	Louise Brough, Margaret Osborne du Pont
1949	Pancho Gonzales, Frank Parker	Louise Brough, Margaret Osborne du Pont
1950	John Bromwich, Adrian Quist	Louise Brough, Margaret Osborne du Pont
1951	Ken McGregor, Frank Sedgman	Doris Hart, Shirley Fry
1952	Ken McGregor, Frank Sedgman	Doris Hart, Shirley Fry
1953	Ken Rosewall, Lew Hoad	Doris Hart, Shirley Fry
1954	Rex Hartwig, Mervyn Rose	Louise Brough, Margaret Osborne du Pont
1955	Rex Hartwig, Lew Hoad	Angela Mortimer, Anne Shilcock
1956	Ken Rosewall, Lew Hoad	Angela Buxton, Althea Gibson
1957	Budge Patty, Gardnar Mulloy	Althea Gibson, Darlene Hard
1958	Sven Davidson, Ulf Schmidt	Maria Bueno, Althea Gibson
1959	Roy Emerson, Neale Fraser	Jeanne Arth, Darlene Hard
1960	Rafael Osuna, Dennis Ralston	Maria Bueno, Darlene Hard
1961	Roy Emerson, Neale Fraser	Karen Hantze, Billie Jean Moffitt
1962	Bob Hewitt, Fred Stolle	Karen Hantze Susman, Billie Jean Moffitt
1963	Rafael Osuna, Antonio Palafox	Maria Bueno, Darlene Hard
1964	Bob Hewitt, Fred Stolle	Margaret Smith, Leslie Turner
1965	John Newcombe, Tony Roche	Maria Bueno, Billie Jean Moffitt
1966	John Newcombe, Ken Fletcher	Maria Bueno, Nancy Richey
1967	Bob Hewitt, Frew McMillan	Rosemary Casals, Billie Jean Moffitt King
1968	John Newcombe, Tony Roche	Rosemary Casals, Billie Jean King
1969	John Newcombe, Tony Roche	Margaret Smith Court, Judy Tegart
1970	John Newcombe, Tony Roche	Rosemary Casals, Billie Jean King
1971	Rod Laver, Roy Emerson	Rosemary Casals, Billie Jean King
1972	Bob Hewitt, Frew McMillan	Billie Jean King, Betty Stove
1973	Jimmy Connors, Ilie Nastase	Rosemary Casals, Billie Jean King
1974	John Newcombe, Tony Roche	Evonne Goolagong, Peggy Michel
1975	Vitas Gerulaitis, Sandy Mayer	Ann Kiyomura, Kazuko Sawamatsu
1976	Brian Gottfried, Raul Ramirez	Chris Evert, Martina Navratilova
1977	Ross Case, Geoff Masters	Helen Gourlay Cawley, Joanne Russell
1978	Bob Hewitt, Frew McMillan	Kerry Reid, Wendy Turnbull
1979	John McEnroe, Peter Fleming	Billie Jean King, Martina Navratilova
1980	Peter McNamara, Paul McNamee	Kathy Jordan, Anne Smith
1981	John McEnroe, Peter Fleming	Martina Navratilova, Pam Shriver
1982	Peter McNamara, Paul McNamee	Martina Navratilova, Pam Shriver
1983	John McEnroe, Peter Fleming	Martina Navratilova, Pam Shriver
1984	John McEnroe, Peter Fleming	Martina Navratilova, Pam Shriver
1985	Heinz Gunthardt, Balazs Taroczy	Kathy Jordan, Elizabeth Smylie
1986	Joakim Nystrom, Mats Wilander	Martina Navratilova, Pam Shriver
1987	Robert Seguso, Ken Flach	Claudia Kohde-Kilsche, Helena Sukova
1988	Robert Seguso, Ken Flach	Steffi Graf, Gabriela Sabatini
1989	John Fitzgerald, Anders Jarryd	Jana Novotna, Helena Sukova
1990	Rick Leach, Jim Pugh	Jana Novotna, Helena Sukova
1991	John Fitzgerald, Anders Jarryd	Larisa Savchenko, Natasha Zvereva
1992	John McEnroe, Michael Stich	Gigi Fernandez, Natasha Zvereva
1993	Todd Woodbridge, Mark Woodforde	Gigi Fernandez, Natasha Zvereva
1994	Todd Woodbridge, Mark Woodforde	Gigi Fernandez, Natasha Zvereva
1995	Todd Woodbridge, Mark Woodforde	Arantxa Sánchez Vicario, Jana Novotna

All-England (Wimbledon) Tennis Championships—Doubles (continued)

YEAR	MEN	WOMEN
1996	Todd Woodbridge, Mark Woodforde	Helena Sukova, Martina Hingis
1997	Todd Woodbridge, Mark Woodforde	Gigi Fernandez, Natasha Zvereva
1998	Jacco Eltingh, Paul Haarhuis	Martina Hingis, Jana Novotna
1999	Mahesh Bhupathi, Leander Paes	Lindsay Davenport, Corina Morariu
2000	Todd Woodbridge, Mark Woodforde	Venus Williams, Serena Williams
2001	Donald Johnson, Jared Palmer	Lisa Raymond, Rennae Stubbs
2002	Todd Woodbridge, Jonas Bjorkman	Venus Williams, Serena Williams
2003	Todd Woodbridge, Jonas Bjorkman	Kim Clijsters, Ai Sugiyama
2004	Todd Woodbridge, Jonas Bjorkman	Cara Black, Rennae Stubbs
2005	Stephen Huss, Wesley Moodie	Cara Black, Liezel Huber

United States Open Tennis Championships—Singles

YEAR	MEN	WOMEN
1881	Richard Sears (USA)	
1882	Richard Sears (USA)	
1883	Richard Sears (USA)	
1884	Richard Sears (USA)	
1885	Richard Sears (USA)	
1886	Richard Sears (USA)	
1887	Richard Sears (USA)	Ellen Hansell (USA)
1888	Henry Slocum, Jr. (USA)	Bertha Townsend (USA)
1889	Henry Slocum, Jr. (USA)	Bertha Townsend (USA)
1890	Oliver Campbell (USA)	Ellen Roosevelt (USA)
1891	Oliver Campbell (USA)	Mabel Cahill (USA)
1892	Oliver Campbell (USA)	Mabel Cahill (USA)
1893	Robert Wrenn (USA)	Aline Terry (USA)
1894	Robert Wrenn (USA)	Helen Helwig (USA)
1895	Fred Hovey (USA)	Juliette Atkinson (USA)
1896	Robert Wrenn (USA)	Elisabeth Moore (USA)
1897	Robert Wrenn (USA)	Juliette Atkinson (USA)
1898	Malcom Whitman (USA)	Juliette Atkinson (USA)
1899	Malcom Whitman (USA)	Marion Jones (USA)
1900	Malcom Whitman (USA)	Myrtle McAteer (USA)
1901	William Larned (USA)	Elisabeth Moore (USA)
1902	William Larned (USA)	Marion Jones (USA)
1903	Laurie Doherty (GBR)	Elisabeth Moore (USA)
1904	Holcombe Ward (USA)	May Sutton (USA)
1905	Beals Wright (USA)	Elisabeth Moore (USA)
1906	Bill Clothier (USA)	Helen Homans (USA)
1907	William Larned (USA)	Evelyn Sears (USA)
1908	William Larned (USA)	Maud Barger-Wallach (USA)
1909	William Larned (USA)	Hazel Hotchkiss (USA)
1910	William Larned (USA)	Hazel Hotchkiss (USA)
1911	William Larned (USA)	Hazel Hotchkiss (USA)
1912	Maurice McLoughlin (USA)	Mary Browne (USA)
1913	Maurice McLoughlin (USA)	Mary Browne (USA)
1914	R. Norris Williams (USA)	Mary Browne (USA)
1915	Bill Johnston (USA)	Molla Bjurstedt (NOR)
1916	R. Norris Williams (USA)	Molla Bjurstedt (NOR)
1917	Lindley Murray (USA)	Molla Bjurstedt (NOR)
1918	Lindley Murray (USA)	Molla Bjurstedt (NOR)
1919	Bill Johnston (USA)	Hazel Hotchkiss Wightman (USA)
1920	Bill Tilden (USA)	Molla Bjurstedt Mallory (USA)
1921	Bill Tilden (USA)	Molla Bjurstedt Mallory (USA)
1922	Bill Tilden (USA)	Molla Bjurstedt Mallory (USA)
1923	Bill Tilden (USA)	Helen Wills (USA)
1924	Bill Tilden (USA)	Helen Wills (USA)
1925	Bill Tilden (USA)	Helen Wills (USA)
1926	René Lacoste (FRA)	Molla Bjurstedt Mallory (USA)
1927	René Lacoste (FRA)	Helen Wills (USA)
1928	Henri Cochet (FRA)	Helen Wills (USA)
1929	Bill Tilden (USA)	Helen Wills (USA)
1930	John Doeg (USA)	Betty Nuthall (GBR)
1931	Ellsworth Vines (USA)	Helen Wills Moody (USA)
1932	Ellsworth Vines (USA)	Helen Jacobs (USA)

United States Open Tennis Championships—Singles (continued)

YEAR	MEN	WOMEN
1933	Fred Perry (GBR)	Helen Jacobs (USA)
1934	Fred Perry (GBR)	Helen Jacobs (USA)
1935	Wilmer Allison (USA)	Helen Jacobs (USA)
1936	Fred Perry (GBR)	Alice Marble (USA)
1937	Don Budge (USA)	Anita Lizana (CHI)
1938	Don Budge (USA)	Alice Marble (USA)
1939	Bobby Riggs (USA)	Alice Marble (USA)
1940	Don McNeill (USA)	Alice Marble (USA)
1941	Bobby Riggs (USA)	Sarah Palfrey Cooke (USA)
1942	Ted Schroeder (USA)	Pauline Betz (USA)
1943	Joe Hunt (USA)	Pauline Betz (USA)
1944	Frank Parker (USA)	Pauline Betz (USA)
1945	Frank Parker (USA)	Sarah Palfrey Cooke (USA)
1946	Jack Kramer (USA)	Pauline Betz (USA)
1947	Jack Kramer (USA)	Louise Brough (USA)
1948	Pancho Gonzales (USA)	Margaret du Pont (USA)
1949	Pancho Gonzales (USA)	Margaret du Pont (USA)
1950	Arthur Larsen (USA)	Margaret du Pont (USA)
1951	Frank Sedgman (AUS)	Maureen Connolly (USA)
1952	Frank Sedgman (AUS)	Maureen Connolly (USA)
1953	Tony Trabert (USA)	Maureen Connolly (USA)
1954	Vic Seixas (USA)	Doris Hart (USA)
1955	Tony Trabert (USA)	Doris Hart (USA)
1956	Ken Rosewall (AUS)	Shirley Fry (USA)
1957	Mal Anderson (AUS)	Althea Gibson (USA)
1958	Ashley Cooper (AUS)	Althea Gibson (USA)
1959	Neale Fraser (AUS)	Maria Bueno (BRA)
1960	Neale Fraser (AUS)	Darlene Hard (USA)
1961	Roy Emerson (AUS)	Darlene Hard (USA)
1962	Rod Laver (AUS)	Margaret Smith (AUS)
1963	Rafael Osuna (MEX)	Maria Bueno (BRA)
1964	Roy Emerson (AUS)	Maria Bueno (BRA)
1965	Manuel Santana (SPA)	Margaret Smith (AUS)
1966	Fred Stolle (AUS)	Maria Bueno (BRA)
1967	John Newcombe (AUS)	Billie Jean King (USA)
1968[1]	Arthur Ashe (USA)	Virginia Wade (GBR); Margaret Smith Court (AUS)
1969[1]	Rod Laver (AUS); Stan Smith (USA)	Margaret Smith Court (AUS)
1970	Ken Rosewall (AUS)	Margaret Smith Court (AUS)
1971	Stan Smith (USA)	Billie Jean King (USA)
1972	Ilie Nastase (ROM)	Billie Jean King (USA)
1973	John Newcombe (AUS)	Margaret Smith Court (AUS)
1974	Jimmy Connors (USA)	Billie Jean King (USA)
1975	Manuel Orantes (SPA)	Chris Evert (USA)
1976	Jimmy Connors (USA)	Chris Evert (USA)
1977	Guillermo Vilas (ARG)	Chris Evert (USA)
1978	Jimmy Connors (USA)	Chris Evert (USA)
1979	John McEnroe (USA)	Tracy Austin (USA)
1980	John McEnroe (USA)	Chris Evert Lloyd (USA)
1981	John McEnroe (USA)	Tracy Austin (USA)
1982	Jimmy Connors (USA)	Chris Evert Lloyd (USA)
1983	Jimmy Connors (USA)	Martina Navratilova (USA)
1984	John McEnroe (USA)	Martina Navratilova (USA)
1985	Ivan Lendl (TCH)	Hana Mandlikova (TCH)
1986	Ivan Lendl (TCH)	Martina Navratilova (USA)
1987	Ivan Lendl (TCH)	Martina Navratilova (USA)
1988	Mats Wilander (SWE)	Steffi Graf (FRG)
1989	Boris Becker (FRG)	Steffi Graf (FRG)
1990	Pete Sampras (USA)	Gabriela Sabatini (ARG)
1991	Stefan Edberg (SWE)	Monica Seles (YUG)
1992	Stefan Edberg (SWE)	Monica Seles (YUG)
1993	Pete Sampras (USA)	Steffi Graf (GER)
1994	Andre Agassi (USA)	Arantxa Sánchez Vicario (SPA)
1995	Pete Sampras (USA)	Steffi Graf (GER)
1996	Pete Sampras (USA)	Steffi Graf (GER)
1997	Patrick Rafter (AUS)	Martina Hingis (SUI)
1998	Patrick Rafter (AUS)	Lindsay Davenport (USA)
1999	Andre Agassi (USA)	Serena Williams (USA)
2000	Marat Safin (RUS)	Venus Williams (USA)

United States Open Tennis Championships—Singles (continued)

YEAR	MEN	WOMEN
2001	Lleyton Hewitt (AUS)	Venus Williams (USA)
2002	Pete Sampras (USA)	Serena Williams (USA)
2003	Andy Roddick (USA)	Justine Henin-Hardenne (BEL)
2004	Roger Federer (SUI)	Svetlana Kuznetsova (RUS)
2005	*to be held in August and September*	

[1]In 1968 and 1969 both amateur and open championships were held. Ashe won both men's competitions in 1968; Smith won the amateur championship in 1969. Court won the women's amateur competition in 1968 and both championships in 1969. Thereafter the championships were open.

United States Open Tennis Championships—Doubles

YEAR	MEN	WOMEN
1881	Clarence Clark, Fred Taylor	
1882	Richard Sears, James Dwight	
1883	Richard Sears, James Dwight	
1884	Richard Sears, James Dwight	
1885	Richard Sears, Joseph Clark	
1886	Richard Sears, James Dwight	
1887	Richard Sears, James Dwight	
1888	Oliver Campbell, Valentine Hall	
1889	Henry Slocum, Howard Taylor	Bertha Townsend, Margarette Ballard
1890	Valentine Hall, Clarence Hobart	Ellen Roosevelt, Grace Roosevelt
1891	Oliver Campbell, Robert Huntington	Mabel Cahill, Mrs. W. Fellowes Morgan
1892	Oliver Campbell, Robert Huntington	Mabel Cahill, Adeline McKinley
1893	Clarence Hobart, Fred Hovey	Aline Terry, Hattie Butler
1894	Clarence Hobart, Fred Hovey	Helen Helwig, Juliette Atkinson
1895	Malcom Chace, Robert Wrenn	Helen Helwig, Juliette Atkinson
1896	Carr Neel, Samuel Neel	Elisabeth Moore, Juliette Atkinson
1897	Leo Ware, George Sheldon	Juliette Atkinson, Kathleen Atkinson
1898	Leo Ware, George Sheldon	Juliette Atkinson, Kathleen Atkinson
1899	Holcombe Ward, Dwight Davis	Jane Craven, Myrtle McAteer
1900	Holcombe Ward, Dwight Davis	Edith Parker, Hallie Champlin
1901	Holcombe Ward, Dwight Davis	Juliette Atkinson, Myrtle McAteer
1902	Reginald Doherty, Hugh Doherty	Juliette Atkinson, Marion Jones
1903	Reginald Doherty, Hugh Doherty	Elisabeth Moore, Carrie Neely
1904	Holcombe Ward, Beals Wright	Mary Sutton, Miriam Hall
1905	Holcombe Ward, Beals Wright	Helen Homans, Carrie Neely
1906	Holcombe Ward, Beals Wright	Mrs. L.S. Coe, Mrs. D.S. Platt
1907	Fred Alexander, Harold Hackett	Marie Weimer, Carrie Neely
1908	Fred Alexander, Harold Hackett	Evelyn Sears, Margaret Curtis
1909	Fred Alexander, Harold Hackett	Hazel Hotchkiss, Edith Rotch
1910	Fred Alexander, Harold Hackett	Hazel Hotchkiss, Edith Rotch
1911	Raymond Little, Gustave Touchard	Hazel Hotchkiss, Eleanora Sears
1912	Maurice McLoughlin, Thomas Bundy	Dorothy Green, Mary Browne
1913	Maurice McLoughlin, Thomas Bundy	Mary Browne, Mrs. R.H. Williams
1914	Maurice McLoughlin, Thomas Bundy	Mary Browne, Mrs. R.H. Williams
1915	William Johnston, Clarence Griffin	Hazel Hotchkiss Wightman, Eleanora Sears
1916	William Johnston, Clarence Griffin	Molla Bjurstedt, Eleanora Sears
1917	Fred Alexander, Harold Throckmorton	Molla Bjurstedt, Eleanora Sears
1918	Bill Tilden, Vincent Richards	Marion Zinderstein, Eleanor Goss
1919	Norman Brookes, Gerald Patterson	Marion Zinderstein, Eleanor Goss
1920	William Johnston, Clarence Griffin	Marion Zinderstein, Eleanor Goss
1921	Bill Tilden, Vincent Richards	Mary Browne, Mrs. R.H. Williams
1922	Bill Tilden, Vincent Richards	Marion Zinderstein Jessup, Helen Wills
1923	Bill Tilden, Brian Norton	Kathleen McKane, Phyllis Covell
1924	Howard Kinsey, Robert Kinsey	Hazel Hotchkiss Wightman, Helen Wills
1925	Richard Williams, Vincent Richards	Mary Browne, Helen Wills
1926	Richard Williams, Vincent Richards	Elizabeth Ryan, Eleanor Goss
1927	Bill Tilden, Frank Hunter	Kathleen McKane Godfree, Ermyntrude Harvey
1928	George Lott, John Hennessey	Hazel Hotchkiss Wightman, Helen Wills
1929	George Lott, John Doeg	Phoebe Watson, Peggy Michell
1930	George Lott, John Doeg	Betty Nuthall, Sarah Palfrey
1931	Wilmer Allison, John Van Ryn	Betty Nuthall, Eileen Whittingstall
1932	Ellsworth Vines, Keith Gledhill	Helen Jacobs, Sarah Palfrey
1933	George Lott, Lester Stoefen	Betty Nuthall, Freda James
1934	George Lott, Lester Stoefen	Helen Jacobs, Sarah Palfrey

United States Open Tennis Championships—Doubles (continued)

YEAR	MEN	WOMEN
1935	Wilmer Allison, John Van Ryn	Helen Jacobs, Sarah Palfrey Fabyan
1936	Don Budge, Gene Mako	Marjorie Van Ryn, Carolin Babcock
1937	Gottfried von Cramm, Henner Henkel	Sarah Palfrey Fabyan, Alice Marble
1938	Don Budge, Gene Mako	Sarah Palfrey Fabyan, Alice Marble
1939	Adrian Quist, John Bromwich	Sarah Palfrey Fabyan, Alice Marble
1940	Jack Kramer, Ted Schroeder	Sarah Palfrey Fabyan, Alice Marble
1941	Jack Kramer, Ted Schroeder	Sarah Palfrey Fabyan, Margaret Osborne
1942	Gardnar Mulloy, Billy Talbert	Louise Brough, Margaret Osborne
1943	Jack Kramer, Frank Parker	Louise Brough, Margaret Osborne
1944	Don McNeill, Bob Falkenburg	Louise Brough, Margaret Osborne
1945	Gardnar Mulloy, Billy Talbert	Louise Brough, Margaret Osborne
1946	Gardnar Mulloy, Billy Talbert	Louise Brough, Margaret Osborne
1947	Jack Kramer, Ted Schroeder	Louise Brough, Margaret Osborne
1948	Gardnar Mulloy, Billy Talbert	Louise Brough, Margaret Osborne du Pont
1949	John Bromwich, Billy Sidwell	Louise Brough, Margaret Osborne du Pont
1950	John Bromwich, Frank Sedgman	Louise Brough, Margaret Osborne du Pont
1951	Ken McGregor, Frank Sedgman	Shirley Fry, Doris Hart
1952	Mervyn Rose, Vic Seixas	Shirley Fry, Doris Hart
1953	Mervyn Rose, Rex Hartwig	Shirley Fry, Doris Hart
1954	Vic Seixas, Tony Trabert	Shirley Fry, Doris Hart
1955	Kosei Kamo, Atushi Miyagi	Louise Brough, Margaret Osborne du Pont
1956	Lew Hoad, Ken Rosewall	Louise Brough, Margaret Osborne du Pont
1957	Ashley Cooper, Neale Fraser	Louise Brough, Margaret Osborne du Pont
1958	Alex Olmedo, Hamilton Richardson	Jeanne Arth, Darlene Hard
1959	Neale Fraser, Roy Emerson	Jeanne Arth, Darlene Hard
1960	Neale Fraser, Roy Emerson	Darlene Hard, Maria Bueno
1961	Charles McKinley, Dennis Ralston	Darlene Hard, Lesley Turner
1962	Rafael Osuna, Antonio Palafox	Darlene Hard, Maria Bueno
1963	Charles McKinley, Dennis Ralston	Robyn Ebbern, Margaret Smith
1964	Charles McKinley, Dennis Ralston	Billie Jean Moffitt, Karen Susman
1965	Roy Emerson, Fred Stolle	Carole Caldwell Graebner, Nancy Richey
1966	Roy Emerson, Fred Stolle	Maria Bueno, Nancy Richey
1967	John Newcombe, Tony Roche	Billie Jean Moffitt King, Rosemary Casals
1968[1]	Robert Lutz, Stan Smith	Maria Bueno, Margaret Smith Court
1969[1]	Ken Rosewall, Fred Stolle;	Françoise Durr, Darlene Hard;
	Dick Crealy, Allan Stone	Margaret Smith Court, Virginia Wade
1970	Pierre Barthes, Nikki Pilic	Margaret Smith Court, Judy Dalton
1971	John Newcombe, Roger Taylor	Rosemary Casals, Judy Dalton
1972	Cliff Drysdale, Roger Taylor	Françoise Durr, Betty Stove
1973	Owen Davidson, John Newcombe	Margaret Smith Court, Virginia Wade
1974	Robert Lutz, Stan Smith	Billie Jean King, Rosemary Casals
1975	Jimmy Connors, Ilie Nastase	Margaret Smith Court, Virginia Wade
1976	Tom Okker, Marty Riessen	Delina Boshoff, Ilana Kloss
1977	Bob Hewitt, Frew McMillan	Martina Navratilova, Betty Stove
1978	Robert Lutz, Stan Smith	Martina Navratilova, Billie Jean King
1979	John McEnroe, Peter Fleming	Wendy Turnbull, Betty Stove
1980	Robert Lutz, Stan Smith	Martina Navratilova, Billie Jean King
1981	John McEnroe, Peter Fleming	Kathy Jordan, Anne Smith
1982	Kevin Curren, Steve Denton	Rosemary Casals, Wendy Turnbull
1983	John McEnroe, Peter Fleming	Martina Navratilova, Pam Shriver
1984	John Fitzgerald, Tomas Smid	Martina Navratilova, Pam Shriver
1985	Ken Flach, Robert Seguso	Claudia Kohde-Kilsch, Helena Sukova
1986	Andres Gómez, Slobodan Zivojinovic	Martina Navratilova, Pam Shriver
1987	Stefan Edberg, Anders Jarryd	Martina Navratilova, Pam Shriver
1988	Sergio Casal, Emilio Sánchez	Gigi Fernandez, Robin White
1989	John McEnroe, Mark Woodforde	Martina Navratilova, Hana Mandlikova
1990	Pieter Aldrich, Danie Visser	Martina Navratilova, Gigi Fernandez
1991	John Fitzgerald, Anders Jarryd	Pam Shriver, Natasha Zvereva
1992	Jim Grabb, Richey Reneberg	Gigi Fernandez, Natasha Zvereva
1993	Ken Flach, Rick Leach	Arantxa Sánchez Vicario, Helena Sukova
1994	Paul Haarhuis, Jacco Eltingh	Arantxa Sánchez Vicario, Jana Novotna
1995	Todd Woodbridge, Mark Woodforde	Gigi Fernandez, Natasha Zvereva
1996	Todd Woodbridge, Mark Woodforde	Gigi Fernandez, Natasha Zvereva
1997	Yevgeny Kafelnikov, Daniel Vacek	Lindsay Davenport, Jana Novotna
1998	Sandon Stolle, Cyril Suk	Martina Hingis, Jana Novotna
1999	Sebastian Lareau, Alex O'Brien	Venus Williams, Serena Williams
2000	Lleyton Hewitt, Max Mirnyi	Julie Halard-Decugis, Ai Sugiyama
2001	Wayne Black, Kevin Ullyet	Lisa Raymond, Rennae Stubbs

United States Open Tennis Championships—Doubles (continued)

YEAR	MEN	WOMEN
2002	Mahesh Bhupathi, Max Mirnyi	Virginia Ruano Pascual, Paola Suárez
2003	Jonas Bjorkman, Todd Woodbridge	Virginia Ruano Pascual, Paola Suárez
2004	Mark Knowles, Daniel Nestor	Virginia Ruano Pascual, Paola Suárez
2005	*to be held in August and September*	

[1]*In 1968 and 1969 both amateur and open championships were held. Lutz and Smith won both men's competitions in 1968; Crealy and Stone took the men's amateur championships in 1969. Bueno and Court won both women's competitions in 1968; Court and Wade took the women's amateur championships in 1969. Thereafter the championships were open.*

Davis Cup

YEAR	WINNER	RUNNER-UP	RESULTS	YEAR	WINNER	RUNNER-UP	RESULTS
1900	United States	British Isles	3–0	1957	Australia	United States	3–2
1901	*not held*			1958	United States	Australia	3–2
1902	United States	British Isles	3–2	1959	Australia	United States	3–2
1903	British Isles[1]	United States	4–1	1960	Australia	Italy	4–1
1904	British Isles	Belgium	5–0	1961	Australia	Italy	5–0
1905	British Isles	United States	5–0	1962	Australia	Mexico	5–0
1906	British Isles	United States	5–0	1963	United States	Australia	3–2
1907	Australasia[2]	British Isles	3–2	1964	Australia	United States	3–2
1908	Australasia	United States	3–2	1965	Australia	Spain	4–1
1909	Australasia	United States	5–0	1966	Australia	India	4–1
1910	*not held*			1967	Australia	Spain	4–1
1911	Australasia	United States	5–0	1968	United States	Australia	4–1
1912	British Isles	Australia	3–2	1969	United States	Romania	5–0
1913	United States	British Isles	3–2	1970	United States	West Germany	5–0
1914	Australasia	United States	3–2	1971	United States	Romania	3–2
1915–18	*not held*			1972	United States	Romania	3–2
1919	Australasia	British Isles	4–1	1973	Australia	United States	5–0
1920	United States	Australasia	5–0	1974	South Africa[3]	India	
1921	United States	Japan	5–0	1975	Sweden	Czechoslovakia	3–2
1922	United States	Australasia	4–1	1976	Italy	Chile	4–1
1923	United States	Australasia	4–1	1977	Australia	Italy	3–1
1924	United States	Australasia	5–0	1978	United States	United Kingdom	4–1
1925	United States	France	5–0	1979	United States	Italy	5–0
1926	United States	France	4–1	1980	Czechoslovakia	Italy	4–1
1927	France	United States	3–2	1981	United States	Argentina	3–1
1928	France	United States	4–1	1982	United States	France	4–1
1929	France	United States	3–2	1983	Australia	Sweden	3–2
1930	France	United States	4–1	1984	Sweden	United States	4–1
1931	France	United Kingdom	3–2	1985	Sweden	West Germany	3–2
1932	France	United States	3–2	1986	Australia	Sweden	3–2
1933	United Kingdom	France	3–2	1987	Sweden	India	5–0
1934	United Kingdom	United States	4–1	1988	West Germany	Sweden	4–1
1935	United Kingdom	United States	5–0	1989	West Germany	Sweden	3–2
1936	United Kingdom	Australia	3–2	1990	United States	Australia	3–2
1937	United States	United Kingdom	4–1	1991	France	United States	3–1
1938	United States	Australia	3–2	1992	United States	Switzerland	3–1
1939	Australia	United States	3–2	1993	Germany	Australia	4–1
1940–45	*not held*			1994	Sweden	Russia	4–1
1946	United States	Australia	5–0	1995	United States	Russia	3–2
1947	United States	Australia	4–1	1996	France	Sweden	3–2
1948	United States	Australia	5–0	1997	Sweden	United States	5–0
1949	United States	Australia	4–1	1998	Sweden	Italy	4–1
1950	Australia	United States	4–1	1999	Australia	France	3–2
1951	Australia	United States	3–2	2000	Spain	Australia	3–1
1952	Australia	United States	4–1	2001	France	Australia	3–2
1953	Australia	United States	3–2	2002	Russia	France	3–2
1954	United States	Australia	3–2	2003	Australia	Spain	3–1
1955	Australia	United States	5–0	2004	Spain	United States	3–2
1956	Australia	United States	5–0	2005	*to be played 2–4 December*		

[1]*Included Ireland up to 1922.*   [2]*Included Australia and New Zealand up to 1923.*   [3]*Forfeit; India withdrew from final.*

Fed Cup

YEAR	WINNER	RUNNER-UP	RESULTS	YEAR	WINNER	RUNNER-UP	RESULTS
1963	United States	Australia	2–1	1985	Czechoslovakia	United States	2–1
1964	Australia	United States	2–1	1986	United States	Czechoslovakia	3–0
1965	Australia	United States	2–1	1987	West Germany	United States	2–1
1966	United States	West Germany	3–0	1988	Czechoslovakia	USSR	2–1
1967	United States	United Kingdom	2–0	1989	United States	Spain	3–0
1968	Australia	The Netherlands	3–0	1990	United States	USSR	2–1
1969	United States	Australia	2–1	1991	Spain	United States	2–1
1970	Australia	West Germany	3–0	1992	Germany	Spain	2–1
1971	Australia	United Kingdom	3–0	1993	Spain	Australia	3–0
1972	South Africa	United Kingdom	2–1	1994	Spain	United States	3–0
1973	Australia	South Africa	3–0	1995	Spain	United States	3–2
1974	Australia	United States	2–1	1996	United States	Spain	5–0
1975	Czechoslovakia	Australia	3–0	1997	France	The Netherlands	4–1
1976	United States	Australia	2–1	1998	Spain	Switzerland	3–2
1977	United States	Australia	2–1	1999	United States	Russia	4–1
1978	United States	Australia	2–1	2000	United States	Spain	5–0
1979	United States	Australia	3–0	2001	Belgium	Russia	2–1
1980	United States	Australia	3–0	2002	Slovakia	Spain	3–1
1981	United States	United Kingdom	3–0	2003	France	United States	4–1
1982	United States	West Germany	3–0	2004	Russia	France	3–2
1983	Czechoslovakia	West Germany	2–1	2005	*to be played in November*		
1984	Czechoslovakia	Australia	2–1				

Track & Field

The world governing body for track and field, or athletics, is the **International Association of Athletic Federations** (IAAF), founded in 1912. The sport includes relay running, a number of individual running, jumping, and throwing events, and one event (the decathlon for men and the heptathlon for women) that includes all three activities. The best-known occasion for most track-and-field athletics is the **Olympic Games** held every four years. The World Cup (inaugurated 1977) is a finals-only competition for national, hemispheric, and continental teams. In 1983, however, the first officially recognized non-Olympic world athletics championships were held.

A long-distance event that has special status is the **marathon race**, the standard distance for which is 42,195 m (26 mi 385 yd).

IAAF Web site: <www.iaaf.org>.

Outdoor Track & Field World Records

men

EVENT	RECORD HOLDER (NATIONALITY)	PERFORMANCE	DATE
100 m	Asafa Powell (JAM)[2]	9.77 sec	14 Jun 2005
200 m	Michael Johnson (USA)	19.32 sec	1 Aug 1996
400 m	Michael Johnson (USA)	43.18 sec	26 Aug 1999
800 m	Wilson Kipketer (DEN)	1 min 41.11 sec	24 Aug 1997
1,000 m	Noah Ngeny (KEN)	2 min 11.96 sec	5 Sep 1999
1,500 m	Hicham El Guerrouj (MAR)	3 min 26.00 sec	14 Jul 1998
1 mile	Hicham El Guerrouj (MAR)	3 min 43.13 sec	7 Jul 1999
3,000 m	Daniel Komen (KEN)	7 min 20.67 sec	1 Sep 1996
5,000 m	Kenenisa Bekele (ETH)	12 min 37.35 sec	31 May 2004
10,000 m	Kenenisa Bekele (ETH)	26 min 20.31 sec	8 Jun 2004
marathon[1]	Paul Tergat (KEN)	2 hr 4 min 55 sec	28 Sep 2003
110-m hurdles	Liu Xiang (CHN)	12.91 sec	27 Aug 2004
400-m hurdles	Kevin Young (USA)	46.78 sec	6 Aug 1992
20-km walk	Jefferson Pérez (ECU)	1 hr 17 min 21 sec	23 Aug 2003
50-km walk	Robert Korzeniowski (POL)	3 hr 36 min 3 sec	27 Aug 2003
steeplechase	Saif Saeed Shaheen (QAT)	7 min 53.63 sec	3 Sep 2004
4 × 100-m relay	United States	37.40 sec	21 Aug 1993
4 × 400-m relay	United States	2 min 54.20 sec	22 Jul 1998
high jump	Javier Sotomayor (CUB)	2.45 m (8 ft ½ in)	27 Jul 1993
long jump	Mike Powell (USA)	8.95 m (29 ft 4½ in)	30 Aug 1991
triple jump	Jonathan Edwards (GBR)	18.29 m (60 ft ¼ in)	7 Aug 1995
pole vault	Sergey Bubka (UKR)	6.14 m (20 ft 1¾ in)	31 Jul 1994
shot put	Randy Barnes (USA)	23.12 m (75 ft 10¼ in)	20 May 1990
discus throw	Jürgen Schult (GDR)	74.08 m (243 ft)	6 Jun 1986
hammer throw	Yury Sedykh (URS)	86.74 m (284 ft 7 in)	30 Aug 1986
javelin throw	Jan Zelezny (CZE)	98.48 m (323 ft 1 in)	25 May 1996
decathlon	Roman Sebrle (CZE)	9,026 pt	27 May 2001

Outdoor Track & Field World Records (continued)

women

EVENT	RECORD HOLDER (NATIONALITY)	PERFORMANCE	DATE
100 m	Florence Griffith-Joyner (USA)	10.49 sec	16 Jul 1988
200 m	Florence Griffith-Joyner (USA)	21.34 sec	29 Sep 1988
400 m	Marita Koch (GDR)	47.60 sec	6 Oct 1985
800 m	Jarmila Kratochvilova (TCH)	1 min 53.28 sec	26 Jul 1983
1,000 m	Svetlana Masterkova (RUS)	2 min 28.98 sec	23 Aug 1996
1,500 m	Qu Yunxia (CHN)	3 min 50.46 sec	11 Sep 1993
1 mile	Svetlana Masterkova (RUS)	4 min 12.56 sec	14 Aug 1996
3,000 m	Wang Junxia (CHN)	8 min 6.11 sec	13 Sep 1993
5,000 m	Elvan Abeylegesse (TUR)	14 min 24.68 sec	11 Jun 2004
10,000 m	Wang Junxia (CHN)	29 min 31.78 sec	8 Sep 1993
marathon[1]	Paula Radcliffe (GBR)	2 hr 15 min 25 sec	13 Apr 2003
100-m hurdles	Iordanka Donkova (BUL)	12.21 sec	20 Aug 1988
400-m hurdles	Yuliya Pechenkina (RUS)	52.34 sec	8 Aug 2003
20-km walk	Olimpiada Ivanova (RUS)[2]	1 hr 25 min 41 sec	7 Aug 2005
steeplechase	Gulnara Samitova (RUS)	9 min 1.59 sec	4 Jul 2004
4 × 100-m relay	East Germany	41.37 sec	6 Oct 1985
4 × 400-m relay	USSR	3 min 15.17 sec	1 Oct 1988
high jump	Stefka Kostadinova (BUL)	2.09 m (6 ft 10¼ in)	30 Aug 1987
long jump	Galina Chistyakova (URS)	7.52 m (24 ft 8¼ in)	11 Jun 1988
triple jump	Inessa Kravets (UKR)	15.50 m (50 ft 10¼ in)	10 Aug 1995
pole vault	Yelena Isinbayeva (RUS)[2]	5.01 m (16 ft 5¼ in)	12 Aug 2005
shot put	Natalya Lisovskaya (URS)	22.63 m (74 ft 3 in)	7 Jun 1987
discus throw	Gabriele Reinsch (GDR)	76.80 m (252 ft)	9 Jul 1988
hammer throw	Tatyana Lysenko (RUS)[2]	77.06 m (252 ft 10 in)	15 Jul 2005
javelin throw	Osleidys Menéndez (CUB)[2]	71.70 m (235 ft 3 in)	14 Aug 2005
heptathlon	Jackie Joyner-Kersee (USA)	7,291 pt	24 Sep 1988
decathlon	Austra Skujyte (LTU)[2]	8,366 points	15 Apr 2005

[1]Not an officially ratified event; best performance on record. [2]Pending ratification.

Indoor Track & Field World Records

men

EVENT	RECORD HOLDER (NATIONALITY)	PERFORMANCE	DATE
50 m	Donovan Bailey (CAN)	5.56 sec	9 Feb 1996
60 m	Maurice Greene (USA)	6.39 sec	3 Mar 2001
200 m	Frank Fredericks (NAM)	19.92 sec	18 Feb 1996
400 m	Kerron Clement (USA)	44 min 57 sec	12 Mar 2005
800 m	Wilson Kipketer (DEN)	1 min 42.67 sec	9 Mar 1997
1,000 m	Wilson Kipketer (DEN)	2 min 14.96 sec	20 Feb 2000
1,500 m	Hicham El Guerrouj (MAR)	3 min 31.18 sec	2 Feb 1997
1 mile	Hicham El Guerrouj (MAR)	3 min 48.45 sec	12 Feb 1997
3,000 m	Daniel Komen (KEN)	7 min 24.90 sec	6 Feb 1998
5,000 m	Kenenisa Bekele (ETH)	12 min 49.60 sec	20 Feb 2004
50-m hurdles	Mark McKoy (CAN)	6.25 sec	5 Mar 1986
60-m hurdles	Colin Jackson (GBR)	7.30 sec	6 Mar 1994
5-km walk	Mikhail Shchennikov (RUS)	18 min 7.08 sec	14 Feb 1995
4 × 200-m relay	Great Britain & Northern Ireland	1 min 22.11 sec	3 Mar 1991
4 × 400-m relay	United States	3 min 2.83 sec	7 Mar 1999
4 × 800-m relay	United States	7 min 13.94 sec	6 Feb 2000
high jump	Javier Sotomayor (CUB)	2.43 m (7 ft 11½ in)	4 Mar 1989
long jump	Carl Lewis (USA)	8.79 m (28 ft 10¼ in)	27 Jan 1984
triple jump	Aliecer Urrutia (CUB)	17.83 m (58 ft 6 in)	1 Mar 1997
	Christian Olsson (SWE)		7 Mar 2004
pole vault	Sergey Bubka (UKR)	6.15 m (20 ft 2 in)	21 Feb 1993
shot put	Randy Barnes (USA)	22.66 m (74 ft 4¼ in)	20 Jan 1989
heptathlon	Dan O'Brien (USA)	6,476 pt	14 Mar 1993

women

EVENT	RECORD HOLDER (NATIONALITY)	PERFORMANCE	DATE
50 m	Irina Privalova (RUS)	5.96 sec	9 Feb 1995
60 m	Irina Privalova (RUS)	6.92 sec	11 Feb 1993
200 m	Merlene Ottey (JAM)	21.87 sec	13 Feb 1993
400 m	Jarmila Kratochvilova (TCH)	49.59 sec	7 Mar 1982
800 m	Jolanda Ceplak (SLO)	1 min 55.82 sec	3 Mar 2002
1,000 m	Maria Mutola (MOZ)	2 min 30.94 sec	25 Feb 1999

Indoor Track & Field World Records (continued)

women (continued)

EVENT	RECORD HOLDER (NATIONALITY)	PERFORMANCE	DATE
1,500 m	Regina Jacobs (USA)	3 min 59.98 sec	1 Feb 2003
1 mile	Doina Melinte (ROM)	4 min 17.14 sec	9 Feb 1990
3,000 m	Berhane Adere (ETH)	8 min 29.15 sec	3 Feb 2002
5,000 m	Tirunesh Dibaba (ETH)	14 min 32.93 sec	29 Jan 2005
50-m hurdles	Cornelia Oschkenat (GDR)	6.58 sec	20 Feb 1988
60-m hurdles	Lyudmila Engquist (URS)	7.69 sec	4 Feb 1990
3-km walk	Claudia Stef (ROM)	11 min 40.33 sec	30 Jan 1999
4 × 200-m relay	Russia	1 min 32.41 sec	29 Jan 2005
4 × 400-m relay	Russia	3 min 23.88 sec	7 Mar 2004
4 × 800-m relay	Russia	8 min 18.71 sec	4 Feb 1994
high jump	Heike Henkel (GER)	2.07 m (6 ft 9½ in)	8 Feb 1992
long jump	Heike Drechsler (GDR)	7.37 m (24 ft 2¼ in)	13 Feb 1988
triple jump	Tatyana Lebedeva (RUS)	15.36 m (50 ft 4¾ in)	6 Mar 2004
pole vault	Yelena Isinbayeva (RUS)	4.90 m (16 ft ¾ in)	6 Mar 2005
shot put	Helena Fibingerova (TCH)	22.50 m (73 ft 10 in)	19 Feb 1977
pentathlon	Irina Belova (UNT)	4,991 pt	15 Feb 1992

World Track & Field Championships—Men

The next championships are scheduled to be held in 2007.

100 M
1983	Carl Lewis (USA)
1987	Carl Lewis (USA)
1991	Carl Lewis (USA)
1993	Linford Christie (GBR)
1995	Donovan Bailey (CAN)
1997	Maurice Greene (USA)
1999	Maurice Greene (USA)
2001	Maurice Greene (USA)
2003	Kim Collins (SKN)
2005	Justin Gatlin (USA)

200 M
1983	Calvin Smith (USA)
1987	Calvin Smith (USA)
1991	Michael Johnson (USA)
1993	Frank Fredericks (NAM)
1995	Michael Johnson (USA)
1997	Ato Boldon (TRI)
1999	Maurice Greene (USA)
2001	Konstadinos Kederis (GRE)
2003	John Capel (USA)
2005	Justin Gatlin (USA)

400 M
1983	Bert Cameron (JAM)
1987	Thomas Schoenlebe (GDR)
1991	Antonio Pettigrew (USA)
1993	Michael Johnson (USA)
1995	Michael Johnson (USA)
1997	Michael Johnson (USA)
1999	Michael Johnson (USA)
2001	Avard Moncur (BAH)
2003	Jerome Young (USA)
2005	Jeremy Wariner (USA)

800 M
1983	Willi Wülbeck (FRG)
1987	Billy Konchellah (KEN)
1991	Billy Konchellah (KEN)
1993	Paul Ruto (KEN)
1995	Wilson Kipketer (DEN)
1997	Wilson Kipketer (DEN)
1999	Wilson Kipketer (DEN)
2001	André Bucher (SUI)
2003	Djabir Saïd-Guerni (ALG)

800 M (CONTINUED)
2005	Rashid Ramzi (BRN)

1,500 M
1983	Steve Cram (GBR)
1987	Abdi Bile (SOM)
1991	Noureddine Morceli (ALG)
1993	Noureddine Morceli (ALG)
1995	Noureddine Morceli (ALG)
1997	Hicham El Guerrouj (MAR)
1999	Hicham El Guerrouj (MAR)
2001	Hicham El Guerrouj (MAR)
2003	Hicham El Guerrouj (MAR)
2005	Rashid Ramzi (BRN)

5,000 M
1983	Eamonn Coghlan (IRL)
1987	Said Aouita (MAR)
1991	Yobes Ondieki (KEN)
1993	Ismael Kirui (KEN)
1995	Ismael Kirui (KEN)
1997	Daniel Komen (KEN)
1999	Salah Hissou (MAR)
2001	Richard Limo (KEN)
2003	Eliud Kipchoge (KEN)
2005	Benjamin Limo (KEN)

10,000 M
1983	Alberto Cova (ITA)
1987	Paul Kipkoech (KEN)
1991	Moses Tanui (KEN)
1993	Haile Gebrselassie (ETH)
1995	Haile Gebrselassie (ETH)
1997	Haile Gebrselassie (ETH)
1999	Haile Gebrselassie (ETH)
2001	Charles Kamathi (KEN)
2003	Kenenisa Bekele (ETH)
2005	Kenenisa Bekele (ETH)

STEEPLECHASE
1983	Patriz Ilg (FRG)
1987	Francesco Panetta (ITA)
1991	Moses Kiptanui (KEN)
1993	Moses Kiptanui (KEN)
1995	Moses Kiptanui (KEN)
1997	Wilson Boit Kipketer (KEN)

STEEPLECHASE (CONTINUED)
1999	Christopher Koskei (KEN)
2001	Reuben Kosgei (KEN)
2003	Saif Saaeed Shaheen (QAT)
2005	Saif Saaeed Shaheen (QAT)

110-M HURDLES
1983	Greg Foster (USA)
1987	Greg Foster (USA)
1991	Greg Foster (USA)
1993	Colin Jackson (GBR)
1995	Allen Johnson (USA)
1997	Allen Johnson (USA)
1999	Colin Jackson (GBR)
2001	Allen Johnson (USA)
2003	Allen Johnson (USA)
2005	Ladji Doucouré (FRA)

400-M HURDLES
1983	Edwin Moses (USA)
1987	Edwin Moses (USA)
1991	Samuel Matete (ZAM)
1993	Kevin Young (USA)
1995	Derrick Adkins (USA)
1997	Stéphane Diagana (FRA)
1999	Fabrizio Mori (ITA)
2001	Felix Sánchez (DOM)
2003	Felix Sánchez (DOM)
2005	Bershawn Jackson (USA)

MARATHON
1983	Robert de Castella (AUS)
1987	Douglas Wakiihuri (KEN)
1991	Hiromi Taniguchi (JPN)
1993	Mark Plaatjes (USA)
1995	Martín Fiz (ESP)
1997	Abel Antón (ESP)
1999	Abel Antón (ESP)
2001	Gezahegne Abera (ETH)
2003	Jaouad Gharib (MAR)
2005	Jaouad Gharib (MAR)

20-KM WALK
1983	Ernesto Canto (MEX)
1987	Maurizio Damilano (ITA)
1991	Maurizio Damilano (ITA)

World Track & Field Championships—Men (continued)

20-KM WALK (CONTINUED)
1993 Valentí Massana (ESP)
1995 Michele Didoni (ITA)
1997 Daniel García (MEX)
1999 Ilya Markov (RUS)
2001 Roman Rasskazov (RUS)
2003 Jefferson Pérez (ECU)
2005 Jefferson Pérez (ECU)

50-KM WALK
1983 Ronald Weigel (GDR)
1987 Hartwig Gauder (GDR)
1991 Aleksandr Potashov (URS)
1993 Jesús Angel García (ESP)
1995 Valentin Kononen (FIN)
1997 Robert Korzeniowski (POL)
1999 Ivano Brugnetti (ITA)
2001 Robert Korzeniowski (POL)
2003 Robert Korzeniowski (POL)
2005 Sergey Kirdyapkin (RUS)

4 X 100-M RELAY
1983 United States
1987 United States
1991 United States
1993 United States
1995 Canada
1997 Canada
1999 United States
2001 United States
2003 United States
2005 France

4 X 400-M RELAY
1983 USSR
1987 United States
1991 United Kingdom
1993 United States
1995 United States
1997 United States
1999 United States
2001 United States
2003 France
2005 United States

HIGH JUMP
1983 Gennady Avdeyenko (URS)
1987 Patrik Sjöberg (SWE)
1991 Charles Austin (USA)
1993 Javier Sotomayor (CUB)
1995 Troy Kemp (BAH)
1997 Javier Sotomayor (CUB)

HIGH JUMP (CONTINUED)
1999 Vyacheslav Voronin (RUS)
2001 Martin Buss (GER)
2003 Jacques Freitag (RSA)
2005 Yuri Krymarenko (UKR)

POLE VAULT
1983 Sergey Bubka (URS)
1987 Sergey Bubka (URS)
1991 Sergey Bubka (URS)
1993 Sergey Bubka (UKR)
1995 Sergey Bubka (UKR)
1997 Sergey Bubka (UKR)
1999 Maksim Tarasov (RUS)
2001 Dmitri Markov (AUS)
2003 Giuseppe Gibilisco (ITA)
2005 Rens Blom (NED)

LONG JUMP
1983 Carl Lewis (USA)
1987 Carl Lewis (USA)
1991 Mike Powell (USA)
1993 Mike Powell (USA)
1995 Iván Pedroso (CUB)
1997 Iván Pedroso (CUB)
1999 Iván Pedroso (CUB)
2001 Iván Pedroso (CUB)
2003 Dwight Phillips (USA)
2005 Dwight Phillips (USA)

TRIPLE JUMP
1983 Zdzislaw Hoffman (POL)
1987 Khristo Markov (BUL)
1991 Kenny Harrison (USA)
1993 Mike Conley (USA)
1995 Jonathan Edwards (GBR)
1997 Yoelbi Quesada (CUB)
1999 Charles Michael Friedek (GER)
2001 Jonathan Edwards (GBR)
2003 Christian Olsson (SWE)
2005 Walter Davis (USA)

SHOT PUT
1983 Edward Sarul (POL)
1987 Werner Günthör (SUI)
1991 Werner Günthör (SUI)
1993 Werner Günthör (SUI)
1995 John Godina (USA)
1997 John Godina (USA)
1999 C.J. Hunter (USA)
2001 John Godina (USA)

SHOT PUT (CONTINUED)
2003 Andrey Mikhnevich (BLR)
2005 Adam Nelson (USA)

DISCUS THROW
1983 Imrich Bugar (TCH)
1987 Jürgen Schult (GDR)
1991 Lars Riedel (GER)
1993 Lars Riedel (GER)
1995 Lars Riedel (GER)
1997 Lars Riedel (GER)
1999 Anthony Washington (USA)
2001 Lars Riedel (GER)
2003 Virgilijus Alekna (LTU)
2005 Virgilijus Alekna (LTU)

HAMMER THROW
1983 Sergey Litvinov (URS)
1987 Sergey Litvinov (URS)
1991 Yury Sedykh (URS)
1993 Andrey Abduvaliyev (TJK)
1995 Andrey Abduvaliyev (TJK)
1997 Heinz Weis (GER)
1999 Karsten Kobs (GER)
2001 Szymon Ziolkowski (POL)
2003 Ivan Tikhon (BLR)
2005 Ivan Tikhon (BLR)

JAVELIN THROW
1983 Detlef Michel (GDR)
1987 Seppo Räty (FIN)
1991 Kimmo Kinnunen (FIN)
1993 Jan Zelezny (CZE)
1995 Jan Zelezny (CZE)
1997 Marius Corbett (RSA)
1999 Aki Parviainen (FIN)
2001 Jan Zelezny (CZE)
2003 Sergey Makarov (RUS)
2005 Andrus Varnik (EST)

DECATHLON
1983 Daley Thompson (GBR)
1987 Torsten Voss (GDR)
1991 Dan O'Brien (USA)
1993 Dan O'Brien (USA)
1995 Dan O'Brien (USA)
1997 Tomas Dvorak (CZE)
1999 Tomas Dvorak (CZE)
2001 Tomas Dvorak (CZE)
2003 Tom Pappas (USA)
2005 Bryan Clay (USA)

World Track & Field Championships—Women
The next championships are scheduled to be held in 2007.

100 M
1983 Marlies Göhr (GDR)
1987 Silke Gladisch (GDR)
1991 Katrin Krabbe (GER)
1993 Gail Devers (USA)
1995 Gwen Torrence (USA)
1997 Marion Jones (USA)
1999 Marion Jones (USA)
2001 Zhanna Pintusevich (UKR)
2003 Torri Edwards (USA)
2005 Lauryn Williams (USA)

200 M
1983 Marita Koch (GDR)
1987 Silke Gladisch (GDR)
1991 Katrin Krabbe (GER)
1993 Merlene Ottey (JAM)
1995 Merlene Ottey (JAM)
1997 Zhanna Pintusevich (UKR)
1999 Inger Miller (USA)
2001 Marion Jones (USA)
2003 Anastasiya Kapachinskaya (RUS)
2005 Allyson Felix (USA)

400 M
1983 Jarmila Kratochvilova (TCH)
1987 Olga Bryzgina (URS)
1991 Marie-José Pérec (FRA)
1993 Jearl Miles (USA)
1995 Marie-José Pérec (FRA)
1997 Cathy Freeman (AUS)
1999 Cathy Freeman (AUS)
2001 Amy Mbacke Thiam (SEN)
2003 Ana Guevara (MEX)
2005 Tonique Williams-Darling (BAH)

World Track & Field Championships—Women (continued)

800 M
1983	Jarmila Kratochvilova (TCH)
1987	Sigrun Wodars (GDR)
1991	Liliya Nurutdinova (URS)
1993	Maria Mutola (MOZ)
1995	Ana Quirot (CUB)
1997	Ana Quirot (CUB)
1999	Ludmila Formanova (CZE)
2001	Maria Mutola (MOZ)
2003	Maria Mutola (MOZ)
2005	Zulia Calatayud (CUB)

1,500 M
1983	Mary Decker (USA)
1987	Tatyana Samolenko (URS)
1991	Hassiba Boulmerka (ALG)
1993	Liu Dong (CHN)
1995	Hassiba Boulmerka (ALG)
1997	Carla Sacramento (POR)
1999	Svetlana Masterkova (RUS)
2001	Gabriela Szabo (ROM)
2003	Tatyana Tomashova (RUS)
2005	Tatyana Tomashova (RUS)

3,000 M[1]
1983	Mary Decker (USA)
1987	Tatyana Samolenko (URS)
1991	Tatyana Dorovskikh (URS)
1993	Qu Yunxia (CHN)
1995	Sonia O'Sullivan (IRL)
1997	Gabriela Szabo (ROM)
1999	Gabriela Szabo (ROM)
2001	Olga Yegorova (RUS)
2003	Tirunesh Dibaba (ETH)
2005	Tirunesh Dibaba (ETH)

10,000 M[2]
1987	Ingrid Kristiansen (NOR)
1991	Liz McColgan (GBR)
1993	Wang Junxia (CHN)
1995	Fernanda Ribeiro (POR)
1997	Sally Barsosio (KEN)
1999	Gete Wami (ETH)
2001	Derartu Tulu (ETH)
2003	Berhane Adere (ETH)
2005	Tirunesh Dibaba (ETH)

STEEPLECHASE
2005	Dorcus Inzikuru (UGA)

100-M HURDLES
1983	Bettine Jahn (GDR)
1987	Ginka Zagorcheva (BUL)
1991	Ludmila Narozhilenko (URS)
1993	Gail Devers (USA)
1995	Gail Devers (USA)
1997	Ludmila Engquist (SWE)
1999	Gail Devers (USA)
2001	Anjanette Kirkland (USA)
2003	Perdita Felicien (CAN)
2005	Michelle Perry (USA)

400-M HURDLES
1983	Yekaterina Fesenko (URS)
1987	Sabine Busch (GDR)
1991	Tatyana Ledovskaya (URS)
1993	Sally Gunnell (GBR)

400-M HURDLES (CONTINUED)
1995	Kim Batten (USA)
1997	Nezha Bidouane (MAR)
1999	Daimí Pernía (CUB)
2001	Nezha Bidouane (MAR)
2003	Jana Pittman (AUS)
2005	Yuliya Pechonkina (RUS)

MARATHON
1983	Grete Waitz (NOR)
1987	Rosa Mota (POR)
1991	Wanda Panfil (POL)
1993	Asari Junko (JPN)
1995	Maria Machado (POR)
1997	Hiromi Suzuki (JPN)
1999	Jong Song Ok (PRK)
2001	Lidia Simon (ROM)
2003	Catherine Ndereba (KEN)
2005	Paula Radcliffe (GBR)

10-KM WALK[2]
1987	Irina Strakhova (URS)
1991	Alina Ivanova (URS)
1993	Sari Essayeh (FIN)
1995	Irina Stankina (RUS)
1997	Annarita Sidoti (ITA)

20-KM RACE WALK[3]
1999	Liu Hongyu (CHN)
2001	Olimpiada Ivanova (RUS)
2003	Yelena Nikolayeva (RUS)
2005	Olimpiada Ivanova (RUS)

4 X 100-M RELAY
1983	East Germany
1987	United States
1991	Jamaica
1993	Russia
1995	United States
1997	United States
1999	Bahamas
2001	Germany
2003	France
2005	United States

4 X 400-M RELAY
1983	East Germany
1987	East Germany
1991	USSR
1993	United States
1995	United States
1997	Germany
1999	Russia
2001	Jamaica
2003	United States
2005	Russia

HIGH JUMP
1983	Tamara Bykova (URS)
1987	Stefka Kostadinova (BUL)
1991	Heike Henkel (GER)
1993	Ioamnet Quintero (CUB)
1995	Stefka Kostadinova (BUL)
1997	Hanne Haugland (NOR)
1999	Inga Babakova (UKR)
2001	Hestrie Cloete (RSA)
2003	Hestrie Cloete (RSA)
2005	Kajsa Bergqvist (SWE)

POLE VAULT[3]
1999	Stacy Dragila (USA)
2001	Stacy Dragila (USA)
2003	Svetlana Feofanova (RUS)
2005	Yelena Isinbayeva (RUS)

LONG JUMP
1983	Heike Daute (GDR)
1987	Jackie Joyner-Kersee (USA)
1991	Jackie Joyner-Kersee (USA)
1993	Heike Drechsler (GER)
1995	Fiona May (ITA)
1997	Ludmila Galkina (RUS)
1999	Niurka Montalvo (ESP)
2001	Fiona May (ITA)
2003	Eunice Barber (FRA)
2005	Tianna Madison (USA)

TRIPLE JUMP[4]
1993	Anna Biryukova (RUS)
1995	Inessa Kravets (UKR)
1997	Sarka Kasparkova (CZE)
1999	Paraskevi Tsiamita (GRE)
2001	Tatyana Lebedeva (RUS)
2003	Tatyana Lebedeva (RUS)
2005	Trecia Smith (JAM)

SHOT PUT
1983	Helena Fibingerova (TCH)
1987	Natalya Lisovskaya (URS)
1991	Huang Zhihong (CHN)
1993	Huang Zhihong (CHN)
1995	Astrid Kumbernuss (GER)
1997	Astrid Kumbernuss (GER)
1999	Astrid Kumbernuss (GER)
2001	Yanina Korolchik (BLR)
2003	Svetlana Krivelyova (RUS)
2005	Nadezhda Ostapchuk (BLR)

DISCUS THROW
1983	Martina Opitz (GDR)
1987	Martina Hellmann (GDR)
1991	Tsvetanka Khristova (BUL)
1993	Olga Burova (RUS)
1995	Ellina Zvereva (BLR)
1997	Beatrice Faumuina (NZL)
1999	Franka Dietzsch (GER)
2001	Ellina Zvereva (BLR)
2003	Irina Yachenko (BLR)
2005	Franka Dietzsch (GER)

HAMMER THROW[3]
1999	Mihaela Melinte (ROM)
2001	Yipsi Moreno (CUB)
2003	Yipsi Moreno (CUB)
2005	Olga Kuzenkova (RUS)

JAVELIN THROW
1983	Tiina Lillak (FIN)
1987	Fatima Whitbread (GBR)
1991	Xu Demei (CHN)
1993	Trine Hattestad (NOR)
1995	Natalya Shikolenko (BLR)
1997	Trine Hattestad (NOR)
1999	Mirela Tzelili (GRE)

World Track & Field Championships—Women (continued)

JAVELIN THROW (CONTINUED)
2001 Osleidys Menéndez (CUB)
2003 Mirela Manjani (GRE)
2005 Osleidys Menéndez (CUB)

HEPTATHLON
1983 Ramona Neubert (GDR)
1987 Jackie Joyner-Kersee (USA)
1991 Sabine Braun (GER)
1993 Jackie Joyner-Kersee (USA)
1995 Ghada Shouaa (SYR)

HEPTATHLON (CONTINUED)
1997 Sabine Braun (GER)
1999 Eunice Barber (FRA)
2001 Yelena Prokhorova (RUS)
2003 Carolina Klüft (SWE)
2005 Carolina Klüft (SWE)

¹Became 5,000 m in 1995.   ²Event added in 1987.   ³Event added in 1999.   ⁴Event added in 1993.

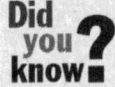

Did you know? The first athlete to run a mile in less than four minutes was Roger Bannister of England. He broke the four-minute barrier with a time of 3 min 59.4 sec in a dual meet at Oxford on 6 May 1954. Bannister became a neurologist in 1963, published papers on the physiology of exercise, heat illness, and neurological subjects, and was knighted in 1975.

IAAF World Cup—Men

The next IAAF World Cup competition is scheduled to be held 16–17 September 2006. No competition was held in 2004.

YEAR	WINNER
100 M	
1977	Steve Williams (USA)
1979	James Sanford (USA)
1981	Allan Wells (EUR)
1985	Ben Johnson (AME)
1989	Linford Christie (GBR)
1992	Linford Christie (GBR)
1994	Linford Christie (GBR)
1998	Obadele Thompson (AME)
2002	Uchenna Emedolu (AFR)
200 M	
1977	Clancy Edwards (USA)
1979	Silvio Leonard (AME)
1981	Melvin Lattany (USA)
1985	Robson Caetano da Silva (AME)
1989	Robson Caetano da Silva (AME)
1992	Robson Caetano da Silva (AME)
1994	John Regis (GBR)
1998	Frank Fredericks (AFR)
2002	Francis Obikwelu (EUR)
400 M	
1977	Alberto Juantorena (AME)
1979	Kashief Hassan (AFR)
1981	Cliff Wiley (USA)
1985	Mike Franks (USA)
1989	Roberto Hernández (AME)
1992	Sunday Bada (AFR)
1994	Antonio Pettigrew (USA)
1998	Iwan Thomas (GBR)
2002	Michael Blackwood (AME)
800 M	
1977	Alberto Juantorena (AME)
1979	James Maina (AFR)
1981	Sebastian Coe (EUR)
1985	Sammy Koskei (AFR)

YEAR	WINNER
800 M (CONT.)	
1989	Tom McKean (GBR)
1992	David Sharpe (GBR)
1994	Mark Everett (USA)
1998	Nils Schumann (GER)
2002	Antonio Manuel Reina (ESP)
1,500 M	
1977	Steve Ovett (EUR)
1979	Thomas Wessinghage (EUR)
1981	Steve Ovett (EUR)
1985	Omer Khalifa (AFR)
1989	Abdi Bile (AFR)
1992	Mohammed Suleiman (ASI)
1994	Noureddine Morceli (AFR)
1998	Laban Rotich (AFR)
2002	Bernard Lagat (AFR)
3,000 M	
1998	Dieter Baumann (GER)
2002	Craig Mottram (OCE)
5,000 M	
1977	Miruts Yifter (AFR)
1979	Miruts Yifter (AFR)
1981	Eamonn Coghlan (EUR)
1985	Doug Padilla (USA)
1989	Said Aouita (AFR)
1992	Fita Bayesa (AFR)
1994	Brahim Lahlafi (AFR)
1998	Daniel Komen (AFR)
2002	Alberto García (ESP)
10,000 M	
1977	Miruts Yifter (AFR)
1979	Miruts Yifter (AFR)
1981	Werner Schildhauer (GDR)
1985	Wodajo Bulti (AFR)

YEAR	WINNER
10,000 M (CONT.)	
1989	Salvatore Antibo (EUR)
1992	Addis Abebe (AFR)
1994	Khalid Skah (AFR)
STEEPLECHASE	
1977	Michael Karst (FRG)
1979	Henry Rono (AFR)
1981	Boguslaw Maminski (EUR)
1985	Julius Kariuki (AFR)
1989	Julius Kariuki (AFR)
1992	Philip Barkutwo (AFR)
1994	Moses Kiptanui (AFR)
1998	Damian Kallabis (GER)
2002	Wilson Boit Kipketer (AFR)
110-M HURDLES	
1977	Thomas Munkelt (GDR)
1979	Reynaldo Nehemiah (USA)
1981	Greg Foster (USA)
1985	Tony Campbell (USA)
1989	Roger Kingdom (USA)
1992	Colin Jackson (GBR)
1994	Tony Jarrett (GBR)
1998	Falk Balzer (GER)
2002	Anier García (AME)
400-M HURDLES	
1977	Edwin Moses (USA)
1979	Edwin Moses (USA)
1981	Edwin Moses (USA)
1985	Andre Phillips (USA)
1989	David Patrick (USA)
1992	Samuel Matete (AFR)
1994	Samuel Matete (AFR)
1998	Samuel Matete (AFR)
2002	James Carter (USA)
4 X 100-M RELAYS	
1977	United States
1979	Americas

IAAF World Cup—Men (continued)

YEAR	WINNER	YEAR	WINNER	YEAR	WINNER
4 X 100-M RELAYS (CONT.)		**HIGH JUMP (CONT.)**		**DISCUS THROW**	
1981	Europe	1994	Javier Sotomayor (AME)	1977	Wolfgang Schmidt (GDR)
1985	United States	1998	Charles Austin (USA)	1979	Wolfgang Schmidt (GDR)
1989	United States	2002	Yaroslav Rybakov (EUR)	1981	Armin Lemme (GDR)
1992	United States			1985	Georgy Kolnoochenko
1994	Great Britain	**POLE VAULT**			(URS)
1998	Great Britain	1977	Mike Tully (USA)	1989	Jürgen Schult (GDR)
2002	United States	1979	Mike Tully (USA)	1992	Anthony Washington (USA)
		1981	Konstantin Volkov (URS)	1994	Vladimir Dubrovshchik
4 X 400-M RELAYS		1985	Sergey Bubka (URS)		(EUR)
1977	West Germany	1989	Philippe Collet (EUR)	1998	Virgilijus Alekna (EUR)
1979	United States	1992	Igor Potapovich (UNT[1])	2002	Róbert Fazekas (EUR)
1981	United States	1994	Okkert Brits (AFR)		
1985	United States	1998	Maksim Tarasov (EUR)	**JAVELIN THROW**	
1989	Americas	2002	Okkert Brits (AFR)	1977	Michael Wessing (FRG)
1992	Africa			1979	Wolfgang Hanisch (FRG)
1994	Great Britain	**LONG JUMP**		1981	Dainis Kula (URS)
1998	United States	1977	Arnie Robinson (USA)	1985	Uwe Hohn (GDR)
2002	Americas	1979	Larry Myricks (USA)	1989	Steve Backley (GBR)
		1981	Carl Lewis (USA)	1992	Jan Zelezny (EUR)
TRIPLE JUMP		1985	Mike Conley (USA)	1994	Steve Backley (GBR)
1977	João de Oliveira (AME)	1989	Larry Myricks (USA)	1998	Steve Backley (GBR)
1979	João de Oliveira (AME)	1992	Iván Pedroso (AME)	2002	Sergey Makarov (EUR)
1981	João de Oliveira (AME)	1994	Fred Salle (GBR)		
1985	Willie Banks (USA)	1998	Iván Pedroso (AME)	**TEAM**	
1989	Mike Conley (USA)	2002	Savanté Stringfellow (USA)	1977	East Germany
1992	Jonathan Edwards (GBR)			1979	United States
1994	Yoelbi Quesada (AME)	**SHOT PUT**		1981	Europe
1998	Charles Friedek (GER)	1977	Udo Beyer (GDR)	1985	United States
2002	Jonathan Edwards (GBR)	1979	Udo Beyer (GDR)	1989	United States
		1981	Udo Beyer (GDR)	1992	Africa
HIGH JUMP		1985	Ulf Timmermann (GDR)	1994	Africa
1977	Rolf Beilschmidt (GDR)	1989	Ulf Timmermann (GDR)	1998	Africa
1979	Franklin Jacobs (USA)	1992	Mike Stulce (USA)	2002	Africa
1981	Tyke Peacock (USA)	1994	C.J. Hunter (USA)		
1985	Patrik Sjöberg (EUR)	1998	John Godina (USA)		
1989	Patrik Sjöberg (EUR)	2002	Adam Nelson (USA)		
1992	Yury Sergeyenko (UNT[1])				

[1]*Unified Team, consisting of athletes from the Commonwealth of Independent States plus Georgia.*

IAAF World Cup—Women

The next IAAF World Cup competition is scheduled to be held 16–17 September 2006. No competition was held in 2004.

YEAR	WINNER	YEAR	WINNER	YEAR	WINNER
100 M		**400 M**		**1,500 M**	
1977	Marlies Oelsner (GDR)	1977	Irina Szewinska (EUR)	1977	Tatyana Kazankina
1979	Evelyn Ashford (USA)	1979	Marita Koch (GDR)		(URS)
1981	Evelyn Ashford (USA)	1981	Jarmila Kratochvilova (EUR)	1979	Christiane Wartenburg
1985	Marlies Göhr (GDR)	1985	Marita Koch (GDR)		(GDR)
1989	Sheila Echols (USA)	1989	Ana Quirot (AME)	1981	Tamara Sorokina (URS)
1992	Natalya Voronova (UNT[1])	1992	Jearl Miles (USA)	1985	Hildegard Körner (GDR)
1994	Irina Privalova (EUR)	1994	Irina Privalova (EUR)	1989	Paula Ivan (EUR)
1998	Marion Jones (USA)	1998	Falilat Ogunkoya (AFR)	1992	Yekaterina Podkopayeva
2002	Marion Jones (USA)	2002	Ana Guevara (AME)		(UNT[1])
				1994	Hassiba Boulmerka (AFR)
200 M		**800 M**		1998	Svetlana Masterkova
1977	Irina Szewinska (EUR)	1977	Totka Petrova (EUR)		(RUS)
1979	Evelyn Ashford (USA)	1979	Nikolina Shtereva (EUR)	2002	Süreyya Ayhan (EUR)
1981	Evelyn Ashford (USA)	1981	Lyudmila Veselkova (URS)		
1985	Marita Koch (GDR)	1985	Christine Wachtel (GDR)		
1989	Silke Möller (GDR)	1989	Ana Quirot (AME)		
1992	Marie-José Pérec (EUR)	1992	Maria Mutola (AFR)		
1994	Merlene Ottey (AME)	1994	Maria Mutola (AFR)		
1998	Marion Jones (USA)	1998	Maria Mutola (AFR)		
2002	Debbie Ferguson (AME)	2002	Maria Mutola (AFR)		

IAAF World Cup—Women (continued)

YEAR	WINNER
3,000 M	
1977	Grete Waitz (EUR)
1979	Svetlana Ulmasova (URS)
1981	Angelika Zauber (GDR)
1985	Ulrike Bruns (GDR)
1989	Yvonne Murray (EUR)
1992	Derartu Tulu (AFR)
1994	Yvonne Murray (GBR)
1998	Gabriela Szabo (EUR)
2002	Berhane Adere (AFR)
5,000 M	
1998	Sonia O'Sullivan (EUR)
2002	Olga Yegorova (RUS)
10,000 M	
1985	Aurora Cunha (EUR)
1989	Kathrin Ullrich (GDR)
1992	Derartu Tulu (AFR)
1994	Elana Meyer (AFR)
100-M HURDLES	
1977	Grazyna Rabsztyn (EUR)
1979	Grazyna Rabsztyn (EUR)
1981	Tatyana Anisimova (URS)
1985	Cornelia Oschkenat (GDR)
1989	Cornelia Oschkenat (GDR)
1992	Aliuska López (AME)
1994	Aliuska López (AME)
1998	Glory Alozie (AFR)
2002	Gail Devers (USA)
400-M HURDLES	
1979	Bärbel Klepp (GDR)
1981	Ellen Neumann (GDR)
1985	Sabine Busch (GDR)
1989	Sandra Farmer-Patrick (USA)
1992	Sandra Farmer-Patrick (USA)
1994	Sally Gunnell (GBR)
1998	Nezha Bidouane (AFR)
2002	Yuliya Pechonkina (RUS)
4 X 100-M RELAYS	
1977	Europe Select
1979	Europe Select
1981	East Germany
1985	East Germany

YEAR	WINNER
4 X 100-M RELAYS (CONT.)	
1989	East Germany
1992	Asia
1994	Africa
1998	United States
2002	Americas
4 X 400-M RELAYS	
1977	East Germany
1979	East Germany
1981	East Germany
1985	East Germany
1989	Americas
1992	Americas
1994	Great Britain
1998	Germany
2002	Americas
TRIPLE JUMP	
1994	Anna Biryukova (EUR)
1998	Olga Vasdeki (EUR)
2002	Françoise Mbango Etone (AFR)
HIGH JUMP	
1977	Rosemarie Ackermann (GDR)
1979	Debbie Brill (AME)
1981	Ulrike Meyfarth (EUR)
1985	Stefka Kostadinova (URS)
1989	Silvia Costa (AME)
1992	Ioamnet Quintero (AME)
1994	Britta Bilac (EUR)
1998	Monica Iagar-Dinescu (EUR)
2002	Hestrie Cloete (AFR)
LONG JUMP	
1977	Lyn Jacenko (OCE)
1979	Anita Stukane (URS)
1981	Sigrid Ulbricht (GDR)
1985	Heike Daute Drechsler (GDR)
1989	Galina Chistyakova (URS)
1992	Heike Drechsler (GER)
1994	Inessa Kravets (EUR)
1998	Heike Drechsler (GER)
2002	Tatyana Kotova (RUS)

YEAR	WINNER
SHOT PUT	
1977	Helena Fibingerova (EUR)
1979	Ilona Slupianek (GDR)
1981	Ilona Slupianek (GDR)
1985	Natalya Lisovskaya (URS)
1989	Zhihong Huang (ASI)
1992	Belsis Laza (AME)
1994	Zhihong Huang (ASI)
1998	Vita Pavlysh (EUR)
2002	Irina Korzhanenko (RUS)
DISCUS THROW	
1977	Faina Melnik (URS)
1979	Evelin Jahl (GDR)
1981	Evelin Jahl (GDR)
1985	Martina Optiz (GDR)
1989	Ilke Wyludda (GDR)
1992	Maritza Marten (AME)
1994	Ilke Wyludda (EUR)
1998	Franka Dietzsch (GER)
2002	Beatrice Faumuina (OCE)
JAVELIN THROW	
1977	Ruth Fuchs (GDR)
1979	Ruth Fuchs (GDR)
1981	Antoaneta Todorova (EUR)
1985	Olga Gavrilova (URS) *
1989	Petra Felke (GDR)
1992	Tessa Sanderson (GBR)
1994	Trine Hattestad (EUR)
1998	Joanna Stone (OCE)
2002	Osleidys Menéndez (AME)
TEAM	
1977	Europe Select
1979	East Germany
1981	East Germany
1985	East Germany
1989	East Germany
1992	Unified Team[1]
1994	Europe
1998	United States
2002	Russia

[1]*Unified Team, consisting of athletes from the Commonwealth of Independent States plus Georgia.*

World Cross Country Championships

Men's competition held since 1903, women's since 1967. Table shows results from the past 20 years.

men (12,000 meters)

YEAR	INDIVIDUAL (NATIONALITY)	TEAM	YEAR	INDIVIDUAL (NATIONALITY)	TEAM
1986	John Ngugi (KEN)	Kenya	1996	Paul Tergat (KEN)	Kenya
1987	John Ngugi (KEN)	Kenya	1997	Paul Tergat (KEN)	Kenya
1988	John Ngugi (KEN)	Kenya	1998	Paul Tergat (KEN)	Kenya
1989	John Ngugi (KEN)	Kenya	1999	Paul Tergat (KEN)	Kenya
1990	Khalid Skah (MAR)	Kenya	2000	Mohammed Mourhit (BEL)	Kenya
1991	Khalid Skah (MAR)	Kenya	2001	Mohammed Mourhit (BEL)	Kenya
1992	John Ngugi (KEN)	Kenya	2002	Kenenisa Bekele (ETH)	Kenya
1993	William Sigei (KEN)	Kenya	2003	Kenenisa Bekele (ETH)	Kenya
1994	William Sigei (KEN)	Kenya	2004	Kenenisa Bekele (ETH)	Ethiopia
1995	Paul Tergat (KEN)	Kenya	2005	Kenenisa Bekele (ETH)	Ethiopia

World Cross Country Championships (continued)

women (8,000 meters)

YEAR	INDIVIDUAL (NATIONALITY)	TEAM	YEAR	INDIVIDUAL (NATIONALITY)	TEAM
1986	Zola Budd (GBR)	England	1996	Gete Wami (ETH)	Kenya
1987	Annette Sargent (FRA)	United States	1997	Derartu Tulu (ETH)	Ethiopia
1988	Ingrid Kristiansen (NOR)	USSR	1998	Sonia O'Sullivan (IRE)	Kenya
1989	Annette Sargent (FRA)	USSR	1999	Gete Wami (ETH)	Ethiopia
1990	Lynn Jennings (USA)	USSR	2000	Derartu Tulu (ETH)	Ethiopia
1991	Lynn Jennings (USA)	Kenya	2001	Paula Radcliffe (GBR)	Kenya
1992	Lynn Jennings (USA)	Kenya	2002	Paula Radcliffe (GBR)	Ethiopia
1993	Albertina Dias (POR)	Kenya	2003	Werknesh Kidane (ETH)	Ethiopia
1994	Hellen Chepngeno (KEN)	Portugal	2004	Benita Johnson (AUS)	Ethiopia
1995	Derartu Tulu (ETH)	Kenya	2005	Tirunesh Dibaba (ETH)	Ethiopia

Volleyball

World volleyball championships for men were inaugurated in 1949. Women's competition began in 1952. These biennial championships are organized by the Fédération Internationale de Volleyball (FIVB; founded 1947). Indoor volleyball has been included in the Olympic Games since 1964 and beach volleyball since 1996.

FIVB Web site: <www.fivb.org>.

World Volleyball Championships

YEAR	MEN	WOMEN	YEAR[1]	MEN	WOMEN
1949	USSR		1980[1]	USSR	USSR
1952	USSR	USSR	1982	USSR	China
1956	Czechoslovakia	USSR	1984[1]	United States	China
1960	USSR	USSR	1986	United States	China
1962	USSR	Japan	1988[1]	United States	USSR
1964[1]	USSR	Japan	1990	Italy	USSR
1966	Czechoslovakia	Japan	1992[1]	Brazil	Cuba
1967	*not held*	Japan	1994	Italy	Cuba
1968[1]	USSR	USSR	1996[1]	The Netherlands	Cuba
1970	East Germany	USSR	1998	Italy	Cuba
1972[1]	Japan	USSR	2000[1]	Yugoslavia	Cuba
1974	Poland	Japan	2002	Brazil	Italy
1976[1]	Poland	Japan	2004[1]	Brazil	China
1978	USSR	Cuba			

[1]*Olympic champions, considered world champions.*

Weight Lifting

World weight lifting is overseen by the International Weightlifting Federation (IWF; founded 1905). The first men's international weight lifting competition was held in London in 1891; the sport was also included in the first modern Olympic Games in 1896. By the 1930s championship events consisted of the snatch, clean and jerk, and press, which was eliminated in 1972. Women's world championships have been held since 1987, and women's competition was added to the Olympics in 2000. In 1998 the IWF established new weight classes (eight for men and seven for women) as well as a new world standard for each class in determining world records.

IWF Web site: <www.iwf.net>.

Weight Lifting World Records

Total weight for snatch and clean & jerk. World standards were reset on 1 Jan 1998 and have not been achieved in some men's events.

men

WEIGHT CLASS	WINNER (NATIONALITY)	PERFORMANCE	DATE
56 kg (123 lb)	Halil Mutlu (TUR)	305 kg (672 lb)	16 Sep 2000
62 kg (137 lb)	*world standard*	325 kg (716.5 lb)	1 Jan 1998
69 kg (152 lb)	Galabin Boevski (BUL)	357 kg (787 lb)	24 Nov 1999
77 kg (170 lb)	Plamen Zhelyazkov (BUL)	377 kg (831 lb)	27 Mar 2002
85 kg (187 lb)	*world standard*	395 kg (871 lb)	1 Jan 1998
94 kg (207 lb)	*world standard*	417 kg (919 lb)	1 Jan 1998
105 kg (231.5 lb)	*world standard*	440 kg (970 lb)	1 Jan 1998
+105 kg (+231.5 lb)	Hossein Rezazadeh (IRI)	472 kg (1041 lb)	26 Sep 2000

Weight Lifting World Records (continued)

women

WEIGHT CLASS	WINNER (NATIONALITY)	PERFORMANCE	DATE
48kg (106 lb)	Nurcan Taylan (TUR)	210 kg (463 lb)	14 Aug 2004
53 kg (117 lb)	Yang Xia (CHN)	225 kg (496 lb)	18 Sep 2000
58 kg (128 lb)	Wang Li (CHN)	240 kg (529 lb)	10 Aug 2003
63 kg (139 lb)	Liu Xia (CHN)	247.5 kg (545 lb)	12 Sep 2003
69 kg (152 lb)	Liu Chunhong (CHN)	275 kg (606 lb)	19 Aug 2004
75 kg (165 lb)	Liu Chunhong (CHN)	273 kg (602 lb)	23 May 2005
+75 kg (+165 lb)	Tang Gonghong (CHN)	305 kg (672 lb)	21 Aug 2004

World Weight Lifting Champions, 2004

Next competition scheduled to be held 9–21 Nov 2005 in Doha, Qatar.

men

WEIGHT CLASS	WINNER (NATIONALITY)	PERFORMANCE
56 kg (123 lb)	Halil Mutlu (TUR)	295 kg (650 lb)
62 kg (137 lb)	Shi Zhiyong (CHN)	325 kg (717 lb)
69 kg (152 lb)	Zhang Guozheng (CHN)	347.5 kg (766.1 lb)
77 kg (170 lb)	Taner Sagir (TUR)	375 kg (827 lb)
85 kg (187 lb)	George Asanidze (GEO)	382.5 kg (843.3 lb)
94 kg (207 lb)	Milen Dobrev (BUL)	407.5 kg (898.4 lb)
105 kg (231 lb)	Dmitry Berestov (RUS)	425 kg (937 lb)
105+ kg (231+ lb)	Hossein Reza Zadeh (IRI)	472.5 kg (1041.7 lb)

women

WEIGHT CLASS	WINNER (NATIONALITY)	PERFORMANCE
48 kg (106 lb)	Nurcan Taylan (TUR)	210 kg (463 lb)
53 kg (117 lb)	Udomporn Polsak (THA)	222.5 kg (490.5 lb)
58 kg (128 lb)	Chen Yanqing (CHN)	237.5 kg (523.6 lb)
63 kg (139 lb)	Nataliya Skakun (UKR)	242.5 kg (534.6 lb)
69 kg (152 lb)	Liu Chunhong (CHN)	275 kg (606 lb)
75 kg (165 lb)	Pawina Thongsuk (THA)	272.5 kg (600.8 lb)
75+ kg (165+ lb)	Tang Gonghong (CHN)	305 kg (672 lb)

Wrestling

Greco-Roman wrestling involves holds made only above the waist and forbids wrapping the legs about an opponent when the wrestlers go down. **Freestyle (catch-as-catch-can)** permits holds above the waist and leg grips and is won by a pin-fall (in which the opponent must be held down for a measurable length of time). In Japanese **sumo** the object is to propel the opponent out of a ring about 4.6 m (15 ft) in diameter or to force him to touch the ground with any part of his body other than the soles of his feet. The wrestlers wear only loincloths and grip each other by the belt.

The first official amateur wrestling **world championship** was organized by the Fédération Interna-tionale de Lutte Amateur (FILA; founded 1913, reconstituted 1921; now called the **International Federation of Associated Wrestling Styles**). Although Greco-Roman style wrestling championships were held in 1910 and 1920–22, they were in effect (like the championships of 1923–49 in fact) open European championships, and the first actual world Greco-Roman wrestling championships were not held until 1950. World amateur **freestyle wrestling championships** were first held in 1951.

Related Web sites: International Federation of Associated Wrestling Styles <www.fila-wrestling.com>; sumo <www.sumo.or.jp/eng>.

World Wrestling Championships—Greco-Roman Style

The maximum weight in some classes was revised in 1962, 1969, 1985, 1997, and 2002. The 2005 competition is scheduled to be held 26 September–2 October in Budapest, Hungary.

YEAR	WINNER (NATIONALITY)	YEAR	WINNER (NATIONALITY)	YEAR	WINNER (NATIONALITY)
48 kg		**48 kg (continued)**		**48 kg (continued)**	
1969	Gheorghe Berceanu (ROM)	1972[1]	Gheorghe Berceanu (ROM)	1976[1]	Aleksey Shumakov (URS)
1970	Gheorghe Berceanu (ROM)	1973	Vladimir Zubkov (URS)	1977	Aleksey Shumakov (URS)
		1974	Vladimir Zubkov (URS)	1978	Constantin Alexandru (ROM)
1971	Vladimir Zubkov (URS)	1975	Vladimir Zubkov (URS)		

World Wrestling Championships—Greco-Roman Style (continued)

YEAR	WINNER (NATIONALITY)
48 kg (continued)	
1979	Constantin Alexandru (ROM)
1980[1]	Saksylik Ushkempirov (URS)
1981	Saksylik Ushkempirov (URS)
1982	Temo Kazarashvili (URS)
1983	Bratan Tsenov (BUL)
1984[1]	Vincenzo Maenza (ITA)
1985	Magyatdin Allakhverdiyev (URS)
1986	Magyatdin Allakhverdiyev (URS)
1987	Magyatdin Allakhverdiyev (URS)
1988[1]	Vincenzo Maenza (ITA)
1989	Oleg Kucherenko (URS)
1990	Oleg Kucherenko (URS)
1991	Gooun Duk-Yong (KOR)
1992[1]	Oleg Kucherenko (UNT)[2]
1993	Wilber Sánchez (CUB)
1994	Wilber Sánchez (CUB)
1995	Sim Kwon Ho (KOR)
1996[1]	Sim Kwon Ho (KOR)
1997	*discontinued*
55 kg	
1950	Bengt Johansson (SWE)
1952[1]	Boris Gurevich (URS)
1953	Boris Gurevich (URS)
1955	Ignazio Fabra (ITA)
1956[1]	Nikolay Solovyov (URS)
1958	Boris Gurevich (URS)
1960[1]	Dumitru Pirvulescu (ROM)
1961	Armais Sayadov (URS)
1962	Sergey Rybalko (URS)
1963	Borivoje Vukov (YUG)
1964[1]	Tsutomu Hanahara (JPN)
1965	Sergey Rybalko (URS)
1966	Angel Keresov (BUL)
1967	Vladimir Bakulin (URS)
1968[1]	Petar Kirov (BUL)
1969	Feerooz Aluzadeh (IRI)
1970	Petar Kirov (BUL)
1971	Petar Kirov (BUL)
1972[1]	Petar Kirov (BUL)
1973	Nicu Ginga (ROM)
1974	Petar Kirov (BUL)
1975	Vitaly Konstantinov (URS)
1976[1]	Vitaly Konstantinov (URS)
1977	Nicu Ginga (ROM)
1978	Vakhtang Blagidze (URS)
1979	Lajos Racz (HUN)
1980[1]	Vakhtang Blagidze (URS)
1981	Vakhtang Blagidze (URS)
1982	Benur Pashayan (URS)
1983	Benur Pashayan (URS)
1984[1]	Atsuji Miyahara (JPN)
1985	Jon Ronningen (NOR)
1986	Sergey Dudayev (URS)
1987	Pedro Favier Roque (CUB)
1988[1]	Jon Ronningen (NOR)
1989	Aleksandr Ignatenko (URS)
1990	Aleksandr Ignatenko (URS)

YEAR	WINNER (NATIONALITY)
55 kg (continued)	
1991	Raul Martínez (CUB)
1992[1]	Jon Ronningen (NOR)
1993	Raul Martínez (CUB)
1994	Alfred Ter-Mkrtchyan (GER)
1995	Samvel Danielane (RUS)
1996[1]	Armen Nazaryan (ARM)
1997	Ercan Yildiz (TUR)
1998	Sim Kwon Ho (KOR)
1999	Lazaro Rivas (CUB)
2000[1]	Sim Kwon Ho (KOR)
2001	Hassan Rangraz (IRI)
2002	Gaidar Mamedaliev (RUS)
2003	Dariusz Jablonski (POL)
2004[1]	Istvan Majoros (HUN)
60 kg	
1950	Ali Mahmoud Hassan (EGY)
1952[1]	Imre Hodos (HUN)
1953	Artyom Teryan (URS)
1955	Vladimir Stashkevich (URS)
1956[1]	Konstantin Vyrupayev (URS)
1958	Oleg Karavayev (URS)
1960[1]	Oleg Karavayev (URS)
1961	Oleg Karavayev (URS)
1962	Masamitsu Ichiguchi (JPN)
1963	Janos Varga (HUN)
1964[1]	Masamitsu Ichiguchi (JPN)
1965	Ion Chernya (ROM)
1966	Fritz Stange (FRG)
1967	Ion Baciu (ROM)
1968[1]	Janos Varga (HUN)
1969	Rustam Kazakov (URS)
1970	Janos Varga (HUN)
1971	Rustam Kazakov (URS)
1972[1]	Rustam Kazakov (URS)
1973	Jozef Lipien (POL)
1974	Farhat Mustafin (URS)
1975	Farhat Mustafin (URS)
1976[1]	Pertti Olavi Ukkola (FIN)
1977	Pertti Olavi Ukkola (FIN)
1978	Shamil Serikov (URS)
1979	Shamil Serikov (URS)
1980[1]	Shamil Serikov (URS)
1981	Pasquale Passarelli (FRG)
1982	Piotr Michalik (POL)
1983	Masaki Ito (JPN)
1984[1]	Pasquale Passarelli (FRG)
1985	Stoyan Balov (BUL)
1986	Emil Ivanov (BUL)
1987	Patrice Mourier (FRA)
1988[1]	Andras Sike (HUN)
1989	Emil Ivanov (BUL)
1990	Rifat Yildiz (GER)
1991	Rifat Yildiz (GER)
1992[1]	An Han-Bong (KOR)
1993	Agazi Manukyan (ARM)
1994	Yury Melnichenko (KAZ)
1995	Dennis Hall (USA)
1996[1]	Yury Melnichenko (KAZ)
1997	Yury Melnichenko (KAZ)
1998	Kim In Sub (KOR)

YEAR	WINNER (NATIONALITY)
60 kg (continued)	
1999	Kim In Sub (KOR)
2000[1]	Armen Nazaryan (BUL)
2001	Dilshod Aripov (UZB)
2002	Armen Nazarian (BUL)
2003	Armen Nazarian (BUL)
2004[1]	Jung Ji Hyun (KOR)
66 kg	
1950	Olle Anderberg (SWE)
1952[1]	Yakov Punkin (URS)
1953	Olle Anderberg (SWE)
1955	Imre Polyak (HUN)
1956[1]	Rauno Leonhard Mäkinen (FIN)
1958	Imre Polyak (HUN)
1960[1]	Muzahir Sille (TUR)
1961	Hamid Mansour Mustafa (EGY)
1962	Imre Polyak (HUN)
1963	Gennady Sapunov (URS)
1964[1]	Imre Polyak (HUN)
1965	Yury Grigoryev (URS)
1966	Roman Rurua (URS)
1967	Roman Rurua (URS)
1968[1]	Roman Rurua (URS)
1969	Roman Rurua (URS)
1970	Hideo Fujimoto (JPN)
1971	Georgi Markov (BUL)
1972[1]	Georgi Markov (BUL)
1973	Kazimierz Lipien (POL)
1974	Kazimierz Lipien (POL)
1975	Nelson Davidyan (URS)
1976[1]	Kazimierz Lipien (POL)
1977	Laszlo Reczi (HUN)
1978	Boris Kramarenko (URS)
1979	Istvan Toth (HUN)
1980[1]	Stylianos Migiakis (GRE)
1981	Istvan Toth (HUN)
1982	Ryszard Swierad (POL)
1983	Hannu Lahtinen (FIN)
1984[1]	Kim Weon-Kee (KOR)
1985	Zhivko Vangelov Atanasov (BUL)
1986	Komandar Madshidov (URS)
1987	Zhivko Vangelov Atanasov (BUL)
1988[1]	Komandar Madshidov (URS)
1989	Komandar Madshidov (URS)
1990	Mario Olivera (CUB)
1991	Sergey Martinov (URS)
1992[1]	Akif Mehmet Pirim (TUR)
1993	Sergey Martinov (RUS)
1994	Sergey Martinov (RUS)
1995	Sergey Martinov (RUS)
1996[1]	Wlodzimierz Zawadzki (POL)
1997	Seref Eroglu (TUR)
1998	Makhidar Manukyan (KAZ)
1999	Makhidar Manukyan (KAZ)
2000[1]	Varteres Samurgashev (RUS)
2001	Vaghinak Galustyan (ARM)
2002	Jimmy Samuelsson (SWE)

World Wrestling Championships—Greco-Roman Style (continued)

YEAR	WINNER (NATIONALITY)
66 kg (continued)	
2003	Manuchar Kvirkvelia (GEO)
2004[1]	Farid Mansurov (AZE)
69 kg	
1950	Jozsef Gal (HUN)
1952[1]	Shazam Safin (URS)
1953	Gustav Freij (SWE)
1955	Grigory Gamarnik (URS)
1956[1]	Kyösti Emil Lehtonen (FIN)
1958	Riza Dogan (TUR)
1960[1]	Avtandil Koridze (URS)
1961	Avtandil Koridze (URS)
1962	Kazim Ayvaz (TUR)
1963	Stevan Horvat (YUG)
1964[1]	Kazim Ayvaz (TUR)
1965	Gennady Sapunov (URS)
1966	Stevan Horvat (YUG)
1967	Eero Tapio (FIN)
1968[1]	Muneji Mumemura (JPN)
1969	Simion Popescu (ROM)
1970	Roman Rurua (URS)
1971	Sreten Damjanovic (YUG)
1972[1]	Shamil Khisamutdinov (URS)
1973	Shamil Khisamutdinov (URS)
1974	Nelson Davidyan (URS)
1975	Shamil Khisamutdinov (URS)
1976[1]	Suren Nalbandyan (URS)
1977	Heinz-Helmut Wehling (GDR)
1978	Stefan Rusu (ROM)
1979	Andrzej Supron (POL)
1980[1]	Stefan Rusu (ROM)
1981	Gennady Yermilov (URS)
1982	Gennady Yermilov (URS)
1983	Tapio Sipila (FIN)
1984[1]	Vlado Lisjak (YUG)
1985	Stefan Negrisan (ROM)
1986	Levon Dzulfalakyan (URS)
1987	Aslaudin Abayev (URS)
1988[1]	Levon Dzulfalakyan (URS)
1989	Claudio Passarelli (FRG)
1990	Islam Doguchiyev (RUS)
1991	Islam Doguchiyev (RUS)
1992[1]	Attila Repka (HUN)
1993	Islam Doguchiyev (RUS)
1994	Islam Doguchiyev (RUS)
1995	Rustam Adzhy (UKR)
1996[1]	Ryszard Wolny (POL)
1997	Son Sang-Pil (KOR)
1998	Aleksandr Tretyakov (RUS)
1999	Son Sang-Pil (KOR)
2000[1]	Filiberto Ascuy Aguilera (CUB)
2001	Filiberto Ascuy Aguilera (CUB)
2002	*discontinued*
74 kg	
1950	Matti Siimanainen (FIN)
1952[1]	Miklos Szilvasi (HUN)
1953	Georgy Chatvorgian (URS)
1955	Vladimir Maneyev (URS)

YEAR	WINNER (NATIONALITY)
74 kg (continued)	
1956[1]	Mithat Bayrak (TUR)
1958	Kazim Ayvaz (TUR)
1960[1]	Mithat Bayrak (TUR)
1961	Valeriu Bularca (ROM)
1962	Anatoly Kolesov (URS)
1963	Anatoly Kolesov (URS)
1964[1]	Anatoly Kolesov (URS)
1965	Anatoly Kolesov (URS)
1966	Viktor Igumenov (URS)
1967	Viktor Igumenov (URS)
1968[1]	Rudolph Vesper (GDR)
1969	Viktor Igumenov (URS)
1970	Viktor Igumenov (URS)
1971	Viktor Igumenov (URS)
1972[1]	Viteslav Macha (TCH)
1973	Ivan Kolev (BUL)
1974	Viteslav Macha (TCH)
1975	Anatoly Bykov (URS)
1976[1]	Anatoly Bykov (URS)
1977	Viteslav Macha (TCH)
1978	Arif Niftulayev (URS)
1979	Ferenc Kocsis (HUN), Iyanko Chopov (BUL)[3]
1980[1]	Ferenc Kocsis (HUN)
1981	Aleksandr Kudryavtsev (URS)
1982	Stefan Rusa (ROM)
1983	Mikhail Mamiashvili (URS)
1984[1]	Jouko Johann Salomaki (FIN)
1985	Mikhail Mamiashvili (URS)
1986	Mikhail Mamiashvili (URS)
1987	Jouko Johann Salomaki (FIN)
1988[1]	Kim Young-Nam (KOR)
1989	Daulet Turlykhanov (URS)
1990	Mnazakan Iskandaryan (RUS)
1991	Mnazakan Iskandaryan (RUS)
1992[1]	Mnazakan Iskandaryan (UNT)[2]
1993	Nestor Alamanza (CUB)
1994	Mnazakan Iskandaryan (RUS)
1995	Yvon Riemer (FRA)
1996[1]	Filiberto Ascuy Aguilera (CUB)
1997	Marko Yli-Hannuksela (FIN)
1998	Bakhtiar Bayseytov (KAZ)
1999	Nazmi Avluca (TUR)
2000[1]	Murat Kardanov (RUS)
2001	Ara Abrahamian (SWE)
2002	Varteres Samourgashev (RUS)
2003	Aleksey Glushkov (RUS)
2004[1]	Alexander Dokturishvili (UZB)
84 kg	
1950	Axel Grönberg (SWE)
1952[1]	Axel Grönberg (SWE)
1953	Givi Kartoziya (URS)

YEAR	WINNER (NATIONALITY)
84 kg (continued)	
1955	Givi Kartoziya (URS)
1956[1]	Givi Kartoziya (URS)
1958	Givi Kartoziya (URS)
1960[1]	Dimitar Dobrev (BUL)
1961	Vasily Zenin (URS)
1962	Tevfik Kis (TUR)
1963	Tevfik Kis (TUR)
1964[1]	Branislav Simic (YUG)
1965	Rimantes Bogdanas (URS)
1966	Valentin Olenik (URS)
1967	Laszlo Sillai (HUN)
1968[1]	Lothar Metz (GDR)
1969	Petar Krumov (BUL)
1970	Anatoly Nazarenko (URS)
1971	Csaba Hegedus (HUN)
1972[1]	Csaba Hegedus (HUN)
1973	Leonid Liberman (URS)
1974	Anatoly Nazarenko (URS)
1975	Anatoly Nazarenko (URS)
1976[1]	Momir Petkovic (YUG)
1977	Vladimir Cheboksarov (URS)
1978	Ion Draica (ROM)
1979	Gennady Korban (URS)
1980[1]	Gennady Korban (URS)
1981	Gennady Korban (URS)
1982	Taymuraz Abkhasava (URS)
1983	Taymuraz Abkhasava (URS)
1984[1]	Ion Draica (ROM)
1985	Bogdan Daras (POL)
1986	no award
1987	Tibor Komaromi (HUN)
1988[1]	Mikhail Mamiashvili (URS)
1989	Tibor Komaromi (HUN)
1990	Peter Farkas (HUN)
1991	Peter Farkas (HUN)
1992[1]	Peter Farkas (HUN)
1993	Hamza Yerlikaya (TUR)
1994	Thomas Zander (GER)
1995	Hamza Yerlikaya (TUR)
1996[1]	Hamza Yerlikaya (TUR)
1997	Sergey Tsvir (RUS)
1998	Aleksandr Menshikov (RUS)
1999	Luiz Enrique Mendez Lazo (CUB)
2000[1]	Hamza Yerlikaya (TUR)
2001	Muhran Vakhtangadze (GEO)
2002	Ara Abrahamian (SWE)
2003	Gocha Ziziashvilly (ISR)
2004[1]	Alexei Michine (RUS)
90 kg	
1950	Muharrem Candas (TUR)
1952[1]	Kelpo Olavi Gröndahl (FIN)
1953	August Englas (URS)
1955	Valentin Nikolayev (URS)
1956[1]	Valentin Nikolayev (URS)
1958	Rostom Abashidze (URS)
1960[1]	Tevfik Kis (TUR)
1961	Gyorgy Gurics (HUN)
1962	Rostom Abashidze (URS)

World Wrestling Championships—Greco-Roman Style (continued)

YEAR	WINNER (NATIONALITY)
90 kg (continued)	
1963	Rostom Abashidze (URS)
1964[1]	Boyan Radev (BUL)
1965	Valery Anisimov (URS)
1966	Boyan Radev (BUL)
1967	Nikolay Yakovenko (URS)
1968[1]	Boyan Radev (BUL)
1969	Aleksandr Yurkevich (URS)
1970	Valery Rezantsev (URS)
1971	Valery Rezantsev (URS)
1972[1]	Valery Rezantsev (URS)
1973	Valery Rezantsev (URS)
1974	Valery Rezantsev (URS)
1975	Valery Rezantsev (URS)
1976[1]	Valery Rezantsev (URS)
1977	Frank Andersson (SWE)
1978	Stoyan Nikolov Ivanov (BUL)
1979	Frank Andersson (SWE)
1980[1]	Norbert Nottny (HUN)
1981	Igor Kanygin (URS)
1982	Frank Andersson (SWE)
1983	Igor Kanygin (URS)
1984[1]	Steven Fraser (USA)
1985	Michael Houck (USA)
1986	Andrzej Malina (POL)
1987	Vladimir Popov (URS)
1988[1]	Atanas Komchev (BUL)
1989	Maik Bullmann (GDR)
1990	Maik Bullmann (GER)
1991	Maik Bullmann (GER)
1992[1]	Maik Bullmann (GER)
1993	Georgy Koguchavilli (RUS)
1994	Georgy Koguchavilli (RUS)
1995	Hakki Basar (TUR)
1996[1]	Vyacheslav Oleynyk (UKR)
1997	*discontinued*
96 kg	
1950	Bertil Antonsson (SWE)
1952[1]	Johannes Kotkas (URS)
1953	Bertil Antonsson (SWE)
1955	Aleksandr Mazur (URS)
1956[1]	Anatoly Parfenov (URS)
1958	Ivan Bogdan (URS)
1960[1]	Ivan Bogdan (URS)
1961	Ivan Bogdan (URS)
1962	Istvan Kozma (HUN)

YEAR	WINNER (NATIONALITY)
96 kg (continued)	
1963	Anatoly Roshchin (URS)
1964[1]	Istvan Kozma (HUN)
1965	Nikolay Shmakov (URS)
1966	Istvan Kozma (HUN)
1967	Istvan Kozma (HUN)
1968[1]	Istvan Kozma (HUN)
1969	Nikolay Yakovenko (URS)
1970	Per Oskar Svensson (SWE)
1971	Per Oskar Svensson (SWE)
1972[1]	Nicolae Martinescu (ROM)
1973	Nikolay Balboshin (URS)
1974	Nikolay Balboshin (URS)
1975	Kamen Losanov (BUL)
1976[1]	Nikolay Balboshin (URS)
1977	Nikolay Balboshin (URS)
1978	Nikolay Balboshin (URS)
1979	Nikolay Balboshin (URS)
1980[1]	Georgi Raykov-Petkov (BUL)
1981	Michail Saladze (URS)
1982	Roman Wroclawski (POL)
1983	Andrey Dimitrov (BUL)
1984[1]	Vasile Andrei (ROM)
1985	Andrey Dimitrov (BUL)
1986	Tamas Gaspar (HUN)
1987	Guram Guedekhaorui (URS)
1988[1]	Andrzej Wronski (POL)
1989	Gerhard Himmel (FRG)
1990	Sergey Demyashkevich (URS)
1991	Hector Milian (CUB)
1992[1]	Hector Milian (CUB)
1993	Mikael Ljungberg (SWE)
1994	Andrzej Wronski (POL)
1995	Mikael Ljungberg (SWE)
1996[1]	Andrzej Wronski (POL)
1997	Georgy Koguchavilli (RUS)
1998	Georgy Koguchavilli (RUS)
1999	Georgy Koguchavilli (RUS)
2000[1]	Mikael Ljungberg (SWE)
2001	Aleksandr Bezruchkin (RUS)
2002	Mehmet Oezal (TUR)

YEAR	WINNER (NATIONALITY)
96 kg (continued)	
2003	Martin Lidberg (SWE)
2004[1]	Karam Ibrahim (EGY)
120 kg	
1969	Anatoly Roshchin (URS)
1970	Anatoly Roshchin (URS)
1971	Aleksandar Tomov (BUL)
1972[1]	Anatoly Roshchin (URS)
1973	Aleksandar Tomov (BUL)
1974	Aleksandar Tomov (BUL)
1975	Aleksandar Tomov (BUL)
1976[1]	Aleksandr Kolchinsky (URS)
1977	Nikola Dinev (BUL)
1978	Aleksandr Kolchinsky (URS)
1979	Aleksandar Tomov (BUL)
1980[1]	Aleksandr Kolchinsky (URS)
1981	Refik Memisevic (YUG)
1982	Nikola Dinev (BUL)
1983	Yevgeny Artyukhin (URS)
1984[1]	Jeffrey Blatnick (USA)
1985	Igor Rostorotsky (URS)
1986	Tomas Johansson (SWE)
1987	Igor Rostorotsky (URS)
1988[1]	Aleksandr Karelin (URS)
1989	Aleksandr Karelin (URS)
1990	Aleksandr Karelin (URS)
1991	Aleksandr Karelin (URS)
1992[1]	Aleksandr Karelin (UNT)[2]
1993	Aleksandr Karelin (RUS)
1994	Aleksandr Karelin (RUS)
1995	Aleksandr Karelin (RUS)
1996[1]	Aleksandr Karelin (RUS)
1997	Aleksandr Karelin (RUS)
1998	Aleksandr Karelin (RUS)
1999	Aleksandr Karelin (RUS)
2000[1]	Rulon Gardner (USA)
2001	Rulon Gardner (USA)
2002	Dremiel D. Byers (USA)
2003	Khassen Baroyev (RUS)
2004[1]	Khassen Baroyev (RUS)

[1]*Olympic champions, recognized as world champions (for earlier Olympic champions, see Olympic Games).* [2]*Unified Team, consisting of athletes from the Commonwealth of Independent States plus Georgia.* [3]*Tied.*

World Wrestling Championships—Freestyle

The maximum weight in some classes was revised in 1962, 1969, 1985, 1997, and 2002. The 2005 competition is scheduled for 26 September–2 October in Budapest, Hungary.

YEAR	WINNER (NATIONALITY)
48 kg	
1969	Ibrahim Javadi (IRI)
1970	Ibrahim Javadi (IRI)
1971	Ibrahim Javadi (IRI)
1972[1]	Roman Dmitriyev (URS)
1973	Roman Dmitriyev (URS)
1974	Hassan Issaev (Murselov) (BUL)

YEAR	WINNER (NATIONALITY)
48 kg (continued)	
1975	Hassan Issaev (BUL)
1976[1]	Hassan Issaev (BUL)
1977	Anatoly Beloglazov (URS)
1978	Sergey Kornilayev (URS)
1979	Sergey Kornilayev (URS)
1980[1]	Claudio Pollio (ITA)
1981	Sergey Kornilayev (URS)

YEAR	WINNER (NATIONALITY)
48 kg (continued)	
1982	Sergey Kornilayev (URS)
1983	Kim Hwan Cher (PRK)
1984[1]	Robert Weaver (USA)
1985	Kim Chol Hwan (PRK)
1986	Li Yae-sik (PRK)
1987	Li Yae-sik (PRK)
1988[1]	Takashi Kobayashi (JPN)

World Wrestling Championships—Freestyle (continued)

YEAR	WINNER (NATIONALITY)
48 kg (continued)	
1989	Kim Jong-shin (KOR)
1990	Aldo Martínez (CUB)
1991	Vugar Orudzhev (URS)
1992[1]	Kim II (PRK)
1993	Alexis Vila (CUB)
1994	Alexis Vila (CUB)
1995	Vugar Orudzhev (RUS)
1996[1]	Kim II (PRK)
1997	*discontinued*
55 kg	
1951	Ali Yucel (TUR)
1952[1]	Hasan Gemici (TUR)
1954	Huseyin Akbas (TUR)
1956[1]	Mirian Tsalkalamanidze (URS)
1957	Mehmet Kartal (TUR)
1959	Ali Aliyev (URS)
1960[1]	Ahmet Bilek (TUR)
1961	Ali Aliyev (URS)
1962	Ali Aliyev (URS)
1963	Cemal Yanilmaz (TUR)
1964[1]	Yoshikatsu Yoshida (JPN)
1965	Yoshikatsu Yoshida (JPN)
1966	Chang-Sun Chang (KOR)
1967	Shigeo Nakata (JPN)
1968[1]	Shigeo Nakata (JPN)
1969	Richard Joseph Sanders (USA)
1970	Ali Riza Alan (TUR)
1971	Mohammad Ghorbani (IRI)
1972[1]	Kiyomi Kato (JPN)
1973	Ibrahim Javadi (IRI)
1974	Yuji Takada (JPN)
1975	Yuji Takada (JPN)
1976[1]	Yuji Takada (JPN)
1977	Yuji Takada (JPN)
1978	Anatoly Beloglazov (URS)
1979	Yuji Takada (JPN)
1980[1]	Anatoly Beloglazov (URS)
1981	Toshio Asakura (JPN)
1982	Hartmut Reich (GDR)
1983	Valentin Iordanov (BUL)
1984[1]	Saban Trstena (YUG)
1985	Valentin Iordanov (BUL)
1986	Kim Yong-sik (PRK)
1987	Valentin Iordanov (BUL)
1988[1]	Mitsuru Sato (JPN)
1989	Valentin Iordanov (BUL)
1990	Majid Torkan (IRI)
1991	Larry Zeke Jones (USA)
1992[1]	Li Hak-Son (PRK)
1993	Valentin Iordanov (BUL)
1994	Valentin Iordanov (BUL)
1995	Valentin Iordanov (BUL)
1996[1]	Valentin Iordanov (BUL)
1997	Wilfredo Garcia Quintana (CUB)
1998	Samuel Henson (USA)
1999	Kim Woo Yong (KOR)
2000[1]	Namik Abdullayev (AZE)
2001	Herman Kontoyev (BLR)
2002	Rene Montero Rosales (CUB)
2003	Dilshod Mansurov (UZB)
2004	Mavlet Batirov (RUS)

YEAR	WINNER (NATIONALITY)
60 kg	
1951	Nasuh Akar (TUR)
1952[1]	Shohachi Ishii (JPN)
1954	Mustafa Dagistanli (TUR)
1956[1]	Mustafa Dagistanli (TUR)
1957	Huseyin Akbas (TUR)
1959	Huseyin Akbas (TUR)
1960[1]	Terrence McCann (USA)
1961	Mohamad Ebrahim Saifpour Saidabadi (IRI)
1962	Huseyin Akbas (TUR)
1963	Aydyn Ibragimov (URS)
1964[1]	Yojiro Uetake (JPN)
1965	Tomiaki Fukuda (JPN)
1966	Ali Aliyev (URS)
1967	Ali Aliyev (URS)
1968[1]	Yojiro Uetake (JPN)
1969	Tadamichi Tanaka (JPN)
1970	Hideaki Yanagida (JPN)
1971	Hideaki Yanagida (JPN)
1972[1]	Hideaki Yanagida (JPN)
1973	Moshen Faravashi (IRI)
1974	Vladimir Yumin (URS)
1975	Masao Arai (JPN)
1976[1]	Vladmir Yumin (URS)
1977	Tadashi Sasaki (JPN)
1978	Hideaki Tomiyama (JPN)
1979	Hideaki Tomiyama (JPN)
1980[1]	Sergey Beloglazov (URS)
1981	Sergey Beloglazov (URS)
1982	Anatoly Beloglazov (URS)
1983	Sergey Beloglazov (URS)
1984[1]	Hideaki Tomiyama (JPN)
1985	Sergey Beloglazov (URS)
1986	Sergey Beloglazov (URS)
1987	Sergey Beloglazov (URS)
1988[1]	Sergey Beloglazov (URS)
1989	Kim Sik-seung (PRK)
1990	Alejandro Puerto (CUB)
1991	Sergey Smal (URS)
1992[1]	Alejandro Puerto (CUB)
1993	Terry Brands (USA)
1994	Alejandro Puerto (CUB)
1995	Terry Brands (USA)
1996[1]	Kendall Cross (USA)
1997	Mohammad Talaee (IRI)
1998	Ali Reza Dabir (IRI)
1999	Harun Dogan (TUR)
2000[1]	Ali Reza Dabir (IRI)
2001	Guivi Sissaouri (CAN)
2002	Aram Markaryan (ARM)
2003	Abdullaev Arif Yadulla (AZE)
2004[1]	Yandro Miguel Quintana (CUB)
66 kg	
1951	Nurettin Zafer (TUR)
1952[1]	Bayram Sit (TUR)
1954	Shozo Sasahara (JPN)
1956[1]	Shozo Sasahara (JPN)
1957	Mustafa Dagistanli (TUR)
1959	Mustafa Dagistanli (TUR)
1960[1]	Mustafa Dagistanli (TUR)
1961	Vladimir Rubashvili (URS)
1962	Osamu Watanabe (JPN)
1963	Osamu Watanabe (JPN)
1964[1]	Osamu Watanabe (JPN)

YEAR	WINNER (NATIONALITY)
66 kg (continued)	
1965	Mohamad Ebrahim Saifpour Saidabadi (IRI)
1966	Masaaki Kaneko (JPN)
1967	Masaaki Kaneko (JPN)
1968[1]	Masaaki Kaneko (JPN)
1969	Takeo Morita (JPN)
1970	Shamseddin Seyed-Abbassi (IRI)
1971	Sagalav Abdulbekov (URS)
1972[1]	Sagalav Abdulbekov (URS)
1973	Sagalav Abdulbekov (URS)
1974	Zeveg Oydov (MGL)
1975	Zeveg Oydov (MGL)
1976[1]	Yang Jung-Mo (KOR)
1977	Vladimir Yumin (URS)
1978	Vladimir Yumin (URS)
1979	Vladimir Yumin (URS)
1980[1]	Magomedgasan Abushev (URS)
1981	Simeon Sterev (BUL)
1982	Sergey Beloglazov (URS)
1983	Viktor Alekseyev (URS)
1984[1]	Randy Lewis (USA)
1985	Viktor Alekseyev (URS)
1986	Hassar Issayev (URS)
1987	John Smith (USA)
1988[1]	John Smith (USA)
1989	John Smith (USA)
1990	John Smith (USA)
1991	John Smith (USA)
1992[1]	John Smith (USA)
1993	Thomas Brands (USA)
1994	Magomed Azizov (RUS)
1995	Elbrus Tedeyev (UKR)
1996[1]	Thomas Brands (USA)
1997	Abbas Hajd Kenari (IRI)
1998	Serafim Barzakov (BUL)
1999	Elbrus Tedeyev (UKR)
2000[1]	Murad Umakhanov (RUS)
2001	Serafim Barzakov (BUL)
2002	Elbrus Tedeyev (UKR)
2003	Irbek Farniyev (RUS)
2004[1]	Elbrus Tedeyev (UKR)
69 kg	
1951	Olle Anderberg (SWE)
1952[1]	Olle Anderberg (SWE)
1954	Djahanbakte Tovfighe (IRI)
1956[1]	Emam Goudarzi Habibi (IRI)
1957	Alimbeg Bestayev (URS)
1959	Vladimir Sinyavsky (URS)
1960[1]	Shelby Wilson (USA)
1961	Mohammad Sanatkaran (IRI)
1962	Eniu Valchev-Dimov (BUL)
1963	Iwao Horiuchi (JPN)
1964[1]	Eniu Valchev-Dimov (BUL)
1965	Abdullah Movahed Ardabili (IRI)
1966	Abdullah Movahed Ardabili (IRI)
1967	Abdullah Movahed Ardabili (IRI)
1968[1]	Abdullah Movahed Ardabili (IRI)

World Wrestling Championships—Freestyle (continued)

YEAR	WINNER (NATIONALITY)
69 kg (continued)	
1969	Abdullah Movahed Ardabili (IRI)
1970	Abdullah Movahed Ardabili (IRI)
1971	Danny Mack Gable (USA)
1972[1]	Danny Mack Gable (USA)
1973	Lloyd Keaser (USA)
1974	Nasrula Nasrullayev (URS)
1975	Pavel Pinigin (URS)
1976[1]	Pavel Pinigin (URS)
1977	Pavel Pinigin (URS)
1978	Pavel Pinigin (URS)
1979	Mikhail Kharachura (URS)
1980[1]	Saipulla Absaidov (URS)
1981	Saipulla Absaidov (URS)
1982	Mikhail Kharachura (URS)
1983	Arsen Fadzayev (URS)
1984[1]	You In-Tak (KOR)
1985	Arsen Fadzayev (URS)
1986	Arsen Fadzayev (URS)
1987	Arsen Fadzayev (URS)
1988[1]	Arsen Fadzayev (URS)
1989	Boris Bovdayev (URS)
1990	Arsen Fadzayev (URS)
1991	Arsen Fadzayev (URS)
1992[1]	Arsen Fadzayev (UNT)[2]
1993	Akbar Fallah (IRI)
1994	Alexander Leipold (GER)
1995	Araik Gevorkian (ARM)
1996[1]	Vadim Bogiyev (RUS)
1997	Araik Gevorkian (ARM)
1998	Araik Gevorkian (ARM)
1999	Daniel Igali (CAN)
2000[1]	Daniel Igali (CAN)
2001	Nikolay Paslar (BUL)
2002	*discontinued*
74 kg	
1951	Celal Atik (TUR)
1952[1]	William Thomas Smith (USA)
1954	Vakhtang Balavadze (URS)
1956[1]	Mitsuo Ikeda (JPN)
1957	Vakhtang Balavadze (URS)
1959	Emam Goudarzi Habibi (IRI)
1960[1]	Douglas Blubaugh (USA)
1961	Emam Goudarzi Habibi (IRI)
1962	Emam Goudarzi Habibi (IRI)
1963	Guliko Sagaradze (URS)
1964[1]	Ismail Ogan (TUR)
1965	Guliko Sagaradze (URS)
1966	Mahmut Atalay (TUR)
1967	Daniel Sauton-Robin (FRA)
1968[1]	Mahmut Atalay (TUR)
1969	Zarbeg Beriashvili (URS)
1970	Wayne Wells (USA)
1971	Yury Gusov (URS)
1972[1]	Wayne Turner Wells (USA)
1973	Mansoor Barzegar (IRI)
1974	Ruslan Ashuraliyev (URS)
1975	Ruslan Ashuraliyev (URS)
1976[1]	Jiichiro Date (JPN)

YEAR	WINNER (NATIONALITY)
74 kg (continued)	
1977	Stanley Dziedzic (USA)
1978	Leroy Kemp (USA)
1979	Leroy Kemp (USA)
1980[1]	Valentin Raychev (BUL)
1981	Martin Knosp (FRG)
1982	Leroy Kemp (USA)
1983	David Schultz (USA)
1984[1]	David Schultz (USA)
1985	Raul Cascaret Fonseca (CUB)
1986	Raul Cascaret Fonseca (CUB)
1987	Adlan Varayev (URS)
1988[1]	Kenneth Monday (USA)
1989	Kenneth Monday (USA)
1990	Rahmat Sukra (BUL)
1991	Amir Reza Khadem Azghadi (IRI)
1992[1]	Park Jang-Soon (KOR)
1993	Park Jang-Soon (KOR)
1994	Turan Ceylan (TUR)
1995	Buvaysa Saytyev (RUS)
1996[1]	Buvaysa Saytyev (RUS)
1997	Buvaysa Saytyev (RUS)
1998	Buvaysa Saytyev (RUS)
1999	Adam Saytyev (RUS)
2000[1]	Brandon Slay (USA)
2001	Buvaysa Saytyev (RUS)
2002	Mehdi Hajizadeh Jouibari (IRI)
2003	Buvaysa Saytyev (RUS)
2004[1]	Buvaysa Saytyev (RUS)
84 kg	
1951	Haydar Zafer (TUR)
1952[1]	David Tsimakurdze (URS)
1954	Abbas Zandi (IRI)
1956[1]	Nikola Stanchev (BUL)
1957	Nabi Soruri (IRI)
1959	Georgy Skhirtladze (URS)
1960[1]	Hassan Gungor (TUR)
1961	Mansoor Mehdizadeh (IRI)
1962	Mansoor Mehdizadeh (IRI)
1963	Prodan Gardzhev (BUL)
1964[1]	Prodan Gardzhev (BUL)
1965	Mansoor Mehdizadeh (IRI)
1966	Prodan Gardzhev (BUL)
1967	Boris Gurevich (URS)
1968[1]	Boris Gurevich (URS)
1969	Fred Fozzard (USA)
1970	Yury Shakhmuradov (URS)
1971	Levan Tediashvili (URS)
1972[1]	Levan Tediashvili (URS)
1973	Vasily Syulzhin (URS)
1974	Viktor Novozhilov (URS)
1975	Adolf Seger (FRG)
1976[1]	John Allan Peterson (USA)
1977	Adolf Seger (FRG)
1978	Magomed Aratsilov (URS)
1979	Istvan Kovacs (HUN)
1980[1]	Ismail Abilov (BUL)
1981	Christopher Campbell (USA)
1982	Tajmuraz Dzgoyev (URS)
1983	Tajmuraz Dzgoyev (URS)
1984[1]	Mark Schultz (USA)

YEAR	WINNER (NATIONALITY)
84 kg (continued)	
1985	Mark Schultz (USA)
1986	Vladimir Modozyan (URS)
1987	Mark Schultz (USA)
1988[1]	Han Myung-Woo (KOR)
1989	Elmadi Jabrailov (URS)
1990	Jozef Lohyna (TCH)
1991	Kevin Jackson (USA)
1992[1]	Kevin Jackson (USA)
1993	Sabahattin Ozturk (TUR)
1994	Lukman Jabrailov (MDA)
1995	Kevin Jackson (USA)
1996[1]	Khadshimurad Magomedov (RUS)
1997	Leslie Gutches (USA)
1998	Ali Reza Heydari (IRI)
1999	Yoel Romero Palacio (CUB)
2000[1]	Adam Saytyev (RUS)
2001	Khadshimurad Magomedov (RUS)
2002	Adam Saytyev (RUS)
2003	Sazhid Sazhidov (RUS)
2004[1]	Cael Sanderson (USA)
90 kg	
1951	Yasar Dogu (TUR)
1952[1]	Viking Palm (SWE)
1954	Arsen Englas (URS)
1956[1]	Gholamreza Takhti (IRI)
1957	Petko Sirakov Atanasov (BUL)
1959	Gholamreza Takhti (IRI)
1960[1]	Ismet Atli (TUR)
1961	Gholamreza Takhti (IRI)
1962	Aleksandr Medved (URS)
1963	Aleksandr Medved (URS)
1964[1]	Aleksandr Medved (URS)
1965	Ahmet Ayik (TUR)
1966	Aleksandr Medved (URS)
1967	Ahmet Ayik (TUR)
1968[1]	Ahmet Ayik (TUR)
1969	Boris Gurevich (URS)
1970	Gennady Strakhov (URS)
1971	Rusi Petrov (BUL)
1972[1]	Benjamin Lee Peterson (USA)
1973	Levan Tediashvili (URS)
1974	Levan Tediashvili (URS)
1975	Levan Tediashvili (URS)
1976[1]	Levan Tediashvili (URS)
1977	Anatoly Prokopchuk (URS)
1978	Uwe Neupert (GDR)
1979	Khasan Ortsuyev (URS)
1980[1]	Sanasar Oganisyan (URS)
1981	Sanasar Oganisyan (URS)
1982	Uwe Neupert (GDR)
1983	Pyotr Naniyev (URS)
1984[1]	Edward Banach (USA)
1985	William Scherr (USA)
1986	Macharbek Khadartsev (URS)
1987	Macharbek Khadartsev (URS)
1988[1]	Macharbek Khadartsev (URS)

World Wrestling Championships—Freestyle (continued)

YEAR	WINNER (NATIONALITY)
90 kg (continued)	
1989	Macharbek Khadartsev (URS)
1990	Macharbek Khadartsev (URS)
1991	Macharbek Khadartsev (URS)
1992[1]	Macharbek Khadartsev (UNT)[2]
1993	Melvin Douglas (USA)
1994	Rasul Khadem Azghadi (IRI)
1995	Rasul Khadem Azghadi (IRI)
1996[1]	Rasul Khadem Azghadi (IRI)
1997	*discontinued*
96 kg	
1951	Bertil Antonsson (SWE)
1952[1]	Arsen Mekokishvili (URS)
1954	Arsen Mekokishvili (URS)
1956[1]	Hamit Kaplan (TUR)
1957	Hamit Kaplan (TUR)
1959	Lyutvi Akhmedov (BUL)
1960[1]	Wilfried Dietrich (FRG)
1961	Wilfried Dietrich (FRG)
1962	Aleksandr Ivanitsky (URS)
1963	Aleksandr Ivanitsky (URS)
1964[1]	Aleksandr Ivanitsky (URS)
1965	Aleksandr Ivanitsky (URS)
1966	Aleksandr Ivanitsky (URS)
1967	Aleksandr Medved (URS)
1968[1]	Aleksandr Medved (URS)
1969	Shota Lomidze (URS)
1970	Vladimir Gulyutkin (URS)
1971	Shota Lomidze (URS)
1972[1]	Ivan Yarygin (URS)
1973	Ivan Yarygin (URS)
1974	Vladimir Gulyutkin (URS)
1975	Khorloo Bayanmunkh (MGL)

YEAR	WINNER (NATIONALITY)
96 kg (continued)	
1976[1]	Ivan Yarygin (URS)
1977	Aslanbek Bisultanov (URS)
1978	Harald Buettner (GDR)
1979	Ilya Mate (URS)
1980[1]	Ilya Mate (URS)
1981	Roland Gehrke (GDR)
1982	Ilya Mate (URS)
1983	Aslan Khadartzev (URS)
1984[1]	Louis Banach (USA)
1985	Leri Khabelov (URS)
1986	Aslan Khadartzev (URS)
1987	Leri Khabelov (URS)
1988[1]	Vasile Puscasu (ROM)
1989	Ahmed Atavov (URS)
1990	Leri Khabelov (URS)
1991	Leri Khabelov (URS)
1992[1]	Leri Khabelov (UNT)[2]
1993	Leri Khabelov (RUS)
1994	Arawat Sabejew (GER)
1995	Kurt Angle (USA)
1996[1]	Kurt Angle (USA)
1997	Kuramagomed Kuramagòmedov (RUS)
1998	Abbas Jadidi (IRI)
1999	Sagid Murtasaliyev (RUS)
2000[1]	Sagid Murtasaliyev (RUS)
2001	Georgy Gogchelidze (RUS)
2002	Eldar Kurtanidze (GEO)
2003	Eldar Kurtanidze (GEO)
2004[1]	Khasimurat Gatsalov (RUS)
120 kg	
1969	Aleksandr Medved (URS)
1970	Aleksandr Medved (URS)
1971	Aleksandr Medved (URS)
1972[1]	Aleksandr Medved (URS)
1973	Soslan Andiyev (URS)
1974	Simon Ladislav (ROM)

YEAR	WINNER (NATIONALITY)
120 kg (continued)	
1975	Soslan Andiyev (URS)
1976[1]	Soslan Andiyev (URS)
1977	Soslan Andiyev (URS)
1978	Soslan Andiyev (URS)
1979	Salman Khasimikov (URS)
1980[1]	Soslan Andiyev (URS)
1981	Salman Khasimikov (URS)
1982	Salman Khasimikov (URS)
1983	Salman Khasimikov (URS)
1984[1]	Bruce Baumgartner (USA)
1985	David Gobedzhishvili (URS)
1986	Bruce Baumgartner (USA)
1987	Aslan Khadartzev (URS)
1988[1]	David Gobedzhishvili (URS)
1989	Ali Reza Soleimani (IRI)
1990	David Gobedzhishvili (URS)
1991	Andreas Schröder (GER)
1992[1]	Bruce Baumgartner (USA)
1993	Bruce Baumgartner (USA)
1994	Mahmut Demir (TUR)
1995	Bruce Baumgartner (USA)
1996[1]	Mahmut Demir (TUR)
1997	Zekeriya Guclu (TUR)
1998	Alexis Rodríguez Valera (CUB)
1999	Stephen Neal (USA)
2000[1]	David Musulbes (RUS)
2001	David Musulbes (RUS)
2002	David Musulbes (RUS)
2003	Artur Taymazov (UZB)
2004[1]	Artur Taymazov (UZB)

[1]*Olympic champions, recognized as world champions (for earlier Olympic champions, see Olympic Games).* [2]*Unified Team, consisting of athletes from the Commonwealth of Independent States plus Georgia.*

2004—06 Sumo Tournaments

TOURNAMENT	LOCATION	DATE	WINNER	WINNER'S RECORD
Nagoya Basho (Nagoya tournament)	Nagoya	4–18 Jul 2004	Asashoryu	13–2
Aki Basho (autumn tournament)	Tokyo	12–26 Sep 2004	Kaio	13–2
Kyushu Basho (Kyushu tournament)	Fukuoka	14–28 Nov 2004	Asashoryu	13–2
Hatsu Basho (New Year's tournament)	Tokyo	9–23 Jan 2005	Asashoryu	15–0
Haru Basho (spring tournament)	Osaka	13–27 Mar 2005	Asashoryu	14–1
Natsu Basho (summer tournament)	Tokyo	8–22 May 2005	Asashoryu	15–0
Nagoya Basho (Nagoya tournament)	Nagoya	10–24 Jul 2005	Asashoryu	13–2
Aki Basho (autumn tournament)	Tokyo	11–25 Sep 2005		
Kyushu Basho (Kyushu tournament)	Fukuoka	13–27 Nov 2005		
Hatsu Basho (New Year's tournament)	Tokyo	8–22 Jan 2006		
Haru Basho (spring tournament)	Osaka	12–26 Mar 2006		
Natsu Basho (summer tournament)	Tokyo	7–21 May 2006		
Nagoya Basho (Nagoya tournament)	Nagoya	9–23 Jul 2006		
Aki Basho (autumn tournament)	Tokyo	10–24 Sep 2006		
Kyushu Basho (Kyushu tournament)	Fukuoka	12–26 Nov 2006		

INDEX

Page numbers in **boldface** indicate main subject references; references in *italics* indicate illustrations. Photographs are on the plates after page 192; flags and maps of the world are on the plates after page 960.

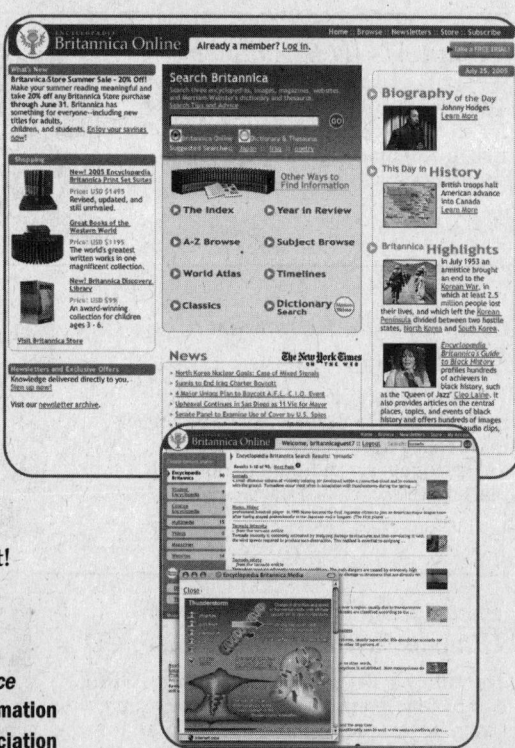

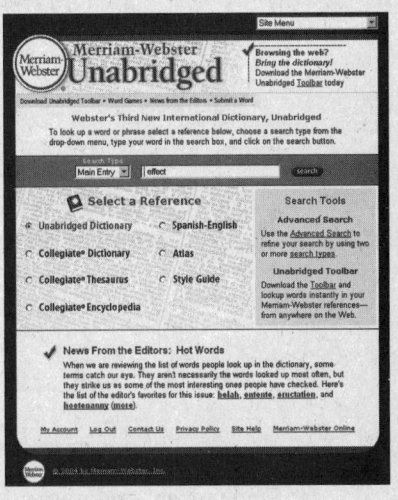
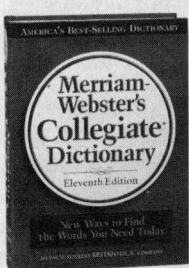

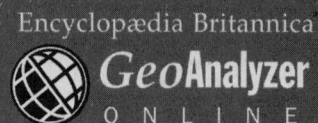
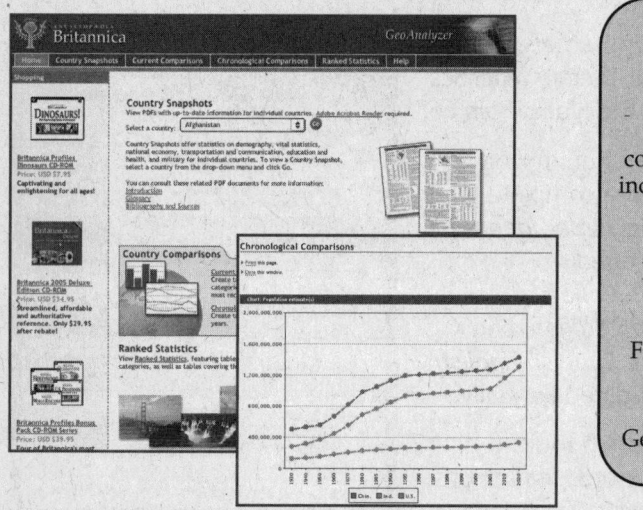